START HERE

YOU'RE HOLDING THE BESTSELLING BOOK OF ALL TIME.

Welcome to the Bible!
We've made a film for you to watch before you get stuck in.
Head to gnbyouthedition.co.uk/welcome

WHAT'S INSIDE...

NAME:

IF YOU'VE GOT A FAVOURITE BIBLE VERSE, WRITE IT HERE.

PEOPLE WHO HAVE IMPACTED YOUR LIFE.

GRAB A FRIEND (OR TWO...)

AND ASK THEM TO WRITE POSITIVE WORDS THAT DESCRIBE YOU HERE.

THIS IS A LIST...

Fill the lines with things that really matter to you.

ON THIS LINE, DRAW YOUR LIFE JOURNEY UP UNTIL THIS POINT, AND MARK IT WITH IMPORTANT MOMENTS.

THE GALLERY OF
MEANINGFUL MOMENTS

Cover this space by sticking in things that remind you of times when you encountered God or had a significant moment with him. It could be leaves from walks, letters from friends, wristbands from events... anything!

GOD
↘ ●

X MARKS THE SPOT...

So go ahead and draw an X somewhere on this page that represents your relationship with God. How close to him, or far away, do you feel? Mark it with today's date. Whenever you come back to this page, see if you feel any different and draw another X.

WHY

· READ THE ·

BIBLE?

The Bible has something to say about almost all the questions we might be asking - whether about our relationships, our purpose here on earth or how to live a good life. People in really tough situations have read the Bible and found themselves changed. God speaks to us through the Bible, bringing a message of hope, love, forgiveness, freedom and purpose. We learn that nothing can ever separate us from God's love, and we find out more about this God who loves us unconditionally and can make a difference to us today.

The Bible is one of the most influential historical documents of all time and has been transforming people's lives for thousands of years. To hear some stories of how it's still changing people's lives today, go to gnbyouthedition.co.uk/stories

WHAT IS THE BIBLE?

The Bible is more like a library than one book. It's a whole collection of books that tell us who God is and how we fit into the big story of life. It can help to shape our lives today and make a difference to the way we view our identity. We find out that God loves and cares about us and has a plan for our lives.

Take a quick look at the 'What's inside' page (p. 2). You'll see that the Bible is split into two parts called the Old Testament and the New Testament. The Old Testament tells us about the Jewish people's history and the way they understood God. The New Testament is the story of Jesus and the difference he makes to our understanding of the same God.

There are loads of different types of books in the Bible. Just as you might have a favourite film genre - such as action, sci-fi or comedy - there might be some biblical genres that interest you more than others. There are songs, poems, stories, letters and much more to unpack.

CHECK THEM OUT!

However, the whole Bible is one big story with a common theme that runs throughout all the little stories. (A fancy word for this kind of big story is 'metanarrative'.)

Old Testament

THE LAW
The first five books of the Bible tell the story of the origins of God's...

people, the Israelites, and outline the laws they were to keep.

HISTORY
These books outline the historical events in the story of the Israelites.

POETRY
These books are full of wisdom for daily life, as well as poetry and songs...

that span all kinds of human emotions and life experiences.

PROPHETS
These books are packed with the messages God gave to...

particular people, to pass on to the Israelites.

New Testament

GOSPELS
The first four books of the New Testament are...

all about the life, miracles and teaching of Jesus.

HISTORY
The book of Acts tells us how the church spread the good news.

LETTERS
These are letters written to the early church...

covering different issues and giving guidance on following Jesus.

PROPHECY
The book of Revelation is full of imagery and symbolism.

HOW TO
USE THIS BIBLE

Sometimes, getting the most out of the Bible depends on the type of person God created you to be.

ARE YOU A
CREATIVE PERSON?

MAKE USE OF THE SPACE!

COLOUR, DRAW AND IMAGINE.

HIGHLIGHT GREAT VERSES AND MAKE THE MOST OF THE INTERACTIONS.

ARE YOU A REFLECTIVE PERSON?

Always allow yourself time to

STOP AND THINK.

Use the space to write out your thoughts, and ask loads of questions about what you read.

THERE'S ALWAYS MORE TO FIND OUT.

ARE YOU AN ACTIVE PERSON?

Feel free to take this Bible around with you!

IT DOESN'T HAVE TO BE READ IN YOUR ROOM.

Carry it with you when you're exploring new places, and read it there.

Are you a
TALKER?

This book has loads in it to chat about.

GET TOGETHER WITH MATES and talk through what you read.

Write down questions as you read, and try to answer them.

ARE YOU A BIT OF EVERYTHING?

Use the Bible differently depending on how you feel at the time.

THERE'S NO RIGHT WAY TO DO IT!

The book you are reading and
the chapters on these pages.

Page number.

2 Chron.
Ezra
Nehem.
Esther
Job

The verse number you are reading.

A list of books either before or after this one.

The chapter number you are reading.

PSALM 104

Use this space to

– DOODLE –

DIFFERENT

IMAGES

that are used in Psalm
104. Reflect on God as
Creator while you do it.

There are different things for you
to do in the margins. Some are creative,
some will make you think and some just
leave room for you to do your own thing!

Extra information about the text

14 He knows what we are made of;
      he remembers that we are dust.

15 As for us, our life is like grass.
      We grow and flourish like a wild flower;
16   then the wind blows on it, and it is gone —
          no one sees it again.
17 But for those who honour the LORD, his love lasts for ever,
      and his goodness endures for all generations
18 of those who are true to his covenant
      and who faithfully obey his commands.

19 The LORD placed his throne in heaven;
      he is king over all.
20 Praise the LORD, you strong and mighty angels,
      who obey his commands,
      who listen to what he says.
21 Praise the LORD, all you heavenly powers,
      you servants of his, who do his will!
22 Praise the LORD, all his creatures
      in all the places he rules.
      Praise the LORD, my soul!

In Praise of the Creator

104 ¹Praise the LORD, my soul!
      O LORD, my God, how great you are!
      You are clothed with majesty and glory;
2   you cover yourself with light.
      You have spread out the heavens like a tent
3   and built your home on the waters above.*
      You use the clouds as your chariot
      and ride on the wings of the wind.
4 You use the winds as your messengers
      and flashes of lightning as your servants.

5 You have set the earth firmly on its foundations,
      and it will never be moved.
6 You placed the ocean over it like a robe,
      and the water covered the mountains.
7 When you rebuked the waters, they fled;
      they rushed away when they heard your shout of command.
8 They flowed over the mountains and into the valleys,
      to the place you had made for them.
9 You set a boundary they can never pass,
      to keep them from covering the earth again.

10 You make springs flow in the valleys,
      and rivers run between the hills.
11 They provide water for the wild animals;
      there the wild donkeys quench their thirst.
12 In the trees near by,
      the birds make their nests and sing.

13 From the sky you send rain on the hills,
      and the earth is filled with your blessings.
14 You make grass grow for the cattle

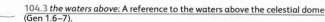

104.3 *the waters above*: A reference to the waters above the celestial dome
(Gen 1.6–7).

MAKE A NOTE

FAVOURITE BIBLE VERSES

write your favourite verses here

HOW TO READ THE BIBLE

On this page are a bunch of ideas to help you engage with the Bible. If you're finding it hard to get going, here are some top tips to start you off.

READ THE GOSPEL OF MARK

It's short, snappy and all about Jesus.
(Don't worry if you can't read it all in one go, though.)

PROVERBS IS FULL OF WISDOM FOR LIFE

... and you can read just one verse at a time.

THE PSALMS SPAN THE WHOLE RANGE OF HUMAN EMOTION

... and their poetic style makes them easy to read. Perhaps start with a short one, like Psalm 23.

CHECK OUT THE BIBLE READING PLANS ON PAGES 19-20

To find out how to connect with God through the Bible and prayer, head to gnbyouthedition.co.uk/connectbible and gnbyouthedition.co.uk/connectprayer to watch a couple of

FILMS

WE MADE ABOUT IT.

GOT 5 MINUTES?

If you've only got a few minutes, that's cool, but it might be worth picking a story from the Gospels or a psalm to focus on - something punchy and short. The key is not to spend the whole time reading. Make space before and afterwards to process what you've read, and be creative.

GOT 15 MINUTES?

15 minutes is a good amount of time to go through a chapter of the Bible. It's probably best not to grab any chapter at random, though. Maybe start at the beginning of a new book? Pray first, read a chapter, stop for a minute, then read it again. On the second time, underline, ask questions, colour and imagine! And it's always good to ask: what does this mean for me?

GOT 30 MINUTES?

If you have a bit longer, you can read a longer chapter, or a few chapters back to back. Or you can go really deep on one chapter, or even one verse. Having more time means you can focus on reflecting more. Try memorising a few verses, or close your eyes and keep repeating a passage, pulling out different words. If you make a habit of meditating like this, it could change your life!

THE BIBLE:

HOW IT CAME TOGETHER

So, how did the Bible come together? Who put all of the books in order and why were those ones chosen?

WELL, HERE'S A SNAPSHOT.

The early Christians (in churches that sprang up after Jesus' resurrection and ascension to heaven) needed guidance on how to live their lives as followers of Jesus. They used both the Jewish holy scriptures (which we call the Old Testament) and also stories of eyewitnesses' experiences with Jesus.

The Old Testament was based on oral history - stories passed down from generation to generation. Once the Jews were in exile, it seemed important to make sure all their laws and stories were written down, and so the Old Testament was gradually put together.

Regarding the eyewitnesses' stories of Jesus, the believers realised that once these people had died, their stories would be lost, so many people tried to put them down in writing. There were also letters written by church leaders such as Paul and Peter to answer the early believers' questions and to encourage them as they worked out how to live the Christian life.

However, after the first century AD, lots of less reliable books began to appear, causing confusion. In AD367, a bishop called Athanasius put together a list of the most trustworthy books and letters to read. His list was backed up by two councils of important people in the cities of Rome and Carthage, and that list formed the New Testament we have today.

You can find out more detail about how the Bible was put together (and how reliable it is) by heading to gnbyouthedition.co.uk/bibletogether to

WATCH A FILM

WE MADE ABOUT IT.

THE
BIG QUESTIONS

Got big questions about faith, God or the Bible? Make a note of them here.

_____
_____
_____
_____
_____
_____
_____
_____
_____
_____
_____
_____
_____
_____
_____
_____

Finding answers to these big questions is called 'apologetics' and we've made a couple of films to get you thinking about it. Go to gnbyouthedition.co.uk/apologetics1 and gnbyouthedition.co.uk/apologetics2.

TIMELINE

— OF THE —

BIBLE STORY

The Bible is one great big dramatic story that covers thousands of years of history. It can sometimes be difficult to work out what is going on where, but here is a timeline of highlights. It's hard to be exact on dates, so we've put down our best estimates.

To watch a short film unpacking the biblical timeline, go to gnbyouthedition.co.uk/timeline

THE BEGINNING
DATE: ??? - ???

WHERE IN THE BIBLE: GENESIS 1-2
God creates the earth. God makes human beings, and all is well. But humankind gives into temptation and so evil comes into the world.

WHERE IN THE BIBLE: GENESIS 6-9
God decides to restart humanity as people have become too evil. He chooses Noah and his family to be the start of a reset earth.

THE FLOOD
DATE: SOMETIME BEFORE 1800BC

ABRAHAM AND
THE ISRAELITES
DATE: AROUND 1800-1500BC

WHERE IN THE BIBLE: GENESIS 12-36
God chooses Abraham as the man to kick-start a new nation, who will be God's representatives on earth. Abraham has Isaac, who has Jacob, who has twelve sons including Joseph. Their descendants are known as the Israelites.

WHERE IN THE BIBLE: EXODUS 1-13
Through Joseph, the Israelites move to Egypt, but generations later they end up as slaves. Under Moses' leadership, the Israelites escape Egypt to pursue the land that God promised to Abraham.

EGYPT
AND EXODUS
DATE: AROUND 1500-1400BC

WANDERING IN THE DESERT
DATE: AROUND 1400-1300BC

WHERE IN THE BIBLE: EXODUS 14 TO JOSHUA
The journey to the promised land isn't really very long, but the Israelites get lost because of their disobedience to God. From Exodus to the book of Joshua, we see how the Israelites live in the desert.

WHERE IN THE BIBLE: JOSHUA AND JUDGES
With Joshua in command, the Israelites conquer the promised land, but they are still a mess - forgetting about God and disobeying his commands. So God sends a series of leaders called judges, to rescue them from their enemies and remind them of the God they serve.

THE PROMISED LAND
AND THE TIME OF THE JUDGES
DATE: FROM AROUND 1300BC

DAVID & THE TIME OF THE KINGS

DATE: UP TO AROUND 930BC

WHERE IN THE BIBLE: 1 AND 2 SAMUEL; 1 KINGS 1-11; 2 CHRONICLES 1-9
The Israelites call out for a king, and so, reluctantly, God appoints Saul. Saul starts well but then begins to disobey God, so David is chosen instead. When Saul dies, David becomes king and does a great job! After David, King Solomon reigns and builds the temple of God. During this time, many of the Psalms and Proverbs may have been written.

WHERE IN THE BIBLE: 1 KINGS 12-13 AND 2 CHRONICLES 10-12
Solomon's son Rehoboam becomes king, but he is cruel and so the northern tribes of Israel revolt against him, choosing another man, Jeroboam, to be their king. Therefore, the nation splits into two - Israel in the north and Judah in the south.

A DIVIDED KINGDOM

DATE: UP TO AROUND 850BC

THE TIME OF THE PROPHETS AND EXILE

DATE: AROUND 850-400BC

WHERE IN THE BIBLE: 2 KINGS TO MALACHI
Throughout the rest of the Old Testament, we see a series of (mostly) evil kings taking God's people further away from him. So God sends prophets to warn and encourage his people. But eventually both Israel and Judah are captured and sent into exile. The people of Judah are allowed to return home from around 535BC, though still under foreign rule. Ezra and Nehemiah lead the rebuilding of the temple and city walls.

WHERE IN THE BIBLE: NOWHERE!
Malachi is the last prophet in the Old Testament, writing around 450-420BC. Between then and the New Testament, we have no more prophecies - but God's people are waiting for a promised saviour.

SILENGE

DATE: AROUND 400-6BC

THE
SAVIOUR
DATE: AROUND 6BC-AD27

WHERE IN THE BIBLE: THE GOSPELS
- MATTHEW, MARK, LUKE AND JOHN
After a long wait, Jesus bursts onto the scene. During his short life he teaches, heals and performs many miracles, proving to his followers that he is the long-awaited saviour. But his job isn't finished until he dies on the cross and rises again from death. In doing so, he defeats the powers of evil and sin.

WHERE IN THE BIBLE: ACTS
After Jesus ascends to heaven, his disciples receive the gift of the Holy Spirit. God's people, the church, spread quickly throughout the Middle East and beyond, into Asia Minor (modern-day Turkey) and Europe.

ACTS AND
THE CHURCH
DATE: AROUND AD27-100

PAUL
THE MISSIONARY
DATE: AROUND AD35-65

WHERE IN THE BIBLE: ACTS 9-28
Saul, a kind of terrorist trying to destroy the church, sees a vision of Jesus and converts to Christianity. Saul, also known as Paul, travels around Asia Minor and Europe, preaching about Jesus and setting up new churches. He ends up writing about 40% of our New Testament.

WHERE IN THE BIBLE: ROMANS TO JUDE
Much of the New Testament consists of letters written by Paul, Peter, James and John to various churches in Asia Minor and Europe. They served to encourage and warn the new believers, and are still great for us to read today.

THE
LETTERS
DATE: AROUND AD40-100

THE END
DATE: ???-???

WHERE IN THE BIBLE: REVELATION
The final book, written by a man called John, speaks partly of a time we haven't yet experienced - an ending where there is no more death or pain. Right now, we are living somewhere before the very end of Revelation!

HOW DO I
BECOME A CHRISTIAN?

A Christian is someone who follows Jesus. Living as a Christian means saying 'yes' to this journey every day. It's saying 'yes' to something that will not always be easy, might look different from the world around you, but which promises to be an amazing adventure!

If you have never considered yourself Christian, or would like to renew your commitment to living as a follower of Jesus, you might want to pray a prayer a bit like this - a prayer that invites Jesus into your life:

FATHER GOD, THANK YOU THAT YOU LOVE ME. JESUS, THANK YOU THAT YOU DIED AND ROSE AGAIN FOR ME. I AM SORRY FOR WHEN I HAVE NOT DONE THE RIGHT THING. PLEASE FILL ME WITH YOUR HOLY SPIRIT SO THAT I CAN LIVE LIFE AS A FOLLOWER OF YOU. AMEN.

GOD + PEOPLE =
CHURCH

As human beings, we are not meant to live out our lives, and our faith, alone.

Instead, we were created to
LIVE IN RELATIONSHIP
with others - with our friends, family and those around us.

We are designed to learn to love and follow Jesus alongside others and to pray, serve, support, love and connect with each other in community.

THIS COMMUNITY,
THIS BODY OF PEOPLE,
IS THE CHURCH!

A lot of the time we think church is just a building, but it is so much more than that - it is the people of God. God wants us to journey together, and this is why it's so important to get plugged into church.

BIBLE STUDY

_____
_____
_____
_____
_____
_____
_____
_____
_____
_____
_____

MINI STUDY

○ **DAY 1:** Read Mark 1-2

QUESTIONS TO THINK ABOUT:
Mark launches straight into Jesus' public ministry at the start of his Gospel. Why do you think he writes this way?

Which healing stands out to you most, and why?

What was revolutionary about what Jesus said and did in Mark 2.18-27?

○ **DAY 2:** Read Mark 3-4

QUESTIONS TO THINK ABOUT:
What do these passages say about Jesus' authority (the way he can give a command and be obeyed straight away)?

Why did Jesus tell parables? What do they mean?

○ **DAY 3:** Read Mark 5-7

QUESTIONS TO THINK ABOUT:
What do you think the people Jesus interacted with thought of him?

What do you think Jesus means in Mark 7.15?

AN OVERVIEW OF THE WHOLE BIBLE

○ **DAY 1:** Read Genesis 1-2

○ **DAY 2:** Read Genesis 3

○ **DAY 3:** Read Genesis 6-8

○ **DAY 4:** Read Genesis 12.1-5; 18.1-15; 17.1-22; 21.1-7

○ **DAY 5:** Read Genesis 37 and 41

○ **DAY 6:** Read Exodus 2-3

○ **DAY 7:** Read Exodus 12.1-42; 13.17-14.31

○ **DAY 8:** Read Exodus 20.1-21

○ **DAY 9:** Read Joshua 1 and 3

○ **DAY 10:** Read Joshua 8 and 11

○ **DAY 11:** Read Judges 13 and 16

○ **DAY 12:** Read 1 Samuel 1 and 3.1-21

○ **DAY 13:** Read 1 Samuel 8.1-10.1 and chapter 15

○ **DAY 14:** Read 1 Samuel 17

READING PLAN

○ **DAY 1:** Read Luke 1-2

THE BIRTH OF JESUS

Head to gnbyouthedition.co.uk/day1 to watch a short film.

○ **DAY 2:** Read John 1.1-18

WHO JESUS WAS

Head to gnbyouthedition.co.uk/day2 to watch a short film.

○ **DAY 3:** Read Luke 4.14-44

THE START OF JESUS' WORK ON EARTH

○ **DAY 4:** Read Matthew 5-6

SOME OF JESUS' CORE TEACHING

○ **DAY 5:** Read John 3

JESUS TEACHES ABOUT GOD'S LOVE

Head to gnbyouthedition.co.uk/day5 to watch a short film.

○ DAY 4: Read Mark 8-9
QUESTIONS TO THINK ABOUT:
What did Jesus say about the importance of his death, in Mark 8.31-38?

What was the significance of Jesus' transfiguration, in Mark 9.2-13?

○ DAY 5: Read Mark 10-12
QUESTIONS TO THINK ABOUT:
Which of the events in these chapters would have been most impactful to witness?

What does 'the great commandment' in Mark 12.29-30 mean for you today?

○ DAY 6: Read Mark 13-14
QUESTIONS TO THINK ABOUT:
What do you make of chapter 13 and the prophecies that Jesus speaks?

What comments can you make about Jesus' attitude in the run-up to his death?

○ DAY 7: Read Mark 15-16
QUESTIONS TO THINK ABOUT:
Which details of the crucifixion do you think are most significant?

What would it have been like to be present at each of Jesus' appearances after his resurrection?

○ DAY 15: Read 2 Samuel 5-6

○ DAY 16: Read 1 Kings 3, 6 and 8

○ DAY 17: Read 2 Kings 17 and 25

○ DAY 18: Read Esther 3-4 and 7

○ DAY 19: Read Psalms 23 and 51

○ DAY 20: Read Isaiah 52.13-53.12

○ DAY 21: Read Matthew 1.18-2.23; Luke 2

○ DAY 22: Read Matthew 5-7

○ DAY 23: Read Matthew 8-9

○ DAY 24: Read John 18-19

○ DAY 25: Read John 20-21

○ DAY 26: Read Acts 2

○ DAY 27: Read Acts 9.1-3

○ DAY 28: Read Romans 3 and 8

○ DAY 29: Read 1 Corinthians 12-13

○ DAY 30: Read Hebrews 11

○ DAY 31: Read Revelation 21-22

○ DAY 6: Read John 5

JESUS' POWER AND MIRACLES

○ DAY 7: Read John 15

JESUS TALKS ABOUT THE LIFE OF A CHRISTIAN
Head to gnbyouthedition.co.uk/day7 to watch a short film.

○ DAY 8: Read Matthew 26-27

JESUS IS ARRESTED AND KILLED

○ DAY 9: Read John 20 & Luke 24

JESUS RISES FROM THE DEAD

○ DAY 10: Read Acts 2

THE HOLY SPIRIT AND THE BIRTH OF THE CHURCH
Head to gnbyouthedition.co.uk/day10 to watch a short film.

THE BOOK OF
GENESIS

WRITTEN: PROBABLY 600-400BC
(USING STORIES FROM A MUCH EARLIER TIME)

WHAT YOU NEED TO KNOW:

The book of Genesis (meaning 'origin' in Greek) takes us from the very beginning of the world, through to the arrival of the Israelites in Egypt with Joseph. In it we find themes of creation, sin and mistakes, promises and covenants (agreements with God), and we see how God chose to use one man to kick-start his plan for humanity. The story starts with a perfect world, before things quickly go wrong. Right away we see God putting in place a plan to save humanity, which will eventually be fulfilled in Jesus. Genesis begins with a poetic description of creation and introduces a God who (unlike the gods that non-Israelites believed in) is personal and loving, and wants to work with humanity to restore the world to what it was created to be.

WHY READ IT?

This book is action-packed. Here we have the stories of creation, Adam and Eve, the tower of Babel, Noah and the ark, Abraham, Jacob wrestling with God, Joseph and his fancy coat, and two nations being saved from famine. This is the book to read to find out how the story starts, and to learn about a God who creates, gives purpose, and sets the greatest promise into motion.

HERE ARE SOME OF THE
· KEY ·
CHARACTERS

IN GENESIS. NEXT TO EACH OF THEIR NAMES, WRITE A SHORT SUMMARY OF THEIR STORY.

○ ADAM
_____
_____
_____

○ NOAH
_____
_____
_____

○ ABRAHAM
_____
_____
_____
_____

○ JOSEPH
_____
_____
_____
_____

| CREATION (?) | NOAH AND THE FLOOD | ABRAHAM (1800BC) | ISAAC | JACOB | JOSEPH | 1500BC |

GENESIS

In the beginning,
God spoke the universe
into creation.

WE MADE A

≥ **FILM** ≤

ABOUT IT!

Head to
gnbyouthedition.co.uk/creation
to watch it.

The Story of Creation

1 In the beginning, when God created the universe,* ²the earth was formless and desolate. The raging ocean that covered everything was engulfed in total darkness, and the Spirit of God* was moving over the water. ³Then God commanded, "Let there be light" — and light appeared. ⁴God was pleased with what he saw. Then he separated the light from the darkness, ⁵and he named the light "Day" and the darkness "Night". Evening passed and morning came — that was the first day.

⁶⁻⁷Then God commanded, "Let there be a dome to divide the water and to keep it in two separate places" — and it was done. So God made a dome, and it separated the water under it from the water above it. ⁸He named the dome "Sky". Evening passed and morning came — that was the second day.

⁹Then God commanded, "Let the water below the sky come together in one place, so that the land will appear" — and it was done. ¹⁰He named the land "Earth", and the water which had come together he named "Sea". And God was pleased with what he saw. ¹¹Then he commanded, "Let the earth produce all kinds of plants, those that bear grain and those that bear fruit" — and it was done. ¹²So the earth produced all kinds of plants, and God was pleased with what he saw. ¹³Evening passed and morning came — that was the third day.

¹⁴Then God commanded, "Let lights appear in the sky to separate day from night and to show the time when days, years, and religious festivals* begin; ¹⁵they will shine in the sky to give light to the earth" — and it was done. ¹⁶So God made the two larger lights, the sun to rule over the day and the moon to rule over the night; he also made the stars. ¹⁷He placed the lights in the sky to shine on the earth, ¹⁸to rule over the day and the night, and to separate light from darkness. And God was pleased with what he saw. ¹⁹Evening passed and morning came — that was the fourth day.

²⁰Then God commanded, "Let the water be filled with many kinds of living beings, and let the air be filled with birds." ²¹So God created the great sea monsters, all kinds of creatures that live in the water, and all kinds of birds. And God was pleased with what he saw. ²²He blessed them all and told the creatures that live in the water to reproduce, and to fill the sea, and he told the birds to increase in number. ²³Evening passed and morning came — that was the fifth day.

²⁴Then God commanded, "Let the earth produce all kinds of animal life: domestic and wild, large and small" — and it was done. ²⁵So God made them all, and he was pleased with what he saw.

²⁶Then God said, "And now we will make human beings; they will be like us and resemble us. They will have power over the fish, the birds, and all animals, domestic and wild,* large and small." ²⁷So God created human beings, making them to be like himself. He created them male and female, ²⁸blessed them, and said, "Have many children, so that your descendants will live all over the earth and bring it under their control. I am putting you in charge of the fish, the birds, and all the wild animals. ²⁹I have provided all kinds of grain and all kinds of fruit for you to eat;

....

1.1 *In the beginning… the universe*; or *In the beginning God created the universe*; or *When God began to create the universe*.
1.2 *the Spirit of God*; or *the power of God*; or *a wind from God*; or *an awesome wind*.
1.14 *religious festivals*; or *seasons*.
1.26 One ancient translation *animals, domestic and wild*; Hebrew *domestic animals and all the earth*.

23

Genesis
....
Exodus
Leviticus
Num.
Deuter.
Joshua

[30] but for all the wild animals and for all the birds I have provided grass and leafy plants for food" — and it was done. [31] God looked at everything he had made, and he was very pleased. Evening passed and morning came — that was the sixth day.

2 And so the whole universe was completed. [2] By the seventh day God finished what he had been doing and stopped working. [3] He blessed the seventh day and set it apart as a special day, because by that day he had completed his creation* and stopped working. [4] And that is how the universe was created.

The Garden of Eden

When the LORD God made the universe, [5] there were no plants on the earth and no seeds had sprouted, because he had not sent any rain, and there was no one to cultivate the land; [6] but water would come up from beneath the surface and water the ground.

[7] Then the LORD God took some soil from the ground and formed a man* out of it; he breathed life-giving breath into his nostrils and the man began to live.

[8] Then the LORD God planted a garden in Eden, in the East, and there he put the man he had formed. [9] He made all kinds of beautiful trees grow there and produce good fruit. In the middle of the garden stood the tree that gives life and the tree that gives knowledge of what is good and what is bad.*

[10] A stream flowed in Eden and watered the garden; beyond Eden it divided into four rivers. [11] The first river is the Pishon; it flows round the country of Havilah. [12] (Pure gold is found there and also rare perfume and precious stones.) [13] The second river is the Gihon; it flows round the country of Cush.* [14] The third river is the Tigris, which flows east of Assyria, and the fourth river is the Euphrates.

[15] Then the LORD God placed the man in the Garden of Eden to cultivate it and guard it. [16] He said to him, "You may eat the fruit of any tree in the garden, [17] except the tree that gives knowledge of what is good and what is bad.* You must not eat the fruit of that tree; if you do, you will die the same day."

[18] Then the LORD God said, "It is not good for the man to live alone. I will make a suitable companion to help him." [19] So he took some soil from the ground and formed all the animals and all the birds. Then he brought them to the man to see what he would name them; and that is how they all got their names. [20] So the man named all the birds and all the animals; but not one of them was a suitable companion to help him.

[21] Then the LORD God made the man fall into a deep sleep, and while he was sleeping, he took out one of the man's ribs and closed up the flesh. [22] He formed a woman out of the rib and brought her to him. [23] Then the man said,

"At last, here is one of my own kind —
Bone taken from my bone, and flesh from my flesh.
'Woman' is her name because she was taken out of man."*
[24] That is why a man leaves his father and mother and is united with his wife, and they become one.

GENESIS 1.1

GOD THE CREATOR!

2.3 by that day he had completed his creation; or on that day he completed his creation.
2.7 ground… man: The Hebrew words for "man" and "ground" have similar sounds.
2.9; 2.17 knowledge of what is good and what is bad; or knowledge of everything.
2.13 Cush (of Mesopotamia); or Ethiopia.
2.23 woman… man: The Hebrew words for "woman" and "man" have similar sounds.

25 The man and the woman were both naked, but they were not embarrassed.

Human Disobedience

3 Now the snake was the most cunning animal that the LORD God had made. The snake asked the woman, "Did God really tell you not to eat fruit from any tree in the garden?"

2 "We may eat the fruit of any tree in the garden," the woman answered, 3 "except the tree in the middle of it. God told us not to eat the fruit of that tree or even touch it; if we do, we will die."

4 The snake replied, "That's not true; you will not die. 5 God said that, because he knows that when you eat it you will be like God* and know what is good and what is bad."*

6 The woman saw how beautiful the tree was and how good its fruit would be to eat, and she thought how wonderful it would be to become wise. So she took some of the fruit and ate it. Then she gave some to her husband, and he also ate it. 7 As soon as they had eaten it, they were given understanding and realized that they were naked; so they sewed fig leaves together and covered themselves.

8 That evening they heard the LORD God walking in the garden, and they hid from him among the trees. 9 But the LORD God called out to the man, "Where are you?"

10 He answered, "I heard you in the garden; I was afraid and hid from you, because I was naked."

11 "Who told you that you were naked?" God asked. "Did you eat the fruit that I told you not to eat?"

12 The man answered, "The woman you put here with me gave me the fruit, and I ate it."

13 The LORD God asked the woman, "Why did you do this?"

She replied, "The snake tricked me into eating it."

God Pronounces Judgement

14 Then the LORD God said to the snake, "You will be punished for this; you alone of all the animals must bear this curse: from now on you will crawl on your belly, and you will have to eat dust as long as you live. 15 I will make you and the woman hate each other; her offspring and yours will always be enemies. Her offspring will crush your head, and you will bite her offspring's* heel."

16 And he said to the woman, "I will increase your trouble in pregnancy and your pain in giving birth. In spite of this, you will still have desire for your husband, yet you will be subject to him."

17 And he said to the man, "You listened to your wife and ate the fruit which I told you not to eat. Because of what you have done, the ground will be under a curse. You will have to work hard all your life to make it produce enough food for you. 18 It will produce weeds and thorns, and you will have to eat wild plants. 19 You will have to work hard and sweat to make the soil produce anything, until you go back to the soil from which you were formed. You were made from soil, and you will become soil again."

20 Adam* named his wife Eve,* because she was the mother of all human beings. 21 And the LORD God made clothes out of animal skins for Adam and his wife, and he clothed them.

....

3.5 *God*; or *the gods*.
3.5 *know what is good and what is bad*; or *know everything*.
3.15 *her offspring's*; or *their*.
3.20 *Adam*: This name in Hebrew means "humanity".
3.20 *Eve*: This name sounds similar to the Hebrew word for "living", which is rendered in this context as "human beings".

Genesis
··········

Exodus
Leviticus
Num.
Deuter.
Joshua

Adam and Eve are Sent Out of the Garden

22 Then the LORD God said, "Now the man has become like one of us and has knowledge of what is good and what is bad.* He must not be allowed to take fruit from the tree that gives life, eat it, and live for ever." 23 So the LORD God sent him out of the Garden of Eden and made him cultivate the soil from which he had been formed. 24 Then at the east side of the garden he put living creatures and a flaming sword which turned in all directions. This was to keep anyone from coming near the tree that gives life.

Cain and Abel

4 Then Adam had intercourse with his wife, and she became pregnant. She bore a son and said, "By the LORD's help I have acquired a son." So she named him Cain.* 2 Later she gave birth to another son, Abel. Abel became a shepherd, but Cain was a farmer. 3 After some time, Cain brought some of his harvest and gave it as an offering to the LORD. 4 Then Abel brought the first lamb born to one of his sheep, killed it, and gave the best parts of it as an offering. The LORD was pleased with Abel and his offering, 5 but he rejected Cain and his offering. Cain became furious, and he scowled in anger. 6 Then the LORD said to Cain, "Why are you angry? Why that scowl on your face? 7 If you had done the right thing, you would be smiling;* but because you have done evil, sin is crouching at your door. It wants to rule you, but you must overcome it."

8 Then Cain said to his brother Abel, "Let's go out in the fields."* When they were out in the fields, Cain turned on his brother and killed him.

9 The LORD asked Cain, "Where is your brother Abel?"

He answered, "I don't know. Am I supposed to take care of my brother?"

10 Then the LORD said, "Why have you done this terrible thing? Your brother's blood is crying out to me from the ground, like a voice calling for revenge. 11 You are placed under a curse and can no longer farm the soil. It has soaked up your brother's blood as if it had opened its mouth to receive it when you killed him. 12 If you try to grow crops, the soil will not produce anything; you will be a homeless wanderer on the earth."

13 And Cain said to the LORD, "This punishment is too hard for me to bear. 14 You are driving me off the land and away from your presence. I will be a homeless wanderer on the earth, and anyone who finds me will kill me."

15 But the LORD answered, "No. If anyone kills you, seven lives will be taken in revenge." So the LORD put a mark on Cain to warn anyone who met him not to kill him. 16 And Cain went away from the LORD's presence and lived in a land called "Wandering", which is east of Eden.

The Descendants of Cain

17 Cain and his wife had a son and named him Enoch. Then Cain built a city and named it after his son. 18 Enoch had a son named Irad, who was the father of Mehujael, and Mehujael had a son named Methushael, who was the father of Lamech. 19 Lamech had two wives, Adah and Zillah. 20 Adah gave birth to Jabal, who was the

---

3.22 *knowledge of what is good and what is bad; or knowledge of everything.*
4.1 *Cain: This name sounds like the Hebrew for "acquired".*
4.7 *you would be smiling; or I would have accepted your offering.*
4.8 *Some ancient translations Let's go out in the fields; Hebrew does not have these words.*

ancestor of those who raise livestock and live in tents. [21] His brother was Jubal, the ancestor of all musicians who play the harp and the flute. [22] Zillah gave birth to Tubal Cain, who made all kinds of tools* out of bronze and iron. The sister of Tubal Cain was Naamah. [23] Lamech said to his wives,

"Adah and Zillah, listen to me: I have killed a young man
          because he struck me.
[24] If seven lives are taken to pay for killing Cain,
    77 will be taken if anyone kills me."

Seth and Enosh
[25] Adam and his wife had another son. She said, "God has given me a son to replace Abel, whom Cain killed." So she named him Seth.* [26] Seth had a son whom he named Enosh. It was then that people began using the Lord's holy name in worship.

The Descendants of Adam
(1 Chr 1.1–4)

5 This is the list of the descendants of Adam. (When God created human beings, he made them like himself. [2] He created them male and female, blessed them, and named them "Humanity".) [3] When Adam was 130 years old, he had a son who was like him, and he named him Seth. [4] After that, Adam lived another 800 years. He had other children [5] and died at the age of 930.

[6] When Seth was 105, he had a son, Enosh, [7] and then lived another 807 years. He had other children [8] and died at the age of 912.

[9] When Enosh was ninety, he had a son, Kenan, [10] and then lived another 815 years. He had other children [11] and died at the age of 905.

[12] When Kenan was seventy, he had a son, Mahalalel, [13] and then lived another 840 years. He had other children [14] and died at the age of 910.

[15] When Mahalalel was 65, he had a son, Jared, [16] and then lived another 830 years. He had other children [17] and died at the age of 895.

[18] When Jared was 162, he had a son, Enoch, [19] and then lived another 800 years. He had other children [20] and died at the age of 962.

[21] When Enoch was 65, he had a son, Methuselah. [22] After that, Enoch lived in fellowship with God for 300 years and had other children. [23] He lived to be 365 years old. [24] He spent his life in fellowship with God, and then he disappeared, because God took him away.

[25] When Methuselah was 187, he had a son, Lamech, [26] and then lived another 782 years. He had other children [27] and died at the age of 969.

[28] When Lamech was 182, he had a son, [29] and said, "From the very ground on which the Lord put a curse, this child will bring us relief from all our hard work"; so he named him Noah.* [30] Lamech lived another 595 years. He had other children [31] and died at the age of 777.

[32] After Noah was 500 years old, he had three sons, Shem, Ham, and Japheth.

....

4.22 *who made all kinds of tools*; one ancient translation *ancestor of all metalworkers*.
4.25 *Seth*: This name sounds like the Hebrew for "has given".
5.29 *Noah*: This name sounds like the Hebrew for "relief".

GENESIS 6, 7

27

Genesis

..........:

Exodus
Leviticus
Num.
Deuter.
Joshua

Human Wickedness

6 When the human race had spread all over the world, and daughters were being born, [2]some of the heavenly beings* saw that these young women were beautiful, so they took the ones they liked. [3]Then the LORD said, "I will not allow people to live for ever; they are mortal. From now on they will live no longer than 120 years." [4]In those days, and even later, there were giants on the earth who were descendants of human women and the heavenly beings.* They were the great heroes and famous men of long ago.

[5]When the LORD saw how wicked everyone on earth was and how evil their thoughts were all the time, [6]he was sorry that he had ever made them and put them on the earth. He was so filled with regret [7]that he said, "I will wipe out these people I have created, and also the animals and the birds, because I am sorry that I made any of them." [8]But the LORD was pleased with Noah.

Noah

[9-10]This is the story of Noah. He had three sons, Shem, Ham, and Japheth. Noah had no faults and was the only good man of his time. He lived in fellowship with God, [11]but everyone else was evil in God's sight, and violence had spread everywhere. [12]God looked at the world and saw that it was evil, for the people were all living evil lives.

[13]God said to Noah, "I have decided to put an end to the whole human race. I will destroy them completely, because the world is full of their violent deeds. [14]Build a boat for yourself out of good timber; make rooms in it and cover it with tar inside and out. [15]Make it 133 metres long, 22 metres wide, and thirteen metres high. [16]Make a roof* for the boat and leave a space of 44 centimetres between the roof and the sides. Build it with three decks and put a door in the side. [17]I am going to send a flood on the earth to destroy every living being. Everything on the earth will die, [18]but I will make a covenant with you. Go into the boat with your wife, your sons, and their wives. [19-20]Take into the boat with you a male and a female of every kind of animal and of every kind of bird, in order to keep them alive. [21]Take along all kinds of food for you and for them." [22]Noah did everything that God commanded.

The Flood

7 The LORD said to Noah, "Go into the boat with your whole family; I have found that you are the only one in all the world who does what is right. [2]Take with you seven pairs of each kind of ritually clean animal, but only one pair of each kind of unclean animal. [3]Take also seven pairs of each kind of bird. Do this so that every kind of animal and bird will be kept alive to reproduce again on the earth. [4]Seven days from now I am going to send rain that will fall for forty days and nights, in order to destroy all the living beings that I have made." [5]And Noah did everything that the LORD commanded.

[6]Noah was 600 years old when the flood came on the earth. [7]He and his wife, and his sons and their wives, went into the boat to escape the flood. [8]A male and a female of every kind of animal and bird, whether ritually clean or unclean, [9]went into

6.2; 6.4 *heavenly beings*; or *sons of the gods*; or *sons of God.*
6.16 *roof*; or *window.*

the boat with Noah, as God had commanded. [10] Seven days later the flood came.

[11] When Noah was 600 years old, on the seventeenth day of the second month all the outlets of the vast body of water beneath the earth burst open, all the floodgates of the sky were opened, [12] and rain fell on the earth for forty days and nights. [13] On that same day Noah and his wife went into the boat with their three sons, Shem, Ham, and Japheth, and their wives. [14] With them went every kind of animal, domestic and wild, large and small, and every kind of bird. [15] A male and a female of each kind of living being went into the boat with Noah, [16] as God had commanded. Then the LORD shut the door behind Noah.

[17] The flood continued for forty days, and the water became deep enough for the boat to float. [18] The water became deeper, and the boat drifted on the surface. [19] It became so deep that it covered the highest mountains; [20] it went on rising until it was about seven metres above the tops of the mountains. [21] Every living being on the earth died — every bird, every animal, and every person. [22] Everything on earth that breathed died. [23] The LORD destroyed all living beings on the earth — human beings, animals, and birds. The only ones left were Noah and those who were with him in the boat. [24] The water did not start going down for 150 days.

The End of the Flood

8 God had not forgotten Noah and all the animals with him in the boat; he caused a wind to blow, and the water started going down. [2] The outlets of the water beneath the earth and the floodgates of the sky were closed. The rain stopped, [3] and the water gradually went down for 150 days. [4] On the seventeenth day of the seventh month the boat came to rest on a mountain in the Ararat range. [5] The water kept going down, and on the first day of the tenth month the tops of the mountains appeared.

[6] After forty days Noah opened a window [7] and sent out a raven. It did not come back, but kept flying around until the water was completely gone. [8] Meanwhile, Noah sent out a dove to see if the water had gone down, [9] but since the water still covered all the land, the dove did not find a place to alight. It flew back to the boat, and Noah reached out and took it in. [10] He waited another seven days and sent out the dove again. [11] It returned to him in the evening with a fresh olive leaf in its beak. So Noah knew that the water had gone down. [12] Then he waited another seven days and sent out the dove once more; this time it did not come back.

[13] When Noah was 601 years old, on the first day of the first month, the water was gone. Noah removed the covering of the boat, looked round, and saw that the ground was getting dry. [14] By the 27th day of the second month the earth was completely dry.

[15] God said to Noah, [16] "Go out of the boat with your wife, your sons, and their wives. [17] Take all the birds and animals out with you, so that they may reproduce and spread over all the earth." [18] So Noah went out of the boat with his wife, his sons, and their wives. [19] All the animals and birds went out of the boat in groups of their own kind.

Noah Offers a Sacrifice

[20] Noah built an altar to the LORD; he took one of each kind of ritually clean animal and bird, and burnt them whole as a sacrifice on the altar. [21] The odour of the sacrifice pleased the LORD, and he said to himself, "Never again will I put the earth under a curse

GENESIS 8.20

Noah chose to

MAKE
— SPACE —
FOR GOD

in the chaos of a
flood-torn world.

Altars were traditionally
made out of stone.

WHY NOT MAKE
A SMALL ALTAR

from stones and pebbles,
or even sticks that
you find lying around?
As you build it, consciously
make space for God to
meet with you.

GENESIS 8, 9

29

Genesis
....
Exodus
Leviticus
Num.
Deuter.
Joshua

because of what people do; I know that from the time they are young their thoughts are evil. Never again will I destroy all living beings, as I have done this time. ²²As long as the world exists, there will be a time for planting and a time for harvest. There will always be cold and heat, summer and winter, day and night."

God's Covenant with Noah

9 God blessed Noah and his sons and said, "Have many children, so that your descendants will live all over the earth. ²All the animals, birds, and fish will live in fear of you. They are all placed under your power. ³Now you can eat them, as well as green plants; I give them all to you for food. ⁴The one thing you must not eat is meat with blood still in it; I forbid this because the life is in the blood. ⁵If anyone takes human life, he will be punished. I will punish with death any animal that takes a human life. ⁶Human beings were made like God, so whoever murders one of them will be killed by someone else.

⁷"You must have many children, so that your descendants will live all over the earth."

⁸God said to Noah and his sons, ⁹"I am now making my covenant with you and with your descendants, ¹⁰and with all living beings — all birds and all animals — everything that came out of the boat with you. ¹¹With these words I make my covenant with you: I promise that never again will all living beings be destroyed by a flood; never again will a flood destroy the earth. ¹²As a sign of this everlasting covenant which I am making with you and with all living beings, ¹³I am putting my bow in the clouds. It will be the sign of my covenant with the world. ¹⁴Whenever I cover the sky with clouds and the rainbow appears, ¹⁵I will remember my promise to you and to all the animals that a flood will never again destroy all living beings. ¹⁶When the rainbow appears in the clouds, I will see it and remember the everlasting covenant between me and all living beings on earth. ¹⁷That is the sign of the promise which I am making to all living beings."

Noah and his Sons

¹⁸The sons of Noah who went out of the boat were Shem, Ham, and Japheth. (Ham was the father of Canaan.) ¹⁹These three sons of Noah were the ancestors of all the people on earth.

²⁰Noah, who was a farmer, was the first man to plant a vineyard. ²¹After he drank some of the wine, he became drunk, took off his clothes, and lay naked in his tent. ²²When Ham, the father of Canaan, saw that his father was naked, he went out and told his two brothers. ²³Then Shem and Japheth took a robe and held it behind them on their shoulders. They walked backwards into the tent and covered their father, keeping their faces turned away so as not to see him naked. ²⁴When Noah was sober again and learnt what his youngest son had done to him, ²⁵he said,

"A curse on Canaan!
He will be a slave to his brothers.
²⁶ Give praise to the LORD, the God of Shem!
Canaan will be the slave of Shem.
²⁷ May God cause Japheth* to increase!
May his descendants live with the people of Shem!
Canaan will be the slave of Japheth."

²⁸After the flood Noah lived for 350 years ²⁹and died at the age of 950.

9.27 *Japheth*: This name sounds like the Hebrew for "increase".

COVENANT

GENESIS 9.11;
GENESIS 17.7;
HEBREWS 10.16

Search for the Oxford or Cambridge Dictionary definition of 'covenant' and write the definition here.

The Descendants of Noah's Sons
(1 Chr 1.5–23)

10 These are the descendants of Noah's sons, Shem, Ham, and Japheth. These three had sons after the flood. ²The sons of Japheth — Gomer, Magog, Madai, Javan, Tubal, Meshech, and Tiras — were the ancestors of the peoples who bear their names. ³The descendants of Gomer were the people of Ashkenaz, Riphath, and Togarmah. ⁴The descendants of Javan were the people of Elishah, Spain, Cyprus, and Rhodes; ⁵they were the ancestors of the people who live along the coast and on the islands. These are the descendants of Japheth, living in their different tribes and countries, each group speaking its own language.

⁶The sons of Ham — Cush, Egypt, Libya and Canaan — were the ancestors of the peoples who bear their names. ⁷The descendants of Cush were the people of Seba, Havilah, Sabtah, Raamah, and Sabteca. The descendants of Raamah were the people of Sheba and Dedan. ⁸Cush had a son named Nimrod, who became the world's first great conqueror. ⁹By the LORD's help he was a great hunter, and that is why people say, "May the LORD make you as great a hunter as Nimrod!" ¹⁰At first his kingdom included Babylon, Erech, and Accad, all three of them in Babylonia. ¹¹From that land he went to Assyria and built the cities of Nineveh, Rehoboth Ir, Calah, ¹²and Resen, which is between Nineveh and the great city of Calah.

¹³The descendants of Egypt were the people of Lydia, Anam, Lehab, Naphtuh, ¹⁴Pathrus, Casluh, and of Crete, from whom the Philistines are descended.*

¹⁵Canaan's sons — Sidon, the eldest, and Heth — were the ancestors of the peoples who bear their names. ¹⁶Canaan was also the ancestor of the Jebusites, the Amorites, the Girgashites, ¹⁷the Hivites, the Arkites, the Sinites, ¹⁸the Arvadites, the Zemarites, and the Hamathites. The different tribes of the Canaanites spread out, ¹⁹until the Canaanite borders reached from Sidon southwards to Gerar near Gaza, and eastwards to Sodom, Gomorrah, Admah, and Zeboiim near Lasha. ²⁰These are the descendants of Ham, living in their different tribes and countries, each group speaking its own language.

²¹Shem, the elder brother of Japheth, was the ancestor of all the Hebrews. ²²Shem's sons — Elam, Asshur, Arpachshad, Lud, and Aram — were the ancestors of the peoples who bear their names. ²³The descendants of Aram were the people of Uz, Hul, Gether, and Meshek. ²⁴Arpachshad was the father of Shelah, who was the father of Eber. ²⁵Eber had two sons: one was named Peleg,* because during his time the people of the world were divided; and the other was named Joktan. ²⁶The descendants of Joktan were the people of Almodad, Sheleph, Hazarmaveth, Jerah, ²⁷Hadoram, Uzal, Diklah, ²⁸Obal, Abimael, Sheba, ²⁹Ophir, Havilah, and Jobab. All of them were descended from Joktan. ³⁰The land in which they lived extended from Mesha to Sephar in the eastern hill country. ³¹These are the descendants of Shem, living in their different tribes and countries, each group speaking its own language.

³²All these peoples are the descendants of Noah, nation by nation, according to their different lines of descent. After the flood all the nations of the earth were descended from the sons of Noah.

....

10.14 Probable text *and of Crete… descended*; Hebrew *from whom the Philistines are descended, and Crete.*
10.25 *Peleg*: This name sounds like the Hebrew for "divide".

31

Genesis
....

Exodus
Leviticus
Num.
Deuter.
Joshua

The Tower of Babylon

11 At first, the people of the whole world had only one language and used the same words. [2] As they wandered about in the East, they came to a plain in Babylonia and settled there. [3] They said to one another, "Come on! Let's make bricks and bake them hard." So they had bricks to build with and tar to hold them together. [4] They said, "Now let's build a city with a tower that reaches the sky, so that we can make a name for ourselves and not be scattered all over the earth."

[5] Then the LORD came down to see the city and the tower which those men had built, [6] and he said, "Now then, these are all one people and they speak one language; this is just the beginning of what they are going to do. Soon they will be able to do anything they want! [7] Let us go down and mix up their language so that they will not understand one another." [8] So the LORD scattered them all over the earth, and they stopped building the city. [9] The city was called Babylon,* because there the LORD mixed up the language of all the people, and from there he scattered them all over the earth.

The Descendants of Shem
(1 Chr 1.24–27)

[10] These are the descendants of Shem. Two years after the flood, when Shem was 100 years old, he had a son, Arpachshad. [11] After that, he lived another 500 years and had other children.

[12] When Arpachshad was 35 years old, he had a son, Shelah; [13] after that, he lived another 403 years and had other children.

[14] When Shelah was thirty years old, he had a son, Eber; [15] after that, he lived another 403 years and had other children.

[16] When Eber was 34 years old, he had a son, Peleg; [17] after that, he lived another 430 years and had other children.

[18] When Peleg was thirty years old, he had a son, Reu; [19] after that, he lived another 209 years and had other children.

[20] When Reu was 32 years old, he had a son, Serug; [21] after that, he lived another 207 years and had other children.

[22] When Serug was thirty years old, he had a son, Nahor; [23] after that, he lived another 200 years and had other children.

[24] When Nahor was 29 years old, he had a son, Terah; [25] after that, he lived another 119 years and had other children.

[26] After Terah was seventy years old, he became the father of Abram, Nahor, and Haran.

The Descendants of Terah

[27] These are the descendants of Terah, who was the father of Abram, Nahor, and Haran. Haran was the father of Lot, [28] and Haran died in his native city, Ur in Babylonia, while his father was still living. [29] Abram married Sarai, and Nahor married Milcah, the daughter of Haran, who was also the father of Iscah. [30] Sarai was not able to have children.

[31] Terah took his son Abram, his grandson Lot, who was the son of Haran, and his daughter-in-law Sarai, Abram's wife, and with them he left the city of Ur in Babylonia to go to the land of Canaan. They went as far as Haran and settled there. [32] Terah died there at the age of 205.

God's Call to Abram

12 The LORD said to Abram, "Leave your country, your relatives, and your father's home, and go to a land that I am going

11.9 *Babylon*: This name sounds like the Hebrew for "mixed up".

TURN THESE LINES INTO A PICTURE OF SOMETHING.

to show you. [2] I will give you many descendants, and they will become a great nation. I will bless you and make your name famous, so that you will be a blessing.
[3] I will bless those who bless you,
But I will curse those who curse you.
And through you I will bless all the nations."*

[4] When Abram was 75 years old, he started out from Haran, as the LORD had told him to do; and Lot went with him. [5] Abram took his wife Sarai, his nephew Lot, and all the wealth and all the slaves they had acquired in Haran, and they started out for the land of Canaan.

When they arrived in Canaan, [6] Abram travelled through the land until he came to the sacred tree of Moreh, the holy place at Shechem. (At that time the Canaanites were still living in the land.) [7] The LORD appeared to Abram and said to him, "This is the country that I am going to give to your descendants." Then Abram built an altar there to the LORD, who had appeared to him. [8] After that, he moved on south to the hill country east of the city of Bethel and set up his camp between Bethel on the west and Ai on the east. There also he built an altar and worshipped the LORD. [9] Then he moved on from place to place, going towards the southern part of Canaan.

Abram in Egypt

[10] But there was a famine in Canaan, and it was so bad that Abram went farther south to Egypt, to live there for a while. [11] When he was about to cross the border into Egypt, he said to his wife Sarai, "You are a beautiful woman. [12] When the Egyptians see you, they will assume that you are my wife, and so they will kill me and let you live. [13] Tell them that you are my sister; then because of you they will let me live and treat me well." [14] When he crossed the border into Egypt, the Egyptians did see that his wife was beautiful. [15] Some of the court officials saw her and told the king how beautiful she was; so she was taken to his palace. [16] Because of her the king treated Abram well and gave him flocks of sheep and goats, cattle, donkeys, slaves, and camels.

[17] But because the king had taken Sarai, the LORD sent terrible diseases on him and on the people of his palace. [18] Then the king sent for Abram and asked him, "What have you done to me? Why didn't you tell me that she was your wife? [19] Why did you say that she was your sister, and let me take her as my wife? Here is your wife; take her and get out!" [20] The king gave orders to his men, so they took Abram and put him out of the country, together with his wife and everything he owned.

Abram and Lot Separate

13 Abram went north out of Egypt to the southern part of Canaan with his wife and everything he owned, and Lot went with him. [2] Abram was a very rich man, with sheep, goats, and cattle, as well as silver and gold. [3] Then he left there and moved from place to place, going towards Bethel. He reached the place between Bethel and Ai where he had camped before [4] and had built an altar. There he worshipped the LORD.

[5] Lot also had sheep, goats, and cattle, as well as his own family and servants. [6] And so there was not enough pasture land for the two of them to stay together, because they had too many animals.

....

12.3 *And through… nations;* or *All the nations will ask me to bless them as I have blessed you.*

[7] So quarrels broke out between the men who took care of Abram's animals and those who took care of Lot's animals. (At that time the Canaanites and the Perizzites were still living in the land.) [8] Then Abram said to Lot, "We are relatives, and your men and my men shouldn't be quarrelling. [9] So let's separate. Choose any part of the land you want. You go one way, and I'll go the other." [10] Lot looked round and saw that the whole Jordan Valley, all the way to Zoar, had plenty of water, like the Garden of the LORD* or like the land of Egypt. (This was before the LORD had destroyed the cities of Sodom and Gomorrah.) [11] So Lot chose the whole Jordan Valley for himself and moved away towards the east. That is how the two men parted. [12] Abram stayed in the land of Canaan, and Lot settled among the cities in the valley and camped near Sodom, [13] whose people were wicked and sinned against the LORD.

Abram Moves to Hebron

[14] After Lot had left, the LORD said to Abram, "From where you are, look carefully in all directions. [15] I am going to give you and your descendants all the land that you see, and it will be yours for ever. [16] I am going to give you so many descendants that no one will be able to count them all; it would be as easy to count all the specks of dust on earth! [17] Now, go and look over the whole land, because I am going to give it all to you." [18] So Abram moved his camp and settled near the sacred trees of Mamre at Hebron, and there he built an altar to the LORD.

Abram Rescues Lot

14 Four kings, Amraphel of Babylonia, Arioch of Ellasar, Chedorlaomer of Elam, and Tidal of Goiim, [2] went to war against five other kings: Bera of Sodom, Birsha of Gomorrah, Shinab of Admah, Shemeber of Zeboiim, and the king of Bela (or Zoar). [3] These five kings had formed an alliance and joined forces in the Valley of Siddim, which is now the Dead Sea. [4] They had been under the control of Chedorlaomer for twelve years, but in the thirteenth year they rebelled against him. [5] In the fourteenth year Chedorlaomer and his allies came with their armies and defeated the Rephaim in Ashteroth Karnaim, the Zuzim in Ham, the Emim in the plain of Kiriathaim, [6] and the Horites in the mountains of Edom, pursuing them as far as Elparan on the edge of the desert. [7] Then they turned round and came back to Kadesh (then known as Enmishpat). They conquered all the land of the Amalekites and defeated the Amorites who lived in Hazazon Tamar.

[8] Then the kings of Sodom, Gomorrah, Admah, Zeboiim, and Bela drew up their armies for battle in the Valley of Siddim and fought [9] against the kings of Elam, Goiim, Babylonia, and Ellasar, five kings against four. [10] The valley was full of tar pits, and when the kings of Sodom and Gomorrah tried to run away from the battle, they fell into the pits; but the other three kings escaped to the mountains. [11] The four kings took everything in Sodom and Gomorrah, including the food, and went away. [12] Lot, Abram's nephew, was living in Sodom, so they took him and all his possessions.

[13] But a man escaped and reported all this to Abram, the Hebrew, who was living near the sacred trees belonging to Mamre the Amorite. Mamre and his brothers Eshcol and Aner were Abram's

....

13.10 *Garden of the LORD*: a reference to the Garden of Eden.

allies. [14] When Abram heard that his nephew had been captured, he called together all the fighting men in his camp, 318 in all, and pursued the four kings all the way to Dan. [15] There he divided his men into groups, attacked the enemy by night, and defeated them. He chased them as far as Hobah, north of Damascus, [16] and recovered the loot that had been taken. He also brought back his nephew Lot and his possessions, together with the women and the other prisoners.

Melchizedek Blesses Abram

[17] When Abram came back from his victory over Chedorlaomer and the other kings, the king of Sodom went out to meet him in the Valley of Shaveh (also called the King's Valley). [18] And Melchizedek, who was king of Salem and also a priest of the Most High God, brought bread and wine to Abram, [19] blessed him, and said, "May the Most High God, who made heaven and earth, bless Abram! [20] May the Most High God, who gave you victory over your enemies, be praised!" And Abram gave Melchizedek a tenth of all the loot he had recovered.

[21] The king of Sodom said to Abram, "Keep the loot, but give me back all my people."

[22] Abram answered, "I solemnly swear before the LORD, the Most High God, Maker of heaven and earth, [23] that I will not keep anything of yours, not even a thread or a sandal strap. Then you can never say, 'I am the one who made Abram rich.' [24] I will take nothing for myself. I will accept only what my men have used. But let my allies, Aner, Eshcol, and Mamre, take their share."

God's Covenant with Abram

15 After this, Abram had a vision and heard the LORD say to him, "Do not be afraid, Abram. I will shield you from danger and give you a great reward."

[2] But Abram answered, "Sovereign LORD, what good will your reward do me, since I have no children? My only heir is Eliezer of Damascus.* [3] You have given me no children, and one of my slaves will inherit my property."

[4] Then he heard the LORD speaking to him again: "This slave Eliezer will not inherit your property; your own son will be your heir." [5] The LORD took him outside and said, "Look at the sky and try to count the stars; you will have as many descendants as that."

[6] Abram put his trust in the LORD, and because of this the LORD was pleased with him and accepted him.

[7] Then the LORD said to him, "I am the LORD, who led you out of Ur in Babylonia, to give you this land as your own."

[8] But Abram asked, "Sovereign LORD, how can I know that it will be mine?"

[9] He answered, "Bring me a cow, a goat, and a ram, each of them three years old, and a dove and a pigeon." [10] Abram brought the animals to God, cut them in half, and placed the halves opposite each other in two rows; but he did not cut up the birds. [11] Vultures came down on the bodies, but Abram drove them off.

[12] When the sun was going down, Abram fell into a deep sleep, and fear and terror came over him. [13] The LORD said to him, "Your descendants will be strangers in a foreign land; they will be slaves there and will be treated cruelly for 400 years. [14] But I will punish the nation that enslaves them, and when they leave that foreign land, they will take great wealth with them. [15] You yourself will

---

GENESIS 15.5

God's promises for us far

OUTWEIGH THE
DREAMS

we might have.

God's promise for
Abraham was of
uncountable descendants.

Go outside when it is
dark and the stars are
out, and reflect on the
fact that God and
his promises are
much greater than
you could imagine.

GENESIS 15–17

35

Genesis

·········

Exodus

Leviticus

Num.

Deuter.

Joshua

live to a ripe old age, die in peace, and be buried. [16] It will be four generations before your descendants come back here, because I will not drive out the Amorites until they become so wicked that they must be punished."

[17] When the sun had set and it was dark, a smoking fire-pot and a flaming torch suddenly appeared and passed between the pieces of the animals. [18] Then and there the LORD made a covenant with Abram. He said, "I promise to give your descendants all this land from the border of Egypt to the River Euphrates, [19] including the lands of the Kenites, the Kenizzites, the Kadmonites, [20] the Hittites, the Perizzites, the Rephaim, [21] the Amorites, the Canaanites, the Girgashites, and the Jebusites."

Hagar and Ishmael

16 Abram's wife Sarai had not borne him any children. But she had an Egyptian slave woman named Hagar, [2] and so she said to Abram, "The LORD has kept me from having children. Why don't you sleep with my slave? Perhaps she can have a child for me." Abram agreed with what Sarai said. [3] So she gave Hagar to him to be his concubine. (This happened after Abram had lived in Canaan for ten years.) [4] Abram had intercourse with Hagar, and she became pregnant. When she found out that she was pregnant, she became proud and despised Sarai.

[5] Then Sarai said to Abram, "It's your fault that Hagar despises me.* I myself gave her to you, and ever since she found out that she was pregnant, she has despised me. May the LORD judge which of us is right, you or me!"

[6] Abram answered, "Very well, she is your slave and under your control; do whatever you want with her." Then Sarai treated Hagar so cruelly that she ran away.

[7] The angel of the LORD met Hagar at a spring in the desert on the road to Shur [8] and said, "Hagar, slave of Sarai, where have you come from and where are you going?"

She answered, "I am running away from my mistress."

[9] He said, "Go back to her and be her slave." [10] Then he said, "I will give you so many descendants that no one will be able to count them. [11] You are going to have a son, and you will name him Ishmael,* because the LORD has heard your cry of distress. [12] But your son will live like a wild donkey; he will be against everyone, and everyone will be against him. He will live apart from all his relatives."

[13] Hagar asked herself, "Have I really seen God and lived to tell about it?"* So she called the LORD who had spoken to her "A God who Sees". [14] That is why people call the well between Kadesh and Bered "The Well of the Living One who Sees Me".

[15] Hagar bore Abram a son, and he named him Ishmael. [16] Abram was 86 years old at the time.

Circumcision, the Sign of the Covenant

17 When Abram was 99 years old, the LORD appeared to him and said, "I am the Almighty God. Obey me and always do what is right. [2] I will make my covenant with you and give you many descendants." [3] Abram bowed down with his face touching the ground, and God said, [4] "I make this covenant with you: I promise that you will be the ancestor of many nations. [5] Your

---

16.5 *It's your fault… me;* or *May you suffer for this wrong done against me.*
16.11 *Ishmael:* This name in Hebrew means "God hears".
16.13 Probable text *lived to tell about it?*; Hebrew unclear.

name will no longer be Abram, but Abraham,* because I am making you the ancestor of many nations. ⁶I will give you many descendants, and some of them will be kings. You will have so many descendants that they will become nations.

⁷"I will keep my promise to you and to your descendants in future generations as an everlasting covenant. I will be your God and the God of your descendants. ⁸I will give to you and to your descendants this land in which you are now a foreigner. The whole land of Canaan will belong to your descendants for ever, and I will be their God."

⁹God said to Abraham, "You also must agree to keep the covenant with me, both you and your descendants in future generations. ¹⁰You and your descendants must all agree to circumcise every male among you. ¹¹⁻¹²From now on you must circumcise every baby boy when he is eight days old, including slaves born in your homes and slaves bought from foreigners. This will show that there is a covenant between you and me. ¹³Each one must be circumcised, and this will be a physical sign to show that my covenant with you is everlasting. ¹⁴Any male who has not been circumcised will no longer be considered one of my people, because he has not kept the covenant with me."

¹⁵God said to Abraham, "You must no longer call your wife Sarai; from now on her name is Sarah.* ¹⁶I will bless her, and I will give you a son by her. I will bless her, and she will become the mother of nations, and there will be kings among her descendants."

¹⁷Abraham bowed down with his face touching the ground, but he began to laugh when he thought, "Can a man have a child when he is a hundred years old? Can Sarah have a child at ninety?" ¹⁸He asked God, "Why not let Ishmael be my heir?"

¹⁹But God said, "No. Your wife Sarah will bear you a son and you will name him Isaac.* I will keep my covenant with him and with his descendants for ever. It is an everlasting covenant. ²⁰I have heard your request about Ishmael, so I will bless him and give him many children and many descendants. He will be the father of twelve princes, and I will make a great nation of his descendants. ²¹But I will keep my covenant with your son Isaac, who will be born to Sarah about this time next year." ²²When God finished speaking to Abraham, he left him.

²³On that same day Abraham obeyed God and circumcised his son Ishmael and all the other males in his household, including the slaves born in his home and those he had bought. ²⁴Abraham was 99 years old when he was circumcised, ²⁵and his son Ishmael was thirteen. ²⁶They were both circumcised on the same day, ²⁷together with all Abraham's slaves.

A Son is Promised to Abraham

18 The LORD appeared to Abraham at the sacred trees of Mamre. As Abraham was sitting at the entrance of his tent during the hottest part of the day, ²he looked up and saw three men standing there. As soon as he saw them, he ran out to meet them. Bowing down with his face touching the ground, ³he said, "Sirs, please do not pass by my home without stopping; I am here to serve you. ⁴Let me bring some water for you to wash your feet; you can rest here beneath this tree. ⁵I will also bring a bit

17.5 *Abraham*: This name sounds like the Hebrew for "ancestor of many nations".
17.15 *Sarah*: This name in Hebrew means "princess".
17.19 *Isaac*: This name in Hebrew means "he laughs".

Genesis
....

Exodus
Leviticus
Num.
Deuter.
Joshua

of food; it will give you strength to continue your journey. You have honoured me by coming to my home, so let me serve you."

They replied, "Thank you; we accept."

[6] Abraham hurried into the tent and said to Sarah, "Quick, take a sack of your best flour, and bake some bread." [7] Then he ran to the herd and picked out a calf that was tender and fat, and gave it to a servant, who hurried to get it ready. [8] He took some cream, some milk, and the meat, and set the food before the men. There under the tree he served them himself, and they ate.

[9] Then they asked him, "Where is your wife Sarah?"

"She is there in the tent," he answered.

[10] One of them said, "Nine months from now* I will come back, and your wife Sarah will have a son."

Sarah was behind him, at the door of the tent, listening. [11] Abraham and Sarah were very old, and Sarah had stopped having her monthly periods. [12] So Sarah laughed to herself and said, "Now that I am old and worn out, can I still enjoy sex? And besides, my husband is old too."

[13] Then the LORD asked Abraham, "Why did Sarah laugh and say, 'Can I really have a child when I am so old?' [14] Is anything too hard for the LORD? As I said, nine months from now I will return, and Sarah will have a son."

[15] Because Sarah was afraid, she denied it. "I didn't laugh," she said.

"Yes, you did," he replied. "You laughed."

Abraham Pleads for Sodom

[16] Then the men left and went to a place where they could look down at Sodom, and Abraham went with them to send them on their way. [17] And the LORD said to himself, "I will not hide from Abraham what I am going to do. [18] His descendants will become a great and mighty nation, and through him I will bless all the nations.* [19] I have chosen him in order that he may command his sons and his descendants to obey me and to do what is right and just. If they do, I will do everything for him that I have promised."

[20] Then the LORD said to Abraham, "There are terrible accusations against Sodom and Gomorrah, and their sin is very great. [21] I must go down to find out whether or not the accusations which I have heard are true."

[22] Then the two men left and went on towards Sodom, but the LORD remained with Abraham. [23] Abraham approached the LORD and asked, "Are you really going to destroy the innocent with the guilty? [24] If there are fifty innocent people in the city, will you destroy the whole city? Won't you spare it in order to save the fifty? [25] Surely you won't kill the innocent with the guilty. That's impossible! You can't do that. If you did, the innocent would be punished along with the guilty. That is impossible. The judge of all the earth has to act justly."

[26] The LORD answered, "If I find fifty innocent people in Sodom, I will spare the whole city for their sake."

[27] Abraham spoke again: "Please forgive my boldness in continuing to speak to you, Lord. I am only a man and have no right to say anything. [28] But perhaps there will be only 45 innocent people instead of fifty. Will you destroy the whole city because there are five too few?"

18.10 *Nine months from now*; or *This time next year.*
18.18 *through... nations*; or *all the nations will ask me to bless them as I have blessed him.*

STOP READING AND PRAY FOR ONE MINUTE.

It doesn't matter what it's about - just talk to God!

The Lord answered, "I will not destroy the city if I find 45 innocent people."

29 Abraham spoke again: "Perhaps there will be only forty."

He replied, "I will not destroy it if there are forty."

30 Abraham said, "Please don't be angry, Lord, but I must speak again. What if there are only thirty?"

He said, "I will not do it if I find thirty."

31 Abraham said, "Please forgive my boldness in continuing to speak to you, Lord. Suppose that only twenty are found?"

He said, "I will not destroy the city if I find twenty."

32 Abraham said, "Please don't be angry, Lord, and I will speak just once more. What if only ten are found?"

He said, "I will not destroy it if there are ten." 33 After he had finished speaking with Abraham, the Lord went away, and Abraham returned home.

The Sinfulness of Sodom

19 When the two angels came to Sodom that evening, Lot was sitting at the city gate. As soon as he saw them, he got up and went to meet them. He bowed down before them 2 and said, "Sirs, I am here to serve you. Please come to my house. You can wash your feet and stay the night. In the morning you can get up early and go on your way."

But they answered, "No, we will spend the night here in the city square."

3 He kept on urging them, and finally they went with him to his house. Lot ordered his servants to bake some bread and prepare a fine meal for the guests. When it was ready, they ate it.

4 Before the guests went to bed, the men of Sodom surrounded the house. All the men of the city, both young and old, were there. 5 They called out to Lot and asked, "Where are the men who came to stay with you tonight? Bring them out to us!" The men of Sodom wanted to have sex with them.

6 Lot went outside and closed the door behind him. 7 He said to them, "Friends, I beg you, don't do such a wicked thing! 8 Look, I have two daughters who are still virgins. Let me bring them out to you, and you can do whatever you want with them. But don't do anything to these men; they are guests in my house, and I must protect them."

9 But they said, "Get out of our way, you foreigner! Who are you to tell us what to do? Out of our way, or we will treat you worse than them." They pushed Lot back and moved up to break down the door. 10 But the two men inside reached out, pulled Lot back into the house, and shut the door. 11 Then they struck all the men outside with blindness, so that they couldn't find the door.

Lot Leaves Sodom

12 The two men said to Lot, "If you have anyone else here — sons, daughters, sons-in-law, or any other relatives living in the city — get them out of here, 13 because we are going to destroy this place. The Lord has heard the terrible accusations against these people and has sent us to destroy Sodom."

14 Then Lot went to the men that his daughters were going to marry, and said, "Hurry up and get out of here; the Lord is going to destroy this place." But they thought he was joking.

15 At dawn the angels tried to make Lot hurry. "Quick!" they said. "Take your wife and your two daughters and get out, so that you will not lose your lives when the city is destroyed." 16 Lot hesitated. The Lord, however, had pity on him; so the men took

39

Genesis
·········:·

Exodus
Leviticus
Num.
Deuter.
Joshua

him, his wife, and his two daughters by the hand and led them out of the city. [17] Then one of the angels said, "Run for your lives! Don't look back and don't stop in the valley. Run to the hills, so that you won't be killed."

[18] But Lot answered, "No, please don't make us do that, sir. [19] You have done me a great favour and saved my life. But the hills are too far away; the disaster will overtake me, and I will die before I get there. [20] Do you see that little town? It is near enough. Let me go over there — you can see it is just a small place — and I will be safe."

[21] He answered, "All right, I agree. I won't destroy that town. [22] Hurry! Run! I can't do anything until you get there."

Because Lot called it small, the town was named Zoar.*

The Destruction of Sodom and Gomorrah

[23] The sun was rising when Lot reached Zoar. [24] Suddenly the LORD rained burning sulphur on the cities of Sodom and Gomorrah [25] and destroyed them and the whole valley, along with all the people there and everything that grew on the land. [26] But Lot's wife looked back and was turned into a pillar of salt.

[27] Early the next morning Abraham hurried to the place where he had stood in the presence of the LORD. [28] He looked down at Sodom and Gomorrah and the whole valley and saw smoke rising from the land, like smoke from a huge furnace. [29] But when God destroyed the cities of the valley where Lot was living, he kept Abraham in mind and allowed Lot to escape to safety.

The Origin of the Moabites and Ammonites

[30] Because Lot was afraid to stay in Zoar, he and his two daughters moved up into the hills and lived in a cave. [31] The elder daughter said to her sister, "Our father is getting old, and there are no men in the whole world* to marry us so that we can have children. [32] Come on, let's make our father drunk, so that we can sleep with him and have children by him." [33] That night they gave him wine to drink, and the elder daughter had intercourse with him. But he was so drunk that he didn't know it.

[34] The next day the elder daughter said to her sister, "I slept with him last night; now let's make him drunk again tonight, and you sleep with him. Then each of us will have a child by our father." [35] So that night they made him drunk, and the younger daughter had intercourse with him. Again he was so drunk that he didn't know it. [36] In this way both of Lot's daughters became pregnant by their own father. [37] The elder daughter had a son, whom she named Moab.* He was the ancestor of the present-day Moabites. [38] The younger daughter also had a son, whom she named Benammi.* He was the ancestor of the present-day Ammonites.

Abraham and Abimelech

20 Abraham moved from Mamre to the southern part of Canaan and lived between Kadesh and Shur. Later, while he was living in Gerar, [2] he said that his wife Sarah was his sister. So King Abimelech of Gerar had Sarah brought to him. [3] One night

....

19.22 *Zoar*: This name sounds like the Hebrew for "small".
19.31 *the whole world*; or *this land*.
19.37 *Moab*: This name sounds like the Hebrew for "from my father".
19.38 *Benammi*: This name in Hebrew means "son of my relative" and sounds like the Hebrew for "Ammonite".

God appeared to him in a dream and said: "You are going to die, because you have taken this woman; she is already married."

⁴But Abimelech had not come near her, and he said, "Lord, I am innocent! Would you destroy me and my people? ⁵Abraham himself said that she was his sister, and she said the same thing. I did this with a clear conscience, and I have done no wrong."

⁶God replied in the dream, "Yes, I know that you did it with a clear conscience; so I kept you from sinning against me and did not let you touch her. ⁷But now, give the woman back to her husband. He is a prophet, and he will pray for you, so that you will not die. But if you do not give her back, I warn you that you are going to die, you and all your people."

⁸Early the next morning Abimelech called all his officials and told them what had happened, and they were terrified. ⁹Then Abimelech called Abraham and asked, "What have you done to us? What wrong have I done to you to make you bring this disaster on me and my kingdom? No one should ever do what you have done to me. ¹⁰Why did you do it?"

¹¹Abraham answered, "I thought that there would be no one here who has reverence for God and that they would kill me to get my wife. ¹²She really is my sister. She is the daughter of my father, but not of my mother, and I married her. ¹³So when God sent me from my father's house into foreign lands, I said to her, 'You can show how loyal you are to me by telling everyone that I am your brother.'"

¹⁴Then Abimelech gave Sarah back to Abraham, and at the same time he gave him sheep, cattle, and slaves. ¹⁵He said to Abraham, "Here is my whole land; live anywhere you like." ¹⁶He said to Sarah, "I am giving your brother a thousand pieces of silver as proof to all who are with you that you are innocent; everyone will know that you have done no wrong."

¹⁷⁻¹⁸Because of what had happened to Sarah, Abraham's wife, the LORD had made it impossible for any woman in Abimelech's palace to have children. So Abraham prayed for Abimelech, and God healed him. He also healed his wife and his slave women, so that they could have children.

The Birth of Isaac

21 The LORD blessed Sarah, as he had promised, ²and she became pregnant and bore a son to Abraham when he was old. The boy was born at the time God had said he would be born. ³Abraham named him Isaac, ⁴and when Isaac was eight days old, Abraham circumcised him, as God had commanded. ⁵Abraham was a hundred years old when Isaac was born. ⁶Sarah said, "God has brought me joy and laughter.* Everyone who hears about it will laugh with me." ⁷Then she added, "Who would have said to Abraham that Sarah would nurse children? Yet I have borne him a son in his old age."

⁸The child grew, and on the day that he was weaned, Abraham gave a great feast.

Hagar and Ishmael are Sent Away

⁹One day Ishmael, whom Hagar the Egyptian had borne to Abraham, was playing with* Sarah's son Isaac.* ¹⁰Sarah saw them

....

21.6 *laughter*: The name Isaac in Hebrew means "he laughs" (see also 17.17–19).
21.9 *playing with*; or *making fun of*.
21.9 Some ancient translations *with Sarah's son Isaac*; Hebrew does not have these words.

Genesis
....

Exodus
Leviticus
Num.
Deuter.
Joshua

and said to Abraham, "Send this slave and her son away. The son of this woman must not get any part of your wealth, which my son Isaac should inherit." [11] This troubled Abraham very much, because Ishmael was also his son. [12] But God said to Abraham, "Don't be worried about the boy and your slave Hagar. Do whatever Sarah tells you, because it is through Isaac that you will have the descendants I have promised. [13] I will also give many children to the son of the slave woman, so that they will become a nation. He too is your son."

[14] Early the next morning Abraham gave Hagar some food and a leather bag full of water. He put the child on her back and sent her away. She left and wandered about in the wilderness of Beersheba. [15] When the water was all gone, she left the child under a bush [16] and sat down about a hundred metres away. She said to herself, "I can't bear to see my child die." While she was sitting there, she* began to cry.

[17] God heard the boy crying, and from heaven the angel of God spoke to Hagar, "What are you troubled about, Hagar? Don't be afraid. God has heard the boy crying. [18] Get up, go and pick him up, and comfort him. I will make a great nation out of his descendants." [19] Then God opened her eyes, and she saw a well. She went and filled the leather bag with water and gave some to the boy. [20] God was with the boy as he grew up; he lived in the wilderness of Paran and became a skilful hunter. [21] His mother found an Egyptian wife for him.

The Agreement between Abraham and Abimelech

[22] At that time Abimelech went with Phicol, the commander of his army, and said to Abraham, "God is with you in everything you do. [23] So make a vow here in the presence of God that you will not deceive me, my children, or my descendants. I have been loyal to you, so promise that you will also be loyal to me and to this country in which you are living."

[24] Abraham said, "I promise."

[25] Abraham complained to Abimelech about a well which the servants of Abimelech had seized. [26] Abimelech said, "I don't know who did this. You didn't tell me about it, and this is the first I have heard of it." [27] Then Abraham gave some sheep and cattle to Abimelech, and the two of them made an agreement. [28] Abraham separated seven lambs from his flock, [29] and Abimelech asked him, "Why did you do that?"

[30] Abraham answered, "Accept these seven lambs. By doing this, you admit that I am the one who dug this well." [31] And so the place was called Beersheba,* because it was there that the two of them made a vow.

[32] After they had made this agreement at Beersheba, Abimelech and Phicol went back to Philistia. [33] Then Abraham planted a tamarisk tree in Beersheba and worshipped the LORD, the Everlasting God. [34] Abraham lived in Philistia for a long time.

God Commands Abraham to Offer Isaac

22 Some time later God tested Abraham; he called to him, "Abraham!" And Abraham answered, "Yes, here I am!"

[2] "Take your son," God said, "your only son, Isaac, whom you love so much, and go to the land of Moriah. There on a mountain that I will show you, offer him as a sacrifice to me."

....

21.16 *she*; one ancient translation *the child*.
21.31 *Beersheba*: This name in Hebrew means "Well of the Vow" or "Well of Seven" (see also 26.33).

GENESIS 22.1-14

There are many details in the Bible that seem insignificant at first glance but, when you look deeper, are very profound.

Take this story.

Abraham tells Isaac that God will provide a lamb. However, after being stopped by the angel, Abraham finds a ram instead. Is this a mistake, or could it be a

• REFERENCE TO •

SOMETHING ELSE?

God doesn't provide a lamb for Abraham. But centuries later, on a hill in the same area, the 'lamb of God' - Jesus - is finally sacrificed for all human beings.

[3] Early the next morning Abraham cut some wood for the sacrifice, loaded his donkey, and took Isaac and two servants with him. They started out for the place that God had told him about. [4] On the third day Abraham saw the place in the distance. [5] Then he said to the servants, "Stay here with the donkey. The boy and I will go over there and worship, and then we will come back to you."

[6] Abraham made Isaac carry the wood for the sacrifice, and he himself carried a knife and live coals for starting the fire. As they walked along together, [7] Isaac said, "Father!"

He answered, "Yes, my son?"

Isaac asked, "I see that you have the coals and the wood, but where is the lamb for the sacrifice?"

[8] Abraham answered, "God himself will provide one." And the two of them walked on together.

[9] When they came to the place which God had told him about, Abraham built an altar and arranged the wood on it. He tied up his son and placed him on the altar, on top of the wood. [10] Then he picked up the knife to kill him. [11] But the angel of the LORD called to him from heaven, "Abraham, Abraham!"

He answered, "Yes, here I am."

[12] "Don't hurt the boy or do anything to him," he said. "Now I know that you honour and obey God, because you have not kept back your only son from him."

[13] Abraham looked round and saw a ram caught in a bush by its horns. He went and got it and offered it as a burnt offering instead of his son. [14] Abraham named that place "The LORD Provides".* And even today people say, "On the LORD's mountain he provides."*

[15] The angel of the LORD called to Abraham from heaven a second time, [16] "I make a vow by my own name — the LORD is speaking — that I will richly bless you. Because you did this and did not keep back your only son from me, [17] I promise that I will give you as many descendants as there are stars in the sky or grains of sand along the seashore. Your descendants will conquer their enemies. [18] All the nations will ask me to bless them as I have blessed your descendants — all because you obeyed my command." [19] Abraham went back to his servants, and they went together to Beersheba, where Abraham settled.

The Descendants of Nahor

[20] Some time later Abraham learnt that Milcah had borne eight children to his brother Nahor: [21] Uz the firstborn, Buz his brother, Kemuel the father of Aram, [22] Chesed, Hazo, Pildash, Jidlaph, and Bethuel, [23] Rebecca's father. Milcah bore these eight sons to Nahor, Abraham's brother. [24] Reumah, Nahor's concubine, bore Tebah, Gaham, Tahash, and Maacah.

Sarah Dies and Abraham Buys a Burial Ground

23 Sarah lived to be 127 years old. [2] She died in Hebron in the land of Canaan, and Abraham mourned her death.

[3] He left the place where his wife's body was lying, went to the Hittites, and said, [4] "I am a foreigner living here among you; sell me some land, so that I can bury my wife."

[5] They answered, [6] "Listen to us, sir. We look upon you as a mighty leader; bury your wife in the best grave that we have. Any of us would be glad to give you a grave, so that you can bury her."

....

22.14 *Provides*; or *Sees*.
22.14 *provides*; or *is seen*.

43

Genesis

....

Exodus

Leviticus

Num.

Deuter.

Joshua

[7] Then Abraham bowed before them [8] and said, "If you are willing to let me bury my wife here, please ask Ephron son of Zohar [9] to sell me Machpelah Cave, which is near the edge of his field. Ask him to sell it to me for its full price, here in your presence, so that I can own it as a burial ground."

[10] Ephron himself was sitting with the other Hittites at the meeting place at the city gate; he answered in the hearing of everyone there, [11] "Listen, sir; I will give you the whole field and the cave that is in it. Here in the presence of my own people, I will give it to you, so that you can bury your wife."

[12] But Abraham bowed before the Hittites [13] and said to Ephron, so that everyone could hear, "May I ask you, please, to listen. I will buy the whole field. Accept my payment, and I will bury my wife there."

[14] Ephron answered, [15] "Sir, land worth only 400 pieces of silver — what is that between us? Bury your wife in it." [16] Abraham agreed and weighed out the amount that Ephron had mentioned in the hearing of the people — 400 pieces of silver, according to the standard weights used by the merchants.

[17] That is how the property which had belonged to Ephron at Machpelah, east of Mamre, became Abraham's. It included the field, the cave which was in it, and all the trees in the field up to the edge of the property. [18] It was recognized as Abraham's property by all the Hittites who were there at the meeting.

[19] Then Abraham buried his wife Sarah in that cave in the land of Canaan. [20] So the field which had belonged to the Hittites, and the cave in it, became the property of Abraham for a burial ground.

A Wife for Isaac

24 Abraham was now very old, and the LORD had blessed him in everything he did. [2] He said to his oldest servant, who was in charge of all that he had, "Place your hand between my thighs* and make a vow. [3] I want you to make a vow in the name of the LORD, the God of heaven and earth, that you will not choose a wife for my son from the people here in Canaan. [4] You must go back to the country where I was born and get a wife for my son Isaac from among my relatives."

[5] But the servant asked, "What if the young woman will not leave home to come with me to this land? Shall I send your son back to the land you came from?"

[6] Abraham answered, "Make sure that you don't send my son back there! [7] The LORD, the God of heaven, brought me from the home of my father and from the land of my relatives, and he solemnly promised me that he would give this land to my descendants. He will send his angel before you, so that you can get a wife there for my son. [8] If the young woman is not willing to come with you, you will be free from this promise. But you must not under any circumstances take my son back there." [9] So the servant put his hand between the thighs of Abraham, his master, and made a vow to do what Abraham had asked.

[10] The servant, who was in charge of Abraham's property, took ten of his master's camels and went to the city where Nahor had lived in northern Mesopotamia. [11] When he arrived, he made the camels kneel down at the well outside the city. It was late afternoon, the time when women came out to get water. [12] He prayed, "LORD, God of my master Abraham, give me success

24.2 *Place... thighs*: This was the way in which a vow was made absolutely unchangeable.

today and keep your promise to my master. [13] Here I am at the well where the young women of the city will be coming to get water. [14] I will say to one of them, 'Please, lower your jar and let me have a drink.' If she says, 'Drink, and I will also bring water for your camels,' may she be the one that you have chosen for your servant Isaac. If this happens, I will know that you have kept your promise to my master."

[15] Before he had finished praying, Rebecca arrived with a water jar on her shoulder. She was the daughter of Bethuel, who was the son of Abraham's brother Nahor and his wife Milcah. [16] She was a very beautiful young woman and still a virgin. She went down to the well, filled her jar, and came back. [17] The servant ran to meet her and said, "Please give me a drink of water from your jar."

[18] She said, "Drink, sir," and quickly lowered her jar from her shoulder and held it while he drank. [19] When he had finished, she said, "I will also bring water for your camels and let them have all they want." [20] She quickly emptied her jar into the animals' drinking-trough and ran to the well to get more water, until she had watered all his camels. [21] The man kept watching her in silence, to see if the LORD had given him success.

[22] When she had finished, the man took an expensive gold ring and put it in her nose and put two large gold bracelets on her arms. [23] He said, "Please tell me who your father is. Is there room in his house for my men and me to spend the night?"

[24] "My father is Bethuel son of Nahor and Milcah," she answered. [25] "There is plenty of straw and fodder at our house, and there is a place for you to stay."

[26] Then the man knelt down and worshipped the LORD. [27] He said, "Praise the LORD, the God of my master Abraham, who has faithfully kept his promise to my master. The LORD has led me straight to my master's relatives."

[28] The young woman ran to her mother's house and told the whole story. [29] Now Rebecca had a brother named Laban, and he ran outside to go to the well where Abraham's servant was. [30] Laban had seen the nose-ring and the bracelets on his sister's arms and had heard her say what the man had told her. He went to Abraham's servant, who was standing by his camels at the well, [31] and said, "Come home with me. You are a man whom the LORD has blessed. Why are you standing out here? I have a room ready for you in my house, and there is a place for your camels."

[32] So the man went into the house, and Laban unloaded the camels and gave them straw and fodder. Then he brought water for Abraham's servant and his men to wash their feet. [33] When food was brought, the man said, "I will not eat until I have said what I have to say."

Laban said, "Go on and speak."

[34] "I am the servant of Abraham," he began. [35] "The LORD has greatly blessed my master and made him a rich man. He has given him flocks of sheep and goats, cattle, silver, gold, male and female slaves, camels, and donkeys. [36] Sarah, my master's wife, bore him a son when she was old, and my master has given everything he owns to him. [37] My master made me promise with a vow to obey his command. He said, 'Do not choose a wife for my son from the young women in the land of Canaan. [38] Instead, go to my father's people, to my relatives, and choose a wife for him.' [39] And I asked my master, 'What if she will not come with me?' [40] He answered, 'The LORD, whom I have always obeyed, will send his angel with you and give you success. You will get for my son a wife from my own people, from my father's family. [41] There

45

Genesis

....

Exodus

Leviticus

Num.

Deuter.

Joshua

is only one way for you to be free from your vow: if you go to my relatives and they refuse you, then you will be free.'

⁴²"When I came to the well today, I prayed, 'LORD, God of my master Abraham, please give me success in what I am doing. ⁴³Here I am at the well. When a young woman comes out to get water, I will ask her to give me a drink of water from her jar. ⁴⁴If she agrees and also offers to bring water for my camels, may she be the one that you have chosen as the wife for my master's son.' ⁴⁵Before I had finished my silent prayer, Rebecca came with a water jar on her shoulder and went down to the well to get water. I said to her, 'Please give me a drink.' ⁴⁶She quickly lowered her jar from her shoulder and said, 'Drink, and I will also water your camels.' So I drank, and she watered the camels. ⁴⁷I asked her, 'Who is your father?' And she answered, 'My father is Bethuel son of Nahor and Milcah.' Then I put the ring in her nose and the bracelets on her arms. ⁴⁸I knelt down and worshipped the LORD. I praised the LORD, the God of my master Abraham, who had led me straight to my master's relative, where I found his daughter for my master's son. ⁴⁹Now, if you intend to fulfil your responsibility towards my master and treat him fairly, please tell me; if not, say so, and I will decide what to do."

⁵⁰Laban and Bethuel answered, "Since this matter comes from the LORD, it is not for us to make a decision. ⁵¹Here is Rebecca; take her and go. Let her become the wife of your master's son, as the LORD himself has said." ⁵²When the servant of Abraham heard this, he bowed down and worshipped the LORD. ⁵³Then he brought out clothing and silver and gold jewellery, and gave them to Rebecca. He also gave expensive gifts to her brother and to her mother.

⁵⁴Then Abraham's servant and the men with him ate and drank, and spent the night there. When they got up in the morning, he said, "Let me go back to my master."

⁵⁵But Rebecca's brother and her mother said, "Let her stay with us a week or ten days, and then she may go."

⁵⁶But he said, "Don't make us stay. The LORD has made my journey a success; let me go back to my master."

⁵⁷They answered, "Let's call her and find out what she has to say." ⁵⁸So they called Rebecca and asked, "Do you want to go with this man?"

"Yes," she answered.

⁵⁹So they let Rebecca and her old family servant go with Abraham's servant and his men. ⁶⁰And they gave Rebecca their blessing in these words:

"May you, sister, become the mother of millions!
May your descendants conquer the cities of their
enemies!"

⁶¹Then Rebecca and her young women got ready and mounted the camels to go with Abraham's servant, and they all started out.

⁶²Isaac had come into the wilderness of* "The Well of the Living One who Sees Me" and was staying in the southern part of Canaan. ⁶³He went out in the early evening to take a walk in the fields and saw camels coming. ⁶⁴When Rebecca saw Isaac, she got down from her camel ⁶⁵and asked Abraham's servant, "Who is that man walking towards us in the field?"

"He is my master," the servant answered. So she took her scarf and covered her face.

....

24.62 Some ancient translations *into the wilderness of;* Hebrew *from coming.*

⁶⁶ The servant told Isaac everything he had done. ⁶⁷ Then Isaac brought Rebecca into the tent that his mother Sarah had lived in, and she became his wife. Isaac loved Rebecca, and so he was comforted for the loss of his mother.

Other Descendants of Abraham
(1 Chr 1.32–33)

25 Abraham married another wife, whose name was Keturah. ² She bore him Zimran, Jokshan, Medan, Midian, Ishbak, and Shuah. ³ Jokshan was the father of Sheba and Dedan, and the descendants of Dedan were the Asshurim, the Letushim, and the Leummim. ⁴ The sons of Midian were Ephah, Epher, Hanoch, Abida, and Eldaah. All these were Keturah's descendants.

⁵ Abraham left everything he owned to Isaac; ⁶ but while he was still alive, he gave presents to the sons his other wives had borne him. Then he sent these sons to the land of the East, away from his son Isaac.

The Death and Burial of Abraham

⁷⁻⁸ Abraham died at the ripe old age of 175. ⁹ His sons Isaac and Ishmael buried him in Machpelah Cave, in the field east of Mamre that had belonged to Ephron son of Zohar the Hittite. ¹⁰ It was the field that Abraham had bought from the Hittites; both Abraham and his wife Sarah were buried there. ¹¹ After the death of Abraham, God blessed his son Isaac, who lived near "The Well of the Living One who Sees Me".

The Descendants of Ishmael
(1 Chr 1.28–31)

¹² Ishmael, whom Hagar, the Egyptian slave of Sarah, bore to Abraham, ¹³ had the following sons, listed in the order of their birth: Nebaioth, Kedar, Adbeel, Mibsam, ¹⁴ Mishma, Dumah, Massa, ¹⁵ Hadad, Tema, Jetur, Naphish, and Kedemah. ¹⁶ They were the ancestors of twelve tribes, and their names were given to their villages and camping places. ¹⁷ Ishmael was 137 years old when he died. ¹⁸ The descendants of Ishmael lived in the territory between Havilah and Shur, to the east of Egypt on the way to Assyria. They lived apart from the other descendants of Abraham.

The Birth of Esau and Jacob

¹⁹ This is the story of Abraham's son Isaac. ²⁰ Isaac was forty years old when he married Rebecca, the daughter of Bethuel (an Aramean from Mesopotamia) and sister of Laban. ²¹ Because Rebecca had no children, Isaac prayed to the LORD for her. The LORD answered his prayer, and Rebecca became pregnant. ²² She was going to have twins, and before they were born, they struggled against each other in her womb. She said, "Why should something like this happen to me?" So she went to ask the LORD for an answer.

²³ The LORD said to her,

"Two nations are within you;
You will give birth to two rival peoples.
One will be stronger than the other;
The older will serve the younger."

²⁴ The time came for her to give birth, and she had twin sons. ²⁵ The first one was reddish, and his skin was like a hairy robe, so he was named Esau.* ²⁶ The second one was born holding on

25.25 *Esau*: This name is taken to refer to Seir, the territory later inhabited by Esau's descendants; Seir sounds like the Hebrew for "hairy".

tightly to the heel of Esau, so he was named Jacob.* Isaac was sixty years old when they were born.

Esau Sells his Rights as the Firstborn Son

²⁷The boys grew up, and Esau became a skilled hunter, a man who loved the outdoor life, but Jacob was a quiet man who stayed at home. ²⁸Isaac preferred Esau, because he enjoyed eating the animals Esau killed, but Rebecca preferred Jacob.

²⁹One day while Jacob was cooking some bean soup, Esau came in from hunting. He was hungry ³⁰and said to Jacob, "I'm starving; give me some of that red stuff." (That is why he was called Edom.*)

³¹Jacob answered, "I will give it to you if you give me your rights as the firstborn son."

³²Esau said, "All right! I am about to die; what good will my rights do me then?"

³³Jacob answered, "First make a vow that you will give me your rights."

Esau made the vow and gave his rights to Jacob. ³⁴Then Jacob gave him some bread and some of the soup. He ate and drank and then got up and left. That was all Esau cared about his rights as the firstborn son.

Isaac Lives at Gerar

26 There was another famine in the land besides the earlier one during the time of Abraham. Isaac went to Abimelech, king of the Philistines, at Gerar. ²The Lᴏʀᴅ had appeared to Isaac and had said, "Do not go to Egypt; stay in this land, where I tell you to stay. ³Live here, and I will be with you and bless you. I am going to give all this territory to you and to your descendants. I will keep the promise I made to your father Abraham. ⁴I will give you as many descendants as there are stars in the sky, and I will give them all this territory. All the nations will ask me to bless them as I have blessed your descendants. ⁵I will bless you, because Abraham obeyed me and kept all my laws and commands."

⁶So Isaac lived at Gerar. ⁷When the men there asked about his wife, he said that she was his sister. He would not admit that she was his wife, because he was afraid that the men there would kill him to get Rebecca, who was very beautiful. ⁸When Isaac had been there for some time, King Abimelech looked down from his window and saw Isaac and Rebecca making love. ⁹Abimelech sent for Isaac and said, "So she is your wife! Why did you say she was your sister?"

He answered, "I thought I would be killed if I said she was my wife."

¹⁰"What have you done to us?" Abimelech said. "One of my men might easily have slept with your wife, and you would have been responsible for our guilt." ¹¹Abimelech warned all the people: "Anyone who ill-treats this man or his wife will be put to death."

¹²Isaac sowed seed in that land, and that year he harvested a hundred times as much as he had sown, because the Lᴏʀᴅ blessed him. ¹³He continued to prosper and became a very rich man. ¹⁴Because he had many herds of sheep and cattle and many servants, the Philistines were jealous of him. ¹⁵So they filled in all the wells which the servants of his father Abraham had dug while Abraham was alive.

25.26 *Jacob*: This name sounds like the Hebrew for "heel".
25.30 *Edom*: This name sounds like the Hebrew for "red".

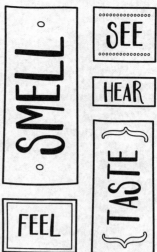

WRITE HERE WHAT YOU

SMELL · SEE · HEAR · FEEL · TASTE

RIGHT AT THIS MOMENT.

[16] Then Abimelech said to Isaac, "Leave our country. You have become more powerful than we are." [17] So Isaac left and set up his camp in the Valley of Gerar, where he stayed for some time. [18] He dug once again the wells which had been dug during the time of Abraham and which the Philistines had stopped up after Abraham's death. Isaac gave the wells the same names that his father had given them.

[19] Isaac's servants dug a well in the valley and found water. [20] The shepherds of Gerar quarrelled with Isaac's shepherds and said, "This water belongs to us." So Isaac named the well "Quarrel". [21] Isaac's servants dug another well, and there was a quarrel about that one also, so he named it "Enmity". [22] He moved away from there and dug another well. There was no dispute about this one, so he named it "Freedom". He said, "Now the LORD has given us freedom to live in the land, and we will be prosperous here."

[23] Isaac left and went to Beersheba. [24] That night the LORD appeared to him and said, "I am the God of your father Abraham. Do not be afraid; I am with you. I will bless you and give you many descendants because of my promise to my servant Abraham." [25] Isaac built an altar there and worshipped the LORD. Then he set up his camp there, and his servants dug another well.

The Agreement between Isaac and Abimelech

[26] Abimelech came from Gerar with Ahuzzath his adviser and Phicol the commander of his army to see Isaac. [27] So Isaac asked, "Why have you now come to see me, when you were so unfriendly to me before and made me leave your country?"

[28] They answered, "Now we know that the LORD is with you, and we think that there should be a solemn agreement between us. We want you to promise [29] that you will not harm us, just as we did not harm you. We were kind to you and let you leave peacefully. Now it is clear that the LORD has blessed you." [30] Isaac prepared a feast for them, and they ate and drank. [31] Early next morning each man made his promise and sealed it with a vow. Isaac said goodbye to them, and they parted as friends.

[32] On that day Isaac's servants came and told him about the well which they had dug. They said, "We have found water." [33] He named the well "Vow". That is how the city of Beersheba* got its name.

Esau's Foreign Wives

[34] When Esau was forty years old, he married two Hittite women, Judith the daughter of Beeri, and Basemath the daughter of Elon. [35] They made life miserable for Isaac and Rebecca.

Isaac Blesses Jacob

27 Isaac was now old and had become blind. He sent for his elder son Esau and said to him, "My son!"

"Yes," he answered.

[2] Isaac said, "You see that I am old and may die soon. [3] Take your bow and arrows, go out into the country, and kill an animal for me. [4] Cook me some of that tasty food that I like, and bring it to me. After I have eaten it, I will give you my final blessing before I die."

[5] While Isaac was talking to Esau, Rebecca was listening. So when Esau went out to hunt, [6] she said to Jacob, "I have just heard

....

26.33 *Beersheba*: This name in Hebrew means "Well of the Vow" or "Well of Seven" (see also 21.31).

49

Genesis
....

Exodus
Leviticus
Num.
Deuter.
Joshua

your father say to Esau, [7]'Bring me an animal and cook it for me. After I have eaten it, I will give you my blessing in the presence of the Lord before I die.' [8]Now, my son," Rebecca continued, "listen to me and do what I say. [9]Go to the flock and pick out two fat young goats, so that I can cook them and make some of that food your father likes so much. [10]You can take it to him to eat, and he will give you his blessing before he dies."

[11]But Jacob said to his mother, "You know that Esau is a hairy man, but I have smooth skin. [12]Perhaps my father will touch me and find out that I am deceiving him; in this way I will bring a curse on myself instead of a blessing."

[13]His mother answered, "Let any curse against you fall on me, my son; just do as I say, and go and get the goats for me." [14]So he went to get them and brought them to her, and she cooked the kind of food that his father liked. [15]Then she took Esau's best clothes, which she kept in the house, and put them on Jacob. [16]She put the skins of the goats on his arms and on the hairless part of his neck. [17]She handed him the tasty food, together with the bread she had baked.

[18]Then Jacob went to his father and said, "Father!"

"Yes," he answered. "Which of my sons are you?"

[19]Jacob answered, "I am your elder son Esau; I have done as you told me. Please sit up and eat some of the meat that I have brought you, so that you can give me your blessing."

[20]Isaac said, "How did you find it so quickly, my son?"

Jacob answered, "The Lord your God helped me to find it."

[21]Isaac said to Jacob, "Please come closer so that I can touch you. Are you really Esau?" [22]Jacob moved closer to his father, who felt him and said, "Your voice sounds like Jacob's voice, but your arms feel like Esau's arms." [23]He did not recognize Jacob, because his arms were hairy like Esau's. He was about to give him his blessing, [24]but asked again, "Are you really Esau?"

"I am," he answered.

[25]Isaac said, "Bring me some of the meat. After I have eaten it, I will give you my blessing." Jacob brought it to him, and he also brought him some wine to drink. [26]Then his father said to him, "Come closer and kiss me, my son." [27]As he came up to kiss him, Isaac smelt his clothes — so he gave him his blessing. He said, "The pleasant smell of my son is like the smell of a field which the Lord has blessed. [28]May God give you dew from heaven and make your fields fertile! May he give you plenty of corn and wine! [29]May nations be your servants, and may peoples bow down before you. May you rule over all your relatives, and may your mother's descendants bow down before you. May those who curse you be cursed, and may those who bless you be blessed."

Esau Begs for Isaac's Blessing

[30]Isaac finished giving his blessing, and as soon as Jacob left, his brother Esau came in from hunting. [31]He also cooked some tasty food and took it to his father. He said, "Please, father, sit up and eat some of the meat that I have brought you, so that you can give me your blessing."

[32]"Who are you?" Isaac asked.

"Your elder son Esau," he answered.

[33]Isaac began to tremble and shake all over, and he asked, "Who was it, then, who killed an animal and brought it to me? I ate it just before you came. I gave him my final blessing, and so it is his for ever."

34 When Esau heard this, he cried out loudly and bitterly and said, "Give me your blessing also, father!"

35 Isaac answered, "Your brother came and deceived me. He has taken away your blessing."

36 Esau said, "This is the second time that he has cheated me. No wonder his name is Jacob.* He took my rights as the firstborn son, and now he has taken away my blessing. Haven't you saved a blessing for me?"

37 Isaac answered, "I have already made him master over you, and I have made all his relatives his slaves. I have given him corn and wine. Now there is nothing that I can do for you, my son!"

38 Esau continued to plead with his father: "Have you only one blessing, father? Bless me too, father!" He began to cry.

39 Then Isaac said to him,

"No dew from heaven for you,
No fertile fields for you.
40 You will live by your sword,
But be your brother's slave.
Yet when you rebel,*
You will break away from his control."

41 Esau hated Jacob, because his father had given Jacob the blessing. He thought, "The time to mourn my father's death is near; then I will kill Jacob."

42 But when Rebecca heard about Esau's plan, she sent for Jacob and said, "Listen, your brother Esau is planning to get even with you and kill you. 43 Now, my son, do what I say. Go at once to my brother Laban in Haran, 44 and stay with him for a while, until your brother's anger cools down 45 and he forgets what you have done to him. Then I will send someone to bring you back. Why should I lose both my sons on the same day?"

Isaac Sends Jacob to Laban

46 Rebecca said to Isaac, "I am sick and tired of Esau's foreign wives. If Jacob also marries one of these Hittite women, I might as well die."

28 Isaac called Jacob, greeted him, and said to him, "Don't marry a Canaanite woman. 2 Go instead to Mesopotamia, to the home of your grandfather Bethuel, and marry one of the young women there, one of your uncle Laban's daughters. 3 May Almighty God bless your marriage and give you many children, so that you will become the father of many nations! 4 May he bless you and your descendants as he blessed Abraham, and may you take possession of this land, in which you have lived and which God gave to Abraham!" 5 Isaac sent Jacob away to Mesopotamia, to Laban, who was the son of Bethuel the Aramean and the brother of Rebecca, the mother of Jacob and Esau.

Esau Takes Another Wife

6 Esau learnt that Isaac had blessed Jacob and sent him away to Mesopotamia to find a wife. He also learnt that when Isaac blessed him, he commanded him not to marry a Canaanite woman. 7 He found out that Jacob had obeyed his father and mother and had gone to Mesopotamia. 8 Esau then understood that his father Isaac did not approve of Canaanite women. 9 So he went to Ishmael son of Abraham and married his daughter Mahalath, who was the sister of Nebaioth.

....

27.36 *Jacob*: This name sounds like the Hebrew for "cheat".
27.40 *rebel*; or *grow restless*.

Jacob's Dream at Bethel

¹⁰ Jacob left Beersheba and started towards Haran. ¹¹ At sunset he came to a holy place* and camped there. He lay down to sleep, resting his head on a stone. ¹² He dreamt that he saw a stairway reaching from earth to heaven, with angels going up and coming down on it. ¹³ And there was the LORD standing beside him.* "I am the LORD, the God of Abraham and Isaac," he said. "I will give to you and to your descendants this land on which you are lying. ¹⁴ They will be as numerous as the specks of dust on the earth. They will extend their territory in all directions, and through you and your descendants I will bless all the nations.* ¹⁵ Remember, I will be with you and protect you wherever you go, and I will bring you back to this land. I will not leave you until I have done all that I have promised you."

¹⁶ Jacob woke up and said, "The LORD is here! He is in this place, and I didn't know it!" ¹⁷ He was afraid and said, "What a terrifying place this is! It must be the house of God; it must be the gate that opens into heaven."

¹⁸ Jacob got up early next morning, took the stone that was under his head, and set it up as a memorial. Then he poured olive oil on it to dedicate it to God. ¹⁹ He named the place Bethel.* (The town there was once known as Luz.) ²⁰ Then Jacob made a vow to the LORD: "If you will be with me and protect me on the journey I am making and give me food and clothing, ²¹ and if I return safely to my father's home, then you will be my God. ²² This memorial stone which I have set up will be the place where you are worshipped, and I will give you a tenth of everything you give me."

Jacob Arrives at Laban's Home

29 Jacob continued on his way and went towards the land of the East. ² Suddenly he came upon a well out in the fields with three flocks of sheep lying round it. The flocks were watered from this well, which had a large stone over the opening. ³ Whenever all the flocks came together there, the shepherds would roll the stone back and water them. Then they would put the stone back in place.

⁴ Jacob asked the shepherds, "My friends, where are you from?"

"From Haran," they answered.

⁵ He asked, "Do you know Laban, grandson of Nahor?"

"Yes, we do," they answered.

⁶ "Is he well?" he asked.

"He is well," they answered. "Look, here comes his daughter Rachel with his flock."

⁷ Jacob said, "Since it is still broad daylight and not yet time to bring the flocks in, why don't you water them and take them back to pasture?"

⁸ They answered, "We can't do that until all the flocks are here and the stone has been rolled back; then we will water the flocks."

⁹ While Jacob was still talking to them, Rachel arrived with the flock. ¹⁰ When Jacob saw Rachel with his uncle Laban's flock, he went to the well, rolled the stone back, and watered the sheep. ¹¹ Then he kissed her and began to cry for joy. ¹² He told her, "I am your father's relative, the son of Rebecca."

Genesis

Exodus
Leviticus
Num.
Deuter.
Joshua

GENESIS 28.13

• I am the •

LORD

28.11 *a holy place*; or *a place*.
28.13 *beside him*; or *on it*.
28.14 *through you… nations*; or *all the nations will ask me to bless them as I have blessed you and your descendants*.
28.19 *Bethel*: This name in Hebrew means "house of God".

She ran to tell her father; [13] and when he heard the news about his nephew Jacob, he ran to meet him, hugged him and kissed him, and brought him into the house. When Jacob told Laban everything that had happened, [14] Laban said, "Yes, indeed, you are my own flesh and blood." Jacob stayed there a whole month.

Jacob Serves Laban for Rachel and Leah

[15] Laban said to Jacob, "You shouldn't work for me for nothing just because you are my relative. How much pay do you want?" [16] Laban had two daughters; the elder was named Leah, and the younger Rachel. [17] Leah had lovely* eyes, but Rachel was shapely and beautiful.

[18] Jacob was in love with Rachel, so he said, "I will work seven years for you, if you will let me marry Rachel."

[19] Laban answered, "I would rather give her to you than to anyone else; stay here with me." [20] Jacob worked seven years so that he could have Rachel, and the time seemed like only a few days to him, because he loved her.

[21] Then Jacob said to Laban, "The time is up; let me marry your daughter." [22] So Laban gave a wedding feast and invited everyone. [23] But that night, instead of Rachel, he took Leah to Jacob, and Jacob had intercourse with her. [24] (Laban gave his slave woman Zilpah to his daughter Leah as her maid.) [25] Not until the next morning did Jacob discover that it was Leah. He went to Laban and said, "Why did you do this to me? I worked to get Rachel. Why have you tricked me?"

[26] Laban answered, "It is not the custom here to give the younger daughter in marriage before the elder. [27] Wait until the week's marriage celebrations are over, and I will give you Rachel, if you will work for me another seven years."

[28] Jacob agreed, and when the week of marriage celebrations was over, Laban gave him his daughter Rachel as his wife. [29] (Laban gave his slave woman Bilhah to his daughter Rachel as her maid.) [30] Jacob had intercourse with Rachel also, and he loved her more than Leah. Then he worked for Laban another seven years.

The Children Born to Jacob

[31] When the LORD saw that Leah was loved less than Rachel, he made it possible for her to have children, but Rachel remained childless. [32] Leah became pregnant and gave birth to a son. She said, "The LORD has seen my trouble, and now my husband will love me"; so she named him Reuben.* [33] She became pregnant again and gave birth to another son. She said, "The LORD has given me this son also, because he heard that I was not loved"; so she named him Simeon.* [34] Once again she became pregnant and gave birth to another son. She said, "Now my husband will be bound more tightly to me, because I have borne him three sons"; so she named him Levi.* [35] Then she became pregnant again and gave birth to another son. She said, "This time I will praise the LORD"; so she named him Judah.* Then she stopped having children.

30 But Rachel had not borne Jacob any children, and so she became jealous of her sister and said to Jacob, "Give me children, or I will die."

....

29.17 *lovely*; or *weak*.
29.32 *Reuben*: This name sounds like the Hebrew for "see, a son" and "has seen my trouble".
29.33 *Simeon*: This name sounds like the Hebrew for "hear".
29.34 *Levi*: This name sounds like the Hebrew for "bound".
29.35 *Judah*: This name sounds like the Hebrew for "praise".

[2] Jacob became angry with Rachel and said, "I can't take the place of God. He is the one who keeps you from having children." [3] She said, "Here is my slave Bilhah; sleep with her, so that she can have a child for me. In this way I can become a mother through her." [4] So she gave Bilhah to her husband, and he had intercourse with her. [5] Bilhah became pregnant and bore Jacob a son. [6] Rachel said, "God has judged in my favour. He has heard my prayer and has given me a son"; so she named him Dan.* [7] Bilhah became pregnant again and bore Jacob a second son. [8] Rachel said, "I have fought a hard fight with my sister, but I have won"; so she named him Naphtali.*

[9] When Leah realized that she had stopped having children, she gave her slave Zilpah to Jacob as his wife. [10] Then Zilpah bore Jacob a son. [11] Leah said, "I have been lucky"; so she named him Gad.* [12] Zilpah bore Jacob another son, [13] and Leah said, "How happy I am! Now women will call me happy"; so she named him Asher.*

[14] During the wheat harvest Reuben went into the fields and found mandrakes,* which he brought to his mother Leah. Rachel said to Leah, "Please give me some of your son's mandrakes."

[15] Leah answered, "Isn't it enough that you have taken away my husband? Now you are even trying to take away my son's mandrakes."

Rachel said, "If you will give me your son's mandrakes, you can sleep with Jacob tonight."

[16] When Jacob came in from the fields in the evening, Leah went out to meet him and said, "You are going to sleep with me tonight, because I have paid for you with my son's mandrakes." So he had intercourse with her that night.

[17] God answered Leah's prayer, and she became pregnant and bore Jacob a fifth son. [18] Leah said, "God has given me my reward, because I gave my slave to my husband"; so she named her son Issachar.* [19] Leah became pregnant again and bore Jacob a sixth son. [20] She said, "God has given me a fine gift. Now my husband will accept me, because I have borne him six sons"; so she named him Zebulun.* [21] Later she bore a daughter, whom she named Dinah.

[22] Then God remembered Rachel; he answered her prayer and made it possible for her to have children. [23] She became pregnant and gave birth to a son. She said, "God has taken away my disgrace by giving me a son. [24] May the LORD give me another son"; so she named him Joseph.*

Jacob's Bargain with Laban

[25] After the birth of Joseph, Jacob said to Laban, "Let me go, so that I can return home. [26] Give me my wives and children that I have earned by working for you, and I will leave. You know how well I have served you."

GENESIS 29.35

JUDAH
– MEANS –
'PRAISE'.

In the midst of Leah's heartache, God brought something good.

It is important to praise God even if life is tough.

On this page,

WRITE THINGS TO PRAISE GOD FOR.

Make them creative!

30.6 *Dan*: This name sounds like the Hebrew for "judge in favour".
30.8 *Naphtali*: This name sounds like the Hebrew for "fight".
30.11 *Gad*: This name in Hebrew means "luck".
30.13 *Asher*: This name in Hebrew means "happy".
30.14 *mandrakes*: Plants which were believed to produce fertility and were used as love-charms.
30.18 *Issachar*: This name sounds like the Hebrew for "a man is hired" and "there is reward".
30.20 *Zebulun*: This name sounds like the Hebrew for "accept" and "gift".
30.24 *Joseph*: This name sounds like the Hebrew for "may he give another" and "he has taken away".

27 Laban said to him, "Let me say this: I have learnt by divination that the Lord has blessed me because of you. 28 Name your wages, and I will pay them."

29 Jacob answered, "You know how I have worked for you and how your flocks have prospered under my care. 30 The little you had before I came has grown enormously, and the Lord has blessed you wherever I went.* Now it is time for me to look out for my own interests."

31 "What shall I pay you?" Laban asked.

Jacob answered, "I don't want any wages. I will continue to take care of your flocks if you agree to this suggestion: 32 Let me go through all your flocks today and take every black lamb* and every spotted or speckled young goat. That is all the wages I want. 33 In the future you can easily find out if I have been honest. When you come to check up on my wages, if I have any goat that isn't speckled or spotted or any sheep that isn't black, you will know that it has been stolen."

34 Laban answered, "Agreed. We will do as you suggest." 35 But that day Laban removed the male goats that had stripes or spots and all the females that were speckled and spotted or which had white on them; he also removed all the black sheep. He put his sons in charge of them, 36 and then went away from Jacob with this flock as far as he could travel in three days. Jacob took care of the rest of Laban's flocks.

37 Jacob got green branches of poplar, almond, and plane trees and stripped off some of the bark so that the branches had white stripes on them. 38 He placed these branches in front of the flocks at their drinking troughs. He put them there, because the animals mated when they came to drink. 39 So when the goats bred in front of the branches, they produced young that were streaked, speckled, and spotted.

40 Jacob kept the sheep separate from the goats and made them face in the direction of the streaked and black animals of Laban's flock. In this way he built up his own flock and kept it apart from Laban's.

41 When the healthy animals were mating, Jacob put the branches in front of them at the drinking troughs, so that they would breed among the branches. 42 But he did not put the branches in front of the weak animals. Soon Laban had all the weak animals, and Jacob all the healthy ones. 43 In this way Jacob became very wealthy. He had many flocks, slaves, camels, and donkeys.

Jacob Flees from Laban

31 Jacob heard that Laban's sons were saying, "Jacob has taken everything that belonged to our father. All his wealth has come from what our father owned." 2 He also saw that Laban was no longer as friendly as he had been earlier. 3 Then the Lord said to him, "Go back to the land of your fathers and to your relatives. I will be with you."

4 So Jacob sent word to Rachel and Leah to meet him in the field where his flocks were. 5 He said to them, "I have noticed that your father is not as friendly towards me as he used to be; but my father's God has been with me. 6 You both know that I have worked for your father with all my strength. 7 Yet he has cheated

....

30.30 *wherever I went*; or *because of me.*
30.32 One ancient translation *every black lamb*; Hebrew *every spotted and speckled lamb, and every black lamb.*

me and changed my wages ten times. But God did not let him harm me. [8] Whenever Laban said, 'The speckled goats shall be your wages,' all the flocks produced speckled young. When he said, 'The striped goats shall be your wages,' all the flocks produced striped young. [9] God has taken flocks away from your father and given them to me.

[10] "During the breeding season I had a dream, and I saw that the male goats that were mating were striped, spotted, and speckled. [11] The angel of God spoke to me in the dream and said, 'Jacob!' 'Yes,' I answered. [12] 'Look,' he continued, 'all the male goats that are mating are striped, spotted, and speckled. I am making this happen because I have seen all that Laban is doing to you. [13] I am the God who appeared to you at Bethel, where you dedicated a stone as a memorial by pouring olive oil on it and where you made a vow to me. Now get ready to go back to the land where you were born.'"

[14] Rachel and Leah answered Jacob, "There is nothing left for us to inherit from our father. [15] He treats us like foreigners. He sold us, and now he has spent all the money he was paid for us. [16] All this wealth which God has taken from our father belongs to us and to our children. Do whatever God has told you."

[17-18] So Jacob got ready to go back to his father in the land of Canaan. He put his children and his wives on the camels, and drove all his flocks ahead of him, with everything that he had acquired in Mesopotamia. [19] Laban had gone to shear his sheep, and during his absence Rachel stole the household gods that belonged to her father. [20] Jacob deceived Laban by not letting him know that he was leaving. [21] He took everything he owned and left in a hurry. He crossed the River Euphrates and started for the hill country of Gilead.

Laban Pursues Jacob

[22] Three days later Laban was told that Jacob had fled. [23] He took his men with him and pursued Jacob for seven days until he caught up with him in the hill country of Gilead. [24] In a dream that night God came to Laban and said to him, "Be careful not to threaten Jacob in any way." [25] Jacob had set up his camp on a mountain, and Laban set up his camp with his relatives in the hill country of Gilead.

[26] Laban said to Jacob, "Why did you deceive me and carry off my daughters like women captured in war? [27] Why did you deceive me and slip away without telling me? If you had told me, I would have sent you on your way with rejoicing and singing to the music of tambourines and harps. [28] You did not even let me kiss my grandchildren and my daughters goodbye. That was a foolish thing to do! [29] I have the power to do you harm, but last night the God of your father warned me not to threaten you in any way. [30] I know that you left because you were so anxious to get back home, but why did you steal my household gods?"

[31] Jacob answered, "I was afraid, because I thought that you might take your daughters away from me. [32] But if you find that anyone here has your gods, he will be put to death. Here, with our men as witnesses, look for anything that belongs to you and take what is yours." Jacob did not know that Rachel had stolen Laban's gods.

[33] Laban went and searched Jacob's tent; then he went into Leah's tent, and the tent of the two slave women, but he did not find his gods. Then he went into Rachel's tent. [34] Rachel had taken the household gods and put them in a camel's saddlebag and

Genesis

Exodus

Leviticus

Num.

Deuter.

Joshua

TURN THESE SHAPES INTO

SOMETHING ELSE.

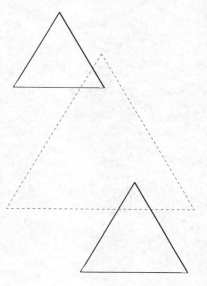

was sitting on them. Laban searched through the whole tent, but did not find them. [35] Rachel said to her father, "Do not be angry with me, sir, but I am not able to stand up in your presence; I am having my monthly period." Laban searched but did not find his household gods.

[36] Then Jacob lost his temper. "What crime have I committed?" he asked angrily. "What law have I broken that gives you the right to hunt me down? [37] Now that you have searched through all my belongings, what household article have you found that belongs to you? Put it out here where your men and mine can see it, and let them decide which one of us is right. [38] I have been with you now for twenty years; your sheep and your goats have not failed to reproduce, and I have not eaten any rams from your flocks. [39] Whenever a sheep was killed by wild animals, I always bore the loss myself. I didn't take it to you to show that it was not my fault. You demanded that I make good anything that was stolen during the day or during the night. [40] Many times I suffered from the heat during the day and from the cold at night. I was not able to sleep. [41] It was like that for the whole twenty years I was with you. For fourteen years I worked to win your two daughters — and six years for your flocks. And even then, you changed my wages ten times. [42] If the God of my fathers, the God of Abraham and Isaac, had not been with me, you would have already sent me away empty-handed. But God has seen my trouble and the work I have done, and last night he gave his judgement."

The Agreement between Jacob and Laban

[43] Laban answered Jacob, "These young women are my daughters; their children belong to me, and these flocks are mine. In fact, everything you see here belongs to me. But since I can do nothing to keep my daughters and their children, [44] I am ready to make an agreement with you. Let us make a pile of stones to remind us of our agreement."

[45] So Jacob took a stone and set it up as a memorial. [46] He told his men to gather some rocks and pile them up. Then they ate a meal beside the pile of rocks. [47] Laban named it Jegar Sahadutha,* while Jacob named it Galeed.* [48] Laban said to Jacob, "This pile of rocks will be a reminder for both of us." That is why that place was named Galeed. [49] Laban also said, "May the LORD keep an eye on us while we are separated from each other." So the place was also named Mizpah.* [50] Laban went on, "If you ill-treat my daughters or if you marry other women, even though I don't know about it, remember that God is watching us. [51] Here are the rocks that I have piled up between us, and here is the memorial stone. [52] Both this pile and this memorial stone are reminders. I will never go beyond this pile to attack you, and you must never go beyond it or beyond this memorial stone to attack me. [53] The God of Abraham and the God of Nahor* will judge between us." Then, in the name of the God whom his father Isaac worshipped, Jacob solemnly vowed to keep this promise. [54] He killed an animal, which he offered as a sacrifice on the mountain, and he invited his men to the meal. After they had eaten, they

---

31.47 *Jegar Sahadutha*: This name in Aramaic means "a pile to remind us".
31.47 *Galeed*: This name in Hebrew means "a pile to remind us".
31.49 *Mizpah*: This name sounds like the Hebrew for "place from which to watch".
31.53 *Abraham… Nahor*: Abraham was Jacob's grandfather and Nahor was Laban's grandfather.

spent the night on the mountain. [55] Early the next morning Laban kissed his grandchildren and his daughters goodbye, and left to go back home.

Jacob Prepares to Meet Esau

32 As Jacob went on his way, some angels met him. [2] When he saw them, he said, "This is God's camp"; so he called the place Mahanaim.*

[3] Jacob sent messengers ahead of him to his brother Esau in the country of Edom. [4] He instructed them to say: "I, Jacob, your obedient servant, report to my master Esau that I have been staying with Laban and that I have delayed my return until now. [5] I own cattle, donkeys, sheep, goats, and slaves. I am sending you word, sir, in the hope of gaining your favour."

[6] When the messengers came back to Jacob, they said, "We went to your brother Esau, and he is already on his way to meet you. He has 400 men with him." [7] Jacob was frightened and worried. He divided into two groups the people who were with him, and also his sheep, goats, cattle, and camels. [8] He thought, "If Esau comes and attacks the first group, the other may be able to escape."

[9] Then Jacob prayed, "God of my grandfather Abraham and God of my father Isaac, hear me! You told me, LORD, to go back to my land and to my relatives, and you would make everything go well for me. [10] I am not worth all the kindness and faithfulness that you have shown me, your servant. I crossed the Jordan with nothing but a walking stick, and now I have come back with these two groups. [11] Save me, I pray, from my brother Esau. I am afraid — afraid that he is coming to attack us and destroy us all, even the women and children. [12] Remember that you promised to make everything go well for me and to give me more descendants than anyone could count, as many as the grains of sand along the seashore."

[13-15] After spending the night there, Jacob chose from his livestock as a present for his brother Esau: 200 female goats and twenty males, 200 female sheep and twenty males, thirty milk camels with their young, forty cows and ten bulls, twenty female donkeys and ten males. [16] He divided them into herds and put one of his servants in charge of each herd. He said to them, "Go ahead of me, and leave a space between each herd and the one behind it." [17] He ordered the first servant, "When my brother Esau meets you and asks, 'Who is your master? Where are you going? Who owns these animals in front of you?' [18] you must answer, 'They belong to your servant Jacob. He sends them as a present to his master Esau. Jacob himself is just behind us.'"
[19] He gave the same order to the second, the third, and to all the others who were in charge of the herds: "This is what you must say to Esau when you meet him. [20] You must say, 'Yes, your servant Jacob is just behind us.'" Jacob was thinking, "I will win him over with the gifts, and when I meet him, perhaps he will forgive me." [21] He sent the gifts on ahead of him and spent that night in camp.

Jacob Wrestles at Peniel

[22] That same night Jacob got up, took his two wives, his two concubines, and his eleven children, and crossed the River Jabbok.

....

32.2 *Mahanaim*: This name in Hebrew means "two camps".

Finish the sentence below:

I AM...

_____

_____

_____

_____

_____

_____

_____

_____

_____

_____

_____

_____

_____

_____

_____

_____

_____

23 After he had sent them across, he also sent across all that he owned, 24 but he stayed behind, alone.

Then a man came and wrestled with him until just before daybreak. 25 When the man saw that he was not winning the struggle, he struck Jacob on the hip, and it was thrown out of joint. 26 The man said, "Let me go; daylight is coming."

"I won't, unless you bless me," Jacob answered.

27 "What is your name?" the man asked.

"Jacob," he answered.

28 The man said, "Your name will no longer be Jacob. You have struggled with God and with men, and you have won; so your name will be Israel."*

29 Jacob said, "Now tell me your name."

But he answered, "Why do you want to know my name?" Then he blessed Jacob.

30 Jacob said, "I have seen God face to face, and I am still alive"; so he named the place Peniel.* 31 The sun rose as Jacob was leaving Peniel, and he was limping because of his hip. 32 Even today the descendants of Israel do not eat the muscle which is on the hip joint, because it was on this muscle that Jacob was struck.

Jacob Meets Esau

33 Jacob saw Esau coming with his 400 men, so he divided the children among Leah, Rachel, and the two concubines. 2 He put the concubines and their children first, then Leah and her children, and finally Rachel and Joseph at the rear. 3 Jacob went ahead of them and bowed down to the ground seven times as he approached his brother. 4 But Esau ran to meet him, threw his arms round him, and kissed him. They were both crying. 5 When Esau looked round and saw the women and the children, he asked, "Who are these people with you?"

"These, sir, are the children whom God has been good enough to give me," Jacob answered. 6 Then the concubines came up with their children and bowed down; 7 then Leah and her children came, and last of all Joseph and Rachel came and bowed down.

8 Esau asked, "What about that other group I met? What did that mean?"

Jacob answered, "It was to gain your favour."

9 But Esau said, "I have enough, my brother; keep what you have."

10 Jacob said, "No, please, if I have gained your favour, accept my gift. To see your face is for me like seeing the face of God, now that you have been so friendly to me. 11 Please accept this gift which I have brought for you; God has been kind to me and given me everything I need." Jacob kept on urging him until he accepted.

12 Esau said, "Let's prepare to leave. I will go ahead of you."

13 Jacob answered, "You know that the children are weak, and I must think of the sheep and cattle with their young. If they are driven hard for even one day, the whole herd will die. 14 Please go on ahead of me, and I will follow slowly, going as fast as I can with the livestock and the children until I catch up with you in Edom."

15 Esau said, "Then let me leave some of my men with you."

But Jacob answered, "There is no need for that for I only want to gain your favour."* 16 So that day Esau started on his way back

....

32.28 *Israel*: This name sounds like the Hebrew for "he struggles with God" or "God struggles".

32.30 *Peniel*: This name sounds like the Hebrew for "the face of God".

33.15 *for I only want to gain your favour*; or *if it's all right with you*.

Genesis

Exodus
Leviticus
Num.
Deuter.
Joshua

to Edom. ¹⁷But Jacob went to Sukkoth, where he built a house for himself and shelters for his livestock. That is why the place was named Sukkoth.*

¹⁸On his return from Mesopotamia Jacob arrived safely at the city of Shechem in the land of Canaan and set up his camp in a field near the city. ¹⁹He bought that part of the field from the descendants of Hamor father of Shechem for a hundred pieces of silver. ²⁰He put up an altar there and named it after El, the God of Israel.

The Rape of Dinah

34 One day Dinah, the daughter of Jacob and Leah, went to visit some of the Canaanite women. ²When Shechem son of Hamor the Hivite, who was chief of that region, saw her, he took her and raped her. ³But he found the young woman so attractive that he fell in love with her and tried to win her affection.* ⁴He said to his father, "I want you to get this woman for me as my wife."

⁵Jacob learnt that his daughter had been disgraced, but because his sons were out in the fields with his livestock, he did nothing until they came back. ⁶Shechem's father Hamor went out to talk with Jacob, ⁷just as Jacob's sons were coming in from the fields. When they heard about it, they were shocked and furious that Shechem had done such a thing and had insulted the people of Israel by raping Jacob's daughter. ⁸Hamor said to him, "My son Shechem has fallen in love with your daughter; please let him marry her. ⁹Let us make an agreement that there will be intermarriage between our people and yours. ¹⁰Then you may stay here in our country with us; you may live anywhere you wish, trade freely, and own property."

¹¹Then Shechem said to Dinah's father and brothers, "Do me this favour, and I will give you whatever you want. ¹²Tell me what presents you want, and set the payment for the bride as high as you wish; I will give you whatever you ask, if you will only let me marry her."

¹³Because Shechem had disgraced their sister Dinah, Jacob's sons answered Shechem and his father Hamor in a deceitful way. ¹⁴They said to him, "We cannot let our sister marry a man who is not circumcised; that would be a disgrace for us. ¹⁵We can agree only on the condition that you become like us by circumcising all your males. ¹⁶Then we will agree to intermarriage. We will settle among you and become one people with you. ¹⁷But if you will not accept our terms and be circumcised, we will take her and leave."

¹⁸These terms seemed fair to Hamor and his son Shechem, ¹⁹and the young man lost no time in doing what was suggested, because he was in love with Jacob's daughter. He was the most important member of his family.

²⁰Hamor and his son Shechem went to the meeting place at the city gate and spoke to the people of the town: ²¹"These men are friendly; let them live in the land with us and travel freely. The land is large enough for them also. Let us marry their daughters and give them ours in marriage. ²²But these men will agree to live among us and be one people with us only on condition that we circumcise all our males, as they are circumcised. ²³Won't all their livestock and everything else they own be ours? So let us agree that they can live among us." ²⁴All the citizens of the city agreed with what Hamor and Shechem proposed, and all the males were circumcised.

33.17 *Sukkoth*: This name in Hebrew means "shelters".
34.3 *tried to win her affection*; or *comforted her*.

25 Three days later, when the men were still sore from their circumcision, two of Jacob's sons, Simeon and Levi, the brothers of Dinah, took their swords, went into the city without arousing suspicion, and killed all the men, 26 including Hamor and his son Shechem. Then they took Dinah from Shechem's house and left. 27 After the slaughter Jacob's other sons looted the town to take revenge for their sister's disgrace. 28 They took the flocks, the cattle, the donkeys, and everything else in the city and in the fields. 29 They took everything of value, captured all the women and children, and carried off everything in the houses.

30 Jacob said to Simeon and Levi, "You have brought trouble on me; now the Canaanites, the Perizzites, and everybody else in the land will hate me. I haven't many men; if they all band together against me and attack me, our whole family will be destroyed."

31 But they answered, "We cannot let our sister be treated like a common whore."

God Blesses Jacob at Bethel

35 God said to Jacob, "Go to Bethel at once, and live there. Build an altar there to me, the God who appeared to you when you were running away from your brother Esau."

2 So Jacob said to his family and to all who were with him, "Get rid of the foreign gods that you have; purify yourselves and put on clean clothes. 3 We are going to leave here and go to Bethel, where I will build an altar to the God who helped me in the time of my trouble and who has been with me everywhere I have gone." 4 So they gave Jacob all the foreign gods that they had and also the earrings that they were wearing. He buried them beneath the oak tree near Shechem.

5 When Jacob and his sons started to leave, great fear fell on the people of the nearby towns, and they did not pursue them. 6 Jacob came with all his people to Luz, which is now known as Bethel, in the land of Canaan. 7 He built an altar there and named the place after the God of Bethel, because God had revealed himself to him there when he was running away from his brother. 8 Rebecca's nurse Deborah died and was buried beneath the oak south of Bethel. So it was named "Oak of Weeping".

9 When Jacob returned from Mesopotamia, God appeared to him again and blessed him. 10 God said to him, "Your name is Jacob, but from now on it will be Israel." So God named him Israel. 11 And God said to him, "I am Almighty God. Have many children. Nations will be descended from you, and you will be the ancestor of kings. 12 I will give you the land which I gave to Abraham and to Isaac, and I will also give it to your descendants after you." 13 Then God left him. 14 There, where God had spoken to him, Jacob set up a memorial stone and consecrated it by pouring wine and olive oil on it. 15 He named the place Bethel.

The Death of Rachel

16 Jacob and his family left Bethel, and when they were still some distance from Ephrath, the time came for Rachel to have her baby, and she was having difficult labour. 17 When her labour pains were at their worst, the midwife said to her, "Don't be afraid, Rachel; it's another boy." 18 But she was dying, and as she breathed her last, she named her son Benoni,* but his father named him Benjamin.*

....

35.18 *Benoni*: This name in Hebrew means "son of my sorrow".
35.18 *Benjamin*: This name in Hebrew means "son who will be fortunate".

GENESIS 35, 36

61

Genesis

·········:·

Exodus
Leviticus
Num.
Deuter.
Joshua

[19]When Rachel died, she was buried beside the road to Ephrath, now known as Bethlehem. [20]Jacob set up a memorial stone there, and it still marks Rachel's grave to this day. [21]Jacob moved on and set up his camp on the other side of the tower of Eder.

The Sons of Jacob
(1 Chr 2.1–2)

[22]While Jacob was living in that land, Reuben had sexual intercourse with Bilhah, one of his father's concubines; Jacob heard about it and was furious.*

Jacob had twelve sons. [23]The sons of Leah were Reuben (Jacob's eldest son), Simeon, Levi, Judah, Issachar, and Zebulun. [24]The sons of Rachel were Joseph and Benjamin. [25]The sons of Rachel's slave Bilhah were Dan and Naphtali. [26]The sons of Leah's slave Zilpah were Gad and Asher. These sons were born in Mesopotamia.

The Death of Isaac
[27]Jacob went to his father Isaac at Mamre, near Hebron, where Abraham and Isaac had lived. [28]Isaac lived to be 180 years old [29]and died at a ripe old age; and his sons Esau and Jacob buried him.

The Descendants of Esau
(1 Chr 1.34–37)

36 These are the descendants of Esau, also called Edom. [2]Esau married Canaanite women: Adah, the daughter of Elon the Hittite; Oholibamah, the daughter of Anah son* of Zibeon the Hivite; [3]and Basemath, the daughter of Ishmael and sister of Nebaioth. [4]Adah bore Eliphaz; Basemath bore Reuel; [5]and Oholibamah bore Jeush, Jalam, and Korah. All these sons were born to Esau in the land of Canaan.

[6]Then Esau took his wives, his sons, his daughters, and all the people of his house, together with all his livestock and all the possessions he had acquired in the land of Canaan, and went away from his brother Jacob to another land. [7]He left because the land where he and Jacob were living was not able to support them; they had too much livestock and could no longer stay together. [8]So Esau lived in the hill country of Edom.

[9]These are the descendants of Esau, the ancestor of the Edomites. [10-13]Esau's wife Adah bore him one son, Eliphaz, and Eliphaz had five sons: Teman, Omar, Zepho, Gatam, and Kenaz. And by another wife, Timna, he had one more son, Amalek.

Esau's wife Basemath bore him one son, Reuel, and Reuel had four sons: Nahath, Zerah, Shammah, and Mizzah.

[14]Esau's wife Oholibamah, the daughter of Anah son* of Zibeon, bore him three sons: Jeush, Jalam, and Korah.

[15]These are the tribes descended from Esau. Esau's first son Eliphaz was the ancestor of the following tribes: Teman, Omar, Zepho, Kenaz, [16]Korah, Gatam, and Amalek. These were all descendants of Esau's wife Adah.

[17]Esau's son Reuel was the ancestor of the following tribes: Nahath, Zerah, Shammah, and Mizzah. These were all descendants of Esau's wife Basemath.

35.22 One ancient translation *and was furious*; Hebrew does not have these words.
36.2; 36.14 Some ancient translations *son*; Hebrew *daughter*; or *granddaughter*.

¹⁸The following tribes were descended from Esau by his wife Oholibamah, the daughter of Anah: Jeush, Jalam, and Korah. ¹⁹All these tribes were descended from Esau.

The Descendants of Seir
(1 Chr 1.38–42)

²⁰⁻²¹The original inhabitants of the land of Edom were divided into tribes which traced their ancestry to the following descendants of Seir, a Horite: Lotan, Shobal, Zibeon, Anah, Dishon, Ezer, and Dishan.

²²Lotan was the ancestor of the clans of Hori and Heman. (Lotan had a sister named Timna.)

²³Shobal was the ancestor of the clans of Alvan, Manahath, Ebal, Shepho, and Onam.

²⁴Zibeon had two sons, Aiah and Anah. (This is the Anah who found the hot springs in the wilderness when he was taking care of his father's donkeys.) ²⁵⁻²⁶Anah was the father of Dishon, who was the ancestor of the clans of Hemdan, Eshban, Ithran, and Cheran. Anah also had a daughter named Oholibamah.

²⁷Ezer was the ancestor of the clans of Bilhan, Zaavan, and Akan.

²⁸Dishan was the ancestor of the clans of Uz and Aran.

²⁹⁻³⁰These are the Horite tribes in the land of Edom: Lotan, Shobal, Zibeon, Anah, Dishon, Ezer, and Dishan.

The Kings of Edom
(1 Chr 1.43–54)

³¹⁻³⁹Before there were any kings in Israel, the following kings ruled over the land of Edom in succession:

Bela son of Beor from Dinhabah
Jobab son of Zerah from Bozrah
Husham from the region of Teman
Hadad son of Bedad from Avith (he defeated the
    Midianites in a battle in the country of Moab)
Samlah from Masrekah
Shaul from Rehoboth-on-the-River
Baal Hanan son of Achbor
Hadad from Pau (his wife was Mehetabel, the daughter of
    Matred and granddaughter of Mezahab).

⁴⁰⁻⁴³Esau was the ancestor of the following Edomite tribes: Timna, Alvah, Jetheth, Oholibamah, Elah, Pinon, Kenaz, Teman, Mibzar, Magdiel, and Iram. The area where each of these tribes lived was known by the name of the tribe.

Joseph and his Brothers

37 Jacob continued to live in the land of Canaan, where his father had lived, ²and this is the story of Jacob's family.

Joseph, a young man of seventeen, took care of the sheep and goats with his brothers, the sons of Bilhah and Zilpah, his father's concubines. He brought bad reports to his father about what his brothers were doing.

³Jacob loved Joseph more than all his other sons, because he had been born to him when he was old. He made a long robe with full sleeves* for him. ⁴When his brothers saw that their father loved Joseph more than he loved them, they hated their brother so much that they would not speak to him in a friendly manner.

⁵One night Joseph had a dream, and when he told his brothers about it, they hated him even more. ⁶He said, "Listen to the dream

....

37.3 *robe with full sleeves*; or *decorated robe*.

Genesis

Exodus
Leviticus
Num.
Deuter.
Joshua

I had. ⁷We were all in the field tying up sheaves of wheat, when my sheaf got up and stood up straight. Yours formed a circle round mine and bowed down to it."

⁸"Do you think you are going to be a king and rule over us?" his brothers asked. So they hated him even more because of his dreams and because of what he said about them.

⁹Then Joseph had another dream and said to his brothers, "I had another dream, in which I saw the sun, the moon, and eleven stars bowing down to me."

¹⁰He also told the dream to his father, and his father scolded him: "What kind of a dream is that? Do you think that your mother, your brothers, and I are going to come and bow down to you?" ¹¹Joseph's brothers were jealous of him, but his father kept thinking about the whole matter.

Joseph is Sold and Taken to Egypt

¹²One day when Joseph's brothers had gone to Shechem to take care of their father's flock, ¹³Jacob said to Joseph, "I want you to go to Shechem, where your brothers are taking care of the flock."

Joseph answered, "I am ready."

¹⁴His father said, "Go and see if your brothers are safe and if the flock is all right; then come back and tell me." So his father sent him on his way from the Valley of Hebron.

Joseph arrived at Shechem ¹⁵and was wandering about in the country when a man saw him and asked him, "What are you looking for?"

¹⁶"I am looking for my brothers, who are taking care of their flock," he answered. "Can you tell me where they are?"

¹⁷The man said, "They have already left. I heard them say that they were going to Dothan." So Joseph went after his brothers and found them at Dothan.

¹⁸They saw him in the distance, and before he reached them, they plotted against him and decided to kill him. ¹⁹They said to one another, "Here comes that dreamer. ²⁰Come on now, let's kill him and throw his body into one of the dry wells. We can say that a wild animal killed him. Then we will see what becomes of his dreams."

²¹Reuben heard them and tried to save Joseph. "Let's not kill him," he said. ²²"Just throw him into this well in the wilderness, but don't hurt him." He said this, planning to save him from them and send him back to his father. ²³When Joseph came up to his brothers, they ripped off his long robe with full sleeves.* ²⁴Then they took him and threw him into the well, which was dry.

²⁵While they were eating, they suddenly saw a group of Ishmaelites travelling from Gilead to Egypt. Their camels were loaded with spices and resins. ²⁶Judah said to his brothers, "What will we gain by killing our brother and covering up the murder? ²⁷Let's sell him to these Ishmaelites. Then we won't have to hurt him; after all, he is our brother, our own flesh and blood." His brothers agreed, ²⁸and when some Midianite traders came by, the brothers* pulled Joseph out of the well and sold him for twenty pieces of silver to the Ishmaelites, who took him to Egypt.

²⁹When Reuben came back to the well and found that Joseph was not there, he tore his clothes in sorrow. ³⁰He returned to his brothers and said, "The boy is not there! What am I going to do?"

37.23 *robe with full sleeves*; or *decorated robe*.
37.28 *the brothers*; Hebrew *they*.

GENESIS 37.19

Joseph was

— KNOWN AS THE —

'DREAMER'

because God spoke to him through dreams and visions. Where you are right now, why not ask God in prayer to give you a vision or dream for your life.

write some thoughts here

³¹ Then they killed a goat and dipped Joseph's robe in its blood. ³² They took the robe to their father and said, "We found this. Does it belong to your son?"

³³ He recognized it and said, "Yes, it is his! Some wild animal has killed him. My son Joseph has been torn to pieces!" ³⁴ Jacob tore his clothes in sorrow and put on sackcloth. He mourned for his son a long time. ³⁵ All his sons and daughters came to comfort him, but he refused to be comforted and said, "I will go down to the world of the dead still mourning for my son." So he continued to mourn for his son Joseph.

³⁶ Meanwhile, in Egypt, the Midianites had sold Joseph to Potiphar, one of the king's officers, who was the captain of the palace guard.

Judah and Tamar

38 About that time Judah left his brothers and went to stay with a man named Hirah, who was from the town of Adullam. ² There Judah met a young Canaanite woman whose father was named Shua. He married her, ³ and she bore him a son, whom he named Er. ⁴ She became pregnant again and bore another son and named him Onan. ⁵ Again she had a son and named him Shelah. Judah was at Achzib when the boy was born.

⁶ For his first son Er, Judah got a wife whose name was Tamar. ⁷ Er's conduct was evil, and it displeased the LORD, so the LORD killed him. ⁸ Then Judah said to Er's brother Onan, "Go and sleep with your brother's widow. Fulfil your obligation to her as her husband's brother, so that your brother may have descendants." ⁹ But Onan knew that the children would not belong to him, so whenever he had intercourse with his brother's widow, he let the semen spill on the ground, so that there would be no children for his brother. ¹⁰ What he did displeased the LORD, and the LORD killed him also. ¹¹ Then Judah said to his daughter-in-law Tamar, "Return to your father's house and remain a widow until my son Shelah grows up." He said this because he was afraid that Shelah would be killed, as his brothers had been. So Tamar went back home.

¹² After some time Judah's wife died. When he had finished the time of mourning, he and his friend Hirah of Adullam went to Timnah, where his sheep were being sheared. ¹³ Someone told Tamar that her father-in-law was going to Timnah to shear his sheep. ¹⁴ So she changed from the widow's clothes she had been wearing, covered her face with a veil, and sat down at the entrance to Enaim, a town on the road to Timnah. As she well knew, Judah's youngest son Shelah had now grown up, and yet she had not been given to him in marriage.

¹⁵ When Judah saw her, he thought that she was a prostitute, because she had her face covered. ¹⁶ He went over to her at the side of the road and said, "All right, how much do you charge?" (He did not know that she was his daughter-in-law.)

She said, "What will you give me?"

¹⁷ He answered, "I will send you a young goat from my flock."

She said, "All right, if you will give me something to keep as a pledge until you send the goat."

¹⁸ "What shall I give you as a pledge?" he asked.

She answered, "Your seal with its cord and the stick you are carrying." He gave them to her. Then they had intercourse, and she became pregnant. ¹⁹ Tamar went home, took off her veil, and put her widow's clothes back on.

²⁰ Judah sent his friend Hirah to take the goat and get back from the woman the articles he had pledged, but Hirah could not

GENESIS 38, 39

65

Genesis
···········

Exodus
Leviticus
Num.
Deuter.
Joshua

find her. ²¹He asked some men at Enaim, "Where is the prostitute who was here by the road?"

"There has never been a prostitute here," they answered.

²²He returned to Judah and said, "I couldn't find her. The men of the place said that there had never been a prostitute there."

²³Judah said, "Let her keep the things. We don't want people to laugh at us. I did try to pay her, but you couldn't find her."

²⁴About three months later someone said to Judah, "Your daughter-in-law Tamar has been acting like a whore, and now she is pregnant."

Judah ordered, "Take her out and burn her to death."

²⁵As she was being taken out, she sent word to her father-in-law: "I am pregnant by the man who owns these things. Look at them and see whose they are — this seal with its cord and this stick."

²⁶Judah recognized them and said, "She is in the right. I have failed in my obligation to her — I should have given her to my son Shelah in marriage." And Judah never had intercourse with her again.

²⁷When the time came for her to give birth, it was discovered that she was going to have twins. ²⁸While she was in labour, one of them put out an arm; the midwife caught it, tied a red thread round it, and said, "This one was born first." ²⁹But he pulled his arm back, and his brother was born first. Then the midwife said, "So this is how you break your way out!" So he was named Perez.* ³⁰Then his brother was born with the red thread on his arm, and he was named Zerah.*

Joseph and Potiphar's Wife

39 Now the Ishmaelites had taken Joseph to Egypt and sold him to Potiphar, one of the king's officers, who was the captain of the palace guard. ²The LORD was with Joseph and made him successful. He lived in the house of his Egyptian master, ³who saw that the LORD was with Joseph and had made him successful in everything he did. ⁴Potiphar was pleased with him and made him his personal servant; so he put him in charge of his house and everything he owned. ⁵From then on, because of Joseph the LORD blessed the household of the Egyptian and everything that he had in his house and in his fields. ⁶Potiphar handed over everything he had to the care of Joseph and did not concern himself with anything except the food he ate.

Joseph was well-built and good-looking, ⁷and after a while his master's wife began to desire Joseph and asked him to go to bed with her. ⁸He refused and said to her, "Look, my master does not have to concern himself with anything in the house, because I am here. He has put me in charge of everything he has. ⁹I have as much authority in this house as he has, and he has not kept back anything from me except you. How then could I do such an immoral thing and sin against God?" ¹⁰Although she asked Joseph day after day, he would not go to bed with her.

¹¹But one day when Joseph went into the house to do his work, none of the house servants was there. ¹²She caught him by his robe and said, "Come to bed with me." But he escaped and ran outside, leaving his robe in her hand. ¹³When she saw that he had left his robe and had run out of the house, ¹⁴she called to her house servants and said, "Look at this! This Hebrew that my husband

38.29 *Perez*: This name in Hebrew means "breaking out".
38.30 *Zerah*: This name sounds like a Hebrew word for the red brightness of dawn.

brought to the house is insulting us. He came into my room and tried to rape me, but I screamed as loud as I could. [15] When he heard me scream, he ran outside, leaving his robe beside me."

[16] She kept his robe with her until Joseph's master came home. [17] Then she told him the same story: "That Hebrew slave that you brought here came into my room and insulted me. [18] But when I screamed, he ran outside, leaving his robe beside me."

[19] Joseph's master was furious [20] and had Joseph arrested and put in the prison where the king's prisoners were kept, and there he stayed. [21] But the LORD was with Joseph and blessed him, so that the jailer was pleased with him. [22] He put Joseph in charge of all the other prisoners and made him responsible for everything that was done in the prison. [23] The jailer did not have to look after anything for which Joseph was responsible, because the LORD was with Joseph and made him succeed in everything he did.

Joseph Interprets the Prisoners' Dreams

40 Some time later the king of Egypt's wine steward and his chief baker offended the king. [2] He was angry with these two officials [3] and put them in prison in the house of the captain of the guard, in the same place where Joseph was being kept. [4] They spent a long time in prison, and the captain assigned Joseph as their servant.

[5] One night there in prison the wine steward and the chief baker each had a dream, and the dreams had different meanings. [6] When Joseph came to them in the morning, he saw that they were upset. [7] He asked them, "Why do you look so worried today?"

[8] They answered, "Each of us had a dream, and there is no one here to explain what the dreams mean."

"It is God who gives the ability to interpret dreams," Joseph said. "Tell me your dreams."

[9] So the wine steward said, "In my dream there was a grapevine in front of me [10] with three branches on it. As soon as the leaves came out, the blossoms appeared, and the grapes ripened. [11] I was holding the king's cup; so I took the grapes and squeezed them into the cup and gave it to him."

[12] Joseph said, "This is what it means: the three branches are three days. [13] In three days the king will release you, pardon you, and restore you to your position. You will give him his cup as you did before when you were his wine steward. [14] But please remember me when everything is going well for you, and please be kind enough to mention me to the king and help me to get out of this prison. [15] After all, I was kidnapped from the land of the Hebrews, and even here in Egypt I didn't do anything to deserve being put in prison."

[16] When the chief baker saw that the interpretation of the wine steward's dream was favourable, he said to Joseph, "I had a dream too; I was carrying three bread baskets on my head. [17] In the top basket there were all kinds of pastries for the king, and the birds were eating them."

[18] Joseph answered, "This is what it means: the three baskets are three days. [19] In three days the king will release you — and have your head cut off! Then he will hang your body on a pole, and the birds will eat your flesh."

[20] On his birthday three days later the king gave a banquet for all his officials; he released his wine steward and his chief baker and brought them before his officials. [21] He restored the wine steward to his former position, [22] but he executed the chief baker. It all happened just as Joseph had said. [23] But the wine steward never gave Joseph another thought — he forgot all about him.

Genesis

Exodus
Leviticus
Num.
Deuter.
Joshua

Joseph Interprets the King's Dreams

41 After two years had passed, the king of Egypt dreamt that he was standing by the River Nile, [2] when seven cows, fat and sleek, came up out of the river and began to feed on the grass. [3] Then seven other cows came up; they were thin and bony. They came and stood by the other cows on the river bank, [4] and the thin cows ate up the fat cows. Then the king woke up. [5] He fell asleep again and had another dream. Seven ears of corn, full and ripe, were growing on one stalk. [6] Then seven other ears of corn sprouted, thin and scorched by the desert wind, [7] and the thin ears of corn swallowed the full ones. The king woke up and realized that he had been dreaming. [8] In the morning he was worried, so he sent for all the magicians and wise men of Egypt. He told them his dreams, but no one could explain them to him.

[9] Then the wine steward said to the king, "I must confess today that I have done wrong. [10] You were angry with the chief baker and me, and you put us in prison in the house of the captain of the guard. [11] One night each of us had a dream, and the dreams had different meanings. [12] A young Hebrew was there with us, a slave of the captain of the guard. We told him our dreams, and he interpreted them for us. [13] Things turned out just as he said: you restored me to my position, but you executed the baker."

[14] The king sent for Joseph, and he was immediately brought from the prison. After he had shaved and changed his clothes, he came into the king's presence. [15] The king said to him, "I have had a dream, and no one can explain it. I have been told that you can interpret dreams."

[16] Joseph answered, "I cannot, Your Majesty, but God will give a favourable interpretation."

[17] The king said, "I dreamt that I was standing on the bank of the Nile, [18] when seven cows, fat and sleek, came up out of the river and began feeding on the grass. [19] Then seven other cows came up which were thin and bony. They were the poorest cows I have ever seen anywhere in Egypt. [20] The thin cows ate up the fat ones, [21] but no one would have known it, because they looked just as bad as before. Then I woke up. [22] I also dreamt that I saw seven ears of corn which were full and ripe, growing on one stalk. [23] Then seven ears of corn sprouted, thin and scorched by the desert wind, [24] and the thin ears of corn swallowed the full ones. I told the dreams to the magicians, but none of them could explain them to me."

[25] Joseph said to the king, "The two dreams mean the same thing; God has told you what he is going to do. [26] The seven fat cows are seven years, and the seven full ears of corn are also seven years; they have the same meaning. [27] The seven thin cows which came up later and the seven thin ears of corn scorched by the desert wind are seven years of famine. [28] It is just as I told you — God has shown you what he is going to do. [29] There will be seven years of great plenty in all the land of Egypt. [30] After that, there will be seven years of famine, and all the good years will be forgotten, because the famine will ruin the country. [31] The time of plenty will be entirely forgotten, because the famine which follows will be so terrible. [32] The repetition of your dream means that the matter is fixed by God and that he will make it happen in the near future.

[33] "Now you should choose some man with wisdom and insight and put him in charge of the country. [34] You must also appoint other officials and take a fifth of the crops during the seven years of plenty. [35] Order them to collect all the food during the good

GENESIS 41.16

Ultimately, Joseph realised that

HE COULDN'T DO

ANYTHING

- it was God who was working through him.

Write the words 'God can' and, around these words, write all the things that you believe God can do.

years that are coming, and give them authority to store up corn in the cities and guard it. [36] The food will be a reserve supply for the country during the seven years of famine which are going to come on Egypt. In this way the people will not starve."

Joseph is Made Governor over Egypt

[37] The king and his officials approved this plan, [38] and he said to them, "We will never find a better man than Joseph, a man who has God's Spirit in him." [39] The king said to Joseph, "God has shown you all this, so it is obvious that you have greater wisdom and insight than anyone else. [40] I will put you in charge of my country, and all my people will obey your orders. Your authority will be second only to mine. [41] I now appoint you governor over all Egypt." [42] The king removed from his finger the ring engraved with the royal seal and put it on Joseph's finger. He put a fine linen robe on him, and placed a gold chain round his neck. [43] He gave him the second royal chariot to ride in, and his guard of honour went ahead of him and cried out, "Make way! Make way!" And so Joseph was appointed governor over all Egypt. [44] The king said to him, "I am the king — and no one in all Egypt shall so much as lift a hand or a foot without your permission." [45-46] He gave Joseph the Egyptian name Zaphenath Paneah, and he gave him a wife, Asenath, the daughter of Potiphera, a priest in the city of Heliopolis.

Joseph was thirty years old when he began to serve the king of Egypt. He left the king's court and travelled all over the land. [47] During the seven years of plenty the land produced abundant crops, [48] all of which Joseph collected and stored in the cities. In each city he stored the food from the fields around it. [49] There was so much corn that Joseph stopped measuring it — it was like the sand of the sea.

[50] Before the years of famine came, Joseph had two sons by Asenath. [51] He said, "God has made me forget all my sufferings and all my father's family"; so he named his first son Manasseh.* [52] He also said, "God has given me children in the land of my trouble"; so he named his second son Ephraim.*

[53] The seven years of plenty that the land of Egypt had enjoyed came to an end, [54] and the seven years of famine began, just as Joseph had said. There was famine in every other country, but there was food throughout Egypt. [55] When the Egyptians began to be hungry, they cried out to the king for food. So he ordered them to go to Joseph and do what he told them. [56] The famine grew worse and spread over the whole country, so Joseph opened all the storehouses and sold corn to the Egyptians. [57] People came to Egypt from all over the world to buy corn from Joseph, because the famine was severe everywhere.

Joseph's Brothers Go to Egypt to Buy Corn

42 When Jacob learnt that there was corn in Egypt, he said to his sons, "Why don't you do something? [2] I hear that there is corn in Egypt; go there and buy some to keep us from starving to death." [3] So Joseph's ten half-brothers went to buy corn in Egypt, [4] but Jacob did not send Joseph's full-brother Benjamin with them, because he was afraid that something might happen to him.

[5] The sons of Jacob came with others to buy corn, because there was famine in the land of Canaan. [6] Joseph, as governor

41.51 *Manasseh*: This name sounds like the Hebrew for "cause to forget".
41.52 *Ephraim*: This name sounds like the Hebrew for "give children".

Genesis
·········:·

Exodus
Leviticus
Num.
Deuter.
Joshua

of the land of Egypt, was selling corn to people from all over the world. So Joseph's brothers came and bowed down before him with their faces to the ground. [7]When Joseph saw his brothers, he recognized them, but he acted as if he did not know them. He asked them harshly, "Where do you come from?"

"We have come from Canaan to buy food," they answered.

[8]Although Joseph recognized his brothers, they did not recognize him. [9]He remembered the dreams he had dreamt about them and said, "You are spies; you have come to find out where our country is weak."

[10]"No, sir," they answered. "We have come as your slaves, to buy food. [11]We are all brothers. We are not spies, sir, we are honest men."

[12]Joseph said to them, "No! You have come to find out where our country is weak."

[13]They said, "We were twelve brothers in all, sir, sons of the same man in the land of Canaan. One brother is dead, and the youngest is now with our father."

[14]"It is just as I said," Joseph answered. "You are spies. [15]This is how you will be tested: I swear by the name of the king that you will never leave unless your youngest brother comes here. [16]One of you must go and get him. The rest of you will be kept under guard until the truth of what you say can be tested. Otherwise, as sure as the king lives, you are spies." [17]Then he put them in prison for three days.

[18]On the third day Joseph said to them, "I am a God-fearing man, and I will spare your lives on one condition. [19]To prove that you are honest, one of you will stay in the prison where you have been kept; the rest of you may go and take back to your starving families the corn that you have bought. [20]Then you must bring your youngest brother to me. This will prove that you have been telling the truth, and I will not put you to death."

They agreed to this [21]and said to one another, "Yes, now we are suffering the consequences of what we did to our brother; we saw the great trouble he was in when he begged for help, but we would not listen. That is why we are in this trouble now."

[22]Reuben said, "I told you not to harm the boy, but you wouldn't listen. And now we are being paid back for his death." [23]Joseph understood what they said, but they did not know it, because they had been speaking to him through an interpreter. [24]Joseph left them and began to cry. When he was able to speak again, he came back, picked out Simeon, and had him tied up in front of them.

Joseph's Brothers Return to Canaan

[25]Joseph gave orders to fill his brothers' packs with corn, to put each man's money back in his sack, and to give them food for the journey. This was done. [26]The brothers loaded their donkeys with the corn they had bought, and then they left. [27]At the place where they spent the night, one of them opened his sack to feed his donkey and found his money at the top of the sack. [28]"My money has been returned to me," he called to his brothers. "Here it is in my sack!" Their hearts sank, and in fear they asked one another, "What has God done to us?"

[29]When they came to their father Jacob in Canaan, they told him all that had happened to them: [30]"The governor of Egypt spoke harshly to us and accused us of spying against his country. [31]'We are not spies,' we answered, 'we are honest men. [32]We were twelve brothers in all, sons of the same father. One brother is dead, and the youngest is still in Canaan with our father.' [33]The man

answered, 'This is how I will find out if you are honest men: one of you will stay with me; the rest will take corn for your starving families and leave. [34] Bring your youngest brother to me. Then I will know that you are not spies, but honest men; I will give your brother back to you, and you can stay here and trade.'"

[35] Then when they emptied out their sacks, every one of them found his bag of money; and when they saw the money, they and their father Jacob were afraid. [36] Their father said to them, "Do you want to make me lose all my children? Joseph is gone; Simeon is gone; and now you want to take away Benjamin. I am the one who suffers!"

[37] Reuben said to his father, "If I do not bring Benjamin back to you, you can kill my two sons. Put him in my care, and I will bring him back."

[38] But Jacob said, "My son cannot go with you; his brother is dead, and he is the only one left. Something might happen to him on the way. I am an old man, and the sorrow you would cause me would kill me."

Joseph's Brothers Return to Egypt with Benjamin

43 The famine in Canaan got worse, [2] and when the family of Jacob had eaten all the corn which had been brought from Egypt, Jacob said to his sons, "Go back and buy a little food for us."

[3] Judah said to him, "The man sternly warned us that we would not be admitted to his presence unless we had our brother with us. [4] If you are willing to send our brother with us, we will go and buy food for you. [5] If you are not willing, we will not go, because the man told us we would not be admitted to his presence unless our brother was with us."

[6] Jacob said, "Why did you cause me so much trouble by telling the man that you had another brother?"

[7] They answered, "The man kept asking about us and our family, 'Is your father still living? Have you got another brother?' We had to answer his questions. How could we know that he would tell us to bring our brother with us?"

[8] Judah said to his father, "Send the boy with me, and we will leave at once. Then none of us will starve to death. [9] I will pledge my own life, and you can hold me responsible for him. If I do not bring him back to you safe and sound, I will always bear the blame. [10] If we had not waited so long, we could have been there and back twice by now."

[11] Their father said to them, "If that is how it has to be, then take the best products of the land in your packs as a present for the governor: a little resin, a little honey, spices, pistachio nuts, and almonds. [12] Take with you also twice as much money, because you must take back the money that was returned in the top of your sacks. Maybe it was a mistake. [13] Take your brother and return at once. [14] May Almighty God cause the man to have pity on you, so that he will give Benjamin and your other brother back to you. As for me, if I must lose my children, I must lose them."

[15] So the brothers took the gifts and twice as much money, and set out for Egypt with Benjamin. There they presented themselves to Joseph. [16] When Joseph saw Benjamin with them, he said to the servant in charge of his house, "Take these men to my house. They are going to eat with me at noon, so kill an animal and prepare it." [17] The servant did as he was commanded and took the brothers to Joseph's house.

[18] As they were being brought to the house, they were afraid and thought, "We are being brought here because of the money that

GENESIS 43, 44

71

Genesis
....
Exodus
Leviticus
Num.
Deuter.
Joshua

was returned in our sacks the first time. They will suddenly attack us, take our donkeys, and make us his slaves." ¹⁹So at the door of the house, they said to the servant in charge, ²⁰"If you please, sir, we came here once before to buy food. ²¹When we set up camp on the way home, we opened our sacks, and each man found his money in the top of his sack — every bit of it. We have brought it back to you. ²²We have also brought some more money with us to buy more food. We do not know who put our money back in our sacks."

²³The servant said, "Don't worry. Don't be afraid. Your God, the God of your father, must have put the money in your sacks for you. I received your payment." Then he brought Simeon to them.

²⁴The servant took the brothers into the house. He gave them water so that they could wash their feet, and he fed their donkeys. ²⁵They got their gifts ready to present to Joseph when he arrived at noon, because they had been told that they were to eat with him. ²⁶When Joseph got home, they took the gifts into the house to him and bowed down to the ground before him. ²⁷He asked about their health and then said, "You told me about your old father — how is he? Is he still alive and well?"

²⁸They answered, "Your humble servant, our father, is still alive and well." And they knelt and bowed down before him.

²⁹When Joseph saw his brother Benjamin, he said, "So this is your youngest brother, the one you told me about. God bless you, my son." ³⁰Then Joseph left suddenly, because his heart was full of tender feelings for his brother. He was about to break down, so he went to his room and cried. ³¹After he had washed his face, he came out, and controlling himself, he ordered the meal to be served. ³²Joseph was served at one table and his brothers at another. The Egyptians who were eating there were served separately, because they considered it beneath their dignity to eat with Hebrews. ³³The brothers had been seated at table, facing Joseph, in the order of their age from the eldest to the youngest. When they saw how they had been seated, they looked at one another in amazement. ³⁴Food was served to them from Joseph's table, and Benjamin was served five times as much as the rest of them. So they ate and drank with Joseph until they were drunk.

The Missing Cup

44 Joseph commanded the servant in charge of his house, "Fill the men's sacks with as much food as they can carry, and put each man's money in the top of his sack. ²Put my silver cup in the top of the youngest brother's sack, together with the money for his corn." He did as he was told. ³Early in the morning the brothers were sent on their way with their donkeys. ⁴When they had gone only a short distance from the city, Joseph said to the servant in charge of his house, "Hurry after those men. When you catch up with them, ask them, 'Why have you paid back evil for good? ⁵Why did you steal my master's silver cup?* It is the one he drinks from, the one he uses for divination. You have committed a serious crime!' "

⁶When the servant caught up with them, he repeated these words. ⁷They answered him, "What do you mean, sir, by talking like this? We swear that we have done no such thing. ⁸You know that we brought back to you from the land of Canaan the money we found in the top of our sacks. Why then should we steal silver or gold from your master's house? ⁹Sir, if any one of us is found

....

44.5 One ancient translation *Why did you steal my master's silver cup?*; Hebrew does not have these words.

to have it, he will be put to death, and the rest of us will become your slaves."

[10] He said, "I agree; but only the one who has taken the cup will become my slave, and the rest of you can go free." [11] So they quickly lowered their sacks to the ground, and each man opened his sack. [12] Joseph's servant searched carefully, beginning with the eldest and ending with the youngest, and the cup was found in Benjamin's sack. [13] The brothers tore their clothes in sorrow, loaded their donkeys, and returned to the city.

[14] When Judah and his brothers came to Joseph's house, he was still there. They bowed down before him, [15] and Joseph said, "What have you done? Didn't you know that a man in my position could find you out by practising divination?"

[16] "What can we say to you, sir?" Judah answered. "How can we argue? How can we clear ourselves? God has uncovered our guilt. All of us are now your slaves and not just the one with whom the cup was found."

[17] Joseph said, "Oh, no! I would never do that! Only the one who had the cup will be my slave. The rest of you may go back safe and sound to your father."

Judah Pleads for Benjamin

[18] Judah went up to Joseph and said, "Please, sir, allow me to speak with you freely. Don't be angry with me; you are like the king himself. [19] Sir, you asked us, 'Have you got a father or another brother?' [20] We answered, 'We have a father who is old and a younger brother, born to him in his old age. The boy's brother is dead, and he is the only one of his mother's children still alive; his father loves him very much.' [21] Sir, you told us to bring him here, so that you could see him, [22] and we answered that the boy could not leave his father; if he did, his father would die. [23] Then you said, 'You will not be admitted to my presence again unless your youngest brother comes with you.'

[24] "When we went back to our father, we told him what you had said. [25] Then he told us to return and buy a little food. [26] We answered, 'We cannot go; we will not be admitted to the man's presence unless our youngest brother is with us. We can go only if our youngest brother goes also.' [27] Our father said to us, 'You know that my wife Rachel bore me only two sons. [28] One of them has already left me. He must have been torn to pieces by wild animals, because I have not seen him since he left. [29] If you take this one from me now and something happens to him, the sorrow you would cause me would kill me, old as I am.'

[30-31] "And now, sir," Judah continued, "if I go back to my father without the boy, as soon as he sees that the boy is not with me, he will die. His life is wrapped up with the life of the boy, and he is so old that the sorrow we would cause him would kill him. [32] What is more, I pledged my life to my father for the boy. I told him that if I did not bring the boy back to him, I would bear the blame all my life. [33] And now, sir, I will stay here as your slave in place of the boy; let him go back with his brothers. [34] How can I go back to my father if the boy is not with me? I cannot bear to see this disaster come upon my father."

Joseph Tells his Brothers Who he Is

45 Joseph was no longer able to control his feelings in front of his servants, so he ordered them all to leave the room. No one else was with him when Joseph told his brothers who he was. [2] He cried with such loud sobs that the Egyptians heard it, and the news was taken to the king's palace. ³ Joseph said to his brothers, "I am Joseph. Is my father still alive?" But when his brothers heard this, they were so terrified that they could not answer. ⁴ Then Joseph said to them, "Please come closer." They did, and he said, "I am your brother Joseph, whom you sold into Egypt. ⁵ Now do not be upset or blame yourselves because you sold me here. It was really God who sent me ahead of you to save people's lives. ⁶ This is only the second year of famine in the land; there will be five more years in which there will be neither ploughing nor reaping. ⁷ God sent me ahead of you to rescue you in this amazing way and to make sure that you and your descendants survive. ⁸ So it was not really you who sent me here, but God. He has made me the king's highest official. I am in charge of his whole country; I am the ruler of all Egypt.

⁹ "Now hurry back to my father and tell him that this is what his son Joseph says: 'God has made me ruler of all Egypt; come to me without delay. ¹⁰ You can live in the region of Goshen, where you can be near me — you, your children, your grandchildren, your sheep, your goats, your cattle, and everything else that you have. ¹¹ If you are in Goshen, I can take care of you. There will still be five years of famine; and I do not want you, your family, and your livestock to starve.' "

¹² Joseph continued, "Now all of you, and you too, Benjamin, can see that I am really Joseph. ¹³ Tell my father how powerful I am here in Egypt and tell him about everything that you have seen. Then hurry and bring him here."

¹⁴ He threw his arms round his brother Benjamin and began to cry; Benjamin also cried as he hugged him. ¹⁵ Then, still weeping, he embraced each of his brothers and kissed them. After that, his brothers began to talk with him.

¹⁶ When the news reached the palace that Joseph's brothers had come, the king and his officials were pleased. ¹⁷ He said to Joseph, "Tell your brothers to load their animals and to return to the land of Canaan. ¹⁸ Let them get their father and their families and come back here. I will give them the best land in Egypt, and they will have more than enough to live on. ¹⁹ Tell them also to take wagons with them from Egypt for their wives and small children and to bring their father with them. ²⁰ They are not to worry about leaving their possessions behind; the best in the whole land of Egypt will be theirs."

²¹ Jacob's sons did as they were told. Joseph gave them wagons, as the king had ordered, and food for the journey. ²² He also gave each of them a change of clothes, but he gave Benjamin 300 pieces of silver and five changes of clothes. ²³ He sent his father ten donkeys loaded with the best Egyptian goods and ten donkeys loaded with corn, bread, and other food for the journey. ²⁴ He sent his brothers off and as they left, he said to them, "Don't quarrel on the way."

²⁵ They left Egypt and went back home to their father Jacob in Canaan. ²⁶ "Joseph is still alive!" they told him. "He is the ruler of all Egypt!" Jacob was stunned and could not believe them.

²⁷ But when they told him all that Joseph had said to them, and when he saw the wagons which Joseph had sent to take him to Egypt, he recovered from the shock. ²⁸ "My son Joseph is still alive!" he said. "This is all I could ask for! I must go and see him before I die."

Jacob and his Family Go to Egypt

46 Jacob packed up all he had and went to Beersheba, where he offered sacrifices to the God of his father Isaac. ² God spoke to him in a vision at night and called, "Jacob, Jacob!"

TURN THESE SHAPES INTO

SOMETHING
ELSE.

"Yes, here I am," he answered.

³"I am God, the God of your father," he said. "Do not be afraid to go to Egypt; I will make your descendants a great nation there. ⁴I will go with you to Egypt, and I will bring your descendants back to this land. Joseph will be with you when you die."

⁵Jacob set out from Beersheba. His sons put him, their small children, and their wives in the wagons which the king of Egypt had sent. ⁶They took their livestock and the possessions they had acquired in Canaan and went to Egypt. Jacob took all his descendants with him: ⁷his sons, his grandsons, his daughters, and his granddaughters.

⁸The members of Jacob's family who went to Egypt with him were his eldest son Reuben ⁹and Reuben's sons: Hanoch, Pallu, Hezron, and Carmi. ¹⁰Simeon and his sons: Jemuel, Jamin, Ohad, Jachin, Zohar, and Shaul, the son of a Canaanite woman. ¹¹Levi and his sons: Gershon, Kohath, and Merari. ¹²Judah and his sons: Shelah, Perez, and Zerah. (Judah's other sons, Er and Onan, had died in Canaan.) Perez' sons were Hezron and Hamul. ¹³Issachar and his sons: Tola, Puah, Jashub, and Shimron. ¹⁴Zebulun and his sons: Sered, Elon, and Jahleel. ¹⁵These are the sons that Leah had borne to Jacob in Mesopotamia, besides his daughter Dinah. In all, his descendants by Leah numbered 33.

¹⁶Gad and his sons: Zephon, Haggi, Shuni, Ezbon, Eri, Arod, and Areli. ¹⁷Asher and his sons: Imnah, Ishvah, Ishvi, Beriah, and their sister Serah. Beriah's sons were Heber and Malchiel. ¹⁸These sixteen are the descendants of Jacob by Zilpah, the slave woman whom Laban gave to his daughter Leah.

¹⁹Jacob's wife Rachel bore him two sons: Joseph and Benjamin. ²⁰In Egypt Joseph had two sons, Manasseh and Ephraim, by Asenath, the daughter of Potiphera, a priest in Heliopolis. ²¹Benjamin's sons were Bela, Becher, Ashbel, Gera, Naaman, Ehi, Rosh, Muppim, Huppim, and Ard. ²²These fourteen are the descendants of Jacob by Rachel.

²³Dan and his son Hushim. ²⁴Naphtali and his sons: Jahzeel, Guni, Jezer, and Shillem. ²⁵These seven are the descendants of Jacob by Bilhah, the slave woman whom Laban gave to his daughter Rachel.

²⁶The total number of the direct descendants of Jacob who went to Egypt was 66, not including his sons' wives. ²⁷Two sons were born to Joseph in Egypt, bringing to seventy the total number of Jacob's family who went there.

Jacob and his Family in Egypt

²⁸Jacob sent Judah ahead to ask Joseph to meet them in Goshen. When they arrived, ²⁹Joseph got in his chariot and went to Goshen to meet his father. When they met, Joseph threw his arms round his father's neck and cried for a long time. ³⁰Jacob said to Joseph, "I am ready to die, now that I have seen you and know that you are still alive."

³¹Then Joseph said to his brothers and the rest of his father's family, "I must go and tell the king that my brothers and all my father's family, who were living in Canaan, have come to me. ³²I will tell him that you are shepherds and take care of livestock and that you have brought your flocks and herds and everything else that belongs to you. ³³When the king calls for you and asks what your occupation is, ³⁴be sure to tell him that you have taken care of livestock all your lives, just as your ancestors did. In this way he will let you live in the region of Goshen." Joseph said this because Egyptians will have nothing to do with shepherds.

GENESIS 47

75

Genesis
.........:.
Exodus
Leviticus
Num.
Deuter.
Joshua

47 So Joseph took five of his brothers and went to the king. He said, "My father and my brothers have come from Canaan with their flocks, their herds, and all that they own. They are now in the region of Goshen." ²He then presented his brothers to the king. ³The king asked them, "What is your occupation?"

"We are shepherds, sir, just as our ancestors were," they answered. ⁴"We have come to live in this country, because in the land of Canaan the famine is so severe that there is no pasture for our flocks. Please give us permission to live in the region of Goshen." ⁵The king said to Joseph, "Now that your father and your brothers have arrived, ⁶the land of Egypt is theirs. Let them settle in the region of Goshen, the best part of the land. And if there are any capable men among them, put them in charge of my own livestock."

⁷Then Joseph brought his father Jacob and presented him to the king. Jacob gave the king his blessing, ⁸and the king asked him, "How old are you?"

⁹Jacob answered, "My life of wandering has lasted 130 years. Those years have been few and difficult, unlike the long years of my ancestors in their wanderings." ¹⁰Jacob gave the king a farewell blessing and left. ¹¹Then Joseph settled his father and his brothers in Egypt, giving them property in the best of the land near the city of Rameses, as the king had commanded. ¹²Joseph provided food for his father, his brothers, and all the rest of his father's family, including the very youngest.

The Famine

¹³The famine was so severe that there was no food anywhere, and the people of Egypt and Canaan became weak with hunger. ¹⁴As they bought corn, Joseph collected all the money and took it to the palace. ¹⁵When all the money in Egypt and Canaan was spent, the Egyptians came to Joseph and said, "Give us food! Don't let us die. Do something! Our money is all gone."

¹⁶Joseph answered, "Bring your livestock; I will give you food in exchange for it if your money is all gone." ¹⁷So they brought their livestock to Joseph, and he gave them food in exchange for their horses, sheep, goats, cattle, and donkeys. That year he supplied them with food in exchange for all their livestock.

¹⁸The following year they came to him and said, "We will not hide the fact from you, sir, that our money is all gone and our livestock belongs to you. There is nothing left to give you except our bodies and our lands. ¹⁹Don't let us die. Do something! Don't let our fields be deserted. Buy us and our land in exchange for food. We will be the king's slaves, and he will own our land. Give us corn to keep us alive and seed to sow in our fields."

²⁰Joseph bought all the land in Egypt for the king. Every Egyptian was forced to sell his land, because the famine was so severe; and all the land became the king's property. ²¹Joseph made slaves of the people from one end of Egypt to the other. ²²The only land he did not buy was the land that belonged to the priests. They did not have to sell their lands, because the king gave them an allowance to live on. ²³Joseph said to the people, "You see, I have now bought you and your lands for the king. Here is seed for you to sow in your fields. ²⁴At the time of harvest you must give a fifth to the king. You can use the rest for seed and for food for yourselves and your families."

²⁵They answered, "You have saved our lives; you have been good to us, sir, and we will be the king's slaves." ²⁶So Joseph made

it a law for the land of Egypt that a fifth of the harvest should belong to the king. This law still remains in force today. Only the lands of the priests did not become the king's property.

Jacob's Last Request

27 The Israelites lived in Egypt in the region of Goshen, where they became rich and had many children. 28 Jacob lived in Egypt for seventeen years, until he was 147 years old. 29 When the time drew near for him to die, he called for his son Joseph and said to him, "Place your hand between my thighs* and make a solemn vow that you will not bury me in Egypt. 30 I want to be buried where my fathers are; carry me out of Egypt and bury me where they are buried."

Joseph answered, "I will do as you say."

31 Jacob said, "Make a vow that you will." Joseph made the vow, and Jacob gave thanks there on his bed.

Jacob Blesses Ephraim and Manasseh

48 Some time later Joseph was told that his father was ill. So he took his two sons, Manasseh and Ephraim, and went to see Jacob. 2 When Jacob was told that his son Joseph had come to see him, he gathered his strength and sat up in bed. 3 Jacob said to Joseph, "Almighty God appeared to me at Luz in the land of Canaan and blessed me. 4 He said to me, 'I will give you many children, so that your descendants will become many nations; I will give this land to your descendants as their possession for ever.'"

5 Jacob continued, "Joseph, your two sons, who were born to you in Egypt before I came here, belong to me; Ephraim and Manasseh are just as much my sons as Reuben and Simeon. 6 If you have any more sons, they will not be considered mine; the inheritance they get will come through Ephraim and Manasseh. 7 I am doing this because of your mother Rachel. To my great sorrow she died in the land of Canaan, not far from Ephrath, as I was returning from Mesopotamia. I buried her there beside the road to Ephrath." (Ephrath is now known as Bethlehem.)

8 When Jacob saw Joseph's sons, he asked, "Who are these boys?"

9 Joseph answered, "These are my sons, whom God has given me here in Egypt."

Jacob said, "Bring them to me so that I may bless them." 10 Jacob's eyesight was failing because of his age, and he could not see very well. Joseph brought the boys to him, and he hugged them and kissed them. 11 Jacob said to Joseph, "I never expected to see you again, and now God has even let me see your children." 12 Then Joseph took them from Jacob's lap and bowed down before him with his face to the ground.

13 Joseph put Ephraim at Jacob's left and Manasseh at his right. 14 But Jacob crossed his hands, and put his right hand on the head of Ephraim, even though he was the younger, and his left hand on the head of Manasseh, who was the elder. 15 Then he blessed Joseph:*

"May the God whom my fathers Abraham and Isaac
    served bless these boys!
May God, who has led me to this very day, bless them!

....

47.29 *Place... thighs*: See 24.2.
48.15 *Joseph*: In blessing Ephraim and Manasseh, Jacob was in fact blessing Joseph.

Genesis

....

Exodus

Leviticus

Num.

Deuter.

Joshua

16 May the angel, who has rescued me from all harm, bless
them!
May my name and the name of my fathers
Abraham and Isaac live on through these boys!
May they have many children,
many descendants!"

17 Joseph was upset when he saw that his father had put his
right hand on Ephraim's head; so he took his father's hand to
move it from Ephraim's head to the head of Manasseh. 18 He said
to his father, "Not that way, father. This is the elder boy; put your
right hand on his head."

19 His father refused, saying, "I know, my son, I know. Manasseh's
descendants will also become a great people. But his younger
brother will be greater than he, and his descendants will become
great nations."

20 So he blessed them that day, saying, "The Israelites will use
your names when they pronounce blessings. They will say, 'May
God make you like Ephraim and Manasseh.' " In this way Jacob
put Ephraim before Manasseh.

21 Then Jacob said to Joseph, "As you see, I am about to die,
but God will be with you and will take you back to the land of your
ancestors. 22 It is to you and not to your brothers that I am giving
Shechem, that fertile region which I took from the Amorites with
my sword and my bow."

The Last Words of Jacob

49 Jacob called for his sons and said, "Gather round, and I will
tell you what will happen to you in the future:

2 "Come together and listen, sons of Jacob.
Listen to your father Israel.

3 "Reuben, my firstborn, you are my strength
And the first child of my manhood,
The proudest and strongest of all my sons.
4 You are like a raging flood,
But you will not be the most important,
For you slept with my concubine
And dishonoured your father's bed.

5 "Simeon and Levi are brothers.
They use their weapons to commit violence.
6 I will not join in their secret talks,
Nor will I take part in their meetings,
For they killed men in anger
And they crippled bulls for sport.
7 A curse be on their anger, because it is so fierce,
And on their fury, because it is so cruel.
I will scatter them throughout the land of Israel.
I will disperse them among its people.

8 "Judah, your brothers will praise you.
You hold your enemies by the neck.
Your brothers will bow down before you.
9 Judah is like a lion,
Killing his victim and returning to his den,
Stretching out and lying down.
No one dares disturb him.
10 Judah will hold the royal sceptre,
And his descendants will always rule.

FILL THIS SPACE HOWEVER YOU LIKE...

Nations will bring him tribute*
And bow in obedience before him.
11 He ties his young donkey to a grapevine,
To the very best of the vines.
He washes his clothes in blood-red wine.
12 His eyes are bloodshot from drinking wine,
His teeth white from drinking milk.*

13 "Zebulun will live beside the sea.
His shore will be a haven for ships.
His territory will reach as far as Sidon.

14 "Issachar is no better than a donkey
That lies stretched out between its saddlebags.
15 But he sees that the resting place is good
And that the land is delightful.
So he bends his back to carry the load
And is forced to work as a slave.

16 "Dan will be a ruler for his people.
They will be like the other tribes of Israel.
17 Dan will be a snake at the side of the road,
A poisonous snake beside the path,
That strikes at the horse's heel,
So that the rider is thrown off backwards.

18 "I wait for your deliverance, LORD.

19 "Gad will be attacked by a band of robbers,
But he will turn and pursue them.

20 "Asher's land will produce rich food.
He will provide food fit for a king.

21 "Naphtali is a deer that runs free,
Who bears lovely fawns.*

22 "Joseph is like a wild donkey by a spring,
A wild colt on a hillside.*
23 His enemies attack him fiercely
And pursue him with their bows and arrows.
24 But his bow remains steady,
And his arms are made strong*
By the power of the Mighty God of Jacob,
By the Shepherd, the Protector of Israel.
25 It is your father's God who helps you,
The Almighty God who blesses you
With blessings of rain from above
And of deep waters from beneath the ground,
Blessings of many cattle and children,

....

49.10 Probable text Nations... tribute; Hebrew unclear.
49.12 His eyes... milk; or His eyes are darker than wine, his teeth are whiter
than milk.
49.21 Naphtali... fawns; or Naphtali is a spreading tree that puts out lovely
branches.
49.22 Joseph... hillside; or Joseph is like a tree by a spring, a fruitful tree
that spreads over a wall.
49.24 But... strong; or But their bows were broken and splintered, the
muscles of their arms torn apart.

GENESIS 49, 50

79

Genesis

Exodus
Leviticus
Num.
Deuter.
Joshua

26 Blessings of corn and flowers,*
Blessings of ancient mountains,*
Delightful things from everlasting hills.
May these blessings rest on the head of Joseph,
On the brow of the one set apart from his brothers.

27 "Benjamin is like a vicious wolf.
Morning and evening he kills and devours."

28 These are the twelve tribes of Israel, and this is what their father said as he spoke a suitable word of farewell to each son.

The Death and Burial of Jacob
29 Then Jacob commanded his sons, "Now that I am going to join my people in death, bury me with my fathers in the cave that is in the field of Ephron the Hittite, 30 at Machpelah, east of Mamre, in the land of Canaan. Abraham bought this cave and field from Ephron for a burial ground. 31 That is where they buried Abraham and his wife Sarah; that is where they buried Isaac and his wife Rebecca; and that is where I buried Leah. 32 The field and the cave in it were bought from the Hittites. Bury me there." 33 When Jacob had finished giving instructions to his sons, he lay down again and died.

50 Joseph threw himself on his father, crying and kissing his face. 2 Then Joseph gave orders to embalm his father's body. 3 It took forty days, the normal time for embalming. The Egyptians mourned for him seventy days.

4 When the time of mourning was over, Joseph said to the king's officials, "Please take this message to the king: 5 'When my father was about to die, he made me promise him that I would bury him in the tomb which he had prepared in the land of Canaan. So please let me go and bury my father, and then I will come back.'"

6 The king answered, "Go and bury your father, as you promised you would."

7 So Joseph went to bury his father. All the king's officials, the senior men of his court, and all the leading men of Egypt went with Joseph. 8 His family, his brothers, and the rest of his father's family all went with him. Only their small children and their sheep, goats, and cattle stayed in the region of Goshen. 9 Men in chariots and men on horseback also went with him; it was a huge group.

10 When they came to the threshing place at Atad east of the Jordan, they mourned loudly for a long time, and Joseph performed mourning ceremonies for seven days. 11 When the citizens of Canaan saw those people mourning at Atad, they said, "What a solemn ceremony of mourning the Egyptians are holding!" That is why the place was named Abel Mizraim.*

12 So Jacob's sons did as he had commanded them; 13 they carried his body to Canaan and buried it in the cave at Machpelah, east of Mamre, in the field which Abraham had bought from Ephron the Hittite for a burial ground. 14 After Joseph had buried his father, he returned to Egypt with his brothers and all who had gone with him for the funeral.

49.26 Probable text corn and flowers; Hebrew your fathers are mightier than.
49.26 One ancient translation ancient mountains; Hebrew my ancestors to.
50.11 Abel Mizraim: This name sounds like the Hebrew for "mourning of the Egyptians".

GENESIS 50.20

God has the ability
to turn evil plots
into good. Have
there been dark
times in your life?
How might God

- BE ABLE TO -

REFRAME

them to bring his own
glory and goodness
out of them?

Joseph Reassures his Brothers

¹⁵ After the death of their father, Joseph's brothers said, "What if Joseph still hates us and plans to pay us back for all the harm we did to him?" ¹⁶ So they sent a message to Joseph: "Before our father died, ¹⁷ he told us to ask you, 'Please forgive the crime your brothers committed when they wronged you.' Now please forgive us the wrong that we, the servants of your father's God, have done." Joseph cried when he received this message.

¹⁸ Then his brothers themselves came and bowed down before him. "Here we are before you as your slaves," they said.

¹⁹ But Joseph said to them, "Don't be afraid; I can't put myself in the place of God. ²⁰ You plotted evil against me, but God turned it into good, in order to preserve the lives of many people who are alive today because of what happened. ²¹ You have nothing to fear. I will take care of you and your children." So he reassured them with kind words that touched their hearts.

The Death of Joseph

²² Joseph continued to live in Egypt with his father's family; he was 110 years old when he died. ²³ He lived to see Ephraim's children and grandchildren. He also lived to receive the children of Machir son of Manasseh into the family. ²⁴ He said to his brothers, "I am about to die, but God will certainly take care of you and lead you out of this land to the land he solemnly promised to Abraham, Isaac, and Jacob." ²⁵ Then Joseph asked his people to make a vow. "Promise me," he said, "that when God leads you to that land, you will take my body with you." ²⁶ So Joseph died in Egypt at the age of 110. They embalmed his body and put it in a coffin.

THE BOOK OF

EXODUS

WRITTEN: PROBABLY 600-400BC
(USING STORIES FROM A MUCH EARLIER TIME)

WHY READ IT?

Exodus is all about God's power to rescue people. It's also about the relationship that God wants to have with his people. It's a key part of biblical history but, more than that, it teaches us about God's power to defend those who believe in him.

WHAT YOU NEED TO KNOW:

Genesis ends with the Israelites settling in Egypt under the Pharaoh, and Joseph as his second-in-command. However, Exodus begins with a different scene - a new Pharaoh and the Israelites being forced into slavery. Exodus tells of the Israelites' miraculous escape from their oppressors and their attempt to reach the Promised Land. However, a journey that should have taken a few days ended up taking 40 years, because of their disobedience to God. In Exodus we are also introduced to the Ten Commandments, as well as the Tent of the Lord's Presence (sometimes called the tabernacle), where Moses and the other priests could meet with God.

Moses, even though he admitted to being shy and not good at speaking, was chosen by God to lead his people.

DRAW A
FIGURE OF
MOSES

and label it with some of the leadership skills that you see in him here.

500BC ——— ISRAEL IN EGYPT ——— EXODUS ——— 1400BC

JOSEPH   MOSES, AARON, MIRIAM   WILDERNESS

The Israelites are Treated Cruelly in Egypt

1 The sons of Jacob who went to Egypt with him, each with his family, were ²Reuben, Simeon, Levi, Judah, ³Issachar, Zebulun, Benjamin, ⁴Dan, Naphtali, Gad, and Asher. ⁵The total number of these people directly descended from Jacob was seventy.* His son Joseph was already in Egypt. ⁶In the course of time Joseph, his brothers, and all the rest of that generation died, ⁷but their descendants, the Israelites, had many children and became so numerous and strong that Egypt was filled with them.

⁸Then, a new king, who knew nothing about Joseph, came to power in Egypt. ⁹He said to his people, "These Israelites are so numerous and strong that they are a threat to us. ¹⁰In case of war they might join our enemies in order to fight against us, and might escape from* the country. We must find some way to keep them from becoming even more numerous." ¹¹So the Egyptians put slave-drivers over them to crush their spirits with hard labour. The Israelites built the cities of Pithom and Rameses to serve as supply centres for the king. ¹²But the more the Egyptians oppressed the Israelites, the more they increased in number and the further they spread through the land. The Egyptians came to fear the Israelites ¹³⁻¹⁴and made their lives miserable by forcing them into cruel slavery. They made them work on their building projects and in their fields, and they had no mercy on them.

¹⁵Then the king of Egypt spoke to Shiphrah and Puah, the two midwives who helped the Hebrew women. ¹⁶"When you help the Hebrew women give birth," he said to them, "kill the baby if it is a boy; but if it is a girl, let it live." ¹⁷But the midwives feared God and so did not obey the king; instead, they let the boys live. ¹⁸So the king sent for the midwives and asked them, "Why are you doing this? Why are you letting the boys live?"

¹⁹They answered, "The Hebrew women are not like Egyptian women; they give birth easily, and their babies are born before either of us gets there." ²⁰⁻²¹Because the midwives feared God, he was good to them and gave them families of their own. And the Israelites continued to increase and become strong. ²²Finally the king issued a command to all his people: "Take every newborn Hebrew boy and throw him into the Nile, but let all the girls live."

The Birth of Moses

2 During this time a man from the tribe of Levi married a woman of his own tribe, ²and she bore him a son. When she saw what a fine baby he was, she hid him for three months. ³But when she could not hide him any longer, she took a basket made of reeds and covered it with tar to make it watertight. She put the baby in it and then placed it in the tall grass at the edge of the river. ⁴The baby's sister stood some distance away to see what would happen to him.

⁵The king's daughter came down to the river to bathe, while her servants walked along the bank. Suddenly she noticed the basket in the tall grass and sent a slave woman to get it. ⁶The princess opened it and saw a baby boy. He was crying, and she felt sorry for him. "This is one of the Hebrew babies," she said.

⁷Then his sister asked her, "Shall I go and call a Hebrew woman to act as a wet nurse?"

⁸"Please do," she answered. So the girl went and brought the baby's own mother. ⁹The princess told the woman, "Take this

1.5 One ancient translation *75* (see Acts 7.14).
1.10 *escape from*; or *take control of*.

Exodus

Leviticus
Num.
Deuter.
Joshua
Judges

baby and nurse him for me, and I will pay you." So she took the baby and nursed him. [10] Later, when the child was old enough, she took him to the king's daughter, who adopted him as her own son. She said to herself, "I pulled him out of the water, and so I name him Moses."*

Moses Escapes to Midian

[11] When Moses had grown up, he went out to visit his people, the Hebrews, and he saw how they were forced to do hard labour. He even saw an Egyptian kill a Hebrew, one of Moses' own people. [12] Moses looked all round, and when he saw that no one was watching, he killed the Egyptian and hid his body in the sand. [13] The next day he went back and saw two Hebrew men fighting. He said to the one who was in the wrong, "Why are you beating up a fellow-Hebrew?"

[14] The man answered, "Who made you our ruler and judge? Are you going to kill me just as you killed that Egyptian?" Then Moses was afraid and said to himself, "People have found out what I have done." [15-16] When the king heard about what had happened, he tried to have Moses killed, but Moses fled and went to live in the land of Midian.

One day, when Moses was sitting by a well, seven daughters of Jethro, the priest of Midian, came to draw water and fill the troughs for their father's sheep and goats. [17] But some shepherds drove Jethro's daughters away. Then Moses went to their rescue and watered their animals for them. [18] When they returned to their father, he asked, "Why have you come back so early today?"

[19] "An Egyptian rescued us from the shepherds," they answered, "and he even drew water for us and watered our animals."

[20] "Where is he?" he asked his daughters. "Why did you leave the man out there? Go and invite him to eat with us."

[21] So Moses agreed to live there, and Jethro gave him his daughter Zipporah in marriage, [22] who bore him a son. Moses said to himself, "I am a foreigner in this land, and so I name him Gershom."*

[23] Years later the king of Egypt died, but the Israelites were still groaning under their slavery and cried out for help. Their cry went up to God, [24] who heard their groaning and remembered his covenant with Abraham, Isaac, and Jacob. [25] He saw the slavery of the Israelites and was concerned for them.*

God Calls Moses

3 One day while Moses was taking care of the sheep and goats of his father-in-law Jethro, the priest of Midian, he led the flock across the desert and came to Sinai, the holy mountain. [2] There the angel of the LORD appeared to him as a flame coming from the middle of a bush. Moses saw that the bush was on fire but that it was not burning up. [3] "This is strange," he thought. "Why isn't the bush burning up? I will go closer and see."

[4] When the LORD saw that Moses was coming closer, he called to him from the middle of the bush and said, "Moses! Moses!"

He answered, "Yes, here I am."

[5] God said, "Do not come any closer. Take off your sandals, because you are standing on holy ground. [6] I am the God of your

---

2.10 *Moses*: This name sounds like the Hebrew for "pull out".
2.22 *Gershom*: This name sounds like the Hebrew for "foreigner".
2.25 *was concerned for them*; one ancient translation *revealed himself to them*.

ancestors, the God of Abraham, Isaac, and Jacob." So Moses covered his face, because he was afraid to look at God.

⁷Then the Lord said, "I have seen how cruelly my people are being treated in Egypt; I have heard them cry out to be rescued from their slave-drivers. I know all about their sufferings, ⁸and so I have come down to rescue them from the Egyptians and to bring them out of Egypt to a spacious land, one which is rich and fertile and in which the Canaanites, the Hittites, the Amorites, the Perizzites, the Hivites, and the Jebusites now live. ⁹I have indeed heard the cry of my people, and I see how the Egyptians are oppressing them. ¹⁰Now I am sending you to the king of Egypt so that you can lead my people out of his country."

¹¹But Moses said to God, "I am nobody. How can I go to the king and bring the Israelites out of Egypt?"

¹²God answered, "I will be with you, and when you bring the people out of Egypt, you will worship me on this mountain. That will be the proof that I have sent you."

¹³But Moses replied, "When I go to the Israelites and say to them, 'The God of your ancestors sent me to you,' they will ask me, 'What is his name?' So what can I tell them?"

¹⁴God said, "I am who I am. This is what you must say to them: 'The one who is called I AM* has sent me to you.' ¹⁵Tell the Israelites that I, the Lord, the God of their ancestors, the God of Abraham, Isaac, and Jacob, have sent you to them. This is my name for ever; this is what all future generations are to call me. ¹⁶Go and gather the leaders of Israel together and tell them that I, the Lord, the God of their ancestors, the God of Abraham, Isaac, and Jacob, appeared to you. Tell them that I have come to them and have seen what the Egyptians are doing to them. ¹⁷I have decided that I will bring them out of Egypt, where they are being treated cruelly, and will take them to a rich and fertile land — the land of the Canaanites, the Hittites, the Amorites, the Perizzites, the Hivites, and the Jebusites.

¹⁸"My people will listen to what you say to them. Then you must go with the leaders of Israel to the king of Egypt and say to him, 'The Lord, the God of the Hebrews, has revealed himself to us. Now allow us to travel for three days into the desert to offer sacrifices to the Lord, our God.' ¹⁹I know that the king of Egypt will not let you go unless he is forced to do so. ²⁰But I will use my power and will punish Egypt by doing terrifying things there. After that he will let you go.

²¹"I will make the Egyptians respect you so that when my people leave, they will not go empty-handed. ²²Every Israelite woman will go to her Egyptian neighbours and to any Egyptian woman living in her house and will ask for clothing and for gold and silver jewellery. The Israelites will put these things on their sons and daughters and carry away the wealth of the Egyptians."

God Gives Moses Miraculous Power

4 Then Moses answered the Lord, "But suppose the Israelites do not believe me and will not listen to what I say. What shall I do if they say that you did not appear to me?"

²So the Lord asked him, "What are you holding?"

"A stick," he answered.

EXODUS 3.14

God loves to

BREAK INTO THE

ORDINARY.

Moses was doing a really familiar job and was in an ordinary place at an ordinary time. It was there that he encountered God.

On your next walk to school or your next well-known journey, ask God in prayer to speak to you through something ordinary. It could be a bush...

3.14 *I am who I am... I AM*; or *I will be who I will be... I WILL BE.* "I am" sounds like the Hebrew name Yahweh, traditionally transliterated as Jehovah. This name is represented in this translation by "the Lord" in capital letters, following a usage which is widespread in English versions.

EXODUS 4

85

Exodus
....

Leviticus
Num.
Deuter.
Joshua
Judges

³ The Lord said, "Throw it on the ground." When Moses threw it down, it turned into a snake, and he ran away from it. ⁴ Then the Lord said to Moses, "Bend down and pick it up by the tail." So Moses bent down and caught it, and it became a stick again. ⁵ The Lord said, "Do this to prove to the Israelites that the Lord, the God of their ancestors, the God of Abraham, Isaac, and Jacob, has appeared to you."

⁶ The Lord spoke to Moses again, "Put your hand inside your robe." Moses obeyed; and when he took his hand out, it was diseased, covered with white spots, like snow. ⁷ Then the Lord said, "Put your hand inside your robe again." He did so, and when he took it out this time, it was healthy, just like the rest of his body. ⁸ The Lord said, "If they will not believe you or be convinced by the first miracle, then this one will convince them. ⁹ If in spite of these two miracles they still will not believe you, and if they refuse to listen to what you say, take some water from the Nile and pour it on the ground. The water will turn into blood."

¹⁰ But Moses said, "No, Lord, don't send me. I have never been a good speaker, and I haven't become one since you began to speak to me. I am a poor speaker, slow and hesitant."

¹¹ The Lord said to him, "Who gives man his mouth? Who makes him deaf or dumb? Who gives him sight or makes him blind? It is I, the Lord. ¹² Now, go! I will help you to speak, and I will tell you what to say."

¹³ But Moses answered, "No, Lord, please send someone else."

¹⁴ At this the Lord became angry with Moses and said, "What about your brother Aaron, the Levite? I know that he can speak well. In fact, he is now coming to meet you and will be glad to see you. ¹⁵ You can speak to him and tell him what to say. I will help both of you to speak, and I will tell you both what to do. ¹⁶ He will be your spokesman and speak to the people for you. Then you will be like God, telling him what to say. ¹⁷ Take this stick with you; for with it you will perform miracles."

Moses Returns to Egypt

¹⁸ Then Moses went back to Jethro, his father-in-law, and said to him, "Please let me go back to my relatives in Egypt to see if they are still alive." Jethro agreed and said goodbye to him.

¹⁹ While Moses was still in Midian, the Lord said to him, "Go back to Egypt, for all those who wanted to kill you are dead." ²⁰ So Moses took his wife and his sons, put them on a donkey, and set out with them for Egypt, carrying the stick that God had told him to take.

²¹ Again the Lord said to Moses, "Now that you are going back to Egypt, be sure to perform before the king all the miracles which I have given you the power to do. But I will make the king stubborn, and he will not let the people go. ²² Then you must tell him that I, the Lord, say, 'Israel is my firstborn son. ²³ I told you to let my son go, so that he might worship me, but you refused. Now I am going to kill your firstborn son.' "

²⁴ At a camping place on the way to Egypt, the Lord met Moses and tried to kill him. ²⁵⁻²⁶ Then Zipporah, his wife, took a sharp stone, cut off the foreskin of her son, and touched Moses' feet* with it. Because of the rite of circumcision she said to Moses, "You are a husband of blood to me." And so the Lord spared Moses' life.

²⁷ Meanwhile the Lord had said to Aaron, "Go into the desert to meet Moses." So he went to meet him at the holy mountain;

4.25–26 *feet*: This reference to "feet" is thought by some to be a euphemism for the genitals.

and when he met him, he kissed him. ²⁸Then Moses told Aaron everything that the LORD had said when he told him to return to Egypt; he also told him about the miracles which the LORD had ordered him to perform. ²⁹So Moses and Aaron went to Egypt and gathered all the Israelite leaders together. ³⁰Aaron told them everything that the LORD had said to Moses, and then Moses performed all the miracles in front of the people. ³¹They believed, and when they heard that the LORD had come to them and had seen how they were being treated cruelly, they bowed down and worshipped.

Moses and Aaron before the King of Egypt

5 Then Moses and Aaron went to the king of Egypt and said, "The LORD, the God of Israel, says, 'Let my people go, so that they can hold a festival in the desert to honour me.'"

²"Who is the LORD?" the king demanded. "Why should I listen to him and let Israel go? I do not know the LORD; and I will not let Israel go."

³Moses and Aaron replied, "The God of the Hebrews has revealed himself to us. Allow us to travel for three days into the desert to offer sacrifices to the LORD our God. If we don't do so, he will kill us with disease or by war."

⁴The king said to Moses and Aaron, "What do you mean by making the people neglect their work? Get those slaves back to work! ⁵You people have become more numerous than the Egyptians. And now you want to stop working!"

⁶That same day the king commanded the Egyptian slave-drivers and the Israelite foremen: ⁷"Stop giving the people straw for making bricks. Make them go and find it for themselves. ⁸But still require them to make the same number of bricks as before, not one brick less. They haven't enough work to do, and that is why they keep asking me to let them go and offer sacrifices to their God! ⁹Make these people work harder and keep them busy, so that they won't have time to listen to a pack of lies."

¹⁰The slave-drivers and the Israelite foremen went out and said to the Israelites, "The king has said that he will not supply you with any more straw. ¹¹He says that you must go and get it for yourselves wherever you can find it, but you must still make the same number of bricks." ¹²So the people went all over Egypt looking for straw. ¹³The slave-drivers kept trying to force them to make the same number of bricks every day as they had made when they were given straw. ¹⁴The Egyptian slave-drivers beat the Israelite foremen, whom they had put in charge of the work. They demanded, "Why aren't you people making the same number of bricks as you made before?"

¹⁵Then the foremen went to the king and complained, "Why do you do this to us, Your Majesty? ¹⁶We are given no straw, but we are still ordered to make bricks! And now we are being beaten. It is your people that are at fault."

¹⁷The king answered, "You are lazy and don't want to work, and that is why you ask me to let you go and offer sacrifices to the LORD. ¹⁸Now get back to work! You will not be given any straw, but you must still make the same number of bricks." ¹⁹The foremen realized that they were in trouble when they were told that they had to make the same number of bricks every day as they had made before.

²⁰As they were leaving, they met Moses and Aaron, who were waiting for them. ²¹They said to Moses and Aaron, "The LORD has seen what you have done and will punish you for making the king and his officers hate us. You have given them an excuse to kill us."

EXODUS 5, 6

87

Exodus
....
Leviticus
Num.
Deuter.
Joshua
Judges

Moses Complains to the Lord

22 Then Moses turned to the Lord again and said, "Lord, why do you ill-treat your people? Why did you send me here? 23 Ever since I went to the king to speak for you, he has treated them cruelly. And you have done nothing to help them!"

6 Then the Lord said to Moses, "Now you are going to see what I will do to the king. I will force him to let my people go. In fact, I will force him to drive them out of his land."

God Calls Moses

2 God spoke to Moses and said, "I am the Lord. 3 I appeared to Abraham, to Isaac, and to Jacob as Almighty God, but I did not make myself known to them by my holy name, the Lord.* 4 I also made my covenant with them, promising to give them the land of Canaan, the land in which they had lived as foreigners. 5 Now I have heard the groaning of the Israelites, whom the Egyptians have enslaved, and I have remembered my covenant. 6 So tell the Israelites that I say to them, 'I am the Lord; I will rescue you and set you free from your slavery to the Egyptians. I will raise my mighty arm to bring terrible punishment upon them, and I will save you. 7 I will make you my own people, and I will be your God. You will know that I am the Lord your God when I set you free from slavery in Egypt. 8 I will bring you to the land that I solemnly promised to give to Abraham, Isaac, and Jacob; and I will give it to you as your own possession. I am the Lord.'" 9 Moses told this to the Israelites, but they would not listen to him, because their spirit had been broken by their cruel slavery.

10 Then the Lord said to Moses, 11 "Go and tell the king of Egypt that he must let the Israelites leave his land."

12 But Moses replied, "Even the Israelites will not listen to me, so why should the king? I am such a poor speaker."

13 The Lord commanded Moses and Aaron: "Tell the Israelites and the king of Egypt that I have ordered you to lead the Israelites out of Egypt."

The Family Record of Moses and Aaron

14 Reuben, Jacob's firstborn, had four sons: Hanoch, Pallu, Hezron, and Carmi; they were the ancestors of the clans that bear their names. 15 Simeon had six sons: Jemuel, Jamin, Ohad, Jachin, Zohar, and Shaul, the son of a Canaanite woman; they were the ancestors of the clans that bear their names. 16 Levi had three sons: Gershon, Kohath, and Merari; they were the ancestors of the clans that bear their names. Levi lived 137 years. 17 Gershon had two sons: Libni and Shimei, and they had many descendants. 18 Kohath had four sons: Amram, Izhar, Hebron, and Uzziel. Kohath lived 133 years. 19 Merari had two sons: Mahli and Mushi. These are the clans of Levi with their descendants.

20 Amram married his father's sister Jochebed, who bore him Aaron and Moses. Amram lived 137 years. 21 Izhar had three sons: Korah, Nepheg, and Zichri. 22 Uzziel also had three sons: Mishael, Elzaphan, and Sithri.

23 Aaron married Elisheba, the daughter of Amminadab and sister of Nahshon; she bore him Nadab, Abihu, Eleazar, and Ithamar. 24 Korah had three sons: Assir, Elkanah, and Abiasaph; they were the ancestors of the divisions of the clan of Korah. 25 Eleazar, Aaron's son, married one of Putiel's daughters, who bore him Phinehas. These were the heads of the families and the clans of the tribe of Levi.

EXODUS 6.6-7

• I AM THE •

LORD.

I WILL

SAVE

{ YOU }

6.3 *the Lord*: See 3.14.

26 Aaron and Moses were the ones to whom the LORD said, "Lead the tribes of Israel out of Egypt." 27 They were the men who told the king of Egypt to free the Israelites.

The LORD's Command to Moses and Aaron

28 When the LORD spoke to Moses in the land of Egypt, 29 he said, "I am the LORD. Tell the king of Egypt everything I tell you."

30 But Moses answered, "You know that I am such a poor speaker; why should the king listen to me?"

7 The LORD said, "I am going to make you like God to the king, and your brother Aaron will speak to him as your prophet. 2 Tell Aaron everything I command you, and he will tell the king to let the Israelites leave his country. 3-4 But I will make the king stubborn, and he will not listen to you, no matter how many terrifying things I do in Egypt. Then I will bring severe punishment on Egypt and lead the tribes of my people out of the land. 5 The Egyptians will then know that I am the LORD, when I raise my hand against them and bring the Israelites out of their country." 6 Moses and Aaron did what the LORD commanded. 7 At the time when they spoke to the king, Moses was eighty years old, and Aaron was 83.

Aaron's Stick

8 The LORD said to Moses and Aaron, 9 "If the king demands that you prove yourselves by performing a miracle, tell Aaron to take his stick and throw it down in front of the king, and it will turn into a snake." 10 So Moses and Aaron went to the king and did as the LORD had commanded. Aaron threw his stick down in front of the king and his officers, and it turned into a snake. 11 Then the king called for his wise men and magicians, and by their magic they did the same thing. 12 They threw down their sticks, and the sticks turned into snakes. But Aaron's stick swallowed theirs. 13 The king, however, remained stubborn and, just as the LORD had said, the king would not listen to Moses and Aaron.

Disasters Strike Egypt
Blood

14 Then the LORD said to Moses, "The king is very stubborn and refuses to let the people go. 15 So go and meet him in the morning when he goes down to the Nile. Take with you the stick that was turned into a snake, and wait for him on the bank of the river. 16 Then say to the king, 'The LORD, the God of the Hebrews, sent me to tell you to let his people go, so that they can worship him in the desert. But until now you have not listened. 17 Now, Your Majesty, the LORD says that you will find out who he is by what he is going to do. Look, I am going to strike the surface of the river with this stick, and the water will be turned into blood. 18 The fish will die, and the river will stink so much that the Egyptians will not be able to drink from it.' "

19 The LORD said to Moses, "Tell Aaron to take his stick and hold it out over all the rivers, canals, and pools in Egypt. The water will become blood, and all over the land there will be blood, even in the wooden tubs and stone jars."

20 Then Moses and Aaron did as the LORD commanded. In the presence of the king and his officers, Aaron raised his stick and struck the surface of the river, and all the water in it was turned into blood. 21 The fish in the river died, and it smelt so bad that the Egyptians could not drink from it. There was blood everywhere in Egypt. 22 Then the king's magicians did the same thing by means

EXODUS 7, 8

89

Exodus

Leviticus

Num.

Deuter.

Joshua

Judges

of their magic, and the king was as stubborn as ever. Just as the LORD had said, the king refused to listen to Moses and Aaron. ²³ Instead, he turned and went back to his palace without paying any attention even to this. ²⁴ All the Egyptians dug along the bank of the river for drinking water, because they were not able to drink water from the river.

²⁵ Seven days passed after the LORD struck the river.

Frogs

8 Then the LORD said to Moses, "Go to the king and tell him that the LORD says, 'Let my people go, so that they can worship me. ² If you refuse, I will punish your country by covering it with frogs. ³ The Nile will be so full of frogs that they will leave it and go into your palace, your bedroom, your bed, the houses of your officials and your people, and even into your ovens and baking pans. ⁴ They will jump up on you, your people, and all your officials.' "

⁵ The LORD said to Moses, "Tell Aaron to hold out his stick over the rivers, the canals, and the pools, and make frogs come up and cover the land of Egypt." ⁶ So Aaron held it out over all the water, and the frogs came out and covered the land. ⁷ But the magicians used magic, and they too made frogs come up on the land.

⁸ The king called for Moses and Aaron and said, "Pray to the LORD to take away these frogs, and I will let your people go, so that they can offer sacrifices to the LORD."

⁹ Moses replied, "I will be glad to pray for you. Just set the time when I am to pray for you, your officers, and your people. Then you will be rid of the frogs, and there will be none left except in the Nile."

¹⁰ The king answered, "Pray for me tomorrow."

Moses said, "I will do as you ask, and then you will know that there is no other god like the LORD, our God. ¹¹ You, your officials, and your people will be rid of the frogs, and there will be none left except in the Nile." ¹² Then Moses and Aaron left the king, and Moses prayed to the LORD to take away the frogs which he had brought on the king. ¹³ The LORD did as Moses asked, and the frogs in the houses, the courtyards, and the fields died. ¹⁴ The Egyptians piled them up in great heaps, until the land stank with them. ¹⁵ When the king saw that the frogs were dead, he became stubborn again and, just as the LORD had said, the king would not listen to Moses and Aaron.

Gnats

¹⁶ The LORD said to Moses, "Tell Aaron to strike the ground with his stick, and all over the land of Egypt the dust will change into gnats." ¹⁷ So Aaron struck the ground with his stick, and all the dust in Egypt was turned into gnats, which covered the people and the animals. ¹⁸ The magicians tried to use their magic to make gnats appear, but they failed. There were gnats everywhere, ¹⁹ and the magicians said to the king, "God has done this!" But the king was stubborn and, just as the LORD had said, the king would not listen to Moses and Aaron.

Flies

²⁰ The LORD said to Moses, "Early tomorrow morning go and meet the king as he goes to the river, and tell him that the LORD says, 'Let my people go, so that they can worship me. ²¹ I warn you that if you refuse, I will punish you by sending flies on you, your officials, and your people. The houses of the Egyptians will be full of flies, and the ground will be covered with them. ²² But

I will spare the region of Goshen, where my people live, so that there will be no flies there. I will do this so that you will know that I, the LORD, am at work in this land. ²³ I will make a distinction* between my people and your people. This miracle will take place tomorrow.'" ²⁴ The LORD sent great swarms of flies into the king's palace and the houses of his officials. The whole land of Egypt was brought to ruin by the flies.

²⁵ Then the king called for Moses and Aaron and said, "Go and offer sacrifices to your God here in this country."

²⁶ "It would not be right to do that," Moses answered, "because the Egyptians would be offended by our sacrificing the animals that we offer to the LORD our God. If we use these animals and offend the Egyptians by sacrificing them where they can see us, they will stone us to death. ²⁷ We must travel three days into the desert to offer sacrifices to the LORD our God, just as he commanded us."

²⁸ The king said, "I will let you go to sacrifice to the LORD, your God, in the desert, if you do not go very far. Pray for me."

²⁹ Moses answered, "As soon as I leave, I will pray to the LORD that tomorrow the flies will leave you, your officials, and your people. But you must not deceive us again and prevent the people from going to sacrifice to the LORD."

³⁰ Moses left the king and prayed to the LORD, ³¹ and the LORD did as Moses asked. The flies left the king, his officials, and his people; not one fly remained. ³² But even this time the king became stubborn, and again he would not let the people go.

Death of the Animals

9 The LORD said to Moses, "Go to the king and tell him that the LORD, the God of the Hebrews, says, 'Let my people go, so that they may worship me. ² If you again refuse to let them go, ³ I will punish you by sending a terrible disease on all your animals — your horses, donkeys, camels, cattle, sheep, and goats. ⁴ I will make a distinction between the animals of the Israelites and those of the Egyptians, and no animal that belongs to the Israelites will die. ⁵ I, the LORD, have set tomorrow as the time when I will do this.'"

⁶ The next day the LORD did as he had said, and all the animals of the Egyptians died, but not one of the animals of the Israelites died. ⁷ The king asked what had happened and was told that none of the animals of the Israelites had died. But he was stubborn and would not let the people go.

Boils

⁸ Then the LORD said to Moses and Aaron, "Take a few handfuls of ashes from a furnace; Moses shall throw them into the air in front of the king. ⁹ They will spread out like fine dust over all the land of Egypt, and everywhere they will produce boils that become open sores on the people and the animals." ¹⁰ So they got some ashes and stood before the king; Moses threw them into the air, and they produced boils that became open sores on the people and the animals. ¹¹ The magicians were not able to appear before Moses, because they were covered with boils, like all the other Egyptians. ¹² But the LORD made the king stubborn and, just as the LORD had said, the king would not listen to Moses and Aaron.

Hail

¹³ The LORD then said to Moses, "Early tomorrow morning meet with the king and tell him that the LORD, the God of the Hebrews,

8.23 Some ancient translations *a distinction*; Hebrew *redemption*.

says, 'Let my people go, so that they may worship me. [14] This time I will punish not only your officials and your people, but I will punish you as well, so that you may know that there is no one like me in all the world. [15] If I had raised my hand to strike you and your people with disease, you would have been completely destroyed. [16] But to show you my power I have let you live so that my fame might spread over the whole world. [17] Yet you are still arrogant and refuse to let my people go. [18] This time tomorrow I will cause a heavy hailstorm, such as Egypt has never known in all its history. [19] Now give orders for your livestock and everything else you have in the open to be put under shelter. Hail will fall on the people and animals left outside unprotected, and they will all die.' " [20] Some of the king's officials were afraid because of what the LORD had said, and they brought their slaves and animals indoors for shelter. [21] Others, however, paid no attention to the LORD's warning and left their slaves and animals out in the open.

[22] Then the LORD said to Moses, "Raise your hand towards the sky, and hail will fall over the whole land of Egypt — on the people, the animals, and all the plants in the fields." [23] So Moses raised his stick towards the sky, and the LORD sent thunder and hail, and lightning struck the ground. The LORD sent [24] a heavy hailstorm, with lightning flashing to and fro. It was the worst storm that Egypt had ever known in all its history. [25] All over Egypt the hail struck down everything in the open, including all the people and all the animals. It beat down all the plants in the fields and broke all the trees. [26] The region of Goshen, where the Israelites lived, was the only place where there was no hail.

[27] The king sent for Moses and Aaron and said, "This time I have sinned; the LORD is in the right, and my people and I are in the wrong. [28] Pray to the LORD! We have had enough of this thunder and hail! I promise to let you go; you don't have to stay here any longer."

[29] Moses said to him, "As soon as I go out of the city, I will lift up my hands in prayer to the LORD. The thunder will stop, and there will be no more hail, so that you may know that the earth belongs to the LORD. [30] But I know that you and your officials do not yet fear the LORD God."

[31] The flax and the barley were ruined, because the barley was ripe, and the flax was budding. [32] But none of the wheat was ruined, because it ripens later.

[33] Moses left the king, went out of the city, and lifted up his hands in prayer to the LORD. The thunder, the hail, and the rain all stopped. [34] When the king saw what had happened, he sinned again. He and his officials remained as stubborn as ever [35] and, just as the LORD had foretold through Moses, the king would not let the Israelites go.

Locusts

10 Then the LORD said to Moses, "Go and see the king. I have made him and his officials stubborn, in order that I may perform these miracles among them [2] and in order that you may be able to tell your children and grandchildren how I made fools of the Egyptians when I performed the miracles. All of you will know that I am the LORD."

[3] So Moses and Aaron went to the king and said to him, "The LORD, the God of the Hebrews, says 'How much longer will you refuse to submit to me? Let my people go, so that they may worship me. [4] If you keep on refusing, then I will bring locusts into your country tomorrow. [5] There will be so many that they

TURN THESE LINES INTO A PICTURE OF SOMETHING.

will completely cover the ground. They will eat everything that the hail did not destroy, even the trees that are left. ⁶They will fill your palaces and the houses of all your officials and all your people. They will be worse than anything your ancestors ever saw.' " Then Moses turned and left.

⁷The king's officials said to him, "How long is this man going to give us trouble? Let the Israelite men go, so that they can worship the LORD their God. Don't you realize that Egypt is ruined?"

⁸So Moses and Aaron were brought back to the king, and he said to them, "You may go and worship the LORD your God. But exactly who will go?"

⁹Moses answered, "We will all go, including our children and our old people. We will take our sons and daughters, our sheep and goats, and our cattle, because we must hold a festival to honour the LORD."

¹⁰The king said, "I swear by the LORD that I will never let you take your women and children! It is clear that you are plotting to revolt. ¹¹No! Only the men may go and worship the LORD if that is what you want." With that, Moses and Aaron were driven out of the king's presence.

¹²Then the LORD said to Moses, "Raise your hand over the land of Egypt to bring the locusts. They will come and eat everything that grows, everything that has survived the hail." ¹³So Moses raised his stick, and the LORD caused a wind from the east to blow on the land all that day and all that night. By morning it had brought the locusts. ¹⁴They came in swarms and settled over the whole country. It was the largest swarm of locusts that had ever been seen or that ever would be seen again. ¹⁵They covered the ground until it was black with them; they ate everything that the hail had left, including all the fruit on the trees. Not a green thing was left on any tree or plant in all the land of Egypt.

¹⁶Then the king hurriedly called Moses and Aaron and said, "I have sinned against the LORD your God and against you. ¹⁷Now forgive my sin this once and pray to the LORD your God to take away this fatal punishment from me." ¹⁸Moses left the king and prayed to the LORD. ¹⁹And the LORD changed the east wind into a very strong west wind, which picked up the locusts and blew them into the Gulf of Suez.* Not one locust was left in all Egypt. ²⁰But the LORD made the king stubborn, and he did not let the Israelites go.

Darkness

²¹The LORD then said to Moses, "Raise your hand towards the sky, and a darkness thick enough to be felt will cover the land of Egypt." ²²Moses raised his hand towards the sky, and there was total darkness throughout Egypt for three days. ²³The Egyptians could not see each other, and no one left his house during that time. But the Israelites had light where they were living.

²⁴The king called Moses and said, "You may go and worship the LORD; even your women and children may go with you. But your sheep, goats, and cattle must stay here."

²⁵Moses answered, "Then you would have to provide us with animals for sacrifices and burnt offerings to offer to the LORD our God. ²⁶No, we will take our animals with us; not one will be left behind. We ourselves must select the animals with which to worship the LORD our God. And until we get there, we will not know what animals to sacrifice to him."

10.19 *Gulf of Suez*: See Red Sea in 13.18.

EXODUS 10–12

93

Exodus
....

Leviticus
Num.
Deuter.
Joshua
Judges

²⁷The Lord made the king stubborn, and he would not let them go. ²⁸He said to Moses, "Get out of my sight! Don't let me ever see you again! On the day I do, you will die!"

²⁹"You are right," Moses answered. "You will never see me again."

Moses Announces the Death of the Firstborn

11 Then the Lord said to Moses, "I will send only one more punishment on the king of Egypt and his people. After that he will let you leave. In fact, he will drive all of you out of here. ²Now speak to the people of Israel and tell all of them to ask their neighbours for gold and silver jewellery." ³The Lord made the Egyptians respect the Israelites. Indeed, the officials and all the people considered Moses to be a very great man.

⁴Moses then said to the king, "The Lord says, 'At about midnight I will go through Egypt, ⁵and every firstborn son in Egypt will die, from the king's son, who is heir to the throne, to the son of the slave woman who grinds corn. The firstborn of all the cattle will die also. ⁶There will be loud crying all over Egypt, such as there has never been before or ever will be again. ⁷But not even a dog will bark at the Israelites or their animals. Then you will know that I, the Lord, make a distinction between the Egyptians and the Israelites.'" ⁸Moses concluded by saying, "All your officials will come to me and bow down before me, and they will beg me to take all my people and go away. After that, I will leave." Then in great anger Moses left the king.

⁹The Lord had said to Moses, "The king will continue to refuse to listen to you, in order that I may do more of my miracles in Egypt." ¹⁰Moses and Aaron performed all these miracles before the king, but the Lord made him stubborn, and he would not let the Israelites leave his country.

The Passover

12 The Lord spoke to Moses and Aaron in Egypt: ²"This month is to be the first month of the year for you. ³Give these instructions to the whole community of Israel: on the tenth day of this month each man must choose either a lamb or a young goat for his household. ⁴If his family is too small to eat a whole animal, he and his next-door neighbour may share an animal, in proportion to the number of people and the amount that each person can eat. ⁵You may choose either a sheep or a goat, but it must be a one-year-old male without any defects. ⁶Then, on the evening of the fourteenth day of the month, the whole community of Israel will kill the animals. ⁷The people are to take some of the blood and put it on the doorposts and above the doors of the houses in which the animals are to be eaten. ⁸That night the meat is to be roasted, and eaten with bitter herbs and with bread made without yeast. ⁹Do not eat any of it raw or boiled, but eat it roasted whole, including the head, the legs, and the internal organs. ¹⁰You must not leave any of it until morning; if any is left over, it must be burnt. ¹¹You are to eat it quickly, for you are to be dressed for travel, with your sandals on your feet and your stick in your hand. It is the Passover Festival to honour me, the Lord.

¹²"On that night I will go through the land of Egypt, killing every firstborn male, both human and animal, and punishing all the gods of Egypt. I am the Lord. ¹³The blood on the doorposts will be a sign to mark the houses in which you live. When I see the blood, I will pass over you and will not harm you when I punish the Egyptians. ¹⁴You must celebrate this day as a religious festival

to remind you of what I, the LORD, have done. Celebrate it for all time to come."

The Festival of Unleavened Bread

15 The LORD said, "For seven days you must not eat any bread made with yeast — eat only unleavened bread. On the first day you are to get rid of all the yeast in your houses, for if anyone during those seven days eats bread made with yeast, he shall no longer be considered one of my people. 16 On the first day and again on the seventh day you are to meet for worship. No work is to be done on those days, but you may prepare food. 17 Keep this festival, because it was on this day that I brought your tribes out of Egypt. For all time to come you must celebrate this day as a festival. 18 From the evening of the fourteenth day of the first month to the evening of the 21st day, you must not eat any bread made with yeast. 19-20 For seven days no yeast must be found in your houses, for if anyone, native-born or foreign, eats bread made with yeast, he shall no longer be considered one of my people."

The First Passover

21 Moses called for all the leaders of Israel and said to them, "Each of you is to choose a lamb or a young goat and kill it, so that your families can celebrate Passover. 22 Take a sprig of hyssop, dip it in the bowl containing* the animal's blood, and wipe the blood on the doorposts and the beam above the door of your house. Not one of you is to leave the house until morning. 23 When the LORD goes through Egypt to kill the Egyptians, he will see the blood on the beams and the doorposts and will not let the Angel of Death enter your houses and kill you. 24 You and your children must obey these rules for ever. 25 When you enter the land that the LORD has promised to give you, you must perform this ritual. 26 When your children ask you, 'What does this ritual mean?' 27 you will answer, 'It is the sacrifice of Passover to honour the LORD, because he passed over the houses of the Israelites in Egypt. He killed the Egyptians, but spared us.'"

The Israelites knelt down and worshipped. 28 Then they went and did what the LORD had commanded Moses and Aaron.

The Death of the Firstborn

29 At midnight the LORD killed all the firstborn sons in Egypt, from the king's son, who was heir to the throne, to the son of the prisoner in the dungeon; all the firstborn of the animals were also killed. 30 That night, the king, his officials, and all the other Egyptians were awakened. There was loud crying throughout Egypt, because there was not one home in which there was not a dead son. 31 That same night the king sent for Moses and Aaron and said, "Get out, you and your Israelites! Leave my country; go and worship the LORD, as you asked. 32 Take your sheep, goats, and cattle, and leave. Also pray for a blessing on me."

33 The Egyptians urged the people to hurry and leave the country; they said, "We will all be dead if you don't leave." 34 So the people filled their baking pans with unleavened dough, wrapped them in clothing, and carried them on their shoulders. 35 The Israelites had done as Moses had said, and had asked the Egyptians for gold and silver jewellery and for clothing. 36 The LORD made the Egyptians respect the people and give them what they asked for. In this way the Israelites carried away the wealth of the Egyptians.

12.22 *dip it in the bowl containing*; or *put it on the threshold covered with.*

Exodus

Leviticus
Num.
Deuter.
Joshua
Judges

The Israelites Leave Egypt

37 The Israelites set out on foot from Rameses for Sukkoth. There were about 600,000 men, not counting women and children. 38 A large number of other people and many sheep, goats, and cattle also went with them. 39 They baked unleavened bread from the dough that they had brought out of Egypt, for they had been driven out of Egypt so suddenly that they did not have time to get their food ready or to prepare leavened dough.

40 The Israelites had lived in Egypt for 430 years. 41 On the day the 430 years ended, all the tribes of the LORD's people left Egypt. 42 It was a night when the LORD kept watch to bring them out of Egypt; this same night is dedicated to the LORD for all time to come as a night when the Israelites must keep watch.

Regulations about Passover

43 The LORD said to Moses and Aaron, "These are the Passover regulations: no foreigner shall eat the Passover meal, 44 but any slave that you have bought may eat it if you circumcise him first. 45 No temporary resident or hired worker may eat it. 46 The whole meal must be eaten in the house in which it was prepared; it must not be taken outside. And do not break any of the animal's bones. 47 The whole community of Israel must celebrate this festival, 48 but no uncircumcised man may eat it. If a foreigner has settled among you and wants to celebrate Passover to honour the LORD, you must first circumcise all the males of his household. He is then to be treated like a native-born Israelite and may join in the festival. 49 The same regulations apply to native-born Israelites and to foreigners who settle among you." 50 All the Israelites obeyed and did what the LORD had commanded Moses and Aaron. 51 On that day the LORD brought the Israelite tribes out of Egypt.

Dedication of the Firstborn

13 The LORD said to Moses, 2 "Dedicate all the firstborn males to me, for every firstborn male Israelite and every firstborn male animal belongs to me."

The Festival of Unleavened Bread

3 Moses said to the people, "Remember this day — the day on which you left Egypt, the place where you were slaves. This is the day the LORD brought you out by his great power. No leavened bread is to be eaten. 4 You are leaving Egypt on this day in the first month, the month of Abib. 5 The LORD solemnly promised your ancestors to give you the land of the Canaanites, the Hittites, the Amorites, the Hivites, and the Jebusites. When he brings you into that rich and fertile land, you must celebrate this festival in the first month of every year. 6 For seven days you must eat unleavened bread and on the seventh day there is to be a festival to honour the LORD. 7 For seven days you must not eat any bread made with yeast; there must be no yeast or leavened bread anywhere in your land. 8 When the festival begins, explain to your sons that you do all this because of what the LORD did for you when you left Egypt. 9 This observance will be a reminder, like something tied on your hand or on your forehead; it will remind you to continue to recite and study the Law of the LORD, because the LORD brought you out of Egypt by his great power. 10 Celebrate this festival at the appointed time each year.

The Firstborn

11 "The LORD will bring you into the land of the Canaanites, which he solemnly promised to you and your ancestors. When

THE LAW

EXODUS 13.9;
DEUTERONOMY 29.29

DEFINITION: The body of divine commandments as expressed in the Bible or other religious texts. (oxforddictionaries.com)

he gives it to you, [12] you must offer every firstborn male to the LORD. Every firstborn male of your animals belongs to the LORD, [13] but you must buy back from him every firstborn male donkey by offering a lamb in its place. If you do not want to buy back the donkey, break its neck. You must buy back every firstborn male child of yours. [14] In the future, when your son asks what this observance means, you will answer him, 'By using great power the LORD brought us out of Egypt, the place where we were slaves. [15] When the king of Egypt was stubborn and refused to let us go, the LORD killed every firstborn male in the land of Egypt, both human and animal. That is why we sacrifice every firstborn male animal to the LORD, but buy back our firstborn sons. [16] This observance will be a reminder, like something tied on our hands or on our foreheads; it will remind us that the LORD brought us out of Egypt by his great power.' "

The Pillar of Cloud and the Pillar of Fire

[17] When the king of Egypt let the people go, God did not take them by the road that goes up the coast to Philistia, although it was the shortest way. God thought, "I do not want the people to change their minds and return to Egypt when they see that they are going to have to fight." [18] Instead, he led them in a roundabout way through the desert towards the Red Sea.* The Israelites were armed for battle.

[19] Moses took the body of Joseph with him, as Joseph had made the Israelites solemnly promise to do. Joseph had said, "When God rescues you, you must carry my body with you from this place."

[20] The Israelites left Sukkoth and camped at Etham on the edge of the desert. [21] During the day the LORD went in front of them in a pillar of cloud to show them the way, and during the night he went in front of them in a pillar of fire to give them light, so that they could travel night and day. [22] The pillar of cloud was always in front of the people during the day, and the pillar of fire at night.

Crossing the Red Sea

14 Then the LORD said to Moses, [2] "Tell the Israelites to turn back and camp in front of Pi Hahiroth, between Migdol and the Red Sea, near Baal Zephon. [3] The king will think that the Israelites are wandering about in the country and are closed in by the desert. [4] I will make him stubborn, and he will pursue you, and my victory over the king and his army will bring me honour. Then the Egyptians will know that I am the LORD." The Israelites did as they were told.

[5] When the king of Egypt was told that the people had escaped, he and his officials changed their minds and said, "What have we done? We have let the Israelites escape, and we have lost them as our slaves!" [6] The king got his war chariot and his army ready. [7] He set out with all his chariots, including the 600 finest, commanded by their officers. [8] The LORD made the king stubborn, and he pursued the Israelites, who were leaving triumphantly.* [9] The Egyptian army, with all the horses, chariots, and drivers, pursued them and caught up with them where they were camped by the Red Sea near Pi Hahiroth and Baal Zephon.

13.18 *Red Sea*: (in Hebrew literally "Sea of Reeds") evidently referred to (1) a series of lakes and marshes between the head of the Gulf of Suez and the Mediterranean, the region generally regarded as the site of the events described in Exodus 13, and was also used to designate (2) the Gulf of Suez, and (3) the Gulf of Aqaba.
14.8 *triumphantly*; or *under the protection of the LORD*.

EXODUS 14, 15

97

Exodus
....
Leviticus
Num.
Deuter.
Joshua
Judges

[10] When the Israelites saw the king and his army marching against them, they were terrified and cried out to the LORD for help. [11] They said to Moses, "Weren't there any graves in Egypt? Did you have to bring us out here in the desert to die? Look what you have done by bringing us out of Egypt! [12] Didn't we tell you before we left that this would happen? We told you to leave us alone and let us go on being slaves of the Egyptians. It would be better to be slaves there than to die here in the desert."

[13] Moses answered, "Don't be afraid! Stand your ground, and you will see what the LORD will do to save you today; you will never see these Egyptians again. [14] The LORD will fight for you, and there is no need for you to do anything."

[15] The LORD said to Moses, "Why are you crying out for help? Tell the people to move forward. [16] Lift up your stick and hold it out over the sea. The water will divide, and the Israelites will be able to walk through the sea on dry ground. [17] I will make the Egyptians so stubborn that they will go in after them, and I will gain honour by my victory over the king, his army, his chariots, and his drivers. [18] When I defeat them, the Egyptians will know that I am the LORD."

[19] The angel of God, who had been in front of the army of Israel, moved and went to the rear. The pillar of cloud also moved until it was [20] between the Egyptians and the Israelites. The cloud made it dark for the Egyptians, but gave light to the people of Israel,* and so the armies could not come near each other all night.

[21] Moses held out his hand over the sea, and the LORD drove the sea back with a strong east wind. It blew all night and turned the sea into dry land. The water was divided, [22] and the Israelites went through the sea on dry ground, with walls of water on both sides. [23] The Egyptians pursued them and went after them into the sea with all their horses, chariots, and drivers. [24] Just before dawn the LORD looked down from the pillar of fire and cloud at the Egyptian army and threw them into a panic. [25] He made the wheels of their chariots get stuck, so that they moved with great difficulty. The Egyptians said, "The LORD is fighting for the Israelites against us. Let's get out of here!"

[26] The LORD said to Moses, "Hold out your hand over the sea, and the water will come back over the Egyptians and their chariots and drivers." [27] So Moses held out his hand over the sea, and at daybreak the water returned to its normal level. The Egyptians tried to escape from the water, but the LORD threw them into the sea. [28] The water returned and covered the chariots, the drivers, and all the Egyptian army that had followed the Israelites into the sea; not one of them was left. [29] But the Israelites walked through the sea on dry ground, with walls of water on both sides.

[30] On that day the LORD saved the people of Israel from the Egyptians, and the Israelites saw them lying dead on the seashore. [31] When the Israelites saw the great power with which the LORD had defeated the Egyptians, they stood in awe of the LORD; and they had faith in the LORD and in his servant Moses.

The Song of Moses

15 Then Moses and the Israelites sang this song to the LORD:
"I will sing to the LORD, because he has won a glorious
victory;
he has thrown the horses and their riders into the sea.

14.20 Probable text *The cloud… Israel*; Hebrew unclear.

EXODUS 15

In response to all the specific things God had done, the Israelites wrote an impromptu song. When we sing in worship, we

REFLECT
— ON GOD'S —
GOODNESS.

Many of these songs are general praise to God, but it is sometimes good to get specific.

WRITE A
SONG OR POEM
about the specific things God has done in your life. It's a great way to praise him!

² The LORD is my strong defender;
  he is the one who has saved me.
He is my God, and I will praise him,
  my father's God, and I will sing about his greatness.
³ The LORD is a warrior;
  the LORD is his name.

⁴ "He threw Egypt's army and its chariots into the sea;
  the best of its officers were drowned in the Red Sea.
⁵ The deep sea covered them;
  they sank to the bottom like a stone.

⁶ "Your right hand, LORD, is awesome in power;
  it breaks the enemy in pieces.
⁷ In majestic triumph you overthrow your foes;
  your anger blazes out and burns them up like straw.
⁸ You blew on the sea and the water piled up high;
  it stood up straight like a wall;
  the deepest part of the sea became solid.
⁹ The enemy said, 'I will pursue them and catch them;
  I will divide their wealth and take all I want;
  I will draw my sword and take all they have.'
¹⁰ But one breath from you, LORD, and the Egyptians were
  drowned;
  they sank like lead in the terrible water.

¹¹ "LORD, who among the gods is like you?
  Who is like you, wonderful in holiness?
  Who can work miracles and mighty acts like yours?
¹² You stretched out your right hand,
  and the earth swallowed our enemies.
¹³ Faithful to your promise, you led the people you had
  rescued;
  by your strength you guided them to your sacred land.
¹⁴ The nations have heard, and they tremble with fear;
  the Philistines are seized with terror.
¹⁵ The leaders of Edom are terrified;
  Moab's mighty men are trembling;
  the people of Canaan lose their courage.
¹⁶ Terror and dread fall upon them.
They see your strength, O LORD,
  and stand helpless with fear
  until your people have marched past —
  the people you set free from slavery.
¹⁷ You bring them in and plant them on your mountain,
  the place that you, LORD, have chosen for your home,
  the Temple that you yourself have built.
¹⁸ You, LORD, will be king for ever and ever."

The Song of Miriam

¹⁹ The Israelites walked through the sea on dry ground. But
when the Egyptian chariots with their horses and drivers went into
the sea, the LORD brought the water back, and it covered them.
²⁰ The prophet Miriam, Aaron's sister, took her tambourine, and
all the women followed her, playing tambourines and dancing.
²¹ Miriam sang for them:

  "Sing to the LORD, because he has won a glorious victory;
    he has thrown the horses and their riders into the
      sea."

99

Exodus

Leviticus
Num.
Deuter.
Joshua
Judges

Bitter Water

22 Then Moses led the people of Israel away from the Red Sea into the desert of Shur. For three days they walked through the desert, but found no water. 23 Then they came to a place called Marah, but the water there was so bitter that they could not drink it. That is why it was named Marah.* 24 The people complained to Moses and asked, "What are we going to drink?" 25 Moses prayed earnestly to the Lord, and the Lord showed him a piece of wood, which he threw into the water; and the water became fit to drink.

There the Lord gave them laws to live by, and there he also tested them. 26 He said, "If you will obey me completely by doing what I consider right and by keeping my commands, I will not punish you with any of the diseases that I brought on the Egyptians. I am the Lord, the one who heals you."

27 Next they came to Elim, where there were twelve springs and seventy palm trees; there they camped by the water.

The Manna and the Quails

16 The whole Israelite community set out from Elim, and on the fifteenth day of the second month after they had left Egypt, they came to the desert of Sin, which is between Elim and Sinai. 2 There in the desert they all complained to Moses and Aaron 3 and said to them, "We wish that the Lord had killed us in Egypt. There we could at least sit down and eat meat and as much other food as we wanted. But you have brought us out into this desert to starve us all to death."

4 The Lord said to Moses, "Now I am going to make food rain down from the sky for all of you. The people must go out every day and gather enough for that day. In this way I can test them to find out if they will follow my instructions. 5 On the sixth day they are to bring in twice as much as usual and prepare it."

6 So Moses and Aaron said to all the Israelites, "This evening you will know that it was the Lord who brought you out of Egypt. 7 In the morning you will see the dazzling light of the Lord's presence. He has heard your complaints against him — yes, against him, because we are only carrying out his instructions." 8 Then Moses said, "It is the Lord who will give you meat to eat in the evening and as much bread as you want in the morning, because he has heard how much you have complained against him. When you complain against us, you are really complaining against the Lord."

9 Moses said to Aaron, "Tell the whole community to come and stand before the Lord, because he has heard their complaints." 10 As Aaron spoke to the whole community, they turned towards the desert, and suddenly the dazzling light of the Lord appeared in a cloud. 11 The Lord said to Moses, 12 "I have heard the complaints of the Israelites. Tell them that at twilight they will have meat to eat, and in the morning they will have all the bread they want. Then they will know that I, the Lord, am their God."

13 In the evening a large flock of quails flew in, enough to cover the camp, and in the morning there was dew all round the camp. 14 When the dew evaporated, there was something thin and flaky on the surface of the desert. It was as delicate as frost. 15 When the Israelites saw it, they didn't know what it was and asked each other, "What is it?"

Moses said to them, "This is the food that the Lord has given you to eat. 16 The Lord has commanded that each of you is to gather as much of it as he needs, two litres for each member of his household."

15.23 *Marah*: This name in Hebrew means "bitter".

[17] The Israelites did this, some gathering more, others less. [18] When they measured it, those who gathered much did not have too much, and those who gathered less did not have too little. Each had gathered just what he needed. [19] Moses said to them, "No one is to keep any of it for tomorrow." [20] But some of them did not listen to Moses and saved part of it. The next morning it was full of worms and smelt rotten, and Moses was angry with them. [21] Every morning each one gathered as much as he needed; and when the sun grew hot, what was left on the ground melted.

[22] On the sixth day they gathered twice as much food, four litres for each person. All the leaders of the community came and told Moses about it, [23] and he said to them, "The LORD has commanded that tomorrow is a holy day of rest, dedicated to him. Bake today what you want to bake and boil what you want to boil. Whatever is left should be put aside and kept for tomorrow." [24] As Moses had commanded, they kept what was left until the next day; it did not spoil or get worms in it. [25] Moses said, "Eat this today, because today is the Sabbath, a day of rest dedicated to the LORD, and you will not find any food outside the camp. [26] You must gather food for six days, but on the seventh day, the day of rest, there will be none."

[27] On the seventh day some of the people went out to gather food, but they did not find any. [28] Then the LORD said to Moses, "How much longer will you people refuse to obey my commands? [29] Remember that I, the LORD, have given you a day of rest, and that is why on the sixth day I will always give you enough food for two days. Everyone is to stay where he is on the seventh day and not leave his home." [30] So the people did no work on the seventh day.

[31] The people of Israel called the food manna.[*] It was like a small white seed, and tasted like biscuits made with honey. [32] Moses said, "The LORD has commanded us to save some manna, to be kept for our descendants, so that they can see the food which he gave us to eat in the desert when he brought us out of Egypt." [33] Moses said to Aaron, "Take a jar, put two litres of manna in it, and place it in the LORD's presence to be kept for our descendants." [34] As the LORD had commanded Moses, Aaron put it in front of the Covenant Box, so that it could be kept. [35] The Israelites ate manna for the next forty years, until they reached the land of Canaan, where they settled. [36] (The standard dry measure then in use equalled twenty litres.)

Water from the Rock
(Num 20.1–13)

17 The whole Israelite community left the desert of Sin, moving from one place to another at the command of the LORD. They made camp at Rephidim, but there was no water there to drink. [2] They complained to Moses and said, "Give us water to drink."

Moses answered, "Why are you complaining? Why are you putting the LORD to the test?"

[3] But the people were very thirsty and continued to complain to Moses. They said, "Why did you bring us out of Egypt? To kill us and our children and our livestock with thirst?"

[4] Moses prayed earnestly to the LORD and said, "What can I do with these people? They are almost ready to stone me."

16.31 *manna*: This word sounds like the Hebrew for "what is it?" (see verse 15).

EXODUS 17, 18

101

Exodus
....
Leviticus
Num.
Deuter.
Joshua
Judges

[5] The LORD said to Moses, "Take some of the leaders of Israel with you, and go on ahead of the people. Take along the stick with which you struck the Nile. [6] I will stand before you on a rock at Mount Sinai. Strike the rock, and water will come out of it for the people to drink." Moses did so in the presence of the leaders of Israel.

[7] The place was named Massah and Meribah,* because the Israelites complained and put the LORD to the test when they asked, "Is the LORD with us or not?"

War with the Amalekites

[8] The Amalekites came and attacked the Israelites at Rephidim. [9] Moses said to Joshua, "Pick out some men to go and fight the Amalekites tomorrow. I will stand on top of the hill holding the stick that God told me to carry." [10] Joshua did as Moses commanded him and went out to fight the Amalekites, while Moses, Aaron, and Hur went up to the top of the hill. [11] As long as Moses held up his arms, the Israelites won, but when he put his arms down, the Amalekites started winning. [12] When Moses' arms grew tired, Aaron and Hur brought a stone for him to sit on, while they stood beside him and held up his arms, holding them steady until the sun went down. [13] In this way Joshua totally defeated the Amalekites.

[14] Then the LORD said to Moses, "Write an account of this victory, so that it will be remembered. Tell Joshua that I will completely destroy the Amalekites." [15] Moses built an altar and named it "The LORD is my Banner". [16] He said, "Hold high the banner of the LORD!* The LORD will continue to fight against the Amalekites for ever!"

Jethro Visits Moses

18 Moses' father-in-law Jethro, the priest of Midian, heard about everything that God had done for Moses and the people of Israel when he led them out of Egypt. [2] So he came to Moses, bringing with him Moses' wife Zipporah, who had been left behind, [3] and Gershom and Eliezer, her two sons. (Moses had said, "I have been a foreigner in a strange land"; so he had named one son Gershom.* [4] He had also said, "The God of my father helped me and saved me from being killed by the king of Egypt"; so he had named the other son Eliezer.*) [5] Jethro came with Moses' wife and her two sons into the desert where Moses was camped at the holy mountain. [6] He had sent word to Moses that they were coming, [7] so Moses went out to meet him, bowed before him, and kissed him. They asked about each other's health and then went into Moses' tent. [8] Moses told Jethro everything that the LORD had done to the king and the people of Egypt in order to rescue the Israelites. He also told him about the hardships the people had faced on the way and how the LORD had saved them. [9] When Jethro heard all this, he was happy [10] and said, "Praise the LORD, who saved you from the king and the people of Egypt! Praise the LORD, who saved his people from slavery! [11] Now I know that the LORD is greater than all the gods, because he did this when the Egyptians treated the Israelites with such contempt." [12] Then Jethro brought an offering to be burnt whole and other sacrifices to be offered to God; and Aaron and all the leaders of Israel went with him to eat the sacred meal as an act of worship.

EXODUS 17.12

This story is a

BEAUTIFUL
- EXAMPLE -

of friendship and service. Aaron and Hur held Moses' arms up when he physically couldn't do it alone. Get together with two friends and discuss some of the following questions.

What does this story teach you about friendship?

In what ways can you support each other better through tough times?

Is there anything that you can lift up in prayer for each other right now?

17.7 *Massah… Meribah*: These names in Hebrew mean "testing" and "complaining".
17.16 Probable text *Hold… LORD*; Hebrew unclear.
18.3 *Gershom*: This name sounds like the Hebrew for "foreigner".
18.4 *Eliezer*: This name sounds like the Hebrew for "God helps me".

The Appointment of Judges
(Deut 1.9–18)

13 The next day Moses was settling disputes among the people, and he was kept busy from morning till night. 14 When Jethro saw everything that Moses had to do, he asked, "What is all this that you are doing for the people? Why are you doing this all alone, with people standing here from morning till night to consult you?"

15 Moses answered, "I must do this because the people come to me to learn God's will. 16 When two people have a dispute, they come to me, and I decide which one of them is right, and I tell them God's commands and laws."

17 Then Jethro said, "You are not doing it the right way. 18 You will wear yourself out and these people as well. This is too much for you to do alone. 19 Now let me give you some good advice, and God will be with you. It is right for you to represent the people before God and bring their disputes to him. 20 You should teach them God's commands and explain to them how they should live and what they should do. 21 But in addition, you should choose some capable men and appoint them as leaders of the people: leaders of thousands, hundreds, fifties, and tens. They must be God-fearing men who can be trusted and who cannot be bribed. 22 Let them serve as judges for the people on a permanent basis. They can bring all the difficult cases to you, but they themselves can decide all the smaller disputes. That will make it easier for you, as they share your burden. 23 If you do this, as God commands, you will not wear yourself out, and all these people can go home with their disputes settled."

24 Moses took Jethro's advice 25 and chose capable men from among all the Israelites. He appointed them as leaders of thousands, hundreds, fifties, and tens. 26 They served as judges for the people on a permanent basis, bringing the difficult cases to Moses but deciding the smaller disputes themselves.

27 Then Moses said goodbye to Jethro, and Jethro went back home.

The Israelites at Mount Sinai

19 1-2 The people of Israel left Rephidim, and on the first day of the third month after they had left Egypt they came to the desert of Sinai. There they set up camp at the foot of Mount Sinai, 3 and Moses went up the mountain to meet with God.

The LORD called to him from the mountain and told him to say to the Israelites, Jacob's descendants: 4 "You saw what I, the LORD, did to the Egyptians and how I carried you as an eagle carries her young on her wings, and brought you here to me. 5 Now, if you will obey me and keep my covenant, you will be my own people. The whole earth is mine, but you will be my chosen people, 6 a people dedicated to me alone, and you will serve me as priests." 7 So Moses went down and called the leaders of the people together and told them everything that the LORD had commanded him. 8 Then all the people answered together, "We will do everything that the LORD has said," and Moses reported this to the LORD.

9 The LORD said to Moses, "I will come to you in a thick cloud, so that the people will hear me speaking with you and will believe you from now on."

Moses told the LORD what the people had answered, 10 and the LORD said to him, "Go to the people and tell them to spend today and tomorrow purifying themselves for worship. They must wash their clothes 11 and be ready the day after tomorrow. On that

EXODUS 19, 20

103

Exodus
....
Leviticus
Num.
Deuter.
Joshua
Judges

day I will come down on Mount Sinai, where all the people can see me. ¹²Mark a boundary round the mountain that the people must not cross, and tell them not to go up the mountain or even get near it. If anyone sets foot on it, he is to be put to death; ¹³he must either be stoned or shot with arrows, without anyone touching him. This applies to both men and animals; they must be put to death. But when the trumpet is blown, then the people are to go up to the mountain."

¹⁴Then Moses came down the mountain and told the people to get ready for worship. So they washed their clothes, ¹⁵and Moses said to them, "Be ready by the day after tomorrow and don't have sexual intercourse in the meantime."

¹⁶On the morning of the third day there was thunder and lightning, a thick cloud appeared on the mountain, and a very loud trumpet blast was heard. All the people in the camp trembled with fear. ¹⁷Moses led them out of the camp to meet God, and they stood at the foot of the mountain. ¹⁸The whole of Mount Sinai was covered with smoke, because the LORD had come down on it in fire. The smoke went up like the smoke of a furnace, and all the people trembled violently. ¹⁹The sound of the trumpet became louder and louder. Moses spoke, and God answered him with thunder. ²⁰The LORD came down on the top of Mount Sinai and called Moses to the top of the mountain. Moses went up ²¹and the LORD said to him, "Go down and warn the people not to cross the boundary to come and look at me; if they do, many of them will die. ²²Even the priests who come near me must purify themselves, or I will punish them."

²³Moses said to the LORD, "The people cannot come up, because you commanded us to consider the mountain sacred and to mark a boundary round it."

²⁴The LORD replied, "Go down and bring Aaron back with you. But the priests and the people must not cross the boundary to come up to me, or I will punish them." ²⁵Moses then went down to the people and told them what the LORD had said.

The Ten Commandments
(Deut 5.1–21)

20 God spoke, and these were his words: ²"I am the LORD your God who brought you out of Egypt, where you were slaves.

³"Worship no god but me.

⁴"Do not make for yourselves images of anything in heaven or on earth or in the water under the earth. ⁵Do not bow down to any idol or worship it, because I am the LORD your God and I tolerate no rivals. I bring punishment on those who hate me and on their descendants down to the third and fourth generation. ⁶But I show my love to thousands of generations* of those who love me and obey my laws.

⁷"Do not use my name for evil purposes, for I, the LORD your God, will punish anyone who misuses my name.

⁸"Observe the Sabbath and keep it holy. ⁹You have six days in which to do your work, ¹⁰but the seventh day is a day of rest dedicated to me. On that day no one is to work — neither you, your children, your slaves, your animals, nor the foreigners who live in your country. ¹¹In six days I, the LORD, made the earth, the sky, the sea, and everything in them, but on the seventh day I rested. That is why I, the LORD, blessed the Sabbath and made it holy.

....
20.6 *thousands of generations*; or *thousands*.

12 "Respect your father and your mother, so that you may live a long time in the land that I am giving you.

13 "Do not commit murder.

14 "Do not commit adultery.

15 "Do not steal.

16 "Do not accuse anyone falsely.

17 "Do not desire another man's house; do not desire his wife, his slaves, his cattle, his donkeys, or anything else that he owns."

The People's Fear
(Deut 5.22–33)

18 When the people heard the thunder and the trumpet blast and saw the lightning and the smoking mountain, they trembled with fear and stood a long way off. 19 They said to Moses, "If you speak to us, we will listen; but we are afraid that if God speaks to us, we will die."

20 Moses replied, "Don't be afraid; God has only come to test you and make you keep on obeying him, so that you will not sin." 21 But the people continued to stand a long way off, and only Moses went near the dark cloud where God was.

Laws about Altars

22 The LORD commanded Moses to say to the Israelites: "You have seen how I, the LORD, have spoken to you from heaven. 23 Do not make for yourselves gods of silver or gold to be worshipped in addition to me. 24 Make an altar of earth for me, and on it sacrifice your sheep and your cattle as offerings to be completely burnt and as fellowship offerings. In every place that I set aside for you to worship me, I will come to you and bless you. 25 If you make an altar of stone for me, do not build it out of cut stones, because when you use a chisel on stones, you make them unfit for my use. 26 Do not build an altar for me with steps leading up to it; if you do, you will expose yourselves as you go up the steps.

The Treatment of Slaves
(Deut 15.12–18)

21 "Give the Israelites the following laws: 2 If you buy a Hebrew slave, he shall serve you for six years. In the seventh year he is to be set free without having to pay anything. 3 If he was unmarried when he became your slave, he is not to take a wife with him when he leaves; but if he was married when he became your slave, he may take his wife with him. 4 If his master gave him a wife and she bore him sons or daughters, the woman and her children belong to the master, and the man shall leave by himself. 5 But if the slave declares that he loves his master, his wife, and his children and does not want to be set free, 6 then his master shall take him to the place of worship. There he is to make him stand against the door or the doorpost and pierce his ear. Then he will be his slave for life.

7 "If a man sells his daughter as a slave, she is not to be set free, as male slaves are. 8 If she is sold to someone who intends to make her his wife, but he doesn't like her, then she is to be sold back to her father; her master cannot sell her to foreigners, because he has treated her unfairly. 9 If a man buys a female slave to give to his son, he is to treat her like a daughter. 10 If a man takes a second wife, he must continue to give his first wife the same amount of food and clothing and the same rights that she had before. 11 If he does not fulfil these duties to her, he must set her free and not receive any payment.

EXODUS 21, 22

105

Exodus
....
Leviticus
Num.
Deuter.
Joshua
Judges

Laws about Violent Acts

[12] "Whoever hits someone and kills him is to be put to death. [13] But if it was an accident and he did not mean to kill him, he can escape to a place which I will choose for you, and there he will be safe. [14] But when anyone gets angry and deliberately kills someone else, he is to be put to death, even if he has run to my altar for safety.

[15] "Whoever hits his father or his mother is to be put to death.

[16] "Whoever kidnaps someone, either to sell him or to keep him as a slave, is to be put to death.

[17] "Whoever curses his father or his mother is to be put to death.

[18-19] "If there is a fight and one person hits another with a stone or with their fist, but does not kill them, they are not to be punished. If the one who was hit has to stay in bed, but later is able to get up and walk outside with the help of a stick, the one who hit them is to pay for their lost time and take care of them until they get well.

[20] "If a slave owner takes a stick and beats his slave, whether male or female, and the slave dies on the spot, the slave owner is to be punished. [21] But if the slave does not die for a day or two, the master is not to be punished. The loss of his property is punishment enough.

[22] "If some men are fighting and hurt a pregnant woman so that she loses her child, but she is not injured in any other way, the one who hurt her is to be fined whatever amount the woman's husband demands, subject to the approval of the judges. [23] But if the woman herself is injured, the punishment shall be life for life, [24] eye for eye, tooth for tooth, hand for hand, foot for foot, [25] burn for burn, wound for wound, bruise for bruise.

[26] "If someone hits his male or female slave in the eye and puts it out, he is to free the slave as payment for the eye. [27] If he knocks out a tooth, he is to free the slave as payment for the tooth.

The Responsibility of Owners

[28] "If a bull gores someone to death, it is to be stoned, and its flesh shall not be eaten; but its owner is not to be punished. [29] But if the bull had been in the habit of attacking people and its owner had been warned, but did not keep it penned up — then if it gores someone to death, it is to be stoned, and its owner is to be put to death also. [30] However, if the owner is allowed to pay a fine to save his life, he must pay the full amount required. [31] If the bull kills a boy or a girl, the same rule applies. [32] If the bull kills a male or female slave, its owner shall pay the owner of the slave thirty pieces of silver, and the bull shall be stoned to death.

[33] "If someone takes the cover off a pit or if he digs one and does not cover it, and a bull or a donkey falls into it, [34] he must pay for the animal. He is to pay the money to the owner and may keep the dead animal. [35] If someone's bull kills someone else's bull, the two of them shall sell the live bull and divide the money; they shall also divide up the meat from the dead animal. [36] But if it was known that the bull had been in the habit of attacking and its owner did not keep it penned up, he must make good the loss by giving the other man a live bull, but he may keep the dead animal.

Laws about Repayment

22 "If someone steals a cow or a sheep and kills it or sells it, he must pay five cows for one cow and four sheep for one sheep. [2-4] He must pay for what he stole. If he owns nothing, he shall be sold as a slave to pay for what he has stolen. If the stolen animal, whether a cow, a donkey, or a sheep, is found alive in his possession, he shall pay two for one.

"If a thief is caught breaking into a house at night and is killed, the one who killed him is not guilty of murder. But if it happens during the day, he is guilty of murder.

5 "If someone lets his animals graze in a field or a vineyard and they stray away and eat up the crops* growing in someone else's field, he must make good the loss with the crops from his own fields or vineyards.

6 "If someone starts a fire in his own field and it spreads through the weeds to someone else's field and burns up corn that is growing or that has been cut and stacked, the one who started the fire is to pay for the damage.

7 "If anyone agrees to keep someone else's money or other valuables for him and they are stolen from his house, the thief, if found, shall repay double. 8 But if the thief is not found, the one who was keeping the valuables is to be brought to the place of worship and there he must take an oath that he has not stolen the other one's property.

9 "In every case of a dispute about property, whether it involves cattle, donkeys, sheep, clothing, or any other lost object, the two people claiming the property shall be taken to the place of worship. The one whom God declares to be guilty shall pay double to the other one.

10 "If someone agrees to keep a neighbour's donkey, cow, sheep, or other animal for him, and the animal dies or is injured or is carried off in a raid, and if there was no witness, 11 the man must go to the place of worship and take an oath that he has not stolen the other man's animal. If the animal was not stolen, the owner shall accept the loss, and the other man need not repay him; 12 but if the animal was stolen, the man must repay the owner. 13 If it was killed by wild animals, the man is to bring the remains as evidence; he need not pay for what has been killed by wild animals.

14 "If anyone borrows an animal from someone else and it is injured or dies when its owner is not present, he must pay for it. 15 But if that happens when the owner is present, he need not repay. If it is a hired animal, the loss is covered by the hiring charge.

Moral and Religious Laws

16 "If a man seduces a virgin who is not engaged, he must pay the bride price for her and marry her. 17 But if her father refuses to let him marry her, he must pay the father a sum of money equal to the bride price for a virgin.

18 "Put to death any woman who practises magic.

19 "Put to death any man who has sexual relations with an animal.

20 "Condemn to death anyone who offers sacrifices to any god except to me, the Lord.

21 "Do not ill-treat or oppress a foreigner; remember that you were foreigners in Egypt. 22 Do not ill-treat any widow or orphan. 23 If you do, I, the Lord, will answer them when they cry out to me for help, 24 and I will be angry and kill you in war. Your wives will become widows, and your children will be fatherless.

25 "If you lend money to any of my people who are poor, do not act like a moneylender and require him to pay interest. 26 If

··

22.5 *If… crops*; or *If someone burns off a field or a vineyard, and lets the fire get out of control and burn up the crops.*

Exodus
....
Leviticus
Num.
Deuter.
Joshua
Judges

you take someone's cloak as a pledge that he will pay you, you must give it back to him before the sun sets, 27because it is the only covering he has to keep him warm. What else can he sleep in? When he cries out to me for help, I will answer him because I am merciful.

28"Do not speak evil of God,* and do not curse a leader of your people.

29"Give me the offerings from your corn, your wine, and your olive oil when they are due.

"Give me your firstborn sons. 30Give me the firstborn of your cattle and your sheep. Let the firstborn male stay with its mother for seven days, and on the eighth day offer it to me.

31"You are my people, so you must not eat the meat of any animal that has been killed by wild animals; instead, give it to the dogs.

Justice and Fairness

23 "Do not spread false rumours, and do not help a guilty person by giving false evidence. 2Do not follow the majority when they do wrong or when they give evidence that perverts justice. 3Do not show partiality to a poor person at his trial.

4"If you happen to see your enemy's cow or donkey running loose, take it back to him. 5If his donkey has fallen under its load, help him get the donkey to its feet again; don't just walk off.

6"Do not deny justice to a poor person when he appears in court. 7Do not make false accusations, and do not put an innocent person to death, for I will condemn anyone who does such an evil thing. 8Do not accept a bribe, for a bribe makes people blind to what is right and ruins the cause of those who are innocent.

9"Do not ill-treat a foreigner; you know how it feels to be a foreigner, because you were foreigners in Egypt.

The Seventh Year and the Seventh Day

10"For six years sow your field and gather in what it produces. 11But in the seventh year let it rest, and do not harvest anything that grows on it. The poor may eat what grows there, and the wild animals can have what is left. Do the same with your vineyards and your olive trees.

12"Work six days a week, but do no work on the seventh day, so that your slaves and the foreigners who work for you and even your animals can rest.

13"Listen to everything that I, the LORD, have said to you. Do not pray to other gods; do not even mention their names.

The Three Great Festivals
(Ex 34.18–26; Deut 16.1–17)

14"Celebrate three festivals a year to honour me. 15In the month of Abib, the month in which you left Egypt, celebrate the Festival of Unleavened Bread in the way that I commanded you. Do not eat any bread made with yeast during the seven days of this festival. Never come to worship me without bringing an offering.

16"Celebrate the Harvest Festival when you begin to harvest your crops.

"Celebrate the Festival of Shelters in the autumn, when you gather the fruit from your vineyards and orchards. 17Every year at these three festivals all your men must come to worship me, the LORD your God.

22.28 *God*; or *the judges*.

¹⁸"Do not offer bread made with yeast when you sacrifice an animal to me. The fat of animals sacrificed to me during these festivals is not to be left until the following morning.

¹⁹"Each year bring to the house of the LORD your God the first corn that you harvest.

"Do not cook a young sheep or goat in its mother's milk.

Promises and Instructions

²⁰"I will send an angel ahead of you to protect you as you travel and to bring you to the place which I have prepared. ²¹Pay attention to him and obey him. Do not rebel against him, for I have sent him, and he will not pardon such rebellion. ²²But if you obey him and do everything I command, I will fight against all your enemies. ²³My angel will go ahead of you and take you into the land of the Amorites, the Hittites, the Perizzites, the Canaanites, the Hivites, and the Jebusites, and I will destroy them. ²⁴Do not bow down to their gods or worship them, and do not adopt their religious practices. Destroy their gods and break down their sacred stone pillars. ²⁵If you worship me, the LORD your God, I will bless you with food and water and take away all your illnesses. ²⁶In your land no woman will have a miscarriage or be without children. I will give you long lives.

²⁷"I will make the people who oppose you afraid of me; I will bring confusion among the people against whom you fight, and I will make all your enemies turn and run from you. ²⁸I will throw your enemies into a panic;* I will drive out the Hivites, the Canaanites, and the Hittites as you advance. ²⁹I will not drive them out within one year; if I did, the land would become deserted, and the wild animals would be too many for you. ³⁰Instead, I will drive them out little by little, until there are enough of you to take possession of the land. ³¹I will make the borders of your land extend from the Gulf of Aqaba to the Mediterranean Sea and from the desert to the Euphrates River. I will give you power over the inhabitants of the land, and you will drive them out as you advance. ³²Do not make any agreement with them or with their gods. ³³Do not let those people live in your country; if you do, they will make you sin against me. If you worship their gods, it will be a fatal trap for you."

The Covenant is Sealed

24 The LORD said to Moses, "Come up the mountain to me, you and Aaron, Nadab, Abihu, and seventy of the leaders of Israel; and while you are still some distance away, bow down in worship. ²You alone, and none of the others, are to come near me. The people are not even to come up the mountain."

³Moses went and told the people all the LORD's commands and all the ordinances, and all the people answered together, "We will do everything that the LORD has said." ⁴Moses wrote down all the LORD's commands. Early the next morning he built an altar at the foot of the mountain and set up twelve stones, one for each of the twelve tribes of Israel. ⁵Then he sent young men, and they burnt sacrifices to the LORD and sacrificed some cattle as fellowship offerings. ⁶Moses took half the blood of the animals and put it in bowls; and the other half he threw against the altar. ⁷Then he took the book of the covenant, in which the LORD's commands were written, and read it aloud to the people. They said, "We will obey the LORD and do everything that he has commanded."

23.28 *I will… panic*; or *I will send hornets among your enemies.*

[8] Then Moses took the blood in the bowls and threw it on the people. He said, "This is the blood that seals the covenant which the LORD made with you when he gave all these commands." [9] Moses, Aaron, Nadab, Abihu, and seventy of the leaders of Israel went up the mountain [10] and they saw the God of Israel. Beneath his feet was what looked like a pavement of sapphire, as blue as the sky. [11] God did not harm these leading men of Israel; they saw God, and then they ate and drank together.

Moses on Mount Sinai

[12] The LORD said to Moses, "Come up the mountain to me, and while you are here, I will give you two stone tablets which contain all the laws that I have written for the instruction of the people." [13] Moses and his helper Joshua got ready, and Moses began* to go up the holy mountain. [14] Moses said to the leaders, "Wait here in the camp for us until we come back. Aaron and Hur are here with you; and so whoever has a dispute to settle can go to them." [15] Moses went up Mount Sinai, and a cloud covered it. [16-17] The dazzling light of the LORD's presence came down on the mountain. To the Israelites the light looked like a fire burning on top of the mountain. The cloud covered the mountain for six days, and on the seventh day the LORD called to Moses from the cloud. [18] Moses went on up the mountain into the cloud. There he stayed for forty days and nights.

Offerings for the Sacred Tent
(Ex 35.4–9)

25 The Lord said to Moses, [2] "Tell the Israelites to make an offering to me. Receive whatever offerings anyone wishes to give. [3] These offerings are to be: gold, silver, and bronze; [4] fine linen; blue, purple, and red wool; cloth made of goats' hair; [5] rams' skin dyed red; fine leather; acacia wood; [6] oil for the lamps; spices for the anointing oil and for the sweet-smelling incense; [7] carnelians and other jewels to be set in the ephod* of the High Priest and in his breastpiece. [8] The people must make a sacred tent for me, so that I may live among them. [9] Make it and all its furnishings according to the plan that I will show you.

The Covenant Box
(Ex 37.1–9)

[10] "Make a box out of acacia wood, 110 centimetres long, 66 centimetres wide, and 66 centimetres high. [11] Cover it with pure gold inside and out and put a gold border all round it. [12] Make four carrying rings of gold for it and attach them to its four legs, with two rings on each side. [13] Make carrying poles of acacia wood and cover them with gold [14] and put them through the rings on each side of the box. [15] The poles are to be left in the rings and must not be taken out. [16] Then put in the box the two stone tablets that I will give you, on which the commandments are written. [17] "Make a lid of pure gold, 110 centimetres long and 66 centimetres wide. [18] Make two winged creatures of hammered gold, [19] one for each end of the lid. Make them so that they form one piece with the lid. [20] The winged creatures are to face each

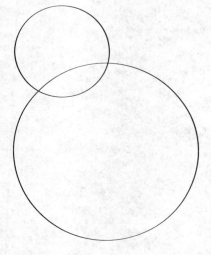

TURN THESE SHAPES INTO

SOMETHING
ELSE.

24.13 *Moses began*; one ancient translation *they began.*
25.7 *ephod*: In most contexts the term ephod refers to a type of garment, in certain respects resembling a waistcoat. It was made of costly and colourful cloth and to it was attached a kind of pouch containing the Urim and Thummim, two objects used in determining God's will.

other across the lid, and their outspread wings are to cover it. ²¹Put the two stone tablets inside the box and put the lid on top of it. ²²I will meet you there, and from above the lid between the two winged creatures I will give you all my laws for the people of Israel.

The Table for the Bread Offered to God
(Ex 37.10–16)

²³"Make a table out of acacia wood, 88 centimetres long, 44 centimetres wide, and 66 centimetres high. ²⁴Cover it with pure gold and put a gold border round it. ²⁵Make a rim 75 millimetres wide round it and a gold border round the rim. ²⁶Make four carrying rings of gold for it and put them at the four corners, where the legs are. ²⁷The rings to hold the poles for carrying the table are to be placed near the rim. ²⁸Make the poles of acacia wood and cover them with gold. ²⁹Make plates, cups, jars, and bowls to be used for the wine offerings. All of these are to be made of pure gold. ³⁰The table is to be placed in front of the Covenant Box, and on the table there is always to be the sacred bread offered to me.

The Lampstand
(Ex 37.17–24)

³¹"Make a lampstand of pure gold. Make its base and its shaft of hammered gold; its decorative flowers, including buds and petals, are to form one piece with it. ³²Six branches shall extend from its sides, three from each side. ³³Each of the six branches is to have three decorative flowers shaped like almond blossoms with buds and petals. ³⁴The shaft of the lampstand is to have four decorative flowers shaped like almond blossoms with buds and petals. ³⁵There is to be one bud below each of the three pairs of branches. ³⁶The buds, the branches, and the lampstand are to be a single piece of pure hammered gold. ³⁷Make seven lamps for the lampstand and set them up so that they shine towards the front. ³⁸Make its tongs and trays of pure gold. ³⁹Use 35 kilogrammes of pure gold to make the lampstand and all this equipment. ⁴⁰Take care to make them according to the plan that I showed you on the mountain.

The Tent of the LORD's Presence
(Ex 36.8–38)

26 "Make the interior of the sacred Tent, the Tent of my presence, out of ten pieces of fine linen woven with blue, purple, and red wool. Embroider them with figures of winged creatures. ²Make each piece the same size, twelve metres long and two metres wide. ³Sew five of them together in one set, and do the same with the other five. ⁴Make loops of blue cloth on the edge of the outside piece in each set. ⁵Put fifty loops on the first piece of the first set and fifty loops matching them on the last piece of the second set. ⁶Make fifty gold hooks with which to join the two sets into one piece.

⁷"Make a cover for the Tent out of eleven pieces of cloth made of goats' hair. ⁸Make them all the same size, thirteen metres long and two metres wide. ⁹Sew five of them together in one set, and the other six in another set. Fold the sixth piece double over the front of the Tent. ¹⁰Put fifty loops on the edge of the last piece of one set, and fifty loops on the edge of the other set. ¹¹Make fifty bronze hooks and put them in the loops to join the two sets so as to form one cover. ¹²Hang the extra half-piece over the back of the Tent. ¹³The extra fifty centimetres on each side of the length is to hang over the sides of the Tent to cover it.

SOMETHING ELSE

EXODUS 26

The Tent of the Lord's Presence (also called the tabernacle) was so much more than a big tent! The Hebrew word for it is mishkan, which means

• 'DWELLING •

PLACE'.

This tent was the place where the presence of God dwelt.

EXODUS 26, 27

111

Exodus

. . . .

Leviticus

Num.

Deuter.

Joshua

Judges

[14] "Make two more coverings, one of rams' skin dyed red and the other of fine leather, to serve as the outer cover.

[15] "Make upright frames for the Tent out of acacia wood. [16] Each frame is to be four metres long and 66 centimetres wide, [17] with two matching projections, so that the frames can be joined together. All the frames are to have these projections. [18] Make twenty frames for the south side [19] and forty silver bases to go under them, two bases under each frame to hold its two projections. [20] Make twenty frames for the north side of the Tent [21] and forty silver bases, two under each frame. [22] For the back of the Tent on the west, make six frames, [23] and two frames for the corners. [24] These corner frames are to be joined at the bottom and connected all the way to the top. The two frames that form the two corners are to be made in this way. [25] So there will be eight frames with their sixteen silver bases, two under each frame.

[26] "Make fifteen crossbars of acacia wood, five for the frames on one side of the Tent, [27] five for the frames on the other side, and five for the frames on the west end, at the back. [28] The middle crossbar, set halfway up the frames, is to extend from one end of the Tent to the other. [29] Cover the frames with gold and fit them with gold rings to hold the crossbars, which are also to be covered with gold. [30] Set up the Tent according to the plan that I showed you on the mountain.

[31] "Make a curtain of fine linen woven with blue, purple, and red wool. Embroider it with figures of winged creatures. [32] Hang it on four posts of acacia wood covered with gold, fitted with hooks, and set in four silver bases. [33] Place the curtain under the row of hooks in the roof of the Tent, and behind the curtain put the Covenant Box containing the two stone tablets. The curtain will separate the Holy Place from the Most Holy Place. [34] Put the lid on the Covenant Box. [35] Outside the Most Holy Place put the table against the north side of the Tent and the lampstand against the south side.

[36] "For the entrance of the Tent make a curtain of fine linen woven with blue, purple, and red wool and decorated with embroidery. [37] For this curtain make five posts of acacia wood covered with gold and fitted with gold hooks; make five bronze bases for these posts.

The Altar
(Ex 38.1–7)

27 "Make an altar out of acacia wood. It is to be square, 2.2 metres long and 2.2 metres wide, and it is to be 1.3 metres high. [2] Make projections at the top of the four corners. They are to form one piece with the altar, and the whole is to be covered with bronze. [3] Make pans for the greasy ashes, and make shovels, bowls, hooks, and firepans. All this equipment is to be made of bronze. [4] Make a bronze grating and put four bronze carrying rings on its corners. [5] Put the grating under the rim of the altar, so that it reaches halfway up the altar. [6] Make carrying poles of acacia wood, cover them with bronze, [7] and put them in the rings on each side of the altar when it is carried. [8] Make the altar out of boards and leave it hollow, according to the plan that I showed you on the mountain.

The Enclosure for the Tent of the LORD's Presence
(Ex 38.9–20)

[9] "For the Tent of my presence make an enclosure out of fine linen curtains. On the south side the curtains are to be 44 metres

long, [10] supported by twenty bronze posts in twenty bronze bases, with hooks and rods made of silver. [11] The same is to be done on the north side of the enclosure. [12] On the west side there are to be curtains 22 metres long, with ten posts and ten bases. [13] On the east side, where the entrance is, the enclosure is also to be 22 metres wide. [14-15] On each side of the entrance there are to be 6.6 metres of curtains, with three posts and three bases. [16] For the entrance itself there is to be a curtain nine metres long made of fine linen woven with blue, purple, and red wool, and decorated with embroidery. It is to be supported by four posts in four bases. [17] All the posts round the enclosure are to be connected with silver rods, and their hooks are to be made of silver and their bases of bronze. [18] The enclosure is to be 44 metres long, 22 metres wide, and 2.2 metres high. The curtains are to be made of fine linen and the bases of bronze. [19] All the equipment that is used in the Tent and all the pegs for the Tent and for the enclosure are to be made of bronze.

Taking Care of the Lamp
(Lev 24.1–4)

[20] "Command the people of Israel to bring you the best olive oil for the lamp, so that it can be lit each evening. [21] Aaron and his sons are to set up the lamp in the Tent of my presence outside the curtain which is in front of the Covenant Box. There in my presence it is to burn from evening until morning. This command is to be kept for ever by the Israelites and their descendants.

Garments for the Priests
(Ex 39.1–7)

28 "Summon your brother Aaron and his sons, Nadab, Abihu, Eleazar, and Ithamar. Separate them from the people of Israel, so that they may serve me as priests. [2] Make priestly garments for your brother Aaron, to provide him with dignity and beauty. [3] Call all the skilled workers to whom I have given ability, and tell them to make Aaron's clothes, so that he may be dedicated as a priest in my service. [4] Tell them to make a breastpiece, an ephod, a robe, an embroidered shirt, a turban, and a sash. They are to make these priestly garments for your brother Aaron and his sons, so that they can serve me as priests. [5] The skilled workers are to use blue, purple, and red wool, gold thread, and fine linen.

[6] "They are to make the ephod of blue, purple, and red wool, gold thread, and fine linen, decorated with embroidery. [7] Two shoulder straps, by which it can be fastened, are to be attached to the sides. [8] A finely woven belt made of the same materials is to be attached to the ephod so as to form one piece with it. [9] Take two carnelian stones and engrave on them the names of the twelve sons of Jacob, [10] in the order of their birth, with six on one stone and six on the other. [11] Get a skilful jeweller to engrave on the two stones the names of the sons of Jacob, and mount the stones in gold settings. [12] Put them on the shoulder straps of the ephod to represent the twelve tribes of Israel. In this way Aaron will carry their names on his shoulders, so that I, the LORD, will always remember my people. [13] Make two gold settings [14] and two chains of pure gold twisted like cords, and attach them to the settings.

The Breastpiece
(Ex 39.8–21)

[15] "Make a breastpiece for the High Priest to use in determining God's will. It is to be made of the same materials as the ephod

EXODUS 28

113

Exodus

Leviticus
Num.
Deuter.
Joshua
Judges

and with similar embroidery. ¹⁶It is to be square and folded double, 22 centimetres long and 22 centimetres wide. ¹⁷Mount four rows of precious stones on it; in the first row mount a ruby, a topaz, and a garnet; ¹⁸in the second row, an emerald, a sapphire, and a diamond; ¹⁹in the third row, a turquoise, an agate, and an amethyst; ²⁰and in the fourth row, a beryl, a carnelian, and a jasper. These are to be mounted in gold settings. ²¹Each of these twelve stones is to have engraved on it the name of one of the sons of Jacob, to represent the tribes of Israel. ²²For the breastpiece make chains of pure gold, twisted like cords. ²³Make two gold rings and attach them to the upper corners of the breastpiece, ²⁴and fasten the two gold cords to the two rings. ²⁵Fasten the other two ends of the cords to the two settings, and in this way attach them in front to the shoulder straps of the ephod. ²⁶Then make two rings of gold and attach them to the lower corners of the breastpiece on the inside edge next to the ephod. ²⁷Make two more gold rings and attach them to the lower part of the front of the two shoulder straps of the ephod near the seam and above the finely woven belt. ²⁸Tie the rings of the breastpiece to the rings of the ephod with a blue cord, so that the breastpiece rests above the belt and does not come loose.

²⁹"When Aaron enters the Holy Place, he will wear this breastpiece engraved with the names of the tribes of Israel, so that I, the LORD, will always remember my people. ³⁰Put the Urim and Thummim* in the breastpiece, so that Aaron will carry them when he comes into my holy presence. At such times he must always wear this breastpiece, so that he can determine my will for the people of Israel.

The Other Priestly Garments
(Ex 39.22–31)

³¹"The robe that goes under the ephod is to be made entirely of blue wool. ³²It is to have a hole for the head, and this hole is to be reinforced with a woven binding to keep it from tearing. ³³⁻³⁴All round its lower hem put pomegranates of blue, purple, and red wool, alternating with gold bells. ³⁵Aaron is to wear this robe when he serves as priest. When he comes into my presence in the Holy Place or when he leaves it, the sound of the bells will be heard, and he will not be killed.

³⁶"Make an ornament of pure gold and engrave on it 'Dedicated to the LORD'. ³⁷Tie it to the front of the turban with a blue cord. ³⁸Aaron is to wear it on his forehead, so that I, the LORD, will accept all the offerings that the Israelites dedicate to me, even if the people commit some error in offering them.

³⁹"Weave Aaron's shirt of fine linen and make a turban of fine linen and also a sash decorated with embroidery.

⁴⁰"Make shirts, sashes, and caps for Aaron's sons, to provide them with dignity and beauty. ⁴¹Put these clothes on your brother Aaron and his sons. Then ordain them and dedicate them by anointing them with olive oil, so that they may serve me as priests. ⁴²Make linen shorts for them, reaching from the waist to the thighs, so that they will not expose themselves. ⁴³Aaron and his sons must always wear them when they go into the Tent of my presence or approach the altar to serve as priests in the Holy Place, so that they will not be killed for exposing themselves. This is a permanent rule for Aaron and his descendants.

28.30 *Urim and Thummim*: Two objects used by the priest to determine God's will; it is not known precisely how they were used.

Instructions for Ordaining Aaron and his Sons as Priests
(Lev 8.1–36)

29 "This is what you are to do to Aaron and his sons to dedicate them as priests in my service. Take one young bull and two rams without any defects. [2] Use the best wheat flour, but no yeast, and make some bread with olive oil, some without it, and some in the form of biscuits brushed with oil. [3] Put them in a basket and offer them to me when you sacrifice the bull and the two rams.

[4] "Bring Aaron and his sons to the entrance of the Tent of my presence, and tell them to take a ritual bath. [5] Then dress Aaron in the priestly garments — the shirt, the robe that goes under the ephod, the ephod, the breastpiece, and the belt. [6] Put the turban on him and tie on it the sacred sign of dedication engraved 'Dedicated to the LORD'. [7] Then take the anointing oil, pour it on his head, and anoint him.

[8] "Bring his sons and put shirts on them; [9] put sashes round their waists and tie caps on their heads. That is how you are to ordain Aaron and his sons. They and their descendants are to serve me as priests for ever.

[10] "Bring the bull to the front of the Tent of my presence and tell Aaron and his sons to put their hands on its head. [11] Kill the bull there in my holy presence at the entrance of the Tent. [12] Take some of the bull's blood and with your finger put it on the projections of the altar. Then pour out the rest of the blood at the base of the altar. [13] Next, take all the fat which covers the internal organs, the best part of the liver, and the two kidneys with the fat on them and burn them on the altar as an offering to me. [14] But burn the bull's flesh, its skin, and its intestines outside the camp. This is an offering to take away the sins of the priests.

[15] "Take one of the rams and tell Aaron and his sons to put their hands on its head. [16] Kill it, and take its blood and throw it against all four sides of the altar. [17] Cut the ram in pieces; wash its internal organs and its hind legs, and put them on top of the head and the other pieces. [18] Burn the whole ram on the altar as a food offering. The odour of this offering pleases me.

[19] "Take the other ram — the ram used for dedication — and tell Aaron and his sons to put their hands on its head. [20] Kill it, and take some of its blood and put it on the lobes of the right ears of Aaron and his sons, on the thumbs of their right hands and on the big toes of their right feet. Throw the rest of the blood against all four sides of the altar. [21] Take some of the blood that is on the altar and some of the anointing oil, and sprinkle it on Aaron and his clothes and on his sons and their clothes. He, his sons, and their clothes will then be dedicated to me.

[22] "Cut away the ram's fat, the fat tail, the fat covering the internal organs, the best part of the liver, the two kidneys with the fat on them, and the right thigh. [23] From the basket of bread which has been offered to me, take one loaf of each kind: one loaf made with olive oil and one made without it and one biscuit. [24] Put all this food in the hands of Aaron and his sons and tell them to dedicate it to me as a special gift. [25] Then take it from them and burn it on the altar, on top of the burnt offering, as a food offering to me. The odour of this offering pleases me.

[26] "Take the breast of this ram and dedicate it to me as a special gift. This part of the animal will be yours.

[27] "When a priest is ordained, the breast and the thigh of the ram being used for the ordination are to be dedicated to me as a special gift and set aside for the priests. [28] It is my unchanging

EXODUS 29, 30

115

Exodus

....

Leviticus
Num.
Deuter.
Joshua
Judges

decision that when my people make their fellowship offerings, the breast and the thigh of the animal belong to the priests. This is the people's gift to me, the LORD.

29 "Aaron's priestly garments are to be handed on to his sons after his death, for them to wear when they are ordained. 30 The son of Aaron who succeeds him as priest and who goes into the Tent of my presence to serve in the Holy Place is to wear these garments for seven days.

31 "Take the meat of the ram used for the ordination of Aaron and his sons and boil it in a holy place. 32 At the entrance of the Tent of my presence they are to eat it along with the bread left in the basket. 33 They shall eat what was used in the ritual of forgiveness at their ordination. Only priests may eat this food, because it is sacred. 34 If some of the meat or some of the bread is not eaten by morning, it is to be burnt; it is not to be eaten, for it is sacred.

35 "Perform the rites of ordination for Aaron and his sons for seven days exactly as I have commanded you. 36 Each day you must offer a bull as a sacrifice, so that sin may be forgiven. This will purify the altar. Then anoint it with olive oil to make it holy. 37 Do this every day for seven days. Then the altar will be completely holy, and anyone or anything that touches it will be harmed by the power of its holiness.*

The Daily Offerings
(Num 28.1–8)

38 "Every day for all time to come, sacrifice on the altar two one-year-old lambs. 39 Sacrifice one of the lambs in the morning and the other in the evening. 40 With the first lamb offer one kilogramme of fine wheat flour mixed with one litre of pure olive oil. Pour out one litre of wine as an offering. 41 Sacrifice the second lamb in the evening, and offer with it the same amounts of flour, olive oil, and wine as in the morning. This is a food offering to me, the LORD, and its odour pleases me. 42 For all time to come, this burnt offering is to be offered in my presence at the entrance of the Tent of my presence. That is where I will meet my people and speak to you. 43 There I will meet the people of Israel, and the dazzling light of my presence will make the place holy. 44 I will make the Tent and the altar holy, and I will set Aaron and his sons apart to serve me as priests. 45 I will live among the people of Israel, and I will be their God. 46 They will know that I am the LORD their God who brought them out of Egypt so that I could live among them. I am the LORD their God.

The Altar for Burning Incense
(Ex 37.25–28)

30 "Make an altar out of acacia wood, for burning incense. 2 It is to be square, 45 centimetres long and 45 centimetres wide, and it is to be ninety centimetres high. Its projections at the four corners are to form one piece with it. 3 Cover its top, all four sides, and its projections with pure gold, and put a gold border round it. 4 Make two gold carrying rings for it and attach them below the border on two sides to hold the poles with which it is to be carried. 5 Make these poles of acacia wood and cover them with gold. 6 Put this altar outside the curtain which hangs in front of the Covenant Box. That is the place where I will meet you. 7 Every morning when Aaron

29.37 be harmed by the power of its holiness: It was believed that ordinary people or things would be harmed by touching something holy.

EXODUS 30.1-8

Incense had a really important role in worship. It was a

SYMBOL
– OF –
PRAYER

rising to God (see Psalm 141.2) but was also something that God wanted as part of an offering.

In 2 Corinthians 2.15, Paul says that we are like incense.

GO AND FIND SOMETHING SWEET OR NICE-SMELLING

in your house and offer a prayer to God as you enjoy the scent.

comes to get the lamps ready, he is to burn sweet-smelling incense on it. [8] He must do the same when he lights the lamps in the evening. This offering of incense is to continue without interruption for all time to come. [9] Do not offer on this altar any forbidden incense, any animal offering, or any grain offering, and do not pour out any wine offering on it. [10] Once a year Aaron is to perform the ritual for purifying the altar by putting on its four projections the blood of the animal sacrificed for sin. This is to be done every year for all time to come. This altar is to be completely holy, dedicated to me, the Lord."

The Tax for the Tent of the Lord's Presence

[11] The Lord said to Moses, [12] "When you take a census of the people of Israel, each man is to pay me a price for his life, so that no disaster will come on him while the census is being taken. [13] Everyone included in the census must pay the required amount of money, weighed according to the official standard. Everyone must pay this as an offering to me. [14] Everyone being counted in the census, that is, every man twenty years old or older, is to pay me this amount. [15] The rich man is not to pay more, nor the poor man less, when they pay this amount for their lives. [16] Collect this money from the people of Israel and spend it for the upkeep of the Tent of my presence. This tax will be the payment for their lives, and I will remember to protect them."

The Bronze Basin

[17] The Lord said to Moses, [18] "Make a bronze basin with a bronze base. Place it between the Tent and the altar, and put water in it. [19] Aaron and his sons are to use the water to wash their hands and feet [20] before they go into the Tent or approach the altar to offer the food offering. Then they will not be killed. [21] They must wash their hands and feet, so that they will not die. This is a rule which they and their descendants are to observe for ever."

The Anointing Oil

[22] The Lord said to Moses, [23] "Take the finest spices — six kilogrammes of liquid myrrh, three kilogrammes of sweet-smelling cinnamon, three kilogrammes of sweet-smelling cane, [24] and six kilogrammes of cassia (all weighed according to the official standard). Add four litres of olive oil, [25] and make a sacred anointing oil, mixed like perfume. [26] Use it to anoint the Tent of my presence, the Covenant Box, [27] the table and all its equipment, the lampstand and its equipment, the altar for burning incense, [28] the altar for burning offerings, together with all its equipment, and the washbasin with its base. [29] Dedicate these things in this way, and they will be completely holy, and anyone or anything that touches them will be harmed by the power of their holiness.* [30] Then anoint Aaron and his sons, and ordain them as priests in my service. [31] Say to the people of Israel, 'This holy anointing oil is to be used in my service for all time to come. [32] It must not be poured on ordinary men, and you must not use the same formula to make any mixture like it. It is holy, and you must treat it as holy. [33] Whoever makes any like it or uses any of it on anyone who is not a priest will no longer be considered one of my people.' "

The Incense

[34] The Lord said to Moses, "Take an equal part of each of the following sweet spices — stacte, onycha, galbanum, and pure

30.29 *harmed by the power of their holiness*: See 29.37.

EXODUS 30–32

117

Exodus

Leviticus
Num.
Deuter.
Joshua
Judges

frankincense. [35] Use them to make incense, mixed like perfume. Add salt to keep it pure and holy. [36] Beat part of it into a fine powder, take it into the Tent of my presence, and sprinkle it in front of the Covenant Box. Treat this incense as completely holy. [37] Do not use the same formula to make any incense like it for yourselves. Treat it as a holy thing dedicated to me. [38] If anyone makes any like it for use as perfume, he will no longer be considered one of my people."

Workers to make the Tent of the LORD's Presence
(Ex 35.30—36.1)

31 The LORD said to Moses, [2] "I have chosen Bezalel, the son of Uri and grandson of Hur, from the tribe of Judah, [3] and I have filled him with my power.* I have given him understanding, skill, and ability for every kind of artistic work — [4] for planning skilful designs and working them in gold, silver, and bronze; [5] for cutting jewels to be set; for carving wood; and for every other kind of artistic work. [6] I have also selected Oholiab son of Ahisamach, from the tribe of Dan, to work with him. I have also given great ability to all the other skilled workers, so that they can make everything I have commanded to be made: [7] the Tent of my presence, the Covenant Box and its lid, all the furnishings of the Tent, [8] the table and its equipment, the lampstand of pure gold and all its equipment, the altar for burning incense, [9] the altar for burnt offerings and all its equipment, the washbasin and its base, [10] the magnificent priestly garments for Aaron and his sons to use when they serve as priests, [11] the anointing oil, and the sweet-smelling incense for the Holy Place. In making all these things, they are to do exactly as I have commanded you."

Sabbath, the Day of Rest

[12] The LORD commanded Moses [13] to say to the people of Israel, "Keep the Sabbath, my day of rest, because it is a sign between you and me for all time to come, to show that I, the LORD, have made you my own people. [14] You must keep the day of rest, because it is sacred. Whoever does not keep it, but works on that day, is to be put to death. [15] You have six days in which to do your work, but the seventh day is a solemn day of rest dedicated to me. Whoever does any work on that day is to be put to death. [16] The people of Israel are to keep this day as a sign of the covenant. [17] It is a permanent sign between the people of Israel and me, because I, the LORD, made heaven and earth in six days, and on the seventh day I stopped working and rested."

[18] When God had finished speaking to Moses on Mount Sinai, he gave him the two stone tablets on which God himself had written the commandments.

The Gold Bull Calf
(Deut 9.6–29)

32 When the people saw that Moses had not come down from the mountain but was staying there a long time, they gathered round Aaron and said to him, "We do not know what has happened to this man Moses, who led us out of Egypt; so make us a god* to lead us."

[2] Aaron said to them, "Take off the gold earrings which your wives, your sons, and your daughters are wearing, and bring them

31.3 *power;* or *spirit.*
32.1 *a god;* or *some gods.*

DOODLE HERE...

to me." ³So all the people took off their gold earrings and brought them to Aaron. ⁴He took the earrings, melted them, poured the gold into a mould, and made a gold bull calf.

The people said, "Israel, this is our god, who led us out of Egypt!"

⁵Then Aaron built an altar in front of the gold bull calf and announced, "Tomorrow there will be a festival to honour the LORD." ⁶Early the next morning they brought some animals to burn as sacrifices and others to eat as fellowship offerings. The people sat down to a feast, which turned into an orgy of drinking and sex.

⁷The LORD said to Moses, "Go back down at once, because your people, whom you led out of Egypt, have sinned and rejected me. ⁸They have already left the way that I commanded them to follow; they have made a bull calf out of melted gold and have worshipped it and offered sacrifices to it. They are saying that this is their god, who led them out of Egypt. ⁹I know how stubborn these people are. ¹⁰Now, don't try to stop me. I am angry with them, and I am going to destroy them. Then I will make you and your descendants into a great nation."

¹¹But Moses pleaded with the LORD his God and said, "LORD, why should you be so angry with your people, whom you rescued from Egypt with great might and power? ¹²Why should the Egyptians be able to say that you led your people out of Egypt, planning to kill them in the mountains and destroy them completely? Stop being angry; change your mind and do not bring this disaster on your people. ¹³Remember your servants Abraham, Isaac, and Jacob. Remember the solemn promise you made to them to give them as many descendants as there are stars in the sky and to give their descendants all that land you promised would be their possession for ever." ¹⁴So the LORD changed his mind and did not bring on his people the disaster he had threatened.

¹⁵Moses went back down the mountain, carrying the two stone tablets with the commandments written on both sides. ¹⁶God himself had made the tablets and had engraved the commandments on them.

¹⁷Joshua heard the people shouting and said to Moses, "I hear the sound of battle in the camp."

¹⁸Moses said, "That doesn't sound like a shout of victory or a cry of defeat; it's the sound of singing."

¹⁹When Moses came close enough to the camp to see the bull calf and to see the people dancing, he was furious. There at the foot of the mountain, he threw down the tablets he was carrying and broke them. ²⁰He took the bull calf which they had made, melted it, ground it into fine powder, and mixed it with water. Then he made the people of Israel drink it. ²¹He said to Aaron, "What did these people do to you, that you have made them commit such a terrible sin?"

²²Aaron answered, "Don't be angry with me; you know how determined these people are to do evil. ²³They said to me, 'We don't know what has happened to this man Moses, who brought us out of Egypt; so make us a god to lead us.' ²⁴I asked them to bring me their gold ornaments, and those who had any took them off and gave them to me. I threw the ornaments into the fire and out came this bull calf!"

²⁵Moses saw that Aaron had let the people get out of control and make fools of themselves in front of their enemies. ²⁶So he stood at the gate of the camp and shouted, "Everyone who is on the LORD's side come over here!" So all the Levites gathered round him, ²⁷and he said to them, "The LORD God of Israel commands every one of you to put on his sword and go through the camp

EXODUS 32, 33   119

Exodus
........∴

Leviticus
Num.
Deuter.
Joshua
Judges

from this gate to the other and kill his brothers, his friends, and his neighbours." [28] The Levites obeyed, and killed about 3,000 men that day. [29] Moses said to the Levites, "Today you have consecrated yourselves* as priests in the service of the LORD by killing your sons and brothers, so the LORD has given you his blessing."

[30] The next day Moses said to the people, "You have committed a terrible sin. But now I will again go up the mountain to the LORD; perhaps I can obtain forgiveness for your sin." [31] Moses then returned to the LORD and said, "These people have committed a terrible sin. They have made a god out of gold and worshipped it. [32] Please forgive their sin; but if you won't, then remove my name from the book in which you have written the names of your people."

[33] The LORD answered, "It is those who have sinned against me whose names I will remove from my book. [34] Now go, lead the people to the place I told you about. Remember that my angel will guide you, but the time is coming when I will punish these people for their sin."

[35] So the LORD sent a disease on the people, because they had caused Aaron to make the gold bull calf.

The LORD Orders Israel to Leave Mount Sinai

33 The LORD said to Moses, "Leave this place, you and the people you brought out of Egypt, and go to the land that I promised to give to Abraham, Isaac, and Jacob and to their descendants. [2] I will send an angel to guide you, and I will drive out the Canaanites, the Amorites, the Hittites, the Perizzites, the Hivites, and the Jebusites. [3] You are going to a rich and fertile land. But I will not go with you myself, because you are a stubborn people, and I might destroy you on the way."

[4] When the people heard this, they began to mourn and did not wear jewellery any more. [5] For the LORD had commanded Moses to say to them, "You are a stubborn people. If I were to go with you even for a moment, I would completely destroy you. Now take off your jewellery, and I will decide what to do with you." [6] So after they left Mount Sinai, the people of Israel no longer wore jewellery.

The Tent of the LORD's Presence

[7] Whenever the people of Israel set up camp, Moses would take the sacred Tent and put it up some distance away from the camp. It was called the Tent of the LORD's presence, and anyone who wanted to consult the LORD would go out to it. [8] Whenever Moses went out there, the people would stand at the door of their tents and watch Moses until he entered it. [9] After Moses had gone in, the pillar of cloud would come down and stay at the door of the Tent, and the LORD would speak to Moses from the cloud. [10] As soon as the people saw the pillar of cloud at the door of the Tent, they would bow down. [11] The LORD would speak with Moses face to face, just as someone speaks with a friend. Then Moses would return to the camp. But the young man who was his helper, Joshua son of Nun, stayed in the Tent.

The LORD Promises to be with his People

[12] Moses said to the LORD, "It is true that you have told me to lead these people to that land, but you did not tell me whom you

....
32.29 Some ancient translations *Today you have consecrated yourselves*; Hebrew *Consecrate yourselves today*; or *You have been consecrated today*.

would send with me. You have said that you know me well and are pleased with me. [13] Now if you are, tell me your plans, so that I may serve you and continue to please you. Remember also that you have chosen this nation to be your own."

[14] The LORD said, "I will go with you, and I will give you victory."

[15] Moses replied, "If you do not go with us, don't make us leave this place. [16] How will anyone know that you are pleased with your people and with me if you do not go with us? Your presence with us will distinguish us from any other people on earth."

[17] The LORD said to Moses, "I will do just as you have asked, because I know you very well and I am pleased with you."

[18] Then Moses requested, "Please, let me see the dazzling light of your presence."

[19] The LORD answered, "I will make all my splendour pass before you and in your presence I will pronounce my sacred name. I am the LORD, and I show compassion and pity on those I choose. [20] I will not let you see my face, because no one can see me and stay alive, [21] but here is a place beside me where you can stand on a rock. [22] When the dazzling light of my presence passes by, I will put you in an opening in the rock and cover you with my hand until I have passed by. [23] Then I will take my hand away, and you will see my back but not my face."

The Second Set of Stone Tablets
(Deut 10.1–5)

34 The LORD said to Moses, "Cut two stone tablets like the first ones, and I will write on them the words that were on the first tablets, which you broke. [2] Be ready tomorrow morning, and come up Mount Sinai to meet me there at the top. [3] No one is to come up with you; no one is to be seen on any part of the mountain; and no sheep or cattle are to graze at the foot of the mountain." [4] So Moses cut two more stone tablets, and early the next morning he carried them up Mount Sinai, just as the LORD had commanded.

[5] The LORD came down in a cloud, stood with him there, and pronounced his holy name, the LORD.* [6] The LORD then passed in front of him and called out, "I, the LORD, am a God who is full of compassion and pity, who is not easily angered and who shows great love and faithfulness. [7] I keep my promise for thousands of generations* and forgive evil and sin; but I will not fail to punish children and grandchildren to the third and fourth generation for the sins of their parents."

[8] Moses quickly bowed down to the ground and worshipped. [9] He said, "Lord, if you really are pleased with me, I ask you to go with us. These people are stubborn, but forgive our evil and our sin, and accept us as your own people."

The Covenant is Renewed
(Ex 23.14–19; Deut 7.1–5; 16.1–17)

[10] The LORD said to Moses, "I now make a covenant with the people of Israel. In their presence I will do great things such as have never been done anywhere on earth among any of the nations. All the people will see what great things I, the LORD, can do, because I am going to do an awesome thing for you. [11] Obey the laws that I am giving you today. I will drive out the Amorites, the Canaanites, the Hittites, the Perizzites, the Hivites, and the

EXODUS 34.10

- I will do -
GREAT
THINGS
such as have
NEVER
been done anywhere
ON EARTH

34.5 *the LORD:* See 3.14.
34.7 *thousands of generations*; or *thousands*.

EXODUS 34

121

Exodus
............:

Leviticus
Num.
Deuter.
Joshua
Judges

Jebusites, as you advance. ¹²Do not make any treaties with the people of the country into which you are going, because this could be a fatal trap for you. ¹³Instead, tear down their altars, destroy their sacred pillars, and cut down the symbols of their goddess Asherah.

¹⁴"Do not worship any other god, because I, the LORD, tolerate no rivals. ¹⁵Do not make any treaties with the people of the country, because when they worship their pagan gods and sacrifice to them, they will invite you to join them, and you will be tempted to eat the food they offer to their gods. ¹⁶Your sons might marry those foreign women, who would lead them to be unfaithful to me and to worship their pagan gods.

¹⁷"Do not make and worship gods of metal.

¹⁸"Keep the Festival of Unleavened Bread. As I have commanded you, eat unleavened bread for seven days in the month of Abib, because it was in that month that you left Egypt.

¹⁹"Every firstborn son and firstborn male domestic animal belongs to me, ²⁰but you are to buy back every firstborn donkey by offering a lamb in its place. If you do not buy it back, break its neck. Buy back every firstborn son.

"No one is to appear before me without an offering.

²¹"You have six days in which to do your work, but do not work on the seventh day, not even during ploughing time or harvest.

²²"Keep the Harvest Festival when you begin to harvest the first crop of your wheat, and keep the Festival of Shelters in the autumn when you gather your fruit.

²³"Three times a year all your men must come to worship me, the LORD, the God of Israel. ²⁴After I have driven out the nations before you and extended your territory, no one will try to conquer your country during the three festivals.

²⁵"Do not offer bread made with yeast when you sacrifice an animal to me. Do not keep until the following morning any part of the animal killed at the Passover Festival.

²⁶"Each year bring to the house of the LORD the first corn that you harvest.

"Do not cook a young sheep or goat in its mother's milk."

²⁷The LORD said to Moses, "Write these words down, because it is on the basis of these words that I am making a covenant with you and with Israel." ²⁸Moses stayed there with the LORD forty days and nights, eating and drinking nothing. He wrote on the tablets the words of the covenant — the Ten Commandments.

Moses Goes Down from Mount Sinai

²⁹When Moses went down from Mount Sinai carrying the Ten Commandments, his face was shining because he had been speaking with the LORD; but he did not know it. ³⁰Aaron and all the people looked at Moses and saw that his face was shining, and they were afraid to go near him. ³¹But Moses called them, and Aaron and all the leaders of the community went to him, and Moses spoke to them. ³²After that, all the people of Israel gathered round him, and Moses gave them all the laws that the LORD had given him on Mount Sinai. ³³When Moses had finished speaking to them, he covered his face with a veil. ³⁴Whenever Moses went into the Tent of the LORD's presence to speak to the LORD, he took the veil off. When he came out, he would tell the people of Israel everything that he had been commanded to say, ³⁵and they would see that his face was shining. Then he would put the veil back on until the next time he went to speak to the LORD.

Regulations for the Sabbath

35 Moses called together the whole community of the people of Israel and said to them, "This is what the LORD has commanded you to do: ²You have six days in which to do your work, but the seventh day is to be sacred, a solemn day of rest dedicated to me, the LORD. Anyone who does any work on that day is to be put to death. ³Do not even light a fire in your homes on the Sabbath."

Offerings for the Sacred Tent
(Ex 25.1–9)

⁴Moses said to all the people of Israel, "This is what the LORD has commanded: ⁵Make an offering to the LORD. Everyone who wishes to do so is to bring an offering of gold, silver, or bronze; ⁶fine linen; blue, purple, and red wool; cloth made of goats' hair; ⁷rams' skin dyed red; fine leather; acacia wood; ⁸oil for the lamps; spices for the anointing oil and for the sweet-smelling incense; ⁹carnelians and other jewels to be set in the High Priest's ephod and in his breastpiece."

Articles for the Tent of the LORD's Presence
(Ex 39.32–43)

¹⁰"All the skilled workers among you are to come and make everything that the LORD commanded: ¹¹the Tent, its covering and its outer covering, its hooks and its frames, its crossbars, its posts, and its bases; ¹²the Covenant Box, its poles, its lid, and the curtain to screen it off; ¹³the table, its poles, and all its equipment; the bread offered to God; ¹⁴the lampstand for the light and its equipment; the lamps with their oil; ¹⁵the altar for burning incense and its poles; the anointing oil; the sweet-smelling incense; the curtain for the entrance of the Tent; ¹⁶the altar on which to burn offerings, with its bronze grating attached, its poles, and all its equipment; the washbasin and its base; ¹⁷the curtains for the enclosure, its posts and bases; the curtain for the entrance of the enclosure; ¹⁸the pegs and ropes for the Tent and the enclosure; ¹⁹and the magnificent garments the priests are to wear when they serve in the Holy Place — the sacred clothes for Aaron the priest and for his sons."

The People Bring their Offerings

²⁰All the people of Israel left, ²¹and everyone who wished to do so brought an offering to the LORD for making the Tent of the LORD's presence. They brought everything needed for use in worship and for making the priestly garments. ²²All who wanted to, both men and women, brought decorative pins, earrings, rings, necklaces, and all kinds of gold jewellery and dedicated them to the LORD. ²³Everyone who had fine linen; blue, purple, or red wool; cloth of goats' hair; rams' skin dyed red; or fine leather, brought it. ²⁴All who were able to contribute silver or bronze brought their offering for the LORD, and all who had acacia wood which could be used for any of the work brought it. ²⁵All the skilled women brought fine linen thread and thread of blue, purple, and red wool, which they had made. ²⁶They also made thread of goats' hair. ²⁷The leaders brought carnelians and other jewels to be set in the ephod and the breastpiece ²⁸and spices and oil for the lamps, for the anointing oil, and for the sweet-smelling incense. ²⁹All the people of Israel who wanted to brought their offering to the LORD for the work which he had commanded Moses to do.

EXODUS 35, 36

123

Exodus
....
Leviticus
Num.
Deuter.
Joshua
Judges

Workers to Make the Tent of the LORD's Presence
(Ex 31.1–11)

[30] Moses said to the Israelites, "The LORD has chosen Bezalel, the son of Uri and grandson of Hur, from the tribe of Judah. [31] God has filled him with his power* and given him skill, ability, and understanding for every kind of artistic work, [32] for planning skilful designs and working them in gold, silver and bronze; [33] for cutting jewels to be set; for carving wood; and for every other kind of artistic work. [34] The LORD has given to him and to Oholiab son of Ahisamach, from the tribe of Dan, the ability to teach their crafts to others. [35] He has given them skill in all kinds of work done by engravers, designers, and weavers of fine linen; blue, purple, and red wool; and other cloth. They are able to do all kinds of work and are skilful designers.

36 "Bezalel, Oholiab, and all the other workers to whom the LORD has given skill and understanding, who know how to make everything needed to build the sacred Tent, are to make everything just as the LORD has commanded."

The People Bring Many Gifts

[2] Moses called Bezalel, Oholiab, and all the other skilled men to whom the LORD had given ability and who were willing to help, and Moses told them to start working. [3] They received from him all the offerings which the Israelites had brought for constructing the sacred Tent. But the people of Israel continued to bring Moses their offerings every morning. [4] Then the skilled men who were doing the work went [5] and reported to Moses, "The people are bringing more than is needed for the work which the LORD commanded to be done."

[6] So Moses sent a command throughout the camp that no one was to make any further contribution for the sacred Tent; so the people did not bring any more. [7] What had already been brought was more than enough to finish all the work.

Making the Tent of the LORD's Presence
(Ex 26.1–37)

[8] The most skilled men among those doing the work made the Tent of the LORD's presence. They made it out of ten pieces of fine linen woven with blue, purple, and red wool and embroidered with figures of winged creatures. [9] Each piece was the same size, twelve metres long and two metres wide. [10] They sewed five of them together in one set and did the same with the other five. [11] They made loops of blue cloth on the edge of the outside piece in each set. [12] They put fifty loops on the first piece of the first set and fifty loops matching them on the last piece of the second set. [13] They made fifty gold hooks, with which to join the two sets into one piece.

[14] Then they made a cover for the Tent out of eleven pieces of cloth made of goats' hair. [15] They made them all the same size, thirteen metres long and two metres wide. [16] They sewed five of them together in one set and the other six in another set. [17] They put fifty loops on the edge of the last piece of one set and fifty loops on the edge of the other set. [18] They made fifty bronze hooks to join the two sets, so as to form one cover. [19] They made two more coverings, one of rams' skin dyed red and the other of fine leather, to serve as an outer cover.

35.31 *power;* or *spirit.*

TURN THESE SHAPES INTO
SOMETHING
ELSE.

²⁰They made upright frames of acacia wood for the Tent. ²¹Each frame was four metres tall and 66 centimetres wide, ²²with two matching projections, so that the frames could be joined together. All the frames had these projections. ²³They made twenty frames for the south side ²⁴and forty silver bases to go under them, two bases under each frame to hold its two projections. ²⁵They made twenty frames for the north side of the Tent ²⁶and forty silver bases, two under each frame. ²⁷For the back of the Tent, on the west, they made six frames ²⁸and two frames for the corners. ²⁹These corner frames were joined at the bottom and connected all the way to the top. The two frames that formed the two corners were made in this way. ³⁰So there were eight frames and sixteen silver bases, two under each frame.

³¹They made fifteen crossbars of acacia wood, five for the frames on one side of the Tent, ³²five for the frames on the other side, and five for the frames on the west end, at the back. ³³The middle crossbar, set halfway up the frames, extended from one end of the Tent to the other. ³⁴They covered the frames with gold and fitted them with gold rings to hold the crossbars, which were also covered with gold.

³⁵They made a curtain of fine linen, woven with blue, purple, and red wool and embroidered it with figures of winged creatures. ³⁶They made four posts of acacia wood to hold the curtain, covered them with gold, and fitted them with gold hooks. Then they made four silver bases to hold the posts. ³⁷For the entrance of the Tent they made a curtain of fine linen woven with blue, purple, and red wool and decorated with embroidery. ³⁸For this curtain they made five posts fitted with hooks, covered their tops and their rods with gold, and made five bronze bases for the posts.

Making the Covenant Box
(Ex 25.10–22)

37 Bezalel made the Covenant Box out of acacia wood, 110 centimetres long, 66 centimetres wide, and 66 centimetres high. ²He covered it with pure gold inside and out and put a gold border all round it. ³He made four carrying rings of gold for it and attached them to its four feet, with two rings on each side. ⁴He made carrying poles of acacia wood, covered them with gold, ⁵and put them through the rings on each side of the box. ⁶He made a lid of pure gold, 110 centimetres long and 66 centimetres wide. ⁷He made two winged creatures of hammered gold, ⁸one for each end of the lid. He made them so that they formed one piece with the lid. ⁹The winged creatures faced each other across the lid, and their outspread wings covered it.

Making the Table for the Bread Offered to God
(Ex 25.23–30)

¹⁰He made the table out of acacia wood, 88 centimetres long, 44 centimetres wide, and 66 centimetres high. ¹¹He covered it with pure gold and put a gold border round it. ¹²He made a rim 75 millimetres wide round it and put a gold border round the rim. ¹³He made four carrying rings of gold for it and put them at the four corners, where the legs were. ¹⁴The rings to hold the poles for carrying the table were placed near the rim. ¹⁵He made the poles of acacia wood and covered them with gold. ¹⁶He made the dishes of pure gold for the table: the plates, the cups, the jars, and the bowls to be used for the wine offering.

EXODUS 37, 38

125

Exodus

....

Leviticus

Num.

Deuter.

Joshua

Judges

Making the Lampstand
(Ex 25.31–40)

¹⁷He made the lampstand of pure gold. He made its base and its shaft of hammered gold; its decorative flowers, including buds and petals, formed one piece with it.

¹⁸Six branches extended from its sides, three from each side. ¹⁹Each of the six branches had three decorative flowers shaped like almond blossoms with buds and petals. ²⁰The shaft of the lampstand had four decorative flowers shaped like almond blossoms with buds and petals. ²¹There was one bud below each of the three pairs of branches. ²²The buds, the branches, and the lampstand were a single piece of pure hammered gold. ²³He made seven lamps for the lampstand, and he made its tongs and trays of pure gold. ²⁴He used 35 kilogrammes of pure gold to make the lampstand and all its equipment.

Making the Altar for Burning Incense
(Ex 30.1–5)

²⁵He made an altar out of acacia wood, for burning incense. It was square, 45 centimetres long and 45 centimetres wide, and it was ninety centimetres high. Its projections at the four corners formed one piece with it. ²⁶He covered its top, all four sides, and its projections with pure gold and put a gold border round it. ²⁷He made two gold carrying rings for it and attached them below the border on the two sides, to hold the poles with which it was to be carried. ²⁸He made the poles of acacia wood and covered them with gold.

Making the Anointing Oil and the Incense
(Ex 30.22–38)

²⁹He also made the sacred anointing oil and the pure sweet-smelling incense, mixed like perfume.

Making the Altar for Burning Offerings
(Ex 27.1–8)

38 For burning offerings, he made an altar out of acacia wood. It was square, 2.2 metres long and 2.2 metres wide, and it was 1.3 metres high. ²He made the projections at the top of the four corners, so that they formed one piece with the altar. He covered it all with bronze. ³He also made all the equipment for the altar: the pans, the shovels, the bowls, the hooks, and the firepans. All this equipment was made of bronze. ⁴He made a bronze grating and put it under the rim of the altar, so that it reached halfway up the altar. ⁵He made four carrying rings and put them on the four corners. ⁶He made carrying poles of acacia wood, covered them with bronze, ⁷and put them in the rings on each side of the altar. The altar was made of boards and was hollow.

Making the Bronze Basin
(Ex 30.18)

⁸He made the bronze basin and its bronze base out of the mirrors belonging to the women who served at the entrance of the Tent of the LORD's presence.

The Enclosure for the Tent of the LORD's Presence
(Ex 27.9–19)

⁹For the Tent of the LORD's presence he made the enclosure out of fine linen curtains. On the south side the curtains were 44

metres long, [10] supported by twenty bronze posts in twenty bronze bases, with hooks and rods made of silver. [11] The enclosure was the same on the north side. [12] On the west side there were curtains 22 metres long, with ten posts and ten bases and with hooks and rods made of silver. [13] On the east side, where the entrance was, the enclosure was also 22 metres wide. [14-15] On each side of the entrance there were 6.6 metres of curtains, with three posts and three bases. [16] All the curtains round the enclosure were made of fine linen. [17] The bases for the posts were made of bronze, and the hooks, the rods, and the covering of the tops of the posts were made of silver. All the posts round the enclosure were connected with silver rods. [18] The curtain for the entrance of the enclosure was made of fine linen woven with blue, purple, and red wool and decorated with embroidery. It was nine metres long and two metres high, like the curtains of the enclosure. [19] It was supported by four posts in four bronze bases. Their hooks, the covering of their tops, and their rods were made of silver. [20] All the pegs for the Tent and for the surrounding enclosure were made of bronze.

Metals Used in the Tent of the LORD's Presence

[21] Here is a list of the amounts of the metals used in the Tent of the LORD's presence, where the two stone tablets were kept on which the Ten Commandments were written. The list was ordered by Moses and made by the Levites who worked under the direction of Ithamar son of Aaron the priest.

[22] Bezalel, the son of Uri and grandson of Hur, from the tribe of Judah, made everything that the LORD had commanded. [23] His helper, Oholiab son of Ahisamach, from the tribe of Dan, was an engraver, a designer, and a weaver of fine linen and of blue, purple, and red wool.

[24] All the gold that had been dedicated to the LORD for the sacred Tent weighed one tonne, weighed according to the official standard. [25] The silver from the census of the community weighed 3.43 tonnes, weighed according to the official standard. [26] This amount equalled the total paid by all persons enrolled in the census, each one paying the required amount, weighed according to the official standard. There were 603,550 men twenty years old or older enrolled in the census. [27] Of the silver, 3.4 tonnes were used to make the hundred bases for the sacred Tent and for the curtain, 34 kilogrammes for each base. [28] With the remaining thirty kilogrammes of silver Bezalel made the rods, the hooks for the posts, and the covering for their tops. [29] The bronze which was dedicated to the LORD amounted to 2.425 tonnes. [30] With it he made the bases for the entrance of the Tent of the LORD's presence, the bronze altar with its bronze grating, all the equipment for the altar, [31] the bases for the surrounding enclosure and for the entrance of the enclosure, and all the pegs for the Tent and the surrounding enclosure.

Making the Garments for the Priests
(Ex 28.1–14)

39 With the blue, purple, and red wool they made the magnificent garments which the priests were to wear when they served in the Holy Place. They made the priestly garments for Aaron, as the LORD had commanded Moses.

[2] They made the ephod of fine linen; blue, purple, and red wool; and gold thread. [3] They hammered out sheets of gold and cut them into thin strips to be worked into the fine linen and into the blue, purple, and red wool. [4] They made two shoulder straps

Exodus
··········:·

Leviticus
Num.
Deuter.
Joshua
Judges

for the ephod and attached them to its sides, so that it could be fastened. [5] The finely woven belt, made of the same materials, was attached to the ephod so as to form one piece with it, as the Lord had commanded Moses. [6] They prepared the carnelians and mounted them in gold settings; they were skilfully engraved with the names of the twelve sons of Jacob. [7] They put them on the shoulder straps of the ephod to represent the twelve tribes of Israel, just as the Lord had commanded Moses.

Making the Breastpiece
(Ex 28.15–30)

[8] They made the breastpiece of the same materials as the ephod and with similar embroidery. [9] It was square and folded double, 22 centimetres long and 22 centimetres wide. [10] They mounted four rows of precious stones on it: in the first row they mounted a ruby, a topaz, and a garnet; [11] in the second row, an emerald, a sapphire, and a diamond; [12] in the third row, a turquoise, an agate, and an amethyst; [13] and in the fourth row, a beryl, a carnelian, and a jasper. These were mounted in gold settings. [14] Each of the twelve stones had engraved on it the name of one of the sons of Jacob, in order to represent the twelve tribes of Israel. [15] For the breastpiece they made chains of pure gold, twisted like cords. [16] They made two gold settings and two gold rings and attached the two rings to the upper corners of the breastpiece. [17] They fastened the two gold cords to the two rings [18] and fastened the other two ends of the cords to the two settings and in this way attached them in front to the shoulder straps of the ephod. [19] They made two rings of gold and attached them to the lower corners of the breastpiece, on the inside edge next to the ephod. [20] They made two more gold rings and attached them to the lower part of the front of the two shoulder straps of the ephod, near the seam and above the finely woven belt. [21] Just as the Lord had commanded Moses, they tied the rings of the breastpiece to the rings of the ephod with a blue cord, so that the breastpiece rested above the belt and did not come loose.

Making the Other Priestly Garments
(Ex 28.31–43)

[22] The robe that goes under the ephod was made entirely of blue wool. [23] The hole for the head was reinforced with a woven binding to keep it from tearing. [24-26] All round its lower hem they put pomegranates of fine linen and of blue, purple, and red wool, alternating with bells of pure gold, just as the Lord had commanded Moses.

[27] They made the shirts for Aaron and his sons, [28] and the turban, the caps, the linen shorts, [29] and the sash of fine linen and of blue, purple, and red wool, decorated with embroidery, as the Lord had commanded Moses. [30] They made the ornament, the sacred sign of dedication, out of pure gold, and they engraved on it "Dedicated to the Lord". [31] They tied it to the front of the turban with a blue cord, just as the Lord had commanded Moses.

The Completion of the Work
(Ex 35.10–19)

[32] All the work on the Tent of the Lord's presence was finally completed. The Israelites made everything just as the Lord had commanded Moses. [33] They brought to Moses the Tent and all its equipment, its hooks, its frames, its crossbars, its posts, and its bases; [34] the covering of rams' skin dyed red; the covering of

EXODUS 40

When everything
was made right, the

GLORY

— OF GOD'S PRESENCE —

filled the tabernacle.
Close your eyes and, for
two minutes, imagine
how it would have
looked. Imagine the
cloud of pure light
during the day and the
great fire at night.
How would you respond?
What would you do?

write some
thoughts here ↙

fine leather; the curtain; [35] the Covenant Box containing the stone tablets, its poles, and its lid; [36] the table and all its equipment, and the bread offered to God; [37] the lampstand of pure gold, its lamps, all its equipment, and the oil for the lamps; [38] the gold altar; the anointing oil; the sweet-smelling incense; the curtain for the entrance of the Tent; [39] the bronze altar with its bronze grating, its poles, and all its equipment; the washbasin and its base; [40] the curtains for the enclosure and its posts and bases; the curtain for the entrance of the enclosure and its ropes; the pegs for the Tent; all the equipment to be used in the Tent; [41] and the magnificent garments the priests were to wear in the Holy Place — the sacred clothes for Aaron the priest and for his sons. [42] The Israelites had done all the work just as the Lord had commanded Moses. [43] Moses examined everything and saw that they had made it all just as the Lord had commanded. So Moses blessed them.

Setting Up and Dedicating the Tent of the Lord's Presence

40 The Lord said to Moses, [2] "On the first day of the first month set up the Tent of the Lord's presence. [3] Place in it the Covenant Box containing the Ten Commandments and put the curtain in front of it. [4] Bring in the table and place the equipment on it. Also bring in the lampstand and set up the lamps on it. [5] Put the gold altar for burning incense in front of the Covenant Box and hang the curtain at the entrance of the Tent. [6] Put in front of the Tent the altar for burning offerings. [7] Put the washbasin between the Tent and the altar and fill it with water. [8] Put up the surrounding enclosure and hang the curtain at its entrance.

[9] "Then dedicate the Tent and all its equipment by anointing it with the sacred oil, and it will be holy. [10] Next, dedicate the altar and all its equipment by anointing it, and it will be completely holy. [11] Also dedicate the washbasin and its base in the same way.

[12] "Bring Aaron and his sons to the entrance of the Tent, and tell them to take a ritual bath. [13] Dress Aaron in the priestly garments, anoint him, and in this way consecrate him, so that he can serve me as priest. [14] Bring his sons and put the shirts on them. [15] Then anoint them, just as you anointed their father, so that they can serve me as priests. This anointing will make them priests for all time to come."

[16] Moses did everything just as the Lord had commanded. [17] So on the first day of the first month of the second year after they left Egypt, the Tent of the Lord's presence was set up. [18] Moses put down its bases, set up its frames, attached its crossbars, and put up its posts. [19] He spread out the covering over the Tent and put the outer covering over it, just as the Lord had commanded. [20] Then he took the two stone tablets and put them in the Covenant Box. He put the poles in the rings of the box and put the lid on it. [21] Then he put the box in the Tent and hung up the curtain. In this way he screened off the Covenant Box, just as the Lord had commanded.

[22] He put the table in the Tent, on the north side outside the curtain, [23] and placed on it the bread offered to the Lord, just as the Lord had commanded. [24] He put the lampstand in the Tent, on the south side, opposite the table, [25] and there in the Lord's presence he lit the lamps, just as the Lord had commanded. [26] He put the gold altar in the Tent, in front of the curtain, [27] and burnt the sweet-smelling incense, just as the Lord had commanded. [28] He hung the curtain at the entrance of the Tent, [29] and there in front of the curtain he placed the altar for burning offerings.

129

Exodus
....
Leviticus
Num.
Deuter.
Joshua
Judges

On it he sacrificed the burnt offering and the grain offering, just as the LORD had commanded. 30 He put the washbasin between the Tent and the altar and filled it with water. 31 Moses, Aaron, and his sons washed their hands and their feet there 32 whenever they went into the Tent or to the altar, just as the LORD had commanded. 33 Moses set up the enclosure round the Tent and the altar and hung the curtain at the entrance of the enclosure. So he finished all the work.

The Cloud over the Tent of the LORD's Presence
(Num 9.15–23)

34 Then the cloud covered the Tent and the dazzling light of the LORD's presence filled it. 35 Because of this, Moses could not go into the Tent. 36 The Israelites moved their camp to another place only when the cloud lifted from the Tent. 37 As long as the cloud stayed there, they did not move their camp. 38 During all their wanderings they could see the cloud of the LORD's presence over the Tent during the day and a fire burning above it during the night.

THE BOOK OF
LEVITICUS

PROBABLY 600-400BC
(USING STORIES FROM A MUCH EARLIER TIME)

WHAT YOU NEED TO KNOW:

Leviticus gets its name from the Levites, who were one of the 12 tribes of Israel. The Levites were set apart as priests - the people who helped others to connect with God. Aaron, Moses' brother, was the chief Levite and the first high priest. There are 610 laws outlined in Leviticus. These laws were put in place both to help the Israelites to be holy in God's eyes and to protect them against danger and disease. Many other local tribes died out during the timespan of the Old Testament, but God's people were set apart both spiritually and physically.

WHY READ IT?

Leviticus can be difficult to read, but it is essential. Leviticus teaches us about the importance of holiness to God. 'Holy' means 'set apart', and God wants his people to be known as set apart from the rest of the world. Leviticus also shows us how much effort was needed for the Israelites to be right with God, making us even more grateful and in awe of what Jesus (known in the letter to the Hebrews as the great high priest) did when he gave his life for us.

Aaron was
CHOSEN
• BY GOD •

as the high priest, who oversaw the work of the Levites. Write down what the role of the Levites was, and why it was so important for the Israelites.

1400BC

WILDERNESS

1300BC

LEVITICUS 1, 2

131

Leviticus

....

Num.

Deuter.

Joshua

Judges

Ruth

Sacrifices Burnt Whole

1 The LORD called to Moses from the Tent of the LORD's presence and gave him the following rules ² for the Israelites to observe when they offer their sacrifices.

When anyone offers an animal sacrifice, it may be one of his cattle or one of his sheep or goats. ³ If he is offering one of his cattle as a burnt offering, he must bring a bull without any defects. He must present it at the entrance of the Tent of the LORD's presence so that the LORD will accept him. ⁴ The man shall put his hand on its head, and it will be accepted as a sacrifice to take away his sins. ⁵ He shall kill the bull there, and the Aaronite priests shall present the blood to the LORD and then throw it against all four sides of the altar which is at the entrance of the Tent. ⁶ Then he shall skin the animal and cut it up, ⁷ and the priests shall arrange firewood on the altar and light it. ⁸ They shall put on the fire the pieces of the animal, including the head and the fat. ⁹ The man must wash the internal organs and the hind legs, and the officiating priest will burn the whole sacrifice on the altar. The smell of this food offering is pleasing to the LORD.

¹⁰ If the man is offering one of his sheep or goats, it must be a male without any defects. ¹¹ He shall kill it on the north side of the altar, and the priests shall throw its blood on all four sides of the altar. ¹² After the man cuts it up, the officiating priest shall put on the fire all the parts, including the head and the fat. ¹³ The man must wash the internal organs and the hind legs, and the priest will present the sacrifice to the LORD and burn all of it on the altar. The smell of this food offering is pleasing to the LORD.

¹⁴ If the man is offering a bird as a burnt offering, it must be a dove or a pigeon. ¹⁵ The priest shall present it at the altar, wring its neck, and burn its head on the altar. Its blood shall be drained out against the side of the altar. ¹⁶ He shall remove the crop and its contents and throw them away on the east side of the altar where the ashes are put. ¹⁷ He shall take hold of its wings and tear its body open, without tearing the wings off, and then burn it whole on the altar. The smell of this food offering is pleasing to the LORD.

Grain Offerings

2 When anyone presents an offering of grain to the LORD, he must first grind it into flour. He must put olive oil and incense on it ² and bring it to the Aaronite priests. The officiating priest shall take a handful of the flour and oil and all of the incense and burn it on the altar as a token that it has all been offered to the LORD. The smell of this food offering is pleasing to the LORD. ³ The rest of the grain offering belongs to the priests; it is very holy, since it is taken from the food offered to the LORD.

⁴ If the offering is bread baked in an oven, it must be made without yeast. It may be thick loaves made of flour mixed with olive oil or biscuits brushed with olive oil.

⁵ If the offering is bread cooked on a griddle, it is to be made of flour mixed with olive oil but without yeast. ⁶ Crumble it up and pour the oil on it when you present it as an offering.

⁷ If the offering is bread cooked in a pan, it is to be made of flour and olive oil. ⁸ Bring it as an offering to the LORD and present it to the priest, who will take it to the altar. ⁹ The priest will take part of it as a token that it has all been offered to the LORD, and he will burn it on the altar. The smell of this food offering is pleasing to the LORD. ¹⁰ The rest of the offering belongs to the priests; it is very holy, since it is taken from the food offered to the LORD.

LEVITICUS 1

The Hebrew word Corban means 'offering', and implies 'drawing near' to God. To give up an animal as an offering was a way for the Israelites to

• DRAW NEAR •

TO GOD,

but it was also a symbol of God drawing near to them. Because Jesus died, giving up his own life, we don't need to make these sorts of offerings any more. However, God still wants us to draw near to him. James 4.8 tells us that when we do so, he will draw near to us.

[11] None of the grain offerings which you present to the LORD may be made with yeast; you must never use yeast or honey in food offered to the LORD. [12] An offering of the first corn that you harvest each year shall be brought to the LORD, but it is not to be burnt on the altar. [13] Put salt on every grain offering, because salt represents the covenant between you and God. (You must put salt on all your offerings.) [14] When you bring to the LORD an offering of the first corn harvested, offer roasted grain or ground meal. [15] Add olive oil and put incense on it. [16] The priest will burn that part of the meal and oil that is to serve as a token, and also all the incense, as a food offering to the LORD.

Fellowship Offerings

3 When anyone offers one of his cattle as a fellowship offering, it is to be a bull or a cow without any defects. [2] The man shall put his hand on the head of the animal and kill it at the entrance of the Tent of the LORD's presence. The Aaronite priests shall throw the blood against all sides of the altar [3] and present the following parts of the animal as a food offering to the LORD: all the fat on the internal organs, [4] the kidneys and the fat on them, and the best part of the liver. [5] The priests shall burn all this on the altar along with the burnt offerings. The smell of this food offering is pleasing to the LORD.

[6] If a sheep or goat is used as a fellowship offering, it may be male or female, but it must be without any defects. [7] If a man offers a sheep, [8] he shall put his hand on its head and kill it in front of the Tent. The priests shall throw its blood against all four sides of the altar [9] and present the following parts of the animal as a food offering to the LORD: the fat, the entire fat tail cut off near the backbone, all the fat covering the internal organs, [10] the kidneys and the fat on them, and the best part of the liver. [11] The officiating priest shall burn all this on the altar as a food offering to the LORD.

[12] If a man offers a goat, [13] he shall put his hand on its head and kill it in front of the Tent. The priests shall throw its blood against all four sides of the altar [14] and present the following parts as a food offering to the LORD: all the fat on the internal organs, [15] the kidneys and the fat on them, and the best part of the liver. [16] The priest shall burn all this on the altar as a food offering pleasing to the LORD. All the fat belongs to the LORD. [17] No Israelite may eat any fat or any blood; this is a rule to be kept for ever by all Israelites wherever they live.

Offerings for Unintentional Sins

4 The LORD commanded Moses [2] to tell the people of Israel that anyone who sinned and broke any of the LORD's commands without intending to, would have to observe the following rules.

[3] If it is the High Priest who sins and so brings guilt on the people, he shall present a young bull without any defects and sacrifice it to the LORD for his sin. [4] He shall bring the bull to the entrance of the Tent, put his hand on its head, and kill it there in the LORD's presence. [5] Then the High Priest shall take some of the bull's blood and carry it into the Tent. [6] He shall dip his finger in the blood and sprinkle it in front of the sacred curtain seven times. [7] Then he shall put some of the blood on the projections at the corners of the incense altar in the Tent. He shall pour out the rest of the blood at the base of the altar used for burning sacrifices, which is at the entrance of the Tent. [8] From this bull he shall take all the fat, the fat on the internal organs, [9] the kidneys

and the fat on them, and the best part of the liver. [10] The priest shall take this fat and burn it on the altar used for the burnt offerings, just as he does with the fat from the animal killed for the fellowship offering. [11] But he shall take its skin, all its flesh, its head, its legs, and its internal organs including the intestines, [12] carry it all outside the camp to the ritually clean place where the ashes are poured out, and there he shall burn it on a wood fire.

[13] If it is the whole community of Israel that sins and becomes guilty of breaking one of the LORD's commands without intending to, [14] then as soon as the sin becomes known, the community shall bring a young bull as a sin offering. They shall bring it to the Tent of the LORD's presence; [15] the leaders of the community shall put their hands on its head, and it shall be killed there. [16] The High Priest shall take some of the bull's blood into the Tent, [17] dip his finger in it, and sprinkle it in front of the curtain seven times. [18] He shall put some of the blood on the projections at the corners of the incense altar inside the Tent and pour out the rest of it at the base of the altar used for burning sacrifices, which is at the entrance of the Tent. [19] Then he shall take all its fat and burn it on the altar. [20] He shall do the same thing with this bull as he does with the bull for the sin offering, and in this way he shall make the sacrifice for the people's sin, and they will be forgiven. [21] Then he shall take the bull outside the camp and burn it, just as he burns the bull offered for his own sin. This is an offering to take away the sin of the community.

[22] If it is a ruler who sins and becomes guilty of breaking one of the LORD's commands without intending to, [23] then as soon as his attention is called to the sin, he shall bring as his offering a male goat without any defects. [24] He shall put his hand on its head and kill it on the north side of the altar, where the animals for the burnt offerings are killed. This is an offering to take away sin. [25] The priest shall dip his finger in the blood of the animal, put it on the projections at the corners of the altar, and pour out the rest of it at the base of the altar. [26] Then he shall burn all its fat on the altar, just as he burns the fat of the animals killed for the fellowship offerings. In this way the priest shall offer the sacrifice for the sin of the ruler, and he will be forgiven.

[27] If it is one of the common people who sins and becomes guilty of breaking one of the LORD's commands without intending to, [28] then as soon as his attention is called to the sin, he shall bring as his offering a female goat without any defects. [29] He shall put his hand on its head and kill it on the north side of the altar, where the animals for the burnt offerings are killed. [30] The priest shall dip his finger in the blood of the animal, put it on the projections at the corners of the altar, and pour out the rest of it at the base of the altar. [31] Then he shall remove all its fat, just as the fat is removed from the animals killed for the fellowship offerings, and he shall burn it on the altar so that the smell pleases the LORD. In this way the priest shall offer the sacrifice for the man's sin, and he will be forgiven.

[32] If a man brings a sheep as a sin offering, it must be a female without any defects. [33] He shall put his hand on its head and kill it on the north side of the altar, where the animals for the burnt offerings are killed. [34] The priest shall dip his finger in the blood of the animal, put it on the projections at the corners of the altar, and pour out the rest of it at the base of the altar. [35] Then he shall remove all its fat, just as the fat is removed from the sheep killed for the fellowship offerings, and he shall burn it on the altar along with the food offerings given to the LORD. In this way the priest shall offer the sacrifice for the man's sin, and he will be forgiven.

On a scale **FROM 1 TO 10,** how easy are you finding it to read the Bible currently?

Think of one way you can go up a number on the scale.

10
9 **8**
7
5 **6**
4
3 **2**
1

Cases Requiring Sin Offerings

5 Sin offerings are required in the following cases. If someone is officially summoned to give evidence in court and does not give information about something he has seen or heard, he must suffer the consequences.

2 If someone unintentionally touches anything ritually unclean, such as a dead animal, he is unclean and guilty as soon as he realizes what he has done.

3 If someone unintentionally touches anything of human origin that is unclean, whatever it may be, he is guilty as soon as he realizes what he has done.

4 If someone makes a careless vow, no matter what it is about, he is guilty as soon as he realizes what he has done.

5 When a person is guilty, he must confess the sin, 6 and as the penalty for his sin he must bring to the LORD a female sheep or goat as an offering. The priest shall offer the sacrifice for the man's sin.

7 If a man cannot afford a sheep or a goat, he shall bring to the LORD as the payment for his sin two doves or two pigeons, one for a sin offering and the other for a burnt offering. 8 He shall bring them to the priest, who will first offer the bird for the sin offering. He will break its neck without pulling off its head 9 and sprinkle some of its blood against the side of the altar. The rest of the blood will be drained out at the base of the altar. This is an offering to take away sin. 10 Then he shall offer the second bird as a burnt offering, according to the regulations. In this way the priest shall offer the sacrifice for the man's sin, and he will be forgiven.

11 If a man cannot afford two doves or two pigeons, he shall bring one kilogramme of flour as a sin offering. He shall not put any olive oil or any incense on it, because it is a sin offering, not a grain offering. 12 He shall bring it to the priest, who will take a handful of it as a token that it has all been offered to the LORD, and he will burn it on the altar as a food offering. It is an offering to take away sin. 13 In this way the priest shall offer the sacrifice for the man's sin, and he will be forgiven. The rest of the flour belongs to the priest, just as in the case of a grain offering.

Repayment Offerings

14 The LORD gave the following regulations to Moses. 15 If anyone sins unintentionally by failing to hand over the payments that are sacred to the LORD, he shall bring as his repayment offering to the LORD a male sheep or goat without any defects. Its value is to be determined according to the official standard. 16 He must make the payments he has failed to hand over and must pay an additional twenty per cent. He shall give it to the priest, and the priest shall offer the animal as a sacrifice for the man's sin, and he will be forgiven.

17 If anyone sins unintentionally by breaking any of the LORD's commands, he is guilty and must pay the penalty. 18 He must bring to the priest as a repayment offering a male sheep or goat without any defects. Its value is to be determined according to the official standard. The priest shall offer the sacrifice for the sin which the man committed unintentionally, and he will be forgiven. 19 It is a repayment offering for the sin he committed against the LORD.

6 The LORD gave the following regulations to Moses. 2 An offering is to be made if anyone sins against the LORD by refusing to return what a fellow-Israelite has left as a deposit or by stealing something from him or by cheating him 3 or by lying

LEVITICUS 6

135

Leviticus
············

Num.
Deuter.
Joshua
Judges
Ruth

about something that has been lost and swearing that he did not find it. [4-5] When a man sins in any of these ways, he must repay whatever he got by dishonest means. On the day he is found guilty, he must repay the owner in full, plus an additional twenty per cent. [6] He shall bring to the priest as his repayment offering to the LORD a male sheep or goat without any defects. Its value is to be determined according to the official standard. [7] The priest shall offer the sacrifice for the man's sin, and he will be forgiven.

Sacrifices Burnt Whole

[8] The LORD commanded Moses [9] to give Aaron and his sons the following regulations for burnt offerings. A burnt offering is to be left on the altar all night long, and the fire is to be kept burning. [10] Then the priest, wearing his linen robe and linen shorts, shall remove the greasy ashes left on the altar and put them at the side of the altar. [11] Then he shall change his clothes and take the ashes outside the camp to a ritually clean place. [12] The fire on the altar must be kept burning and never allowed to go out. Every morning the priest shall put firewood on it, arrange the burnt offering on it, and burn the fat of the fellowship offering. [13] The fire must always be kept burning on the altar and never allowed to go out.

Grain Offerings

[14] The following are the regulations for grain offerings. An Aaronite priest shall present the grain offering to the LORD in front of the altar. [15] Then he shall take a handful of the flour and oil, and the incense on it, and burn it on the altar as a token that all of it has been offered to the LORD. The smell of this offering is pleasing to the LORD. [16-17] The priests shall eat the rest of it. It shall be made into bread baked without yeast and eaten in a holy place, the courtyard of the Tent of the LORD's presence. The LORD has given it to the priests as their part of the food offerings. It is very holy, like the sin offerings and the repayment offerings. [18] For all time to come any of the male descendants of Aaron may eat it as their continuing share of the food offered to the LORD. Anyone else who touches a food offering will be harmed by the power of its holiness.

[19] The LORD gave Moses the following regulations [20] for the ordination of an Aaronite priest. On the day he is ordained, he shall present as an offering to the LORD one kilogramme of flour (the same amount as the daily grain offering), half in the morning and half in the evening. [21] It is to be mixed with oil and cooked on a griddle and then crumbled and presented as a grain offering, a smell pleasing to the LORD. [22] For all time to come this offering is to be made by every descendant of Aaron who is serving as High Priest. It shall be completely burnt as a sacrifice to the LORD. [23] No part of a grain offering that a priest makes may be eaten; all of it must be burnt.

Sin Offerings

[24] The LORD commanded Moses [25] to give Aaron and his sons the following regulations for sin offerings. The animal for a sin offering shall be killed on the north side of the altar, where the animals for the burnt offerings are killed. This is a very holy offering. [26] The priest who sacrifices the animal shall eat it in a holy place, the courtyard of the Tent of the LORD's presence. [27] Anyone or anything that touches the flesh of the animal will be harmed by the power of its holiness. If any article of clothing

136

Leviticus

∴ . . . .

Genesis
Exodus

LEVITICUS 6, 7

is spattered with the animal's blood, it must be washed in a holy place. ²⁸Any clay pot in which the meat is boiled must be broken, and if a metal pot is used, it must be scrubbed and rinsed with water. ²⁹Any male of the priestly families may eat this offering; it is very holy. ³⁰But if any of the blood is brought into the Tent and used in the ritual to take away sin, the animal must not be eaten; it must be burnt.

Repayment Offerings

7 The following are the regulations for repayment offerings, which are very holy. ²The animal for this offering is to be killed on the north side of the altar, where the animals for the burnt offerings are killed, and its blood is to be thrown against all four sides of the altar. ³All its fat shall be removed and offered on the altar: the fat tail, the fat covering the internal organs, ⁴the kidneys and the fat on them, and the best part of the liver. ⁵The priest shall burn all the fat on the altar as a food offering to the LORD. It is a repayment offering. ⁶Any male of the priestly families may eat it, but it must be eaten in a holy place, because it is very holy.

⁷There is one regulation that applies to both the sin offering and the repayment offering: the meat belongs to the priest who offers the sacrifice. ⁸The skin of an animal offered as a burnt offering belongs to the priest who offers the sacrifice. ⁹Every grain offering that has been baked in an oven or prepared in a pan or on a griddle belongs to the priest who has offered it to God. ¹⁰But all uncooked grain offerings, whether mixed with oil or dry, belong to all the Aaronite priests and must be shared equally among them.

Fellowship Offerings

¹¹The following are the regulations for the fellowship offerings presented to the LORD. ¹²If a man makes this offering as a thank-offering to God, he shall present, together with the animal to be sacrificed, an offering of bread made without yeast: either thick loaves made of flour mixed with olive oil or biscuits brushed with olive oil or cakes made of flour mixed with olive oil. ¹³In addition, he shall offer loaves of bread baked with yeast. ¹⁴He shall present one part of each kind of bread as a special contribution to the LORD; it belongs to the priest who takes the blood of the animal and throws it against the altar. ¹⁵The flesh of the animal must be eaten on the day it is sacrificed; none of it may be left until the next morning.

¹⁶If a man brings a fellowship offering in fulfilment of a vow or as his own freewill offering, not all of it has to be eaten on the day it is offered, but any that is left over may be eaten on the following day. ¹⁷Any meat that still remains on the third day must be burnt. ¹⁸If any of it is eaten on the third day, God will not accept the man's offering. The offering will not be counted to his credit but will be considered unclean, and whoever eats it will suffer the consequences. ¹⁹If the meat comes into contact with anything ritually unclean, it must not be eaten, but must be burned.

Anyone who is ritually clean may eat the meat, ²⁰but if anyone who is not clean eats it, he shall no longer be considered one of God's people. ²¹Also, if anyone eats the meat of this offering after he has touched anything ritually unclean, whether from a man or an animal, he shall no longer be considered one of God's people.

²²The LORD gave Moses the following regulations ²³for the people of Israel. No fat of cattle, sheep, or goats shall be eaten. ²⁴The fat of an animal that has died a natural death or has been killed by a wild animal must not be eaten, but it may be used for any other

LEVITICUS 7, 8

137

Leviticus
....

Num.
Deuter.
Joshua
Judges
Ruth

purpose. [25] Anyone who eats the fat of an animal that may be offered as a food offering to the Lord will no longer be considered one of God's people. [26] No matter where the Israelites live, they must never use the blood of birds or animals for food. [27] Anyone who breaks this law will no longer be considered one of God's people.

[28] The Lord gave Moses the following regulations [29] for the people of Israel. Whoever offers a fellowship offering must bring part of it as a special gift to the Lord, [30] bringing it with his own hands as a food offering. He shall bring the fat of the animal with its breast and present it as a special gift to the Lord. [31] The priest shall burn the fat on the altar, but the breast shall belong to the priests. [32] The right hind leg of the animal shall be given as a special contribution [33] to the priest who offers the blood and the fat of the fellowship offering. [34] The breast of the animal is a special gift, and the right hind leg is a special contribution that the Lord has taken from the people of Israel and given to the priests. This is what the people of Israel must give to the priests for all time to come. [35] This is the part of the food offered to the Lord that was given to Aaron and his sons on the day they were ordained as priests. [36] On that day the Lord commanded the people of Israel to give them this part of the offering. It is a regulation that the people of Israel must obey for all time to come.

[37] These, then, are the regulations for the burnt offerings, the grain offerings, the sin offerings, the repayment offerings, the ordination offerings, and the fellowship offerings. [38] There on Mount Sinai in the desert, the Lord gave these commands to Moses on the day he told the people of Israel to make their offerings.

The Ordination of Aaron and his Sons
(Ex 29.1–37)

8 The Lord said to Moses, [2] "Take Aaron and his sons to the entrance of the Tent of my presence and bring the priestly garments, the anointing oil, the young bull for the sin offering, the two rams, and the basket of unleavened bread. [3] Then call the whole community together there."

[4] Moses did as the Lord had commanded, and when the community had assembled, [5] he said to them, "What I am now about to do is what the Lord has commanded."

[6] Moses brought Aaron and his sons forward and told them to take a ritual bath. [7] He put the shirt and the robe on Aaron and the sash round his waist. He put the ephod on him and fastened it by putting its finely woven belt round his waist. [8] He put the breastpiece on him and put the Urim and Thummim* in it. [9] He placed the turban on his head, and on the front of it he put the gold ornament, the sacred sign of dedication, just as the Lord had commanded him.

[10] Then Moses took the anointing oil and put it on the Tent of the Lord's presence and everything that was in it, and in this way he dedicated it all to the Lord. [11] He took some of the oil and sprinkled it seven times on the altar and its equipment and on the basin and its base, in order to dedicate them to the Lord. [12] He ordained Aaron by pouring some of the anointing oil on his head. [13] Next, Moses brought the sons of Aaron forward and put shirts on them, put sashes round their waists, and tied caps on their heads, just as the Lord had commanded.

....

8.8 *Urim and Thummim*: Two objects used by the priest to determine God's will; it is not known precisely how they were used.

[14] Then Moses brought the young bull for the sin offering, and Aaron and his sons put their hands on its head. [15] Moses killed it and took some of the blood, and with his finger put it on the projections at the corners of the altar, in order to dedicate it. He then poured out the rest of the blood at the base of the altar. In this way he dedicated it and purified it. [16] Moses took all the fat on the internal organs, the best part of the liver, and the kidneys with the fat on them, and burnt it all on the altar. [17] He took the rest of the bull, including its skin, flesh, and intestines, and burnt it outside the camp, just as the LORD had commanded.

[18] Next, Moses brought the ram for the burnt offering, and Aaron and his sons put their hands on its head. [19] Moses killed it and threw the blood on all four sides of the altar. [20-21] He cut the ram in pieces, washed the internal organs and the hind legs with water, and burnt the head, the fat, and all the rest of the ram on the altar, just as the LORD had commanded. This burnt offering was a food offering, and the smell was pleasing to the LORD.

[22] Then Moses brought the second ram, which was for the ordination of priests, and Aaron and his sons put their hands on its head. [23] Moses killed it and took some of the blood and put it on the lobe of Aaron's right ear, on the thumb of his right hand, and on the big toe of his right foot. [24] Then he brought Aaron's sons forward and put some of the blood on the lobes of their right ears, on the thumbs of their right hands, and on the big toes of their right feet. Moses then threw the rest of the blood on all four sides of the altar. [25] He took the fat, the fat tail, all the fat covering the internal organs, the best part of the liver, the kidneys with the fat on them, and the right hind leg. [26] Then he took one loaf of bread from the basket of unleavened bread dedicated to the LORD, one loaf made with oil, and one biscuit, and he put them on top of the fat and the right hind leg. [27] He put all this food in the hands of Aaron and his sons, and they presented it as a special gift to the LORD. [28] Then Moses took the food from them and burnt it on the altar, on top of the burnt offering, as an ordination offering. This was a food offering, and the smell was pleasing to the LORD. [29] Then Moses took the breast and presented it as a special gift to the LORD. It was Moses' part of the ordination ram. Moses did everything just as the LORD had commanded.

[30] Moses took some of the anointing oil and some of the blood that was on the altar and sprinkled them on Aaron and his sons and on their clothes. In this way he consecrated them and their clothes to the LORD.

[31] Moses said to Aaron and his sons, "Take the meat to the entrance of the Tent of the LORD's presence, boil it, and eat it there with the bread that is in the basket of ordination offerings, just as the LORD commanded. [32] Burn up any meat or bread that is left over. [33] You shall not leave the entrance of the Tent for seven days, until your ordination rites are completed. [34] The LORD commanded us to do what we have done today, in order to take away your sin. [35] You must stay at the entrance of the Tent day and night for seven days, doing what the LORD has commanded. If you don't, you will die. This is what the LORD has commanded me." [36] So Aaron and his sons did everything that the LORD had commanded through Moses.

Aaron Offers Sacrifices

9 The day after the ordination rites were completed, Moses called Aaron and his sons and the leaders of Israel. [2] He said to Aaron, "Take a young bull and a ram without any defects and offer them to the LORD, the bull for a sin offering and the ram for a burnt offering. [3] Then tell the people of Israel to take a male goat for a sin offering, a one-year-old calf, and a one-year-old lamb without any defects for a burnt offering, ⁴and a bull and a ram for a fellowship offering. They are to sacrifice them to the LORD with the grain offering mixed with oil. They must do this because the LORD will appear to them today."

⁵They brought to the front of the Tent everything that Moses had commanded, and the whole community assembled there to worship the LORD. ⁶Moses said, "The LORD has commanded you to do all this, so that the dazzling light of his presence can appear to you." ⁷Then he said to Aaron, "Go to the altar and offer the sin offering and the burnt offering to take away your sins and the sins of the people. Present this offering to take away the sins of the people, just as the LORD commanded."

⁸Aaron went to the altar and killed the young bull which was for his own sin offering. ⁹His sons brought him the blood, and he dipped his finger in it, put some of it on the projections at the corners of the altar, and poured out the rest of it at the base of the altar. ¹⁰Then he burnt on the altar the fat, the kidneys, and the best part of the liver, just as the LORD had commanded Moses. ¹¹But he burnt the meat and the skin outside the camp.

¹²He killed the animal which was for his own burnt offering. His sons brought him the blood, and he threw it on all four sides of the altar. ¹³They handed him the head and the other pieces of the animal, and he burnt them on the altar. ¹⁴Then he washed the internal organs and the hind legs and burnt them on the altar on top of the rest of the burnt offering.

¹⁵After that, he presented the people's offerings. He took the goat that was to be offered for the people's sins, killed it, and offered it, as he had done with his own sin offering. ¹⁶He also brought the animal for the burnt offering and offered it according to the regulations. ¹⁷He presented the grain offering and took a handful of flour and burnt it on the altar. (This was in addition to the daily burnt offering.) ¹⁸He killed the bull and the ram as a fellowship offering for the people. His sons brought him the blood, and he threw it on all four sides of the altar. ¹⁹Aaron put the fat parts of the bull and the ram ²⁰on top of the breasts of the animals and carried it all to the altar. He burnt the fat on the altar ²¹and presented the breasts and the right hind legs as the special gift to the LORD for the priests, as Moses had commanded.

²²When Aaron had finished all the sacrifices, he raised his hands over the people and blessed them, and then stepped down. ²³Moses and Aaron went into the Tent of the LORD's presence, and when they came out, they blessed the people, and the dazzling light of the LORD's presence appeared to all the people. ²⁴Suddenly the LORD sent a fire, and it consumed the burnt offering and the fat parts on the altar. When the people saw it, they all shouted and bowed down with their faces to the ground.

The Sin of Nadab and Abihu

10 Aaron's sons Nadab and Abihu, each took his firepan, put live coals in it, added incense, and presented it to the LORD. But this fire was not holy, because the LORD had not commanded them to present it. ²Suddenly the LORD sent fire, and it burnt them to death there in the presence of the LORD. ³Then Moses said to Aaron, "This is what the LORD was speaking about when he said, 'All who serve me must respect my holiness; I will reveal my glory to my people.'"* But Aaron remained silent.

10.3 *I will reveal my glory to my people;* or *my people must honour me.*

LEVITICUS 10.3

GOD IS HOLY

⁴ Moses called Mishael and Elzaphan, the sons of Uzziel, Aaron's uncle, and said to them, "Come here and carry your cousins' bodies away from the sacred Tent and put them outside the camp." ⁵ So they came and took hold of the clothing on the corpses and carried them outside the camp, just as Moses had commanded.

⁶ Then Moses said to Aaron and to his sons Eleazar and Ithamar, "Do not leave your hair uncombed or tear your clothes to show that you are in mourning. If you do, you will die, and the LORD will be angry with the whole community. But all your fellow-Israelites are allowed to mourn this death caused by the fire which the LORD sent. ⁷ Do not leave the entrance of the Tent or you will die, because you have been consecrated by the anointing oil of the LORD." So they did as Moses said.

Rules for Priests

⁸ The LORD said to Aaron, ⁹ "You and your sons are not to enter the Tent of my presence after drinking wine or beer; if you do, you will die. This is a law to be kept by all your descendants. ¹⁰ You must distinguish between what belongs to God and what is for general use, between what is ritually clean and what is unclean. ¹¹ You must teach the people of Israel all the laws which I have given to you through Moses."

¹² Moses said to Aaron and his two remaining sons, Eleazar and Ithamar, "Take the grain offering that is left over from the food offered to the LORD, make unleavened bread with it and eat it beside the altar, because this offering is very holy. ¹³ Eat it in a holy place; it is the part that belongs to you and your sons from the food offered to the LORD. That is what the LORD commanded me. ¹⁴ But you and your families may eat the breast and the hind leg that are presented as the special gift and the special contribution to the LORD for the priests. You may eat them in any ritually clean place. These offerings have been given to you and your children as the part that belongs to you from the fellowship offerings of the people of Israel. ¹⁵ They shall bring the hind leg and the breast at the time the fat is presented as a food offering to the LORD. These parts belong to you and your children for ever, just as the LORD commanded."

¹⁶ Moses asked about the goat for the sin offering and learnt that it had already been burnt. This made him angry with Eleazar and Ithamar, and he demanded, ¹⁷ "Why didn't you eat the sin offering in a sacred place? It is very holy, and the LORD has given it to you in order to take away the sin of the community. ¹⁸ Since its blood was not brought into the sacred tent, you should have eaten the sacrifice there, as I commanded."

¹⁹ Aaron answered, "If I had eaten the sin offering today, would the LORD have approved? The people presented their sin offering to the LORD today, and they brought their burnt offering, but still these terrible things have happened to me." ²⁰ When Moses heard this, he was satisfied.

Animals that may be Eaten
(Deut 14.3–21)

11 The Lord gave Moses and Aaron the following regulations ² for the people of Israel. You may eat any land animal ³ that has divided hoofs and that also chews the cud, ⁴⁻⁶ but you must not eat camels, rock-badgers, or rabbits. They must be considered unclean; they chew the cud, but do not have divided hoofs. ⁷ Do not eat pigs. They must be considered unclean; they have divided hoofs, but do not chew the cud. ⁸ Do not eat these animals or even touch their dead bodies; they are unclean.

141

Leviticus

Num.
Deuter.
Joshua
Judges
Ruth

⁹You may eat any kind of fish that has fins and scales, ¹⁰but anything living in the water that does not have fins and scales must not be eaten. ¹¹Such creatures must be considered unclean. You must not eat them or even touch their dead bodies. ¹²You must not eat anything that lives in the water and does not have fins and scales.

¹³⁻¹⁹You must not eat any of the following birds: eagles, owls, hawks, falcons; buzzards, vultures, crows; ostriches; seagulls, storks, herons, pelicans, cormorants;* hoopoes; or bats.

²⁰All winged insects are unclean, ²¹except those that hop. ²²You may eat locusts, crickets, or grasshoppers. ²³But all other small things that have wings and also crawl must be considered unclean.

²⁴⁻²⁸Whoever touches the dead bodies of the following animals will be unclean until evening: all animals with hoofs, unless their hoofs are divided and they chew the cud, and all four-footed animals with paws. Whoever carries their dead bodies must wash his clothes, but he will still be unclean until evening.

²⁹⁻³⁰Moles, rats, mice, and lizards must be considered unclean. ³¹Whoever touches them or their dead bodies will be unclean until evening. ³²And if their dead bodies fall on anything, it will be unclean. This applies to any article of wood, cloth, leather, or sacking, no matter what it is used for. It shall be dipped in water, but it will remain unclean until evening. ³³And if their bodies fall into a clay pot, everything that is in it shall be unclean, and you must break the pot. ³⁴Any food which could normally be eaten, but on which water from such a pot has been poured, will be unclean, and anything drinkable in such a pot is unclean. ³⁵Anything on which the dead bodies fall is unclean; a clay stove or oven shall be broken, ³⁶but a spring or a cistern remains clean, although anything else that touches their dead bodies is unclean. ³⁷If one of them falls on seed that is going to be sown, the seed remains clean. ³⁸But if the seed is soaking in water and one of them falls on it, the seed is unclean.

³⁹If any animal that may be eaten dies, anyone who touches it will be unclean until evening. ⁴⁰And if anyone eats any part of the animal, he must wash his clothes, but he will still be unclean until evening; anyone who carries the dead body must wash his clothes, but he will still be unclean until evening.

⁴¹You must not eat any of the small animals that move on the ground, ⁴²whether they crawl, or walk on four legs, or have many legs. ⁴³Do not make yourselves unclean by eating any of these. ⁴⁴I am the LORD your God, and you must keep yourselves holy, because I am holy. ⁴⁵I am the LORD who brought you out of Egypt so that I could be your God. You must be holy, because I am holy.

⁴⁶This, then, is the law about animals and birds, about everything that lives in the water, and everything that moves on the ground. ⁴⁷You must be careful to distinguish between what is ritually clean and unclean, between animals that may be eaten and those that may not.

The Purification of Women after Childbirth

12 The LORD gave Moses the following regulations ²for the people of Israel. For seven days after a woman gives birth to a son, she is ritually unclean, as she is during her monthly period. ³On the eighth day, the child shall be circumcised. ⁴Then it will be 33 more days before she is ritually clean from her loss of blood;

11.13–19 The identification of some of the birds in verses 13–19 is uncertain.

she must not touch anything that is holy or enter the sacred Tent until the time of her purification is completed.

⁵For fourteen days after a woman gives birth to a daughter, she is ritually unclean, as she is during her monthly period. Then it will be 66 more days before she is ritually clean from her loss of blood.

⁶When the time of her purification is completed, whether for a son or daughter, she shall bring to the priest at the entrance of the Tent of the LORD's presence a one-year-old lamb for a burnt offering and a pigeon or a dove for a sin offering. ⁷The priest shall present her offering to the Lord and perform the ritual to take away her impurity, and she will be ritually clean. This, then, is what a woman must do after giving birth.

⁸If the woman cannot afford a lamb, she shall bring two doves or two pigeons, one for a burnt offering and the other for a sin offering, and the priest shall perform the ritual to take away her impurity, and she will be ritually clean.

Laws concerning Skin Diseases

13 The LORD gave Moses and Aaron these regulations. ²If anyone has a sore on his skin or a boil or an inflammation which could develop into a dreaded skin disease, he shall be brought to the Aaronite priest. ³The priest shall examine the sore, and if the hairs in it have turned white and the sore appears to be deeper than the surrounding skin, it is a dreaded skin disease, and the priest shall pronounce the person unclean. ⁴But if the sore is white and does not appear to be deeper than the skin round it and the hairs have not turned white, the priest shall isolate the person for seven days. ⁵The priest shall examine him again on the seventh day, and if in his opinion the sore looks the same and has not spread, he shall isolate him for another seven days. ⁶The priest shall examine him again on the seventh day, and if the sore has faded and has not spread, he shall pronounce him ritually clean; it is only a sore. The person shall wash his clothes and be ritually clean. ⁷But if the sore spreads after the priest has examined him and pronounced him clean, he must appear before the priest again. ⁸The priest will examine him again, and if it has spread, he shall pronounce him unclean; it is a dreaded skin disease.

⁹If anyone has a dreaded skin disease, he shall be brought to the priest, ¹⁰who will examine him. If there is a white sore on his skin which turns the hairs white and is full of pus, ¹¹it is a chronic skin disease. The priest shall pronounce him unclean; there is no need to isolate him, because he is obviously unclean. ¹²If the skin disease spreads and covers the person from head to foot, ¹³the priest shall examine him again. If he finds that it actually has covered the whole body, he shall pronounce the person ritually clean. If his whole skin has turned white, he is ritually clean. ¹⁴But from the moment an open sore appears, he is unclean. ¹⁵The priest shall examine him again, and if he sees an open sore, he shall pronounce him unclean. An open sore means a dreaded skin disease, and the person is unclean. ¹⁶But when the sore heals and becomes white again, the person shall go to the priest, ¹⁷who will examine him again. If the sore has turned white, he is ritually clean, and the priest shall pronounce him clean.

¹⁸If anyone has a boil that has healed ¹⁹and if afterwards a white swelling or a reddish-white spot appears where the boil was, he shall go to the priest. ²⁰The priest shall examine him, and if the spot seems to be deeper than the surrounding skin and the hairs in it have turned white, he shall pronounce him unclean. It

DRAW A CIRCLE BELOW.

Inside the circle, draw your reaction to what's written on this page.

Leviticus

Num.
Deuter.
Joshua
Judges
Ruth

is a dreaded skin disease that has started in the boil. [21]But if the priest examines it and finds that the hairs in it have not turned white and that it is not deeper than the surrounding skin, but is light in colour, the priest shall isolate him for seven days. [22]If the spot spreads, the priest shall pronounce him unclean; he is diseased. [23]But if it remains unchanged and does not spread, it is only the scar left from the boil, and the priest shall pronounce him ritually clean.

[24]In the case of a person who has been burnt, if the raw flesh becomes white or reddish-white, [25]the priest shall examine him. If the hairs in the spot have turned white and it appears deeper than the surrounding skin, it is a dreaded skin disease that has started in the burn, and the priest shall pronounce him unclean. [26]But if the hairs in it have not turned white and it is not deeper than the surrounding skin, but is light in colour, the priest shall isolate him for seven days. [27]The priest shall examine him again on the seventh day, and if it is spreading, it is a dreaded skin disease, and the priest shall pronounce him unclean. [28]But if the spot remains unchanged and does not spread and is light in colour, it is not a dreaded skin disease. The priest shall pronounce him ritually clean, because it is only a scar from the burn.

[29]When a man or a woman has a sore on the head or the chin, [30]the priest shall examine it. If it seems to be deeper than the surrounding skin and the hairs in it are yellowish and thin, it is a dreaded skin disease, and he shall pronounce the person unclean. [31]If, when the priest examines him, the sore does not appear to be deeper than the surrounding skin, but there are still no healthy hairs in it, he shall isolate him for seven days. [32]The priest shall examine the sore again on the seventh day, and if it has not spread and there are no yellowish hairs in it and it does not seem to be deeper than the surrounding skin, [33]the person shall shave the head except the area round the sore. The priest shall then isolate him for another seven days. [34]On the seventh day the priest shall again examine the sore, and if it has not spread and does not seem to be deeper than the surrounding skin, he shall pronounce him ritually clean. The person shall wash his clothes, and he will be clean. [35]But if the sore spreads after he has been pronounced clean, [36]the priest shall examine him again. If the sore has spread, he need not look for yellowish hairs; the person is obviously unclean. [37]But if in the priest's opinion the sore has not spread and healthy hairs are growing in it, the sore has healed, and the priest shall pronounce him ritually clean.

[38]When a man or a woman has white spots on the skin, [39]the priest shall examine that person. If the spots are dull white, it is only a blemish that has broken out on the skin; the person is ritually clean.

[40-41]If a man loses his hair at the back or the front of his head, this does not make him unclean. [42]But if a reddish-white sore appears on the bald spot, it is a dreaded skin disease. [43]The priest shall examine him, and if there is a reddish-white sore, [44]the priest shall pronounce him unclean, because of the dreaded skin disease on his head.

[45]A person who has a dreaded skin disease must wear torn clothes, leave his hair uncombed, cover the lower part of his face, and call out, "Unclean, unclean!" [46]He remains unclean as long as he has the disease, and he must live outside the camp, away from others.

Laws concerning Mildew

47 When there is mildew* on clothing, whether wool or linen, 48 or on any piece of linen or wool cloth or on leather or anything made of leather, 49 if it is greenish or reddish, it is a spreading mildew and must be shown to the priest. 50 The priest shall examine it and put the object away for seven days. 51 He shall examine it again on the seventh day, and if the mildew has spread, the object is unclean. 52 The priest shall burn it, because it is a spreading mildew which must be destroyed by fire.

53 But if, when he examines it, the priest finds that the mildew has not spread on the object, 54 he shall order it to be washed and put away for another seven days. 55 Then he shall examine it, and if the mildew has not changed colour, even though it has not spread, it is still unclean; you must burn the object, whether the rot is on the front or the back. 56 But if, when the priest examines it again, the mildew has faded, he shall tear it out of the clothing or leather. 57 Then, if the mildew reappears, it is spreading again, and the owner shall burn the object. 58 If he washes the object and the spot disappears, he shall wash it again, and it will be ritually clean.

59 This, then, is the law about mildew on clothing, whether it is wool or linen, or on linen or wool cloth or on anything made of leather; this is how the decision is made as to whether it is ritually clean or unclean.

Purification after Having Skin Diseases

14 The LORD gave Moses 2 the following regulations about the ritual purification of a person cured of a dreaded skin disease. On the day he is to be pronounced clean, he shall be brought to the priest, 3 and the priest shall take him outside the camp and examine him. If the disease is healed, 4 the priest shall order two ritually clean birds to be brought, together with a piece of cedar wood, a red cord, and a sprig of hyssop. 5 Then the priest shall order one of the birds to be killed over a clay bowl containing fresh spring water. 6 He shall take the other bird and dip it, together with the cedar wood, the red cord, and the hyssop, in the blood of the bird that was killed. 7 He shall sprinkle the blood seven times on the person who is to be purified from his skin disease, and then he shall pronounce him clean. He shall let the live bird fly away over the open fields. 8 The person shall wash his clothes, shave off all his hair, and have a bath; he will then be ritually clean. He may enter the camp, but he must live outside his tent for seven days. 9 On the seventh day he shall again shave his head, his beard, his eyebrows, and all the rest of the hair on his body; he shall wash his clothes and have a bath, and then he will be ritually clean.

10 On the eighth day he shall bring two male lambs and one female lamb a year old that are without any defects, three kilogrammes of flour mixed with olive oil, and a third of a litre of olive oil. 11 The priest shall take the person and these offerings to the entrance of the Tent of the LORD's presence. 12 Then the priest shall take one of the male lambs and together with the one-third of a litre of oil he shall offer it as a repayment offering. He shall present them as a special gift to the LORD for the priest. 13 He shall kill the lamb in the place where the animals for the sin offerings and the burnt offerings are killed. He must do this

13.47 *mildew*: The Hebrew word for "dreaded skin disease" and "mildew" is the same.

Leviticus

···········

Num.

Deuter.

Joshua

Judges

Ruth

because the repayment offering, like the sin offering, belongs to the priest and is very holy. [14] The priest shall take some of the blood of the lamb and put it on the lobe of the right ear, on the thumb of the right hand, and on the big toe of the right foot of the one who is to be declared ritually clean. [15] The priest shall take some of the olive oil and pour it in the palm of his own left hand, [16] dip a finger of his right hand in it, and sprinkle some of it seven times there in the LORD's presence. [17] He shall take some of the oil that is in the palm of his hand and some of the blood of the lamb and put them on the lobe of the right ear, on the thumb of the right hand, and on the big toe of the right foot of the one who is to be declared ritually clean. [18] He shall put the rest of the oil that is in the palm of his hand on the person's head. In this way he shall perform the ritual of purification.

[19] Then the priest shall offer the sin offering and perform the ritual of purification. After that, he shall kill the animal for the burnt offering [20] and offer it with the grain offering on the altar. In this way the priest shall perform the ritual of purification, and the person will be ritually clean.

[21] If he is poor and cannot afford any more, he shall bring for his purification only one male lamb as his repayment offering, a special gift to the LORD for the priest. He shall bring only one kilogramme of flour mixed with olive oil for a grain offering and a third of a litre of olive oil. [22] He shall also bring two doves or two pigeons, one for the sin offering and one for the burnt offering. [23] On the eighth day of his purification he shall bring them to the priest at the entrance of the Tent. [24] The priest shall take the lamb and the olive oil and present them as a special gift to the LORD for the priest. [25] He shall kill the lamb and take some of the blood and put it on the lobe of the person's right ear, on the thumb of his right hand, and on the big toe of his right foot. [26] The priest shall pour some of the oil into the palm of his own left hand [27] and with a finger of his right hand sprinkle some of it seven times there in the LORD's presence. [28] He shall put some of the oil on the same places as he put the blood: on the lobe of the person's right ear, on the thumb of his right hand, and on the big toe of his right foot. [29] The rest of the oil that is in his palm he shall put on the person's head and in this way perform the ritual of purification. [30] Then he shall offer one of the doves or pigeons [31] as the sin offering and the other as the burnt offering with the grain offering. In this way the priest shall perform the ritual of purification. [32] This is the law for the one who has a dreaded skin disease but who cannot afford the normal offerings required for his purification.

Mildew in Houses

[33] The LORD gave Moses and Aaron [34-35] the following regulations about houses affected by spreading mildew. (These were to apply after the people of Israel entered the land of Canaan, which the LORD was going to give them as their possession.) If someone finds that the LORD has sent mildew on his house, then he must go and tell the priest about it. [36] The priest shall order everything to be moved out of the house before he goes to examine the mildew; otherwise everything in the house will be declared unclean. Then he shall go to the house [37] and examine the mildew. If there are greenish or reddish spots that appear to be eating into the wall, [38] he shall leave the house and lock it up for seven days. [39] On the seventh day he shall return and examine it again. If the mildew has spread, [40] he shall order the stones on which the mildew is

found to be removed and thrown into some unclean place outside the city. ⁴¹After that he must have all the interior walls scraped and the plaster dumped in an unclean place outside the city. ⁴²Then other stones are to be used to replace the stones that were removed, and new plaster will be used to cover the walls.

⁴³If the mildew breaks out again in the house after the stones have been removed and the house has been scraped and plastered, ⁴⁴the priest shall go and look. If it has spread, the house is unclean. ⁴⁵It must be torn down, and its stones, its wood, and all its plaster must be carried out of the city to an unclean place. ⁴⁶Anyone who enters the house while it is locked up will be unclean until evening. ⁴⁷Anyone who lies down or eats in the house must wash his clothes.

⁴⁸If, when the priest comes to look, the mildew has not reappeared after the house has been replastered, he shall pronounce the house ritually clean, because the mildew has been completely removed. ⁴⁹To purify the house, he shall take two birds, some cedar wood, a red cord, and a sprig of hyssop. ⁵⁰He shall kill one of the birds over a clay bowl containing fresh spring water. ⁵¹Then he shall take the cedar wood, the hyssop, the red cord, and the live bird and shall dip them in the blood of the bird that was killed and in the fresh water. And he shall sprinkle the house seven times. ⁵²In this way he shall purify the house with the bird's blood, the fresh water, the live bird, the cedar wood, the hyssop, and the red cord. ⁵³Then he shall let the live bird fly away outside the city over the open fields. In this way he shall perform the ritual of purification for the house, and it will be ritually clean.

⁵⁴These are the laws about dreaded skin diseases; ⁵⁵⁻⁵⁶sores, boils, or inflammations; and about mildew in clothes or houses. ⁵⁷These laws determine when something is unclean and when it is clean.

Unclean Bodily Discharges

15 The LORD gave Moses and Aaron the following regulations ²for the people of Israel. When any man has a discharge from his penis, the discharge is unclean, ³whether the penis runs with it or is stopped up by it. ⁴Any bed on which he sits or lies is unclean. ⁵Anyone who touches his bed ⁶or sits on anything the man has sat on must wash his clothes and have a bath, and he remains unclean until evening. ⁷Anyone who touches the man with the discharge must wash his clothes and have a bath, and he remains unclean until evening. ⁸If the man with the discharge spits on anyone who is ritually clean, that person must wash his clothes and have a bath, and he remains unclean until evening. ⁹Any saddle or seat on which the man with the discharge sits is unclean. ¹⁰Anyone who touches anything on which the man sat is unclean until evening. Anyone who carries anything on which the man sat must wash his clothes and have a bath, and he remains unclean until evening. ¹¹If a man who has a discharge touches someone without first having washed his hands, that person must wash his clothes and have a bath, and he remains unclean until evening. ¹²Any clay pot that the man touches must be broken, and any wooden bowl that he touches must be washed.

¹³After the man is cured of his discharge, he must wait seven days and then wash his clothes and bathe in fresh spring water, and he will be ritually clean. ¹⁴On the eighth day he shall take two doves or two pigeons to the entrance of the Tent of the LORD's presence and give them to the priest. ¹⁵The priest shall offer

LEVITICUS 15, 16

147

Leviticus

···········:·

Num.

Deuter.

Joshua

Judges

Ruth

one of them as a sin offering and the other as a burnt offering. In this way he will perform the ritual of purification for the man.

16 When a man has an emission of semen, he must bathe his whole body, and he remains unclean until evening. 17 Anything made of cloth or leather on which the semen falls must be washed, and it remains unclean until evening. 18 After sexual intercourse both the man and the woman must have a bath, and they remain unclean until evening.

19 When a woman has her monthly period, she remains unclean for seven days. Anyone who touches her is unclean until evening. 20 Anything on which she sits or lies during her monthly period is unclean. 21-23 Anyone who touches her bed or anything on which she has sat must wash his clothes and have a bath, and he remains unclean until evening. 24 If a man has sexual intercourse with her during her period, he is contaminated by her impurity and remains unclean for seven days, and any bed on which he lies is unclean.

25 If a woman has a flow of blood for several days outside her monthly period or if her flow continues beyond her regular period, she remains unclean as long as the flow continues, just as she is during her monthly period. 26 Any bed on which she lies and anything on which she sits during this time is unclean. 27 Anyone who touches them is unclean and must wash his clothes and have a bath; he remains unclean until evening. 28 After her flow stops, she must wait seven days, and then she will be ritually clean. 29 On the eighth day she shall take two doves or two pigeons to the priest at the entrance of the Tent of the LORD's presence. 30 The priest shall offer one of them as a sin offering and the other as a burnt offering, and in this way he will perform the ritual of purification for her.

31 The LORD told Moses to warn the people of Israel about their uncleanness, so that they would not defile the Tent of his presence, which was in the middle of the camp. If they did, they would be killed.

32 These are the regulations about a man who has a discharge or an emission of semen, 33 a woman during her monthly period, or a man who has sexual intercourse with a woman who is ritually unclean.

The Day of Atonement

16 The LORD spoke to Moses after the death of the two sons of Aaron who were killed when they offered unholy fire to the LORD. 2 He said, "Tell your brother Aaron that only at the proper time is he to go behind the curtain into the Most Holy Place, because that is where I appear in a cloud above the lid on the Covenant Box. If he disobeys, he will be killed. 3 He may enter the Most Holy Place only after he has brought a young bull for a sin offering and a ram for a burnt offering."

4 Then the LORD gave the following instructions. Before Aaron goes into the Most Holy Place, he must have a bath and put on the priestly garments: the linen robe and shorts, the belt, and the turban.

5 The community of Israel shall give Aaron two male goats for a sin offering and a ram for a burnt offering. 6 He shall offer a bull as a sacrifice to take away his own sins and those of his family. 7 Then he shall take the two goats to the entrance of the Tent of the LORD's presence. 8 There he shall draw lots, using two stones, one marked "for the LORD" and the other "for Azazel".* 9 Aaron

---

16.8 Azazel: The meaning of this Hebrew word is unknown; it may be the name of a desert demon.

LEVITICUS 16

Offerings were very important in the Old Testament (see Deuteronomy 12). We don't need to sacrifice animals to God today, but there are still things we can give up to him.

DECORATE
– THESE –
PAGES

with all the different things you could offer to God (for example, your time, your money, your gifts...).

148

Leviticus

⫶⫶⫶⫶⫶⫶⫶⫶

Genesis

Exodus

LEVITICUS 16

shall sacrifice the goat chosen by lot for the LORD and offer it as a sin offering. [10] The goat chosen for Azazel shall be presented alive to the LORD and sent off into the desert to Azazel, in order to take away the sins of the people.

[11] When Aaron sacrifices the bull as the sin offering for himself and his family, [12] he shall take a firepan full of burning coals from the altar and two handfuls of fine incense and bring them into the Most Holy Place. [13] There in the LORD's presence he shall put the incense on the fire, and the smoke of the incense will hide the lid of the Covenant Box so that he will not see it and die. [14] He shall take some of the bull's blood and with his finger sprinkle it on the front of the lid and then sprinkle some of it seven times in front of the Covenant Box.

[15] After that, he shall kill the goat for the sin offering for the people, bring its blood into the Most Holy Place, and sprinkle it on the lid and then in front of the Covenant Box, as he did with the bull's blood. [16] In this way he will perform the ritual to purify the Most Holy Place from the uncleanness of the people of Israel and from all their sins. He must do this to the Tent, because it stands in the middle of the camp, which is ritually unclean. [17] From the time Aaron enters the Most Holy Place to perform the ritual of purification until he comes out, there must be no one in the Tent. When he has performed the ritual for himself, his family, and the whole community, [18] he must then go out to the altar for burnt offerings and purify it. He must take some of the bull's blood and some of the goat's blood and put it all over the projections at the corners of the altar. [19] With his finger he must sprinkle some of the blood on the altar seven times. In this way he is to purify it from the sins of the people of Israel and make it holy.

The Scapegoat

[20] When Aaron has finished performing the ritual to purify the Most Holy Place, the rest of the Tent of the LORD's presence, and the altar, he shall present to the LORD the live goat chosen for Azazel.* [21] He shall put both his hands on the goat's head and confess over it all the evils, sins, and rebellions of the people of Israel, and so transfer them to the goat's head. Then the goat is to be driven off into the desert by someone appointed to do it. [22] The goat will carry all their sins away with him into some uninhabited land.

[23] Then Aaron shall go into the Tent, take off the priestly garments that he had put on before entering the Most Holy Place, and leave them there. [24] He must bathe in a holy place and put on his own clothes. After that, he shall go out and offer the burnt offering to remove his own sins and those of the people. [25] He shall burn on the altar the fat of the animal for the sin offering. [26] The man who drove the goat into the desert to Azazel must wash his clothes and have a bath before he comes back into camp. [27] The bull and the goat used for the sin offering, whose blood was brought into the Most Holy Place to take away sin, shall be carried outside the camp and burnt. Skin, meat, and intestines shall all be burnt. [28] The one who burns them must wash his clothes and have a bath before he returns to camp.

Observing the Day of Atonement

[29] The following regulations are to be observed for all time to come. On the tenth day of the seventh month the Israelites and the

16.20 *Azazel*: The meaning of this Hebrew word is unknown; it may be the name of a desert demon.

149

Leviticus

....

Num.
Deuter.
Joshua
Judges
Ruth

foreigners living among them must fast and must not do any work. [30] On that day the ritual is to be performed to purify them from all their sins, so that they will be ritually clean. [31] That day is to be a very holy day, one on which they fast and do no work at all. These regulations are to be observed for all time to come. [32] The High Priest, properly ordained and consecrated to succeed his father, is to perform the ritual of purification. He shall put on the priestly garments [33] and perform the ritual to purify the Most Holy Place, the rest of the Tent of the LORD's presence, the altar, the priests, and all the people of the community. [34] These regulations are to be observed for all time to come. This ritual must be performed once a year to purify the people of Israel from all their sins.

So Moses* did as the Lord had commanded.

The Sacredness of Blood

17 The Lord commanded Moses [2] to give Aaron and his sons and all the people of Israel the following regulations. [3-4] An Israelite who kills a cow or a sheep or a goat as an offering to the LORD anywhere except at the entrance of the Tent of the LORD's presence has broken the Law. He has shed blood and shall no longer be considered one of God's people. [5] The meaning of this command is that the people of Israel shall now bring to the LORD the animals which they used to kill in the open country. They shall now bring them to the priest at the entrance of the Tent and kill them as fellowship offerings. [6] The priest shall throw the blood against the sides of the altar at the entrance of the Tent and burn the fat to produce a smell that is pleasing to the LORD. [7] The people of Israel must no longer be unfaithful to the LORD by killing their animals in the fields as sacrifices to the goat-demons. The people of Israel must keep this regulation for all time to come.

[8] Any Israelite or any foreigner living in the community who offers a burnt offering or any other sacrifice [9] as an offering to the LORD anywhere except at the entrance of the Tent shall no longer be considered one of God's people.

[10] If any Israelite or any foreigner living in the community eats meat with blood still in it, the LORD will turn against him and no longer consider him one of his people. [11] The life of every living thing is in the blood, and that is why the LORD has commanded that all blood be poured out on the altar to take away the people's sins. Blood, which is life, takes away sins. [12] That is why the LORD has told the people of Israel that neither they nor any foreigner living among them shall eat any meat with blood still in it.

[13] If any Israelite or any foreigner living in the community hunts an animal or a bird which is ritually clean, he must pour out its blood on the ground and cover it with earth. [14] The life of every living thing is in the blood, and that is why the LORD has told the people of Israel that they shall not eat any meat with blood still in it and that anyone who does so will no longer be considered one of his people.

[15] Any person, Israelite or foreigner, who eats meat from an animal that has died a natural death or has been killed by wild animals must wash his clothes, have a bath, and wait until evening before he is ritually clean. [16] If he does not, he must suffer the consequences.

Forbidden Sexual Practices

18 The LORD told Moses [2] to say to the people of Israel, "I am the LORD your God. [3] Do not follow the practices of the

16.34 *Moses*; or *Aaron*.

HOLY

LEVITICUS 19.2;
PSALM 30.4

What do you
think it means?

What does someone
else think it means?

Now go and look up
the definition.

people of Egypt, where you once lived, or of the people in the land of Canaan, where I am now taking you. ⁴Obey my laws and do what I command. I am the LORD your God. ⁵Follow the practices and the laws that I give you; you will save your life by doing so. I am the LORD."

⁶The LORD gave the following regulations. Do not have sexual intercourse with any of your relatives. ⁷Do not disgrace your father by having intercourse with your mother. You must not disgrace your own mother. ⁸Do not disgrace your father by having intercourse with any of his other wives. ⁹Do not have intercourse with your sister or your stepsister, whether or not she was brought up in the same house with you. ¹⁰Do not have intercourse with your granddaughter; that would be a disgrace to you. ¹¹Do not have intercourse with a half-sister; she, too, is your sister. ¹²⁻¹³Do not have intercourse with an aunt, whether she is your father's sister or your mother's sister. ¹⁴Do not have intercourse with your uncle's wife; she, too, is your aunt. ¹⁵Do not have intercourse with your daughter-in-law ¹⁶or with your brother's wife. ¹⁷Do not have intercourse with the daughter or granddaughter of a woman with whom you have had intercourse; they may be related to you, and that would be incest. ¹⁸Do not take your wife's sister as one of your wives, as long as your wife is living.

¹⁹Do not have intercourse with a woman during her monthly period, because she is ritually unclean. ²⁰Do not have intercourse with another man's wife; that would make you ritually unclean. ²¹Do not hand over any of your children to be used in the worship of the god Molech, because that would bring disgrace on the name of God, the LORD. ²²No man is to have sexual relations with another man; God hates that. ²³No man or woman is to have sexual relations with an animal; that perversion makes you ritually unclean.

²⁴Do not make yourselves unclean by any of these acts, for that is how the pagans made themselves unclean, those pagans who lived in the land before you and whom the LORD is driving out so that you can go in. ²⁵Their actions made the land unclean, and so the LORD is punishing the land and making it reject the people who lived there. ²⁶⁻²⁷They did all these disgusting things and made the land unclean, but you must not do them. All of you, whether Israelites or foreigners living with you, must keep the LORD's laws and commands, ²⁸and then the land will not reject you, as it rejected the pagans who lived there before you. ²⁹You know that whoever does any of these disgusting things will no longer be considered one of God's people.

³⁰And the LORD said, "Obey the commands I give and do not follow the practices of the people who lived in the land before you, and do not make yourselves unclean by doing any of these things. I am the LORD your God."

Laws of Holiness and Justice

19 The LORD told Moses ²to say to the community of Israel, "Be holy, because I, the LORD your God, am holy. ³Each of you must respect his mother and his father, and must keep the Sabbath, as I have commanded. I am the LORD your God.

⁴"Do not abandon me and worship idols; do not make gods of metal and worship them. I am the LORD your God.

⁵"When you kill an animal for a fellowship offering, keep the regulations that I have given you, and I will accept the offering. ⁶The meat must be eaten on the day the animal is killed or on the next day. Any meat left on the third day must be burnt, ⁷because

LEVITICUS 19

151

Leviticus

....

Num.
Deuter.
Joshua
Judges
Ruth

it is ritually unclean, and if anyone eats it, I will not accept the offering. ⁸Anyone who eats it will be guilty of treating as ordinary what is dedicated to me, and he will no longer be considered one of my people.

⁹"When you harvest your fields, do not cut the corn at the edges of the fields, and do not go back to cut the ears of corn that were left. ¹⁰Do not go back through your vineyard to gather the grapes that were missed or to pick up the grapes that have fallen; leave them for poor people and foreigners. I am the LORD your God.

¹¹"Do not steal or cheat or lie. ¹²Do not make a promise in my name if you do not intend to keep it; that brings disgrace on my name. I am the LORD your God.

¹³"Do not take advantage of anyone or rob him. Do not hold back the wages of someone you have hired, not even for one night. ¹⁴Do not curse a deaf man or put something in front of a blind man so as to make him stumble over it. Obey me; I am the LORD your God.

¹⁵"Be honest and just when you make decisions in legal cases; do not show favouritism to the poor or fear the rich. ¹⁶Do not spread lies about anyone, and when someone is on trial for his life, speak out if your testimony can help him. I am the LORD.

¹⁷"Do not bear a grudge against anyone, but settle your differences with him, so that you will not commit a sin because of him.* ¹⁸Do not take revenge on anyone or continue to hate him, but love your neighbour as you love yourself. I am the LORD.

¹⁹"Obey my commands. Do not crossbreed domestic animals. Do not plant two kinds of seed in the same field. Do not wear clothes made of two kinds of material.

²⁰"If a slave woman is the recognized concubine of a man and she has not been paid for and freed, then if another man has sexual relations with her, they will be punished but not* put to death, since she is a slave. ²¹The man shall bring a ram to the entrance of the Tent of my presence as his repayment offering, ²²and with it the priest shall perform the ritual of purification to remove the man's sin, and God will forgive him.

²³"When you come into the land of Canaan and plant any kind of fruit tree, consider the fruit ritually unclean for the first three years. During that time you must not eat it. ²⁴In the fourth year all the fruit shall be dedicated as an offering to show your gratitude to me,* the LORD. ²⁵But in the fifth year you may eat the fruit. If you do all this, your trees will bear more fruit. I am the LORD your God.

²⁶"Do not eat any meat with blood still in it. Do not practise any kind of magic. ²⁷Do not cut the hair on the sides of your head or trim your beard ²⁸or tattoo yourselves or cut gashes in your body to mourn for the dead. I am the LORD.

²⁹"Do not disgrace your daughters by making them temple prostitutes;* if you do, you will turn to other gods and the land will be full of immorality. ³⁰Keep the Sabbath, and honour the place where I am worshipped. I am the LORD.

³¹"Do not go for advice to people who consult the spirits of the dead. If you do, you will be ritually unclean. I am the LORD your God.

³²"Show respect for old people and honour them. Reverently obey me; I am the LORD.

....

19.17 *so... him*; or *so that you do not commit this sin against him.*
19.20 *they... not*; or *an investigation will be made but they will not be.*
19.24 *to show your gratitude to me*; or *in praise of me.*
19.29 *temple prostitutes*: These women were found in Canaanite temples, where fertility gods were worshipped. It was believed that intercourse with these prostitutes assured fertile fields and herds.

152

Leviticus

⁘⋯⋯⋯

Genesis
Exodus

LEVITICUS 19, 20

33 "Do not ill-treat foreigners who are living in your land. 34 Treat them as you would a fellow-Israelite, and love them as you love yourselves. Remember that you were once foreigners in the land of Egypt. I am the LORD your God.

35 "Do not cheat anyone by using false measures of length, weight, or quantity. 36 Use honest scales, honest weights, and honest measures. I am the LORD your God, and I brought you out of Egypt. 37 Obey all my laws and commands. I am the LORD."

Penalties for Disobedience

20 The LORD told Moses 2 to say to the people of Israel, "Any of you or any foreigner living among you who gives any of his or her children to be used in the worship of the god Molech shall be stoned to death by the whole community. 3 If anyone gives one of his children to Molech and makes my sacred Tent unclean and disgraces my holy name, I will turn against him and will no longer consider him one of my people. 4 But if the community ignores what he has done and does not put him to death, 5 I myself will turn against the man and his whole family and against all who join him in being unfaithful to me and worshipping Molech. I will no longer consider them my people.

6 "If anyone goes for advice to people who consult the spirits of the dead, I will turn against him and will no longer consider him one of my people. 7 Keep yourselves holy, because I am the LORD your God. 8 Obey my laws, because I am the LORD and I make you holy."

9 The LORD gave the following regulations. Anyone who curses his father or his mother shall be put to death; he is responsible for his own death.

10 If a man commits adultery with the wife of a fellow-Israelite, both he and the woman shall be put to death. 11 A man who has intercourse with one of his father's wives disgraces his father, and both he and the woman shall be put to death. They are responsible for their own death. 12 If a man has intercourse with his daughter-in-law, they shall both be put to death. They have committed incest and are responsible for their own death. 13 If a man has sexual relations with another man, they have done a disgusting thing, and both shall be put to death. They are responsible for their own death. 14 If a man marries a woman and her mother, all three shall be burnt to death because of the disgraceful thing they have done; such a thing must not be permitted among you. 15 If a man has sexual relations with an animal, he and the animal shall be put to death. 16 If a woman tries to have sexual relations with an animal, she and the animal shall be put to death. They are responsible for their own death.

17 If a man marries his sister or half-sister, they shall be publicly disgraced and driven out of the community. He has had intercourse with his sister and must suffer the consequences. 18 If a man has intercourse with a woman during her monthly period, both of them are to be driven out of the community, because they have broken the regulations about ritual uncleanness.

19 If a man has intercourse with his aunt, both of them must suffer the consequences for incest. 20 If a man has intercourse with his uncle's wife, he disgraces his uncle, and he and the woman will pay the penalty; neither of them will have children. 21 If a man marries his brother's wife, they will die childless. He has done a ritually unclean thing and has disgraced his brother.

22 The LORD said, "Keep all my laws and commands, so that you will not be rejected by the land of Canaan, into which I am bringing you. 23 Do not adopt the customs of people who live

LEVITICUS 20, 21

153

Leviticus
..........:.

Num.
Deuter.
Joshua
Judges
Ruth

there; I am driving out those pagans so that you can enter the land. They have disgusted me with all their evil practices. ²⁴But I have promised you this rich and fertile land as your possession, and I will give it to you. I am the LORD your God, and I have set you apart from the other nations. ²⁵So then, you must make a clear distinction between animals and birds that are ritually clean and those that are not. Do not eat unclean animals or birds. I have declared them unclean, and eating them would make you unclean. ²⁶You shall be holy and belong only to me, because I am the LORD and I am holy. I have set you apart from the other nations so that you would belong to me alone.

²⁷"Any man or woman who consults the spirits of the dead shall be stoned to death; any person who does this is responsible for his own death."

The Holiness of the Priests

21 The LORD commanded Moses to say to the Aaronite priests, "No priest is to make himself ritually unclean by taking part in the funeral ceremonies when a relative dies, ²unless it is his mother, father, son, daughter, brother, ³or unmarried sister living in his house. ⁴He shall not make himself unclean at the death of those related to him by marriage.*

⁵"No priest shall shave any part of his head or trim his beard or cut gashes on his body to show that he is in mourning. ⁶He must be holy and must not disgrace my name. He offers food offerings to me, and he must be holy. ⁷A priest shall not marry a woman who has been a prostitute or a woman who is not a virgin or who is divorced; he is holy. ⁸The people must consider the priest holy, because he presents the food offerings to me. I am the LORD; I am holy and I make my people holy. ⁹If a priest's daughter becomes a prostitute, she disgraces her father; she shall be burnt to death.

¹⁰"The High Priest has had the anointing oil poured on his head and has been consecrated to wear the priestly garments, so he must not leave his hair uncombed or tear his clothes to show that he is in mourning. ¹¹⁻¹²He has been dedicated to me and is not to make himself ritually unclean nor is he to defile my sacred Tent by leaving it and entering a house where there is a dead person, even if it is his own father or mother. ¹³He shall marry a virgin, ¹⁴not a widow or a divorced woman or a woman who has been a prostitute. He shall marry only a virgin from his own clan. ¹⁵Otherwise, his children, who ought to be holy, will be ritually unclean. I am the LORD and I have set him apart as the High Priest."

¹⁶The LORD commanded Moses ¹⁷to say to Aaron, "None of your descendants who has any physical defect may present the food offering to me. This applies for all time to come. ¹⁸No man with any physical defect may make the offering: no one who is blind, lame, disfigured, or deformed; ¹⁹no one with a crippled hand or foot; ²⁰no one who is a hunchback or a dwarf; no one with any eye or skin disease; and no eunuch. ²¹No descendant of Aaron the priest who has any physical defect may present the food offering to me. ²²Such a man may eat the food offered to me, both the holy food offering and the very holy food offering, ²³but because he has a physical defect, he shall not come near the sacred curtain or approach the altar. He must not profane these holy things, because I am the LORD and I make them holy."

²⁴This, then, is what Moses said to Aaron, the sons of Aaron, and to all the people of Israel.

....

21.4 Verse 4 in Hebrew is unclear.

LEVITICUS 22.2

Much of Leviticus
revolves around the
fact that God is holy.
– HOLY MEANS –
'SET APART'.

God is set apart because
he is perfect. Take
a moment to close this
book and reflect on how
magnificent, holy
and perfect God is.

The Holiness of the Offerings

22 The LORD commanded Moses ²to say to Aaron and his sons, "You must not bring disgrace on my holy name, so treat with respect the sacred offerings that the people of Israel dedicate to me. I am the LORD. ³If any of your descendants, while he is ritually unclean, comes near the sacred offerings which the people of Israel have dedicated to me, he can never again serve at the altar. This applies for all time to come. I am the LORD.

⁴"None of the descendants of Aaron who has a dreaded skin disease or a discharge may eat any of the sacred offerings until he is ritually clean. Any priest is unclean if he touches anything which is unclean through contact with a corpse or if he has an emission of semen ⁵or if he has touched an unclean animal or person. ⁶Any priest who becomes unclean remains unclean until evening, and even then he may not eat any of the sacred offerings until he has had a bath. ⁷After the sun sets he is clean, and then he may eat the sacred offerings, which are his food. ⁸He shall not eat the meat of any animal that has died a natural death or has been killed by wild animals; it will make him unclean. I am the LORD.

⁹"All priests shall observe the regulations that I have given. Otherwise, they will be guilty and die, because they have disobeyed the sacred regulations. I am the LORD and I make them holy.

¹⁰"Only a member of a priestly family may eat any of the sacred offerings; no one else may eat them — not even someone staying with a priest or hired by him. ¹¹But a priest's slaves, bought with his own money or born in his home, may eat the food the priest receives. ¹²A priest's daughter who marries someone who is not a priest may not eat any of the sacred offerings. ¹³But a widowed or divorced daughter who has no children and who has returned to live in her father's house as a dependant may eat the food her father receives as a priest. Only a member of a priestly family may eat any of it.

¹⁴"If any person who is not a member of a priestly family eats any of the sacred offerings without intending to, he must repay the priest its full value plus an additional twenty per cent. ¹⁵The priests shall not profane the sacred offerings ¹⁶by letting any unauthorized person eat them; this would bring guilt and punishment on such a person. I am the LORD and I make the offerings holy."

¹⁷The LORD commanded Moses ¹⁸to give Aaron and his sons and all the people of Israel the following regulations. When any Israelite or any foreigner living in Israel presents a burnt offering, whether in fulfilment of a vow or as a freewill offering, the animal must not have any defects. ¹⁹To be accepted, it must be a male without any defects. ²⁰If you offer any animal that has any defect, the LORD will not accept it. ²¹When anyone presents a fellowship offering to the LORD, whether in fulfilment of a vow or as a freewill offering, the animal must be without any defect if it is to be accepted. ²²Do not offer to the LORD any animal that is blind or crippled or mutilated, or that has a running sore or a skin eruption or scabs. Do not offer any such animals on the altar as a food offering. ²³As a freewill offering you may offer an animal that is stunted or not perfectly formed, but it is not acceptable in fulfilment of a vow. ²⁴Do not offer to the LORD any animal whose testicles have been crushed, cut, bruised, or torn off. This is not permitted in your land.

²⁵Do not offer as a food offering any animal obtained from a foreigner. Such animals are considered defective and are not acceptable.

²⁶⁻²⁷When a calf or a lamb or a kid is born, it must not be taken from its mother for seven days, but after that it is acceptable as

LEVITICUS 22, 23

155

Leviticus
............:

Num.
Deuter.
Joshua
Judges
Ruth

a food offering. [28] Do not sacrifice a cow and its calf or a sheep and its lamb or a goat and its kid on the same day. [29] When you offer a sacrifice of thanksgiving to the Lord, follow the rules so that you will be accepted; [30] eat it the same day and leave none of it until the next morning.

[31] The Lord said, "Obey my commands; I am the Lord. [32] Do not bring disgrace on my holy name; all the people of Israel must acknowledge me to be holy. I am the Lord and I make you holy; [33] and I brought you out of Egypt to become your God. I am the Lord."

The Religious Festivals

23 The Lord gave Moses [2] the following regulations for the religious festivals, when the people of Israel are to gather for worship. [3] You have six days in which to do your work, but remember that the seventh day, the Sabbath, is a day of rest. On that day do not work, but gather for worship. The Sabbath belongs to the Lord, no matter where you live. [4] Proclaim the following festivals at the appointed times.

Passover and Unleavened Bread
(Num 28.16–25)

[5] The Passover, celebrated to honour the Lord, begins at sunset on the fourteenth day of the first month. [6] On the fifteenth day the Festival of Unleavened Bread begins, and for seven days you must not eat any bread made with yeast. [7] On the first of these days you shall gather for worship and do none of your daily work. [8] Offer your food offerings to the Lord for seven days. On the seventh day you shall again gather for worship, but you shall do none of your daily work.

[9-10] When you come into the land that the Lord is giving you and you harvest your corn, take the first sheaf to the priest. [11] He shall present it as a special offering to the Lord, so that you may be accepted. The priest shall present it the day after the Sabbath. [12] On the day you present the offering of corn, also sacrifice as a burnt offering a one-year-old male lamb that has no defects. [13] With it you shall present two kilogrammes of flour mixed with olive oil as a food offering. The smell of this offering is pleasing to the Lord. You shall also present with it an offering of one litre of wine. [14] Do not eat any of the new corn, whether raw, roasted, or baked into bread, until you have brought this offering to God. This regulation is to be observed by all your descendants for all time to come.

The Harvest Festival
(Num 28.26–31)

[15] Count seven full weeks from the day after the Sabbath on which you bring your sheaf of corn to present to the Lord. [16] On the fiftieth day, the day after the seventh Sabbath, present to the Lord another new offering of corn. [17] Each family is to bring two loaves of bread and present them to the Lord as a special gift. Each loaf shall be made of two kilogrammes of flour baked with yeast and shall be presented to the Lord as an offering of the first corn to be harvested. [18] And with the bread the community is to present seven one-year-old lambs, one bull, and two rams, none of which may have any defects. They shall be offered as a burnt offering to the Lord, together with a grain offering and a wine offering. The smell of this offering is pleasing to the Lord. [19] Also offer one male goat as a sin offering and two one-year-old male lambs as a fellowship offering. [20] The priest shall present the bread

with the two lambs as a special gift to the LORD for the priests. These offerings are holy. ²¹On that day do none of your daily work, but gather for worship. Your descendants are to observe this regulation for all time to come, no matter where they live.

²²When you harvest your fields, do not cut the corn at the edges of the fields, and do not go back to cut the ears of corn that were left; leave them for poor people and foreigners. The LORD is your God.

The New Year Festival
(Num 29.1–6)

²³⁻²⁴On the first day of the seventh month observe a special day of rest, and come together for worship when the trumpets sound. ²⁵Present a food offering to the LORD and do none of your daily work.

The Day of Atonement
(Num 29.7–11)

²⁶⁻²⁷The tenth day of the seventh month is the day when the annual ritual is to be performed to take away the sins of the people. On that day do not eat anything at all; come together for worship, and present a food offering to the Lord. ²⁸Do no work on that day, because it is the day for performing the ritual to take away sin. ²⁹Anyone who eats anything on that day will no longer be considered one of God's people. ³⁰And if anyone does any work on that day, the LORD himself will put him to death. ³¹This regulation applies to all your descendants, no matter where they live. ³²From sunset on the ninth day of the month to sunset on the tenth observe this day as a special day of rest, during which nothing may be eaten.

The Festival of Shelters
(Num 29.12–40)

³³⁻³⁴The Festival of Shelters begins on the fifteenth day of the seventh month and continues for seven days. ³⁵On the first of these days come together for worship and do none of your daily work. ³⁶Each day for seven days you shall present a food offering. On the eighth day come together again for worship and present a food offering. It is a day for worship, and you shall do no work.

³⁷(These are the religious festivals on which you honour the LORD by gathering together for worship and presenting food offerings, burnt offerings, grain offerings, sacrifices, and wine offerings, as required day by day. ³⁸These festivals are in addition to the regular Sabbaths, and these offerings are in addition to your regular gifts, your offerings in fulfilment of vows, and your freewill offerings that you give to the LORD.)

³⁹When you have harvested your fields, celebrate this festival for seven days, beginning on the fifteenth day of the seventh month. The first day shall be a special day of rest. ⁴⁰On that day take some of the best fruit from your trees, take palm branches and the branches of leafy trees, and begin a religious festival to honour the LORD your God. ⁴¹Celebrate it for seven days. This regulation is to be kept by your descendants for all time to come. ⁴²All the people of Israel shall live in shelters for seven days, ⁴³so that your descendants may know that the LORD made the people of Israel live in simple shelters when he led them out of Egypt. He is the LORD your God.

⁴⁴So in this way Moses gave the people of Israel the regulations for observing the religious festivals to honour the LORD.

Leviticus
....
Num.
Deuter.
Joshua
Judges
Ruth

Taking Care of the Lamps
(Ex 27.20–21)

24 The LORD told Moses [2] to give the following orders to the people of Israel: Bring pure olive oil of the finest quality for the lamps in the Tent, so that a light may be kept burning regularly. [3] Each evening Aaron shall light them and keep them burning until morning, there in the LORD's presence outside the curtain in front of the Covenant Box, which is in the Most Holy Place. This regulation is to be observed for all time to come. [4] Aaron shall take care of the lamps on the lampstand of pure gold and must see that they burn regularly in the LORD's presence.

The Bread Offered to God

[5] Take twelve kilogrammes of flour and bake twelve loaves of bread. [6] Put the loaves in two rows, six in each row, on the table covered with pure gold, which is in the LORD's presence. [7] Put some pure incense on each row, as a token food offering to the LORD to take the place of the bread. [8] Every Sabbath, for all time to come, the bread must be placed in the presence of the LORD. This is Israel's duty for ever. [9] The bread belongs to Aaron and his descendants, and they shall eat it in a holy place, because this is a very holy part of the food offered to the LORD for the priests.

An Example of Just and Fair Punishment

[10-11] There was a man whose father was an Egyptian and whose mother was an Israelite named Shelomith, the daughter of Dibri from the tribe of Dan. There in the camp this man quarrelled with an Israelite. During the quarrel he cursed God, so they took him to Moses, [12] put him under guard, and waited for the LORD to tell them what to do with him.

[13] The LORD said to Moses, [14] "Take that man out of the camp. Everyone who heard him curse shall put his hands on the man's head to testify that he is guilty, and then the whole community shall stone him to death. [15] Then tell the people of Israel that anyone who curses God must suffer the consequences [16] and be put to death. Any Israelite or any foreigner living in Israel who curses the LORD shall be stoned to death by the whole community.

[17] "Anyone who commits murder shall be put to death, [18] and anyone who kills an animal belonging to someone else must replace it. The principle is a life for a life.

[19] "If anyone injures another person, whatever he has done shall be done to him. [20] If he breaks a bone, one of his bones shall be broken; if he blinds him in one eye, one of his eyes shall be blinded; if he knocks out a tooth, one of his teeth shall be knocked out. Whatever injury he causes another person shall be done to him in return. [21] Whoever kills an animal shall replace it, but whoever kills a human being shall be put to death. [22] This law applies to all of you, to Israelites and to foreigners living among you, because I am the LORD your God."

[23] When Moses had said this to the people of Israel, they took the man outside the camp and stoned him to death. In this way the people of Israel did what the LORD had commanded Moses.

The Seventh Year
(Deut 15.1–11)

25 The LORD spoke to Moses on Mount Sinai and commanded him [2] to give the following regulations to the people of Israel. When you enter the land that the LORD is giving you, you shall honour the LORD by not cultivating the land every seventh year. ³You shall sow your fields, prune your vineyards, and gather your crops for six years. ⁴But the seventh year is to be a year of complete rest for the land, a year dedicated to the LORD. Do not sow your fields or prune your vineyards. ⁵Do not even harvest the corn that grows by itself without being sown, and do not gather the grapes from your unpruned vines; it is a year of complete rest for the land. ⁶Although the land has not been cultivated during that year, it will provide food for you, your slaves, your hired men, the foreigners living with you, ⁷your domestic animals, and the wild animals in your fields. Everything that it produces may be eaten.

The Year of Restoration

⁸Count seven times seven years, a total of 49 years. ⁹Then, on the tenth day of the seventh month, the Day of Atonement, send someone to blow a trumpet throughout the whole land. ¹⁰In this way you shall set the fiftieth year apart and proclaim freedom to all the inhabitants of the land. During this year all property that has been sold shall be restored to the original owner or his descendants, and anyone who has been sold as a slave shall return to his family. ¹¹You shall not sow your fields or harvest the corn that grows by itself or gather the grapes in your unpruned vineyards. ¹²The whole year shall be sacred for you; you shall eat only what the fields produce of themselves.

¹³In this year all property that has been sold shall be restored to its original owner. ¹⁴So when you sell land to your fellow-Israelite or buy land from him, do not deal unfairly. ¹⁵The price is to be fixed according to the number of years the land can produce crops before the next Year of Restoration. ¹⁶If there are many years, the price shall be higher, but if there are only a few years, the price shall be lower, because what is being sold is the number of crops the land can produce. ¹⁷Do not cheat a fellow-Israelite, but obey the LORD your God.

The Problem of the Seventh Year

¹⁸Obey all the LORD's laws and commands, so that you may live in safety in the land. ¹⁹The land will produce its crops, and you will have all you want to eat and will live in safety.

²⁰But someone may ask what there will be to eat during the seventh year, when no fields are sown and no crops gathered. ²¹The LORD will bless the land in the sixth year so that it will produce enough food for two years. ²²When you sow your fields in the eighth year, you will still be eating what you harvested during the sixth year, and you will have enough to eat until the crops you plant that year are harvested.

Restoration of Property

²³Your land must not be sold on a permanent basis, because you do not own it; it belongs to God, and you are like foreigners who are allowed to make use of it.

²⁴When land is sold, the right of the original owner to buy it back must be recognized. ²⁵If an Israelite becomes poor and is forced to sell his land, his closest relative is to buy it back. ²⁶Anyone who has no relative to buy it back may later become prosperous and have enough to buy it back. ²⁷In that case he must pay to the man who bought it a sum that will make up for the years remaining until the next Year of Restoration, when he would in any event recover his land. ²⁸But if he does not have enough money to buy the land back, it remains under the control of the man who bought it until the next Year of Restoration. In that year it will be returned to its original owner.

LEVITICUS 25.8

The Year of Restoration (also called the Jubilee) was a countercultural celebration in which debts were forgiven and slaves freed. It was about

GENEROSITY &
FORGIVENESS.

Make a note of two people, one you might need to forgive and one you can be generous to. This week, forgive and be generous to them.

 1.

 2.

LEVITICUS 25

159

Leviticus

...........:-

Num.

Deuter.

Joshua

Judges

Ruth

29 If someone sells a house in a walled city, he has the right to buy it back during the first full year from the date of sale. 30 But if he does not buy it back within the year, he loses the right of repurchase, and the house becomes the permanent property of the purchaser and his descendants; it will not be returned in the Year of Restoration. 31 But houses in unwalled villages are to be treated like fields; the original owner has the right to buy them back, and they are to be returned in the Year of Restoration. 32 However, Levites have the right to buy back at any time their property in the cities assigned to them. 33 If a house in one of these cities is sold by a Levite and is not bought back, it must be returned in the Year of Restoration,* because the houses which the Levites own in their cities are their permanent property among the people of Israel. 34 But the pasture land round the Levite cities shall never be sold; it is their property for ever.

Loans to the Poor

35 If a fellow-Israelite living near you becomes poor and cannot support himself or herself, you must provide for them as you would for hired servants, so that they can continue to live near you. 36 Do not charge them any interest, but obey God and let your fellow-Israelites live near you. 37 Do not make them pay interest on the money you lend them, and do not make a profit on the food you sell them. 38 This is the command of the LORD your God, who brought you out of Egypt in order to give you the land of Canaan and to be your God.

Release of Slaves

39 If a fellow-Israelite living near you becomes so poor that he sells himself to you as a slave, you shall not make him do the work of a slave. 40 He shall stay with you as a hired servant and serve you until the next Year of Restoration. 41 At that time he and his children shall leave you and return to his family and to the property of his ancestors. 42 The people of Israel are the LORD's slaves, and he brought them out of Egypt; they must not be sold into slavery. 43 Do not treat them harshly, but obey your God. 44 If you need slaves, you may buy them from the nations round you. 45 You may also buy the children of the foreigners who are living among you. Such children born in your land may become your property, 46 and you may leave them as an inheritance to your sons, whom they must serve as long as they live. But you must not treat any of your fellow-Israelites harshly.

47 Suppose a foreigner living with you becomes rich, while a fellow-Israelite becomes poor and sells himself as a slave to that foreigner or to a member of his family. 48 After he is sold, he still has the right to be bought back. One of his brothers 49 or his uncle or his cousin or another of his close relatives may buy him back; or if he himself earns enough, he may buy his own freedom. 50 He must consult the one who bought him, and they must count the years from the time he sold himself until the next Year of Restoration and must set the price for his release on the basis of the wages paid to a hired servant. 51-52 He must refund a part of the purchase price according to the number of years left, 53 as if he had been hired on an annual basis. His master must not treat him harshly. 54 If he is not set free in any of these ways, he and his children must be set free in the next Year of Restoration. 55 An Israelite cannot be a permanent slave, because the people of Israel are the LORD's slaves. He brought them out of Egypt; he is the LORD their God.

....

25.33 Probable text *If a house… Restoration*; Hebrew unclear.

160

Leviticus

.:.........

Genesis

Exodus

LEVITICUS 26

Blessings for Obedience
(Deut 7.12–24; 28.1–14)

26 The LORD said, "Do not make idols or set up statues, stone pillars, or carved stones to worship. I am the LORD your God. ² Keep the religious festivals and honour the place where I am worshipped. I am the LORD.

³ "If you live according to my laws and obey my commands, ⁴ I will send you rain at the right time, so that the land will produce crops and the trees will bear fruit. ⁵ Your crops will be so plentiful that you will still be harvesting corn when it is time to pick grapes, and you will still be picking grapes when it is time to sow corn. You will have all that you want to eat, and you will live in safety in your land.

⁶ "I will give you peace in your land, and you will sleep without being afraid of anyone. I will get rid of the dangerous animals in the land, and there will be no more war there. ⁷ You will be victorious over your enemies; ⁸ five of you will be able to defeat a hundred, and a hundred will be able to defeat 10,000. ⁹ I will bless you and give you many children; I will keep my part of the covenant that I made with you. ¹⁰ Your harvests will be so plentiful that they will last for a year, and even then you will have to throw away what is left of the old harvest to make room for the new. ¹¹ I will live among you in my sacred tent, and I will never turn away from you. ¹² I will be with you; I will be your God, and you will be my people. ¹³ I, the LORD your God, brought you out of Egypt so that you would no longer be slaves. I broke the power that held you down and I let you walk with your head held high."

Punishment for Disobedience
(Deut 28.15–68)

¹⁴ The LORD said, "If you will not obey my commands, you will be punished. ¹⁵ If you refuse to obey my laws and commands and break the covenant I have made with you, ¹⁶ I will punish you. I will bring disaster on you — incurable diseases and fevers that will make you blind and cause your life to waste away. You will sow your seed, but it will do you no good, because your enemies will conquer you and eat what you have grown. ¹⁷ I will turn against you, so that you will be defeated, and those who hate you will rule over you; you will be so terrified that you will run when no one is chasing you.

¹⁸ "If even after all this you still do not obey me, I will increase your punishment seven times. ¹⁹ I will break your stubborn pride; there will be no rain, and your land will be dry and as hard as iron. ²⁰ All your hard work will do you no good, because your land will not produce crops and the trees will not bear fruit.

²¹ "If you still continue to resist me and refuse to obey me, I will again increase your punishment seven times. ²² I will send dangerous animals among you, and they will kill your children, destroy your livestock, and leave so few of you that your roads will be deserted.

²³ "If after all this punishment you still do not listen to me, but continue to defy me, ²⁴ then I will turn on you and punish you seven times harder than before. ²⁵ I will bring war on you to punish you for breaking our covenant, and if you gather in your cities for safety, I will send incurable diseases among you, and you will be forced to surrender to your enemies. ²⁶ I will cut off your food supply, so that ten women will need only one oven to bake all the bread they have. They will ration it out, and when you have eaten it all, you will still be hungry.

²⁷ "If after all this you still continue to defy me and refuse to obey me, ²⁸ then in my anger I will turn on you and again make

LEVITICUS 26, 27

161

Leviticus

............:.

Num.
Deuter.
Joshua
Judges
Ruth

your punishment seven times worse than before. 29 Your hunger will be so great that you will eat your own children. 30 I will destroy your places of worship on the hills, tear down your incense altars, and throw your dead bodies on your fallen idols. In utter disgust 31 I will turn your cities into ruins, destroy your places of worship, and refuse to accept your sacrifices. 32 I will destroy your land so completely that the enemies who occupy it will be shocked at the destruction. 33 I will bring war on you and scatter you in foreign lands. Your land will be deserted, and your cities left in ruins. 34-35 Then the land will enjoy the years of complete rest that you would not give it; it will lie abandoned and get its rest while you are in exile in the land of your enemies.

36 "I will make those of you who are in exile so terrified that the sound of a leaf blowing in the wind will make you run. You will run as if you were being pursued in battle, and you will fall when there is no enemy near you. 37 You will stumble over one another when no one is chasing you, and you will be unable to fight against any enemy. 38 You will die in exile, swallowed up by the land of your enemies. 39 The few of you who survive in the land of your enemies will waste away because of your own sin and the sin of your ancestors.

40 "But your descendants will confess their sins and the sins of their ancestors, who resisted me and rebelled against me, 41 and made me turn against them and send them into exile in the land of their enemies. At last, when your descendants are humbled and they have paid the penalty for their sin and rebellion, 42 I will remember my covenant with Jacob and with Isaac and with Abraham, and I will renew my promise to give my people the land. 43 First, however, the land must be rid of its people, so that it can enjoy its complete rest, and they must pay the full penalty for having rejected my laws and my commands. 44 But even then, when they are still in the land of their enemies, I will not completely abandon or destroy them. That would put an end to my covenant with them, and I am the LORD their God. 45 I will renew the covenant that I made with their ancestors when I showed all the nations my power by bringing my people out of Egypt, in order that I, the LORD, might be their God."

46 All these are the laws and commands that the LORD gave to Moses on Mount Sinai for the people of Israel.

Laws concerning Gifts to the LORD

27 The LORD gave Moses 2 the following regulations for the people of Israel. When a person has been given to the LORD in fulfilment of a special vow, that person may be set free by the payment of the following sums of money, 3-7 according to the official standard:

— adult male, twenty to sixty years old: fifty pieces of silver
— adult female: thirty pieces of silver
— young male, five to twenty years old: twenty pieces of silver
— young female: ten pieces of silver
— infant male under five: five pieces of silver
— infant female: three pieces of silver
— male above sixty years of age: fifteen pieces of silver
— female above sixty: ten pieces of silver.

8 If anyone who made the vow is too poor to pay the standard price, he or she shall bring the person to the priest, and the priest will set a lower price, according to the ability of that person to pay.

⁹ If the vow concerns an animal that is acceptable as an offering to the Lord, then every gift made to the Lord is sacred, ¹⁰ and anyone who made the vow may not substitute another animal for it. If he does, both animals belong to the Lord. ¹¹ But if the vow concerns a ritually unclean animal, which is not acceptable as an offering to the Lord, the man shall take the animal to the priest. ¹² The priest shall fix a price for it, according to its good or bad qualities, and the price will be final. ¹³ If the person wishes to buy it back, he must pay the price plus an additional twenty per cent.

¹⁴ When someone dedicates his house to the Lord, the priest shall fix the price according to its good or bad points, and the price will be final. ¹⁵ If the one who dedicated the house wishes to buy it back, he must pay the price plus an additional twenty per cent.

¹⁶ If someone dedicates part of his land to the Lord, the price shall be fixed according to the amount of seed it takes to sow it, at the rate of ten pieces of silver for every twenty kilogrammes of barley. ¹⁷ If he dedicates the land immediately after a Year of Restoration, the full price applies. ¹⁸ If he dedicates it later, the priest shall estimate the cash value according to the number of years left until the next Year of Restoration, and fix a reduced price. ¹⁹ If the one who dedicated the field wishes to buy it back, he or she must pay the price plus an additional twenty per cent. ²⁰ If they sell the field to someone else without first buying it back from the Lord, they lose the right to buy it back. ²¹ At the next Year of Restoration the field will become the Lord's permanent property; it shall belong to the priests.

²² If someone dedicates to the Lord a field that he has bought, ²³ the priest shall estimate its value according to the number of years until the next Year of Restoration, and the person must pay the price that very day; the money belongs to the Lord. ²⁴ At the Year of Restoration the field shall be returned to the original owner or to his descendants.

²⁵ All prices shall be fixed according to the official standard.

²⁶ The firstborn of an animal already belongs to the Lord, so no one may dedicate it to him as a freewill offering. A calf, a lamb, or a kid belongs to the Lord, ²⁷ but the firstborn of an unclean animal may be bought back at the standard price plus an additional twenty per cent. If it is not bought back, it may be sold to someone else at the standard price.

²⁸ No one may sell or buy back what he has unconditionally dedicated* to the Lord, whether it is a human being, an animal, or land. It belongs permanently to the Lord. ²⁹ Not even a human being who has been unconditionally dedicated may be bought back; he must be put to death.

³⁰ One-tenth of all the produce of the land, whether grain or fruit, belongs to the Lord. ³¹ If a man wishes to buy any of it back, he must pay the standard price plus an additional twenty per cent. ³² One out of every ten domestic animals belongs to the Lord. When the animals are counted, every tenth one belongs to the Lord. ³³ The owner may not arrange the animals so that the poor animals are chosen, and he may not make any substitutions. If he does substitute one animal for another, then both animals will belong to the Lord and may not be bought back.

³⁴ These are the commands that the Lord gave Moses on Mount Sinai for the people of Israel.

....

27.28 *unconditionally dedicated*: Anything dedicated in this way belonged completely to the Lord and could not be used; it had to be destroyed.

THE BOOK OF
NUMBERS

PROBABLY 600-400BC
(USING STORIES FROM A MUCH EARLIER TIME)

WHY READ IT?

Every generation, including yours, must choose to take its stand with God. Even though a whole generation was forbidden by God to enter the Promised Land because of their disobedience, a new generation was being raised up to claim the inheritance. Like the Israelites, we often switch between obedience and rebellion. This book teaches us the results of these two choices.

WHAT YOU NEED TO KNOW:

The book of Numbers does contain quite a few numbers (for example, it records the number of Israelites who were wandering in the wilderness with Moses). But really it is about how a group of unruly and uneducated people were trained and matured into the people God wanted them to be. Numbers takes us on the journey of the Israelites caught in the wilderness, continuing to switch between obeying God and disobeying him. Regardless of their behaviour, God continued to show favour and faithfulness to his people.

Find the story of

CALEB
AND
JOSHUA

in chapters 13-14.
Summarise the story here. ↗

Find all the moments in Numbers when the Israelites make mistakes, and put a mark next to them. Then find the moments when God provides for the Israelites and, in another colour, put a mark next to them.

1400BC — SPIES SENT INTO CANAAN — 1300BC

WILDERNESS   AARON AND MIRIAM DIE

164

Num.

Genesis
Exodus
Leviticus

NUMBERS 1

NUMBERS 1-2

• DON'T BE •
PUT OFF
BY THE TITLE

- this isn't just a book full of numbers! There are lots of numbers in the first two chapters because God commanded a census to be taken, to see how big Israel's army was. In fact, in Hebrew (the original language of the Old Testament), this book isn't called Numbers at all. It's called Bemidbar, meaning 'In the desert'. It is a book about God's people wandering through the desert towards a promise.

The First Census of Israel

1 On the first day of the second month in the second year after the people of Israel left Egypt, the LORD spoke to Moses there in the Tent of his presence in the Sinai Desert. He said, ²"You and Aaron are to take a census of the people of Israel by clans and families. List the names of all the men ³twenty years old or older who are fit for military service. ⁴Ask one clan chief from each tribe to help you." ⁵⁻¹⁶ These are the men, leaders within their tribes, who were chosen from the community for this work:

Tribe	Clan chief
Reuben	Elizur son of Shedeur
Simeon	Shelumiel son of Zurishaddai
Judah	Nahshon son of Amminadab
Issachar	Nethanel son of Zuar
Zebulun	Eliab son of Helon
Ephraim	Elishama son of Ammihud
Manasseh	Gamaliel son of Pedahzur
Benjamin	Abidan son of Gideoni
Dan	Ahiezer son of Ammishaddai
Asher	Pagiel son of Ochran
Gad	Eliasaph son of Deuel
Naphtali	Ahira son of Enan

¹⁷With the help of these twelve men Moses and Aaron ¹⁸called together the whole community on the first day of the second month and registered all the people by clans and families. The names of all the men twenty years old or older were recorded and counted, ¹⁹as the LORD had commanded. In the Sinai Desert, Moses registered the people. ²⁰⁻⁴⁶The men twenty years old or older who were fit for military service were registered by name according to clan and family, beginning with the tribe of Reuben, Jacob's eldest son. The totals were as follows:

Tribe	Number
Reuben	46,500
Simeon	59,300
Gad	45,650
Judah	74,600
Issachar	54,400
Zebulun	57,400
Ephraim	40,500
Manasseh	32,200
Benjamin	35,400
Dan	62,700
Asher	41,500
Naphtali	53,400
Total:	603,550

⁴⁷The Levites were not registered with the other tribes, ⁴⁸because the LORD had said to Moses, ⁴⁹"When you take a census of the men fit for military service, do not include the tribe of Levi. ⁵⁰Instead, put the Levites in charge of the Tent of my presence and all its equipment. They shall carry it and its equipment, serve in it, and set up their camp round it. ⁵¹Whenever you move your camp, the Levites shall take the Tent down and set it up again at each new camping place. Anyone else who comes near the Tent shall be put to death. ⁵²The rest of the Israelites shall set

165

Num.

....

Deuter.
Joshua
Judges
Ruth
1 Sam.

up camp, company by company, each man with his own group and under his own banner. [53] But the Levites shall camp round the Tent to guard it, so that no one may come near and cause my anger to strike the community of Israel." [54] So the people of Israel did everything that the LORD had commanded Moses.

The Arrangement of the Tribes in Camp

2 The LORD gave Moses and Aaron the following instructions. [2] When the Israelites set up camp, each man will camp under the banner of his division and the flag of his own clan. The camp is to be set up all round the Tent.

[3-9] On the east side, those under the banner of the division of Judah shall camp in their groups, under their leaders, as follows:

Tribe	Leader	Number
Judah	Nahshon son of Amminadab	74,600
Issachar	Nethanel son of Zuar	54,400
Zebulun	Eliab son of Helon	57,400
	Total:	186,400

The division of Judah shall march first.

[10-16] On the south, those under the banner of the division of Reuben shall camp in their groups, under their leaders, as follows:

Tribe	Leader	Number
Reuben	Elizur son of Shedeur	46,500
Simeon	Shelumiel son of Zurishaddai	59,300
Gad	Eliasaph son of Deuel	45,650
	Total:	151,450

The division of Reuben shall march second.

[17] Then, between the first two divisions and the last two the Levites are to march carrying the Tent. Each division shall march in the same order as they camp, each in position under its banner.

[18-24] On the west, those under the banner of the division of Ephraim shall camp in their groups, under their leaders, as follows:

Tribe	Leader	Number
Ephraim	Elishama son of Ammihud	40,500
Manasseh	Gamaliel son of Pedahzur	32,200
Benjamin	Abidan son of Gideoni	35,400
	Total:	108,100

The division of Ephraim shall march third.

[25-31] On the north, those under the banner of the division of Dan shall camp in their groups, under their leaders, as follows:

Tribe	Leader	Number
Dan	Ahiezer son of Ammishaddai	62,700
Asher	Pagiel son of Ochran	41,500
Naphtali	Ahira son of Enan	53,400
	Total:	157,600

The division of Dan shall march last.

[32] The total number of the people of Israel enrolled in the divisions, group by group, was 603,550. [33] As the LORD had commanded Moses, the Levites were not registered with the rest of the Israelites.

34 So the people of Israel did everything the LORD had commanded Moses. They camped, each under his own banner, and they marched, each with his own clan.

Aaron's Sons

3 This is the family of Aaron and Moses at the time the LORD spoke to Moses on Mount Sinai. 2 Aaron had four sons: Nadab, the eldest, Abihu, Eleazar, and Ithamar. 3 They were anointed and ordained as priests, 4 but Nadab and Abihu were killed when they offered unholy fire to the LORD in the Sinai Desert. They had no children, so Eleazar and Ithamar served as priests during Aaron's lifetime.

The Levites are Appointed to Serve the Priests

5 The LORD said to Moses, 6 "Bring forward the tribe of Levi and appoint them as servants of Aaron the priest. 7 They shall do the work required for the Tent of my presence and perform duties for the priests and for the whole community. 8 They shall take charge of all the equipment of the Tent and perform the duties for the rest of the Israelites. 9 The only responsibility the Levites have is to serve Aaron and his sons. 10 You shall appoint Aaron and his sons to carry out the duties of the priesthood; anyone else who tries to do so shall be put to death."

11 The LORD said to Moses, 12-13 "The Levites are now to be mine. When I killed all the firstborn of the Egyptians, I consecrated as my own the eldest son of each Israelite family and the firstborn of every animal. Now, instead of having the firstborn sons of Israel as my own, I have the Levites; they will belong to me. I am the LORD."

The Census of the Levites

14 In the Sinai Desert the LORD commanded Moses 15 to register the Levites by clans and families, enrolling every male a month old or older, 16 and Moses did so. 17-20 Levi had three sons: Gershon, Kohath, and Merari, who were the ancestors of the clans that bear their names. Gershon had two sons: Libni and Shimei; Kohath had four sons: Amram, Izhar, Hebron, and Uzziel; and Merari had two sons: Mahli and Mushi. They were the ancestors of the families that bear their names.

21 The clan of Gershon was composed of the families of Libni and Shimei. 22 The total number of males one month old or older that were enrolled was 7,500. 23 This clan was to camp on the west behind the Tent, 24 with Eliasaph son of Lael as chief of the clan. 25 They were responsible for the Tent, its inner cover, its outer cover, the curtain for the entrance, 26 the curtains for the court which is round the Tent and the altar, and the curtain for the entrance of the court. They were responsible for all the service connected with these items.

27 The clan of Kohath was composed of the families of Amram, Izhar, Hebron, and Uzziel. 28 The total number of males one month old or older that were enrolled was 8,600. 29 This clan was to camp on the south side of the Tent, 30 with Elizaphan son of Uzziel as chief of the clan. 31 They were responsible for the Covenant Box, the table, the lampstand, the altars, the utensils the priests use in the Holy Place, and the curtain at the entrance to the Most Holy Place. They were responsible for all the service connected with these items.

32 The chief of the Levites was Eleazar son of Aaron the priest. He was in charge of those who carried out the duties in the Holy Place.

NUMBERS 3, 4

167

Num.

....

Deuter.
Joshua
Judges
Ruth
1 Sam.

³³ The clan of Merari was composed of the families of Mahli and Mushi. ³⁴ The total number of males one month old or older that were enrolled was 6,200. ³⁵ This clan was to camp on the north side of the Tent, with Zuriel son of Abihail as chief of the clan. ³⁶ They were assigned responsibility for the frames for the Tent, its bars, posts, bases, and all its fittings. They were responsible for all the service connected with these items. ³⁷ They were also responsible for the posts, bases, pegs, and ropes for the outer court.

³⁸ Moses and Aaron and his sons were to camp in front of the Tent on the east. They were responsible for carrying out the services performed in the Holy Place for the people of Israel. Anyone else who tried to do so was to be put to death. ³⁹ The total number of all the Levite males one month old or older that Moses enrolled by clans at the command of the LORD, was 22,000.

The Levites Take the Place of the Firstborn Sons

⁴⁰⁻⁴¹ The LORD said to Moses, "All of Israel's firstborn sons belong to me. So register by name every firstborn male Israelite, one month old or older. But in place of them I claim all the Levites as mine! I am the LORD! I also claim the livestock of the Levites in place of all the firstborn of the livestock." ⁴² Moses obeyed, and registered all the firstborn males ⁴³ one month old or older; the total was 22,273.

⁴⁴ The LORD said to Moses, ⁴⁵ "Now dedicate the Levites as mine in place of all the firstborn Israelite sons, and dedicate the livestock of the Levites in place of the firstborn of the Israelites' livestock. ⁴⁶ Since the firstborn Israelite sons outnumber the Levites by 273, you must buy back the extra sons. ⁴⁷ For each one pay five pieces of silver, according to the official standard, ⁴⁸ and give this money to Aaron and his sons." ⁴⁹ Moses obeyed and took ⁵⁰ the 1,365 pieces of silver ⁵¹ and gave them to Aaron and his sons.

The Duties of the Levite Clan of Kohath

4 The LORD told Moses ² to take a census of the Levite clan of Kohath by sub-clans and families, ³ and to register all the men between the ages of thirty and fifty who were qualified to work in the Tent of the LORD's presence. ⁴ Their service involves the most holy things.

⁵ The LORD gave Moses the following instructions. When it is time to break camp, Aaron and his sons shall enter the Tent, take down the curtain in front of the Covenant Box, and cover the Box with it. ⁶ They shall put a fine leather cover over it, spread a blue cloth on top, and then insert the carrying poles.

⁷ They shall spread a blue cloth over the table for the bread offered to the LORD and put on it the dishes, the incense bowls, the offering bowls, and the jars for the wine offering. There shall always be bread on the table. ⁸ They shall spread a red cloth over all this, put a fine leather cover over it, and then insert the carrying poles.

⁹ They shall take a blue cloth and cover the lampstand, with its lamps, tongs, trays, and all the olive oil containers. ¹⁰ They shall wrap it and all its equipment in a fine leather cover and place it on a carrying frame.

¹¹ Next they shall spread a blue cloth over the gold altar, put a fine leather cover over it, and then insert the carrying poles. ¹² They shall take all the utensils used in the Holy Place, wrap them in a blue cloth, put a fine leather cover over them, and place them on a carrying frame. ¹³ They shall remove the greasy ashes from

168

Num.

∴ ⋮ ⋯

Genesis
Exodus
Leviticus

NUMBERS 4

the altar and spread a purple cloth over it. [14] They shall put on it all the equipment used in the service at the altar: firepans, hooks, shovels, and basins. Then they shall put a fine leather cover over it and insert the carrying poles. [15] When it is time to break camp, the clan of Kohath shall come to carry the sacred objects only after Aaron and his sons have finished covering them and all their equipment. The clan of Kohath must not touch the sacred objects, or they will die.

These are the responsibilities of the clan of Kohath whenever the Tent is moved.

[16] Eleazar son of Aaron the priest shall be responsible for the whole Tent and for the oil for the lamps, the incense, the grain offerings, the anointing oil, and everything else in the Tent that has been consecrated to the LORD.

[17] The LORD said to Moses and Aaron, [18] "Do not let the clan of Kohath [19] be killed by coming near these most sacred objects. To prevent this happening, Aaron and his sons shall go in and assign each man his task and tell him what to carry. [20] But if the Kohathites enter the Tent and see the priests preparing the sacred objects for moving,* they will die."

The Duties of the Levite Clan of Gershon

[21] The LORD told Moses [22] to take a census of the Levite clan of Gershon by sub-clans and families, [23] and to register all the men between the ages of thirty and fifty who were qualified to work in the Tent of the LORD's presence. [24] They shall be responsible for carrying the following objects: [25] the Tent, its inner cover, its outer cover, the fine leather cover on top of it, the curtain for the entrance, [26] the curtains and ropes for the court that is round the Tent and the altar, the curtains for the entrance of the court, and all the fittings used in setting up these objects. They shall perform all the tasks required for these things. [27] Moses and Aaron shall see to it that the Gershonites perform all the duties and carry everything that Aaron and his sons assign to them. [28] These are the responsibilities of the Gershon clan in the Tent; they shall carry them out under the direction of Ithamar son of Aaron the priest.

The Duties of the Levite Clan of Merari

[29] The LORD told Moses to take a census of the Levite clan of Merari by sub-clans and families, [30] and to register all the men between the ages of thirty and fifty who were qualified to work in the Tent of the LORD's presence. [31] They shall be responsible for carrying the frames, bars, posts, and bases of the Tent, [32] and the posts, bases, pegs, and ropes of the court round the Tent, with all the fittings used in setting them up. Each man will be responsible for carrying specific items. [33] These are the responsibilities of the Merari clan in their service in the Tent: they shall carry them out under the direction of Ithamar son of Aaron the priest.

The Census of the Levites

[34-48] Following the LORD's command, Moses, Aaron, and the leaders of the community took a census of the three Levite clans, Kohath, Gershon, and Merari. They did this by sub-clans and families and registered all the men between the ages of thirty and fifty who were qualified to work in the Tent of the LORD's presence, as follows:

4.20 *see... moving*; or *see the sacred objects even for a moment.*

Num.
....

Deuter.
Joshua
Judges
Ruth
1 Sam.

Clan	Number
Kohath	2,750
Gershon	2,630
Merari	3,200
Total:	8,580

[49] Each man was registered as the LORD had commanded Moses; and at the command of the LORD given through Moses, each man was assigned responsibility for his task of serving or carrying.

Unclean People

5 The LORD said to Moses, [2] "Command the people of Israel to expel from the camp everyone with a dreaded skin disease or a bodily discharge and everyone who is unclean by contact with a corpse. [3] Send all these ritually unclean people out, so that they will not defile the camp, where I live among my people." [4] The Israelites obeyed and expelled them all from the camp.

Repayment for Wrongs Done

[5] The LORD gave Moses [6] the following instructions for the people of Israel. When anyone is unfaithful to the LORD and commits a wrong against someone, [7] he must confess his sin and make full repayment, plus an additional twenty per cent, to the person he has wronged. [8] But if that person has died and has no near relative to whom payment can be made, it shall be given to the LORD for the priest. This payment is in addition to the ram used to perform the ritual of purification for the guilty person. [9] Also every special contribution which the Israelites offer to the LORD belongs to the priest to whom they present it. [10] Each priest shall keep the offerings presented to him.

Cases of Wives with Suspicious Husbands

[11] The LORD commanded Moses [12-14] to give the Israelites the following instructions. It may happen that a man becomes suspicious that his wife is unfaithful to him and has defiled herself by having intercourse with another man. But the husband may not be certain, for his wife may have kept it secret — there was no witness, and she was not caught in the act. Or it may happen that a husband becomes suspicious of his wife, even though she has not been unfaithful. [15] In either case the man shall take his wife to the priest. He shall also take the required offering of one kilogramme of barley flour, but he shall not pour any olive oil on it or put any incense on it, because it is an offering from a suspicious husband, made to bring the truth to light.

[16] The priest shall bring the woman forward and make her stand in front of the altar. [17] He shall pour some holy water into a clay bowl and take some of the earth that is on the floor of the Tent of the LORD's presence and put it in the water to make it bitter. [18] Then he shall loosen the woman's hair and put the offering of flour in her hands. In his hands the priest shall hold the bowl containing the bitter water that brings a curse. [19] Then the priest shall make the woman agree to this oath spoken by the priest: "If you have not committed adultery, you will not be harmed by the curse that this water brings. [20] But if you have committed adultery, [21] may the LORD make your name a curse among your people. May he cause your genital organs to shrink and your stomach to swell up. [22] May this water enter your stomach and cause it to swell up and your genital organs to shrink."

170

Num.

Genesis
Exodus
Leviticus

NUMBERS 5, 6

The woman shall respond, "I agree; may the LORD do so."

23 Then the priest shall write this curse down and wash the writing off into the bowl of bitter water. 24 Before he makes the woman drink the water, which may then cause her bitter pain, 25 the priest shall take the offering of flour out of the woman's hands, hold it out in dedication to the LORD, and present it on the altar. 26 Then he shall take a handful of it as a token offering and burn it on the altar. Finally, he shall make the woman drink the water. 27 If she has committed adultery, the water will cause bitter pain; her stomach will swell up and her genital organs will shrink. Her name will become a curse among her people. 28 But if she is innocent, she will not be harmed and will be able to bear children.

29-30 This is the law in cases where a man is jealous and becomes suspicious that his wife has committed adultery. The woman shall be made to stand in front of the altar, and the priest shall perform this ritual. 31 The husband shall be free of guilt, but the woman, if guilty, must suffer the consequences.

Rules for Nazirites

6 The LORD commanded Moses 2 to give the following instructions to the people of Israel. Any men or women who make a special vow to become Nazirites and dedicate themselves to the LORD 3 shall abstain from wine and beer. They shall not drink any kind of drink made from grapes or eat any grapes or raisins. 4 As long as they are Nazirites, they shall not eat anything that comes from a grapevine, not even the seeds or skins of grapes.

5 As long as they are under the Nazirite vow, they must not cut their hair or shave. They are bound by the vow for the full time that they are dedicated to the LORD, and they shall let their hair grow. 6-7 Their hair is the sign of their dedication to God, and so they must not defile themselves by going near a corpse, not even that of their father, mother, brother, or sister. 8 As long as they are Nazirites, they are consecrated to the LORD.

9 If the consecrated hair of a Nazirite is defiled because he or she is right beside someone who suddenly dies, they must wait seven days and then shave off their hair; and so they become ritually clean. 10 On the eighth day they shall bring two doves or two pigeons to the priest at the entrance of the Tent of the LORD's presence. 11 The priest shall offer one as a sin offering and the other as a burnt offering, to perform the ritual of purification for them because of their contact with a corpse. On the same day they shall reconsecrate their hair 12 and rededicate to the LORD their time as Nazirites. The previous period of time doesn't count, because their consecrated hair was defiled. As a repayment offering they shall bring a one-year-old lamb.

13 When Nazirites complete their vows, they shall perform this ritual. They shall go to the entrance of the Tent 14 and present to the LORD three animals without any defects: a one-year-old male lamb for a burnt offering, a one-year-old ewe lamb for a sin offering, and a ram for a fellowship offering. 15 They shall also offer a basket of bread made without yeast: thick loaves made of flour mixed with olive oil and biscuits brushed with olive oil, and in addition the required offerings of corn and wine.

16 The priest shall present all these to the LORD and offer the sin offering and the burnt offering. 17 He shall sacrifice the ram to the LORD as a fellowship offering, and offer it with the basket of bread; he shall also present the offerings of corn and wine. 18 At the entrance of the Tent the Nazirite shall shave off his or her hair and put it on the fire on which the fellowship offering is being burnt.

NUMBERS 6, 7

171

Num.

....

Deuter.
Joshua
Judges
Ruth
1 Sam.

¹⁹ Then, when the shoulder of the ram is boiled, the priest shall take it and put it, together with one thick loaf of bread and one biscuit from the basket, into the hands of the Nazirite. ²⁰ Next, the priest shall present them as a special gift to the LORD; they are a sacred offering for the priest, in addition to the breast and the leg of the ram which by law belong to the priest. After that, the Nazirite may drink wine.

²¹ These are the regulations for Nazirites; but if a Nazirite promises an offering beyond what his or her vow requires them to give, they must fulfil exactly the promise they made.

The Priestly Blessing

²² The LORD commanded Moses ²³ to tell Aaron and his sons to use the following words in blessing the people of Israel:

²⁴ May the LORD bless you and take care of you;

²⁵ May the LORD be kind and gracious to you;

²⁶ May the LORD look on you with favour and give you peace.

²⁷ And the LORD said, "If they pronounce my name as a blessing upon the people of Israel, I will bless them."

The Offerings of the Leaders

7 On the day Moses finished setting up the Tent of the LORD's presence, he anointed and dedicated the Tent and all its equipment, and the altar and all its equipment. ² Then the clan chiefs who were leaders in the tribes of Israel, the same men who were in charge of the census, ³ brought their offerings to the LORD: six wagons and twelve oxen, a wagon for every two leaders and an ox for each leader. After they had presented them, ⁴ the LORD said to Moses, ⁵ "Accept these gifts for use in the work to be done for the Tent; give them to the Levites according to the work they have to do." ⁶ So Moses gave the wagons and the oxen to the Levites. ⁷ He gave two wagons and four oxen to the Gershonites, ⁸ and four wagons and eight oxen to the Merarites. All their work was to be done under the direction of Ithamar son of Aaron. ⁹ But Moses gave no wagons or oxen to the Kohathites, because the sacred objects they took care of had to be carried on their shoulders.

¹⁰ The leaders also brought offerings to celebrate the dedication of the altar. When they were ready to present their gifts at the altar, ¹¹ the LORD said to Moses, "Tell them that each day for a period of twelve days one of the leaders is to present his gifts for the dedication of the altar."

¹²⁻⁸³ They presented their offerings in the following order:

Day	Tribe	Leader
1st	Judah	Nahshon son of Amminadab
2nd	Issachar	Nethanel son of Zuar
3rd	Zebulun	Eliab son of Helon
4th	Reuben	Elizur son of Shedeur
5th	Simeon	Shelumiel son of Zurishaddai
6th	Gad	Eliasaph son of Deuel
7th	Ephraim	Elishama son of Ammihud
8th	Manasseh	Gamaliel son of Pedahzur
9th	Benjamin	Abidan son of Gideoni
10th	Dan	Ahiezer son of Ammishaddai
11th	Asher	Pagiel son of Ochran
12th	Naphtali	Ahira son of Enan

The offerings each one brought were identical: one silver bowl weighing 1.5 kilogrammes and one silver basin weighing 800

NUMBERS 6.24

May the
LORD
bless you
AND
TAKE
CARE
- of you -

grammes, by the official standard, both of them full of flour mixed with oil for the grain offering; one gold dish weighing 110 grammes, full of incense; one young bull, one ram, and a one-year-old lamb, for the burnt offering; one goat for the sin offering; and two bulls, five rams, five goats, and five one-year-old lambs for the fellowship offering.

84-88 The totals of the offerings brought by the twelve leaders for the dedication of the altar were as follows:
— twelve silver bowls and twelve silver basins weighing a total of 27.6 kilogrammes
— twelve gold dishes weighing a total of 1.32 kilogrammes, filled with incense
— twelve bulls, twelve rams, and twelve one-year-old lambs, together with the grain offerings that go with them, for the burnt offerings
— twelve goats for the sin offerings
— 24 bulls, sixty rams, sixty goats, sixty one-year-old lambs, for the fellowship offerings.

89 When Moses went into the Tent to talk with the LORD, he heard the LORD speaking to him from above the lid on the Covenant Box, between the two winged creatures.

Placing the Lamps

8 The LORD said to Moses, 2 "Tell Aaron that when he puts the seven lamps on the lampstand, he should place them so that the light shines towards the front." 3 Aaron obeyed and placed the lamps facing the front of the lampstand. 4 From top to bottom the lampstand was made of hammered gold, according to the pattern that the LORD had shown Moses.

The Purification and Dedication of the Levites

5 The LORD said to Moses, 6 "Separate the Levites from the rest of the people of Israel and purify them 7 in the following way: sprinkle them with the water of purification and tell them to shave their whole bodies and to wash their clothes. Then they will be ritually clean. 8 Then they are to take a young bull and the required grain offering of flour mixed with olive oil; and you are to take another bull for the sin offering. 9 Then assemble the whole community of Israel and make the Levites stand in front of the Tent of my presence. 10 The people of Israel are to place their hands on the heads of the Levites, 11 and then Aaron shall dedicate the Levites to me as a special gift from the Israelites, so that they may do my work. 12 The Levites shall then put their hands on the heads of the two bulls; one is to be offered as a sin offering and the other as a burnt offering, in order to perform the ritual of purification for the Levites.

13 "Dedicate the Levites as a special gift to me, and put Aaron and his sons in charge of them. 14 Separate the Levites in this way from the rest of the Israelites, so that they will belong to me. 15 After you have purified and dedicated the Levites, they will be qualified to work in the Tent. 16 I have claimed them in the place of all the firstborn sons of the Israelites, and they belong to me alone. 17 When I killed all the firstborn in Egypt, I consecrated as my own the eldest son of each Israelite family and the firstborn of every animal. 18 I am now taking the Levites instead of all the firstborn of the Israelites, 19 and I assign the Levites to Aaron and his sons, as a gift from the Israelites, to work in the Tent for the people of Israel and to protect the Israelites from the disaster that would strike them if they came too near the Holy Place."

Num.

....

Deuter.

Joshua

Judges

Ruth

1 Sam.

²⁰So Moses, Aaron, and all the people of Israel dedicated the Levites, as the LORD commanded Moses. ²¹The Levites purified themselves and washed their clothes, and Aaron dedicated them as a special gift to the LORD. He also performed the ritual of purification for them. ²²The people did everything the LORD had commanded Moses concerning the Levites. And so the Levites were qualified to work in the Tent under Aaron and his sons.

²³The LORD said to Moses, ²⁴"From the age of 25 each Levite shall perform his duties in the Tent of my presence, ²⁵and at the age of fifty he shall retire. ²⁶After that, he may help his fellow-Levites in performing their duties in the Tent, but he must not perform any service by himself. This is how you are to regulate the duties of the Levites."

The Second Passover

9 The LORD spoke to Moses in the Sinai Desert in the first month of the second year after the people of Israel had left Egypt. He said, ²⁻³"On the fourteenth day of this month, beginning at sunset, the people of Israel are to observe the Passover according to all the rules and regulations for it." ⁴So Moses told the people to observe the Passover, ⁵and on the evening of the fourteenth day of the first month they did so in the Sinai Desert. The people did everything just as the LORD had commanded Moses.

⁶But there were some people who were ritually unclean because they had touched a corpse, and they were not able to keep the Passover on that day. They went to Moses and Aaron ⁷and said, "We are unclean because we have touched a corpse, but why should we be excluded from presenting the LORD's offering with the rest of the Israelites?"

⁸Moses answered, "Wait until I receive instructions from the LORD."

⁹The LORD told Moses ¹⁰to say to the people of Israel, "When any of you or your descendants are unclean from touching a corpse or are far away on a journey, but still want to keep the Passover, ¹¹you are permitted to observe it one month later instead, on the evening of the fourteenth day of the second month. Celebrate it with unleavened bread and bitter herbs. ¹²Do not leave any of the food until the following morning and do not break any of the animal's bones. Observe the Passover according to all the regulations. ¹³But anyone who is ritually clean and not away on a journey and who does not observe the Passover, shall no longer be considered one of my people, because he did not present the offering to me at the appointed time. He must suffer the consequences of his sin.

¹⁴"If foreigners living among you want to keep the Passover, they must observe it according to all the rules and regulations. The same law applies to everyone, whether native or foreigner."

The Fiery Cloud
(Ex 40.34–38)

¹⁵⁻¹⁶On the day the Tent of the Lord's presence was set up, a cloud came and covered it. At night the cloud looked like fire. ¹⁷Whenever the cloud lifted, the people of Israel broke camp, and they set up camp again in the place where the cloud came down. ¹⁸The people broke camp at the command of the LORD, and at his command they set up camp. As long as the cloud stayed over the Tent, they stayed in the same camp. ¹⁹When the cloud stayed over the Tent for a long time, they obeyed the LORD and did not move on. ²⁰Sometimes the cloud remained over the Tent for only a few

174

Num.

Genesis
Exodus
Leviticus

NUMBERS 9, 10

days; in any case, they remained in camp or moved, according to the command of the LORD. [21] Sometimes the cloud remained only from evening until morning, and they moved on as soon as the cloud lifted. Whenever the cloud lifted, they moved on. [22] Whether it was two days, a month, a year, or longer, as long as the cloud remained over the Tent, they did not move on; but when it lifted, they moved. [23] They set up camp and broke camp in obedience to the commands which the LORD gave through Moses.

The Silver Trumpets

10 The LORD said to Moses, [2] "Make two trumpets of hammered silver to use for calling the people together and for breaking camp. [3] When long blasts are sounded on both trumpets, the whole community is to gather round you at the entrance to the Tent of my presence. [4] But when only one trumpet is sounded, then only the leaders of the clans are to gather round you. [5] When short blasts are sounded, the tribes camped on the east will move out. [6] When short blasts are sounded a second time, the tribes on the south will move out. So short blasts are to be sounded to break camp, [7] but in order to call the community together, long blasts are to be sounded. [8] The trumpets are to be blown by Aaron's sons, the priests.

"The following rule is to be observed for all time to come. [9] When you are at war in your land, defending yourselves against an enemy who has attacked you, sound the signal for battle on these trumpets. I, the LORD your God, will help you and save you from your enemies. [10] Also on joyful occasions — at your New Moon Festivals and your other religious festivals — you are to blow the trumpets when you present your burnt offerings and your fellowship offerings. Then I will help you. I am the LORD your God."

The Israelites Break Camp

[11] On the twentieth day of the second month in the second year after the people left Egypt, the cloud over the Tent of the LORD's presence lifted, [12] and the Israelites started on their journey out of the Sinai Desert. The cloud came to rest in the wilderness of Paran.

[13] They began to march at the command of the LORD through Moses, [14] and each time they moved, they were in the same order. Those under the banner of the division led by the tribe of Judah started out first, company by company, with Nahshon son of Amminadab in command. [15] Nethanel son of Zuar was in command of the tribe of Issachar, [16] and Eliab son of Helon was in command of the tribe of Zebulun.

[17] Then the Tent would be taken down, and the clans of Gershon and Merari, who carried it, would start out.

[18] Next, those under the banner of the division led by the tribe of Reuben would start out, company by company, with Elizur son of Shedeur in command. [19] Shelumiel son of Zurishaddai was in command of the tribe of Simeon, [20] and Eliasaph son of Deuel was in command of the tribe of Gad.

[21] Then the Levite clan of Kohath would start out, carrying the sacred objects. By the time they arrived at the next camp, the Tent had been set up again.

[22] Next, those under the banner of the division led by the tribe of Ephraim would start out, company by company, with Elishama son of Ammihud in command. [23] Gamaliel son of Pedahzur was in command of the tribe of Manasseh, [24] and Abidan son of Gideoni was in command of the tribe of Benjamin.

[25] Finally, those under the banner of the division led by the tribe of Dan, serving as the rearguard of all the divisions, would start

Num.
..........:..

Deuter.
Joshua
Judges
Ruth
1 Sam.

out, company by company, with Ahiezer son of Ammishaddai in command. [26] Pagiel son of Ochran was in command of the tribe of Asher, [27] and Ahira son of Enan was in command of the tribe of Naphtali. [28] This, then, was the order of march, company by company, whenever the Israelites broke camp and set out.

[29] Moses said to his brother-in-law Hobab son of Jethro the Midianite, "We are about to start out for the place which the LORD said he would give us. He has promised to make Israel prosperous, so come with us, and we will share our prosperity with you."

[30] Hobab answered, "No, I am going back to my native land."

[31] "Please don't leave us," Moses said. "You know where we can camp in the wilderness, and you can be our guide. [32] If you come with us, we will share with you all the blessings that the LORD gives us."

The People Set Out

[33] When the people left Sinai, the holy mountain, they travelled for three days. The LORD's Covenant Box always went ahead of them to find a place for them to camp. [34] As they moved on from each camp, the cloud of the LORD was over them by day. [35] Whenever the Covenant Box started out, Moses would say, "Arise, LORD; scatter your enemies and put to flight those who hate you!" [36] And whenever it stopped, he would say, "Return, LORD, to the thousands of families of Israel."*

The Place Named Taberah

11 The people began to complain to the LORD about their troubles. When the LORD heard them, he was angry and sent fire on the people. It burnt among them and destroyed one end of the camp. [2] The people cried out to Moses for help; he prayed to the LORD, and the fire died down. [3] So the place was named Taberah,* because there the fire of the LORD burnt among them.

Moses Chooses Seventy Leaders

[4] There were some foreigners travelling with the Israelites. They had a strong craving for meat, and even the Israelites themselves began to complain: "If only we could have some meat! [5] In Egypt we used to eat all the fish we wanted, and it cost us nothing. Remember the cucumbers, the watermelons, the leeks, the onions, and the garlic we had? [6] But now our strength is gone. There is nothing at all to eat — nothing but this manna day after day!"

[7] (Manna was like small seeds, whitish yellow in colour. [8-9] It fell on the camp at night along with the dew. The next morning the people would go round and gather it, grind it or pound it into flour, and then boil it and make it into flat cakes. It tasted like bread baked with olive oil.)

[10] Moses heard all the people complaining as they stood about in groups at the entrances of their tents. He was distressed because the LORD was angry with them, [11] and he said to the LORD, "Why have you treated me so badly? Why are you displeased with me? Why have you given me the responsibility for all these people? [12] I didn't create them or bring them to birth! Why should you ask me to act like a nurse and carry them in my arms like babies all the way to the land you promised to their ancestors? [13] Where

---

NUMBERS 11.1-3

God is always the same. However, it can sometimes seem like the God we read about in the Old Testament is different from the one in the New Testament.

CHECK OUT THIS

FILM

ON THE SUBJECT.

Head to
gnbyouthedition.co.uk/samegod

10.36 Return… Israel; or Return, LORD, you who are like an army of millions for Israel.

11.3 Taberah: This name sounds like the Hebrew for "burning".

176

Num.

.:.......

Genesis
Exodus
Leviticus

NUMBERS 11

could I get enough meat for all these people? They keep whining and asking for meat. [14] I can't be responsible for all these people by myself; it's too much for me! [15] If you are going to treat me like this, take pity on me and kill me, so that I won't have to endure your cruelty any longer."

[16] The Lord said to Moses, "Assemble seventy respected men who are recognized as leaders of the people, bring them to me at the Tent of my presence, and tell them to stand there beside you. [17] I will come down and speak with you there, and I will take some of the spirit I have given you and give it to them. Then they can help you to bear the responsibility for these people, and you will not have to bear it alone. [18] Now tell the people, 'Purify yourselves for tomorrow; you will have meat to eat. The Lord has heard you whining and saying that you wished you had some meat and that you were better off in Egypt. Now the Lord will give you meat, and you will have to eat it. [19] You will have to eat it not just for one or two days, or five, or ten, or even twenty days, [20] but for a whole month, until it comes out of your ears, until you are sick of it. This will happen because you have rejected the Lord who is here among you and have complained to him that you should never have left Egypt.'"

[21] Moses said to the Lord, "Here I am leading 600,000 people, and you say that you will give them enough meat for a month? [22] Could enough cattle and sheep be killed to satisfy them? Are all the fish in the sea enough for them?"

[23] "Is there a limit to my power?" the Lord answered. "You will soon see whether what I have said will happen or not!"

[24] So Moses went out and told the people what the Lord had said. He assembled seventy of the leaders and placed them round the Tent. [25] Then the Lord came down in the cloud and spoke to him. He took some of the spirit he had given to Moses and gave it to the seventy leaders. When the spirit came on them, they began to shout like prophets, but not for long.

[26] Two of the seventy leaders, Eldad and Medad, had stayed in the camp and had not gone out to the Tent. There in the camp the spirit came on them, and they too began to shout like prophets. [27] A young man ran out to tell Moses what Eldad and Medad were doing.

[28] Then Joshua son of Nun, who had been Moses' helper since he was a young man, spoke up and said to Moses, "Stop them, sir!"

[29] Moses answered, "Are you concerned about my interests? I wish that the Lord would give his Spirit to all his people and make all of them shout like prophets!" [30] Then Moses and the seventy leaders of Israel went back to camp.

The Lord Sends Quails

[31] Suddenly the Lord sent a wind that brought quails from the sea, flying less than a metre above the ground. They settled on the camp and all round it for many kilometres in every direction.[*] [32] So all that day, all night, and all the next day, the people worked catching quails; no one gathered less than a thousand kilogrammes. They spread them out to dry all round the camp. [33] While there was still plenty of meat for them to eat, the Lord became angry with the people and caused an epidemic to break out among them. [34] That place was named Kibroth Hattaavah

11.31 *sea, flying... direction*; or *sea. They settled in the camp and all round it for many kilometres in every direction, until they were piled up nearly a metre deep on the ground.*

Num.

Deuter.
Joshua
Judges
Ruth
1 Sam.

(which means "Graves of Craving"), because there they buried the people who had craved meat. [35] From there the people moved to Hazeroth, where they made camp.

Miriam is Punished

12 Moses had married a Cushite* woman, and Miriam and Aaron criticized him for it. [2] They said, "Has the LORD spoken only through* Moses? Hasn't he also spoken through* us?" The LORD heard what they said. [3] (Moses was a humble man, more humble than anyone else on earth.)

[4] Suddenly the LORD said to Moses, Aaron, and Miriam, "I want the three of you to come out to the Tent of my presence." They went, [5] and the LORD came down in a pillar of cloud, stood at the entrance of the Tent, and called out, "Aaron! Miriam!" The two of them stepped forward, [6] and the LORD said, "Now hear what I have to say! When there are prophets among you,* I reveal myself to them in visions and speak to them in dreams. [7] It is different when I speak with my servant Moses; I have put him in charge of all my people Israel.* [8] So I speak to him face to face, clearly and not in riddles; he has even seen my form! How dare you speak against my servant Moses?"

[9] The LORD was angry with them; and so as he departed [10] and the cloud left the Tent, Miriam's skin was suddenly covered with a dreaded disease and turned as white as snow. When Aaron looked at her and saw that she was covered with the disease, [11] he said to Moses, "Please, sir, do not make us suffer this punishment for our foolish sin. [12] Don't let her become like something born dead with half its flesh eaten away."

[13] So Moses cried out to the LORD, "O God, heal her!"

[14] The LORD answered, "If her father had spat in her face, she would have to bear her disgrace for seven days. So let her be shut out of the camp for a week, and after that she can be brought back in." [15] Miriam was shut out of the camp for seven days, and the people did not move on until she was brought back in. [16] Then they left Hazeroth and set up camp in the wilderness of Paran.

The Spies
(Deut 1.19–33)

13 The LORD said to Moses, [2] "Choose one of the leaders from each of the twelve tribes and send them as spies to explore the land of Canaan, which I am giving to the Israelites." [3-15] Moses obeyed and from the wilderness of Paran he sent out leaders, as follows:

Tribe	Leader
Reuben	Shammua son of Zaccur
Simeon	Shaphat son of Hori
Judah	Caleb son of Jephunneh
Issachar	Igal son of Joseph
Ephraim	Hoshea son of Nun
Benjamin	Palti son of Raphu
Zebulun	Gaddiel son of Sodi
Manasseh	Gaddi son of Susi

12.1 *Cushite* (compare Hab 3.7); or *Midianite*; or *Ethiopian*.
12.2 *through*; or *to*.
12.6 Some ancient translations *When… you*; Hebrew unclear.
12.7 *I have put… Israel*; or *he can be trusted with all my affairs*.

178

Num.

Genesis
Exodus
Leviticus

NUMBERS 13, 14

NUMBERS 13.30

Caleb (whose name means 'faithful dog') had a different mindset from most of the other spies. Where the others had an attitude of fear because of the giants, he had an attitude of courage and boldness, because he knew that even one person with God has the majority.

Write down
- SOME OF THE -
'GIANTS'
you are facing (such as exams, or a worrying situation for a family member or friend). Knowing that God is on your side, what could your attitude be as you face these giants?

Tribe	Leader
Dan	Ammiel son of Gemalli
Asher	Sethur son of Michael
Naphtali	Nahbi son of Vophsi
Gad	Geuel son of Machi

16 These are the spies Moses sent to explore the land. He changed the name of Hoshea son of Nun to Joshua.

17 When Moses sent them out, he said to them, "Go north from here into the southern part of the land of Canaan and then on into the hill country. 18 Find out what kind of country it is, how many people live there, and how strong they are. 19 Find out whether the land is good or bad and whether the people live in open towns or in fortified cities. 20 Find out whether the soil is fertile and whether the land is wooded. And be sure to bring back some of the fruit that grows there." (It was the season when grapes were beginning to ripen.)

21 So the men went north and explored the land from the wilderness of Zin in the south all the way to Rehob, near Hamath Pass in the north. 22 They went first into the southern part of the land and came to Hebron, where the clans of Ahiman, Sheshai, and Talmai, the descendants of a race of giants called the Anakim, lived. (Hebron was founded seven years before Zoan in Egypt.) 23 They came to the Valley of Eshcol, and there they cut off a branch which had one bunch of grapes on it so heavy that it took two men to carry it on a pole between them. They also brought back some pomegranates and figs. 24 (That place was named the Valley of Eshcol* because of the bunch of grapes the Israelites cut off there.)

25 After exploring the land for forty days, the spies returned 26 to Moses, Aaron, and the whole community of Israel at Kadesh in the wilderness of Paran. They reported what they had seen and showed them the fruit they had brought. 27 They said to Moses, "We explored the land and found it to be rich and fertile; and here is some of its fruit. 28 But the people who live there are powerful, and their cities are very large and well fortified. Even worse, we saw the descendants of the giants there. 29 Amalekites live in the southern part of the land; Hittites, Jebusites, and Amorites live in the hill country; and Canaanites live by the Mediterranean Sea and along the River Jordan."

30 Caleb silenced the people who were complaining against* Moses, and said, "We should attack now and take the land; we are strong enough to conquer it."

31 But the men who had gone with Caleb said, "No, we are not strong enough to attack them; the people there are more powerful than we are." 32 So they spread a false report among the Israelites about the land they had explored. They said, "That land doesn't even produce enough to feed the people who live there. Everyone we saw was very tall, 33 and we even saw giants there, the descendants of Anak. We felt as small as grasshoppers, and that is how we must have looked to them."

The People Complain

14 All night long the people cried out in distress. 2 They complained against Moses and Aaron, and said, "It would have been better to die in Egypt or even here in the wilderness!

13.24 *Eshcol*: This name in Hebrew means "bunch of grapes".
13.30 *complaining against*; or *gathered round*.

NUMBERS 14

179

Num.

·········:

Deuter.

Joshua

Judges

Ruth

1 Sam.

³Why is the Lord taking us into that land? We will be killed in battle, and our wives and children will be captured. Wouldn't it be better to go back to Egypt?" ⁴So they said to one another, "Let's choose a leader and go back to Egypt!"

⁵Then Moses and Aaron bowed to the ground in front of all the people. ⁶And Joshua son of Nun and Caleb son of Jephunneh, two of the spies, tore their clothes in sorrow ⁷and said to the people, "The land we explored is an excellent land. ⁸If the Lord is pleased with us, he will take us there and give us that rich and fertile land. ⁹Do not rebel against the Lord and don't be afraid of the people who live there. We will conquer them easily. The Lord is with us and has defeated the gods who protected them; so don't be afraid." ¹⁰The whole community was threatening to stone them to death, but suddenly the people saw the dazzling light of the Lord's presence appear over the tent.

Moses Prays for the People

¹¹The Lord said to Moses, "How much longer will these people reject me? How much longer will they refuse to trust in me, even though I have performed so many miracles among them? ¹²I will send an epidemic and destroy them, but I will make you the father of a nation that is larger and more powerful than they are!"

¹³But Moses said to the Lord, "You brought these people out of Egypt by your power. When the Egyptians hear what you have done to your people, ¹⁴they will tell it to the people who live in this land. These people have already heard that you, Lord, are with us, that you are plainly seen when your cloud stops over us, and that you go before us in a pillar of cloud by day and a pillar of fire by night. ¹⁵Now if you kill all your people, the nations who have heard of your fame will say ¹⁶that you killed your people in the wilderness because you were not able to bring them into the land you promised to give them. ¹⁷So now Lord, I pray, show us your power and do what you promised when you said, ¹⁸'I, the Lord, am not easily angered, and I show great love and faithfulness and forgive sin and rebellion. Yet I will not fail to punish children and grandchildren to the third and fourth generation for the sins of their parents.' ¹⁹And now, Lord, according to the greatness of your unchanging love, forgive, I pray, the sin of these people, just as you have forgiven them ever since they left Egypt."

²⁰The Lord answered, "I will forgive them, as you have asked. ²¹But I promise that as surely as I live and as surely as my presence fills the earth, ²²none of these people will live to enter that land. They have seen the dazzling light of my presence and the miracles that I performed in Egypt and in the wilderness, but they have tried my patience over and over again and have refused to obey me. ²³They will never enter the land which I promised to their ancestors. None of those who have rejected me will ever enter it. ²⁴But because my servant Caleb has a different attitude and has remained loyal to me, I will bring him into the land which he explored, and his descendants will possess the land ²⁵in whose valleys the Amalekites and the Canaanites now live. Turn back tomorrow and go into the wilderness in the direction of the Gulf of Aqaba."

The Lord Punishes the People for Complaining

²⁶The Lord said to Moses and Aaron, ²⁷"How much longer are these wicked people going to complain against me? I have heard enough of these complaints! ²⁸Now give them this answer: 'I swear that as surely as I live, I will do to you just what you have asked.

180

Num.

Genesis
Exodus
Leviticus

NUMBERS 14, 15

I, the Lord, have spoken. ²⁹You will die and your corpses will be scattered across this wilderness. Because you have complained against me, none of you over twenty years of age will enter that land. ³⁰I promised to let you live there, but not one of you will, except Caleb and Joshua. ³¹You said that your children would be captured, but I will bring them into the land that you rejected, and it will be their home. ³²You will die here in this wilderness. ³³Your children will wander in the wilderness for forty years, suffering for your unfaithfulness, until the last one of you dies. ³⁴You will suffer the consequences of your sin for forty years, one year for each of the forty days you spent exploring the land. You will know what it means to have me against you! ³⁵I swear that I will do this to you wicked people who have gathered together against me. Here in the wilderness every one of you will die. I, the Lord, have spoken.' "

³⁶⁻³⁷The men Moses had sent to explore the land brought back a false report which caused the people to complain against the Lord. And so the Lord struck them with a disease, and they died. ³⁸Of the twelve spies only Joshua and Caleb survived.

The First Attempt to Invade the Land
(Deut 1.41–46)

³⁹When Moses told the Israelites what the Lord had said, they mourned bitterly. ⁴⁰Early the next morning they started out to invade the hill country, saying, "Now we are ready to go to the place which the Lord told us about. We admit that we have sinned."

⁴¹But Moses said, "Then why are you disobeying the Lord now? You will not succeed! ⁴²Don't go. The Lord is not with you, and your enemies will defeat you. ⁴³When you face the Amalekites and the Canaanites, you will die in battle; the Lord will not be with you, because you have refused to follow him."

⁴⁴Yet they still dared to go up into the hill country, even though neither the Lord's Covenant Box nor Moses left the camp. ⁴⁵Then the Amalekites and the Canaanites who lived there attacked and defeated them, and pursued them as far as Hormah.

Laws about Sacrifice

15 The Lord gave Moses ²the following regulations for the people of Israel to observe in the land that he was going to give them. ³A bull, a ram, a sheep, or a goat may be presented to the Lord as a burnt offering or as a sacrifice in fulfilment of a vow or as a freewill offering or as an offering at your regular religious festivals; the smell of these food offerings is pleasing to the Lord. ⁴⁻⁵Whoever presents a sheep or a goat as a burnt offering to the Lord is to bring with each animal a kilogramme of flour mixed with one litre of olive oil as a grain offering, together with one litre of wine. ⁶When a ram is offered, two kilogrammes of flour mixed with 1.5 litres of olive oil are to be presented as a grain offering, ⁷together with 1.5 litres of wine. The smell of these sacrifices is pleasing to the Lord. ⁸When a bull is offered to the Lord as a burnt offering or as a sacrifice in fulfilment of a vow or as a fellowship offering, ⁹a grain offering of three kilogrammes of flour mixed with two litres of olive oil is to be presented, ¹⁰together with two litres of wine. The smell of this sacrifice is pleasing to the Lord.

¹¹That is what shall be offered with each bull, ram, sheep, or goat. ¹²When more than one animal is offered, the accompanying offering is to be increased proportionately. ¹³All native Israelites are to do this when they present a food offering, a smell pleasing

NUMBERS 15

181

Num.

Deuter.
Joshua
Judges
Ruth
1 Sam.

to the LORD. [14]And if at any time foreigners living among you, whether on a temporary or a permanent basis, make a food offering, a smell that pleases the LORD, they are to observe the same regulations. [15]For all time to come, the same* rules are binding on you and on the foreigners who live among you. You and they are alike in the LORD's sight; [16]the same laws and regulations apply to you and to them.

[17]The LORD gave Moses [18]the following regulations for the people of Israel to observe in the land that he was going to give them. [19]When any food produced there is eaten, some of it is to be set aside as a special contribution to the LORD. [20]When you bake bread, the first loaf of the first bread made from the new corn is to be presented as a special contribution to the LORD. This is to be presented in the same way as the special contribution you make from the corn you thresh. [21]For all time to come, this special gift is to be given to the LORD from the bread you bake.

[22]But suppose someone unintentionally fails to keep some of these regulations which the LORD has given Moses. [23]And suppose that in the future the community fails to do everything that the LORD commanded through Moses. [24]If the mistake was made because of the ignorance of the community, they are to offer a bull as a burnt offering, a smell that pleases the LORD, with the proper grain offering and wine offering. In addition, they are to offer a male goat as a sin offering. [25]The priest shall perform the ritual of purification for the community, and they will be forgiven, because the mistake was unintentional and they brought their sin offering as a food offering to the LORD. [26]The whole community of Israel and the foreigners living among them will be forgiven, because everyone was involved in the mistake.

[27]If an individual sins unintentionally, he is to offer a one-year-old female goat as a sin offering. [28]At the altar the priest shall perform the ritual of purification to purify the person from his sin, and he will be forgiven. [29]The same regulation applies to all who unintentionally commit a sin, whether they are native Israelites or resident foreigners.

[30]But any person who sins deliberately, whether he is a native or a foreigner, is guilty of treating the LORD with contempt, and he shall be put to death, [31]because he has rejected what the LORD said and has deliberately broken one of his commands. He is responsible for his own death.

The Man who Broke the Sabbath
[32]Once, while the Israelites were still in the wilderness, a man was found gathering firewood on the Sabbath. [33]He was taken to Moses, Aaron, and the whole community, [34]and was put under guard, because it was not clear what should be done with him. [35]Then the LORD said to Moses, "The man must be put to death; the whole community is to stone him to death outside the camp." [36]So the whole community took him outside the camp and stoned him to death, as the LORD had commanded.

Rules about Tassels
[37]The LORD commanded Moses [38]to say to the people of Israel: "Make tassels on the corners of your garments and put a blue cord on each tassel. You are to do this for all time to come. [39]The tassels will serve as reminders, and each time you see them you

NUMBERS 15.37

In this passage, God commands his people to wear tassels to remind them of his commands and his ways. It also reminded them that

THEY WERE

– SET –

APART

and living differently.

Take a

PIECE OF STRING

and tie some knots in it. (It won't look as good as a tassel, but it will do!) For each knot, think of a way that you think God might be calling you to live differently from people who don't believe in God. Keep this 'tassel' in your Bible.

15.15 Some ancient translations *the same*; Hebrew *the congregation the same*.

182

Num.

.:. ....

Genesis
Exodus
Leviticus

NUMBERS 15, 16

will remember all my commands and obey them; then you will not turn away from me and follow your own wishes and desires. [40] The tassels will remind you to keep all my commands, and you will belong completely to me. [41] I am the LORD your God; I brought you out of Egypt to be your God. I am the LORD."

The Rebellion of Korah, Dathan, and Abiram

16 [1-2] Korah son of Izhar, from the Levite clan of Kohath, rebelled against the leadership of Moses. He was joined by three members of the tribe of Reuben — Dathan and Abiram, the sons of Eliab, and On son of Peleth — and by 250 other Israelites, well-known leaders chosen by the community. [3] They assembled before Moses and Aaron and said to them, "You have gone too far! All the members of the community belong to the LORD, and the LORD is with all of us. Why, then, Moses, do you set yourself above the LORD's community?"

[4] When Moses heard this, he threw himself on the ground and prayed. [5] Then he said to Korah and his followers, "Tomorrow morning the LORD will show us who belongs to him; he will let the one who belongs to him, that is, the one he has chosen, approach him at the altar. [6-7] Tomorrow morning you and your followers take firepans, put live coals and incense on them, and take them to the altar. Then we will see which of us the LORD has chosen. You Levites are the ones who have gone too far!"

[8] Moses continued to speak to Korah. "Listen, you Levites! [9] Do you consider it a small matter that the God of Israel has set you apart from the rest of the community, so that you can approach him, perform your service in the LORD's Tent, and minister to the community and serve them? [10] He has let you and all the other Levites have this honour — and now you are trying to get the priesthood too! [11] When you complain against Aaron, it is really against the LORD that you and your followers are rebelling."

[12] Then Moses sent for Dathan and Abiram, but they said, "We will not come! [13] Isn't it enough that you have brought us out of the fertile land of Egypt to kill us here in the wilderness? Do you also have to lord it over us? [14] You certainly have not brought us into a fertile land or given us fields and vineyards as our possession, and now you are trying to deceive us. We will not come!"

[15] Moses was angry and said to the LORD, "Do not accept any offerings these men bring. I have not wronged any of them; I have not even taken one of their donkeys."

[16] Moses said to Korah, "Tomorrow you and your 250 followers must come to the Tent of the LORD's presence; Aaron will also be there. [17] Each of you will take his firepan, put incense on it, and then present it at the altar." [18] So every man took his firepan, put live coals and incense on it, and stood at the entrance of the Tent with Moses and Aaron. [19] Then Korah gathered the whole community, and they stood facing Moses and Aaron at the entrance of the Tent. Suddenly the dazzling light of the LORD's presence appeared to the whole community, [20] and the LORD said to Moses and Aaron, [21] "Stand back from these people, and I will destroy them immediately."

[22] But Moses and Aaron bowed down with their faces to the ground and said, "O God, you are the source of all life. When one person sins, do you get angry with the whole community?"

[23] The LORD said to Moses, [24] "Tell the people to move away from the tents of Korah, Dathan, and Abiram."

[25] Then Moses, accompanied by the leaders of Israel, went to Dathan and Abiram. [26] He said to the people, "Stand away from

NUMBERS 16
183
Num.
....
Deuter.
Joshua
Judges
Ruth
1 Sam.

the tents of these wicked men and don't touch anything that belongs to them. Otherwise, you will be wiped out with them for all their sins." 27 So they moved away from the tents of Korah, Dathan, and Abiram.

Dathan and Abiram had come out and were standing at the entrance of their tents, with their wives and children. 28 Moses said to the people, "This is how you will know that the LORD has sent me to do all these things and that it is not by my own choice that I have done them. 29 If these men die a natural death without some punishment from God, then the LORD did not send me. 30 But if the LORD does something unheard of, and the earth opens up and swallows them with all they own, so that they go down alive to the world of the dead, you will know that these men have rejected the LORD."

31 As soon as he had finished speaking, the ground under Dathan and Abiram split open 32 and swallowed them and their families, together with all of Korah's followers and their possessions. 33 So they went down alive to the world of the dead, with their possessions. The earth closed over them, and they vanished. 34 All the people of Israel who were there fled when they heard their cry. They shouted, "Run! The earth might swallow us too!"

35 Then the LORD sent a fire that blazed out and burnt up the 250 men who had presented the incense.

The Firepans

36 Then the LORD said to Moses, 37 "Tell Eleazar son of Aaron the priest to remove the bronze firepans from the remains of the men who have been burnt, and scatter the coals from the firepans somewhere else, because the firepans are holy. 38 They became holy when they were presented at the LORD's altar. So take the firepans of these men who were put to death for their sin, beat them into thin plates, and make a covering for the altar. It will be a warning to the people of Israel." 39 So Eleazar the priest took the firepans and had them beaten into thin plates to make a covering for the altar. 40 This was a warning to the Israelites that no one who was not a descendant of Aaron should come to the altar to burn incense for the LORD. Otherwise he would be destroyed like Korah and his men. All this was done as the LORD had commanded Eleazar through Moses.

Aaron Saves the People

41 The next day the whole community complained against Moses and Aaron and said, "You have killed some of the LORD's people." 42 After they had all gathered to protest to Moses and Aaron, they turned towards the Tent and saw that the cloud was covering it and that the dazzling light of the LORD's presence had appeared. 43 Moses and Aaron went and stood in front of the Tent, 44 and the LORD said to Moses, 45 "Stand back from these people, and I will destroy them on the spot!"

The two of them bowed down with their faces to the ground, 46 and Moses said to Aaron, "Take your firepan, put live coals from the altar in it, and put some incense on the coals. Then hurry with it to the people and perform the ritual of purification for them. Hurry! The LORD's anger has already broken out and an epidemic has already begun." 47 Aaron obeyed, took his firepan and ran into the middle of the assembled people. When he saw that the plague had already begun, he put the incense on the coals and performed the ritual of purification for the people. 48 This stopped the plague, and he was left standing between the living and the

184

Num.

Genesis
Exodus
Leviticus

NUMBERS 16–18

TURN THESE
LINES INTO A
PICTURE OF
SOMETHING.

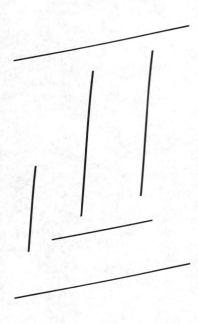

dead. [49] The number of people who died was 14,700, not counting those who died in Korah's rebellion. [50] When the plague had stopped, Aaron returned to Moses at the entrance of the Tent.

Aaron's Stick

17 The LORD said to Moses, [2] "Tell the people of Israel to give you twelve sticks, one from the leader of each tribe. Write each man's name on his stick [3] and then write Aaron's name on the stick representing Levi. There will be one stick for each tribal leader. [4] Take them to the Tent of my presence and put them in front of the Covenant Box, where I meet you. [5] Then the stick of the man I have chosen will sprout. In this way I will put a stop to the constant complaining of these Israelites against you."

[6] So Moses spoke to the Israelites, and each of their leaders gave him a stick, one for each tribe, twelve in all, and Aaron's stick was put with them. [7] Moses then put all the sticks in the Tent in front of the LORD's Covenant Box.

[8] The next day, when Moses went into the Tent, he saw that Aaron's stick, representing the tribe of Levi, had sprouted. It had budded, blossomed, and produced ripe almonds! [9] Moses took all the sticks and showed them to the Israelites. They saw what had happened, and each leader took his own stick back. [10] The LORD said to Moses, "Put Aaron's stick back in front of the Covenant Box. It is to be kept as a warning to the rebel Israelites that they will die unless their complaining stops." [11] Moses did as the LORD commanded.

[12] The people of Israel said to Moses, "Then that's the end of us! [13] If anyone who even comes near the Tent must die, then we are all as good as dead!"

Duties of Priests and Levites

18 The LORD said to Aaron, "You, your sons, and the Levites must suffer the consequences of any guilt connected with serving in the Tent of my presence; but only you and your sons will suffer the consequences of service in the priesthood. [2] Bring in your relatives, the tribe of Levi, to work with you and help you while you and your sons are serving at the Tent. [3] They are to fulfil their duties to you and their responsibilities for the Tent, but they must not have any contact with sacred objects in the Holy Place or with the altar. If they do, both they and you will be put to death. [4] They are to work with you and fulfil their responsibilities for all the service in the Tent, but no unqualified person may work with you. [5] You and your sons alone must fulfil the responsibilities for the Holy Place and the altar, so that my anger will not again break out against the people of Israel. [6] I am the one who has chosen your relatives the Levites from among the Israelites as a gift to you. They are dedicated to me, so that they can carry out their duties in the Tent. [7] But you and your sons alone shall fulfil all the responsibilities of the priesthood that concern the altar and what is in the Most Holy Place. These things are your responsibility, because I have given you the gift of the priesthood. Any unqualified person who comes near the sacred objects shall be put to death."

The Share of the Priests

[8] The LORD said to Aaron, "Remember that I am giving you all the special contributions made to me that are not burnt as sacrifices. I am giving them to you and to your descendants as the part assigned to you for ever. [9] Of the most sacred offerings not burnt on the altar, the following belong to you: the grain offerings, the sin offerings, and the repayment offerings. Everything that

NUMBERS 18

185

Num.

.........:

Deuter.
Joshua
Judges
Ruth
1 Sam.

is presented to me as a sacred offering belongs to you and your sons. ¹⁰ You must eat these things in a holy place, and only males may eat them; consider them holy.

¹¹ "In addition, any other special contributions that the Israelites present to me shall be yours. I am giving them to you, your sons, and your daughters for all time to come. Every member of your family who is ritually clean may eat them.

¹² "I am giving you all the best of the first produce which the Israelites give me each year: olive oil, wine, and corn. ¹³ It all belongs to you. Every member of your family who is ritually clean may eat it.

¹⁴ "Everything in Israel that has been unconditionally dedicated to me belongs to you.

¹⁵ "Every firstborn child or animal that the Israelites present to me belongs to you. But you must accept payment to buy back every firstborn child, and must also accept payment for every firstborn animal that is ritually unclean. ¹⁶ Children shall be bought back at the age of one month for the fixed price of five pieces of silver, according to the official standard. ¹⁷ But the firstborn of cows, sheep, and goats are not to be bought back; they belong completely to me and are to be sacrificed. Throw their blood against the altar and burn their fat as a food offering, a smell pleasing to me. ¹⁸ The meat from them belongs to you, like the breast and the right hind leg of the special offering.

¹⁹ "I am giving to you, to your sons, and to your daughters, for all time to come, all the special contributions which the Israelites present to me. This is an unbreakable covenant that I have made with you and your descendants."

²⁰ The LORD said to Aaron, "You will not receive any property that can be inherited, and no part of the land of Israel will be assigned to you. I, the LORD, am all you need."

The Share of the Levites

²¹ The LORD said, "I have given to the Levites every tithe that the people of Israel present to me. This is in payment for their service in taking care of the Tent of my presence. ²² The other Israelites must no longer approach the Tent and in this way bring on themselves the penalty of death. ²³ From now on only the Levites will take care of the Tent and bear the full responsibility for it. This is a permanent rule that applies also to your descendants. The Levites shall have no permanent property in Israel, ²⁴ because I have given to them as their possession the tithe which the Israelites present to me as a special contribution. That is why I told them that they would have no permanent property in Israel."

The Levites' Tithe

²⁵ The LORD commanded Moses ²⁶ to say to the Levites: "When you receive from the Israelites the tithe that the LORD gives you as your possession, you must present a tenth of it as a special contribution to the LORD. ²⁷ This special contribution will be considered as the equivalent of the offering which the farmer makes of new corn and new wine. ²⁸ In this way you also will present the special contribution that belongs to the LORD from all the tithes which you receive from the Israelites. You are to give this special contribution for the LORD to Aaron the priest. ²⁹ Give it from the best that you receive. ³⁰ When you have presented the best part, you may keep the rest, just as the farmer keeps what is left after he makes his offering. ³¹ You and your families may eat the rest anywhere, because it is your wages for your service in

186

Num.

∴········

Genesis
Exodus
Leviticus

NUMBERS 18, 19

the Tent. [32] You will not become guilty when you eat it, as long as you have presented the best of it to the LORD. But be sure not to profane the sacred gifts of the Israelites by eating any of the gifts before the best part is offered; if you do, you will be put to death."

Ashes of the Red Cow

19 The LORD commanded Moses and Aaron [2] to give the Israelites the following regulations. Bring to Moses and Aaron a red cow which has no defects and which has never been put to work, [3] and they will give it to Eleazar the priest. It is to be taken outside the camp and killed in his presence.* [4] Then Eleazar is to take some of its blood and with his finger sprinkle it seven times in the direction of the Tent. [5] The whole animal, including skin, meat, blood, and intestines, is to be burnt in the presence of the priest. [6] Then he is to take some cedar wood, a sprig of hyssop, and a red cord and throw them into the fire. [7] After that, he is to wash his clothes and pour water over himself, and then he may enter the camp; but he remains ritually unclean until evening. [8] The man who burnt the cow must also wash his clothes and pour water over himself, but he also remains unclean until evening. [9] Then a man who is ritually clean is to collect the ashes of the cow and put them in a ritually clean place outside the camp, where they are to be kept for the Israelite community to use in preparing the water for removing ritual uncleanness. This ritual is performed to remove sin. [10] The man who collected the ashes must wash his clothes, but he remains unclean until evening. This regulation is valid for all time to come, both for the Israelites and for the foreigners living among them.

Contact with a Corpse

[11] Whoever touches a corpse is ritually unclean for seven days. [12] He must purify himself with the water for purification on the third day and on the seventh day, and then he will be clean. But if he does not purify himself on both the third and the seventh day, he will not be clean. [13] Whoever touches a corpse and does not purify himself remains unclean, because the water for purification has not been thrown over him. He defiles the LORD's Tent, and he will no longer be considered one of God's people.

[14] If someone dies in a tent, anyone who is in the tent at the time of death or who enters it becomes ritually unclean for seven days. [15] Every jar and pot in the tent that has no lid* on it also becomes unclean. [16] If someone touches a person who has been killed or has died a natural death out of doors or if someone touches a human bone or a grave, he becomes unclean for seven days.

[17] To remove the uncleanness, some ashes from the red cow which was burnt to remove sin shall be taken and put in a pot, and fresh water added. [18] In the first case, someone who is ritually clean is to take a sprig of hyssop, dip it in the water, and sprinkle the tent, everything in it, and the people who were there. In the second case, someone who is ritually clean is to sprinkle the water on the man who had touched the human bone or the dead body or the grave. [19] On the third day and on the seventh the person who is ritually clean is to sprinkle the water on the unclean person. On the seventh day he is to purify the man, who, after washing his clothes and pouring water over himself, becomes ritually clean at sunset.

....

19.3 *It... presence*; or *He is to take it outside to the east of the camp and kill it*.
19.15 *no lid*; or *no lid fastened*.

Num.

Deuter.
Joshua
Judges
Ruth
1 Sam.

²⁰ Anyone who has become ritually unclean and does not purify himself remains unclean, because the water for purification has not been thrown over him. He defiles the LORD's Tent and will no longer be considered one of God's people. ²¹ You are to observe this rule for all time to come. The person who sprinkles the water for purification must also wash his clothes; anyone who touches the water remains ritually unclean until evening. ²² Whatever an unclean person touches is unclean, and anyone else who touches it remains unclean until evening.

Events at Kadesh
(Ex 17.1–7)

20 In the first month the whole community of Israel came to the wilderness of Zin and camped at Kadesh. There Miriam died and was buried.

² There was no water where they camped, so the people gathered round Moses and Aaron ³ and complained: "It would have been better if we had died in front of the LORD's Tent along with our fellow-Israelites. ⁴ Why have you brought us out into this wilderness? Just so that we can die here with our animals? ⁵ Why did you bring us out of Egypt into this miserable place where nothing will grow? There's no corn, no figs, no grapes, no pomegranates. There is not even any water to drink!" ⁶ Moses and Aaron moved away from the people and stood at the entrance of the Tent. They bowed down with their faces to the ground, and the dazzling light of the LORD's presence appeared to them.

⁷ The LORD said to Moses, ⁸ "Take the stick that is in front of the Covenant Box, and then you and Aaron assemble the whole community. There in front of them all speak to that rock over there, and water will gush out of it. In this way you will bring water out of the rock for the people, for them and their animals to drink." ⁹ Moses went and got the stick, as the LORD had commanded.

¹⁰ He and Aaron assembled the whole community in front of the rock, and Moses said, "Listen, you rebels! Do we have to get water out of this rock for you?" ¹¹ Then Moses raised the stick and struck the rock twice with it, and a great stream of water gushed out, and all the people and animals drank.

¹² But the LORD reprimanded Moses and Aaron. He said, "Because you did not have enough faith to acknowledge my holy power before the people of Israel, you will not lead them into the land that I promised to give them."

¹³ This happened at Meribah,* where the people of Israel complained against the LORD and where he showed them that he was holy.

The King of Edom Refuses to Let Israel Pass

¹⁴ Moses sent messengers from Kadesh to the king of Edom. They said, "This message is from your kinsmen, the tribes of Israel. You know the hardships we have suffered, ¹⁵ how our ancestors went to Egypt, where we lived many years. The Egyptians ill-treated our ancestors and us, ¹⁶ and we cried to the LORD for help. He heard our cry and sent an angel, who led us out of Egypt. Now we are at Kadesh, a town at the border of your territory. ¹⁷ Please permit us to pass through your land. We and our cattle will not leave the road or go into your fields or vineyards, and we will not drink from your wells. We will stay on the main road* until we are out of your territory."

20.13 *Meribah*: This name in Hebrew means "complaining".
20.17 *main road*; or *king's highway*.

READ THIS PASSAGE

AGAIN

BUT SLOWER,

taking time to soak
in what is going on.

188

Num.

.·:········

Genesis
Exodus
Leviticus

NUMBERS 20, 21

¹⁸But the Edomites answered, "We refuse to let you pass through our country! If you try, we will march out and attack you." ¹⁹The people of Israel said, "We will stay on the main road, and if we or our animals drink any of your water, we will pay for it — all we want is to pass through." ²⁰The Edomites repeated, "We refuse!" and they marched out with a powerful army to attack the people of Israel. ²¹Because the Edomites would not let the Israelites pass through their territory, the Israelites turned and went another way.

The Death of Aaron

²²The whole community of Israel left Kadesh and arrived at Mount Hor, ²³on the border of Edom. There the Lord said to Moses and Aaron, ²⁴"Aaron is not going to enter the land which I promised to give to Israel; he is going to die, because the two of you rebelled against my command at Meribah. ²⁵Take Aaron and his son Eleazar up Mount Hor, ²⁶and there remove Aaron's priestly robes and put them on Eleazar. Aaron is going to die there." ²⁷Moses did what the Lord had commanded. They went up Mount Hor in the sight of the whole community, ²⁸and Moses removed Aaron's priestly robes and put them on Eleazar. There on the top of the mountain Aaron died, and Moses and Eleazar came back down. ²⁹The whole community learnt that Aaron had died, and they all mourned for him for thirty days.

Victory over the Canaanites

21 When the Canaanite king of Arad in the southern part of Canaan heard that the Israelites were coming by way of Atharim, he attacked them and captured some of them. ²Then the Israelites made a vow to the Lord: "If you will let us conquer these people, we will unconditionally dedicate* them and their cities to you and will destroy them." ³The Lord heard them and helped them to conquer the Canaanites. So the Israelites completely destroyed them and their cities, and named the place Hormah.*

The Snake Made of Bronze

⁴The Israelites left Mount Hor by the road that leads to the Gulf of Aqaba, in order to go round the territory of Edom. But on the way the people lost their patience ⁵and spoke against God and Moses. They complained, "Why did you bring us out of Egypt to die in this desert, where there is no food or water? We can't stand any more of this miserable food!" ⁶Then the Lord sent poisonous snakes among the people, and many Israelites were bitten and died. ⁷The people came to Moses and said, "We sinned when we spoke against the Lord and against you. Now pray to the Lord to take these snakes away." So Moses prayed for the people. ⁸Then the Lord told Moses to make a metal snake and put it on a pole, so that anyone who was bitten could look at it and be healed. ⁹So Moses made a bronze snake and put it on a pole. Anyone who had been bitten would look at the bronze snake and be healed.

From Mount Hor to the Valley of the Moabites

¹⁰The Israelites moved on and camped at Oboth. ¹¹After leaving that place, they camped at the ruins of Abarim in the

....

21.2 *unconditionally dedicate*: Anything dedicated in this way belonged completely to the Lord and could not be used; it had to be destroyed.
21.3 *Hormah*: This name in Hebrew means "destruction".

NUMBERS 21   189

Num.

....

Deuter.
Joshua
Judges
Ruth
1 Sam.

wilderness east of Moabite territory. ¹²Then they camped in the
Valley of Zered. ¹³From there they moved again and camped on
the north side of the River Arnon, in the wilderness which extends
into Amorite territory. (The Arnon was the border between the
Moabites and the Amorites.) ¹⁴That is why *The Book of the* LORD's
Battles speaks of "...the town of Waheb in the area of Suphah,
and the valleys; the River Arnon, ¹⁵and the slope of the valleys
that extend to the town of Ar and towards the border of Moab."

¹⁶From there they went on to a place called Wells, where the
LORD said to Moses, "Bring the people together, and I will give
them water." ¹⁷At that time the people of Israel sang this song:

"Wells, produce your water;
And we will greet it with a song —
¹⁸ The well dug by princes
And by leaders of the people,
Dug with a royal sceptre
And with their sticks."

They moved from the wilderness to Mattanah, ¹⁹and from there
they went on to Nahaliel, and from Nahaliel to Bamoth, ²⁰and
from Bamoth to the valley in the territory of the Moabites, below
the top of Mount Pisgah, looking out over the desert.

Victory over King Sihon and King Og
(Deut 2.26—3.11)

²¹Then the people of Israel sent messengers to the Amorite
king Sihon to say: ²²"Let us pass through your land. We and our
cattle will not leave the road and go into your fields or vineyards,
and we will not drink water from your wells; we will stay on the
main road* until we are out of your territory." ²³But Sihon would
not permit the people of Israel to pass through his territory. He
gathered his army and went out to Jahaz in the wilderness and
attacked the Israelites. ²⁴But the Israelites killed many of the
enemy in battle and occupied their land from the River Arnon
north to the Jabbok, that is, to the Ammonites, because the
Ammonite border was strongly defended.* ²⁵So the people of
Israel captured all the Amorite cities, including Heshbon and all
the surrounding towns, and settled in them. ²⁶Heshbon was the
capital city of the Amorite king Sihon, who had fought against
the former king of Moab and had captured all his land as far as
the River Arnon. ²⁷That is why the poets sing,

"Come to Heshbon, to King Sihon's city!
We want to see it rebuilt and restored.
²⁸ Once from this city of Heshbon
Sihon's army went forth like a fire;
It destroyed the city of Ar in Moab
And devoured* the hills of the upper Arnon.
²⁹ How terrible for you, people of Moab!
You worshippers of Chemosh are brought to ruin!
Your god let the men become refugees,
And the women became captives of the Amorite king.
³⁰ But now their descendants are destroyed,
All the way from Heshbon to Dibon,
From Nashim to Nophah, near Medeba."*

21.22 *main road*; or *king's highway.*
21.24 *because... strongly defended*; some ancient translations *as far as
Jazer on the Ammonite border.*
21.28 One ancient translation *devoured*; Hebrew *the lords of.*
21.30 Verse 30 in Hebrew is unclear.

Colour these shapes.

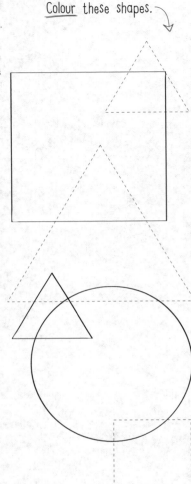

31 So the people of Israel settled in the territory of the Amorites, 32 and Moses sent men to find the best way to attack the city of Jazer. The Israelites captured it and its surrounding towns and drove out the Amorites living there.

33 Then the Israelites turned and took the road to Bashan, and King Og of Bashan marched out with his army to attack them at Edrei. 34 The LORD said to Moses, "Do not be afraid of him. I will give you victory over him, all his people, and his land. Do to him what you did to Sihon, the Amorite king who ruled at Heshbon." 35 So the Israelites killed Og, his sons, and all his people, leaving no survivors, and then they occupied his land.

The King of Moab Sends for Balaam

22 The Israelites moved on and set up camp in the plains of Moab east of the Jordan and opposite Jericho.

2 When the king of Moab, Balak son of Zippor, heard what the Israelites had done to the Amorites and how many Israelites there were, 3 he and all his people became terrified. 4 The Moabites said to the leaders of the Midianites, "This horde will soon destroy everything round us, like a bull eating the grass in a pasture." So King Balak 5 sent messengers to summon Balaam son of Beor, who was at Pethor near the River Euphrates in the land of Amaw. They brought him this message from Balak: "I want you to know that a whole nation has come from Egypt; its people are spreading out everywhere and threatening to take over our land. 6 They outnumber us, so please come and put a curse on them for me. Then perhaps we will be able to defeat them and drive them out of the land. I know that when you pronounce a blessing, people are blessed, and when you pronounce a curse, they are placed under a curse."

7 So the Moabite and Midianite leaders took with them the payment for the curse, went to Balaam, and gave him Balak's message. 8 Balaam said to them, "Spend the night here, and tomorrow I will report to you whatever the LORD tells me." So the Moabite leaders stayed with Balaam.

9 God came to Balaam and asked, "Who are these men that are staying with you?"

10 He answered, "King Balak of Moab has sent them to tell me 11 that a people who came from Egypt has spread out over the whole land. He wants me to curse them for him, so that he can fight them and drive them out."

12 God said to Balaam, "Do not go with these men, and do not put a curse on the people of Israel, because they have my blessing."

13 The next morning Balaam went to Balak's messengers and said, "Go back home; the LORD has refused to let me go with you." 14 So they returned to Balak and told him that Balaam had refused to come with them.

15 Then Balak sent a larger number of leaders, who were more important than the first. 16 They went to Balaam and gave him this message from Balak: "Please don't let anything prevent you from coming to me! 17 I will reward you richly and do anything you say. Please come and curse these people for me."

18 But Balaam answered, "Even if Balak gave me all the silver and gold in his palace, I could not disobey the command of the LORD my God in even the smallest matter. 19 But please stay the night, as the others did, so that I may learn whether or not the LORD has something else to tell me."

20 That night God came to Balaam and said, "If these men have come to ask you to go with them, get ready to go, but do

Num.

..........:.

Deuter.

Joshua

Judges

Ruth

1 Sam.

only what I tell you." [21] So the next morning Balaam saddled his donkey and went with the Moabite leaders.

Balaam and his Donkey

[22] God was angry that Balaam was going, and as Balaam was riding along on his donkey, accompanied by his two servants, the angel of the LORD stood in the road to bar his way. [23] When the donkey saw the angel standing there holding a sword, it left the road and turned into the fields. Balaam beat the donkey and brought it back on to the road. [24] Then the angel stood where the road narrowed between two vineyards and had a stone wall on each side. [25] When the donkey saw the angel, it moved over against the wall and crushed Balaam's foot against it. Again Balaam beat the donkey. [26] Once more the angel moved ahead; he stood in a narrow place where there was no room at all to pass on either side. [27] This time, when the donkey saw the angel, it lay down. Balaam lost his temper and began to beat the donkey with his stick. [28] Then the LORD gave the donkey the power of speech, and it said to Balaam, "What have I done to you? Why have you beaten me these three times?"

[29] Balaam answered, "Because you have made a fool of me! If I had a sword, I would kill you."

[30] The donkey replied, "Am I not the same donkey on which you have ridden all your life? Have I ever treated you like this before?"

"No," he answered.

[31] Then the LORD let Balaam see the angel standing there with his sword; and Balaam threw himself face downwards on the ground. [32] The angel demanded, "Why have you beaten your donkey three times like this? I have come to bar your way, because you should not be making this journey.* [33] But your donkey saw me and turned aside three times. If it hadn't, I would have killed you and spared the donkey."

[34] Balaam replied, "I have sinned. I did not know that you were standing in the road to oppose me; but now if you think it is wrong for me to go on, I will return home."

[35] But the angel said, "Go on with these men, but say only what I tell you to say." So Balaam went on with them.

Balak Welcomes Balaam

[36] When Balak heard that Balaam was coming, he went to meet him at Ar, a city on the River Arnon at the border of Moab. [37] Balak said to him, "Why didn't you come when I sent for you the first time? Did you think I wasn't able to reward you enough?"

[38] Balaam answered, "I came, didn't I? But now, what power have I got? I can say only what God tells me to say." [39] So Balaam went with Balak to the town of Huzoth, [40] where Balak slaughtered cattle and sheep and gave some of the meat to Balaam and the leaders who were with him.

Balaam's First Prophecy

[41] Next morning Balak took Balaam up to Bamoth Baal, from where Balaam could see a part of the people of Israel.

23 He said to Balak, "Build seven altars here for me, and bring me seven bulls and seven rams."

[2] Balak did as he was told, and he and Balaam offered a bull and a ram on each altar. [3] Then Balaam said to Balak, "Stand here by your burnt offering, while I go to see whether or not the

22.32 Probable text *you should… journey*; Hebrew unclear.

192

Num.

Genesis
Exodus
Leviticus

NUMBERS 23

LORD will meet me. I will tell you whatever he reveals to me." So he went alone to the top of a hill, ⁴and God met him. Balaam said to him, "I have built the seven altars and offered a bull and a ram on each."

⁵The LORD told Balaam what to say and sent him back to Balak to give him his message. ⁶So he went back and found Balak still standing by his burnt offering, with all the leaders of Moab. ⁷Balaam uttered this prophecy:

"Balak king of Moab has brought me
From Syria, from the eastern mountains.
'Come and speak for me,' he said.
'Put a curse on the people of Israel.'
⁸ How can I curse what God has not cursed,
Or speak of doom when the LORD has not?
⁹ From the high rocks I can see them;
I can watch them from the hills.
They are a nation that lives alone;
They know they are blessed more than other nations.
¹⁰ The descendants of Israel are like the dust —
There are too many of them to be counted.
Let me end my days like one of God's people;
Let me die in peace like the righteous."

¹¹Then Balak said to Balaam, "What have you done to me? I brought you here to curse my enemies, but all you have done is bless them."

¹²He answered, "I can say only what the LORD tells me to say."

Balaam's Second Prophecy

¹³Then Balak said to Balaam, "Come with me to another place from which you can see only some of the Israelites. Curse them for me from there." ¹⁴He took him to the field of Zophim on the top of Mount Pisgah. There also he built seven altars and offered a bull and a ram on each of them.

¹⁵Balaam said to Balak, "Stand here by your burnt offering, and I will meet God over there."

¹⁶The LORD met Balaam, told him what to say, and sent him back to Balak to give him his message. ¹⁷So he went back and found Balak still standing by his burnt offering, with the leaders of Moab. Balak asked what the LORD had said, ¹⁸and Balaam uttered this prophecy:

"Come, Balak son of Zippor,
And listen to what I have to say.
¹⁹ God is not like men, who lie;
He is not a human who changes his mind.
Whatever he promises, he does;
He speaks, and it is done.
²⁰ I have been instructed to bless,
And when God blesses, I cannot call it back.
²¹ I foresee that Israel's future
Will bring her no misfortune or trouble.
The LORD their God is with them;
They proclaim that he is their king.
²² God has brought them out of Egypt;
He fights for them like a wild ox.
²³ There is no magic charm, no witchcraft,
That can be used against the nation of Israel.*

NUMBERS 23.19

GOD SPEAKS, and it is DONE

23.23 There... Israel; or No magic charms are used in Israel, no witchcraft is practised there.

NUMBERS 23, 24

193

Num.

....

Deuter.

Joshua

Judges

Ruth

1 Sam.

Now people will say about Israel,
'Look what God has done!'
24 The nation of Israel is like a mighty lion:
It doesn't rest until it has torn and devoured,
Until it has drunk the blood of those it has killed."
25 Then Balak said to Balaam, "You refuse to curse the people of Israel, but at least don't bless them!"
26 Balaam answered, "Didn't I tell you that I had to do everything that the LORD told me?"

Balaam's Third Prophecy

27 Balak said, "Come with me, and I will take you to another place. Perhaps God will be willing to let you curse them for me from there." 28 So he took Balaam to the top of Mount Peor overlooking the desert. 29 Balaam said to him, "Build seven altars for me here and bring me seven bulls and seven rams." 30 Balak did as he was told, and offered a bull and a ram on each altar.

24 By now Balaam knew that the LORD wanted him to bless the people of Israel, so he did not go to look for omens, as he had done before. He turned towards the desert 2 and saw the people of Israel camped tribe by tribe. The Spirit of God took control of him, 3 and he uttered this prophecy:
"The message of Balaam son of Beor,
The words of the man who can see clearly,*
4 Who can hear what God is saying.
With staring eyes I see in a trance
A vision from Almighty God.
5 The tents of Israel are beautiful,
6 Like long rows of palms
Or gardens beside a river,
Like aloes planted by the LORD
Or cedars beside the water.
7 They will have abundant rainfall
And plant their seed in well-watered fields.*
Their king shall be greater than Agag,
And his rule shall be extended far and wide.
8 God brought them out of Egypt;
He fights for them like a wild ox.
They devour their enemies,
Crush their bones, smash their arrows.
9 The nation is like a mighty lion;
When it is sleeping, no one dares wake it.
Whoever blesses Israel will be blessed,
And whoever curses Israel will be cursed."
10 Balak clenched his fists in anger and said to Balaam, "I called you to curse my enemies, but three times now you have blessed them instead. 11 Now go off home! I promised to reward you, but the LORD has kept you from getting the reward."
12 Balaam answered, "I told the messengers you sent to me that 13 even if you gave me all the silver and gold in your palace, I could not disobey the command of the LORD by doing anything of myself. I will say only what the LORD tells me to say."

Balaam's Final Prophecies

14 Balaam said to Balak, "Now I am going back to my own people, but before I go, I am warning you what the people of

24.3 *who can see clearly; or whose eyes are closed.*
24.7 One ancient translation *They... fields;* Hebrew unclear.

194

Num.

⁝⁝⁝⁝⁝⁝⁝

Genesis
Exodus
Leviticus

NUMBERS 24, 25

Israel will do to your people in the future." ¹⁵ Then he uttered this prophecy:

"The message of Balaam son of Beor,
The words of the man who can see clearly,*
¹⁶ Who can hear what God is saying
And receive the knowledge that comes from the Most
    High.
With staring eyes I see in a trance
A vision from Almighty God.
¹⁷ I look into the future,
And I see the nation of Israel.
A king, like a bright star, will arise in that nation.
Like a comet he will come from Israel.
He will strike the leaders of Moab
And beat down all the people of Seth.*
¹⁸ He will conquer his enemies in Edom
And make their land his property,
While Israel continues victorious.
¹⁹ The nation of Israel will trample them down
And wipe out the last survivors."

²⁰ Then in his vision Balaam saw the Amalekites and uttered this prophecy:

"Amalek was the most powerful nation of all,
But at the end it will perish for ever."
²¹ In his vision he saw the Kenites, and uttered this prophecy:
"The place where you live is secure,
Safe as a nest set high on a cliff,
²² But you Kenites will be destroyed
When Assyria takes you captive."*
²³ Balaam uttered this prophecy:
"Who are these people gathering in the north?*
²⁴ Invaders will sail from Cyprus;
They will conquer Assyria and Eber,
But they, in turn, will perish for ever."

²⁵ Then Balaam got ready and went back home, and Balak went on his way.

The People of Israel at Peor

25 When the Israelites were camped in the Valley of Acacia, the men began to have sexual intercourse with the Moabite women who were there. ² These women invited them to sacrificial feasts, where the god of Moab was worshipped. The Israelites ate the food and worshipped the god ³ Baal of Peor. So the LORD was angry with them ⁴ and said to Moses, "Take all the leaders of Israel and, in obedience to me, execute them in broad daylight,* and then I will no longer be angry with the people." ⁵ Moses said to the officials, "Each of you is to kill every man in your tribe who has become a worshipper of Baal of Peor."

⁶ One of the Israelites took a Midianite woman into his tent in the sight of Moses and the whole community, while they were mourning at the entrance of the Tent of the LORD's presence. ⁷ When Phinehas, the son of Eleazar and grandson of Aaron the

....

24.15 *who can see clearly*; or *whose eyes are closed*.
24.17 *the people of Seth*; or *who are proud and violent*.
24.22 Verse 22 in Hebrew is unclear.
24.23 Probable text *Who... north*; Hebrew unclear.
25.4 *in broad daylight*; or *publicly*.

Num.

...........:.

Deuter.

Joshua

Judges

Ruth

1 Sam.

priest, saw this, he got up and left the assembly. He took a spear, [8]followed the man and the woman into the tent, and drove the spear through both of them. In this way the epidemic that was destroying Israel was stopped, [9]but it had already killed 24,000 people.

[10]The Lord said to Moses, [11]"Because of what Phinehas has done, I am no longer angry with the people of Israel. He refused to tolerate the worship of any god but me, and that is why I did not destroy them in my anger. [12]So tell him that I am making a covenant with him that is valid for all time to come. [13]He and his descendants are permanently established as priests, because he did not tolerate any rivals to me and brought about forgiveness for the people's sin."

[14]The name of the Israelite who was killed with the Midianite woman was Zimri son of Salu, the head of a family in the tribe of Simeon. [15]The woman's name was Cozbi. Zur, her father, was chief of a group of Midianite clans.

[16]The Lord commanded Moses, [17]"Attack the Midianites and destroy them, [18]because of the evil they did to you when they deceived you at Peor, and because of Cozbi, who was killed at the time of the epidemic at Peor."

The Second Census

26 After the epidemic the Lord said to Moses and Eleazar son of Aaron, [2]"Take a census by families of the whole community of Israel, of all men twenty years old or older who are fit for military service." [3-4]Moses and Eleazar obeyed, and called together all the men of that age group. They assembled in the plains of Moab across the River Jordan from Jericho.

These were the Israelites who came out of Egypt:

[5]The tribe of Reuben (Reuben was the eldest son of Jacob): the clans of Hanoch, Pallu, [6]Hezron, and Carmi. [7]These clans numbered 43,730 men. [8]The descendants of Pallu were Eliab [9]and his sons Nemuel, Dathan, and Abiram. (These are the Dathan and Abiram who were chosen by the community. They defied Moses and Aaron and joined the followers of Korah when they rebelled against the Lord. [10]The ground opened and swallowed them, and they died with Korah and his followers when fire destroyed 250 men; they became a warning to the people. [11]But the sons of Korah were not killed.)

[12]The tribe of Simeon: the clans of Nemuel, Jamin, Jachin, [13]Zerah, and Shaul. [14]These clans numbered 22,200 men.

[15]The tribe of Gad: the clans of Zephon, Haggi, Shuni, [16]Ozni, Eri, [17]Arod, and Areli. [18]These clans numbered 40,500 men.

[19-21]The tribe of Judah: the clans of Shelah, Perez, Zerah, Hezron, and Hamul. (Two of Judah's sons, Er and Onan, had died in the land of Canaan.) [22]These clans numbered 76,500 men.

[23]The tribe of Issachar: the clans of Tola, Puah, [24]Jashub, and Shimron. [25]These clans numbered 64,300 men.

[26]The tribe of Zebulun: the clans of Sered, Elon, and Jahleel. [27]These clans numbered 60,500 men.

[28]The tribes of Joseph, who was the father of two sons, Manasseh and Ephraim.

[29]The tribe of Manasseh: Machir son of Manasseh was the father of Gilead, and the following clans traced their ancestry to Gilead: [30]the clans of Iezer, Helek, [31]Asriel, Shechem, [32]Shemida, and Hepher. [33]Zelophehad son of Hepher had no sons, but only daughters; their names were Mahlah, Noah, Hoglah, Milcah, and Tirzah. [34]These clans numbered 52,700 men.

196

Num.

Genesis
Exodus
Leviticus

NUMBERS 26, 27

35 The tribe of Ephraim: the clans of Shuthelah, Becher, and Tahan. 36 The clan of Eran traced its descent from Shuthelah. 37 These clans numbered 32,500 men.

These are the clans descended from Joseph.

38 The tribe of Benjamin: the clans of Bela, Ashbel, Ahiram, 39 Shephupham, and Hupham. 40 The clans of Ard and Naaman traced their descent from Bela. 41 These clans numbered 45,600 men.

42 The tribe of Dan: the clan of Shuham, 43 which numbered 64,400 men.

44 The tribe of Asher: the clans of Imnah, Ishvi, and Beriah. 45 The clans of Heber and Malchiel traced their descent from Beriah. 46 Asher had a daughter named Serah. 47 These clans numbered 53,400 men.

48 The tribe of Naphtali: the clans of Jahzeel, Guni, 49 Jezer, and Shillem. 50 These clans numbered 45,400 men.

51 The total number of the Israelite men was 601,730.

52 The LORD said to Moses, 53 "Divide the land among the tribes, according to their size. 54-56 Divide the land by drawing lots, and give a large share to a large tribe and a small one to a small tribe."

57 The tribe of Levi consisted of the clans of Gershon, Kohath, and Merari. 58 Their descendants included the sub-clans of Libni, Hebron, Mahli, Mushi, and Korah. Kohath was the father of Amram, 59 who was married to Levi's daughter Jochebed, who was born in Egypt. She bore Amram two sons, Aaron and Moses, and a daughter, Miriam. 60 Aaron had four sons, Nadab, Abihu, Eleazar, and Ithamar. 61 Nadab and Abihu died when they offered unholy fire to the LORD. 62 The male Levites who were one month old or older numbered 23,000. They were listed separately from the rest of the Israelites, because they were not given any property in Israel.

63 All these clans were listed by Moses and Eleazar when they took a census of the Israelites in the plains of Moab across the River Jordan from Jericho. 64 There was not even one man left among those whom Moses and Aaron had listed in the first census in the Sinai Desert. 65 The LORD had said that all of them would die in the wilderness, and except for Caleb son of Jephunneh and Joshua son of Nun they all did.

The Daughters of Zelophehad

27 Mahlah, Noah, Hoglah, Milcah, and Tirzah were the daughters of Zelophehad son of Hepher, son of Gilead, son of Machir, son of Manasseh, son of Joseph. 2 They went and stood before Moses, Eleazar the priest, the leaders, and the whole community at the entrance of the Tent of the LORD's presence and said, 3 "Our father died in the wilderness without leaving any sons. He was not among the followers of Korah, who rebelled against the LORD; he died because of his own sin. 4 Just because he had no sons, why should our father's name disappear from Israel? Give us property among our father's relatives."

5 Moses presented their case to the LORD, 6 and the LORD said to him, 7 "What the daughters of Zelophehad request is right; give them property among their father's relatives. Let his inheritance pass on to them. 8 Tell the people of Israel that whenever a man dies without leaving a son, his daughter is to inherit his property. 9 If he has no daughter, his brothers are to inherit it. 10 If he has no brothers, his father's brothers are to inherit it. 11 If he has no brothers or uncles, then his nearest relative is to inherit it and hold it as his own property. The people of Israel are to

NUMBERS 27, 28

197

Num.

....

Deuter.
Joshua
Judges
Ruth
1 Sam.

observe this as a legal requirement, just as I, the LORD, have commanded you."

Joshua is Chosen as Successor to Moses
(Deut 31.1–8)

[12] The LORD said to Moses, "Go up the Abarim Mountains and look out over the land that I am giving to the Israelites. [13] After you have seen it, you will die, as your brother Aaron did, [14] because both of you rebelled against my command in the wilderness of Zin. When the whole community complained against me at Meribah, you refused to acknowledge my holy power before them." (Meribah is the spring at Kadesh in the wilderness of Zin.)

[15] Moses prayed, [16] "LORD God, source of all life, appoint, I pray, a man who can lead the people [17] and can command them in battle, so that your community will not be like sheep without a shepherd."

[18] The LORD said to Moses, "Take Joshua son of Nun, a capable man, and place your hands on his head. [19] Make him stand in front of Eleazar the priest and the whole community, and there before them all proclaim him as your successor. [20] Give him some of your own authority, so that the whole community of Israel will obey him. [21] He will depend on Eleazar the priest, who will learn my will by using the Urim and Thummim.* In this way Eleazar will direct Joshua and the whole community of Israel in all their affairs." [22] Moses did as the LORD had commanded him. He made Joshua stand before Eleazar the priest and the whole community. [23] As the LORD had commanded, Moses put his hands on Joshua's head and proclaimed him as his successor.

The Regular Offerings
(Ex 29.38–46)

28 The LORD commanded Moses [2] to instruct the Israelites to present to God at the appointed times the required food offerings that are pleasing to him.

[3] These are the food offerings that are to be presented to the LORD: for the daily burnt offering, two one-year-old male lambs without any defects. [4] Offer the first lamb in the morning, and the second in the evening, [5] each with a grain offering of one kilogramme of flour, mixed with one litre of the best olive oil. [6] This is the daily offering that is completely burnt, which was first offered at Mount Sinai as a food offering, a smell pleasing to the LORD. [7] As the wine offering with the first lamb, pour out at the altar one litre of wine. [8] In the evening offer the second lamb in the same way as the morning offering, together with its wine offering. It also is a food offering, a smell pleasing to the LORD.

The Sabbath Offering

[9] On the Sabbath day offer two one-year-old male lambs without any defects, two kilogrammes of flour mixed with olive oil as a grain offering, and the wine offering. [10] This burnt offering is to be offered every Sabbath in addition to the daily offering with its wine offering.

The Offering on the First Day of the Month

[11] Present a burnt offering to the LORD at the beginning of each month: two young bulls, one ram, seven one-year-old male

27.21 *Urim and Thummim*: Two objects used by the priest to determine God's will; it is not known precisely how they were used.

NUMBERS 28-29

God spoke to Moses about the importance of holding feasts in his name. These were to be regular times of celebration for different reasons throughout the year. Feasts helped the Israelites to recognise that they were set apart and that the God they served was good.

Why not take some food (a meal or a snack) and, as you eat, thank God for his goodness. Even better, invite a couple of

FRIENDS OVER FOR A
TAKEAWAY

and, as you eat together, have a conversation about God.

lambs, all without any defects. ^{12}As a grain offering, offer flour mixed with olive oil: with each bull, three kilogrammes of flour; with the ram, two kilogrammes; ^{13}and with each lamb, one kilogramme. These burnt offerings are food offerings, a smell pleasing to the LORD. ^{14}The proper wine offering is two litres of wine with each bull, 1.5 litres with the ram, and one litre with each lamb. This is the regulation for the burnt offering for the first day of each month throughout the year. ^{15}And in addition to the daily burnt offering with its wine offering, offer one male goat as a sin offering.

The Offerings at the Festival of Unleavened Bread
(Lev 23.5–14)

^{16}The Passover Festival in honour of the LORD is to be held on the fourteenth day of the first month. ^{17}On the fifteenth day a religious festival begins which lasts seven days, during which only bread prepared without yeast is to be eaten. ^{18}On the first day of the festival you are to gather for worship, and no work is to be done. ^{19}Offer a burnt offering as a food offering to the LORD: two young bulls, one ram, and seven one-year-old male lambs, all without any defects. ^{20}Offer the proper grain offering of flour mixed with olive oil: three kilogrammes with each bull, two kilogrammes with the ram, ^{21}and one kilogramme with each lamb. ^{22}Also offer one male goat as a sin offering, and in this way perform the ritual of purification for the people. ^{23}Offer these in addition to the regular morning burnt offering. ^{24}In the same way, for seven days offer to the LORD a food offering, a smell pleasing to him. Offer this in addition to the daily burnt offering and wine offering. ^{25}Meet for worship on the seventh day and do no work.

The Offerings at the Harvest Festival
(Lev 23.15–22)

^{26}On the first day of the Harvest Festival, when you present the offering of new corn to the LORD, you are to gather for worship, and no work is to be done. ^{27}Offer a burnt offering as a smell pleasing to the LORD: two young bulls, one ram, and seven one-year-old male lambs, all without any defects. ^{28}Offer the proper grain offering of flour mixed with olive oil: three kilogrammes with each bull, two kilogrammes with the ram, ^{29}and one kilogramme with each lamb. ^{30}Also offer one male goat as a sin offering, and in this way perform the ritual of purification for the people. ^{31}Offer these and the wine offering in addition to the daily burnt offering and grain offering.

The Offerings at the New Year Festival
(Lev 23.23–25)

29 On the first day of the seventh month you are to gather for worship, and no work is to be done. On that day trumpets are to be blown. ^{2}Present a burnt offering to the LORD, a smell pleasing to him: one young bull, one ram, and seven one-year-old male lambs, all without any defects. ^{3}Offer the proper grain offering of flour mixed with olive oil: three kilogrammes of flour with the bull, two kilogrammes with the ram, ^{4}and one kilogramme with each lamb. ^{5}Also offer one male goat as a sin offering, and in this way perform the ritual of purification for the people. ^{6}Offer these in addition to the regular burnt offering for the first day of the month with its grain offering, and the daily burnt offering with its grain offering and wine offering. These food offerings are a smell pleasing to the LORD.

NUMBERS 29

199

Num.

Deuter.

Joshua

Judges

Ruth

1 Sam.

The Offerings at the Day of Atonement
(Lev 23.26–32)

⁷Gather for worship on the tenth day of the seventh month; eat no food and do no work. ⁸Offer a burnt offering to the LORD, a smell pleasing to him: one young bull, one ram, and seven one-year-old male lambs, all without any defects. ⁹Offer the proper grain offering of flour mixed with olive oil: three kilogrammes of flour with the bull, two kilogrammes with the ram, ¹⁰and one kilogramme with each lamb. ¹¹Also offer one male goat as a sin offering, in addition to the goat offered in the ritual of purification for the people, and the daily burnt offering with its grain offering and wine offering.

The Offerings at the Festival of Shelters
(Lev 23.33–44)

¹²Gather for worship on the fifteenth day of the seventh month. Celebrate this festival in honour of the LORD for seven days and do no work. ¹³On this first day offer a food offering to the LORD, a smell pleasing to him: thirteen young bulls, two rams, and fourteen one-year-old male lambs, all without any defects. ¹⁴Offer the proper grain offering of flour mixed with olive oil: three kilogrammes of flour with each bull, two kilogrammes with each ram, ¹⁵and one kilogramme with each lamb, with the required wine offerings. ¹⁶Also offer one male goat as a sin offering. Offer these in addition to the daily burnt offering with its grain offering and wine offering.

¹⁷On the second day offer twelve young bulls, two rams, and fourteen one-year-old male lambs, all without any defects. ¹⁸⁻¹⁹Offer with them all the other offerings required for the first day.

²⁰On the third day offer eleven young bulls, two rams, and fourteen one-year-old male lambs, all without any defects. ²¹⁻²²Offer with them all the other offerings required for the first day.

²³On the fourth day offer ten young bulls, two rams, and fourteen one-year-old male lambs, all without any defects. ²⁴⁻²⁵Offer with them all the other offerings required for the first day.

²⁶On the fifth day offer nine young bulls, two rams, and fourteen one-year-old male lambs, all without any defects. ²⁷⁻²⁸Offer with them all the other offerings required for the first day.

²⁹On the sixth day offer eight young bulls, two rams, and fourteen one-year-old male lambs, all without any defects. ³⁰⁻³¹Offer with them all the other offerings required for the first day.

³²On the seventh day offer seven young bulls, two rams, and fourteen one-year-old male lambs, all without any defects. ³³⁻³⁴Offer with them all the other offerings required for the first day.

³⁵On the eighth day gather for worship and do no work. ³⁶Offer a burnt offering as a food offering to the LORD, a smell pleasing to him: one young bull, one ram, and seven one-year-old male lambs, all without any defects. ³⁷⁻³⁸Offer with them all the other offerings required for the first day.

³⁹These are the regulations concerning the burnt offerings, grain offerings, wine offerings, and fellowship offerings that you are to make to the LORD at your appointed festivals. These are in addition to the offerings you give in fulfilment of a vow or as freewill offerings.

Num.

Genesis
Exodus
Leviticus

FILL THIS SPACE HOWEVER YOU LIKE...

40 So Moses told the people of Israel everything that the LORD had commanded him.

Rules about Vows

30 Moses gave the following instructions to the leaders of the tribes of Israel. 2 When a man makes a vow to give something to the LORD or takes an oath to abstain from something, he must not break his promise, but must do everything that he said he would.

3 When a young woman still living in her father's house makes a vow to give something to the LORD or promises to abstain from something, 4 she must do everything that she vowed or promised unless her father raises an objection when he hears about it. 5 But if her father forbids her to fulfil the vow when he hears about it, she is not required to keep it. The LORD will forgive her, because her father refused to let her keep it.

6 If an unmarried woman makes a vow, whether deliberately or carelessly, or promises to abstain from something, and then marries, 7 she must do everything that she vowed or promised unless her husband raises an objection when he hears about it. 8 But if her husband forbids her to fulfil the vow when he hears about it, she is not required to keep it. The LORD will forgive her.

9 A widow or a divorced woman must keep every vow she makes and every promise to abstain from something.

10 If a married woman makes a vow or promises to abstain from something, 11 she must do everything that she vowed or promised unless her husband raises an objection when he hears about it. 12 But if her husband forbids her to fulfil the vow when he hears about it, she is not required to keep it. The LORD will forgive her, because her husband prevented her from keeping her vow. 13 Her husband has the right to affirm or to annul any vow or promise that she has made. 14 But if, by the day after he hears of the vow, he has raised no objection, she must do everything that she has vowed or promised. He has affirmed the vow by not objecting on the day he heard of it. 15 But if he later annuls the vow, he must suffer the consequences for the failure to fulfil the vow.

16 These are the rules that the LORD gave Moses concerning vows made by an unmarried woman living in her father's house or by a married woman.

The Holy War against Midian

31 The LORD said to Moses, 2 "Punish the Midianites for what they did to the people of Israel. After you have done that, you will die."

3 So Moses said to the people, "Get ready for war, so that you can attack Midian and punish them for what they did to the LORD. 4 From each tribe of Israel send a thousand men to war."

5 So a thousand men were chosen from each tribe, a total of 12,000 men ready for battle. 6 Moses sent them to war under the command of Phinehas son of Eleazar the priest, who took charge of the sacred objects and the trumpets for giving signals. 7 They attacked Midian, as the LORD had commanded Moses, and killed all the men, 8 including the five kings of Midian: Evi, Rekem, Zur, Hur, and Reba. They also killed Balaam son of Beor.

9 The people of Israel captured the Midianite women and children, took their cattle and their flocks, plundered all their wealth, 10 and burnt all their cities and camps. 11 They took all the loot that they had captured, including the prisoners and the animals, 12 and brought them to Moses and Eleazar and to the

NUMBERS 31

201

Num.

....

Deuter.
Joshua
Judges
Ruth
1 Sam.

community of the people of Israel, who were at the camp on the plains of Moab across the Jordan from Jericho.

The Army Returns

13 Moses, Eleazar, and all the other leaders of the community went out of the camp to meet the army. 14 Moses was angry with the officers, the commanders of battalions and companies, who had returned from the war. 15 He asked them, "Why have you kept all the women alive? 16 Remember that it was the women who followed Balaam's instructions and at Peor led the people to be unfaithful to the LORD. That was what brought the epidemic on the LORD's people. 17 So now kill every boy and kill every woman who has had sexual intercourse, 18 but keep alive for yourselves all the girls and all the women who are virgins. 19 Now all of you who have killed anyone or have touched a corpse must stay outside the camp for seven days. On the third day and on the seventh day purify yourselves and the women you have captured. 20 You must also purify every piece of clothing and everything made of leather, goats' hair, or wood."

21 Eleazar the priest said to the men who had returned from battle, "These are the regulations that the LORD has given to Moses. 22-23 Everything that will not burn, such as gold, silver, bronze, iron, tin, or lead, is to be purified by passing it through fire. Everything else is to be purified by the water for purification. 24 On the seventh day you must wash your clothes; then you will be ritually clean and will be permitted to enter the camp."

Division of the Loot

25 The LORD said to Moses, 26 "You and Eleazar, together with the other leaders of the community, are to count everything that has been captured, including the prisoners and the animals. 27 Divide what was taken into two equal parts, one part for the soldiers and the other part for the rest of the community. 28 From the part that belongs to the soldiers, withhold as a tax for the LORD one out of every 500 prisoners and the same proportion of the cattle, donkeys, sheep, and goats. 29 Give them to Eleazar the priest as a special contribution to the LORD. 30 From the part given to the rest of the people, take one out of every fifty prisoners and the same proportion of the cattle, donkeys, sheep, and goats. Give them to the Levites who are in charge of the LORD's Tent." 31 Moses and Eleazar did what the LORD commanded.

32-35 The following is a list of what was captured by the soldiers, in addition to what they kept for themselves: 675,000 sheep and goats, 72,000 cattle, 61,000 donkeys, and 32,000 virgins. 36-40 The half-share of the soldiers was 337,500 sheep and goats, of which 675 were the tax for the LORD; 36,000 cattle for the soldiers, of which 72 were the tax for the LORD; 30,500 donkeys for the soldiers, of which 61 were the tax for the LORD; and 16,000 virgins for the soldiers, of which 32 were the tax for the LORD. 41 So Moses gave Eleazar the tax as a special contribution to the LORD, as the LORD had commanded.

42-46 The share of the community was the same as that for the soldiers: 337,500 sheep and goats, 36,000 cattle, 30,500 donkeys, and 16,000 virgins. 47 From this share Moses took one out of every fifty prisoners and animals, and as the LORD had commanded, gave them to the Levites who were in charge of the LORD's Tent.

48 Then the officers who had commanded the army went to Moses 49 and reported, "Sir, we have counted the soldiers under our command and not one of them is missing. 50 So we are bringing

202

NUMBERS 31, 32

Num.

Genesis
Exodus
Leviticus

the gold ornaments, armlets, bracelets, rings, earrings, and necklaces that each of us has taken. We offer them to the LORD as a payment for our lives, so that he will protect us." [51]Moses and Eleazar received the gold, all of which was in the form of ornaments. [52]The total contribution of the officers weighed nearly 200 kilogrammes. [53]Those who were not officers kept the loot they had taken. [54]So Moses and Eleazar took the gold to the Tent, so that the LORD would protect the people of Israel.

The Tribes East of the Jordan
(Deut 3.12–22)

32 The tribes of Reuben and Gad had a lot of livestock. When they saw how suitable the land of Jazer and Gilead was for cattle, [2]they went to Moses, Eleazar, and the other leaders of the community and said, [3-4]"This region which the LORD has helped the Israelites to occupy — the towns of Ataroth, Dibon, Jazer, Nimrah, Heshbon, Elealeh, Sibmah, Nebo, and Beon — is good land for livestock, and we have so much livestock. [5]Please give us this land as our property, and do not make us cross the River Jordan and settle there."

[6]Moses replied, "Do you want to stay here while your fellow-Israelites go to war? [7]How dare you try to discourage the people of Israel from crossing the Jordan into the land which the LORD has given them? [8]That is what your fathers did when I sent them from Kadesh Barnea to explore the land. [9]They went as far as the Valley of Eshcol and saw the land, but when they returned, they discouraged the people from entering the land which the LORD had given them. [10]The LORD was angry that day and made a promise: [11]'I swear that because they did not remain loyal to me, none of the men twenty years old or older who came out of Egypt will enter the land that I promised to Abraham, Isaac, and Jacob.' [12]This included everyone, except Caleb son of Jephunneh the Kenizzite and Joshua son of Nun; they remained loyal to the LORD. [13]The LORD was angry with the people and made them wander in the wilderness for forty years until that whole generation that had displeased him was dead. [14]And now you have taken your fathers' place, a new generation of sinful men ready to bring down the fierce anger of the LORD on Israel again. [15]If you people of Reuben and Gad refuse to follow him now, he will once again abandon all these people in the wilderness, and you will be responsible for their destruction."

[16]They approached Moses and said, "First, allow us to build stone enclosures here for our sheep and fortified towns for our dependants. [17]Then we will be ready to go with our fellow-Israelites into battle and lead the attack until we have settled them in the land that will be theirs. In the meantime, our dependants can live here in the fortified towns, safe from the people of this land. [18]We will not return to our homes until all the other Israelites have taken possession of the land assigned to them. [19]We will not take possession of any property among them on the other side of the Jordan, because we have received our share here east of the Jordan."

[20]Moses answered, "If you really mean what you say, then here in the presence of the LORD get ready to go into battle. [21]All your fighting men are to cross the Jordan and under the command of the LORD they are to attack our enemies until the LORD defeats them [22]and takes possession of the land. After that, you may return, because you will have fulfilled your obligation to the LORD and to your fellow-Israelites. Then the LORD will acknowledge that this land east of the Jordan is yours. [23]But if you do not keep your promise, I warn you that you will be sinning against

203

Num.

....

Deuter.
Joshua
Judges
Ruth
1 Sam.

the LORD. Make no mistake about it; you will be punished for your sin. 24 So build your towns and the enclosures for your sheep, but do what you have promised!"

25 The men of Gad and Reuben said, "Sir, we will do as you command. 26 Our wives and children and our cattle and sheep will remain here in the towns of Gilead. 27 But all of us are ready to go into battle under the LORD's command. We will cross the Jordan and fight, just as you have said."

28 So Moses gave these commands to Eleazar, Joshua, and the other leaders of Israel: 29 "If the men of Gad and Reuben cross the Jordan ready for battle at the LORD's command and if with their help you are able to conquer the land, then give them the land of Gilead as their property. 30 But if they do not cross the Jordan and go into battle with you, they are to receive their share of the property in the land of Canaan, as you do."

31 The men of Gad and Reuben answered, "Sir, we will do as the LORD has commanded. 32 Under his command we will cross into the land of Canaan and go into battle, so that we can retain our property here east of the Jordan."

33 So Moses assigned to the tribes of Gad and Reuben and to half the tribe of Manasseh all the territory of King Sihon of the Amorites and King Og of Bashan, including the towns and the country round them. 34 The tribe of Gad rebuilt the fortified towns of Dibon, Ataroth, Aroer, 35 Atroth Shophan, Jazer, Jogbehah, 36 Beth Nimrah, and Beth Haran. 37 The tribe of Reuben rebuilt Heshbon, Elealeh, Kiriathaim, 38 Nebo, Baal Meon (this name was changed), and Sibmah. They gave new names to the towns they rebuilt.

39 The clan of Machir son of Manasseh invaded the land of Gilead, occupied it, and drove out the Amorites who were there. 40 So Moses gave Gilead to the clan of Machir, and they lived there. 41 Jair, of the tribe of Manasseh, attacked and captured some villages and named them "Villages of Jair". 42 Nobah attacked and captured Kenath and its villages, and he renamed it Nobah, after himself.

The Journey from Egypt to Moab

33 The following account gives the names of the places where the Israelites set up camp after they left Egypt in their tribes under the leadership of Moses and Aaron. 2 At the command of the LORD, Moses wrote down the name of the place each time they set up camp.

3 The people of Israel left Egypt on the fifteenth day of the first month of the year, the day after the first Passover. Under the LORD's protection they left the city of Rameses in full view of the Egyptians, 4 who were burying the firstborn sons that the LORD had killed. By doing this, the LORD showed that he was more powerful than the gods of Egypt.

5 The people of Israel left Rameses and set up camp at Sukkoth. 6 Their next camp was at Etham on the edge of the desert. 7 From there they turned back to Pi Hahiroth, east of Baal Zephon, and camped near Migdol. 8 They left Pi Hahiroth and passed through the Red Sea into the desert of Shur; after a three days' march they camped at Marah. 9 From there they went to Elim, where they camped, because there were twelve springs of water and seventy palm trees there.

10 They left Elim and camped near the Gulf of Suez. 11 Their next camp was in the desert of Sin. 12 Then they camped at Dophkah, 13 and after that at Alush. 14 Next was Rephidim, where there was no water for them to drink.

NUMBERS 33

It was important for Moses to record the journey the Israelites took, all the way from Egypt. Similarly, it is important on the

JOURNEY
– OF –
LIFE

to remember where we have come from and how far God has taken us.

DRAW A LINE
on this page, representing the highs and lows of your journey with God. Mark significant moments on the line.

204

Num.

Genesis
Exodus
Leviticus

NUMBERS 33, 34

15-37 From Rephidim to Mount Hor they set up camp at the following places: the Sinai Desert, Kibroth Hattaavah (or "Graves of Craving"), Hazeroth, Rithmah, Rimmon Perez, Libnah, Rissah, Kehelathah, Mount Shepher, Haradah, Makheloth, Tahath, Terah, Mithkah, Hashmonah, Moseroth, Bene Jaakan, Hor Haggidgad, Jotbathah, Abronah, Eziongeber, the wilderness of Zin (that is, Kadesh), and Mount Hor, at the edge of the land of Edom.

38-39 At the command of the LORD, Aaron the priest climbed Mount Hor. At the age of 123 he died there on the first day of the fifth month of the fortieth year after the Israelites had left Egypt.

40 The king of Arad in southern Canaan heard that the Israelites were coming.

41-49 From Mount Hor to the plains of Moab the Israelites set up camp at the following places: Zalmonah, Punon, Oboth, the ruins of Abarim in the territory of Moab, Dibon Gad, Almon Diblathaim, the Abarim Mountains near Mount Nebo, and in the plains of Moab across the River Jordan from Jericho, between Beth Jeshimoth and the Valley of Acacia.

Instructions before Crossing the Jordan

50 There in the plains of Moab across the Jordan from Jericho the LORD gave Moses 51 the following instructions for Israel: "When you cross the Jordan into the land of Canaan, 52 you must drive out all the inhabitants of the land. Destroy all their stone and metal idols and all their places of worship. 53 Occupy the land and settle in it, because I am giving it to you. 54 Divide the land among the various tribes and clans by drawing lots, giving a large piece of property to a large clan and a small one to a small clan. 55 But if you do not drive out the inhabitants of the land, those that are left will be as troublesome as splinters in your eyes and thorns in your sides, and they will fight against you. 56 If you do not drive them out, I will destroy you, as I planned to destroy them."

The Boundaries of the Land

34 The LORD gave Moses 2 the following instructions for the people of Israel: "When you enter Canaan, the land which I am giving you, the borders of your territory will be as follows. 3 The southern border will extend from the wilderness of Zin along the border of Edom. It will begin on the east at the southern end of the Dead Sea. 4 Then it will turn southwards towards Akrabbim Pass and continue on through Zin as far south as Kadesh Barnea. Then it will turn north-west to Hazar Addar and on to Azmon, 5 where it will turn towards the valley at the border of Egypt and end at the Mediterranean.

6 "The western border will be the Mediterranean Sea.

7 "The northern border will follow a line from the Mediterranean to Mount Hor 8 and from there to Hamath Pass. It will continue to Zedad 9 and to Ziphron, and will end at Hazar Enan.

10 "The eastern border will follow a line from Hazar Enan to Shepham. 11 It will then go south to Harbel, east of Ain, and on to the hills on the eastern shore of Lake Galilee, 12 then south along the River Jordan to the Dead Sea.

"These will be the four borders of your land."

13 So Moses said to the Israelites, "This is the land that you will receive by drawing lots, the land that the LORD has assigned to the nine and a half tribes. 14 The tribes of Reuben and Gad and the eastern half of Manasseh have received their property, divided according to their families, 15 on the eastern side of the Jordan, opposite Jericho."

205

Num.
....

Deuter.
Joshua
Judges
Ruth
1 Sam.

The Leaders Responsible for Dividing the Land

16 The LORD said to Moses, 17 "Eleazar the priest and Joshua son of Nun will divide the land for the people. 18 Take also one leader from each tribe to help them divide it." 19-28 These are the men the LORD chose:

Tribe	Leader
Judah	Caleb son of Jephunneh
Simeon	Shelumiel son of Ammihud
Benjamin	Elidad son of Chislon
Dan	Bukki son of Jogli
Manasseh	Hanniel son of Ephod
Ephraim	Kemuel son of Shiphtan
Zebulun	Elizaphan son of Parnach
Issachar	Paltiel son of Azzan
Asher	Ahihud son of Shelomi
Naphtali	Pedahel son of Ammihud

29 These are the men that the LORD assigned to divide the property for the people of Israel in the land of Canaan.

The Cities Assigned to the Levites

35 In the plains of Moab across the Jordan from Jericho the LORD said to Moses, 2 "Tell the Israelites that from the property they receive they must give the Levites some cities to live in and pasture land round the cities. 3 These cities will belong to the Levites, and they will live there. The pasture land will be for their cattle and all their other animals. 4 The pasture land is to extend outwards from the city walls 450 metres in each direction, 5 so that there is a square area measuring 900 metres on each side, with the city in the middle. 6 You are to give the Levites six cities of refuge to which a man can escape if he kills someone accidentally. In addition, give them 42 other cities 7 with their pasture land, making a total of 48. 8 The number of Levite cities in each tribe is to be determined according to the size of its territory."

The Cities of Refuge
(Deut 19.1–13; Josh 20.1–9)

9 The LORD told Moses 10 to say to the people of Israel: "When you cross the River Jordan and enter the land of Canaan, 11 you are to choose cities of refuge to which a man can escape if he kills someone accidentally. 12 There he will be safe from the dead person's relative who seeks revenge. No one accused of manslaughter is to be put to death without a public trial. 13 Choose six cities, 14 three east of the Jordan and three in the land of Canaan. 15 These will serve as cities of refuge for Israelites and for foreigners who are temporary or permanent residents. Anyone who kills someone accidentally can escape to one of them.

16-18 "If, however, anyone uses a weapon of iron or stone or wood to kill someone, he is guilty of murder and is to be put to death. 19 The dead person's nearest relative has the responsibility for putting the murderer to death. When he finds him, he is to kill him.

20 "If anyone hates someone and kills him by pushing him down or by throwing something at him 21 or by striking him with his fist, he is guilty of murder and is to be put to death. The dead man's nearest relative has the responsibility for putting the murderer to death. When he finds him, he is to kill him.

22 "But suppose anyone accidentally kills someone he does not hate, whether by pushing him down or by throwing something at

206

Num.

:········

Genesis

Exodus

Leviticus

NUMBERS 35, 36

him. ²³ Or suppose that, without looking, anyone throws a stone that kills someone whom he did not intend to hurt and who was not his enemy. ²⁴ In such cases the community shall judge in favour of the one who caused the death and not in favour of the dead person's relative who is seeking revenge. ²⁵ The community is to rescue the one guilty of manslaughter from the dead person's relative, and they are to return him to the city of refuge to which he had escaped. He must live there until the death of the man who is then High Priest. ²⁶ If the one guilty of manslaughter leaves the city of refuge to which he has escaped ²⁷ and if the dead person's relative finds him and kills him, this act of revenge is not murder. ²⁸ The person guilty of manslaughter must remain in the city of refuge until the death of the High Priest, but after that he may return home. ²⁹ These rules apply to you and your descendants wherever you may live.

³⁰ "Anyone accused of murder may be found guilty and put to death only on the evidence of two or more witnesses; the evidence of one witness is not sufficient to support an accusation of murder. ³¹ A murderer must be put to death. He cannot escape this penalty by the payment of money. ³² If someone has fled to a city of refuge, do not allow him to make a payment in order to return home before the death of the High Priest. ³³ If you did this, you would defile the land where you are living. Murder defiles the land, and except by the death of the murderer there is no way to perform the ritual of purification for the land where someone has been murdered. ³⁴ Do not defile the land where you are living, because I am the LORD and I live among the people of Israel."

The Inheritance of Married Women

36 The heads of the families in the clan of Gilead, the son of Machir and grandson of Manasseh son of Joseph, went to Moses and the other leaders. ² They said, "The LORD commanded you to distribute the land to the people of Israel by drawing lots. He also commanded you to give the property of our relative Zelophehad to his daughters. ³ But remember, if they marry men of another tribe, their property will then belong to that tribe, and the total allotted to us will be reduced. ⁴ In the Year of Restoration, when all property that has been sold is restored to its original owners, the property of Zelophehad's daughters will be permanently added to the tribe into which they marry and will be lost to our tribe."

⁵ So Moses gave the people of Israel the following command from the LORD. He said, "What the tribe of Manasseh says is right, ⁶ and so the LORD says that the daughters of Zelophehad are free to marry anyone they wish but only within their own tribe. ⁷ The property of every Israelite will remain attached to his tribe. ⁸ Every woman who inherits property in an Israelite tribe must marry a man belonging to that tribe. In this way all Israelites will inherit the property of their ancestors, ⁹ and the property will not pass from one tribe to another. Each tribe will continue to possess its own property."

¹⁰⁻¹¹ So Mahlah, Tirzah, Hoglah, Milcah, and Noah, the daughters of Zelophehad, did as the LORD had commanded Moses, and they married their cousins. ¹² They married within the clans of the tribe of Manasseh son of Joseph, and their property remained in their father's tribe.

¹³ These are the rules and regulations that the LORD gave the Israelites through Moses in the plains of Moab across the River Jordan from Jericho.

THE BOOK OF
DEUTERONOMY

WRITTEN: PROBABLY 800-500BC (USING STORIES FROM A MUCH EARLIER TIME)

WHAT YOU NEED TO KNOW:

Deuteronomy is a record of three big sermons given by Moses to a new generation of Israelites who were preparing to enter the Promised Land. The first is found in chapters 1-4 and is about how the Israelites' disobedience led to their wandering in the desert; it teaches the importance of obedience. The second sermon is found in chapters 5-26 and is about the commandments and the law. The third is found in chapters 29-33 and is a reminder of God's blessings; it also describes how a new leader, Joshua, is to take over from Moses.

WHY READ IT?

Deuteronomy shows us the last words of Moses before he dies, and in it we see much more about God's tenderness and care than in the other first books of the Bible. We know that God disciplines us and wants us to live correctly, but Moses teaches that this is because he loves us and wants what is best for us.

SUMMARISE
THE JOURNEY...
of the Israelites from Genesis until the death of Moses.

Genesis →

Moses ←

The first five books of the Bible, known in Judaism as the Torah (or 'teachings'), are about a journey with God. If you were to summarise your life so far as a journey, what would you say? Write your thoughts below.

_____
_____
_____
_____
_____
_____
_____
_____
_____
_____
_____
_____
_____
_____

1400BC → JOSHUA CHOSEN AS LEADER 1300BC →
WILDERNESS   MOSES DIES

208

Deuter.

:·········

Genesis
Exodus
Leviticus
Num.

DEUTERONOMY 1

Introduction

1 In this book are the words that Moses spoke to the people of Israel when they were in the wilderness east of the River Jordan. They were in the Jordan Valley near Suph, between the town of Paran on one side and the towns of Tophel, Laban, Hazeroth, and Dizahab on the other. [2] (It takes eleven days to travel from Mount Sinai to Kadesh Barnea by way of the hill country of Edom.) [3] On the first day of the eleventh month of the fortieth year after they had left Egypt, Moses told the people everything the LORD had commanded him to tell them. [4] This was after the LORD* had defeated King Sihon of the Amorites, who ruled in the town of Heshbon, and King Og of Bashan, who ruled in the towns of Ashtaroth and Edrei. [5] It was while the people were east of the Jordan in the territory of Moab that Moses began to explain God's laws and teachings.

He said, [6] "When we were at Mount Sinai, the LORD our God said to us, 'You have stayed long enough at this mountain. [7] Break camp and move on. Go to the hill country of the Amorites and to all the surrounding regions — to the Jordan Valley, to the hill country and the lowlands, to the southern region, and to the Mediterranean coast. Go to the land of Canaan and on beyond the Lebanon Mountains as far as the great River Euphrates. [8] All of this is the land which I, the LORD, promised to give to your ancestors, Abraham, Isaac, and Jacob, and to their descendants. Go and occupy it.'"

Moses Appoints Judges
(Ex 18.13–27)

[9] Moses said to the people, "While we were still at Mount Sinai, I told you, 'The responsibility for leading you is too much for me. I can't do it alone. [10] The LORD your God has made you as numerous as the stars in the sky. [11] May the LORD, the God of your ancestors, make you increase a thousand times more and make you prosperous, as he promised! [12] But how can I alone bear the heavy responsibility for settling your disputes? [13] Choose some wise, understanding, and experienced men from each tribe, and I will put them in charge of you.' [14] And you agreed that this was a good thing to do. [15] So I took the wise and experienced leaders you chose from your tribes, and I placed them in charge of you. Some were responsible for a thousand people, some for a hundred, some for fifty, and some for ten. I also appointed other officials throughout the tribes.

[16] "At that time I instructed them, 'Listen to the disputes that come up among your people. Judge every dispute fairly, whether it concerns only your own people or involves foreigners who live among you. [17] Show no partiality in your decisions; judge everyone on the same basis, no matter who they are. Do not be afraid of anyone, for the decisions you make come from God. If any case is too difficult for you, bring it to me, and I will decide it.' [18] At the same time I gave you instructions for everything else you were to do.

The Spies are Sent Out from Kadesh Barnea
(Num 13.1–33)

[19] "We did what the LORD our God commanded us. We left Mount Sinai and went through that vast and fearful desert on the way to the hill country of the Amorites. When we reached Kadesh

---

1.4 *the* LORD; or *Moses.*

Barnea, 20-21 I said, 'You have now come to the hill country of the Amorites, which the LORD our God, the God of our ancestors, is giving us. Look, there it is. Go and occupy it as he commanded. Do not hesitate or be afraid.'

22 "But you came to me and said, 'Let's send men ahead of us to spy out the land, so that they can tell us the best route to take and what kind of cities are there.'

23 "That seemed a good thing to do, so I selected twelve men, one from each tribe. 24 They went into the hill country as far as the Valley of Eshcol and explored it. 25 They brought us back some fruit they found there, and reported that the land which the LORD our God was giving us was very fertile.

26 "But you rebelled against the command of the LORD your God, and you would not enter the land. 27 You grumbled to one another: 'The LORD hates us. He brought us out of Egypt just to hand us over to these Amorites, so that they could kill us. 28 Why should we go there? We are afraid. The men we sent tell us that the people there are stronger and taller than we are, and that they live in cities with walls that reach the sky. They saw giants there!'

29 "But I said, 'Don't be afraid of those people. 30 The LORD your God will lead you, and he will fight for you, just as you saw him do in Egypt 31 and in the desert. You saw how he brought you safely all the way to this place, just as a father would carry his son.' 32 But in spite of what I said, you still would not trust the LORD, 33 even though he always went ahead of you to find a place for you to camp. To show you the way, he went in front of you in a pillar of fire by night and in a pillar of cloud by day.

The LORD Punishes Israel
(Num 14.20—45)

34 "The LORD heard your complaints and became angry, and so he solemnly declared, 35 'Not one of you from this evil generation will enter the fertile land that I promised to give your ancestors. 36 Only Caleb son of Jephunneh will enter it. He has remained faithful to me, and I will give him and his descendants the land that he has explored.' 37 Because of you the LORD also became angry with me and said, 'Not even you, Moses, will enter the land. 38 But strengthen the determination of your helper, Joshua son of Nun. He will lead Israel to occupy the land.'

39 "Then the LORD said to all of us, 'Your children, who are still too young to know right from wrong, will enter the land — the children you said would be seized by your enemies. I will give the land to them, and they will occupy it. 40 But as for you people, turn round and go back into the desert along the road to the Gulf of Aqaba.'

41 "You replied, 'Moses, we have sinned against the LORD. But now we will attack, just as the LORD our God commanded us.' Then each one of you got ready to fight, thinking it would be easy to invade the hill country.

42 "But the LORD said to me, 'Warn them not to attack, for I will not be with them, and their enemies will defeat them.' 43 I told you what the LORD had said, but you paid no attention. You rebelled against him, and in your pride you marched into the hill country. 44 Then the Amorites who lived in those hills came out against you like a swarm of bees. They chased you as far as Hormah and defeated you there in the hill country of Edom. 45 So you cried out to the LORD for help, but he would not listen to you or pay any attention to you.

TURN THESE SHAPES INTO
SOMETHING
ELSE.

210

Deuter.

Genesis
Exodus
Leviticus
Num.

DEUTERONOMY 1, 2

The Years in the Desert

46"So then, after we had stayed at Kadesh for a long time,

2 we finally turned and went into the desert, along the road to the Gulf of Aqaba, as the LORD had commanded, and we spent a long time wandering about in the hill country of Edom.

2"Then the LORD told me 3that we had spent enough time wandering about in those hills and that we should go north. 4He told me to give you the following instructions: 'You are about to go through the hill country of Edom, the territory of your distant relatives, the descendants of Esau. They will be afraid of you, 5but you must not start a war with them, because I am not going to give you so much as a square metre of their land. I have given Edom to Esau's descendants. 6You may buy food and water from them.'

7"Remember how the LORD your God has blessed you in everything that you have done. He has taken care of you as you wandered through this vast desert. He has been with you these forty years, and you have had everything you needed.

8"So we moved on and left the road that goes from the towns of Elath and Eziongeber to the Dead Sea, and we turned north-east towards Moab. 9The LORD said to me, 'Don't trouble the people of Moab, the descendants of Lot, or start a war against them. I have given them the city of Ar, and I am not going to give you any of their land.'"

10(A mighty race of giants called the Emim used to live in Ar. They were as tall as the Anakim, another race of giants. 11Like the Anakim they were also known as Rephaim; but the Moabites called them Emim. 12The Horites used to live in Edom, but the descendants of Esau chased them out, destroyed their nation, and settled there themselves, just as the Israelites later chased their enemies out of the land that the LORD gave them.)

13"Then we crossed the River Zered as the LORD told us to do. 14This was 38 years after we had left Kadesh Barnea. All the fighting men of that generation had died, as the LORD had said they would. 15The LORD kept on opposing them until he had destroyed them all.

16"After they had all died, 17the LORD said to us, 18'Today you are to pass through the territory of Moab by way of Ar. 19You will then be near the land of the Ammonites, the descendants of Lot. Don't trouble them or start a war against them, because I am not going to give you any of the land that I have given them.'"

20(This territory is also known as the land of the Rephaim, the name of the people who used to live there; the Ammonites called them Zamzummim. 21They were as tall as the Anakim. There were many of them, and they were a mighty race. But the LORD destroyed them, so that the Ammonites took over their land and settled there. 22The LORD had done the same thing for the Edomites, the descendants of Esau, who live in the hill country of Edom. He destroyed the Horites, so that the Edomites took over their land and settled there, where they still live. 23The land along the Mediterranean coast had been settled by people from the island of Crete. They had destroyed the Avvim, the original inhabitants, and had taken over all their land as far south as the city of Gaza.)

24"After we had passed through Moab, the LORD said to us, 'Now, start out and cross the River Arnon. I am placing in your power Sihon, the Amorite king of Heshbon, along with his land. Attack him, and begin occupying his land. 25From today on I will make people everywhere afraid of you. Everyone will tremble with fear at the mention of your name.'

Deuter.

....

Joshua

Judges

Ruth

1 Sam.

2 Sam.

Israel Defeats King Sihon
(Num 21.21–30)

26 "Then I sent messengers from the desert of Kedemoth to King Sihon of Heshbon with the following offer of peace: 27 'Let us pass through your country. We will go straight through and not leave the road. 28 We will pay for the food we eat and the water we drink. All we want to do is to pass through your country, 29 until we cross the River Jordan into the land that the LORD our God is giving us. The descendants of Esau, who live in Edom, and the Moabites, who live in Ar, allowed us to pass through their territory.'

30 "But King Sihon would not let us pass through his country. The LORD your God had made him stubborn and rebellious, so that we could defeat him and take his territory, which we still occupy.

31 "Then the LORD said to me, 'Look, I have made King Sihon and his land helpless before you; take his land and occupy it.' 32 Sihon came out with all his men to fight us near the town of Jahaz, 33 but the LORD our God put him in our power, and we killed him, his sons, and all his men. 34 At the same time we captured and destroyed every town, and put everyone to death, men, women, and children. We left no survivors. 35 We took the livestock and plundered the towns. 36 The LORD our God let us capture all the towns from Aroer, on the edge of the valley of the Arnon, and the city in the middle of that valley, all the way to Gilead. No town had walls too strong for us. 37 But we did not go near the territory of the Ammonites or to the banks of the River Jabbok or to the towns of the hill country or to any other place where the LORD our God had commanded us not to go.

Israel Conquers King Og
(Num 21.31–35)

3 "Next, we moved north towards the region of Bashan, and King Og came out with all his men to fight us near the town of Edrei. 2 But the LORD said to me, 'Don't be afraid of him. I am going to give him, his men, and all his territory to you. Do the same to him as you did to Sihon the Amorite king who ruled in Heshbon.'

3 "So the LORD also placed King Og and his people in our power, and we slaughtered them all. 4 At the same time we captured all his towns — there was not one that we did not take. In all we captured sixty towns — the whole region of Argob, where King Og of Bashan ruled. 5 All these towns were fortified with high walls, gates, and bars to lock the gates, and there were also many villages without walls. 6 We destroyed all the towns and put to death all the men, women, and children, just as we did in the towns that belonged to King Sihon of Heshbon. 7 We took the livestock and plundered the towns.

8 "At that time we took from those two Amorite kings the land east of the River Jordan, from the River Arnon to Mount Hermon. 9 (Mount Hermon is called Sirion by the Sidonians, and Senir by the Amorites.) 10 We took all the territory of King Og of Bashan: the cities on the plateau, the regions of Gilead and of Bashan, as far east as the towns of Salecah and Edrei."

11 (King Og was the last of the Rephaim. His coffin,* made of stone,* was four metres long and almost two metres wide according to standard measurements. It can still be seen in the Ammonite city of Rabbah.)

....

3.11 coffin; or bed.
3.11 stone; or iron.

The Tribes that Settled East of the Jordan
(Num 32.1–42)

12"When we took possession of the land, I assigned to the tribes of Reuben and Gad the territory north of the town of Aroer near the River Arnon and part of the hill country of Gilead, along with its towns. 13 To half the tribe of Manasseh I assigned the rest of Gilead and also all of Bashan, where Og had ruled, that is, the entire Argob region."

(Bashan was known as the land of the Rephaim. 14 Jair, from the tribe of Manasseh, took the entire region of Argob, that is, Bashan, as far as the border of Geshur and Maacah. He named the villages after himself, and they are still known as the villages of Jair.)

15"I assigned Gilead to the clan of Machir of the tribe of Manasseh. 16 And to the tribes of Reuben and Gad I assigned the territory from Gilead to the River Arnon. The middle of the river was their southern boundary, and their northern boundary was the River Jabbok, part of which formed the Ammonite border. 17 On the west their territory extended to the River Jordan, from Lake Galilee in the north down to the Dead Sea in the south and to the foot of Mount Pisgah on the east.

18"At the same time, I gave them the following instructions: 'The LORD our God has given you this land east of the Jordan to occupy. Now arm your fighting men and send them across the Jordan ahead of the other tribes of Israel, to help them to occupy their land. 19 Only your wives, children, and livestock — I know you have a lot of livestock — will remain behind in the towns that I have assigned to you. 20 Help your fellow-Israelites until they occupy the land that the LORD is giving them west of the Jordan and until the LORD lets them live there in peace, as he has already done here for you. After that, you may return to this land which I have assigned to you.'

21"Then I instructed Joshua: 'You have seen all that the LORD your God did to those two kings, Sihon and Og; and he will do the same to everyone else whose land you invade. 22 Don't be afraid of them, for the LORD your God will fight for you.'

Moses is not Permitted to Enter Canaan

23"At that time I earnestly prayed, 24 'Sovereign LORD, I know that you have shown me only the beginning of the great and wonderful things you are going to do. There is no god in heaven or on earth who can do the mighty things that you have done! 25 Let me cross the River Jordan, LORD, and see the fertile land on the other side, the beautiful hill country and the Lebanon Mountains.'

26"But because of you people the LORD was angry with me and would not listen. Instead, he said, 'That's enough! Don't mention this again! 27 Go to the peak of Mount Pisgah and look to the north and to the south, to the east and to the west. Look carefully at what you see, because you will never go across the Jordan. 28 Give Joshua his instructions. Strengthen his determination, because he will lead the people across to occupy the land that you see.'

29"So we remained in the valley opposite the town of Bethpeor."

Moses Urges Israel to be Obedient

4 Then Moses said to the people, "Obey all the laws that I am teaching you, and you will live and occupy the land which the LORD, the God of your ancestors, is giving you. 2 Do not add anything to what I command you, and do not take anything away. Obey the commands of the LORD your God

DEUTERONOMY 4

213

Deuter.
..........:
Joshua
Judges
Ruth
1 Sam.
2 Sam.

that I have given you. ³You yourselves saw what the Lord did at Mount Peor. He destroyed everyone who worshipped Baal there, ⁴but those of you who were faithful to the Lord your God are still alive today.

⁵"I have taught you all the laws, as the Lord my God told me to do. Obey them in the land that you are about to invade and occupy. ⁶Obey them faithfully, and this will show the people of other nations how wise you are. When they hear of all these laws, they will say, 'What wisdom and understanding this great nation has!'

⁷"No other nation, no matter how great, has a god who is so near when they need him as the Lord our God is to us. He answers us whenever we call for help. ⁸No other nation, no matter how great, has laws so just as those that I have taught you today. ⁹Be on your guard! Make certain that you do not forget, as long as you live, what you have seen with your own eyes. Tell your children and your grandchildren ¹⁰about the day you stood in the presence of the Lord your God at Mount Sinai,* when he said to me, 'Assemble the people. I want them to hear what I have to say, so that they will learn to obey me as long as they live and so that they will teach their children to do the same.'

¹¹"Tell your children how you went and stood at the foot of the mountain which was covered with thick clouds of dark smoke and fire blazing up to the sky. ¹²Tell them how the Lord spoke to you from the fire, how you heard him speaking but did not see him in any form at all. ¹³He told you what you must do to keep the covenant he made with you — you must obey the Ten Commandments, which he wrote on two stone tablets. ¹⁴The Lord told me to teach you all the laws that you are to obey in the land that you are about to invade and occupy.

Warning against Idolatry

¹⁵"When the Lord spoke to you from the fire on Mount Sinai, you did not see any form. For your own good, then, make certain ¹⁶that you do not sin by making for yourselves an idol in any form at all — whether man or woman, ¹⁷animal or bird, ¹⁸reptile or fish. ¹⁹Do not be tempted to worship and serve what you see in the sky — the sun, the moon, and the stars. The Lord your God has given these to all other peoples for them to worship. ²⁰But you are the people he rescued from Egypt, that blazing furnace. He brought you out to make you his own people, as you are today. ²¹Because of you the Lord your God was angry with me and solemnly declared that I would not cross the River Jordan to enter the fertile land which he is giving you. ²²I will die in this land and never cross the river, but you are about to go across and occupy that fertile land. ²³Be certain that you do not forget the covenant that the Lord your God made with you. Obey his command not to make yourselves any kind of idol, ²⁴because the Lord your God is like a flaming fire; he tolerates no rivals.

²⁵"Even when you have been in the land a long time and have children and grandchildren, do not sin by making for yourselves an idol in any form at all. This is evil in the Lord's sight, and it will make him angry. ²⁶I call heaven and earth as witnesses against you today that, if you disobey me, you will soon disappear from the land. You will not live very long in the land across the Jordan that you are about to occupy. You will be completely destroyed. ²⁷The Lord will scatter you among

DEUTERONOMY 4.7

NO OTHER NATION, NO MATTER HOW GREAT, HAS A GOD WHO IS SO NEAR WHEN THEY NEED HIM AS THE LORD OUR GOD IS TO US

4.10 *Sinai*; or *Horeb*.

other nations, where only a few of you will survive. [28] There you will serve gods made by human hands, gods of wood and stone, gods that cannot see or hear, eat or smell. [29] There you will look for the LORD your God, and if you search for him with all your heart, you will find him. [30] When you are in trouble and all those things happen to you, then you will finally turn to the LORD and obey him. [31] He is a merciful God. He will not abandon you or destroy you, and he will not forget the covenant that he himself made with your ancestors.

[32] "Search the past, the time before you were born, all the way back to the time when God created humanity on the earth. Search the entire earth. Has anything as great as this ever happened before? Has anyone ever heard of anything like this? [33] Have any people ever lived after hearing a god speak to them from a fire, as you have? [34] Has any god ever dared to go and take a people from another nation and make them his own, as the LORD your God did for you in Egypt? Before your very eyes he used his great power and strength; he brought plagues and war, worked miracles and wonders, and caused terrifying things to happen. [35] The LORD has shown you this, to prove to you that he alone is God and that there is no other. [36] He let you hear his voice from heaven so that he could instruct you; and here on earth he let you see his holy fire, and he spoke to you from it. [37] Because he loved your ancestors, he chose you, and by his great power he himself brought you out of Egypt. [38] As you advanced, he drove out nations greater and more powerful than you, so that he might bring you in and give you their land, the land which still belongs to you. [39] So remember today and never forget: the LORD is God in heaven and on earth. There is no other god. [40] Obey all his laws that I have given you today, and all will go well with you and your descendants. You will continue to live in the land which the LORD your God is giving you to be yours for ever."

The Cities of Refuge East of the Jordan

[41] Then Moses set aside three cities east of the River Jordan [42] to which a man could escape and be safe if he had accidentally killed someone who had not been his enemy. He could escape to one of these cities and not be put to death. [43] For the tribe of Reuben there was the city of Bezer, on the desert plateau; for the tribe of Gad there was Ramoth, in the territory of Gilead; and for the tribe of Manasseh there was Golan, in the territory of Bashan.

Introduction to the Giving of God's Law

[44] Moses gave God's laws and teachings to the people of Israel. [45-46] It was after they had come out of Egypt and were in the valley east of the River Jordan, opposite the town of Bethpeor, that he gave them these laws. This was in the territory that had belonged to King Sihon of the Amorites, who had ruled in the town of Heshbon. Moses and the people of Israel defeated him when they came out of Egypt. [47] They occupied his land and the land of King Og of Bashan, the other Amorite king who lived east of the Jordan. [48] This land extended from the town of Aroer, on the edge of the River Arnon, all the way north to Mount Sirion,* that is, Mount Hermon. [49] It also included all the region east of the River Jordan as far south as the Dead Sea and east to the foot of Mount Pisgah.

....

4.48 One ancient translation *Sirion*; Hebrew *Sion*.

DEUTERONOMY 5

215

Deuter.
...........:

Joshua
Judges
Ruth
1 Sam.
2 Sam.

The Ten Commandments
(Ex 20.1–17)

5 Moses called together all the people of Israel and said to them, "People of Israel, listen to all the laws that I am giving you today. Learn them and be sure that you obey them. ² At Mount Sinai the LORD our God made a covenant, ³ not only with our fathers, but with all of us who are living today. ⁴ There on the mountain the LORD spoke to you face-to-face from the fire. ⁵ I stood between you and the LORD at that time to tell you what he said, because you were afraid of the fire and would not go up the mountain.

"The LORD said, ⁶ 'I am the LORD your God, who rescued you from Egypt, where you were slaves.

⁷ " 'Worship no god but me.

⁸ " 'Do not make for yourselves images of anything in heaven or on earth or in the water under the earth. ⁹ Do not bow down to any idol or worship it, for I am the LORD your God and I tolerate no rivals. I bring punishment on those who hate me and on their descendants down to the third and fourth generation. ¹⁰ But I show my love to thousands of generations* of those who love me and obey my laws.

¹¹ " 'Do not use my name for evil purposes, for I, the LORD your God, will punish anyone who misuses my name.

¹² " 'Observe the Sabbath and keep it holy, as I, the LORD your God, have commanded you. ¹³ You have six days in which to do your work, ¹⁴ but the seventh day is a day of rest dedicated to me. On that day no one is to work — neither you, your children, your slaves, your animals, nor the foreigners who live in your country. Your slaves must rest just as you do. ¹⁵ Remember that you were slaves in Egypt, and that I, the LORD your God, rescued you by my great power and strength. That is why I command you to observe the Sabbath.

¹⁶ " 'Respect your father and your mother, as I, the LORD your God, command you, so that all may go well with you and so that you may live a long time in the land that I am giving you.

¹⁷ " 'Do not commit murder.

¹⁸ " 'Do not commit adultery.

¹⁹ " 'Do not steal.

²⁰ " 'Do not accuse anyone falsely.

²¹ " 'Do not desire another man's wife; do not desire his house, his land, his slaves, his cattle, his donkeys, or anything else that he owns.'

²² "These are the commandments the LORD gave to all of you when you were gathered at the mountain. When he spoke with a mighty voice from the fire and from the thick clouds, he gave these commandments and no others. Then he wrote them on two stone tablets and gave them to me.

The People's Fear
(Ex 20.18–21)

²³ "When the whole mountain was on fire and you heard the voice from the darkness, your leaders and the chiefs of your tribes came to me ²⁴ and said, 'The LORD our God showed us his greatness and his glory when we heard him speak from the fire! Today we have seen that it is possible for a human being to continue to live, even though God has spoken to him. ²⁵ But why should we risk death again? That terrible fire will destroy us. We

....

5.10 *thousands of generations*; or *thousands.*

216

Deuter.

Genesis
Exodus
Leviticus
Num.

DEUTERONOMY 5, 6

DEUTERONOMY 6.5

Draw in each of these boxes something that represents

– YOUR –
HEART,
YOUR SOUL
– AND YOUR –
STRENGTH.

are sure to die if we hear the LORD our God speak again. ²⁶ Has any human being ever lived after hearing the living God speak from a fire? ²⁷ Go back, Moses, and listen to everything that the LORD our God says. Then return and tell us what he said to you. We will listen and obey.'

²⁸ "When the LORD heard this, he said to me, 'I have heard what these people said, and they are right. ²⁹ If only they would always feel like this! If only they would always honour me and obey all my commands, so that everything would go well with them and their descendants for ever. ³⁰ Go and tell them to return to their tents. ³¹ But you, Moses, stay here with me, and I will give you all my laws and commands. Teach them to the people, so that they will obey them in the land that I am giving them.'

³² "People of Israel, be sure that you do everything that the LORD your God has commanded you. Do not disobey any of his laws. ³³ Obey them all, so that everything will go well with you and so that you will continue to live in the land that you are going to occupy.

The Great Commandment

6 "These are all the laws that the LORD your God commanded me to teach you. Obey them in the land that you are about to enter and occupy. ² As long as you live, you and your descendants are to honour the LORD your God and obey all his laws that I am giving you, so that you may live in that land a long time. ³ Listen to them, people of Israel, and obey them! Then all will go well with you, and you will become a mighty nation and live in that rich and fertile land, just as the LORD, the God of our ancestors, has promised.

⁴ "Israel, remember this! The LORD — and the LORD alone — is our God.* ⁵ Love the LORD your God with all your heart, with all your soul, and with all your strength. ⁶ Never forget these commands that I am giving you today. ⁷ Teach them to your children. Repeat them when you are at home and when you are away, when you are resting and when you are working. ⁸ Tie them on your arms and wear them on your foreheads as a reminder. ⁹ Write them on the doorposts of your houses and on your gates.

Warning against Disobedience

¹⁰ "Just as the LORD your God promised your ancestors, Abraham, Isaac, and Jacob, he will give you a land with large and prosperous cities which you did not build. ¹¹ The houses will be full of good things which you did not put in them, and there will be wells that you did not dig, and vineyards and olive orchards that you did not plant. When the LORD brings you into this land and you have all you want to eat, ¹² make certain that you do not forget the LORD who rescued you from Egypt, where you were slaves. ¹³ Honour the LORD your God, worship only him, and make your promises in his name alone. ¹⁴ Do not worship other gods, any of the gods of the peoples around you. ¹⁵ If you do worship other gods, the LORD's anger will come against you like fire and will destroy you completely, because the LORD your God, who is present with you, tolerates no rivals.

¹⁶ "Do not put the LORD your God to the test, as you did at Massah. ¹⁷ Be sure that you obey all the laws that he has given you. ¹⁸ Do what the LORD says is right and good, and all will go

6.4 *The LORD... is our God*; or *The LORD, our God, is the only God*; or *The LORD our God is one.*

Deuter.

....

Joshua

Judges

Ruth

1 Sam.

2 Sam.

well with you. You will be able to take possession of the fertile land that the LORD promised your ancestors, [19] and you will drive out your enemies, as he promised.

[20] "In time to come your children will ask you, 'Why did the LORD our God command us to obey all these laws?' [21] Then tell them, 'We were slaves of the king of Egypt, and the LORD rescued us by his great power. [22] With our own eyes we saw him work miracles and do terrifying things to the Egyptians and to their king and to all his officials. [23] He freed us from Egypt to bring us here and give us this land, as he had promised our ancestors he would. [24] Then the LORD our God commanded us to obey all these laws and to honour him. If we do, he will always watch over our nation and keep it prosperous. [25] If we faithfully obey everything that God has commanded us, he will be pleased with us.'*

The Lord's Own People
(Ex 34.11–16)

7 "The LORD your God will bring you into the land which you are going to occupy, and he will drive many nations out of it. As you advance, he will drive out seven nations larger and more powerful than you: the Hittites, the Girgashites, the Amorites, the Canaanites, the Perizzites, the Hivites, and the Jebusites. [2] When the LORD your God places these people in your power and you defeat them, you must put them all to death. Do not make an alliance with them or show them any mercy. [3] Do not marry any of them, and do not let your children marry any of them, [4] because then they would lead your children away from the LORD to worship other gods. If that happens, the LORD will be angry with you and destroy you at once. [5] So then, tear down their altars, break their sacred stone pillars in pieces, cut down the symbols of their goddess Asherah, and burn their idols. [6] Do this because you belong to the LORD your God. From all the peoples on earth he chose you to be his own special people.

[7] "The LORD did not love you and choose you because you outnumbered other peoples; you were the smallest nation on earth. [8] But the LORD loved you and wanted to keep the promise that he made to your ancestors. That is why he saved you by his great might and set you free from slavery to the king of Egypt. [9] Remember that the LORD your God is the only God and that he is faithful. He will keep his covenant and show his constant love to a thousand generations of those who love him and obey his commands, [10] but he will not hesitate to punish those who hate him. [11] So now, obey what you have been taught; obey all the laws that I have given you today.

The Blessings of Obedience
(Deut 28.1–14)

[12] "If you listen to these commands and obey them faithfully, then the LORD your God will continue to keep his covenant with you and will show you his constant love, as he promised your ancestors. [13] He will love you and bless you, so that you will increase in number and have many children; he will bless your fields, so that you will have corn, wine, and olive oil; and he will bless you by giving you a lot of cattle and sheep. He will give you all these blessings in the land that he promised your ancestors he would give to you. [14] No people in the world will be as richly blessed as

6.25 *If we faithfully... with us*; or *The right thing for us to do is to obey faithfully everything that God has commanded us.*

218

Deuter.

⋮⋯⋯⋯

Genesis
Exodus
Leviticus
Num.

DEUTERONOMY 7, 8

you. None of you nor any of your livestock will be sterile. ¹⁵ The LORD will protect you from all sickness, and he will not bring on you any of the dreadful diseases that you experienced in Egypt, but he will bring them on all your enemies. ¹⁶ Destroy every nation that the LORD your God places in your power, and do not show them any mercy. Do not worship their gods, for that would be fatal.

¹⁷ "Do not tell yourselves that these peoples outnumber you and that you cannot drive them out. ¹⁸ Do not be afraid of them; remember what the LORD your God did to the king of Egypt and to all his people. ¹⁹ Remember the terrible plagues that you saw with your own eyes, the miracles and wonders, and the great power and strength by which the LORD your God set you free. In the same way that he destroyed the Egyptians, he will destroy all these people that you now fear. ²⁰ He will even cause panic* among them and will destroy those who escape and go into hiding. ²¹ So do not be afraid of these people. The LORD your God is with you; he is a great God and one to be feared. ²² Little by little he will drive out these nations as you advance. You will not be able to destroy them all at once, for, if you did, the number of wild animals would increase and be a threat to you. ²³ The LORD will put your enemies in your power and make them panic until they are destroyed. ²⁴ He will put their kings in your power. You will kill them, and they will be forgotten. No one will be able to stop you; you will destroy everyone. ²⁵ Burn their idols. Do not desire the silver or gold that is on them, and do not take it for yourselves. If you do, that will be fatal, because the LORD hates idolatry. ²⁶ Do not bring any of these idols into your homes, or the same curse will be on you that is on them. You must hate and despise these idols, because they are under the LORD's curse.

A Good Land to be Possessed

8 "Obey faithfully all the laws that I have given you today, so that you may live, increase in number, and occupy the land which the LORD promised to your ancestors. ² Remember how the LORD your God led you on this long journey through the desert these past forty years, sending hardships to test you, so that he might know what you intended to do and whether you would obey his commands. ³ He made you go hungry, and then he gave you manna to eat, food that you and your ancestors had never eaten before. He did this to teach you that human beings must not depend on bread alone to sustain them, but on everything that the LORD says. ⁴ During these forty years your clothes have not worn out, nor have your feet swollen up. ⁵ Remember that the LORD your God corrects and punishes you just as a father disciplines his children. ⁶ So then, do as the LORD has commanded you: live according to his laws and obey him. ⁷ The LORD your God is bringing you into a fertile land — a land that has rivers and springs, and underground streams gushing out into the valleys and hills; ⁸ a land that produces wheat and barley, grapes, figs, pomegranates, olives, and honey. ⁹ There you will never go hungry or ever be in need. Its rocks have iron in them, and from its hills you can mine copper. ¹⁰ You will have all you want to eat, and you will give thanks to the LORD your God for the fertile land that he has given you.

Warnings against Forgetting the Lord

¹¹ "Make certain that you do not forget the LORD your God; do not fail to obey any of his laws that I am giving you today. ¹² When

---

7.20 *cause panic*; or *send hornets*, or *send plagues*.

DEUTERONOMY 8, 9

219

Deuter.

....

Joshua
Judges
Ruth
1 Sam.
2 Sam.

you have all you want to eat and have built good houses to live in [13] and when your cattle and sheep, your silver and gold, and all your other possessions have increased, [14] make sure that you do not become proud and forget the LORD your God who rescued you from Egypt, where you were slaves. [15] He led you through that vast and terrifying desert where there were poisonous snakes and scorpions. In that dry and waterless land he made water flow out of solid rock for you. [16] In the desert he gave you manna to eat, food that your ancestors had never eaten. He sent hardships on you to test you, so that in the end he could bless you with good things. [17] So then, you must never think that you have made yourselves wealthy by your own power and strength. [18] Remember that it is the LORD your God who gives you the power to become rich. He does this because he is still faithful today to the covenant that he made with your ancestors. [19] Never forget the LORD your God or turn to other gods to worship and serve them. If you do, then I warn you today that you will certainly be destroyed. [20] If you do not obey the LORD, then you will be destroyed just like those nations that he is going to destroy as you advance.

The People's Disobedience
(Ex 32.1–35)

9 "Listen, people of Israel! Today you are about to cross the River Jordan and occupy the land belonging to nations greater and more powerful than you. Their cities are large, with walls that reach the sky. [2] The people themselves are tall and strong; they are giants, and you have heard it said that no one can stand against them. [3] But now you will see for yourselves that the LORD your God will go ahead of you like a raging fire. He will defeat them as you advance, so that you will drive them out and destroy them quickly, as he promised.

[4] "After the LORD your God has driven them out for you, do not say to yourselves that he brought you in to possess this land because you deserved it. No, the LORD is going to drive these people out for you because they are wicked. [5] It is not because you are good and do what is right that the LORD is letting you take their land. He will drive them out because they are wicked and because he intends to keep the promise that he made to your ancestors, Abraham, Isaac, and Jacob. [6] You can be sure that the LORD is not giving you this fertile land because you deserve it. No, you are a stubborn people.

[7] "Never forget how you made the LORD your God angry in the desert. From the day that you left Egypt until the day you arrived here, you have rebelled against him. [8] Even at Mount Sinai you made the LORD angry — angry enough to destroy you. [9] I went up the mountain to receive the stone tablets on which was written the covenant that the LORD had made with you. I stayed there forty days and nights and did not eat or drink anything. [10] Then the LORD gave me the two stone tablets on which he had written with his own hand what he had said to you from the fire on the day that you were gathered there at the mountain. [11] Yes, after those forty days and nights the LORD gave me the two stone tablets on which he had written the covenant.

[12] "Then the LORD said to me, 'Go down the mountain at once, because your people, whom you led out of Egypt, have become corrupt and have done evil. They have already turned away from what I commanded them to do, and they have made an idol for themselves.'

[13] "The LORD also said to me, 'I know how stubborn these people are. [14] Don't try to stop me. I intend to destroy them so that no

DECORATE THESE SHAPES IN RELATION TO YOUR MOOD.

220

Deuter.

Genesis
Exodus
Leviticus
Num.

DEUTERONOMY 9, 10

one will remember them any longer. Then I will make you the father of a nation larger and more powerful than they are.'

15 "So I turned and went down the mountain, carrying the two stone tablets on which the covenant was written. Flames of fire were coming from the mountain. 16 I saw that you had already disobeyed the command that the LORD your God had given you, and that you had sinned against him by making yourselves a metal idol in the form of a bull calf. 17 So there in front of you I threw the stone tablets down and broke them to pieces. 18 Then once again I lay face downwards in the LORD's presence for forty days and nights and did not eat or drink anything. I did this because you had sinned against the LORD and had made him angry. 19 I was afraid of the LORD's fierce anger, because he was furious enough to destroy you; but once again the LORD listened to me. 20 The LORD was also angry enough with Aaron to kill him, so I prayed for Aaron at the same time. 21 I took that sinful thing that you had made — that metal bull calf — and threw it into the fire. Then I broke it in pieces, ground it to dust, and threw the dust into the stream that flowed down the mountain.

22 "You also made the LORD your God angry when you were at Taberah, Massah, and Kibroth Hattaavah. 23 And when he sent you from Kadesh Barnea with orders to go and take possession of the land that he was giving you, you rebelled against him; you did not trust him or obey him. 24 Ever since I have known you, you have rebelled against the LORD.

25 "So I lay face downwards in the LORD's presence those forty days and nights, because I knew that he was determined to destroy you. 26 And I prayed, 'Sovereign LORD, don't destroy your own people, the people you rescued and brought out of Egypt by your great strength and power. 27 Remember your servants, Abraham, Isaac, and Jacob, and do not pay any attention to the stubbornness, wickedness, and sin of this people. 28 Otherwise, the Egyptians will say that you were unable to take your people into the land that you had promised them. They will say that you took your people out into the desert to kill them, because you hated them. 29 After all, these are the people whom you chose to be your own and whom you brought out of Egypt by your great power and might.'

Moses Receives the Commandments Again
(Ex 34.1–10)

10 "Then the LORD said to me, 'Cut two stone tablets like the first ones and make a wooden box to put them in. Come up to me on the mountain, 2 and I will write on those tablets what I wrote on the tablets that you broke, and then you are to put them in the box.'

3 "So I made a box of acacia wood and cut two stone tablets like the first ones and took them up the mountain. 4 Then the LORD wrote on those tablets the same words that he had written the first time, the Ten Commandments that he gave you when he spoke from the fire on the day you were gathered at the mountain. The LORD gave me the tablets, 5 and I turned and went down the mountain. Then, just as the LORD had commanded, I put them in the box that I had made — and they have been there ever since."

6 (The Israelites set out from the wells that belonged to the people of Jaakan, and went to Moserah. There Aaron died and was buried, and his son Eleazar succeeded him as priest. 7 From there they went to Gudgodah and then on to Jotbathah,

DEUTERONOMY 10, 11

221

Deuter.

....

Joshua
Judges
Ruth
1 Sam.
2 Sam.

a well-watered place. [8] At the mountain* the LORD appointed the men of the tribe of Levi to be in charge of the Covenant Box, to serve him as priests, and to pronounce blessings in his name. And these are still their duties. [9] That is why the tribe of Levi received no land as the other tribes did; what they received was the privilege of being the LORD's priests, as the LORD your God promised.)

[10] "I stayed on the mountain forty days and nights, as I did the first time. The LORD listened to me once more and agreed not to destroy you. [11] Then he told me to go and lead you, so that you could take possession of the land that he had promised to give to your ancestors.

What God Demands

[12] "Now, people of Israel, listen to what the LORD your God demands of you: worship the LORD and do all that he commands. Love him, serve him with all your heart, [13] and obey all his laws. I am giving them to you today for your benefit. [14] To the LORD belong even the highest heavens; the earth is his also, and everything on it. [15] But the LORD's love for your ancestors was so strong that he chose you instead of any other people, and you are still his chosen people. [16] So then, from now on be obedient to the LORD and stop being stubborn. [17] The LORD your God is supreme over all gods and over all powers. He is great and mighty, and he is to be feared. He does not show partiality, and he does not accept bribes. [18] He makes sure that orphans and widows are treated fairly; he loves the foreigners who live with our people, and gives them food and clothes. [19] So then, show love for those foreigners, because you were once foreigners in Egypt. [20] Obey the LORD your God and worship only him. Be faithful to him and make your promises in his name alone. [21] Praise him — he is your God, and you have seen with your own eyes the great and astounding things that he has done for you. [22] When your ancestors went to Egypt, there were only seventy of them. But now the LORD your God has made you as numerous as the stars in the sky.

The LORD's Greatness

11 "Love the LORD your God and always obey all his laws. [2] Remember today what you have learned about the LORD through your experiences with him. It was you, not your children, who had these experiences. You saw the LORD's greatness, his power, his might, [3] and his miracles. You saw what he did to the king of Egypt and to his entire country. [4] You saw how the LORD completely wiped out the Egyptian army, along with their horses and chariots, by drowning them in the Red Sea when they were pursuing you. [5] You know what the LORD did for you in the desert before you arrived here. [6] You recall what he did to Dathan and Abiram, the sons of Eliab of the tribe of Reuben. In the sight of everyone the earth opened up and swallowed them, along with their families, their tents, and all their servants and animals. [7] Yes, you are the ones who have seen all these great things that the LORD has done.

The Blessings of the Promised Land

[8] "Obey all the laws that I have given you today. Then you will be able to cross the river and occupy the land that you are about to enter. [9] And you will live a long time in the rich and

10.8 *the mountain;* or *that time.*

222

Deuter.

⋮⋯⋯⋯

Genesis
Exodus
Leviticus
Num.

DEUTERONOMY 11, 12

DEUTERONOMY 11.26-28

Moses sets out in these verses a really simple choice, which you'll find throughout the Old Testament - obey and be blessed, or disobey and invite God's judgement. But God's love always prevails, which is why in Deuteronomy 8.5 he refers to this judgement as 'discipline'. Discipline is meant to be based on love, not anger - to help people see right from wrong.

• GOD IS A •

GOOD PARENT

who disciplines his children out of love. (Hosea 11.1 is the first place in the Old Testament where we find God speaking as a father.)

fertile land that the LORD promised to give your ancestors and their descendants. [10] The land that you are about to occupy is not like the land of Egypt, where you lived before. There, when you sowed seed, you had to work hard to irrigate the fields; [11] but the land that you are about to enter is a land of mountains and valleys, a land watered by rain. [12] The LORD your God takes care of this land and watches over it throughout the year.

[13] "So then, obey the commands that I have given you today; love the LORD your God and serve him with all your heart. [14] If you do, he will send rain on your land when it is needed, in the autumn and in the spring, so that there will be corn, wine, and olive oil for you, [15] and grass for your livestock. You will have all the food you want. [16] Do not let yourselves be led away from the LORD to worship and serve other gods. [17] If you do, the LORD will become angry with you. He will hold back the rain, and your ground will become too dry for crops to grow. Then you will soon die there, even though it is a good land that he is giving you.

[18] "Remember these commands and cherish them. Tie them on your arms and wear them on your foreheads as a reminder. [19] Teach them to your children. Talk about them when you are at home and when you are away, when you are resting and when you are working. [20] Write them on the doorposts of your houses and on your gates. [21] Then you and your children will live a long time in the land that the LORD your God promised to give to your ancestors. You will live there as long as there is a sky above the earth.

[22] "Obey faithfully all the laws that I have given you: Love the LORD your God, do everything he commands, and be faithful to him. [23] Then he will drive out all those nations as you advance, and you will occupy the land belonging to nations greater and more powerful than you. [24] All the ground that you march over will be yours. Your territory will extend from the desert in the south to the Lebanon Mountains in the north, and from the River Euphrates in the east to the Mediterranean Sea in the west. [25] Wherever you go in that land, the LORD your God will make the people fear you, as he has promised, and no one will be able to stop you.

[26] "Today I am giving you the choice between a blessing and a curse — [27] a blessing, if you obey the commands of the LORD your God that I am giving you today; [28] but a curse, if you disobey these commands and turn away to worship other gods that you have never worshipped before. [29] When the LORD brings you into the land that you are going to occupy, you are to proclaim the blessing from Mount Gerizim and the curse from Mount Ebal. [30] (These two mountains are west of the River Jordan in the territory of the Canaanites who live in the Jordan Valley. They are towards the west, not far from the sacred trees of Moreh near the town of Gilgal.) [31] You are about to cross the River Jordan and occupy the land that the LORD your God is giving you. When you take it and settle there, [32] be sure to obey all the laws that I am giving you today.

The One Place for Worship

12 "Here are the laws that you are to obey as long as you live in the land that the LORD, the God of your ancestors, is giving you. Listen to them! [2] In the land that you are taking, destroy all the places where the people worship their gods on high mountains, on hills, and under green trees. [3] Tear down their altars and smash their sacred stone pillars to pieces. Burn their symbols of the goddess Asherah and chop down their idols, so that they will never again be worshipped at those places.

Deuter.

Joshua
Judges
Ruth
1 Sam.
2 Sam.

4 "Do not worship the LORD your God in the way that these people worship their gods. 5 Out of the territory of all your tribes the LORD will choose the one place where the people are to come into his presence and worship him. 6 There you are to offer your sacrifices that are to be burnt and your other sacrifices, your tithes and your offerings, the gifts that you promise to the LORD, your freewill offerings, and the firstborn of your cattle and sheep. 7 There, in the presence of the LORD your God, who has blessed you, you and your families will eat and enjoy the good things that you have worked for.

8 "When that time comes, you must not do as you have been doing. Until now you have all been worshipping as you please, 9 because you have not yet entered the land that the LORD your God is giving you, where you can live in peace. 10 When you cross the River Jordan, the LORD will let you occupy the land and live there. He will keep you safe from all your enemies, and you will live in peace. 11 The LORD will choose a single place where he is to be worshipped, and there you must bring to him everything that I have commanded: your sacrifices that are to be burnt and your other sacrifices, your tithes and your offerings, and those special gifts that you have promised to the LORD. 12 Be joyful there in his presence, together with your children, your servants, and the Levites who live in your towns; remember that the Levites will have no land of their own. 13 You are not to offer your sacrifices wherever you choose; 14 you must offer them only in the one place that the LORD will choose in the territory of one of your tribes. Only there are you to offer your sacrifices that are to be burnt and do all the other things that I have commanded you.

15 "But you are free to kill and eat your animals wherever you live. You may eat as many as the LORD gives you. All of you, whether ritually clean or unclean, may eat them, just as you would eat the meat of deer or antelope. 16 But you must not use their blood as food; you must pour it out on the ground like water. 17 Nothing that you offer to the LORD is to be eaten in the places where you live: neither the tithes of your corn, your wine, or your olive oil, nor the firstborn of your cattle and sheep, the gifts that you promise to the LORD, your freewill offerings, or any other offerings. 18 You and your children, together with your servants and the Levites who live in your towns, are to eat these offerings only in the presence of the LORD your God, in the one place of worship chosen by the LORD your God. And you are to be happy there over everything that you have done. 19 Be sure, also, not to neglect the Levites, as long as you live in your land.

20 "When the LORD your God enlarges your territory, as he has promised, you may eat meat whenever you wish. 21 If the one place of worship is too far away, then, whenever you wish, you may kill any of the cattle or sheep that the LORD has given you, and you may eat the meat at home, as I have told you. 22 Anyone, ritually clean or unclean, may eat that meat, just as he would eat the meat of deer or antelope. 23 Only do not eat meat with blood still in it, for the life is in the blood, and you must not eat the life with the meat. 24 Do not use the blood for food; instead pour it out on the ground like water. 25 If you obey this command, the LORD will be pleased, and all will go well for you and your descendants. 26 Take to the one place of worship your offerings and the gifts that you have promised the LORD. 27 Offer there the sacrifices which are to be completely burnt on the LORD's altar. Also offer those sacrifices in which you eat the meat and pour the blood out on the altar. 28 Obey faithfully everything that I have commanded you, and all

DEUTERONOMY 12.6-7

The whole deal around sacrificing animals and what it meant can be tough to get your head around. So we

MADE A SHORT

≽ FILM ≼

ABOUT IT.

Head to gnbyouthedition.co.uk/sacrifice to watch it.

224

Deuter.

·:········

Genesis
Exodus
Leviticus
Num.

DEUTERONOMY 12–14

will go well for you and your descendants for ever, because you will be doing what is right and what pleases the LORD your God.

Warning against Idolatry

29 "The LORD your God will destroy the nations as you invade their land, and you will occupy it and settle there. 30 After the LORD destroys those nations, make sure that you don't follow their religious practices, because that would be fatal. Don't try to find out how they worship their gods, so that you can worship in the same way. 31 Do not worship the LORD your God in the way they worship their gods, for in the worship of their gods they do all the disgusting things that the LORD hates. They even sacrifice their children in the fires on their altars.

32 "Do everything that I have commanded you; do not add anything to it or take anything from it.

13 "Prophets or interpreters of dreams may promise a miracle or a wonder, 2 in order to lead you to worship and serve gods that you have not worshipped before. Even if what they promise comes true, 3 do not pay any attention to them. The LORD your God is using them to test you, to see if you love the LORD with all your heart. 4 Follow the LORD and honour him; obey him and keep his commands; worship him and be faithful to him. 5 But put to death any interpreters of dreams or prophets who tell you to rebel against the LORD, who rescued you from Egypt, where you were slaves. Such people are evil and are trying to lead you away from the life that the LORD has commanded you to live. They must be put to death, in order to rid yourselves of this evil.

6 "Even your brother or your son or your daughter or the wife you love or your closest friend may secretly encourage you to worship other gods, gods that you and your ancestors have never worshipped. 7 One of them may encourage you to worship the gods of the people who live near you or the gods of those who live far away. 8 But do not let him or her persuade you; do not even listen to them. Show them no mercy or pity, and do not protect them. 9 Kill them! Be the first to stone them, and then let everyone else stone them too. 10 Stone them to death! They tried to lead you away from the LORD your God, who rescued you from Egypt, where you were slaves. 11 Then all the people of Israel will hear what happened; they will be afraid, and no one will ever again do such an evil thing.

12 "When you are living in the towns that the LORD your God gives you, you may hear 13 that some worthless people of your nation have misled the people of their town to worship gods that you have never worshipped before. 14 If you hear such a rumour, investigate it thoroughly; and if it is true that this evil thing did happen, 15 then kill all the people in that town and all their livestock too. Destroy that town completely. 16 Bring together all the possessions of the people who live there and pile them up in the town square. Then burn the town and everything in it as an offering to the LORD your God. It must be left in ruins for ever and never again be rebuilt. 17 Do not keep for yourselves anything that was condemned to destruction, and then the LORD will turn from his fierce anger and show you mercy. He will be merciful to you and make you a numerous people, as he promised your ancestors, 18 if you obey all his commands that I have given you today, and do what he requires.

A Forbidden Mourning Practice

14 "You are the people of the LORD your God. So when you mourn for the dead, don't gash yourselves or shave the front of your head, as other people do. ²You belong to the LORD your God; he has chosen you to be his own people from among all the peoples who live on earth.

Clean and Unclean Animals
(Lev 11.1–47)

³"Do not eat anything that the LORD has declared unclean. ⁴You may eat these animals: cattle, sheep, goats, ⁵deer, wild sheep, wild goats, or antelopes — ⁶any animals that have divided hoofs and that also chew the cud. ⁷But no animals may be eaten unless they have divided hoofs and also chew the cud. You may not eat camels, rabbits, or rock-badgers. They must be considered unclean; they chew the cud but do not have divided hoofs. ⁸Do not eat pigs. They must be considered unclean; they have divided hoofs but do not chew the cud. Do not eat any of these animals or even touch their dead bodies.

⁹"You may eat any kind of fish that has fins and scales, ¹⁰but anything living in the water that does not have fins and scales may not be eaten; it must be considered unclean.

¹¹"You may eat any clean bird. ¹²⁻¹⁸But these are the kinds of birds you are not to eat: eagles, owls, hawks, falcons; buzzards, vultures, crows; ostriches; seagulls, storks, herons, pelicans, cormorants;* hoopoes; and bats.

¹⁹"All winged insects are unclean; do not eat them. ²⁰You may eat any clean insect.

²¹"Do not eat any animal that dies a natural death. You may let the foreigners who live among you eat it, or you may sell it to other foreigners. But you belong to the LORD your God; you are his people.

"Do not cook a young sheep or goat in its mother's milk.

The Law of the Tithe

²²"Set aside a tithe — a tenth of all that your fields produce each year. ²³Then go to the one place where the LORD your God has chosen to be worshipped; and there in his presence eat the tithes of your corn, wine, and olive oil, and the firstborn of your cattle and sheep. Do this so that you may learn to honour the LORD your God always. ²⁴If the place of worship is too far from your home for you to carry there the tithe of the produce that the LORD has blessed you with, then do this: ²⁵Sell your produce and take the money with you to the one place of worship. ²⁶Spend it on whatever you want — beef, lamb, wine, beer — and there, in the presence of the LORD your God, you and your families are to eat and enjoy yourselves.

²⁷"Do not neglect the Levites who live in your towns; they have no property of their own. ²⁸At the end of every third year bring the tithe of all your crops and store it in your towns. ²⁹This food is for the Levites, since they own no property, and for the foreigners, orphans, and widows who live in your towns. They are to come and get all they need. Do this, and the LORD your God will bless you in everything you do.

The Seventh Year
(Lev 25.1–7)

15 "At the end of every seventh year you are to cancel the debts of those who owe you money. ²This is how it is to be done. All who have lent money to a fellow-Israelite are to

---

14.12–18 The identification of some of these birds is uncertain.

226

DEUTERONOMY 15, 16

Deuter.

.:........

Genesis
Exodus
Leviticus
Num.

cancel the debt; they must not try to collect the money; the LORD himself has declared the debt cancelled. ³You may collect what a foreigner owes you, but you must not collect what any of your own people owe you.

⁴"The LORD your God will bless you in the land that he is giving you. Not one of your people will be poor ⁵if you obey him and carefully observe everything that I command you today. ⁶The LORD will bless you, as he has promised. You will lend money to many nations, but you will not have to borrow from any; you will have control over many nations, but no nation will have control over you.

⁷"If in any of the towns in the land that the LORD your God is giving you there is a fellow-Israelite in need, then do not be selfish and refuse to help him. ⁸Instead, be generous and lend him as much as he needs. ⁹Do not refuse to lend him something, just because the year when debts are cancelled is near. Do not let such an evil thought enter your mind. If you refuse to make the loan, he will cry out to the LORD against you, and you will be held guilty. ¹⁰Give to him freely and unselfishly, and the LORD will bless you in everything you do. ¹¹There will always be some Israelites who are poor and in need, and so I command you to be generous to them.

The Treatment of Slaves
(Ex 21.1–11)

¹²"If a fellow-Israelite sells himself or herself* to you as a slave, you are to release them after they have served you for six years. When the seventh year comes, you must let them go free. ¹³When you set them free, do not send them away empty-handed. ¹⁴Give to them generously from what the LORD has blessed you with — sheep, corn, and wine. ¹⁵Remember that you were slaves in Egypt and the LORD your God set you free; that is why I am now giving you this command.

¹⁶"But your slave may not want to leave; he may love you and your family and be content to stay. ¹⁷Then take him to the door of your house and there pierce his ear; he will then be your slave for life. Treat your female slave in the same way. ¹⁸Do not be resentful when you set a slave free; after all, the slave has served you for six years at half the cost of a hired servant.* Do this, and the LORD your God will bless you in all that you do.

The Firstborn Cattle and Sheep

¹⁹"Set aside for the LORD your God all the firstborn males of your cattle and sheep; don't use any of these cattle for work and don't shear any of these sheep. ²⁰Each year you and your family are to eat them in the LORD's presence at the one place of worship. ²¹But if there is anything wrong with the animals, if they are crippled or blind or have any other serious defect, you must not sacrifice them to the LORD your God. ²²You may eat such animals at home. All of you, whether ritually clean or unclean, may eat them, just as you eat deer or antelope. ²³But do not use their blood for food; instead, you must pour it out on the ground like water.

The Passover
(Ex 12.1–20)

16 "Honour the LORD your God by celebrating Passover in the month of Abib; it was on a night in that month that

15.12 *sells himself or herself*; or *is sold*.
15.18 *at half... servant*; or *and has worked twice as hard as a hired servant*.

he rescued you from Egypt. [2] Go to the one place of worship and slaughter there one of your sheep or cattle for the Passover meal to honour the LORD your God. [3] When you eat this meal, do not eat bread prepared with yeast. For seven days you are to eat bread prepared without yeast, as you did when you had to leave Egypt in such a hurry. Eat this bread — it will be called the bread of suffering — so that as long as you live you will remember the day you came out of Egypt, that place of suffering. [4] For seven days no one in your land is to have any yeast in the house; and the meat of the animal killed on the evening of the first day must be eaten that same night.

[5-6] "Slaughter the Passover animals at the one place of worship — and nowhere else in the land that the LORD your God will give you. Do it at sunset, the time of day when you left Egypt. [7] Boil the meat and eat it at the one place of worship; and the next morning return home. [8] For the next six days you are to eat bread prepared without yeast, and on the seventh day assemble to worship the LORD your God, and do no work on that day.

The Harvest Festival
(Ex 34.22; Lev 23.15–21)

[9] "Count seven weeks from the time that you begin to harvest the corn, [10] and then celebrate the Harvest Festival, to honour the LORD your God, by bringing him a freewill offering in proportion to the blessing he has given you. [11] Be joyful in the LORD's presence, together with your children, your servants, and the Levites, foreigners, orphans, and widows who live in your towns. Do this at the one place of worship. [12] Be sure that you obey these commands; do not forget that you were slaves in Egypt.

The Festival of Shelters
(Lev 23.33–43)

[13] "After you have threshed all your corn and pressed all your grapes, celebrate the Festival of Shelters for seven days. [14] Enjoy it with your children, your servants, and the Levites, foreigners, orphans, and widows who live in your towns. [15] Honour the LORD your God by celebrating this festival for seven days at the one place of worship. Be joyful, because the LORD has blessed your harvest and your work.

[16] "All the men of your nation are to come to worship the LORD three times a year at the one place of worship: at Passover, Harvest Festival, and the Festival of Shelters. Each man is to bring a gift [17] as he is able, in proportion to the blessings that the LORD your God has given him.

The Administration of Justice

[18] "Appoint judges and other officials in every town that the LORD your God gives you. These men are to judge the people impartially. [19] They are not to be unjust or show partiality in their judgements; and they are not to accept bribes, for gifts blind the eyes even of wise and honest men, and cause them to give wrong decisions. [20] Always be fair and just, so that you will occupy the land that the LORD your God is giving you and will continue to live there.

[21] "When you make an altar for the LORD your God, do not put beside it a wooden symbol of the goddess Asherah. [22] And do not set up any stone pillar for idol worship; the LORD hates them.

17 "Do not sacrifice to the LORD your God cattle or sheep that have any defects; the LORD hates this.

FILL THIS SPACE HOWEVER YOU LIKE...

[2] "Suppose you hear that in one of your towns some man or woman has sinned against the LORD and broken his covenant [3] by worshipping and serving other gods or the sun or the moon or the stars, contrary to the LORD's command. [4] If you hear such a report, then investigate it thoroughly. If it is true that this evil thing has happened in Israel, [5] then take that person outside the town and stone him to death. [6] However, he may be put to death only if two or more witnesses testify against him; he is not to be put to death if there is only one witness. [7] The witnesses are to throw the first stones, and then the rest of the people are to stone that person; in this way you will get rid of this evil.

[8] "It may be that some cases will be too difficult for the local judges to decide, such as certain cases of property rights or of bodily injury or those cases that involve a distinction between murder and manslaughter. When this happens, go to the one place of worship chosen by the LORD your God, [9] and present your case to the levitical priests and to the judge who is in office at that time, and let them decide the case. [10] They will give their decision, and you are to do exactly as they tell you. [11] Accept their verdict and follow their instructions in every detail. [12] Anyone who dares to disobey either the judge or the priest on duty is to be put to death; in this way you will remove this evil from Israel. [13] Then everyone will hear of it and be afraid, and no one else will dare to act in such a way.

Instructions Concerning a King

[14] "After you have taken possession of the land that the LORD your God is going to give you and have settled there, then you will decide you need a king like all the nations round you. [15] Make sure that the man you choose to be king is the one whom the LORD has chosen. He must be one of your own people; do not make a foreigner your king. [16] The king is not to have a large number of horses for his army, and he is not to send people to Egypt to buy horses,* because the LORD has said that his people are never to return there. [17] The king is not to have many wives, because this would make him turn away from the LORD; and he is not to make himself rich with silver and gold. [18] When he becomes king, he is to have a copy of the book of God's laws and teachings made from the original copy kept by the levitical priests. [19] He is to keep this book near him and read from it all his life, so that he will learn to honour the LORD and to obey faithfully everything that is commanded in it. [20] This will keep him from thinking that he is better than his fellow-Israelites and from disobeying the LORD's commands in any way. Then he will reign for many years, and his descendants will rule Israel for many generations.

The Share of the Priests

18 "The priestly tribe of Levi is not to receive any share of land in Israel; instead, they are to live on the offerings and other sacrifices given to the LORD. [2] They are to own no land, as the other tribes do; their share is the privilege of being the LORD's priests, as the LORD has promised.

[3] "Whenever cattle or sheep are sacrificed, the priests are to be given the shoulder, the jaw, and the stomach. [4] They are to receive the first share of the corn, wine, olive oil, and wool. [5] The LORD chose from all your tribes the tribe of Levi to serve him as priests for ever.

....

17.16 *to buy horses*; or *in exchange for horses.*

6 "Any Levite who wants to may come from any town in Israel to the one place of worship 7 and may serve there as a priest of the LORD his God, like the other Levites who are serving there. 8 He is to receive the same amount of food as the other priests, and he may keep whatever his family sends him.*

Warning against Pagan Practices

9 "When you come into the land that the LORD your God is giving you, don't follow the disgusting practices of the nations that are there. 10 Don't sacrifice your children in the fires on your altars; and don't let your people practise divination or look for omens or use spells 11 or charms, and don't let them consult the spirits of the dead. 12 The LORD your God hates people who do these disgusting things, and that is why he is driving those nations out of the land as you advance. 13 Be completely faithful to the LORD."

The Promise to Send a Prophet

14 Then Moses said, "In the land you are about to occupy, people follow the advice of those who practise divination and look for omens, but the LORD your God does not allow you to do this. 15 Instead, he will send you a prophet like me from among your own people, and you are to obey him.*

16 "On the day that you were gathered at Mount Sinai, you begged not to hear the LORD speak again or to see his fiery presence any more, because you were afraid you would die. 17 So the LORD said to me, 'They have made a wise request. 18 I will send them a prophet like you from among their own people; I will tell him what to say, and he* will tell the people everything I command. 19 He will speak in my name, and I* will punish anyone who refuses to obey him. 20 But if any prophet dares to speak a message in my name when I did not command him to do so, he must die for it, and so must any prophet who speaks in the name of other gods.'

21 "You may wonder how you can tell when a prophet's message does not come from the LORD. 22 If a prophet speaks in the name of the LORD and what he says does not come true, then it is not the LORD's message. That prophet has spoken on his own authority, and you are not to fear him.

The Cities of Refuge
(Num 35.9–34; Josh 20.1–9)

19 "After the LORD your God has destroyed the people whose land he is giving you and after you have taken their cities and houses and settled there, 2-3 divide the territory into three parts, each with a city that can be easily reached. Then anyone who kills someone will be able to escape to one of them for protection. 4 If someone accidentally kills someone who is not an enemy, he may escape to any of these cities and be safe. 5 For example, if two men go into the forest together to cut wood and if, as one of them is chopping down a tree, the head of the axe comes off the handle and kills the other, he can run to one of those three cities and be safe. 6 If there were only one city, the distance to it might be too great, and the relative who is responsible for taking revenge for the killing might catch him and in his anger

18.8 Probable text *and he may keep… sends him*; Hebrew unclear.
18.15 *a prophet… him*; or *prophets… them*.
18.18 *a prophet… him… he*; or *prophets… them… they*.
18.19 *He will speak… and I*; or *When a prophet speaks in my name, I*.

230

Deuter.

Genesis
Exodus
Leviticus
Num.

DEUTERONOMY 19, 20

kill an innocent neighbour. After all, it was by accident that he killed his neighbour who was not his enemy. [7]This is why I order you to set aside three cities.

[8]"When the Lord your God enlarges your territory, as he told your ancestors he would, and gives you all the land he has promised, [9]then you are to select three more cities. (He will give you this land if you do everything that I command you today and if you love the Lord your God and live according to his teachings.) [10]Do this, so that innocent people will not die and so that you will not be guilty of putting them to death in the land that the Lord is giving you.

[11]"But suppose someone deliberately murders an enemy in cold blood and then escapes to one of those cities for protection. [12]In that case, the leaders of his own town are to send for him and hand him over to the relative responsible for taking revenge for the murder, so that he may be put to death. [13]Show him no mercy. Rid Israel of this murderer, so that all will go well with you.

Ancient Boundaries

[14]"Do not move your neighbour's boundary mark, established long ago in the land that the Lord your God is giving you.

Concerning Witnesses

[15]"One witness is not enough to convict a man of a crime; at least two witnesses are necessary to prove that a man is guilty. [16]If someone tries to harm someone else by false accusation, [17]both are to go to the one place of worship and be judged by the priests and judges who are then in office. [18]The judges will investigate the case thoroughly; and if someone has made a false accusation against a fellow-Israelite, [19]that person is to receive the punishment the accused would have received. In this way you will get rid of this evil. [20]Then everyone else will hear what happened; they will be afraid, and no one will ever again do such an evil thing. [21]In such cases show no mercy; the punishment is to be a life for a life, an eye for an eye, a tooth for a tooth, a hand for a hand, and a foot for a foot.

Concerning War

20 "When you go out to fight against your enemies and you see chariots and horses and an army that outnumbers yours, do not be afraid of them. The Lord your God, who rescued you from Egypt, will be with you. [2]Before you start fighting, a priest is to come forward and say to the army, [3]'Men of Israel, listen! Today you are going into battle. Do not be afraid of your enemies, or lose courage, or panic. [4]The Lord your God is going with you, and he will give you victory.'

[5]"Then the officers will address the men and say, 'Is there any man here who has just built a house, but has not yet dedicated it? If so, he is to go home. Otherwise, if he is killed in battle, someone else will dedicate his house. [6]Is there any man here who has just planted a vineyard, but has not yet had the chance to harvest its grapes? If so, he is to go home. Otherwise, if he is killed in battle, someone else will enjoy the wine. [7]Is there anyone here who is engaged to be married? If so, he is to go home. Otherwise, if he is killed in battle, someone else will marry the woman he is engaged to.'

[8]"The officers will also say to the men, 'Is there any man here who has lost his nerve and is afraid? If so, he is to go home. Otherwise, he will destroy the morale of the others.' [9]When the

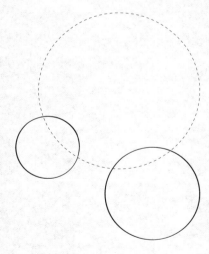

TURN THESE SHAPES INTO

SOMETHING ELSE.

Deuter.

....

Joshua

Judges

Ruth

1 Sam.

2 Sam.

officers have finished speaking to the army, leaders are to be chosen for each unit. [10]"When you go to attack a city, first give its people a chance to surrender. [11]If they open the gates and surrender, they are all to become your slaves and do forced labour for you. [12]But if the people of that city will not surrender, but choose to fight, surround it with your army. [13]Then, when the LORD your God lets you capture the city, kill every man in it. [14]You may, however, take for yourselves the women, the children, the livestock, and everything else in the city. You may use everything that belongs to your enemies. The LORD has given it to you. [15]That is how you are to deal with those cities that are far away from the land you will settle in.

[16]"But when you capture cities in the land that the LORD your God is giving you, kill everyone. [17]Completely destroy all the people: the Hittites, the Amorites, the Canaanites, the Perizzites, the Hivites, and the Jebusites, as the LORD ordered you to do. [18]Kill them, so that they will not make you sin against the LORD by teaching you to do all the disgusting things that they do in the worship of their gods.

[19]"When you are trying to capture a city, do not cut down its fruit trees, even though the siege lasts a long time. Eat the fruit, but do not destroy the trees; the trees are not your enemies. [20]You may cut down the other trees and use them in the siege mounds until the city is captured.

Concerning Unsolved Murders

21 "Suppose someone is found murdered in a field in the land that the LORD your God is going to give you, and you do not know who killed him. [2]Your leaders and judges are to go out and measure the distance from the place where the body was found to each of the nearby towns. [3]Then the leaders of the town nearest to where the body was found are to select a young cow that has never been used for work. [4]They are to take it down to a spot near a stream that never runs dry and where the ground has never been ploughed or planted, and there they are to break its neck. [5]The levitical priests are to go there also, because they are to decide every legal case involving violence. The LORD your God has chosen them to serve him and to pronounce blessings in his name. [6]Then all the leaders from the town nearest the place where the murdered person was found are to wash their hands over the cow [7]and say, 'We did not murder this person, and we do not know who did it. [8]LORD, forgive your people Israel, whom you rescued from Egypt. Forgive us and do not hold us responsible for the murder of an innocent person.' [9]And so, by doing what the LORD requires, you will not be held responsible for the murder.

Concerning Women Prisoners of War

[10]"When the LORD your God gives you victory in battle and you take prisoners, [11]you may see among them a beautiful woman that you like and want to marry. [12]Take her to your home, where she will shave her head,* cut her fingernails, [13]and change her clothes. She is to stay in your home and mourn for her parents for a month; after that, you may marry her. [14]Later, if you no longer want her, you are to let her go free. Since you forced her to have intercourse with you, you cannot treat her as a slave and sell her.

....

21.12 *shave her head*; or *trim her hair.*

232

Deuter.

....

Genesis
Exodus
Leviticus
Num.

DEUTERONOMY 21, 22

Concerning the First Son's Inheritance

15 "Suppose a man has two wives and they both bear him sons, but the first son is not the child of his favourite wife. 16 When the man decides how he is going to divide his property among his children, he is not to show partiality to the son of his favourite wife by giving him the share that belongs to the firstborn son. 17 He is to give a double share of his possessions to his first son, even though he is not the son of his favourite wife. A man must acknowledge his first son and give him the share he is legally entitled to.

Concerning a Disobedient Son

18 "Suppose someone has a son who is stubborn and rebellious, a son who will not obey his parents, even though they punish him. 19 His parents are to take him before the leaders of the town where he lives and make him stand trial. 20 They are to say to them, 'Our son is stubborn and rebellious and refuses to obey us; he wastes money and is a drunkard.' 21 Then the men of the city are to stone him to death, and so you will get rid of this evil. Everyone in Israel will hear what has happened and be afraid.

Various Laws

22 "If someone has been put to death for a crime and his body is hung on a post, 23 it is not to remain there overnight. It must be buried the same day, because a dead body hanging on a post brings God's curse on the land. Bury the body, so that you will not defile the land that the LORD your God is giving you.

22 "If you see a fellow-Israelite's cow or sheep running loose, do not ignore it; take it back to him. 2 But if its owner lives a long way off or if you don't know who owns it, then take it home with you. When its owner comes looking for it, give it to him. 3 Do the same thing if you find a donkey, a piece of clothing, or anything else that your fellow-Israelite may have lost.

4 "If a fellow-Israelite's donkey or cow has fallen down, don't ignore it; help him to get the animal to its feet again.

5 "Women are not to wear men's clothing, and men are not to wear women's clothing; the LORD your God hates people who do such things.

6 "If you happen to find a bird's nest in a tree or on the ground with the mother bird sitting either on the eggs or with her young, you are not to take the mother bird. 7 You may take the young birds, but you must let the mother bird go, so that you will live a long and prosperous life.

8 "When you build a new house, be sure to put a railing round the edge of the roof. Then you will not be responsible if someone falls off and is killed.

9 "Do not plant any crop in the same field as your grapevines; if you do, you are forbidden to use either the grapes or the produce of the other crop.

10 "Do not hitch an ox and a donkey together for ploughing.

11 "Do not wear cloth made by weaving wool and linen together.

12 "Sew tassels on the four corners of your clothes.

Laws Concerning Sexual Purity

13 "Suppose a man marries a woman and later he decides he doesn't want her. 14 So he makes up false charges against her, accusing her of not being a virgin when they got married.

15 "If this happens, the woman's parents are to take the bloodstained wedding sheet that proves she was a virgin, and

DEUTERONOMY 22, 23

233

Deuter.

..........:

Joshua

Judges

Ruth

1 Sam.

2 Sam.

they are to show it in court to the town leaders. [16] Her father will say to them, 'I gave my daughter to this man in marriage, and now he doesn't want her. [17] He has made false charges against her, saying that she was not a virgin when he married her. But here is the proof that my daughter was a virgin; look at the bloodstains on the wedding sheet!' [18] Then the town leaders are to take the husband and beat him. [19] They are also to fine him a hundred pieces of silver and give the money to the woman's father, because the man has brought disgrace on an Israelite woman. Moreover, she will continue to be his wife, and he can never divorce her as long as he lives.

[20] "But if the charge is true and there is no proof that she was a virgin, [21] then they are to take her out to the entrance of her father's house, where the men of her city are to stone her to death. She has done a shameful thing among our people by having intercourse before she was married, while she was still living in her father's house. In this way you will get rid of this evil.

[22] "If a man is caught having intercourse with another man's wife, both of them are to be put to death. In this way you will get rid of this evil.

[23] "Suppose a man is caught in a town having intercourse with a woman who is engaged to someone else. [24] You are to take them outside the town and stone them to death. The woman is to die because she did not cry out for help, although she was in a town, where she could have been heard. And the man is to die because he had intercourse with a woman who was engaged. In this way you will get rid of this evil.

[25] "Suppose a man out in the countryside rapes a woman who is engaged to someone else. Then only the man is to be put to death; [26] nothing is to be done to the woman, because she has not committed a sin worthy of death. This case is the same as when one man attacks another man and murders him. [27] The man raped the engaged woman in the countryside, and although she cried for help, there was no one to help her.

[28] "Suppose a man is caught raping a young woman who is not engaged. [29] He is to pay her father the bride price of fifty pieces of silver, and she is to become his wife, because he forced her to have intercourse with him. He can never divorce her as long as he lives.

[30] "No man is to disgrace his father by having intercourse with any of his father's wives.

Exclusion from the LORD's People

23 "No man who has been castrated or whose penis has been cut off may be included among the LORD's people.

[2] "No one born out of wedlock or any descendant of such a person, even in the tenth generation, may be included among the LORD's people.

[3] "No Ammonite or Moabite — or any of their descendants, even in the tenth generation — may be included among the LORD's people. [4] They refused to provide you with food and water when you were on your way out of Egypt, and they hired Balaam son of Beor, from the city of Pethor in Mesopotamia, to curse you. [5] But the LORD your God would not listen to Balaam; instead he turned the curse into a blessing, because he loved you. [6] As long as you are a nation, never do anything to help these nations or to make them prosperous.

[7] "Do not despise the Edomites; they are your relatives. And do not despise the Egyptians; you once lived in their land. [8] From the third generation onward their descendants may be included among the LORD's people.

234

Deuter.

⋮⋯⋯⋯

Genesis

Exodus

Leviticus

Num.

DEUTERONOMY 23, 24

Keeping the Military Camp Clean

9 "When you are in camp in time of war, you are to avoid anything that would make you ritually unclean. 10 If a man becomes unclean because he has had a wet dream during the night, he is to go outside the camp and stay there. 11 Towards evening he is to wash himself, and at sunset he may come back into camp.

12 "You are to have a place outside the camp where you can go when you need to relieve yourselves. 13 Carry a stick as part of your equipment, so that when you have a bowel movement you can dig a hole and cover it up. 14 Keep your camp ritually clean, because the LORD your God is with you in your camp to protect you and to give you victory over your enemies. Do not do anything indecent that would cause the LORD to turn his back on you.

Various Laws

15 "If a slave runs away from his or her owner and comes to you for protection, do not send them back. 16 They may live in any of your towns that they choose, and you are not to treat them harshly.

17 "No Israelite, man or woman, is to become a temple prostitute. 18 Also, no money earned in this way may be brought into the house of the LORD your God in fulfilment of a vow. The LORD hates temple prostitutes.

19 "When you lend money or food or anything else to a fellow-Israelite, do not charge him interest. 20 You may charge interest on what you lend to a foreigner, but not on what you lend to a fellow-Israelite. Obey this rule, and the LORD your God will bless everything you do in the land that you are going to occupy.

21 "When you make a vow to the LORD your God, do not put off doing what you promised; the LORD will hold you to your vow, and it is a sin not to keep it. 22 It is no sin not to make a vow to the LORD, 23 but if you make one voluntarily, be sure that you keep it.

24 "When you walk along a path in someone else's vineyard, you may eat all the grapes you want, but you must not carry any away in a container. 25 When you walk along a path in someone else's cornfield, you may eat all the corn you can pull off with your hands, but you must not cut any corn with a sickle.

Divorce and Remarriage

24 "Suppose a man marries a woman and later decides that he doesn't want her, because he finds something about her that he doesn't like.* So he writes out divorce papers, gives them to her, and sends her away from his home. 2 Then suppose she marries another man, 3 and he also decides that he doesn't want her, so he also writes out divorce papers, gives them to her, and sends her away from his home. Or suppose her second husband dies. 4 In either case, her first husband is not to marry her again; he is to consider her defiled. If he married her again, it would be offensive to the LORD. You are not to commit such a terrible sin in the land that the LORD your God is giving you.

Various Laws

5 "When a man is newly married, he is not to be drafted into military service or any other public duty; he is to be excused from duty for one year, so that he can stay at home and make his wife happy.*

24.1 *something… like; or that she is guilty of some shameful conduct.*
24.5 *make his wife happy; or be happy with his wife.*

DEUTERONOMY 24, 25

235

Deuter.

Joshua
Judges
Ruth
1 Sam.
2 Sam.

[6] "When you lend someone something, you are not to take as security his millstones used for grinding his corn. This would take away the family's means of preparing food to keep alive.

[7] "Whoever kidnaps a fellow-Israelite and takes him or her as a slave or sells them into slavery is to be put to death. In this way you will get rid of this evil.

[8] "When you are suffering from a dreaded skin disease, be sure to do exactly what the levitical priests tell you; follow the instructions that I have given them. [9] Remember what the LORD your God did to Miriam as you were coming from Egypt.

[10] "When you lend a neighbour something, do not go into his house to get the garment he is going to give you as security; [11] wait outside and let him bring it to you himself. [12] If he is poor, do not keep it overnight; [13] return it to him each evening, so that he can have it to sleep in. Then he will be grateful, and the LORD your God will be pleased with you.

[14] "Do not cheat poor and needy hired servants, whether fellow-Israelites or foreigners living in one of your towns. [15] Each day before sunset pay them for that day's work; they need the money and have counted on getting it. If you do not pay them, they will cry out against you to the LORD, and you will be guilty of sin.

[16] "Parents are not to be put to death for crimes committed by their children, and children are not to be put to death for crimes committed by their parents; people are to be put to death only for crimes they themselves have committed.

[17] "Do not deprive foreigners and orphans of their rights; and do not take a widow's garment as security for a loan. [18] Remember that you were slaves in Egypt and that the LORD your God set you free; that is why I have given you this command.

[19] "When you gather your crops and fail to bring in some of the corn that you have cut, do not go back for it; it is to be left for the foreigners, orphans, and widows, so that the LORD your God will bless you in everything you do. [20] When you have picked your olives once, do not go back and get those that are left; they are for the foreigners, orphans, and widows. [21] When you have gathered your grapes once, do not go back over the vines a second time; the grapes that are left are for the foreigners, orphans, and widows. [22] Never forget that you were slaves in Egypt; that is why I have given you this command.

25 "Suppose two Israelites go to court to settle a dispute, and one is declared innocent and the other guilty. [2] If the guilty person is sentenced to be beaten, the judge is to make him lie face downwards and have him whipped. The number of lashes will depend on the crime he has committed. [3] He may be given as many as forty lashes, but no more; more than that would humiliate him publicly.

[4] "Do not muzzle an ox when you are using it to thresh corn.

Duty to a Dead Brother

[5] "If two brothers live on the same property and one of them dies, leaving no son, then his widow is not to be married to someone outside the family; it is the duty of the dead man's brother to marry her. [6] The first son that they have will be considered the son of the dead man, so that his family line will continue in Israel. [7] But if the dead man's brother does not want to marry her, she is to go before the town leaders and say, 'My husband's brother will not do his duty; he refuses to give his brother a descendant among the people of Israel.' [8] Then the town leaders are to summon him and speak to him. If he

DEUTERONOMY 24.17-18

In Deuteronomy, when God gives out a law, he often also reminds people of what he has done for them. There is nothing we can do for God or others that is greater than what

– GOD HAS DONE –

FOR US.

When you think of what God asks you to do (for example, read the Bible, tell your friends about Jesus, love the poor) what are your natural responses? What should your perspective be when reading verses like these?

236
DEUTERONOMY 25, 26

Deuter.

·:········

Genesis
Exodus
Leviticus
Num.

still refuses to marry her, [9]his brother's widow is to go up to him in the presence of the town leaders, take off one of his sandals, spit in his face, and say, 'This is what happens to the man who refuses to give his brother a descendant.' [10]His family will be known in Israel as 'the family of the man who had his sandal pulled off.'

Other Laws

[11]"If two men are having a fight and the wife of one tries to help her husband by grabbing hold of the other man's genitals, [12]show her no mercy; cut off her hand.

[13-14]"Do not cheat when you use weights and measures. [15]Use true and honest weights and measures, so that you may live a long time in the land that the LORD your God is giving you. [16]The LORD hates people who cheat.

The Command to Kill the Amalekites

[17]"Remember what the Amalekites did to you as you were coming from Egypt. [18]They had no fear of God, and so they attacked you from the rear when you were tired and exhausted, and killed all who were straggling behind. [19]So then, when the LORD your God has given you the land and made you safe from all your enemies who live around you, be sure to kill all the Amalekites, so that no one will remember them any longer. Do not forget!

Harvest Offerings

26 "After you have occupied the land that the LORD your God is giving you and have settled there, [2]each of you must place in a basket the first part of each crop that you harvest and you must take it with you to the one place of worship. [3]Go to the priest in charge at that time and say to him, 'I now acknowledge to the LORD my God that I have entered the land that he promised our ancestors to give us.'

[4]"The priest will take the basket from you and place it before the altar of the LORD your God. [5]Then, in the LORD's presence you will recite these words: 'My ancestor was a wandering Aramean, who took his family to Egypt to live. They were few in number when they went there, but they became a large and powerful nation. [6]The Egyptians treated us harshly and forced us to work as slaves. [7]Then we cried out for help to the LORD, the God of our ancestors. He heard us and saw our suffering, hardship, and misery. [8]By his great power and strength he rescued us from Egypt. He worked miracles and wonders, and caused terrifying things to happen. [9]He brought us here and gave us this rich and fertile land. [10]So now I bring to the LORD the first part of the harvest that he has given me.'

"Then set the basket down in the LORD's presence and worship there. [11]Be grateful for the good things that the LORD your God has given you and your family; and let the Levites and the foreigners who live among you join in the celebration.

[12]"Every third year give the tithe — a tenth of your crops — to the Levites, the foreigners, the orphans, and the widows, so that in every community they will have all they need to eat. When you have done this, [13]say to the LORD, 'None of the sacred tithe is left in my house; I have given it to the Levites, the foreigners, the orphans, and the widows, as you commanded me to do. I have not disobeyed or forgotten any of your commands concerning the tithe. [14]I have not eaten any of it when I was mourning; I have

Deuter.
....
Joshua
Judges
Ruth
1 Sam.
2 Sam.

not taken any of it out of my house when I was ritually unclean; and I have not given any of it as an offering for the dead.* I have obeyed you, O LORD; I have done everything you commanded concerning the tithe. ¹⁵ Look down from your holy place in heaven and bless your people Israel; bless also the rich and fertile land that you have given us, as you promised our ancestors.'

The LORD's Own People

¹⁶ "Today the LORD your God commands you to obey all his laws; so obey them faithfully with all your heart. ¹⁷ Today you have acknowledged the LORD as your God; you have promised to obey him, to keep all his laws, and to do all that he commands. ¹⁸ Today the LORD has accepted you as his own people, as he promised you; and he commands you to obey all his laws. ¹⁹ He will make you greater than any other nation that he has created, and you will bring praise and honour to his name.* You will be his own people, as he promised."

God's Laws Written on Stones

27 Then Moses, together with the leaders of Israel, said to the people, "Obey all the instructions that I am giving you today. ² On the day you cross the River Jordan and enter the land that the LORD your God is giving you, you are to set up some large stones, cover them with plaster, ³ and write on them all these laws and teachings. When you have entered the rich and fertile land that the LORD, the God of your ancestors, promised you, ⁴ and you are on the other side of the Jordan, set up these stones on Mount Ebal, as I am instructing you today, and cover them with plaster. ⁵ Build an altar there made of stones that have had no iron tools used on them, ⁶ because any altar you build for the LORD your God must be made of uncut stones. There you are to offer the sacrifices that are to be burnt, ⁷ and there you are to sacrifice and eat your fellowship offerings and be grateful in the presence of the LORD your God. ⁸ On the stones covered with plaster write clearly every word of God's laws."

⁹ Then Moses, together with the levitical priests, said to all the people of Israel, "Give me your attention, people of Israel, and listen to me. Today you have become the people of the LORD your God; ¹⁰ so obey him and keep all his laws that I am giving you today."

The Curses on Disobedience

¹¹ Then Moses said to the people of Israel, ¹² "After you have crossed the Jordan, the following tribes are to stand on Mount Gerizim when the blessings are pronounced on the people: Simeon, Levi, Judah, Issachar, Joseph, and Benjamin. ¹³ And the following tribes will stand on Mount Ebal when the curses are pronounced: Reuben, Gad, Asher, Zebulun, Dan, and Naphtali. ¹⁴ The Levites will speak these words in a loud voice:

¹⁵ " 'God's curse on anyone who makes an idol of stone, wood, or metal and secretly worships it; the LORD hates idolatry.'

"And all the people will answer, 'Amen!'

¹⁶ " 'God's curse on anyone who dishonours his father or mother.'

"And all the people will answer, 'Amen!'

¹⁷ " 'God's curse on anyone who moves a neighbour's boundary mark.'

26.14 *for the dead*; or *to the dead.*
26.19 *bring praise… name*; or *receive praise and honour.*

238

DEUTERONOMY 27, 28

Deuter.

Genesis
Exodus
Leviticus
Num.

"And all the people will answer, 'Amen!'

18 " 'God's curse on anyone who leads a blind person in the wrong direction.'

"And all the people will answer, 'Amen!'

19 " 'God's curse on anyone who deprives foreigners, orphans, and widows of their rights.'

"And all the people will answer, 'Amen!'

20 " 'God's curse on anyone who disgraces his father by having intercourse with any of his father's wives.'

"And all the people will answer, 'Amen!'

21 " 'God's curse on anyone who has sexual relations with an animal.'

"And all the people will answer, 'Amen!'

22 " 'God's curse on anyone who has intercourse with his sister or half sister.'

"And all the people will answer, 'Amen!'

23 " 'God's curse on anyone who has intercourse with his mother-in-law.'

"And all the people will answer, 'Amen!'

24 " 'God's curse on anyone who secretly commits murder.'

"And all the people will answer, 'Amen!'

25 " 'God's curse on anyone who accepts money to murder an innocent person.'

"And all the people will answer, 'Amen!'

26 " 'God's curse on anyone who does not obey all of God's laws and teachings.'

"And all the people will answer, 'Amen!'

The Blessings of Obedience
(Lev 26.3–13; Deut 7.12–24)

28 "If you obey the LORD your God and faithfully keep all his commands that I am giving you today, he will make you greater than any other nation on earth. 2 Obey the LORD your God and all these blessings will be yours:

3 "The LORD will bless your towns and your fields.

4 "The LORD will bless you with many children, with abundant crops, and with many cattle and sheep.

5 "The LORD will bless your corn crops and the food you prepare from them.

6 "The LORD will bless everything you do.

7 "The LORD will defeat your enemies when they attack you. They will attack from one direction, but they will run from you in all directions.

8 "The LORD your God will bless your work and fill your barns with corn. He will bless you in the land that he is giving you.

9 "If you obey the LORD your God and do everything he commands, he will make you his own people, as he has promised. 10 Then all the peoples on earth will see that the LORD has chosen you to be his own people, and they will be afraid of you. 11 The LORD will give you many children, many cattle, and abundant crops in the land that he promised your ancestors to give you. 12 He will send rain in season from his rich storehouse in the sky and bless all your work, so that you will lend to many nations, but you will not have to borrow from any. 13 The LORD your God will make you the leader among the nations and not a follower; you will always prosper and never fail if you obey faithfully all his commands that I am giving you today. 14 But you must never disobey them in any way, or worship and serve other gods.

· CHANGE ·
LOCATION
before continuing
TO READ.

Deuter.

....

Joshua
Judges
Ruth
1 Sam.
2 Sam.

The Consequences of Disobedience
(Lev 26.14–46)

15 "But if you disobey the LORD your God and do not faithfully keep all his commands and laws that I am giving you today, all these evil things will happen to you:

16 "The LORD will curse your towns and your fields.

17 "The LORD will curse your corn crops and the food you prepare from them.

18 "The LORD will curse you by giving you only a few children, poor crops, and few cattle and sheep.

19 "The LORD will curse everything you do.

20 "If you do evil and reject the LORD, he will bring on you disaster, confusion, and trouble in everything you do, until you are quickly and completely destroyed. 21 He will send disease after disease on you until there is not one of you left in the land that you are about to occupy. 22 The LORD will strike you with infectious diseases, with swelling and fever; he will send drought and scorching winds to destroy your crops. These disasters will be with you until you die. 23 No rain will fall, and your ground will become as hard as iron. 24 Instead of rain, the LORD will send down duststorms and sandstorms until you are destroyed.

25 "The LORD will give your enemies victory over you. You will attack them from one direction, but you will run from them in all directions, and all the people on earth will be terrified when they see what happens to you. 26 When you die, birds and wild animals will come and eat your bodies, and there will be no one to scare them off. 27 The LORD will send boils on you, as he did on the Egyptians. He will make your bodies break out with sores. You will be covered with scabs, and you will itch, but there will be no cure. 28 The LORD will make you lose your mind; he will strike you with blindness and confusion. 29 You will grope about in broad daylight like a blind person, and you will not be able to find your way. You will not prosper in anything you do. You will be constantly oppressed and robbed, and there will be no one to help you.

30 "You will be engaged to a young woman — but someone else will marry her. You will build a house — but never live in it. You will plant a vineyard — but never eat its grapes. 31 Your cattle will be butchered before your very eyes, but you will not eat any of the meat. Your donkeys will be dragged away while you look on, and they will not be given back to you. Your sheep will be given to your enemies, and there will be no one to help you. 32 Your sons and daughters will be given as slaves to foreigners while you look on. Every day you will strain your eyes, looking in vain for your children to return. 33 A foreign nation will take all the crops that you have worked so hard to grow, while you receive nothing but constant oppression and harsh treatment. 34 Your sufferings will make you lose your mind. 35 The LORD will cover your legs with incurable, painful sores; boils will cover you from head to foot.

36 "The LORD will take you and your king away to a foreign land, where neither you nor your ancestors ever lived before; there you will serve gods made of wood and stone. 37 In the countries to which the LORD will scatter you, the people will be shocked at what has happened to you; they will make fun of you and ridicule you.

38 "You will sow plenty of seed, but reap only a small harvest, because the locusts will eat your crops. 39 You will plant vineyards and take care of them, but you will not gather their grapes or drink wine from them, because worms will eat the vines. 40 Olive trees will grow everywhere in your land, but you will not have any olive oil, because the olives will drop off. 41 You will have

sons and daughters, but you will lose them, because they will be taken away as prisoners of war. ⁴²All your trees and crops will be devoured by insects.

⁴³"Foreigners who live in your land will gain more and more power, while you gradually lose yours. ⁴⁴They will have money to lend you, but you will have none to lend them. In the end they will be your rulers.

⁴⁵"All these disasters will come on you, and they will be with you until you are destroyed, because you did not obey the LORD your God and keep all the laws that he gave you. ⁴⁶They will be the evidence of God's judgement on you and your descendants for ever. ⁴⁷The LORD blessed you in every way, but you would not serve him with glad and joyful hearts. ⁴⁸So then, you will serve the enemies that the LORD is going to send against you. You will be hungry, thirsty, and naked — in need of everything. The LORD* will oppress you harshly until you are destroyed. ⁴⁹The LORD will bring against you a nation from the ends of the earth, a nation whose language you do not know. They will swoop down on you like an eagle. ⁵⁰They will be ruthless and show no mercy to anyone, young or old. ⁵¹They will eat your livestock and your crops, and you will starve to death. They will not leave you any corn, wine, olive oil, cattle, or sheep; and you will die. ⁵²They will attack every town in the land that the LORD your God is giving you, and the high, fortified walls in which you trust will fall.

⁵³"When your enemies are besieging your towns, you will become so desperate for food that you will even eat the children that the LORD your God has given you. ⁵⁴⁻⁵⁵Even the most refined man of noble birth will become so desperate during the siege that he will eat some of his own children because he has no other food. He will not even give any to his brother or to the wife he loves or to any of his children who are left. ⁵⁶⁻⁵⁷Even the most refined woman of noble birth, so rich that she has never had to walk anywhere, will behave in the same way. When the enemy besieges her town, she will become so desperate for food that she will secretly eat her newborn child and the afterbirth as well. She will not share them with the husband she loves or with any of her children.

⁵⁸"If you do not obey faithfully all God's teachings that are written in this book and if you do not honour the wonderful and awesome name of the LORD your God, ⁵⁹he will send on you and on your descendants incurable diseases and horrible epidemics that can never be stopped. ⁶⁰He will bring on you once again all the dreadful diseases you experienced in Egypt, and you will never recover. ⁶¹He will also send all kinds of diseases and epidemics that are not mentioned in this book of God's laws and teachings, and you will be destroyed. ⁶²Although you become as numerous as the stars in the sky, only a few of you will survive, because you did not obey the LORD your God. ⁶³Just as the LORD took delight in making you prosper and in making you increase in number, so he will take delight in destroying you and in bringing ruin on you. You will be uprooted from the land that you are about to occupy.

⁶⁴"The LORD will scatter you among all the nations, from one end of the earth to the other, and there you will serve gods made of wood and stone, gods that neither you nor your ancestors have ever worshipped before. ⁶⁵You will find no peace anywhere, no place to call your own; the LORD will overwhelm you with anxiety, hopelessness, and despair. ⁶⁶Your life will always be in danger. Day

28.48 *The* LORD; or *Your enemies.*

Deuter.

..........:.

Joshua
Judges
Ruth
1 Sam.
2 Sam.

and night you will be filled with terror, and you will live in constant fear of death. [67]Your hearts will pound with fear at everything you see. Every morning you will wish for evening; every evening you will wish for morning. [68]The LORD will send you back to Egypt in ships, even though he* said that you would never have to go there again. There you will try to sell yourselves to your enemies as slaves, but no one will want to buy you."

The LORD's Covenant with Israel in the Land of Moab

29 These are the terms of the covenant that the LORD commanded Moses to make with the people of Israel in the land of Moab; all this was in addition to the covenant which the LORD had made with them at Mount Sinai.

[2]Moses called together all the people of Israel and said to them, "You saw for yourselves what the LORD did to the king of Egypt, to his officials, and to his entire country. [3]You saw the terrible plagues, the miracles, and the great wonders that the LORD performed. [4]But to this very day he has not let you understand what you have experienced. [5]For forty years the LORD led you through the desert, and your clothes and sandals never wore out. [6]You did not have bread to eat or wine or beer to drink, but the LORD provided for your needs in order to teach you that he is your God. [7]And when we came to this place, King Sihon of Heshbon and King Og of Bashan came out to fight against us. But we defeated them, [8]took their land, and divided it among the tribes of Reuben and Gad, and half the tribe of Manasseh. [9]Obey faithfully all the terms of this covenant, so that you will be successful in everything you do.

[10]"Today you are standing in the presence of the LORD your God, all of you — your leaders and officials, your men, [11]women, and children, and the foreigners who live among you and cut wood and carry water for you. [12]You are here today to enter into this covenant that the LORD your God is making with you and to accept its obligations, [13]so that the LORD may now confirm you as his people and be your God, as he promised you and your ancestors, Abraham, Isaac, and Jacob. [14]You are not the only ones with whom the LORD is making this covenant with its obligations. [15]He is making it with all of us who stand here in his presence today and also with our descendants who are not yet born.

[16]"You remember what life was like in Egypt and what it was like to travel through the territory of other nations. [17]You saw their disgusting idols made of wood, stone, silver, and gold. [18]Make sure that no man, woman, family, or tribe standing here today turns from the LORD our God to worship the gods of other nations. This would be like a root that grows to be a bitter and poisonous plant. [19]Make sure that there is no one here today who hears these solemn demands and yet convinces himself that all will be well with him, even if he stubbornly goes his own way. That would destroy all of you, good and evil alike. [20]The LORD will not forgive such a man. Instead, the LORD's burning anger will flame up against him, and all the disasters written in this book will fall on him until the LORD has destroyed him completely. [21]The LORD will make an example of him before all the tribes of Israel and will bring disaster on him in accordance with all the curses listed in the covenant that is written in this book of the LORD's teachings.

[22]"In future generations your descendants and foreigners from distant lands will see the disasters and sufferings that the LORD

....

28.68 *he*; or *I*.

242

Deuter.

Genesis
Exodus
Leviticus
Num.

DEUTERONOMY 29, 30

has brought on your land. ²³ The fields will be a barren waste, covered with sulphur and salt; nothing will be planted, and not even weeds will grow there. Your land will be like the cities of Sodom and Gomorrah, of Admah and Zeboiim, which the LORD destroyed when he was furiously angry. ²⁴ Then the whole world will ask, 'Why did the LORD do this to their land? What was the reason for his fierce anger?' ²⁵ And the answer will be, 'It is because the LORD's people broke the covenant they had made with him, the God of their ancestors, when he brought them out of Egypt. ²⁶ They served other gods that they had never worshipped before, gods that the LORD had forbidden them to worship. ²⁷ And so the LORD became angry with his people and brought on their land all the disasters written in this book. ²⁸ The LORD became furiously angry, and in his great anger he uprooted them from their land and threw them into a foreign land, and there they are today.'

²⁹ "There are some things that the LORD our God has kept secret; but he has revealed his Law, and we and our descendants are to obey it for ever.

THE LAW

EXODUS 13.9;
DEUTERONOMY 29.29

DEFINITION: The body of divine commandments as expressed in the Bible or other religious texts. (oxforddictionaries.com)

Conditions for Restoration and Blessing

30 "I have now given you a choice between a blessing and a curse. When all these things have happened to you, and you are living among the nations where the LORD your God has scattered you, you will remember the choice I gave you. ² If you and your descendants will turn back to the LORD and with all your heart obey his commands that I am giving you today, ³ then the LORD your God will have mercy on you. He will bring you back from the nations where he has scattered you, and he will make you prosperous again. ⁴ Even if you are scattered to the farthest corners of the earth, the LORD your God will gather you together and bring you back, ⁵ so that you may again take possession of the land where your ancestors once lived. And he will make you more prosperous and more numerous than your ancestors ever were. ⁶ The LORD your God will give you and your descendants obedient hearts, so that you will love him with all your heart, and you will continue to live in that land. ⁷ He will turn all these curses against your enemies, who hated you and oppressed you, ⁸ and you will again obey him and keep all his commands that I am giving you today. ⁹ The LORD will make you prosperous in all that you do; you will have many children and a lot of livestock, and your fields will produce abundant crops. He will be as glad to make you prosperous as he was to make your ancestors prosperous, ¹⁰ but you will have to obey him and keep all his laws that are written in this book of his teachings. You will have to turn to him with all your heart.

¹¹ "The command that I am giving you today is not too difficult or beyond your reach. ¹² It is not up in the sky. You do not have to ask, 'Who will go up and bring it down for us, so that we can hear it and obey it?' ¹³ Nor is it on the other side of the ocean. You do not have to ask, 'Who will go across the ocean and bring it to us, so that we may hear it and obey it?' ¹⁴ No, it is here with you. You know it and can quote it, so now obey it.

¹⁵ "Today I am giving you a choice between good and evil, between life and death. ¹⁶ If you obey the commands of the LORD your God,* which I give you today, if you love him, obey him, and keep all his laws, then you will prosper and become a nation of

----

30.16 One ancient translation *If you obey the commands of the LORD your God*; Hebrew does not have these words.

many people. The LORD your God will bless you in the land that you are about to occupy. [17]But if you disobey and refuse to listen, and are led away to worship other gods, [18]you will be destroyed — I warn you here and now. You will not live long in that land across the Jordan that you are about to occupy. [19]I am now giving you the choice between life and death, between God's blessing and God's curse, and I call heaven and earth to witness the choice you make. Choose life. [20]Love the LORD your God, obey him and be faithful to him, and then you and your descendants will live long in the land that he promised to give your ancestors, Abraham, Isaac, and Jacob."

Joshua Becomes Moses' Successor
(Num 27.12–23)

31 Moses continued speaking to the people of Israel, [2]and said, "I am now 120 years old and am no longer able to be your leader. And besides this, the LORD has told me that I will not cross the Jordan. [3]The LORD your God himself will go before you and destroy the nations living there, so that you can occupy their land; and Joshua will be your leader, as the LORD has said. [4]The LORD will destroy those people, just as he defeated Sihon and Og, kings of the Amorites, and destroyed their country. [5]The LORD will give you victory over them, and you are to treat them exactly as I have told you. [6]Be determined and confident. Do not be afraid of them. Your God, the LORD himself, will be with you. He will not fail you or abandon you."

[7]Then Moses called Joshua and said to him in the presence of all the people of Israel, "Be determined and confident; you are the one who will lead these people to occupy the land that the LORD promised to their ancestors. [8]The LORD himself will lead you and be with you. He will not fail you or abandon you, so do not lose courage or be afraid."

The Law is to be Read Every Seven Years

[9]So Moses wrote down God's Law and gave it to the levitical priests, who were in charge of the LORD's Covenant Box, and to the leaders of Israel. [10]He commanded them, "At the end of every seven years, when the year that debts are cancelled comes round, read this aloud at the Festival of Shelters. [11]Read it to the people of Israel when they come to worship the LORD your God at the one place of worship. [12]Call together all the men, women, and children, and the foreigners who live in your towns, so that everyone may hear it and learn to honour the LORD your God and to obey his teachings faithfully. [13]In this way your descendants who have never heard the Law of the LORD your God will hear it. And so they will learn to obey him as long as they live in the land that you are about to occupy across the Jordan."

The LORD's Last Instruction to Moses

[14]Then the LORD said to Moses, "You haven't much longer to live. Call Joshua and bring him to the Tent, so that I may give him his instructions." Moses and Joshua went to the Tent, [15]and the LORD appeared to them there in a pillar of cloud that stood by the door of the Tent.

[16]The LORD said to Moses, "You will soon die, and after your death the people will become unfaithful to me and break the covenant that I made with them. They will abandon me and worship the pagan gods of the land they are about to enter. [17]When that happens, I will become angry with them; I will

DEUTERONOMY 30.19

God calls his people to choose life over death by following him.

Where you are right now, why not consciously choose life.

TAKE FIVE
DEEP BREATHS.

On each breath in and out, say a quiet 'yes' to God and his purposes in your life.

244

Deuter.

⋮⋯⋯⋯

Genesis
Exodus
Leviticus
Num.

DEUTERONOMY 31, 32

abandon them, and they will be destroyed. Many terrible disasters will come upon them, and then they will realize that these things are happening to them because I, their God, am no longer with them. [18] And I will refuse to help them then, because they have done evil and worshipped other gods.

[19] "Now, write down this song. Teach it to the people of Israel, so that it will stand as evidence against them. [20] I will take them into this rich and fertile land, as I promised their ancestors. There they will have all the food they want, and they will live comfortably. But they will turn away and worship other gods. They will reject me and break my covenant, [21] and many terrible disasters will come on them. But this song will still be sung, and it will stand as evidence against them. Even now, before I take them into the land that I promised to give them, I know what they are thinking."

[22] That same day Moses wrote down the song and taught it to the people of Israel.

[23] Then the LORD spoke to Joshua son of Nun and said to him, "Be confident and determined. You will lead the people of Israel into the land that I promised them, and I will be with you."

[24] Moses wrote God's Law in a book, taking care not to leave out anything. [25] When he finished, he said to the levitical priests, who were in charge of the LORD's Covenant Box, [26] "Take this book of God's Law and place it beside the Covenant Box of the LORD your God, so that it will remain there as a witness against his people. [27] I know how stubborn and rebellious they are. They have rebelled against the LORD during my lifetime, and they will rebel even more after I am dead. [28] Assemble all your tribal leaders and officials before me, so that I can tell them these things; I will call heaven and earth to be my witnesses against them. [29] I know that after my death the people will become wicked and reject what I have taught them. And in time to come they will meet with disaster, because they will have made the LORD angry by doing what he has forbidden."

The Song of Moses

[30] Then Moses recited the entire song while all the people of Israel listened.

32 "Earth and sky, hear my words,
listen closely to what I say.
[2] My teaching will fall like drops of rain
and form on the earth like dew.
My words will fall like showers on young plants,
like gentle rain on tender grass.
[3] I will praise the name of the LORD,
and his people will tell of his greatness.

[4] "The LORD is your mighty defender,
perfect and just in all his ways;
Your God is faithful and true;
he does what is right and fair.
[5] But you are unfaithful, unworthy to be his people,*
a sinful and deceitful nation.
[6] Is this the way you should treat the LORD,
you foolish, senseless people?
He is your father, your Creator,
he made you into a nation.

32.5 Probable text *But you... people*; Hebrew unclear.

7 "Think of the past, of the time long ago;
   ask your parents to tell you what happened,
   ask the old people to tell of the past.
8 The Most High assigned nations their lands;
   he determined where peoples should live.
He assigned to each nation a heavenly being,
9   but Jacob's descendants he chose for himself.

10 "He found them wandering through the desert,
   a desolate, windswept wilderness.
He protected them and cared for them,
   as he would protect himself.
11 Like an eagle teaching its young to fly,*
   catching them safely on its spreading wings,
   the LORD kept Israel from falling.
12 The LORD alone led his people
   without the help of a foreign god.

13 "He let them rule the highlands,
   and they ate what grew in the fields.
They found wild honey among the rocks;
   their olive trees flourished in stony ground.
14 Their cows and goats gave plenty of milk;
   they had the best sheep, goats, and cattle,
   the finest wheat, and the choicest wine.

15 "The LORD's people grew rich, but rebellious;
   they were fat and stuffed with food.
They abandoned God their Creator
   and rejected their mighty saviour.
16 Their idolatry made the LORD jealous;
   the evil they did made him angry.
17 They sacrificed to gods that are not real,
   new gods their ancestors had never known,
   gods that Israel had never obeyed,
18 They forgot their God, their mighty saviour,
   the one who had given them life.

19 "When the LORD saw this, he was angry
   and rejected his sons and daughters.
20 'I will no longer help them,' he said;
   'then I will see what happens to them,
   those stubborn, unfaithful people.
21 With their idols they have made me angry,
   jealous with their so-called gods,
   gods that are really not gods.
So I will use a so-called nation to make them angry;
   I will make them jealous with a nation of fools.
22 My anger will flame up like fire
   and burn everything on earth.
It will reach to the world below*
   and consume the roots of the mountains.

23 "'I will bring on them endless disasters
   and use all my arrows against them.

....

32.11 teaching its young to fly; or watching over its young.
32.22 the world below: This refers to the world of the dead.

246

DEUTERONOMY 32

Deuter.

Genesis
Exodus
Leviticus
Num.

24 They will die from hunger and fever;
    they will die from terrible diseases.
  I will send wild animals to attack them,
    and poisonous snakes to bite them.
25 War will bring death in the streets;
    terrors will strike in the homes.
  Young men and young women will die;
    neither babies nor old people will be spared.
26 I would have destroyed them completely,
    so that no one would remember them.
27 But I could not let their enemies boast
    that they had defeated my people,
    when it was I myself who had crushed them.'

28 "Israel is a nation without sense;
    they have no wisdom at all.
29 They fail to see why they were defeated;
    they cannot understand what happened.
30 Why were a thousand defeated by one,
    and 10,000 by only two?
  The Lord, their God, had abandoned them;
    their mighty God had given them up.
31 Their enemies know that their own gods are weak,
    not mighty like Israel's God.
32 Their enemies, corrupt as Sodom and Gomorrah,
    are like vines that bear bitter and poisonous grapes,
33   like wine made from the venom of snakes.

34 "The Lord remembers what their enemies have done;
    he waits for the right time to punish them.
35 The Lord will take revenge and punish them;
    the time will come when they will fall;
    the day of their doom is near.
36 The Lord will rescue his people
    when he sees that their strength is gone.
  He will have mercy on those who serve him,
    when he sees how helpless they are.
37 Then the Lord will ask his people,
    'Where are those mighty gods you trusted?
38 You fed them with the fat of your sacrifices
    and offered them wine to drink.
  Let them come and help you now;
    let them run to your rescue.

39 "'I, and I alone, am God;
    no other god is real.
  I kill and I give life, I wound and I heal,
    and no one can oppose what I do.
40 As surely as I am the living God,
    I raise my hand and I vow
41   that I will sharpen my flashing sword
    and see that justice is done.
  I will take revenge on my enemies
    and punish those who hate me.
42 My arrows will drip with their blood,
    and my sword will kill all who oppose me.
  I will spare no one who fights against me;
    even the wounded and prisoners will die.'

DEUTERONOMY 32, 33

247

Deuter.

....

Joshua

Judges

Ruth

1 Sam.

2 Sam.

[43] "Nations, you must praise the Lord's people —
   he punishes all who kill them.
He takes revenge on his enemies
   and forgives the sins of his people."

[44] Moses and Joshua son of Nun recited this song, so that the people of Israel could hear it.

Moses' Final Instructions

[45] When Moses had finished giving God's teachings to the people, [46] he said, "Make sure you obey all these commands that I have given you today. Repeat them to your children, so that they may faithfully obey all God's teachings. [47] These teachings are not empty words; they are your very life. Obey them and you will live long in that land across the Jordan that you are about to occupy."

[48] That same day the Lord said to Moses, [49] "Go to the Abarim Mountains in the land of Moab opposite the city of Jericho; climb Mount Nebo and look at the land of Canaan that I am about to give the people of Israel. [50] You will die on that mountain as your brother Aaron died on Mount Hor, [51] because both of you were unfaithful to me in the presence of the people of Israel. When you were at the waters of Meribah, near the town of Kadesh in the wilderness of Zin, you dishonoured me in the presence of the people. [52] You will look at the land from a distance, but you will not enter the land that I am giving the people of Israel."

Moses Blesses the Tribes of Israel

33 These are the blessings that Moses, the man of God, pronounced on the people of Israel before he died.

[2] The Lord came from Mount Sinai;
   he rose like the sun over Edom
   and shone on his people from Mount Paran.
   10,000 angels were with him,
   a flaming fire at his right hand.*
[3] The Lord loves his people*
   and protects those who belong to him.
So we bow at* his feet
   and obey his commands.
[4] We obey the Law that Moses gave us,
   our nation's most treasured possession.
[5] The Lord became king of his people Israel
   when their tribes and leaders were gathered together.

[6] Moses said about the tribe of Reuben:
   "May Reuben never die out,
   Although their people are few."

[7] About the tribe of Judah he said:
   "Lord, listen to their cry for help;
Unite them again with the other tribes.
Fight for them, Lord,
And help them against their enemies."*

33.2 Probable text *10,000… right hand*; Hebrew unclear.
33.3 One ancient translation *his people*; Hebrew *the peoples*.
33.3 Probable text *bow at*; Hebrew unclear.
33.7 Probable text *Fight for… enemies*; Hebrew *The tribe of Judah will fight for itself, and the Lord will help it against its enemies*.

DEUTERONOMY 33

Choosing to

- BLESS -

PEOPLE

is really important.
Write a list of people
that you would love God
to bless. Pray for each
of them as you read
down your list.

_____

_____

_____

_____

_____

_____

_____

_____

_____

_____

_____

_____

_____

_____

_____

248

Deuter.

Genesis
Exodus
Leviticus
Num.

DEUTERONOMY 33

8 About the tribe of Levi he said:
"You, LORD, reveal your will by the Urim and
Thummim*
Through your faithful servants, the Levites;
You put them to the test at Massah
And proved them true at the waters of Meribah.
9 They showed greater loyalty to you
Than to parents, brothers, or children.
They obeyed your commands
And were faithful to your covenant.
10 They will teach your people to obey your Law;
They will offer sacrifices on your altar.
11 Lord, help their tribe to grow strong;
Be pleased with what they do.
Crush all their enemies;
Let them never rise again."

12 About the tribe of Benjamin he said:
"This is the tribe the LORD loves and protects;
He guards them all the day long,
And he dwells in their midst."*

13 About the tribe of Joseph he said:
"May the LORD bless their land with rain
And with water from under the earth.
14 May their land be blessed with sun-ripened fruit,
Rich with the best fruits of each season.
15 May their ancient hills be covered with choice fruit.
16 May their land be filled with all that is good,
Blessed by the goodness of the LORD,
Who spoke from the burning bush.
May these blessings come to the tribe of Joseph,
Because he was the leader among his brothers.
17 Joseph has the strength of a bull,
The horns of a wild ox.
His horns are Manasseh's thousands
And Ephraim's 10,000s.
With them he gores the nations
And pushes them to the ends of the earth."

18 About the tribes of Zebulun and Issachar he said:
"May Zebulun be prosperous in their trade on the sea,
And may Issachar's wealth increase at home.
19 They invite foreigners to their mountain
And offer the right sacrifices there.
They get their wealth from the sea
And from the sand along the shore."

20 About the tribe of Gad he said:
"Praise God, who made their territory large.
Gad waits like a lion
To tear off an arm or a scalp.
21 They took the best of the land for themselves;
A leader's share was assigned to them.

33.8 *Urim and Thummim*: Two objects used by the priest to determine God's will; it is not known precisely how they were used.
33.12 *And he... midst*; or *They live under his protection.*

DEUTERONOMY 33, 34

249

Deuter.

............:.

Joshua
Judges
Ruth
1 Sam.
2 Sam.

They obeyed the LORD's commands and laws
When the leaders of Israel were gathered together."*

[22] About the tribe of Dan he said:
"Dan is a young lion;
He leaps out from Bashan."

[23] About the tribe of Naphtali he said:
"Naphtali is richly blessed by the LORD's good favour;
Their land reaches to the south from Lake Galilee."

[24] About the tribe of Asher he said:
"Asher is blessed more than the other tribes.
May he be the favourite of his brothers,
And may his land be rich with olive trees.
[25] May his towns be protected with iron gates,
And may he always live secure."

[26] People of Israel, no god is like your God,
   riding in splendour across the sky,
   riding through the clouds to come to your aid.
[27] God has always been your defence;
   his eternal arms are your support.
He drove out your enemies as you advanced,
   and told you to destroy them all.
[28] So Jacob's descendants live in peace,
   secure in a land full of corn and wine,
   where dew from the sky waters the ground.
[29] Israel, how happy you are!
   There is no one like you,
   a nation saved by the LORD.
The LORD himself is your shield and your sword,
   to defend you and give you victory.
Your enemies will come begging for mercy,
   and you will trample them down.

The Death of Moses

34 Moses went up from the plains of Moab to Mount Nebo, to the top of Mount Pisgah east of Jericho, and there the LORD showed him the whole land: the territory of Gilead as far north as the town of Dan; [2] the entire territory of Naphtali; the territories of Ephraim and Manasseh; the territory of Judah as far west as the Mediterranean Sea; [3] the southern part of Judah; and the plain that reaches from Zoar to Jericho, the city of palm trees. [4] Then the LORD said to Moses, "This is the land that I promised Abraham, Isaac, and Jacob I would give to their descendants. I have let you see it, but I will not let you go there."

[5] So Moses, the LORD's servant, died there in the land of Moab, as the LORD had said he would. [6] The LORD buried him in a valley in Moab, opposite the town of Bethpeor, but to this day no one knows the exact place of his burial. [7] Moses was 120 years old when he died; he was as strong as ever, and his eyesight was still good. [8] The people of Israel mourned for him for thirty days in the plains of Moab.

[9] Joshua son of Nun was filled with wisdom, because Moses had appointed him to be his successor. The people of Israel obeyed

33.21 One ancient translation *When the leaders… together*; Hebrew unclear.

Joshua and kept the commands that the LORD had given them through Moses.

10 There has never been a prophet in Israel like Moses; the LORD spoke with him face to face. 11 No other prophet has ever done miracles and wonders like those that the LORD sent Moses to perform against the king of Egypt, his officials, and the entire country. 12 No other prophet has been able to do the great and terrifying things that Moses did in the sight of all Israel.

THE BOOK OF
JOSHUA

WRITTEN: PROBABLY 700-500BC

WHY READ IT?

The book of Joshua shows that God is faithful to each of his promises, even if it takes a long time for them to come about. It teaches us to be patient and that we can trust God to keep his word. Ultimately, he is in charge.

WHAT YOU NEED TO KNOW:

Joshua took over from Moses as leader of the Israelites, and this book sees him lead the people as they fight for and conquer the Promised Land. After walking in the desert for 40 years, the Israelites finally got to enter this new homeland, Canaan. However, before they could settle in the land, they had to fight many battles against enemies there, and the book of Joshua shows how God faithfully helped them. It's a book about God's fulfilled promises and highlights his authority, power and might.

IF YOU KNEW THAT GOD WAS BACKING YOU 100%, WHAT WOULD YOU DO FOR HIM?

Joshua was a

GODLY
• LEADER •

In different colours and sizes, write what you think a godly leader would be like and act like.

300BC — **ENTRY TO CANAAN** — **JOSHUA DIES** — 1200BC
JOSHUA LEADS — **THE ISRAELITES FIGHT THEIR ENEMIES**

252

Joshua

Genesis
Exodus
Leviticus
Num.
Deuter.

JOSHUA 1.9

DON'T BE afraid

OR DISCOURAGED,

FOR I AM

with YOU

God Commands Joshua to Conquer Canaan

1 After the death of the LORD's servant Moses, the LORD spoke to Moses' helper, Joshua son of Nun. [2] He said, "My servant Moses is dead. Get ready now, you and all the people of Israel, and cross the River Jordan into the land that I am giving them. [3] As I told Moses, I have given you and all my people the entire land that you will be marching over. [4] Your borders will reach from the desert in the south to the Lebanon Mountains in the north; from the great River Euphrates in the east, through the Hittite country, to the Mediterranean Sea in the west. [5] Joshua, no one will be able to defeat you as long as you live. I will be with you as I was with Moses. I will always be with you; I will never abandon you. [6] Be determined and confident, for you will be the leader of these people as they occupy this land which I promised their ancestors. [7] Just be determined, be confident; and make sure that you obey the whole Law that my servant Moses gave you. Do not neglect any part of it and you will succeed wherever you go. [8] Be sure that the book of the Law is always read in your worship. Study it day and night, and make sure that you obey everything written in it. Then you will be prosperous and successful. [9] Remember that I have commanded you to be determined and confident! Don't be afraid or discouraged, for I, the LORD your God, am with you wherever you go."

Joshua Gives Orders to the People

[10] Then Joshua ordered the leaders to [11] go through the camp and say to the people, "Get some food ready, because in three days you are going to cross the River Jordan to occupy the land that the LORD your God is giving you."

[12] Joshua said to the tribes of Reuben and Gad and to half the tribe of Manasseh, [13] "Remember how Moses, the LORD's servant, told you that the LORD your God would give you this land on the east side of the Jordan as your home. [14] Your wives, your children, and your livestock will stay here, but your soldiers, armed for battle, will cross over ahead of their fellow-Israelites in order to help them [15] until they have occupied the land west of the Jordan that the LORD your God has given them. When he has given safety to all the tribes of Israel, then you may come back and settle here in your own land east of the Jordan, which Moses, the LORD's servant, gave to you."

[16] They answered Joshua, "We will do everything you have told us and will go wherever you send us. [17] We will obey you, just as we always obeyed Moses, and may the LORD your God be with you as he was with Moses! [18] Whoever questions your authority or disobeys any of your orders will be put to death. Be determined and confident!"

Joshua Sends Spies into Jericho

2 Then Joshua sent two spies from the camp at Acacia with orders to go and secretly explore the land of Canaan, especially the city of Jericho. When they came to the city, they went to spend the night in the house of a prostitute named Rahab. [2] The king of Jericho heard that some Israelites had come that night to spy out the country, [3] so he sent word to Rahab: "The men in your house have come to spy out the whole country! Bring them out!"

[4-6] "Some men did come to my house," she answered, "but I don't know where they were from. They left at sunset before the city gate was closed. I didn't find out where they were going, but if

JOSHUA 2, 3

253

Joshua

Judges
Ruth
1 Sam.
2 Sam.
1 Kings

you start after them quickly, you can catch them." (Now Rahab had taken the two spies up on the roof and hidden them under some stalks of flax that she had put there.) [7]The king's men left the city, and then the gate was shut. They went looking for the Israelite spies as far as the place where the road crosses the Jordan.

[8]Before the spies settled down for the night, Rahab went up on the roof [9]and said to them, "I know that the LORD has given you this land. Everyone in the country is terrified of you. [10]We have heard how the LORD dried up the Red Sea in front of you when you were leaving Egypt. We have also heard how you killed Sihon and Og, the two Amorite kings east of the Jordan. [11]We were afraid as soon as we heard about it; we have all lost our courage because of you. The LORD your God is God in heaven above and here on earth. [12]Now swear by him that you will treat my family as kindly as I have treated you, and give me some sign that I can trust you. [13]Promise me that you will save my father and mother, my brothers and sisters, and all their families! Don't let us be killed!"

[14]The men said to her, "May God take our lives if we don't do as we say!* If you do not tell anyone what we have been doing, we promise you that when the LORD gives us this land, we will treat you well."

[15]Rahab lived in a house built into the city wall, so she let the men down from the window by a rope. [16]"Go into the hill country," she said, "or the king's men will find you. Hide there for three days until they come back. After that you can go on your way."

[17]The men said to her, "We will keep the promise that you have made us give. [18]This is what you must do. When we invade your land, tie this red cord to the window you let us down from. Get your father and mother, your brothers, and all your father's family together in your house. [19]If anyone goes out of the house, his death will be his own fault, and we will not be responsible; but if anyone in the house with you is harmed, then we will be responsible. [20]However, if you tell anyone what we have been doing, then we will not have to keep our promise which you have made us give you." [21]She agreed and sent them away. When they had gone, she tied the red cord to the window.

[22]The spies went into the hills and hid. The king's men looked for them all over the countryside for three days, but they did not find them, so they returned to Jericho. [23]Then the two spies came down from the hills, crossed the river, and went back to Joshua. They told him everything that had happened, [24]and then said, "We are sure that the LORD has given us the whole country. All the people there are terrified of us."

The People of Israel Cross the Jordan

3 The next morning Joshua and all the people of Israel got up early, left the camp at Acacia, and went to the Jordan, where they camped while waiting to cross it. [2]Three days later the leaders went through the camp [3]and said to the people, "When you see the priests carrying the Covenant Box of the LORD your God, break camp and follow them. [4]You have never been here before, so they will show you the way to go. But do not get near the Covenant Box; stay about a kilometre behind it."

[5]Joshua said to the people, "Purify yourselves, because tomorrow the LORD will perform miracles among you." [6]Then he told the priests to take the Covenant Box and go with it ahead of the people. They did as he said.

....

2.14 *May God... say*; or *We will protect you if you protect us.*

JOSHUA 2

Use the space below to
sum up the

STORY
– OF –
RAHAB

and the two spies.
Illustrate it, write a poem,
draw stick men...
whatever you like!

254

Joshua

⋮

Genesis
Exodus
Leviticus
Num.
Deuter.

JOSHUA 3, 4

[7] The LORD said to Joshua, "What I do today will make all the people of Israel begin to honour you as a great man, and they will realize that I am with you as I was with Moses. [8] Tell the priests carrying the Covenant Box that when they reach the river, they must wade in and stand near the bank."

[9] Then Joshua said to the people, "Come here and listen to what the LORD your God has to say. [10] As you advance, he will surely drive out the Canaanites, the Hittites, the Hivites, the Perizzites, the Girgashites, the Amorites, and the Jebusites. You will know that the living God is among you [11] when the Covenant Box of the Lord of all the earth crosses the Jordan ahead of you. [12] Now choose twelve men, one from each of the tribes of Israel. [13] When the priests who carry the Covenant Box of the LORD of all the earth put their feet in the water, the Jordan will stop flowing, and the water coming downstream will pile up in one place."

[14-15] It was harvest time, and the river was in flood.

When the people left the camp to cross the Jordan, the priests went ahead of them, carrying the Covenant Box. As soon as the priests stepped into the river, [16] the water stopped flowing and piled up, far upstream at Adam, the city beside Zarethan. The flow downstream to the Dead Sea was completely cut off, and the people were able to cross over near Jericho. [17] While the people walked across on dry ground, the priests carrying the LORD's Covenant Box stood on dry ground in the middle of the Jordan until all the people had crossed over.

Memorial Stones are Set Up

4 When the whole nation had crossed the Jordan, the LORD said to Joshua, [2] "Choose twelve men, one from each tribe, [3] and command them to take twelve stones out of the middle of the Jordan, from the very place where the priests were standing. Tell them to carry these stones with them and to put them down where you camp tonight."

[4] Then Joshua called the twelve men he had chosen, [5] and said, "Go into the Jordan ahead of the Covenant Box of the LORD your God. Each one of you take a stone on your shoulder, one for each of the tribes of Israel. [6] These stones will remind the people of what the LORD has done. In the future, when your children ask what these stones mean to you, [7] you will tell them that the water of the Jordan stopped flowing when the LORD's Covenant Box crossed the river. These stones will always remind the people of Israel of what happened here."

[8] The men followed Joshua's orders. As the LORD had commanded Joshua, they took twelve stones from the middle of the Jordan, one for each of the tribes of Israel, carried them to the camping place, and put them down there. [9] Joshua also set up twelve stones in the middle of the Jordan, where the priests carrying the Covenant Box had stood. (Those stones are still there.) [10] The priests stood in the middle of the Jordan until everything had been done that the LORD ordered Joshua to tell the people to do. This is what Moses had commanded.

The people hurried across the river. [11] When they were all on the other side, the priests with the LORD's Covenant Box went on ahead of the people. [12] The men of the tribes of Reuben and Gad and of half the tribe of Manasseh, ready for battle, crossed ahead of the rest of the people, as Moses had told them to do. [13] In the presence of the LORD about 40,000 men ready for war crossed over to the plain near Jericho. [14] What the LORD did that day made the people of Israel consider Joshua a great man. They honoured him all his life, just as they had honoured Moses.

¹⁵ Then the LORD told Joshua ¹⁶ to command the priests carrying the Covenant Box to come up out of the Jordan. ¹⁷ Joshua did so, ¹⁸ and when the priests reached the river bank, the river began flowing once more and flooded its banks again.

¹⁹ The people crossed the Jordan on the tenth day of the first month and made camp at Gilgal, east of Jericho. ²⁰ There Joshua set up the twelve stones taken from the Jordan. ²¹ He said to the people of Israel, "In the future, when your children ask you what these stones mean, ²² you will tell them about the time when Israel crossed the Jordan on dry ground. ²³ Tell them that the LORD your God dried up the water of the Jordan for you until you had crossed, just as he dried up the Red Sea for us. ²⁴ Because of this everyone on earth will know how great the LORD's power is, and you will honour the LORD your God for ever."

5 All the Amorite kings west of the Jordan and all the Canaanite kings along the Mediterranean Sea heard that the LORD had dried up the Jordan until the people of Israel had crossed it. They became afraid and lost their courage because of the Israelites.

The Circumcision at Gilgal

² Then the LORD told Joshua, "Make some knives out of flint and circumcise the Israelites." ³ So Joshua did as the LORD had commanded, and he circumcised the Israelites at a place called Circumcision Hill. ⁴⁻⁶ When the people of Israel left Egypt, all the males were already circumcised. However, during the forty years the people spent crossing the desert, none of the baby boys had been circumcised. Also, by the end of that time all the men who were of fighting age when they left Egypt had died because they had disobeyed the LORD. Just as he had sworn, they were not allowed to see the rich and fertile land that he had promised their ancestors. ⁷ The sons of these men had never been circumcised, and it was this new generation that Joshua circumcised.

⁸ After the circumcision was completed, the whole nation stayed in the camp until the wounds had healed. ⁹ The LORD said to Joshua, "Today I have removed from you the disgrace of being slaves in Egypt." That is why the place was named Gilgal,* the name it still has.

¹⁰ While the Israelites were camping at Gilgal on the plain near Jericho, they observed Passover on the evening of the fourteenth day of the month. ¹¹ The next day was the first time they ate food grown in Canaan: roasted grain and bread made without yeast. ¹² The manna stopped falling then, and the Israelites no longer had any. From that time on they ate food grown in Canaan.

Joshua and the Man with a Sword

¹³ While Joshua was near Jericho, he suddenly saw a man standing in front of him, holding a sword. Joshua went up to him and asked, "Are you one of our soldiers, or an enemy?"

¹⁴ "Neither," the man answered. "I am here as the commander of the LORD's army."

Joshua threw himself on the ground in worship and said, "I am your servant, sir. What do you want me to do?"

¹⁵ And the commander of the LORD's army told him, "Take your sandals off; you are standing on holy ground." And Joshua did as he was told.

....

5.9 *Gilgal*: This name sounds like the Hebrew for "removed".

JOSHUA 6

There's no way the
Israelites could have
brought down Jericho by
themselves. Can you
think of a time when
you were tempted to
sort things out yourself
rather than trusting in
God? Grab a pen and
circle the word 'Jericho'

– SEVEN –

TIMES.

Each time, think of a
different situation
where God came
through for you or one
where you would like to
trust him more.

JERICHO

The Fall of Jericho

6 The gates of Jericho were kept shut and guarded to keep the Israelites out. No one could enter or leave the city. ²The LORD said to Joshua, "I am putting into your hands Jericho, with its king and all its brave soldiers. ³You and your soldiers are to march round the city once a day for six days. ⁴Seven priests, each carrying a trumpet, are to go in front of the Covenant Box. On the seventh day you and your soldiers are to march round the city seven times while the priests blow the trumpets. ⁵Then they are to sound one long note. As soon as you hear it, all the people are to give a loud shout, and the city walls will collapse. Then the whole army will go straight into the city."

⁶Joshua called the priests and said to them, "Take the Covenant Box, and seven of you go in front of it, carrying trumpets." ⁷Then he ordered the people to start marching round the city, with an advance guard going on ahead of the LORD's Covenant Box.

⁸⁻⁹So, just as Joshua had ordered, an advance guard started out ahead of the priests who were blowing trumpets; behind these came the priests who were carrying the Covenant Box, followed by a rearguard. All this time the trumpets were sounding. ¹⁰But Joshua had ordered the people not to shout, not to say a word until he gave the order. ¹¹So he told this group of men to take the LORD's Covenant Box round the city once. Then they came back to camp and spent the night there.

¹²⁻¹³Joshua got up early the next morning, and for the second time the priests and soldiers marched round the city in the same order as the day before: first, the advance guard; next, the seven priests blowing the seven trumpets; then, the priests carrying the LORD's Covenant Box; and finally, the rearguard. All this time the trumpets were sounding. ¹⁴On this second day they again marched round the city once and then returned to camp. They did this for six days.

¹⁵On the seventh day they got up at daybreak and marched seven times round the city in the same way — this was the only day that they marched round it seven times. ¹⁶The seventh time round, when the priests were about to sound the trumpets, Joshua ordered the people to shout, and he said, "The LORD has given you the city! ¹⁷The city and everything in it must be totally destroyed as an offering to the LORD. Only the prostitute Rahab and her household will be spared, because she hid our spies. ¹⁸But you are not to take anything that is to be destroyed; if you do, you will bring trouble and destruction on the Israelite camp. ¹⁹Everything made of silver, gold, bronze, or iron is set apart for the LORD. It is to be put in the LORD's treasury."

²⁰So the priests blew the trumpets. As soon as the people heard it, they gave a loud shout, and the walls collapsed. Then all the army went straight up the hill into the city and captured it. ²¹With their swords they killed everyone in the city, men and women, young and old. They also killed the cattle, sheep, and donkeys.

²²Joshua then told the two men who had served as spies, "Go into the prostitute's house and bring her and her family out, as you promised her." ²³So they went and brought Rahab out, along with her father and mother, her brothers, and the rest of her family. They took them all, family and slaves, to safety near the Israelite camp. ²⁴Then they set fire to the city and burnt it to the ground, along with everything in it, except the things made of gold, silver, bronze, and iron, which they took and put in the LORD's treasury. ²⁵But Joshua spared the lives of the prostitute Rahab and all her relatives, because she had hidden the two

spies that he had sent to Jericho. (Her descendants have lived in Israel to this day.)

26 At that time Joshua issued a solemn warning: "Anyone who tries to rebuild the city of Jericho will be under the LORD's curse.

Whoever lays the foundation will lose his eldest son;
Whoever builds the gates will lose his youngest."

27 So the LORD was with Joshua, and his fame spread through the whole country.

Achan's Sin

7 The LORD's command to Israel not to take from Jericho anything that was to be destroyed was not obeyed. A man named Achan disobeyed that order, and so the LORD was furious with the Israelites. (Achan was the son of Carmi and grandson of Zabdi, and belonged to the clan of Zerah, a part of the tribe of Judah.)

2 Joshua sent some men from Jericho to Ai, a city east of Bethel, near Bethaven, with orders to go and explore the land. When they had done so, 3 they reported back to Joshua: "There is no need for everyone to attack Ai. Send only about two or three thousand men. Don't send the whole army up there to fight; it is not a large city." 4 So about 3,000 Israelites made the attack, but they were forced to retreat. 5 The men of Ai chased them from the city gate as far as some quarries and killed about 36 of them on the way down the hill. Then the Israelites lost their courage and were afraid.

6 Joshua and the leaders of Israel tore their clothes in grief, threw themselves to the ground before the LORD's Covenant Box, and lay there till evening, with dust on their heads to show their sorrow. 7 And Joshua said, "Sovereign LORD! Why did you bring us across the Jordan at all? To hand us over to the Amorites? To destroy us? Why didn't we just stay on the other side of the Jordan? 8 What can I say, O Lord, now that Israel has retreated from the enemy? 9 The Canaanites and everyone else in the country will hear about it. They will surround us and kill every one of us! And then what will you do to protect your honour?"

10 The LORD said to Joshua, "Get up! Why are you lying on the ground like this? 11 Israel has sinned! They have broken the agreement with me that I ordered them to keep. They have taken some of the things condemned to destruction. They stole them, lied about it, and put them with their own things. 12 This is why the Israelites cannot stand against their enemies. They retreat from them because they themselves have now been condemned to destruction! I will not stay with you any longer unless you destroy the things you were ordered not to take! 13 Get up! Purify the people and get them ready to come before me. Tell them to be ready tomorrow, because I, the LORD God of Israel, have this to say: 'Israel, you have in your possession some things that I ordered you to destroy! You cannot stand against your enemies until you get rid of these things!' 14 So tell them that in the morning they will be brought forward, tribe by tribe. The tribe that I pick out will then come forward, clan by clan. The clan that I pick out will come forward, family by family. The family that I pick out will come forward, one by one. 15 The one who is then picked out and found with the condemned goods will be burnt, along with his family and everything he owns, for he has brought terrible shame on Israel and has broken my covenant."

16 Early the next morning Joshua brought Israel forward, tribe by tribe, and the tribe of Judah was picked out. 17 He brought the

tribe of Judah forward, clan by clan, and the clan of Zerah was picked out. Then he brought the clan of Zerah forward, family by family, and the family of Zabdi was picked out. [18] He then brought Zabdi's family forward, one by one, and Achan, the son of Carmi and grandson of Zabdi, was picked out. [19] Joshua said to him, "My son, tell the truth here before the LORD, the God of Israel, and confess. Tell me now what you have done. Don't try to hide it from me."

[20] "It's true," Achan answered. "I have sinned against the LORD, Israel's God, and this is what I did. [21] Among the things we seized I saw a beautiful Babylonian cloak, about two kilogrammes of silver, and a bar of gold weighing over half a kilogramme. I wanted them so much that I took them. You will find them buried inside my tent, with the silver at the bottom."

[22] So Joshua sent some men, who ran to the tent and found that the condemned things really were buried there, with the silver at the bottom. [23] They brought them out of the tent, took them to Joshua and all the Israelites, and laid them down in the presence of the LORD. [24] Joshua, along with all the people of Israel, seized Achan, the silver, the cloak, and the bar of gold, together with Achan's sons and daughters, his cattle, donkeys, and sheep, his tent, and everything else he owned; and they took them to Trouble Valley. [25] And Joshua said, "Why have you brought such trouble on us? The LORD will now bring trouble on you!" All the people then stoned Achan to death; they also stoned and burnt his family and possessions. [26] They put a huge pile of stones over him, which is there to this day. That is why that place is still called Trouble Valley.

Then the LORD was no longer furious.

The Capture and Destruction of Ai

8 The LORD said to Joshua, "Take all the soldiers with you and go on up to Ai. Don't be afraid or discouraged. I will give you victory over the king of Ai; his people, city, and land will be yours. [2] You are to do to Ai and its king what you did to Jericho and its king, but this time you may keep its goods and livestock for yourselves. Prepare to attack the city by surprise from the rear."

[3] So Joshua got ready to go to Ai with all his soldiers. He picked out 30,000 of his best troops and sent them out at night [4] with these orders: "Hide on the other side of the city, but not too far away from it; be ready to attack. [5] My men and I will approach the city. When the men of Ai come out against us, we will turn and run, just as we did the first time. [6] They will pursue us until we have led them away from the city. They will think that we are running away from them, as we did before. [7] Then you will come out of hiding and capture the city. The LORD your God will give it to you. [8] After you have taken the city, set it on fire, just as the LORD has commanded. These are your orders." [9] So Joshua sent them out, and they went to their hiding place and waited there, west of Ai, between Ai and Bethel. Joshua spent the night in camp.

[10] Early in the morning Joshua got up and called the soldiers together. Then he and the leaders of Israel led them to Ai. [11] The soldiers with him went towards the main entrance to the city and set up camp on the north side, with a valley between themselves and Ai. [12] He took about 5,000 men and put them in hiding west of the city, between Ai and Bethel. [13] The soldiers were arranged for battle with the main camp north of the city and the rest of the men to the west. Joshua spent the night in the valley. [14] When the king of Ai saw Joshua's men, he acted quickly. He and all his

JOSHUA 8

259

Joshua

Judges
Ruth
1 Sam.
2 Sam.
1 Kings

men went out towards the Jordan Valley to fight the Israelites at the same place as before, not knowing that he was about to be attacked from the rear. ¹⁵ Joshua and his men pretended that they were retreating, and ran away towards the barren country. ¹⁶ All the men in the city had been called together to go after them, and as they pursued Joshua, they kept getting farther away from the city. ¹⁷ Every man in Ai* went after the Israelites, and the city was left wide open, with no one to defend it.

¹⁸ Then the Lord said to Joshua, "Point your spear at Ai; I am giving it to you." Joshua did as he was told, ¹⁹ and as soon as he lifted his hand, the men who had been hiding got up quickly, ran into the city and captured it. They immediately set the city on fire. ²⁰ When the men of Ai looked back, they saw the smoke rising to the sky. There was no way for them to escape, because the Israelites who had run towards the barren country now turned round to attack them. ²¹ When Joshua and his men saw that the others had taken the city and that it was on fire, they turned round and began killing the men of Ai. ²² The Israelites in the city now came down to join the battle. So the men of Ai found themselves completely surrounded by Israelites, and they were all killed. No one got away, and no one lived through it ²³ except the king of Ai. He was captured and taken to Joshua.

²⁴ The Israelites killed every one of the enemy in the barren country where they had chased them. Then they went back to Ai and killed everyone there. ²⁵⁻²⁶ Joshua kept his spear pointed at Ai and did not put it down until every person there had been killed. The whole population of Ai was killed that day — 12,000 men and women. ²⁷ The Israelites kept for themselves the livestock and goods captured in the city, as the Lord had told Joshua. ²⁸ Joshua burnt Ai and left it in ruins. It is still like that today. ²⁹ He hanged the king of Ai from a tree and left his body there until evening. At sunset Joshua gave orders for the body to be removed, and it was thrown down at the entrance to the city gate. They covered it with a huge pile of stones, which is still there today.

The Law is Read at Mount Ebal

³⁰ Then Joshua built on Mount Ebal an altar to the Lord, the God of Israel. ³¹ He made it according to the instructions that Moses, the Lord's servant, had given the Israelites, as it says in the Law of Moses: "an altar made of stones which have not been cut with iron tools." On it they offered burnt sacrifices to the Lord, and they also presented their fellowship offerings. ³² There, with the Israelites looking on, Joshua made on the stones* a copy of the Law which Moses had written. ³³ The Israelites, with their leaders, officers, and judges, as well as the foreigners among them, stood on two sides of the Lord's Covenant Box, facing the levitical priests who carried it. Half the people stood with their backs to Mount Gerizim and the other half with their backs to Mount Ebal. The Lord's servant Moses had commanded them to do this when the time came for them to receive the blessing. ³⁴ Joshua then read aloud the whole Law, including the blessings and the curses, just as they are written in the book of the Law. ³⁵ Every one of the commandments of Moses was read by Joshua to the whole gathering, which included women and children, as well as the foreigners living among them.

8.17 One ancient translation *Ai*; Hebrew *Ai and Bethel*.
8.32 *the stones*; or *stones*.

260

Joshua

Genesis
Exodus
Leviticus
Num.
Deuter.

JOSHUA 9

The Gibeonites Deceive Joshua

9 The victories of Israel became known to all the kings west of the Jordan — in the hills, in the foothills, and all along the coastal plain of the Mediterranean Sea as far north as Lebanon; these were the kings of the Hittites, the Amorites, the Canaanites, the Perizzites, the Hivites, and the Jebusites. ²They all came together and joined forces to fight against Joshua and the Israelites.

³But the people of Gibeon, who were Hivites, heard what Joshua had done to Jericho and Ai, ⁴and they decided to deceive him. They went and got some food and loaded their donkeys with worn-out sacks and patched-up wineskins. ⁵They put on ragged clothes and worn-out sandals that had been mended. The bread they took with them was dry and mouldy. ⁶Then they went to the camp at Gilgal and said to Joshua and the Israelites, "We have come from a distant land. We want you to make a treaty with us."

⁷But the Israelites said, "Why should we make a treaty with you? Maybe you live nearby."

⁸They said to Joshua, "We are at your service."

Joshua asked them, "Who are you? Where do you come from?"

⁹Then they told him this story: "We have come from a very distant land, sir, because we have heard of the LORD your God. We have heard about everything that he did in Egypt ¹⁰and what he did to the two Amorite kings east of the Jordan: King Sihon of Heshbon and King Og of Bashan, who lived in Ashtaroth. ¹¹Our leaders and all the people that live in our land told us to get some food ready for a journey and to go and meet you. We were told to put ourselves at your service and ask you to make a treaty with us. ¹²Look at our bread. When we left home with it and started out to meet you, it was still warm. But look! Now it is dry and mouldy. ¹³When we filled these wineskins, they were new, but look! They are torn. Our clothes and sandals are worn out from the long journey."

¹⁴The Israelites accepted some food from them, but did not consult the LORD about it. ¹⁵Joshua made a treaty of friendship with the people of Gibeon and allowed them to live. The leaders of the community of Israel gave their solemn promise to keep the treaty.

¹⁶Three days after the treaty had been made, the Israelites learnt that these people did indeed live nearby. ¹⁷So the people of Israel started out and three days later arrived at the cities where these people lived: Gibeon, Chephirah, Beeroth, and Kiriath Jearim. ¹⁸But the Israelites could not kill them, because their leaders had made a solemn promise to them in the name of the LORD, Israel's God. All the people complained to the leaders about this, ¹⁹but they answered, "We have made our solemn promise to them in the name of the LORD God of Israel. Now we cannot harm them. ²⁰We must let them live because of our promise; if we don't, God will punish us. ²¹Let them live, but they will have to cut wood and carry water for us." This was what the leaders suggested.

²²Joshua ordered the people of Gibeon to be brought to him, and he asked them, "Why did you deceive us and tell us that you were from far away, when you live right here? ²³Because you did this, God has condemned you. Your people will always be slaves, cutting wood and carrying water for the sanctuary of my God."

²⁴They answered, "We did it, sir, because we learnt that it was really true that the LORD your God had commanded his servant Moses to give you the whole land and to kill the people living in it as you advanced. We did it because we were terrified of you; we

Joshua

Judges
Ruth
1 Sam.
2 Sam.
1 Kings

were in fear of our lives. ²⁵Now we are in your power; do with us what you think is right." ²⁶So this is what Joshua did: he protected them and did not allow the people of Israel to kill them. ²⁷But at the same time he made them slaves, to cut wood and carry water for the people of Israel and for the LORD's altar. To this day they have continued to do this work in the place where the LORD has chosen to be worshipped.

The Amorites are Defeated

10 Adonizedek, the king of Jerusalem,* heard that Joshua had captured and totally destroyed Ai and had killed its king, just as he had done to Jericho and its king. He also heard that the people of Gibeon had made peace with the Israelites and were living among them. ²The people of Jerusalem were greatly alarmed at this because Gibeon was as large as any of the cities that had a king; it was larger than Ai, and its men were good fighters. ³So Adonizedek sent the following message to King Hoham of Hebron, King Piram of Jarmuth, King Japhia of Lachish, and to King Debir of Eglon: ⁴"Come and help me attack Gibeon, because its people have made peace with Joshua and the Israelites." ⁵These five Amorite kings, the kings of Jerusalem, Hebron, Jarmuth, Lachish, and Eglon, joined forces, surrounded Gibeon, and attacked it.

⁶The men of Gibeon sent word to Joshua at the camp in Gilgal: "Do not abandon us, sir! Come at once and help us! Save us! All the Amorite kings in the hill country have joined forces and have attacked us!"

⁷So Joshua and his whole army, including the best troops, started out from Gilgal. ⁸The LORD said to Joshua, "Do not be afraid of them. I have already given you the victory. Not one of them will be able to stand against you." ⁹All night Joshua and his army marched from Gilgal to Gibeon, and they made a surprise attack on the Amorites. ¹⁰The LORD made the Amorites panic at the sight of Israel's army. The Israelites slaughtered them at Gibeon and pursued them down the mountain pass at Beth Horon, keeping up the attack as far south as Azekah and Makkedah. ¹¹While the Amorites were running down the pass from the Israelite army, the LORD made large hailstones fall down on them all the way to Azekah. More were killed by the hailstones than by the Israelites.

¹²On the day that the LORD gave the men of Israel victory over the Amorites, Joshua spoke to the LORD. In the presence of the Israelites he said,

"Sun, stand still over Gibeon;
Moon, stop over Aijalon Valley."

¹³The sun stood still and the moon did not move until the nation had conquered its enemies. This is written in *The Book of Jashar*. The sun stood still in the middle of the sky and did not go down for a whole day. ¹⁴Never before, and never since, has there been a day like it, when the LORD obeyed a human being. The LORD fought on Israel's side!

¹⁵After this, Joshua and his army went back to the camp at Gilgal.

Joshua Captures the Five Amorite Kings

¹⁶The five Amorite kings, however, had escaped and were hiding in the cave at Makkedah. ¹⁷Someone found them, and Joshua was told where they were hiding. ¹⁸He said, "Roll some

10.1 *Jerusalem*: At that time it was a Jebusite city.

List some

QUESTIONS

you have about
faith here.

_____

_____

_____

_____

_____

_____

_____

_____

_____

_____

_____

_____

_____

_____

_____

_____

_____

_____

_____

big stones in front of the entrance to the cave. Place some guards there, [19] but don't stay there yourselves. Keep on after the enemy and attack them from the rear; don't let them get to their cities! The LORD your God has given you victory over them." [20] Joshua and the men of Israel slaughtered them, although some managed to find safety inside their city walls and were not killed. [21] Then all of Joshua's men came back safe to him at the camp at Makkedah.

No one in the land dared even to speak against the Israelites. [22] Then Joshua said, "Open the entrance to the cave and bring those five kings out to me." [23] So the cave was opened, and the kings of Jerusalem, Hebron, Jarmuth, Lachish, and Eglon were brought out [24] and taken to Joshua. Joshua then called all the men of Israel to him and ordered the officers who had gone with him to come and put their feet on the necks of the kings. They did so. [25] Then Joshua said to his officers, "Don't be afraid or discouraged. Be determined and confident because this is what the LORD is going to do to all your enemies." [26] Then Joshua killed the kings and hanged them on five trees, where their bodies stayed until evening. [27] At sunset Joshua gave orders, and their bodies were taken down and thrown into the same cave where they had hidden earlier. Large stones were placed at the entrance to the cave, and they are still there.

Joshua Captures More Amorite Territory

[28] Joshua attacked and captured Makkedah and its king that day. He put everyone in the city to death; no one was left alive. He did to the king of Makkedah what he had done to the king of Jericho.

[29] After this, Joshua and his army went on from Makkedah to Libnah and attacked it. [30] The LORD also gave the Israelites victory over this city and its king. They spared no one, but killed every person in it. They did to the king what they had done to the king of Jericho.

[31] After this, Joshua and his army went on from Libnah to Lachish, surrounded it and attacked it. [32] The LORD gave the Israelites victory over Lachish on the second day of the battle. Just as they had done at Libnah, they spared no one, but killed every person in the city. [33] King Horam of Gezer came to the aid of Lachish, but Joshua defeated him and his army and left none of them alive.

[34] Next, Joshua and his army went on from Lachish to Eglon, surrounded it and attacked it. [35] They captured it the same day and put everyone there to death, just as they had done at Lachish.

[36] After this, Joshua and his army went from Eglon up into the hills to Hebron, attacked it [37] and captured it. They killed the king and everyone else in the city as well as in the nearby towns. Joshua condemned the city to total destruction, just as he had done to Eglon. No one in it was left alive.

[38] Then Joshua and his army turned back to Debir and attacked it. [39] He captured it, with its king and all the nearby towns. They put everyone there to death. Joshua did to Debir and its king what he had done to Hebron and to Libnah and its king.

[40] Joshua conquered the whole land. He defeated the kings of the hill country, the eastern slopes, and the western foothills, as well as those of the dry country in the south. He spared no one; everyone was put to death. This was what the LORD God of Israel had commanded. [41] Joshua's campaign took him from Kadesh Barnea in the south to Gaza near the coast, including all the area

Joshua

....

Judges
Ruth
1 Sam.
2 Sam.
1 Kings

of Goshen, and as far north as Gibeon. ⁴²Joshua conquered all these kings and their territory in one campaign because the Lord, Israel's God, was fighting for Israel. ⁴³After this, Joshua and his army went back to the camp at Gilgal.

Joshua Defeats Jabin and his Allies

11 When the news of Israel's victories reached King Jabin of Hazor, he sent word to King Jobab of Madon, to the kings of Shimron and Achshaph, ²and to the kings in the hill country in the north, in the Jordan Valley south of Lake Galilee, in the foothills, and on the coast near Dor. ³He also sent word to the Canaanites on both sides of the Jordan, to the Amorites, the Hittites, the Perizzites, and the Jebusites in the hill country, as well as to the Hivites who lived at the foot of Mount Hermon in the land of Mizpah. ⁴They came with all their soldiers — an army with as many men as there are grains of sand on the seashore. They also had many horses and chariots. ⁵All these kings joined forces and came together and set up camp at Merom Brook to fight against Israel.

⁶The Lord said to Joshua, "Do not be afraid of them. By this time tomorrow I will have killed all of them for Israel. You are to cripple their horses and burn their chariots." ⁷So Joshua and all his men attacked them by surprise at Merom Brook. ⁸The Lord gave the Israelites victory over them; the Israelites attacked and pursued them as far north as Misrephoth Maim and Sidon, and as far east as the valley of Mizpah. The fight continued until none of the enemy was left alive. ⁹Joshua did to them what the Lord had commanded: he crippled their horses and burnt their chariots.

¹⁰Joshua then turned back, captured Hazor and killed its king. (At that time Hazor was the most powerful of all those kingdoms.) ¹¹They put everyone there to death; no one was left alive, and the city was burnt.

¹²Joshua captured all these cities and their kings, putting everyone to death, just as Moses, the Lord's servant, had commanded. ¹³However, the Israelites did not burn any of the cities built on mounds, except Hazor, which Joshua did burn. ¹⁴The people of Israel took all the valuables and livestock from these cities and kept them for themselves. But they put every person to death; no one was left alive. ¹⁵The Lord had given his commands to his servant Moses, Moses had given them to Joshua, and Joshua obeyed them. He did everything that the Lord had commanded Moses.

The Territory Taken by Joshua

¹⁶Joshua captured all the land — the hill country and foothills, both north and south, all the area of Goshen and the dry country south of it, as well as the Jordan Valley. ¹⁷⁻¹⁸The territory extended from Mount Halak in the south near Edom, as far as Baalgad in the north, in the valley of Lebanon south of Mount Hermon. Joshua was at war with the kings of this territory for a long time, but he captured them all and put them to death. ¹⁹The only city that made peace with the people of Israel was Gibeon, where some of the Hivites lived. All the others were conquered in battle. ²⁰The Lord had made them determined to fight the Israelites, so that they would be condemned to total destruction and all be killed without mercy. This was what the Lord had commanded Moses.

²¹At this time Joshua went and destroyed the race of giants called the Anakim who lived in the hill country — in Hebron,

264

Joshua

·:········

Genesis
Exodus
Leviticus
Num.
Deuter.

JOSHUA 11–13

Debir, Anab, and in all the hill country of Judah and Israel. Joshua completely destroyed them and their cities. 22 None of the Anakim were left in the land of Israel; a few, however, were left in Gaza, Gath, and Ashdod.

23 Joshua captured the whole land, as the LORD had commanded Moses. Joshua gave it to the Israelites as their own and divided it into portions, one for each tribe.

So the people rested from war.

The Kings Defeated by Moses

12 The people of Israel had already conquered and occupied the land east of the Jordan, from the Arnon Valley up the Jordan Valley and as far north as Mount Hermon. They defeated two kings. 2 One was Sihon, the Amorite king who ruled at Heshbon. His kingdom included half of Gilead: from Aroer (on the edge of the valley of the Arnon) and the city in* the middle of that valley, as far as the River Jabbok, the border of Ammon; 3 it included the Jordan Valley from Lake Galilee south to Beth Jeshimoth (east of the Dead Sea) and on towards the foot of Mount Pisgah.

4 They also defeated King Og of Bashan, who was one of the last of the Rephaim; he ruled at Ashtaroth and Edrei. 5 His kingdom included Mount Hermon, Salecah, and all of Bashan as far as the boundaries of Geshur and Maacah, as well as half of Gilead, as far as the territory of King Sihon of Heshbon.

6 These two kings were defeated by Moses and the people of Israel. Moses, the LORD's servant, gave their land to the tribes of Reuben and Gad and to half the tribe of Manasseh, to be their possession.

The Kings Defeated by Joshua

7 Joshua and the people of Israel defeated all the kings in the territory west of the Jordan, from Baalgad in the valley of Lebanon to Mount Halak in the south near Edom. Joshua divided this land among the tribes and gave it to them as a permanent possession. 8 This portion included the hill country, the western foothills, the Jordan Valley and its foothills, the eastern slopes, and the dry country in the south. This land had been the home of the Hittites, the Amorites, the Canaanites, the Perizzites, the Hivites, and the Jebusites. 9 The people of Israel defeated the kings of the following cities: Jericho, Ai (near Bethel), 10 Jerusalem, Hebron, 11 Jarmuth, Lachish, 12 Eglon, Gezer, 13 Debir, Geder, 14 Hormah, Arad, 15 Libnah, Adullam, 16 Makkedah, Bethel, 17 Tappuah, Hepher, 18 Aphek, Lasharon, 19 Madon, Hazor, 20 Shimron Meron, Achshaph, 21 Taanach, Megiddo, 22 Kedesh, Jokneam (in Carmel), 23 Dor (on the coast), Goiim (in Galilee*), 24 and Tirzah — 31 kings in all.

The Land Still to be Taken

13 Joshua was now very old. The LORD said to him, "You are very old, but there is still much land to be taken: 2 all the territory of Philistia and Geshur, 3 as well as all the territory of the Avvim to the south. (The land from the stream of Shihor, at the Egyptian border, as far north as the border of Ekron was considered Canaanite; the kings of the Philistines lived at Gaza, Ashdod, Ashkelon, Gath, and Ekron.) 4 There is still all the Canaanite country, and Mearah (which belonged to the

12.2 Probable text (see 13.16; Deut 2.36) *the city in*; Hebrew does not have these words.
12.23 One ancient translation *Galilee*; Hebrew *Gilgal*.

265

Joshua
...........:

Judges
Ruth
1 Sam.
2 Sam.
1 Kings

Sidonians), as far as Aphek, at the Amorite border; [5] the land of the Gebalites; all of Lebanon to the east, from Baalgad, which is south of Mount Hermon, to Hamath Pass. [6] This includes all the territory of the Sidonians, who live in the hill country between the Lebanon Mountains and Misrephoth Maim. I will drive all these peoples out as the people of Israel advance. You must divide the land among the Israelites, just as I have commanded you to do. [7] Now then, divide this land among the other nine tribes and half of the tribe of Manasseh, for them to possess as their own."

The Division of the Territory East of the Jordan
[8] The tribes of Reuben and Gad and the other half of the tribe of Manasseh had already received the land that Moses, the LORD's servant, had given them; it was on the east side of the River Jordan. [9] Their territory extended to Aroer (on the edge of the Arnon Valley) and the city in the middle of that valley and included all the plateau from Medeba to Dibon. [10] It went as far as the border of Ammon and included all the cities that had been ruled by the Amorite king Sihon, who had ruled at Heshbon. [11] It included Gilead, the regions of Geshur and Maacah, all Mount Hermon, and all of Bashan as far as Salecah. [12] It included the kingdom of Og, the last of the Rephaim, who had ruled at Ashtaroth and Edrei. Moses had defeated these people and driven them out. [13] However, the Israelites did not drive out the people of Geshur and Maacah; they still live in Israel.

[14] Moses had given no land to the tribe of Levi. As the LORD had told Moses, they were to receive as their possession a share of the sacrifices burnt on the altar to the LORD God of Israel.

The Territory Assigned to Reuben
[15] Moses had given a part of the land to the families of the tribe of Reuben as their possession. [16] Their territory extended to Aroer (on the edge of the Arnon Valley) and the city in the middle of that valley and included all the plateau round Medeba. [17] It included Heshbon and all the cities on the plateau: Dibon, Bamoth Baal, Beth Baalmeon, [18] Jahaz, Kedemoth, Mephaath, [19] Kiriathaim, Sibmah, Zerethshahar on the hill in the valley, [20] Bethpeor, the slopes of Mount Pisgah, and Beth Jeshimoth. [21] It included all the cities of the plateau and the whole kingdom of the Amorite king Sihon, who had ruled at Heshbon. Moses defeated him, as well as the rulers of Midian: Evi, Rekem, Zur, Hur, and Reba. All of them had ruled the land for King Sihon. [22] Among those whom the people of Israel killed was the fortune teller Balaam son of Beor. [23] The Jordan was the western border of the tribe of Reuben. These were the cities and towns given to the families of the tribe of Reuben as their possession.

The Territory Assigned to Gad
[24] Moses had also given a part of the land to the families of the tribe of Gad as their possession. [25] Their territory included Jazer and all the cities of Gilead, half the land of Ammon as far as Aroer, which is east of Rabbah; [26] their land extended from Heshbon to Ramath Mizpeh and Betonim, from Mahanaim to the border of Lodebar. [27] In the Jordan Valley it included Beth Haram, Bethnimrah, Sukkoth, and Zaphon, the rest of the kingdom of King Sihon of Heshbon. Their western border was the River Jordan as far north as Lake Galilee. [28] These were the cities and towns given to the families of the tribe of Gad as their possession.

266

JOSHUA 14, 15

Joshua

Genesis
Exodus
Leviticus
Num.
Deuter.

The Territory Assigned to East Manasseh

²⁹ Moses had given a part of the land to the families of half the tribe of Manasseh as their possession. ³⁰ Their territory extended to Mahanaim and included all of Bashan — the whole kingdom of Og, the king of Bashan, as well as all sixty of the villages of Jair in Bashan. ³¹ It included half of Gilead, as well as Ashtaroth and Edrei, the capital cities of Og's kingdom in Bashan. All this was given to half the families descended from Machir son of Manasseh.

³² That is how Moses divided the land east of Jericho and the Jordan when he was in the plains of Moab. ³³ But Moses did not assign any land to the tribe of Levi. He told them that their possession was to be a share of the offerings to the LORD God of Israel.

The Division of the Territory West of the Jordan

14 What follows is an account of how the land of Canaan west of the Jordan was divided among the people of Israel. Eleazar the priest, Joshua son of Nun, and the leaders of the families of the Israelite tribes divided it among the population. ² As the LORD had commanded Moses, the territories of the nine and a half tribes west of the Jordan were determined by drawing lots.* ³⁻⁴ Moses had already assigned the land east of the Jordan to the other two and a half tribes. (The descendants of Joseph were divided into two tribes: Manasseh and Ephraim.) However, Moses gave the Levites no portion of the territory. Instead, they received cities to live in, with fields for their cattle and flocks. ⁵ The people of Israel divided the land as the LORD had commanded Moses.

Hebron is Given to Caleb

⁶ One day some people from the tribe of Judah came to Joshua at Gilgal. One of them, Caleb son of Jephunneh the Kenizzite, said to him, "You know what the LORD said in Kadesh Barnea about you and me to Moses, the man of God. ⁷ I was forty years old when the LORD's servant Moses sent me from Kadesh Barnea to spy out this land. I brought an honest report back to him. ⁸ The men who went with me, however, made our people afraid. But I faithfully obeyed the LORD my God. ⁹ Because I did, Moses promised me that my children and I would certainly receive as our possession the land which I walked over. ¹⁰ But now, look. It has been 45 years since the LORD said that to Moses. That was when Israel was going through the desert, and the LORD, as he promised, has kept me alive ever since. Look at me! I am 85 years old ¹¹ and I'm just as strong today as I was when Moses sent me out. I am still strong enough for war or for anything else. ¹² Now then, give me the hill country that the LORD promised me on that day when my men and I reported. We told you then that the race of giants called the Anakim were there in large walled cities. Maybe the LORD will be with me, and I will drive them out, just as the LORD said."

¹³ Joshua blessed Caleb son of Jephunneh and gave him the city of Hebron as his possession. ¹⁴ Hebron still belongs to the descendants of Caleb son of Jephunneh the Kenizzite, because he faithfully obeyed the LORD, the God of Israel. ¹⁵ Before this, Hebron was called the city of Arba. (Arba had been the greatest of the Anakim.)

There was now peace in the land.

14.2 *drawing lots*: This was usually done by using specially marked stones to determine God's will.

JOSHUA 15

267

Joshua

..........:

Judges
Ruth
1 Sam.
2 Sam.
1 Kings

The Territory Assigned to Judah

15 The families of the tribe of Judah received a part of the land described as follows:

The land reached south to the southernmost point of the wilderness of Zin, at the border of Edom. [2] This southern border ran from the south end of the Dead Sea, [3] went southwards from the Akrabbim Pass and on to Zin. It ran south of Kadesh Barnea, past Hezron and up to Addar, turned towards Karka, [4] went on to Azmon, and followed the stream on the border of Egypt to the Mediterranean Sea, where the border ended. That was the southern border of Judah.

[5] The eastern border was the Dead Sea, all the way up to the inlet where the Jordan empties into it.

The northern border began there, [6] extended up to Beth Hoglah, and went north of the ridge overlooking the Jordan Valley. Then it went up to the Stone of Bohan (Bohan was a son of Reuben), [7] from Trouble Valley up to Debir, and then turned north towards Gilgal, which faces Adummim Pass on the south side of the valley. It then went on to the springs of Enshemesh, out to Enrogel, [8] and up through the Valley of Hinnom on the south side of the hill where the Jebusite city of Jerusalem was located. The border then proceeded up to the top of the hill on the west side of the Valley of Hinnom, at the northern end of the Valley of Rephaim. [9] From there it went to the Springs of Nephtoah and out to the cities near Mount Ephron. There it turned towards Baalah (or Kiriath Jearim), [10] where it circled west of Baalah towards the hill country of Edom, went on the north side of Mount Jearim (or Chesalon), down to Beth Shemesh, and on past Timnah. [11] The border then went out to the hill north of Ekron, turned towards Shikkeron, past Mount Baalah, and on to Jamnia. It ended at the Mediterranean Sea, [12] which formed the western border.

Within these borders lived the people of the families of Judah.

Caleb Conquers Hebron and Debir
(Judg 1.11–15)

[13] As the Lord commanded Joshua, part of the territory of Judah was given to Caleb son of Jephunneh, from the tribe of Judah. He received Hebron, the city belonging to Arba, father of Anak. [14] Caleb drove the descendants of Anak out of the city — the clans of Sheshai, Ahiman, and Talmai. [15] From there he went to attack the people living in Debir. (This city used to be called Kiriath Sepher.) [16] Caleb said, "I will give my daughter Achsah in marriage to the man who succeeds in capturing Kiriath Sepher." [17] Othniel, the son of Caleb's brother Kenaz, captured the city, so Caleb gave him his daughter Achsah in marriage. [18] On the wedding day Othniel urged her* to ask her father for a field. She got down from her donkey, and Caleb asked her what she wanted. [19] She answered, "I want some pools of water. The land you have given me is in the dry country." So Caleb gave her the upper and lower springs.

The Cities of Judah

[20] This is the land that the families of the tribe of Judah received as their possession. [21] The cities farthest south that belonged to them, those that were near the border of Edom, were Kabzeel, Eder, Jagur, [22] Kinah, Dimonah, Adadah, [23] Kedesh, Hazor, Ithnan,

---

15.18 Probable text (see Judg 1.14) *Othniel urged her*; Hebrew *she urged Othniel.*

268

Joshua

⋅:⋯⋯⋯

Genesis
Exodus
Leviticus
Num.
Deuter.

JOSHUA 15, 16

24 Ziph, Telem, Bealoth, 25 Hazor Hadattah, Kerioth Hezron (or Hazor), 26 Amam, Shema, Moladah, 27 Hazar Gaddah, Heshmon, Bethpelet, 28 Hazar Shual, Beersheba, Biziothiah, 29 Baalah, Iim, Ezem, 30 Eltolad, Chesil, Hormah, 31 Ziklag, Madmannah, Sansannah, 32 Lebaoth, Shilhim, Ain, and Rimmon: 29 cities in all, along with the towns round them.

33 The cities in the foothills were Eshtaol, Zorah, Ashnah, 34 Zanoah, Engannim, Tappuah, Enam, 35 Jarmuth, Adullam, Socoh, Azekah, 36 Shaaraim, Adithaim, Gederah, and Gederothaim: fourteen cities, along with the towns round them.

37 There were also Zenan, Hadashah, Migdalgad, 38 Dilean, Mizpah, Joktheel, 39 Lachish, Bozkath, Eglon, 40 Cabbon, Lahmam, Chitlish, 41 Gederoth, Bethdagon, Naamah, and Makkedah: sixteen cities, along with the towns round them.

42 There were also Libnah, Ether, Ashan, 43 Iphtah, Ashnah, Nezib, 44 Keilah, Achzib, and Mareshah: nine cities, along with the towns round them.

45 There was Ekron with its towns and villages, 46 and all the cities and towns near Ashdod, from Ekron to the Mediterranean Sea.

47 There were Ashdod and Gaza, with their towns and villages, reaching to the stream on the border of Egypt and the coast of the Mediterranean Sea.

48 In the hill country there were Shamir, Jattir, Socoh, 49 Dannah, Kiriath Sepher (or Debir), 50 Anab, Eshtemoa, Anim, 51 Goshen, Holon, and Giloh: eleven cities, along with the towns round them.

52 There were Arab, Dumah, Eshan, 53 Janim, Beth Tappuah, Aphekah, 54 Humtah, Hebron, and Zior: nine cities, along with the towns round them.

55 There were Maon, Carmel, Ziph, Juttah, 56 Jezreel, Jokdeam, Zanoah, 57 Kain, Gibeah, and Timnah: ten cities, along with the towns round them.

58 There were Halhul, Bethzur, Gedor, 59 Maarath, Bethanoth, and Eltekon: six cities, along with the towns round them.

60 There were Kiriath Baal (or Kiriath Jearim) and Rabbah: two cities, along with the towns round them.

61 In the desert there were Beth Arabah, Middin, Secacah, 62 Nibshan, the city of Salt, and Engedi: six cities, along with the towns round them.

63 But the people of Judah were not able to drive out the Jebusites, who lived in Jerusalem. The Jebusites still live there with the people of Judah.

The Territory Assigned to Ephraim and West Manasseh

16 The southern boundary of the land assigned to the descendants of Joseph started from the Jordan near Jericho, at a point east of the springs of Jericho, and went into the desert. It went from Jericho up into the hill country as far as Bethel. 2 From Bethel it went to Luz, passing on to Ataroth Addar, where the Archites lived. 3 It then went west to the area of the Japhletites, as far as the area of Lower Beth Horon. It went on from there to Gezer and ended at the Mediterranean Sea.

4 The descendants of Joseph, the tribes of Ephraim and West Manasseh, received this land as their possession.

Ephraim

5 This was the territory of the Ephraimite families: their border ran from Ataroth Addar eastwards to Upper Beth Horon, 6 and from there to the Mediterranean Sea. Michmethath was on their north. East of there the border bent towards Taanath Shiloh and

went past it on the east to Janoah. [7] Then it went down from Janoah to Ataroth and Naarah, reaching Jericho and ending at the Jordan. [8] The border went west from Tappuah to the stream of Kanah and ended at the Mediterranean Sea. This was the land given to the families of the tribe of Ephraim as their possession, [9] along with some towns and villages that were within the borders of Manasseh, but given to the Ephraimites. [10] But they did not drive out the Canaanites who lived in Gezer, so the Canaanites have lived among the Ephraimites to this day, but they have been forced to work as slaves.

West Manasseh

17 A part of the land west of the Jordan was assigned to some of the families descended from Joseph's elder son Manasseh. Machir, the father of Gilead, was Manasseh's eldest son and a military hero, so Gilead and Bashan, east of the Jordan, were assigned to him. [2] Land west of the Jordan was assigned to the rest of the families of Manasseh: Abiezer, Helek, Asriel, Shechem, Hepher, and Shemida. These were male descendants of Manasseh son of Joseph, and they were heads of families. [3] Zelophehad, son of Hepher, son of Gilead, son of Machir, son of Manasseh, did not have any sons, but only daughters. Their names were Mahlah, Noah, Hoglah, Milcah, and Tirzah. [4] They went to Eleazar the priest and to Joshua son of Nun and to the leaders, and said, "The LORD commanded Moses to give us, as well as our male relatives, a part of the land to possess." So, as the LORD had commanded, they were given land along with their male relatives. [5] That is why Manasseh received ten shares in addition to Gilead and Bashan on the east side of the Jordan, [6] since his female descendants as well as his male descendants were assigned land. The land of Gilead was assigned to the rest of the descendants of Manasseh.

[7] The territory of Manasseh reached from Asher to Michmethath, east of Shechem. The border then went south to include the people of Entappuah. [8] The land round Tappuah belonged to Manasseh, but the town of Tappuah, on the border, belonged to the descendants of Ephraim. [9] The border then went down to the stream of Kanah. The cities south of the stream belonged to Ephraim, even though they were in the territory of Manasseh. The border of Manasseh proceeded along the north side of the stream and ended at the Mediterranean Sea. [10] Ephraim was to the south, and Manasseh was to the north, with the Mediterranean Sea as their western border. Asher was to the north-west, and Issachar to the north-east. [11] Within the territories of Issachar and Asher, Manasseh possessed Beth Shan and Ibleam, along with their surrounding towns, as well as Dor (the one on the coast),* Endor, Taanach, Megiddo, and their surrounding towns. [12] The people of Manasseh, however, were not able to drive out the people living in those cities, so the Canaanites continued to live there. [13] Even when the Israelites became stronger, they did not drive out all the Canaanites, but they did force them to work for them.

Ephraim and West Manasseh Request More Land

[14] The descendants of Joseph said to Joshua, "Why have you given us only one part of the land to possess as our own? There are very many of us because the LORD has blessed us."

[15] Joshua answered, "If there are so many of you and the hill country of Ephraim is too small for you, then go into the forests

17.11 Probable text *Dor (the one on the coast);* Hebrew unclear.

Colour these shapes.

270

Joshua

⁝ ┄┄┄┄

Genesis
Exodus
Leviticus
Num.
Deuter.

JOSHUA 17, 18

and clear ground for yourselves in the land of the Perizzites and the Rephaim."

16 They replied, "The hill country is not big enough for us, but the Canaanites in the plains have iron chariots, both those who live in Beth Shan and its surrounding towns and those who live in the Valley of Jezreel."

17 Joshua said to the tribes of Ephraim and West Manasseh, "There are indeed many of you, and you are very powerful. You shall have more than one share. 18 The hill country will be yours. Even though it is a forest, you will clear it and take possession of it from one end to the other. As for the Canaanites, you will drive them out, even though they do have iron chariots and are a strong people."

The Division of the Rest of the Land

18 After they had conquered the land, the entire community of Israel assembled at Shiloh and set up the Tent of the LORD's presence. 2 There were still seven tribes of the people of Israel who had not yet been assigned their share of the land. 3 So Joshua said to the people of Israel, "How long are you going to wait before you go in and take the land that the LORD, the God of your ancestors, has given you? 4 Let me have three men from each tribe. I will send them out over the whole country to map out the territory that they would like to have as their possession. Then they are to come back to me. 5 The land will be divided among them in seven parts; Judah will stay in its territory in the south, and Joseph in its territory in the north. 6 Write down a description of these seven divisions and bring it to me. Then I will draw lots* to consult the LORD our God for you. 7 The Levites, however, will not receive a share of the land with the rest of you, because their share is to serve as the LORD's priests. And of course, the tribes of Gad, Reuben, and East Manasseh have already received their land east of the Jordan, which Moses, the LORD's servant, gave to them."

8 The men went on their way to map out the land after Joshua had given them these instructions: "Go all over the land and map it out, and come back to me. And then here in Shiloh I will consult the LORD for you by drawing lots." 9 So the men went all over the land and set down in writing how they divided it into seven parts, making a list of the towns. Then they went back to Joshua in the camp at Shiloh. 10 Joshua drew lots to consult the LORD for them, and assigned each of the remaining tribes of Israel a certain part of the land.

The Territory Assigned to Benjamin

11 The territory belonging to the families of the tribe of Benjamin was the first to be assigned. Their land lay between the tribes of Judah and Joseph. 12 On the north their border began at the Jordan and then went up the slope north of Jericho and westwards through the hill country as far as the desert of Bethaven. 13 The border then went to the slope on the south side of Luz (also called Bethel), then down to Ataroth Addar, on the mountain south of Lower Beth Horon. 14 The border then went in another direction, turning south from the western side of this mountain and going to Kiriath Baal (or Kiriath Jearim), which belongs to the tribe of Judah. This was the western border. 15 The southern border started on the edge of Kiriath Jearim and went* to the Springs of

18.6 *draw lots*: See 14.2.
18.15 Probable text *and went*; Hebrew *and went westwards*.

JOSHUA 18, 19

271

Joshua

....

Judges
Ruth
1 Sam.
2 Sam.
1 Kings

Nephtoah. [16] It then went down to the foot of the mountain that overlooks the Valley of Hinnom, at the north end of the Valley of Rephaim. It then went south through the Valley of Hinnom, south of the Jebusite ridge, towards Enrogel. [17] It then turned north to Enshemesh and then on to Geliloth, opposite Adummim Pass. The border then went down to the Stone of Bohan (Bohan was a son of Reuben) [18] and passed north of the ridge overlooking the Jordan Valley. It then went down into the valley, [19] passing north of the ridge of Beth Hoglah, and ended at the northern inlet on the Dead Sea, where the River Jordan empties into it. This was the southern border. [20] The Jordan was the eastern border. These were the borders of the land which the families of the tribe of Benjamin received as their possession.

[21] The cities belonging to the families of the tribe of Benjamin were Jericho, Beth Hoglah, Emek Keziz, [22] Beth Arabah, Zemaraim, Bethel, [23] Avvim, Parah, Ophrah, [24] Chepharammoni, Ophni, and Geba: twelve cities, along with the towns round them. [25] There were also Gibeon, Ramah, Beeroth, [26] Mizpah, Chephirah, Mozah, [27] Rekem, Irpeel, Taralah, [28] Zela, Haeleph, Jebus (or Jerusalem), Gibeah, and Kiriath Jearim: fourteen cities, along with the towns round them. This is the land which the families of the tribe of Benjamin received as their possession.

The Territory Assigned to Simeon

19 The second assignment made was for the families of the tribe of Simeon. Its territory extended into the land assigned to the tribe of Judah. [2] It included Beersheba, Sheba, Moladah, [3] Hazar Shual, Balah, Ezem, [4] Eltolad, Bethul, Hormah, [5] Ziklag, Beth Marcaboth, Hazar Susah, [6] Beth Lebaoth, and Sharuhen: thirteen cities, along with the towns round them.

[7] There were also Ain, Rimmon, Ether, and Ashan: four cities, along with the towns round them. [8] This included all the towns round these cities as far as Baalath Beer (or Ramah), in the south. This was the land which the families of the tribe of Simeon received as their possession. [9] Since Judah's assignment was larger than was needed, part of its territory was given to the tribe of Simeon.

The Territory Assigned to Zebulun

[10] The third assignment made was for the families of the tribe of Zebulun. The land which they received reached as far as Sarid. [11] From there the border went west to Mareal, touching Dabbesheth and the stream east of Jokneam. [12] On the other side of Sarid it went east to the border of Chisloth Tabor, then to Daberath and up to Japhia. [13] It continued east from there to Gath Hepher and Ethkazin, turning in the direction of Neah on the way to Rimmon. [14] On the north the border turned towards Hannathon, ending at the Valley of Iphtahel. [15] It included Kattath, Nahalal, Shimron, Idalah, and Bethlehem: twelve cities, along with the towns round them. [16] These cities and their towns were in the land which the families of the tribe of Zebulun received as their possession.

The Territory Assigned to Issachar

[17] The fourth assignment made was for the families of the tribe of Issachar. [18] Its area included Jezreel, Chesulloth, Shunem, [19] Hapharaim, Shion, Anaharath, [20] Rabbith, Kishion, Ebez, [21] Remeth, Engannim, Enhaddah, and Bethpazzez. [22] The border also touched Tabor, Shahazumah, and Beth Shemesh, ending at the Jordan. It included sixteen cities along with the towns round

272

Joshua

Genesis
Exodus
Leviticus
Num.
Deuter.

JOSHUA 19

DOODLE HERE...

them. 23 These cities and their towns were in the land which the families of the tribe of Issachar received as their possession.

The Territory Assigned to Asher

24 The fifth assignment made was for the families of the tribe of Asher. 25 Its area included Helkath, Hali, Beten, Achshaph, 26 Allam Melech, Amad, and Mishal. On the west it touched Carmel and Shihor Libnath. 27 As it turned east, the border went to Bethdagon, touching Zebulun and the Valley of Iphtahel on the way north to Bethemek and Neiel. It continued north to Cabul, 28 Ebron, Rehob, Hammon, and Kanah, as far as Sidon. 29 The border then turned to Ramah, reaching the fortified city of Tyre; then it turned to Hosah and ended at the Mediterranean Sea. It included Mahalab, Achzib, 30 Ummah, Aphek, and Rehob: 22 cities, along with the towns round them. 31 These cities and their towns were in the land which the families of the tribe of Asher received as their possession.

The Territory Assigned to Naphtali

32 The sixth assignment made was for the families of the tribe of Naphtali. 33 Its border went from Heleph to the oak in Zaanannim, on to Adaminekeb and to Jamnia, as far as Lakkum, and ended at the Jordan. 34 There the border turned west to Aznoth Tabor, from there to Hukkok, touching Zebulun on the south, Asher on the west, and the Jordan* on the east. 35 The fortified cities were Ziddim, Zer, Hammath, Rakkath, Chinnereth, 36 Adamah, Ramah, Hazor, 37 Kedesh, Edrei, Enhazor, 38 Yiron, Migdalel, Horem, Bethanath, and Beth Shemesh: nineteen cities, along with the towns round them. 39 These cities and their towns were in the land which the families of the tribe of Naphtali received as their possession.

The Territory Assigned to Dan

40 The seventh assignment made was for the families of the tribe of Dan. 41 Its area included Zorah, Eshtaol, Irshemesh, 42 Shaalbim, Aijalon, Ithlah, 43 Elon, Timnah, Ekron, 44 Eltekeh, Gibbethon, Baalath, 45 Jehud, Beneberak, Gathrimmon, 46 Mejarkon, and Rakkon, as well as the territory round Joppa. 47 When the people of Dan lost their land, they went to Laish and attacked it. They captured it, killed its people, and claimed it for themselves. They settled there and changed the name of the city from Laish to Dan, naming it after their ancestor Dan. 48 These cities and their towns were in the land which the families of the tribe of Dan received as their possession.

The Final Assignment of the Land

49 When the people of Israel finished dividing up the land, they gave Joshua son of Nun a part of the land as his own. 50 As the Lord had commanded, they gave him the city he asked for: Timnath Serah, in the hill country of Ephraim. He rebuilt the city and settled there.

51 Eleazar the priest, Joshua son of Nun, and the leaders of the families of the tribes of Israel assigned these parts of the land by drawing lots* to consult the Lord at Shiloh, at the entrance of the Tent of the Lord's presence. In this way they finished dividing the land.

19.34 One ancient translation *the Jordan*; Hebrew *Judah at the Jordan*.
19.51 *drawing lots*: See 14.2.

Joshua

....

Judges

Ruth

1 Sam.

2 Sam.

1 Kings

The Cities of Refuge
(Num 35.9–34)

20 Then the LORD told Joshua [2] to say to the people of Israel, "Choose the cities of refuge that I commanded Moses to tell you about. [3] A person who kills someone accidentally can go there and escape the one who is looking for revenge. [4] He or she can run away to one of these cities, go to the place of judgement at the entrance to the city, and explain to the leaders what happened. Then they will let him or her into the city and give them a place to stay in, so that they can stay there. [5] If the one looking for revenge follows them there, the people of the city must not hand them over to them. They must protect them because they killed the person accidentally and not out of anger. [6] They may stay in the city until they have received a public trial and until the death of the man who is then the High Priest. Then they may go back home to their own town, from which they had run away."

[7] So, on the west side of the Jordan they set aside Kedesh in Galilee, in the hill country of Naphtali; Shechem, in the hill country of Ephraim; and Hebron, in the hill country of Judah. [8] East of the Jordan, on the desert plateau east of Jericho, they chose Bezer in the territory of Reuben; Ramoth in Gilead, in the territory of Gad; and Golan in Bashan, in the territory of Manasseh. [9] These were the cities of refuge chosen for all the people of Israel and for any foreigner living among them. Anyone who killed a person accidentally could find protection there from the one looking for revenge; no one could be killed without first receiving a public trial.

The Cities of the Levites

21 The leaders of the Levite families went to Eleazar the priest, Joshua son of Nun, and to the heads of the families of all the tribes of Israel. [2] There at Shiloh in the land of Canaan they said to them, "The LORD commanded through Moses that we were to be given cities to live in, as well as pasture land round them for our livestock." [3] So in accordance with the LORD's command the people of Israel gave the Levites certain cities and pasture lands out of their own territories.

[4] The families of the Levite clan of Kohath were the first to be assigned cities. The families who were descended from Aaron the priest were assigned thirteen cities from the territories of Judah, Simeon, and Benjamin. [5] The rest of the clan of Kohath was assigned ten cities from the territories of Ephraim, Dan, and West Manasseh.

[6] The clan of Gershon was assigned thirteen cities from the territories of Issachar, Asher, Naphtali, and East Manasseh.

[7] The families of the clan of Merari were assigned twelve cities from the territories of Reuben, Gad, and Zebulun.

[8] By drawing lots,* the people of Israel assigned these cities and their pasture lands to the Levites, as the LORD had commanded through Moses.

[9] These are the names of the cities from the territories of Judah and Simeon which were given [10] to the descendants of Aaron who were of the clan of Kohath, which was descended from Levi. Their assignment was the first to be made. [11] They were given the city of Arba (Arba was Anak's father), now called Hebron, in the hill country of Judah, along with the pasture land surrounding it. [12] However, the fields of the city, as well as its towns, had already been given to Caleb son of Jephunneh as his possession.

....

21.8 *drawing lots*: See 14.2.

274

Joshua

∴┄┄┄┄┄┄

Genesis
Exodus
Leviticus
Num.
Deuter.

JOSHUA 21, 22

13 In addition to Hebron (one of the cities of refuge), the following cities were assigned to the descendants of Aaron the priest: Libnah, 14 Jattir, Eshtemoa, 15 Holon, Debir, 16 Ain, Juttah, and Beth Shemesh, with their pasture lands: nine cities from the tribes of Judah and Simeon. 17 From the territory of Benjamin they were given four cities: Gibeon, Geba, 18 Anathoth, and Almon, with their pasture lands. 19 Thirteen cities in all, with their pasture lands, were given to the priests, the descendants of Aaron.

20 The other families of the Levite clan of Kohath were assigned some cities from the territory of Ephraim. 21 They were given four cities: Shechem and its pasture lands in the hill country of Ephraim (one of the cities of refuge), Gezer, 22 Kibzaim, and Beth Horon, with their pasture lands. 23 From the territory of Dan they were given four cities: Eltekeh, Gibbethon, 24 Aijalon, and Gathrimmon, with their pasture lands. 25 From the territory of West Manasseh they were given two cities: Taanach and Gathrimmon, with their pasture lands. 26 These families of the clan of Kohath received ten cities in all, with their pasture lands.

27 Another group of Levites, the clan of Gershon, received from the territory of East Manasseh two cities: Golan in Bashan (one of the cities of refuge) and Beeshterah, with their pasture lands. 28 From the territory of Issachar they received four cities: Kishion, Daberath, 29 Jarmuth, and Engannim, with their pasture lands. 30 From the territory of Asher they received four cities: Mishal, Abdon, 31 Helkath, and Rehob, with their pasture lands. 32 From the territory of Naphtali they received three cities: Kedesh in Galilee, with its pasture lands (one of the cities of refuge), Hammoth Dor, and Kartan, with their pasture lands. 33 The various families of the clan of Gershon received a total of thirteen cities with their pasture lands.

34 The rest of the Levites, the clan of Merari, received from the territory of Zebulun four cities: Jokneam, Kartah, 35 Dimnah, and Nahalal, with their pasture lands. 36 From the territory of Reuben they received four cities: Bezer, Jahaz, 37 Kedemoth, and Mephaath, with their pasture lands. 38 From the tribe of Gad they received four cities: Ramoth in Gilead, with its pasture lands (one of the cities of refuge), Mahanaim, 39 Heshbon, and Jazer, with their pasture lands. 40 So the clan of Merari was assigned a total of twelve cities.

41-42 From the land that the people of Israel possessed, a total of 48 cities, with the pasture lands round them, was given to the Levites.

Israel Takes Possession of the Land

43 So the LORD gave to Israel all the land that he had solemnly promised their ancestors he would give them. When they had taken possession of it, they settled down there. 44 The LORD gave them peace throughout the land, just as he had promised their ancestors. Not one of all their enemies had been able to stand against them, because the LORD gave the Israelites the victory over all their enemies. 45 The LORD kept every one of the promises that he had made to the people of Israel.

Joshua Sends the Eastern Tribes Home

22 Then Joshua called together the people of the tribes of Reuben, Gad, and East Manasseh. 2 He said to them, "You have done everything that Moses the LORD's servant ordered you to do, and you have obeyed all my commands. 3 All this time you have never once deserted your fellow-Israelites. You have been

JOSHUA 21.43-45

Read Genesis 15.18-21 to see where God originally promised the Israelites that they would have a land of their own. Finally, after generations of wandering, the Israelites had

• MADE IT •

HOME.

Joshua

············

Judges
Ruth
1 Sam.
2 Sam.
1 Kings

careful to obey the commands of the LORD your God. ⁴Now, as he promised, the LORD your God has given your fellow-Israelites peace. So go back home to the land which you claimed for your own, the land on the east side of the Jordan, that Moses, the LORD's servant, gave you. ⁵Make sure you obey the law that Moses commanded you: love the LORD your God, do his will, obey his commandments, be faithful to him, and serve him with all your heart and soul." ⁶⁻⁸Joshua sent them home with his blessing and with these words: "You are going back home very rich, with a lot of livestock, silver, gold, bronze, iron, and many clothes. Share with your fellow-tribesmen what you took from your enemies." Then they left for home.

Moses had given land east of the Jordan to one half of the tribe of Manasseh, but to the other half Joshua had given land west of the Jordan, along with the other tribes.

⁹So the people of the tribes of Reuben, Gad, and East Manasseh went back home. They left the rest of the people of Israel at Shiloh in the land of Canaan and started out for their own land, the land of Gilead, which they had taken as the LORD had commanded them through Moses.

The Altar by the Jordan

¹⁰When the tribes of Reuben, Gad, and East Manasseh arrived at Geliloth, still on the west side* of the Jordan, they built a large, impressive altar there by the river. ¹¹The rest of the people of Israel were told, "Listen! The people of the tribes of Reuben, Gad, and East Manasseh have built an altar at Geliloth, on our side of the Jordan!" ¹²When the people of Israel heard this, the whole community came together at Shiloh to go to war against the eastern tribes.

¹³Then the people of Israel sent Phinehas, the son of Eleazar the priest, to the people of the tribes of Reuben, Gad, and East Manasseh in the land of Gilead. ¹⁴Ten leading men went with Phinehas, one from each of the western tribes and each one the head of a family among the clans. ¹⁵They came to the land of Gilead, to the people of Reuben, Gad, and East Manasseh, ¹⁶and speaking for the whole community of the LORD, they said to them, "Why have you done this evil thing against the God of Israel? You have rebelled against the LORD by building this altar for yourselves! You are no longer following him! ¹⁷Remember our sin at Peor, when the LORD punished his own people with an epidemic? We are still suffering because of that. Wasn't that sin enough? ¹⁸Are you going to refuse to follow him now? If you rebel against the LORD today, he will be angry with everyone in Israel tomorrow. ¹⁹Now then, if your land is not fit to worship in, come over into the LORD's land, where his Tent is. Claim some land among us. But don't rebel against the LORD or make rebels out of us by building an altar in addition to the altar of the LORD our God. ²⁰Remember how Achan son of Zerah refused to obey the command about the things condemned to destruction; the whole community of Israel was punished for that. Achan was not the only one who died because of his sin."

²¹The people of the tribes of Reuben, Gad, and East Manasseh answered the heads of the families of the western tribes: ²²"The Mighty One is God! He is the LORD! The Mighty One is God! He is the LORD! He knows why we did this, and we want you to know too! If we rebelled and did not keep faith with the LORD, do not

---

22.10 *still on the west side*; or *on the east side.*

276

Joshua

..:..........

Genesis
Exodus
Leviticus
Num.
Deuter.

JOSHUA 22, 23

let us live any longer! [23] If we disobeyed the LORD and built our own altar to burn sacrifices on or to use for grain offerings or fellowship offerings, let the LORD himself punish us. [24] No! We did it because we were afraid that in the future your descendants would say to ours, 'What do you have to do with the LORD, the God of Israel? [25] He made the Jordan a boundary between us and you people of Reuben and Gad. You have nothing to do with the LORD.' Then your descendants might make our descendants stop worshipping the LORD. [26] So we built an altar, not to burn sacrifices or make offerings, [27] but instead, as a sign for our people and yours, and for the generations after us, that we do indeed worship the LORD before his sacred Tent with our offerings to be burnt and with sacrifices and fellowship offerings. This was to keep your descendants from saying that ours have nothing to do with the LORD. [28] It was our idea that, if this should ever happen, our descendants could say, 'Look! Our ancestors made an altar just like the LORD's altar. It was not for burning offerings or for sacrifice, but as a sign for our people and yours.' [29] We would certainly not rebel against the LORD or stop following him now by building an altar to burn offerings on or for grain offerings or sacrifices. We would not build any other altar than the altar of the LORD our God that stands in front of the Tent of his presence."

[30] Phinehas the priest and the ten leading men of the community who were with him, the heads of families of the western tribes, heard what the people of the tribes of Reuben, Gad, and East Manasseh had to say, and they were satisfied. [31] Phinehas, the son of Eleazar the priest, said to them, "Now we know that the LORD is with us. You have not rebelled against him, and so you have saved the people of Israel from the LORD's punishment."

[32] Then Phinehas and the leaders left the people of Reuben and Gad in the land of Gilead and went back to Canaan, to the people of Israel, and reported to them. [33] The Israelites were satisfied and praised God. They no longer talked about going to war to devastate the land where the people of Reuben and Gad had settled.

[34] The people of Reuben and Gad said, "This altar is a witness to all of us that the LORD is God." And so they named it "Witness".

Joshua's Farewell Address

23 Much later the LORD gave Israel security from their enemies around them. By that time Joshua was very old, [2] so he called all Israel, the elders, leaders, judges, and officers of the people, and said, "I am very old now. [3] You have seen everything that the LORD your God has done to all these nations because of you. The LORD your God has been fighting for you. [4] I have assigned as the possession of your tribes the land of the nations that are still left, as well as of all the nations that I have already conquered, from the River Jordan in the east to the Mediterranean Sea in the west. [5] The LORD your God will make them retreat from you, and he will drive them away as you advance. You shall have their land, as the LORD your God has promised you. [6] So be careful to obey and do everything that is written in the book of the Law of Moses. Do not neglect any part of it, [7] and then you will not associate with these peoples left among you or speak the names of their gods or use those names in taking vows or worship those gods or bow down to them. [8] Instead, be faithful to the LORD, as you have been till now. [9] The LORD has driven great and powerful nations out as you advanced and no one has ever been able to stand against you. [10] Any one of you can make a thousand men

JOSHUA 23, 24   277

Joshua
....
Judges
Ruth
1 Sam.
2 Sam.
1 Kings

run away, because the LORD your God is fighting for you, just as he promised. [11]Be careful, then, to love the LORD your God. [12]If you are disloyal and join with the nations that are still left among you and intermarry with them, [13]you may be sure that the LORD your God will no longer drive these nations out as you advance. Rather, they will be as dangerous for you as a trap or a pit and as painful as a whip on your back or thorns in your eyes. And this will last until none of you are left in this good land which the LORD your God has given you.

[14]"Now my time has come to die. Every one of you knows in his heart and soul that the LORD your God has given you all the good things that he promised. Every promise he made has been kept; not one has failed. [15]But just as he kept every promise that he made to you, so he will carry out every threat. [16]If you do not keep the covenant which the LORD your God commanded you to keep and if you serve and worship other gods, then in his anger he will punish you, and soon none of you will be left in this good land that he has given you."

Joshua Speaks to the People at Shechem

24 Joshua gathered all the tribes of Israel together at Shechem. He called the elders, the leaders, the judges, and the officers of Israel, and they came into the presence of God. [2]Joshua said to all the people, "This is what the LORD, the God of Israel, has to say: 'Long ago your ancestors lived on the other side of the River Euphrates and worshipped other gods. One of those ancestors was Terah, the father of Abraham and Nahor. [3]Then I took Abraham, your ancestor, from the land beyond the Euphrates and led him through the whole land of Canaan. I gave him many descendants. I gave him Isaac, [4]and to Isaac I gave Jacob and Esau. I gave Esau the hill country of Edom as his possession, but your ancestor Jacob and his children went down to Egypt. [5]Later I sent Moses and Aaron, and I brought great trouble on Egypt. But I led you out; [6]I brought your ancestors out of Egypt, and the Egyptians pursued them with chariots and cavalry. But when your ancestors got to the Red Sea [7]they cried out to me for help, and I put darkness between them and the Egyptians. I made the sea come rolling over the Egyptians and drown them. You know what I did to Egypt.

"'You lived in the desert a long time. [8]Then I brought you to the land of the Amorites, who lived on the east side of the Jordan. They fought you, but I gave you victory over them. You took their land, and I destroyed them as you advanced. [9]Then the king of Moab, Balak son of Zippor, fought against you. He sent word to Balaam son of Beor and asked him to put a curse on you. [10]But I would not listen to Balaam, so he blessed you, and in this way I rescued you from Balak. [11]You crossed the Jordan and came to Jericho. The men of Jericho fought against you, as did the Amorites, the Perizzites, the Canaanites, the Hittites, the Girgashites, the Hivites, and the Jebusites. But I gave you victory over them all. [12]As you advanced, I threw them into panic in order to drive out the two Amorite kings. Your swords and bows had nothing to do with it. [13]I gave you a land that you had never cultivated and cities that you had not built. Now you are living there and eating grapes from vines that you did not plant, and olives from trees that you did not plant.'

[14]"Now then," Joshua continued, "honour the LORD and serve him sincerely and faithfully. Get rid of the gods which your ancestors used to worship in Mesopotamia and in Egypt, and serve only the

278

Joshua

· :· ········

Genesis
Exodus
Leviticus
Num.
Deuter.

JOSHUA 24

JOSHUA 24.14-24

The Israelites often gave higher importance to things that weren't God. Turn this Bible

- UPSIDE -

DOWN.

Write down some things that you can sometimes prioritise over your relationship with God. Now, flip the Bible the right way up and write 'God' at the top as a sign that you are recommitting yourself to putting him first.

LORD. [15] If you are not willing to serve him, decide today whom you will serve, the gods your ancestors worshipped in Mesopotamia or the gods of the Amorites, in whose land you are now living. As for my family and me, we will serve the LORD."

[16] The people replied, "We would never leave the LORD to serve other gods! [17] The LORD our God brought our fathers and us out of slavery in Egypt, and we saw the miracles that he performed. He kept us safe wherever we went among all the nations through which we passed. [18] As we advanced into this land, the LORD drove out all the Amorites who lived here. So we also will serve the LORD; he is our God."

[19] Joshua said to the people, "But you may not be able to serve the LORD. He is a holy God and will not forgive your sins. He will tolerate no rivals, [20] and if you leave him to serve foreign gods, he will turn against you and punish you. He will destroy you, even though he was good to you before."

[21] The people said to Joshua, "No! We will serve the LORD."

[22] Joshua said to them, "You are your own witnesses to the fact that you have chosen to serve the LORD."

"Yes," they said, "we are witnesses."

[23] "Then get rid of those foreign gods that you have," he demanded, "and pledge your loyalty to the LORD, the God of Israel."

[24] The people then said to Joshua, "We will serve the LORD our God. We will obey his commands."

[25] So Joshua made a covenant for* the people that day, and there at Shechem he gave them laws and rules to follow. [26] Joshua wrote these commands in the book of the Law of God. Then he took a large stone and set it up under the oak tree in the LORD's sanctuary. [27] He said to all the people, "This stone will be our witness. It has heard all the words that the LORD has spoken to us. So it will be a witness against you, to keep you from rebelling against your God." [28] Then Joshua sent the people away, and they all returned to their own part of the land.

Joshua and Eleazar Die

[29] After that, the LORD's servant Joshua son of Nun died at the age of 110. [30] They buried him on his own land at Timnath Serah in the hill country of Ephraim north of Mount Gaash.

[31] As long as Joshua lived, the people of Israel served the LORD, and after his death they continued to do so as long as those leaders were alive who had seen for themselves everything that the LORD had done for Israel.

[32] The body of Joseph, which the people of Israel had brought from Egypt, was buried at Shechem, in the piece of land that Jacob had bought from the sons of Hamor, the father of Shechem, for a hundred pieces of silver. This land was inherited by Joseph's descendants.

[33] Eleazar son of Aaron died and was buried at Gibeah, the town in the hill country of Ephraim which had been given to his son Phinehas.

24.25 *for*; or *with*.

THE BOOK OF

JUDGES

WRITTEN: PROBABLY AROUND 800-700BC
(USING STORIES FROM A MUCH EARLIER TIME)

WHY READ IT?

The book of Judges includes some epic stories that could each be made into its own feature film. Here we begin to learn what the world looks like when people, rather than God, are in charge. If you want to learn some lessons about leadership (both good and bad) and what happens when we step away from God's guidelines for right living, this is an important read.

In this space, write a list of the judges that you read about. For each judge, note one of their key

LEADERSHIP
QUALITIES

WHAT YOU NEED TO KNOW:

The story told in Judges takes us on from the death of Joshua. The Israelites had arrived in the Promised Land, but even when God had given them everything they had asked for, they still found it easy to forget him. So God raised up leaders, called judges, to unite the nation and remind them who they served. However, God's people were stuck in a cycle. They would reject God, God would punish them, they would cry out, and God would send a leader to rescue them.
Then the cycle would start all over again.

What are some of the cycles that you see in your own life? Perhaps there are mistakes you keep making or something that God continually speaks to you about.

Draw some spirals here and, in each one, write a word to describe these cycles.

200BC — GOD APPOINTS JUDGES — DEBORAH — GIDEON — SAMSON

280

Judges

Exodus
Leviticus
Num.
Deuter.
Joshua

JUDGES 1

JUDGES 1.29–2.12

As you read these verses, you see Israel

BEGINNING TO

COMPROMISE

on what God asked them to do. Each one of these actions may have seemed small at the time, but as they built up they knocked Israel completely off track from what God had in store for them.

On these pages, write a list of the last few things that God spoke to you about or asked you to do. When you have done this, circle one of them and go and do something towards it immediately.

_____

_____

_____

_____

_____

The Tribes of Judah and Simeon Capture Adonibezek

1 After Joshua's death the people of Israel asked the LORD, "Which of our tribes should be the first to go and attack the Canaanites?"

2 The LORD answered, "The tribe of Judah will go first. I am giving them control of the land."

3 The people of Judah said to the people of Simeon, "Go with us into the territory assigned to us, and we will fight the Canaanites together. Then we will go with you into the territory assigned to you." So the tribes of Simeon 4 and Judah went into battle together. The LORD gave them victory over the Canaanites and the Perizzites, and they defeated 10,000 men at Bezek. 5 They found Adonibezek there and fought against him. 6 He ran away, but they chased him, caught him, and cut off his thumbs and big toes. 7 Adonibezek said, "Seventy kings with their thumbs and big toes cut off have picked up scraps under my table. God has now done to me what I did to them." He was taken to Jerusalem, where he died.

The Tribe of Judah Conquers Jerusalem and Hebron

8 The men of Judah attacked Jerusalem and captured it. They killed its people and set fire to the city. 9 After this they went on to fight the Canaanites who lived in the hill country, in the foothills, and in the dry country to the south. 10 They marched against the Canaanites living in the city of Hebron, which used to be called Kiriath Arba. There they defeated the clans of Sheshai, Ahiman, and Talmai.

Othniel Conquers the City of Debir
(Josh 15.13–19)

11 From there the men of Judah marched against the city of Debir, at that time called Kiriath Sepher. 12 One of them, called Caleb, said, "I will give my daughter Achsah in marriage to the man who succeeds in capturing Kiriath Sepher." 13 Othniel, the son of Caleb's younger brother Kenaz, captured the city, so Caleb gave him his daughter Achsah in marriage. 14 On the wedding day Othniel urged her* to ask her father for a field. She got down from her donkey, and Caleb asked her what she wanted. 15 She answered, "I want some pools of water. The land you have given me is in the dry country." So Caleb gave her the upper and lower springs.

The Victories of the Tribes of Judah and Benjamin

16 The descendants of Moses' father-in-law, the Kenite, went on with the people of Judah from Jericho, the city of palm trees, into the barren country south of Arad in Judah. There they settled among the Amalekites.* 17 The people of Judah went with the people of Simeon, and together they defeated the Canaanites who lived in the city of Zephath. They put a curse on the city, destroyed it, and named it Hormah.* 18-19 The LORD helped the people of Judah, and they took possession of the hill country. But they did not capture* Gaza, Ashkelon, or Ekron, with their surrounding territories. These people living along the coast had iron chariots, and so the people of Judah were not able to drive

1.14 Some ancient translations *Othniel urged her*; Hebrew *she urged Othniel.*
1.16 Some ancient translations *Amalekites*; Hebrew *people.*
1.17 *Hormah*: This name in Hebrew means "destruction".
1.18–19 One ancient translation *But they did not capture*; Hebrew *And they captured.*

them out. ²⁰ As Moses had commanded, Hebron was given to Caleb, who drove out of the city the three clans descended from Anak. ²¹ But the people of the tribe of Benjamin did not drive out the Jebusites living in Jerusalem, and the Jebusites have continued to live there with the people of Benjamin ever since.

The Tribes of Ephraim and Manasseh Conquer Bethel

²²⁻²³ The tribes of Ephraim and Manasseh went to attack the city of Bethel, at that time called Luz. The LORD helped them. They sent spies to the city, ²⁴ who saw a man leaving and said to him, "Show us how to get into the city, and we won't hurt you." ²⁵ So he showed them, and the people of Ephraim and Manasseh killed everyone in the city, except this man and his family. ²⁶ He later went to the land of the Hittites, built a city there, and named it Luz, which is still its name.

People who were not Driven Out by the Israelites

²⁷ The tribe of Manasseh did not drive out the people living in the cities of Beth Shan, Taanach, Dor, Ibleam, Megiddo, and the nearby towns; the Canaanites continued to live there. ²⁸ When the Israelites became stronger, they forced the Canaanites to work for them, but still they did not drive them all out.

²⁹ The tribe of Ephraim did not drive out the Canaanites living in the city of Gezer, and so the Canaanites continued to live there with them.

³⁰ The tribe of Zebulun did not drive out the people living in the cities of Kitron and Nahalal, and so the Canaanites continued to live there with them and were forced to work for them.

³¹ The tribe of Asher did not drive out the people living in the cities of Acco, Sidon, Ahlab, Achzib, Helbah, Aphek, and Rehob. ³² The people of Asher lived with the local Canaanites, since they did not drive them out.

³³ The tribe of Naphtali did not drive out the people living in the cities of Beth Shemesh and Bethanath. The people of Naphtali lived with the local Canaanites, but forced them to work for them.

³⁴ The Amorites forced the people of the tribe of Dan into the hill country and did not let them come down to the plain. ³⁵ The Amorites continued to live at Aijalon, Shaalbim, and Mount Heres, but the tribes of Ephraim and Manasseh kept them under their rule and forced them to work for them.

³⁶ North of Sela, the Edomite* border ran through Akrabbim Pass.

The Angel of the LORD at Bochim

2 The angel of the LORD went from Gilgal to Bochim and said to the Israelites, "I took you out of Egypt and brought you to the land that I promised to your ancestors. I said, 'I will never break my covenant with you. ² You must not make any covenant with the people who live in this land. You must tear down their altars.' But you have not done what I told you. You have done just the opposite! ³ So I tell you now that I will not drive these people out as you advance. They will be your enemies,* and you will be trapped by the worship of their gods." ⁴ When the angel had said this, all the people of Israel began to cry, ⁵ and that is why the place is called Bochim.* There they offered sacrifices to the LORD.

1.36 One ancient translation *Edomite*; Hebrew *Amorite*.
2.3 Some ancient translations *enemies*; Hebrew *sides*.
2.5 *Bochim*: This name in Hebrew means "those who cry".

The Death of Joshua

⁶Joshua sent the people of Israel on their way, and each man went to take possession of his own share of the land. ⁷As long as Joshua lived, the people of Israel served the LORD, and after his death they continued to do so as long as the leaders were alive who had seen for themselves all the great things that the LORD had done for Israel. ⁸The LORD's servant Joshua son of Nun died at the age of 110. ⁹He was buried in his own part of the land at Timnath Serah in the hill country of Ephraim north of Mount Gaash. ¹⁰That whole generation also died, and the next generation forgot the LORD and what he had done for Israel.

Israel Stops Worshipping the LORD

¹¹Then the people of Israel sinned against the LORD and began to serve the Baals. ¹²They stopped worshipping the LORD, the God of their ancestors, the God who had brought them out of Egypt, and they began to worship other gods, the gods of the peoples round them. They bowed down to them and made the LORD angry. ¹³They stopped worshipping the LORD and served the Baals and the Astartes. ¹⁴And so the LORD became furious with Israel and let raiders attack and rob them. He let enemies all around overpower them, and the Israelites could no longer protect themselves. ¹⁵Every time they went into battle, the LORD was against them, just as he had said he would be. They were in great distress.

¹⁶Then the LORD gave the Israelites leaders who saved them from the raiders. ¹⁷But the Israelites paid no attention to their leaders. Israel was unfaithful to the LORD and worshipped other gods. Their fathers had obeyed the LORD's commands, but this new generation soon stopped doing so. ¹⁸Whenever the LORD gave Israel a leader, the LORD would help that leader and would save the people from their enemies as long as that leader lived. The LORD would have mercy on them because they groaned under their suffering and oppression. ¹⁹But when the leader died, the people used to return to the old ways and behave worse than the previous generation. They would serve and worship other gods, and refused to give up their own evil ways. ²⁰Then the LORD would become furious with Israel and say, "This nation has broken the covenant that I commanded their ancestors to keep. Because they have not obeyed me, ²¹I will no longer drive out any of the nations that were still in the land when Joshua died. ²²I will use them to find out whether or not these Israelites will follow my ways, as their ancestors did." ²³So the LORD allowed those nations to remain in the land; he did not give Joshua victory over them, nor did he drive them out soon after Joshua's death.

The Nations Remaining in the Land

3 So then, the LORD left some nations in the land to test the Israelites who had not been through the wars in Canaan. ²He did this only in order to teach each generation of Israelites about war, especially those who had never been in battle before. ³Those left in the land were the five Philistine cities, all the Canaanites, the Sidonians, and the Hivites who lived in the Lebanon Mountains from Mount Baal Hermon as far as Hamath Pass. ⁴They were to be a test for Israel, to find out whether or not the Israelites would obey the commands that the LORD had given their ancestors through Moses. ⁵And so the people of Israel settled down among the Canaanites, the Hittites, the Amorites, the Perizzites, the Hivites, and the Jebusites. ⁶They intermarried with them and worshipped their gods.

Judges
....
Ruth
1 Sam.
2 Sam.
1 Kings
2 Kings

Othniel

7 The people of Israel forgot the LORD their God; they sinned against him and worshipped the idols of Baal and Asherah. **8** So the LORD became angry with Israel and let King Cushan Rishathaim of Mesopotamia conquer them, and he ruled over them for eight years. **9** Then the Israelites cried out to the LORD, and he sent a man who freed them. This was Othniel, the son of Caleb's younger brother Kenaz. **10** The Spirit of the LORD came upon him, and he became Israel's leader. Othniel went to war, and the LORD gave him victory over the king of Mesopotamia. **11** There was peace in the land for forty years, and then Othniel died.

Ehud

12 The people of Israel sinned against the LORD again. Because of this the LORD made King Eglon of Moab stronger than Israel. **13** Eglon joined the Ammonites and the Amalekites; they defeated Israel and captured Jericho, the city of palm trees. **14** The Israelites were subject to Eglon for eighteen years.

15 Then the Israelites cried out to the LORD, and he sent a man to free them. This was Ehud, a left-handed man, who was the son of Gera, from the tribe of Benjamin. The people of Israel sent Ehud to King Eglon of Moab with gifts for him. **16** Ehud had made himself a double-edged sword nearly fifty centimetres long. He had it fastened on his right side under his clothes. **17** Then he took the gifts to Eglon, who was a very fat man. **18** When Ehud had given him the gifts, he told the men who had carried them to go back home. **19** But Ehud himself turned back at the carved stones near Gilgal, went back to Eglon, and said, "Your Majesty, I have a secret message for you."

So the king ordered his servants, "Leave us alone!" And they all went out.

20 Then, as the king was sitting there alone in his cool room on the roof, Ehud went over to him and said, "I have a message from God for you." The king stood up. **21** With his left hand Ehud took the sword from his right side and plunged it into the king's belly. **22** The whole sword went in, handle and all, and the fat covered it up. Ehud did not pull it out of the king's belly, and it stuck out behind, between his legs.* **23** Then Ehud went outside, closed the doors behind him, locked them, **24** and left. The servants came and saw that the doors were locked, but they only thought that the king was inside, relieving himself. **25** They waited as long as they thought they should, but when he still did not open the door, they took the key and opened it. And there was their master, lying dead on the floor.

26 Ehud got away while they were waiting. He went past the carved stones and escaped to Seirah. **27** When he arrived there in the hill country of Ephraim, he blew a trumpet to call the men of Israel to battle; then he led them down from the hills. **28** He said, "Follow me! The LORD has given you victory over your enemies, the Moabites." So they followed Ehud down and captured the place where the Moabites were to cross the Jordan; they did not allow a single man to cross. **29** That day they killed about 10,000 of the best Moabite soldiers; none of them escaped. **30** That day the Israelites defeated Moab, and there was peace in the land for eighty years.

Shamgar

31 The next leader was Shamgar son of Anath. He too rescued Israel, and did so by killing 600 Philistines with an ox goad.

....

3.22 Probable text *it stuck… legs*; Hebrew unclear.

JUDGES 4

Deborah was the
only female judge
and is one of the

• FIRST FEMALE •

LEADERS

recorded in the Bible.
As you read chapter 4
you see a woman who
is both strong and
courageous.
But this is also a story
about leadership: it
shows that you don't
have to be the loudest
or strongest person for
God to use you in the
greatest way. God
doesn't always use the
most obvious person.
Here he uses the
unexpected - two
women - to rescue
Israel. The battle is won
through the quiet
bravery of individuals
and their faithfulness
to what God is asking
them to do.

Deborah and Barak

4 After Ehud died, the people of Israel sinned against the LORD again. [2] So the LORD let them be conquered by Jabin, a Canaanite king who ruled in the city of Hazor. The commander of his army was Sisera, who lived at Harosheth-of-the-Gentiles. [3] Jabin had 900 iron chariots, and he ruled the people of Israel with cruelty and violence for twenty years. Then the people of Israel cried out to the LORD for help.

[4] Now Deborah, the wife of Lappidoth, was a prophet, and she was serving as a judge for the Israelites at that time. [5] She used to sit under a certain palm tree between Ramah and Bethel in the hill country of Ephraim, and the people of Israel would go there for her decisions. [6] One day she sent for Barak son of Abinoam from the city of Kedesh in Naphtali and said to him, "The LORD, the God of Israel, has given you this command: 'Take 10,000 men from the tribes of Naphtali and Zebulun and lead them to Mount Tabor. [7] I will bring Sisera, the commander of Jabin's army, to fight against you at the River Kishon. He will have his chariots and soldiers, but I will give you victory over him.' "

[8] Then Barak replied, "I will go if you go with me, but if you don't go with me, I won't go either."

[9] She answered, "All right, I will go with you, but you won't get any credit for the victory, because the LORD will hand Sisera over to a woman." So Deborah set off for Kedesh with Barak. [10] Barak called the tribes of Zebulun and Naphtali to Kedesh, and 10,000 men followed him. Deborah went with him.

[11] In the meantime Heber the Kenite had set up his tent close to Kedesh near the oak tree at Zanannim. He had moved away from the other Kenites, the descendants of Hobab, the brother-in-law of Moses.

[12] When Sisera learnt that Barak had gone up to Mount Tabor, [13] he called out his 900 iron chariots and all his men, and sent them from Harosheth-of-the-Gentiles to the River Kishon.

[14] Then Deborah said to Barak, "Go! The LORD is leading you! Today he has given you victory over Sisera." So Barak went down from Mount Tabor with his 10,000 men. [15] When Barak attacked with his army, the LORD threw Sisera into confusion together with all his chariots and men. Sisera got down from his chariot and fled on foot. [16] Barak pursued the chariots and the army to Harosheth-of-the-Gentiles, and Sisera's whole army was killed. Not a man was left.

[17] Sisera ran away to the tent of Jael, the wife of Heber the Kenite, because King Jabin of Hazor was at peace with Heber's family. [18] Jael went out to meet Sisera and said to him, "Come in, sir; come into my tent. Don't be afraid." So he went in, and she hid him behind a curtain.* [19] He said to her, "Please give me a drink of water; I'm thirsty." She opened a leather bag of milk, gave him a drink, and hid him again. [20] Then he told her, "Stand at the door of the tent, and if anyone comes and asks you if someone is here, say no."

[21] Sisera was so tired that he fell sound asleep. Then Jael took a hammer and a tent peg, went up to him quietly, and killed him by driving the peg right through the side of his head and into the ground. [22] When Barak came looking for Sisera, Jael went out to meet him and said to him, "Come here! I'll show you the man you're looking for." So he went in with her, and there was Sisera on the ground, dead, with the tent peg through his head.

4.18 *hid him behind a curtain;* or *covered him with a rug.*

23 That day God gave the Israelites victory over Jabin, the Canaanite king. 24 They pressed harder and harder against him until they destroyed him.

The Song of Deborah and Barak

5 On that day Deborah and Barak son of Abinoam sang this song:

2 Praise the LORD!
    The Israelites were determined to fight;
    the people gladly volunteered.
3 Listen, you kings!
    Pay attention, you rulers!
I will sing, I will play music
    to Israel's God, the LORD.
4 LORD, when you left the mountains of Seir,
    when you came out of the region of Edom,
    the earth shook, and rain fell from the sky.
    Yes, water poured down from the clouds.

5 The mountains quaked before the LORD of Sinai,
    before the LORD, the God of Israel.

6 In the days of Shamgar son of Anath,
    in the days of Jael,
caravans no longer went through the land,
    and travellers used the side roads.
7 The towns of Israel stood abandoned, Deborah;
    they stood empty until you came,*
    came like a mother for Israel.
8 Then there was war in the land
    when the Israelites chose new gods.
Of the 40,000 men in Israel,
    did anyone carry shield or spear?
9 My heart is with the commanders of Israel,
    with the people who gladly volunteered.
    Praise the LORD!
10 Tell of* it, you that ride on white donkeys,
    sitting on saddles,
    and you that must walk wherever you go.
11 Listen! The noisy crowds round the wells
    are telling of the LORD's victories,
    the victories of Israel's people!

Then the LORD's people marched down from their cities.*
12 Lead on, Deborah, lead on!
    Lead on! Sing a song! Lead on!
Forward, Barak son of Abinoam,
    lead your captives away!
13 Then the faithful ones came down to their leaders;
    the LORD's people came to him* ready to fight.
14 They came* from Ephraim into the valley,*

5.7 *abandoned, Deborah… you came;* or *abandoned; they stood empty until I, Deborah, came.*
5.10 *Tell of;* or *Think about.*
5.11 *from their cities;* or *to their gates.*
5.13 One ancient translation *him;* Hebrew *me.*
5.14 Probable text *They came;* Hebrew *Their root.*
5.14 One ancient translation *into the valley;* Hebrew *in Amalek.*

behind the tribe of Benjamin and its people.
The commanders came down from Machir,
    the officers down from Zebulun.
15 The leaders of Issachar came with Deborah;
    yes, Issachar came and Barak too,
    and they followed him into the valley.
But the tribe of Reuben was divided;
    they could not decide whether to come.
16 Why did they stay behind with the sheep?
    To listen to shepherds calling the flocks?
Yes, the tribe of Reuben was divided;
    they could not decide whether to come.
17 The tribe of Gad stayed east of the Jordan,
    and the tribe of Dan remained by the ships.
The tribe of Asher stayed by the coast;
    they remained along the shore.
18 But the people of Zebulun and Naphtali
    risked their lives on the battlefield.

19 At Taanach, by the stream of Megiddo,
    the kings came and fought;
the kings of Canaan fought,
    but they took no silver away.
20 The stars fought from the sky;
    as they moved across the sky,
    they fought against Sisera.
21 A flood in the Kishon swept them away —
    the onrushing River Kishon.
I shall march, march on, with strength!
22 Then the horses came galloping on,
    stamping the ground with their hooves.

23 "Put a curse on Meroz," says the angel of the Lord,
    "a curse, a curse on those who live there.
They did not come to help the Lord,
    come as soldiers to fight for him."

24 The most fortunate of women is Jael,
    the wife of Heber the Kenite —
    the most fortunate of women who live in tents.
25 Sisera asked for water, but she gave him milk;
    she brought him cream in a beautiful bowl.
26 She took a tent peg in one hand,
    a workman's hammer in the other;
she struck Sisera and crushed his skull;
    she pierced him through the head.
27 He sank to his knees,
    fell down and lay still at her feet.
At her feet he sank to his knees and fell;
    he fell to the ground, dead.

28 Sisera's mother looked out of the window;
    she gazed* from behind the lattice.
"Why is his chariot so late in coming?" she asked.
    "Why are his horses so slow to return?"
29 Her wisest ladies answered her,
    and she told herself over and over,

5.28 Some ancient translations *gazed*; Hebrew *cried out*.

JUDGES 5, 6

287

Judges

....

Ruth

1 Sam.

2 Sam.

1 Kings

2 Kings

30 "They are only finding things to capture and divide,
 a woman or two for every soldier,
 rich cloth for Sisera,
 embroidered pieces for the neck of the queen."*

31 May all your enemies die like that, O LORD,
 but may your friends shine like the rising sun!

And there was peace in the land for forty years.

Gideon

6 Once again the people of Israel sinned against the LORD, so he let the people of Midian rule them for seven years. ² The Midianites were stronger than Israel, and the people of Israel hid from them in caves and other safe places in the hills. ³ Whenever the Israelites sowed any seed, the Midianites would come with the Amalekites and the desert tribes and attack them. ⁴ They would camp on the land and destroy the crops as far south as the area round Gaza. They would take all the sheep, cattle, and donkeys, and leave nothing for the Israelites to live on. ⁵ They would come with their livestock and tents, as thick as locusts. They and their camels were too many to count. They came and devastated the land, ⁶ and Israel was helpless against them.

⁷ Then the people of Israel cried out to the LORD for help against the Midianites, ⁸ and he sent them a prophet who brought them this message from the LORD, the God of Israel: "I brought you out of slavery in Egypt. ⁹ I rescued you from the Egyptians and from the people who fought against you here in this land. I drove them out as you advanced, and I gave you their land. ¹⁰ I told you that I am the LORD your God and that you should not worship the gods of the Amorites, whose land you are now living in. But you did not listen to me."

¹¹ Then the LORD's angel came to the village of Ophrah and sat under the oak tree that belonged to Joash, a man of the clan of Abiezer. His son Gideon was threshing some wheat secretly in a winepress, so that the Midianites would not see him. ¹² The LORD's angel appeared to him there and said, "The LORD is with you, brave and mighty man!"

¹³ Gideon said to him, "If I may ask, sir, why has all this happened to us if the LORD is with us? What about all the wonderful things that our fathers told us the LORD used to do — how he brought them out of Egypt? The LORD has abandoned us and left us to the mercy of the Midianites."

¹⁴ Then the LORD ordered him, "Go with all your great strength and rescue Israel from the Midianites. I myself am sending you."

¹⁵ Gideon replied, "But LORD, how can I rescue Israel? My clan is the weakest in the tribe of Manasseh, and I am the least important member of my family."

¹⁶ The LORD answered, "You can do it because I will help you. You will crush the Midianites as easily as if they were only one man."

¹⁷ Gideon replied, "If you are pleased with me, give me some proof that you are really the LORD. ¹⁸ Please do not leave until I bring you an offering of food."

He said, "I will stay until you come back."

¹⁹ So Gideon went into his house and cooked a young goat and used ten kilogrammes of flour to make bread without any yeast. He put the meat in a basket and the broth in a pot, brought

....

5.30 Probable text *queen*; Hebrew *plunder*.

288

Judges

Exodus
Leviticus
Num.
Deuter.
Joshua

JUDGES 6

TURN THESE LINES INTO A PICTURE OF SOMETHING.

them to the Lord's angel under the oak tree, and gave them to him. ²⁰The angel ordered him, "Put the meat and the bread on this rock, and pour the broth over them." Gideon did so. ²¹Then the Lord's angel reached out and touched the meat and the bread with the end of the stick he was holding. Fire came out of the rock and burnt up the meat and the bread. Then the angel disappeared.

²²Gideon then realized that it was the Lord's angel he had seen, and he said in terror, "Sovereign Lord! I have seen your angel face to face!"

²³But the Lord said to him, "Peace. Don't be afraid. You will not die." ²⁴Gideon built an altar to the Lord there and named it "The Lord is Peace". (It is still standing at Ophrah, which belongs to the clan of Abiezer.)

²⁵That night the Lord told Gideon, "Take your father's bull and another bull seven years old,* tear down your father's altar to Baal, and cut down the symbol of the goddess Asherah, which is beside it. ²⁶Build a well-constructed altar to the Lord your God on top of this mound. Then take the second bull* and burn it whole as an offering, using for firewood the symbol of Asherah you have cut down." ²⁷So Gideon took ten of his servants and did what the Lord had told him. He was too afraid of his family and the people of the town to do it by day, so he did it at night.

²⁸When the people of the town got up early the next morning, they found that the altar to Baal and the symbol of Asherah had been cut down, and that the second bull had been burnt on the altar that had been built there. ²⁹They asked each other, "Who did this?" They investigated and found out that Gideon son of Joash had done it. ³⁰Then they said to Joash, "Bring your son out here, so that we can kill him! He tore down the altar to Baal and cut down the symbol of Asherah beside it."

³¹But Joash said to all those who confronted him, "Are you standing up for Baal? Are you defending him? Anyone who stands up for him will be killed before morning. If Baal is a god, let him defend himself. It is his altar that was torn down." ³²From then on Gideon was known as Jerubbaal,* because Joash said, "Let Baal defend himself; it is his altar that was torn down."

³³Then all the Midianites, the Amalekites, and the desert tribes assembled, crossed the River Jordan, and camped in the Valley of Jezreel. ³⁴The Spirit of the Lord took control of Gideon, and he blew a trumpet to call the men of the clan of Abiezer to follow him. ³⁵He sent messengers throughout the territory of both parts of Manasseh to call them to follow him. He sent messengers to the tribes of Asher, Zebulun, and Naphtali, and they also came to join him.

³⁶Then Gideon said to God, "You say that you have decided to use me to rescue Israel. ³⁷Well, I am putting some wool on the ground where we thresh the wheat. If in the morning there is dew only on the wool but not on the ground, then I will know that you are going to use me to rescue Israel." ³⁸That is exactly what happened. When Gideon got up early the next morning, he squeezed the wool and wrung enough dew out of it to fill a bowl with water. ³⁹Then Gideon said to God, "Don't be angry with me; let me speak just once more. Please let me make one more test with the wool. This time let the wool be dry, and the ground be

6.25 *bull and another bull seven years old*; or *bull, the seven-year-old one.*
6.26 *the second bull*; or *the bull.*
6.32 *Jerubbaal*: This name in Hebrew means "Let Baal defend himself."

JUDGES 6, 7

289

Judges
....

Ruth
1 Sam.
2 Sam.
1 Kings
2 Kings

wet." ⁴⁰ That night God did that very thing. The next morning the wool was dry, but the ground was wet with dew.

Gideon Defeats the Midianites

7 One day Gideon and all his men got up early and camped beside the Spring of Harod. The Midianite camp was in the valley to the north of them by Moreh Hill.

² The LORD said to Gideon, "The men you have are too many for me to give them victory over the Midianites. They might think that they had won by themselves, and so give me no credit. ³ Announce to the people, 'Anyone who is afraid should go back home, and we will stay here at Mount Gilead.'" So 22,000 went back, but 10,000 stayed.

⁴ Then the LORD said to Gideon, "You still have too many men. Take them down to the water, and I will separate them for you there. If I tell you a man should go with you, he will go. If I tell you a man should not go with you, he will not go." ⁵ Gideon took the men down to the water, and the LORD said to him, "Separate everyone who laps up the water with his tongue like a dog, from everyone who gets down on his knees to drink." ⁶ There were 300 men who scooped up water in their hands and lapped it; all the others got down on their knees to drink. ⁷ The LORD said to Gideon, "I will rescue you and give you victory over the Midianites with the 300 men who lapped the water. Tell everyone else to go home." ⁸ So Gideon sent all the Israelites home, except the 300, who kept all the supplies and trumpets. The Midianite camp was below them in the valley.

⁹ That night the LORD commanded Gideon, "Get up and attack the camp; I am giving you victory over it. ¹⁰ But if you are afraid to attack, go down to the camp with your servant Purah. ¹¹ You will hear what they are saying, and then you will have the courage to attack." So Gideon and his servant Purah went down to the edge of the enemy camp. ¹² The Midianites, the Amalekites, and the desert tribesmen were spread out in the valley like a swarm of locusts, and they had as many camels as there were grains of sand on the seashore.

¹³ When Gideon arrived, he heard a man telling a friend about a dream. He was saying, "I dreamt that a loaf of barley bread rolled into our camp and hit a tent. The tent collapsed and lay flat on the ground."

¹⁴ His friend replied, "It's the sword of the Israelite, Gideon son of Joash! It can't mean anything else! God has given him victory over Midian and our whole army!"

¹⁵ When Gideon heard about the man's dream and what it meant, he fell to his knees and worshipped the LORD. Then he went back to the Israelite camp and said, "Get up! The LORD is giving you victory over the Midianite army!" ¹⁶ He divided his 300 men into three groups and gave each man a trumpet and a jar with a torch inside it. ¹⁷ He told them, "When I get to the edge of the camp, watch me, and do what I do. ¹⁸ When my group and I blow our trumpets, then you blow yours all round the camp and shout, 'For the LORD and for Gideon!'"

¹⁹ Gideon and his hundred men came to the edge of the camp a short while before midnight, just after the guard had been changed. Then they blew the trumpets and broke the jars they were holding, ²⁰ and the other two groups did the same. They all held the torches in their left hands, the trumpets in their right, and shouted, "A sword for the LORD and for Gideon!" ²¹ Every man stood in his place round the camp, and the whole enemy army ran

290

Judges

∴ ┈┈┈┈

Exodus

Leviticus

Num.

Deuter.

Joshua

JUDGES 7, 8

away yelling. [22] While Gideon's men were blowing their trumpets, the LORD made the enemy troops attack each other with their swords. They ran towards Zarethan as far as Beth Shittah, as far as the town of Abel Meholah near Tabbath.

[23] Then men from the tribes of Naphtali, Asher, and both parts of Manasseh were called out, and they pursued the Midianites. [24] Gideon sent messengers through all the hill country of Ephraim to say, "Come down and fight the Midianites. Hold the River Jordan and the streams as far as Bethbarah, to keep the Midianites from crossing them." The men of Ephraim were called together, and they held the River Jordan and the streams as far as Bethbarah. [25] They captured the two Midianite chiefs, Oreb and Zeeb; they killed Oreb at Oreb Rock, and Zeeb at the Winepress of Zeeb. They continued to pursue the Midianites and brought the heads of Oreb and Zeeb to Gideon, who was now east of the Jordan.

The Final Defeat of the Midianites

8 Then the men of Ephraim said to Gideon, "Why didn't you call us when you went to fight the Midianites? Why did you treat us like this?" They complained bitterly about it.

[2] But he said, "What I was able to do is nothing compared with what you have done. Even the little that you men of Ephraim did is worth more than what my whole clan has done. [3] After all, through the power of God you killed the two Midianite chiefs, Oreb and Zeeb. What have I done to compare with that?" When he said this, they were no longer so angry.

[4] By this time Gideon and his 300 men had come to the River Jordan and had crossed it. They were exhausted, but were still pursuing the enemy. [5] When they arrived at Sukkoth, he said to the men of the town, "Please give my men some loaves of bread. They are exhausted, and I am pursuing Zebah and Zalmunna, the Midianite kings." [6] But the leaders of Sukkoth said, "Why should we give your army any food? You haven't captured Zebah and Zalmunna yet." [7] So Gideon said, "All right! When the LORD has handed Zebah and Zalmunna over to me, I will beat you with thorns and briars from the desert!" [8] Gideon went on to Penuel and made the same request of the people there, but the men of Penuel gave the same answer as the men of Sukkoth. [9] So he said to them, "I am going to come back safe and sound, and when I do, I will tear your tower down!"

[10] Zebah and Zalmunna were at Karkor with their army. Of the whole army of desert tribesmen, only about 15,000 were left; 120,000 soldiers had been killed. [11] Gideon went along the road by the edge of the desert, east of Nobah and Jogbehah, and attacked the army by surprise. [12] The two Midianite kings, Zebah and Zalmunna, ran away, but he pursued them and captured them, and caused their whole army to panic.

[13] When Gideon was returning from the battle by way of Heres Pass, [14] he captured a young man from Sukkoth and questioned him. The young man wrote down for Gideon the names of the 77 leading men of Sukkoth. [15] Then Gideon went to the men of Sukkoth and said, "Remember when you refused to help me? You said that you couldn't give any food to my exhausted army because I hadn't captured Zebah and Zalmunna yet. Well, here they are!" [16] He then took thorns and briars from the desert and used them to punish the leaders of Sukkoth. [17] He also tore down the tower at Penuel and killed the men of that city.

[18] Then Gideon asked Zebah and Zalmunna, "What about the men you killed at Tabor?"

JUDGES 8, 9

291

Judges

....

Ruth

1 Sam.

2 Sam.

1 Kings

2 Kings

They answered, "They looked like you — every one of them like the son of a king."

¹⁹ Gideon said, "They were my brothers, my own mother's sons. I solemnly swear that if you had not killed them, I would not kill you." ²⁰ Then he said to Jether, his eldest son, "Go ahead, kill them!" But the boy did not draw his sword. He hesitated, because he was still only a boy.

²¹ Then Zebah and Zalmunna said to Gideon, "Come on, kill us yourself. It takes a man to do a man's job." So Gideon killed them and took the ornaments that were on the necks of their camels.

²² After that, the Israelites said to Gideon, "Be our ruler — you and your descendants after you. You have saved us from the Midianites."

²³ Gideon answered, "I will not be your ruler, nor will my son. The LORD will be your ruler." ²⁴ But he went on to say, "Let me ask one thing of you. Every one of you give me the earrings you took." (The Midianites, like other desert people, wore gold earrings.)

²⁵ The people answered, "We'll be glad to give them to you." They spread out a cloth, and everyone put on it the earrings that he had taken. ²⁶ The gold earrings that Gideon received weighed nearly twenty kilogrammes, and this did not include the ornaments, necklaces, and purple clothes that the kings of Midian wore, nor the collars that were round the necks of their camels. ²⁷ Gideon made an idol from the gold and put it in his home town, Ophrah. All the Israelites abandoned God and went there to worship the idol. It was a trap for Gideon and his family.

²⁸ So Midian was defeated by the Israelites and was no longer a threat. The land was at peace for forty years, until Gideon died.

The Death of Gideon

²⁹ Gideon went back to his own home and lived there. ³⁰ He had seventy sons, because he had many wives. ³¹ He also had a concubine in Shechem; she bore him a son, and he named him Abimelech. ³² Gideon son of Joash died at a ripe old age and was buried in the tomb of his father Joash, at Ophrah, the town of the clan of Abiezer.

³³ After Gideon's death the people of Israel were again unfaithful to God and worshipped the Baals. They made Baal-of-the-Covenant their god, ³⁴ and no longer served the LORD their God, who had saved them from all their enemies round them. ³⁵ They were not grateful to the family of Gideon for all the good that he had done for Israel.

Abimelech

9 Gideon's son Abimelech went to the town of Shechem, where all his mother's relatives lived, and told them ² to ask the men of Shechem, "Which would you prefer? To be governed by all seventy of Gideon's sons or by just one man? Remember that Abimelech is your own flesh and blood." ³ His mother's relatives talked to the men of Shechem about this for him, and the men of Shechem decided to follow Abimelech because he was their relative. ⁴ They gave him seventy pieces of silver from the temple of Baal-of-the-Covenant, and with this money he hired a bunch of worthless scoundrels to join him. ⁵ He went to his father's house at Ophrah, and there on the top of a single stone he killed his seventy brothers, Gideon's sons. But Jotham, Gideon's youngest son, hid and was not killed. ⁶ Then all the men of Shechem and Bethmillo got together and went to the sacred oak tree at Shechem, where they made Abimelech king.

JUDGES 8.22-27

We see in verse 27 that, somewhere amid Gideon's success,

– GOD SLIPPED FROM –

THE CENTRE

of his life.

When things go well for you, what is your most common reaction?

Do you think we recognise God enough when things go well? Why or why not?

Why do you think things seem so different for Gideon between verses 23 and 27?

How do we keep ourselves on track when God does something amazing for us?

292

Judges

. . . .

Exodus
Leviticus
Num.
Deuter.
Joshua

JUDGES 9

[7] When Jotham heard about this, he went and stood on top of Mount Gerizim and shouted out to them, "Listen to me, you men of Shechem, and God may listen to you! [8] Once upon a time the trees got together to choose a king for themselves. They said to the olive tree, 'Be our king.' [9] The olive tree answered, 'In order to govern you, I would have to stop producing my oil, which is used to honour gods and human beings.' [10] Then the trees said to the fig tree, 'You come and be our king.' [11] But the fig tree answered, 'In order to govern you, I would have to stop producing my good sweet fruit.' [12] So the trees then said to the grapevine, 'You come and be our king.' [13] But the vine answered, 'In order to govern you, I would have to stop producing my wine, that makes gods and human beings happy.' [14] So then all the trees said to the thorn bush, 'You come and be our king.' [15] The thorn bush answered, 'If you really want to make me your king, then come and take shelter in my shade. If you don't, fire will blaze out of my thorny branches and burn up the cedars of Lebanon.'

[16] "Now then," Jotham continued, "were you really honest and sincere when you made Abimelech king? Did you respect Gideon's memory and treat his family properly, as his actions deserved? [17] Remember that my father fought for you. He risked his life to save you from the Midianites. [18] But today you turned against my father's family. You killed his sons — seventy men on a single stone — and just because Abimelech, his son by his servant woman, is your relative, you have made him king of Shechem. [19] Now then, if what you did today to Gideon and his family was sincere and honest, then be happy with Abimelech and let him be happy with you. [20] But if not, may fire blaze out from Abimelech and burn up the men of Shechem and Bethmillo. May fire blaze out from the men of Shechem and Bethmillo and burn Abimelech up." [21] Then because he was afraid of his brother Abimelech, Jotham ran away and went to live at Beer.

[22] Abimelech ruled Israel for three years. [23] Then God made Abimelech and the men of Shechem hostile to each other, and they rebelled against him. [24] This happened so that Abimelech and the men of Shechem, who encouraged him to murder Gideon's seventy sons, would pay for their crime. [25] The men of Shechem put men in ambush against Abimelech on the mountain tops, and they robbed everyone who passed their way. Abimelech was told about this.

[26] Then Gaal son of Ebed came to Shechem with his brothers, and the men of Shechem put their confidence in him. [27] They all went out into their vineyards and picked the grapes, made wine from them, and held a festival. They went into the temple of their god, where they ate and drank and spoke scornfully of Abimelech. [28] Gaal said, "What kind of men are we in Shechem? Why are we serving Abimelech? Who is he, anyway? The son of Gideon! And Zebul takes orders from him, but why should we serve him? Be loyal to your ancestor Hamor, who founded your clan! [29] I wish I were leading this people! I would get rid of Abimelech! I would say* to him, 'Reinforce your army, come on out and fight!'"

[30] Zebul, the ruler of the city, became angry when he heard what Gaal had said. [31] He sent messengers to Abimelech at Arumah* to say, "Gaal son of Ebed and his brothers have come to Shechem, and they are not going to let you into the city. [32] Now then, you and your men should move by night and hide in the fields. [33] Get

9.29 One ancient translation I would say; Hebrew He said.
9.31 Probable text Arumah; Hebrew unclear.

JUDGES 9, 10

293

Judges

....

Ruth
1 Sam.
2 Sam.
1 Kings
2 Kings

up tomorrow morning at sunrise and make a sudden attack on the city. Then when Gaal and his men come out against you, hit them as hard as you can!"

³⁴ So Abimelech and all his men made their move at night and hid outside Shechem in four groups. ³⁵ When Abimelech and his men saw Gaal come out and stand at the city gate, they got up from their hiding places. ³⁶ Gaal saw them and said to Zebul, "Look! There are men coming down from the mountain tops!"

"Those are not men," Zebul answered. "They are just shadows on the mountains."

³⁷ Gaal said again, "Look! There are men coming down the crest of the mountain and one group is coming along the road from the oak tree of the fortune tellers!"

³⁸ Then Zebul said to him, "Where is all your big talk now? You were the one who asked why we should serve this man Abimelech. These are the men you were treating so scornfully. Go on out now and fight them." ³⁹ Gaal led the men of Shechem out and fought Abimelech. ⁴⁰ Gaal fled, and Abimelech pursued him. Many were wounded, even at the city gate. ⁴¹ Abimelech lived in Arumah, and Zebul drove Gaal and his brothers out of Shechem, so that they could no longer live there.

⁴² The next day Abimelech found out that the people of Shechem were planning to go out into the fields, ⁴³ so he took his men, divided them into three groups, and hid in the fields, waiting. When he saw the people coming out of the city, he came out of hiding to kill them. ⁴⁴ While Abimelech and his group hurried forward to guard the city gate, the other two companies attacked the people in the fields and killed them all. ⁴⁵ The fighting continued all day long. Abimelech captured the city, killed its people, tore it down, and covered the ground with salt.

⁴⁶ When all the leading men in the fort at Shechem heard about this, they sought safety in the stronghold of the temple of Baal-of-the-Covenant. ⁴⁷ Abimelech was told that they had gathered there, ⁴⁸ so he went up to Mount Zalmon with his men. There he took an axe, cut a branch off a tree, and put it on his shoulder. He told his men to be quick and do the same thing. ⁴⁹ So every man cut off a branch of a tree; then they followed Abimelech and piled the wood up against the stronghold. They set it on fire, with the people inside, and all the people of the fort died — about a thousand men and women.

⁵⁰ Then Abimelech went to Thebez, surrounded that city, and captured it. ⁵¹ There was a strong tower there, and every man and woman in the city, including the leaders, ran to it. They locked themselves in and went up to the roof. ⁵² When Abimelech came to attack the tower, he went up to the door to set the tower on fire. ⁵³ But a woman threw a millstone down on his head and fractured his skull. ⁵⁴ Then he quickly called the young man who was carrying his weapons and ordered, "Draw your sword and kill me. I don't want it said that a woman killed me." So the young man ran him through, and he died. ⁵⁵ When the Israelites saw that Abimelech was dead, they all went home.

⁵⁶ In this way God paid Abimelech back for the crime that he committed against his father in killing his seventy brothers. ⁵⁷ God also made the men of Shechem suffer for their wickedness, just as Jotham, Gideon's son, said they would when he cursed them.

Tola

10 After Abimelech's death Tola, the son of Puah and grandson of Dodo, came to free Israel. He was from the tribe of

294

Judges

·:········

Exodus
Leviticus
Num.
Deuter.
Joshua

Issachar and lived at Shamir in the hill country of Ephraim. [2] He was Israel's leader for 23 years. Then he died and was buried at Shamir.

Jair

[3] After Tola came Jair from Gilead. He led Israel for 22 years. [4] He had thirty sons who rode thirty donkeys. They had thirty cities in the land of Gilead, which are still called the villages of Jair. [5] Jair died and was buried at Kamon.

Jephthah

[6] Once again the Israelites sinned against the LORD by worshipping the Baals and the Astartes, as well as the gods of Syria, of Sidon, of Moab, of Ammon, and of Philistia. They abandoned the LORD and stopped worshipping him. [7] So the LORD became angry with the Israelites, and let the Philistines and the Ammonites conquer them. [8] For eighteen years they oppressed and persecuted all the Israelites who lived in Amorite country east of the River Jordan in Gilead. [9] The Ammonites even crossed the Jordan to fight the tribes of Judah, Benjamin, and Ephraim. Israel was in great distress.

[10] Then the Israelites cried out to the LORD and said, "We have sinned against you, for we left you, our God, and worshipped the Baals."

[11] The LORD gave them this answer: "The Egyptians, the Amorites, the Ammonites, the Philistines, [12] the Sidonians, the Amalekites, and the Maonites oppressed you in the past, and you cried out to me. Did I not save you from them? [13] But you still left me and worshipped other gods, so I am not going to rescue you again. [14] Go and cry out to the gods you have chosen. Let them rescue you when you get into trouble."

[15] But the people of Israel said to the LORD, "We have sinned. Do whatever you like, but please, save us today." [16] So they got rid of their foreign gods and worshipped the LORD; and he became troubled over Israel's distress.

[17] Then the Ammonite army prepared for battle and made camp in Gilead. The people of Israel came together and camped at Mizpah in Gilead. [18] There the people and the leaders of the Israelite tribes asked one another, "Who will lead the fight against the Ammonites? Whoever does will be the leader of everyone in Gilead."

11 Jephthah, a brave soldier from Gilead, was the son of a prostitute. His father Gilead [2] had other sons by his wife, and when they grew up, they forced Jephthah to leave home. They said to him, "You will not inherit anything from our father; you are the son of another woman." [3] Jephthah fled from his brothers and lived in the land of Tob. There he attracted a group of worthless men, and they went round with him.

[4] It was some time later that the Ammonites went to war against Israel. [5] When this happened, the leaders of Gilead went to bring Jephthah back from the land of Tob. [6] They said, "Come and lead us, so that we can fight the Ammonites."

[7] But Jephthah answered, "You hated me so much that you forced me to leave my father's house. Why come to me now that you're in trouble?"

[8] They said to Jephthah, "We are turning to you now because we want you to go with us and fight the Ammonites and lead all the people of Gilead."

[9] Jephthah said to them, "If you take me back home to fight the Ammonites and the LORD gives me victory, I will be your ruler."

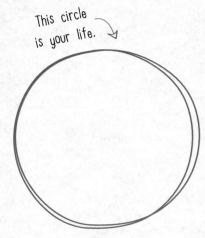

This circle is your life.

What's at the centre of it?

IS IT GOD?

295

Judges

············⋮·

Ruth
1 Sam.
2 Sam.
1 Kings
2 Kings

[10] They replied, "We agree. The LORD is our witness." [11] So Jephthah went with the leaders of Gilead, and the people made him their ruler and leader. Jephthah stated his terms at Mizpah in the presence of the LORD.

[12] Then Jephthah sent messengers to the king of Ammon to say, "What is your quarrel with us? Why have you invaded our country?" [13] The king of Ammon answered Jephthah's messengers, "When the Israelites came out of Egypt, they took away my land from the River Arnon to the River Jabbok and the River Jordan. Now you must give it back peacefully."

[14] Jephthah sent messengers back to the king of Ammon [15] with this answer: "It is not true that Israel took away the land of Moab or the land of Ammon. [16] This is what happened: when the Israelites left Egypt, they went through the desert to the Gulf of Aqaba and came to Kadesh. [17] Then they sent messengers to the king of Edom to ask permission to go through his land. But the king of Edom would not let them. They also asked the king of Moab, but neither would he let them go through his land. So the Israelites stayed at Kadesh. [18] Then they went on through the desert, going round the land of Edom and the land of Moab until they came to the east side of Moab, on the other side of the River Arnon. They made camp there, but they did not cross the Arnon because it was the boundary of Moab. [19] Then the Israelites sent messengers to Sihon, the Amorite king of Heshbon, and asked him for permission to go through his country to their own land. [20] But Sihon would not let Israel do it. He brought his whole army together, made camp at Jahaz, and attacked Israel. [21] But the LORD, the God of Israel, gave the Israelites victory over Sihon and his army. So the Israelites took possession of all the territory of the Amorites who lived in that country. [22] They occupied all the Amorite territory from the Arnon in the south to the Jabbok in the north and from the desert on the east to the Jordan on the west. [23] So it was the LORD, the God of Israel, who drove out the Amorites for his people, the Israelites. [24] Are you going to try to take it back? You can keep whatever your god Chemosh has given you. But we are going to keep everything that the LORD, our God, has given us. [25] Do you think you are any better than Balak son of Zippor, king of Moab? He never challenged Israel, did he? Did he ever go to war against us? [26] For 300 years Israel has occupied Heshbon and Aroer, and the towns round them, and all the cities on the banks of the River Arnon. Why haven't you taken them back in all this time? [27] No, I have not done you any wrong. You are doing wrong by making war on me. The LORD is the judge. He will decide today between the Israelites and the Ammonites." [28] But the king of Ammon paid no attention to this message from Jephthah.

[29] Then the Spirit of the LORD came upon Jephthah. He went through Gilead and Manasseh and returned to Mizpah in Gilead and went on to Ammon. [30] Jephthah promised the LORD: "If you give me victory over the Ammonites, [31] I will burn as an offering the first person that comes out of my house to meet me, when I come back from the victory. I will offer that person to you as a sacrifice."

[32] So Jephthah crossed the river to fight the Ammonites, and the LORD gave him victory. [33] He struck at them from Aroer to the area round Minnith, twenty cities in all, and as far as Abel Keramim. There was a great slaughter, and the Ammonites were defeated by Israel.

Jephthah's Daughter

[34] When Jephthah went back home to Mizpah, there was his daughter coming out to meet him, dancing and playing the

296

Judges

·:·········

Exodus
Leviticus
Num.
Deuter.
Joshua

JUDGES 11, 12

tambourine. She was his only child. [35] When he saw her, he tore his clothes in sorrow and said, "Oh, my daughter! You are breaking my heart! Why must it be you that causes me pain? I have made a solemn promise to the LORD, and I cannot take it back!"

[36] She said to him, "If you have made a promise to the LORD, do what you said you would do to me, since the LORD has given you revenge on your enemies, the Ammonites." [37] But she asked her father, "Do this one thing for me. Leave me alone for two months, so that I can go with my friends to wander in the mountains and grieve that I must die a virgin." [38] He told her to go and sent her away for two months. She and her friends went up into the mountains and grieved because she was going to die unmarried and childless. [39] After two months she came back to her father. He did what he had promised the LORD, and she died still a virgin.

This was the origin of the custom in Israel [40] that the young women would go away for four days every year to grieve for the daughter of Jephthah of Gilead.

Jephthah and the Ephraimites

12 The men of Ephraim prepared for battle; they crossed the River Jordan to Zaphon and said to Jephthah, "Why did you cross the border to fight the Ammonites without calling us to go with you? We'll burn the house down over your head!" [2] But Jephthah said to them, "My people and I had a serious quarrel with the Ammonites. I did call you, but you would not rescue me from them. [3] When I saw that you were not going to, I risked my life and crossed the border to fight them, and the LORD gave me victory over them. So why are you coming to fight me now?" [4] Then Jephthah brought all the men of Gilead together, fought the men of Ephraim and defeated them. (The Ephraimites had said, "You Gileadites in Ephraim and Manasseh, you are deserters from Ephraim!") [5] In order to keep the Ephraimites from escaping, the Gileadites captured the places where the Jordan could be crossed. When any Ephraimite who was trying to escape asked permission to cross, the men of Gilead would ask, "Are you an Ephraimite?" If he said, "No," [6] they would tell him to say "Shibboleth". But he would say "Sibboleth", because he could not pronounce it correctly. Then they would seize him and kill him there at one of the crossings of the Jordan. At that time 42,000 of the Ephraimites were killed.

[7] Jephthah led Israel for six years. Then he died and was buried in his home town* in Gilead.

Ibzan, Elon, and Abdon

[8] After Jephthah, Ibzan from Bethlehem led Israel. [9] He had thirty sons and thirty daughters. He gave his daughters in marriage outside the clan and brought thirty women from outside the clan for his sons to marry. Ibzan led Israel for seven years, [10] then he died and was buried at Bethlehem.

[11] After Ibzan, Elon from Zebulun led Israel for ten years. [12] Then he died and was buried at Aijalon in the territory of Zebulun.

[13] After Elon, Abdon son of Hillel from Pirathon led Israel. [14] He had forty sons and thirty grandsons, who rode on seventy donkeys. Abdon led Israel for eight years, [15] then he died and was buried at Pirathon in the territory of Ephraim in the hill country of the Amalekites.

....

12.7 One ancient translation *his home town*; Hebrew *the towns*.

The Birth of Samson

13 The Israelites sinned against the LORD again, and he let the Philistines rule them for forty years.

[2] At that time there was a man named Manoah from the town of Zorah. He was a member of the tribe of Dan. His wife had never been able to have children. [3] The LORD's angel appeared to her and said, "You have never been able to have children, but you will soon be pregnant and have a son. [4] Take care not to drink any wine or beer, or eat any forbidden food; [5] and after your son is born, you must never cut his hair, because from the day of his birth he will be dedicated to God as a Nazirite.* He will begin the work of rescuing Israel from the Philistines."

[6] Then the woman went and said to her husband, "A man of God has come to me, and he looked as frightening as the angel* of God. I didn't ask him where he came from, and he didn't tell me his name. [7] But he did tell me that I would become pregnant and have a son. He told me not to drink any wine or beer, or eat any forbidden food, because the boy is to be dedicated to God as a Nazirite as long as he lives."

[8] Then Manoah prayed to the LORD, "Please, LORD, let the man of God that you sent come back to us and tell us what we must do with the boy when he is born."

[9] God did what Manoah asked, and his angel came back to the woman while she was sitting in the fields. Her husband Manoah was not with her, [10] so she ran at once and said to him, "Look! The man who came to me the other day has appeared to me again."

[11] Manoah got up and followed his wife. He went to the man and asked, "Are you the man who was talking to my wife?"

"Yes," he answered.

[12] Then Manoah asked, "When your words come true, what must the boy do? What kind of a life must he lead?"

[13] The LORD's angel answered, "Your wife must be sure to do everything that I have told her. [14] She must not eat anything that comes from the grapevine; she must not drink any wine or beer, or eat any forbidden food. She must do everything that I have told her."

[15-16] Manoah did not know that it was the LORD's angel, so he said to him, "Please do not go yet. Let us cook a young goat for you."

But the angel said, "If I do stay, I will not eat your food. But if you want to prepare it, burn it as an offering to the LORD."

[17] Manoah replied, "Tell us your name, so that we can honour you when your words come true."

[18] The angel asked, "Why do you want to know my name? It is a name of wonder."*

[19] So Manoah took a young goat and some grain, and offered them on the rock altar to the LORD who works wonders.* [20-21] While the flames were going up from the altar, Manoah and his wife saw the LORD's angel go up towards heaven in the flames. Manoah realized then that the man had been the LORD's angel, and he and his wife threw themselves face downwards on the ground. They never saw the angel again.

[22] Manoah said to his wife, "We are sure to die, because we have seen God!"

....

13.5 *Nazirite*: A person who showed devotion to God by taking vows not to drink wine or beer or cut their hair or touch corpses (see Num 6.1–8).
13.6 *the angel*; or *an angel*.
13.18 *name of wonder*; or *mysterious name*.
13.19 Some ancient translations *who works wonders*; Hebrew *and working wonders while Manoah and his wife watched*.

298

Judges

Exodus
Leviticus
Num.
Deuter.
Joshua

JUDGES 14

Samson was gifted
and God had

BIG PLANS
FOR HIM,

but he kept using his
gifting to benefit himself
rather than to honour
God or others.

Think of one thing you're
good at. Go and use that
gift to encourage someone
else today: it might be
drawing something, playing
Fifa with someone, cooking
for them or just listening
to them.

Put down your Bible and use
what you're good at to
benefit someone else now.

²³ But his wife answered, "If the LORD had wanted to kill us, he would not have accepted our offerings; he would not have shown us all this or told us such things now."

²⁴ The woman gave birth to a son and named him Samson. The child grew and the LORD blessed him. ²⁵ And the LORD's power began to strengthen him while he was between Zorah and Eshtaol in the Camp of Dan.

Samson and the Woman from Timnah

14 One day Samson went down to Timnah, where he noticed a certain Philistine woman. ² He went back home and said to his father and mother, "There is a Philistine woman down at Timnah who has caught my attention. Get her for me; I want to marry her."

³ But his father and mother asked him, "Why do you have to go to those heathen Philistines to get a wife? Can't you find a girl in our own clan, among all our people?"

But Samson said to his father, "She is the one I want you to get for me. I like her."

⁴ His parents did not know that it was the LORD who was leading Samson to do this, for the LORD was looking for a chance to fight the Philistines. At this time the Philistines were ruling Israel.

⁵ So Samson went down to Timnah with his father and mother. As they were going through the vineyards there, he heard a young lion roaring. ⁶ Suddenly the power of the LORD made Samson strong, and he tore the lion apart with his bare hands, as if it were a young goat. But he did not tell his parents what he had done.

⁷ Then he went and talked to the woman, and he liked her. ⁸ A few days later Samson went back to marry her. On the way he left the road to look at the lion he had killed, and he was surprised to find a swarm of bees and some honey inside the dead body. ⁹ He scraped the honey out into his hands and ate it as he walked along. Then he went to his father and mother and gave them some. They ate it, but Samson did not tell them that he had taken the honey from the dead body of a lion.

¹⁰ His father went to the woman's house, and Samson gave a banquet there. This was a custom among the young men. ¹¹ When the Philistines saw him, they sent thirty young men to stay with him. ¹²⁻¹³ Samson said to them, "Let me ask you a riddle. I'll bet each one of you a piece of fine linen and a change of fine clothes that you can't tell me its meaning before the seven days of the wedding feast are over."

"Tell us your riddle," they said. "Let's hear it."

¹⁴ He said,

"Out of the eater came something to eat;
    Out of the strong came something sweet."
Three days later they had still not solved the riddle.

¹⁵ On the fourth* day they said to Samson's wife, "Trick your husband into telling us what the riddle means. If you don't, we'll set fire to your father's house and burn you with it.* You two invited us so that you could rob us, didn't you?"

¹⁶ So Samson's wife went to him in tears and said, "You don't love me! You just hate me! You asked my friends a riddle and didn't tell me what it means!"

He said, "Look, I haven't even told my father and mother. Why should I tell you?" ¹⁷ She cried about it for the whole seven days

14.15 Some ancient translations *fourth*; Hebrew *seventh*.
14.15 *set fire… you with it*; or *burn you and your family*.

JUDGES 14, 15

299

Judges

..........:.

Ruth
1 Sam.
2 Sam.
1 Kings
2 Kings

of the feast. But on the seventh day he told her what the riddle meant, for she nagged him about it so much. Then she told the Philistines. ¹⁸So on the seventh day, before Samson went into the bedroom,* the men of the city said to him,

"What could be sweeter than honey?
What could be stronger than a lion?"

Samson replied,

"If you hadn't been ploughing with my cow,
You wouldn't know the answer now."

¹⁹Suddenly the power of the LORD made him strong, and he went down to Ashkelon, where he killed thirty men, stripped them, and gave their fine clothes to the men who had solved the riddle. After that, he went back home, furious about what had happened, ²⁰and his wife was given to the man that had been his best man at the wedding.

15 Some time later Samson went to visit his wife during the wheat harvest and took her a young goat. He said to her father, "I want to go to my wife's room."

But he wouldn't let him go in. ²He said to Samson, "I really thought that you hated her, so I gave her to your friend. But her younger sister is prettier, anyway. You can have her, instead."

³Samson said, "This time I'm not going to be responsible for what I do to the Philistines!" ⁴So he went and caught 300 foxes. Two by two, he tied their tails together and put torches in the knots. ⁵Then he set fire to the torches and turned the foxes loose in the Philistine cornfields. In this way he burnt up not only the corn that had been harvested but also the corn that was still in the fields, and the olive orchards as well. ⁶When the Philistines asked who had done this, they learnt that Samson had done it because his father-in-law, a man from Timnah, had given Samson's wife to a friend of Samson's. So the Philistines went and burnt the woman to death and burnt down her father's house.*

⁷Samson told them, "So this is how you act! I swear that I won't stop until I pay you back!" ⁸He attacked them fiercely and killed many of them. Then he went and stayed in the cave in the cliff at Etam.

Samson Defeats the Philistines

⁹The Philistines came and made camp in Judah, and attacked the town of Lehi. ¹⁰The men of Judah asked them, "Why are you attacking us?"

They answered, "We came to take Samson prisoner and to treat him as he treated us." ¹¹So 3,000 men of Judah went to the cave in the cliff at Etam and said to Samson, "Don't you know that the Philistines are our rulers? What have you done to us?"

He answered, "I did to them just what they did to me."

¹²They said, "We have come here to tie you up, so that we can hand you over to them."

Samson said, "Give me your word that you won't kill me yourselves."

¹³"All right," they said, "we are only going to tie you up and hand you over to them. We won't kill you." So they tied him up with two new ropes and brought him back from the cliff.

¹⁴When he got to Lehi, the Philistines came running towards him, shouting at him. Suddenly the power of the LORD made him

---

14.18 Probable text *bedroom*; Hebrew *sun*.
15.6 *burnt the woman… house*; or *burnt the woman and her family to death*.

300

Judges

·⋮········

Exodus
Leviticus
Num.
Deuter.
Joshua

JUDGES 15, 16

strong, and he broke the ropes round his arms and hands as if they were burnt thread. [15] Then he found the jawbone of a donkey that had recently died. He bent down and picked it up, and killed a thousand men with it. [16] So Samson sang,

"With the jawbone of a donkey I killed a thousand men;
    With the jawbone of a donkey I piled them up in piles."*

[17] After that, he threw the jawbone away. The place where this happened was named Ramath Lehi.*

[18] Then Samson became very thirsty, so he called to the LORD and said, "You gave me this great victory; am I now going to die of thirst and be captured by these heathen Philistines?" [19] Then God opened a hollow place in the ground there at Lehi, and water came out of it. Samson drank it and began to feel much better. So the spring was named Hakkore;* it is still there at Lehi.

[20] Samson led Israel for twenty years while the Philistines ruled the land.

Samson at Gaza

16 One day Samson went to the Philistine city of Gaza, where he met a prostitute and went to bed with her. [2] The people of Gaza found out that Samson was there, so they surrounded the place and waited for him all night long at the city gate. They were quiet all night, thinking to themselves, "We'll wait until daybreak, and then we'll kill him." [3] But Samson stayed in bed only until midnight. Then he got up and took hold of the city gate and pulled it up — doors, posts, lock, and all. He put them on his shoulders and carried them all the way to the top of the hill overlooking Hebron.

Samson and Delilah

[4] After this, Samson fell in love with a woman named Delilah, who lived in the Valley of Sorek. [5] The five Philistine kings went to her and said, "Trick Samson into telling you why he is so strong and how we can overpower him, tie him up, and make him helpless. Each one of us will give you 1,100 pieces of silver."

[6] So Delilah said to Samson, "Please tell me what makes you so strong. If someone wanted to tie you up and make you helpless, how could he do it?"

[7] Samson answered, "If they tie me up with seven new bowstrings that are not dried out, I'll be as weak as anybody else."

[8] So the Philistine kings brought Delilah seven new bowstrings that were not dried out, and she tied Samson up. [9] She had some men waiting in another room, so she shouted, "Samson! The Philistines are coming!" But he snapped the bowstrings just as thread breaks when fire touches it. So they still did not know the secret of his strength.

[10] Delilah said to Samson, "Look, you've been making a fool of me and not telling me the truth. Please tell me how someone could tie you up."

[11] He answered, "If they tie me with new ropes that have never been used, I'll be as weak as anybody else."

[12] So Delilah got some new ropes and tied him up. Then she shouted, "Samson! The Philistines are coming!" The men were waiting in another room. But he snapped the ropes off his arms like thread.

....

15.16 *piles*: This word sounds like the Hebrew for "donkey".
15.17 *Ramath Lehi*: This name in Hebrew means "Jawbone Hill".
15.19 *Hakkore*: This name in Hebrew means "caller".

JUDGES 16

301

Judges

Ruth

1 Sam.

2 Sam.

1 Kings

2 Kings

¹³ Delilah said to Samson, "You're still making a fool of me and not telling me the truth. Tell me how someone could tie you up."

He answered, "If you weave my seven locks of hair into a loom, and make it tight with a peg, I'll be as weak as anybody else."

¹⁴ Delilah then lulled him to sleep, took his seven locks of hair, and wove them into the loom.* She made it tight with a peg and shouted, "Samson! The Philistines are coming!" But he woke up and pulled his hair loose from the loom.

¹⁵ So she said to him, "How can you say you love me, when you don't mean it? You've made a fool of me three times, and you still haven't told me what makes you so strong." ¹⁶ She kept on asking him, day after day. He got so sick and tired of her nagging him about it ¹⁷ that he finally told her the truth. "My hair has never been cut," he said. "I have been dedicated to God as a Nazirite* from the time I was born. If my hair were cut, I would lose my strength and be as weak as anybody else."

¹⁸ When Delilah realized that he had told her the truth, she sent a message to the Philistine kings and said, "Come back just once more. He has told me the truth." Then they came and brought the money with them. ¹⁹ Delilah lulled Samson to sleep in her lap and then called a man, who cut off* Samson's seven locks of hair. Then she began to torment him, for he had lost his strength. ²⁰ Then she shouted, "Samson! The Philistines are coming!" He woke up and thought, "I'll get loose and go free, as always." He did not know that the LORD had left him. ²¹ The Philistines captured him and put his eyes out. They took him to Gaza, chained him with bronze chains, and put him to work grinding at the mill in the prison. ²² But his hair started growing again.

The Death of Samson

²³ The Philistine kings met together to celebrate and offer a great sacrifice to their god Dagon. They sang, "Our god has given us victory over our enemy Samson!" ²⁴⁻²⁵ They were enjoying themselves, so they said, "Call Samson, and let's make him entertain us!"* When they brought Samson out of the prison, they made him entertain them* and made him stand between the pillars. When the people saw him, they sang praise to their god: "Our god has given us victory over our enemy, who devastated our land and killed so many of us!" ²⁶ Samson said to the boy who was leading him by the hand, "Let me touch the pillars that hold up the building. I want to lean on them." ²⁷ The building was crowded with men and women. All five Philistine kings were there, and there were about 3,000 men and women on the roof, watching Samson entertain them.*

²⁸ Then Samson prayed, "Sovereign LORD, please remember me; please, God, give me my strength just once more, so that with this one blow I can get even with the Philistines for putting out my two eyes." ²⁹ So Samson took hold of the two middle pillars holding up the building. Putting one hand on each pillar, he pushed against them ³⁰ and shouted, "Let me die with the Philistines!" He pushed with all his might, and the building fell down on the five kings and everyone else. Samson killed more people at his death than he had killed during his life.

16.14 One ancient translation *and make it tight* (in verse 13) ... *into the loom* (in verse 14); Hebrew does not have these words.
16.17 *Nazirite*: See 13.5.
16.19 Probable text *who cut off*; Hebrew *and she cut off*.
16.24–25 *make him entertain us*; or *make fun of him*.
16.24–25 *made him entertain them*; or *jeered at him*.
16.27 *entertain them*; or *and jeering at him*.

302

Judges

∴⋯⋯⋯

Exodus
Leviticus
Num.
Deuter.
Joshua

JUDGES 16–18

[31] His brothers and the rest of his family came down to get his body. They took him back and buried him between Zorah and Eshtaol in the tomb of his father Manoah. He had been Israel's leader for twenty years.

Micah's Idols

17 There was once a man named Micah, who lived in the hill country of Ephraim. [2] He said to his mother, "When someone stole those 1,100 pieces of silver from you, you put a curse on the thief. I heard you do it. Look, I have the money. I am the one who took it."

His mother said, "May the LORD bless you, my son!" [3] He gave the money back to his mother, and she said, "To stop the curse from falling on my son, I myself am solemnly dedicating the silver to the LORD. It will be used to make a wooden idol covered with silver. So now I will give the pieces of silver back to you." [4] Then he gave them back to his mother. She took 200 of the pieces of silver and gave them to a metalworker, who made an idol, carving it from wood and covering it with the silver. It was placed in Micah's house.

[5] This man Micah had his own place of worship. He made some idols and an ephod, and appointed one of his sons as his priest. [6] There was no king in Israel at that time; all the people did just as they pleased.

[7] At that same time there was a young Levite who had been living in the town of Bethlehem in Judah. [8] He left Bethlehem to find somewhere else to live. While he was travelling, he came to Micah's house in the hill country of Ephraim. [9] Micah asked him, "Where do you come from?"

He answered, "I am a Levite from Bethlehem in Judah. I am looking for somewhere to live."

[10] Micah said, "Stay with me. Be my adviser and priest, and I will give you ten pieces of silver a year, some clothes, and your food."* [11] The young Levite agreed to stay with Micah and became like a son to him. [12] Micah appointed him as his priest, and he lived in Micah's home. [13] Micah said, "Now that I have a Levite as my priest, I know that the LORD will make things go well for me."

Micah and the Tribe of Dan

18 There was no king in Israel at that time. In those days the tribe of Dan was looking for territory to claim and occupy because they had not yet received any land of their own among the tribes of Israel. [2] So the people of Dan chose five qualified* men out of all the families in the tribe and sent them from the towns of Zorah and Eshtaol with instructions to explore the land. When they arrived in the hill country of Ephraim, they stayed at Micah's house. [3] While they were there, they recognized the accent of the young Levite, so they went up to him and asked, "What are you doing here? Who brought you here?"

[4] He answered, "I have an arrangement with Micah, who pays me to serve as his priest."

[5] They said to him, "Please ask God if we are going to be successful on our journey."

[6] The priest answered, "You have nothing to worry about. The LORD is taking care of you on this journey."

17.10 Probable text *your food*; Hebrew *your food. So the Levite went.*
18.2 *qualified*; or *brave*.

[7] So the five men left and went to the town of Laish. They saw how safely the people there were living, like the Sidonians. They were a peaceful, quiet people, with no disputes with anyone; they had all they needed.* They lived far away from the Sidonians and had no dealings with any other people. [8] When the five men returned to Zorah and Eshtaol, their countrymen asked them what they had found out. [9] "Come on," they replied. "Let's attack Laish. We saw the land, and it's very good. Don't stay here doing nothing; hurry! Go on in and take it over! [10] When you get there, you will find that the people don't suspect a thing. It is a big country; it has everything a person could want, and God has given it to you."

[11] So 600 men from the tribe of Dan left Zorah and Eshtaol, ready for battle. [12] They went up and made camp west of Kiriath Jearim in Judah. That is why the place is still called Camp of Dan. [13] They went on from there and came to Micah's house in the hill country of Ephraim.

[14] Then the five men who had gone to explore the country round Laish said to their companions, "Did you know that here in one of these houses there is a wooden idol covered with silver? There are also other idols and an ephod. What do you think we should do?" [15] So they went into Micah's house, where the young Levite lived, and asked the Levite how he was getting on. [16] Meanwhile the 600 soldiers from Dan, ready for battle, were standing at the gate. [17] The five spies went straight on into the house and took the wooden idol covered with silver, the other idols, and the ephod, while the priest stayed at the gate with the 600 armed men.

[18] When the men went into Micah's house and took the sacred objects, the priest asked them, "What are you doing?"

[19] They said, "Keep quiet. Don't say a word. Come with us and be our priest and adviser. Wouldn't you rather be a priest for a whole Israelite tribe than for the family of one man?" [20] This made the priest very happy, so he took the sacred objects and went along with them.

[21] They turned round and started off, with their children, their livestock, and their belongings going ahead. [22] They had travelled a good distance from the house when Micah called his neighbours out for battle. They caught up with the men from Dan [23] and shouted at them. The men from Dan turned round and asked Micah, "What's the matter? Why all this mob?"

[24] Micah answered, "What do you mean, 'What's the matter?' You take my priest and the gods that I made, and walk off! What have I got left?"

[25] The men from Dan said, "You had better not say anything else unless you want these men to get angry and attack you. Then you and your whole family would die." [26] Then they went on. Micah saw that they were too strong for him, so he turned and went back home.

[27-28] After the men from Dan had taken the priest and the things that Micah had made, they went and attacked Laish, that town of peaceful, quiet people which was in the same valley as Bethrehob. They killed the inhabitants and burnt the town. There was no one to save them, because Laish was a long way from Sidon, and they had no dealings with any other people. The men from Dan rebuilt the town and settled down there. [29] They changed its name from Laish to Dan, after their ancestor Dan, the son of Jacob. [30] The men from Dan set up the idol to be worshipped, and

---

18.7 Probable text *They were… needed*; Hebrew unclear.

304

Judges

Exodus
Leviticus
Num.
Deuter.
Joshua

JUDGES 18, 19

JUDGES 19

THIS STORY
– IS –
AWFUL.

It's difficult to read and hard to make sense of, but as we read chapter 20 we see God's heart for justice in the things of this world which just should not be, and how one evil act can escalate with many ending up hurt.

Visit some news websites and, in the space on the opposite page,

WRITE HEADLINES THAT CATCH YOUR ATTENTION.

As you do this, pray for healing, justice and God's involvement in these stories. Pray for those who have been hurt as a result of other people's choices.

Jonathan, the son of Gershom and grandson of Moses, served as a priest for the tribe of Dan, and his descendants served as their priests until the people were taken away into exile. ³¹ Micah's idol remained there all the time that the Tent where God was worshipped remained at Shiloh.

The Levite and his Concubine

19 In those days, before Israel had a king, there was a Levite living far back in the hill country of Ephraim. He took a woman from Bethlehem in Judah to be his concubine, ² but she became angry with him, went back to her father's house in Bethlehem, and stayed there four months. ³ Then the man decided to go after her and try to persuade her to return to him. He took his servant and two donkeys with him. The woman showed the Levite into the house, and when her father saw him, he gave him a warm welcome. ⁴ The father insisted that he stay, and so he stayed for three days. The couple had their meals and spent the nights there. ⁵ On the morning of the fourth day they woke up early and got ready to go. But the woman's father said to the Levite, "Have something to eat first. It will do you good. You can go later."

⁶ So the two men sat down and ate and drank together. Then the woman's father said to him, "Please spend the night here and enjoy yourself."

⁷ The Levite got up to go, but the father urged him to stay, so he spent another night there. ⁸ Early in the morning of the fifth day he started to leave, but the woman's father said, "Eat something, please. Wait until later in the day." So the two men ate together.

⁹ When the man, his concubine, and the servant once more started to leave, the father said, "Look, it's almost evening now; you might as well stay all night. It will be dark soon; stay here and have a good time. Tomorrow you can get up early for your journey and go home."

¹⁰⁻¹¹ But the man did not want to spend another night there, so he and his concubine started on their way, with their servant and two donkeys with pack saddles. It was late in the day when they came near Jebus (that is, Jerusalem), so the servant said to his master, "Why don't we stop and spend the night here in this Jebusite city?"

¹²⁻¹³ But his master said, "We're not going to stop in a city where the people are not Israelites. We'll pass on and go a little farther and spend the night at Gibeah or Ramah." ¹⁴ So they went past Jebus and continued on their way. It was sunset when they came to Gibeah in the territory of the tribe of Benjamin. ¹⁵ They turned off the road to go and spend the night there. They went into the city and sat down in the square, but no one offered to take them home for the night.

¹⁶ While they were there, an old man came by at the end of a day's work in the fields. He was originally from the hill country of Ephraim, but he was now living in Gibeah. (The other people there were from the tribe of Benjamin.) ¹⁷ The old man noticed the traveller in the city square and asked him, "Where do you come from? Where are you going?"

¹⁸ The Levite answered, "We have been to Bethlehem in Judah, and now we are on our way home* deep in the hill country of Ephraim. No one will put us up for the night, ¹⁹ even though we have fodder and straw for our donkeys, as well as bread and

19.18 One ancient translation *home*; Hebrew *to the house of the LORD*.

Judges

....

Ruth

1 Sam.

2 Sam.

1 Kings

2 Kings

wine for my concubine and me and for my servant. We have everything we need."

20 The old man said, "You are welcome in my home! I'll take care of you; you don't have to spend the night in the square." 21 So he took them home with him and fed their donkeys. His guests washed their feet and had a meal.

22 They were enjoying themselves when all of a sudden some sexual perverts from the town surrounded the house and started beating on the door. They said to the old man, "Bring out that man that came home with you! We want to have sex with him!"

23 But the old man went outside and said to them, "No, my friends! Please! Don't do such an evil, immoral thing! This man is my guest. 24 Look! Here is his concubine and my own daughter, who is a virgin. I'll bring them out now, and you can have them. Do with them whatever you want. But don't do such an awful thing to this man!" 25 But the men would not listen to him. So the Levite took his concubine and put her outside with them. They raped her and abused her all night long and didn't stop until morning.

26 At dawn the woman came and fell down at the door of the old man's house, where her husband was. She was still there when daylight came. 27 Her husband got up that morning, and when he opened the door to go on his way, he found his concubine lying in front of the house with her hands reaching for the door. 28 He said, "Get up. Let's go." But there was no answer. So he put her body across the donkey and started on his way home. 29 When he arrived, he went into the house and got a knife. He took his concubine's body, cut it into twelve pieces, and sent one piece to each of the twelve tribes of Israel. 30 Everyone who saw it said, "We have never heard of such a thing! Nothing like this has ever happened since the Israelites left Egypt! We have to do something about this! What will it be?"

Israel Prepares for War

20 All the people of Israel from Dan in the north to Beersheba in the south, as well as from the land of Gilead in the east, answered the call. They gathered in one body in the LORD's presence at Mizpah. 2 The leaders of all the tribes of Israel were present at this gathering of God's people, and there were 400,000 foot soldiers. 3 Meanwhile the people of Benjamin heard that all the other Israelites had gathered at Mizpah.

The Israelites asked, "Tell us, how was this crime committed?" 4 The Levite whose concubine had been murdered answered, "My concubine and I went to Gibeah in the territory of Benjamin to spend the night. 5 The men of Gibeah came to attack me and surrounded the house at night. They intended to kill me; instead they raped my concubine, and she died. 6 I took her body, cut it in pieces, and sent one piece to each of the twelve tribes of Israel. These people have committed an evil and immoral act among us. 7 All of you here are Israelites. What are we going to do about this?"

8 All the people stood up together and said, "None of us, whether he lives in a tent or in a house, will go home. 9 This is what we will do: we will draw lots and choose some men to attack Gibeah.* 10 One tenth of the men in Israel will provide food for the army, and the others will go and punish Gibeah* for this immoral act that they have committed in Israel." 11 So all the men in Israel assembled with one purpose — to attack the town.

....

20.9 One ancient translation to attack Gibeah; Hebrew to Gibeah.
20.10 One ancient translation Gibeah; Hebrew Geba.

306

Judges

.::.........

Exodus

Leviticus

Num.

Deuter.

Joshua

JUDGES 20

¹² The Israelite tribes sent messengers all through the territory of the tribe of Benjamin to say, "What is this crime that you have committed? ¹³ Now hand over those perverts in Gibeah, so that we can kill them and remove this evil from Israel." But the people of Benjamin paid no attention to the other Israelites. ¹⁴ From all the cities of Benjamin they came to Gibeah to fight against the other people of Israel. ¹⁵⁻¹⁶ They called out 26,000 soldiers from their cities that day. Besides these, the citizens of Gibeah gathered 700 specially chosen men* who were left handed. Every one of them could sling a stone at a strand of hair and never miss. ¹⁷ The rest of the Israelite tribes gathered 400,000 trained soldiers.

The War against the Benjaminites

¹⁸ The Israelites went to the place of worship at Bethel, and there they asked God, "Which tribe should attack the Benjaminites first?"

The LORD answered, "The tribe of Judah."

¹⁹ So the Israelites started out the next morning and made camp near the city of Gibeah. ²⁰ They went to attack the army of Benjamin, and placed the soldiers in position facing the city. ²¹ The army of Benjamin came out of the city, and before the day was over they had killed 22,000 Israelite soldiers. ²²⁻²³ Then the Israelites went to the place of worship and mourned in the presence of the LORD until evening. They asked him, "Should we go again into battle against our brothers the Benjaminites?"

The LORD answered, "Yes."

So the Israelite army was encouraged, and they placed their soldiers in the same position as they had been the day before. ²⁴ They marched against the army of Benjamin a second time. ²⁵ And for the second time the Benjaminites came out of Gibeah, and this time they killed 18,000 trained Israelite soldiers. ²⁶ Then all the people of Israel went up to Bethel and mourned. They sat there in the LORD's presence and did not eat until evening. They offered fellowship sacrifices and burnt some sacrifices whole — all in the presence of the LORD. ²⁷⁻²⁸ God's Covenant Box was there at Bethel in those days, and Phinehas, the son of Eleazar and grandson of Aaron, was in charge of it. The people asked the LORD, "Should we go out to fight our brothers the Benjaminites again, or should we give up?"

The LORD answered, "Fight. Tomorrow I will give you victory over them."

²⁹ So the Israelites put some soldiers in hiding round Gibeah. ³⁰ Then for the third successive day they marched against the army of Benjamin and placed their soldiers in battle position facing Gibeah, as they had done before. ³¹ The Benjaminites came out to fight and were led away from the city. As before, they began killing some Israelites in the open country on the road to Bethel and on the road to Gibeah. They killed about thirty Israelites. ³² The Benjaminites said, "We've beaten them just as we did before."

But the Israelites had planned to retreat and lead them away from the city on to the roads. ³³ So when the main army of the Israelites pulled back and regrouped at Baaltamar, the men surrounding Gibeah suddenly rushed out of their hiding places in the rocky country round the city.* ³⁴ 10,000 men, specially chosen out of all Israel, attacked Gibeah, and the fighting was hard. The Benjaminites had not realized that they were about

---

20.15–16 Some ancient translations *men*; Hebrew *men. In all this number there were 700 specially chosen men.*
20.33 One ancient translation *the city* (that is, Gibeah); Hebrew *Geba.*

JUDGES 20, 21

307

Judges
........:.

Ruth
1 Sam.
2 Sam.
1 Kings
2 Kings

to be destroyed. [35] The LORD gave Israel victory over the army of Benjamin. The Israelites killed 25,100 of the enemy that day, [36] and the Benjaminites realized they were defeated.

How the Israelites Won

The main body of the Israelite army had retreated from the Benjaminites because they were relying on the men that they had put in hiding round Gibeah. [37] These men ran quickly towards Gibeah; they spread out in the city and killed everyone there. [38] The main Israelite army and the men in hiding had arranged a signal. When they saw a big cloud of smoke going up from the town, [39] the Israelites out on the battlefield were to turn round. By this time the Benjaminites had already killed the thirty Israelites. They told themselves, "Yes, we've beaten them just as we did before." [40] Then the signal appeared; a cloud of smoke began to go up from the town. The Benjaminites looked behind them and were amazed to see the whole city going up in flames. [41] Then the Israelites turned round, and the Benjaminites were thrown into a panic because they realized that they were about to be destroyed. [42] They retreated from the Israelites and ran towards the open country, but they could not escape. They were caught between the main army and the men who were now coming out of the city,* and they were destroyed. [43] The Israelites had the enemy trapped, and without stopping they pursued them as far as a point east of Gibeah, killing them as they went.* [44] 80,000 of the best Benjaminite soldiers were killed. [45] The others turned and ran towards the open country to the Rock of Rimmon. 5,000 of them were killed along the road. The Israelites continued to pursue the rest to Gidom, killing 2,000. [46] In all, 25,000 Benjaminites were killed that day — all of them brave soldiers.

[47] But 600 men were able to escape to the open country to the Rock of Rimmon, and they stayed there four months. [48] The Israelites turned back against the rest of the Benjaminites and killed them all — men, women, and children, and animals as well. They burnt every town in the area.

Wives for the Tribe of Benjamin

21 When the Israelites had gathered at Mizpah, they had made a solemn promise to the LORD: "None of us will allow a Benjaminite to marry a daughter of ours." [2] So now the people of Israel went to Bethel and sat there in the presence of God until evening. Loudly and bitterly they mourned: [3] "LORD God of Israel, why has this happened? Why is the tribe of Benjamin about to disappear from Israel?"

[4] Early the next morning the people built an altar there, offered fellowship sacrifices and burnt some sacrifices whole. [5] They asked, "Is there any group out of all the tribes of Israel that did not go to the gathering in the LORD's presence at Mizpah?" (They had taken a solemn oath that anyone who had not gone to Mizpah would be put to death.) [6] The people of Israel felt sorry for their brothers the Benjaminites and said, "Today Israel has lost one of its tribes. [7] What shall we do to provide wives for the men of Benjamin who are left? We have made a solemn promise to the LORD that we will not give them any of our daughters."

[8] When they asked if there was some group out of the tribes of Israel that had not gone to the gathering at Mizpah, they found

....

20.42 Probable text *city*; Hebrew *cities*.
20.43 Verse 43 in Hebrew is unclear.

out that no one from Jabesh in Gilead had been there; ⁹at the roll call of the army no one from Jabesh had responded. ¹⁰So the assembly sent 12,000 of their bravest men with the orders, "Go and kill everyone in Jabesh, including the women and children. ¹¹Kill all the males, and also every woman who is not a virgin." ¹²Among the people in Jabesh they found 400 young virgins, so they brought them to the camp at Shiloh, which is in the land of Canaan.

¹³Then the whole assembly sent word to the Benjaminites who were at the Rock of Rimmon and offered to end the war. ¹⁴The Benjaminites came back, and the other Israelites gave them the girls from Jabesh whom they had not killed. But there were not enough of them.

¹⁵The people felt sorry for the Benjaminites because the LORD had broken the unity of the tribes of Israel. ¹⁶So the leaders of the gathering said, "There are no more women in the tribe of Benjamin. What shall we do to provide wives for the men who are left? ¹⁷Israel must not lose one of its twelve tribes. We must find a way for the tribe of Benjamin to survive, ¹⁸but we cannot allow them to marry our daughters, because we have put a curse on anyone of us who allows a Benjaminite to marry one of our daughters."

¹⁹Then they thought, "The yearly festival of the LORD at Shiloh is coming soon." (Shiloh is north of Bethel, south of Lebonah, and east of the road between Bethel and Shechem.) ²⁰They said to the Benjaminites, "Go and hide in the vineyards ²¹and watch. When the young women of Shiloh come out to dance during the festival, you come out of the vineyards. Each of you take a wife by force from among them and take her back to the territory of Benjamin with you. ²²If their fathers or brothers come to you* and protest, you* can say, 'Please let us keep them, because we did not take them from you in battle to be our wives. And since you did not give them to us, you are not guilty of breaking your promise.' "

²³The Benjaminites did this; each of them chose a wife from the women who were dancing at Shiloh and carried her away. Then they went back to their own territory, rebuilt their towns, and lived there. ²⁴At the same time the rest of the Israelites left, and every man went back to his own tribe and family and to his own property.

²⁵There was no king in Israel at that time. All the people did just as they pleased.

21.22 One ancient translation *you*; Hebrew *us*.
21.22 Probable text *you*; Hebrew *we*.

THE BOOK OF

RUTH

WRITTEN: PROBABLY BETWEEN 500 AND 400BC

FAMILY LOYALTY · KINDNESS ·

WHAT YOU NEED TO KNOW:

Ruth is a story about family, love, kindness and redemption, which took place in the midst of the unstable time of the judges. (Head to the book of Judges to find out more about them!) Ruth, the focus of the story, was not one of the Israelites but was a foreigner. After some tragic events, she was faced with a difficult choice to make, which led her to move to a new land with her mother-in-law, Naomi. Throughout the story, we see that Ruth, despite being a non-Israelite, was accepted into God's people.

As you read the story of Ruth, pick out verses that link back to these themes.

WHY READ IT?

Ruth gives us hope that even when circumstances are tough, like they were in the time of the judges, kindness and loyalty can still come out on top - through the courageous actions of ordinary people.

LIST THE ACTS OF KINDNESS OR COMPASSION THAT RUTH & BOAZ SHOWED.

_____
_____
_____
_____
_____

1200BC

RUTH AND NAOMI GO TO BETHLEHEM

RUTH MARRIES BOAZ

310

Ruth

.·: ....

Leviticus

Num.

Deuter.

Joshua

Judges

RUTH 1

RUTH 1.16-18

Imagine you're Ruth. Your spouse has died and your life has been

- TURNED -
UPSIDE-DOWN.

These are your two choices: go back home to people who love you or go somewhere completely foreign, to a different culture where you only know one person (Naomi). What would you do? Why do you think Ruth made the choice she did?

write some thoughts here

Elimelech and his Family Move to Moab

1 ¹⁻² Long ago, in the days before Israel had a king, there was a famine in the land. So a man named Elimelech, who belonged to the clan of Ephrath and who lived in Bethlehem in Judah, went with his wife Naomi and their two sons Mahlon and Chilion to live for a while in the country of Moab. While they were living there, ³ Elimelech died, and Naomi was left alone with her two sons, ⁴ who married Moabite women, Orpah and Ruth. About ten years later ⁵ Mahlon and Chilion also died, and Naomi was left all alone, without husband or sons.

Naomi and Ruth Return to Bethlehem

⁶ Some time later Naomi heard that the LORD had blessed his people by giving them a good harvest; so she got ready to leave Moab with her daughters-in-law. ⁷ They started out together to go back to Judah, but on the way ⁸ she said to them, "Go back home and stay with your mothers. May the LORD be as good to you as you have been to me and to those who have died. ⁹ And may the LORD make it possible for each of you to marry again and have a home."

So Naomi kissed them goodbye. But they started crying ¹⁰ and said to her, "No! We will go with you to your people."

¹¹ "You must go back, my daughters," Naomi answered. "Why do you want to come with me? Do you think I could have sons again for you to marry? ¹² Go back home, for I am too old to get married again. Even if I thought there was still hope, and so got married tonight and had sons, ¹³ would you wait until they had grown up? Would this keep you from marrying someone else? No, my daughters, you know that's impossible. The LORD has turned against me, and I feel very sorry for you."*

¹⁴ Again they started crying. Then Orpah kissed her mother-in-law goodbye and went back home,* but Ruth held on to her. ¹⁵ So Naomi said to her, "Ruth, your sister-in-law has gone back to her people and to her god.* Go back home with her."

¹⁶ But Ruth answered, "Don't ask me to leave you! Let me go with you. Wherever you go, I will go; wherever you live, I will live. Your people will be my people, and your God will be my God. ¹⁷ Wherever you die, I will die, and that is where I will be buried. May the LORD's worst punishment come upon me if I let anything but death* separate me from you!"

¹⁸ When Naomi saw that Ruth was determined to go with her, she said nothing more.

¹⁹ They went on until they came to Bethlehem. When they arrived, the whole town got excited, and the women there exclaimed, "Is this really Naomi?"

²⁰ "Don't call me Naomi," she answered; "call me Marah,* because Almighty God has made my life bitter. ²¹ When I left here, I had plenty, but the LORD has brought me back without a thing. Why call me Naomi when the LORD Almighty has condemned me and sent me trouble?"

²² This, then, was how Naomi came back from Moab with Ruth, her Moabite daughter-in-law. The barley harvest was just beginning when they arrived in Bethlehem.

....

1.13 *sorry for you*; or *bitter about what has happened to you*.
1.14 One ancient translation *and went back home*; Hebrew does not have these words.
1.15 *god*; or *gods*.
1.17 *anything but death*; or *even death*.
1.20 *Naomi… Marah*: In Hebrew Naomi means "pleasant" and Marah means "bitter".

RUTH 2

311

Ruth

1 Sam.
2 Sam.
1 Kings
2 Kings
1 Chron.

Ruth Works in the Field of Boaz

2 Naomi had a relative named Boaz, a rich and influential man who belonged to the family of her husband Elimelech. [2] One day Ruth said to Naomi, "Let me go to the fields to gather the corn that the harvest workers leave. I am sure to find someone who will let me work with him."

Naomi answered, "Go ahead, my daughter."

[3] So Ruth went out to the fields and walked behind the workers, picking up the corn which they left. It so happened that she was in a field that belonged to Boaz.

[4] Some time later Boaz himself arrived from Bethlehem and greeted the workers. "The LORD be with you!" he said.

"The LORD bless you!" they answered.

[5] Boaz asked the man in charge, "Who is that young woman?"

[6] The man answered, "She is the young woman from Moab who came back with Naomi. [7] She asked me to let her follow the workers and pick up the corn. She has been working since early morning and has just now stopped to rest for a while under the shelter."

[8] Then Boaz said to Ruth, "Let me give you some advice. Don't pick up corn anywhere except in this field. Work with the women here; [9] watch them to see where they are reaping and stay with them. I have ordered my men not to molest you. And whenever you are thirsty, go and drink from the water jars that they have filled."

[10] Ruth bowed down with her face touching the ground, and said to Boaz, "Why should you be so concerned about me? Why should you be so kind to a foreigner?"

[11] Boaz answered, "I have heard about everything that you have done for your mother-in-law since your husband died. I know how you left your father and mother and your own country and how you came to live among a people you had never known before. [12] May the LORD reward you for what you have done. May you have a full reward from the LORD God of Israel, to whom you have come for protection!"

[13] Ruth answered, "You are very kind* to me, sir. You have made me feel better by speaking gently to me, even though I am not the equal of one of your servants."

[14] At mealtime Boaz said to Ruth, "Come and have a piece of bread, and dip it in the sauce." So she sat with the workers, and Boaz passed some roasted grain to her. She ate until she was satisfied, and she still had some food left over. [15-16] After she had left to go on picking up corn, Boaz ordered the workers, "Let her pick it up even where the bundles are lying, and don't say anything to stop her. Besides that, pull out some corn from the bundles and leave it for her to pick up."

[17] So Ruth went on gathering corn in the field until evening, and when she had beaten it out, she found she had nearly ten kilogrammes. [18] She took the corn back into town and showed her mother-in-law how much she had gathered. She also gave her the food left over from the meal. [19] Naomi asked her, "Where did you gather all this? Whose field have you been working in? May God bless the man who took an interest in you!"

So Ruth told Naomi that she had been working in a field belonging to a man named Boaz.

[20] "May the LORD bless Boaz!" Naomi exclaimed. "The LORD always keeps his promises to the living and the dead." And she went on, "That man is a close relative of ours, one of those responsible for taking care of us."

RUTH 2.3

Go back to Leviticus and read chapter 23 verse 22. Ruth is benefiting from this law in practice, as someone who is both

FOREIGN
AND POOR.

Think about something you could do to leave extra for those who have little - for example, putting aside some pocket money each month to donate to charity.

2.13 *You are very kind*; or *Please be kind*.

312

Ruth
∴∙········

Leviticus
Num.
Deuter.
Joshua
Judges

RUTH 2–4

²¹Then Ruth said, "Best of all, he told me to keep picking up corn with his workers until they finish the harvest."

²²Naomi said to Ruth, "Yes, my daughter, it will be better for you to work with the women in Boaz' field. You might be molested if you went to someone else's field." ²³So Ruth worked with them and gathered corn until all the barley and wheat had been harvested. And she continued to live with her mother-in-law.

Ruth Finds a Husband

3 Some time later Naomi said to Ruth, "I must find a husband for you, so that you will have a home of your own. ²Remember that this man Boaz, whose women you have been working with, is our relative. Now listen. This evening he will be threshing the barley. ³So wash yourself, put on some perfume, and get dressed in your best clothes. Then go where he is threshing, but don't let him know you are there until he has finished eating and drinking. ⁴Be sure to notice where he lies down, and after he falls asleep, go and lift the covers and lie down at his feet. He will tell you what to do."

⁵Ruth answered, "I will do everything you say."

⁶So Ruth went to the threshing place and did just what her mother-in-law had told her. ⁷When Boaz had finished eating and drinking, he was in a good mood. He went to the pile of barley and lay down to sleep. Ruth slipped over quietly, lifted the covers and lay down at his feet. ⁸During the night he woke up suddenly, turned over, and was surprised to find a woman lying at his feet. ⁹"Who are you?" he asked.

"It's Ruth, sir," she answered. "Because you are a close relative, you are responsible for taking care of me. So please marry me."

¹⁰"The LORD bless you," he said. "You are showing even greater family loyalty in what you are doing now than in what you did for your mother-in-law. You might have gone looking for a young man, either rich or poor, but you didn't. ¹¹Now don't worry, Ruth. I will do everything you ask; as everyone in town knows, you are a fine woman. ¹²It is true that I am a close relative and am responsible for you, but there is a man who is a closer relative than I am. ¹³Stay here the rest of the night, and in the morning we will find out whether or not he will take responsibility for you. If so, well and good; if not, then I swear by the living LORD that I will take the responsibility. Now lie down and stay here till morning."

¹⁴So she lay there at his feet, but she got up before it was light enough for her to be seen, because Boaz did not want anyone to know that she had been there. ¹⁵Boaz said to her, "Take off your cloak and spread it out here." She did, and he poured out nearly twenty kilogrammes of barley and helped her to lift it on her shoulder. Then she returned to the town with it. ¹⁶When she arrived home, her mother-in-law asked her, "How did you get on, my daughter?"

Ruth told her everything that Boaz had done for her. ¹⁷She added, "He told me I must not come back to you empty-handed, so he gave me all this barley."

¹⁸Naomi said to her, "Now be patient, Ruth, until you see how this all turns out. Boaz will not rest today until he settles the matter."

Boaz Marries Ruth

4 Boaz went to the meeting place at the town gate and sat down there. Then Elimelech's nearest relative, the man whom Boaz had mentioned, came by, and Boaz called to him, "Come

RUTH 3.9

There was a law in these days that said

• IF A MAN •

DIED,

leaving his wife without a child, then his brother would marry her and take care of her. As a close relative of Ruth, Boaz had a responsibility to look after her in this way.

RUTH 4

313

Ruth
..........:

1 Sam.
2 Sam.
1 Kings
2 Kings
1 Chron.

over here, my friend, and sit down." So he went over and sat down. [2] Then Boaz got ten of the leaders of the town and asked them to sit down there too. When they were seated, [3] he said to his relative, "Now that Naomi has come back from Moab, she wants to sell the field that belonged to our relative Elimelech, [4] and I think you ought to know about it. Now then, if you want it, buy it in the presence of these men sitting here. But if you don't want it, say so, because the right to buy it belongs first to you and then to me."

The man said, "I will buy it."

[5] Boaz said, "Very well, but if you buy the field from Naomi, then you are also buying Ruth,* the Moabite widow, so that the field will stay in the dead man's family."

[6] The man answered, "In that case I will give up my right to buy the field, because it would mean that my own children would not inherit it. You buy it; I would rather not."

[7] Now in those days, to settle a sale or an exchange of property, it was the custom for the seller to take off his sandal and give it to the buyer. In this way the Israelites showed that the matter was settled.

[8] So when the man said to Boaz, "You buy it," he took off his sandal and gave it to Boaz.* [9] Then Boaz said to the leaders and all the others there, "You are all witnesses today that I have bought from Naomi everything that belonged to Elimelech and to his sons Chilion and Mahlon. [10] In addition, Ruth the Moabite, Mahlon's widow, becomes my wife. This will keep the property in the dead man's family, and his family line will continue among his people and in his town. You are witnesses to this today."

[11] The leaders and the others said, "Yes, we are witnesses. May the LORD make your wife become like Rachel and Leah, who bore many children to Jacob. May you become rich in the clan of Ephrath and famous in Bethlehem. [12] May the children that the LORD will give you by this young woman make your family like the family of Perez, the son of Judah and Tamar."

Boaz and his Descendants

[13] So Boaz took Ruth home as his wife. The LORD blessed her, and she became pregnant and had a son. [14] The women said to Naomi, "Praise the LORD! He has given you a grandson today to take care of you. May the boy become famous in Israel! [15] Your daughter-in-law loves you, and has done more for you than seven sons. And now she has given you a grandson, who will bring new life to you and give you security in your old age." [16] Naomi took the child, held him close,* and took care of him.

[17] The women of the neighbourhood named the boy Obed. They told everyone, "A son has been born to Naomi!"

Obed became the father of Jesse, who was the father of David.

[18-22] This is the family line from Perez to David: Perez, Hezron, Ram, Amminadab, Nahshon, Salmon, Boaz, Obed, Jesse, David.

....

4.5 Some ancient translations *Naomi... Ruth*; Hebrew *Naomi and from Ruth.*
4.8 One ancient translation *and gave it to Boaz*; Hebrew does not have these words.
4.16 *held him close*; or *adopted him*.

THE BOOK OF

1 SAMUEL

WRITTEN: PROBABLY 600-400BC
(USING STORIES FROM A MUCH EARLIER TIME)

FIND A GREEN PEN. AS YOU READ THROUGH 1 SAMUEL, USE YOUR GREEN PEN TO MARK OUT STORIES IN WHICH FOLLOWING GOD'S WAY OF DOING THINGS WAS MORE SUCCESSFUL THAN CHOOSING WHAT MIGHT HAVE MADE SENSE TO HUMANS.

WHAT YOU NEED TO KNOW:

This book is set between the time of the judges and the time when kings began to rule in Israel. Here we are introduced to Samuel, who was the final judge and a prophet (someone used by God to speak to the nation). The Israelites went to Samuel to ask for a king. Neither Samuel nor God was keen on this idea, as God was intended to be Israel's only king. However, God allowed their request and Saul became their first king.

The Israelites were a bit behind other nations in the way they lived at this time - their main enemies, the Philistines, were cultured, had better technology and were rich. But the most important thing is not money or power, but having a strong desire to follow God's ways. When Saul messed up, it was David, 'the kind of man God wants', who replaced him as king.

WHY READ IT?

There are some amazing stories in this book. Through them we see how easily we can make decisions, one choice at a time, that take us away from God. (For us, that might mean choices about who we spend the most time with, or what places we visit.) But there is always a way back to God. Here we see that people who follow him closely can beat all the odds, whether they're up against power, wealth, birth, opportunity or even popular opinion.

David was the second king of Israel and his rise to power shaped him into the king, leader and person that God wanted him to become.

NOTE HERE

some of the character-building and character-defining moments from his life and the character qualities they will have built.

_____
_____
_____
_____
_____
_____
_____

PROPHET
SAMUEL

DAVID FIGHTS
GOLIATH

SAUL DI

KING SAUL

SAMUEL DIES

Elkanah and his Family at Shiloh

1 There was a man named Elkanah, from the tribe of Ephraim, who lived in the town of Ramah in the hill country of Ephraim. He was the son of Jeroham and grandson of Elihu, and belonged to the family of Tohu, a part of the clan of Zuph. ²Elkanah had two wives, Hannah and Peninnah. Peninnah had children, but Hannah had none. ³Every year Elkanah went from Ramah to worship and offer sacrifices to the LORD Almighty at Shiloh, where Hophni and Phinehas, the two sons of Eli, were priests of the LORD. ⁴Each time Elkanah offered his sacrifice, he would give one share of the meat to Peninnah and one share to each of her children. ⁵And even though he loved Hannah very much he would give her only one share, because* the LORD had kept her from having children. ⁶Peninnah, her rival, would torment and humiliate her, because the LORD had kept her childless. ⁷This went on year after year; whenever they went to the house of the LORD, Peninnah would upset Hannah so much that she would cry and refuse to eat anything. ⁸Her husband Elkanah would ask her, "Hannah, why are you crying? Why won't you eat? Why are you always so sad? Don't I mean more to you than ten sons?"

Hannah and Eli

⁹⁻¹⁰One day, after they had finished their meal in the house of the LORD at Shiloh, Hannah got up. She was deeply distressed, and she cried bitterly as she prayed to the LORD. Meanwhile, Eli the priest was sitting in his place by the door. ¹¹Hannah made a solemn promise: "Almighty LORD, look at me, your servant! See my trouble and remember me! Don't forget me! If you give me a son, I promise that I will dedicate him to you for his whole life and that he will never have his hair cut."*

¹²Hannah continued to pray to the LORD for a long time, and Eli watched her lips. ¹³She was praying silently; her lips were moving, but she made no sound. So Eli thought that she was drunk, ¹⁴and said to her, "Stop making a drunken show of yourself! Stop your drinking and sober up!"

¹⁵"No, I'm not drunk, sir," she answered. "I haven't been drinking! I am desperate, and I have been praying, pouring out my troubles to the LORD. ¹⁶Don't think I am a worthless woman. I have been praying like this because I'm so miserable."

¹⁷"Go in peace," Eli said, "and may the God of Israel give you what you have asked him for."

¹⁸"May you always think kindly of me," she replied. Then she went away, ate some food, and was no longer sad.

Samuel's Birth and Dedication

¹⁹The next morning Elkanah and his family got up early, and after worshipping the LORD, they went back home to Ramah. Elkanah had intercourse with his wife Hannah, and the LORD answered her prayer. ²⁰So it was that she became pregnant and gave birth to a son. She named him Samuel,* and explained, "I asked the LORD for him."

²¹The time came again for Elkanah and his family to go to Shiloh and offer to the LORD the yearly sacrifice and the special sacrifice he had promised. ²²But this time Hannah did not go. She

---

1.5 *And... because*; or *To Hannah, however, he would give a special share, because he loved her very much, even though.*
1.11 *never have his hair cut*: A sign of dedication to the LORD (see Num 6.5).
1.20 *Samuel*: This name, which in Hebrew means "name of God", is here related to the Hebrew verb for "ask".

316

1 Sam.

Num.
Deuter.
Joshua
Judges
Ruth

1 SAMUEL 1, 2

1 SAMUEL 2

Hannah's greatest dream was to have a son, and when her

DREAM
— CAME —
TRUE

she gave him back to God.

In the space on these pages, write a **LETTER TO GOD** outlining some of your dreams for your life. Spend some time praying over them and hand them back to God.

_____

_____

_____

_____

_____

_____

_____

told her husband, "As soon as the child is weaned, I will take him to the house of the LORD, where he will stay all his life."

23 Elkanah answered, "All right, do whatever you think best; stay at home until you have weaned him. And may the LORD make your* promise come true." So Hannah stayed at home and nursed her child.

24 After she had weaned him, she took him to Shiloh, taking along a three-year-old bull,* ten kilogrammes of flour, and a leather bag full of wine. She took Samuel, young as he was, to the house of the LORD at Shiloh. 25 After they had killed the bull, they took the child to Eli. 26 Hannah said to him, "Excuse me, sir. Do you remember me? I am the woman you saw standing here, praying to the LORD. 27 I asked him for this child, and he gave me what I asked for. 28 So I am dedicating him to the LORD. As long as he lives, he will belong to the LORD."

Then they* worshipped the LORD there.

Hannah's Prayer

2 Hannah prayed:
"The LORD has filled my heart with joy;
　　how happy I am because of what he has done!
I laugh at my enemies;
　　how joyful I am because God has helped me!

2 "No one is holy like the LORD;
　　there is none like him,
　　no protector like our God.
3 Stop your loud boasting;
　　silence your proud words.
For the LORD is a God who knows,
　　and he judges all that people do.
4 The bows of strong soldiers are broken,
　　but the weak grow strong.
5 The people who once were well fed
　　now hire themselves out to get food,
　　but the hungry are hungry no more.
The childless wife has borne seven children,
　　but the mother of many is left with none.
6 The LORD kills and restores to life;
　　he sends people to the world of the dead
　　and brings them back again.
7 He makes some poor and others rich;
　　he humbles some and makes others great.
8 He lifts the poor from the dust
　　and raises the needy from their misery.
He makes them companions of princes
　　and puts them in places of honour.
The foundations of the earth belong to the LORD;
　　on them he has built the world.

9 "He protects the lives of his faithful people,
　　but the wicked disappear in darkness;
　　a man does not triumph by his own strength.
10 The LORD's enemies will be destroyed;
　　he will thunder against them from heaven.

....

1.23 Some ancient translations *your*; Hebrew *his*.
1.24 Some ancient translations *a three-year-old bull*; Hebrew *three bulls*.
1.28 Some ancient translations *they*; Hebrew *he*.

The Lord will judge the whole world;
    he will give power to his king,
    he will make his chosen king victorious."

¹¹ Then Elkanah went back home to Ramah, but the boy Samuel stayed in Shiloh and served the Lord under the priest Eli.

The Sons of Eli

¹² The sons of Eli were scoundrels. They paid no attention to the Lord ¹³ or to the regulations concerning what the priests could demand from the people. Instead, when anyone was offering a sacrifice, the priest's servant would come with a three-pronged fork. While the meat was still cooking, ¹⁴ he would stick the fork into the cooking pot, and whatever the fork brought out belonged to the priest. All the Israelites who came to Shiloh to offer sacrifices were treated like this. ¹⁵ In addition, even before the fat was taken off and burnt, the priest's servant would come and say to the one offering the sacrifice, "Give me some meat for the priest to roast; he won't accept boiled meat from you, only raw meat."

¹⁶ If the person answered, "Let us do what is right and burn the fat first; then take what you want," the priest's servant would say, "No! Give it to me now! If you don't, I will have to take it by force!"

¹⁷ This sin of the sons of Eli was extremely serious in the Lord's sight, because they treated the offerings to the Lord with such disrespect.

Samuel at Shiloh

¹⁸ In the meantime the boy Samuel continued to serve the Lord, wearing a sacred linen apron. ¹⁹ Each year his mother would make a little robe and take it to him when she accompanied her husband to offer the yearly sacrifice. ²⁰ Then Eli would bless Elkanah and his wife, and say to Elkanah, "May the Lord give you other children by this woman to take the place of the one you dedicated to him."

After that they would go back home.

²¹ The Lord did bless Hannah, and she had three more sons and two daughters. The boy Samuel grew up in the service of the Lord.

Eli and his Sons

²² Eli was now very old. He kept hearing about everything his sons were doing to the Israelites and that they were even sleeping with the women who worked at the entrance to the Tent of the Lord's presence. ²³ So he said to them, "Why are you doing these things? Everybody tells me about the evil you are doing. ²⁴ Stop it, my sons! This is an awful thing the people of the Lord are talking about! ²⁵ If anyone sins against someone else, God can defend him; but who can defend someone who sins against the Lord?"

But they would not listen to their father, for the Lord had decided to kill them.

²⁶ The boy Samuel continued to grow and to gain favour both with the Lord and with people.

The Prophecy against Eli's Family

²⁷ A prophet came to Eli with this message from the Lord: "When your ancestor Aaron and his family were slaves of the king of Egypt, I revealed myself to Aaron. ²⁸ From all the tribes of Israel I chose his family to be my priests, to serve at the altar, to burn the incense, and to wear the ephod to consult me. And I gave them the right to keep a share of the sacrifices burnt on the altar.

1 Sam.

2 Sam.
1 Kings
2 Kings
1 Chron.
2 Chron.

318

1 Sam.

∴ ⋯⋯⋯

Num.
Deuter.
Joshua
Judges
Ruth

1 SAMUEL 2, 3

²⁹Why, then, do you look with greed* at the sacrifices and offerings which I require from my people? Why, Eli, do you honour your sons more than me by letting them fatten themselves on the best parts of all the sacrifices my people offer to me? ³⁰I, the LORD God of Israel, promised in the past that your family and your clan would serve me as priests for all time. But now I say that I won't have it any longer! Instead, I will honour those who honour me, and I will treat with contempt those who despise me. ³¹Listen, the time is coming when I will kill all the young men in your family and your clan, so that no man in your family will live to be old. ³²You will be troubled and look with envy* on all the blessings I will give to the other people of Israel, but no one in your family will ever again live to old age. ³³Yet I will keep one of your descendants alive, and he will serve me as priest. But he* will become blind and lose all hope, and all your other descendants will die a violent death. ³⁴When your two sons Hophni and Phinehas both die on the same day, this will show you that everything I have said will come true. ³⁵I will choose a priest who will be faithful to me and do everything I want him to. I will give him descendants, who will always serve in the presence of my chosen king. ³⁶Any of your descendants who survive will have to go to that priest and ask him for money and food, and beg to be allowed to help the priests, in order to have something to eat."

The LORD Appears to Samuel

3 In those days, when the boy Samuel was serving the LORD under the direction of Eli, there were very few messages from the LORD, and visions from him were quite rare. ²One night Eli, who was now almost blind, was sleeping in his own room; ³Samuel was sleeping in the sanctuary, where the sacred Covenant Box was. Before dawn, while the lamp was still burning, ⁴the LORD called Samuel. He answered, "Yes, sir!" ⁵and ran to Eli and said, "You called me, and here I am."

But Eli answered, "I didn't call you; go back to bed." So Samuel went back to bed.

⁶⁻⁷The LORD called Samuel again. The boy did not know that it was the LORD, because the LORD had never spoken to him before. So he got up, went to Eli, and said, "You called me, and here I am."

But Eli answered, "My son, I didn't call you; go back to bed."

⁸The LORD called Samuel a third time; he got up, went to Eli, and said, "You called me, and here I am."

Then Eli realized that it was the LORD who was calling the boy, ⁹so he said to him, "Go back to bed; and if he calls you again, say, 'Speak, LORD, your servant is listening.'" So Samuel went back to bed.

¹⁰The LORD came and stood there, and called as he had before, "Samuel! Samuel!"

Samuel answered, "Speak; your servant is listening."

¹¹The LORD said to him, "Some day I am going to do something to the people of Israel that is so terrible that everyone who hears about it will be stunned. ¹²On that day I will carry out all my threats against Eli's family, from beginning to end. ¹³I have already told him* that I am going to punish his family for ever because his sons have spoken evil things against me. Eli knew

⋯⋯⋯⋯⋯⋯⋯⋯⋯⋯⋯⋯⋯⋯⋯⋯⋯⋯⋯⋯⋯⋯⋯⋯⋯⋯

2.29 One ancient translation *look with greed*; Hebrew unclear.
2.32 Probable text *look with envy*; Hebrew unclear.
2.33 One ancient translation *he*; Hebrew *you*.
3.13 One ancient translation *I have already told him*; Hebrew *I will tell him*.

1 Sam.

....

2 Sam.

1 Kings

2 Kings

1 Chron.

2 Chron.

they were doing this, but he did not stop them. [14] So I solemnly declare to the family of Eli that no sacrifice or offering will ever be able to remove the consequences of this terrible sin."

[15] Samuel stayed in bed until morning; then he got up and opened the doors of the house of the LORD. He was afraid to tell Eli about the vision. [16] Eli called him, "Samuel, my boy!"

"Yes, sir," answered Samuel.

[17] "What did the LORD tell you?" Eli asked. "Don't keep anything from me. God will punish you severely if you don't tell me everything he said." [18] So Samuel told him everything; he did not keep anything back. Eli said, "He is the LORD; he will do whatever seems best to him."

[19] As Samuel grew up, the LORD was with him and made everything that Samuel said come true. [20] So all the people of Israel, from one end of the country to the other, knew that Samuel was indeed a prophet of the LORD. [21] The LORD continued to reveal himself at Shiloh, where he had appeared to Samuel and had spoken to him. And when Samuel spoke, all Israel listened.

The Capture of the Covenant Box

4 At that time the Philistines gathered to go to war against Israel, so* the Israelites set out to fight them. The Israelites set up their camp at Ebenezer and the Philistines at Aphek. [2] The Philistines attacked, and after fierce fighting they defeated the Israelites and killed about 4,000 men on the battlefield. [3] When the survivors came back to camp, the leaders of Israel said, "Why did the LORD let the Philistines defeat us today? Let's go and bring the LORD's Covenant Box from Shiloh, so that he* will go with us and save us from our enemies." [4] So they sent messengers to Shiloh and fetched the Covenant Box of the LORD Almighty, who is enthroned above the winged creatures. And Eli's two sons, Hophni and Phinehas, came along with the Covenant Box.

[5] When the Covenant Box arrived, the Israelites gave such a loud shout of joy that the earth shook. [6] The Philistines heard the shouting and said, "Listen to all that shouting in the Hebrew camp! What does it mean?" When they found out that the LORD's Covenant Box had arrived in the Hebrew camp, [7] they were afraid, and said, "A god has come into their camp! We're lost! Nothing like this has ever happened to us before! [8] Who can save us from those powerful gods? They are the gods who slaughtered the Egyptians in the desert! [9] Be brave, Philistines! Fight like men, or we will become slaves to the Hebrews, just as they were our slaves. So fight like men!"

[10] The Philistines fought hard and defeated the Israelites, who went running to their homes. There was a great slaughter: 30,000 Israelite soldiers were killed. [11] God's Covenant Box was captured, and Eli's sons, Hophni and Phinehas, were both killed.

The Death of Eli

[12] A man from the tribe of Benjamin ran all the way from the battlefield to Shiloh and arrived there the same day. To show his grief, he had torn his clothes and put earth on his head. [13] Eli, who was very anxious about the Covenant Box, was sitting on a seat beside the road, staring. The man spread the news throughout the town, and everyone cried out in fear. [14] Eli heard the noise

....

4.1 One ancient translation *the Philistines... so*; Hebrew does not have these words.
4.3 *he*; or *it*.

320

1 Sam.

·:·········

Num.
Deuter.
Joshua
Judges
Ruth

1 SAMUEL 4, 5

and asked, "What is all this noise about?" The man hurried to Eli to tell him the news. [15] (Eli was now 98 years old and almost completely blind.) [16] The man said, "I have escaped from the battle and have run all the way here today."

Eli asked him, "What happened, my son?"

[17] The messenger answered, "Israel ran away from the Philistines; it was a terrible defeat for us! Besides that, your sons Hophni and Phinehas were killed, and God's Covenant Box was captured!"

[18] When the man mentioned the Covenant Box, Eli fell backwards from his seat beside the gate. He was so old and fat that the fall broke his neck, and he died. He had been a leader in Israel for forty years.

The Death of the Widow of Phinehas

[19] Eli's daughter-in-law, the wife of Phinehas, was pregnant, and it was almost time for her baby to be born. When she heard that God's Covenant Box had been captured and that her father-in-law and her husband were dead, she suddenly went into labour and gave birth. [20] As she was dying, the women helping her said to her, "Be brave! You have a son!" But she paid no attention and did not answer. [21] She named the boy Ichabod,* explaining, "God's glory has left Israel" — referring to the capture of the Covenant Box and the death of her father-in-law and her husband. [22] "God's glory has left Israel," she said, "because God's Covenant Box has been captured."

The Covenant Box among the Philistines

5 After the Philistines captured the Covenant Box, they carried it from Ebenezer to their city of Ashdod, [2] took it into the temple of their god Dagon, and set it up beside his statue. [3] Early next morning the people of Ashdod saw that the statue of Dagon had fallen face downwards on the ground in front of the LORD's Covenant Box. So they lifted it up and put it back in its place. [4] Early the following morning they saw that the statue had again fallen down in front of the Covenant Box. This time its head and both its arms were broken off and were lying in the doorway; only the body was left. [5] (That is why even today the priests of Dagon and all his worshippers in Ashdod step over that place and do not walk on it.)

[6] The LORD punished the people of Ashdod severely and terrified them. He punished them and the people in the surrounding territory by causing them to have tumours.* [7] When they saw what was happening, they said, "The God of Israel is punishing us and our god Dagon. We can't let the Covenant Box stay here any longer." [8] So they sent messengers and called together all five of the Philistine kings and asked them, "What shall we do with the Covenant Box of the God of Israel?"

"Take it over to Gath," they answered; so they took it to Gath, another Philistine city. [9] But after it arrived there, the LORD punished that city too and caused a great panic. He punished them with tumours which developed in all the people of the city, young and old alike. [10] So they sent the Covenant Box to Ekron, another Philistine city; but when it arrived there, the people cried out, "They have brought the Covenant Box of the God of Israel here, in order to kill us all!" [11] So again they sent for all the Philistine

1 SAMUEL 5-6

The Covenant Box represented God's own presence, so it's not surprising that Dagon, the Philistine god, ended up

BOWING
• FACE DOWN •

before the Covenant Box in his own temple! When the box was returned to the Israelites, the Philistines seemed to have a bit more respect for God and how powerful he was. However, the Israelites still didn't get it: 70 of the men thought they could look inside, forgetting that their God wasn't just another statue.

4.21 *Ichabod*: This name in Hebrew means "no glory".
5.6 *tumours*: The association of tumours with an abundance of mice suggests that this was a case of bubonic plague (see 6.5).

kings and said, "Send the Covenant Box of Israel back to its own place, so that it won't kill us and our families." There was panic throughout the city because God was punishing them so severely. [12] Even those who did not die developed tumours and the people cried out to their gods for help.

The Return of the Covenant Box

6 After the LORD's Covenant Box had been in Philistia for seven months, [2] the people called the priests and the magicians and asked, "What shall we do with the Covenant Box of the LORD? If we send it back where it belongs, what shall we send with it?"

[3] They answered, "If you return the Covenant Box of the God of Israel, you must, of course, send with it a gift to him to pay for your sin. The Covenant Box must not go back without a gift. In this way you will be healed, and you will find out why he has kept on punishing you."

[4] "What gift shall we send him?" the people asked.

They answered, "Five gold models of tumours and five gold mice, one of each for each Philistine king. The same plague was sent on all of you and on the five kings. [5] You must make these models of the tumours and of the mice that are ravaging your country, and you must give honour to the God of Israel. Perhaps he will stop punishing you, your gods, and your land. [6] Why should you be stubborn, as the king of Egypt and the Egyptians were? Don't forget how God made fools of them until they let the Israelites leave Egypt. [7] So prepare a new wagon and two cows that have never been yoked; hitch them to the wagon and drive their calves back to the barn. [8] Take the LORD's Covenant Box, put it on the wagon, and place in a box beside it the gold models that you are sending to him as a gift to pay for your sins. Start the wagon on its way and let it go by itself. [9] Then watch it go; if it goes towards the town of Beth Shemesh, this means that it is the God of the Israelites who has sent this terrible disaster on us. But if it doesn't, then we will know that he did not send the plague; it was only a matter of chance."

[10] They did what they were told: they took two cows and hitched them to the wagon, and shut the calves in the barn. [11] They put the Covenant Box in the wagon, together with the box containing the gold models of the mice and of the tumours. [12] The cows started off on the road to Beth Shemesh and headed straight towards it, without turning off the road. They were mooing as they went. The five Philistine kings followed them as far as the border of Beth Shemesh.

[13] The people of Beth Shemesh were harvesting wheat in the valley, when suddenly they looked up and saw the Covenant Box. They were overjoyed at the sight. [14] The wagon came to a field belonging to a man named Joshua, who lived in Beth Shemesh, and it stopped there near a large rock. The people chopped up the wooden wagon and killed the cows and offered them as a burnt sacrifice to the LORD. [15] The Levites lifted off the Covenant Box of the LORD and the box with the gold models in it, and placed them on the large rock. Then the people of Beth Shemesh offered burnt sacrifices and other sacrifices to the LORD. [16] The five Philistine kings watched them do this and then went back to Ekron that same day.

[17] The Philistines sent the five gold tumours to the LORD as a gift to pay for their sins, one each for the cities of Ashdod, Gaza, Ashkelon, Gath, and Ekron. [18] They also sent gold mice, one for each of the cities ruled by the five Philistine kings, both

322

1 Sam.

⫶⫶⫶⫶⫶⫶⫶

Num.
Deuter.
Joshua
Judges
Ruth

1 SAMUEL 6, 7

the fortified towns and the villages without walls. The large rock in the field of Joshua of Beth Shemesh, on which they placed the LORD's Covenant Box, is still there as a witness to what happened.

[19] The LORD killed seventy of the men of Beth Shemesh because they looked inside the Covenant Box. And the people mourned because the LORD had caused such a great slaughter among them.

The Covenant Box at Kiriath Jearim

[20] So the men of Beth Shemesh said, "Who can stand before the LORD, this holy God? Where can we send him to get him away from us?" [21] They sent messengers to the people of Kiriath Jearim to say, "The Philistines have returned the LORD's Covenant Box. Come down and fetch it."

7 So the people of Kiriath Jearim fetched the LORD's Covenant Box and took it to the house of a man named Abinadab, who lived on a hill. They consecrated his son Eleazar to be in charge of it.

Samuel Rules Israel

[2] The Covenant Box of the LORD stayed in Kiriath Jearim a long time, some twenty years. During this time all the Israelites cried to the LORD for help.

[3] Samuel said to the people of Israel, "If you are going to turn to the LORD with all your hearts, you must get rid of all the foreign gods and the images of the goddess Astarte. Dedicate yourselves completely to the LORD and worship only him, and he will rescue you from the power of the Philistines." [4] So the Israelites got rid of their idols of Baal and Astarte, and worshipped only the LORD.

[5] Then Samuel sent for all the Israelites to meet at Mizpah, saying, "I will pray to the LORD for you there." [6] So they all gathered at Mizpah. They drew some water and poured it out as an offering to the LORD and fasted that whole day. They said, "We have sinned against the LORD." (It was at Mizpah that Samuel settled disputes among the Israelites.)

[7] When the Philistines heard that the Israelites had gathered at Mizpah, the five Philistine kings started out with their men to attack them. The Israelites heard about it and were afraid, [8] and said to Samuel, "Keep praying to the LORD our God to save us from the Philistines." [9] Samuel killed a young lamb and burnt it whole as a sacrifice to the LORD. Then he prayed to the LORD to help Israel, and the LORD answered his prayer. [10] While Samuel was offering the sacrifice, the Philistines moved forward to attack; but just then the LORD thundered from heaven against them. They became completely confused and fled in panic. [11] The Israelites marched out from Mizpah and pursued the Philistines almost as far as Bethcar, killing them along the way.

[12] Then Samuel took a stone, set it up between Mizpah and Shen, and said, "The LORD has helped us all the way" — and he named it "Stone of Help". [13] So the Philistines were defeated, and the LORD prevented them from invading Israel's territory as long as Samuel lived. [14] All the cities which the Philistines had captured between Ekron and Gath were returned to Israel, and so Israel got back all its territory. And there was peace also between the Israelites and the Canaanites.

[15] Samuel ruled Israel as long as he lived. [16] Every year he would go round to Bethel, Gilgal, and Mizpah, and in these places he would settle disputes. [17] Then he would go back to his home in Ramah, where also he would serve as judge. In Ramah he built an altar to the LORD.

1 Sam.

..........:.

2 Sam.
1 Kings
2 Kings
1 Chron.
2 Chron.

The People Ask for a King

8 When Samuel grew old, he made his sons judges in Israel. [2]The elder son was named Joel and the younger one Abijah; they were judges in Beersheba. [3]But they did not follow their father's example; they were interested only in making money, so they accepted bribes and did not decide cases honestly.

[4]Then all the leaders of Israel met together, went to Samuel in Ramah, [5]and said to him, "Look, you are getting old and your sons don't follow your example. So then, appoint a king to rule over us, so that we will have a king, as other countries have." [6]Samuel was displeased with their request for a king; so he prayed to the LORD, [7]and the LORD said, "Listen to everything the people say to you. You are not the one they have rejected; I am the one they have rejected as their king. [8]Ever since I brought them out of Egypt, they have turned away from me and worshipped other gods; and now they are doing to you what they have always done to me. [9]So then, listen to them, but give them strict warnings and explain how their kings will treat them."

[10]Samuel told the people who were asking him for a king everything that the LORD had said to him. [11]"This is how your king will treat you," Samuel explained. "He will make soldiers of your sons; some of them will serve in his war chariots, others in his cavalry, and others will run before his chariots. [12]He will make some of them officers in charge of a thousand men, and others in charge of fifty men. Your sons will have to plough his fields, harvest his crops, and make his weapons and the equipment for his chariots. [13]Your daughters will have to make perfumes for him and work as his cooks and his bakers. [14]He will take your best fields, vineyards, and olive groves, and give them to his officials. [15]He will take a tenth of your corn and of your grapes for his court officers and other officials. [16]He will take your servants and your best cattle* and donkeys, and make them work for him. [17]He will take a tenth of your flocks. And you yourselves will become his slaves. [18]When that time comes, you will complain bitterly because of your king, whom you yourselves chose, but the LORD will not listen to your complaints."

[19]The people paid no attention to Samuel, but said "No! We want a king, [20]so that we will be like other nations, with our own king to rule us and to lead us out to war and to fight our battles." [21]Samuel listened to everything they said and then went and told the LORD. [22]The LORD answered, "Do what they want and give them a king." Then Samuel told all the men of Israel to go back home.

Saul Meets Samuel

9 There was a wealthy and influential man named Kish, from the tribe of Benjamin; he was the son of Abiel and grandson of Zeror, and belonged to the family of Becorath, a part of the clan of Aphiah. [2]He had a son named Saul, a handsome man in the prime of life. Saul was a head taller than anyone else in Israel and more handsome as well.

[3]Some donkeys belonging to Kish had wandered off, so he said to Saul, "Take one of the servants with you and go and look for the donkeys." [4]They went through the hill country of Ephraim and the region of Shalishah, but did not find them; so they went on through the region of Shaalim, but the donkeys were not there. Then they went through the territory of Benjamin, but still did not find them. [5]When they came into the region of Zuph, Saul

8.16 One ancient translation *cattle*; Hebrew *young men*.

1 Sam.

∴........

Num.
Deuter.
Joshua
Judges
Ruth

said to his servant, "Let's go back home, or my father might stop thinking about the donkeys and start worrying about us."

6 The servant answered, "Wait! In this town there is a holy man who is highly respected because everything he says comes true. Let's go to him, and maybe he can tell us where we can find the donkeys."

7 "If we go to him, what can we give him?" Saul asked. "There is no food left in our packs, and we haven't anything to give him, have we?"

8 The servant answered, "I have a small silver coin. I can give him that, and then he will tell us where we can find them."

9-11 Saul replied, "A good idea! Let's go." So they went to the town where the holy man lived. As they were going up the hill to the town, they met some young women who were coming out to draw water. They asked these women, "Is the seer in town?"

(At that time a prophet was called a seer, and so whenever someone wanted to ask God a question, he would say, "Let's go to the seer.")

12-13 "Yes, he is," the young women answered. "In fact, he is just ahead of you. If you hurry, you will catch up with him. As soon as you go into the town, you will find him. He arrived in town today because the people are going to offer a sacrifice on the altar on the hill. The people who are invited won't start eating until he gets there, because he has to bless the sacrifice first. If you go now, you will find him before he goes up the hill to eat."

14 So Saul and his servant went on to the town, and as they were going in, they saw Samuel coming out towards them on his way to the place of worship.

15 Now on the previous day the Lord had said to Samuel, 16 "Tomorrow about this time I will send you a man from the tribe of Benjamin; anoint him as ruler of my people Israel, and he will rescue them from the Philistines. I have seen the suffering of my people and have heard their cries for help."

17 When Samuel caught sight of Saul, the Lord said to him, "This is the man I told you about. He will rule my people." 18 Then Saul went over to Samuel, who was near the gate, and asked, "Tell me, where does the seer live?"

19 Samuel answered, "I am the seer. Go on ahead of me to the place of worship. Both of you are to eat with me today. Tomorrow morning I will answer all your questions and send you on your way. 20 As for the donkeys that were lost three days ago, don't worry about them; they have already been found. But who is it that the people of Israel want so much?* It is you — you and your father's family."

21 Saul answered, "I belong to the tribe of Benjamin, the smallest tribe in Israel, and my family is the least important one in the tribe. Why, then, do you talk like this to me?"

22 Then Samuel led Saul and his servant into the large room and gave them a place at the head of the table where the guests, about thirty in all, were seated. 23 Samuel said to the cook, "Bring the piece of meat I gave you, which I told you to set aside." 24 So the cook brought the choice piece of the leg and placed it before Saul. Samuel* said, "Look, here is the piece that was kept for you. Eat it. I saved it for you to eat at this time with the people I invited."*

9.20 who is it... much?; or who is to have the most desirable thing in Israel?
9.24 Some ancient translations Samuel; Hebrew He (that is, the cook).
9.24 Probable text I saved it... invited; Hebrew unclear.

1 Sam.
....
2 Sam.
1 Kings
2 Kings
1 Chron.
2 Chron.

So Saul ate with Samuel that day. [25]When they went down from the place of worship to the town, they made up a bed for Saul* on the roof,* [26]and he slept there.*

Samuel Anoints Saul as Ruler

At dawn Samuel called to Saul on the roof, "Get up, and I will send you on your way." Saul got up, and he and Samuel went out to the street together. [27]When they arrived at the edge of the town, Samuel said to Saul, "Tell the servant to go on ahead of us." The servant left, and Samuel continued, "Stay here a minute, and I will tell you what God has said."

10 Then Samuel took a jar of olive oil and poured it on Saul's head, kissed him, and said, "The LORD anoints you as ruler of his people Israel. You will rule his people and protect them from all their enemies. And this is the proof to you that the LORD has chosen you* to be the ruler of his people: [2]when you leave me today, you will meet two men near Rachel's tomb at Zelzah in the territory of Benjamin. They will tell you that the donkeys you were looking for have been found, so that your father isn't worried any more about them but about you, and he keeps asking, 'What shall I do about my son?' [3]You will go on from there until you come to the sacred tree at Tabor, where you will meet three men on their way to offer a sacrifice to God at Bethel. One of them will be leading three young goats, another one will be carrying three loaves of bread, and the third one will have a leather bag full of wine. [4]They will greet you and offer you two of the loaves, which you are to accept. [5]Then you will go to the Hill of God in Gibeah, where there is a Philistine camp. At the entrance to the town you will meet a group of prophets coming down from the altar on the hill, playing harps, drums, flutes, and lyres. They will be dancing and shouting. [6]Suddenly the Spirit of the LORD will take control of you, and you will join in their religious dancing and shouting and will become a different person. [7]When these things happen, do whatever God leads you to do. [8]You will go ahead of me to Gilgal, where I will meet you and offer burnt sacrifices and fellowship sacrifices. Wait there seven days until I come and tell you what to do."

[9]When Saul turned to leave Samuel, God gave Saul a new nature. And everything Samuel had told him happened that day. [10]When Saul and his servant arrived at Gibeah, a group of prophets met him. Suddenly the Spirit of God took control of him, and he joined in their ecstatic dancing and shouting. [11]People who had known him before saw him doing this and asked one another, "What has happened to the son of Kish? Has Saul become a prophet?" [12]A man who lived there asked, "How about these other prophets — who do you think their fathers are?" This is how the saying originated, "Has even Saul become a prophet?" [13]When Saul finished his ecstatic dancing and shouting, he went to the altar on the hill.

[14]Saul's uncle saw him and the servant, and he asked them, "Where have you been?"

....

9.25 One ancient translation *they made up a bed for Saul*; Hebrew *he spoke with Saul.*
9.25 *on the roof*: At that time houses had flat roofs, and it was common for people to sleep on them.
9.26 Some ancient translations *and he slept there*; Hebrew *and they got up early.*
10.1 Some ancient translations *as ruler of his people... the LORD has chosen you*; Hebrew does not have these words.

326

1 Sam.

:·········

Num.
Deuter.
Joshua
Judges
Ruth

1 SAMUEL 10, 11

"Looking for the donkeys," Saul answered. "When we couldn't find them, we went to see Samuel."

[15] "And what did he tell you?" Saul's uncle asked.

[16] "He told us that the animals had been found," Saul answered — but he did not tell his uncle what Samuel had said about his becoming king.

Saul is Acclaimed as King

[17] Samuel called the people together for a religious gathering at Mizpah [18] and said to them, "The LORD, the God of Israel, says, 'I brought you out of Egypt and rescued you from the Egyptians and all the other peoples who were oppressing you. [19] I am your God, the one who rescues you from all your troubles and difficulties, but today you have rejected me and have asked me to give you a king. Very well, then, gather yourselves before the LORD by tribes and by clans.' "

[20] Then Samuel made each tribe come forward, and the LORD picked the tribe of Benjamin. [21] Then Samuel made the families of the tribe of Benjamin come forward, and the family of Matri was picked out. Then the men of the family of Matri came forward,* and Saul son of Kish was picked out. They looked for him, but when they could not find him, [22] they asked the LORD, "Is there still someone else?"

The LORD answered, "Saul is over there, hiding behind the supplies."

[23] So they ran and brought Saul out to the people, and they could see that he was a head taller than anyone else. [24] Samuel said to the people, "Here is the man the LORD has chosen! There is no one else among us like him."

All the people shouted, "Long live the king!"

[25] Samuel explained to the people the rights and duties of a king, and then wrote them in a book, which he deposited in a holy place. Then he sent everyone home. [26] Saul also went back home to Gibeah. Some powerful men,* whose hearts God had touched, went with him. [27] But some worthless people said, "How can this fellow do us any good?" They despised Saul and did not bring him any gifts.

Saul Defeats the Ammonites

11 About a month later King Nahash of Ammon led his army against the town of Jabesh in the territory of Gilead and besieged it. The men of Jabesh said to Nahash, "Make a treaty with us, and we will accept you as our ruler."

[2] Nahash answered, "I will make a treaty with you on one condition: I will put out everyone's right eye and so bring disgrace on all Israel."

[3] The leaders of Jabesh said, "Give us seven days to send messengers throughout the land of Israel. If no one will help us, then we will surrender to you."

[4] The messengers arrived at Gibeah, where Saul lived, and when they told the news, the people started crying in despair. [5] Saul was just coming in from the field with his oxen, and he asked, "What's wrong? Why is everyone crying?" They told him what the messengers from Jabesh had reported. [6] When Saul heard this, the Spirit of God took control of him, and he became furious.

....

10.21 One ancient translation *Then the men of the family of Matri came forward*; Hebrew does not have these words.
10.26 One ancient translation *Some powerful men*; Hebrew *The army.*

1 SAMUEL 11, 12

327

1 Sam.

....

2 Sam.
1 Kings
2 Kings
1 Chron.
2 Chron.

[7]He took two oxen, cut them in pieces, and sent messengers to carry the pieces throughout the land of Israel with this warning: "Whoever does not follow Saul and Samuel into battle will have this done to his oxen!"

The people of Israel were afraid of what the LORD might do, and all of them, without exception, came out together. [8]Saul gathered them at Bezek: there were 300,000 from Israel and 30,000 from Judah. [9]They said to the messengers from Jabesh, "Tell your people that before noon tomorrow they will be rescued." When the people of Jabesh received the message, they were overjoyed [10]and said to Nahash, "Tomorrow we will surrender to you, and you can do with us whatever you wish."

[11]That night Saul divided his men into three groups, and at dawn they rushed into the enemy camp and attacked the Ammonites. By noon they had slaughtered them. The survivors scattered, each man running off by himself.

[12]Then the people of Israel said to Samuel, "Where are the people who said that Saul should not be our king? Hand them over to us, and we will kill them!"

[13]But Saul said, "No one will be put to death today, for this is the day the LORD rescued Israel." [14]And Samuel said to them, "Let us all go to Gilgal and once more proclaim Saul as our king." [15]So they all went to Gilgal, and there at the holy place they proclaimed Saul king. They offered fellowship sacrifices, and Saul and all the people of Israel celebrated the event.

Samuel Addresses the People

12 Then Samuel said to the people of Israel, "I have done what you asked me to do. I have given you a king to rule you, [2]and now you have him to lead you. As for me, I am old and grey, and my sons are with you. I have been your leader from my youth until now. [3]Here I am. If I have done anything wrong, accuse me now in the presence of the LORD and the king he has chosen. Have I taken anybody's cow or anybody's donkey? Have I cheated or oppressed anyone? Have I accepted a bribe from anyone? If I have done any of these things, I will pay back what I have taken."

[4]The people answered, "No, you have not cheated us or oppressed us; you have not taken anything from anyone."

[5]Samuel replied, "The LORD and the king he has chosen are witnesses today that you have found me to be completely innocent."

"Yes, the LORD is our witness," they answered.

[6]Samuel continued, "The LORD is the one who chose Moses and Aaron and who brought your ancestors out of Egypt. [7]Now stand where you are, and I will accuse you before the LORD by reminding you* of all the mighty actions the LORD did to save you and your ancestors. [8]When Jacob and his family went to Egypt and the Egyptians oppressed them,* your ancestors cried to the LORD for help, and he sent Moses and Aaron, who brought them out of Egypt and settled them in this land. [9]But the people forgot the LORD their God, and so he let the Philistines and the king of Moab and Sisera, commander of the army of the city of Hazor, fight against your ancestors and conquer them. [10]Then they

....

12.7 One ancient translation *by reminding you*; Hebrew does not have these words.
12.8 One ancient translation *and the Egyptians oppressed them*; Hebrew does not have these words.

328

1 Sam.

Num.
Deuter.
Joshua
Judges
Ruth

1 SAMUEL 12, 13

1 SAMUEL 12.12-25

The Israelites asked for a king (see 1 Samuel 8), but it was only God who was meant to rule them.

CUT OUT

– OR –

DRAW

some pictures of things that people have made 'kings' in our culture - things that we worship instead of God.

Stick them in the space on these pages and pray that God will show you any things in your life that you worship instead of God.

cried to the LORD for help and said, 'We have sinned, because we turned away from you, LORD, and worshipped the idols of Baal and Astarte. Rescue us from our enemies, and we will worship you!' [11] And the LORD sent Gideon, Barak,* Jephthah, and finally me. Each of us rescued you from your enemies, and you lived in safety. [12] But when you saw that King Nahash of Ammon was about to attack you, you rejected the LORD as your king and said to me, 'We want a king to rule us.'

[13] "Now here is the king you chose; you asked for him, and now the LORD has given him to you. [14] All will go well with you if you honour the LORD your God, serve him, listen to him, and obey his commands, and if you and your king follow him. [15] But if you do not listen to the LORD but disobey his commands, he will be against you and your king.* [16] So then, stand where you are, and you will see the great thing which the LORD is going to do. [17] It's the dry season, isn't it? But I will pray, and the LORD will send thunder and rain. When this happens, you will realize that you committed a great sin against the LORD when you asked him for a king."

[18] So Samuel prayed, and on that same day the LORD sent thunder and rain. Then all the people became afraid of the LORD and of Samuel, [19] and they said to Samuel, "Please, sir, pray to the LORD your God for us, so that we won't die. We now realize that, besides all our other sins, we have sinned by asking for a king."

[20] "Don't be afraid," Samuel answered. "Even though you have done such an evil thing, do not turn away from the LORD, but serve him with all your heart. [21] Don't go after* false gods; they cannot help you or save you, for they are not real. [22] The LORD has made a solemn promise, and he will not abandon you, for he has decided to make you his own people. [23] As for me, the LORD forbid that I should sin against him by no longer praying for you. Instead, I will teach you what is good and right for you to do. [24] Obey the LORD and serve him faithfully with all your heart. Remember the great things he has done for you. [25] But if you continue to sin, you and your king will be destroyed."

War against the Philistines

13 * [2] Saul picked 3,000 men, keeping 2,000 of them with him in Michmash and in the hill country of Bethel and sending 1,000 with his son Jonathan to Gibeah, in the territory of the tribe of Benjamin. The rest of the men Saul sent home.

[3] Jonathan killed the Philistine commander* in Geba, and all the Philistines heard about it. Then Saul sent messengers to call the Hebrews to war by blowing a trumpet throughout the whole country. [4] All the Israelites were told that Saul had killed the Philistine commander and that the Philistines hated them. So the people answered the call to join Saul at Gilgal.

[5] The Philistines assembled to fight the Israelites; they had 30,000 war chariots, 6,000 horsemen, and as many soldiers as there are grains of sand on the seashore. They went to Michmash, east of Bethaven, and camped there. [6] Then they launched a strong attack against the Israelites, putting them in a desperate situation. Some of the Israelites hid in caves and holes or among

12.11 Some ancient translations *Barak*; Hebrew *Bedan*.
12.15 One ancient translation *your king*; Hebrew *your ancestors*.
12.21 Some ancient translations *after*; Hebrew *because after*.
13.1 One ancient translation does not have verse 1; Hebrew has as verse 1 *Saul was… years old when he became king, and he was king of Israel for two years.* The Hebrew text is defective at two points in this verse.
13.3 *killed the Philistine commander*; or *defeated the Philistines camping*.

↖ stick them here

1 SAMUEL 13, 14

329

1 Sam.

⋯⋯⋯⋮⋯

2 Sam.
1 Kings
2 Kings
1 Chron.
2 Chron.

the rocks or in pits and wells; [7]others crossed the River Jordan into the territories of Gad and Gilead.

Saul was still at Gilgal, and the people with him were trembling with fear. [8]He waited seven days for Samuel, as Samuel had instructed him to do, but Samuel still had not come to Gilgal. The people began to desert Saul, [9]so he said to them, "Bring me the burnt sacrifices and the fellowship sacrifices." He offered a burnt sacrifice, [10]and just as he was finishing, Samuel arrived. Saul went out to meet him and welcome him, [11]but Samuel said, "What have you done?"

Saul answered, "The people were deserting me, and you had not come when you said you would; besides that, the Philistines are gathering at Michmash. [12]So I thought, 'The Philistines are going to attack me here in Gilgal, and I have not tried to win the LORD's favour.' So I felt I had to offer a sacrifice."

[13]"That was a foolish thing to do," Samuel answered. "You have not obeyed the command the LORD your God gave you. If you had obeyed, he would have let you and your descendants rule over Israel for ever. [14]But now your rule will not continue. Because you have disobeyed him, the LORD will find the kind of man he wants and make him ruler of his people."

[15]Samuel left Gilgal and went on his way. The rest of the people followed Saul as he went to join his soldiers. They went from Gilgal* to Gibeah in the territory of Benjamin. Saul inspected his troops, about 600 men. [16]Saul, his son Jonathan, and their men camped in Geba in the territory of Benjamin; the Philistine camp was at Michmash. [17]The Philistine soldiers went out on raids from their camp in three groups: one group went towards Ophrah in the territory of Shual, [18]another went towards Beth Horon, and the other one went to the border overlooking the Valley of Zeboim and the wilderness.

[19]There were no blacksmiths in Israel because the Philistines were determined to keep the Hebrews from making swords and spears. [20](The Israelites had to go to the Philistines to get their ploughs, hoes, axes, and sickles* sharpened; [21]the charge was one small coin for sharpening axes and for repairing ox goads,* and two coins for sharpening ploughs or hoes.) [22]And so on the day of battle none of the Israelite soldiers except Saul and his son Jonathan had swords or spears.

[23]The Philistines sent a group of soldiers to defend the pass of Michmash.

Jonathan's Daring Deed

14 One day Jonathan said to the young man who carried his weapons, "Let's go across to the Philistine camp." But Jonathan did not tell his father Saul, [2]who was camping under a pomegranate tree in Migron, not far from Gibeah; he had about 600 men with him. [3](The priest carrying the ephod was Ahijah, the son of Ichabod's brother Ahitub, who was the son of Phinehas and grandson of Eli, the priest of the LORD in Shiloh.) The men did not know that Jonathan had left.

[4]In the pass of Michmash, which Jonathan had to go through to get over to the Philistine camp, there were two large jagged rocks, one on each side of the pass: one was called Bozez and

13.15 Some ancient translations *on his way... went from Gilgal*; Hebrew does not have these words.
13.20 One ancient translation *sickles*; Hebrew *ploughs*.
13.21 Probable text *the charge... repairing ox goads*; Hebrew unclear.

stick them here

330

1 Sam.

⋮··········

Num.

Deuter.

Joshua

Judges

Ruth

1 SAMUEL 14

the other Seneh. [5] One was on the north side of the pass, facing Michmash, and the other was on the south side, facing Geba.

[6] Jonathan said to the young man, "Let's cross over to the camp of those heathen Philistines. Maybe the LORD will help us; if he does, nothing can keep him from giving us the victory, no matter how few of us there are."

[7] The young man answered, "Whatever you want to do,* I'm with you."

[8] "All right," Jonathan said. "We will go across and let the Philistines see us. [9] If they tell us to wait for them to come to us, then we will stay where we are. [10] But if they tell us to go to them, then we will, because that will be the sign that the LORD has given us victory over them."

[11] So they let the Philistines see them, and the Philistines said, "Look! Some Hebrews are coming out of the holes they have been hiding in!" [12] Then they called out to Jonathan and the young man, "Come on up here! We have something to tell* you!"

Jonathan said to the young man, "Follow me. The LORD has given Israel victory over them." [13] Jonathan climbed up out of the pass on his hands and knees, and the young man followed him. Jonathan attacked the Philistines and knocked them down, and the young man killed them. [14] In that first slaughter Jonathan and the young man killed about twenty men in an area of about a quarter of a hectare.* [15] All the Philistines in the countryside were terrified; the raiders and the soldiers in the camp trembled with fear; the earth shook, and there was great panic.

The Defeat of the Philistines

[16] Saul's men on watch at Gibeah in the territory of Benjamin saw the Philistines running in confusion. [17] So Saul said to his men, "Count the soldiers and find out who is missing." They did so and found that Jonathan and the young man who carried his weapons were missing. [18] "Bring the ephod* here," Saul said to Ahijah the priest. (On that day Ahijah was carrying it in front of the people of Israel.)* [19] As Saul was speaking to the priest, the confusion in the Philistine camp got worse and worse, so Saul said to him, "There's no time to consult the LORD!" [20] Then he and his men marched into battle against the Philistines, who were fighting each other in complete confusion. [21] Some Hebrews, who had been on the Philistine side and had gone with them to the camp, changed sides again* and joined Saul and Jonathan. [22] Others, who had been hiding in the hills of Ephraim, heard that the Philistines were running away, so they also joined in and attacked the Philistines, [23] fighting all the way beyond Bethaven. The LORD saved Israel that day.

Events after the Battle

[24] The Israelites were weak with hunger that day, because Saul, with a solemn oath, had given the order: "A curse be on anyone who eats any food today before I take revenge on my enemies." So nobody had eaten anything all day. [25] They all* came into

··

14.7 One ancient translation you want to do; Hebrew you want to do. Turn.
14.12 tell; or show.
14.14 Probable text in an area of about a quarter of a hectare; Hebrew unclear.
14.18 One ancient translation ephod (see 2.28); Hebrew Covenant Box.
14.18 One ancient translation On that day... Israel; Hebrew Because on that day God's Covenant Box and the people of Israel.
14.21 Some ancient translations changed sides again; Hebrew around also.
14.25 Probable text They all; Hebrew All the land.

1 SAMUEL 14

331

1 Sam.

....

2 Sam.
1 Kings
2 Kings
1 Chron.
2 Chron.

a wooded area and found honey everywhere. [26] The woods were full of honey, but no one ate any of it because they were all afraid of Saul's curse. [27] But Jonathan had not heard his father threaten the people with a curse; so he reached out with the stick he was carrying, dipped it in a honeycomb, and ate some honey. At once he felt much better. [28] But one of the men said, "We are all weak with hunger, but your father threatened us and said, 'A curse be on anyone who eats any food today.'"

[29] Jonathan answered, "What a terrible thing my father has done to our people! See how much better I feel because I ate some honey! [30] How much better it would have been today if our people had eaten the food they took when they defeated the enemy. Just think how many more Philistines they would have killed!"

[31] That day the Israelites defeated the Philistines, fighting all the way from Michmash to Aijalon. By this time the Israelites were very weak with hunger, [32] and so they rushed over to what they had captured from the enemy, took sheep and cattle, slaughtered them on the spot, and ate the meat with the blood still in it. [33] Saul was told, "Look, the people are sinning against the LORD by eating meat with the blood in it."

"You are traitors!" Saul cried out. "Roll a big stone over here* to me." [34] Then he gave another order: "Go among the people and tell them all to bring their cattle and sheep here. They are to slaughter them and eat them here; they must not sin against the LORD by eating meat with blood in it." So that night they all brought their cattle and slaughtered them there. [35] Saul built an altar to the LORD, the first one that he built.

[36] Saul said to his men, "Let's go down and attack the Philistines in the night, plunder them until dawn, and kill them all."

"Do whatever you think best," they answered.

But the priest said, "Let's consult God first."

[37] So Saul asked God, "Shall I attack the Philistines? Will you give us victory?" But God did not answer that day. [38] Then Saul said to the leaders of the people, "Come here and find out what sin was committed today. [39] I promise by the living LORD, who gives Israel victory, that the guilty one will be put to death, even if he is my son Jonathan." But no one said anything. [40] Then Saul said to them, "All of you stand over there, and Jonathan and I will stand over here."

"Do whatever you think best," they answered.

[41] Saul said to the LORD, the God of Israel, "LORD, why have you not answered me today? LORD, God of Israel, answer me by the sacred stones. If the guilt is Jonathan's or mine, answer by the Urim; but if it belongs to your people Israel,* answer by the Thummim."* The answer indicated Jonathan and Saul; and the people were cleared. [42] Then Saul said, "Decide between my son Jonathan and me." And Jonathan was indicated. [43] Then Saul asked Jonathan, "What have you done?"

Jonathan answered, "I ate a little honey with the stick I was holding. Here I am — I am ready to die."

[44] Saul said to him, "May God strike me dead if you are not put to death!"

[45] But the people said to Saul, "Will Jonathan, who won this great victory for Israel, be put to death? No! We promise by the

....

14.33 One ancient translation *here*; Hebrew *today*.
14.41 Some ancient translations *answer me by the sacred stones... your people Israel*; Hebrew does not have these words.
14.41 *Urim... Thummim*: Two stones used by the priest to determine God's will; it is not known precisely how they were used.

332

1 Sam.

·:········

Num.
Deuter.
Joshua
Judges
Ruth

1 SAMUEL 14, 15

living LORD that he will not lose even a hair from his head. What he did today was done with God's help." So the people saved Jonathan from being put to death.

⁴⁶After that, Saul stopped pursuing the Philistines, and they went back to their own territory.

Saul's Reign and Family

⁴⁷After Saul became king of Israel, he fought against all his enemies everywhere: the people of Moab, of Ammon, and of Edom, the kings of Zobah, and the Philistines. Wherever he fought he was victorious.* ⁴⁸He fought heroically and defeated even the people of Amalek. He saved the Israelites from all attacks.

⁴⁹Saul's sons were Jonathan, Ishvi, and Malchishua. His elder daughter was named Merab, and the younger one Michal. ⁵⁰His wife was Ahinoam, the daughter of Ahimaaz; his army commander was his cousin Abner, the son of his uncle Ner. ⁵¹Saul's father Kish and Abner's father Ner were sons of Abiel.

⁵²As long as he lived, Saul had to fight fiercely against the Philistines. So whenever he found a man who was strong or brave, he would enlist him in his army.

War against the Amalekites

15 Samuel said to Saul, "I am the one whom the LORD sent to anoint you king of his people Israel. Now listen to what the LORD Almighty says. ²He is going to punish the people of Amalek because their ancestors opposed the Israelites when they were coming from Egypt. ³Go and attack the Amalekites and completely destroy everything they have. Don't leave a thing; kill all the men, women, children, and babies; the cattle, sheep, camels, and donkeys."

⁴Saul called his forces together and inspected them at Telem: there were 200,000 soldiers from Israel and 10,000 from Judah. ⁵Then he and his men went to the city of Amalek and waited in ambush in a dry riverbed. ⁶He sent a warning to the Kenites, a people whose ancestors had been kind to the Israelites when they came from Egypt: "Go away and leave the Amalekites, so that I won't kill you along with them." So the Kenites left.

⁷Saul defeated the Amalekites, fighting all the way from Havilah to Shur, east of Egypt; ⁸he captured King Agag of Amalek alive and killed all the people. ⁹But Saul and his men spared Agag's life and did not kill the best sheep and cattle, the best calves and lambs,* or anything else that was good; they destroyed only what was useless or worthless.*

Saul is Rejected as King

¹⁰The LORD said to Samuel, ¹¹"I am sorry that I made Saul king; he has turned away from me and disobeyed my commands." Samuel was angry, and all night long he pleaded with the LORD. ¹²Early the following morning he went off to find Saul. He heard that Saul had gone to the town of Carmel, where he had built a monument to himself, and then had gone on to Gilgal. ¹³Samuel went up to Saul, who greeted him, saying, "The LORD bless you, Samuel! I have obeyed the LORD's command."

¹⁴Samuel asked, "Why, then, do I hear cattle mooing and sheep bleating?"

....

14.47 One ancient translation *was victorious*; Hebrew *acted wickedly*.
15.9 One ancient translation *the best calves and lambs*; Hebrew unclear.
15.9 Some ancient translations *useless or worthless*; Hebrew unclear.

¹⁵Saul answered, "My men took them from the Amalekites. They kept the best sheep and cattle to offer as a sacrifice to the Lord your God, and the rest we have destroyed completely."*

¹⁶"Stop," Samuel ordered, "and I will tell you what the Lord said to me last night."

"Tell me," Saul said.

¹⁷Samuel answered, "Even though you consider yourself of no importance, you are the leader of the tribes of Israel. The Lord anointed you king of Israel, ¹⁸and he sent you out with orders to destroy those wicked people of Amalek. He told you to fight until you had killed them all. ¹⁹Why, then, did you not obey him? Why did you rush to seize the loot, and so do what displeases the Lord?"

²⁰"I did obey the Lord," Saul replied. "I went out as he told me to, brought back King Agag, and killed all the Amalekites. ²¹But my men did not kill the best sheep and cattle that they captured; instead, they brought them here to Gilgal to offer as a sacrifice to the Lord your God."

²²Samuel said, "Which does the Lord prefer: obedience or offerings and sacrifices? It is better to obey him than to sacrifice the best sheep to him. ²³Rebellion against him is as bad as witchcraft, and arrogance is as sinful as idolatry. Because you rejected the Lord's command, he has rejected you as king."

²⁴"Yes, I have sinned," Saul replied. "I disobeyed the Lord's command and your instructions. I was afraid of my men and did what they wanted. ²⁵But now I beg you, forgive my sin and go back with me, so that I can worship the Lord."

²⁶"I will not go back with you," Samuel answered. "You rejected the Lord's command, and he has rejected you as king of Israel."

²⁷Then Samuel turned to leave, but Saul caught hold of his cloak, and it tore. ²⁸Samuel said to him, "The Lord has torn the kingdom of Israel away from you today and given it to someone who is a better man than you. ²⁹Israel's majestic God does not lie or change his mind. He is not a human being — he does not change his mind."

³⁰"I have sinned," Saul replied. "But at least show me respect in front of the leaders of my people and all Israel. Go back with me so that I can worship the Lord your God." ³¹So Samuel went back with him, and Saul worshipped the Lord.

³²"Bring King Agag here to me," Samuel ordered. Agag came to him, trembling with fear, thinking to himself, "What a bitter thing it is to die!"* ³³Samuel said, "As your sword has made many mothers childless, so now will your mother become childless." And he cut Agag to pieces in front of the altar in Gilgal.

³⁴Then Samuel went to Ramah, and King Saul went home to Gibeah. ³⁵As long as Samuel lived, he never again saw the king; but he grieved over him. The Lord was sorry that he had made Saul king of Israel.

David is Anointed King

16 The Lord said to Samuel, "How long will you go on grieving over Saul? I have rejected him as king of Israel. But now get some olive oil and go to Bethlehem, to a man named Jesse, because I have chosen one of his sons to be king."

²"How can I do that?" Samuel asked. "If Saul hears about it, he will kill me!"

Colour these shapes.

....

15.15 *destroyed completely:* These animals had been unconditionally dedicated to the Lord and had to be destroyed (see Lev 27.28).
15.32 *trembling with fear… die;* or *confidently, thinking to himself, "Surely the bitter danger of death is past!"*

334

1 Sam.

. :. . . . .

Num.
Deuter.
Joshua
Judges
Ruth

1 SAMUEL 16, 17

The LORD answered, "Take a calf with you and say that you are there to offer a sacrifice to the LORD. ³Invite Jesse to the sacrifice, and I will tell you what to do. You will anoint as king the man I tell you to."

⁴Samuel did what the LORD told him to do and went to Bethlehem, where the city leaders came trembling to meet him and asked, "Is this a peaceful visit, seer?"

⁵"Yes," he answered. "I have come to offer a sacrifice to the LORD. Purify yourselves and come with me." He also told Jesse and his sons to purify themselves, and he invited them to the sacrifice.

⁶When they arrived, Samuel saw Jesse's son Eliab and said to himself, "This man standing here in the LORD's presence is surely the one he has chosen." ⁷But the LORD said to him, "Pay no attention to how tall and handsome he is. I have rejected him, because I do not judge as people judge. They look at the outward appearance, but I look at the heart."

⁸Then Jesse called his son Abinadab and brought him to Samuel. But Samuel said, "No, the LORD hasn't chosen him either." ⁹Jesse then brought Shammah. "No, the LORD hasn't chosen him either," Samuel said. ¹⁰In this way Jesse brought seven of his sons to Samuel. And Samuel said to him, "No, the LORD hasn't chosen any of these." ¹¹Then he asked him, "Have you any more sons?"

Jesse answered, "There is still the youngest, but he is out taking care of the sheep."

"Tell him to come here," Samuel said. "We won't offer the sacrifice until he comes." ¹²So Jesse sent for him. He was a handsome, healthy young man, and his eyes sparkled. The LORD said to Samuel, "This is the one — anoint him!" ¹³Samuel took the olive oil and anointed David in front of his brothers. Immediately the Spirit of the LORD took control of David and was with him from that day on. Then Samuel returned to Ramah.

David in Saul's Court

¹⁴The LORD's spirit left Saul, and an evil spirit sent by the LORD tormented him. ¹⁵His servants said to him, "We know that an evil spirit sent by God is tormenting you. ¹⁶So give us the order, sir, and we will look for a man who knows how to play the harp. Then when the evil spirit comes on you, the man can play his harp, and you will be all right again."

¹⁷Saul ordered them, "Find me a man who plays well and bring him to me."

¹⁸One of his attendants said, "Jesse, of the town of Bethlehem, has a son who is a good musician. He is also a brave and handsome man, a good soldier, and an able speaker. The LORD is with him."

¹⁹So Saul sent messengers to Jesse to say, "Send me your son David, the one who takes care of the sheep." ²⁰Jesse sent David to Saul with a young goat, a donkey loaded with bread, and a leather bag full of wine. ²¹David came to Saul and entered his service. Saul liked him very much and chose him as the man to carry his weapons. ²²Then Saul sent a message to Jesse: "I like David. Let him stay here in my service." ²³From then on, whenever the evil spirit sent by God came on Saul, David would get his harp and play it. The evil spirit would leave, and Saul would feel better and be all right again.

Goliath Challenges the Israelites

17 The Philistines gathered for battle in Socoh, a town in Judah; they camped at a place called Ephes Dammim, between Socoh and Azekah. ²Saul and the Israelites assembled

335

1 Sam.

....

2 Sam.
1 Kings
2 Kings
1 Chron.
2 Chron.

and camped in the Valley of Elah, where they got ready to fight the Philistines. ³The Philistines lined up on one hill and the Israelites on another, with a valley between them.

⁴A man named Goliath, from the city of Gath, came out from the Philistine camp to challenge the Israelites. He was nearly three metres* tall ⁵and wore bronze armour that weighed about 57 kilogrammes and a bronze helmet. ⁶His legs were also protected by bronze armour, and he carried a bronze javelin slung over his shoulder. ⁷His spear was as thick as the bar on a weaver's loom, and its iron head weighed about seven kilogrammes. A soldier walked in front of him carrying his shield. ⁸Goliath stood and shouted at the Israelites, "What are you doing there, lined up for battle? I am a Philistine, you slaves of Saul! Choose one of your men to fight me. ⁹If he wins and kills me, we will be your slaves; but if I win and kill him, you will be our slaves. ¹⁰Here and now I challenge the Israelite army. I dare you to pick someone to fight me!" ¹¹When Saul and his men heard this, they were terrified.

David in Saul's Camp

¹²David was the son of Jesse, who was an Ephrathite from Bethlehem in Judah. Jesse had eight sons, and at the time Saul was king, he was already a very old man.* ¹³His three eldest sons had gone with Saul to war. The eldest was Eliab, the next was Abinadab, and the third was Shammah. ¹⁴David was the youngest son, and while the three eldest brothers stayed with Saul, ¹⁵David would go back to Bethlehem from time to time, to take care of his father's sheep.

¹⁶Goliath challenged the Israelites every morning and evening for forty days.

¹⁷One day Jesse said to David, "Take ten kilogrammes of this roasted grain and these ten loaves of bread, and hurry with them to your brothers in the camp. ¹⁸And take these ten cheeses to the commanding officer. Find out how your brothers are getting on and bring back something to show that you saw them and that they are well. ¹⁹King Saul, your brothers, and all the other Israelites are in the Valley of Elah fighting the Philistines."

²⁰David got up early the next morning, left someone else in charge of the sheep, took the food, and went as Jesse had told him to. He arrived at the camp just as the Israelites were going out to their battle line, shouting the war cry. ²¹The Philistine and the Israelite armies took up positions for battle, facing each other. ²²David left the food with the officer in charge of the supplies, ran to the battle line, went to his brothers, and asked how they were getting on. ²³As he was talking to them, Goliath came forward and challenged the Israelites as he had done before. And David heard him. ²⁴When the Israelites saw Goliath, they ran away in terror. ²⁵"Look at him!" they said to each other. "Listen to his challenge! King Saul has promised to give a big reward to the man who kills him; the king will also give him his daughter to marry and will not require his father's family to pay taxes."*

²⁶David asked the men who were near him, "What will the man get who kills this Philistine and frees Israel from this disgrace?

17.4 Hebrew *nearly three metres*; one ancient Hebrew manuscript and one ancient translation *about two metres.*
17.12 Some ancient translations *a very old man*; Hebrew unclear.
17.25 *to pay taxes*; or *either to pay taxes or serve him.*

336

1 Sam.

Num.
Deuter.
Joshua
Judges
Ruth

After all, who is this heathen Philistine to defy the army of the living God?" ²⁷They told him what would be done for the man who killed Goliath.

²⁸Eliab, David's eldest brother, heard David talking to the men. He was angry with David and said, "What are you doing here? Who is taking care of those sheep of yours out there in the wilderness? You cheeky brat, you! You just came to watch the fighting!"

²⁹"Now what have I done?" David asked. "Can't I even ask a question?" ³⁰He turned to another man and asked him the same question, and every time he asked, he got the same answer.

³¹Some men heard what David had said, and they told Saul, who sent for him. ³²David said to Saul, "Your Majesty, no one should be afraid of this Philistine! I will go and fight him."

³³"No," answered Saul. "How could you fight him? You're just a boy, and he has been a soldier all his life!"

³⁴"Your Majesty," David said, "I take care of my father's sheep. Whenever a lion or a bear carries off a lamb, ³⁵I go after it, attack it, and rescue the lamb. And if the lion or bear turns on me, I grab it by the throat and beat it to death. ³⁶I have killed lions and bears, and I will do the same to this heathen Philistine, who has defied the army of the living God. ³⁷The LORD has saved me from lions and bears; he will save me from this Philistine."

"All right," Saul answered. "Go, and the LORD be with you." ³⁸He gave his own armour to David for him to wear: a bronze helmet, which he put on David's head, and a coat of armour. ³⁹David strapped Saul's sword over the armour and tried to walk, but he couldn't, because he wasn't used to wearing them. "I can't fight with all this," he said to Saul. "I'm not used to it." So he took it all off. ⁴⁰He took his shepherd's stick and then picked up five smooth stones from the stream and put them in his bag. With his sling ready, he went out to meet Goliath.

David Defeats Goliath

⁴¹The Philistine started walking towards David, with his shield-bearer walking in front of him. He kept coming closer, ⁴²and when he got a good look at David, he was filled with scorn for him because he was just a nice, good-looking boy. ⁴³He said to David, "What's that stick for? Do you think I'm a dog?" And he called down curses from his god on David. ⁴⁴"Come on," he challenged David, "and I will give your body to the birds and animals to eat."

⁴⁵David answered, "You are coming against me with sword, spear, and javelin, but I come against you in the name of the LORD Almighty, the God of the Israelite armies, which you have defied. ⁴⁶This very day the LORD will put you in my power; I will defeat you and cut off your head. And I will give the bodies of the Philistine soldiers to the birds and animals to eat. Then the whole world will know that Israel has a God, ⁴⁷and everyone here will see that the LORD does not need swords or spears to save his people. He is victorious in battle, and he will put all of you in our power."

⁴⁸Goliath started walking towards David again, and David ran quickly towards the Philistine battle line to fight him. ⁴⁹He put his hand into his bag and took out a stone, which he slung at Goliath. It hit him on the forehead and broke his skull, and Goliath fell face downwards on the ground. ⁵⁰And so, without a sword, David defeated and killed Goliath with a sling and a stone! ⁵¹He ran to him, stood over him, took Goliath's sword out of its sheath, and cut off his head and killed him.

When the Philistines saw that their hero was dead, they ran away. ⁵²The men of Israel and Judah shouted and ran after them,

1 SAMUEL 17.40

Go for a walk and find three stones. Hold them in your hand as you keep walking, and

THINK OF THREE

'GIANTS'

that you would like God to fight for you. They might be fears, difficult situations or obstacles. After you have prayed, release the stones.

1 Sam.

..........:.

2 Sam.
1 Kings
2 Kings
1 Chron.
2 Chron.

pursuing them all the way to Gath* and to the gates of Ekron. The Philistines fell wounded all along the road that leads to Shaaraim, as far as Gath and Ekron. ⁵³When the Israelites came back from pursuing the Philistines, they looted their camp. ⁵⁴David picked up Goliath's head and took it to Jerusalem, but he kept Goliath's weapons in his own tent.

David is Presented to Saul

⁵⁵When Saul saw David going out to fight Goliath, he asked Abner, the commander of his army, "Abner, whose son is he?"

"I have no idea, Your Majesty," Abner answered.

⁵⁶"Then go and find out," Saul ordered.

⁵⁷So when David returned to camp after killing Goliath, Abner took him to Saul. David was still carrying Goliath's head. ⁵⁸Saul asked him, "Young man, whose son are you?"

"I am the son of your servant Jesse from Bethlehem," David answered.

18 Saul and David finished their conversation. After that, Saul's son Jonathan was deeply attracted to David and came to love him as much as he loved himself. ²Saul kept David with him from that day on and did not let him go back home. ³Jonathan swore eternal friendship with David because of his deep affection for him. ⁴He took off the robe he was wearing and gave it to David, together with his armour and also his sword, bow, and belt. ⁵David was successful in all the missions on which Saul sent him, and so Saul made him an officer in his army. This pleased all of Saul's officers and men.

Saul Becomes Jealous of David

⁶As David was returning after killing Goliath and as the soldiers were coming back home, women from every town in Israel came out to meet King Saul. They were singing joyful songs, dancing, and playing tambourines and lyres. ⁷In their celebration the women sang, "Saul has killed thousands, but David tens of thousands." ⁸Saul did not like this, and he became very angry. He said, "For David they claim tens of thousands, but only thousands for me. They will be making him king next!" ⁹And so he was jealous and suspicious of David from that day on.

¹⁰The next day an evil spirit from God suddenly took control of Saul, and he raved in his house like a madman. David was playing the harp, as he did every day, and Saul was holding a spear. ¹¹"I'll pin him to the wall," Saul said to himself, and he threw the spear at him twice; but David dodged each time.

¹²Saul was afraid of David because the LORD was with David but had abandoned him. ¹³So Saul sent him away and put him in command of a thousand men. David led his men in battle ¹⁴and was successful in all he did, because the LORD was with him. ¹⁵Saul noticed David's success and became even more afraid of him. ¹⁶But everyone in Israel and Judah loved David because he was such a successful leader.

David Marries Saul's Daughter

¹⁷Then Saul said to David, "Here is my elder daughter Merab. I will give her to you as your wife on condition that you serve me as a brave and loyal soldier, and fight the LORD's battles." (Saul was thinking that in this way the Philistines would kill David, and he would not have to do it himself.)

....

17.52 One ancient translation *Gath*; Hebrew *a valley*.

338

1 Sam.

·:········

Num.
Deuter.
Joshua
Judges
Ruth

1 SAMUEL 18, 19

18 David answered, "Who am I and what is my family that I should become the king's son-in-law?" 19 But when the time came for Merab to be given to David, she was given instead to a man named Adriel from Meholah.

20 Saul's daughter Michal, however, fell in love with David, and when Saul heard of this, he was pleased. 21 He said to himself, "I'll give Michal to David; I will use her to trap him, and he will be killed by the Philistines." So for the second time Saul said to David, "You will be my son-in-law." 22 He ordered his officials to speak privately to David and tell him, "The king is pleased with you and all his officials like you; now is a good time for you to marry his daughter."

23 So they told David this, and he answered, "It's a great honour to become the king's son-in-law, too great for someone poor and insignificant like me."

24 The officials told Saul what David had said, 25 and Saul ordered them to tell David: "All the king wants from you as payment for the bride is the foreskins of a hundred dead Philistines, as revenge on his enemies." (This was how Saul planned to have David killed by the Philistines.) 26 Saul's officials reported to David what Saul had said, and David was delighted with the thought of becoming the king's son-in-law. Before the day set for the wedding, 27 David and his men went and killed 200 Philistines. He took their foreskins to the king and counted them all out to him, so that he might become his son-in-law. So Saul had to give his daughter Michal in marriage to David.

28 Saul realized clearly that the LORD was with David and also that his daughter Michal loved him. 29 So he became even more afraid of David and was his enemy as long as he lived.

30 The Philistine armies would come and fight, but in every battle David was more successful than any of Saul's other officers. As a result David became very famous.

David is Persecuted by Saul

19 Saul told his son Jonathan and all his officials that he planned to kill* David. But Jonathan was very fond of David, 2 and so he said to him, "My father is trying to kill you. Please be careful tomorrow morning; hide in some secret place and stay there. 3 I will go and stand by my father in the field where you are hiding, and I will speak to him about you. If I find out anything, I will let you know."

4 Jonathan praised David to Saul and said, "Sir, don't do wrong to your servant David. He has never done you any wrong; on the contrary, everything he has done has been a great help to you. 5 He risked his life when he killed Goliath, and the LORD won a great victory for Israel. When you saw it, you were glad. Why, then, do you now want to do wrong to an innocent man and kill David for no reason at all?"

6 Saul was convinced by what Jonathan said and made a vow in the LORD's name that he would not kill David. 7 So Jonathan called David and told him everything; then he took him to Saul, and David served the king as he had before.

8 War with the Philistines broke out again. David attacked them and defeated them so thoroughly that they fled.

9 One day an evil spirit from the LORD took control of Saul. He was sitting in his house with his spear in his hand, and David was there, playing his harp. 10 Saul tried to pin David to the wall

···

19.1 *that he planned to kill*; or *to kill*.

1 Sam.

....

2 Sam.
1 Kings
2 Kings
1 Chron.
2 Chron.

with his spear, but David dodged, and the spear stuck in the wall. David ran away and escaped.

¹¹ That same night Saul sent some men to watch David's house and kill him the next morning. Michal, David's wife, warned him, "If you don't get away tonight, tomorrow you will be dead." ¹² She let him down from a window, and he ran away and escaped. ¹³ Then she took the household idol, laid it on the bed, put a pillow made of goats'-hair at its head, and put a cover over it. ¹⁴ When Saul's men came to get David, Michal told them that he was ill. ¹⁵ But Saul sent them back to see David for themselves. He ordered them, "Carry him here in his bed, and I will kill him." ¹⁶ They went inside and found the household idol in the bed and the goats'-hair pillow at its head. ¹⁷ Saul asked Michal, "Why have you tricked me like this and let my enemy escape?"

She answered, "He said he would kill me if I didn't help him to escape."

¹⁸ David escaped and went to Samuel in Ramah and told him everything that Saul had done to him. Then he and Samuel went to Naioth and stayed there. ¹⁹ Saul was told that David was in Naioth in Ramah, ²⁰ so he sent some men to arrest him. They saw* the group of prophets dancing and shouting, with Samuel as their leader. Then the Spirit of God took control of Saul's men, and they also began to dance and shout. ²¹ When Saul heard of this, he sent more messengers, and they also began to dance and shout. He sent messengers the third time, and the same thing happened to them. ²² Then he himself started out for Ramah. When he came to the large well in Secu, he asked where Samuel and David were and was told that they were at Naioth. ²³ As he was going there, the Spirit of God took control of him also, and he danced and shouted all the way to Naioth. ²⁴ He took off his clothes and danced and shouted in Samuel's presence, and lay naked all that day and all that night. (This is how the saying originated, "Has even Saul become a prophet?")

Jonathan Helps David

20 Then David fled from Naioth in Ramah and went to Jonathan. "What have I done?" he asked. "What crime have I committed? What wrong have I done to your father to make him want to kill me?"

² Jonathan answered, "God forbid that you should die! My father tells me everything he does, important or not, and he would not hide this from me. It isn't true!"

³ But David answered,* "Your father knows very well how much you like me, and he has decided not to let you know what he plans to do, because you would be deeply hurt. I swear to you by the living LORD that I am only a step away from death!"

⁴ Jonathan said, "I'll do anything you want."

⁵ "Tomorrow is the New Moon Festival," David replied, "and I am supposed to eat with the king. But if it's all right with you, I will go and hide in the fields until the evening of the day after tomorrow. ⁶ If your father notices that I am not at table, tell him that I begged your permission to hurry home to Bethlehem, since it's the time for the annual sacrifice there for my whole family. ⁷ If he says, 'All right,' I will be safe; but if he becomes angry, you will know that he is determined to harm me. ⁸ Please do me this favour, and keep the sacred promise you

....

19.20 Some ancient translations *They saw*; Hebrew *He saw*.
20.3 One ancient translation *answered*; Hebrew *made a vow again*.

340

1 Sam.

:·:·········

Num.
Deuter.
Joshua
Judges
Ruth

1 SAMUEL 20

made to me. But if I'm guilty, kill me yourself! Why take me to your father to be killed?"

⁹"Don't even think such a thing!" Jonathan answered. "If I knew for certain that my father was determined to harm you, wouldn't I tell you?"

¹⁰David then asked, "Who will let me know if your father answers you angrily?"

¹¹"Let's go out to the fields," Jonathan answered. So they went, ¹²and Jonathan said to David, "May the LORD God of Israel be our witness!* At this time tomorrow and on the following day I will question my father. If his attitude towards you is good, I will send you word. ¹³If he intends to harm you, may the LORD strike me dead if I don't let you know about it and get you safely away. May the LORD be with you as he was with my father! ¹⁴And if I remain alive, please keep your sacred promise and be loyal to me; but if I die,* ¹⁵show the same kind of loyalty to my family for ever. And when the LORD has completely destroyed all your enemies, ¹⁶may our promise to each other still be unbroken. If it is broken, the LORD will punish you."*

¹⁷Once again Jonathan made David promise to love him, for Jonathan loved David as much as he loved himself. ¹⁸Then Jonathan said to him, "Since tomorrow is the New Moon Festival, your absence will be noticed if you aren't at the meal. ¹⁹The day after tomorrow your absence will be noticed* even more; so go to the place where you hid the other time, and hide behind the pile of stones there.* ²⁰I will then shoot three arrows at it, as though it were a target. ²¹Then I will tell my servant to go and find them. And if I tell him, 'Look, the arrows are on this side of you; get them,' that means that you are safe and can come out. I swear by the living LORD that you will be in no danger. ²²But if I tell him, 'The arrows are on the other side of you,' then leave, because the LORD is sending you away. ²³As for the promise we have made to each other, the LORD will make sure that we will keep it for ever."

²⁴So David hid in the fields. At the New Moon Festival, King Saul came to the meal ²⁵and sat in his usual place by the wall. Abner sat next to him, and Jonathan sat opposite him.* David's place was empty, ²⁶but Saul said nothing that day, because he thought, "Something has happened to him, and he is not ritually pure." ²⁷On the following day, the day after the New Moon Festival, David's place was still empty, and Saul asked Jonathan, "Why didn't David come to the meal either yesterday or today?"

²⁸Jonathan answered, "He begged me to let him go to Bethlehem. ²⁹'Please let me go,' he said, 'because our family is celebrating the sacrificial feast in town, and my brother ordered me to be there. So then, if you are my friend, let me go and see my relatives.' That is why he isn't in his place at your table."

³⁰Saul was furious with Jonathan and said to him, "How rebellious and faithless your mother was! Now I know you are taking sides with David and are disgracing yourself and that mother of yours! ³¹Don't you realize that as long as David is

....

20.12 One ancient translation be our witness; Hebrew does not have these words.
20.14 Some ancient translations if I die; Hebrew that I may not die.
20.16 Verses 15–16 in Hebrew are unclear.
20.19 Some ancient translations your absence will be noticed; Hebrew go down.
20.19 Probable text the pile of stones there; Hebrew the Ezel Stone.
20.25 One ancient translation sat opposite him; Hebrew stood up.

1 SAMUEL 20, 21

341

1 Sam.

....

2 Sam.
1 Kings
2 Kings
1 Chron.
2 Chron.

alive, you will never be king of this country? Now go and bring him here — he must die!"

32 "Why should he die?" Jonathan replied. "What has he done?"

33 At that, Saul threw his spear at Jonathan to kill him, and Jonathan realized that his father was really determined to kill David. 34 Jonathan got up from the table in a rage and ate nothing that day — the second day of the New Moon Festival. He was deeply distressed about David, because Saul had insulted him. 35 The following morning Jonathan went to the fields to meet David, as they had agreed. He took a young boy with him 36 and said to him, "Run and find the arrows I'm going to shoot." The boy ran, and Jonathan shot an arrow beyond him. 37 When the boy reached the place where the arrow had fallen, Jonathan shouted to him, "The arrow is further on! 38 Don't just stand there! Hurry up!" The boy picked up the arrow and returned to his master, 39 not knowing what it all meant; only Jonathan and David knew. 40 Jonathan gave his weapons to the boy and told him to take them back to the town.

41 After the boy had left, David got up from behind the pile of stones,* fell on his knees and bowed with his face to the ground three times. Both he and Jonathan were crying as they kissed each other; David's grief was even greater than Jonathan's.* 42 Then Jonathan said to David, "God be with you. The Lord will make sure that you and I, and your descendants and mine, will for ever keep the sacred promise we have made to each other." Then David left, and Jonathan went back to the town.

David Flees from Saul

21 David went to the priest Ahimelech in Nob. Ahimelech came out trembling to meet him and asked, "Why did you come here all by yourself?"

2 "I am here on the king's business," David answered. "He told me not to let anyone know what he sent me to do. As for my men, I have told them to meet me at a certain place. 3 Now, then, what supplies have you got? Give me five loaves of bread or anything else you have."

4 The priest said, "I haven't any ordinary bread, only sacred bread; you can have it if your men haven't had sexual relations recently."

5 "Of course they haven't," answered David. "My men always keep themselves ritually pure even when we go out on an ordinary mission; how much more this time when we are on a special mission!"

6 So the priest gave David the sacred bread, because the only bread he had was the loaves offered to God, which had been removed from the sacred table and replaced by fresh bread.

7 (Saul's chief herdsman, Doeg, who was from Edom, happened to be there that day, because he had to fulfil a religious obligation.)

8 David said to Ahimelech, "Have you got a spear or a sword you can give me? The king's orders made me leave in such a hurry that I didn't have time to get my sword or any other weapon."

9 Ahimelech answered, "I have the sword of Goliath the Philistine, whom you killed in the Valley of Elah; it is behind the ephod, wrapped in a cloth. If you want it, take it — it's the only weapon here."

---

1 SAMUEL 21

David spent years
— RUNNING AND —
HIDING
from Saul, largely
because Saul envied
David and felt
threatened by him.

How do we react when
we see other people
who are better at
things than we are?

Do you ever feel
threatened by people
who are really good at
something you enjoy?
Why or why not?

How does God want us
to react when
someone is better at
something than we
are? How can we
improve our reactions?

20.41 Probable text *the pile of stones*; Hebrew *the south*.
20.41 Probable text *David's grief was even greater than Jonathan's*; Hebrew unclear.

342

1 Sam.

Num.
Deuter.
Joshua
Judges
Ruth

1 SAMUEL 22

There are more than a few passages in the Bible which are difficult to understand, and this is one of them! So how do we approach tough passages?

WATCH THIS

⇒ **FILM** ⇐

ON THE SUBJECT.

Head to
gnbyouthedition.co.uk/toughpassages

"Give it to me," David said. "There is not a better sword anywhere!"

10 So David left, fleeing from Saul, and went to King Achish of Gath. 11 The king's officials said to Achish, "Isn't this David, the king of his country? This is the man about whom the women sang, as they danced, 'Saul has killed thousands, but David has killed tens of thousands.'"

12 Their words made a deep impression on David, and he became very much afraid of King Achish. 13 So whenever they were around, David pretended to be insane and acted like a madman when they tried to restrain him; he would scribble on the city* gates and dribble down his beard. 14 So Achish said to his officials, "Look! The man is mad! Why did you bring him to me? 15 Haven't I got enough madmen already? Why bring another one to annoy me with his daft actions right here in my own house?"

The Slaughter of the Priests

22 David fled from the city of Gath and went to a cave near the town of Adullam. When his brothers and the rest of the family heard that he was there, they joined him. 2 People who were oppressed or in debt or dissatisfied went to him, about 400 men in all, and he became their leader.

3 David went on from there to Mizpah in Moab and said to the king of Moab, "Please let my father and mother come and stay with you until I find out what God is going to do for me." 4 So David left his parents with the king of Moab, and they stayed there as long as David was hiding in the cave.

5 Then the prophet Gad came to David and said, "Don't stay here; go at once to the land of Judah." So David left and went to the forest of Hereth.

6 One day Saul was in Gibeah, sitting under a tamarisk tree on a hill, with his spear in his hand, and all his officers were standing round him. He was told that David and his men had been found, 7 and he said to his officers, "Listen, men of Benjamin! Do you think that David will give fields and vineyards to all of you, and make you officers in his army? 8 Is that why you are plotting against me? Not one of you told me that my own son had made an alliance with David. No one is concerned about me or tells me that David, one of my own men, is at this moment looking for a chance to kill me, and that my son has encouraged him!"

9 Doeg was standing there with Saul's officers, and he said, "I saw David when he went to Ahimelech son of Ahitub in Nob. 10 Ahimelech asked the Lord what David should do, and then he gave David some food and the sword of Goliath the Philistine."

11 So King Saul sent for the priest Ahimelech and all his relatives, who were also priests in Nob, and they came to him. 12 Saul said to Ahimelech, "Listen, Ahimelech!"

"At your service, sir," he answered.

13 Saul asked him, "Why are you and David plotting against me? Why did you give him some food and a sword, and consult God for him? Now he has turned against me and is waiting for a chance to kill me!"

14 Ahimelech answered, "David is the most faithful officer you have! He is your own son-in-law, captain of* your bodyguard, and

21.13 *city*; or *palace*.
22.14 Some ancient translations *captain of*; Hebrew *he turned to*.

1 Sam.

2 Sam.
1 Kings
2 Kings
1 Chron.
2 Chron.

highly respected by everyone in the royal court. ¹⁵Yes, I consulted God for him, and it wasn't the first time.* As for plotting against you, Your Majesty must not accuse me or anyone else in my family. I don't know anything about this matter!"

¹⁶The king said, "Ahimelech, you and all your relatives must die." ¹⁷Then he said to the guards standing near him, "Kill the LORD's priests! They conspired with David and did not tell me that he had run away, even though they knew it all along." But the guards refused to lift a hand to kill the LORD's priests. ¹⁸So Saul said to Doeg, "You kill them!" — and Doeg killed them all. On that day he killed 85 priests who were qualified to carry the ephod. ¹⁹Saul also ordered all the other inhabitants of Nob, the city of priests, to be put to death: men and women, children and babies, cattle, donkeys, and sheep — they were all killed.

²⁰But Abiathar, one of Ahimelech's sons, escaped, and went and joined David. ²¹He told him how Saul had slaughtered the priests of the LORD. ²²David said to him, "When I saw Doeg there that day, I knew that he would be sure to tell Saul. So I am responsible* for the death of all your relatives. ²³Stay with me and don't be afraid. Saul wants to kill both you and me, but you will be safe with me."

David Saves the Town of Keilah

23 David heard that the Philistines were attacking the town of Keilah and were stealing the newly harvested corn. ²So he asked the LORD, "Shall I go and attack the Philistines?"

"Yes," the LORD answered. "Attack them and save Keilah."

³But David's men said to him, "We have enough to be afraid of here in Judah; it will be much worse if we go to Keilah and attack the Philistine forces!" ⁴So David consulted the LORD again, and the LORD said to him, "Go and attack Keilah, because I will give you victory over the Philistines." ⁵So David and his men went to Keilah and attacked the Philistines; they killed many of them and took their livestock. And that was how David saved the town.

⁶When Abiathar son of Ahimelech escaped and joined David in Keilah, he took the ephod with him.

⁷Saul was told that David had gone to Keilah, and he said, "God has put him in my power. David has trapped himself by going into a walled town with fortified gates." ⁸So Saul called his troops to war, to march against Keilah and besiege David and his men.

⁹When David heard that Saul was planning to attack him, he said to the priest Abiathar, "Bring the ephod here." ¹⁰Then David said, "LORD, God of Israel, I have heard that Saul is planning to come to Keilah and destroy it on account of me, your servant. ¹¹Will the citizens of Keilah hand me over to Saul? Will Saul really come, as I have heard? LORD, God of Israel, I beg you to answer me!"

The LORD answered, "Saul will come."

¹²"And will the citizens of Keilah hand my men and me over to Saul?" David asked again.

"They will," the LORD answered.

¹³So David and his men — about 600 in all — left Keilah at once and kept on the move. When Saul heard that David had escaped from Keilah, he gave up his plan.

22.15 *Yes, I consulted… time*; or *Now, have I done something wrong today by consulting God for him? Not at all!*
22.22 Some ancient translations *I am responsible*; Hebrew *I have turned.*

David in the Hill Country

¹⁴David stayed in hiding in the hill country, in the wilderness near Ziph. Saul was always trying to find him, but God did not hand David over to him. ¹⁵David saw that Saul was out to kill him.

David was at Horesh, in the wilderness near Ziph. ¹⁶Jonathan went to him there and encouraged him with assurances of God's protection, ¹⁷saying to him, "Don't be afraid. My father Saul won't be able to harm you. He knows very well that you are the one who will be the king of Israel and that I will be next in rank to you." ¹⁸The two of them made a sacred promise of friendship to each other. David stayed at Horesh, and Jonathan went home.

¹⁹Some people from Ziph went to Saul at Gibeah and said, "David is hiding in our territory at Horesh on Mount Hachilah, in the southern part of the Judean wilderness. ²⁰We know, Your Majesty, how much you want to capture him; so come to our territory, and we will make sure that you catch him."

²¹Saul answered, "May the Lord bless you for being so kind to me! ²²Go and make sure once more; find out for certain where he is and who has seen him there. I hear that he is very cunning. ²³Find out exactly the places where he hides, and be sure to bring back a report to me straight away. Then I will go with you, and if he is still in the region, I will hunt him down, even if I have to search the whole land of Judah."

²⁴So they left and returned to Ziph ahead of Saul. David and his men were in the wilderness of Maon, in a desolate valley in the southern part of the Judean wilderness. ²⁵Saul and his men set out to look for David, but he heard about it and went to a rocky hill in the wilderness of Maon and stayed there. When Saul heard about this, he went after David. ²⁶Saul and his men were on one side of the hill, separated from David and his men, who were on the other side. They were hurrying to get away from Saul and his men, who were closing in on them and were about to capture them. ²⁷Just then a messenger arrived and said to Saul, "Come back at once! The Philistines are invading the country!" ²⁸So Saul stopped pursuing David and went to fight the Philistines. That is why that place is called Separation Hill. ²⁹David left and went to the region of Engedi, where he stayed in hiding.

David Spares Saul's Life

24 When Saul came back from fighting the Philistines, he was told that David was in the wilderness near Engedi. ²Saul took 3,000 of the best soldiers in Israel and went looking for David and his men east of Wild Goat Rocks. ³He came to a cave close to some sheep pens by the road and went in to relieve himself. It happened to be the very cave in which David and his men were hiding far back in the cave. ⁴They said to him, "This is your chance! The Lord has told you that he would put your enemy in your power and you could do to him whatever you wanted to." David crept over and cut off a piece of Saul's robe without Saul's knowing it. ⁵But then David's conscience began to trouble him, ⁶and he said to his men, "May the Lord keep me from doing any harm to my master, whom the Lord chose as king! I must not harm him in the least, because he is the king chosen by the Lord!" ⁷So David convinced his men that they should not attack Saul.

Saul got up, left the cave, and started on his way. ⁸Then David went out after him and called to him, "Your Majesty!" Saul turned round, and David bowed down to the ground in respect ⁹and said, "Why do you listen to people who say that I am trying to harm you? ¹⁰You can see for yourself that just now in the cave the Lord

1 SAMUEL 24, 25

345

1 Sam.
....

2 Sam.
1 Kings
2 Kings
1 Chron.
2 Chron.

put you in my power. Some of my men told me to kill you, but I felt sorry for you and said that I would not harm you in the least, because you are the one whom the LORD chose to be king. [11] Look, my father, look at the piece of your robe I am holding! I could have killed you, but instead I only cut this off. This should convince you that I have no thought of rebelling against you or of harming you. You are hunting me down to kill me, even though I have not done you any wrong. [12] May the LORD judge which one of us is wrong! May he punish you for your action against me, for I will not harm you in the least. [13] You know the old saying, 'Evil is done only by evil people.' And so I will not harm you. [14] Look at what the king of Israel is trying to kill! Look at what he is chasing! A dead dog, a flea! [15] The LORD will judge, and he will decide which one of us is wrong. May he look into the matter, defend me, and save me from you."

[16] When David had finished speaking, Saul said, "Is that really you, David my son?" And he started crying. [17] Then he said to David, "You are right, and I am wrong. You have been so good to me, while I have done such wrong to you! [18] Today you have shown how good you are to me, because you did not kill me, even though the LORD put me in your power. [19] How often does a man catch his enemy and then let him get away unharmed? The LORD bless you for what you have done to me today! [20] Now I am sure that you will be king of Israel and that the kingdom will continue under your rule. [21] But promise me in the LORD's name that you will spare my descendants, so that my name and my family's name will not be completely forgotten." [22] David promised that he would.

Then Saul went back home, and David and his men went back to their hiding place.

The Death of Samuel

25 Samuel died, and all the Israelites came together and mourned for him. Then they buried him at his home in Ramah.

David and Abigail

After this, David went to the wilderness of Paran. [2-3] There was a man of the clan of Caleb named Nabal, who was from the town of Maon, and who owned land near the town of Carmel. He was a very rich man, the owner of 3,000 sheep and 1,000 goats. His wife Abigail was beautiful and intelligent, but he was a mean, bad-tempered man.

Nabal was shearing his sheep in Carmel, [4] and David, who was in the wilderness, heard about it, [5] so he sent ten young men with orders to go to Carmel, find Nabal, and give him his greetings. [6] He instructed them to say to Nabal: "David sends you greetings, my friend, with his best wishes for you, your family, and all that is yours. [7] He heard that you were shearing your sheep, and he wants you to know that your shepherds have been with us and we did not harm them. Nothing that belonged to them was stolen all the time they were at Carmel. [8] Just ask them, and they will tell you. We have come on a feast day, and David asks you to receive us kindly. Please give what you can to us your servants and to your dear friend David."

[9] David's men delivered this message to Nabal in David's name. Then they waited there, [10] and Nabal finally answered, "David? Who is he? I've never heard of him! The country is full of runaway slaves nowadays! [11] I'm not going to take my bread and water, and the animals I have slaughtered for my shearers, and give them to people who come from I don't know where!"

346

1 Sam.

Num.
Deuter.
Joshua
Judges
Ruth

1 SAMUEL 25

¹² David's men went back to him and told him what Nabal had said. ¹³ "Buckle on your swords!" he ordered, and they all did. David also buckled on his sword and left with about 400 of his men, leaving 200 behind with the supplies.

¹⁴ One of Nabal's servants said to Nabal's wife Abigail, "Have you heard? David sent some messengers from the wilderness with greetings for our master, but he insulted them. ¹⁵ Yet they were very good to us; they never bothered us, and all the time we were with them in the fields, nothing that belonged to us was stolen. ¹⁶ They protected us day and night the whole time we were with them looking after our flocks. ¹⁷ Please think this over and decide what to do. This could be disastrous for our master and all his family. He is so pigheaded that he won't listen to anybody!"

¹⁸ Abigail quickly collected 200 loaves of bread, two leather bags full of wine, five roasted sheep, seventeen kilogrammes of roasted grain, a hundred bunches of raisins, and 200 cakes of dried figs, and loaded them on donkeys. ¹⁹ Then she said to the servants, "You go on ahead and I will follow you." But she said nothing to her husband.

²⁰ She was riding her donkey round a bend on a hillside when suddenly she met David and his men coming towards her. ²¹ David had been thinking, "Why did I ever protect that fellow's property out here in the wilderness? Not a thing that belonged to him was stolen, and this is how he pays me back for the help I gave him! ²² May God strike me* dead if I don't kill every last one of those men before morning!"

²³ When Abigail saw David, she quickly dismounted and threw herself on the ground ²⁴ at David's feet, and said to him, "Please, sir, listen to me! Let me take the blame. ²⁵ Please, don't pay any attention to Nabal, that good-for-nothing! He is exactly what his name means — a fool!* I wasn't there when your servants arrived, sir. ²⁶ It is the LORD who has kept you from taking revenge and killing your enemies. And now I swear to you by the living LORD that your enemies and all who want to harm you will be punished like Nabal. ²⁷ Please, sir, accept this present I have brought you, and give it to your men. ²⁸ Please forgive me, sir, for any wrong I have done. The LORD will make you king, and your descendants also, because you are fighting his battles; and you will not do anything evil* as long as you live. ²⁹ If anyone should attack you and try to kill you, the LORD your God will keep you safe, as someone guards a precious treasure. As for your enemies, however, he will throw them away, as someone hurls stones with a sling. ³⁰ And when the LORD has done all the good things he has promised you and has made you king of Israel, ³¹ then you will not have to feel regret or remorse, sir, for having killed without cause or for having taken your own revenge. And when the LORD has blessed you, sir, please do not forget me."

³² David said to her, "Praise the LORD, the God of Israel, who sent you today to meet me! ³³ Thank God for your good sense and for what you have done today in keeping me from the crime of murder and from taking my own revenge. ³⁴ The LORD has kept me from harming you. But I swear by the living God of Israel that if you had not hurried to meet me, all of Nabal's men would have been dead by morning!" ³⁵ Then David accepted what she had brought him and said to her, "Go back home and don't worry. I will do what you want."

1 SAMUEL 25.29

THE LORD YOUR GOD will keep you SAFE

25.22 One ancient translation *me*; Hebrew *my enemies*.
25.25 *a fool*: This is the meaning of the Hebrew name Nabal.
25.28 *you will not do anything evil*; or *no evil will happen to you*.

1 SAMUEL 25, 26

347

1 Sam.

....

2 Sam.
1 Kings
2 Kings
1 Chron.
2 Chron.

36 Abigail went back to Nabal, who was at home having a feast fit for a king. He was drunk and in a good mood, so she did not tell him anything until the next morning. 37 Then, after he had sobered up, she told him everything. He suffered a stroke and was completely paralysed. 38 Some ten days later the LORD struck Nabal and he died.

39 When David heard that Nabal had died, he said, "Praise the LORD! He has taken revenge on Nabal for insulting me and has kept me his servant from doing wrong. The LORD has punished Nabal for his evil."

Then David sent a proposal of marriage to Abigail. 40 His servants went to her at Carmel and said to her, "David sent us to take you to him to be his wife."

41 Abigail bowed down to the ground and said, "I am his servant, ready to wash the feet of his servants." 42 She rose quickly and mounted her donkey. Accompanied by her five maids, she went with David's servants and became his wife.

43 David had married Ahinoam from Jezreel, and now Abigail also became his wife. 44 Meanwhile, Saul had given his daughter Michal, who had been David's wife, to Palti son of Laish, who was from the town of Gallim.

David Spares Saul's Life Again

26 Some men from Ziph came to Saul at Gibeah and told him that David was hiding on Mount Hachilah at the edge of the Judean wilderness. 2 Saul went at once with 3,000 of the best soldiers in Israel to the wilderness of Ziph to look for David, 3 and camped by the road on Mount Hachilah. David was still in the wilderness, and when he learnt that Saul had come to look for him, 4 he sent spies and found out that Saul was indeed there. 5 He went at once and located the exact place where Saul and Abner son of Ner, commander of Saul's army, slept. Saul slept inside the camp, and his men camped round him.

6 Then David asked Ahimelech the Hittite, and Abishai the brother of Joab (their mother was Zeruiah), "Which of you two will go to Saul's camp with me?"

"I will," Abishai answered.

7 So that night David and Abishai entered Saul's camp and found Saul sleeping in the centre of the camp with his spear stuck in the ground near his head. Abner and the troops were sleeping round him. 8 Abishai said to David, "God has put your enemy in your power tonight. Now let me plunge his own spear through him and pin him to the ground with just one blow — I won't have to strike twice!"

9 But David said, "You must not harm him! The LORD will certainly punish whoever harms his chosen king. 10 By the living LORD," David continued, "I know that the LORD himself will kill Saul, either when his time comes to die a natural death or when he dies in battle. 11 The LORD forbid that I should try to harm the one whom the LORD has made king! Let's take his spear and his water jar, and go." 12 So David took the spear and the water jar from just beside Saul's head, and he and Abishai left. No one saw or knew what had happened or even woke up — they were all sound asleep, because the LORD had sent a heavy sleep on them all.

13 Then David crossed over to the other side of the valley to the top of the hill, a safe distance away, 14 and shouted to Saul's troops and to Abner, "Abner! Can you hear me?"

"Who is that shouting and waking up the king?" Abner asked.

15 David answered, "Abner, aren't you the greatest man in Israel? So why aren't you protecting your master, the king? Just

348

1 Sam.

⁝ ....

Num.

Deuter.

Joshua

Judges

Ruth

1 SAMUEL 26, 27

now someone entered the camp to kill your master. ¹⁶ You failed in your duty, Abner! I swear by the living LORD that all of you deserve to die, because you have not protected your master, whom the LORD made king. Look! Where is the king's spear? Where is the water jar that was beside his head?"

¹⁷ Saul recognized David's voice and asked, "David, is that you, my son?"

"Yes, Your Majesty," David answered. ¹⁸ And he added, "Why, sir, are you still pursuing me, your servant? What have I done? What crime have I committed? ¹⁹ Your Majesty, listen to what I have to say. If it is the LORD who has turned you against me, an offering to him will make him change his mind; but if human beings have done it, may the LORD's curse fall on them. For they have driven me out from the LORD's land to a country where I can only worship foreign gods. ²⁰ Don't let me be killed on foreign soil, away from the LORD. Why should the king of Israel come to kill a flea like me? Why should he hunt me down like a wild bird?"

²¹ Saul answered, "I have done wrong. Come back, David, my son! I will never harm you again, because you have spared my life tonight. I have been a fool! I have done a terrible thing!"

²² David replied, "Here is your spear, Your Majesty. Let one of your men come over and get it. ²³ The LORD rewards those who are faithful and righteous. Today he put you in my power, but I did not harm you, whom the LORD made king. ²⁴ Just as I have spared your life today, may the LORD do the same to me and free me from all troubles!"

²⁵ Saul said to David, "God bless you, my son! You will succeed in everything you do!"

So David went on his way, and Saul returned home.

David among the Philistines

27 David said to himself, "One of these days Saul will kill me. The best thing for me to do is to escape to Philistia. Then Saul will give up looking for me in Israel, and I will be safe." ² So David and his 600 men went over at once to Achish son of Maoch, king of Gath. ³ David and his men settled there in Gath with their families. David had his two wives with him, Ahinoam from Jezreel, and Abigail, Nabal's widow, from Carmel. ⁴ When Saul heard that David had fled to Gath, he gave up trying to find him.

⁵ David said to Achish, "If you are my friend, let me have a small town to live in. There is no need, sir, for me to live with you in the capital city." ⁶ So Achish gave him the town of Ziklag, and for this reason Ziklag has belonged to the kings of Judah ever since. ⁷ David lived in Philistia for sixteen months.

⁸ During that time David and his men would attack the people of Geshur, Girzi, and Amalek, who had been living in the region a very long time. He would raid their land as far as Shur, all the way down to Egypt, ⁹ killing all the men and women and taking the sheep, cattle, donkeys, camels, and even the clothes. Then he would come back to Achish, ¹⁰ who would ask him, "Where did you go on a raid this time?" and David would tell him that he had gone to the southern part of Judah or to the territory of the clan of Jerahmeel or to the territory where the Kenites lived. ¹¹ David would kill everyone, men and women, so that no one could go back to Gath and report what he and his men had really done. This is what David did the whole time he lived in Philistia. ¹² But Achish trusted David and said to himself, "He is hated so much by his own people the Israelites that he will have to serve me all his life."

28

Some time later, the Philistines gathered their troops to fight Israel, and Achish said to David, "Of course you understand that you and your men are to fight on my side."

[2] "Of course," David answered. "I am your servant, and you will see for yourself what I can do."

Achish said, "Good! I will make you my permanent bodyguard."

Saul Consults a Medium

[3] Now Samuel had died, and all the Israelites had mourned for him and had buried him in his own city of Ramah. Saul had forced all the fortune tellers and mediums to leave Israel.

[4] The Philistine troops assembled and camped near the town of Shunem; Saul gathered the Israelites and camped at Mount Gilboa. [5] When Saul saw the Philistine army, he was terrified, [6] and so he asked the LORD what to do. But the LORD did not answer him at all, either by dreams or by the use of Urim and Thummim or by prophets. [7] Then Saul ordered his officials, "Find me a woman who is a medium, and I will go and consult her."

"There is one in Endor," they answered.

[8] So Saul disguised himself; he put on different clothes, and after dark he went with two of his men to see the woman. "Consult the spirits for me and tell me what is going to happen," he said to her. "Call up the spirit of the man I name."

[9] The woman answered, "Surely you know what King Saul has done, how he forced the fortune tellers and mediums to leave Israel.* Why, then, are you trying to trap me and get me killed?"

[10] Then Saul made a sacred vow. "By the living LORD I promise that you will not be punished for doing this," he told her.

[11] "Whom shall I call up for you?" the woman asked.

"Samuel," he answered.

[12] When the woman saw Samuel, she screamed and said to Saul, "Why have you tricked me? You are King Saul!"

[13] "Don't be afraid!" the king said to her. "What do you see?"

"I see a spirit coming up from the earth," she answered.

[14] "What does it look like?" he asked.

"It's an old man coming up," she answered. "He is wearing a cloak."

Then Saul knew that it was Samuel, and he bowed to the ground in respect.

[15] Samuel said to Saul, "Why have you disturbed me? Why did you make me come back?"

Saul answered, "I am in great trouble! The Philistines are at war with me, and God has abandoned me. He doesn't answer me any more, either by prophets or by dreams. And so I have called you, for you to tell me what I must do."

[16] Samuel said, "Why do you call me when the LORD has abandoned you and become your enemy? [17] The LORD has done to you what he told you through me: he has taken the kingdom away from you and given it to David instead. [18] You disobeyed the LORD's command and did not completely destroy the Amalekites and all they had. That is why the LORD is doing this to you now. [19] He will hand you and Israel over to the Philistines. Tomorrow you and your sons will join me, and the LORD will also hand the army of Israel over to the Philistines."

[20] At once Saul fell down and lay stretched out on the ground, terrified by what Samuel had said. He was weak, because he had

1 Sam.

2 Sam.
1 Kings
2 Kings
1 Chron.
2 Chron.

28.9 he forced... Israel; or he put to death the fortune tellers and mediums in Israel.

350

1 Sam.

Num.
Deuter.
Joshua
Judges
Ruth

1 SAMUEL 28–30

not eaten anything all day and all night. ²¹The woman went over to him and saw that he was terrified, so she said to him, "Please, sir, I risked my life by doing what you asked. ²²Now please do what I ask. Let me prepare some food for you. You must eat so that you will be strong enough to travel."

²³Saul refused and said he would not eat anything. But his officers also urged him to eat. He finally gave in, got up from the ground, and sat on the bed. ²⁴The woman quickly killed a calf which she had been fattening. Then she took some flour, prepared it, and baked some bread without yeast. ²⁵She set the food before Saul and his officers, and they ate it. And they left that same night.

David is Rejected by the Philistines

29 The Philistines brought all their troops together at Aphek, while the Israelites camped at the spring in the Valley of Jezreel. ²The five Philistine kings marched out with their units of a hundred and of a thousand men; David and his men marched in the rear with King Achish. ³The Philistine commanders saw them and asked, "What are these Hebrews doing here?"

Achish answered, "This is David, an official of King Saul of Israel. He has been with me for quite a long time now. He has done nothing I can find fault with since the day he came over to me."

⁴But the Philistine commanders were angry with Achish and said to him, "Send that fellow back to the town you gave him. Don't let him go into battle with us; he might turn against us during the fighting. What better way is there for him to win back his master's favour than by the death of our men? ⁵After all, this is David, the one about whom the women sang, as they danced, 'Saul has killed thousands, but David has killed tens of thousands.'"

⁶Achish called David and said to him, "I swear by the living GOD of Israel that you have been loyal to me; and I would be pleased to let you go with me and fight in this battle. I have not found any fault in you from the day you came over to me. But the other kings don't approve of you. ⁷So go back home in peace, and don't do anything that would displease them."

⁸David answered, "What have I done wrong, sir? If, as you say, you haven't found any fault in me since the day I started serving you, why shouldn't I go with you, my master and king, and fight your enemies?"

⁹"I agree," Achish replied. "I consider you as loyal as an angel of God. But the other kings have said that you can't go with us into battle. ¹⁰So then, David, tomorrow morning all of you who left Saul and came over to me will have to get up early and leave as soon as it's light."

¹¹So David and his men started out early the following morning to go back to Philistia, and the Philistines went on to Jezreel.

The War against the Amalekites

30 Two days later David and his men arrived back at Ziklag. The Amalekites had raided southern Judah and attacked Ziklag. They had burnt down the town ²and captured all the women; they had not killed anyone, but had taken everyone with them when they left. ³When David and his men arrived, they found that the town had been burnt down and that their wives, sons, and daughters had been carried away. ⁴David and his men started crying and did not stop until they were completely exhausted. ⁵Even David's two wives, Ahinoam and Abigail, had been taken away.

1 Sam.
..........:
2 Sam.
1 Kings
2 Kings
1 Chron.
2 Chron.

[6] David was now in great trouble, because his men were all very bitter about losing their children, and they were threatening to stone him; but the LORD his God gave him courage. [7] David said to the priest Abiathar son of Ahimelech, "Bring me the ephod," and Abiathar brought it to him. [8] David asked the LORD, "Shall I go after those raiders? And will I catch them?"

He answered, "Go after them; you will catch them and rescue the captives."

[9] So David and his 600 men started out, and when they arrived at the brook of Besor, some of them stayed there. [10] David continued on his way with 400 men; the other 200 men were too tired to cross the brook and so stayed behind. [11] The men with David found an Egyptian out in the country and brought him to David. They gave him some food and water, [12] some dried figs, and two bunches of raisins. After he had eaten, his strength returned; he had not had anything to eat or drink for three full days. [13] David asked him, "Who is your master, and where are you from?"

"I am an Egyptian, the slave of an Amalekite," he answered. "My master left me behind three days ago because I was ill. [14] We had raided the territory of the Cherethites in the southern part of Judah and the territory of the clan of Caleb, and we burnt down Ziklag."

[15] "Will you lead me to those raiders?" David asked him.

He answered, "I will if you promise me in God's name that you will not kill me or hand me over to my master." [16] And he led David to them.

The raiders were scattered all over the place, eating, drinking, and celebrating because of the enormous amount of loot they had captured from Philistia and Judah. [17] At dawn the next day David attacked them and fought until evening. Except for 400 young men who mounted camels and got away, none of them escaped. [18] David rescued everyone and everything the Amalekites had taken, including his two wives; [19] nothing at all was missing. David got back all his men's sons and daughters, and all the loot the Amalekites had taken. [20] He also recovered all the flocks and herds; his men drove all the livestock in front of them* and said, "This belongs to David!"

[21] Then David went back to the 200 men who had been too weak to go with him and had stayed behind at the brook of Besor. They came forward to meet David and his men, and David went up to them and greeted them warmly. [22] But some mean and worthless men who had gone with David said, "They didn't go with us, and so we won't give them any of the loot. They can take their wives and children and go away."

[23] But David answered, "My brothers, you can't do this with what the LORD has given us! He kept us safe and gave us victory over the raiders. [24] No one can agree with what you say! All must share alike: whoever stays behind with the supplies gets the same share as the one who goes into battle." [25] David made this a rule, and it has been followed in Israel ever since.

[26] When David returned to Ziklag, he sent part of the loot to his friends, the leaders of Judah, with the message, "Here is a present for you from the loot we took from the LORD's enemies." [27] He sent it to the people in Bethel, to the people in Ramah in the southern part of Judah, and to the people in the towns of Jattir, [28] Aroer, Siphmoth, Eshtemoa, [29] and Racal; to the clan of Jerahmeel, to the Kenites, [30] and to the people in the towns of

....

30.20 Probable text *his men... front of them*; Hebrew unclear.

352

1 Sam.

Num.
Deuter.
Joshua
Judges
Ruth

TURN THESE LINES INTO A PICTURE OF SOMETHING.

Hormah, Borashan, Athach, [31] and Hebron. He sent it to all the places where he and his men had roamed.

The Death of Saul and his Sons
(1 Chr 10.1–12)

31 The Philistines fought a battle against the Israelites on Mount Gilboa. Many Israelites were killed there, and the rest of them, including King Saul and his sons, fled. [2] But the Philistines caught up with them and killed three of Saul's sons, Jonathan, Abinadab, and Malchishua. [3] The fighting was heavy round Saul, and he himself was hit by enemy arrows and badly wounded. [4] He said to the young man carrying his weapons, "Draw your sword and kill me, so that these godless Philistines won't gloat over me and kill me." But the young man was too terrified to do it. So Saul took his own sword and threw himself on it. [5] The young man saw that Saul was dead, so he too threw himself on his own sword and died with Saul. [6] And that is how Saul, his three sons, and the young man died; all of Saul's men died that day. [7] When the Israelites on the other side of the Valley of Jezreel and east of the River Jordan heard that the Israelite army had fled and that Saul and his sons had been killed, they abandoned their towns and fled. Then the Philistines came and occupied them.

[8] The day after the battle the Philistines went to plunder the corpses, and they found the bodies of Saul and his three sons lying on Mount Gilboa. [9] They cut off Saul's head, stripped off his armour, and sent messengers with them throughout Philistia to tell the good news to their idols and to their people. [10] Then they put his weapons in the temple of the goddess Astarte, and they nailed his body to the wall of the city of Beth Shan.

[11] When the people of Jabesh in Gilead heard what the Philistines had done to Saul, [12] the bravest men started out and marched all night to Beth Shan. They took down the bodies of Saul and his sons from the wall, brought them back to Jabesh, and burnt them there. [13] Then they took the bones and buried them under the tamarisk tree in the town, and fasted for seven days.

THE BOOK OF
2 SAMUEL

WRITTEN: PROBABLY 600-400BC
(USING STORIES FROM A MUCH EARLIER TIME)

KEY CHARACTER:

Nathan the prophet appears twice in 2 Samuel, in chapters 7 and 12. He was the person God chose to guide and challenge David. In chapter 12 we see the wisdom and discernment that Nathan used to challenge David. This is a great lesson about courage and about leading people who are in authority over you.

WHY READ IT?

This is the close-up story of an excellent leader, a man who completely loved God but who was human and kept getting things wrong. David betrayed others and experienced betrayal. It was not until he messed up that he really understood what God's love and forgiveness meant. The story shows that human weaknesses don't stop us from being great leaders and passionate about God.

ON A PIECE OF PAPER, WRITE DOWN SOME OF THE

BIGGER MISTAKES

THAT YOU'VE MADE.

AFTER THINKING ABOUT THEM, GO AND

DESTROY

THE PIECE OF PAPER.

IT'S NOT UNTIL WE MAKE SOME MASSIVE MISTAKES THAT WE REALISE WHAT

GOD'S LOVE

WILL COVER - AND THEN WE CAN MOVE AWAY FROM MAKING THOSE MISTAKES AGAIN.

WHAT YOU NEED TO KNOW:

2 Samuel is the sequel to 1 Samuel - they were originally one book. 1 Samuel tells how David became king and 2 Samuel is about how he ruled. David was an excellent king, and Israel started to become a strong force, but David had his weaknesses and the longer he ruled, the more complicated things got. The book starts with David ruling first Judah in the south and then Israel in the north. David defeated the Jebusites and took their city, Jerusalem, thought to be unconquerable. God promised that David's descendants would always be on the throne of Israel - a pointer towards Jesus.

KING DAVID

DAVID AND BATHSHEBA

ABSALOM (DAVID'S SON) REBELS

ABSALOM DIES

354

2 Sam.

Deuter.
Joshua
Judges
Ruth
1 Sam.

2 SAMUEL 1

David Learns of Saul's Death

1 After Saul's death David came back from his victory over the Amalekites and stayed in Ziklag for two days. [2] The next day a young man arrived from Saul's camp. To show his grief, he had torn his clothes and put earth on his head. He went to David and bowed to the ground in respect. [3] David asked him, "Where have you come from?"

"I have escaped from the Israelite camp," he answered.

[4] "Tell me what happened," David said.

"Our army ran away from the battle," he replied, "and many of our men were killed. Saul and his son Jonathan were also killed."

[5] "How do you know that Saul and Jonathan are dead?" David asked him.

[6] He answered, "I happened to be on Mount Gilboa, and I saw that Saul was leaning on his spear and that the chariots and horsemen of the enemy were closing in on him. [7] Then he turned round, saw me, and called to me. I answered, 'Yes, sir!' [8] He asked who I was, and I told him that I was an Amalekite. [9] Then he said, 'Come here and kill me! I have been badly wounded, and I'm about to die.' [10] So I went up to him and killed him, because I knew that he would die anyway as soon as he fell. Then I took the crown from his head and the bracelet from his arm, and I have brought them to you, sir."

[11] David tore his clothes in sorrow, and all his men did the same. [12] They grieved and mourned and fasted until evening for Saul and Jonathan and for Israel, the people of the LORD, because so many had been killed in battle.

[13] David asked the young man who had brought him the news, "Where are you from?"

He answered, "I'm an Amalekite, but I live in your country."

[14] David asked him, "How is it that you dared to kill the LORD's chosen king?" [15] Then David called one of his men and said, "Kill him!" The man struck the Amalekite and mortally wounded him, [16] and David said to the Amalekite, "You brought this on yourself. You condemned yourself when you admitted that you killed the one whom the LORD chose to be king."

David's Lament for Saul and Jonathan

[17] David sang this lament for Saul and his son Jonathan, [18] and ordered it* to be taught to the people of Judah. (It is recorded in *The Book of Jashar*.)

[19] "On the hills of Israel our leaders are dead!
    The bravest of our soldiers have fallen!
[20] Do not announce it in Gath
    or in the streets of Ashkelon.
Do not make the women of Philistia glad;
    do not let the daughters of pagans rejoice.

[21] "May no rain or dew fall on Gilboa's hills;
    may its fields be always barren!
For the shields of the brave lie there in disgrace;
    the shield of Saul is no longer polished with oil.
[22] Jonathan's bow was deadly,
    the sword of Saul was merciless,
    striking down the mighty, killing the enemy.

1.18 One ancient translation *it*; Hebrew *the bow*.

355

2 Sam.

....

1 Kings
2 Kings
1 Chron.
2 Chron.
Ezra

23 "Saul and Jonathan, so wonderful and dear;
together in life, together in death;
swifter than eagles, stronger than lions.

24 "Women of Israel, mourn for Saul!
He clothed you in rich scarlet dresses
and adorned you with jewels and gold.

25 "The brave soldiers have fallen,
they were killed in battle.
Jonathan lies dead in the hills.

26 "I grieve for you, my brother Jonathan;
how dear you were to me!
How wonderful was your love for me,
better even than the love of women.

27 "The brave soldiers have fallen,
their weapons abandoned and useless."

David is Made King of Judah

2 After this, David asked the Lord, "Shall I go and take control of one of the towns of Judah?"

"Yes," the Lord answered.

"Which one?" David asked.

"Hebron," the Lord said. 2 So David went to Hebron, taking with him his two wives: Ahinoam, who was from Jezreel, and Abigail, Nabal's widow, who was from Carmel. 3 He also took his men and their families, and they settled in the towns round Hebron. 4 Then the men of Judah came to Hebron and anointed David as king of Judah.

When David heard that the people of Jabesh in Gilead had buried Saul, 5 he sent some men there with the message: "May the Lord bless you for showing your loyalty to your king by burying him. 6 And now may the Lord be kind and faithful to you. I too will treat you well because of what you have done. 7 Be strong and brave! Saul your king is dead, and the people of Judah have anointed me as their king."

Ishbosheth is Made King of Israel

8 The commander of Saul's army, Abner son of Ner, had fled with Saul's son Ishbosheth across the Jordan to Mahanaim. 9 There Abner made Ishbosheth king of the territories of Gilead, Asher,* Jezreel, Ephraim, and Benjamin, and indeed over all Israel. 10 He was forty years old when he was made king of Israel, and he ruled for two years.

But the tribe of Judah was loyal to David, 11 and he ruled in Hebron over Judah for seven and a half years.

War between Israel and Judah

12 Abner and the officials of Ishbosheth went from Mahanaim to the city of Gibeon. 13 Joab, whose mother was Zeruiah, and David's other officials met them at the pool, where they all sat down, one group on one side of the pool and the other group on the opposite side. 14 Abner said to Joab, "Let's get some of the young men from each side to fight an armed contest."

....

2.9 One ancient translation *Asher*; Hebrew *Assyria*.

356

2 Sam.

Deuter.
Joshua
Judges
Ruth
1 Sam.

2 SAMUEL 2, 3

JOIN THE DOTS

below to make a picture.

"All right," Joab answered.

15 So twelve men, representing Ishbosheth and the tribe of Benjamin, fought twelve of David's men. 16 Each man caught his opponent by the head and plunged his sword into his opponent's side, so that all 24 of them fell down dead together. And so that place in Gibeon is called "Field of Swords".

17 Then a furious battle broke out, and Abner and the Israelites were defeated by David's men. 18 The three sons of Zeruiah were there: Joab, Abishai, and Asahel. Asahel, who could run as fast as a wild deer, 19 started chasing Abner, running straight for him. 20 Abner looked back and said, "Is that you, Asahel?"

"Yes," he answered.

21 "Stop chasing me!" Abner said. "Run after one of the soldiers and take what he has." But Asahel kept on chasing him. 22 Once more Abner said to him, "Stop chasing me! Why force me to kill you? How could I face your brother Joab?" 23 But Asahel would not give up; so Abner, with a backward thrust* of his spear, struck him through the belly so that the spear came out at his back. Asahel dropped to the ground dead, and everyone who came to the place where he was lying stopped and stood there.

24 But Joab and Abishai started out after Abner, and at sunset they came to the hill of Ammah, which is to the east of Giah on the road to the wilderness of Gibeon. 25 The men from the tribe of Benjamin gathered round Abner again and took their stand on the top of a hill. 26 Abner called out to Joab, "Do we have to go on fighting for ever? Can't you see that in the end there will be nothing but bitterness? We are your fellow-countrymen. How long will it be before you order your men to stop chasing us?"

27 "I swear by the living God," Joab answered, "that if you had not spoken, my men would have kept on chasing you until tomorrow morning." 28 Then Joab blew the trumpet as a signal for his men to stop pursuing the Israelites; and so the fighting stopped.

29 Abner and his men marched through the Jordan Valley all that night; they crossed the River Jordan, and after marching all the next morning, they arrived back at Mahanaim.

30 When Joab gave up the chase, he gathered all his men and found that nineteen of them were missing, in addition to Asahel. 31 David's men had killed 360 of Abner's men from the tribe of Benjamin. 32 Joab and his men took Asahel's body and buried it in the family tomb at Bethlehem. Then they marched all night and at dawn arrived back at Hebron.

3 The fighting between the forces supporting Saul's family and those supporting David went on for a long time. As David became stronger and stronger, his opponents became weaker and weaker.

David's Sons

2 The following six sons, in the order of their birth, were born to David at Hebron: Amnon, whose mother was Ahinoam, from Jezreel; 3 Chileab, whose mother was Abigail, Nabal's widow, from Carmel; Absalom, whose mother was Maacah, the daughter of King Talmai of Geshur; 4 Adonijah, whose mother was Haggith; Shephatiah, whose mother was Abital; 5 Ithream, whose mother was Eglah. All of these sons were born in Hebron.

2.23 Probable text with a backward thrust; Hebrew unclear.

2 SAMUEL 3

357

2 Sam.

....

1 Kings
2 Kings
1 Chron.
2 Chron.
Ezra

Abner Joins David

⁶ As the fighting continued between David's forces and the forces loyal to Saul's family, Abner became more and more powerful among Saul's followers.

⁷ One day Ishbosheth son of Saul accused Abner of sleeping with Saul's concubine Rizpah, the daughter of Aiah. ⁸ This made Abner furious. "Do you think that I would betray Saul? Do you really think I'm serving Judah?" he exclaimed. "From the very first I have been loyal to the cause of your father Saul, his brothers, and his friends, and I have saved you from being defeated by David; yet today you find fault with me about a woman! ⁹⁻¹⁰ The LORD promised David that he would take the kingdom away from Saul and his descendants and would make David king of both Israel and Judah, from one end of the country to the other. Now may God strike me dead if I don't make this come true!" ¹¹ Ishbosheth was so afraid of Abner that he could not say a word.

¹² Abner sent messengers to David, who at that time was at Hebron,* to say, "Who is going to rule this land? Make an agreement with me, and I will help you win all Israel over to your side."

¹³ "Good!" David answered. "I will make an agreement with you on one condition: you must bring Saul's daughter Michal to me when you come to see me." ¹⁴ And David also sent messengers to Ishbosheth to say, "Give me back my wife Michal. I paid a hundred Philistine foreskins in order to marry her." ¹⁵ So Ishbosheth took her away from her husband Paltiel son of Laish. ¹⁶ Paltiel followed her all the way to the town of Bahurim, crying as he went. But when Abner said, "Go back home," he did.

¹⁷ Abner went to the leaders of Israel and said to them, "For a long time you have wanted David to be your king. ¹⁸ Now here is your chance. Remember that the LORD has said, 'I will use my servant David to rescue my people Israel from the Philistines and from all their other enemies.' " ¹⁹ Abner spoke also to the people of the tribe of Benjamin and then went to Hebron to tell David what the people of Benjamin and of Israel had agreed to do.

²⁰ When Abner came to David at Hebron with twenty men, David gave a feast for them. ²¹ Abner told David, "I will go now and win all Israel over to Your Majesty. They will accept you as king, and then you will get what you have wanted and will rule over the whole land." David gave Abner a guarantee of safety and sent him on his way.

Abner is Murdered

²² Later on Joab and David's other officials returned from a raid, bringing a large amount of loot with them. Abner, however, was no longer there at Hebron with David, because David had sent him away with a guarantee of safety. ²³ When Joab and his men arrived, he was told that Abner had come to King David and had been sent away with a guarantee of safety. ²⁴ So Joab went to the king and said to him, "What have you done? Abner came to you — why did you let him go like that? ²⁵ He came here to deceive you and to find out everything you do and everywhere you go. Surely you know that!"

²⁶ After leaving David, Joab sent messengers to get Abner, and they brought him back from the well of Sirah; but David knew nothing about it. ²⁷ When Abner arrived in Hebron, Joab took him aside at the gate, as though he wanted to speak privately

....

3.12 One ancient translation *at Hebron*; Hebrew *where he (Abner) was*.

358

2 Sam.

Deuter.
Joshua
Judges
Ruth
1 Sam.

2 SAMUEL 3, 4

with him, and there he stabbed him in the belly. And so Abner was murdered because he had killed Joab's brother Asahel. [28] When David heard the news, he said, "The LORD knows that my subjects and I are completely innocent of the murder of Abner. [29] May the punishment for it fall on Joab and all his family! In every generation may there be some man in his family who has gonorrhoea or a dreaded skin disease or is fit only to do a woman's work or is killed in battle or hasn't enough to eat!" [30] So Joab and his brother Abishai took revenge on Abner for killing their brother Asahel in the battle at Gibeon.

Abner is Buried

[31] Then David ordered Joab and his men to tear their clothes, wear sackcloth, and mourn for Abner. And at the funeral King David himself walked behind the coffin. [32] Abner was buried at Hebron, and the king wept aloud at the grave, and so did all the people. [33] David sang this lament for Abner:

"Why did Abner have to die like a fool?
[34] His hands were not tied,
And his feet were not bound;
He died like someone killed by criminals!"
And the people wept for him again.

[35] All day long the people tried to get David to eat something, but he made a solemn promise, "May God strike me dead if I eat anything before the day is over!" [36] They took note of this and were pleased. Indeed, everything the king did pleased the people. [37] All David's people and all the people in Israel understood that the king had no part in the murder of Abner. [38] The king said to his officials, "Don't you realize that this day a great leader in Israel has died? [39] Even though I am the king chosen by God, I feel weak today. These sons of Zeruiah are too violent for me. May the LORD punish these criminals as they deserve!"

Ishbosheth is Murdered

4 When Saul's son Ishbosheth heard that Abner had been killed in Hebron, he was afraid, and all the people of Israel were alarmed. [2] Ishbosheth had two officers who were leaders of raiding parties, Baanah and Rechab, sons of Rimmon, from Beeroth in the tribe of Benjamin. (Beeroth is counted as part of Benjamin. [3] Its original inhabitants had fled to Gittaim, where they have lived ever since.)

[4] Another descendant of Saul was Jonathan's son Mephibosheth, who was five years old when Saul and Jonathan were killed. When the news about their death came from the city of Jezreel, his nurse picked him up and fled; but she was in such a hurry that she dropped him, and he became crippled.

[5] Rechab and Baanah set out for Ishbosheth's house and arrived there about noon, while he was taking his midday rest. [6] The woman at the door had become drowsy while she was sifting wheat and had fallen asleep, so Rechab and Baanah slipped in.* [7] Once inside, they went to Ishbosheth's bedroom, where he was sound asleep, and killed him. Then they cut off his head, took it with them, and walked all night through the Jordan Valley. [8] They presented the head to King David at Hebron and said to him, "Here is the head of Ishbosheth, the son of your enemy Saul,

---

4.6 Verse 6 follows one ancient translation; Hebrew *They went on into the house carrying wheat, and struck him in the belly. Then Rechab and his brother Baanah escaped.*

2 SAMUEL 4, 5

359

2 Sam.

....

1 Kings
2 Kings
1 Chron.
2 Chron.
Ezra

who tried to kill you. Today the Lord has allowed Your Majesty to take revenge on Saul and his descendants." [9] David answered them, "I make a vow by the living Lord, who has saved me from all dangers! [10] The messenger who came to me at Ziklag and told me of Saul's death thought he was bringing good news. I seized him and had him put to death. That was the reward I gave him for his good news! [11] How much worse it will be for evil men who murder an innocent man asleep in his own house! I will now take revenge on you for murdering him and will wipe you off the face of the earth!" [12] David gave the order, and his soldiers killed Rechab and Baanah and cut off their hands and feet, which they hung up near the pool in Hebron. They took Ishbosheth's head and buried it in Abner's tomb there at Hebron.

David Becomes King of Israel and Judah
(1 Chr 11.1–9; 14.1–7)

5 Then all the tribes of Israel came to David at Hebron and said to him, "We are your own flesh and blood. [2] In the past, even when Saul was still our king, you led the people of Israel in battle, and the Lord promised you that you would lead his people and be their ruler." [3] So all the leaders of Israel came to King David at Hebron. He made a sacred alliance with them, they anointed him, and he became king of Israel. [4] David was thirty years old when he became king, and he ruled for forty years. [5] He ruled in Hebron over Judah for seven and a half years, and in Jerusalem over all Israel and Judah for 33 years.

[6] The time came when King David and his men set out to attack Jerusalem. The Jebusites, who lived there, thought that David would not be able to conquer the city, and so they said to him, "You will never get in here; even the blind and the crippled could keep you out." [7] (But David did capture their fortress of Zion, and it became known as "David's City".)

[8] That day David said to his men, "Does anybody here hate the Jebusites as much as I do? Enough to kill them? Then go up through the water tunnel and attack those poor blind cripples." (That is why it is said, "The blind and the crippled cannot enter the Lord's house.")*

[9] After capturing the fortress, David lived in it and named it "David's City". He built the city round it, starting at the place where land was filled in on the east side of the hill. [10] He grew stronger all the time, because the Lord God Almighty was with him.

[11] King Hiram of Tyre sent a trade mission to David; he provided him with cedar logs and with carpenters and stonemasons to build a palace. [12] And so David realized that the Lord had established him as king of Israel and was making his kingdom prosperous for the sake of his people.

[13] After moving from Hebron to Jerusalem, David took more concubines and wives, and had more sons and daughters. [14] The following children were born to him in Jerusalem: Shammua, Shobab, Nathan, Solomon, [15] Ibhar, Elishua, Nepheg, Japhia, [16] Elishama, Eliada, and Eliphelet.

Victory over the Philistines
(1 Chr 14.8–17)

[17] The Philistines were told that David had been made king of Israel, so their army set out to capture him. When David heard of it, he went down to a fortified place. [18] The Philistines arrived

....

5.8 Verse 8 in Hebrew is unclear.

360

2 Sam.

⋮

Deuter.
Joshua
Judges
Ruth
1 Sam.

2 SAMUEL 5, 6

at the Valley of Rephaim and occupied it. [19] David asked the LORD, "Shall I attack the Philistines? Will you give me the victory?"

"Yes, attack!" the LORD answered. "I will give you the victory!"

[20] So David went to Baal Perazim and there he defeated the Philistines. He said, "The LORD has broken through my enemies like a flood." And so that place is called Baal Perazim.* [21] When the Philistines fled, they left their idols behind, and David and his men carried them away.

[22] Then the Philistines went back to the Valley of Rephaim and occupied it again. [23] Once more David consulted the LORD, who answered, "Don't attack them from here, but go round and get ready to attack them from the other side, near the balsam trees. [24] When you hear the sound of marching in the treetops, then attack because I will be marching ahead of you to defeat the Philistine army." [25] David did what the LORD had commanded, and was able to drive the Philistines back from Geba all the way to Gezer.

The Covenant Box is Brought to Jerusalem
(1 Chr 13.1–14; 15.25—16.6, 43)

6 Once more David called together the best soldiers in Israel, a total of 30,000 men, [2] and led them to Baalah* in Judah, in order to bring from there God's Covenant Box, bearing the name of the LORD Almighty, who is enthroned above the winged creatures. [3] They took it from Abinadab's home on the hill and placed it on a new cart. Uzzah and Ahio, sons of Abinadab, were guiding the cart, [4] with Ahio walking in front. [5] David and all the Israelites were dancing and singing with all their might* to honour the LORD. They were playing harps, lyres, drums, rattles, and cymbals.

[6] As they came to the threshing place of Nacon, the oxen stumbled, and Uzzah reached out and took hold of the Covenant Box. [7] At once the LORD God became angry with Uzzah and killed him because of his irreverence.* Uzzah died there beside the Covenant Box, [8] and so that place has been called Perez Uzzah* ever since. David was furious because the LORD had punished Uzzah in anger.

[9] Then David was afraid of the LORD and said, "How can I take the Covenant Box with me now?" [10] So he decided not to take it with him to Jerusalem; instead, he turned off the road and took it to the house of Obed Edom, a native of the city of Gath. [11] It stayed there three months, and the LORD blessed Obed Edom and his family.

[12] King David heard that because of the Covenant Box the LORD had blessed Obed Edom's family and all that he had; so he fetched the Covenant Box from Obed's house to take it to Jerusalem with a great celebration. [13] After the men carrying the Covenant Box had gone six steps, David made them stop while he offered the LORD a sacrifice of a bull and a fattened calf. [14] David, wearing only a linen cloth round his waist, danced with all his might to honour the LORD. [15] And so he and all the Israelites took the Covenant Box up to Jerusalem with shouts of joy and the sound of trumpets.

....

5.20 *Baal Perazim*: This name in Hebrew means "Lord of the Breakthrough".
6.2 Probable text (see 1 Chr 13.6) *to Baalah*; Hebrew *from Baaley*, or *from the leaders*.
6.5 One ancient translation (and see 1 Chr 13.8) *and singing with all their might*; Hebrew *with all the fir trees*.
6.7 Probable text *his irreverence*; Hebrew unclear.
6.8 *Perez Uzzah*: This name in Hebrew means "Punishment of Uzzah".

2 SAMUEL 6, 7

361

2 Sam.

....

1 Kings
2 Kings
1 Chron.
2 Chron.
Ezra

[16] As the Box was being brought into the city, Michal, Saul's daughter, looked out of the window and saw King David dancing and jumping around in the sacred dance, and she was disgusted with him. [17] They brought the Box and put it in its place in the Tent that David had set up for it. Then he offered sacrifices and fellowship offerings to the LORD. [18] When he had finished offering the sacrifices, he blessed the people in the name of the LORD Almighty [19] and distributed food to them all. He gave each man and woman in Israel a loaf of bread, a piece of roasted meat,* and some raisins. Then everyone went home.

[20] Afterwards, when David went home to greet his family, Michal came out to meet him. "The king of Israel made a big name for himself today!" she said. "He exposed himself like a fool in the sight of the servant women of his officials!"

[21] David answered, "I was dancing to honour the LORD, who chose me instead of your father and his family to make me the leader of his people Israel. And I will go on dancing to honour the LORD, [22] and will disgrace myself even more. You* may think I am nothing, but those women will think highly of me!"

[23] Michal, Saul's daughter, never had any children.

Nathan's Message to David
(1 Chr 17.1–15)

7 King David was settled in his palace, and the LORD kept him safe from all his enemies. [2] Then the king said to the prophet Nathan, "Here I am living in a house built of cedar, but God's Covenant Box is kept in a tent!"

[3] Nathan answered, "Do whatever you have in mind, because the LORD is with you." [4] But that night the LORD said to Nathan, [5] "Go and tell my servant David that I say to him, 'You are not the one to build a temple for me to live in. [6] From the time I rescued the people of Israel from Egypt until now, I have never lived in a temple; I have travelled round living in a tent. [7] In all my travelling with the people of Israel I never asked any of the leaders* that I appointed why they had not built me a temple made of cedar.'

[8] "So tell my servant David that I, the LORD Almighty, say to him, 'I took you from looking after sheep in the fields and made you the ruler of my people Israel. [9] I have been with you wherever you have gone, and I have defeated all your enemies as you advanced. I will make you as famous as the greatest leaders in the world. [10-11] I have chosen a place for my people Israel and have settled them there, where they will live without being oppressed any more. Ever since they entered this land, they have been attacked by violent people, but this will not happen again. I promise to keep you safe from all your enemies and to give you descendants. [12] When you die and are buried with your ancestors, I will make one of your sons king and will keep his kingdom strong. [13] He will be the one to build a temple for me, and I will make sure that his dynasty continues for ever. [14] I will be his father, and he will be my son. When he does wrong, I will punish him as a father punishes his son. [15] But I will not withdraw my support from him as I did from Saul, whom I removed so that you could be king. [16] You will always have descendants, and I will make your kingdom last for ever. Your dynasty will never end.'"

[17] Nathan told David everything that God had revealed to him.

....

6.19 *a piece of roasted meat*; or *a cake of dates*.
6.22 One ancient translation *You*; Hebrew *I*.
7.7 Probable text (see 1 Chr 17.6) *leaders*; Hebrew *tribes*.

362

2 Sam.

Deuter.
Joshua
Judges
Ruth
1 Sam.

2 SAMUEL 7, 8

David's Prayer of Thanksgiving
(1 Chr 17.16–27)

18 Then King David went into the Tent of the LORD's presence, sat down and prayed, "I am not worthy of what you have already done for me, Sovereign LORD, nor is my family. 19 Yet now you are doing even more, Sovereign LORD; you have made promises about my descendants in the years to come. And you let a man see this,* Sovereign LORD! 20 What more can I say to you! You know me, your servant. 21 It was your will and purpose to do this; you have done all these great things in order to teach me. 22 How great you are, Sovereign LORD! There is none like you; we have always known that you alone are God. 23 There is no other nation on earth like Israel, whom you rescued from slavery to make them your own people. The great and wonderful things you did for them* have spread your fame throughout the world. You drove out* other nations and their gods as your people advanced, the people whom you set free from Egypt to be your own. 24 You have made Israel your own people for ever, and you, LORD, have become their God.

25 "And now, LORD God, fulfil for all time the promise you made about me and my descendants, and do what you said you would. 26 Your fame will be great, and people will for ever say, 'The LORD Almighty is God over Israel.' And you will preserve my dynasty for all time. 27 Almighty LORD, God of Israel! I have the courage to pray this prayer to you, because you have revealed all this to me, your servant, and have told me that you will make my descendants kings.

28 "And now, Sovereign LORD, you are God; you always keep your promises, and you have made this wonderful promise to me. 29 I ask you to bless my descendants so that they will continue to enjoy your favour. You, Sovereign LORD, have promised this, and your blessing will rest on my descendants for ever."

David's Military Victories
(1 Chr 18.1–17)

8 Some time later King David attacked the Philistines again, defeated them, and ended their control over the land.*

2 Then he defeated the Moabites. He made the prisoners lie down on the ground and put two out of every three of them to death. So the Moabites became his subjects and paid taxes to him.

3 Then he defeated the king of the Syrian state of Zobah, Hadadezer son of Rehob, as Hadadezer was on his way to restore his control over the territory by the upper Euphrates. 4 David captured 1,700 of his horsemen and 20,000 of his foot soldiers. He kept enough horses for a hundred chariots and crippled all the rest.

5 When the Syrians of Damascus sent an army to help King Hadadezer, David attacked it and killed 22,000 men. 6 Then he set up military camps in* their territory, and they became his subjects and paid taxes to him. The LORD made David victorious everywhere. 7 David captured the gold shields carried by Hadadezer's officials and took them to Jerusalem. 8 He also took a great quantity of bronze from Betah and Berothai, cities ruled by Hadadezer.

9 King Toi of Hamath heard that David had defeated all of Hadadezer's army. 10 So he sent his son Joram to greet King

7.19 Probable text *you let a man see this*; Hebrew *this is a law for human beings*.
7.23 Probable text *them*; Hebrew *you* (plural).
7.23 One ancient translation (and see 1 Chr 17.21) *You drove out*; Hebrew *for your land*.
8.1 Probable text *over the land*; Hebrew unclear.
8.6 *set up military camps in*; or *placed military commanders over*.

2 SAMUEL 8, 9

363

2 Sam.

1 Kings
2 Kings
1 Chron.
2 Chron.
Ezra

David and congratulate him on his victory over Hadadezer, against whom Toi had fought many times. Joram took David presents made of gold, silver, and bronze. ¹¹King David dedicated them for use in worship, along with the silver and gold he took from the nations he had conquered — ¹²Edom, Moab, Ammon, Philistia, and Amalek — as well as part of the loot he had taken from Hadadezer.

¹³David became even more famous when he returned from killing 18,000 Edomites in the Valley of Salt. ¹⁴He set up military camps* throughout Edom, and the people there became his subjects. The LORD made David victorious everywhere.

¹⁵David ruled over all Israel and made sure that his people were always treated fairly and justly. ¹⁶Joab, whose mother was Zeruiah, was the commander of the army; Jehoshaphat son of Ahilud was in charge of the records; ¹⁷Zadok son of Ahitub and Ahimelech son of Abiathar were priests; Seraiah was the court secretary; ¹⁸Benaiah son of Jehoiada was in charge of* David's bodyguard and David's sons were priests.

David and Mephibosheth

9 One day David asked, "Is there anyone left of Saul's family? If there is, I would like to show him kindness for Jonathan's sake."

²There was a servant of Saul's family named Ziba, and he was told to go to David. "Are you Ziba?" the king asked.

"At your service, sir," he answered.

³The king asked him, "Is there anyone left of Saul's family to whom I can show loyalty and kindness, as I promised God I would?"

Ziba answered, "There is still one of Jonathan's sons. He is crippled."

⁴"Where is he?" the king asked.

"At the home of Machir son of Ammiel in Lodebar," Ziba answered. ⁵So King David sent for him.

⁶When Mephibosheth, the son of Jonathan and grandson of Saul, arrived, he bowed down before David in respect. David said, "Mephibosheth," and he answered, "At your service, sir."

⁷"Don't be afraid," David replied. "I will be kind to you for the sake of your father Jonathan. I will give you back all the land that belonged to your grandfather Saul, and you will always be welcome at my table."

⁸Mephibosheth bowed again and said, "I am no better than a dead dog, sir! Why should you be so good to me?"

⁹Then the king called Ziba, Saul's servant, and said, "I am giving Mephibosheth, your master's grandson, everything that belonged to Saul and his family. ¹⁰You, your sons, and your servants will farm the land for your master Saul's family and bring in the harvest, to provide food for them. But Mephibosheth himself will always be a guest at my table." (Ziba had fifteen sons and twenty servants.)

¹¹Ziba answered, "I will do everything Your Majesty commands."

So Mephibosheth ate at the king's* table, just like one of the king's sons. ¹²Mephibosheth had a young son named Mica. All the members of Ziba's family became servants of Mephibosheth. ¹³So Mephibosheth, who was crippled in both feet, lived in Jerusalem, eating all his meals at the king's table.

2 SAMUEL 9

This story is an example of a 'foreshadowing' - a shadow in the Old Testament of what Jesus would do in the New Testament. David was loving, forgiving and kind to Mephibosheth, not because of what Mephibosheth had done but because of a promise that David made. In the same way, Jesus doesn't love us because we are worthy but

• BECAUSE HE •

PROMISED

'to give his life to redeem many people' (Mark 10.45). (See 2 Samuel 19.24-30 for more about Mephibosheth.)

8.14 *set up military camps*; or *placed military commanders*.
8.18 Some ancient translations *was in charge of*; Hebrew does not have these words.
9.11 One ancient translation *the king's*; Hebrew *my*.

364

2 Sam.

⋮........

Deuter.

Joshua

Judges

Ruth

1 Sam.

David Defeats the Ammonites and the Syrians
(1 Chr 19.1–19)

10 Some time later King Nahash of Ammon died, and his son Hanun became king. ²King David said, "I must show loyal friendship to Hanun, as his father Nahash did to me." So David sent messengers to express his sympathy.

When they arrived in Ammon, ³the Ammonite leaders said to the king, "Do you think that it is in your father's honour that David has sent these men to express sympathy to you? Of course not! He has sent them here as spies to explore the city, so that he can conquer us!"

⁴Hanun seized David's messengers, shaved off one side of their beards, cut off their clothes at the hips, and sent them away. ⁵They were too ashamed to return home. When David heard about what had happened, he sent word that they should stay in Jericho and not return until their beards had grown again.

⁶The Ammonites realized that they had made David their enemy, so they hired 20,000 Syrian soldiers from Bethrehob and Zobah, 12,000 men from Tob, and the king of Maacah with a thousand men. ⁷David heard of it and sent Joab against them with the whole army. ⁸The Ammonites marched out and took up their position at the entrance to Rabbah, their capital city, while the others, both the Syrians and the men from Tob and Maacah, took up their position in the open countryside.

⁹Joab saw that the enemy troops would attack him in front and from the rear, so he chose the best of Israel's soldiers and put them in position facing the Syrians. ¹⁰He placed the rest of his troops under the command of his brother Abishai, who put them in position facing the Ammonites. ¹¹Joab said to him, "If you see that the Syrians are defeating me, come and help me, and if the Ammonites are defeating you, I will go and help you. ¹²Be strong and courageous! Let's fight hard for our people and for the cities of our God. And may the LORD's will be done!"

¹³Joab and his men advanced to attack, and the Syrians fled. ¹⁴When the Ammonites saw the Syrians running away, they fled from Abishai and retreated into the city. Then Joab turned back from fighting the Ammonites and went back to Jerusalem.

¹⁵The Syrians realized that they had been defeated by the Israelites, so they called all their troops together. ¹⁶King Hadadezer sent for the Syrians who were on the east side of the River Euphrates, and they came to Helam under the command of Shobach, commander of the army of King Hadadezer of Zobah. ¹⁷When David heard of it, he gathered the Israelite troops, crossed the River Jordan, and marched to Helam, where the Syrians took up their position facing him. The fighting began, ¹⁸and the Israelites drove the Syrian army back. David and his men killed 700 Syrian chariot drivers and 40,000 horsemen, and they wounded Shobach, the enemy commander, who died on the battlefield. ¹⁹When the kings who were subject to Hadadezer realized that they had been defeated by the Israelites, they made peace with them and became their subjects. And the Syrians were afraid to help the Ammonites any more.

David and Bathsheba

11 The following spring, at the time of the year when kings usually go to war, David sent out Joab with his officers and the Israelite army; they defeated the Ammonites and besieged the city of Rabbah. But David himself stayed in Jerusalem.

2 Sam.
....

1 Kings
2 Kings
1 Chron.
2 Chron.
Ezra

² One day, late in the afternoon, David got up from his nap and went to the palace roof. As he walked about up there, he saw a woman having a bath. She was very beautiful. ³ So he sent a messenger to find out who she was, and learnt that she was Bathsheba, the daughter of Eliam and the wife of Uriah the Hittite. ⁴ David sent messengers to fetch her; they brought her to him and he made love to her. (She had just finished her monthly ritual of purification.) Then she went back home. ⁵ Afterwards she discovered that she was pregnant and sent a message to David to tell him.

⁶ David then sent a message to Joab: "Send me Uriah the Hittite." So Joab sent him to David. ⁷ When Uriah arrived, David asked him if Joab and the troops were well, and how the fighting was going. ⁸ Then he said to Uriah, "Go home and rest a while." Uriah left, and David sent a present to his home. ⁹ But Uriah did not go home; instead he slept at the palace gate with the king's guards. ¹⁰ When David heard that Uriah had not gone home, he asked him, "You have just returned after a long absence; why didn't you go home?"

¹¹ Uriah answered, "The men of Israel and Judah are away at the war, and the Covenant Box is with them; my commander Joab and his officers are camping out in the open. How could I go home, eat and drink, and sleep with my wife? By all that's sacred, I swear that I could never do such a thing!"

¹² So David said, "Then stay here the rest of the day, and tomorrow I'll send you back." So Uriah stayed in Jerusalem that day and the next. ¹³ David invited him to supper and made him drunk. But again that night Uriah did not go home; instead he slept on his blanket* in the palace guardroom.

¹⁴ The next morning David wrote a letter to Joab and sent it by Uriah. ¹⁵ He wrote: "Put Uriah in the front line, where the fighting is heaviest, then retreat and let him be killed." ¹⁶ So while Joab was besieging the city, he sent Uriah to a place where he knew the enemy was strong. ¹⁷ The enemy troops came out of the city and fought Joab's forces; some of David's officers were killed, and so was Uriah.

¹⁸ Then Joab sent a report to David telling him about the battle, ¹⁹ and he instructed the messenger, "After you have told the king all about the battle, ²⁰ he may get angry and ask you, 'Why did you go so near the city to fight them? Didn't you realize that they would shoot arrows from the walls? ²¹ Don't you remember how Abimelech son of Gideon was killed? It was at Thebez, where a woman threw a millstone down from the wall and killed him. Why, then, did you go so near the wall?' If the king asks you this, tell him, 'Your officer Uriah was also killed.'"

²² So the messenger went to David and told him what Joab had commanded him to say. ²³ He said, "Our enemies were stronger than we were and came out of the city to fight us in the open, but we drove them back to the city gate. ²⁴ Then they shot arrows at us from the wall, and some of Your Majesty's officers were killed; your officer Uriah was also killed."

²⁵ David said to the messenger, "Encourage Joab and tell him not to be upset, since you never can tell who will die in battle. Tell him to launch a stronger attack on the city and capture it."

²⁶ When Bathsheba heard that her husband had been killed, she mourned for him. ²⁷ When the time of mourning was over, David sent for her to come to the palace; she became his wife and bore him a son. But the LORD was not pleased with what David had done.

....

11.13 *blanket*; or *bunk*.

366

2 Sam.

Deuter.
Joshua
Judges
Ruth
1 Sam.

2 SAMUEL 12

2 SAMUEL 12.1-15

Nathan asked David difficult questions to help him get closer to God.

Arrange to meet someone who you think is wise but loving, and ask them to talk to you honestly about your character. Be ready to

HEAR THE

ANSWERS!

(Do make sure your parent or guardian knows who you're meeting.)

Nathan's Message and David's Repentance

12 The LORD sent the prophet Nathan to David. Nathan went to him and said, "There were two men who lived in the same town; one was rich and the other poor. [2] The rich man had many cattle and sheep, [3] while the poor man had only one lamb, which he had bought. He took care of it, and it grew up in his home with his children. He would feed it with some of his own food, let it drink from his cup, and hold it in his lap. The lamb was like a daughter to him. [4] One day a visitor arrived at the rich man's home. The rich man didn't want to kill one of his own animals to prepare a meal for him; instead, he took the poor man's lamb and cooked a meal for his guest."

[5] David was very angry with the rich man and said, "I swear by the living LORD that the man who did this ought to die! [6] For having done such a cruel thing, he must pay back four times as much as he took."

[7] "You are that man," Nathan said to David. "And this is what the LORD God of Israel says: 'I made you king of Israel and rescued you from Saul. [8] I gave you his kingdom and his wives; I made you king over Israel and Judah. If this had not been enough, I would have given you twice as much. [9] Why, then, have you disobeyed my commands? Why did you do this evil thing? You had Uriah killed in battle; you let the Ammonites kill him, and then you took his wife! [10] Now, in every generation some of your descendants will die a violent death because you have disobeyed me and have taken Uriah's wife. [11] I swear to you that I will cause someone from your own family to bring trouble on you. You will see it when I take your wives from you and give them to another man; and he will have intercourse with them in broad daylight. [12] You sinned in secret, but I will make this happen in broad daylight for all Israel to see.'"

[13] "I have sinned against the LORD," David said.

Nathan replied, "The LORD forgives you; you will not die. [14] But because you have shown such contempt for the LORD in doing this, your child will die." [15] Then Nathan went home.

David's Son Dies

The LORD caused the child that Uriah's wife had borne to David to become very ill. [16] David prayed to God that the child would get well. He refused to eat anything, and every night he went into his room and spent the night lying on the floor. [17] His court officials went to him and tried to make him get up, but he refused and would not eat anything with them. [18] A week later the child died, and David's officials were afraid to tell him the news. They said, "While the child was living, David wouldn't answer us when we spoke to him. How can we tell him that his child is dead? He might do himself some harm!"

[19] When David noticed them whispering to each other, he realized that the child had died. So he asked them, "Is the child dead?"

"Yes, he is," they answered.

[20] David got up from the floor, had a bath, combed his hair, and changed his clothes. Then he went and worshipped in the house of the LORD. When he returned to the palace, he asked for food and ate it as soon as it was served. [21] "We don't understand this," his officials said to him. "While the child was alive, you wept for him and would not eat; but as soon as he died, you got up and ate!"

[22] "Yes," David answered, "I did fast and weep while he was still alive. I thought that the LORD might be merciful to me and not

2 SAMUEL 12, 13

367

2 Sam.

....

1 Kings
2 Kings
1 Chron.
2 Chron.
Ezra

let the child die. ²³But now that he is dead, why should I fast? Could I bring the child back to life? I will some day go to where he is, but he can never come back to me."

Solomon is Born

²⁴Then David comforted his wife Bathsheba. He had intercourse with her, and she bore a son, whom David named Solomon. The LORD loved the boy ²⁵and commanded the prophet Nathan to name the boy Jedidiah,* because the LORD loved him.

David Captures Rabbah
(1 Chr 20.1–3)

²⁶Meanwhile Joab continued his campaign against Rabbah, the capital city of Ammon, and was about to capture it. ²⁷He sent messengers to David to report: "I have attacked Rabbah and have captured its water supply. ²⁸Now gather the rest of your forces, attack the city and take it yourself. I don't want to get the credit for capturing it." ²⁹So David gathered his forces, went to Rabbah, attacked it, and conquered it. ³⁰From the head of the idol of the Ammonite god Molech* David took a gold crown which weighed about 35 kilogrammes and had a jewel in it. David took the jewel and put it in his own crown.* He also took a large amount of loot from the city ³¹and put its people to work with saws, iron hoes, and iron axes, and forced them to work at* making bricks. He did the same to the people of all the other towns of Ammon. Then he and his men returned to Jerusalem.

Amnon and Tamar

13 David's son Absalom had a beautiful unmarried sister named Tamar. Amnon, another of David's sons, fell in love with her. ²He was so much in love with her that he became ill, because it seemed impossible for him to have her; as a virgin, she was kept from meeting men. ³But he had a friend, a very shrewd man named Jonadab, the son of David's brother Shammah. ⁴Jonadab said to Amnon, "You are the king's son, yet day after day I see you looking sad. What's the matter?"

"I'm in love with Tamar, the sister of my half-brother Absalom," he answered.

⁵Jonadab said to him, "Pretend that you are ill and go to bed. When your father comes to see you, say to him, 'Please ask my sister Tamar to come and feed me. I want her to prepare the food here where I can see her, and then serve it to me herself.' " ⁶So Amnon pretended that he was ill and went to bed.

King David went to see him, and Amnon said to him, "Please let Tamar come and make a few cakes here where I can see her, and then serve them to me herself."

⁷So David sent word to Tamar in the palace: "Go to Amnon's house and prepare some food for him." ⁸She went there and found him in bed. She took some dough, prepared it, and made some cakes there where he could see her. Then she baked the cakes ⁹and emptied them out of the pan for him to eat, but he wouldn't. He said, "Send everyone away" — and they all left. ¹⁰Then he said to her, "Bring the cakes here to my bed and serve them to me yourself." She took the cakes and went over to him.

....

12.25 *Jedidiah*: This name in Hebrew means "Beloved of the LORD".
12.30 *idol of the Ammonite god Molech*; or *Ammonite king*.
12.30 *jewel... crown*; or *crown and put it on his own head*.
12.31 Probable text (see 1 Chr 20.3) *work at*; Hebrew *pass through*.

[11] As she offered them to him, he grabbed her and said, "Come to bed with me!"

[12] "No," she said. "Don't force me to do such a degrading thing! That's awful! [13] How could I ever hold up my head in public again? And you — you would be completely disgraced in Israel. Please, speak to the king, and I'm sure that he will give me to you." [14] But he would not listen to her; and since he was stronger than she was, he overpowered her and raped her.

[15] Then Amnon was filled with a deep hatred for her; he hated her now even more than he had loved her before. He said to her, "Get out!"

[16] "No," she answered. "To send me away like this is a greater crime* than what you just did!"

But Amnon would not listen to her; [17] he called in his personal servant and said, "Get this woman out of my sight! Throw her out and lock the door!" [18] The servant put her out and locked the door.

Tamar was wearing a long robe with full sleeves,* the usual clothing for an unmarried princess in those days.* [19] She sprinkled ashes on her head, tore her robe, and with her face buried in her hands went away crying. [20] When her brother Absalom saw her, he asked, "Has Amnon molested you? Please, sister, don't let it upset you so much. He is your half-brother, so don't tell anyone about it." So Tamar lived in Absalom's house, sad and lonely.

[21] When King David heard what had happened, he was furious. [22] And Absalom hated Amnon so much for having raped his sister Tamar that he would no longer even speak to him.

Absalom's Revenge

[23] Two years later Absalom was having his sheep sheared at Baal Hazor, near the town of Ephraim, and he invited all the king's sons to be there. [24] He went to King David and said, "Your Majesty, I am having my sheep sheared. Will you and your officials come and take part in the festivities?"

[25] "No, my son," the king answered. "It would be too much trouble for you if we all went." Absalom insisted, but the king would not give in, and he asked Absalom to leave.

[26] But Absalom said, "Well, then, will you at least let my brother Amnon come?"

"Why should he?" the king asked. [27] But Absalom kept on insisting until David finally let Amnon and all his other sons go with Absalom.

Absalom prepared a banquet fit for a king* [28] and instructed his servants: "Notice when Amnon has had too much to drink, and then when I give the order, kill him. Don't be afraid. I will take the responsibility myself. Be brave and don't hesitate!" [29] So the servants followed Absalom's instructions and killed Amnon. All the rest of David's sons mounted their mules and fled.

[30] While they were on their way home, David was told: "Absalom has killed all your sons — not one of them is left!" [31] The king stood up, tore his clothes in sorrow, and threw himself to the ground. The servants who were there with him tore their clothes also. [32] But Jonadab, the son of David's brother Shammah, said, "Your Majesty, they haven't killed all your sons. Only Amnon is

13.16 Probable text *To send me... crime*; Hebrew unclear.
13.18 *long robe with full sleeves*; or *decorated robe* (see Gen 37.3).
13.18 Probable text *in those days*; Hebrew *garments*.
13.27 Some ancient translations *Absalom prepared a banquet fit for a king*; Hebrew does not have these words.

369

2 Sam.

1 Kings
2 Kings
1 Chron.
2 Chron.
Ezra

dead. You could tell by looking at Absalom that he had made up his mind to do this from the time that Amnon raped his sister Tamar. ³³ So don't believe the news that all your sons are dead; only Amnon was killed."

³⁴ In the meantime Absalom had fled.

Just then the soldier on sentry duty saw a large crowd coming down the hill on the road from Horonaim.* He went to the king and reported what he had seen.* ³⁵ Jonadab said to David, "Those are your sons coming, just as I said they would." ³⁶ As soon as he finished saying this, David's sons came in; they started crying, and David and his officials also wept bitterly.

³⁷⁻³⁸ Absalom fled and went to the king of Geshur, Talmai son of Ammihud, and stayed there three years. David mourned a long time for his son Amnon; ³⁹ but when he got over Amnon's death, he was filled with longing for his son Absalom.

Joab Arranges for Absalom's Return

14 Joab knew that King David missed Absalom very much, ² so he sent for a clever woman who lived in Tekoa. When she arrived, he said to her, "Pretend that you are in mourning; put on your mourning clothes, and don't comb your hair. Act like a woman who has been in mourning for a long time. ³ Then go to the king and say to him what I tell you to say." Then Joab told her what to say.

⁴ The woman went to the king, bowed down to the ground in respect, and said, "Help me, Your Majesty!"

⁵ "What do you want?" he asked her.

"I am a poor widow, sir," she answered. "My husband is dead. ⁶ Sir, I had two sons, and one day they got into a quarrel out in the fields, where there was no one to separate them, and one of them killed the other. ⁷ And now, sir, all my relatives have turned against me and are demanding that I hand my son over to them, so that they can kill him for murdering his brother. If they do this, I will be left without a son. They will destroy my last hope and leave my husband without a son to keep his name alive."

⁸ "Go back home," the king answered, "and I will take care of the matter."

⁹ "Your Majesty," she said, "whatever you do, my family and I will take the blame; you and the royal family are innocent."

¹⁰ The king replied, "If anyone threatens you, bring him to me, and he will never trouble you again."

¹¹ She said, "Your Majesty, please pray to the LORD your God, so that my relative who is responsible for avenging the death of my son will not commit a greater crime by killing my other son."

"I promise by the living LORD," David replied, "that your son will not be harmed in the least."

¹² "Please, Your Majesty, let me say just one more thing," the woman said.

"All right," he answered.

¹³ She said to him, "Why have you done such a wrong to God's people? You have not allowed your own son to return from exile, and so you have condemned yourself by what you have just said. ¹⁴ We will all die; we are like water spilt on the ground, which can't be gathered again. Even God does not bring the dead back to life, but the king can at least find a way to bring a man back from

370

2 SAMUEL 14

2 Sam.

Deuter.
Joshua
Judges
Ruth
1 Sam.

exile.* ¹⁵ Now, Your Majesty, the reason I have come to speak to you is that the people threatened me, and so I said to myself that I would speak to you in the hope that you would do what I ask. ¹⁶ I thought you would listen to me and save me from the one who is trying to kill my son and me and so remove us from the land God gave his people. ¹⁷ I said to myself that your promise, sir, would make me safe, because the king is like God's angel and can distinguish good from evil.* May the LORD your God be with you!"

¹⁸ The king answered, "I'm going to ask you a question, and you must tell me the whole truth."

"Ask me anything, Your Majesty," she answered.

¹⁹ "Did Joab put you up to this?" he asked her.

She answered, "I swear by all that is sacred, Your Majesty, that there is no way to avoid answering your question.* It was indeed your officer Joab who told me what to do and what to say. ²⁰ But he did it in order to straighten out this whole matter. Your Majesty is as wise as the angel of God and knows everything that happens."

²¹ Later on the king said to Joab, "I have decided to do what you want. Go and get the young man Absalom and bring him back here."

²² Joab threw himself to the ground in front of David in respect, and said, "God bless you, Your Majesty! Now I know that you are pleased with me, because you have granted my request." ²³ Then he got up and went to Geshur and brought Absalom back to Jerusalem. ²⁴ The king, however, gave orders that Absalom should not live in the palace. "I don't want to see him," the king said. So Absalom lived in his own house and did not appear before the king.

Absalom is Reconciled to David

²⁵ There was no one in Israel as famous for his good looks as Absalom; he had no defect from head to foot. ²⁶ His hair was very thick, and he had to cut it once a year, when it grew too long and heavy. It would weigh more than two kilogrammes according to the royal standard of weights. ²⁷ Absalom had three sons and one daughter named Tamar, a very beautiful woman.

²⁸ Absalom lived two years in Jerusalem without seeing the king. ²⁹ Then he sent for Joab, to ask him to go to the king for him; but Joab would not come. Again Absalom sent for him, and again Joab refused to come. ³⁰ So Absalom said to his servants, "Look, Joab's field is next to mine, and it has barley growing in it. Go and set fire to it." So they went and set the field on fire.

³¹ Joab went to Absalom's house and demanded, "Why did your servants set fire to my field?"

³² Absalom answered, "Because you wouldn't come when I sent for you. I wanted you to go to the king and ask him from me: 'Why did I leave Geshur and come here? It would have been better for me to have stayed there.'" And Absalom went on, "I want you to arrange for me to see the king, and if I'm guilty, then let him put me to death."

³³ So Joab went to King David and told him what Absalom had said. The king sent for Absalom, who went to him and bowed down to the ground in front of him. The king welcomed him with a kiss.

14.14 Probable text *Even God… from exile*; Hebrew unclear.
14.17 *can distinguish good from evil*; or *knows everything*.
14.19 *there is… question*; or *you are absolutely right*.

2 SAMUEL 15

371

2 Sam.

1 Kings
2 Kings
1 Chron.
2 Chron.
Ezra

Absalom Plans Rebellion

15 After this, Absalom provided a chariot and horses for himself, and an escort of fifty men. [2] He would get up early and go and stand by the road at the city gate. Whenever someone came there with a dispute that he wanted the king to settle, Absalom would call him over and ask him where he was from. And after the man had told him what tribe he was from, [3] Absalom would say, "Look, the law is on your side, but there is no representative of the king to hear your case." [4] And he would add, "How I wish I were a judge! Then anyone who had a dispute or a claim could come to me, and I would give him justice." [5] When the man approached Absalom to bow down before him, Absalom would reach out, take hold of him, and kiss him. [6] Absalom did this with every Israelite who came to the king for justice, and so he won their loyalty.

[7] After four* years Absalom said to King David, "Sir, let me go to Hebron and keep a promise I made to the Lord. [8] While I was living in Geshur in Syria, I promised the Lord that if he would take me back to Jerusalem, I would worship him in Hebron."*

[9] "Go in peace," the king said. So Absalom went to Hebron. [10] But he sent messengers to all the tribes of Israel to say, "When you hear the sound of trumpets, shout, 'Absalom has become king at Hebron!'" [11] There were 200 men who at Absalom's invitation had gone from Jerusalem with him; they knew nothing of the plot and went in all good faith. [12] And while he was offering sacrifices, Absalom also sent to the town of Gilo for Ahithophel, who was one of King David's advisers. The plot against the king gained strength, and Absalom's followers grew in number.

David Flees from Jerusalem

[13] A messenger reported to David, "The Israelites are pledging their loyalty to Absalom."

[14] So David said to all his officials who were with him in Jerusalem, "We must get away at once if we want to escape from Absalom! Hurry! Or else he will soon be here and defeat us and kill everyone in the city!"

[15] "Yes, Your Majesty," they answered. "We are ready to do whatever you say." [16] So the king left, accompanied by all his family and officials, except for ten concubines, whom he left behind to take care of the palace.

[17] As the king and all his men were leaving the city, they stopped at the last house. [18] All his officials stood* next to him as the royal bodyguard passed by in front of him. The 600 soldiers who had followed him from Gath also passed by, [19] and the king said to Ittai, their leader, "Why are you going with us? Go back and stay with the new king. You are a foreigner, a refugee away from your own country. [20] You have lived here only a short time, so why should I make you wander round with me? I don't even know where I'm going. Go back and take your fellow-countrymen with you — and may the Lord be kind and faithful to you."*

[21] But Ittai answered, "Your Majesty, I swear to you in the Lord's name that I will always go with you wherever you go, even if it means death."

15.7 Some ancient translations *four*; Hebrew *forty*.
15.8 One ancient translation *in Hebron*; Hebrew does not have these words.
15.18 Probable text *stood*; Hebrew *passed*.
15.20 One ancient translation *and may the Lord be kind and faithful to you*; Hebrew *kindness and faithfulness*.

---

2 SAMUEL 15

Absalom betrayed his father David, and his betrayal

STARTED
– WITH –
SMALL ACTIONS.

Make a list of all that you have said or done in the last 24 hours that might somehow have betrayed someone else. Find an object for each one of these things and

STICK THEM IN
THESE PAGES

or draw a picture of them, asking God for forgiveness.

stick them here

372

2 Sam.

Deuter.
Joshua
Judges
Ruth
1 Sam.

2 SAMUEL 15, 16

²²"Fine!" David answered. "March on!" So Ittai went on with all his men and their dependants. ²³The people cried loudly as David's followers left. The king crossed the brook of Kidron, followed by his men, and together they went out towards the wilderness.

²⁴Zadok the priest was there, and with him were the Levites, carrying the sacred Covenant Box. They set it down* and didn't pick it up again until all the people had left the city. The priest Abiathar was there too.* ²⁵Then the king said to Zadok, "Take the Covenant Box back to the city. If the LORD is pleased with me, some day he will let me come back to see it and the place where it stays. ²⁶But if he isn't pleased with me — well, then, let him do to me what he wishes." ²⁷And he went on to say to Zadok, "Look,* take your son Ahimaaz and Abiathar's son Jonathan and go back to the city in peace. ²⁸Meanwhile, I will wait at the river crossings in the wilderness until I receive news from you." ²⁹So Zadok and Abiathar took the Covenant Box back into Jerusalem and stayed there.

³⁰David went on up the Mount of Olives weeping; he was barefoot and had his head covered as a sign of grief. All who followed him covered their heads and wept also. ³¹When David was told* that Ahithophel had joined Absalom's rebellion, he prayed, "Please, LORD, turn Ahithophel's advice into nonsense!"

³²When David reached the top of the hill, where there was a place of worship, his trusted friend Hushai the Archite met him with his clothes torn and with earth on his head. ³³David said to him, "You will be of no help to me if you come with me, ³⁴but you can help me by returning to the city and telling Absalom that you will now serve him as faithfully as you served his father. And do all you can to oppose any advice that Ahithophel gives. ³⁵The priests Zadok and Abiathar will be there; tell them everything you hear in the king's palace. ³⁶They have their sons Ahimaaz and Jonathan with them, and you can send them to me with all the information you gather."

³⁷So Hushai, David's friend, returned to the city just as Absalom was arriving.

David and Ziba

16 When David had gone a little beyond the top of the hill, he was suddenly met by Ziba, the servant of Mephibosheth, who had with him a couple of donkeys loaded with 200 loaves of bread, a hundred bunches of raisins, a hundred bunches of fresh fruit, and a leather bag full of wine. ²King David asked him, "What are you going to do with all that?"

Ziba answered, "The donkeys are for Your Majesty's family to ride, the bread and the fruit are for the men to eat, and the wine is for them to drink when they get tired in the wilderness."

³"Where is Mephibosheth, the grandson of your master Saul?" the king asked him.

"He is staying in Jerusalem," Ziba answered, "because he is convinced that the Israelites will now restore to him the kingdom of his grandfather Saul."

⁴The king said to Ziba, "Everything that belonged to Mephibosheth is yours."

"I am your servant," Ziba replied. "May I always please Your Majesty!"

15.24 Probable text *set it down*; Hebrew *poured it out*.
15.24 Probable text *was there too*; Hebrew *went up*.
15.27 Some ancient translations *Look*; Hebrew *Are you the seer?*
15.31 One ancient translation *was told*; Hebrew *told*.

2 Sam.

1 Kings
2 Kings
1 Chron.
2 Chron.
Ezra

David and Shimei

[5] When King David arrived at Bahurim, one of Saul's relatives, Shimei son of Gera, came out to meet him, cursing him as he came. [6] Shimei started throwing stones at David and his officials, even though David was surrounded by his men and his bodyguard. [7] Shimei cursed him and said, "Get out! Get out! Murderer! Criminal! [8] You took Saul's kingdom, and now the LORD is punishing you for murdering so many of Saul's family. The LORD has given the kingdom to your son Absalom, and you are ruined, you murderer!"

[9] Abishai, whose mother was Zeruiah, said to the king, "Your Majesty, why do you let this dog curse you? Let me go over there and cut off his head!"

[10] "This is none of your business," the king said to Abishai and his brother Joab. "If he curses me because the LORD told him to, who has the right to ask why he does it?" [11] And David said to Abishai and to all his officials, "My own son is trying to kill me; so why should you be surprised at this Benjaminite? The LORD told him to curse; so leave him alone and let him do it. [12] Perhaps the LORD will notice my misery* and give me some blessings to take the place of his curse." [13] So David and his men continued along the road. Shimei kept up with them, walking on the hillside; he was cursing and throwing stones and earth at them as he went. [14] The king and all his men were worn out when they reached the Jordan,* and there they rested.

Absalom in Jerusalem

[15] Absalom and all the Israelites with him entered Jerusalem, and Ahithophel was with them. [16] When Hushai, David's trusted friend, met Absalom, he shouted, "Long live the king! Long live the king!"

[17] "What has happened to your loyalty to your friend David?" Absalom asked him. "Why didn't you go with him?"

[18] Hushai answered, "How could I? I am on the side of the one chosen by the LORD, by these people, and by all the Israelites. I will stay with you. [19] After all, whom should I serve, if not my master's son? As I served your father, so now I will serve you."

[20] Then Absalom turned to Ahithophel and said, "Now that we are here, what do you advise us to do?"

[21] Ahithophel answered, "Go and have intercourse with your father's concubines whom he left behind to take care of the palace. Then everyone in Israel will know that your father regards you as his enemy, and your followers will be greatly encouraged." [22] So they set up a tent for Absalom on the palace roof, and in the sight of everyone Absalom went in and had intercourse with his father's concubines.

[23] Any advice that Ahithophel gave in those days was accepted as though it were the very word of God; both David and Absalom followed it.

Hushai Misleads Absalom

17 Not long after that, Ahithophel said to Absalom, "Let me choose 12,000 men, and tonight I will set out after David. [2] I will attack him while he is tired and discouraged. He will be frightened, and all his men will run away. I will kill only the king [3] and then bring back all his men to you, like a bride returning

---

16.12 Some ancient translations *misery*; Hebrew *wickedness*.
16.14 One ancient translation *the Jordan*; Hebrew does not have these words.

2 Sam.

Deuter.
Joshua
Judges
Ruth
1 Sam.

to her husband. You want to kill only one man;* the rest of the people will be safe." ⁴This seemed like good advice to Absalom and all the Israelite leaders.

⁵Absalom said, "Now call Hushai, and let us hear what he has to say." ⁶When Hushai arrived, Absalom said to him, "This is the advice that Ahithophel has given us; shall we follow it? If not, you tell us what to do."

⁷Hushai answered, "The advice Ahithophel gave you this time is no good. ⁸You know that your father David and his men are hard fighters and that they are as fierce as a mother bear robbed of her cubs. Your father is an experienced soldier and does not stay with his men at night. ⁹Just now he is probably hiding in a cave or some other place. As soon as David attacks your men, whoever hears about it will say that your men have been defeated. ¹⁰Then even the bravest men, as fearless as lions, will be afraid because everyone in Israel knows that your father is a great soldier and that his men are hard fighters. ¹¹My advice is that you bring all the Israelites together from one end of the country to the other, as many as the grains of sand on the seashore, and that you lead them personally in battle. ¹²We will find David wherever he is, and attack him before he knows what's happening. Neither he nor any of his men will survive. ¹³If he retreats into a city, our people will all bring ropes and just pull the city* into the valley below. Not a single stone will be left there on top of the hill."

¹⁴Absalom and all the Israelites said, "Hushai's advice is better than Ahithophel's." The LORD had decided that Ahithophel's good advice would not be followed, so that disaster would come on Absalom.

David is Warned and Escapes

¹⁵Then Hushai told the priests Zadok and Abiathar what advice he had given to Absalom and the Israelite leaders and what advice Ahithophel had given. ¹⁶Hushai added, "Quick, now! Send a message to David not to spend the night at the river crossings in the wilderness, but to cross the Jordan at once, so that he and his men won't all be caught and killed."

¹⁷Abiathar's son Jonathan and Zadok's son Ahimaaz were waiting at the spring of Enrogel, on the outskirts of Jerusalem, because they did not dare to be seen entering the city. A servant woman would regularly go and tell them what was happening, and then they would go and tell King David. ¹⁸But one day a boy happened to see them, and he told Absalom; so they hurried off to hide in the house of a certain man in Bahurim. He had a well near his house, and they got down into it. ¹⁹The man's wife took a covering, spread it over the opening of the well and scattered grain over it, so that no one would notice anything. ²⁰Absalom's officials came to the house and asked the woman, "Where are Ahimaaz and Jonathan?"

"They crossed the river," she answered.

The men looked for them but could not find them, and so they returned to Jerusalem. ²¹After they left, Ahimaaz and Jonathan came up out of the well and went and reported to King David. They told him what Ahithophel had planned against him and said, "Hurry up and cross the river." ²²So David and his men started crossing the Jordan, and by daybreak they had all gone across.

17.3 One ancient translation *like a bride... only one man*; Hebrew *like the return of the whole, so is the man you seek.*
17.13 Some ancient translations *the city*; Hebrew *him.*

2 Sam.

.........:.

1 Kings

2 Kings

1 Chron.

2 Chron.

Ezra

²³When Ahithophel saw that his advice had not been followed, he saddled his donkey and went back to his own city. After putting his affairs in order, he hanged himself. He was buried in the family grave.

²⁴David had reached the town of Mahanaim by the time Absalom and the Israelites had crossed the Jordan. ²⁵(Absalom had put Amasa in command of the army in the place of Joab. Amasa was the son of Jether the Ishmaelite;* his mother was Abigail, the daughter of Nahash and the sister of Joab's mother Zeruiah.) ²⁶Absalom and his men camped in the land of Gilead.

²⁷When David arrived at Mahanaim, he was met by Shobi son of Nahash, from the city of Rabbah in Ammon, and by Machir son of Ammiel, from Lodebar, and by Barzillai, from Rogelim in Gilead. ²⁸⁻²⁹They brought bowls, clay pots, and bedding, and also food for David and his men: wheat, barley, meal, roasted grain, beans, peas,* honey, cheese, cream, and some sheep. They knew that David and his men would be hungry, thirsty, and tired in the wilderness.

Absalom is Defeated and Killed

18 King David brought all his men together, divided them into units of a thousand and of a hundred, and placed officers in command of them. ²Then he sent them out in three groups, with Joab and Joab's brother Abishai and Ittai from Gath, each in command of a group. And the king said to his men, "I will go with you myself."

³"You mustn't go with us," they answered. "It won't make any difference to the enemy if the rest of us turn and run, or even if half of us are killed; but you are worth 10,000 of us. It will be better if you stay here in the city and send us help."

⁴"I will do whatever you think best," the king answered. Then he stood by the side of the gate as his men marched out in units of a thousand and of a hundred. ⁵He gave orders to Joab, Abishai, and Ittai: "For my sake don't harm the young man Absalom." And all the troops heard David give this command to his officers.

⁶David's army went out into the countryside and fought the Israelites in the forest of Ephraim. ⁷The Israelites were defeated by David's men; it was a terrible defeat, with 20,000 men killed that day. ⁸The fighting spread over the countryside, and more men died in the forest than were killed in battle.

⁹Suddenly Absalom met some of David's men. Absalom was riding a mule, and as it went under a large oak tree, Absalom's head got caught in the branches. The mule ran on and Absalom was left hanging in mid air. ¹⁰One of David's men saw him and reported to Joab, "Sir, I saw Absalom hanging in an oak tree!"

¹¹Joab answered, "If you saw him, why didn't you kill him on the spot? I myself would have given you ten pieces of silver and a belt."

¹²But the man answered, "Even if you gave me a thousand pieces of silver, I wouldn't lift a finger against the king's son. We all heard the king command you and Abishai and Ittai, 'For my sake don't harm the young man Absalom.' ¹³But if I had disobeyed the king and killed Absalom, the king would have heard about it — he hears about everything — and you would not have defended me."

¹⁴"I'm not going to waste any more time with you," Joab said. He took three spears and plunged them into Absalom's chest

---

17.25 One ancient translation (and see 1 Chr 2.17) *Ishmaelite*; Hebrew *Israelite*.

17.28–29 Some ancient translations *peas*; Hebrew *peas and roasted grain*.

376

2 Sam.

Deuter.
Joshua
Judges
Ruth
1 Sam.

2 SAMUEL 18

while he was still alive, hanging in the oak tree. [15] Then ten of Joab's soldiers closed in on Absalom and finished killing him.

[16] Joab ordered the trumpet to be blown to stop the fighting, and his troops came back from pursuing the Israelites. [17] They took Absalom's body, threw it into a deep pit in the forest, and covered it with a huge pile of stones. All the Israelites fled to their own homes.

[18] During his lifetime Absalom had built a monument for himself in King's Valley, because he had no son to keep his name alive. So he named it after himself, and to this day it is known as Absalom's Monument.

David is Told of Absalom's Death

[19] Then Ahimaaz son of Zadok said to Joab, "Let me run to the king with the good news that the LORD has saved him from his enemies."

[20] "No," Joab said, "today you will not take any good news. Some other day you may do so, but not today, for the king's son is dead." [21] Then he said to his Ethiopian slave, "Go and tell the king what you have seen." The slave bowed and ran off.

[22] Ahimaaz insisted, "I don't care what happens; please let me take the news also."

"Why do you want to do it, my son?" Joab asked. "You will get no reward for it."

[23] "Whatever happens," Ahimaaz said again, "I want to go."

"Then go," Joab said. So Ahimaaz ran off down the road through the Jordan Valley, and soon he passed the slave.

[24] David was sitting in the space between the inner and outer gates of the city. The watchman went up to the top of the wall and stood on the roof of the gateway; he looked out and saw a man running alone. [25] He called down and told the king, and the king said, "If he is alone, he is bringing good news." The runner came nearer and nearer.

[26] Then the watchman saw another man running alone, and he called down to the gatekeeper, "Look! There's another man running!"

The king answered, "This one also is bringing good news."

[27] The watchman said, "I can see that the first man runs like Ahimaaz."

"He's a good man," the king said, "and he is bringing good news."

[28] Ahimaaz called out a greeting to the king, threw himself down to the ground before him, and said, "Praise the LORD your God, who has given you victory over the men who rebelled against Your Majesty!"

[29] "Is the young man Absalom safe?" the king asked.

Ahimaaz answered, "Sir, when your officer Joab sent me, I saw a great commotion, but I couldn't tell what it was."

[30] "Stand over there," the king said; and he went over and stood there.

[31] Then the Ethiopian slave arrived and said to the king, "I have good news for Your Majesty! Today the LORD has given you victory over all who rebelled against you!"

[32] "Is the young man Absalom safe?" the king asked.

The slave answered, "I wish that what has happened to him would happen to all your enemies, sir, and to all who rebel against you."

[33] The king was overcome with grief. He went up to the room over the gateway and wept. As he went, he cried, "O my son! My son Absalom! Absalom, my son! If only I had died in your place, my son! Absalom, my son!"

2 SAMUEL 19

377

2 Sam.
....
1 Kings
2 Kings
1 Chron.
2 Chron.
Ezra

Joab Reprimands David

19 Joab was told that King David was weeping and mourning for Absalom. [2] And so the joy of victory was turned into sadness for all David's troops that day, because they heard that the king was mourning for his son. [3] They went back into the city quietly, like soldiers who are ashamed because they are running away from battle. [4] The king covered his face and cried loudly, "O my son! My son Absalom! Absalom, my son!"

[5] Joab went to the king's house and said to him, "Today you have humiliated your men — the men who saved your life and the lives of your sons and daughters and of your wives and concubines. [6] You oppose those who love you and support those who hate you! You have made it clear that your officers and men mean nothing to you. I can see that you would be quite happy if Absalom were alive today and all of us were dead. [7] Now go and reassure your men. I swear by the LORD's name that if you don't, not one of them will be with you by tomorrow morning. That would be the worst disaster you have suffered in all your life." [8] Then the king got up, and went out and sat near the city gate. His men heard that he was there, and they all gathered round him.

David Starts Back to Jerusalem

Meanwhile all the Israelites had fled to their own homes. [9] All over the country they started quarrelling among themselves. "King David saved us from our enemies," they said to one another. "He rescued us from the Philistines, but now he has fled from Absalom and left the country. [10] We anointed Absalom as our king, but he has been killed in battle. So why doesn't somebody try to bring King David back?"

[11] The news of what the Israelites were saying reached King David.* So he sent the priests Zadok and Abiathar to ask the leaders of Judah, "Why should you be the last to help bring the king back to his palace? [12] You are my relatives, my own flesh and blood; why should you be the last to bring me back?" [13] David also told them to say to Amasa, "You are my relative. From now on I am putting you in charge of the army in place of Joab. May God strike me dead if I don't!" [14] David's words won the complete loyalty of all the men of Judah, and they sent him word to return with all his officials.

[15] On his way back the king was met at the River Jordan by the men of Judah, who had come to Gilgal to escort him across the river. [16] At the same time the Benjaminite Shimei son of Gera from Bahurim hurried to the Jordan to meet King David. [17] He had with him a thousand men from the tribe of Benjamin. And Ziba, the servant of Saul's family, also came with his fifteen sons and twenty servants, and they arrived at the Jordan before the king. [18] They crossed* the river to escort the royal party across and to do whatever the king wanted.

David Shows Kindness to Shimei

As the king was getting ready to cross, Shimei threw himself down in front of him [19] and said, "Your Majesty, please forget the wrong I did that day you left Jerusalem. Don't hold it against me or think about it any more. [20] I know, sir, that I have sinned, and this is why I am the first one from the northern tribes to come and meet Your Majesty today."

19.11 Some ancient translations *The news… David*; Hebrew *The news… David, to his palace*, and places this sentence at the end of the verse.
19.18 Probable text *They crossed*; Hebrew *The crossing crossed*.

2 SAMUEL 19.1-8

Do you think Joab was

- A LITTLE -

HARSH

to David? Why or why not? What do you think Joab was getting at? How can we be better at controlling our emotions when they might affect other people badly?

378

2 Sam.

Deuter.
Joshua
Judges
Ruth
1 Sam.

2 SAMUEL 19

[21] Abishai son of Zeruiah spoke up: "Shimei should be put to death because he cursed the one whom the LORD chose as king."

[22] But David said to Abishai and his brother Joab, "Who asked your opinion? Are you going to give me trouble? I am the one who is king of Israel now, and no Israelite will be put to death today." [23] And he said to Shimei, "I give you my word that you will not be put to death."

David Shows Kindness to Mephibosheth

[24] Then Mephibosheth, Saul's grandson, came down to meet the king. He had not washed his feet, trimmed his beard, or washed his clothes from the time the king left Jerusalem until he returned victorious. [25] When Mephibosheth arrived from* Jerusalem to meet the king, the king said to him, "Mephibosheth, you didn't go with me. Why not?"

[26] He answered, "As you know, Your Majesty, I am crippled. I told my servant to saddle my donkey so that I could ride along with you, but he betrayed me. [27] He lied about me to Your Majesty, but you are like God's angel, so do what seems right to you. [28] All my father's family deserved to be put to death by Your Majesty, but you gave me the right to eat at your table. I have no right to ask for any more favours from Your Majesty."

[29] The king answered, "You don't have to say anything more. I have decided that you and Ziba will share Saul's property."

[30] "Let Ziba have it all," Mephibosheth answered. "It's enough for me that Your Majesty has come home safely."

David Shows Kindness to Barzillai

[31] Barzillai, from Gilead, had also come down from Rogelim to escort the king across the Jordan. [32] Barzillai was a very old man, eighty years old. He was very rich and had supplied the king with food while he was staying at Mahanaim. [33] The king said to him, "Come with me to Jerusalem, and I will take care of you."

[34] But Barzillai answered, "I haven't long to live; why should I go with Your Majesty to Jerusalem? [35] I am already eighty years old, and nothing gives me pleasure any more. I can't taste what I eat and drink, and I can't hear the voices of singers. I would only be a burden to Your Majesty. [36] I don't deserve such a great reward. So I will go just a little way with you beyond the Jordan. [37] Then let me go back home and die near my parents' grave. Here is my son Chimham, who will serve you; take him with you, Your Majesty, and do for him as you think best."

[38] The king answered, "I will take him with me and do for him whatever you want. And I will do for you anything you ask." [39] Then David and all his men crossed the Jordan. He kissed Barzillai and gave him his blessing, and Barzillai went back home.

Judah and Israel Argue over the King

[40] When the king had crossed, escorted by all the people of Judah and half the people of Israel, he went on to Gilgal, and Chimham went with him. [41] Then all the Israelites went to the king and said to him, "Your Majesty, why did our brothers, the men of Judah, think they had the right to take you away and escort you, your family, and your men across the Jordan?"

[42] The men of Judah answered, "We did it because the king is one of us. So why should this make you angry? He hasn't paid for our food nor has he given us anything."

....

19.25 One ancient translation *from*; Hebrew *at*.

2 Sam.

1 Kings
2 Kings
1 Chron.
2 Chron.
Ezra

43 The Israelites replied, "We have ten times as many claims on King David as you have, even if he is one of you. Why do you look down on us? Don't forget that we were the first to talk about bringing the king back!"

But the men of Judah were more violent in making their claims than the men of Israel.

Sheba's Rebellion

20 There happened to be in Gilgal a worthless character named Sheba son of Bikri, of the tribe of Benjamin. He blew the trumpet and called out, "Down with David! We won't follow him! Men of Israel, let's go home!" 2 So the Israelites deserted David and went with Sheba, but the men of Judah remained loyal and followed David from the Jordan to Jerusalem.

3 When David arrived at his palace in Jerusalem, he took the ten concubines he had left to take care of the palace, and put them under guard. He provided for their needs, but did not have intercourse with them. They were kept confined for the rest of their lives, living like widows.

4 The king said to Amasa, "Call the men of Judah together and be back here with them by the day after tomorrow." 5 Amasa went to call them, but he did not get back by the time the king had set. 6 So the king said to Abishai, "Sheba will give us more trouble than Absalom. Take my men and go after him, or else he may occupy some fortified towns and escape from us." 7 So Joab's men, the royal bodyguard, and all the other soldiers left Jerusalem with Abishai to go after Sheba. 8 When they reached the large rock at Gibeon, Amasa met them. Joab was dressed for battle, with a sword in its sheath fastened to his belt. As he came forward, the sword fell out. 9 Joab said to Amasa, "How are you, my friend?" and took hold of his beard with his right hand in order to kiss him. 10 Amasa was not on guard against the sword that Joab was holding in his other hand, and Joab stabbed him in the belly, and his entrails spilt out on the ground. He died immediately, and Joab did not have to strike again.

Then Joab and his brother Abishai went on after Sheba. 11 One of Joab's men stood by Amasa's body and called out, "Everyone who is for Joab and David follow Joab!" 12 Amasa's body, covered with blood, was lying in the middle of the road. Joab's man saw that everybody was stopping, so he dragged the body from the road into the field and threw a blanket over it. 13 After the body had been removed from the road, everyone followed Joab in pursuit of Sheba.

14 Sheba passed through the territory of all the tribes of Israel and came to the city of Abel Beth Maacah, and all the members of the clan of Bikri* assembled and followed him into the city. 15 Joab's men heard that Sheba was there, and so they went and besieged the city. They built ramps of earth against the outer wall and also began to dig under the wall to make it fall down. 16 There was a wise woman in the city who shouted from the wall, "Listen! Listen! Tell Joab to come here; I want to speak with him." 17 Joab went, and she asked, "Are you Joab?"

"Yes, I am," he answered.

"Listen to me, sir," she said.

"I'm listening," he answered.

18 She said, "Long ago they used to say, 'Go and get your answer in the city of Abel' — and that's just what they did. 19 Ours is a great city, one of the most peaceful and loyal in Israel. Why are you trying to destroy it? Do you want to ruin what belongs to the LORD?"

20.14 Probable text Bikri; Hebrew Beri.

380

2 Sam.

Deuter.
Joshua
Judges
Ruth
1 Sam.

2 SAMUEL 20, 21

²⁰"Never!" Joab answered. "I will never ruin or destroy your city! ²¹That is not our plan. A man named Sheba son of Bikri, who is from the hill country of Ephraim, started a rebellion against King David. Hand over this one man, and I will withdraw from the city."

"We will throw his head over the wall to you," she said. ²²Then she went to the people of the city with her plan, and they cut off Sheba's head and threw it over the wall to Joab. He blew the trumpet as a signal for his men to leave the city, and they went back home. And Joab returned to Jerusalem to the king.

David's Officials

²³Joab was in command of the army of Israel; Benaiah son of Jehoiada was in charge of David's bodyguard; ²⁴Adoniram was in charge of the forced labour; Jehoshaphat son of Ahilud was in charge of the records; ²⁵Sheva was the court secretary; Zadok and Abiathar were the priests, ²⁶and Ira from the town of Jair was also one of David's priests.

Saul's Descendants are Put to Death

21 During David's reign there was a severe famine which lasted for three full years. So David consulted the LORD about it, and the LORD said, "Saul and his family are guilty of murder; he put the people of Gibeon to death." ²(The people of Gibeon were not Israelites; they were a small group of Amorites whom the Israelites had promised to protect, but Saul had tried to destroy them because of his zeal for the people of Israel and Judah.) ³So David summoned the people of Gibeon and said to them, "What can I do for you? I want to make up for the wrong that was done to you, so that you will bless the LORD's people."

⁴They answered, "Our quarrel with Saul and his family can't be settled with silver or gold, nor do we want to kill any Israelite."

"What, then, do you think I should do for you?" David asked.

⁵They answered, "Saul wanted to destroy us and leave none of us alive anywhere in Israel. ⁶So hand over seven of his male descendants, and we will hang them before the LORD at Gibeah, the town of Saul, the LORD's chosen king."

"I will hand them over," the king answered.

⁷But because of the sacred promise that he and Jonathan had made to each other, David spared Jonathan's son Mephibosheth, the grandson of Saul. ⁸However, he took Armoni and Mephibosheth, the two sons that Rizpah the daughter of Aiah had borne to Saul; he also took the five sons of Saul's daughter Merab, whom she had borne to Adriel son of Barzillai, who was from Meholah. ⁹David handed them over to the people of Gibeon, who hanged them on the mountain before the LORD — and all seven of them died together. It was late in the spring, at the beginning of the barley harvest, when they were put to death.

¹⁰Then Saul's concubine Rizpah, the daughter of Aiah, used sackcloth to make a shelter for herself on the rock where the corpses were, and she stayed there from the beginning of harvest until the autumn rains came. During the day she would keep the birds away from the corpses, and at night she would protect them from wild animals.

¹¹When David heard what Rizpah had done, ¹²he went and got the bones of Saul and of his son Jonathan from the people of Jabesh in Gilead. (They had stolen them from the public square in Beth Shan, where the Philistines had hanged the bodies on the day they killed Saul on Mount Gilboa.) ¹³David took the bones of Saul and Jonathan and also gathered up the bones of the seven

2 Sam.

....

1 Kings
2 Kings
1 Chron.
2 Chron.
Ezra

men who had been hanged. ¹⁴ Then they buried the bones of Saul and Jonathan in the grave of Saul's father Kish, in Zela in the territory of Benjamin, doing all that the king had commanded. And after that, God answered their prayers for the country.

Battles against Philistine Giants
(1 Chr 20.4–8)

¹⁵ There was another war between the Philistines and Israel, and David and his men went and fought the Philistines. During one of the battles David grew tired. ¹⁶ A giant named Ishbibenob, who was carrying a bronze spear that weighed about 3.5 kilogrammes and who was wearing a new sword, thought he could kill David. ¹⁷ But Abishai son of Zeruiah came to David's help, attacked the giant, and killed him. Then David's men made David promise that he would never again go out with them to battle. "You are the hope of Israel, and we don't want to lose you," they said.

¹⁸ After this there was a battle with the Philistines at Gob, during which Sibbecai from Hushah killed a giant named Saph.

¹⁹ There was another battle with the Philistines at Gob, and Elhanan son of Jair* from Bethlehem killed Goliath from Gath, whose spear had a shaft as thick as the bar on a weaver's loom.

²⁰ Then there was another battle at Gath, where there was a giant who loved to fight. He had six fingers on each hand and six toes on each foot. ²¹ He defied the Israelites, and Jonathan, the son of David's brother Shammah, killed him.

²² These four were descendants of the giants of Gath, and they were killed by David and his men.

David's Song of Victory
(Ps 18)

22 When the LORD saved David from Saul and his other enemies, David sang this song to the LORD:

² The LORD is my protector;
   he is my strong fortress.
³ My God is my protection,
   and with him I am safe.
He protects me like a shield;
   he defends me and keeps me safe.
He is my saviour;
   he protects me and saves me from violence.
⁴ I call to the LORD,
   and he saves me from my enemies.
Praise the LORD!

⁵ The waves of death were all round me;
   the waves of destruction rolled over me.
⁶ The danger of death was round me,
   and the grave set its trap for me.
⁷ In my trouble I called to the LORD;
   I called to my God for help.
In his temple he heard my voice;
   he listened to my cry for help.

⁸ Then the earth trembled and shook;
   the foundations of the sky rocked and quivered
   because God was angry!

21.19 Probable text (see 1 Chr 20.5) *Jair*; Hebrew *Jaareoregim*.

⁹ Smoke poured out of his nostrils,
 a consuming flame and burning coals from his mouth.
¹⁰ He tore the sky apart and came down,
 with a dark cloud under his feet.
¹¹ He flew swiftly on his winged creature;
 he travelled on the wings of the wind.
¹² He covered himself with darkness;
 thick clouds, full of* water, surrounded him;
¹³ burning coals flamed up from the lightning before him.

¹⁴ Then the LORD thundered from the sky,
 and the voice of Almighty God was heard.
¹⁵ He shot his arrows and scattered his enemies;
 with flashes of lightning he sent them running.
¹⁶ The floor of the ocean was laid bare,
 and the foundations of the earth were uncovered
when the LORD rebuked his enemies
 and roared at them in anger.

¹⁷ The LORD reached down from above and took hold of me;
 he pulled me out of the deep waters.
¹⁸ He rescued me from my powerful enemies
 and from all those who hate me —
 they were too strong for me.
¹⁹ When I was in trouble, they attacked me,
 but the LORD protected me.
²⁰ He helped me out of danger;
 he saved me because he was pleased with me.

²¹ The LORD rewards me because I do what is right;
 he blesses me because I am innocent.
²² I have obeyed the law of the LORD;
 I have not turned away from my God.
²³ I have observed all his laws;
 I have not disobeyed his commands.
²⁴ He knows that I am faultless,
 that I have kept myself from doing wrong.
²⁵ And so he rewards me because I do what is right,
 because he knows that I am innocent.

²⁶ O LORD, you are faithful to those who are faithful to you,
 and completely good to those* who are perfect.
²⁷ You are pure to those who are pure,
 but hostile to those who are wicked.
²⁸ You save those who are humble,
 but you humble those who are proud.

²⁹ You, LORD, are my light;
 you dispel my darkness.
³⁰ You give me strength to attack my enemies
 and power to overcome their defences.

³¹ This God — how perfect are his deeds,
 how dependable his words!
He is like a shield
 for all who seek his protection.

2 SAMUEL 22.29

YOU DISPEL MY DARKNESS

22.12 Some ancient translations (and see Ps 18.11) *full of*; Hebrew unclear.
22.26 Probable text (see Ps 18.25) *those*; Hebrew *the strong*.

383

2 Sam.
..........:.

1 Kings
2 Kings
1 Chron.
2 Chron.
Ezra

32 The Lord alone is God;
    God alone is our defence.
33 This God is my strong refuge;
    he makes* my pathway safe.
34 He makes me sure-footed as a deer;
    he keeps me safe on the mountains.
35 He trains me for battle,
    so that I can use the strongest bow.

36 O Lord, you protect me and save me;
    your help has made me great.
37 You have kept me from being captured,
    and I have never fallen.
38 I pursue my enemies and defeat them;
    I do not stop until I destroy them.
39 I strike them down, and they cannot rise;
    they lie defeated before me.
40 You give me strength for the battle
    and victory over my enemies.
41 You make my enemies run from me;
    I destroy those who hate me.
42 They look for help, but no one saves them;
    they call to the Lord, but he does not answer.
43 I crush them, and they become like dust;
    I trample on them like mud in the streets.

44 You saved me from my rebellious people
    and maintained my rule over the nations;
    people I did not know have now become my subjects.
45 Foreigners bow before me;
    when they hear me, they obey.
46 They lose their courage
    and come trembling* from their fortresses.

47 The Lord lives! Praise my defender!
    Proclaim the greatness of the strong God who saves me!
48 He gives me victory over my enemies;
    he subdues the nations under me
49 and saves me from my foes.

    O Lord, you give me victory over my enemies
    and protect me from violent men.
50 And so I praise you among the nations;
    I sing praises to you.
51 God gives great victories to his king;
    he shows constant love to the one he has chosen,
    to David and his descendants for ever.

David's Last Words

23 David son of Jesse was the man whom God made great, whom the God of Jacob chose to be king, and who was the composer of beautiful songs for Israel. These are David's last words:

2 The Spirit of the Lord speaks through me;
    his message is on my lips.

22.33 Probable text (see Ps 18.32) *he makes*; Hebrew unclear.
22.46 Probable text (see Ps 18.45) *come trembling*; Hebrew *come ready to fight*.

384

2 Sam.

Deuter.
Joshua
Judges
Ruth
1 Sam.

2 SAMUEL 23

3 The God of Israel has spoken;
   the protector of Israel said to me:
"The king who rules with justice,
   who rules in obedience to God,
4 is like the sun shining on a cloudless dawn,
   the sun that makes the grass sparkle after rain."

5 And that is how God will bless my descendants,
   because he has made an eternal covenant with me,
   an agreement that will not be broken,
   a promise that will not be changed.
That is all I desire;
   that will be my victory,
   and God will surely bring it about.
6 But godless people are like thorns that are thrown away;
   no one can touch them with bare hands.
7 You must use an iron tool or a spear;
   they will be burnt completely.*

David's Famous Soldiers
(1 Chr 11.10–41)

8 These are the names of David's famous soldiers: the first was Josheb Basshebeth from Tachemon, who was the leader of "The Three";* he fought with his spear* against 800 men and killed them all in one battle.

9 The second of the famous three was Eleazar son of Dodo, of the clan of Ahoh. One day he and David challenged the Philistines who had gathered for battle. The Israelites fell back, 10 but he stood his ground and fought the Philistines until his hand was so stiff that he could not let go of his sword. The LORD won a great victory that day. After it was over, the Israelites returned to where Eleazar was and stripped the armour from the dead.

11 The third of the famous three was Shammah son of Agee, from Harar. The Philistines had gathered at Lehi, where there was a field of peas. The Israelites fled from the Philistines, 12 but Shammah stood his ground in the field, defended it, and killed the Philistines. The LORD won a great victory that day.

13 Near the beginning of harvest time* three of "The Thirty" went down to the cave of Adullam, where David was, while a band of Philistines was camping in the Valley of Rephaim. 14 At that time David was on a fortified hill, and a group of Philistines had occupied Bethlehem. 15 David felt homesick and said, "How I wish someone would bring me a drink of water from the well by the gate at Bethlehem!" 16 The three famous soldiers forced their way through the Philistine camp, drew some water from the well, and brought it back to David. But he would not drink it; instead he poured it out as an offering to the LORD 17 and said, "LORD, I could never drink this! It would be like drinking the blood of these men who risked their lives!" So he refused to drink it.

Those were the brave deeds of the three famous soldiers.

18 Joab's brother Abishai (their mother was Zeruiah) was the leader of "The Famous Thirty". He fought with his spear against 300 men and killed them, and became famous among "The

---

23.7 Verses 6–7 in Hebrew are unclear.
23.8 One ancient translation "The Three"; Hebrew the third.
23.8 Probable text (see 1 Chr 11.11) he fought with his spear; Hebrew unclear.
23.13 Probable text Near the beginning of harvest time; Hebrew unclear.

2 SAMUEL 23, 24

385

2 Sam.

....

1 Kings
2 Kings
1 Chron.
2 Chron.
Ezra

Thirty".* [19] He was the most famous of "The Thirty"* and became their leader, but he was not as famous as "The Three".

[20] Benaiah son of Jehoiada, from Kabzeel, was another famous soldier; he did many brave deeds, including killing two great Moabite warriors. He once went down into a pit on a snowy day and killed a lion. [21] He also killed an Egyptian, a huge man who was armed with a spear. Benaiah attacked him with his club, snatched the spear from the Egyptian's hand, and killed him with it. [22] Those were the brave deeds of Benaiah, who was one of "The Thirty".* [23] He was outstanding among them, but was not as famous as "The Three". David put him in charge of his bodyguard.

[24-39] Other members of "The Thirty" included:

Asahel, Joab's brother
Elhanan son of Dodo from Bethlehem
Shammah and Elika from Harod
Helez from Pelet
Ira son of Ikkesh from Tekoa
Abiezer from Anathoth
Mebunnai from Hushah
Zalmon from Ahoh
Maharai from Netophah
Heleb son of Baanah from Netophah
Ittai son of Ribai from Gibeah in Benjamin
Benaiah from Pirathon
Hiddai from the valleys near Gaash
Abialbon from Arabah
Azmaveth from Bahurim
Eliahba from Shaalbon
The sons of Jashen
Jonathan
Shammah from Harar
Ahiam son of Sharar from Harar
Eliphelet son of Ahasbai from Maacah
Eliam son of Ahithophel from Gilo
Hezro from Carmel
Paarai from Arab
Igal son of Nathan from Zobah
Bani from Gad
Zelek from Ammon
Naharai from Beeroth, Joab's armour bearer
Ira and Gareb from Jattir
Uriah the Hittite.

There were 37 famous soldiers in all.

David Takes a Census
(1 Chr 21.1–27)

24 The LORD was angry with Israel once more, and he made David bring trouble on them. The LORD said to him, "Go and count the people of Israel and Judah." [2] So David gave orders to Joab, the commander of his army: "Go with your officers through all the tribes of Israel from one end of the country to the other, and count the people. I want to know how many there are."

[3] But Joab answered the king, "Your Majesty, may the LORD your God make the people of Israel a hundred times more numerous than they are now, and may you live to see him do it. But why does Your Majesty want to do this?" [4] But the king made Joab

23.18 One ancient translation "The Thirty"; Hebrew "The Three".
23.19; 23.22 Probable text "The Thirty"; Hebrew "The Three".

2 Sam.

Deuter.
Joshua
Judges
Ruth
1 Sam.

and his officers obey his order; they left his presence and went out to count the people of Israel.

⁵ They crossed the Jordan and camped south of Aroer, the city in the middle of the valley, in the territory of Gad.* From there they went north to Jazer, ⁶ and on to Gilead and to Kadesh, in Hittite territory.* Then they went to Dan, and from Dan they went* west to Sidon. ⁷ Then they went south to the fortified city of Tyre, on to all the cities of the Hivites and the Canaanites, and finally to Beersheba, in the southern part of Judah. ⁸ So after nine months and twenty days they returned to Jerusalem, having travelled through the whole country. ⁹ They reported to the king the total number of men capable of military service: 800,000 in Israel and 500,000 in Judah.

¹⁰ But after David had taken the census, his conscience began to trouble him, and he said to the Lord, "I have committed a terrible sin in doing this! Please forgive me. I have acted foolishly."

¹¹⁻¹² The Lord said to Gad, David's prophet, "Go and tell David that I am giving him three choices. I will do whichever he chooses." The next morning, after David got up, ¹³ Gad went to him, told him what the Lord had said, and asked, "Which is it to be? Three* years of famine in your land or three months of running away from your enemies or three days of an epidemic in your land? Now think it over, and tell me what answer to take back to the Lord."

¹⁴ David answered, "I am in a desperate situation! But I don't want to be punished by human beings. Let the Lord himself be the one to punish us, for he is merciful." ¹⁵ So the Lord sent an epidemic on Israel, which lasted from that morning until the time that he had chosen. From one end of the country to the other 70,000 Israelites died. ¹⁶ When the Lord's angel was about to destroy Jerusalem, the Lord changed his mind about punishing the people and said to the angel who was killing them, "Stop! That's enough!" The angel was by the threshing place of Araunah, a Jebusite.

¹⁷ David saw the angel who was killing the people, and said to the Lord, "I am the guilty one. I am the one who did wrong. What have these poor people done? You should punish me and my family."

¹⁸ That same day Gad went to David and said to him, "Go up to Araunah's threshing place and build an altar to the Lord." ¹⁹ David obeyed the Lord's command and went as Gad had told him. ²⁰ Araunah looked down and saw the king and his officials coming up to him. He threw himself on the ground in front of David ²¹ and asked, "Your Majesty, why are you here?"

David answered, "To buy your threshing place and build an altar for the Lord, in order to stop the epidemic."

²² "Take it, Your Majesty," Araunah said, "and offer to the Lord whatever you wish. Here are these oxen to burn as an offering on the altar; here are their yokes and the threshing boards to use as fuel." ²³ Araunah gave it all to the king* and said to him, "May the Lord your God accept your offering."

²⁴ But the king answered, "No, I will pay you for it. I will not offer to the Lord my God sacrifices that have cost me nothing." And he bought the threshing place and the oxen for fifty pieces of silver. ²⁵ Then he built an altar to the Lord and offered burnt offerings and fellowship offerings. The Lord answered his prayer, and the epidemic in Israel was stopped.

....

24.5 Probable text *Aroer... Gad*; Hebrew unclear.
24.6 One ancient translation *Kadesh, in Hittite territory*; Hebrew *to the land of Tahtim, Hodshi.*
24.6 Probable text *and from Dan they went*; Hebrew unclear.
24.13 Some ancient translations (and see 1 Chr 21.12) *Three*; Hebrew *Seven.*
24.23 Probable text *to the king*; Hebrew *to the king the king.*

THE BOOK OF
1 KINGS

WRITTEN: PROBABLY AROUND 650-530BC

WHAT YOU NEED TO KNOW:

1 and 2 Kings were originally one book, spanning about 400 years in total. Solomon, David's son, rules as king in much of this book. He was incredibly wise and led the nation into a time of great wealth. After his death, the kingdom divided into two - Israel in the north and Judah in the south. The book talks about good kings and bad kings, judged not by their wealth but by their loyalty to God. It is thought that this book was partly written while the Jews were in exile, as an explanation of why the nation had fallen apart. The prophet Elijah is a key character in the second half of the book, calling the nation back to God.

WHY READ IT?

Solomon began his reign with power and fame, but he started to believe in his own brilliance and forgot about God. Then it all went wrong. Here we watch as kings either think they know better than God and let their pride rule, or love God and lead their people well. We also see what it looks like to stand up for God in a nation where those who love God are in the minority.

Write down here the ways in which your life would

LOOK
· DIFFERENT ·

if your success wasn't measured by how much you achieved or your popularity but by whether or not you followed God.

OBG · DAVID DIES · KING SOLOMON · TEMPLE BUILT · JUDAH AND ISRAEL SPLIT · PROPHET ELIJAH · 850BC

388

1 Kings

:·:········

Joshua
Judges
Ruth
1 Sam.
2 Sam.

1 KINGS 1

King David in his Old Age

1 King David was now a very old man, and although his servants covered him with blankets, he could not keep warm. [2] So his officials said to him, "Your Majesty, let us find a young woman to stay with you and take care of you. She will lie close to you and keep you warm." [3] A search was made all over Israel for a beautiful young woman, and in Shunem they found such a woman named Abishag, and brought her to the king. [4] She was very beautiful, and waited on the king and took care of him, but he did not have intercourse with her.

Adonijah Claims the Throne

[5-6] Now that Absalom was dead, Adonijah, the son of David and Haggith, was the eldest surviving son. He was a very handsome man. David had never reprimanded him about anything, and he was ambitious to be king. He provided for himself chariots, horses, and an escort of fifty men. [7] He talked with Joab (whose mother was Zeruiah) and with Abiathar the priest, and they agreed to support his cause. [8] But Zadok the priest, Benaiah son of Jehoiada, Nathan the prophet, Shimei, Rei, and David's bodyguard were not on Adonijah's side.

[9] One day Adonijah offered a sacrifice of sheep, bulls, and fattened calves at Snake Rock, near the spring of Enrogel. He invited the other sons of King David and the king's officials who were from Judah to come to this sacrificial feast, [10] but he did not invite his half brother Solomon or Nathan the prophet, or Benaiah, or the king's bodyguard.

Solomon is Made King

[11] Then Nathan went to Bathsheba, Solomon's mother, and asked her, "Haven't you heard that Haggith's son Adonijah has made himself king? And King David doesn't know anything about it! [12] If you want to save your life and the life of your son Solomon, I would advise you [13] to go at once to King David and ask him, 'Your Majesty, didn't you solemnly promise me that my son Solomon would succeed you as king? How is it, then, that Adonijah has become king?'" [14] And Nathan added, "Then, while you are still talking with King David, I will come in and confirm your story."

[15] So Bathsheba went to see the king in his bedroom. He was very old, and Abishag, the woman from Shunem, was taking care of him. [16] Bathsheba bowed low before the king, and he asked, "What do you want?"

[17] She answered, "Your Majesty, you made me a solemn promise in the name of the LORD your God that my son Solomon would be king after you. [18] But Adonijah has already become king, and you don't know anything about it. [19] He has offered a sacrifice of many bulls, sheep, and fattened calves, and he invited your sons, and Abiathar the priest, and Joab the commander of your army to the feast, but he did not invite your son Solomon. [20] Your Majesty, all the people of Israel are looking to you to tell them who is to succeed you as king. [21] If you don't, as soon as you are dead my son Solomon and I will be treated as traitors."

[22] She was still speaking, when Nathan arrived at the palace. [23] The king was told that the prophet was there, and Nathan went in and bowed low before the king. [24] Then he said, "Your Majesty, have you announced that Adonijah would succeed you as king? [25] This very day he has gone and offered a sacrifice of many bulls, sheep, and fattened calves. He invited all your sons,

1 KINGS 1

389

1 Kings
2 Kings
1 Chron.
2 Chron.
Ezra
Nehem.

Joab the commander of your army,* and Abiathar the priest, and just now they are feasting with him and shouting, 'Long live King Adonijah!' 26 But he did not invite me, sir, or Zadok the priest, or Benaiah, or Solomon. 27 Did Your Majesty approve all this and not even tell your officials who is to succeed you as king?"

28 King David said, "Ask Bathsheba to come back in" — and she came and stood before him. 29 Then he said to her, "I promise you by the living LORD, who has rescued me from all my troubles, 30 that today I will keep the promise I made to you in the name of the LORD, the God of Israel, that your son Solomon would succeed me as king."

31 Bathsheba bowed low and said, "May my lord the king live for ever!"

32 Then King David sent for Zadok, Nathan, and Benaiah. When they came in, 33 he said to them, "Take my court officials with you; let my son Solomon ride my own mule, and escort him down to the spring of Gihon, 34 where Zadok and Nathan are to anoint him as king of Israel. Then blow the trumpet and shout, 'Long live King Solomon!' 35 Follow him back here when he comes to sit on my throne. He will succeed me as king, because he is the one I have chosen to be the ruler of Israel and Judah."

36 "It shall be done," answered Benaiah, "and may the LORD your God confirm it. 37 As the LORD has been with Your Majesty, may he also be with Solomon, and make his reign even more prosperous than yours."

38 So Zadok, Nathan, Benaiah, and the royal bodyguard put Solomon on King David's mule, and escorted him to the spring of Gihon. 39 Zadok took the container of olive oil which he had brought from the Tent of the LORD's presence, and anointed Solomon. They blew the trumpet, and all the people shouted, "Long live King Solomon!" 40 Then they all followed him back, shouting for joy and playing flutes, making enough noise to shake the ground.

41 As Adonijah and all his guests were finishing the feast, they heard the noise. And when Joab heard the trumpet, he asked, "What's the meaning of all that noise in the city?" 42 Before he finished speaking, Jonathan, the son of the priest Abiathar, arrived. "Come in," Adonijah said. "You're a good man — you must be bringing good news."

43 "I'm afraid not," Jonathan answered. "His Majesty King David has made Solomon king. 44 He sent Zadok, Nathan, Benaiah, and the royal bodyguard to escort him. They made him ride on the king's mule, 45 and Zadok and Nathan anointed him as king at the spring of Gihon. Then they went into the city, shouting for joy, and the people are now in an uproar. That's the noise you just heard. 46 Solomon is now the king. 47 What is more, the court officials went in to pay their respects to His Majesty King David, and said, 'May your God make Solomon even more famous than you, and may Solomon's reign be even more prosperous than yours.' Then King David bowed in worship on his bed 48 and prayed, 'Let us praise the LORD, the God of Israel, who has today made one of my descendants succeed me as king, and has let me live to see it!' "

49 Then Adonijah's guests were afraid, and they all got up and left, each going his own way. 50 Adonijah, in great fear of Solomon, went to the Tent of the LORD's presence and took hold of the corners

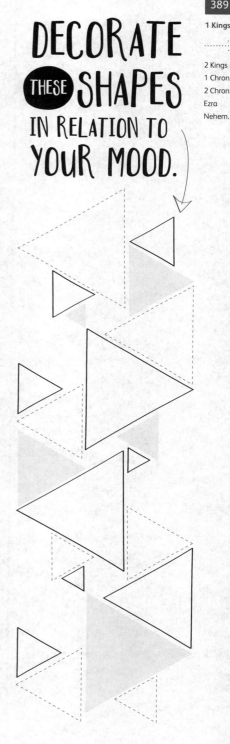

DECORATE THESE SHAPES IN RELATION TO YOUR MOOD.

1.25 One ancient translation Joab the commander of your army; Hebrew your army commanders.

390

1 Kings

Joshua
Judges
Ruth
1 Sam.
2 Sam.

1 KINGS 1, 2

of the altar.* [51] King Solomon was told that Adonijah was afraid of him and that he was holding on to the corners of the altar and had said, "First, I want King Solomon to swear to me that he will not have me put to death."

[52] Solomon replied, "If he is loyal, not even a hair on his head will be touched; but if he is not, he will die." [53] King Solomon then sent for Adonijah and had him brought down from the altar. Adonijah went to the king and bowed low before him, and the king said to him, "You may go home."

David's Last Instructions to Solomon

2 When David was about to die, he called his son Solomon and gave him his last instructions: [2] "My time to die has come. Be confident and determined, [3] and do what the LORD your God orders you to do. Obey all his laws and commands, as written in the Law of Moses, so that wherever you go you may prosper in everything you do. [4] If you obey him, the LORD will keep the promise he made when he told me that my descendants would rule Israel as long as they were careful to obey his commands faithfully with all their heart and soul.

[5] "There is something else. You remember what Joab did to me by killing the two commanders of Israel's armies, Abner son of Ner and Amasa son of Jether. You remember how he murdered them in time of peace in revenge for deaths they had caused in time of war. He killed innocent men* and now I bear the responsibility for what he did, and I suffer* the consequences. [6] You know what to do; you must not let him die a natural death.

[7] "But show kindness to the sons of Barzillai from Gilead and take care of them, because they were kind to me when I was fleeing from your brother Absalom.

[8] "There is also Shimei son of Gera, from the town of Bahurim in Benjamin. He cursed me bitterly the day I went to Mahanaim, but when he met me at the River Jordan, I gave him my solemn promise in the name of the LORD that I would not have him killed. [9] But you must not let him go unpunished. You know what to do, and you must see to it that he is put to death."

The Death of David

[10] David died and was buried in David's City. [11] He had been king of Israel for forty years, ruling seven years in Hebron and 33 years in Jerusalem. [12] Solomon succeeded his father David as king, and his royal power was firmly established.

The Death of Adonijah

[13] Then Adonijah, whose mother was Haggith, went to Bathsheba, who was Solomon's mother. "Is this a friendly visit?" she asked.

"It is," he answered, [14] and then he added, "I have something to ask of you."

"What is it?" she asked.

[15] He answered, "You know that I should have become king and that everyone in Israel expected it. But it happened differently, and my brother became king, because it was the LORD's will. [16] And now I have one request to make; please do not refuse me."

....

1.50 *corners of the altar*: Small projections at the four corners of the altar that looked like horns. Anyone holding on to them was safe from being killed.
2.5 Some ancient translations *innocent men*; Hebrew *men in battle*.
2.5 Some ancient translations *I bear... and I suffer*; Hebrew *he bears... and he suffers*.

1 KINGS 2
391

1 Kings

2 Kings
1 Chron.
2 Chron.
Ezra
Nehem.

"What is it?" Bathsheba asked.

¹⁷He answered, "Please ask King Solomon — I know he won't refuse you — to let me have Abishag, the woman from Shunem, as my wife."

¹⁸"Very well," she answered. "I will speak to the king for you."

¹⁹So Bathsheba went to the king to speak to him on behalf of Adonijah. The king stood up to greet his mother and bowed to her. Then he sat on his throne and had another one brought in on which she sat at his right. ²⁰She said, "I have a small favour to ask of you; please do not refuse me."

"What is it, mother?" he asked. "I will not refuse you."

²¹She answered, "Let your brother Adonijah have Abishag as his wife."

²²"Why do you ask me to give Abishag to him?" the king asked. "You might as well ask me to give him the throne too. After all, he is my elder brother, and Abiathar the priest and Joab are on his side!"* ²³Then Solomon made a solemn promise in the LORD's name, "May God strike me dead if I don't make Adonijah pay with his life for asking this! ²⁴The LORD has firmly established me on the throne of my father David; he has kept his promise and given the kingdom to me and my descendants. I swear by the living LORD that Adonijah will die this very day!"

²⁵So King Solomon gave orders to Benaiah, who went out and killed Adonijah.

Abiathar's Banishment and Joab's Death

²⁶Then King Solomon said to Abiathar the priest, "Go to your country home in Anathoth. You deserve to die, but I will not have you put to death now, for you were in charge of the LORD's Covenant Box while you were with my father David, and you shared in all his troubles." ²⁷Then Solomon dismissed Abiathar from serving as a priest of the LORD, and so he made what the LORD had said in Shiloh about the priest Eli and his descendants come true.

²⁸Joab heard what had happened. (He had supported Adonijah, but not Absalom.) So he fled to the Tent of the LORD's presence and took hold of the corners of the altar.* ²⁹When the news reached King Solomon that Joab had fled to the Tent and was by the altar, Solomon sent a messenger to Joab to ask him why he had fled to the altar. Joab answered that he had fled to the LORD because he was afraid of Solomon. So King Solomon sent Benaiah* to kill Joab. ³⁰He went to the Tent of the LORD's presence and said to Joab, "The king orders you to come out."

"No," Joab answered. "I will die here."

Benaiah went back to the king and told him what Joab had said.

³¹"Do what Joab says," Solomon answered. "Kill him and bury him. Then neither I nor any other of David's descendants will any longer be held responsible for what Joab did when he killed innocent men. ³²The LORD will punish Joab for those murders, which he committed* without my father David's knowledge. Joab killed two innocent men who were better men than he: Abner, commander of the army of Israel, and Amasa, commander of the army of Judah. ³³The punishment for their murders will fall

2.22 Some ancient translations *and Abiathar the priest... on his side*; Hebrew unclear.
2.28 *corners of the altar*: See 1.50.
2.29 One ancient translation *Solomon sent a messenger... sent Benaiah*; Hebrew *Solomon sent Benaiah*.
2.32 *will punish... committed*; or *will kill Joab, because he committed those murders*.

392

1 Kings

Joshua
Judges
Ruth
1 Sam.
2 Sam.

1 KINGS 2, 3

1 KINGS 3.5

What would you
answer if you were
asked this question?

Why did Solomon's
– REQUEST FOR –
WISDOM
please God? Are
there any areas where
you regularly make
unwise decisions?
What are they?

on Joab and on his descendants for ever. But the LORD will always give success to David's descendants who sit on his throne."

³⁴ So Benaiah went to the Tent of the LORD's presence and killed Joab, and he was buried at his home in the open country. ³⁵ The king made Benaiah commander of the army in Joab's place and put Zadok the priest in Abiathar's place.

The Death of Shimei

³⁶ Then the king sent for Shimei and said to him, "Build a house for yourself here in Jerusalem. Live in it and don't leave the city. ³⁷ If you ever leave and go beyond the brook of Kidron, you will certainly die — and you yourself will be to blame."

³⁸ "Very well, Your Majesty," Shimei answered. "I will do what you say." So he lived in Jerusalem a long time.

³⁹ Three years later, however, two of Shimei's slaves ran away to the king of Gath, Achish son of Maacah. When Shimei heard that they were in Gath, ⁴⁰ he saddled his donkey and went to King Achish in Gath, to find his slaves. He found them and brought them back home. ⁴¹ When Solomon heard what Shimei had done, ⁴² he sent for him and said, "I made you promise in the LORD's name not to leave Jerusalem. And I warned you that if you ever did, you would certainly die. Did you not agree to it and say that you would obey me? ⁴³ Why, then, have you broken your promise and disobeyed my command? ⁴⁴ You know very well all the wrong that you did to my father David. The LORD will punish you for it. ⁴⁵ But he will bless me and he will make David's kingdom secure for ever."

⁴⁶ Then the king gave orders to Benaiah, who went out and killed Shimei. Solomon was now in complete control.

Solomon Prays for Wisdom
(2 Chr 1.3–12)

3 Solomon made an alliance with the king of Egypt by marrying his daughter. He brought her to live in David's City until he had finished building his palace, the Temple, and the wall round Jerusalem. ² A temple had not yet been built for the LORD, and so the people were still offering sacrifices at many different altars. ³ Solomon loved the LORD and followed the instructions of his father David, but he also slaughtered animals and offered them as sacrifices on various altars.

⁴ On one occasion he went to Gibeon to offer sacrifices because that was where the most famous altar was. He had offered hundreds of burnt offerings there in the past. ⁵ That night the LORD appeared to him in a dream and asked him, "What would you like me to give you?"

⁶ Solomon answered, "You always showed great love for my father David, your servant, and he was good, loyal, and honest in his relations with you. And you have continued to show him your great and constant love by giving him a son who today rules in his place. ⁷ O LORD God, you have let me succeed my father as king, even though I am very young and don't know how to rule. ⁸ Here I am among the people you have chosen to be your own, a people who are so many that they cannot be counted. ⁹ So give me the wisdom I need to rule your people with justice and to know the difference between good and evil. Otherwise, how would I ever be able to rule this great people of yours?"

¹⁰ The LORD was pleased that Solomon had asked for this, ¹¹ and so he said to him, "Because you have asked for the wisdom to rule justly, instead of long life for yourself or riches or the death of your enemies, ¹² I will do what you have asked. I will give you more

1 KINGS 3, 4

393

1 Kings

....

2 Kings

1 Chron.

2 Chron.

Ezra

Nehem.

wisdom and understanding than anyone has ever had before or will ever have again. ¹³ I will also give you what you have not asked for: all your life you will have wealth and honour, more than that of any other king. ¹⁴ And if you obey me and keep my laws and commands, as your father David did, I will give you a long life."

¹⁵ Solomon woke up and realized that God had spoken to him in the dream. Then he went to Jerusalem and stood in front of the LORD's Covenant Box and offered burnt offerings and fellowship offerings to the LORD. After that he gave a feast for all his officials.

Solomon Judges a Difficult Case

¹⁶ One day two prostitutes came and presented themselves before King Solomon. ¹⁷ One of them said, "Your Majesty, this woman and I live in the same house, and I gave birth to a baby boy at home while she was there. ¹⁸ Two days after my child was born she also gave birth to a baby boy. Only the two of us were there in the house — no one else was present. ¹⁹ Then one night she accidentally rolled over on her baby and smothered it. ²⁰ She got up during the night, took my son from my side while I was asleep, and carried him to her bed; then she put the dead child in my bed. ²¹ The next morning, when I woke up and was going to feed my baby, I saw that it was dead. I looked at it more closely and saw that it was not my child."

²² But the other woman said, "No! The living child is mine, and the dead one is yours!"

The first woman answered, "No! The dead child is yours, and the living one is mine!"

And so they argued before the king.

²³ Then King Solomon said, "Each of you claims that the living child is hers and that the dead child belongs to the other one." ²⁴ He sent for a sword, and when it was brought, ²⁵ he said, "Cut the living child in two and give each woman half of it."

²⁶ The real mother, her heart full of love for her son, said to the king, "Please, Your Majesty, don't kill the child! Give it to her!"

But the other woman said, "Don't give it to either of us; go ahead and cut it in two."

²⁷ Then Solomon said, "Don't kill the child! Give it to the first woman — she is its real mother."

²⁸ When the people of Israel heard of Solomon's decision, they were all filled with deep respect for him, because they knew then that God had given him the wisdom to settle disputes fairly.

Solomon's Officials

4 Solomon was king of all Israel, ² and these were his high officials:

The priest: Azariah son of Zadok

³ The court secretaries: Elihoreph and Ahijah, sons of Shisha
In charge of the records: Jehoshaphat son of Ahilud

⁴ Commander of the army: Benaiah son of Jehoiada
Priests: Zadok and Abiathar

⁵ Chief of the district governors: Azariah son of Nathan
Royal adviser: the priest Zabud son of Nathan

⁶ In charge of the palace servants: Ahishar
In charge of the forced labour: Adoniram son of Abda.

⁷ Solomon appointed twelve men as district governors in Israel. They were to provide food from their districts for the king and his household, each man being responsible for one month out of the year. ⁸ The following are the names of these twelve officers and the districts they were in charge of:

394

1 Kings

∴.........

Joshua
Judges
Ruth
1 Sam.
2 Sam.

1 KINGS 4

Benhur: the hill country of Ephraim

9 Bendeker: the cities of Makaz, Shaalbim, Beth Shemesh, Elon, and Beth Hanan

10 Benhesed: the cities of Arubboth and Socoh and all the territory of Hepher

11 Benabinadab, who was married to Solomon's daughter Taphath: the whole region of Dor

12 Baana son of Ahilud: the cities of Taanach, Megiddo, and all the region near Beth Shan, near the town of Zarethan, south of the town of Jezreel, as far as the city of Abel Meholah and the city of Jokmeam

13 Bengeber: the city of Ramoth in Gilead, and the villages in Gilead belonging to the clan of Jair, a descendant of Manasseh, and the region of Argob in Bashan, sixty large towns in all, fortified with walls and with bronze bars on the gates

14 Ahinadab son of Iddo: the district of Mahanaim

15 Ahimaaz, who was married to Basemath, another of Solomon's daughters: the territory of Naphtali

16 Baana son of Hushai: the region of Asher and the town of Bealoth

17 Jehoshaphat son of Paruah: the territory of Issachar

18 Shimei son of Ela: the territory of Benjamin

19 Geber son of Uri: the region of Gilead, which had been ruled by King Sihon of the Amorites and King Og of Bashan.

Besides these twelve, there was one governor over the whole land.

Solomon's Prosperous Reign

20 The people of Judah and Israel were as numerous as the grains of sand on the seashore; they ate and drank, and were happy. 21 Solomon's kingdom included all the nations from the River Euphrates to Philistia and the Egyptian border. They paid him taxes and were subject to him all his life.

22 The supplies Solomon needed each day were 5,000 litres of fine flour and 10,000 litres of meal; 23 ten stall-fed cattle, twenty pasture-fed cattle, and a hundred sheep, besides deer, gazelles, roebucks, and poultry.

24 Solomon ruled over all the land west of the River Euphrates, from Tiphsah on the Euphrates as far west as the city of Gaza. All the kings west of the Euphrates were subject to him, and he was at peace with all the neighbouring countries. 25 As long as he lived, the people throughout Judah and Israel lived in safety, each family with its own grapevines and fig trees.

26 Solomon had 40,000 stalls for his chariot horses and 12,000 cavalry horses. 27 His twelve governors, each one in the month assigned to him, supplied the food King Solomon needed for himself and for all who ate in the palace; they always supplied everything needed. 28 Each governor also supplied his share of barley and straw, where it was needed,* for the chariot horses and the draught animals.

29 God gave Solomon unusual wisdom and insight, and knowledge too great to be measured. 30 Solomon was wiser than the wise men of the East or the wise men of Egypt. 31 He was the wisest of all men: wiser than Ethan the Ezrahite, and Heman, Calcol, and Darda, the sons of Mahol, and his fame

....

4.28 *where it was needed*; or *wherever King Solomon was.*

1 KINGS 4–6

395

1 Kings

2 Kings
1 Chron.
2 Chron.
Ezra
Nehem.

spread throughout all the neighbouring countries. [32] He composed 3,000 proverbs and more than a thousand songs. [33] He spoke of trees and plants, from the Lebanon cedars to the hyssop that grows on walls; he talked about animals, birds, reptiles, and fish. [34] Kings all over the world heard of his wisdom and sent people to listen to him.

Solomon Prepares to Build the Temple
(2 Chr 2.1–18)

5 King Hiram of Tyre had always been a friend of David's, and when he heard that Solomon had succeeded his father David as king he sent ambassadors to him. [2] Solomon sent back this message to Hiram: [3] "You know that because of the constant wars my father David had to fight against the enemy countries all round him, he could not build a temple for the worship of the LORD his God until the LORD had given him victory over all his enemies. [4] But now the LORD my God has given me peace on all my borders. I have no enemies, and there is no danger of attack. [5] The LORD promised my father David, 'Your son, whom I will make king after you, will build a temple for me.' And I have now decided to build that temple for the worship of the LORD my God. [6] So send your men to Lebanon to cut down cedars for me. My men will work with them, and I will pay your men whatever you decide. As you well know, my men don't know how to cut down trees as well as yours do."

[7] Hiram was extremely pleased when he received Solomon's message, and he said, "Praise the LORD today for giving David such a wise son to succeed him as king of that great nation!" [8] Then Hiram sent Solomon the following message: "I have received your message and I am ready to do what you ask. I will provide the cedars and the pine trees. [9] My men will bring the logs down from Lebanon to the sea, and will tie them together in rafts to float them down the coast to the place you choose. There my men will untie them, and your men will take charge of them. On your part, I would like you to supply the food for my men."

[10] So Hiram supplied Solomon with all the cedar and pine logs that he wanted, [11] and Solomon provided Hiram with 2,000 tonnes of wheat and 400,000 litres* of pure olive oil every year to feed his men.

[12] The LORD kept his promise and gave Solomon wisdom. There was peace between Hiram and Solomon, and they made a treaty with each other.

[13] King Solomon drafted 30,000 men as forced labour from all over Israel, [14] and put Adoniram in charge of them. He divided them into three groups of 10,000 men, and each group spent one month in Lebanon and two months back home. [15] Solomon also had 80,000 men in the hill country quarrying stone, with 70,000 men to carry it, [16] and he placed 3,300 foremen in charge of them to supervise their work. [17] At King Solomon's command they quarried fine large stones for the foundation of the Temple. [18] Solomon's and Hiram's workmen and men from the city of Byblos prepared the stones and the timber to build the Temple.

Solomon Builds the Temple

6 480 years after the people of Israel left Egypt, during the fourth year of Solomon's reign over Israel, in the second

---

5.11 Some ancient translations (and see 2 Chr 2.10) *400,000 litres*; Hebrew *4,000 litres*.

396

1 Kings

Joshua
Judges
Ruth
1 Sam.
2 Sam.

1 KINGS 6

1 KINGS 6

Up to this point, God's presence was with his people in the Covenant Box (also known as the ark of the covenant), but here God is getting

• A NEW •

HOME.

The temple will be the place where God's presence lives with Israel. This is why Jews would travel from around the world to visit the temple.

month, the month of Ziv, Solomon began work on the Temple. [2] Inside it was 27 metres long, nine metres wide, and 13.5 metres high. [3] The entrance room was 4.5 metres deep and nine metres wide, as wide as the sanctuary itself. [4] The walls of the Temple had openings in them, narrower on the outside than on the inside. [5] Against the outside walls, on the sides and the back of the Temple, a three-storied annexe was built, each storey 2.2 metres high. [6] Each room in the lowest storey was 2.2 metres wide, in the middle storey 2.7 metres wide, and in the top storey 3.1 metres wide. The temple wall on each floor was thinner than on the floor below so that the rooms could rest on the wall without having their beams built into it.

[7] The stones with which the Temple was built had been prepared at the quarry, so that there was no noise made by hammers, axes, or any other iron tools as the Temple was being built.

[8] The entrance to the lowest* storey of the annexe was on the south side of the Temple, with stairs leading up to the second and third storeys. [9] So King Solomon finished building the Temple. He put in a ceiling made of beams and boards of cedar. [10] The three-storied annexe, each storey* 2.2 metres high, was built against the outside walls of the Temple, and was joined to them by cedar beams.

[11] The LORD said to Solomon, [12] "If you obey all my laws and commands, I will do for you what I promised your father David. [13] I will live among my people Israel in this Temple that you are building, and I will never abandon them."

[14] So Solomon finished building the Temple.

The Interior Furnishings of the Temple
(2 Chr 3.8–14)

[15] The inside walls were covered with cedar panels from the floor to the ceiling, and the floor was made of pine. [16] An inner room, called the Most Holy Place, was built in the rear of the Temple. It was nine metres long and was partitioned off by cedar boards reaching from the floor to the ceiling.* [17] The room in front of the Most Holy Place was eighteen metres long. [18] The cedar panels were decorated with carvings of gourds and flowers; the whole interior was covered with cedar, so that the stones of the walls could not be seen.

[19] In the rear of the Temple an inner room was built, where the LORD's Covenant Box was to be placed. [20] This inner room was nine metres long, nine metres wide, and nine metres high, all covered with pure gold. The altar was covered with cedar panels.* [21] The inside of the Temple was covered with gold, and gold chains were placed across the entrance of the inner room, which was also covered with gold. [22] The whole interior of the Temple was covered with gold, as well as the altar in the Most Holy Place.

[23] Two winged creatures were made of olive wood and placed in the Most Holy Place, each one 4.4 metres tall. [24-26] Both were of the same size and shape. Each had two wings, each wing 2.2 metres long, so that the distance from one wing tip to the other was 4.4 metres. [27] They were placed side by side in the Most Holy Place, so that two of their outstretched wings touched each other

6.8 Some ancient translations *lowest*; Hebrew *middle*.
6.10 Probable text *three-storied annexe, each storey*; Hebrew *three-storied annexe*.
6.16 One ancient translation *ceiling*; Hebrew *walls*.
6.20 Verse 20 in Hebrew is unclear.

397

1 Kings

··········:·

2 Kings
1 Chron.
2 Chron.
Ezra
Nehem.

in the middle of the room, and the other two wings touched the walls. ²⁸The two winged creatures were covered with gold.

²⁹The walls of the main room and of the inner room were all decorated with carved figures of winged creatures, palm trees, and flowers. ³⁰Even the floor was covered with gold.

³¹A double door made of olive wood was set in place at the entrance of the Most Holy Place; the top of the doorway was a pointed arch. ³²The doors were decorated with carved figures of winged creatures, palm trees, and flowers. The doors, the winged creatures, and the palm trees were covered with gold. ³³For the entrance to the main room a rectangular door-frame of olive wood was made. ³⁴There were two folding doors made of pine ³⁵and decorated with carved figures of winged creatures, palm trees, and flowers, which were evenly covered with gold.

³⁶An inner court was built in front of the Temple, enclosed with walls which had one layer of cedar beams for every three layers of stone.

³⁷The foundation of the Temple was laid in the second month, the month of Ziv, in the fourth year of Solomon's reign. ³⁸In the eighth month, the month of Bul, in the eleventh year of Solomon's reign, the Temple was completely finished exactly as it had been planned. It had taken Solomon seven years to build it.

Solomon's Palace

7 Solomon also built a palace for himself, and it took him thirteen years. ²⁻³The Hall of the Forest of Lebanon* was 44 metres long, 22 metres wide, and 13.5 metres high. It had three* rows of cedar pillars, fifteen in each row, with cedar beams resting on them. The ceiling was of cedar, extending over storerooms, which were supported by the pillars. ⁴In each of the two side walls there were three rows of windows. ⁵The doorways and the windows* had rectangular frames, and the three rows of windows in each wall faced the opposite rows.

⁶The Hall of Columns was 22 metres long and 13.5 metres wide. It had a covered porch, supported by columns.

⁷The Throne Room, also called the Hall of Judgement, where Solomon decided cases, had cedar panels from the floor to the rafters.*

⁸Solomon's own quarters, in another court behind the Hall of Judgement, were made like the other buildings. He also built the same kind of house for his wife, the daughter of the king of Egypt.

⁹All these buildings and the great court were made of fine stones from the foundations to the eaves. The stones were prepared at the quarry and cut to measure, with their inner and outer sides trimmed with saws. ¹⁰The foundations were made of large stones prepared at the quarry, some of them 3.5 metres long and others four metres long. ¹¹On top of them were other stones, cut to measure, and cedar beams. ¹²The palace court, the inner court of the Temple, and the entrance room of the Temple had walls with one layer of cedar beams for every three layers of cut stones.

....

7.2–3 Hall of the Forest of Lebanon: A large ceremonial hall in the palace, probably so called because it was panelled in cedar.
7.2–3 One ancient translation *three*; Hebrew *four*.
7.5 One ancient translation *windows*; Hebrew *doorposts*.
7.7 Some ancient translations *rafters*; Hebrew *floor*.

398

1 Kings

Joshua
Judges
Ruth
1 Sam.
2 Sam.

1 KINGS 7

Huram's Task

¹³ King Solomon sent for a man named Huram, a craftsman living in the city of Tyre, who was skilled in bronze work. ¹⁴ His father, who was no longer living, was from Tyre, and had also been a skilled bronze craftsman; his mother was from the tribe of Naphtali. Huram was an intelligent and experienced craftsman. He accepted King Solomon's invitation to be in charge of all the bronze work.

The Two Bronze Columns
(2 Chr 3.15–17)

¹⁵ Huram cast two bronze columns, each one eight metres tall and 5.3 metres in circumference,* and placed them at the entrance of the Temple. ¹⁶ He also made two bronze capitals, each one 2.2 metres tall, to be placed on top of the columns. ¹⁷ The top of each column was decorated with a design of interwoven chains,* ¹⁸ and two rows of bronze pomegranates.

¹⁹ The capitals were shaped like lilies, 1.8 metres tall, ²⁰ and were placed on a rounded section which was above the chain design. There were 200 pomegranates in two rows round each* capital.

²¹ Huram placed these two bronze columns in front of the entrance of the Temple: the one on the south side was named Jachin,* and the one on the north was named Boaz.* ²² The lily-shaped bronze capitals were on top of the columns.

And so the work on the columns was completed.

The Bronze Tank
(2 Chr 4.2–5)

²³ Huram made a round tank of bronze, 2.2 metres deep, 4.4 metres in diameter, and 13.2 metres in circumference. ²⁴ All round the outer edge of the rim of the tank* were two rows of bronze gourds, which had been cast all in one piece with the rest of the tank. ²⁵ The tank rested on the backs of twelve bronze bulls that faced outwards, three facing in each direction. ²⁶ The sides of the tank were 75 millimetres thick. Its rim was like the rim of a cup, curving outwards like the petals of a lily. The tank held about 40,000 litres.

The Bronze Carts

²⁷ Huram also made ten bronze carts; each was 1.8 metres long, 1.8 metres wide, and 1.3 metres high. ²⁸ They were made of square panels which were set in frames, ²⁹ with the figures of lions, bulls, and winged creatures on the panels; and on the frames, above and underneath the lions and bulls, there were spiral figures in relief. ³⁰ Each cart had four bronze wheels with bronze axles. At the four corners were bronze supports for a basin; the supports were decorated with spiral figures in relief. ³¹ There was a circular frame on top for the basin. It projected upwards 45 centimetres from the top of the cart and eighteen centimetres down into it. It had carvings round it. ³² The wheels were 66 centimetres high; they were under the panels, and the axles were of one piece with

---

7.15 Some ancient translations *each one... circumference*; Hebrew *the first column was 8 metres tall and the second column was 5.3 metres in circumference.*
7.17 Verse 17 in Hebrew is unclear.
7.20 One ancient translation *each*; Hebrew *the second.*
7.21 *Jachin*: This name sounds like the Hebrew for "he (God) establishes".
7.21 *Boaz*: This name sounds like the Hebrew for "by his (God's) strength".
7.24 Probable text *All round... tank*; Hebrew unclear.

the carts. 33 The wheels were like chariot wheels; their axles, rims, spokes, and hubs were all of bronze. 34 There were four supports at the bottom corners of each cart, which were of one piece with the cart. 35 There was a 22 centimetre band round the top of each cart; its supports and the panels were of one piece with the cart. 36 The supports and panels were decorated with figures of winged creatures, lions, and palm trees, wherever there was space for them, with spiral figures all round. 37 This, then, is how the carts were made; they were all alike, having the same size and shape.

38 Huram also made ten basins, one for each cart. Each basin was 1.8 metres in diameter, and held about 800 litres. 39 He placed five of the carts on the south side of the Temple, and the other five on the north side; the tank he placed at the south-east corner.

Summary List of Temple Furnishings
(2 Chr 4.11—5.1)

40-45 Huram also made pots, shovels, and bowls. He completed all his work for King Solomon for the LORD's Temple. This is what he made:

The two columns
The two bowl-shaped capitals on top of the columns
The design of interwoven chains on each capital
The 400 bronze pomegranates, in two rows of a hundred each round the design on each capital
The ten carts
The ten basins
The tank
The twelve bulls supporting the tank
The pots, shovels, and bowls.

All this equipment for the Temple, which Huram made for King Solomon, was of polished bronze. 46 The king had it all made in the foundry between Sukkoth and Zarethan, in the Jordan Valley. 47 Solomon did not have these bronze objects weighed, because there were too many of them, and so their weight was never determined.

48 Solomon also had gold furnishings made for the Temple: the altar, the table for the bread offered to God, 49 the ten lampstands that stood in front of the Most Holy Place, five on the south side and five on the north; the flowers, lamps, and tongs; 50 the cups, lamp snuffers, bowls, dishes for incense, and the pans used for carrying live coals; and the hinges for the doors of the Most Holy Place and of the outer doors of the Temple. All these furnishings were made of gold.

51 When King Solomon finished all the work on the Temple, he placed in the temple storerooms all the things that his father David had dedicated to the LORD — the silver, gold, and other articles.

The Covenant Box is Brought to the Temple
(2 Chr 5.2—6.2)

8 Then King Solomon summoned all the leaders of the tribes and clans of Israel to come to him in Jerusalem in order to take the LORD's Covenant Box from Zion, David's City, to the Temple. 2 They all assembled during the Festival of Shelters in the seventh month, in the month of Ethanim. 3 When all the leaders had gathered, the priests lifted the Covenant Box 4 and carried it to the Temple. The Levites and the priests also moved the Tent of the LORD's presence and all its equipment to the Temple. 5 King Solomon and all the people of Israel assembled in front of the Covenant Box and sacrificed a large number of

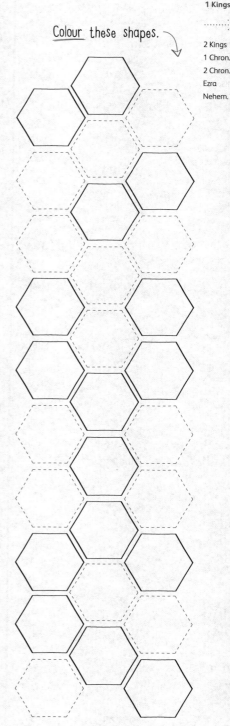

Colour these shapes.

400

1 Kings

⋮⋯⋯⋯⋯

Joshua
Judges
Ruth
1 Sam.
2 Sam.

1 KINGS 8

sheep and cattle — too many to count. [6] Then the priests carried the Covenant Box into the Temple and put it in the Most Holy Place, beneath the winged creatures. [7] Their outstretched wings covered the box and the poles it was carried by. [8] The ends of the poles could be seen by anyone standing directly in front of the Most Holy Place, but from nowhere else. (The poles are still there today.) [9] There was nothing inside the Covenant Box except the two stone tablets which Moses had placed there at Mount Sinai, when the LORD made a covenant with the people of Israel as they were coming from Egypt.

[10] As the priests were leaving the Temple, it was suddenly filled with a cloud [11] shining with the dazzling light of the LORD's presence, and they could not go back in to perform their duties. [12] Then Solomon prayed:

"You, LORD, have placed the sun in the sky,*
    yet you have chosen to live in clouds and darkness.
[13] Now I have built a majestic temple for you,
    a place for you to live in for ever."

Solomon's Address to the People
(2 Chr 6.3–11)

[14] As the people stood there, King Solomon turned to face them, and he asked God's blessing on them. [15] He said, "Praise the LORD God of Israel! He has kept the promise he made to my father David, when he said, [16] 'From the time I brought my people out of Egypt, I have not chosen any city in all the land of Israel in which a temple should be built where I would be worshipped. But I chose you, David, to rule my people.' "

[17] And Solomon continued, "My father David planned to build a temple for the worship of the LORD God of Israel, [18] but the LORD said to him, 'You were right in wanting to build a temple for me, [19] but you will never build it. It is your son, your own son, who will build my temple.'

[20] "And now the LORD has kept his promise. I have succeeded my father as king of Israel, and I have built the Temple for the worship of the LORD God of Israel. [21] I have also provided a place in the Temple for the Covenant Box containing the stone tablets of the covenant which the LORD made with our ancestors when he brought them out of Egypt."

Solomon's Prayer
(2 Chr 6.12–42)

[22] Then in the presence of the people Solomon went and stood in front of the altar, where he raised his arms [23] and prayed, "LORD God of Israel, there is no god like you in heaven above or on earth below! You keep your covenant with your people and show them your love when they live in wholehearted obedience to you. [24] You have kept the promise you made to my father David; today every word has been fulfilled. [25] And now, LORD God of Israel, I pray that you will also keep the other promise you made to my father when you told him that there would always be one of his descendants ruling as king of Israel, provided they obeyed you as carefully as he did. [26] So now, O God of Israel, let everything come true that you promised to my father David, your servant.

[27] "But can you, O God, really live on earth? Not even all heaven is large enough to hold you, so how can this Temple that I have built be large enough? [28] LORD my God, I am your servant. Listen to my

8.12 One ancient translation *You… sky*; Hebrew does not have these words.

1 KINGS 8

401

1 Kings
....

2 Kings
1 Chron.
2 Chron.
Ezra
Nehem.

prayer, and grant the requests I make to you today. [29] Watch over this Temple day and night, this place where you have chosen to be worshipped. Hear me when I face this Temple and pray. [30] Hear my prayers and the prayers of your people when they face this place and pray. In your home in heaven hear us and forgive us.

[31] "When a person is accused of wronging another and is brought to your altar in this Temple to take an oath that he is innocent, [32] O LORD, listen in heaven and judge your servants. Punish the guilty one as he deserves, and acquit the one who is innocent.

[33] "When your people Israel are defeated by their enemies because they have sinned against you, and then when they turn to you and come to this Temple, humbly praying to you for forgiveness, [34] listen to them in heaven. Forgive the sins of your people, and bring them back to the land which you gave to their ancestors.

[35] "When you hold back the rain because your people have sinned against you, and then when they repent and face this Temple, humbly praying to you, [36] listen to them in heaven. Forgive the sins of the king and of the people of Israel. Teach them to do what is right. Then, O LORD, send rain on this land of yours, which you gave to your people as a permanent possession.

[37] "When there is famine in the land or an epidemic, or the crops are destroyed by scorching winds or swarms of locusts, or when your people are attacked by their enemies, or when there is disease or sickness among them, [38] listen to their prayers. If any of your people Israel, out of heartfelt sorrow, stretch out their hands in prayer towards this Temple, [39] hear their prayer. Listen to them in your home in heaven, forgive them, and help them. You alone know the thoughts of the human heart. Deal with each person as he deserves, [40] so that your people may obey you all the time they live in the land which you gave to our ancestors.

[41-42] "When a foreigner who lives in a distant land hears of your fame and of the great things you have done for your people, and comes to worship you and to pray at this Temple, [43] listen to his prayer. In heaven, where you live, hear him and do what he asks you to do, so that all the peoples of the world may know you and obey you, as your people Israel do. Then they will know that this Temple I have built is the place where you are to be worshipped.

[44] "When you command your people to go into battle against their enemies and they pray to you, wherever they are, facing this city which you have chosen and this Temple which I have built for you, [45] listen to their prayers. Hear them in heaven, and give them victory.

[46] "When your people sin against you — and there is no one who does not sin — and in your anger you let their enemies defeat them and take them as prisoners to some other land, even if that land is far away, [47] listen to your people's prayers. If there in that land they repent and pray to you, confessing how sinful and wicked they have been, hear their prayers, O LORD. [48] If in that land they truly and sincerely repent, and pray to you as they face towards this land which you gave to our ancestors, this city which you have chosen, and this Temple which I have built for you, [49] then listen to their prayers. In your home in heaven hear them and be merciful to them. [50] Forgive all their sins and their rebellion against you, and make their enemies treat them with kindness. [51] They are your own people, whom you brought out of Egypt, that blazing furnace.

[52] "Sovereign LORD, may you always look with favour on your people Israel and their king, and hear their prayer whenever they

402

1 Kings

Joshua
Judges
Ruth
1 Sam.
2 Sam.

1 KINGS 8, 9

call to you for help. [53] You chose them from all the peoples to be your own people, as you told them through your servant Moses when you brought our ancestors out of Egypt."

The Final Prayer

[54] After Solomon had finished praying to the LORD, he stood up in front of the altar, where he had been kneeling with uplifted hands. [55] In a loud voice he asked God's blessings on all the people assembled there. He said, [56] "Praise the LORD who has given his people peace, as he promised he would. He has kept all the generous promises he made through his servant Moses. [57] May the LORD our God be with us, as he was with our ancestors; may he never leave us, or abandon us; [58] may he make us obedient to him, so that we will always live as he wants us to live, and keep all the laws and commands he gave our ancestors. [59] May the LORD our God remember at all times this prayer and these petitions I have made to him. May he always be merciful to the people of Israel and to their king, according to their daily needs. [60] And so all the nations of the world will know that the LORD alone is God — there is no other. [61] May you, his people, always be faithful to the LORD our God, obeying all his laws and commands, as you do today."

The Dedication of the Temple
(2 Chr 7.4–10)

[62] Then King Solomon and all the people there offered sacrifices to the LORD. [63] He sacrificed 22,000 head of cattle and 120,000 sheep as fellowship offerings. And so the king and all the people dedicated the Temple. [64] That same day he also consecrated the central part of the courtyard, the area in front of the Temple, and then he offered there the sacrifices burnt whole, the grain offerings, and the fat of the animals for the fellowship offerings. He did this because the bronze altar was too small for all these offerings.

[65] There at the Temple, Solomon and all the people of Israel celebrated the Festival of Shelters for seven* days. There was a huge crowd of people from as far away as Hamath Pass in the north and the Egyptian border in the south. [66] On the eighth day Solomon sent the people home. They all praised him and went home happy because of all the blessings that the LORD had given his servant David and his people Israel.

God Appears to Solomon Again
(2 Chr 7.11–22)

9 After King Solomon had finished building the Temple and the palace and everything else he wanted to build, [2] the LORD appeared to him again, as he had in Gibeon. [3] The LORD said to him, "I have heard your prayer. I consecrate this Temple which you have built as the place where I shall be worshipped for ever. I will watch over it and protect it for all time. [4] If you will serve me in honesty and integrity, as your father David did, and if you obey my laws and do everything I have commanded you, [5] I will keep the promise I made to your father David when I told him that Israel would always be ruled by his descendants. [6] But if you or your descendants stop following me, if you disobey the laws and commands I have given you, and worship other gods, [7] then I will remove my people Israel from the land that I have given them. I will also abandon this Temple which I have consecrated

1 KINGS 9.1–9

The temple went on
to be destroyed
in 587BC by King
Nebuchadnezzar II, then

REBUILT,
• AND DESTROYED •
again by the
Romans in AD70.

8.65 One ancient translation *seven*; Hebrew *fourteen*.

1 KINGS 9

403

1 Kings

2 Kings
1 Chron.
2 Chron.
Ezra
Nehem.

as the place where I am to be worshipped. People everywhere will ridicule Israel and treat her with contempt. ⁸This Temple will become a pile of ruins,* and everyone who passes by will be shocked and amazed. 'Why did the LORD do this to this land and this Temple?' they will ask. ⁹People will answer, 'It is because they abandoned the LORD their God, who brought their ancestors out of Egypt. They gave their allegiance to other gods and worshipped them. That is why the LORD has brought this disaster on them.'"

Solomon's Agreement with Hiram
(2 Chr 8.1–2)

¹⁰It took Solomon twenty years to build the Temple and his palace. ¹¹King Hiram of Tyre had provided him with all the cedar and pine and with all the gold he wanted for this work. After it was finished, King Solomon gave Hiram twenty towns in the region of Galilee. ¹²Hiram went to see them, and he did not like them. ¹³So he said to Solomon, "So these, my brother, are the towns you have given me!" For this reason the area is still called Cabul.* ¹⁴Hiram had sent Solomon more than four tonnes of gold.

Further Achievements of Solomon
(2 Chr 8.3–18)

¹⁵King Solomon used forced labour to build the Temple and the palace, to fill in land on the east side of the city, and to build the city wall. He also used it to rebuild the cities of Hazor, Megiddo, and Gezer. ¹⁶(The king of Egypt had attacked Gezer and captured it, killing its inhabitants and setting fire to the city. Then he gave it as a wedding present to his daughter when she married Solomon, ¹⁷and Solomon rebuilt it.) Using his forced labour, Solomon also rebuilt Lower Beth Horon, ¹⁸Baalath, Tamar in the Judean wilderness, ¹⁹the cities where his supplies were kept, the cities for his horses and chariots, and everything else he wanted to build in Jerusalem, in Lebanon, and elsewhere in his kingdom. ²⁰⁻²¹For his forced labour Solomon used the descendants of the people of Canaan whom the Israelites had not killed when they took possession of their land. These included Amorites, Hittites, Perizzites, Hivites, and Jebusites, whose descendants continue to be slaves down to the present time. ²²Solomon did not make slaves of Israelites; they served as his soldiers, officers, commanders, chariot captains, and horsemen.

²³There were 550 officials in charge of the forced labour working on Solomon's various building projects.

²⁴Solomon filled in the land on the east side of the city, after his wife, the daughter of the king of Egypt, had moved from David's City to the palace Solomon built for her.

²⁵Three times a year Solomon offered burnt offerings and fellowship offerings on the altar he had built to the LORD. He also burnt incense* to the LORD. And so he finished building the Temple.

²⁶King Solomon also built a fleet of ships at Eziongeber, which is near Elath, on the shore of the Gulf of Aqaba, in the land of Edom. ²⁷King Hiram sent some experienced seamen from his fleet to serve with Solomon's men. ²⁸They sailed to the land of Ophir, and brought back to Solomon more than fourteen tonnes of gold.

9.8 Some ancient translations *a pile of ruins*; Hebrew *high*.
9.13 *Cabul*: This name sounds like "ke-bal", the Hebrew for "worthless".
9.25 Hebrew has two additional words, the meaning of which is unclear.

404

1 Kings

Joshua
Judges
Ruth
1 Sam.
2 Sam.

1 KINGS 10

The Visit of the Queen of Sheba
(2 Chr 9.1–12)

10 The queen of Sheba heard of Solomon's fame,* and she travelled to Jerusalem to test him with difficult questions. ²She brought with her a large group of attendants, as well as camels loaded with spices, jewels, and a large amount of gold. When she and Solomon met, she asked him all the questions that she could think of. ³He answered them all; there was nothing too difficult for him to explain. ⁴The queen of Sheba heard Solomon's wisdom and saw the palace he had built. ⁵She saw the food that was served at his table, the living quarters for his officials, the organization of his palace staff and the uniforms they wore, the servants who waited on him at feasts, and the sacrifices he offered in the Temple. It left her breathless and amazed. ⁶She said to King Solomon, "What I heard in my own country about you* and your wisdom is true! ⁷But I couldn't believe it until I had come and seen it all for myself. But I didn't hear even half of it; your wisdom and wealth are much greater than what I was told. ⁸How fortunate are your wives!* And how fortunate your servants, who are always in your presence and are privileged to hear your wise sayings! ⁹Praise the LORD your God! He has shown how pleased he is with you by making you king of Israel. Because his love for Israel is eternal, he has made you their king so that you can maintain law and justice."

¹⁰She presented to King Solomon the gifts she had brought: more than four tonnes of gold and a very large amount of spices and jewels. The amount of spices she gave him was by far the greatest that he ever received at any time.

¹¹(Hiram's fleet, which had brought gold from Ophir, also brought from there a large amount of juniper wood and jewels. ¹²Solomon used the wood to build railings in the Temple and the palace, and also to make harps and lyres for the musicians. It was the finest juniper wood ever imported into Israel; none like it has ever been seen again.)

¹³King Solomon gave the queen of Sheba everything she asked for, besides all the other customary gifts that he had generously given her. Then she and her attendants returned to the land of Sheba.

King Solomon's Wealth
(2 Chr 9.13–28)

¹⁴Every year King Solomon received almost 23 tonnes of gold ¹⁵in addition to the taxes* paid by merchants, the profits from trade, and tribute paid by the Arabian kings and the governors of the Israelite districts.

¹⁶Solomon made 200 large shields, and had each one overlaid with almost seven kilogrammes of gold. ¹⁷He also made 300 smaller shields, overlaying each one of them with almost two kilogrammes of gold. He had all these shields placed in the Hall of the Forest of Lebanon.*

¹⁸He also had a large throne made. Part of it was covered with ivory and the rest of it was covered with the finest gold. ¹⁹⁻²⁰The throne had six steps leading up to it, with the figure of a lion at

10.1 Probable text (see 2 Chr 9.1) *Solomon's fame*; Hebrew *Solomon's fame concerning the name of the LORD.*
10.6 *you*; or *your deeds.*
10.8 Some ancient translations *wives*; Hebrew *men.*
10.15 Some ancient translations *taxes*; Hebrew *men.*
10.17 *Hall of the Forest of Lebanon*: See 7.2–3.

1 Kings

2 Kings

1 Chron.

2 Chron.

Ezra

Nehem.

each end of every step, a total of twelve lions. At the back of the throne was the figure of a bull's head, and beside each of the two arms was the figure of a lion. No throne like this had ever existed in any other kingdom.

21 All of Solomon's drinking cups were made of gold, and all the utensils in the Hall of the Forest of Lebanon were of pure gold. No silver was used, since it was not considered valuable in Solomon's day. 22 He had a fleet of ocean-going ships sailing with Hiram's fleet. Every three years his fleet would return, bringing gold, silver, ivory, apes, and monkeys.

23 King Solomon was richer and wiser than any other king, 24 and the whole world wanted to come and listen to the wisdom that God had given him. 25 Everyone who came brought him a gift — articles of silver and gold, robes, weapons, spices, horses, and mules. This continued year after year.

26 Solomon built up a force of 1,400 chariots and 12,000 cavalry horses. Some of them he kept in Jerusalem and the rest he stationed in various other cities. 27 During his reign silver was as common in Jerusalem as stone, and cedar was as plentiful as ordinary sycomore in the foothills of Judah. 28 The king's agents controlled the export of horses from Musri* and Cilicia,* 29 and the export of chariots from Egypt. They supplied the Hittite and Syrian kings with horses and chariots, selling chariots for 600 pieces of silver each and horses for 150 each.

Solomon Turns Away from God

11 Solomon loved many foreign women. Besides the daughter of the king of Egypt he married Hittite women and women from Moab, Ammon, Edom, and Sidon. 2 He married them even though the Lord had commanded the Israelites not to intermarry with these people, because they would cause the Israelites to give their loyalty to other gods. 3 Solomon married 700 princesses and also had 300 concubines. They made him turn away from God 4 and by the time he was old they had led him into the worship of foreign gods. He was not faithful to the Lord his God, as his father David had been. 5 He worshipped Astarte the goddess of Sidon, and Molech the disgusting god of Ammon. 6 He sinned against the Lord and was not true to him as his father David had been. 7 On the mountain east of Jerusalem he built a place to worship Chemosh, the disgusting god of Moab, and a place to worship Molech, the disgusting god of Ammon. 8 He also built places of worship where all his foreign wives could burn incense and offer sacrifices to their own gods.

9-10 Even though the Lord, the God of Israel, had appeared to Solomon twice and had commanded him not to worship foreign gods, Solomon did not obey the Lord, but turned away from him. So the Lord was angry with Solomon 11 and said to him, "Because you have deliberately broken your covenant with me and disobeyed my commands, I promise that I will take the kingdom away from you and give it to one of your officials. 12 However, for the sake of your father David I will not do this in your lifetime, but during the reign of your son. 13 And I will not take the whole kingdom away from him; instead, I will leave him one tribe for the sake of my servant David and for the sake of Jerusalem, the city I have made my own."

10.28 Probable text *Musri*; Hebrew *Egypt*.
10.28 *Musri and Cilicia*: Two ancient countries in what is now south-east Turkey, which were centres of horse breeding in Solomon's time.

406

1 Kings

Joshua
Judges
Ruth
1 Sam.
2 Sam.

Solomon's Enemies

[14] So the LORD caused Hadad, of the royal family of Edom, to turn against Solomon. [15-16] Long before this, when David had conquered Edom, Joab the commander of his army had gone there to bury the dead. He and his men remained in Edom six months, and during that time they killed every male in Edom [17] except Hadad and some of his father's Edomite servants, who escaped to Egypt. (At that time Hadad was just a child.) [18] They left Midian and went to Paran, where some other men joined them. Then they travelled to Egypt and went to the king, who gave Hadad some land and a house and provided him with food. [19] Hadad won the friendship of the king, and the king gave his sister-in-law, the sister of Queen Tahpenes, to Hadad in marriage. [20] She bore him a son, Genubath, who was brought up by the queen in the palace, where he lived with the king's sons.

[21] When the news reached Hadad in Egypt that David had died and that Joab the commander of the army was dead, Hadad said to the king, "Let me go back to my own country."

[22] "Why?" the king asked. "Have I failed to give you something? Is that why you want to go back home?"

"Just let me go," Hadad answered the king. And he went back to his country.*

As king of Edom, Hadad was an evil, bitter enemy of Israel.*

[23] God also caused Rezon son of Eliada to turn against Solomon. Rezon had fled from his master, King Hadadezer of Zobah, [24] and had become the leader of a gang of outlaws. (This happened after David had defeated Hadadezer and had slaughtered his Syrian allies.) Rezon and his men went and lived in Damascus, where his men made him king of Syria. [25] He was an enemy of Israel during the lifetime of Solomon.

God's Promise to Jeroboam

[26] Another man who turned against King Solomon was one of his officials, Jeroboam son of Nebat, from Zeredah in Ephraim. His mother was a widow named Zeruah. [27] This is the story of the revolt. Solomon was filling in the land on the east side of Jerusalem and repairing the city walls. [28] Jeroboam was an able young man, and when Solomon noticed how hard he worked, he put him in charge of all the forced labour in the territory of the tribes of Manasseh and Ephraim. [29] One day, as Jeroboam was travelling from Jerusalem, the prophet Ahijah, from Shiloh, met him alone on the road in the open country. [30] Ahijah took off the new robe he was wearing, tore it into twelve pieces, [31] and said to Jeroboam, "Take ten pieces for yourself, because the LORD, the God of Israel, says to you, 'I am going to take the kingdom away from Solomon, and I will give you ten tribes. [32] Solomon will keep one tribe, for the sake of my servant David and for the sake of Jerusalem, the city I have chosen to be my own from the whole land of Israel. [33] I am going to do this because Solomon has rejected me and has* worshipped foreign gods: Astarte, the goddess of Sidon; Chemosh, the god of Moab; and Molech, the god of Ammon. Solomon has* disobeyed me; he has done wrong, and has not kept my laws and

JOIN THE DOTS

below to make a picture.

• • •

• • •

• • •

• • •

• • •

• • •

11.22 One ancient translation *And he went back to his country*; Hebrew does not have these words.
11.22 One ancient translation *As king... Israel*; in Hebrew this sentence, with some differences, comes at the end of verse 25.
11.33 Some ancient translations *Solomon has... and has*; Hebrew *they have... and have.*
11.33 Some ancient translations *Solomon has*; Hebrew *They have.*

1 KINGS 11, 12

407

1 Kings

2 Kings
1 Chron.
2 Chron.
Ezra
Nehem.

commands as his father David did. [34] But I will not take the whole kingdom away from Solomon, and I will keep him in power as long as he lives. This I will do for the sake of my servant David, whom I chose and who obeyed my laws and commands. [35] I will take the kingdom away from Solomon's son and will give you ten tribes, [36] but I will let Solomon's son keep one tribe, so that I will always have a descendant of my servant David ruling in Jerusalem, the city I have chosen as the place where I am worshipped. [37] Jeroboam, I will make you king of Israel, and you will rule over all the territory that you want. [38] If you obey me completely, live by my laws, and win my approval by doing what I command, as my servant David did, I will always be with you. I will make you king of Israel and will make sure that your descendants rule after you, just as I have done for David. [39] Because of Solomon's sin I will punish the descendants of David, but not for all time.' "

[40] And so Solomon tried to kill Jeroboam, but he escaped to King Shishak of Egypt and stayed there until Solomon's death.

The Death of Solomon
(2 Chr 9.29-31)

[41] Everything else that Solomon did, his career and his wisdom, are all recorded in *The History of Solomon*. [42] He was king in Jerusalem over all Israel for forty years. [43] He died and was buried in David's City, and his son Rehoboam succeeded him as king.

The Northern Tribes Revolt
(2 Chr 10.1-19)

12 Rehoboam went to Shechem, where all the people of northern Israel had gathered to make him king. [2] When Jeroboam son of Nebat, who had gone to Egypt to escape from King Solomon, heard this news, he returned from* Egypt. [3] The people of the northern tribes sent for him, and then they all went together to Rehoboam and said to him, [4] "Your father Solomon treated us harshly and placed heavy burdens on us. If you make these burdens lighter and make life easier for us, we will be your loyal subjects."

[5] "Come back in three days and I will give you my answer," he replied. So they left.

[6] King Rehoboam consulted the older men who had served as his father Solomon's advisers. "What answer do you advise me to give these people?" he asked.

[7] They replied, "If you want to serve this people well, give a favourable answer to their request, and they will always serve you loyally."

[8] But he ignored the advice of the older men and went instead to the young men who had grown up with him and who were now his advisers. [9] "What do you advise me to do?" he asked. "What shall I say to the people who are asking me to make their burdens lighter?"

[10] They replied, "This is what you should tell them: 'My little finger is thicker than my father's waist!' [11] Tell them, 'My father placed heavy burdens on you; I will make them even heavier. He beat you with a whip; I'll flog you with a horsewhip!' "

[12] Three days later Jeroboam and all the people returned to King Rehoboam, as he had instructed them. [13] The king ignored the advice of the older men and spoke harshly to the people,

---

12.2 Some ancient translations (and see 2 Chr 10.2) *returned from*; Hebrew *remained in*.

408

1 Kings

Joshua
Judges
Ruth
1 Sam.
2 Sam.

1 KINGS 12

¹⁴as the younger men had advised. He said, "My father placed heavy burdens on you; I will make them even heavier. He beat you with a whip; I'll flog you with a horsewhip!" ¹⁵It was the will of the LORD to bring about what he had spoken to Jeroboam son of Nebat through the prophet Ahijah from Shiloh. This is why the king did not pay any attention to the people.

¹⁶When the people saw that the king would not listen to them, they shouted, "Down with David and his family! What have they ever done for us? People of Israel, let's go home! Let Rehoboam look out for himself!"

So the people of Israel rebelled, ¹⁷leaving Rehoboam as king only of the people who lived in the territory of Judah.

¹⁸Then King Rehoboam sent Adoniram, who was in charge of the forced labour, to go to the Israelites, but they stoned him to death. At this, Rehoboam hurriedly got into his chariot and escaped to Jerusalem. ¹⁹Ever since that time the people of the northern kingdom of Israel have been in rebellion against the dynasty of David.

²⁰When the people of Israel heard that Jeroboam had returned from Egypt, they invited him to a meeting of the people and made him king of Israel. Only the tribe of Judah remained loyal to David's descendants.

Shemaiah's Prophecy
(2 Chr 11.1–4)

²¹When Rehoboam arrived in Jerusalem, he called together 180,000 of the best soldiers from the tribes of Judah and Benjamin. He intended to go to war and restore his control over the northern tribes of Israel. ²²But God told the prophet Shemaiah ²³to give this message to Rehoboam and to all the people of the tribes of Judah and Benjamin: ²⁴"Do not attack your own brothers, the people of Israel. Go home, all of you. What has happened is my will." They all obeyed the LORD's command and went back home.

Jeroboam Turns Away from the LORD

²⁵King Jeroboam of Israel fortified the town of Shechem in the hill country of Ephraim and lived there for a while. Then he left and fortified the town of Penuel. ²⁶⁻²⁷He said to himself, "As things are now, if my people go to Jerusalem and offer sacrifices to the LORD in the Temple there, they will transfer their allegiance to King Rehoboam of Judah and will kill me."

²⁸After thinking it over, he made two bull calves of gold and said to his people, "You have been going long enough to Jerusalem to worship. People of Israel, here are your gods who brought you out of Egypt!" ²⁹He placed one of the gold bull calves in Bethel and the other in Dan. ³⁰And so the people sinned, going to worship in Bethel and in Dan.* ³¹Jeroboam also built places of worship on hilltops, and he chose priests from families who were not of the tribe of Levi.

Worship at Bethel is Condemned

³²Jeroboam also instituted a religious festival on the fifteenth day of the eighth month, like the festival in Judah. On the altar in Bethel he offered sacrifices to the gold bull calves he had made, and he placed there in Bethel the priests serving at the places of worship he had built. ³³And on the fifteenth day of the eighth

---

12.30 One ancient translation *in Bethel and in Dan*; Hebrew *in Dan*.

1 KINGS 12, 13

409

1 Kings

2 Kings
1 Chron.
2 Chron.
Ezra
Nehem.

month, the day that he himself had set, he went to Bethel and offered a sacrifice on the altar in celebration of the festival he had instituted for the people of Israel.

13 At the LORD's command a prophet from Judah went to Bethel and arrived there as Jeroboam stood at the altar to offer the sacrifice. [2] Following the LORD's command, the prophet denounced the altar: "O altar, altar, this is what the LORD says: A child, whose name will be Josiah, will be born to the family of David. He will slaughter on you the priests serving at the pagan altars who offer sacrifices on you, and he will burn human bones on you." [3] And the prophet went on to say, "This altar will fall apart, and the ashes on it will be scattered. Then you will know that the LORD has spoken through me."

[4] When King Jeroboam heard this, he pointed at him and ordered, "Seize that man!" At once the king's arm became paralysed so that he couldn't pull it back. [5] The altar suddenly fell apart and the ashes spilt to the ground, as the prophet had predicted in the name of the LORD. [6] King Jeroboam said to the prophet, "Please pray for me to the LORD your God, and ask him to heal my arm!"

The prophet prayed to the LORD, and the king's arm was healed. [7] Then the king said to the prophet, "Come home with me and have something to eat. I will reward you for what you have done."

[8] The prophet answered, "Even if you gave me half your wealth, I would not go with you or eat or drink anything with you. [9] The LORD has commanded me not to eat or drink a thing, and not to return home the same way I came." [10] So he did not go back the same way he had come, but by another road.

The Old Prophet of Bethel

[11] At that time there was an old prophet living in Bethel. His sons* came and told him what the prophet from Judah had done in Bethel that day and what he had said to King Jeroboam. [12] "Which way did he go when he left?" the old prophet asked them. They showed him* the road [13] and he told them to saddle his donkey for him. They did so, and he rode off [14] down the road after the prophet from Judah and found him sitting under an oak. "Are you the prophet from Judah?" he asked.

"I am," the man answered.

[15] "Come home and have a meal with me," he said.

[16] But the prophet from Judah answered, "I can't go home with you or accept your hospitality. And I won't eat or drink anything with you here, [17] because the LORD has commanded me not to eat or drink a thing, and not to return home the same way I came."

[18] Then the old prophet from Bethel said to him, "I, too, am a prophet just like you, and at the LORD's command an angel told me to take you home with me and offer you my hospitality." But the old prophet was lying.

[19] So the prophet from Judah went home with the old prophet and had a meal with him. [20] As they were sitting at the table, the word of the LORD came to the old prophet, [21] and he cried out to the prophet from Judah, "The LORD says that you disobeyed him and did not do what he commanded. [22] Instead, you returned and ate a meal in a place he had ordered you not to eat in. Because of this you will be killed, and your body will not be buried in your family grave."

13.11 Some ancient translations *sons*; Hebrew *son*.
13.12 Some ancient translations *showed him*; Hebrew *saw*.

410

1 Kings

Joshua
Judges
Ruth
1 Sam.
2 Sam.

1 KINGS 13, 14

1 KINGS 13.33-34

Who you follow is really important. Go into a café or fast food place and

GET IN THE

QUEUE.

Order exactly the same as the person in front of you (as long as you're not allergic to it!). As you eat or drink, think about who you are influenced by and how they impact your life and your choices.

23 After they had finished eating, the old prophet saddled the donkey for the prophet from Judah, 24 who rode off. On the way, a lion met him and killed him. His body lay on the road, and the donkey and the lion stood beside it. 25 Some men passed by and saw the body on the road, with the lion standing near by. They went on into Bethel and reported what they had seen.

26 When the old prophet heard about it, he said, "That is the prophet who disobeyed the LORD's command! And so the LORD sent the lion to attack and kill him, just as the LORD said he would." 27 Then he said to his sons, "Saddle my donkey for me." They did so, 28 and he rode off and found the prophet's body lying on the road, with the donkey and the lion still standing by it. The lion had not eaten the body or attacked the donkey. 29 The old prophet picked up the body, put it on the donkey, and brought it back to Bethel to mourn over it and bury it. 30 He buried it in his own family grave, and he and his sons mourned over it, saying, "Oh my brother, my brother!" 31 After the burial, the prophet said to his sons, "When I die, bury me in this grave and lay my body next to his. 32 The words that he spoke at the LORD's command against the altar in Bethel and against all the places of worship in the towns of Samaria will surely come true."

Jeroboam's Fatal Sin

33 King Jeroboam of Israel still did not turn from his evil ways, but continued to choose priests from ordinary families to serve at the altars he had built. He ordained as priest anyone who wanted to be one. 34 This sin on his part brought about the ruin and total destruction of his dynasty.

The Death of Jeroboam's Son

14 At that time King Jeroboam's son Abijah fell ill. 2 Jeroboam said to his wife, "Disguise yourself so that no one will recognize you, and go to Shiloh, where the prophet Ahijah lives, the one who said I would be king of Israel. 3 Take him ten loaves of bread, some cakes, and a jar of honey. Ask him what is going to happen to our son, and he will tell you."

4 So she went to Ahijah's home in Shiloh. Old age had made Ahijah blind. 5 The LORD had told him that Jeroboam's wife was coming to ask him about her son, who was ill. And the LORD told Ahijah what to say.

When Jeroboam's wife arrived, she pretended to be someone else. 6 But when Ahijah heard her coming in the door, he said, "Come in. I know you are Jeroboam's wife. Why are you pretending to be someone else? I have bad news for you. 7 Go and tell Jeroboam that this is what the LORD, the God of Israel, says to him: 'I chose you from among the people and made you the ruler of my people Israel. 8 I took the kingdom away from David's descendants and gave it to you. But you have not been like my servant David, who was completely loyal to me, obeyed my commands, and did only what I approve of. 9 You have committed far greater sins than those who ruled before you. You have rejected me and have aroused my anger by making idols and metal images to worship. 10 Because of this I will bring disaster on your dynasty and will kill all your male descendants, young and old alike. I will get rid of your family; they will be swept away like dung. 11 Any members of your family who die in the city will be eaten by dogs, and any who die in the open country will be eaten by vultures. I, the LORD, have spoken.'"

12 And Ahijah went on to say to Jeroboam's wife, "Now go back home. As soon as you enter the town your son will die. 13 All the

1 Kings

2 Kings
1 Chron.
2 Chron.
Ezra
Nehem.

people of Israel will mourn for him and bury him. He will be the only member of Jeroboam's family who will be properly buried, because he is the only one with whom the LORD, the God of Israel, is pleased. [14] The LORD is going to place a king over Israel who will put an end to Jeroboam's dynasty.* [15] The LORD will punish Israel, and she will shake like a reed shaking in a stream. He will uproot the people of Israel from this good land which he gave to their ancestors, and he will scatter them beyond the River Euphrates, because they have aroused his anger by making idols of the goddess Asherah. [16] The LORD will abandon Israel because Jeroboam sinned and led the people of Israel into sin."

[17] Jeroboam's wife went back to Tirzah. Just as she entered her home, the child died. [18] The people of Israel mourned for him and buried him, as the LORD had said through his servant, the prophet Ahijah.

The Death of Jeroboam

[19] Everything else that King Jeroboam did, the wars he fought and how he ruled, are all recorded in *The History of the Kings of Israel*. [20] Jeroboam ruled as king for 22 years. He died and was buried, and his son Nadab succeeded him as king.

King Rehoboam of Judah
(2 Chr 11.5—12.15)

[21] Solomon's son Rehoboam was 41 years old when he became king of Judah, and he ruled for seventeen years in Jerusalem, the city which the LORD had chosen from all the territory of Israel as the place where he was to be worshipped. Rehoboam's mother was Naamah from Ammon.

[22] The people of Judah sinned against the LORD and did more to arouse his anger against them than all their ancestors had done. [23] They built places of worship for false gods, and put up stone pillars and symbols of Asherah to worship on the hills and under shady trees. [24] Worst of all, there were men and women who served as prostitutes at those pagan places of worship. The people of Judah practised all the shameful things done by the people whom the LORD had driven out of the land as the Israelites advanced into the country.x [25] In the fifth year of Rehoboam's reign King Shishak of Egypt attacked Jerusalem. [26] He took away all the treasures in the Temple and in the palace, including the gold shields Solomon had made. [27] To replace them, King Rehoboam made bronze shields and entrusted them to the officers responsible for guarding the palace gates. [28] Every time the king went to the Temple, the guards carried the shields, and then returned them to the guardroom.

[29] Everything else that King Rehoboam did is recorded in *The History of the Kings of Judah*. [30] During all this time Rehoboam and Jeroboam were constantly at war with each other. [31] Rehoboam died and was buried in the royal tombs in David's City, and his son Abijah succeeded him as king.

King Abijah of Judah
(2 Chr 13.1—14.1)

15 In the eighteenth year of the reign of King Jeroboam of Israel, Abijah became king of Judah, [2] and he ruled for three years in Jerusalem. His mother was Maacah, the daughter of Absalom. [3] He committed the same sins as his father and was not

14.14 Hebrew has five additional words, the meaning of which is unclear.

412

1 Kings

:········

Joshua
Judges
Ruth
1 Sam.
2 Sam.

1 KINGS 15

completely loyal to the LORD his God, as his great-grandfather David had been. [4] But for David's sake, the LORD his God gave Abijah a son to rule after him in Jerusalem and to keep Jerusalem secure. [5] The LORD did this because David had done what pleased him and had never disobeyed any of his commands, except in the case of Uriah the Hittite. [6] The war which had begun between Rehoboam and Jeroboam continued throughout Abijah's lifetime. [7] And everything else that Abijah did is recorded in *The History of the Kings of Judah.*

[8] Abijah died and was buried in David's City, and his son Asa succeeded him as king.

King Asa of Judah
(2 Chr 15.16—16.6)

[9] In the twentieth year of the reign of King Jeroboam of Israel, Asa became king of Judah, [10] and he ruled for 41 years in Jerusalem. His grandmother was Maacah, the daughter of Absalom. [11] Asa did what pleased the LORD, as his ancestor David had done. [12] He expelled from the country all the male and female prostitutes serving at the pagan places of worship, and he removed all the idols his predecessors had made. [13] He removed his grandmother Maacah from her position as queen mother, because she had made an obscene idol of the fertility goddess Asherah. Asa cut down the idol and burnt it in the valley of the Kidron. [14] Even though Asa did not destroy all the pagan places of worship, he remained faithful to the LORD all his life. [15] He placed in the Temple all the objects his father had dedicated to God, as well as the gold and silver objects that he himself dedicated.

[16] King Asa of Judah and King Baasha of Israel were constantly at war with each other as long as they were in power. [17] Baasha invaded Judah and started to fortify Ramah in order to cut off all traffic in and out of Judah. [18] So King Asa took all the silver and gold that was left in the Temple and the palace, and sent it by some of his officials to Damascus, to King Benhadad of Syria, the son of Tabrimmon and grandson of Hezion, with this message: [19] "Let us be allies, as our fathers were. This silver and gold is a present for you. Now break your alliance with King Baasha of Israel, so that he will have to pull his troops out of my territory."

[20] King Benhadad agreed to Asa's proposal and sent his commanding officers and their armies to attack the cities of Israel. They captured Ijon, Dan, Abel Beth Maacah, the area near Lake Galilee, and the whole territory of Naphtali. [21] When King Baasha heard what had happened, he stopped fortifying Ramah and went to Tirzah.

[22] Then King Asa sent out an order throughout all Judah requiring everyone, without exception, to help carry away from Ramah the stones and timber that Baasha had been using to fortify it. With this material Asa fortified Mizpah and Geba, a city in the territory of Benjamin.

[23] Everything else that King Asa did, his brave deeds and the towns he fortified, are all recorded in *The History of the Kings of Judah.* But in his old age he was crippled by a foot disease. [24] Asa died and was buried in the royal tombs in David's City, and his son Jehoshaphat succeeded him as king.

King Nadab of Israel

[25] In the second year of the reign of King Asa of Judah, King Jeroboam's son Nadab became king of Israel, and he ruled for two years. [26] Like his father before him, he sinned against the LORD and led Israel into sin.

1 KINGS 15, 16

413

1 Kings

2 Kings
1 Chron.
2 Chron.
Ezra
Nehem.

[27]Baasha son of Ahijah, of the tribe of Issachar, plotted against Nadab and killed him as Nadab and his army were besieging the city of Gibbethon in Philistia. [28]This happened during the third year of the reign of King Asa of Judah. And so Baasha succeeded Nadab as king of Israel. [29]At once he began killing all the members of Jeroboam's family. In accordance with what the LORD had said through his servant, the prophet Ahijah from Shiloh, all Jeroboam's family were killed; not one survived. [30]This happened because Jeroboam aroused the anger of the LORD, the God of Israel, by the sins that he committed and that he caused Israel to commit.

[31]Everything else that Nadab did is recorded in *The History of the Kings of Israel.* [32]King Asa of Judah and King Baasha of Israel were constantly at war with each other as long as they were in power.

King Baasha of Israel

[33]In the third year of the reign of King Asa of Judah, Baasha son of Ahijah became king of all Israel, and he ruled in Tirzah for 24 years. [34]Like King Jeroboam before him, he sinned against the LORD and led Israel into sin.

16 The LORD spoke to the prophet Jehu son of Hanani and gave him this message for Baasha: [2]"You were a nobody, but I made you the leader of my people Israel. And now you have sinned like Jeroboam and have led my people into sin. Their sins have aroused my anger, [3]and so I will do away with you and your family, just as I did with Jeroboam. [4]Any members of your family who die in the city will be eaten by dogs, and any who die in the open country will be eaten by vultures."

[5]Everything else that Baasha did and all his brave deeds are recorded in *The History of the Kings of Israel.* [6]Baasha died and was buried in Tirzah, and his son Elah succeeded him as king.

[7]That message from the LORD against Baasha and his family was given by the prophet Jehu because of the sins that Baasha committed against the LORD. He aroused the LORD's anger not only because of the evil he did, just as King Jeroboam had done before him, but also because he killed all Jeroboam's family.

King Elah of Israel

[8]In the 26th year of the reign of King Asa of Judah, Elah son of Baasha became king of Israel, and he ruled in Tirzah for two years. [9]Zimri, one of his officers who was in charge of half the king's chariots, plotted against him. One day in Tirzah, Elah was getting drunk in the home of Arza, who was in charge of the palace. [10]Zimri entered the house, assassinated Elah, and succeeded him as king. This happened in the 27th year of the reign of King Asa of Judah.

[11]As soon as Zimri became king he killed off all the members of Baasha's family. Every male relative and friend was put to death. [12]And so, in accordance with what the LORD had said against Baasha through the prophet Jehu, Zimri killed all the family of Baasha. [13]Because of their idolatry and because they led Israel into sin, Baasha and his son Elah had aroused the anger of the LORD, the God of Israel. [14]Everything else that Elah did is recorded in *The History of the Kings of Israel.*

King Zimri of Israel

[15]In the 27th year of the reign of King Asa of Judah, Zimri ruled in Tirzah over Israel for seven days. The Israelite troops

414

1 Kings

⋮⋯⋯⋯

Joshua
Judges
Ruth
1 Sam.
2 Sam.

1 KINGS 16, 17

were besieging the city of Gibbethon in Philistia, [16] and when they heard that Zimri had plotted against the king and assassinated him, then and there they all proclaimed their commander Omri king of Israel. [17] Omri and his troops left Gibbethon and went and besieged Tirzah. [18] When Zimri saw that the city had fallen, he went into the palace's inner fortress, set the palace on fire, and died in the flames. [19] This happened because of his sins against the LORD. Like his predecessor Jeroboam he displeased the LORD by his own sins and by leading Israel into sin. [20] Everything else that Zimri did, including the account of his conspiracy, is recorded in *The History of the Kings of Israel.*

King Omri of Israel

[21] The people of Israel were divided: some of them wanted to make Tibni son of Ginath king, and the others were in favour of Omri. [22] In the end, those in favour of Omri won; Tibni died and Omri became king. [23] So in the 31st year of the reign of King Asa of Judah, Omri became king of Israel, and he ruled for twelve years. The first six years he ruled in Tirzah, [24] and then he bought the hill of Samaria for 6,000 pieces of silver from a man named Shemer. Omri fortified the hill, built a town there, and named it Samaria, after Shemer, the former owner of the hill.

[25] Omri sinned against the LORD more than any of his predecessors. [26] Like Jeroboam before him, he aroused the anger of the LORD, the God of Israel, by his sins and by leading the people into sin and idolatry. [27] Everything else that Omri did and all his accomplishments are recorded in *The History of the Kings of Israel.* [28] Omri died and was buried in Samaria, and his son Ahab succeeded him as king.

King Ahab of Israel

[29] In the 38th year of the reign of King Asa of Judah, Ahab son of Omri became king of Israel, and he ruled in Samaria for 22 years. [30] He sinned against the LORD more than any of his predecessors. [31] It was not enough for him to sin like King Jeroboam; he went further and married Jezebel, the daughter of King Ethbaal of Sidon, and worshipped Baal. [32] He built a temple to Baal in Samaria, made an altar for him, and put it in the temple. [33] He also put up an image of the goddess Asherah. He did more to arouse the anger of the LORD, the God of Israel, than all the kings of Israel before him. [34] During his reign Hiel from Bethel rebuilt Jericho. As the LORD had foretold through Joshua son of Nun, Hiel lost his eldest son Abiram when he laid the foundation of Jericho, and his youngest son Segub when he built the gates.

Elijah and the Drought

17 A prophet named Elijah, from Tishbe in Gilead, said to King Ahab, "In the name of the LORD, the living God of Israel, whom I serve, I tell you that there will be no dew or rain for the next two or three years until I say so."

[2] Then the LORD said to Elijah, [3] "Leave this place and go east and hide yourself near the brook of Cherith, east of the Jordan. [4] The brook will supply you with water to drink, and I have commanded ravens to bring you food there."

[5] Elijah obeyed the LORD's command, and went and stayed by the brook of Cherith. [6] He drank water from the brook, and ravens brought him bread and meat every morning and every evening. [7] After a while the brook dried up because of the lack of rain.

1 Kings
2 Kings
1 Chron.
2 Chron.
Ezra
Nehem.

Elijah and the Widow in Zarephath

[8] Then the LORD said to Elijah, [9] "Now go to the town of Zarephath, near Sidon, and stay there. I have commanded a widow who lives there to feed you." [10] So Elijah went to Zarephath, and as he came to the gate of the town, he saw a widow gathering firewood. "Please bring me a drink of water," he said to her. [11] And as she was going to get it, he called out, "And please bring me some bread, too."

[12] She answered, "By the living LORD your God I swear that I haven't got any bread. All I have is a handful of flour in a bowl and a drop of olive oil in a jar. I came here to gather some firewood to take back home and prepare what little I have for my son and me. That will be our last meal, and then we will starve to death."

[13] "Don't worry," Elijah said to her. "Go ahead and prepare your meal. But first make a small loaf from what you have and bring it to me, and then prepare the rest for you and your son. [14] For this is what the LORD, the God of Israel, says: 'The bowl will not run out of flour or the jar run out of oil before the day that I, the LORD, send rain.'"

[15] The widow went and did as Elijah had told her, and all of them had enough food for many days. [16] As the LORD had promised through Elijah, the bowl did not run out of flour nor did the jar run out of oil.

[17] Some time later the widow's son fell ill; he got worse and worse, and finally he died. [18] She said to Elijah, "Man of God, why did you do this to me? Did you come here to remind God of my sins and so cause my son's death?"

[19] "Give the boy to me," Elijah said. He took the boy from her arms, carried him upstairs to the room where he was staying, and laid him on the bed. [20] Then he prayed aloud, "O LORD my God, why have you done such a terrible thing to this widow? She has been kind enough to take care of me, and now you kill her son!" [21] Then Elijah stretched himself out on the boy three times and prayed, "O LORD my God, restore this child to life!" [22] The LORD answered Elijah's prayer; the child started breathing again and revived.

[23] Elijah took the boy back downstairs to his mother and said to her, "Look, your son is alive!"

[24] She answered, "Now I know that you are a man of God and that the LORD really speaks through you!"

Elijah and the Prophets of Baal

18 After some time, in the third year of the drought, the LORD said to Elijah, "Go and present yourself to King Ahab, and I will send rain." [2] So Elijah started out.

The famine in Samaria was at its worst, [3] so Ahab called in Obadiah, who was in charge of the palace. (Obadiah was a devout worshipper of the LORD, [4] and when Jezebel was killing the LORD's prophets, Obadiah took a hundred of them, hid them in caves in two groups of fifty, and provided them with food and water.) [5] Ahab said to Obadiah, "Let us go and look* at every spring and every riverbed in the land to see if we can find enough grass to keep the horses and mules alive. Maybe we won't have to kill any of our animals." [6] They agreed on which part of the land each one would explore, and set off in different directions.

[7] As Obadiah was on his way, he suddenly met Elijah. He recognized him, bowed low before him, and asked, "Is it really you, sir?"

18.5 One ancient translation *Let us go and look*; Hebrew *You go and look*.

READ THIS PASSAGE

AGAIN

BUT SLOWER,

taking time to soak in what is going on.

8 "Yes, I'm Elijah," he answered. "Go and tell your master the king that I am here."

9 Obadiah answered, "What have I done that you want to put me in danger of being killed by King Ahab? 10 By the living LORD, your God, I swear that the king has made a search for you in every country in the world. Whenever the ruler of a country reported that you were not in his country, Ahab would require that ruler to swear that you could not be found. 11 And now you want me to go and tell him that you are here? 12 What if the Spirit of the LORD carries you off to some unknown place as soon as I leave? Then, when I tell Ahab that you are here, and he can't find you, he will put me to death. Remember that I have been a devout worshipper of the LORD ever since I was a boy. 13 Haven't you heard that when Jezebel was killing the prophets of the LORD I hid a hundred of them in caves, in two groups of fifty, and supplied them with food and water? 14 So how can you order me to go and tell the king that you are here? He will kill me!"

15 Elijah answered, "By the living LORD, whom I serve, I promise that I will present myself to the king today."

16 So Obadiah went to King Ahab and told him, and Ahab set off to meet Elijah. 17 When Ahab saw him, he said, "So there you are — the worst troublemaker in Israel!"

18 "I'm not the troublemaker," Elijah answered. "You are — you and your father. You are disobeying the LORD's commands and worshipping the idols of Baal. 19 Now order all the people of Israel to meet me at Mount Carmel. Bring along the 450 prophets of Baal and the 400 prophets of the goddess Asherah who are supported by Queen Jezebel."

20 So Ahab summoned all the Israelites and the prophets of Baal to meet at Mount Carmel. 21 Elijah went up to the people and said, "How much longer will it take you to make up your minds? If the LORD is God, worship him; but if Baal is God, worship him!" But the people didn't say a word. 22 Then Elijah said, "I am the only prophet of the LORD still left, but there are 450 prophets of Baal. 23 Bring two bulls; let the prophets of Baal take one, kill it, cut it in pieces, and put it on the wood — but don't light the fire. I will do the same with the other bull. 24 Then let the prophets of Baal pray to their god, and I will pray to the LORD, and the one who answers by sending fire — he is God."

The people shouted their approval.

25 Then Elijah said to the prophets of Baal, "Since there are so many of you, you take a bull and prepare it first. Pray to your god, but don't set fire to the wood."

26 They took the bull that was brought to them, prepared it, and prayed to Baal until noon. They shouted, "Answer us, Baal!" and kept dancing round the altar they had built. But no answer came.

27 At noon Elijah started making fun of them: "Pray louder! He is a god! Maybe he is daydreaming or relieving himself, or perhaps he's gone on a journey! Or maybe he's sleeping, and you've got to wake him up!" 28 So the prophets prayed louder and cut themselves with knives and daggers, according to their ritual, until blood flowed. 29 They kept on ranting and raving until the middle of the afternoon; but no answer came, not a sound was heard.

30 Then Elijah said to the people, "Come closer to me," and they all gathered round him. He set about repairing the altar of the LORD which had been torn down. 31 He took twelve stones, one for each of the twelve tribes named after the sons of Jacob, the man to whom the LORD had given the name Israel. 32 With these stones he rebuilt the altar for the worship of the LORD. He dug a trench

1 KINGS 18, 19

417

1 Kings

2 Kings

1 Chron.

2 Chron.

Ezra

Nehem.

round it, large enough to hold almost fourteen litres of water.
[33] Then he placed the wood on the altar, cut the bull in pieces, and
laid it on the wood. He said, "Fill four jars with water and pour it
on the offering and the wood." They did so, [34] and he said, "Do
it again" — and they did. "Do it once more," he said — and they
did. [35] The water ran down round the altar and filled the trench.

[36] At the hour of the afternoon sacrifice the prophet Elijah
approached the altar and prayed, "O LORD, the God of Abraham,
Isaac, and Jacob, prove now that you are the God of Israel and
that I am your servant and have done all this at your command.
[37] Answer me, LORD, answer me, so that this people will know that
you, the LORD, are God, and that you are bringing them back to
yourself."[*]

[38] The LORD sent fire down, and it burnt up the sacrifice, the wood,
and the stones, scorched the earth and dried up the water in the
trench. [39] When the people saw this, they threw themselves on the
ground and exclaimed, "The LORD is God; the LORD alone is God!"

[40] Elijah ordered, "Seize the prophets of Baal; don't let any of
them get away!" The people seized them all, and Elijah led them
down to the River Kishon and killed them.

The End of the Drought

[41] Then Elijah said to King Ahab, "Now, go and eat. I hear
the roar of rain approaching." [42] While Ahab went to eat, Elijah
climbed to the top of Mount Carmel, where he bowed down to
the ground, with his head between his knees. [43] He said to his
servant, "Go and look towards the sea."

The servant went and returned, saying, "I didn't see anything."
Seven times in all Elijah told him to go and look. [44] The seventh
time he returned and said, "I saw a little cloud no bigger than
a man's hand, coming up from the sea."

Elijah ordered his servant, "Go to King Ahab and tell him to get
into his chariot and go back home before the rain stops him."

[45] In a little while the sky was covered with dark clouds, the
wind began to blow, and heavy rain began to fall. Ahab got into
his chariot and started back to Jezreel. [46] The power of the LORD
came on Elijah; he fastened his clothes tight round his waist and
ran ahead of Ahab all the way to Jezreel.

Elijah on Mount Sinai

19 King Ahab told his wife Jezebel everything that Elijah had
done and how he had put all the prophets of Baal to death.
[2] She sent a message to Elijah: "May the gods strike me dead if
by this time tomorrow I don't do the same thing to you that you
did to the prophets." [3] Elijah was afraid, and fled for his life; he
took his servant and went to Beersheba in Judah.

Leaving the servant there, [4] Elijah walked a whole day into the
wilderness. He stopped and sat down in the shade of a tree and
wished he would die. "It's too much, LORD," he prayed. "Take away
my life; I might as well be dead!"

[5] He lay down under the tree and fell asleep. Suddenly an angel
touched him and said, "Wake up and eat." [6] He looked round, and
saw a loaf of bread and a jar of water near his head. He ate and
drank, and lay down again. [7] The LORD's angel returned and woke
him up a second time, saying, "Get up and eat, or the journey
will be too much for you." [8] Elijah got up, ate and drank, and the

---

18.37 *you are bringing them back to yourself*; or *you yourself made them
turn away from you.*

1 KINGS 19.9-13

GO FOR A WALK

and ask God to

SPEAK

– TO –

YOU.

It's likely that it will be in a 'soft whisper', so keep your ears and eyes open!

On your walk, pick up something that catches your eye and stick it on to this page, or draw a picture of it if it's too big. Write next to it something that you think God said to you.

stick something here ➘

food gave him enough strength to walk forty days to Sinai, the holy mountain. [9] There he went into a cave to spend the night. Suddenly the LORD spoke to him, "Elijah, what are you doing here?"

[10] He answered, "LORD God Almighty, I have always served you — you alone. But the people of Israel have broken their covenant with you, torn down your altars, and killed all your prophets. I am the only one left — and they are trying to kill me!"

[11] "Go out and stand before me on top of the mountain," the LORD said to him. Then the LORD passed by and sent a furious wind that split the hills and shattered the rocks — but the LORD was not in the wind. The wind stopped blowing, and then there was an earthquake — but the LORD was not in the earthquake. [12] After the earthquake, there was a fire — but the LORD was not in the fire. And after the fire, there was the soft whisper of a voice.

[13] When Elijah heard it, he covered his face with his cloak and went out and stood at the entrance of the cave. A voice said to him, "Elijah, what are you doing here?"

[14] He answered, "LORD God Almighty, I have always served you — you alone. But the people of Israel have broken their covenant with you, torn down your altars, and killed all your prophets. I am the only one left — and they are trying to kill me."

[15] The LORD said, "Return to the wilderness near Damascus, then enter the city and anoint Hazael as king of Syria; [16] anoint Jehu son of Nimshi as king of Israel, and anoint Elisha son of Shaphat from Abel Meholah to succeed you as prophet. [17] Anyone who escapes being put to death by Hazael will be killed by Jehu, and anyone who escapes Jehu will be killed by Elisha. [18] Yet I will leave 7,000 people alive in Israel — all those who are loyal to me and have not bowed to Baal or kissed his idol."

The Call of Elisha

[19] Elijah left and found Elisha ploughing with a team of oxen; there were eleven teams ahead of him, and he was ploughing with the last one. Elijah took off his cloak and put it on Elisha. [20] Elisha then left his oxen, ran after Elijah, and said, "Let me kiss my father and mother goodbye, and then I will go with you."

Elijah answered, "All right, go back. I'm not stopping you!"*

[21] Then Elisha went to his team of oxen, killed them, and cooked the meat, using the yoke as fuel for the fire. He gave the meat to the people, and they ate it. Then he went and followed Elijah as his helper.

War with Syria

20 King Benhadad of Syria gathered all his troops, and supported by 32 other rulers with their horses and chariots, he marched up, laid siege to Samaria, and launched attacks against it. [2] He sent messengers into the city to King Ahab of Israel to say, "King Benhadad demands that [3] you surrender to him your silver and gold, your women and the strongest of your children."

[4] "Tell my lord, King Benhadad, that I agree; he can have me and everything I own," Ahab answered.

[5] Later the messengers came back to Ahab with another demand from Benhadad: "I sent you word that you were to hand over to me your silver and gold, your women and your children. [6] Now, however, I will send my officers to search your palace and the

19.20 *All right… you;* or *Go on, but come back, because what I have just done to you is important.*

419

1 Kings
....

2 Kings
1 Chron.
2 Chron.
Ezra
Nehem.

homes of your officials, and to take everything they* consider valuable. They will be there about this time tomorrow."

⁷King Ahab called in all the leaders of the country and said, "You see that this man wants to ruin us. He sent me a message demanding my wives and children, my silver and gold, and I agreed."

⁸The leaders and the people answered, "Don't pay any attention to him; don't give in."

⁹So Ahab replied to Benhadad's messengers, "Tell my lord the king that I agreed to his first demand, but I cannot agree to the second."

The messengers left and then returned with another message ¹⁰from Benhadad: "I will bring enough men to destroy this city of yours and carry off the rubble in their hands. May the gods strike me dead if I don't!"

¹¹King Ahab answered, "Tell King Benhadad that a real soldier does his boasting *after* a battle, not before it."

¹²Benhadad received Ahab's answer as he and his allies, the other rulers, were drinking in their tents. He ordered his men to get ready to attack the city, so they moved into position.

¹³Meanwhile, a prophet went to King Ahab and said, "The Lord says, 'Don't be afraid of that huge army! I will give you victory over it today, and you will know that I am the Lord.'"

¹⁴"Who will lead the attack?" Ahab asked.

The prophet answered, "The Lord says that the young soldiers under the command of the district governors are to do it."

"Who will command the main force?" the king asked.

"You," the prophet answered.

¹⁵So the king called out the young soldiers who were under the district commanders, 232 in all. Then he called out the Israelite army, a total of 7,000 men.

¹⁶The attack began at noon, as Benhadad and his 32 allies were getting drunk in their tents. ¹⁷The young soldiers advanced first. Scouts sent out by Benhadad reported to him that a group of soldiers was coming out of Samaria. ¹⁸He ordered, "Take them alive, no matter whether they are coming to fight or to ask for peace."

¹⁹The young soldiers led the attack, followed by the Israelite army, ²⁰and each one killed the man he fought. The Syrians fled, with the Israelites in hot pursuit, but Benhadad escaped on horseback, accompanied by some of the cavalry. ²¹King Ahab took to the field, captured* the horses and chariots, and inflicted a severe defeat on the Syrians.

²²Then the prophet went to King Ahab and said, "Go back and build up your forces, and make careful plans, because the king of Syria will attack again next spring."

The Second Syrian Attack

²³King Benhadad's officials said to him, "The gods of Israel are mountain gods, and that is why the Israelites defeated us. But we will certainly defeat them if we fight them in the plains. ²⁴Now, remove the 32 rulers from their commands and replace them with field commanders. ²⁵Then call up an army as large as the one that deserted you, with the same number of horses and chariots. We will fight the Israelites in the plains, and this time we will defeat them."

20.6 Some ancient translations *they*; Hebrew *you*.
20.21 One ancient translation *captured*; Hebrew *destroyed*.

420

1 Kings

: :

Joshua
Judges
Ruth
1 Sam.
2 Sam.

1 KINGS 20

King Benhadad agreed and followed their advice. ²⁶The following spring he called up his men and marched with them to the city of Aphek to attack the Israelites. ²⁷The Israelites were called up and equipped; they marched out and camped in two groups facing the Syrians. The Israelites looked like two small flocks of goats compared with the Syrians, who spread out over the countryside.

²⁸A prophet went to King Ahab and said, "This is what the LORD says: 'Because the Syrians say that I am a god of the hills and not of the plains, I will give you victory over their huge army, and you and your people will know that I am the LORD.' "

²⁹For seven days the Syrians and the Israelites stayed in their camps, facing each other. On the seventh day they started fighting, and the Israelites killed a hundred thousand Syrians. ³⁰The survivors fled into the city of Aphek, where the city walls fell on 27,000 of them.

Benhadad also escaped into the city and took refuge in the back room of a house. ³¹His officials went to him and said, "We have heard that the Israelite kings are merciful. Give us permission to go to the king of Israel with sackcloth round our waists and ropes round our necks, and maybe he will spare your life." ³²So they wrapped sackcloth round their waists and ropes round their necks, went to Ahab and said, "Your servant Benhadad pleads with you for his life."

Ahab answered, "Is he still alive? Good! He's like a brother to me!"

³³Benhadad's officials were watching for a good sign, and when Ahab said "brother", they took it up at once, and said, "As you say, Benhadad is your brother!"

"Bring him to me," Ahab ordered. When Benhadad arrived, Ahab invited him to get in the chariot with him. ³⁴Benhadad said to him, "I will restore to you the towns my father took from your father, and you may set up a commercial centre for yourself in Damascus, just as my father did in Samaria."

Ahab replied, "On these terms, then, I will set you free." He made a treaty with him and let him go.

A Prophet Condemns Ahab

³⁵At the LORD's command a member of a group of prophets ordered a fellow-prophet to hit him. But he refused, ³⁶so he said to him, "Because you have disobeyed the LORD's command, a lion will kill you as soon as you leave me." And as soon as he left, a lion came along and killed him.

³⁷Then this same prophet went to another man and said, "Hit me!" This man did so; he hit him a hard blow and hurt him. ³⁸The prophet bandaged his face with a cloth, to disguise himself, and went and stood by the road, waiting for the king of Israel to pass. ³⁹As the king was passing by, the prophet called out to him and said, "Your Majesty, I was fighting in the battle when a soldier brought a captured enemy to me and said, 'Guard this man; if he escapes, you will pay for it with your life or else pay a fine of 3,000 pieces of silver.' ⁴⁰But I got busy with other things, and the man escaped."

The king answered, "You have pronounced your own sentence, and you will have to pay the penalty."

⁴¹The prophet tore the cloth from his face, and at once the king recognized him as one of the prophets. ⁴²The prophet then said to the king, "This is the word of the LORD: 'Because you allowed the man to escape whom I had ordered to be killed, you will pay for it with your life, and your army will be destroyed for letting his army escape.' "

⁴³The king went back home to Samaria, worried and depressed.

1 Kings

2 Kings
1 Chron.
2 Chron.
Ezra
Nehem.

Naboth's Vineyard

21 Near King Ahab's palace in Jezreel there was a vineyard owned by a man named Naboth. [2] One day Ahab said to Naboth, "Let me have your vineyard; it is close to my palace, and I want to use the land for a vegetable garden. I will give you a better vineyard for it, or, if you prefer, I will pay you a fair price."

[3] "I inherited this vineyard from my ancestors," Naboth replied. "The Lord forbid that I should let you have it!"

[4] Ahab went home, depressed and angry over what Naboth had said to him. He lay down on his bed, facing the wall, and would not eat. [5] His wife Jezebel went to him and asked, "Why are you so depressed? Why won't you eat?"

[6] He answered, "Because of what Naboth said to me. I offered to buy his vineyard, or, if he preferred, to give him another one for it, but he told me that I couldn't have it!"

[7] "Well, are you the king or aren't you?" Jezebel replied. "Get out of bed, cheer up and eat. I will get you Naboth's vineyard!"

[8] Then she wrote some letters, signed them with Ahab's name, sealed them with his seal, and sent them to the officials and leading citizens of Jezreel. [9] The letters said: "Proclaim a day of fasting, call the people together, and give Naboth the place of honour. [10] Get a couple of scoundrels to accuse him to his face of cursing God and the king. Then take him out of the city and stone him to death."

[11] The officials and leading citizens of Jezreel did what Jezebel had commanded. [12] They proclaimed a day of fasting, called the people together, and gave Naboth the place of honour. [13] The two scoundrels publicly accused him of cursing God and the king, and so he was taken outside the city and stoned to death. [14] The message was sent to Jezebel: "Naboth has been put to death."

[15] As soon as Jezebel received the message, she said to Ahab, "Naboth is dead. Now go and take possession of the vineyard which he refused to sell to you." [16] At once Ahab went to the vineyard to take possession of it.

[17] Then the Lord said to Elijah, the prophet from Tishbe, [18] "Go to King Ahab of Samaria. You will find him in Naboth's vineyard, about to take possession of it. [19] Tell him that I, the Lord, say to him, 'After murdering the man, are you taking over his property as well?' Tell him that this is what I say: 'In the very place that the dogs licked up Naboth's blood they will lick up your blood!'"

[20] When Ahab saw Elijah, he said, "Have you caught up with me, my enemy?"

"Yes, I have," Elijah answered. "You have devoted yourself completely to doing what is wrong in the Lord's sight. [21] So the Lord says to you, 'I will bring disaster on you. I will do away with you and get rid of every male in your family, young and old alike. [22] Your family will become like the family of King Jeroboam son of Nebat and like the family of King Baasha son of Ahijah, because you have stirred up my anger by leading Israel into sin.' [23] And concerning Jezebel, the Lord says that dogs will eat her body in the city of Jezreel. [24] Any of your relatives who die in the city will be eaten by dogs, and any who die in the open country will be eaten by vultures."

[25] (There was no one else who had devoted himself so completely to doing wrong in the Lord's sight as Ahab — all at the urging of his wife Jezebel. [26] He committed the most shameful sins by worshipping idols, as the Amorites had done, whom the Lord had driven out of the land as the people of Israel advanced.)

422

1 Kings

Joshua
Judges
Ruth
1 Sam.
2 Sam.

1 KINGS 21, 22

1 KINGS 22.1-9

Having people in your life who speak truth is vital.

Take a

PIECE

– OF –

STRING

and think of a friend who speaks truth to you. Think of any times when they have told you a harsh truth, and

TIE A KNOT

for each one. Tape the string to this page.

↖ *tape string here*

27 When Elijah finished speaking, Ahab tore his clothes, took them off, and put on sackcloth. He refused food, slept in the sackcloth, and went about gloomy and depressed.
28 The LORD said to the prophet Elijah, 29 "Have you noticed how Ahab has humbled himself before me? Since he has done this, I will not bring disaster on him during his lifetime; it will be during his son's lifetime that I will bring disaster on Ahab's family."

The Prophet Micaiah Warns Ahab
(2 Chr 18.2–27)

22 There was peace between Israel and Syria for the next two years, 2 but in the third year King Jehoshaphat of Judah went to see King Ahab of Israel.
3 Ahab asked his officials, "Why is it that we have not done anything to get back Ramoth in Gilead from the king of Syria? It belongs to us!" 4 And Ahab asked Jehoshaphat, "Will you go with me to attack Ramoth?"
"I am ready when you are," Jehoshaphat answered, "and so are my soldiers and my cavalry. 5 But first let's consult the LORD."
6 So Ahab called in the prophets, about 400 of them, and asked them, "Should I go and attack Ramoth, or not?"
"Attack it," they answered. "The Lord will give you victory."
7 But Jehoshaphat asked, "Isn't there another prophet through whom we can consult the LORD?"
8 Ahab answered, "There is one more, Micaiah son of Imlah. But I hate him, because he never prophesies anything good for me; it's always something bad."
"You shouldn't say that!" Jehoshaphat replied.
9 Then Ahab called in a court official and told him to go and fetch Micaiah at once.
10 The two kings, dressed in their royal robes, were sitting on their thrones at the threshing place just outside the gate of Samaria, and all the prophets were prophesying in front of them. 11 One of them, Zedekiah son of Chenaanah, made iron horns and said to Ahab, "This is what the LORD says: 'With these you will fight the Syrians and totally defeat them.'" 12 All the other prophets said the same thing. "March against Ramoth and you will win," they said. "The LORD will give you victory."
13 Meanwhile, the official who had gone to get Micaiah said to him, "All the other prophets have prophesied success for the king, and you had better do the same."
14 But Micaiah answered, "By the living LORD I promise that I will say what he tells me to!"
15 When he appeared before King Ahab, the king asked him, "Micaiah, should King Jehoshaphat and I go and attack Ramoth, or not?"
"Attack!" Micaiah answered. "Of course you'll win. The LORD will give you victory."
16 But Ahab replied, "When you speak to me in the name of the LORD, tell the truth! How many times do I have to tell you that?"
17 Micaiah answered, "I can see the army of Israel scattered over the hills like sheep without a shepherd. And the LORD said, 'These men have no leader; let them go home in peace.'"
18 Ahab said to Jehoshaphat, "Didn't I tell you that he never prophesies anything good for me? It's always something bad!"
19 Micaiah went on: "Now listen to what the LORD says! I saw the LORD sitting on his throne in heaven, with all his angels standing beside him. 20 The LORD asked, 'Who will deceive Ahab so that he will go and be killed at Ramoth?' Some of the angels said one

1 KINGS 22

423

1 Kings

· · · · · · · · · ·

2 Kings
1 Chron.
2 Chron.
Ezra
Nehem.

thing, and others said something else, [21] until a spirit stepped forward, approached the LORD, and said, 'I will deceive him.' [22] 'How?' the LORD asked. The spirit replied, 'I will go and make all Ahab's prophets tell lies.' The LORD said, 'Go and deceive him. You will succeed.'"

[23] And Micaiah concluded: "This is what has happened. The LORD has made these prophets of yours lie to you. But he himself has decreed that you will meet with disaster!"

[24] Then the prophet Zedekiah went up to Micaiah, slapped his face, and asked, "Since when did the LORD's spirit leave me and speak to you?"

[25] "You will find out when you go into some back room to hide," Micaiah replied.

[26] Then King Ahab ordered one of his officers, "Arrest Micaiah and take him to Amon, the governor of the city, and to Prince Joash. [27] Tell them to throw him in prison and to put him on bread and water until I return safely."

[28] "If you return safely," Micaiah exclaimed, "then the LORD has not spoken through me!" And he added, "Listen, everyone, to what I have said!"

The Death of Ahab
(2 Chr 18.28–34)

[29] Then King Ahab of Israel and King Jehoshaphat of Judah went to attack the city of Ramoth in Gilead. [30] Ahab said to Jehoshaphat, "As we go into battle, I will disguise myself, but you wear your royal garments." So the king of Israel went into battle in disguise.

[31] The king of Syria had ordered his 32 chariot commanders to attack no one else except the king of Israel. [32] So when they saw King Jehoshaphat, they all thought that he was the king of Israel, and they turned to attack him. But when he cried out, [33] they realized that he was not the king of Israel, and they stopped their attack. [34] By chance, however, a Syrian soldier shot an arrow which struck King Ahab between the joints of his armour. "I'm wounded!" he cried out to his chariot driver. "Turn round and pull out of the battle!"

[35] While the battle raged on, King Ahab remained propped up in his chariot, facing the Syrians. The blood from his wound ran down and covered the bottom of the chariot, and at evening he died. [36] Near sunset the order went out through the Israelite ranks: "Every man go back to his own country and city!"

[37] So died King Ahab. His body was taken to Samaria and buried. [38] His chariot was cleaned up at the pool of Samaria, where dogs licked up his blood and prostitutes washed themselves, as the LORD had said would happen.

[39] Everything else that King Ahab did, including an account of his palace decorated with ivory and all the cities he built, is recorded in *The History of the Kings of Israel.* [40] At his death his son Ahaziah succeeded him as king.

King Jehoshaphat of Judah
(2 Chr 20.31—21.1)

[41] In the fourth year of the reign of King Ahab of Israel, Jehoshaphat son of Asa became king of Judah [42] at the age of 35, and he ruled in Jerusalem for 25 years. His mother was Azubah, the daughter of Shilhi. [43] Like his father Asa before him, he did what was right in the sight of the LORD; but the places of worship were not destroyed, and the people continued to offer

424

1 Kings

.:........

Joshua
Judges
Ruth
1 Sam.
2 Sam.

1 KINGS 22

sacrifices and burn incense there. ⁴⁴Jehoshaphat made peace with the king of Israel.

⁴⁵Everything else that Jehoshaphat did, all his bravery and his battles, are recorded in *The History of the Kings of Judah.* ⁴⁶He got rid of all the male and female prostitutes serving at the pagan altars who were still left from the days of his father Asa.

⁴⁷The land of Edom had no king; it was ruled by a deputy appointed by the king of Judah.

⁴⁸King Jehoshaphat built ocean-going ships to sail to the land of Ophir for gold; but they were wrecked at Eziongeber and never sailed. ⁴⁹Then King Ahaziah of Israel offered to let his men sail with Jehoshaphat's men, but Jehoshaphat refused the offer.

⁵⁰Jehoshaphat died and was buried in the royal tombs in David's City, and his son Jehoram succeeded him as king.

King Ahaziah of Israel

⁵¹In the seventeenth year of the reign of King Jehoshaphat of Judah, Ahaziah son of Ahab became king of Israel, and he ruled in Samaria for two years. ⁵²He sinned against the LORD, following the wicked example of his father Ahab, his mother Jezebel, and King Jeroboam, who had led Israel into sin. ⁵³He worshipped and served Baal, and like his father before him, he aroused the anger of the LORD, the God of Israel.

THE BOOK OF

2 KINGS

WRITTEN: PROBABLY AROUND 650-530BC

KEY CHARACTER:

Josiah (chapters 22-23) was only eight years old when he became king but he was an excellent ruler. He followed God and is described as being like King David; he also made some pretty bold moves for God. Spend some time reflecting on the ways in which you let your age dictate your expectations of how and when God will use you.

WHY READ IT?

While many of the kings got things wrong, the book gives some examples of brilliant kings who demonstrated what it means to follow God in a tricky world. This was a pretty dark time for God's people, but even when things appeared to be at their worst, and God seemed to be very quiet, he had not forgotten them. He was waiting in the wings to make it all right again.

DOODLE HERE...

WHAT YOU NEED TO KNOW:

2 Kings continues from where 1 Kings left off. When the prophet Elijah was taken to heaven, Elisha took up his ministry. Many kings continued to make bad choices until, finally, God's people were conquered. First the northern kingdom of Israel fell to the Assyrians. Later, the southern kingdom of Judah fell to the Babylonians, and the capital city Jerusalem came under Babylonian rule. At this point, many of God's people were captured and taken to Babylon as slaves - a really important event known as the exile. The nation of Israel rose to power after escaping from Egypt, but then returned to slavery as God removed his protection from them.

God's people experienced slavery at several times through their journey, but this was not God's

ORIGINAL PLAN
FOR HIS
PEOPLE.

Slavery is not gone and forgotten today.

Go and research modern-day slavery on the internet, and spend some time praying about the stories that you find.

850BC → ELIJAH TAKEN TO HEAVEN — ELISHA — ISRAEL FALLS TO ASSYRIA — JUDAH FALLS TO BABYLON (586BC)

Elijah and King Ahaziah

1 After the death of King Ahab of Israel, the country of Moab rebelled against Israel.

[2] King Ahaziah of Israel fell off the balcony on the roof of his palace in Samaria and was seriously injured. So he sent some messengers to consult Baalzebub, the god of the Philistine city of Ekron, in order to find out whether or not he would recover. [3] But an angel of the LORD commanded Elijah, the prophet from Tishbe, to go and meet the messengers of King Ahaziah and ask them, "Why are you going to consult Baalzebub, the god of Ekron? Is it because you think there is no god in Israel? [4] Tell the king that the LORD says, 'You will not recover from your injuries; you will die!'"

Elijah did as the LORD commanded, [5] and the messengers returned to the king. "Why have you come back?" he asked.

[6] They answered, "We were met by a man who told us to come back and tell you that the LORD says to you, 'Why are you sending messengers to consult Baalzebub, the god of Ekron? Is it because you think there is no god in Israel? You will not recover from your injuries; you will die!'"

[7] "What did the man look like?" the king asked.

[8] "He was wearing a cloak made of animal skins, tied with[*] a leather belt," they answered.

"It's Elijah!" the king exclaimed.

[9] Then he sent an officer with fifty men to get Elijah. The officer found him sitting on a hill and said to him, "Man of God, the king orders you to come down."

[10] "If I am a man of God," Elijah answered, "may fire come down from heaven and kill you and your men!" At once fire came down and killed the officer and his men.

[11] The king sent another officer with fifty men, who went up[*] and said to Elijah, "Man of God, the king orders you to come down at once!"

[12] "If I am a man of God," Elijah answered, "may fire come down from heaven and kill you and your men!" At once the fire of God came down and killed the officer and his men.

[13] Once more the king sent an officer with fifty men. He went up the hill, fell on his knees in front of Elijah, and pleaded, "Man of God, be merciful to me and my men. Spare our lives! [14] The two other officers and their men were killed by fire from heaven; but please be merciful to me!"

[15] The angel of the LORD said to Elijah, "Go down with him, and don't be afraid." So Elijah went with the officer to the king [16] and said to him, "This is what the LORD says: 'Because you sent messengers to consult Baalzebub, the god of Ekron — as if there were no god in Israel to consult — you will not get well; you will die!'"

[17] Ahaziah died, as the LORD had said through Elijah. Ahaziah had no sons, so his brother[*] Joram succeeded him as king in the second year of the reign of Jehoram son of Jehoshaphat, king of Judah.

[18] Everything else that King Ahaziah did is recorded in *The History of the Kings of Israel*.

Elijah is Taken Up to Heaven

2 The time came for the LORD to take Elijah up to heaven in a whirlwind. Elijah and Elisha set out from Gilgal, [2] and on the

....
1.8 *was wearing… with*; or *was a hairy man and wore.*
1.11 One ancient translation *went up*; Hebrew *answered.*
1.17 Some ancient translations *his brother*; Hebrew does not have these words.

2 KINGS 2

427

2 Kings

....

1 Chron.
2 Chron.
Ezra
Nehem.
Esther

way Elijah said to Elisha, "Now stay here; the LORD has ordered me to go to Bethel."

But Elisha answered, "I swear by my loyalty to the living LORD and to you that I will not leave you." So they went on to Bethel. ³A group of prophets who lived there went to Elisha and asked him, "Do you know that the LORD is going to take your master away from you today?"

"Yes, I know," Elisha answered. "But let's not talk about it." ⁴Then Elijah said to Elisha, "Now stay here; the LORD has ordered me to go to Jericho."

But Elisha answered, "I swear by my loyalty to the living LORD and to you that I will not leave you." So they went on to Jericho. ⁵A group of prophets who lived there went to Elisha and asked him, "Do you know that the LORD is going to take your master away from you today?"

"Yes, I know," Elisha answered. "But let's not talk about it." ⁶Then Elijah said to Elisha, "Now stay here; the LORD has ordered me to go to the River Jordan."

But Elisha answered, "I swear by my loyalty to the living LORD and to you that I will not leave you." So they went on, ⁷and fifty of the prophets followed them to the Jordan. Elijah and Elisha stopped by the river, and the fifty prophets stood a short distance away. ⁸Then Elijah took off his cloak, rolled it up, and struck the water with it; the water divided, and he and Elisha crossed to the other side on dry ground. ⁹There, Elijah said to Elisha, "Tell me what you want me to do for you before I am taken away."

"Let me receive the share of your power that will make me your successor,"* Elisha answered.

¹⁰"That is a difficult request to grant," Elijah replied. "But you will receive it if you see me as I am being taken away from you; if you don't see me, you won't receive it."

¹¹They kept talking as they walked on; then suddenly a chariot of fire pulled by horses of fire came between them, and Elijah was taken up to heaven by a whirlwind. ¹²Elisha saw it and cried out to Elijah, "My father, my father! Mighty defender of Israel! You are gone!" And he never saw Elijah again. ¹³Then he picked up Elijah's cloak that had fallen from him, and went back and stood on the bank of the Jordan. ¹⁴He struck the water with Elijah's cloak, and said, "Where is the LORD, the God of Elijah?" Then he struck the water again, and it divided, and he walked over to the other side. ¹⁵The fifty prophets from Jericho saw him and said, "The power of Elijah is on Elisha!" They went to meet him, bowed down before him, ¹⁶and said, "There are fifty of us here, all strong men. Let us go and look for your master. Maybe the Spirit of the LORD has carried him away and left him on some mountain or in some valley."

"No, you must not go," Elisha answered.

¹⁷But they insisted until he gave in and let them go. The fifty of them went and looked high and low for Elijah for three days, but didn't find him. ¹⁸Then they returned to Elisha, who had waited at Jericho, and he said to them, "Didn't I tell you not to go?"

Miracles of Elisha

¹⁹Some men from Jericho went to Elisha and said, "As you know, sir, this is a fine city, but the water is bad and causes miscarriages."

2.9 *the share... successor*: Elisha asked for the share that the firstborn son inherited by law from his father (see Deut 21.17).

2 KINGS 2.1-12

Elisha desperately wanted some of what Elijah displayed - to be able to interact with God in the same way as him - so he made sure that he

STUCK CLOSE
TO HIM.

Find a youth leader or friend who you think displays something that you would like more of in your life, and arrange to spend some time with them to learn more from them. (Make sure that your parents or guardians are happy with this!)

428

2 Kings

Judges
Ruth
1 Sam.
2 Sam.
1 Kings

2 KINGS 2, 3

20 "Put some salt in a new bowl, and bring it to me," he ordered. They brought it to him, 21 and he went to the spring, threw the salt in the water, and said, "This is what the LORD says: 'I make this water pure, and it will not cause any more deaths or miscarriages.'" 22 And that water has been pure ever since, just as Elisha said it would be.

23 Elisha left Jericho to go to Bethel, and on the way some boys came out of a town and made fun of him. "Get out of here, baldy!" they shouted.

24 Elisha turned round, glared at them, and cursed them in the name of the LORD. Then two she-bears came out of the woods and tore 42 of the boys to pieces.

25 Elisha went on to Mount Carmel, and later returned to Samaria.

War between Israel and Moab

3 In the eighteenth year of the reign of King Jehoshaphat of Judah, Joram son of Ahab became king of Israel, and he ruled in Samaria for twelve years. 2 He sinned against the LORD, but he was not as bad as his father or his mother Jezebel; he pulled down the image his father had made for the worship of Baal. 3 Yet, like King Jeroboam son of Nebat before him, he led Israel into sin, and would not stop.

4 King Mesha of Moab bred sheep, and every year he gave as tribute to the king of Israel 100,000 lambs, and the wool from 100,000 sheep. 5 But when King Ahab of Israel died, Mesha rebelled against Israel. 6 At once King Joram left Samaria and gathered all his troops. 7 He sent word to King Jehoshaphat of Judah: "The king of Moab has rebelled against me; will you join me in war against him?"

"I will," King Jehoshaphat replied. "I am at your disposal, and so are my men and my horses. 8 What route shall we take for the attack?"

"We will go the long way, through the wilderness of Edom," Joram answered.

9 So King Joram and the kings of Judah and Edom set out. After marching for seven days, they ran out of water, and there was none left for the men or the pack animals. 10 "We're done for!" King Joram exclaimed. "The LORD has put the three of us at the mercy of the king of Moab!"

11 King Jehoshaphat asked, "Is there a prophet here through whom we can consult the LORD?"

An officer of King Joram's forces answered, "Elisha son of Shaphat is here. He was Elijah's assistant."

12 "He is a true prophet," King Jehoshaphat said. So the three kings went to Elisha.

13 "Why should I help you?" Elisha said to the king of Israel. "Go and consult those prophets that your father and mother consulted."

"No!" Joram replied. "It is the LORD who has put us three kings at the mercy of the king of Moab."

14 Elisha answered, "By the living LORD, whom I serve, I swear that I would have nothing to do with you if I didn't respect your ally King Jehoshaphat of Judah. 15 Now get me a musician."

As the musician played his harp, the power of the LORD came on Elisha, 16 and he said, "This is what the LORD says: 'Dig ditches all over this dry stream bed. 17 Even though you will not see any rain or wind, this stream bed will be filled with water, and you, your livestock, and your pack animals will have plenty to drink.'"

2 KINGS 3, 4

429

2 Kings

1 Chron.
2 Chron.
Ezra
Nehem.
Esther

[18] And Elisha continued, "But this is an easy thing for the LORD to do; he will also give you victory over the Moabites. [19] You will conquer all their beautiful fortified cities; you will cut down all their fruit trees, stop all their springs, and ruin all their fertile fields by covering them with stones."

[20] The next morning, at the time of the regular morning sacrifice, water came flowing from the direction of Edom, and covered the ground.

[21] When the Moabites heard that the three kings had come to attack them, all the men who could bear arms, from the oldest to the youngest, were called out and stationed at the border. [22] When they got up the following morning, the sun was shining on the water, making it look as red as blood. [23] "It's blood!" they exclaimed. "The three enemy armies must have fought and killed each other! Let's go and loot their camp!"

[24] But when they reached the camp, the Israelites attacked them and drove them back. The Israelites kept up the pursuit,* slaughtering the Moabites [25] and destroying their cities. As they passed a fertile field, every Israelite would throw a stone on it until finally all the fields were covered; they also stopped up the springs and cut down the fruit trees. At last only the capital city of Kir Heres* was left, and the slingers surrounded it and attacked it.

[26] When the king of Moab realized that he was losing the battle, he took 700 swordsmen with him and tried to force his way through the enemy lines and escape to the king of Syria,* but he failed. [27] So he took his eldest son, who was to succeed him as king, and offered him on the city wall as a sacrifice to the god of Moab. The Israelites were terrified* and so they drew back from the city and returned to their own country.

Elisha Helps a Poor Widow

4 The widow of a member of a group of prophets went to Elisha and said, "Sir, my husband has died! As you know, he was a God-fearing man, but now a man he owed money to has come to take away my two sons as slaves in payment for my husband's debt."

[2] "What shall I do for you?" he asked. "Tell me, what have you got at home?"

"Nothing at all, except a small jar of olive oil," she answered.

[3] "Go to your neighbours and borrow as many empty jars as you can," Elisha told her. [4] "Then you and your sons go into the house, close the door, and start pouring oil into the jars. Set each one aside as soon as it is full."

[5] So the woman went into her house with her sons, closed the door, took the small jar of olive oil, and poured oil into the jars as her sons brought them to her. [6] When they had filled all the jars, she asked if there were any more. "That was the last one," one of her sons answered. And the olive oil stopped flowing. [7] She went back to Elisha, the prophet, who said to her, "Sell the olive oil and pay all your debts, and there will be enough money left over for you and your sons to live on."

....

3.24 One ancient translation *kept up the pursuit*; Hebrew unclear.
3.25 Probable text *only the capital city of Kir Heres*; Hebrew unclear.
3.26 One ancient translation *Syria*; Hebrew *Edom*.
3.27 *terrified*: either because of what Chemosh, the god of the Moabites, might do, or because of what the LORD, the God of the Israelites, might do.

430

2 Kings

Judges
Ruth
1 Sam.
2 Sam.
1 Kings

2 KINGS 4

Colour these shapes.

Elisha and the Rich Woman from Shunem

8 One day Elisha went to Shunem, where a rich woman lived. She invited him to a meal, and from then on every time he went to Shunem he would have his meals at her house. 9 She said to her husband, "I am sure that this man who comes here so often is a holy man. 10 Let's build a small room on the roof, put a bed, a table, a chair, and a lamp in it, and he can stay there whenever he visits us."

11 One day Elisha returned to Shunem and went up to his room to rest. 12 He told his servant Gehazi to go and call the woman. When she came, 13 he said to Gehazi, "Ask her what I can do for her in return for all the trouble she has had in providing for our needs. Maybe she would like me to go to the king or the army commander and put in a good word for her."

"I have all I need here among my own people," she answered.

14 Elisha asked Gehazi, "What can I do for her then?"

He answered, "Well, she has no son, and her husband is an old man."

15 "Tell her to come here," Elisha ordered. She came and stood in the doorway, 16 and Elisha said to her, "By this time next year you will be holding a son in your arms."

"Oh!" she exclaimed. "Please, sir, don't lie to me. You are a man of God!"

17 But, as Elisha had said, at about that time the following year she gave birth to a son.

18 Some years later, at harvest time, the boy went out one morning to join his father, who was in the field with the harvest workers. 19 Suddenly he cried out to his father, "My head hurts! My head hurts!"

"Carry the boy to his mother," the father said to a servant. 20 The servant carried the boy back to his mother, who held him in her lap until noon, at which time he died. 21 She carried him up to Elisha's room, put him on the bed and left, closing the door behind her. 22 Then she called her husband and said to him, "Send a servant here with a donkey. I need to go to the prophet Elisha. I'll be back as soon as I can."

23 "Why do you have to go today?" her husband asked. "It's neither a Sabbath nor a New Moon Festival."*

"Never mind," she answered. 24 Then she had the donkey saddled, and ordered the servant, "Make the donkey go as fast as it can, and don't slow down, unless I tell you to." 25 So she set out, and went to Mount Carmel, where Elisha was.

Elisha saw her coming while she was still some distance away, and said to his servant Gehazi, "Look — there comes the woman from Shunem! 26 Hurry to her and find out if everything is all right with her, her husband, and her son."

She told Gehazi that everything was all right, 27 but when she came to Elisha she bowed down before him and took hold of his feet. Gehazi was about to push her away, but Elisha said, "Leave her alone. Can't you see she's deeply distressed? And the LORD has not told me a thing about it."

28 The woman said to him, "Sir, did I ask you for a son? Didn't I tell you not to raise my hopes?"

29 Elisha turned to Gehazi and said, "Hurry! Take my stick and go. Don't stop to greet anyone you meet, and if anyone greets you, don't take time to answer. Go straight to the house and hold my stick over the boy."

4.23 *Sabbath... New Moon Festival*: Such holy days were thought to be the best time to consult a prophet.

2 KINGS 4, 5

431

2 Kings

1 Chron.
2 Chron.
Ezra
Nehem.
Esther

30 The woman said to Elisha, "I swear by my loyalty to the living LORD and to you that I will not leave you!" So the two of them started back together. 31 Gehazi went on ahead and held Elisha's stick over the child, but there was no sound or any other sign of life. So he went back to meet Elisha and said, "The boy didn't wake up."

32 When Elisha arrived, he went alone into the room and saw the boy lying dead on the bed. 33 He closed the door and prayed to the LORD. 34 Then he lay down on the boy, placing his mouth, eyes, and hands on the boy's mouth, eyes, and hands. As he lay stretched out over the boy, the boy's body started to get warm. 35 Elisha got up, walked about the room, and then went back and again stretched himself over the boy. The boy sneezed seven times, and then opened his eyes. 36 Elisha called Gehazi and told him to call the boy's mother. When she came in, he said to her, "Here's your son." 37 She fell at Elisha's feet, with her face touching the ground; then she took her son and left.

Two More Miracles

38 Once, when there was a famine throughout the land, Elisha returned to Gilgal. While he was teaching a group of prophets, he told his servant to put a big pot on the fire and make some stew for them. 39 One of them went out in the fields to get some herbs. He found a wild vine, and picked as many gourds as he could carry. He brought them back and sliced them up into the stew, not knowing what they were. 40 The stew was poured out for the men to eat, but as soon as they tasted it they exclaimed to Elisha, "It's poisoned!" — and wouldn't eat it. 41 Elisha asked for some meal, threw it into the pot, and said, "Pour out some more stew for them." And then there was nothing wrong with it.

42 Another time, a man came from Baal Shalishah, bringing Elisha twenty loaves of bread made from the first barley harvested that year, and some freshly-cut ears of corn. Elisha told his servant to feed the group of prophets with this, 43 but he answered, "Do you think this is enough for a hundred men?"

Elisha replied, "Give it to them to eat, because the LORD says that they will eat and still have some left over." 44 So the servant set the food before them, and, as the LORD had said, they all ate and there was still some left over.

Naaman is Cured

5 Naaman, the commander of the Syrian army, was highly respected and esteemed by the king of Syria, because through Naaman the LORD had given victory to the Syrian forces. He was a great soldier, but he suffered from a dreaded skin disease. 2 In one of their raids against Israel, the Syrians had carried off a little Israelite girl, who became a servant of Naaman's wife. 3 One day she said to her mistress, "I wish that my master could go to the prophet who lives in Samaria! He would cure him of his disease." 4 When Naaman heard of this, he went to the king and told him what the girl had said. 5 The king said, "Go to the king of Israel and take this letter to him."

So Naaman set out, taking 30,000 pieces of silver, 6,000 pieces of gold, and ten changes of fine clothes. 6 The letter that he took read: "This letter will introduce my officer Naaman. I want you to cure him of his disease."

7 When the king of Israel read the letter, he tore his clothes in dismay and exclaimed, "How can the king of Syria expect

432

2 Kings

⁖ ········

Judges
Ruth
1 Sam.
2 Sam.
1 Kings

2 KINGS 5

me to cure this man? Does he think that I am God,* with the power of life and death? It's plain that he is trying to start a quarrel with me!"

⁸ When the prophet Elisha heard what had happened, he sent word to the king: "Why are you so upset? Send the man to me, and I'll show him that there is a prophet in Israel!"

⁹ So Naaman went with his horses and chariot, and stopped at the entrance to Elisha's house. ¹⁰ Elisha sent a servant out to tell him to go and wash himself seven times in the River Jordan, and he would be completely cured of his disease. ¹¹ But Naaman left in a rage, saying, "I thought that he would at least come out to me, pray to the LORD his God, wave his hand over the diseased spot,* and cure me! ¹² Besides, aren't the rivers Abana and Pharpar, back in Damascus, better than any river in Israel? I could have washed in them and been cured!"

¹³ His servants went up to him and said, "Sir, if the prophet had told you to do something difficult, you would have done it. Now why can't you just wash yourself, as he said, and be cured?" ¹⁴ So Naaman went down to the Jordan, dipped himself in it seven times, as Elisha had instructed, and he was completely cured. His flesh became firm and healthy, like that of a child. ¹⁵ He returned to Elisha with all his men and said, "Now I know that there is no god but the God of Israel; so please, sir, accept a gift from me."

¹⁶ Elisha answered, "By the living LORD, whom I serve, I swear that I will not accept a gift."

Naaman insisted that he accept it, but he would not. ¹⁷ So Naaman said, "If you won't accept my gift, then let me have two mule-loads of earth to take home with me,* because from now on I will not offer sacrifices or burnt offerings to any god except the LORD. ¹⁸ So I hope that the LORD will forgive me when I accompany my king to the temple of Rimmon, the god of Syria, and worship him. Surely the LORD will forgive me!"

¹⁹ "Go in peace," Elisha said. And Naaman left.

He had gone only a short distance, ²⁰ when Elisha's servant Gehazi said to himself, "My master has let Naaman get away without paying a thing! He should have accepted what that Syrian offered him. By the living LORD, I will run after him and get something from him." ²¹ So he set off after Naaman. When Naaman saw a man running after him, he got down from his chariot to meet him, and asked, "Is something wrong?"

²² "No," Gehazi answered. "But my master sent me to tell you that just now two members of the group of prophets in the hill country of Ephraim arrived, and he would like you to give them 3,000 pieces of silver and two changes of fine clothes."

²³ "Please take 6,000 pieces of silver," Naaman replied. He insisted on it, tied up the silver in two bags, gave them and two changes of fine clothes to two of his servants, and sent them on ahead of Gehazi. ²⁴ When they reached the hill where Elisha lived, Gehazi took the two bags and carried them into the house. Then he sent Naaman's servants back. ²⁵ He went back into the house, and Elisha asked him, "Where have you been?"

"Oh, nowhere, sir," he answered.

²⁶ But Elisha said, "Wasn't I there in spirit when the man got out of his chariot to meet you? This is no time to accept money and

······································

5.7 *God;* or *a god.*
5.11 *the diseased spot;* or *this place.*
5.17 *earth to take home with me:* It was then believed that a god could be worshipped only on his own land.

2 KINGS 5, 6

433

2 Kings
·········
1 Chron.
2 Chron.
Ezra
Nehem.
Esther

clothes, olive groves and vineyards, sheep and cattle, or servants! 27 And now Naaman's disease will come upon you, and you and your descendants will have it for ever!"

When Gehazi left, he had the disease — his skin was as white as snow.

The Recovery of the Axe Head

6 One day the group of prophets that Elisha was in charge of complained to him, "The place where we live is too small! 2 Give us permission to go to the Jordan and cut down some trees, so that we can build a place to live."

"All right," Elisha answered.

3 One of them urged him to go with them; he agreed, 4 and they set out together. When they arrived at the Jordan, they began to work. 5 As one of them was cutting down a tree, suddenly his iron axe head fell in the water. "What shall I do, sir?" he exclaimed to Elisha. "It was a borrowed axe!"

6 "Where did it fall?" Elisha asked.

The man showed him the place, and Elisha cut off a stick, threw it in the water, and made the axe head float. 7 "Take it out," he ordered, and the man bent down and picked it up.

The Syrian Army is Defeated

8 The king of Syria was at war with Israel. He consulted his officers and chose a place to set up his camp. 9 But Elisha sent word to the king of Israel, warning him not to go near that place, because the Syrians were waiting in ambush there. 10 So the king of Israel warned the people who lived in that place, and they were on guard. This happened several times.

11 The Syrian king became greatly upset over this; he called in his officers and asked them, "Which one of you is on the side of the king of Israel?"

12 One of them answered, "No one is, Your Majesty. The prophet Elisha tells the king of Israel what you say even in the privacy of your own room."

13 "Find out where he is," the king ordered, "and I will capture him."

When he was told that Elisha was in Dothan, 14 he sent a large force there with horses and chariots. They reached the town at night and surrounded it. 15 Early the next morning Elisha's servant got up, went out of the house, and saw the Syrian troops with their horses and chariots surrounding the town. He went back to Elisha and exclaimed, "We are doomed, sir! What shall we do?"

16 "Don't be afraid," Elisha answered. "We have more on our side than they have on theirs." 17 Then he prayed, "O Lord, open his eyes and let him see!" The Lord answered his prayer, and Elisha's servant looked up and saw the hillside covered with horses and chariots of fire all round Elisha.

18 When the Syrians attacked, Elisha prayed, "O Lord, strike these men blind!" The Lord answered his prayer and struck them blind. 19 Then Elisha went to them and said, "You are on the wrong road; this is not the town you are looking for. Follow me, and I will lead you to the man you are after." And he led them to Samaria.

20 As soon as they had entered the city, Elisha prayed, "Open their eyes, Lord, and let them see." The Lord answered his prayer; he restored their sight, and they saw that they were inside Samaria.

21 When the king of Israel saw the Syrians, he asked Elisha, "Shall I kill them, sir? Shall I kill them?"

2 KINGS 6.1-7

This is an

ODD STORY

– TO INCLUDE –

in the Bible! Talk these questions through with friends:

Why do you think this story of the axe head was included?

Do you think there is a deeper learning point beneath the story you've read?

If so, what do you think it might be, and how could you apply it to your life?

434

2 Kings

⋮

Judges
Ruth
1 Sam.
2 Sam.
1 Kings

2 KINGS 6, 7

22 "No," he answered. "Not even soldiers you had captured in combat would you put to death. Give them something to eat and drink, and let them return to their king." 23 So the king of Israel provided a great feast for them; and after they had eaten and drunk, he sent them back to the king of Syria. From then on the Syrians stopped raiding the land of Israel.

The Siege of Samaria

24 Some time later King Benhadad of Syria led his entire army against Israel and laid siege to the city of Samaria. 25 As a result of the siege the food shortage in the city was so severe that a donkey's head cost eighty pieces of silver, and 200 grammes of dove's dung* cost five pieces of silver.

26 The king of Israel was walking by on the city wall when a woman cried out, "Help me, Your Majesty!"

27 He replied, "If the LORD won't help you, what help can I provide? Have I got any wheat or wine? 28 What's your trouble?"

She answered, "The other day this woman here suggested that we eat my child, and then eat her child the next day. 29 So we cooked my son and ate him. The next day I told her that we would eat her son, but she had hidden him!"

30 Hearing this, the king tore his clothes in dismay, and the people who were close to the wall could see that he was wearing sackcloth under his clothes. 31 He exclaimed, "May God strike me dead if Elisha is not beheaded before the day is over!" 32 And he sent a messenger to get Elisha.

Meanwhile, Elisha was at home with some elders who were visiting him. Before the king's messenger arrived, Elisha said to the elders, "That murderer is sending someone to kill me! Now, when he gets here, shut the door and don't let him come in. The king himself will be just behind him." 33 He had hardly finished saying this, when the king* arrived and said, "It's the LORD who has brought this trouble on us! Why should I wait any longer for him to do something?"

7 Elisha answered, "Listen to what the LORD says! By this time tomorrow you will be able to buy in Samaria three kilogrammes of the best wheat or six kilogrammes of barley for one piece of silver."

2 The personal attendant of the king said to Elisha, "That can't happen — not even if the LORD himself were to send grain* at once!"

"You will see it happen, but you will never eat any of the food," Elisha replied.

The Syrian Army Leaves

3 Four men who were suffering from a dreaded skin disease were outside the gates of Samaria, and they said to one another, "Why should we wait here until we die? 4 It's no use going into the city, because we would starve to death in there; but if we stay here, we'll die also. So let's go to the Syrian camp; the worst they can do is kill us, but maybe they will spare our lives." 5 So, as it began to get dark, they went to the Syrian camp, but when they reached it, no one was there. 6 The Lord had made the Syrians hear what sounded like the advance of a large army, with horses and

....

6.25 dove's dung: This may be a popular term for a vegetable such as wild onions.
6.33 Probable text king; Hebrew messenger.
7.2 grain; or rain.

2 KINGS 7, 8

435

2 Kings

1 Chron.
2 Chron.
Ezra
Nehem.
Esther

chariots, and the Syrians thought that the king of Israel had hired Hittite and Egyptian kings and their armies to attack them. [7]So that evening the Syrians had fled for their lives, abandoning their tents, horses, and donkeys, and leaving the camp just as it was.

[8]When the four men reached the edge of the camp, they went into a tent, ate and drank what was there, grabbed the silver, gold, and clothing they found, and went off and hid them; then they returned, entered another tent, and did the same thing. [9]But then they said to each other, "We shouldn't be doing this! We have good news and we shouldn't keep it to ourselves. If we wait until morning to tell it, we are sure to be punished. Let's go at once and tell the king's officers!" [10]So they left the Syrian camp, went back to Samaria and called out to the guards at the gates: "We went to the Syrian camp and didn't see or hear anybody; the horses and donkeys have not been untied, and the tents are just as the Syrians left them."

[11]The guards announced the news, and it was reported in the palace. [12]It was still night, but the king got out of bed and said to his officials, "I'll tell you what the Syrians are planning! They know about the famine here, so they have left their camp to go and hide in the countryside. They think that we will leave the city to find food, and then they will take us alive and capture the city."

[13]One of his officials said, "The people here in the city are doomed anyway, like those that have already died. So let's send some men with five of the horses that are left, so that we can find out what has happened."* [14]They chose some men, and the king sent them in two chariots with instructions to go and find out what had happened to the Syrian army. [15]The men went as far as the Jordan, and all along the road they saw the clothes and equipment that the Syrians had abandoned as they fled. Then they returned and reported to the king. [16]The people of Samaria rushed out and looted the Syrian camp. And, as the LORD had said, three kilogrammes of the best wheat or six kilogrammes of barley were sold for one piece of silver.

[17]It so happened that the king of Israel had put the city gate under the command of the officer who was his personal attendant. The officer was trampled to death there by the people and died, as Elisha had predicted when the king went to see him. [18]Elisha had told the king that by that time the following day three kilogrammes of the best wheat or six kilogrammes of barley would be sold in Samaria for one piece of silver, [19]to which the officer had answered, "That can't happen — not even if the LORD himself were to send grain* at once!" And Elisha had replied, "You will see it happen, but you will never eat any of the food." [20]And that is just what happened to him — he died, trampled to death by the people at the city gate.

The Woman from Shunem Returns

8 Now Elisha had told the woman who lived in Shunem, whose son he had brought back to life, that the LORD was sending a famine on the land, which would last for seven years, and that she should leave with her family and go and live somewhere else. [2]She had followed his instructions, and had gone with her family to live in Philistia for the seven years.

[3]At the end of the seven years, she returned to Israel and went to the king to ask for her house and her land to be restored to

7.13 Verse 13 in Hebrew is unclear.
7.19 grain; or rain.

436

2 Kings

Judges
Ruth
1 Sam.
2 Sam.
1 Kings

2 KINGS 8

her. ⁴She found the king talking with Gehazi, Elisha's servant; the king wanted to know about Elisha's miracles. ⁵While Gehazi was telling the king how Elisha had brought a dead person back to life, the woman made her appeal to the king. Gehazi said to him, "Your Majesty, here is the woman and here is her son whom Elisha brought back to life!" ⁶In answer to the king's question, she confirmed Gehazi's story, and so the king called an official and told him to give back to her everything that was hers, including the value of all the crops that her fields had produced during the seven years she had been away.

Elisha and King Benhadad of Syria

⁷Elisha went to Damascus at a time when King Benhadad of Syria was ill. When the king was told that Elisha was there, ⁸he said to Hazael, one of his officials, "Take a gift to the prophet, and ask him to consult the LORD to find out whether or not I am going to get well." ⁹So Hazael loaded forty camels with all kinds of the finest products of Damascus and went to Elisha. When Hazael met him, he said, "Your servant King Benhadad has sent me to ask you whether or not he will recover from his illness."

¹⁰Elisha answered, "The LORD has revealed to me that he will die; but go to him and tell him that he will recover." ¹¹Then Elisha stared at him with a horrified look on his face until Hazael became ill at ease. Suddenly Elisha burst into tears. ¹²"Why are you crying, sir?" Hazael asked.

"Because I know the horrible things you will do against the people of Israel," Elisha answered. "You will set their fortresses on fire, slaughter their finest young men, batter their children to death, and rip open their pregnant women."

¹³"How could I ever be that powerful?" Hazael asked. "I'm a nobody!"

"The LORD has shown me that you will be king of Syria," Elisha replied.

¹⁴Hazael went back to Benhadad, who asked him, "What did Elisha say?"

"He told me that you would certainly get well," Hazael answered. ¹⁵But on the following day Hazael took a blanket, soaked it in water, and smothered the king.

And Hazael succeeded Benhadad as king of Syria.

King Jehoram of Judah
(2 Chr 21.1–20)

¹⁶In the fifth year of the reign of Joram son of Ahab as king of Israel,* Jehoram son of Jehoshaphat became king of Judah ¹⁷at the age of 32, and he ruled in Jerusalem for eight years. ¹⁸His wife was Ahab's daughter, and like the family of Ahab he followed the evil ways of the kings of Israel. He sinned against the LORD, ¹⁹but the LORD was not willing to destroy Judah, because he had promised his servant David that his descendants would always continue to rule.

²⁰During Jehoram's reign Edom revolted against Judah and became an independent kingdom. ²¹So Jehoram set out with all his chariots for Zair, where the Edomite army surrounded them. During the night he and his chariot commanders managed to break out and escape, and his soldiers scattered to their homes.

8.16 Some ancient translations *Israel*; Hebrew *Israel, Jehoshaphat being king of Judah*.

2 KINGS 8, 9

437

2 Kings

1 Chron.

2 Chron.

Ezra

Nehem.

Esther

22 Edom has been independent of* Judah ever since. During this same period the city of Libnah also revolted. 23 Everything else that Jehoram did is recorded in *The History of the Kings of Judah*. 24 Jehoram died and was buried in the royal tombs in David's City, and his son Ahaziah succeeded him as king.

King Ahaziah of Judah
(2 Chr 22.1–6)

25 In the twelfth year of the reign of Joram son of Ahab as king of Israel, Ahaziah son of Jehoram became king of Judah 26 at the age of 22, and he ruled in Jerusalem for one year. His mother was Athaliah, the daughter of King Ahab and granddaughter of King Omri of Israel. 27 Since Ahaziah was related to King Ahab by marriage, he sinned against the LORD, just as Ahab's family did.

28 King Ahaziah joined King Joram of Israel in a war against King Hazael of Syria. The armies clashed at Ramoth in Gilead, and Joram was wounded in battle. 29 He returned to the city of Jezreel to recover from his wounds, and Ahaziah went there to visit him.

Jehu is Anointed King of Israel

9 Meanwhile the prophet Elisha called one of the young prophets and said to him, "Get ready and go to Ramoth in Gilead. Take this jar of olive oil with you, 2 and when you get there look for Jehu, the son of Jehoshaphat and grandson of Nimshi. Take him to a private room away from his companions, 3 pour this olive oil on his head, and say, 'The LORD proclaims that he anoints you king of Israel.' Then leave there as fast as you can."

4 So the young prophet went to Ramoth, 5 where he found the army officers in a conference. He said, "Sir, I have a message for you."

Jehu asked, "Which one of us are you speaking to?"

"To you, sir," he replied. 6 Then the two of them went indoors, and the young prophet poured the olive oil on Jehu's head and said to him, "The LORD, the God of Israel, proclaims: 'I anoint you king of my people Israel. 7 You are to kill your master the king, that son of Ahab, so that I may punish Jezebel for murdering my prophets and my other servants. 8 All Ahab's family and descendants are to die; I will get rid of every male in his family, young and old alike. 9 I will treat his family as I did the families of King Jeroboam of Israel and of King Baasha of Israel. 10 Jezebel will not be buried; her body will be eaten by dogs in the territory of Jezreel.' " After saying this, the young prophet left the room and fled.

11 Jehu went back to his fellow-officers, who asked him, "Is everything all right? What did that crazy fellow want with you?"

"You know what he wanted," Jehu answered.

12 "No we don't!" they replied. "Tell us what he said!"

"He told me that the LORD proclaims: 'I anoint you king of Israel.' "

13 At once Jehu's fellow-officers spread their cloaks at the top of the steps for Jehu to stand on, blew trumpets, and shouted, "Jehu is king!"

King Joram of Israel is Killed

14-15 Then Jehu plotted against King Joram, who was in Jezreel, where he had gone to recover from the wounds which he had received in the battle at Ramoth against King Hazael of Syria. So Jehu said to his fellow-officers, "If you are with me, make

8.22 *independent of*; or *in revolt against*.

438

2 Kings

Judges
Ruth
1 Sam.
2 Sam.
1 Kings

sure that no one slips out of Ramoth to go and warn the people in Jezreel." [16] Then he got into his chariot and set off for Jezreel. Joram had still not recovered, and King Ahaziah of Judah was there, visiting him.

[17] A guard on duty in the watchtower at Jezreel saw Jehu and his men approaching. "I see some men riding up!" he called out.

Joram replied, "Send a rider to find out if they are friends or enemies."

[18] The messenger rode out to Jehu and said to him, "The king wants to know if you come as a friend."

"That's none of your business!" Jehu answered. "Fall in behind me."

The guard on the watchtower reported that the messenger had reached the group but was not returning. [19] Another messenger was sent out, who asked Jehu the same question. Again Jehu answered, "That's none of your business! Fall in behind me."

[20] Once more the guard reported that the messenger had reached the group but was not returning. And he added, "The leader of the group is driving his chariot like a madman, just like Jehu!"

[21] "Get my chariot ready," King Joram ordered. It was done, and he and King Ahaziah rode out, each in his own chariot, to meet Jehu. They met him at the field which had belonged to Naboth. [22] "Are you coming in peace?" Joram asked him.

"How can there be peace," Jehu answered, "when we still have all the witchcraft and idolatry that your mother Jezebel started?"

[23] "It's treason, Ahaziah!" Joram cried out, as he turned his chariot round and fled. [24] Jehu drew his bow, and with all his strength shot an arrow that struck Joram in the back and pierced his heart. Joram fell dead in his chariot, [25] and Jehu said to his aide Bidkar, "Get his body and throw it in the field that belonged to Naboth. Remember that when you and I were riding together behind King Joram's father Ahab, the LORD spoke these words against Ahab: [26] 'I saw the murder of Naboth and his sons yesterday. And I promise that I will punish you here in this same field.' So take Joram's body," Jehu ordered his aide, "and throw it in the field that belonged to Naboth, so as to fulfil the LORD's promise."

King Ahaziah of Judah is Killed

[27] King Ahaziah saw what happened, so he fled in his chariot towards the town of Beth Haggan, pursued by Jehu. "Kill him too!" Jehu ordered his men, and they wounded him* as he drove his chariot on the road up to Gur, near the town of Ibleam. But he managed to keep going until he reached the city of Megiddo, where he died. [28] His officials took his body back to Jerusalem in a chariot and buried him in the royal tombs in David's City.

[29] Ahaziah had become king of Judah in the eleventh year that Joram son of Ahab was king of Israel.

Queen Jezebel is Killed

[30] Jehu arrived in Jezreel. Jezebel, having heard what had happened, put on eyeshadow, arranged her hair, and stood looking down at the street from a window in the palace. [31] As Jehu came through the gate, she called out, "You Zimri!* You assassin! Why are you here?"

9.27 Some ancient translations *and they wounded him*; Hebrew does not have these words.
9.31 *Zimri*: An Israelite army officer who assassinated the king of Israel (see 1 Kgs 16.8–12).

2 KINGS 9, 10

439

2 Kings

1 Chron.
2 Chron.
Ezra
Nehem.
Esther

[32] Jehu looked up and shouted, "Who is on my side?" Two or three palace officials looked down at him from a window, [33] and Jehu said to them, "Throw her down!" They threw her down, and her blood spattered the wall and the horses. Jehu drove his horses and chariot over her body, [34] entered the palace, and had a meal. Only then did he say, "Take that cursed woman and bury her; after all, she is a king's daughter." [35] But the men who went out to bury her found nothing except her skull, and the bones of her hands and feet. [36] When they reported this to Jehu, he said, "This is what the Lord said would happen, when he spoke through his servant Elijah: 'Dogs will eat Jezebel's body in the territory of Jezreel. [37] Her remains will be scattered there like dung, so that no one will be able to identify them.'"

The Descendants of Ahab are Killed

10 There were seventy descendants of King Ahab living in the city of Samaria. Jehu wrote a letter and sent copies to the rulers of the city,* to the leading citizens, and to the guardians of Ahab's descendants. The letter read: [2] "You are in charge of the king's descendants and you have at your disposal chariots, horses, weapons, and fortified cities. So then, as soon as you receive this letter, [3] you are to choose the best qualified of the king's descendants, make him king, and fight to defend him."

[4] The rulers of Samaria were terrified. "How can we oppose Jehu," they said, "when neither King Joram nor King Ahaziah could?" [5] So the officer in charge of the palace and the official in charge of the city, together with the leading citizens and the guardians, sent this message to Jehu: "We are your servants and we are ready to do anything you say. But we will not make anyone king; do whatever you think best."

[6] Jehu wrote them another letter: "If you are with me, and are ready to follow my orders, bring the heads of King Ahab's descendants to me at Jezreel by this time tomorrow."

The seventy descendants of King Ahab were under the care of the leading citizens of Samaria, who were bringing them up. [7] When Jehu's letter was received, the leaders of Samaria killed all seventy of Ahab's descendants, put their heads in baskets, and sent them to Jehu at Jezreel.

[8] When Jehu was told that the heads of Ahab's descendants had been brought, he ordered them to be piled up in two heaps at the city gate and to be left there until the following morning. [9] In the morning, he went out to the gate and said to the people who were there, "I was the one who plotted against King Joram and killed him; you are not responsible for that. But who killed all these? [10] This proves that everything that the Lord said about the descendants of Ahab will come true. The Lord has done what he promised through his prophet Elijah." [11] Then Jehu put to death all the other relatives of Ahab living in Jezreel, and all his officers, close friends, and priests; not one of them was left alive.

The Relatives of King Ahaziah are Killed

[12] Jehu left Jezreel to go to Samaria. On the way, at a place called "Shepherds' Camp", [13] he met some relatives of the late King Ahaziah of Judah and asked them, "Who are you?"

"Ahaziah's relatives," they answered. "We are going to Jezreel to pay our respects to the children of Queen Jezebel and to the rest of the royal family." [14] Jehu ordered his men, "Take them alive!"

10.1 Some ancient translations *the city*; Hebrew *Jezreel*.

2 KINGS 10

You can't help but notice that there's

• A LOT OF •

KILLING

in some parts of the Bible! War and bloodshed were a normal part of life during these times. People even believed that their gods showed their power through death and by helping people win wars. That's why it's even more amazing when God shows himself as a God of mercy and love – it makes him totally different from those other gods.

440

2 Kings

⋮⋯⋯

Judges
Ruth
1 Sam.
2 Sam.
1 Kings

2 KINGS 10

They seized them, and he put them to death near a pit there. There were 42 people in all, and not one of them was left alive.

All Remaining Relatives of Ahab are Killed

[15] Jehu started out again, and on his way he was met by Jonadab son of Rechab. Jehu greeted him and said, "You and I think alike. Will you support me?"

"I will," Jonadab answered.

"Give me your hand, then," Jehu replied. They clasped hands, and Jehu helped him up into the chariot, [16] saying, "Come with me and see for yourself how devoted I am to the LORD." And they rode on together to Samaria. [17] When they arrived there, Jehu killed all of Ahab's relatives, not sparing even one. This is what the LORD had told Elijah would happen.

The Worshippers of Baal are Killed

[18] Jehu called the people of Samaria together and said, "King Ahab served the god Baal a little, but I will serve him much more. [19] Call together all the prophets of Baal, all his worshippers, and all his priests. No one is excused; I am going to offer a great sacrifice to Baal, and whoever is not present will be put to death." (This was a trick on the part of Jehu by which he meant to kill all the worshippers of Baal.) [20] Then Jehu ordered, "Proclaim a day of worship in honour of Baal!" The proclamation was made, [21] and Jehu sent word throughout all the land of Israel. All who worshipped Baal came; not one of them failed to come. They all went into the temple of Baal, filling it from one end to the other. [22] Then Jehu ordered the priest in charge of the sacred robes to bring the robes out and give them to the worshippers. [23] After that, Jehu himself went into the temple with Jonadab son of Rechab and said to the people there, "Make sure that only worshippers of Baal are present and that no worshipper of the LORD has come in." [24] Then he and Jonadab went in to offer sacrifices and burnt offerings to Baal. He had stationed eighty men outside the temple and had instructed them: "You are to kill all these people; anyone who lets one of them escape will pay for it with his life!"

[25] As soon as Jehu had presented the offerings, he said to the guards and officers, "Go in and kill them all; don't let anyone escape!" They went in with drawn swords, killed them all, and dragged the bodies outside. Then they went on into the inner sanctuary of the temple, [26] brought out the sacred pillar that was there, and burnt it. [27] So they destroyed the sacred pillar and the temple, and turned the temple into a latrine — which it still is today.

[28] That was how Jehu wiped out the worship of Baal in Israel. [29] But he imitated the sin of King Jeroboam, who led Israel into the sin of worshipping the gold bull calves he set up in Bethel and in Dan. [30] The LORD said to Jehu, "You have done to Ahab's descendants everything I wanted you to do. So I promise you that your descendants, down to the fourth generation, will be kings of Israel." [31] But Jehu did not obey with all his heart the law of the LORD, the God of Israel; instead, he followed the example of Jeroboam, who led Israel into sin.

The Death of Jehu

[32] At that time the LORD began to reduce the size of Israel's territory. King Hazael of Syria conquered all the Israelite territory [33] east of the Jordan, as far south as the town of Aroer on the

2 KINGS 10, 11

441

2 Kings

1 Chron.
2 Chron.
Ezra
Nehem.
Esther

River Arnon — this included the territories of Gilead and Bashan, where the tribes of Gad, Reuben, and East Manasseh lived.

³⁴Everything else that Jehu did, including his brave deeds, is recorded in *The History of the Kings of Israel*. ³⁵He died and was buried in Samaria, and his son Jehoahaz succeeded him as king. ³⁶Jehu had ruled in Samaria as king of Israel for 28 years.

Queen Athaliah of Judah
(2 Chr 22.10—23.15)

11 As soon as King Ahaziah's mother Athaliah learnt of her son's murder, she gave orders for all the members of the royal family to be killed. ²Only Ahaziah's son Joash escaped. He was about to be killed with the others, but was rescued by his aunt Jehosheba, who was King Jehoram's daughter and Ahaziah's half-sister. She took him and his nurse into a bedroom in the Temple and hid him from Athaliah, so that he was not killed. ³For six years Jehosheba took care of the boy and kept him hidden in the Temple, while Athaliah ruled as queen.

⁴But in the seventh year Jehoiada the priest sent for the officers in charge of the royal bodyguard and of the palace guards, and told them to come to the Temple, where he made them agree under oath to what he planned to do. He showed them King Ahaziah's son Joash ⁵and gave them the following orders: "When you come on duty on the Sabbath, one third of you are to guard the palace; ⁶another third are to stand guard at the Sur Gate, and the other third are to stand guard at the gate behind the other guards.* ⁷The two groups that go off duty on the Sabbath are to stand guard at the Temple to protect the king. ⁸You are to guard King Joash with drawn swords and stay with him wherever he goes. Anyone who comes near you is to be killed."

⁹The officers obeyed Jehoiada's instructions and brought their men to him — those going off duty on the Sabbath and those going on duty. ¹⁰He gave the officers the spears* and shields that had belonged to King David and had been kept in the Temple, ¹¹and he stationed the men with drawn swords all round the front of the Temple, to protect the king. ¹²Then Jehoiada led Joash out, placed the crown on his head, and gave him a copy of the laws governing kingship. Then Joash was anointed and proclaimed king. The people clapped their hands and shouted, "Long live the king!"

¹³Queen Athaliah heard the noise being made by the guards and the people, so she hurried to the Temple, where the crowd had gathered. ¹⁴There she saw the new king standing by the column at the entrance of the Temple, as was the custom. He was surrounded by the officers and the trumpeters, and the people were all shouting joyfully and blowing trumpets. Athaliah tore her clothes in distress and shouted, "Treason! Treason!"

¹⁵Jehoiada did not want Athaliah killed in the temple area, so he ordered the army officers: "Take her out between the rows of guards, and kill anyone who tries to rescue her." ¹⁶They seized her, took her to the palace, and there at the Horse Gate they killed her.

Jehoiada's Reforms
(2 Chr 23.16–21)

¹⁷The priest Jehoiada made King Joash and the people enter into a covenant with the LORD that they would be the LORD's

11.6 Hebrew has an additional word, the meaning of which is unclear.
11.10 Some ancient translations (and see 2 Chr 23.9) *spears*; Hebrew *spear*.

442

2 Kings

⋮ ⋯⋯⋯

Judges
Ruth
1 Sam.
2 Sam.
1 Kings

2 KINGS 11, 12

people; he also made a covenant between the king and the people. ¹⁸ Then the people went to the temple of Baal and tore it down; they smashed the altars and the idols, and killed Mattan, the priest of Baal, in front of the altars.

Jehoiada put guards on duty at the Temple, ¹⁹ and then he, the officers, the royal bodyguard, and the palace guards escorted the king from the Temple to the palace, followed by all the people. Joash entered by the Guard Gate and took his place on the throne. ²⁰ All the people were filled with happiness, and the city was quiet, now that Athaliah had been killed in the palace.

²¹ Joash became king of Judah at the age of seven.

King Joash of Judah
(2 Chr 24.1–16)

12 In the seventh year of the reign of King Jehu of Israel, Joash became king of Judah, and he ruled in Jerusalem for forty years. His mother was Zibiah from the city of Beersheba. ² Throughout his life he did what pleased the LORD, because Jehoiada the priest instructed him. ³ However, the pagan places of worship were not destroyed, and the people continued to offer sacrifices and burn incense there.

⁴ Joash called the priests and ordered them to save up the money paid in connection with the sacrifices in the Temple, both the dues paid for the regular sacrifices and the money given as freewill gifts. ⁵ Each priest was to be responsible for the money brought by those he served, and the money was to be used to repair the Temple, as needed.

⁶ But by the 23rd year of Joash's reign the priests still had not made any repairs to the Temple. ⁷ So he called in Jehoiada and the other priests and asked them, "Why aren't you repairing the Temple? From now on you are not to keep the money you receive; you must hand it over, so that the repairs can be made." ⁸ The priests agreed to this and also agreed not to make the repairs in the Temple.

⁹ Then Jehoiada took a box, made a hole in the lid, and placed the box by the altar, on the right side as one enters the Temple. The priests on duty at the entrance put in the box all the money given by the worshippers. ¹⁰ Whenever there was a large amount of money in the box, the royal secretary and the High Priest would come, melt down the silver, and weigh it.* ¹¹ After recording the exact amount, they would hand the silver over to the men in charge of the work in the Temple, and these would pay the carpenters, the builders, ¹² the masons, and the stonecutters, buy the timber and the stones used in the repairs, and pay all other necessary expenses. ¹³ None of the money, however, was used to pay for making silver cups, bowls, trumpets, or tools for tending the lamps, or any other article of silver or of gold. ¹⁴ It was all used to pay the workers and to buy the materials used in the repairs. ¹⁵ The men in charge of the work were thoroughly honest, so there was no need to require them to account for the funds. ¹⁶ The money given for the repayment offerings and for the offerings for sin was not deposited in the box; it belonged to the priests.

¹⁷ At that time King Hazael of Syria attacked the city of Gath and conquered it; then he decided to attack Jerusalem. ¹⁸ King Joash of Judah took all the offerings that his predecessors Jehoshaphat,

<hr>

12.10 *melt down the silver, and weigh it*; or *count the money, and tie it up in bags*.

2 KINGS 12, 13

443

2 Kings

1 Chron.
2 Chron.
Ezra
Nehem.
Esther

Jehoram, and Ahaziah had dedicated to the LORD, added to them his own offerings and all the gold in the treasuries of the Temple and the palace, and sent them all as a gift to King Hazael, who then led his army away from Jerusalem.

¹⁹ Everything else that King Joash did is recorded in *The History of the Kings of Judah*.

²⁰⁻²¹ King Joash's officials plotted against him, and two of them, Jozacar son of Shimeath and Jehozabad son of Shomer, killed him at the house built on the land that was filled in on the east side of Jerusalem, on the road that goes down to Silla. Joash was buried in the royal tombs in David's City, and his son Amaziah succeeded him as king.

King Jehoahaz of Israel

13 In the 23rd year of the reign of Joash son of Ahaziah as king of Judah, Jehoahaz son of Jehu became king of Israel, and he ruled in Samaria for seventeen years. ² Like King Jeroboam before him he sinned against the LORD and led Israel into sin; he never gave up his evil ways. ³ So the LORD was angry with Israel, and he allowed King Hazael of Syria and his son Benhadad to defeat Israel time after time. ⁴ Then Jehoahaz prayed to the LORD, and the LORD, seeing how harshly the king of Syria was oppressing the Israelites, answered his prayer. ⁵ The LORD sent Israel a leader, who freed them from the Syrians, and so the Israelites lived in peace, as before. ⁶ But they still did not give up the sins into which King Jeroboam had led Israel, but kept on* committing them; and the image of the goddess Asherah remained in Samaria.

⁷ Jehoahaz had no armed forces left except fifty horsemen, ten chariots, and 10,000 men on foot, because the king of Syria had destroyed the rest, trampling them down like dust.

⁸ Everything else that Jehoahaz did and all his brave deeds are recorded in *The History of the Kings of Israel*. ⁹ He died and was buried in Samaria, and his son Jehoash succeeded him as king.

King Jehoash of Israel

¹⁰ In the 37th year of the reign of King Joash of Judah, Jehoash son of Jehoahaz became king of Israel, and he ruled in Samaria for sixteen years. ¹¹ He too sinned against the LORD and followed the evil example of King Jeroboam, who had led Israel into sin. ¹² Everything else that Jehoash did, including his bravery in the war against King Amaziah of Judah, is recorded in *The History of the Kings of Israel*. ¹³ Jehoash died and was buried in the royal tombs in Samaria, and his son Jeroboam II succeeded him as king.

The Death of Elisha

¹⁴ The prophet Elisha fell ill with a fatal disease, and as he lay dying King Jehoash of Israel went to visit him. "My father, my father!" he exclaimed as he wept. "You have been the mighty defender of Israel!"

¹⁵ "Get a bow and some arrows," Elisha ordered him. Jehoash got them, ¹⁶ and Elisha told him to get ready to shoot. The king did so, and Elisha placed his hands on the king's hands. ¹⁷ Then, following the prophet's instructions, the king opened the window that faced towards Syria. "Shoot the arrow!" Elisha ordered. As soon as the king shot the arrow, the prophet exclaimed, "You are the LORD's arrow, with which he will win victory over Syria. You will fight the Syrians in Aphek until you defeat them."

13.6 Some ancient translations *kept on*; Hebrew *he kept on*.

---

2 KINGS 13.14-19

This is a really
– INTERESTING –
STORY
when we think about what we expect of God and whether our prayers and hopes are too small.

- -

When you ask God for something, what are your expectations?

- -

How do you feel, knowing that the impact of King Jehoash's future depended upon his own determination and persistence?

- -

What might you take from this story when you are dreaming about how God might want to use your life?

444

2 Kings

Judges
Ruth
1 Sam.
2 Sam.
1 Kings

2 KINGS 13, 14

[18] Then Elisha told the king to take the other arrows and strike the ground with them. The king struck the ground three times, and then stopped. [19] This made Elisha angry, and he said to the king, "You should have struck five or six times, and then you would have won complete victory over the Syrians; but now you will defeat them only three times."

[20] Elisha died and was buried.

Every year bands of Moabites used to invade the land of Israel. [21] Once, during a funeral, one of those bands was seen, and the people threw the corpse into Elisha's tomb and ran off.* As soon as the body came into contact with Elisha's bones, the man came back to life and stood up.

War between Israel and Syria

[22] King Hazael of Syria oppressed the Israelites during all of Jehoahaz' reign, [23] but the LORD was kind and merciful to them. He would not let them be destroyed, but helped them, because of his covenant with Abraham, Isaac, and Jacob. He has never forgotten his people.

[24] At the death of King Hazael of Syria his son Benhadad became king. [25] Then King Jehoash of Israel defeated Benhadad three times and recaptured the cities that had been taken by Benhadad during the reign of Jehoahaz, the father of Jehoash.

King Amaziah of Judah
(2 Chr 25.1–24)

14 In the second year of the reign of Jehoash son of Jehoahaz as king of Israel, Amaziah son of Joash became king of Judah [2] at the age of 25, and he ruled in Jerusalem for 29 years. His mother was Jehoaddin, from Jerusalem. [3] He did what was pleasing to the LORD, but he was not like his ancestor King David; instead, he did what his father Joash had done. [4] He did not tear down the pagan places of worship, and the people continued to offer sacrifices and burn incense there.

[5] As soon as Amaziah was firmly in power, he executed the officials who had killed his father, the king. [6] However, he did not kill their children but followed what the LORD had commanded in the Law of Moses: "Parents are not to be put to death for crimes committed by their children, and children are not to be put to death for crimes committed by their parents; a person is to be put to death only for a crime he himself has committed."

[7] Amaziah killed 10,000 Edomite soldiers in Salt Valley; he captured the city of Sela in battle and called it Joktheel, the name it still has.

[8] Then Amaziah sent messengers to King Jehoash of Israel, challenging him to fight.* [9] But King Jehoash sent back the following reply: "Once a thorn bush on the Lebanon Mountains sent a message to a cedar: 'Give your daughter in marriage to my son.' A wild animal passed by and trampled the bush down. [10] Now Amaziah, you have defeated the Edomites, and you are filled with pride. Be satisfied with your fame and stay at home. Why stir up trouble that will only bring disaster on you and your people?"

[11] But Amaziah refused to listen, so King Jehoash marched out with his men and fought against him at Beth Shemesh in Judah. [12] Amaziah's army was defeated, and all his soldiers fled to their homes. [13] Jehoash took Amaziah prisoner, advanced on Jerusalem,

---

13.21 One ancient translation *and ran off*; Hebrew *and he ran off*.
14.8 *challenging him to fight*; or *inviting him to a conference*.

2 Kings

1 Chron.
2 Chron.
Ezra
Nehem.
Esther

and tore down the city wall from Ephraim Gate to the Corner Gate, a distance of nearly 200 metres. [14] He took all the silver and gold he could find, all the temple equipment and all the palace treasures, and carried them back to Samaria. He also took hostages with him.

[15] Everything else that Jehoash did, including his bravery in the war against King Amaziah of Judah, is recorded in *The History of the Kings of Israel*. [16] Jehoash died and was buried in the royal tombs in Samaria, and his son Jeroboam II succeeded him as king.

The Death of King Amaziah of Judah
(2 Chr 25.25–28)

[17] King Amaziah of Judah lived fifteen years after the death of King Jehoash of Israel. [18] Everything else that Amaziah did is recorded in *The History of the Kings of Judah*.

[19] There was a plot in Jerusalem to assassinate Amaziah, so he fled to the city of Lachish, but his enemies followed him there and killed him. [20] His body was carried back to Jerusalem on a horse and was buried in the royal tombs in David's City. [21] The people of Judah then crowned his sixteen-year-old son Uzziah as king. [22] Uzziah reconquered and rebuilt Elath after his father's death.

King Jeroboam II of Israel

[23] In the fifteenth year of the reign of Amaziah son of Joash as king of Judah, Jeroboam son of Jehoash became king of Israel, and he ruled in Samaria for 41 years. [24] He sinned against the LORD, following the wicked example of his predecessor King Jeroboam son of Nebat, who led Israel into sin. [25] He reconquered all the territory that had belonged to Israel, from Hamath Pass in the north to the Dead Sea in the south. This was what the LORD, the God of Israel, had promised through his servant the prophet Jonah son of Amittai, from Gath Hepher.

[26] The LORD saw the terrible* suffering of the Israelites; there was no one at all to help them. [27] But it was not the LORD's purpose to destroy Israel completely and for ever, so he rescued them through King Jeroboam II.

[28] Everything else that Jeroboam II did, his brave battles, and how he restored Damascus and Hamath to Israel,* are all recorded in *The History of the Kings of Israel*. [29] Jeroboam died and was buried in the royal tombs, and his son Zechariah succeeded him as king.

King Uzziah of Judah
(2 Chr 26.1–23)

15 In the 27th year of the reign of King Jeroboam II of Israel, Uzziah son of Amaziah became king of Judah [2] at the age of sixteen, and he ruled in Jerusalem for 52 years. His mother was Jecoliah from Jerusalem. [3] Following the example of his father, he did what was pleasing to the LORD. [4] But the pagan places of worship were not destroyed, and the people continued to offer sacrifices and burn incense there. [5] The LORD struck Uzziah with a dreaded skin disease that stayed with him the rest of his life. He lived in a house on his own, relieved of all duties, while his son Jotham governed the country.

[6] Everything else that Uzziah did is recorded in *The History of the Kings of Judah*. [7] Uzziah died and was buried in the royal burial ground in David's City, and his son Jotham succeeded him as king.

14.26 Some ancient translations *terrible*; Hebrew *rebellious*.
14.28 One ancient translation *to Israel*; Hebrew *for Judah in Israel*.

446

2 Kings

⋮⋯⋯⋯⋯

Judges
Ruth
1 Sam.
2 Sam.
1 Kings

2 KINGS 15

King Zechariah of Israel

[8] In the 38th year of the reign of King Uzziah of Judah, Zechariah son of Jeroboam II became king of Israel, and he ruled in Samaria for six months. [9] He, like his predecessors, sinned against the LORD. He followed the wicked example of King Jeroboam son of Nebat, who led Israel into sin. [10] Shallum son of Jabesh conspired against King Zechariah, assassinated him at Ibleam,* and succeeded him as king.

[11] Everything else that Zechariah did is recorded in *The History of the Kings of Israel.*

[12] So the promise was fulfilled which the LORD had made to King Jehu: "Your descendants, down to the fourth generation,* will be kings of Israel."

King Shallum of Israel

[13] In the 39th year of the reign of King Uzziah of Judah, Shallum son of Jabesh became king of Israel, and he ruled in Samaria for one month.

[14] Menahem son of Gadi went from Tirzah to Samaria, assassinated Shallum, and succeeded him as king. [15] Everything else that Shallum did, including an account of his conspiracy, is recorded in *The History of the Kings of Israel.* [16] As Menahem was on his way from Tirzah, he completely destroyed the city of Tappuah,* its inhabitants, and the surrounding territory, because the city did not surrender to him. He even ripped open the bellies of all the pregnant women.

King Menahem of Israel

[17] In the 39th year of the reign of King Uzziah of Judah, Menahem son of Gadi became king of Israel, and he ruled in Samaria for ten years. [18] He sinned against the LORD, for until the day of his death he followed the wicked example of King Jeroboam son of Nebat, who led Israel into sin till the day of his death. [19] Tiglath Pileser, the emperor of Assyria, invaded Israel, and Menahem gave him 34 tonnes of silver to gain his support in strengthening Menahem's power over the country. [20] Menahem got the money from the rich men of Israel by forcing each one to contribute fifty pieces of silver. So Tiglath Pileser went back to his own country.

[21] Everything else that Menahem did is recorded in *The History of the Kings of Israel.* [22] He died and was buried, and his son Pekahiah succeeded him as king.

King Pekahiah of Israel

[23] In the fiftieth year of the reign of King Uzziah of Judah, Pekahiah son of Menahem became king of Israel, and he ruled in Samaria for two years. [24] He sinned against the LORD, following the wicked example of King Jeroboam son of Nebat, who led Israel into sin. [25] An officer of Pekahiah's forces, Pekah son of Remaliah, plotted with fifty men from Gilead, assassinated Pekahiah in the palace's inner fortress* in Samaria, and succeeded him as king.

[26] Everything else that Pekahiah did is recorded in *The History of the Kings of Israel.*

....

15.10 One ancient translation *at Ibleam*; Hebrew *before people.*
15.12 *fourth generation*: Zechariah was Jehu's great-great-grandson.
15.16 One ancient translation *Tappuah*; Hebrew *Tiphsah.*
15.25 Hebrew has two additional words, the meaning of which is unclear.

2 KINGS 15, 16

447

2 Kings
................:

1 Chron.
2 Chron.
Ezra
Nehem.
Esther

King Pekah of Israel

²⁷In the 52nd year of the reign of King Uzziah of Judah, Pekah son of Remaliah became king of Israel, and he ruled in Samaria for twenty years. ²⁸He sinned against the LORD, following the wicked example of King Jeroboam son of Nebat, who led Israel into sin.

²⁹It was while Pekah was king that Tiglath Pileser, the emperor of Assyria, captured the cities of Ijon, Abel Beth Maacah, Janoah, Kedesh, and Hazor, and the territories of Gilead, Galilee, and Naphtali, and took the people to Assyria as prisoners.

³⁰In the twentieth year of the reign of Jotham son of Uzziah as king of Judah, Hoshea son of Elah plotted against King Pekah, assassinated him, and succeeded him as king. ³¹Everything else that Pekah did is recorded in *The History of the Kings of Israel*.

King Jotham of Judah
(2 Chr 27.1–9)

³²In the second year of the reign of Pekah son of Remaliah as king of Israel, Jotham son of Uzziah became king of Judah ³³at the age of 25, and he ruled in Jerusalem for sixteen years. His mother was Jerusha, the daughter of Zadok. ³⁴Following the example of his father Uzziah, Jotham did what was pleasing to the LORD. ³⁵But the pagan places of worship were not destroyed, and the people continued to offer sacrifices and burn incense there. It was Jotham who built the North Gate of the Temple.

³⁶Everything else that Jotham did is recorded in *The History of the Kings of Judah*. ³⁷It was while he was king that the LORD first sent King Rezin of Syria and King Pekah of Israel to attack Judah. ³⁸Jotham died and was buried in the royal tombs in David's City, and his son Ahaz succeeded him as king.

King Ahaz of Judah
(2 Chr 28.1–27)

16 In the seventeenth year of the reign of Pekah son of Remaliah as king of Israel, Ahaz son of Jotham became king of Judah ²at the age of twenty, and he ruled in Jerusalem for sixteen years. He did not follow the good example of his ancestor King David; instead, he did what was not pleasing to the LORD his God ³and followed the example of the kings of Israel. He even sacrificed his own son as a burnt offering to idols, imitating the disgusting practice of the people whom the LORD had driven out of the land as the Israelites advanced. ⁴At the pagan places of worship, on the hills, and under every shady tree, Ahaz offered sacrifices and burnt incense.

⁵King Rezin of Syria and King Pekah of Israel attacked Jerusalem and besieged it, but could not defeat Ahaz. ⁶(At the same time, the king of Edom* regained control of the city of Elath, and drove out the Judeans who lived there. The Edomites settled in Elath, and still live there.) ⁷Ahaz sent men to Tiglath Pileser, the emperor of Assyria, with this message: "I am your devoted servant. Come and rescue me from the kings of Syria and of Israel, who are attacking me." ⁸Ahaz took the silver and gold from the Temple and the palace treasury and sent it as a present to the emperor. ⁹Tiglath Pileser, in answer to Ahaz' plea, marched out with his army against Damascus, captured it, killed King Rezin, and took the people to Kir as prisoners.

¹⁰When King Ahaz went to Damascus to meet Emperor Tiglath Pileser, he saw the altar there and sent back to Uriah the priest an

---

16.6 Probable text *the king of Edom*; Hebrew *King Rezin of Syria*.

448

2 Kings

⋮·········

Judges
Ruth
1 Sam.
2 Sam.
1 Kings

2 KINGS 16, 17

exact model of it, down to the smallest details. [11]So Uriah built an altar just like it, and finished it before Ahaz returned. [12]On his return from Damascus, Ahaz saw that the altar was finished, [13]so he burnt animal sacrifices and grain offerings on it, and poured a wine offering and the blood of a fellowship offering on it. [14]The bronze altar dedicated to the LORD was between the new altar and the Temple, so Ahaz moved it to the north side of his new altar. [15]Then he ordered Uriah: "Use this large altar of mine for the morning burnt offerings and the evening grain offerings, for the burnt offerings and grain offerings of the king and the people, and for the people's wine offerings. Pour on it the blood of all the animals that are sacrificed. But keep the bronze altar for me to use for divination." [16]Uriah did as the king commanded.

[17]King Ahaz took apart the bronze carts used in the Temple and removed the basins that were on them; he also took the bronze tank from the backs of the twelve bronze bulls, and placed it on a stone foundation. [18]And in order to please the Assyrian emperor, Ahaz also removed from the Temple the platform for the royal throne and closed up the king's private entrance to the Temple.*

[19]Everything else that King Ahaz did is recorded in *The History of the Kings of Judah*. [20]Ahaz died and was buried in the royal tombs in David's City, and his son Hezekiah succeeded him as king.

King Hoshea of Israel

17 In the twelfth year of the reign of King Ahaz of Judah, Hoshea son of Elah became king of Israel, and he ruled in Samaria for nine years. [2]He sinned against the LORD, but not as much as the kings who had ruled Israel before him. [3]Emperor Shalmaneser of Assyria made war against him; Hoshea surrendered to Shalmaneser and paid him tribute every year. [4]But one year Hoshea sent messengers to So, king of Egypt,* asking for his help, and stopped paying the annual tribute to Assyria. When Shalmaneser learnt of this, he had Hoshea arrested and put in prison.

The Fall of Samaria

[5]Then Shalmaneser invaded Israel and besieged Samaria. In the third year of the siege, [6]which was the ninth year of the reign of Hoshea, the Assyrian emperor* captured Samaria, took the Israelites to Assyria as prisoners, and settled some of them in the city of Halah, some near the River Habor in the district of Gozan, and some in the cities of Media.

[7]Samaria fell because the Israelites sinned against the LORD their God, who had rescued them from the king of Egypt and had led them out of Egypt. They worshipped other gods, [8]followed the customs of the people whom the LORD had driven out as his people advanced, and adopted customs introduced by the kings of Israel.* [9]The Israelites did* things that the LORD their God disapproved of. They built pagan places of worship in all their towns, from the smallest village to the largest city. [10]On all the hills and under every shady tree they put up stone pillars and images of the goddess Asherah, [11]and they burnt incense on all the pagan altars, following the practice of the people whom the

....

16.18 Verse 18 in Hebrew is unclear.
17.4 *So, king of Egypt*; or *the king of Egypt at Sais.*
17.6 *Assyrian emperor*: Probably Sargon II, the successor of Shalmaneser.
17.8 Probable text *and adopted... Israel*; Hebrew unclear.
17.9 *did*; or *said.*

LORD had driven out of the land. They aroused the LORD's anger with all their wicked deeds [12] and disobeyed the LORD's command not to worship idols.

[13] The LORD had sent his messengers and prophets to warn Israel and Judah: "Abandon your evil ways and obey my commands, which are contained in the Law I gave to your ancestors and which I handed on to you through my servants the prophets." [14] But they would not obey; they were stubborn like their ancestors, who had not trusted in the LORD their God. [15] They refused to obey his instructions, they did not keep the covenant he had made with their ancestors, and they disregarded his warnings. They worshipped worthless idols and became worthless themselves, and they followed the customs of the surrounding nations, disobeying the LORD's command not to imitate them. [16] They broke all the laws of the LORD their God and made two metal bull calves to worship; they also made an image of the goddess Asherah, worshipped the stars, and served the god Baal. [17] They sacrificed their sons and daughters as burnt offerings to pagan gods; they consulted mediums and fortune tellers, and they devoted themselves completely to doing what is wrong in the LORD's sight, and so aroused his anger. [18] The LORD was angry with the Israelites and banished them from his sight, leaving only the kingdom of Judah.

[19] But even the people of Judah did not obey the laws of the LORD their God; they imitated the customs adopted by the people of Israel. [20] The LORD rejected all the Israelites, punishing them and handing them over to cruel enemies until at last he had banished them from his sight.

[21] After the LORD had separated Israel from Judah, the Israelites made Jeroboam son of Nebat their king. Jeroboam made them abandon the LORD and led them into terrible sins. [22] They followed Jeroboam and continued to practise all the sins he had committed, [23] until at last the LORD banished them from his sight, as he had warned through his servants the prophets that he would do. So the people of Israel were taken into exile to Assyria, where they still live.

The Assyrians Settle in Israel

[24] The emperor of Assyria took people from the cities of Babylon, Cuth, Ivvah, Hamath, and Sepharvaim, and settled them in the cities of Samaria,* in place of the exiled Israelites. They took possession of these cities and lived there. [25] When they first settled there, they did not worship the LORD, and so he sent lions, which killed some of them. [26] The emperor of Assyria was told that the people he had settled in the cities of Samaria did not know the law of the god of that land, and so the god had sent lions, which were killing them. [27] So the emperor commanded: "Send back one of the priests we brought as prisoners; make him* go back and live there, in order to teach the people the law of the god of that land." [28] So an Israelite priest who had been deported from Samaria went and lived in Bethel, where he taught the people how to worship the LORD.

[29] But the people who settled in Samaria continued to make their own idols, and they placed them in the shrines that the Israelites had built. Each different group made idols in the cities they were living in: [30] The people of Babylon made idols of the god Succoth Benoth; the people of Cuth, idols of Nergal; the people of Hamath,

17.24 *Samaria*: The name of its capital city was applied to the territory of the former kingdom of Israel.
17.27 Some ancient translations *him*; Hebrew *them*.

EXILE

2 KINGS 17.23;
1 CHRONICLES 5.22;
ISAIAH 14.1

Search for the Oxford or Cambridge Dictionary definition of 'exile' and write the definition here.

1 Chron.
2 Chron.
Ezra
Nehem.
Esther

idols of Ashima; [31] the people of Ivvah, idols of Nibhaz and Tartak; and the people of Sepharvaim sacrificed their children as burnt offerings to their gods Adrammelech and Anammelech. [32] These people also worshipped the LORD and chose from among their own number all sorts of people to serve as priests at the pagan places of worship and to offer sacrifices for them there. [33] So they worshipped the LORD, but they also worshipped their own gods according to the customs of the countries from which they had come.

[34] They still carry on their old customs to this day. They do not worship the LORD nor do they obey the laws and commands which he gave to the descendants of Jacob, whom he named Israel. [35] The LORD had made a covenant with them and had ordered them: "Do not worship other gods; do not bow down to them or serve them or offer sacrifices to them. [36] You shall obey me, the LORD, who brought you out of Egypt with great power and strength; you are to bow down to me and offer sacrifices to me. [37] You shall always obey the laws and commands that I wrote for you. You shall not obey other gods, [38] and you shall not forget the covenant I made with you. [39] You shall obey me, the LORD your God, and I will rescue you from your enemies." [40] But those people would not listen, and they continued to follow their old customs.

[41] So those people worshipped the LORD, but they also worshipped their idols; and to this day their descendants continue to do the same.

King Hezekiah of Judah
(2 Chr 29.1–2; 31.1)

18 In the third year of the reign of Hoshea son of Elah as king of Israel, Hezekiah son of Ahaz became king of Judah [2] at the age of 25, and he ruled in Jerusalem for 29 years. His mother was Abijah, the daughter of Zechariah. [3] Following the example of his ancestor King David, he did what was pleasing to the LORD. [4] He destroyed the pagan places of worship, broke the stone pillars, and cut down the images of the goddess Asherah. He also broke in pieces the bronze snake that Moses had made, which was called Nehushtan. Up to that time the people of Israel had burnt incense in its honour. [5] Hezekiah trusted in the LORD, the God of Israel; Judah never had another king like him, either before or after his time. [6] He was faithful to the LORD and never disobeyed him, but carefully kept all the commands that the LORD had given Moses. [7] So the LORD was with him, and he was successful in everything he did. He rebelled against the emperor of Assyria and refused to submit to him. [8] He defeated the Philistines, and raided their settlements, from the smallest village to the largest city, including Gaza and its surrounding territory.

[9] In the fourth year of Hezekiah's reign — which was the seventh year of King Hoshea's reign over Israel — Emperor Shalmaneser of Assyria invaded Israel and besieged Samaria. [10] In the third year of the siege, Samaria fell; this was the sixth year of Hezekiah's reign, and the ninth year of Hoshea's reign. [11] The Assyrian emperor* took the Israelites to Assyria as prisoners and settled some of them in the city of Halah, some near the River Habor in the district of Gozan, and some in the cities of Media.

[12] Samaria fell because the Israelites did not obey the LORD their God, but broke the covenant he had made with them and disobeyed all the laws given by Moses, the servant of the LORD. They would not listen and they would not obey.

18.11 *Assyrian emperor*: See 17.6.

2 KINGS 18.6

HE WAS

faithful

TO THE

LORD

- AND NEVER -

disobeyed

him

2 Kings

....

1 Chron.

2 Chron.

Ezra

Nehem.

Esther

The Assyrians Threaten Jerusalem
(2 Chr 32.1–19; Is 36.1–22)

¹³ In the fourteenth year of the reign of King Hezekiah, Sennacherib, the emperor of Assyria, attacked the fortified cities of Judah and conquered them. ¹⁴ Hezekiah sent a message to Sennacherib, who was in Lachish: "I have done wrong; please stop your attack, and I will pay whatever you demand." The emperor's answer was that Hezekiah should send him ten tonnes of silver and one tonne of gold. ¹⁵ Hezekiah sent him all the silver in the Temple and in the palace treasury; ¹⁶ he also stripped the gold from the temple doors and the gold with which he himself had covered the doorposts, and he sent it all to Sennacherib. ¹⁷ The Assyrian emperor sent a large army from Lachish to attack Hezekiah at Jerusalem; it was commanded by his three highest officials. When they arrived at Jerusalem, they occupied the road where the clothmakers work, by the ditch that brings water from the upper pond. ¹⁸ Then they sent for King Hezekiah, and three of his officials went out to meet them: Eliakim son of Hilkiah, who was in charge of the palace; Shebna, the court secretary; and Joah son of Asaph, who was in charge of the records. ¹⁹ One of the Assyrian officials told them that the emperor wanted to know what made King Hezekiah so confident. ²⁰ He demanded, "Do you think that words can take the place of military skill and might? Who do you think will help you rebel against Assyria? ²¹ You are expecting Egypt to help you, but that would be like using a reed as a walking stick — it would break and jab your hand. That is what the king of Egypt is like when anyone relies on him."

²² The Assyrian official went on, "Or will you tell me that you are relying on the Lord your God? It was the Lord's shrines and altars that Hezekiah destroyed, when he told the people of Judah and Jerusalem to worship only at the altar in Jerusalem. ²³ I will make a bargain with you in the name of the emperor. I will give you 2,000 horses if you can find that many men to ride them! ²⁴ You are no match for even the lowest ranking Assyrian official, and yet you expect the Egyptians to send you chariots and horsemen! ²⁵ Do you think I have attacked your country and destroyed it without the Lord's help? The Lord himself told me to attack it and destroy it."

²⁶ Then Eliakim, Shebna, and Joah told the official, "Speak Aramaic to us, sir. We understand it. Don't speak Hebrew; all the people on the wall are listening."

²⁷ He replied, "Do you think you and the king are the only ones the emperor sent me to say all these things to? No, I am also talking to the people who are sitting on the wall, who will have to eat their excrement and drink their urine, just as you will."

²⁸ Then the official stood up and shouted in Hebrew, "Listen to what the emperor of Assyria is telling you! ²⁹ He warns you not to let Hezekiah deceive you. Hezekiah can't save you. ³⁰ And don't let him persuade you to rely on the Lord. Don't think that the Lord will save you, and that he will stop our Assyrian army from capturing your city. ³¹ Don't listen to Hezekiah. The emperor of Assyria commands you to come out of the city and surrender. You will all be allowed to eat grapes from your own vines, and figs from your own trees, and to drink water from your own wells — ³² until the emperor resettles you in a country much like your own, where there are vineyards to give wine and there is corn for making bread; it is a land of olives, olive oil, and honey. If you do what he commands, you will not die, but live. Don't let Hezekiah fool you into thinking that the Lord will rescue you. ³³ Did the gods

452

2 Kings

∴ ⋯⋯

Judges
Ruth
1 Sam.
2 Sam.
1 Kings

2 KINGS 18, 19

of any other nations save their countries from the emperor of Assyria? ³⁴Where are they now, the gods of Hamath and Arpad? Where are the gods of Sepharvaim, Hena, and Ivvah? Did anyone save Samaria? ³⁵When did any of the gods of all these countries ever save their country from our emperor? Then what makes you think the LORD can save Jerusalem?"

³⁶The people kept quiet, just as King Hezekiah had told them to; they did not say a word. ³⁷Then Eliakim, Shebna, and Joah tore their clothes in grief, and went and reported to the king what the Assyrian official had said.

The King Asks Isaiah's Advice
(Is 37.1-7)

19 As soon as King Hezekiah heard their report, he tore his clothes in grief, put on sackcloth, and went to the Temple of the LORD. ²He sent Eliakim, the official in charge of the palace, Shebna, the court secretary, and the senior priests to the prophet Isaiah son of Amoz. They also were wearing sackcloth. ³This is the message which he told them to give Isaiah: "Today is a day of suffering; we are being punished and are in disgrace. We are like a woman who is ready to give birth, but is too weak to do it. ⁴The Assyrian emperor has sent his chief official to insult the living God. May the LORD your God hear these insults and punish those who spoke them. So pray to God for those of our people who survive."

⁵When Isaiah received King Hezekiah's message, ⁶he sent back this answer: "The LORD tells you not to let the Assyrians frighten you with their claims that he cannot save you. ⁷The LORD will cause the emperor to hear a rumour that will make him go back to his own country, and the LORD will have him killed there."

The Assyrians Send Another Threat
(Is 37.8-20)

⁸The Assyrian official learnt that the emperor had left Lachish and was fighting against the nearby city of Libnah; so he went there to consult him. ⁹Word reached the Assyrians that the Egyptian army, led by King Tirhakah of Ethiopia, was coming to attack them. When the emperor heard this, he sent a letter to King Hezekiah of Judah ¹⁰to say to him, "The god you are trusting in has told you that you will not fall into my hands, but don't let that deceive you. ¹¹You have heard what an Assyrian emperor does to any country he decides to destroy. Do you think that you can escape? ¹²My ancestors destroyed the cities of Gozan, Haran, and Rezeph, and killed the people of Betheden who lived in Telassar, and none of their gods could save them. ¹³Where are the kings of the cities of Hamath, Arpad, Sepharvaim, Hena, and Ivvah?"

¹⁴King Hezekiah took the letter from the messengers and read it. Then he went to the Temple, placed the letter there in the presence of the LORD, ¹⁵and prayed, "O LORD, the God of Israel, enthroned above the winged creatures, you alone are God, ruling all the kingdoms of the world. You created the earth and the sky. ¹⁶Now, LORD, look at what is happening to us. Listen to all the things that Sennacherib is saying to insult you, the living God. ¹⁷We all know, LORD, that the emperors of Assyria have destroyed many nations, made their lands desolate, ¹⁸and burnt up their gods — which were no gods at all, only images of wood and stone made by human hands. ¹⁹Now, LORD our God, rescue us from the Assyrians, so that all the nations of the world will know that only you, O LORD, are God."

Isaiah's Message to the King
(Is 37.21–38)

20 Then Isaiah sent a message telling King Hezekiah that in answer to the king's prayer 21 the LORD had said, "The city of Jerusalem laughs at you, Sennacherib, and despises you. 22 Whom do you think you have been insulting and ridiculing? You have been disrespectful to me, the holy God of Israel. 23 You sent your messengers to boast to me that with all your chariots you had conquered the highest mountains of Lebanon. You boasted that there you cut down the tallest cedars and the finest cypress trees and that you reached the deepest parts of the forests. 24 You boasted that you dug wells and drank water in foreign lands and that the feet of your soldiers tramped the River Nile dry.

25 "Have you never heard that I planned all this long ago? And now I have carried it out. I gave you the power to turn fortified cities into piles of rubble. 26 The people who lived there were powerless; they were frightened and stunned. They were like grass in a field or weeds growing on a roof when the hot east wind blasts them.*

27 "But I know everything about you, what you do and where you go. I know how you rage against me. 28 I have received the report of that rage and that pride of yours, and now I will put a hook through your nose and a bit in your mouth, and take you back by the same road you came."

29 Then Isaiah said to King Hezekiah, "This is a sign of what will happen. This year and next you will have only wild grain to eat, but the following year you will be able to sow your corn and harvest it, and plant vines and eat grapes. 30 Those in Judah who survive will flourish like plants that send roots deep into the ground and produce fruit. 31 There will be people in Jerusalem and on Mount Zion who will survive, because the LORD is determined to make this happen.

32 "This is what the LORD has said about the Assyrian emperor: 'He will not enter this city or shoot a single arrow against it. No soldiers with shields will come near the city, and no siege mounds will be built round it. 33 He will go back by the same road he came, without entering this city. I, the LORD, have spoken. 34 I will defend this city and protect it, for the sake of my own honour and because of the promise I made to my servant David.'"

35 That night an angel of the LORD went to the Assyrian camp and killed 185,000 soldiers. At dawn the next day, there they lay, all dead! 36 Then the Assyrian emperor Sennacherib withdrew and returned to Nineveh. 37 One day, when he was worshipping in the temple of his god Nisroch, two of his sons, Adrammelech and Sharezer, killed him with their swords, and then escaped to the land of Ararat. Another of his sons, Esarhaddon, succeeded him as emperor.

King Hezekiah's Illness and Recovery
(Is 38.1–8, 21–22; 2 Chr 32.24–26)

20 About this time King Hezekiah fell ill and almost died. The prophet Isaiah son of Amoz went to see him and said to him, "The LORD tells you that you are to put everything in order, because you will not recover. Get ready to die."

2 Hezekiah turned his face to the wall and prayed: 3 "Remember, LORD, that I have served you faithfully and loyally, and that I have

19.26 Probable text when the hot east wind blasts them; Hebrew blasted before they are grown.

JOIN THE DOTS
below to make a picture.

2 Kings
....
1 Chron.
2 Chron.
Ezra
Nehem.
Esther

454

2 Kings

Judges
Ruth
1 Sam.
2 Sam.
1 Kings

2 KINGS 20

always tried to do what you wanted me to." And he began to cry bitterly.

⁴Isaiah left the king, but before he had passed through the central courtyard of the palace the LORD told him ⁵to go back to Hezekiah, ruler of the LORD's people, and say to him, "I, the LORD, the God of your ancestor David, have heard your prayer and seen your tears. I will heal you, and in three days you will go to the Temple. ⁶I will let you live fifteen years longer. I will rescue you and this city of Jerusalem from the emperor of Assyria. I will defend this city, for the sake of my own honour and because of the promise I made to my servant David."

⁷Then Isaiah told the king's attendants to put on his boil a paste made of figs, and he would get well.* ⁸King Hezekiah asked, "What is the sign to prove that the LORD will heal me and that three days later I will be able to go to the Temple?"

⁹Isaiah replied, "The LORD will give you a sign to prove that he will keep his promise. Now, would you prefer the shadow on the stairway to go forward ten steps or go back ten steps?"*

¹⁰Hezekiah answered, "It's easy to make the shadow go forward ten steps!* Make it go back ten steps."*

¹¹Isaiah prayed to the LORD, and the LORD made the shadow go back ten steps* on the stairway* set up by King Ahaz.

Messengers from Babylonia
(Is 39.1–8)

¹²About that same time the king of Babylonia, Merodach Baladan, the son of Baladan, heard that King Hezekiah had been ill, so he sent him a letter and a present. ¹³Hezekiah welcomed the messengers and showed them his wealth — his silver and gold, his spices and perfumes, and all his military equipment. There was nothing in his storerooms or anywhere in his kingdom that he did not show them. ¹⁴Then the prophet Isaiah went to King Hezekiah and asked, "Where did these men come from and what did they say to you?"

Hezekiah answered, "They came from a very distant country, from Babylonia."

¹⁵"What did they see in the palace?"

"They saw everything. There is nothing in the storerooms that I didn't show them."

¹⁶Isaiah then said to the king, "The LORD Almighty says that ¹⁷a time is coming when everything in your palace, everything that your ancestors have stored up to this day, will be carried off to Babylonia. Nothing will be left. ¹⁸Some of your own direct descendants will be taken away and made eunuchs to serve in the palace of the king of Babylonia."

¹⁹King Hezekiah understood this to mean that there would be peace and security during his lifetime, so he replied, "The message you have given me from the LORD is good."

The End of Hezekiah's Reign
(2 Chr 32.32–33)

²⁰Everything else that King Hezekiah did, his brave deeds, and an account of how he built a reservoir and dug a tunnel to bring

. . . .
20.7 One ancient translation (and see Is 38.21) figs, and he would get well; Hebrew figs. They did so, and he got well.
20.9 stairway... steps... steps; or sundial... divisions... divisions.
20.10; 20.11 steps; or divisions.
20.11 stairway; or sundial. Archaeological evidence suggests that the stairway referred to in this passage was one specially constructed to tell the time.

2 KINGS 20, 21   455

2 Kings

1 Chron.
2 Chron.
Ezra
Nehem.
Esther

water into the city, are all recorded in *The History of the Kings of Judah.* ²¹Hezekiah died, and his son Manasseh succeeded him as king.

King Manasseh of Judah
(2 Chr 33.1–20)

21 Manasseh was twelve years old when he became king of Judah, and he ruled in Jerusalem for 55 years. His mother was Hephzibah. ²Following the disgusting practices of the nations whom the LORD had driven out of the land as his people advanced, Manasseh sinned against the LORD. ³He rebuilt the pagan places of worship that his father Hezekiah had destroyed; he built altars for the worship of Baal and made an image of the goddess Asherah, as King Ahab of Israel had done. Manasseh also worshipped the stars. ⁴He built pagan altars in the Temple, the place that the LORD had said was where he should be worshipped. ⁵In the two courtyards of the Temple he built altars for the worship of the stars. ⁶He sacrificed his son as a burnt offering. He practised divination and magic and consulted* fortune tellers and mediums. He sinned greatly against the LORD and stirred up his anger. ⁷He placed the symbol of the goddess Asherah in the Temple, the place about which the LORD had said to David and his son Solomon: "Here in Jerusalem, in this Temple, is the place that I have chosen out of all the territory of the twelve tribes of Israel as the place where I am to be worshipped. ⁸And if the people of Israel will obey all my commands and keep the whole Law that my servant Moses gave them, then I will not allow them to be driven out of the land that I gave to their ancestors." ⁹But the people of Judah did not obey the LORD, and Manasseh led them to commit even greater sins than those committed by the nations whom the LORD had driven out of the land as his people advanced.

¹⁰Through his servants the prophets the LORD said, ¹¹"King Manasseh has done these disgusting things, things far worse than what the Canaanites did; and with his idols he has led the people of Judah into sin. ¹²So I, the LORD God of Israel, will bring such a disaster on Jerusalem and Judah that everyone who hears about it will be stunned. ¹³I will punish Jerusalem as I did Samaria, as I did King Ahab of Israel and his descendants. I will wipe Jerusalem clean of its people, as clean as a plate that has been wiped and turned upside down. ¹⁴I will abandon the people who survive, and will hand them over to their enemies, who will conquer them and plunder their land. ¹⁵I will do this to my people because they have sinned against me and have stirred up my anger from the time their ancestors came out of Egypt to this day."

¹⁶Manasseh killed so many innocent people that the streets of Jerusalem were flowing with blood; he did this in addition to leading the people of Judah into idolatry, causing them to sin against the LORD.

¹⁷Everything else that Manasseh did, including the sins he committed, is recorded in *The History of the Kings of Judah.* ¹⁸Manasseh died and was buried in the palace garden, the garden of Uzza, and his son Amon succeeded him as king.

King Amon of Judah
(2 Chr 33.21–25)

¹⁹Amon was 22 years old when he became king of Judah, and he ruled in Jerusalem for two years. His mother was Meshullemeth,

21.6 *consulted; or brought back.*

456

2 Kings

Judges
Ruth
1 Sam.
2 Sam.
1 Kings

the daughter of Haruz, from the town of Jotbah. [20] Like his father Manasseh, he sinned against the LORD; [21] he imitated his father's actions, and he worshipped the idols that his father had worshipped. [22] He rejected the LORD, the God of his ancestors, and disobeyed the LORD's commands.

[23] Amon's officials plotted against him and assassinated him in the palace. [24] The people of Judah killed Amon's assassins and made his son Josiah king.

[25] Everything else that Amon did is recorded in *The History of the Kings of Judah*. [26] Amon was buried in the tomb in the garden of Uzza, and his son Josiah succeeded him as king.

King Josiah of Judah
(2 Chr 34.1–2)

22 Josiah was eight years old when he became king of Judah, and he ruled in Jerusalem for 31 years. His mother was Jedidah, the daughter of Adaiah, from the town of Bozkath. [2] Josiah did what was pleasing to the LORD; he followed the example of his ancestor King David, strictly obeying all the laws of God.

The Book of the Law is Discovered
(2 Chr 34.8–28)

[3] In the eighteenth year of his reign, King Josiah sent the court secretary Shaphan, the son of Azaliah and grandson of Meshullam, to the Temple with the order: [4] "Go to the High Priest Hilkiah and get a report on the amount of money that the priests on duty at the entrance to the Temple have collected from the people. [5] Tell him to give the money to the men who are in charge of the repairs in the Temple. They are to pay [6] the carpenters, the builders, and the masons, and buy the timber and the stones used in the repairs. [7] The men in charge of the work are thoroughly honest, so there is no need to require them to account for the funds."

[8] Shaphan delivered the king's order to Hilkiah, and Hilkiah told him that he had found the book of the Law in the Temple. Hilkiah gave him the book, and Shaphan read it. [9] Then he went back to the king and reported: "Your servants have taken the money that was in the Temple and have handed it over to the men in charge of the repairs." [10] And then he said, "I have here a book that Hilkiah gave me." And he read it aloud to the king.

[11] When the king heard the book being read, he tore his clothes in dismay, [12] and gave the following order to Hilkiah the priest, to Ahikam son of Shaphan, to Achbor son of Micaiah, to Shaphan, the court secretary, and to Asaiah, the king's attendant: [13] "Go and consult the LORD for me and for all the people of Judah about the teachings of this book. The LORD is angry with us because our ancestors have not done what this book says must be done."

[14] Hilkiah, Ahikam, Achbor, Shaphan, and Asaiah went to consult a woman named Huldah, a prophet who lived in the newer part of Jerusalem. (Her husband Shallum, the son of Tikvah and grandson of Harhas, was in charge of the temple robes.) They described to her what had happened, [15] and she told them to go back to the king and give him [16] the following message from the LORD: "I am going to punish Jerusalem and all its people, as written in the book that the king has read. [17] They have rejected me and have offered sacrifices to other gods, and so have stirred up my anger by all they have done. My anger is aroused against Jerusalem, and it will not die down. [18] As for the king himself, this is what I, the LORD God of Israel, say: you listened to what is written in the book, [19] and you repented and humbled yourself before me, tearing your clothes and

---

2 KINGS 22.8-13

Take a highlighter and go through all the bits of the Bible that you have read most recently.

Highlight all the verses

THAT
CHALLENGE
– YOU –

in the way you live. Pray that God will help you to do what these verses are asking of you.

2 KINGS 22, 23

457

2 Kings

1 Chron.
2 Chron.
Ezra
Nehem.
Esther

weeping, when you heard how I threatened to punish Jerusalem and its people. I will make it a terrifying sight, a place whose name people will use as a curse. But I have heard your prayer, [20] and the punishment which I am going to bring on Jerusalem will not come until after your death. I will let you die in peace."

The men returned to King Josiah with this message.

Josiah Does Away with Pagan Worship
(2 Chr 34.3–7, 29–33)

23 King Josiah summoned all the leaders of Judah and Jerusalem, [2] and together they went to the Temple, accompanied by the priests and the prophets and all the rest of the people, rich and poor alike. Before them all, the king read aloud the whole book of the covenant which had been found in the Temple. [3] He stood by the royal column and made a covenant with the LORD to obey him, to keep his laws and commands with all his heart and soul, and to put into practice the demands attached to the covenant, as written in the book. And all the people promised to keep the covenant.

[4] Then Josiah ordered the High Priest Hilkiah, his assistant priests, and the guards on duty at the entrance to the Temple to bring out of the Temple all the objects used in the worship of Baal, of the goddess Asherah, and of the stars. The king burnt all these objects outside the city near the valley of the Kidron, and then had the ashes taken to Bethel. [5] He removed from office the priests that the kings of Judah had ordained to offer sacrifices* on the pagan altars in the cities of Judah and in places near Jerusalem — all the priests who offered sacrifices to Baal, to the sun, the moon, the planets, and the stars. [6] He removed from the Temple the symbol of the goddess Asherah, took it out of the city to the valley of the Kidron, burnt it, pounded its ashes to dust, and scattered it over the public burial ground. [7] He destroyed the living quarters in the Temple occupied by the temple prostitutes.* (It was there that women wove robes used in the worship of Asherah.) [8] He brought to Jerusalem the priests who were in the cities of Judah, and throughout the whole country he desecrated the altars where they had offered sacrifices. He also tore down the altars dedicated to the goat-demons near the gate built by Joshua, the city governor, which was to the left of the main gate as one enters the city. [9] Those priests were not allowed to serve in the Temple, but they could eat the unleavened bread provided for their fellow-priests.

[10] King Josiah also desecrated Topheth, the pagan place of worship in the Valley of Hinnom, so that no one could sacrifice his son or daughter as a burnt offering to the god Molech. [11] He also removed the horses that the kings of Judah had dedicated to the worship of the sun, and he burnt the chariots used in this worship. (These were kept in the temple courtyard, near the gate and not far from the living quarters of Nathan Melech, a high official.) [12] The altars which the kings of Judah had built on the palace roof above King Ahaz' quarters, King Josiah tore down, along with the altars put up by King Manasseh in the two courtyards of the Temple; he smashed the altars to bits* and threw them into the valley of the Kidron. [13] Josiah desecrated the altars that

....

23.5 Some ancient translations *to offer sacrifices*; Hebrew *and he offered sacrifices*.
23.7 *temple prostitutes*: Men and women who practised prostitution in the worship of fertility gods.
23.12 Probable text *smashed… to bits*; Hebrew unclear.

458

2 Kings

Judges
Ruth
1 Sam.
2 Sam.
1 Kings

2 KINGS 23

King Solomon had built east of Jerusalem, south of the Mount of Olives,* for the worship of disgusting idols — Astarte the goddess of Sidon, Chemosh the god of Moab, and Molech the god of Ammon. [14] King Josiah broke the stone pillars to pieces, cut down the symbols of the goddess Asherah, and the ground where they had stood he covered with human bones.

[15] Josiah also tore down the place of worship in Bethel which had been built by King Jeroboam son of Nebat, who led Israel into sin. Josiah pulled down the altar, broke its stones into pieces,* and pounded them to dust; he also burnt the image of Asherah. [16] Then Josiah looked round and saw some tombs there on the hill; he had the bones taken out of them and burnt on the altar. In this way he desecrated the altar, doing what the prophet had predicted long before during the festival as King Jeroboam was standing by the altar. King Josiah looked round and saw the tomb of the prophet* who had made this prediction. [17] "Whose tomb is that?" he asked.

The people of Bethel answered, "It is the tomb of the prophet who came from Judah and predicted these things that you have done to this altar."

[18] "Leave it as it is," Josiah ordered. "His bones are not to be moved."

So his bones were not moved, neither were those of the prophet who had come from Samaria.

[19] In every city of Israel King Josiah tore down all the pagan places of worship which had been built by the kings of Israel, who thereby aroused the LORD's anger. He did to all those altars what he had done in Bethel. [20] He killed all the pagan priests on the altars where they served, and he burnt human bones on every altar. Then he returned to Jerusalem.

Josiah Celebrates the Passover
(2 Chr 35.1–19)

[21] King Josiah ordered the people to celebrate the Passover in honour of the LORD their God, as written in the book of the covenant. [22] No Passover like this one had ever been celebrated by any of the kings of Israel or of Judah, since the time when judges ruled the nation. [23] Now at last, in the eighteenth year of the reign of Josiah, the Passover was celebrated in Jerusalem.

Other Changes Made by Josiah

[24] In order to enforce the laws written in the book that the High Priest Hilkiah had found in the Temple, King Josiah removed from Jerusalem and the rest of Judah all the mediums and fortune tellers, and all the household gods, idols, and all other pagan objects of worship. [25] There had never been a king like him before, who served the LORD with all his heart, mind, and strength, obeying all the Law of Moses; nor has there been a king like him since.

[26] But the LORD's fierce anger had been aroused against Judah by what King Manasseh had done, and even now it did not die down. [27] The LORD said, "I will do to Judah what I have done to Israel: I will banish the people of Judah from my sight, and I will reject Jerusalem, the city I chose, and the Temple, the place I said was where I should be worshipped."

23.13 *Mount of Olives*: Hebrew here refers to it as "Mount of Destruction" or "Mount of Sin".
23.15 One ancient translation *broke its stones into pieces*; Hebrew *burnt the altar*.
23.16 One ancient translation *during the festival… the prophet*; Hebrew does not have these words.

The End of Josiah's Reign
(2 Chr 35.20—36.1)

28 Everything else that King Josiah did is recorded in *The History of the Kings of Judah*. 29 While Josiah was king, King Neco of Egypt led an army to the River Euphrates to help the emperor of Assyria. King Josiah tried to stop the Egyptian army at Megiddo and was killed in battle. 30 His officials placed his body in a chariot and took it back to Jerusalem, where he was buried in the royal tombs.

The people of Judah chose Josiah's son Joahaz and anointed him king.

King Joahaz of Judah
(2 Chr 36.2–4)

31 Joahaz was 23 years old when he became king of Judah, and he ruled in Jerusalem for three months. His mother was Hamutal, the daughter of Jeremiah from the city of Libnah. 32 Following the example of his ancestors, he sinned against the LORD. 33 His reign ended when King Neco of Egypt took him prisoner in Riblah, in the land of Hamath, and made Judah pay 3.4 tonnes of silver and 34 kilogrammes of gold as tribute. 34 King Neco made Josiah's son Eliakim king of Judah as successor to Josiah, and changed his name to Jehoiakim. Joahaz was taken to Egypt by King Neco, and there he died.

King Jehoiakim of Judah
(2 Chr 36.5–8)

35 King Jehoiakim collected a tax from the people in proportion to their wealth, in order to raise the amount needed to pay the tribute demanded by the king of Egypt.

36 Jehoiakim was 25 years old when he became king of Judah, and he ruled in Jerusalem for eleven years. His mother was Zebidah, the daughter of Pedaiah from the town of Rumah. 37 Following the example of his ancestors, Jehoiakim sinned against the LORD.

24 While Jehoiakim was king, King Nebuchadnezzar of Babylonia invaded Judah, and for three years Jehoiakim was forced to submit to his rule; then he rebelled. 2 The LORD sent armed bands of Babylonians, Syrians, Moabites, and Ammonites against Jehoiakim to destroy Judah, as the LORD had said through his servants the prophets that he would do. 3 This happened at the LORD's command, in order to banish the people of Judah from his sight because of all the sins that King Manasseh had committed, 4 and especially because of all the innocent people he had killed. The LORD could not forgive Manasseh for that.

5 Everything else that Jehoiakim did is recorded in *The History of the Kings of Judah*. 6 Jehoiakim died, and his son Jehoiachin succeeded him as king.

7 The king of Egypt and his army never marched out of Egypt again, because the king of Babylonia now controlled all the territory that had belonged to Egypt, from the River Euphrates to the northern border of Egypt.

King Jehoiachin of Judah
(2 Chr 36.9–10)

8 Jehoiachin was eighteen years old when he became king of Judah, and he ruled in Jerusalem for three months. His mother was Nehushta, the daughter of Elnathan from Jerusalem. 9 Following the example of his father, Jehoiachin sinned against the LORD.

460

2 Kings

Judges
Ruth
1 Sam.
2 Sam.
1 Kings

2 KINGS 24, 25

READ THIS
PASSAGE,

CLOSE THE BOOK

& REFLECT
ON WHAT

HAPPENED IN THE

PASSAGE.

[10] It was during his reign that the Babylonian army, commanded by King Nebuchadnezzar's officers, marched against Jerusalem and besieged it. [11] During the siege Nebuchadnezzar himself came to Jerusalem, [12] and King Jehoiachin, along with his mother, his sons, his officers, and the palace officials, surrendered to the Babylonians. In the eighth year of Nebuchadnezzar's reign he took Jehoiachin prisoner [13] and carried off to Babylon all the treasures in the Temple and the palace. As the LORD had foretold, Nebuchadnezzar broke up all the gold utensils which King Solomon had made for use in the Temple. [14] Nebuchadnezzar carried away as prisoners the people of Jerusalem, all the royal princes, and all the leading men, 10,000 in all. He also deported all the skilled workmen, including the blacksmiths, leaving only the poorest of the people behind in Judah.

[15] Nebuchadnezzar took Jehoiachin to Babylon as a prisoner, together with Jehoiachin's mother, his wives, his officials, and the leading men of Judah. [16] Nebuchadnezzar deported all the important men to Babylonia, 7,000 in all, and 1,000 skilled workers, including the blacksmiths, all of them able-bodied men fit for military duty.

[17] Nebuchadnezzar made Jehoiachin's uncle Mattaniah king of Judah and changed his name to Zedekiah.

King Zedekiah of Judah
(2 Chr 36.11–12; Jer 52.1–3a)

[18] Zedekiah was 21 years old when he became king of Judah, and he ruled in Jerusalem for eleven years. His mother was Hamutal, the daughter of Jeremiah from the city of Libnah. [19] King Zedekiah sinned against the LORD, just as King Jehoiakim had done. [20] The LORD became so angry with the people of Jerusalem and Judah that he banished them from his sight.

The Fall of Jerusalem
(2 Chr 36.13–21; Jer 52.3b–11)

25 Zedekiah rebelled against King Nebuchadnezzar of Babylonia, so Nebuchadnezzar came with all his army and attacked Jerusalem on the tenth day of the tenth month of the ninth year of Zedekiah's reign. They set up camp outside the city, built siege walls round it, [2] and kept it under siege until Zedekiah's eleventh year. [3] On the ninth day of the fourth month* of that same year, when the famine was so bad that the people had nothing left to eat, [4] the city walls were broken through. Although the Babylonians were surrounding the city, all the soldiers escaped during the night. They left by way of the royal garden, went through the gateway connecting the two walls, and fled in the direction of the Jordan Valley. [5] But the Babylonian army pursued King Zedekiah, captured him in the plains near Jericho, and all his soldiers deserted him. [6] Zedekiah was taken to King Nebuchadnezzar, who was in the city of Riblah, and there Nebuchadnezzar passed sentence on him. [7] While Zedekiah was looking on, his sons were put to death; then Nebuchadnezzar had Zedekiah's eyes put out, placed him in chains, and took him to Babylon.

The Destruction of the Temple
(Jer 52.12–23)

[8] On the seventh day of the fifth month of the nineteenth year of King Nebuchadnezzar of Babylonia, Nebuzaradan, adviser to

25.3 Probable text (see Jer 52.6) *the fourth month*; Hebrew *the month*.

2 KINGS 25

461

2 Kings
·········:·

1 Chron.
2 Chron.
Ezra
Nehem.
Esther

the king and commander of his army, entered Jerusalem. [9] He burnt down the Temple, the palace, and the houses of all the important people in Jerusalem, [10] and his soldiers tore down the city walls. [11] Then Nebuzaradan took away to Babylonia the people who were left in the city, the remaining skilled workmen,[*] and those who had deserted to the Babylonians. [12] But he left in Judah some of the poorest people, who owned no property, and put them to work in the vineyards and fields.

[13] The Babylonians broke in pieces the bronze columns and the carts that were in the Temple, together with the large bronze tank, and they took all the bronze to Babylon. [14] They also took away the shovels and the ash containers used in cleaning the altar, the tools used in tending the lamps, the bowls used for catching the blood from the sacrifices, the bowls used for burning incense, and all the other bronze articles used in the temple service. [15] They took away everything that was made of gold or silver, including the small bowls and the pans used for carrying live coals. [16] The bronze objects that King Solomon had made for the Temple — the two columns, the carts, and the large tank — were too heavy to weigh. [17] The two columns were identical: each one was eight metres high, with a bronze capital on top, 1.3 metres high. All round each capital was a bronze grating decorated with pomegranates made of bronze.

The People of Judah are Taken to Babylonia
(Jer 52.24–27)

[18] In addition, Nebuzaradan, the commanding officer, took away as prisoners Seraiah the High Priest, Zephaniah the priest next in rank, and the three other important temple officials. [19] From the city he took the officer who had been in command of the troops, five of the king's personal advisers who were still in the city, the commander's assistant, who was in charge of military records, and sixty other important men. [20] Nebuzaradan took them to the king of Babylonia, who was in the city of Riblah [21] in the territory of Hamath. There the king had them beaten and put to death.

So the people of Judah were carried away from their land into exile.

Gedaliah, Governor of Judah
(Jer 40.7–9; 41.1–3)

[22] King Nebuchadnezzar of Babylonia made Gedaliah, the son of Ahikam and grandson of Shaphan, governor of Judah, and placed him in charge of all those who had not been taken away to Babylonia. [23] When the Judean officers and soldiers who had not surrendered heard about this, they joined Gedaliah at Mizpah. These officers were Ishmael son of Nethaniah, Johanan son of Kareah, Seraiah son of Tanhumeth, from the town of Netophah, and Jezaniah from Maacah. [24] Gedaliah said to them, "I give you my word that there is no need for you to be afraid of the Babylonian officials. Settle in this land, serve the king of Babylonia, and all will go well with you."

[25] But in the seventh month of that year, Ishmael, the son of Nethaniah and grandson of Elishama, a member of the royal family, went to Mizpah with ten men, attacked Gedaliah and killed him. He also killed the Israelites and Babylonians who were there with him. [26] Then all the Israelites, rich and poor alike, together with the army officers, left and went to Egypt, because they were afraid of the Babylonians.

· ·

25.11 Probable text (see Jer 52.15) *skilled workmen*; Hebrew *crowd*.

462

2 Kings

⋮⋯⋯⋯⋯

Judges
Ruth
1 Sam.
2 Sam.
1 Kings

2 KINGS 25

Jehoiachin is Released from Prison
(Jer 52.31–34)

²⁷In the year that Evilmerodach became king of Babylonia, he showed kindness to King Jehoiachin of Judah by releasing him from prison. This happened on the 27th day of the twelfth month of the 37th year after Jehoiachin had been taken away as prisoner. ²⁸Evilmerodach treated him kindly, and gave him a position of greater honour than he gave the other kings who were exiles with him in Babylonia. ²⁹So Jehoiachin was permitted to change from his prison clothes and to dine at the king's table for the rest of his life. ³⁰Each day, for as long as he lived, he was given a regular allowance for his needs.

THE BOOK OF
1 CHRONICLES

WRITTEN: LATER THAN 1 AND 2 KINGS (PROBABLY 350-300BC)

KEY CHARACTER:

Chapter 11 gives the names of David's most trusted soldiers - 'The Three' and another 'Famous Thirty'. These were his elite fighters who he kept close to him because he knew that they would lay down their lives for him. They showed strength, bravery and commitment, and were willing to give everything for what they believed in.

In this space, doodle some of your life's highlights and times when you have seen God being faithful to you.
Use it as a celebration of your story.

WHAT YOU NEED TO KNOW:

1 and 2 Chronicles were originally one book, thought to have been written after the Jews had returned from exile in Babylon. This book is more interested in story than historical accuracy, intended as an encouragement to the Jewish people. It highlights the times when people did follow God rather than when they weren't faithful to him, and shows the lessons learned from history. The writer focuses on God's promises, people's achievements and the origin of worship and the Temple.

WHY READ IT?

This book is a cheery recap of Israel's history, up to the death of King David. It opens with a long list of names, but this is to give some context to the people's story. It's an encouragement to see God's faithfulness to people who keep going even when things go wrong.

NG SAUL DIES

DAVID BECOMES KING

KING DAVID DIES

960BC

464

1 Chron.

Ruth
1 Sam.
2 Sam.
1 Kings
2 Kings

1 CHRONICLES 1

1 CHRONICLES 1.1-27

Lists of names can be hard work to read. Here you have a direct line from Adam to Abraham. Matthew chapter 1 tells us that there's a direct line from Abraham to Jesus, so this is the first part of the link

• FROM ADAM •

TO JESUS,

who is described as the second Adam in 1 Corinthians 15.47.

From Adam to Abraham
(Gen 5.1–32; 10.1–32; 11.10–26)

1 Adam was the father of Seth, Seth was the father of Enosh, Enosh the father of Kenan, ²Kenan the father of Mahalalel, Mahalalel the father of Jared. ³Jared was the father of Enoch, who was the father of Methuselah; Methuselah was the father of Lamech, ⁴who was the father of Noah. Noah had three sons: Shem, Ham, and Japheth.

⁵The sons of Japheth — Gomer, Magog, Madai, Javan, Tubal, Meshech, and Tiras — were the ancestors of the peoples who bear their names. ⁶The descendants of Gomer were the people of Ashkenaz, Riphath, and Togarmah. ⁷The descendants of Javan were the people of Elishah, Spain, Cyprus, and Rhodes.

⁸The sons of Ham — Cush, Egypt, Libya, and Canaan — were the ancestors of the peoples who bear their names. ⁹The descendants of Cush were the people of Seba, Havilah, Sabtah, Raamah, and Sabteca. The descendants of Raamah were the people of Sheba and Dedan. ¹⁰(Cush had a son named Nimrod, who became the world's first great conqueror.) ¹¹The descendants of Egypt were the people of Lydia, Anam, Lehab, Naphtuh, ¹²Pathrus, Casluh, and of Crete (from whom the Philistines were descended). ¹³Canaan's sons — Sidon, the eldest, and Heth — were the ancestors of the peoples who bear their names. ¹⁴Canaan was also the ancestor of the Jebusites, the Amorites, Girgashites, ¹⁵Hivites, Arkites, Sinites, ¹⁶Arvadites, Zemarites, and Hamathites.

¹⁷Shem's sons — Elam, Asshur, Arpachshad, Lud, Aram, Uz, Hul, Gether, and Meshek — were the ancestors of the peoples who bear their names. ¹⁸Arpachshad was the father of Shelah, who was the father of Eber. ¹⁹Eber had two sons; one was named Peleg,* because during his time the people of the world were divided, and the other was named Joktan. ²⁰The descendants of Joktan were the people of Almodad, Sheleph, Hazarmaveth, Jerah, ²¹Hadoram, Uzal, Diklah, ²²Ebal, Abimael, Sheba, ²³Ophir, Havilah, and Jobab.

²⁴The family line from Shem to Abram is as follows: Shem, Arpachshad, Shelah, ²⁵Eber, Peleg, Reu, ²⁶Serug, Nahor, Terah, ²⁷and Abram (also known as Abraham).

The Descendants of Ishmael
(Gen 25.12–16)

²⁸Abraham had two sons, Isaac and Ishmael. ²⁹The sons of Ishmael became the heads of twelve tribes: Nebaioth (from the name of Ishmael's eldest son), Kedar, Adbeel, Mibsam, ³⁰Mishma, Dumah, Massa, Hadad, Tema, ³¹Jetur, Naphish, and Kedemah.

³²Abraham had a concubine named Keturah, who bore him six sons: Zimran, Jokshan, Medan, Midian, Ishbak, and Shuah. Jokshan had two sons: Sheba and Dedan. ³³Midian had five sons: Ephah, Epher, Hanoch, Abida, and Eldaah.

The Descendants of Esau
(Gen 36.1–19)

³⁴Abraham's son Isaac had two sons, Esau and Jacob. ³⁵Esau's sons were Eliphaz, Reuel, Jeush, Jalam, and Korah. ³⁶Eliphaz became the ancestor of the following tribes: Teman, Omar, Zephi, Gatam, Kenaz, Timna, and Amalek. ³⁷And Reuel became the ancestor of the tribes of Nahath, Zerah, Shammah, and Mizzah.

1.19 *Peleg*: This name sounds like the Hebrew for "divide".

1 Chron.

· · · · · · · ·⟶

2 Chron.

Ezra

Nehem.

Esther

Job

The Original Inhabitants of Edom
(Gen 36.20–30)

38-42 The original inhabitants of Edom were descended from the following sons of Seir:

> Lotan, who was the ancestor of the clans of Hori and Homam. (Lotan had a sister named Timna.)

> Shobal, who was the ancestor of the clans of Alvan, Manahath, Ebal, Shephi, and Onam.

> Zibeon, who had two sons, Aiah and Anah. Anah was the father of Dishon, and Dishon was the ancestor of the clans of Hamran, Eshban, Ithran, and Cheran.

> Ezer, who was the ancestor of the clans of Bilhan, Zaavan, and Jaakan.

> Dishan, who was the ancestor of the clans of Uz and Aran.

The Kings of Edom
(Gen 36.31–43)

43-50 The following kings ruled the land of Edom one after the other, in the time before there were any kings in Israel:

> Bela son of Beor from Dinhabah

> Johab son of Zerah from Bozrah

> Husham from the region of Teman

> Hadad son of Bedad from Avith (he defeated the Midianites in a battle in the country of Moab)

> Samlah from Masrekah

> Shaul from Rehoboth-on-the-River

> Baal Hanan son of Achbor

> Hadad from Pau (his wife was Mehetabel, the daughter of Matred and granddaughter of Mezahab).

51 The people of Edom were divided into the following tribes: Timna, Alvah, Jetheth, 52 Oholibamah, Elah, Pinon, 53 Kenaz, Teman, Mibzar, 54 Magdiel, and Iram.

The Descendants of Judah

2 Jacob had twelve sons: Reuben, Simeon, Levi, Judah, Issachar, Zebulun, 2 Dan, Joseph, Benjamin, Naphtali, Gad, and Asher.
3 Judah had five sons in all. By his wife Bathshua, a Canaanite, he had three sons: Er, Onan, and Shelah. His eldest son, Er, was so evil that the LORD killed him. 4 By his daughter-in-law Tamar, Judah had two more sons, Perez and Zerah.
5 Perez had two sons, Hezron and Hamul. 6 His brother Zerah had five sons: Zimri, Ethan, Heman, Calcol, and Darda. 7 Achan* son of Carmi, one of Zerah's descendants, brought disaster on the people of Israel by keeping loot that had been devoted to God.
8 Ethan had one son, Azariah.

The Family Tree of King David

9 Hezron had three sons: Jerahmeel, Ram, and Caleb.
10 The family line from Ram to Jesse is as follows: Ram, Amminadab, Nahshon (a prominent man of the tribe of Judah), 11 Salmon, Boaz, 12 Obed, and Jesse.
13 Jesse had seven sons. In order of age they were: Eliab, Abinadab, Shammah, 14 Nethanel, Raddai, 15 Ozem, and David.
16 He also had two daughters, Zeruiah and Abigail.

2.7 *Achan*: This is his name in Josh 7.1. The Hebrew text here calls him "Achar", which means "disaster".

466   1 CHRONICLES 2

1 Chron.

Ruth
1 Sam.
2 Sam.
1 Kings
2 Kings

Jesse's daughter Zeruiah had three sons: Abishai, Joab, and Asahel. [17]His other daughter Abigail married Jether, a descendant of Ishmael, and they had a son named Amasa.

The Descendants of Hezron
[18]Hezron's son Caleb married Azubah and had a daughter named Jerioth. She had* three sons: Jesher, Shobab, and Ardon. [19]After the death of Azubah, Caleb married Ephrath, and they had a son named Hur. [20]Hur's son was Uri, and his grandson was Bezalel.

[21]When Hezron was sixty years old, he married Machir's daughter, the sister of Gilead. They had a son named Segub, [22]and Segub had a son named Jair. Jair ruled* 23 cities in the territory of Gilead. [23]But the kingdoms of Geshur and Aram conquered sixty towns there, including the villages of Jair and Kenath, and the towns near by. All the people who lived there were descendants of Machir, the father of Gilead. [24]After Hezron died, his son Caleb married Ephrath, his father's widow.* They had a son named Ashhur, who founded the town of Tekoa.

The Descendants of Jerahmeel
[25]Jerahmeel, the eldest son of Hezron, had five sons: Ram, the eldest, Bunah, Oren, Ozem, and Ahijah. [26-27]Ram had three sons: Maaz, Jamin, and Eker. Jerahmeel had another wife, a woman named Atarah, and they had a son, Onam. [28]Onam had two sons, Shammai and Jada, and Shammai also had two sons, Nadab and Abishur.

[29]Abishur married a woman named Abihail, and they had two sons, Ahban and Molid. [30]Abishur's brother Nadab had two sons, Seled and Appaim, but Seled died without having any sons. [31]Appaim was the father of Ishi, Ishi was the father of Sheshan, and Sheshan the father of Ahlai.

[32]Jada, the brother of Shammai, had two sons, Jether and Jonathan, but Jether died without having any sons. [33]Jonathan had two sons, Peleth and Zaza. All these were descendants of Jerahmeel.

[34]Sheshan had no sons, only daughters. He had an Egyptian servant named Jarha, [35]to whom he gave one of his daughters in marriage. They had a son named Attai. [36]The family line from Attai to Elishama is as follows: Attai, Nathan, Zabad, [37]Ephlal, Obed, [38]Jehu, Azariah, [39]Helez, Eleasah, [40]Sismai, Shallum, [41]Jekamiah, and Elishama.

Other Descendants of Caleb
[42]The eldest son of Caleb, Jerahmeel's brother, was named Mesha. Mesha was the father of Ziph, who was the father of Mareshah, who was the father of Hebron.* [43]Hebron had four sons: Korah, Tappuah, Rekem, and Shema. [44]Shema was the father of Raham and the grandfather of Jorkeam. Rekem, Shema's brother, was the father of Shammai, [45]who was the father of Maon, who was the father of Bethzur.

[46]Caleb had a concubine named Ephah, and by her he had three more sons: Haran, Moza, and Gazez. Haran also had a son named Gazez.

2.18 Some ancient translations *had a daughter… She had*; Hebrew unclear.
2.22 *ruled*; or *owned*.
2.24 Some ancient translations *his son… widow*; Hebrew unclear.
2.42 Probable text *father of Mareshah… Hebron*; Hebrew unclear.

1 Chron.
....
2 Chron.
Ezra
Nehem.
Esther
Job

JOIN THE DOTS

below to make a picture.

47(A man named Jahdai had six sons: Regem, Jotham, Geshan, Pelet, Ephah, and Shaaph.)

48Caleb had another concubine, Maacah, who bore him two sons, Sheber and Tirhanah. 49Later she had two more sons: Shaaph, who founded the town of Madmannah; and Shevah, who founded the towns of Machbenah and Gibea.

In addition, Caleb had a daughter named Achsah.

50The following are also descendants of Caleb.

Hur was the eldest son of Caleb and his wife Ephrath. Hur's son Shobal founded Kiriath Jearim, 51his second son Salma founded Bethlehem, and his third son Hareph founded Bethgader.

52Shobal, the founder of Kiriath Jearim, was the ancestor of the people of Haroeh, of half the inhabitants of Menuhoth, 53and of the following clans that lived in Kiriath Jearim: the Ithrites, Puthites, Shumathites, and Mishraites. (The people of the cities of Zorah and Eshtaol were members of these clans.)

54Salma, the founder of Bethlehem, was the ancestor of the people of Netophath, of Atroth Beth Joab, and of the Zorites, who were one of the two clans in Manahath.

55(The following clans of experts in writing and copying documents lived in the town of Jabez: the Tirathites, Shimeathites, and Sucathites. They were Kenites who had intermarried with the Rechabites.)

King David's Children

3 1-3The following, in order of age, are David's sons who were born while he was in Hebron:

Amnon, whose mother was Ahinoam from Jezreel

Daniel, whose mother was Abigail from Carmel

Absalom, whose mother was Maacah, daughter of King Talmai of Geshur

Adonijah, whose mother was Haggith

Shephatiah, whose mother was Abital

Ithream, whose mother was Eglah.

4All six were born in Hebron during the seven and a half years that David ruled there.

In Jerusalem he ruled as king for 33 years, 5and many sons were born to him there.

His wife Bathsheba, daughter of Ammiel, bore him four sons: Shimea, Shobab, Nathan, and Solomon.

6He had nine other sons: Ibhar, Elishua, Elpelet, 7Nogah, Nepheg, Japhia, 8Elishama, Eliada, and Eliphelet. 9In addition to all these sons, David had sons by his concubines. He also had a daughter, Tamar.

The Descendants of King Solomon

10This is the line of King Solomon's descendants from father to son: Solomon, Rehoboam, Abijah, Asa, Jehoshaphat, 11Jehoram, Ahaziah, Joash, 12Amaziah, Uzziah, Jotham, 13Ahaz, Hezekiah, Manasseh, 14Amon, and Josiah. 15Josiah had four sons: Johanan, Jehoiakim, Zedekiah, and Joahaz. 16Jehoiakim had two sons: Jehoiachin and Zedekiah.

The Descendants of King Jehoiachin

17These are the descendants of King Jehoiachin, who was taken prisoner by the Babylonians. Jehoiachin had seven sons: Shealtiel, 18Malchiram, Pedaiah, Shenazzar, Jekamiah, Hoshama, and Nedabiah. 19Pedaiah had two sons, Zerubbabel and Shimei. Zerubbabel was the father of two sons, Meshullam and Hananiah,

468

1 Chron.

Ruth
1 Sam.
2 Sam.
1 Kings
2 Kings

1 CHRONICLES 3, 4

and one daughter, Shelomith. ²⁰He had five other sons: Hashubah, Ohel, Berechiah, Hasadiah, and Jushab Hesed.

²¹Hananiah had two sons, Pelatiah and Jeshaiah. Jeshaiah was the father of Rephaiah, who was the father of Arnan, the father of Obadiah, the father of Shecaniah.* ²²Shecaniah had one son, Shemaiah, and five grandsons: Hattush, Igal, Bariah, Neariah, and Shaphat. ²³Neariah had three sons: Elioenai, Hizkiah, and Azrikam. ²⁴Elioenai had seven sons: Hodaviah, Eliashib, Pelaiah, Akkub, Johanan, Delaiah, and Anani.

The Descendants of Judah

4 These are some of the descendants of Judah: Perez, Hezron, Carmi, Hur, and Shobal. ²Shobal was the father of Reaiah, who was the father of Jahath, the father of Ahumai and Lahad, the ancestors of the people who lived in Zorah.

³⁻⁴Hur was the eldest son of his father Caleb's wife Ephrath, and his descendants founded the city of Bethlehem. Hur had three sons: Etam, Penuel, and Ezer. Etam had three sons:* Jezreel, Ishma, and Idbash, and one daughter, Hazzelelponi. Penuel founded the city of Gedor, and Ezer founded Hushah.

⁵Ashhur, who founded the town of Tekoa, had two wives, Helah and Naarah. ⁶He and Naarah had four sons: Ahuzzam, Hepher, Temeni, and Haahashtari. ⁷Ashhur and Helah had three sons: Zereth, Izhar, and Ethnan.

⁸Koz was the father of Anub and Zobebah, and the ancestor of the clans descended from Aharhel son of Harum.

⁹There was a man named Jabez, who was the most respected member of his family. His mother had given him the name Jabez,* because his birth had been very painful. ¹⁰But Jabez prayed to the God of Israel, "Bless me, God, and give me much land. Be with me and keep me from anything evil that might cause me pain." And God gave him what he prayed for.

Other Family Lists

¹¹Caleb, the brother of Shuhah, had a son, Mehir. Mehir was the father of Eshton, ¹²who had three sons: Bethrapha, Paseah, and Tehinnah. Tehinnah was the founder of the city of Nahash. The descendants of these men lived in Recah.

¹³Kenaz had two sons, Othniel and Seraiah. Othniel also had two sons, Hathath and Meonothai.* ¹⁴Meonothai was the father of Ophrah.

Seraiah was the father of Joab, the founder of the Valley of Craftsmen, where all the people were skilled workmen.

¹⁵Caleb son of Jephunneh had three sons: Iru, Elah, and Naam. And Elah was the father of Kenaz.

¹⁶Jehallelel had four sons: Ziph, Ziphah, Tiria, and Asarel.

¹⁷⁻¹⁸Ezrah had four sons: Jether, Mered, Epher, and Jalon. Mered married Bithiah, a daughter of the king of Egypt, and they had a daughter, Miriam, and two sons, Shammai and Ishbah. Ishbah founded the town of Eshtemoa. Mered also married a woman from the tribe of Judah, and they had three sons: Jered, who founded the town of Gedor; Heber, founder of the town of Soco; and Jekuthiel, founder of the town of Zanoah.

3.21 Verse 21 in Hebrew is unclear.
4.3–4 Some ancient translations *sons*; Hebrew *fathers*.
4.9 *Jabez*: This name sounds like the Hebrew for "pain".
4.13 Some ancient translations *Meonothai*; Hebrew does not have this name.

1 CHRONICLES 4

469

1 Chron.

2 Chron.

Ezra

Nehem.

Esther

Job

¹⁹Hodiah married the sister of Naham. Their descendants founded the clan of Garm, which lived in the town of Keilah, and the clan of Maacath, which lived in the town of Eshtemoa.*
²⁰Shimon had four sons: Amnon, Rinnah, Benhanan, and Tilon. Ishi had two sons: Zoheth and Benzoheth.

The Descendants of Shelah
²¹Shelah was one of Judah's sons. His descendants included Er, who founded the town of Lecah; Laadah, founder of the town of Mareshah; the clan of linen weavers, who lived in the town of Beth Ashbea; ²²Jokim and the people who lived in the town of Cozeba; and Joash and Saraph, who married Moabite women and then settled in Bethlehem.* (These traditions are very old.) ²³They were potters in the service of the king and lived in the towns of Netaim and Gederah.

The Descendants of Simeon
²⁴Simeon had five sons: Nemuel, Jamin, Jarib, Zerah, and Shaul. ²⁵Shaul's son was Shallum, his grandson was Mibsam, and his great-grandson was Mishma. ²⁶Then from Mishma the line descended through Hammuel, Zaccur, and Shimei. ²⁷Shimei had sixteen sons and six daughters, but his relatives had fewer children, and the tribe of Simeon did not grow as much as the tribe of Judah did.

²⁸Down to the time of King David the descendants of Simeon lived in the following towns: Beersheba, Moladah, Hazarshual, ²⁹Bilhah, Ezem, Tolad, ³⁰Bethuel, Hormah, Ziklag, ³¹Beth Marcaboth, Hazarsusim, Bethbiri, and Shaaraim. ³²They also lived in five other places: Etam, Ain, Rimmon, Tochen, and Ashan, ³³and the surrounding villages, as far south-west as the town of Baalath. These are the records which they kept of their families and of the places where they lived.

³⁴⁻³⁸The following men were the heads of their clans:

Meshobab, Jamlech, Joshah son of Amaziah, Joel,

Jehu (the son of Joshibiah, the son of Seraiah, the son of Asiel),

Elioenai, Jaakobah, Jeshohaiah, Asaiah, Adiel, Jesimiel, Benaiah,

Ziza (the son of Shiphi, the son of Allon, a descendant of Jedaiah, Shimri, and Shemaiah).

Because their families continued to grow, ³⁹they spread out westwards almost to Gerar* and pastured their sheep on the eastern side of the valley in which that city is located. ⁴⁰They found plenty of fertile pasture lands there in a stretch of open country that was quiet and peaceful. The people who had lived there before were Hamites.

⁴¹In the time of King Hezekiah of Judah, the men named above went to Gerar and destroyed the tents and huts of the people who lived there.* They drove the people out and settled there permanently because there was plenty of pasture for their sheep. ⁴²500 other members of the tribe of Simeon went east to Edom. They were led by the sons of Ishi: Pelatiah, Neariah, Rephaiah, and Uzziel. ⁴³There they killed the surviving Amalekites, and they have lived there ever since.

....

4.19 Verse 19 in Hebrew is unclear.
4.22 Probable text settled in Bethlehem; Hebrew unclear.
4.39 Some ancient translations Gerar; Hebrew Gedor.
4.41 the tents and huts... there; or the tents of the people who lived there, and the Meunites also.

470

1 Chron.

Ruth
1 Sam.
2 Sam.
1 Kings
2 Kings

EXILE

2 KINGS 17.23;
1 CHRONICLES 5.22;
ISAIAH 14.1

Search for the Oxford
or Cambridge Dictionary
definition of 'exile'
and write the
definition here. ➘

_____

_____

_____

_____

_____

_____

_____

_____

_____

_____

_____

_____

_____

_____

_____

_____

The Descendants of Reuben

5 These are the descendants of Reuben, the eldest of Jacob's sons. (Because he had intercourse with one of his father's concubines, he lost the rights belonging to the firstborn son, and those rights were given to Joseph. [2] It was the tribe of Judah, however, that became the strongest and provided a ruler for all the tribes.) [3] Reuben, the eldest of Jacob's sons, had four sons: Hanoch, Pallu, Hezron, and Carmi.

[4-6] These are the descendants of Joel from generation to generation: Shemaiah, Gog, Shimei, Micah, Reaiah, Baal, and Beerah. The Assyrian emperor, Tiglath Pileser, captured Beerah, a leader of the tribe, and deported him.

[7] The family records list the following clan leaders in the tribe of Reuben: Jeiel, Zechariah, [8] and Bela, the son of Azaz and grandson of Shema, of the clan of Joel. This clan lived in Aroer and in the territory from there north to Nebo and Baal Meon. [9] They had large herds in the land of Gilead, and so they occupied the land as far east as the desert that stretches all the way to the River Euphrates.

[10] In the time of King Saul the tribe of Reuben attacked the Hagrites, killed them in battle, and occupied their land in the eastern part of Gilead.

The Descendants of Gad

[11] The tribe of Gad lived to the north of Reuben in the land of Bashan as far east as Salecah. [12] Joel was the founder of the leading clan, and Shapham of the second most important clan. Janai and Shaphat were founders of other clans in Bashan. [13] The other members of the tribe belonged to the following seven clans: Michael, Meshullam, Sheba, Jorai, Jacan, Zia, and Eber. [14] They were descendants of Abihail son of Huri, whose ancestors were traced back as follows: Abihail, Huri, Jaroah, Gilead, Michael, Jeshishai, Jahdo, Buz. [15] Ahi, the son of Abdiel and grandson of Guni, was head of these clans. [16] They lived in the territory of Bashan and Gilead, in the towns there and all over the pasture lands of Sharon. [17] (These records were compiled in the days of King Jotham of Judah and King Jeroboam II of Israel.)

The Armies of the Eastern Tribes

[18] In the tribes of Reuben, Gad, and East Manasseh there were 44,760 soldiers, well trained in the use of shields, swords, and bows. [19] They went to war against the Hagrite tribes of Jetur, Naphish, and Nodab. [20] They put their trust in God and prayed to him for help, and God answered their prayers and made them victorious over the Hagrites and their allies. [21] They captured from the enemy 50,000 camels, 250,000 sheep, and 2,000 donkeys, and took 100,000 prisoners of war. [22] They killed many of the enemy, because the war was God's will. And they went on living in that territory until the exile.*

The People of East Manasseh

[23] The people of East Manasseh settled in the territory of Bashan as far north as Baal Hermon, Senir, and Mount Hermon, and their population increased greatly. [24] The following were the heads of their clans: Epher, Ishi, Eliel, Azriel, Jeremiah, Hodaviah,

....

5.22 *the exile*: About 733 BC the Assyrians conquered northern Israel and the Israelite territory east of the River Jordan and deported the people (see 2 Kgs 15.29).

471

1 Chron.

2 Chron.
Ezra
Nehem.
Esther
Job

and Jahdiel. They were all outstanding soldiers, well-known leaders of their clans.

The Eastern Tribes are Deported

25 But the people were unfaithful to the God of their ancestors and deserted him to worship the gods of the nations whom God had driven out of the land. 26 So God made Emperor Pul of Assyria (also known as Tiglath Pileser) invade their country. He deported the tribes of Reuben, Gad, and East Manasseh and settled them permanently in Halah, Habor, and Hara, and by the River Gozan.

The Family Line of the High Priests

6 Levi had three sons: Gershon, Kohath, and Merari. 2 Kohath had four sons: Amram, Izhar, Hebron, and Uzziel. 3 Amram had two sons, Aaron and Moses, and one daughter, Miriam.

Aaron had four sons: Nadab, Abihu, Eleazar, and Ithamar. 4 The descendants of Eleazar from generation to generation are as follows: Phinehas, Abishua, 5 Bukki, Uzzi, 6 Zerahiah, Meraioth, 7 Amariah, Ahitub, 8 Zadok, Ahimaaz, 9 Azariah, Johanan, 10 Azariah (the one who served in the Temple which King Solomon built in Jerusalem), 11 Amariah, Ahitub, 12 Zadok, Shallum, 13 Hilkiah, Azariah, 14 Seraiah, Jehozadak. 15 King Nebuchadnezzar deported Jehozadak along with the other people of Judah and Jerusalem whom the LORD sent into exile.

Other Descendants of Levi

16 Levi had three sons: Gershon, Kohath, and Merari. 17 Each of them also had sons. Gershon was the father of Libni and Shimei; 18 Kohath was the father of Amram, Izhar, Hebron, and Uzziel; 19 and Merari was the father of Mahli and Mushi.

20 These are the descendants of Gershon from generation to generation: Libni, Jahath, Zimmah, 21 Joah, Iddo, Zerah, Jeatherai. 22 These are the descendants of Kohath from generation to generation: Amminadab, Korah, Assir, 23 Elkanah, Ebiasaph, Assir, 24 Tahath, Uriel, Uzziah, Shaul. 25 Elkanah had two sons, Amasai and Ahimoth. 26 These are Ahimoth's descendants from generation to generation: Elkanah, Zophai, Nahath, 27 Eliab, Jeroham, Elkanah. 28 Samuel had two sons: Joel,* the elder, and Abijah, the younger. 29 These are the descendants of Merari from generation to generation: Mahli, Libni, Shimei, Uzzah, 30 Shimea, Haggiah, Asaiah.

The Temple Musicians

31 These are the men whom King David put in charge of the music at the place of worship in Jerusalem after the Covenant Box was moved there. 32 They took regular turns of duty at the Tent of the LORD's presence during the time before King Solomon built the Temple. 33 The family lines of those who held this office are as follows:

The clan of Kohath: Heman, the leader of the first choir, was the son of Joel. His family line went back to Jacob as follows: Heman, Joel, Samuel, 34 Elkanah, Jeroham, Eliel, Toah, 35 Zuph, Elkanah, Mahath, Amasai, 36 Elkanah, Joel, Azariah, Zephaniah, 37 Tahath, Assir, Ebiasaph, Korah, 38 Izhar, Kohath, Levi, Jacob.

1 CHRONICLES 6

The tribe of Levi were the family of Moses and his brother Aaron, who was the first high priest. As priests, they were set apart with a

• SPECIAL •
CALLING

from God and direct access to him. This meant that the purity of their line was really important.

6.28 Some ancient translations (see also 1 Sam 8.2) *Joel*; Hebrew does not have this name.

472

1 Chron.

Ruth

1 Sam.

2 Sam.

1 Kings

2 Kings

1 CHRONICLES 6

[39] Asaph was leader of the second choir. His family line went back to Levi as follows: Asaph, Berechiah, Shimea, [40] Michael, Baaseiah, Malchijah, [41] Ethni, Zerah, Adaiah, [42] Ethan, Zimmah, Shimei, [43] Jahath, Gershon, Levi.

[44] Ethan of the clan of Merari was the leader of the third choir. His family line went back to Levi as follows: Ethan, Kishi, Abdi, Malluch, [45] Hashabiah, Amaziah, Hilkiah, [46] Amzi, Bani, Shemer, [47] Mahli, Mushi, Merari, Levi.

[48] The other Levites were assigned all the other duties at the place of worship.

The Descendants of Aaron

[49] Aaron and his descendants presented the offerings of incense and offered the sacrifices that were burnt on the altar. They were responsible for all the worship in the Most Holy Place and for the sacrifices by which God forgives Israel's sins. They did all this in accordance with the instructions given by Moses, God's servant. [50] This is the line of Aaron's descendants: Eleazar, Phinehas, Abishua, [51] Bukki, Uzzi, Zerahiah, [52] Meraioth, Amariah, Ahitub, [53] Zadok, Ahimaaz.

Where the Levites Lived

[54] This is the territory assigned to the descendants of Aaron of the clan of Kohath. They received the first share of the land assigned to the Levites. [55] This included Hebron in the territory of Judah and the pasture lands round it. [56] The fields and villages, however, that belonged to the city were assigned to Caleb son of Jephunneh. [57-59] The following towns were assigned to Aaron's descendants: Hebron, a city of refuge,* Jattir, and the towns of Libnah, Eshtemoa, Hilen, Debir, Ashan, and Beth Shemesh, with their pasture lands. [60] In the territory of Benjamin they were assigned the following towns with their pasture lands: Geba, Alemeth, and Anathoth. This made a total of thirteen towns for all their families to live in. [61] Ten towns in the territory of West Manasseh were assigned by lot to the rest of the clan of Kohath, family by family.

[62] To the clan of Gershon, family by family, were assigned thirteen towns in the territories of Issachar, Asher, Naphtali, and East Manasseh in Bashan. [63] In the same way, twelve towns in the territories of Reuben, Gad, and Zebulun were assigned to the clan of Merari, family by family. [64] In this way the people of Israel assigned towns for the Levites to live in, together with the pasture lands round the towns. [65] (The towns in the territories of Judah, Simeon, and Benjamin, mentioned above, were also assigned by drawing lots.)

[66] Some of the families of the clan of Kohath were assigned towns and pasture lands in the territory of Ephraim: [67] Shechem, the city of refuge in the hills of Ephraim, Gezer, [68] Jokmeam, Beth Horon, [69] Aijalon, and Gath Rimmon. [70] In the territory of West Manasseh they were assigned the towns of Aner and Bileam with the surrounding pasture lands.

[71] The families of the clan of Gershon were assigned the following towns, with the surrounding pasture lands:

In the territory of East Manasseh: Golan in Bashan, and Ashtaroth.

[72] In the territory of Issachar: Kedesh, Daberath, [73] Ramoth, and Anem.

6.57–59 *city of refuge*: If anyone accidentally killed someone, he could escape to one of these cities and be safe from revenge (see Josh 20.1–9).

1 CHRONICLES 6, 7

473

1 Chron.

2 Chron.
Ezra
Nehem.
Esther
Job

⁷⁴ In the territory of Asher: Mashal, Abdon, ⁷⁵ Hukok, and Rehob.
⁷⁶ In the territory of Naphtali: Kedesh in Galilee, Hammon, and Kiriathaim.

⁷⁷ The remaining families of the clan of Merari were assigned the following towns with the surrounding pasture lands:

In the territory of Zebulun: Rimmono and Tabor.

⁷⁸ In the territory of Reuben, east of the River Jordan beyond Jericho: Bezer on the plateau, Jahzah, ⁷⁹ Kedemoth, and Mephaath.

⁸⁰ In the territory of Gad: Ramoth in Gilead, Mahanaim, ⁸¹ Heshbon, and Jazer.

The Descendants of Issachar

7 Issachar had four sons: Tola, Puah, Jashub, and Shimron.
² Tola had six sons: Uzzi, Rephaiah, Jeriel, Jahmai, Ibsam, and Shemuel. They were heads of families of the clan of Tola and were famous soldiers. At the time of King David their descendants numbered 22,600.
³ Uzzi had one son, Izrahiah. Izrahiah and his four sons, Michael, Obadiah, Joel, and Isshiah, were all heads of families. ⁴ They had so many wives and children that their descendants were able to provide 36,000 men for military service.
⁵ The official records of all the families of the tribe of Issachar listed 87,000 men eligible for military service.

The Descendants of Benjamin and Dan

⁶ Benjamin had three sons: Bela, Becher, and Jediael.
⁷ Bela had five sons: Ezbon, Uzzi, Uzziel, Jerimoth, and Iri. They were heads of families in the clan and were all famous soldiers. Their descendants included 22,034 men eligible for military service.
⁸ Becher had nine sons: Zemirah, Joash, Eliezer, Elioenai, Omri, Jeremoth, Abijah, Anathoth, and Alemeth. ⁹ The official record of their descendants by families listed 20,200 men eligible for military service.
¹⁰ Jediael had one son, Bilhan, and Bilhan had seven sons: Jeush, Benjamin, Ehud, Chenaanah, Zethan, Tarshish, and Ahishahar.
¹¹ They were heads of families in the clan and were all famous soldiers. Their descendants included 17,200 men eligible for military service. ¹² Shuppim and Huppim also belonged to this tribe.
Dan had one son, Hushim.*

The Descendants of Naphtali

¹³ Naphtali had four sons: Jahziel, Guni, Jezer, and Shallum. (They were descendants of Bilhah.*)

The Descendants of Manasseh

¹⁴ By his Aramean concubine, Manasseh had two sons, Asriel and Machir. Machir was the father of Gilead. ¹⁵ Machir found a wife for Huppim and one for Shuppim. His sister's name was Maacah. Machir's second son was Zelophehad, and he had only daughters.
¹⁶ Maacah, Machir's wife, gave birth to two sons, whom they named Peresh and Sheresh. Peresh had two sons, Ulam and Rakem, ¹⁷ and Ulam had a son named Bedan. These are all descendants of Gilead, the son of Machir and grandson of Manasseh.

7.12 Probable text *Shuppim… Hushim* (see Gen 46.23; Num 26.39, 42); Hebrew *And Shuppim and Huppim, sons of Ir; Hushim son of Aher.*
7.13 *Bilhah*: A concubine of Jacob and the mother of his two sons Dan and Naphtali.

474

1 Chron.

∴⋯⋯

Ruth
1 Sam.
2 Sam.
1 Kings
2 Kings

1 CHRONICLES 7, 8

¹⁸ Gilead's sister Hammolecheth had three sons: Ishod, Abiezer, and Mahlah. ¹⁹ (Shemida had four sons: Ahian, Shechem, Likhi, and Aniam.)

The Descendants of Ephraim

²⁰ These are the descendants of Ephraim from generation to generation: Shuthelah, Bered, Tahath, Eleadah, Tahath, ²¹ Zabad, Shuthelah. Ephraim had two other sons besides Shuthelah: Ezer and Elead, who were killed when they tried to steal the livestock belonging to the native inhabitants of Gath. ²² Their father Ephraim mourned for them for many days, and his relatives came to comfort him. ²³ Then he had intercourse with his wife again, and she became pregnant and had a son. They named him Beriah,* because of the trouble that had come to their family.

²⁴ Ephraim had a daughter named Sheerah. She built the towns of Upper and Lower Beth Horon, and Uzzen Sheerah.

²⁵ Ephraim also had a son named Rephah, whose descendants were as follows: Resheph, Telah, Tahan, ²⁶ Ladan, Ammihud, Elishama, ²⁷ Nun, Joshua.

²⁸ The territory which they took and settled in included Bethel and the towns round it, as far east as Naaran and as far west as Gezer and the towns round it. It also included the cities of Shechem and Ayyah, and the towns round them.

²⁹ The descendants of Manasseh controlled the cities of Beth Shan, Taanach, Megiddo, and Dor, and the towns round them.

All these are the places where the descendants of Joseph son of Jacob lived.

The Descendants of Asher

³⁰ These are the descendants of Asher. He had four sons: Imnah, Ishvah, Ishvi, and Beriah; and one daughter, Serah.

³¹ Beriah had two sons, Heber and Malchiel. (Malchiel founded the city of Birzaith.)

³² Heber had three sons: Japhlet, Shomer, and Hotham; and one daughter, Shua.

³³ Japhlet also had three sons: Pasach, Bimhal, and Ashvath.

³⁴ His brother Shomer had three sons: Rohgah, Jehubbah, and Aram.

³⁵ His brother Hotham* had four sons: Zophah, Imna, Shelesh, and Amal.

³⁶ The descendants of Zophah were Suah, Harnepher, Shual, Beri, Imrah, ³⁷ Bezer, Hod, Shamma, Shilshah, Ithran, and Beera.

³⁸ The descendants of Jether were Jephunneh, Pispa, and Ara, ³⁹ and the descendants of Ulla were Arah, Hanniel, and Rizia.

⁴⁰ All these were descendants of Asher. They were heads of families, famous fighting men, outstanding leaders. Asher's descendants included 26,000 men eligible for military service.

The Descendants of Benjamin

8 Benjamin had five sons. In order of age they were Bela, Ashbel, Aharah, ² Nohah, and Rapha.

³ The descendants of Bela were Addar, Gera, Abihud, ⁴ Abishua, Naaman, Ahoah, ⁵ Gera, Shephuphan, and Huram.

⁶⁻⁷ The descendants of Ehud were Naaman, Ahijah, and Gera. They were heads of families that lived in Geba, but which were

⋯⋯⋯⋯⋯⋯⋯⋯⋯⋯⋯⋯⋯⋯⋯⋯⋯⋯⋯⋯⋯⋯⋯⋯⋯⋯

7.23 *Beriah*: This name sounds like the Hebrew for "in trouble".
7.35 Probable text (see verse 32) *Hotham*; Hebrew *Helem*.

1 CHRONICLES 8

475

1 Chron.
....
2 Chron.
Ezra
Nehem.
Esther
Job

forced out and went to live in Manahath. Gera, the father of Uzza and Ahihud, led them in this move.

8-9 Shaharaim divorced two wives, Hushim and Baara. Later, when he lived in the country of Moab, he married Hodesh and had seven sons: Jobab, Zibia, Mesha, Malcam, 10 Jeuz, Sachia, and Mirmah. His sons all became heads of families.

11 He also had two sons by Hushim: Abitub and Elpaal.

12 Elpaal had three sons: Eber, Misham, and Shemed. It was Shemed who built the cities of Ono and Lod and the surrounding villages.

The Benjaminites in Gath and Aijalon

13 Beriah and Shema were heads of families that settled in the city of Aijalon and drove out the people who lived in the city of Gath. 14 Beriah's descendants included Ahio, Shashak, Jeremoth, 15 Zebadiah, Arad, Eder, 16 Michael, Ishpah, and Joha.

The Benjaminites in Jerusalem

17 Elpaal's descendants included Zebadiah, Meshullam, Hizki, Heber, 18 Ishmerai, Izliah, and Jobab.

19 Shimei's descendants included Jakim, Zichri, Zabdi, 20 Elienai, Zillethai, Eliel, 21 Adaiah, Beraiah, and Shimrath.

22 Shashak's descendants included Ishpan, Eber, Eliel, 23 Abdon, Zichri, Hanan, 24 Hananiah, Elam, Anthothijah, 25 Iphdeiah, and Penuel.

26 Jeroham's descendants included Shamsherai, Shehariah, Athaliah, 27 Jaareshiah, Elijah, and Zichri.

28 These were the ancestral heads of families and their principal descendants who lived in Jerusalem.

The Benjaminites in Gibeon and Jerusalem

29 Jeiel* founded the city of Gibeon and settled there. His wife was named Maacah, 30 and his eldest son, Abdon. His other sons were Zur, Kish, Baal, Ner,* Nadab, 31 Gedor, Ahio, Zechariah, 32 and Mikloth, the father of Shimeah. Their descendants lived in Jerusalem near other families of their clan.

The Family of King Saul

33 Ner was the father of Kish, and Kish was the father of King Saul. Saul had four sons: Jonathan, Malchishua, Abinadab, and Eshbaal.* 34 Jonathan was the father of Meribbaal,* who was the father of Micah.

35 Micah had four sons: Pithon, Melech, Tarea, and Ahaz. 36 Ahaz was the father of Jehoaddah, who was the father of three sons: Alemeth, Azmaveth, and Zimri. Zimri was the father of Moza, 37 Moza the father of Binea, Binea of Raphah, Raphah of Eleasah, and Eleasah of Azel.

38 Azel had six sons: Azrikam, Bocheru, Ishmael, Sheariah, Obadiah, and Hanan. 39 Azel's brother Eshek had three sons: Ulam, Jeush, and Eliphelet.

40 Ulam's sons were outstanding soldiers and archers. He had 150 sons and grandsons in all. All those named above were members of the tribe of Benjamin.

....

8.29 Probable text (and see 9.35) *Jeiel*; Hebrew does not have this name.
8.30 One ancient translation (and see 9.36) *Ner*; Hebrew does not have this name.
8.33 *Eshbaal*: Called Ishbosheth in 2 Sam 2.8 and elsewhere in 2 Sam.
8.34 *Meribbaal*: Called Mephibosheth in 2 Sam 4.4 and elsewhere in 2 Sam.

476

1 Chron.

Ruth
1 Sam.
2 Sam.
1 Kings
2 Kings

1 CHRONICLES 9

1 CHRONICLES 9.17-21

Some people had the job of standing guard at the gates and deciding who was allowed to access the

PRESENCE

– OF –

GOD.

Now that Jesus has died and risen from the dead, access to God's presence is open to everyone, through faith in him.

In the space on these pages, **DRAW A CLOSED GATE AND AN OPEN GATE,** and spend some time praying for all the people you'd like to see meet God for themselves.

The People who Returned from Captivity

9 All the people of Israel were listed according to their families, and this information was recorded in *The Book of the Kings of Israel.*

The people of Judah had been deported to Babylon as punishment for their sins. ²The first to return to their property in the cities included Israelite citizens, priests, Levites, and temple workers. ³People from the tribes of Judah, Benjamin, Ephraim, and Manasseh went to live in Jerusalem.

⁴⁻⁶There were 690 families of the tribe of Judah who lived in Jerusalem.

The descendants of Judah's son Perez had as their leader Uthai, the son of Ammihud and grandson of Omri. His other ancestors included Imri and Bani.

The descendants of Judah's son Shelah had as their leader Asaiah, who was the head of his family.

The descendants of Judah's son Zerah had Jeuel as their leader.

⁷⁻⁸The following members of the tribe of Benjamin lived in Jerusalem:

Sallu son of Meshullam, who was the son of Hodaviah, the son of Hassenuah

Ibneiah son of Jeroham

Elah, the son of Uzzi and grandson of Michri

Meshullam son of Shephatiah, who was the son of Reuel, the son of Ibnijah.

⁹There were 956 families of this tribe living there. All the men named above were heads of families.

The Priests who Lived in Jerusalem

¹⁰⁻¹²The following priests lived in Jerusalem:

Jedaiah, Jehoiarib, and Jachin

Azariah son of Hilkiah (the chief official in the Temple), whose ancestors included Meshullam, Zadok, Meraioth, and Ahitub

Adaiah son of Jeroham, whose ancestors included Pashhur and Malchijah

Maasai son of Adiel, whose ancestors included Jahzerah, Meshullam, Meshillemith, and Immer.

¹³The priests who were heads of families totalled 1,760. They were experts in all the work carried on in the Temple.

The Levites who Lived in Jerusalem

¹⁴⁻¹⁶The following Levites lived in Jerusalem:

Shemaiah son of Hasshub, whose ancestors included Azrikam and Hashabiah, of the clan of Merari

Bakbakkar, Heresh, and Galal

Mattaniah son of Mica, whose ancestors included Zichri and Asaph

Obadiah son of Shemaiah, whose ancestors included Galal and Jeduthun

Berechiah, the son of Asa and grandson of Elkanah, who lived in the territory that belonged to the town of Netophah.

The Temple Guards who Lived in Jerusalem

¹⁷The following temple guards lived in Jerusalem: Shallum, Akkub, Talmon, and Ahiman. Shallum was their leader. ¹⁸Down to that time members of their clans had been stationed at the

1 Chron.
....
2 Chron.
Ezra
Nehem.
Esther
Job

eastern entrance to the King's Gate.* Formerly they had stood guard at the gates to the camps of the Levites.

¹⁹Shallum, the son of Kore and grandson of Ebiasaph, together with his fellow-members of the clan of Korah, was responsible for guarding the entrance to the Tent of the LORD's presence, just as their ancestors had been when they were in charge of the LORD's camp. ²⁰Phinehas son of Eleazar — may the LORD be with him! — had supervised them at one time.

²¹Zechariah son of Meshelemiah was also a guard at the entrance to the Tent of the LORD's presence.

²²In all, 212 men were chosen as guards for the entrances and gates. They were registered according to the villages where they lived. It was King David and the prophet Samuel who had put their ancestors in these responsible positions. ²³They and their descendants continued to guard the gates to the Temple. ²⁴There was a gate facing in each direction, north, south, east, and west, and each had a chief guard. ²⁵These guards were assisted by their relatives, who lived in the villages and who had to take turns at guard duty for seven days at a time. ²⁶The four chief guards were Levites and had the final responsibility. They were also responsible for the rooms in the Temple and for the supplies kept there. ²⁷They lived near the Temple, because it was their duty to guard it and to open the gates every morning.

The Other Levites

²⁸Other Levites were responsible for the utensils used in worship. They checked them out and checked them back in every time they were used. ²⁹Others were in charge of the other sacred equipment, and of the flour, wine, olive oil, incense, and spices. ³⁰But the responsibility for mixing the spices belonged to the priests.

³¹A Levite named Mattithiah, eldest son of Shallum, of the clan of Korah, was responsible for preparing the baked offerings.* ³²Members of the clan of Kohath were responsible for preparing the sacred bread* for the Temple every Sabbath.

³³Some Levite families were responsible for the temple music. The heads of these families lived in some of the temple buildings and were free from other duties, because they were on call day and night.

³⁴The men named above were heads of Levite families, according to their ancestral lines. They were the leaders who lived in Jerusalem.

The Ancestors and Descendants of King Saul
(1 Chr 8.29–38)

³⁵Jeiel founded the city of Gibeon and settled there. His wife was named Maacah. ³⁶His eldest son was Abdon, and his other sons were Zur, Kish, Baal, Ner, Nadab, ³⁷Gedor, Ahio, Zechariah, and Mikloth, ³⁸the father of Shimeah. Their descendants lived in Jerusalem near other families of their clan.

³⁹Ner was the father of Kish, and Kish was the father of Saul. Saul had four sons: Jonathan, Malchishua, Abinadab, and Eshbaal.* ⁴⁰Jonathan was the father of Meribbaal,* who was the father of

. . . .

9.18 *King's Gate*: The east gate of the Temple, through which the king usually entered.
9.31 *baked offerings*: Thin cakes of flour and olive oil which were baked and then presented as offerings to God (see Lev 2.4–6).
9.32 *sacred bread*: Twelve loaves of bread which were placed on a table in the Temple each Sabbath as an offering to God (see Lev 24.5–9).
9.39 *Eshbaal*: Called Ishbosheth in 2 Sam 2.8 and elsewhere in 2 Sam.
9.40 *Meribbaal*: Called Mephibosheth in 2 Sam 4.4 and elsewhere in 2 Sam.

478

1 Chron.

∴ ┄┄┄┄

Ruth
1 Sam.
2 Sam.
1 Kings
2 Kings

1 CHRONICLES 9–11

Micah. [41] Micah had four sons: Pithon, Melech, Tarea, and Ahaz.* [42] Ahaz was the father of Jarah, who was the father of three sons: Alemeth, Azmaveth, and Zimri. Zimri was the father of Moza, [43] Moza the father of Binea, Binea of Rephaiah, Rephaiah of Eleasah, and Eleasah of Azel.

[44] Azel had six sons: Azrikam, Bocheru, Ishmael, Sheariah, Obadiah, and Hanan.

The Death of King Saul
(1 Sam 31.1–13)

10 The Philistines fought a battle against the Israelites on Mount Gilboa. Many Israelites were killed there, and the rest of them, including King Saul and his sons, fled. [2] But the Philistines caught up with them and killed three of Saul's sons, Jonathan, Abinadab, and Malchishua. [3] The fighting was heavy round Saul, and he was hit by enemy arrows and badly wounded. [4] He said to the young man carrying his weapons, "Draw your sword and kill me, to keep these godless Philistines from gloating over me." But the young man was too terrified to do it. So Saul took his own sword and threw himself on it. [5] The young man saw that Saul was dead, so he too threw himself on his sword and died. [6] So Saul and his three sons all died together and none of his descendants ever ruled. [7] When the Israelites who lived in the Valley of Jezreel heard that the army had fled and that Saul and his sons had died, they abandoned their towns and ran off. Then the Philistines came and occupied them.

[8] The day after the battle, the Philistines went to plunder the corpses, and they found the bodies of Saul and his sons lying on Mount Gilboa. [9] They cut off Saul's head, stripped off his armour, and sent messengers with them throughout Philistia to tell the good news to their idols and to their people. [10] They put his weapons in one of their temples and hung his head in the temple of their god Dagon. [11] When the people of Jabesh in Gilead heard what the Philistines had done to Saul, [12] the bravest men went and fetched the bodies of Saul and his sons and took them to Jabesh. They buried them there under an oak and fasted for seven days.

[13] Saul died because he was unfaithful to the LORD. He disobeyed the LORD's commands; he tried to find guidance by consulting the spirits of the dead [14] instead of consulting the LORD. So the LORD killed him and gave control of the kingdom to David son of Jesse.

David Becomes King of Israel and Judah
(2 Sam 5.1–10)

11 All the people of Israel went to David at Hebron and said to him, "We are your own flesh and blood. [2] In the past, even when Saul was still our king, you led the people of Israel in battle, and the LORD your God promised you that you would lead his people and be their ruler." [3] So all the leaders of Israel came to King David at Hebron. He made a sacred alliance with them, they anointed him, and he became king of Israel, just as the LORD had promised through Samuel.

[4] King David and all the Israelites went and attacked the city of Jerusalem. It was then known as Jebus, and the Jebusites, the original inhabitants of the land, were still living there. [5] The Jebusites told David he would never get inside the city, but

9.41 Some ancient translations *Ahaz* (see 1 Chr 8.35); Hebrew does not have this name.

1 CHRONICLES 11

479

1 Chron.

2 Chron.
Ezra
Nehem.
Esther
Job

David captured their fortress of Zion, and it became known as "David's City". ⁶David said, "The first man to kill a Jebusite will be commander of the army!" Joab, whose mother was Zeruiah, led the attack and became commander. ⁷Because David went to live in the fortress, it came to be called "David's City". ⁸He rebuilt the city, starting at the place where land was filled in on the east side of the hill, and Joab restored the rest of the city. ⁹David grew stronger and stronger, because the LORD Almighty was with him.

David's Famous Soldiers
(2 Sam 23.8–39)

¹⁰This is the list of David's famous soldiers. Together with the rest of the people of Israel, they helped him to become king, as the LORD had promised, and they kept his kingdom strong.

¹¹First was Jashobeam of the clan of Hachmon, the leader of "The Three".* He fought with his spear against 300 men and killed them all in one battle. ¹²Next among the famous "Three" was Eleazar son of Dodo, of the clan of Ahoh. ¹³He fought on David's side against the Philistines at the battle of Pas Dammim. He was in a barley field when the Israelites started to run away, ¹⁴so he and his men made a stand in the middle of the field and fought the Philistines. The LORD gave him a great victory.

¹⁵One day three of the thirty leading soldiers went to a rock where David was staying near the cave of Adullam, while a band of Philistines was camping in the Valley of Rephaim. ¹⁶At that time David was on a fortified hill, and a group of Philistines had occupied Bethlehem. ¹⁷David got homesick and said, "How I wish someone would bring me a drink of water from the well by the gate in Bethlehem!" ¹⁸The three famous soldiers forced their way through the Philistine camp, drew some water from the well, and brought it back to David. But he would not drink it; instead he poured it out as an offering to the LORD ¹⁹and said, "I could never drink this! It would be like drinking the blood of these men who risked their lives!" So he refused to drink it. These were the brave deeds of the three famous soldiers.

²⁰Joab's brother Abishai was the leader of "The Famous Thirty".* He fought with his spear against 300 men and killed them, and became famous among "The Thirty".* ²¹He was the most famous of "The Thirty"* and became their leader, but he was not as famous as "The Three".

²²Benaiah son of Jehoiada from Kabzeel was a famous soldier; he did many brave deeds, including killing two great Moabite warriors. He once went down into a pit on a snowy day and killed a lion. ²³He also killed an Egyptian, a huge man over two metres tall, who was armed with a gigantic spear. Benaiah attacked him with a club, snatched the spear from the Egyptian's hand, and killed him with it. ²⁴Those were the brave deeds of Benaiah, who was one of "The Thirty".* ²⁵He was outstanding among "The Thirty", but not as famous as "The Three". David put him in charge of his bodyguard.

²⁶⁻⁴⁷These are the other outstanding soldiers:

11.11 One ancient translation (see also 2 Sam 23.8) *"The Three"*; Hebrew *"The Thirty"*.
11.20 One ancient translation *Thirty*; Hebrew *Three*.
11.20 One ancient translation (see also 2 Sam 23.18) *"The Thirty"*; Hebrew *"The Three"*.
11.21 Probable text (see 2 Sam 23.19) *most famous of "The Thirty"*; Hebrew unclear.
11.24 Probable text *"The Thirty"*; Hebrew *"The Three"*.

1 CHRONICLES

How do God and wars mix?
Head to
gnbyouthedition.co.uk/war

TO SEE A

FILM

WE MADE ABOUT IT.

480

1 Chron.

⁝⁖⁙⁖⁙⁖

Ruth
1 Sam.
2 Sam.
1 Kings
2 Kings

1 CHRONICLES 11, 12

Asahel, Joab's brother
Elhanan son of Dodo from Bethlehem
Shammoth from Harod
Helez from Pelet
Ira son of Ikkesh from Tekoa
Abiezer from Anathoth
Sibbecai from Hushah
Ilai from Ahoh
Maharai from Netophah
Heled son of Baanah from Netophah
Ithai son of Ribai from Gibeah in Benjamin
Benaiah from Pirathon
Hurai from the valleys near Gaash
Abiel from Arbah
Azmaveth from Bahurum
Eliahba from Shaalbon
Hashem* from Gizon
Jonathan son of Shagee from Harar
Ahiam son of Sachar from Harar
Eliphal son of Ur
Hepher from Mecherah
Ahijah from Pelon
Hezro from Carmel
Naarai son of Ezbai
Joel brother of Nathan
Mibhar son of Hagri
Zelek from Ammon
Naharai, Joab's armour-bearer, from Beeroth
Ira and Gareb from Jattir
Uriah the Hittite
Zabad son of Ahlai
Adina son of Shiza (a leading member of the tribe of
    Reuben, with his own group of thirty soldiers)
Hanan son of Maacah
Joshaphat from Mithan
Uzzia from Ashterah
Shamma and Jeiel, sons of Hotham, from Aroer
Jediael and Joha, sons of Shimri, from Tiz
Eliel from Mahavah
Jeribai and Joshaviah, sons of Elnaam
Ithmah from Moab
Eliel, Obed, and Jaasiel from Zobah.*

David's Early Followers from the Tribe of Benjamin

12 David was living in Ziklag, where he had gone to escape from King Saul. There he was joined by many experienced, reliable soldiers, ²members of the tribe of Benjamin, to which Saul belonged. They could shoot arrows and sling stones either right handed or left handed. ³⁻⁷They were under the command of Ahiezer and Joash, sons of Shemaah, from Gibeah.

These were the soldiers:
Jeziel and Pelet, sons of Azmaveth
Beracah and Jehu from Anathoth
Ishmaiah from Gibeon, a famous soldier and one of the
    leaders of "The Thirty"
Jeremiah, Jahaziel, Johannan, and Jozabad, from Gederah

11.26–47 Probable text *Hashem*; Hebrew *the sons of Hashem*.
11.26–47 Probable text *from Zobah*; Hebrew unclear.

481

1 Chron.

....

2 Chron.

Ezra

Nehem.

Esther

Job

Eluzai, Jerimoth, Bealiah, Shemariah, and Shephatiah,
   from Hariph
Elkanah, Isshiah, Azarel, Joezer, and Jashobeam, of the
   clan of Korah
Joelah and Zebadiah, sons of Jeroham, from Gedor.

David's Followers from the Tribe of Gad

[8] These are the names of the famous, experienced soldiers from the tribe of Gad who joined David's troops when he was at the desert fort. They were experts with shields and spears, as fierce-looking as lions and as quick as mountain deer. [9-13] They were ranked in the following order: Ezer, Obadiah, Eliab, Mishmannah, Jeremiah, Attai, Eliel, Johanan, Elzabad, Jeremiah, and Machbannai.

[14] Some of these men from the tribe of Gad were senior officers in command of a thousand men, and others were junior officers in command of a hundred. [15] In the first month of one year, the time when the River Jordan overflowed its banks, they crossed the river, scattering the people who lived in the valleys both east and west of the river.

Followers from Benjamin and Judah

[16] Once a group of men from the tribes of Benjamin and Judah went out to the fort where David was. [17] David went to meet them and said, "If you are coming as friends to help me, you are welcome here. Join us! But if you intend to betray me to my enemies, even though I have not tried to hurt you, the God of our ancestors will know it and punish you."

[18] God's Spirit took control of one of them, Amasai, who later became the commander of "The Thirty", and he called out,

"David son of Jesse, we are yours!
Success to you and those who help you!
God is on your side."

David welcomed them and made them officers in his army.

Followers from Manasseh

[19] Some soldiers from the tribe of Manasseh went over to David's side when he was marching out with the Philistines to fight King Saul. Actually he did not help the Philistines, for their kings were afraid that he would betray them to his former master Saul, so they sent him back to Ziklag. [20] These are the soldiers from Manasseh who went over to David's side when he was returning: Adnah, Jozabad, Jediael, Michael, Jozabad, Elihu, and Zillethai. In Manasseh they had all commanded units of a thousand men. [21] They served David as officers over his troops,* because they were all outstanding soldiers. Later they were officers in the Israelite army. [22] Almost every day new men joined David's forces, so that his army was soon enormous.

List of David's Forces

[23-37] When David was at Hebron, many trained soldiers joined his army to help make him king in place of Saul, as the LORD had promised. Their numbers were as follows:

Judah: 6,800 well-equipped men, armed with shields and
   spears;
Simeon: 7,100 well-trained men;

....

12.21 *They served David… troops*; or *They helped David fight against the bands of raiders.*

482

1 Chron.

Ruth
1 Sam.
2 Sam.
1 Kings
2 Kings

1 CHRONICLES 12, 13

1 CHRONICLES 13.1-11

God's actions here can
seem harsh; even

– DAVID WAS –

ANGRY.

The problem was
compromise: the
Covenant Box was never
meant to be put on
wheels, let alone
touched (see Numbers
4.15). One small
compromise at a
time, the Israelites
had forgotten what
God had said.

Are there areas of your
life where compromise
has crept in? What are
they? What three
things could you do to
make sure you are
sticking to what God is
asking of you in every
part of your life?

1.

2.

3.

Levi: 4,600 men;
Followers of Jehoiada, descendant of Aaron: 3,700 men;
Relatives of Zadok, an able young fighter: 22 leading men;
Benjamin (Saul's own tribe): 3,000 men (most of the
    people of Benjamin had remained loyal to Saul);
Ephraim: 20,800 men famous in their own clans;
West Manasseh: 18,000 men chosen to go and make
    David king;
Issachar: 200 leaders, together with the men under their
    command (these leaders knew what Israel should do
    and the best time to do it);
Zebulun: 50,000 loyal and reliable men ready to fight,
    trained to use all kinds of weapons;
Naphtali: 1,000 leaders, together with 37,000 men armed
    with shields and spears;
Dan: 28,600 trained men;
Asher: 40,000 men ready for battle;
Tribes east of the Jordan — Reuben, Gad, and East Manasseh:
    120,000 men trained to use all kinds of weapons.

[38] All these soldiers, ready for battle, went to Hebron, determined to make David king over all Israel. All the rest of the people of Israel were united in the same purpose. [39] They spent three days there with David, feasting on the food and drink which other Israelites had prepared for them. [40] From as far away as the northern tribes of Issachar, Zebulun, and Naphtali, people came bringing donkeys, camels, mules, and oxen loaded with food — flour, figs, raisins, wine, and olive oil. They also brought cattle and sheep to kill and eat. All this was an expression of the joy that was felt throughout the whole country.

The Covenant Box is Moved from Kiriath Jearim
(2 Sam 6.1–11)

13 King David consulted with all the officers in command of units of a thousand men and units of a hundred men. [2] Then he announced to all the people of Israel, "If you give your approval and if it is the will of the LORD our God, let us send messengers to the rest of our people and to the priests and Levites in their towns, and tell them to assemble here with us. [3] Then we will go and fetch God's Covenant Box, which was ignored while Saul was king." [4] The people were pleased with the suggestion and agreed to it.

[5] So David assembled the people of Israel from all over the country, from the Egyptian border in the south to Hamath Pass in the north, in order to bring the Covenant Box from Kiriath Jearim to Jerusalem. [6] David and the people went to the city of Baalah, that is, to Kiriath Jearim, in the territory of Judah, to fetch the Covenant Box of God, which bears the name of the LORD enthroned above the winged creatures. [7] At Abinadab's house they brought out the Covenant Box and put it on a new cart. Uzzah and Ahio guided the cart, [8] while David and all the people danced with all their might to honour God. They sang and played musical instruments — harps, drums, cymbals, and trumpets.

[9] As they came to the threshing place of Chidon, the oxen stumbled, and Uzzah stretched out his hand and took hold of the Covenant Box. [10] At once the LORD became angry with Uzzah and killed him for touching the box. He died there in God's presence, [11] and so that place has been called Perez Uzzah* ever since. David was furious because the LORD had punished Uzzah in anger.

13.11 *Perez Uzzah*: This name in Hebrew means "Punishment of Uzzah".

1 CHRONICLES 13–15

483

1 Chron.

2 Chron.
Ezra
Nehem.
Esther
Job

¹²Then David was afraid of God and said, "How can I take the Covenant Box with me now?" ¹³So David did not take it with him to Jerusalem. Instead, he left it at the house of a man named Obed Edom, a native of the city of Gath. ¹⁴It stayed there three months, and the LORD blessed Obed Edom's family and everything that belonged to him.

David's Activities in Jerusalem
(2 Sam 5.11–16)

14 King Hiram of Tyre sent a trade mission to David; he provided him with cedar logs and with stonemasons and carpenters to build a palace. ²And so David realized that the LORD had established him as king of Israel and was making his kingdom prosperous for the sake of his people.

³There in Jerusalem, David married more wives and had more sons and daughters. ⁴The following children were born to him in Jerusalem: Shammua, Shobab, Nathan, Solomon, ⁵Ibhar, Elishua, Elpelet, ⁶Nogah, Nepheg, Japhia, ⁷Elishama, Beeliada,* and Eliphelet.

Victory over the Philistines
(2 Sam 5.17–25)

⁸When the Philistines heard that David had now been made king over the whole country of Israel, their army went out to capture him. So David marched out to meet them. ⁹The Philistines arrived at the Valley of Rephaim and began plundering. ¹⁰David asked God, "Shall I attack the Philistines? Will you give me the victory?"

The LORD answered, "Yes, attack! I will give you the victory!"

¹¹So David attacked them at Baal Perazim and defeated them. He said, "God has used me to break through the enemy army like a flood." So that place is called Baal Perazim.* ¹²When the Philistines fled, they left their idols behind, and David gave orders for them to be burnt.

¹³Soon the Philistines returned to the valley and started plundering it again. ¹⁴Once more David consulted God, who answered, "Don't attack them from here, but go round and get ready to attack them from the other side, near the balsam trees. ¹⁵When you hear the sound of marching in the treetops, then attack, because I will be marching ahead of you to defeat the Philistine army." ¹⁶David did what God had commanded, and so he drove the Philistines back from Gibeon all the way to Gezer. ¹⁷David's fame spread everywhere, and the LORD made every nation afraid of him.

Getting Ready to Move the Covenant Box

15 For his own use, David built houses in David's City.* He also prepared a place for God's Covenant Box and put up a tent for it. ²Then he said, "Only Levites should carry the Covenant Box, because they are the ones the LORD chose to carry it and to serve him for ever." ³So David summoned all the people of Israel to Jerusalem in order to bring the Covenant Box to the place he had prepared for it. ⁴Next he sent for the descendants of Aaron and for the Levites. ⁵From the Levite clan of Kohath came Uriel,

---

14.7 *Beeliada*: Called Eliada in 3.8.
14.11 *Baal Perazim*: This name in Hebrew means "Lord of the Breakthrough".
15.1 *David's city*: That part of Jerusalem which David had captured from the original inhabitants, the Jebusites (see 2 Sam 5.6–10).

484

1 Chron.

⋮⋯⋯⋯

Ruth
1 Sam.
2 Sam.
1 Kings
2 Kings

1 CHRONICLES 15, 16

in charge of 120 members of his clan; [6] from the clan of Merari came Asaiah, in charge of 220; [7] from the clan of Gershon, Joel, in charge of 130; [8] from the clan of Elizaphan, Shemaiah, in charge of 200; [9] from the clan of Hebron, Eliel, in charge of eighty; [10] and from the clan of Uzziel, Amminadab, in charge of 112.

[11] David called in the priests Zadok and Abiathar and the six Levites, Uriel, Asaiah, Joel, Shemaiah, Eliel, and Amminadab. [12] He said to the Levites, "You are the leaders of the Levite clans. Purify yourselves and your fellow-Levites, so that you can bring the Covenant Box of the LORD God of Israel to the place I have prepared for it. [13] Because you were not there to carry it the first time, the LORD our God punished us for not worshipping him as we should have done."

[14] Then the priests and the Levites purified themselves in order to move the Covenant Box of the LORD God of Israel. [15] The Levites carried it on poles on their shoulders, as the LORD had commanded through Moses.

[16] David commanded the leaders of the Levites to assign various Levites to sing and to play joyful music on harps and cymbals. [17-21] From the clans of singers they chose the following men to play the brass cymbals: Heman son of Joel, his relative Asaph son of Berechiah, and Ethan son of Kushaiah, of the clan of Merari. To assist them they chose the following Levites to play the high-pitched harps: Zechariah, Jaaziel, Shemiramoth, Jehiel, Unni, Eliab, Maaseiah, and Benaiah.

To play the low-pitched harps they chose the following Levites: Mattithiah, Eliphelehu, Mikneiah, Azaziah, and the temple guards, Obed Edom and Jeiel.

[22] Because of his skill in music Chenaniah was chosen to be in charge of the levitical musicians. [23-24] Berechiah and Elkanah, along with Obed Edom and Jehiah, were chosen as guards for the Covenant Box. The priests Shebaniah, Joshaphat, Nethanel, Amasai, Zechariah, Benaiah, and Eliezer were chosen to blow trumpets in front of the Covenant Box.

Moving the Covenant Box to Jerusalem
(2 Sam 6.12–22)

[25] So King David, the leaders of Israel, and the military commanders went to the house of Obed Edom to fetch the Covenant Box, and they had a great celebration. [26] They sacrificed seven bulls and seven sheep, to make sure that God would help the Levites who were carrying the Covenant Box. [27] David was wearing a robe made of the finest linen, and so were the musicians, Chenaniah their leader, and the Levites who carried the Box. David also wore a linen ephod. [28] So all the Israelites accompanied the Covenant Box up to Jerusalem with shouts of joy, the sound of trumpets, horns, and cymbals, and the music of harps.

[29] As the Box was being brought into the city, Michal, Saul's daughter, looked out of the window and saw King David dancing and leaping for joy, and she was disgusted with him.

16 They took the Covenant Box to the tent which David had prepared for it and put it inside. Then they offered sacrifices and fellowship offerings to God. [2] After David had finished offering the sacrifices, he blessed the people in the name of the LORD [3] and distributed food to them all. He gave each man and woman in Israel a loaf of bread, a piece of roasted meat,* and some raisins.

⋯⋯⋯⋯⋯⋯⋯⋯⋯⋯⋯⋯⋯⋯⋯⋯⋯⋯⋯⋯⋯⋯⋯⋯⋯⋯⋯⋯

16.3 *a piece of roasted meat*; or *a cake of dates.*

1 Chron.

2 Chron.
Ezra
Nehem.
Esther
Job

⁴David appointed some of the Levites to lead the worship of the LORD, the God of Israel, in front of the Covenant Box, by singing and praising him. ⁵Asaph was appointed leader, with Zechariah as his assistant. Jeiel, Shemiramoth, Jehiel, Mattithiah, Eliab, Benaiah, Obed Edom, and Jeiel were to play harps. Asaph was to sound the cymbals, ⁶and two priests, Benaiah and Jahaziel, were to blow trumpets regularly in front of the Covenant Box. ⁷It was then that David first gave Asaph and his fellow-Levites the responsibility for singing praises to the LORD.

A Song of Praise
(Ps 105.1–15; 96.1–13; 106.1, 47–48)

⁸ Give thanks to the LORD, proclaim his greatness;
    tell the nations what he has done.
⁹ Sing praise to the LORD;
    tell the wonderful things he has done.
¹⁰ Be glad that we belong to him;
    let all who worship him rejoice!
¹¹ Go to the LORD for help,
    and worship him continually.
¹²⁻¹³ You descendants of Jacob, God's servant,
    descendants of Israel, whom God chose,
    remember the miracles that God performed
    and the judgements that he gave.
¹⁴ The LORD is our God;
    his commands are for all the world.
¹⁵ Never forget God's covenant,
    which he made to last for ever,
¹⁶ the covenant he made with Abraham,
    the promise he made to Isaac.
¹⁷ The LORD made a covenant with Jacob,
    one that will last for ever.
¹⁸ "I will give you the land of Canaan," he said.
    "It will be your own possession."

¹⁹ God's people were few in number,
    strangers in the land of Canaan.
²⁰ They wandered from country to country,
    from one kingdom to another.
²¹ But God let no one oppress them;
    to protect them, he warned the kings:
²² "Don't harm my chosen servants;
    do not touch my prophets."

²³ Sing to the LORD, all the world!
    Proclaim every day the good news that he has saved us.
²⁴ Proclaim his glory to the nations,
    his mighty deeds to all peoples.
²⁵ The LORD is great and is to be highly praised;
    he is to be honoured more than all the gods.
²⁶ The gods of all other nations are only idols,
    but the LORD created the heavens.
²⁷ Glory and majesty surround him,
    power and joy fill his Temple.

²⁸ Praise the LORD, all people on earth,
    praise his glory and might.
²⁹ Praise the LORD's glorious name;
    bring an offering and come into his Temple.

486

1 Chron.

⋮········

Ruth
1 Sam.
2 Sam.
1 Kings
2 Kings

1 CHRONICLES 16, 17

Bow down before the Holy One when he appears;*
30   tremble before him, all the earth!
The earth is set firmly in place and cannot be moved.
31 Be glad, earth and sky!
  Tell the nations that the LORD is king.
32 Roar, sea, and every creature in you;
  be glad, fields, and everything in you!
33 The trees in the woods will shout for joy
  when the LORD comes to rule the earth.

34 Give thanks to the LORD, because he is good;
  his love is eternal.
35 Say to him, "Save us, O God our Saviour;
  gather us together; rescue us from the nations,
  so that we may be thankful
  and praise your holy name."
36 Praise the LORD, the God of Israel!
Praise him now and for ever!

Then all the people said, "Amen", and praised the LORD.

Worship at Jerusalem and Gibeon
37 King David put Asaph and his fellow-Levites in permanent charge of the worship that was held at the place where the Covenant Box was kept. They were to perform their duties there day by day. 38 Obed Edom son of Jeduthun and 68 men of his clan were to assist them. Hosah and Obed Edom were in charge of guarding the gates.

39 Zadok the priest and his fellow-priests, however, were in charge of the worship of the LORD at the place of worship in Gibeon. 40 Every morning and evening they were to burn sacrifices whole on the altar in accordance with what was written in the Law which the LORD gave to Israel. 41 There with them were Heman and Jeduthun and the others who were specifically chosen to sing praises to the LORD for his eternal love. 42 Heman and Jeduthun also had charge of the trumpets and cymbals and the other instruments which were played when the songs of praise were sung. The members of Jeduthun's clan were in charge of guarding the gates.

43 Then everyone went home, and David went home to spend some time with his family.

Nathan's Message to David
(2 Sam 7.1–17)

17 King David was now living in his palace. One day he sent for the prophet Nathan and said to him, "Here I am living in a house built of cedar, but the LORD's Covenant Box is kept in a tent!"

2 Nathan answered, "Do whatever you have in mind, because God is with you."

3 But that night God said to Nathan, 4 "Go and tell my servant David that I say to him, 'You are not the one to build a temple for me to live in. 5 From the time I rescued the people of Israel from Egypt until now, I have never lived in a temple; I have always lived in tents and moved from place to place. 6 In all my travelling with the people of Israel I never asked any of the leaders that I appointed why they had not built me a temple made of cedar.'

16.29 *when he appears*; or *in garments of worship*.

1 CHRONICLES 17, 18

487

1 Chron.

········

2 Chron.

Ezra

Nehem.

Esther

Job

7"So tell my servant David that I, the LORD Almighty, say to him, 'I took you from looking after sheep in the fields and made you the ruler of my people Israel. 8 I have been with you wherever you have gone, and I have defeated all your enemies as you advanced. I will make you as famous as the greatest leaders in the world. 9-10 I have chosen a place for my people Israel and have settled them there, where they will live without being oppressed any more. Ever since they entered this land they have been attacked by violent people, but this will not happen again. I promise to defeat all your enemies and to give you descendants. 11 When you die and are buried with your ancestors, I will make one of your sons king and will keep his kingdom strong. 12 He will be the one to build a temple for me, and I will make sure that his dynasty continues for ever. 13 I will be his father and he will be my son. I will not withdraw my support from him as I did from Saul, whom I removed so that you could be king. 14 I will put him in charge of my people and my kingdom for ever. His dynasty will never end.'"

15 Nathan told David everything that God had revealed to him.

David's Prayer of Thanksgiving
(2 Sam 7.18–29)

16 Then King David went into the Tent of the LORD's presence, sat down, and prayed, "I am not worthy of what you have already done for me, LORD God, nor is my family. 17 Yet now you are doing even more; you have made promises about my descendants in the years to come, and you, LORD God, are already treating me like a great man.* 18 What more can I say to you! You know me well, and yet you honour me, your servant. 19 It was your will and purpose to do this for me and to show me my future greatness. 20 LORD, there is none like you; we have always known that you alone are God. 21 There is no other nation on earth like Israel, whom you rescued from slavery to make them your own people. The great and wonderful things you did for them spread your fame throughout the world. You rescued your people from Egypt and drove out other nations as your people advanced. 22 You have made Israel your own people for ever, and you, LORD, have become their God.

23 "And now, O LORD, fulfil for all time the promise you made about me and my descendants, and do what you said you would. 24 Your fame will be great, and people will for ever say, 'The LORD Almighty is God over Israel.' And you will preserve my dynasty for all time. 25 I have the courage to pray this prayer to you, my God, because you have revealed all this to me, your servant, and have told me that you will make my descendants kings. 26 You, LORD, are God, and you have made this wonderful promise to me. 27 I ask you to bless my descendants so that they will continue to enjoy your favour. You, LORD, have blessed them, and your blessing will rest on them for ever."

David's Military Victories
(2 Sam 8.1–18)

18 Some time later King David attacked the Philistines again and defeated them. He took out of their control the city of Gath and its surrounding villages. 2 He also defeated the Moabites, who became his subjects and paid taxes to him.

3 Next, David attacked King Hadadezer of the Syrian state of Zobah, near the territory of Hamath, because Hadadezer was

····················

17.17 Probable text and you, LORD God... man; Hebrew unclear.

1 CHRONICLES 17.20

LORD,
- there is -
NONE
LIKE YOU
- we have -
ALWAYS
KNOWN THAT
- you alone -
ARE GOD

488

1 Chron.

⋮

Ruth
1 Sam.
2 Sam.
1 Kings
2 Kings

1 CHRONICLES 18, 19

trying to gain control of the territory by the upper Euphrates. [4] David captured a thousand of his chariots, 7,000 horsemen, and 20,000 foot soldiers. He kept enough horses for a hundred chariots and crippled all the rest.

[5] When the Syrians of Damascus sent an army to help King Hadadezer, David attacked it and killed 22,000 men. [6] Then he set up military camps in their territory, and they became his subjects and paid taxes to him. The LORD made David victorious everywhere. [7] David captured the gold shields carried by Hadadezer's officials and took them to Jerusalem. [8] He also took a great quantity of bronze from Tibhath and Kun, cities ruled by Hadadezer. (Solomon later used this bronze to make the tank, the columns, and the bronze utensils for the Temple.)

[9] King Toi of Hamath heard that David had defeated Hadadezer's entire army. [10] So he sent his son Joram to greet King David and congratulate him for his victory over Hadadezer, against whom Toi had fought many times. Joram brought David presents made of gold, silver, and bronze. [11] King David dedicated them for use in worship, along with the silver and gold he took from the nations he conquered — Edom, Moab, Ammon, Philistia, and Amalek.

[12] Abishai, whose mother was Zeruiah, defeated the Edomites in the Valley of Salt and killed 18,000 of them. [13] He set up military camps throughout Edom, and the people there became King David's subjects. The LORD made David victorious everywhere.

[14] David ruled over all Israel and made sure that his people were always treated fairly and justly. [15] Abishai's brother Joab was commander of the army; Jehoshaphat son of Ahilud was in charge of the records; [16] Zadok son of Ahitub and Ahimelech son of Abiathar were priests; Seraiah* was court secretary; [17] Benaiah son of Jehoiada was in charge of David's bodyguard; and King David's sons held high positions in his service.

David Defeats the Ammonites and the Syrians
(2 Sam 10.1–19)

19 Some time later King Nahash of Ammon died, and his son Hanun became king. [2] King David said, "I must show loyal friendship to Hanun, as his father Nahash did to me." So David sent messengers to express his sympathy.

When they arrived in Ammon and called on King Hanun, [3] the Ammonite leaders said to the king, "Do you think that it is in your father's honour that David has sent these men to express sympathy to you? Of course not! He has sent them here as spies to explore the land, so that he can conquer it!"

[4] Hanun seized David's messengers, shaved off their beards, cut off their clothes at the hips, and sent them away. [5] They were too ashamed to return home. When David heard what had happened, he sent word for them to stay in Jericho and not return until their beards had grown again.

[6] King Hanun and the Ammonites realized that they had made David their enemy, so they paid 34 tonnes of silver to hire chariots and charioteers from Upper Mesopotamia and from the Syrian states of Maacah and Zobah. [7] The 32,000 chariots they hired and the army of the king of Maacah came and camped near Medeba. The Ammonites too came out from all their cities and got ready to fight.

[8] When David heard what was happening, he sent out Joab and the whole army. [9] The Ammonites marched out and took

---

18.16 Probable text (see 2 Sam 8.17) *Seraiah*; Hebrew *Shavsha*.

1 CHRONICLES 19, 20

489

1 Chron.

....

2 Chron.

Ezra

Nehem.

Esther

Job

up their position at the entrance to Rabbah, their capital city, and the kings who had come to help took up their position in the open countryside. [10] Joab saw that the enemy troops would attack him in front and from the rear, so he chose the best of Israel's soldiers and put them in position facing the Syrians. [11] He placed the rest of his troops under the command of his brother Abishai, who put them in position facing the Ammonites. [12] Joab said to him, "If you see that the Syrians are defeating me, come and help me, and if the Ammonites are defeating you, I will go and help you. [13] Be strong and courageous! Let's fight hard for our people and for the cities of our God. And may the LORD's will be done."

[14] Joab and his men advanced to attack, and the Syrians fled. [15] When the Ammonites saw the Syrians running away, they fled from Abishai and retreated into the city. Then Joab went back to Jerusalem.

[16] The Syrians realized that they had been defeated by the Israelites, so they brought troops from the Syrian states on the east side of the River Euphrates and placed them under the command of Shobach, commander of the army of King Hadadezer of Zobah. [17] When David heard of it, he gathered the Israelite troops, crossed the Jordan, and put them in position facing the Syrians. The fighting began, [18] and the Israelites drove the Syrian army back. David and his men killed 7,000 Syrian chariot drivers and 40,000 foot soldiers. They also killed the Syrian commander, Shobach. [19] When the kings who were subject to Hadadezer realized that they had been defeated by Israel, they made peace with David and became his subjects. The Syrians were never again willing to help the Ammonites.

David Captures Rabbah
(2 Sam 12.26–31)

20 The following spring, at the time of the year when kings usually go to war, Joab led out the army and invaded the land of Ammon; King David, however, stayed in Jerusalem. They besieged the city of Rabbah, attacked it, and destroyed it. [2] The Ammonite idol Molech* had a gold crown which weighed about 34 kilogrammes. In it there was a jewel, which David took and put in his own crown. He also took a large amount of loot from the city. [3] He took the people of the city and put them to work with saws, iron hoes, and axes. He did the same to the people of all the other towns of Ammon. Then he and his men returned to Jerusalem.

Battles against Philistine Giants
(2 Sam 21.15–22)

[4] Later on, war broke out again with the Philistines at Gezer. This was when Sibbecai from Hushah killed a giant named Sippai, and the Philistines were defeated.

[5] There was another battle with the Philistines, and Elhanan son of Jair killed Lahmi, the brother of Goliath from Gath, whose spear had a shaft as thick as the bar on a weaver's loom.

[6] Another battle took place at Gath, where there was a giant with six fingers on each hand and six toes on each foot. He was a descendant of the ancient giants. [7] He defied the Israelites, and Jonathan, the son of David's brother Shammah, killed him.

[8] These three, who were killed by David and his men, were descendants of the giants at Gath.

....

20.2 *Ammonite idol Molech*; or *Ammonite king*.

David Takes a Census
(2 Sam 24.1–25)

21 Satan wanted to bring trouble on the people of Israel, so he made David decide to take a census. [2] David gave orders to Joab and the other officers, "Go through Israel, from one end of the country to the other, and count the people. I want to know how many there are."

[3] Joab answered, "May the LORD make the people of Israel a hundred times more numerous than they are now! Your Majesty, they are all your servants. Why do you want to do this and make the whole nation guilty?" [4] But the king made Joab obey the order. Joab went out, travelled through the whole country of Israel, and then returned to Jerusalem. [5] He reported to King David the total number of men capable of military service: 1,100,000 in Israel, and 470,000 in Judah. [6] Because Joab disapproved of the king's command, he did not take any census of the tribes of Levi and Benjamin.

[7] God was displeased with what had been done, so he punished Israel. [8] David said to God, "I have committed a terrible sin in doing this! Please forgive me. I have acted foolishly."

[9] Then the LORD said to Gad, David's prophet, [10] "Go and tell David that I am giving him three choices. I will do whichever he chooses."

[11] Gad went to David, told him what the LORD had said, and asked, "Which is it to be? [12] Three years of famine? Or three months of running away from the armies of your enemies? Or three days during which the LORD attacks you with his sword and sends an epidemic on your land, using his angel to bring death throughout Israel? What answer shall I give the LORD?"

[13] David replied to Gad, "I am in a desperate situation! But I don't want to be punished by people. Let the LORD himself be the one to punish me, because he is merciful."

[14] So the LORD sent an epidemic on the people of Israel, and 70,000 of them died. [15] Then he sent an angel to destroy Jerusalem, but he changed his mind and said to the angel, "Stop! That's enough!" The angel was standing by the threshing place of Araunah, a Jebusite.

[16] David saw the angel standing in mid air, holding his sword in his hand, ready to destroy Jerusalem. Then David and the leaders of the people — all of whom were wearing sackcloth — bowed low, with their faces touching the ground. [17] David prayed, "O God, I am the one who did wrong. I am the one who ordered the census. What have these poor people done? LORD, my God, punish me and my family, and spare your people."

[18] The angel of the LORD told Gad to command David to go and build an altar to the LORD at Araunah's threshing place. [19] David obeyed the LORD's command and went, as Gad had told him to. [20] There at the threshing place Araunah and his four sons were threshing wheat, and when they saw the angel, the sons ran and hid. [21] As soon as Araunah saw King David approaching, he left the threshing place and bowed low, with his face touching the ground. [22] David said to him, "Sell me your threshing place, so that I can build an altar to the LORD, to stop the epidemic. I'll give you the full price."

[23] "Take it, Your Majesty," Araunah said, "and do whatever you wish. Here are these oxen to burn as an offering on the altar, and here are the threshing boards to use as fuel, and wheat to give as an offering. I give it all to you."

[24] But the king answered, "No, I will pay you the full price. I will not give as an offering to the LORD something that belongs to you,

1 CHRONICLES 21, 22

491

1 Chron.

……….:.

2 Chron.

Ezra

Nehem.

Esther

Job

something that costs me nothing." ²⁵ And he paid Araunah 600 gold coins for the threshing place. ²⁶ He built an altar to the LORD there and offered burnt offerings and fellowship offerings. He prayed, and the LORD answered him by sending fire from heaven to burn the sacrifices on the altar.

²⁷ The LORD told the angel to put his sword away, and the angel obeyed. ²⁸ David saw by this that the LORD had answered his prayer, so he offered sacrifices on the altar at Araunah's threshing place. ²⁹ The Tent of the LORD's presence which Moses had made in the wilderness, and the altar on which sacrifices were burnt were still at the place of worship at Gibeon at this time; ³⁰ but David was not able to go there to worship God, because he was afraid of the sword of the LORD's angel.

22 So David said, "This is where the Temple of the LORD God will be. Here is the altar where the people of Israel are to offer burnt offerings."

Preparations for Building the Temple

² King David gave orders for all the foreigners living in the land of Israel to assemble, and he put them to work. Some of them prepared stone blocks for building the Temple. ³ He supplied a large amount of iron for making nails and clamps for the wooden gates, and so much bronze that no one could weigh it. ⁴ He arranged for the people of Tyre and Sidon to bring him a large number of cedar logs. ⁵ David thought, "The Temple that my son Solomon is to build must be splendid and world-famous. But he is young and inexperienced, so I must make preparations for it." So David got large amounts of the materials ready before he died.

⁶ He sent for his son Solomon and commanded him to build a temple for the LORD, the God of Israel. ⁷ David said to him, "My son, I wanted to build a temple to honour the LORD my God. ⁸ But the LORD told me that I had killed too many people and fought too many wars. And so, because of all the bloodshed I have caused, he would not let me build a temple for him. ⁹ He did, however, make me a promise. He said, 'You will have a son who will rule in peace, because I will give him peace from all his enemies. His name will be Solomon,* because during his reign I will give Israel peace and security. ¹⁰ He will build a temple for me. He will be my son, and I will be his father. His dynasty will rule Israel for ever.' "

¹¹ David continued, "Now, my son, may the LORD your God be with you, and may he keep his promise to make you successful in building a temple for him. ¹² And may the LORD your God give you insight and wisdom so that you may govern Israel according to his Law. ¹³ If you obey all the laws which the LORD gave to Moses for Israel, you will be successful. Be determined and confident, and don't let anything make you afraid. ¹⁴ As for the Temple, by my efforts I have accumulated more than 3,400 tonnes of gold and over 34,000 tonnes of silver to be used in building it. Besides that, there is an unlimited supply of bronze and iron. I also have wood and stone ready, but you must get more. ¹⁵ You have many workmen. There are men to work in the stone quarries, and there are masons and carpenters, as well as a large number of craftsmen of every sort who can work ¹⁶ with gold, silver, bronze, and iron. Now begin the work, and may the LORD be with you."

¹⁷ David commanded all the leaders of Israel to help Solomon. ¹⁸ He said, "The LORD your God has been with you and given you

---

22.9 *Solomon*: This name is formed from the Hebrew word "shalom", which means "peace and security".

peace on all sides. He let me conquer all the people who used to live in this land, and they are now subject to you and to the LORD. ¹⁹Now serve the LORD your God with all your heart and soul. Start building the Temple, so that you can place in it the Covenant Box of the LORD and all the other sacred objects used in worshipping him."

23 When David was very old, he made his son Solomon king of Israel.

The Work of the Levites

²King David brought together all the Israelite leaders and all the priests and Levites. ³He took a census of all the male Levites aged thirty or older. The total was 38,000. ⁴The king assigned 24,000 to administer the work of the Temple, 6,000 to keep records and decide disputes, ⁵4,000 to do guard duty, and 4,000 to praise the LORD, using the musical instruments provided by the king for this purpose.

⁶David divided the Levites into three groups, according to their clans: Gershon, Kohath, and Merari.

⁷Gershon had two sons: Ladan and Shimei. ⁸Ladan had three sons: Jehiel, Zetham, and Joel, ⁹who were the heads of the clans descended from Ladan. (Shimei had three sons: Shelomoth, Haziel, and Haran.)* ¹⁰⁻¹¹Shimei had four sons: Jahath, Zina, Jeush, and Beriah, in order of age. Jeush and Beriah did not have many descendants, so they were counted as one clan.

¹²Kohath had four sons: Amram, Izhar, Hebron, and Uzziel. ¹³His eldest son, Amram, was the father of Aaron and Moses. (Aaron and his descendants were set apart to be in charge of the sacred objects for ever, to burn incense in the worship of the LORD, to serve him, and to bless the people in his name. ¹⁴But the sons of Moses, the man of God, were included among the Levites.) ¹⁵Moses had two sons, Gershom and Eliezer. ¹⁶The leader among Gershom's sons was Shebuel. ¹⁷Eliezer had only one son, Rehabiah, but Rehabiah had many descendants.

¹⁸Kohath's second son, Izhar, had a son, Shelomith, the head of the clan. ¹⁹Kohath's third son, Hebron, had four sons: Jeriah, Amariah, Jahaziel, and Jekameam. ²⁰Kohath's fourth son, Uzziel, had two sons, Micah and Isshiah.

²¹Merari had two sons, Mahli and Mushi. Mahli also had two sons, Eleazar and Kish, ²²but Eleazar died without having any sons, only daughters. His daughters married their cousins, the sons of Kish. ²³Merari's second son, Mushi, had three sons: Mahli, Eder, and Jeremoth.

²⁴These were the descendants of Levi, by clans and families, every one of them registered by name. Each of his descendants, twenty years of age or older, had a share in the work of the LORD's Temple.

²⁵David said, "The LORD God of Israel has given peace to his people, and he himself will live in Jerusalem for ever. ²⁶So there is no longer any need for the Levites to carry the Tent of the LORD's presence and all the equipment used in worship." ²⁷On the basis of David's final instructions all Levites were registered for service when they reached the age of twenty, ²⁸and were assigned the following duties: to help the priests descended from Aaron with the temple worship, to take care of its courtyards and its rooms, and to keep undefiled everything that is sacred; ²⁹to be responsible for

23.9 *Shimei... Haran*: The relation of this list to the list of Shimei's sons in verse 10 is not clear.

1 Chron.

....

2 Chron.

Ezra

Nehem.

Esther

Job

the bread offered to God, the flour used in offerings, the wafers made without yeast, the baked offerings, and the flour mixed with olive oil; to weigh and measure the temple offerings; [30] and to praise and glorify the LORD every morning and every evening [31] and whenever offerings to the LORD are burnt on the Sabbath, the New Moon Festival, and other festivals. Rules were made specifying the number of Levites assigned to do this work each time. The Levites were assigned the duty of worshipping the LORD for all time. [32] They were given the responsibility of taking care of the Tent of the LORD's presence and the Temple, and of assisting their relatives, the priests descended from Aaron, in the temple worship.

The Work Assigned to the Priests

24 These are the groups to which the descendants of Aaron belong. Aaron had four sons: Nadab, Abihu, Eleazar, and Ithamar. [2] Nadab and Abihu died before their father did, and left no descendants, so their brothers Eleazar and Ithamar became priests. [3] King David organized the descendants of Aaron into groups according to their duties. He was assisted in this by Zadok, a descendant of Eleazar, and by Ahimelech, a descendant of Ithamar. [4] The descendants of Eleazar were organized into sixteen groups, while the descendants of Ithamar were organized into eight; this was done because there were more male heads of families among the descendants of Eleazar. [5] Since there were temple officials and spiritual leaders among the descendants of both Eleazar and Ithamar, assignments were made by drawing lots. [6] The descendants of Eleazar and of Ithamar took turns in drawing lots. Then they were registered by Shemaiah son of Nethanel, a Levite secretary. The king, his officials, the priest Zadok, Ahimelech son of Abiathar, and the heads of the priestly families and of the Levite families, were all witnesses.

[7-18] This is the order in which the 24 family groups were given their assignments:

1. Jehoiarib
2. Jedaiah
3. Harim
4. Seorim
5. Malchijah
6. Mijamin
7. Hakkoz
8. Abijah
9. Jeshua
10. Shecaniah
11. Eliashib
12. Jakim
13. Huppah
14. Jeshebeab
15. Bilgah
16. Immer
17. Hezir
18. Happizzez
19. Pethahiah
20. Jehezkel
21. Jachin
22. Gamul
23. Delaiah
24. Maaziah

1 CHRONICLES 24.1-19

Write a list of your

- SPIRITUAL -

FAMILY

- the people around you who encourage your faith. Write down their role in your spiritual life and what they invest in you. Then write down what you might be able to contribute to others spiritually as well.

_____

_____

_____

_____

_____

_____

_____

_____

_____

_____

_____

_____

_____

_____

_____

_____

_____

_____

1 Chron.

Ruth
1 Sam.
2 Sam.
1 Kings
2 Kings

19 These men were registered according to their assignments for going to the Temple and performing the duties established by their ancestor Aaron in obedience to the commands of the LORD God of Israel.

The List of the Levites

20 These are other heads of families descended from Levi:
Jehdeiah, a descendant of Amram through Shebuel;
21 Isshiah, a descendant of Rehabiah;
22 Jahath, a descendant of Izhar through Shelomith;
23 Jeriah, Amariah, Jehaziel, and Jekameam, sons of Hebron, in order of age;
24 Shamir, a descendant of Uzziel through Micah;
25 Zechariah, a descendant of Uzziel through Isshiah, Micah's brother;
26 Mahli, Mushi, and Jaaziah, descendants of Merari. 27 Jaaziah had three sons: Shoham, Zaccur, and Ibri. 28-29 Mahli had two sons, Eleazar and Kish. Eleazar had no sons, but Kish had one son, Jerahmeel. 30 Mushi had three sons: Mahli, Eder, and Jeremoth. These are the families of the Levites.
31 The head of each family and one of his younger brothers drew lots for their assignments, just as their relatives, the priests descended from Aaron, had done. King David, Zadok, Ahimelech, and the heads of families of the priests and of the Levites were witnesses.

The Temple Musicians

25 King David and the leaders of the Levites chose the following Levite clans to lead the services of worship: Asaph, Heman, and Jeduthun. They were to proclaim God's messages, accompanied by the music of harps and cymbals. This is the list of persons chosen to lead the worship, with the type of service that each group performed:
2 The four sons of Asaph: Zaccur, Joseph, Nethaniah, and Asharelah. They were under the direction of Asaph, who proclaimed God's messages whenever the king commanded.
3 The six sons of Jeduthun: Gedaliah, Zeri, Jeshaiah, Shimei, Hashabiah, and Mattithiah. Under the direction of their father they proclaimed God's message, accompanied by the music of harps, and sang praise and thanks to the LORD.
4 The fourteen sons of Heman: Bukkiah, Mattaniah, Uzziel, Shebuel, Jerimoth, Hananiah, Hanani, Eliathah, Giddalti, Romamti Ezer, Joshbekashah, Mallothi, Hothir, and Mahazioth. 5 God gave to Heman, the king's prophet, these fourteen sons and also three daughters, as he had promised, in order to give power to Heman. 6 All his sons played cymbals and harps under their father's direction, to accompany the temple worship. And Asaph, Jeduthun, and Heman were under orders from the king.
7 All these 24 men were experts; and their fellow-Levites were trained musicians. There were 288 men in all.
8 To determine the assignment of duties they all drew lots, whether they were young or old, experts or beginners.
9-31 These 288 men were divided according to families into 24 groups of twelve, with a leader in charge of each group. This is the order in which they were on duty:

1. Joseph of the family of Asaph
2. Gedaliah
3. Zaccur

4. Zeri
5. Nethaniah
6. Bukkiah
7. Asharelah
8. Jeshaiah
9. Mattaniah
10. Shimei
11. Uzziel
12. Hashabiah
13. Shebuel
14. Mattithiah
15. Jerimoth
16. Hananiah
17. Joshbekashah
18. Hanani
19. Mallothi
20. Eliathah
21. Hothir
22. Giddalti
23. Mahazioth
24. Romamti Ezer

The Temple Guards

26 These are the assignments of work for the Levites who served as temple guards. From the clan of Korah there was Meshelemiah son of Kore, of the family of Asaph. ²He had seven sons, listed in order of age: Zechariah, Jediael, Zebadiah, Jathniel, ³Elam, Jehohanan, and Eliehoenai.

⁴There was also Obed Edom, whom God blessed by giving him eight sons, listed in order of age: Shemaiah, Jehozabad, Joah, Sachar, Nethanel, ⁵Ammiel, Issachar, and Peullethai.

⁶⁻⁷Obed Edom's eldest son, Shemaiah, had six sons: Othni, Rephael, Obed, Elzabad, Elihu, and Semachiah. They were important men in their clan because of their great ability; the last two were especially talented.

⁸Obed Edom's family furnished a total of 62 highly qualified men for this work.

⁹Meshelemiah's family furnished eighteen qualified men.

¹⁰From the clan of Merari there was Hosah, who had four sons: Shimri (his father made him the leader, even though he was not the eldest son), ¹¹Hilkiah, Tebaliah, and Zechariah. In all there were thirteen members of Hosah's family who were temple guards.

¹²The temple guards were divided into groups, according to families, and they were assigned duties in the Temple, just as the other Levites were. ¹³Each family, regardless of size, drew lots to see which gate it would be responsible for. ¹⁴Shelemiah drew the east gate, and his son Zechariah, a man who always gave good advice, drew the north gate. ¹⁵Obed Edom was allotted the south gate, and his sons were allotted to guard the storerooms. ¹⁶Shuppim and Hosah were allotted the west gate and the Shallecheth Gate on the upper road. Guard duty was divided into assigned periods, one after another. ¹⁷On the east, six guards were on duty each day, on the north, four, and on the south, four. Four guards were stationed at the storerooms daily, two at each storeroom. ¹⁸Near the western pavilion there were four guards by the road and two at the pavilion itself. ¹⁹This is the assignment of guard duty to the clan of Korah and the clan of Merari.

496

1 Chron.

⫶┈┈┈┈

Ruth
1 Sam.
2 Sam.
1 Kings
2 Kings

1 CHRONICLES 26, 27

Other Temple Duties

20 Others of their fellow-Levites* were in charge of the temple treasury and the storerooms for gifts dedicated to God. 21 Ladan, one of the sons of Gershon, was the ancestor of several family groups, including the family of his son Jehiel. 22 Ladan's two other sons, Zetham and Joel, had charge of the temple treasury and storerooms.

23 Duties were also assigned to the descendants of Amram, Izhar, Hebron, and Uzziel.

24 Shebuel, of the clan of Moses' son Gershom, was the chief official responsible for the temple treasury. 25 Through Gershom's brother Eliezer he was related to Shelomith. Eliezer was the father of Rehabiah, who was the father of Jeshiah, the father of Joram, the father of Zichri, the father of Shelomith. 26 Shelomith and the members of his family were in charge of all the gifts dedicated to God by King David, the heads of families, leaders of clan groups, and army officers. 27 They took some of the loot they captured in battle and dedicated it for use in the Temple. 28 Shelomith and his family were in charge of everything that had been dedicated for use in the Temple, including the gifts brought by the prophet Samuel, by King Saul, by Abner son of Ner, and by Joab son of Zeruiah.

Duties of Other Levites

29 Among the descendants of Izhar, Chenaniah and his sons were assigned administrative duties: keeping records and settling disputes for the people of Israel.

30 Among the descendants of Hebron, Hashabiah and 1,700 of his relatives, all outstanding men, were put in charge of the administration of all religious and civil matters in Israel west of the River Jordan. 31 Jeriah was the leader of the descendants of Hebron. In the fortieth year that David was king, an investigation was made of the family line of Hebron's descendants, and outstanding soldiers belonging to this family were found living at Jazer in the territory of Gilead. 32 King David chose 2,700 outstanding heads of families from Jeriah's relatives and put them in charge of administering all religious and civil matters in Israel east of the River Jordan — the territories of Reuben, Gad, and East Manasseh.

Military and Civil Organization

27 This is the list of the Israelite heads of families and clan leaders and their officials who administered the work of the kingdom. Each month of the year a different group of 24,000 men was on duty under the commander for that month.

2-15 The following were the commanders for each month:

First month: Jashobeam son of Zabdiel (he was a member of the clan of Perez, a part of the tribe of Judah)

Second month: Dodai, a descendant of Ahohi (Mikloth was his second in command)*

Third month: Benaiah son of Jehoiada the priest; he was the leader of "The Thirty" (his son Ammizabad succeeded him as commander of this group)

Fourth month: Asahel, brother of Joab (his son Zebadiah succeeded him)

Fifth month: Shamhuth, a descendant of Izhar

26.20 One ancient translation fellow-Levites; Hebrew Levites, Ahijah.
27.2–15 Probable text Mikloth... command; Hebrew unclear.

1 CHRONICLES 27

497

1 Chron.

···········

2 Chron.

Ezra

Nehem.

Esther

Job

Sixth month: Ira son of Ikkesh from Tekoa

Seventh month: Helez, an Ephraimite from Pelon

Eighth month: Sibbecai from Hushah (he was a member of the clan of Zerah, a part of the tribe of Judah)

Ninth month: Abiezer from Anathoth in the territory of the tribe of Benjamin

Tenth month: Maharai from Netophah (he was a member of the clan of Zerah)

Eleventh month: Benaiah from Pirathon in the territory of the tribe of Ephraim

Twelfth month: Heldai from Netophah (he was a descendant of Othniel).

Administration of the Tribes of Israel

16-22 This is the list of the administrators of the tribes of Israel:

Tribe	Administrator
Reuben	Eliezer son of Zichri
Simeon	Shephatiah son of Maacah
Levi	Hashabiah son of Kemuel
Aaron	Zadok
Judah	Elihu, one of King David's brothers
Issachar	Omri son of Michael
Zebulun	Ishmaiah son of Obadiah
Naphtali	Jeremoth son of Azriel
Ephraim	Hoshea son of Azaziah
West Manasseh	Joel son of Pedaiah
East Manasseh	Iddo son of Zechariah
Benjamin	Jaasiel son of Abner
Dan	Azarel son of Jeroham

23 King David did not take a census of the people who were under the age of twenty, because of the LORD's promise to make the people of Israel as numerous as the stars in the sky. 24 Joab, whose mother was Zeruiah, began to take a census, but he did not complete it. God punished Israel because of this census, so the final figures were never recorded in King David's official records.

Administrators of the Royal Property

25-31 This is the list of those who administered the royal property:

Royal storerooms: Azmaveth son of Adiel

Local storerooms: Jonathan son of Uzziah

Farm labour: Ezri son of Chelub

Vineyards: Shimei from Ramah

Wine cellars: Zabdi from Shepham

Olives and sycomore trees (in the western foothills): Baal Hanan from Geder

Olive oil storage: Joash

Cattle in the Plain of Sharon: Shirtai from Sharon

Cattle in the valleys: Shaphat son of Adlai

Camels: Obil, an Ishmaelite

Donkeys: Jehdeiah from Meronoth

Sheep and goats: Jaziz, a Hagrite.

David's Personal Advisers

32 Jonathan, King David's uncle, was a skilful adviser and a scholar. He and Jehiel son of Hachmoni were in charge of the education of the king's sons. 33 Ahithophel was adviser to the king, and Hushai the Archite was the king's friend and counsellor.

498

1 CHRONICLES 27, 28

1 Chron.

⁝⁝⁝⁝⁝⁝⁝⁝

Ruth
1 Sam.
2 Sam.
1 Kings
2 Kings

³⁴After Ahithophel died, Abiathar and Jehoiada son of Benaiah became advisers. Joab was commander of the royal army.

David's Instructions for the Temple

28 King David commanded all the officials of Israel to assemble in Jerusalem. So all the officials of the tribes, the officials who administered the work of the kingdom, the leaders of the clans, the supervisors of the property and livestock that belonged to the king and his sons — indeed all the palace officials, leading soldiers, and important men — gathered in Jerusalem. ²David stood before them and addressed them: "My friends, listen to me. I wanted to build a permanent home for the Covenant Box, the footstool of the LORD our God. I have made preparations for building a temple to honour him, ³but he has forbidden me to do it, because I am a soldier and have shed too much blood. ⁴The LORD, the God of Israel, chose me and my descendants to rule Israel for ever. He chose the tribe of Judah to provide leadership, and out of Judah he chose my father's family. From all that family it was his pleasure to take me and make me king over all Israel. ⁵He gave me many sons, and out of them all he chose Solomon to rule over Israel, the LORD's kingdom.

⁶"The LORD said to me, 'Your son Solomon is the one who will build my Temple. I have chosen him to be my son, and I will be his father. ⁷I will make his kingdom last for ever if he continues to obey carefully all my laws and commands as he does now.'

⁸"So now, my people, and in the presence of our God and of this assembly of all Israel, the LORD's people, I charge you to obey carefully everything that the LORD our God has commanded us, so that you may continue to possess this good land and so that you may hand it on to succeeding generations for ever."

⁹And to Solomon he said, "My son, I charge you to acknowledge your father's God and to serve him with an undivided heart and a willing mind. He knows all our thoughts and desires. If you go to him, he will accept you; but if you turn away from him, he will abandon you for ever. ¹⁰You must realize that the LORD has chosen you to build his holy Temple. Now do it — and do it with determination."

¹¹David gave Solomon the plans for all the temple buildings, for the storerooms and all the other rooms, and for the Most Holy Place, where sins are forgiven. ¹²He also gave him the plans for all he had in mind for the courtyards and the rooms around them, and for the storerooms for the temple equipment and the gifts dedicated to the LORD. ¹³David also gave him the plans for organizing the priests and Levites to perform their duties, to do the work of the Temple, and to take care of all the temple utensils. ¹⁴He gave instructions as to how much silver and gold was to be used for making the utensils, ¹⁵for each lamp and lampstand, ¹⁶for the silver tables, and for each gold table on which were placed the loaves of bread offered to God. ¹⁷He also gave instructions as to how much pure gold was to be used in making forks, bowls, and jars, how much silver and gold in making dishes, ¹⁸and how much pure gold in making the altar on which incense was burnt and in making the chariot for the winged creatures that spread their wings over the LORD's Covenant Box. ¹⁹King David said, "All this is contained in the plan written according to the instructions which the LORD himself gave me to carry out."

²⁰King David said to his son Solomon, "Be confident and determined. Start the work and don't let anything stop you. The

1 CHRONICLES 28, 29

499

1 Chron.

2 Chron.
Ezra
Nehem.
Esther
Job

LORD God, whom I serve, will be with you. He will not abandon you, but he will stay with you until you finish the work to be done on his Temple. [21] The priests and the Levites have been assigned duties to perform in the Temple. Workers with every kind of skill are eager to help you, and all the people and their leaders are at your command."

Gifts for Building the Temple

29 King David announced to the whole assembly: "My son Solomon is the one whom God has chosen, but he is still young and lacks experience. The work to be done is tremendous, because this is not a palace for people but a temple for the LORD God. [2] I have made every effort to prepare materials for the Temple — gold, silver, bronze, iron, timber, precious stones and gems, stones for mosaics, and quantities of marble. [3] Over and above all this that I have provided, I have given silver and gold from my personal property because of my love for God's Temple. [4] I have given more than a hundred tonnes of the finest gold and almost 240 tonnes of pure silver for decorating the walls of the Temple [5] and for all the objects which the skilled workers are to make. Now who else is willing to give a generous offering to the LORD?"

[6] Then the heads of the clans, the officials of the tribes, the commanders of the army, and the administrators of the royal property volunteered to give [7] the following for the work on the Temple: more than 170 tonnes of gold, over 340 tonnes of silver, almost 620 tonnes of bronze, and more than 3,400 tonnes of iron. [8] Those who had precious stones gave them to the temple treasury, which was administered by Jehiel of the Levite clan of Gershon. [9] The people had given willingly to the LORD, and they were happy that so much had been given. King David also was extremely happy.

David Praises God

[10] There in front of the whole assembly King David praised the LORD. He said, "LORD God of our ancestor Jacob, may you be praised for ever and ever! [11] You are great and powerful, glorious, splendid, and majestic. Everything in heaven and earth is yours, and you are king, supreme ruler over all. [12] All riches and wealth come from you; you rule everything by your strength and power; and you are able to make anyone great and strong. [13] Now, our God, we give you thanks, and we praise your glorious name.

[14] "Yet my people and I cannot really give you anything, because everything is a gift from you, and we have only given back what is yours already. [15] You know, O LORD, that we pass through life like exiles and strangers, as our ancestors did. Our days are like a passing shadow, and we cannot escape death. [16] O LORD, our God, we have brought together all this wealth to build a temple to honour your holy name, but it all came from you and all belongs to you. [17] I know that you test everyone's heart and are pleased with people of integrity. In honesty and sincerity I have willingly given all this to you, and I have seen how your people who are gathered here have been happy to bring offerings to you. [18] LORD God of our ancestors Abraham, Isaac, and Jacob, keep such devotion for ever strong in your people's hearts and keep them always faithful to you. [19] Give my son Solomon a wholehearted desire to obey everything that you command and to build the Temple for which I have made these preparations."

[20] Then David commanded the people, "Praise the LORD your God!" And the whole assembly praised the LORD, the God of their

1 CHRONICLES 29.11

EVERYTHING
··· in ···
HEAVEN
& EARTH
· is yours ·

1 Chron.

....

Ruth
1 Sam.
2 Sam.
1 Kings
2 Kings

ancestors, and they bowed low and gave honour to the LORD and also to the king.

21 The following day they killed animals as sacrifices, dedicating them to the LORD, and then gave them to the people to eat. In addition, they sacrificed a thousand bulls, a thousand rams, and a thousand lambs, which they burnt whole on the altar. They also brought the offerings of wine. 22 So that day they were very happy as they ate and drank in the presence of the LORD.

For a second time they proclaimed Solomon king. In the name of the LORD they anointed him as their ruler and Zadok as priest. 23 So Solomon succeeded his father David on the throne which the LORD had established. He was a successful king, and the whole nation of Israel obeyed him. 24 All the officials and soldiers, and even all of David's other sons promised to be loyal to Solomon as king. 25 The LORD made the whole nation stand in awe of Solomon, and he made him more glorious than any other king that had ruled Israel.

Summary of David's Reign

26 David son of Jesse ruled over all Israel 27 for forty years. He ruled in Hebron for seven years and in Jerusalem for 33. 28 He died at a ripe old age, wealthy and respected, and his son Solomon succeeded him as king. 29 The history of King David from beginning to end is recorded in the records of the three prophets, Samuel, Nathan, and Gad. 30 The records tell how he ruled, how powerful he was, and all the things that happened to him, to Israel, and to the surrounding kingdoms.

THE BOOK OF

2 CHRONICLES

WRITTEN: LATER THAN 1 AND 2 KINGS (PROBABLY 350-300BC)

WHAT YOU NEED TO KNOW:

2 Chronicles is a direct follow-on from 1 Chronicles. While 1 Chronicles covered the rule and reign of David, this book moves on to look at the rule of Solomon in a very positive way - mostly ignoring his weaknesses. However, it also records the defeat of the northern and southern parts of the kingdom before the exile. There is a lot of detail about the building of Solomon's temple. This may be because, before the exile, the temple was destroyed. The people who returned from Babylon had to build it all over again, and would need these instructions!

In this book is a list of the good kings who ruled over the people of Israel. As you read through,

UNDERLINE SOME OF THE

POSITIVE

CHOICES

and actions that the kings made, to help the nation become more like the God that they served.

WHY READ IT?

Although 2 Chronicles is a retelling of 1 and 2 Kings, it highlights different stories, aspects and themes. The point of this book is not necessarily historical accuracy, but the lessons that might be learned from the experiences that the people of Israel have been through, and God's faithfulness throughout.

KEY CHARACTER:

Solomon was known for his wisdom as well as his power and wealth (see chapter 1). Even the Queen of Sheba came from miles away to see what all the fuss was about. Solomon was an incredible king, and this book tells you all the good bits of his reign. He did make plenty of mistakes as well, but you'll need to read 1 Kings 11 to find out about them.

KING SOLOMON BUILDS THE TEMPLE

JUDAH FALLS TO BABYLON

960BC

JUDAH AND ISRAEL SPLIT

(586BC)

King Solomon Prays for Wisdom
(1 Kgs 3.1–15)

1 Solomon, the son of King David, took firm control of the kingdom of Israel, and the LORD his God blessed him and made him very powerful.

[2] King Solomon gave an order to all the officers in charge of units of a thousand men and of a hundred men, all the government officials, all the heads of families, and all the rest of the people, [3] commanding them to go with him to the place of worship at Gibeon. They went there because that was where the Tent of the LORD's presence was located, which Moses, the LORD's servant, had made in the wilderness. [4] (The Covenant Box, however, was in Jerusalem, kept in a tent which King David had set up when he brought the Box from Kiriath Jearim.) [5] The bronze altar which had been made by Bezalel, the son of Uri and grandson of Hur, was also in Gibeon in front of the Tent of the LORD's presence. King Solomon and all the people worshipped the LORD there. [6] In front of the Tent the king worshipped the LORD by offering sacrifices on the bronze altar; he had a thousand animals killed and burnt whole on it.

[7] That night God appeared to Solomon and asked, "What would you like me to give you?"

[8] Solomon answered, "You always showed great love for my father David, and now you have let me succeed him as king. [9] O LORD God, fulfil the promise you made to my father. You have made me king over a people who are so many that they cannot be counted, [10] so give me the wisdom and knowledge I need to rule over them. Otherwise, how would I ever be able to rule this great people of yours?"

[11] God replied to Solomon, "You have made the right choice. Instead of asking for wealth or treasure or fame or the death of your enemies or even for long life for yourself, you have asked for wisdom and knowledge so that you can rule my people, over whom I have made you king. [12] I will give you wisdom and knowledge. And in addition, I will give you more wealth, treasure, and fame than any king has ever had before or will ever have again."

King Solomon's Power and Wealth
(1 Kgs 10.26–29)

[13] So Solomon left* the place of worship at Gibeon, where the Tent of the LORD's presence was, and returned to Jerusalem. There he ruled over Israel. [14] He built up a force of 1,400 chariots and 12,000 cavalry horses. Some of them he kept in Jerusalem, and the rest he stationed in various other cities. [15] During his reign silver and gold became as common in Jerusalem as stone, and cedar was as plentiful as ordinary sycamore. [16] The king's agents controlled the export of horses from Musri* and Cilicia,* [17] and the export of chariots from Egypt. They supplied the Hittite and Syrian kings with horses and chariots, selling chariots for 600 pieces of silver each and horses for 150 each.*

Preparations for Building the Temple
(1 Kgs 5.1–18)

2 King Solomon decided to build a temple where the LORD would be worshipped, and also to build a palace for himself. [2] He

---

1.13 Some ancient translations *left*; Hebrew *came to*.
1.16 Probable text *Musri*; Hebrew *Egypt*.
1.16 *Musri and Cilicia*: Two ancient countries in what is now south-east Turkey which were centres of horse breeding in Solomon's time.
1.17 Verses 16–17 in Hebrew are unclear.

2 CHRONICLES 2, 3

503

2 Chron.

Ezra
Nehem.
Esther
Job
Psalms

put 70,000 men to work transporting materials, and 80,000 to work quarrying stone. There were 3,600 others responsible for supervising the work.

[3] Solomon sent a message to King Hiram of Tyre: "Do business with me as you did with my father, King David, when you sold him cedar logs for building his palace. [4] I am building a temple to honour the LORD my God. It will be a holy place where my people and I will worship him by burning incense of fragrant spices, where we will present offerings of sacred bread to him continuously, and where we will offer burnt offerings every morning and evening, as well as on Sabbaths, New Moon Festivals, and other holy days honouring the LORD our God. He has commanded Israel to do this for ever. [5] I intend to build a great temple, because our God is greater than any other god. [6] Yet no one can really build a temple for God, because even all the vastness of heaven cannot contain him. How then can I build a temple that would be anything more than a place to burn incense to God? [7] Now send me a man with skill in engraving, in working gold, silver, bronze, and iron, and in making blue, purple and red cloth. He will work with the craftsmen of Judah and Jerusalem whom my father David selected. [8] I know how skilful your woodmen are, so send me cedar, cypress, and juniper logs from Lebanon. I am ready to send my men to assist yours [9] in preparing large quantities of timber, because this temple I intend to build will be large and magnificent. [10] As provisions for your workmen, I will send you 2,000 tonnes of wheat, 2,000 tonnes of barley, 400,000 litres of wine, and 400,000 litres of olive oil."

[11] King Hiram sent Solomon a letter in reply. He wrote, "Because the LORD loves his people, he has made you their king. [12] Praise the LORD God of Israel, Creator of heaven and earth! He has given King David a wise son, full of understanding and skill, who now plans to build a temple for the LORD and a palace for himself. [13] I am sending you a wise and skilful master craftsman named Huram. [14] His mother was a member of the tribe of Dan and his father was a native of Tyre. He knows how to make things out of gold, silver, bronze, iron, stone, and wood. He can work with blue, purple, and red cloth, and with linen. He can do all sorts of engraving and can follow any design suggested to him. Let him work with your skilled workers and with those who worked for your father, King David. [15] So now send us the wheat, barley, wine, and olive oil that you promised. [16] In the mountains of Lebanon we will cut down all the cedars you need, bind them together in rafts, and float them by sea as far as Joppa. From there you can take them to Jerusalem."

Construction of the Temple Begins
(1 Kgs 6.1–38)

[17] King Solomon took a census of all the foreigners living in the land of Israel, similar to the census his father David had taken. There were 153,600 resident foreigners. [18] He assigned 70,000 of them to transport materials and 80,000 to cut stones in the mountains, and appointed 3,600 supervisors to make sure the work was done.

3 King David, Solomon's father, had already prepared a place for the Temple. It was in Jerusalem, on Mount Moriah, where the LORD appeared to David, the place which Araunah the Jebusite had used as a threshing place. King Solomon began the construction [2] in the second month of the fourth year that he was king. [3] The Temple which King Solomon built was 27 metres long and nine

2 CHRONICLES 2.11-16

We see here that God uses creative people to express his beauty and power.

DECORATE
– THESE –
PAGES

in a way that says something about the character of God.

504

2 Chron.

1 Sam.
2 Sam.
1 Kings
2 Kings
1 Chron.

2 CHRONICLES 3, 4

metres wide. ⁴ The entrance room was the full width of the Temple, nine metres, and was 54 metres high. The inside of the room was overlaid with pure gold. ⁵ The main room was panelled with cedar and overlaid with fine gold, in which were worked designs of palm trees and chain patterns. ⁶ The king decorated the Temple with beautiful precious stones and with gold imported from the land of Parvaim. ⁷ He used the gold to overlay the temple walls, the rafters, the thresholds, and the doors. On the walls the workers carved designs of winged creatures. ⁸ The inner room, called the Most Holy Place, was nine metres long and nine metres wide, which was the full width of the Temple. Over twenty tonnes of gold were used to cover the walls of the Most Holy Place; ⁹ 570 grammes of gold were used for making nails, and the walls of the upper rooms were also covered with gold.

¹⁰ The king also ordered his workers to make two winged creatures out of metal, cover them with gold, and place them in the Most Holy Place, ¹¹⁻¹³ where they stood side by side facing the entrance. Each had two wings, each wing 2.2 metres long, which were spread out so that they touched each other in the centre of the room and reached the wall on either side of the room, stretching across the full width of about nine metres. ¹⁴ A curtain for the Most Holy Place was made of linen and of other material, which was dyed blue, purple, and red, with designs of the winged creatures worked into it.

The Two Bronze Columns
(1 Kgs 7.15–22)

¹⁵ The king made two columns, each one 15.5 metres tall, and placed them in front of the Temple. Each one had a capital 2.2 metres tall. ¹⁶ The tops of the columns were decorated with a design of interwoven chains and 100 bronze pomegranates.* ¹⁷ The columns were set at the sides of the temple entrance: the one on the south side was named Jachin,* and the one on the north side was named Boaz.*

Equipment for the Temple
(1 Kgs 7.23–51)

4 King Solomon had a bronze altar made, which was nine metres square and 4.5 metres high. ² He also made a round tank of bronze, 2.2 metres deep, 4.5 metres in diameter, and 13.2 metres in circumference. ³ All round the outer edge of the rim of the tank* were two rows of decorations, one above the other. The decorations were in the shape of bulls, which had been cast all in one piece with the rest of the tank. ⁴ The tank rested on the backs of twelve bronze bulls that faced outwards, three facing in each direction. ⁵ The sides of the tank were 75 millimetres thick. Its rim was like the rim of a cup, curving outwards like the petals of a flower. The tank held about 60,000 litres. ⁶ They also made ten basins, five to be placed on the south side of the Temple and five on the north side. They were to be used to rinse the parts of the animals that were burnt as sacrifices. The water in the large tank was for the priests to use for washing.

⁷⁻⁸ They made ten gold lampstands according to the usual pattern, and ten tables, and placed them in the main room of

3.16 Verse 16 in Hebrew is unclear.
3.17 Jachin: This name sounds like the Hebrew for "he (God) establishes".
3.17 Boaz: This name sounds like the Hebrew for "by his (God's) strength".
4.3 Probable text All round... tank; Hebrew unclear.

2 CHRONICLES 4, 5

505

2 Chron.

············:·

Ezra
Nehem.
Esther
Job
Psalms

the Temple, five lampstands and five tables on each side. They also made a hundred gold bowls.

⁹They made an inner courtyard for the priests, and also an outer courtyard. The doors in the gates between the courtyards were covered with bronze. ¹⁰The tank was placed near the south-east corner of the Temple.

¹¹⁻¹⁶Huram also made pots, shovels, and bowls. He completed all the objects that he had promised King Solomon he would make for the Temple:

The two columns
The two bowl-shaped capitals on top of the columns
The design of interwoven chains on each capital
The 400 bronze pomegranates arranged in two rows
    round the design of each capital
The ten* carts
The ten basins
The tank
The twelve bulls supporting the tank
The pots, shovels, and forks.

Huram the master craftsman made all these objects* out of polished bronze, as King Solomon had commanded, for use in the Temple of the Lord.

¹⁷The king had them all made in the foundry between Sukkoth and Zeredah* in the Jordan Valley. ¹⁸So many objects were made that no one determined the total weight of the bronze used.

¹⁹King Solomon also had gold furnishings made for the Temple: the altar and the tables for the bread offered to God; ²⁰the lampstands and the lamps of fine gold that were to burn in front of the Most Holy Place, according to plan; ²¹the flower decorations, the lamps, and the tongs; ²²the lamp snuffers, the bowls, the dishes for incense, and the pans used for carrying live coals. All these objects were made of pure gold. The outer doors of the Temple and the doors to the Most Holy Place were overlaid with gold.

5 When King Solomon finished all the work on the Temple, he placed in the temple storerooms all the things that his father David had dedicated to the Lord — the silver, gold, and other articles.

The Covenant Box is Brought to the Temple
(1 Kgs 8.1–9)

²Then King Solomon summoned all the leaders of the tribes and clans of Israel to assemble in Jerusalem, in order to take the Lord's Covenant Box from Zion, David's City, to the Temple. ³They all assembled at the time of the Festival of Shelters. ⁴When all the leaders had gathered, then the Levites lifted the Covenant Box ⁵and carried it to the Temple. The priests and the Levites also moved the Tent of the Lord's presence and all its equipment to the Temple. ⁶King Solomon and all the people of Israel assembled in front of the Covenant Box and sacrificed a large number of sheep and cattle — too many to count. ⁷Then the priests carried the Covenant Box of the Lord into the Temple and put it in the Most Holy Place, beneath the winged creatures. ⁸Their outstretched wings covered the Box and the carrying poles. ⁹The ends of the poles could be seen by anyone standing directly in front of the

4.11–16 Probable text (see 1 Kgs 7.40–45) ten; Hebrew he made.
4.11–16 One ancient translation all these objects; Hebrew all their objects.
4.17 Zeredah; or Zarethan (see 1 Kgs 7.46).

506

2 Chron.

⋮········

1 Sam.
2 Sam.
1 Kings
2 Kings
1 Chron.

2 CHRONICLES 5, 6

Most Holy Place, but from nowhere else. (The poles are still there today.) [10] There was nothing inside the Covenant Box except the two stone tablets which Moses had placed there at Mount Sinai, when the LORD made a covenant with the people of Israel as they were coming from Egypt.

The Glory of the Lord

[11-14] All the priests present, regardless of the group to which they belonged, had consecrated themselves. And all the Levite musicians — Asaph, Heman, and Jeduthun, and the members of their clans — were wearing linen clothing. The Levites stood near the east side of the altar with cymbals and harps, and with them were 120 priests playing trumpets. The singers were accompanied in perfect harmony by trumpets, cymbals, and other instruments, as they praised the LORD, singing:

"Praise the LORD, because he is good,
And his love is eternal."

As the priests were leaving the Temple, it was suddenly filled with a cloud shining with the dazzling light of the LORD's presence, and they could not continue the service of worship.

Solomon's Address to the People
(1 Kgs 8.12–21)

6 Then King Solomon prayed,
"LORD, you have chosen to live in clouds and darkness.
[2] Now I have built a majestic temple for you,
a place for you to live in for ever."

[3] All the people of Israel were standing there. The king turned to face them and asked God's blessing on them. [4] He said, "Praise the LORD God of Israel! He has kept the promise he made to my father David when he said to him, [5] 'From the time I brought my people out of Egypt until now, I did not choose any city in the land of Israel as the place to build a temple where I would be worshipped, and I did not choose anyone to lead my people Israel. [6] But now I have chosen Jerusalem as the place where I will be worshipped, and you, David, to rule my people.'"

[7] And Solomon continued, "My father David planned to build a temple for the worship of the LORD God of Israel, [8] but the LORD said to him, 'You were right in wanting to build a temple for me, [9] but you will never build it. It is your son, your own son, who will build my temple.'

[10] "Now the LORD has kept his promise: I have succeeded my father as king of Israel, and I have built a temple for the worship of the LORD God of Israel. [11] I have placed in the Temple the Covenant Box, which contains the stone tablets of the covenant which the LORD made with the people of Israel."

Solomon's Prayer
(1 Kgs 8.22–53)

[12] Then in the presence of the people Solomon went and stood in front of the altar and raised his arms in prayer. [13] (Solomon had made a bronze platform and put it in the middle of the courtyard. It was 2.2 metres square and 1.3 metres high. He mounted this platform, knelt down where everyone could see him, and raised his hands towards heaven.) [14] He prayed, "LORD God of Israel, in all heaven and earth there is no god like you. You keep your covenant with your people and show them your love when they live in wholehearted obedience to you. [15] You have kept the promise you made to my father David; today every word has been fulfilled.

2 Chron.

Ezra

Nehem.

Esther

Job

Psalms

¹⁶ Now, LORD God of Israel, keep the other promise you made to my father when you told him that there would always be one of his descendants ruling as king of Israel, provided that they carefully obeyed your Law just as he did. ¹⁷ So now, LORD God of Israel, let everything come true that you promised to your servant David.

¹⁸ "But can you, O God, really live on earth among men and women? Not even all heaven is large enough to hold you, so how can this Temple that I have built be large enough? ¹⁹ LORD my God, I am your servant. Listen to my prayer and grant the requests I make to you. ²⁰ Watch over this Temple day and night. You have promised that this is where you will be worshipped, so hear me when I face this Temple and pray. ²¹ Hear my prayers and the prayers of your people Israel when they face this place and pray. In your home in heaven hear us and forgive us.

²² "When a person is accused of wronging another and is brought to your altar in this Temple to take an oath that he is innocent, ²³ O LORD, listen in heaven and judge your servants. Punish the guilty one as he deserves and acquit the one who is innocent.

²⁴ "When your people Israel are defeated by their enemies because they have sinned against you and then when they turn to you and come to this Temple, humbly praying to you for forgiveness, ²⁵ listen to them in heaven. Forgive the sins of your people and bring them back to the land which you gave to them and to their ancestors.

²⁶ "When you hold back the rain because your people have sinned against you and then when they repent and face this Temple, humbly praying to you, ²⁷ O LORD, listen to them in heaven and forgive the sins of your servants, the people of Israel, and teach them to do what is right. Then, O LORD, send rain on this land of yours, which you gave to your people as a permanent possession.

²⁸ "When there is famine in the land or an epidemic or the crops are destroyed by scorching winds or swarms of locusts, or when your people are attacked by their enemies, or when there is disease or sickness among them, ²⁹ listen to their prayers. If any of your people Israel, out of heartfelt sorrow, stretch out their hands in prayer towards this Temple, ³⁰ hear their prayer. Listen to them in your home in heaven and forgive them. You alone know the thoughts of the human heart. Deal with each person as he deserves, ³¹ so that your people may honour you and obey you all the time they live in the land which you gave to our ancestors.

³² "When foreigners who live in a distant land hear how great and powerful you are and how you are always ready to act, and then they come to pray at this Temple, ³³ listen to their prayers. In heaven, where you live, hear them and do what they ask you to do, so that all the peoples of the world may know you and obey you, as your people Israel do. Then they will know that this Temple I have built is where you are to be worshipped.

³⁴ "When you command your people to go into battle against their enemies and they pray to you, wherever they are, facing this city which you have chosen and this Temple which I have built for you, ³⁵ listen to their prayers. Hear them in heaven and give them victory.

³⁶ "When your people sin against you — and there is no one who does not sin — and in your anger you let their enemies defeat them and take them as prisoners to some other land, even if that land is far away, ³⁷ listen to your people's prayers. If there in that land they repent and pray to you, confessing how sinful and wicked they have been, hear their prayers, O LORD. ³⁸ If in

Write here what you will be praying about this week.

2 Chron.

1 Sam.
2 Sam.
1 Kings
2 Kings
1 Chron.

that land they truly and sincerely repent and pray to you as they face towards this land which you gave to our ancestors, this city which you have chosen, and this Temple which I have built for you, ³⁹ then listen to their prayers. In your home in heaven hear them and be merciful to them and forgive all the sins of your people.

⁴⁰ "Now, O my God, look on us and listen to the prayers offered in this place. ⁴¹ Rise up now, Lord God, and with the Covenant Box, the symbol of your power, enter the Temple and stay here for ever. Bless your priests in all they do, and may all your people be happy because of your goodness to them. ⁴² Lord God, do not reject the king you have chosen. Remember the love you had for your servant David."*

The Dedication of the Temple
(1 Kgs 8.62–66)

7 When King Solomon finished his prayer, fire came down from heaven and burnt up the sacrifices that had been offered, and the dazzling light of the Lord's presence filled the Temple. ² Because the Temple was full of the dazzling light, the priests could not enter it. ³ When the people of Israel saw the fire fall from heaven and the light fill the Temple, they fell face downwards on the pavement, worshipping God and praising him for his goodness and his eternal love. ⁴ Then Solomon and all the people offered sacrifices to the Lord. ⁵ He sacrificed 22,000 head of cattle and 120,000 sheep as fellowship offerings. And so he and all the people dedicated the Temple. ⁶ The priests stood in the places that were assigned to them, and facing them stood the Levites, praising the Lord with the musical instruments that King David had provided and singing the hymn, "His Love is Eternal!" as they had been commissioned by David. The priests blew trumpets while all the people stood.

⁷ Solomon consecrated the central part of the courtyard, the area in front of the Temple, and then offered there the sacrifices burnt whole, the grain offerings, and the fat from the fellowship offerings. He did this because the bronze altar which he had made was too small for all these offerings.

⁸ Solomon and all the people of Israel celebrated the Festival of Shelters for seven days. There was a huge crowd of people from as far away as Hamath Pass in the north and the Egyptian border in the south. ⁹ They had spent seven days for the dedication of the altar and then seven more days for the festival. On the last day they had a closing celebration, ¹⁰ and on the following day, the 23rd day of the seventh month, Solomon sent the people home. They were happy about all the blessings that the Lord had given to his people Israel, to David, and to Solomon.

God Appears to Solomon Again
(1 Kgs 9.1–9)

¹¹ After King Solomon had finished the Temple and the palace, successfully completing all his plans for them, ¹² the Lord appeared to him at night. He said to him, "I have heard your prayer, and I accept this Temple as the place where sacrifices are to be offered to me. ¹³ Whenever I hold back the rain or send locusts to eat up the crops or send an epidemic on my people, ¹⁴ if they pray to me and repent and turn away from the evil they have been doing, then I will hear them in heaven, forgive their sins, and make their land prosperous again. ¹⁵ I will watch over this Temple and

6.42 the love you… David; or your servant David's loyal service.

2 CHRONICLES 7, 8

509

2 Chron.
....

Ezra
Nehem.
Esther
Job
Psalms

be ready to hear all the prayers that are offered here, [16] because I have chosen it and consecrated it as the place where I will be worshipped for ever. I will watch over it and protect it for all time. [17] If you serve me faithfully as your father David did, obeying my laws and doing everything I have commanded you, [18] I will keep the promise I made to your father David when I told him that Israel would always be ruled by his descendants. [19] But if you and your people ever disobey the laws and commands I have given you, and worship other gods, [20] then I will remove you from the land that I gave you, and I will abandon this Temple that I have consecrated as the place where I am to be worshipped. People everywhere will ridicule it and treat it with contempt.

[21] "The Temple is now greatly honoured, but then everyone who passes by it will be amazed and will ask, 'Why did the LORD do this to this land and this Temple?' [22] People will answer, 'It is because they abandoned the LORD their God, who brought their ancestors out of Egypt. They gave their allegiance to other gods and worshipped them. That is why the LORD has brought this disaster on them.'"

Solomon's Achievements
(1 Kgs 9.10–28)

8 It took Solomon twenty years to build the Temple and his palace. [2] He also rebuilt the cities that King Hiram had given him, and sent Israelites to settle in them. [3] He captured the territory of Hamath and Zobah [4] and fortified the city of Palmyra in the desert. He rebuilt all the cities in Hamath that were centres for storing supplies. [5] Solomon also rebuilt the following cities: Upper Beth Horon and Lower Beth Horon (fortified cities with gates that could be barred), [6] the city of Baalath, all the cities where he stored supplies, and the cities where his horses and chariots were stationed. He carried out all his plans for building in Jerusalem, in Lebanon, and throughout the territory that he ruled over. [7-8] Solomon employed in forced labour all the descendants of the people of Canaan whom the Israelites had not killed when they took possession of the land. These included Hittites, Amorites, Perizzites, Hivites, and Jebusites, whose descendants continue to be slaves down to the present time. [9] Israelites were not used in forced labour, but served as soldiers, officers, chariot commanders, and horsemen. [10] There were 250 officials in charge of the forced labour working on the various building projects.

[11] Solomon moved his wife, the daughter of the king of Egypt, from David's City to a house he built for her. He said, "She must not live in the palace of King David of Israel, because any place where the Covenant Box has been is holy."

[12] Solomon offered sacrifices to the LORD on the altar which he had built in front of the Temple. [13] He offered burnt offerings according to the requirements of the Law of Moses for each holy day: Sabbaths, New Moon Festivals, and the three annual festivals — the Festival of Unleavened Bread, the Harvest Festival, and the Festival of Shelters. [14] Following the rules laid down by his father David, he organized the daily work of the priests and of the Levites who assisted the priests in singing hymns and in doing their work. He also organized the temple guards in sections for performing their daily duties at each gate, in accordance with the commands of David, the man of God. [15] The instructions which David had given the priests and the Levites concerning the storehouses and other matters were carried out in detail.

510

2 Chron.
⋮⋯⋯⋯⋮

1 Sam.
2 Sam.
1 Kings
2 Kings
1 Chron.

2 CHRONICLES 8, 9

¹⁶By this time all Solomon's projects had been completed. From the laying of the foundation of the Lord's Temple to its completion, all the work had been successful. ¹⁷Then Solomon went to Eziongeber and Elath, ports on the shore of the Gulf of Aqaba, in the land of Edom. ¹⁸King Hiram sent him ships under the command of his own officers and crewed by experienced sailors. They sailed with Solomon's officers to the land of Ophir and brought back to Solomon more than fifteen tonnes of gold.

The Visit of the Queen of Sheba
(1 Kgs 10.1–13)

9 The queen of Sheba heard of King Solomon's fame, and she travelled to Jerusalem to test him with difficult questions. She brought with her a large group of attendants, as well as camels loaded with spices, jewels, and a large amount of gold. When she and Solomon met, she asked him all the questions that she could think of. ²He answered them all; there was nothing too difficult for him to explain. ³The queen of Sheba heard Solomon's wisdom and saw the palace he had built. ⁴She saw the food that was served at his table, the living quarters for his officials, the organization of his palace staff and the uniforms they wore, the clothing of the servants who waited on him at feasts, and the sacrifices he offered* in the Temple. It left her breathless and amazed.

⁵She said to the king, "What I heard in my own country about you* and your wisdom is true! ⁶I did not believe what they told me until I came and saw for myself. I had not heard of even half your wisdom. You are even wiser than people say. ⁷How fortunate are those who serve you, who are always in your presence and are privileged to hear your wise sayings! ⁸Praise the Lord your God! He has shown how pleased he is with you by making you king, to rule in his name. Because he loves his people Israel and wants to preserve them for ever, he has made you their king so that you can maintain law and justice."

⁹She presented to King Solomon the gifts she had brought: more than four tonnes of gold and a very large amount of spices and jewels. There have never been any other spices as fine as those that the queen of Sheba gave to King Solomon.

¹⁰(The men of King Hiram and of King Solomon who brought gold from Ophir also brought juniper wood and jewels. ¹¹Solomon used the wood to make stairs for the Temple and for his palace, and to make harps and lyres for the musicians. Nothing like that had ever been seen before in the land of Judah.)

¹²King Solomon gave the queen of Sheba everything she asked for. This was in addition to what he gave her in exchange for the gifts* she brought to him. Then she and her attendants returned to the land of Sheba.

King Solomon's Wealth
(1 Kgs 10.14–25)

¹³Every year King Solomon received almost 23 tonnes of gold, ¹⁴in addition to the taxes paid by the traders and merchants. The kings of Arabia and the governors of the Israelite districts also brought him silver and gold. ¹⁵Solomon made 200 large shields,

2 CHRONICLES 9

Solomon had committed himself to

– PUTTING GOD –

FIRST

and pursuing wisdom. This meant that when other people came to look at his life close up, they were left 'breathless and amazed'.

Spend some time examining your own life.

If someone came and looked at your life close up, what would they find? What would it tell them about God?

9.4 Probable text (see 1 Kgs 10.5) *sacrifices he offered*; Hebrew *his upper rooms*.
9.5 *you*; or *your deeds*.
9.12 Probable text *he gave her in exchange for the gifts*; Hebrew unclear.

2 Chron.

Ezra
Nehem.
Esther
Job
Psalms

each of which was covered with about seven kilogrammes of beaten gold, [16] and 300 smaller shields, each covered with about three kilogrammes of beaten gold. He had them all placed in the Hall of the Forest of Lebanon.*

[17] The king also had a large throne made. Part of it was covered with ivory and the rest of it was covered with pure gold. [18] Six steps led up to the throne, and there was a footstool attached to it, covered with gold. There were arms on each side of the throne, and the figure of a lion stood at each side. [19] Twelve figures of lions were on the steps, one at either end of each step. No throne like this had ever existed in any other kingdom.

[20] All King Solomon's cups were made of gold, and all the utensils in the Hall of the Forest of Lebanon were of pure gold. Silver was not considered valuable in Solomon's day. [21] He had a fleet of ocean-going ships sailing with King Hiram's fleet. Every three years his fleet would return, bringing gold, silver, ivory, apes, and monkeys.

[22] King Solomon was richer and wiser than any other king in the world. [23] They all consulted him, to hear the wisdom that God had given him. [24] Each of them brought Solomon gifts — articles of silver and gold, robes, weapons, spices, horses, and mules. This continued year after year.

[25] King Solomon also had 4,000 stalls for his chariots and horses, and had 12,000 cavalry horses. Some of them he kept in Jerusalem and the rest he stationed in various other cities. [26] He was supreme ruler of all the kings in the territory from the River Euphrates to Philistia and the Egyptian border. [27] During his reign silver was as common in Jerusalem as stone, and cedar was as plentiful as ordinary sycamore in the foothills of Judah. [28] Solomon imported horses from Musri* and from every other country.

Summary of Solomon's Reign
(1 Kgs 11.41–43)

[29] The rest of the history of Solomon from beginning to end is recorded in *The History of Nathan the Prophet*, in *The Prophecy of Ahijah of Shiloh*, and in *The Visions of Iddo the Prophet*, which also deal with the reign of King Jeroboam of Israel. [30] Solomon ruled in Jerusalem over all Israel for forty years. [31] He died and was buried in David's City, and his son Rehoboam succeeded him as king.

The Northern Tribes Revolt
(1 Kgs 12.1–20)

10 Rehoboam went to Shechem, where all the people of northern Israel had gathered to make him king. [2] When Jeroboam son of Nebat, who had gone to Egypt to escape from King Solomon, heard this news, he returned home. [3] The people of the northern tribes sent for him, and they all went together to Rehoboam and said to him, [4] "Your father placed heavy burdens on us. If you make these burdens lighter and make life easier for us, we will be your loyal subjects."

[5] Rehoboam replied, "Give me three days to consider the matter. Then come back." So the people left.

[6] King Rehoboam consulted the older men who had served as his father Solomon's advisers. "What answer do you advise me to give these people?" he asked.

....

9.16 *Hall of the Forest of Lebanon*: A large ceremonial hall in the palace, probably so called because it was panelled in cedar.
9.28 Probable text (see 1.16) *Musri*; Hebrew *Egypt*.

2 Chron.

1 Sam.
2 Sam.
1 Kings
2 Kings
1 Chron.

[7] They replied, "If you are kind to these people and try to please them by giving a considerate answer, they will always serve you loyally."

[8] But he ignored the advice of the older men and went instead to the young men who had grown up with him and who were now his advisers. [9] "What do you advise me to do?" he asked. "What shall I say to the people who are asking me to make their burdens lighter?"

[10] They replied, "This is what you should tell them: 'My little finger is thicker than my father's waist.' [11] Tell them, 'My father placed heavy burdens on you; I will make them even heavier. He beat you with a whip; I'll flog you with a horsewhip!'"

[12] Three days later Jeroboam and all the people returned to King Rehoboam, as he had instructed them. [13] The king ignored the advice of the older men and spoke harshly to the people, [14] as the younger men had advised. He said, "My father placed heavy burdens on you; I will make them even heavier. He beat you with a whip; I'll flog you with a horsewhip!" [15] It was the will of the LORD God to bring about what he had spoken to Jeroboam son of Nebat through the prophet Ahijah from Shiloh. This is why the king did not pay any attention to the people.

[16] When the people saw that the king would not listen to them, they shouted, "Down with David and his family! What have they ever done for us? People of Israel, let's go home! Let Rehoboam look out for himself!"

So the people of Israel rebelled, [17] leaving Rehoboam as king only of the people who lived in the territory of Judah.

[18] Then King Rehoboam sent Adoniram, who was in charge of the forced labour, to go to the Israelites, but they stoned him to death. At this, Rehoboam hurriedly got into his chariot and escaped to Jerusalem. [19] Ever since that time the people of the northern kingdom of Israel have been in rebellion against the dynasty of David.

Shemaiah's Prophecy
(1 Kgs 12.21–24)

11 When King Rehoboam arrived in Jerusalem, he called together 180,000 of the best soldiers from the tribes of Benjamin and Judah. He intended to go to war and restore his control over the northern tribes of Israel. [2] But the LORD told the prophet Shemaiah [3] to give this message to King Rehoboam and to all the people of the tribes of Judah and Benjamin: [4] "Do not attack your fellow-Israelites. Go home, all of you. What has happened is my will." They obeyed the LORD's command and did not go to fight Jeroboam.

Rehoboam Fortifies the Cities

[5] Rehoboam remained in Jerusalem and had fortifications built for the following cities of Judah and Benjamin: [6] Bethlehem, Etam, Tekoa, [7] Bethzur, Soco, Adullam, [8] Gath, Mareshah, Ziph, [9] Adoraim, Lachish, Azekah, [10] Zorah, Aijalon, and Hebron. [11] He had them strongly fortified and appointed a commander for each of them, and in each one he placed supplies of food, olive oil, and wine, [12] and also shields and spears. In this way he kept Judah and Benjamin under his control.

Priests and Levites Come to Judah

[13] From all the territory of Israel priests and Levites came south to Judah. [14] The Levites abandoned their pastures and other land

2 Chron.

············:·

Ezra
Nehem.
Esther
Job
Psalms

and moved to Judah and Jerusalem, because King Jeroboam of Israel and his successors would not let them serve as priests of the LORD. [15] Jeroboam appointed priests of his own to serve at the pagan places of worship and to worship demons and the idols he made in the form of bull calves. [16] From all the tribes of Israel people who sincerely wanted to worship the LORD, the God of Israel, followed the Levites to Jerusalem, so that they could offer sacrifices to the LORD, the God of their ancestors. [17] This strengthened the kingdom of Judah, and for three years they supported Rehoboam son of Solomon and lived as they had under the rule of King David and King Solomon.

Rehoboam's Family

[18] Rehoboam married Mahalath, whose father was Jerimoth son of David, and whose mother was Abihail, the daughter of Eliab and granddaughter of Jesse. [19] They had three sons, Jeush, Shemariah, and Zaham. [20] Later he married Maacah, the daughter of Absalom, and they had four sons: Abijah, Attai, Ziza, and Shelomith. [21] In all, Rehoboam had eighteen wives and sixty concubines, and he fathered 28 sons and sixty daughters. Of all his wives and concubines he loved Maacah best, [22] and he favoured her son Abijah over all his other children, choosing him as the one to succeed him as king. [23] Rehoboam wisely assigned responsibilities to his sons, and stationed them throughout Judah and Benjamin in the fortified cities. He provided generously for them and also secured many wives for them.

An Egyptian Invasion of Judah
(1 Kgs 14,25–28)

12 As soon as Rehoboam had established his authority as king, he and all his people abandoned the Law of the LORD. [2] In the fifth year of Rehoboam's reign their disloyalty to the LORD was punished. King Shishak of Egypt attacked Jerusalem [3] with an army of 1,200 chariots, 60,000 horsemen, and more soldiers than could be counted, including Libyan, Sukkite, and Ethiopian troops. [4] He captured the fortified cities of Judah and advanced as far as Jerusalem.

[5] Shemaiah the prophet went to King Rehoboam and the Judean leaders who had gathered in Jerusalem to escape Shishak. He said to them, "This is the LORD's message to you: 'You have abandoned me, so now I have abandoned you to Shishak.' "

[6] The king and the leaders admitted that they had sinned, and they said, "What the LORD is doing is just."

[7] When the LORD saw this, he spoke again to Shemaiah and said to him, "Because they admit their sin, I will not destroy them. But when Shishak attacks, they will barely survive. Jerusalem will not feel the full force of my anger, [8] but Shishak will conquer them, and they will learn the difference between serving me and serving earthly rulers."

[9] King Shishak came to Jerusalem and took the treasures from the Temple and from the palace. He took everything, including the gold shields that King Solomon had made. [10] To replace them, Rehoboam made bronze shields and entrusted them to the officers responsible for guarding the palace gates. [11] Every time the king went to the Temple, the guards carried the shields and then returned them to the guardroom. [12] Because he submitted to the LORD, the LORD's anger did not completely destroy him, and things went well for Judah.

2 Chron.

1 Sam.
2 Sam.
1 Kings
2 Kings
1 Chron.

Summary of Rehoboam's Reign

¹³Rehoboam ruled in Jerusalem and increased his power as king. He was 41 years old when he became king, and he ruled for seventeen years in Jerusalem, the city which the LORD had chosen from all the territory of Israel as the place where he was to be worshipped. Rehoboam's mother was Naamah, from the land of Ammon. ¹⁴He did what was evil, because he did not try to find the LORD's will.

¹⁵Rehoboam's acts from beginning to end and his family records are found in *The History of Shemaiah the Prophet* and *The History of Iddo the Prophet*. Rehoboam and Jeroboam were constantly at war with each other. ¹⁶Rehoboam died and was buried in the royal tombs in David's City and his son Abijah succeeded him as king.

Abijah's War with Jeroboam
(1 Kgs 15.1–8)

13 In the eighteenth year of the reign of King Jeroboam of Israel, Abijah became king of Judah, ²and he ruled for three years in Jerusalem. His mother was Micaiah daughter of Uriel, from the city of Gibeah.

War broke out between Abijah and Jeroboam. ³Abijah raised an army of 400,000 soldiers, and Jeroboam opposed him with an army of 800,000.

⁴The armies met in the hill country of Ephraim. King Abijah went up Mount Zemaraim and called out to Jeroboam and the Israelites: "Listen to me!" he said. ⁵"Don't you know that the LORD, the God of Israel, made an unbreakable covenant with David, giving him and his descendants kingship over Israel for ever? ⁶Jeroboam son of Nebat rebelled against Solomon, his king. ⁷Later he gathered together a group of worthless scoundrels, and they forced their will on Rehoboam son of Solomon, who was too young and inexperienced to resist them. ⁸Now you propose to fight against the royal authority that the LORD gave to David's descendants. You have a huge army and have with you the gold bull calves that Jeroboam made to be your gods. ⁹You drove out the LORD's priests, the descendants of Aaron, and you drove out the Levites. In their place you appointed priests in the same way that other nations do. Anybody who comes along with a bull or seven sheep can get himself consecrated as a priest of those so-called gods of yours.

¹⁰"But we still serve the LORD our God and have not abandoned him. Priests descended from Aaron perform their duties, and Levites assist them. ¹¹Every morning and every evening they offer him incense and animal sacrifices burnt whole. They present the offerings of bread on a table that is ritually clean, and every evening they light the lamps on the gold lampstand. We do what the LORD has commanded, but you have abandoned him. ¹²God himself is our leader and his priests are here with trumpets, ready to blow them and call us to battle against you. People of Israel, don't fight against the LORD, the God of your ancestors! You can't win!"

¹³Meanwhile Jeroboam had sent some of his troops to ambush the Judean army from the rear, while the rest faced them from the front. ¹⁴The Judeans looked round and saw that they were surrounded. They cried to the LORD for help, and the priests blew the trumpets. ¹⁵The Judeans gave a loud shout, and led by Abijah, they attacked; God defeated Jeroboam and the Israelite army. ¹⁶The Israelites fled from the Judeans, and God let the Judeans overpower them. ¹⁷Abijah and his army dealt the Israelites

2 CHRONICLES 13–15

515

2 Chron.

Ezra
Nehem.
Esther
Job
Psalms

a crushing defeat — half a million of Israel's best soldiers were killed. [18] And so the people of Judah were victorious over Israel, because they relied on the LORD, the God of their ancestors.

[19] Abijah pursued Jeroboam's army and occupied some of his cities: Bethel, Jeshanah, and Ephron, and the villages near each of these cities. [20] Jeroboam never regained his power during Abijah's reign. Finally the LORD struck him down, and he died.

[21] Abijah, however, grew more powerful. He had fourteen wives and fathered 22 sons and sixteen daughters. [22] The rest of the history of Abijah, what he said and what he did, is written in *The History of Iddo the Prophet.*

King Asa Defeats the Ethiopians

14 King Abijah died and was buried in the royal tombs in David's City. His son Asa succeeded him as king, and under Asa the land enjoyed peace for ten years. [2] Asa pleased the LORD, his God, by doing what was right and good. [3] He removed the foreign altars and the pagan places of worship, broke down the sacred stone columns, and cut down the symbols of the goddess Asherah. [4] He commanded the people of Judah to do the will of the LORD, the God of their ancestors, and to obey his teachings and commands. [5] Because he abolished the pagan places of worship and the incense altars from all the cities of Judah, the kingdom was at peace under his rule. [6] He built fortifications for the cities of Judah during this time, and for several years there was no war, because the LORD gave him peace. [7] He said to the people of Judah, "Let us fortify the cities by building walls and towers, and gates that can be shut and barred. We have control of the land because we have done the will of the LORD our God. He has protected us and given us security on every side." And so they built and prospered. [8] King Asa had an army of 300,000 men from Judah, armed with shields and spears, and 280,000 men from Benjamin, armed with shields and bows. All of them were brave, well-trained men.

[9] An Ethiopian named Zerah invaded Judah with an army of a million men and 300 chariots and advanced as far as Mareshah. [10] Asa went out to fight him, and both sides took up their positions in the Valley of Zephathah near Mareshah. [11] Asa prayed to the LORD his God, "O LORD, you can help a weak army as easily as a powerful one. Help us now, O LORD our God, because we are relying on you, and in your name we have come out to fight against this huge army. LORD, you are our God; no one can hope to defeat you."

[12] The LORD defeated the Ethiopian army when Asa and the Judean army attacked them. They fled, [13] and Asa and his troops pursued them as far as Gerar. So many of the Ethiopians were killed that the army was unable to rally and fight.* They were overpowered by the LORD and his army, and the army took large amounts of loot. [14] Then they were able to destroy the cities in the area around Gerar, because the people there were terrified of the LORD. The army plundered all those cities and captured large amounts of loot. [15] They also attacked the camps of some shepherds, capturing large numbers of sheep and camels. Then they returned to Jerusalem.

Asa's Reforms

15 The Spirit of God came upon Azariah son of Oded, [2] and he went to meet King Asa. He called out, "Listen to me,

---

14.13 *So many of the Ethiopians… fight;* or *The Ethiopians were completely defeated; not one of them was left alive.*

King Asa, and all you people of Judah and Benjamin! The LORD is with you as long as you are with him. If you look for him, he will let you find him, but if you turn away, he will abandon you. [3] For a long time Israel lived without the true God, without priests to teach them, and without a law. [4] But when trouble came, they turned to the LORD, the God of Israel. They searched for him and found him. [5] In those days no one could come and go in safety, because there was trouble and disorder in every land. [6] One nation oppressed another nation, and one city oppressed another city, because God was bringing trouble and distress on them. [7] But you must be strong and not be discouraged. The work that you do will be rewarded."

[8] When Asa heard the prophecy that Azariah son of* Oded had spoken, he was encouraged. He did away with all the idols in the land of Judah and Benjamin and all the idols in the cities he had captured in the hill country of Ephraim. He also repaired the altar of the LORD that stood in the temple courtyard.

[9] Many people had come over to Asa's side from Ephraim, Manasseh, and Simeon, and were living in his kingdom, because they had seen that the LORD was with him. Asa summoned all of them and the people of Judah and Benjamin. [10] They assembled in Jerusalem in the third month of the fifteenth year that Asa was king. [11] On that day they offered sacrifices to the LORD from the loot they had brought back: 700 head of cattle and 7,000 sheep. [12] They made a covenant in which they agreed to worship the LORD, the God of their ancestors, with all their heart and soul. [13] Anyone, young or old, male or female, who did not worship him was to be put to death. [14] In a loud voice they took an oath in the LORD's name that they would keep the covenant, and then they shouted and blew trumpets. [15] All the people of Judah were happy because they had made this covenant with all their heart. They took delight in worshipping the LORD, and he accepted them and gave them peace on every side.

[16] King Asa removed his grandmother Maacah from her position as queen mother, because she had made an obscene idol of the fertility goddess Asherah. Asa cut down the idol, chopped it up, and burnt the pieces in the valley of the Kidron. [17] Even though Asa did not destroy all the pagan places of worship in the land, he remained faithful to the LORD all his life. [18] He placed in the Temple all the objects his father Abijah had dedicated to God, as well as the gold and silver objects that he himself dedicated. [19] There was no more war until the 35th year of his reign.

Troubles with Israel
(1 Kgs 15.17–22)

16 In the 36th year of the reign of King Asa of Judah, King Baasha of Israel invaded Judah and started to fortify Ramah in order to cut off all traffic in and out of Judah. [2] So Asa took silver and gold from the treasuries of the Temple and the palace and sent it to Damascus, to King Benhadad of Syria, with this message: [3] "Let us be allies, as our fathers were. This silver and gold is a present for you. Now break your alliance with King Baasha of Israel so that he will have to pull his troops out of my territory."

[4] Benhadad agreed to Asa's proposal and sent his commanding officers and their armies to attack the cities of Israel. They

15.8 Some ancient translations *Azariah son of*; Hebrew does not have these words.

2 CHRONICLES 16, 17

517

2 Chron.

Ezra
Nehem.
Esther
Job
Psalms

captured Ijon, Dan, Abel Beth Maacah, and all the cities of Naphtali where supplies were stored. [5] When King Baasha heard what was happening, he stopped fortifying Ramah and abandoned the work. [6] Then King Asa gathered men from throughout Judah and ordered them to carry off the stones and timber that Baasha had been using at Ramah, and they used them to fortify the cities of Geba and Mizpah.

The Prophet Hanani

[7] At that time the prophet Hanani went to King Asa and said, "Because you relied on the king of Syria instead of relying on the LORD your God, the army of the king of Israel* has escaped from you. [8] Didn't the Ethiopians and the Libyans have large armies with many chariots and horsemen? But because you relied on the LORD, he gave you victory over them. [9] The LORD keeps close watch over the whole world, to give strength to those whose hearts are loyal to him. You have acted foolishly, and so from now on you will always be at war." [10] This made Asa so angry with the prophet that he had him put in chains. It was at this same time that Asa began treating some of the people cruelly.

The End of Asa's Reign
(1 Kgs 15.23–24)

[11] All the events of Asa's reign from beginning to end are recorded in *The History of the Kings of Judah and Israel*. [12] In the 39th year that Asa was king, he was crippled by a severe foot disease; but even then he did not turn to the LORD for help, but to doctors. [13] Two years later he died [14] and was buried in the rock tomb which he had carved out for himself in David's City. They used spices and perfumed oils to prepare his body for burial, and they built a huge bonfire to mourn his death.

Jehoshaphat Becomes King

17 Jehoshaphat succeeded his father Asa as king and strengthened his position against Israel. [2] He stationed troops in the fortified cities of Judah, in the Judean countryside, and in the cities which Asa had captured in the territory of Ephraim. [3] The LORD blessed Jehoshaphat because he followed the example of his father's early life and did not worship Baal. [4] He served his father's God, obeyed God's commands, and did not act in the way the kings of Israel did. [5] The LORD gave Jehoshaphat firm control over the kingdom of Judah, and all the people brought him gifts, so that he became wealthy and highly honoured. [6] He took pride in serving the LORD and destroyed all the pagan places of worship and the symbols of the goddess Asherah in Judah.

[7] In the third year of his reign he sent out the following officials to teach in the cities of Judah: Benhail, Obadiah, Zechariah, Nethanel, and Micaiah. [8] They were accompanied by nine Levites and two priests. The Levites were Shemaiah, Nethaniah, Zebadiah, Asahel, Shemiramoth, Jehonathan, Adonijah, Tobijah, and Tobadonijah; and the priests were Elishama and Jehoram. [9] They took the book of the Law of the LORD and went through all the towns of Judah, teaching it to the people.

Jehoshaphat's Greatness

[10] The LORD made all the surrounding kingdoms afraid to go to war against King Jehoshaphat. [11] Some of the Philistines brought

16.7 One ancient translation *Israel*; Hebrew *Syria*.

2 CHRONICLES 16.9

THE LORD
- keeps close -
watch OVER THE WHOLE WORLD,
- to give -
strength TO THOSE WHOSE HEARTS
are loyal to him

518

2 Chron.

1 Sam.
2 Sam.
1 Kings
2 Kings
1 Chron.

2 CHRONICLES 17, 18

Jehoshaphat a large amount of silver and other gifts, and some Arabs brought him 7,700 sheep and 7,700 goats. ¹²So Jehoshaphat continued to grow more and more powerful. Throughout Judah he built fortifications and cities, ¹³where supplies were stored in huge amounts.

In Jerusalem he stationed outstanding officers, ¹⁴according to their clans. Adnah was the commander of the troops from the clans of Judah, and he had 300,000 soldiers under him. ¹⁵Second in rank was Jehohanan, with 280,000 soldiers, ¹⁶and third was Amasiah son of Zichri, with 200,000. (Amasiah had volunteered to serve the LORD.) ¹⁷The commander of the troops from the clans of Benjamin was Eliada, an outstanding soldier, in command of 200,000 men armed with shields and bows. ¹⁸His second in command was Jehozabad with 180,000 men, well equipped for battle. ¹⁹These men served the king in Jerusalem, and in addition he stationed other soldiers in the other fortified cities of Judah.

The Prophet Micaiah Warns Ahab
(1 Kgs 22.1–28)

18 When King Jehoshaphat of Judah became rich and famous, he arranged a marriage between a member of his family and the family of King Ahab of Israel. ²A number of years later Jehoshaphat went to the city of Samaria to visit Ahab. To honour Jehoshaphat and those with him, Ahab had a large number of sheep and cattle slaughtered for a feast. He tried to persuade Jehoshaphat to join him in attacking the city of Ramoth in Gilead. ³He asked, "Will you go with me to attack Ramoth?"

Jehoshaphat replied, "I am ready when you are, and so is my army. We will join you." ⁴Then he added, "But first let's consult the LORD."

⁵So Ahab called in the prophets, about 400 of them, and asked them, "Should I go and attack Ramoth, or not?"

"Attack it," they answered. "God will give you victory."

⁶But Jehoshaphat asked, "Isn't there another prophet through whom we can consult the LORD?"

⁷Ahab answered, "There is one more, Micaiah son of Imlah. But I hate him because he never prophesies anything good for me; it's always something bad."

"You shouldn't say that!" Jehoshaphat replied.

⁸So King Ahab called in a court official and told him to go and fetch Micaiah at once.

⁹The two kings, dressed in their royal robes, were sitting on their thrones at the threshing place just outside the gate of Samaria, and all the prophets were prophesying in front of them. ¹⁰One of them, Zedekiah son of Chenaanah, made iron horns and said to Ahab, "This is what the LORD says, 'With these you will fight the Syrians and totally defeat them.'" ¹¹All the other prophets said the same thing. "March against Ramoth and you will win," they said. "The LORD will give you victory."

¹²Meanwhile, the official who had gone to fetch Micaiah said to him, "All the other prophets have prophesied success for the king, and you had better do the same."

¹³But Micaiah answered, "By the living LORD, I will say what my God tells me to!"

¹⁴When he appeared before King Ahab, the king asked him, "Micaiah, should King Jehoshaphat and I go and attack Ramoth, or not?"

"Attack!" Micaiah answered. "Of course you'll win. The LORD will give you victory."

¹⁵ But Ahab replied, "When you speak to me in the name of the LORD, tell the truth! How many times do I have to tell you that?"

¹⁶ Micaiah answered, "I can see the army of Israel scattered over the hills like sheep without a shepherd. And the LORD said, 'These men have no leader; let them go home in peace.'"

¹⁷ Ahab said to Jehoshaphat, "I told you that he never prophesies anything good for me; it's always something bad!"

¹⁸ Micaiah went on: "Now listen to what the LORD says! I saw the LORD sitting on his throne in heaven, with all his angels standing beside him. ¹⁹ The LORD asked, 'Who will deceive Ahab so that he will go and get killed at Ramoth?' Some of the angels said one thing, and others said something else, ²⁰ until a spirit stepped forward, approached the LORD, and said, 'I will deceive him.' 'How?' the LORD asked. ²¹ The spirit replied, 'I will go and make all Ahab's prophets tell lies.' The LORD said, 'Go and deceive him. You will succeed.'"

²² And Micaiah concluded: "This is what has happened. The LORD has made these prophets of yours lie to you. But he himself has decreed that you will meet with disaster!"

²³ Then the prophet Zedekiah went up to Micaiah, slapped his face, and asked, "Since when did the LORD's spirit leave me and speak to you?"

²⁴ "You will find out when you go into some back room to hide," Micaiah replied.

²⁵ Then King Ahab ordered one of his officers, "Arrest Micaiah and take him to Amon, the governor of the city, and to Prince Joash. ²⁶ Tell them to throw him in prison and to put him on bread and water until I return safely."

²⁷ "If you return safely," Micaiah exclaimed, "then the LORD has not spoken through me!" And he added, "Listen, everyone, to what I have said!"

The Death of Ahab
(1 Kgs 22.29–35)

²⁸ Then King Ahab of Israel and King Jehoshaphat of Judah went to attack the city of Ramoth in Gilead. ²⁹ Ahab said to Jehoshaphat, "As we go into battle, I will disguise myself, but you wear your royal garments." So the king of Israel went into battle in disguise.

³⁰ The king of Syria had ordered his chariot commanders to attack no one else except the king of Israel. ³¹ So when they saw King Jehoshaphat, they all thought that he was the king of Israel, and they turned to attack him. But Jehoshaphat gave a shout, and the LORD God rescued him and turned the attack away from him. ³² The chariot commanders saw that he was not the king of Israel, so they stopped pursuing him. ³³ By chance, however, a Syrian soldier shot an arrow which struck King Ahab between the joints of his armour. "I'm wounded!" he cried out to his chariot driver. "Turn round and pull out of the battle!" ³⁴ While the battle raged on, King Ahab remained propped up in his chariot, facing the Syrians. At sunset he died.

A Prophet Reprimands Jehoshaphat

19 King Jehoshaphat of Judah returned safely to his palace in Jerusalem. ² A prophet, Jehu son of Hanani, went to meet the king and said to him, "Do you think it is right to help those who are wicked and to take the side of those who hate the LORD? What you have done has brought the LORD's anger on you. ³ But even so, there is some good in you. You have removed all

520

2 Chron.

⋮·········

1 Sam.
2 Sam.
1 Kings
2 Kings
1 Chron.

2 CHRONICLES 19, 20

the symbols of the goddess Asherah which people worshipped, and you have tried to follow God's will."

Jehoshaphat's Reforms

[4] Even though King Jehoshaphat lived in Jerusalem, he travelled regularly among the people, from Beersheba in the south to the edge of the hill country of Ephraim in the north, in order to call the people back to the LORD, the God of their ancestors. [5] He appointed judges in each of the fortified cities of Judah [6] and instructed them: "Be careful in pronouncing judgement; you are not acting on human authority, but on the authority of the LORD, and he is with you when you pass sentence. [7] Honour the LORD and act carefully, because the LORD our God does not tolerate fraud or partiality or the taking of bribes."

[8] In Jerusalem Jehoshaphat appointed Levites, priests, and some of the leading citizens as judges in cases involving a violation of the Law of the LORD or legal disputes between inhabitants of the city.* [9] He gave them the following instructions: "You must perform your duties in reverence for the LORD, faithfully obeying him in everything you do. [10] Whenever your fellow-citizens from any of the cities bring before you a case of homicide or any other violation of a law or commandment, you must instruct them carefully how to conduct themselves during the trial, so that they do not become guilty of sinning against the LORD. Unless you do, you and your fellow-citizens will feel the force of the LORD's anger. But if you do your duty, you will not be guilty. [11] Amariah the High Priest will have final authority in all religious cases, and Zebadiah son of Ishmael, governor of Judah, will have final authority in all civil cases. The Levites have the responsibility of seeing that the decisions of the courts are carried out. Be courageous and carry out these instructions, and may the LORD be on the side of the right!"

War against Edom

20 Some time later the armies of Moab and Ammon, together with their allies, the Meunites,* invaded Judah. [2] Some messengers came and announced to King Jehoshaphat: "A large army from Edom has come from the other side of the Dead Sea to attack you. They have already captured Hazazon Tamar." (This is another name for Engedi.) [3] Jehoshaphat was frightened and prayed to the LORD for guidance. Then he gave orders for a fast to be observed throughout the country. [4] From every city of Judah people hurried to Jerusalem to ask the LORD for guidance, [5] and they and the people of Jerusalem gathered in the new courtyard of the Temple. King Jehoshaphat went and stood before them [6] and prayed aloud, "O LORD God of our ancestors, you rule in heaven over all the nations of the world. You are powerful and mighty, and no one can oppose you. [7] You are our God. When your people Israel moved into this land, you drove out the people who were living here and gave the land to the descendants of Abraham, your friend, to be theirs for ever. [8] They have lived here and have built a temple to honour you, knowing [9] that if any disaster struck them to punish them — a war,* an epidemic, or a famine — then they could come and stand in front of this Temple where you are worshipped. They

19.8 Some ancient translations *between... city*; Hebrew unclear.
20.1 One ancient translation *Meunites*; Hebrew *Ammonites*.
20.9 *struck... war*; or *struck them — a devastating war*.

2 CHRONICLES 20

521

2 Chron.
....
Ezra
Nehem.
Esther
Job
Psalms

could pray to you in their trouble, and you would hear them and rescue them.

¹⁰"Now the people of Ammon, Moab, and Edom have attacked us. When our ancestors came out of Egypt, you did not allow them to enter those lands, so our ancestors went round them and did not destroy them. ¹¹This is how they repay us — they come to drive us out of the land that you gave us. ¹²You are our God! Punish them, for we are helpless in the face of this large army that is attacking us. We do not know what to do, but we look to you for help."

¹³All the men of Judah, with their wives and children, were standing there at the Temple. ¹⁴The Spirit of the LORD came upon a Levite who was present in the crowd. His name was Jahaziel son of Zechariah; he was a member of the clan of Asaph and was descended from Asaph through Mattaniah, Jeiel, and Benaiah. ¹⁵Jahaziel said, "Your Majesty and all you people of Judah and Jerusalem, the LORD says that you must not be discouraged or be afraid to face this large army. The battle depends on God, not on you. ¹⁶Attack them tomorrow as they come up the pass at Ziz. You will meet them at the end of the valley that leads to the wild country near Jeruel. ¹⁷You will not have to fight this battle. Just take up your positions and wait; you will see the LORD give you victory. People of Judah and Jerusalem, do not hesitate or be afraid. Go out to battle, and the LORD will be with you!"

¹⁸Then King Jehoshaphat bowed low, with his face touching the ground, and all the people bowed with him and worshipped the LORD. ¹⁹The members of the Levite clans of Kohath and Korah stood up and with a loud shout praised the LORD, the God of Israel.

²⁰Early the next morning the people went out to the wild country near Tekoa. As they were starting out, Jehoshaphat addressed them with these words: "People of Judah and Jerusalem! Put your trust in the LORD your God, and you will stand firm. Believe what his prophets tell you, and you will succeed." ²¹After consulting with the people, the king ordered some musicians to put on the robes they wore on sacred occasions and to march ahead of the army, singing: "Praise the LORD! His love is eternal!"

²²When they began to sing, the LORD threw the invading armies into a panic. ²³The Ammonites and the Moabites attacked the Edomite army and completely destroyed it, and then they turned on each other in savage fighting. ²⁴When the Judean army reached a tower that was in the desert, they looked towards the enemy and saw that they were all lying on the ground, dead. Not one had escaped.

²⁵Jehoshaphat and his troops moved in to take the loot, and they found many cattle,* supplies, clothing, and other valuable objects. They spent three days gathering the loot, but there was so much that they could not take everything. ²⁶On the fourth day they assembled in the Valley of Beracah and praised the LORD for all he had done. That is why the valley is called "Beracah".* ²⁷Jehoshaphat led his troops back to Jerusalem in triumph, because the LORD had defeated their enemies. ²⁸When they reached the city, they marched to the Temple, to the music of harps and trumpets. ²⁹Every nation that heard how the LORD had defeated Israel's enemies was terrified, ³⁰so Jehoshaphat ruled in peace, and God gave him security on every side.

20.25 One ancient translation *cattle*; Hebrew *among them*.
20.26 *Beracah*: This name in Hebrew means "praise".

2 CHRONICLES 20.20-24

When we worship and pray,

STUFF

HAPPENS.

In this story, worshipping and praying was all that the Judean army had to do, and God sorted out the battle they were in.

Play some worship music and turn up the volume; pray out loud, talking to God about battles you feel that you are facing, and ask him to fight for you.

522

2 Chron.

⋮

1 Sam.
2 Sam.
1 Kings
2 Kings
1 Chron.

2 CHRONICLES 20, 21

The End of Jehoshaphat's Reign
(1 Kgs 22.41–50)

31 Jehoshaphat had become king of Judah at the age of 35 and had ruled in Jerusalem for 25 years. His mother was Azubah, the daughter of Shilhi. 32 Like his father Asa before him, he did what was right in the sight of the LORD; 33 but the pagan places of worship were not destroyed. The people still did not turn wholeheartedly to the worship of the God of their ancestors.

34 Everything else that Jehoshaphat did, from the beginning of his reign to its end, is recorded in *The History of Jehu Son of Hanani*, which is a part of *The History of the Kings of Israel*.

35 At one time King Jehoshaphat of Judah made an alliance with King Ahaziah of Israel, who did many wicked things. 36 At the port of Eziongeber they built ocean-going ships. 37 But Eliezer son of Dodavahu, from the town of Mareshah, warned Jehoshaphat, "Because you have made an alliance with Ahaziah, the LORD will destroy what you have built." And the ships were wrecked and never sailed.

21 Jehoshaphat died and was buried in the royal tombs in David's City and his son Jehoram succeeded him as king.

King Jehoram of Judah
(2 Kgs 8.17–24)

2 Jehoram son of King Jehoshaphat of Judah had six brothers: Azariah, Jehiel, Zechariah, Azariahu, Michael, and Shephatiah. 3 Their father gave them large amounts of gold, silver, and other valuable possessions, and placed each one in charge of one of the fortified cities of Judah. But because Jehoram was the eldest, Jehoshaphat made him his successor. 4 When Jehoram was in firm control of the kingdom, he had all his brothers killed, and also some Israelite officials.

5 Jehoram became king at the age of 32, and he ruled in Jerusalem for eight years. 6 He followed the wicked example of King Ahab and the other kings of Israel, because he had married one of Ahab's daughters. He sinned against the LORD, 7 but the LORD was not willing to destroy the dynasty of David, because he had made a covenant with David and promised that his descendants would always continue to rule.

8 During Jehoram's reign Edom revolted against Judah and became an independent kingdom. 9 So Jehoram and his officers set out with chariots and invaded Edom. There the Edomite army surrounded them, but during the night they managed to break out and escape. 10 Edom has been independent of* Judah ever since. During this same period, the city of Libnah also revolted, because Jehoram had abandoned the LORD, the God of his ancestors. 11 He even built pagan places of worship in the Judean highlands and led the people of Judah and Jerusalem to sin against the LORD.

12 The prophet Elijah sent Jehoram a letter, which read as follows: "The LORD, the God of your ancestor David, condemns you, because you did not follow the example of your father, King Jehoshaphat, or that of your grandfather, King Asa. 13 Instead, you have followed the example of the kings of Israel and have led the people of Judah and Jerusalem into being unfaithful to God, just as Ahab and his successors led Israel into unfaithfulness. You even murdered your brothers, who were better men than you are. 14 As a result, the LORD will severely punish your people, your children, and your wives, and will destroy your possessions.

....

21.10 *independent of*; or *in revolt against*.

2 CHRONICLES 21, 22

523

2 Chron.

....

Ezra
Nehem.
Esther
Job
Psalms

¹⁵You yourself will suffer a painful disease of the intestines that will grow worse day by day."

¹⁶Some Philistines and Arabs lived near where some Ethiopians had settled along the coast. The LORD incited them to go to war against Jehoram. ¹⁷They invaded Judah, looted the royal palace, and carried off as prisoners all the king's wives and sons except Ahaziah, his youngest son.

¹⁸Then after all this, the LORD brought on the king a painful disease of the intestines. ¹⁹For almost two years it grew steadily worse until finally the king died in agony. His subjects did not light a bonfire in mourning for him as had been done for his ancestors.

²⁰Jehoram had become king at the age of 32 and had ruled in Jerusalem for eight years. Nobody was sorry when he died. They buried him in David's City, but not in the royal tombs.

King Ahaziah of Judah
(2 Kgs 8.25–29; 9.21–28)

22 Some Arabs had led a raid and killed all King Jehoram's sons except Ahaziah, the youngest. So now the people of Jerusalem made Ahaziah king as his father's successor. ²⁻³Ahaziah became king at the age of 22,* and he ruled in Jerusalem for one year. Ahaziah also followed the example of King Ahab's family, since his mother Athaliah — the daughter of King Ahab and granddaughter of King Omri of Israel — gave him advice that led him into evil. ⁴He sinned against the LORD, because after his father's death other members of King Ahab's family became his advisers, and they led to his downfall. ⁵Following their advice, he joined King Joram of Israel in a war against King Hazael of Syria. The armies clashed at Ramoth in Gilead, and Joram was wounded in battle. ⁶He returned to the city of Jezreel to recover from his wounds, and Ahaziah went there to visit him.

⁷God used this visit to Joram to bring about Ahaziah's downfall. While Ahaziah was there, he and Joram were confronted by a man named Jehu son of Nimshi, whom the LORD had chosen to destroy the dynasty of Ahab. ⁸As Jehu was carrying out God's sentence on the dynasty, he came across a group made up of Judean leaders and of Ahaziah's nephews that had accompanied Ahaziah on his visit. Jehu killed them all. ⁹A search was made for Ahaziah, and he was found hiding in Samaria. They took him to Jehu and put him to death. But they did bury his body out of respect for his grandfather King Jehoshaphat, who had done all he could to serve the LORD.

No member of Ahaziah's family was left who could rule the kingdom.

Queen Athaliah of Judah
(2 Kgs 11.1–3)

¹⁰As soon as King Ahaziah's mother Athaliah learnt of her son's murder, she gave orders for all the members of the royal family of Judah to be killed. ¹¹Ahaziah had a half-sister, Jehosheba, who was married to a priest named Jehoiada. She secretly rescued one of Ahaziah's sons, Joash, took him away from the other princes who were about to be murdered and hid him and a nurse in a bedroom at the Temple. By keeping him hidden, she saved him from death at the hands of Athaliah. ¹²For six years he remained there in hiding, while Athaliah ruled as queen.

....

22.2–3 Some ancient translations (and see 2 Kgs 8.26) *22*; Hebrew *42*.

524

2 Chron.

⋮

1 Sam.
2 Sam.
1 Kings
2 Kings
1 Chron.

2 CHRONICLES 23

The Revolt against Athaliah
(2 Kgs 11.4–16)

23 After waiting six years Jehoiada the priest decided that it was time to take action. He made a pact with five army officers: Azariah son of Jeroham, Ishmael son of Jehohanan, Azariah son of Obed, Maaseiah son of Adaiah, and Elishaphat son of Zichri. ² They travelled to all the cities of Judah and brought back with them to Jerusalem the Levites and all the heads of the clans.

³ They all gathered in the Temple, and there they made a covenant with Joash, the king's son. Jehoiada said to them, "Here is the son of the late king! He is now to be king, as the Lord promised that King David's descendants would be. ⁴ This is what we will do. When the priests and Levites come on duty on the Sabbath, one third of them will guard the temple gates, ⁵ another third will guard the royal palace, and the rest will be stationed at the Foundation Gate. All the people will assemble in the temple courtyard. ⁶ No one is to enter the temple buildings except the priests and the Levites who are on duty. They may enter, because they are consecrated, but the rest of the people must obey the Lord's instructions and stay outside. ⁷ The Levites are to stand guard round the king, with their swords drawn, and are to stay with the king wherever he goes. Anyone who tries to enter the Temple is to be killed."

⁸ The Levites and the people of Judah carried out Jehoiada's instructions. The men were not dismissed when they went off duty on the Sabbath, so the commanders had available both those coming on duty and those going off. ⁹ Jehoiada gave the officers the spears and shields that had belonged to King David and had been kept in the Temple. ¹⁰ He stationed the men with drawn swords all round the front of the Temple, to protect the king. ¹¹ Then Jehoiada led Joash out, placed the crown on his head, and gave him a copy of the laws governing kingship. And so he was made king. Jehoiada the priest and his sons anointed Joash, and everyone shouted, "Long live the king!"

¹² Athaliah heard the people cheering for the king, so she hurried to the Temple, where the crowd had gathered. ¹³ There she saw the new king at the temple entrance, standing by the column reserved for kings and surrounded by the army officers and the trumpeters. All the people were shouting joyfully and blowing trumpets, and the temple musicians with their instruments were leading the celebration. She tore her clothes in distress and shouted, "Treason! Treason!"

¹⁴ Jehoiada did not want Athaliah killed in the temple area, so he called out the army officers and said, "Take her out between the rows of guards, and kill anyone who tries to rescue her." ¹⁵ They seized her, took her to the palace, and there at the Horse Gate they killed her.

Jehoiada's Reforms
(2 Kgs 11.17–20)

¹⁶ The priest Jehoiada got King Joash and the people to join him in making a covenant that they would be the Lord's people. ¹⁷ Then they all went to the temple of Baal and tore it down. They smashed the altars and idols there and killed Mattan, the priest of Baal, in front of the altars. ¹⁸ Jehoiada put the priests and Levites in charge of the work of the Temple. They were to carry out the duties assigned to them by King David and to burn the sacrifices offered to the Lord in accordance with the Law of Moses. They were also in charge of the music and the celebrations. ¹⁹ Jehoiada

also put guards on duty at the temple gates to keep out anyone who was ritually unclean. ²⁰The army officers, the leading citizens, the officials, and all the rest of the people joined Jehoiada in a procession that brought the king from the Temple to the palace. They entered by the main gate, and the king took his place on the throne. ²¹All the people were filled with happiness, and the city was quiet, now that Athaliah had been killed.

King Joash of Judah
(2 Kgs 12.1–16)

24 Joash became king of Judah at the age of seven, and he ruled in Jerusalem for forty years. His mother was Zibiah from the city of Beersheba. ²He did what was pleasing to the LORD as long as Jehoiada the priest was alive. ³Jehoiada chose two wives for King Joash, and they bore him sons and daughters.

⁴After he had been king for a while, Joash decided to have the Temple repaired. ⁵He ordered the priests and the Levites to go to the cities of Judah and collect from all the people enough money to make the annual repairs on the Temple. He told them to act promptly, but the Levites delayed, ⁶so he called in Jehoiada, their leader, and demanded, "Why haven't you seen to it that the Levites collect from Judah and Jerusalem the tax which Moses, the servant of the LORD, required the people* to pay for support of the Tent of the LORD's presence?"

⁷(The followers of Athaliah, that corrupt woman,* had damaged the Temple and had used many of the sacred objects in the worship of Baal.)

⁸The king ordered the Levites to make a box for contributions and to place it at the temple gate. ⁹They sent word throughout Jerusalem and Judah for everyone to bring to the LORD the tax which Moses, God's servant, had first collected in the wilderness. ¹⁰This pleased the people and their leaders, and they brought their tax money and filled the box with it. ¹¹Every day the Levites would take the box to the royal official who was in charge of it. Whenever it was full, the royal secretary and the High Priest's representative would take the money out and return the box to its place. And so they collected a large sum of money.

¹²The king and Jehoiada would give the money to those who were in charge of repairing the Temple, and they hired stonemasons, carpenters, and metalworkers to make the repairs. ¹³All of them worked hard, and they restored the Temple to its original condition, as solid as ever. ¹⁴When the repairs were finished, the remaining gold and silver was given to the king and Jehoiada, who used it to have bowls and other utensils made for the Temple.

Jehoiada's Policies are Reversed

As long as Jehoiada was alive, sacrifices were offered regularly at the Temple. ¹⁵After reaching the very old age of 130, he died. ¹⁶They buried him in the royal tombs in David's City in recognition of the service he had done for the people of Israel, for God, and for the Temple.

¹⁷But once Jehoiada was dead, the leaders of Judah persuaded King Joash to listen to them instead. ¹⁸So the people stopped worshipping in the Temple of the LORD, the God of their ancestors,

24.6 Probable text *required the people*; Hebrew unclear.
24.7 *that corrupt woman*; or *whom she corrupted*.

Write your to-do list here.

Pray that God would be with you through each thing you have to do.

526

2 Chron.

1 Sam.
2 Sam.
1 Kings
2 Kings
1 Chron.

2 CHRONICLES 24, 25

and began to worship idols and the images of the goddess Asherah. Their guilt for these sins brought the Lord's anger on Judah and Jerusalem. [19] The Lord sent prophets to warn them to return to him, but the people refused to listen. [20] Then the Spirit of God took control of Zechariah son of Jehoiada the priest. He stood where the people could see him and called out, "The Lord God asks why you have disobeyed his commands and are bringing disaster on yourselves! You abandoned him, so he has abandoned you!" [21] King Joash joined in a conspiracy against Zechariah, and on the king's orders the people stoned Zechariah in the temple courtyard. [22] The king forgot about the loyal service that Zechariah's father Jehoiada had given him, and he had Zechariah killed. As Zechariah was dying, he called out, "May the Lord see what you are doing and punish you!"

The End of Joash's Reign

[23] When autumn came that year, the Syrian army attacked Judah and Jerusalem, killed all the leaders, and took large amounts of loot back to Damascus. [24] The Syrian army was small, but the Lord let them defeat a much larger Judean army because the people had abandoned him, the Lord God of their ancestors. In this way King Joash was punished. [25] He was severely wounded, and when the enemy withdrew, two of his officials plotted against him and killed him in his bed to avenge the murder of the son* of Jehoiada the priest. He was buried in David's City, but not in the royal tombs. [26] (Those who plotted against him were Zabad, the son of an Ammonite woman named Shimeath, and Jehozabad, the son of a Moabite woman named Shimrith). [27] The *Commentary on the Book of Kings* contains the stories of the sons of Joash, the prophecies spoken against him, and the record of how he rebuilt the Temple. His son Amaziah succeeded him as king.

King Amaziah of Judah
(2 Kgs 14.2–6)

25 Amaziah became king at the age of 25, and he ruled in Jerusalem for 29 years. His mother was Jehoaddin from Jerusalem. [2] He did what was pleasing to the Lord, but did it reluctantly. [3] As soon as he was firmly in power, he executed the officials who had murdered his father. [4] He did not, however, execute their children, but followed what the Lord had commanded in the Law of Moses: "Parents are not to be put to death for crimes committed by their children, and children are not to be put to death for crimes committed by their parents; a person is to be put to death only for a crime he himself has committed."

War against Edom
(2 Kgs 14.7)

[5] King Amaziah organized all the men of the tribes of Judah and Benjamin into army units, according to the clans they belonged to, and placed officers in command of units of a thousand and units of a hundred. This included all men twenty years of age or older, 300,000 in all. They were picked troops, ready for battle, skilled in using spears and shields. [6] In addition, he hired 100,000 soldiers from Israel at a cost of about 3.4 tonnes of silver. [7] But a prophet went to the king and said to him, "Don't take these Israelite soldiers with you. The Lord is not with these troops from the Northern Kingdom. [8] You may think that they will make you

....

24.25 Some ancient translations *son*; Hebrew *sons*.

527

2 Chron.
....

Ezra
Nehem.
Esther
Job
Psalms

stronger* in battle, but it is God who has the power to give victory or defeat, and he will let your enemies defeat you."

⁹Amaziah asked the prophet, "But what about all that silver I have already paid for them?"

The prophet replied, "The Lord can give you back more than that!" ¹⁰So Amaziah sent the hired troops away and told them to go home. At this they went home, bitterly angry with the people of Judah.

¹¹Amaziah summoned up his courage and led his army to the Valley of Salt. There they fought and killed 10,000 Edomite soldiers ¹²and captured another 10,000. They took the prisoners to the top of the cliff at the city of Sela and threw them off, so that they were killed on the rocks below.

¹³Meanwhile the Israelite soldiers that Amaziah had not allowed to go into battle with him attacked the Judean cities between Samaria and Beth Horon, killed 3,000 men, and captured quantities of loot.

¹⁴When Amaziah returned from defeating the Edomites, he brought their idols back with him, set them up, worshipped them, and burnt incense to them. ¹⁵This made the Lord angry, so he sent a prophet to Amaziah. The prophet demanded, "Why have you worshipped foreign gods that could not even save their own people from your power?"

¹⁶"Since when," Amaziah interrupted, "have we made you adviser to the king? Stop talking, or I'll have you killed!"

The prophet stopped, but not before saying, "Now I know that God has decided to destroy you because you have done all this and have ignored my advice."

War against Israel
(2 Kgs 14.8–20)

¹⁷King Amaziah of Judah and his advisers plotted against Israel. He then sent a message to King Jehoash of Israel, who was the son of Jehoahaz and grandson of Jehu, challenging him to fight.* ¹⁸Jehoash sent this answer to Amaziah: "Once, a thorn bush in the Lebanon Mountains sent a message to a cedar: 'Give your daughter in marriage to my son.' A wild animal passed by and trampled the bush down. ¹⁹Now Amaziah, you boast that you have defeated the Edomites, but I advise you to stay at home. Why stir up trouble that will only bring disaster on you and your people?"

²⁰But Amaziah refused to listen. It was God's will for Amaziah to be defeated, because he had worshipped the Edomite idols. ²¹So King Jehoash of Israel went into battle against King Amaziah of Judah. They met at Beth Shemesh in Judah, ²²the Judean army was defeated, and the soldiers fled to their homes. ²³Jehoash captured Amaziah and took him to Jerusalem. There he tore down the city wall from Ephraim Gate to the Corner Gate, a distance of nearly 200 metres. ²⁴He took back to Samaria as loot all the gold and silver in the Temple, the temple equipment guarded by the descendants of Obed Edom, and the palace treasures. He also took hostages with him.

²⁵King Amaziah of Judah outlived King Jehoash of Israel by fifteen years. ²⁶All the other things that Amaziah did from the beginning to the end of his reign are recorded in *The History of the Kings of Judah and Israel.* ²⁷Ever since the time when he rebelled

....

25.8 Some ancient translations *You may... stronger*; Hebrew unclear.
25.17 *challenging him to fight*; or *inviting him to a conference.*

528

2 Chron.

1 Sam.
2 Sam.
1 Kings
2 Kings
1 Chron.

2 CHRONICLES 25, 26

2 CHRONICLES 26.16-21

King Uzziah had let pride
creep in, so he started
to believe he was

- MORE -
IMPORTANT

and significant than
he actually was. Are
there areas where we
think about ourselves more
than other people or God?
What was the result
of Uzziah's pride?
Why do you think God
reacted so strongly?

write some
thoughts here

against the LORD, there had been a plot against him in Jerusalem. Finally he fled to the city of Lachish, but his enemies followed him there and killed him. [28] His body was carried to Jerusalem on a horse, and he was buried in the royal tombs in David's City.

King Uzziah of Judah
(2 Kgs 14.21–22; 15.1–7)

26 All the people of Judah chose Amaziah's sixteen-year-old son Uzziah to succeed his father as king. [2] (It was after the death of Amaziah that Uzziah recaptured Elath and rebuilt the city.)

[3] Uzziah became king at the age of sixteen, and he ruled in Jerusalem for 52 years. His mother was Jecoliah from Jerusalem. [4] Following the example of his father, he did what was pleasing to the LORD. [5] As long as Zechariah, his religious adviser, was living, he served the LORD faithfully, and God blessed him.

[6] Uzziah went to war against the Philistines. He tore down the walls of the cities of Gath, Jamnia, and Ashdod, and built fortified cities near Ashdod and in the rest of Philistia. [7] God helped him to defeat the Philistines, the Arabs living at Gurbaal, and the Meunites. [8] The Ammonites paid tribute to Uzziah, and he became so powerful that his fame spread even to Egypt.

[9] Uzziah strengthened the fortifications of Jerusalem by building towers at the Corner Gate, at the Valley Gate, and where the wall turned. [10] He also built fortified towers in the open country and dug many cisterns, because he had large herds of livestock in the western foothills and plains. Because he loved farming, he encouraged the people to plant vineyards in the hill country and to farm the fertile land.

[11] He had a large army ready for battle. Its records were kept by his secretaries Jeiel and Maaseiah under the supervision of Hananiah, a member of the king's staff. [12] The army was commanded by 2,600 officers. [13] Under them were 307,500 soldiers able to fight effectively for the king against his enemies. [14] Uzziah supplied the army with shields, spears, helmets, coats of armour, bows and arrows, and stones for slinging. [15] In Jerusalem his inventors made equipment for shooting arrows and for throwing large stones from the towers and corners of the city wall. His fame spread everywhere, and he became very powerful because of the help he received from God.

Uzziah is Punished for his Pride

[16] But when King Uzziah became strong, he grew arrogant, and that led to his downfall. He defied the LORD his God by going into the Temple to burn incense on the altar of incense. [17] Azariah the priest, accompanied by eighty strong and courageous priests, followed the king [18] to resist him. They said, "Uzziah! You have no right to burn incense to the LORD. Only the priests who are descended from Aaron have been consecrated to do this. Leave this holy place. You have offended the LORD God, and you no longer have his blessing."

[19] Uzziah was standing there in the Temple beside the incense altar and was holding an incense burner. He became angry with the priests, and immediately a dreaded skin disease broke out on his forehead. [20] Azariah and the other priests stared at the king's forehead in horror, and then forced him to leave the Temple. He hurried to get out, because the LORD had punished him.

[21] For the rest of his life King Uzziah was ritually unclean because of his disease. Unable to enter the Temple again, he lived in his

2 Chron.

Ezra
Nehem.
Esther
Job
Psalms

own house, relieved of all duties, while his son Jotham governed the country. [22] The prophet Isaiah son of Amoz recorded all the other things that King Uzziah did during his reign. [23] Uzziah died and was buried in the royal burial ground, but because of his disease he was not buried in the royal tombs. His son Jotham succeeded him as king.

King Jotham of Judah
(2 Kgs 15.32–38)

27 Jotham became king at the age of 25, and he ruled in Jerusalem for sixteen years. His mother was Jerushah, the daughter of Zadok. [2] He did what was pleasing to the LORD, just as his father had done; but unlike his father he did not sin by burning incense* in the Temple. The people, however, went on sinning.

[3] It was Jotham who built the North Gate of the Temple and did extensive work on the city wall in the area of Jerusalem called Ophel. [4] In the mountains of Judah he built cities, and in the forests he built forts and towers. [5] He fought against the king of Ammon and his army and defeated them. Then he forced the Ammonites to pay him the following tribute each year for three years: 3.4 tonnes of silver, 1,000 tonnes of wheat, and 1,000 tonnes of barley. [6] Jotham grew powerful because he faithfully obeyed the LORD his God. [7] The other events of Jotham's reign, his wars, and his policies, are all recorded in *The History of the Kings of Israel and Judah*. [8] Jotham was 25 years old when he became king, and he ruled in Jerusalem for sixteen years. [9] He died and was buried in David's City and his son Ahaz succeeded him as king.

King Ahaz of Judah
(2 Kgs 16.1–4)

28 Ahaz became king at the age of twenty, and he ruled in Jerusalem for sixteen years. He did not follow the good example of his ancestor King David; instead, he did what was not pleasing to the LORD [2] and followed the example of the kings of Israel. He had metal images of Baal made, [3] burnt incense in the Valley of Hinnom, and even sacrificed his own sons as burnt offerings to idols, imitating the disgusting practice of the people whom the LORD had driven out of the land as the Israelites advanced. [4] At the pagan places of worship, on the hills, and under every shady tree Ahaz offered sacrifices and burnt incense.

War with Syria and Israel
(2 Kgs 16.5)

[5-6] Because King Ahaz sinned, the LORD his God let the king of Syria defeat him and take a large number of Judeans back to Damascus as prisoners. The LORD also let the king of Israel, Pekah son of Remaliah, defeat Ahaz and kill 120,000 of the bravest Judean soldiers in one day. The LORD, the God of their ancestors, permitted this to happen, because the people of Judah had abandoned him. [7] An Israelite soldier named Zichri killed King Ahaz' son Maaseiah, the palace administrator Azrikam, and Elkanah, who was second in command to the king. [8] Even though the Judeans were their own relatives, the Israelite army captured 200,000 women and children as prisoners and took them back to Samaria, along with large amounts of loot.

27.2 *he did not sin by burning incense*; or *he did not take part in the worship*.

2 Chron.

1 Sam.
2 Sam.
1 Kings
2 Kings
1 Chron.

The Prophet Oded

⁹A man named Oded, a prophet of the LORD, lived in the city of Samaria. He met the returning Israelite army with its Judean prisoners as it was about to enter the city, and he said, "The LORD God of your ancestors was angry with Judah and let you defeat them, but now he has heard of the vicious way you slaughtered them. ¹⁰And now you intend to make the men and women of Jerusalem and Judah your slaves. Don't you know that you also have committed sins against the LORD your God? ¹¹Listen to me! These prisoners are your brothers and sisters. Let them go, or the LORD will punish you in his anger."

¹²Four of the leading men of the Northern Kingdom, Azariah son of Jehohanan, Berechiah son of Meshillemoth, Jehizkiah son of Shallum, and Amasa son of Hadlai also opposed the actions of the army. ¹³They said, "Don't bring those prisoners here! We have already sinned against the LORD and made him angry enough to punish us. Now you want to do something that will increase our guilt." ¹⁴So then the army handed the prisoners and the loot over to the people and their leaders, ¹⁵and the four men were appointed to provide the prisoners with clothing from the captured loot. They gave them clothes and sandals to wear, gave them enough to eat and drink, and put olive oil on their wounds. Those who were too weak to walk were put on donkeys, and all the prisoners were taken back to Judean territory at Jericho, the city of palm trees. Then the Israelites returned home to Samaria.

Ahaz Asks Assyria for Help
(2 Kgs 16.7–9)

¹⁶⁻¹⁷The Edomites began to raid Judah again and captured many prisoners, so King Ahaz asked Tiglath Pileser, the emperor of Assyria, to send help. ¹⁸At this same time the Philistines were raiding the towns in the western foothills and in southern Judah. They captured the cities of Beth Shemesh, Aijalon, and Gederoth, and the cities of Soco, Timnah, and Gimzo with their villages, and settled there permanently. ¹⁹Because King Ahaz of Judah had violated the rights of his people and had defied the LORD, the LORD brought troubles on Judah. ²⁰The Assyrian emperor, instead of helping Ahaz, opposed him and caused him trouble. ²¹So Ahaz took the gold from the Temple, the palace, and the homes of the leaders of the people, and gave it to the emperor, but even this did not help.

The Sins of Ahaz

²²When his troubles were at their worst, that man Ahaz sinned against the LORD more than ever. ²³He offered sacrifices to the gods of the Syrians, who had defeated him. He said, "The Syrian gods helped the kings of Syria, so if I sacrifice to them, they may help me too." This brought disaster on him and on his nation. ²⁴In addition, he took all the temple equipment and broke it in pieces. He closed the Temple and set up altars in every part of Jerusalem. ²⁵In every city and town in Judah, he built pagan places of worship, where incense was to be burnt to foreign gods. In this way he brought on himself the anger of the LORD, the God of his ancestors.

²⁶All the other events of his reign, from beginning to end, are recorded in *The History of the Kings of Judah and Israel.* ²⁷King Ahaz died and was buried in Jerusalem, but not in the royal tombs. His son Hezekiah succeeded him as king.

King Hezekiah of Judah
(2 Kgs 18.1–3)

29 Hezekiah became king of Judah at the age of 25, and he ruled in Jerusalem for 29 years. His mother was Abijah, the daughter of Zechariah. [2] Following the example of his ancestor King David, he did what was pleasing to the LORD.

The Purification of the Temple

[3] In the first month of the year after Hezekiah became king, he re-opened the gates of the Temple and had them repaired. [4] He assembled a group of priests and Levites in the east courtyard of the Temple [5] and spoke to them there. He said, "You Levites are to consecrate yourselves and purify the Temple of the LORD, the God of your ancestors. Remove from the Temple everything that defiles it. [6] Our ancestors were unfaithful to the LORD our God and did what was displeasing to him. They abandoned him and turned their backs on the place where he dwells. [7] They closed the doors of the Temple, let the lamps go out, and failed to burn incense or offer burnt offerings in the Temple of the God of Israel. [8] Because of this the LORD has been angry with Judah and Jerusalem, and what he has done to them has shocked and frightened everyone. You know this very well. [9] Our fathers were killed in battle, and our wives and children have been taken away as prisoners.

[10] "I have now decided to make a covenant with the LORD, the God of Israel, so that he will no longer be angry with us. [11] My sons, do not lose any time. You are the ones that the LORD has chosen to burn incense to him and to lead the people in worshipping him."

[12-14] The following Levites were there:

From the clan of Kohath, Mahath son of Amasai and Joel son of Azariah

From the clan of Merari, Kish son of Abdi and Azariah son of Jehallelel

From the clan of Gershon, Joah son of Zimnah and Eden son of Joah

From the clan of Elizaphan, Shimri and Jeuel

From the clan of Asaph, Zechariah and Mattaniah

From the clan of Heman, Jehuel and Shimei

From the clan of Jeduthun, Shemaiah and Uzziel.

[15] These men assembled their fellow-Levites, and they all made themselves ritually clean. Then, as the king had commanded them to do, they began to make the Temple ritually clean, according to the Law of the LORD.* [16] The priests went inside the Temple to purify it, and they carried out into the temple courtyard everything that was ritually unclean. From there the Levites took it all outside the city to the valley of the Kidron. [17] The work was begun on the first day of the first month, and by the eighth day they had finished it all, including the entrance room to the Temple. Then they worked for the next eight days, until the sixteenth of the month, preparing the Temple for worship.

The Temple is Rededicated

[18] The Levites made the following report to King Hezekiah: "We have completed the ritual purification of the whole Temple, including the altar for burnt offerings, the table for the sacred bread, and all their equipment. [19] We have also brought back all

....

29.15 *Then, as the king… LORD*; or *Then they began to make the Temple ritually clean, as the king, who was acting at the LORD's command, had ordered them to do.*

532

2 Chron.

1 Sam.
2 Sam.
1 Kings
2 Kings
1 Chron.

2 CHRONICLES 29, 30

the equipment which King Ahaz took away during those years he was unfaithful to God, and we have rededicated it. It is all in front of the Lord's altar."

²⁰ Without delay King Hezekiah assembled the leading men of the city, and together they went to the Temple. ²¹ As an offering to take away the sins of the royal family and of the people of Judah and to purify the Temple, they took seven bulls, seven sheep, seven lambs, and seven goats. The king told the priests, who were descendants of Aaron, to offer the animals as sacrifices on the altar. ²² The priests killed the bulls first, then the sheep, and then the lambs, and sprinkled the blood of each sacrifice on the altar. ²³ Finally they took the goats to the king and to the other worshippers, who laid their hands on them. ²⁴ Then the priests killed the goats and poured their blood on the altar as a sacrifice to take away the sin of all the people, for the king had commanded burnt offerings and sin offerings to be made for all Israel.

²⁵ The king followed the instructions that the Lord had given to King David through Gad, the king's prophet, and through the prophet Nathan; he stationed Levites in the Temple, with harps and cymbals, ²⁶ instruments like those that King David had used. The priests also stood there with trumpets. ²⁷ Hezekiah gave the order for the burnt offering to be presented; and as the offering began, the people sang praise to the Lord, and the musicians began to play the trumpets and all the other instruments. ²⁸ Everyone who was there joined in worship, and the singing and the rest of the music continued until all the sacrifices had been burnt. ²⁹ Then King Hezekiah and all the people knelt down and worshipped God. ³⁰ The king and the leaders of the nation told the Levites to sing to the Lord the songs of praise that were written by David and by Asaph the prophet. So everyone sang with great joy as they knelt and worshipped God.

³¹ Hezekiah said to the people, "Now that you are ritually clean, bring sacrifices as offerings of thanksgiving to the Lord." They obeyed, and some of them also voluntarily brought animals to be sacrificed as burnt offerings. ³² They brought seventy bulls, 100 sheep, and 200 lambs as burnt offerings for the Lord; ³³ they also brought 600 bulls and 3,000 sheep as sacrifices for the people to eat. ³⁴ Since there were not enough priests to kill all these animals, the Levites helped them until the work was finished. By then more priests had made themselves ritually clean. (The Levites were more faithful in keeping ritually clean than the priests were.) ³⁵ In addition to offering the sacrifices that were burnt whole, the priests were responsible for burning the fat that was offered from the sacrifices which the people ate, and for pouring out the wine that was presented with the burnt offerings.

And so worship in the Temple was begun again. ³⁶ King Hezekiah and the people were happy, because God had helped them to do all this so quickly.

Preparations for Passover

30 ¹⁻³ The people had not been able to celebrate the Passover Festival at the proper time, in the first month, because not enough priests were ritually clean and not many people had assembled in Jerusalem. So King Hezekiah, his officials, and the people of Jerusalem agreed to celebrate it in the second month, and the king sent word to all the people of Israel and Judah. He took special care to send letters to the tribes of Ephraim and Manasseh, inviting them to come to the Temple in Jerusalem to celebrate the Passover in honour of the Lord, the God of Israel.

533

2 Chron.

Ezra
Nehem.
Esther
Job
Psalms

[4] The king and the people were pleased with their plan, [5] so they invited all the Israelites, from Dan in the north to Beersheba in the south, to come together in Jerusalem and celebrate the Passover according to the Law, in larger numbers than ever before. [6] Messengers went out at the command of the king and his officials through all Judah and Israel with the following invitation:

"People of Israel, you have survived the Assyrian conquest of the land. Now return to the LORD, the God of Abraham, Isaac, and Jacob, and he will return to you. [7] Do not be like your ancestors and your fellow-Israelites who were unfaithful to the LORD their God. As you can see, he punished them severely. [8] Do not be stubborn as they were, but obey the LORD. Come to the Temple in Jerusalem, which the LORD your God has made holy for ever, and worship him so that he will no longer be angry with you. [9] If you return to the LORD, then those who have taken your relatives away as prisoners will take pity on them and let them come back home. The LORD your God is kind and merciful, and if you return to him, he will accept you."

[10] The messengers went to every city in the territory of the tribes of Ephraim and Manasseh, and as far north as the tribe of Zebulun, but people laughed at them and ridiculed them. [11] Still, there were some from the tribes of Asher, Manasseh, and Zebulun who were willing to come to Jerusalem. [12] God was also at work in Judah and united the people in their determination to obey his will by following the commands of the king and his officials.

Passover is Celebrated

[13] A great number of people gathered in Jerusalem in the second month to celebrate the Festival of Unleavened Bread. [14] They took all the altars that had been used in Jerusalem for offering sacrifices and burning incense and threw them into the valley of the Kidron. [15] And on the fourteenth day of the month they killed the lambs for the Passover sacrifice. The priests and Levites who were not ritually clean were so ashamed that they dedicated themselves to the LORD, and now they could sacrifice burnt offerings in the Temple. [16] They took their places in the Temple according to the instructions in the Law of Moses, the man of God. The Levites gave the blood of the sacrifices to the priests, who sprinkled it on the altar. [17] Because many of the people were not ritually clean, they could not kill the Passover lambs, so the Levites did it for them, and dedicated the lambs to the LORD. [18] In addition, many of those who had come from the tribes of Ephraim, Manasseh, Issachar, and Zebulun had not performed the ritual of purification, and so they were observing Passover improperly. King Hezekiah offered this prayer for them: [19] "O LORD, the God of our ancestors, in your goodness forgive those who are worshipping you with all their heart, even though they are not ritually clean." [20] The LORD answered Hezekiah's prayer; he forgave the people and did not harm them. [21] For seven days the people who had gathered in Jerusalem celebrated the Festival of Unleavened Bread with great joy, and day after day the Levites and the priests praised the LORD with all their strength.* [22] Hezekiah praised the Levites for their skill in conducting the worship of the LORD.

A Second Celebration

After the seven days during which they offered sacrifices in praise of the LORD, the God of their ancestors, [23] they all decided

---

30.21 Probable text *with all their strength*; Hebrew *with mighty instruments*.

534

2 Chron.

1 Sam.
2 Sam.
1 Kings
2 Kings
1 Chron.

2 CHRONICLES 30, 31

This is a space to write down some of your goals!

GOALS FOR 1 WEEK...

GOALS FOR 1 MONTH...

GOALS FOR 1 YEAR...

to celebrate for another seven days. So they celebrated with joy. 24 King Hezekiah contributed 1,000 bulls and 7,000 sheep for the people to kill and eat, and the officials gave them another thousand bulls and 10,000 sheep. A large number of priests went through the ritual of purification. 25 So everyone was happy — the people of Judah, the priests, the Levites, the people who had come from the north, and the foreigners who had settled permanently in Israel and Judah. 26 The city of Jerusalem was filled with joy, because nothing like this had happened since the days of King Solomon, the son of David. 27 The priests and the Levites asked the LORD's blessing on the people. In his home in heaven God heard their prayers and accepted them.

Hezekiah Reforms Religious Life

31 After the festival ended, all the people of Israel went to every city in Judah and broke the stone pillars, cut down the symbols of the goddess Asherah, and destroyed the altars and the pagan places of worship. They did the same thing throughout the rest of Judah, and the territories of Benjamin, Ephraim, and Manasseh; then they all returned home.

2 King Hezekiah re-established the organization of the priests and Levites, under which they each had specific duties. These included offering the burnt offerings and the fellowship offerings, taking part in the temple worship, and giving praise and thanks in the various parts of the Temple. 3 From his own flocks and herds he provided animals for the burnt offerings each morning and evening, and for those offered on the Sabbath, at the New Moon Festival, and at the other festivals which are required by the Law of the LORD. 4 In addition, the king told the people of Jerusalem to bring the offerings to which the priests and the Levites were entitled, so that they could give all their time to the requirements of the Law of the LORD. 5 As soon as the order was given, the people of Israel brought gifts of their finest corn, wine, olive oil, honey, and other farm produce, and they also brought the tithes* of everything they had. 6 All the people who lived in the cities of Judah brought tithes of their cattle and sheep, and they also brought large quantities of gifts, which they dedicated to the LORD their God. 7 The gifts started arriving in the third month and continued to pile up for the next four months. 8 When King Hezekiah and his officials saw how much had been given, they praised the LORD and praised his people Israel. 9 The king spoke to the priests and the Levites about these gifts, 10 and Azariah the High Priest, a descendant of Zadok, said to him, "Since the people started bringing their gifts to the Temple, there has been enough to eat and a large surplus besides. We have all this because the LORD has blessed his people."

11 On the king's orders they prepared storerooms in the Temple area 12 and put all the gifts and tithes in them for safe-keeping. They placed a Levite named Conaniah in charge and made his brother Shimei his assistant. 13 Ten Levites were assigned to work under them: Jehiel, Azaziah, Nahath, Asahel, Jerimoth, Jozabad, Eliel, Ismachiah, Mahath, and Benaiah. All this was done under the authority of King Hezekiah and Azariah the High Priest. 14 Kore son of Imnah, a Levite who was chief guard at the East Gate of the Temple, was in charge of receiving the gifts offered to the LORD and of distributing them. 15 In the other cities where priests lived, he was faithfully assisted in this by other Levites: Eden,

31.5 *gifts... tithes*: The gifts were for the priests, and the tithes for the Levites (see Num 18).

Miniamin, Jeshua, Shemaiah, Amariah, and Shecaniah. They distributed the food equally to their fellow-Levites according to what their duties were, [16] and not by clans. They gave a share to all males thirty* years of age or older who had daily responsibilities in the Temple in accordance with their positions. [17] The priests were assigned their duties by clans, and the Levites twenty years of age or older were assigned theirs by work groups. [18] They were all registered together with their wives, children, and other dependants, because they were required to be ready to perform their sacred duties at any time. [19] Among the priests who lived in the cities assigned to Aaron's descendants, or in the pasture lands belonging to these cities, there were responsible men who distributed the food to all the males in the priestly families and to everyone who was on the rolls of the Levite clans.

[20] Throughout all Judah, King Hezekiah did what was right and what was pleasing to the LORD his God. [21] He was successful, because everything he did for the Temple or in observance of the Law, he did in a spirit of complete loyalty and devotion to his God.

The Assyrians Threaten Jerusalem
(2 Kgs 18.13–37; 19.14–19, 35–37; Is 36.1–22; 37.8–38)

32 After these events, in which King Hezekiah served the LORD faithfully, Sennacherib, the emperor of Assyria, invaded Judah. He besieged the fortified cities and gave orders for his army to break their way through the walls. [2] When Hezekiah saw that Sennacherib intended to attack Jerusalem also, [3-4] he and his officials decided to cut off the supply of water outside the city in order to prevent the Assyrians from having any water when they got near Jerusalem. The officials led a large number of people out and stopped up all the springs, so that no more water flowed out of them. [5] The king strengthened the city's defences by repairing the wall, building towers on it,* and building an outer wall. In addition, he repaired the defences built on the land that was filled in on the east side of the old part of Jerusalem. He also had a large number of spears and shields made. [6] He placed all the men in the city under the command of army officers and ordered them to assemble in the open square at the city gate. He said to them, [7]"Be determined and confident, and don't be afraid of the Assyrian emperor or of the army he is leading. We have more power on our side than he has on his. [8] He has human power, but we have the LORD our God to help us and to fight our battles." The people were encouraged by these words of their king.

[9] Some time later, while Sennacherib and his army were still at Lachish, he sent the following message to Hezekiah and the people of Judah who were with him in Jerusalem: [10]"I, Sennacherib, Emperor of Assyria, ask what gives you people the confidence to remain in Jerusalem under siege. [11] Hezekiah tells you that the LORD your God will save you from our power, but Hezekiah is deceiving you and will let you die of hunger and thirst. [12] He is the one who destroyed the LORD's shrines and altars and then told the people of Judah and Jerusalem to worship and burn incense at one altar only. [13] Don't you know what my ancestors and I have done to the people of other nations? Did the gods of any other nation save their people from the emperor of Assyria? [14] When did any of the gods of all those countries ever save their country from us? Then

---

31.16 Probable text *thirty*; Hebrew *three*.
32.5 Some ancient translations *building towers on it*; Hebrew *building on the towers*.

2 Chron.

1 Sam.
2 Sam.
1 Kings
2 Kings
1 Chron.

what makes you think that your god can save you? [15] Now don't let Hezekiah deceive you or mislead you like that. Don't believe him! No god of any nation has ever been able to save his people from any Assyrian emperor. So certainly this god of yours can't save you!"

[16] The Assyrian officials said even worse things about the LORD God and Hezekiah, the LORD's servant. [17] The letter that the emperor wrote defied the LORD, the God of Israel. It said, "The gods of the nations have not saved their people from my power, and neither will Hezekiah's god save his people from me." [18] The officials shouted this in Hebrew in order to frighten and discourage the people of Jerusalem who were on the city wall, so that it would be easier to capture the city. [19] They talked about the God of Jerusalem in the same way that they talked about the gods of the other peoples, idols made by human hands.

[20] Then King Hezekiah and the prophet Isaiah son of Amoz prayed to God and cried out to him for help. [21] The LORD sent an angel that killed the soldiers and officers of the Assyrian army. So the emperor went back to Assyria disgraced. One day when he was in the temple of his god, some of his sons killed him with their swords.

[22] In this way the LORD rescued King Hezekiah and the people of Jerusalem from the power of Sennacherib, the emperor of Assyria, and also from their other enemies. He let the people live in peace* with all the neighbouring countries. [23] Many people came to Jerusalem, bringing offerings to the LORD and gifts to Hezekiah, so that from then on all the nations held Hezekiah in honour.

Hezekiah's Illness and Pride
(2 Kgs 20.1–3, 12–19; Is 38.1–3; 39.1–8)

[24] About this time King Hezekiah fell ill and almost died. He prayed, and the LORD gave him a sign that he would recover. [25] But Hezekiah was too proud to show gratitude for what the LORD had done for him, and Judah and Jerusalem suffered for it. [26] Finally, however, Hezekiah and the people of Jerusalem humbled themselves, and so the LORD did not punish the people until after Hezekiah's death.

Hezekiah's Wealth and Splendour

[27] King Hezekiah became very wealthy, and everyone held him in honour. He had storerooms built for his gold, silver, precious stones, spices, shields, and other valuable objects. [28] In addition, he had storehouses built for his corn, wine, and olive oil; barns for his cattle; and enclosures for his sheep. [29] Besides all this, God gave him sheep and cattle and so much other wealth that he built many cities. [30] It was King Hezekiah who blocked the outlet for the Spring of Gihon and channelled the water to flow through a tunnel to a point inside the walls of Jerusalem. Hezekiah succeeded in everything he did, [31] and even when the Babylonian ambassadors came to inquire about the unusual event that had happened in the land, God let Hezekiah go his own way only in order to test his character.

The End of Hezekiah's Reign
(2 Kgs 20.20–21)

[32] Everything else that King Hezekiah did and his devotion to the LORD are recorded in *The Vision of the Prophet Isaiah Son of Amoz* and in *The History of the Kings of Judah and Israel.* [33] Hezekiah

---

32.22 Some ancient translations *He let the people live in peace*; Hebrew *He led the people.*

2 CHRONICLES 32, 33

537

2 Chron.

⋯⋯⋯

Ezra

Nehem.

Esther

Job

Psalms

died and was buried in the upper section of the royal tombs. All the people of Judah and Jerusalem paid him great honour at his death. His son Manasseh succeeded him as king.

King Manasseh of Judah
(2 Kgs 21.1–9)

33 Manasseh was twelve years old when he became king of Judah, and he ruled in Jerusalem for 55 years. ² Following the disgusting practices of the nations whom the LORD had driven out of the land as his people advanced, Manasseh sinned against the LORD. ³ He rebuilt the pagan places of worship that his father Hezekiah had destroyed. He built altars for the worship of Baal, made images of the goddess Asherah, and worshipped the stars. ⁴ He built pagan altars in the Temple, the place that the LORD had said was where he should be worshipped for ever. ⁵ In the two courtyards of the Temple he built altars for the worship of the stars. ⁶ He sacrificed his sons in the Valley of Hinnom as burnt offerings. He practised divination and magic and consulted fortune tellers and mediums. He sinned greatly against the LORD and stirred up his anger. ⁷ He placed an image in the Temple, the place about which God had said to David and his son Solomon: "Here in Jerusalem, in this Temple, is the place that I have chosen out of all the territory of the twelve tribes of Israel as the place where I am to be worshipped. ⁸ And if the people of Israel will obey all my commands and keep the whole Law that my servant Moses gave them, then I will not allow them to be driven out of the land that I gave to their ancestors." ⁹ Manasseh led the people of Judah to commit even greater sins than those committed by the nations whom the LORD had driven out of the land as his people advanced.

Manasseh Repents

¹⁰ Although the LORD warned Manasseh and his people, they refused to listen. ¹¹ So the LORD let the commanders of the Assyrian army invade Judah. They captured Manasseh, stuck hooks in him, put him in chains, and took him to Babylon. ¹² In his suffering he became humble, turned to the LORD his God, and begged him for help. ¹³ God accepted Manasseh's prayer and answered it by letting him go back to Jerusalem and rule again. This convinced Manasseh that the LORD was God.

¹⁴ After this, Manasseh increased the height of the outer wall on the east side of David's City, from a point in the valley near the spring of Gihon north to the Fish Gate and the area of the city called Ophel. He also stationed an army officer in command of a unit of troops in each of the fortified cities of Judah. ¹⁵ He removed from the Temple the foreign gods and the image that he had placed there, and the pagan altars that were on the hill where the Temple stood and in other places in Jerusalem; he took all these things outside the city and threw them away. ¹⁶ He also repaired the altar where the LORD was worshipped, and he sacrificed fellowship offerings and thanksgiving offerings on it. He commanded all the people of Judah to worship the LORD, the God of Israel. ¹⁷ Although the people continued to offer sacrifices at other places of worship, they offered them only to the LORD.

The End of Manasseh's Reign
(2 Kgs 21.17–18)

¹⁸ Everything else that Manasseh did, the prayer he made to his God, and the messages of the prophets who spoke to him in the name of the LORD, the God of Israel, are all recorded in

The History of the Kings of Israel. [19] The king's prayer and God's answer to it, and an account of the sins he committed before he repented — the evil he did, the pagan places of worship and the symbols of the goddess Asherah that he made and the idols that he worshipped — are all recorded in *The History of the Prophets.* [20] Manasseh died and was buried at the palace, and his son Amon succeeded him as king.

King Amon of Judah
(2 Kgs 21.19–26)

[21] Amon was 22 years old when he became king of Judah, and he ruled in Jerusalem for two years. [22] Like his father Manasseh, he sinned against the LORD, and he worshipped the idols that his father had worshipped. [23] But unlike his father, he did not become humble and turn to the LORD; he was even more sinful than his father had been.

[24] Amon's officials plotted against him and assassinated him in the palace. [25] The people of Judah killed Amon's assassins and made his son Josiah king.

King Josiah of Judah
(2 Kgs 22.1–2)

34 Josiah was eight years old when he became king of Judah, and he ruled in Jerusalem for 31 years. [2] He did what was pleasing to the LORD; he followed the example of his ancestor King David, strictly obeying all the laws of God.

Josiah Attacks Pagan Worship

[3] In the eighth year that Josiah was king, while he was still very young, he began to worship the God of his ancestor King David. Four years later he began to destroy the pagan places of worship, the symbols of the goddess Asherah, and all the other idols. [4] Under his direction the altars where Baal was worshipped were smashed, and the incense altars near them were torn down. They ground to dust the images of Asherah and all the other idols and then scattered the dust on the graves of the people who had sacrificed to them. [5] He burnt the bones of the pagan priests on the altars where they had worshipped. By doing all this, he made Judah and Jerusalem ritually clean again. [6] He did the same thing in the cities and the devastated areas of Manasseh, Ephraim, and Simeon, and as far north as Naphtali. [7] Throughout the territory of the Northern Kingdom he smashed the altars and the symbols of Asherah, ground the idols to dust, and broke in pieces all the incense altars. Then he returned to Jerusalem.

The Book of the Law is Discovered
(2 Kgs 22.3–20)

[8] In the eighteenth year of his reign, after he had purified the land and the Temple by ending pagan worship, King Josiah sent three men to repair the Temple of the LORD God: Shaphan son of Azaliah, Maaseiah, the governor of Jerusalem, and Joah son of Joahaz, a high official. [9] The money that the Levite guards had collected in the Temple was handed over to Hilkiah the High Priest. (It had been collected from the people of Ephraim and Manasseh and the rest of the Northern Kingdom, and from the people of Judah, Benjamin, and Jerusalem.) [10] This money was then handed over to the three men in charge of the temple repairs, and they gave it to [11] the carpenters and the builders to buy the stones and the timber used to repair the buildings

2 CHRONICLES 34

539

2 Chron.

Ezra
Nehem.
Esther
Job
Psalms

that the kings of Judah had allowed to decay. [12] The men who did the work were thoroughly honest. They were supervised by four Levites: Jahath and Obadiah of the clan of Merari, and Zechariah and Meshullam of the clan of Kohath. (The Levites were all skilful musicians.) [13] Other Levites were in charge of transporting materials and supervising the workmen on various jobs, and others kept records or served as guards.

[14] While the money was being taken out of the storeroom, Hilkiah found the book of the Law of the LORD, the Law that God had given to Moses. [15] He said to Shaphan, "I have found the book of the Law here in the Temple." He gave Shaphan the book, [16] and Shaphan took it to the king. He reported, "We have done everything that you commanded. [17] We have taken the money that was kept in the Temple and handed it over to the workmen and their supervisors." [18] Then he added, "I have here a book that Hilkiah gave me." And he read it aloud to the king.

[19] When the king heard the book being read, he tore his clothes in dismay [20] and gave the following order to Hilkiah, to Ahikam son of Shaphan, to Abdon* son of Micaiah, to Shaphan, the court secretary, and to Asaiah, the king's attendant: [21] "Go and consult the LORD for me and for the people who still remain in Israel and Judah. Find out about the teachings of this book. The LORD is angry with us because our ancestors have not obeyed the word of the LORD and have not done what this book says must be done."

[22] At the king's command, Hilkiah and the others went to consult a woman named Huldah, a prophet who lived in the newer part of Jerusalem. (Her husband Shallum, the son of Tikvah and grandson of Harhas, was in charge of the temple robes.) They described to her what had happened, [23] and she told them to go back to the king and give him [24] the following message from the LORD: "I am going to punish Jerusalem and all its people with the curses written in the book that was read to the king. [25] They have rejected me and have offered sacrifices to other gods, and so have stirred up my anger by all they have done. My anger is aroused against Jerusalem, and it will not die down. [26] As for the king himself, this is what I, the LORD God of Israel, say: You listened to what is written in the book, [27] and you repented and humbled yourself before me, tearing your clothes and weeping, when you heard how I threatened to punish Jerusalem and its people. I have heard your prayer, [28] and the punishment which I am going to bring on Jerusalem will not come until after your death. I will let you die in peace."

The men returned to King Josiah with this message.

Josiah Makes a Covenant to Obey the LORD
(2 Kgs 23.1–20)

[29] King Josiah summoned all the leaders of Judah and Jerusalem, [30] and together they went to the Temple, accompanied by the priests and the Levites and all the rest of the people, rich and poor alike. Before them all, the king read aloud the whole book of the covenant, which had been found in the Temple. [31] He stood by the royal column* and made a covenant with the LORD to obey him, to keep his laws and commands with all his heart and soul, and to put into practice the demands attached to the covenant, as written in the book. [32] He made the people of Benjamin and

34.20 *Abdon*: Achbor in 2 Kgs 22.12.
34.31 Probable text (see 2 Kgs 23.3) *by the royal column*; Hebrew *in his place*.

2 CHRONICLES 34.29-33

Would you be able to tell God that you want to obey him with

ALL OF YOUR

HEART

and soul?

Think through what this might mean for your lifestyle - the way you speak, think and act.

For the next 24 hours, try to obey God in all that you say - not just what you think about other people but also about yourself.

540

2 Chron.

.·:········

1 Sam.
2 Sam.
1 Kings
2 Kings
1 Chron.

2 CHRONICLES 34, 35

everyone else present in Jerusalem promise to keep the covenant. And so the people of Jerusalem obeyed the requirements of the covenant they had made with the God of their ancestors. [33] King Josiah destroyed all the disgusting idols that were in the territory belonging to the people of Israel, and as long as he lived, he required the people to serve the LORD, the God of their ancestors.

Josiah Celebrates the Passover
(2 Kgs 23.21–23)

35 King Josiah celebrated the Passover at Jerusalem in honour of the LORD; on the fourteenth day of the first month they killed the animals for the festival. [2] He assigned to the priests the duties they were to perform in the Temple and encouraged them to do them well. [3] He also gave these instructions to the Levites, the teachers of Israel, who were dedicated to the LORD: "Put the sacred Covenant Box in the Temple that King Solomon, the son of David, built. You are no longer to carry it from place to place, but you are to serve the LORD your God and his people Israel. [4] Take your places in the Temple by clans, according to the responsibilities assigned to you by King David and his son King Solomon, [5] and arrange yourselves so that some of you will be available to help each family of the people of Israel. [6] You are to kill the Passover lambs and goats. Now make yourselves ritually clean and prepare the sacrifices in order that your fellow-Israelites may follow the instructions which the LORD gave through Moses."

[7] For the use of the people at the Passover, King Josiah contributed from his own herds and flocks 30,000 sheep, lambs, and young goats, and 3,000 bulls. [8] His officials also made contributions for the people, the priests, and the Levites to use. And the officials in charge of the Temple — Hilkiah, the High Priest, Zechariah, and Jehiel — gave the priests 2,600 lambs and young goats and 300 bulls for sacrifices during the festival. [9] The leaders of the Levites — Conaniah, Shemaiah and his brother Nethanel, Hashabiah, Jeiel, and Jozabad — contributed 5,000 lambs and young goats and 500 bulls for the Levites to offer as sacrifices.

[10] When everything was arranged for the Passover, the priests and the Levites took their places, as commanded by the king. [11] After the lambs and goats had been killed, the Levites skinned them, and the priests sprinkled the blood on the altar. [12] Then they divided among the people, by family groups, the animals for burnt offerings, so that they could offer them according to the instructions in the Law of Moses. [13] The Levites roasted the Passover sacrifices over the fire, according to the regulations, and boiled the sacred offerings in pots, cauldrons, and pans, and quickly distributed the meat to the people. [14] After this was done, the Levites provided meat for themselves and for the priests descended from Aaron, for the priests were kept busy until night, burning the animals that were burnt whole and the fat of the sacrifices. [15] The following musicians of the Levite clan of Asaph were in the places assigned to them by King David's instructions: Asaph, Heman, and Jeduthun, the king's prophet. The guards at the temple gates did not need to leave their posts, because the other Levites prepared the Passover for them. [16] So, as King Josiah had commanded, everything was done that day for the worship of the LORD, the keeping of the Passover Festival, and the offering of burnt offerings on the altar. [17] For seven days all the people of Israel who were present celebrated the Passover and the Festival of Unleavened Bread. [18] Since the days of the prophet Samuel, the Passover had never been celebrated like

2 CHRONICLES 35, 36

541

2 Chron.

Ezra
Nehem.
Esther
Job
Psalms

this. None of the former kings had ever celebrated a Passover like this one celebrated by King Josiah, the priests, the Levites, and the people of Judah, Israel, and Jerusalem [19] in the eighteenth year of Josiah's reign.

The End of Josiah's Reign
(2 Kgs 23.28–30)

[20] After King Josiah had done all this for the Temple, King Neco of Egypt led an army to fight at Carchemish on the River Euphrates. Josiah tried to stop him, [21] but Neco sent Josiah this message: "This war I am fighting does not concern you, King of Judah. I have not come to fight you, but to fight my enemies, and God has told me to hurry. God is on my side, so don't oppose me, or he will destroy you." [22] But Josiah was determined to fight. He refused to listen to what God was saying through King Neco, so he disguised himself and went into battle on the plain of Megiddo.

[23] During the battle King Josiah was struck by Egyptian arrows. He ordered his servants, "Take me away; I'm badly hurt!" [24] They lifted him out of his chariot, placed him in a second chariot which he had there, and took him to Jerusalem. There he died and was buried in the royal tombs. All the people of Judah and Jerusalem mourned his death.

[25] The prophet Jeremiah composed a lament for King Josiah. It has become a custom in Israel for the singers, both men and women, to use this song when they mourn for him. The song is found in the collection of laments.

[26] Everything that Josiah did — his devotion to the LORD, his obedience to the Law, [27] and his history from beginning to end — is all recorded in *The History of the Kings of Israel and Judah*.

King Joahaz of Judah
(2 Kgs 23.30–35)

36 The people of Judah chose Josiah's son Joahaz and anointed him king in Jerusalem. [2] Joahaz was 23 years old when he became king of Judah, and he ruled in Jerusalem for three months. [3] King Neco of Egypt took him prisoner and made Judah pay 3.4 tonnes of silver and 34 kilogrammes of gold as tribute. [4] Neco made Joahaz' brother Eliakim king of Judah and changed his name to Jehoiakim. Joahaz was taken to Egypt by Neco.

King Jehoiakim of Judah
(2 Kgs 23.36—24.7)

[5] Jehoiakim was 25 years old when he became king of Judah, and he ruled in Jerusalem for eleven years. He sinned against the LORD his God. [6] King Nebuchadnezzar of Babylonia invaded Judah, captured Jehoiakim, and took him to Babylonia in chains. [7] Nebuchadnezzar carried off some of the treasures of the Temple and put them in his palace in Babylon. [8] Everything that Jehoiakim did, including his disgusting practices and the evil he committed, is recorded in *The History of the Kings of Israel and Judah*. His son Jehoiachin succeeded him as king.

King Jehoiachin of Judah
(2 Kgs 24.8–17)

[9] Jehoiachin was eighteen* years old when he became king of Judah, and he ruled in Jerusalem for three months and ten

36.9 Some ancient translations (and see 2 Kgs 24.8) *eighteen*; Hebrew *eight*.

542

2 Chron.

⋮

1 Sam.
2 Sam.
1 Kings
2 Kings
1 Chron.

2 CHRONICLES 36

2 CHRONICLES 36.13-21

This passage is

• A BIG •

DEAL.

God's people were driven out of Jerusalem, the place that God had promised would be theirs as long as they followed him. The temple was destroyed, which was the place where God's presence rested with them. In this one attack, they lost a key part of who they were, and things would never be the same again.

days. He too sinned against the LORD. ¹⁰When spring came, King Nebuchadnezzar took Jehoiachin to Babylonia as a prisoner, and carried off the treasures of the Temple. Then Nebuchadnezzar made Jehoiachin's uncle* Zedekiah king of Judah and Jerusalem.

King Zedekiah of Judah
(2 Kgs 24.18–20; Jer 52.1–3a)

¹¹Zedekiah was 21 years old when he became king of Judah, and he ruled in Jerusalem for eleven years. ¹²He sinned against the LORD and did not listen humbly to the prophet Jeremiah, who spoke the word of the LORD.

The Fall of Jerusalem
(2 Kgs 25.1–21; Jer 52.3b–11)

¹³Zedekiah rebelled against King Nebuchadnezzar, who had forced him to swear in God's name that he would be loyal. He stubbornly refused to repent and return to the LORD, the God of Israel. ¹⁴In addition, the leaders of Judah, the priests, and the people followed the sinful example of the nations round them in worshipping idols, and so they defiled the Temple, which the LORD himself had made holy. ¹⁵The LORD, the God of their ancestors, had continued to send prophets to warn his people, because he wanted to spare them and the Temple. ¹⁶But they ridiculed God's messengers, ignoring his words and laughing at his prophets, until at last the LORD's anger against his people was so great that there was no escape.

¹⁷So the LORD brought the king of Babylonia to attack them. The king killed the young men of Judah, even in the Temple. He had no mercy on anyone, young or old, man or woman, sick or healthy. God handed them all over to him. ¹⁸The king of Babylonia looted the Temple, the temple treasury, and the wealth of the king and his officials, and took everything back to Babylon. ¹⁹He burnt down the Temple and the city, with all its palaces and its wealth, and broke down the city wall. ²⁰He took all the survivors to Babylonia, where they served him and his descendants as slaves until the rise of the Persian Empire. ²¹And so what the LORD had foretold through the prophet Jeremiah was fulfilled: "The land will lie desolate for seventy years, to make up for the Sabbath rest* that has not been observed."

Cyrus Commands the Jews to Return
(Ezra 1.1–4)

²²In the first year that Cyrus of Persia was emperor,* the LORD made what he had said through the prophet Jeremiah come true. He prompted Cyrus to issue the following command and send it out in writing to be read aloud everywhere in his empire:

²³"This is the command of Cyrus, Emperor of Persia. The LORD, the God of Heaven, has made me ruler over the whole world and has given me the responsibility of building a temple for him in Jerusalem in Judah. Now, all of you who are God's people, go there, and may the LORD your God be with you."

....

36.10 Some ancient translations (and see 2 Kgs 24.17) *uncle*; Hebrew *brother*.
36.21 *Sabbath rest*: A reference to the requirement of the Law that every seventh year the land was not to be farmed (see Lev 25.1–7).
36.22 *emperor*: King Cyrus of Persia occupied the city of Babylon in 539 BC and began to reign as the emperor of Babylonia.

THE BOOK OF

EZRA

WRITTEN: AROUND 400-300BC

WHAT YOU NEED TO KNOW:

The book of Ezra records some pretty significant events in the history of God's people. Earlier in the Bible, we read that there was a temple in Jerusalem, which was extremely important to the Judeans (people of Judah). The temple was destroyed when those people were exiled to Babylon. Years later, the Persians conquered the Babylonians, and this is where Ezra starts. The book tells how the Judeans were permitted to return to Jerusalem to rebuild the temple (under the guidance of Zerubbabel), but faced opposition when trying to do so. It goes on to show Ezra reorganising religious life and encouraging the people to place their focus firmly back on God.

IMAGINE THAT YOUR SCHOOL OR CHURCH WAS TOTALLY UNDER GOD'S CONTROL. WHAT WOULD IT LOOK LIKE? WHAT WOULD BE DIFFERENT ABOUT IT?

_____

_____

_____

_____

_____

_____

WHY READ IT?

Here we can read all about the importance of putting God first, and coming back to him if we have fallen away. Ezra shows us how God restores what has been broken and fulfils all his promises.

TURN THESE RECTANGLES INTO

IDENTITY CARDS

FOR ZERUBBABEL AND EZRA, WRITING DOWN THE THINGS THEY DID AND WHAT THEY WERE LIKE.

537BC   **TEMPLE REBUILT**   **456BC**

JEWS RETURN FROM EXILE TO JERUSALEM

EZRA RETURNS TO JERUSALEM

EZRA 1.2-4

This was

• A BIG •

DEAL.

A few decades before, the Babylonians had come along and destroyed the temple of God in Jerusalem and had forced the people of Judah to leave their homeland. After that, the Persians overcame the Babylonians, and the Jews became part of the Persian Empire. In a surprising turn of events, Cyrus, the Emperor of Persia, allowed the Jews to return home and rebuild their temple.

Cyrus Commands the Jews to Return

1 In the first year that Cyrus of Persia was emperor,* the LORD made what he had said through the prophet Jeremiah come true. He prompted Cyrus to issue the following command and send it out in writing to be read aloud everywhere in his empire:

2 "This is the command of Cyrus, Emperor of Persia. The LORD, the God of Heaven, has made me ruler over the whole world and has given me the responsibility of building a temple for him in Jerusalem in Judah. 3 May God be with all of you who are his people. You are to go to Jerusalem and rebuild the Temple of the LORD, the God of Israel, the God who is worshipped in Jerusalem. 4 If any of his people in exile need help to return, their neighbours are to give them this help. They are to provide them with silver and gold, supplies and pack animals, as well as offerings to present in the Temple of God in Jerusalem."

5 Then the heads of the clans of the tribes of Judah and Benjamin, the priests and Levites, and everyone else whose heart God had moved got ready to go and rebuild the LORD's Temple in Jerusalem. 6 All their neighbours helped them by giving them many things: silver utensils, gold, supplies, pack animals, other valuables, and offerings for the Temple.

7 Cyrus gave them back the bowls and cups that King Nebuchadnezzar had taken from the Temple in Jerusalem and had put in the temple of his gods. 8 He handed them over to Mithredath, chief of the royal treasury, who made an inventory of them for Sheshbazzar, the governor of Judah, 9-10 as follows:

gold bowls for offerings	30
silver bowls for offerings	1,000
other bowls	29
small gold bowls	30
small silver bowls	410
other utensils	1,000

11 In all there were 5,400 gold and silver bowls and other articles which Sheshbazzar took with him when he and the other exiles went from Babylon to Jerusalem.

The List of Those who Returned from Exile
(Neh 7.4–73)

2 Many of the exiles left the province of Babylon and returned to Jerusalem and Judah, all to their own cities. Their families had been living in exile in Babylonia ever since King Nebuchadnezzar had taken them there as prisoners. 2 Their leaders were Zerubbabel, Joshua, Nehemiah, Seraiah, Reelaiah, Mordecai, Bilshan, Mispar, Bigvai, Rehum, and Baanah.

This is the list of the clans of Israel, with the number of those from each clan who returned from exile:
3-20 Parosh — 2,172
    Shephatiah — 372
    Arah — 775
    Pahath Moab (descendants of Jeshua and Joab)
    — 2,812
    Elam — 1,254
    Zattu — 945
    Zaccai — 760

1.1 *emperor*: King Cyrus of Persia occupied the city of Babylon in 539 BC and began to reign as the emperor of Babylonia.

EZRA 2

545

Ezra
....

Nehem.
Esther
Job
Psalms
Proverbs

Bani — 642
Bebai — 623
Azgad — 1,222
Adonikam — 666
Bigvai — 2,056
Adin — 454
Ater (also called Hezekiah) — 98
Bezai — 323
Jorah — 112
Hashum — 223
Gibbar — 95

21-35 People whose ancestors had lived in the following towns also returned:

Bethlehem — 123
Netophah — 56
Anathoth — 128
Azmaveth — 42
Kiriath Jearim, Chephirah, and Beeroth — 743
Ramah and Geba — 621
Michmash — 122
Bethel and Ai — 223
Nebo — 52
Magbish — 156
The other Elam — 1,254
Harim — 320
Lod, Hadid, and Ono — 725
Jericho — 345
Senaah — 3,630

36-39 This is the list of the priestly clans that returned from exile:

Jedaiah (descendants of Jeshua) — 973
Immer — 1,052
Pashhur — 1,247
Harim — 1,017

40-42 Clans of Levites who returned from exile:

Jeshua and Kadmiel (descendants of Hodaviah) — 74
Temple musicians (descendants of Asaph) — 128
Temple guards (descendants of Shallum, Ater, Talmon,
    Akkub, Hatita, and Shobai) — 139

43-54 Clans of temple workmen who returned from exile:

Ziha, Hasupha, Tabbaoth,
Keros, Siaha, Padon,
Lebanah, Hagabah, Akkub,
Hagab, Shamlai, Hanan,
Giddel, Gahar, Reaiah,
Rezin, Nekoda, Gazzam,
Uzza, Paseah, Besai,
Asnah, Meunim, Nephisim,
Bakbuk, Hakupha, Harhur,
Bazluth, Mehida, Harsha,
Barkos, Sisera, Temah,
Neziah, and Hatipha.

55-57 Clans of Solomon's servants who returned from exile:

Sotai, Hassophereth, Peruda,
Jaalah, Darkon, Giddel,
Shephatiah, Hattil, Pochereth Hazzebaim, and Ami.

58 The total number of descendants of the temple workmen and of Solomon's servants who returned from exile was 392.

59-60 There were 652 belonging to the clans of Delaiah, Tobiah, and Nekoda who returned from the towns of Tel Melah, Tel Harsha,

Cherub, Addan, and Immer; but they could not prove that they were descendants of Israelites.

61-62 The following priestly clans could find no record to prove their ancestry: Habaiah, Hakkoz, and Barzillai. (The ancestor of the priestly clan of Barzillai had married a woman from the clan of Barzillai of Gilead and had taken the name of his father-in-law's clan.) Since they were unable to prove who their ancestors were, they were not accepted as priests. 63 The Jewish governor told them that they could not eat the food offered to God until there was a priest who could use the Urim and Thummim.*

64-67 Total number of exiles who returned — 42,360
  Their male and female servants — 7,337
  Male and female musicians — 200
  Horses — 736
  Mules — 245
  Camels — 435
  Donkeys — 6,720

68 When the exiles arrived at the Lord's Temple in Jerusalem, some of the leaders of the clans gave freewill offerings to help rebuild the Temple on its old site. 69 They gave as much as they could for this work, and the total came to 500 kilogrammes of gold, 2.8 tonnes of silver, and 100 robes for priests.

70 The priests, the Levites, and some of the people settled in or near Jerusalem;* the musicians, the temple guards, and the temple workmen settled in nearby towns; and the rest of the Israelites settled in the towns where their ancestors had lived.

Worship Begins Again

3 By the seventh month the people of Israel were all settled in their towns. Then they all assembled in Jerusalem, 2 and Joshua son of Jehozadak, his fellow-priests, and Zerubbabel son of Shealtiel, together with his relatives, rebuilt the altar of the God of Israel, so that they could burn sacrifices on it according to the instructions written in the Law of Moses, the man of God. 3 Even though* the returning exiles were afraid of the people who were living in the land, they rebuilt the altar where it had stood before. Then they began once again to burn on it the regular morning and evening sacrifices. 4 They celebrated the Festival of Shelters according to the regulations; each day they offered the sacrifices required for that day; 5 and in addition they offered the regular sacrifices to be burnt whole and those to be offered at the New Moon Festival and at all the other regular assemblies at which the Lord is worshipped, as well as all the offerings that were given to the Lord voluntarily. 6 Although the people had not yet started to rebuild the Temple, they began on the first day of the seventh month to burn sacrifices to the Lord.

The Rebuilding of the Temple Begins

7 The people gave money to pay the stonemasons and the carpenters and gave food, drink, and olive oil to be sent to the cities of Tyre and Sidon in exchange for cedar trees from Lebanon, which were to be brought by sea to Joppa. All this was done with the permission of Cyrus, emperor of Persia. 8 So in the second

2.63 *Urim and Thummim*: Two objects used by the priest to determine God's will; it is not known precisely how they were used.
2.70 One ancient translation *in or near Jerusalem*; Hebrew does not have these words.
3.3 *Even though*; or *Because*.

Ezra
....

Nehem.
Esther
Job
Psalms
Proverbs

month of the year after they came back to the site of the Temple in Jerusalem, they began work. Zerubbabel, Joshua, and the rest of their fellow-countrymen, the priests, and the Levites, in fact all the exiles who had come back to Jerusalem, joined in the work. All the Levites twenty years of age or older were put in charge of the work of rebuilding the Temple. [9] The Levite Jeshua and his sons and relatives, and Kadmiel and his sons (the clan of Hodaviah)* joined together in taking charge of the rebuilding of the Temple. (They were helped by the Levites of the clan of Henadad.)

[10] When the builders started to lay the foundation of the Temple, the priests in their robes took their places with trumpets in their hands, and the Levites of the clan of Asaph stood there with cymbals. They praised the LORD according to the instructions handed down from the time of King David. [11] They sang the LORD's praises, repeating the refrain:

"The LORD is good, and his love for Israel is eternal."
Everyone shouted with all his might, praising the LORD, because the work on the foundation of the Temple had been started. [12] Many of the older priests, Levites, and heads of clans had seen the first Temple, and as they watched the foundation of this Temple being laid, they cried and wailed. But the others who were there shouted for joy. [13] No one could distinguish between the joyful shouts and the crying, because the noise they made was so loud that it could be heard far and wide.

Opposition to the Rebuilding of the Temple

4 The enemies of the people of Judah and Benjamin heard that those who had returned from exile were rebuilding the Temple of the LORD, the God of Israel. [2] So they went to see Zerubbabel and the heads of the clans and said, "Let us join you in building the Temple. We worship the same God you worship, and we have been offering sacrifices to him ever since Esarhaddon, emperor of Assyria, sent us here to live."

[3] Zerubbabel, Joshua, and the heads of the clans said to them, "We don't need your help to build a temple for the LORD our God. We will build it ourselves, just as Cyrus, emperor of Persia, commanded us."

[4] Then the people who had been living in the land tried to discourage and frighten the Jews and keep them from building. [5] They also bribed Persian government officials to work against them. They kept on doing this throughout the reign of Cyrus and into the reign of Darius.*

Opposition to the Rebuilding of Jerusalem

[6] At the beginning of the reign of Xerxes the emperor, the enemies of the people living in Judah and Jerusalem brought written charges against them.

[7] Again, in the reign of Artaxerxes, emperor of Persia, Bishlam, Mithredath, Tabeel, and their associates wrote a letter to the emperor. The letter was written in Aramaic* and was to be translated when read.*

....

3.9 Probable text (see 2.40) *Hodaviah*; Hebrew *Judah*.
4.5 *Darius*: The account of these events is continued at verse 24. The material in verses 6–23 describes events which took place almost a century later.
4.7 *Aramaic*: From 4.8 to 6.18 this book is not in Hebrew, but Aramaic, the official language of the Persian Empire.
4.7 *The letter... read*; or *It was in Aramaic and was written in the Aramaic script.*

548

Ezra
·:········

2 Sam.
1 Kings
2 Kings
1 Chron.
2 Chron.

EZRA 4, 5

[8] Also Rehum, the governor, and Shimshai, the secretary of the province, wrote the following letter to Artaxerxes about Jerusalem: [9] "From Rehum, the governor, from Shimshai, secretary of the province, from their associates, the judges, and from all the other officials, who are men originally from Erech, Babylon, and Susa in the land of Elam, [10] together with the other peoples whom the great and powerful Ashurbanipal moved from their homes and settled in the city of Samaria and elsewhere in the province of West Euphrates."*

[11] This is the text of the letter:

"To Emperor Artaxerxes from his servants, the men of West Euphrates.

[12] "We want Your Majesty to know that the Jews who came here from your other territories have settled in Jerusalem and are rebuilding that evil and rebellious city. They have begun to rebuild the walls and will soon finish them. [13] Your Majesty, if this city is rebuilt and its walls are completed, the people will stop paying taxes, and your royal revenues will decrease. [14] Now, because we are under obligation to Your Majesty, we do not want to see this happen, and so we suggest [15] that you order a search to be made in the records your ancestors kept. If you do, you will discover that this city has always been rebellious and that from ancient times it has given trouble to kings and to rulers of provinces. Its people have always been hard to govern. This is why the city was destroyed. [16] We therefore are convinced that if this city is rebuilt and its walls are completed, Your Majesty will no longer be able to control the province of West Euphrates."

[17] The emperor sent this answer:

"To Rehum, the governor, to Shimshai, secretary of the province, and to their associates who live in Samaria and in the rest of West Euphrates, greetings.

[18] "The letter which you sent has been translated and read to me. [19] I gave orders for an investigation to be made, and it has indeed been found that from ancient times Jerusalem has revolted against royal authority and that it has been full of rebels and troublemakers. [20] Powerful kings have reigned there and have ruled over the entire province of West Euphrates, collecting taxes and revenue. [21] Therefore you are to issue orders that those men are to stop rebuilding the city until I give further commands. [22] Do this at once, so that no more harm may be done to my interests."

[23] As soon as this letter from Artaxerxes was read to Rehum, Shimshai, and their associates, they hurried to Jerusalem and forced the Jews to stop rebuilding the city.

Work on the Temple Begins Again

[24] Work on the Temple had been stopped and had remained at a standstill until the second year of the reign of Darius, emperor of Persia.

5 At that time two prophets, Haggai and Zechariah son of Iddo, began to speak in the name of the God of Israel to the Jews who lived in Judah and Jerusalem. [2] When Zerubbabel son of Shealtiel and Joshua son of Jehozadak heard their messages, they began to rebuild the Temple in Jerusalem, and the two prophets helped them.

....

4.10 *province of West Euphrates*: Under Persian rule the land of Judah was part of this large Persian province west of the River Euphrates.

Ezra
....

Nehem.
Esther
Job
Psalms
Proverbs

[3] Almost at once Tattenai, governor of West Euphrates, Shethar Bozenai, and their fellow-officials came to Jerusalem and demanded: "Who gave you orders to build this Temple and equip it?" [4] They* also asked for the names of all the men who were helping to build the Temple. [5] But God was watching over the Jewish leaders, and the Persian officials decided to take no action until they could write to Darius and receive a reply. [6] This is the report that they sent to the emperor:

[7] "To Emperor Darius, may you rule in peace.

[8] "Your Majesty should know that we went to the province of Judah and found that the Temple of the great God is being rebuilt with large stone blocks and with wooden beams set in the wall. The work is being done with great care and is moving ahead steadily.

[9] "We then asked the leaders of the people to tell us who had given them authority to rebuild the Temple and to equip it. [10] We also asked them their names so that we could inform you who the leaders of this work are.

[11] "They answered, 'We are servants of the God of heaven and earth, and we are rebuilding the Temple which was originally built and equipped many years ago by a powerful king of Israel. [12] But because our ancestors made the God of Heaven angry, he let them be conquered by King Nebuchadnezzar of Babylonia, a king of the Chaldean dynasty. The Temple was destroyed, and the people were taken into exile in Babylonia. [13] Then in the first year of the reign of King Cyrus as emperor of Babylonia, Cyrus issued orders for the Temple to be rebuilt. [14] He restored the gold and silver temple utensils which Nebuchadnezzar had taken from the Temple in Jerusalem and had placed in the temple in Babylon. Cyrus handed these utensils over to a man named Sheshbazzar, whom he appointed governor of Judah. [15] The emperor told him to take them and return them to the Temple in Jerusalem, and to rebuild the Temple where it had stood before. [16] So Sheshbazzar came and laid its foundation; construction has continued from then until the present, but the Temple is still not finished.'

[17] "Now, if it please Your Majesty, let a search be made in the royal records in Babylon to find whether or not Cyrus gave orders for this Temple in Jerusalem to be rebuilt, and then inform us what your will is in this matter."

Cyrus' Order is Rediscovered

6 So Darius the emperor issued orders for a search to be made in the royal records that were kept in Babylon. [2] But it was in the city of Ecbatana in the province of Media that a scroll was found, containing the following record:

[3] "In the first year of his reign Cyrus the emperor commanded that the Temple in Jerusalem be rebuilt as a place where sacrifices are made and offerings are burnt. The Temple is to be 27 metres high and 27 metres wide. [4] The walls are to be built with one layer of wood on top of every three layers of stone. All expenses are to be paid by the royal treasury. [5] Also the gold and silver utensils which King Nebuchadnezzar brought to Babylon from the Temple in Jerusalem are to be returned to their proper place in the Jerusalem Temple."

Darius Orders the Work to Continue

[6] Then Darius sent the following reply:

....

5.4 Some ancient translations *They*; Aramaic *We*.

550

Ezra

2 Sam.
1 Kings
2 Kings
1 Chron.
2 Chron.

EZRA 6

EZRA 6.15-16

For the next week,

DEDICATE
EVERYTHING

you do to God.
Pray beforehand and
thank him afterwards.

In the space below, write
some of the everyday
things that you will
dedicate to him.

_____

_____

_____

_____

_____

_____

_____

_____

_____

_____

_____

_____

_____

_____

_____

"To Tattenai, governor of West Euphrates, Shethar Bozenai, and your fellow-officials in West Euphrates.

"Stay away from the Temple [7] and do not interfere with its construction. Let the governor of Judah and the Jewish leaders rebuild the Temple of God where it stood before. [8] I hereby command you to help them rebuild it. Their expenses are to be paid promptly out of the royal funds received from taxes in West Euphrates, so that the work is not interrupted. [9] Day by day, without fail, you are to give the priests in Jerusalem whatever they tell you they need: young bulls, sheep, or lambs to be burnt as offerings to the God of Heaven, or wheat, salt, wine, or olive oil. [10] This is to be done so that they can offer sacrifices that are acceptable to the God of Heaven and pray for his blessing on me and my sons. [11] I further command that if anyone disobeys this order, a wooden beam is to be torn out of his house, sharpened at one end, and then driven through his body. And his house is to be made a rubbish heap. [12] May the God who chose Jerusalem as the place where he is to be worshipped overthrow any king or nation that defies this command and tries to destroy the Temple there. I, Darius, have given this order. It is to be fully obeyed."

The Temple is Dedicated

[13] Then Tattenai the governor, Shethar Bozenai, and their fellow-officials did exactly as the emperor had commanded. [14] The Jewish leaders made good progress with the building of the Temple, encouraged by the prophets Haggai and Zechariah. They completed the Temple as they had been commanded by the God of Israel and by Cyrus, Darius, and Artaxerxes, emperors of Persia. [15] They finished the Temple on the third day of the month Adar in the sixth year of the reign of Darius the emperor. [16] Then the people of Israel — the priests, the Levites, and all the others who had returned from exile — joyfully dedicated the Temple. [17] For the dedication they offered 100 bulls, 200 sheep, and 400 lambs as sacrifices, and twelve goats as offerings for sin, one for each tribe of Israel. [18] They also organized the priests and the Levites for the temple services in Jerusalem, according to the instructions contained in the book of Moses.

The Passover

[19] The people who had returned from exile celebrated Passover on the fourteenth day of the first month of the following year. [20] All the priests and the Levites had purified themselves and were ritually clean. The Levites killed the animals for the Passover sacrifices for all the people who had returned, for the priests, and for themselves. [21] The sacrifices were eaten by all the Israelites who had returned from exile and by all those who had given up the pagan ways of the other people who were living in the land and who had come to worship the LORD God of Israel. [22] For seven days they joyfully celebrated the Festival of Unleavened Bread. They were full of joy because the LORD had made the emperor of Assyria* favourable to them, so that he supported them in their work of rebuilding the Temple of the God of Israel.

6.22 *emperor of Assyria*: Apparently a reference to the Persian emperor who then also ruled the territory once occupied by Assyria, Israel's ancient enemy.

Ezra

Nehem.
Esther
Job
Psalms
Proverbs

Ezra Arrives in Jerusalem

7 Many years later, when Artaxerxes was emperor of Persia, there was a man named Ezra. He traced his ancestors back to Aaron, the High Priest, as follows: Ezra was the son of Seraiah, son of Azariah, son of Hilkiah, [2]son of Shallum, son of Zadok, son of Ahitub, [3]son of Amariah, son of Azariah, son of Meraioth, [4]son of Zerahiah, son of Uzzi, son of Bukki, [5]son of Abishua, son of Phinehas, son of Eleazar, son of Aaron.

[6-7]Ezra was a scholar with a thorough knowledge of the Law which the LORD, the God of Israel, had given to Moses. Because Ezra had the blessing of the LORD his God, the emperor gave him everything he asked for. In the seventh year of the reign of Artaxerxes, Ezra set out from Babylonia for Jerusalem with a group of Israelites which included priests, Levites, temple musicians, temple guards, and workmen. [8-9]They left Babylonia on the first day of the first month, and with God's help they arrived in Jerusalem on the first day of the fifth month. [10]Ezra had devoted his life to studying the Law of the LORD, to practising it, and to teaching all its laws and regulations to the people of Israel.

The Document which Artaxerxes Gave to Ezra

[11]Artaxerxes gave the following document to Ezra, the priest and scholar, who had a thorough knowledge of the laws and commands which the LORD had given to Israel:

[12]"From Artaxerxes* the emperor to Ezra the priest, scholar in the Law of the God of Heaven.*

[13]"I command that throughout my empire all the Israelite people, priests, and Levites that so desire be permitted to go with you to Jerusalem. [14]I, together with my seven counsellors, send you to investigate the conditions in Jerusalem and Judah in order to see how well the Law of your God, which has been entrusted to you, is being obeyed. [15]You are to take with you the gold and silver offerings which I and my counsellors desire to give to the God of Israel, whose Temple is in Jerusalem. [16]You are also to take all the silver and gold which you collect throughout the province of Babylon and the offerings which the Israelite people and their priests give for the Temple of their God in Jerusalem.

[17]"You are to spend this money carefully and buy bulls, rams, lambs, corn, and wine and offer them on the altar of the Temple in Jerusalem. [18]You may use the silver and gold that is left over for whatever you and your people desire, in accordance with the will of your God. [19]You are to present to God in Jerusalem all the utensils that have been given to you for use in the temple services. [20]And anything else which you need for the Temple, you may get from the royal treasury.

[21]"I command all the treasury officials in the province of West Euphrates to provide promptly for Ezra, the priest and scholar in the Law of the God of Heaven, everything he asks you for, [22]up to a limit of 3.4 tonnes of silver, ten tonnes of wheat, 2,000 litres of wine, 2,000 litres of olive oil, and as much salt as necessary. [23]You must be careful to provide everything which the God of Heaven requires for his Temple, and so make sure that he is never angry with me or with those who reign after me. [24]You are forbidden to collect any taxes from the priests, Levites, musicians, guards, workmen, or anyone else connected with this Temple.

7.12 Verses 12–26 are in Aramaic (see also 4.7).
7.12 Aramaic has an additional word, the meaning of which is unclear.

552

Ezra

⋮⋯⋯⋯

2 Sam.
1 Kings
2 Kings
1 Chron.
2 Chron.

EZRA 7, 8

25 "You, Ezra, using the wisdom which your God has given you, are to appoint administrators and judges to govern all the people in West Euphrates who live by the Law of your God. You must teach that Law to anyone who does not know it. 26 If anyone disobeys the laws of your God or the laws of the empire, he is to be punished promptly: by death or by exile or by confiscation of his property or by imprisonment."

Ezra Praises God

27 Ezra said, "Praise the LORD, the God of our ancestors! He has made the emperor willing to honour in this way the Temple of the LORD in Jerusalem. 28 By God's grace I have won the favour of the emperor, of his counsellors, and of all his powerful officials; the LORD my God has given me courage, and I have been able to persuade many of the heads of the clans of Israel to return with me."

The People who Returned from Exile

8 This is the list of the heads of the clans who had been in exile in Babylonia and who returned with Ezra to Jerusalem when Artaxerxes was emperor:

2-14 Gershom, of the clan of Phinehas
Daniel, of the clan of Ithamar
Hattush son of Shecaniah, of the clan of David
Zechariah, of the clan of Parosh, with 150 men of his clan
(there were records of their ancestry)
Eliehoenai son of Zerahiah, of the clan of Pahath Moab,
with 200 men
Shecaniah son of Jahaziel, of the clan of Zattu,* with 300
men
Ebed son of Jonathan, of the clan of Adin, with fifty men
Jeshaiah son of Athaliah, of the clan of Elam, with seventy
men
Zebadiah son of Michael, of the clan of Shephatiah, with
eighty men
Obadiah son of Jehiel, of the clan of Joab, with 218 men
Shelomith son of Josiphiah, of the clan of Bani,* with 160
men
Zechariah son of Bebai, of the clan of Bebai, with 28 men
Johanan son of Hakkatan, of the clan of Azgad, with 110
men
Eliphelet, Jeuel, and Shemaiah, of the clan of Adonikam,
with sixty men (they returned at a later date)
Uthai and Zaccur, of the clan of Bigvai, with seventy
men.

Ezra Finds Levites for the Temple

15 I assembled the entire group by the canal that runs to the town of Ahava, and we camped there three days. I found that there were priests in the group, but no Levites. 16 I sent for nine of the leaders: Eliezer, Ariel, Shemaiah, Elnathan, Jarib, Elnathan, Nathan, Zechariah, and Meshullam, and for two teachers, Joiarib and Elnathan. 17 I sent them to Iddo, head of the community at Casiphia, to ask him and his associates, the temple workmen,

....

8.2–14 One ancient translation (see also 2.8) *Zattu*; Hebrew does not have this name.
8.2–14 One ancient translation (see also 2.10) *Bani*; Hebrew does not have this name.

Ezra
....

Nehem.
Esther
Job
Psalms
Proverbs

to send us people to serve God in the Temple. [18] Through God's grace they sent us Sherebiah, an able man, a Levite from the clan of Mahli, and eighteen of his sons and brothers came with him. [19] They also sent Hashabiah and Jeshaiah of the clan of Merari, with twenty of their relatives. [20] In addition there were 220 temple workmen whose ancestors had been designated by King David and his officials to assist the Levites. They were all listed by name.

Ezra Leads the People in Fasting and Prayer

[21] There by the Ahava Canal I gave orders for us all to fast and humble ourselves before our God and to ask him to lead us on our journey and protect us and our children and all our possessions. [22] I would have been ashamed to ask the emperor for a troop of cavalry to guard us from any enemies during our journey, because I had told him that our God blesses everyone who trusts him, but that he is displeased with and punishes anyone who turns away from him. [23] So we fasted and prayed for God to protect us, and he answered our prayers.

The Gifts for the Temple

[24] From among the leading priests I chose Sherebiah, Hashabiah, and ten others. [25] Then I weighed out the silver, the gold, and the utensils which the emperor, his advisers and officials, and the people of Israel had given to be used in the Temple, and I gave it to the priests. [26-27] This is what I gave them:

silver — 22 tonnes
100 silver utensils — seventy kilogrammes
gold — 3.4 tonnes
twenty gold bowls — 8.4 kilogrammes
two fine bronze bowls, equal in value to gold bowls.

[28] I said to them, "You are sacred to the LORD, the God of your ancestors, and so are all the silver and gold utensils brought to him as freewill offerings. [29] Guard them carefully until you reach the Temple. There in the priests' room weigh them and hand them over to the leaders of the priests and of the Levites, and to the leaders of the people of Israel in Jerusalem." [30] So the priests and the Levites took charge of the silver, the gold, and the utensils, to take them to the Temple in Jerusalem.

The Return to Jerusalem

[31] It was on the twelfth day of the first month that we left the Ahava Canal to go to Jerusalem. Our God was with us and protected us from enemy attacks and from ambush as we travelled. [32] When we reached Jerusalem, we rested for three days. [33] Then on the fourth day we went to the Temple, weighed the silver, the gold, and the utensils, and handed them over to Meremoth the priest, son of Uriah. With him were Eleazar son of Phinehas and two Levites, Jozabad son of Jeshua and Noadiah son of Binnui. [34] Everything was counted and weighed, and a complete record was made at the same time.

[35] All those who had returned from exile then brought offerings to be burnt as sacrifices to the God of Israel. They offered twelve bulls for all Israel, 96 rams, and 77 lambs; they also offered twelve goats to purify themselves from sin. All these animals were burnt as sacrifices to the LORD. [36] They also took the document the emperor had given them and gave it to the governors and officials of the province of West Euphrates, who then gave their support to the people and the temple worship.

Ezra
: ········

2 Sam.
1 Kings
2 Kings
1 Chron.
2 Chron.

NO MATTER WHAT
YOU HAVE DONE,

GOD'S

FORGIVENESS

IS NEVER-ENDING

FOR YOU.

Ezra Learns of Intermarriages with Non-Jews

9 After all this had been done, some of the leaders of the people of Israel came and told me that the people, the priests, and the Levites had not kept themselves separate from the people in the neighbouring countries of Ammon, Moab, and Egypt or from the Canaanites, Hittites, Perizzites, Jebusites, and Amorites. They were doing the same disgusting things that those people did. [2] Jewish men were marrying foreign women, and so God's holy people had become contaminated. The leaders and officials were the chief offenders. [3] When I heard this, I tore my clothes in despair, tore my hair and my beard, and sat down crushed with grief. [4] I sat there grieving until the time for the evening sacrifice to be offered, and people began to gather round me — all those who were frightened because of what the God of Israel had said about the sins of those who had returned from exile.

[5] When the time came for the evening sacrifice, I got up from where I had been grieving, and still wearing my torn clothes, I knelt in prayer and stretched out my hands to the LORD my God. [6] I said, "O God, I am too ashamed to raise my head in your presence. Our sins pile up, high above our heads; they reach as high as the heavens. [7] From the days of our ancestors until now, we, your people, have sinned greatly. Because of our sins we, our kings, and our priests have fallen into the hands of foreign kings, and we have been slaughtered, robbed, and carried away as prisoners. We have been totally disgraced, as we still are today. [8] Now for a short time, O LORD our God, you have been gracious to us and have let some of us escape from slavery and live in safety in this holy place. You have freed us from slavery and given us new life. [9] We were slaves, but you did not leave us in slavery. You made the emperors of Persia favour us and permit us to go on living and to rebuild your Temple, which was in ruins, and to find safety here in Judah and Jerusalem.

[10] "But now, O God, what can we say after all that has happened? We have again disobeyed the commands [11] that you gave us through your servants, the prophets. They told us that the land we were going to occupy was an impure land because the people who lived in it filled it from one end to the other with disgusting, filthy actions. [12] They told us that we were never to intermarry with those people and never to help them prosper or succeed if we wanted to enjoy the land and pass it on to our descendants for ever. [13] Even after everything that has happened to us in punishment for our sins and wrongs, we know that you, our God, have punished us less than we deserve and have allowed us to survive. [14] Then how can we ignore your commandments again and intermarry with these wicked people? If we do, you will be so angry that you will destroy us completely and let no one survive. [15] LORD God of Israel, you are just, but you have let us survive. We confess our guilt to you; we have no right to come into your presence."

The Plan for Ending Mixed Marriages

10 While Ezra was bowing in prayer in front of the Temple, weeping and confessing these sins, a large group of Israelites — men, women, and children — gathered round him, weeping bitterly. [2] Then Shecaniah son of Jehiel, of the clan of Elam, said to Ezra, "We have broken faith with God by marrying foreign women, but even so there is still hope for Israel. [3] Now we must make a solemn promise to our God that we will send

Ezra
....

Nehem.
Esther
Job
Psalms
Proverbs

these women and their children away. We will do what you and the others who honour God's commands advise us to do. We will do what God's Law demands. ⁴ It is your responsibility to act. We are behind you, so go ahead and get it done."

⁵ So Ezra began by making the leaders of the priests, of the Levites, and of the rest of the people take an oath that they would do what Shecaniah had proposed. ⁶ Then he went from in front of the Temple into the living quarters of Jehohanan son of Eliashib, and spent the night* there grieving over the unfaithfulness of the exiles. He did not eat or drink anything.

⁷ A message was sent throughout Jerusalem and Judah that all those who had returned from exile were to meet in Jerusalem ⁸ by order of the leaders of the people. If anyone failed to come within three days, all his property would be confiscated, and he would lose his right to be a member of the community. ⁹ Within the three days, on the twentieth day of the ninth month, all the men living in the territory of Judah and Benjamin came to Jerusalem and assembled in the temple square. It was raining hard, and because of the weather and the importance of the meeting everyone was trembling.

¹⁰ Ezra the priest stood up and spoke to them. He said, "You have been faithless and have brought guilt on Israel by marrying foreign women. ¹¹ Now then, confess your sins to the Lord, the God of your ancestors, and do what pleases him. Separate yourselves from the foreigners living in our land and get rid of your foreign wives."

¹² The people shouted in answer, "We will do whatever you say." ¹³ But they added, "The crowd is too big, and it's raining hard. We can't stand here in the open like this. This isn't something that can be done in one or two days, because so many of us are involved in this sin. ¹⁴ Let our officials stay in Jerusalem and take charge of the matter. Then let anyone who has a foreign wife come at a set time, together with the leaders and the judges of his city. In this way God's anger over this situation will be turned away." ¹⁵ No one was opposed to the plan except Jonathan son of Asahel and Jahzeiah son of Tikvah, who had the support of Meshullam and of Shabbethai, a Levite.

¹⁶ The returned exiles accepted the plan, so Ezra the priest appointed* men from among the heads of the clans and recorded their names. On the first day of the tenth month they began their investigation, ¹⁷ and within the next three months they investigated all the cases of men with foreign wives.

The Men who had Foreign Wives

¹⁸ This is the list of the men who had foreign wives:

Priests, listed by clans:
    Clan of Joshua and his brothers, sons of Jehozadak:
        Maaseiah, Eliezer, Jarib, and Gedaliah. ¹⁹ They promised
        to divorce their wives, and they offered a ram as
        a sacrifice for their sins.
²⁰ Clan of Immer: Hanani and Zebadiah
²¹ Clan of Harim: Maaseiah, Elijah, Shemaiah, Jehiel, and
    Uzziah
²² Clan of Pashhur: Elioenai, Maaseiah, Ishmael, Nethanel,
    Jozabad, and Elasah.

....

10.6 One ancient translation *spent the night*; Hebrew *went*.
10.16 Some ancient translations *appointed*; Hebrew unclear.

Ezra

2 Sam.
1 Kings
2 Kings
1 Chron.
2 Chron.

23 Levites:
     Jozabad, Shimei, Kelaiah (also called Kelita), Pethahiah, Judah, and Eliezer.

24 Musicians:
     Eliashib.

Temple guards:
     Shallum, Telem, and Uri.

25 Others:
     Clan of Parosh: Ramiah, Izziah, Malchijah, Mijamin, Eleazar, Malchijah, and Benaiah
26   Clan of Elam: Mattaniah, Zechariah, Jehiel, Abdi, Jeremoth, and Elijah
27   Clan of Zattu: Elioenai, Eliashib, Mattaniah, Jeremoth, Zabad, and Aziza
28   Clan of Bebai: Jehohanan, Hananiah, Zabbai, and Athlai
29   Clan of Bani: Meshullam, Malluch, Adaiah, Jashub, Sheal, and Jeremoth
30   Clan of Pahath Moab: Adna, Chelal, Benaiah, Maaseiah, Mattaniah, Bezalel, Binnui, and Manasseh
31-32   Clan of Harim: Eliezer, Isshijah, Malchijah, Shemaiah, Shimeon, Benjamin, Malluch, and Shemariah
33   Clan of Hashum: Mattenai, Mattattah, Zabad, Eliphelet, Jeremai, Manasseh, and Shimei
34-37   Clan of Bani: Maadai, Amram, Uel, Benaiah, Bedeiah, Cheluhi, Vaniah, Meremoth, Eliashib, Mattaniah, Mattenai, and Jaasu
38-42   Clan of Binnui: Shimei, Shelemiah, Nathan, Adaiah, Machnadebai, Shashai, Sharai, Azarel, Shelemiah, Shemariah, Shallum, Amariah, and Joseph
43   Clan of Nebo: Jeiel, Mattithiah, Zabad, Zebina, Jaddai, Joel, and Benaiah.
44 All these men had foreign wives. They divorced them and sent them and their children away.*

10.44 Verse 44 in Hebrew is unclear.

THE BOOK OF
NEHEMIAH

WRITTEN: AROUND 400-300BC

WHAT YOU NEED TO KNOW:

The book of Nehemiah is set in Jerusalem shortly after the rebuilding of the temple, which is described in the book of Ezra. Many of God's people were still in exile in Babylon, under the rule of the Persian empire. This book tells how Nehemiah, cupbearer to the Persian king, asked for permission to rebuild the broken-down walls of Jerusalem. Permission was granted, and we see the walls being rebuilt, as well as God's people rededicating themselves to God.

WHY READ IT?

There are many themes throughout this book that can link up with our lives today, including working with others, social action and looking out for those who are less fortunate. It also lets us know that we can always return to God, and it shows us an example of people standing firm when facing opposition and discouragement.

Nehemiah was determined to rebuild Jerusalem's walls.

DOODLE
HIM BELOW.

Then jot down why he was so passionate about the building project, and the things he did that showed his dedication to it.

City walls were a sign of protection. They were the first defence against any potential invaders, so the fact that Jerusalem's walls were broken down showed that the city was vulnerable. Jerusalem was believed to be God's holy city, so the broken walls also suggested that God was weak and could be defeated. Nehemiah knew this was not true of God, and he wanted to restore Jerusalem as a respectable city once again.

445BC

CITY WALLS REBUILT

432BC

NEHEMIAH RETURNS
TO JERUSALEM

LAW REINSTATED

558

Nehem.

....

1 Kings
2 Kings
1 Chron.
2 Chron.
Ezra

NEHEMIAH 1, 2

1

This is the account of what Nehemiah son of Hacaliah accomplished.

Nehemiah's Concern for Jerusalem

In the month of Kislev in the twentieth year that Artaxerxes was emperor of Persia, I, Nehemiah, was in Susa, the capital city. [2] Hanani, one of my brothers, arrived from Judah with another group, and I asked them about Jerusalem and about our fellow-Jews who had returned from exile in* Babylonia. [3] They told me that those who had survived and were back in the homeland* were in great difficulty and that the foreigners who lived near by looked down on them. They also told me that the walls of Jerusalem were still broken down and that the gates had not been restored since the time they were burnt. [4] When I heard all this, I sat down and wept.

For several days I mourned and did not eat. I prayed to God, [5] "Lord God of Heaven! You are great, and we stand in fear of you. You faithfully keep your covenant with those who love you and do what you command. [6] Look at me, Lord, and hear my prayer, as I pray day and night for your servants, the people of Israel. I confess that we, the people of Israel, have sinned. My ancestors and I have sinned. [7] We have acted wickedly against you and have not done what you commanded. We have not kept the laws which you gave us through Moses, your servant. [8] Remember now what you told Moses: 'If you people of Israel are unfaithful to me, I will scatter you among the other nations. [9] But then if you turn back to me and do what I have commanded you, I will bring you back to the place where I have chosen to be worshipped, even though you are scattered to the ends of the earth.'

[10] "Lord, these are your servants, your own people. You rescued them by your great power and strength. [11] Listen now to my prayer and to the prayers of all your other servants who want to honour you. Give me success today and make the emperor merciful to me."

In those days I was the emperor's wine steward.

Nehemiah Goes to Jerusalem

2

One day four months later, when Emperor Artaxerxes was dining, I took the wine to him. He had never seen me look sad before, [2] so he asked, "Why are you looking so sad? You aren't ill, so it must be that you're unhappy."

I was startled [3] and answered, "May Your Majesty live for ever! How can I help looking sad when the city where my ancestors are buried is in ruins and its gates have been destroyed by fire?"

[4] The emperor asked, "What is it that you want?"

I prayed to the God of Heaven, [5] and then I said to the emperor, "If Your Majesty is pleased with me and is willing to grant my request, let me go to the land of Judah, to the city where my ancestors are buried, so that I can rebuild the city."

[6] The emperor, with the empress sitting at his side, approved my request. He asked me how long I would be gone and when I would return, and I told him.

[7] Then I asked him to grant me the favour of giving me letters to the governors of West Euphrates Province,* instructing them

....

1.2 *had returned from exile in*; or *had not been exiled to.*
1.3 *had survived and… homeland*; or *had remained in the homeland and had not gone into exile.*
2.7 *West Euphrates Province*: Under Persian rule the land of Israel was part of this large Persian province west of the River Euphrates.

Nehem.

..........:.

Esther
Job
Psalms
Proverbs
Eccles.

to let me travel to Judah. [8] I asked also for a letter to Asaph, keeper of the royal forests, instructing him to supply me with timber for the gates of the fort that guards the Temple, for the city walls, and for the house I was to live in. The emperor gave me all I asked for, because God was with me.

[9] The emperor sent some army officers and a troop of horsemen with me, and I made the journey to West Euphrates. There I gave the emperor's letters to the governors. [10] But Sanballat, from the town of Beth Horon, and Tobiah, an official in the province of Ammon, heard that someone had come to work for the good of the people of Israel, and they were highly indignant.

[11] I went on to Jerusalem, and for three days [12] I did not tell anyone what God had inspired me to do for Jerusalem. Then in the middle of the night I got up and went out, taking a few of my companions with me. The only animal we took was the donkey that I rode on. [13] It was still night as I left the city through the Valley Gate on the west and went south past Dragon's Fountain to the Rubbish Gate. As I went, I inspected the broken walls of the city and the gates that had been destroyed by fire. [14] Then on the east side of the city I went north to the Fountain Gate and the King's Pool. The donkey I was riding could not find any path through the rubble, [15] so I went down into the valley of the Kidron and rode along, looking at the wall. Then I returned the way I had come and went back into the city through the Valley Gate.

[16] None of the local officials knew where I had been or what I had been doing. So far I had not said anything to any of my fellow-Jews — the priests, the leaders, the officials, or anyone else who would be taking part in the work. [17] But now I said to them, "See what trouble we are in because Jerusalem is in ruins and its gates are destroyed! Let's rebuild the city walls and put an end to our disgrace." [18] And I told them how God had been with me and helped me, and what the emperor had said to me.

They responded, "Let's start rebuilding!" And they got ready to start the work.

[19] When Sanballat, Tobiah, and an Arab named Geshem heard what we were planning to do, they laughed at us and said, "What do you think you're doing? Are you going to rebel against the emperor?"

[20] I answered, "The God of Heaven will give us success. We are his servants, and we are going to start building. But you have no right to any property in Jerusalem, and you have no share in its traditions."

Rebuilding the Wall of Jerusalem

3 This is how the city wall was rebuilt.* The High Priest Eliashib and his fellow-priests rebuilt the Sheep Gate, dedicated it, and put the gates in place. They dedicated the wall as far as the Tower of the Hundred and the Tower of Hananel.

[2] The men of Jericho built the next section.

Zaccur son of Imri built the next section.

[3] The clan of Hassenaah built the Fish Gate. They put the beams and the gates in place, and put in the bolts and bars for locking the gate.

....

3.1 *city wall was rebuilt*: According to the following report, the rebuilding of the wall started at the middle of the north side and proceeded anti-clockwise round the city. Many of the places mentioned cannot be identified.

560

Nehem.

....

1 Kings
2 Kings
1 Chron.
2 Chron.
Ezra

NEHEMIAH 3

NEHEMIAH 3

DRAW A WALL

in the space on these pages by doodling a brick for each person or group of people who helped to

REBUILD

– THE –

WALLS

of Jerusalem. It took a lot of people working together to rebuild the walls and gates - Nehemiah couldn't do it all by himself.

Often, teaming up with other people can help us to do more and go further for God than if we act alone.

[4] Meremoth, the son of Uriah and grandson of Hakkoz, built the next section.

Meshullam, the son of Berechiah and grandson of Meshezabel, built the next section.

Zadok son of Baana built the next section.

[5] The men of Tekoa built the next section, but the leading men of the town refused to do the manual labour assigned to them by the supervisors.

[6] Joiada son of Paseah and Meshullam son of Besodeiah rebuilt Jeshanah Gate.* They put the beams and the gates in place, and put in the bolts and bars for locking the gate.

[7] Melatiah from Gibeon, Jadon from Meronoth, and the men of Gibeon and Mizpah built the next section, as far as the residence of the governor of West Euphrates.

[8] Uzziel son of Harhaiah, a goldsmith, built the next section. Hananiah, a maker of perfumes, built the next section, as far as Broad Wall.

[9] Rephaiah son of Hur, ruler of half the Jerusalem District, built the next section.

[10] Jedaiah son of Harumaph built the next section, which was near his own house. Hattush son of Hashabneiah built the next section.

[11] Malchijah son of Harim and Hasshub son of Pahath Moab built both the next section and the Tower of the Ovens.

[12] Shallum son of Hallohesh, ruler of the other half of the Jerusalem District, built the next section. (His daughters helped with the work.)

[13] Hanun and the inhabitants of the city of Zanoah rebuilt the Valley Gate. They put the gates in place, put in the bolts and the bars for locking the gate, and repaired the wall for 440 metres, as far as the Rubbish Gate.

[14] Malchijah son of Rechab, ruler of the Beth Haccherem District, rebuilt the Rubbish Gate. He put the gates in place, and put in the bolts and the bars for locking the gate.

[15] Shallum son of Colhozeh, ruler of the Mizpah District, rebuilt the Fountain Gate. He covered the gateway, put the gates in place, and put in the bolts and the bars. At the Pool of Shelah he built the wall next to the royal garden, as far as the steps leading down from David's City.

[16] Nehemiah son of Azbuk, ruler of half the Bethzur District, built the next section, as far as David's tomb, the pool, and the barracks.

Levites who Worked on the Wall

[17] The following Levites rebuilt the next several sections of the wall:

Rehum son of Bani built the next section;

Hashabiah, ruler of half the Keilah District, built the next section on behalf of his district;

[18] Bavvai son of Henadad, ruler of the other half of the Keilah District, built the next section;

[19] Ezer son of Jeshua, ruler of Mizpah, built the next section in front of the armoury, as far as the place where the wall turns;

[20] Baruch son of Zabbai built the next section, as far as the entrance to the house of the High Priest Eliashib;

[21] Meremoth, the son of Uriah and grandson of Hakkoz, built the next section, up to the far end of Eliashib's house.

....

3.6 *Jeshanah Gate*; or the *Old Gate*.

NEHEMIAH 3, 4

561

Nehem.
....

Esther
Job
Psalms
Proverbs
Eccles.

Priests who Worked on the Wall

²²The following priests rebuilt the next several sections of the wall:

Priests from the area around Jerusalem built the next section;

²³Benjamin and Hasshub built the next section, which was in front of their houses;

Azariah, the son of Maaseiah and grandson of Ananiah, built the next section, which was in front of his house;

²⁴Binnui son of Henadad built the next section, from Azariah's house to the corner of the wall;

²⁵⁻²⁶Palal son of Uzai built the next section, beginning at the corner of the wall and the tower of the upper palace near the court of the guard;

Pedaiah son of Parosh built the next section, to a point on the east near the Water Gate and the tower guarding the Temple. (This was near that part of the city called Ophel, where the temple workmen lived.)

Other Builders

²⁷The men of Tekoa built the next section, their second one, from a point opposite the large tower guarding the Temple as far as the wall near Ophel.

²⁸A group of priests built the next section, going north from the Horse Gate, each one building in front of his own house.

²⁹Zadok son of Immer built the next section, which was in front of his house.

Shemaiah son of Shecaniah, keeper of the East Gate, built the next section.

³⁰Hananiah son of Shelemiah and Hanun, the sixth son of Zalaph, built the next section, their second one.

Meshullam son of Berechiah built the next section, which was in front of his house.

³¹Malchijah, a goldsmith, built the next section, as far as the building used by the temple workmen and the merchants, which was by the Miphkad* Gate, near the room on top of the north-east corner of the wall.

³²The goldsmiths and the merchants built the last section, from the room at the corner as far as the Sheep Gate.

Nehemiah Overcomes Opposition to his Work

4 When Sanballat heard that we Jews had begun rebuilding the wall, he was furious and began to ridicule us. ²In front of his companions and the Samaritan troops he said, "What do these miserable Jews think they're doing? Do they intend to rebuild the city? Do they think that by offering sacrifices they can finish the work in one day? Can they make building stones out of heaps of burnt rubble?"

³Tobiah was standing there beside him, and he added, "What kind of wall could they ever build? Even a fox could knock it down!"

⁴I prayed, "Listen to them mocking us, O God! Let their ridicule fall on their own heads. Let them be robbed of everything they have, and let them be taken as prisoners to a foreign land. ⁵Don't forgive the evil they do and don't forget their sins, for they have insulted us who are building."

⁶So we went on rebuilding the wall, and soon it was half its full height, because the people were eager to work.

....

3.31 *Miphkad*; or *Mustering*, or *Watch*.

562

Nehem.

········

1 Kings
2 Kings
1 Chron.
2 Chron.
Ezra

NEHEMIAH 4, 5

[7]Sanballat, Tobiah, and the people of Arabia, Ammon, and Ashdod heard that we were making progress in rebuilding the wall of Jerusalem and that the gaps in the wall were being closed, and they were very angry. [8]So they all plotted together to come and attack Jerusalem and create confusion, [9]but we prayed to our God and kept men on guard against them day and night.

[10]The people of Judah had a song they sang:

"We grow weak carrying burdens;
There's so much rubble to take away.
How can we build the wall today?"

[11]Our enemies thought we would not see them or know what was already happening upon us, killing us and putting an end to our work. [12]But time after time Jews who were living among our enemies came to warn us of the plans our enemies were making against us.* [13]So I armed the people with swords, spears, and bows, and stationed them by clans behind the wall, wherever it was still unfinished.

[14]I saw that the people were worried, so I said to them and to their leaders and officials, "Don't be afraid of our enemies. Remember how great and terrifying the Lord is, and fight for your fellow-countrymen, your children, your wives, and your homes." [15]Our enemies heard that we had found out what they were plotting, and they realized that God had defeated their plans. Then all of us went back to rebuilding the wall.

[16]From then on half my men worked and half stood guard, wearing coats of armour and armed with spears, shields, and bows. And our leaders gave their full support to the people [17]who were rebuilding the wall. Even those who carried building materials worked with one hand and kept a weapon in the other, [18]and everyone who was building kept a sword strapped to his waist. The man who was to sound the alarm on the bugle stayed with me. [19]I told the people and their officials and leaders, "The work is spread out over such a distance that we are widely separated from one another on the wall. [20]If you hear the bugle, gather round me. Our God will fight for us." [21]So every day, from dawn until the stars came out at night, half of us worked on the wall, while the other half stood guard with spears.

[22]During this time I told the men in charge that they and all their helpers had to stay in Jerusalem at night, so that we could guard the city at night as well as work in the daytime. [23]I didn't take off my clothes even at night, neither did any of my companions nor my servants nor my bodyguard. And we all kept our weapons to hand.*

Oppression of the Poor

5 Some time later many of the people, both men and women, began to complain against their fellow-Jews. [2]Some said, "We have large families, we need corn to keep us alive."

[3]Others said, "We have had to mortgage our fields and vineyards and houses to get enough corn to keep us from starving."

[4]Still others said, "We had to borrow money to pay the royal tax on our fields and vineyards. [5]We are of the same race as our fellow-Jews. Aren't our children just as good as theirs? But we have to make slaves of our children. Some of our daughters have already been sold as slaves. We are helpless because our fields and vineyards have been taken away from us."

4.12 Probable text *the plans our enemies were making against us*; Hebrew unclear.
4.23 Probable text *weapons to hand*; Hebrew unclear.

NEHEMIAH 5, 6   563

Nehem.

Esther
Job
Psalms
Proverbs
Eccles.

⁶When I heard their complaints, I was angry ⁷and decided to act. I denounced the leaders and officials of the people and told them, "You are oppressing your fellow-Jews!"

I called a public assembly to deal with the problem ⁸and said, "As far as we have been able, we have been buying back our Jewish relatives who had to sell themselves to foreigners. Now you are forcing your own relatives to sell themselves to you, their own people!" The leaders were silent and could find nothing to say.

⁹Then I said, "What you are doing is wrong! You ought to obey God and do what's right. Then you would not give our enemies, the Gentiles, any reason to ridicule us. ¹⁰I have let the people borrow money and corn from me, and so have my companions and the people who work for me. Now let's give up all our claims to repayment. ¹¹Cancel all the debts* they owe you — money or corn or wine or olive oil. And give them back their fields, vineyards, olive groves, and houses at once!"

¹²The leaders replied, "We'll do as you say. We'll give the property back and not try to collect the debts."

I called in the priests and made the leaders swear in front of them to keep the promise they had just made. ¹³Then I took off the sash* I was wearing round my waist and shook it out. "This is how God will shake any of you who don't keep your promise," I said. "God will take away your houses and everything you own, and will leave you with nothing."

Everyone who was present said, "Amen!" and praised the LORD. And the leaders kept their promise.

Nehemiah's Unselfishness

¹⁴During all the twelve years that I was governor of the land of Judah, from the twentieth year that Artaxerxes was emperor until his 32nd year, neither my relatives nor I ate the food I was entitled to have as governor. ¹⁵Every governor who had been in office before me had been a burden to the people and had demanded forty silver coins a day* for food and wine. Even their servants had oppressed the people. But I acted differently, because I honoured God. ¹⁶I put all my energy into rebuilding the wall and did not acquire any property. Everyone who worked for me joined in the rebuilding. ¹⁷I regularly fed at my table 150 of the Jewish people and their leaders, besides all the people who came to me from the surrounding nations. ¹⁸Every day I served one ox, six of the best sheep, and many chickens, and every ten days I provided a fresh supply of wine. But I knew what heavy burdens the people had to bear, so I did not claim the allowance that the governor is entitled to.

¹⁹I pray you, O God, remember to my credit everything that I have done for this people.

Plots against Nehemiah

6 Sanballat, Tobiah, Geshem, and the rest of our enemies heard that we had finished building the wall and that there were no gaps left in it, although we still had not set up the gates in the gateways. ²So Sanballat and Geshem sent me a message, suggesting that I meet with them in one of the villages in the

NEHEMIAH 6

Nehemiah faced a lot of opposition to the rebuilding of the wall. (Take a look at chapter 4 too.) How did he respond? Have you ever

- FACED -

OPPOSITION

for doing something for God? What did you do? How might you overcome opposition in the future?

5.11 One ancient translation *debts*; Hebrew unclear.
5.13 *sash*: Clothing in those days had no pockets, so small items were tucked into the sash that was worn like a belt around the waist. Shaking it out was a symbol of losing everything.
5.15 One ancient translation *a day*; Hebrew unclear.

564

Nehem.

∴ ∙∙∙∙∙∙∙∙

1 Kings
2 Kings
1 Chron.
2 Chron.
Ezra

NEHEMIAH 6, 7

Plain of Ono. This was a trick of theirs to try to harm me. ³I sent messengers to say to them, "I am doing important work and can't go down there. I am not going to let the work stop just to go and see you."

⁴They sent me the same message four times, and each time I sent them the same reply.

⁵Then Sanballat sent one of his servants to me with a fifth message, this one in the form of an unsealed letter.* ⁶It read:

"Geshem tells me that a rumour is going round among the neighbouring peoples that you and the Jewish people intend to revolt and that this is why you are rebuilding the wall. He also says you plan to make yourself king ⁷and that you have arranged for some prophets to proclaim in Jerusalem that you are the king of Judah. His Majesty is certain to hear about this, so I suggest that you and I meet to talk the situation over."

⁸I sent a reply to him: "Nothing of what you are saying is true. You have made it all up yourself."

⁹They were trying to frighten us into stopping work. I prayed, "But now, God, make me strong!"

¹⁰About this time I went to visit Shemaiah, the son of Delaiah and grandson of Mehetabel, who was unable to leave his house. He said to me, "You and I must go and hide together in the Holy Place of the Temple and lock the doors, because they are coming to kill you. Any night now they will come to kill you."

¹¹I answered, "I'm not the kind of person that runs and hides. Do you think I would try to save my life by hiding in the Temple? I won't do it."

¹²When I thought it over, I realized that God had not spoken to Shemaiah, but that Tobiah and Sanballat had bribed him to give me this warning. ¹³They hired him to frighten me into sinning, so that they could ruin my reputation and humiliate me.

¹⁴I prayed, "God, remember what Tobiah and Sanballat have done and punish them. Remember that woman Noadiah and all the other prophets who tried to frighten me."

The Conclusion of the Work

¹⁵After 52 days of work the entire wall was finished on the 25th day of the month of Elul. ¹⁶When our enemies in the surrounding nations heard this, they realized that they had lost face, since everyone knew that the work had been done with God's help.

¹⁷During all this time the Jewish leaders had been in correspondence with Tobiah. ¹⁸Many people in Judah were on his side because of his Jewish father-in-law, Shecaniah son of Arah. In addition, his son Jehohanan had married the daughter of Meshullam son of Berechiah. ¹⁹People would talk in front of me about all the good deeds Tobiah had done and would tell him everything I said. And he kept sending me letters to try to frighten me.

7 And now the wall had been rebuilt, the gates had all been put in place, and the temple guards, the members of the sacred choir, and the other Levites had been assigned their work. ²I put two men in charge of governing the city of Jerusalem: my brother Hanani and Hananiah, commanding officer of the fortress. Hananiah was a reliable and God-fearing man without an equal. ³I told them not to have the gates of Jerusalem opened

6.5 *unsealed letter*: Leaving a letter unsealed was a deliberate way of making certain that its contents would become widely known.

NEHEMIAH 7

565

Nehem.

....

Esther
Job
Psalms
Proverbs
Eccles.

in the morning until well after sunrise and to have them closed and barred before the guards went off duty at sunset. I also told them to appoint guards from among the people who lived in Jerusalem and to assign some of them to specific posts and others to patrol the area round their own houses.

The List of Those who Returned from Exile
(Ezra 2.1–70)

⁴ Jerusalem was a large city, but not many people were living in it, and not many houses had been built yet. ⁵ God inspired me to assemble the people and their leaders and officials and to check their family records. I located the records of those who had first returned from captivity, and this is the information I found:

⁶ Many of the exiles left the province of Babylon and returned to Jerusalem and Judah, each to his own city. Their families had been living in exile in Babylonia ever since King Nebuchadnezzar had taken them there as prisoners. ⁷ Their leaders were Zerubbabel, Joshua, Nehemiah, Azariah, Raamiah, Nahamani, Mordecai, Bilshan, Mispereth, Bigvai, Nehum, and Baanah.

⁸⁻²⁵ This is the list of the clans of Israel, with the number of those from each clan who returned from exile:

Parosh — 2,172
Shephatiah — 372
Arah — 652
Pahath Moab (descendants of Jeshua and Joab) — 2,818
Elam — 1,254
Zattu — 845
Zaccai — 760
Binnui — 648
Bebai — 628
Azgad — 2,322
Adonikam — 667
Bigvai — 2,067
Adin — 655
Ater (also called Hezekiah) — 98
Hashum — 328
Bezai — 324
Hariph — 112
Gibeon — 95

²⁶⁻³⁸ People whose ancestors had lived in the following towns also returned:

Bethlehem and Netophah — 188
Anathoth — 128
Beth Azmaveth — 42
Kiriath Jearim, Chephirah, and Beeroth — 743
Ramah and Geba — 621
Michmash — 122
Bethel and Ai — 123
The other Nebo — 52
The other Elam — 1,254
Harim — 320
Jericho — 345
Lod, Hadid, and Ono — 721
Senaah — 3,930

³⁹⁻⁴² This is the list of the priestly clans that returned from exile:

Jedaiah (descendants of Jeshua) — 973
Immer — 1,052
Pashhur — 1,247
Harim — 1,017

566

Nehem.

....

1 Kings
2 Kings
1 Chron.
2 Chron.
Ezra

NEHEMIAH 7

43-45 Clans of Levites who returned from exile:
Jeshua and Kadmiel (descendants of Hodaviah) — 74
Temple musicians (descendants of Asaph) — 148
Temple guards (descendants of Shallum, Ater, Talmon,
Akkub, Hatita, and Shobai) — 138
46-56 Clans of temple workmen who returned from exile:
Ziha, Hasupha, Tabbaoth,
Keros, Sia, Padon,
Lebana, Hagaba, Shalmai,
Hanan, Giddel, Gahar,
Reaiah, Rezin, Nekoda,
Gazzam, Uzza, Paseah,
Besai, Meunim, Nephushesim,
Bakbuk, Hakupha, Harhur,
Bazlith, Mehida, Harsha,
Barkos, Sisera, Temah,
Neziah, and Hatipha.
57-59 Clans of Solomon's servants who returned from exile:
Sotai, Sophereth, Perida,
Jaalah, Darkon, Giddel,
Shephatiah, Hattil, Pochereth Hazzebaim, and Amon.
60 The total number of descendants of the temple workmen
and of Solomon's servants who returned from exile was 392.
61-62 There were 642 belonging to the clans of Delaiah, Tobiah,
and Nekoda who returned from the towns of Tel Melah, Tel Harsha,
Cherub, Addon, and Immer; but they could not prove that they
were descendants of Israelites.
63-64 The following priestly clans could find no record to prove
their ancestry: Hobaiah, Hakkoz, and Barzillai. (The ancestor of
the priestly clan of Barzillai had married a woman from the clan
of Barzillai of Gilead and taken the name of his father-in-law's
clan.) Since they were unable to prove who their ancestors were,
they were not accepted as priests. 65 The Jewish governor told
them that they could not eat the food offered to God until there
was a priest who could use the Urim and Thummim.*
66-69 Total number of exiles who returned — 42,360
Their male and female servants — 7,337
Male and female musicians — 245
Horses — 736
Mules — 245
Camels — 435
Donkeys — 6,720
70-72 Many of the people contributed to help pay the cost of
restoring the Temple:

The governor	8 kilogrammes of gold
	50 ceremonial bowls
	530 robes for priests
Heads of clans	168 kilogrammes of gold
	1.25 tonnes of silver
The rest of the people	168 kilogrammes of gold
	140 kilogrammes of silver
	67 robes for priests

73 The priests, the Levites, the temple guards, the musicians,
many of the ordinary people, the temple workmen — all the people
of Israel — settled in the towns and cities of Judah.

....

7.65 *Urim and Thummim*: Two objects used by the priest to determine
God's will; it is not known precisely how they were used.

NEHEMIAH 8

567

Nehem.

Esther
Job
Psalms
Proverbs
Eccles.

Ezra Reads the Law to the People

8 By the seventh month the people of Israel were all settled in their towns. On the first day of that month they all assembled in Jerusalem, in the square just inside the Water Gate. They asked Ezra, the priest and scholar of the Law which the LORD had given Israel through Moses, to get the book of the Law. [2] So Ezra brought it to the place where the people had gathered — men, women, and the children who were old enough to understand. [3] There in the square by the gate he read the Law to them from dawn until noon, and they all listened attentively.

[4] Ezra was standing on a wooden platform that had been built for the occasion. The following men stood at his right: Mattithiah, Shema, Anaiah, Uriah, Hilkiah, and Maaseiah; and the following stood at his left: Pedaiah, Mishael, Malchijah, Hashum, Hashbaddanah, Zechariah, and Meshullam.

[5] As Ezra stood there on the platform high above the people, they all kept their eyes fixed on him. As soon as he opened the book, they all stood up. [6] Ezra said, "Praise the LORD, the great God!"

All the people raised their arms in the air and answered, "Amen! Amen!" They knelt in worship, with their faces to the ground.

[7] Then they rose and stood in their places, and the following Levites explained the Law to them: Jeshua, Bani, Sherebiah, Jamin, Akkub, Shabbethai, Hodiah, Maaseiah, Kelita, Azariah, Jozabad, Hanan, and Pelaiah. [8] They gave an oral translation* of God's Law and explained* it so that the people could understand it.

[9] When the people heard what the Law required, they were so moved that they began to cry. So Nehemiah, who was the governor, Ezra, the priest and scholar of the Law, and the Levites who were explaining the Law told all the people, "This day is holy to the LORD your God, so you are not to mourn or cry. [10] Now go home and have a feast. Share your food and wine with those who haven't enough. Today is holy to our Lord, so don't be sad. The joy that the LORD gives you will make you strong."

[11] The Levites went about calming the people and telling them not to be sad on such a holy day. [12] So all the people went home and ate and drank joyfully and shared what they had with others, because they understood what had been read to them.

The Festival of Shelters

[13] The next day the heads of the clans, together with the priests and the Levites, went to Ezra to study the teachings of the Law. [14] They discovered that the Law, which the LORD gave through Moses, ordered the people of Israel to live in temporary shelters during the Festival of Shelters. [15] So they gave the following instructions and sent them* all through Jerusalem and the other cities and towns: "Go out to the hills and get branches from pines, olives, myrtles, palms, and other trees to make shelters according to the instructions written in the Law."

[16] So the people got branches and built shelters on the flat roofs of their houses, in their yards, in the temple courtyard, and in the public squares by the Water Gate and by the Ephraim Gate.

NEHEMIAH 8.10

THE **JOY** ... THAT THE ... **LORD** GIVES YOU WILL MAKE YOU **STRONG**

8.8 *translation*: The Law was written in Hebrew, but in Babylonia the Jews had adopted Aramaic as the language for daily life. Because of this a translation was necessary.
8.8 *They gave... explained*; or *They read God's Law and then translated it, explaining.*
8.15 Probable text *So they... sent them*; Hebrew *It also ordered that the following instructions be sent.*

568

Nehem.

1 Kings
2 Kings
1 Chron.
2 Chron.
Ezra

[17]All the people who had come back from captivity built shelters and lived in them. This was the first time it had been done since the days of Joshua son of Nun, and everybody was excited and happy. [18]From the first day of the festival to the last they read a part of God's Law every day. They celebrated for seven days, and on the eighth day there was a closing ceremony, as required in the Law.

The People Confess their Sins

9 [1-2]On the 24th day of the same month the people of Israel assembled to fast in order to show sorrow for their sins. They had already separated themselves from all foreigners. They wore sackcloth and put dust on their heads as signs of grief. Then they stood and began to confess the sins that they and their ancestors had committed. [3]For about three hours the Law of the LORD their God was read to them, and for the next three hours they confessed their sins and worshipped the LORD their God.

[4]There was a platform for the Levites, and on it stood Jeshua, Bani, Kadmiel, Shebaniah, Bunni, Sherebiah, Bani, and Chenani. They prayed aloud to the LORD their God.

[5]The following Levites gave a call to worship: Jeshua, Kadmiel, Bani, Hashabneiah, Sherebiah, Hodiah, Shebaniah, and Pethahiah. They said:

"Stand up and praise the LORD your God;
  praise him for ever and ever!
Let everyone praise his glorious name,
  although no human praise is great enough."

The Prayer of Confession

[6]And then the people of Israel prayed this prayer:
"You, LORD, you alone are LORD;
  you made the heavens and the stars of the sky.
You made land and sea and everything in them;
  you gave life to all.
The heavenly powers bow down and worship you.
[7] You, LORD God, chose Abram
  and led him out of Ur in Babylonia;
  you changed his name to Abraham.
[8] You found that he was faithful to you,
  and you made a covenant with him.
You promised to give him the land of the Canaanites,
  the land of the Hittites and the Amorites,
  the land of the Perizzites, the Jebusites, and the
    Girgashites,
  to be a land where his descendants would live.
You kept your promise, because you are faithful.

[9] "You saw how our ancestors suffered in Egypt;
  you heard their call for help at the Red Sea.
[10] You worked amazing miracles against the king,
  against his officials and the people of his land,
  because you knew how they oppressed your people.
You won then the fame you still have today.
[11] Through the sea you made a path for your people
  and led them through on dry ground.
Those who pursued them drowned in deep water,
  as a stone sinks in the raging sea.
[12] With a cloud you led them in daytime,
  and at night you lighted their way with fire.

NEHEMIAH 9

569

Nehem.

Esther
Job
Psalms
Proverbs
Eccles.

¹³ At Mount Sinai you came down from heaven;
  you spoke to your people
  and gave them good laws and sound teachings.
¹⁴ You taught them to keep your Sabbaths holy,
  and through your servant Moses you gave them your
    laws.

¹⁵ "When they were hungry, you gave them bread from
    heaven,
  and water from a rock when they were thirsty.
  You told them to take control of the land
    which you had promised to give them.
¹⁶ But our ancestors grew proud and stubborn
  and refused to obey your commands.
¹⁷ They refused to obey; they forgot all you did;
  they forgot the miracles you had performed.
  In their pride they chose a leader
    to take them back to slavery in Egypt.
  But you are a God who forgives;
    you are gracious and loving, slow to be angry.
  Your mercy is great; you did not forsake them.
¹⁸ They made an idol in the shape of a bull calf
  and said it was the god who led them from Egypt!
  How much they insulted you, LORD!
¹⁹ But you did not abandon them there in the desert,
    for your mercy is great.
  You did not take away the cloud or the fire
    that showed them the path by day and night.
²⁰ In your goodness you told them what they should do;
  you fed them with manna and gave them water to drink.
²¹ Through forty years in the desert
  you provided all that they needed;
    their clothing never wore out,
  and their feet were not swollen with pain.

²² "You let them conquer nations and kingdoms,
    lands that bordered their own.
  They conquered the land of Heshbon, where Sihon ruled,
    and the land of Bashan, where Og was king.
²³ You gave them as many children as there are stars in the
    sky,
  and let them conquer and live in the land
    that you had promised their ancestors to give them.
²⁴ They conquered the land of Canaan;
  you overcame the people living there.
  You gave your people the power to do as they pleased
    with the people and kings of Canaan.
²⁵ Your people captured fortified cities,
    fertile land, houses full of wealth,
    cisterns already dug,
    olive trees, fruit trees, and vineyards.
  They ate all they wanted and grew fat;
    they enjoyed all the good things you gave them.

²⁶ "But your people rebelled and disobeyed you;
    they turned their backs on your Law.
  They killed the prophets who warned them,
    who told them to turn back to you.
  They insulted you time after time,

NEHEMIAH 9

No matter how hard we try, we will always make mistakes. It's impossible to live up to God's standards perfectly. However, God has

UNDESERVED (AND UNENDING)

love and forgiveness for us.

Ask God if there's anything in your life that you should own up to and confess. In pencil, **WRITE IT DOWN** to say that you're sorry, then grab a rubber and rub it out as a sign of God's forgiveness for you.

570

Nehem.

......

1 Kings
2 Kings
1 Chron.
2 Chron.
Ezra

NEHEMIAH 9, 10

27 so you let their enemies conquer and rule them.
In their trouble they called to you for help,
and you answered them from heaven.
In your great mercy you sent them leaders
who rescued them from their foes.
28 When peace returned, they sinned again,
and again you let their enemies conquer them.
Yet when they repented and asked you to save them,
in heaven you heard, and time after time
you rescued them in your great mercy.
29 You warned them to obey your teachings,
but in pride they rejected your laws,
although keeping your Law is the way to life.
Obstinate and stubborn, they refused to obey.
30 Year after year you patiently warned them.
You inspired your prophets to speak,
but your people were deaf,
so you let them be conquered by other nations.
31 And yet, because your mercy is great,
you did not forsake or destroy them.
You are a gracious and merciful God!

32 "O God, our God, how great you are!
How terrifying, how powerful!
You faithfully keep your covenant promises.
From the time when Assyrian kings oppressed us,
even till now, how much we have suffered!
Our kings, our leaders, our priests and prophets,
our ancestors, and all our people have suffered.
Remember how much we have suffered!
33 You have done right to punish us;
you have been faithful, even though we have sinned.
34 Our ancestors, our kings, leaders, and priests
have not kept your Law.
They did not listen to your commands and warnings.
35 With your blessing, kings ruled your people
when they lived in the broad, fertile land you gave
them;
but they failed to turn from sin and serve you.
36 And now we are slaves in the land that you gave us,
this fertile land which gives us food.
37 What the land produces goes to the kings
that you put over us because we sinned.
They do as they please with us and our livestock,
and we are in deep distress!"

The People Sign an Agreement

38 Because of all that has happened, we, the people of Israel,
hereby make a solemn written agreement, and our leaders, our
Levites, and our priests put their seals to it.

10 The first to sign was the governor, Nehemiah son of
Hacaliah, and then Zedekiah signed. The following also
signed:

2-8 *Priests:*
Seraiah, Azariah, Jeremiah,
Pashhur, Amariah, Malchijah,
Hattush, Shebaniah, Malluch,
Harim, Meremoth, Obadiah,

NEHEMIAH 10

571

Nehem.
....
Esther
Job
Psalms
Proverbs
Eccles.

Daniel, Ginnethon, Baruch,
Meshullam, Abijah, Mijamin,
Maaziah, Bilgai, and Shemaiah.

9-13 *Levites:*
Jeshua son of Azaniah,
Binnui of the clan of Henadad,
Kadmiel, Shebaniah, Hodiah,
Kelita, Pelaiah, Hanan,
Mica, Rehob, Hashabiah,
Zaccur, Sherebiah, Shebaniah,
Hodiah, Bani, and Beninu.

14-27 *Leaders of the people:*
Parosh, Pahath Moab,
Elam, Zattu, Bani,
Bunni, Azgad, Bebai,
Adonijah, Bigvai, Adin,
Ater, Hezekiah, Azzur,
Hodiah, Hashum, Bezai,
Hariph, Anathoth, Nebai,
Magpiash, Meshullam, Hezir,
Meshezabel, Zadok, Jaddua,
Pelatiah, Hanan, Anaiah,
Hoshea, Hananiah, Hasshub,
Hallohesh, Pilha, Shobek,
Rehum, Hashabnah, Maaseiah,
Ahiah, Hanan, Anan,
Malluch, Harim, and Baanah.

The Agreement

28 We, the people of Israel, the priests, the Levites, the temple guards, the temple musicians, the temple workmen, and all others who in obedience to God's Law have separated themselves from the foreigners living in our land, we, together with our wives and all our children old enough to understand, 29 do hereby join with our leaders in an oath, under penalty of a curse if we break it, that we will live according to God's Law, which God gave through his servant Moses; that we will obey all that the LORD, our Lord, commands us; and that we will keep all his laws and requirements.

30 We will not intermarry with the foreigners living in our land.

31 If foreigners bring corn or anything else to sell to us on the Sabbath or on any other holy day, we will not buy from them. Every seventh year we will not farm the land, and we will cancel all debts.

32 Every year we will each contribute five grammes of silver to help pay the expenses of the Temple.

33 We will provide for the temple worship the following: the sacred bread, the daily grain offering, the animals to be burnt each day as sacrifices, the sacred offerings for Sabbaths, New Moon Festivals, and other festivals, the other sacred offerings, the offerings to take away the sins of Israel, and anything else needed for the Temple.

34 We, the people, priests, and Levites, will draw lots each year to determine which clans are to provide wood to burn the sacrifices offered to the LORD our God, according to the requirements of the Law.

35 We will take to the Temple each year an offering of the first corn we harvest and of the first fruit that ripens on our trees.

572

Nehem.

∴.........

1 Kings
2 Kings
1 Chron.
2 Chron.
Ezra

NEHEMIAH 10, 11

36 The first son born to each of us we will take to the priests in the Temple and there, as required by the Law, dedicate him to God. We will also dedicate the first calf born to each of our cows, and the first lamb or kid born to each of our sheep or goats. 37 We will take to the priests in the Temple the dough made from the first corn harvested each year and our other offerings of wine, olive oil, and all kinds of fruit.

We will take to the Levites, who collect tithes in our farming villages, the tithes from the crops that grow on our land. 38 Priests who are descended from Aaron are to be with the Levites when tithes are collected, and for use in the Temple the Levites are to take to the temple storerooms one tenth of all the tithes they collect. 39 The people of Israel and the Levites are to take the contributions of corn, wine, and olive oil to the storerooms where the utensils for the Temple are kept and where the priests who are on duty, the temple guards, and the members of the temple choir have their quarters.

We will not neglect the house of our God.

The People who Lived in Jerusalem

11 The leaders settled in Jerusalem, and the rest of the people drew lots to choose one family out of every ten to go and live in the holy city of Jerusalem, while the rest were to live in the other cities and towns. 2 The people praised anyone else who volunteered to live in Jerusalem. 3 In the other towns and cities the people of Israel, the priests, the Levites, the temple workmen, and the descendants of Solomon's servants lived on their own property in their own towns.

The following is the list of the leading citizens of the province of Judah who lived in Jerusalem:

4 *Members of the tribe of Judah:*

Athaiah, the son of Uzziah and grandson of Zechariah. His other ancestors included Amariah, Shephatiah, and Mahalalel, descendants of Judah's son Perez.

5 Maaseiah, the son of Baruch and grandson of Colhozeh. His other ancestors included Hazaiah, Adaiah, Joiarib, and Zechariah, descendants of Judah's son Shelah.

6 Of the descendants of Perez, 468 outstanding men lived in Jerusalem.

7 *Members of the tribe of Benjamin:*

Sallu, the son of Meshullam and grandson of Joed. His other ancestors included Pedaiah, Kolaiah, Maaseiah, Ithiel, and Jeshaiah.

8 Gabbai and Sallai, close relatives* of Sallu.

In all, 928 Benjaminites lived in Jerusalem. 9 Joel son of Zichri was their leader, and Judah son of Hassenuah was the second senior official in the city.

10 *Priests:*

Jedaiah son of Joiarib, and Jachin.

11 Seraiah, the son of Hilkiah and grandson of Meshullam. His ancestors included Zadok, Meraioth, and Ahitub, who was the High Priest. 12 In all, 822 members of this clan served in the Temple.

....

11.8 One ancient translation *close relatives*; Hebrew *after him.*

NEHEMIAH 11

573

Nehem.

Esther
Job
Psalms
Proverbs
Eccles.

Adaiah, the son of Jeroham and grandson of Pelaliah. His ancestors included Amzi, Zechariah, Pashhur, and Malchijah. [13] In all, 242 members of this clan were heads of families.

Amashsai, the son of Azarel and grandson of Ahzai. His ancestors included Meshillemoth and Immer. [14] There were 128 members of this clan who were outstanding soldiers. Their leader was Zabdiel, a member of a leading family.*

[15] *Levites:*

Shemaiah, the son of Hasshub and grandson of Azrikam. His ancestors included Hashabiah and Bunni.

[16] Shabbethai and Jozabad, prominent Levites in charge of the work outside the Temple.

[17] Mattaniah, the son of Mica and grandson of Zabdi, a descendant of Asaph. He led the temple choir in singing the prayer of thanksgiving.

Bakbukiah, who was Mattaniah's assistant.

Abda, the son of Shammua and grandson of Galal, a descendant of Jeduthun.

[18] In all, 284 Levites lived in the holy city of Jerusalem.

[19] *Temple guards:*

Akkub, Talmon, and their relatives, 172 in all.

[20] The rest of the people of Israel and the remaining priests and Levites lived on their own property in the other cities and towns of Judah. [21] The temple workmen lived in the part of Jerusalem called Ophel and worked under the supervision of Ziha and Gishpa.

[22] The supervisor of the Levites who lived in Jerusalem was Uzzi, the son of Bani and grandson of Hashabiah. His ancestors included Mattaniah and Mica, and he belonged to the clan of Asaph, the clan that was responsible for the music in the temple services. [23] There were royal regulations stating how the clans should take turns in leading the temple music each day.

[24] Pethahiah son of Meshezabel, of the clan of Zerah and the tribe of Judah, represented the people of Israel at the Persian court.

The People in Other Towns and Cities

[25] Many of the people lived in towns near their farms. Those who were of the tribe of Judah lived in Kiriath Arba, Dibon, and Jekabzeel, and in the villages near these cities. [26] They also lived in the cities of Jeshua, Moladah, Bethpelet, [27] and Hazarshual, and in Beersheba and the villages around it. [28] They lived in the city of Ziklag, in Meconah and its villages, [29] in Enrimmon, in Zorah, in Jarmuth, [30] in Zanoah, in Adullam, and in the villages near these towns. They lived in Lachish and on the farms near by, and in Azekah and its villages. That is to say, the people of Judah lived in the territory between Beersheba in the south and the Valley of Hinnom in the north.

[31] The people of the tribe of Benjamin lived in Geba, Michmash, Ai, Bethel and the nearby villages, [32] Anathoth, Nob, Ananiah, [33] Hazor, Ramah, Gittaim, [34] Hadid, Zeboim, Neballat, [35] Lod, and Ono, and in the Valley of Craftsmen. [36] Some groups of Levites that had lived in the territory of Judah were assigned to live with the people of Benjamin.

....

11.14 *a member of a leading family*; or *son of Haggedolim.*

574

Nehem.

⋮ ⋯⋯⋯

1 Kings
2 Kings
1 Chron.
2 Chron.
Ezra

NEHEMIAH 12

List of Priests and Levites

12 The following is a list of the priests and Levites who returned from exile with Zerubbabel son of Shealtiel and with the High Priest Joshua:

2-7 *Priests:*

> Seraiah, Jeremiah, Ezra,
> Amariah, Malluch, Hattush,
> Shecaniah, Rehum, Meremoth,
> Iddo, Ginnethoi, Abijah,
> Mijamin, Maadiah, Bilgah,
> Shemaiah, Joiarib, Jedaiah,
> Sallu, Amok, Hilkiah, and Jedaiah.

These men were leaders among all their fellow-priests in the days of Joshua.

8 *Levites:*

> The following were in charge of the singing of hymns of thanksgiving: Jeshua, Binnui, Kadmiel, Sherebiah, Judah, and Mattaniah.
> 9 The following formed the choir that sang the responses: Bakbukiah, Unno, and their fellow-Levites.

Descendants of the High Priest Joshua

10 Joshua was the father of Joiakim; Joiakim was the father of Eliashib; Eliashib was the father of Joiada; 11 Joiada was the father of Jonathan; and Jonathan was the father of Jaddua.

Heads of the Priestly Clans

12-21 When Joiakim was High Priest, the following priests were the heads of the priestly clans:

Priest	Clan
Meraiah	Seraiah
Hananiah	Jeremiah
Meshullam	Ezra
Jehohanan	Amariah
Jonathan	Malluchi
Joseph	Shebaniah
Adna	Harim
Helkai	Meraioth
Zechariah	Iddo
Meshullam	Ginnethon
Zichri	Abijah
...*	Miniamin
Piltai	Moadiah
Shammua	Bilgah
Jehonathan	Shemaiah
Mattenai	Joiarib
Uzzi	Jedaiah
Kallai	Sallai
Eber	Amok
Hashabiah	Hilkiah
Nethanel	Jedaiah

⋯⋯⋯⋯⋯⋯⋯⋯⋯⋯⋯⋯⋯⋯⋯⋯⋯⋯⋯⋯⋯⋯⋯⋯⋯⋯

12.12–21 In Hebrew a name is missing from the list.

Record of the Priestly and Levite Families

22 A record was kept of the heads of the Levite families and of the priestly families during the lifetimes of the following High Priests: Eliashib, Joiada, Jonathan, and Jaddua. This record was finished when Darius was emperor of Persia.

23 The heads of the Levite families, however, were recorded in the official records only until the time of Jonathan, the grandson of Eliashib.

Assignment of Duties in the Temple

24 Under the direction of Hashabiah, Sherebiah, Jeshua, Binnui,* and Kadmiel, the Levites were organized into groups. Two groups at a time praised God responsively and gave thanks to him, in accordance with the instructions given by King David, the man of God.

25 The following temple guards were in charge of guarding the storerooms by the gates to the Temple: Mattaniah, Bakbukiah, Obadiah, Meshullam, Talmon, and Akkub.

26 These people lived during the time of Joiakim, the son of Joshua and grandson of Jehozadak, and the time of Nehemiah the governor, and the time of Ezra, the priest who was a scholar of the Law.

Nehemiah Dedicates the City Wall

27 When the city wall of Jerusalem was dedicated, the Levites were brought in from wherever they were living, so that they could join in celebrating the dedication with songs of thanksgiving and with the music of cymbals and harps. 28 The Levite families of singers gathered from the area where they had settled round Jerusalem and from the towns round Netophah, 29 and from Bethgilgal, Geba, and Azmaveth. 30 The priests and the Levites performed ritual purification for themselves, the people, the gates, and the city wall.

31 I assembled the leaders of Judah on top of the wall and put them in charge of two large groups to march round the city, giving thanks to God.

The first group went to the right on top of the wall towards the Rubbish Gate.* 32 Hoshaiah marched behind the singers, followed by half the leaders of Judah. 33-35 The following priests, blowing trumpets, marched next: Azariah, Ezra, Meshullam, Judah, Benjamin, Shemaiah, and Jeremiah. Next came Zechariah, the son of Jonathan and grandson of Shemaiah. (His ancestors also included Mattaniah, Micaiah, and Zaccur, of the clan of Asaph.) 36 He was followed by other members of his clan — Shemaiah, Azarel, Milalai, Gilalai, Maai, Nethanel, Judah, and Hanani — all of whom carried musical instruments of the kind played by King David, the man of God. Ezra the scholar led this group in the procession. 37 At the Fountain Gate they went up the steps that led to David's City, past David's palace, and back to the wall at the Water Gate, on the east side of the city.

38 The other group of those who gave thanks went to the left along the top of the wall, and I followed with half the people. We marched past the Tower of the Ovens to the Broad Wall, 39 and from there we went past Ephraim Gate, Jeshanah

TURN THESE LINES INTO A PICTURE OF SOMETHING.

576

Nehem.

1 Kings
2 Kings
1 Chron.
2 Chron.
Ezra

NEHEMIAH 12, 13

Gate,* the Fish Gate, the Tower of Hananel, and the Tower of the Hundred, to the Sheep Gate. We ended our march near the gate to the Temple.

40 So both the groups that were giving thanks to God reached the temple area.

In addition to the leaders who were with me, 41 my group included the following priests, blowing trumpets: Eliakim, Maaseiah, Miniamin, Micaiah, Elioenai, Zechariah, and Hananiah; 42 and they were followed by Maaseiah, Shemaiah, Eleazar, Uzzi, Jehohanan, Malchijah, Elam, and Ezer. The singers, led by Jezrahiah, sang at the top of their voices.

43 That day many sacrifices were offered, and the people were full of joy because God had made them very happy. The women and the children joined in the celebration, and the noise they all made could be heard far and wide.

Providing for Worship in the Temple

44 At that time men were put in charge of the storerooms where contributions for the Temple were kept, including the tithes and the first corn and fruit that ripened each year. These men were responsible for collecting from the farms near the various cities the contributions for the priests and the Levites which the Law required. All the people of Judah were pleased with the priests and the Levites, 45 because they performed the ceremonies of purification and the other rituals that God had commanded. The temple musicians and the temple guards also performed their duties in accordance with the regulations made by King David and his son Solomon. 46 From the time of King David and the musician Asaph long ago, the musicians have led songs of praise and thanksgiving to God. 47 In the time of Zerubbabel and also in the time of Nehemiah, all the people of Israel gave daily gifts for the support of the temple musicians and the temple guards. The people gave a sacred offering to the Levites, and the Levites gave the required portion to the priests.

Separation from Foreigners

13 When the Law of Moses was being read aloud to the people, they came to the passage that said that no Ammonite or Moabite was ever to be permitted to join God's people. 2 This was because the people of Ammon and Moab did not give food and water to the Israelites on their way out of Egypt. Instead, they paid money to Balaam to curse Israel, but our God turned the curse into a blessing. 3 When the people of Israel heard this law read, they excluded all foreigners from the community.

Nehemiah's Reforms

4 The priest Eliashib, who was in charge of the temple storerooms, had for a long time been on good terms with Tobiah. 5 He allowed Tobiah to use a large room that was intended only for storing offerings of corn and incense, the equipment used in the Temple, the offerings for the priests, and the tithes of corn, wine, and olive oil given to the Levites, to the temple musicians, and to the temple guards. 6 While this was going on, I was not in Jerusalem, because in the 32nd year that Artaxerxes* was

12.39 Ephraim Gate, Jeshanah Gate; or Ephraim Gate (also called the Old Gate).
13.6 Artaxerxes: As emperor of Persia, Artaxerxes also had the title "King of Babylon".

NEHEMIAH 13   577

Nehem.
....
Esther
Job
Psalms
Proverbs
Eccles.

king of Babylon I had gone back to report to him. After some time I received his permission [7]and returned to Jerusalem. There I was shocked to find that Eliashib had allowed Tobiah to use a room in the Temple. [8]I was furious and threw out all Tobiah's belongings. [9]I gave orders for the rooms to be ritually purified and for the temple equipment, grain offerings, and incense to be put back.

[10]I also learnt that the temple musicians and other Levites had left Jerusalem and gone back to their farms, because the people had not been giving them enough to live on. [11]I reprimanded the officials for letting the Temple be neglected. And I brought the Levites and musicians back to the Temple and put them to work again. [12]Then all the people of Israel again started bringing to the temple storerooms their tithes of corn, wine, and olive oil. [13]I put the following men in charge of the storerooms: Shelemiah, a priest; Zadok, a scholar of the Law; and Pedaiah, a Levite. Hanan, the son of Zaccur and grandson of Mattaniah, was to be their assistant. I knew I could trust these men to be honest in distributing the supplies to their fellow-workers.

[14]Remember, my God, all these things that I have done for your Temple and its worship.

[15]At that time I saw people in Judah pressing juice from grapes on the Sabbath. Others were loading corn, wine, grapes, figs, and other things on their donkeys and taking them into Jerusalem; I warned them not to sell anything on the Sabbath. [16]Some people from the city of Tyre were living in Jerusalem, and they brought fish and all kinds of goods into the city to sell to our people on the Sabbath. [17]I reprimanded the Jewish leaders and said, "Look at the evil you're doing! You're making the Sabbath unholy. [18]This is exactly why God punished your ancestors when he brought destruction on this city. And yet you insist on bringing more of God's anger down on Israel by profaning the Sabbath."

[19]So I gave orders for the city gates to be shut at the beginning of every Sabbath, as soon as evening* began to fall, and not to be opened again until the Sabbath was over. I stationed some of my men at the gates to make sure that nothing was brought into the city on the Sabbath. [20]Once or twice merchants who sold all kinds of goods spent Friday night outside the city walls. [21]I warned them, "It's no use waiting out there for morning to come. If you try this again, I'll use force against you." From then on they did not come back on the Sabbath. [22]I ordered the Levites to purify themselves and to go and guard the gates to make sure that the Sabbath was kept holy.

Remember me, O God, for this also, and spare me because of your great love.

[23]At that time I also discovered that many of the Jewish men had married women from Ashdod, Ammon, and Moab. [24]Half their children spoke the language of Ashdod or some other language and didn't know how to speak our language. [25]I reprimanded the men, called down curses on them, beat them, and pulled out their hair. Then I made them take an oath in God's name that never again would they or their children intermarry with foreigners. [26]I said, "It was foreign women that made King Solomon sin. He was a man who was greater than any of the kings of other nations. God loved him and made him king over all Israel, and yet he fell into this sin. [27]Are we

----

13.19 *evening*: The Jewish day begins at sunset.

then to follow your example and disobey our God by marrying foreign women?"

28 Joiada was the son of Eliashib the High Priest, but one of Joiada's sons married the daughter of Sanballat, from the town of Beth Horon, so I made Joiada leave Jerusalem.

29 Remember, O God, how those people defiled both the office of priest and the covenant you made with the priests and the Levites.

30 I purified the people from everything foreign; I prepared regulations for the priests and the Levites so that each one would know his duty; 31 I arranged for the wood used for burning the offerings to be brought at the proper times, and for the people to bring their offerings of the first corn and the first fruits that ripened.

Remember all this, O God, and give me credit for it.

THE BOOK OF

ESTHER

WRITTEN: AROUND 400-300BC

WHAT YOU NEED TO KNOW:

Esther is the gripping story of a Jewish girl who became the queen of Persia and rescued her people by foiling a plot to wipe out the Jews. It's a story of courage, intrigue and danger, but most of all it's a story of God working through the actions and lives of his people to bring about an amazing rescue. The book tells the story of how the Jews end up in danger of being entirely wiped out, but through Esther's influence they are permitted to live in peace and restore their land.

WHY READ IT?

Esther is an incredible story, with many unexpected twists and turns, but it also shows us that God can place us in situations for a purpose and that he can use us to achieve his aims.

Esther and Mordecai were passionate about standing up for the rights and the lives of their people, the Jews.

What are you passionate about?

What might God be asking you to stand up for?

_____
_____
_____
_____
_____
_____
_____
_____
_____
_____
_____
_____
_____
_____

ESTHER a Jewish girl who was raised to the highest position in society as the queen of Persia. With the help and guidance of Mordecai, her bravery and cleverness helped her save her people.

MORDECAI Esther's cousin, who adopted her when she was orphaned. Mordecai worked in the king's government. He was also faithful to God, even when his faithfulness put him in danger.

HAMAN a man who became prime minister of Persia and wanted to wipe out the Jews.

483BC — ESTHER BECOMES QUEEN OF PERSIA — PLOT TO KILL THE JEWS — JEWS SAVED — 472BC

580

Esther

.:.........

2 Kings
1 Chron.
2 Chron.
Ezra
Nehem.

Queen Vashti Defies King Xerxes

1 [1-2] From his royal throne in Persia's capital city of Susa, King Xerxes ruled over 127 provinces, all the way from India to Ethiopia.

[3] In the third year of his reign he gave a banquet for all his officials and administrators. The armies of Persia and Media were present, as well as the governors and noblemen of the provinces. [4] For six whole months he made a show of the riches of the imperial court with all its splendour and majesty.

[5] After that, the king gave a banquet for all the people in the capital city of Susa, rich and poor alike. It lasted a whole week and was held in the gardens of the royal palace. [6] The courtyard there was decorated with blue and white cotton curtains, tied by cords of fine purple linen to silver rings on marble columns. Couches made of gold and silver had been placed in the courtyard, which was paved with white marble, red feldspar, shining mother-of-pearl, and blue turquoise. [7] Drinks were served in gold cups, no two of them alike, and the king was generous with the royal wine. [8] There were no limits on the drinks; the king had given orders to the palace servants that everyone could have as much as he wanted.*

[9] Meanwhile, inside the royal palace Queen Vashti was giving a banquet for the women.

[10] On the seventh day of his banquet the king was drinking and feeling merry, so he called in the seven eunuchs who were his personal servants, Mehuman, Biztha, Harbona, Bigtha, Abagtha, Zethar, and Carkas. [11] He ordered them to bring in Queen Vashti, wearing her royal crown. The queen was a beautiful woman, and the king wanted to show off her beauty to the officials and all his guests. [12] But when the servants told Queen Vashti of the king's command, she refused to come. This made the king furious.

[13] Now it was the king's custom to ask for expert opinion on questions of law and order, so he called for his advisers, who would know what should be done. [14] Those he most often turned to for advice were Carshena, Shethar, Admatha, Tarshish, Meres, Marsena, and Memucan — seven officials of Persia and Media who held the highest offices in the kingdom. [15] He said to these men, "I, King Xerxes, sent my servants to Queen Vashti with a command, and she refused to obey it! What does the law say that we should do with her?"

[16] Then Memucan declared to the king and his officials: "Queen Vashti has insulted not only the king but also his officials — in fact, every man in the empire! [17] Every woman in the empire will begin to look down on her husband as soon as she hears what the queen has done. They'll say, 'King Xerxes commanded Queen Vashti to come to him, and she refused.' [18] When the wives of the royal officials of Persia and Media hear about the queen's behaviour they will be telling their husbands about it before the day is out. Wives everywhere will have no respect for their husbands, and husbands will be angry with their wives. [19] If it please Your Majesty, issue a royal proclamation that Vashti may never again appear before the king. Order it to be written into the laws of Persia and Media, so that it can never be changed. Then give her place as queen to some better woman. [20] When your proclamation is made known all over this huge empire, every

---

1.8 *There were no limits… wanted*; or *But no one was forced to drink; the king had given orders to the palace servants that everyone could have as much or as little as he wanted.*

581

Esther

....

Job
Psalms
Proverbs
Eccles.
Songs

woman will treat her husband with proper respect, whether he's rich or poor."

²¹ The king and his officials liked this idea, and the king did what Memucan suggested. ²² To each of the royal provinces he sent a message in the language and the system of writing of that province, saying* that every husband should be the master of his home and speak with final authority.

Esther Becomes Queen

2 Later, even after the king's anger had cooled down, he kept thinking about what Vashti had done and about his proclamation against her. ² So some of the king's advisers who were close to him suggested, "Why don't you make a search to find some beautiful young virgins? ³ You can appoint officials in every province of the empire and order them to bring all these beautiful young women to your harem here in Susa, the capital city. Put them in the care of Hegai, the eunuch who is in charge of your women, and let them be given a beauty treatment. ⁴ Then take the young woman you like best and make her queen in Vashti's place."

The king thought this was good advice, so he followed it.

⁵ There in Susa lived a Jew named Mordecai son of Jair; he was from the tribe of Benjamin and was a descendant of Kish and Shimei. ⁶ When King Nebuchadnezzar of Babylon took King Jehoiachin of Judah into exile from Jerusalem, along with a group of captives, Mordecai was among them. ⁷ He had a cousin, Esther, whose Hebrew name was Hadassah; she was a beautiful young woman, and had a good figure. At the death of her parents, Mordecai had adopted her and brought her up as his own daughter.

⁸ When the king had issued his new proclamation and many young women were being brought to Susa, Esther was among them. She too was put in the royal palace in the care of Hegai, who had charge of the harem. ⁹ Hegai liked Esther, and she won his favour. He lost no time in beginning her beauty treatment of massage and special diet. He gave her the best place in the harem and assigned seven young women specially chosen from the royal palace to serve her.

¹⁰ Now, on the advice of Mordecai, Esther had kept it secret that she was Jewish. ¹¹ Every day Mordecai would walk to and fro in front of the courtyard of the harem, in order to find out how she was getting on and what was going to happen to her.

¹² The regular beauty treatment for the women lasted a year — massages with oil of myrrh for six months and with oil of balsam for six more. After that, each young woman would be taken in turn to King Xerxes. ¹³ When she went from the harem to the palace, she could wear whatever she wanted. ¹⁴ She would go there in the evening, and the next morning she would be taken to another harem and put in the care of Shaashgaz, the eunuch in charge of the king's concubines. She would not go to the king again unless he liked her enough to ask for her by name.

¹⁵ The time came for Esther to go to the king. Esther — the daughter of Abihail and the cousin of Mordecai, who had adopted her as his daughter; Esther — admired by everyone who saw her. When her turn came, she wore just what Hegai, the eunuch in charge of the harem, advised her to wear. ¹⁶ So in Xerxes' seventh year as king, in the tenth month, the month of Tebeth, Esther was brought to King Xerxes in the royal palace. ¹⁷ The king liked

1.22 *saying*; or *in order*.

582

Esther

....

2 Kings
1 Chron.
2 Chron.
Ezra
Nehem.

ESTHER 2, 3

her more than any of the other women, and more than any of the others she won his favour and affection. He placed the royal crown on her head and made her queen in place of Vashti. [18] Then the king gave a great banquet in Esther's honour and invited all his officials and administrators. He proclaimed a holiday* for the whole empire and distributed gifts worthy of a king.

Mordecai Saves the King's Life

[19] Meanwhile Mordecai had been appointed by the king to an administrative position. [20] As for Esther, she had still not let it be known that she was Jewish. Mordecai had told her not to tell anyone, and she obeyed him in this, just as she had obeyed him when she was a little girl under his care.

[21] During the time that Mordecai held office in the palace, Bigthana and Teresh, two of the palace eunuchs who guarded the entrance to the king's rooms, became hostile to King Xerxes and plotted to assassinate him. [22] Mordecai learnt about it and told Queen Esther, who then told the king what Mordecai had found out. [23] There was an investigation, and it was discovered that the report was true, so both men were hanged on the gallows. The king ordered an account of this to be written down in the official records of the empire.

Haman Plots to Destroy the Jews

3 Some time later King Xerxes promoted a man named Haman to the position of prime minister. Haman was the son of Hammedatha, a descendant of Agag.* [2] The king ordered all the officials in his service to show their respect for Haman by kneeling and bowing to him. They all did so, except for Mordecai, who refused to do it. [3] The other officials in the royal service asked him why he was disobeying the king's command; [4] day after day they urged him to give in, but he would not listen to them. "I am a Jew," he explained, "and I cannot bow to Haman." So they told Haman about this, wondering if he would tolerate Mordecai's conduct. [5] Haman was furious when he realized that Mordecai was not going to kneel and bow to him, [6] and when he learnt that Mordecai was a Jew, he decided to do more than punish Mordecai alone. He made plans to kill every Jew in the whole Persian Empire.

[7] In the twelfth year of King Xerxes' rule, in the first month, the month of Nisan, Haman ordered the lots to be cast ("purim", they were called) to find out the right day and month to carry out his plot. The thirteenth day of the twelfth month, the month of Adar, was decided on.

[8] So Haman told the king, "There is a certain race of people scattered all over your empire and found in every province. They observe customs that are not like those of any other people. Moreover, they do not obey the laws of the empire, so it is not in your best interests to tolerate them. [9] If it please Your Majesty, issue a decree that they are to be put to death. If you do, I guarantee that I will be able to put more than 340 tonnes of silver into the royal treasury for the administration of the empire."

[10] The king took off his ring, which was used to stamp proclamations and make them official, and gave it to the enemy of the Jewish people, Haman son of Hammedatha, the descendant

----

2.18 *holiday*; or *remission of taxes.*
3.1 *Agag*: An Amalekite king; his people were traditional enemies of the people of Israel.

of Agag. [11] The king told him, "The people and their money are yours; do as you like with them."

[12] So on the thirteenth day of the first month Haman called the king's secretaries and dictated a proclamation to be translated into every language and system of writing used in the empire and to be sent to all the rulers, governors, and officials. It was issued in the name of King Xerxes and stamped with his ring. [13] Runners took this proclamation to every province of the empire. It contained the instructions that on a single day, the thirteenth day of Adar, all Jews — young and old, women and children — were to be killed. They were to be slaughtered without mercy and their belongings were to be taken. [14] The contents of the proclamation were to be made public in every province, so that everyone would be prepared when that day came.

[15] At the king's command the decree was made public in the capital city of Susa, and runners carried the news to the provinces. The king and Haman sat down and had a drink while the city of Susa was being thrown into confusion.

Mordecai Asks for Esther's Help

4 When Mordecai learnt of all that had been done, he tore his clothes in anguish. Then he dressed in sackcloth, covered his head with ashes, and walked through the city, wailing loudly and bitterly, [2] until he came to the entrance of the palace. He did not go in because no one wearing sackcloth was allowed inside. [3] Throughout all the provinces, wherever the king's proclamation was made known, there was loud mourning among the Jews. They fasted, wept and wailed, and most of them put on sackcloth and lay in ashes.

[4] When Esther's young women and eunuchs told her what Mordecai was doing, she was deeply disturbed. She sent Mordecai some clothes to put on instead of the sackcloth, but he would not accept them. [5] Then she called Hathach, one of the palace eunuchs appointed as her servant by the king, and told him to go to Mordecai and find out what was happening and why. [6] Hathach went to Mordecai in the city square at the entrance of the palace. [7] Mordecai told him everything that had happened to him and just how much money Haman had promised to put into the royal treasury if all the Jews were killed. [8] He gave Hathach a copy of the proclamation that had been issued in Susa, ordering the destruction of the Jews. Mordecai asked him to take it to Esther, explain the situation to her, and ask her to go and plead with the king and beg him to have mercy on her people. [9] Hathach did this, [10] and Esther gave him this message to take back to Mordecai: [11] "If anyone, man or woman, goes to the inner courtyard and sees the king without being summoned, that person must die. That is the law; everyone, from the king's advisers to the people in the provinces, knows that. There is only one way to get round this law: if the king holds out his gold sceptre to someone, then that person's life is spared. But it has been a month since the king sent for me."

[12] When Mordecai received Esther's message, [13] he sent her this warning: "Don't imagine that you are safer than any other Jew just because you are in the royal palace. [14] If you keep quiet at a time like this, help will come from heaven to the Jews, and they will be saved, but you will die and your father's family will come to an end. Yet who knows — maybe it was for a time like this that you were made queen!"

[15] Esther sent Mordecai this reply: [16] "Go and gather all the Jews in Susa together; hold a fast and pray for me. Don't eat or

ESTHER 4.14

Mordecai suggested that Esther had been made queen - 'FOR A TIME -

LIKE THIS'.

Where do you go? Who do you talk to? Have you considered that God might have placed you there for a reason? Spend some time praying about what this may look like.

write some thoughts here

584

Esther

·········

2 Kings
1 Chron.
2 Chron.
Ezra
Nehem.

ESTHER 4–6

drink anything for three days and nights. My young women and I will be doing the same. After that, I will go to the king, even though it is against the law. If I must die for doing it, I will die."
[17] Mordecai then left and did everything that Esther had told him to do.

Esther Invites the King and Haman to a Banquet

5 On the third day of her fast Esther put on her royal robes and went and stood in the inner courtyard of the palace, facing the throne room. The king was inside, seated on the royal throne, facing the entrance. [2] When the king saw Queen Esther standing outside, she won his favour, and he held out to her the gold sceptre. She then came up and touched the tip of it. [3] "What is it, Queen Esther?" the king asked. "Tell me what you want, and you shall have it — even if it is half my empire."

[4] Esther replied, "If it please Your Majesty, I would like you and Haman to be my guests tonight at a banquet I am preparing for you."

[5] The king then ordered Haman to come quickly, so that they could be Esther's guests. So the king and Haman went to Esther's banquet. [6] Over the wine the king asked her, "Tell me what you want, and you shall have it. I will grant your request, even if you ask for half my empire."

[7] Esther replied, [8] "If Your Majesty is kind enough to grant my request, I would like you and Haman to be my guests tomorrow at another banquet that I will prepare for you. At that time I will tell you what I want."

Haman Plots to Kill Mordecai

[9] When Haman left the banquet he was happy and in a good mood. But then he saw Mordecai at the entrance of the palace, and when Mordecai did not rise or show any sign of respect as he passed, Haman was furious with him. [10] But he controlled himself and went home. Then he invited his friends to his house and asked his wife Zeresh to join them. [11] He boasted to them how rich he was, how many sons he had, how the king had promoted him to high office, and how much more important he was than any of the king's other officials. [12] "What is more," Haman went on, "Queen Esther gave a banquet for no one but the king and me, and we are invited back tomorrow. [13] But none of this means a thing to me as long as I see that Jew Mordecai sitting at the entrance of the palace."

[14] So his wife and all his friends suggested, "Why don't you have a gallows built, 22 metres tall? Tomorrow morning you can ask the king to have Mordecai hanged on it, and then you can go to the banquet happy."

Haman thought this was a good idea, so he had the gallows built.

The King Honours Mordecai

6 That same night the king could not get to sleep, so he ordered the official records of the empire to be brought and read to him. [2] The part they read included the account of how Mordecai had uncovered a plot to assassinate the king — the plot made by Bigthana and Teresh, the two palace eunuchs who had guarded the king's rooms. [3] The king asked, "How have we honoured and rewarded Mordecai for this?"

His servants answered, "Nothing has been done for him."

[4] "Are any of my officials in the palace?" the king asked.

Now Haman had just entered the courtyard; he had come to ask the king to have Mordecai hanged on the gallows that was now ready. ⁵ So the servants answered, "Haman is here, waiting to see you."

"Show him in," said the king.

⁶ So Haman came in, and the king said to him, "There is someone I wish very much to honour. What should I do for this man?"

Haman thought to himself, "Now who could the king want to honour so much? Me, of course."

⁷⁻⁸ So he answered the king, "Order royal robes to be brought for this man — robes that you yourself wear. Order a royal ornament* to be put on your own horse. ⁹ Then get one of your highest noblemen to dress the man in these robes and lead him, mounted on the horse, through the city square. Let the nobleman announce as they go: 'See how the king rewards a person he wishes to honour!'"

¹⁰ Then the king said to Haman, "Hurry and get the robes and the horse, and provide these honours for Mordecai the Jew. Do everything for him that you have suggested. You will find him sitting at the entrance of the palace."

¹¹ So Haman got the robes and the horse, and he put the robes on Mordecai. Mordecai got on the horse, and Haman led him through the city square, announcing to the people as they went: "See how the king rewards a man he wishes to honour!"

¹² Mordecai then went back to the palace entrance while Haman hurried home, covering his face in embarrassment. ¹³ He told his wife and all his friends everything that had happened to him. Then she and those wise friends of his said to him, "You are beginning to lose power to Mordecai. He is a Jew, and you cannot overcome him. He will certainly defeat you."

Haman is Put to Death

¹⁴ While they were still talking, the palace eunuchs arrived in a hurry to take Haman to Esther's banquet.

7 And so the king and Haman went to eat with Esther ² for a second time. Over the wine the king asked her again, "Now, Queen Esther, what do you want? Tell me and you shall have it. I'll even give you half the empire."

³ Queen Esther answered, "If it please Your Majesty to grant my humble request, my wish is that I may live and that my people may live. ⁴ My people and I have been sold for slaughter. If it were nothing more serious than being sold into slavery, I would have kept quiet and not bothered you about it;* but we are about to be destroyed — exterminated!"

⁵ Then King Xerxes asked Queen Esther, "Who dares to do such a thing? Where is this man?"

⁶ Esther answered, "Our enemy, our persecutor, is this evil man Haman!"

Haman stared at the king and queen in terror. ⁷ The king got up in a fury, left the room, and went outside to the palace gardens. Haman could see that the king was determined to punish him for this, so he stayed behind to beg Queen Esther for his life. ⁸ He had just thrown himself down on Esther's couch to beg for mercy, when the king came back into the room from the gardens. Seeing this, the king cried out, "Is this man going to rape the queen right here in front of me, in my own palace?"

6.7–8 *ornament*: Probably a type of crown.
7.4 Probable text *and not… it*; Hebrew unclear.

586

Esther

2 Kings
1 Chron.
2 Chron.
Ezra
Nehem.

ESTHER 7, 8

DECORATE THESE SHAPES IN RELATION TO YOUR MOOD.

The king had no sooner said this than the eunuchs covered Haman's head. [9] Then one of them, who was named Harbonah, said, "Haman even went so far as to build a gallows at his house so that he could hang Mordecai, who saved Your Majesty's life. And it's 22 metres tall!"

"Hang Haman on it!" the king commanded.

[10] So Haman was hanged on the gallows that he had built for Mordecai. Then the king's anger cooled down.

The Jews are Told to Fight Back

8 That same day King Xerxes gave Queen Esther all the property of Haman, the enemy of the Jews. Esther told the king that Mordecai was related to her, and from then on Mordecai was allowed to enter the king's presence. [2] The king took off his ring with his seal on it (which he had taken back from Haman) and gave it to Mordecai. Esther put Mordecai in charge of Haman's property.

[3] Then Esther spoke to the king again, throwing herself at his feet and crying. She begged him to do something to stop the evil plot that Haman, the descendant of Agag,* had made against the Jews. [4] The king held out the gold sceptre to her, so she stood up and said, [5] "If it please Your Majesty, and if you care about me and if it seems right to you, please issue a proclamation to prevent Haman's orders from being carried out — those orders that the son of Hammedatha the descendant of Agag gave for the destruction of all the Jews in the empire. [6] How can I endure it if this disaster comes on my people, and my own relatives are killed?"

[7] King Xerxes then said to Queen Esther and Mordecai, the Jew, "Look, I have hanged Haman for his plot against the Jews, and I have given Esther his property. [8] But a proclamation issued in the king's name and stamped with the royal seal cannot be revoked. You may, however, write to the Jews whatever you wish; and you may write it in my name and stamp it with the royal seal."

[9] This happened on the 23rd day of the third month, the month of Sivan. Mordecai called the king's secretaries and dictated letters to the Jews and to the governors, administrators, and officials of all the 127 provinces from India to Ethiopia. The letters were written to each province in its own language and system of writing and to the Jews in their language and system of writing. [10] Mordecai had the letters written in the name of King Xerxes, and he stamped them with the royal seal. They were delivered by riders mounted on fast horses from the royal stables.

[11] These letters explained that the king would allow the Jews in every city to organize themselves for self-defence. If armed men of any nationality in any province attacked the Jewish men, their children or their women, the Jews could fight back and destroy the attackers; they could slaughter them to the last man and take their possessions. [12] This decree was to take effect throughout the Persian Empire on the day set for the slaughter of the Jews, the thirteenth of Adar, the twelfth month. [13] It was to be proclaimed as law and made known to everyone in every province, so that the Jews would be ready to take revenge on their enemies when that day came. [14] At the king's command the riders mounted royal horses and rode off at top speed. The decree was also made public in Susa, the capital city.

[15] Mordecai left the palace, wearing royal robes of blue and white, a cloak of fine purple linen, and a magnificent gold crown.

8.3 *Agag*: See 3.1.

Then the streets of Susa rang with cheers and joyful shouts. [16] For the Jews there was joy and relief, happiness and a sense of victory. [17] In every city and province, wherever the king's proclamation was read, the Jews held a joyful holiday with feasting and happiness. In fact, many other people became Jews, because they were afraid of them now.

The Jews Destroy their Enemies

9 The thirteenth day of Adar came, the day on which the royal proclamation was to take effect, the day when the enemies of the Jews were hoping to get them in their power. But instead, the Jews triumphed over them. [2] In the Jewish quarter of every city* in the empire the Jews organized themselves to attack anyone who tried to harm them. People everywhere were afraid of them, and no one could stand against them. [3] In fact, all the provincial officials — governors, administrators, and royal representatives — helped the Jews because they were all afraid of Mordecai. [4] It was well known throughout the empire that Mordecai was now a powerful man in the palace and was growing more powerful. [5] So the Jews could do what they wanted with their enemies. They attacked them with swords and slaughtered them.

[6] In Susa, the capital city itself, the Jews killed 500 people. [7-10] Among them were the ten sons of Haman son of Hammedatha, the enemy of the Jews: Parshandatha, Dalphon, Aspatha, Poratha, Adalia, Aridatha, Parmashta, Arisai, Aridai, and Vaizatha. However, there was no looting.

[11] That same day the number of people killed in Susa was reported to the king. [12] He then said to Queen Esther, "In Susa alone the Jews have killed 500 people, including Haman's ten sons. What must they have done out in the provinces! What do you want now? You shall have it. Tell me what else you want, and you shall have it."

[13] Esther answered, "If it please Your Majesty, let the Jews in Susa do again tomorrow what they were allowed to do today. And order the bodies of Haman's ten sons to be hung from the gallows." [14] The king ordered this to be done, and the proclamation was issued in Susa. The bodies of Haman's ten sons were publicly displayed. [15] On the fourteenth day of Adar the Jews of Susa got together again and killed 300 more people in the city. But again, they did no looting.

[16] The Jews in the provinces also organized and defended themselves. They rid themselves of their enemies by killing 75,000 people who hated them. But they did no looting. [17] This was on the thirteenth day of Adar. On the next day, the fourteenth, there was no more killing, and they made it a joyful day of feasting. [18] The Jews of Susa, however, made the fifteenth a holiday, since they had slaughtered their enemies on the thirteenth and fourteenth and then stopped on the fifteenth. [19] This is why Jews who live in small towns observe the fourteenth day of the month of Adar as a joyous holiday, a time for feasting and giving gifts of food to one another.

The Festival of Purim

[20] Mordecai had these events written down and sent letters to all the Jews, near and far, throughout the Persian Empire, [21] telling them to observe the fourteenth and fifteenth days of Adar as holidays every year. [22] These were the days on which the

....

9.2 *In the Jewish quarter of every city*; or *In every Jewish city.*

588

Esther

⁝⸱⸳⸳⸳⸳⸳

2 Kings
1 Chron.
2 Chron.
Ezra
Nehem.

ESTHER 9, 10

Jews had rid themselves of their enemies; this was a month that had been turned from a time of grief and despair into a time of joy and happiness. They were told to observe these days with feasts and parties, giving gifts of food to one another and to the poor. [23] So the Jews followed Mordecai's instructions, and the celebration became an annual custom.

[24] Haman son of Hammedatha — the descendant of Agag and the enemy of the Jewish people — had cast lots (or "purim", as they were called) to determine the day for destroying the Jews; he had planned to wipe them out. [25] But Esther went to the king, and the king issued written orders with the result that Haman suffered the fate he had planned for the Jews — he and his sons were hanged from the gallows. [26] That is why the holidays are called Purim. Because of Mordecai's letter and because of all that had happened to them, [27] the Jews made it a rule for themselves, their descendants, and anyone who might become a Jew, that at the proper time each year these two days would be regularly observed according to Mordecai's instructions. [28] It was resolved that every Jewish family of every future generation in every province and every city should remember and observe the days of Purim for all time to come.

[29] Then Queen Esther, the daughter of Abihail, along with Mordecai, also wrote a letter, putting her full authority behind the letter about Purim, which Mordecai had written earlier. [30] The letter was addressed to all the Jews, and copies were sent to all the 127 provinces of the Persian Empire. It wished the Jews peace and security [31] and directed them and their descendants to observe the days of Purim at the proper time, just as they had adopted rules for the observance of fasts and times of mourning. This was commanded by both Mordecai and Queen Esther. [32] Esther's command, confirming the rules for Purim, was written down on a scroll.

The Greatness of Xerxes and Mordecai

10 King Xerxes imposed forced labour on the people of the coastal regions of his empire as well as on those of the interior. [2] All the great and wonderful things he did, as well as the whole story of how he promoted Mordecai to high office, are recorded in the official records of the kings of Persia and Media. [3] Mordecai the Jew was second in rank only to King Xerxes himself. He was honoured and well liked by his fellow-Jews. He worked for the good of his people and for the security of all their descendants.

THE BOOK OF

JOB

WRITTEN: PROBABLY 600-500BC

write some thoughts here

KEY CHARACTER:

After Job has stopped talking (at the end of chapter 31), it is Elihu who then speaks up. At first he is only a bystander in the conversation, but he carries a lot of wisdom. He is also the youngest member of the group and is respectful of the other men's ages, but his speech shows that you don't have to be old to be wise.

WHAT YOU NEED TO KNOW:

The name Job means 'persecuted' or 'afflicted', and that's really what this book is about. It is a poetic dialogue between Job and his friends about what happens when everything goes wrong. Job is totally committed to God, and his wealth at the beginning of the story suggests that God has rewarded him for his faithfulness. Yet disaster hits Job and his family, so how is it that God would let this happen to such a good man? The book of Job is more about asking questions than about getting answers.

WHY READ IT?

This is a book that asks some very real questions about how we feel when life seems to fall apart, and about where God is in it all. It is honest about pain, about faith, and about what it's like to have people around you who are a negative influence when you are at your weakest point. At the end of the story, God steps in and responds to Job - but asks questions of his own rather than giving answers!

(DO THIS WHEN YOU'RE HAVING A ROUGH TIME...)

Take a coloured pen and look through some of Job's words. Underline the things he says that reflect the way you're feeling at the moment.

WE DON'T KNOW WHEN THE STORY OF JOB IS SET, BUT WE THINK BEFORE THE TIME OF ABRAHAM

590

Job

1 Chron.
2 Chron.
Ezra
Nehem.
Esther

JOB 1

JOB 1.6-12

The story of Job is
a window into the world
of suffering. But can
there even be a God if
there is suffering?

CHECK OUT THIS

at gnbyouthedition.co.uk/suffering

Satan Tests Job

1 There was a man named Job, living in the land of Uz,* who worshipped God and was faithful to him. He was a good man, careful not to do anything evil. ² He had seven sons and three daughters, ³ and owned 7,000 sheep, 3,000 camels, 1,000 head of cattle, and 500 donkeys. He also had a large number of servants and was the richest man in the East.

⁴ Job's sons used to take it in turns to give a feast, to which all the others would come, and they always invited their three sisters to join them. ⁵ The morning after each feast, Job would get up early and offer sacrifices for each of his children in order to purify them. He always did this because he thought that one of them might have sinned by insulting God unintentionally.

⁶ When the day came for the heavenly beings* to appear before the LORD, Satan* was there among them. ⁷ The LORD asked him, "What have you been doing?"

Satan answered, "I have been walking here and there, roaming round the earth."

⁸ "Did you notice my servant Job?" the LORD asked. "There is no one on earth as faithful and good as he is. He worships me and is careful not to do anything evil."

⁹ Satan replied, "Would Job worship you if he got nothing out of it? ¹⁰ You have always protected him and his family and everything he owns. You bless everything he does, and you have given him enough cattle to fill the whole country. ¹¹ But now suppose you take away everything he has — he will curse you to your face!"

¹² "All right," the LORD said to Satan, "everything he has is in your power, but you must not hurt Job himself." So Satan left.

Job's Children and Wealth are Destroyed

¹³ One day when Job's children were having a feast at the home of their eldest brother, ¹⁴ a messenger came running to Job. "We were ploughing the fields with the oxen," he said, "and the donkeys were in a nearby pasture. ¹⁵ Suddenly the Sabeans* attacked and stole them all. They killed every one of your servants except me. I am the only one who escaped to tell you."

¹⁶ Before he had finished speaking, another servant came and said, "Lightning struck the sheep and the shepherds and killed them all. I am the only one who escaped to tell you."

¹⁷ Before he had finished speaking, another servant came and said, "Three bands of Chaldean* raiders attacked us, took away the camels, and killed all your servants except me. I am the only one who escaped to tell you."

¹⁸ Before he had finished speaking, another servant came and said, "Your children were having a feast at the home of your eldest son, ¹⁹ when a storm swept in from the desert. It blew the house down and killed them all. I am the only one who escaped to tell you."

²⁰ Then Job stood up and tore his clothes in grief. He shaved his head and threw himself face downwards on the ground. ²¹ He said, "I was born with nothing, and I will die with nothing. The LORD gave, and now he has taken away. May his name be praised!"

²² In spite of everything that had happened, Job did not sin by blaming God.

....

1.1 *Uz*: An area whose exact location is unknown.
1.6 *heavenly beings*: Supernatural beings who serve God in heaven.
1.6 *Satan*: A supernatural being whose name indicates he was regarded as the opponent of humanity.
1.15 *Sabeans*: A tribe of wandering raiders from the south.
1.17 *Chaldean*(s): A tribe of wandering raiders from the north.

JOB 2, 3

591

Job

....

Psalms
Proverbs
Eccles.
Songs
Isaiah

Satan Tests Job Again

2 When the day came for the heavenly beings to appear before the LORD again, Satan was there among them. [2] The LORD asked him, "Where have you been?"

Satan answered, "I have been walking here and there, roaming round the earth."

[3] "Did you notice my servant Job?" the LORD asked. "There is no one on earth as faithful and good as he is. He worships me and is careful not to do anything evil. You persuaded me to let you attack him for no reason at all, but Job is still as faithful as ever."

[4] Satan replied, "A person will give up everything in order to stay alive. [5] But now suppose you hurt his body — he will curse you to your face!"

[6] So the LORD said to Satan, "All right, he is in your power, but you are not to kill him."

[7] Then Satan left the LORD's presence and made sores break out all over Job's body. [8] Job went and sat by the rubbish heap and took a piece of broken pottery to scrape his sores. [9] His wife said to him, "You are still as faithful as ever, aren't you? Why don't you curse God and die?"

[10] Job answered, "You are talking nonsense! When God sends us something good, we welcome it. How can we complain when he sends us trouble?" In spite of everything he suffered, Job said nothing against God.

Job's Friends Come

[11] Three of Job's friends were Eliphaz, from the city of Teman, Bildad, from the land of Shuah, and Zophar, from the land of Naamah. When they heard how much Job had been suffering, they decided to go and comfort him. [12] While they were still a long way off they saw Job, but did not recognize him. When they did, they began to weep and wail, tearing their clothes in grief and throwing dust into the air and on their heads. [13] Then they sat there on the ground with him for seven days and nights without saying a word, because they saw how much he was suffering.

Job's Complaint to God

3 Finally Job broke the silence and cursed the day on which he had been born.

Job

2-3 O God, put a curse on the day I was born;
  put a curse on the night when I was conceived!
4 Turn that day into darkness, God.
 Never again remember that day;
  never again let light shine on it.
5 Make it a day of gloom and thick darkness;
  cover it with clouds, and blot out the sun.
6 Blot that night out of the year,
  and never let it be counted again;
7 make it a barren, joyless night.
8 Tell the sorcerers to curse that day,
  those who know how to control Leviathan.*
9 Keep the morning star from shining;
  give that night no hope of dawn.

3.8 *Leviathan*: Some take this to be the crocodile, others a legendary monster. Magicians were thought to be able to make him cause eclipses of the sun.

592

Job

1 Chron.
2 Chron.
Ezra
Nehem.
Esther

JOB 3, 4

10 Curse that night for letting me be born,
   for exposing me to trouble and grief.
11 I wish I had died in my mother's womb
   or died the moment I was born.
12 Why did my mother hold me on her knees?
   Why did she feed me at her breast?
13 If I had died then, I would be at rest now,
14   sleeping like the kings and rulers
     who rebuilt ancient palaces.
15 Then I would be sleeping like princes
   who filled their houses with gold and silver,
16   or sleeping like a stillborn child.
17 In the grave wicked people stop their evil,
   and tired workers find rest at last.
18 Even prisoners enjoy peace,
   free from shouts and harsh commands.
19 Everyone is there, the famous and the unknown,
   and slaves at last are free.

20 Why let people go on living in misery?
   Why give light to those in grief?
21 They wait for death, but it never comes;
   they prefer a grave to any treasure.
22 They are not happy till they are dead and buried;
23   God keeps their future hidden
     and hems them in on every side.
24 Instead of eating, I mourn,
   and I can never stop groaning.
25 Everything I fear and dread comes true.
26 I have no peace, no rest,
   and my troubles never end.

The First Dialogue
(4.1—14.22)

Eliphaz

4 1-2 Job, will you be annoyed if I speak?
   I can't keep quiet any longer.
3 You have taught many people
   and given strength to feeble hands.
4 When someone stumbled, weak and tired,
   your words encouraged him to stand.
5 Now it's your turn to be in trouble,
   and you are too stunned to face it.
6 You worshipped God, and your life was blameless;
   and so you should have confidence and hope.
7 Think back now. Name a single case
   where a righteous person met with disaster.
8 I have seen people plough fields of evil
   and sow wickedness like seed;
   now they harvest wickedness and evil.
9 Like a storm, God destroys them in his anger.
10 The wicked roar and growl like lions,
   but God silences them and breaks their teeth.
11 Like lions with nothing to kill and eat,
   they die, and all their children are scattered.

JOB 4, 5

593

Job
....
Psalms
Proverbs
Eccles.
Songs
Isaiah

JOIN THE DOTS
below to make a picture.

¹² Once a message came quietly,
　　so quietly I could hardly hear it.
¹³ Like a nightmare it disturbed my sleep.
¹⁴ 　I trembled and shuddered;
　　my whole body shook with fear.
¹⁵ A light breeze touched my face,
　　and my hair bristled with fright.
¹⁶ I could see something standing there;
　　I stared, but couldn't tell what it was.
　　Then I heard a voice out of the silence:
¹⁷ "Can anyone be righteous in the sight of* God
　　or be pure before* his Creator?
¹⁸ God does not trust his heavenly servants;
　　he finds fault even with his angels.
¹⁹ Do you think he will trust a creature of clay,
　　a thing of dust that can be crushed like a moth?
²⁰ Someone may be alive in the morning,
　　but die unnoticed before evening comes.
²¹ All that he has is taken away;
　　he dies, still lacking wisdom."

5 Call out, Job. See if anyone answers.
　　Is there any angel to whom you can turn?
² To worry yourself to death with resentment
　　would be a foolish, senseless thing to do.
³ I have seen fools who looked secure,
　　but I called down a sudden curse on their homes.
⁴ Their children can never find safety;
　　no one stands up to defend them in court.
⁵ Hungry people will eat the fool's crops —
　　even the grain growing among thorns* —
　　and thirsty people will envy his wealth.
⁶ Evil does not grow in the soil,
　　nor does trouble grow out of the ground.
⁷ No indeed! People bring trouble on themselves,
　　as surely as sparks fly up from a fire.*

⁸ If I were you, I would turn to God
　　and present my case to him.
⁹ We cannot understand the great things he does,
　　and to his miracles there is no end.
¹⁰ He sends rain on the land
　　and he waters the fields.
¹¹ Yes, it is God who raises the humble
　　and gives joy to all who mourn.
¹²⁻¹³ He upsets the plans of cunning people,
　　and traps the wise in their own schemes,
　　so that nothing they do succeeds;
¹⁴ 　even at noon they grope in darkness.
¹⁵ But God saves the poor* from death;
　　he saves the needy from oppression.
¹⁶ He gives hope to the poor and silences the wicked.

4.17 righteous in the sight of; or more righteous than.
4.17 be pure before; or be more pure than.
5.5 Probable text even… thorns; Hebrew unclear.
5.7 sparks fly up from a fire; or birds fly up to the sky.
5.15 Probable text poor; Hebrew unclear.

594

Job

1 Chron.
2 Chron.
Ezra
Nehem.
Esther

JOB 5, 6

17 Happy is the person whom God corrects!
    Do not resent it when he rebukes you.
18 God bandages the wounds he makes;
    his hand hurts you, and his hand heals.
19 Time after time he will save you from harm;
20   when famine comes, he will keep you alive,
    and in war protect you from death.
21 God will rescue you from slander;
    he will save you when destruction comes.
22 You will laugh at violence and hunger
    and not be afraid of wild animals.
23 The fields you plough will be free of rocks;
    wild animals will never attack you.
24 Then you will live at peace in your tent;
    when you look at your sheep, you will find them safe.
25 You will have as many children
    as there are blades of grass in a pasture.
26 Like wheat that ripens till harvest time,
    you will live to a ripe old age.
27 Job, we have learnt this by long study.
    It is true, so now accept it.

Job

6 1-2 If my troubles and griefs were weighed on scales,
3   they would weigh more than the sands of the sea,
    so my wild words should not surprise you.
4 Almighty God has pierced me with arrows,
    and their poison spreads through my body.
    God has lined up his terrors against me.

5 A donkey is content when eating grass,
    and a cow is quiet when eating hay.
6 But who can eat tasteless, unsalted food?
    What flavour is there in the white of an egg?
7 I have no appetite for food like that,
    and everything I eat makes me sick.*

8 Why won't God give me what I ask?
    Why won't he answer my prayer?
9 If only he would go ahead and kill me!
10 If I knew he would, I would leap for joy,
    no matter how great my pain.
    I know that God is holy;
    I have never opposed what he commands.
11 What strength have I got to keep on living?
    Why go on living when I have no hope?
12 Am I made of stone? Is my body bronze?
13 I have no strength left to save myself;
    there is nowhere I can turn for help.

14 In trouble* like this I need loyal friends —
    whether I've forsaken God or not.
15 But you, my friends, you deceive me like streams
    that go dry when no rain comes.

6.7 Probable text *sick*; Hebrew unclear.
6.14 Probable text *trouble*; Hebrew unclear.

16 The streams are choked with snow and ice,
17   but in the heat they disappear,
   and the stream beds lie bare and dry.
18 Caravans get lost looking for water;
   they wander and die in the desert.
19 Caravans from Sheba and Tema search,
20   but their hope dies beside dry streams.
21 You are like* those streams to me,*
   you see my fate and draw back in fear.
22 Have I asked you to give me a gift
   or to bribe someone on my behalf
23   or to save me from some enemy or tyrant?

24 All right, teach me; tell me my faults.
   I will be quiet and listen to you.
25 Honest words are convincing,
   but you are talking nonsense.
26 You think I am talking nothing but wind;
   then why do you answer my words of despair?
27 You would even throw dice for orphan slaves
   and make yourselves rich off your closest friends!
28 Look me in the face. I won't lie.
29 You have gone far enough. Stop being unjust.
   Don't condemn me. I'm in the right.
30 But you think I am lying —
   you think I can't tell right from wrong.

7 Human life is like forced army service,
   like a life of hard manual labour,
2   like slaves longing for cool shade;
   like workers waiting for their pay.
3 Month after month I have nothing to live for;
   night after night brings me grief.
4 When I lie down to sleep, the hours drag;
   I toss all night and long for dawn.
5 My body is full of worms;
   it is covered with scabs;
   pus runs out of my sores.
6 My days pass by without hope,
   pass faster than a weaver's shuttle.*

7 Remember, O God, my life is only a breath;
   my happiness has already ended.
8 You see me now, but never again.
   If you look for me, I'll be gone.
9-10 Like a cloud that fades and is gone,
   people die and never return;
   they are forgotten by all who knew them.
11 No! I can't be quiet!
   I am angry and bitter.
   I have to speak.

6.21 Probable text *like*; Hebrew *because*.
6.21 Some ancient translations *and one*; Hebrew manuscript *to me*; most
Hebrew manuscripts have two different expressions: *nothing* in the text
and *to him* in the margin.
7.6 *weaver's shuttle*: A small device in the loom which carries threads to
and fro rapidly in weaving cloth.

596

Job

1 Chron.
2 Chron.
Ezra
Nehem.
Esther

JOB 7, 8

Write here what you
will be praying about
this week.

_____

_____

_____

_____

_____

_____

_____

_____

_____

_____

_____

_____

_____

_____

_____

_____

_____

_____

_____

_____

_____

_____

12 Why do you keep me under guard?
    Do you think I am a sea monster?*
13 I lie down and try to rest;
    I look for relief from my pain.
14 But you — you terrify me with dreams;
    you send me visions and nightmares
15   until I would rather be strangled
    than live in this miserable body.
16 I give up; I am tired of living.
    Leave me alone. My life makes no sense.

17 Why are human beings so important to you?
    Why pay attention to what they do?
18 You inspect them every morning
    and test them every minute.
19 Won't you look away long enough
    for me to swallow my spittle?
20 Are you harmed by my sin, you jailer?
    Why use me for your target practice?
    Am I so great a burden to you?
21 Can't you ever forgive my sin?
    Can't you pardon the wrong I do?
    Soon I will be in my grave,
    and I'll be gone when you look for me.

Bildad

8 1-2 Are you finally through with your windy speech?
     3 God never twists justice;
    he never fails to do what is right.
4 Your children must have sinned against God,
    and so he punished them as they deserved.
5 But turn now and plead with Almighty God;
6   if you are so honest and pure,
    then God will come and help you
    and restore your household as your reward.
7 All the wealth you lost will be nothing
    compared with what God will give you then.

8 Look for a moment at ancient wisdom;
    consider the truths our ancestors learnt.
9 Our life is short, we know nothing at all;
    we pass like shadows across the earth.
10 But let the wise ancestors teach you;
    listen to what they had to say:

11 "Reeds can't grow where there is no water;
    they are never found outside a swamp.
12 If the water dries up, they are the first to wither,
    while still too small to be cut and used.
13 Godless men are like those reeds;
    their hope is gone, once God is forgotten.
14 They trust a thread — a spider's web.
15   If they lean on a web, will it hold them up?
    If they grab for a thread, will it help them stand?"

7.12 *sea monster*: A reference to ancient stories in which sea monsters had
to be guarded so that they would not escape and do damage.

JOB 8, 9

597

Job
....

Psalms
Proverbs
Eccles.
Songs
Isaiah

16 The wicked sprout like weeds in the sun,
   like weeds that spread all through the garden.
17 Their roots wrap round the stones
   and hold fast to* every rock.
18 But then pull them up —
   no one will ever know they were there.
19 Yes, that's all the joy wicked people have;
   others now come and take their places.

20 But God will never abandon the faithful
   or ever give help to evil people.
21 He will let you laugh and shout again,
22   but he will bring disgrace on those who hate you,
   and the homes of the wicked will vanish.

Job

9

1-2 Yes, I've heard all that before.
   But how can a human being win a case against God?
3 How can anyone argue with him?
   He can ask a thousand questions
   that no one could ever answer.*
4 God is so wise and powerful;
   no one can stand up against him.
5 Without warning he moves mountains
   and in anger he destroys them.
6 God sends earthquakes and shakes the ground;
   he rocks the pillars that support the earth.
7 He can keep the sun from rising,
   and the stars from shining at night.
8 No one helped God spread out the heavens
   or trample the sea monster's back.*
9 God hung the stars in the sky — the Great Bear,
   Orion, the Pleiades, and the stars of the south.
10 We cannot understand the great things he does,
   and to his miracles there is no end.

11 God passes by, but I cannot see him.
12 He takes what he wants, and no one can stop him;
   no one dares ask him, "What are you doing?"
13 God's anger is constant. He crushed his enemies
   who helped Rahab,* the sea monster, oppose him.
14 So how can I find words to answer God?
15 Though I am innocent, all I can do
   is beg for mercy from God my judge.
16 Yet even then, if he lets me speak,
   I can't believe he would listen to me.
17 He sends storms to batter and bruise me
   without any reason at all.
18 He won't let me get my breath;
   he has filled my life with bitterness.
19 Should I try force? Try force on God?

JOB 9

Job felt a

- MILLION -

MILES

away from God because
of his circumstances.

When was the last
time you felt distant
from God?

What do you do
when you can't hear
God's voice?

How do your
circumstances affect
the way you see God?

8.17 Probable text hold fast to; Hebrew see.
9.3 He can ask... answer; or Someone could ask him a thousand questions,
and he would not answer.
9.8 trample the sea monster's back: A reference to ancient stories in which
a sea monster was killed and then trampled on (see also 26.13).
9.13 Rahab: A legendary sea monster which represented the forces of
chaos and evil.

598

Job

∴|⋯⋯⋯

1 Chron.
2 Chron.
Ezra
Nehem.
Esther

JOB 9, 10

Should I take him to court? Could anyone make him go?*
20 I am innocent and faithful, but my words sound guilty,
and everything I say seems to condemn me.
21-22 I am innocent, but I no longer care.
I am sick of living. Nothing matters;
innocent or guilty, God will destroy us.
23 When an innocent person suddenly dies,
God laughs.
24 God gave the world to the wicked.
He made all the judges blind.
And if God didn't do it, who did?

25 My days race by, not one of them good.
26 My life passes like the swiftest boat,
as fast as an eagle swooping down on a rabbit.
27-28 If I smile and try to forget my pain,
all my suffering comes back to haunt me;
I know that God does hold me guilty.
29 Since I am held guilty, why should I bother?
30 No soap can wash away my sins.
31 God throws me into a pit of filth,
and even my clothes are ashamed of me.
32 If God were human, I could answer him;
we could go to court to decide our quarrel.
33 But there is no one to step between us —
no one to judge both God and me.
34 Stop punishing me, God!
Keep your terrors away!
35 I am not afraid. I am going to talk
because I know my own heart.

10 I am tired of living.
Listen to my bitter complaint.
2 Don't condemn me, God.
Tell me! What is the charge against me?
3 Is it right for you to be so cruel?
To despise what you yourself have made?
And then to smile on the schemes of wicked people?
4 Do you see things as we do?
5 Is your life as short as ours?
6 Then why do you track down all my sins
and hunt down every fault I have?
7 You know that I am not guilty,
that no one can save me from you.

8 Your hands formed and shaped me,
and now* those same hands destroy me.
9 Remember that you made me from clay;*
are you going to crush me back to dust?
10 You gave my father strength to beget me;
you made me grow in my mother's womb.
11 You formed my body with bones and sinews
and covered the bones with muscles and skin.
12 You have given me life and constant love,
and your care has kept me alive.

....
9.19 Probable text *make him go*; Hebrew *make me go*.
10.8 Some ancient translations *and now*; Hebrew *together*.
10.9 One ancient translation *from clay*; Hebrew *like clay*.

Job

Psalms
Proverbs
Eccles.
Songs
Isaiah

¹³ But now I know that all that time
  you were secretly planning to harm me.
¹⁴ You were watching to see if I would sin,
  so that you could refuse to forgive me.
¹⁵ As soon as I sin, I'm in trouble with you,
  but when I do right, I get no credit.
  I am miserable and covered with shame.*
¹⁶ If I have any success at all,
  you hunt me down like a lion;
  to hurt me you even work miracles.
¹⁷ You always have some witness against me;
  your anger towards me grows and grows;
  you always plan some new attack.

¹⁸ Why, God, did you let me be born?
  I should have died before anyone saw me.
¹⁹ To go from the womb straight to the grave
  would have been as good as never existing.
²⁰ Isn't my life almost over? Leave me alone!
  Let me enjoy the time I have left.
²¹ I am going soon and will never come back —
  going to a land that is dark and gloomy,
²² a land of darkness, shadows, and confusion,
  where the light itself is darkness.

Zophar

11 ¹⁻²Will no one answer all this nonsense?
  Does talking so much put you in the right?
³ Job, do you think we can't answer you?
  That your mocking words will leave us speechless?
⁴ You claim that what you say is true;
  you claim you are pure in the sight of God.
⁵ How I wish God would answer you!
⁶ He would tell you there are many sides to wisdom;
  there are things too deep for human knowledge.
  God is punishing you less than you deserve.

⁷ Can you discover the limits and bounds
  of the greatness and power of God?
⁸ The sky is no limit for God,
  but it lies beyond your reach.
God knows the world of the dead,
  but you do not know it.
⁹ God's greatness is broader than the earth,
  wider than the sea.
¹⁰ If God arrests you and brings you to trial,
  who is there to stop him?
¹¹ God knows which people are worthless;
  he sees all their evil deeds.
¹² Stupid people will start being wise
  when wild donkeys are born tame.

¹³ Put your heart right, Job. Reach out to God.
¹⁴ Put away evil and wrong from your home.
¹⁵ Then face the world again, firm and courageous.

10.15 Probable text *covered with shame*; Hebrew *see my shame*.

600

Job

1 Chron.
2 Chron.
Ezra
Nehem.
Esther

JOB 11, 12

16 Then all your troubles will fade from your memory,
    like floods that are past and remembered no more.
17 Your life will be brighter than sunshine at noon,
    and life's darkest hours will shine like the dawn.
18 You will live secure and full of hope;
    God will protect you and give you rest.
19 You won't be afraid of your enemies;
    many people will ask you for help.
20 But the wicked will look round in despair
    and find that there is no way to escape.
    Their one hope is that death will come.

Job

12 1-2 Yes, you are the voice of the people.
    When you die, wisdom will die with you.
3 But I have as much sense as you have;
    I am in no way inferior to you;
    everyone knows all that you have said.
4 Even my friends laugh at me now;
    they laugh, although I am righteous and blameless;
    but there was a time when God answered my prayers.
5 You have no troubles, and yet you make fun of me;
    you hit someone who is about to fall.
6 But thieves and godless people live in peace,
    though their only god is their own strength.

7 Even birds and animals have much they could teach
    you;
8   ask the creatures of earth and sea for their wisdom.
9 All of them know that the LORD's hand made them.
10 It is God who directs the lives of his creatures;
    everyone's life is in his power.
11 But just as your tongue enjoys tasting food,
    your ears enjoy hearing words.

12-13 Old people have wisdom,
    but God has wisdom and power.
    Old people have insight;
    God has insight and power to act.
14 When God tears down, who can rebuild,
    and who can free those God imprisons?
15 Drought comes when God withholds rain;
    floods come when he turns water loose.

16 God is strong and always victorious;
    both deceived and deceiver are in his power.
17 He takes away the wisdom of rulers
    and makes leaders act like fools.
18 He dethrones kings and makes them prisoners;
19   he humbles priests and men of power.
20 He silences those who are trusted,
    and takes the wisdom of old people away.
21 He disgraces those in power
    and puts an end to the strength of rulers.
22 He sends light to places dark as death.
23 He makes nations strong and great,
    but then he defeats and destroys them.

JOB 12.16

· · · GOD IS · · ·
STRONG
AND ALWAYS
VICTORIOUS

24 He makes their leaders foolish
   and lets them wander confused and lost;
25   they grope in the dark and stagger like drunkards.

13

1-2 Everything you say, I have heard before.
   I understand it all; I know as much as you do.
   I'm not your inferior.
3 But my dispute is with God, not you;
   I want to argue my case with him.
4 You cover up your ignorance with lies;
   you are like doctors who can't heal anyone.
5 Say nothing, and someone may think you are wise!

6 Listen while I state my case.
7   Why are you lying?
   Do you think your lies will benefit God?
8 Are you trying to defend him?
   Are you going to argue his case in court?
9 If God looks at you closely, will he find anything good?
   Do you think you can fool God as you fool others?
10 Even though your prejudice is hidden,
    he will reprimand you,
11   and his power will fill you with terror.
12 Your proverbs are as useless as ashes;
    your arguments crumble like clay.
13 Be quiet and give me a chance to speak,
    and let the results be what they will.

14 I am* ready to risk my life.
15 I've lost all hope, so what if God kills me?
   I am going to state my case to him.
16 It may even be that my boldness will save me,
   since no wicked person would dare to face God.
17 Now listen to my words of explanation.
18 I am ready to state my case,
   because I know I am in the right.

19 Are you coming to accuse me, God?
   If you do, I am ready to be silent and die.
20 Let me ask for two things; agree to them,
   and I will not try to hide from you;
21   stop punishing me, and don't crush me with terror.

22 Speak first, O God, and I will answer.
   Or let me speak, and you answer me.
23 What are my sins? What wrongs have I done?
   What crimes am I charged with?

24 Why do you avoid me?
   Why do you treat me like an enemy?
25 Are you trying to frighten me? I'm nothing but a leaf;
   you are attacking a piece of dry straw.

26 You bring bitter charges against me,
   even for what I did when I was young.
27 You bind chains on my feet;
   you watch every step I take,

....

13.14 One ancient translation *I am*; Hebrew *Why am I…?*

602

Job

.:........

1 Chron.
2 Chron.
Ezra
Nehem.
Esther

JOB 13, 14

and even examine my footprints.
28 As a result, I crumble like rotten wood,
like a moth-eaten coat.

14 We are all born weak and helpless.
All lead the same short, troubled life.
2 We grow and wither as quickly as flowers;
we disappear like shadows.
3 Will you even look at me, God,
or put me on trial and judge me?
4 Nothing clean can ever come
from anything as unclean as human beings.
5 The length of their lives is decided beforehand —
the number of months they will live.
You have settled it, and it can't be changed.
6 Look away from them and leave them alone;*
let them enjoy their hard life — if they can.*

7 There is hope for a tree that has been cut down;
it can come back to life and sprout.
8 Even though its roots grow old,
and its stump dies in the ground,
9 with water it will sprout like a young plant.
10 But people die, and that is the end of them;
they die, and where are they then?
11 Like rivers that stop running,
and lakes that go dry,
12 people die, never to rise.
They will never wake up while the sky endures;
they will never stir from their sleep.

13 I wish you would hide me in the world of the dead;
let me be hidden until your anger is over,
and then set a time to remember me.
14 If people die, can they come back to life?
But I will wait for better times,
wait till this time of trouble is ended.
15 Then you will call, and I will answer,
and you will be pleased with me, your creature.
16 Then you will watch every step I take,
but you will not keep track of my sins.
17 You will forgive them and put them away;
you will wipe out all the wrongs I have done.

18 There comes a time when mountains fall
and solid cliffs are moved away.
19 Water will wear down rocks,
and heavy rain will wash away the soil;
so you destroy our hope for life.
20 You overpower someone and send him away for ever;
his face is twisted in death.
21 His sons win honour, but he never knows it,
nor is he told when they are disgraced.
22 He feels only the pain of his own body
and the grief of his own mind.

....

14.6 One Hebrew manuscript *and leave them alone*; most Hebrew
manuscripts *so that they may rest.*
14.6 *let them... can*; or *until they finish their day of hard work.*

The Second Dialogue
(15.1—21.34)

Eliphaz

15
¹⁻² Empty words, Job! Empty words!
³ No wise person would talk as you do
or defend himself with such meaningless words.
⁴ If you had your way, no one would fear God;
no one would pray to him.
⁵ Your wickedness is evident by what you say;
you are trying to hide behind clever words.
⁶ There is no need for me to condemn you;
you are condemned by every word you speak.

⁷ Do you think you were the first person born?
Were you there when God made the mountains?
⁸ Did you overhear the plans God made?
Does human wisdom belong to you alone?
⁹ There is nothing you know that we don't know.
¹⁰ We learnt our wisdom from grey-haired people —
those born before your father.

¹¹ God offers you comfort; why still reject it?
We have spoken for him with calm, even words.
¹² But you are excited and glare at us in anger.
¹³ You are angry with God and denounce him.

¹⁴ Can any human being be really pure?
Can anyone be right with God?
¹⁵ Why, God does not trust even his angels;
even they are not pure in his sight.
¹⁶ And people drink evil as if it were water;
yes, they are corrupt; they are worthless.

¹⁷ Now listen, Job, to what I know.
¹⁸ Those who are wise have taught me truths
which they learnt from their ancestors,
and they kept no secrets hidden.
¹⁹ Their land was free from foreigners;
there was no one to lead them away from God.

²⁰ The wicked who oppress others
will be in torment as long as they live.
²¹ Voices of terror will scream in their ears,
and robbers attack when they think they are safe.
²² They have no hope of escaping from darkness,
for somewhere a sword is waiting to kill them,
²³ and vultures* are waiting* to eat their corpses.
They know their future is dark;
²⁴ disaster, like a powerful king,
is waiting to attack them.

²⁵ That is the fate of those
who shake their fists at God
and defy the Almighty.
²⁶⁻²⁷ They are proud and rebellious;

15.23 One ancient translation *vultures*; Hebrew *where is he?*
15.23 One ancient translation *are waiting*; Hebrew *he wanders.*

604

Job

1 Chron.
2 Chron.
Ezra
Nehem.
Esther

JOB 15, 16

List some

QUESTIONS

you have about
faith here.

_____

_____

_____

_____

_____

_____

_____

_____

_____

_____

they stubbornly hold up their shields
and rush to fight against God.

28 They are the ones who captured cities
and seized houses whose owners had fled,
but war will destroy those cities and houses.
29 They will not remain rich for long;
nothing they own will last.
Even their shadows* will vanish,
30 and they will not escape from darkness.
They will be like trees
whose branches are burnt by fire,
whose blossoms* are blown away by the wind.
31 If they are foolish enough to trust in evil,
then evil will be their reward.
32 Before their time is up they will wither,*
wither like a branch and never be green again.
33 They will be like vines that lose their unripe grapes;
like olive trees that drop their blossoms.
34 There will be no descendants for godless people,
and fire will destroy the homes built by bribery.
35 These are the ones who plan trouble and do evil;
their hearts are always full of deceit.

Job

16 1-2 I have heard words like that before;
the comfort you give is only torment.
3 Are you going to keep on talking for ever?
Do you always have to have the last word?
4 If you were in my place and I in yours,
I could say everything you are saying.
I could shake my head wisely
and drown you with a flood of words.
5 I could strengthen you with advice
and keep talking to comfort you.

6 But nothing I say helps,
and being silent does not calm my pain.
7 You have worn me out, God;
you have let my family be killed.
8 You have seized me; you are my enemy.
I am skin and bones,
and people take that as proof of my guilt.*
9 In anger God tears me limb from limb;
he glares at me with hate.
10 People sneer at me;
they crowd round me and slap my face.
11 God has handed me over to evil people.
12 I was living in peace,
but God took me by the throat
and battered me and crushed me.
God uses me for target practice

....

15.29 One ancient translation *shadow*; Hebrew unclear.
15.30 One ancient translation *blossoms*; Hebrew *mouth*.
15.32 Some ancient translations *wither*; Hebrew *be filled*.
16.8 Verses 7–8 in Hebrew are unclear.

JOB 16, 17

605

Job
················

Psalms
Proverbs
Eccles.
Songs
Isaiah

13 and shoots arrows at me from every side —
   arrows that pierce and wound me;
   and even then he shows no pity.
14 He wounds me again and again;
   he attacks like a soldier gone mad with hate.

15 I mourn and wear clothes made of sackcloth,
   and I sit here in the dust defeated.
16 I have cried until my face is red,
   and my eyes are swollen and circled with shadows,
17 but I am not guilty of any violence,
   and my prayer to God is sincere.

18 O Earth, don't hide the wrongs done to me!
   Don't let my call for justice be silenced!
19 There is someone in heaven
   to stand up for me and take my side.
20 My friends scorn me;
   my eyes pour out tears to God.
21 I want someone to plead with God for me,
   as one pleads for a friend.
22 My years are passing now,
   and I walk the road of no return.

17

The end of my life is near. I can hardly breathe;
there is nothing left for me but the grave.
2 I watch how bitterly everyone mocks me.
3 I am being honest, God. Accept my word.
   There is no one else to support what I say.
4 You have closed their minds to reason;
   don't let them triumph over me now.
5 In the old proverb someone betrays his friends for money,
   and his children suffer for it.*
6 And now people use this proverb against me;
   they come and spit in my face.
7 My grief has almost made me blind;
   my arms and legs are as thin as shadows.
8 Those who claim to be honest are shocked,
   and they all condemn me as godless.
9 Those who claim to be respectable
   are more and more convinced they are right.
10 But if all of them came and stood before me,
   I would not find even one of them wise.

11 My days have passed; my plans have failed;
   my hope is gone.
12 But my friends say night is daylight;
   they say that light is near,
   but I know I remain in darkness.
13 My only hope is the world of the dead,
   where I will lie down to sleep in the dark.
14 I will call the grave my father,
   and the worms that eat me
   I will call my mother and my sisters.
15 Where is there any hope for me?
   Who sees any?

17.5 *someone... suffer for it;* or *someone entertains his friends while his children go hungry.*

606

Job

1 Chron.
2 Chron.
Ezra
Nehem.
Esther

JOB 18

Job's friends
made some really

- UNHELPFUL -

COMMENTS.

Write your name on this
page and, around it, write
the names of your friends.
<u>Underline</u> the names of
your friends who speak
positively to you when
things are difficult, and
give you hope.

your name
here
⌐

- -

16 Hope will not go with me*
  when I go down to the world of the dead.

Bildad

18 1-2 Job, can't people like you ever be quiet?
     If you stopped to listen, we could talk to you.
  3 What makes you think we are as stupid as cattle?
  4 You are only hurting yourself with your anger.
    Will the earth be deserted because you are angry?
    Will God move mountains to satisfy you?
  5 The light of the wicked will still be put out;
    its flame will never burn again.
  6 The lamp in their tents will be darkened.
  7 Their steps were firm, but now they stumble;
    they fall — victims of their own advice.
  8 They walk into a net, and their feet are caught;
  9   a trap catches their heels and holds them.
  10 On the ground a snare is hidden;
     a trap has been set in their path.

  11 All round them terror is waiting;
     it follows them at every step.
  12 They used to be rich, but now they go hungry;
     disaster stands and waits at their side.
  13 A deadly disease spreads over their bodies
     and causes their arms and legs to rot.
  14 They are torn from the tents where they lived secure,
     and are dragged off to face King Death.
  15 Now anyone may live in their tents —*
     after sulphur is sprinkled to disinfect them!*
  16 Their roots and branches are withered and dry.
  17 Their fame is ended at home and abroad;
     no one remembers them any more.
  18 They will be driven out of the land of the living,
     driven from light into darkness.
  19 They have no descendants, no survivors.
  20 From east to west, all who hear of their fate
     shudder and tremble with fear.
  21 That is the fate of wicked people,
     the fate of those who care nothing for God.

Job

19 1-2 Why do you keep tormenting me with words?
     3 Time after time you insult me
       and show no shame for the way you abuse me.
  4 Even if I have done wrong,
    how does that hurt you?
  5 You think you are better than I am,
    and regard my troubles as proof of my guilt.
  6 Can't you see it is God who has done this?
    He has set a trap to catch me.

17.16 One ancient translation *with me*; Hebrew unclear.
18.15 *Now anyone may live in their tents*; Hebrew unclear.
18.15 *to disinfect them*: Sulphur was used in the ancient world as
a disinfectant and to clean rooms that had contained corpses.

7 I protest against his violence,
  but no one is listening;
  no one hears my cry for justice.
8 God has blocked the way, and I can't get through;
  he has hidden my path in darkness.
9 He has taken away all my wealth
  and destroyed my reputation.
10 He batters me from every side.
  He uproots my hope
  and leaves me to wither and die.
11 God is angry and rages against me;
  he treats me like his worst enemy.
12 He sends his army to attack me;
  they dig trenches and lay siege to my tent.

13 God has made my own family forsake me;
  I am a stranger to those who knew me;
14 my relatives and friends are gone.
15 Those who were guests in my house have forgotten me;
  my servant women treat me like a stranger and
    a foreigner.
16 When I call a servant, he doesn't answer —
  even when I beg him to help me.
17 My wife can't stand the smell of my breath,
  and my own brothers won't come near me.
18 Children despise me and laugh when they see me.
19 My closest friends look at me with disgust;
  those I loved most have turned against me.
20 My skin hangs loose on my bones;
  I have barely escaped with my life.*

21 You are my friends! Take pity on me!
  The hand of God has struck me down.
22 Why must you persecute me as God does?
  Haven't you tormented me enough?

23 How I wish that someone would remember my words
  and record them in a book!
24 Or with a chisel carve my words in stone
  and write them so that they would last for ever.*
25 But I know there is someone in heaven
  who will come at last to my defence.
26 Even after my skin is eaten by disease,
  while still in this body* I will see God.*
27 I will see him with my own eyes,
  and he will not be a stranger.

  My courage failed because you said,
28 "How can we torment him?"
  You looked for some excuse to attack me.
29 But now, be afraid of the sword —
  the sword that brings God's wrath on sin,
  so that you will know there is one who judges.*

19.20 Verse 20 in Hebrew is unclear.
19.24 last for ever; or be on record.
19.26 while still in this body; or although not in this body.
19.26 Verse 26 in Hebrew is unclear.
19.29 one who judges; or a judgement.

Zophar

20

¹⁻² Job, you upset me. Now I'm impatient to answer.
   ³ What you have said is an insult,
   but I know how to reply to you.

⁴ Surely you know that from ancient times,
   when human beings were first placed on earth,
⁵   no wicked people have been happy for long.
⁶ They may grow great, towering to the sky,
   so great that their heads reach the clouds,
⁷   but they will be blown away like dust.
Those who used to know them
   will wonder where they have gone.
⁸ They will vanish like a dream, like a vision at night,
   and never be seen again.
⁹ The wicked will disappear from the place where they used
   to live;
¹⁰   and their children will make good what they stole from
   the poor.
¹¹ Their bodies used to be young and vigorous,
   but soon they will turn to dust.

¹²⁻¹³ Evil tastes so good to them
   that they keep some in their mouths to enjoy its
   flavour.
¹⁴ But in their stomachs the food turns bitter,
   as bitter as any poison could be.
¹⁵ The wicked vomit up the wealth they stole;
   God takes it back, even out of their stomachs.
¹⁶ What evil people swallow is like poison;
   it kills them like the bite of a deadly snake.
¹⁷ They will not live to see rivers of olive oil*
   or streams that flow with milk and honey.
¹⁸ They will have to give up all they have worked for;
   they will have no chance to enjoy their wealth,
¹⁹   because they oppressed and neglected the poor
   and seized houses someone else had built.
²⁰ Their greed is never satisfied.
²¹ When they eat, there is nothing left over,
   but now their prosperity comes to an end.
²² At the height of their success
   all the weight of misery will crush them.
²³ Let them eat all they want!
   God will punish them in fury and anger.
²⁴ When they try to escape from an iron sword,
   a bronze bow will shoot them down.
²⁵ Arrows stick through their bodies;
   the shiny points drip with their blood,
   and terror grips their hearts.
²⁶ Everything they have saved is destroyed;
   a fire not lit by human hands
   burns them and all their families.
²⁷ Heaven reveals their sin,
   and the earth gives testimony against them.
²⁸ All their wealth will be destroyed
   in the flood of God's anger.

20.17 Probable text *They will... olive oil*; Hebrew unclear.

Job

Psalms
Proverbs
Eccles.
Songs
Isaiah

29 This is the fate of the wicked,
the fate that God assigns to them.

Job
21

1-2 Listen to what I am saying;
that is all the comfort I ask from you.
3 Give me a chance to speak and then,
when I am through, sneer if you like.

4 My quarrel is not with mortals;
I have good reason to be impatient.
5 Look at me. Isn't that enough
to make you stare in shocked silence?
6 When I think of what has happened to me,
I am stunned, and I tremble and shake.

7 Why does God let evil people live,
let them grow old and prosper?
8 They have children and grandchildren,
and live to watch them all grow up.
9 God does not bring disaster on their homes;
they never have to live in terror.
10 Yes, all their cattle breed
and give birth without trouble.
11 Their children run and play like lambs
12 and dance to the music of harps and flutes.
13 They live out their lives in peace
and quietly die without suffering.

14 The wicked tell God to leave them alone;
they don't want to know his will for their lives.
15 They think there is no need to serve God
nor any advantage in praying to him.
16 They claim they succeed by their own strength,
but their way of thinking I can't accept.

17 Was a wicked person's light ever put out?
Did one of them ever meet with disaster?
Did God ever punish the wicked in anger
18 and blow them away like straw in the wind,
or like dust carried away in a storm?

19 You claim God punishes a child for the sins of his father.
No! Let God punish the sinners themselves;
let him show that he does it because of *their* sins.
20 Let sinners bear their own punishment;
let them feel the wrath of Almighty God.
21 When our lives are over,
do we really care whether our children are happy?
22 Can anyone teach God,
who judges even those in high places?

23-24 Some people stay healthy till the day they die;
they die happy and at ease,
their bodies well nourished.
25 Others have no happiness at all;
they live and die with bitter hearts.

610

Job

1 Chron.
2 Chron.
Ezra
Nehem.
Esther

JOB 21, 22

²⁶ But all alike die and are buried;
    they all are covered with worms.

²⁷ I know what spiteful thoughts you have.
²⁸ You ask, "Where are the houses of great people now,
    those who practised evil?"
²⁹ Haven't you talked with people who travel?
    Don't you know the reports they bring back?
³⁰ On the day God is angry and punishes,
    it is the wicked who are always spared.
³¹ There is no one to accuse the wicked
    or pay them back for all they have done.
³² When they are carried to the graveyard,
    to their well-guarded tombs,
³³   thousands join the funeral procession,
    and even the earth lies gently on their bodies.

³⁴ And you! You try to comfort me with nonsense!
    Every answer you give is a lie!

The Third Dialogue
(22.1—27.23)

Eliphaz

22 ¹⁻² Is there anyone, even the wisest,
    who could ever be of use to God?
³ Does your doing right benefit God,
    or does your being good help him at all?
⁴ It is not because you stand in awe of God
    that he reprimands you and brings you to trial.
⁵ No, it's because you have sinned so much;
    it's because of all the evil you do.
⁶ To make your brother repay you the money he owed,
    you took away his clothes and left him nothing to
    wear.
⁷ You refused water to those who were tired,
    and refused to feed those who were hungry.
⁸ You used your power and your position
    to take over the whole land.
⁹ You not only refused to help widows,
    but you also robbed and ill-treated orphans.
¹⁰ So now there are pitfalls all round you,
    and suddenly you are full of fear.
¹¹ It has grown so dark that you cannot see,
    and a flood overwhelms you.

¹² Doesn't God live in the highest heavens
    and look down on the stars, even though they are high?
¹³ And yet you ask, "What does God know?
    He is hidden by clouds — how can he judge us?"
¹⁴ You think the thick clouds keep him from seeing,
    as he walks on the dome of the sky.

¹⁵ Are you determined to walk in the paths
    that evil people have always followed?
¹⁶ Even before their time had come,
    they were washed away by a flood.
¹⁷ These are the ones who rejected God
    and believed that he could do nothing to them.

611

Job

.........:

Psalms
Proverbs
Eccles.
Songs
Isaiah

¹⁸ And yet it was God who made them prosperous —
   I can't understand the thoughts of the wicked.
¹⁹ Good people are glad and the innocent laugh
   when they see the wicked punished.
²⁰ All that the wicked own is destroyed,
   and fire burns up anything that is left.

²¹ Now, Job, make peace with God
   and stop treating him like an enemy;
   if you do, then he will bless you.
²² Accept the teaching he gives;
   keep his words in your heart.
²³ Yes, you must humbly* return to God
   and put an end to all the evil
   that is done in your house.
²⁴ Throw away your gold;
   dump your finest gold in the dry stream bed.
²⁵ Let Almighty God be your gold,
   and let him be silver, piled high for you.
²⁶ Then you will always trust in God
   and find that he is the source of your joy.
²⁷ When you pray, he will answer you,
   and you will keep the vows you made.
²⁸ You will succeed in all you do,
   and light will shine on your path.
²⁹ God brings down the proud*
   and saves the humble.
³⁰ He will rescue you if you are innocent,*
   if what you do is right.*

Job

23 ¹⁻² I still rebel and complain against God;
   I can't hold back my groaning.
³ How I wish I knew where to find him,
   and knew how to go where he is.
⁴ I would state my case before him
   and present all the arguments in my favour.
⁵ I want to know what he would say
   and how he would answer me.
⁶ Would God use all his strength against me?
   No, he would listen as I spoke.
⁷ I am honest; I could reason with God;
   he would declare me innocent* once and for all.

⁸ I have searched in the east, but God is not there;
   I have not found him when I searched in the west.
⁹ God has been at work in the north and the south,
   but still I have not seen him.
¹⁰ Yet God knows every step I take;
   if he tests me, he will find me pure.
¹¹ I follow faithfully the road he chooses,
   and never wander to either side.

JOB 23.1-5

FIND A TISSUE

to represent sadness.
Write on it all of the
things that you are

STRUGGLING
– WITH –

at the moment and all of

THE QUESTIONS

that you have for God
in whatever situations
you are facing.
Pray about them.

22.23 One ancient translation *humbly*; Hebrew *be built up.*
22.29 Probable text *proud*; Hebrew unclear.
22.30 Some ancient translations *innocent*; Hebrew *not innocent.*
22.30 Verse 30 in Hebrew is unclear.
23.7 *he would declare me innocent*; or *then my rights would be safe.*

612

Job

1 Chron.
2 Chron.
Ezra
Nehem.
Esther

JOB 23, 24

¹² I always do what God commands;
  I follow his will, not my own desires.

¹³ He never changes. No one can oppose him
  or stop him from doing what he wants to do.
¹⁴ He will fulfil what he has planned for me;
  that plan is just one of the many he has;
¹⁵ I tremble with fear before him.
¹⁶⁻¹⁷ Almighty God has destroyed my courage.
  It is God, not the dark, that makes me afraid —
    even though the darkness has made me blind.

24 Why doesn't God set a time for judging,
  a day of justice for those who serve him?

² People move boundary stones to get more land;
  they steal sheep and put them with their own flocks.
³ They take donkeys that belong to orphans,
  and keep a widow's ox till she pays her debts.
⁴ They prevent the poor from getting their rights
  and force the needy to run and hide.

⁵ So the poor, like wild donkeys,
  search for food in the dry wilderness;
  nowhere else can they find food for their children.
⁶ They have to harvest fields they don't own,*
  and gather grapes in the vineyards of the wicked.
⁷ At night they sleep with nothing to cover them,
  nothing to keep them from the cold.
⁸ They are drenched by the rain that falls on the
    mountains,
  and they huddle beside the rocks for shelter.

⁹ Evil people make slaves of fatherless infants
  and take the children of the poor in payment for
    debts.
¹⁰ But the poor must go out with no clothes to protect
    them;
  they must go hungry while harvesting wheat.
¹¹ They press olives for oil, and grapes for wine,
  but they themselves are thirsty.
¹² In the cities the wounded and dying cry out,
  but God ignores their prayers.

¹³ There are those who reject the light;
  they don't understand it or go where it leads.
¹⁴ At dawn the murderer gets up
  and goes out to kill the poor,
  and at night he steals.
¹⁵ The adulterer waits for twilight to come;
  he covers his face so that no one can see him.
¹⁶ At night thieves break into houses,
  but by day they hide and avoid the light.
¹⁷ They fear the light of day,
  but darkness holds no terror for them.

....

24.6 *fields they don't own*: Having been cheated out of their own land, the
poor are forced to work for others for very small pay.

[Zophar]*
18 The wicked are swept away by floods,
and the land they own is under God's curse;
they no longer go to work in their vineyards.
19 As snow vanishes in heat and drought,
so sinners vanish from the land of the living.
20 Not even their mothers remember them now;
they are eaten by worms and destroyed like fallen trees.
21 That happens because they ill-treated widows
and showed no kindness to childless women.
22 God, in his strength, destroys the mighty;
God acts — and the wicked die.
23 God may let them live secure,
but keeps an eye on them all the time.
24 For a while the wicked prosper,
but then they wither like weeds,
like ears of corn that have been cut off.
25 Can anyone deny that this is so?
Can anyone prove that my words are not true?

Bildad
25 1-2 God is powerful; all must stand in awe of him;
he keeps his heavenly kingdom in peace.
3 Can anyone count the angels who serve him?
Is there any place where God's light does not shine?
4 Can anyone be righteous or pure in God's sight?
5 In his eyes even the moon is not bright,
nor the stars pure.
6 Then what about a human being, that worm, that insect?
What is a human life worth in God's eyes?

Job
26 1-2 What a fine help you are to me —
poor, weak man that I am!
3 You give such good advice
and share your knowledge with a fool like me!
4 Who do you think will hear all your words?
Who inspired you to speak like this?

[Bildad]*
5 The spirits of the dead tremble
in the waters under the earth.
6 The world of the dead lies open to God;
no covering shields it from his sight.
7 God stretched out the northern sky
and hung the earth in empty space.
8 It is God who fills the clouds with water
and keeps them from bursting with the weight.
9 He hides the full moon behind a cloud.
10 He divided light from darkness
by a circle drawn on the face of the sea.

KINGDOM

JOB 25.1-2;
MATTHEW 16.19

Search for the Oxford
or Cambridge Dictionary
definition of 'kingdom'
and write the
definition here.

_____
_____
_____
_____
_____
_____
_____
_____
_____
_____
_____
_____
_____
_____
_____
_____
_____
_____
_____

24.18 heading Zophar is not named in the text, but this speech is usually assigned to him.
26.5 heading Bildad is not named in the text, but this speech is usually assigned to him.

¹¹ When he threatens the pillars that hold up the sky,
they shake and tremble with fear.
¹² It is his strength that conquered the sea;*
by his skill he destroyed the monster Rahab.*
¹³ It is his breath that made the sky clear,
and his hand that killed the escaping monster.*
¹⁴ But these are only hints of his power,
only the whispers that we have heard.
Who can know how truly great God is?

Job

27 ¹⁻² I swear by the living Almighty God,
who refuses me justice and makes my life bitter —
³ as long as God gives me breath,
⁴ my lips will never say anything evil,
my tongue will never tell a lie.
⁵ I will never say that you men are right;
I will insist on my innocence to my dying day.
⁶ I will never give up my claim to be right;
my conscience is clear.

⁷ May all who oppose me and fight against me
be punished like the wicked and the unrighteous.
⁸ What hope is there for the godless
in the hour when God demands their life?
⁹ When trouble comes, will God hear their cries?
¹⁰ They should have desired the joy he gives;
they should have constantly prayed to him.

¹¹ Let me teach you how great is God's power,
and explain what Almighty God has planned.
¹² But no, after all, you have seen for yourselves;
so why do you talk such nonsense?

[Zophar]*
¹³ This is how Almighty God
punishes wicked, violent people.
¹⁴ They may have many sons,
but all will be killed in war;
their children never have enough to eat.
¹⁵ Those who survive will die from disease,
and even their widows will not mourn their death.
¹⁶ The wicked may have too much silver to count
and more clothes than anyone needs;
¹⁷ but some good person will wear the clothes,
and some honest person will get the silver.
¹⁸ The wicked build houses like a spider's web*
or like the hut of a slave guarding the fields.

26.12 *conquered the sea*: A reference to an ancient story in which the sea fought against God.
26.12 *Rahab*: See 9.13.
26.13 *escaping monster*: See 9.8.
27.13 heading *Zophar* is not named in the text, but this speech is usually assigned to him.
27.18 Some ancient translations *spider's web*; Hebrew *moth* or *bird's nest*.

JOB 27, 28

615

Job
....

Psalms
Proverbs
Eccles.
Songs
Isaiah

¹⁹ One last time* they will lie down rich,
   and when they wake up, they will find their wealth gone.
²⁰ Terror will strike like a sudden flood;
   a wind in the night will blow them away;
²¹   the east wind will sweep them from their homes;
²²   it will blow down on them without pity
   while they try their best to escape.
²³ The wind howls at them as they run,
   frightening them with destructive power.

In Praise of Wisdom*

28 There are mines where silver is dug;
   There are places where gold is refined.
² Miners dig iron out of the ground
   And melt copper out of the stones.
³ They explore the deepest darkness.
   They search the depths of the earth
   And dig for rocks in the darkness.
⁴ Far from where anyone lives
   Or human feet ever travel,
   They dig the shafts of mines.
   There they work in loneliness,
   Clinging to ropes in the pits.
⁵ Food grows out of the earth,
   But underneath the same earth
   All is torn up and crushed.
⁶ The stones of the earth contain sapphires,
   And its dust contains gold.
⁷ No hawk sees the roads to the mines,
   And no vulture ever flies over them.
⁸ No lion or other fierce beast
   Ever travels those lonely roads.

⁹ Miners dig the hardest rocks,
   Dig mountains away at their base.
¹⁰ As they tunnel through the rocks,
   They discover precious stones.
¹¹ They dig to the sources of* rivers
   And bring to light what is hidden.
¹² But where can wisdom be found?
   Where can we learn to understand?

¹³ Wisdom is not to be found among mortals;
   No one knows its true value.
¹⁴ The depths of the oceans and seas
   Say that wisdom is not found there.
¹⁵ It cannot be bought with silver or gold.
¹⁶ The finest gold and jewels
   Cannot equal its value.
¹⁷ It is worth more than gold,
   Than a gold vase or finest glass.
¹⁸ The value of wisdom is more
   Than coral or crystal or rubies.

....

27.19 Some ancient translations *One last time*; Hebrew *They will not be gathered.*
Ch. 28 heading The Hebrew text does not indicate who is speaking in this chapter.
28.11 Some ancient translations *dig to the sources of*; Hebrew *bind from trickling.*

Job

1 Chron.
2 Chron.
Ezra
Nehem.
Esther

DOODLE HERE...

19 The finest topaz and the purest gold
   Cannot compare with the value of wisdom.

20 Where, then, is the source of wisdom?
   Where can we learn to understand?
21 No living creature can see it,
   Not even a bird in flight.
22 Even death and destruction
   Admit they have heard only rumours.

23 God alone knows the way,
   Knows the place where wisdom is found,
24 Because he sees the ends of the earth,
   Sees everything under the sky.
25 When God gave the wind its power
   And determined the size of the sea;
26 When God decided where the rain would fall,
   And the path that the thunderclouds travel;
27 It was then he saw wisdom and tested its worth —
   He gave it his approval.

28 God said to human beings,
   "To be wise, you must have reverence for the Lord.
   To understand, you must turn from evil."

Job's Final Statement of his Case

29 Job began speaking again.

Job
2 If only my life could once again
   be as it was when God watched over me.
3 God was always with me then
   and gave me light as I walked through the darkness.
4 Those were the days when I was prosperous,
   and the friendship of God protected my home.
5 Almighty God was with me then,
   and I was surrounded by all my children.
6 My cows and goats gave plenty of milk,
   and my olive trees grew in the rockiest soil.
7 Whenever the city elders met
   and I took my place among them,
8   young men stepped aside as soon as they saw me,
   and old men stood up to show me respect.
9 The leaders of the people would stop talking;
10   even the most important men kept silent.

11 Everyone who saw me or heard of me
   had good things to say about what I had done.
12 When the poor cried out, I helped them;
   I gave help to orphans who had nowhere to turn.
13 Those who were in deepest misery praised me,
   and I helped widows find security.
14 I have always acted justly and fairly.
15 I was eyes for the blind,
   and feet for the lame.
16 I was like a father to the poor
   and took the side of strangers in trouble.
17 I destroyed the power of cruel men
   and rescued their victims.

18 I always expected to live a long life
  and to die at home in comfort.
19 I was like a tree whose roots always have water
  and whose branches are wet with dew.
20 Everyone was always praising me,
  and my strength never failed me.
21 When I gave advice, people were silent
  and listened carefully to what I said;
22   they had nothing to add when I had finished.
My words sank in like drops of rain;
23   everyone welcomed them
  just as farmers welcome rain in spring.
24 I smiled on them when they had lost confidence;
  my cheerful face encouraged them.
25 I took charge and made the decisions;
  I led them as a king leads his troops,
  and gave them comfort in their despair.

30 But men younger than I am make fun of me now!
  Their fathers have always been so worthless
  that I wouldn't let them help my dogs guard sheep.
2 They were a bunch of worn-out men,
  too weak to do any work for me.
3 They were so poor and hungry
  that they would gnaw dry roots —
  at night, in wild, desolate places.
4 They pulled up the plants of the desert and ate them,
  even the tasteless roots of the broom tree!
5 Everyone drove them away with shouts,
  as if they were shouting at thieves.
6 They had to live in caves,
  in holes dug in the sides of cliffs.
7 Out in the wilds they howled like animals
  and huddled together under the bushes.
8 A worthless bunch of nameless nobodies!
  They were driven out of the land.

9 Now they come and laugh at me;
  I am nothing but a joke to them.
10 They treat me with disgust;
  they think they are too good for me,
  and even come and spit in my face.
11 Because God has made me weak and helpless,
  they turn against me with all their fury.
12 This mob attacks me head-on;
  they send me running; they prepare their final assault.
13 They cut off my escape and try to destroy me;
  and there is no one to stop* them.
14 They pour through the holes in my defences
  and come crashing down on top of me;
15 I am overcome with terror;
  my dignity is gone like a puff of wind,
  and my prosperity like a cloud.

16 Now I am about to die;
  there is no relief for my suffering.

On a scale
FROM 1 TO 10,
how easy are you
finding it to read the
Bible currently?

Think of one way you
can go up a number on
the scale.

10
9 8
7
5 6
4
3 2
1

30.13 Probable text *stop*; Hebrew *help*.

618

Job

1 Chron.
2 Chron.
Ezra
Nehem.
Esther

JOB 30, 31

¹⁷ At night my bones all ache;
 the pain that gnaws me never stops.
¹⁸ God seizes me by my collar
 and twists my clothes out of shape.
¹⁹ He throws me down in the mud;
 I am no better than dirt.

²⁰ I call to you, O God, but you never answer;
 and when I pray, you pay no attention.
²¹ You are treating me cruelly;
 you persecute me with all your power.
²² You let the wind blow me away;
 you toss me about in a raging storm.
²³ I know you are taking me off to my death,
 to the fate in store for everyone.
²⁴ Why do you attack a ruined man,
 one who can do nothing but beg for pity?*
²⁵ Didn't I weep with people in trouble
 and feel sorry for those in need?
²⁶ I hoped for happiness and light,
 but trouble and darkness came instead.
²⁷ I am torn apart by worry and pain;
 I have had day after day of suffering.
²⁸ I go about in gloom, without any sunshine;
 I stand up in public and plead for help.
²⁹ My voice is as sad and lonely
 as the cries of a jackal or an ostrich.
³⁰ My skin has turned dark; I am burning with fever.
³¹ Where once I heard joyful music,
 now I hear only mourning and weeping.

31 I have made a solemn promise
 never to look with lust at a woman.

² What does Almighty God do to us?
 How does he repay human deeds?
³ He sends disaster and ruin
 to those who do wrong.
⁴ God knows everything I do;
 he sees every step I take.
⁵ I swear I have never acted wickedly
 and never tried to deceive others.
⁶ Let God weigh me on honest scales,
 and he will see how innocent I am.
⁷ If I have turned from the right path
 or let myself be attracted to evil,
 if my hands are stained with sin,
⁸ then let my crops be destroyed,
 or let others eat the food I grow.

⁹ If I have been attracted to my neighbour's wife,
 and waited, hidden, outside her door,
¹⁰ then let my wife cook another man's food
 and sleep in another man's bed.
¹¹ Such wickedness should be punished by death.
¹² It would be like a destructive, hellish fire,
 consuming everything I have.

30.24 Verse 24 in Hebrew is unclear.

JOB 31

619

Job

....

Psalms

Proverbs

Eccles.

Songs

Isaiah

13 When any of my servants complained against me,
   I would listen and treat them fairly.
14 If I did not, how could I then face God?
   What could I say when God came to judge me?
15 The same God who created me
   created my servants also.

16 I have never refused to help the poor;
   never have I let widows live in despair
17   or let orphans go hungry while I ate.
18 All my life I have taken care of them.*

19 When I found someone in need,
   too poor to buy clothes,
20   I would give him clothing made of wool
   that had come from my own flock of sheep.
   Then he would praise me with all his heart.

21 If I have ever cheated an orphan,
   knowing I could win in court,
22   then may my arms be broken;
   may they be torn from my shoulders.
23 Because I fear God's punishment,
   I could never do such a thing.

24 I have never trusted in riches
25   or taken pride in my wealth.
26 I have never worshipped the sun in its brightness
   or the moon in all its beauty.
27 I have not been led astray to honour them
   by kissing my hand in reverence to them.
28 Such a sin should be punished by death;
   it denies Almighty God.

29 I have never been glad when my enemies suffered,
   or pleased when they met with disaster;
30   I never sinned by praying for their death.
31 All those who work for me know
   that I have always welcomed strangers.
32 I invited travellers into my home
   and never let them sleep in the streets.

33 Others try to hide their sins,
   but I have never concealed mine.
34 I have never feared what people would say;
   I have never kept quiet or stayed indoors
   because I feared their scorn.

35 Will no one listen to what I am saying?
   I swear that every word is true.
   Let Almighty God answer me.

   If the charges my opponent brings against me
   were written down so that I could see them,
36 I would wear them proudly on my shoulder
   and place them on my head like a crown.

....

31.18 *All my life... them;* Hebrew unclear.

620

Job

1 Chron.
2 Chron.
Ezra
Nehem.
Esther

JOB 31, 32

37 I would tell God everything I have done,
and hold my head high in his presence.

38 If I have stolen the land I farm
and taken it from its rightful owners —
39 if I have eaten the food that grew there
but let the farmers that grew it starve —
40 then instead of wheat and barley,
may weeds and thistles grow.

The words of Job are ended.

Elihu's Speech
(32.1—37.24)

32 Because Job was convinced of his own innocence, the
three men gave up trying to answer him. 2 But a bystander
named Elihu could not control his anger any longer, because Job
was justifying himself and blaming God. (Elihu was the son of
Barakel, a descendant of Buz, and belonged to the clan of Ram.)
3 He was also angry with Job's three friends. They could find no
way to answer Job, and this made it appear that God was in the
wrong. 4 Because Elihu was the youngest one there, he had waited
until everyone finished speaking. 5 When he saw that the three
men could not answer Job, he was angry 6 and began to speak.

Elihu
I am young, and you are old,
so I was afraid to tell you what I think.
7 I told myself that you ought to speak,
that you older men should share your wisdom.
8 But it is the Spirit of Almighty God
that comes to human beings and gives them wisdom.
9 It is not growing old that makes people wise
or helps them to know what is right.
10 So now I want you to listen to me;
let me tell you what I think.

11 I listened patiently while you were speaking
and waited while you searched for wise phrases.
12 I paid close attention and heard you fail;
you have not disproved what Job has said.
13 How can you claim you have discovered wisdom?
God must answer Job, for you have failed.
14 Job was speaking to you, not to me,
but I would never answer as you did.

15 Words have failed them, Job;
they have no answer for you.
16 Shall I go on waiting when they are silent?
They stand there with nothing more to say.
17 No, I will give my own answer now
and tell you what I think.
18 I can hardly wait to speak.
I can't hold back the words.
19 If I don't get a chance to speak,
I will burst like a wineskin full of new wine.
20 I can't stand it; I have to speak.
21 I will not take sides in this debate;
I am not going to flatter anyone.

JOB 32

It was Job's youngest
friend who was the
most helpful and
spoke most wisely.

Get your

CLOSEST

FEW FRIENDS TOGETHER

and come up with some
helpful guidelines about
how you will speak to
each other and about
each other. (For example,
'We will never say
anything negative about
someone that we haven't
first said to their face
in private.')

JOB 32, 33

621

Job

Psalms
Proverbs
Eccles.
Songs
Isaiah

²² I don't know how to flatter,
  and God would quickly punish me if I did.

33

And now, Job, listen carefully
  to all that I have to say.
² I am ready to say what's on my mind.
³ All my words are sincere,
  and I am speaking the truth.
⁴ God's Spirit made me and gave me life.

⁵ Answer me if you can. Prepare your arguments.
⁶ You and I are the same in God's sight,
  both of us were formed from clay.
⁷ So you have no reason to fear me;
  I will not overpower you.

⁸ Now this is what I heard you say:
⁹ "I am not guilty; I have done nothing wrong.
  I am innocent and free from sin.
¹⁰ But God finds excuses for attacking me
  and treats me like an enemy.
¹¹ He binds chains on my feet;
  he watches every move I make."

¹² But I tell you, Job, you are wrong.
  God is greater than any human being.
¹³ Why do you accuse God
  of never answering our complaints?
¹⁴ Although God speaks again and again,
  no one pays attention to what he says.
¹⁵ At night when people are asleep,
  God speaks in dreams and visions.
¹⁶ He makes them listen to what he says,
  and they are frightened at his warnings.
¹⁷ God speaks to make them stop their sinning
  and to save them from becoming proud.
¹⁸ He will not let them be destroyed;
  he saves them from death itself.
¹⁹ God corrects people by sending sickness
  and filling their bodies with pain.
²⁰ Those who are sick lose their appetites,
  and even the finest food looks revolting.
²¹ Their bodies waste away to nothing;
  you can see all their bones;
²² they are about to go to the world of the dead.

²³ Perhaps an angel may come to their aid —
  one of God's thousands of angels,
  who remind us of our duty.
²⁴ In mercy the angel will say, "Release them!
  They are not to go down to the world of the dead.
  Here is the ransom to set them free."
²⁵ Their bodies will grow young and strong again;
²⁶ when they pray, God will answer;
  they will worship God with joy;
  God will set things right for them again.
²⁷ Each one will say in public, "I have sinned.
  I have not done right, but God spared me.

28 He kept me from going to the world of the dead,
and I am still alive."

29 God does all this again and again;
30   he saves a person's life,
and gives him the joy of living.

31 Now, Job, listen to what I am saying;
be quiet and let me speak.
32 But if you have something to say, let me hear it;
I would gladly admit you are in the right.
33 But if not, be quiet and listen to me,
and I will teach you how to be wise.

34

1-2 You men are so wise, so clever;
listen now to what I am saying.
3 You know good food when you taste it,
but not wise words when you hear them.
4 It is up to us to decide the case.
5 Job claims that he is innocent,
that God refuses to give him justice.
6 He asks, "How could I lie and say I am wrong?
I am fatally wounded, but I am sinless."

7 Have you ever seen anyone like this man Job?
He never shows respect for God.
8 He likes the company of evil people
and goes about with sinners.
9 He says that it never does any good
to try to follow God's will.

10 Listen to me, you men who understand!
Will Almighty God do what is wrong?
11 He rewards people for what they do
and treats them as they deserve.
12 Almighty God does not do evil;
he is never unjust to anyone.
13 Did God get his power from someone else?
Did someone put him in charge of the world?
14 If God took back the breath of life,
15   then everyone living would die
and turn into dust again.

16 Now listen to me, if you are wise.
17 Are you condemning the righteous God?
Do you think that *he* hates justice?
18 God condemns kings and rulers
when they are worthless or wicked.
19 He does not take the side of rulers
nor favour the rich against the poor,
for he created everyone.
20 Someone may suddenly die at night.
God strikes people down and they perish;
he kills the mighty with no effort at all.
21 He watches every step we take.
22 There is no darkness dark enough
to hide a sinner from God.

JOB 34, 35

623

Job

Psalms
Proverbs
Eccles.
Songs
Isaiah

23 God does not need to set a time*
   for us to go and be judged by him.
24 He does not need an investigation
   to remove leaders and replace them with others.
25 Because he knows what they do
   he overthrows them and crushes them by night.
26 He punishes sinners where all can see it,
27   because they have stopped following him
   and ignored all his commands.
28 They forced the poor to cry out to God,
   and he heard their calls for help.

29 If God decided to do nothing at all,
   no one could criticize him.
   If he hid his face, we would be helpless.
30 There would be nothing that nations could do
   to keep godless oppressors from ruling them.

31 Job, have you confessed your sins to God
   and promised not to sin again?
32 Have you asked God to show you your faults,
   and have you agreed to stop doing evil?
33 Since you object to what God does,
   can you expect him to do what you want?
   The decision is yours, not mine;
   tell us now what you think.

34 Any sensible person will surely agree;
   and the wise who hear me will say
35   that Job is speaking from ignorance
   and that nothing he says makes sense.
36 Think through everything that Job says;
   you will see that he talks like an evil man.
37 To his sins he adds rebellion;
   in front of us all he mocks God.

35 1-2 It is not right, Job, for you to say
   that you are innocent in God's sight,
3 or to ask God, "How does my sin affect you?
   What have I gained by not sinning?"
4 I am going to answer you and your friends too.

5 Look at the sky! See how high the clouds are!
6 If you sin, that does no harm to God.
   If you do wrong many times, does that affect him?
7 Do you help God by being so righteous?
   There is nothing God needs from you.
8 Others suffer from your sins,
   and the good you do helps them.

9 When people are oppressed, they groan;
   they cry for someone to save them.
10 But they don't turn to God, their Creator,
   who gives them hope in their darkest hours.
11 They don't turn to God, who makes us wise,
   wiser than any animal or bird.

DECORATE
(THESE) SHAPES
IN RELATION TO
YOUR MOOD.

624

Job

1 Chron.
2 Chron.
Ezra
Nehem.
Esther

JOB 35, 36

12 They cry for help, but God doesn't answer,
   for they are proud and evil.
13 It is useless for them to cry out;
   Almighty God does not see or hear them.

14 Job, you say you can't see God;
   but wait patiently — your case is before him.
15 You think that God does not punish,
   that he pays little attention to sin.
16 It is useless for you to go on talking;
   it is clear you don't know what you are saying.

36

1-2 Be patient and listen a little longer
   to what I am saying on God's behalf.
3 My knowledge is wide; I will use what I know
   to show that God, my Creator, is just.
4 Nothing I say to you is false;
   you see before you a truly wise man.

5 How strong God is! He despises no one;
   there is nothing he doesn't understand.
6 He does not let sinners live on,
   and he always treats the poor with justice.
7 He protects those who are righteous;
   he allows them to rule like kings
   and lets them be honoured for ever.
8 But if people are bound in chains,
   suffering for what they have done,
9   God shows them their sins and their pride.
10 He makes them listen to his warning
   to turn away from evil.
11 If they obey God and serve him,
   they live out their lives in peace and prosperity.
12 But if not, they will die in ignorance
   and cross the stream into the world of the dead.

13 Those who are godless keep on being angry,
   and even when punished, they don't pray for help.
14 They die while they are still young,
   worn out by a life of disgrace.
15 But God teaches people through suffering
   and uses distress to open their eyes.

16 God brought you out of trouble,
   and let you enjoy security;
   your table was piled high with food.
17 But now you are being punished as you deserve.
18 Be careful not to let bribes deceive you,
   or riches lead you astray.
19 It will do you no good to cry out for help;
   all your strength can't help you now.
20 Don't wish for night to come,
   the time when nations will perish.
21 Be careful not to turn to evil;
   your suffering was sent to keep you from it.

22 Remember how great is God's power;
   he is the greatest teacher of all.

Job

Psalms
Proverbs
Eccles.
Songs
Isaiah

²³ No one can tell God what to do
    or accuse him of doing evil.
²⁴ He has always been praised for what he does;
    you also must praise him.
²⁵ Everyone has seen what he has done;
    but we can only watch from a distance.*
²⁶ We cannot fully know his greatness
    or count the number of his years.

²⁷ It is God who takes water from the earth
    and turns it into drops of rain.
²⁸ He lets the rain pour from the clouds
    in showers for the whole human race.
²⁹ No one knows how the clouds move
    or how the thunder roars
    through the sky, where God dwells.
³⁰ He sends lightning through all the sky,
    but the depths of the sea remain dark.
³¹ This is how he feeds* the people
    and provides an abundance of food.
³² He seizes the lightning with his hands
    and commands it to hit the mark.
³³ Thunder announces the approaching storm,
    and the cattle know it is coming.

37

The storm makes my heart beat wildly.
² Listen, all of you, to the voice of God,
    to the thunder that comes from his mouth.
³ He sends the lightning across the sky,
    from one end of the earth to the other.
⁴ Then the roar of his voice is heard,
    the majestic sound of thunder,
    and all the while the lightning flashes.
⁵ At God's command amazing things happen,
    wonderful things that we can't understand.
⁶ He commands snow to fall on the earth,
    and sends torrents of drenching rain.
⁷ He brings our work to a stop;
    he shows us what he can do.*
⁸ The wild animals go to their dens.
⁹ The storm winds come from the south,
    and the biting cold from the north.
¹⁰ The breath of God freezes the waters,
    and turns them to solid ice.
¹¹ Lightning flashes from the clouds,*
¹²   as they move at God's will.
    They do all that God commands,
    everywhere throughout the world.
¹³ God sends rain to water the earth;
    he may send it to punish us,
    or to show us his favour.

¹⁴ Pause a moment, Job, and listen;
    consider the wonderful things God does.

....

36.25 *but we can only watch from a distance*; or *no one understands it all.*
36.31 Probable text *feeds*; Hebrew *judges.*
37.7 One ancient translation *them what he can do*; Hebrew *this to those whom he has made.*
37.11 Verse 11 in Hebrew is unclear.

626

Job

1 Chron.
2 Chron.
Ezra
Nehem.
Esther

JOB 37, 38

¹⁵ Do you know how God gives the command
    and makes lightning flash from the clouds?
¹⁶ Do you know how clouds float in the sky,
    the work of God's amazing skill?
¹⁷ No, you can only suffer in the heat
    when the south wind oppresses the land.
¹⁸ Can you help God stretch out the sky
    and make it as hard as polished metal?
¹⁹ Teach us what to say to God;
    our minds are blank; we have nothing to say.
²⁰ I won't ask to speak with God;
    why should I give him a chance to destroy me?

²¹ And now the light in the sky is dazzling,
    too bright for us to look at it;
    and the sky has been swept clean by the wind.
²² A golden glow is seen in the north,
    and the glory of God fills us with awe.
²³ God's power is so great that we cannot come near him;
    he is righteous and just in his dealings with us.
²⁴ No wonder, then, that everyone stands in awe of him,
    and that he ignores those who claim to be wise.

The Lord Answers Job

38 Then out of the storm the Lord spoke to Job.

The Lord
² Who are you to question my wisdom
    with your ignorant, empty words?
³ Now stand up straight
    and answer the questions I ask you.
⁴ Were you there when I made the world?
    If you know so much, tell me about it.
⁵ Who decided how large it would be?
    Who stretched the measuring line over it?
    Do you know all the answers?
⁶ What holds up the pillars that support the earth?
    Who laid the cornerstone of the world?
⁷ In the dawn of that day the stars sang together,
    and the heavenly beings* shouted for joy.
⁸ Who closed the gates to hold back the sea*
    when it burst from the womb of the earth?
⁹ It was I who covered the sea with clouds
    and wrapped it in darkness.
¹⁰ I marked a boundary for the sea
    and kept it behind bolted gates.
¹¹ I told it, "So far and no farther!
    Here your powerful waves must stop."
¹² Job, have you ever in all your life
    commanded a day to dawn?
¹³ Have you ordered the dawn to seize the earth
    and shake the wicked from their hiding places?
¹⁴ Daylight makes the hills and valleys stand out
    like the folds of a garment,
    clear as the imprint of a seal on clay.

JOB 38-39

Read chapters 38-39
and, on this page,

RECREATE

- THE -

IMAGES

that you find most striking.

38.7 *heavenly beings*: See 1.6.
38.8 *to hold back the sea*: See 26.12.

627

Job

....

Psalms
Proverbs
Eccles.
Songs
Isaiah

15 The light of day is too bright for the wicked
   and restrains them from deeds of violence.

16 Have you been to the springs in the depths of the sea?
   Have you walked on the floor of the ocean?
17 Has anyone ever shown you the gates
   that guard the dark world of the dead?
18 Have you any idea how big the world is?
   Answer me if you know.

19 Do you know where the light comes from
   or what the source of darkness is?
20 Can you show them how far to go,
   or send them back again?
21 I am sure you can, because you're so old
   and were there when the world was made!

22 Have you ever visited the storerooms,
   where I keep the snow and the hail?
23 I keep them ready for times of trouble,
   for days of battle and war.
24 Have you been to the place where the sun comes up,
   or the place from which the east wind blows?

25 Who dug a channel for the pouring rain
   and cleared the way for the thunderstorm?
26 Who makes rain fall where no one lives?
27 Who waters the dry and thirsty land,
   so that grass springs up?
28 Does either the rain or the dew have a father?
29 Who is the mother of the ice and the frost,
30   which turn the waters to stone
   and freeze the face of the sea?

31 Can you tie the Pleiades together
   or loosen the bonds that hold Orion?
32 Can you guide the stars season by season
   and direct the Great and the Little Bear?
33 Do you know the laws that govern the skies,
   and can you make them apply to the earth?

34 Can you shout orders to the clouds
   and make them drench you with rain?
35 And if you command the lightning to flash,
   will it come to you and say, "At your service"?
36 Who tells the ibis* when the Nile will flood,
   or who tells the cock that rain will fall?*
37 Who is wise enough to count the clouds
   and tilt them over to pour out the rain,
38   rain that hardens the dust into lumps?

39 Do you find food for lions to eat,
   and satisfy hungry young lions
40   when they hide in their caves,
   or lie in wait in their dens?

....

38.36 *ibis*: A bird in ancient Egypt that was believed to announce the
flooding of the River Nile.
38.36 Verse 36 in Hebrew is unclear.

628

Job

·:········

1 Chron.
2 Chron.
Ezra
Nehem.
Esther

JOB 38, 39

41 Who is it that feeds the ravens
    when they wander about hungry,
    when their young cry to me for food?

39 Do you know when mountain goats are born?
    Have you watched wild deer give birth?
2 Do you know how long they carry their young?
    Do you know the time for their birth?
3 Do you know when they will crouch down
    and bring their young into the world?
4 In the wilds their young grow strong;
    they go away and don't come back.

5 Who gave the wild donkeys their freedom?
    Who turned them loose and let them roam?
6 I gave them the desert to be their home,
    and let them live on the salt plains.
7 They keep far away from the noisy cities,
    and no one can tame them and make them work.
8 The mountains are the pastures where they feed,
    where they search for anything green to eat.

9 Will a wild ox work for you?
    Is he willing to spend the night in your stable?
10 Can you hold one with a rope and make him plough?
    Or make him pull a harrow in your fields?
11 Can you rely on his great strength
    and expect him to do your heavy work?
12 Do you expect him to bring in your harvest
    and gather the grain from your threshing place?

13 How fast the wings of an ostrich beat!
    But no ostrich can fly like a stork.*
14 The ostrich leaves her eggs on the ground
    for the heat in the soil to warm them.
15 She is unaware that a foot may crush them
    or a wild animal break them.
16 She acts as if the eggs were not hers,
    and is unconcerned that her efforts were wasted.
17 It was I who made her foolish
    and did not give her wisdom.
18 But when she begins to run,*
    she can laugh at any horse and rider.

19 Was it you, Job, who made horses so strong
    and gave them their flowing manes?
20 Did you make them leap like locusts
    and frighten people with their snorting?
21 They eagerly paw the ground in the valley;
    they rush into battle with all their strength.
22 They do not know the meaning of fear,
    and no sword can turn them back.
23 The weapons which their riders carry
    rattle and flash in the sun.
24 Trembling with excitement, the horses race ahead;
    when the trumpet blows, they can't stand still.

....

39.13 Verse 13 in Hebrew is unclear.
39.18 Probable text *run*; Hebrew unclear.

629

Job
....

Psalms
Proverbs
Eccles.
Songs
Isaiah

25 At each blast of the trumpet they snort;
    they can smell a battle before they get near,
    and they hear the officers shouting commands.

26 Does a hawk learn from you how to fly
    when it spreads its wings towards the south?
27 Does an eagle wait for your command
    to build its nest high in the mountains?
28 It makes its home on the highest rocks
    and makes the sharp peaks its fortress.
29 From there it watches near and far
    for something to kill and eat.
30 Around dead bodies the eagles gather,
    and the young eagles drink the blood.

40

1-2 Job, you challenged Almighty God;
    will you give up now, or will you answer?

Job

3-4 I spoke foolishly, LORD. What can I answer?
    I will not try to say anything else.
 5 I have already said more than I should.

6 Then out of the storm the LORD spoke to Job once again.

The LORD

 7 Stand up straight now,
    and answer my questions.
 8 Are you trying to prove that I am unjust —
    to put me in the wrong and yourself in the right?
 9 Are you as strong as I am?
    Can your voice thunder as loud as mine?
10 If so, stand up in your honour and pride;
    clothe yourself with majesty and glory.
11 Look at those who are proud;
    pour out your anger and humble them.
12 Yes, look at them and bring them down;
    crush the wicked where they stand.
13 Bury them all in the ground;
    bind them in the world of the dead.
14 Then I will be the first to praise you
    and admit that you won the victory yourself.

15 Look at the monster Behemoth;*
    I created him and I created you.
    He eats grass like a cow,
16   but what strength there is in his body,
    and what power there is in his muscles!
17 His tail stands up like a cedar,
    and the muscles in his legs are strong.
18 His bones are as strong as bronze,
    and his legs are like iron bars.

19 The most amazing of all my creatures!
    Only his Creator can defeat him.

40.15 Behemoth: Some identify this with the hippopotamus, others with
a legendary creature.

630

Job

1 Chron.
2 Chron.
Ezra
Nehem.
Esther

JOB 40, 41

²⁰ Grass to feed him grows
    on the hills where wild beasts play.*
²¹ He lies down under the thorn bushes,
    and hides among the reeds in the swamp.
²² The thorn bushes and the willows by the stream
    give him shelter in their shade.
²³ He is not afraid of a rushing river;
    he is calm when the Jordan dashes in his face.
²⁴ Who can blind his eyes and capture him?
    Or who can catch his snout in a trap?

41 Can you catch Leviathan* with a fish-hook
    or tie his tongue down with a rope?
² Can you put a rope through his snout
    or put a hook through his jaws?
³ Will he beg you to let him go?
    Will he plead with you for mercy?
⁴ Will he make an agreement with you
    and promise to serve you for ever?
⁵ Will you tie him up like a pet bird,
    like something to amuse your servant women?
⁶ Will fishermen bargain over him?
    Will merchants cut him up to sell?
⁷ Can you fill his hide with fishing spears
    or pierce his head with a harpoon?
⁸ Touch him once and you'll never try it again;
    you'll never forget the fight!

⁹ Anyone who sees Leviathan
    loses courage and falls to the ground.
¹⁰ When he is aroused, he is fierce;
    no one would dare to stand before him.
¹¹ Who can attack him and still be safe?
    No one in all the world can do it.*

¹² Let me tell you about Leviathan's legs
    and describe how great and strong he is.
¹³ No one can tear off his outer coat
    or pierce the armour* he wears.
¹⁴ Who can make him open his jaws,
    ringed with those terrifying teeth?
¹⁵ His back* is made of rows of shields,
    fastened together and hard as stone.
¹⁶ Each one is joined so tight to the next,
    not even a breath can come between.
¹⁷ They all are fastened so firmly together
    that nothing can ever pull them apart.
¹⁸ Light flashes when he sneezes,
    and his eyes glow like the rising sun.
¹⁹ Flames blaze from his mouth,
    and streams of sparks fly out.
²⁰ Smoke comes pouring out of his nose,
    like smoke from weeds burning under a pot.

40.20 Verse 20 in Hebrew is unclear.
41.1 *Leviathan*: See 3.8.
41.11 Verse 11 in Hebrew is unclear.
41.13 One ancient translation *armour*; Hebrew *bridle*.
41.15 Some ancient translations *back*; Hebrew *pride*.

631

Job

....

Psalms
Proverbs
Eccles.
Songs
Isaiah

21 His breath starts fires burning;
  flames leap out of his mouth.
22 His neck is so powerful
  that all who meet him are terrified.
23 There is not a weak spot in his skin;
  it is as hard and unyielding as iron.
24 His stony heart is without fear,
  as unyielding and hard as a millstone.
25 When he rises up, even the strongest* are frightened;
  they are helpless with fear.
26 There is no sword that can wound him;
  no spear or arrow or lance that can harm him.
27 For him iron is as flimsy as straw,
  and bronze as soft as rotten wood.
28 There is no arrow that can make him run;
  rocks thrown at him are like bits of straw.
29 To him a club is a piece of straw,
  and he laughs when men throw spears.
30 The scales on his belly are like jagged pieces of pottery;
  they tear up the muddy ground like a threshing-sledge.*
31 He churns up the sea like boiling water
  and makes it bubble like a pot of oil.
32 He leaves a shining path behind him
  and turns the sea to white foam.
33 There is nothing on earth to compare with him;
  he is a creature that has no fear.
34 He looks down on even the proudest animals;
  he is king of all wild beasts.

42

Then Job answered the LORD.

Job

2 I know, LORD, that you are all-powerful;
  that you can do everything you want.
3 You ask how I dare question your wisdom
  when I am so very ignorant.
  I talked about things I did not understand,
  about marvels too great for me to know.
4 You told me to listen while you spoke
  and to try to answer your questions.
5 In the past I knew only what others had told me,
  but now I have seen you with my own eyes.
6 So I am ashamed of all I have said
  and repent in dust and ashes.

Conclusion

7 After the LORD had finished speaking to Job, he said to Eliphaz, "I am angry with you and your two friends, because you did not speak the truth about me, as my servant Job did. 8 Now take seven bulls and seven rams to Job and offer them as a sacrifice for yourselves. Job will pray for you, and I will answer his prayer and not disgrace you as you deserve. You did not speak the truth about me as he did."

9 Eliphaz, Bildad, and Zophar did what the LORD had told them to do, and the LORD answered Job's prayer.

41.25 *strongest*; or *gods*.
41.30 *threshing-sledge*(s): These had sharp pieces of iron or stone fastened beneath them.

Fill in the blank:

GOD IS

¹⁰Then, after Job had prayed for his three friends, the LORD made him prosperous again and gave him twice as much as he had had before. ¹¹All Job's brothers and sisters and former friends came to visit him and feasted with him in his house. They expressed their sympathy and comforted him for all the troubles the LORD had brought on him. Each of them gave him some money and a gold ring.

¹²The LORD blessed the last part of Job's life even more than he had blessed the first. Job owned 14,000 sheep, 6,000 camels, 2,000 head of cattle, and 1,000 donkeys. ¹³He was the father of seven sons and three daughters. ¹⁴He called the eldest daughter Jemimah, the second Keziah, and the youngest Keren Happuch.* ¹⁵There were no other women in the whole world as beautiful as Job's daughters. Their father gave them a share of the inheritance along with their brothers.

¹⁶Job lived 140 years after this, long enough to see his grandchildren and great-grandchildren. ¹⁷And then he died at a very great age.

42.14 In Hebrew the names of Job's daughters suggest beauty both by their sound and by their meaning. *Jemimah* means "dove"; *Keziah* means "cassia", a variety of cinnamon used as a perfume; and *Keren Happuch* means a small box used for eye make-up.

THE BOOK OF

PSALMS

WRITTEN: OVER A VERY LONG TIME PERIOD
- ALMOST THE WHOLE OF OLD TESTAMENT HISTORY

We can read all about the events in King David's life in 1 and 2 Samuel, 1 Kings and 1 Chronicles, but some of the Psalms give us an insight to how he felt during those times. Write down all of the emotions you find as you read through the Psalms he wrote.

_____
_____
_____
_____
_____
_____
_____

WHAT YOU NEED TO KNOW:

Psalms is a big book of poems and songs about God and to God. They cover every situation - joy and celebration, war and facing enemies, exploring our purpose and identity, and appreciating nature. There are passages of thankfulness, praise and worship to God, as well as cries for help. The people who wrote the Psalms were honest about their emotions and weren't afraid to write it all down. When reading the Psalms, bear in mind that they were meant to be sung and not read: it's a bit like sitting and reading the lyrics to your favourite songs.

WHY READ IT?

Psalms shows us that we can bring all of our emotions and situations to God. We can talk to God however we are feeling - angry, upset, confused, fearful, happy or excited - and even if we are feeling one of these emotions because of him. The Psalms also show us that whether we feel near to God or far from him, he hears us and wants us to talk to him.

THE PSALMS DISPLAY EVERY KIND OF HUMAN EMOTION, FROM JOY TO SADNESS, AND FEAR TO THANKFULNESS. EVERY TIME YOU TURN TO THIS PAGE, DRAW A FACE ON A CIRCLE AND PRAY TO GOD ABOUT HOW YOU'RE FEELING.

THE PSALMS WERE WRITTEN BY LOTS OF PEOPLE AND COVER A LONG TIMESPAN – BETWEEN 1400 AND 586BC!

Book One
Psalms 1—41

True Happiness

1 ¹ Happy are those
   who reject the advice of evil people,
   who do not follow the example of sinners
   or join those who have no use for God.
² Instead, they find joy in obeying the Law of the LORD,
   and they study it day and night.
³ They are like trees that grow beside a stream,
   that bear fruit at the right time,
   and whose leaves do not dry up.
   They succeed in everything they do.

⁴ But evil people are not like this at all;
   they are like straw that the wind blows away.
⁵ Sinners will be condemned by God
   and kept apart from God's own people.
⁶ The righteous are guided and protected by the LORD,
   but the evil are on the way to their doom.

God's Chosen King

2 ¹ Why do the nations plan rebellion?
   Why do people make their useless plots?
² Their kings revolt,
   their rulers plot together against the LORD
   and against the king he chose.
³ "Let us free ourselves from their rule," they say;
   "let us throw off their control."

⁴ From his throne in heaven the Lord laughs
   and mocks their feeble plans.
⁵ Then he warns them in anger
   and terrifies them with his fury.
⁶ "On Zion, my sacred hill," he says,
   "I have installed my king."

⁷ "I will announce," says the king, "what the LORD has
      declared.
   He said to me: 'You are my son;
   today I have become your father.
⁸ Ask, and I will give you all the nations;
   the whole earth will be yours.
⁹ You will break them with an iron rod;
   you will shatter them in pieces like a clay pot.'"

¹⁰ Now listen to this warning, you kings;
   learn this lesson, you rulers of the world:
¹¹ Serve the LORD with fear;
¹²   tremble and bow down to him;*
   or else his anger will be quickly aroused,
   and you will suddenly die.
   Happy are all who go to him for protection.

2.12 Probable text *tremble… him*; some other possible texts *with trembling kiss his feet* and *with trembling kiss the Son* and *tremble and kiss the mighty one*; Hebrew unclear.

PSALMS 3, 4

635

Psalms

Proverbs
Eccles.
Songs
Isaiah
Jerem.

Morning Prayer for Help*

3 ¹I have so many enemies, LORD,
so many who turn against me!
² They talk about me and say,
"God will not help him."

³ But you, O LORD, are always my shield from danger;
you give me victory
and restore my courage.
⁴ I call to the LORD for help,
and from his sacred hill* he answers me.

⁵ I lie down and sleep,
and all night long the LORD protects me.
⁶ I am not afraid of the thousands of enemies
who surround me on every side.

⁷ Come, LORD! Save me, my God!
You punish all my enemies
and leave them powerless to harm me.
⁸ Victory comes from the LORD —
may he bless his people.

Evening Prayer for Help*

4 ¹Answer me when I pray,
O God, my defender!
When I was in trouble, you helped me.
Be kind to me now and hear my prayer.

² How long will you people insult me?
How long will you love what is worthless
and go after what is false?

³ Remember that the LORD has chosen the righteous for his
own,
and he hears me when I call to him.

⁴ Tremble with fear and stop sinning;
think deeply about this,
when you lie in silence on your beds.
⁵ Offer the right sacrifices to the LORD,
and put your trust in him.

⁶ There are many who pray:
"Give us more blessings, O LORD.
Look on us with kindness!"
⁷ But the joy that you have given me
is more than they will ever have
with all their corn and wine.

⁸ When I lie down, I go to sleep in peace;
you alone, O LORD, keep me perfectly safe.

PSALM 3

A number of the psalms that David wrote talk about wicked people and enemies. For example, this psalm was written after David ran away from his own son, Absalom, who was trying to violently

• TAKE THE •

THRONE

from him. (Read more about it in 2 Samuel 15-19.) David addresses the fact that there is evil in the world but also acknowledges God's place in it all. Underline any bits where David talks about God; what do they show you?

Ps 3 *Hebrew title*: A psalm by David, after he ran away from his son
Absalom.
3.4 *sacred hill*: See 2.6.
Ps 4 *Hebrew title*: A psalm by David.

636

Psalms

·:·········

2 Chron.
Ezra
Nehem.
Esther
Job

PSALMS 5, 6

A Prayer for Protection*

5 ¹Listen to my words, O LORD,
and hear my sighs.
² Listen to my cry for help,
my God and king!

I pray to you, O LORD;
³ you hear my voice in the morning;
at sunrise I offer my prayer*
and wait for your answer.

⁴ You are not a God who is pleased with wrongdoing;
you allow no evil in your presence.
⁵ You cannot stand the sight of the proud;
you hate all wicked people.
⁶ You destroy all liars
and despise violent, deceitful people.

⁷ But because of your great love
I can come into your house;
I can worship in your holy Temple
and bow down to you in reverence.
⁸ LORD, I have so many enemies!
Lead me to do your will;
make your way plain for me to follow.

⁹ What my enemies say can never be trusted;
they only want to destroy.
Their words are flattering and smooth,
but full of deadly deceit.
¹⁰ Condemn and punish them, O God;
may their own plots cause their ruin.
Drive them out of your presence
because of their many sins
and their rebellion against you.

¹¹ But all who find safety in you will rejoice;
they can always sing for joy.
Protect those who love you;
because of you they are truly happy.
¹² You bless those who obey you, LORD;
your love protects them like a shield.

A Prayer for Help in Time of Trouble*

6 ¹LORD, don't be angry and rebuke me!
Don't punish me in your anger!
² I am worn out, O LORD; have pity on me!
Give me strength; I am completely exhausted
³ and my whole being is deeply troubled.
How long, O LORD, will you wait to help me?

⁴ Come and save me, LORD;
in your mercy rescue me from death.
⁵ In the world of the dead you are not remembered;
no one can praise you there.

Ps 5; Ps 6 *Hebrew title:* A psalm by David.
5.3 *prayer;* or *sacrifice.*

PSALMS 6, 7

637

Psalms

Proverbs
Eccles.
Songs
Isaiah
Jerem.

6 I am worn out with grief;
 every night my bed is damp from my weeping;
 my pillow is soaked with tears.
7 I can hardly see;
 my eyes are so swollen
 from the weeping caused by my enemies.

8 Keep away from me, you evil people!
 The LORD hears my weeping;
9 he listens to my cry for help
 and will answer my prayer.
10 My enemies will know the bitter shame of defeat;
 in sudden confusion they will be driven away.

A Prayer for Justice*

7 1 O LORD, my God, I come to you for protection;
 rescue me and save me from all who pursue me,
2 or else like a lion they will carry me off
 where no one can save me,
 and there they will tear me to pieces.

3-4 O LORD, my God, if I have wronged anyone,
 if I have betrayed a friend
 or without cause done violence to my enemy* —
 if I have done any of these things —
5 then let my enemies pursue me and catch me,
 let them cut me down and kill me
 and leave me lifeless on the ground!

6 Rise in your anger, O LORD!
 Stand up against the fury of my enemies;
 rouse yourself and help me!
 Justice is what you demand,
7 so bring together all the peoples round you,
 and rule over them from above.*
8 You are the judge of the whole human race.
 Judge in my favour, O LORD;
 you know that I am innocent.
9 You are a righteous God
 and judge our thoughts and desires.
 Stop the wickedness of evildoers
 and reward those who are good.

10 God is my protector;
 he saves those who obey him.
11 God is a righteous judge
 and always condemns the wicked.
12 If they do not change their ways,
 God will sharpen his sword.
 He bends his bow and makes it ready;
13 he takes up his deadly weapons
 and aims his burning arrows.

Ps 7 *Hebrew title*: A song which David sang to the LORD because of Cush the Benjaminite.
7.3–4 *without… enemy*; or *shown mercy to someone who wronged me unjustly*.
7.7 Probable text *rule over them from above*; Hebrew *return above over them*.

638

Psalms

---

2 Chron.
Ezra
Nehem.
Esther
Job

PSALMS 7–9

14 See how wicked people think up evil;
	they plan trouble and practise deception.
15 But in the traps they set for others,
	they themselves get caught.
16 So they are punished by their own evil
	and are hurt by their own violence.

17 I thank the LORD for his justice,
	I sing praises to the LORD, the Most High.

God's Glory and Human Dignity*

8 ¹O LORD, our Lord,
	your greatness is seen in all the world!
Your praise reaches up to the heavens;
2	it is sung by children and babies.
You are safe and secure from all your enemies;
	you stop anyone who opposes you.

3 When I look at the sky, which you have made,
	at the moon and the stars, which you set in their places
		—
4 what are human beings, that you think of them;
	mere mortals, that you care for them?

5 Yet you made them inferior only to yourself;*
	you crowned them with glory and honour.
6 You appointed them rulers over everything you made;
	you placed them over all creation:
7	sheep and cattle, and the wild animals too;
8	the birds and the fish
	and the creatures in the seas.

9 O LORD, our Lord,
	your greatness is seen in all the world!

Thanksgiving to God for his Justice*

9 ¹I will praise you, LORD, with all my heart;
	I will tell of all the wonderful things you have done.
2 I will sing with joy because of you.
	I will sing praise to you, Almighty God.

3 My enemies turn back when you appear;
	they fall down and die.
4 You are fair and honest in your judgements,
	and you have judged in my favour.

5 You have condemned the heathen
	and destroyed the wicked;
	they will be remembered no more.
6 Our enemies are finished for ever;
	you have destroyed their cities,
	and they are completely forgotten.

7 But the LORD is king for ever;
	he has set up his throne for judgement.

PSALM 9.1

I WILL
praise you,
LORD,
WITH ALL MY
HEART

Ps 8; Ps 9 *Hebrew title*: A psalm by David.
8.5 *yourself*; or *the gods*, or *the angels*.

639

Psalms

....

Proverbs
Eccles.
Songs
Isaiah
Jerem.

8 He rules the world with righteousness;
   he judges the nations with justice.

9 The Lord is a refuge for the oppressed,
   a place of safety in times of trouble.
10 Those who know you, Lord, will trust you;
   you do not abandon anyone who comes to you.

11 Sing praise to the Lord, who rules in Zion!
   Tell every nation what he has done!
12 God remembers those who suffer;
   he does not forget their cry,
   and he punishes those who wrong them.

13 Be merciful to me, O Lord!
   See the sufferings my enemies cause me!
   Rescue me from death, O Lord,
14   that I may stand before the people of Jerusalem
   and tell them all the things for which I praise you.
   I will rejoice because you saved me.

15 The heathen have dug a pit and fallen in;
   they have been caught in their own trap.
16 The Lord has revealed himself by his righteous
      judgements,
   and the wicked are trapped by their own deeds.

17 Death is the destiny of all the wicked,
   of all those who reject God.
18 The needy will not always be neglected;
   the hope of the poor will not be crushed for ever.

19 Come, Lord! Do not let human beings defy you!
   Bring the heathen before you
   and pronounce judgement on them.
20 Make them afraid, O Lord;
   make them know that they are only mortal beings.

A Prayer for Justice

10 1 Why are you so far away, O Lord?
   Why do you hide yourself when we are in trouble?
2 The wicked are proud and persecute the poor;
   catch them in the traps they have made.

3 The wicked are proud of their evil desires;
   the greedy curse and reject the Lord.
4 The wicked do not care about the Lord;
   in their pride they think that God doesn't matter.

5 The wicked succeed in everything.
   They cannot understand God's judgements;
   they sneer at their enemies.
6 They say to themselves, "I will never fail;
   I will never be in trouble."

7 Their speech is filled with curses, lies, and threats;
   they are quick to speak hateful, evil words.

8 They hide themselves in the villages,
   waiting to murder innocent people.

640

Psalms

⁙ ·········

2 Chron.
Ezra
Nehem.
Esther
Job

PSALMS 10, 11

They spy on their helpless victims;
9   they wait in their hiding places like lions.
They lie in wait for the poor;
  they catch them in their traps and drag them away.

10 The helpless victims lie crushed;
  brute strength has defeated them.
11 The wicked say to themselves, "God doesn't care!
  He has closed his eyes and will never see me!"

12 O Lord, punish those wicked people!
  Remember those who are suffering!
13 How can the wicked despise God
  and say to themselves, "He will not punish me"?

14 But you do see; you take notice of trouble and suffering
  and are always ready to help.
The helpless commit themselves to you;
  you have always helped the needy.

15 Break the power of wicked and evil people;
  punish them for the wrong they have done
  until they do it no more.

16 The Lord is king for ever and ever.
  Those who worship other gods
  will vanish from his land.

17 You will listen, O Lord, to the prayers of the lowly;
  you will give them courage.
18 You will hear the cries of the oppressed and the orphans;
  you will judge in their favour,
  so that mortal men may cause terror no more.

Confidence in the Lord*

11 ¹I trust in the Lord for safety.
  How foolish of you to say to me,
"Fly away like a bird to the mountains,*
2   because the wicked have drawn their bows and aimed
    their arrows
  to shoot from the shadows at good people.
3 There is nothing a good person can do
  when everything falls apart."

4 The Lord is in his holy temple;
  he has his throne in heaven.
He watches people everywhere
  and knows what they are doing.
5 He examines the good and the wicked alike;
  the lawless he hates with all his heart.

6 He sends down flaming coals* and burning sulphur on the
  wicked;
  he punishes them with scorching winds.

Ps 11 *Hebrew title*: By David.
11.1 Some ancient translations *like a bird to the mountains*; Hebrew *bird, to
your* (plural) *mountains*.
11.6 One ancient translation *coals*; Hebrew *traps*.

PSALMS 11–14

641

Psalms

Proverbs

Eccles.

Songs

Isaiah

Jerem.

7 The Lord is righteous and loves good deeds;
    those who do them will live in his presence.

A Prayer for Help*

12 1 Help us, Lord!
    There is not a good person left;
    honest people can no longer be found.
2 All of them lie to one another;
    they deceive each other with flattery.

3 Silence those flattering tongues, O Lord!
    Close those boastful mouths that say,
4 "With our words we get what we want.
    We will say what we wish,
    and no one can stop us."

5 "But now I will come," says the Lord,
    "because the needy are oppressed
    and the persecuted groan in pain.
    I will give them the security they long for."

6 The promises of the Lord can be trusted;
    they are as genuine as silver
    refined seven times in the furnace.

7-8 The wicked are everywhere,
    and everyone praises what is evil.
    Keep us always safe, O Lord,
    and preserve us from such people.

A Prayer for Help*

13 1 How much longer will you forget me, Lord?
    For ever?
    How much longer will you hide yourself from me?
2 How long must I endure trouble?
    How long will sorrow fill my heart day and night?
    How long will my enemies triumph over me?

3 Look at me, O Lord my God, and answer me.
    Restore my strength; don't let me die.
4 Don't let my enemies say, "We have defeated him."
    Don't let them gloat over my downfall.

5 I rely on your constant love;
    I will be glad, because you will rescue me.
6 I will sing to you, O Lord,
    because you have been good to me.

Human Wickedness*
(Ps 53)

14 1 Fools say to themselves,
    "There is no God."
    They are all corrupt,
    and they have done terrible things;
    there is no one who does what is right.

Ps 12; Ps 13 *Hebrew title*: A psalm by David.
Ps 14 *Hebrew title*: By David.

642

Psalms

·:·········

2 Chron.
Ezra
Nehem.
Esther
Job

PSALMS 14–16

2 The LORD looks down from heaven at human beings
to see if there are any who are wise,
any who worship him.
3 But they have all gone wrong;
they are all equally bad.
Not one of them does what is right,
not a single one.

4 "Don't they know?" asks the LORD.
"Are all these evildoers ignorant?
They live by robbing my people,
and they never pray to me."

5 But then they will be terrified,
for God is with those who obey him.
6 Evildoers frustrate the plans of the humble,
but the LORD is their protection.

7 How I pray that victory
will come to Israel from Zion.
How happy the people of Israel will be
when the LORD makes them prosperous again!

What God Requires*

15 1 LORD, who may enter your Temple?
Who may worship on Zion, your sacred hill?*

2 Those who obey God in everything
and always do what is right,
whose words are true and sincere,
3   and who do not slander others.
They do no wrong to their friends
nor spread rumours about their neighbours.
4 They despise those whom God rejects,
but honour those who obey the LORD.
They always do what they promise,
no matter how much it may cost.
5 They make loans without charging interest
and cannot be bribed to testify against the innocent.

Whoever does these things will always be secure.

A Prayer of Confidence*

16 1 Protect me, O God; I trust in you for safety.
2 I say to the LORD, "You are my Lord;
all the good things I have come from you."

3 How excellent are the LORD's faithful people!
My greatest pleasure is to be with them.

4 Those who rush to other gods
bring many troubles on themselves.*
I will not take part in their sacrifices;
I will not worship their gods.

Ps 15; Ps 16 *Hebrew title:* A psalm by David.
15.1 *sacred hill:* See 2.6.
16.4 Probable text *Those… themselves;* Hebrew unclear.

PSALMS 16, 17

643

Psalms
............:
Proverbs
Eccles.
Songs
Isaiah
Jerem.

⁵ You, Lord, are all I have,
   and you give me all I need;
   my future is in your hands.
⁶ How wonderful are your gifts to me;
   how good they are!

⁷ I praise the Lord, because he guides me,
   and in the night my conscience warns me.
⁸ I am always aware of the Lord's presence;
   he is near, and nothing can shake me.

⁹ And so I am thankful and glad,
   and I feel completely secure,
¹⁰ because you protect me from the power of death.
   I have served you faithfully,
   and you will not abandon me to the world of the dead.

¹¹ You will show me the path that leads to life;
   your presence fills me with joy
   and brings me pleasure for ever.

The Prayer of an Innocent Person*

17 ¹ Listen, O Lord, to my plea for justice;
   pay attention to my cry for help!
   Listen to my honest prayer.
² You will judge in my favour,
   because you know what is right.

³ You know my heart.
   You have come to me at night;
   you have examined me completely
   and found no evil desire in me.
⁴ I speak no evil as others do;
   I have obeyed your command
   and have not followed paths of violence.
⁵ I have always walked in your way
   and have never strayed from it.

⁶ I pray to you, O God, because you answer me;
   so turn to me and listen to my words.
⁷ Reveal your wonderful love and save me;
   at your side I am safe from my enemies.

⁸ Protect me as you would your very eyes;
   hide me in the shadow of your wings
⁹   from the attacks of the wicked.

   Deadly enemies surround me;
¹⁰   they have no pity and speak proudly.
¹¹ They are round me now, wherever I turn,
   watching for a chance to pull me down.
¹² They are like lions, waiting for me,
   wanting to tear me to pieces.

¹³ Come, Lord! Oppose my enemies and defeat them!
   Save me from the wicked by your sword;
¹⁴   save me from those who in this life have all they want.

Ps 17 *Hebrew title*: A prayer by David.

644

Psalms

2 Chron.

Ezra

Nehem.

Esther

Job

PSALMS 17, 18

PSALM 18.2

Fill in the blanks with your

- OWN -

THOUGHTS.

THE LORD IS...

THE
LORD
IS...

THE LORD IS...

THE
LORD
IS...

Punish them with the sufferings you have stored up for
them;
may there be enough for their children
and some left over for their children's children!

15 But I will see you, because I have done no wrong;
and when I awake, your presence will fill me with joy.

David's Song of Victory*
(2 Sam 22.1–51)

18 ¹How I love you, LORD!
You are my defender.

2 The LORD is my protector;
he is my strong fortress.
My God is my protection,
and with him I am safe.
He protects me like a shield;
he defends me and keeps me safe.
3 I call to the LORD,
and he saves me from my enemies.
Praise the LORD!

4 The danger of death was all round me;
the waves of destruction rolled over me.
5 The danger of death was round me,
and the grave set its trap for me.
6 In my trouble I called to the LORD;
I called to my God for help.
In his temple he heard my voice;
he listened to my cry for help.

7 Then the earth trembled and shook;
the foundations of the mountains rocked and quivered,
because God was angry.
8 Smoke poured out of his nostrils,
a consuming flame and burning coals from his mouth.
9 He tore the sky apart and came down
with a dark cloud under his feet.
10 He flew swiftly on a winged creature,
he travelled on the wings of the wind.
11 He covered himself with darkness;
thick clouds, full of water, surrounded him.
12 Hailstones and flashes of fire
came from the lightning before him
and broke through the dark clouds.

13 Then the LORD thundered from the sky;
and the voice of the Most High was heard.*
14 He shot his arrows and scattered his enemies;
with flashes of lightning he sent them running.
15 The floor of the ocean was laid bare,
and the foundations of the earth were uncovered,

Ps 18 *Hebrew title*: The words that David, the LORD's servant, sang to the
LORD on the day the LORD saved him from Saul and all his other enemies.
18.13 One ancient translation (and see 2 Sam 22.14) *was heard*; Hebrew
was heard hailstones and flashes of fire.

645

Psalms

Proverbs
Eccles.
Songs
Isaiah
Jerem.

when you rebuked your enemies, Lord,
and roared at them in anger.

16 The Lord reached down from above and took hold of me;
he pulled me out of the deep waters.
17 He rescued me from my powerful enemies
and from all those who hate me —
they were too strong for me.
18 When I was in trouble, they attacked me,
but the Lord protected me.
19 He helped me out of danger;
he saved me because he was pleased with me.

20 The Lord rewards me because I do what is right;
he blesses me because I am innocent.
21 I have obeyed the law of the Lord;
I have not turned away from my God.
22 I have observed all his laws;
I have not disobeyed his commands.
23 He knows that I am faultless,
that I have kept myself from doing wrong.
24 And so he rewards me because I do what is right,
because he knows that I am innocent.

25 O Lord, you are faithful to those who are faithful to
you;
completely good to those who are perfect.
26 You are pure to those who are pure,
but hostile to those who are wicked.
27 You save those who are humble,
but you humble those who are proud.

28 O Lord, you give me light;
you dispel my darkness.
29 You give me strength to attack my enemies
and power to overcome their defences.

30 This God — how perfect are his deeds!
How dependable his words!
He is like a shield
for all who seek his protection.
31 The Lord alone is God;
God alone is our defence.
32 He is the God who makes me strong,
who makes my pathway safe.
33 He makes me sure-footed as a deer;
he keeps me safe on the mountains.
34 He trains me for battle,
so that I can use the strongest bow.

35 O Lord, you protect me and save me;
your care has made me great,
and your power has kept me safe.
36 You have kept me from being captured,
and I have never fallen.
37 I pursue my enemies and catch them;
I do not stop until I destroy them.
38 I strike them down, and they cannot rise;
they lie defeated before me.

646

Psalms

⋮···········

2 Chron.
Ezra
Nehem.
Esther
Job

PSALMS 18, 19

39 You give me strength for the battle
  and victory over my enemies.
40 You make my enemies run from me;
  I destroy those who hate me.
41 They cry for help, but no one saves them;
  they call to the LORD, but he does not answer.
42 I crush them, so that they become like dust
  which the wind blows away.
  I trample on them like mud in the streets.

43 You saved me from a rebellious people
  and made me ruler over the nations;
  people I did not know have now become my subjects.
44 Foreigners bow before me;
  when they hear me, they obey.
45 They lose their courage
  and come trembling from their fortresses.

46 The LORD lives! Praise my defender!
  Proclaim the greatness of the God who saves me.
47 He gives me victory over my enemies;
  he subdues the nations under me
48 and saves me from my foes.
  O LORD, you give me victory over my enemies
  and protect me from violent people.
49 And so I praise you among the nations;
  I sing praises to you.

50 God gives great victories to his king;
  he shows constant love to the one he has chosen,
  to David and his descendants for ever.

God's Glory in Creation*

19 ¹How clearly the sky reveals God's glory!
  How plainly it shows what he has done!
2 Each day announces it to the following day;
  each night repeats it to the next.
3 No speech or words are used,
  no sound is heard;
4 yet their message* goes out to all the world
  and is heard to the ends of the earth.
  God made a home in the sky for the sun;
5 it comes out in the morning like a happy bridegroom,
  like an athlete eager to run a race.
6 It starts at one end of the sky
  and goes across to the other.
  Nothing can hide from its heat.

The Law of the LORD

7 The law of the LORD is perfect;
  it gives new strength.
  The commands of the LORD are trustworthy,
  giving wisdom to those who lack it.
8 The laws of the LORD are right,
  and those who obey them are happy.

··

Ps 19 *Hebrew title*: A psalm by David.
19.4 Some ancient translations *message*; Hebrew *line*.

647

Psalms

Proverbs
Eccles.
Songs
Isaiah
Jerem.

The commands of the LORD are just
and give understanding to the mind.
9 Reverence for the LORD is good;
it will continue for ever.
The judgements of the LORD are just;
they are always fair.
10 They are more desirable than the finest gold;
they are sweeter than the purest honey.
11 They give knowledge to me, your servant;
I am rewarded for obeying them.

12 No one can see his own errors;
deliver me, LORD, from hidden faults!
13 Keep me safe, also, from wilful sins;
don't let them rule over me.
Then I shall be perfect
and free from the evil of sin.

14 May my words and my thoughts be acceptable to you,
O LORD, my refuge and my redeemer!

A Prayer for Victory*

20 1 May the LORD answer you when you are in trouble!
May the God of Jacob protect you!
2 May he send you help from his Temple
and give you aid from Mount Zion.
3 May he accept all your offerings
and be pleased with all your sacrifices.
4 May he give you what you desire
and make all your plans succeed.
5 Then we will shout for joy over your victory
and celebrate your triumph by praising our God.
May the LORD answer all your requests.

6 Now I know that the LORD gives victory to his chosen king;
he answers him from his holy heaven
and by his power gives him great victories.
7 Some trust in their war chariots
and others in their horses,
but we trust in the power of the LORD our God.
8 Such people will stumble and fall,
but we will rise and stand firm.

9 Give victory to the king, O LORD;
answer* us when we call.

Praise for Victory*

21 1 The king is glad, O LORD, because you gave him strength;
he rejoices because you made him victorious.
2 You have given him his heart's desire;
you have answered his request.

3 You came to him with great blessings
and set a crown of gold on his head.

Ps 20; Ps 21 *Hebrew title*: A psalm by David.
20.9 Some ancient translations *answer*; Hebrew *he will answer*.

648

Psalms

2 Chron.
Ezra
Nehem.
Esther
Job

PSALMS 21, 22

4 He asked for life, and you gave it,
    a long and lasting life.
5 His glory is great because of your help;
    you have given him fame and majesty.
6 Your blessings are with him for ever
    and your presence fills him with joy.

7 The king trusts in the LORD Almighty;
    and because of the LORD's constant love
    he will always be secure.
8 The king will capture all his enemies;
    he will capture everyone who hates him.
9 He will destroy them like a blazing fire
    when he appears.

The LORD will devour them in his anger,
    and fire will consume them.
10 None of their descendants will survive;
    the king will kill them all.

11 They make their plans, and plot against him,
    but they will not succeed.
12 He will shoot his arrows at them
    and make them turn and run.

13 We praise you, LORD, for your great strength!
    We will sing and praise your power.

A Cry of Anguish and a Song of Praise*

22 1 My God, my God, why have you abandoned me?
    I have cried desperately for help,
    but still it does not come.
2 During the day I call to you, my God,
    but you do not answer;
I call at night,
    but get no rest.
3 But you are enthroned as the Holy One,
    the one whom Israel praises.
4 Our ancestors put their trust in you;
    they trusted you, and you saved them.
5 They called to you and escaped from danger;
    they trusted you and were not disappointed.

6 But I am no longer a human being; I am a worm,
    despised and scorned by everyone!
7 All who see me jeer at me;
    they stick out their tongues and shake their heads.
8 "You relied on the LORD," they say.
    "Why doesn't he save you?
If the LORD likes you,
    why doesn't he help you?"

9 It was you who brought me safely through birth,
    and when I was a baby, you kept me safe.
10 I have relied on you since the day I was born,
    and you have always been my God.

PSALM 22

Grab a

− COLOURED −

PENCIL

and highlight verses 1, 7, 8, 16, 17 and 18. Now go look up Mark 15.20, 27, 29 and 34, and Matthew 27.35 and 43. Do you notice any similarities?

This psalm was written 1000 years before Jesus lived and died, yet the passages have a lot in common. Amazing, right?

Ps 22 *Hebrew title*: A psalm by David.

PSALMS 22

649

Psalms

....

Proverbs

Eccles.

Songs

Isaiah

Jerem.

11 Do not stay away from me!
    Trouble is near,
    and there is no one to help.
12 Many enemies surround me like bulls;
    they are all round me,
    like fierce bulls from the land of Bashan.
13 They open their mouths like lions,
    roaring and tearing at me.

14 My strength is gone,
    gone like water spilt on the ground.
    All my bones are out of joint;
    my heart is like melted wax.
15 My throat* is as dry as dust,
    and my tongue sticks to the roof of my mouth.
    You have left me for dead in the dust.

16 An evil gang is round me;
    like a pack of dogs they close in on me;
    they tear at* my hands and feet.
17 All my bones can be seen.
    My enemies look at me and stare.
18 They gamble for my clothes
    and divide them among themselves.

19 O Lord, don't stay away from me!
    Come quickly to my rescue!
20 Save me from the sword;
    save my life from these dogs.
21 Rescue me from these lions;
    I am helpless* before these wild bulls.

22 I will tell my people what you have done;
    I will praise you in their assembly:
23 "Praise him, you servants of the Lord!
    Honour him, you descendants of Jacob!
    Worship him, you people of Israel!
24 He does not neglect the poor or ignore their suffering;
    he does not turn away from them,
    but answers when they call for help."

25 In the full assembly I will praise you for what you have
        done;
    in the presence of those who worship you
    I will offer the sacrifices I promised.
26 The poor will eat as much as they want;
    those who come to the Lord will praise him.
    May they prosper for ever!

27 All nations will remember the Lord.
    From every part of the world they will turn to him;
    all races will worship him.

....

22.15 Probable text *throat*; Hebrew *strength*.
22.16 Some ancient translations *they tear at*; others *they tie*; Hebrew *like a lion*.
22.21 Some ancient translations *I am helpless*; Hebrew *you answered me*.

650

Psalms

2 Chron.
Ezra
Nehem.
Esther
Job

PSALMS 22–24

PSALM 23

Look after an egg for a
day, then come back to
this page... Looked after
an egg yet? No?
Stop reading and

GO AND FIND
AN EGG.

Yes? Read on...

What did you have to do
to look after your egg?
How did you go about
protecting it? What did
this teach you about God
being our shepherd and
looking after his sheep?

write some
thoughts here

28 The LORD is king,
    and he rules the nations.

29 All proud people will bow down to him;*
    all mortals will bow down before him.
30 Future generations will serve him;
    they will speak of the Lord to the coming generation.
31 People not yet born will be told:
    "The Lord saved his people."

The LORD our Shepherd*

23 ¹ The LORD is my shepherd;
      I have everything I need.
² He lets me rest in fields of green grass
    and leads me to quiet pools of fresh water.
³ He gives me new strength.
  He guides me in the right paths,
    as he has promised.
⁴ Even if I go through the deepest darkness,
    I will not be afraid, LORD,
  for you are with me.
  Your shepherd's rod and staff protect me.

⁵ You prepare a banquet for me,
    where all my enemies can see me;
  you welcome me as an honoured guest
    and fill my cup to the brim.
⁶ I know that your goodness and love will be with me all my
    life;
  and your house will be my home as long as I live.

The Great King*

24 ¹ The world and all that is in it belong to the LORD;
      the earth and all who live on it are his.
² He built it on the deep waters beneath the earth
    and laid its foundations in the ocean depths.

³ Who has the right to go up the LORD's hill?*
    Who may enter his holy Temple?
⁴ Those who are pure in act and in thought,
    who do not worship idols
    or make false promises.
⁵ The LORD will bless them and save them;
    God will declare them innocent.
⁶ Such are the people who come to God,
    who come into the presence of the God of Jacob.

⁷ Fling wide the gates,
    open the ancient doors,
    and the great king will come in.
⁸ Who is this great king?
  He is the LORD, strong and mighty,
    the LORD, victorious in battle.

Psalms
....
Proverbs
Eccles.
Songs
Isaiah
Jerem.

[9] Fling wide the gates,
     open the ancient doors,
     and the great king will come in.
[10] Who is this great king?
     The triumphant LORD — he is the great king!

A Prayer for Guidance and Protection*

25 [1] To you, O LORD, I offer my prayer;
      [2] in you, my God, I trust.
     Save me from the shame of defeat;
        don't let my enemies gloat over me!
[3] Defeat does not come to those who trust in you,
     but to those who are quick to rebel against you.

[4] Teach me your ways, O LORD;
     make them known to me.
[5] Teach me to live according to your truth,
     for you are my God, who saves me.
     I always trust in you.

[6] Remember, O LORD, your kindness and constant love
     which you have shown from long ago.
[7] Forgive the sins and errors of my youth.
     In your constant love and goodness,
        remember me, LORD!

[8] Because the LORD is righteous and good,
     he teaches sinners the path they should follow.
[9] He leads the humble in the right way
     and teaches them his will.
[10] With faithfulness and love he leads
     all who keep his covenant and obey his commands.

[11] Keep your promise, LORD, and forgive my sins,
     for they are many.
[12] Those who have reverence for the LORD
     will learn from him the path they should follow.
[13] They will always be prosperous,
     and their children will possess the land.
[14] The LORD is the friend of those who obey him
     and he affirms his covenant with them.

[15] I look to the LORD for help at all times,
     and he rescues me from danger.
[16] Turn to me, LORD, and be merciful to me,
     because I am lonely and weak.
[17] Relieve me of my worries
     and save me from all my troubles.
[18] Consider my distress and suffering
     and forgive all my sins.

[19] See how many enemies I have;
     see how much they hate me.
[20] Protect me and save me;
     keep me from defeat.
     I come to you for safety.

Ps 25 *Hebrew title*: By David.

652

Psalms

2 Chron.
Ezra
Nehem.
Esther
Job

PSALMS 25–27

21 May my goodness and honesty preserve me,
because I trust in you.

22 From all their troubles, O God,
save your people Israel!

The Prayer of a Good Person*

26 ¹Declare me innocent, O Lord,
because I do what is right
and trust you completely.
² Examine me and test me, Lord;
judge my desires and thoughts.
³ Your constant love is my guide;
your faithfulness always leads me.*

⁴ I do not keep company with worthless people;
I have nothing to do with hypocrites.
⁵ I hate the company of the evil
and avoid the wicked.

⁶ Lord, I wash my hands to show that I am innocent
and march in worship round your altar.
⁷ I sing a hymn of thanksgiving
and tell of all your wonderful deeds.

⁸ I love the house where you live, O Lord,
the place where your glory dwells.
⁹ Do not destroy me with the sinners;
spare me from the fate of murderers —
10   those who do evil all the time
and are always ready to take bribes.

¹¹ As for me, I do what is right;
be merciful to me and save me!

¹² I am safe from all dangers;
in the assembly of his people I praise the Lord.

A Prayer of Praise*

27 ¹The Lord is my light and my salvation;
I will fear no one.
The Lord protects me from all danger;
I will never be afraid.

² When evil people attack me and try to kill me,
they stumble and fall.
³ Even if a whole army surrounds me,
I will not be afraid;
even if enemies attack me,
I will still trust God.*

⁴ I have asked the Lord for one thing;
one thing only do I want:
to live in the Lord's house all my life,

PSALM 27.1

I WILL FEAR NO ONE

Ps 26; Ps 27 *Hebrew title: By David.*
26.3 *your faithfulness always leads me;* or *I live in loyalty to you.*
27.3 *still trust God;* or *not lose courage.*

PSALMS 27, 28

653

Psalms
...........:
Proverbs
Eccles.
Songs
Isaiah
Jerem.

to marvel there at his goodness,
and to ask for his guidance.
5 In times of trouble he will shelter me;
he will keep me safe in his Temple
and make me secure on a high rock.
6 So I will triumph over my enemies around me.
With shouts of joy I will offer sacrifices in his Temple;
I will sing, I will praise the LORD.

7 Hear me, LORD, when I call to you!
Be merciful and answer me!
8 When you said, "Come and worship me,"
I answered, "I will come, LORD;
9   don't hide yourself from me!"

Don't be angry with me;
don't turn your servant away.
You have been my help;
don't leave me, don't abandon me,
O God, my saviour.
10 My father and mother may abandon me,
but the LORD will take care of me.

11 Teach me, LORD, what you want me to do,
and lead me along a safe path,
because I have many enemies.
12 Don't abandon me to my enemies,
who attack me with lies and threats.

13 I know that I will live to see
the LORD's goodness in this present life.
14 Trust in the LORD.
Have faith, do not despair.
Trust in the LORD.

A Prayer for Help*

28 1 O LORD, my defender, I call to you.
Listen to my cry!
If you do not answer me,
I will be among those who go down to the world of the
dead.
2 Hear me when I cry to you for help,
when I lift my hands towards your holy Temple.
3 Do not condemn me with the wicked,
with those who do evil —
those whose words are friendly,
but who have hatred in their hearts.

4 Punish them for what they have done,
for the evil they have committed.
Punish them for all their deeds;
give them what they deserve!
5 They take no notice of what the LORD has done
or of what he has made;
so he will punish them
and destroy them for ever.

Ps 28 *Hebrew title*: By David.

654

Psalms

⋮········

2 Chron.

Ezra

Nehem.

Esther

Job

PSALMS 28–30

6 Give praise to the LORD;
  he has heard my cry for help.
7 The LORD protects and defends me;
  I trust in him.
He gives me help and makes me glad;
  I praise him with joyful songs.

8 The LORD protects his people;
  he defends and saves his chosen king.
9 Save your people, LORD,
  and bless those who are yours.
Be their shepherd,
  and take care of them for ever.

The Voice of the LORD in the Storm*

29 1 Praise the LORD, you heavenly beings;
  praise his glory and power.
2 Praise the LORD's glorious name;
  bow down before the Holy One when he appears.*

3 The voice of the LORD is heard on the seas;
  the glorious God thunders,
  and his voice echoes over the ocean.
4 The voice of the LORD is heard
  in all its might and majesty.

5 The voice of the LORD breaks the cedars,
  even the cedars of Lebanon.
6 He makes the mountains of Lebanon jump like calves
  and makes Mount Hermon leap like a young bull.

7 The voice of the LORD makes the lightning flash.
8 His voice makes the desert shake;
  he shakes the desert of Kadesh.
9 The LORD's voice shakes the oaks*
  and strips the leaves from the trees
  while everyone in his Temple shouts, "Glory to God!"

10 The LORD rules over the deep waters;
  he rules as king for ever.
11 The LORD gives strength to his people
  and blesses them with peace.

A Prayer of Thanksgiving*

30 1 I praise you, LORD, because you have saved me
  and kept my enemies from gloating over me.
2 I cried to you for help, O LORD my God,
  and you healed me;
3   you kept me from the grave.
I was on my way to the depths below,*
  but you restored my life.

....

Ps 29 *Hebrew title*: A psalm by David.
29.2 *when he appears*; or *in garments of worship*; or *in his beautiful Temple*.
29.9 Probable text *shakes the oaks*; Hebrew *makes the deer give birth*.
Ps 30 *Hebrew title*: A song for the dedication of the Temple; a psalm by David.
30.3 *the depths below*: The world of the dead (see 6.5).

Psalms
Proverbs
Eccles.
Songs
Isaiah
Jerem.

⁴ Sing praise to the LORD,
  all his faithful people!
Remember what the Holy One has done,
  and give him thanks!
⁵ His anger lasts only a moment,
  his goodness for a lifetime.
Tears may flow in the night,
  but joy comes in the morning.

⁶ I felt secure and said to myself,
  "I will never be defeated."
⁷ You were good to me, LORD;
  you protected me like a mountain fortress.
But then you hid yourself from me,
  and I was afraid.

⁸ I called to you, LORD;
  I begged for your help:
⁹ "What will you gain from my death?
  What profit from my going to the grave?
Are dead people able to praise you?
  Can they proclaim your unfailing goodness?
¹⁰ Hear me, LORD, and be merciful!
  Help me, LORD!"

¹¹ You have changed my sadness into a joyful dance;
  you have taken away my sorrow
  and surrounded me with joy.
¹² So I will not be silent;
  I will sing praise to you.
LORD, you are my God,
  I will give you thanks for ever.

A Prayer of Trust in God*

31 ¹ I come to you, LORD, for protection;
  never let me be defeated.
You are a righteous God;
  save me, I pray!
² Hear me! Save me now!
Be my refuge to protect me;
  my defence to save me.

³ You are my refuge and defence;
  guide me and lead me as you have promised.
⁴ Keep me safe from the trap that has been set for me;
  shelter me from danger.
⁵ I place myself in your care.
You will save me, LORD;
  you are a faithful God.

⁶ You hate those who worship false gods,
  but I trust in you.
⁷ I will be glad and rejoice
  because of your constant love.
You see my suffering;
  you know my trouble.

Ps 31 *Hebrew title*: A psalm by David.

HOLY

LEVITICUS 19.2;
PSALM 30.4

What do you
think it means?

What does someone
else think it means?

Now go and look up
the definition.

656

Psalms

2 Chron.
Ezra
Nehem.
Esther
Job

PSALMS 31

8 You have not let my enemies capture me;
  you have given me freedom to go where I wish.

9 Be merciful to me, LORD,
  for I am in trouble;
  my eyes are tired from so much crying;
  I am completely worn out.
10 I am exhausted by sorrow,
  and weeping has shortened my life.
  I am weak from all my troubles;*
  even my bones are wasting away.

11 All my enemies, and especially my neighbours,
  treat me with contempt;
  those who know me are afraid of me;
  when they see me in the street, they run away.
12 Everyone has forgotten me, as though I were dead;
  I am like something thrown away.
13 I hear many enemies whispering;
  terror is all round me.
  They are making plans against me,
  plotting to kill me.

14 But my trust is in you, O LORD;
  you are my God.
15 I am always in your care;
  save me from my enemies,
  from those who persecute me.
16 Look on your servant with kindness;
  save me in your constant love.
17 I call to you, LORD;
  don't let me be disgraced.
  May the wicked be disgraced;
  may they go silently down to the world of the dead.
18 Silence those liars —
  all the proud and arrogant
  who speak with contempt about the righteous.

19 How wonderful are the good things
  you keep for those who honour you!
  Everyone knows how good you are,
  how securely you protect those who trust you.
20 You hide them in the safety of your presence
  from the plots of others;
  in a safe shelter you hide them
  from the insults of their enemies.

21 Praise the LORD!
  How wonderfully he showed his love for me
  when I was surrounded and attacked!
22 I was afraid and thought
  that he had driven me out of his presence.
  But he heard my cry,
  when I called to him for help.

23 Love the LORD, all his faithful people.
  The LORD protects the faithful,

....
31.10 Some ancient translations *troubles*; Hebrew *iniquity*.

PSALMS 31–33

657

Psalms

Proverbs
Eccles.
Songs
Isaiah
Jerem.

but punishes the proud as they deserve.
24 Be strong, be courageous,
all you that hope in the LORD.

Confession and Forgiveness*

32 1Happy are those whose sins are forgiven,
whose wrongs are pardoned.
2 Happy is the one whom the LORD does not accuse of doing
wrong
and who is free from all deceit.

3 When I did not confess my sins,
I was worn out from crying all day long.
4 Day and night you punished me, LORD;
my strength was completely drained,
as moisture is dried up by the summer heat.

5 Then I confessed my sins to you;
I did not conceal my wrongdoings.
I decided to confess them to you,
and you forgave all my sins.

6 So all your loyal people should pray to you in times of need;*
when a great flood of trouble comes rushing in,
it will not reach them.
7 You are my hiding place;
you will save me from trouble.
I sing aloud of your salvation,
because you protect me.

8 The LORD says, "I will teach you the way you should go;
I will instruct you and advise you.
9 Don't be stupid like a horse or a mule,
which must be controlled with a bit and bridle
to make it submit."

10 The wicked will have to suffer,
but those who trust in the LORD
are protected by his constant love.
11 You that are righteous, be glad and rejoice
because of what the LORD has done.
You that obey him, shout for joy!

A Song of Praise

33 1All you that are righteous,
shout for joy for what the LORD has done;
praise him, all you that obey him.
2 Give thanks to the LORD with harps,
sing to him with stringed instruments.
3 Sing a new song to him,
play the harp with skill, and shout for joy!

4 The words of the LORD are true
and all his works are dependable.
5 The LORD loves what is righteous and just;
his constant love fills the earth.

Ps 32 Hebrew title: A poem by David.
32.6 Some ancient translations need; Hebrew finding only.

PSALM 34

USE
– THIS –
SPACE

to write your own
PSALM, POEM OR LETTER
to God.

6 The LORD created the heavens by his command,
the sun, moon, and stars by his spoken word.
7 He gathered all the seas into one place;
he shut up the ocean depths in storerooms.

8 Worship the LORD, all the earth!
Honour him, all peoples of the world!
9 When he spoke, the world was created;
at his command everything appeared.

10 The LORD frustrates the purposes of the nations;
he keeps them from carrying out their plans.
11 But his plans endure for ever;
his purposes last eternally.
12 Happy is the nation whose God is the LORD;
happy are the people he has chosen for his own!

13 The LORD looks down from heaven
and sees the whole human race.
14 From where he rules, he looks down
on all who live on earth.
15 He forms all their thoughts
and knows everything they do.

16 A king does not win because of his powerful army;
a soldier does not triumph because of his strength.
17 War horses are useless for victory;
their great strength cannot save.

18 The LORD watches over those who obey him,
those who trust in his constant love.
19 He saves them from death;
he keeps them alive in times of famine.

20 We put our hope in the LORD;
he is our protector and our help.
21 We are glad because of him;
we trust in his holy name.

22 May your constant love be with us, LORD,
as we put our hope in you.

In Praise of God's Goodness*

34 1 I will always thank the LORD;
I will never stop praising him.
2 I will praise him for what he has done;
may all who are oppressed listen and be glad!
3 Proclaim with me the LORD's greatness;
let us praise his name together!

4 I prayed to the LORD, and he answered me;
he freed me from all my fears.
5 The oppressed look to him and are glad;
they will never be disappointed.
6 The helpless call to him, and he answers;
he saves them from all their troubles.

Ps 34 *Hebrew title*: By David, who left the presence of Abimelech after
pretending to be mad and being sent away by him.

PSALMS 34, 35

659

Psalms

....

Proverbs
Eccles.
Songs
Isaiah
Jerem.

7 His angel guards those who honour the Lord
    and rescues them from danger.

8 Find out for yourself how good the Lord is.
    Happy are those who find safety with him.
9 Honour the Lord, all his people;
    those who obey him have all they need.
10 Even lions go hungry for lack of food,
    but those who obey the Lord lack nothing good.

11 Come, my young friends, and listen to me,
    and I will teach you to honour the Lord.
12 Would you like to enjoy life?
    Do you want long life and happiness?
13 Then hold back from speaking evil
    and from telling lies.
14 Turn away from evil and do good;
    strive for peace with all your heart.

15 The Lord watches over the righteous
    and listens to their cries;
16 but he opposes those who do evil,
    so that when they die, they are soon forgotten.
17 The righteous call to the Lord, and he listens;
    he rescues them from all their troubles.
18 The Lord is near to those who are discouraged;
    he saves those who have lost all hope.

19 Good people suffer many troubles,
    but the Lord saves them from them all;
20 the Lord preserves them completely;
    not one of their bones is broken.
21 Evil will kill the wicked;
    those who hate the righteous will be punished.

22 The Lord will save his people;
    those who go to him for protection will be spared.

A Prayer for Help*

35 1 Oppose those who oppose me, Lord,
    and fight those who fight against me!
2 Take your shield and armour
    and come to my rescue.
3 Lift up your spear and your axe
    against those who pursue me.
    Promise that you will save me.

4 May those who try to kill me
    be defeated and disgraced!
    May those who plot against me
    be turned back and confused!
5 May they be like straw blown by the wind
    as the angel of the Lord pursues them!
6 May their path be dark and slippery
    while the angel of the Lord strikes them down!

Ps 35 *Hebrew title*: By David.

660

Psalms

:: · · · · · · ·

2 Chron.

Ezra

Nehem.

Esther

Job

PSALMS 35

7 Without any reason they laid a trap for me
  and dug a deep hole to catch me.
8 But destruction will catch them before they know it;
  they will be caught in their own trap
  and fall to their destruction!

9 Then I will be glad because of the LORD;
  I will be happy because he saved me.
10 With all my heart I will say to the LORD,
  "There is no one like you.
  You protect the weak from the strong,
  the poor from the oppressor."

11 Evil people testify against me
  and accuse me of crimes I know nothing about.
12 They pay me back evil for good,
  and I sink in despair.
13 But when they were sick, I dressed in mourning;
  I deprived myself of food;
  I prayed with my head bowed low,
14   as I would pray for a friend or a brother.
  I went about bent over in mourning,
  as one who mourns for his mother.

15 But when I was in trouble, they were all glad
  and gathered round to mock me;
  strangers beat me
  and kept striking me.
16 Like those who would mock a cripple,*
  they glared at me with hate.

17 How much longer, Lord, will you just look on?
  Rescue me from their attacks;
  save my life from these lions!
18 Then I will thank you in the assembly of your people;
  I will praise you before them all.

19 Don't let my enemies, those liars,
  gloat over my defeat.
  Don't let those who hate me for no reason
  smirk with delight over my sorrow.

20 They do not speak in a friendly way;
  instead they invent all kinds of lies about peace-loving
    people.
21 They accuse me, shouting,
  "We saw what you did!"
22 But you, O LORD, have seen this.
  So don't be silent, Lord;
  don't keep yourself far away!
23 Rouse yourself, O Lord, and defend me;
  rise up, my God, and plead my cause.
24 You are righteous, O LORD, so declare me innocent;
  don't let my enemies gloat over me.
25 Don't let them say to themselves,
  "We are rid of him!
  That's just what we wanted!"

....
35.16 Probable text *Like those... cripple*; Hebrew unclear.

PSALMS 35–37

661

Psalms

....

Proverbs
Eccles.
Songs
Isaiah
Jerem.

26 May those who gloat over my suffering
   be completely defeated and confused;
   may those who claim to be better than I am
   be covered with shame and disgrace.

27 May those who want to see me acquitted
   shout for joy and say again and again,
   "How great is the LORD!
   He is pleased with the success of his servant."
28 Then I will proclaim your righteousness,
   and I will praise you all day long.

Human Wickedness*

36
¹Sin speaks to the wicked deep in their hearts;
   they reject God and have no reverence for him.
² Because they think so highly of themselves,
   they think that God will not discover their sin and
      condemn it.
³ Their speech is wicked and full of lies;
   they no longer do what is wise and good.
⁴ They make evil plans as they lie in bed;
   nothing they do is good,
   and they never reject anything evil.

The Goodness of God

⁵ LORD, your constant love reaches the heavens;
   your faithfulness extends to the skies.
⁶ Your righteousness is towering like the mountains;
   your justice is like the depths of the sea.
   People and animals are in your care.

⁷ How precious, O God, is your constant love!
   We find* protection under the shadow of your wings.
⁸ We feast on the abundant food you provide;
   you let us drink from the river of your goodness.
⁹ You are the source of all life,
   and because of your light we see the light.

¹⁰ Continue to love those who know you
   and to do good to those who are righteous.
¹¹ Do not let proud people attack me
   or the wicked make me run away.
¹² See where evil people have fallen.
   There they lie, unable to rise.

The Destiny of the Wicked and of the Good*

37
¹Don't be worried on account of the wicked;
   don't be jealous of those who do wrong.
² They will soon disappear like grass that dries up;
   they will die like plants that wither.

³ Trust in the LORD and do good;
   live in the land and be safe.

Ps 36 Hebrew title: By David, the LORD's servant.
36.7 precious, O God, is... find; or precious is your constant love! Gods and
people find.
Ps 37 Hebrew title: By David.

662

Psalms

·:·········

2 Chron.
Ezra
Nehem.
Esther
Job

PSALMS 37

Write the

DATE

AND A

SENTENCE

about how you
are doing below.

Whenever you return to
this page, write the
date and an update on
how you are doing.

___ / / _____

_____

_____

___ / / _____

_____

_____

___ / / _____

_____

_____

___ / / _____

_____

_____

___ / / _____

_____

4 Seek your happiness in the LORD,
    and he will give you your heart's desire.

5 Give yourself to the LORD;
    trust in him, and he will help you;
6 he will make your righteousness shine like the noonday sun.

7 Be patient and wait for the LORD to act;
    don't be worried about those who prosper
    or those who succeed in their evil plans.

8 Don't give in to worry or anger;
    it only leads to trouble.
9 Those who trust in the LORD will possess the land,
    but the wicked will be driven out.

10 Soon the wicked will disappear;
    you may look for them, but you won't find them;
11 the humble will possess the land
    and enjoy prosperity and peace.

12 The wicked plot against good people
    and glare at them with hate.
13 But the Lord laughs at wicked people,
    because he knows they will soon be destroyed.

14 The wicked draw their swords and bend their bows
    to kill the poor and needy,
    to slaughter those who do what is right;
15 but they will be killed by their own swords,
    and their bows will be smashed.

16 The little that a good person owns
    is worth more than the wealth of all the wicked,
17 because the LORD will take away the strength of the wicked,
    but protect those who are good.

18 The LORD takes care of those who obey him,
    and the land will be theirs for ever.
19 They will not suffer when times are bad;
    they will have enough in time of famine.
20 But the wicked will die;
    the enemies of the LORD will vanish like wild flowers;
    they will disappear like smoke.

21 The wicked borrow and never pay back,
    but good people are generous with their gifts.
22 Those who are blessed by the LORD will possess the land,
    but those who are cursed by him will be driven out.

23 The LORD guides people in the way they should go
    and protects those who please him.
24 If they fall, they will not stay down,
    because the LORD will help them up.

25 I am old now; I have lived a long time,
    but I have never seen good people abandoned by the
    LORD
    or their children begging for food.

663

Psalms
....
Proverbs
Eccles.
Songs
Isaiah
Jerem.

²⁶ At all times they give freely and lend to others,
    and their children are a blessing.

²⁷ Turn away from evil and do good,
    and your descendants will always live in the land;
²⁸ for the LORD loves what is right
    and does not abandon his faithful people.
    He protects them for ever,
    but the descendants of the wicked will be driven out.
²⁹ The righteous will possess the land
    and live in it for ever.

³⁰ The words of good people are wise,
    and they are always fair.
³¹ They keep the law of their God in their hearts
    and never depart from it.

³² Wicked people watch good people
    and try to kill them;
³³ but the LORD will not abandon them to their enemy's power
    or let them be condemned when they are on trial.

³⁴ Put your hope in the LORD and obey his commands;
    he will honour you by giving you the land,
    and you will see the wicked driven out.

³⁵ I once knew a wicked and ruthless person;
    he towered over everyone like a cedar of Lebanon;*
³⁶ but later I* passed by, and he wasn't there;
    I looked for him, but couldn't find him.

³⁷ Notice good people, observe the righteous;
    peaceful people have descendants,
³⁸ but sinners are completely destroyed,
    and their descendants are wiped out.

³⁹ The LORD saves the righteous
    and protects them in times of trouble.
⁴⁰ He helps them and rescues them;
    he saves them from the wicked,
    because they go to him for protection.

The Prayer of a Sufferer*

38 ¹ O LORD, don't punish me in your anger!
    ² You have wounded me with your arrows;
    you have struck me down.
³ Because of your anger, I am in great pain;
    my whole body is diseased because of my sins.
⁴ I am drowning in the flood of my sins;
    they are a burden too heavy to bear.

⁵ Because I have been foolish,
    my sores stink and rot.
⁶ I am bowed down, I am crushed;
    I mourn all day long.

37.35 One ancient translation *like a cedar of Lebanon*; Hebrew unclear.
37.36 Some ancient translations *I*; Hebrew *he*.
Ps 38 *Hebrew title*: A psalm by David; a lament.

664

Psalms

·:········

2 Chron.
Ezra
Nehem.
Esther
Job

PSALMS 38, 39

⁷ I am burning with fever
    and I am near to death.
⁸ I am worn out and utterly crushed;
    my heart is troubled, and I groan with pain.

⁹ O Lord, you know what I long for;
    you hear all my groans.
¹⁰ My heart is pounding, my strength is gone,
    and my eyes have lost their brightness.
¹¹ My friends and neighbours will not come near me,
    because of my sores;
    even my family keeps away from me.
¹² Those who want to kill me lay traps for me,
    and those who want to hurt me threaten to ruin me;
    they never stop plotting against me.

¹³ I am like the deaf and cannot hear,
    like the dumb and cannot speak.
¹⁴ I am like those who do not answer,
    because they cannot hear.

¹⁵ But I trust in you, O LORD;
    and you, O Lord my God, will answer me.
¹⁶ Don't let my enemies gloat over my distress;
    don't let them boast about my downfall!
¹⁷ I am about to fall
    and am in constant pain.

¹⁸ I confess my sins;
    they fill me with anxiety.
¹⁹ My enemies are healthy and strong;
    there are many who hate me for no reason.
²⁰ Those who pay back evil for good
    are against me because I try to do right.

²¹ Do not abandon me, O LORD;
    do not stay away, my God!
²² Help me now, O Lord my saviour!

The Confession of a Sufferer*

39 ¹ I said, "I will be careful what I do
    and will not let my tongue make me sin;
I will not say anything
    while evil people are near."
² I kept quiet, not saying a word,
    not even about anything good!
But my suffering only grew worse,
³   and I was overcome with anxiety.
The more I thought, the more troubled I became;
    I could not keep from asking:
⁴ "LORD, how long will I live?
    When will I die?
    Tell me how soon my life will end."

⁵ How short you have made my life!
    In your sight my lifetime seems nothing.

Ps 39 *Hebrew title*: A psalm by David.

665

Psalms

....

Proverbs
Eccles.
Songs
Isaiah
Jerem.

Indeed every living being is no more than a puff of wind,
6   no more than a shadow.
All they do is for nothing;
    they gather wealth, but don't know who will get it.

7 What, then, can I hope for, Lord?
    I put my hope in you.
8 Save me from all my sins,
    and don't let fools laugh at me.
9 I will keep quiet, I will not say a word,
    for you are the one who made me suffer like this.
10 Don't punish me any more!
    I am about to die from your blows.
11 You punish our sins by your rebukes,
    and like a moth you destroy what we love.
Indeed we are no more than a puff of wind!

12 Hear my prayer, LORD,
    and listen to my cry;
    come to my aid when I weep.
Like all my ancestors
    I am only your guest for a little while.
13 Leave me alone so that I may have some happiness
    before I go away and am no more.

A Song of Praise*

40 ¹ I waited patiently for the LORD's help;
    then he listened to me and heard my cry.
² He pulled me out of a dangerous pit,
    out of the deadly quicksand.
He set me safely on a rock
    and made me secure.
³ He taught me to sing a new song,
    a song of praise to our God.
Many who see this will take warning
    and will put their trust in the LORD.

⁴ Happy are those who trust the LORD,
    who do not turn to idols
    or join those who worship false gods.
⁵ You have done many things for us, O LORD our God;
    there is no one like you!
You have made many wonderful plans for us.
I could never speak of them all —
    their number is so great!

⁶ You do not want sacrifices and offerings;
    you do not ask for animals burnt whole on the altar
    or for sacrifices to take away sins.
Instead, you have given me ears to hear you,
⁷   and so I answered, "Here I am;
    your instructions for me are in the book of the Law.*
⁸ How I love to do your will, my God!
    I keep your teaching in my heart."

....

Ps 40 *Hebrew title*: A psalm by David.
40.7 *your instructions… Law*; or *my devotion to you is recorded in your book.*

666

Psalms

2 Chron.
Ezra
Nehem.
Esther
Job

PSALMS 40, 41

PSALM 40.12-17

Throughout the book of Psalms, the writers are

— EXTREMELY —

HONEST

about their emotions and the troubles they're going through. How often are you honest about your feelings when speaking with God? Do your prayers reflect how you're actually feeling?

9 In the assembly of all your people, LORD,
    I told the good news that you save us.
    You know that I will never stop telling it.
10 I have not kept the news of salvation to myself;
    I have always spoken of your faithfulness and help.
    In the assembly of all your people I have not been silent
    about your loyalty and constant love.

11 LORD, I know you will never stop being merciful to me.
    Your love and loyalty will always keep me safe.

A Prayer for Help
(Ps 70)

12 I am surrounded by many troubles —
    too many to count!
    My sins have caught up with me,
    and I can no longer see;
    they are more than the hairs of my head,
    and I have lost my courage.
13 Save me, LORD! Help me now!
14 May those who try to kill me
    be completely defeated and confused.
    May those who are happy because of my troubles
    be turned back and disgraced.
15 May those who jeer at me
    be dismayed by their defeat.

16 May all who come to you
    be glad and joyful.
    May all who are thankful for your salvation
    always say, "How great is the LORD!"

17 I am weak and poor, O Lord,
    but you have not forgotten me.
    You are my saviour and my God —
    hurry to my aid!

A Prayer in Sickness*

41 ¹Happy are those who are concerned for the poor;
    the LORD will help them when they are in trouble.
2 The LORD will protect them and preserve their lives;
    he will make them happy in the land;
    he will not abandon them to the power of their enemies.
3 The LORD will help them when they are sick
    and will restore them to health.

4 I said, "I have sinned against you, LORD;
    be merciful to me and heal me."
5 My enemies say cruel things about me.
    They want me to die and be forgotten.
6 Those who come to see me are not sincere;
    they gather bad news about me
    and then go out and tell it everywhere.
7 All who hate me whisper to each other about me,
    they imagine the worst about* me.

Ps 41 *Hebrew title: A psalm by David.*
41.7 *imagine the worst about; or make evil plans to harm.*

667

Psalms

Proverbs
Eccles.
Songs
Isaiah
Jerem.

[8] They say, "He is fatally ill;
    he will never leave his bed again."
[9] Even my best friend, the one I trusted most,
    the one who shared my food,
    has turned against me.

[10] Be merciful to me, LORD, and restore my health,
    and I will pay my enemies back.
[11] They will not triumph over me,
    and I will know that you are pleased with me.
[12] You will help me, because I do what is right;
    you will keep me in your presence for ever.

[13] Praise the LORD, the God of Israel!
    Praise him now and for ever!

Amen! Amen!

Book Two
Psalms 42—72

The Prayer of Someone in Exile*

42 [1] As a deer longs for a stream of cool water,
    so I long for you, O God.
[2] I thirst for you, the living God;
    when can I go and worship in your presence?
[3] Day and night I cry,
    and tears are my only food;
  all the time my enemies ask me,
    "Where is your God?"

[4] My heart breaks when I remember the past,
    when I went with the crowds to the house of God
    and led them as they walked along,
    a happy crowd, singing and shouting praise to God.
[5] Why am I so sad?
    Why am I so troubled?
  I will put my hope in God,
    and once again I will praise him,
    my saviour and my God.

[6-7] Here in exile my heart is breaking,
    and so I turn my thoughts to him.
  He has sent waves of sorrow over my soul;
    chaos roars at me like a flood,
    like waterfalls thundering down to the Jordan
    from Mount Hermon and Mount Mizar.
[8] May the LORD show his constant love during the day,
    so that I may have a song at night,
    a prayer to the God of my life.

[9] To God, my defender, I say,
    "Why have you forgotten me?
  Why must I go on suffering
    from the cruelty of my enemies?"

Ps 42 *Hebrew title*: A poem by the clan of Korah.

668

Psalms

·:········

2 Chron.
Ezra
Nehem.
Esther
Job

PSALMS 42–44

10 I am crushed by their insults,
    as they keep on asking me,
    "Where is your God?"

11 Why am I so sad?
    Why am I so troubled?
    I will put my hope in God,
    and once again I will praise him,
    my saviour and my God.

The Prayer of Someone in Exile
(Continuation of Ps 42)

43 ¹ O God, declare me innocent,
    and defend my cause against the ungodly;
    deliver me from lying and evil people!
² You are my protector;
    why have you abandoned me?
    Why must I go on suffering
    from the cruelty of my enemies?

³ Send your light and your truth;
    may they lead me
    and bring me back to Zion, your sacred hill,*
    and to your Temple, where you live.
⁴ Then I will go to your altar, O God;
    you are the source of my happiness.
    I will play my harp and sing praise to you,
    O God, my God.

⁵ Why am I so sad?
    Why am I so troubled?
    I will put my hope in God,
    and once again I will praise him,
    my saviour and my God.

A Prayer for Protection*

44 ¹ With our own ears we have heard it, O God —
    our ancestors have told us about it,
    about the great things you did in their time,
    in the days of long ago:
² how you yourself drove out the heathen
    and established your people in their land;
    how you punished the other nations
    and caused your own to prosper.
³ Your people did not conquer the land with their swords;
    they did not win it by their own power;
    it was by your power and your strength,
    by the assurance of your presence,
    which showed that you loved them.

⁴ You are my king and my God;
    you give* victory to your people,
⁵   and by your power we defeat our enemies.
⁶ I do not trust in my bow
    or in my sword to save me;

43.3 *sacred hill*: See 2.6.
Ps 44 *Hebrew title*: A poem by the clan of Korah.
44.4 Some ancient translations *and my God; you give*; Hebrew *O God; give*.

PSALMS 44, 45

669

Psalms

Proverbs
Eccles.
Songs
Isaiah
Jerem.

7 but you have saved us from our enemies
   and defeated those who hate us.
8 We will always praise you
   and give thanks to you for ever.

9 But now you have rejected us and let us be defeated;
   you no longer march out with our armies.
10 You made us run from our enemies,
   and they took for themselves what was ours.
11 You allowed us to be slaughtered like sheep;
   you scattered us in foreign countries.
12 You sold your own people for a small price
   as though they had little value.*

13 Our neighbours see what you did to us,
   and they mock us and laugh at us.
14 You have made us an object of contempt among the
      nations;
   they shake their heads at us in scorn.
15 I am always in disgrace;
   I am covered with shame
16 from hearing the sneers and insults
   of my enemies and those who hate me.

17 All this has happened to us,
   even though we have not forgotten you
   or broken the covenant you made with us.
18 We have not been disloyal to you;
   we have not disobeyed your commands.
19 Yet you left us helpless among wild animals;
   you abandoned us in deepest darkness.

20 If we had stopped worshipping our God
   and prayed to a foreign god,
21 you would surely have discovered it,
   because you know our secret thoughts.
22 But it is on your account that we are being killed all the
      time,
   that we are treated like sheep to be slaughtered.

23 Wake up, Lord! Why are you asleep?
   Rouse yourself! Don't reject us for ever!
24 Why are you hiding from us?
   Don't forget our suffering and trouble!

25 We fall crushed to the ground;
   we lie defeated in the dust.
26 Come to our aid!
   Because of your constant love save us!

A Royal Wedding Song*

45 1 Beautiful words fill my mind,
   as I compose this song for the king.
   Like the pen of a good writer
   my tongue is ready with a poem.

44.12 as... value; or and made no profit from the sale.
Ps 45 Hebrew title: A poem by the clan of Korah; a love song.

670

Psalms

·ː········

2 Chron.
Ezra
Nehem.
Esther
Job

PSALMS 45, 46

2 You are the most handsome of men;
  you are an eloquent speaker.
  God has always blessed you.
3 Buckle on your sword, mighty king;
  you are glorious and majestic.

4 Ride on in majesty to victory
  for the defence of truth and justice!*
  Your strength will win you great victories!
5 Your arrows are sharp,
  they pierce the hearts of your enemies;
  nations fall down at your feet.

6 The kingdom that God has given you*
  will last for ever and ever.
  You rule over your people with justice;
7   you love what is right and hate what is evil.
  That is why God, your God, has chosen you
  and has poured out more happiness on you
  than on any other king.
8 The perfume of myrrh and aloes is on your clothes;
  musicians entertain you in palaces decorated with ivory.
9 Among the ladies of your court are daughters of kings,
  and on the right of your throne stands the queen,
  wearing ornaments of finest gold.

10 Bride of the king, listen to what I say —
  forget your people and your relatives.
11 Your beauty will make the king desire you;
  he is your master, so you must obey him.
12 The people of Tyre will bring you gifts;
  rich people will try to win your favour.

13 The princess is in the palace — how beautiful she is!
  Her gown is made of gold thread.
14 In her colourful gown she is led to the king,
  followed by her bridesmaids,
  and they also are brought to him.
15 With joy and gladness they come
  and enter the king's palace.

16 You, my king, will have many sons
  to succeed your ancestors as kings,
  and you will make them rulers over the whole earth.
17 My song will keep your fame alive for ever,
  and everyone will praise you for all time to come.

God is with Us*

46 ¹God is our shelter and strength,
  always ready to help in times of trouble.
2 So we will not be afraid, even if the earth is shaken
  and mountains fall into the ocean depths;
3 even if the seas roar and rage,
  and the hills are shaken by the violence.

....
45.4 Probable text *and justice*; Hebrew *and meekness of justice*.
45.6 *The kingdom that God has given you*; or *Your kingdom, O God*; or *Your divine kingdom*.
Ps 46 *Hebrew title*: A song by the clan of Korah.

671

Psalms

Proverbs
Eccles.
Songs
Isaiah
Jerem.

⁴ There is a river that brings joy to the city of God,
　　to the sacred house of the Most High.
⁵ God is in that city, and it will never be destroyed;
　　at early dawn he will come to its aid.
⁶ Nations are terrified, kingdoms are shaken;
　　God thunders, and the earth dissolves.

⁷ The Lord Almighty is with us;
　　the God of Jacob is our refuge.

⁸ Come and see what the Lord has done.
　　See what amazing things he has done on earth.
⁹ He stops wars all over the world;
　　he breaks bows, destroys spears,
　　and sets shields on fire.
¹⁰ "Stop fighting," he says, "and know that I am God,
　　supreme among the nations,
　　supreme over the world."

¹¹ The Lord Almighty is with us;
　　the God of Jacob is our refuge.

The Supreme Ruler*

47 ¹ Clap your hands for joy, all peoples!
　　Praise God with loud songs!
² The Lord, the Most High, is to be feared;
　　he is a great king, ruling over all the world.
³ He gave us victory over the peoples;
　　he made us rule over the nations.
⁴ He chose for us the land where we live,
　　the proud possession of his people, whom he loves.

⁵ God goes up to his throne.
　　There are shouts of joy and the blast of trumpets,
　　as the Lord goes up.
⁶ Sing praise to God;
　　sing praise to our king!
⁷ God is king over all the world;
　　praise him with songs!

⁸ God sits on his sacred throne;
　　he rules over the nations.
⁹ The rulers of the nations assemble
　　with the people* of the God of Abraham.
　　More powerful than all armies is he;
　　he rules supreme.

Zion, the City of God*

48 ¹ The Lord is great and is to be highly praised
　　in the city of our God, on his sacred hill.*
² Zion, the mountain of God, is high and beautiful;
　　the city of the great king brings joy to all the world.
³ God has shown that there is safety with him
　　inside the fortresses of the city.

PSALM 46.10

Close this book right
now and spend
two minutes resting.

**SAY HELLO
TO GOD.**

Ps 47 *Hebrew title*: A psalm by the clan of Korah.
47.9 *Probable text* with the people; *Hebrew* the people.
Ps 48 *Hebrew title*: A psalm by the clan of Korah; a song.
48.1 *sacred hill*: See 2.6.

672

Psalms

2 Chron.
Ezra
Nehem.
Esther
Job

PSALMS 48, 49

⁴ The kings gathered together
  and came to attack Mount Zion.
⁵ But when they saw it, they were amazed;
  they were afraid and ran away.
⁶ There they were seized with fear and anguish,
  like a woman about to bear a child,
⁷ like ships tossing in a furious storm.

⁸ We have heard what God has done,
  and now we have seen it
  in the city of our God, the LORD Almighty;
he will keep the city safe for ever.

⁹ Inside your Temple, O God,
  we think of your constant love.
¹⁰ You are praised by people everywhere,
  and your fame extends over all the earth.
  You rule with justice;
¹¹ let the people of Zion be glad!
  You give right judgements;
  let there be joy in the cities of Judah!

¹² People of God, walk round Zion and count the towers;
¹³ take notice of the walls and examine the fortresses,
  so that you may tell the next generation:
¹⁴ "This God is our God for ever and ever;
  he will lead us for all time to come."

The Foolishness of Trusting in Riches*

49

¹ Hear this, everyone!
  Listen, all people everywhere,
² great and small alike,
  rich and poor together.
³ My thoughts will be clear;
  I will speak words of wisdom.
⁴ I will turn my attention to proverbs
  and explain their meaning as I play the harp.

⁵ I am not afraid in times of danger
  when I am surrounded by enemies,
⁶ by evil people who trust in their riches
  and boast of their great wealth.
⁷ A person can never redeem himself;
  he cannot pay God the price for his life,
⁸ because the payment for a human life is too great.
  What he could pay would never be enough
⁹ to keep him from the grave,
  to let him live for ever.

¹⁰ Anyone can see that even the wise die,
  as well as the foolish and stupid.
  They all leave their riches to their descendants.
¹¹ Their graves* are their homes for ever;
  there they stay for all time,
  though they once had lands of their own.

Ps 49 *Hebrew title*: A psalm by the clan of Korah.
49.11 Some ancient translations *graves*; Hebrew *inner thoughts*.

¹² No one's greatness can save him from death;
he will still die like the animals.

¹³ See what happens to those who trust in themselves,
the fate of those* who are satisfied with their wealth —
¹⁴ they are doomed to die like sheep,
and Death will be their shepherd.
The righteous will triumph over them,
as their bodies quickly decay
in the world of the dead far from their homes.*
¹⁵ But God will rescue me;
he will save me from the power of death.

¹⁶ Don't be upset when someone becomes rich,
when his wealth grows even greater;
¹⁷ he cannot take it with him when he dies;
his wealth will not go with him to the grave.
¹⁸ Even if he is satisfied with this life
and is praised because he is successful,
¹⁹ he will join all his ancestors in death,
where the darkness lasts for ever.
²⁰ His greatness cannot save him from death;
he will still die like the animals.

True Worship*

50 ¹ The Almighty God, the LORD, speaks;
he calls to the whole earth from east to west.
² God shines from Zion,
the city perfect in its beauty.

³ Our God is coming, but not in silence;
a raging fire is in front of him,
a furious storm is round him.
⁴ He calls heaven and earth as witnesses
to see him judge his people.
⁵ He says, "Gather my faithful people to me,
those who made a covenant with me by offering
a sacrifice."
⁶ The heavens proclaim that God is righteous,
that he himself is judge.

⁷ "Listen, my people, and I will speak;
I will testify against you, Israel.
I am God, your God.
⁸ I do not reprimand you because of your sacrifices
and the burnt offerings you always bring me.
⁹ And yet I do not need bulls from your farms
or goats from your flocks;
¹⁰ all the animals in the forest are mine
and the cattle on thousands of hills.
¹¹ All the wild birds are mine
and all living things in the fields.

¹² "If I were hungry, I would not ask you for food,
for the world and everything in it is mine.

FILL THIS SPACE HOWEVER YOU LIKE...

49.13 One ancient translation *the fate of those*; Hebrew *after them*.
49.14 *in... homes*; Hebrew unclear.
Ps 50 *Hebrew title*: A psalm by Asaph.

674

Psalms

·:·········

2 Chron.
Ezra
Nehem.
Esther
Job

PSALMS 50, 51

¹³ Do I eat the flesh of bulls
　　or drink the blood of goats?
¹⁴ Let the giving of thanks be your sacrifice to God,*
　　and give the Almighty all that you promised.
¹⁵ Call to me when trouble comes;
　　I will save you,
　　and you will praise me."

¹⁶ But God says to the wicked,
　　"Why should you recite my commandments?
　　Why should you talk about my covenant?
¹⁷ You refuse to let me correct you;
　　you reject my commands.
¹⁸ You become the friend of every thief you see
　　and you associate with adulterers.

¹⁹ "You are always ready to speak evil;
　　you never hesitate to tell lies.
²⁰ You are ready to accuse your own relatives
　　and to find fault with them.
²¹ You have done all this, and I have said nothing,
　　so you thought that I was like you.
　　But now I reprimand you
　　and make the matter plain to you.

²² "Listen to this, you that ignore me,
　　or I will destroy you,
　　and there will be no one to save you.
²³ Giving thanks is the sacrifice that honours me,
　　and I will surely save all who obey me."

A Prayer for Forgiveness*

51 ¹ Be merciful to me, O God,
　　because of your constant love.
　　Because of your great mercy wipe away my sins!
² Wash away all my evil
　　and make me clean from my sin!

³ I recognize my faults;
　　I am always conscious of my sins.
⁴ I have sinned against you — only against you —
　　and done what you consider evil.
　　So you are right in judging me;
　　you are justified in condemning me.
⁵ I have been evil from the day I was born;
　　from the time I was conceived, I have been sinful.

⁶ Sincerity and truth are what you require;
　　fill my mind with your wisdom.
⁷ Remove my sin, and I will be clean;
　　wash me, and I will be whiter than snow.
⁸ Let me hear the sounds of joy and gladness;
　　and though you have crushed me and broken me,
　　I will be happy once again.
⁹ Close your eyes to my sins and wipe out all my evil.

....

50.14 *Let the giving... to God*; or *Offer your thanksgiving sacrifice to God.*
Ps 51 *Hebrew title*: A psalm by David, after the prophet Nathan had spoken
to him about his adultery with Bathsheba.

PSALMS 51–53

675

Psalms

....

Proverbs
Eccles.
Songs
Isaiah
Jerem.

¹⁰ Create a pure heart in me, O God,
   and put a new and loyal spirit in me.
¹¹ Do not banish me from your presence;
   do not take your Holy Spirit away from me.
¹² Give me again the joy that comes from your salvation,
   and make me willing to obey you.
¹³ Then I will teach sinners your commands,
   and they will turn back to you.

¹⁴ Spare my life, O God, and save me,*
   and I will gladly proclaim your righteousness.
¹⁵ Help me to speak, Lord, and I will praise you.

¹⁶ You do not want sacrifices, or I would offer them;
   you are not pleased with burnt offerings.
¹⁷ My sacrifice is a humble spirit, O God;
   you will not reject a humble and repentant heart.

¹⁸ O God, be kind to Zion and help her;
   rebuild the walls of Jerusalem.
¹⁹ Then you will be pleased with proper sacrifices
   and with our burnt offerings;
   and bulls will be sacrificed on your altar.

God's Judgement and Grace*

52

¹ Why do you boast, great one, of your evil?
   God's faithfulness is eternal.
² You make plans to ruin others;
   your tongue is like a sharp razor.
   You are always inventing lies.
³ You love evil more than good and falsehood more than truth.
⁴ You love to hurt people with your words, you liar!

⁵ So God will ruin you for ever;
   he will take hold of you and snatch you from your home;
   he will remove you from the world of the living.
⁶ Righteous people will see this and be afraid;
   then they will laugh at you and say,
⁷ "Look, here is someone who did not depend on God for
      safety,
   but trusted instead in his great wealth
   and looked for security in being wicked."

⁸ But I am like an olive tree growing in the house of God;
   I trust in his constant love for ever and ever.
⁹ I will always thank you, God, for what you have done;
   in the presence of your people
   I will proclaim that you are good.

Human Wickedness*
(Ps 14)

53

¹ Fools say to themselves,
   "There is no God."

....

51.14 *Spare my life... me*; or *O God my saviour, keep me from the crime of murder.*
Ps 52 *Hebrew title: A poem by David, after Doeg the Edomite went to Saul and told him that David had gone to the house of Ahimelech.*
Ps 53 *Hebrew title: A poem by David.*

676

Psalms

2 Chron.
Ezra
Nehem.
Esther
Job

PSALMS 53–55

PSALM 54

This prayer for protection was written by David while he was running away from King Saul, who wanted to

KILL

• HIM. •

(Read more in 1 Samuel 21-23.) Do you see God as your protector?

They are all corrupt,
and they have done terrible things;
there is no one who does what is right.
2 God looks down from heaven at the human race
to see if there are any who are wise,
any who worship him.
3 But they have all turned away;
they are all equally bad.
Not one of them does what is right,
not a single one.

4 "Don't they know?" God asks.
"Are these evildoers ignorant?
They live by robbing my people,
and they never pray to me."

5 But then they will be terrified,
as they have never been before,
for God will scatter the bones of the enemies of his
people.
God has rejected them,
and so Israel will totally defeat them.

6 How I pray that victory
will come to Israel from Zion.
How happy the people of Israel will be
when God makes them prosperous again!

A Prayer for Protection from Enemies*

54 1 Save me by your power, O God;
set me free by your might!
2 Hear my prayer, O God;
listen to my words!
3 Proud men are coming to attack me;
cruel men are trying to kill me —
men who do not care about God.

4 But God is my helper.
The Lord is my defender.
5 May God use their own evil to punish my enemies.
He will destroy them because he is faithful.

6 I will gladly offer you a sacrifice, O Lord;
I will give you thanks
because you are good.
7 You have rescued me from all my troubles,
and I have seen my enemies defeated.

The Prayer of Someone Betrayed by a Friend*

55 1 Hear my prayer, O God;
don't turn away from my plea!
2 Listen to me and answer me;
I am worn out by my worries.
3 I am terrified by the threats of my enemies,
crushed by the oppression of the wicked.

Ps 54 *Hebrew title*: A poem by David, after the men from Ziph went to Saul and told him that David was hiding in their territory.
Ps 55 *Hebrew title*: A poem by David.

Psalms
....

Proverbs
Eccles.
Songs
Isaiah
Jerem.

They bring trouble on me;
   they are angry with me and hate me.

4 I am terrified,
   and the terrors of death crush me.
5 I am gripped by fear and trembling;
   I am overcome with horror.
6 I wish I had wings, like a dove.
   I would fly away and find rest.
7 I would fly far away
   and make my home in the desert.
8 I would quickly find myself a shelter
   from the raging wind and the storm.
9 Confuse the speech of my enemies, O Lord!

   I see violence and riots in the city,
10   surrounding it day and night,
   filling it with crime and trouble.
11 There is destruction everywhere;
   the streets are full of oppression and fraud.

12 If it were an enemy that mocked me,
   I could endure it;
   if it were an opponent boasting over me,
   I could hide myself from him.
13 But it is you, my companion,
   my colleague and close friend.
14 We had intimate talks with each other
   and worshipped together in the Temple.
15 May my enemies die before their time;
   may they go down alive into the world of the dead!
   Evil is in their homes and in their hearts.

16 But I call to the LORD God for help,
   and he will save me.
17 Morning, noon, and night
   my complaints and groans go up to him,
   and he will hear my voice.
18 He will bring me safely back
   from the battles that I fight
   against so many enemies.
19 God, who has ruled from eternity,
   will hear me and defeat them;
   for they refuse to change,
   and they do not fear him.

20 My former companion attacked his friends;
   he broke his promises.
21 His words were smoother than cream,
   but there was hatred in his heart;
   his words were as soothing as oil,
   but they cut like sharp swords.

22 Leave your troubles with the LORD,
   and he will defend you;
   he never lets honest people be defeated.

23 But you, O God, will bring those murderers and liars to
   their graves

678

Psalms

·:········

2 Chron.
Ezra
Nehem.
Esther
Job

PSALMS 55–57

before half their life is over.
As for me, I will trust in you.

A Prayer of Trust in God*

56 [1] Be merciful to me, O God,
because I am under attack;
my enemies persecute me all the time.
[2] All day long my opponents attack me.
There are so many who fight against me.
[3] When I am afraid, O LORD Almighty,
I put my trust in you.
[4] I trust in God and am not afraid;
I praise him for what he has promised.
What can a mere human being do to me?

[5] My enemies make trouble for me all day long;
they are always planning how to hurt me!
[6] They gather in hiding places
and watch everything I do,
hoping to kill me.
[7] Punish* them, O God, for their evil;
defeat those people in your anger!

[8] You know how troubled I am;
you have kept a record of my tears.
Aren't they listed in your book?
[9] The day I call to you,
my enemies will be turned back.
I know this: God* is on my side —
[10] the LORD, whose promises I praise.
[11] In him I trust, and I will not be afraid.
What can a mere human being do to me?

[12] O God, I will offer you what I have promised;
I will give you my offering of thanksgiving,
[13] because you have rescued me from death
and kept me from defeat.
And so I walk in the presence of God,
in the light that shines on the living.

A Prayer for Help*

57 [1] Be merciful to me, O God, be merciful,
because I come to you for safety.
In the shadow of your wings I find protection
until the raging storms are over.

[2] I call to God, the Most High,
to God, who supplies my every need.
[3] He will answer from heaven and save me;
he will defeat my oppressors.
God will show me his constant love and faithfulness.

Ps 56 *Hebrew title*: A psalm by David, after the Philistines captured him in Gath.
56.7 Probable text *Punish*; Hebrew *Save*.
56.9 *I know this: God*; or *Because I know that God*.
Ps 57 *Hebrew title*: A psalm by David, after he fled from Saul in the cave.

PSALMS 57, 58

679

Psalms

Proverbs
Eccles.
Songs
Isaiah
Jerem.

⁴ I am surrounded by enemies,
   who are like lions hungry for human flesh.
Their teeth are like spears and arrows;
   their tongues are like sharp swords.

⁵ Show your greatness in the sky, O God,
   and your glory over all the earth.

⁶ My enemies have spread a net to catch me;
   I am overcome with distress.
They dug a pit in my path,
   but fell into it themselves.

⁷ I have complete confidence, O God;
   I will sing and praise you!
⁸ Wake up, my soul!
   Wake up, my harp and lyre!
   I will wake up the sun.
⁹ I will thank you, O Lord, among the nations.
   I will praise you among the peoples.
¹⁰ Your constant love reaches the heavens;
   your faithfulness touches the skies.
¹¹ Show your greatness in the sky, O God,
   and your glory over all the earth.

A Prayer for God to Punish the Wicked*

58 ¹Do you rulers* ever give a just decision?
   Do you judge everyone fairly?
² No! You think only of the evil you can do,
   and commit crimes of violence in the land.

³ Evildoers go wrong all their lives;
   they tell lies from the day they are born.
⁴ They are full of poison like snakes;
   they stop up their ears like a deaf cobra,
⁵ which does not hear the voice of the snake charmer,
   or the chant of the clever magician.

⁶ Break the teeth of these fierce lions, O God.
⁷ May they disappear like water draining away;
   may they be crushed like weeds on a path.*
⁸ May they be like snails that dissolve into slime;
   may they be like a baby born dead that never sees the
      light.
⁹ Before they know it, they are cut down like weeds;
   in his fierce anger God will blow them away
      while they are still living.*

¹⁰ The righteous will be glad when they see sinners
      punished;
   they will wade through the blood of the wicked.
¹¹ People will say, "The righteous are indeed rewarded;
   there is indeed a God who judges the world."

GLORY

PSALM 57.11;
EZEKIEL 3.12;
JOHN 17.4

Search for the Oxford
or Cambridge Dictionary
definition of 'glory'
and write the
definition here.

_____
_____
_____
_____
_____
_____
_____
_____
_____
_____
_____
_____
_____
_____
_____
_____

Ps 58 *Hebrew title*: A psalm by David.
58.1 *rulers*; or *gods*.
58.7 Probable text *may... path*; Hebrew unclear.
58.9 Verse 9 in Hebrew is unclear.

680

Psalms

2 Chron.
Ezra
Nehem.
Esther
Job

PSALMS 59

A Prayer for Safety*

59 ¹Save me from my enemies, my God;
protect me from those who attack me!
² Save me from those evil people;
rescue me from those murderers!

³ Look! They are waiting to kill me;
cruel people are gathering against me.
It is not because of any sin or wrong I have done,
⁴ nor because of any fault of mine, O LORD,
that they hurry to their places.

⁵ Rise, LORD God Almighty, and come to my aid;
see for yourself, God of Israel!
Wake up and punish the heathen;
show no mercy to evil traitors!

⁶ They come back in the evening,
snarling like dogs as they go about the city.
⁷ Listen to their insults and threats.
Their tongues are like swords in their mouths,
yet they think that no one hears them.

⁸ But you laugh at them, LORD;
you mock all the heathen.
⁹ I have confidence in your strength;
you are my refuge, O God.
¹⁰ My God loves me and will come to me;
he will let me see my enemies defeated.

¹¹ Do not kill them, O God, or my people may forget.
Scatter them by your strength and defeat them,
O Lord, our protector.
¹² Sin is on their lips; all their words are sinful;
may they be caught in their pride!
Because they curse and lie,
¹³ destroy them in your anger;
destroy them completely.
Then everyone will know that God rules in Israel,
that his rule extends over all the earth.

¹⁴ My enemies come back in the evening,
snarling like dogs as they go about the city,
¹⁵ like dogs roaming about for food
and growling if they do not find enough.

¹⁶ But I will sing about your strength;
every morning I will sing aloud of your constant love.
You have been a refuge for me,
a shelter in my time of trouble.
¹⁷ I will praise you, my defender.
My refuge is God,
the God who loves me.

Ps 59 *Hebrew title*: A psalm by David, after Saul sent men to watch his house in order to kill him.

A Prayer for Deliverance*

60 [1] You have rejected us, God, and defeated us;
you have been angry with us — but now turn back to
us.*

[2] You have made the land tremble, and you have cut it
open;
now heal its wounds, because it is falling apart.

[3] You have made your people suffer greatly;
we stagger around as though we were drunk.

[4] You have warned those who show you reverence,
so that they might escape destruction.

[5] Save us by your might; answer our prayer,
so that the people you love may be rescued.

[6] From his sanctuary* God has said,
"In triumph I will divide Shechem
and distribute the Valley of Sukkoth to my people.

[7] Gilead is mine, and Manasseh too;
Ephraim is my helmet
and Judah my royal sceptre.

[8] But I will use Moab as my washbasin
and I will throw my sandals on Edom,
as a sign that I own it.
Did the Philistines think they would shout in triumph over
me?"

[9] Who, O God, will take me into the fortified city?
Who will lead me to Edom?

[10] Have you really rejected us?
Aren't you going to march out with our armies?

[11] Help us against the enemy;
human help is worthless.

[12] With God on our side we will win;
he will defeat our enemies.

A Prayer for Protection*

61 [1] Hear my cry, O God;
listen to my prayer!

[2] In despair and far from home
I call to you!

Take me to a safe refuge,
[3] for you are my protector,
my strong defence against my enemies.

[4] Let me live in your sanctuary all my life;
let me find safety under your wings.

[5] You have heard my promises, O God,
and you have given me what belongs to those who
honour you.

[6] Add many years to the king's life;
let him live on and on!

....

Ps 60 *Hebrew title*: A psalm by David, for teaching, when he fought against
the Arameans from Naharaim and from Zobah, and Joab turned back and
killed 12,000 Edomites in the Valley of Salt.
60.1 *angry with us... us*; or *angry with us and turned your back on us.*
60.6 *From his sanctuary*; or *In his holiness.*
Ps 61 *Hebrew title*: By David.

682

Psalms

⫶⫶·········

2 Chron.
Ezra
Nehem.
Esther
Job

PSALMS 61–63

7 May he rule for ever in your presence, O God;
    protect him with your constant love and faithfulness.

8 So I will always sing praises to you,
    as I offer you daily what I have promised.

Confidence in God's Protection*

62 ¹ I wait patiently for God to save me;
    I depend on him alone.
² He alone protects and saves me;
    he is my defender,
    and I shall never be defeated.

³ How much longer will all of you attack someone
    who is no stronger than a broken-down fence?
⁴ You only want to bring him down from his place of honour;
    you take pleasure in lies.
You speak words of blessing,
    but in your heart you curse him.

⁵ I depend on God alone;
    I put my hope in him.
⁶ He alone protects and saves me;
    he is my defender,
    and I shall never be defeated.
⁷ My salvation and honour depend on God;
    he is my strong protector;
    he is my shelter.

⁸ Trust in God at all times, my people.
    Tell him all your troubles,
    for he is our refuge.

⁹ Human beings are all like a puff of breath;
    great and small alike are worthless.
Put them on the scales, and they weigh nothing;
    they are lighter than a mere breath.
¹⁰ Don't put your trust in violence;
    don't hope to gain anything by robbery;
even if your riches increase,
    don't depend on them.

¹¹ More than once I have heard God say
    that power belongs to him
¹²   and that his love is constant.
You yourself, O Lord, reward everyone according to his deeds.

Longing for God*

63 ¹ O God, you are my God,
    and I long for you.
My whole being desires you;
    like a dry, worn-out, and waterless land,
    my soul is thirsty for you.
² Let me see you in the sanctuary;
    let me see how mighty and glorious you are.
³ Your constant love is better than life itself,

....

Ps 62 *Hebrew title:* A psalm by David.
Ps 63 *Hebrew title:* A psalm by David, when he was in the desert of Judah.

PSALMS 63–65

683

Psalms

....

Proverbs
Eccles.
Songs
Isaiah
Jerem.

and so I will praise you.
⁴ I will give you thanks as long as I live;
    I will raise my hands to you in prayer.
⁵ My soul will feast and be satisfied,
    and I will sing glad songs of praise to you.

⁶ As I lie in bed, I remember you;
    all night long I think of you,
⁷ because you have always been my help.
    In the shadow of your wings I sing for joy.
⁸ I cling to you,
    and your hand keeps me safe.

⁹ Those who are trying to kill me
    will go down into the world of the dead.
¹⁰ They will be killed in battle,
    and their bodies eaten by wolves.
¹¹ Because God gives him victory,
    the king will rejoice.
    Those who make promises in God's name will praise him,
    but the mouths of liars will be shut.

A Prayer for Protection*

64 ¹ I am in trouble, God — listen to my prayer!
    I am afraid of my enemies — save my life!
² Protect me from the plots of the wicked,
    from evil mobs.
³ They sharpen their tongues like swords
    and aim cruel words like arrows.
⁴ They are quick to spread their shameless lies;
    they destroy good people with cowardly slander.
⁵ They encourage each other in their evil plots;
    they plan where to place their traps.
    "No one can see them," they say.
⁶ They make evil plans and say,
    "We have planned a perfect crime."
    The human heart and mind are a mystery.

⁷ But God shoots his arrows at them,
    and suddenly they are wounded.
⁸ He will destroy them because of those words;*
    all who see them will shake their heads.
⁹ They will all be afraid;
    they will think about what God has done
    and tell about his deeds.
¹⁰ All righteous people will rejoice
    because of what the LORD has done.
    They will find safety in him;
    all good people will praise him.

Praise and Thanksgiving*

65 ¹ O God, it is right for us to praise you in Zion
    and keep our promises to you,
² because you answer prayers.

Ps 64 *Hebrew title*: A psalm by David.
64.8 *Probable text* He will destroy them because of those words; *Hebrew*
They will destroy him, those words are against them.
Ps 65 *Hebrew title*: A psalm by David; a song.

684

Psalms

2 Chron.
Ezra
Nehem.
Esther
Job

PSALMS 65, 66

PSALM 66

Make a

LIST
– OF –

THANKFULNESS!

(Write down a bunch
of things you're thankful
to God for.)

_____

_____

_____

_____

_____

_____

_____

_____

_____

_____

_____

_____

_____

_____

_____

_____

People everywhere will come to you
3   on account of their sins.
Our faults defeat us,*
   but you forgive them.
4 Happy are those whom you choose,
   whom you bring to live in your sanctuary.
We shall be satisfied with the good things of your house,
   the blessings of your sacred Temple.

5 You answer us by giving us victory
   and you do wonderful things to save us.
People all over the world
   and across the distant seas trust in you.
6 You set the mountains in place by your strength,
   showing your mighty power.
7 You calm the roar of the seas
   and the noise of the waves;
   you calm the uproar of the peoples.
8 The whole world stands in awe
   of the great things that you have done.
Your deeds bring shouts of joy
   from one end of the earth to the other.

9 You show your care for the land by sending rain;
   you make it rich and fertile.
You fill the streams with water;
   you provide the earth with crops.
This is how you do it:
10   you send abundant rain on the ploughed fields
   and soak them with water;
you soften the soil with showers
   and cause the young plants to grow.
11 What a rich harvest your goodness provides!
   Wherever you go there is plenty.
12 The pastures are filled with flocks;
   the hillsides are full of joy.
13 The fields are covered with sheep;
   the valleys are full of wheat.
Everything shouts and sings for joy.

A Song of Praise and Thanksgiving*
66 1 Praise God with shouts of joy, all people!
   2   Sing to the glory of his name;
   offer him glorious praise!
3 Say to God, "How wonderful are the things you do!
   Your power is so great
   that your enemies bow down in fear before you.
4 Everyone on earth worships you;
   they sing praises to you,
   they sing praises to your name."

5 Come and see what God has done,
   his wonderful acts for mankind.
6 He changed the sea into dry land;
   our ancestors crossed the river on foot.
There we rejoiced because of what he did.

....
65.3 One ancient translation us; Hebrew me.
Ps 66 Hebrew title: A song.

PSALMS 66, 67

685

Psalms

Proverbs
Eccles.
Songs
Isaiah
Jerem.

7 He rules for ever by his might
    and keeps his eyes on the nations.
    Let no rebels rise against him.
8 Praise our God, all nations;
    let your praise be heard.
9 He has kept us alive
    and has not allowed us to fall.

10 You have put us to the test, God;
    as silver is purified by fire
    so you have tested us.
11 You let us fall into a trap
    and placed heavy burdens on our backs.
12 You let our enemies trample over us;
    we went through fire and flood,
    but now you have brought us to a place of safety.*

13 I will bring burnt offerings to your house;
    I will offer you what I promised.
14 I will give you what I said I would
    when I was in trouble.
15 I will offer sheep to be burnt on the altar;
    I will sacrifice bulls and goats,
    and the smoke will go up to the sky.

16 Come and listen, all who honour God,
    and I will tell you what he has done for me.
17 I cried to him for help;
    I praised him with songs.
18 If I had ignored my sins,
    the Lord would not have listened to me.
19 But God has indeed heard me;
    he has listened to my prayer.

20 I praise God,
    because he did not reject my prayer
    or keep back his constant love from me.

A Song of Thanksgiving*

67 1 God, be merciful to us and bless us;
    look on us with kindness,
2 so that the whole world may know your will;
    so that all nations may know your salvation.

3 May the peoples praise you, O God;
    may all the peoples praise you!

4 May the nations be glad and sing for joy,
    because you judge the peoples with justice
    and guide every nation on earth.

5 May the peoples praise you, O God;
    may all the peoples praise you!

6 The land has produced its harvest;
    God, our God, has blessed us.

66.12 Some ancient translations *safety*; Hebrew *overflowing*.
Ps 67 *Hebrew title*: A psalm; a song.

686

Psalms

2 Chron.
Ezra
Nehem.
Esther
Job

PSALMS 67, 68

7 God has blessed us;
may all people everywhere honour him.

A National Song of Triumph*

68 1 God rises up and scatters his enemies.
Those who hate him run away in defeat.
2 As smoke is blown away, so he drives them off;
as wax melts in front of the fire,
so do the wicked perish in God's presence.
3 But the righteous are glad and rejoice in his presence;
they are happy and shout for joy.

4 Sing to God, sing praises to his name;
prepare a way for him who rides on the clouds.*
His name is the LORD — be glad in his presence!

5 God, who lives in his sacred Temple,
cares for orphans and protects widows.
6 He gives the lonely a home to live in
and leads prisoners out into happy freedom,
but rebels will have to live in a desolate land.

7 O God, when you led your people,
when you marched across the desert,
8 the earth shook, and the sky poured down rain,
because of the coming of the God of Sinai,*
the coming of the God of Israel.
9 You caused abundant rain to fall
and restored your worn-out land;
10 your people made their home there;
in your goodness you provided for the poor.

11 The Lord gave the command,
and many women carried the news:
12 "Kings and their armies are running away!"
The women at home divided what was captured:
13 figures of doves covered with silver,
whose wings glittered with fine gold.
(Why did some of you stay among the sheep pens on the
day of battle?)
14 When Almighty God scattered the kings on Mount
Zalmon,
he caused snow to fall there.

15 What a mighty mountain is Bashan,
a mountain of many peaks!
16 Why from your mighty peaks do you look with scorn
on the mountain* on which God chose to live?
The LORD will live there for ever!

17 With his many thousands of mighty chariots
the Lord comes from Sinai* into the holy place.

....

Ps 68 *Hebrew title*: A psalm by David; a song.
68.4 *on the clouds*; or *across the desert*.
68.8 *God of Sinai*: As the people of Israel went from Egypt to Canaan, God
revealed himself to them at Mount Sinai (see Ex 19.16–25).
68.16 *mountain*: See 2.6.
68.17 Probable text *comes from Sinai*; Hebrew *in them, Sinai*.

Psalms

Proverbs
Eccles.
Songs
Isaiah
Jerem.

18 He goes up to the heights,
    taking many captives with him;
    he receives gifts from rebellious people.
The LORD God will live there.

19 Praise the Lord,
    who carries our burdens day after day;
    he is the God who saves us.
20 Our God is a God who saves;
    he is the LORD, our Lord,
    who rescues us from death.

21 God will surely break the heads of his enemies,
    of those who persist in their sinful ways.
22 The Lord has said, "I will bring your enemies back from
        Bashan;
    I will bring them back from the depths of the ocean,
23 so that you may wade in their blood,
    and your dogs may lap up as much as they want."

24 O God, your march of triumph is seen by all,
    the procession of God, my king, into his sanctuary.
25 The singers are in front, the musicians are behind,
    in between are the young women beating the
        tambourines.
26 "Praise God in the meeting of his people;
    praise the LORD, all you descendants of Jacob!"
27 First comes Benjamin, the smallest tribe,
    then the leaders of Judah with their group,
    followed by the leaders of Zebulun and Naphtali.

28 Show your power, O God,
    the power you have used on our behalf
29   from your Temple in Jerusalem,
    where kings bring gifts to you.
30 Rebuke Egypt, that wild animal in the reeds;
    rebuke the nations, that herd of bulls with their calves,
    until they all bow down and offer you their silver.
Scatter those people who love to make war!*
31 Ambassadors* will come from Egypt;
    the Ethiopians will raise their hands in prayer to God.

32 Sing to God, kingdoms of the world,
    sing praise to the Lord,
33   to him who rides in the sky,
    the ancient sky.
Listen to him shout with a mighty roar.
34 Proclaim God's power;
    his majesty is over Israel,
    his might is in the skies.
35 How awesome is God as he comes from his sanctuary —
    the God of Israel!
He gives strength and power to his people.

Praise God!

68.30 Verse 30 in Hebrew is unclear.
68.31 Some ancient translations *Ambassadors*; Hebrew unclear.

688

Psalms

2 Chron.
Ezra
Nehem.
Esther
Job

PSALMS 69

A Cry for Help*

69

¹Save me, O God!
The water is up to my neck;

² I am sinking in deep mud,
and there is no solid ground;
I am out in deep water,
and the waves are about to drown me.
³ I am worn out from calling for help,
and my throat is aching.
I have strained my eyes,
looking for your help.

⁴ Those who hate me for no reason
are more numerous than the hairs of my head.
My enemies tell lies against me;
they are strong and want to kill me.
They made me give back things I did not steal.
⁵ My sins, O God, are not hidden from you;
you know how foolish I have been.
⁶ Don't let me bring shame on those who trust in you,
Sovereign Lord Almighty!
Don't let me bring disgrace to those who worship you,
O God of Israel!
⁷ It is for your sake that I have been insulted
and that I am covered with shame.
⁸ I am like a stranger to my relatives,
like a foreigner to my family.

⁹ My devotion to your Temple burns in me like a fire;
the insults which are hurled at you fall on me.
¹⁰ I humble myself* by fasting,
and people insult me;
¹¹ I dress myself in clothes of mourning,
and they laugh at me.
¹² They talk about me in the streets,
and drunkards make up songs about me.

¹³ But as for me, I will pray to you, Lord;
answer me, God, at a time you choose.
Answer me because of your great love,
because you keep your promise to save.
¹⁴ Save me from sinking in the mud;
keep me safe from my enemies,
safe from the deep water.
¹⁵ Don't let the flood come over me;
don't let me drown in the depths
or sink into the grave.

¹⁶ Answer me, Lord, in the goodness of your constant love;
in your great compassion turn to me!
¹⁷ Don't hide yourself from your servant;
I am in great trouble — answer me now!
¹⁸ Come to me and save me;
rescue me from my enemies.

Ps 69 *Hebrew title*: By David.
69.10 Some ancient translations *humble myself*; Hebrew *cry*.

PSALMS 69, 70

689

Psalms
·········
Proverbs
Eccles.
Songs
Isaiah
Jerem.

19 You know how I am insulted,
   how I am disgraced and dishonoured;
   you see all my enemies.
20 Insults have broken my heart,
   and I am in despair.
   I had hoped for sympathy, but there was none;
   for comfort, but I found none.
21 When I was hungry, they gave me poison;
   when I was thirsty, they offered me vinegar.
22 May their banquets cause their ruin;
   may their sacred feasts cause their downfall.
23 Strike them with blindness!
   Make their backs always weak!
24 Pour out your anger on them;
   let your indignation overtake them.
25 May their camps be left deserted;
   may no one be left alive in their tents.
26 They persecute those whom you have punished;
   they talk about the sufferings of those you have wounded.
27 Keep a record of all their sins;
   don't let them have any part in your salvation.
28 May their names be erased from the book of the living;
   may they not be included in the list of your people.

29 But I am in pain and despair;
   lift me up, O God, and save me!

30 I will praise God with a song;
   I will proclaim his greatness by giving him thanks.
31 This will please the LORD more than offering him cattle,
   more than sacrificing a full-grown bull.
32 When the oppressed see this, they will be glad;
   those who worship God will be encouraged.
33 The LORD listens to those in need
   and does not forget his people in prison.

34 Praise God, O heaven and earth,
   seas and all creatures in them.
35 He will save Jerusalem
   and rebuild the towns of Judah.
   His people will live there and possess the land;
36   the descendants of his servants will inherit it,
   and those who love him will live there.

A Prayer for Help*
(Ps 40.13–17)

70 1 Save me, O God!
   LORD, help me now!
2 May those who try to kill me
   be defeated and confused.
   May those who are happy because of my troubles
   be turned back and disgraced.
3 May those who jeer at me
   be dismayed by their defeat.

4 May all who come to you
   be glad and joyful.

Ps 70 *Hebrew title*: A psalm by David; a lament.

WHAT DOES 'SALVATION' MEAN?
Finish the mindmap below.

Deliverance
from sin and
its consequences,
believed by
Christians to be
brought about
by faith in Christ.
(oxforddictionaries.com)

SALVATION

PSALM 70.4; LUKE 1.78

May all who are thankful for your salvation
    always say, "How great is God!"

5 I am weak and poor;
    come to me quickly, O God.
  You are my saviour, O Lord —
    hurry to my aid!

An Old Person's Prayer

71 1 Lord, I have come to you for protection;
    never let me be defeated!
2 Because you are righteous, help me and rescue me.
    Listen to me and save me!
3 Be my secure shelter
    and a strong fortress* to protect me;
    you are my refuge and defence.

4 My God, rescue me from the wicked,
    from the power of those who are cruel and evil.
5 Sovereign Lord, I put my hope in you;
    I have trusted in you since I was young.
6 I have relied on you all my life;
    you have protected* me since the day I was born.
    I will always praise you.

7 My life has been an example to many,
    because you have been my strong defender.
8 All day long I praise you
    and proclaim your glory.
9 Do not reject me now that I am old;
    do not abandon me now that I am feeble.
10 My enemies want to kill me;
    they talk and plot against me.
11 They say, "God has abandoned him;
    let's go after him and catch him;
    there is no one to rescue him."

12 Don't stay so far away, O God;
    my God, hurry to my aid!
13 May those who attack me
    be defeated and destroyed.
  May those who try to hurt me
    be shamed and disgraced.
14 I will always put my hope in you;
    I will praise you more and more.
15 I will tell of your goodness;
    all day long I will speak of your salvation,
    though it is more than I can understand.
16 I will go in the strength of the Lord God;
    I will proclaim your goodness, yours alone.

17 You have taught me ever since I was young,
    and I still tell of your wonderful acts.
18 Now that I am old and my hair is grey,
    do not abandon me, O God!

71.3 One ancient translation *a strong fortress*; Hebrew *to go always you commanded.*
71.6 Some ancient translations *protected*; Hebrew unclear.

PSALMS 71, 72

691

Psalms

Proverbs
Eccles.
Songs
Isaiah
Jerem.

Be with me while I proclaim your power and might
to all generations to come.

19 Your righteousness, God, reaches the skies.
You have done great things;
there is no one like you.
20 You have sent troubles and suffering on me,
but you will restore my strength;
you will keep me from the grave.
21 You will make me greater than ever;
you will comfort me again.

22 I will indeed praise you with the harp;
I will praise your faithfulness, my God.
On my harp I will play hymns to you,
the Holy One of Israel.
23 I will shout for joy as I play for you;
with my whole being I will sing
because you have saved me.
24 I will speak of your righteousness all day long,
because those who tried to harm me
have been defeated and disgraced.

A Prayer for the King*

72

1 Teach the king to judge with your righteousness,
O God;
share with him your own justice,
2 so that he will rule over your people with justice
and govern the oppressed with righteousness.
3 May the land enjoy prosperity;
may it experience righteousness.
4 May the king judge the poor fairly;
may he help the needy
and defeat their oppressors.
5 May your people worship you as long as the sun shines,
as long as the moon gives light, for ages to come.

6 May the king be like rain on the fields,
like showers falling on the land.
7 May righteousness flourish in his lifetime,
and may prosperity last as long as the moon gives light.

8 His kingdom will reach from sea to sea,
from the Euphrates to the ends of the earth.
9 The peoples of the desert will bow down before him;
his enemies will throw themselves to the ground.
10 The kings of Spain and of the islands will offer him gifts;
the kings of Sheba and Seba* will bring him offerings.
11 All kings will bow down before him;
all nations will serve him.

12 He rescues the poor who call to him,
and those who are needy and neglected.
13 He has pity on the weak and poor;
he saves the lives of those in need.

Ps 72 *Hebrew title*: By Solomon.
72.10 *Sheba and Seba*: Sheba was towards the south in Arabia and Seba
was on the opposite side of the Red Sea.

692

Psalms

.:........

2 Chron.
Ezra
Nehem.
Esther
Job

PSALMS 72, 73

14 He rescues them from oppression and violence;
    their lives are precious to him.

15 Long live the king!
    May he be given gold from Sheba*;
    may prayers be said for him at all times;
    may God's blessings be on him always!
16 May there be plenty of corn in the land;
    may the hills be covered with crops,
        as fruitful as those of Lebanon.
    May the cities be filled with people,
        like fields full of grass.
17 May the king's name never be forgotten;
    may his fame last as long as the sun.
    May all nations ask God to bless them
        as he has blessed the king.*

18 Praise the Lord, the God of Israel!
    He alone does these wonderful things.
19 Praise his glorious name for ever!
    May his glory fill the whole world.

Amen! Amen!

20 This is the end of the prayers of David son of Jesse.

Book Three
Psalms 73—89

The Justice of God*
73 ¹God is indeed good to Israel,
    to those who have pure hearts.
2 But I had nearly lost confidence;
    my faith was almost gone
3 because I was jealous of the proud
    when I saw that things go well for the wicked.

4 They do not suffer pain;
    they are strong and healthy.
5 They do not suffer as other people do;
    they do not have the troubles that others have.
6 And so they wear pride like a necklace
    and violence like a robe;
7 their hearts pour out evil,*
    and their minds are busy with wicked schemes.
8 They laugh at other people and speak of evil things;
    they are proud and make plans to oppress others.
9 They speak evil of God in heaven
    and give arrogant orders to everyone on earth,
10 so that even God's people turn to them
    and eagerly believe whatever they say.*
11 They say, "God will not know;
    the Most High will not find out."

72.15 *Sheba and Seba*: Sheba was towards the south in Arabia and Seba was on the opposite side of the Red Sea.
72.17 *as he… king*; or *and may they wish happiness for the king.*
Ps 73 *Hebrew title*: By Asaph.
73.7 Some ancient translations *their hearts pour out evil*; Hebrew unclear.
73.10 Verse 10 in Hebrew is unclear.

PSALMS 73, 74

693

Psalms

..........:

Proverbs
Eccles.
Songs
Isaiah
Jerem.

12 That is what the wicked are like.
   They have plenty and are always getting more.

13 Is it for nothing, then, that I have kept myself pure
   and have not committed sin?
14 O God, you have made me suffer all day long;
   every morning you have punished me.

15 If I had said such things,
   I would not be acting as one of your people.
16 I tried to think this problem through,
   but it was too difficult for me
17 until I went into your Temple.
   Then I understood what will happen to the wicked.

18 You will put them in slippery places
   and make them fall to destruction!
19 They are instantly destroyed;
   they go down to a horrible end.
20 They are like a dream that goes away in the morning;
   when you rouse yourself, O Lord, they disappear.

21 When my thoughts were bitter
   and my feelings were hurt,
22 I was as stupid as an animal;
   I did not understand you.
23 Yet I always stay close to you,
   and you hold me by the hand.
24 You guide me with your instruction
   and at the end you will receive me with honour.
25 What else have I in heaven but you?
   Since I have you, what else could I want on earth?
26 My mind and my body may grow weak,
   but God is my strength;
   he is all I ever need.

27 Those who abandon you will certainly perish;
   you will destroy those who are unfaithful to you.
28 But as for me, how wonderful to be near God,
   to find protection with the Sovereign LORD
   and to proclaim all that he has done!

A Prayer for National Deliverance*

74 1 Why have you abandoned us like this, O God?
   Will you be angry with your own people for ever?
2 Remember your people, whom you chose for yourself long
   ago,
   whom you brought out of slavery to be your own tribe.
   Remember Mount Zion, where once you lived.
3 Walk over these total ruins;
   our enemies have destroyed everything in the Temple.

4 Your enemies have shouted in triumph in your Temple;
   they have placed their flags there as signs of victory.
5 They looked like woodmen
   cutting down trees with their axes.*

PSALM 73.26

GOD
is my
STRENGTH

....

Ps 74 *Hebrew title*: A poem by Asaph.
74.5 Verse 5 in Hebrew is unclear.

694

Psalms

·:········

2 Chron.

Ezra

Nehem.

Esther

Job

PSALMS 74, 75

⁶ They smashed all the wooden panels
    with their axes and sledgehammers.
⁷ They wrecked your Temple and set it on fire;
    they desecrated the place where you are worshipped.
⁸ They wanted to crush us completely;
    they burnt down every holy place in the land.

⁹ All our sacred symbols are gone;
    there are no prophets left,
    and no one knows how long this will last.
¹⁰ How long, O God, will our enemies laugh at you?
    Will they insult your name for ever?
¹¹ Why have you refused to help us?
    Why do you keep your hands behind you?*

¹² But you have been our king from the beginning, O God;
    you have saved us many times.
¹³ With your mighty strength you divided the sea
    and smashed the heads of the sea monsters;
¹⁴ you crushed the heads of the monster Leviathan*
    and fed his body to desert animals.*
¹⁵ You made springs and fountains flow;
    you dried up large rivers.
¹⁶ You created the day and the night;
    you set the sun and the moon in their places;
¹⁷ you set the limits of the earth;
    you made summer and winter.

¹⁸ But remember, O Lᴏʀᴅ, that your enemies laugh at you,
    that they are godless and despise you.
¹⁹ Don't abandon your helpless people to their cruel enemies;
    don't forget your persecuted people!

²⁰ Remember the covenant you made with us.
    There is violence in every dark corner of the land.
²¹ Don't let the oppressed be put to shame;
    let those poor and needy people praise you.

²² Rouse yourself, God, and defend your cause!
    Remember that godless people laugh at you all day long.
²³ Don't forget the angry shouts of your enemies,
    the continuous noise made by your foes.

God the Judge*

75 ¹ We give thanks to you, O God, we give thanks to you!
    We proclaim how great you are
    and tell of* the wonderful things you have done.

² "I have set a time for judgement," says God,
    "and I will judge with fairness.

74.11 Probable text *Why do you keep your hands behind you*; Hebrew unclear.
74.14 *Leviathan*: A legendary monster which was a symbol of the forces of chaos and evil.
74.14 *animals*; or *people*.
Ps 75 Hebrew title: *A psalm by Asaph; a song.*
75.1 Some ancient translations *We proclaim how great you are and tell of*; Hebrew *Your name is near and they tell of.*

PSALMS 75, 76

695

Psalms

Proverbs
Eccles.
Songs
Isaiah
Jerem.

3 Though every living creature tremble
   and the earth itself be shaken,
   I will keep its foundations firm.
4 I tell the wicked not to be arrogant;
5   I tell them to stop their boasting."

6 Judgement does not come from the east or from the west,
   from the north or from the south;*
7 it is God who is the judge,
   condemning some and acquitting others.
8 The LORD holds a cup in his hand,
   filled with the strong wine of his anger.
   He pours it out, and all the wicked drink it;
   they drink it down to the last drop.

9 But I will never stop speaking of the God of Jacob
   or singing praises to him.
10 He will break the power of the wicked,
   but the power of the righteous will be increased.

God the Victor*

76 ¹ God is known in Judah;
   his name is honoured in Israel.
2 He has his home in Jerusalem;
   he lives on Mount Zion.
3 There he broke the arrows of the enemy,
   their shields and swords, yes, all their weapons.

4 How glorious you are, O God!
   How majestic, as you return from the mountains
   where you defeated your foes.
5 Their brave soldiers have been stripped of all they had
   and now are sleeping the sleep of death;
   all their strength and skill was useless.
6 When you threatened them, O God of Jacob,
   the horses and their riders fell dead.

7 But you, LORD, are feared by all.
   No one can stand in your presence
   when you are angry.
8 You made your judgement known from heaven;
   the world was afraid and kept silent,
9 when you rose up to pronounce judgement,
   to save all the oppressed on earth.

10 Human anger only results in more praise for you;
   those who survive the wars will keep your festivals.*

11 Give the LORD your God what you promised him;
   bring gifts to him, all you nearby nations.
   God makes everyone fear him;
12   he humbles proud princes
   and terrifies great kings.

75.6 Probable text *from the north or from the south*; Hebrew *from the wilderness of the mountains.*
Ps 76 *Hebrew title*: A psalm by Asaph; a song.
76.10 One ancient translation *will keep your festivals*; verse 10 in Hebrew is unclear.

696

Psalms

2 Chron.
Ezra
Nehem.
Esther
Job

PSALMS 77, 78

WHAT IS GOD
SPEAKING
TO YOU
ABOUT FROM THIS
PASSAGE?
WRITE IT HERE.

Comfort in Time of Distress*

77 [1] I cry aloud to God;
  I cry aloud, and he hears me.
[2] In times of trouble I pray to the Lord;
  all night long I lift my hands in prayer,
  but I cannot find comfort.
[3] When I think of God, I sigh;
  when I meditate, I feel discouraged.

[4] He keeps me awake all night;
  I am so worried that I cannot speak.
[5] I think of days gone by
  and remember years of long ago.
[6] I spend the night in deep thought;*
  I meditate, and this is what I ask myself:
[7] "Will the Lord always reject us?
  Will he never again be pleased with us?
[8] Has he stopped loving us?
  Does his promise no longer stand?
[9] Has God forgotten to be merciful?
  Has anger taken the place of his compassion?"
[10] Then I said, "What hurts me most is this —
  that God is no longer powerful."*

[11] I will remember your great deeds, LORD;
  I will recall the wonders you did in the past.
[12] I will think about all that you have done;
  I will meditate on all your mighty acts.

[13] Everything you do, O God, is holy.
  No god is as great as you.
[14] You are the God who works miracles;
  you showed your might among the nations.
[15] By your power you saved your people,
  the descendants of Jacob and of Joseph.

[16] When the waters saw you, O God, they were afraid,
  and the depths of the sea trembled.
[17] The clouds poured down rain;
  thunder crashed from the sky,
  and lightning flashed in all directions.
[18] The crash of your thunder rolled out,
  and flashes of lightning lit up the world;
  the earth trembled and shook.
[19] You walked through the waves;
  you crossed the deep sea,
  but your footprints could not be seen.
[20] You led your people like a shepherd,
  with Moses and Aaron in charge.

God and his People*

78 [1] Listen, my people, to my teaching,
  and pay attention to what I say.
[2] I am going to use wise sayings

Ps 77; Ps 78 *Hebrew title*: A psalm by Asaph.
77.6 Some ancient translations *deep thought*; Hebrew *song*.
77.10 Verse 10 in Hebrew is unclear.

Psalms
....

Proverbs
Eccles.
Songs
Isaiah
Jerem.

and explain mysteries from the past,
3 things we have heard and known,
things that our ancestors told us.
4 We will not keep them from our children;
we will tell the next generation
about the LORD's power and his great deeds
and the wonderful things he has done.

5 He gave laws to the people of Israel
and commandments to the descendants of Jacob.
He instructed our ancestors
to teach his laws to their children,
6 so that the next generation might learn them
and in turn should tell their children.
7 In this way they also would put their trust in God
and not forget what he has done,
but always obey his commandments.
8 They would not be like their ancestors,
a rebellious and disobedient people,
whose trust in God was never firm
and who did not remain faithful to him.
9 The Ephraimites, armed with bows and arrows,
ran away on the day of battle.
10 They did not keep their covenant with God;
they refused to obey his law.
11 They forgot what he had done,
the miracles they had seen him perform.
12 While their ancestors watched, God performed miracles
in the plain of Zoan in the land of Egypt.
13 He divided the sea and took them through it;
he made the waters stand like walls.
14 By day he led them with a cloud
and all night long with the light of a fire.
15 He split rocks open in the desert
and gave them water from the depths.
16 He caused a stream to come out of the rock
and made water flow like a river.

17 But they continued to sin against God,
and in the desert they rebelled against the Most High.
18 They deliberately put God to the test
by demanding the food they wanted.
19 They spoke against God and said,
"Can God supply food in the desert?
20 It is true that he struck the rock,
and water flowed out in a torrent;
but can he also provide us with bread
and give his people meat?"

21 And so the LORD was angry when he heard them;
he attacked his people with fire,
and his anger against them grew,
22 because they had no faith in him
and did not believe that he would save them.
23 But he spoke to the sky above
and commanded its doors to open;
24 he gave them grain from heaven,
by sending down manna for them to eat.

698

Psalms
⋮·········

2 Chron.
Ezra
Nehem.
Esther
Job

PSALMS 78

25 So they ate the food of angels,
    and God gave them all they wanted.
26 He also caused the east wind to blow,
    and by his power he stirred up the south wind;
27 and to his people he sent down birds,
    as many as the grains of sand on the shore;
28 they fell in the middle of the camp
    all round the tents.
29 So the people ate and were satisfied;
    God gave them what they wanted.
30 But they had not yet satisfied their craving
    and were still eating,
31 when God became angry with them
    and killed their strongest men,
    the best young men of Israel.

32 In spite of all this the people kept sinning;
    in spite of his miracles they did not trust him.
33 So he ended their days like a breath
    and their lives with sudden disaster.
34 Whenever he killed some of them,
    the rest would turn to him;
    they would repent and pray earnestly to him.
35 They remembered that God was their protector,
    that the Almighty came to their aid.
36 But their words were all lies;
    nothing they said was sincere.
37 They were not loyal to him;
    they were not faithful to their covenant with him.

38 But God was merciful to his people.
    He forgave their sin
    and did not destroy them.
    Many times he held back his anger
    and restrained his fury.
39 He remembered that they were only mortal beings,
    like a wind that blows by and is gone.

40 How often they rebelled against him in the desert;
    how many times they made him sad!
41 Again and again they put God to the test
    and brought pain to the Holy God of Israel.
42 They forgot his great power
    and the day when he saved them from their enemies
43 and performed his mighty acts and miracles
    in the plain of Zoan in the land of Egypt.
44 He turned the rivers into blood,
    and the Egyptians had no water to drink.
45 He sent flies among them, that tormented them,
    and frogs that ruined their land.
46 He sent locusts to eat their crops
    and to destroy their fields.
47 He killed their grapevines with hail
    and their fig trees with frost.
48 He killed their cattle with hail
    and their flocks with lightning.*

78.48 *hail... lightning;* or *terrible disease... deadly plague.*

PSALMS 78

699

Psalms
............:.
Proverbs
Eccles.
Songs
Isaiah
Jerem.

49 He caused them great distress
   by pouring out his anger and fierce rage,
   which came as messengers of death.
50 He did not restrain his anger
   or spare their lives,
   but killed them with a plague.
51 He killed the firstborn sons
   of all the families of Egypt.

52 Then he led his people out like a shepherd
   and guided them through the desert.
53 He led them safely, and they were not afraid;
   but the sea came rolling over their enemies.
54 He brought them to his holy land,
   to the mountains which he himself conquered.
55 He drove out the inhabitants as his people advanced;
   he divided their land among the tribes of Israel
   and gave their homes to his people.

56 But they rebelled against Almighty God
   and put him to the test.
   They did not obey his commandments,
57   but were rebellious and disloyal like their ancestors,
   unreliable as a crooked arrow.
58 They angered him with their heathen places of worship,
   and with their idols they made him furious.
59 God was angry when he saw it,
   so he rejected his people completely.
60 He abandoned his tent in Shiloh,*
   the home where he had lived among us.
61 He allowed our enemies to capture the Covenant Box,
   the symbol of his power and glory.
62 He was angry with his own people
   and let them be killed by their enemies.
63 Young men were killed in war,
   and young women had no one to marry.
64 Priests died by violence,
   and their widows were not allowed to mourn.

65 At last the Lord woke up as though from sleep;
   he was like a strong man excited by wine.
66 He drove his enemies back
   in lasting and shameful defeat.
67 But he rejected the descendants of Joseph;
   he did not select the tribe of Ephraim.
68 Instead he chose the tribe of Judah
   and Mount Zion, which he dearly loves.
69 There he built his Temple
   like his home in heaven;
   he made it firm like the earth itself,
   secure for all time.

70 He chose his servant David;
   he took him from the pastures,
71   where he looked after his flocks,

....

78.60 *Shiloh*: The central place of worship for the people of Israel before
the time of King David.

2 Chron.
Ezra
Nehem.
Esther
Job

MERCY

PSALM 80.3;

ISAIAH 55.1;

JEREMIAH 30.18

What do you
think it means?

What does someone
else think it means?

Now go and look up
the definition.

and he made him king of Israel,
the shepherd of the people of God.
72 David took care of them with unselfish devotion
and led them with skill.

A Prayer for the Nation's Deliverance*

79
1 O God, the heathen have invaded your land.
They have desecrated your holy Temple
and left Jerusalem in ruins.
2 They left the bodies of your people for the vultures,
the bodies of your servants for wild animals to eat.
3 They shed your people's blood like water;
blood flowed like water all through Jerusalem,
and no one was left to bury the dead.
4 The surrounding nations insult us;
they laugh at us and mock us.

5 LORD, will you be angry with us for ever?
Will your anger continue to burn like fire?
6 Turn your anger on the nations that do not worship you,
on the people who do not pray to you.
7 For they have killed your people;
they have ruined your country.

8 Do not punish us for the sins of our ancestors.
Have mercy on us now;
we have lost all hope.
9 Help us, O God, and save us;
rescue us and forgive our sins
for the sake of your own honour.
10 Why should the nations ask us,
"Where is your God?"
Let us see you punish the nations
for shedding the blood of your servants.

11 Listen to the groans of the prisoners,
and by your great power free those who are condemned
to die.
12 Lord, pay the other nations back seven times
for all the insults they have hurled at you.
13 Then we, your people, the sheep of your flock,
will thank you for ever
and praise you for all time to come.

A Prayer for the Nation's Restoration*

80
1 Listen to us, O Shepherd of Israel;
hear us, leader of your flock.
Seated on your throne above the winged creatures,
2 reveal yourself to the tribes of Ephraim, Benjamin, and
Manasseh.
Show us your strength;
come and save us!

3 Bring us back, O God!
Show us your mercy, and we will be saved!

Ps 79 *Hebrew title*: A psalm by Asaph.
Ps 80 *Hebrew title*: A psalm by Asaph; a testimony.

PSALMS 80, 81

701

Psalms

Proverbs
Eccles.
Songs
Isaiah
Jerem.

⁴ How much longer, LORD God Almighty,
   will you be angry with your people's prayers?
⁵ You have given us sorrow to eat,
   a large cup of tears to drink.
⁶ You let the surrounding nations fight over our land;
   our enemies insult us.

⁷ Bring us back, Almighty God!
   Show us your mercy, and we will be saved!

⁸ You brought a grapevine out of Egypt;
   you drove out other nations and planted it in their land.
⁹ You cleared a place for it to grow;
   its roots went deep, and it spread out over the whole land.
¹⁰ It covered the hills with its shade;
   its branches overshadowed the giant cedars.
¹¹ It extended its branches to the Mediterranean Sea
   and as far as the River Euphrates.
¹² Why did you break down the fences round it?
   Now anyone passing by can steal its grapes;
¹³   wild pigs trample it down,
   and wild animals feed on it.

¹⁴ Turn to us, Almighty God!
   Look down from heaven at us;
   come and save your people!
¹⁵ Come and save this grapevine that you planted,
   this young vine you made grow so strong!

¹⁶ Our enemies have set it on fire and cut it down;
   look at them in anger and destroy them!
¹⁷ Preserve and protect the people you have chosen,
   the nation you made so strong.
¹⁸ We will never turn away from you again;
   keep us alive, and we will praise you.

¹⁹ Bring us back, LORD God Almighty.
   Show us your mercy, and we will be saved.

A Song for a Festival*

81 ¹ Shout for joy to God our defender;
   sing praise to the God of Jacob!
² Start the music and beat the tambourines;
   play pleasant music on the harps and the lyres.
³ Blow the trumpet for the festival,
   when the moon is new and when the moon is full.
⁴ This is the law in Israel,
   an order from the God of Jacob.
⁵ He gave it to the people of Israel
   when he attacked the land of Egypt.

   I hear an unknown voice saying,
⁶ "I took the burdens off your backs;
   I let you put down your loads of bricks.
⁷ When you were in trouble, you called to me, and I saved you.
   From my hiding place in the storm, I answered you.
   I put you to the test at the springs of Meribah.

Ps 81 *Hebrew title*: By Asaph.

702

Psalms

2 Chron.

Ezra

Nehem.

Esther

Job

PSALMS 81–83

8 Listen, my people, to my warning;
  Israel, how I wish you would listen to me!
9 You must never worship another god.
10 I am the LORD your God,
   who brought you out of Egypt.
   Open your mouth, and I will feed you.

11 "But my people would not listen to me;
   Israel would not obey me.
12 So I let them go their stubborn ways
   and do whatever they wanted.
13 How I wish my people would listen to me;
   how I wish they would obey me!
14 I would quickly defeat their enemies
   and conquer all their foes.
15 Those who hate me would bow in fear before me;
   their punishment would last for ever.
16 But I would feed you with the finest wheat
   and satisfy you with wild honey."

God the Supreme Ruler*

82 1 God presides in the heavenly council;
   in the assembly of the gods he gives his decision:
2 "You must stop judging unjustly;
   you must no longer be partial to the wicked!
3 Defend the rights of the poor and the orphans;
   be fair to the needy and the helpless.
4 Rescue them from the power of the wicked.

5 "How ignorant you are! How stupid!
   You are completely corrupt,
   and justice has disappeared from the world.
6 'You are gods,' I said;
   'all of you are children of the Most High.'
7 But you will die like mortals;
   your life will end like that of any prince."

8 Come, O God, and rule the world;
   all the nations are yours.

A Prayer for the Defeat of Israel's Enemies*

83 1 O God, do not keep silent;
   do not be still, do not be quiet!
2 Look! Your enemies are in revolt,
   and those who hate you are rebelling.
3 They are making secret plans against your people;
   they are plotting against those you protect.
4 "Come," they say, "let us destroy their nation,
   so that Israel will be forgotten for ever."

5 They agree on their plan
   and form an alliance against you:
6 the people of Edom and the Ishmaelites;
   the people of Moab and the Hagrites;
7 the people of Gebal, Ammon, and Amalek,
   and of Philistia and Tyre.

Ps 82 Hebrew title: A psalm by Asaph.
Ps 83 Hebrew title: A psalm by Asaph; a song.

PSALMS 83, 84

703

Psalms
............:.

Proverbs
Eccles.
Songs
Isaiah
Jerem.

8 Assyria has also joined them
as a strong ally of the Ammonites and Moabites, the
descendants of Lot.

9 Do to them what you did to the Midianites,
and to Sisera and Jabin at the River Kishon.
10 You defeated them at Endor,
and their bodies rotted on the ground.
11 Do to their leaders what you did to Oreb and Zeeb;
defeat all their rulers as you did Zebah and Zalmunna,
12 who said, "We will take for our own
the land that belongs to God."

13 Scatter them like dust, O God,
like straw blown away by the wind.
14 As fire burns the forest,
as flames set the hills on fire,
15 chase them away with your storm
and terrify them with your fierce winds.
16 Cover their faces with shame, O LORD,
and make them acknowledge your power.
17 May they be defeated and terrified for ever;
may they die in complete disgrace.
18 May they know that you alone are the LORD,
supreme ruler over all the earth.

Longing for God's House*

84 1 How I love your Temple, LORD Almighty!
2 How I want to be there!
I long to be in the LORD's Temple.
With my whole being I sing for joy
to the living God.
3 Even the sparrows have built a nest,
and the swallows have their own home;
they keep their young near your altars,
LORD Almighty, my king and my God.
4 How happy are those who live in your Temple,
always singing praise to you.

5 How happy are those whose strength comes from you,
who are eager to make the pilgrimage to Mount Zion.
6 As they pass through the dry valley of Baca,
it becomes a place of springs;
the autumn rain fills it with pools.
7 They grow stronger as they go;
they will see the God of gods on Zion.

8 Hear my prayer, LORD God Almighty.
Listen, O God of Jacob!
9 Bless our king, O God,
the king you have chosen.

10 One day spent in your Temple
is better than a thousand anywhere else;
I would rather stand at the gate of the house of my God
than live in the homes of the wicked.

Ps 84 *Hebrew title*: A psalm by the clan of Korah.

704

Psalms

2 Chron.
Ezra
Nehem.
Esther
Job

PSALM 86.7

In times of trouble, who or what do you turn to? What's the

- FIRST -

THING

you do? What would it look like for God to be the first person you turn to?

write some
thoughts here

11 The LORD is our protector and glorious king,
      blessing us with kindness and honour.
   He does not refuse any good thing
      to those who do what is right.
12 LORD Almighty, how happy are those who trust in you!

A Prayer for the Nation's Welfare*

85 1 LORD, you have been merciful to your land;
        you have made Israel prosperous again.
2 You have forgiven your people's sins
      and pardoned all their wrongs.
3 You stopped being angry with them
      and held back your furious rage.

4 Bring us back, O God our saviour,
      and stop being displeased with us!
5 Will you be angry with us for ever?
      Will your anger never cease?
6 Make us strong again,
      and we, your people, will praise you.
7 Show us your constant love, O LORD,
      and give us your saving help.

8 I am listening to what the LORD God is saying;
      he promises peace to us, his own people,
      if we do not go back to our foolish ways.
9 Surely he is ready to save those who honour him,
      and his saving presence will remain in our land.

10 Love and faithfulness will meet;
      righteousness and peace will embrace.
11 Human loyalty will reach up from the earth,
      and God's righteousness will look down from heaven.
12 The LORD will make us prosperous,
      and our land will produce rich harvests.
13 Righteousness will go before the LORD
      and prepare the path for him.

A Prayer for Help*

86 1 Listen to me, LORD, and answer me,
        for I am helpless and weak.
2 Save me from death, because I am loyal to you;
      save me, for I am your servant and I trust in you.

3 You are my God, so be merciful to me;
      I pray to you all day long.
4 Make your servant glad, O Lord,
      because my prayers go up to you.
5 You are good to us and forgiving,
      full of constant love for all who pray to you.

6 Listen, LORD, to my prayer;
      hear my cries for help.
7 I call to you in times of trouble,
      because you answer my prayers.

Ps 85 *Hebrew title*: A psalm by the clan of Korah.
Ps 86 *Hebrew title*: A prayer by David.

PSALMS 86–88

705

Psalms
....
Proverbs
Eccles.
Songs
Isaiah
Jerem.

8 There is no god like you, O Lord,
    not one has done what you have done.
9 All the nations that you have created
    will come and bow down to you;
    they will praise your greatness.
10 You are mighty and do wonderful things;
    you alone are God.

11 Teach me, Lord, what you want me to do,
    and I will obey you faithfully;
    teach me to serve you with complete devotion.
12 I will praise you with all my heart, O Lord my God;
    I will proclaim your greatness for ever.
13 How great is your constant love for me!
    You have saved me from the grave itself.
14 The proud are coming against me, O God;
    a cruel gang is trying to kill me —
    people who pay no attention to you.
15 But you, O Lord, are a merciful and loving God,
    always patient, always kind and faithful.
16 Turn to me and have mercy on me;
    strengthen me and save me,
    because I serve you, just as my mother did.
17 Show me proof of your goodness, Lord;
    those who hate me will be ashamed
    when they see that you have given me comfort and
        help.

In Praise of Jerusalem*

87 1 The Lord built his city on the sacred hill;*
     2   more than any other place in Israel
    he loves the city of Jerusalem.
3 Listen, city of God,
    to the wonderful things he says about you:

4 "I will include Egypt and Babylonia
    when I list the nations that obey me;
    I will number among the inhabitants of Jerusalem
    the people of Philistia, Tyre, and Ethiopia."

5 Of Zion it will be said
    that all nations belong there
    and that the Almighty will make her strong.
6 The Lord will write a list of the peoples
    and include them all as citizens of Jerusalem.
7 They dance and sing,
    "In Zion is the source of all our blessings."

A Cry for Help*

88 1 Lord God, my saviour, I cry out all day,
    and at night I come before you.
    2 Hear my prayer;
    listen to my cry for help!

Ps 87 *Hebrew title*: A psalm by the clan of Korah; a song.
87.1 *sacred hill*: See 2.6.
Ps 88 *Hebrew title*: A psalm by the clan of Korah; a song. A poem by Heman
the Ezrahite.

706

Psalms

∴ ········

2 Chron.
Ezra
Nehem.
Esther
Job

PSALMS 88, 89

3 So many troubles have fallen on me
    that I am close to death.
4 I am like all others who are about to die;
    all my strength is gone.*
5 I am abandoned among the dead;
    I am like the slain lying in their graves,
those you have forgotten completely,
    who are beyond your help.
6 You have thrown me into the depths of the tomb,
    into the darkest and deepest pit.
7 Your anger lies heavy on me,
    and I am crushed beneath its waves.

8 You have caused my friends to abandon me;
    you have made me repulsive to them.
I am closed in and cannot escape;
9   my eyes are weak from suffering.
LORD, every day I call to you
    and lift my hands to you in prayer.

10 Do you perform miracles for the dead?
    Do they rise up and praise you?
11 Is your constant love spoken of in the grave
    or your faithfulness in the place of destruction?
12 Are your miracles seen in that place of darkness
    or your goodness in the land of the forgotten?

13 LORD, I call to you for help;
    every morning I pray to you.
14 Why do you reject me, LORD?
    Why do you turn away from me?
15 Ever since I was young, I have suffered and been near
    death;
    I am worn out* from the burden of your punishments.
16 Your furious anger crushes me;
    your terrible attacks destroy me.
17 All day long they surround me like a flood;
    they close in on me from every side.
18 You have made even my closest friends abandon me,
    and darkness is my only companion.

A Hymn in Time of National Trouble*

89 1 O LORD, I will always sing of your constant love;
    I will proclaim your faithfulness for ever.
2 I know that your love will last for all time,
    that your faithfulness is as permanent as the sky.
3 You said, "I have made a covenant with the man I chose;
    I have promised my servant David,
4 'A descendant of yours will always be king;
    I will preserve your dynasty for ever.'"

5 The heavens sing of the wonderful things you do;
    the holy ones sing of your faithfulness, LORD.
6 No one in heaven is like you, LORD;
    none of the heavenly beings is your equal.

··

88.4 *all my strength is gone*; or *there is no help for me.*
88.15 Probable text *I am worn out*; Hebrew unclear.
Ps 89 *Hebrew title*: A poem by Ethan the Ezrahite.

PSALMS 89

707

Psalms

Proverbs
Eccles.
Songs
Isaiah
Jerem.

7 You are feared in the council of the holy ones;
  and all of them stand in awe of you.

8 LORD God Almighty, none is as mighty as you;
  in all things you are faithful, O LORD.

9 You rule over the powerful sea;
  you calm its angry waves.

10 You crushed the monster Rahab* and killed it;
  with your mighty strength you defeated your
    enemies.

11 Heaven is yours, the earth also;
  you made the world and everything in it.

12 You created the north and the south;
  Mount Tabor and Mount Hermon sing to you for joy.

13 How powerful you are!
  How great is your strength!

14 Your kingdom is founded on righteousness and justice;
  love and faithfulness are shown in all you do.

15 How happy are the people who worship you with
    songs,
  who live in the light of your kindness!

16 Because of you they rejoice all day long,
  and they praise you for your goodness.

17 You give us great victories;
  in your love you make us triumphant.

18 You, O LORD, chose our protector;
  you, the Holy God of Israel, gave us our king.

God's Promise to David

19 In a vision long ago you said to your faithful servants,
  "I have given help to a famous soldier;
  I have given the throne to one I chose from the
    people.

20 I have made my servant David king
  by anointing him with holy oil.

21 My strength will always be with him,
  my power will make him strong.

22 His enemies will never succeed against him;
  the wicked will not defeat him.

23 I will crush his foes
  and kill everyone who hates him.

24 I will love him and be loyal to him;
  I will make him always victorious.

25 I will extend his kingdom
  from the Mediterranean to the River Euphrates.

26 He will say to me,
  'You are my father and my God;
  you are my protector and saviour.'

27 I will make him my firstborn son,
  the greatest of all kings.

28 I will always keep my promise to him,
  and my covenant with him will last for ever.

29 His dynasty will be as permanent as the sky;
  a descendant of his will always be king.

....

89.10 *Rahab*: A legendary sea monster which represented the forces of chaos and evil.

708

Psalms

⋮⋯⋯⋯

2 Chron.

Ezra

Nehem.

Esther

Job

PSALMS 89

30 "But if his descendants disobey my law
and do not live according to my commands,
31 if they disregard my instructions
and do not keep my commandments,
32 then I will punish them for their sins;
I will make them suffer for their wrongs.
33 But I will not stop loving David
or fail to keep my promise to him.
34 I will not break my covenant with him
or take back even one promise I made him.

35 "Once and for all I have promised by my holy name:
I will never lie to David.
36 He will always have descendants,
and I will watch over his kingdom as long as the sun
shines.
37 It will be as permanent as the moon,
that faithful witness in the sky."

Lament over the Defeat of the King
38 But you are angry with your chosen king;
you have deserted and rejected him.
39 You have broken your covenant with your servant
and thrown his crown in the mud.
40 You have torn down the walls of his city
and left his forts in ruins.
41 All who pass by steal his belongings;
all his neighbours laugh at him.
42 You have given the victory to his enemies;
you have made them all happy.
43 You have made his weapons useless
and let him be defeated in battle.
44 You have taken away his royal sceptre*
and hurled his throne to the ground.
45 You have made him old before his time
and covered him with disgrace.

A Prayer for Deliverance
46 LORD, will you hide yourself for ever?
How long will your anger burn like fire?
47 Remember how short my life is;
remember that you created all of us mortal!
48 Who can live and never die?
How can human beings keep themselves from the
grave?

49 Lord, where are the former proofs of your love?
Where are the promises you made to David?
50 Don't forget how I, your servant, am insulted,
how I endure all the curses* of the heathen.
51 Your enemies insult your chosen king, O LORD!
They insult him wherever he goes.

52 Praise the LORD for ever!

Amen! Amen!

....

89.44 Probable text *royal sceptre*; Hebrew *purity*.
89.50 Probable text *curses*; Hebrew *crowds*.

PSALMS 90, 91

709

Psalms

Proverbs
Eccles.
Songs
Isaiah
Jerem.

Book Four
Psalms 90—106

Of God and Humanity*

90 [1] O Lord, you have always been our home.
[2] Before you created the hills
or brought the world into being,
you were eternally God,
and will be God for ever.

[3] You tell us to return to what we were;
you change us back to dust.
[4] A thousand years to you are like one day;
they are like yesterday, already gone,
like a short hour in the night.
[5] You carry us away like a flood;
we last no longer than a dream.
We are like weeds that sprout in the morning,
[6] that grow and burst into bloom,
then dry up and die in the evening.

[7] We are destroyed by your anger;
we are terrified by your fury.
[8] You place our sins before you,
our secret sins where you can see them.

[9] Our life is cut short by your anger;
it fades away like a whisper.
[10] Seventy years is all we have —
eighty years, if we are strong;
yet all they bring us is trouble and sorrow;
life is soon over, and we are gone.

[11] Who has felt the full power of your anger?
Who knows what fear your fury can bring?
[12] Teach us how short our life is,
so that we may become wise.

[13] How much longer will your anger last?
Have pity, O LORD, on your servants!
[14] Fill us each morning with your constant love,
so that we may sing and be glad all our life.
[15] Give us now as much happiness as the sadness you gave us
during all our years of misery.
[16] Let us, your servants, see your mighty deeds;
let our descendants see your glorious might.
[17] LORD our God, may your blessings be with us.
Give us success in all we do!

God our Protector

91 [1] Whoever goes to the LORD for safety,
whoever remains under the protection of the Almighty,
[2] can say to him,
"You are my defender and protector.
You are my God; in you I trust."
[3] He will keep you safe from all hidden dangers
and from all deadly diseases.

Ps 90 *Hebrew title*: A prayer by Moses, the man of God.

710

Psalms

2 Chron.
Ezra
Nehem.
Esther
Job

PSALMS 91, 92

4 He will cover you with his wings;
   you will be safe in his care;
   his faithfulness will protect and defend you.
5 You need not fear any dangers at night
   or sudden attacks during the day
6   or the plagues that strike in the dark
   or the evils that kill in daylight.

7 A thousand may fall dead beside you,
   10,000 all round you,
   but you will not be harmed.
8 You will look and see
   how the wicked are punished.

9 You have made the LORD your* defender,
   the Most High your protector,
10 and so no disaster will strike you,
   no violence will come near your home.
11 God will put his angels in charge of you
   to protect you wherever you go.
12 They will hold you up with their hands
   to keep you from hurting your feet on the stones.
13 You will trample down lions and snakes,
   fierce lions and poisonous snakes.

14 God says, "I will save those who love me
   and will protect those who acknowledge me as LORD.
15 When they call to me, I will answer them;
   when they are in trouble, I will be with them.
   I will rescue them and honour them.
16 I will reward them with long life;
   I will save them."

A Song of Praise*

92 1 How good it is to give thanks to you, O LORD,
   to sing in your honour, O Most High God,
2 to proclaim your constant love every morning
   and your faithfulness every night,
3 with the music of stringed instruments
   and with melody on the harp.
4 Your mighty deeds, O LORD, make me glad;
   because of what you have done, I sing for joy.

5 How great are your actions, LORD!
   How deep are your thoughts!
6 This is something a fool cannot know;
   a stupid person cannot understand:
7 the wicked may grow like weeds,
   those who do wrong may prosper;
   yet they will be totally destroyed,
8   because you, LORD, are supreme for ever.

9 We know that your enemies will die,
   and all the wicked will be defeated.
10 You have made me as strong as a wild ox;
   you have blessed me with happiness.

91.9 Probable text *your*; Hebrew *my*.
Ps 92 *Hebrew title*: A psalm; a song for the Sabbath.

11 I have seen the defeat of my enemies
    and heard the cries of the wicked.

12 The righteous will flourish like palm trees;
    they will grow like the cedars of Lebanon.
13 They are like trees planted in the house of the LORD,
    that flourish in the Temple of our God,
14   that still bear fruit in old age
    and are always green and strong.
15 This shows that the LORD is just,
    that there is no wrong in my protector.

God the King

93 1 The LORD is king.
    He is clothed with majesty and strength.
    The earth is set firmly in place
    and cannot be moved.
2 Your throne, O LORD, has been firm from the beginning,
    and you existed before time began.

3 The ocean depths raise their voice, O LORD;
    they raise their voice and roar.
4 The LORD rules supreme in heaven,
    greater than the roar of the ocean,
    more powerful than the waves of the sea.

5 Your laws are eternal, LORD,
    and your Temple is holy indeed,
    for ever and ever.

God the Judge of All

94 1 LORD, you are a God who punishes;
    reveal your anger!
2 You are the judge of all;
    rise and give the proud what they deserve!
3 How much longer will the wicked be glad?
    How much longer, LORD?
4 How much longer will criminals be proud
    and boast about their crimes?

5 They crush your people, LORD;
    they oppress those who belong to you.
6 They kill widows and orphans,
    and murder the strangers who live in our land.
7 They say, "The LORD does not see us;
    the God of Israel does not notice."

8 My people, how can you be such stupid fools?
    When will you ever learn?
9 God made our ears — can't he hear?
    He made our eyes — can't he see?
10 He scolds the nations — won't he punish them?*
    He is the teacher of all — hasn't he any knowledge?
11 The LORD knows what they think;
    he knows how senseless their reasoning is.

PSALM 93

FILL
- THIS -
SPACE

with words you would use
to describe God. Decorate
them, doodle around them,
make them colourful!

94.10 *them?*; or *our wicked leaders?*

712

Psalms

2 Chron.
Ezra
Nehem.
Esther
Job

PSALMS 94, 95

12 LORD, how happy are those you instruct,
the ones to whom you teach your law!
13 You give them rest from days of trouble
until a pit is dug to trap the wicked.
14 The LORD will not abandon his people;
he will not desert those who belong to him.
15 Justice will again be found in the courts,
and all righteous people will support it.

16 Who stood up for me against the wicked?
Who took my side against the evildoers?
17 If the LORD had not helped me,
I would have gone quickly to the land of silence.*
18 I said, "I am falling";
but your constant love, O LORD, held me up.
19 Whenever I am anxious and worried,
you comfort me and make me glad.

20 You have nothing to do with corrupt judges,
who make injustice legal,
21 who plot against good people
and sentence the innocent to death.
22 But the LORD defends me;
my God protects me.
23 He will punish them for their wickedness
and destroy them for their sins;
the LORD our God will destroy them.

A Song of Praise

95 1 Come, let us praise the LORD!
Let us sing for joy to God, who protects us!
2 Let us come before him with thanksgiving
and sing joyful songs of praise.
3 For the LORD is a mighty God,
a mighty king over all the gods.
4 He rules over the whole earth,
from the deepest caves to the highest hills.
5 He rules over the sea, which he made;
the land also, which he himself formed.

6 Come, let us bow down and worship him;
let us kneel before the LORD, our Maker!
7 He is our God;
we are the people he cares for,
the flock for which he provides.

Listen today to what he says:
8 "Don't be stubborn, as your ancestors were at Meribah,
as they were that day in the desert at Massah.
9 There they put me to the test and tried me,
although they had seen what I did for them.
10 For forty years I was disgusted with those people.
I said, 'How disloyal they are!
They refuse to obey my commands.'
11 I was angry and made a solemn promise:
'You will never enter the land
where I would have given you rest.'"

94.17 *land of silence*: The world of the dead (see 6.5).

PSALMS 96, 97   713

Psalms

Proverbs
Eccles.
Songs
Isaiah
Jerem.

God the Supreme King
(1 Chr 16.23–33)

96 [1] Sing a new song to the LORD!
Sing to the LORD, all the world!
[2] Sing to the LORD, and praise him!
Proclaim every day the good news that he has saved
us.
[3] Proclaim his glory to the nations,
his mighty deeds to all peoples.

[4] The LORD is great and is to be highly praised;
he is to be honoured more than all the gods.
[5] The gods of all other nations are only idols,
but the LORD created the heavens.
[6] Glory and majesty surround him;
power and beauty fill his Temple.

[7] Praise the LORD, all people on earth;
praise his glory and might.
[8] Praise the LORD's glorious name;
bring an offering and come into his Temple.
[9] Bow down before the Holy One when he appears;*
tremble before him, all the earth!

[10] Say to all the nations, "The LORD is king!
The earth is set firmly in place and cannot be moved;
he will judge the peoples with justice."
[11] Be glad, earth and sky!
Roar, sea, and every creature in you;
[12] be glad, fields, and everything in you!
The trees in the woods will shout for joy
[13] when the LORD comes to rule the earth.
He will rule the peoples of the world
with justice and fairness.

God the Supreme Ruler

97 [1] The LORD is king! Earth, be glad!
Rejoice, you islands of the seas!
[2] Clouds and darkness surround him;
he rules with righteousness and justice.
[3] Fire goes in front of him
and burns up his enemies round him.
[4] His lightning lights up the world;
the earth sees it and trembles.
[5] The hills melt like wax before the LORD,
before the Lord of all the earth.
[6] The heavens proclaim his righteousness,
and all the nations see his glory.

[7] Everyone who worships idols is put to shame;
all the gods bow down* before the LORD.
[8] The people of Zion are glad,
and the cities of Judah rejoice
because of your judgements, O LORD.
[9] LORD Almighty, you are ruler of all the earth;
you are much greater than all the gods.

96.9 *when he appears*; or *in garments of worship.*
97.7 *all the gods bow down*; or *bow down, all gods.*

714

Psalms

⋮⋯⋯⋯⋯

2 Chron.
Ezra
Nehem.
Esther
Job

PSALMS 97–99

10 The LORD loves those who hate evil;*
   he protects the lives of his people;
   he rescues them from the power of the wicked.
11 Light shines on the righteous,
   and gladness on the good.
12 All you that are righteous be glad
   because of what the LORD has done!
   Remember what the holy God has done,
   and give thanks to him.

God the Ruler of the World*

98 ¹ Sing a new song to the LORD;
   he has done wonderful things!
   By his own power and holy strength
   he has won the victory.
² The LORD announced his victory;
   he made his saving power known to the nations.
³ He kept his promise to the people of Israel
   with loyalty and constant love for them.
   All people everywhere have seen the victory of our
      God.

⁴ Sing for joy to the LORD, all the earth;
   praise him with songs and shouts of joy!
⁵ Sing praises to the LORD!
   Play music on the harps!
⁶ Blow trumpets and horns,
   and shout for joy to the LORD, our king.

⁷ Roar, sea, and every creature in you;
   sing, earth, and all who live on you!
⁸ Clap your hands, you rivers;
   you hills, sing together with joy before the LORD,
⁹   because he comes to rule the earth.
   He will rule the peoples of the world
      with justice and fairness.

God the Supreme King

99 ¹ The LORD is king;
   and the people tremble.
   He is enthroned above the winged creatures
   and the earth shakes.
² The LORD is mighty in Zion;
   he is supreme over all the nations.
³ Everyone will praise his great and majestic name.
   Holy is he!

⁴ Mighty king,* you love what is right;
   you have established justice in Israel;
   you have brought righteousness and fairness.
⁵ Praise the LORD our God;
   worship before his throne!
   Holy is he!

97.10 Probable text *The LORD loves those who hate evil*; Hebrew *Hate evil,
you who love the LORD.*
Ps 98 *Hebrew title*: A psalm.
99.4 Probable text *Mighty king*; Hebrew *The might of the king.*

PSALMS 99–101

715

Psalms

Proverbs
Eccles.
Songs
Isaiah
Jerem.

⁶ Moses and Aaron were his priests,
   and Samuel was one who prayed to him;
   they called to the LORD, and he answered them.
⁷ He spoke to them from the pillar of cloud;
   they obeyed the laws and commands that he gave
      them.

⁸ O LORD, our God, you answered your people;
   you showed them that you are a God who forgives,
   even though you punished them for their sins.
⁹ Praise the LORD our God,
   and worship at his sacred hill!*
The LORD our God is holy.

A Hymn of Praise*

100 ¹Sing to the LORD, all the world!
   ² Worship the LORD with joy;
   come before him with happy songs!

³ Acknowledge that the LORD is God.
   He made us, and we belong to him;
   we are his people, we are his flock.

⁴ Enter the temple gates with thanksgiving,
   go into its courts with praise.
   Give thanks to him and praise him.

⁵ The LORD is good;
   his love is eternal
   and his faithfulness lasts for ever.

A King's Promise*

101 ¹My song is about loyalty and justice,
   and I sing it to you, O LORD.
² My conduct will be faultless.
   When will you come to me?

I will live a pure life in my house,
³   and will never tolerate evil.
I hate the actions of those who turn away from God;
   I will have nothing to do with them.
⁴ I will not be dishonest,*
   and will have no dealings with evil.*
⁵ I will get rid of anyone
   who whispers evil things about someone else;
I will not tolerate anyone
   who is proud and arrogant.

⁶ I will approve of those who are faithful to God
   and will let them live in my palace.
Those who are completely honest
   will be allowed to serve me.

PSALM 99.9

THE LORD OUR GOD IS HOLY

99.9 *sacred hill*: See 2.6.
Ps 100 *Hebrew title*: A psalm of thanksgiving.
Ps 101 *Hebrew title*: A psalm by David.
101.4 *not be dishonest*; or *stay away from dishonest people*.
101.4 *evil*; or *evil people*.

716

Psalms

2 Chron.

Ezra

Nehem.

Esther

Job

PSALMS 101, 102

7 No liar will live in my palace;
     no hypocrite will remain in my presence.
8 Day after day I will destroy
     the wicked in our land;
  I will expel all who are evil
     from the city of the LORD.

The Prayer of a Troubled Youth*

102 1 Listen to my prayer, O LORD,
       and hear my cry for help!
2 When I am in trouble,
     don't turn away from me!
  Listen to me,
     and answer me quickly when I call!

3 My life is disappearing like smoke;
     my body is burning like fire.
4 I am beaten down like dry grass;
     I have lost my desire for food.
5 I groan aloud;
     I am nothing but skin and bones.
6 I am like a wild bird in the desert,
     like an owl in abandoned ruins.
7 I lie awake;
     I am like a lonely bird on a housetop.
8 All day long my enemies insult me;
     those who mock me use my name in cursing.

9-10 Because of your anger and fury,
     ashes are my food,
     and my tears are mixed with my drink.
  You picked me up and threw me away.
11 My life is like the evening shadows;
     I am like dry grass.

12 But you, O LORD, are king for ever;
     all generations will remember you.
13 You will rise and take pity on Zion;
     the time has come to have mercy on her;
     this is the right time.
14 Your servants love her,
     even though she is destroyed;
  they have pity on her,
     even though she is in ruins.

15 The nations will fear the LORD;
     all the kings of the earth will fear his power.
16 When the LORD rebuilds Zion,
     he will reveal his greatness.
17 He will hear his forsaken people
     and listen to their prayer.

18 Write down for the coming generation what the LORD has
       done,
     so that people not yet born will praise him.

Ps 102 *Hebrew title*: A prayer by a weary sufferer who pours out his
complaints to the LORD.

PSALMS 102, 103

717

Psalms

Proverbs
Eccles.
Songs
Isaiah
Jerem.

¹⁹ The LORD looked down from his holy place on high,
  he looked down from heaven to earth.
²⁰ He heard the groans of prisoners
  and set free those who were condemned to die.
²¹ And so his name will be proclaimed in Zion,
  and he will be praised in Jerusalem
²² when nations and kingdoms come together
  and worship the LORD.

²³ The LORD has made me weak while I am still young;
  he has shortened my life.
²⁴ O God, do not take me away now
  before I grow old.

O LORD, you live for ever;
²⁵ long ago you created the earth,
  and with your own hands you made the heavens.
²⁶ They will disappear, but you will remain;
  they will all wear out like clothes.
  You will discard them like clothes,
  and they will vanish.
²⁷ But you are always the same,
  and your life never ends.
²⁸ Our children will live in safety,
  and under your protection
  their descendants will be secure.

The Love of God*

103 ¹ Praise the LORD, my soul!
  All my being, praise his holy name!
² Praise the LORD, my soul,
  and do not forget how kind he is.
³ He forgives all my sins
  and heals all my diseases.
⁴ He keeps me from the grave
  and blesses me with love and mercy.
⁵ He fills my life* with good things,
  so that I stay young and strong like an eagle.

⁶ The LORD judges in favour of the oppressed
  and gives them their rights.
⁷ He revealed his plans to Moses
  and let the people of Israel see his mighty deeds.
⁸ The LORD is merciful and loving,
  slow to become angry and full of constant love.
⁹ He does not keep on rebuking;
  he is not angry for ever.
¹⁰ He does not punish us as we deserve
  or repay us according to our sins and wrongs.
¹¹ As high as the sky is above the earth,
  so great is his love for those who honour him.
¹² As far as the east is from the west,
  so far does he remove our sins from us.
¹³ As a father is kind to his children,
  so the LORD is kind to those who honour him.

Ps 103 *Hebrew title*: By David.
103.5 Probable text *my life*; Hebrew unclear.

718

Psalms

2 Chron.
Ezra
Nehem.
Esther
Job

PSALMS 103, 104

PSALM 104

Use this space to

— DOODLE —

DIFFERENT

IMAGES

that are used in Psalm 104. Reflect on God as Creator while you do it.

¹⁴ He knows what we are made of;
    he remembers that we are dust.

¹⁵ As for us, our life is like grass.
    We grow and flourish like a wild flower;
¹⁶   then the wind blows on it, and it is gone —
    no one sees it again.
¹⁷ But for those who honour the LORD, his love lasts for ever,
    and his goodness endures for all generations
¹⁸ of those who are true to his covenant
    and who faithfully obey his commands.

¹⁹ The LORD placed his throne in heaven;
    he is king over all.
²⁰ Praise the LORD, you strong and mighty angels,
    who obey his commands,
    who listen to what he says.
²¹ Praise the LORD, all you heavenly powers,
    you servants of his, who do his will!
²² Praise the LORD, all his creatures
    in all the places he rules.
    Praise the LORD, my soul!

In Praise of the Creator

104 ¹ Praise the LORD, my soul!
    O LORD, my God, how great you are!
    You are clothed with majesty and glory;
²   you cover yourself with light.
    You have spread out the heavens like a tent
³   and built your home on the waters above.*
    You use the clouds as your chariot
    and ride on the wings of the wind.
⁴ You use the winds as your messengers
    and flashes of lightning as your servants.

⁵ You have set the earth firmly on its foundations,
    and it will never be moved.
⁶ You placed the ocean over it like a robe,
    and the water covered the mountains.
⁷ When you rebuked the waters, they fled;
    they rushed away when they heard your shout of command.
⁸ They flowed over the mountains and into the valleys,
    to the place you had made for them.
⁹ You set a boundary they can never pass,
    to keep them from covering the earth again.

¹⁰ You make springs flow in the valleys,
    and rivers run between the hills.
¹¹ They provide water for the wild animals;
    there the wild donkeys quench their thirst.
¹² In the trees near by,
    the birds make their nests and sing.

¹³ From the sky you send rain on the hills,
    and the earth is filled with your blessings.
¹⁴ You make grass grow for the cattle

104.3 *the waters above*: A reference to the waters above the celestial dome (Gen 1.6–7).

and plants for human beings to use,
so that they can grow their crops
15 and produce wine to make them happy,
olive oil to make them cheerful,
and bread to give them strength.

16 The cedars of Lebanon get plenty of rain —
the LORD's own trees, which he planted.
17 There the birds build their nests;
the storks nest in the fir trees.
18 The wild goats live in the high mountains,
and the rock-badgers hide in the cliffs.

19 You created the moon to mark the months;
the sun knows the time to set.
20 You made the night, and in the darkness
all the wild animals come out.
21 The young lions roar while they hunt,
looking for the food that God provides.
22 When the sun rises, they go back
and lie down in their dens.
23 Then people go out to do their work
and keep working until evening.

24 LORD, you have made so many things!
How wisely you made them all!
The earth is filled with your creatures.
25 There is the ocean, large and wide,
where countless creatures live,
large and small alike.
26 The ships sail on it, and in it plays Leviathan,
that sea monster which you made.*

27 All of them depend on you
to give them food when they need it.
28 You give it to them, and they eat it;
you provide food, and they are satisfied.
29 When you turn away, they are afraid;
when you take away your breath, they die
and go back to the dust from which they came.
30 But when you give them breath,* they are created;
you give new life to the earth.

31 May the glory of the LORD last for ever!
May the LORD be happy with what he has made!
32 He looks at the earth, and it trembles;
he touches the mountains, and they pour out smoke.

33 I will sing to the LORD all my life;
as long as I live I will sing praises to my God.
34 May he be pleased with my song,
for my gladness comes from him.

35 May sinners be destroyed from the earth;
may the wicked be no more.

104.26 in it plays... made; or Leviathan is there, that sea monster you
made to amuse you.
104.30 give them breath; or send out your spirit.

720

Psalms

2 Chron.
Ezra
Nehem.
Esther
Job

PSALMS 104, 105

DECORATE (THESE) SHAPES IN RELATION TO YOUR MOOD.

Praise the LORD, my soul!
Praise the LORD!

God and his People
(1 Chr 16.8–22)

105 ¹ Give thanks to the LORD, proclaim his greatness;
tell the nations what he has done.
² Sing praise to the LORD;
tell of the wonderful things he has done.
³ Be glad that we belong to him;
let all who worship him rejoice.
⁴ Go to the LORD for help;
and worship him continually.
⁵⁻⁶ You descendants of Abraham, his servant;
you descendants of Jacob, the man he chose:
remember the miracles that God performed
and the judgements that he gave.

⁷ The LORD is our God;
his commands are for all the world.
⁸ He will keep his covenant for ever,
his promises for a thousand generations.
⁹ He will keep the agreement he made with Abraham
and his promise to Isaac.
¹⁰ The LORD made a covenant with Jacob,
one that will last for ever.
¹¹ "I will give you the land of Canaan," he said.
"It will be your own possession."

¹² God's people were few in number,
strangers in the land of Canaan.
¹³ They wandered from country to country,
from one kingdom to another.
¹⁴ But God let no one oppress them;
to protect them, he warned the kings:
¹⁵ "Don't harm my chosen servants;
do not touch my prophets."

¹⁶ The LORD sent famine to their country
and took away all their food.
¹⁷ But he sent a man ahead of them,
Joseph, who had been sold as a slave.
¹⁸ His feet were kept in chains,
and an iron collar was round his neck,
¹⁹ until what he had predicted came true.
The word of the LORD proved him right.
²⁰ Then the king of Egypt had him released;
the ruler of nations set him free.
²¹ He put him in charge of his government
and made him ruler over all the land,
²² with power over the king's officials
and authority to instruct his advisers.

²³ Then Jacob went to Egypt
and settled in that country.
²⁴ The LORD gave many children to his people
and made them stronger than their enemies.
²⁵ He made the Egyptians hate his people
and treat his servants with deceit.

PSALMS 105, 106

721

Psalms

....

Proverbs
Eccles.
Songs
Isaiah
Jerem.

26 Then he sent his servant Moses,
  and Aaron, whom he had chosen.
27 They did God's mighty acts
  and performed miracles in Egypt.
28 God sent darkness on the country,
  but the Egyptians did not obey* his command.
29 He turned their rivers into blood
  and killed all their fish.
30 Their country was overrun with frogs,
  even the palace was filled with them.
31 God commanded, and flies and gnats
  swarmed throughout the whole country.
32 He sent hail and lightning on their land
  instead of rain;
33 he destroyed their grapevines and fig trees
  and broke down all the trees.
34 He commanded, and the locusts came,
  countless millions of them;
35 they ate all the plants in the land;
  they ate all the crops.
36 He killed the firstborn sons
  of all the families of Egypt.

37 Then he led the Israelites out;
  they carried silver and gold,
  and all of them were healthy and strong.
38 The Egyptians were afraid of them
  and were glad when they left.
39 God put a cloud over his people
  and a fire at night to give them light.
40 They* asked, and he sent quails;
  he gave them food from heaven to satisfy them.
41 He opened a rock, and water gushed out,
  flowing through the desert like a river.
42 He remembered his sacred promise
  to Abraham his servant.

43 So he led his chosen people out,
  and they sang and shouted for joy.
44 He gave them the lands of other peoples
  and let them take over their fields,
45 so that his people would obey his laws
  and keep all his commands.

  Praise the LORD!

The LORD's Goodness to his People

106 ¹Praise the LORD!

  Give thanks to the LORD, because he is good;
    his love is eternal.
2 Who can tell all the great things he has done?
  Who can praise him enough?
3 Happy are those who obey his commands,
  who always do what is right.

....

105.28 Some ancient translations *did not obey*; Hebrew *obeyed*.
105.40 Some ancient translations *They*; Hebrew *He*.

722

Psalms

2 Chron.
Ezra
Nehem.
Esther
Job

PSALMS 106

⁴ Remember me, LORD, when you help your people;
  include me when you save them.
⁵ Let me see the prosperity of your people
  and share in the happiness of your nation,
  in the glad pride of those who belong to you.

⁶ We have sinned as our ancestors did;
  we have been wicked and evil.
⁷ Our ancestors in Egypt did not understand God's
    wonderful acts;
  they forgot the many times he showed them his love,
  and they rebelled against the Almighty* at the Red
    Sea.
⁸ But he saved them, as he had promised,
  in order to show his great power.
⁹ He gave a command to the Red Sea,
  and it dried up;
  he led his people across on dry land.
¹⁰ He saved them from those who hated them;
  he rescued them from their enemies.
¹¹ But the water drowned their enemies;
  not one of them was left.
¹² Then his people believed his promises
  and sang praises to him.

¹³ But they quickly forgot what he had done
  and acted without waiting for his advice.
¹⁴ They were filled with craving in the desert
  and put God to the test;
¹⁵ so he gave them what they asked for,
  but also sent a terrible disease among them.

¹⁶ There in the desert they were jealous of Moses
  and of Aaron, the LORD's holy servant.
¹⁷ Then the earth opened up and swallowed Dathan
  and buried Abiram and his family;
¹⁸ fire came down on their followers
  and burnt up those wicked people.

¹⁹ They made a gold bull calf at Sinai
  and worshipped that idol;
²⁰ they exchanged the glory of God
  for the image of an animal that eats grass.
²¹ They forgot the God who had saved them
  by his mighty acts in Egypt.
²² What wonderful things he did there!
  What amazing things at the Red Sea!
²³ When God said that he would destroy his people,
  his chosen servant, Moses, stood up against God
  and prevented his anger from destroying them.

²⁴ Then they rejected the pleasant land,
  because they did not believe God's promise.
²⁵ They stayed in their tents and grumbled
  and would not listen to the LORD.
²⁶ So he gave them a solemn warning
  that he would make them die in the desert

106.7 Probable text the Almighty; Hebrew the sea.

27 and scatter their descendants among the heathen,
   letting them die in foreign countries.

28 Then at Peor, God's people joined in the worship of
   Baal,
   and ate sacrifices offered to dead gods.
29 They stirred up the LORD's anger by their actions,
   and a terrible disease broke out among them.
30 But Phinehas stood up and punished the guilty,
   and the plague was stopped.
31 This has been remembered in his favour ever since
   and will be for all time to come.

32 At the springs of Meribah the people made the LORD
   angry,
   and Moses was in trouble on their account.
33 They made him so bitter
   that he spoke without stopping to think.

34 They did not kill the heathen,
   as the LORD had commanded them to do,
35 but they intermarried with them
   and adopted their pagan ways.
36 God's people worshipped idols,
   and this caused their destruction.
37 They offered their own sons and daughters
   as sacrifices to the idols of Canaan.
38 They killed those innocent children,
   and the land was defiled by those murders.
39 They made themselves impure by their actions
   and were unfaithful to God.

40 So the LORD was angry with his people;
   he was disgusted with them.
41 He abandoned them to the power of the heathen,
   and their enemies ruled over them.
42 They were oppressed by their enemies
   and were in complete subjection to them.
43 Many times the LORD rescued his people,
   but they chose to rebel against him
   and sank deeper into sin.
44 Yet the LORD heard them when they cried out,
   and he took notice of their distress.
45 For their sake he remembered his covenant,
   and because of his great love he relented.
46 He made all their oppressors
   feel sorry for them.

47 Save us, O LORD our God,
   and bring us back from among the nations,
so that we may be thankful
   and praise your holy name.

48 Praise the LORD, the God of Israel;
   praise him now and for ever!
   Let everyone say, "Amen!"

Praise the LORD!

724

Psalms

⋮⋯⋯⋯

2 Chron.
Ezra
Nehem.
Esther
Job

PSALMS 107

- Know that -
IT'S OK
to come to God no
matter how you're
FEELING.

Book Five
Psalms 107—150

In Praise of God's Goodness

107 ¹ "Give thanks to the LORD, because he is good;
his love is eternal!"
² Repeat these words in praise to the LORD,
all you whom he has saved.
He has rescued you from your enemies
³ and has brought you back from foreign countries,
from east and west, from north and south.*

⁴ Some wandered in the trackless desert
and could not find their way to a city to live in.
⁵ They were hungry and thirsty
and had given up all hope.
⁶ Then in their trouble they called to the LORD,
and he saved them from their distress.
⁷ He led them by a straight road
to a city where they could live.
⁸ They must thank the LORD for his constant love,
for the wonderful things he did for them.
⁹ He satisfies those who are thirsty
and fills the hungry with good things.

¹⁰ Some were living in gloom and darkness,
prisoners suffering in chains,
¹¹ because they had rebelled against the commands of
Almighty God
and had rejected his instructions.
¹² They were worn out from hard work;
they would fall down, and no one would help.
¹³ Then in their trouble they called to the LORD,
and he saved them from their distress.
¹⁴ He brought them out of their gloom and darkness
and broke their chains in pieces.
¹⁵ They must thank the LORD for his constant love,
for the wonderful things he did for them.
¹⁶ He breaks down doors of bronze
and smashes iron bars.

¹⁷ Some were fools, suffering because of their sins
and because of their evil;
¹⁸ they couldn't stand the sight of food
and were close to death.
¹⁹ Then in their trouble they called to the LORD,
and he saved them from their distress.
²⁰ He healed them with his command
and saved them from the grave.
²¹ They must thank the LORD for his constant love,
for the wonderful things he did for them.
²² They must thank him with sacrifices,
and with songs of joy must tell all that he has done.

²³ Some sailed over the ocean in ships,
earning their living on the seas.

107.3 Probable text *south*; Hebrew *the Mediterranean Sea* (meaning
"west").

725

Psalms

....

Proverbs

Eccles.

Songs

Isaiah

Jerem.

24 They saw what the LORD can do,
  his wonderful acts on the seas.
25 He commanded, and a mighty wind began to blow
  and stirred up the waves.
26 The ships were lifted high in the air
  and plunged down into the depths.
  In such danger the sailors lost their courage;
27   they stumbled and staggered like drunken men —
  all their skill was useless.
28 Then in their trouble they called to the LORD,
  and he saved them from their distress.
29 He calmed the raging storm,
  and the waves became quiet.
30 They were glad because of the calm,
  and he brought them safe to the port they wanted.
31 They must thank the LORD for his constant love,
  for the wonderful things he did for them.
32 They must proclaim his greatness in the assembly of the
    people
  and praise him before the council of the leaders.

33 The LORD made rivers dry up completely
  and stopped springs from flowing.
34 He made rich soil become a salty wilderness
  because of the wickedness of those who lived there.
35 He changed deserts into pools of water
  and dry land into flowing springs.
36 He let hungry people settle there,
  and they built a city to live in.
37 They sowed the fields and planted grapevines
  and reaped an abundant harvest.
38 He blessed his people, and they had many children;
  he kept their herds of cattle from decreasing.

39 When God's people were defeated and humiliated
  by cruel oppression and suffering,
40 he showed contempt for their oppressors
  and made them wander in trackless deserts.
41 But he rescued the needy from their misery
  and made their families increase like flocks.
42 The righteous see this and are glad,
  but all the wicked are put to silence.

43 May those who are wise think about these things;
  may they consider the LORD's constant love.

A Prayer for Help against Enemies*
(Ps 57.7–11; 60.5–12)

108 1 I have complete confidence, O God!
  I will sing and praise you!
  Wake up, my soul!
2   Wake up, my harp and lyre!
  I will wake up the sun.
3 I will thank you, O LORD, among the nations.
  I will praise you among the peoples.
4 Your constant love reaches above the heavens;
  your faithfulness touches the skies.

....

Ps 108 *Hebrew title*: A psalm by David; a song.

726

Psalms

⋮⋯⋯⋯⋯

2 Chron.
Ezra
Nehem.
Esther
Job

PSALMS 108, 109

5 Show your greatness in the sky, O God,
  and your glory over all the earth.
6 Save us by your might; answer my prayer,
  so that the people you love may be rescued.

7 From his sanctuary* God has said,
  "In triumph I will divide Shechem
  and distribute the Valley of Sukkoth to my people.
8 Gilead is mine, and Manasseh too;
  Ephraim is my helmet
  and Judah my royal sceptre.
9 But I will use Moab as my washbasin
  and I will throw my sandals on Edom,
  as a sign that I own it.
  I will shout in triumph over the Philistines."

10 Who, O God, will take me into the fortified city?
  Who will lead me to Edom?
11 Have you really rejected us?
  Aren't you going to march out with our armies?
12 Help us against the enemy;
  human help is worthless.
13 With God on our side we will win;
  he will defeat our enemies.

The Complaint of Someone in Trouble*

109 1 I praise you, God; don't remain silent!
2 Wicked people and liars have attacked me.
  They tell lies about me
3   and they say evil things about me,
  attacking me for no reason.
4 They oppose me, even though I love them
  and have prayed for them.*
5 They pay me back evil for good
  and hatred for love.

6 Choose some corrupt judge to try my enemy,
  and let one of his own enemies accuse him.
7 May he be tried and found guilty;
  may even his prayer be considered a crime!
8 May his life soon be ended;
  may someone else take his job!
9 May his children become orphans,
  and his wife a widow!
10 May his children be homeless beggars;
  may they be driven from* the ruins they live in!
11 May his creditors take away all his property,
  and may strangers get everything he worked for.
12 May no one ever be kind to him
  or care for the orphans he leaves behind.
13 May all his descendants die,
  and may his name be forgotten in the next generation.
14 May the LORD remember the evil of his ancestors
  and never forgive his mother's sins.

108.7 *From his sanctuary*; or *In his holiness*.
Ps 109 *Hebrew title*: A psalm by David.
109.4 Probable text *have prayed for them*; Hebrew unclear.
109.10 One ancient translation *be driven from*; Hebrew *seek*.

PSALMS 109, 110

727

Psalms

Proverbs
Eccles.
Songs
Isaiah
Jerem.

¹⁵ May the LORD always remember their sins,
but may they themselves be completely forgotten!

¹⁶ That man never thought of being kind;
he persecuted and killed
the poor, the needy, and the helpless.
¹⁷ He loved to curse — may he be cursed!
He hated to give blessings — may no one bless him!
¹⁸ He cursed as naturally as he dressed himself;
may his own curses soak into his body like water
and into his bones like oil!
¹⁹ May they cover him like clothes
and always be round him like a belt!

²⁰ LORD, punish my enemies in that way —
those who say such evil things against me!
²¹ But my Sovereign LORD, help me as you have promised,
and rescue me because of the goodness of your love.
²² I am poor and needy;
I am hurt to the depths of my heart.
²³ Like an evening shadow I am about to vanish;
I am blown away like an insect.
²⁴ My knees are weak from lack of food;
I am nothing but skin and bones.
²⁵ When people see me, they laugh at me;
they shake their heads in scorn.

²⁶ Help me, O LORD my God;
because of your constant love, save me!
²⁷ Make my enemies know
that you are the one who saves me.
²⁸ They may curse me, but you will bless me.
May my persecutors be defeated,*
and may I, your servant, be glad.
²⁹ May my enemies be covered with disgrace;
may they wear their shame like a robe.

³⁰ I will give loud thanks to the LORD;
I will praise him in the assembly of the people,
³¹ because he defends the poor
and saves them from those who condemn them to
death.

The LORD and his Chosen King*

110 ¹ The LORD said to my lord,
"Sit here at my right
until I put your enemies under your feet."
² From Zion the LORD will extend your royal power.
"Rule over your enemies," he says.
³ On the day you fight your enemies,
your people will volunteer.
Like the dew of early morning
your young men will come to you on the sacred hills.*

109.28 One ancient translation *May my persecutors be defeated*; Hebrew
They persecuted me and were defeated.
Ps 110 *Hebrew title*: A psalm by David.
110.3 Verse 3 in Hebrew is unclear.

728

Psalms

2 Chron.
Ezra
Nehem.
Esther
Job

PSALMS 110–112

4 The Lord made a solemn promise and will not take it back:
"You will be a priest for ever
in the priestly order of Melchizedek."*

5 The Lord is at your right side;
when he becomes angry, he will defeat kings.
6 He will pass judgement on the nations
and fill the battlefield with corpses;
he will defeat kings all over the earth.
7 The king will drink from the stream by the road,
and strengthened, he will stand victorious.

In Praise of the Lord

111 ¹Praise the Lord!

With all my heart I will thank the Lord
in the assembly of his people.
2 How wonderful are the things the Lord does!
All who are delighted with them want to understand
them.
3 All he does is full of honour and majesty;
his righteousness is eternal.

4 The Lord does not let us forget his wonderful actions;
he is kind and merciful.
5 He provides food for those who honour him;
he never forgets his covenant.
6 He has shown his power to his people
by giving them the lands of foreigners.

7 In all he does he is faithful and just;
all his commands are dependable.
8 They last for all time;
they were given in truth and righteousness.
9 He set his people free
and made an eternal covenant with them.
Holy and mighty is he!
10 The way to become wise is to honour the Lord;*
he gives sound judgement to all who obey his
commands.
He is to be praised for ever.

The Happiness of a Good Person

112 ¹Praise the Lord!

Happy is the person who honours the Lord,
who takes pleasure in obeying his commands.
2 The good man's children will be powerful in the land;
his descendants will be blessed.
3 His family will be wealthy and rich,
and he will be prosperous for ever.

4 Light shines in the darkness for good people,
for those who are merciful, kind, and just.

110.4 in... Melchizedek; or like Melchizedek; or in the line of succession to
Melchizedek.
111.10 The way... the Lord; or The most important part of wisdom is
honouring the Lord.

729

Psalms

Proverbs
Eccles.
Songs
Isaiah
Jerem.

⁵ Happy is the person who is generous with his loans,
 who runs his business honestly.
⁶ A good person will never fail;
 he will always be remembered.

⁷ He is not afraid of receiving bad news;
 his faith is strong, and he trusts in the Lord.
⁸ He is not worried or afraid;
 he is certain to see his enemies defeated.
⁹ He gives generously to the needy,
 and his kindness never fails;
 he will be powerful and respected.
¹⁰ The wicked see this and are angry;
 they glare in hate and disappear;
 their hopes are gone for ever.

In Praise of the Lord's Goodness

113 ¹Praise the Lord!

You servants of the Lord,
 praise his name!
² May his name be praised,
 now and for ever.
³ From the east to the west
 praise the name of the Lord!
⁴ The Lord rules over all nations;
 his glory is above the heavens.

⁵ There is no one like the Lord our God.
 He lives in the heights above,
⁶ but he bends down
 to see the heavens and the earth.
⁷ He raises the poor from the dust;
 he lifts the needy from their misery
⁸ and makes them companions of princes,
 the princes of his people.
⁹ He honours the childless wife in her home;
 he makes her happy by giving her children.

Praise the Lord!

A Passover Song

114 ¹When the people of Israel left Egypt,
 when Jacob's descendants left that foreign land,
² Judah became the Lord's holy people,
 Israel became his own possession.

³ The Red Sea looked and ran away;
 the River Jordan stopped flowing.
⁴ The mountains skipped like goats;
 the hills jumped about like lambs.

⁵ What happened, Sea, to make you run away?
 And you, O Jordan, why did you stop flowing?
⁶ You mountains, why did you skip like goats?
 You hills, why did you jump about like lambs?

⁷ Tremble, earth, at the Lord's coming,
 at the presence of the God of Jacob,

PSALM 112.9

This is your

ACTION PLAN

SPACE.

Write below how you
could help others. Then...
go and do it!

730

Psalms

2 Chron.
Ezra
Nehem.
Esther
Job

PSALMS 114–116

8 who changes rocks into pools of water
  and solid cliffs into flowing springs.

The One True God

115 ¹To you alone, O LORD, to you alone,
  and not to us, must glory be given
  because of your constant love and faithfulness.

² Why should the nations ask us,
  "Where is your God?"
³ Our God is in heaven;
  he does whatever he wishes.
⁴ Their gods are made of silver and gold,
  formed by human hands.
⁵ They have mouths, but cannot speak,
  and eyes, but cannot see.
⁶ They have ears, but cannot hear,
  and noses, but cannot smell.
⁷ They have hands, but cannot feel,
  and feet, but cannot walk;
  they cannot make a sound.
⁸ May all who made them and who trust in them
  become* like the idols they have made.

⁹ Trust in the LORD, you people of Israel.
  He helps you and protects you.
¹⁰ Trust in the LORD, you priests of God.
  He helps you and protects you.
¹¹ Trust in the LORD, all you that worship him.
  He helps you and protects you.

¹² The LORD remembers us and will bless us;
  he will bless the people of Israel
  and all the priests of God.
¹³ He will bless everyone who honours him,
  the great and the small alike.

¹⁴ May the LORD give you children —
  you and your descendants!
¹⁵ May you be blessed by the LORD,
  who made heaven and earth!

¹⁶ Heaven belongs to the LORD alone,
  but he gave the earth to the human race.
¹⁷ The LORD is not praised by the dead,
  by any who go down to the land of silence.*
¹⁸ But we, the living, will give thanks to him
  now and for ever.

  Praise the LORD!

Someone Saved from Death Praises God

116 ¹I love the LORD, because he hears me;
  he listens to my prayers.

115.8 *May all… become*; or *All who made them and who trust in them will
become.*
115.17 *land of silence*: The world of the dead (see 6.5).

PSALMS 116–118

731

Psalms

Proverbs
Eccles.
Songs
Isaiah
Jerem.

2 He listens to me
  every time I call to him.
3 The danger of death was all round me;
  the horrors of the grave closed in on me;
  I was filled with fear and anxiety.
4 Then I called to the LORD,
  "I beg you, LORD, save me!"

5 The LORD is merciful and good;
  our God is compassionate.
6 The LORD protects the helpless;
  when I was in danger, he saved me.
7 Be confident, my heart,
  because the LORD has been good to me.

8 The LORD saved me from death;
  he stopped my tears
  and kept me from defeat.
9 And so I walk in the presence of the LORD
  in the world of the living.
10 I kept on believing, even when I said,
  "I am completely crushed,"
11 even when I was afraid and said,
  "No one can be trusted."

12 What can I offer the LORD
  for all his goodness to me?
13 I will bring a wine offering to the LORD,
  to thank him for saving me.
14 In the assembly of all his people
  I will give him what I have promised.

15 How painful it is to the LORD
  when one of his people dies!
16 I am your servant, LORD;
  I serve you, just as my mother did.
  You have saved me from death.
17 I will give you a sacrifice of thanksgiving
  and offer my prayer to you.
18-19 In the assembly of all your people,
  in the sanctuary of your Temple in Jerusalem,
  I will give you what I have promised.

  Praise the LORD!

In Praise of the LORD

117 1 Praise the LORD, all nations!
  Praise him, all peoples!
2 His love for us is strong
  and his faithfulness is eternal.

  Praise the LORD!

A Prayer of Thanks for Victory

118 1 Give thanks to the LORD, because he is good,
  and his love is eternal.
2 Let the people of Israel say,
  "His love is eternal."

³ Let the priests of God say,
   "His love is eternal."
⁴ Let all who worship him say,
   "His love is eternal."

⁵ In my distress I called to the LORD;
   he answered me and set me free.
⁶ The LORD is with me, I will not be afraid;
   what can anyone do to me?
⁷ It is the LORD who helps me,
   and I will see my enemies defeated.
⁸ It is better to trust in the LORD
   than to depend on human beings.
⁹ It is better to trust in the LORD
   than to depend on human leaders.

¹⁰ Many enemies were round me;
   but I destroyed them by the power of the LORD!
¹¹ They were round me on every side;
   but I destroyed them by the power of the LORD!
¹² They swarmed round me like bees,
   but they burnt out as quickly as a fire among thorns;
   by the power of the LORD I destroyed them.
¹³ I was fiercely attacked and was being defeated,
   but the LORD helped me.
¹⁴ The LORD makes me powerful and strong;
   he has saved me.

¹⁵ Listen to the glad shouts of victory in the tents of God's
      people:
   "The LORD's mighty power has done it!
¹⁶   His power has brought us victory —
   his mighty power in battle!"

¹⁷ I will not die; instead, I will live
   and proclaim what the LORD has done.
¹⁸ He has punished me severely,
   but he has not let me die.

¹⁹ Open to me the gates of the Temple;
   I will go in and give thanks to the LORD!
²⁰ This is the gate of the LORD;
   only the righteous can come in.

²¹ I praise you, LORD, because you heard me,
   because you have given me victory.

²² The stone which the builders rejected as worthless
   turned out to be the most important of all.
²³ This was done by the LORD;
   what a wonderful sight it is!
²⁴ This is the day of the LORD's victory;
   let us be happy, let us celebrate!
²⁵ Save us, LORD, save us!
   Give us success, O LORD!

²⁶ May God bless the one who comes in the name of the
   LORD!

PSALMS 118, 119

733

Psalms

Proverbs
Eccles.
Songs
Isaiah
Jerem.

From the Temple of the LORD we bless you.
27 The LORD is God; he has been good to us.
   With branches in your hands, start the festival
      and march round the altar.

28 You are my God, and I give you thanks;
      I will proclaim your greatness.

29 Give thanks to the LORD, because he is good,
      and his love is eternal.

The Law of the LORD

119

¹ Happy are those whose lives are faultless,
   who live according to the law of the LORD.
² Happy are those who follow his commands,
   who obey him with all their heart.
³ They never do wrong;
   they walk in the LORD's ways.
⁴ LORD, you have given us your laws
   and told us to obey them faithfully.
⁵ How I hope that I shall be faithful
   in keeping your instructions!
⁶ If I pay attention to all your commands,
   then I will not be put to shame.
⁷ As I learn your righteous judgements,
   I will praise you with a pure heart.
⁸ I will obey your laws;
   never abandon me!

Obedience to the Law of the LORD

⁹ How can young people keep their lives pure?
   By obeying your commands.
¹⁰ With all my heart I try to serve you;
   keep me from disobeying your commandments.
¹¹ I keep your law in my heart,
   so that I will not sin against you.
¹² I praise you, O LORD;
   teach me your ways.
¹³ I will repeat aloud
   all the laws you have given.
¹⁴ I delight in following your commands
   more than in having great wealth.
¹⁵ I study your instructions;
   I examine your teachings.
¹⁶ I take pleasure in your laws;
   your commands I will not forget.

Happiness in the Law of the LORD

¹⁷ Be good to me, your servant,
   so that I may live and obey your teachings.
¹⁸ Open my eyes, so that I may see
   the wonderful truths in your law.
¹⁹ I am here on earth for just a little while;
   do not hide your commands from me.
²⁰ My heart aches with longing;
   I want to know your judgements at all times.
²¹ You reprimand the proud;
   cursed are those who disobey your commands.

PSALM 119

Psalm 119 is broken into 22 different sections, one for each letter of the Hebrew alphabet. (The psalms were written in Hebrew.) Within each section, every sentence begins with the same letter of the alphabet. However, we don't see this when we read the psalm in our

• OWN • LANGUAGE.

Why not grab a piece of paper and have a go at writing your own psalm in this style, using the English alphabet?

734

Psalms

⠒⠄⠄⠄⠄⠄⠄⠄

2 Chron.

Ezra

Nehem.

Esther

Job

PSALMS 119

22 Free me from their insults and scorn,
  because I have kept your laws.
23 The rulers meet and plot against me,
  but I will study your teachings.
24 Your instructions give me pleasure;
  they are my advisers.

Determination to Obey the Law of the LORD

25 I lie defeated in the dust;
  revive me, as you have promised.
26 I confessed all I have done, and you answered me;
  teach me your ways.
27 Help me to understand your laws,
  and I will meditate on your wonderful teachings.*
28 I am overcome by sorrow;
  strengthen me, as you have promised.
29 Keep me from going the wrong way,
  and in your goodness teach me your law.
30 I have chosen to be obedient;
  I have paid attention to your judgements.
31 I have followed your instructions, LORD;
  don't let me be put to shame.
32 I will eagerly obey your commands,
  because you will give me more understanding.

A Prayer for Understanding

33 Teach me, LORD, the meaning of your laws,
  and I will obey them at all times.
34 Explain your law to me, and I will obey it;
  I will keep it with all my heart.
35 Keep me obedient to your commandments,
  because in them I find happiness.
36 Give me the desire to obey your laws
  rather than to get rich.
37 Keep me from paying attention to what is worthless;
  be good to me, as you have promised.
38 Keep your promise to me, your servant —
  the promise you make to those who obey you.
39 Save me from the insults I fear;
  how wonderful are your judgements!
40 I want to obey your commands;
  give me new life, for you are righteous.

Trusting the Law of the LORD

41 Show me how much you love me, LORD,
  and save me according to your promise.
42 Then I can answer those who insult me
  because I trust in your word.
43 Enable me to speak the truth at all times,
  because my hope is in your judgements.
44 I will always obey your law,
  for ever and ever.
45 I will live in perfect freedom,
  because I try to obey your teachings.
46 I will announce your commands to kings
  and I will not be ashamed.

119.27 *teachings*; or *deeds*.

Psalms

....

Proverbs

Eccles.

Songs

Isaiah

Jerem.

[47] I find pleasure in obeying your commands,
because I love them.
[48] I respect and love your commandments;
I will meditate on your instructions.

Confidence in the Law of the LORD

[49] Remember your promise to me, your servant;
it has given me hope.
[50] Even in my suffering I was comforted
because your promise gave me life.
[51] The proud are always scornful of me,
but I have not departed from your law.
[52] I remember your judgements of long ago,
and they bring me comfort, O LORD.
[53] When I see the wicked breaking your law,
I am filled with anger.
[54] During my brief earthly life
I compose songs about your commands.
[55] In the night I remember you, LORD,
and I think about your law.
[56] I find my happiness
in obeying your commands.

Devotion to the Law of the LORD

[57] You are all I want, O LORD;
I promise to obey your laws.
[58] I ask you with all my heart
to have mercy on me, as you have promised!
[59] I have considered my conduct,
and I promise to follow your instructions.
[60] Without delay I hurry
to obey your commands.
[61] The wicked have laid a trap for me,
but I do not forget your law.
[62] In the middle of the night I wake up
to praise you for your righteous judgements.
[63] I am a friend of all who serve you,
of all who obey your laws.
[64] LORD, the earth is full of your constant love;
teach me your commandments.

The Value of the Law of the LORD

[65] You have kept your promise, LORD,
and you are good to me, your servant.
[66] Give me wisdom and knowledge,
because I trust in your commands.
[67] Before you punished me, I used to go wrong,
but now I obey your word.
[68] How good you are — how kind!
Teach me your commands.
[69] The proud have told lies about me,
but with all my heart I obey your instructions.
[70] They have no understanding,
but I find pleasure in your law.
[71] My punishment was good for me,
because it made me learn your commands.
[72] The law that you gave means more to me
than all the money in the world.

2 Chron.
Ezra
Nehem.
Esther
Job

DECORATE THESE SHAPES IN RELATION TO YOUR MOOD.

The Justice of the Law of the LORD

73 You created me, and you keep me safe;
   give me understanding, so that I may learn your laws.
74 Those who honour you will be glad when they see me,
   because I trust in your promise.
75 I know that your judgements are righteous, LORD,
   and that you punished me because you are faithful.
76 Let your constant love comfort me,
   as you have promised me, your servant.
77 Have mercy on me, and I will live
   because I take pleasure in your law.
78 May the proud be ashamed for falsely accusing me;
   as for me, I will meditate on your instructions.
79 May those who honour you come to me —
   all those who know your commands.
80 May I perfectly obey your commandments
   and be spared the shame of defeat.

A Prayer for Deliverance

81 I am worn out, LORD, waiting for you to save me;
   I place my trust in your word.
82 My eyes are tired from watching for what you promised,
   while I ask, "When will you help me?"
83 I am as useless as a discarded wineskin;
   yet I have not forgotten your commands.
84 How much longer must I wait?
   When will you punish those who persecute me?
85 The proud, who do not obey your law,
   have dug pits to trap me.
86 Your commandments are all trustworthy;
   people persecute me with lies — help me!
87 They have almost succeeded in killing me,
   but I have not neglected your commands.
88 Because of your constant love be good to me,
   so that I may obey your laws.

Faith in the Law of the LORD

89 Your word, O LORD, will last for ever;
   it is eternal in heaven.
90 Your faithfulness endures through all the ages;
   you have set the earth in place, and it remains.
91 All things remain to this day because of your command,
   because they are all your servants.
92 If your law had not been the source of my joy,
   I would have died from my sufferings.
93 I will never neglect your instructions,
   because by them you have kept me alive.
94 I am yours — save me!
   I have tried to obey your commands.
95 The wicked are waiting to kill me,
   but I will meditate on your laws.
96 I have learnt that everything has limits;
   but your commandment is perfect.

Love for the Law of the LORD

97 How I love your law!
   I think about it all day long.
98 Your commandment is with me all the time
   and makes me wiser than my enemies.

PSALMS 119

737

Psalms

Proverbs
Eccles.
Songs
Isaiah
Jerem.

99 I understand more than all my teachers,
  because I meditate on your instructions.
100 I have greater wisdom than those who are old,
  because I obey your commands.
101 I have avoided all evil conduct,
  because I want to obey your word.
102 I have not neglected your instructions,
  for you yourself are my teacher.
103 How sweet is the taste of your instructions —
  sweeter even than honey!
104 I gain wisdom from your laws,
  and so I hate all bad conduct.

Light from the Law of the LORD
105 Your word is a lamp to guide me
  and a light for my path.
106 I will keep my solemn promise
  to obey your just instructions.
107 My sufferings, LORD, are terrible indeed;
  keep me alive, as you have promised.
108 Accept my prayer of thanks, O LORD,
  and teach me your commands.
109 I am always ready to risk my life;
  I* have not forgotten your law.
110 The wicked lay a trap for me,
  but I have not disobeyed your commands.
111 Your commandments are my eternal possession;
  they are the joy of my heart.
112 I have decided to obey your laws
  until the day I die.

Safety in the Law of the LORD
113 I hate those who are not completely loyal to you,
  but I love your law.
114 You are my defender and protector;
  I put my hope in your promise.
115 Go away from me, you sinful people.
  I will obey the commands of my God.
116 Give me strength, as you promised, and I shall live;
  don't let me be disappointed in my hope!
117 Hold me, and I will be safe,
  and I will always pay attention to your commands.
118 You reject everyone who disobeys your laws;
  their deceitful schemes are useless.
119 You treat all the wicked like rubbish,
  and so I love your instructions.
120 Because of you I am afraid;
  I am filled with fear because of your judgements.

Obedience to the Law of the LORD
121 I have done what is right and good;
  don't abandon me to my enemies!
122 Promise that you will help your servant;
  don't let the arrogant oppress me!
123 My eyes are tired from watching for your saving help,
  for the deliverance you promised.

119.109 *I am always ready to risk my life; I;* or *My life is in constant danger, but I.*

124 Treat me according to your constant love,
and teach me your commands.
125 I am your servant; give me understanding,
so that I may know your teachings.
126 LORD, it is time for you to act,
because people are disobeying your law.
127 I love your commands more than gold,
more than the finest gold.
128 And so I follow all your instructions;*
I hate all wrong ways.

Desire to Obey the Law of the LORD
129 Your teachings are wonderful;
I obey them with all my heart.
130 The explanation of your teachings gives light
and brings wisdom to the ignorant.
131 In my desire for your commands
I pant with open mouth.
132 Turn to me and have mercy on me
as you do on all those who love you.
133 As you have promised, keep me from falling;
don't let me be overcome by evil.
134 Save me from those who oppress me,
so that I may obey your commands.
135 Bless me with your presence
and teach me your laws.
136 My tears pour down like a river,
because people do not obey your law.

The Justice of the Law of the LORD
137 You are righteous, LORD,
and your laws are just.
138 The rules that you have given
are completely fair and right.
139 My anger burns in me like a fire,
because my enemies disregard your commands.
140 How certain your promise is!
How I love it!
141 I am unimportant and despised,
but I do not neglect your teachings.
142 Your righteousness will last for ever,
and your law is always true.
143 I am filled with trouble and anxiety,
but your commandments bring me joy.
144 Your instructions are always just;
give me understanding, and I shall live.

A Prayer for Deliverance
145 With all my heart I call to you;
answer me, LORD, and I will obey your commands!
146 I call to you;
save me, and I will keep your laws.
147 Before sunrise I call to you for help;
I place my hope in your promise.
148 All night long I lie awake,
to meditate on your instructions.

....

119.128 Some ancient translations *all your instructions*; Hebrew unclear.

149 Because your love is constant, hear me, O LORD;
  show your mercy, and preserve my life!
150 My cruel persecutors are coming closer,
  people who never keep your law.
151 But you are near to me, LORD,
  and all your commands are permanent.
152 Long ago I learnt about your instructions;
  you made them to last for ever.

A Plea for Help

153 Look at my suffering, and save me,
  because I have not neglected your law.
154 Defend my cause, and set me free;
  save me, as you have promised.
155 The wicked will not be saved,
  for they do not obey your laws.
156 But your compassion, LORD, is great;
  show your mercy and save me!
157 I have many enemies and oppressors,
  but I do not fail to obey your laws.
158 When I look at those traitors, I am filled with disgust,
  because they do not keep your commands.
159 See how I love your instructions, LORD.
  Your love never changes, so save me!
160 The heart of your law is truth,
  and all your righteous judgements are eternal.

Dedication to the Law of the LORD

161 Powerful people attack me unjustly,
  but I respect your law.
162 How happy I am because of your promises —
  as happy as someone who finds rich treasure.
163 I hate and detest all lies,
  but I love your law.
164 Seven times each day I thank you
  for your righteous judgements.
165 Those who love your law have perfect security,
  and there is nothing that can make them fall.
166 I wait for you to save me, LORD,
  and I do what you command.
167 I obey your teachings;
  I love them with all my heart.
168 I obey your commands and your instructions;
  you see everything I do.

A Prayer for Help

169 Let my cry for help reach you, LORD!
  Give me understanding, as you have promised.
170 Listen to my prayer,
  and save me according to your promise!
171 I will always praise you,
  because you teach me your laws.
172 I will sing about your law,
  because your commands are just.
173 Always be ready to help me,
  because I follow your commands.
174 How I long for your saving help, O LORD!
  I find happiness in your law.

740

Psalms

2 Chron.
Ezra
Nehem.
Esther
Job

PSALMS 119–122

PSALM 121

Underline any bits of Psalm 121 that

JUMP
- OUT -

to you. What do they make you think of? How does this psalm make you see God?

write some thoughts here

175 Give me life, so that I may praise you;
  may your instructions help me.
176 I wander about like a lost sheep;
  so come and look for me, your servant,
  because I have not neglected your laws.

A Prayer for Help

120 ¹When I was in trouble, I called to the LORD,
  and he answered me.
² Save me, LORD,
  from liars and deceivers.

³ You liars, what will God do to you?
  How will he punish you?
⁴ With a soldier's sharp arrows,
  with red-hot charcoal!

⁵ Living among you is as bad as living in Meshech
  or among the people of Kedar.*
⁶ I have lived too long
  with people who hate peace!
⁷ When I speak of peace,
  they are for war.

The LORD our Protector

121 ¹I look to the mountains;
  where will my help come from?
² My help will come from the LORD,
  who made heaven and earth.

³ He will not let you fall;
  your protector is always awake.
⁴ The protector of Israel
  never dozes or sleeps.
⁵ The LORD will guard you;
  he is by your side to protect you.
⁶ The sun will not hurt you during the day,
  nor the moon during the night.

⁷ The LORD will protect you from all danger;
  he will keep you safe.
⁸ He will protect you as you come and go
  now and for ever.

In Praise of Jerusalem*

122 ¹I was glad when they said to me,
  "Let us go to the LORD's house."
² And now we are here,
  standing inside the gates of Jerusalem!

³ Jerusalem is a city restored
  in beautiful order and harmony.
⁴ This is where the tribes come,
  the tribes of Israel,

120.5 *Meshech… Kedar:* Two distant regions, whose people were regarded as savages.
Ps 122 *Hebrew title:* By David.

PSALMS 122–125

741

Psalms
....
Proverbs
Eccles.
Songs
Isaiah
Jerem.

to give thanks to the Lord
according to his command.
⁵ Here the kings of Israel
sat to judge their people.

⁶ Pray for the peace of Jerusalem:
"May those who love you prosper.
⁷ May there be peace inside your walls
and safety in your palaces."
⁸ For the sake of my relatives and friends
I say to Jerusalem, "Peace be with you!"
⁹ For the sake of the house of the Lord our God
I pray for your prosperity.

A Prayer for Mercy

123 ¹ Lord, I look up to you,
up to heaven, where you rule.
² As a servant depends on his master,
as a maid depends on her mistress,
so we will keep looking to you, O Lord our God,
until you have mercy on us.

³ Be merciful to us, Lord, be merciful;
we have been treated with so much contempt.
⁴ We have been mocked too long by the rich
and scorned by proud oppressors.

God the Protector of his People*

124 ¹ What if the Lord had not been on our side?
Answer, O Israel!

² "If the Lord had not been on our side
when our enemies attacked us,
³ then they would have swallowed us alive
in their furious anger against us;
⁴ then the flood would have carried us away,
the water would have covered us,
⁵ the raging torrent would have drowned us."

⁶ Let us thank the Lord,
who has not let our enemies destroy us.
⁷ We have escaped like a bird from a hunter's trap;
the trap is broken, and we are free!
⁸ Our help comes from the Lord,
who made heaven and earth.

The Security of God's People

125 ¹ Those who trust in the Lord are like Mount Zion,
which can never be shaken, never be moved.
² As the mountains surround Jerusalem,
so the Lord surrounds his people
now and for ever.

³ The wicked will not always rule over the land of the
righteous;
if they did, the righteous themselves might do evil.

Ps 124 *Hebrew title*: By David.

742

Psalms

⋮⋯⋯⋯

2 Chron.
Ezra
Nehem.
Esther
Job

PSALMS 125–128

⁴ LORD, do good to those who are good,
to those who obey your commands.
⁵ But when you punish the wicked,
punish also those who abandon your ways.

Peace be with Israel!

A Prayer for Deliverance

126 ¹ When the LORD brought us back to Jerusalem,*
it was like a dream!
² How we laughed, how we sang for joy!
Then the other nations said about us,
"The LORD did great things for them."
³ Indeed he did great things for us;
how happy we were!

⁴ LORD, make us prosperous again,*
just as the rain brings water back to dry riverbeds.
⁵ Let those who wept as they sowed their seed,
gather the harvest with joy!

⁶ Those who wept as they went out carrying the seed
will come back singing for joy,
as they bring in the harvest.

In Praise of God's Goodness*

127 ¹ If the LORD does not build the house,
the work of the builders is useless;
if the LORD does not protect the city,
it is useless for the sentries to stand guard.
² It is useless to work so hard for a living,
getting up early and going to bed late.
For the LORD provides for those he loves,
while they are asleep.

³ Children are a gift from the LORD;
they are a real blessing.
⁴ The sons a man has when he is young
are like arrows in a soldier's hand.
⁵ Happy is the man who has many such arrows.
He will never be defeated
when he meets his enemies in the place of judgement.

The Reward of Obedience to the LORD

128 ¹ Happy are those who obey the LORD,
who live by his commands.

² Your work will provide for your needs;
you will be happy and prosperous.
³ Your wife will be like a fruitful vine in your home,
and your children will be like young olive trees round
your table.
⁴ A man who obeys the LORD
will surely be blessed like this.

126.1 *brought us back to Jerusalem;* or *made Jerusalem prosperous again.*
126.4 *make... again;* or *take us back to our land.*
Ps 127 *Hebrew title:* By Solomon.

PSALMS 128–131

743

Psalms

Proverbs
Eccles.
Songs
Isaiah
Jerem.

5 May the LORD bless you from Zion!
  May you see Jerusalem prosper
    all the days of your life!
6 May you live to see your grandchildren!

  Peace be with Israel!

A Prayer against Israel's Enemies

129 [1] Israel, tell us how your enemies have persecuted
    you
    ever since you were young.

2 "Ever since I was young,
    my enemies have persecuted me cruelly,
    but they have not overcome me.
3 They cut deep wounds in my back
    and made it like a ploughed field.
4 But the LORD, the righteous one,
    has freed me from slavery."

5 May everyone who hates Zion
    be defeated and driven back.
6 May they all be like grass growing on the housetops,
    which dries up before it can grow;
7 no one gathers it up
    or carries it away in bundles.
8 No one who passes by will say,
    "May the LORD bless you!
    We bless you in the name of the LORD."

A Prayer for Help

130 [1] From the depths of my despair I call to you, LORD.
    2 Hear my cry, O Lord;
    listen to my call for help!
3 If you kept a record of our sins,
    who could escape being condemned?
4 But you forgive us,
    so that we should stand in awe of you.

5 I wait eagerly for the LORD's help,
    and in his word I trust.
6 I wait for the Lord
    more eagerly than watchmen wait for the dawn —
    than watchmen wait for the dawn.

7 Israel, trust in the LORD,
    because his love is constant
    and he is always willing to save.
8 He will save his people Israel
    from all their sins.

A Prayer of Humble Trust*

131 [1] LORD, I have given up my pride
    and turned away from my arrogance.
    I am not concerned with great matters
    or with subjects too difficult for me.

Ps 131 *Hebrew title*: By David.

744

Psalms

⋮⋯⋯⋯

2 Chron.

Ezra

Nehem.

Esther

Job

PSALMS 131–133

2 Instead, I am content and at peace.
   As a child lies quietly in its mother's arms,
      so my heart is quiet within me.
3 Israel, trust in the LORD
   now and for ever!

In Praise of the Temple

132 ¹ LORD, do not forget David
      and all the hardships he endured.
2 Remember, LORD, what he promised,
   the vow he made to you, the Mighty God of Jacob:
3 "I will not go home or go to bed;
4   I will not rest or sleep,
5   until I provide a place for the LORD,
      a home for the Mighty God of Jacob."

6 In Bethlehem we heard about the Covenant Box,
   and we found it in the fields of Jearim.
7 We said, "Let us go to the LORD's house;
   let us worship before his throne."

8 Come to the Temple, LORD, with the Covenant Box,
      the symbol of your power,
      and stay here for ever.
9 May your priests do always what is right;
      may your people shout for joy!

10 You made a promise to your servant David;
      do not reject your chosen king, LORD.
11 You made a solemn promise to David —
   a promise you will not take back:
   "I will make one of your sons king,
      and he will rule after you.
12 If your sons are true to my covenant
   and to the commands I give them,
      their sons, also, will succeed you for all time as kings."

13 The LORD has chosen Zion;
      he wants to make it his home:
14 "This is where I will live for ever;
      this is where I want to rule.
15 I will richly provide Zion with all she needs;
      I will satisfy her poor with food.
16 I will bless her priests in all they do,
      and her people will sing and shout for joy.
17 Here I will make one of David's descendants a great king;
      here I will preserve the rule of my chosen king.
18 I will cover his enemies with shame,
      but his kingdom will prosper and flourish."

In Praise of Living in Peace*

133 ¹ How wonderful it is, how pleasant,
      for God's people to live together in harmony!
2 It is like the precious anointing oil
      running down from Aaron's head and beard,
      down to the collar of his robes.

⋯⋯⋯⋯⋯⋯⋯⋯⋯⋯⋯⋯⋯⋯⋯⋯⋯⋯⋯⋯⋯⋯⋯⋯⋯⋯⋯⋯⋯⋯⋯⋯⋯⋯⋯⋯

Ps 133 *Hebrew title*: By David.

PSALMS 133–135

745

Psalms

Proverbs
Eccles.
Songs
Isaiah
Jerem.

3 It is like the dew on Mount Hermon,
   falling on the hills of Zion.
   That is where the LORD has promised his blessing —
   life that never ends.

A Call to Praise God

134 ¹Come, praise the LORD,
   all his servants,
   all who serve in his Temple at night.
² Raise your hands in prayer in the Temple,
   and praise the LORD!

³ May the LORD, who made heaven and earth,
   bless you from Zion!

A Hymn of Praise

135 ¹Praise the LORD!

   Praise his name, you servants of the LORD,
²   who stand in the LORD's house,
   in the Temple of our God.
³ Praise the LORD, because he is good;
   sing praises to his name, because he is kind.*
⁴ He chose Jacob for himself,
   the people of Israel for his own.

⁵ I know that our LORD is great,
   greater than all the gods.
⁶ He does whatever he wishes
   in heaven and on earth,
   in the seas and in the depths below.
⁷ He brings storm clouds from the ends of the earth;
   he makes lightning for the storms,
   and he brings out the wind from his storeroom.

⁸ In Egypt he killed all the firstborn
   of people and animals alike.
⁹ There he performed miracles and wonders
   to punish the king and all his officials.
¹⁰ He destroyed many nations
   and killed powerful kings:
¹¹ Sihon, king of the Amorites,
   Og, king of Bashan,
   and all the kings in Canaan.
¹² He gave their lands to his people;
   he gave them to Israel.

¹³ LORD, you will always be proclaimed as God;
   all generations will remember you.
¹⁴ The LORD will defend his people;
   he will take pity on his servants.

¹⁵ The gods of the nations are made of silver and gold;
   they are formed by human hands.
¹⁶ They have mouths, but cannot speak,
   and eyes, but cannot see.

TURN THESE SHAPES INTO

SOMETHING ELSE.

135.3 *he is kind*; or *it is pleasant to do so.*

746

Psalms

2 Chron.
Ezra
Nehem.
Esther
Job

PSALMS 135, 136

¹⁷ They have ears, but cannot hear;
      they are not even able to breathe.
¹⁸ May all who made them and who trust in them
      become* like the idols they have made!

¹⁹ Praise the Lord, people of Israel;
      praise him, you priests of God!
²⁰ Praise the Lord, you Levites;
      praise him, all you that worship him!
²¹ Praise the Lord in Zion,
      in Jerusalem, his home.

      Praise the Lord!

A Hymn of Thanksgiving

136 ¹Give thanks to the Lord, because he is good;
      his love is eternal.
² Give thanks to the greatest of all gods;
      his love is eternal.
³ Give thanks to the mightiest of all lords;
      his love is eternal.

⁴ He alone performs great miracles;
      his love is eternal.
⁵ By his wisdom he made the heavens;
      his love is eternal;
⁶ he built the earth on the deep waters;
      his love is eternal.
⁷ He made the sun and the moon;
      his love is eternal;
⁸ the sun to rule over the day;
      his love is eternal;
⁹ the moon and the stars to rule over the night;
      his love is eternal.

¹⁰ He killed the firstborn sons of the Egyptians;
      his love is eternal.
¹¹ He led the people of Israel out of Egypt;
      his love is eternal;
¹² with his strong hand, his powerful arm;
      his love is eternal.
¹³ He divided the Red Sea;
      his love is eternal;
¹⁴ he led his people through it;
      his love is eternal;
¹⁵ but he drowned the king of Egypt and his army;
      his love is eternal.

¹⁶ He led his people through the desert;
      his love is eternal.
¹⁷ He killed powerful kings;
      his love is eternal;
¹⁸ he killed famous kings;
      his love is eternal;
¹⁹ Sihon, king of the Amorites;
      his love is eternal;

──────────────────────────────

135.18 *May all... become*; or *All who made them and who trust in them will become.*

747

Psalms
....
Proverbs
Eccles.
Songs
Isaiah
Jerem.

20 and Og, king of Bashan;
   his love is eternal.
21 He gave their lands to his people;
   his love is eternal;
22 he gave them to Israel, his servant;
   his love is eternal.
23 He did not forget us when we were defeated;
   his love is eternal;
24 he freed us from our enemies;
   his love is eternal.
25 He gives food to every living creature;
   his love is eternal.

26 Give thanks to the God of heaven;
   his love is eternal.

A Lament of Israelites in Exile

137 ¹ By the rivers of Babylon we sat down;
   there we wept when we remembered Zion.
² On the willows near by
   we hung up our harps.
³ Those who captured us told us to sing;
   they told us to entertain them:
   "Sing us a song about Zion."

⁴ How can we sing a song to the LORD
   in a foreign land?
⁵ May I never be able to play the harp again
   if I forget you, Jerusalem!
⁶ May I never be able to sing again
   if I do not remember you,
   if I do not think of you as my greatest joy!

⁷ Remember, LORD, what the Edomites did
   the day Jerusalem was captured.
   Remember how they kept saying,
   "Tear it down to the ground!"

⁸ Babylon, you will be destroyed.
   Happy are those who pay you back
   for what you have done to us —
⁹ who take your babies
   and smash them against a rock.

A Prayer of Thanksgiving*

138 ¹ I thank you, LORD, with all my heart;
   I sing praise to you before the gods.
² I face your holy Temple,
   bow down, and praise your name
   because of your constant love and faithfulness,
   because you have shown that your name and your
   commands are supreme.*
³ You answered me when I called to you;
   with your strength you strengthened me.

Ps 138 *Hebrew title*: By David.
138.2 Probable text *your name and your commands are supreme*; Hebrew
your command is greater than all your name.

748

Psalms

2 Chron.
Ezra
Nehem.
Esther
Job

PSALMS 138, 139

PSALM 139

Write a verse here that

STANDS
– OUT –
TO YOU

from Psalm 139.

DECORATE IT

with patterns and
colour as you think and
pray about what it
means for you.

⁴ All the kings in the world will praise you, Lord,
   because they have heard your promises.
⁵ They will sing about what you have done
   and about your great glory.
⁶ Even though you are so high above,
   you care for the lowly,
   and the proud cannot hide from you.

⁷ When I am surrounded by troubles,
   you keep me safe.
   You oppose my angry enemies
   and save me by your power.
⁸ You will do everything you have promised;
   Lord, your love is eternal.
   Complete the work that you have begun.

God's Complete Knowledge and Care*

139 ¹ Lord, you have examined me and you know me.
   ² You know everything I do;
   from far away you understand all my thoughts.
³ You see me, whether I am working or resting;
   you know all my actions.
⁴ Even before I speak,
   you already know what I will say.
⁵ You are all round me on every side;
   you protect me with your power.
⁶ Your knowledge of me is too deep;
   it is beyond my understanding.

⁷ Where could I go to escape from you?
   Where could I get away from your presence?
⁸ If I went up to heaven, you would be there;
   if I lay down in the world of the dead, you would be
      there.
⁹ If I flew away beyond the east
   or lived in the farthest place in the west,
¹⁰ you would be there to lead me,
   you would be there to help me.
¹¹ I could ask the darkness to hide me
   or the light round me to turn into night,
¹² but even darkness is not dark for you,
   and the night is as bright as the day.
   Darkness and light are the same to you.

¹³ You created every part of me;
   you put me together in my mother's womb.
¹⁴ I praise you because you are to be feared;
   all you do is strange and wonderful.
   I know it with all my heart.
¹⁵ When my bones were being formed,
   carefully put together in my mother's womb,
   when I was growing there in secret,
   you knew that I was there —
¹⁶   you saw me before I was born.
   The days allotted to me
   had all been recorded in your book,
   before any of them ever began.

Ps 139 *Hebrew title*: A psalm by David.

PSALMS 139, 140

749

Psalms

....

Proverbs
Eccles.
Songs
Isaiah
Jerem.

¹⁷ O God, how difficult I find your thoughts;*
    how many of them there are!
¹⁸ If I counted them, they would be more than the grains of
    sand.
    When I awake, I am still with you.

¹⁹ O God, how I wish you would kill the wicked!
    How I wish violent people would leave me alone!
²⁰ They say wicked things about you;
    they speak evil things against your name.*
²¹ O Lord, how I hate those who hate you!
    How I despise those who rebel against you!
²² I hate them with a total hatred;
    I regard them as my enemies.

²³ Examine me, O God, and know my mind;
    test me, and discover my thoughts.
²⁴ Find out if there is any evil in me
    and guide me in the everlasting way.*

A Prayer for Protection*

140 ¹ Save me, Lord, from evildoers;
    keep me safe from violent people.
² They are always plotting evil,
    always stirring up quarrels.
³ Their tongues are like deadly snakes;
    their words are like a cobra's poison.

⁴ Protect me, Lord, from the power of the wicked;
    keep me safe from violent people
    who plot my downfall.
⁵ The proud have set a trap for me;
    they have laid their snares
    and along the path they have set traps to catch me.

⁶ I say to the Lord, "You are my God."
    Hear my cry for help, Lord!
⁷ My Sovereign Lord, my strong defender,
    you have protected me in battle.
⁸ Lord, don't give the wicked what they want;
    don't let their plots succeed.

⁹ Don't let my enemies be victorious;*
    make their threats against me fall back on them.
¹⁰ May red-hot coals fall on them;
    may they be thrown into a pit and never get out.
¹¹ May those who accuse others falsely not succeed;
    may evil overtake violent people and destroy them.

¹² Lord, I know that you defend the cause of the poor
    and the rights of the needy.
¹³ The righteous will praise you indeed;
    they will live in your presence.

....

139.17 *how difficult I find your thoughts*; or *how precious are your thoughts to me.*
139.20 Probable text *they speak… name*; Hebrew unclear.
139.24 *the everlasting way*; or *the ways of my ancestors.*
Ps 140 *Hebrew title*: A psalm by David.
140.9 Probable text *Don't let my enemies be victorious*; Hebrew unclear.

An Evening Prayer*

141

1 I call to you, LORD; help me now!
   Listen to me when I call to you.
2 Receive my prayer as incense,
   my uplifted hands as an evening sacrifice.

3 LORD, place a guard at my mouth,
   a sentry at the door of my lips.
4 Keep me from wanting to do wrong
   and from joining evil people in their wickedness.
   May I never take part in their feasts.

5 Good people may punish me and rebuke me in
      kindness,
   but I will never accept honour from evil people,
   because I am always praying against their evil deeds.
6 When their rulers are thrown down from rocky cliffs,
   the people will admit that my words were true.
7 Like wood that is split and chopped into bits,
   so their bones are scattered at the edge of the grave.*

8 But I keep trusting in you, my Sovereign LORD.
   I seek your protection;
   don't let me die!
9 Protect me from the traps they have set for me,
   from the snares of those evildoers.
10 May the wicked fall into their own traps
   while I go by unharmed.

A Prayer for Help*

142

1 I call to the LORD for help;
   I plead with him.
2 I bring him all my complaints;
   I tell him all my troubles.
3 When I am ready to give up,
   he knows what I should do.
   In the path where I walk,
   my enemies have hidden a trap for me.
4 When I look beside me,
   I see that there is no one to help me,
   no one to protect me.
   No one cares for me.

5 LORD, I cry to you for help;
   you, LORD, are my protector;
   you are all I want in this life.
6 Listen to my cry for help,
   for I am sunk in despair.
   Save me from my enemies;
   they are too strong for me.
7 Set me free from my distress;*
   then in the assembly of your people I will praise you
   because of your goodness to me.

Ps 141 *Hebrew title*: A psalm by David.
141.7 Verses 5–7 in Hebrew are unclear.
Ps 142 *Hebrew title*: A poem by David, when he was in the cave; a prayer.
142.7 *distress*; or *prison*.

PSALMS 143, 144

751

Psalms

Proverbs
Eccles.
Songs
Isaiah
Jerem.

A Prayer for Help*

143

[1] LORD, hear my prayer!
In your righteousness listen to my plea;
answer me in your faithfulness!
[2] Don't put me, your servant, on trial;
no one is innocent in your sight.

[3] My enemies have hunted me down
and completely defeated me.
They have put me in a dark prison,
and I am like those who died long ago.
[4] So I am ready to give up;
I am in deep despair.

[5] I remember the days gone by;
I think about all that you have done,
I bring to mind all your deeds.
[6] I lift up my hands to you in prayer;
like dry ground my soul is thirsty for you.

[7] Answer me now, LORD!
I have lost all hope.
Don't hide yourself from me,
or I will be among those who go down to the world of
the dead.
[8] Remind me each morning of your constant love,
for I put my trust in you.
My prayers go up to you;
show me the way I should go.

[9] I go to you for protection, LORD;
rescue me from my enemies.
[10] You are my God;
teach me to do your will.
Be good to me, and guide me on a safe path.

[11] Rescue me, LORD, as you have promised;
in your goodness save me from my troubles!
[12] Because of your love for me, kill my enemies
and destroy all my oppressors,
for I am your servant.

A King Thanks God for Victory*

144

[1] Praise the LORD, my protector!
He trains me for battle
and prepares me for war.
[2] He is my protector and defender,
my shelter and saviour,
in whom I trust for safety.
He subdues the nations under me.

[3] LORD, what are mortals, that you notice them;
mere mortals, that you pay attention to them?
[4] They are like a puff of wind;
their days are like a passing shadow.

Ps 143 *Hebrew title*: A psalm by David.
Ps 144 *Hebrew title*: By David.

752

Psalms

2 Chron.
Ezra
Nehem.
Esther
Job

PSALMS 144, 145

PSALM 145

Finish the mindmap below with all your thoughts about the

CHARACTER
- OF GOD. -

CHARACTER
OF GOD

⁵ O Lord, tear the sky apart and come down;
    touch the mountains, and they will pour out smoke.
⁶ Send flashes of lightning and scatter your enemies;
    shoot your arrows and send them running.
⁷ Reach down from above,
    pull me out of the deep water, and rescue me;
    save me from the power of foreigners,
⁸ who never tell the truth
    and lie even under oath.

⁹ I will sing you a new song, O God;
    I will play the harp and sing to you.
¹⁰ You give victory to kings
    and rescue your servant David.
¹¹ Save me from my cruel enemies;
    rescue me from the power of foreigners,
    who never tell the truth
    and lie even under oath.

¹² May our sons in their youth
    be like plants that grow up strong.
    May our daughters be like stately pillars
    which adorn the corners of a palace.
¹³ May our barns be filled
    with crops of every kind.
    May the sheep in our fields
    bear young by the tens of thousands.
¹⁴ May our cattle reproduce plentifully
    without miscarriage or loss.
    May there be no cries of distress in our streets.

¹⁵ Happy is the nation of whom this is true;
    happy are the people whose God is the Lord!

A Hymn of Praise*

145 ¹ I will proclaim your greatness, my God and king;
    I will thank you for ever and ever.
² Every day I will thank you;
    I will praise you for ever and ever.
³ The Lord is great and is to be highly praised;
    his greatness is beyond understanding.

⁴ What you have done will be praised from one generation
        to the next;
    they will proclaim your mighty acts.
⁵ They will speak of your glory and majesty,
    and I will meditate on your wonderful deeds.
⁶ People will speak of your mighty deeds,
    and I will proclaim your greatness.
⁷ They will tell about all your goodness
    and sing about your kindness.
⁸ The Lord is loving and merciful,
    slow to become angry and full of constant love.
⁹ He is good to everyone
    and has compassion on all he made.

Ps 145 *Hebrew title*: A song of praise by David.

PSALMS 145, 146

753

Psalms

Proverbs
Eccles.
Songs
Isaiah
Jerem.

¹⁰ All your creatures, LORD, will praise you,
　　and all your people will give you thanks.
¹¹ They will speak of the glory of your royal power
　　and tell of your might,
¹² so that everyone will know your mighty deeds
　　and the glorious majesty of your kingdom.
¹³ Your rule is eternal,
　　and you are king for ever.

　　The LORD is faithful to his promises,
　　　and he is merciful in all his acts.
¹⁴ He helps those who are in trouble;
　　he lifts those who have fallen.

¹⁵ All living things look hopefully to you,
　　and you give them food when they need it.
¹⁶ You give them enough
　　and satisfy the needs of all.

¹⁷ The LORD is righteous in all he does,
　　merciful in all his acts.
¹⁸ He is near to those who call to him,
　　who call to him with sincerity.
¹⁹ He supplies the needs of those who honour him;
　　he hears their cries and saves them.
²⁰ He protects everyone who loves him,
　　but he will destroy the wicked.

²¹ I will always praise the LORD;
　　let all his creatures praise his holy name for ever.

In Praise of God the Saviour

146 ¹Praise the LORD!
　　Praise the LORD, my soul!
² I will praise him as long as I live;
　　I will sing to my God all my life.

³ Don't put your trust in human leaders;
　　no human being can save you.
⁴ When they die, they return to the dust;
　　on that day all their plans come to an end.

⁵ Happy are those who have the God of Jacob to help
　　them
　　and who depend on the LORD their God,
⁶ 　the Creator of heaven, earth, and sea,
　　and all that is in them.
　He always keeps his promises;
⁷ 　he judges in favour of the oppressed
　　and gives food to the hungry.

　The LORD sets prisoners free
⁸ 　and gives sight to the blind.
　He lifts those who have fallen;
　　he loves his righteous people.
⁹ He protects the strangers who live in our land;
　　he helps widows and orphans,
　　but takes the wicked to their ruin.

754

Psalms
·:·········

2 Chron.
Ezra
Nehem.
Esther
Job

PSALMS 146, 147

10 The LORD is king for ever.
Your God, O Zion, will reign for all time.

Praise the LORD!

In Praise of God the Almighty

147 [1] Praise the LORD!

It is good to sing praise to our God;
it is pleasant and right to praise him.
2 The LORD is restoring Jerusalem;
he is bringing back the exiles.
3 He heals the broken-hearted
and bandages their wounds.

4 He has decided the number of the stars
and calls each one by name.
5 Great and mighty is our Lord;
his wisdom cannot be measured.
6 He raises the humble,
but crushes the wicked to the ground.

7 Sing hymns of praise to the LORD;
play music on the harp to our God.
8 He spreads clouds over the sky;
he provides rain for the earth
and makes grass grow on the hills.
9 He gives animals their food
and feeds the young ravens when they call.

10 His pleasure is not in strong horses,
nor his delight in brave soldiers;
11 but he takes pleasure in those who honour him,
in those who trust in his constant love.

12 Praise the LORD, O Jerusalem!
Praise your God, O Zion!
13 He keeps your gates strong;
he blesses your people.
14 He keeps your borders safe
and satisfies you with the finest wheat.

15 He gives a command to the earth,
and what he says is quickly done.
16 He spreads snow like a blanket
and scatters frost like dust.
17 He sends hail like gravel;
no one can endure the cold he sends!
18 Then he gives a command, and the ice melts;
he sends the wind, and the water flows.

19 He gives his message to his people,
his instructions and laws to Israel.
20 He has not done this for other nations;
they do not know his laws.

Praise the LORD!

PSALMS 148, 149

755

Psalms

Proverbs
Eccles.
Songs
Isaiah
Jerem.

A Call for the Universe to Praise God

148
¹ Praise the LORD!

Praise the LORD from heaven,
   you that live in the heights above.
² Praise him, all his angels,
   all his heavenly armies.

³ Praise him, sun and moon;
   praise him, shining stars.
⁴ Praise him, highest heavens,
   and the waters above the sky.*

⁵ Let them all praise the name of the LORD!
He commanded, and they were created;
⁶   by his command they were fixed in their places for
      ever,
   and they cannot disobey.*

⁷ Praise the LORD from the earth,
   sea monsters and all ocean depths;
⁸ lightning and hail, snow and clouds,
   strong winds that obey his command.

⁹ Praise him, hills and mountains,
   fruit trees and forests;
¹⁰ all animals, tame and wild,
   reptiles and birds.

¹¹ Praise him, kings and all peoples,
   princes and all other rulers;
¹² young women and young men,
   old people and children too.

¹³ Let them all praise the name of the LORD!
His name is greater than all others;
   his glory is above earth and heaven.
¹⁴ He made his nation strong,
   so that all his people praise him —
   the people of Israel, so dear to him.

Praise the LORD!

A Hymn of Praise

149
¹ Praise the LORD!

Sing a new song to the LORD;
   praise him in the assembly of his faithful people!
² Be glad, Israel, because of your Creator;
   rejoice, people of Zion, because of your king!
³ Praise his name with dancing;
   play drums and harps in praise of him.

⁴ The LORD takes pleasure in his people;
   he honours the humble with victory.

148.4 *waters above the sky*: See Gen 1.6–7.
148.6 *by his command... disobey*; or *he has fixed them in their places for all
time, by a command that lasts for ever.*

756

Psalms

2 Chron.
Ezra
Nehem.
Esther
Job

PSALM 150

This psalm sums up what the entire book was created to be! Each psalm was designed to be a song, with the words

• PUT TO •

MUSIC.

The music would have emphasised the feelings portrayed by the words. Look up the lyrics to your favourite song. That's a bit what it's like when we read the Psalms - they are song lyrics without the music.

[5] Let God's people rejoice in their triumph
and sing joyfully all night long.
[6] Let them shout aloud as they praise God,
with their sharp swords in their hands
[7] to defeat the nations
and to punish the peoples;
[8] to bind their kings in chains,
their leaders in chains of iron;
[9] to punish the nations as God has commanded.
This is the victory of God's people.

Praise the LORD!

Praise the LORD!

150 [1] Praise the LORD!
Praise God in his Temple!
Praise his strength in heaven!
[2] Praise him for the mighty things he has done.
Praise his supreme greatness.

[3] Praise him with trumpets.
Praise him with harps and lyres.
[4] Praise him with drums and dancing.
Praise him with harps and flutes.
[5] Praise him with cymbals.
Praise him with loud cymbals.
[6] Praise the LORD, all living creatures!

Praise the LORD!

THE BOOK OF
PROVERBS

WRITTEN: OVER A LONG PERIOD OF TIME, POSSIBLY COLLECTED AROUND 800-700BC

WHAT YOU NEED TO KNOW:

Proverbs is like a little library of parables and wise advice for living. Many of the proverbs are said to have been written by King Solomon, who was renowned for his wisdom. This is not a book of instructions or enforced rules; instead it is a collection of guidelines and thoughts on how to live in a way that pleases God, loving God's path and making wise decisions.

WHY READ IT?

There's loads of great advice and wisdom in this book that is still applicable to us today. The book helps us to think about how to be wise in our own lives. The proverbs cover things like speaking well of others, not being greedy, being calm, loving God and putting others first.

SPOTLIGHT:

You can read about an example of Solomon's wisdom in 1 Kings 3.16-28, which tells the story of two women and their argument.

As you read Proverbs, UNDERLINE ANY VERSES that particularly STAND OUT TO YOU.

Pray that God would HELP YOU TO LIVE OUT the advice in those verses.

THE PROVERBS WERE WRITTEN BY A NUMBER OF AUTHORS, BETWEEN AROUND 900 AND 700BC

758

Proverbs

Ezra
Nehem.
Esther
Job
Psalms

PROVERBS 1

The Value of Proverbs

1 The proverbs of Solomon, son of David and king of Israel.
² Here are proverbs that will help you to recognize wisdom and good advice, and understand sayings with deep meaning. ³ They can teach you how to live intelligently and how to be honest, just, and fair. ⁴ They can make an inexperienced person clever and teach young people how to be resourceful. ⁵ These proverbs can even add to the knowledge of the wise and give guidance to the educated, ⁶ so that they can understand the hidden meanings of proverbs and the problems that the wise raise.

Advice to Young People

⁷ To have knowledge, you must first have reverence for the LORD.* Stupid people have no respect for wisdom and refuse to learn.

⁸ Pay attention to what your father and mother tell you, my child. ⁹ Their teaching will improve your character as a handsome turban or a necklace improves your appearance.

¹⁰ When sinners tempt you, my child, don't give in. ¹¹ Suppose they say, "Come on; let's find someone to kill! Let's attack some innocent people for the fun of it! ¹² They may be alive and well when we find them, but they'll be dead when we're through with them! ¹³ We'll find all kinds of riches and fill our houses with loot! ¹⁴ Come and join us, and we'll all share what we steal."

¹⁵ Don't go with people like that, my child. Stay away from them. ¹⁶ They can't wait to do something bad. They're always ready to kill. ¹⁷ It does no good to spread a net when the bird you want to catch is watching, ¹⁸ but people like that are setting a trap for themselves, a trap in which they will die. ¹⁹ Robbery always claims the life of the robber — this is what happens to* anyone who lives by violence.

Wisdom Calls

²⁰ Listen! Wisdom is calling out in the streets and market places, ²¹ calling loudly at the city gates and wherever people come together:

²² "Foolish people! How long do you want to be foolish? How long will you enjoy pouring scorn on knowledge? Will you never learn? ²³ Listen when I reprimand you; I will give you good advice and share my knowledge with you. ²⁴ I have been calling you, inviting you to come, but you would not listen. You paid no attention to me. ²⁵ You have ignored all my advice and have not been willing to let me correct you. ²⁶ So when you get into trouble, I will laugh at you. I will mock you when terror strikes — ²⁷ when it comes on you like a storm, bringing fierce winds of trouble, and you are in pain and misery. ²⁸ Then you will call for wisdom, but I will not answer. You may look for me everywhere, but you will not find me. ²⁹ You have never had any use for knowledge and have always refused to obey the LORD. ³⁰ You have never wanted my advice or paid any attention when I corrected you. ³¹ So then, you will get what you deserve, and your own actions will make you sick. ³² Inexperienced people die because they reject wisdom. Stupid people are destroyed by their own lack of concern. ³³ But whoever listens to me will have security. He will be safe, with no reason to be afraid."

....

1.7 *To... LORD*; or *The most important part of knowledge is having reverence for the LORD.*
1.19 One ancient translation *what happens to*; Hebrew *the path of.*

The Rewards of Wisdom

2 Learn what I teach you, my child, and never forget what I tell you to do. ²Listen to what is wise and try to understand it. ³Yes, beg for knowledge; plead for insight. ⁴Look for it as hard as you would for silver or some hidden treasure. ⁵If you do, you will know what it means to fear the LORD and you will succeed in learning about God. ⁶It is the LORD who gives wisdom; from him come knowledge and understanding. ⁷He provides help and protection for those who are righteous and honest. ⁸He protects those who treat others fairly, and guards those who are devoted to him.

⁹If you listen to me, you will know what is right, just, and fair. You will know what you should do. ¹⁰You will become wise, and your knowledge will give you pleasure. ¹¹Your insight and understanding will protect you ¹²and prevent you from doing the wrong thing. They will keep you away from people who stir up trouble by what they say — ¹³those who have abandoned a righteous life to live in the darkness of sin, ¹⁴those who find pleasure in doing wrong and who enjoy senseless evil, ¹⁵unreliable people who cannot be trusted.

¹⁶You will be able to resist any immoral woman who tries to seduce you with her smooth talk, ¹⁷who is faithless to her own husband and forgets her sacred vows. ¹⁸If you go to her house, you are travelling the road to death. To go there is to approach the world of the dead. ¹⁹No one who visits her ever comes back. He never returns to the road to life. ²⁰So you must follow the example of good people and live a righteous life. ²¹Righteous people — people of integrity — will live in this land of ours. ²²But God will snatch the wicked from the land and pull sinners out of it like plants from the ground.

Advice to Young People

3 Don't forget what I teach you, my child. Always remember what I tell you to do. ²My teaching will give you a long and prosperous life. ³Never let go of loyalty and faithfulness. Tie them round your neck; write them on your heart. ⁴If you do this, both God and people will be pleased with you.

⁵Trust in the LORD with all your heart. Never rely on what you think you know. ⁶Remember the LORD in everything you do, and he will show you the right way. ⁷Never let yourself think that you are wiser than you are; simply obey the LORD and refuse to do wrong. ⁸If you do, it will be like good medicine, healing your wounds and easing your pains. ⁹Honour the LORD by making him an offering from the best of all that your land produces. ¹⁰If you do, your barns will be filled with grain, and you will have too much wine to be able to store it all.

¹¹When the LORD corrects you, my child, pay close attention and take it as a warning. ¹²The LORD corrects those he loves, as parents correct a child of whom they are proud. ¹³Happy is anyone who becomes wise — who gains understanding. ¹⁴There is more profit in it than there is in silver; it is worth more to you than gold. ¹⁵Wisdom is more valuable than jewels; nothing you could want can compare with it. ¹⁶Wisdom offers you long life, as well as wealth and honour. ¹⁷Wisdom can make your life pleasant and lead you safely through it. ¹⁸Those who become wise are happy; wisdom will give them life.

¹⁹ The LORD created the earth by his wisdom;
    by his knowledge he set the sky in place.
²⁰ His wisdom caused the rivers to flow
    and the clouds to give rain to the earth.

PROVERBS 3.5

TRUST ... in the ... LORD with all your HEART

760

Proverbs

⋮········

Ezra
Nehem.
Esther
Job
Psalms

PROVERBS 3, 4

²¹ Hold on to your wisdom and insight, my child. Never let them get away from you. ²² They will provide you with life — a pleasant and happy life. ²³ You can go safely on your way and never even stumble. ²⁴ You will not be afraid when you go to bed, and you will sleep soundly through the night. ²⁵ You will not have to worry about sudden disasters, such as come on the wicked like a storm. ²⁶ The LORD will keep you safe. He will not let you fall into a trap.

²⁷ Whenever you possibly can, do good to those who need it. ²⁸ Never tell your neighbours to wait until tomorrow if you can help them now. ²⁹ Don't plan anything that will hurt your neighbours; they live beside you, trusting you. ³⁰ Don't argue with others for no reason when they have never done you any harm. ³¹ Don't be jealous of violent people or decide to act as they do, ³² because the LORD hates people who do evil, but he takes righteous people into his confidence. ³³ The LORD puts a curse on the homes of the wicked, but blesses the homes of the righteous. ³⁴ He has no use for conceited people, but shows favour to those who are humble. ³⁵ Wise people will gain an honourable reputation, but stupid people will only add to their own disgrace.

The Benefits of Wisdom

4 Listen to what your father teaches you, my children. Pay attention, and you will have understanding. ² What I am teaching you is good, so remember it all. ³ When I was only a little boy, my parents' only son, ⁴ my father would teach me. He would say, "Remember what I say and never forget it. Do as I tell you, and you will live. ⁵ Get wisdom and insight! Do not forget or ignore what I say. ⁶ Do not abandon wisdom, and she will protect you; love her, and she will keep you safe. ⁷ Getting wisdom is the most important thing you can do. Whatever else you get, get insight. ⁸ Love wisdom, and she will make you great. Embrace her,* and she will bring you honour. ⁹ She will be your crowning glory."

¹⁰ Listen to me, my child. Take seriously what I am telling you, and you will live a long life. ¹¹ I have taught you wisdom and the right way to live. ¹² Nothing will stand in your way if you walk wisely, and you will not stumble when you run. ¹³ Always remember what you have learnt. Your education is your life — guard it well. ¹⁴ Do not go where evil people go. Do not follow the example of the wicked. ¹⁵ Don't do it! Keep away from evil! Refuse it and go on your way. ¹⁶ Wicked people cannot sleep unless they have done something wrong. They lie awake unless they have hurt someone. ¹⁷ Wickedness and violence are like food and drink to them.

¹⁸ The road the righteous travel is like the sunrise, getting brighter and brighter until daylight has come. ¹⁹ The road of the wicked, however, is dark as night. They fall, but cannot see what they have stumbled over.

²⁰ Pay attention to what I say, my child. Listen to my words. ²¹ Never let them get away from you. Remember them and keep them in your heart. ²² They will give life and health to anyone who understands them. ²³ Be careful how you think; your life is shaped by your thoughts. ²⁴ Never say anything that isn't true. Have nothing to do with lies and misleading words. ²⁵ Look straight ahead with honest confidence; don't hang your head in shame. ²⁶ Plan carefully what you do, and whatever you do will turn out right. ²⁷ Avoid evil and walk straight ahead. Don't go one step off the right way.

4.8 Embrace her; or Prize her highly.

Warning against Adultery

5 Pay attention, my child, and listen to my wisdom and insight. ² Then you will know how to behave properly, and your words will show that you have knowledge. ³ The lips of another man's wife may be as sweet as honey and her kisses as smooth as olive oil, ⁴ but when it is all over, she leaves you nothing but bitterness and pain. ⁵ She will take you down to the world of the dead; the road she walks is the road to death. ⁶ She does not stay on the road to life; but wanders off, and does not realize what is happening.

⁷ Now listen to me, my children, and never forget what I am saying. ⁸ Keep away from such a woman! Don't even go near her door! ⁹ If you do, others will gain the respect that you once had, and you will die young at the hands of merciless people. ¹⁰ Yes, strangers will take all your wealth, and what you have worked for will belong to someone else. ¹¹ You will lie groaning on your deathbed, your flesh and muscles being eaten away, ¹² and you will say, "Why would I never learn? Why would I never let anyone correct me? ¹³ I wouldn't listen to my teachers. I paid no attention to them. ¹⁴ And suddenly I found myself* publicly disgraced."

¹⁵ Be faithful to your own wife and give your love to her alone. ¹⁶ Children that you have by other women will do you no good. ¹⁷ Your children should grow up to help you, not strangers. ¹⁸ So be happy with your wife and find your joy with the woman you married — ¹⁹ pretty and graceful as a deer. Let her charms keep you happy; let her surround you with her love. ²⁰ Why should you give your love to another woman, my son? Why should you prefer the charms of another man's wife? ²¹ The LORD sees everything you do. Wherever you go, he is watching. ²² The sins of the wicked are a trap. They get caught in the net of their own sin. ²³ They die because they have no self-control. Their utter stupidity will send them to their graves.

More Warnings

6 Have you promised to be responsible for someone else's debts, my child? ² Have you been caught by your own words, trapped by your own promises? ³ Well then, my child, you are in that person's power, but this is how to get out of it: hurry to him, and beg him to release you. ⁴ Don't let yourself go to sleep or even stop to rest. ⁵ Get out of the trap like a bird or a deer escaping from a hunter.

⁶ Lazy people should learn a lesson from the way ants live. ⁷ They have no leader, chief, or ruler, ⁸ but they store up their food during the summer, getting ready for winter. ⁹ How long is the lazy man going to lie in bed? When is he ever going to get up? ¹⁰ "I'll just take a short nap," he says; "I'll fold my hands and rest a while." ¹¹ But while he sleeps, poverty will attack him like an armed robber.

¹² Worthless, wicked people go around telling lies. ¹³ They wink and make gestures to deceive you, ¹⁴ all the while planning evil in their perverted minds, stirring up trouble everywhere. ¹⁵ Because of this, disaster will strike them without warning, and they will be fatally wounded.

¹⁶⁻¹⁹ There are seven things that the LORD hates and cannot tolerate:

> a proud look,
> a lying tongue,
> hands that kill innocent people,

5.14 *And suddenly... myself*; or *I was about to be.*

762

Proverbs

Ezra
Nehem.
Esther
Job
Psalms

PROVERBS 6, 7

a mind that thinks up wicked plans,
feet that hurry off to do evil,
a witness who tells one lie after another,
and someone who stirs up trouble among friends.

Warning against Adultery

20 Do what your father tells you, my son, and never forget what your mother taught you. 21 Keep their words with you always, locked in your heart. 22 Their teaching will lead you when you travel, protect you at night, and advise you during the day. 23 Their instructions are a shining light; their correction can teach you how to live. 24 It can keep you away from bad women, from the seductive words of other men's wives. 25 Don't be tempted by their beauty; don't be trapped by their flirting eyes. 26 A man can hire a prostitute for the price of a loaf of bread, but adultery will cost him all he has.

27 Can you carry fire against your chest without burning your clothes? 28 Can you walk on hot coals without burning your feet? 29 It is just as dangerous to sleep with another man's wife. Whoever does it will suffer. 30 People don't despise a thief if he steals food when he is hungry;* 31 yet if he is caught, he must pay back seven times more — he must give up everything he has. 32 But a man who commits adultery hasn't any sense. He is just destroying himself. 33 He will be dishonoured and beaten up; he will be permanently disgraced. 34 A husband is never angrier than when he is jealous; his revenge knows no limits. 35 He will not accept any payment; no amount of gifts will satisfy his anger.

7 Remember what I say, my child, and never forget what I tell you to do. 2 Do what I say, and you will live. Be as careful to follow my teaching as you are to protect your eyes. 3 Keep my teaching with you all the time; write it on your heart. 4 Treat wisdom as your sister, and insight as your closest friend. 5 They will keep you away from other men's wives, from women with seductive words.

The Immoral Woman

6 Once I was looking out of the window of my house, 7 and I saw many inexperienced young men, but noticed one foolish fellow in particular. 8 He was walking along the street near the corner where a certain woman lived. He was passing near her house 9 in the evening after it was dark. 10 And then she met him; she was dressed like a prostitute and was making plans. 11 She was a bold and shameless woman who always walked the streets 12 or stood waiting at a corner, sometimes in the streets, sometimes in the market place. 13 She threw her arms round the young man, kissed him, looked him straight in the eye, and said, 14 "I made my offerings today and have the meat from the sacrifices. 15 So I came out looking for you. I wanted to find you, and here you are! 16 I've covered my bed with sheets of coloured linen from Egypt. 17 I've perfumed it with myrrh, aloes, and cinnamon. 18 Come on! Let's make love all night long. We'll be happy in each other's arms. 19 My husband isn't at home. He's gone away on a long journey. 20 He took plenty of money with him and won't be back for two weeks." 21 So she tempted him with her charms, and he gave in to her smooth talk. 22 Suddenly he was going with her like an ox on the way to be slaughtered, like a deer prancing into a trap*

6.30 People don't despise... hungry; or Don't people despise... hungry?
7.22 Probable text like a deer prancing into a trap; Hebrew unclear.

PROVERBS 7, 8

763

Proverbs
···········:

Eccles.
Songs
Isaiah
Jerem.
Lamen.

²³ where an arrow would pierce its heart. He was like a bird going into a net — he did not know that his life was in danger.

²⁴ Now then, my sons, listen to me. Pay attention to what I say. ²⁵ Do not let such a woman win your heart; don't go wandering after her. ²⁶ She has been the ruin of many men and caused the death of too many to count. ²⁷ If you go to her house, you are on the way to the world of the dead. It is a short cut to death.

In Praise of Wisdom

8 Listen! Wisdom is calling out.
    Reason is making herself heard.
² On the hilltops near the road
    and at the crossroads she stands.
³ At the entrance to the city,
    beside the gates, she calls:
⁴ "I appeal to all of you;
    I call to everyone on earth.
⁵ Are you immature? Learn to be mature.
    Are you foolish? Learn to have sense.
⁶ Listen to my excellent words;
    all I tell you is right.
⁷ What I say is the truth;
    lies are hateful to me.
⁸ Everything I say is true;
    nothing is false or misleading.
⁹ To those with insight, it is all clear;
    to the well-informed, it is all plain.
¹⁰ Choose my instruction instead of silver;
    choose knowledge rather than the finest gold.

¹¹ "I am Wisdom, I am better than jewels;
    nothing you want can compare with me.
¹² I am Wisdom, and I have insight;
    I have knowledge and sound judgement.
¹³ To honour the LORD is to hate evil;
    I hate pride and arrogance,
    evil ways and false words.
¹⁴ I make plans and carry them out.
    I have understanding, and I am strong.
¹⁵ I help kings to govern
    and rulers to make good laws.
¹⁶ Every ruler on earth governs with my help,
    officials and nobles alike.
¹⁷ I love those who love me;
    whoever looks for me can find me.
¹⁸ I have riches and honour to give,
    prosperity and success.
¹⁹ What you get from me is better than the finest gold,
    better than the purest silver.
²⁰ I walk the way of righteousness;
    I follow the paths of justice,
²¹ giving wealth to those who love me,
    filling their houses with treasures.

²² "The LORD created me first of all,
    the first of his works, long ago.
²³ I was made in the very beginning,
    at the first, before the world began.

764

Proverbs

Ezra
Nehem.
Esther
Job
Psalms

PROVERBS 8, 9

PROVERBS 8.35

The character
speaking in this verse
is called 'wisdom'.

DRAW CIRCLES

to represent different
areas of your life
that you'd like

GOD'S
WISDOM

for. Label the circles and
colour them in while
praying for God's wisdom
in each area.

24 I was born before the oceans,
  when there were no springs of water.
25 I was born before the mountains,
  before the hills were set in place,
26 before God made the earth and its fields
  or even the first handful of soil.
27 I was there when he set the sky in place,
  when he stretched the horizon across the ocean,
28 when he placed the clouds in the sky,
  when he opened the springs of the ocean
29 and ordered the waters of the sea
  to rise no further than he said.
  I was there when he laid the earth's foundations.
30 I was beside him like an architect,*
  I was his daily source of joy,
  always happy in his presence —
31 happy with the world
  and pleased with the human race.

32 "Now, young people, listen to me.
  Do as I say, and you will be happy.
33 Listen to what you are taught.
  Be wise; do not neglect it.
34 Those who listen to me will be happy —
  those who stay at my door every day,
  waiting at the entrance to my home.
35 Those who find me find life,
  and the LORD will be pleased with them.
36 Those who do not find me hurt themselves;
  anyone who hates me loves death."

Wisdom and Stupidity

9 Wisdom has built her house and made seven pillars for it. 2 She
  has had an animal killed for a feast, mixed spices in the wine,
and laid the table. 3 She has sent her servant women to call out
from the highest place in the town: 4 "Come in, ignorant people!"
And to the foolish she says, 5 "Come, eat my food and drink the
wine that I have mixed. 6 Leave the company of ignorant people,
and live. Follow the way of knowledge."

7 If you correct conceited people, you will only be insulted. If
you reprimand evil people, you will only get hurt. 8 Never correct
conceited people; they will hate you for it. But if you correct the
wise, they will respect you. 9 Anything you say to the wise will
make them wiser. Whatever you tell the righteous will add to
their knowledge.

10 To be wise you must first have reverence for the LORD. If you
know the Holy One, you have understanding. 11 Wisdom will add
years to your life. 12 You are the one who will profit if you have
wisdom, and if you reject it, you are the one who will suffer.

13 Stupidity is like a loud, ignorant, shameless woman.* 14 She
sits at the door of her house or on a seat in the highest part of the
town, 15 and calls out to people passing by, who are minding their
own business: 16 "Come in, ignorant people!" To the foolish she says,
17 "Stolen water is sweeter. Stolen bread tastes better." 18 Her victims
do not know that the people die who go to her house, that those
who have already entered are now deep in the world of the dead.

8.30 *an architect*; or *a little child.*
9.13 Verse 13 in Hebrew is unclear.

PROVERBS 10

765

Proverbs

Eccles.
Songs
Isaiah
Jerem.
Lamen.

Solomon's Proverbs

10 These are Solomon's proverbs:

Wise children make their fathers proud of them; foolish ones bring their mothers grief.

² Wealth that you get by dishonesty will do you no good, but honesty can save your life.

³ The LORD will not let good people go hungry, but he will keep the wicked from getting what they want.

⁴ Being lazy will make you poor, but hard work will make you rich.

⁵ A sensible person gathers the crops when they are ready; it is a disgrace to sleep through the time of harvest.

⁶ Good people will receive blessings. The words of the wicked hide a violent nature.

⁷ Good people will be remembered as a blessing, but the wicked will soon be forgotten.

⁸ Sensible people accept good advice. People who talk foolishly will come to ruin.

⁹ Honest people are safe and secure, but the dishonest will be caught.

¹⁰ Someone who holds back the truth causes trouble, but one who openly criticizes works for peace.*

¹¹ A good person's words are a fountain of life, but a wicked person's words hide a violent nature.

¹² Hate stirs up trouble, but love overlooks all offences.

¹³ Intelligent people talk sense, but stupid people need to be punished.

¹⁴ The wise get all the knowledge they can, but when fools speak, trouble is not far off.

¹⁵ Wealth protects the rich; poverty destroys the poor.

¹⁶ The reward for doing good is life, but sin leads only to more sin.

¹⁷ People who listen when they are corrected will live, but those who will not admit that they are wrong are in danger.

¹⁸ Anyone who hides hatred is a liar. Anyone who spreads gossip is a fool.

¹⁹ The more you talk, the more likely you are to sin. If you are wise, you will keep quiet.

²⁰ A good person's words are like pure silver; a wicked person's ideas are worthless.

²¹ A good person's words will benefit many people, but you can kill yourself with stupidity.

²² It is the LORD's blessing that makes you wealthy. Hard work can make you no richer.*

²³ It is foolish to enjoy doing wrong. Intelligent people take pleasure in wisdom.

²⁴ The righteous get what they want, but the wicked will get what they fear most.

²⁵ Storms come, and the wicked are blown away, but honest people are always safe.

²⁶ Never get a lazy person to do something for you; he will be as irritating as vinegar on your teeth or smoke in your eyes.

²⁷ Obey the LORD, and you will live longer. The wicked die before their time.

²⁸ The hopes of good people lead to joy, but wicked people can look forward to nothing.

....

10.10 One ancient translation *but one... peace*; Hebrew repeats verse 8b.
10.22 *Hard work... richer*; or *And the LORD does not add sorrow to your wealth.*

766

Proverbs

·:········

Ezra
Nehem.
Esther
Job
Psalms

PROVERBS 10, 11

²⁹ The LORD protects honest people, but destroys those who do wrong.

³⁰ Righteous people will always have security, but the wicked will not survive in the land.

³¹ Righteous people speak wisdom, but the tongue that speaks evil will be stopped.

³² Righteous people know the kind thing to say, but the wicked are always saying things that hurt.

11 The LORD hates people who use dishonest scales. He is happy with honest weights.

² People who are proud will soon be disgraced. It is wiser to be modest.

³ If you are good, you are guided by honesty. People who can't be trusted are destroyed by their own dishonesty.

⁴ Riches will do you no good on the day you face death, but honesty can save your life.

⁵ Honesty makes a good person's life easier, but the wicked will cause their own downfall.

⁶ Righteousness rescues those who are honest, but those who can't be trusted are trapped by their own greed.

⁷ When the wicked die, their hope dies with them. Confidence placed in riches comes to nothing.

⁸ The righteous are protected from trouble; it comes to the wicked instead.

⁹ You can be ruined by the talk of godless people, but the wisdom of the righteous can save you.

¹⁰ A city is happy when honest people have good fortune, and there are joyful shouts when the wicked die.

¹¹ A city becomes great when the righteous give it their blessing; but a city is brought to ruin by the words of the wicked.

¹² It is foolish to speak scornfully of others. If you are sensible, you will keep quiet.

¹³ No one who gossips can be trusted with a secret, but you can put confidence in someone who is trustworthy.

¹⁴ A nation will fall if it has no guidance. Many advisers mean security.

¹⁵ If you promise to pay a stranger's debt, you will regret it. You are better off if you don't get involved.

¹⁶ A gracious woman is respected, but a woman without virtue is a disgrace.

Lazy people will never have money,* but aggressive people will get rich.

¹⁷ You do yourself a favour when you are kind. If you are cruel, you only hurt yourself.

¹⁸ Wicked people do not really gain anything, but if you do what is right, you are certain to be rewarded.

¹⁹ Anyone who is determined to do right will live, but anyone who insists on doing wrong will die.

²⁰ The LORD hates evil-minded people, but loves those who do right.

²¹ You can be sure that evil people will be punished, but the righteous will escape.

²² Beauty in a woman without good judgement is like a gold ring in a pig's snout.

²³ What good people want always results in good; when the wicked get what they want, everyone is angry.*

11.16 One ancient translation *but a woman… money*; Hebrew does not have these words.
11.23 *everyone is angry*; or *God punishes them*.

²⁴ Some people spend their money freely and still grow richer. Others are cautious, and yet grow poorer.

²⁵ Be generous, and you will be prosperous. Help others, and you will be helped.

²⁶ People curse someone who hoards grain, waiting for a higher price, but they praise the one who puts it up for sale.

²⁷ If your goals are good, you will be respected, but if you are looking for trouble, that is what you will get.

²⁸ Those who depend on their wealth will fall like the leaves of autumn, but the righteous will prosper like the leaves of summer.

²⁹ Those who bring trouble on their families will have nothing at the end.
Foolish people will always be servants to the wise.

³⁰ Righteousness* gives life, but violence* takes it away.

³¹ Those who are good are rewarded here on earth, so you can be sure that wicked and sinful people will be punished.

12 Those who love knowledge want to be told when they are wrong. It is stupid to hate being corrected.

² The LORD is pleased with good people, but condemns those who plan evil.

³ Wickedness does not give security, but righteous people stand firm.

⁴ A good wife is her husband's pride and joy; but a wife who brings shame on her husband is like a cancer in his bones.

⁵ Honest people will treat you fairly; the wicked only want to deceive you.

⁶ The words of the wicked are murderous, but the words of the righteous rescue those who are threatened.

⁷ The wicked meet their downfall and leave no descendants, but the families of the righteous live on.

⁸ If you are intelligent, you will be praised; if you are stupid, people will look down on you.

⁹ It is better to be an ordinary person working for a living than to play the part of someone great but go hungry.

¹⁰ Good people take care of their animals, but wicked people are cruel to theirs.

¹¹ A hard-working farmer has plenty to eat, but it is stupid to waste time on useless projects.

¹² All that wicked people want is to find evil things to do, but the righteous stand firm.*

¹³ The wicked are trapped by their own words, but honest people get themselves out of trouble.

¹⁴ Your reward depends on what you say and what you do; you will get what you deserve.

¹⁵ Stupid people always think they are right. Wise people listen to advice.

¹⁶ When a fool is annoyed, he quickly lets it be known. Sensible people will ignore an insult.

¹⁷ When you tell the truth, justice is done, but lies lead to injustice.

¹⁸ Thoughtless words can wound as deeply as any sword, but wisely spoken words can heal.

¹⁹ A lie has a short life, but truth lives on for ever.

²⁰ Those who plan evil are in for a rude surprise, but those who work for good will find happiness.

RIGHTEOUSNESS

PROVERBS 11.30;
HOSEA 10.12;
2 PETER 3.13

DEFINITION: The quality of being morally right or justifiable.
(oxforddictionaries.com)

....

11.30 One ancient translation *Righteousness*; Hebrew *A righteous person*.
11.30 Probable text *violence*; Hebrew *a wise person*.
12.12 Verse 12 in Hebrew is unclear.

768

Proverbs

⫶········

Ezra
Nehem.
Esther
Job
Psalms

PROVERBS 12, 13

²¹Nothing bad happens to righteous people, but the wicked have nothing but trouble.

²²The LORD hates liars, but is pleased with those who keep their word.

²³Sensible people keep quiet about what they know, but stupid people advertise their ignorance.

²⁴Hard work will give you power; being lazy will make you a slave.

²⁵Worry can rob you of happiness, but kind words will cheer you up.

²⁶The righteous person is a guide to his friend, but the path of the wicked leads them astray.

²⁷If you are lazy, you will never get what you are after, but if you work hard, you will get a fortune.*

²⁸Righteousness is the road to life; wickedness* is the road to death.

13 A wise son pays attention when his father corrects him, but an arrogant person never admits he is wrong.

²Good people will be rewarded for what they say, but those who are deceitful are hungry for violence.

³Be careful what you say and protect your life. A careless talker destroys himself.

⁴No matter how much a lazy person may want something, he will never get it. A hard worker will get everything he wants.

⁵Honest people hate lies, but the words of wicked people are shameful and disgraceful.

⁶Righteousness protects the innocent; wickedness is the downfall of sinners.

⁷Some people pretend to be rich, but have nothing. Others pretend to be poor, but own a fortune.

⁸The rich have to use their money to save their lives, but no one threatens the poor.

⁹The righteous are like a light shining brightly; the wicked are like a lamp flickering out.

¹⁰Arrogance causes nothing but trouble. It is wiser to ask for advice.

¹¹The more easily you get your wealth, the sooner you will lose it. The harder it is to earn, the more you will have.

¹²When hope is crushed, the heart is crushed, but a wish come true fills you with joy.

¹³If you refuse good advice, you are asking for trouble; follow it and you are safe.

¹⁴The teachings of the wise are a fountain of life; they will help you escape when your life is in danger.

¹⁵Intelligence wins respect, but those who can't be trusted are on the road to ruin.*

¹⁶Sensible people always think before they act, but stupid people advertise their ignorance.

¹⁷Unreliable messengers cause trouble, but those who can be trusted bring peace.

¹⁸Someone who will not learn will be poor and disgraced. Anyone who listens to correction is respected.

¹⁹How good it is to get what you want! Stupid people refuse to turn away from evil.

²⁰Keep company with the wise and you will become wise. If you make friends with stupid people, you will be ruined.

....

12.27 Verse 27 in Hebrew is unclear.
12.28 One ancient translation *wickedness*; Hebrew *path*.
13.15 One ancient translation *road to ruin*; Hebrew *permanent road*.

Proverbs

Eccles.
Songs
Isaiah
Jerem.
Lamen.

²¹ Trouble follows sinners everywhere, but righteous people will be rewarded with good things.

²² Good people will have wealth to leave to their grandchildren, but the wealth of sinners will go to the righteous.

²³ Unused fields could yield plenty of food for the poor, but unjust people keep them from being farmed.*

²⁴ If you don't punish your son, you don't love him. If you do love him, you will correct him.

²⁵ The righteous have enough to eat, but the wicked are always hungry.

14 Homes are made by the wisdom of women, but are destroyed by foolishness.

² Be honest and you show that you have reverence for the LORD; be dishonest and you show that you do not.

³ Proud fools talk too much; the words of the wise protect them.

⁴ Without any oxen to pull the plough your barn will be empty, but with them it will be full of corn.*

⁵ A reliable witness always tells the truth, but an unreliable one tells nothing but lies.

⁶ Conceited people can never become wise, but intelligent people learn easily.

⁷ Stay away from foolish people; they have nothing to teach you.

⁸ Why is a clever person wise? Because he knows what to do. Why is a stupid person foolish? Because he only thinks he knows.

⁹ Foolish people don't care if they sin, but good people want to be forgiven.*

¹⁰ Your joy is your own; your bitterness is your own. No one can share them with you.

¹¹ A good person's house will still be standing after an evildoer's house has been destroyed.

¹² What you think is the right road may lead to death.

¹³ Laughter may hide sadness. When happiness is gone, sorrow is always there.

¹⁴ Bad people will get what they deserve. Good people will be rewarded for their deeds.*

¹⁵ A fool will believe anything; sensible people watch their step.

¹⁶ Wise people are careful to stay out of trouble, but stupid people are careless and act too quickly.

¹⁷ People with a hot temper do foolish things; wiser people remain calm.*

¹⁸ Ignorant people get what their foolishness deserves, but the clever are rewarded with knowledge.

¹⁹ Evil people will have to bow down to the righteous and humbly beg their favour.

²⁰ No one likes the poor, not even their neighbours, but the rich have many friends.

²¹ If you want to be happy, be kind to the poor; it is a sin to despise anyone.

²² You will earn the trust and respect of others if you work for good; if you work for evil, you are making a mistake.

²³ Work and you will earn a living; if you sit around talking you will be poor.

13.23 Verse 23 in Hebrew is unclear.
14.4 your barn will be... corn; or you may grow a little corn, but with them you can grow much more.
14.9 Verse 9 in Hebrew is unclear.
14.14 Probable text for their deeds; Hebrew from upon them.
14.17 One ancient translation remain calm; Hebrew are hated.

DOODLE HERE...

770

Proverbs

∴ ⋯⋯

Ezra
Nehem.
Esther
Job
Psalms

PROVERBS 14, 15

²⁴Wise people are rewarded with wealth, but fools are known by* their foolishness.

²⁵A witness saves lives when he tells the truth; when he tells lies, he betrays people.

²⁶Reverence for the LORD gives confidence and security to a man and his family.

²⁷Do you want to avoid death? Reverence for the LORD is a fountain of life.

²⁸A king's greatness depends on how many people he rules; without them he is nothing.

²⁹If you stay calm, you are wise, but if you have a hot temper, you only show how stupid you are.

³⁰Peace of mind makes the body healthy, but jealousy is like a cancer.

³¹If you oppress poor people, you insult the God who made them; but kindness shown to the poor is an act of worship.

³²Wicked people bring about their own downfall by their evil deeds, but good people are protected by their integrity.*

³³Wisdom is in every thought of intelligent people; fools know nothing* about wisdom.

³⁴Righteousness makes a nation great; sin is a disgrace to any nation.

³⁵Kings are pleased with competent officials, but they punish those who fail them.

15 A gentle answer quietens anger, but a harsh one stirs it up. ²When wise people speak, they make knowledge attractive, but stupid people spout nonsense.

³The LORD sees what happens everywhere; he is watching us, whether we do good or evil.

⁴Kind words bring life, but cruel words crush your spirit.

⁵It is foolish to ignore what your father taught you; it is wise to accept his correction.

⁶Righteous people keep their wealth, but the wicked lose theirs when hard times come.

⁷Knowledge is spread by people who are wise, not by fools.

⁸The LORD is pleased when good people pray, but hates the sacrifices that the wicked bring him.

⁹The LORD hates the ways of evil people, but loves those who do what is right.

¹⁰If you do what is wrong, you will be severely punished; you will die if you do not let yourself be corrected.

¹¹Not even the world of the dead can keep the LORD from knowing what is there; how then can people hide their thoughts from God?

¹²Conceited people do not like to be corrected; they never ask for advice from those who are wiser.

¹³When people are happy, they smile, but when they are sad, they look depressed.

¹⁴Intelligent people want to learn, but stupid people are satisfied with ignorance.

¹⁵The life of the poor is a constant struggle, but happy people always enjoy life.

¹⁶Better to be poor and fear the LORD than to be rich and in trouble.

¹⁷Better to eat vegetables with people you love than to eat the finest meat where there is hate.

⋯⋯⋯

14.24 Probable text *are known by*; Hebrew unclear.
14.32 Some ancient translations *integrity*; Hebrew *death*.
14.33 One ancient translation *nothing*; Hebrew does not have this word.

PROVERBS 15, 16

771

Proverbs
...........:.
Eccles.
Songs
Isaiah
Jerem.
Lamen.

¹⁸ Hot tempers cause arguments, but patience brings peace.

¹⁹ If you are lazy, you will meet difficulty everywhere, but if you are honest, you will have no trouble.

²⁰ Wise children make their fathers happy. Only fools despise their mothers.

²¹ Stupid people are happy with their foolishness, but the wise will do what is right.

²² Get all the advice you can, and you will succeed; without it you will fail.

²³ What a joy it is to find just the right word for the right occasion!

²⁴ Wise people walk the road that leads upwards to life, not the road that leads downwards to death.

²⁵ The LORD will destroy the homes of arrogant men, but he will protect a widow's property.

²⁶ The LORD hates evil thoughts, but he is pleased with friendly words.

²⁷ If you try to make a profit dishonestly, you will get your family into trouble. Don't take bribes and you will live longer.

²⁸ Good people think before they answer. Evil people have a quick reply, but it causes trouble.

²⁹ When good people pray, the LORD listens, but he ignores those who are evil.

³⁰ Smiling faces make you happy, and good news makes you feel better.

³¹ If you pay attention when you are corrected, you are wise.

³² If you refuse to learn, you are hurting yourself. If you accept correction, you will become wiser.

³³ Reverence for the LORD is an education in itself. You must be humble before you can ever receive honours.

16

We may make our plans, but God has the last word.*

² You may think everything you do is right, but the LORD judges your motives.

³ Ask the LORD to bless your plans, and you will be successful in carrying them out.

⁴ Everything the LORD has made has its destiny; and the destiny of the wicked is destruction.

⁵ The LORD hates everyone who is arrogant; he will never let them escape punishment.

⁶ Be loyal and faithful, and God will forgive your sin. Obey the LORD and nothing evil will happen to you.

⁷ When you please the LORD, you can make* your enemies into friends.

⁸ It is better to have a little, honestly earned, than to have a large income gained dishonestly.

⁹ You may make your plans, but God directs your actions.

¹⁰ The king speaks with divine authority; his decisions are always right.

¹¹ The LORD wants weights and measures to be honest and every sale to be fair.

¹² Kings cannot tolerate evil,* because justice is what makes a government strong.

¹³ A king wants to hear the truth and will favour those who speak it.

¹⁴ A wise person will try to keep the king happy; if the king becomes angry, someone may die.

....

16.1 *God… word*; or *God inspires our words.*
16.7 *you can make*; or *he will make.*
16.12 *Kings… evil*; or *It is intolerable for kings to do evil.*

772
Proverbs

Ezra
Nehem.
Esther
Job
Psalms

PROVERBS 16.24

Think about

THREE

FRIENDS

you could encourage with a kind word. List their names here and write down what you would like to say. Over the next week, speak these words to them.

1.

2.

3.

15 The king's favour is like the clouds that bring rain in the springtime — life is there.

16 It is better — much better — to have wisdom and knowledge than gold and silver.

17 Those who are good travel a road that avoids evil; so watch where you are going — it may save your life.

18 Pride leads to destruction, and arrogance to downfall.

19 It is better to be humble and stay poor than to be one of the arrogant and get a share of their loot.

20 Pay attention to what you are taught, and you will be successful; trust in the LORD and you will be happy.

21 A wise, mature person is known for his understanding. The more pleasant his words, the more persuasive he is.

22 Wisdom is a fountain of life to the wise, but trying to educate stupid people is a waste of time.

23 Intelligent people think before they speak; what they say is then more persuasive.

24 Kind words are like honey — sweet to the taste and good for your health.

25 What you think is the right road may lead to death.

26 A labourer's appetite makes him work harder, because he wants to satisfy his hunger.

27 Evil people look for ways to harm others; even their words burn with evil.

28 Gossip is spread by wicked people; they stir up trouble and break up friendships.

29 Violent people deceive their friends and lead them to disaster.

30 Watch out for people who grin and wink at you; they have thought of something evil.

31 Long life is the reward of the righteous; grey hair is a glorious crown.

32 It is better to be patient than powerful. It is better to win control over yourself than over whole cities.

33 People cast lots to learn God's will, but God himself determines the answer.

17 Better to eat a dry crust of bread with peace of mind than to have a banquet in a house full of trouble.

2 A shrewd servant will gain authority over a master's worthless son and receive a part of the inheritance.

3 Gold and silver are tested by fire, and a person's heart is tested by the LORD.

4 Evil people listen to evil ideas, and liars listen to lies.

5 If you laugh at poor people, you insult the God who made them. You will be punished if you take pleasure in someone's misfortune.

6 Grandparents are proud of their grandchildren, just as children are proud of their parents.

7 Respected people do not tell lies, and fools have nothing worthwhile to say.

8 Some people think a bribe works like magic; they believe it can do anything.

9 If you want people to like you, forgive them when they wrong you. Remembering wrongs can break up a friendship.

10 An intelligent person learns more from one rebuke than a fool learns from being beaten a hundred times.

11 Death will come like a cruel messenger to wicked people who are always stirring up trouble.

12 It is better to meet a mother bear robbed of her cubs than to meet some fool busy with a stupid project.

¹³ If you repay good with evil, you will never get evil out of your house.

¹⁴ The start of an argument is like the first break in a dam; stop it before it goes any further.

¹⁵ Condemning the innocent or letting the wicked go — both are hateful to the Lord.

¹⁶ It does a fool no good to spend money on an education, because he has no common sense.

¹⁷ Friends always show their love. What are relatives for if not to share trouble?

¹⁸ Only someone with no sense would promise to be responsible for someone else's debts.

¹⁹ To like sin is to like making trouble. If you brag all the time,* you are asking for trouble.

²⁰ Anyone who thinks and speaks evil can expect to find nothing good — only disaster.

²¹ There is nothing but sadness and sorrow for parents whose children do foolish things.

²² Being cheerful keeps you healthy. It is slow death to be gloomy all the time.

²³ Corrupt judges accept secret bribes, and then justice is not done.

²⁴ An intelligent person aims at wise action, but a fool starts off in many directions.

²⁵ Foolish children bring grief to their fathers and bitter regrets to their mothers.

²⁶ It is not right to make an innocent person pay a fine; justice is perverted when good people are punished.

²⁷ Those who are sure of themselves do not talk all the time. People who stay calm have real insight. ²⁸ After all, even a fool may be thought wise and intelligent if he stays quiet and keeps his mouth shut.

18 People who do not get along with others are interested only in themselves; they will disagree with what everyone else knows is right.

² A fool does not care whether he understands a thing or not; all he wants to do is to show how clever he is.

³ Sin and shame go together. Lose your honour, and you will get scorn in its place.

⁴ A person's words can be a source of wisdom, deep as the ocean, fresh as a flowing stream.

⁵ It is not right to favour the guilty and prevent the innocent from receiving justice.

⁶ When some fool starts an argument, he is asking for a beating.

⁷ When a fool speaks, he is ruining himself; he gets caught in the trap of his own words.

⁸ Gossip is so tasty — how we love to swallow it!

⁹ A lazy person is as bad as someone who is destructive.

¹⁰ The Lord is like a strong tower, where the righteous can go and be safe. ¹¹ Rich people, however, imagine that their wealth protects them like high, strong walls round a city.

¹² No one is respected unless he is humble; arrogant people are on the way to ruin.

¹³ Listen before you answer. If you don't you are being stupid and insulting.

¹⁴ Your will to live can sustain you when you are sick, but if you lose it, your last hope is gone.

....

17.19 *brag... time*; or *make a show of your wealth.*

774

Proverbs

‥⋮⋯⋯⋯

Ezra
Nehem.
Esther
Job
Psalms

PROVERBS 18, 19

15 Intelligent people are always eager and ready to learn.

16 Do you want to meet an important person? Take a gift and it will be easy.

17 The first to speak in court always seems right until his opponent begins to question him.

18 If two powerful men are opposing each other in court, casting lots can settle the issue.

19 Help your relatives and they will protect you like a strong city wall,* but if you quarrel with them, they will close their doors to you.

20 You will have to live with the consequences of everything you say. 21 What you say can preserve life or destroy it; so you must accept the consequences of your words.

22 Find a wife and you find a good thing; it shows that the LORD is good to you.

23 When the poor speak, they have to beg politely, but when the rich answer, they are rude.

24 Some friendships do* not last, but some friends are more loyal than brothers.

19 It is better to be poor but honest than to be a lying fool. 2 Enthusiasm without knowledge is not good; impatience will get you into trouble.

3 Some people ruin themselves by their own stupid actions and then blame the LORD.

4 Rich people are always finding new friends, but the poor cannot keep the few they have.

5 If you tell lies in court, you will be punished — there will be no escape.

6 Everyone tries to gain the favour of important people; everyone claims the friendship of those who give out favours.

7 Even the relatives of a poor person have no use for him; no wonder he has no friends. No matter how hard he tries, he cannot win any.*

8 Do yourself a favour and learn all you can; then remember what you learn and you will prosper.

9 No one who tells lies in court can escape punishment; he is doomed.

10 Fools should not live in luxury, and slaves should not rule over noblemen.

11 If you are sensible, you will control your temper. When someone wrongs you, it is a great virtue to ignore it.

12 The king's anger is like the roar of a lion, but his favour is like welcome rain.

13 Stupid children can bring their parents to ruin. A nagging wife is like water going drip-drip-drip.

14 A man can inherit a house and money from his parents, but only the LORD can give him a sensible wife.

15 Be lazy if you want to; sleep on, but you will go hungry.

16 Keep God's laws and you will live longer; if you ignore them, you will die.

17 When you give to the poor, it is like lending to the LORD, and the LORD will pay you back.

18 Discipline your children while they are young enough to learn. If you don't, you are helping them to destroy themselves.*

⋯⋯⋯⋯⋯⋯⋯⋯⋯⋯⋯⋯⋯⋯⋯⋯⋯⋯⋯⋯⋯⋯⋯⋯⋯⋯

18.19 Some ancient translations *Help... wall*; Hebrew unclear.
18.24 Some ancient translations *Some friendships do*; Hebrew *Someone with friends does.*
19.7 Probable text *No matter... any*; Hebrew unclear.
19.18 *If you... themselves*; or *But don't beat them so hard that you kill them.*

Proverbs

Eccles.
Songs
Isaiah
Jerem.
Lamen.

¹⁹ If someone has a hot temper, let him take the consequences. If you get him out of trouble once, you will have to do it again.*

²⁰ If you listen to advice and are willing to learn, one day you will be wise.

²¹ People may plan all kinds of things, but the LORD's will is going to be done.

²² It is a disgrace to be greedy;* poor people are better off than liars.

²³ Obey the LORD and you will live a long life, content and safe from harm.

²⁴ Some people are too lazy to put food in their own mouths.

²⁵ Arrogance should be punished, so that people who don't know any better can learn a lesson. If you are wise, you will learn when you are corrected.

²⁶ Only a shameful, disgraceful person would ill-treat his father or turn his mother away from his home.

²⁷ Son, when you stop learning, you will soon neglect what you already know.

²⁸ There is no justice where a witness is determined to hurt someone. Wicked people love the taste of evil.

²⁹ A conceited fool is sure to get a beating.

20 Drinking too much makes you loud and foolish. It's stupid to get drunk.

² Fear an angry king as you would a growling lion; making him angry is suicide.

³ Any fool can start arguments; the honourable thing is to stay out of them.

⁴ A farmer who is too lazy to plough his fields at the right time will have nothing to harvest.

⁵ A person's thoughts are like water in a deep well, but someone with insight can draw them out.

⁶ Everyone talks about how loyal and faithful he is, but just try to find someone who really is!

⁷ Children are fortunate if they have a father who is honest and does what is right.

⁸ The king sits in judgement and knows evil when he sees it.

⁹ Can anyone really say that his conscience is clear, that he has got rid of his sin?

¹⁰ The LORD hates people who use dishonest weights and measures.

¹¹ Even children show what they are by what they do; you can tell if they are honest and good.

¹² The LORD has given us eyes to see with and ears to listen with.

¹³ If you spend your time sleeping, you will be poor. Keep busy and you will have plenty to eat.

¹⁴ The customer always complains that the price is too high, but then he goes off and brags about the bargain he got.

¹⁵ If you know what you are talking about, you have something more valuable than gold or jewels.

¹⁶ Anyone stupid enough to promise to be responsible for a stranger's debts ought to have his own property held to guarantee payment.

¹⁷ What you get by dishonesty you may enjoy like the finest food, but sooner or later it will be like a mouthful of sand.

....

19.19 *get him out... again;* or *try to get him out of trouble, you only make things worse.*
19.22 *It... greedy;* or *Loyalty is what is desired in a person.*

776

Proverbs

Ezra
Nehem.
Esther
Job
Psalms

PROVERBS 20, 21

18 Get good advice and you will succeed; don't go charging into battle without a plan.

19 A gossip can never keep a secret. Stay away from people who talk too much.

20 If you curse your parents, your life will end like a lamp that goes out in the dark.

21 The more easily you get your wealth, the less good it will do you.

22 Don't take it on yourself to repay a wrong. Trust the LORD and he will make it right.

23 The LORD hates people who use dishonest scales and weights.

24 The LORD has determined our path; how then can anyone understand the direction his own life is taking?

25 Think carefully before you promise an offering to God. You might regret it later.

26 A wise king will find out who is doing wrong, and will punish him without pity.

27 The LORD gave us mind and conscience; we cannot hide from ourselves.

28 A king will remain in power as long as his rule is honest, just, and fair.

29 We admire the strength of youth and respect the grey hair of age.

30 Sometimes it takes a painful experience to make us change our ways.

21 The LORD controls the mind of a king as easily as he directs the course of a stream.

2 You may think that everything you do is right, but remember that the LORD judges your motives.

3 Do what is right and fair; that pleases the LORD more than bringing him sacrifices.

4 Wicked people are controlled by their conceit and arrogance, and this is sinful.

5 Plan carefully and you will have plenty; if you act too quickly, you will never have enough.

6 The riches you get by dishonesty soon disappear, but not before they lead you into the jaws of death.

7 The wicked are doomed by their own violence; they refuse to do what is right.

8 Guilty people walk a crooked path; the innocent do what is right.

9 Better to live on the roof than share the house with a nagging wife.

10 Wicked people are always hungry for evil; they have no mercy on anyone.

11 When someone who is conceited gets his punishment, even an unthinking person learns a lesson. One who is wise will learn from what he is taught.

12 God, the righteous one, knows what goes on in the homes of the wicked, and he will bring the wicked down to ruin.

13 If you refuse to listen to the cry of the poor, your own cry for help will not be heard.

14 If someone is angry with you, a gift given secretly will calm him down.

15 When justice is done, good people are happy, but evil people are brought to despair.

16 Death is waiting for anyone who wanders away from good sense.

17 Indulging in luxuries, wine, and rich food will never make you wealthy.

PROVERBS 21, 22

777

Proverbs

Eccles.
Songs
Isaiah
Jerem.
Lamen.

18 The wicked bring on themselves the suffering they try to cause good people.

19 Better to live out in the desert than with a nagging, complaining wife.

20 Wise people live in wealth and luxury, but stupid people spend their money as fast as they get it.

21 Be kind and honest and you will live a long life; others will respect you and treat you fairly.

22 A shrewd general can take a city defended by strong men, and destroy the walls they relied on.

23 If you want to stay out of trouble, be careful what you say.

24 Show me a conceited person and I will show you someone who is arrogant, proud, and inconsiderate.

25 Lazy people who refuse to work are only killing themselves; 26 all they do is think about what they would like to have. The righteous, however, can give, and give generously.

27 The LORD hates it when wicked people offer him sacrifices, especially if they do it from evil motives.

28 The testimony of a liar is not believed, but the word of someone who thinks matters through is accepted.

29 Righteous people are sure of themselves; the wicked have to pretend as best they can.

30 Human wisdom, brilliance, insight — they are of no help if the LORD is against you.

31 You can get horses ready for battle, but it is the LORD who gives victory.

22 If you have to choose between a good reputation and great wealth, choose a good reputation.

2 The rich and the poor have this in common: the LORD made them both.

3 Sensible people will see trouble coming and avoid it, but an unthinking person will walk right into it and regret it later.

4 Obey the LORD, be humble, and you will get riches, honour, and a long life.

5 If you love your life, stay away from the traps that catch the wicked along the way.

6 Teach children how they should live, and they will remember it all their lives.

7 Poor people are slaves of the rich. Borrow money and you are the lender's slave.

8 If you sow the seeds of injustice, disaster will spring up, and your oppression of others will end.

9 Be generous and share your food with the poor. You will be blessed for it.

10 Get rid of a conceited person, and then there will be no more arguments, quarrelling, or calling of names.

11 If you love purity of heart and graciousness of speech, the king will be your friend.

12 The LORD sees to it that truth is kept safe by disproving the words of liars.

13 Lazy people stay at home; they say a lion might get them if they go outside.

14 Adultery is a trap — it catches those with whom the LORD is angry.

15 Children just naturally do silly, careless things, but a good spanking will teach them how to behave.

16 If you make gifts to rich people or oppress the poor to get rich, you will become poor yourself.

PROVERBS 22.1

Would you rather be
- KNOWN FOR BEING -
SUPER-RICH
or for being a
good person? Why?
Why do you think
this proverb tells
us to choose a
good reputation?

The Thirty Wise Sayings

[17] Listen, and I will teach you what the wise have said. Study their teachings, [18] and you will be glad if you remember them and can quote them. [19] I want you to put your trust in the LORD; that is why I am going to tell them to you now. [20] I have written down thirty sayings for you. They contain knowledge and good advice, [21] and will teach you what the truth really is. Then when you are sent to find it out, you will bring back the right answer.

The First Saying

[22] Don't take advantage of the poor just because you can; don't take advantage of those who stand helpless in court. [23] The LORD will argue their case for them and threaten the life of anyone who threatens theirs.

The Second Saying

[24] Don't make friends with people who have hot, violent tempers. [25] You might learn their habits and not be able to change.

The Third Saying

[26] Don't promise to be responsible for someone else's debts. [27] If you should be unable to pay, they will take away even your bed.

The Fourth Saying

[28] Never move an old boundary mark that your ancestors established.

The Fifth Saying

[29] Show me someone who does a good job, and I will show you someone who is better than most and worthy of the company of kings.

The Sixth Saying

23 When you sit down to eat with someone important, keep in mind who he is.* [2] If you have a big appetite, restrain yourself. [3] Don't be greedy for the fine food he serves; he may be trying to trick you.

The Seventh Saying

[4] Be wise enough not to wear yourself out trying to get rich. [5] Your money can be gone in a flash, as if it had grown wings and flown away like an eagle.

The Eighth Saying

[6] Don't eat at the table of a stingy person or be greedy for the fine food he serves. [7] "Come on and have some more," he says, but he doesn't mean it. What he thinks is what he really is. [8] You will vomit up what you have eaten, and all your flattery will be wasted.

The Ninth Saying

[9] Don't try to talk sense to a fool; he can't appreciate it.

The Tenth Saying

[10] Never move an old boundary mark or take over land owned by orphans. [11] The LORD is their powerful defender, and he will argue their case against you.

....

23.1 *keep... is;* or *notice carefully what is before you.*

PROVERBS 23, 24

779

Proverbs
..........:
Eccles.
Songs
Isaiah
Jerem.
Lamen.

The Eleventh Saying
¹²Pay attention to your teacher and learn all you can.

The Twelfth Saying
¹³Don't hesitate to discipline children. A good spanking won't kill them. ¹⁴As a matter of fact, it may save their lives.

The Thirteenth Saying
¹⁵Son, if you become wise, I will be very happy. ¹⁶I will be proud when I hear you speaking words of wisdom.

The Fourteenth Saying
¹⁷Don't be envious of sinful people; let reverence for the LORD be the concern of your life. ¹⁸If it is, you have a bright future.

The Fifteenth Saying
¹⁹Listen, my child, be wise and give serious thought to the way you live. ²⁰Don't associate with people who drink too much wine or stuff themselves with food. ²¹Drunkards and gluttons will be reduced to poverty. If all you do is eat and sleep, you will soon be wearing rags.

The Sixteenth Saying
²²Listen to your father; without him you would not exist. When your mother is old, show her your appreciation.
²³Truth, wisdom, learning, and good sense — these are worth paying for, but too valuable for you to sell.
²⁴A righteous man's father has good reason to be happy. You can take pride in a wise son.
²⁵Make your father and mother proud of you; give your mother that happiness.

The Seventeenth Saying
²⁶Pay close attention, son, and let my life be your example. ²⁷Prostitutes and immoral women are a deadly trap. ²⁸They wait for you like robbers and cause many men to be unfaithful.

The Eighteenth Saying
²⁹⁻³⁰Show me someone who drinks too much, who has to try out some new drink, and I will show you someone miserable and sorry for himself, always causing trouble and always complaining. His eyes are bloodshot, and he has bruises that could have been avoided. ³¹Don't let wine tempt you, even though it is rich red, though it sparkles in the cup, and it goes down smoothly. ³²The next morning you will feel as if you had been bitten by a poisonous snake. ³³Weird sights will appear before your eyes, and you will not be able to think or speak clearly. ³⁴You will feel as if you were out on the ocean, sea-sick, swinging high up in the rigging of a tossing ship. ³⁵"I must have been hit," you will say; "I must have been beaten up, but I don't remember it. Why can't I wake up? I need another drink."

The Nineteenth Saying
24 Don't be envious of evil people, and don't try to make friends with them. ²Causing trouble is all they ever think about; every time they open their mouth someone is going to be hurt.

780

Proverbs

Ezra
Nehem.
Esther
Job
Psalms

PROVERBS 24

TURN THESE LINES INTO A PICTURE OF SOMETHING.

The Twentieth Saying
³ Homes are built on the foundation of wisdom and understanding.* ⁴ Where there is knowledge, the rooms are furnished with valuable, beautiful things.

The 21st Saying
⁵ Being wise is better than being strong;* yes, knowledge is more important than strength. ⁶ After all, you must make careful plans before you fight a battle, and the more good advice you get, the more likely you are to win.

The 22nd Saying
⁷ Wise sayings are too deep for stupid people to understand. They have nothing to say when important matters are being discussed.

The 23rd Saying
⁸ If you are always planning evil, you will earn a reputation as a troublemaker. ⁹ Any scheme a fool thinks up is sinful. People hate a person who has nothing but scorn for others.

The 24th Saying
¹⁰ If you are weak in a crisis, you are weak indeed.

The 25th Saying
¹¹ Don't hesitate to rescue someone who is about to be executed unjustly. ¹² You may say that it is none of your business, but God knows and judges your motives. He keeps watch on you; he knows. And he will reward you according to what you do.

The 26th Saying
¹³ Son, eat honey; it is good. And just as honey from the comb is sweet on your tongue, ¹⁴ you may be sure that wisdom is good for the soul. Get wisdom and you have a bright future.

The 27th Saying
¹⁵ Don't be like the wicked who scheme to rob honest people or to take away their homes. ¹⁶ No matter how often honest people fall, they always get up again; but disaster destroys the wicked.

The 28th Saying
¹⁷ Don't be glad when your enemies meet disaster, and don't rejoice when they stumble. ¹⁸ The LORD will know if you are gloating, and he will not like it; and then he might not punish them.

The 29th Saying
¹⁹ Don't let evil people worry you; don't be envious of them. ²⁰ A wicked person has no future — nothing to look forward to.

The Thirtieth Saying
²¹ Have reverence for the LORD, my child, and honour the king. Have nothing to do with people who rebel against them; ²² such people could be ruined in a moment. Do you realize the disaster that God or the king can cause?

24.3 *Homes… understanding*; or *It takes care to lay the foundations of a house, and skill to build it.*
24.5 Some ancient translations *Being wise is better than being strong*; Hebrew *A person is wise in strength.*

PROVERBS 24, 25

781

Proverbs

....

Eccles.
Songs
Isaiah
Jerem.
Lamen.

More Wise Sayings

²³ The wise have also said these things:

It is wrong for judges to be prejudiced. ²⁴ If they pronounce a guilty person innocent, they will be cursed and hated by everyone. ²⁵ Judges who punish the guilty, however, will be prosperous and enjoy a good reputation.

²⁶ An honest answer is a sign of true friendship.

²⁷ Don't build your house and establish a home until your fields are ready, and you are sure that you can earn a living.

²⁸ Don't give evidence against someone else without good reason, or say misleading things about him. ²⁹ Don't say, "I'll do to him just what he did to me! I'll get even with him!"

³⁰ I walked through the fields and vineyards of a lazy, stupid person. ³¹ They were full of thorn bushes and overgrown with weeds. The stone wall round them had fallen down. ³² I looked at this, thought about it, and learned a lesson from it: ³³ have a nap and sleep if you want to. Fold your hands and rest awhile, ³⁴ but while you are asleep, poverty will attack you like an armed robber.

More of Solomon's Proverbs

25 Here are more of Solomon's proverbs, copied by men at the court of King Hezekiah of Judah.

² We honour God for what he conceals; we honour kings for what they explain.

³ You never know what a king is thinking; his thoughts are beyond us, like the heights of the sky or the depths of the ocean.

⁴ Take the impurities out of silver and the artist can produce a thing of beauty. ⁵ Keep evil advisers away from the king and his government will be known for its justice.

⁶ When you stand before the king, don't try to impress him and pretend to be important. ⁷ It is better to be asked to take a higher position than to be told to give your place to someone more important.

⁸ Don't be too quick to go to court about something you have seen. If another witness later proves you wrong, what will you do then?

⁹ If you and your neighbour have a difference of opinion, settle it between yourselves and do not reveal any secrets. ¹⁰ Otherwise everyone will learn that you can't keep a secret, and you will never live down the shame.

¹¹ An idea well expressed is like a design of gold, set in silver.

¹² A warning given by an experienced person to someone willing to listen is more valuable than gold rings or jewellery made of the finest gold.

¹³ A reliable messenger is refreshing to the one who sends him, like cold water in the heat of harvest time.

¹⁴ People who promise things that they never give are like clouds and wind that bring no rain.

¹⁵ Patient persuasion can break down the strongest resistance and can even convince rulers.

¹⁶ Never eat more honey than you need; too much may make you vomit. ¹⁷ Don't visit your neighbours too often; they may get tired of you and come to hate you.

¹⁸ A false accusation is as deadly as a sword, a club, or a sharp arrow.

¹⁹ Depending on an unreliable person in a crisis is like trying to chew with a loose tooth or walk with a crippled foot.

²⁰ Singing to a person who is depressed is like taking off his clothes on a cold day or like rubbing salt in a wound.

782

Proverbs

Ezra
Nehem.
Esther
Job
Psalms

PROVERBS 25, 26

²¹ If your enemies are hungry, feed them; if they are thirsty, give them a drink. ²² You will make them burn with shame, and the LORD will reward you.

²³ Gossip brings anger just as surely as the north wind brings rain.

²⁴ Better to live on the roof than share the house with a nagging wife.

²⁵ Finally, hearing good news from a distant land is like a drink of cold water when you are dry and thirsty.

²⁶ A good person who gives in to someone who is evil reminds you of a polluted spring or a poisoned well.

²⁷ Too much honey is bad for you, and so is trying to win too much praise.*

²⁸ If you cannot control your anger, you are as helpless as a city without walls, open to attack.

26 Praise for a fool is out of place, like snow in summer or rain at harvest time.

² Curses cannot hurt you unless you deserve them. They are like birds that fly by and never settle.

³ You have to whip a horse, you have to bridle a donkey, and you have to beat a fool.

⁴ If you answer a silly question, you are just as silly as the person who asked it.

⁵ Give a silly answer to a silly question, and the one who asked it will realize that he's not as clever as he thinks.

⁶ If you let a fool deliver a message, you might as well cut off your own feet; you are asking for trouble.

⁷ A fool can use a proverb about as well as crippled people can use their legs.

⁸ Praising someone who is stupid makes as much sense as tying a stone in a sling.

⁹ A fool quoting a wise saying reminds you of a drunk trying to pick a thorn out of his hand.

¹⁰ An employer who hires any fool that comes along is only hurting everybody concerned.*

¹¹ A fool doing some stupid thing a second time is like a dog going back to its vomit.

¹² The most stupid fool is better off than someone who thinks he is wise when he is not.

¹³ Why don't lazy people ever get out of the house? What are they afraid of? Lions?

¹⁴ Lazy people turn over in bed. They get no farther than a door swinging on its hinges.

¹⁵ Some people are too lazy to put food in their own mouths.

¹⁶ A lazy person will think he is more intelligent than seven people who can give good reasons for their opinions.

¹⁷ Getting involved in an argument that is none of your business is like going down the street and grabbing a dog by the ears.

¹⁸⁻¹⁹ Someone who misleads someone else and then claims that he was only joking is like a mad person playing with a deadly weapon.

²⁰ Without wood, a fire goes out; without gossip, quarrelling stops.

²¹ Charcoal keeps the embers glowing, wood keeps the fire burning, and troublemakers keep arguments alive.

²² Gossip is so tasty! How we love to swallow it!

....

25.27 Probable text *and so... praise*; Hebrew unclear.
26.10 Verse 10 in Hebrew is unclear.

783

Proverbs

Eccles.
Songs
Isaiah
Jerem.
Lamen.

23 Insincere* talk that hides what you are really thinking is like a fine glaze* on a cheap clay pot.

24 A hypocrite hides hatred behind flattering words. 25 They may sound fine, but don't believe him, because his heart is filled to the brim with hate. 26 He may disguise his hatred, but everyone will see the evil things he does.

27 People who set traps for others get caught themselves. People who start landslides get crushed.

28 You have to hate someone to want to hurt him with lies. Insincere talk brings nothing but ruin.

27 Never boast about tomorrow. You don't know what will happen between now and then.

2 Let other people praise you — even strangers; never do it yourself.

3 The weight of stone and sand is nothing compared to the trouble that stupidity can cause.

4 Anger is cruel and destructive, but it is nothing compared to jealousy.

5 Better to correct someone openly than to let him think you don't care for him at all.

6 Friends mean well, even when they hurt you. But when an enemy puts an arm round your shoulder — watch out!

7 When you are full, you will refuse honey, but when you are hungry, even bitter food tastes sweet.

8 Anyone away from home is like a bird away from its nest.

9 Perfume and fragrant oils make you feel happier, but trouble shatters your peace of mind.*

10 Do not forget your friends or your father's friends. If you are in trouble, don't ask a relative for help; a neighbour near by can help you more than relatives who are far away.

11 Be wise, my child, and I will be happy; I will have an answer for anyone who criticizes me.

12 Sensible people will see trouble coming and avoid it, but an unthinking person will walk right into it and regret it later.

13 Anyone stupid enough to promise to be responsible for a stranger's debts* deserves to have his own property held to guarantee payment.

14 You might as well curse your friends as wake them up early in the morning with a loud greeting.

15 A nagging wife is like water going drip-drip-drip on a rainy day. 16 How can you keep her quiet? Have you ever tried to stop the wind or ever tried to hold a handful of oil?*

17 People learn from one another, just as iron sharpens iron.

18 Take care of a fig tree and you will have figs to eat. Servants who take care of their master will be honoured.

19 It is your own face that you see reflected in the water and it is your own self that you see in your heart.

20 Human desires are like the world of the dead — there is always room for more.

21 Fire tests gold and silver; a person's reputation can also be tested.

22 Even if you beat fools until they're half dead, you still can't beat their foolishness out of them.

PROVERBS 27.17

List some friends here who could be the 'iron' to sharpen you, walk alongside you in your faith and help you to

— BECOME THE —

BEST

you can be for God. Who do you think you could help to grow in the same way? Get in touch with some of these friends and pray together that God would help you to build each other up in your friendship.

_____

_____

_____

_____

_____

_____

_____

26.23 One ancient translation Insincere; Hebrew Burning.
26.23 Probable text fine glaze; Hebrew unrefined silver.
27.9 One ancient translation but trouble... mind; Hebrew unclear.
27.13 One ancient translation stranger's debts; Hebrew stranger's debts or those of an immoral woman.
27.16 Probable text or ever... oil; Hebrew unclear.

784

Proverbs

Ezra
Nehem.
Esther
Job
Psalms

PROVERBS 27, 28

²³ Look after your sheep and cattle as carefully as you can, ²⁴ because wealth is not permanent. Not even nations last for ever. ²⁵ You cut the hay and then cut the grass on the hillsides while the next crop of hay is growing. ²⁶ You can make clothes from the wool of your sheep and buy land with the money you get from selling some of your goats. ²⁷ The rest of the goats will provide milk for you and your family, and for your servant women as well.

28

The wicked run when no one is chasing them, but an honest person is as brave as a lion.

² When a nation sins, it will have one ruler after another. But a nation will be strong and endure when it has intelligent, sensible leaders.

³ Someone in authority who oppresses poor people is like a driving rain that destroys the crops.

⁴ If you have no regard for the law, you are on the side of the wicked; but if you obey it, you are against them.

⁵ Evil people do not know what justice is, but those who worship the LORD understand it well.

⁶ Better to be poor and honest than rich and dishonest.

⁷ A young man who obeys the law is intelligent. One who makes friends with good-for-nothings is a disgrace to his father.

⁸ If you get rich by charging interest and taking advantage of people, your wealth will go to someone who is kind to the poor.

⁹ If you do not obey the law, God will find your prayers too hateful to hear.

¹⁰ If you trick an honest person into doing evil, you will fall into your own trap.

The innocent will be well rewarded.

¹¹ Rich people always think they are wise, but a poor person who has insight into character knows better.

¹² When good people come to power, everybody celebrates, but when bad people rule, people stay in hiding.

¹³ You will never succeed in life if you try to hide your sins. Confess them and give them up; then God will show mercy to you.

¹⁴ Always obey the LORD and you will be happy. If you are stubborn, you will be ruined.

¹⁵ Poor people are helpless against a wicked ruler; he is as dangerous as a growling lion or a prowling bear.

¹⁶ A ruler without good sense will be a cruel tyrant. One who hates dishonesty will rule a long time.

¹⁷ Someone guilty of murder is digging his own grave as fast as he can. Don't try to stop him.

¹⁸ Be honest and you will be safe. If you are dishonest, you will suddenly fall.

¹⁹ A hard-working farmer has plenty to eat. People who waste time will always be poor.

²⁰ Honest people will lead a full, happy life. But if you are in a hurry to get rich, you are going to be punished.

²¹ Prejudice is wrong. But some judges will do wrong to get even the smallest bribe.

²² Selfish people are in such a hurry to get rich that they do not know when poverty is about to strike.

²³ Correct someone, and afterwards he will appreciate it more than flattery.

²⁴ Anyone who thinks it isn't wrong to steal from his parents is no better than a common thief.

²⁵ Selfishness only causes trouble. You are much better off to trust the LORD.

PROVERBS 28, 29

785

Proverbs

Eccles.
Songs
Isaiah
Jerem.
Lamen.

26 It is foolish to follow your own opinions. Be safe, and follow the teachings of wiser people.

27 Give to the poor and you will never be in need. If you close your eyes to the poor, many people will curse you.

28 People stay in hiding when the wicked come to power. But when they fall from power, the righteous will rule again.

29

If you get more stubborn every time you are corrected, one day you will be crushed and never recover.

2 Show me a righteous ruler and I will show you a happy people. Show me a wicked ruler and I will show you a miserable people.

3 If you appreciate wisdom, your father will be proud of you. It is a foolish waste to spend money on prostitutes.

4 When the king is concerned with justice, the nation will be strong, but when he is only concerned with money, he will ruin his country.

5 If you flatter your friends, you set a trap for yourself.*

6 Evil people are trapped in their own sins, while honest people are happy and free.

7 A good person knows the rights of the poor, but wicked people cannot understand such things.

8 People with no regard for others can throw whole cities into turmoil. Those who are wise keep things calm.

9 When an intelligent person brings a lawsuit against a fool, the fool only laughs and becomes loud and abusive.

10 Bloodthirsty people hate anyone who's honest, but righteous people will protect* the life of such a person.

11 Stupid people express their anger openly, but sensible people are patient and hold it back.

12 If a ruler pays attention to false information, all his officials will be liars.

13 A poor person and his oppressor have this in common — the LORD gave eyes to both of them.

14 If a king defends the rights of the poor, he will rule for a long time.

15 Correction and discipline are good for children. If they have their own way, they will make their mothers ashamed of them.

16 When evil people are in power, crime increases. But the righteous will live to see the downfall of such people.

17 Discipline your children and you can always be proud of them. They will never give you reason to be ashamed.

18 A nation without God's guidance is a nation without order. Happy are those who keep God's law!

19 You cannot correct servants just by talking to them. They may understand you, but they will pay no attention.

20 There is more hope for a stupid fool than for someone who speaks without thinking.

21 If you give your servants everything they want from childhood on, some day they will take over everything you own.*

22 People with quick tempers cause a lot of quarrelling and trouble.

23 Arrogance will bring your downfall, but if you are humble, you will be respected.

24 A thief's partner is his own worst enemy. He will be punished if he tells the truth in court, and God will curse him if he doesn't.

....

29.5 *yourself*; or *them*.
29.10 Probable text *protect*; Hebrew *seek*.
29.21 *they... own*; or *you will not be able to control them*.

786

Proverbs

Ezra
Nehem.
Esther
Job
Psalms

PROVERBS 29, 30

²⁵ It is dangerous to be concerned with what others think of you, but if you trust the LORD, you are safe.

²⁶ Everybody wants the good will of the ruler, but only from the LORD can you get justice.

²⁷ The righteous hate the wicked, and the wicked hate the righteous.

The Words of Agur

30 These are the solemn words of Agur son of Jakeh:
"God is not with me, God is not with me,
and I am helpless.*
² I am more like an animal than a human being;
I do not have the sense a human being should have.
³ I have never learned any wisdom,
and I know nothing at all about God.
⁴ Who has ever mastered heavenly knowledge?
Who has ever caught the wind in his hand?
Or wrapped up water in a piece of cloth?
Or fixed the boundaries of the earth?
Who is he, if you know? Who is his son?

⁵ "God keeps every promise he makes. He is like a shield for all who seek his protection. ⁶ If you claim that he said something that he never said, he will reprimand you and show that you are a liar."

More Proverbs

⁷ I ask you, God, to let me have two things before I die: ⁸ keep me from lying, and let me be neither rich nor poor. So give me only as much food as I need. ⁹ If I have more, I might say that I do not need you. But if I am poor, I might steal and bring disgrace on my God.

¹⁰ Never criticize servants to their master. You will be cursed and suffer for it.

¹¹ There are people who curse their fathers and do not show their appreciation for their mothers.

¹² There are people who think they are pure when they are as filthy as they can be.

¹³ There are people who think they are so good — oh, how good they think they are!

¹⁴ There are people who take cruel advantage of the poor and needy; that is the way they make their living.

¹⁵ A leech has two daughters, and both are named "Give me!"
There are four things that are never satisfied:
¹⁶ the world of the dead,
a woman without children,
dry ground that needs rain,
and a fire burning out of control.

¹⁷ Those who make fun of their father or despise their mother in her old age* ought to be eaten by vultures or have their eyes picked out by wild ravens.

¹⁸ There are four things that are too mysterious for me to understand:
¹⁹ an eagle flying in the sky,
a snake moving on a rock,
a ship finding its way over the sea,
and a man and a woman falling in love.

. . . .

30.1 Probable text *"God... helpless*; Hebrew unclear.
30.17 One ancient translation *mother in her old age*; Hebrew *mother's obedience*.

20 This is how an unfaithful wife acts: she commits adultery, has a bath, and says, "But I haven't done anything wrong!"

21 There are four things that the earth itself cannot tolerate:

22 a slave who becomes a king,
a fool who has all he wants to eat,

23 a hateful woman who gets married,
and a servant woman who takes the place of her mistress.

24 There are four animals in the world that are small, but very, very clever:

25 Ants: they are weak, but they store up their food in the summer.

26 Rock-badgers: they are not strong either, but they make their homes among the rocks.

27 Locusts: they have no king, but they move in formation.

28 Lizards: you can hold one in your hand, but you can find them in palaces.

29 There are four things that are impressive to watch as they walk:

30 lions, strongest of all animals and afraid of none;

31 goats,
strutting cocks,
and kings in front of their people.*

32 If you have been foolish enough to be arrogant and plan evil, stop and think! 33 If you churn milk, you get butter. If you hit someone's nose, it bleeds. If you stir up anger, you get into trouble.

Advice to a King

31 These are the solemn words which King Lemuel's mother said to him:

2 "You are my own dear son, the answer to my prayers. What shall I tell you? 3 Don't spend all your energy on sex and all your money on women; they have destroyed kings. 4 Listen, Lemuel. Kings should not drink wine or have a craving for alcohol. 5 When they drink, they forget the laws and ignore the rights of people in need. 6 Alcohol is for people who are dying, for those who are in misery. 7 Let them drink and forget their poverty and unhappiness.

8 "Speak up for people who cannot speak for themselves. Protect the rights of all who are helpless. 9 Speak for them and be a righteous judge. Protect the rights of the poor and needy."

The Capable Wife

10 How hard it is to find a capable wife! She is worth far more than jewels!

11 Her husband puts his confidence in her, and he will never be poor.

12 As long as she lives, she does him good and never harm.

13 She keeps herself busy making wool and linen cloth.

14 She brings home food from out-of-the-way places, as merchant ships do.

15 She gets up before daylight to prepare food for her family and to tell her servant women what to do.

16 She looks at land and buys it, and with money she has earned she plants a vineyard.

17 She is a hard worker, strong and industrious.

18 She knows the value of everything she makes, and works late into the night.

19 She spins her own thread and weaves her own cloth.

30.31 Verse 31 in Hebrew is unclear.

788

Proverbs

Ezra
Nehem.
Esther
Job
Psalms

PROVERBS 31

Write a note here for your {FUTURE SELF} to read.

²⁰ She is generous to the poor and needy.

²¹ She doesn't worry when it snows, because her family has warm clothing.

²² She makes bedspreads and wears clothes of fine purple linen.

²³ Her husband is well known, one of the leading citizens.

²⁴ She makes clothes and belts, and sells them to merchants.

²⁵ She is strong and respected and not afraid of the future.

²⁶ She speaks with a gentle wisdom.

²⁷ She is always busy and looks after her family's needs.

²⁸ Her children show their appreciation, and her husband praises her.

²⁹ He says, "Many women are good wives, but you are the best of them all."

³⁰ Charm is deceptive and beauty disappears, but a woman who honours the LORD should be praised.

³¹ Give her credit for all she does. She deserves the respect of everyone.

THE BOOK OF
EGGLESIASTES

WRITTEN: PROBABLY BETWEEN 450 AND 180BC

WHAT YOU NEED TO KNOW:

Ecclesiastes is considered a wisdom book, like Proverbs. Throughout the book, the writer wrestles with the meaning of life. The content is unusual and, while it can appear rather gloomy and down-beat, it puts human life into perspective in the light of eternity. There is a lot of debate around who wrote it. Solomon is traditionally suggested as the author, but it was probably written long after his reign. One theory is that Ecclesiastes is a piece of royal fiction, by a writer taking on the persona of a king.

WHY READ IT?

This book honestly addresses some big questions in a poetic way. Looking at life, death and purpose, the writer puts life in perspective while giving us words to say to God when everything feels hopeless. It can be seen as a book about the meaninglessness of life without God.

WRITE OUT HERE THE TOP FIVE
PIECES OF WISDOM
THAT YOU FIND IN THIS BOOK.

1. _____
2. _____
3. _____
4. _____
5. _____

DECORATE
THESE SHAPES
IN RELATION TO
YOUR MOOD.

WE'RE NOT SURE WHEN EGGLESIASTES WAS WRITTEN
BUT IT'S LIKELY TO HAVE BEEN AFTER 450BG

790

Eccles.

Nehem.
Esther
Job
Psalms
Proverbs

ECCLESIASTES 1, 2

Life is Useless

1 These are the words of the Philosopher, David's son, who was king in Jerusalem.

[2] It is useless, useless, said the Philosopher. Life is useless, all useless. [3] You spend your life working, labouring, and what do you have to show for it? [4] Generations come and generations go, but the world stays just the same. [5] The sun still rises, and it still goes down, going wearily back to where it must start all over again. [6] The wind blows south, the wind blows north — round and round and back again. [7] Every river flows into the sea, but the sea is not yet full. The water returns to where the rivers began, and starts all over again. [8] Everything leads to weariness — a weariness too great for words. Our eyes can never see enough to be satisfied; our ears can never hear enough. [9] What has happened before will happen again. What has been done before will be done again. There is nothing new in the whole world. [10] "Look," they say, "here is something new!" But no, it has all happened before, long before we were born. [11] No one remembers what has happened in the past, and no one in days to come will remember what happens between now and then.

The Philosopher's Experience

[12] I, the Philosopher, have been king over Israel in Jerusalem. [13] I determined that I would examine and study all the things that are done in this world.

God has laid a miserable fate upon us. [14] I have seen everything done in this world, and I tell you, it is all useless. It is like chasing the wind. [15] You can't straighten out what is crooked; you can't count things that aren't there.

[16] I told myself, "I have become a great man, far wiser than anyone who ruled Jerusalem before me. I know what wisdom and knowledge really are." [17] I was determined to learn the difference between knowledge and foolishness, wisdom and madness. But I found out that I might as well be chasing the wind. [18] The wiser you are, the more worries you have; the more you know, the more it hurts.

2 I decided to enjoy myself and find out what happiness is. But I found that this is useless, too. [2] I discovered that laughter is foolish, that pleasure does you no good. [3] Driven on by my desire for wisdom, I decided to cheer myself up with wine and have a good time. I thought that this might be the best way people can spend their short lives on earth.

[4] I accomplished great things. I built myself houses and planted vineyards. [5] I planted gardens and orchards, with all kinds of fruit trees in them; [6] I dug ponds to irrigate them. [7] I bought many slaves, and there were slaves born in my household. I owned more livestock than anyone else who had ever lived in Jerusalem. [8] I also piled up silver and gold from the royal treasuries of the lands I ruled. Men and women sang to entertain me, and I had all the women a man could want.

[9] Yes, I was great, greater than anyone else who had ever lived in Jerusalem, and my wisdom never failed me. [10] Anything I wanted, I got. I did not deny myself any pleasure. I was proud of everything I had worked for, and all this was my reward. [11] Then I thought about all that I had done and how hard I had worked doing it, and I realized that it didn't mean a thing. It was like chasing the wind — of no use at all. [12] After all, a king can only do what previous kings have done.

So I started thinking about what it meant to be wise or reckless or foolish. [13] Oh, I know, "Wisdom is better than foolishness, just

ECCLESIASTES 2, 3

791

Eccles.
....

Songs
Isaiah
Jerem.
Lamen.
Ezekiel

as light is better than darkness. [14] The wise can see where they are going, and fools cannot." But I also know that the same fate is waiting for us all. [15] I thought to myself, "I will suffer the same fate as fools. So what have I gained from being so wise?" "Nothing," I answered, "not a thing." [16] No one remembers the wise, and no one remembers fools. In days to come, we will all be forgotten. We must all die — wise and foolish alike. [17] So life came to mean nothing to me, because everything in it had brought me nothing but trouble. It had all been useless; I had been chasing the wind.

[18] Nothing that I had worked for and earned meant a thing to me, because I knew that I would have to leave it to my successor, [19] and he might be wise, or he might be foolish — who knows? Yet he will own everything I have worked for, everything my wisdom has earned for me in this world. It is all useless. [20] So I came to regret that I had worked so hard. [21] You work for something with all your wisdom, knowledge, and skill, and then you have to leave it all to someone who hasn't had to work for it. It is useless, and it isn't right! [22] You work and worry your way through life, and what do you have to show for it? [23] As long as you live, everything you do brings nothing but worry and heartache. Even at night your mind can't rest. It is all useless.

[24] The best thing anyone can do is to eat and drink and enjoy what he has earned. And yet, I realized that even this comes from God. [25] How else could you have anything to eat or enjoy yourself at all? [26] God gives wisdom, knowledge, and happiness to those who please him, but he makes sinners work, earning and saving, so that what they get can be given to those who please him. It is all useless. It is like chasing the wind.

A Time for Everything

3 Everything that happens in this world happens at the time God chooses.
[2] He sets the time for birth and the time for death,
   the time for planting and the time for pulling up,
[3]   the time for killing and the time for healing,
   the time for tearing down and the time for building.
[4] He sets the time for sorrow and the time for joy,
   the time for mourning and the time for dancing,
[5]   the time for making love and the time for not making love,
   the time for kissing and the time for not kissing.
[6] He sets the time for finding and the time for losing,
   the time for saving and the time for throwing away,
[7]   the time for tearing and the time for mending,
   the time for silence and the time for talk.
[8] He sets the time for love and the time for hate,
   the time for war and the time for peace.

[9] What do we gain from all our work? [10] I know the heavy burdens that God has laid on us. [11] He has set the right time for everything. He has given us a desire to know the future, but never gives us the satisfaction of fully understanding what he does. [12] So I realized that all we can do is to be happy and do the best we can while we are still alive. [13] All of us should eat and drink and enjoy what we have worked for. It is God's gift.

[14] I know that everything God does will last for ever. You can't add anything to it or take anything away from it. And one thing God does is to make us stand in awe of him. [15] Whatever happens or can happen has already happened before. God makes the same thing happen again and again.

READ THIS PASSAGE

OVER & OVER

AGAIN.

EACH TIME YOU READ,
EMPHASISE A DIFFERENT
WORD IN THE PASSAGE.

792

Eccles.

·:········

Nehem.
Esther
Job
Psalms
Proverbs

ECCLESIASTES 3–5

Injustice in the World

16 In addition, I have also noticed that in this world you find wickedness where justice and right ought to be. 17 I told myself, "God is going to judge the righteous and the evil alike, because every thing, every action, will happen at its own set time."* 18 I concluded that God is testing us, to show us that we are no better than animals. 19 After all, the same fate awaits human beings and animals alike. One dies just like the other. They are both the same kind of creature. A human being is no better off than an animal, because life has no meaning for either. 20 They are both going to the same place — the dust. They both came from it; they will both go back to it. 21 How can anyone be sure that the human spirit goes upwards while an animal's spirit goes down into the ground? 22 So I realized then that the best thing we can do is to enjoy what we have worked for. There is nothing else we can do.* There is no way for us to know what will happen after we die.

4 Then I looked again at all the injustice that goes on in this world. The oppressed were weeping, and no one would help them. No one would help them, because their oppressors had power on their side. 2 I envy those who are dead and gone; they are better off than those who are still alive. 3 But better off than either are those who have never been born, who have never seen the injustice that goes on in this world.

4 I have also learnt why people work so hard to succeed: it is because they envy their neighbours. But it is useless. It is like chasing the wind. 5 They say that anyone would be a fool to fold his hands and let himself starve to death. 6 Perhaps so, but it is better to have only a little, with peace of mind, than to be busy all the time with both hands, trying to catch the wind.

7 I have noticed something else in life that is useless. 8 Here is a man who lives alone. He has no son, no brother, yet he is always working, never satisfied with the wealth he has. For whom is he working so hard and denying himself any pleasure? This is useless, too — and a miserable way to live.

9 Two are better off than one, because together they can work more effectively. 10 If one of them falls down, the other can help him up. But if someone is alone and falls, it's just too bad, because there is no one to help him. 11 If it is cold, two can sleep together and stay warm, but how can you keep warm by yourself? 12 Two people can resist an attack that would defeat one person alone. A rope made of three cords is hard to break.

13-14 A man may rise from poverty to become king of his country, or go from prison to the throne, but if in his old age he is too foolish to take advice, he is not as well off as a young man who is poor but intelligent. 15 I thought about all the people who live in this world, and I realized that somewhere among them there is a young man who will take the king's place. 16 There may be no limit to the number of people a king rules; when he is gone, no one will be grateful for what he has done. It is useless. It is like chasing the wind.

Don't Make Rash Promises

5 Be careful about going to the Temple. It is better to go there to learn than to offer sacrifices as foolish people do, people

3.17 Probable text *its own set time*; Hebrew *its own set time there.*
3.22 *what we have... do;* or *our work, because we are going to have to do it anyway.*

ECCLESIASTES 5, 6   793

Eccles.

....

Songs
Isaiah
Jerem.
Lamen.
Ezekiel

who don't know right from wrong. ²Think before you speak, and don't make any rash promises to God. He is in heaven and you are on earth, so don't say any more than you have to. ³The more you worry, the more likely you are to have bad dreams, and the more you talk, the more likely you are to say something foolish. ⁴So when you make a promise to God, keep it as quickly as possible. He has no use for a fool. Do what you promise to do. ⁵Better not to promise at all than to make a promise and not keep it. ⁶Don't let your own words lead you into sin, so that you have to tell God's priest that you didn't mean it. Why make God angry with you? Why let him destroy what you have worked for? ⁷No matter how much you dream, how much useless work you do, or how much you talk, you must still stand in awe of God.

Life is Useless

⁸Don't be surprised when you see that the government oppresses the poor and denies them justice and their rights. Every official is protected by the one over him, and both are protected by still higher officials.

⁹Even a king depends on the harvest.*

¹⁰If you love money, you will never be satisfied; if you long to be rich, you will never get all you want. It is useless. ¹¹The richer you are, the more mouths you must feed. All you gain is the knowledge that you are rich. ¹²Workers may or may not have enough to eat, but at least they can get a good night's sleep. The rich, however, have so much that they stay awake worrying.

¹³Here is a terrible thing that I have seen in this world: people save up their money for a time when they may need it,* ¹⁴and then lose it all in some unlucky deal and end up with nothing left to pass on to their children. ¹⁵We leave this world just as we entered it — with nothing. In spite of all our work there is nothing we can take with us. ¹⁶It isn't right! We go just as we came. We labour, trying to catch the wind, and what do we get? ¹⁷We have to live our lives in darkness and grief,* worried, angry, and sick.

¹⁸This is what I have found out: the best thing anyone can do is to eat and drink and enjoy what he has worked for during the short life that God has given him; this is man's fate. ¹⁹If God gives a man wealth and property and lets him enjoy them, he should be grateful and enjoy what he has worked for. It is a gift from God. ²⁰Since God has allowed him to be happy, he will not worry too much about how short life is.

6 I have noticed that in this world a serious injustice is done. ²God will give someone wealth, honour, and property, yes, everything he wants, but then will not let him enjoy it. Some stranger will enjoy it instead. It is useless, and it's all wrong. ³A person may have a hundred children and live a long time, but no matter how long he lives, if he does not get his share of happiness and does not receive a decent burial, then I say that a baby born dead is better off. ⁴It does that baby no good to be born; it disappears into darkness, where it is forgotten. ⁵It never sees the light of day or knows what life is like, but at least it has found rest — ⁶more so than the man who never enjoys life, though he may live 2,000 years. After all, both of them are going to the same place.

....

5.9 Verse 9 in Hebrew is unclear.
5.13 *for... it*; or *to their own hurt*.
5.17 Some ancient translations *in darkness and grief*; Hebrew *eating in darkness*.

794

Eccles.

Nehem.
Esther
Job
Psalms
Proverbs

ECCLESIASTES 7.20

Write one list of all the

- GOOD -
DECISIONS

you have made this week
and another list of all
the bad decisions you
have made.

GOOD	BAD
_____	_____
_____	_____
_____	_____
_____	_____
_____	_____
_____	_____
_____	_____
_____	_____
_____	_____
_____	_____
_____	_____

Isn't it amazing that
Jesus knows all
of this and loves you
just the same?

7 People do all their work just to get something to eat, but they never have enough. 8 How are the wise better off than fools? What good does it do the poor to know how to face life? 9 It is useless; it is like chasing the wind. It is better to be satisfied with what you have than to be always wanting something else.

10 Everything that happens was already determined long ago, and we all know that you* cannot argue with someone who is stronger than you are. 11 The longer you argue, the more useless it is, and you are no better off. 12 How can anyone know what is best for us in this short, useless life of ours — a life that passes like a shadow? How can we know what will happen in the world after we die?

Thoughts about Life

7 A good reputation is better than expensive perfume; and the day you die is better than the day you are born.

2 It is better to go to a home where there is mourning than to one where there is a party, because the living should always remind themselves that death is waiting for us all.

3 Sorrow is better than laughter; it may sadden your face, but it sharpens your understanding.

4 Someone who is always thinking about happiness is a fool. A wise person thinks about death.

5 It is better to have wise people reprimand you than to have stupid people sing your praises.

6 When a fool laughs, it is like thorns crackling in a fire. It doesn't mean a thing.

7 You may be wise, but if you cheat someone, you are acting like a fool. If you take a bribe, you ruin your character.

8 The end of anything is better than its beginning.
Patience is better than pride.

9 Keep your temper under control; it is foolish to harbour a grudge.

10 Never ask, "Oh, why were things so much better in the old days?" It's not an intelligent question.

11 Everyone who lives ought to be wise; it is as good as receiving an inheritance 12 and will give you as much security as money can. Wisdom keeps you safe — this is the advantage of knowledge.

13 Think about what God has done. How can anyone straighten out what God has made crooked? 14 When things are going well for you, be glad, and when trouble comes, just remember: God sends both happiness and trouble; you never know what is going to happen next.*

15 My life has been useless, but in it I have seen everything. Some good people may die while others live on, even though they are evil. 16 So don't be too good or too wise — why kill yourself? 17 But don't be too wicked or too foolish, either — why die before you have to? 18 Avoid both extremes. If you have reverence for God, you will be successful anyway.

19 Wisdom does more for a person than ten rulers can do for a city.

20 There is no one on earth who does what is right all the time and never makes a mistake.

21 Don't pay attention to everything people say — you may hear your servant insulting you, 22 and you know yourself that you have insulted other people many times.

....

6.10 and we… you; or and our nature is already known; you.
7.14 you… next; or you cannot find fault with him.

ECCLESIASTES 7–9

795

Eccles.

·········

Songs
Isaiah
Jerem.
Lamen.
Ezekiel

²³ I used my wisdom to test all of this. I was determined to be wise, but it was beyond me. ²⁴ How can anyone discover what life means? It is too deep for us, too hard to understand. ²⁵ But I devoted myself to knowledge and study; I was determined to find wisdom and the answers to my questions, and to learn how wicked and foolish stupidity is.

²⁶ I found something more bitter than death — the woman who is like a trap. The love she offers you will catch you like a net; and her arms round you will hold you like a chain. A man who pleases God can get away, but she will catch the sinner. ²⁷ Yes, said the Philosopher, I found this out little by little while I was looking for answers. ²⁸ I have looked for other answers but have found none. I found one man in a thousand that I could respect, but not one woman. ²⁹ This is all that I have learnt: God made us plain and simple, but we have made ourselves very complicated.

8 Only the wise know what things really mean. Wisdom makes them smile and makes their frowns disappear.

Obey the King

² Do what the king says,* and don't make any rash promises to God. ³ The king can do anything he likes, so depart from his presence; don't stay in such a dangerous place. ⁴ The king acts with authority, and no one can challenge what he does. ⁵ As long as you obey his commands, you are safe, and a wise person knows how and when to do it. ⁶ There is a right time and a right way to do everything, but we know so little! ⁷ None of us knows what is going to happen, and there is no one to tell us. ⁸ No one can keep from dying or put off the day of death. That is a battle we cannot escape; we cannot cheat our way out.

The Wicked and the Righteous

⁹ I saw all this when I thought about the things that are done in this world, a world where some people have power and others have to suffer under them. ¹⁰ Yes, I have seen the wicked buried and in their graves, but on the way back from the cemetery people praise them in the very city where they did their evil. It is useless.*

¹¹ Why do people commit crimes so readily? Because crime is not punished quickly enough. ¹² A sinner may commit a hundred crimes and still live. Oh yes, I know what they say: "If you obey God, everything will be all right, ¹³ but it will not go well for the wicked. Their life is like a shadow and they will die young, because they do not obey God." ¹⁴ But this is nonsense. Look at what happens in the world: sometimes the righteous get the punishment of the wicked, and the wicked get the reward of the righteous. I say it is useless.

¹⁵ So I am convinced that we should enjoy ourselves, because the only pleasure we have in this life is eating and drinking and enjoying ourselves. We can at least do this as we labour during the life that God has given us in this world.

¹⁶ Whenever I tried to become wise and learn what goes on in the world, I realized that you could stay awake night and day ¹⁷ and never be able to understand what God is doing. However hard you try, you will never find out. The wise may claim to know, but they don't.

9 I thought long and hard about all this and saw that God controls the actions of wise and righteous people, even their

---

8.2 Some ancient translations *Do what the king says*; Hebrew unclear.
8.10 Verse 10 in Hebrew is unclear.

796

Eccles.

·:·········

Nehem.
Esther
Job
Psalms
Proverbs

ECCLESIASTES 9, 10

love and their hate. No one knows anything about what lies ahead. [2] It makes no difference.* The same fate comes to the righteous and the wicked, to the good and the bad,* to those who are religious and those who are not, to those who offer sacrifices and those who do not. A good person is no better off than a sinner; one who takes an oath is no better off than one who does not. [3] One fate comes to all alike, and this is as wrong as anything that happens in this world. As long as people live, their minds are full of evil and madness, and suddenly they die. [4] But anyone who is alive in the world of the living has some hope; a live dog is better off than a dead lion. [5] Yes, the living know they are going to die, but the dead know nothing. They have no further reward; they are completely forgotten. [6] Their loves, their hates, their passions, all died with them. They will never again take part in anything that happens in this world.

[7] Go ahead — eat your food and be happy; drink your wine and be cheerful. It's all right with God. [8] Always look happy and cheerful. [9] Enjoy life with the woman you love, as long as you live the useless life that God has given you in this world. Enjoy every useless day of it, because that is all you will get for all your trouble. [10] Work hard at whatever you do, because there will be no action, no thought, no knowledge, no wisdom in the world of the dead — and that is where you are going.

[11] I realized another thing, that in this world fast runners do not always win the race, and the brave do not always win the battle. The wise do not always earn a living, intelligent people do not always get rich, and capable people do not always rise to high positions. Bad luck happens to everyone. [12] You never know when your time is coming. Like birds suddenly caught in a trap, like fish caught in a net, we are trapped at some evil moment when we least expect it.

Thoughts on Wisdom and Foolishness

[13] There is something else I saw, a good example of how wisdom is regarded in this world. [14] There was a little town without many people in it. A powerful king attacked it. He surrounded it and prepared to break through the walls. [15] Someone lived there who was poor, but so clever that he could have saved the town. But no one thought about him.* [16] I have always said that wisdom is better than strength, but no one thinks of the poor as wise or pays any attention to what they say. [17] It is better to listen to the quiet words of a wise person than to the shouts of a ruler at a council of fools. [18] Wisdom does more good than weapons, but one sinner can undo a lot of good.

10 Dead flies can make a whole bottle of perfume stink, and a little stupidity can cancel out the greatest wisdom. [2] It is natural for the wise to do the right thing and for fools to do the wrong thing. [3] Their stupidity will be evident even to strangers they meet along the way; they let everyone know that they are fools.

[4] If your ruler becomes angry with you, do not hand in your resignation; serious wrongs may be pardoned if you keep calm.*

....

9.2 *people, even their… difference*; or *people, but no one knows whether it is out of love or hate.* [2] *It makes no difference what lies ahead of us.*
9.2 Some ancient translations *and the bad*; Hebrew does not have these words.
9.15 *he could have… him*; or *he saved the town. But later on no one remembered him.*
10.4 *keep calm*; or *submit to him.*

Eccles.

....

Songs
Isaiah
Jerem.
Lamen.
Ezekiel

5 Here is an injustice I have seen in the world — an injustice caused by rulers. 6 Stupid people are given positions of authority while the rich are ignored. 7 I have seen slaves on horseback while noblemen go on foot like slaves.

8 If you dig a pit, you fall in it; if you break through a wall, a snake bites you. 9 If you work in a stone quarry, you get hurt by stones. If you split wood, you get hurt doing it. 10 If your axe is blunt and you don't sharpen it, you have to work harder to use it. It is more sensible to plan ahead. 11 Knowing how to charm a snake is of no use if you let the snake bite first. 12 What the wise say brings them honour, but fools are destroyed by their own words. 13 They start out with silly talk and end up with pure madness. 14 A fool talks on and on.

No one knows what is going to happen next, and no one can tell us what will happen after we die.

15 Only someone too stupid to find his way home would wear himself out with work.

16 A country is in trouble when its king is a youth and its leaders feast all night long. 17 But a country is fortunate to have a king who makes his own decisions and leaders who eat at the proper time, who control themselves and don't get drunk.

18 When someone is too lazy to repair his roof, it will leak, and the house will fall in.

19 Feasting makes you happy and wine cheers you up, but you can't have either without money.

20 Don't criticize the king, even silently, and don't criticize the rich, even in the privacy of your bedroom. A bird might carry the message and tell them what you said.

What a Wise Person Does

11 Invest your money in foreign trade, and one of these days you will make a profit. 2 Put your investments in several places — many places, in fact — because you never know what kind of bad luck you are going to have in this world.

3 No matter in which direction a tree falls, it will lie where it fell. When the clouds are full, it rains. 4 If you wait until the wind and the weather are just right, you will never sow anything and never harvest anything. 5 God made everything, and you can no more understand what he does than you understand how new life begins in the womb of a pregnant woman. 6 Do your sowing in the morning and in the evening, too. You never know whether it will all grow well or whether one sowing will do better than the other.

7 It is good to be able to enjoy the pleasant light of day. 8 Be grateful for every year you live. No matter how long you live, remember that you will be dead much longer. There is nothing at all to look forward to.

Advice to Young People

9 Young people, enjoy your youth. Be happy while you are still young. Do what you want to do, and follow your heart's desire. But remember that God is going to judge you for whatever you do.

10 Don't let anything worry you or cause you pain. You aren't going to be young very long.

12 So remember your Creator* while you are still young, before those dismal days and years come when you will say, "I don't enjoy life." 2 That is when the light of the sun, the

12.1 The Hebrew expression for *your Creator* sounds like the Hebrew for *your grave.*

ECCLESIASTES 11.9-10

Write out here what your life might

- LOOK -

LIKE

if you did what was written in Ecclesiastes 11.9-10.

_____

_____

_____

_____

_____

_____

_____

_____

_____

_____

_____

_____

_____

moon, and the stars will grow dim for you, and the rain clouds will never pass away. [3] Then your arms, that have protected you, will tremble, and your legs, now strong, will grow weak. Your teeth will be too few to chew your food, and your eyes too dim to see clearly. [4] Your ears will be deaf to the noise of the street. You will barely be able to hear the mill as it grinds or music as it plays, but even the song of a bird will wake you from sleep. [5] You will be afraid of high places, and walking will be dangerous. Your hair will turn white; you will hardly be able to drag yourself along, and all desire will have gone.

We are going to our final resting place, and then there will be mourning in the streets. [6] The silver chain will snap, and the golden lamp will fall and break; the rope at the well will break, and the water jar will be shattered. [7] Our bodies will return to the dust of the earth, and the breath of life will go back to God, who gave it to us.

[8] Useless, useless, said the Philosopher. It is all useless.

The Summing Up

[9] But because the Philosopher was wise, he kept on teaching the people what he knew. He studied proverbs and honestly tested their truth. [10] The Philosopher tried to find comforting words, but the words he wrote were honest. [11] The sayings of the wise are like the sharp sticks that shepherds use to guide sheep, and collected proverbs are as lasting as firmly driven nails. They have been given by God, the one Shepherd of us all.

[12] My child, there is something else to watch out for. There is no end to the writing of books, and too much study will wear you out.

[13] After all this, there is only one thing to say: have reverence for God, and obey his commands, because this is all that human beings were created for. [14] God is going to judge everything we do, whether good or bad, even things done in secret.

THE BOOK OF

SONG OF SONGS

WRITTEN: PROBABLY BETWEEN 400 AND 100BC, BUT COULD BE MUCH EARLIER

WHAT YOU NEED TO KNOW:

This book is very different from other books of the Bible! Song of Songs is a series of love poems written as a celebration of human love between a man and a woman. As the book goes on, their love grows stronger, and the poems are full of word-pictures that describe their sexual relationship. This book was considered so rude that, in ancient Israel, men weren't allowed to read it until they were 30.

WHY READ IT?

This book is a demonstration of how being in love, in a God-honouring relationship, can enhance your relationship with God. It also shows that romantic relationships are not to be entered into lightly. The name 'Song of Songs' means 'the greatest song', which emphasises that these relationships are very special and need to be taken seriously.

Song of Songs shows us what romantic love looks like.

Go through and circle some of the adjectives that the man and woman use to describe each other.

Why do you think that a book like this might be included in the Bible?

What do you think God might be wanting us to know?

_____

_____

_____

_____

_____

_____

_____

_____

_____

_____

_____

_____

_____

LOVE

SONG OF SONGS COULD HAVE BEEN WRITTEN ANYTIME BETWEEN 900 AND 100BC!

1 The most beautiful of songs, by Solomon.*

The First Song

The Woman
² Your lips cover me with kisses;
    your love is better than wine.
³ There is a fragrance about you;
    the sound of your name recalls it.
    No woman could help loving you.
⁴ Take me with you, and we'll run away;
    be my king and take me to your room.
We will be happy together,
    drink deep, and lose ourselves in love.
    No wonder all women love you!
⁵ Women of Jerusalem, I am dark but* beautiful,
    dark as the desert tents of Kedar,
    but beautiful as the curtains in Solomon's palace.
⁶ Don't look down on me because of my colour,
    because the sun has tanned me.
My brothers were angry with me
    and made me work in the vineyard.
    I had no time to care for myself.
⁷ Tell me, my love,
    Where will you lead your flock to graze?
    Where will they rest from the noonday sun?
Why should I need to look for you
    among the flocks of the other shepherds?*

The Man
⁸ Don't you know the place, loveliest of women?
Go and follow the flock;
    find pasture for your goats
    near the tents of the shepherds.

⁹ You, my love, excite men
    as a mare excites the stallions of Pharaoh's chariots.
¹⁰ Your hair is beautiful upon your cheeks
    and falls along your neck like jewels.
¹¹ But we will make for you a chain of gold
    with ornaments of silver.

The Woman
¹² My king was lying on his couch,
    and my perfume filled the air with fragrance.
¹³ My lover has the scent of myrrh
    as he lies upon my breasts.
¹⁴ My lover is like the wild flowers
    that bloom in the vineyards at Engedi.

The Man
¹⁵ How beautiful you are, my love;
    how your eyes shine with love!

The Woman
¹⁶ How handsome you are, my dearest;

1.1 *by Solomon*; or *dedicated to Solomon*, or *about Solomon*.
1.5 *but*; or *and*.
1.7 Probable text *Why should I... shepherds*; Hebrew unclear.

Songs

....

Isaiah
Jerem.
Lamen.
Ezekiel
Daniel

how you delight me!
The green grass will be our bed;
17 the cedars will be the beams of our house,
and the cypress trees the ceiling.

2 I am only a wild flower in Sharon,
a lily in a mountain valley.

The Man
2 Like a lily among thorns
is my darling among women.

The Woman
3 Like an apple tree among the trees of the forest,
so is my dearest compared with other men.
I love to sit in its shadow,
and its fruit is sweet to my taste.
4 He brought me to his banqueting hall
and raised the banner of love over me.
5 Restore my strength with raisins
and refresh me with apples!
I am weak from passion.
6 His left hand is under my head,
and his right hand caresses me.
7 Promise me, women of Jerusalem;
swear by the swift deer and the gazelles
that you will not interrupt our love.

The Second Song

The Woman
8 I hear my lover's voice.
He comes running over the mountains,
racing across the hills to me.
9 My lover is like a gazelle,
like a young stag.
There he stands beside the wall.
He looks in through the window
and glances through the lattice.
10 My lover speaks to me.

The Man
Come then, my love;
my darling, come with me.
11 The winter is over; the rains have stopped;
12 in the countryside the flowers are in bloom.
This is the time for singing;
the song of doves is heard in the fields.
13 Figs are beginning to ripen;
the air is fragrant with blossoming vines.
Come then, my love;
my darling, come with me.
14 You are like a dove that hides
in the crevice of a rock.
Let me see your lovely face
and hear your enchanting voice.

15 Catch the foxes, the little foxes,
before they ruin our vineyard in bloom.

Colour these shapes. ↘

The Woman
16 My lover is mine, and I am his.
    He feeds his flock among the lilies
17   until the morning breezes blow
    and the darkness disappears.
    Return, my darling, like a gazelle,
    like a stag on the mountains of Bether.*

3 Asleep on my bed, night after night
    I dreamt of the one I love;
    I was looking for him, but couldn't find him.
2 I went wandering through the city,
    through its streets and alleys.
    I looked for the one I love.
    I looked, but couldn't find him.
3 The watchmen patrolling the city saw me.
    I asked them, "Have you found my lover?"
4 As soon as I left them, I found him.
    I held him and wouldn't let him go
    until I took him to my mother's house,
    to the room where I was born.

5 Promise me, women of Jerusalem;
    swear by the swift deer and the gazelles
    that you will not interrupt our love.

The Third Song

The Woman
6 What is this coming from the desert like a column of smoke,
    fragrant with incense and myrrh,
    the incense sold by the traders?
7 Solomon is coming, carried on his throne;
    sixty soldiers form the bodyguard,
    the finest soldiers in Israel.
8 All of them are skilful with the sword;
    they are battle-hardened veterans.
    Each of them is armed with a sword,
    on guard against a night attack.
9 King Solomon is carried on a throne
    made of the finest wood.
10 Its posts are covered with silver;
    over it is cloth embroidered with gold.
    Its cushions are covered with purple cloth,
    lovingly woven by the women of Jerusalem.
11 Women of Zion, come and see King Solomon.
    He is wearing the crown that his mother placed on his
        head
    on his wedding day,
    on the day of his gladness and joy.

The Man
4 How beautiful you are, my love!
    How your eyes shine with love behind your veil.
    Your hair dances, like a flock of goats
    bounding down the hills of Gilead.
2 Your teeth are as white as sheep
    that have just been shorn and washed.

2.17 *mountains of Bether*; or *rugged mountains*.

SONG OF SONGS 4, 5

803

Songs
....

Isaiah
Jerem.
Lamen.
Ezekiel
Daniel

Not one of them is missing;
  they are all perfectly matched.
3 Your lips are like a scarlet ribbon;
  how lovely they are when you speak.
Your cheeks glow behind your veil.
4 Your neck is like the tower of David,
  round and smooth,*
  with a necklace like a thousand shields hung round it.
5 Your breasts are like gazelles,
  twin deer feeding among lilies.
6 I will stay on the hill of myrrh,
  the hill of incense,
  until the morning breezes blow
  and the darkness disappears.
7 How beautiful you are, my love;
  how perfect you are!

8 Come with me from the Lebanon Mountains, my bride;
  come with me from Lebanon.
Come down from the top of Mount Amana,
  from Mount Senir and Mount Hermon,
  where the lions and leopards live.
9 The look in your eyes, my sweetheart and bride,
  and the necklace you are wearing
  have stolen my heart.
10 Your love delights me,
  my sweetheart and bride.
Your love is better than wine;
  your perfume more fragrant than any spice.
11 The taste of honey is on your lips, my darling;
  your tongue is milk and honey for me.
Your clothing has all the fragrance of Lebanon.

12 My sweetheart, my bride, is a secret garden,
  a walled garden, a private spring;
13   there the plants flourish.
They grow like an orchard of pomegranate trees
  and bear the finest fruits.
There is no lack of henna and nard,
14   of saffron, calamus, and cinnamon,
  or incense of every kind.
Myrrh and aloes grow there
  with all the most fragrant perfumes.
15 Fountains water the garden,
  streams of flowing water,
  brooks gushing down from the Lebanon Mountains.

The Woman
16 Wake up, North Wind.
South Wind, blow on my garden;
  fill the air with fragrance.
Let my lover come to his garden
  and eat the best of its fruits.

The Man
5 I have entered my garden,
  my sweetheart, my bride.

. . . .
4.4 *round and smooth*; Hebrew unclear.

I am gathering my spices and myrrh;
I am eating my honey and honeycomb;
I am drinking my wine and milk.

The Women
Eat, lovers, and drink
until you are drunk with love!

The Fourth Song

The Woman
² While I slept, my heart was awake.
I dreamt my lover knocked at the door.

The Man
Let me come in, my darling,
my sweetheart, my dove.
My head is wet with dew,
and my hair is damp from the mist.

The Woman
³ I have already undressed;
why should I get dressed again?
I have washed my feet;
why should I get them dirty again?

⁴ My lover put his hand to the door,
and I was thrilled that he was near.
⁵ I was ready to let him come in.
My hands were covered with myrrh,
my fingers with liquid myrrh,
as I grasped the handle of the door.
⁶ I opened the door for my lover,
but he had already gone.
How I wanted to hear his voice!
I looked for him, but couldn't find him;
I called to him, but heard no answer.

⁷ The watchmen patrolling the city found me;
they struck me and bruised me;
the guards at the city wall tore off my cape.
⁸ Promise me, women of Jerusalem,
that if you find my lover,
you will tell him I am weak from passion.

The Women
⁹ Most beautiful of women,
is your lover different from everyone else?
What is there so wonderful about him
that we should give you our promise?

The Woman
¹⁰ My lover is handsome and strong;
he is one in 10,000.
¹¹ His face is bronzed and smooth;
his hair is wavy,
black as a raven.
¹² His eyes are as beautiful as doves by a flowing brook,

SONG OF SONGS 5, 6

805

Songs

Isaiah
Jerem.
Lamen.
Ezekiel
Daniel

doves washed in milk and standing by the stream.*

13 His cheeks are as lovely as a garden
    that is full of herbs and spices.
  His lips are like lilies,
    wet with liquid myrrh.
14 His hands are well formed,
    and he wears rings set with gems.
  His body is like smooth ivory,*
    with sapphires set in it.
15 His thighs are columns of alabaster
    set in sockets of gold.
  He is majestic, like the Lebanon Mountains
    with their towering cedars.
16 His mouth is sweet to kiss;
    everything about him enchants me.
  This is what my lover is like,
    women of Jerusalem.

The Women

6 Most beautiful of women,
    where has your lover gone?
  Tell us which way your lover went,
    so that we can help you find him.

The Woman

2 My lover has gone to his garden,
    where the balsam trees grow.
  He is feeding his flock in the garden
    and gathering lilies.
3 My lover is mine, and I am his;
    he feeds his flock among the lilies.

The Fifth Song

The Man

4 My love, you are as beautiful as Jerusalem,
    as lovely as the city of Tirzah,
    as breathtaking as these great cities.*
5 Turn your eyes away from me;
    they are holding me captive.
  Your hair dances, like a flock of goats
    bounding down the hills of Gilead.
6 Your teeth are as white as a flock of sheep
    that have just been washed.
  Not one of them is missing;
    they are all perfectly matched.
7 Your cheeks glow behind your veil.
8 Let the king have sixty queens, eighty concubines,
    young women without number!
9 But I love only one,
    and she is as lovely as a dove.
  She is her mother's only daughter,
    her mother's favourite child.
  All women look at her and praise her;
    queens and concubines sing her praises.

SONG OF SONGS 6

Draw

- TWO LARGE -

CIRCLES

in the margins of these pages. If you were to get into a romantic relationship, what characteristics would you want the other person to have? (Think about their inside rather than their outside!) Write these things in one of the circles. In the other circle, write down the characteristics that you would like God to grow in you, if you were in that relationship. Spend some time thinking about this circle, and pray that God would continue to shape you into this kind of person, whether you are in a relationship or not.

....

5.12 *and standing by the stream*; Hebrew unclear.
5.14 *like smooth ivory*; Hebrew unclear.
6.4 *as breathtaking as… cities*; Hebrew unclear.

806

Songs

·:·········

Esther
Job
Psalms
Proverbs
Eccles.

SONG OF SONGS 6, 7

¹⁰ Who is this whose glance is like the dawn?
　　She is beautiful and bright,
　　　　as dazzling as the sun or the moon.*
¹¹ I have come down among the almond trees
　　to see the young plants in the valley,
　　to see the new leaves on the vines
　　and the blossoms on the pomegranate trees.
¹² I am trembling; you have made me as eager for love
　　as a chariot driver is for battle.*

The Women
¹³ Dance, dance,* girl of Shulam.
　　Let us watch you as you dance.

The Woman
　　Why do you want to watch me
　　　　as I dance between the rows of onlookers?

The Man
7 What a wonderful woman you are!
　　How beautiful are your feet in sandals.
　　The curve of your thighs
　　　　is like the work of an artist.
² A bowl is there,
　　that never runs out of spiced wine.
　A sheaf of wheat is there,
　　surrounded by lilies.
³ Your breasts are like twin deer,
　　like two gazelles.
⁴ Your neck is like a tower of ivory.
　Your eyes are like the pools in the city of Heshbon,
　　near the gate of that great city.
　Your nose is as lovely as the tower of Lebanon
　　that stands guard at Damascus.
⁵ Your head is held high like Mount Carmel.
　Your braided hair shines like the finest satin;
　its beauty* could hold a king captive.

⁶ How pretty you are, how beautiful;
　　how complete the delights of your love.
⁷ You are as graceful as a palm tree,
　　and your breasts are clusters of dates.
⁸ I will climb the palm tree
　　and pick its fruit.
　To me your breasts are like bunches of grapes,
　　your breath like the fragrance of apples,
⁹　and your mouth like the finest wine.

The Woman
　　Then let the wine flow straight to my lover,
　　　　flowing over his lips and teeth.*
¹⁰ I belong to my lover, and he desires me.
¹¹ Come, darling, let's go out to the countryside

6.10 *as dazzling as... moon*; Hebrew unclear.
6.12 Verse 12 in Hebrew is unclear.
6.13 *Dance, dance*; or *Come back, come back*.
7.5 *beauty*; Hebrew unclear.
7.9 Some ancient translations *lips and teeth*; Hebrew *lips of those who sleep*.

SONG OF SONGS 7, 8

807

Songs

Isaiah
Jerem.
Lamen.
Ezekiel
Daniel

and spend the night in the villages.*
¹² We will get up early and look at the vines
to see whether they've started to grow,
whether the blossoms are opening
and the pomegranate trees are in bloom.
There I will give you my love.
¹³ You can smell the scent of mandrakes,
and all the pleasant fruits are near our door.
Darling, I have kept for you
the old delights and the new.

8 I wish that you were my brother,
that my mother had nursed you at her breast.
Then, if I met you in the street,
I could kiss you and no one would mind.
² I would take you to my mother's house,
where you could teach me love.
I would give you spiced wine,
my pomegranate wine to drink.

³ Your left hand is under my head,
and your right hand caresses me.

⁴ Promise me, women of Jerusalem,
that you will not interrupt our love.

The Sixth Song

The Women
⁵ Who is this coming from the desert,
arm in arm with her lover?

The Woman
Under the apple tree I woke you,
in the place where you were born.
⁶ Close your heart to every love but mine;
hold no one in your arms but me.
Love is as powerful as death;
passion is as strong as death itself.
It bursts into flame
and burns like a raging fire.
⁷ Water cannot put it out;
no flood can drown it.
But if anyone tried to buy love with wealth,
contempt is all they would get.

The Woman's Brothers
⁸ We have a young sister,
and her breasts are still small.
What will we do for her
when a young man comes courting?
⁹ If she is a wall,
we will build her a silver tower.
But if she is a gate,
we will protect her with panels of cedar.

7.11 *villages*; or *fields*.

The Woman

10 I am a wall,
      and my breasts are its towers.
   My lover knows that with him
      I find contentment and peace.

The Man

11 Solomon has a vineyard
      in a place called Baal Hamon.
   There are farmers who rent it from him;
      each one pays a thousand silver coins.
12 Solomon is welcome to his thousand coins,
      and the farmers to 200 as their share;
   I have a vineyard of my own!

13 Let me hear your voice from the garden, my love;
      my companions are waiting to hear you speak.

The Woman

14 Come to me, my lover, like a gazelle,
      like a young stag on the mountains where spices grow.

THE BOOK OF

ISAIAH

WRITTEN: PROBABLY IN THREE PARTS,
THE EARLIEST BETWEEN 800 AND 700BC

Read about the calling of Isaiah in chapter 6.
What do you think are some of the characteristics
that define someone as a 'prophet'?

_____

_____

_____

_____

_____

_____

Underline all the prophecies that could

RELATE TO

JESUS

in the book of Isaiah.

WHAT YOU NEED TO KNOW:

Isaiah is the first of the Bible's 'Major Prophets'
(meaning 'longest' rather than 'most important'). A
prophet is someone who is specially gifted and
inspired to speak words from God. Prophecy is more
than just predicting the future; it is about
revealing God's love and plans for his people. As
the kings of Israel and Judah pulled people further
and further away from God, God sent prophets to
warn his people of what would happen if they
continued to live apart from him. Isaiah prophesied
about the kingdoms of Judah and Israel, as well as
the surrounding powerful nations.

The book of Isaiah is divided into three main parts.
It starts with messages of judgement and warning
(chapters 1-39), but then switches to words of love
and hope (chapters 40-55 and 56-66). In several
chapters throughout the book, we hear Isaiah
speaking of a coming saviour, a Messiah who will
save the Israelites from their sinful ways.

WHY READ IT?

Isaiah is a great book to read to understand the
calling and purpose of a prophet. Chapter 6 shows us
God's calling of Isaiah. Then come several messages
from God to the Israelites and their neighbours.
Although there are some harsh words in the first
half of the book, the second half - containing the
prophecies of hope and of a coming Messiah - is
life-giving and hopeful for us today, too.

734BC

ISRAEL FALLS
TO ASSYRIA

JUDAH FALLS
TO BABYLON

JEWS RETURN
FROM EXILE

515BC

ISAIAH 1.18

Grab a red pen or pencil and
SCRIBBLE A RED PATCH
on this page. Then compare
this colour to the white
space around it. This is the
difference that Jesus
makes in your life when

— HE —

FORGIVES

YOU

for all your mistakes,
past and future.

scribble!

1 This book contains the messages about Judah and Jerusalem which God revealed to Isaiah son of Amoz during the time when Uzziah, Jotham, Ahaz, and Hezekiah were kings of Judah.

God Reprimands his People

²The LORD said, "Earth and sky, listen to what I am saying! The children I brought up have rebelled against me. ³Cattle know who owns them, and donkeys know where their master feeds them. But that is more than my people Israel know. They don't understand at all."

⁴You are doomed, you sinful nation, you corrupt and evil people! Your sins drag you down! You have rejected the LORD, the holy God of Israel, and have turned your backs on him. ⁵Why do you keep on rebelling? Do you want to be punished even more? Israel, your head is already covered with wounds, and your heart and mind are sick. ⁶From head to foot there is not a healthy spot on your body. You are covered with bruises and sores and open wounds. Your wounds have not been cleaned or bandaged. No ointment has been put on them.

⁷Your country has been devastated, and your cities have been burnt to the ground. While you look on, foreigners take over your land and bring everything to ruin. ⁸Jerusalem alone is left, a city under siege — as defenceless as a guard's hut in a vineyard or a shed in a cucumber field. ⁹If the LORD Almighty had not let some of the people survive, Jerusalem would have been totally destroyed, just as Sodom and Gomorrah were.

¹⁰Jerusalem, your rulers and your people are like those of Sodom and Gomorrah. Listen to what the LORD is saying to you. Pay attention to what our God is teaching you. ¹¹He says, "Do you think I want all these sacrifices you keep offering to me? I have had more than enough of the sheep you burn as sacrifices and of the fat of your fine animals. I am tired of the blood of bulls and sheep and goats. ¹²Who asked you to bring me all this when you come to worship me? Who asked you to do all this tramping about in my Temple? ¹³It's useless to bring your offerings. I am disgusted with the smell of the incense you burn. I cannot stand your New Moon Festivals, your Sabbaths, and your religious gatherings; they are all corrupted by your sins. ¹⁴I hate your New Moon Festivals and holy days; they are a burden that I am tired of bearing.

¹⁵"When you lift your hands in prayer, I will not look at you. No matter how much you pray, I will not listen, for your hands are covered with blood. ¹⁶Wash yourselves clean. Stop all this evil that I see you doing. Yes, stop doing evil ¹⁷and learn to do right. See that justice is done — help those who are oppressed, give orphans their rights, and defend widows."

¹⁸The LORD says, "Now, let's settle the matter. You are stained red with sin, but I will wash you as clean as snow.* Although your stains are deep red, you will be as white as wool.* ¹⁹If you will only obey me, you will eat the good things the land produces. ²⁰But if you defy me, you are doomed to die. I, the LORD, have spoken."

The Sinful City

²¹The city that once was faithful is behaving like a whore! At one time it was filled with righteous people, but now only murderers

---

1.18 *sin, but... snow*; or *sin; do you think I will wash you as clean as snow?*
1.18 *Although your... wool*; or *Your stains are deep red; do you think you will be as white as wool?*

ISAIAH 1, 2

811

Isaiah

....

Jerem.

Lamen.

Ezekiel

Daniel

Hosea

remain. [22] Jerusalem, you were once like silver, but now you are worthless; you were like good wine, but now you are only water. [23] Your leaders are rebels and friends of thieves; they are always accepting gifts and bribes. They never defend orphans in court or listen when widows present their case.

[24] So now, listen to what the Lord Almighty, Israel's powerful God, is saying: "I will take revenge on you, my enemies, and you will cause me no more trouble. [25] I will take action against you. I will purify you just as metal is refined, and will remove all your impurity. [26] I will give you rulers and advisers like those you had long ago. Then Jerusalem will be called the righteous, faithful city."

[27] Because the Lord is righteous, he will save Jerusalem and everyone there who repents. [28] But he will crush everyone who sins and rebels against him; he will kill everyone who forsakes him.

[29] You will be sorry that you ever worshipped trees and planted sacred gardens.* [30] You will wither like a dying oak, like a garden that no one waters. [31] Just as straw is set on fire by a spark, so powerful people will be destroyed by their own evil deeds, and no one will be able to stop the destruction.

Everlasting Peace
(Mic 4.1–3)

2 This is the message which God gave to Isaiah son of Amoz about Judah and Jerusalem:

[2] In days to come
the mountain where the Temple stands
will be the highest one of all,
towering above all the hills.
Many nations will come streaming to it,
[3] and their people will say,
"Let us go up the hill of the Lord,*
to the Temple of Israel's God.
He will teach us what he wants us to do;
we will walk in the paths he has chosen.
For the Lord's teaching comes from Jerusalem;
from Zion he speaks to his people."

[4] He will settle disputes among great nations.
They will hammer their swords into ploughs
and their spears into pruning knives.
Nations will never again go to war,
never prepare for battle again.
[5] Now, descendants of Jacob, let us walk in the light which the Lord gives us!

Arrogance will be Destroyed

[6] O God, you have forsaken your people, the descendants of Jacob! The land is full of magic practices from the east and from Philistia.* The people follow foreign customs. [7] Their land is full of silver and gold, and there is no end to their treasures. Their land is full of horses, and there is no end to their chariots. [8] Their land

....

1.29 *sacred gardens*: People believed that dedicating a garden to a fertility god would cause him to bless their crops.
2.3 *hill of the Lord*: Mount Zion, the hill in Jerusalem on which the Temple was built.
2.6 Probable text *The land… Philistia*; Hebrew unclear.

812

Isaiah

Job
Psalms
Proverbs
Eccles.
Songs

is full of idols, and they worship objects that they have made with their own hands.

⁹Everyone will be humiliated and disgraced. Do not forgive them, LORD!

¹⁰They will hide in caves in the rocky hills or dig holes in the ground to try to escape from the LORD's anger and to hide from his power and glory! ¹¹A day is coming when human pride will be ended and human arrogance destroyed. Then the LORD alone will be exalted. ¹²On that day the LORD Almighty will humble everyone who is powerful, everyone who is proud and conceited. ¹³He will destroy the tall cedars of Lebanon and all the oaks in the land of Bashan. ¹⁴He will level the high mountains and hills, ¹⁵every high tower, and the walls of every fortress. ¹⁶He will sink even the largest and most beautiful ships. ¹⁷⁻¹⁸Human pride will be ended, and human arrogance will be destroyed. Idols will completely disappear, and the LORD alone will be exalted on that day.

¹⁹People will hide in caves in the rocky hills or dig holes in the ground to try to escape from the LORD's anger and to hide from his power and glory, when he comes to shake the earth. ²⁰When that day comes, they will throw away the gold and silver idols they have made, and abandon them to the moles and the bats. ²¹When the LORD comes to shake the earth, people will hide in holes and caves in the rocky hills to try to escape from his anger and to hide from his power and glory.

²²Put no more confidence in mortals. What are they worth?

Chaos in Jerusalem

3 Now the Lord, the Almighty LORD, is about to take away from Jerusalem and Judah everything and everyone that the people depend on. He is going to take away their food and their water, ²their heroes and their soldiers, their judges and their prophets, their fortune tellers and their statesmen, ³their military and civilian leaders, their politicians and everyone who uses magic to control events. ⁴The LORD will let the people be governed by immature boys. ⁵Everyone will take advantage of everyone else. Young people will not respect their elders, and worthless people will not respect their superiors.

⁶A time will come when the members of a clan will choose one of their number and say to him, "You at least have something to wear, so be our leader in this time of trouble."

⁷But he will answer, "Not me! I can't help you. I haven't any food or clothes either. Don't make me your leader!"

⁸Yes, Jerusalem is doomed! Judah is collapsing! Everything they say and do is against the LORD; they openly insult God himself. ⁹Their prejudices will be held against them. They sin as openly as the people of Sodom did. They are doomed, and they have brought it on themselves.

¹⁰The righteous will be happy,* and things will go well for them. They will be able to enjoy what they have worked for. ¹¹But evil people are doomed; what they have done to others will now be done to them.

¹²Moneylenders oppress my people, and their creditors cheat them.

My people, your leaders are misleading you, so that you do not know which way to turn.

3.10 Probable text *The righteous will be happy*; Hebrew *Say to the righteous.*

ISAIAH 3–5

813

Isaiah

Jerem.

Lamen.

Ezekiel

Daniel

Hosea

The Lord Judges his People

[13] The Lord is ready to state his case; he is ready to judge his people.* [14] The Lord is bringing the elders and leaders of his people to judgement. He makes this accusation: "You have plundered vineyards, and your houses are full of what you have taken from the poor. [15] You have no right to crush my people and take advantage of the poor. I, the Sovereign Lord Almighty, have spoken."

A Warning to the Women of Jerusalem

[16] The Lord said, "Look how proud the women of Jerusalem are! They walk along with their noses in the air. They are always flirting. They take dainty little steps, and the bracelets on their ankles jingle. [17] But I will punish them — I will shave their heads and leave them bald."

[18] A day is coming when the Lord will take away from the women of Jerusalem everything they are so proud of — the ornaments they wear on their ankles, on their heads, on their necks, [19] and on their wrists. He will take away their veils [20] and their hats; the magic charms they wear on their arms and at their waists; [21] the rings they wear on their fingers and in their noses; [22] all their fine robes, gowns, cloaks, and purses; [23] their revealing garments, their linen handkerchiefs, and the scarves and long veils they wear on their heads.

[24] Instead of using perfumes, they will stink; instead of fine belts, they will wear coarse ropes; instead of having beautiful hair, they will be bald; instead of fine clothes, they will be dressed in rags; their beauty will be turned to shame!

[25] The men of the city, yes, even the strongest men, will be killed in war. [26] The city gates will mourn and cry, and the city itself will be like a woman sitting on the ground, stripped naked.

4 When that time comes, seven women will grab hold of one man and say, "We can feed and clothe ourselves, but please let us say you are our husband, so that we won't have to endure the shame of being unmarried."

Jerusalem will be Restored

[2] The time is coming when the Lord will make every plant and tree in the land grow large and beautiful. All the people of Israel who survive will take delight and pride in the crops that the land produces. [3] Everyone who is left in Jerusalem, whom God has chosen for survival, will be called holy. [4] By his power the Lord will judge and purify the nation and wash away the guilt of Jerusalem and the blood that has been shed there. [5] Then over Mount Zion and over all who are gathered there, the Lord will send a cloud in the daytime and smoke and a bright flame at night. God's glory will cover and protect the whole city. [6] His glory will shade the city from the heat of the day and make it a place of safety, sheltered from the rain and storm.

The Song of the Vineyard

5 Listen while I sing you this song,
  a song of my friend and his vineyard:
  My friend had a vineyard
    on a very fertile hill.
[2] He dug the soil and cleared it of stones;
    he planted the finest vines.

3.13 Some ancient translations *his people*; Hebrew *the peoples*.

814

Isaiah

: ....

Job
Psalms
Proverbs
Eccles.
Songs

ISAIAH 5

He built a tower to guard them,
    dug a pit for treading the grapes.
He waited for the grapes to ripen,
    but every grape was sour.
³ So now my friend says, "You people who live in Jerusalem and Judah, judge between my vineyard and me. ⁴ Is there anything I failed to do for it? Then why did it produce sour grapes and not the good grapes I expected?

⁵ "This is what I am going to do to my vineyard; I will take away the hedge round it, break down the wall that protects it, and let wild animals eat it and trample it down. ⁶ I will let it be overgrown with weeds. I will not prune the vines or hoe the ground; instead I will let briars and thorns cover it. I will even forbid the clouds to let rain fall on it."

⁷ Israel is the vineyard of the LORD Almighty;
    the people of Judah are the vines he planted.
He expected them to do what was good,
    but instead they committed murder.
He expected them to do what was right,
    but their victims cried out for justice.

The Evil that People Do

⁸ You are doomed! You buy more houses and fields to add to those you already have. Soon there will be nowhere for anyone else to live, and you alone will live in the land. ⁹ I have heard the LORD Almighty say, "All these big, fine houses will be empty ruins. ¹⁰ The grapevines growing on ten hectares of land will yield only eight litres of wine. 180 litres of seed will produce only eighteen litres of corn."

¹¹ You are doomed! You get up early in the morning to start drinking, and you spend long evenings getting drunk. ¹² At your feasts you have harps and tambourines and flutes — and wine. But you don't understand what the LORD is doing, ¹³ and so you will be carried away as prisoners. Your leaders will starve to death, and the common people will die of thirst. ¹⁴ The world of the dead is hungry for them, and it opens its mouth wide. It gulps down the nobles of Jerusalem along with the noisy crowd of common people.

¹⁵ Everyone will be disgraced, and all who are proud will be humbled. ¹⁶ But the LORD Almighty shows his greatness by doing what is right, and he reveals his holiness by judging his people. ¹⁷ In the ruins of the cities lambs will eat grass and young goats will find pasture.*

¹⁸ You are doomed! You are unable to break free from your sins. ¹⁹ You say, "Let the LORD hurry up and do what he says he will, so that we can see it. Let Israel's holy God carry out his plans; let's see what he has in mind."

²⁰ You are doomed! You call evil good and call good evil. You turn darkness into light and light into darkness. You make what is bitter sweet, and what is sweet you make bitter.

²¹ You are doomed! You think you are wise, so very clever.

²² You are doomed! Heroes of the wine bottle! Brave and fearless when it comes to mixing drinks! ²³ But for just a bribe you let the guilty go free, and you prevent the innocent from getting justice. ²⁴ So now, just as straw and dry grass shrivel and burn in the fire, your roots will rot and your blossoms will dry up and blow away, because you have rejected what the

....

5.17 Verse 17 in Hebrew is unclear.

ISAIAH 5, 6

815

Isaiah
.......................:
Jerem.
Lamen.
Ezekiel
Daniel
Hosea

Lord Almighty, Israel's holy God, has taught us. 25 The Lord is angry with his people and has stretched out his hand to punish them. The mountains will shake, and the bodies of those who die will be left in the streets like rubbish. Yet even then the Lord's anger will not be ended, but his hand will still be stretched out to punish.

26 The Lord gives a signal to call for a distant nation.* He whistles for them to come from the ends of the earth. And here they come, swiftly, quickly! 27 None of them grows tired; none of them stumbles. They never doze or sleep. Not a belt is loose; not a sandal strap is broken. 28 Their arrows are sharp, and their bows are ready to shoot. Their horses' hooves are as hard as flint, and their chariot-wheels turn like a whirlwind. 29 The soldiers roar like lions that have killed an animal and are carrying it off where no one can take it away from them.

30 When that day comes, they will roar over Israel as loudly as the sea. Look at this country! Darkness and distress! The light is swallowed by darkness.

God Calls Isaiah to be a Prophet

6 In the year that King Uzziah died, I saw the Lord. He was sitting on his throne, high and exalted, and his robe filled the whole Temple. 2 Round him flaming creatures were standing, each of which had six wings. Each creature covered its face with two wings, and its body with two, and used the other two for flying. 3 They were calling out to each other:

"Holy, holy, holy!
The Lord Almighty is holy!
His glory fills the world."

4 The sound of their voices made the foundation of the Temple shake, and the Temple itself was filled with smoke.

5 I said, "There is no hope for me! I am doomed because every word that passes my lips is sinful, and I live among a people whose every word is sinful. And yet, with my own eyes, I have seen the King, the Lord Almighty!"

6 Then one of the creatures flew down to me, carrying a burning coal that he had taken from the altar with a pair of tongs. 7 He touched my lips with the burning coal and said, "This has touched your lips, and now your guilt is gone, and your sins are forgiven."

8 Then I heard the Lord say, "Whom shall I send? Who will be our messenger?"

I answered, "I will go! Send me!"

9 So he told me to go and give the people this message: "No matter how much you listen, you will not understand. No matter how much you look, you will not know what is happening." 10 Then he said to me, "Make the minds of these people dull, their ears deaf, and their eyes blind, so that they cannot see or hear or understand. If they did, they might turn to me and be healed."

11 I asked, "How long will it be like this, Lord?"

He answered, "Until the cities are ruined and empty — until the houses are uninhabited — until the land itself is a desolate waste. 12 I will send the people far away and make the whole land desolate. 13 Even if one person out of ten remains in the land, he too will be destroyed; he will be like the stump of an oak tree that has been cut down."

(The stump represents a new beginning for God's people.)

....
5.26 Probable text *a distant nation*; Hebrew *distant nations*.

ISAIAH 6

In the Old Testament there are LOADS of prophecies - where someone is called by God to bring a special message to his people. What does it all mean?

WE MADE A

FILM

ABOUT IT.

Head to
gnbyouthedition.co.uk/prophecy
to watch it.

ISAIAH 6.8

Read Isaiah 6.8
and then pray a

SIMILAR PRAYER

TO GOD.

Ask him where he might want to send you - this week, this year, and in your whole life.

816

Isaiah

⁖⋯⋯

Job
Psalms
Proverbs
Eccles.
Songs

ISAIAH 7

A Message for King Ahaz

7 When King Ahaz, the son of Jotham and grandson of Uzziah, ruled Judah, war broke out. Rezin, king of Syria, and Pekah son of Remaliah, king of Israel, attacked Jerusalem, but were unable to capture it.

² When word reached the king of Judah that the armies of Syria were already in the territory of Israel, he and all his people were so terrified that they trembled like trees shaking in the wind.

³ The LORD said to Isaiah, "Take your son Shear Jashub,* and go to meet King Ahaz. You will find him on the road where the cloth makers work, at the end of the ditch that brings water from the upper pool. ⁴ Tell him to keep alert, to stay calm, and not to be frightened or disturbed. The anger of King Rezin and his Syrians and of King Pekah is no more dangerous than the smoke from two smouldering sticks. ⁵ Syria, together with Israel and its king, has made a plot. ⁶ They intend to invade Judah, terrify the people into joining their side, and then put Tabeel's son on the throne.

⁷ "But I, the LORD, declare that this will never happen. ⁸ Why? Because Syria is no stronger than Damascus, its capital city, and Damascus is no stronger than King Rezin. As for Israel, within 65 years it will be too shattered to survive as a nation. ⁹ Israel is no stronger than Samaria, its capital city, and Samaria is no stronger than King Pekah.

"If your faith is not enduring, you will not endure."

The Sign of Immanuel

¹⁰ The LORD sent another message to Ahaz: ¹¹ "Ask the LORD your God to give you a sign. It can be from deep in the world of the dead or from high up in heaven."

¹² Ahaz answered, "I will not ask for a sign. I refuse to put the LORD to the test."

¹³ To that Isaiah replied, "Listen, now, descendants of King David. It's bad enough for you to wear out the patience of people — must you wear out God's patience too? ¹⁴ Well then, the Lord himself will give you a sign: a young woman* who is pregnant will have a son and will name him 'Immanuel.'* ¹⁵ By the time he is old enough to make his own decisions, people will be drinking milk and eating honey.* ¹⁶ Even before that time comes, the lands of those two kings who terrify you will be deserted.

¹⁷ "The LORD is going to bring on you, on your people, and on the whole royal family, days of trouble worse than any that have come since the kingdom of Israel separated from Judah — he is going to bring the king of Assyria.

¹⁸ "When that time comes, the LORD will whistle as a signal for the Egyptians to come like flies from the farthest branches of the Nile, and for the Assyrians to come from their land like bees. ¹⁹ They will swarm in the rugged valleys and in the caves in the rocks, and they will cover every thorn bush and every pasture.

⋯⋯⋯⋯⋯⋯⋯⋯⋯⋯⋯⋯⋯⋯⋯⋯⋯⋯⋯⋯⋯⋯⋯⋯⋯⋯⋯⋯

7.3 *Shear Jashub*: This name in Hebrew means "A few will come back" (see 10.20–22).

7.14 *young woman*: The Hebrew word here translated "young woman" is not the specific term for "virgin", but refers to any young woman of marriageable age. The use of "virgin" in Mt 1.23 reflects a Greek translation of the Old Testament, made some 500 years after Isaiah.

7.14 *Immanuel*: This name in Hebrew means "God is with us".

7.15 *milk and honey*: These foods were associated with the earlier days of Israel's history.

ISAIAH 7, 8

817

Isaiah

............⁝

Jerem.
Lamen.
Ezekiel
Daniel
Hosea

²⁰"When that time comes, the Lord will hire a barber from across the Euphrates — the emperor of Assyria! — and he will shave off your beards, and the hair on your heads and your bodies.

²¹"When that time comes, even if a farmer has been able to save only one young cow and two goats, ²²they will give so much milk that he will have all he needs. Yes, the few survivors left in the land will have milk and honey to eat.

²³"When that time comes, the fine vineyards, each with a thousand vines and each worth a thousand pieces of silver, will be overgrown with thorn bushes and briars. ²⁴People will go hunting there with bows and arrows. Yes, the whole country will be full of briars and thorn bushes. ²⁵All the hills where crops used to grow will be so overgrown with thorns that no one will go there. It will be a place where cattle and sheep graze."

Isaiah's Son as a Sign to the People

8 The LORD said to me, "Take a large piece of writing material and write on it in large letters:* 'Quick Loot, Fast Plunder'. ²Get two reliable men, the priest Uriah and Zechariah son of Jeberechiah, to serve as witnesses."

³Some time later my wife became pregnant. When our son was born, the LORD said to me, "Name him 'Quick-Loot-Fast-Plunder'. ⁴Before the boy is old enough to say 'Mummy' and 'Daddy', all the wealth of Damascus and all the loot of Samaria will be carried off by the king of Assyria."

The Emperor of Assyria is Coming

⁵The LORD spoke to me again. ⁶He said, "Because these people have rejected the quiet waters from the brook of Shiloah,* and tremble* before King Rezin and King Pekah, ⁷I, the Lord, will bring the emperor of Assyria and all his forces to attack Judah. They will advance like the flood waters of the River Euphrates, overflowing all its banks. ⁸They will sweep through Judah in a flood, rising shoulder high and covering everything."

God is with us! His outspread wings protect the land.*

⁹Gather together in fear, you nations! Listen, you distant parts of the earth. Get ready to fight, but be afraid! Yes, get ready, but be afraid! ¹⁰Make your plans! But they will never succeed. Talk as much as you like! But it is all useless, because God is with us.

The LORD Warns the Prophet

¹¹With his great power the LORD warned me not to follow the path which the people were following. He said, ¹²"Do not join in the schemes of the people and do not be afraid of the things that they fear. ¹³Remember that I, the LORD Almighty, am holy; I am the one you must fear. ¹⁴Because of my awesome holiness I am like a stone that people stumble over; I am like a trap that will catch the people of the kingdoms of Judah and Israel and the people of Jerusalem. ¹⁵Many will stumble; they will fall and be crushed. They will be caught in a trap."

....

8.1 *large letters*; or *letters that everyone can read.*
8.6 *brook of Shiloah*: A stream which flowed from the large spring on the eastern side of Jerusalem.
8.6 Probable text *tremble*; Hebrew *rejoice.*
8.8 *everything." God... land*; or *everything. They will spread out over the land. God be with us!"*

818

Isaiah

Job
Psalms
Proverbs
Eccles.
Songs

ISAIAH 8, 9

Circle your
**FAVOURITE
PASSAGE**
on this page.

Warning against Consulting the Dead

16 You, my disciples are to guard and preserve the messages that God has given me. 17 The LORD has hidden himself from his people, but I trust him and place my hope in him.

18 Here I am with the children the LORD has given me. The LORD Almighty, whose throne is on Mount Zion, has sent us as living messages to the people of Israel.

19 But people will tell you to ask for messages from fortune tellers and mediums, who chirp and mutter. They will say, "After all, people should ask for messages from the spirits and consult the dead on behalf of the living."

20 You are to answer them, "Listen to what the LORD is teaching you! Don't listen to mediums — what they tell you cannot keep trouble away."*

A Time of Trouble

21 The people will wander through the land, discouraged and hungry. In their hunger and their anger they will curse their king and their God. They may look up to the sky 22 or stare at the ground, but they will see nothing but trouble and darkness, terrifying darkness into which they are being driven.

9 There will be no way for them to escape from this time of trouble.

The Future King

The land of the tribes of Zebulun and Naphtali was once disgraced, but the future will bring honour to this region, from the Mediterranean eastwards to the land on the other side of the Jordan, and even to Galilee itself, where the foreigners live.

2 The people who walked in darkness
    have seen a great light.
They lived in a land of shadows,
    but now light is shining on them.
3 You have given them great joy,* LORD;
    you have made them happy.
They rejoice in what you have done,
    as people rejoice when they harvest their corn
    or when they divide captured wealth.
4 For you have broken the yoke that burdened them
    and the rod that beat their shoulders.
You have defeated the nation
    that oppressed and exploited your people,
    just as you defeated the army of Midian long ago.
5 The boots of the invading army
    and all their bloodstained clothing
    will be destroyed by fire.
6 A child is born to us!
    A son is given to us!
    And he will be our ruler.
He will be called, "Wonderful* Counsellor",
    "Mighty God", "Eternal Father",
    "Prince of Peace".
7 His royal power will continue to grow;
    his kingdom will always be at peace.

8.20 Verse 20 in Hebrew is unclear.
9.3 Probable text *You have given them great joy*; Hebrew *You have increased the nation.*
9.6 *Wonderful*; or *Wise*.

819

Isaiah

Jerem.
Lamen.
Ezekiel
Daniel
Hosea

He will rule as King David's successor,
basing his power on right and justice,
from now until the end of time.
The LORD Almighty is determined to do all this.

The LORD will Punish Israel
[8] The Lord has pronounced judgement on the kingdom of Israel, on the descendants of Jacob. [9] All the people of Israel, everyone who lives in the city of Samaria, will know that he has done this. Now they are proud and arrogant. They say, [10] "The brick buildings have fallen down, but we will replace them with stone buildings. The beams of sycamore wood have been cut down, but we will replace them with the finest cedar."

[11] The LORD has stirred up their enemies* to attack them. [12] Syria on the east and Philistia on the west have opened their mouths to devour Israel. Yet even so the LORD's anger is not ended; his hand is still stretched out to punish.

[13] The people of Israel have not repented; even though the LORD Almighty has punished them, they have not returned to him. [14] In a single day the LORD will punish Israel's leaders and its people; he will cut them off, head and tail. [15] The old and honourable men are the head — and the tail is the prophets whose teachings are lies! [16] Those who lead these people have misled them and totally confused them. [17] And so the Lord will not let any of the young men escape, and he will not show pity to any of the widows and orphans, because all the people are godless and wicked and everything they say is evil. Yet even so the LORD's anger will not be ended, but his hand will still be stretched out to punish.

[18] The wickedness of the people burns like a fire that destroys thorn bushes and thistles. It burns like a forest fire that sends up columns of smoke. [19] Because the LORD Almighty is angry, his punishment burns like a fire throughout the land and destroys the people, and it is everyone for himself. [20] Everywhere in the country people snatch and eat any bit of food they can find, but their hunger is never satisfied. They even eat their own children! [21] The people of Manasseh and the people of Ephraim attack each other, and together they attack Judah. Yet even so the LORD's anger is not ended; his hand is still stretched out to punish.

10 You are doomed! You make unjust laws that oppress my people. [2] That is how you prevent the poor from having their rights and from getting justice. That is how you take the property that belongs to widows and orphans. [3] What will you do when God punishes you? What will you do when he brings disaster on you from a distant country? Where will you run to find help? Where will you hide your wealth? [4] You will be killed in battle or dragged off as prisoners. Yet even so the LORD's anger will not be ended; his hand will still be stretched out to punish.

The Emperor of Assyria as the Instrument of God
[5] The LORD said, "Assyria! I use Assyria like a club to punish those with whom I am angry. [6] I sent Assyria to attack a godless nation, people who have made me angry. I sent them to loot and steal and trample on the people like dirt in the streets."

[7] But the Assyrian emperor has his own violent plans in mind. He is determined to destroy many nations. [8] He boasts, "Every one of my commanders is a king! [9] I conquered the cities of Calno and Carchemish, the cities of Hamath and Arpad. I conquered

9.11 Probable text *their enemies*; Hebrew *the enemies of Rezin*.

820

Isaiah

·:·········

Job
Psalms
Proverbs
Eccles.
Songs

Samaria and Damascus. [10] I stretched out my hand to punish those kingdoms that worship idols, idols more numerous than those of Jerusalem and Samaria. [11] I have destroyed Samaria and all its idols, and I will do the same to Jerusalem and the images that are worshipped there."

[12] But the Lord says, "When I finish what I am doing on Mount Zion and in Jerusalem, I will punish the emperor of Assyria for all his boasting and all his pride."

[13] The emperor of Assyria boasts, "I have done it all myself. I am strong and wise and clever. I wiped out the boundaries between nations and took the supplies they had stored. Like a bull I have trampled on the people who live there. [14] The nations of the world were like a bird's nest, and I gathered their wealth as easily as gathering eggs. Not a wing fluttered to scare me off; no beak opened to scream at me!"

[15] But the LORD says, "Can an axe claim to be greater than the man who uses it? Is a saw more important than the man who saws with it? A club doesn't lift up a man; a man lifts up a club."

[16] The LORD Almighty is going to send disease to punish those who are now well fed. In their bodies there will be a fire that burns and burns. [17] God, the light of Israel, will become a fire. Israel's holy God will become a flame, which in a single day will burn up everything, even the thorns and thistles. [18] The rich forests and farmlands will be totally destroyed, in the same way that a fatal sickness destroys a person. [19] There will be so few trees left that even a child will be able to count them.

A Few will Come Back

[20] A time is coming when the people of Israel who have survived will no longer rely on the nation that almost destroyed them. They will truly put their trust in the LORD, Israel's holy God. [21] A few of the people of Israel will come back to their mighty God. [22] Even though now there are as many people of Israel as there are grains of sand by the sea, only a few will come back. Destruction is in store for the people, and it is fully deserved. [23] Yes, throughout the whole country the Sovereign LORD Almighty will bring destruction, as he said he would.

The LORD will Punish Assyria

[24] The Sovereign LORD Almighty says to his people who live in Zion, "Do not be afraid of the Assyrians, even though they oppress you as the Egyptians used to do. [25] In only a little while I will finish punishing you, and then I will destroy them. [26] I, the LORD Almighty, will beat them with my whip as I beat the people of Midian at the Rock of Oreb. I will punish Assyria as I punished Egypt. [27] When that time comes, I will free you from the power of Assyria, and their yoke will no longer be a burden on your shoulders."*

The Invader Attacks

[28] The enemy army has captured the city of Ai!* They have passed through Migron! They left their supplies at Michmash! [29] They have crossed the pass and are spending the night at Geba! The people in the town of Ramah are terrified, and the people in

10.27 Hebrew has three additional words, the meaning of which is unclear.
10.28 Ai: This and the other places mentioned in verses 28–32 were located near Jerusalem, along the way by which an invader would come to attack from the north.

ISAIAH 10, 11

821

Isaiah

Jerem.
Lamen.
Ezekiel
Daniel
Hosea

King Saul's town of Gibeah have run away. ³⁰Shout, people of Gallim! Listen, people of Laishah! Answer, people of Anathoth! ³¹The people of Madmenah and Gebim are running for their lives. ³²Today the enemy are in the town of Nob, and there they are shaking their fists at Mount Zion, at the city of Jerusalem.

³³The LORD Almighty will bring them crashing down like branches cut off a tree. The proudest and highest of them will be cut down and humiliated. ³⁴The LORD will cut them down as trees in the heart of the forest are cut down with an axe, as even the finest trees of Lebanon fall!

The Peaceful Kingdom

11 The royal line of David is like a tree that has been cut down; but just as new branches sprout from a stump, so a new king will arise from among David's descendants.
² The Spirit of the LORD will give him wisdom,
   and the knowledge and skill to rule his people.
He will know the LORD's will and honour him,
³   and find pleasure in obeying him.
He will not judge by appearance or hearsay;
⁴   he will judge the poor fairly
   and defend the rights of the helpless.
At his command the people will be punished,
   and evil persons will die.
⁵ He will rule his people with justice and integrity.

⁶ Wolves and sheep will live together in peace,
   and leopards will lie down with young goats.
Calves and lion cubs will feed* together,
   and little children will take care of them.
⁷ Cows and bears will eat together,
   and their calves and cubs will lie down in peace.
Lions will eat straw as cattle do.
⁸ Even a baby will not be harmed
   if it plays near a poisonous snake.
⁹ On Zion, God's sacred hill,
   there will be nothing harmful or evil.
The land will be as full of knowledge of the LORD
   as the seas are full of water.

The Exiled People will Return

¹⁰A day is coming when the new king from the royal line of David will be a symbol to the nations. They will gather in his royal city and give him honour. ¹¹When that day comes, the Lord will once again use his power and bring back home those of his people who are left in Assyria and Egypt, in the lands of Pathros, Ethiopia, Elam, Babylonia, and Hamath, and in the coastlands and on the islands of the sea. ¹²The LORD will raise a signal flag to show the nations that he is gathering together again the scattered people of Israel and Judah and bringing them back from the four corners of the earth. ¹³The kingdom of Israel will not be jealous of Judah any more, and Judah will not be the enemy of Israel. ¹⁴Together they will attack the Philistines on the west and plunder the people who live to the east. They will conquer the people of Edom and Moab, and the people of Ammon will obey them. ¹⁵The LORD will dry up the Gulf of Suez, and he will bring a hot wind to dry up the Euphrates, leaving only seven tiny streams, so that anyone will be

....

11.6 Some ancient translations *will feed*; Hebrew *and well-fed cattle.*

822

Isaiah

········

Job
Psalms
Proverbs
Eccles.
Songs

ISAIAH 11–13

able to walk across. ¹⁶There will be a highway out of Assyria for those of his people Israel who have survived there, just as there was for their ancestors when they left Egypt.

Hymn of Thanksgiving

12 A day is coming when people will sing,
"I praise you, Lord! You were angry with me,
but now you comfort me and are angry no longer.
² God is my saviour;
I will trust him and not be afraid.
The Lord gives me power and strength;
he is my saviour.
³ As fresh water brings joy to the thirsty,
so God's people rejoice when he saves them."

⁴A day is coming when people will sing,
"Give thanks to the Lord! Call for him to help you!
Tell all the nations what he has done!
Tell them how great he is!
⁵ Sing to the Lord because of the great things he has done.
Let the whole world hear the news.
⁶ Let everyone who lives in Zion shout and sing!
Israel's holy God is great,
and he lives among his people."

God will Punish Babylon

13 This is a message about Babylon, which Isaiah son of Amoz received from God.

²On the top of a barren hill raise the battle flag! Shout to the soldiers and raise your arm as the signal for them to attack the gates of the proud city. ³The Lord has called out his proud and confident soldiers to fight a holy war and punish those he is angry with.

⁴Listen to the noise on the mountains — the sound of a great crowd of people, the sound of nations and kingdoms gathering. The Lord of Armies is preparing his troops for battle. ⁵They are coming from far-off countries at the ends of the earth. In his anger the Lord is coming to devastate the whole country.

⁶Howl in pain! The day of the Lord is near, the day when the Almighty brings destruction. ⁷Everyone's hands will hang limp, and everyone's courage will fail. ⁸They will all be terrified and overcome with pain, like the pain of a woman in labour. They will look at each other in fear, and their faces will burn with shame. ⁹The day of the Lord is coming — that cruel day of his fierce anger and fury. The earth will be made a wilderness, and every sinner will be destroyed. ¹⁰Every star and every constellation will stop shining, the sun will be dark when it rises, and the moon will give no light.

¹¹The Lord says, "I will bring disaster on the earth and punish all wicked people for their sins. I will humble everyone who is proud and punish everyone who is arrogant and cruel. ¹²Those who survive will be scarcer than gold. ¹³I will make the heavens tremble, and the earth will be shaken out of its place on that day when I, the Lord Almighty, show my anger.

¹⁴"The foreigners living in Babylon will run away to their own countries, scattering like deer escaping from hunters, like sheep without a shepherd. ¹⁵Anyone who is caught will be stabbed to death. ¹⁶While they look on helplessly, their babies will be battered to death, their houses will be looted, and their wives will be raped."

ISAIAH 13, 14

823

Isaiah
....

Jerem.
Lamen.
Ezekiel
Daniel
Hosea

[17]The LORD says, "I am stirring up the Medes* to attack Babylon. They care nothing for silver and are not tempted by gold. [18]With their bows and arrows they will kill the young men. They will show no mercy to babies and take no pity on children. [19]Babylonia is the most beautiful kingdom of all; it is the pride of its people. But I, the LORD, will overthrow Babylon as I did Sodom and Gomorrah! [20]No one will ever live there again. No wandering Arab will ever pitch his tent there, and no shepherd will ever pasture his flock there. [21]It will be a place where desert animals live and where owls build their nests. Ostriches will live there, and wild goats will prance through the ruins. [22]The towers and palaces will echo with the cries of hyenas and jackals. Babylon's time has come! Her days are almost over."

The Return from Exile

14 The LORD will once again be merciful to his people Israel and choose them as his own. He will let them live in their own land again, and foreigners will come and live there with them. [2]Many nations will help the people of Israel to return to the land which the LORD gave them, and there the nations will serve Israel as slaves. Those who once captured Israel will now be captured by Israel, and the people of Israel will rule over those who once oppressed them.

The King of Babylonia in the World of the Dead

[3]The LORD will give the people of Israel relief from their pain and suffering, and from the hard work they were forced to do. [4]When he does this, they are to mock the king of Babylonia and say:

"The cruel king has fallen! He will never oppress anyone again! [5]The LORD has ended the power of the evil rulers [6]who angrily oppressed the peoples and never stopped persecuting the nations they had conquered. [7]Now at last the whole world enjoys rest and peace, and everyone sings for joy. [8]The cypress trees and the cedars of Lebanon rejoice over the fallen king, because there is no one to cut them down, now that he is gone!

[9]"The world of the dead is getting ready to welcome the king of Babylonia. The ghosts of those who were powerful on earth are stirring about. The ghosts of kings are rising from their thrones. [10]They all call out to him, 'Now you are as weak as we are! You are one of us! [11]You used to be honoured with the music of harps, but now here you are in the world of the dead. You lie on a bed of maggots and are covered with a blanket of worms.'

[12]"King of Babylonia, bright morning star, you have fallen from heaven! In the past you conquered nations, but now you have been thrown to the ground. [13]You were determined to climb up to heaven and to place your throne above the highest stars. You thought you would sit like a king on that mountain in the north where the gods assemble. [14]You said you would climb to the tops of the clouds and be like the Almighty. [15]But instead, you have been brought down to the deepest part of the world of the dead.

[16]"The dead will stare and gape at you. They will ask, 'Is this the man who shook the earth and made kingdoms tremble? [17]Is this the man who destroyed cities and turned the world into a desert? Is this the man who never freed his prisoners or let them go home?' [18]All the kings of the earth lie in their magnificent tombs, [19]but you have no tomb, and your corpse is

EXILE

2 KINGS 17.23;
1 CHRONICLES 5.22;
ISAIAH 14.1

Search for the Oxford or Cambridge Dictionary definition of 'exile' and write the definition here.

_____

_____

_____

_____

_____

_____

_____

_____

_____

_____

_____

_____

_____

_____

_____

13.17 *Medes*: People of a nation north-east of Babylonia, which became part of the Persian empire.

824

Isaiah

Job
Psalms
Proverbs
Eccles.
Songs

ISAIAH 14, 15

ISAIAH 15

God used Isaiah to prophesy not just to the Israelites but to all surrounding areas.

God deals with people of all nations and all backgrounds and all tribes at all times. The

• ISRAELITES WERE •

GOD'S EXAMPLE

to other nations of who the true God was.

thrown out to rot. It is covered by the bodies of soldiers killed in battle, thrown with them into a rocky pit, and trampled down. [20] Because you ruined your country and killed your own people, you will not be buried like other kings. None of your evil family will survive. [21] Let the slaughter begin! The sons of this king will die because of their ancestors' sins. None of them will ever rule the earth or cover it with cities."

God will Destroy Babylon

[22] The LORD Almighty says, "I will attack Babylon and bring it to ruin. I will leave nothing — no children, no survivors at all. I, the LORD, have spoken. [23] I will turn Babylon into a marsh, and owls will live there. I will sweep Babylon with a broom that will sweep everything away. I, the LORD Almighty, have spoken."

God will Destroy the Assyrians

[24] The LORD Almighty has sworn an oath: "What I have planned will happen. What I have determined to do will be done. [25] I will destroy the Assyrians in my land of Israel and trample upon them on my mountains. I will free my people from the Assyrian yoke and from the burdens they have had to bear. [26] This is my plan for the world, and my arm is stretched out to punish the nations." [27] The LORD Almighty is determined to do this; he has stretched out his arm to punish, and no one can stop him.

God will Destroy the Philistines

[28] This is a message that was proclaimed in the year that King Ahaz died.

[29] People of Philistia, the rod that beat you is broken, but you have no reason to be glad. When one snake dies, a worse one comes in its place. A snake's egg hatches a flying dragon. [30] The LORD will be a shepherd to the poor of his people and will let them live in safety. But he will send a terrible famine on you Philistines, and it will not leave any of you alive.

[31] Howl and cry for help, all you Philistine cities! Be terrified, all of you! A cloud of dust is coming from the north — it is an army with no cowards in its ranks.

[32] How shall we answer the messengers that come to us from Philistia? We will tell them that the LORD has established Zion and that his suffering people will find safety there.

God will Destroy Moab

15 This is a message about Moab.
The cities of Ar and Kir are destroyed in a single night, and silence covers the land of Moab. [2] The people of Dibon* climb the hill to weep at the shrine. The people of Moab wail in grief over the cities of Nebo and Medeba; they have shaved their heads and their beards in grief. [3] The people in the streets are dressed in sackcloth; in the city squares and on the housetops people mourn and cry. [4] The people of Heshbon and Elealeh cry out, and their cry can be heard as far away as Jahaz. Even the soldiers tremble; their courage is gone. [5] My heart cries out for Moab! The people have fled to the town of Zoar, and to Eglath Shelishiyah. Some climb the road to Luhith, weeping as they go; some escape to Horonaim, grieving loudly. [6] The brook of Nimrim is dry, the grass beside it has withered, and nothing green is left. [7] The people go across the Valley of Willows, trying to escape with

15.2 Probable text *people of Dibon*; Hebrew *people and Dibon*.

ISAIAH 15–17

825

Isaiah

· · · · · · · · ·

Jerem.
Lamen.
Ezekiel
Daniel
Hosea

all their possessions. [8] Everywhere at Moab's borders the sound of crying is heard. It is heard at the towns of Eglaim and Beerelim. [9] At the town of Dibon the river is red with blood, and God has something even worse in store for the people there. Yes, there will be a bloody slaughter of everyone left in Moab.

Moab's Hopeless Situation

16 From the city of Sela in the desert the people of Moab send a lamb as a present to the one who rules in Jerusalem. [2] They wait on the banks of the River Arnon and move aimlessly to and fro, like birds driven from their nest.

[3] They say to the people of Judah, "Tell us what to do. Protect us like a tree that casts a cool shadow in the heat of noon, and let us rest in your shade. We are refugees; hide us where no one can find us. [4] Let us stay in your land. Protect us from those who want to destroy us."

(Oppression and destruction will end, and those who are devastating the country will be gone. [5] Then one of David's descendants will be king, and he will rule the people with faithfulness and love. He will be quick to do what is right, and he will see that justice is done.)

[6] The people of Judah say, "We have heard how proud the people of Moab are. We know that they are arrogant and conceited, but their boasts are empty."

[7] The people of Moab will weep because of the troubles they suffer. They will all weep when they remember the fine food they used to eat in the city of Kir Heres. They will be driven to despair. [8] The farms near Heshbon and the vineyards of Sibmah are destroyed — those vineyards whose wine used to make the rulers of the nations drunk. At one time the vines spread as far as the city of Jazer, and eastwards into the desert, and westwards to the other side of the Dead Sea. [9] Now I weep for Sibmah's vines as I weep for Jazer. My tears fall for Heshbon and Elealeh, because there is no harvest to make the people glad. [10] No one is happy now in the fertile fields. No one shouts or sings in the vineyards. No one tramples grapes to make wine; the shouts of joy are ended.* [11] I groan with sadness for Moab, with grief for Kir Heres. [12] The people of Moab wear themselves out going to their mountain shrines and to their temples to pray, but it will do them no good.

[13] That is the message the LORD gave earlier about Moab. [14] And now the LORD says, "In exactly three years Moab's great wealth will disappear. Of its many people, only a few will survive, and they will be weak."

God will Punish Syria and Israel

17 The LORD said, "Damascus will not be a city any longer; it will be only a pile of ruins. [2] The cities of Syria will be deserted for ever.* They will be a pasture for sheep and cattle, and no one will drive them away. [3] Israel will be defenceless, and Damascus will lose its independence. Those Syrians who survive will be in disgrace like the people of Israel. I, the LORD Almighty, have spoken."

[4] The LORD said, "A day is coming when Israel's greatness will come to an end, and its wealth will be replaced by poverty. [5] Israel will be like a field where the corn has been cut and harvested,

· ·

16.10 One ancient translation *the shouts of joy are ended*; Hebrew *I have ended the shouts of joy.*
17.2 One ancient translation *The cities… for ever*; Hebrew *The cities of Aroer are deserted.*

as desolate as a field in the valley of Rephaim when it has been picked bare. [6] Only a few people will survive, and Israel will be like an olive tree from which all the olives have been picked except two or three at the very top, or a few that are left on the lower branches. I, the Lord God of Israel, have spoken."

[7] When that day comes, people will turn for help to their Creator, the holy God of Israel. [8] They will no longer rely on the altars they made with their own hands, or trust in their own handiwork — symbols of the goddess Asherah and altars for burning incense.

[9] When that day comes, well-defended cities will be deserted and left in ruins like the cities that the Hivites and the Amorites* abandoned as they fled from the people of Israel.

[10] Israel, you have forgotten the God who rescues you and who protects you like a mighty rock. Instead, you plant sacred gardens* in order to worship a foreign god. [11] But even if they sprouted and blossomed the very morning you planted them, there would still be no harvest. There would be only trouble and incurable pain.

Enemy Nations are Defeated

[12] Powerful nations are in commotion with a sound like the roar of the sea, like the crashing of huge waves. [13] The nations advance like rushing waves, but God reprimands them and they retreat, driven away like dust on a hillside, like straw in a whirlwind. [14] In the evening they cause terror, but by morning they are gone. That is the fate of everyone who plunders our land.

God will Punish Ethiopia

18 Beyond the rivers of Ethiopia there is a land where the sound of wings is heard. [2] From that land ambassadors come down the Nile in boats made of reeds. Go back home, swift messengers! Take a message back to your land divided by rivers, to your strong and powerful nation, to your tall and smooth-skinned people, who are feared all over the world.

[3] Listen, everyone who lives on earth! Look for a signal flag to be raised on the tops of the mountains! Listen for the blowing of the bugle! [4] The Lord said to me, "I will look down from heaven as quietly as the dew forms in the warm nights of harvest time, as serenely as the sun shines in the heat of the day. [5] Before the grapes are gathered, when the blossoms have all fallen and the grapes are ripening, the enemy will destroy the Ethiopians as easily as a knife cuts branches from a vine. [6] The corpses of their soldiers will be left exposed to the birds and the wild animals. In summer the birds will feed on them, and in winter, the animals."

[7] A time is coming when the Lord Almighty will receive offerings from this land divided by rivers, this strong and powerful nation, this tall and smooth-skinned people, who are feared all over the world. They will come to Mount Zion, where the Lord Almighty is worshipped.

God will Punish Egypt

19 This is a message about Egypt.
The Lord is coming to Egypt, riding swiftly on a cloud. The Egyptian idols tremble before him, and the people of Egypt lose their courage. [2] The Lord says, "I will stir up civil war in Egypt and turn brother against brother and neighbour against neighbour.

17.9 One ancient translation *the Hivites and the Amorites*; Hebrew *woodland and hill country*.
17.10 *sacred gardens*: See 1.29.

ISAIAH 19, 20

827

Isaiah

....

Jerem.
Lamen.
Ezekiel
Daniel
Hosea

Rival cities will fight each other, and rival kings will struggle for power. ³I am going to frustrate the plans of the Egyptians and destroy their morale. They will ask their idols to help them, and they will go and consult mediums and ask the spirits of the dead for advice. ⁴I will hand the Egyptians over to a tyrant, to a cruel king who will rule them. I, the LORD Almighty, have spoken."

⁵The water will be low in the Nile, and the river will gradually dry up. ⁶The channels of the river will stink as they slowly go dry. Reeds and rushes will wither, ⁷and all the crops sown along the banks of the Nile will dry up and be blown away. ⁸Everyone who earns his living by fishing in the Nile will groan and cry; their hooks and their nets will be useless. ⁹Those who make linen cloth will be in despair; ¹⁰weavers and skilled workers will be broken and depressed.

¹¹The leaders of the city of Zoan are fools! Egypt's wisest people give stupid advice! How dare they tell the king that they are successors to the ancient scholars and kings? ¹²King of Egypt, where are those clever advisers of yours? Perhaps they can tell you what plans the LORD Almighty has for Egypt. ¹³The leaders of Zoan and Memphis are fools. They were supposed to lead the nation, but they have misled it. ¹⁴The LORD has made them give confusing advice. As a result, Egypt does everything wrong and staggers like a drunken man slipping on his own vomit. ¹⁵No one in Egypt, rich or poor, important or unknown, can offer help.

Egypt will Worship the LORD

¹⁶A time is coming when the people of Egypt will be as timid as women. They will tremble in terror when they see that the LORD Almighty has stretched out his hand to punish them. ¹⁷The people of Egypt will be terrified of Judah every time they are reminded of the fate that the LORD Almighty has prepared for them.

¹⁸When that time comes, the Hebrew language will be spoken in five Egyptian cities. The people there will take their oaths in the name of the LORD Almighty. One of the cities will be called, "City of the Sun".

¹⁹When that time comes, there will be an altar to the LORD in the land of Egypt and a stone pillar dedicated to him at the Egyptian border. ²⁰They will be symbols of the LORD Almighty's presence in Egypt. When the people there are oppressed and call out to the LORD for help, he will send someone to rescue them. ²¹The LORD will reveal himself to the Egyptian people, and then they will acknowledge and worship him, and bring him sacrifices and offerings. They will make solemn promises to him and do what they promise. ²²The LORD will punish the Egyptians, but then he will heal them. They will turn to him, and he will hear their prayers and heal them.

²³When that time comes, there will be a highway between Egypt and Assyria. The people of those two countries will travel to and fro between them, and the two nations will worship together. ²⁴When that time comes, Israel will rank with Egypt and Assyria, and these three nations will be a blessing to all the world. ²⁵The LORD Almighty will bless them and say, "I will bless you, Egypt, my people; you, Assyria, whom I created; and you, Israel, my chosen people."

The Sign of the Naked Prophet

20 Under the orders of Sargon, emperor of Assyria, the commander-in-chief of the Assyrian army attacked the Philistine city of Ashdod. ²Three years earlier the LORD had told

828

Isaiah

Job
Psalms
Proverbs
Eccles.
Songs

ISAIAH 20, 21

Isaiah son of Amoz to take off his sandals and the sackcloth he was wearing. He obeyed and went about naked and barefoot. ³When Ashdod was captured, the LORD said, "My servant Isaiah has been going about naked and barefoot for three years. This is a sign of what will happen to Egypt and Ethiopia. ⁴The emperor of Assyria will lead away naked the prisoners he captures from those two countries. Young and old, they will walk barefoot and naked, with their buttocks exposed, bringing shame on Egypt. ⁵Those who have put their trust in Ethiopia and have boasted about Egypt will be disillusioned, their hopes shattered. ⁶When that time comes, the people who live along the coast of Philistia will say, 'Look at what has happened to the people we relied on to protect us from the emperor of Assyria! How will we ever survive?'"

A Vision of the Fall of Babylon

21 This is a message about Babylonia.
Like a whirlwind sweeping across the desert, disaster will come from a terrifying land. ²I have seen a vision of cruel events, a vision of betrayal and destruction.

Army of Elam, attack! Army of Media, lay siege to the cities! God will put an end to the suffering which Babylon has caused.

³What I saw and heard in the vision has filled me with terror and pain, pain like that of a woman in labour. ⁴My head is spinning, and I am trembling with fear. I had been longing for evening to come, but it has brought me nothing but terror.

⁵In the vision a banquet is ready; rugs are spread for the guests to sit on. They are eating and drinking. Suddenly the command rings out: "Officers! Prepare your shields!"

⁶Then the Lord said to me, "Go and post a sentry, and tell him to report what he sees. ⁷If he sees men coming on horseback, two by two, and men riding on donkeys and camels, he is to observe them carefully."

⁸The sentry calls out, "Sir, I have been standing guard at my post day and night."

⁹Suddenly, here they come! Men on horseback, two by two. The sentry gives the news, "Babylon has fallen! All the idols they worshipped lie shattered on the ground."

¹⁰My people Israel, you have been threshed like wheat, but now I have announced to you the good news that I have heard from the LORD Almighty, the God of Israel.

A Message about Edom

¹¹This is a message about Edom.
Someone calls to me from Edom, "Sentry, how soon will the night be over? Tell me how soon it will end."

¹²I answer, "Morning is coming, but night will come again. If you want to ask again, come back and ask."

A Message about Arabia

¹³This is a message about Arabia.
You people of Dedan, whose caravans camp in the barren country of Arabia, ¹⁴give water to the thirsty people who come to you. You people of the land of Tema, give food to the refugees. ¹⁵People are fleeing to escape from swords that are ready to kill them, from bows that are ready to shoot, from all the dangers of war.

¹⁶Then the Lord said to me, "In exactly one year the greatness of the tribes of Kedar will be at an end. ¹⁷The bowmen are the bravest men of Kedar, but few of them will be left. I, the LORD God of Israel, have spoken."

TURN THESE SHAPES INTO **SOMETHING ELSE.**

Isaiah
. . . .

Jerem.
Lamen.
Ezekiel
Daniel
Hosea

A Message about Jerusalem

22 This is a message about the Valley of Vision.
What is happening? Why are all the people of the city celebrating on the roofs of the houses? ²The whole city is in an uproar, filled with noise and excitement.

Your people who died in this war did not die fighting. ³All your leaders ran away and were captured before they shot a single arrow. ⁴Now leave me alone to weep bitterly over all those of my people who have died. Don't try to comfort me. ⁵This is a time of panic, defeat, and confusion in the Valley of Vision, and the Sovereign Lord Almighty has sent it on us. The walls of our city have been battered down, and cries for help have echoed among the hills.

⁶The soldiers from the land of Elam came riding on horseback, armed with bows and arrows. Soldiers from the land of Kir had their shields ready. ⁷The fertile valleys of Judah were filled with chariots; soldiers on horseback stood in front of Jerusalem's gates. ⁸All Judah's defences crumbled.

When that happened, you brought weapons out of the arsenal. ⁹⁻¹⁰You found the places where the walls of Jerusalem needed repair. You inspected all the houses in Jerusalem and tore some of them down to get stones to repair the city walls. In order to store water, ¹¹you built a reservoir inside the city to hold the water flowing down from the old pool. But you paid no attention to God, who planned all this long ago and who caused it to happen.

¹²The Sovereign Lord Almighty was calling you then to weep and mourn, to shave your heads and wear sackcloth. ¹³Instead, you laughed and celebrated. You killed sheep and cattle to eat, and you drank wine. You said, "We might as well eat and drink! Tomorrow we'll be dead."

¹⁴The Sovereign Lord Almighty himself spoke to me and said, "This evil will never be forgiven them as long as they live. I, the Sovereign Lord Almighty, have spoken."

A Warning to Shebna

¹⁵The Sovereign Lord Almighty told me to go to Shebna, the manager of the royal household, and say to him, ¹⁶"Who do you think you are? What right have you to carve a tomb for yourself out of the rocky hillside? ¹⁷You may be important, but the Lord will pick you up and throw you away. ¹⁸He will pick you up like a ball and throw you into a much larger country. You will die there beside the chariots you were so proud of. You are a disgrace to your master's household. ¹⁹The Lord will remove you from office and bring you down from your high position."

²⁰The Lord said to Shebna, "When that happens, I will send for my servant Eliakim son of Hilkiah. ²¹I will put your official robe and belt on him and give him all the authority you have had. He will be like a father to the people of Jerusalem and Judah. ²²I will give him complete authority under the king, the descendant of David. He will have the keys of office; what he opens, no one will shut, and what he shuts, no one will open. ²³I will fasten him firmly in place like a peg, and he will be a source of honour to his whole family.

²⁴"But all his relatives and dependants will become a burden to him. They will hang on him like pots and bowls hanging from a peg! ²⁵When that happens, the peg that was firmly fastened will work loose and fall. And that will be the end of everything that was hanging on it." The Lord has spoken.

830

Isaiah

.·:·........

Job
Psalms
Proverbs
Eccles.
Songs

ISAIAH 23, 24

A Message about Phoenicia

23 This is a message about Tyre.

Howl with grief, you sailors out on the ocean! Your home port of Tyre has been destroyed; its houses and its harbour are in ruins. As your ships return from Cyprus, you learn the news. [2] Wail, you merchants of Sidon! You sent men [3] across the sea to buy and sell the corn that grew in Egypt and to do business with all the nations.

[4] City of Sidon, you are disgraced! The sea and the great ocean depths disown you and say, "I never had any children. I never brought up sons or daughters."

[5] Even the Egyptians will be shocked and dismayed when they learn that Tyre has been destroyed.

[6] Howl with grief, you people of Phoenicia! Try to escape to Spain! [7] Can this be the joyful city of Tyre, founded so long ago? Is this the city that sent settlers across the sea to establish colonies? [8] Who was it that planned to bring all this on Tyre, that imperial city, whose merchant princes were the most honoured men on earth? [9] The LORD Almighty planned it. He planned it in order to put an end to their pride in what they had done and to humiliate their honoured ones.

[10] Go and farm the land, you people in the colonies in Spain! There is no one to protect you any more.* [11] The LORD has stretched out his hand over the sea and overthrown kingdoms. He has ordered the Phoenician centres of commerce to be destroyed. [12] City of Sidon, your happiness has ended, and your people are oppressed. Even if they escape to Cyprus, they will still not be safe.

[13] (It was the Babylonians, not the Assyrians, who let the wild animals overrun Tyre. It was the Babylonians who put up siege towers, tore down the fortifications of Tyre, and left the city in ruins.*)

[14] Howl with grief, you sailors out on the ocean! The city you relied on has been destroyed.

[15] A time is coming when Tyre will be forgotten for seventy years, the lifetime of a king. When those years are over, Tyre will be like the prostitute in the song:

[16] Take your harp, go round the town,
 you poor forgotten whore!
 Play and sing your songs again
 to bring men back once more.

[17] When the seventy years are over, the LORD will let Tyre go back to her old trade, and she will hire herself out to all the kingdoms of the world. [18] The money she earns by commerce will be dedicated to the LORD. She will not store it away, but those who worship the LORD will use her money to buy the food and the clothing they need.

The LORD will Punish the Earth

24 The LORD is going to devastate the earth and leave it desolate. He will twist the earth's surface and scatter its people. [2] Everyone will meet the same fate — the priests and the people, slaves and masters, buyers and sellers, lenders and borrowers, rich and poor. [3] The earth will lie shattered and ruined. The LORD has spoken and it will be done.

[4] The earth dries up and withers; the whole world grows weak; both earth and sky decay. [5] The people have defiled the earth by

---

23.10 Verse 10 in Hebrew is unclear.
23.13 Verse 13 in Hebrew is unclear.

ISAIAH 24, 25

831

Isaiah

Jerem.
Lamen.
Ezekiel
Daniel
Hosea

breaking God's laws and by violating the covenant he made to last for ever. [6] So God has pronounced a curse on the earth. Its people are paying for what they have done. Fewer and fewer remain alive. [7] The grapevines wither, and wine is becoming scarce. Everyone who was once happy is now sad, [8] and the joyful music of their harps and drums has ceased. [9] There is no more happy singing over wine; no one enjoys its taste any more. [10] In the city everything is in chaos, and people lock themselves in their houses for safety. [11] People shout in the streets because there is no more wine. Happiness is gone for ever; it has been banished from the land. [12] The city is in ruins, and its gates have been broken down. [13] This is what will happen in every nation all over the world. It will be like the end of harvest, when the olives have been beaten off every tree and the last grapes picked from the vines.

[14] Those who survive will sing for joy. Those in the west will tell how great the LORD is, [15] and those in the east will praise him. The people who live along the sea will praise the LORD, the God of Israel. [16] From the most distant parts of the world we will hear songs in praise of Israel, the righteous nation.

But there is no hope for me! I am wasting away! Traitors continue to betray, and their treachery grows worse and worse. [17] Listen to me, everyone! There are terrors, pits, and traps waiting for you. [18] Anyone who tries to escape from the terror will fall into a pit, and anyone who escapes from the pit will be caught in a trap. Torrents of rain will pour from the sky, and earth's foundations will shake. [19] The earth will crack and shatter and split open. [20] The earth itself will stagger like a drunken man and sway like a hut in a storm. The world is weighed down by its sins; it will collapse and never rise again.

[21] A time is coming when the LORD will punish the powers above and the rulers of the earth. [22] God will crowd kings together like prisoners in a pit. He will shut them in prison until the time of their punishment comes. [23] The moon will grow dark, and the sun will no longer shine, for the LORD Almighty will be king. He will rule in Jerusalem on Mount Zion, and the leaders of the people will see his glory.

A Hymn of Praise

25 LORD, you are my God;
   I will honour you and praise your name.
   You have done amazing things;
      you have faithfully carried out
      the plans you made long ago.
[2] You have turned cities into ruins
      and destroyed their fortifications.
   The palaces which our enemies built
      are gone for ever.
[3] The people of powerful nations will praise you;
      you will be feared in the cities of cruel nations.
[4] The poor and the helpless have fled to you
      and have been safe in times of trouble.
   You give them shelter from storms
      and shade from the burning heat.
   Cruel enemies attack like a winter storm,*
[5]   like drought in a dry land.

....

25.4 Probable text *winter storm*; Hebrew *storm against a wall*.

832

Isaiah

Job
Psalms
Proverbs
Eccles.
Songs

ISAIAH 25.8

The
— Sovereign —
LORD
WILL DESTROY DEATH
for ever!
He will
WIPE
AWAY
— the tears —
FROM EVERYONE'S
EYES

But you, LORD, have silenced our enemies;
 you silence the shouts of cruel people,
 as a cloud cools a hot day.

God Prepares a Banquet

⁶ Here on Mount Zion the LORD Almighty will prepare a banquet for all the nations of the world — a banquet of the richest food and the finest wine. ⁷ Here he will suddenly remove the cloud of sorrow that has been hanging over all the nations. ⁸ The Sovereign LORD will destroy death for ever! He will wipe away the tears from everyone's eyes and take away the disgrace his people have suffered throughout the world. The LORD himself has spoken!

⁹ When it happens, everyone will say, "He is our God! We have put our trust in him, and he has rescued us. He is the LORD! We have put our trust in him, and now we are happy and joyful because he has saved us."

God will Punish Moab

¹⁰ The LORD will protect Mount Zion, but the people of Moab will be trampled down, just as straw is trampled in manure. ¹¹ They will stretch out their hands as if they were trying to swim, but God will humiliate them, and their hands will sink helplessly. ¹² He will destroy the fortresses of Moab with their high walls and bring them tumbling down into the dust.

God will Give his People Victory

26 A day is coming when the people will sing this song in the land of Judah:
 Our city is strong!
 God himself defends its walls!
² Open the city gates
 and let the faithful nation enter,
 the nation whose people do what is right.
³ You, LORD, give perfect peace
 to those who keep their purpose firm
 and put their trust in you.
⁴ Trust in the LORD for ever;
 he will always protect us.
⁵ He has humbled those who were proud;
 he destroyed the strong city they lived in,
 and sent its walls crashing into the dust.
⁶ Those who were oppressed walk over it now
 and trample it under their feet.

⁷ LORD, you make the path smooth for good people;
 the road they travel is level.
⁸ We follow your will and put our hope in you;
 you are all that we desire.
⁹ At night I long for you with all my heart;
 when you judge the earth and its people,
 they will all learn what justice is.
¹⁰ Even though you are kind to the wicked,
 they never learn to do what is right.
 Even here in a land of righteous people they still do wrong;
 they refuse to recognize your greatness.
¹¹ Your enemies do not know that you will punish them.
 LORD, put them to shame and let them suffer;
 let them suffer the punishment you have prepared.
 Show them how much you love your people.

833

Isaiah
..........:.

Jerem.
Lamen.
Ezekiel
Daniel
Hosea

¹² You will give us prosperity, LORD;
everything that we achieve
is the result of what you do.*
¹³ LORD our God, we have been ruled by others,
but you alone are our LORD.
¹⁴ Now they are dead and will not live again;
their ghosts will not rise,
for you have punished them and destroyed them.
No one remembers them any more.
¹⁵ LORD, you have made our nation grow,
enlarging its territory on every side,
and this has brought you honour.
¹⁶ You punished your people, LORD,
and in anguish they prayed to you.*
¹⁷ You, LORD, have made us cry out,
as a woman in labour cries out in pain.
¹⁸ We were in pain and agony,
but we gave birth to nothing.
We have won no victory for our land;
we have accomplished nothing.*

¹⁹ Those of our people who have died will live again!
Their bodies will come back to life.
All those sleeping in their graves
will wake up and sing for joy.
As the sparkling dew refreshes the earth,
so the LORD will revive those who have long been dead.

Judgement and Restoration

²⁰ Go into your houses, my people, and shut the door behind you. Hide yourselves for a little while until God's anger is over. ²¹ The LORD is coming from his heavenly dwelling place to punish the people of the earth for their sins. The murders that were secretly committed on the earth will be revealed, and the ground will no longer hide those who have been killed.

27 On that day the LORD will use his powerful and deadly sword to punish Leviathan, that wriggling, twisting dragon, and to kill the monster* that lives in the sea.

² On that day the LORD will say of his pleasant vineyard, ³ "I watch over it and water it continually. I guard it night and day so that no one will harm it. ⁴ I am no longer angry with the vineyard. If only there were thorns and briars to fight against, then I would burn them up completely. ⁵ But if the enemies of my people want my protection, let them make peace with me. Yes, let them make peace with me."

⁶ In days to come the people of Israel, the descendants of Jacob, will take root like a tree, and they will blossom and bud. The earth will be covered with the fruit they produce.

⁷ Israel has not been punished by the LORD as severely as its enemies, nor lost as many people. ⁸ The LORD punished his people by sending them into exile. He took them away with a cruel wind from the east.* ⁹ But Israel's sins will be forgiven only when the

....

26.12 *everything that... do*; or *you treat us according to what we do.*
26.16 Verse 16 in Hebrew is unclear.
26.18 *We have won... nothing*; Hebrew unclear.
27.1 *Leviathan... monster*: Legendary monsters which were symbols of the nations oppressing Israel.
27.8 Verse 8 in Hebrew is unclear.

834

Isaiah
·:·········

Job
Psalms
Proverbs
Eccles.
Songs

ISAIAH 27, 28

stones of pagan altars are ground up like chalk, and no more incense altars or symbols of the goddess Asherah are left.

¹⁰The fortified city lies in ruins. It is deserted like an empty wilderness. It has become a pasture for cattle, where they can rest and graze. ¹¹The branches of the trees are withered and broken, and women gather them for firewood. Because the people have understood nothing, God their Creator will not pity them or show them any mercy.

¹²On that day, from the Euphrates to the Egyptian border, the LORD will gather his people one by one, like someone separating the wheat from the chaff.

¹³When that day comes, a trumpet will be blown to call back from Assyria and Egypt all the Israelites who are in exile there. They will come and worship the LORD in Jerusalem, on his sacred hill.*

A Warning to the Northern Kingdom

28 The kingdom of Israel is doomed! Its glory is fading like the crowns of flowers on the heads of its drunken leaders. Their proud heads are well perfumed, but there they lie, dead drunk. ²The Lord has someone strong and powerful ready to attack them, someone who will come like a hailstorm, like a torrent of rain, like a rushing, overpowering flood, and will overwhelm the land. ³The pride of those drunken leaders will be trampled underfoot. ⁴The fading glory of those proud leaders will disappear like the first figs of the season, picked and eaten as soon as they are ripe.

⁵A day is coming when the LORD Almighty will be like a glorious crown of flowers for his people who survive. ⁶He will give a sense of justice to those who serve as judges, and courage to those who defend the city gates from attack.

Isaiah and the Drunken Prophets of Judah

⁷Even the prophets and the priests are so drunk that they stagger. They have drunk so much wine and liquor that they stumble in confusion. The prophets are too drunk to understand the visions that God sends, and the priests are too drunk to decide the cases that are brought to them. ⁸The tables where they sit are all covered with vomit, and not a clean spot is left.

⁹They complain about me. They say, "Who does that man think he's teaching? Who needs his message? It's only good for babies that have just been weaned! ¹⁰He is trying to teach us letter by letter, line by line, lesson by lesson."

¹¹If you won't listen to me, then God will use foreigners speaking some strange-sounding language to teach you a lesson. ¹²He offered rest and comfort to all of you, but you refused to listen to him. ¹³That is why the LORD is going to teach you letter by letter, line by line, lesson by lesson. Then you will stumble with every step you take. You will be wounded, trapped, and taken prisoner.

A Cornerstone for Zion

¹⁴Now you arrogant ones who rule here in Jerusalem over this people, listen to what the LORD is saying. ¹⁵You boast that you have made a treaty with death and reached an agreement with the world of the dead. You are certain that disaster will spare you when it comes, because you depend on lies and deceit to keep you safe. ¹⁶This, now, is what the Sovereign LORD says: "I am placing

---

27.13 *sacred hill*: See 2.3.

in Zion a foundation that is firm and strong. In it I am putting a solid cornerstone on which are written the words, 'Faith that is firm is also patient.' 17 Justice will be the measuring line for the foundation, and honesty will be its plumb line."

Hailstorms will sweep away all the lies you depend on, and floods will destroy your security. 18 The treaty you have made with death will be abolished, and your agreement with the world of the dead will be cancelled. When disaster sweeps down, you will be overcome. 19 It will strike you again and again, morning after morning. You will have to bear it day and night. Each new message from God will bring new terror! 20 You will be like the person in the proverb, who tries to sleep in a bed too short to stretch out on, with a blanket too narrow to wrap himself in. 21 The LORD will fight as he did at Mount Perazim and in the valley of Gibeon, in order to do what he intends to do — strange as his actions may seem. He will complete his work, his mysterious work.

22 Don't laugh at the warning I am giving you! If you do, it will be even harder for you to escape. I have heard the LORD Almighty's decision to destroy the whole country.

God's Wisdom

23 Listen to what I am saying; pay attention to what I am telling you. 24 No farmer goes on constantly ploughing his fields and getting them ready for sowing. 25 Once he has prepared the soil, he sows the seeds of herbs such as dill and cumin. He sows rows of wheat and barley,* and at the edges of his fields he sows other grain. 26 He knows how to do his work, because God has taught him. 27 He never uses a heavy club to beat out dill seeds or cumin seeds; instead he uses light sticks of the proper size. 28 He does not ruin the wheat by threshing it endlessly, and he knows how to thresh it by driving a cart over it without bruising the grains. 29 All this wisdom comes from the LORD Almighty. The plans God makes are wise, and they always succeed!

The Fate of Jerusalem

29 God's altar, Jerusalem itself, is doomed! The city where David camped is doomed! Let another year or two come and go, with its feasts and festivals, 2 and then God will bring disaster on the city that is called "God's altar". There will be weeping and wailing, and the whole city will be like an altar covered with blood. 3 God will attack the city, surround it, and besiege it. 4 Jerusalem will be like a ghost struggling to speak from under the ground, a muffled voice coming from the dust.

5 Jerusalem, all the foreigners who attack you will be blown away like dust, and their terrifying armies will fly away like straw. Suddenly and unexpectedly 6 the LORD Almighty will rescue you with violent thunderstorms and earthquakes. He will send tempests and raging fire; 7 then all the armies of the nations attacking the city of God's altar, all their weapons and equipment — everything — will vanish like a dream, like something imagined in the night. 8 All the nations that assemble to attack Jerusalem will be like a starving person who dreams he is eating and wakes up hungry, or like someone dying of thirst who dreams he is drinking and wakes with a dry throat.

28.25 Hebrew has an additional word, the meaning of which is unclear.

FAITH

ISAIAH 28.16;
HEBREWS 11.1

What do you
think it means?

What does someone
else think it means?

Now go and look up
the definition.

Disregarded Warnings

9 Go ahead and be stupid! Go ahead and be blind! Get drunk without any wine! Stagger without drinking a drop! 10 The LORD has made you drowsy, ready to fall into a deep sleep. The prophets should be the eyes of the people, but God has blindfolded them. 11 The meaning of every prophetic vision will be hidden from you; it will be like a sealed scroll. If you take it to someone who knows how to read and ask him to read it to you, he will say he can't because it is sealed. 12 If you give it to someone who can't read and ask him to read it to you, he will answer that he doesn't know how.

13 The Lord said, "These people claim to worship me, but their words are meaningless, and their hearts are somewhere else. Their religion is nothing but human rules and traditions, which they have simply memorized. 14 So I will startle them with one unexpected blow after another. Those who are wise will turn out to be fools, and all their cleverness will be useless."

Hope for the Future

15 Those who try to hide their plans from the LORD are doomed! They carry out their schemes in secret and think no one will see them or know what they are doing. 16 They turn everything upside down. Which is more important, the potter or the clay? Can a thing which someone has made say to its maker, "You didn't make me"? Or "You don't know what you are doing"?

17 As the saying goes, before long the dense forest will become farmland, and the farmland will go back to forest.

18 When that day comes, the deaf will be able to hear a book being read aloud, and the blind, who have been living in darkness, will open their eyes and see. 19 Poor and humble people will once again find the happiness which the LORD, the holy God of Israel, gives. 20 It will be the end of those who oppress others and show contempt for God. Every sinner will be destroyed. 21 God will destroy those who slander others, those who prevent the punishment of criminals, and those who tell lies to keep honest men from getting justice.

22 So now the LORD, the God of Israel, who rescued Abraham from trouble, says, "My people, you will not be disgraced any longer, and your faces will no longer be pale with shame. 23 When you see the children that I will give you, then you will acknowledge that I am the holy God of Israel. You will honour me and stand in awe of me. 24 Foolish people will learn to understand, and those who are always grumbling will be glad to be taught."

A Useless Treaty with Egypt

30 The LORD has spoken: "Those who rule Judah are doomed because they rebel against me. They follow plans that I did not make, and sign treaties against my will, piling one sin on another. 2 They go to Egypt for help without asking for my advice. They want Egypt to protect them, so they put their trust in Egypt's king. 3 But the king will be powerless to help them, and Egypt's protection will end in disaster. 4 Although their ambassadors have already arrived at the Egyptian cities of Zoan and Hanes, 5 the people of Judah will regret that they ever trusted that unreliable nation, a nation that fails them when they expect help."

6 This is God's message about the animals of the southern desert: "The ambassadors travel through dangerous country, where lions live and where there are poisonous snakes and flying dragons. They load their donkeys and camels with expensive

Isaiah

Jerem.
Lamen.
Ezekiel
Daniel
Hosea

gifts for a nation that cannot give them any help. [7]The help that Egypt gives is useless. So I have nicknamed Egypt, 'The Harmless Dragon' ".

The Disobedient People

[8]God told me to write down in a book what the people are like, so that there would be a permanent record of how evil they are. [9]They are always rebelling against God, always lying, always refusing to listen to the LORD's teachings. [10]They tell the prophets to keep quiet. They say, "Don't talk to us about what's right. Tell us what we want to hear. Let us keep our illusions. [11]Get out of our way and stop blocking our path. We don't want to hear about your holy God of Israel."

[12]But this is what the holy God of Israel says: "You ignore what I tell you and rely on violence and deceit. [13]You are guilty. You are like a high wall with a crack running down it; suddenly you will collapse. [14]You will be shattered like a clay pot, so badly broken that there is no piece big enough to pick up hot coals with, or to scoop water from a cistern."

[15]The Sovereign LORD, the holy God of Israel, says to the people, "Come back and quietly trust in me. Then you will be strong and secure." But you refuse to do it! [16]Instead, you plan to escape from your enemies by riding fast horses. And you are right — escape is what you will have to do! You think your horses are fast enough, but those who pursue you will be faster! [17]A thousand of you will run away when you see one enemy soldier, and five soldiers will be enough to make you all run away. Nothing will be left of your army except a lonely flagstaff on the top of a hill! [18]And yet the LORD is waiting to be merciful to you. He is ready to take pity on you because he always does what is right. Happy are those who put their trust in the LORD.

God will Bless his People

[19]You people who live in Jerusalem will not weep any more. The LORD is compassionate, and when you cry to him for help, he will answer you. [20]The Lord will make you go through hard times, but he himself will be there to teach you, and you will not have to search for him any more. [21]If you wander off the road to the right or the left, you will hear his voice behind you saying, "Here is the road. Follow it." [22]You will take your idols plated with silver and your idols covered with gold, and will throw them away like filth, shouting, "Out of my sight!" [23]Whenever you sow your seeds, the LORD will send rain to make them grow and will give you a rich harvest, and your livestock will have plenty of pasture. [24]The oxen and donkeys that plough your fields will eat the finest and best fodder. [25]On the day when the forts of your enemies are captured and their people are killed, streams of water will flow from every mountain and every hill. [26]The moon will be as bright as the sun, and the sun will be seven times brighter than usual, like the light of seven days in one. This will all happen when the LORD bandages and heals the wounds he has given his people.

God will Punish Assyria

[27]The LORD's power and glory can be seen in the distance. Fire and smoke show his anger. He speaks, and his words burn like fire. [28]He sends the wind in front of him like a flood that carries everything away. It sweeps nations to destruction and puts an end to their evil plans. [29]But you, God's people, will be happy and sing as you do on the night of a sacred festival. You will be

ISAIAH 30.15

God told the Israelites that they would find security if only they would return and

TRUST
- IN HIM -

but they wouldn't obey. In the two boxes labelled 'return' and 'trust', write down what these words mean to you and how they can lead you to be strong and secure in God.

RETURN

TRUST

838

Isaiah

Job
Psalms
Proverbs
Eccles.
Songs

ISAIAH 30–32

as happy as those who walk to the music of flutes on their way to the Temple of the LORD, the defender of Israel. ³⁰The LORD will let everyone hear his majestic voice and feel the force of his anger. There will be flames, cloudbursts, hailstones, and torrents of rain. ³¹The Assyrians will be terrified when they hear the LORD's voice and feel the force of his punishment. ³²As the LORD strikes them again and again, his people will keep time with the music of drums and harps. God himself will fight against the Assyrians. ³³Long ago a place was prepared where a huge fire will burn the emperor of Assyria. It is deep and wide, and piled high with wood. The LORD will breathe out a stream of flame to set it on fire.

God will Protect Jerusalem

31 Those who go to Egypt for help are doomed! They are relying on Egypt's vast military strength — horses, chariots, and soldiers. But they do not rely on the LORD, the holy God of Israel, or ask him for help. ²He knows what he is doing! He sends disaster. He carries out his threats to punish evil men and those who protect them. ³The Egyptians are not gods — they are only human. Their horses are not supernatural. When the LORD acts, the strong nation will crumble, and the weak nation it helped will fall. Both of them will be destroyed.

⁴The LORD said to me, "No matter how shepherds yell and shout, they can't scare away a lion from an animal that it has killed; in the same way, there is nothing that can keep me, the LORD Almighty, from protecting Mount Zion. ⁵Just as a bird hovers over its nest to protect its young, so I, the LORD Almighty, will protect Jerusalem and defend it."

⁶The LORD said, "People of Israel, you have sinned against me and opposed me. But now, come back to me! ⁷A time is coming when all of you will throw away the sinful idols you made out of silver and gold. ⁸Assyria will be destroyed in war, but not by human power. The Assyrians will run from battle, and their young men will be made slaves. ⁹Their emperor will run away in terror, and the officers will be so frightened that they will abandon their battle flags." The LORD has spoken — the LORD who is worshipped in Jerusalem and whose fire burns there for sacrifices.

A King with Integrity

32 Some day there will be a king who rules with integrity, and national leaders who govern with justice. ²Each of them will be like a shelter from the wind and a place to hide from storms. They will be like streams flowing in a desert, like the shadow of a giant rock in a barren land. ³Their eyes and ears will be open to the needs of the people. ⁴They will not be impatient any longer, but they will act with understanding and will say what they mean. ⁵No one will think that a fool is honourable or say that a scoundrel is honest. ⁶A fool speaks foolishly and thinks up evil things to do. What he does and what he says are an insult to the LORD, and he never feeds the hungry or gives thirsty people anything to drink. ⁷A stupid person is evil and does evil things; he plots to ruin the poor with lies and to prevent them getting their rights. ⁸But an honourable person acts honestly and stands firm for what is right.

Judgement and Restoration

⁹You women who live an easy life, free from worries, listen to what I am saying. ¹⁰You may be satisfied now, but this time

ISAIAH 32, 33

839

Isaiah
··········:⟩
Jerem.
Lamen.
Ezekiel
Daniel
Hosea

next year you will be in despair because there will be no grapes for you to gather. [11] You have been living an easy life, free from worries; but now, tremble with fear! Strip off your clothes and tie rags round your waist. [12] Beat your breasts in grief because the fertile fields and the vineyards have been destroyed, [13] and thorn bushes and briars are growing on my people's land. Weep for all the houses where people were happy and for the city that was full of life. [14] Even the palace will be abandoned and the capital city totally deserted. Homes and the forts that guarded them will be in ruins for ever. Wild donkeys will roam there, and sheep will find pasture there.

[15] But once more God will send us his Spirit. The waste land will become fertile, and fields will produce rich crops. [16] Everywhere in the land righteousness and justice will be done. [17] Because everyone will do what is right, there will be peace and security for ever. [18] God's people will be free from worries, and their homes peaceful and safe. [19] (But hail will fall on the forests, and the city will be torn down.) [20] How happy everyone will be with plenty of water for the crops and safe pasture everywhere for the donkeys and cattle.

A Prayer for Help

33 Our enemies are doomed! They have robbed and betrayed, although no one has robbed them or betrayed them. But their time to rob and betray will end, and they themselves will become victims of robbery and treachery.

[2] LORD, have mercy on us. We have put our hope in you. Protect us day by day and save us in times of trouble. [3] When you fight for us, nations run away from the noise of battle. [4] Their belongings are pounced upon and taken as loot.

[5] How great the LORD is! He rules over everything. He will fill Jerusalem with justice and integrity [6] and give stability to the nation. He always protects his people and gives them wisdom and knowledge. Their greatest treasure is their reverence for the LORD.

[7] The brave are calling for help. The ambassadors who tried to bring about peace are crying bitterly. [8] The highways are so dangerous that no one travels on them. Treaties are broken and agreements are violated. No one is respected any more. [9] The land lies idle and deserted. The forests of Lebanon have withered, the fertile valley of Sharon is like a desert, and in Bashan and on Mount Carmel the leaves are falling from the trees.

The LORD Warns his Enemies

[10] The LORD says to the nations, "Now I will act. I will show how powerful I am. [11] You make worthless plans and everything you do is useless. My spirit is like a fire that will destroy you.* [12] You will crumble like rocks burnt to make lime, like thorns burnt to ashes. [13] Let everyone near and far hear what I have done and acknowledge my power."

[14] The sinful people of Zion are trembling with fright. They say, "God's judgement is like a fire that burns for ever. Can any of us survive a fire like that?" [15] You can survive if you say and do what is right. Don't use your power to cheat the poor and don't accept bribes. Don't join with those who plan to commit murder or to do other evil things. [16] Then you will be safe; you will be as secure as if you were in a strong fortress. You will have food to eat and water to drink.

··

33.11 One ancient translation *My spirit… you*; Hebrew *You are destroying yourselves.*

840

Isaiah

Job
Psalms
Proverbs
Eccles.
Songs

ISAIAH 33, 34

The Glorious Future

¹⁷Once again you will see a king ruling in splendour over a land that stretches in all directions. ¹⁸Your old fears of foreign tax collectors and spies will be only a memory. ¹⁹You will no longer see any arrogant foreigners who speak a language that you can't understand. ²⁰Look at Zion, the city where we celebrate our religious festivals. Look at Jerusalem! What a safe place it will be to live in! It will be like a tent that is never moved, whose pegs are never pulled up and whose ropes never break. ²¹The LORD will show us his glory. We will live beside broad rivers and streams, but hostile ships will not sail on them.* ²²⁻²³All the rigging on those ships is useless; the sails cannot be spread! We will seize all the wealth of enemy armies, and there will be so much that even the lame can have a share. The LORD himself will be our king; he will rule over us and protect us. ²⁴No one who lives in our land will ever again complain of being ill, and all sins will be forgiven.

God will Punish his Enemies

34 Come, people of all nations! Gather round and listen. Let the whole earth and everyone living on it come here and listen. ²The LORD is angry with all the nations and all their armies. He has condemned them to destruction. ³Their corpses will not be buried, but will lie there rotting and stinking; and the mountains will be red with blood. ⁴The sun, moon, and stars will crumble to dust. The sky will disappear like a scroll being rolled up, and the stars will fall like leaves dropping from a vine or a fig tree.

⁵The LORD has prepared his sword in heaven, and now it will strike Edom, those people whom he has condemned to destruction. ⁶His sword will be covered with their blood and fat, like the blood and fat of lambs and goats that are sacrificed. The LORD will offer this sacrifice in the city of Bozrah; he will make this a great slaughter in the land of Edom. ⁷The people will fall like wild oxen and young bulls, and the earth will be red with blood and covered with fat. ⁸This is the time when the LORD will rescue Zion and take vengeance on her enemies.

⁹The rivers of Edom will turn into tar, and the soil will turn into sulphur. The whole country will burn like tar. ¹⁰It will burn day and night, and smoke will rise from it for ever. The land will lie waste age after age, and no one will ever travel through it again. ¹¹Owls and ravens will take over the land. The LORD will make it a barren waste again, as it was before the creation. ¹²There will be no king to rule the country, and the leaders will all be gone.* ¹³Thorns and thistles will grow up in all the palaces and walled towns, and jackals and owls will live in them. ¹⁴Wild animals will roam there, and demons will call to each other. The night monster* will come there looking for a place to rest. ¹⁵Owls will build their nests, lay eggs, hatch their young, and care for them there. Vultures will gather there, one after another.

¹⁶Search in the LORD's book of living creatures and read what it says. Not one of these creatures will be missing, and not one will be without its mate. The LORD has commanded it to be so; he himself will bring them together. ¹⁷It is the LORD who will divide the land among them and give each of them a share. They will live in the land age after age, and it will belong to them for ever.

33.21 Verse 21 in Hebrew is unclear.
34.12 Verse 12 in Hebrew begins with a word, the meaning of which is unclear.
34.14 *night monster*: A female demon, believed to live in desolate places.

ISAIAH 35, 36

841

Isaiah

Jerem.
Lamen.
Ezekiel
Daniel
Hosea

The Road of Holiness

35 The desert will rejoice,
and flowers will bloom in the wilderness.
² The desert will sing and shout for joy;
it will be as beautiful as the Lebanon Mountains
and as fertile as the fields of Carmel and Sharon.
Everyone will see the LORD's splendour,
see his greatness and power.

³ Give strength to hands that are tired
and to knees that tremble with weakness.
⁴ Tell everyone who is discouraged,
"Be strong and don't be afraid!
God is coming to your rescue,
coming to punish your enemies."

⁵ The blind will be able to see,
and the deaf will hear.
⁶ The lame will leap and dance,
and those who cannot speak will shout for joy.
Streams of water will flow through the desert;
⁷   the burning sand will become a lake,
and dry land will be filled with springs.
Where jackals used to live,
marsh grass and reeds will grow.

⁸ There will be a highway there,
called "The Road of Holiness".
No sinner will ever travel that road;
no fools will mislead those who follow it.*
⁹ No lions will be there;
no fierce animals will pass that way.
Those whom the LORD has rescued
will travel home by that road.
¹⁰ They will reach Jerusalem with gladness,
singing and shouting for joy.
They will be happy for ever,
for ever free from sorrow and grief.

The Assyrians Threaten Jerusalem
(2 Kgs 18.13–27; 2 Chr 32.1–19)

36 In the fourteenth year that Hezekiah was king of Judah, Sennacherib, the emperor of Assyria, attacked the fortified cities of Judah and captured them. ² Then he ordered his chief official to go from Lachish to Jerusalem with a large military force to demand that King Hezekiah should surrender. The official occupied the road where the clothmakers work, by the ditch that brings water from the upper pond. ³ Three Judeans came out to meet him: the official in charge of the palace, Eliakim son of Hilkiah; the court secretary, Shebna; and the official in charge of the records, Joah son of Asaph. ⁴ The Assyrian official told them that the emperor wanted to know what made King Hezekiah so confident. ⁵ He demanded, "Do you think that words can take the place of military skill and might? Who do you think will help you rebel against Assyria? ⁶ You are expecting Egypt to help you, but that would be like using a reed as a walking stick — it would break and jab your hand. That is what the king of Egypt is like when anyone relies on him."

....

35.8 Probable text *no fools… follow it*; Hebrew unclear.

ISAIAH 35

Isaiah speaks here of a time when God's people will return from exile. However, it can also be seen as a prophecy relating to the distant future, when all humankind will be redeemed - so it could apply to us. One of the images is of a desert blooming into life. In the blank areas on these pages,

BLOOM
- SOME -
LIFE!

842

Isaiah

Job
Psalms
Proverbs
Eccles.
Songs

ISAIAH 36, 37

[7]The Assyrian official went on, "Or will you tell me that you are relying on the LORD your God? It was the LORD's shrines and altars that Hezekiah destroyed when he told the people of Judah and Jerusalem to worship at one altar only. [8]I will make a bargain with you in the name of the emperor. I will give you 2,000 horses if you can find that many riders. [9]You are no match for even the lowest ranking Assyrian official, and yet you expect the Egyptians to send you chariots and cavalry. [10]Do you think I have attacked your country and destroyed it without the LORD's help? The LORD himself told me to attack it and destroy it."

[11]Then Eliakim, Shebna, and Joah said to the official, "Speak Aramaic to us. We understand it. Don't speak Hebrew; all the people on the wall are listening."

[12]He replied, "Do you think you and the king are the only ones the emperor sent me to say all these things to? No, I am also talking to the people who are sitting on the wall, who will have to eat their excrement and drink their urine, just as you will."

[13]Then the official stood up and shouted in Hebrew, "Listen to what the emperor of Assyria is telling you. [14]He warns you not to let Hezekiah deceive you. Hezekiah can't save you. [15]And don't let him persuade you to rely on the LORD. Don't think that the LORD will save you and that he will stop our Assyrian army from capturing your city. [16]Don't listen to Hezekiah! The emperor of Assyria commands you to come out of the city and surrender. You will all be allowed to eat grapes from your own vines and figs from your own trees, and to drink water from your own wells — [17]until the emperor resettles you in a country much like your own, where there are vineyards to give wine and there is corn for making bread. [18]Don't let Hezekiah fool you into thinking that the LORD will rescue you. Did the gods of any other nations save their countries from the emperor of Assyria? [19]Where are they now, the gods of Hamath and Arpad? Where are the gods of Sepharvaim? Did anyone save Samaria? [20]When did any of the gods of all these countries ever save their country from our emperor? Then what makes you think the LORD can save Jerusalem?"

[21]The people kept quiet, just as King Hezekiah had told them to; they did not say a word. [22]Then Eliakim, Shebna, and Joah tore their clothes in grief and went and reported to the king what the Assyrian official had said.

The King Asks Isaiah's Advice
(2 Kgs 19.1–7)

37 As soon as King Hezekiah heard their report, he tore his clothes in grief, put on sackcloth, and went to the Temple of the LORD. [2]He sent Eliakim, the official in charge of the palace, Shebna, the court secretary, and the senior priests to the prophet Isaiah son of Amoz. They also were wearing sackcloth. [3]This is the message which he told them to give to Isaiah: "Today is a day of suffering; we are being punished and are in disgrace. We are like a woman who is ready to give birth, but is too weak to do it. [4]The Assyrian emperor has sent his chief official to insult the living God. May the LORD your God hear these insults and punish those who spoke them. So pray to God for those of our people who survive."

[5]When Isaiah received King Hezekiah's message, [6]he sent back this answer: "The LORD tells you not to let the Assyrians frighten you by their claims that he cannot save you. [7]The LORD will cause the emperor to hear a rumour that will make him go back to his own country, and the LORD will have him killed there."

ISAIAH 37

843

Isaiah
............:

Jerem.
Lamen.
Ezekiel
Daniel
Hosea

The Assyrians Send Another Threat
(2 Kgs 19.8–19)

⁸ The Assyrian official learnt that the emperor had left Lachish and was fighting against the nearby city of Libnah; so he went there to consult him. ⁹ Word reached the Assyrians that the Egyptian army, led by King Tirhakah of Ethiopia, was coming to attack them. When the emperor heard this, he sent a letter to King Hezekiah ¹⁰ of Judah to say to him, "The god you are trusting in has told you that you will not fall into my hands, but don't let that deceive you. ¹¹ You have heard what an Assyrian emperor does to any country he decides to destroy. Do you think that you can escape? ¹² My ancestors destroyed the cities of Gozan, Haran, and Rezeph, and killed the people of Betheden who lived in Telassar, and none of their gods could save them. ¹³ Where are the kings of the cities of Hamath, Arpad, Sepharvaim, Hena, and Ivvah?"

¹⁴ King Hezekiah took the letter from the messengers and read it. Then he went to the Temple, placed the letter there in the presence of the Lord, ¹⁵ and prayed, ¹⁶ "Almighty Lord, God of Israel, enthroned above the winged creatures, you alone are God, ruling all the kingdoms of the world. You created the earth and the sky. ¹⁷ Now, Lord, hear us and look at what is happening to us. Listen to all the things that Sennacherib is saying to insult you, the living God. ¹⁸ We all know, Lord, that the emperors of Assyria have destroyed many nations, made their lands desolate, ¹⁹ and burnt up their gods — which were no gods at all, only images of wood and stone made by human hands. ²⁰ Now, Lord our God, rescue us from the Assyrians, so that all the nations of the world will know that you alone are God."

Isaiah's Message to the King
(2 Kgs 19.20–37)

²¹ Then Isaiah sent a message telling King Hezekiah that in answer to the king's prayer ²² the Lord had said, "The city of Jerusalem laughs at you, Sennacherib, and despises you. ²³ Whom do you think you have been insulting and ridiculing? You have been disrespectful to me, the holy God of Israel. ²⁴ You sent your servants to boast to me that with all your chariots you had conquered the highest mountains of Lebanon. You boasted that there you cut down the tallest cedars and the finest cypress trees, and that you reached the deepest parts of the forests. ²⁵ You boasted that you dug wells and drank water in foreign lands, and that the feet of your soldiers tramped the River Nile dry.

²⁶ "Have you never heard that I planned all this long ago? And now I have carried it out. I gave you the power to turn fortified cities into piles of rubble. ²⁷ The people who lived there were powerless; they were frightened and stunned. They were like grass in a field or weeds growing on a roof when the hot east wind blasts them.*

²⁸ "But I know everything about you, what you do and where you go. I know how you rage against me. ²⁹ I have received the report of that rage and that pride of yours, and now I will put a hook through your nose and a bit in your mouth and will take you back by the road on which you came."

³⁰ Then Isaiah said to King Hezekiah, "This is a sign of what will happen. This year and next you will have only wild grain to eat, but the following year you will be able to sow your corn and harvest it, and plant vines and eat grapes. ³¹ Those in Judah

....

37.27 Probable text *when... them*; Hebrew *blasted before they are grown.*

844

Isaiah

Job
Psalms
Proverbs
Eccles.
Songs

ISAIAH 37, 38

who survive will flourish like plants that send roots deep into the ground and produce fruit. [32] There will be people in Jerusalem and on Mount Zion who will survive, because the LORD Almighty is determined to make this happen.

[33] "This is what the LORD has said about the Assyrian emperor: 'He will not enter this city or shoot a single arrow against it. No soldiers with shields will come near the city, and no siege mounds will be built round it. [34] He will go back by the road on which he came, without entering this city. I, the LORD, have spoken. [35] I will defend this city and protect it, for the sake of my own honour and because of the promise I made to my servant David.' "

[36] An angel of the LORD went to the Assyrian camp and killed 185,000 soldiers. At dawn the next day there they lay, all dead! [37] Then the Assyrian emperor Sennacherib withdrew and returned to Nineveh. [38] One day when he was worshipping in the temple of his god Nisroch, two of his sons, Adrammelech and Sharezer, killed him with their swords and then escaped to the land of Ararat. Another of his sons, Esarhaddon, succeeded him as emperor.

King Hezekiah's Illness and Recovery
(2 Kgs 20.1–11; 2 Chr 32.24–26)

38 About this time King Hezekiah fell ill and almost died. The prophet Isaiah son of Amoz went to see him and said to him, "The LORD tells you that you are to put everything in order because you will not recover. Get ready to die."

[2] Hezekiah turned his face to the wall and prayed: [3] "Remember, LORD, that I have served you faithfully and loyally, and that I have always tried to do what you wanted me to." And he began to cry bitterly.

[4] Then the LORD commanded Isaiah [5] to go back to Hezekiah and say to him, "I, the LORD, the God of your ancestor David, have heard your prayer and seen your tears; I will let you live fifteen years longer. [6] I will rescue you and this city of Jerusalem from the emperor of Assyria, and I will continue to protect the city."

[21]* Isaiah told the king to put a paste made of figs on his boil, and he would get well. [22] Then King Hezekiah asked, "What is the sign to prove that I will be able to go to the Temple?"

[7] Isaiah replied, "The LORD will give you a sign to prove that he will keep his promise. [8] On the stairway built by King Ahaz, the LORD will make the shadow go back ten steps." And the shadow moved back ten steps.*

[9] After Hezekiah recovered from his illness, he wrote this song of praise:

[10] I thought that in the prime of life
    I was going to the world of the dead,
    Never to live out my life.
[11] I thought that in this world of the living
    I would never again see the LORD
    Or any living person.
[12] My life was cut off and ended,
    Like a tent that is taken down,
    Like cloth that is cut from a loom.
    I thought that God was ending my life.*

....

38.21 Verses 21–22 are moved here from the end of the chapter (see 2 Kgs 20.6–9).
38.8 *stairway... ten steps... steps*; or *sundial... ten degrees... degrees* (see 2 Kgs 20.9–11).
38.12 *I thought... my life*; Hebrew unclear.

ISAIAH 38—40

845

Isaiah
....

Jerem.
Lamen.
Ezekiel
Daniel
Hosea

13 All night I cried out with pain,
   As if a lion were breaking my bones.
   I thought that God was ending my life.*
14 My voice was thin and weak,
   And I moaned like a dove.
   My eyes grew tired from looking to heaven.
   Lord, rescue me from all this trouble.
15 What can I say? The LORD has done this.
   My heart is bitter, and I cannot sleep.

16 Lord, I will live for you, for you alone;
   Heal me and let me live.*
17 My bitterness will turn into peace.
   You save* my life from all danger;
   You forgive all my sins.
18 No one in the world of the dead can praise you;
   The dead cannot trust in your faithfulness.
19 It is the living who praise you,
   As I praise you now.
   Parents tell their children how faithful you are.
20 LORD, you have healed me.
   We will play harps and sing your praise,
   Sing praise in your Temple as long as we live.*

Messengers from Babylonia
(2 Kgs 20.12–19)

39 About this time, the king of Babylonia, Merodach Baladan, son of Baladan, heard that King Hezekiah had been ill, so he sent him a letter and a present. 2 Hezekiah welcomed the messengers and showed them his wealth — his silver and gold, his spices and perfumes, and all his military equipment. There was nothing in his storerooms or anywhere in his kingdom that he did not show them. 3 Then the prophet Isaiah went to King Hezekiah and asked, "Where did they come from and what did they say to you?"

Hezekiah answered, "They came from a very distant country, from Babylonia."

4 "What did they see in the palace?"

"They saw everything. There is nothing in the storerooms that I didn't show them."

5 Isaiah then told the king, "The LORD Almighty says that 6 a time is coming when everything in your palace, everything that your ancestors have stored up to this day, will be carried off to Babylonia. Nothing will be left. 7 Some of your own direct descendants will be taken away and made eunuchs to serve in the palace of the king of Babylonia."

8 King Hezekiah understood this to mean that there would be peace and security during his lifetime, so he replied, "The message you have given me from the LORD is good."

Words of Hope

40 "Comfort my people," says our God. "Comfort them!
   2   Encourage the people of Jerusalem.
   Tell them they have suffered long enough

....

38.13 Verse 13 in Hebrew is unclear.
38.16 Verses 15–16 in Hebrew are unclear.
38.17 Some ancient translations save; Hebrew love.
38.20 Verses 21–22 are placed after verse 6.

846

Isaiah
·:········

Job
Psalms
Proverbs
Eccles.
Songs

ISAIAH 40

Read Isaiah 40

THREE TIMES

TODAY

- in the morning,
afternoon and evening.

Each time, write down on
this page one thing from
the chapter that stands
out to you.

Morning:

Afternoon:

Evening:

and their sins are now forgiven.*
I have punished them in full for all their sins."

3 A voice cries out,
"Prepare in the wilderness a road for the LORD!
   Clear the way in the desert for our God!
4 Fill every valley;
   level every mountain.
The hills will become a plain,
   and the rough country will be made smooth.
5 Then the glory of the LORD will be revealed,
   and the whole human race will see it.
The LORD himself has promised this."

6 A voice cries out, "Proclaim a message!"
"What message shall I proclaim?" I ask.
"Proclaim that all human beings are like grass;
   they last no longer than wild flowers.
7 Grass withers and flowers fade,
   when the LORD sends the wind blowing over them.
People are no more enduring than grass.
8 Yes, grass withers and flowers fade,
   but the word of our God endures for ever."

9 Jerusalem, go up on a high mountain
   and proclaim the good news!
Call out with a loud voice, Zion;
   announce the good news!*
Speak out and do not be afraid.
Tell the towns of Judah
   that their God is coming!

10 The Sovereign LORD is coming to rule with power,
   bringing with him the people he has rescued.*
11 He will take care of his flock like a shepherd;
   he will gather the lambs together
   and carry them in his arms;
   he will gently lead their mothers.

Israel's Incomparable God
12 Can anyone measure the ocean by handfuls
   or measure the sky with his hands?
Can anyone hold the soil of the earth in a cup
   or weigh the mountains and hills on scales?
13 Can anyone tell the LORD what to do?
   Who can teach him or give him advice?
14 With whom does God consult
   in order to know and understand
   and to learn how things should be done?

15 To the LORD the nations are nothing,
   no more than a drop of water;
   the distant islands are as light as dust.

....

40.2 *and their sins are now forgiven*; or *they have paid for what they did.*
40.9 *Jerusalem, go up... news!*; or *Go up on a high mountain and proclaim
the good news to Jerusalem! Call out with a loud voice and announce the
good news to Zion!*
40.10 *the people he has rescued*; or *the rewards he has for his people.*

16 All the animals in the forests of Lebanon
   are not enough for a sacrifice to our God,
   and its trees are too few to kindle the fire.
17 The nations are nothing at all to him.

18 To whom can God be compared?
   How can you describe what he is like?
19 He is not like an idol that workmen make,
   that metalworkers cover with gold
   and set in a base of silver.
20 The man who cannot afford silver or gold*
   chooses wood that will not rot.
   He finds a skilful craftsman
   to make an image that won't fall down.

21 Do you not know?
   Were you not told long ago?
   Have you not heard how the world began?
22 It was made by the one who sits on his throne
   above the earth and beyond the sky;
   the people below look as tiny as ants.
   He stretched out the sky like a curtain,
   like a tent in which to live.
23 He brings down powerful rulers
   and reduces them to nothing.
24 They are like young plants,
   just set out and barely rooted.
   When the LORD sends a wind,
   they dry up and blow away like straw.

25 To whom can the holy God be compared?
   Is there anyone else like him?
26 Look up at the sky!
   Who created the stars you see?
   The one who leads them out like an army,
   he knows how many there are
   and calls each one by name!
   His power is so great —
   not one of them is ever missing!
27 Israel, why then do you complain
   that the LORD doesn't know your troubles
   or care if you suffer injustice?
28 Don't you know? Haven't you heard?
   The LORD is the everlasting God;
   he created all the world.
   He never grows tired or weary.
   No one understands his thoughts.
29 He strengthens those who are weak and tired.
30 Even those who are young grow weak;
   young people can fall exhausted.
31 But those who trust in the LORD for help
   will find their strength renewed.
   They will rise on wings like eagles;
   they will run and not get weary;
   they will walk and not grow weak.

40.20 Verses 19–20a in Hebrew are unclear.

848

Isaiah

Job
Psalms
Proverbs
Eccles.
Songs

ISAIAH 41

DECORATE THESE SHAPES IN RELATION TO YOUR MOOD.

God's Assurance to Israel

41 God says,
"Be silent and listen to me, you distant lands!
Get ready to present your case in court;
   you will have your chance to speak.
Let us come together to decide who is right.

2 "Who was it that brought the conqueror from the east,*
   and makes him triumphant wherever he goes?
Who gives him victory over kings and nations?
   His sword strikes them down as if they were dust.
   His arrows scatter them like straw before the wind.
3 He follows in pursuit and marches safely on,
   so fast that he hardly touches the ground!
4 Who was it that made this happen?
   Who has determined the course of history?
I, the LORD, was there at the beginning,
   and I, the LORD, will be there at the end.

5 "The people of distant lands have seen what I have done;
   they are frightened and tremble with fear.
   So they all assemble and come.
6 The craftsmen help and encourage one another.
7 The carpenter says to the goldsmith, 'Well done!'
   The man who beats the idol smooth
   encourages the one who nails it together.
They say, 'The soldering is good' —
   and they fasten the idol in place with nails.

8 "But you, Israel my servant,
   you are the people that I have chosen,
   the descendants of Abraham, my friend.
9 I brought you from the ends of the earth;
   I called you from its farthest corners
   and said to you, 'You are my servant.'
I did not reject you, but chose you.
10 Do not be afraid — I am with you!
   I am your God — let nothing terrify you!
I will make you strong and help you;
   I will protect you and save you.

11 "Those who are angry with you
   will know the shame of defeat.
Those who fight against you will die
12   and will disappear from the earth.
13 I am the LORD your God;
   I strengthen you and say,
   'Do not be afraid; I will help you.'"

14 The LORD says,
"Small and weak as you are, Israel,
   don't be afraid; I will help you.
I, the holy God of Israel, am the one who saves you.
15 I will make you like a threshing board,
   with spikes that are new and sharp.
You will thresh mountains and destroy them;
   hills will crumble into dust.

41.2 *the conqueror from the east*: Cyrus, the emperor of Persia (see 45.1).

ISAIAH 41

849

Isaiah

···········⟩

Jerem.

Lamen.

Ezekiel

Daniel

Hosea

16 You will toss them in the air;
   the wind will carry them off,
   and they will be scattered by the storm.
Then you will be happy because I am your God;
   you will praise me, the holy God of Israel.

17 "When my people in their need look for water,
   when their throats are dry with thirst,
then I, the Lord, will answer their prayer;
   I, the God of Israel, will never abandon them.
18 I will make rivers flow among barren hills
   and springs of water run in the valleys.
I will turn the desert into pools of water
   and the dry land into flowing springs.
19 I will make cedars grow in the desert,
   and acacias and myrtles and olive trees.
Forests will grow in barren land,
   forests of pine and juniper and cypress.
20 People will see this and know
   that I, the Lord, have done it.
They will come to understand
   that Israel's holy God has made it happen."

The Lord's Challenge to False Gods

21 The Lord, the king of Israel, has this to say:
   "You gods of the nations, present your case.
   Bring the best arguments you have!
22 Come here and predict what will happen,
   so that we will know it when it takes place.
Explain to the court the events of the past,
   and tell us what they mean.
23 Tell us what the future holds —
   then we will know that you are gods!
Do something good or bring some disaster;
   fill us with fear and awe!
24 You and all you do are nothing;
   those who worship you are disgusting!

25 "I have chosen a man who lives in the east;*
   I will bring him to attack from the north.
He tramples on rulers as if they were mud,
   like a potter trampling clay.
26 Which of you predicted that this would happen,
   so that we could say that you were right?
None of you said a word about it;
   no one heard you say a thing!
27 I, the Lord, was the first to tell Zion the news;
   I sent a messenger to Jerusalem to say,
   'Your people are coming! They are coming home!'*
28 When I looked among the gods,
   none of them had a thing to say;
   not one could answer the questions I asked.
29 All these gods are useless;
   they can do nothing at all —
   these idols are weak and powerless."

···

41.25 *a man who lives in the east:* See 41.2.
41.27 Verse 27 in Hebrew is unclear.

The Lord's Servant

42 The Lord says,
"Here is my servant, whom I strengthen —
the one I have chosen, with whom I am pleased.
I have filled him with my Spirit,
and he will bring justice to every nation.
2 He will not shout or raise his voice
or make loud speeches in the streets.
3 He will not break off a bent reed
or put out a flickering lamp.
He will bring lasting justice to all.
4 He will not lose hope or courage;
he will establish justice on the earth.
Distant lands eagerly wait for his teaching."

5 God created the heavens and stretched them out;
he fashioned the earth and all that lives there;
he gave life and breath to all its people.
And now the Lord God says to his servant,
6 "I, the Lord, have called you and given you power
to see that justice is done on earth.
Through you I will make a covenant with all peoples;
through you I will bring light to the nations.
7 You will open the eyes of the blind
and set free those who sit in dark prisons.

8 "I alone am the Lord your God.
No other god may share my glory;
I will not let idols share my praise.
9 The things I predicted have now come true.
Now I will tell you of new things
even before they begin to happen."

A Song of Praise

10 Sing a new song to the Lord;
sing his praise, all the world!
Praise him, you that sail the sea;
praise him, all creatures of the sea!
Sing, distant lands and all who live there!
11 Let the desert and its towns praise God;
let the people of Kedar praise him!
Let those who live in the city of Sela
shout for joy from the tops of the mountains!
12 Let those who live in distant lands
give praise and glory to the Lord!
13 The Lord goes out to fight like a warrior;
he is ready and eager for battle.
He gives a war cry, a battle shout;
he shows his power against his enemies.

God Promises to Help his People

14 God says,
"For a long time I kept silent;
I did not answer my people.
But now the time to act has come;
I cry out like a woman in labour.
15 I will destroy the hills and mountains
and dry up the grass and trees.

ISAIAH 42, 43

851

Isaiah

Jerem.
Lamen.
Ezekiel
Daniel
Hosea

I will turn the river valleys into deserts*
    and dry up the pools of water.
16 "I will lead my blind people
    by roads they have never travelled.
I will turn their darkness into light
    and make rough country smooth before them.
These are my promises,
    and I will keep them without fail.
17 All who trust in idols,
    who call images their gods,
    will be humiliated and disgraced."

Israel's Failure to Learn
18 The LORD says,
  "Listen, you deaf people!
  Look closely, you that are blind!
19 Is anyone more blind than my servant,
    more deaf than the messenger I send?
20 Israel, you have seen so much,
    but what has it meant to you?
You have ears to hear with,
    but what have you really heard?"

21 The LORD is a God who is eager to save,
    so he exalted his laws and teachings,
    and he wanted his people to honour them.
22 But now his people have been plundered;
    they are locked up in dungeons
    and hidden away in prisons.
They were robbed and plundered,
    with no one to come to their rescue.

23 Will any of you listen to this?
    From now on will you listen with care?
24 Who gave Israel up to the looters?
    It was the LORD himself, against whom we sinned!
We would not live as he wanted us to live
    or obey the teachings he gave us.
25 So he made us feel the force of his anger
    and suffer the violence of war.
Like fire his anger burned throughout Israel,
    but we never knew what was happening;
    we learnt from it nothing at all.

God Promises to Rescue his People
43 Israel, the LORD who created you says,
  "Do not be afraid — I will save you.
I have called you by name — you are mine.
2 When you pass through deep waters, I will be with you;
    your troubles will not overwhelm you.
When you pass through fire, you will not be burnt;
    the hard trials that come will not hurt you.
3 For I am the LORD your God,
    the holy God of Israel, who saves you.
I will give up Egypt to set you free;
    I will give up Ethiopia and Seba.

Circle your
FAVOURITE
PASSAGE
on this page.

42.15 Probable text *deserts*; Hebrew *coastlands*.

852

Isaiah

·:·· ········

Job
Psalms
Proverbs
Eccles.
Songs

ISAIAH 43

⁴ I will give up whole nations to save your life,
    because you are precious to me
    and because I love you and give you honour.
⁵ Do not be afraid — I am with you!

"From the distant east and the farthest west,
    I will bring your people home.
⁶ I will tell the north to let them go
    and the south not to hold them back.
Let my people return from distant lands,
    from every part of the world.
⁷ They are my own people,
    and I created them to bring me glory."

Israel is the LORD's Witness

⁸ God says,
    "Summon my people to court.
    They have eyes, but they are blind;
    they have ears, but they are deaf!
⁹ Summon the nations to come to the trial.
    Which of their gods can predict the future?
    Which of them foretold what is happening
        now?
Let these gods bring in their witnesses
    to prove that they are right,
    to testify to the truth of their words.

¹⁰ "People of Israel, you are my witnesses;
    I chose you to be my servant,
so that you would know me and believe in me
    and understand that I am the only God.
Besides me there is no other god;
    there never was and never will be.

¹¹ "I alone am the LORD,
    the only one who can save you.
¹² I predicted what would happen,
    and then I came to your aid.
No foreign god has ever done this;
    you are my witnesses.
¹³ I am God and always will be.
No one can escape from my power;
    no one can change what I do."

Escape from Babylon

¹⁴ Israel's holy God, the LORD who saves you, says,
    "To save you, I will send an army against Babylon;
    I will break down the city gates,
    and the shouts of her people will turn into crying.
¹⁵ I am the LORD, your holy God.
    I created you, Israel, and I am your king."

¹⁶ Long ago the LORD made a road through the sea,
    a path through the swirling waters.
¹⁷ He led a mighty army to destruction,
    an army of chariots and horses.
Down they fell, never to rise,
    snuffed out like the flame of a lamp!

Isaiah

Jerem.
Lamen.
Ezekiel
Daniel
Hosea

JOIN THE DOTS
below to make a picture.

¹⁸ But the LORD says,
"Do not cling to events of the past
or dwell on what happened long ago.
¹⁹ Watch for the new thing I am going to do.
It is happening already — you can see it now!
I will make a road through the wilderness
and give you streams of water there.
²⁰ Even the wild animals will honour me;
jackals and ostriches will praise me
when I make rivers flow in the desert
to give water to my chosen people.
²¹ They are the people I made for myself,
and they will sing my praises!"

Israel's Sin
²² The LORD says,
"But you were tired of me, Israel;
you did not worship me.
²³ You did not bring me your burnt offerings of sheep;
you did not honour me with your sacrifices.
I did not burden you by demanding offerings
or wear you out by asking for incense.
²⁴ You didn't buy incense for me
or satisfy me with the fat of your animals.
Instead you burdened me with your sins;
you wore me out with the wrongs you committed.
²⁵ And yet, I am the God who forgives your sins,
and I do this because of who I am.
I will not hold your sins against you.

²⁶ "Let us go to court; bring your accusation!
Present your case to prove you are in the right!
²⁷ Your earliest ancestor* sinned;
your leaders sinned against me,
²⁸ and your rulers profaned* my sanctuary.
So I brought destruction on Israel;
I let my own people be insulted."

The LORD is the Only God
44 The LORD says,
"Listen now, Israel, my servant,
my chosen people, the descendants of Jacob.
² I am the LORD who created you;
from the time you were born, I have helped you.
Do not be afraid; you are my servant,
my chosen people whom I love.

³ "I will give water to the thirsty land
and make streams flow on the dry ground.
I will pour out my spirit on your children
and my blessing on your descendants.
⁴ They will thrive like well-watered grass,
like willows by streams of running water.

43.27 *your earliest ancestor*: A reference either to Jacob or to Abraham, or possibly to Adam.
43.28 One ancient translation *your rulers profaned*; Hebrew *I profaned the rulers of*.

854

ISAIAH 44

Isaiah

⋮⋯⋯⋯

Job
Psalms
Proverbs
Eccles.
Songs

5 "One by one, people will say, 'I am the LORD's.'
They will come to join the people of Israel.
They will each mark the name of the LORD on their
arms
and call themselves members of God's people."

6 The LORD, who rules and protects Israel,
the LORD Almighty, has this to say:
"I am the first, the last, the only God;
there is no other god but me.
7 Could anyone else have done what I did?
Who could have predicted all that would happen
from the very beginning to the end of time?*
8 Do not be afraid, my people!
You know that from ancient times until now
I have predicted all that would happen,
and you are my witnesses.
Is there any other god?
Is there some powerful god I never heard of?"

Idolatry is Ridiculed

9 All those who make idols are worthless, and the gods they prize
so highly are useless. Those who worship these gods are blind and
ignorant — and they will be disgraced. 10 It's no good making
a metal image to worship as a god! 11 Everyone who worships it
will be humiliated. The people who make idols are human beings
and nothing more. Let them come and stand trial — they will be
terrified and will suffer disgrace.

12 The metalworker takes a piece of metal and works with it
over a fire. His strong arm swings a hammer to pound the metal
into shape. As he works, he gets hungry, thirsty, and tired.

13 The carpenter measures the wood. He outlines a figure with
chalk, carves it out with his tools, and makes it in the form of
a man, a handsome human figure, to be placed in his house.
14 He might cut down cedars to use, or choose oak or cypress
wood from the forest. Or he might plant a laurel-tree and wait
for the rain to make it grow. 15 A person uses part of a tree for
fuel and part of it for making an idol. With one part he builds
a fire to warm himself and bake bread; with the other part he
makes a god and worships it. 16 With some of the wood he
makes a fire; he roasts meat, eats it, and is satisfied. He warms
himself and says, "How nice and warm! What a beautiful fire!"
17 The rest of the wood he makes into an idol, and then he
bows down and worships it. He prays to it and says, "You are
my god — save me!"

18 Such people are too stupid to know what they are doing. They
close their eyes and their minds to the truth. 19 The maker of idols
hasn't the wit or the sense to say, "Some of the wood I burnt up.
I baked some bread on the embers and I roasted meat and ate it.
And the rest of the wood I made into an idol. Here I am bowing
down to a block of wood!"

20 It makes as much sense* as eating ashes. His foolish ideas
have so misled him that he is beyond help. He won't admit
to himself that the idol he holds in his hand is not a god at
all.

⋯⋯⋯⋯⋯⋯⋯⋯⋯⋯⋯⋯⋯⋯⋯⋯⋯⋯⋯⋯⋯⋯⋯⋯⋯⋯⋯⋯⋯⋯⋯⋯⋯⋯⋯⋯⋯

44.7 Verse 7 in Hebrew is unclear.
44.20 It makes as much sense; or It will do as much good.

ISAIAH 44, 45

855

Isaiah

Jerem.
Lamen.
Ezekiel
Daniel
Hosea

The LORD, the Creator and Saviour

²¹ The LORD says,
"Israel, remember this;
    remember that you are my servant.
I created you to be my servant,
    and I will never forget you.
²² I have swept your sins away like a cloud.
    Come back to me; I am the one who saves you."

²³ Shout for joy, you heavens!
    Shout, deep places of the earth!
Shout for joy, mountains, and every tree of the
       forest!
The LORD has shown his greatness
    by saving his people Israel.

²⁴ "I am the LORD, your saviour;
I am the one who created you.
I am the LORD, the Creator of all things.
    I alone stretched out the heavens;
    when I made the earth, no one helped me.
²⁵ I make fools of fortune tellers
    and frustrate the predictions of astrologers.
    The words of the wise I refute
    and show that their wisdom is foolishness.
²⁶ But when my servant makes a prediction,
    when I send a messenger to reveal my plans,
    I make those plans and predictions come true.
I tell Jerusalem that people will live there again,
    and the cities of Judah that they will be rebuilt.
    Those cities will rise from the ruins.
²⁷ With a word of command I dry up the ocean.
²⁸ I say to Cyrus, 'You are the one who will rule for me;
    you will do what I want you to do:
    you will order Jerusalem to be rebuilt
    and the Temple foundations to be laid.'"

The LORD Appoints Cyrus

45 The LORD has chosen Cyrus to be king!
He has appointed him to conquer nations;
    he sends him to strip kings of their power;
    the LORD will open the gates of cities for him.
To Cyrus the LORD says,
² "I myself will prepare your way,
    levelling mountains and hills.
I will break down bronze gates
    and smash their iron bars.
³ I will give you treasures from dark, secret places;
    then you will know that I am the LORD,
    and that the God of Israel has called you by name.
⁴ I appoint you to help my servant Israel,
    the people that I have chosen.
I have given you great honour,
    although you do not know me.

⁵ "I am the LORD; there is no other god.
I will give you the strength you need,
    although you do not know me.

856

Isaiah

....

Job
Psalms
Proverbs
Eccles.
Songs

ISAIAH 45

ISAIAH 45.9

Isaiah compares us to a
clay pot created by God,

– THE –
MASTER
POTTER.

FIND SOMETHING
MOULDABLE

- playdough, clay,
Plasticine, maybe even
Lego - and create a
small person.

6 I do this so that everyone
  from one end of the world to the other
  may know that I am the LORD
  and that there is no other god.
7 I create both light and darkness;
  I bring both blessing and disaster.
  I, the LORD, do all these things.
8 I will send victory from the sky like rain;
  the earth will open to receive it
  and will blossom with freedom and justice.
  I, the LORD, will make this happen."

The LORD of Creation and History

9 Does a clay pot dare to argue with its maker,
  a pot that is like all the others?
  Does the clay ask the potter what he is doing?
  Does the pot complain that its maker has no skill?
10 Does anyone dare to say to his parents,
  "Why did you make me like this?"
11 The LORD, the holy God of Israel,
  the one who shapes the future, says:
  "You have no right to question me about my children
  or to tell me what I ought to do!
12 I am the one who made the earth
  and created the human race to live there.
  By my power I stretched out the heavens;
  I control the sun, the moon, and the stars.
13 I myself have stirred Cyrus to action
  to fulfil my purpose and put things right.
  I will straighten every road that he travels.
  He will rebuild my city, Jerusalem,
  and set my captive people free.
  No one has hired him or bribed him to do this."
  The LORD Almighty has spoken.

14 The LORD says to Israel,
  "The wealth of Egypt and Ethiopia will be yours,
  and the tall men of Seba will be your slaves;
  they will follow you in chains.
  They will bow down to you and confess,
  'God is with you — he alone is God.
15 The God of Israel, who saves his people,
  is a God who conceals himself.
16 Those who make idols will all be ashamed;
  all of them will be disgraced.
17 But Israel is saved by the LORD,
  and her victory lasts for ever;
  her people will never be disgraced.'"

18 The LORD created the heavens —
  he is the one who is God!
  He formed and made the earth —
  he made it firm and lasting.
  He did not make it a desolate waste,
  but a place for people to live in.
  It is he who says, "I am the LORD,
  and there is no other god.
19 I have not spoken in secret
  or kept my purpose hidden.

ISAIAH 45, 46

857

Isaiah
....
Jerem.
Lamen.
Ezekiel
Daniel
Hosea

I did not require the people of Israel
   to look for me in a desolate waste.
I am the LORD, and I speak the truth;
   I make known what is right."

The LORD of the World and the Idols of Babylon

20 The LORD says,
   "Come together, people of the nations,
      all who survive the fall of the empire;
      present yourselves for the trial!
The people who parade with their idols of wood
      and pray to gods that cannot save them —
      those people know nothing at all!
21 Come and present your case in court;
      let the defendants consult one another.
Who predicted long ago what would happen?
Was it not I, the LORD, the God who saves his people?
      There is no other god.

22 "Turn to me now and be saved,
      people all over the world!
I am the only God there is.
23 My promise is true,
      and it will not be changed.
I solemnly promise by all that I am:
      Everyone will come and kneel before me
      and vow to be loyal to me.

24 "They will say that only through me
      are victory and strength to be found;
      but all who hate me will suffer disgrace.
25 I, the LORD, will rescue all the descendants of Jacob,
      and they will give me praise.

46

   "This is the end for Babylon's gods!
   Bel and Nebo once were worshipped,
   but now they are loaded on donkeys,
   a burden for the backs of tired animals.
2   The idols cannot save themselves;
      they are captured and carried away.
This is the end for Babylon's gods!

3 "Listen to me, descendants of Jacob,
      all who are left of my people.
I have cared for you from the time you were born.
4 I am your God and will take care of you
      until you are old and your hair is grey.
I made you and will care for you;
      I will give you help and rescue you.

5 "With whom will you compare me?" says the LORD.
      "Is there anyone else like me?
6 People open their purses and pour out gold;
      they weigh out silver on the scales.
They hire a goldsmith to make a god;
      then they bow down and worship it!
7 They lift it to their shoulders and carry it;
      they put it in place, and there it stands,
      unable to move from where it is.

> If anyone prays to it, it cannot answer
> or save him from disaster.

8 "Remember this, you sinners;
> consider what I have done.
9 Remember what happened long ago;
> acknowledge that I alone am God
> and that there is no one else like me.
10 From the beginning I predicted the outcome;
> long ago I foretold what would happen.
> I said that my plans would never fail,
> that I would do everything I intended to do.
11 I am calling a man to come from the east;*
> he will swoop down like a hawk
> and accomplish what I have planned.
> I have spoken, and it will be done.

12 "Listen to me, you stubborn people
> who think that victory is far away.
13 I am bringing the day of victory near —
> it is not far away at all.
> My triumph will not be delayed.
> I will save Jerusalem
> and bring honour to Israel there."

Judgement on Babylon

47 The LORD says,
> "Babylon, come down from your throne,
> and sit in the dust on the ground.
> You were once like a virgin, a city unconquered,
> but you are soft and delicate no longer!
> You are now a slave!
2 Turn the millstone! Grind the flour!
> Off with your veil! Strip off your fine clothes!
> Lift up your skirts to cross the streams!*
3 People will see you naked;
> they will see you humbled and shamed.
> I will take vengeance, and no one will stop me."

4 The holy God of Israel sets us free —
> his name is the LORD Almighty.

5 The LORD says to Babylon,
> "Sit in silence and darkness;
> no more will they call you the queen of nations!
6 I was angry with my people;
> I treated them as no longer mine:
> I put them in your power,
> and you showed them no mercy;
> even the aged you treated harshly.
7 You thought you would always be a queen,
> and did not take these things to heart
> or think how it all would end.

8 "Listen to this, you lover of pleasure,
> you that think you are safe and secure.

46.11 *a man to come from the east*: See 41.2.
47.2 *cross the streams*: This probably refers to going into exile.

You claim you are as great as God —
that there is no one else like you.
You thought that you would never be a widow
or suffer the loss of your children.
9 But in a moment, in a single day,
both of these things will happen.
In spite of all the magic you use,
you will lose your husband and children.

10 "You felt sure of yourself in your evil;
you thought that no one could see you.
Your wisdom and knowledge led you astray,
and you said to yourself, 'I am God —
there is no one else like me.'
11 Disaster will come upon you,
and none of your magic can stop it.
Ruin will come on you suddenly —
ruin you never dreamt of!
12 Keep all your magic spells and charms;
you have used them since you were young.
Perhaps they will be of some help to you;
perhaps you can frighten your enemies.
13 You are powerless in spite of the advice you get.
Let your astrologers come forward and save you —
those people who study the stars,
who map out the zones of the heavens
and tell you from month to month
what* is going to happen to you.

14 "They will be like bits of straw,
and a fire will burn them up!
They will not even be able to save themselves —
the flames will be too hot for them,
not a cosy fire to warm themselves by.
15 That is all the good they will do you —
those astrologers you've consulted all your life.
They all will leave you and go their own way,
and none will be left to save you."

God is LORD of the Future

48 Listen to this, people of Israel,
you that are descended from Judah:
You swear by the name of the LORD
and claim to worship the God of Israel —
but you don't mean a word you say.
2 And yet you are proud to say
that you are citizens of the holy city
and that you depend on Israel's God,
whose name is the LORD Almighty.

3 The LORD says to Israel,
"Long ago I predicted what would take place;
then suddenly I made it happen.
4 I knew that you would prove to be stubborn,
as rigid as iron and unyielding as bronze.
5 And so I predicted your future long ago,
announcing events before they took place,

47.13 Some ancient translations *what*; Hebrew *from what*.

860

Isaiah

Job
Psalms
Proverbs
Eccles.
Songs

ISAIAH 48

to prevent you from claiming
that your idols and images made them happen.

6 "All I foretold has now taken place;
   you have to admit my predictions were right.
Now I will tell you of new things to come,
   events that I did not reveal before.
7 Only now am I making them happen;
   nothing like this took place in the past.
If it had, you would claim that you knew all about it.
8 I knew that you couldn't be trusted,
   that you have always been known as a rebel.
That is why you never heard of this at all,
   why no word of it ever came to your ears.

9 "In order that people will praise my name,
   I am holding my anger in check;
   I am keeping it back and will not destroy you.
10 I have tested you in the fire of suffering,
   as silver is refined in a furnace.
But I have found that you are worthless.
11 What I do is done for my own sake —
   I will not let my name be dishonoured
   or let anyone else share the glory
   that should be mine and mine alone."

Cyrus, the LORD's Chosen Leader
12 The LORD says,
   "Listen to me, Israel, the people I have called!
I am God, the first, the last, the only God!
13 My hands made the earth's foundations
   and spread the heavens out.
When I summon earth and sky,
   they come at once and present themselves.

14 "Assemble and listen, all of you!
None of the gods could predict
   that the man I have chosen would attack Babylon;
   he will do what I want him to do.
15 I am the one who spoke and called him;
   I led him out and gave him success.

16 "Now come close to me and hear what I say.
   From the beginning I have spoken openly,
   and have always made my words come true."
(Now the Sovereign LORD has given me his power and sent me.)

The LORD's Plan for his People
17 The holy God of Israel,
   the LORD who saves you, says:
"I am the LORD your God,
   the one who wants to teach you for your own good
   and direct you in the way you should go.

18 "If only you had listened to my commands!
Then blessings would have flowed for you
   like a stream that never goes dry!
Victory would have come to you
   like the waves that roll on the shore.

861

Isaiah

....

Jerem.
Lamen.
Ezekiel
Daniel
Hosea

¹⁹ Your descendants would be as numerous as grains of
sand,
and I would have made sure they were never
destroyed."

²⁰ Go out from Babylon, go free!
Shout the news gladly; make it known everywhere:
"The Lord has saved his servant Israel!"
²¹ When the Lord led his people through a hot, dry desert,
they did not suffer from thirst.
He made water come from a rock for them;
he split the rock open, and water flowed out.

²² "There is no safety for sinners," says the Lord.

Israel, a Light to the Nations

49 Listen to me, distant nations,
you people who live far away!
Before I was born, the Lord chose me
and appointed me to be his servant.
² He made my words as sharp as a sword.
With his own hand he protected me.*
He made me like an arrow,
sharp and ready for use.
³ He said to me, "Israel, you are my servant;
because of you, people will praise me."

⁴ I said, "I have worked, but how hopeless it is!
I have used up my strength, but have accomplished
nothing."
Yet I can trust the Lord to defend my cause;
he will reward me for what I do.

⁵ Before I was born, the Lord appointed me;
he made me his servant to bring back his people,
to bring back the scattered people of Israel.
The Lord gives me honour;
he is the source of my strength.

⁶ The Lord said to me,
"I have a greater task for you, my servant.
Not only will you restore to greatness
the people of Israel who have survived,
but I will also make you a light to the nations —
so that all the world may be saved."

⁷ Israel's holy God and saviour says
to the one who is deeply despised,
who is hated by the nations
and is the servant of rulers:
"Kings will see you released
and will rise to show their respect;
princes also will see it,
and they will bow low to honour you."

This will happen because the Lord has chosen his servant;
the holy God of Israel keeps his promises.

49.2 *With his own hand... me*; or *He kept me hidden in his hand.*

862

Isaiah

∴∙∙∙∙∙∙∙∙

Job
Psalms
Proverbs
Eccles.
Songs

ISAIAH 49

The Restoration of Jerusalem

8 The LORD says to his people,
"When the time comes to save you, I will show you favour
and answer your cries for help.
I will guard and protect you
and through you make a covenant with all peoples.
I will let you settle once again
in your land that is now laid waste.
9 I will say to the prisoners, 'Go free!'
and to those who are in darkness,
'Come out to the light!'
They will be like sheep that graze on the hills;
10 they will never be hungry or thirsty.
Sun and desert heat will not hurt them,
for they will be led by one who loves them.
He will lead them to springs of water.

11 "I will make a highway across the mountains
and prepare a road for my people to travel.
12 My people will come from far away,
from the north and the west,
and from Aswan* in the south."

13 Sing, heavens! Shout for joy, earth!
Let the mountains burst into song!
The LORD will comfort his people;
he will have pity on his suffering people.

14 But the people of Jerusalem said,
"The LORD has abandoned us!
He has forgotten us."
15 So the LORD answers,
"Can a woman forget her own baby
and not love the child she bore?
Even if a mother should forget her child,
I will never forget you.
16 Jerusalem, I can never forget you!
I have written your name on the palms of my hands.

17 "Those who will rebuild you are coming soon,
and those who destroyed you will leave.
18 Look around and see what is happening!
Your people are assembling — they are coming home!
As surely as I am the living God,
you will be proud of your people,
as proud as a bride is of her jewels.

19 "Your country was ruined and desolate —
but now it will be too small
for those who are coming to live there.
And those who left you in ruins
will be far removed from you.
20 Your people who were born in exile
will one day say to you,
'This land is too small —
we need more room to live in!'

ISAIAH 49.16

God says that he has written the name of Jerusalem on his hands to show that

HE WON'T FORGET

- HIS PEOPLE -

there. Take a pen and write the name of someone important to you on your hand. Commit to praying for them today.

49.12 *Aswan*: A city in southern Egypt, where a large Jewish community had settled.

21 Then you will say to yourself,
  'Who bore all these children for me?
  I lost my children and could have no more.
  I was exiled and driven away —
    who brought these children up?
  I was left all alone —
    where did these children come from?' "

22 The Sovereign Lord says to his people:
  "I will signal to the nations,
    and they will bring your children home.
23 Kings will be like fathers to you;
    queens will be like mothers.
  They will bow low before you and honour you;
    they will humbly show their respect for you.
  Then you will know that I am the Lord;
    no one who waits for my help will be disappointed."

24 Can you take away a soldier's loot?
    Can you rescue the prisoners of a tyrant?

25 The Lord replies,
  "That is just what is going to happen.
  The soldier's prisoners will be taken away,
    and the tyrant's loot will be seized.
  I will fight against whoever fights you,
    and I will rescue your children.
26 I will make your oppressors kill each other;
    they will be drunk with murder and rage.
  Then the whole human race will know that I am the
      Lord,
    the one who saves you and sets you free.
  They will know that I am Israel's powerful God."

50 The Lord says,
  "Do you think I sent my people away
    like a man who divorces his wife?
  Where, then, are the papers of divorce?
  Do you think I sold you into captivity
    like a man who sells his children as slaves?
  No, you went away captive because of your sins;
    you were sent away because of your crimes.

2 "Why did my people fail to respond
    when I went to them to save them?
  Why did they not answer when I called?
  Am I too weak to save them?
  I can dry up the sea with a command
    and turn rivers into a desert,
    so that the fish in them die for lack of water.
3 I can make the sky turn dark,
    as if it were in mourning for the dead."

The Obedience of the Lord's Servant
4 The Sovereign Lord has taught me what to say,
    so that I can strengthen the weary.
  Every morning he makes me eager
    to hear what he is going to teach me.

5 The LORD has given me understanding,
    and I have not rebelled
    or turned away from him.
6 I bared my back to those who beat me.
    I did not stop them when they insulted me,
    when they pulled out the hairs of my beard
    and spat in my face.

7 But their insults cannot hurt me
    because the Sovereign LORD gives me help.
  I brace myself to endure them.
    I know that I will not be disgraced,
8   for God is near,
    and he will prove me innocent.
  Does anyone dare to bring charges against me?
    Let us go to court together!
    Let him bring his accusation!
9 The Sovereign LORD himself defends me —
    who, then, can prove me guilty?
  All my accusers will disappear;
    they will vanish like moth-eaten cloth.

10 All of you that honour the LORD
    and obey the words of his servant,
  the path you walk may be dark indeed,
    but trust in the LORD, rely on your God.
11 All of you that plot to destroy others
    will be destroyed by your own plots.
  The LORD himself will make this happen;
    you will suffer a miserable fate.

Words of Comfort to Jerusalem

51 The LORD says,
    "Listen to me, you that want to be saved,
    you that come to me for help.
  Think of the rock from which you came,
    the quarry from which you were dug.
2 Think of your ancestor, Abraham,
    and of Sarah, from whom you are descended.
  When I called Abraham, he was childless,
    but I blessed him and gave him children;
    I made his descendants numerous.

3 "I will show compassion to Jerusalem,
    to all who live in her ruins.
  Though her land is a desert, I will make it a garden,
    like the garden I planted in Eden.
  Joy and gladness will be there,
    and songs of praise and thanks to me.

4 "Listen to me, my people,
    listen to what I say:
  I give my teaching to the nations;
    my laws will bring them light.
5 I will come quickly and save them;
    the time of my victory is near.
  I myself will rule over the nations.
    Distant lands wait for me to come;
    they wait with hope for me to save them.

ISAIAH 51

865

Isaiah

....

Jerem.

Lamen.

Ezekiel

Daniel

Hosea

⁶ Look up at the heavens; look at the earth!
   The heavens will disappear like smoke;
   the earth will wear out like old clothing,
   and all its people will die like flies.
  But the deliverance I bring will last for ever;
   my victory will be final.

⁷ "Listen to me, you that know what is right,
   who have my teaching fixed in your hearts.
  Do not be afraid when people taunt and insult you;
⁸   they will vanish like moth-eaten clothing!
  But the deliverance I bring will last for ever;
   my victory will endure for all time."

⁹ Wake up, LORD, and help us!
  Use your power and save us;
   use it as you did in ancient times.
  It was you that cut the sea monster Rahab* to pieces.
¹⁰ It was you also who dried up the sea
   and made a path through the water,
   so that those you were saving could cross.
¹¹ Those whom you have rescued
   will reach Jerusalem with gladness,
   singing and shouting for joy.
  They will be happy for ever,
   for ever free from sorrow and grief.

¹² The LORD says,
  "I am the one who strengthens you.
   Why should you fear mortals,
   who are no more enduring than grass?
¹³ Have you forgotten the LORD who made you,
   who stretched out the heavens
   and laid the earth's foundations?
  Why should you live in constant fear
   of the fury of those who oppress you,
   of those who are ready to destroy you?
  Their fury can no longer touch you.
¹⁴ Those who are prisoners will soon be set free;
   they will live a long life
   and have all the food they need.

¹⁵ "I am the LORD your God;
   I stir up the sea
   and make its waves roar.
  My name is the LORD Almighty!
¹⁶ I stretched out* the heavens
   and laid the earth's foundations;
  I say to Jerusalem, 'You are my people!
   I have given you my teaching,
   and I protect you with my hand.'"

The End of Jerusalem's Suffering
¹⁷ Jerusalem, wake up!
   Rouse yourself and get up!

....

51.9 *Rahab*: A legendary sea monster, which represented the forces of chaos and evil, and was sometimes a symbol of Egypt.
51.16 One ancient translation *stretched out*; Hebrew *planted*.

866

Isaiah

Job
Psalms
Proverbs
Eccles.
Songs

ISAIAH 51, 52

You have drunk the cup of punishment
that the LORD in his anger gave you to drink;
you drank it down, and it made you stagger.
18 There is no one to lead you,
no one among your people
to take you by the hand.

19 A double disaster has fallen on you:
your land has been devastated by war,
and your people have starved.
There is no one to show you sympathy.
20 At the corner of every street
your people collapse from weakness;
they are like deer caught in a hunter's net.
They have felt the force of God's anger.

21 You suffering people of Jerusalem,
you that stagger as though you were drunk,
22 the LORD your God defends you and says,
"I am taking away the cup
that I gave you in my anger.
You will no longer have to drink
the wine that makes you stagger.
23 I will give it to those who oppressed you,
to those who made you lie down in the streets
and trampled on you as if you were dirt."

God will Rescue Jerusalem

52 Jerusalem, be strong and great again!
Holy city of God, clothe yourself with splendour!
The heathen will never enter your gates again.
2 Shake yourself free, Jerusalem!
Rise from the dust and sit on your throne!
Undo the chains that bind you,
captive people of Zion!

3 The Sovereign LORD says to his people, "When you became slaves, no money was paid for you; in the same way nothing will be paid to set you free. 4 When you went to live in Egypt as foreigners, you did so of your own free will; Assyria, however, took you away by force and paid nothing for you. 5 And now in Babylonia the same thing has happened: you are captives, and nothing was paid for you. Those who rule over you boast and brag and constantly show contempt for me. 6 In time to come you will acknowledge that I am God and that I have spoken to you."

7 How wonderful it is to see
a messenger coming across the mountains,
bringing good news, the news of peace!
He announces victory and says to Zion,
"Your God is king!"
8 Those who guard the city are shouting,
shouting together for joy!
They can see with their own eyes
the return of the LORD to Zion!

9 Break into shouts of joy,
you ruins of Jerusalem!

ISAIAH 52, 53

867

Isaiah

....

Jerem.
Lamen.
Ezekiel
Daniel
Hosea

The LORD will rescue his city
and comfort his people.

10 The LORD will use his holy power;
he will save his people,
and all the world will see it.

11 Make sure you leave Babylonia,
all you that carry the temple equipment!
Touch no forbidden thing;*
keep yourselves holy and leave.

12 This time you will not have to leave in a hurry;
you will not be trying to escape.
The LORD your God will lead you
and protect you on every side.

The Suffering Servant

13 The LORD says,
"My servant will succeed in his task;
he will be highly honoured.*

14 Many people were shocked when they saw him;
he was so disfigured that he hardly looked human.

15 But now many nations will marvel at him,
and kings will be speechless with amazement.
They will see and understand
something they had never known."

53 The people reply,
"Who would have believed what we now report?
Who could have seen the LORD's hand in this?

2 It was the will of the LORD that his servant
should grow like a plant taking root in dry ground.
He had no dignity or beauty
to make us take notice of him.
There was nothing attractive about him,
nothing that would draw us to him.

3 We despised him and rejected him;
he endured suffering and pain.
No one would even look at him —
we ignored him as if he were nothing.

4 "But he endured the suffering that should have been
ours,
the pain that we should have borne.
All the while we thought that his suffering
was punishment sent by God.

5 But because of our sins he was wounded,
beaten because of the evil we did.
We are healed by the punishment he suffered,
made whole by the blows he received.

6 All of us were like sheep that were lost,
each of us going his own way.
But the LORD made the punishment fall on him,
the punishment all of us deserved.

7 "He was treated harshly, but endured it humbly;
he never said a word.

ISAIAH 53.5

- We are -
HEALED
... by the ...
PUNISHMENT
HE SUFFERED,
- made -
WHOLE
... by the ...
BLOWS HE
RECEIVED

....

52.11 *forbidden thing*: Any object that was considered ritually unclean.
52.13 *he will be highly honoured*; or *he will be restored to greatness and honour.*

868

Isaiah

Job
Psalms
Proverbs
Eccles.
Songs

ISAIAH 53, 54

Like a lamb about to be slaughtered,
like a sheep about to be sheared,
he never said a word.
8 He was arrested and sentenced and led off to die,
and no one cared about his fate.
He was put to death for the sins of our people.
9 He was placed in a grave with the wicked,
he was buried with the rich,
even though he had never committed a crime
or ever told a lie."

10 The LORD says,
"It was my will that he should suffer;
his death was a sacrifice to bring forgiveness.
And so he will see his descendants;
he will live a long life,
and through him my purpose will succeed.
11 After a life of suffering, he will again have joy;
he will know that he did not suffer in vain.
My devoted servant, with whom I am pleased,
will bear the punishment of many
and for his sake I will forgive them.
12 And so I will give him a place of honour,
a place among the great and powerful.
He willingly gave his life
and shared the fate of evil men.
He took the place of many sinners
and prayed that they might be forgiven."*

The LORD's Love for Israel

54 Jerusalem, you have been like a childless woman,
but now you can sing and shout for joy.
Now you will have more children
than a woman whose husband never left her!
2 Make the tent you live in larger;
lengthen its ropes and strengthen the pegs!
3 You will extend your boundaries on all sides;
your people will get back the land
that the other nations now occupy.
Cities now deserted will be filled with people.

4 Do not be afraid — you will not be disgraced again;
you will not be humiliated.
You will forget your unfaithfulness as a young wife,
and your desperate loneliness as a widow.
5 Your Creator will be like a husband to you —
the LORD Almighty is his name.
The holy God of Israel will save you —
he is the ruler of all the world.

6 Israel, you are like a young wife,
deserted by her husband and deeply distressed.
But the LORD calls you back to him and says:
7 "For one brief moment I left you;
with deep love I will take you back.

....

53.12 *prayed that they might be forgiven*; or *suffered the punishment they
deserved.*

ISAIAH 54, 55

869

Isaiah
....
Jerem.
Lamen.
Ezekiel
Daniel
Hosea

8 I turned away angry for only a moment,
  but I will show you my love for ever."
So says the LORD who saves you.

9 "In the time of Noah I promised
  never again to flood the earth.
Now I promise not to be angry with you again;
  I will not reprimand or punish you.
10 The mountains and hills may crumble,
  but my love for you will never end;
  I will keep for ever my promise of peace."
So says the LORD who loves you.

The Future Jerusalem
11 The LORD says,
  "O Jerusalem, you suffering, helpless city,
    with no one to comfort you,
  I will rebuild your foundations with precious stones.
12 I will build your towers with rubies,
    your gates with stones that glow like fire,
    and the wall around you with jewels.

13 "I myself will teach your people,
    and give them prosperity and peace.
14 Justice and right will make you strong.
    You will be safe from oppression and terror.
15 Whoever attacks you
    does it without my consent;
    whoever fights against you will fall.

16 "I create the blacksmith,
    who builds a fire and forges weapons.
  I also create the soldier,
    who uses the weapons to kill.
17 But no weapon will be able to hurt you;
    you will have an answer for all who accuse you.
  I will defend my servants
    and give them victory."
The LORD has spoken.

God's Offer of Mercy
55 The LORD says,
  "Come, everyone who is thirsty —
    here is water!
Come, you that have no money —
    buy corn and eat!
Come! Buy wine and milk —
    it will cost you nothing!
2 Why spend money on what does not satisfy?
    Why spend your wages and still be hungry?
Listen to me and do what I say,
    and you will enjoy the best food of all.

3 "Listen now, my people, and come to me;
    come to me, and you will have life!
  I will make a lasting covenant with you
    and give you the blessings I promised to David.
4 I made him a leader and commander of nations,

MERCY

PSALM 80.3;
ISAIAH 55.1;
JEREMIAH 30.18

What do you
think it means?

What does someone
else think it means?

Now go and look up
the definition.

870

Isaiah

⁚·········

Job
Psalms
Proverbs
Eccles.
Songs

ISAIAH 55, 56

and through him I showed them my power.
⁵ Now you will summon foreign nations;
    at one time they did not know you,
    but now they will come running to join you!
I, the LORD your God, the holy God of Israel,
    will make all this happen;
    I will give you honour and glory."

⁶ Turn to the LORD and pray to him,
    now that he is near.
⁷ Let the wicked leave their way of life
    and change their way of thinking.
Let them turn to the LORD, our God;
    he is merciful and quick to forgive.
⁸ "My thoughts," says the LORD, "are not like yours,
    and my ways are different from yours.
⁹ As high as the heavens are above the earth,
    so high are my ways and thoughts above yours.

¹⁰ "My word is like the snow and the rain
    that come down from the sky to water the earth.
They make the crops grow
    and provide seed for sowing and food to eat.
¹¹ So also will be the word that I speak —
    it will not fail to do what I plan for it;
    it will do everything I send it to do.

¹² "You will leave Babylon with joy;
    you will be led out of the city in peace.
The mountains and hills will burst into singing,
    and the trees will shout for joy.
¹³ Cypress trees will grow where now there are briars;
    myrtle trees will come up in place of thorns.
This will be a sign that will last for ever,
    a reminder of what I, the LORD, have done."

God's People will Include All Nations

56 The LORD says to his people, "Do what is just and right, for soon I will save you. ²I will bless those who always observe the Sabbath and do not misuse it. I will bless those who do nothing evil."

³A foreigner who has joined the LORD's people should not say, "The LORD will not let me worship with his people."

A man who has been castrated should never think that because he cannot have children, he can never be part of God's people. ⁴The LORD says to such a man, "If you honour me by observing the Sabbath and if you do what pleases me and faithfully keep my covenant, ⁵then your name will be remembered in my Temple and among my people longer than if you had sons and daughters. You will never be forgotten."

⁶And the LORD says to those foreigners who become part of his people, who love him and serve him, who observe the Sabbath and faithfully keep his covenant: ⁷"I will bring you to Zion, my sacred hill,* give you joy in my house of prayer, and accept the sacrifices you offer on my altar. My Temple will be called a house of prayer for the people of all nations."

....

56.7 *sacred hill*: See 2.3.

ISAIAH 56, 57

871

Isaiah
·········›

Jerem.
Lamen.
Ezekiel
Daniel
Hosea

[8] The Sovereign Lord, who has brought his people Israel home from exile, has promised that he will bring still other people to join them.

Israel's Leaders are Condemned

[9] The Lord has told the foreign nations to come like wild animals and devour his people. [10] He says, "All the leaders, who are supposed to warn my people, are blind! They know nothing. They are like watchdogs that don't bark — they only lie about and dream. How they love to sleep! [11] They are like greedy dogs that never get enough. These leaders have no understanding. They each do as they please and seek their own advantage. [12] 'Let's get some wine,' these drunkards say, 'and drink all we can hold! Tomorrow will be even better than today!' "

Israel's Idolatry is Condemned

57 Good people die, and no one understands or even cares. But when they die, no calamity can hurt them. [2] Those who live good lives find peace and rest in death.

[3] Come here to be judged, you sinners! You are no better than sorcerers, adulterers, and prostitutes. [4] Who are you making fun of? Who are you liars jeering at? [5] You worship the fertility gods by having sex under those sacred trees of yours. You offer your children as sacrifices in the rocky caves near the bed of a stream. [6] You take smooth stones from there and worship them as gods. You pour out wine as offerings to them and bring them grain offerings. Do you think I am pleased with all this? [7] You go to the high mountains to offer sacrifices and have sex. [8] You set up your obscene idols just inside your front doors. You forsake me; you take off your clothes and climb into your large beds with your lovers, whom you pay to sleep with you. And there you satisfy your lust. [9] You put on your perfumes and ointments and go to worship the god Molech. To find gods to worship, you send messengers far and wide, even to the world of the dead. [10] You wear yourselves out looking for other gods, but you never give up. You think your obscene idols give you strength, and so you never grow weak.

[11] The Lord says, "Who are these gods that make you afraid, so that you tell me lies and forget me completely? Have you stopped honouring me because I have kept silent for so long? [12] You think that what you do is right, but I will expose your conduct, and your idols will not be able to help you. [13] When you cry for help, let those idols of yours save you! A puff of wind will carry them off! But those who trust in me will live in the land and will worship me in my Temple."

God's Promise of Help and Healing

[14] The Lord says, "Let my people return to me. Remove every obstacle from their path! Build the road, and make it ready!

[15] "I am the high and holy God, who lives for ever. I live in a high and holy place, but I also live with people who are humble and repentant, so that I can restore their confidence and hope. [16] I gave my people life, and I will not continue to accuse them or be angry with them for ever.* [17] I was angry with them because of their sin and greed, and so I punished them and abandoned them. But they were stubborn and kept on going their own way.

....

57.16 *I gave my people... for ever;* or *I will not continue to accuse them or be angry with them for ever, for then they would die — the very people to whom I gave life.*

872

Isaiah

Job
Psalms
Proverbs
Eccles.
Songs

[18] "I have seen how they acted, but I will heal them. I will lead them and help them, and I will comfort those who mourn. [19] I offer peace to all, both near and far! I will heal my people. [20] But evil people are like the restless sea, whose waves never stop rolling in, bringing filth and muck. [21] There is no safety for sinners," says the LORD.

True Fasting

58 The LORD says, "Shout as loud as you can! Tell my people Israel about their sins! [2] They worship me every day, claiming that they are eager to know my ways and obey my laws. They say they want me to give them just laws and that they take pleasure in worshipping me."

[3] The people ask, "Why should we fast if the LORD never notices? Why should we go without food if he pays no attention?"

The LORD says to them, "The truth is that at the same time as you fast, you pursue your own interests and oppress your workers. [4] Your fasting makes you violent, and you quarrel and fight. Do you think this kind of fasting will make me listen to your prayers? [5] When you fast, you make yourselves suffer; you bow your heads low like a blade of grass, and spread out sackcloth and ashes to lie on. Is that what you call fasting? Do you think I will be pleased with that?

[6] "The kind of fasting I want is this: remove the chains of oppression and the yoke of injustice, and let the oppressed go free. [7] Share your food with the hungry and open your homes to the homeless poor. Give clothes to those who have nothing to wear, and do not refuse to help your own relatives.

[8] "Then my favour will shine on you like the morning sun, and your wounds will be quickly healed. I will always be with you to save you; my presence will protect you on every side. [9] When you pray, I will answer you. When you call to me, I will respond.

"If you put an end to oppression, to every gesture of contempt, and to every evil word; [10] if you give food to the hungry and satisfy those who are in need, then the darkness around you will turn to the brightness of noon. [11] And I will always guide you and satisfy you with good things. I will keep you strong and well. You will be like a garden that has plenty of water, like a spring of water that never runs dry. [12] Your people will rebuild what has long been in ruins, building again on the old foundations. You will be known as the people who rebuilt the walls, who restored the ruined houses."

The Reward for Keeping the Sabbath

[13] The LORD says, "If you treat the Sabbath as sacred and do not pursue your own interests on that day; if you value my holy day and honour it by not travelling, working, or talking idly on that day, [14] then you will find the joy that comes from serving me. I will make you honoured all over the world, and you will enjoy the land I gave to your ancestor, Jacob. I, the LORD, have spoken."

The Prophet Condemns the People's Sins

59 Don't think that the LORD is too weak to save you or too deaf to hear your call for help! [2] It is because of your sins that he doesn't hear you. It is your sins that separate you from God when you try to worship him. [3] You are guilty of lying, violence, and murder.

[4] You go to court, but you haven't got justice on your side. You depend on lies to win your case. You carry out your plans to hurt others. [5-6] The evil plots you make are as deadly as the eggs of

---

ISAIAH 58.6-7

If you are able to, skip your next meal as an

ACT OF

FASTING.

As you fast, plan how you might be able to live out God's words in Isaiah 58.6-7.

ISAIAH 59, 60

873

Isaiah

....

Jerem.

Lamen.

Ezekiel

Daniel

Hosea

a poisonous snake. Crush an egg, out comes a snake! But your plots will do you no good — they are as useless as clothing made of cobwebs! [7] You are always planning something evil, and you can hardly wait to do it. You never hesitate to murder innocent people. You leave ruin and destruction wherever you go, [8] and no one is safe when you are about. Everything you do is unjust. You follow a crooked path, and no one who walks that path will ever be safe.

The People Confess their Sin

[9] The people say, "Now we know why God does not save us from those who oppress us. We hope for light to walk by, but there is only darkness, [10] and we grope about like blind people. We stumble at noon, as if it were night, as if we were in the dark world of the dead. [11] We are frightened and distressed. We long for God to save us from oppression and wrong, but nothing happens.

[12] "LORD, our crimes against you are many. Our sins accuse us. We are well aware of them all. [13] We have rebelled against you, rejected you, and refused to follow you. We have oppressed others and turned away from you. Our thoughts are false; our words are lies. [14] Justice is driven away, and right cannot come near. Truth stumbles in the public square, and honesty finds no place there. [15] There is so little honesty that those who stop doing evil find themselves the victims of crime."

The LORD Prepares to Rescue his People

The LORD has seen this, and he is displeased that there is no justice. [16] He is astonished to see that there is no one to help the oppressed. So he will use his own power to rescue them and to win the victory. [17] He will wear justice like a coat of armour and saving power like a helmet. He will clothe himself with the strong desire to set things right and to punish and avenge the wrongs that people suffer. [18] He will punish his enemies according to what they have done, even those who live in distant lands. [19] From east to west everyone will fear him and his great power. He will come like a rushing river, like a strong wind.

[20] The LORD says to his people, "I will come to Jerusalem to defend you and to save all of you that turn from your sins. [21] And I make a covenant with you: I have given you my power and my teachings to be yours for ever, and from now on you are to obey me and teach your children and your descendants to obey me for all time to come."

The Future Glory of Jerusalem

60

Arise, Jerusalem, and shine like the sun;
The glory of the LORD is shining on you!
[2] Other nations will be covered by darkness,
But on you the light of the LORD will shine;
The brightness of his presence will be with you.
[3] Nations will be drawn to your light,
And kings to the dawning of your new day.

[4] Look around you and see what is happening:
Your people are gathering to come home!
Your sons will come from far away;
Your daughters will be carried like children.
[5] You will see this and be filled with joy;
You will tremble with excitement.

The wealth of the nations will be brought to you;
From across the sea their riches will come.
6 Great caravans of camels will come, from Midian and
Ephah.
They will come from Sheba, bringing gold and incense.
People will tell the good news of what the LORD has done!
7 All the sheep of Kedar and Nebaioth
Will be brought to you as sacrifices
And offered on the altar to please the LORD.
The LORD will make his Temple more glorious than ever.

8 What are these ships that skim along like clouds,
Like doves returning home?
9 They are ships coming from distant lands,
Bringing God's people home.
They bring with them silver and gold
To honour the name of the LORD,
The holy God of Israel,
Who has made all nations honour his people.

10 The LORD says to Jerusalem,
"Foreigners will rebuild your walls,
And their kings will serve you.
In my anger I punished you,
But now I will show you my favour and mercy.
11 Day and night your gates will be open,
So that the kings of the nations
May bring you their wealth.
12 But nations that do not serve you
Will be completely destroyed.

13 "The wood of the pine, the juniper, and the cypress,
The finest wood from the forests of Lebanon,
Will be brought to rebuild you, Jerusalem,
To make my Temple beautiful,
To make my city glorious.
14 The descendants of those who oppressed you will come
And bow low to show their respect.
All who once despised you will worship at your feet.
They will call you 'The City of the LORD',
'Zion, the City of Israel's Holy God'.

15 "You will no longer be forsaken and hated,
A city deserted and desolate.
I will make you great and beautiful,
A place of joy for ever and ever.
16 Nations and kings will care for you
As a mother nurses her child.
You will know that I, the LORD, have saved you,
That the mighty God of Israel sets you free.

17 "I will bring you gold instead of bronze,
Silver and bronze instead of iron and wood,
And iron instead of stone.
Your rulers will no longer oppress you;
I will make them rule with justice and peace.
18 The sounds of violence will be heard no more;
Destruction will not shatter your country again.

I will protect and defend you like a wall;
You will praise me because I have saved you.

19 "No longer will the sun be your light by day
Or the moon be your light by night;
I, the LORD, will be your eternal light;
The light of my glory will shine on you.
20 Your days of grief will come to an end.
I, the LORD, will be your eternal light,
More lasting than the sun and moon.
21 Your people will all do what is right,
And will possess the land for ever.
I planted them, I made them,
To reveal my greatness to all.
22 Even your smallest and humblest family
Will become as great as a powerful nation.
When the right time comes,
I will make this happen quickly.
I am the LORD!"

The Good News of Deliverance

61 The Sovereign LORD has filled me with his Spirit.
He has chosen me and sent me
To bring good news to the poor,
To heal the broken-hearted,
To announce release to captives
And freedom to those in prison.
2 He has sent me to proclaim
That the time has come
When the LORD will save his people
And defeat their enemies.
He has sent me to comfort all who mourn,
3 To give to those who mourn in Zion
Joy and gladness instead of grief,
A song of praise instead of sorrow.
They will be like trees
That the LORD himself has planted.
They will all do what is right,
And God will be praised for what he has done.
4 They will rebuild cities that have long been in ruins.

5 My people, foreigners will serve you.
They will take care of your flocks
And farm your land and tend your vineyards.
6 And you will be known as the priests of the LORD,
The servants of our God.
You will enjoy the wealth of the nations
And be proud that it is yours.
7 Your shame and disgrace are ended.
You will live in your own land,
And your wealth will be doubled;
Your joy will last for ever.

8 The LORD says,
"I love justice and I hate oppression and crime.
I will faithfully reward my people
And make an eternal covenant with them.
9 They will be famous among the nations;

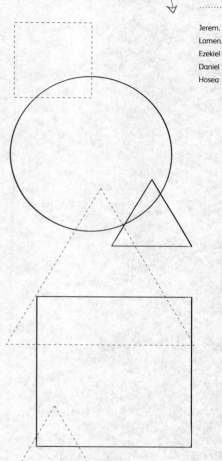

Colour these shapes.

Isaiah

Jerem.

Lamen.

Ezekiel

Daniel

Hosea

876

Isaiah

Job
Psalms
Proverbs
Eccles.
Songs

ISAIAH 61, 62

Everyone who sees them will know
That they are a people whom I have blessed."

10 Jerusalem rejoices because of what the LORD has
done.
She is like a bride dressed for her wedding.
God has clothed her with salvation and victory.
11 As surely as seeds sprout and grow,
The Sovereign LORD will save his people,
And all the nations will praise him.

62 I will speak out to encourage Jerusalem;
I will not be silent until she is saved,
And her victory shines like a torch in the night.
2 Jerusalem, the nations will see you victorious!
All their kings will see your glory.
You will be called by a new name,
A name given by the LORD himself.
3 You will be like a beautiful crown for the LORD.
4 No longer will you be called "Forsaken",
Or your land be called "The Deserted Wife".
Your new name will be "God is Pleased with Her".
Your land will be called "Happily Married",
Because the LORD is pleased with you
And will be like a husband to your land.
5 Like a young man taking a virgin as his bride,
He who formed you will marry you.
As a groom is delighted with his bride,
So your God will delight in you.
6 On your walls, Jerusalem,
I have placed sentries;
They must never be silent day or night.
They must remind the LORD of his promises
And never let him forget them.
7 They must give him no rest until he restores Jerusalem
And makes it a city the whole world praises.

8 The LORD has made a solemn promise,
And by his power he will carry it out:
"Your corn will no longer be food for your enemies,
And foreigners will no longer drink your wine.
9 But you that sowed and harvested the corn
Will eat the bread and praise the LORD.
You that tended and gathered the grapes
Will drink the wine in the courts of my Temple."

10 People of Jerusalem, go out of the city
And build a road for your returning people!
Prepare a highway; clear it of stones!
Put up a signal so that the nations can know
11 That the LORD is announcing to all the earth:
"Tell the people of Jerusalem
That the LORD is coming to save you,
Bringing with him the people he has rescued."
12 You will be called "God's Holy People",
"The People the LORD has Saved".
Jerusalem will be called "The City that God Loves",
"The City that God did not Forsake".

ISAIAH 63, 64

877

Isaiah
....

Jerem.
Lamen.
Ezekiel
Daniel
Hosea

The LORD's Victory over the Nations

63 "Who is this coming from the city of Bozrah in Edom? Who is this so splendidly dressed in red, marching along* in power and strength?"

"It is the LORD, powerful to save, coming to announce his victory."

² "Why is his clothing so red, like that of someone who tramples grapes to make wine?"

³ The LORD answers, "I have trampled the nations like grapes, and no one came to help me. I trampled them in my anger, and their blood has stained all my clothing. ⁴ I decided that the time to save my people had come; it was time to punish their enemies. ⁵ I was amazed when I looked and saw that there was no one to help me. But my anger made me strong, and I won the victory myself. ⁶ In my anger I trampled whole nations and shattered them. I poured out their lifeblood on the ground."

The LORD's Goodness to Israel

⁷ I will tell of the LORD's unfailing love;
 I praise him for all he has done for us.
He has richly blessed the people of Israel
 because of his mercy and constant love.

⁸ The LORD said, "They are my people; they will not deceive me." And so he saved them ⁹ from all their suffering. It was not an angel, but the LORD himself who saved them. In his love and compassion he rescued them. He had always taken care of them in the past, ¹⁰ but they rebelled against him and made his Holy Spirit sad. So the LORD became their enemy and fought against them.

¹¹ But then they* remembered the past, the days of Moses, the servant of the LORD, and they asked, "Where now is the LORD, who saved the leaders of his people from the sea? Where is the LORD, who gave his Spirit to Moses? ¹²⁻¹³ Where is the LORD, who by his power did great things through Moses, dividing the waters of the sea and leading his people through the deep water, to win everlasting fame for himself?"

Led by the LORD, they were as sure-footed as wild horses, and never stumbled. ¹⁴ As cattle are led into a fertile valley, so the LORD gave his people rest. He led his people and brought honour to his name.

A Prayer for Mercy and Help

¹⁵ LORD, look upon us from heaven, where you live in your holiness and glory. Where is your great concern for us? Where is your power? Where are your love and compassion? Do not ignore us. ¹⁶ You are our father. Our ancestors Abraham and Jacob do not acknowledge us, but you, LORD, are our father, the one who has always rescued us. ¹⁷ Why do you let us stray from your ways? Why do you make us so stubborn that we turn away from you? Come back, for the sake of those who serve you, for the sake of the people who have always been yours.

¹⁸ We, your holy people, were driven out by our enemies for a little while: they trampled down your sanctuary.* ¹⁹ You treat us as though you had never been our ruler, as though we had never been your people.

64 Why don't you tear the sky apart and come down? The mountains would see you and shake with fear. ² They would

....

63.1 Some ancient translations *marching along*; Hebrew *bowed down*.
63.11 Probable text *they*; Hebrew *he*.
63.18 Verse 18 in Hebrew is unclear.

878

Isaiah

⁝········

Job
Psalms
Proverbs
Eccles.
Songs

tremble like water boiling over a hot fire. Come and reveal your power to your enemies, and make the nations tremble at your presence! ³There was a time when you came and did terrifying things that we did not expect; the mountains saw you and shook with fear. ⁴No one has ever seen or heard of a God like you, who does such deeds for those who put their hope in him. ⁵You welcome those who find joy in doing what is right, those who remember how you want them to live. You were angry with us, but we went on sinning; in spite of your great anger we have continued to do wrong since ancient times.* ⁶All of us have been sinful; even our best actions are filthy through and through. Because of our sins we are like leaves that wither and are blown away by the wind. ⁷No one turns to you in prayer; no one goes to you for help. You have hidden yourself from us and have abandoned* us because of our sins.

⁸But you are our father, LORD. We are like clay, and you are like the potter. You created us, ⁹so do not be too angry with us or hold our sins against us for ever. We are your people; be merciful to us. ¹⁰Your sacred cities are like a desert; Jerusalem is a deserted ruin, ¹¹and our Temple, the sacred and beautiful place where our ancestors praised you, has been destroyed by fire. All the places we loved are in ruins. ¹²LORD, are you unmoved by all this? Are you going to do nothing and make us suffer more than we can endure?

God's Punishment of the Rebellious

65 The LORD said, "I was ready to answer my people's prayers, but they did not pray. I was ready for them to find me, but they did not even try. The nation did not pray to me, even though I was always ready to answer, 'Here I am; I will help you.' ²I have always been ready to welcome my people, who stubbornly do what is wrong and go their own way. ³They shamelessly keep on making me angry. They offer pagan sacrifices in sacred gardens* and burn incense on pagan altars. ⁴At night they go to caves and tombs to consult the spirits of the dead. They eat pork and drink broth made from meat offered in pagan sacrifices. ⁵And then they say to others, 'Keep away from us; we are too holy for you to touch!' I cannot stand people like that — my anger against them is like a fire that never goes out.

⁶"I have already decided on their punishment, and their sentence is written down. I will not overlook what they have done, but will repay them ⁷for their sins and the sins of their ancestors. They have burnt incense at pagan hill shrines and spoken evil of me. So I will punish them as their past deeds deserve."

⁸The LORD says, "No one destroys good grapes; instead, they make wine with them. Neither will I destroy all my people — I will save those who serve me. ⁹I will bless the Israelites who belong to the tribe of Judah, and their descendants will possess my land of mountains. My chosen people, who serve me, will live there. ¹⁰They will worship me and will lead their sheep and cattle to pasture in the Plain of Sharon in the west and in the Valley of Trouble in the east.

¹¹"But it will be different for you that forsake me, who ignore Zion, my sacred hill,* and worship Gad and Meni, the gods of luck and fate. ¹²It will be your fate to die a violent death, because

---

64.5 Probable text *in spite of... ancient times*; Hebrew unclear.
64.7 Some ancient translations *abandoned*; Hebrew *melted*.
65.3 *sacred gardens*: See 1.29.
65.11 *sacred hill*: See 2.3.

ISAIAH 65, 66

879

Isaiah

....

Jerem.
Lamen.
Ezekiel
Daniel
Hosea

you did not answer when I called you or listen when I spoke. You chose to disobey me and do evil. [13] And so I tell you that those who worship and obey me will have plenty to eat and drink, but you will be hungry and thirsty. They will be happy, but you will be disgraced. [14] They will sing for joy, but you will cry with a broken heart. [15] My chosen people will use your name as a curse. I, the Sovereign LORD, will put you to death. But I will give a new name to those who obey me. [16] Anyone in the land who asks for a blessing will ask to be blessed by the Faithful God. Whoever takes an oath will swear by the name of the Faithful God. The troubles of the past will be gone and forgotten."

The New Creation

[17] The LORD says, "I am making a new earth and new heavens. The events of the past will be completely forgotten. [18] Be glad and rejoice for ever in what I create. The new Jerusalem I make will be full of joy, and her people will be happy. [19] I myself will be filled with joy because of Jerusalem and her people. There will be no weeping there, no calling for help. [20] Babies will no longer die in infancy, and all people will live out their life span. Those who live to be a hundred will be considered young. To die before that would be a sign that I had punished them. [21-22] People will build houses and live in them themselves — they will not be used by someone else. They will plant vineyards and enjoy the wine — it will not be drunk by others. Like trees, my people will live long lives. They will fully enjoy the things that they have worked for. [23] The work they do will be successful, and their children will not meet with disaster. I will bless them and their descendants for all time to come. [24] Even before they finish praying to me, I will answer their prayers. [25] Wolves and lambs will eat together; lions will eat straw, as cattle do, and snakes will no longer be dangerous. On Zion, my sacred hill,* there will be nothing harmful or evil."

The LORD Judges the Nations

66 The LORD says, "Heaven is my throne, and the earth is my footstool. What kind of house, then, could you build for me, what kind of place for me to live in? [2] I myself created the whole universe! I am pleased with those who are humble and repentant, who fear me and obey me.

[3] "The people do as they please. It's all the same to them whether they kill a bull as a sacrifice or sacrifice a human being; whether they sacrifice a lamb or break a dog's neck; whether they present a grain offering or offer pigs' blood; whether they offer incense or pray to an idol. They take pleasure in disgusting ways of worship. [4] So I will bring disaster upon them — the very things they are afraid of — because no one answered when I called or listened when I spoke. They chose to disobey me and do evil."

[5] Listen to what the LORD says, you that fear him and obey him: "Because you are faithful to me, some of your own people hate you and will have nothing to do with you. They mock you and say, 'Let the LORD show his greatness and save you, so that we may see you rejoice.' But they themselves will be disgraced! [6] Listen! That loud noise in the city, that sound in the Temple, is the sound of the LORD punishing his enemies!

[7] "My holy city is like a woman who suddenly gives birth to a child, without ever going into labour. [8] Has anyone ever seen or heard of such a thing? Has a nation ever been born in a day?

ISAIAH 65.17-25

Many prophecies found in Isaiah and the other prophets relate to Jesus. However, many more, such as those towards the end of Isaiah, speak of a time that has not yet come. We are

· STILL ·

WAITING

for these prophecies to be fulfilled, so it is good to know what we are waiting for!

65.25 *sacred hill*: See 2.3.

880

Isaiah

⠇∙∙∙∙∙∙∙

Job
Psalms
Proverbs
Eccles.
Songs

ISAIAH 66

Zion will not have to suffer long, before the nation is born. ⁹Do not think that I will bring my people to the point of birth and not let them be born." The LORD has spoken.

¹⁰ Rejoice with Jerusalem; be glad for her,
    all you that love this city!
Rejoice with her now,
    all you that have mourned for her!
¹¹ You will enjoy her prosperity,
    like a child at its mother's breast.

¹² The LORD says, "I will bring you lasting prosperity; the wealth of the nations will flow to you like a river that never goes dry. You will be like a child that is nursed by its mother, carried in her arms, and treated with love. ¹³ I will comfort you in Jerusalem, as a mother comforts her child. ¹⁴ When you see this happen, you will be glad; it will make you strong and healthy. Then you will know that I, the LORD, help those who obey me, and I show my anger against my enemies."

¹⁵ The LORD will come with fire. He will ride on the wings of a storm to punish those he is angry with. ¹⁶ By fire and sword he will punish all the people of the world whom he finds guilty — and many will be put to death.

¹⁷ The LORD says, "The end is near for those who purify themselves for pagan worship, who go in procession to sacred gardens,* and who eat pork and mice and other disgusting foods. ¹⁸ I know* their thoughts and their deeds. I am coming* to gather the people of all the nations. When they come together, they will see what my power can do ¹⁹ and will know that I am the one who punishes them.

"But I will spare some of them and send them to the nations and the distant lands that have not heard of my fame or seen my greatness and power: to Spain, Libya,* and Lydia, with its skilled archers, and to Tubal and Greece. Among these nations they will proclaim my greatness. ²⁰ They will bring back all your fellow-Israelites from the nations as a gift to me. They will bring them to my sacred hill* in Jerusalem on horses, mules, and camels, and in chariots and wagons, just as Israelites bring grain offerings to the Temple in ritually clean containers. ²¹ I will make some of them priests and Levites.

²² "Just as the new earth and the new heavens will endure by my power, so your descendants and your name will endure. ²³ On every New Moon Festival and every Sabbath, people of every nation will come to worship me here in Jerusalem," says the LORD. ²⁴ "As they leave, they will see the dead bodies of those who have rebelled against me. The worms that eat them will never die, and the fire that burns them will never be put out. The sight of them will be disgusting to the whole human race."

....
66.17 *sacred gardens*: See 1.29.
66.18 Some ancient translations *I know*; Hebrew *I*.
66.18 Some ancient translations *I am coming*; Hebrew *He is coming*.
66.19 One ancient translation *Libya*; Hebrew *Pul*.
66.20 *sacred hill*: See 2.3.

THE BOOK OF

JEREMIAH

WRITTEN: AROUND 626BC ONWARD

WHAT YOU NEED TO KNOW:

God was at the end of his tether with the kingdom of Judah. He had sent many warnings through his prophets, and yet the kings of Judah (except for Josiah, who brought the nation back to God - see 2 Kings 22) continued to ignore God. Jeremiah witnessed the decline of Judah until the destruction of his home at the hands of the Babylonians. He saw the temple being destroyed by enemy forces and his countryfolk being sent into exile. Although he foresaw and prophesied much of this, Jeremiah still had words of hope to offer to the Judeans, even when they were carried off into captivity.

WHY READ IT?

Jeremiah was known as the 'weeping prophet'. He wasn't one to hold back on his emotions. The events going on around him were raw for him and he would often vent his feelings at God. He would cry, get angry and lament in his prayers. Although he brought prophecies of doom and destruction to Judah, he often pleaded with God to change his mind. Jeremiah teaches us that being emotional with God, being angry and upset about the brokenness around us, is good.

What are some of the things you treasure the most?

WRITE THEM DOWN.

How would you feel if, because of other people's actions, these things were destroyed?

_____
_____
_____
_____
_____
_____
_____
_____
_____
_____
_____
_____
_____
_____
_____
_____
_____
_____
_____
_____
_____
_____
_____

626BC

KING JOSIAH

KING JEHOIAKIM

KING ZEDEKIAH

JUDAH FALLS TO BABYLON

(586BC)

882

Jerem.

Psalms
Proverbs
Eccles.
Songs
Isaiah

JEREMIAH 1.7-10

Jeremiah was a

YOUNG
- PERSON -

when God first spoke to
him, but youth wasn't
an excuse not to fulfil
what God was asking
him to do. Around this
page, write the things
you think God might be
asking you to do while
you are still young.

Jeremiah

1 This book is the account of what was said by Jeremiah son of Hilkiah, one of the priests of the town of Anathoth in the territory of Benjamin. [2] The LORD spoke to Jeremiah in the thirteenth year that Josiah son of Amon was king of Judah, [3] and he spoke to him again when Josiah's son Jehoiakim was king. After that, the LORD spoke to him many times, until the eleventh year of the reign of Zedekiah son of Josiah. In the fifth month of that year the people of Jerusalem were taken into exile.

The Call of Jeremiah

[4] The LORD said to me, [5] "I chose you before I gave you life, and before you were born I selected you to be a prophet to the nations."

[6] I answered, "Sovereign LORD, I don't know how to speak; I am too young."

[7] But the LORD said to me, "Do not say that you are too young, but go to the people I send you to, and tell them everything I command you to say. [8] Do not be afraid of them, for I will be with you to protect you. I, the LORD, have spoken!"

[9] Then the LORD stretched out his hand, touched my lips, and said to me, "Listen, I am giving you the words you must speak. [10] Today I give you authority over nations and kingdoms to uproot and to pull down, to destroy and to overthrow, to build and to plant."

Two Visions

[11] The LORD asked me, "Jeremiah, what do you see?"

I answered, "A branch of an almond tree."

[12] "You are right," the LORD said, "and I am watching* to see that my words come true."

[13] Then the LORD spoke to me again. "What else do you see?" he asked.

I answered, "I see a pot boiling in the north, and it is about to tip over this way."

[14] He said to me, "Destruction will boil over from the north on all who live in this land, [15] because I am calling all the nations in the north to come. Their kings will set up their thrones at the gates of Jerusalem and round its walls, and also round the other cities of Judah. [16] I will punish my people because they have sinned; they have abandoned me, have offered sacrifices to other gods, and have made idols and worshipped them. [17] Get ready, Jeremiah; go and tell them everything I command you to say. Do not be afraid of them now, or I will make you even more afraid when you are with them. [18-19] Listen, Jeremiah! Everyone in this land — the kings of Judah, the officials, the priests, and the people — will be against you. But today I am giving you the strength to resist them; you will be like a fortified city, an iron pillar, and a bronze wall. They will not defeat you, for I will be with you to protect you. I, the LORD, have spoken."

God's Care for Israel

2 The LORD told me [2] to proclaim this message to everyone in Jerusalem.

"I remember how faithful you were when you were young,
     how you loved me when we were first married;
  you followed me through the desert,
     through a land that had not been sown.

1.12 *watching*: This word in Hebrew sounds like the Hebrew for "almond".

JEREMIAH 2

883

Jerem.

....

Lamen.
Ezekiel
Daniel
Hosea
Joel

³ Israel, you belonged to me alone;
  you were my sacred possession.
I sent suffering and disaster
  on everyone who hurt you.
I, the LORD, have spoken."

The Sin of Israel's Ancestors

⁴ Listen to the LORD's message, you descendants of Jacob, you tribes of Israel. ⁵ The LORD says:
  "What accusation did your ancestors bring against
    me?
  What made them turn away from me?
  They worshipped worthless idols
    and became worthless themselves.
⁶ They did not care about me,
    even though I rescued them from Egypt
    and led them through the wilderness:
    a land of deserts and sand dunes,
    a dry and dangerous land
    where no one lives
    and no one will even travel.
⁷ I brought them into a fertile land,
    to enjoy its harvests and its other good things.
  But instead they ruined my land;
    they defiled the country I had given them.
⁸ The priests did not ask, 'Where is the LORD?'
  My own priests did not know me.
  The rulers rebelled against me;
    the prophets spoke in the name of Baal
    and worshipped useless idols.

The LORD's Case against his People

⁹ "And so I, the LORD, will state my case against my people
    again.
  I will bring charges against their descendants.
¹⁰ Go west to the island of Cyprus,
    and send someone eastwards to the land of Kedar.
    You will see that nothing like this has ever happened
      before.
¹¹ No other nation has ever changed its gods,
    even though they were not real.
  But my people have exchanged me,
    the God who has brought them honour,
    for gods that can do nothing for them.
¹² And so I command the sky to shake with horror,
    to be amazed and astonished,
¹³   for my people have committed two sins:
  they have turned away from me,
    the spring of fresh water,
  and they have dug cisterns,
    cracked cisterns that can hold no water at all.

The Results of Israel's Unfaithfulness

¹⁴ "Israel is not a slave;
    he was not born into slavery.
    Why then do his enemies hunt him down?
¹⁵ They have roared at him like lions;
    they have made his land a desert,
    and his towns lie in ruins, completely abandoned.

884

Jerem.

.·:·........

Psalms
Proverbs
Eccles.
Songs
Isaiah

JEREMIAH 2

16 Yes, those of Memphis and Tahpanhes
    have cracked his skull.
17 Israel, you brought this on yourself!
    You deserted me, the LORD your God,
    while I was leading you along the way.
18 What do you think you will gain by going to Egypt
    to drink water from the Nile?
    What do you think you will gain by going to Assyria
    to drink water from the Euphrates?
19 Your own evil will punish you,
    and your turning from me will condemn you.
    You will learn how bitter and wrong it is
    to abandon me, the LORD your God,
    and no longer to remain faithful to me.
    I, the Sovereign LORD Almighty, have spoken."

Israel Refuses to Worship the LORD

20 The Sovereign LORD says,
    "Israel, long ago you rejected my authority;
    you refused to obey me and worship me.
    On every high hill
    and under every green tree
    you worshipped fertility gods.
21 I planted you like a choice vine
    from the very best seed.
    But look what you have become!
    You are like a rotten, worthless vine.
22 Even if you washed with the strongest soap,
    I would still see the stain of your guilt.
23 How can you say you have not defiled yourself,
    that you have never worshipped Baal?
    Look how you sinned in the valley;
    see what you have done.
    You are like a wild camel on heat,
    running about loose,
24   rushing into the desert.*
    When she is on heat, who can control her?
    No male that wants her has to trouble himself;
    she is always available at mating time.
25 Israel, don't wear your feet out,
    or let your throat become dry
    from chasing after other gods.
    But you say, 'No! I can't turn back.
    I have loved foreign gods
    and will go after them.'"

Israel Deserves to be Punished

26 The LORD says, "Just as a thief is disgraced when caught,
so all you people of Israel will be disgraced — your kings and
officials, your priests and prophets. 27 You will all be disgraced
— you that say that a tree is your father and that a rock is your
mother. This will happen because you turned away from me
instead of turning to me. But when you are in trouble, you ask
me to come and save you.
28 "Where are the gods that you made for yourselves? When
you are in trouble, let them save you — if they can! Judah, you

2.24 Probable text rushing into the desert; Hebrew a wild donkey used to
the desert.

885

Jerem.

....

Lamen.
Ezekiel
Daniel
Hosea
Joel

have as many gods as you have cities. ²⁹What is your complaint? Why have you rebelled against me? ³⁰I punished you, but it did no good; you would not let me correct you. Like a raging lion, you have murdered your prophets. ³¹People of Israel, listen to what I am saying. Have I been like a desert to you, like a dark and dangerous land? Why, then, do you say that you will do as you please, that you will never come back to me? ³²Does a young woman forget her jewellery, or a bride her wedding dress? But my people have forgotten me for more days than can be counted. ³³You certainly know how to chase after lovers. Even the worst of women can learn from you. ³⁴Your clothes are stained with the blood of the poor and innocent, not with the blood of burglars.

"But in spite of all this, ³⁵you say, 'I am innocent; surely the LORD is no longer angry with me.' But I, the LORD, will punish you because you deny that you have sinned. ³⁶You have cheapened yourself by turning to the gods of other nations. You will be disappointed by Egypt, just as you were by Assyria. ³⁷You will turn away from Egypt, hanging your head in shame. I, the LORD, have rejected those you trust; you will not gain anything from them."

Unfaithful Israel

3 The LORD says, "If a man divorces his wife, and she leaves him and becomes another man's wife, he cannot take her back again. This would completely defile the land. But, Israel, you have had many lovers, and now you want to return to me! ²Look up at the hilltops. Is there any place where you have not acted like a prostitute? You waited for lovers along the roadside, as an Arab waits for victims in the desert. You have defiled the land with your prostitution. ³That is why the rains were held back, and the spring showers did not come. You even look like a prostitute; you have no shame.

⁴"And now you say to me, 'You are my father, and you have loved me ever since I was a child. ⁵You won't always be angry; you won't be cross with me for ever.' Israel, that is what you said, but you did all the evil you could."

Israel and Judah must Repent

⁶When Josiah was king, the LORD said to me, "Have you seen what Israel, that unfaithful woman, has done? She has turned away from me, and on every high hill and under every green tree she has acted like a prostitute. ⁷I thought that after she had done all this, she would surely return to me. But she did not return, and her unfaithful sister Judah saw it all. ⁸Judah also saw that I divorced Israel and sent her away because she had turned from me and had become a prostitute. But Judah, Israel's unfaithful sister, was not afraid. She too became a prostitute ⁹and was not at all ashamed. She defiled the land, and she committed adultery by worshipping stones and trees. ¹⁰And after all this, Judah, Israel's unfaithful sister, only pretended to return to me; she was not sincere. I, the LORD, have spoken."

¹¹Then the LORD told me that, even though Israel had turned away from him, she had proved to be better than unfaithful Judah. ¹²He told me to go and say to Israel, "Unfaithful Israel, come back to me. I am merciful and will not be angry; I will not be angry with you for ever. ¹³Only admit that you are guilty and that you have rebelled against the LORD, your God. Confess that under every green tree you have given your love to foreign gods and that you have not obeyed my commands. I, the LORD, have spoken.

886

Jerem.

⋮⋯⋯⋯

Psalms
Proverbs
Eccles.
Songs
Isaiah

JEREMIAH 3, 4

14 "Unfaithful people, come back; you belong to me. I will take one of you from each town and two from each clan, and I will bring you back to Mount Zion. 15 I will give you rulers who obey me, and they will rule you with wisdom and understanding. 16 Then when you have become numerous in that land, people will no longer talk about my Covenant Box. They will no longer think about it or remember it; they will not even need it, nor will they make another one. 17 When that time comes, Jerusalem will be called 'The Throne of the LORD', and all nations will gather there to worship me. They will no longer do what their stubborn and evil hearts tell them. 18 Israel will join with Judah, and together they will come from exile in the country in the north and will return to the land that I gave your ancestors as a permanent possession."

The Idolatry of God's People

19 The LORD says,

"Israel, I wanted to accept you as my child
        and give you a delightful land,
        the most beautiful land in all the world.
    I wanted you to call me father,
        and never again turn away from me.
20 But like an unfaithful wife,
        you have not been faithful to me.
    I, the LORD, have spoken."

21 A noise is heard on the hilltops:
        it is the people of Israel crying and pleading,
    because they have lived sinful lives
        and have forgotten the LORD their God.
22 Return, all of you who have turned away from the LORD;
        he will heal you and make you faithful.

You say, "Yes, we are coming to the LORD, because he is our God. 23 We were not helped at all by our pagan worship on the hilltops. Help for Israel comes only from the LORD our God. 24 But the worship of Baal, the god of shame, has made us lose flocks and herds, sons and daughters — everything that our ancestors have worked for since ancient times. 25 We should lie down in shame and let our disgrace cover us. We and our ancestors have always sinned against the LORD our God; we have never obeyed his commands."

A Call to Repentance

4 The LORD says, "People of Israel, if you want to turn, then turn back to me. If you are faithful to me and remove the idols I hate, 2 it will be right for you to swear by my name. Then* all the nations will ask me to bless them, and they will praise me."

3 The LORD says to the people of Judah and Jerusalem, "Plough up your unploughed fields; do not sow your seeds among thorns. 4 Keep your covenant with me, your LORD, and dedicate yourselves to me, you people of Judah and Jerusalem. If you don't, my anger will burn like fire because of the evil things you have done. It will burn, and there will be no one to put it out."

....

4.2 *it will be right... name. Then;* or *and if you swear by my name and are truthful, just, and righteous, then.*

Judah is Threatened with Invasion

⁵ Blow the trumpet throughout the land!
  Shout loud and clear!
  Tell the people of Judah and Jerusalem
    to run to the fortified cities.
⁶ Point the way to Zion!
  Run for safety! Don't delay!
  The LORD is bringing disaster
    and great destruction from the north.
⁷ Like a lion coming from its hiding place,
  a destroyer of nations has set out.
  He is coming to destroy Judah.
  The cities of Judah will be left in ruins,
    and no one will live in them.
⁸ So put on sackcloth, and weep and wail
  because the fierce anger of the LORD
  has not turned away from Judah.

⁹ The LORD said, "On that day kings and officials will lose their courage; priests will be shocked and prophets will be astonished."
¹⁰ Then I said, "Sovereign LORD, you have completely deceived the people of Jerusalem! You have said there would be peace, but a sword is at their throats."
¹¹ The time is coming when the people of Jerusalem will be told that a scorching wind is blowing in from the desert towards them. It will not be a gentle wind that only blows away the chaff — ¹²the wind that comes at the LORD's command will be much stronger than that! It is the LORD himself who is pronouncing judgement on his people.

Judah is Surrounded by Enemies

¹³ Look, the enemy is coming like clouds. Their war chariots are like a whirlwind, and their horses are faster than eagles. We are lost! We are doomed!
¹⁴ Jerusalem, wash the evil from your heart, so that you may be saved. How long will you go on thinking sinful thoughts?
¹⁵ Messengers from the city of Dan and from the hills of Ephraim announce the bad news. ¹⁶They have come to warn the nations and to tell Jerusalem that enemies are coming from a country far away. These enemies will shout against the cities of Judah ¹⁷and will surround Jerusalem like men guarding a field, because her people have rebelled against the LORD. The LORD has spoken.
¹⁸ Judah, you have brought this on yourself by the way you have lived and by the things you have done. Your sin has caused this suffering; it has stabbed you through the heart.

Jeremiah's Sorrow for his People

¹⁹ The pain! I can't bear the pain!
  My heart! My heart is beating wildly!
  I can't keep quiet;
  I hear the trumpets
    and the shouts of battle.
²⁰ One disaster follows another;
    the whole country is left in ruins.
  Suddenly our tents are destroyed;
    their curtains are torn to pieces.
²¹ How long must I see the battle raging
    and hear the blasts of trumpets?

TURN THESE LINES INTO A PICTURE OF SOMETHING.

888

Jerem.

:·········

Psalms
Proverbs
Eccles.
Songs
Isaiah

JEREMIAH 4, 5

22 The LORD says, "My people are stupid;
    they don't know me.
They are like foolish children;
    they have no understanding.
They are experts at doing what is evil,
    but failures at doing what is good."

Jeremiah's Vision of the Coming Destruction
23 I looked at the earth — it was a barren waste;
    at the sky — there was no light.
24 I looked at the mountains — they were shaking,
    and the hills were rocking to and fro.
25 I saw that there were no people;
    even the birds had flown away.
26 The fertile land had become a desert;
    its cities were in ruins
    because of the LORD's fierce anger.
27 (The LORD has said that the whole earth will become
a wilderness, but that he will not completely destroy it.)
28 The earth will mourn;
    the sky will grow dark.
The LORD has spoken
    and will not change his mind.
He has made his decision
    and will not turn back.
29 At the noise of the horsemen and bowmen
    everyone will run away.
Some will run to the forest,
    others will climb up among the rocks.
Every town will be left empty,
    and no one will live in them again.
30 Jerusalem, you are doomed!
    Why do you dress in scarlet?
    Why do you put on jewellery and paint your eyes?
You are making yourself beautiful for nothing!
    Your lovers have rejected you
    and want to kill you.
31 I heard a cry, like a woman in labour,
    a scream like a woman bearing her first child.
It was the cry of Jerusalem gasping for breath,
    stretching out her hand and saying,
"I am doomed!
    They are coming to kill me!"

The Sin of Jerusalem
5 People of Jerusalem, run through your streets!
    Look around! See for yourselves!
    Search the market places!
Can you find one person
    who does what is right
    and tries to be faithful to God?
If you can, the LORD will forgive Jerusalem.
2 Even though you claim to worship the LORD,
    you do not mean what you say.
3 Surely the LORD looks for faithfulness.
He struck you, but you paid no attention;
    he crushed you, but you refused to learn.
You were stubborn and would not turn from your
    sins.

⁴ Then I thought, "These are only the poor and ignorant.
They behave foolishly;
they don't know what their God requires,
what the LORD wants them to do.
⁵ I will go to the people in power,
and talk with them.
Surely they know what their God requires,
what the LORD wants them to do."
But all of them have rejected the LORD's authority
and refuse to obey him.
⁶ That is why lions from the forest will kill them;
wolves from the desert will tear them to pieces,
and leopards will prowl through their towns.
If those people go out, they will be torn apart
because their sins are numerous
and time after time they have turned from God.
⁷ The LORD asked, "Why should I forgive the sins of my
people?
They have abandoned me
and have worshipped gods that are not real.
I fed my people until they were full,
but they committed adultery
and spent their time with prostitutes.
⁸ They were like well-fed stallions wild with desire,
each lusting for his neighbour's wife.
⁹ Shouldn't I punish them for these things
and take revenge on a nation such as this?
¹⁰ I will send enemies to cut down my people's vineyards,
but not to destroy them completely.
I will tell them to strip away the branches,
because those branches are not mine.
¹¹ The people of Israel and Judah
have betrayed me completely.
I, the LORD, have spoken."

The LORD Rejects Israel

¹² The LORD's people have denied him and have said, "He won't really do anything.* We won't have hard times; we won't have war or famine." ¹³⁻¹⁴ They have said that the prophets are nothing but windbags and that they have no message from the LORD. The LORD God Almighty said to me, "Jeremiah, because these people have said such things, I will make my words like a fire in your mouth. The people will be like wood, and the fire will burn them up."

¹⁵ People of Israel, the LORD is bringing a nation from afar to attack you. It is a strong and ancient nation, a nation whose language you do not know. ¹⁶ Their bowmen are mighty soldiers who kill without mercy. ¹⁷ They will devour your crops and your food; they will kill your sons and your daughters. They will slaughter your flocks and your herds and destroy your vines and fig trees. The fortified cities in which you trust will be destroyed by their army.

¹⁸ The LORD says, "Yet even in those days I will not completely destroy my people. ¹⁹ When they ask why I did all these things, tell them, Jeremiah, that just as they turned away from me and served foreign gods in their own land, so they will serve strangers in a land that is not theirs."

5.12 *He won't... anything*; or *We don't want anything to do with him.*

890

Jerem.

⋮·········

Psalms
Proverbs
Eccles.
Songs
Isaiah

JEREMIAH 5, 6

God Warns his People

20 The LORD says, "Tell the descendants of Jacob, tell the people of Judah: 21 Pay attention, you foolish and stupid people, who have eyes, but cannot see, and have ears, but cannot hear. 22 I am the LORD; why don't you fear me? Why don't you tremble before me? I placed the sand as the boundary of the sea, a permanent boundary that it cannot cross. The sea may toss, but it cannot go beyond it; the waves may roar, but they cannot break through. 23 But you people! You are stubborn and rebellious; you have turned aside and left me. 24 You never thought to honour me, even though I send the autumn rains and the spring rains and give you the harvest season each year. 25 Instead, your sins have kept these good things from you.

26 "Evildoers live among my people; they lie in wait like those who spread nets to catch birds,* but they have set their traps to catch people. 27 Just as a hunter fills a cage with birds, they have filled their houses with loot. That is why they are powerful and rich, 28 why they are fat and well fed. There is no limit to their evil deeds. They do not give orphans their rights or show justice to the oppressed.

29 "But I, the LORD, will punish them for these things; I will take revenge on this nation. 30 A terrible and shocking thing has happened in the land: 31 prophets speak nothing but lies; priests rule as the prophets command, and my people offer no objections. But what will they do when it all comes to an end?"

Jerusalem is Surrounded by Enemies

6 People of Benjamin, run for safety! Escape from Jerusalem! Sound the trumpet in Tekoa and build a signal fire in Beth Haccherem. Disaster and destruction are about to come from the north. 2 The city of Zion is beautiful, but it will be destroyed; 3 kings will camp there with their armies. They will pitch their tents round the city, and they will each camp wherever they want. 4 They will say, "Prepare to attack Jerusalem! Get ready! We'll attack at noon!" But then they will say, "It's too late, the day is almost over, and the evening shadows are growing long. 5 We'll attack by night; we'll destroy the city's fortresses."

6 The LORD Almighty has ordered these kings to cut down trees and build mounds in order to besiege Jerusalem. He has said, "I will punish this city because it is full of oppression. 7 As a well keeps its water fresh, so Jerusalem keeps its evil fresh. I hear violence and destruction in the city; sickness and wounds are all I see. 8 People of Jerusalem, let these troubles be a warning to you, or else I will abandon you; I will turn your city into a desert, a place where no one lives."

Rebellious Israel

9 The LORD Almighty said to me, "Israel will be stripped clean like a vineyard from which every grape has been picked. So you must rescue everyone you can while there is still time."

10 I answered, "Who would listen to me if I spoke to them and warned them? They are stubborn and refuse to listen to your message; they laugh at what you tell me to say. 11 Your anger against them burns in me too, LORD, and I can't hold it in any longer."

Then the LORD said to me, "Pour out my anger on the children in the streets and on the gatherings of the young people. Husbands

JEREMIAH 6

Jeremiah received these prophecies around 30 years before the Babylonians destroyed Jerusalem in 587BC (see 2 Kings 25 and Jeremiah 39). Many of the prophecies that Jeremiah spoke were

FULFILLED

• IN HIS LIFETIME •

- most of them about the destruction of Judah because of the people's unfaithfulness to God.

5.26 Probable text they... birds; Hebrew unclear.

Jerem.

.........:.

Lamen.

Ezekiel

Daniel

Hosea

Joel

and wives will be taken away, and even the very old will not be spared. [12] Their houses will be given to others, and so will their fields and their wives. I am going to punish the people of this land. [13] Everyone, great and small, tries to make money dishonestly; even prophets and priests cheat the people. [14] They act as if my people's wounds were only scratches. 'All is well,' they say, when all is not well. [15] Were they ashamed because they did these disgusting things? No, they were not at all ashamed; they don't even know how to blush. And so they will fall as others have fallen; when I punish them, that will be the end of them. I, the LORD, have spoken."

Israel Rejects God's Way

[16] The LORD said to his people, "Stand at the crossroads and look. Ask for the ancient paths and where the best road is. Walk on it, and you will live in peace."

But they said, "No, we will not!" [17] Then the LORD appointed watchmen to listen for the trumpet's warning. But they said, "We will not listen."

[18] So the LORD said, "Listen, you nations, and learn what is going to happen to my people. [19] Listen, earth! As punishment for all their schemes I am bringing ruin on these people, because they have rejected my teaching and have not obeyed my words. [20] What do I care about the incense they bring me from Sheba, or the spices from a distant land? I will not accept their offerings or be pleased with their sacrifices. [21] And so I will make these people stumble and fall. Parents and children will die, and so will friends and neighbours."

Invasion from the North

[22] The LORD says, "People are coming from a country in the north; a mighty nation far away is preparing for war. [23] They have taken up their bows and swords; they are cruel and merciless. They sound like the roaring sea, as they ride their horses. They are ready for battle against Jerusalem."

[24] "We have heard the news," say the people of Jerusalem, "and our hands hang limp; we are seized by anguish and pain like a woman in labour. [25] We dare not go to the countryside or walk on the roads, because our enemies are armed and terror is all round us."

[26] The LORD says to his people, "Put on sackcloth and roll in ashes. Mourn with bitter tears as you would for an only son, because the one who comes to destroy you will suddenly attack. [27] Jeremiah, test my people, as you would test metal, and find out what they are like. [28] They are all stubborn rebels, hard as bronze and iron. They are all corrupt, going round and spreading gossip. [29] The furnace burns fiercely, but the waste metals do not melt and run off. It is useless to go on refining my people, because those who are evil are not taken away. [30] They will be called worthless dross, because I, the LORD, have rejected them."

Jeremiah Preaches in the Temple

7 [1-3] The LORD sent me to the gate of the Temple where the people of Judah went in to worship. He told me to stand there and announce what the LORD Almighty, the God of Israel, had to say to them: "Change the way you are living and the things you are doing, and I will let you go on living here. [4] Stop believing those deceitful words, 'We are safe! This is the LORD's Temple, this is the LORD's Temple, this is the LORD's Temple!'

892

Jerem.

:········

Psalms
Proverbs
Eccles.
Songs
Isaiah

JEREMIAH 7

⁵"Change the way you are living and stop doing the things you are doing. Be fair in your treatment of one another. ⁶Stop taking advantage of aliens, orphans, and widows. Stop killing innocent people in this land. Stop worshipping other gods, for that will destroy you. ⁷If you change, I will let you go on living here in the land which I gave your ancestors as a permanent possession.

⁸"Look, you put your trust in deceitful words. ⁹You steal, murder, commit adultery, tell lies under oath, offer sacrifices to Baal, and worship gods that you had not known before. ¹⁰You do these things I hate, and then you come and stand in my presence, in my own Temple, and say, 'We are safe!' ¹¹Do you think that my Temple is a hiding place for robbers? I have seen what you are doing. ¹²Go to Shiloh,* the first place where I chose to be worshipped, and see what I did to it because of the sins of my people Israel. ¹³You have committed all these sins, and even though I spoke to you over and over again, you refused to listen. You would not answer when I called you. ¹⁴And so, what I did to Shiloh I will do to this Temple of mine, in which you trust. Here in this place that I gave to your ancestors and to you, I will do the same thing that I did to Shiloh. ¹⁵I will drive you out of my sight as I drove out your relatives, the people of Israel. I, the LORD, have spoken."

The People's Disobedience

¹⁶The LORD said, "Jeremiah, do not pray for these people. Do not cry or pray on their behalf; do not plead with me, for I will not listen to you. ¹⁷Don't you see what they are doing in the cities of Judah and in the streets of Jerusalem? ¹⁸The children gather firewood, the men build fires, and the women mix dough to bake cakes for the goddess they call the Queen of Heaven. They also pour out wine offerings to other gods, in order to hurt me. ¹⁹But am I really the one they are hurting? No, they are hurting themselves and bringing shame on themselves. ²⁰And so I, the Sovereign LORD, will pour out my fierce anger on this Temple. I will pour it out on people and animals alike, and even on the trees and the crops. My anger will be like a fire that no one can put out.

²¹"My people, some sacrifices you burn completely on the altar, and some you are permitted to eat. But what I, the LORD, say is that you might as well eat them all. ²²I gave your ancestors no commands about burnt offerings or any other kinds of sacrifices, when I brought them out of Egypt. ²³But I did command them to obey me, so that I would be their God and they would be my people. And I told them to live as I had commanded them, so that things would go well for them. ²⁴But they did not obey or pay any attention. Instead, they did whatever their stubborn and evil hearts told them to do, and they became worse instead of better. ²⁵From the day that your ancestors came out of Egypt until this very day, I have kept on sending my servants, the prophets, to you. ²⁶Yet no one listened or paid any attention. Instead, you became more stubborn and rebellious than your ancestors.

²⁷"So, Jeremiah, you will speak all these words to my people, but they will not listen to you; you will call them, but they will not answer. ²⁸You will tell them that their nation does not obey me, the LORD their God, or learn from their punishment. Faithfulness is dead. No longer is it even talked about.

7.12 *Shiloh:* The city where the Covenant Box was kept in the time of Eli (see 1 Sam 1.3). The city was destroyed, probably by the Philistines.

JEREMIAH 7, 8

893

Jerem.
....

Lamen.
Ezekiel
Daniel
Hosea
Joel

Sinful Deeds in the Valley of Hinnom

29 "Mourn, people of Jerusalem;
    cut off your hair and throw it away.
    Sing a funeral song on the hilltops,
       because I, the LORD, am angry,
       and have rejected my people.

30 "The people of Judah have done an evil thing. They have placed their idols, which I hate, in my Temple and have defiled it. 31 In the Valley of Hinnom they have built an altar called Topheth, so that they can sacrifice their sons and daughters in the fire. I did not command them to do this — it did not even enter my mind. 32 And so, the time will come when it will no longer be called Topheth or the Valley of Hinnom, but the Valley of Slaughter. They will bury people there because there will be nowhere else to bury them. 33 The corpses will be food for the birds and wild animals, and there will be no one to scare them off. 34 The land will become a desert. In the cities of Judah and in the streets of Jerusalem I will put an end to the sounds of joy and gladness and to the happy sounds of wedding feasts.

8 "At that time the bones of the kings and of the officials of Judah, as well as the bones of the priests, of the prophets, and of the other people who lived in Jerusalem, will be taken out of their graves. 2 Instead of being gathered and buried, their bones will be like manure lying on the ground. They will be spread out before the sun, the moon, and the stars, which these people have loved and served, and which they have consulted and worshipped. 3 And the people of this evil nation who survive, who live in the places where I have scattered them, will prefer to die rather than to go on living. I, the LORD Almighty, have spoken."

Sin and Punishment

4 The LORD told me to say to his people, "When someone falls down, doesn't he get back up? If someone misses the road, doesn't he turn back? 5 Why then, my people, do you turn away from me without ever turning back? You cling to your idols and refuse to return to me. 6 I listened carefully, but you did not speak the truth. Not one of you has been sorry for his wickedness; not one of you has asked, 'What have I done wrong?' Everyone keeps on going his own way, like a horse rushing into battle. 7 Even storks know when it is time to return; doves, swallows, and thrushes know when it is time to migrate. But, my people, you do not know the laws by which I rule you. 8 How can you say that you are wise, and that you know my laws? Look, the laws have been changed by dishonest scribes. 9 Your wise men are put to shame; they are confused and trapped. They have rejected my words; what wisdom have they got now? 10 So I will give their fields to new owners and their wives to other men. Everyone, great and small, tries to make money dishonestly. Even prophets and priests cheat the people. 11 They act as if my people's wounds were only scratches. 'All is well,' they say, when all is not well. 12 My people, were you ashamed because you did these disgusting things? No, you were not ashamed at all; you don't even know how to blush! And so you will fall as others have fallen; when I punish you, that will be the end of you. I, the LORD, have spoken.

13 "I wanted to gather my people, as a farmer gathers a harvest; but they are like a vine with no grapes, like a fig tree with no figs; even the leaves have withered. Therefore, I have allowed outsiders to take over the land."*

....

8.13 *Therefore... land*; Hebrew unclear.

894

Jerem.

:·········

Psalms
Proverbs
Eccles.
Songs
Isaiah

JEREMIAH 8, 9

¹⁴"Why are we sitting still?" God's people ask. "Come on, we will run to the fortified cities, and die there. The Lord our God has condemned us to die; he has given us poison to drink, because we have sinned against him. ¹⁵We hoped for peace and a time of healing, but it was no use; terror came instead. ¹⁶Our enemies are already in the city of Dan; we hear the snorting of their horses. The whole land trembles when their horses neigh. Our enemies have come to destroy our land and everything in it, our city and all its people."

¹⁷"Watch out!" the Lord says, "I am sending snakes among you, poisonous snakes that cannot be charmed, and they will bite you."

Jeremiah's Sorrow for his People

¹⁸ My sorrow cannot be healed;*
   I am sick at heart.
¹⁹ Listen! Throughout the land
      I hear my people crying out,
"Is the Lord no longer in Zion?
      Is Zion's king no longer there?"
The Lord, their king, replies,
"Why have you made me angry by worshipping your idols
      and by bowing down to your useless foreign gods?"
²⁰ The people cry out,
"The summer is gone, the harvest is over,
      but we have not been saved."

²¹ My heart has been crushed
      because my people are crushed;
   I mourn; I am completely dismayed.
²² Is there no medicine in Gilead?*
      Are there no doctors there?
      Why, then, have my people not been healed?

9 I wish my head were a well of water,
      and my eyes a fountain of tears,
   so that I could cry day and night
      for my people who have been killed.
² I wish I had a place to stay in the desert
      where I could get away from my people.
   They are all unfaithful,
      a mob of traitors.
³ They are always ready to tell lies;
      dishonesty instead of truth rules the land.

The Lord says,
"My people do one evil thing after another,
      and do not acknowledge me as their God."

⁴ Everyone must be on guard against his friend,
      and no one can trust his brother;
   for every brother is as deceitful as Jacob,
      and everyone slanders his friends.
⁵⁻⁶ They all mislead their friends,
      and no one tells the truth;
   they have taught their tongues to lie
      and will not give up their sinning.

8.18 Probable text *My sorrow... healed*; Hebrew unclear.
8.22 *Gilead*: A region east of the Jordan, famous for plants that were used for medicinal purposes.

895

Jerem.
....

Lamen.
Ezekiel
Daniel
Hosea
Joel

They do one violent thing after another,
    and one deceitful act follows another.
The LORD says that his people reject him.
7 Because of this the LORD Almighty says,
    "I will refine my people like metal
        and put them to the test.
My people have done evil —
    what else can I do with them?
8 Their tongues are like deadly arrows;
    they always tell lies.
Everyone speaks friendly words to his neighbour,
    but is really setting a trap for him.
9 Will I not punish them for these things?
    Will I not take revenge on a nation like this?
I, the LORD, have spoken."

10 I said, "I will mourn for the mountains
    and weep for the pastures,
because they have dried up,
    and no one travels through them.
The sound of livestock is no longer heard;
    birds and wild animals have fled and gone."

11 The LORD says, "I will make Jerusalem a pile of ruins,
    a place where jackals live;
the cities of Judah will become a desert,
    a place where no one lives."

12 I asked, "LORD, why is the land devastated and dry as a desert, so that no one travels through it? Who is wise enough to understand this? To whom have you explained it so that he can tell others?"
13 The LORD answered, "This has happened because my people have abandoned the teaching that I gave them. They have not obeyed me or done what I told them. 14 Instead, they have been stubborn and have worshipped the idols of Baal as their ancestors taught them to do. 15 So then, listen to what I, the LORD Almighty, the God of Israel, will do: I will give my people bitter plants to eat and poison to drink. 16 I will scatter them among nations that neither they nor their ancestors have heard about, and I will send armies against them until I have completely destroyed them."

The People of Jerusalem Cry Out for Help

17 The LORD Almighty said,
    "Think about what is happening!
Call for the mourners to come,
    for the women who sing funeral songs."

18 The people said,
    "Tell them to hurry and sing a funeral song for us,
until our eyes fill with tears,
    and our eyelids are wet from crying."

19 Listen to the sound of crying in Zion,
    "We are ruined!
    We are completely disgraced!
We must leave our land;
    our homes have been torn down."

JEREMIAH 9.10

Jeremiah is known as the 'weeping prophet' because he often got very upset about the state of Jerusalem.

What in the world around you makes you so upset that you could

CRY OUT TO GOD?

Write on a piece of kitchen roll, using a felt-tip pen, the things that you see as being wrong in the world around you. Once you have written them down, pray over them.

896

Jerem.

⁚⁚⁚⁚⁚⁚⁚

Psalms
Proverbs
Eccles.
Songs
Isaiah

JEREMIAH 9, 10

²⁰ I said,
"Listen to the LORD, you women,
    and pay attention to his words.
Teach your daughters how to mourn,
    and your friends how to sing a funeral song.
²¹ Death has come in through our windows
    and entered our palaces;
it has cut down the children in the streets
    and the young men in the market places.
²² Dead bodies are scattered everywhere,
    like piles of manure on the fields,
    like corn cut and left behind by the reapers,
    corn that no one gathers.
This is what the LORD has told me to say."

²³ The LORD says,
"The wise should not boast of their wisdom,
    nor the strong of their strength,
    nor the rich of their wealth.
²⁴ If anyone wants to boast,
    he should boast that he knows and understands me,
because my love is constant,
    and I do what is just and right.
These are the things that please me.
I, the LORD, have spoken."

²⁵⁻²⁶ The LORD says, "The time is coming when I will punish the people of Egypt, Judah, Edom, Ammon, Moab, and the desert people, who have their hair cut short.* All these people are circumcised, but have not kept the covenant it symbolizes. None of these people and none of the people of Israel have kept my covenant."

Idolatry and True Worship

10 People of Israel, listen to the message that the LORD has for you. ² He says,
"Do not follow the ways of other nations;
    do not be disturbed by unusual sights in the sky,
    even though other nations are terrified.
³ The religion of these people is worthless.
A tree is cut down in the forest;
    it is carved by the tools of the woodcarver,
⁴   and decorated with silver and gold.
It is fastened down with nails
    to keep it from falling over.
⁵ Such idols are like scarecrows in a field of melons;
    they cannot speak;
they have to be carried
    because they cannot walk.
Do not be afraid of them:
    they can cause you no harm,
    and they can do you no good."

⁶ LORD, there is no one like you;
    you are mighty,
    and your name is great and powerful.

9.25–26 *hair cut short*: The desert people cut their hair short in honour of their god, a pagan practice forbidden to the Israelites (see Lev 19.27).

JEREMIAH 10

897

Jerem.

Lamen.
Ezekiel
Daniel
Hosea
Joel

⁷ Who would not honour you, the king of all nations?
  You deserve to be honoured.
There is no one like you
    among all the wise men of the nations
    or among any of their kings.
⁸ All of them are stupid and foolish.
  What can they learn from wooden idols?*
⁹ Their idols are covered with silver from Spain
    and with gold from Uphaz,
    all the work of artists;
  they are dressed in violet and purple cloth
    woven by skilled weavers.
¹⁰ But you, Lord, are the true God,
    you are the living God
    and the eternal king.
  When you are angry, the world trembles;
    the nations cannot endure your anger.
¹¹ (You people must tell them that the gods who did not make
the earth and the sky will be destroyed. They will no longer exist
anywhere on earth.)

A Hymn of Praise to God

¹² The Lord made the earth by his power;
    by his wisdom he created the world
    and stretched out the heavens.
¹³ At his command the waters above the sky* roar;
  he brings clouds from the ends of the earth.
He makes lightning flash in the rain
    and sends the wind from his storeroom.
¹⁴ At the sight of this, people feel stupid and senseless;
    those who make idols are disillusioned,
    because the gods they make are false and lifeless.
¹⁵ They are worthless and should be despised;
    they will be destroyed when the Lord comes to deal with
      them.
¹⁶ The God of Jacob is not like them;
    he is the one who made everything,
    and he has chosen Israel to be his very own people.
    The Lord Almighty is his name.

The Coming Exile

¹⁷ People of Jerusalem, you are under siege! Gather up your
belongings. ¹⁸ The Lord is going to throw you out of this land; he is
going to crush you until not one of you is left. The Lord has spoken.
¹⁹ The people of Jerusalem cried out,
  "How badly we are hurt!
    Our wounds will not heal.
  And we thought this was something we could endure!
²⁰ Our tents are ruined;
    the ropes that held them have broken.
  Our children have all gone away;
    there is no one left to put up our tents again;
    there is no one to hang their curtains."

²¹ I answered, "Our leaders are stupid;
    they do not ask the Lord for guidance.

10.8 *What can… idols?*; or *What their idols teach is worthless.*
10.13 *waters above the sky*: See Gen 1.6–8.

898

Jerem.

⋮⋯⋯

Psalms
Proverbs
Eccles.
Songs
Isaiah

JEREMIAH 10, 11

This is why they have failed,
and our people have been scattered.
²² Listen! News has come!
There is a great commotion in a nation to the north;
its army will turn the cities of Judah into a desert,
a place where jackals live."

²³ LORD, I know that no one is the master of his own destiny;
no person has control over his own life.
²⁴ Correct your people, LORD;
but do not be too hard on us
or punish us when you are angry;
that would be the end of us.
²⁵ Turn your anger on the nations that do not worship you
and on the people who reject you.
They have killed your people;
they have destroyed us completely
and left our country in ruins.

Jeremiah and the Covenant

11 The LORD said to me, ² "Listen to the terms of the covenant. Tell the people of Judah and of Jerusalem ³ that I, the LORD God of Israel, have placed a curse on everyone who does not obey the terms of this covenant. ⁴ It is the covenant I made with their ancestors when I brought them out of Egypt, the land that was like a blazing furnace to them. I told them to obey me and to do everything that I had commanded. I told them that if they obeyed, they would be my people and I would be their God. ⁵ Then I would keep the promise I made to their ancestors that I would give them the rich and fertile land which they now have."

I said, "Yes, LORD."

⁶ Then the LORD said to me, "Go to the cities of Judah and to the streets of Jerusalem. Proclaim my message there and tell the people to listen to the terms of the covenant and to obey them. ⁷ When I brought their ancestors out of Egypt, I solemnly warned them to obey me, and I have kept on warning the people until this day. ⁸ But they did not listen or obey. Instead, everyone continued to be as stubborn and evil as ever. I had commanded them to keep the covenant, but they refused. So I brought on them all the punishments described in it."

⁹ Then the LORD said to me, "The people of Judah and of Jerusalem are plotting against me. ¹⁰ They have gone back to the sins of their ancestors, who refused to do what I said; they have worshipped other gods. Both Israel and Judah have broken the covenant that I made with their ancestors. ¹¹ So now, I, the LORD, warn them that I am going to bring destruction on them, and they will not escape. And when they cry out to me for help, I will not listen to them. ¹² Then the people of Judah and of Jerusalem will go to the gods to whom they offer sacrifices and will cry out to them for help. But those gods will not be able to save them when this destruction comes. ¹³ The people of Judah have as many gods as they have cities, and the inhabitants of Jerusalem have set up as many altars for sacrifices to that disgusting god Baal as there are streets in the city. ¹⁴ Jeremiah, don't pray to me or plead with me on behalf of these people. When they are in trouble and call to me for help, I will not listen to them."

¹⁵ The LORD says, "The people I love are doing evil things. What right have they to be in my Temple? Do they think they can prevent

JEREMIAH 11, 12

899

Jerem.

....

Lamen.
Ezekiel
Daniel
Hosea
Joel

disaster by making promises* and by offering animal sacrifices? Will that make them happy? [16] I once called them a leafy olive tree, full of beautiful fruit; but now, with a roar like thunder I will set its leaves on fire and break its branches.

[17] "I, the Lord Almighty, planted Israel and Judah; but now I threaten them with disaster. They have brought this on themselves because they have done wrong; they have made me angry by offering sacrifices to Baal."

A Plot against Jeremiah's Life

[18] The Lord informed me of the plots that my enemies were making against me. [19] I was like a trusting lamb taken out to be killed, and I did not know that it was against me that they were planning evil things. They were saying, "Let's chop down the tree while it is still healthy;* let's kill him so that no one will remember him any more."

[20] Then I prayed, "Almighty Lord, you are a just judge; you test people's thoughts and feelings. I have placed my cause in your hands; so let me watch you take revenge on these people."

[21] The people of Anathoth wanted me killed, and they told me that they would kill me if I kept on proclaiming the Lord's message. [22] So the Lord Almighty said, "I will punish them! Their young men will be killed in war; their children will die of starvation. [23] I have set a time for bringing disaster on the people of Anathoth, and when that time comes, none of them will survive."

Jeremiah Questions the Lord

12 "Lord, if I argued my case with you,
    you would prove to be right.
Yet I must question you about matters of justice.
Why are the wicked so prosperous?
    Why do dishonest people succeed?
[2] You plant them, and they take root;
    they grow and bear fruit.
They always speak well of you,
    yet they do not really care about you.
[3] But, Lord, you know me;
    you see what I do,
    and how I love you.
Drag these evil people away like sheep to be butchered;
    guard them until it is time for them to be slaughtered.
[4] How long will our land be dry,
    and the grass in every field be withered?
Animals and birds are dying
    because of the wickedness of our people,
    people who say, 'God doesn't see what we are doing.' "*

[5] The Lord said,
"Jeremiah, if you get tired racing against people,
    how can you race against horses?
If you can't even stand up in open country,
    how will you manage in the jungle by the Jordan?
[6] Even your relatives, members of your own family, have
        betrayed you;
    they join in the attacks against you.

11.15 One ancient translation *promises*; Hebrew *many*.
11.19 Probable text *while it is still healthy*; Hebrew *with its bread*.
12.4 Some ancient translations *what we are doing*; Hebrew *our latter end*.

900

Jerem.

Psalms
Proverbs
Eccles.
Songs
Isaiah

JEREMIAH 12, 13

Did you know, there's

NOTHING

you can do to make

GOD
LOVE
YOU

any more or any less?

Do not trust them, even though they speak friendly words."

The Lord's Sorrow because of his People

7 The Lord says,
"I have abandoned Israel;
    I have rejected my chosen nation.
I have given the people I love
    into the power of their enemies.
8 My chosen people have turned against me;
    like a lion in the forest
they have roared at me,
    and so I hate them.
9 My chosen people are like a bird
    attacked from all sides by hawks.
Call the wild animals
    to come and join in the feast!
10 Many foreign rulers have destroyed my vineyard;
    they have trampled down my fields;
    they have turned my lovely land into a desert.
11 They have made it a wilderness;
    it lies desolate before me.
The whole land has become a desert,
    and no one cares.
12 Across all the desert highlands
    people have come to plunder.
I have sent war to destroy the entire land;
    no one can live in peace.
13 My people sowed wheat, but gathered weeds;
    they have worked hard, but got nothing for it.
Because of my fierce anger
    their crops have failed."

The Lord's Promise to Israel's Neighbours

14 The Lord says, "I have something to say about Israel's neighbours who have ruined the land I gave to my people Israel. I will take those wicked people away from their countries like an uprooted plant, and I will rescue Judah from them. 15 But after I have taken them away, I will have mercy on them; I will bring each nation back to its own land and to its own country. 16 If with all their hearts they will accept the religion of my people and will swear, 'As the Lord lives' — as they once taught my people to swear by Baal — then they will also be a part of my people and will prosper. 17 But if any nation will not obey, then I will completely uproot it and destroy it. I, the Lord, have spoken."

The Linen Shorts

13 The Lord told me to go and buy myself some linen shorts and to put them on; but he told me not to put them in water. 2 So I bought them and put them on. 3 Then the Lord spoke to me again, and said, 4 "Go to the River Euphrates and hide the shorts in a hole in the rocks." 5 So I went and hid them near the Euphrates.

6 Some time later the Lord told me to go back to the Euphrates and get the shorts. 7 So I went back, and when I found the place where I had hidden them, I saw that they were ruined and were no longer any good.

8 Then the Lord spoke to me again. He said, 9 "This is how I will destroy the pride of Judah and the great pride of Jerusalem.

JEREMIAH 13

901

Jerem.

···········

Lamen.

Ezekiel

Daniel

Hosea

Joel

¹⁰These evil people have refused to obey me. They have been as stubborn and wicked as ever, and have worshipped and served other gods. So then, they will become like these shorts that are no longer any good. ¹¹Just as shorts fit tightly round the waist, so I intended all the people of Israel and Judah to hold tightly to me. I did this so that they would be my people and would bring praise and honour to my name; but they would not obey me."

The Wine Jar

¹²The LORD God said to me, "Jeremiah, tell the people of Israel that every wine jar should be filled with wine. They will answer that they know every wine jar should be filled with wine. ¹³Then tell them that I, the LORD, am going to fill the people in this land with wine until they are drunk: the kings, who are David's descendants, the priests, the prophets, and all the people of Jerusalem. ¹⁴Then I will smash them like jars against one another, old and young alike. No pity, compassion, or mercy will stop me from killing them."

Jeremiah Warns against Pride

¹⁵ People of Israel, the LORD has spoken!
   Be humble and listen to him.
¹⁶ Honour the LORD, your God,
      before he brings darkness,
      and you stumble on the mountains;
   before he turns into deep darkness
      the light you hoped for.
¹⁷ If you will not listen,
      I will cry in secret because of your pride;
   I will cry bitterly, and my tears will flow
      because the LORD's people have been taken away as
         captives.

¹⁸The LORD said to me, "Tell the king and his mother to come down from their thrones, because their beautiful crowns have fallen from their heads.* ¹⁹The towns of southern Judah are under siege; no one can get through to them. All the people of Judah have been taken away into exile."

²⁰Jerusalem, look! Your enemies are coming down from the north! Where are the people entrusted to your care, your people you were so proud of? ²¹What will you say when people you thought were your friends conquer you and rule over you?* You will be in pain like a woman giving birth. ²²If you ask why all this has happened to you — why your clothes have been torn off and you have been raped — it is because your sin is so terrible. ²³Can a Nubian change the colour of his skin, or a leopard remove its spots? If they could, then you that do nothing but evil could learn to do what is right. ²⁴The LORD will scatter you like straw that is blown away by the desert wind. ²⁵He has said that this will be your fate. This is what he has decided to do with you, because you have forgotten him and have trusted in false gods. ²⁶The LORD himself will strip off your clothes and expose you to shame. ²⁷He has seen you do the things he hates. He has seen you go after pagan gods on the hills and in the fields, like a man lusting after his neighbour's wife or like a stallion after a mare. People of Jerusalem, you are doomed! When will you ever be pure?

··

13.18 Some ancient translations *from their heads*; Hebrew unclear.
13.21 Probable text *What... over you*; Hebrew unclear.

902

Jerem.

⋮ . . . .

Psalms
Proverbs
Eccles.
Songs
Isaiah

JEREMIAH 14

The Terrible Drought

14 The LORD said to me concerning the drought,
² "Judah is in mourning;
 its cities are dying,
 its people lie on the ground in sorrow,
 and Jerusalem cries out for help.
³ The rich people send their servants for water;
 they go to the cisterns,
 but find no water;
 they come back with their jars empty.
 Discouraged and confused,
 they hide their faces.
⁴ Because there is no rain
 and the ground is dried up,
 the farmers are sick at heart;
 they hide their faces.
⁵ In the field the mother deer
 abandons her newborn fawn
 because there is no grass.
⁶ The wild donkeys stand on the hilltops
 and pant for breath like jackals;
 their eyesight fails them
 because they have no food.
⁷ My people cry out to me,
 'Even though our sins accuse us,
 help us, LORD, as you have promised.
 We have turned away from you many times;
 we have sinned against you.
⁸ You are Israel's only hope;
 you are the one who saves us from disaster.
 Why are you like a stranger in our land,
 like a traveller who stays for only one night?
⁹ Why are you like someone taken by surprise,
 like a soldier powerless to help?
 Surely, LORD, you are with us!
 We are your people;
 do not abandon us.'"

¹⁰ The LORD says about these people, "They love to run away from me, and they will not control themselves. So I am not pleased with them. I will remember the wrongs they have done and punish them because of their sins."

¹¹ The LORD said to me, "Do not ask me to help these people. ¹² Even if they fast, I will not listen to their cry for help; and even if they offer me burnt offerings and grain offerings, I will not be pleased with them. Instead, I will kill them in war and by starvation and disease."

¹³ Then I said, "Sovereign LORD, you know that the prophets are telling the people that there will be no war or starvation, because you have promised, they say, that there will be only peace in our land."

¹⁴ But the LORD replied, "The prophets are telling lies in my name; I did not send them, nor did I give them any orders or speak one word to them. The visions they talk about have not come from me; their predictions are worthless things that they have imagined. ¹⁵ I, the LORD, tell you what I am going to do to those prophets whom I did not send but who speak in my name and say war and starvation will not strike this land — I will kill them in war and by starvation. ¹⁶ The people to whom they have said these things

JEREMIAH 14, 15

903

Jerem.
·········
Lamen.
Ezekiel
Daniel
Hosea
Joel

will be killed in the same way. Their bodies will be thrown out into the streets of Jerusalem, and there will be no one to bury them. This will happen to all of them — including their wives, their sons, and their daughters. I will make them pay for their wickedness."

[17]The LORD commanded me to tell the people about my sorrow and to say:

"May my eyes flow with tears day and night,
    may I never stop weeping,
for my people are deeply wounded
    and are badly hurt.
[18] When I go out into the fields,
    I see the bodies of men killed in war;
when I go into the towns,
    I see people starving to death.
Prophets and priests carry on their work,
    but they don't know what they are doing."[*]

The People Plead with the LORD

[19] LORD, have you completely rejected Judah?
    Do you hate the people of Zion?
Why have you hurt us so badly
    that we cannot be healed?
We looked for peace, but nothing good happened;
    we hoped for healing, but terror came instead.
[20] We have sinned against you, LORD;
    we confess our own sins
    and the sins of our ancestors.
[21] Remember your promises and do not despise us;
    do not bring disgrace on Jerusalem,
    the place of your glorious throne.
Do not break the covenant you made with us.
[22] None of the idols of the nations can send rain;
    the sky by itself cannot make showers fall.
We have put our hope in you, O LORD our God,
    because you are the one who does these things.

Doom for the People of Judah

15 Then the LORD said to me, "Even if Moses and Samuel were standing here pleading with me, I would not show these people any mercy. Make them go away; make them get out of my sight. [2]When they ask you where they should go, tell them that I have said:

Some are doomed to die by disease —
    that's where they will go!
Others are doomed to die in war —
    that's where they will go!
Some are doomed to die of starvation —
    that's where they will go!
Others are doomed to be taken away as prisoners —
    that's where they will go!

[3]I, the LORD, have decided that four terrible things will happen to them: they will be killed in war; their bodies will be dragged off by dogs; birds will eat them, and wild animals will devour what is left over. [4]I will make all the people of the world horrified at them because of what Hezekiah's son Manasseh did in Jerusalem when he was king of Judah."

14.18 Prophets… doing; or *Prophets and priests have been dragged away to a land they know nothing about.*

904

Jerem.

⋮⋯⋯⋯

Psalms
Proverbs
Eccles.
Songs
Isaiah

JEREMIAH 15

⁵The Lord says,
"Who will pity you, people of Jerusalem,
and who will grieve over you?
Who will stop long enough
to ask how you are?
⁶ You people have rejected me;
you have turned your backs on me.
So I stretched out my hand and crushed you
because I was tired of controlling my anger.*
⁷ In every town in the land
I threw you to the wind like straw.
I destroyed you, my people,
I killed your children
because you did not stop your evil ways.
⁸ There are more widows in your land
than grains of sand by the sea.
I killed your young men in their prime
and made their mothers suffer.
I suddenly struck them
with anguish and terror.
⁹ The mother who lost her seven children has fainted,
gasping for breath.
Her daylight has turned to darkness;
she is disgraced and sick at heart.
I will let your enemies kill
those of you who are still alive.
I, the Lord, have spoken."

Jeremiah Complains to the Lord

¹⁰What an unhappy man I am! Why did my mother bring me into the world? I have to quarrel and argue with everyone in the land. I have not lent any money or borrowed any; yet everyone curses me. ¹¹Lord, may all their curses come true if I have not served* you well, if I have not pleaded with you on behalf of my enemies when they were in trouble and distress. ¹²(No one can break iron, especially the iron from the north that is mixed with bronze.)

¹³The Lord said to me, "I will send enemies to carry away the wealth and treasures of my people, in order to punish them for the sins they have committed throughout the land. ¹⁴I will make them serve their enemies in a land they know nothing about, because my anger is like fire, and it will burn for ever."

¹⁵Then I said, "Lord, you understand. Remember me and help me. Let me have revenge on those who persecute me. Do not be so patient with them that they succeed in killing me. Remember that it is for your sake that I am insulted. ¹⁶You spoke to me, and I listened to every word. I belong to you, Lord God Almighty, and so your words filled my heart with joy and happiness. ¹⁷I did not spend my time with other people, laughing and having a good time. In obedience to your orders I stayed by myself and was filled with anger. ¹⁸Why do I keep on suffering? Why are my wounds incurable? Why won't they heal? Do you intend to disappoint me like a stream that goes dry in the summer?"

¹⁹To this the Lord replied, "If you return, I will take you back, and you will be my servant again. If instead of talking nonsense you proclaim a worthwhile message, you will be my prophet

15.6 *you because... anger*; or *you; I was tired of feeling sorry for you.*
15.11 Probable text *Lord, ...served*; Hebrew unclear.

JEREMIAH 15, 16

905

Jerem.

....

Lamen.

Ezekiel

Daniel

Hosea

Joel

again. The people will come back to you, and you will not need to go to them. ²⁰I will make you like a solid bronze wall as far as they are concerned. They will fight against you, but they will not defeat you. I will be with you to protect you and keep you safe. ²¹I will rescue you from the power of wicked and violent people. I, the LORD, have spoken."

The LORD's Will for Jeremiah's Life

16 Again the LORD spoke to me and said, ²"Do not marry or have children in a place like this. ³I will tell you what is going to happen to the children who are born here and to their parents. ⁴They will die of terrible diseases, and no one will mourn for them or bury them. Their bodies will lie like piles of manure on the ground. They will be killed in war or die of starvation, and their bodies will be food for the birds and the wild animals.

⁵"You must not enter a house where there is mourning. Do not grieve for anyone. I will no longer bless my people with peace or show them love and mercy. ⁶The rich and the poor will die in this land, but no one will bury them or mourn for them. No one will gash himself or shave his head to show his grief. ⁷No one will eat or drink with anyone to comfort him when a loved one dies. No one will show sympathy, not even for someone who has lost his father or mother.

⁸"Do not enter a house where people are feasting. Do not sit down with them to eat and drink. ⁹Listen to what I, the LORD Almighty, the God of Israel, have to say. I will silence the sounds of joy and gladness and the happy sounds of wedding feasts. The people here will live to see this happen.

¹⁰"When you tell them all this, they will ask you why I have decided to punish them so harshly. They will ask what crime they are guilty of and what sin they have committed against the LORD their God. ¹¹Then tell them that the LORD has said, 'Your ancestors turned away from me and worshipped and served other gods. They abandoned me and did not obey my teachings. ¹²But you have done even worse than your ancestors. All of you are stubborn and evil, and you do not obey me. ¹³So then, I will throw you out of this land into a land that neither you nor your ancestors have ever known. And there you will serve other gods day and night, and I will show you no mercy.'"

The Return from Exile

¹⁴The LORD says, "The time is coming when people will no longer swear by me as the living God who brought the people of Israel out of the land of Egypt. ¹⁵Instead, they will swear by me as the living God who brought the people of Israel out of a northern land and out of all the other countries where I had scattered them. I will bring them back to their own country, to the land that I gave their ancestors. I, the LORD, have spoken."

The Coming Punishment

¹⁶The LORD says, "I am sending for many fishermen to come and catch these people. Then I will send for many hunters to hunt them down on every mountain and hill and in the caves among the rocks. ¹⁷I see everything they do. Nothing is hidden from me; their sins do not escape my sight. ¹⁸I will make them pay double for their sin and wickedness, because they have defiled my land with idols that are as lifeless as corpses, and have filled it with their false gods."

JEREMIAH 15.20

God promised that he would

– KEEP –

JEREMIAH

SAFE

in the midst of evil people, like a 'bronze wall' against his enemies. On this page

DRAW A WALL

and write on it a prayer thanking God for His promises.

906

Jerem.

Psalms
Proverbs
Eccles.
Songs
Isaiah

JEREMIAH 16, 17

Jeremiah's Prayer of Confidence in the LORD

[19] LORD, you are the one who protects me and gives me strength; you help me in times of trouble. Nations will come to you from the ends of the earth and say, "Our ancestors had nothing but false gods, nothing but useless idols. [20] Can people make their own gods? No, if they did, those would not really be gods."

[21] "So then," says the LORD, "once and for all I will make the nations know my power and my might; they will know that I am the LORD."

The Sin and Punishment of Judah

17 The LORD says, "People of Judah, your sin is written with an iron pen; it is engraved on your hearts with a diamond point and carved on the corners of your altars. [2] Your people worship at the altars and the symbols that have been set up for the goddess Asherah by every green tree, on the hilltops [3] and on the mountains in the open country. I will make your enemies take away your wealth and your treasures because of all the sins you have committed* throughout your land. [4] You will have to give up* the land I gave you, and I will make you serve your enemies in a land you know nothing about, because my anger is like a fire, and it will burn for ever."

Various Sayings

[5] The LORD says,
"I will condemn those
    who turn away from me
and put their trust in human beings,
    in the strength of mortals.
[6] They are like bushes in the desert,
    which grow in the dry wilderness,
on salty ground where nothing else grows.
Nothing good ever happens to them.

[7] "But I will bless those
    who put their trust in me.
[8] They are like trees growing near a stream
    and sending out roots to the water.
They are not afraid when hot weather comes,
    because their leaves stay green;
they have no worries when there is no rain;
    they keep on bearing fruit.

[9] "Who can understand the human heart?
    There is nothing else so deceitful;
    it is too sick to be healed.
[10] I, the LORD, search human minds
    and test human hearts.
I treat each one according to the way he lives,
    according to what he does."

[11] The person who gets money dishonestly
    is like a bird that hatches eggs it didn't lay.
In the prime of life he will lose his riches,
    and in the end he is nothing but a fool.

17.3 Probable text *because of all the sins you have committed*; Hebrew *your high places for sins.*
17.4 Probable text *You… give up*; Hebrew unclear.

JEREMIAH 17, 18

907

Jerem.

....

Lamen.
Ezekiel
Daniel
Hosea
Joel

¹² Our Temple is like a glorious throne,
standing on a high mountain from the beginning.

¹³ Lᴏʀᴅ, you are Israel's hope;
all who abandon you will be put to shame.
They will disappear like names written in the dust,*
because they have abandoned you, the Lᴏʀᴅ,
the spring of fresh water.

Jeremiah Asks the Lᴏʀᴅ for Help

¹⁴ Lᴏʀᴅ, heal me and I will be completely well; rescue me and I will be perfectly safe. You are the one I praise!
¹⁵ The people say to me, "Where are those threats the Lᴏʀᴅ made against us? Let him carry them out now!"
¹⁶ But, Lᴏʀᴅ, I never urged you to bring disaster on them;* I did not wish a time of trouble for them. Lᴏʀᴅ, you know this; you know what I have said. ¹⁷ Do not be a terror to me; you are my place of safety when trouble comes. ¹⁸ Bring disgrace on those who persecute me, but spare me, Lᴏʀᴅ. Fill them with terror, but do not terrify me. Bring disaster on them and break them to pieces.

On Observing the Sabbath

¹⁹ The Lᴏʀᴅ said to me, "Jeremiah, go and announce my message at the People's Gate, through which the kings of Judah enter and leave the city; then go to all the other gates of Jerusalem. ²⁰ Tell the kings and all the people of Judah and everyone who lives in Jerusalem and enters these gates, to listen to what I say. ²¹ Tell them that if they love their lives, they must not carry any load on the Sabbath; they must not carry anything in through the gates of Jerusalem ²² or carry anything out of their houses on the Sabbath. They must not work on the Sabbath; they must observe it as a sacred day, as I commanded their ancestors. ²³ Their ancestors did not listen to me or pay any attention. Instead, they became stubborn; they would not obey me or learn from me.

²⁴ "Tell these people that they must obey all my commands. They must not carry any load in through the gates of this city on the Sabbath. They must observe the Sabbath as a sacred day and must not do any work at all. ²⁵ Then their kings and princes will enter the gates of Jerusalem and have the same royal power that David had. Together with the people of Judah and of Jerusalem, they will ride in chariots and on horses, and the city of Jerusalem will always be filled with people. ²⁶ People will come from the towns of Judah and from the villages round Jerusalem; they will come from the territory of Benjamin, from the foothills, from the mountains, and from southern Judah. They will bring to my Temple burnt offerings and sacrifices, grain offerings and incense, as well as thank-offerings. ²⁷ But they must obey me and observe the Sabbath as a sacred day. They must not carry any load through the gates of Jerusalem on that day, for if they do, I will set the gates of Jerusalem on fire. Fire will burn down the palaces of Jerusalem, and no one will be able to put it out."

Jeremiah at the Potter's House

18 The Lᴏʀᴅ said to me, ² "Go down to the potter's house, where I will give you my message." ³ So I went there

JEREMIAH 17.14

YOU ARE THE { ONE I } PRAISE!

17.13 *disappear… dust;* or *go to the world of the dead.*
17.16 Probable text *bring disaster on them;* Hebrew *from being a shepherd after you.*

908

Jerem.

··········

Psalms
Proverbs
Eccles.
Songs
Isaiah

JEREMIAH 18, 19

and saw the potter working at his wheel. [4] Whenever a piece of pottery turned out imperfect, he would take the clay and make it into something else.

[5] Then the LORD said to me, [6] "Haven't I the right to do with you people of Israel what the potter did with the clay? You are in my hands just like clay in the potter's hands. [7] If at any time I say that I am going to uproot, break down, or destroy any nation or kingdom, [8] but then that nation turns from its evil, I will not do what I said I would. [9] On the other hand, if I say that I am going to plant or build up any nation or kingdom, [10] but then that nation disobeys me and does evil, I will not do what I said I would. [11] Now then, tell the people of Judah and of Jerusalem that I am making plans against them and getting ready to punish them. Tell them to stop living sinful lives — to change their ways and the things they are doing. [12] They will answer, 'No, why should we? We will all be just as stubborn and evil as we want to be.'"

The People Reject the LORD

[13] The LORD says,

"Ask every nation if such a thing
    has ever happened before.
    The people of Israel have done a terrible thing!
[14] Are Lebanon's rocky heights ever without snow?
    Do its cool mountain streams ever run dry?
[15] Yet my people have forgotten me;
    they burn incense to idols.
They have stumbled in the way they should go,
    they no longer follow the old ways;
    they walk on unmarked paths.
[16] They have made this land a thing of horror,
    to be despised for ever.
All who pass by will be shocked at what they see;
    they will shake their heads in amazement.
[17] I will scatter my people before their enemies,
    like dust blown by the east wind.
I will turn my back on them;
    I will not help them when the disaster comes."

A Plot against Jeremiah

[18] Then the people said, "Let's do something about Jeremiah! There will always be priests to instruct us, the wise to give us counsel, and prophets to proclaim God's message. Let's bring charges against him, and stop listening to what he says."

[19] So I prayed, "LORD, hear what I am saying and listen to what my enemies are saying about me. [20] Is evil the payment for good? Yet they have dug a pit for me to fall in. Remember how I came to you and spoke on their behalf, so that you would not deal with them in anger. [21] But now, LORD, let their children starve to death; let them be killed in war. Let the women lose their husbands and children; let the men die of disease and the young men be killed in battle. [22] Send a mob to plunder their homes without warning; make them cry out in terror. They have dug a pit for me to fall in and have set traps to catch me. [23] But, LORD, you know all their plots to kill me. Do not forgive their evil or pardon their sin. Throw them down in defeat and deal with them while you are angry."

The Broken Jar

19 The LORD told me to go and buy a clay jar. He also told me to take some of the elders of the people and some of

JEREMIAH 19, 20

909

Jerem.

....

Lamen.
Ezekiel
Daniel
Hosea
Joel

the older priests, ²and to go through Potsherd Gate out to the Valley of Hinnom. There I was to proclaim the message that he would give me. ³The LORD told me to say, "Kings of Judah and people of Jerusalem, listen to what I, the LORD Almighty, the God of Israel, have to say. I am going to bring such a disaster on this place that everyone who hears about it will be stunned. ⁴I am going to do this because the people have abandoned me and defiled this place by offering sacrifices here to other gods — gods that neither they nor their ancestors nor the kings of Judah have known anything about. They have filled this place with the blood of innocent people, ⁵and they have built altars for Baal in order to burn their children in the fire as sacrifices. I never commanded them to do this; it never even entered my mind. ⁶So then, the time will come when this place will no longer be called Topheth or the Valley of Hinnom. Instead, it will be known as the Valley of Slaughter. ⁷In this place I will frustrate all the plans of the people of Judah and Jerusalem. I will let their enemies triumph over them and kill them in battle. I will give their corpses to the birds and the wild animals as food. ⁸I will bring such terrible destruction on this city that everyone who passes by will be shocked and amazed. ⁹The enemy will surround the city and try to kill its people. The siege will be so terrible that the people inside the city will eat one another and even their own children."

¹⁰Then the LORD told me to break the jar in front of those who had gone with me ¹¹and to tell them that the LORD Almighty had said, "I will break this people and this city, and it will be like this broken clay jar that cannot be put together again. People will bury their dead even in Topheth because there will be nowhere else to bury them. ¹²I promise that I will make this city and its inhabitants like Topheth. ¹³The houses of Jerusalem, the houses of the kings of Judah, and indeed all the houses on whose roofs incense has been burnt to the stars and where wine has been poured out as an offering to other gods — they will all be as unclean as Topheth."

¹⁴Then I left Topheth, where the LORD had sent me to proclaim his message. I went and stood in the court of the Temple and told all the people ¹⁵that the LORD Almighty, the God of Israel, had said, "I am going to bring on this city and on every nearby town all the punishment that I said I would, because you are stubborn and will not listen to what I say."

Jeremiah's Conflict with Pashhur the Priest

20 When the priest Pashhur son of Immer, who was the chief officer of the Temple, heard me proclaim these things, ²he ordered me to be beaten and placed in chains near the upper Benjamin Gate in the Temple. ³The next morning, after Pashhur had released me from the chains, I said to him, "The LORD did not name you Pashhur. The name he has given you is 'Terror Everywhere'. ⁴The LORD himself has said, 'I am going to make you a terror to yourself and to your friends, and you will see them all killed by the swords of their enemies. I am going to put all the people of Judah under the power of the king of Babylonia; he will take some away as prisoners to his country and put others to death. ⁵I will also let their enemies plunder all the wealth of this city and seize all its possessions and property, even the treasures of the kings of Judah, and carry everything off to Babylonia. ⁶As for you, Pashhur, you and all your family will also be captured and taken off to Babylonia. There you will die and be buried, along with all your friends to whom you have told so many lies.'"

910

Jerem.

Psalms
Proverbs
Eccles.
Songs
Isaiah

JEREMIAH 20, 21

DECORATE THESE SHAPES IN RELATION TO YOUR MOOD.

Jeremiah Complains to the LORD

7 LORD, you have deceived me,
  and I was deceived.
You are stronger than I am,
  and you have overpowered me.
Everyone jeers at me;
  they mock me all day long.

8 Whenever I speak, I have to cry out
  and shout, "Violence! Destruction!"
LORD, I am ridiculed and scorned all the time
  because I proclaim your message.
9 But when I say, "I will forget the LORD
  and no longer speak in his name,"
then your message is like a fire
  burning deep within me.
I try my best to hold it in,
  but can no longer keep it back.
10 I hear everybody whispering,
  "Terror is everywhere!
  So let's report him to the authorities!"
Even my close friends wait for my downfall.
"Perhaps he can be tricked," they say;
  "then we can catch him and get revenge."
11 But you, LORD, are on my side, strong and mighty,
  and those who persecute me will fail.
They will be disgraced for ever,
  because they cannot succeed.
Their disgrace will never be forgotten.
12 But, Almighty LORD, you test people justly;
  you know what is in their hearts and minds.
So let me see you take revenge on my enemies,
  for I have placed my cause in your hands.
13 Sing to the LORD!
  Praise the LORD!
He rescues the oppressed from the power of evil people.

14 Curse the day I was born!
Forget the day my mother gave me birth!
15 Curse the one who made my father glad
  by bringing him the news,
  "It's a boy! You have a son!"
16 May he be like those cities
  that the LORD destroyed without mercy.
May he hear cries of pain in the morning
  and the battle alarm at noon,
17 because he didn't kill me before I was born.
Then my mother's womb would have been my grave.
18 Why was I born?
  Was it only to have trouble and sorrow,
  to end my life in disgrace?

Jerusalem's Defeat is Predicted

21 King Zedekiah of Judah sent Pashhur son of Malchiah and the priest Zephaniah son of Maaseiah to me with this request: 2 "Please speak to the LORD for us, because King Nebuchadnezzar of Babylonia and his army are besieging the city. Maybe the LORD will perform one of his miracles for us and force Nebuchadnezzar to retreat."

JEREMIAH 21, 22

911

Jerem.

Lamen.

Ezekiel

Daniel

Hosea

Joel

[3] Then the LORD spoke to me, and I told the men who had been sent to me [4] to tell Zedekiah that the LORD, the God of Israel, had said, "Zedekiah, I am going to defeat your army that is fighting against the king of Babylonia and his army. I will pile up your soldiers' weapons in the centre of the city. [5] I will fight against you with all my might, my anger, my wrath, and my fury. [6] I will kill everyone living in this city; people and animals alike will die of a terrible disease. [7] But as for you, your officials, and the people who survive the war, the famine, and the disease — I will let all of you be captured by King Nebuchadnezzar and by your enemies, who want to kill you. Nebuchadnezzar will put you to death. He will not spare any of you or show mercy or pity to any of you. I, the LORD, have spoken."

[8] Then the LORD told me to say to the people, "Listen! I, the LORD, am giving you a choice between the way that leads to life and the way that leads to death. [9] Anyone who stays in the city will be killed in war or by starvation or disease. But those who go out and surrender to the Babylonians, who are now attacking the city, will not be killed; they will at least escape with their lives. [10] I have made up my mind not to spare this city, but to destroy it. It will be given over to the king of Babylonia and he will burn it to the ground. I, the LORD, have spoken."

Judgement on the Royal House of Judah

[11-12] The LORD told me to give this message to the royal house of Judah, the descendants of David: "Listen to what I, the LORD, am saying. See that justice is done every day. Protect the person who is being cheated from the one who is cheating him. If you don't, the evil you are doing will make my anger burn like a fire that cannot be put out. [13] You, Jerusalem, are sitting* high above the valleys, like a rock rising above the plain. But I will fight against you. You say that no one can attack you or break through your defences. [14] But I will punish you for what you have done. I will set your palace on fire, and the fire will burn down everything round it. I, the LORD, have spoken."

Jeremiah's Message to the Royal House of Judah

22 [1-2] The LORD told me to go to the palace of the king of Judah, the descendant of David, and there tell the king, his officials, and the people of Jerusalem to listen to what the LORD had said: [3] "I, the LORD, command you to do what is just and right. Protect the person who is being cheated from the one who is cheating him. Do not ill-treat or oppress foreigners, orphans, or widows; and do not kill innocent people in this holy place. [4] If you really do as I have commanded, then David's descendants will continue to be kings. And they, together with their officials and their people, will continue to pass through the gates of this palace in chariots and on horses. [5] But if you do not obey my commands, then I swear to you that this palace will fall into ruins. I, the LORD, have spoken.

[6] "To me, Judah's royal palace is as beautiful as the land of Gilead and as the Lebanon Mountains; but I will make it a desolate place where no one lives. [7] I am sending men to destroy it. They will all bring their axes, cut down its beautiful cedar pillars, and throw them into the fire.

[8] "Afterwards many foreigners will pass by and ask one another why I, the LORD, have done such a thing to this great city. [9] Then

21.13 *You, Jerusalem, are sitting*; or *You are enthroned*.

Jerem.

.·.········

Psalms
Proverbs
Eccles.
Songs
Isaiah

Take the opportunity to

VENT

about things that are

BOTHERING
YOU HERE.

When you're done, hand
them over to God.

they will answer that it is because you have abandoned your covenant with me, your God, and have worshipped and served other gods."

Jeremiah's Message concerning Joahaz

¹⁰ People of Judah, do not weep for King Josiah;
     do not mourn his death.
But weep bitterly for Joahaz, his son;
     they are taking him away, never to return,
     never again to see the land where he was born.

¹¹ The LORD says concerning Josiah's son Joahaz, who succeeded his father as king of Judah, "He has gone away from here, never to return. ¹² He will die in the country where they have taken him, and he will never again see this land."

Jeremiah's Message concerning Jehoiakim

¹³ Doomed is the man who builds his house by injustice
     and enlarges it by dishonesty;
who makes his countrymen work for nothing
     and does not pay their wages.
¹⁴ Doomed is the one who says,
     "I will build myself a mansion
     with spacious rooms upstairs."
So he puts windows in his house,
     panels it with cedar,
     and paints it red.
¹⁵ Does it make you a better king
     if you build houses of cedar,
     finer than those of others?
Your father enjoyed a full life.
     He was always just and fair,
     and he prospered in everything he did.
¹⁶ He gave the poor a fair trial,
     and all went well with him.
That is what it means to know the LORD.
¹⁷ But you can only see your selfish interests;
     you kill the innocent
     and violently oppress your people.
The LORD has spoken.
¹⁸ So then, the LORD says about Josiah's son Jehoiakim, king of Judah,
"No one will mourn his death or say,
     'How terrible, my friend, how terrible!'
No one will weep for him or cry,
     'My lord! My king!'
¹⁹ With the funeral honours of a donkey,
     he will be dragged away
     and thrown outside Jerusalem's gates."

Jeremiah's Message about the Fate of Jerusalem

²⁰ People of Jerusalem, go to Lebanon and shout,
     go to the land of Bashan and cry;
call out from the mountains of Moab,
     because all your allies have been defeated.
²¹ The LORD spoke to you when you were prosperous,
     but you refused to listen.
That is what you've done all your life;
     you never would obey the LORD.

Jerem.

....

Lamen.
Ezekiel
Daniel
Hosea
Joel

²² Your leaders will be blown away by the wind,
    your allies taken as prisoners of war,
    your city disgraced and put to shame
    because of all the evil you have done.
²³ You rest secure among the cedars brought from
    Lebanon;
    but how pitiful you'll be when pains strike you,
    pains like those of a woman in labour.

God's Judgement on Jehoiachin

²⁴ The Lord said to King Jehoiachin, son of King Jehoiakim of Judah, "As surely as I am the living God, even if you were the signet ring on my right hand, I would pull you off ²⁵ and give you to people you are afraid of, people who want to kill you. I will give you to King Nebuchadnezzar of Babylonia and his soldiers. ²⁶ I am going to force you and your mother into exile. You will go to a country where neither of you was born, and both of you will die there. ²⁷ You will long to see this country again, but you will never return."

²⁸ I said, "Has King Jehoiachin become like a broken jar that is thrown away and that no one wants? Is that why he and his children have been taken into exile to a land they know nothing about?"

²⁹ O land, land, land!
    Listen to what the Lord has said:
³⁰ "This man is condemned to lose his children,
    to be a man who will never succeed.
He will have no descendants
    who will rule in Judah
    as David's successors.
I, the Lord, have spoken."

Hope for the Future

23 How terrible will be the Lord's judgement on those rulers who destroy and scatter his people! ² This is what the Lord, the God of Israel, says about the rulers who were supposed to take care of his people: "You have not taken care of my people; you have scattered them and driven them away. Now I am going to punish you for the evil you have done. ³ I will gather the rest of my people from the countries where I have scattered them, and I will bring them back to their homeland. They will have many children and increase in number. ⁴ I will appoint rulers to take care of them. My people will no longer be afraid or terrified, and I will not punish them again.* I, the Lord, have spoken."

⁵ The Lord says, "The time is coming when I will choose as king a righteous descendant of David. That king will rule wisely and do what is right and just throughout the land. ⁶ When he is king, the people of Judah will be safe, and the people of Israel will live in peace. He will be called 'The Lord Our Salvation'.

⁷ "The time is coming," says the Lord, "when people will no longer swear by me as the living God who brought the people of Israel out of the land of Egypt. ⁸ Instead, they will swear by me as the living God who brought the people of Israel out of a northern land and out of all the other countries where I had scattered them. Then they will live in their own land."

23.4 I will not punish them again; or not one of them will be missing.

Jeremiah's Message about the Prophets

⁹ My heart is crushed,
  and I am trembling.
Because of the LORD,
  because of his holy words,
  I am like a man who is drunk,
  a man who has had too much wine.
¹⁰ The land is full of people unfaithful to the LORD;
  they live wicked lives and misuse their power.
Because of the LORD's curse the land mourns
  and the pastures are dry.

¹¹ The LORD says,
"The prophets and the priests are godless;
  I have caught them doing evil in the Temple itself.
¹² The paths they follow will be slippery and dark;
  I will make them stumble and fall.
I am going to bring disaster on them;
  the time of their punishment is coming.
I, the LORD, have spoken.
¹³ I have seen the sin of Samaria's prophets:
  they have spoken in the name of Baal
  and have led my people astray.
¹⁴ But I have seen the prophets in Jerusalem do even worse:
  they commit adultery and tell lies;
  they help people to do wrong,
  so that no one stops doing what is evil.
To me, they are all as bad
  as the people of Sodom and Gomorrah.

¹⁵ "So then, this is what I, the LORD Almighty, say about the prophets of Jerusalem:
  I will give them bitter plants to eat
  and poison to drink,
  because they have spread ungodliness throughout the land."

¹⁶ The LORD Almighty said to the people of Jerusalem, "Do not listen to what the prophets say; they are filling you with false hopes. They tell you what they have imagined and not what I have said. ¹⁷ To the people who refuse to listen to what I have said, they keep saying that all will go well with them. And they tell everyone who is stubborn that disaster will never touch him."

¹⁸ I said, "None of these prophets has ever known the LORD's secret thoughts. None of them has ever heard or understood his message, or ever listened or paid attention to what he said. ¹⁹ His anger is a storm, a furious wind that will rage over the heads of the wicked, ²⁰ and it will not end until he has done everything he intends to do. In days to come his people will understand this clearly."

²¹ The LORD said, "I did not send these prophets, but even so they went. I did not give them any message, but still they spoke in my name. ²² If they had known my secret thoughts, then they could have proclaimed my message to my people and could have made them give up the evil lives they live and the wicked things they do.

²³ "I am a God who is everywhere and not in one place only. ²⁴ No one can hide where I cannot see him. Do you not know that I am everywhere in heaven and on earth? ²⁵ I know what those prophets have said who speak lies in my name and claim that

JEREMIAH 23, 24

915

Jerem.
....

Lamen.
Ezekiel
Daniel
Hosea
Joel

I have given them my messages in their dreams. ²⁶How much longer will those prophets mislead my people with the lies they have invented? ²⁷They think that the dreams they tell will make my people forget me, just as their ancestors forgot me and turned to Baal. ²⁸The prophet who has had a dream should say it is only a dream, but the prophet who has heard my message should proclaim that message faithfully. What good is straw compared with wheat? ²⁹My message is like a fire, and like a hammer that breaks rocks in pieces. ³⁰I am against those prophets who take each other's words and proclaim them as my message. ³¹I am also against those prophets who speak their own words and claim they came from me. ³²Listen to what I, the Lord, say! I am against the prophets who tell their dreams that are full of lies. They tell these dreams and lead my people astray with their lies and their boasting. I did not send them or order them to go, and they are of no help at all to the people. I, the Lord, have spoken."

The Lord's Burden

³³The Lord said to me, "Jeremiah, when one of my people or a prophet or a priest asks you, 'What is the Lord's message?' you are to tell him, 'You are a burden* to the Lord, and he is going to get rid of you.' ³⁴If any of my people or a prophet or a priest even uses the words 'the Lord's burden', I will punish them and their families. ³⁵Instead, they should each ask their friends and relatives, 'What answer has the Lord given? What has the Lord said?' ³⁶So they must no longer use the words 'the Lord's burden', because if anyone does, I will make my message a real burden to him. The people have perverted the words of their God, the living God, the Lord Almighty. ³⁷Jeremiah, ask the prophets, 'What answer did the Lord give you? What did the Lord say?' ³⁸And if they disobey my command and use the words 'the Lord's burden', then tell them that ³⁹I will certainly pick them up* and throw them far away from me, both them and the city that I gave to them and their ancestors. ⁴⁰I will bring on them everlasting shame and disgrace that will never be forgotten."

Two Baskets of Figs

24 The Lord showed me two baskets of figs placed in front of the Temple. (This was after King Nebuchadnezzar of Babylonia had taken away Jehoiakim's son, King Jehoiachin of Judah, as a prisoner from Jerusalem to Babylonia, together with the leaders of Judah, the craftsmen, and the skilled workers.) ²The first basket contained good figs, those that ripen early; the other one contained bad figs, too bad to eat. ³Then the Lord said to me, "Jeremiah, what do you see?"

I answered, "Figs. The good ones are very good, and the bad ones are very bad, too bad to eat."

⁴So the Lord said to me, ⁵"I, the Lord, the God of Israel, consider that the people who were taken away to Babylonia are like these good figs, and I will treat them with kindness. ⁶I will watch over them and bring them back to this land. I will build them up and not tear them down; I will plant them and not pull them up. ⁷I will give them the desire to know that I am the Lord. Then they will be my people, and I will be their God, because they will return to me with all their heart.

....

23.33 The Hebrew word for *message* and *burden* is the same.
23.39 The Hebrew verb for *pick up* comes from the same root as the Hebrew word for *message* and *burden*.

916

Jerem.

....

Psalms
Proverbs
Eccles.
Songs
Isaiah

JEREMIAH 24, 25

8 "As for King Zedekiah of Judah, the politicians round him, and the rest of the people of Jerusalem who have stayed in this land or moved to Egypt — I, the LORD, will treat them all like these figs that are too bad to be eaten. 9 I will bring such a disaster on them that all the nations of the world will be terrified. People will mock them, make jokes about them, ridicule them, and use their name as a curse everywhere I scatter them. 10 I will bring war, starvation, and disease on them until there is not one of them left in the land that I gave to them and their ancestors."

The Enemy from the North

25 In the fourth year that Jehoiakim son of Josiah was king of Judah, I received a message from the LORD concerning all the people of Judah. (This was the first year that Nebuchadnezzar was king of Babylonia.) 2 I said to all the people of Judah and of Jerusalem, 3 "For 23 years, from the thirteenth year that Josiah son of Amon was king of Judah until this very day, the LORD has spoken to me, and I have never failed to tell you what he said. But you have paid no attention. 4 You would not listen or pay attention, even though the LORD has continued to send you his servants the prophets. 5 They told you to turn from your wicked way of life and from the evil things you are doing, so that you could go on living in the land that the LORD gave you and your ancestors as a permanent possession. 6 They told you not to worship and serve other gods and not to make the LORD angry by worshipping the idols you had made. If you had obeyed the LORD, then he would not have punished you. 7 But the LORD himself says that you refused to listen to him. Instead, you made him angry with your idols and have brought his punishment on yourselves.

8 "So then, because you would not listen to him, the LORD Almighty says, 9 'I am going to send for all the peoples from the north and for my servant, King Nebuchadnezzar of Babylonia. I am going to bring them to fight against Judah and its inhabitants and against all the neighbouring nations. I am going to destroy this nation and its neighbours and leave them in ruins for ever, a terrible and shocking sight. I, the LORD, have spoken. 10 I will silence their shouts of joy and gladness and the happy sounds of wedding feasts. They will have no oil for their lamps, and there will be no more corn. 11 This whole land will be left in ruins and will be a shocking sight, and the neighbouring nations will serve the king of Babylonia for seventy years. 12 After that I will punish Babylonia and its king for their sin. I will destroy that country and leave it in ruins for ever. 13 I will punish Babylonia with all the disasters that I threatened to bring on the nations when I spoke through Jeremiah — all the disasters recorded in this book. 14 I will pay the Babylonians back for what they have done, and many nations and great kings will make slaves of them.'"

God's Judgement on the Nations

15 The LORD, the God of Israel, said to me, "Here is a wine cup filled with my anger. Take it to all the nations to whom I send you, and make them drink from it. 16 When they drink from it, they will stagger and go out of their minds because of the war I am sending against them."

17 So I took the cup from the LORD's hand, gave it to all the nations to whom the LORD had sent me, and made them drink from it. 18 Jerusalem and all the towns of Judah, together with

JEREMIAH 25

917

Jerem.

⋯⋯⋯⋮⋯

Lamen.
Ezekiel
Daniel
Hosea
Joel

its kings and leaders, were made to drink from it, so that they would become a desert, a terrible and shocking sight, and so that people would use their name as a curse — as they still do.

19-26 Here is the list of all the others who had to drink from the cup:

the king of Egypt, his officials and leaders;
all the Egyptians and all the foreigners in Egypt;
all the kings of the land of Uz;
all the kings of the Philistine cities of Ashkelon, Gaza,
    Ekron, and what remains of Ashdod;
all the people of Edom, Moab, and Ammon;
all the kings of Tyre and Sidon;
all the kings of the Mediterranean lands;
the cities of Dedan, Tema, and Buz;
all the people who cut their hair short;
all the kings of Arabia;
all the kings of the desert tribes;
all the kings of Zimri, Elam, and Media;
all the kings of the north, far and near, one after another.

Every nation on the face of the earth had to drink from it. Last of all, the king of Babylonia will drink from it.

27 Then the LORD said to me, "Tell the people that I, the LORD Almighty, the God of Israel, am commanding them to drink until they are drunk and vomit, until they fall down and cannot get up, because of the war that I am sending against them. 28 And if they refuse to take the cup from your hand and drink from it, then tell them that the LORD Almighty has said that they will still have to drink from it. 29 I will begin my work of destruction in my own city. Do they think they will go unpunished? No, they will be punished, for I am going to send war on all the people on earth. I, the LORD Almighty, have spoken.

30 "You, Jeremiah, must proclaim everything I have said. You must tell these people,

'The LORD will roar from heaven
    and thunder from the heights of heaven.
He will roar against his people;
    he will shout like a man treading grapes.
Everyone on earth will hear him,
31   and the sound will echo to the ends of the earth.
The LORD has a case against the nations.
He will bring all people to trial
    and put the wicked to death.
The LORD has spoken.'"

32 The LORD Almighty says that disaster is coming on one nation after another, and a great storm is gathering at the far ends of the earth. 33 On that day the bodies of those whom the LORD has killed will lie scattered from one end of the earth to the other. No one will mourn for them, and they will not be taken away and buried. They will lie on the ground like piles of manure.

34 Cry, you leaders, you shepherds of my people, cry out loud! Mourn and roll in the dust. The time has come for you to be slaughtered,* and you will be butchered like rams.* 35 There will be no way for you to escape. 36-37 You moan and cry out in distress because the LORD in his anger has destroyed your nation and left your peaceful country in ruins. 38 The LORD has abandoned his

25.34 Hebrew has an additional word, the meaning of which is unclear.
25.34 One ancient translation *rams*; Hebrew *vessels*.

918

Jerem.

⋮⋯⋯⋯

Psalms
Proverbs
Eccles.
Songs
Isaiah

JEREMIAH 25, 26

JEREMIAH 26

After all the damage
was done, God still
promised to restore his
people. God always has

SPACE FOR
REDEMPTION.

He promises to plant and
to build those that have
been in exile.

Wherever you are, look
for a plant, a flower or
a building - symbols of
something built or grown.
As you look at it, thank
God that he is ultimately
a redeemer.

people* like a lion that leaves its cave. The horrors of war and the LORD's fierce anger have turned the country into a desert.

Jeremiah is Brought to Trial

26 Soon after Jehoiakim son of Josiah became king of Judah, [2] the LORD said to me, "Stand in the court of the Temple and proclaim all I have commanded you to say to the people who come from the towns of Judah to worship there. Do not leave out anything. [3] Perhaps the people will listen and give up their evil ways. If they do, then I will change my mind about the destruction I plan to bring on them for all their wicked deeds."

[4] The LORD told me to say to the people, "I, the LORD, have said that you must obey me by following the teaching that I gave you, [5] and by paying attention to the words of my servants, the prophets, whom I have kept on sending to you. You have never obeyed what they said. [6] If you continue to disobey, then I will do to this Temple what I did to Shiloh,* and all the nations of the world will use the name of this city as a curse."

[7] The priests, the prophets, and all the people heard me saying these things in the Temple, [8] and as soon as I had finished all that the LORD had commanded me to speak, they seized me and shouted, "You ought to be killed for this! [9] Why have you said in the LORD's name that this Temple will become like Shiloh and that this city will be destroyed and no one will live in it?" Then the people crowded round me.

[10] When the leaders of Judah heard what had happened, they hurried from the royal palace to the Temple and took their places at the New Gate. [11] Then the priests and the prophets said to the leaders and to the people, "This man deserves to be sentenced to death because he has spoken against our city. You heard him with your own ears."

[12] Then I said, "The LORD sent me to proclaim everything that you heard me say against this Temple and against this city. [13] You must change the way you are living and the things you are doing, and must obey the LORD your God. If you do, he will change his mind about the destruction that he said he would bring on you. [14] As for me, I am in your power! Do with me whatever you think is fair and right. [15] But be sure of this: if you kill me, you and the people of this city will be guilty of killing an innocent man, because it is the LORD who sent me to give you this warning."

[16] Then the leaders and the people said to the priests and the prophets, "This man spoke to us in the name of the LORD our God; he should not be put to death."

[17] After that, some of the elders stood up and said to the people who had assembled, [18] "When Hezekiah was king of Judah, the prophet Micah of Moresheth told all the people that the LORD Almighty had said,

'Zion will be ploughed like a field,
    Jerusalem will become a pile of ruins,
        and the Temple hill will become a forest.'

[19] King Hezekiah and the people of Judah did not put Micah to death. Instead, Hezekiah honoured the LORD and tried to win his favour. And the LORD changed his mind about the disaster that he said he would bring on them. Now we are about to bring a terrible disaster on ourselves."

25.38 *The LORD... people*; or *The LORD's people run away.*
26.6 *Shiloh*: See 7.12.

JEREMIAH 26, 27

919

Jerem.

....

Lamen.
Ezekiel
Daniel
Hosea
Joel

²⁰ (There was another man, Uriah son of Shemaiah from Kiriath Jearim, who spoke in the name of the LORD against this city and nation just as Jeremiah did. ²¹ When King Jehoiakim and his soldiers and officials heard what Uriah had said, the king tried to have him killed. But Uriah heard about it; so he fled in terror and escaped to Egypt. ²² King Jehoiakim, however, sent Elnathan son of Achbor and some other men to Egypt to get Uriah. ²³ They brought him back to King Jehoiakim, who had him killed and his body thrown into the public burial ground.)

²⁴ But because I had the support of Ahikam son of Shaphan, I was not handed over to the people and killed.

Jeremiah Wears an Ox Yoke

27 Soon after Josiah's son Zedekiah became king of Judah, the LORD told me ²to make myself a yoke out of leather straps and wooden crossbars and to put it on my neck. ³ Then the LORD told me to send a message* to the kings of Edom, Moab, Ammon, Tyre, and Sidon through their ambassadors who had come to Jerusalem to see King Zedekiah. ⁴ The LORD Almighty, the God of Israel, told me to command them to tell their kings that the LORD had said: ⁵ "By my great power and strength I created the world, the human race, and all the animals that live on the earth; and I give it to anyone I choose. ⁶ I am the one who has placed all these nations under the power of my servant, King Nebuchadnezzar of Babylonia, and I have made even the wild animals serve him. ⁷ All nations will serve him, and they will serve his son and his grandson until the time comes for his own nation to fall. Then his nation will serve powerful nations and great kings.

⁸ "But if any nation or kingdom will not submit to his rule, then I will punish that nation by war, starvation, and disease until I have let Nebuchadnezzar destroy it completely. ⁹ Do not listen to your prophets or to anyone who claims he can predict the future, either by dreams or by calling up the spirits of the dead or by magic. They all tell you not to submit to the king of Babylonia. ¹⁰ They are deceiving you and will cause you to be taken far away from your country. I will drive you out, and you will be destroyed. ¹¹ But if any nation submits to the king of Babylonia and serves him, then I will let it stay on in its own land, to farm it and live there. I, the LORD, have spoken."

¹² I said the same thing to King Zedekiah of Judah, "Submit to the king of Babylonia. Serve him and his people, and you will live. ¹³ Why should you and your people die in war or of starvation or disease? That is what the LORD has said will happen to any nation that does not submit to the king of Babylonia. ¹⁴ Do not listen to the prophets who tell you not to surrender to him. They are deceiving you. ¹⁵ The LORD himself has said that he did not send them and that they are lying to you in his name. And so he will drive you out, and you will be killed, you and the prophets who are telling you these lies."

¹⁶ Then I told the priests and the people that the LORD had said: "Do not listen to the prophets who say that the temple treasures will soon be brought back from Babylonia. They are lying to you. ¹⁷ Don't listen to them! Submit to the king of Babylonia and you will live! Why should this city become a pile of ruins? ¹⁸ If they are really prophets and if they have my message, let them ask me, the LORD Almighty, not to allow the treasures that remain in the Temple and in the royal palace to be taken to Babylonia."

....

27.3 Probable text *a message*; Hebrew *them*.

920

Jerem.

·:·········

Psalms
Proverbs
Eccles.
Songs
Isaiah

JEREMIAH 27–29

19-20 (When King Nebuchadnezzar took away to Babylonia the king of Judah, Jehoiachin son of Jehoiakim, and the leading men of Judah and Jerusalem, he left the columns, the bronze tank, the carts, and some of the other temple treasures.)

21 "Listen to what I, the LORD Almighty, the God of Israel, say about the treasures that are left in the Temple and in the royal palace in Jerusalem: 22 They will be taken to Babylonia and will remain there until I turn my attention to them. Then I will bring them back and restore them to this place. I, the LORD, have spoken."

Jeremiah and the Prophet Hananiah

28 That same year,* in the fifth month of the fourth year that Zedekiah was king, Hananiah son of Azzur, a prophet from the town of Gibeon, spoke to me in the Temple. In the presence of the priests and of the people he told me 2 that the LORD Almighty, the God of Israel, had said: "I have broken the power of the king of Babylonia. 3 Within two years I will bring back to this place all the temple treasures that King Nebuchadnezzar took to Babylonia. 4 I will also bring back the king of Judah, Jehoiachin son of Jehoiakim, along with all the people of Judah who went into exile in Babylonia. Yes, I will break the power of the king of Babylonia. I, the LORD, have spoken."

5 Then in the presence of the priests and of all the people who were standing in the Temple, I said to Hananiah: 6 "Wonderful! I hope the LORD will do this! I certainly hope he will make your prophecy come true and will bring back from Babylonia all the temple treasures and all the people who were taken away as prisoners. 7 But listen to what I say to you and to the people. 8 The prophets who spoke long ago, before my time and yours, predicted that war, starvation, and disease would come to many nations and powerful kingdoms. 9 But a prophet who predicts peace can only be recognized as a prophet whom the LORD has truly sent when that prophet's predictions come true."

10 Then Hananiah took the yoke off my neck, broke it in pieces, 11 and said in the presence of all the people: "The LORD has said that this is how he will break the yoke that King Nebuchadnezzar has put on the neck of all the nations; and he will do this within two years." Then I left.

12 Some time after this the LORD told me 13 to go and say to Hananiah: "The LORD has said that you may be able to break a wooden yoke, but he* will replace it with an iron yoke. 14 The LORD Almighty, the God of Israel, has said that he will put an iron yoke on all these nations and that they will serve King Nebuchadnezzar of Babylonia. The LORD has said that he will make even the wild animals serve Nebuchadnezzar."

15 Then I told Hananiah this, and added, "Listen, Hananiah! The LORD did not send you, and you are making these people believe a lie. 16 And so the LORD himself says that he is going to get rid of you. Before this year is over you will die because you have told the people to rebel against the LORD."

17 And Hananiah died in the seventh month of that same year.

Jeremiah's Letter to the Jews in Babylonia

29 I wrote a letter to the priests, the prophets, the leaders of the people, and to all the others whom Nebuchadnezzar

28.1 One ancient translation That same year; Hebrew That same year at the beginning of his reign.
28.13 One ancient translation he; Hebrew you.

JEREMIAH 29

921

Jerem.

....

Lamen.
Ezekiel
Daniel
Hosea
Joel

had taken away as prisoners from Jerusalem to Babylonia. ²I wrote it after King Jehoiachin, his mother, the palace officials, the leaders of Judah and of Jerusalem, the craftsmen, and the skilled workmen had been taken into exile. ³I gave the letter to Elasah son of Shaphan and to Gemariah son of Hilkiah, whom King Zedekiah of Judah was sending to King Nebuchadnezzar of Babylonia. It said:

⁴"The LORD Almighty, the God of Israel, says to all those people whom he allowed Nebuchadnezzar to take away as prisoners from Jerusalem to Babylonia: ⁵'Build houses and settle down. Plant gardens and eat what you grow in them. ⁶Marry and have children. Then let your children get married, so that they also may have children. You must increase in numbers and not decrease. ⁷Work for the good of the cities where I have made you go as prisoners. Pray to me on their behalf, because if they are prosperous, you will be prosperous too. ⁸I, the LORD, the God of Israel, warn you not to let yourselves be deceived by the prophets who live among you or by any others who claim they can predict the future. Do not pay any attention to their* dreams. ⁹They are telling you lies in my name. I did not send them. I, the LORD Almighty, have spoken.'

¹⁰"The LORD says, 'When Babylonia's seventy years are over, I will show my concern for you and keep my promise to bring you back home. ¹¹I alone know the plans I have for you, plans to bring you prosperity and not disaster, plans to bring about the future you hope for.* ¹²Then you will call to me. You will come and pray to me, and I will answer you. ¹³You will seek me, and you will find me because you will seek me with all your heart. ¹⁴Yes, I say, you will find me, and I will restore you to your land. I will gather you from every country and from every place to which I have scattered you, and I will bring you back to the land from which I had sent you away into exile. I, the LORD, have spoken.'

¹⁵"You say that the LORD has given you prophets in Babylonia. ¹⁶Listen to what the LORD says about the king who rules the kingdom that David ruled and about the people of this city, that is, your relatives who were not taken away as prisoners with you. ¹⁷The LORD Almighty says, 'I am bringing war, starvation, and disease on them, and I will make them like figs that are too rotten to be eaten. ¹⁸I will pursue them with war, starvation, and disease, and all the nations of the world will be horrified at what they see. Everywhere I scatter them, people will be shocked and terrified at what has happened to them. People will mock them and use their name as a curse. ¹⁹This will happen to them because they did not obey the message that I kept on sending to them through my servants the prophets. They refused to listen. ²⁰All of you whom I sent into exile in Babylonia, listen to what I, the LORD, say.'

²¹"The LORD Almighty, the God of Israel, has spoken about Ahab son of Kolaiah and Zedekiah son of Maaseiah, who are telling you lies in his name. He has said that he will hand them over to the power of King Nebuchadnezzar of Babylonia, who will put them to death before your eyes. ²²When the people who were taken away as prisoners from Jerusalem to Babylonia want to bring a curse on someone, they will say, 'May the LORD treat you like Zedekiah and Ahab, whom the king of Babylonia roasted alive!' ²³This will be their fate because they are guilty

JEREMIAH 29.10-14

Jeremiah 29.11 is a great verse - but it sits with

– OTHER –

GREAT

VERSES

in which God promises to bring back the Israelites from exile.

REWRITE VERSES 11-14 AROUND THESE TWO PAGES!

29.8 Probable text *their*; Hebrew *your*.
29.11 *the future you hope for*; or *a future full of hope*.

922

Jerem.

Psalms
Proverbs
Eccles.
Songs
Isaiah

JEREMIAH 29, 30

of terrible sins — they have committed adultery and have told lies in the LORD's name. This was against the LORD's will; he knows what they have done, and he is a witness against them.* The LORD has spoken."

The Letter of Shemaiah

24-25 The LORD Almighty, the God of Israel, gave me a message for Shemaiah of Nehelam, who had sent a letter in his own name to all the people of Jerusalem and to the priest Zephaniah son of Maaseiah and to all the other priests. In this letter, Shemaiah wrote to Zephaniah:

26 "The LORD made you a priest in place of Jehoiada, and you are now the chief officer* in the Temple. It is your duty to see that every madman who pretends to be a prophet is placed in chains with an iron collar round his neck. 27 Why haven't you done this to Jeremiah of Anathoth, who has been speaking as a prophet to the people? 28 He must be stopped because he told the people in Babylonia that they would be prisoners there a long time and should build houses, settle down, plant gardens, and eat what they grow."

29 Zephaniah read the letter to me, 30 and then the LORD told me 31-32 to send to all the prisoners in Babylon this message about Shemaiah: "I, the LORD, will punish Shemaiah and all his descendants. I did not send him, but he spoke to you as if he were a prophet, and he made you believe lies. He will have no descendants among you. He will not live to see the good things that I am going to do for my people, because he told them to rebel against me. I, the LORD, have spoken."

The LORD's Promises to his People

30 The LORD, the God of Israel, 2 said to me: "Write down in a book everything that I have told you, 3 because the time is coming when I will restore my people, Israel and Judah. I will bring them back to the land that I gave their ancestors, and they will take possession of it again. I, the LORD, have spoken."

4 The LORD says to the people of Israel and Judah:

5 "I heard a cry of terror,
a cry of fear and not of peace.
6 Now stop and think!
Can a man give birth to a child?
Why then do I see every man with his hands on his
stomach
like a woman in labour?
Why is everyone so pale?
7 A terrible day is coming;
no other day can compare with it —
a time of distress for my people,
but they will survive."

8 The LORD Almighty says: "When that day comes, I will break the yoke that is round their necks and remove their chains, and they will no longer be the slaves of foreigners. 9 Instead, they will serve me, the LORD their God, and a descendant of David, whom I will enthrone as king.

10 "My people, do not be afraid;
people of Israel, do not be terrified.

29.23 *done, and he... them*; or *done; he saw them do it.*
29.26 Some ancient translations *officer*; Hebrew *officers.*

Jerem.

Lamen.
Ezekiel
Daniel
Hosea
Joel

I will rescue you from that distant land,
    from the land where you are prisoners.
You will come back home and live in peace;
    you will be secure, and no one will make you afraid.
¹¹ I will come to you and save you.
I will destroy all the nations
    where I have scattered you,
    but I will not destroy you.
I will not let you go unpunished;
    but when I punish you, I will be fair.
I, the LORD, have spoken."

¹² The LORD says to his people,
"Your wounds are incurable,
    your injuries cannot be healed.
¹³ There is no one to take care of you,
    no remedy for your sores,
    no hope of healing for you.
¹⁴ All your lovers have forgotten you;
    they no longer care about you.
I have attacked you like an enemy;
    your punishment has been harsh
    because your sins are many
    and your wickedness is great.
¹⁵ Complain no more about your injuries;
    there is no cure for you.
I punished you like this
    because your sins are many
    and your wickedness is great.
¹⁶ But now, all who devour you will be devoured,
    and all your enemies will be taken away as prisoners.
All who oppress you will be oppressed,
    and all who plunder you will be plundered.
¹⁷ I will make you well again;
    I will heal your wounds,
    though your enemies say,
'Zion is an outcast;
    no one cares about her.'
I, the LORD, have spoken."

¹⁸ The LORD says,
"I will restore my people to their land
    and have mercy on every family;
Jerusalem will be rebuilt,
    and its palace restored.
¹⁹ The people who live there will sing praise;
    they will shout for joy.
By my blessing they will increase in numbers;
    my blessing will bring them honour.
²⁰ I will restore the nation's ancient power
    and establish it firmly again;
    I will punish all who oppress them.
²¹⁻²² Their ruler will come from their own nation,
    their prince from their own people.
He will approach me when I invite him,
    for who would dare come uninvited?
They will be my people,
    and I will be their God.
I, the LORD, have spoken."

MERCY

PSALM 80.3;
ISAIAH 55.1;
JEREMIAH 30.18

What do you
think it means?

What does someone
else think it means?

Now go and look up
the definition.

23-24 The LORD's anger is a storm, a furious wind that will rage over the heads of the wicked. It will not end until he has done all that he intends to do. In days to come his people will understand this clearly.

Israel's Return Home

31 The LORD says, "The time is coming when I will be the God of all the tribes of Israel, and they will be my people. [2] In the desert I showed mercy to those people who had escaped death. When the people of Israel longed for rest, [3] I appeared to them* from far away. People of Israel, I have always loved you, so I continue to show you my constant love. [4] Once again I will rebuild you. Once again you will take up your tambourines and dance joyfully. [5] Once again you will plant vineyards on the hills of Samaria, and those who plant them will eat what the vineyards produce. [6] Yes, the time is coming when watchmen will call out on the hills of Ephraim, 'Let's go up to Zion, to the LORD our God.'"

[7] The LORD says,

"Sing with joy for Israel,
    the greatest of the nations.
Sing your song of praise,
    'The LORD has saved his* people;
    he has rescued all who are left.'
[8] I will bring them from the north
    and gather them from the ends of the earth.
The blind and the lame will come with them,
    pregnant women and those about to give birth.
They will come back a great nation.
[9] My people will return weeping,
    praying as I lead them back.
I will guide them to streams of water,
    on a smooth road where they will not stumble.
I am like a father to Israel,
    and Ephraim is my eldest son."

[10] The LORD says,

"Nations, listen to me,
    and proclaim my words on the far-off shores.
I scattered my people, but I will gather them
    and guard them as a shepherd guards his flock.
[11] I have set Israel's people free
    and have saved them from a mighty nation.
[12] They will come and sing for joy on Mount Zion
    and be delighted with my gifts —
    gifts of corn and wine and olive oil,
    gifts of sheep and cattle.
They will be like a well-watered garden;
    they will have everything they need.
[13] Then the young women will dance and be happy,
    and men, young and old, will rejoice.
I will comfort them and turn their mourning into joy,
    their sorrow into gladness.
[14] I will fill the priests with the richest food
    and satisfy all the needs of my people.
I, the LORD, have spoken."

31.3 One ancient translation *them*; Hebrew *me*.
31.7 Some ancient translations *The LORD… his*; Hebrew LORD, *save your*.

JEREMIAH 31

925

Jerem.

....

Lamen.

Ezekiel

Daniel

Hosea

Joel

The Lord's Mercy on Israel

15 The Lord says,
"A sound is heard in Ramah,
    the sound of bitter weeping.
Rachel is crying for her children;
    they are gone,
    and she refuses to be comforted.
16 Stop your crying
    and wipe away your tears.
All that you have done for your children
    will not go unrewarded;
    they will return from the enemy's land.
17 There is hope for your future;
    your children will come back home.
I, the Lord, have spoken.

18 "I hear the people of Israel say in grief,
    'Lord, we were like an untamed animal,
    but you taught us to obey.
Bring us back;
    we are ready to return to you,
    the Lord our God.
19 We turned away from you,
    but soon we wanted to return.
After you had punished us,
    we hung our heads in grief.
We were ashamed and disgraced,
    because we sinned when we were young.'

20 "Israel, you are my dearest son,
    the child I love best.
Whenever I mention your name,
    I think* of you with love.
My heart goes out to you;
    I will be merciful.
21 Set up signs and mark the road;
    find again the way by which you left.
Come back, people of Israel,
    come home to the towns you left.
22 How long will you hesitate, faithless people?
    I have created something new and different,
        as different as a woman protecting a man."*

The Future Prosperity of God's People

23 The Lord Almighty, the God of Israel, says, "When I restore
the people to their land, they will once again say in the land of
Judah and in its towns,
    'May the Lord bless the sacred hill* of Jerusalem,
        the holy place where he lives.'
24 People will live in Judah and in all its towns, and there will be
farmers, and shepherds with their flocks. 25 I will refresh those
who are weary and will satisfy with food everyone who is weak
from hunger. 26 So then, people will say, 'I went to sleep and
woke up refreshed.'

....

31.20 *I mention... I think*; or *I threaten to punish, I still think*.
31.22 *as different... man*; Hebrew unclear.
31.23 *sacred hill*: Mount Zion, the hill in Jerusalem which formed part of
the Temple and palace area.

926

Jerem.

Psalms
Proverbs
Eccles.
Songs
Isaiah

JEREMIAH 31, 32

27"I, the Lord, say that the time is coming when I will fill the land of Israel and Judah with people and animals. 28And just as I took care to uproot, to pull down, to overthrow, to destroy, and to demolish them, so I will take care to plant them and to build them up. 29When that time comes, people will no longer say,

'The parents ate the sour grapes,
    But the children got the sour taste.'

30Instead, all those who eat sour grapes will have their own teeth set on edge; and they will all die because of their own sin."

31The Lord says, "The time is coming when I will make a new covenant with the people of Israel and with the people of Judah. 32It will not be like the old covenant that I made with their ancestors when I took them by the hand and led them out of Egypt. Although I was like a husband to them, they did not keep that covenant. 33The new covenant that I will make with the people of Israel will be this: I will put my law within them and write it on their hearts. I will be their God, and they will be my people. 34None of them will have to teach his fellow-citizen to know the Lord, because all will know me, from the least to the greatest. I will forgive their sins and I will no longer remember their wrongs. I, the Lord, have spoken."

35 The Lord provides the sun for light by day,
        the moon and the stars to shine at night.
    He stirs up the sea and makes it roar;
        his name is the Lord Almighty.
36 He promises that as long as the natural order lasts,
        so long will Israel be a nation.
37 If one day the sky could be measured
        and the foundations of the earth explored,
        only then would he reject the people of Israel
        because of all they have done.
    The Lord has spoken.

38"The time is coming," says the Lord, "when all Jerusalem will be rebuilt as my city, from Hananel Tower west to the Corner Gate. 39And the boundary line will continue from there on the west to the hill of Gareb and then round to Goah. 40The entire valley, where the dead are buried and refuse is thrown, and all the fields above the brook of Kidron as far as the Horse Gate to the east, will be sacred to me. The city will never again be torn down or destroyed."

Jeremiah Buys a Field

32 The Lord spoke to me in the tenth year that Zedekiah was king of Judah, which was also the eighteenth year of King Nebuchadnezzar of Babylonia. 2At that time the army of the king of Babylonia was attacking Jerusalem, and I was locked up in the courtyard of the royal palace. 3King Zedekiah had imprisoned me there and had accused me of announcing that the Lord had said, "I am going to let the king of Babylonia capture this city, 4and King Zedekiah will not escape. He will be handed over to the king of Babylonia; he will see him face to face and will speak to him in person. 5Zedekiah will be taken to Babylonia, and he will remain there until I deal with him. Even if he fights the Babylonians, he will not be successful. I, the Lord, have spoken."

6The Lord told me 7that Hanamel, my uncle Shallum's son, would come to me with the request to buy his field at Anathoth in the territory of Benjamin, because I was his nearest relative

JEREMIAH 32

927

Jerem.

Lamen.
Ezekiel
Daniel
Hosea
Joel

and had the right to buy it for myself. [8] Then, just as the LORD had said, Hanamel came to me there in the courtyard and asked me to buy the field. So I knew that the LORD had really spoken to me. [9] I bought the field from Hanamel and weighed out the money to him; the price came to seventeen pieces of silver. [10] I signed and sealed the deed, had it witnessed, and weighed out the money on scales. [11] Then I took both copies of the deed of purchase — the sealed copy containing the contract and its conditions, and the open copy — [12] and gave them to Baruch, the son of Neriah and grandson of Mahseiah. I gave them to him in the presence of Hanamel and of the witnesses who had signed the deed of purchase and of the people who were sitting in the courtyard. [13] Before them all I said to Baruch, [14] "The LORD Almighty, the God of Israel, has ordered you to take these deeds, both the sealed deed of purchase and the open copy, and to place them in a clay jar, so that they may be preserved for years to come. [15] The LORD Almighty, the God of Israel, has said that houses, fields, and vineyards will again be bought in this land."

Jeremiah's Prayer

[16] After I had given the deed of purchase to Baruch, I prayed, [17] "Sovereign LORD, you made the earth and the sky by your great power and might; nothing is too difficult for you. [18] You have shown constant love to thousands, but you also punish people for the sins of their parents. You are a great and powerful God; you are the LORD Almighty. [19] You make wise plans and do mighty things; you see everything that people do, and you reward them according to their actions. [20] Long ago, you performed miracles and wonders in Egypt, and you have continued to perform them to this day, both in Israel and among all the other nations, so that you are now known everywhere. [21] By means of miracles and wonders that terrified our enemies, you used your power and might to bring your people Israel out of Egypt. [22] You gave them this rich and fertile land, as you had promised their ancestors. [23] But when they came into this land and took possession of it, they did not obey your commands or live according to your teaching; they did nothing that you had ordered them to do. And so you brought all this destruction on them.

[24] "The Babylonians have built siege mounds round the city to capture it, and they are attacking. War, starvation, and disease will make the city fall into their hands. You can see that all you have said has come true. [25] Yet, Sovereign LORD, you are the one who ordered me to buy the field in the presence of witnesses, even though the city is about to be captured by the Babylonians."

[26] Then the LORD said to me, [27] "I am the LORD, the God of the whole human race. Nothing is too difficult for me. [28] I am going to give this city over to King Nebuchadnezzar of Babylonia and his army; they will capture it [29] and set it on fire. They will burn it down, together with the houses where people have made me angry by burning incense to Baal on the rooftops and by pouring out wine offerings to other gods. [30] From the very beginning of their history the people of Israel and the people of Judah have displeased me and made me angry by what they have done. [31] The people of this city have made me angry and furious from the day it was built. I have decided to destroy it [32] because of all the evil that has been done by the people of Judah and Jerusalem, together with their kings and leaders, their priests and prophets. [33] They turned their backs on me; and though I kept on teaching them, they would not listen and learn. [34] They even placed their

STOP READING AND PRAY FOR ONE MINUTE.

It doesn't matter what it's about - just talk to God!

928

Jerem.

Psalms
Proverbs
Eccles.
Songs
Isaiah

JEREMIAH 32, 33

disgusting idols in the Temple built for my worship, and they have defiled it. [35] They have built altars to Baal in the Valley of Hinnom, to sacrifice their sons and daughters to the god Molech. I did not command them to do this, and it did not even enter my mind that they would do such a thing and make the people of Judah sin."

A Promise of Hope

[36] The LORD, the God of Israel, said to me, "Jeremiah, the people are saying that war, starvation, and disease will make this city fall into the hands of the king of Babylonia. Now listen to what else I have to say. [37] I am going to gather the people from all the countries where I have scattered them in my anger and fury, and I am going to bring them back to this place and let them live here in safety. [38] Then they will be my people, and I will be their God. [39] I will give them a single purpose in life: to honour me for all time, for their own good and the good of their descendants. [40] I will make an eternal covenant with them. I will never stop doing good things for them, and I will make them fear me with all their heart, so that they will never turn away from me. [41] I will take pleasure in doing good things for them, and I will establish them permanently in this land.

[42] "Just as I have brought this disaster on these people, so I am going to give them all the good things that I have promised. [43] The people are saying that this land will be like a desert where neither people nor animals live, and that it will be given over to the Babylonians. But fields will once again be bought in this land. [44] People will buy them, and the deeds will be signed, sealed, and witnessed. This will take place in the territory of Benjamin, in the villages round Jerusalem, in the towns of Judah, and in the towns in the hill country, in the foothills, and in southern Judah. I will restore the people to their land. I, the LORD, have spoken."

Another Promise of Hope

33 While I was still in prison in the courtyard, the LORD's message came to me again. [2] The LORD, who made the earth, who formed it and set it in place, spoke to me. He whose name is the LORD said, [3] "Call to me, and I will answer you; I will tell you wonderful and marvellous things that you know nothing about. [4] I, the LORD, the God of Israel, say that the houses of Jerusalem and the royal palace of Judah will be torn down as a result of the siege and the attack. [5] Some will fight against the Babylonians, who will fill the houses* with the corpses of those whom I am going to strike down in my anger and fury. I have turned away from this city because of the evil things that its people have done. [6] But I will heal this city and its people and restore them to health. I will show them abundant peace and security. [7] I will make Judah and Israel prosperous, and I will rebuild them as they were before. [8] I will purify them from the sins that they have committed against me, and I will forgive their sins and their rebellion. [9] Jerusalem will be a source of joy, honour, and pride to me; and every nation in the world will fear and tremble when they hear about the good things that I do for the people of Jerusalem and about the prosperity that I bring to the city."

[10] The LORD said, "People are saying that this place is like a desert, that it has no people or animals living in it. And they are right; the towns of Judah and the streets of Jerusalem are empty; no people or animals live there. But in these places you will hear

JEREMIAH 33.2-3

The God of the universe promised to tell Jeremiah amazing things that he hadn't thought of. Have you ever asked God for that? Find a friend and talk about the

- WONDERS OF THE -

UNIVERSE

- the many things that humanity has no idea about. Then, if you dare, ask God to speak to you about new and wonderful things.

33.4–5 In verses 4 and 5 *as a result... houses*; Hebrew unclear.

JEREMIAH 33, 34

929

Jerem.

..............:-

Lamen.
Ezekiel
Daniel
Hosea
Joel

again [11] the shouts of gladness and joy and the happy sounds of wedding feasts. You will hear people sing as they bring thank-offerings to my Temple; they will say,

'Give thanks to the LORD Almighty,
    because he is good
    and his love is eternal.'

I will make this land as prosperous as it was before. I, the LORD, have spoken."

[12] The LORD Almighty said, "In this land that is like a desert and where no people or animals live, there will once again be pastures where shepherds can take their sheep. [13] In the towns of the hill country, in the foothills, and in southern Judah, in the territory of Benjamin, in the villages round Jerusalem, and in the towns of Judah, shepherds will once again count their sheep. I, the LORD, have spoken."

[14] The LORD said, "The time is coming when I will fulfil the promise that I made to the people of Israel and Judah. [15] At that time I will choose as king a righteous descendant of David. That king will do what is right and just throughout the land. [16] The people of Judah and of Jerusalem will be rescued and will live in safety. The city will be called 'The LORD Our Salvation'. [17] I, the LORD, promise that there will always be a descendant of David to be king of Israel [18] and that there will always be priests from the tribe of Levi to serve me and to offer burnt offerings, grain offerings, and sacrifices."

[19] The LORD said to me, [20] "I have made a covenant with the day and with the night, so that they always come at their proper times; and that covenant can never be broken. [21] In the same way I have made a covenant with my servant David that he would always have a descendant to be king, and I have made a covenant with the priests from the tribe of Levi that they would always serve me; and those covenants can never be broken. [22] I will increase the number of descendants of my servant David and the number of priests from the tribe of Levi, so that it will be as impossible to count them as it is to count the stars in the sky or the grains of sand on the seashore."

[23] The LORD said to me, [24] "Have you noticed how people are saying that I have rejected Israel and Judah, the two families that I chose? And so they look with contempt on my people and no longer consider them a nation. [25] But I, the LORD, have a covenant with day and night, and I have made the laws that control earth and sky. [26] And just as surely as I have done this, so I will maintain my covenant with Jacob's descendants and with my servant David. I will choose one of David's descendants to rule over the descendants of Abraham, Isaac, and Jacob. I will be merciful to my people and make them prosperous again."

A Message for Zedekiah

34 The LORD spoke to me when King Nebuchadnezzar of Babylonia and his army, supported by troops from all the nations and races that were subject to him, were attacking Jerusalem and its nearby towns. [2] The LORD, the God of Israel, told me to go and say to King Zedekiah of Judah, "I, the LORD, will hand this city over to the king of Babylonia, and he will burn it down. [3] You will not escape; you will be captured and handed over to him. You will see him face to face and talk to him in person; then you will go to Babylonia. [4] Zedekiah, listen to what I say about you. You will not be killed in battle. [5] You will die in peace, and as people burnt incense when they buried your ancestors, who

930

Jerem.

Psalms
Proverbs
Eccles.
Songs
Isaiah

JEREMIAH 34, 35

were kings before you, in the same way they will burn incense for you. They will mourn over you and say, 'Our king is dead!' I, the LORD, have spoken."

[6] Then I gave this message to King Zedekiah in Jerusalem [7] while the army of the king of Babylonia was attacking the city. The army was also attacking Lachish and Azekah, the only other fortified cities left in Judah.

Deceitful Treatment of Slaves

[8] King Zedekiah and the people of Jerusalem had made an agreement to set free [9] their Hebrew slaves, both male and female, so that no one would have a fellow-Israelite as a slave. [10] All the people and their leaders agreed to free their slaves and never to enslave them again. They did set them free, [11] but later they changed their minds, took them back, and forced them to become slaves again.

[12] Then the LORD, [13] the God of Israel, told me to say to the people: "I made a covenant with your ancestors when I rescued them from Egypt and set them free from slavery. I told them that [14] every seven years they were to set free any Hebrew slave who had served them for six years. But your ancestors would not pay any attention to me or listen to what I said. [15] Just a few days ago you changed your minds and did what pleased me. All of you agreed to set your fellow-Israelites free, and you made a covenant in my presence, in the Temple where I am worshipped. [16] But then you changed your minds again and dishonoured me. All of you took back the slaves whom you had set free as they desired, and you forced them into slavery again. [17] So now, I, the LORD, say that you have disobeyed me: you have not given your fellow-Israelites their freedom. Very well, then, I will give you freedom: the freedom to die by war, disease, and starvation. I will make every nation in the world horrified at what I do to you. [18-19] The officials of Judah and of Jerusalem, together with the palace officials, the priests, and all the leaders, made a covenant with me by walking between the two halves of a bull that they had cut in two. But they broke the covenant and did not keep its terms. So I will do to these people what they did to the bull. [20] I will hand them over to their enemies, who want to kill them, and their corpses will be eaten by birds and wild animals. [21] I will also hand over King Zedekiah of Judah and his officials to those who want to kill them. I will hand them over to the Babylonian army, which has stopped its attack against you. [22] I will give the order, and they will return to this city. They will attack it, capture it, and burn it down. I will make the towns of Judah like a desert where no one lives. I, the LORD, have spoken."

Jeremiah and the Rechabites

35 When Jehoiakim son of Josiah was king of Judah, the LORD said to me, [2] "Go to the members of the Rechabite clan and talk to them. Then bring them into one of the rooms in the Temple and offer them some wine." [3] So I took the entire Rechabite clan — Jaazaniah (the son of another Jeremiah, who was Habazziniah's son) and all his brothers and sons — [4] and brought them to the Temple. I took them into the room of the disciples of the prophet Hanan son of Igdaliah. This room was above the room of Maaseiah son of Shallum, an important official in the Temple, and near the rooms of the other officials. [5] Then I placed cups and bowls full of wine before the Rechabites, and I said to them, "Have some wine."

JEREMIAH 35, 36

931

Jerem.

Lamen.
Ezekiel
Daniel
Hosea
Joel

⁶ But they answered, "We do not drink wine. Our ancestor Jonadab son of Rechab told us that neither we nor our descendants were ever to drink any wine. ⁷ He also told us not to build houses or farm the land, and not to plant vineyards or buy them. He commanded us always to live in tents, so that we might remain in this land where we live like strangers. ⁸ We have obeyed all the instructions that Jonadab gave us. We ourselves never drink wine, and neither do our wives, our sons, or our daughters. ⁹⁻¹⁰ We do not build houses for homes — we live in tents — and we own no vineyards, fields, or corn. We have fully obeyed everything that our ancestor Jonadab commanded us. ¹¹ But when King Nebuchadnezzar invaded the country, we decided to come to Jerusalem to get away from the Babylonian and Syrian armies. That is why we are living in Jerusalem."

¹²⁻¹³ Then the LORD Almighty, the God of Israel, told me to go and say to the people of Judah and Jerusalem, "I, the LORD, ask you why you refuse to listen to me and to obey my instructions. ¹⁴ Jonadab's descendants have obeyed his command not to drink wine, and to this very day none of them drink any. But I have kept on speaking to you, and you have not obeyed me. ¹⁵ I have continued to send you all my servants the prophets, and they have told you to give up your evil ways and to do what is right. They warned you not to worship and serve other gods, so that you could go on living in the land that I gave you and your ancestors. But you would not listen to me or pay attention to me. ¹⁶ Jonadab's descendants have obeyed the command that their ancestor gave them, but you people have not obeyed me. ¹⁷ So now, I, the LORD Almighty, the God of Israel, will bring on you people of Judah and of Jerusalem all the destruction that I promised. I will do this because you would not listen when I spoke to you, and you would not answer when I called you."

¹⁸ Then I told the Rechabite clan that the LORD Almighty, the God of Israel, had said, "You have obeyed the command that your ancestor Jonadab gave you; you have followed all his instructions, and you have done everything he commanded you. ¹⁹ So I, the LORD Almighty, the God of Israel, promise that Jonadab son of Rechab will always have a male descendant to serve me."

Baruch Reads the Scroll in the Temple

36 In the fourth year that Jehoiakim son of Josiah was king of Judah, the LORD said to me, ² "Get a scroll and write on it everything that I have told you about Israel and Judah and all the nations. Write everything that I have told you from the time I first spoke to you, when Josiah was king, up to the present. ³ Perhaps when the people of Judah hear about all the destruction that I intend to bring on them, they will turn from their evil ways. Then I will forgive their wickedness and their sins."

⁴ So I called Baruch son of Neriah and dictated to him everything that the LORD had said to me. And Baruch wrote it all down on a scroll. ⁵ Then I gave Baruch the following instructions: "I am no longer allowed to go into the Temple. ⁶ But I want you to go there the next time the people are fasting. You are to read the scroll aloud, so that they will hear everything that the LORD has said to me and that I have dictated to you. Do this where everyone can hear you, including the people of Judah who have come in from their towns. ⁷ Perhaps they will pray to the LORD and turn from their evil ways, because the LORD has threatened this people with his terrible anger and fury." ⁸ So Baruch read the LORD's words in the Temple exactly as I had told him to do.

932

Jerem.

Psalms
Proverbs
Eccles.
Songs
Isaiah

JEREMIAH 36

DOODLE HERE...

9 In the ninth month of the fifth year that Jehoiakim was king of Judah, the people fasted to gain the LORD's favour. The fast was kept by all who lived in Jerusalem and by all who came there from the towns of Judah. 10 Then, while all the people were listening, Baruch read from the scroll everything that I had said. He did this in the Temple, from the room of Gemariah son of Shaphan, the court secretary. His room was in the upper court near the entrance of the New Gate of the Temple.

The Scroll is Read to the Officials

11 Micaiah, the son of Gemariah and grandson of Shaphan, heard Baruch read from the scroll what the LORD had said. 12 Then he went to the royal palace, to the room of the court secretary, where all the officials were in session. Elishama, the court secretary, Delaiah son of Shemaiah, Elnathan son of Achbor, Gemariah son of Shaphan, Zedekiah son of Hananiah, and all the other officials were there. 13 Micaiah told them everything that he had heard Baruch read to the people. 14 Then the officials sent Jehudi (the son of Nethaniah, grandson of Shelemiah, and great-grandson of Cushi) to tell Baruch to bring the scroll that he had read to the people. Baruch brought them the scroll. 15 "Sit down," they said, "and read the scroll to us." So Baruch did. 16 After he had read it, they turned to one another in alarm, and said to Baruch, "We must report this to the king." 17 Then they asked him, "Tell us, now, how did you come to write all this? Did Jeremiah dictate it to you?"

18 Baruch answered, "Jeremiah dictated every word of it to me, and I wrote it down in ink on this scroll."

19 Then they said to him, "You and Jeremiah must go and hide. Don't let anyone know where you are."

The King Burns the Scroll

20 The officials put the scroll in the room of Elishama, the court secretary, and went to the king's court, where they reported everything to the king. 21 Then the king sent Jehudi to get the scroll. He took it from the room of Elishama and read it to the king and all the officials who were standing round him. 22 It was winter and the king was sitting in his winter palace in front of the fire. 23 As soon as Jehudi finished reading three or four columns, the king cut them off with a small knife and threw them into the fire. He kept doing this until the entire scroll was burnt up. 24 But neither the king nor any of his officials who heard all this was afraid or showed any sign of sorrow. 25 Although Elnathan, Delaiah, and Gemariah begged the king not to burn the scroll, he paid no attention to them. 26 Then he ordered Prince Jerahmeel, together with Seraiah son of Azriel and Shelemiah son of Abdeel, to arrest me and my secretary Baruch. But the LORD had hidden us.

Jeremiah Writes Another Scroll

27 After King Jehoiakim had burnt the scroll that I had dictated to Baruch, the LORD told me 28 to take another scroll and write on it everything that had been on the first one. 29 The LORD told me to say to the king, "You have burnt the scroll, and you have asked Jeremiah why he wrote that the king of Babylonia would come and destroy this land and kill its people and its animals. 30 So now, I, the LORD, say to you, King Jehoiakim, that no descendant of yours will ever rule over David's kingdom. Your corpse will be thrown out where it will be exposed to the sun during the day

JEREMIAH 36, 37

933

Jerem.

....

Lamen.

Ezekiel

Daniel

Hosea

Joel

and to the frost at night. [31] I will punish you, your descendants, and your officials because of the sins all of you commit. Neither you nor the people of Jerusalem and of Judah have paid any attention to my warnings, and so I will bring on all of you the disaster that I have threatened."

[32] Then I took another scroll and gave it to my secretary Baruch, and he wrote down everything that I dictated. He wrote everything that had been on the first scroll and similar messages that I dictated to him.

Zedekiah's Request to Jeremiah

37 King Nebuchadnezzar of Babylonia made Zedekiah son of Josiah king of Judah in the place of Jehoiachin son of Jehoiakim. [2] But neither Zedekiah nor his officials nor the people obeyed the message which the LORD had given me.

[3] King Zedekiah sent Jehucal son of Shelemiah and the priest Zephaniah son of Maaseiah to ask me to pray to the LORD our God on behalf of our nation. [4] I had not yet been put in prison and was still moving about freely among the people. [5] The Babylonian army had been besieging Jerusalem, but when they heard that the Egyptian army had crossed the Egyptian border, they retreated.

[6] Then the LORD, the God of Israel, told me [7] to say to Zedekiah, "The Egyptian army is on its way to help you, but it will return home. [8] Then the Babylonians will come back, attack the city, capture it, and burn it down. [9] I, the LORD, warn you not to deceive yourselves into thinking that the Babylonians will not come back, because they will. [10] Even if you defeat the whole Babylonian army, so that only wounded men are left, lying in their tents, those men would still get up and burn this city to the ground."

Jeremiah is Arrested and Imprisoned

[11] The Babylonian army retreated from Jerusalem because the Egyptian army was approaching. [12] So I started to leave Jerusalem and go to the territory of Benjamin to take possession of my share of the family property. [13] But when I reached the Benjamin Gate, the officer in charge of the soldiers on duty there, a man by the name of Irijah, the son of Shelemiah and grandson of Hananiah, stopped me and said, "You are deserting to the Babylonians!"

[14] I answered, "That's not so! I'm not deserting." But Irijah would not listen to me. Instead, he arrested me and took me to the officials. [15] They were furious with me and ordered me to be beaten and locked up in the house of Jonathan, the court secretary, whose house had been made into a prison. [16] I was put in an underground cell and kept there a long time.

[17] Later on King Zedekiah sent for me, and there in the palace he asked me privately, "Is there any message from the LORD?"

"There is," I answered, and added, "You will be handed over to the king of Babylonia." [18] Then I asked, "What crime have I committed against you or your officials or this people, to make you put me in prison? [19] What happened to your prophets who told you that the king of Babylonia would not attack you or the country? [20] And now, Your Majesty, I beg you to listen to me and do what I ask. Please do not send me back to the prison in Jonathan's house. If you do, I will surely die there."

[21] So King Zedekiah ordered me to be locked up in the palace courtyard. I stayed there, and each day I was given a loaf of bread from the bakeries until all the bread in the city was gone.

Jeremiah in a Dry Well

38 Shephatiah son of Mattan, Gedaliah son of Pashhur, Jehucal son of Shelemiah, and Pashhur son of Malchiah heard that I was telling the people that [2] the LORD had said, "Whoever stays on in the city will die in war or of starvation or disease. But those who go out and surrender to the Babylonians will not be killed; they will at least escape with their lives." [3] I was also telling them that the LORD had said, "I am going to give the city to the Babylonian army, and they will capture it."

[4] Then the officials went to the king and said, "This man must be put to death. By talking like this he is making the soldiers in the city lose their courage, and he is doing the same thing to everyone else left in the city. He is not trying to help the people; he only wants to hurt them."

[5] King Zedekiah answered, "Very well, then, do what you wish with him; I can't stop you." [6] So they took me and let me down by ropes into Prince Malchiah's well, which was in the palace courtyard. There was no water in the well, only mud, and I sank down in it.

[7] However, Ebedmelech the Ethiopian, a eunuch who worked in the royal palace, heard that they had put me in the well. At that time the king was holding court at the Benjamin Gate. [8] So Ebedmelech went there and said to the king, [9] "Your Majesty, what these men have done is wrong. They have put Jeremiah in the well, where he is sure to die of starvation, since there is no more food in the city." [10] Then the king ordered Ebedmelech to take with him three men and to pull me out of the well before I died. [11] So Ebedmelech went with the men to the palace storeroom and got some worn-out clothing which he let down to me by ropes. [12] He told me to put the rags under my arms, so that the ropes wouldn't hurt me. I did this, [13] and they pulled me up out of the well. After that I was kept in the courtyard.

Zedekiah Asks Jeremiah's Advice

[14] On another occasion King Zedekiah had me brought to him at the third entrance to the Temple, and he said, "I am going to ask you a question, and I want you to tell me the whole truth."

[15] I answered, "If I tell you the truth, you will put me to death, and if I give you advice, you won't pay any attention."

[16] So King Zedekiah promised me in secret, "I swear by the living God, the God who gave us life, that I will not put you to death or hand you over to the men who want to kill you."

[17] Then I told Zedekiah that the LORD Almighty, the God of Israel, had said, "If you surrender to the king of Babylonia's officers, your life will be spared, and this city will not be burnt down. Both you and your family will be spared. [18] But if you do not surrender, then this city will be handed over to the Babylonians, who will burn it down, and you will not escape from them."

[19] But the king answered, "I am afraid of our countrymen who have deserted to the Babylonians. I may be handed over to them and tortured."

[20] I said, "You will not be handed over to them. I beg you to obey the LORD's message; then all will go well with you, and your life will be spared. [21] But the LORD has shown me in a vision what will happen if you refuse to surrender. [22] In it I saw all the women left in Judah's royal palace being led out to the king of Babylonia's officers. Listen to what they were saying as they went:

'The king's best friends misled him,
  they overruled him.

JEREMIAH 38, 39

935

Jerem.

....

Lamen.
Ezekiel
Daniel
Hosea
Joel

And now that his feet have sunk in the mud,
  his friends have left him.' "
23 Then I added, "All your women and children will be taken out to the Babylonians, and you yourself will not escape from them. You will be taken prisoner by the king of Babylonia, and this city will be burnt to the ground."
24 Zedekiah replied, "Don't let anyone know about this conversation, and your life will not be in danger. 25 If the officials hear that I have talked with you, they will come and ask you what we said. They will promise not to put you to death if you tell them everything. 26 Just tell them you were begging me not to send you back to prison to die there." 27 Then all the officials came and questioned me, and I told them exactly what the king had told me to say. There was nothing else they could do, because no one had overheard the conversation. 28 And I was kept in the palace courtyard until the day Jerusalem was captured.

The Fall of Jerusalem

39 In the tenth month of the ninth year that Zedekiah was king of Judah, King Nebuchadnezzar of Babylonia came with his whole army and attacked Jerusalem. 2 On the ninth day of the fourth month of Zedekiah's eleventh year as king, the city walls were broken through.
3 (When Jerusalem was captured,* all the high officials of the king of Babylonia came and took their places at the Middle Gate, including Nergal Sarezer, Samgar Nebo, Sarsechim, and another Nergal Sarezer.)*
4 When King Zedekiah and all his soldiers saw what was happening, they tried to escape from the city during the night. They left by way of the royal garden, went through the gateway connecting the two walls, and escaped in the direction of the Jordan Valley. 5 But the Babylonian army pursued them and captured Zedekiah in the plains near Jericho. Then they took him to King Nebuchadnezzar, who was in the city of Riblah in the territory of Hamath, and there Nebuchadnezzar passed sentence on him. 6 At Riblah he put Zedekiah's sons to death while Zedekiah was looking on, and he also executed the officials of Judah. 7 After that, he had Zedekiah's eyes put out and had him placed in chains to be taken to Babylonia. 8 Meanwhile, the Babylonians burnt down the royal palace and the houses of the people and tore down the walls of Jerusalem. 9 Finally Nebuzaradan, the commanding officer, took away as prisoners to Babylonia the people who were left in the city, together with those who had deserted to him. 10 He left in the land of Judah some of the poorest people, who owned no property, and he gave them vineyards and fields.

Jeremiah's Release

11 But King Nebuchadnezzar commanded Nebuzaradan, the commanding officer, to give the following order: 12 "Go and find Jeremiah and take good care of him. Do not harm him, but do for him whatever he wants." 13 So Nebuzaradan, together with the high officials Nebushazban and Nergal Sarezer and all the other officers of the king of Babylonia, 14 brought me from the palace courtyard. They put me under the care of Gedaliah, the

JEREMIAH 39

After all the warnings of the prophets, Jerusalem in Judah eventually fell to the Babylonians and God's people went into exile: they were taken to another country to live. However, as God had promised, Jeremiah was

KEPT SAFE
• AND FREE •

to continue prophesying. Imagine how hard it must have been for Jeremiah, knowing that destruction was coming, and watching it all unfurl!

39.3 *When Jerusalem was captured*; these words are moved here from the end of chapter 38.
39.3 The names and titles of these men are unclear.

936

Jerem.

: . . . .

Psalms
Proverbs
Eccles.
Songs
Isaiah

JEREMIAH 39, 40

son of Ahikam and grandson of Shaphan, who was to see that I got home safely. And so I stayed there among the people.

Hope for Ebedmelech

[15] While I was still imprisoned in the palace courtyard, the LORD told me [16] to tell Ebedmelech the Ethiopian that the LORD Almighty, the God of Israel, had said, "Just as I said I would, I am going to bring upon this city destruction and not prosperity. And when this happens, you will be there to see it. [17] But I, the LORD, will protect you, and you will not be handed over to those you fear. [18] I will keep you safe, and you will not be put to death. You will escape with your life because you have put your trust in me. I, the LORD, have spoken."

Jeremiah Stays with Gedaliah

40 The LORD spoke to me after Nebuzaradan, the commanding officer, had set me free at Ramah. I had been taken there in chains, along with all the other people from Jerusalem and Judah who were being taken away as prisoners to Babylonia.

[2] The commanding officer took me aside and said, "The LORD your God threatened this land with destruction, [3] and now he has done what he said he would. All this happened because your people sinned against the LORD and disobeyed him. [4] Now, I am taking the chains off your wrists and setting you free. If you want to go to Babylonia with me, you may do so, and I will take care of you. But if you don't want to go, you don't have to. You have the whole country to choose from, and you may go wherever you wish."

[5] When I did not answer,* Nebuzaradan said, "Go back to Gedaliah, the son of Ahikam and grandson of Shaphan, whom the king of Babylonia has made governor of the towns of Judah. You may stay with him and live among the people, or you may go anywhere you think you should." Then he gave me a present and some food to take with me, and let me go on my way. [6] I went to stay with Gedaliah in Mizpah and lived among the people who were left in the land.

Gedaliah, Governor of Judah
(2 Kgs 25.22–24)

[7] Some of the Judean officers and soldiers had not surrendered. They heard that the king of Babylonia had made Gedaliah governor of the land and had placed him in charge of all those who had not been taken away to Babylonia — the poorest people in the land. [8] So Ishmael son of Nethaniah, Johanan son of Kareah, Seraiah son of Tanhumeth, the sons of Ephai from Netophah, and Jezaniah from Maacah went with their men to Gedaliah at Mizpah. [9] Gedaliah said to them, "I give you my word that there is no need for you to be afraid to surrender to the Babylonians. Settle down in this land, serve the king of Babylonia, and all will go well with you. [10] I myself will stay in Mizpah and be your representative when the Babylonians come here. But you can gather and store up wine, fruit, and olive oil, and live in the villages you occupy." [11] Meanwhile, all the Israelites who were in Moab, Ammon, Edom, and other countries, heard that the king of Babylonia had allowed some Israelites to stay on in Judah and that he had made Gedaliah their governor. [12] So they left the places where they had been scattered, and returned to Judah.

....
40.5 *When I did not answer;* or *Then, before he left.*

Jerem.

Lamen.
Ezekiel
Daniel
Hosea
Joel

They came to Gedaliah at Mizpah, and there they gathered in large amounts of wine and fruit.

Gedaliah is Murdered
(2 Kgs 25.25–26)

¹³ After this, Johanan and the leaders of the soldiers who had not surrendered came to Gedaliah at Mizpah ¹⁴ and said to him, "Don't you know that King Baalis of Ammon has sent Ishmael to murder you?" But Gedaliah did not believe it. ¹⁵ Then Johanan said privately to him, "Let me go and kill Ishmael, and no one will know who did it. Why should he be allowed to murder you? That would cause all the Jews who have gathered round you to be scattered, and it would bring disaster on all the people who are left in Judah."

¹⁶ But Gedaliah answered, "Don't do it! What you are saying about Ishmael is not true!"

41 In the seventh month of that year, Ishmael, the son of Nethaniah and grandson of Elishama, a member of the royal family and one of the king's chief officers, went to Mizpah with ten men to see Gedaliah. While they were all eating a meal together, ² Ishmael and the ten men with him pulled out their swords and killed Gedaliah. ³ Ishmael also killed all the Israelites who were with Gedaliah at Mizpah and the Babylonian soldiers who happened to be there.

⁴ The next day, before anyone knew about Gedaliah's murder, ⁵ eighty men arrived from Shechem, Shiloh, and Samaria. They had shaved off their beards, torn their clothes, and gashed themselves. They were taking corn and incense to offer in the Temple. ⁶ So Ishmael went out from Mizpah to meet them, weeping as he went. When he came to them, he said, "Please come in to see Gedaliah." ⁷ As soon as they were inside the city, Ishmael and his men killed them and threw their bodies in a well.

⁸ But there were ten men in the group who said to Ishmael, "Please don't kill us! We have wheat, barley, olive oil, and honey hidden in the fields." So he spared them. ⁹ The well into which Ishmael threw the bodies of the men he had killed was the large one* that King Asa had dug when he was being attacked by King Baasha of Israel. Ishmael filled the well with the bodies. ¹⁰ Then he made prisoners of the king's daughters and all the rest of the people in Mizpah, whom Nebuzaradan the commanding officer had placed under the care of Gedaliah. Ishmael took them prisoner and started off in the direction of the territory of Ammon.

¹¹ Johanan and all the army leaders with him heard of the crime that Ishmael had committed. ¹² So they went after him with their men and overtook him near the large pool at Gibeon. ¹³ When Ishmael's prisoners saw Johanan and the leaders of the forces with him, they were glad, ¹⁴ and turned and ran to them. ¹⁵ But Ishmael and eight of his men got away from Johanan and escaped to the land of Ammon.

¹⁶ Then Johanan and the leaders of the forces with him took charge of the people whom Ishmael had taken away as prisoners from Mizpah after murdering Gedaliah — soldiers, women, children, and eunuchs. ¹⁷·¹⁸ They were afraid of the Babylonians because Ishmael had murdered Gedaliah, whom the king of

41.9 One ancient translation *was the large one*; Hebrew *by means of Gedaliah*.

938

Jerem.

Psalms
Proverbs
Eccles.
Songs
Isaiah

JEREMIAH 41, 42

JEREMIAH 42.1-6

Army leaders came to
Jeremiah begging him to

PRAY

FOR THEM.

Christians today can
be known as people
who will pray on
behalf of others, too.

This week, ask a friend
who doesn't know about
God what you could
pray about for them.

Babylonia had made governor of the land. So they set out for Egypt, in order to get away from the Babylonians. On the way, they stopped at Chimham, near Bethlehem.

The People Ask Jeremiah to Pray for them

42 Then all the army leaders, including Johanan son of Kareah and Azariah* son of Hoshaiah, came with people of every class ² and said to me, "Please do what we ask you! Pray to the LORD our God for us. Pray for all of us who have survived. Once there were many of us; but now only a few of us are left, as you can see. ³ Pray that the LORD our God will show us the way we should go and what we should do."

⁴ I answered, "Very well, then. I will pray to the LORD our God, just as you have asked, and whatever he says, I will tell you. I will not keep back anything from you."

⁵ Then they said to me, "May the LORD be a true and faithful witness against us if we do not obey all the commands that the LORD our God gives you for us. ⁶ Whether it pleases us or not, we will obey the LORD our God, to whom we are asking you to pray. All will go well with us if we obey him."

The LORD's Answer to Jeremiah's Prayer

⁷ Ten days later the LORD spoke to me; ⁸ so I called together Johanan, all the army leaders who were with him, and all the other people. ⁹ I said to them, "The LORD, the God of Israel, to whom you sent me with your request has said, ¹⁰ 'If you are willing to go on living in this land, then I will build you up and not tear you down; I will plant you and not pull you up. The destruction I brought on you has caused me great sorrow. ¹¹ Stop being afraid of the king of Babylonia. I am with you, and I will rescue you from his power. ¹² Because I am merciful, I will make him have mercy on you and let you go back home. I, the LORD, have spoken.'

¹³⁻¹⁵ "But you people who are left in Judah must not disobey the LORD your God and refuse to live in this land. You must not say, 'No, we will go and live in Egypt, where we won't face war any more or hear the call to battle or go hungry.' If you say this, then the LORD Almighty, the God of Israel, says, 'If you are determined to go and live in Egypt, ¹⁶ then the war that you fear will overtake you, and the hunger you dread will follow you, and you will die there in Egypt. ¹⁷ All the people who are determined to go and live in Egypt will die either in war or of starvation or disease. Not one of them will survive, not one will escape the disaster that I am going to bring on them.'

¹⁸ "The LORD, the God of Israel, says, 'Just as my anger and fury were poured out on the people of Jerusalem, so my fury will be poured out on you if you go to Egypt. You will be a horrifying sight; people will treat you with scorn and use your name as a curse. You will never see this place again.'"

¹⁹ Then I continued, "The LORD has told you people who are left in Judah not to go to Egypt. And so I warn you now ²⁰ that you are making a fatal mistake. You asked me to pray to the LORD our God for you, and you promised that you would do everything that he commands. ²¹ And now I have told you, but you are disobeying everything that the LORD our God sent me to tell you. ²² So then, remember this: you will die in war or of starvation or disease in the land where you want to go and live."

....

42.1 One ancient translation (see also 43.2) *Azariah*; Hebrew *Jezaniah*.

Jerem.

............⁚

Lamen.
Ezekiel
Daniel
Hosea
Joel

Jeremiah is Taken to Egypt

43 I finished telling the people everything that the LORD their God had sent me to tell them. [2] Then Azariah son of Hoshaiah and Johanan son of Kareah and all the other arrogant men said to me, "You are lying. The LORD our God did not send you to tell us not to go and live in Egypt. [3] Baruch son of Neriah has stirred you up against us, so that the Babylonians will gain power over us and can either kill us or take us away to Babylonia." [4] So neither Johanan nor any of the army officers nor any of the people would obey the LORD's command to remain in the land of Judah. [5] Then Johanan and all the army officers took everybody left in Judah away to Egypt, together with all the people who had returned from the nations where they had been scattered: [6] the men, the women, the children, and the king's daughters. They took everyone whom Nebuzaradan the commanding officer had left under the care of Gedaliah, including Baruch and me. [7] They disobeyed the LORD's command and went into Egypt as far as the city of Tahpanhes.

[8] There the LORD said to me, [9] "Get some large stones and bury them in the mortar of the pavement* in front of the entrance to the government building here in the city, and let some of the Israelites see you do it. [10] Then tell them that I, the LORD Almighty, the God of Israel, am going to bring my servant King Nebuchadnezzar of Babylonia to this place, and he* will put his throne over these stones that you* buried, and will spread the royal tent over them. [11] Nebuchadnezzar will come and defeat Egypt. Those people who are doomed to die of disease will die of disease, those doomed to be taken away as prisoners will be taken away as prisoners, and those doomed to be killed in war will be killed in war. [12] I will set fire to the temples of Egypt's gods, and the king of Babylonia will either burn their gods or carry them off. As shepherds pick their clothes clean of lice, so the king of Babylonia will pick the land of Egypt clean and then leave victorious. [13] He will destroy the sacred stone monuments at Heliopolis in Egypt and will burn down the temples of the Egyptian gods."

The LORD's Message to the Israelites in Egypt

44 The LORD spoke to me concerning all the Israelites living in Egypt, in the cities of Migdol, Tahpanhes, and Memphis, and in the southern part of the country. [2] The LORD Almighty, the God of Israel, said, "You yourselves have seen the destruction I brought on Jerusalem and all the other cities of Judah. Even now they are still in ruins, and no one lives in them [3] because their people had done evil and had made me angry. They offered sacrifices to other gods and served gods that neither they nor you nor your ancestors ever worshipped. [4] I kept sending you my servants the prophets, who told you not to do this terrible thing that I hate. [5] But you would not listen or pay any attention. You would not give up your evil practice of sacrificing to other gods. [6] So I poured out my anger and fury on the towns of Judah and on the streets of Jerusalem, and I set them on fire. They were left in ruins and became a horrifying sight, as they are today.

[7] "And so I, the LORD Almighty, the God of Israel, now ask why you are doing such an evil thing to yourselves. Do you want to bring destruction on men and women, children and babies, so

---

43.9 Probable text *bury them… pavement*; Hebrew unclear.
43.10 Some ancient translations *he*; Hebrew *I*.
43.10 Some ancient translations *you*; Hebrew *I*.

940

Jerem.

∴ ·········

Psalms
Proverbs
Eccles.
Songs
Isaiah

JEREMIAH 44

that none of your people will be left? [8]Why do you make me angry by worshipping idols and by sacrificing to other gods here in Egypt, where you have come to live? Are you doing this just to destroy yourselves, so that every nation on earth will treat you with scorn and use your name as a curse? [9]Have you forgotten all the wicked things that have been done in the towns of Judah and in the streets of Jerusalem by your ancestors, by the kings of Judah and their wives, and by you and your wives? [10]But to this day you have not humbled yourselves. You have not honoured me or lived according to all the laws that I gave you and your ancestors.

[11]"So then, I, the LORD Almighty, the God of Israel, will turn against you and destroy all Judah. [12]As for the people of Judah who are left and are determined to go and live in Egypt, I will see to it that all of them are destroyed. All of them, great and small, will die in Egypt, either in war or of starvation. They will be a horrifying sight; people will treat them with scorn and use their name as a curse. [13]I will punish those who live in Egypt, just as I punished Jerusalem — with war, starvation, and disease. [14]None of the people of Judah who are left and have come to Egypt to live will escape or survive. Not one of them will return to Judah, where they long to live once again. No one will return except a few refugees."

[15]Then all the men who knew that their wives offered sacrifices to other gods, and all the women who were standing there, including the Israelites who lived in southern Egypt — a large crowd in all — said to me, [16]"We refuse to listen to what you have told us in the name of the LORD. [17]We will do everything that we said we would. We will offer sacrifices to our goddess, the Queen of Heaven, and we will pour out wine offerings to her, just as we and our ancestors, our king and our leaders, used to do in the towns of Judah and in the streets of Jerusalem. Then we had plenty of food, we were prosperous, and had no troubles. [18]But ever since we stopped sacrificing to the Queen of Heaven and stopped pouring out wine offerings to her, we have had nothing, and our people have died in war and of starvation."

[19]And the women added, "When we baked cakes shaped like the Queen of Heaven, offered sacrifices to her, and poured out wine offerings to her, our husbands approved of what we were doing."

[20]Then I said to all the men and the women who had answered me in this way, [21]"As for the sacrifices which you and your ancestors, your kings and your leaders, and the people of the land offered in the towns of Judah and in the streets of Jerusalem — do you think that the LORD did not know about them or that he forgot them? [22]This very day your land lies in ruins and no one lives in it. It has become a horrifying sight, and people use its name as a curse because the LORD could no longer endure your wicked and evil practices. [23]This present disaster has come on you because you offered sacrifices to other gods and sinned against the LORD by not obeying all his commands."

[24-25]I told all the people, especially the women, what the LORD Almighty, the God of Israel, was saying to the people of Judah living in Egypt: "Both you and your wives have made solemn promises to the Queen of Heaven. You promised that you would offer sacrifices to her and pour out wine offerings to her, and you have kept your promises. Very well, then! Keep your promises! Carry out your vows! [26]But now listen to the vow that I, the LORD, have made in my mighty name to all you Israelites

JEREMIAH 44–46

941

Jerem.

....

Lamen.

Ezekiel

Daniel

Hosea

Joel

in Egypt: never again will I let any of you use my name to make a vow by saying, 'I swear by the living Sovereign Lord!' ²⁷I will see to it that you will not prosper, but will be destroyed. All of you will die, either in war or of disease, until not one of you is left. ²⁸But a few of you will escape death and return from Egypt to Judah. Then the survivors will know whose words have come true, mine or theirs. ²⁹I, the Lord, will give you proof that I will punish you in this place and that my promise to bring destruction on you will come true. ³⁰I will hand over King Hophra of Egypt to his enemies who want to kill him, just as I handed over King Zedekiah of Judah to King Nebuchadnezzar of Babylonia, who was his enemy and wanted to kill him."

God's Promise to Baruch

45 In the fourth year that Jehoiakim son of Josiah was king of Judah, Baruch wrote down what I had dictated to him. Then I told him ²that the Lord, the God of Israel, had said, "Baruch, ³you are saying, 'I give up! The Lord has added sorrow to my troubles. I am worn out from groaning, and I can't find any rest!'

⁴"But I, the Lord, am tearing down what I have built and pulling up what I have planted. I will do this to the entire earth. ⁵Are you looking for special treatment for yourself? Don't do it. I am bringing disaster on the whole human race, but you will at least escape with your life wherever you go. I, the Lord, have spoken."

Egypt's Defeat at Carchemish

46 The Lord spoke to me about the nations, ²beginning with Egypt. This is what he said about the army of King Neco of Egypt, which King Nebuchadnezzar of Babylonia defeated at Carchemish near the River Euphrates in the fourth year that Jehoiakim was king of Judah:

³ "The Egyptian officers shout,
  'Get your shields ready
      and march into battle!
⁴ Harness your horses and mount them!
  Fall in line and put on your helmets!
      Sharpen your spears!
      Put on your armour!'

⁵ "But what do I see?" asks the Lord.
  "They are turning back in terror.
  Their soldiers are beaten back;
      overcome with fear, they run as fast as they can
      and do not look back.
⁶ Those who run fast cannot get away;
      the soldiers cannot escape.
  In the north, by the Euphrates,
      they stumble and fall.
⁷ Who is this that rises like the Nile,
      like a river flooding its banks?
⁸ It is Egypt, rising like the Nile,
      like a river flooding its banks.
  Egypt said, 'I will rise and cover the world;
      I will destroy cities and the people who live there.
⁹ Command the horses to go
      and the chariots to roll!
  Send out the soldiers:
      men from Ethiopia and Libya, carrying shields,
      and skilled archers from Lydia.'"

Jerem.

Psalms
Proverbs
Eccles.
Songs
Isaiah

10 This is the day of the Sovereign LORD Almighty:
today he will take revenge;
today he will punish his enemies.
His sword will eat them until it is full,
and drink their blood until it is satisfied.
Today the Almighty sacrifices his victims
in the north, by the Euphrates.
11 People of Egypt, go to Gilead*
and look for medicine!
All your medicine has proved useless;
nothing can heal you.
12 Nations have heard of your shame;
everyone has heard you cry.
One soldier trips over another,
and both of them fall to the ground.

The Coming of Nebuchadnezzar

13 When King Nebuchadnezzar of Babylonia came to attack
Egypt, the LORD spoke to me. He said,
14 "Proclaim it in the towns of Egypt,
in Migdol, Memphis, and Tahpanhes:
'Get ready to defend yourselves;
all you have will be destroyed in war!
15 Why has your mighty god Apis fallen?
The LORD has struck him down!'
16 Your soldiers have stumbled and fallen;*
each one says to the other,
'Hurry! Let's go home to our people
and escape the enemy's sword!'

17 "Give the king of Egypt a new name —
'Noisy Braggart who Missed his Chance'.
18 I, the LORD Almighty, am king.
I am the living God.
As Mount Tabor towers above the mountains
and Mount Carmel stands high above the sea,
so will be the strength of the one who attacks
you.
19 Get ready to be taken prisoner,
you people of Egypt!
Memphis will be made a desert,
a ruin where no one lives.
20 Egypt is like a splendid cow,
attacked by a stinging fly from the north.
21 Even her hired soldiers
are helpless as calves.
They did not stand and fight;
all of them turned and ran.
The day of their doom had arrived,
the time of their destruction.
22 Egypt runs away, hissing like a snake,
as the enemy's army approaches.
They attack her with axes,
like men cutting down trees
23 and destroying a thick forest.

46.11 *Gilead*: See 8.22.
46.16 Probable text *Your soldiers… fallen*; Hebrew unclear.

JEREMIAH 46, 47

943

Jerem.

....

Lamen.
Ezekiel
Daniel
Hosea
Joel

Their men are too many to count;
    their soldiers outnumber the locusts.
24 The people of Egypt are put to shame;
    they are conquered by the people of the north.
I, the LORD, have spoken."

25 The LORD Almighty, the God of Israel, says, "I am going to punish Amon, the god of Thebes, together with Egypt and its gods and kings. I am going to take the king of Egypt and all who put their trust in him, 26 and hand them over to those who want to kill them, to King Nebuchadnezzar of Babylonia and his army. But later on, people will live in Egypt again, as they did in times past. I, the LORD, have spoken."

The LORD will Save his People

27 "My people, do not be afraid,
    people of Israel, do not be terrified.
I will rescue you from that distant land,
    from the land where you are prisoners.
You will come back home and live in peace;
    you will be secure, and no one will make you afraid.
28 I will come to you and save you.
I will destroy all the nations
    where I have scattered you,
    but I will not destroy you.
I will not let you go unpunished;
    but when I punish you, I will be fair.
I, the LORD, have spoken."

The LORD's Message about Philistia

47 Before the king of Egypt attacked Gaza, the LORD spoke to me about Philistia. 2 He said:
"Look! Waters are rising in the north
    and will rush like a river in flood.
They will cover the land and everything on it,
    cities and the people who live there.
People will call out for help;
    everyone on earth will cry bitterly.
3 They will hear the hoof beats of horses,
    the clatter of chariots,
    the rumble of wheels.
Parents will not turn back for their children;
    their hands will hang limp at their sides.
4 The time has come to destroy Philistia,
    to cut off from Tyre and Sidon
    all the help that remains.
I, the LORD, will destroy the Philistines,
    all who came from the shores of Crete.
5 Great sorrow has come to the people of Gaza,
    and Ashkelon's people are silent.
How long will the rest of Philistia mourn?
6 You cry out, 'Sword of the LORD!
    How long will you go on slashing?
Go back to your scabbard,
    stay there and rest!'
7 But how can it rest,
    when I have given it work to do?
I have commanded it to attack Ashkelon
    and the people who live on the coast."

TURN THESE LINES INTO A PICTURE OF SOMETHING.

944

Jerem.

Psalms
Proverbs
Eccles.
Songs
Isaiah

JEREMIAH 48

The Destruction of Moab

48

This is what the LORD Almighty said about Moab:
"Pity the people of Nebo —
their town is destroyed!
Kiriathaim is captured,
its mighty fortress torn down,
and its people put to shame;
2   the splendour of Moab is gone.
The enemy have captured Heshbon
and plot to destroy the nation of Moab.
The town of Madmen will be silenced;
armies will march against it.
3 The people of Horonaim cry out,
'Violence! Destruction!'

4 "Moab has been destroyed;
listen to the children crying.
5 Hear the sound of their sobs
along the road up to Luhith,
the cries of distress
on the way down to Horonaim.
6 'Quick, run for your lives!' they say.
'Run like a wild desert donkey!'

7 "Moab, you trusted in your strength and your wealth,
but now even you will be conquered;
your god Chemosh will go into exile,
along with his princes and priests.
8 Not a town will escape the destruction;
both valley and plain will be ruined.
I, the LORD, have spoken.
9 Set up a tombstone for Moab;
it will soon be destroyed.
Its towns will be left in ruins,
and no one will live there again."
10 (Curse those who do not do the LORD's work with all their heart! Curse those who do not slash and kill!)

The Cities of Moab are Destroyed

11 The LORD said, "Moab has always lived secure and has never been taken into exile. Moab is like wine left to settle undisturbed and never poured from jar to jar. Its flavour has never been ruined, and it tastes as good as ever.

12 "So now, the time is coming when I will send people to pour Moab out like wine. They will empty its wine jars and break them in pieces. 13 Then the Moabites will be disillusioned with their god Chemosh, just as the Israelites were disillusioned with Bethel, a god in whom they trusted.

14 "Men of Moab, why do you claim to be heroes,
brave soldiers tested in war?
15 Moab and its cities are destroyed;
its finest young men have been slaughtered.
I am the king, the LORD Almighty,
and I have spoken.
16 Moab's doom approaches;
its ruin is coming soon.

17 "Mourn for that nation, you that live near by,
all of you that know its fame.

JEREMIAH 48   945

Jerem.

....

Lamen.
Ezekiel
Daniel
Hosea
Joel

Say, 'Its powerful rule has been broken;
its glory and might are no more.'
¹⁸ You that live in Dibon,
come down from your place of honour
and sit on the ground in the dust;
Moab's destroyer is here
and has left its forts in ruins.
¹⁹ You that live in Aroer,
stand by the road and wait;
ask those who are running away,
find out from them what has happened.
²⁰ 'Moab has fallen,' they will answer,
'weep for it; it is disgraced.
Announce along the River Arnon
that Moab is destroyed!'

²¹ "Judgement has come on the cities of the plateau: on Holon, Jahzah, Mephaath, ²²Dibon, Nebo, Beth Diblathaim, ²³Kiriathaim, Bethgamul, Bethmeon, ²⁴Kerioth, and Bozrah. Judgement has come on all the cities of Moab, far and near. ²⁵Moab's might has been crushed; its power has been destroyed. I, the LORD, have spoken."

Moab will be Humbled

²⁶ The LORD said, "Make Moab drunk, because it has rebelled against me. Moab will roll in its own vomit, and people will laugh. ²⁷Moab, remember how you jeered at the people of Israel? You treated them as though they had been caught with a gang of robbers.

²⁸ "You people who live in Moab, leave your towns! Go and live on the cliffs! Be like the dove that makes its nest in the sides of a ravine. ²⁹Moab is very proud! I have heard how proud, arrogant, and conceited the people are, how much they think of themselves. ³⁰I, the LORD, know of their arrogance. Their boasts amount to nothing, and the things they do will not last. ³¹And so I will weep for everyone in Moab and for the people of Kir Heres. ³²I will cry for the people of Sibmah, even more than for the people of Jazer. City of Sibmah, you are like a vine whose branches reach across the Dead Sea and go as far as Jazer. But now your summer fruits and your grapes have been destroyed. ³³Happiness and joy have been taken away from the fertile land of Moab. I have made the wine stop flowing from the winepresses; there is no one to make the wine and shout for joy.

³⁴ "The people of Heshbon and Elealeh cry out,* and their cry can be heard as far as Jahaz; it can be heard by the people in Zoar, and it is heard as far as Horonaim and Eglath Shelishiyah. Even the brook of Nimrim has dried up. ³⁵I will stop the people of Moab from making burnt offerings at their places of worship and from offering sacrifices to their gods. I, the LORD, have spoken.

³⁶ "So my heart mourns for Moab and for the people of Kir Heres, like someone playing a funeral song on a flute, because everything they owned is gone. ³⁷All of them have shaved their heads and cut off their beards. They have all made gashes on their hands, and everyone is wearing sackcloth. ³⁸On all the housetops of Moab and in all its public squares there is nothing but mourning, because I have broken Moab like a jar that no one wants. ³⁹Moab has been shattered! Cry out! Moab has been

....

48.34 Probable text *Heshbon... cry out*; Hebrew unclear.

946

Jerem.

Psalms
Proverbs
Eccles.
Songs
Isaiah

JEREMIAH 48, 49

disgraced. It is in ruins, and all the surrounding nations jeer at it. I, the LORD, have spoken."

No Escape for Moab

⁴⁰ The LORD has promised that a nation will swoop down on Moab like an eagle with its outspread wings, ⁴¹ and the towns and fortresses will be captured. On that day Moab's soldiers will be as frightened as a woman in labour. ⁴² Moab will be destroyed and will no longer be a nation, because it rebelled against me. ⁴³ Terror, pits, and traps are waiting for the people of Moab. The LORD has spoken. ⁴⁴ Whoever tries to escape the terror will fall into the pits, and whoever climbs out of the pits will be caught in the traps, because the LORD has set the time for Moab's destruction. ⁴⁵ Helpless refugees try to find protection in Heshbon, the city that King Sihon once ruled, but it is in flames.* Fire has burnt up the frontiers and the mountain heights of the war-loving people of Moab. ⁴⁶ Pity the people of Moab! The people who worshipped Chemosh have been destroyed, and their sons and daughters have been taken away as prisoners.

⁴⁷ But in days to come the LORD will make Moab prosperous again. All of this is what the LORD has said will happen to Moab.

The LORD's Judgement on Ammon

49 This is what the LORD said about Ammon: "Where are the men of Israel? Is there no one to defend their land? Why have they let the people who worship Molech take the territory of the tribe of Gad and settle there? ² But the time is coming when I will make the people of the capital city of Rabbah hear the noise of battle, and it will be left in ruins and its villages burnt to the ground. Then Israel will take its land back from those who took it from them. ³ People of Heshbon, cry out! Ai is destroyed! Women of Rabbah, go into mourning! Put on sackcloth and mourn. Run about in confusion. Your god Molech will be taken into exile, together with his priests and princes. ⁴ Why do you unfaithful people boast? Your strength is failing. Why do you trust in your power and say that no one would dare attack you? ⁵ I will bring terror on you from every side. You will all run away. Each one will run for his life, and there will be no one to bring your troops together again.

⁶ "But later on I will make Ammon prosperous again. I, the LORD, have spoken."

The LORD's Judgement on Edom

⁷ This is what the LORD Almighty said about Edom: "Have the people of Edom lost their good judgement? Can their advisers no longer tell them what to do? Has all their wisdom disappeared? ⁸ People of Dedan, turn and run! Hide! I am going to destroy Esau's descendants, because the time has come for me to punish them. ⁹ When people pick grapes, they leave a few on the vines, and when robbers come at night, they take only what they want. ¹⁰ But I* have stripped Esau's descendants completely and uncovered their hiding places, so that they can no longer hide. All the people of Edom are destroyed. Not one of them is left. ¹¹ Leave your orphans with me, and I will take care of them. Your widows can depend on me.

48.45 *Heshbon, the city... flames*; or *the city of Heshbon, but it is in flames and the palace of King Sihon is burning.*
49.9–10 *they leave a few... they take only what they want.* ¹⁰ *But I;* or *they leave nothing... they take everything.* ¹⁰ *And so I.*

JEREMIAH 49

947

Jerem.

..........:.

Lamen.
Ezekiel
Daniel
Hosea
Joel

[12] "If even those who did not deserve to be punished had to drink from the cup of punishment, do you think that you will go unpunished? No, you must drink from the cup! [13] I myself have sworn that the city of Bozrah will become a horrifying sight and a desert; people will jeer at it and use its name as a curse. All the nearby villages will be in ruins for ever. I, the LORD, have spoken."

[14] I said, "Edom, I have received a message from the LORD. He has sent a messenger to tell the nations to assemble their armies and to get ready to attack you. [15] The LORD is going to make you weak, and no one will respect you. [16] Your pride has deceived you. No one fears you as much as you think they do. You live on the rocky cliffs, high on top of the mountain; but even though you live as high up as an eagle, the LORD will bring you down. The LORD has spoken."

[17] The LORD said, "The destruction that will come on Edom will be so terrible that everyone who passes by will be shocked and terrified. [18] The same thing will happen to Edom as happened to Sodom and Gomorrah, when they and the nearby towns were destroyed. No one will ever live there again. I, the LORD, have spoken. [19] Like a lion coming out of the thick woods along the Jordan up to the green pasture land, I will come and make the Edomites run away suddenly from their country. Then the leader I choose will rule the nation. Who can be compared to me? Who would dare challenge me? What ruler could oppose me? [20] So listen to the plan that I have made against the people of Edom, and to what I intend to do to the people of the city of Teman. Even their children will be dragged off, and everyone will be horrified. [21] When Edom falls, there will be such a noise that the entire earth will shake, and the cries of alarm will be heard as far away as the Gulf of Aqaba. [22] The enemy will attack Bozrah like an eagle swooping down with outspread wings. On that day Edom's soldiers will be as frightened as a woman in labour."

The LORD's Judgement on Damascus

[23] This is what the LORD said about Damascus: "The people in the cities of Hamath and Arpad are worried and troubled because they have heard bad news. Anxiety rolls over them like a sea, and they cannot rest. [24] The people of Damascus are weak and have fled in terror. They are in pain and misery like a woman in labour. [25] The famous city that used to be happy* is completely deserted. [26] On that day her young men will be killed in the city streets, and all her soldiers destroyed. [27] I will set the walls of Damascus on fire and will burn down King Benhadad's palaces. I, the LORD Almighty, have spoken."

Judgement on the Tribe of Kedar and the City of Hazor

[28] This is what the LORD said about the tribe of Kedar and the districts controlled by Hazor, which were conquered by King Nebuchadnezzar of Babylonia: "Attack the people of Kedar and destroy that tribe of eastern people! [29] Seize their tents and their flocks, their tent curtains and everything in their tents. Take their camels and tell the people, 'Terror is all round you!'

[30] "People of Hazor, I, the LORD, warn you to run far away and hide. King Nebuchadnezzar of Babylonia has plotted against you, and this is what he says, [31] 'Come on! We'll attack those people that feel safe and secure! Their city has no gates or locks and is completely unprotected.'

49.25 Some ancient translations *happy*; Hebrew *my happiness.*

948

Jerem.

Psalms
Proverbs
Eccles.
Songs
Isaiah

JEREMIAH 49, 50

Colour these shapes.

32 "Take their camels and all their livestock! I will scatter in every direction those people who cut their hair short, and I will bring disaster on them from every side. 33 Hazor will be made a desert for ever, a place where only jackals live. No one will ever live there again. I, the LORD, have spoken."

The LORD's Judgement on Elam

34 Soon after Zedekiah became king of Judah, the LORD Almighty spoke to me about the country of Elam. 35 He said, "I will kill all the archers who have made Elam so powerful. 36 I will make winds blow against Elam from all directions, and I will scatter her people everywhere, until there is no country where her refugees have not gone. 37 I will make the people of Elam afraid of their enemies, who want to kill them. In my great anger I will destroy the people of Elam and send armies against them until I have wiped them out. 38 I will destroy their kings and leaders, and set up my throne there. 39 But later on I will make the people of Elam prosperous again. I, the LORD, have spoken."

Babylon's Capture

50 This is the message that the LORD gave me about the city of Babylon and its people:

2 "Tell the news to the nations! Proclaim it!
 Give the signal and announce the news!
 Do not keep it a secret!
 Babylon has fallen!
 Her god Marduk has been shattered!
 Babylon's idols are put to shame,
  her disgusting images are crushed!

3 "A nation from the north has come to attack Babylonia and will make it a desert. People and animals will run away, and no one will live there."

Israel's Return

4 The LORD says, "When that time comes, the people of both Israel and Judah will come weeping, looking for me, their God. 5 They will ask the way to Zion and then go in that direction. They will make an eternal covenant with me and never break it.

6 "My people are like sheep whose shepherds have let them get lost in the mountains. They have wandered like sheep from one mountain to another, and they have forgotten where their home is. 7 They are attacked by all who find them. Their enemies say, 'They sinned against the LORD, and so what we have done is not wrong. Their ancestors trusted in the LORD, and they themselves should have remained faithful to him.'

8 "People of Israel, run away from Babylonia! Leave the country! Be the first to leave! 9 I am going to stir up a group of strong nations in the north and make them attack Babylonia. They will line up in battle against the country and conquer it. They are skilful hunters, shooting arrows that never miss the mark. 10 Babylonia will be looted, and those who loot it will take everything they want. I, the LORD, have spoken."

Babylon's Fall

11 The LORD says, "People of Babylonia, you plundered my nation. You are happy and glad, going about like a cow threshing corn or like a neighing horse, 12 but your own great city will be humiliated and disgraced. Babylonia will be the least important nation of

JEREMIAH 50

949

Jerem.

Lamen.
Ezekiel
Daniel
Hosea
Joel

all; it will become a dry and waterless desert. [13] Because of my anger no one will live in Babylon; it will be left in ruins, and all who pass by will be shocked and amazed.

[14] "Archers, line up for battle against Babylon and surround it. Shoot all your arrows at Babylon, because it has sinned against me, the LORD. [15] Raise the war cry all round the city! Now Babylon has surrendered. Its walls have been broken through and torn down.* I am taking my revenge on the Babylonians. So take your revenge on them, and treat them as they have treated others. [16] Do not let seeds be sown in that country or let a harvest be gathered. Every foreigner living there will be afraid of the attacking army and will go back home."

Israel's Return

[17] The LORD says, "The people of Israel are like sheep, chased and scattered by lions. First, they were attacked by the emperor of Assyria, and then King Nebuchadnezzar of Babylonia gnawed their bones. [18] Because of this, I, the LORD Almighty, the God of Israel, will punish King Nebuchadnezzar and his country, just as I punished the emperor of Assyria. [19] I will restore the people of Israel to their land. They will eat the food that grows on Mount Carmel and in the region of Bashan, and they will eat all they want of the crops that grow in the territories of Ephraim and Gilead. [20] When that time comes, no sin will be found in Israel and no wickedness in Judah, because I will forgive those people whose lives I have spared. I, the LORD, have spoken."

God's Judgement on Babylonia

[21] The LORD says, "Attack the people of Merathaim and of Pekod. Kill and destroy them.* Do everything I command you. I, the LORD, have spoken. [22] The noise of battle is heard in the land, and there is great destruction. [23] Babylonia hammered the whole world to pieces, and now that hammer is shattered! All the nations are shocked at what has happened to that country. [24] Babylonia, you fought against me, and you have been caught in the trap I set for you, even though you did not know it. [25] I have opened the place where my weapons are stored, and in my anger I have taken them out, because I, the Sovereign LORD Almighty, have work to do in Babylonia. [26] Attack it from every side and break open the places where its grain is stored! Pile up the loot like piles of grain! Destroy the country! Leave nothing at all! [27] Kill all their soldiers! Slaughter them! The people of Babylonia are doomed! The time has come for them to be punished!"

[28] (Refugees escape from Babylonia and come to Jerusalem, and they tell how the LORD our God took revenge for what the Babylonians had done to his Temple.)

[29] "Tell the archers to attack Babylon. Send out everyone who knows how to use the bow and arrow. Surround the city and don't let anyone escape. Pay it back for all it has done, and treat it as it has treated others, because it acted with pride against me, the Holy One of Israel. [30] So its young men will be killed in the city streets, and all its soldiers will be destroyed on that day. I, the LORD, have spoken.

[31] "Babylonia, you are filled with pride, so I, the Sovereign LORD Almighty, am against you! The time has come for me to punish

JEREMIAH 50.19

I WILL RESTORE

50.15 Hebrew has an additional word, the meaning of which is unclear.
50.21 One ancient translation *them*; Hebrew *after them*.

950

Jerem.

Psalms
Proverbs
Eccles.
Songs
Isaiah

JEREMIAH 50

you. [32] Your proud nation will stumble and fall, and no one will help you up. I will set your cities on fire, and everything around will be destroyed."

[33] The LORD Almighty says, "The people of Israel and of Judah are oppressed. All who captured them are guarding them closely and will not let them go. [34] But the one who will rescue them is strong — his name is the LORD Almighty. He himself will take up their cause and will bring peace to the earth, but trouble to the people of Babylonia."

[35] The LORD says,
"Death to Babylonia!
    Death to its people,
        to its rulers, to its men of wisdom.
[36] Death to its lying prophets —
    what fools they are!
Death to its soldiers —
    how terrified they are!
[37] Destroy its horses and chariots!
Death to its hired soldiers —
    how weak they are!
Destroy its treasures;
    plunder and loot.
[38] Bring a drought on its land
    and dry up its rivers.
Babylonia is a land of terrifying idols,
    that have made fools of the people.

[39] "And so Babylon will be haunted by demons and evil spirits,* and by unclean birds. Never again will people live there, not for all time to come. [40] The same thing will happen to Babylon as happened to Sodom and Gomorrah, when I destroyed them and the nearby towns. No one will ever live there again. I, the LORD, have spoken.

[41] "People are coming from a country in the north,
    a mighty nation far away;
        many kings are preparing for war.
[42] They have taken their bows and swords;
    they are cruel and merciless.
They sound like the roaring sea,
    as they ride their horses.
They are ready for battle against Babylonia.
[43] The king of Babylonia hears the news,
    and his hands hang limp.
He is seized by anguish,
    by pain like a woman in labour.

[44] "Like a lion coming out of the thick woods along the Jordan up to the green pasture land, I, the LORD, will come and make the Babylonians run away suddenly from their city. Then the leader I choose will rule the nation. Who can be compared to me? Who would dare challenge me? What ruler could oppose me? [45] So listen to the plan that I have made against the city of Babylon and to what I intend to do to its people. Even their children will be dragged off, and everyone will be horrified. [46] When Babylon falls, there will be such a noise that the entire earth will shake, and the cries of alarm will be heard by the other nations."

....
50.39 *demons and evil spirits*; or *wildcats and jackals*.

JEREMIAH 51

951

Jerem.
....
Lamen.
Ezekiel
Daniel
Hosea
Joel

Further Judgement on Babylonia

51 The LORD says, "I am bringing a destructive wind* against Babylonia and its people. [2] I will send foreigners to destroy Babylonia like a wind that blows straw away. When that day of destruction comes, they will attack from every side and leave the land bare. [3] Don't give its soldiers time to shoot their arrows or to put on their armour. Do not spare the young men! Destroy the whole army! [4] They will be wounded and die in the streets of their cities. [5] I, the LORD God Almighty, have not abandoned Israel and Judah, even though they have sinned against me, the Holy One of Israel. [6] Run away from Babylonia! Run for your lives! Do not be killed because of Babylonia's sin. I am now taking my revenge and punishing it as it deserves. [7] Babylonia was like a gold cup in my hand, making the whole world drunk. The nations drank its wine and went out of their minds. [8] Babylonia has suddenly fallen and is destroyed! Mourn over it! Get medicine for its wounds, and perhaps it can be healed. [9] Foreigners living there said, 'We tried to help Babylonia, but it was too late. Let's leave her now and go back home. God has punished Babylonia with all his might and has destroyed it completely.'"

[10] The LORD says, "My people shout, 'The LORD has shown that we are in the right. Let's go and tell the people in Jerusalem what the LORD our God has done.'"

[11] The LORD has stirred up the kings of Media, because he intends to destroy Babylonia. That is how he will take revenge for the destruction of his Temple.

The attacking officers command, "Sharpen your arrows! Get your shields ready! [12] Give the signal to attack Babylon's walls. Strengthen the guard! Post the sentries! Place men in ambush!"

The LORD has done what he said he would do to the people of Babylonia. [13] That country has many rivers and rich treasures, but its time is up, and its thread of life is cut. [14] The LORD Almighty has sworn by his own life that he will bring many men to attack Babylonia like a swarm of locusts, and they will shout with victory.

A Hymn of Praise to God

[15] The LORD made the earth by his power;
    by his wisdom he created the world
    and stretched out the heavens.
[16] At his command the waters above the sky* roar;
    he brings clouds from the ends of the earth.
    He makes lightning flash in the rain
    and sends the wind from his storeroom.
[17] At the sight of this, people feel stupid and senseless;
    those who make idols are disillusioned
    because the gods they make are false and lifeless.
[18] They are worthless and should be despised;
    they will be destroyed when the LORD comes to deal with
      them.
[19] The God of Jacob is not like them;
    he is the one who made everything,
    and he has chosen Israel to be his very own people.
    The LORD Almighty is his name.

51.1 *destructive wind*; or *destroying spirit*.
51.16 *waters above the sky*: See Gen 1.6–8.

JEREMIAH 51.15-19

With a

- COUPLE OF -

FRIENDS,

read Jeremiah 51.15-19 and then discuss some of these questions:

What are some of the gods we see today, other than religious gods?

This passage says that the Lord is not like other gods. In what ways?

Thinking about modern-day 'gods', how is the God of the Bible different from them?

Jerem.

Psalms
Proverbs
Eccles.
Songs
Isaiah

The Lord's Hammer

20 The Lord says,
"Babylonia, you are my hammer, my weapon of war.
I used you to crush nations and kingdoms,
21   to shatter horses and riders,
       to shatter chariots and their drivers,
22   to kill men and women,
       to slay old and young,
       to kill boys and girls,
23   to slaughter shepherds and their flocks,
       to slaughter ploughmen and their horses,
       to crush rulers and high officials."

Babylonia's Punishment

24 The Lord says, "You will see me repay Babylonia and its people for all the evil they did to Jerusalem. 25 Babylonia, you are like a mountain that destroys the whole world, but I, the Lord, am your enemy. I will take hold of you, level you to the ground, and leave you in ashes. 26 None of the stones from your ruins will ever be used again for building. You will be like a desert for ever. I, the Lord, have spoken.

27 "Give the signal to attack! Blow the trumpet so that the nations can hear! Prepare the nations for war against Babylonia! Tell the kingdoms of Ararat, Minni, and Ashkenaz to attack. Appoint an officer to lead the attack. Bring up the horses like a swarm of locusts. 28 Prepare the nations for war against Babylonia. Send for the kings of Media, their leaders and officials, and the armies of all the countries they control. 29 The earth trembles and shakes because the Lord is carrying out his plan to make Babylonia a desert, where no one lives. 30 The Babylonian soldiers have stopped fighting and remain in their forts. They have lost their courage and have become like women. The city gates are broken down, and the houses are on fire. 31 Messenger after messenger runs to tell the king of Babylonia that his city has been broken into from every side. 32 The enemy have captured the river crossing and have set the fortresses on fire. The Babylonian soldiers have panicked. 33 Soon the enemy will cut them down and trample them like corn on a threshing place. I, the Lord Almighty, the God of Israel, have spoken."

34 The king of Babylonia cut Jerusalem up
       and ate it.
He emptied the city like a jar;
       like a monster he swallowed it.
He took what he wanted
       and threw the rest away.
35 Let the people of Zion say,
"May Babylonia be held responsible
       for the violence done to us!"
Let the people of Jerusalem say,
"May Babylonia be held responsible
       for what we have suffered!"

The Lord will Help Israel

36 And so the Lord said to the people of Jerusalem, "I will take up your cause and will make your enemies pay for what they did to you. I will dry up the source of Babylonia's water and make its rivers go dry. 37 That country will become a pile of ruins where wild animals live. It will be a horrible sight; no one will live there, and all who see it will be terrified. 38 The Babylonians all roar like

953

Jerem.

Lamen.
Ezekiel
Daniel
Hosea
Joel

lions and growl like lion cubs. ³⁹Are they greedy? I will prepare them a feast and make them drunk and happy. They will go to sleep and never wake up. ⁴⁰I will take them to be slaughtered, like lambs, goats, and rams. I, the LORD, have spoken."

Babylon's Fate

⁴¹The LORD says about Babylon: "The city that the whole world praised has been captured! What a horrifying sight Babylon has become to the nations! ⁴²The sea has rolled over Babylon and covered it with roaring waves. ⁴³The towns have become a horrifying sight and are like a waterless desert, where no one lives or even travels. ⁴⁴I will punish Bel, the god of Babylonia, and make him give up his stolen goods; the nations will not worship him any more.

"Babylon's walls have fallen. ⁴⁵People of Israel, run away from there! Run for your life from my fierce anger. ⁴⁶Do not lose courage or be afraid because of the rumours you hear. Every year a different rumour spreads — rumours of violence in the land and of one king fighting another. ⁴⁷And so the time is coming when I will deal with Babylonia's idols. The whole country will be put to shame, and all its people will be killed. ⁴⁸Everything on earth and in the sky will shout for joy when Babylonia falls to the people who come from the north to destroy it. ⁴⁹Babylonia caused the death of people all over the world, and now Babylonia will fall because it caused the death of so many Israelites. I, the LORD, have spoken."

God's Message to the Israelites in Babylonia

⁵⁰The LORD says to his people in Babylonia: "You have escaped death! Now go! Don't wait! Though you are far from home, think about me, your LORD, and remember Jerusalem. ⁵¹You say, 'We've been disgraced and made ashamed; we feel completely helpless because foreigners have taken over the holy places in the Temple.' ⁵²So then, I say that the time is coming when I will deal with Babylon's idols, and the wounded will groan throughout the country. ⁵³Even if Babylon could climb to the sky and build a strong fortress there, I would still send people to destroy it. I, the LORD, have spoken."

Further Destruction of Babylon

⁵⁴The LORD says,
"Listen to the sound of crying in Babylon,
    of mourning for the destruction in the land.
⁵⁵ I am destroying Babylon
    and putting it to silence.
The armies rush in like roaring waves
    and attack with noisy shouts.
⁵⁶ They have come to destroy Babylon;
    its soldiers are captured,
    and their bows are broken.
I am a God who punishes evil,
    and I will treat Babylon as it deserves.
⁵⁷ I will make its rulers drunk —
    men of wisdom, leaders, and soldiers.
They will go to sleep and never wake up.
    I, the king, have spoken,
    I am the LORD Almighty.
⁵⁸ The walls of mighty Babylon will be thrown to the ground,
    and its towering gates burnt down.
The work of the nations is all for nothing;

JOIN THE DOTS
below to make a picture.

954

Jerem.

:········

Psalms
Proverbs
Eccles.
Songs
Isaiah

JEREMIAH 51, 52

their efforts go up in flames.
I, the LORD Almighty, have spoken."

Jeremiah's Message is Sent to Babylonia

⁵⁹King Zedekiah's personal attendant was Seraiah, the son of Neriah and grandson of Mahseiah. In the fourth year that Zedekiah was king of Judah, Seraiah was going to Babylonia with him, and I gave him some instructions. ⁶⁰I wrote in a book an account of all the destruction that would come on Babylonia, as well as all these other things about Babylonia. ⁶¹I told Seraiah, "When you get to Babylon, be sure to read aloud to the people everything that is written here. ⁶²Then pray, 'LORD, you have said that you would destroy this place, so that there would be no living creatures in it, neither people nor animals, and it would be like a desert for ever.' ⁶³Seraiah, when you finish reading this book to the people, then tie it to a stone and throw it into the River Euphrates, ⁶⁴and say, 'This is what will happen to Babylonia — it will sink and never rise again, because of the destruction that the LORD is going to bring on it.'"*

The words of Jeremiah end here.

The Fall of Jerusalem
(2 Kgs 24.18—25.7)

52 Zedekiah was 21 years old when he became king of Judah, and he ruled in Jerusalem for eleven years. His mother's name was Hamutal, the daughter of the Jeremiah who lived in the city of Libnah. ²King Zedekiah sinned against the LORD, just as King Jehoiakim had done. ³The LORD became so angry with the people of Jerusalem and Judah that he banished them from his sight.

Zedekiah rebelled against King Nebuchadnezzar of Babylonia, ⁴and so Nebuchadnezzar came with all his army and attacked Jerusalem on the tenth day of the tenth month of the ninth year of Zedekiah's reign. They set up camp outside the city, built siege walls round it, ⁵and kept it under siege until Zedekiah's eleventh year. ⁶On the ninth day of the fourth month of that same year, when the famine was so bad that the people had nothing left to eat, ⁷the city walls were broken through. Although the Babylonians were surrounding the city, all the soldiers escaped during the night. They left by way of the royal garden, went through the gateway connecting the two walls, and fled in the direction of the Jordan Valley. ⁸But the Babylonian army pursued King Zedekiah, captured him in the plains near Jericho, and all his soldiers deserted him. ⁹Zedekiah was taken to King Nebuchadnezzar, who was in the city of Riblah in the territory of Hamath, and there Nebuchadnezzar passed sentence on him. ¹⁰At Riblah he put Zedekiah's sons to death while Zedekiah was looking on and he also had the officials of Judah executed. ¹¹After that, he had Zedekiah's eyes put out and had him placed in chains and taken to Babylon. Zedekiah remained in prison in Babylon until the day he died.

The Destruction of the Temple
(2 Kgs 25.8–17)

¹²On the tenth day of the fifth month of the nineteenth year of King Nebuchadnezzar of Babylonia, Nebuzaradan, adviser to the king and commander of his army, entered Jerusalem. ¹³He

---

51.64 One ancient translation *on it*; Hebrew *on it and they will become tired out*.

Jerem.

Lamen.
Ezekiel
Daniel
Hosea
Joel

burnt down the Temple, the palace, and the houses of all the important people in Jerusalem; [14] and his soldiers tore down the city walls. [15] Then Nebuzaradan took away to Babylonia* the people who were left in the city, the remaining skilled workmen, and those who had deserted to the Babylonians. [16] But he left in Judah some of the poorest people, who owned no property, and he put them to work in the vineyards and fields.

[17] The Babylonians broke in pieces the bronze columns and the carts that were in the Temple, together with the large bronze tank, and they took all the bronze to Babylon. [18] They also took away the shovels and the ash containers used in cleaning the altar, the tools used in tending the lamps, the bowls used for catching the blood from the sacrifices, the bowls used for burning incense, and all the other bronze articles used in the temple service. [19] They took away everything that was made of gold or silver: the small bowls, the pans used for carrying live coals, the bowls for holding the blood from the sacrifices, the ash containers, the lampstands, the bowls used for incense, and the bowls used for pouring out offerings of wine. [20] The bronze objects that King Solomon had made for the Temple — the two columns, the carts, the large tank, and the twelve bulls that supported it — were too heavy to weigh. [21-22] The two columns were identical: each one was eight metres high and 5.3 metres round. They were hollow, and the metal was 75 millimetres thick. On top of each column was a bronze capital 2.2 metres high, and all round it was a grating decorated with pomegranates, all of which were also made of bronze. [23] On the grating of each column there were a hundred pomegranates in all, and 96 of these were visible from the ground.

The People of Judah are Taken to Babylonia
(2 Kgs 25.18–21, 27–30)

[24] In addition, Nebuzaradan, the commanding officer, took away as prisoners Seraiah the High Priest, Zephaniah the priest next in rank, and the three other important temple officials. [25] From the city he took the officer who had been in command of the troops, seven of the king's personal advisers who were still in the city, the commander's assistant, who was in charge of military records, and sixty other important men. [26] Nebuzaradan took them to the king of Babylonia, who was in the city of Riblah [27] in the territory of Hamath. There the king had them beaten and put to death.

So the people of Judah were carried away from their land into exile. [28] This is the record of the people that Nebuchadnezzar took away as prisoners: in his seventh year as king he carried away 3,023; [29] in his eighteenth year, 832 from Jerusalem; [30] and in his 23rd year, 745 — taken away by Nebuzaradan. In all, 4,600 people were taken away.

[31] In the year that Evil-merodach became king of Babylonia, he showed kindness to King Jehoiachin of Judah by releasing him from prison. This happened on the 25th day of the twelfth month of the 37th year after Jehoiachin had been taken away as a prisoner. [32] Evil-merodach treated him kindly and gave him a position of greater honour than he gave the other kings who were exiles with him in Babylonia. [33] So Jehoiachin was permitted to change from his prison clothes and to dine at the king's table for the rest of his life. [34] Each day for as long as he lived, he was given a regular allowance for his needs.

....

52.15 Probable text Babylonia; Hebrew Babylonia some of the poorest of the people.

THE BOOK OF
LAMENTATIONS

WRITTEN: AROUND THE TIME OF THE EXILE (586-520BC)

WHAT YOU NEED TO KNOW:

Lamentations is a series of five poetic laments, written after the destruction of Jerusalem by the Babylonians. The temple was destroyed and the city laid waste. Lamentations opens with a picture of Jerusalem after it had been attacked. From there on, we see the writer's raw dismay at what has happened to his home. After the lamenting comes praise for God and a plea for God to remember his people in exile.

WHY READ IT?

Lamentations is a man's heart being poured out in a book. However, in the midst of the heartache come hints of hope and security. Even though the destruction that God had promised came to pass, the writer makes space in his lament to praise God and take comfort in his love. Even in the darkest times, there is reason for praise and comfort.

THE CITY OF JERUSALEM IS DESCRIBED IN CHAPTER 1 AS IF IT WAS A WOMAN.

DRAW A PICTURE

OF THE WOMAN JERUSALEM IS REPRESENTED AS BEING.

Underline the moment in Lamentations when the writer finds space for hope and praise.

597BC

JUDAH FALLS
TO BABYLON

JERUSALEM DESTROY

(586BC)

The Sorrows of Jerusalem

1 How lonely lies Jerusalem, once so full of people!
Once honoured by the world, she is now like a widow;
The noblest of cities has fallen into slavery.

2 All night long she cries; tears run down her cheeks.
Of all her former friends, not one is left to comfort her.
Her allies have betrayed her and all are now against her.

3 Judah's people are helpless slaves, forced away from home.*
They live in other lands, with no place to call their own —
Surrounded by enemies, with no way to escape.

4 No one comes to the Temple now to worship on the holy
days.
The young women who sang there suffer, and the
priests can only groan.
The city gates stand empty, and Zion is in agony.

5 Her enemies succeeded; they hold her in their power.
The Lord has made her suffer for all her many sins;
Her children have been captured and taken away.

6 The splendour of Jerusalem is a thing of the past.
Her leaders are like deer that are weak from hunger,
Whose strength is almost gone as they flee from the
hunters.

7 A lonely ruin now, Jerusalem recalls her ancient splendour.
When she fell to the enemy, there was no one to help her;
Her conquerors laughed at her downfall.

8 Her honour is gone; she is naked and held in contempt.
She groans and hides her face in shame.
Jerusalem made herself filthy with terrible sin.

9 Her uncleanness was easily seen, but she showed no
concern for her fate.
Her downfall was terrible; no one can comfort her.
Her enemies have won, and she cries to the Lord for
mercy.

10 Her enemies robbed her of all her treasures.
She saw them enter the Temple itself,
Where the Lord had forbidden Gentiles to go.

11 Her people groan as they look for something to eat;
They exchange their treasures for food to keep
themselves alive.
"Look at me, Lord," the city cries; "see me in my misery."

12 "Look at me!" she cries to everyone who passes by.*
"No one has ever had pain like mine,
Pain that the Lord brought on me in the time of his
anger.

1.3 *are helpless... home;* or *fled from home, from the misery of slavery.*
1.12 *Look... by;* or *May this not happen to you that pass by;* or *Does this
mean nothing to you that pass by?*

LAMENTATIONS 1

Lamen.
....
Ezekiel
Daniel
Hosea
Joel
Amos

Lamentations might have
been written
by Jeremiah as he
- WATCHED THE -
DESTRUCTION
of his city and home.
Imagine you are where
Jeremiah was,
amid destruction.
What would you say to
God in that moment?
Think about homes
and cities in the world
that are currently
being destroyed,
perhaps in places not
far from Jerusalem.
If you were walking
those streets, what
conversation would you
be having with God?

write some
thoughts here

958

Lamen.

....

Proverbs
Eccles.
Songs
Isaiah
Jerem.

LAMENTATIONS 1, 2

13 "He sent fire from above, a fire that burnt inside me.
   He set a trap for me and brought me to the ground.
   Then he abandoned me and left me in constant pain.

14 "He took note of all my sins and tied them all together;
   He hung them round my neck, and I grew weak beneath
      the weight.
   The Lord gave me to my foes, and I was helpless against
      them.

15 "The Lord jeered at all my strongest soldiers;
   He sent an army to destroy my young men.
   He crushed my people like grapes in a winepress.

16 "That is why my eyes are overflowing with tears.
   No one can comfort me; no one can give me courage.
   The enemy has conquered me; my people have nothing
      left.

17 "I stretch out my hands, but no one will help me.
   The LORD has called enemies against me from every side;
   They treat me like some filthy thing.

18 "But the LORD is just, for I have disobeyed him.
   Listen to me, people everywhere; look at me in my pain.
   My young men and women have been taken away captive.

19 "I called to my allies, but they refused to help me.
   The priests and the leaders died in the city streets,
   Looking for food to keep themselves alive.

20 "Look, O LORD, at my agony, at the anguish of my soul!
   My heart is broken in sorrow for my sins.
   There is murder in the streets; even indoors there is death.

21 "Listen* to my groans; there is no one to comfort me.
   My enemies are glad that you brought disaster on me.
   Bring* the day you promised; make my enemies suffer
      as I do.

22 "Condemn them for all their wickedness;
   Punish them as you punished me for my sins.
   I groan in misery, and I am sick at heart."

The LORD's Punishment of Jerusalem

2 The Lord in his anger has covered Zion with darkness.
   Its heavenly splendour he has turned into ruins.
   On the day of his anger he abandoned even his Temple.

2 The Lord destroyed without mercy every village in Judah
   And tore down the forts that defended the land.
   He brought disgrace on the kingdom and its rulers.

3 In his fury he shattered the strength of Israel;
   He refused to help us when the enemy came.
   He raged against us like fire, destroying everything.

....

1.21 One ancient translation Listen; Hebrew They listened.
1.21 One ancient translation Bring; Hebrew You brought.

Lamen.

........:

Ezekiel

Daniel

Hosea

Joel

Amos

⁴ He aimed his arrows at us like an enemy;
   He killed all those who were our joy and delight.
   Here in Jerusalem we felt his burning anger.

⁵ Like an enemy, the Lord has destroyed Israel;
   He has left her forts and palaces in ruins.
   He has brought on the people of Judah unending
      sorrow.

⁶ He smashed to pieces the Temple where we worshipped
      him;
   He has put an end to holy days and Sabbaths.
   King and priest alike have felt the force of his anger.

⁷ The Lord rejected his altar and deserted his holy Temple;
   He allowed the enemy to tear down its walls.
   They shouted in victory where once we had worshipped
      in joy.

⁸ The LORD was determined that the walls of Zion should
      fall;
   He measured them off to make sure of total destruction.
   The towers and walls now lie in ruins together.

⁹ The gates lie buried in rubble, their bars smashed to pieces.
   The king and the noblemen now are in exile.
   The Law is no longer taught, and the prophets have no
      visions from the LORD.

¹⁰ Jerusalem's old men sit on the ground in silence,
   With dust on their heads and sackcloth on their bodies.
   Young women bow their heads to the ground.

¹¹ My eyes are worn out with weeping; my soul is in anguish.
   I am exhausted with grief at the destruction of my
      people.
   Children and babies are fainting in the streets of the city.

¹² Hungry and thirsty, they cry to their mothers;
   They fall in the streets as though they were wounded,
   And slowly die in their mothers' arms.

¹³ O Jerusalem, beloved Jerusalem, what can I say?
   How can I comfort you? No one has ever suffered like this.
   Your disaster is boundless as the ocean; there is no
      possible hope.

¹⁴ Your prophets had nothing to tell you but lies;
   Their preaching deceived you by never exposing your sin.
   They made you think you did not need to repent.

¹⁵ People passing by the city look at you in scorn.
   They shake their heads and laugh at the ruins of
      Jerusalem.
   "Is this that lovely city? Is this the pride of the world?"

¹⁶ All your enemies mock you and glare at you with hate.
   They curl their lips and sneer, "We have destroyed it!
   This is the day we have waited for!"

17 The LORD has finally done what he threatened to do:
   He has destroyed us without mercy, as he warned us
      long ago.
   He gave our enemies victory, gave them joy at our downfall.

18 O Jerusalem, let your very walls cry out to the Lord!*
   Let your tears flow like rivers night and day;
   Wear yourself out with weeping and grief!

19 All through the night get up again and again to cry out to
      the Lord;
   Pour out your heart and beg him for mercy on your
      children —
   Children starving to death on every street corner!

20 Look, O LORD! Why are you punishing us like this?
   Women are eating the bodies of the children they loved!
   Priests and prophets are being killed in the Temple itself!

21 Young and old alike lie dead in the streets,
   Young men and women, killed by enemy swords.
   You slaughtered them without mercy on the day of your
      anger.

22 You invited my enemies to hold a carnival of terror all
      round me,
   And no one could escape on that day of your anger.
   They murdered my children, whom I had reared and loved.

Punishment, Repentance, and Hope

3 I am one who knows what it is to be punished by God.
   2   He drove me deeper and deeper into darkness
   3   And beat me again and again with merciless blows.

4 He has left my flesh open and raw, and has broken my bones.
   5   He has shut me in a prison of misery and anguish.
   6   He has forced me to live in the stagnant darkness of death.

7 He has bound me in chains; I am a prisoner with no hope
      of escape.
   8   I cry aloud for help, but God refuses to listen;
   9   I stagger as I walk; stone walls block me wherever I turn.

10 He waited for me like a bear; he pounced on me like a lion.
   11   He chased me off the road, tore me to pieces, and left me.
   12   He drew his bow and made me the target for his arrows.

13 He shot his arrows deep into my body.
   14   People laugh at me all day long; I am a joke to them all.
   15   Bitter suffering is all he has given me for food and drink.

16 He rubbed my face in the ground and broke my teeth on
      the gravel.
   17   I have forgotten what health and peace and happiness
      are.
   18   I have not much longer to live; my hope in the LORD is gone.

2.18 Probable text *O Jerusalem… Lord*; Hebrew *Their hearts cried out to the Lord, O wall of Jerusalem.*

Lamen.

Ezekiel
Daniel
Hosea
Joel
Amos

19 The thought of my pain, my homelessness, is bitter poison;
20   I think of it constantly and my spirit is depressed.
21   Yet hope returns when I remember this one thing:

22 The Lord's unfailing love and mercy still continue,
23   Fresh as the morning, as sure as the sunrise.
24   The Lord is all I have, and so I put my hope in him.

25 The Lord is good to everyone who trusts in him,
26   So it is best for us to wait in patience — to wait for him
       to save us —
27   And it is best to learn this patience in our youth.

28 When we suffer, we should sit alone in silent patience;
29   We should bow in submission, for there may still be hope.
30   Though beaten and insulted, we should accept it all.

31 The Lord is merciful and will not reject us for ever.
32   He may bring us sorrow, but his love for us is sure and
       strong.
33   He takes no pleasure in causing us grief or pain.

34 The Lord knows when our spirits are crushed in prison;
35   He knows when we are denied the rights he gave us;
36   When justice is perverted in court, he knows.

37 The will of the Lord alone is always carried out.*
38   Good and evil alike take place at his command.
39   Why should we ever complain when we are punished for
       our sin?*

40 Let us examine our ways and turn back to the Lord.
41   Let us open our hearts to God in heaven and pray,
42   "We have sinned and rebelled, and you, O Lord, have
       not forgiven us.

43 "You pursued us and killed us; your mercy was hidden by
       your anger,
44   By a cloud of fury too thick for our prayers to get through.
45   You have made us the refuse heap of the world.

46 "We are insulted and mocked by all our enemies.
47   We have been through disaster and ruin; we live in
       danger and fear.
48   My eyes flow with rivers of tears at the destruction of
       my people.

49 "My tears will pour out in a ceaseless stream
50   Until the Lord looks down from heaven and sees us.
51   My heart is grieved when I see what has happened to
       the women of the city.

52 "I was trapped like a bird by enemies who had no cause to
       hate me.

3.37 The will... out; or No one can make anything happen unless the Lord
is willing.
3.39 Why should... sin?; or Why should we complain about being punished
for sin, as long as we are still alive?

LAMENTATIONS 3.22

• The LORD's •
UNFAILING
LOVE
🏴 AND 🏴
MERCY
• still continue •

LAMENTATIONS 3.24

THE
LORD
is all I have,
{ AND SO }
I put my
HOPE
in him

Lamen.
-:-........

Proverbs
Eccles.
Songs
Isaiah
Jerem.

53 They threw me alive into a pit and closed the opening
    with a stone.
54 Water began to close over me, and I thought death was
    near.

55 "From the bottom of the pit, O LORD, I cried out to you,
56 And when I begged you to listen to my cry, you heard.
57 You answered me and told me not to be afraid.

58 "You came to my rescue, Lord, and saved my life.
59 Judge in my favour; you know the wrongs done against
    me.
60 You know how my enemies hate me and how they plot
    against me.

61 "You have heard them insult me, O LORD; you know all their
    plots.
62 All day long they talk about me and make their plans.
63 From morning till night they jeer at me.

64 "Punish them for what they have done, O LORD;
65 Curse them and fill them with despair!
66 Hunt them down and wipe them off the earth!"

Jerusalem after its Fall

4 Our glittering gold has grown dull;
    the stones of the Temple lie scattered in the streets.

2 Zion's young men were as precious to us as gold,
    but now they are treated like common clay pots.

3 Even a mother wolf will nurse her cubs,
    but my people are like ostriches, cruel to their young.

4 They let their babies die of hunger and thirst;
    children are begging for food that no one will give them.

5 People who once ate the finest foods die starving in the
    streets;
    those raised in luxury are pawing through refuse for
    food.

6 My people have been punished even more than the
    inhabitants of Sodom,
    which met with a sudden downfall at the hands of God.

7 Our princes* were undefiled and pure as snow,
    vigorous and strong, glowing with health.

8 Now they lie unknown in the streets, their faces blackened
    in death;
    their skin, dry as wood, has shrivelled on their bones.

9 Those who died in the war were better off than those who
    died later,
    who starved slowly to death, with no food to keep them
    alive.

....

4.7 *princes*; or *Nazirites*.

Lamen.

....

Ezekiel

Daniel

Hosea

Joel

Amos

10 The disaster that came to my people brought horror;
  loving mothers boiled their own children for food.

11 The LORD turned loose the full force of his fury;
  he lit a fire in Zion that burnt it to the ground.

12 No one anywhere, not even rulers of foreign nations,
  believed that any invader could enter Jerusalem's gates.

13 But it happened because her prophets sinned and her
    priests were guilty
  of causing the death of innocent people.

14 Her leaders wandered through the streets like the blind,
  so stained with blood that no one would touch them.

15 "Go away!" people shouted. "You're defiled! Don't touch me!"
  So they wandered from nation to nation, welcomed by
    no one.

16 The LORD had no more concern for them; he scattered
    them himself.
  He showed no regard for our priests and leaders.

17 For help that never came, we looked until we could look no
    longer.
  We kept waiting for help from a nation that had none to give.

18 The enemy was watching for us; we could not even walk in
    the streets.
  Our days were over; the end had come.

19 Swifter than eagles swooping from the sky, they chased us
    down.
  They tracked us down in the hills; they took us by
    surprise in the desert.

20 They captured the source of our life, the king the LORD had
    chosen,
  the one we had trusted to protect us from every invader.

21 Laugh on, people of Edom and Uz; be glad while you can.
  Your disaster is coming too; you too will stagger naked
    in shame.

22 Zion has paid for her sin; the LORD will not keep us in exile
    any longer.
  But Edom, the LORD will punish you; he will expose your
    guilty deeds.

A Prayer for Mercy

5 Remember, O LORD, what has happened to us.
  Look at us, and see our disgrace.

2 Our property is in the hands of strangers;
  foreigners are living in our homes.

3 Our fathers have been killed by the enemy,
  and now our mothers are widows.

⁴ We must pay for the water we drink;
     we must buy the wood we need for fuel.

⁵ Driven hard like donkeys or camels,
     we are tired, but are allowed no rest.

⁶ To get food enough to stay alive,
     we went begging to Egypt and Assyria.

⁷ Our ancestors sinned, but now they are gone,
     and we are suffering for their sins.

⁸ We are ruled by those who are no better than slaves,
     and no one can save us from their power.

⁹ Murderers roam through the countryside;
     we risk our lives when we look for food.

¹⁰ Hunger has made us burn with fever,
     until our skin is as hot as an oven.

¹¹ Our wives have been raped on Mount Zion itself;
     in every Judean village our daughters have been forced
        to submit.

¹² Our leaders have been taken and hanged;
     our elders are shown no respect.

¹³ Our young men are forced to grind corn like slaves;
     boys go staggering under heavy loads of wood.

¹⁴ The old people no longer sit at the city gate,
     and the young people no longer make music.

¹⁵ Happiness has gone out of our lives;
     grief has taken the place of our dances.

¹⁶ Nothing is left of all we were proud of.
     We sinned, and now we are doomed.

¹⁷ We are sick at our very hearts
     and can hardly see through our tears,

¹⁸ because Mount Zion lies lonely and deserted,
     and wild jackals prowl through its ruins.

¹⁹ But you, O Lᴏʀᴅ, are king for ever,
     and will rule to the end of time.

²⁰ Why have you abandoned us so long?
     Will you ever remember us again?

²¹ Bring us back to you, Lᴏʀᴅ! Bring us back!
     Restore our ancient glory.

²² Or have you rejected us for ever?
     Is there no limit to your anger?

THE BOOK OF
EZEKIEL

WRITTEN: ROUGHLY 590-570BC
(WITH SOME LATER ADDITIONS)

MAKE A LIST OF THE
TOP FIVE
WEIRD THINGS
THAT EZEKIEL DOES IN THIS BOOK.

1. _____
2. _____
3. _____
4. _____
5. _____

WHAT YOU NEED TO KNOW:

Ezekiel was one of 10,000 people taken into exile by the Babylonians after the fall of Jerusalem, and many of his prophecies were spoken while he was in exile. Ezekiel taught that there was still space for God to speak with his people, even in a foreign land. God sometimes called his prophets to act out the prophecies he was giving, and Ezekiel was by far the most creative in doing so! (See chapters 4, 5 and 12 for examples.) Like the other Major Prophets, Ezekiel's calling as a prophet is described early in the book. Then there is an extended section of hard-hitting prophecies against Judah and the surrounding nations for their sins, before the book ends by talking about future hope.

WHY READ IT?

Ezekiel was an incredibly creative prophet. We see him lying on his side for weeks, cutting off his beard and spreading it everywhere, cooking over cow dung and bringing dry bones to life. With Ezekiel we see the cost of the prophetic calling: prophets were not just called to say certain things, but to live a totally different life.

Have there been any events in your life through which you feel God has spoken to you? Write them here.

586BC   570BC

JEWS IN EXILE
IN BABYLON

966

Ezekiel

Eccles.
Songs
Isaiah
Jerem.
Lamen.

EZEKIEL 1.28–2.5

Ezekiel was shown the glory of the Lord,

– FELL FACE –

DOWN

in reverence and then heard God say, 'I want to talk to you.' Read Ezekiel chapter 1, close your eyes and imagine God saying to you, 'I want to talk to you.' What might you say back to him? What might you think?

Ezekiel's First Vision of God
1.1—7.27

God's Throne

1 On the fifth day of the fourth month of the thirtieth year,* I, Ezekiel the priest, son of Buzi, was living with the Jewish exiles by the River Chebar in Babylonia. The sky opened, and I saw a vision of God. (²It was the fifth year since King Jehoiachin had been taken into exile.) ³There in Babylonia beside the River Chebar, I heard the LORD speak to me and I felt his power.

⁴I looked up and saw a storm coming from the north. Lightning was flashing from a huge cloud, and the sky round it was glowing. Where the lightning was flashing, something shone like bronze. ⁵At the centre of the storm, I saw what looked like four living creatures in human form, ⁶but each of them had four faces and four wings. ⁷Their legs were straight, and they had hoofs like those of a bull. They shone like polished bronze. ⁸In addition to their four faces and four wings, they each had four human hands, one under each wing. ⁹Two wings of each creature were spread out so that the creatures formed a square with their wing tips touching. When they moved, they moved as a group without turning their bodies.

¹⁰Each living creature had four different faces: a human face in front, a lion's face at the right, a bull's face at the left, and an eagle's face at the back. ¹¹Two wings* of each creature were raised so that they touched the tips of the wings of the creatures next to it, and their other two wings were folded against their bodies. ¹²Each creature faced all four directions, and so the group could go wherever they wished, without having to turn.

¹³Among* the creatures there was something that looked like a blazing torch, constantly moving. The fire would blaze up and shoot out flashes of lightning. ¹⁴The creatures themselves darted to and fro with the speed of lightning.

¹⁵As I was looking at the four creatures, I saw four wheels touching the ground, one beside each of them.* ¹⁶All four wheels were alike; each one shone like a precious stone, and each had another wheel intersecting it at right angles, ¹⁷so that the wheels could move in any of the four directions. ¹⁸The rims of the wheels were covered with eyes.* ¹⁹Whenever the creatures moved, the wheels moved with them, and if the creatures rose up from the earth, so did the wheels. ²⁰The creatures went wherever they wished, and the wheels did exactly what the creatures did, because the creatures controlled them. ²¹So every time the creatures moved or stopped or rose in the air, the wheels did exactly the same.

²²Above the heads of the creatures there was something that looked like a dome made of dazzling crystal. ²³There under the dome stood the creatures, each stretching out two wings towards the ones next to it and covering its body with the other two wings. ²⁴I heard the noise their wings made in flight; it sounded like the roar of the sea, like the noise of a huge army, like the voice of Almighty God. When they stopped flying, they folded

---

1.1 *thirtieth year*: It is not known to what year this refers.
1.11 Some ancient translations *Two wings*; Hebrew *Their faces, their wings*.
1.13 Some ancient translations *Among*; Hebrew *And the likeness of*.
1.15 Some ancient translations *them*; Hebrew *their faces*.
1.18 Verse 18 in Hebrew is unclear.

their wings, ²⁵ but there was still a sound coming from above the dome over their heads.

²⁶ Above the dome there was something that looked like a throne made of sapphire, and sitting on the throne was a figure that looked like a human being. ²⁷ The figure seemed to be shining like bronze in the middle of a fire. It shone all over with a bright light ²⁸ that had in it all the colours of the rainbow. This was the dazzling light that shows the presence of the LORD.

God Calls Ezekiel to be a Prophet

When I saw this, I fell face downwards on the ground. Then I heard a voice

2 saying, "Mortal man, stand up. I want to talk to you." ² While the voice was speaking, God's Spirit entered me and raised me to my feet, and I heard the voice continue, ³ "Mortal man, I am sending you to the people of Israel. They have rebelled and turned against me and are still rebels, just as their ancestors were. ⁴ They are stubborn and do not respect me, so I am sending you to tell them what I, the Sovereign LORD, am saying to them. ⁵ Whether those rebels listen to you or not, they will know that a prophet has been among them.

⁶ "But you, mortal man, must not be afraid of them or of anything they say. They will defy and despise you; it will be like living among scorpions. Still, don't be afraid of those rebels or of anything they say. ⁷ You will tell them whatever I tell you to say, whether they listen or not. Remember what rebels they are.

⁸ "Mortal man, listen to what I tell you. Don't be rebellious like them. Open your mouth and eat what I am going to give you." ⁹ I saw a hand stretched out towards me, and it was holding a scroll. ¹⁰ The hand unrolled the scroll, and I saw that there was writing on both sides — cries of grief were written there, and wails and groans.

3 God said, "Mortal man, eat this scroll; then go and speak to the people of Israel."

² So I opened my mouth, and he gave me the scroll to eat. ³ He said, "Mortal man, eat this scroll that I give you; fill your stomach with it." I ate it, and it tasted as sweet as honey.

⁴ Then God said, "Mortal man, go to the people of Israel and say to them whatever I tell you to say. ⁵ I am not sending you to a nation that speaks a difficult foreign language, but to the Israelites. ⁶ If I sent you to great nations that spoke difficult languages you didn't understand, they would listen to you. ⁷ But none of the people of Israel will be willing to listen; they will not even listen to me. All of them are stubborn and defiant. ⁸ Now I will make you as stubborn and as tough as they are. ⁹ I will make you as firm as a rock, as hard as a diamond; don't be afraid of those rebels."

¹⁰ God continued, "Mortal man, pay close attention and remember everything I tell you. ¹¹ Then go to your countrymen who are in exile and tell them what I, the Sovereign LORD, am saying to them, whether they pay attention to you or not."

¹² Then God's Spirit lifted me up, and I heard behind me the loud roar of a voice that said, "Praise the glory of the LORD in heaven above!" ¹³ I heard the wings of the creatures beating together in the air, and the noise of the wheels, as loud as an earthquake. ¹⁴ The power of the LORD came on me with great force, and as his Spirit carried me off, I felt bitter and angry. ¹⁵ So I came to Tel Abib beside the River Chebar, where the exiles were living, and for seven days I stayed there, overcome by what I had seen and heard.

GLORY

PSALM 57.11;
EZEKIEL 3.12;
JOHN 17.4

Search for the Oxford or Cambridge Dictionary definition of 'glory' and write the definition here.

Ezekiel
Daniel
Hosea
Joel
Amos
Obadiah

968

Ezekiel

Eccles.
Songs
Isaiah
Jerem.
Lamen.

EZEKIEL 3, 4

The Lord Appoints Ezekiel as a Watchman
(Ezek 33.1–9)

16 After the seven days had passed, the Lord spoke to me. 17 "Mortal man," he said, "I am making you a watchman for the nation of Israel. You will pass on to them the warnings I give you. 18 If I announce that an evil person is going to die but you do not warn him to change his ways so that he can save his life, he will die, still a sinner, and I will hold you responsible for his death. 19 If you do warn an evil man and he doesn't stop sinning, he will die, still a sinner, but your life will be spared.

20 "If a truly good person starts doing evil and I put him in a dangerous situation, he will die if you do not warn him. He will die because of his sins — I will not remember the good he did — and I will hold you responsible for his death. 21 If you do warn a good man not to sin and he listens to you and doesn't sin, he will stay alive, and your life will also be spared."

Ezekiel will be Unable to Talk

22 I felt the powerful presence of the Lord and heard him say to me, "Get up and go out into the valley. I will talk to you there." 23 So I went out into the valley, and there I saw the glory of the Lord, just as I had seen it beside the River Chebar. I fell face downwards on the ground, 24 but God's Spirit entered me and raised me to my feet. The Lord said to me, "Go home and shut yourself up in the house. 25 You will be tied with ropes, mortal man, and you will not be able to go out in public. 26 I will paralyse your tongue so that you won't be able to warn these rebellious people. 27 Then, when I speak to you again and give you back the power of speech, you will tell them what I, the Sovereign Lord, am saying. Some of them will listen, but some will ignore you, for they are a nation of rebels."

Ezekiel Acts Out the Siege of Jerusalem

4 God said, "Mortal man, get a brick, put it in front of you, and scratch lines on it to represent the city of Jerusalem. 2 Then, to represent a siege, put trenches, earthworks, camps, and battering rams all round it. 3 Take an iron pan and set it up like a wall between you and the city. Face the city. It is under siege, and you are the one besieging it. This will be a sign to the nation of Israel.

4-5 "Then lie down on your left side, and I* will place on you the guilt of the nation of Israel. For 390 days you will stay there and suffer because of their guilt. I have sentenced you to one day for each year their punishment will last. 6 When you finish that, turn over on your right side and suffer for the guilt of Judah for forty days — one day for each year of their punishment.

7 "Fix your eyes on the siege of Jerusalem. Shake your fist at the city and prophesy against it. 8 I will tie you up so that you cannot turn from one side to the other until the siege is over.

9 "Now take some wheat, barley, beans, peas, millet, and spelt. Mix them all together and make bread. That is what you are to eat during the 390 days you are lying on your left side. 10 You will be allowed 230 grammes of bread a day, and it will have to last until the next day. 11 You will also have a limited amount of water to drink, two cups a day. 12 You are to build a fire out of dried human excrement, bake bread on the fire, and eat it where everyone can see you."

4.4–5 Probable text I; Hebrew you.

EZEKIEL 4, 5   969
Ezekiel
Daniel
Hosea
Joel
Amos
Obadiah

¹³The LORD said, "This represents the way the Israelites will have to eat food which the Law forbids,* when I scatter them to foreign countries."

¹⁴But I replied, "No, Sovereign LORD! I have never defiled myself. From childhood on I have never eaten meat from any animal that died a natural death or was killed by wild animals. I have never eaten any food considered unclean."

¹⁵So God said, "Very well. I will let you use cow dung instead, and you can bake your bread on that."

¹⁶And he added, "Mortal man, I am going to cut off the supply of bread for Jerusalem. The people there will be distressed and anxious as they measure out the food they eat and the water they drink. ¹⁷They will run out of bread and water; they will be in despair, and they will waste away because of their sins."

Ezekiel Cuts his Hair

5 The LORD said, "Mortal man, take a sharp sword and use it to shave off your beard and all your hair. Then weigh the hair on scales and divide it into three parts. ²Burn a third of it in the city when the siege is over. Take another third and chop it up with your sword as you move about outside the city. Scatter the remaining third to the winds, and I will pursue it with my sword. ³Keep back a few hairs and wrap them in the hem of your clothes. ⁴Then take a few of them out again, throw them in the fire, and let them burn up. From them fire will spread to the whole nation of Israel."

⁵The Sovereign LORD said, "Look at Jerusalem. I put her at the centre of the world, with other countries all round her. ⁶But Jerusalem rebelled against my commands and showed that she was more wicked than the other nations, more disobedient than the countries around her. Jerusalem rejected my commands and refused to keep my laws. ⁷Now listen, Jerusalem, to what I, the Sovereign LORD, am saying. By not obeying my laws or keeping my commands, you have caused more trouble than the nations around you. You have followed the customs of other nations. ⁸And so I, the Sovereign LORD, am telling you that I am your enemy. I will pass judgement on you where all the nations can see it. ⁹Because of all the things you do that I hate, I will punish Jerusalem as I have never done before and will never do again. ¹⁰As a result, parents in Jerusalem will eat their children, and children will eat their parents. I will punish you and scatter in every direction any who are left alive.

¹¹"Therefore, as I am the living God — this is the word of the Sovereign LORD — because you defiled my Temple with all the evil, disgusting things you did, I will cut you down without mercy. ¹²A third of your people will die from sickness and hunger in the city; a third will be cut down by swords outside the city; and I will scatter the last third to the winds and pursue them with a sword.

¹³"You will feel all the force of my anger and rage until I am satisfied. When all this happens, you will be convinced that I, the LORD, have spoken to you because I am outraged at your unfaithfulness. ¹⁴All those from the nations around you who pass by will sneer at you and keep their distance.

¹⁵"When I am angry and furious with you and punish you, all the nations around you will be terrified. They will look at you with disgust and will mock you. ¹⁶I will cut off your supply of food and

4.13 *food which the law forbids*: The Law of Moses prohibited the eating of certain foods as being ritually unclean (see Lev 11).

970

Ezekiel

Eccles.
Songs
Isaiah
Jerem.
Lamen.

EZEKIEL 5–7

Colour these shapes.

let you starve. You* will feel the pains of hunger like sharp arrows sent to destroy you. 17 I will send hunger and wild animals to kill your children, and will send sickness, violence, and war to kill you. I, the LORD, have spoken."

The LORD Condemns Idolatry

6 The LORD spoke to me. 2 "Mortal man," he said, "look towards the mountains of Israel and give them my message. 3 Tell the mountains of Israel to hear the word of the LORD — to hear what I, the Sovereign LORD, am telling the mountains, the hills, the gorges, and the valleys: I will send a sword to destroy the places where people worship idols. 4 The altars will be torn down and the incense altars broken. All the people there will be killed in front of their idols. 5 I will scatter the corpses of the people of Israel; I will scatter their bones all round the altars. 6 All the cities of Israel will be destroyed, so that all their altars and their idols will be smashed to pieces, their incense altars will be shattered, and everything they made will disappear. 7 People will be killed everywhere, and those who survive will acknowledge that I am the LORD.

8 "I will let some escape the slaughter and be scattered among the nations, 9 where they will live in exile. There they will remember me and know that I have punished them and disgraced them,* because their faithless hearts deserted me and they preferred idols to me. And they will be disgusted with themselves because of the evil and degrading things they have done. 10 They will know that I am the LORD and that my warnings were not empty threats."

11 The Sovereign LORD said, "Wring your hands! Stamp your feet! Cry in sorrow because of all the evil, disgusting things the Israelites have done. They are going to die in war, by famine, and by disease. 12 Those far away will fall ill and die; those near by will be killed in war; those who survive will starve to death. They will feel all the force of my anger. 13 Corpses will be scattered among the idols and round the altars, scattered on every high hill, on the top of every mountain, under every green tree and every large oak, in every place where they burnt sacrifices to their idols. Then everyone will know that I am the LORD. 14 Yes, I will stretch out my hand and destroy their country. I will make it a waste from the southern desert to the city of Riblah in the north, not sparing any place where the Israelites live. Then everyone will know that I am the LORD."

The End is Near for Israel

7 The LORD spoke to me. 2 "Mortal man," he said, "this is what I, the Sovereign LORD, am saying to the land of Israel: this is the end for the whole land!

3 "Israel, the end has come. You will feel my anger, because I am judging you for what you have done. I will pay you back for all your disgusting conduct. 4 I will not spare you or show you any mercy. I am going to punish you for the disgusting things you have done, so that you will know that I am the LORD."

5 This is what the Sovereign LORD is saying, "One disaster after another is coming on you. 6 It's all over. This is the end. You are finished. 7 The end is coming for you people who live in the land. The time is near when there will be no more celebrations at the mountain shrines, only confusion.*

5.16 Probable text *You*; Hebrew *They*.
6.9 Some ancient translations *disgraced them*; Hebrew *I am disgraced*.
7.7 Probable text *celebrations… confusion*; Hebrew unclear.

EZEKIEL 7, 8

971

Ezekiel

...........:

Daniel
Hosea
Joel
Amos
Obadiah

[8] "Very soon now you will feel all the force of my anger. I am judging you for what you have done, and I will pay you back for all your disgusting conduct. [9] I will not spare you or show you any mercy. I am going to punish you for the disgusting things you have done, so that you will know that I am the LORD, and that I am the one who punishes you."

[10] The day of disaster is coming for Israel. Violence is flourishing. Pride is at its height.* [11] Violence produces more wickedness. Nothing of theirs will remain, nothing of their wealth, their splendour, or their glory.

[12] The time is coming. The day is near when buying and selling will have no more meaning, because God's punishment will fall on everyone alike. [13] No merchant will live long enough to get back what he has lost, because God's anger is on everyone. Those who are evil cannot survive.* [14] The trumpet sounds, and everyone gets ready. But no one goes off to war, for God's anger will fall on everyone alike.

Punishment for Israel's Sins

[15] There is fighting in the streets, and sickness and hunger in the houses. Anyone who is out in the country will die in the fighting, and anyone in the city will be a victim of sickness and hunger. [16] Some will escape to the mountains like doves frightened from the valleys. All of them will moan over their sins.* [17] Everyone's hands will be weak, and their knees will shake. [18] They will put on sackcloth and they will tremble all over. Their heads will be shaved, and they will all be disgraced. [19] They will throw their gold and silver away in the streets like refuse, because neither silver nor gold can save them when the LORD pours out his fury. They cannot use it to satisfy their desires or fill their stomachs. Gold and silver led them into sin. [20] Once they were proud of their beautiful jewels, but they used them to make disgusting idols. That is why the LORD has made their wealth repulsive to them.

[21] "I will let foreigners rob them," says the LORD, "and lawbreakers will take all their wealth and defile it. [22] I will not interfere when my treasured Temple is profaned, when robbers break into it and defile it.

[23] "Everything is in confusion* — the land is full of murders and the cities are full of violence. [24] I will bring the most evil nations here and let them have your homes. Your strongest men will lose their confidence when I let the nations profane the places where you worship. [25] Despair is coming. You will look for peace and never find it. [26] One disaster will follow another, and a steady stream of bad news will pour in. You will beg the prophets to reveal what they foresee. The priests will have nothing to teach the people, and the elders will have no advice to give. [27] The king will mourn, the prince will give up hope, and the people will shake with fear. I will punish you for all you have done, and will judge you in the same way as you have judged others. This will show you that I am the LORD."

Ezekiel's Second Vision of God
8.1—10.22

Idolatry in Jerusalem

8 On the fifth day of the sixth month of the sixth year of our exile, the leaders of the exiles from Judah were sitting in my

---

7.10 Probable text *Pride is at its height*; Hebrew unclear.
7.13 Verse 13 in Hebrew is unclear.
7.16 Verse 16 in Hebrew is unclear.
7.23 One ancient translation *Everything is in confusion*; Hebrew unclear.

972

Ezekiel

∴ ⋯⋯

Eccles.
Songs
Isaiah
Jerem.
Lamen.

EZEKIEL 8, 9

house with me. Suddenly the power of the Sovereign LORD came on me. [2] I looked up and saw a vision of a fiery human form. From the waist down his body looked like fire, and from the waist up he was shining like polished bronze. [3] He stretched out what seemed to be a hand and seized me by the hair. Then in this vision God's Spirit lifted me high in the air and took me to Jerusalem. He took me to the inner entrance of the north gate of the Temple, where there was an idol that was an outrage to God.

[4] There I saw the dazzling light that shows the presence of Israel's God, just as I had seen it when I was by the River Chebar. [5] God said to me, "Mortal man, look towards the north." I looked, and there near the altar by the entrance of the gateway I saw the idol that was an outrage to God.

[6] God said to me, "Mortal man, do you see what is happening? Look at the disgusting things the people of Israel are doing here, driving me farther and farther away from my holy place. You will see even more disgraceful things than this."

[7] He took me to the entrance of the outer courtyard and showed me a hole in the wall. [8] He said, "Mortal man, break through the wall here." I broke through it and found a door. [9] He said to me, "Go in and look at the evil, disgusting things they are doing there." [10] So I went in and looked. The walls were covered with drawings of snakes and other unclean animals,* and of the other things which the Israelites were worshipping. [11] Seventy Israelite leaders were there, including Jaazaniah son of Shaphan. Each one was holding an incense burner, and smoke was rising from the incense. [12] God asked me, "Mortal man, do you see what the Israelite leaders are doing in secret? They are all worshipping in a room full of images. Their excuse is: 'The LORD doesn't see us! He has abandoned the country.'"

[13] Then the LORD said to me, "You are going to see them do even more disgusting things than that." [14] So he took me to the north gate of the Temple and showed me women weeping over the death of the god Tammuz.*

[15] He asked, "Mortal man, do you see that? You will see even more disgusting things." [16] So he took me to the inner courtyard of the Temple. There near the entrance of the sanctuary, between the altar and the passage, were about 25 men. They had turned their backs to the sanctuary and were bowing low towards the east, worshipping the rising sun.

[17] The LORD said to me, "Mortal man, do you see that? These people of Judah are not satisfied with merely doing all the disgusting things you have seen here and with spreading violence throughout the country. No, they must come and do them here in the Temple itself and make me even more angry. Look how they insult me in the most offensive way possible!* [18] They will feel all the force of my anger. I will not spare them or show them any mercy. They will shout prayers to me as loud as they can, but I will not listen to them."

Jerusalem is Punished

9 Then I heard God shout, "Come here, you men who are going to punish the city. Bring your weapons with you." [2] At once

8.10 *unclean animals*: The Law of Moses prohibited the eating of certain animals as being ritually unclean (see 4.13; Lev 11).
8.14 *Tammuz*: A god who was thought to die when vegetation died and to come to life the next year. Women would mourn his ritual death.
8.17 *in the most offensive way possible*: A reference to a pagan rite of putting a branch to the nose.

EZEKIEL 9, 10

973

Ezekiel

·········

Daniel
Hosea
Joel
Amos
Obadiah

six men came from the outer north gate of the Temple, each one carrying a weapon. With them was a man dressed in linen clothes, carrying something to write with. They all came and stood by the bronze altar.

³ Then the dazzling light of the presence of the God of Israel rose up from the winged creatures,* where it had been, and moved to the entrance of the Temple. The LORD called to the man dressed in linen, ⁴ "Go through the whole city of Jerusalem and put a mark on the forehead of everyone who is distressed and troubled because of all the disgusting things being done in the city."

⁵ And I heard God say to the other men, "Follow him through the city, and kill. Spare no one; have mercy on no one. ⁶ Kill the old men, young men, young women, mothers, and children. But don't touch anyone who has the mark on his forehead. Start here at my Temple." So they began with the leaders who were standing there at the Temple.

⁷ God said to them, "Defile the Temple. Fill its courtyards with corpses. Get to work!" So they began to kill the people in the city.*

⁸ While the killing was going on, I was there alone. I threw myself face downwards on the ground and shouted, "Sovereign LORD, are you so angry with Jerusalem that you are going to kill everyone left in Israel?"

⁹ God answered, "The people of Israel and Judah are guilty of terrible sins. They have committed murder all over the land and have filled Jerusalem with crime. They say that I, the LORD, have abandoned their country and that I don't see them. ¹⁰ But I will not have pity on them; I will do to them what they have done to others."

¹¹ Then the man wearing linen clothes returned and reported to the LORD, "I have carried out your orders."

The Glory of the LORD Leaves the Temple

10 I looked at the dome over the heads of the living creatures* and above them was something that seemed to be a throne made of sapphire. ² God said to the man wearing linen clothes, "Go between the wheels under the creatures and fill your hands with burning coals. Then scatter the coals over the city."

I watched him go. ³ The creatures were standing to the south of the Temple when he went in, and a cloud filled the inner courtyard. ⁴ The dazzling light of the LORD's presence rose up from the creatures and moved to the entrance of the Temple. Then the cloud filled the Temple, and the courtyard was blazing with the light. ⁵ The noise made by the creatures' wings was heard even in the outer courtyard. It sounded like the voice of Almighty God.

⁶ When the LORD commanded the man wearing linen clothes to take some fire from between the wheels that were under the creatures, the man went in and stood by one of the wheels. ⁷ One of the creatures put his hand into the fire that was there among them, picked up some coals, and put them in the hands of the man in linen. The man took the coals and left.

⁸ I saw that each creature had what looked like a human hand under each of its wings. ⁹⁻¹⁰ I also saw that there were four wheels, all alike, one beside each creature. The wheels shone like precious stones, and each one had another wheel which intersected it at

....

9.3 *winged creatures*: See 1.5–12.
9.7 *work!" So they... city.*; or *work! Go on and start killing the people in the city!"*
10.1 *living creatures*: See 1.5–12.

974

Ezekiel

Eccles.
Songs
Isaiah
Jerem.
Lamen.

EZEKIEL 10, 11

right angles. ¹¹When the creatures moved, they could go in any direction without turning. They all moved together in the direction they wanted to go, without having to turn round. ¹²Their bodies, backs, hands, wings, and wheels were covered with eyes. ¹³I heard a voice calling out, "Whirling wheels".

¹⁴Each creature had four faces. The first was the face of a bull, the second a human face, the third the face of a lion, and the fourth the face of an eagle. ¹⁵(They were the same creatures that I had seen by the River Chebar.) When the creatures rose in the air ¹⁶and moved, the wheels went with them. Whenever they spread their wings to fly, the wheels still went with them. ¹⁷When the creatures stopped, the wheels stopped; and when the creatures flew, the wheels went with them, because the creatures controlled them.

¹⁸Then the dazzling light of the LORD's presence left the entrance of the Temple and moved to a place above the creatures. ¹⁹They spread their wings and flew up from the earth while I was watching, and the wheels went with them. They paused at the east gate of the Temple, and the dazzling light was over them. ²⁰I recognized them as the same creatures which I had seen beneath the God of Israel at the River Chebar.

²¹Each of them had four faces, four wings, and what looked like a human hand under each wing. ²²Their faces looked exactly like the faces* I had seen by the River Chebar. Each creature moved straight ahead.

Jerusalem is Condemned

11 God's Spirit lifted me up and took me to the east gate of the Temple. There near the gate I saw 25 men, including Jaazaniah son of Azzur and Pelatiah son of Benaiah, two leaders of the nation.

²God said to me, "Mortal man, these men make evil plans and give bad advice in this city. ³They say, 'We will soon be building houses again.* The city is like a cooking pot, and we are like the meat in it, but at least it protects us from the fire.' ⁴Now then, denounce them, mortal man."

⁵The Spirit of the LORD took control of me, and the LORD told me to give the people this message: "People of Israel, I know what you are saying and what you are planning. ⁶You have murdered so many people here in the city that the streets are full of corpses.

⁷"So this is what I, the Sovereign LORD, am saying to you. This city is indeed a cooking pot, but what is the meat? The corpses of those you have killed! You will not be here — I will throw you out of the city! ⁸Are you afraid of swords? I will bring men with swords to attack you. ⁹I will take you out of the city and hand you over to foreigners. I have sentenced you to death, ¹⁰and you will be killed in battle in your own country. Then everyone will know that I am the LORD. ¹¹This city will not protect you as a pot protects the meat in it. I will punish you wherever you may be in the land of Israel. ¹²You will know that I am the LORD and that while you were keeping the laws of the neighbouring nations, you were breaking *my* laws and disobeying *my* commands."

¹³While I was prophesying, Pelatiah dropped dead. I threw myself face downwards on the ground and shouted, "No, Sovereign LORD! Are you going to kill everyone left in Israel?"

10.22 Probable text *the faces*; Hebrew *the faces and them.*
11.3 *We will… again*; or *We won't be building houses for a while.*

975

Ezekiel
···········
Daniel
Hosea
Joel
Amos
Obadiah

God's Promise to the Exiles

[14] The LORD spoke to me. [15] "Mortal man," he said, "the people who live in Jerusalem are talking about you and your fellow-Israelites who are in exile. They say, 'The exiles are too far away to worship the LORD. He has given us possession of the land.'

[16] "Now tell your fellow-exiles what I am saying. I am the one who sent them to live in far-off nations and scattered them in other countries. Yet, for the time being I will be present with them in the lands where they have gone.

[17] "So tell them what I, the Sovereign LORD, am saying. I will gather them out of the countries where I scattered them, and will give the land of Israel back to them. [18] When they return, they are to get rid of all the filthy, disgusting idols they find. [19] I will give them a new heart and a new mind. I will take away their stubborn heart of stone and will give them an obedient heart. [20] Then they will keep my laws and faithfully obey all my commands. They will be my people, and I will be their God. [21] But I will punish the people who love to worship filthy, disgusting idols. I will punish them for what they have done." The Sovereign LORD has spoken.

God's Glory Leaves Jerusalem

[22] The living creatures began to fly, and the wheels went with them. The dazzling light of the presence of the God of Israel was over them. [23] Then the dazzling light left the city and moved to the mountain east of it. [24] In the vision the Spirit of God lifted me up and brought me back to the exiles in Babylonia. Then the vision faded, [25] and I told the exiles everything that the LORD had shown me.

The Prophet as a Refugee

12 The LORD spoke to me. [2] "Mortal man," he said, "you are living among rebellious people. They have eyes, but they see nothing; they have ears, but they hear nothing, because they are rebellious.

[3] "Now, mortal man, pack a bundle just as a refugee would, and start out before nightfall. Let everyone see you leaving and going to another place. Maybe those rebels will notice you.* [4] While it is still daylight, pack your bundle for exile, so that they can see you, and then let them watch you leave in the evening as if you were going into exile. [5] While they are watching, break a hole through the wall of your house and take your pack out through it. [6] Let them watch you putting your pack on your shoulder and going out into the dark with your eyes covered, so that you can't see where you are going. What you do will be a warning to the Israelites."

[7] I did what the LORD told me to do. That day I packed a bundle as a refugee would, and that evening as it was getting dark I dug a hole in the wall with my hands and went out. While everyone watched, I put the pack on my shoulder and left.

[8] The next morning the LORD spoke to me. [9] "Mortal man," he said, "now that those Israelite rebels are asking you what you're doing, [10] tell them what I, the Sovereign LORD, am saying to them. This message is for the prince ruling in Jerusalem and for all the people who live there. [11] Tell them that what you have done is a sign of what will happen to them — they will be refugees and captives. [12] The prince who is ruling them will shoulder his pack in the dark and escape through a hole that they dig for him in

EZEKIEL 11.19

I WILL
GIVE
THEM A
· new ·
heart
AND A
{ new }
MIND

12.3 *Maybe those... you;* or *Maybe they will then realize that they are rebels.*

976

Ezekiel

.:.........

Eccles.
Songs
Isaiah
Jerem.
Lamen.

EZEKIEL 12, 13

the wall. He will cover his eyes and not see where he is going. [13] But I will spread out my net and trap him in it. Then I will take him to the city of Babylon, where he will die without having seen it. [14] I will scatter in every direction all the members of his court and his advisers and bodyguard, and people will search for them to kill them.

[15] "When I scatter them among the other nations and in foreign countries, they will know that I am the LORD. [16] I will let a few of them survive the war, the famine, and the diseases, so that there among the nations they will realize how disgusting their actions have been and will acknowledge that I am the LORD."

The Sign of the Trembling Prophet

[17] The LORD spoke to me. [18] "Mortal man," he said, "tremble when you eat, and shake with fear when you drink. [19] Tell the whole nation that this is the message of the Sovereign LORD to the people of Jerusalem who are still living in their land: they will tremble when they eat and shake with fear when they drink. Their land will be stripped bare, because everyone who lives there is lawless. [20] Cities that are now full of people will be destroyed, and the country will be made a wilderness. Then they will know that I am the LORD."

A Popular Proverb and an Unpopular Message

[21] The LORD spoke to me. [22] "Mortal man," he said, "why do the people of Israel repeat this proverb: 'Time goes by, and predictions come to nothing'? [23] Now tell them what I, the Sovereign LORD, have to say about that. I will put an end to that proverb. It won't be repeated in Israel any more. Tell them instead: the time has come, and the predictions are coming true!

[24] "Among the people of Israel there will be no more false visions or misleading prophecies. [25] I, the LORD, will speak to them, and what I say will be done. There will be no more delay. In your own lifetime, you rebels, I will do what I have warned you I would do. I have spoken," says the Sovereign LORD.

[26] The LORD said to me, [27] "Mortal man, the Israelites think that your visions and prophecies are about the distant future. [28] So tell them that I, the Sovereign LORD, am saying: there will be no more delay. What I have said will be done. I, the Sovereign LORD, have spoken!"

Prophecy against False Male Prophets

13 The LORD spoke to me. [2] "Mortal man," he said, "denounce the prophets of Israel who make up their own prophecies. Tell them to listen to the word of the LORD."

[3] This is what the Sovereign LORD says: "These foolish prophets are doomed! They provide their own inspiration and invent their own visions. [4] People of Israel, your prophets are as useless as foxes living among the ruins of a city. [5] They don't guard the places where the walls have crumbled, nor do they rebuild the walls, and so Israel cannot be defended when war comes on the day of the LORD. [6] Their visions are false, and their predictions are lies. They claim that they are speaking my message, but I have not sent them. Yet they expect their words to come true! [7] I tell them: those visions you see are false, and the predictions you make are lies. You say that they are my words, but I haven't spoken to you!"

[8] So the Sovereign LORD says to them, "Your words are false, and your visions are lies. I am against you. [9] I am about to punish you prophets who have false visions and make misleading predictions.

You will not be there when my people gather to make decisions; your names will not be included in the list of the citizens of Israel; you will never return to your land. Then you will know that I am the Sovereign LORD.

[10]"The prophets mislead my people by saying that all is well. All is certainly not well! My people have put up a wall of loose stones, and then the prophets have come and covered it with whitewash. [11] Tell the prophets that their wall is going to fall down. I will send a pouring rain. Hailstones will fall on it, and a strong wind will blow against it. [12] The wall will collapse, and everyone will ask you what good the whitewash did."

[13] Now this is what the Sovereign LORD says: "In my anger I will send a strong wind, pouring rain, and hailstones to destroy the wall. [14] I intend to break down the wall they whitewashed, to shatter it, and to leave the foundation stones bare. It will collapse and kill you all. Then everyone will know that I am the LORD.

[15]"The wall and those who covered it with whitewash will feel the force of my anger. Then I will tell you that the wall is gone and so are those who whitewashed it — [16] those prophets who assured Jerusalem that all was well, when all was not well!" The Sovereign LORD has spoken.

Prophecy against False Female Prophets

[17] The LORD said, "Now, mortal man, look at the women among your people who make up predictions. Denounce them [18] and tell them what the Sovereign LORD is saying to them:

"You women are doomed! You sew magic wristbands for everyone and make magic scarves for everyone to wear on their heads, so that they can have power over other people's lives. You want to possess the power of life and death over my people and to use it for your own benefit. [19] You dishonour me in front of my people in order to get a few handfuls of barley and a few pieces of bread. You kill people who don't deserve to die, and you keep people alive who don't deserve to live. So you tell lies to my people, and they believe you."

[20] Now this is what the Sovereign LORD says: "I hate the wristbands that you use in your attempt to control life and death. I will rip them off your arms and set free the people that you were controlling.* [21] I will rip off your scarves and let my people escape from your power once and for all. Then you will know that I am the LORD.

[22]"By your lies you discourage good people, whom I do not wish to hurt. You prevent evil people from giving up evil and saving their lives. [23] So now your false visions and misleading predictions are over. I am rescuing my people from your power, so that you will know that I am the LORD."

God Condemns Idolatry

14 Some of the leaders of the Israelites came to consult me about the LORD's will. [2] Then the LORD spoke to me. [3]"Mortal man," he said, "these men have given their hearts to idols and are letting idols lead them into sin. Do they think I will give them an answer?

[4]"Now speak to them and tell them what I, the Sovereign LORD, am saying to them: every Israelite who has given his heart to idols and lets them lead him into sin and who then comes to

---

13.20 In verse 20 in Hebrew a word occurs twice, the meaning of which is unclear.

978

Ezekiel

Eccles.
Songs
Isaiah
Jerem.
Lamen.

EZEKIEL 14, 15

On a scale

FROM 1 TO 10,

how easy are you finding it to read the Bible currently?

Think of one way you can go up a number on the scale.

10
9 8
7
5 6
    4
3 2
1

consult a prophet, will get an answer from me — the answer that his many idols deserve! [5] All those idols have turned the Israelites away from me, but by my answer I hope to win back their loyalty.

[6] "Now then, tell the Israelites what I, the Sovereign LORD, am saying: turn back and leave your disgusting idols.

[7] "Whenever one of the Israelites or one of the foreigners who live in the Israelite community turns away from me and worships idols, and then goes to consult a prophet, I, the LORD, will give him his answer! [8] I will oppose him. I will make an example of him. I will remove him from the community of my people, so that you will know that I am the LORD.

[9] "If a prophet is deceived into giving a false answer, it is because I, the LORD, have deceived him. I will remove him from the people of Israel. [10] Both the prophet and the one who consults him will get the same punishment. [11] I will do this to keep the Israelites from deserting me and defiling themselves by their sins. They are to be my people, and I will be their God." The Sovereign LORD has spoken.

Noah, Danel, and Job

[12] The LORD spoke to me. [13] "Mortal man," he said, "if a country sins and is unfaithful to me, I will stretch out my hand and destroy its supply of food. I will send a famine and kill people and animals alike. [14] Even if those three men, Noah, Danel,* and Job, were living there, their goodness would save only their own lives." The Sovereign LORD has spoken.

[15] "Or I might send wild animals to kill the people, making the land so dangerous that no one could travel through it, [16] and even if those three men lived there — as surely as I, the Sovereign LORD, am the living God — they would not be able to save even their own children. They would save only their own lives, and the land would become a wilderness.

[17] "Or I might bring war on that country and send destructive weapons to wipe out people and animals alike, [18] and even if those three men lived there — as surely as I, the Sovereign LORD, am the living God — they would not be able to save even their children, but only their own lives.

[19] "If I send an epidemic on that country and in my anger take many lives, killing people and animals, [20] even if Noah, Danel, and Job lived there — as surely as I, the Sovereign LORD, am the living God — they would not be able to save even their own children. Their goodness would save only their own lives."

[21] This is what the Sovereign LORD is saying: "I will send my four worst punishments on Jerusalem — war, famine, wild animals, and disease — to destroy people and animals alike. [22] If anyone does survive and save his children, look at them when they come to you. See how evil they are, and be convinced that the punishment I am bringing on Jerusalem is justified; [23] then you will know that there was good reason for everything I did." The Sovereign LORD has spoken.

A Parable about a Vine

15 The LORD spoke to me. [2] "Mortal man," he said, "how does a vine compare with a tree? What good is a branch of a grapevine compared with the trees of the forest? [3] Can you use it to make anything? Can you even make a peg out of it to hang things on? [4] It is only good for building a fire. And when the ends

....

14.14 *Danel*: or *Daniel*, an ancient hero, known for his righteous life.

EZEKIEL 15, 16

979

Ezekiel
....
Daniel
Hosea
Joel
Amos
Obadiah

are burnt up and the middle is charred, can you make anything out of it? ⁵It was useless even before it was burnt. Now that the fire has burnt it and charred it, it is even more useless."

⁶Now this is what the Sovereign LORD is saying, "Just as a vine is taken from the forest and burnt, so I will take the people who live in Jerusalem ⁷and will punish them. They have escaped one fire, but now fire will burn them up. When I punish them, you will know that I am the LORD. ⁸They have been unfaithful to me, and so I will make the country a wilderness." The Sovereign LORD has spoken.

Jerusalem the Unfaithful

16 The LORD spoke to me again. ²"Mortal man," he said, "point out to Jerusalem what disgusting things she has done. ³Tell Jerusalem what the Sovereign LORD is saying to her:

"You were born in the land of Canaan. Your father was an Amorite, and your mother was a Hittite.* ⁴When you were born, no one cut your umbilical cord or washed you* or rubbed you with salt or wrapped you in cloth. ⁵No one took enough pity on you to do any of these things for you. When you were born, no one loved you. You were thrown out in an open field.

⁶"Then I passed by and saw you squirming in your own blood. You were covered with blood, but I wouldn't let you die. ⁷I made you grow like a healthy plant. You grew strong and tall and became a young woman.* Your breasts were well formed, and your hair had grown, but you were naked.

⁸"As I passed by again, I saw that the time had come for you to fall in love. I covered your naked body with my coat and promised to love you. Yes, I made a marriage covenant with you, and you became mine." This is what the Sovereign LORD says.

⁹"Then I took water and washed the blood off you. I rubbed olive oil on your skin. ¹⁰I dressed you in embroidered gowns and gave you shoes of the best leather, a linen headband, and a silk cloak. ¹¹I put jewels on you — bracelets and necklaces. ¹²I gave you a nose-ring and earrings and a beautiful crown to wear. ¹³You had ornaments of gold and silver, and you always wore clothes of embroidered linen and silk. You ate bread made from the best flour, and had honey and olive oil to eat. Your beauty was dazzling, and you became a queen. ¹⁴You became famous in every nation for your perfect beauty, because I was the one who made you so lovely." This is what the Sovereign LORD says.

¹⁵"But you took advantage of your beauty and fame to sleep with everyone who came along.* ¹⁶You used some of your clothes to decorate your places of worship, and just like a prostitute,* you gave yourself to everyone. ¹⁷You took the silver and gold jewellery that I had given you, used it to make male images, and committed adultery with them. ¹⁸You took the embroidered clothes I gave you and put them on the images, and you offered to the images the olive oil and incense I had given you. ¹⁹I gave you food — the best flour, olive oil, and honey — but you offered it as a sacrifice to win the favour of idols." This is what the Sovereign LORD says.

²⁰"Then you took the sons and the daughters you had borne me and offered them as sacrifices to idols. Wasn't it bad enough to

....

16.3 *Amorite... Hittite*: The Israelites regarded these people as immoral and idolatrous.
16.4 Hebrew has an additional word, the meaning of which is unclear.
16.7 Probable text *young woman*; Hebrew unclear.
16.15 Hebrew has two additional words, the meaning of which is unclear.
16.16 Hebrew has four additional words, the meaning of which is unclear.

980

Ezekiel

∴∙∙∙∙∙∙∙∙∙

Eccles.
Songs
Isaiah
Jerem.
Lamen.

EZEKIEL 16

be unfaithful to me, ²¹without taking my children and sacrificing them to idols? ²²During your disgusting life as a prostitute you never once remembered your childhood — when you were naked, squirming in your own blood."

Jerusalem's Life as a Prostitute

²³The Sovereign Lord said, "You are doomed! Doomed! You did all that evil, and then ²⁴by the side of every road you built places to worship idols and practise prostitution. ²⁵You dragged your beauty through the mud. You offered yourself to everyone who came by, and you were more of a prostitute every day. ²⁶You let your lustful neighbours, the Egyptians, go to bed with you, and you used your prostitution to make me angry.

²⁷"Now I have raised my hand to punish you and to take away your share of my blessing. I have handed you over to the Philistines, who hate you and are disgusted with your immoral actions.

²⁸"Because you were not satisfied by the others, you went running after the Assyrians. You were their prostitute, but they didn't satisfy you either. ²⁹You were also a prostitute for the Babylonians, that nation of merchants, but they didn't satisfy you either."

³⁰*This is what the Sovereign Lord is saying: "You have done all this like a shameless prostitute. ³¹On every street you built places to worship idols and practise prostitution. But you are not out for money like a common prostitute. ³²You are like a woman who commits adultery with strangers instead of loving her husband. ³³A prostitute is paid, but you gave presents to all your lovers and bribed them to come from everywhere to sleep with you. ³⁴You are a special kind of prostitute. No one forced you to become one. You didn't get paid; you paid them! Yes, you are different."

God's Judgement on Jerusalem

³⁵Now then, Jerusalem, you whore! Hear what the Lord is saying.

³⁶This is what the Sovereign Lord says: "You stripped off your clothes and, like a prostitute, you gave yourself to your lovers and to all your disgusting idols, and you killed your children as sacrifices to idols. ³⁷Because of this I will bring all your former lovers together — the ones you liked and the ones you hated. I will bring them round you in a circle, and then I will strip off your clothes and let them see you naked. ³⁸I will condemn you for adultery and murder, and in my anger and fury I will punish you with death. ³⁹I will put you in their power, and they will tear down the places where you engage in prostitution and worship idols. They will take away your clothes and jewels and leave you completely naked.

⁴⁰"They will stir up a crowd to stone you, and they will cut you to pieces with their swords. ⁴¹They will burn your houses down and let crowds of women see your punishment. I will make you stop being a prostitute and make you stop giving gifts to your lovers. ⁴²Then my anger will be over, and I will be calm. I will not be angry or jealous any more. ⁴³You have forgotten how I treated you when you were young, and you have made me angry by all the things you did. That is why I have made you pay for them all. Why did you add sexual immorality to all the other disgusting things you did?" The Sovereign Lord has spoken.

....

16.30 Verse 30 in Hebrew begins with three words, the meaning of which is unclear.

EZEKIEL 16, 17

981

Ezekiel

....

Daniel
Hosea
Joel
Amos
Obadiah

Like Mother, Like Daughter

[44] The LORD said, "People will use this proverb about you, Jerusalem: 'Like mother, like daughter.' [45] You really are your mother's daughter. She detested her husband and her children. You are like your sisters, who hated their husbands and their children. You and your sister cities had a Hittite mother and an Amorite* father.

[46] "Your elder sister is Samaria, in the north, with her villages. Your younger sister, with her villages, is Sodom, in the south. [47] Were you content to follow in their footsteps and copy their disgusting actions? No, in only a little while you were behaving worse than they were in everything you did.

[48] "As surely as I am the living God," the Sovereign LORD says, "your sister Sodom and her villages never did the evil that you and your villages have done. [49] She and her daughters were proud because they had plenty to eat and lived in peace and quiet, but they did not take care of the poor and the underprivileged. [50] They were proud and stubborn and did the things that I hate, so I destroyed them, as you well know.

[51] "Samaria did not sin half as much as you have. You have acted more disgustingly than she ever did. Your corruption makes your sisters look innocent by comparison. [52] And now you will have to endure your disgrace. Your sins are so much worse than those of your sisters that they look innocent beside you. Now blush and bear your shame, because you make your sisters look pure."

Sodom and Samaria will be Restored

[53] The LORD said to Jerusalem, "I will make them prosperous again — Sodom and her villages and Samaria and her villages. Yes, I will make you prosperous too. [54] You will be ashamed of yourself, and your disgrace will show your sisters how well off they are. [55] They will become prosperous again, and you and your villages will also be restored. [56] Didn't you joke about Sodom in those days when you were proud [57] and before the evil you did had been exposed? Now you are just like her — a joke to the Edomites, the Philistines, and your other neighbours who hate you. [58] You must suffer for the obscene, disgusting things you have done." The LORD has spoken.

A Covenant that Lasts for Ever

[59] The Sovereign LORD says, "I will treat you as you deserve, because you ignored your promises and broke the covenant. [60] But I will honour the covenant I made with you when you were young, and I will make a covenant with you that will last for ever. [61] You will remember how you have acted, and be ashamed of it when you get your elder sister and your younger sister back. I will let them be like daughters to you, even though this was not part of my covenant with you. [62] I will renew my covenant with you, and you will know that I am the LORD. [63] I will forgive all the wrongs you have done, but you will remember them and be too ashamed to open your mouth." The Sovereign LORD has spoken.

The Parable of the Eagles and the Vine

17 The LORD spoke to me. [2] "Mortal man," he said, "tell the Israelites a parable [3] to let them know what I, the Sovereign LORD, am saying to them: there was a giant eagle with beautiful feathers and huge wings, spread wide. He flew to the Lebanon

---

16.45 *Hittite... Amorite*: See 16.3.

EZEKIEL 16.48-49

In Genesis 19 we read how God destroyed Sodom because it was such an evil and depraved place. Here in Ezekiel, God makes it clear that the city's biggest crime was

IGNORING
• THE POOR. •

In God's eyes, the way we view and treat those who are less fortunate than us is vital.

982

Ezekiel

⋮⋰⋮

Eccles.
Songs
Isaiah
Jerem.
Lamen.

EZEKIEL 17

Mountains and broke off the top of a cedar tree, ⁴which he carried to a land of commerce, and placed in a city of merchants. ⁵Then he took a young plant from the land of Israel and planted it in a fertile field,* where there was always water to make it grow. ⁶The plant sprouted and became a low, wide-spreading grapevine. The branches grew upward towards the eagle, and the roots grew deep. The vine was covered with branches and leaves.

⁷"There was another giant eagle with huge wings and thick plumage. And now the vine sent its roots towards him and turned its leaves towards him, in the hope that he would give it more water than there was in the garden where it was growing.* ⁸But the vine had already been planted in a fertile, well-watered field so that it could grow leaves and bear grapes and be a magnificent vine.

⁹"So I, the Sovereign Lord, ask: will this vine live and grow? Won't the first eagle pull it up by its roots, pull off the grapes, and break off the branches and let them wither? It will not take much strength or a mighty nation to pull it up. ¹⁰Yes, it is planted, but will it live and grow? Won't it wither when the east wind strikes it? Won't it wither there where it is growing?"

The Parable is Explained

¹¹The Lord said to me, ¹²"Ask these rebels if they know what the parable means. Tell them that the king of Babylonia came to Jerusalem and took the king and his officials back with him to Babylonia. ¹³He took one of the king's family, made a treaty with him, and made him swear to be loyal. He took important men as hostages ¹⁴to keep the nation from rising again and to make sure that the treaty would be kept. ¹⁵But the king of Judah rebelled and sent agents to Egypt to get horses and a large army. Will he succeed? Can he get away with that? He cannot break the treaty and go unpunished!

¹⁶"As surely as I am the living God," says the Sovereign Lord, "this king will die in Babylonia because he broke his oath and the treaty he had made with the king of Babylonia, who put him on the throne. ¹⁷Even the powerful army of the king of Egypt will not be able to help him fight when the Babylonians build earthworks and dig trenches in order to kill many people. ¹⁸He broke his oath and the treaty he had made. He did all these things, and now he will not escape."

¹⁹The Sovereign Lord says, "As surely as I am the living God, I will punish him for breaking the treaty which he swore in my name to keep. ²⁰I will spread out a hunter's net and catch him in it. I will take him to Babylonia and punish him there, because he was unfaithful to me. ²¹His best soldiers will be killed in battle, and the survivors will be scattered in every direction. Then you will know that I, the Lord, have spoken."

God's Promise of Hope

²²This is what the Sovereign Lord says:
"I will take the top of a tall cedar
    and break off a tender sprout;
I will plant it on a high mountain,
²³   on Israel's highest mountain.

17.5 Hebrew has an additional word, the meaning of which is unclear.
17.7 And now the vine… growing; or And now the vine turned away from the garden where it was growing and sent its roots towards him and turned its leaves towards him, in the hope that he would give it water.

EZEKIEL 17, 18

983

Ezekiel
............:·

Daniel
Hosea
Joel
Amos
Obadiah

It will grow branches and bear seed
  and become a magnificent cedar.
Birds of every kind will live there
  and find shelter in its shade.
24 All the trees in the land will know
  that I am the LORD.
I cut down the tall trees
  and make the small trees grow tall.
I wither up the green trees
  and make the dry trees become green.
I, the LORD, have spoken. I will do what I have said I would do."

Individual Responsibility

18 The LORD spoke to me 2 and said, "What is this proverb people keep repeating in the land of Israel?
  'The parents ate the sour grapes,
  But the children got the sour taste.'

3 "As surely as I am the living God," says the Sovereign LORD, "you will not repeat this proverb in Israel any more. 4 The life of every person belongs to me, the life of the parent as well as that of the child. The person who sins is the one who will die.

5 "Suppose there is a truly good man, righteous and honest. 6 He doesn't worship the idols of the Israelites or eat the sacrifices offered at forbidden shrines. He doesn't seduce another man's wife or have intercourse with a woman during her period. 7 He doesn't cheat or rob anyone. He returns what a borrower gives him as security; he feeds the hungry and gives clothing to the naked. 8 He doesn't lend money for profit. He refuses to do evil and gives an honest decision in any dispute. 9 Such a man obeys my commands and carefully keeps my laws. He is righteous, and he will live," says the Sovereign LORD.

10 "Then suppose this man has a son who robs and kills, who does any* of these things 11 that the father never did. He eats sacrifices offered at forbidden shrines and seduces other men's wives. 12 He cheats the poor, he robs, he keeps what a borrower gives him as security. He goes to pagan shrines, worships disgusting idols, 13 and lends money for profit. Will he live? No, he will not. He has done all these disgusting things, and so he will die. He will be to blame for his own death.

14 "Now suppose this second man has a son. He sees all the sins his father practised, but does not follow his example. 15 He doesn't worship the idols of the Israelites or eat the sacrifices offered at forbidden shrines. He doesn't seduce another man's wife 16 or oppress anyone or rob anyone. He returns what a borrower gives him as security. He feeds the hungry and gives clothing to the naked. 17 He refuses to do evil* and doesn't lend money for profit. He keeps my laws and obeys my commands. He will not die because of his father's sins, but he will certainly live. 18 His father, on the other hand, cheated and robbed,* and always did evil to everyone. And so he died because of the sins he himself had committed.

19 "But you ask, 'Why shouldn't the son suffer because of his father's sins?' The answer is that the son did what was right and good. He kept my laws and followed them carefully, and so he

....

18.10 Some ancient translations *who does any*; Hebrew unclear.
18.17 Some ancient translations (see also verse 8) *to do evil*; Hebrew *from the poor.*
18.18 Some ancient translations *robbed*; Hebrew unclear.

984

Ezekiel

.·:········

Eccles.
Songs
Isaiah
Jerem.
Lamen.

EZEKIEL 18, 19

will certainly live. [20] It is the one who sins who will die. A son is not to suffer because of his father's sins, nor a father because of the sins of his son. A good person will be rewarded for doing good, and an evil person will suffer for the evil he does.

[21] "If an evil person stops sinning and keeps my laws, if he does what is right and good, he will not die; he will certainly live. [22] All his sins will be forgiven, and he will live, because he did what is right. [23] Do you think I enjoy seeing an evil person die?" asks the Sovereign LORD. "No, I would rather see him repent and live.

[24] "But if a righteous person stops doing good and starts doing all the evil, disgusting things that evil people do, will he go on living? No! None of the good he did will be remembered. He will die because of his unfaithfulness and his sins.

[25] "But you say, 'What the Lord does isn't right.' Listen to me, you Israelites. Do you think my way of doing things isn't right? It is your way that isn't right. [26] When a righteous person stops doing good and starts doing evil and then dies, he dies because of the evil he has done. [27] When someone evil stops sinning and does what is right and good, he saves his life. [28] He realizes what he is doing and stops sinning, so he will certainly not die, but go on living. [29] And you Israelites say, 'What the Lord does isn't right.' You think my way isn't right, do you? It is your way that isn't right.

[30] "Now I, the Sovereign LORD, am telling you Israelites that I will judge each of you by what you have done. Turn away from all the evil you are doing, and don't let your sin destroy you. [31] Give up all the evil you have been doing, and get yourselves new minds and hearts. Why do you Israelites want to die? [32] I do not want anyone to die," says the Sovereign LORD. "Turn away from your sins and live."

A Song of Sorrow

19 The LORD told me to sing this song of sorrow for two princes of Israel:

[2] What a lioness your mother was!
　　She reared her cubs among the fierce male lions.
[3] She reared a cub and taught him to hunt;
　　　he learnt to eat people.
[4] The nations heard about him
　　　and trapped him in a pit.
　　With hooks they dragged him off to Egypt.
[5] She waited until she saw all hope was gone.
　　Then she reared another of her cubs,
　　　and he grew into a fierce lion.
[6] When he was full-grown,
　　　he prowled with the other lions.
　　He too learnt to hunt and eat people.
[7] He wrecked forts,* he ruined towns.
　　The people of the land were terrified
　　　every time he roared.
[8] The nations gathered to fight him;
　　　people came from everywhere.
　　They spread their hunting nets
　　　and caught him in their trap.
[9] They put him in a cage
　　　and took him to the king of Babylonia.
　　They kept him under guard,
　　　so that his roar would never be heard again
　　　on the hills of Israel.

─────────────────────────────

19.7 One ancient translation *wrecked forts*; Hebrew unclear.

EZEKIEL 19, 20

985

Ezekiel
....
Daniel
Hosea
Joel
Amos
Obadiah

10 Your mother was like a grapevine*
    planted near a stream.
Because there was plenty of water,
    the vine was covered with leaves and fruit.
11 Its branches were strong,
    and grew to be royal sceptres.
The vine grew tall enough to reach the clouds;
    everyone saw how leafy and tall it was.
12 But angry hands pulled it up by the roots
    and threw it to the ground.
The east wind dried up its fruit.
Its branches were broken off;
    they dried up and were burnt.
13 Now it is planted in the desert,
    in a dry and waterless land.
14 The stem of the vine caught fire;
    fire burnt up its branches and fruit.
The branches will never again be strong,
    will never be royal sceptres.
This is a song of sorrow; it has been sung again and again.

The LORD's Will and Human Defiance

20 It was the tenth day of the fifth month of the seventh year of our exile. Some of the leaders of the Israelite community came to consult me about the LORD's will, and they sat down in front of me. 2 Then the LORD spoke to me. 3 "Mortal man," he said, "speak to these leaders and tell them that the Sovereign LORD is saying: you have come to ask my will, have you? As surely as I am the living God, I will not let you ask me anything. I, the Sovereign LORD, have spoken.

4 "Are you ready to pass sentence on them, mortal man? Then do so. Remind them of the disgusting things their ancestors did. 5 Tell them what I am saying. When I chose Israel, I made them a promise. I revealed myself to them in Egypt and told them: I am the LORD your God. 6 It was then that I promised to take them out of Egypt and lead them to a land I had chosen for them, a rich and fertile land, the finest land of all. 7 I told them to throw away the disgusting idols they loved and not to make themselves unclean with the false gods of Egypt, because I am the LORD their God. 8 But they defied me and refused to listen. They did not throw away their disgusting idols or give up the Egyptian gods. I was ready to let them feel the full force of my anger there in Egypt. 9 But I did not, since that would have brought dishonour to my name, for in the presence of the people among whom they were living I had announced to Israel that I was going to lead them out of Egypt.

10 "And so I led them out of Egypt into the desert. 11 I gave them my commands and taught them my laws, which bring life to anyone who obeys them. 12 I made the keeping of the Sabbath a sign of the agreement between us, to remind them that I, the LORD, make them holy. 13 But even in the desert they defied me. They broke my laws and rejected my commands, which bring life to anyone who obeys them. They completely profaned the Sabbath. I was ready to let them feel the force of my anger there in the desert and destroy them. 14 But I did not, since that would have brought dishonour to my name among the nations which had seen me lead Israel out of Egypt. 15 So I made a promise in the desert that I would not take them to the land I had given them,

19.10 Hebrew has an additional word, the meaning of which is unclear.

EZEKIEL 20.5-29

In Ezekiel 20, God recounts the story of Israel's past to

- REMIND -

THEM

who he was and is. On this page, write down the main points of what has happened in the story of God from Genesis 1 to here. You could include creation to start with...

986

Ezekiel
·········
Eccles.
Songs
Isaiah
Jerem.
Lamen.

EZEKIEL 20

a rich and fertile land, the finest land of all. ¹⁶ I made the promise because they had rejected my commands, broken my laws, and profaned the Sabbath — they preferred to worship their idols.

¹⁷"But then I took pity on them. I decided not to kill them there in the desert. ¹⁸ Instead, I warned the young people among them: do not keep the laws your ancestors made; do not follow their customs or defile yourselves with their idols. ¹⁹ I am the LORD your God. Obey my laws and my commands. ²⁰ Make the Sabbath a holy day, so that it will be a sign of the covenant we made, and will remind you that I am the LORD your God.

²¹"But that generation also defied me. They broke my laws and did not keep my commands, which bring life to anyone who obeys them. They profaned the Sabbath. I was ready to let them feel the force of my anger there in the desert and kill them all. ²² But I did not, since that would have brought dishonour to my name among the nations which had seen me bring Israel out of Egypt. ²³ So I made another promise in the desert. I vowed that I would scatter them all over the world. ²⁴ I did this because they had rejected my commands, broken my laws, profaned the Sabbath, and worshipped the same idols their ancestors had served.

²⁵"Then I gave them laws that are not good and commands that do not bring life. ²⁶ I let them defile themselves with their own offerings, and I let them sacrifice their firstborn sons. This was to punish them and show them that I am the LORD.

²⁷"Now then, mortal man, tell the Israelites what I, the Sovereign LORD, am saying to them. This is another way their ancestors insulted me by their unfaithfulness. ²⁸ I brought them to the land I had promised to give them. When they saw the high hills and green trees, they offered sacrifices at all of them. They made me angry by the sacrifices they burnt and by the wine they brought as offerings. ²⁹ I asked them: what are these high places where you go? So they have been called 'High Places'* ever since. ³⁰ Now tell the Israelites what I, the Sovereign LORD, am saying: why must you commit the same sins your ancestors did and go running after their idols? ³¹ Even today you offer the same gifts and defile yourselves with the same idols by sacrificing your children to them in the fire. And then you Israelites still come to ask what my will is! As surely as I, the Sovereign LORD, am the living God, I will not let you ask me anything. ³² You have made up your minds that you want to be like the other nations, like the people who live in other countries and worship trees and rocks. But that will never be.

God Punishes and Forgives

³³"As surely as I, the Sovereign LORD, am the living God, I warn you that in my anger I will rule over you with a strong hand, with all my power. ³⁴ I will show you my power and my anger when I gather you together and bring you back from all the countries where you have been scattered. ³⁵ I will bring you into the 'Desert of the Nations', and there I will condemn you to your face. ³⁶ I will now condemn you just as I condemned your ancestors in the Sinai Desert," says the Sovereign LORD.

³⁷"I will take firm control of you and make you obey my covenant. ³⁸ I will take away from among you those who are rebellious and sinful. I will take them out of the lands where they

20.29 *high places:* Pagan places of worship which the Hebrews were forbidden to use. The Hebrew word translated "High Places" sounds like the Hebrew for "where you go".

Ezekiel

..........:.

Daniel
Hosea
Joel
Amos
Obadiah

are living now, but I will not let them return to the land of Israel. Then you will know that I am the LORD."

39 The Sovereign LORD said, "And now, all you Israelites, please yourselves! Go on and serve your idols! But I warn you that after this you will have to obey me and stop dishonouring my holy name by offering gifts to your idols. 40 There in the land, on my holy mountain,* the high mountain of Israel, all you people of Israel will worship me. I will be pleased with you and will expect you to bring me your sacrifices, your best offerings, and your holy gifts. 41 After I bring you out of the countries where you have been scattered and gather you together, I will accept the sacrifices that you burn, and the nations will see that I am holy. 42 When I bring you back to Israel, the land that I promised I would give to your ancestors, then you will know that I am the LORD. 43 Then you will remember all the disgraceful things you did and how you defiled yourselves. You will be disgusted with yourselves because of all the evil things you did. 44 When I act to protect my honour, you Israelites will know that I am the LORD, because I do not deal with you as your wicked, evil actions deserve." The Sovereign LORD has spoken.

Fire in the South

45 The LORD spoke to me. 46 "Mortal man," he said, "look towards the south. Speak against the south and prophesy against the forest of the south. 47 Tell the southern forest to hear what the Sovereign LORD is saying: look! I am starting a fire, and it will burn up every tree in you, whether green or dry. Nothing will be able to put it out. It will spread from south to north, and everyone will feel the heat of the flames. 48 They will all see that I, the LORD, set it on fire and that no one can put it out."

49 But I protested, "Sovereign LORD, don't make me do it! Everyone is already complaining that I always speak in riddles."

The LORD's Sword

21 The LORD spoke to me. 2 "Mortal man," he said, "denounce Jerusalem. Denounce the places where people worship. Warn the land of Israel 3 that I, the LORD, am saying: I am your enemy. I will draw my sword and kill all of you, good and evil alike. 4 I will use my sword against everyone from south to north. 5 Everyone will know that I, the LORD, have drawn my sword and that I will not put it away.

6 "Mortal man, groan as if your heart is breaking with despair. Groan in sorrow where everyone can watch you. 7 When they ask you why you are groaning, tell them it is because of the news that is coming. When it comes, their hearts will be filled with fear, their hands will hang limp, their courage will fail, and their knees will tremble. The time has come; it is here." The Sovereign LORD has spoken.

8 The LORD said to me, 9 "Mortal man, prophesy. Tell the people what I, the Lord, am saying:

A sword, a sword is sharpened and polished.
10 It is sharpened to kill,
    polished to flash like lightning.
There can be no rejoicing,
    for my people have disregarded every warning and
        punishment.*

....

20.40 *holy mountain*: Mount Zion, the hill in Jerusalem which formed part of the Temple and palace area.
21.10 Probable text *There... punishment*; Hebrew unclear.

988

Ezekiel

Eccles.
Songs
Isaiah
Jerem.
Lamen.

EZEKIEL 21

11 The sword is being polished,
  to make it ready for use.
It is sharpened and polished,
  to be put in the hands of a killer.
12 Howl in grief, mortal man;
  this sword is meant for my people
  and for all the leaders of Israel.
They are going to be killed
  with all the rest of my people.
Beat your breast in despair!
13 I am testing my people,
  and if they refuse to repent,
  all these things will happen to them.*

14 "Now, mortal man, prophesy. Clap your hands, and the sword will strike again and again. It is a sword that kills, a sword that terrifies* and slaughters. 15 It makes my people lose courage and stumble. I am threatening their city with a sword* that flashes like lightning and is ready to kill. 16 Cut to the right and the left, you sharp sword! Cut wherever you turn.* 17 I also will clap my hands, and my anger will be over. I, the LORD, have spoken."

The Sword of the King of Babylonia

18 The LORD spoke to me. 19 "Mortal man," he said, "mark out two roads by which the king of Babylonia can come with his sword. Both of them are to start in the same country. Put up a signpost where the roads fork.* 20 One arm will show the king the way to the Ammonite city of Rabbah, and the other the way to Judah, to the fortified city, Jerusalem. 21 The king of Babylonia stands by the signpost at the fork of the road. To discover which way to go, he shakes the arrows;* he consults his idols; he examines the liver of a sacrificed animal. 22 Now! His right hand holds the arrow marked 'Jerusalem'! It tells him to go and set up battering rams, to shout the battle cry, to place battering rams against the gates, to throw up earthworks, and to dig trenches. 23 The people of Jerusalem won't believe this, because of the treaties they have made. But this prediction is to remind them of their sins and to warn them that they will be captured. 24 This then is what I, the Sovereign LORD, am saying: your sins are exposed. Everyone knows how guilty you are. You show your sins in your every action. You stand condemned, and I will hand you over to your enemies.

25 "You wicked, unholy ruler of Israel, your day, the day of your final punishment, is coming. 26 I, the Sovereign LORD, have spoken. Take off your crown and your turban. Nothing will be the same again. Raise the poor to power! Bring down those who are ruling! 27 Ruin, ruin! Yes, I will make the city a ruin. But this will not happen until the one whom I have chosen to punish the city has come. Then I will give it to him.

A Sword and the Ammonites

28 "Mortal man, prophesy. Announce what I, the Sovereign LORD, am saying to the Ammonites, who are insulting Israel. Say to them:

TURN THESE
LINES INTO A
PICTURE OF
SOMETHING.

21.13 Verse 13 in Hebrew is unclear.
21.14 Some ancient translations *terrifies*; Hebrew unclear.
21.15 Probable text *threatening… sword*; Hebrew unclear.
21.16 Verse 16 in Hebrew is unclear.
21.19 Probable text *Put… fork*; Hebrew unclear.
21.21 *shakes the arrows*: When faced with a decision, people in ancient times would sometimes take a handful of arrows, throw them down, and study the pattern in which they fell, in order to learn what to do.

Ezekiel
....
Daniel
Hosea
Joel
Amos
Obadiah

'A sword is ready to destroy;
    It is polished to kill, to flash like lightning.
29 The visions that you see are false, and the predictions you make are lies. You are wicked and evil, and your day is coming, the day of your final punishment. The sword is going to fall on your necks.

30 " 'Put up the sword! I will judge you in the place where you were created, in the land where you were born. 31 You will feel my anger when I turn it loose on you like a blazing fire. And I will hand you over to brutal men, experts at destruction. 32 You will be destroyed by fire. Your blood will be shed in your own country, and no one will remember you any more.' " The LORD has spoken.

The Crimes of Jerusalem

22 The LORD spoke to me. 2 "Mortal man," he said, "are you ready to judge the city that is full of murderers? Make clear to her all the disgusting things she has done. 3 Tell the city what I, the Sovereign LORD, am saying: because you have murdered so many of your own people and have defiled yourself by worshipping idols, your time is coming. 4 You are guilty of those murders and are defiled by the idols you made, and so your day is coming, your time is up! That is why I have let the nations mock you and all the countries sneer at you. 5 Countries near by and countries far away sneer at you because of your lawlessness. 6 All Israel's leaders trust in their own strength and commit murder. 7 You people in the city do not honour your parents. You cheat foreigners and take advantage of widows and orphans. 8 You have no respect for the holy places, and you don't keep the Sabbath. 9 Some of your people tell lies about others in order to have them put to death. Some of them eat sacrifices offered to idols. Some are always satisfying their lusts. 10 Some of them sleep with their father's wife. Some force women to have intercourse with them during their period. 11 Some commit adultery, and others seduce their daughters-in-law or their half-sisters. 12 Some of your people murder for pay. Some charge interest on the loans they make to their fellow-Israelites and get rich by taking advantage of them. They have forgotten me." The Sovereign LORD has spoken.

13 "I will bring my fist down on your robberies and murders. 14 Do you think you will have any courage left or have strength enough to lift your hand when I am finished with you? I, the LORD, have spoken, and I keep my word. 15 I will scatter your people to every country and nation and will put an end to your evil actions. 16 And so the other nations will dishonour you, but you will know that I am the LORD."

God's Refining Furnace

17 The LORD said to me, 18 "Mortal man, the Israelites are of no use to me. They are like the waste metal — copper, tin, iron, and lead — left over after silver has been refined in a furnace. 19 So now I, the Sovereign LORD, am telling them that they are just as useless as that. I will bring them all together in Jerusalem 20 in the same way that the ore of silver, copper, iron, lead, and tin is put in a refining furnace. My anger and rage will melt them just as fire melts ore. 21 Yes, I will gather them in Jerusalem, build a fire under them, and melt them with my anger. 22 They will be melted in Jerusalem just as silver is melted in a furnace, and then they will know that they are feeling the anger of the LORD."

The Sins of Israel's Leaders

23 The LORD spoke to me again. 24 "Mortal man," he said, "tell the Israelites that their land is unholy, and so I am punishing it in my

990

Ezekiel

⋮ ⋯⋯⋯

Eccles.
Songs
Isaiah
Jerem.
Lamen.

EZEKIEL 22, 23

anger. [25] The leaders* are like lions roaring over the animals they have killed. They kill the people, take all the money and property they can get, and by their murders leave many widows. [26] The priests break my law and have no respect for what is holy. They make no distinction between what is holy and what is not. They do not teach the difference between clean and unclean things, and they ignore the Sabbath. As a result the people of Israel do not respect me. [27] The government officials are like wolves tearing apart the animals they have killed. They commit murder in order to get rich. [28] The prophets have hidden these sins like those covering a wall with whitewash. They see false visions and make false predictions. They claim to speak the word of the Sovereign Lord, but I, the Lord, have not spoken to them. [29] The wealthy cheat and rob. They ill-treat the poor and take advantage of foreigners. [30] I looked for someone who could build a wall, who could stand in the places where the walls have crumbled and defend the land when my anger is about to destroy it, but I could find no one. [31] So I will turn my anger loose on them, and like a fire I will destroy them for what they have done." The Sovereign Lord has spoken.

The Sinful Sisters

23 The Lord spoke to me. [2] "Mortal man," he said, "there were once two sisters. [3] When they were young, living in Egypt, they lost their virginity and became prostitutes. [4] The older one was named Oholah* (she represents Samaria), and the younger one was named Oholibah* (she represents Jerusalem). I married both of them, and they bore me children. [5] Although she was mine, Oholah continued to be a prostitute and was full of lust for her lovers from Assyria. [6] They were soldiers in uniforms of purple, noblemen and high-ranking officers; all of them were handsome young cavalry officers. [7] She was the whore for all the Assyrian officers, and her lust led her to defile herself by worshipping Assyrian idols. [8] She continued what she had begun as a prostitute in Egypt, where she lost her virginity. From the time she was a young woman, men slept with her and treated her like a prostitute. [9] So I handed her over to her Assyrian lovers whom she wanted so much. [10] They stripped her naked, seized her sons and daughters, and then killed her with a sword. Women everywhere gossiped about her fate.

[11] "Even though her sister Oholibah saw this, she was wilder and more of a prostitute than Oholah had ever been. [12] She too was full of lust for the Assyrian noblemen and officers — soldiers in bright uniforms — and for the cavalry officers, all those handsome young men. [13] I saw that she was completely immoral, that the second sister was as bad as the first.

[14-15] "She sank deeper and deeper in her immorality. She was attracted by the images of high Babylonian officials carved into the wall and painted bright red, with sashes round their waists and fancy turbans on their heads. [16] As soon as she saw them, she was filled with lust and sent messengers to them in Babylonia. [17] The Babylonians came to have sex with her. They used her and defiled her so much that finally she became disgusted with them. [18] She exposed herself publicly and let everyone know she was a whore. I was as disgusted with her as I had been with her sister.

. . . .

22.25 One ancient translation *The leaders*; Hebrew *A conspiracy of her prophets*.
23.4 *Oholah*: This name in Hebrew means "her sanctuary".
23.4 *Oholibah*: This name in Hebrew means "my sanctuary is in her".

EZEKIEL 23

991

Ezekiel
....
Daniel
Hosea
Joel
Amos
Obadiah

[19] She became more of a prostitute than ever, acting just as she did as a young woman, when she was a prostitute in Egypt. [20] She was filled with lust for oversexed men who had all the lustfulness of donkeys or stallions." [21] (Oholibah, you wanted to repeat the immorality you were guilty of as a young woman in Egypt, where men played with your breasts and you lost your virginity.)

God's Judgement on the Younger Sister

[22] "Now then, Oholibah, this is what I, the Sovereign Lord, am saying to you. You are tired of those lovers, but I will make them angry with you and bring them to surround you. [23] I will bring all the Babylonians and Chaldeans, men from Pekod, Shoa, and Koa, and all the Assyrians. I will gather all those handsome young noblemen and officers, all those important officials and high-ranking cavalry officers. [24] They will attack you from the north,* bringing a large army with chariots and supply wagons. Protected by shields and helmets, they will surround you. I will hand you over to them, and they will judge you by their own laws. [25] Because I am angry with you, I will let them deal with you in their anger. They will cut off your nose and your ears and kill your children. Yes, they will take your sons and daughters from you and burn them alive. [26] They will tear off your clothes and take your jewels. [27] I will put a stop to your lust and to the obscenities you have committed ever since you were in Egypt. You won't look at any more idols or think about Egypt any more."

[28] This is what the Sovereign Lord says: "I will hand you over to people you hate and are disgusted with. [29] And because they hate you, they will take away everything you have worked for and leave you stripped naked, exposed like a prostitute. Your lust and your prostitution [30] have brought this on you. You were a prostitute for the nations and defiled yourself with their idols. [31] You followed in your sister's footsteps, and so I will give you the same cup of punishment to drink."

[32] The Sovereign Lord says,
"You will drink from your sister's cup;
    it is large and deep.
Everyone will scorn and mock you;
    the cup is full.
[33] It will make you miserable and drunk,
    that cup of fear and ruin,
    your sister Samaria's cup.
[34] You will drink and drain it dry,
    and with its broken pieces
    tear your breast.
I, the Sovereign Lord, have spoken."

[35] Now this is what the Sovereign Lord is saying: "Because you forgot me and turned your back on me, you will suffer for your lust and your prostitution."

God's Judgement on Both Sisters

[36] The Lord said to me, "Mortal man, are you ready to judge Oholah and Oholibah? Accuse them of the disgusting things they have done. [37] They have committed adultery and murder — adultery with idols and murder of the children they bore me. They sacrificed my children to their idols. [38] And that is not all they did. They profaned my Temple and broke the Sabbath, which

....

23.24 One ancient translation *north*; Hebrew unclear.

992

Ezekiel

Eccles.
Songs
Isaiah
Jerem.
Lamen.

EZEKIEL 23, 24

I had established. ³⁹The very day that they killed my children as sacrifices to idols, they came to my Temple and profaned it!

⁴⁰"Again and again they sent messengers to invite men to come from a great distance, and the men came. The two sisters would bathe and put on eye shadow and jewellery. ⁴¹They would sit on a beautiful couch, and in front of them they would have a table covered with good things, including the incense and the olive oil that I had given them. ⁴²The sound of a carefree crowd could be heard, a group of men brought in from the desert. They put bracelets on the women's arms and beautiful crowns on their heads. ⁴³And I said to myself that they were using as a prostitute a woman worn out by adultery.* ⁴⁴They went back to these prostitutes again and again. They went back to Oholah and Oholibah, those immoral women. ⁴⁵Righteous men will condemn them on the charge of adultery and murder, because they practise adultery and their hands are stained with blood."

⁴⁶This is what the Sovereign Lord says: "Bring a mob to terrorize them and rob them. ⁴⁷Let the mob stone them and attack them with swords, kill their children, and burn down their houses. ⁴⁸Throughout the land I will put a stop to immorality, as a warning to every woman not to commit adultery as they did. ⁴⁹And you two sisters — I will punish you for your immorality and your sin of worshipping idols. Then you will know that I am the Sovereign Lord."

The Corroded Cooking Pot

24 On the tenth day of the tenth month of the ninth year of our exile, the Lord spoke to me. ²"Mortal man," he said, "write down today's date, because this is the day that the king of Babylonia is beginning the siege of Jerusalem. ³Tell my rebellious people this parable that I, the Sovereign Lord, have for them:

> Set the pot on the fire
> and fill it up with water.
> ⁴ Put in the best pieces of meat —
>   the shoulders and the legs —
>   fill it with choice bony pieces too.
> ⁵ Use the meat of the finest sheep;
>   pile the wood* under the pot.
> Let the water boil;
>   boil the bones and the meat."

⁶This is what the Sovereign Lord is saying: "The city of murderers is doomed! It is like a corroded pot that is never cleaned. Piece after piece of meat is taken out, and not one is left. ⁷There was murder in the city, but the blood was not spilt on the ground where the dust could hide it; it was spilt on a bare rock. ⁸I have left the blood there, where it cannot be hidden, where it demands angry revenge."

⁹This is what the Sovereign Lord is saying: "The city of murderers is doomed! I myself will pile up the firewood. ¹⁰Bring more wood! Fan the flames! Cook the meat! Boil away the broth!* Burn up the bones! ¹¹Now set the empty bronze pot on the coals and let it get red-hot. Then the pot will be ritually pure again after the corrosion is burnt off, ¹²although all that corrosion will not disappear in the flames.* ¹³Jerusalem, your immoral actions have defiled you.

EZEKIEL 24.1-14

God asked Ezekiel to write down the day's date to mark what he was about to say and do.

On a separate piece of paper, notepad or journal, write down

TODAY'S
DATE

and, at the end of the day, write down anything that God has spoken to you about or done.

23.43 Verses 42–43 in Hebrew are unclear.
24.5 Probable text *wood*; Hebrew *bones*.
24.10 Some ancient translations *Boil away the broth!*; Hebrew unclear.
24.12 Verse 12 in Hebrew begins with two words, the meaning of which is unclear.

EZEKIEL 24, 25

993

Ezekiel

Daniel
Hosea
Joel
Amos
Obadiah

Although I tried to purify you, you remained defiled. You will not be pure again until you have felt the full force of my anger. [14] I, the Sovereign LORD, have spoken. The time has come for me to act. I will not ignore your sins or show pity or be merciful. You will be punished for what you have done." The Sovereign LORD has spoken.

The Death of the Prophet's Wife

[15] The LORD spoke to me. [16] "Mortal man," he said, "with one blow I am going to take away the person you love most. You are not to complain or cry or shed any tears. [17] Don't let your sobbing be heard. Do not go bareheaded or barefoot as a sign of mourning. Don't cover your face or eat the food that mourners eat."

[18] Early in the day I was talking with the people. That evening my wife died, and the next day I did as I had been told. [19] The people asked me, "Why are you acting like this?"

[20] So I said to them, "The LORD spoke to me and told me [21] to give you Israelites this message: you are proud of the strength of the Temple. You like to look at it and to visit it, but the LORD is going to profane it. And the younger members of your families who are left in Jerusalem will be killed in war. [22] Then you will do what I have done. You will not cover your faces or eat the food that mourners eat. [23] You will not go bareheaded or barefoot or mourn or cry. You will waste away because of your sins, and you will groan to one another. [24] Then I will be a sign to you; you will do everything I have done. The LORD says that when this happens, you will know that he is the Sovereign LORD."

[25] The LORD said, "Now, mortal man, I will take away from them the strong Temple that was their pride and joy, which they liked to look at and to visit. And I will take away their sons and daughters. [26] On the day that I do this, someone who escapes the destruction will come and tell you about it. [27] That same day you will get back the power of speech which you had lost, and you will talk with him. In this way you will be a sign to the people, and they will know that I am the LORD."

Prophecy against Ammon

25 The LORD spoke to me. [2] "Mortal man," he said, "denounce the country of Ammon. [3] Tell them to listen to what I, the Sovereign LORD, am saying: you were delighted to see my Temple profaned, to see the land of Israel devastated, to see the people of Judah go into exile. [4] Because you were glad, I will let the tribes from the eastern desert conquer you. They will set up their camps in your country and settle there. They will eat the fruit and drink the milk that should have been yours. [5] I will turn the city of Rabbah into a place to keep camels, and the whole country of Ammon into a place to keep sheep, so that you will know that I am the LORD.

[6] "This is what the Sovereign LORD is saying: you clapped your hands and jumped for joy. You despised the land of Israel. [7] Because you did, I will hand you over to other nations who will rob you and plunder you. I will destroy you so completely that you will not be a nation any more or have a country of your own. Then you will know that I am the LORD."

Prophecy against Moab

[8] The Sovereign LORD said, "Because Moab* has said that Judah is like all the other nations, [9] I will let the cities that defend the

25.8 Some ancient translations *Moab*; Hebrew *Moab and Seir*.

994

Ezekiel

: ˙˙˙˙˙˙˙˙

Eccles.
Songs
Isaiah
Jerem.
Lamen.

EZEKIEL 25, 26

border of Moab be attacked, including even the finest cities — Beth Jeshimoth, Baal Meon, and Kiriathaim. [10] I will let the tribes of the eastern desert conquer Moab, together with Ammon, so that Moab* will no longer be a nation. [11] I will punish Moab, and they will know that I am the LORD."

Prophecy against Edom

[12] The Sovereign LORD said, "The people of Edom took cruel revenge on Judah, and that revenge has brought lasting guilt on Edom. [13] Now I announce that I will punish Edom and kill every person and animal there. I will make it a waste, from the city of Teman to the city of Dedan, and the people will be killed in battle. [14] My people Israel will take revenge on Edom for me, and they will make Edom feel my furious anger. Edom will know what it means to be the object of my revenge." The Sovereign LORD has spoken.

Prophecy against Philistia

[15] The Sovereign LORD said, "The Philistines have taken cruel revenge on their age-long enemies and destroyed them in their hate. [16] And so I am announcing that I will attack the Philistines and wipe them out. I will destroy everyone left living there on the Philistine Plain. [17] I will punish them severely and take full revenge on them. They will feel my anger. Then they will know that I am the LORD."

Prophecy against Tyre

26 On the first day of the... month* of the eleventh year of our exile, the LORD spoke to me. [2] "Mortal man," he said, "this is what the people in the city of Tyre are cheering about. They shout, 'Jerusalem is shattered! Her commercial power is gone! She won't be our rival any more!'

[3] "Now then, this is what I, the Sovereign LORD, am saying: I am your enemy, city of Tyre. I will bring many nations to attack you, and they will come like the waves of the sea. [4] They will destroy your city walls and tear down your towers. Then I will sweep away all the dust and leave only a bare rock. [5] Fishermen will dry their nets on it, there where it stands in the sea. I, the Sovereign LORD, have spoken. The nations will plunder Tyre, [6] and with their swords they will kill those who live in her towns on the mainland. Then Tyre will know that I am the LORD."

[7] The Sovereign LORD says, "I am going to bring the greatest king of all — King Nebuchadnezzar of Babylonia — to attack Tyre. He will come from the north with a huge army, with horses and chariots and with cavalry. [8] Those who live in the towns on the mainland will be killed in the fighting. The enemy will dig trenches, build earthworks, and make a solid wall of shields against you. [9] They will pound in your walls with battering rams and tear down your towers with iron bars. [10] The clouds of dust raised by their horses will cover you. The noise of their horses pulling wagons and chariots will shake your walls as they pass through the gates of the ruined city. [11] Their horsemen will storm through your streets, killing your people with their swords. Your mighty pillars will be thrown to the ground. [12] Your enemies will help themselves to your wealth and merchandise. They will pull down your walls and shatter your luxurious houses. They will take

Ezekiel

Daniel
Hosea
Joel
Amos
Obadiah

the stones and wood and all the rubble, and dump them into the sea. ¹³ I will put an end to all your songs, and I will silence the music of your harps. ¹⁴ I will leave only a bare rock where fishermen can dry their nets. The city will never be rebuilt. I, the Sovereign LORD, have spoken."

¹⁵ The Sovereign LORD has this to say to the city of Tyre: "When you are being conquered, the people who live along the coast will be terrified at the screams of those who are slaughtered. ¹⁶ All the kings of the seafaring nations will come down from their thrones. They will take off their robes and their embroidered clothes and sit trembling on the ground. They will be so terrified at your fate that they will not be able to stop trembling. ¹⁷ They will sing this funeral song for you:

The famous city is destroyed!
Her ships have been swept* from the seas.
The people of this city ruled the seas
And terrified all who lived on the coast.
¹⁸ Now, on the day it has fallen,
The islands are trembling,
And their people are shocked at such destruction."

¹⁹ The Sovereign LORD says: "I will make you as desolate as ruined cities where no one lives. I will cover you with the water of the ocean depths. ²⁰ I will send you down to the world of the dead to join the people who lived in ancient times. I will make you stay in that underground world among eternal ruins, keeping company with the dead. As a result you will never again be inhabited and take your place* in the land of the living. ²¹ I will make you a terrifying example, and that will be the end of you. People may look for you, but you will never be found." The Sovereign LORD has spoken.

A Funeral Song for Tyre

27 The LORD said to me, ²"Mortal man, sing a funeral song for Tyre, ³ that city which stands at the edge of the sea and does business with the people living on every seacoast. Tell her what the Sovereign LORD is saying:

"Tyre, you boasted of your perfect beauty.
⁴ Your home is the sea.
Your builders made you like a beautiful ship;
⁵ They used fir trees from Mount Hermon for timber
And a cedar from Lebanon for your mast.
⁶ They took oak trees from Bashan to make oars;
They made your deck out of pine from Cyprus
And inlaid it with ivory.
⁷ Your sails were made of linen,
Embroidered linen from Egypt,
Easily recognized from afar.
Your awnings were made of finest cloth,
Of purple from the island of Cyprus.
⁸ Your oarsmen were from the cities of Sidon and Arvad.
Your own skilful men were the sailors.
⁹ The ship's carpenters
Were well-trained men from Byblos.
Sailors from every seagoing ship
Did business in your shops.
¹⁰ "Soldiers from Persia, Lydia, and Libya served in your army. They hung their shields and their helmets in your barracks.

FILL THIS SPACE HOWEVER YOU LIKE...

26.17 Some ancient translations *swept*; Hebrew *inhabited*.
26.20 One ancient translation *and take your place*; Hebrew unclear.

996

Ezekiel

:·········

Eccles.
Songs
Isaiah
Jerem.
Lamen.

EZEKIEL 27

They are the men who won glory for you. [11]Soldiers from Arvad guarded your walls, and men from Gamad guarded your towers. They hung their shields on your walls. They are the men who made you beautiful.

[12]"You did business in Spain and took silver, iron, tin, and lead in payment for your abundant goods. [13]You did business in Greece, Tubal, and Meshech and traded your goods for slaves and for articles of bronze. [14]You sold your goods for draught horses, war horses, and mules from Beth Togarmah. [15]The people of Rhodes* traded with you; people of many coastal lands gave you ivory and ebony in exchange for your goods. [16]The people of Syria bought your merchandise and your many products. They gave emeralds, purple cloth, embroidery, fine linen, coral, and rubies in payment for your wares. [17]Judah and Israel paid for your goods with wheat,* honey, olive oil, and spices. [18-19]The people of Damascus bought your merchandise and your products, paying for them with wine from Helbon and wool from Sahar.* They exchanged wrought iron and spices for your goods. [20]The people of Dedan exchanged saddlecloths for your goods. [21]The Arabians and the rulers of the land of Kedar paid for your merchandise with lambs, sheep, and goats. [22]For your goods the merchants of Sheba and Raamah exchanged jewels, gold, and the finest spices. [23]The cities of Haran, Canneh, and Eden, the merchants of Sheba, the cities of Asshur and Chilmad — they all traded with you. [24]They sold you luxurious clothing, purple cloth, and embroidery, brightly coloured carpets, and well-made cords and ropes. [25]Your merchandise was carried in fleets of the largest cargo ships.

"You were like a ship at sea
Loaded with heavy cargo.
[26] When your oarsmen brought you out to sea,
An east wind wrecked you far from land.
[27] All your wealth of merchandise,
All the sailors in your crew,
Your ship's carpenters and your merchants,
Every soldier on board the ship —
All, all were lost at sea
When your ship was wrecked.
[28] The shouts of the drowning sailors
Echoed on the shore.

[29] "Every ship is now deserted,
And every sailor has gone ashore.
[30] They all mourn bitterly for you,
Throwing dust on their heads and rolling in ashes.
[31] They shave their heads for you
And dress themselves in sackcloth.
Their hearts are bitter as they weep.
[32] They chant a funeral song for you:
'Who can be compared to Tyre,
To Tyre now silent in the sea?
[33] When your merchandise went overseas,
You filled the needs of every nation.
Kings were made rich
By the wealth of your goods.

27.15 One ancient translation *Rhodes*; Hebrew *Dedan*.
27.17 Hebrew has two additional words, the meaning of which is unclear.
27.18–19 Hebrew has three additional words, the meaning of which is unclear.

EZEKIEL 27, 28

997

Ezekiel

Daniel
Hosea
Joel
Amos
Obadiah

34 Now you are wrecked in the sea;
  You have sunk to the ocean depths.
  Your goods and all who worked for you
  Have vanished with you in the sea.'
35 "Everyone who lives along the coast is shocked at your fate.
Even their kings are terrified, and fear is written on their faces.
36 You are gone, gone for ever, and merchants all over the world
are terrified, afraid that they will share your fate."

Prophecy against the King of Tyre

28 The LORD spoke to me. 2 "Mortal man," he said, "tell the
ruler of Tyre what I, the Sovereign LORD, am saying to
him: puffed up with pride, you claim to be a god. You say that
like a god you sit on a throne, surrounded by the seas. You may
pretend to be a god, but, no, you are mortal, not divine. 3 You
think you are wiser than Danel,* that no secret can be kept from
you. 4 Your wisdom and skill made you rich with treasures of gold
and silver. 5 You made clever business deals and kept on making
profits. How proud you are of your wealth!

6 "Now then, this is what I, the Sovereign LORD, am saying:
because you think you are as wise as a god, 7 I will bring ruthless
enemies to attack you. They will destroy all the beautiful things
you have acquired by your skill and wisdom. 8 They will kill you
and send you to a watery grave. 9 When they come to kill you, will
you still claim that you are a god? When you face your murderers,
you will be mortal and not at all divine. 10 You will die like a dog
at the hand of godless foreigners. I, the Sovereign LORD, have
given the command."

The Fall of the King of Tyre

11 The LORD spoke to me again. 12 "Mortal man," he said, "grieve
for the fate that is waiting for the king of Tyre. Tell him what
I, the Sovereign LORD, am saying: you were once an example of
perfection. How wise and handsome you were! 13 You lived in
Eden, the garden of God, and wore gems of every kind: rubies and
diamonds; topaz, beryl, carnelian, and jasper; sapphires, emeralds,
and garnets. You had ornaments of gold. They were made for you*
on the day you were created. 14 I put a terrifying angel there to
guard you.* You lived on my holy mountain and walked among
sparkling gems. 15 Your conduct was perfect from the day you
were created until you began to do evil. 16 You were busy buying
and selling, and this led you to violence and sin. So I forced you to
leave my holy mountain, and the angel who guarded you drove
you away from the sparkling gems. 17 You were proud of being
handsome, and your fame made you act like a fool. Because of
this I hurled you to the ground and left you as a warning to other
kings. 18 You did such evil in buying and selling that your places
of worship were corrupted. So I set fire to the city and burnt it to
the ground. All who look at you now see you reduced to ashes.
19 You are gone, gone for ever, and all the nations that had come
to know you are terrified, afraid that they will share your fate."

Prophecy against Sidon

20 The LORD said to me, 21 "Mortal man, denounce the city of
Sidon. 22 Tell the people there what I, the Sovereign LORD, say about

28.3 *Danel*: or *Daniel* (see 14.14).
28.13 Probable text *They were made for you*; Hebrew unclear.
28.14 One ancient translation *I put… you*; Hebrew unclear.

998

Ezekiel

.:.........

Eccles.
Songs
Isaiah
Jerem.
Lamen.

EZEKIEL 28, 29

them: I am your enemy, Sidon; people will praise me because of what I do to you. They will know that I am the LORD, when I show how holy I am by punishing those who live in you. [23] I will send diseases on you and make blood flow in your streets. You will be attacked from every side, and your people will be killed. Then you will know that I am the LORD."

Israel will be Blessed

[24] The LORD said, "None of the surrounding nations that treated Israel with scorn will ever again be like thorns and briars to hurt Israel. And they will know that I am the Sovereign LORD."

[25] The Sovereign LORD said, "I will bring back the people of Israel from the nations where I scattered them, and all the nations will know that I am holy. The people of Israel will live in their own land, the land that I gave to my servant Jacob. [26] They will live there in safety. They will build houses and plant vineyards. I will punish all their neighbours who treated them with scorn, and Israel will be secure. Then they will know that I am the LORD their God."

Prophecy against Egypt

29 On the twelfth day of the tenth month of the tenth year of our exile, the LORD spoke to me. [2] "Mortal man," he said, "denounce the king of Egypt. Tell him how he and all the land of Egypt will be punished. [3] Say that this is what the Sovereign LORD is telling the king of Egypt: I am your enemy, you monster crocodile, lying in the river. You say that the Nile is yours and that you made it.* [4] I am going to put a hook through your jaw and make the fish in your river stick fast to you. Then I will pull you up out of the Nile, with all the fish sticking to you. [5] I will throw you and all those fish into the desert. Your body will fall on the ground and be left unburied. I will give it to the birds and animals for food. [6] Then all the people of Egypt will know that I am the LORD."

The LORD says, "The Israelites relied on you Egyptians for support, but you were no better than a weak stick. [7] When they leaned on you, you broke, pierced their armpits, and made them wrench their backs.* [8] Now then, I, the Sovereign LORD, am telling you that I will get troops to attack you with swords, and they will kill your people and your animals. [9] Egypt will become an empty waste. Then you will know that I am the LORD.

"Because you said that the Nile is yours and you made it, [10] I am your enemy and the enemy of your Nile. I will make all of Egypt an empty waste, from the city of Migdol in the north to the city of Aswan in the south, all the way to the Ethiopian border. [11] No human being or animal will walk through it. For forty years nothing will live there. [12] I will make Egypt the most desolate country in the world. For forty years the cities of Egypt will lie in ruins, ruins worse than those of any other city. I will make the Egyptians refugees. They will flee to every country and live among other peoples."

[13] The Sovereign LORD says, "After forty years I will bring the Egyptians back from the nations where I have scattered them, [14] and I will let them live in southern Egypt, their original home. There they will be a weak kingdom, [15] the weakest kingdom of all, and they will never again rule over other nations. I will make them so unimportant that they will not be able to bend any other

29.3 Some ancient translations *you made it*; Hebrew *you made yourself*.
29.7 One ancient translation *wrench their backs*; Hebrew *make their backs stand*.

EZEKIEL 29, 30

999

Ezekiel
.........·:·
Daniel
Hosea
Joel
Amos
Obadiah

nation to their will. [16] Israel will never again depend on them for help. Egypt's fate will remind Israel how wrong it was to rely on them. Then Israel will know that I am the Sovereign Lord."

King Nebuchadnezzar will Conquer Egypt

[17] On the first day of the first month of the 27th year of our exile, the Lord spoke to me. [18] "Mortal man," he said, "King Nebuchadnezzar of Babylonia launched an attack on Tyre. He made his soldiers carry such heavy loads that their heads were rubbed bald and their shoulders were worn raw, but neither the king nor his army got anything for all their trouble. [19] So now this is what I, the Sovereign Lord, am saying: I am giving the land of Egypt to King Nebuchadnezzar. He will loot and plunder it and carry off all the wealth of Egypt as his army's pay. [20] I am giving him Egypt in payment for his services, because his army was working for me. I, the Sovereign Lord, have spoken.

[21] "When that happens, I will make the people of Israel strong and let you, Ezekiel, speak out where everyone can hear you, so that they will know that I am the Lord."

The Lord will Punish Egypt

30 The Lord spoke again. [2] "Mortal man," he said, "prophesy and announce what I, the Sovereign Lord, am saying. You are to shout these words:

A day of terror is coming!
[3] The day is near, the day when the Lord will act,
A day of clouds and trouble for the nations.
[4] There will be war in Egypt
And great distress in Ethiopia.
Many in Egypt will be killed;
The country will be plundered
And left in ruins.
[5] "That war will also kill the soldiers hired from Ethiopia, Lydia, Libya, Arabia, Kub, and even from among my own people."

[6] The Lord says, "From Migdol in the north to Aswan in the south, all Egypt's defenders will be killed in battle. Egypt's proud army will be destroyed. I, the Sovereign Lord, have spoken. [7] The land will be the most desolate in the world, and its cities will be left totally in ruins. [8] When I set fire to Egypt and all her defenders are killed, then they will know that I am the Lord.

[9] "When that day comes and Egypt is destroyed, I will send messengers in ships to arouse the unsuspecting people of Ethiopia, and they will be terrified. That day is coming!"

[10] The Sovereign Lord says, "I will use King Nebuchadnezzar of Babylonia to put an end to Egypt's wealth. [11] He and his ruthless army will come to devastate the land. They will attack Egypt with swords, and the land will be full of corpses. [12] I will dry up the Nile and put Egypt under the power of evil people. Foreigners will devastate the whole country. I, the Lord, have spoken."

[13] The Sovereign Lord says, "I will destroy the idols and the false gods in Memphis. There will be no one to rule over Egypt, and I will terrify all the people. [14] I will make southern Egypt desolate and set fire to the city of Zoan in the north. I will punish the capital city of Thebes. [15] I will let the city of Pelusium, Egypt's great fortress, feel my fury. I will destroy the wealth of Thebes. [16] I will set fire to Egypt, and Pelusium will be in agony. The walls of Thebes will be broken down, and the city will be flooded.* [17] The young men

----

30.16 One ancient translation *flooded*; Hebrew unclear.

EZEKIEL 30

You might notice that at the start of most chapters in this book, Ezekiel is addressed as 'Mortal man'. The phrase occurs 93 times, and the literal translation from the Hebrew is

• 'SON OF •
MAN'.

However, in Babylonian culture the phrase meant 'one of high culture or class' and 'one with inheritance'. It's interesting that Jesus quite often referred to himself as 'the son of man'.

1000

Ezekiel

⫶ ⋯⋯⋯

Eccles.
Songs
Isaiah
Jerem.
Lamen.

EZEKIEL 30, 31

of the cities of Heliopolis and Bubastis will die in the war, and the other people will be taken prisoner. [18] Darkness will fall on Tahpanhes when I break the power of Egypt and put an end to the strength they were so proud of. A cloud will cover Egypt, and the people of all her cities will be taken prisoner. [19] When I punish Egypt in this way, they will know that I am the LORD."

The Broken Power of the King of Egypt

[20] On the seventh day of the first month of the eleventh year of our exile, the LORD spoke to me. [21] "Mortal man," he said, "I have broken the arm of the king of Egypt. No one has bandaged it or put it in a sling so that it could heal and be strong enough to hold a sword again. [22] Now then, this is what I, the Sovereign LORD, say: I am the enemy of the king of Egypt. I am going to break both his arms — the good one and the one already broken — and the sword will fall from his hand. [23] I am going to scatter the Egyptians throughout the world. [24] Then I will make the arms of the king of Babylonia strong and put my sword in his hands. But I will break the arms of the king of Egypt, and he will groan and die in front of his enemy. [25] Yes, I will weaken him and strengthen the king of Babylonia. When I give him my sword and he points it towards Egypt, everyone will know that I am the LORD. [26] I will scatter the Egyptians throughout the world. Then they will know that I am the LORD."

Egypt is Compared with a Cedar Tree

31 On the first day of the third month of the eleventh year of our exile, the LORD spoke to me. [2] "Mortal man," he said, "say to the king of Egypt and all his people:

How powerful you are!
What can I compare you to?
[3] You are like* a cedar in Lebanon,
With beautiful, shady branches,
A tree so tall it reaches the clouds.*
[4] There was water to make it grow,
And underground rivers to feed it.
They watered the place where the tree was growing
And sent streams to all the trees of the forest.
[5] Because it was well watered,
It grew taller than other trees.
Its branches grew thick and long.
[6] Every kind of bird built nests in its branches;
The wild animals bore their young in its shelter;
The nations of the world rested in its shade.
[7] How beautiful the tree was —
So tall, with such long branches.
Its roots reached down to the deep-flowing streams.
[8] No cedar in God's garden could compare with it.
No fir tree ever had such branches,
And no plane tree such boughs.
No tree in God's own garden was so beautiful.
[9] I made it beautiful, with spreading branches.
It was the envy of every tree in Eden, the garden of God.

[10] "Now then, I, the Sovereign LORD, will tell you what is going to happen to that tree that grew until it reached the clouds.* As it grew taller it grew proud; [11] so I have rejected it and will let

....

31.3 Probable text *You are like*; Hebrew *Assyria is*.
31.3; 31.10 One ancient translation *clouds*; Hebrew *thick branches*.

EZEKIEL 31, 32

1001

Ezekiel
.........⁖

Daniel
Hosea
Joel
Amos
Obadiah

a foreign ruler have it. He will give that tree what it deserves for its wickedness. ¹²Ruthless foreigners will cut it down and leave it. Its branches and broken boughs will fall on every mountain and valley in the country. All the nations that have been living in its shade will go away. ¹³The birds will come and perch on the fallen tree, and the wild animals will walk over its branches. ¹⁴And so from now on, no tree, no matter how well watered it is, will grow as tall as that again or push its top through the clouds* and reach such a height. All of them are doomed to die like mortals, doomed to join those who go down to the world of the dead."

¹⁵This is what the Sovereign Lord says: "On the day when the tree goes to the world of the dead, I will make the underground waters cover it as a sign of mourning. I will hold back the rivers and not let the many streams flow out. Because the tree has died, I will bring darkness over the Lebanon Mountains and make all the trees of the forest wither. ¹⁶When I send it down to the world of the dead, the noise of its downfall will shake the nations. All the trees of Eden and all the choice, well-watered trees of Lebanon who have gone to the world below will be pleased at its downfall. ¹⁷They will go with it to the world of the dead to join those that have already fallen. And all who live under its shadow will be scattered among the nations.*

¹⁸"The tree is the king of Egypt and all his people. Not even the trees in Eden were so tall and impressive. But now, like the trees of Eden, it will go down to the world of the dead and join the ungodly and those killed in battle. I have spoken," says the Sovereign Lord.

The King of Egypt is Compared with a Crocodile

32 On the first day of the twelfth month of the twelfth year of our exile, the Lord spoke to me. ²"Mortal man," he said, "give a solemn warning to the king of Egypt. Give him this message from me: you act like a lion among the nations, but you are more like a crocodile splashing through a river. You muddy the water with your feet and pollute the rivers. ³When many nations gather, I will catch you in my net and let them drag the net ashore. ⁴I will throw you out on the ground and bring all the birds and animals of the world to feed on you. ⁵I will cover mountains and valleys with your rotting corpse. ⁶I will pour out your blood until it spreads over the mountains and fills the streams. ⁷When I destroy you, I will cover the sky and blot out the stars. The sun will hide behind the clouds, and the moon will give no light. ⁸I will put out all the lights of heaven and plunge your world into darkness. I, the Sovereign Lord, have spoken.

⁹"Many nations will be troubled when I spread the news of your destruction through countries you never heard of. ¹⁰What I do to you will shock many nations. When I swing my sword, kings will shudder with fright. On the day you fall, all of them will tremble in fear for their own lives."

¹¹The Sovereign Lord says to the king of Egypt, "You will face the sword of the king of Babylonia. ¹²I will let soldiers from cruel nations draw their swords and kill all your people. All your people and everything else that you are proud of will be destroyed. ¹³I will slaughter your cattle at every water hole. There will be no people or cattle to muddy the water any more. ¹⁴I will let your waters settle and become clear and let your rivers run calm. I, the Sovereign Lord,

---

31.14 One ancient translation *clouds*; Hebrew *thick branches*.
31.17 Probable text *And all... nations*; Hebrew unclear.

1002

Ezekiel

Eccles.
Songs
Isaiah
Jerem.
Lamen.

EZEKIEL 32

DECORATE THESE SHAPES IN RELATION TO YOUR MOOD.

have spoken. [15] When I make Egypt a desolate waste and destroy all who live there, they will know that I am the LORD. [16] This solemn warning will become a funeral song. The women of the nations will sing it to mourn for Egypt and all its people. I, the Sovereign LORD, have spoken."

The World of the Dead

[17] On the fifteenth day of the first month* of the twelfth year of our exile, the LORD spoke to me. [18] "Mortal man," he said, "mourn for all the many people of Egypt. Send them down with the other powerful nations to the world of the dead. [19] Say to them:

"Do you think you are more beautiful than anyone else?
You will go down to the world of the dead
and lie there among the ungodly.

[20] "The people of Egypt will fall with those who are killed in battle. A sword is ready to kill them all.* [21] The greatest heroes and those who fought on the Egyptian side welcome the Egyptians to the world of the dead. They shout: 'The ungodly who were killed in battle have come down here, and here they lie!'

[22] "Assyria is there, with the graves of her soldiers all around. They were all killed in battle, [23] and their graves are in the deepest parts of the world of the dead. All her soldiers fell in battle, and their graves surround her tomb. Yet once they terrified the land of the living.

[24] "Elam is there, with the graves of her soldiers all around. They were all killed in battle, and they went down, uncircumcised, to the world of the dead. In life they spread terror, but now they lie dead and disgraced. [25] Elam lies down among those killed in battle, and the graves of her soldiers are all around her. They are all uncircumcised, all killed in battle. In life they spread terror, but now they lie dead and disgraced, sharing the fate of those killed in battle.

[26] "Meshech and Tubal are there, with the graves of their soldiers all around. They are all uncircumcised, all killed in battle. Yet once they terrified the living. [27] They were not given honourable burial like the heroes of ancient times,* who went fully armed to the world of the dead, their swords placed under their heads and their shields* over their bodies. These heroes were once powerful enough to terrify the living.

[28] "That is how the Egyptians will lie crushed among the uncircumcised who were killed in battle.

[29] "Edom is there with her kings and rulers. They were powerful soldiers, but now they lie in the world of the dead with the uncircumcised who were killed in battle.

[30] "All the princes of the north are there, and so are the Sidonians. Their power once spread terror, but now they go down in disgrace with those killed in battle and are laid to rest, uncircumcised. They share the disgrace of those who go down to the world of the dead.

[31] "The sight of all these who were killed in battle will be a comfort to the king of Egypt and his army," says the Sovereign LORD.

[32] "I made the king of Egypt terrorize the living, but he and all his army will be killed and laid to rest with all the uncircumcised who die in battle." The Sovereign LORD has spoken.

....

32.17 One ancient translation *of the first month*; Hebrew does not have these words.
32.20 Probable text *A sword… all*; Hebrew unclear.
32.27 Some ancient translations *of ancient times*; Hebrew *of the uncircumcised*.
32.27 Probable text *shields*; Hebrew *iniquities*.

Ezekiel

· · · · · · · · · ·

Daniel

Hosea

Joel

Amos

Obadiah

God Appoints Ezekiel as a Watchman
(Ezek 3.16–21)

33 The LORD spoke to me. ²"Mortal man," he said, "tell your people what happens when I bring war to a land. The people of that country choose one of their number to be a watchman. ³When he sees the enemy approaching, he sounds the alarm to warn everyone. ⁴If someone hears it but pays no attention and the enemy comes and kills him, then he is to blame for his own death. ⁵His death is his own fault, because he paid no attention to the warning. If he had paid attention, he could have escaped. ⁶If, however, the watchman sees the enemy coming and does not sound the alarm, the enemy will come and kill those sinners, but I will hold the watchman responsible for their death.

⁷"Now, mortal man, I am making you a watchman for the nation of Israel. You must pass on to them the warnings I give you. ⁸If I announce that an evil person is going to die but you do not warn him to change his ways so that he can save his life, then he will die, still a sinner, and I will hold you responsible for his death. ⁹If you do warn an evil person and he doesn't stop sinning, he will die, still a sinner, but your life will be spared."

Individual Responsibility

¹⁰The LORD spoke to me. "Mortal man," he said, "repeat to the Israelites what they are saying: 'We are burdened with our sins and the wrongs we have done. We are wasting away. How can we live?' ¹¹Tell them that as surely as I, the Sovereign LORD, am the living God, I do not enjoy seeing sinners die. I would rather see them stop sinning and live. Israel, stop the evil you are doing. Why do you want to die?

¹²"Now, mortal man, tell the Israelites that when someone good sins, the good he has done will not save him. If an evil person stops doing evil, he won't be punished, and if a good person starts sinning, his life will not be spared. ¹³I may promise life to someone good, but if he starts thinking that his past goodness is enough and begins to sin, I will not remember any of the good he did. He will die because of his sins. ¹⁴I may warn someone evil that he is going to die, but if he stops sinning and does what is right and good — ¹⁵for example, if he returns the security he took for a loan or gives back what he stole — if he stops sinning and follows the laws that give life, he will not die, but live. ¹⁶I will forgive the sins he has committed, and he will live because he has done what is right and good.

¹⁷"And your people say that what I do isn't right! No, it's their way that isn't right. ¹⁸When someone righteous stops doing good and starts doing evil, he will die for it. ¹⁹When someone evil gives up sinning and does what is right and good, he has saved his life. ²⁰But Israel, you say that what I do isn't right. I am going to judge you by what you do."

The News of Jerusalem's Fall

²¹On the fifth day of the tenth month of the twelfth year of our exile, someone who had escaped from Jerusalem came and told me that the city had fallen. ²²The evening before he came, I had felt the powerful presence of the LORD. When the man arrived the next morning, the LORD gave me back the power of speech.

The Sins of the People

²³The LORD spoke to me. ²⁴"Mortal man," he said, "the people who are living in the ruined cities of the land of Israel are saying:

1004

Ezekiel

....

Eccles.
Songs
Isaiah
Jerem.
Lamen.

EZEKIEL 33, 34

'Abraham was only one man, and he was given the whole land. There are many of us, so now the land is ours.'

²⁵"Tell them what I, the Sovereign LORD, am saying: You eat meat with the blood still in it. You worship idols. You commit murder. What makes you think that the land belongs to you? ²⁶You rely on your swords. Your actions are disgusting. Everyone commits adultery. What makes you think that the land is yours?

²⁷"Tell them that I, the Sovereign LORD, warn them that as surely as I am the living God, the people who live in the ruined cities will be killed. Those living in the country will be eaten by wild animals. Those hiding in the mountains and in caves will die of disease. ²⁸I will make the country a desolate waste, and the power they were so proud of will come to an end. The mountains of Israel will be so wild that no one will be able to travel through them. ²⁹When I punish the people for their sins and make the country a waste, then they will know that I am the LORD."

The Results of the Prophet's Message

³⁰The LORD said, "Mortal man, your people are talking about you when they meet by the city walls or in the doorways of their houses. They say to one another, 'Let's go and hear what word has come from the LORD now.' ³¹So my people crowd in to hear what you have to say, but they don't do what you tell them to do. Loving words are on their lips, but they continue their greedy ways. ³²To them you are nothing more than an entertainer singing love songs or playing a harp. They listen to all your words and don't obey a single one of them. ³³But when all your words come true — and they will come true — then they will know that a prophet has been among them."

The Shepherds of Israel

34 The LORD spoke to me. ²"Mortal man," he said, "denounce the rulers of Israel. Prophesy to them, and tell them what I, the Sovereign LORD, say to them: you are doomed, you shepherds of Israel! You take care of yourselves, but never tend the sheep. ³You drink the milk, wear clothes made from the wool, and kill and eat the finest sheep. But you never tend the sheep. ⁴You have not taken care of the weak ones, healed those that are sick, bandaged those that are hurt, brought back those that wandered off, or looked for those that were lost. Instead, you treated them cruelly. ⁵Because the sheep had no shepherd, they were scattered, and wild animals killed and ate them. ⁶So my sheep wandered over the high hills and the mountains. They were scattered over the face of the earth, and no one looked for them or tried to find them.

⁷"Now, you shepherds, listen to what I, the LORD, am telling you. ⁸As surely as I am the living God, you had better listen to me. My sheep have been attacked by wild animals that killed and ate them because there was no shepherd. My shepherds did not try to find the sheep. They were taking care of themselves and not the sheep. ⁹So listen to me, you shepherds. ¹⁰I, the Sovereign LORD, declare that I am your enemy. I will take my sheep away from you and never again let you be their shepherds; never again will I let you take care only of yourselves. I will rescue my sheep from you and not let you eat them.

The Good Shepherd

¹¹"I, the Sovereign LORD, tell you that I myself will look for my sheep and take care of them ¹²in the same way as shepherds take

care of their sheep that were scattered and are brought together again. I will bring them back from all the places where they were scattered on that dark, disastrous day. ¹³ I will take them out of foreign countries, gather them together, and bring them back to their own land. I will lead them back to the mountains and the streams of Israel and will feed them in pleasant pastures. ¹⁴ I will let them graze in safety in the mountain meadows and the valleys and in all the green pastures of the land of Israel. ¹⁵ I myself will be the shepherd of my sheep, and I will find them a place to rest. I, the Sovereign Lord, have spoken.

¹⁶ "I will look for those that are lost, bring back those that wander off, bandage those that are hurt, and heal those that are sick; but those that are fat and strong I will destroy, because I am a shepherd who does what is right.

¹⁷ "Now then, my flock, I, the Sovereign Lord, tell you that I will judge each of you and separate the good from the bad, the sheep from the goats. ¹⁸ Some of you are not satisfied with eating the best grass; you even trample down what you don't eat! You drink the clear water and muddy what you don't drink! ¹⁹ My other sheep have to eat the grass you trample down and drink the water you muddy.

²⁰ "So now, I, the Sovereign Lord, tell you that I will judge between you strong sheep and the weak sheep. ²¹ You pushed the sick ones aside and butted them away from the flock. ²² But I will rescue my sheep and not let them be ill-treated any more. I will judge each of my sheep and separate the good from the bad. ²³ I will give them a king like my servant David to be their one shepherd, and he will take care of them. ²⁴ I, the Lord, will be their God, and a king like my servant David will be their ruler. I have spoken. ²⁵ I will make a covenant with them that guarantees their security. I will get rid of all the dangerous animals in the land, so that my sheep can live safely in the fields and sleep in the forests.

²⁶ "I will bless them and let them live round my sacred hill.* There I will bless them with showers of rain when they need it. ²⁷ The trees will bear fruit, the fields will produce crops, and everyone will live in safety on his own land. When I break my people's chains and set them free from those who made them slaves, then they will know that I am the Lord. ²⁸ The heathen nations will not plunder them any more, and the wild animals will not kill and eat them. They will live in safety, and no one will terrify them. ²⁹ I will give them fertile fields and put an end to hunger in the land. The other nations will not sneer at them any more. ³⁰ Everyone will know that I protect Israel and that they are my people. I, the Sovereign Lord, have spoken.

³¹ "You, my sheep, the flock that I feed, are my people, and I am your God," says the Sovereign Lord.

God's Punishment of Edom

35 The Lord spoke to me. ² "Mortal man," he said, "denounce the country of Edom. ³ Tell the people what I, the Sovereign Lord, am saying:

"I am your enemy, mountains of Edom!
     I will make you a desolate waste.
⁴ I will leave your cities in ruins
     And your land desolate;
     Then you will know that I am the Lord.

34.26 *sacred hill*: See 20.40.

1006

Ezekiel

∴⋯⋯⋯

Eccles.
Songs
Isaiah
Jerem.
Lamen.

EZEKIEL 35, 36

⁵"You were Israel's constant enemy and let her people be slaughtered in the time of her disaster, the time of final punishment for her sins. ⁶So then — as surely as I, the Sovereign Lord, am the living God — death is your fate, and you cannot escape it. You are guilty of* murder, and murder will follow you. ⁷I will make the hill country of Edom a waste and kill everyone who travels through it. ⁸I will cover the mountains with corpses, and the bodies of those who are killed in battle will cover the hills and valleys. ⁹I will make you desolate for ever, and no one will live in your cities again. Then you will know that I am the Lord.

¹⁰"You said that the two nations, Judah and Israel, together with their lands, belonged to you and that you would possess them, even though I, the Lord, was their God. ¹¹So then, as surely as I, the Sovereign Lord, am the living God, I will pay you back for your anger, your jealousy, and your hatred towards my people. They will know that I am punishing you for what you did to them. ¹²Then you will know that I, the Lord, heard you say with contempt that the mountains of Israel were desolate and that they were yours to devour. ¹³I have heard the wild, boastful way you have talked against me."

¹⁴The Sovereign Lord says, "I will make you so desolate that the whole world will rejoice at your downfall, ¹⁵just as you rejoiced at the devastation of Israel, my own possession. The mountains of Seir, yes, all the land of Edom, will be desolate. Then everyone will know that I am the Lord."

God's Blessing on Israel

36 The Lord said, "Mortal man, speak to the mountains of Israel and tell them to listen to the message which I, ²the Sovereign Lord, have for them: Israel's enemies gloated and said, 'Now those ancient hills are ours!'

³"Prophesy, then, and announce what I, the Sovereign Lord, am saying. When the neighbouring nations captured and plundered the mountains of Israel, all of them insulted Israel. ⁴So now listen to what I, the Sovereign Lord, say to you mountains and hills, to you brooks and valleys, to you places that were left in ruins, and to you deserted cities which were plundered and mocked by all the surrounding nations.

⁵"I, the Sovereign Lord, have spoken out in the heat of my anger against the surrounding nations, and especially against Edom. With glee and contempt, they captured my land and took possession of its pastures.

⁶"So prophesy to the land of Israel; tell the mountains, hills, brooks, and valleys what I, the Sovereign Lord, am saying in jealous anger because of the way the nations have insulted and humiliated them. ⁷I, the Sovereign Lord, solemnly promise that the surrounding nations will be humiliated. ⁸But on the mountains of Israel the trees will again grow leaves and bear fruit for you, my people Israel. You are going to come home soon. ⁹I am on your side, and I will make sure that your land is ploughed again and that seeds are sown there. ¹⁰I will make your population grow. You will live in the cities and rebuild everything that was left in ruins. ¹¹I will make people and cattle increase in number. There will be more of you than ever before, and you will have many children. I will let you live there as you used to live, and I will make you more prosperous than ever. Then you will know that I am the Lord. ¹²I will bring you, my people Israel, back to

EZEKIEL 36.9

GOD IS ON YOUR SIDE

35.6 One ancient translation *are guilty of*; Hebrew *hate*.

EZEKIEL 36

1007

Ezekiel
· · · · · · · · · ·

Daniel
Hosea
Joel
Amos
Obadiah

live again in the land. It will be your own land, and it will never again let your children starve.

¹³ "I, the Sovereign Lᴏʀᴅ, say: it is true that people say that the land eats people, and that it robs the nation of its children. ¹⁴ But from now on it will no longer eat people and rob you of your children. I, the Sovereign Lᴏʀᴅ, have spoken. ¹⁵ The land will no longer have to listen to the nations mocking it or see the peoples sneer at it. The land will no longer rob the nation of its children. I, the Sovereign Lᴏʀᴅ, have spoken."

Israel's New Life

¹⁶ The Lᴏʀᴅ spoke to me. ¹⁷ "Mortal man," he said, "when the Israelites were living in their land, they defiled it by the way they lived and acted. I regarded their behaviour as being as ritually unclean as a woman is during her monthly period.* ¹⁸ I let them feel the force of my anger because of the murders they had committed in the land and because of the idols by which they had defiled it. ¹⁹ I condemned them for the way they lived and acted, and I scattered them through foreign countries. ²⁰ Wherever they went, they brought disgrace on my holy name, because people would say, 'These are the people of the Lᴏʀᴅ, but they had to leave his land.' ²¹ That made me concerned for my holy name, since the Israelites brought disgrace on it everywhere they went.

²² "Now then, give the Israelites the message that I, the Sovereign Lᴏʀᴅ, have for them: what I am going to do is not for the sake of you Israelites, but for the sake of my holy name, which you have disgraced in every country where you have gone. ²³ When I demonstrate to the nations the holiness of my great name — the name you disgraced among them — then they will know that I am the Lᴏʀᴅ. I, the Sovereign Lᴏʀᴅ, have spoken. I will use you to show the nations that I am holy. ²⁴ I will take you from every nation and country and bring you back to your own land. ²⁵ I will sprinkle clean water on you and make you clean from all your idols and everything else that has defiled you. ²⁶ I will give you a new heart and a new mind. I will take away your stubborn heart of stone and give you an obedient heart. ²⁷ I will put my spirit in you and I will see to it that you follow my laws and keep all the commands I have given you. ²⁸ Then you will live in the land I gave your ancestors. You will be my people, and I will be your God. ²⁹ I will save you from everything that defiles you. I will command the corn to be plentiful, so that you will not have any more famines. ³⁰ I will increase the yield of your fruit trees and your fields, so that there will be no more famines to disgrace you among the nations. ³¹ You will remember your evil conduct and the wrongs that you committed, and you will be disgusted with yourselves because of your sins and your iniquities. ³² Israel, I want you to know that I am not doing all this for your sake. I want you to feel the shame and disgrace of what you are doing. I, the Sovereign Lᴏʀᴅ, have spoken."

³³ The Sovereign Lᴏʀᴅ says, "When I make you clean from all your sins, I will let you live in your cities again and let you rebuild the ruins. ³⁴ Everyone who used to walk by your fields saw how overgrown and wild they were, but I will let you farm them again. ³⁵ Everyone will say how this land, which was once a wilderness, has become like the Garden of Eden, and how the cities which were torn down, looted, and left in ruins, are now inhabited and

· ·

36.17 *ritually unclean… period*: This is based on the view of ritual uncleanness described in the Law of Moses (see Lev 15.19).

1008

Ezekiel

Eccles.
Songs
Isaiah
Jerem.
Lamen.

EZEKIEL 37.1-14

God promises to

BRING LIFE
– OUT OF –
DEATH.

Transform the bland circles on these pages to life and creativity!

fortified. ³⁶ Then the neighbouring nations that have survived will know that I, the LORD, rebuild ruined cities and replant waste fields. I, the LORD, have promised that I would do this — and I will."

³⁷ The Sovereign LORD says, "I will once again let the Israelites ask me for help, and I will let them increase in numbers like a flock of sheep. ³⁸ The cities that are now in ruins will then be as full of people as Jerusalem was once full of the sheep which were offered as sacrifices at a festival. Then they will know that I am the LORD."

The Valley of Dry Bones

37 I felt the powerful presence of the LORD, and his Spirit took me and set me down in a valley where the ground was covered with bones. ² He led me all round the valley, and I could see that there were very many bones and that they were very dry. ³ He said to me, "Mortal man, can these bones come back to life?"

I replied, "Sovereign LORD, only you can answer that!"

⁴ He said, "Prophesy to the bones. Tell these dry bones to listen to the word of the LORD. ⁵ Tell them that I, the Sovereign LORD, am saying to them: I am going to put breath into you and bring you back to life. ⁶ I will give you sinews and muscles, and cover you with skin. I will put breath into you and bring you back to life. Then you will know that I am the LORD."

⁷ So I prophesied as I had been told. While I was speaking, I heard a rattling noise, and the bones began to join together. ⁸ While I watched, the bones were covered with sinews and muscles, and then with skin. But there was no breath in the bodies.

⁹ God said to me, "Mortal man, prophesy to the wind.* Tell the wind that the Sovereign LORD commands it to come from every direction, to breathe into these dead bodies, and to bring them back to life."

¹⁰ So I prophesied as I had been told. Breath entered the bodies, and they came to life and stood up. There were enough of them to form an army.

¹¹ God said to me, "Mortal man, the people of Israel are like these bones. They say that they are dried up, without any hope and with no future. ¹² So prophesy to my people Israel and tell them that I, the Sovereign LORD, am going to open their graves. I am going to take them out and bring them back to the land of Israel. ¹³ When I open the graves where my people are buried and bring them out, they will know that I am the LORD. ¹⁴ I will put my breath in them, bring them back to life, and let them live in their own land. Then they will know that I am the LORD. I have promised that I would do this — and I will. I, the LORD, have spoken."

Judah and Israel in One Kingdom

¹⁵ The LORD spoke to me again.

¹⁶ "Mortal man," he said, "take a wooden stick and write on it the words, 'The kingdom of Judah'. Then take another stick and write on it the words, 'The kingdom of Israel'. ¹⁷ Then hold the two sticks end to end in your hand so that they look like one stick. ¹⁸ When your people ask you to tell them what this means, ¹⁹ tell them that I, the Sovereign LORD, am going to take the stick representing Israel and put it with the one that represents Judah. Out of the two I will make one stick and hold it in my hand.

²⁰ "Hold in your hand the two sticks and let the people see them. ²¹ Then tell them that I, the Sovereign LORD, am going to

37.9 *wind*; or *spirit*. The same Hebrew word may mean *wind*, or *spirit*, or *breath*.

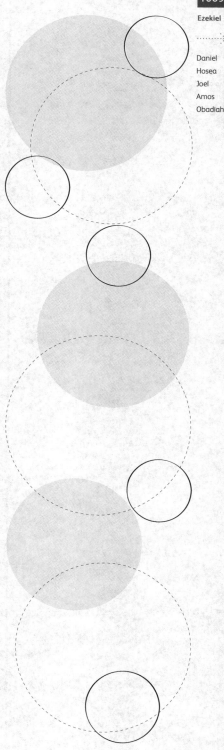

take all my people out of the nations where they have gone, gather them together, and bring them back to their own land. ²² I will unite them into one nation in the land, on the mountains of Israel. They will have one king to rule over them, and they will no longer be divided into two nations or split into two kingdoms. ²³ They will not defile themselves with disgusting idols any more or corrupt themselves with sin. I will free them from all the ways in which they sin and betray me. I will purify them; they will be my people, and I will be their God. ²⁴ A king like my servant David will be their king. They will all be united under one ruler and will obey my laws faithfully. ²⁵ They will live on the land I gave to my servant Jacob, the land where their ancestors lived. They will live there for ever, and so will their children and all their descendants. A king like my servant David will rule over them for ever. ²⁶ I will make a covenant with them that guarantees their security for ever. I will establish them and increase their population, and put my Temple in their land, where it will stay for ever. ²⁷ I will live there with them; I will be their God, and they will be my people. ²⁸ When I place my Temple there to be among them for ever, then the nations will know that I, the LORD, have chosen Israel to be my own people."

Gog as the Instrument of God

38 The LORD spoke to me. ² "Mortal man," he said, "denounce Gog, chief ruler of the nations of Meshech and Tubal in the land of Magog. Denounce him, ³ and tell him that I, the Sovereign LORD, am his enemy. ⁴ I will turn him round, put hooks in his jaws, and drag him and all his troops away. His army, with its horses and uniformed riders, is enormous, and every soldier carries a shield and is armed with a sword. ⁵ Men from Persia, Ethiopia, and Libya are with him, and all have shields and helmets. ⁶ All the fighting men of the lands of Gomer and Beth Togarmah in the north are with him, and so are men from many other nations. ⁷ Tell him to get ready and have all his troops ready at his command. ⁸ After many years I will order him to invade a country where the people were brought back together from many nations and have lived without fear of war. He will invade the mountains of Israel, which were desolate and deserted so long, but where all the people now live in safety. ⁹ He and his army and the many nations with him will attack like a storm and cover the land like a cloud."

¹⁰ This is what the Sovereign LORD says to Gog: "When that time comes, you will start thinking up an evil plan. ¹¹ You will decide to invade a helpless country where the people live in peace and security in unwalled towns that have no defences. ¹² You will plunder and loot the people who live in cities that were once in ruins. They have been gathered from the nations, and now they have livestock and property and live at the crossroads of the world. ¹³ The people of Sheba and Dedan and the merchants from the towns of Spain will ask you, 'Have you assembled your army and attacked in order to loot and plunder? Do you intend to get silver and gold, livestock and property, and to march off with all those spoils?' "

¹⁴ So the Sovereign LORD sent me to tell Gog what he was saying to him: "Now while my people Israel live in security, you will set out* ¹⁵ from your place in the far north, leading a large, powerful army of soldiers from many nations, all of them on horseback. ¹⁶ You will attack my people Israel like a storm moving across the

38.14 One ancient translation *set out*; Hebrew *know*.

1010

Ezekiel

·:········

Eccles.
Songs
Isaiah
Jerem.
Lamen.

EZEKIEL 38, 39

land. When the time comes, I will send you to invade my land in order to show the nations who I am, to show my holiness by what I do through you. [17] You are the one I was talking about long ago, when I announced through my servants, the prophets of Israel, that in days to come I would bring someone to attack Israel." The Sovereign LORD has spoken.

God's Punishment of Gog

[18] The Sovereign LORD says, "On the day when Gog invades Israel, I will be furious. [19] I declare in the heat of my anger that on that day there will be a severe earthquake in the land of Israel. [20] Every fish and bird, every animal large and small, and every human being on the face of the earth will tremble for fear of me. Mountains will fall, cliffs will crumble, and every wall will collapse. [21] I will terrify Gog with all sorts of calamities.* I, the Sovereign LORD, have spoken. His men will turn their swords against one another. [22] I will punish him with disease and bloodshed. Torrents of rain and hail, together with fire and sulphur, will pour down on him and his army and on the many nations that are on his side. [23] In this way I will show all the nations that I am great and that I am holy. They will know then that I am the LORD."

The Defeat of Gog

39 The Sovereign LORD said, "Mortal man, denounce Gog, the chief ruler of the nations of Meshech and Tubal, and tell him that I am his enemy. [2] I will turn him in a new direction and lead him out of the far north until he comes to the mountains of Israel. [3] Then I will knock his bow out of his left hand and his arrows out of his right hand. [4] Gog and his army and his allies will fall dead on the mountains of Israel, and I will let their bodies be food for all the birds and wild animals. [5] They will fall dead in the open field. I, the Sovereign LORD, have spoken. [6] I will start a fire in the land of Magog and along all the coasts where people live undisturbed, and everyone will know that I am the LORD. [7] I will make sure that my people Israel know my holy name, and I will not let my name be disgraced any more. Then the nations will know that I, the LORD, am the Holy God of Israel."

[8] The Sovereign LORD said, "The day I spoke about is certain to come. [9] The people who live in the cities of Israel will go out and collect the abandoned weapons for firewood. They will build fires with the shields, bows, arrows, spears, and clubs, and will have enough to last for seven years. [10] They will not have to gather firewood in the fields or cut down trees in the forest, because they will have the abandoned weapons to burn. They will loot and plunder those who looted and plundered them." The Sovereign LORD has spoken.

The Burial of Gog

[11] The LORD said, "When all this happens, I will give Gog a burial ground there in Israel, in Travellers' Valley, east of the Dead Sea.* Gog and all his army will be buried there, and the valley will be called 'The Valley of Gog's Army'. [12] It will take the Israelites seven months to bury all the corpses and make the land clean again. [13] Everyone in the land will help to bury them, and they will be honoured for this on the day of my victory. I, the Sovereign LORD, have spoken. [14] After the seven months are over, men will be

38.21 One ancient translation *terrify... calamities*; Hebrew unclear.
39.11 Hebrew has four additional words, the meaning of which is unclear.

EZEKIEL 39, 40

1011

Ezekiel

....

Daniel
Hosea
Joel
Amos
Obadiah

chosen to travel through the land in order to find and bury those bodies* remaining on the ground, so that they can make the land clean. [15] As they go up and down the country, every time they find a human bone, they will put a marker beside it so that the grave diggers can come and bury it in the Valley of Gog's Army. [16] (There will be a town near by named after the army.) And so the land will be made clean again."

[17] The Sovereign LORD said to me, "Mortal man, call all the birds and animals to come from all round to eat the sacrifice I am preparing for them. It will be a huge feast on the mountains of Israel, where they can eat meat and drink blood. [18] They are to eat the bodies of soldiers and drink the blood of the rulers of the earth, all of whom will be killed like rams or lambs or goats or fat bulls. [19] When I kill these people like sacrifices, the birds and animals are to eat all the fat they can hold and to drink blood until they are drunk. [20] At my table they will eat all they can hold of horses and their riders and of soldiers and fighting men. I, the Sovereign LORD, have spoken."

The Restoration of Israel

[21] The LORD said, "I will let the nations see my glory and show them how I use my power to carry out my just decisions. [22] The Israelites will know from then on that I am the LORD their God. [23] And the nations will know that the Israelites went into exile because of the sins which they committed against me. I turned away from them and let their enemies defeat them and kill them in battle. [24] I gave them what they deserved for their uncleanness and their wickedness, and I turned away from them."

[25] The Sovereign LORD said, "But now I will be merciful to Jacob's descendants, the people of Israel, and make them prosperous again. I will protect my holy name. [26] When they are once more living in safety in their own land, with no one to threaten them, they will be able to forget how they were disgraced for having betrayed me. [27] In order to show the many nations that I am holy, I will bring my people back from all the countries where their enemies live. [28] Then my people will know that I am the LORD their God. They will know this, because I sent them into captivity and now gather them and bring them back into their own land, not leaving even one of them behind. [29] I will pour out my spirit on the people of Israel and never again turn away from them. I, the Sovereign LORD, have spoken."

A Vision of the Future Temple
40.1—48.35

Ezekiel is Taken to Jerusalem

40 It was the tenth day of the new year, which was the 25th year after we had been taken into exile and the fourteenth year after Jerusalem was captured. On that day I felt the powerful presence of the LORD, and he carried me away. [2] In a vision God took me to the land of Israel and put me on a high mountain. I saw in front of me* a group of buildings that looked like a city. [3] He took me closer, and I saw a man who shone like bronze. He was holding a linen tape measure and a measuring rod and was standing by a gateway.

[4] He said to me, "Watch, mortal man. Listen carefully and pay close attention to everything I show you, because this is

....

39.14 Some ancient translations *those bodies*; Hebrew *the travellers*.
40.2 One ancient translation *in front of me*; Hebrew *in the south*.

1012

Ezekiel

Eccles.
Songs
Isaiah
Jerem.
Lamen.

EZEKIEL 40

Colour these shapes.

why you were brought here. You are to tell the people of Israel everything you see."

The East Gate

⁵ What I saw was the Temple, and there was a wall round it. The man took his measuring rod, which was three metres long, and measured the wall. It was three metres high and three metres thick. ⁶ Then he went to the gateway that faced east. He went up the steps, and at the top he measured the entrance; it was three metres deep.* ⁷ Beyond it there was a passage, which had three guardrooms on each side. Each of the rooms was square, three metres on each side, and the walls between them were 2.5 metres thick. Beyond the guardrooms there was a passage three metres long that led to an entrance room which faced the Temple. ⁸⁻⁹ He measured this room, and found it was four metres deep. It formed that end of the gateway which was nearest the Temple, and at its far end the walls were one metre thick. ¹⁰ (These guardrooms on each side of the passage were all the same size, and the walls between them were all of the same thickness.)

¹¹ Next, the man measured the width of the passage in the gateway. It was 6.5 metres altogether, and the space between the open gates was five metres. ¹² In front of each of the guardrooms there was a low wall fifty centimetres high and fifty centimetres thick. (The rooms were three metres square.) ¹³ Then he measured the distance from the back wall* of one room to the back wall of the room across the passage from it, and it was 12.5 metres. ¹⁴ The room at the far end led out to a courtyard. He measured that room and found it was ten metres wide.* ¹⁵ The total length of the gateway from the outside wall of the gate to the far side of the last room was 25 metres. ¹⁶ There were small openings in the outside walls of all the rooms and also in the inner walls between the rooms. There were palm trees carved on the inner walls that faced the passage.

The Outer Courtyard

¹⁷ The man took me through the gateway into the courtyard. There were thirty rooms built against the outer wall, and in front of them there was an area paved with stones, ¹⁸ which extended round the courtyard. This outer courtyard was at a lower level than the inner courtyard.

¹⁹ There was a gateway at a higher level that led to the inner courtyard. The man measured the distance between the two gateways, and it was fifty metres.*

The North Gate

²⁰ Then the man measured the gateway on the north side that led into the outer courtyard. ²¹ The three guardrooms on each side of the passage, the walls between them, and the entrance room all had the same measurements as those in the east gateway. The total length of the gateway was 25 metres and the width 12.5 metres. ²² The entrance room, the windows, and the carved palm trees were like those in the east gate. Here seven steps led up to the gate, and the entrance room was at the end facing the

40.6 One ancient translation *deep*; Hebrew *deep, one entrance 3 metres deep.*
40.13 Probable text *back wall*; Hebrew *roof.*
40.14 Verse 14 in Hebrew is unclear.
40.19 Hebrew has two additional words, the meaning of which is unclear.

courtyard. ²³Across the courtyard from this north gateway was another gateway leading to the inner courtyard, just as there was on the east side. The man measured the distance between these two gateways, and it was fifty metres.

The South Gate

²⁴Next, the man took me to the south side, and there we saw another gateway. He measured its inner walls and its entrance room, and they were the same as the others. ²⁵There were windows in the rooms of this gateway just as in the others. The total length of the gateway was 25 metres, and the width 12.5 metres. ²⁶Seven steps led up to it, and its entrance room was also at the end facing the courtyard. There were palm trees carved on the inner walls that faced the passage. ²⁷Here, too, there was a gateway leading to the inner courtyard. The man measured the distance to this second gateway, and it was fifty metres.

The Inner Courtyard: the South Gate

²⁸The man took me through the south gateway into the inner courtyard. He measured the gateway, and it was the same size as the gateways in the outer wall. ²⁹⁻³⁰Its guardrooms, its entrance room, and its inner walls were the same size as those in the other gateways. There were also windows in the rooms of this gateway. The total length was 25 metres and the width 12.5 metres. ³¹Its entrance room faced the other courtyard, and palm trees were carved on the walls along the passage. Eight steps led up to this gate.

The Inner Courtyard: the East Gate

³²The man took me through the east gateway into the inner courtyard. He measured the gateway, and it was the same size as the others. ³³Its guardrooms, its entrance room, and its inner walls measured the same as those in the other gateways. There were windows all round, and in the entrance room also. The total length was 25 metres and the width 12.5 metres. ³⁴The entrance room faced the outer courtyard. Palm trees were carved on the walls along the passage. Eight steps led up to this gate.

The Inner Courtyard: the North Gate

³⁵Then the man took me to the north gateway. He measured it, and it was the same size as the others. ³⁶Like them, it also had guardrooms, decorated inner walls, an entrance room, and windows all round. Its total length was 25 metres and its width 12.5 metres. ³⁷The entrance room* faced the outer courtyard. Palm trees were carved on the walls along the passage. Eight steps led up to this gate.

Buildings near the North Gate

³⁸In the outer courtyard there was an annexe attached to the inner gateway on the north side. It opened into the entrance room that faced the courtyard, and there they washed the carcasses of the animals to be burnt whole as sacrifices. ³⁹In this entrance room there were four tables, two on each side of the room. It was on these tables that they killed the animals to be offered as sacrifices, either to be burnt whole or to be sacrifices for sin or as repayment offerings. ⁴⁰Outside the room there were four similar tables, two on either side of the entrance of the north gate. ⁴¹Altogether there

40.37 Some ancient translations *entrance room*; Hebrew *inner wall*.

1014

Ezekiel

.:·········

Eccles.
Songs
Isaiah
Jerem.
Lamen.

EZEKIEL 40, 41

were eight tables on which the animals to be sacrificed were killed: four inside the room and four out in the courtyard. [42] The four tables in the annexe, used to prepare the offerings to be burnt whole, were of cut stone. They were fifty centimetres high, and their tops were 75 centimetres square. All the equipment used in killing the sacrificial animals was kept on these tables. [43] Ledges 25 millimetres wide ran round the edge of the tables. All the meat to be offered in sacrifice was placed on the tables.*

[44] Then he brought me into the inner courtyard. There were two rooms opening on the inner courtyard, one facing south beside the north gateway and the other facing north beside the south gateway.* [45] The man told me that the room which faced south was for the priests who served in the Temple, [46] and the room which faced north was for the priests who served at the altar. All the priests are descended from Zadok; they are the only members of the tribe of Levi who are permitted to go into the LORD's presence to serve him.

The Inner Courtyard and the Temple Building

[47] The man measured the inner courtyard, and it was fifty metres square. The Temple was on the west side, and in front of it was an altar. [48] Then he took me into the entrance room of the Temple. He measured the entrance: it was 2.5 metres deep and seven metres wide,* with walls 1.5 metres thick on either side. [49] Steps led up to the entrance room, which was ten metres wide and six metres deep. There were two columns, one on each side of the entrance.

41 Next, the man took me into the central room, the Holy Place. He measured the passage leading into it: it was three metres deep* [2] and five metres wide, with walls 2.5 metres thick on either side. He measured the room itself: it was twenty metres long, and ten metres wide.

[3] Then he went to the innermost room. He measured the passage leading into it: it was one metre deep and three metres wide, with walls on either side 3.5 metres thick.* [4] He measured the room itself, and it was ten metres square. This room was beyond the central room. Then he said to me, "This is the Most Holy Place."

The Rooms Built against the Temple Walls

[5] The man measured the thickness of the inner wall of the temple building, and it was three metres. Against this wall, all round the Temple, was a series of small rooms two metres wide. [6] These rooms were in three storeys, with thirty rooms on each floor. The Temple's outer wall on each floor was thinner than on the floor below, so that the rooms could rest on the wall without being anchored into it. [7] And so the temple walls, when seen from the outside, seemed to have the same thickness all the way to the top. Against the Temple's outer wall, on the outside of the rooms, two wide stairways were built, so that it was possible to go from the lower storey to the middle and the upper storeys.* [8-11] The outside wall of these rooms was 2.5 metres thick; there was one door into the rooms on

the north side of the Temple, and one into those on the south side. I saw that there was a terrace 2.5 metres wide all round the Temple; it was three metres above the ground and it was level with the foundation of the rooms by the temple walls. Between the terrace and the buildings used by the priests there was an open space ten metres across, along the sides of the Temple.

The Building on the West

12 At the far end of the open space on the west side of the Temple there was a building 45 metres long and 35 metres wide; its walls were 2.5 metres thick all round.

The Total Measurements of the Temple Building

13 The man measured the outside of the Temple, and it was fifty metres long. And from the back of the Temple, across the open space to the far side of the building to the west, the distance was also fifty metres. 14 The distance across the front of the Temple, including the open space on either side, was also fifty metres. 15 He measured the length of the building to the west, including its corridors on both sides, and it was also fifty metres.

Details of the Temple Building

The entrance room of the Temple, the Holy Place, and the Most Holy Place 16 were all panelled with wood from the floor to the windows. These windows could be covered.* 17 The inside walls of the Temple, up as high as above the doors, were completely covered with carvings* 18 of palm trees and winged creatures. Palm trees alternated with creatures, one following the other, all the way round the room. Each creature had two faces: 19 a human face that was turned towards the palm tree on one side, and a lion's face that was turned towards the tree on the other side. It was like this all round the wall, 20 from the floor to above the doors. 21 The doorposts of the Holy Place were square.

The Wooden Altar

In front of the entrance of the Most Holy Place there was something that looked like 22 a wooden altar. It was 1.5 metres high and one metre wide. Its cornerposts, its base,* and its sides were all made of wood. The man said to me, "This is the table which stands in the presence of the LORD."

The Doors

23 There was a door at the end of the passage leading to the Holy Place and one also at the end of the passage leading to the Most Holy Place. 24 They were double doors that swung open in the middle. 25 There were palm trees and winged creatures carved on the doors of the Holy Place, just as there were on the walls. And there was a wooden covering over the outside of the doorway of the entrance room. 26 At the sides of this room there were windows, and the walls were decorated with palm trees.*

Two Buildings near the Temple

42 Then the man took me into the outer courtyard and led me to a building on the north side of the Temple, not far

....
41.16 Verse 16 in Hebrew is unclear.
41.17 Verse 17 in Hebrew is unclear.
41.22 Some ancient translations base; Hebrew length.
41.26 Hebrew has three additional words, the meaning of which is unclear.

1016

Ezekiel

Eccles.
Songs
Isaiah
Jerem.
Lamen.

EZEKIEL 42, 43

EZEKIEL 43.2

Ezekiel compares
God's voice to the

ROAR OF
THE SEA.

If you don't live by the
sea, search online for
sounds of roaring waves
and listen to them with
headphones on. Imagine
what the voice of God
might sound like.

write some
thoughts here ↓

from the building at the west end of the Temple. [2] This building was fifty metres long and 25 metres wide. [3] On one side it faced the space ten metres wide which was alongside the Temple, and on the other side it faced the pavement of the outer court. It was built on three levels, each one set further back than the one below it. [4] Along the north side of this building was a passage five metres wide and fifty metres long,* with entrances on that side. [5] The rooms at the upper level of the building were narrower than those at the middle and lower levels because they were set further back. [6] The rooms at all three levels were on terraces and were not supported by columns like the other buildings in the courtyard. [7-8] At the lower level the outer wall of the building was solid for 25 metres, half its length; and there were rooms in the remaining 25 metres. At the top level there were rooms in the entire length of the building. [9-10] Below these two rooms at the east end of the building, where the wall of the courtyard began,* there was an entrance into the outer courtyard.

At the south* side of the Temple there was an identical building not far from the building at the west end of the Temple. [11] In front of the rooms there was a passage just like the one on the north side. It had the same measurements, the same design, and the same kind of entrances. [12] There was a door under the rooms on the south side of the building, at the east end where the wall began.

[13] The man said to me, "Both these buildings are holy. In them the priests who enter the Lord's presence eat the holiest offerings. Because the rooms are holy, the priests will place the holiest offerings there: the grain offerings and the sacrifices offered for sin or as repayment offerings. [14] When priests have been in the Temple and want to go to the outer courtyard, they must leave in these rooms the holy clothing they wore while serving the Lord. They must put on other clothes before going out to the area where the people gather."

The Measurements of the Temple Area

[15] When the man had finished measuring inside the temple area, he took me out through the east gate and then measured the outside of the area. [16] He took the measuring rod and measured the east side, and it was 250 metres. [17-19] Then he measured the north side, the south side, and the west side; each side had the same length, 250 metres,* [20] so that the wall enclosed a square 250 metres on each side. The wall served to separate what was holy from what was not.

The Lord Returns to the Temple

43 The man took me to the gate that faces east, [2] and there I saw coming from the east the dazzling light of the presence of the God of Israel. God's voice sounded like the roar of the sea, and the earth shone with the dazzling light. [3] This vision was like the one I had seen when God came to destroy Jerusalem, and the one I saw by the River Chebar. Then I threw myself face downwards on the ground. [4] The dazzling light passed through the east gate and went into the Temple.

42.4 Some ancient translations *fifty metres long*; Hebrew *a way of fifty centimetres.*
42.9–10 One ancient translation *where… began*; Hebrew *in the breadth of the wall of the courtyard.*
42.9–10 One ancient translation *south*; Hebrew *east.*
42.17–19 Verses 16–19 in Hebrew are unclear.

EZEKIEL 43

1017

Ezekiel

Daniel
Hosea
Joel
Amos
Obadiah

⁵The Lord's spirit lifted me up and took me into the inner courtyard, where I saw that the Temple was filled with the glory of the Lord. ⁶The man stood beside me there, and I heard the Lord speak to me out of the Temple: ⁷"Mortal man, here is my throne. I will live here among the people of Israel and rule over them for ever. Neither the people of Israel nor their kings will ever again disgrace my holy name by worshipping other gods or by burying the corpses of* their kings in this place. ⁸The kings built the thresholds and doorposts of their palace right against the thresholds and doorposts of my Temple, so that there was only a wall between us. They disgraced my holy name by all the disgusting things they did, and so in my anger I destroyed them. ⁹Now they must stop worshipping other gods and remove the corpses of* their kings. If they do, I will live among them for ever."

¹⁰And the Lord continued, "Mortal man, tell the people of Israel about the Temple, and let them study its plan. Make them ashamed of their sinful actions. ¹¹Then if they are ashamed of what they have done, explain the plan of the Temple to them: its design, its entrances and exits, its shape, the arrangement of everything, and all its rules and regulations. Write all this down for them so that they can see how everything is arranged and can carry out all the rules. ¹²This is the law of the Temple: all the area surrounding it on the top of the mountain is sacred and holy."

The Altar

¹³These are the measurements of the altar, using the same unit of measurement as in measuring the Temple. All round the base of the altar there was a gutter fifty centimetres deep and fifty centimetres wide, with a rim at the outside edge 25 centimetres high. ¹⁴The lowest section of the altar, from the top of the base, was one metre high. The next section was set back from the edge fifty centimetres all round, and was two metres high. The section after that was also set back from the edge fifty centimetres all round. ¹⁵This top section, on which the sacrifices were burnt, was also two metres high. The projections on the four corners were higher than the rest of the top. ¹⁶The top of the altar was a square, six metres on each side. ¹⁷The middle section was also a square, seven metres on each side, with a rim at the outside edge 25 centimetres high. (The gutter was fifty centimetres wide.) The steps going up the altar were on the east side.

The Consecration of the Altar

¹⁸The Sovereign Lord said to me, "Mortal man, listen to what I tell you. When the altar is built, you are to dedicate it by burning sacrifices on it and by sprinkling on it the blood of the animals that were sacrificed. ¹⁹Those priests belonging to the tribe of Levi who are descended from Zadok are the only ones who are to come into my presence to serve me. I, the Sovereign Lord, command this. You will give them a young bull to offer as a sacrifice for sin. ²⁰You are to take some of its blood and put it on the projections on the top corners of the altar, and on the corners of the middle section of the altar, and all round its edges. In this way you will purify the altar and consecrate it. ²¹You are to take the bull that is offered as a sacrifice for sin and burn it at the specified place outside

43.7 *by burying the corpses of*; or *by putting up monuments to.*
43.9 *remove the corpses of*; or *remove the monuments to.*

1018

Ezekiel

⋮·········

Eccles.
Songs
Isaiah
Jerem.
Lamen.

EZEKIEL 43, 44

the temple area. [22] The next day you are to take a male goat without any defects and offer it as a sacrifice for sin. Purify the altar with its blood in the same way as you did with the bull. [23] When you have finished doing that, take a young bull and a young ram, both of them without any defects, [24] and bring them to me. The priests will sprinkle salt on them and burn them as an offering to me. [25] Each day for seven days you are to offer a goat, a bull, and a ram as sacrifices for sin. All of them must be without any defects. [26] For seven days the priests are to consecrate the altar and make it ready for use. [27] When the week is over, the priests are to begin offering on the altar the burnt offerings and the fellowship offerings of the people. Then I will be pleased with all of you. I, the Sovereign LORD, have spoken."

The Use of the East Gate

44 The man led me to the outer gate at the east side of the temple area. The gate was closed, [2] and the LORD said to me, "This gate will stay closed and will never be opened. No human being is allowed to use it, because I, the LORD God of Israel, have entered through it. It is to remain closed. [3] The ruling prince, however, may go there to eat a holy meal in my presence. He is to enter and leave the gateway through the entrance room at the inner end."

Rules for Admission to the Temple

[4] Then the man took me through the north gate to the front of the Temple. As I looked, I saw that the Temple of the LORD was filled with the dazzling light of his presence. I threw myself face downwards on the ground, [5] and the LORD said to me, "Mortal man, pay attention to everything you see and hear. I am going to tell you the rules and regulations for the Temple. Note carefully which persons are allowed to go in and out of the Temple and which persons are not.

[6] "Tell those rebellious people of Israel that I, the Sovereign LORD, will no longer tolerate the disgusting things that they have been doing. [7] They have profaned my Temple by letting uncircumcised foreigners, people who do not obey me, enter the Temple when the fat and the blood of the sacrifices are being offered to me. So my people have broken my covenant by all the disgusting things they have done. [8] They have not taken charge of the sacred rituals in my Temple, but instead have put foreigners in charge.

[9] "I, the Sovereign LORD, declare that no uncircumcised foreigner, no one who disobeys me, will enter my Temple, not even a foreigner who lives among the people of Israel."

The Levites are Excluded from the Priesthood

[10] The LORD said to me, "I am punishing those Levites who, together with the rest of the people of Israel, deserted me and worshipped idols. [11] They may serve me in the Temple by taking charge of the gates and by performing the work of the Temple. They may kill the animals which the people offer for burnt offerings and for sacrifices, and they are to be on duty to serve the people. [12] But because they conducted the worship of idols for the people of Israel and in this way led the people into sin, I, the Sovereign LORD, solemnly swear that they must be punished. [13] They are not to serve me as priests or to go near anything that is holy to me or to enter the Most Holy Place. This is the punishment for the disgusting things they have done.

Ezekiel
....

Daniel
Hosea
Joel
Amos
Obadiah

¹⁴I am assigning to them the menial work that is to be done in the Temple."

The Priests

¹⁵The Sovereign LORD said, "Those priests belonging to the tribe of Levi who are descended from Zadok, however, continued to serve me faithfully in the Temple when the rest of the people of Israel turned away from me. So now they are the ones who are to serve me and come into my presence to offer me the fat and the blood of the sacrifices. ¹⁶They alone will enter my Temple, serve at my altar, and conduct the temple worship. ¹⁷When they enter the gateway to the inner courtyard of the Temple, they are to put on linen clothing. They must not wear anything made of wool when they are on duty in the inner courtyard or in the Temple. ¹⁸So that they won't perspire, they are to wear linen turbans and linen trousers, but no belt. ¹⁹Before they go to the outer courtyard where the people are, they must first take off the clothes they wore on duty in the Temple and leave them in the holy rooms. They are to put on other clothing in order to keep their sacred clothing from harming the people.*

²⁰"Priests must neither shave their heads nor let their hair grow long. They are to keep it a proper length. ²¹Priests must not drink any wine before going into the inner courtyard. ²²No priest may marry a divorced woman; he is to marry only an Israelite virgin or the widow of another priest.

²³"The priests are to teach my people the difference between what is holy and what is not, and between what is ritually clean and what is not. ²⁴When a legal dispute arises, the priests are to decide the case according to my laws. They are to keep the religious festivals according to my rules and regulations, and they are to keep the Sabbaths holy.

²⁵"A priest is not to become ritually unclean by touching a corpse, unless it is one of his parents, one of his children or a brother or an unmarried sister. ²⁶After he has become clean again, he must wait seven days ²⁷and then go into the inner courtyard of the Temple and offer a sacrifice for his purification, so that he can serve in the Temple again. I, the Sovereign LORD, have spoken.

²⁸"The priests have the priesthood as their share of what I have given Israel to be handed down from one generation to another. They are not to hold property in Israel; I am all they need. ²⁹The grain offerings, the sin offerings and the repayment offerings will be the priests' food, and they are to receive everything in Israel that is set apart for me. ³⁰The priests are to have the best of all the first harvest and of everything else that is offered to me. Each time the people bake bread, they are to give the priests the first loaf as an offering, and my blessing will rest on their homes. ³¹The priests must not eat any bird or animal that dies a natural death or is killed by another animal."

The LORD's Portion of the Country

45 When the land is divided to give each tribe a share, one part is to be dedicated to the LORD. It is to be 12.5 kilometres long by ten kilometres* wide. The entire area will be holy. ²In

---

44.19 *harming the people*: It was believed that ordinary people would be harmed by touching something holy.

45.1 One ancient translation *ten kilometres*; Hebrew *five kilometres*.

1020

Ezekiel

.·.··········

Eccles.
Songs
Isaiah
Jerem.
Lamen.

EZEKIEL 45

this area there is to be a square plot of land for the Temple, 250 metres along each side, entirely surrounded by an open space 25 metres wide. [3] Half of this area, a section 12.5 kilometres by five kilometres, is to be measured off; it will contain the Temple, the holiest place of all. [4] It will be a holy part of the country, set aside for the priests who serve the LORD in his Temple. It will contain their houses and the section of land for the Temple. [5] The other half of the area is to be set aside as the possession of the Levites, who do the work in the Temple. There will be towns there for them to live in.*

[6] Next to the holy area, another section, 12.5 kilometres long and 2.5 kilometres wide, is to be set aside for a city where any of the people of Israel may live.

Land for the Prince

[7] Land is also to be set aside for the ruling prince. From the western boundary of the holy area it will extend west to the Mediterranean Sea; and from the eastern boundary it will extend to the eastern border of the country, so that its length will be the same as the length of one of the areas allotted to the tribes of Israel. [8] This area will be the share the ruling prince will have in the land of Israel, so that he will no longer oppress the people, but will let the rest of the country belong to the tribes of Israel.

Rules for the Prince

[9] The Sovereign LORD said, "You have sinned too long, you rulers of Israel! Stop your violence and oppression. Do what is right and just. You must never again drive my people off their land. I, the Sovereign LORD, am telling you this.

[10] "Everyone must use honest weights and measures:

[11] "The *ephah* for dry measure is to be equal to the *bath* for liquid measure. The standard is the *homer*.* The resulting measures are as follows:

 one *homer* == ten *ephahs* == ten *baths*.

[12] "Your weights are to be as follows:

 twenty *gerahs* == one *shekel**

 sixty *shekels* == one *mina*.

[13-15] "This is the basis on which you are to make your offerings:

 Wheat: one sixtieth of your harvest

 Barley: one sixtieth of your harvest

 Olive oil: a hundredth of the yield of your trees.

(Measure it by the *bath*: ten *baths* == one *homer* == one *kor*.)

 Sheep: one sheep out of every 200 from the meadows of
  Israel.

"You are to bring grain offerings, animals to be burnt whole, and animals for fellowship offerings, so that your sins will be forgiven. I, the Sovereign LORD, command it.

[16] "All the people of the land must take* these offerings to the ruling prince of Israel. [17] It will be his duty to provide the animals to be burnt whole, the grain offerings, and the wine offerings for the whole nation of Israel at the New Moon Festivals, the Sabbaths, and the other festivals. He is to provide the sin offerings, the grain

....

45.5 One ancient translation *towns there for them to live in*; Hebrew *twenty rooms*.
45.11 *homer*: A unit of dry or liquid measure, about 175 litres; so an *ephah* or a *bath* would be about 17.5 litres.
45.12 *shekel*: In Ezekiel's time this unit of weight was about 11.4 grammes.
45.16 Probable text *must take*; Hebrew unclear.

EZEKIEL 45, 46

1021

Ezekiel
............:

Daniel
Hosea
Joel
Amos
Obadiah

offerings, the offerings to be burnt whole, and the fellowship offerings, to take away the sins of the people of Israel."

The Festivals
(Ex 12.1–20; Lev 23.33–43)

¹⁸The Sovereign LORD said, "On the first day of the first month you are to sacrifice a bull without any defects and purify the Temple. ¹⁹The priest will take some of the blood of this sin offering and put it on the doorposts of the Temple, on the four corners of the altar, and on the posts of the gateways to the inner courtyard. ²⁰On the seventh day of the month you are to do the same thing on behalf of anyone who sins unintentionally or through ignorance. In this way, you will keep the Temple holy.

²¹"On the fourteenth day of the first month you will begin the celebration of the Passover Festival. For seven days everyone will eat bread made without yeast. ²²On the first day of the festival the ruling prince must offer a bull as a sacrifice for his sins and for those of all the people. ²³On each of the seven days of the festival he is to sacrifice to the LORD seven bulls and seven rams without any defects and burn them whole. He is also to sacrifice a male goat each day as a sin offering. ²⁴For each bull and each ram that is sacrificed, there is to be an offering of 17.5 litres of corn and three litres of olive oil.

²⁵"For the Festival of Shelters, which begins on the fifteenth day of the seventh month, the prince will offer on each of the seven days the same sacrifice for sin, the same offerings to be burnt whole, and the same offerings of corn and olive oil."

The Prince and the Festivals

46 The Sovereign LORD says, "The east gateway to the inner courtyard must be kept closed during the six working days, but it is to be opened on the Sabbath and at the New Moon Festival. ²The ruling prince will go from the outer courtyard into the entrance room by the gateway and stand beside the posts of the gate while the priests burn his sacrifices whole and offer his fellowship offerings. There at the gate he must worship and then go out again. The gate must not be shut until evening. ³Each Sabbath and each New Moon Festival all the people are also to bow down and worship the LORD in front of the gate.

⁴"On the Sabbath the prince is to bring to the LORD, as sacrifices to be burnt whole, six lambs and one ram, all without any defects. ⁵With each ram he is to bring an offering of 17.5 litres of corn, and with each lamb he is to bring whatever he wants to give. For each such grain offering he is to bring three litres of olive oil. ⁶At the New Moon Festival he will offer a young bull, six lambs, and a ram, all without any defects. ⁷With each bull and each ram the offering is to be 17.5 litres of corn, and with each lamb the offering is to be whatever the prince wants to give. Three litres of olive oil are to be offered with each such grain offering of corn. ⁸The prince must leave the entrance room of the gateway and go out by the same way as he went in.

⁹"When the people come to worship the LORD at any festival, those who enter by the north gate are to leave by the south gate after they have worshipped, and those who enter by the south gate are to leave by the north gate. No one may go out by the same way as he entered, but must leave by the opposite gate. ¹⁰The prince is to come in when the people come, and leave when they leave. ¹¹On the feast days and at the festivals the grain offering will be 17.5 litres with each bull or ram, and whatever

1022

Ezekiel

⸫⸳⸳⸳⸳⸳⸳⸳⸳

Eccles.
Songs
Isaiah
Jerem.
Lamen.

EZEKIEL 47.1-12

EZEKIEL 46, 47

God gave Ezekiel a picture of a temple with water flowing out – resulting in beautiful trees, fruits and animals.

DECORATE
– THESE –
PAGES

with rivers, trees and animals as a sign of what happens when God's Spirit is poured out.

the worshipper wants to give with each lamb. Three litres of olive oil are to be offered with each such grain offering.

¹² "When the ruling prince wants to make a voluntary offering to the LORD, either an offering to be burnt whole or a fellowship offering, the east gate to the inner courtyard will be opened for him. He is to make the offering in the same way as he does on the Sabbath, and the gate is to be closed after he goes out again."

The Daily Offering
¹³ The LORD says, "Every morning a one-year-old lamb without any defects is to be burnt whole as an offering to the LORD. This offering must be made every day. ¹⁴ Also an offering of two kilogrammes of flour is to be made every morning, together with one litre of olive oil for mixing with the flour. The rules for this offering to the LORD are to be in force for ever. ¹⁵ The lamb, the flour, and the olive oil are to be offered to the LORD every morning for ever."

The Prince and the Land
¹⁶ The Sovereign LORD commands: "If the ruling prince gives any of the land he owns to one of his sons as a present, it will belong to that son as a part of his family property. ¹⁷ But if the ruling prince gives any of his land to anyone who is in his service, it will become the prince's property again when the Year of Restoration* comes round. It belongs to him, and only he and his sons can own it permanently. ¹⁸ The ruling prince must not take any of the people's property away from them. Any land he gives to his sons must be from the land that is assigned to him, so that he will not oppress any of my people by taking their land."

The Temple Kitchens
¹⁹ Then the man took me to the entrance of the rooms facing north near the gate on the south side of the inner courtyard. These are holy rooms for the priests. He pointed out a place on the west side of the rooms ²⁰ and said, "This is the place where the priests are to boil the meat offered as sacrifices for sin or as repayment offerings, and to bake the offerings of flour, so that nothing holy is carried to the outer courtyard, where it might harm the people."*

²¹⁻²² Then he led me to the outer courtyard and showed me that in each of its four corners there was a smaller* courtyard, twenty metres long and fifteen metres wide. ²³ Each one had a stone wall round it, with fireplaces built against the wall. ²⁴ The man told me, "These are the kitchens where the temple servants are to boil the sacrifices the people offer."

The Stream Flowing from the Temple
47 The man led me back to the entrance of the Temple. Water was coming out from under the entrance and flowing east, the direction the Temple faced. It was flowing down from under the south part of the temple past the south side of the altar. ² The man then took me out of the temple area by way of the north gate and led me round to the gate that faces east.

⸳⸳⸳

46.17 *Year of Restoration*: Every fifty years, all Israelites were required to give freedom to any other Israelites who had become slaves because of debts; they were also to give back to the original owner, or his heirs, any ancestral land that had been sold for debt (see Lev 25.8–55).
46.20 *harm the people*: See 44.19.
46.21–22 One ancient translation *smaller*; Hebrew *enclosed*.

EZEKIEL 47

1023

Ezekiel

....

Daniel
Hosea
Joel
Amos
Obadiah

A small stream of water was flowing out at the south side of the gate. ³With his measuring rod the man measured 500 metres downstream to the east and told me to wade through the stream there. The water came only to my ankles. ⁴Then he measured another 500 metres, and the water came up to my knees. Another 500 metres further down, the water was up to my waist. ⁵He measured 500 metres more, and there the stream was so deep I could not wade through it. It was too deep to cross except by swimming. ⁶He said to me, "Mortal man, note all this carefully."

Then the man took me back to the bank of the river, ⁷and when I got there I saw that there were very many trees on each bank. ⁸He said to me, "This water flows through the land to the east and down into the Jordan Valley and to the Dead Sea. When it flows into the Dead Sea, it replaces the salt water of that sea with fresh water. ⁹Wherever the stream flows, there will be all kinds of animals and fish. The stream will make the water of the Dead Sea fresh, and wherever it flows, it will bring life. ¹⁰From the Springs of Engedi all the way to the Springs of Eneglaim, there will be fishermen on the shore of the sea, and they will spread out their nets there to dry. There will be as many different kinds of fish there as there are in the Mediterranean Sea. ¹¹But the water in the marshes and ponds along the shore will not be made fresh. They will remain there as a source of salt. ¹²On each bank of the stream all kinds of trees will grow to provide food. Their leaves will never wither, and they will never stop bearing fruit. They will have fresh fruit every month, because they are watered by the stream that flows from the Temple. The trees will provide food, and their leaves will be used for healing people."

The Boundaries of the Land

¹³The Sovereign LORD said, "These are the boundaries of the land that is to be divided among the twelve tribes, with the tribe of Joseph receiving two sections.* ¹⁴I solemnly promised your ancestors that I would give them possession of this land; now divide it equally among you.

¹⁵"The northern boundary runs eastwards from the Mediterranean Sea to the city of Hethlon, to Hamath Pass, to the city of Zedad,* ¹⁶to the cities of Berothah and Sibraim (they are located between the territory of the kingdom of Damascus and that of the kingdom of Hamath), and to the city of Ticon (located by the border of the district of Hauran). ¹⁷So the northern boundary runs from the Mediterranean eastwards to the city of Enon, with the border regions of Damascus and Hamath to the north of it.

¹⁸"The eastern boundary runs south from a point between the territory of Damascus and that of Hauran, with the River Jordan forming the boundary between the land of Israel on the west and Gilead on the east, as far as Tamar* on the Dead Sea.

¹⁹"The southern boundary runs south-west from Tamar to the oasis of Kadesh Meribah, and then north-west along the Egyptian border to the Mediterranean Sea.

²⁰"The western boundary is formed by the Mediterranean and runs north to a point west of Hamath Pass.

....

47.13 *two sections*: The tribes of Manasseh and Ephraim, the sons of Joseph, were each given one section.
47.15 One ancient translation *Hamath… Zedad*; Hebrew *Zedad Pass to the city of Hamath.*
47.18 Some ancient translations *Tamar*; Hebrew unclear.

1024

Ezekiel

·:·········

Eccles.
Songs
Isaiah
Jerem.
Lamen.

EZEKIEL 47, 48

21 "Divide this land among your tribes; 22 it is to be your permanent possession. The foreigners who are living among you and who have had children born here are also to receive their share of the land when you divide it. They are to be treated like full Israelite citizens and are to draw lots for shares of the land along with the tribes of Israel. 23 Foreign residents will receive their share with the people of the tribe among whom they are living. I, the Sovereign LORD, have spoken."

The Division of the Land among the Tribes

48 1-7 The northern boundary of the land runs eastwards from the Mediterranean Sea to the city of Hethlon, to Hamath Pass, to the city of Enon, to the boundary between the kingdoms of Damascus and Hamath. Each tribe is to receive one section of land extending from the eastern boundary westwards to the Mediterranean Sea,* in the following order from north to south:

Dan
Asher
Naphtali
Manasseh
Ephraim
Reuben
Judah.

The Special Section in the Centre of the Land

8 The next section of the land is to be set apart for special use. It is to be 12.5 kilometres wide from north to south, and the same length from east to west as the sections given to the tribes. The Temple will be in this section.

9 In the centre of this section, a special area 12.5 kilometres by ten kilometres* is to be dedicated to the LORD. 10 The priests are to have a portion of this holy area. From east to west their portion is to measure 12.5 kilometres, and from north to south, five kilometres. The Temple of the LORD is to be in the middle of this area. 11 This holy area is to be for the priests who are descendants of Zadok. They served me faithfully and did not join the rest of the Israelites in doing wrong, as the other members of the tribe of Levi did. 12 So they are to have a special area next to the area belonging to the Levites, and it will be the holiest of all. 13 The Levites also are to have a special area, south of that of the priests. It too is to be 12.5 kilometres from east to west, by five kilometres from north to south. 14 The area dedicated to the LORD is the best part of all the land, and none of it may be sold or exchanged or transferred to anyone else. It is holy and belongs to the LORD.

15 The part of the special area that is left, 12.5 kilometres by 2.5 kilometres, is not holy, but is for the general use of the people. They may live there and use the land. The city is to be in the centre of it, 16 and it will be a square, measuring 2,250 metres on each side. 17 All round the city on each side there will be an open space 125 metres across. 18 The land that is left after the city has been built in the area immediately to the south of the holy area — five kilometres by 2.5 kilometres on the east and five kilometres by 2.5 kilometres on the west — is to be used as farm land by the people who live in the city. 19 Anyone who lives in the city, no matter which tribe he comes from, may farm that land.

....

48.1–7 One ancient translation extending... Sea; Hebrew having an eastern boundary and a western boundary.
48.9 Probable text (see 45.1) ten kilometres; Hebrew five kilometres.

²⁰ And so the total area in the centre of the section which was set apart will be a square measuring 12.5 kilometres on each side, and it will include the area occupied by the city.

²¹⁻²² To the east and to the west of this area which contains the Temple, the priests' land, the Levites' land, and the city, the remaining land belongs to the ruling prince. It extends eastwards to the eastern boundary and westwards to the Mediterranean Sea, and is bounded on the north by the section belonging to Judah and on the south by the section belonging to Benjamin.

Land for the Other Tribes

²³⁻²⁷ South of this special section, each of the remaining tribes is to receive one section of land running from the eastern boundary westwards to the Mediterranean Sea, in the following order from north to south:

> Benjamin
> Simeon
> Issachar
> Zebulun
> Gad.

²⁸ On the south side of the portion given to the tribe of Gad, the boundary runs south-west from Tamar to the oasis of Kadesh, and then north-west along the Egyptian border to the Mediterranean Sea.

²⁹ The Sovereign LORD said, "That is the way the land is to be divided into sections for the tribes of Israel to possess."

The Gates of Jerusalem

³⁰⁻³⁴ There are twelve entrances to the city of Jerusalem. Each of the four walls measures 2,250 metres and has three gates in it, each named after one of the tribes. The gates in the north wall are named after Reuben, Judah, and Levi; those in the east wall, after Joseph, Benjamin, and Dan; those in the south wall, after Simeon, Issachar, and Zebulun; and those in the west wall are named after Gad, Asher, and Naphtali. ³⁵ The total length of the wall on all four sides of the city is 9,000 metres. The name of the city from now on will be, "The-LORD-is-Here!"

THE BOOK OF
DANIEL

WRITTEN: POSSIBLY BETWEEN 200 AND 150BC

The book of Daniel is about God using a

YOUNG PERSON
DURING CHALLENGING TIMES

How might God want to use you in
some of today's challenging circumstances?

WHAT YOU NEED TO KNOW:

Daniel was a teenager carried off into exile by the
Babylonians. This was the darkest period in Israel's history.
At that time, if a nation was conquered, its neighbours
would take it as a sign that the nation's gods were weak.
However, in Daniel we see a God who is still mightily at
work, even with his people in exile. The book is in two
parts. The first is an account of Daniel's life in Babylon,
including well-known stories such as Shadrach, Meshach and
Abednego in the fiery furnace, Daniel in the lions' den, and
the writing on the wall at Belshazzar's feast. The second
part is full of prophetic visions. It is unclear if these were
written by Daniel or added later. It may be that some of
these visions were not simply for the Israelites at the time,
but for a future we haven't yet entered into.

WHY READ IT?

Daniel was a young person living in a time of
adversity, a believer in God working for a government
that didn't believe in God. His story is one of
resilience and strength under pressure. It is also the
story of God at work even when hope seems lost, a
God who is still able to perform miracles when his
people are scattered. Daniel tells us that whatever
the situation, God is working towards a plan, and he
invites us to join him in it.

597BC   KING NEBUGHADNEZZAR   KING CYRUS

JUDAH FALLS
TO BABYLON   KING BELSHAZZAR   536B

DANIEL 1, 2

1027

Daniel

Hosea
Joel
Amos
Obadiah
Jonah

The Story of Daniel and his Friends
1.1—6.28

The Young Men at Nebuchadnezzar's Court

1 In the third year that Jehoiakim was king of Judah, King Nebuchadnezzar of Babylonia attacked Jerusalem and surrounded the city. [2] The Lord let him capture King Jehoiakim and seize some of the temple treasures. He took some prisoners back with him to the temple of his gods in Babylon, and put the captured treasures in the temple storerooms.

[3] The king ordered Ashpenaz, his chief official, to select from among the Israelite exiles some young men of the royal family and of the noble families. [4] They had to be handsome, intelligent, well trained, quick to learn, and free from physical defects, so that they would be qualified to serve in the royal court. Ashpenaz was to teach them to read and write the Babylonian language. [5] The king also gave orders that every day they were to be given the same food and wine as the members of the royal court. After three years of this training they were to appear before the king. [6] Among those chosen were Daniel, Hananiah, Mishael, and Azariah, all of whom were from the tribe of Judah. [7] The chief official gave them new names: Belteshazzar, Shadrach, Meshach, and Abednego.

[8] Daniel made up his mind not to let himself become ritually unclean by eating the food and drinking the wine of the royal court, so he asked Ashpenaz to help him, [9] and God made Ashpenaz sympathetic to Daniel. [10] Ashpenaz, however, was afraid of the king, so he said to Daniel, "The king has decided what you are to eat and drink, and if you don't look as fit as the other young men, he may kill me."

[11] So Daniel went to the guard whom Ashpenaz had placed in charge of him and his three friends. [12] "Test us for ten days," he said. "Give us vegetables to eat and water to drink. [13] Then compare us with the young men who are eating the food of the royal court, and base your decision on how we look."

[14] He agreed to let them try it for ten days. [15] When the time was up, they looked healthier and stronger than all those who had been eating the royal food. [16] So from then on the guard let them continue to eat vegetables instead of what the king provided.

[17] God gave the four young men knowledge and skill in literature and philosophy. In addition, he gave Daniel skill in interpreting visions and dreams.

[18] At the end of the three years set by the king, Ashpenaz took all the young men to Nebuchadnezzar. [19] The king talked with them all, and Daniel, Hananiah, Mishael, and Azariah impressed him more than any of the others. So they became members of the king's court. [20] No matter what question the king asked, or what problem he raised, these four knew ten times more than any fortune teller or magician in his whole kingdom. [21] Daniel remained at the royal court until Cyrus the emperor of Persia conquered Babylonia.

Nebuchadnezzar's Dream

2 In the second year that Nebuchadnezzar was king, he had a dream. It worried him so much that he couldn't sleep, [2] so he sent for his fortune tellers, magicians, sorcerers, and wizards to come and explain the dream to him. When they came and stood before the king, [3] he said to them, "I'm worried about a dream I have had. I want to know what it means."

DANIEL 1

Daniel and his mates

CHOSE TO BE
SET APART

by eating only vegetables and drinking water.

Go and pour a glass of water (and, if you have any raw vegetables you can eat, take some of them too). As you eat and drink, ask God to give you strength and knowledge that will set you apart from the rest of the world.

1028

Daniel

·:········

Songs
Isaiah
Jerem.
Lamen.
Ezekiel

DANIEL 2

⁴They answered the king in Aramaic,* "May Your Majesty live for ever! Tell us your dream, and we will explain it to you."

⁵The king said to them, "I have made up my mind that you must tell me the dream and then tell me what it means. If you can't, I'll have you torn limb from limb and make your houses a pile of ruins. ⁶But if you can tell me both the dream and its meaning, I will reward you with gifts and great honour. Now then, tell me what the dream was and what it means."

⁷They answered the king again, "If Your Majesty will only tell us what the dream was, we will explain it."

⁸At that, the king exclaimed, "Just as I thought! You are trying to gain time, because you see that I have made up my mind ⁹to give all of you the same punishment if you don't tell me the dream. You have agreed among yourselves to go on telling me lies because you hope that in time things will change. Tell me what the dream was, and then I will know that you can also tell me what it means."

¹⁰The advisers replied, "There is no one on the face of the earth who can tell Your Majesty what you want to know. No king, not even the greatest and most powerful, has ever made such a demand of his fortune tellers, magicians, and wizards. ¹¹What Your Majesty is asking for is so difficult that no one can do it for you except the gods, and they do not live among human beings."

¹²At that, the king flew into a rage and ordered the execution of all the royal advisers in Babylon. ¹³So the order was issued for all of them to be killed, including Daniel and his friends.

God Shows Daniel what the Dream Means

¹⁴Then Daniel went to Arioch, commander of the king's bodyguard, who had been ordered to carry out the execution. Choosing his words carefully, ¹⁵he asked Arioch why the king had issued such a harsh order. So Arioch told Daniel what had happened.

¹⁶Daniel went at once and obtained royal permission for more time, so that he could tell the king what the dream meant. ¹⁷Then Daniel went home and told his friends Hananiah, Mishael, and Azariah what had happened. ¹⁸He told them to pray to the God of heaven for mercy and to ask him to explain the mystery to them so that they would not be killed along with the other advisers in Babylon. ¹⁹Then that same night the mystery was revealed to Daniel in a vision, and he praised the God of heaven:

²⁰ "God is wise and powerful!
　　Praise him for ever and ever.
²¹ He controls the times and the seasons;
　　he makes and unmakes kings;
　　it is he who gives wisdom and understanding.
²² He reveals things that are deep and secret;
　　he knows what is hidden in darkness,
　　and he himself is surrounded by light.
²³ I praise you and honour you, God of my ancestors.
　　You have given me wisdom and strength;
　　　you have answered my prayer
　　　and shown us what to tell the king."

Daniel Tells the King the Dream and Explains it

²⁴So Daniel went to Arioch, whom the king had commanded to execute the royal advisers. He said to him, "Don't put them

2.4 From here to the end of chapter 7, the language used is Aramaic, not Hebrew.

DANIEL 2

1029

Daniel

....

Hosea
Joel
Amos
Obadiah
Jonah

to death. Take me to the king, and I will tell him what his dream means."

²⁵ At once Arioch took Daniel into King Nebuchadnezzar's presence and told the king, "I have found one of the Jewish exiles, who can tell Your Majesty the meaning of your dream."

²⁶ The king said to Daniel (who was also called Belteshazzar), "Can you tell me what I dreamt and what it means?"

²⁷ Daniel replied, "Your Majesty, there is no wizard, magician, fortune teller, or astrologer who can tell you that. ²⁸ But there is a God in heaven, who reveals mysteries. He has informed Your Majesty what will happen in the future. Now I will tell you the dream, the vision you had while you were asleep.

²⁹ "While Your Majesty was sleeping, you dreamt about the future; and God, who reveals mysteries, showed you what is going to happen. ³⁰ Now, this mystery was revealed to me, not because I am wiser than anyone else, but so that Your Majesty may learn the meaning of your dream and understand the thoughts that have come to you.

³¹ "Your Majesty, in your vision you saw standing before you a giant statue, bright and shining, and terrifying to look at. ³² Its head was made of the finest gold; its chest and arms were made of silver; its waist and hips of bronze; ³³ its legs of iron, and its feet partly of iron and partly of clay. ³⁴ While you were looking at it, a great stone broke loose from a cliff without anyone touching it, struck the iron and clay feet of the statue, and shattered them. ³⁵ At once the iron, clay, bronze, silver, and gold crumbled and became like the dust on a threshing place in summer. The wind carried it all away, leaving not a trace. But the stone grew to be a mountain that covered the whole earth.

³⁶ "This was the dream. Now I will tell Your Majesty what it means. ³⁷ Your Majesty, you are the greatest of all kings. The God of heaven has made you emperor and given you power, might, and honour. ³⁸ He has made you ruler of all the inhabited earth and ruler over all the animals and birds. You are the head of gold. ³⁹ After you there will be another empire, not as great as yours, and after that a third, an empire of bronze, which will rule the whole earth. ⁴⁰ And then there will be a fourth empire, as strong as iron, which shatters and breaks everything. And just as iron shatters everything, it will shatter and crush all the earlier empires. ⁴¹ You also saw that the feet and the toes were partly clay and partly iron. This means that it will be a divided empire. It will have something of the strength of iron, because there was iron mixed with the clay. ⁴² The toes — partly iron and partly clay — mean that part of the empire will be strong and part of it weak. ⁴³ You also saw that the iron was mixed with the clay. This means that the rulers of that empire will try to unite their families by intermarriage, but they will not be able to, any more than iron can mix with clay. ⁴⁴ At the time of those rulers the God of heaven will establish a kingdom that will never end. It will never be conquered, but will completely destroy all those empires, and then last for ever. ⁴⁵ You saw how a stone broke loose from a cliff without anyone touching it and how it struck the statue made of iron, bronze, clay, silver, and gold. The great God is telling Your Majesty what will happen in the future. I have told you exactly what you dreamt, and have given you its true meaning."

The King Rewards Daniel

⁴⁶ Then King Nebuchadnezzar bowed to the ground and gave orders for sacrifices and offerings to be made to Daniel. ⁴⁷ The

1030

Daniel

Songs
Isaiah
Jerem.
Lamen.
Ezekiel

DANIEL 3.17-18

This story is amazing! The three men were confident that God would save them, but said that even if he didn't, they would not turn away from him. Sometimes

LIFE

- IS HARD, -

and we have to choose whether to follow God even when things don't go our way. Complete the sentence in the box with something challenging and personal to you.

GOD, I WILL FOLLOW
YOU EVEN IF...

king said, "Your God is the greatest of all gods, the Lord over kings, and the one who reveals mysteries. I know this because you have been able to explain this mystery." [48] Then he gave Daniel a high position, presented him with many splendid gifts, put him in charge of the province of Babylon, and made him the head of all the royal advisers. [49] At Daniel's request the king put Shadrach, Meshach, and Abednego in charge of the affairs of the province of Babylon; Daniel, however, remained at the royal court.

Nebuchadnezzar Commands Everyone to Worship a Gold Statue

3 King Nebuchadnezzar had a gold statue made, 27 metres high and nearly three metres wide, and he had it set up in the plain of Dura in the province of Babylon. [2] Then the king gave orders for all his officials to come together — the princes, governors, lieutenant-governors, commissioners, treasurers, judges, magistrates, and all the other officials of the provinces. They were to attend the dedication of the statue which King Nebuchadnezzar had set up. [3] When all these officials gathered for the dedication and stood in front of the statue, [4] a herald announced in a loud voice, "People of all nations, races, and languages! [5] You will hear the sound of the trumpets, followed by the playing of oboes, lyres, zithers, and harps; and then all the other instruments will join in. As soon as the music starts, you are to bow down and worship the gold statue that King Nebuchadnezzar has set up. [6] Anyone who does not bow down and worship will immediately be thrown into a blazing furnace." [7] And so, as soon as they heard the sound of the instruments, the people of all the nations, races, and languages bowed down and worshipped the gold statue which King Nebuchadnezzar had set up.

Daniel's Three Friends are Accused of Disobedience

[8] It was then that some Babylonians took the opportunity to denounce the Jews. [9] They said to King Nebuchadnezzar, "May Your Majesty live for ever! [10] Your Majesty has issued an order that as soon as the music starts, everyone is to bow down and worship the gold statue, [11] and that anyone who does not bow down and worship it is to be thrown into a blazing furnace. [12] There are some Jews whom you put in charge of the province of Babylon — Shadrach, Meshach, and Abednego — who are disobeying Your Majesty's orders. They do not worship your god or bow down to the statue you set up."

[13] At that, the king flew into a rage and ordered the three men to be brought before him. [14] He said to them, "Shadrach, Meshach, and Abednego, is it true that you refuse to worship my god and to bow down to the gold statue I have set up? [15] Now then, as soon as you hear the sound of the trumpets, oboes, lyres, zithers, harps, and all the other instruments, bow down and worship the statue. If you do not, you will immediately be thrown into a blazing furnace. Do you think there is any god who can save you?"

[16] Shadrach, Meshach, and Abednego answered, "Your Majesty, we will not try to defend ourselves. [17] If the God whom we serve is able to save us from the blazing furnace and from your power, then he will.* [18] But even if he doesn't, Your Majesty may be sure

---

3.17 *If the God... will;* or *If it is true that we refuse to worship your god or bow down to the gold statue you set up, the God whom we serve is able to save us from the blazing furnace and from your power — and he will.*

DANIEL 3, 4

1031

Daniel

....

Hosea
Joel
Amos
Obadiah
Jonah

that we will not worship your god, and we will not bow down to the gold statue that you have set up."

Daniel's Three Friends are Sentenced to Death

¹⁹Then Nebuchadnezzar lost his temper, and his face turned red with anger at Shadrach, Meshach, and Abednego. So he ordered the furnace to be heated seven times hotter than usual. ²⁰And he commanded the strongest men in his army to tie the three men up and throw them into the blazing furnace. ²¹So they tied them up, fully dressed — shirts, robes, caps, and all — and threw them into the blazing furnace. ²²Now because the king had given strict orders for the furnace to be made extremely hot, the flames burnt up the guards who took the men to the furnace. ²³Then Shadrach, Meshach, and Abednego, still tied up, fell into the heart of the blazing fire.

²⁴Suddenly Nebuchadnezzar leapt to his feet in amazement. He asked his officials, "Didn't we tie up three men and throw them into the blazing furnace?"

They answered, "Yes, we did, Your Majesty."

²⁵"Then why do I see four men walking about in the fire?" he asked. "They are not tied up, and they show no sign of being hurt — and the fourth one looks like an angel."*

The Three Men are Released and Promoted

²⁶So Nebuchadnezzar went up to the door of the blazing furnace and called out, "Shadrach! Meshach! Abednego! Servants of the Supreme God! Come out!" And they came out at once. ²⁷All the princes, governors, lieutenant-governors, and other officials of the king gathered to look at the three men, who had not been harmed by the fire. Their hair was not singed, their clothes were not burnt, and there was no smell of smoke on them.

²⁸The king said, "Praise the God of Shadrach, Meshach, and Abednego! He sent his angel and rescued these men who serve and trust him. They disobeyed my orders and risked their lives rather than bow down and worship any god except their own.

²⁹"And now I command that if anyone of any nation, race, or language speaks disrespectfully of the God of Shadrach, Meshach, and Abednego, he is to be torn limb from limb, and his house is to be made a pile of ruins. There is no other god who can rescue like this."

³⁰And the king promoted Shadrach, Meshach, and Abednego to higher positions in the province of Babylon.

Nebuchadnezzar's Second Dream

4 King Nebuchadnezzar sent the following message to the people of all nations, races, and languages in the world:

"Greetings! ²Listen to my account of the wonders and miracles which the Supreme God has shown me.

³ "How great are the wonders God shows us!
    How powerful are the miracles he performs!
    God is king for ever; he will rule for all time.

⁴"I was living comfortably in my palace, enjoying great prosperity. ⁵But I had a frightening dream and saw terrifying visions while I was asleep. ⁶I ordered all the royal advisers in Babylon to be brought to me so that they could tell me what the dream meant. ⁷Then all the fortune tellers, magicians, wizards, and astrologers were brought in, and I told them my dream, but

....

3.25 *an angel*; or *a son of the gods*; or *a son of God.*

1032

Daniel

·:·.........

Songs
Isaiah
Jerem.
Lamen.
Ezekiel

DANIEL 4

they could not explain it to me. [8] Then Daniel came in. (He is also called Belteshazzar, after the name of my god.) The spirit of the holy gods* is in him, so I told him what I had dreamt. I said to him: [9] Belteshazzar, chief of the fortune tellers, I know that the spirit of the holy gods* is in you, and that you understand all mysteries. This is* my dream. Tell me what it means.

[10] "While I was asleep, I had a vision of a huge tree in the middle of the earth. [11] It grew bigger and bigger until it reached the sky and could be seen by everyone in the world. [12] Its leaves were beautiful, and it was loaded down with fruit — enough for the whole world to eat. Wild animals rested in its shade, birds built nests in its branches, and every kind of living being ate its fruit.

[13] "While I was thinking about the vision, I saw coming down from heaven an angel, alert and watchful. [14] He proclaimed in a loud voice, 'Cut the tree down and chop off its branches; strip off its leaves and scatter its fruit. Drive the animals from under it and the birds out of its branches. [15] But leave the stump in the ground with a band of iron and bronze round it. Leave it there in the field with the grass.

" 'Now let the dew fall on this man, and let him live with the animals and the plants. [16] For seven years he will not have a human mind, but the mind of an animal. [17] This is the decision of the alert and watchful angels. So then, let all people everywhere know that the Supreme God has power over human kingdoms and that he can give them to anyone he chooses — even to those who are the least important.'

[18] "This is the dream I had," said King Nebuchadnezzar. "Now, Belteshazzar, tell me what it means. None of my royal advisers could tell me, but you can, because the spirit of the holy gods* is in you."

Daniel Explains the Dream

[19] At this, Daniel, who is also called Belteshazzar, was so alarmed that he could not say anything. The king said to him, "Belteshazzar, don't let the dream and its message alarm you."

Belteshazzar replied, "Your Majesty, I wish that the dream and its explanation applied to your enemies and not to you. [20] The tree, so tall that it reached the sky, could be seen by everyone in the world. [21] Its leaves were beautiful, and it had enough fruit on it to feed the whole world. Wild animals rested under it, and birds made their nests in its branches.

[22] "Your Majesty, you are the tree, tall and strong. You have grown so great that you reach the sky, and your power extends over the whole world. [23] While Your Majesty was watching, an angel came down from heaven and said, 'Cut the tree down and destroy it, but leave the stump in the ground. Wrap a band of iron and bronze round it, and leave it there in the field with the grass. Let the dew fall on this man, and let him live there with the animals for seven years.'

[24] "This, then, is what it means, Your Majesty, and this is what the Supreme God has declared will happen to you. [25] You will be driven away from human society and will live with wild animals. For seven years you will eat grass like an ox, and sleep in the open air, where the dew will fall on you. Then you will admit that the Supreme God controls all human kingdoms, and that he can give them to anyone he chooses. [26] The angel ordered the stump to be

....

4.8; 4.9; 4.18 *gods*; or *God.*
4.9 Probable text *This is*; Aramaic *Visions of.*

DANIEL 4, 5

1033

Daniel
....

Hosea
Joel
Amos
Obadiah
Jonah

left in the ground. This means that you will become king again when you acknowledge that God rules all the world. ²⁷So then, Your Majesty, follow my advice. Stop sinning, do what is right, and be merciful to the poor.* Then you will continue to be prosperous."

²⁸All this did happen to King Nebuchadnezzar. ²⁹Only twelve months later, while he was walking about on the roof of his royal palace in Babylon, ³⁰he said, "Look how great Babylon is! I built it as my capital city to display my power and might, my glory and majesty."

³¹Before the words were out of his mouth, a voice spoke from heaven, "King Nebuchadnezzar, listen to what I say! Your royal power is now taken away from you. ³²You will be driven away from human society, live with wild animals, and eat grass like an ox for seven years. Then you will acknowledge that the Supreme God has power over human kingdoms and that he can give them to anyone he chooses."

³³The words came true immediately. Nebuchadnezzar was driven out of human society and ate grass like an ox. The dew fell on his body, and his hair grew as long as eagles' feathers and his nails as long as birds' claws.

Nebuchadnezzar Praises God

³⁴"When the seven years had passed," said the king, "I looked up at the sky, and my sanity returned. I praised the Supreme God and gave honour and glory to the one who lives for ever.

"He will rule for ever,
and his kingdom will last for all time.
³⁵ He looks on the people of the earth as nothing;
angels in heaven and people on earth
are under his control.
No one can oppose his will
or question what he does.

³⁶"When my sanity returned, my honour, my majesty, and the glory of my kingdom were given back to me. My officials and my noblemen welcomed me, and I was given back my royal power, with even greater honour than before.

³⁷"And now, I, Nebuchadnezzar, praise, honour, and glorify the King of Heaven. Everything he does is right and just, and he can humble anyone who acts proudly."

Belshazzar's Banquet

5 One night King Belshazzar invited a thousand noblemen to a great banquet, and they drank wine together. ²While they were drinking, Belshazzar gave orders to bring in the gold and silver cups and bowls which his father* Nebuchadnezzar had carried off from the Temple in Jerusalem. The king sent for them so that he, his noblemen, his wives, and his concubines could drink out of them. ³At once the gold cups and bowls were brought in, and they all drank wine out of them ⁴and praised gods made of gold, silver, bronze, iron, wood, and stone.

⁵Suddenly a human hand appeared and began writing on the plaster wall of the palace, where the light from the lamps was shining most brightly. And the king saw the hand as it was writing.

....

4.27 *Stop sinning… to the poor*; or *Make up for your sins by doing what is right and by being merciful to the poor.*
5.2 There were several kings of Babylonia between Nebuchadnezzar and Belshazzar. *Father* may mean predecessor, or the name *Nebuchadnezzar* may be used for Nabinodus.

1034

Daniel

Songs
Isaiah
Jerem.
Lamen.
Ezekiel

[6] He turned pale and was so frightened that his knees began to shake. [7] He shouted for someone to bring in the magicians, wizards, and astrologers. When they came in, the king said to them, "Anyone who can read this writing and tell me what it means will be dressed in robes of royal purple, wear a gold chain of honour round his neck, and be the third in power in the kingdom." [8] The royal advisers came forward, but none of them could read the writing or tell the king what it meant. [9] In his distress King Belshazzar grew even paler, and his noblemen had no idea what to do.

[10] The queen mother heard the noise made by the king and his noblemen and entered the banqueting hall. She said, "May Your Majesty live for ever! Please do not be so disturbed and look so pale. [11] There is a man in your kingdom who has the spirit of the holy gods* in him. When your father was king, this man showed good sense, knowledge, and wisdom like the wisdom of the gods. And King Nebuchadnezzar, your father,* made him chief of the fortune tellers, magicians, wizards, and astrologers. [12] He has unusual ability and is wise and skilful in interpreting dreams, solving riddles, and explaining mysteries; so send for this man Daniel, whom the king named Belteshazzar, and he will tell you what all this means."

Daniel Explains the Writing

[13] Daniel was brought at once into the king's presence, and the king said to him, "Are you Daniel, that Jewish exile whom my father the king brought here from Judah? [14] I have heard that the spirit of the holy gods* is in you and that you are skilful and have knowledge and wisdom. [15] The advisers and magicians were brought in to read this writing and tell me what it means, but they could not discover the meaning. [16] Now I have heard that you can find hidden meanings and explain mysteries. If you can read this writing and tell me what it means, you will be dressed in robes of royal purple, wear a gold chain of honour round your neck, and be the third in power in the kingdom."

[17] Daniel replied, "Keep your gifts for yourself or give them to someone else. I will read for Your Majesty what has been written and tell you what it means.

[18] "The Supreme God made your father Nebuchadnezzar a great king and gave him dignity and majesty. [19] He was so great that people of all nations, races, and languages were afraid of him and trembled. If he wanted to kill someone, he did; if he wanted to keep someone alive, he did. He honoured or disgraced anyone he wanted to. [20] But because he became proud, stubborn, and cruel, he was removed from his royal throne and lost his place of honour. [21] He was driven away from human society, and his mind became like that of an animal. He lived with wild donkeys, ate grass like an ox, and slept in the open air with nothing to protect him from the dew. Finally he admitted that the Supreme God controls all human kingdoms and can give them to anyone he chooses.

[22] "But you, his son, have not humbled yourself, even though you knew all this. [23] You acted against the Lord of heaven and brought in the cups and bowls taken from his Temple. You, your noblemen, your wives, and your concubines drank wine out of

5.11; 5.14 *gods*; or *God*.
5.11 There were several kings of Babylonia between Nebuchadnezzar and Belshazzar. *Father* may mean predecessor, or the name *Nebuchadnezzar* may be used for Nabinodus.

DANIEL 5, 6

1035

Daniel
..........:.

Hosea
Joel
Amos
Obadiah
Jonah

them and praised gods made of gold, silver, bronze, iron, wood, and stone — gods that cannot see or hear and that do not know anything. But you did not honour the God who determines whether you live or die and who controls everything you do. ²⁴That is why God has sent the hand to write these words.

²⁵"This is what was written: 'Number, number, weight, divisions.' ²⁶And this is what it means: *number*, God has numbered the days of your kingdom and brought it to an end; ²⁷*weight*, you have been weighed on the scales and found to be too light; ²⁸*divisions*, your kingdom is divided up and given to the Medes and Persians.'"*

²⁹Immediately Belshazzar ordered his servants to dress Daniel in a robe of royal purple and to hang a gold chain of honour round his neck. And he made him the third in power in the kingdom. ³⁰That same night Belshazzar, the king of Babylonia, was killed; ³¹and Darius the Mede, who was then 62 years old, seized the royal power.

Daniel in the Pit of Lions

6 Darius decided to appoint 120 governors to hold office throughout his empire. ²In addition, he chose Daniel and two others to supervise the governors and to look after the king's interests. ³Daniel soon showed that he could do better work than the other supervisors or the governors. Because he was so outstanding, the king considered putting him in charge of the whole empire. ⁴Then the other supervisors and the governors tried to find something wrong with the way Daniel administered the empire, but they couldn't, because Daniel was reliable and did not do anything wrong or dishonest. ⁵They said to one another, "We are not going to find anything of which to accuse Daniel unless it is something in connection with his religion."

⁶So they went to see the king and said, "King Darius, may Your Majesty live for ever! ⁷All of us who administer your empire — the supervisors, the governors, the lieutenant-governors, and the other officials — have agreed that Your Majesty should issue an order and enforce it strictly. Give orders that for thirty days no one be permitted to request anything from any god or from any human being except from Your Majesty. Anyone who violates this order is to be thrown into a pit filled with lions. ⁸So let Your Majesty issue this order and sign it, and it will be in force, a law of the Medes and Persians, which cannot be changed." ⁹And so King Darius signed the order. ¹⁰When Daniel learnt that the order had been signed, he went home. In an upstairs room of his house there were windows that faced towards Jerusalem. There, just as he had always done, he knelt down at the open windows and prayed to God three times a day.

¹¹When Daniel's enemies observed him praying to God, ¹²all of them went together to the king to accuse Daniel. They said, "Your Majesty, you signed an order that for the next thirty days anyone who requested anything from any god or from any human being except you, would be thrown into a pit filled with lions."

The king replied, "Yes, a strict order, a law of the Medes and Persians, which cannot be changed."

¹³Then they said to the king, "Daniel, one of the exiles from Judah, does not respect Your Majesty or obey the order you issued. He prays regularly three times a day."

¹⁴When the king heard this, he was upset and did his best to find some way to rescue Daniel. He kept trying until sunset. ¹⁵Then Daniel's

DANIEL 6

– DRAW –
A LION
ON THIS PAGE!

5.28 *Persians*: In Aramaic the word for "Persians" sounds like the word for "division".

1036

Daniel

Songs
Isaiah
Jerem.
Lamen.
Ezekiel

DANIEL 6, 7

enemies came back to the king and said to him, "Your Majesty knows that according to the laws of the Medes and Persians no order which the king issues can be changed."

16 So the king gave orders for Daniel to be arrested and he was thrown into the pit filled with lions. He said to Daniel, "May your God, whom you serve so loyally, rescue you." 17 A stone was put over the mouth of the pit, and the king placed his own royal seal and the seal of his noblemen on the stone, so that no one could rescue Daniel. 18 Then the king returned to the palace and spent a sleepless night, without food or any form of entertainment.

19 At dawn the king got up and hurried to the pit. 20 When he got there, he called out anxiously, "Daniel, servant of the living God! Was the God you serve so loyally able to save you from the lions?"

21 Daniel answered, "May Your Majesty live for ever! 22 God sent his angel to shut the mouths of the lions so that they would not hurt me. He did this because he knew that I was innocent and because I have not wronged you, Your Majesty."

23 The king was overjoyed and gave orders for Daniel to be pulled up out of the pit. So they pulled him up and saw that he had not been hurt at all, for he trusted God. 24 Then the king gave orders to arrest all the men who had accused Daniel, and they were thrown, together with their wives and their children, into the pit filled with lions. Before they even reached the bottom of the pit, the lions pounced on them and broke all their bones.

25 Then King Darius wrote to the people of all nations, races, and languages on earth:

"Greetings! 26 I command that throughout my empire everyone should fear and respect Daniel's God.

"He is a living God,
and he will rule for ever.
His kingdom will never be destroyed,
and his power will never come to an end.
27 He saves and rescues;
he performs wonders and miracles
in heaven and on earth.
He saved Daniel from being killed by the lions."

28 Daniel prospered during the reign of Darius and the reign of Cyrus the Persian.

Daniel Describes his Visions
7.1—12.13

Daniel's Vision of the Four Beasts

7 In the first year that Belshazzar was king of Babylonia, I had a dream and saw a vision in the night. I wrote the dream down, and this is the record 2 of what I saw that night:

Winds were blowing from all directions and lashing the surface of the ocean. 3 Four huge beasts came up out of the ocean, each one different from the others. 4 The first one looked like a lion, but had wings like an eagle. While I was watching, the wings were torn off. The beast was lifted up and made to stand upright. And then a human mind was given to it.

5 The second beast looked like a bear standing on its hind legs. It was holding three ribs between its teeth, and a voice said to it, "Go on, eat as much meat as you can!"

6 While I was watching, another beast appeared. It looked like a leopard, but on its back there were four wings, like the wings of a bird, and it had four heads. It had a look of authority about it.

⁷As I was watching, a fourth beast appeared. It was powerful, horrible, terrifying. With its huge iron teeth it crushed its victims, and then it trampled on them. Unlike the other beasts, it had ten horns. ⁸While I was staring at the horns, I saw a little horn coming up among the others. It tore out three of the horns that were already there. This horn had human eyes and a mouth that was boasting proudly.

The Vision of the One who has been Living for Ever

⁹While I was looking, thrones were put in place. One who had been living for ever sat down on one of the thrones. His clothes were white as snow, and his hair was like pure wool. His throne, mounted on fiery wheels, was blazing with fire, ¹⁰and a stream of fire was pouring out from it. There were many thousands of people there to serve him, and millions of people stood before him. The court began its session, and the books were opened.

¹¹While I was looking, I could still hear the little horn bragging and boasting. As I watched, the fourth beast was killed, and its body was thrown into the flames and destroyed. ¹²The other beasts had their power taken away, but they were permitted to go on living for a limited time.

¹³During this vision in the night, I saw what looked like a human being. He was approaching me, surrounded by clouds, and he went to the one who had been living for ever and was presented to him. ¹⁴He was given authority, honour, and royal power, so that the people of all nations, races, and languages would serve him. His authority would last for ever, and his kingdom would never end.

The Visions are Explained

¹⁵The visions I saw alarmed me, and I was deeply disturbed.* ¹⁶I went up to one of those standing there and asked him to explain it all. So he told me the meaning. ¹⁷He said, "These four huge beasts are four empires which will arise on earth. ¹⁸And the people of the Supreme God will receive royal power and keep it for ever and ever."

¹⁹Then I wanted to know more about the fourth beast, which was not like any of the others — the terrifying beast which crushed its victims with its bronze claws and iron teeth and then trampled on them. ²⁰And I wanted to know about the ten horns on its head and the horn that had come up afterwards and had made three of the horns fall. It had eyes and a mouth and was boasting proudly. It was more terrifying than any of the others.

²¹While I was looking, that horn made war on God's people and conquered them. ²²Then the one who had been living for ever came and pronounced judgement in favour of* the people of the Supreme God. The time had arrived for God's people to receive royal power.

²³This is the explanation I was given: "The fourth beast is a fourth empire that will be on the earth and will be different from all other empires. It will crush the whole earth and trample it down. ²⁴The ten horns are ten kings who will rule that empire. Then another king will appear; he will be very different from the earlier ones and will overthrow three kings. ²⁵He will speak against the Supreme God and oppress God's people. He will try to change their religious laws and festivals, and God's people will be under his power for 3.5 years. ²⁶Then the heavenly court will sit

DRAW YOUR CURRENT VIEW

- whether it's your desk, your bed, out of the window, the cat... whatever!

7.15 Aramaic has two additional words, the meaning of which is unclear.
7.22 *pronounced judgement in favour of*; or *gave the right to judge to*.

1038

Daniel

Songs
Isaiah
Jerem.
Lamen.
Ezekiel

DANIEL 7, 8

in judgement, take away his power, and destroy him completely. [27] The power and greatness of all the kingdoms on earth will be given to the people of the Supreme God. Their royal power will never end and all rulers on earth will serve and obey them."

[28] This is the end of the account. I was so frightened that I turned pale, and I kept everything to myself.

Daniel's Vision of a Ram and a Goat

8 In the third year that Belshazzar was king, I saw a second vision.* [2] In the vision I suddenly found myself in the walled city of Susa in the province of Elam. I was standing by the River Ulai, [3] and there beside the river I saw a ram that had two long horns, one of which was longer and newer than the other. [4] I watched the ram butting with his horns to the west, the north, and the south. No animal could stop him or escape his power. He did as he pleased and grew arrogant.

[5] While I was wondering what this meant, a goat came rushing out of the west, moving so fast that his feet didn't touch the ground. He had one prominent horn between his eyes. [6] He came towards the ram, which I had seen standing beside the river, and rushed at him with all his force. [7] I watched him attack the ram. He was so angry that he smashed into him and broke the two horns. The ram had no strength to resist. He was thrown to the ground and trampled on, and there was no one who could save him.

[8] The goat grew more and more arrogant, but at the height of his power his horn was broken. In its place four prominent horns came up, each pointing in a different direction. [9] Out of one of these four horns grew a little horn, whose power extended towards the south and the east and towards the Promised Land. [10] It grew strong enough to attack the army of heaven, the stars themselves, and it threw some of them to the ground and trampled on them. [11] It even defied the Prince of the heavenly army, stopped the daily sacrifices offered to him, and desecrated the Temple. [12] People sinned there instead of offering the proper daily sacrifices,* and true religion was thrown to the ground. The horn was successful in everything it did.

[13] Then I heard one angel ask another, "How long will these things that were seen in the vision continue? How long will an awful sin replace the daily sacrifices? How long will the army of heaven and the Temple be trampled on?"

[14] I heard the other angel answer, "It will continue for 2,300 evenings and mornings, during which sacrifices will not be offered. Then the Temple will be restored."

The Angel Gabriel Explains the Vision

[15] I was trying to understand what the vision meant, when suddenly someone was standing in front of me. [16] I heard a voice call out over the River Ulai, "Gabriel, explain to him the meaning of what he saw." [17] Gabriel came and stood beside me, and I was so terrified that I fell to the ground.

He said to me, "Mortal man, understand the meaning. The vision has to do with the end of the world." [18] While he was talking, I fell to the ground unconscious. But he took hold of me, raised me to my feet, [19] and said, "I am showing you what the result of God's anger will be. The vision refers to the time of the end.

[20] "The ram you saw that had two horns represents the kingdoms of Media and Persia. [21] The goat represents the kingdom of Greece,

---

8.1 Beginning at 8.1, the rest of this book is in Hebrew (see 2.4).
8.12 *People… sacrifices*; Hebrew unclear.

DANIEL 8, 9

1039

Daniel

....

Hosea
Joel
Amos
Obadiah
Jonah

and the prominent horn between his eyes is the first king. [22] The four horns that came up when the first horn was broken represent the four kingdoms into which that nation will be divided and which will not be as strong as the first kingdom.

[23] "When the end of those kingdoms is near and they have become so wicked that they must be punished, there will be a stubborn, vicious, and deceitful king. [24] He will grow strong — but not by his own power. He will cause terrible destruction and be successful in everything he does. He will bring destruction on powerful men and on God's own people. [25] Because he is cunning, he will succeed in his deceitful ways. He will be proud of himself and destroy many people without warning. He will even defy the greatest King of all, but he will be destroyed without the use of any human power. [26] This vision about the evening and morning sacrifices which has been explained to you will come true. But keep it secret now, because it will be a long time before it does come true."

[27] I was depressed and ill for several days. Then I got up and went back to the work that the king had assigned to me, but I was puzzled by the vision and could not understand it.

Daniel Prays for his People

9 Darius the Mede, who was the son of Xerxes, ruled over the kingdom of Babylonia. [2] In the first year of his reign, I was studying the sacred books and thinking about the seventy years that Jerusalem would be in ruins, according to what the LORD had told the prophet Jeremiah. [3] And I prayed earnestly to the Lord God, pleading with him, fasting, wearing sackcloth, and sitting in ashes. [4] I prayed to the LORD my God and confessed the sins of my people.

I said, "Lord God, you are great, and we honour you. You are faithful to your covenant and show constant love to those who love you and do what you command.

[5] "We have sinned, we have been evil, we have done wrong. We have rejected what you commanded us to do and have turned away from what you showed us was right. [6] We have not listened to your servants the prophets, who spoke in your name to our kings, our rulers, our ancestors, and our whole nation. [7] You, Lord, always do what is right, but we have always brought disgrace on ourselves. This is true of all of us who live in Judah and in Jerusalem and of all the Israelites whom you scattered in countries near and far because they were unfaithful to you. [8] Our kings, our rulers, and our ancestors have acted shamefully and sinned against you, Lord. [9] You are merciful and forgiving, although we have rebelled against you. [10] We did not listen to you, O LORD our God, when you told us to live according to the laws which you gave us through your servants the prophets. [11] All Israel broke your laws and refused to listen to what you said. We sinned against you, and so you brought on us the curses that are written in the Law of Moses, your servant. [12] You did what you said you would do to us and our rulers. You punished Jerusalem more severely than any other city on earth, [13] giving us all the punishment described in the Law of Moses. But even now, O LORD our God, we have not tried to please you by turning from our sins or by following your truth. [14] You, O LORD our God, were prepared to punish us, and you did, because you always do what is right, and we did not listen to you.

[15] "O Lord our God, you showed your power by bringing your people out of Egypt, and your power is still remembered. We have

1040

Daniel

Songs
Isaiah
Jerem.
Lamen.
Ezekiel

DANIEL 9, 10

sinned; we have done wrong. [16] You have defended us in the past, so do not be angry with Jerusalem any longer. It is your city, your sacred hill.* All the people in the neighbouring countries look down on Jerusalem and on your people because of our sins and the evil our ancestors did. [17] O God, hear my prayer and pleading. Restore your Temple, which has been destroyed; restore it so that everyone will know that you are God. [18] Listen to us, O God; look at us, and see the trouble we are in and the suffering of the city that bears your name. We are praying to you because you are merciful, not because we have done right. [19] Lord, hear us. Lord, forgive us. Lord, listen to us, and act! In order that everyone will know that you are God, do not delay! This city and these people are yours."

Gabriel Explains the Prophecy

[20] I went on praying, confessing my sins and the sins of my people Israel, and pleading with the LORD my God to restore his holy Temple. [21] While I was praying, Gabriel, whom I had seen in the earlier vision, came flying down to where I was. It was the time for the evening sacrifice to be offered. [22] He explained, "Daniel, I have come here to help you understand the prophecy. [23] When you began to plead with God, he answered you. He loves you, and so I have come to tell you the answer. Now pay attention while I explain the vision.

[24] "Seven times seventy years is the length of time God has set for freeing your people and your holy city from sin and evil. Sin will be forgiven and eternal justice established, so that the vision and the prophecy will come true, and the holy Temple* will be rededicated. [25] Note this and understand it: from the time the command is given to rebuild Jerusalem, until God's chosen leader comes, seven times seven years will pass. Jerusalem will be rebuilt with streets and strong defences, and will stand for seven times 62 years, but this will be a time of troubles. [26] And at the end of that time God's chosen leader will be killed unjustly.* The city and the Temple will be destroyed by the invading army of a powerful ruler. The end will come like a flood, bringing the war and destruction which God has prepared. [27] That ruler will have a firm agreement with many people for seven years, and when half this time is past, he will put an end to sacrifices and offerings. The Awful Horror* will be placed on the highest point of the Temple and will remain there until the one who put it there meets the end which God has prepared for him."

Daniel's Vision by the River Tigris

10 (In the third year that Cyrus was emperor of Persia, a message was revealed to Daniel, who is also called Belteshazzar. The message was true but extremely hard to understand.* It was explained to him in a vision.)

[2] At that time, I was mourning for three weeks. [3] I did not eat any rich food or any meat, drink any wine, or comb my hair until the three weeks were past.

[4] On the 24th day of the first month of the year, I was standing on the bank of the mighty River Tigris. [5] I looked up and saw

9.16 *sacred hill*: Mount Zion.
9.24 *Temple*; or *altar*.
9.26 One ancient translation *unjustly*; Hebrew unclear.
9.27 *The Awful Horror*: A pagan image set up in the Jerusalem Temple by foreign conquerors.
10.1 *but extremely hard to understand*; or *and it was about a great war.*

Daniel
....

Hosea
Joel
Amos
Obadiah
Jonah

someone who was wearing linen clothes and a belt of fine gold. [6] His body shone like a jewel. His face was as bright as a flash of lightning, and his eyes blazed like fire. His arms and legs shone like polished bronze, and his voice sounded like the roar of a great crowd.

[7] I was the only one who saw the vision. Those who were with me did not see anything, but they were terrified and ran and hid. [8] I was left there alone, watching this amazing vision. I had no strength left, and my face was so changed that no one could have recognized me. [9] When I heard his voice, I fell to the ground unconscious and lay there face downwards. [10] Then a hand took hold of me and raised me to my hands and knees; I was still trembling.

[11] The angel said to me, "Daniel, God loves you. Stand up and listen carefully to what I am going to say. I have been sent to you." When he had said this, I stood up, still trembling.

[12] Then he said, "Daniel, don't be afraid. God has heard your prayers ever since the first day you decided to humble yourself in order to gain understanding. I have come in answer to your prayer. [13] The angel prince of the kingdom of Persia opposed me for 21 days. Then Michael, one of the chief angels, came to help me, because I had been left there alone in Persia. [14] I have come to make you understand what will happen to your people in the future. This is a vision about the future."

[15] When he said this, I stared at the ground, speechless. [16] Then the angel, who looked like a human being, stretched out his hand and touched my lips. I said to him, "Sir, this vision makes me so weak that I can't stop trembling. [17] I am like a slave standing before his master. How can I talk to you? I have no strength or breath left in me."

[18] Once more he took hold of me, and I felt stronger. [19] He said, "God loves you, so don't let anything worry you or frighten you."

When he had said this, I felt even stronger and said, "Sir, tell me what you have to say. You have made me feel better."

[20-21] He said, "Do you know why I came to you? It is to reveal to you what is written in the Book of Truth. Now I have to go back and fight the guardian angel of Persia. After that, the guardian angel of Greece will appear. There is no one to help me except Michael, Israel's guardian angel.*

11 He is* responsible for helping and defending me. [2] And what I am now going to tell you is true."

The Kingdoms of Egypt and Syria

The angel said, "Three more kings will rule over Persia, followed by a fourth, who will be richer than all the others. At the height of his power and wealth he will challenge the kingdom of Greece.

[3] "Then a heroic king will appear. He will rule over a huge empire and do whatever he wants. [4] But at the height of his power his empire will break up and be divided into four parts. Kings not descended from him will rule in his place, but they will not have the power that he had.

[5] "The king of Egypt will be strong. One of his generals, however, will be even stronger and rule a greater kingdom. [6] After a number of years the king of Egypt will make an alliance with the king of Syria and give him his daughter in marriage. But the alliance

DANIEL 10.19

GOD LOVES YOU,
so don't let
ANYTHING
worry you or frighten you

10.20–21 Probable text *guardian angel*; Hebrew *guardian angel. And I, in the first year of Darius the Mede.*
11.1 One ancient translation *He is*; Hebrew *I am.*

1042

Daniel

Songs
Isaiah
Jerem.
Lamen.
Ezekiel

DANIEL 11

will not last, and she, her husband, her child,* and the servants who went with her will all be killed. [7]Soon afterwards, one of her relatives will become king. He will attack the army of the king of Syria, enter their fortress, and defeat them. [8]He will carry back to Egypt the images of their gods and the articles of gold and silver dedicated to those gods. After several years of peace [9]the king of Syria will invade Egypt, but he will be forced to retreat.

[10]"The sons of the king of Syria will prepare for war and gather a large army. One of them will sweep on like a flood and attack an enemy fortress. [11]In his anger the king of Egypt will go to war against the king of Syria and capture his huge army. [12]He will be proud of his victory and of the many soldiers he has killed, but he will not continue to be victorious.

[13]"The king of Syria will go back and gather a larger army than he had before. When the proper time comes, he will return with a large, well-equipped army. [14]Then many people will rebel against the king of Egypt. And some of the violent from your nation, Daniel, will rebel because of a vision they have seen, but they will be defeated. [15]So the king of Syria will lay siege to a fortified city and capture it. The soldiers of Egypt will not continue to fight; even the best of them will not have enough strength. [16]The Syrian invader will do with them as he pleases, without opposition. He will stand in the Promised Land and have it completely in his power.

[17]"The king of Syria will plan an expedition, using his whole army. Then, in order to destroy his enemy's kingdom, he will make an alliance with him and offer him his daughter* in marriage; but his plan will not succeed. [18]After that he will attack the nations by the sea and conquer many of them. But a foreign leader will defeat him and put an end to his arrogance; indeed he will turn the arrogance of Syria's king back on him.* [19]The king will return to the fortresses of his own land, but he will be defeated, and that will be the end of him.

[20]"He will be followed by another king, who will send an officer to oppress the people with taxes in order to increase the wealth of his kingdom. In a short time that king will be killed, but not publicly and not in battle."

The Evil King of Syria

[21]The angel went on to explain: "The next king of Syria will be an evil man who has no right to be king, but he will come unexpectedly and seize power by trickery. [22]Anyone who opposes him, even God's High Priest, will be swept away and wiped out. [23]By making treaties, he will deceive other nations, and he will grow stronger and stronger, even though he rules only a small nation. [24]He will invade a wealthy province without warning and will do things that none of his ancestors ever did. Then he will divide among his followers the goods and property he has captured in war. He will make plans to attack fortresses, but his time will soon run out.

[25]"He will boldly raise a large army to attack the king of Egypt, who will prepare to fight back with a huge and powerful army. But the king of Egypt will be deceived and will not be successful. [26]His closest advisers will ruin him. Many of his soldiers will be killed, and his army will be wiped out. [27]Then the two kings will

....

11.6 Some ancient translations *her child*; Hebrew *her father*.
11.17 *his daughter*; or *a young woman*.
11.18 Probable text *his arrogance... on him*; Hebrew unclear.

1043

Daniel

·········⠶

Hosea
Joel
Amos
Obadiah
Jonah

sit down to eat at the same table, but their motives will be evil, and they will lie to each other. They will not get what they want, because the time for it has not yet come. ²⁸ The king of Syria will return home with all the loot he has captured, determined to destroy the religion of God's people. He will do as he pleases and then return to his own land.

²⁹ "Later on he will invade Egypt again, but this time things will turn out differently. ³⁰ The Romans will come in ships and oppose him, and he will be frightened.

"Then he will turn back in a rage and try to destroy the religion of God's people. He will follow the advice of those who have abandoned that religion. ³¹ Some of his soldiers will desecrate the Temple. They will stop the daily sacrifices and set up The Awful Horror.* ³² By deceit the king will win the support of those who have already abandoned their religion, but those who follow God will fight back. ³³ Wise leaders of the people will share their wisdom with many others. But for a while some of them will be killed in battle or be burnt to death, and some will be robbed and made prisoners. ³⁴ While the killing is going on, God's people will receive a little help, even though many who join them will do so for selfish reasons. ³⁵ Some of those wise leaders will be killed, but as a result of this the people will be purified. This will continue until the end comes, the time that God has set.

³⁶ "The king of Syria will do as he pleases. He will boast that he is greater than any god, superior even to the Supreme God. He will be able to do this until the time when God punishes him. God will do exactly what he has planned. ³⁷ The king will ignore the god his ancestors served, and also the god that women love. In fact, he will ignore every god, because he will think he is greater than any of them. ³⁸ Instead, he will honour the god who protects fortresses. He will offer gold, silver, jewels, and other rich gifts to a god his ancestors never worshipped. ³⁹ To defend his fortresses, he will use people who worship a foreign god. He will give great honour to those who accept him as ruler, put them into high offices, and give them land as a reward.

⁴⁰ "When the king of Syria's final hour has almost come, the king of Egypt will attack him, and the king of Syria will fight back with all his power, using chariots, horses, and many ships. He will invade many countries, like the waters of a flood. ⁴¹ He will even invade the Promised Land and kill tens of thousands, but the countries of Edom, Moab, and what is left of Ammon will escape. ⁴² When he invades all those countries, even Egypt will not be spared. ⁴³ He will take away Egypt's hidden treasures of gold and silver and its other prized possessions. He will conquer Libya and Ethiopia. ⁴⁴ Then news that comes from the east and the north will frighten him, and he will fight furiously, killing many people. ⁴⁵ He will even set up his huge royal tents between the sea and the mountain on which the Temple stands. But he will die, with no one there to help him."

The Time of the End

12 The angel wearing linen clothes said, "At that time the great angel Michael, who guards your people, will appear. Then there will be a time of troubles, the worst since nations first came into existence. When that time comes, all the people of your nation whose names are written in God's book will be saved. ² Many of those who have already died will live again: some will

11.31 *The Awful Horror*: See 9.27.

1044

Daniel

·:·········

Songs
Isaiah
Jerem.
Lamen.
Ezekiel

DANIEL 12

enjoy eternal life, and some will suffer eternal disgrace. ³The wise leaders will shine with all the brightness of the sky. And those who have taught many people to do what is right will shine like the stars for ever."

⁴He said to me, "And now, Daniel, close the book and put a seal on it until the end of the world. Meanwhile, many people will waste their efforts trying to understand what is happening."

⁵Then I saw two men standing by a river, one on each bank. ⁶One of them asked the angel who was standing further upstream, "How long will it be until these amazing events come to an end?"

⁷The angel raised both hands towards the sky and made a solemn promise in the name of the Eternal God. I heard him say, "It will be 3.5 years. When the persecution of God's people ends, all these things will have happened."

⁸I heard what he said, but I did not understand it. So I asked, "But, sir, how will it all end?"

⁹He answered, "You must go now, Daniel, because these words are to be kept secret and hidden until the end comes. ¹⁰Many people will be purified. Those who are wicked will not understand but will go on being wicked; only those who are wise will understand.

¹¹"From the time the daily sacrifices are stopped, that is, from the time of The Awful Horror,* 1,290 days will pass. ¹²Happy are those who remain faithful until 1,335 days are over!

¹³"And you, Daniel, be faithful to the end. Then you will die, but you will rise to receive your reward at the end of time."

_____

12.11 *The Awful Horror:* See 9.27.

THE BOOK OF

HOSEA

WRITTEN: 715-710BC

WHY READ IT?

This book shows us more about God's heart than perhaps any of the other Old Testament books. It is a tragic, moving, powerful story of his love for the Israelites. It helps us to understand the reasons for God's wrath and judgement and how God never gives up on his people.

WHAT YOU NEED TO KNOW:

The story of Hosea (the first 'Minor Prophet' in the Bible) is a tragic but hope-filled love story. Hosea (a prophet we don't know much about) was called by God to marry a woman called Gomer. Gomer cheated on him and went into prostitution. Hosea bought her back and restored their relationship. The story is a picture of God's relationship with his people. Hosea's whole life is a prophecy and speaks of the heart of God for his people.

This story takes place just before Israel is conquered by the Assyrians. In it, God warns that, although there is a threat looming, if his people turn back to him he will shelter and protect them.

Write down the sort of

EMOTIONS

Hosea must have felt during his relationship with Gomer.

decorate & colour in these hearts

ONAH

HOSEA
IN ISRAEL BEFORE EXILE

(750-722BC)

ISAIAH

AMOS

MICAH

HABAKKUK

1046

Hosea

Isaiah
Jerem.
Lamen.
Ezekiel
Daniel

HOSEA 1, 2

HOSEA 1

Prophets were
sometimes asked by
God to do

• SOMETHING •
PRACTICAL

to show what their
prophecy meant. This is
especially true for
Hosea. He received these
prophecies just before
Israel was conquered by
the Assyrians, and
was shown, maybe
more than any other
prophet, the heart of
God for his people.

1 This is the message which the Lord gave Hosea son of Beeri during the time that Uzziah, Jotham, Ahaz, and Hezekiah were kings of Judah, and Jeroboam son of Jehoash was king of Israel.

Hosea's Wife and Children

² When the Lord first spoke to Israel through Hosea, he said to Hosea, "Go and get married; your wife will be unfaithful, and your children will be just like her.* In the same way, my people have left me and become unfaithful."

³ So Hosea married a woman named Gomer, the daughter of Diblaim. After the birth of their first child, a son, ⁴ the Lord said to Hosea, "Name him 'Jezreel', because it will not be long before I punish the king of Israel for the murders that his ancestor Jehu committed at Jezreel.* I am going to put an end to Jehu's dynasty.* ⁵ And in the Valley of Jezreel I will at that time destroy Israel's military power."

⁶ Gomer had a second child — this time it was a daughter. The Lord said to Hosea, "Name her 'Unloved', because I will no longer show love to the people of Israel or forgive them. ⁷ But to the people of Judah I will show love. I, the Lord their God, will save them, but I will not do it by war — with swords or bows and arrows or with horses and horsemen."

⁸ After Gomer had weaned her daughter, she became pregnant again and had another son. ⁹ The Lord said to Hosea, "Name him 'Not-my-People', because the people of Israel are not my people, and I am not their God."

Israel is to be Restored

¹⁰ The people of Israel will become like the sand of the sea, more than can be counted or measured. Now God says to them, "You are not my people," but the day is coming when he will say to them, "You are the children of the living God!" ¹¹ The people of Judah and the people of Israel will be reunited. They will choose for themselves a single leader, and once again they will grow and prosper in their land. Yes, the day of Jezreel* will be a great day!
2 So call your fellow-Israelites "God's People" and "Loved-by-the-Lord".

Unfaithful Gomer — Unfaithful Israel

² My children, plead with your mother — though she is no longer a wife to me, and I am no longer her husband. Plead with her to stop her adultery and prostitution. ³ If she does not, I will strip her as naked as she was on the day she was born. I will make her like a dry and barren land, and she will die of thirst. ⁴⁻⁵ I will not show mercy to her children; they are the children of a shameless prostitute.* She herself said, "I will go to my lovers — they give me food and water, wool and linen, olive oil and wine."

⁶ So I am going to fence her in with thorn bushes and build a wall to block her way. ⁷ She will run after her lovers but will not catch

1.2 *get married; your wife… her*; or *marry a prostitute, and have children by her who will be just as bad as she is.*
1.4 *Jezreel*: At this city Jehu assassinated the king of Israel and all the rest of the royal family, and became the first king of a new dynasty (see 2 Kgs 9—10).
1.4 *Jehu's dynasty*; or *the kingdom of Israel.*
1.11 *Jezreel*: This name in Hebrew means "God sows" and suggests growth and prosperity.
2.4–5 *the children of a shameless prostitute*; or *as shameless as their mother, a prostitute.*

them. She will look for them but will not find them. Then she will say, "I am going back to my first husband — I was better off then than I am now."

[8] She would never acknowledge that I am the one who gave her the corn, the wine, the olive oil, and all the silver and gold that she used in the worship of Baal. [9] So at harvest time I will take back my gifts of corn and wine, and will take away the wool and the linen I gave her for clothing. [10] I will strip her naked in front of her lovers, and no one will be able to save her from my power. [11] I will put an end to all her festivities — her annual and monthly festivals and her Sabbath celebrations — all her religious meetings. [12] I will destroy her grapevines and her fig trees, which she said her lovers gave her for serving them. I will turn her vineyards and orchards into a wilderness; wild animals will destroy them. [13] I will punish her for the times that she forgot me when she burnt incense to Baal and put on her jewellery to go chasing after her lovers. The LORD has spoken.

The LORD's Love for his People

[14] So I am going to take her into the desert again; there I will win her back with words of love. [15] I will give back to her the vineyards she had and make Trouble Valley a door of hope. She will respond to me there as she did when she was young, when she came from Egypt. [16] Then once again she will call me her husband — she will no longer call me her Baal.* [17] I will never let her speak the name of Baal again.

[18] At that time I will make a covenant with all the wild animals and birds, so that they will not harm my people. I will also remove all weapons of war from the land, all swords and bows, and will let my people live in peace and safety.

[19] Israel, I will make you my wife;
    I will be true and faithful;
    I will show you constant love and mercy
    and make you mine for ever.
[20] I will keep my promise and make you mine,
    and you will acknowledge me as LORD.
[21-22] At that time I will answer the prayers of my people Israel.*
    I will make rain fall on the earth,
    and the earth will produce corn and grapes and olives.
[23] I will establish my people in the land and make them prosper.
    I will show love to those who were called "Unloved",
    and to those who were called "Not-my-People"
    I will say, "You are my people,"
    and they will answer, "You are our God."

Hosea and the Unfaithful Woman

3 The LORD said to me, "Go again* and show your love for a woman who is committing adultery with a lover. You must love her just as I still love the people of Israel, even though they turn to other gods and like to take offerings of raisins to idols."*

[2] So I paid fifteen pieces of silver and 150 kilogrammes of barley to buy her. [3] I told her that for a long time she would have

....

2.16 *Baal*: This title of the Canaanite god means "Lord"; another meaning of the word is "husband".
2.21–22 *Israel*: The Hebrew text here refers to Israel as Jezreel (see 1.4, 11).
3.1 *The LORD ... again*; or *The LORD spoke to me again. He said, "Go ... "*
3.1 *offerings of raisins to idols*: Dried grapes were used in the worship of fertility gods, who were believed to give abundant harvests to their worshippers.

1048

Hosea

᛭᛬᛬᛬᛬᛬᛬᛬

Isaiah
Jerem.
Lamen.
Ezekiel
Daniel

HOSEA 3, 4

to wait for me without being a prostitute or committing adultery; and during this time I would wait for her. ⁴In just this way the people of Israel will have to live for a long time without kings or leaders, without sacrifices or sacred stone pillars, without idols or images to use for divination. ⁵But the time will come when the people of Israel will once again turn to the LORD their God, and to a descendant of David their king. Then they will fear the LORD and will receive his good gifts.

The LORD's Accusation against Israel

4 The LORD has an accusation to bring against the people who live in this land. Listen, Israel, to what he says: "There is no faithfulness or love in the land, and the people do not acknowledge me as God. ²They make promises and break them; they lie, murder, steal, and commit adultery. Crimes increase, and there is one murder after another. ³And so the land will dry up, and everything that lives on it will die. All the animals and birds, and even the fish, will die."

The LORD Accuses the Priests

⁴The LORD says, "Let no one accuse the people or reprimand them — my complaint is against you priests.* ⁵Night and day you blunder on, and the prophets do no better than you. I am going to destroy Israel, your mother. ⁶My people are doomed because they do not acknowledge me. You priests have refused to acknowledge me and have rejected my teaching, and so I reject you and will not acknowledge your sons as my priests.

⁷"The more of you priests there are, the more you sin against me, and so I will turn your honour into disgrace. ⁸You grow rich from the sins of my people, and so you want them to sin more and more. ⁹You will suffer the same punishment as the people! I will punish you and make you pay for the evil you do. ¹⁰You will eat your share of the sacrifices, but still be hungry. You will worship the fertility gods, but still have no children, because you have turned away from me to follow other gods."

The LORD Condemns Pagan Worship

¹¹The LORD says, "Wine, both old and new, is robbing my people of their senses! ¹²They ask for revelations from a piece of wood! A stick tells them what they want to know! They have left me. Like a woman who becomes a prostitute, they have given themselves to other gods. ¹³At sacred places on the mountain tops they offer sacrifices, and on the hills they burn incense under tall, spreading trees, because the shade is so pleasant!

"As a result, your daughters serve as prostitutes, and your daughters-in-law commit adultery. ¹⁴Yet I will not punish them for this, because you yourselves go off with temple prostitutes,* and together with them you offer pagan sacrifices. As the proverb says, 'A people without sense will be ruined.'

¹⁵"Even though you people of Israel are unfaithful to me, may Judah not be guilty of the same thing. Don't worship at Gilgal or Bethaven,* or make promises there in the name of the living LORD.

4.4 Probable text *my complaint is against you priests*; Hebrew *your people are like those with a complaint against the priests.*
4.14 *temple prostitutes*: These women were found in Canaanite temples, where fertility gods were worshipped. It was believed that intercourse with these prostitutes assured fertile fields and herds.
4.15 *Bethaven*: This name means "house of evil" or "house of idolatry" and in this passage refers to the city of Bethel, a name which means "house of God". See also 5.8, 10.5 and 10.8.

HOSEA 4–6

1049

Hosea
...........:

Joel
Amos
Obadiah
Jonah
Micah

¹⁶ The people of Israel are as stubborn as mules. How can I feed them like lambs in a meadow? ¹⁷ The people of Israel are under the spell of idols. Let them go their own way. ¹⁸ After drinking much wine, they delight in their prostitution, preferring disgrace to honour. ¹⁹ They will be carried away as by the wind, and they will be ashamed of their pagan sacrifices.*

5 "Listen to this, you priests! Pay attention, people of Israel! Listen, you that belong to the royal family! You are supposed to judge with justice — so judgement will fall on you! You have become a trap at Mizpah, a net spread on Mount Tabor, ²a deep pit at Acacia City,* and I will punish all of you. ³ I know what Israel is like — she cannot hide from me. She has been unfaithful, and her people are unfit to worship me."

Hosea Warns against Idolatry

⁴ The evil that the people have done prevents them from returning to their God. Idolatry has a powerful hold on them, and they do not acknowledge the Lord. ⁵ The arrogance of the people of Israel cries out against them. Their sins make them stumble and fall, and the people of Judah fall with them. ⁶ They take their sheep and cattle to offer as sacrifices to the Lord, but it does them no good. They cannot find him, for he has left them. ⁷ They have been unfaithful to the Lord; their children do not belong to him. So now they and their lands will soon be destroyed.

War between Judah and Israel

⁸ Blow the war trumpets in Gibeah! Sound the alarm in Ramah! Raise the war cry at Bethaven!* Into battle, men of Benjamin! ⁹ The day of punishment is coming, and Israel will be ruined. People of Israel, this will surely happen!

¹⁰ The Lord says, "I am angry because the leaders of Judah have invaded Israel and stolen land from her. So I will pour out punishment on them like a flood. ¹¹ Israel is suffering oppression; she has lost land that was rightfully hers, because she insisted on going for help to those who had none to give.* ¹² I will bring destruction on Israel and ruin on the people of Judah.

¹³ "When Israel saw how sick she was and when Judah saw her own wounds, then Israel went to Assyria to ask the great emperor for help, but he could not cure them or heal their wounds. ¹⁴ I will attack the people of Israel and Judah like a lion. I myself will tear them to pieces and then leave them. When I drag them off, no one will be able to save them.

¹⁵ "I will abandon my people until they have suffered enough for their sins and come looking for me. Perhaps in their suffering they will try to find me."

The People's Insincere Repentance

6 The people say, "Let's return to the Lord! He has hurt us, but he will be sure to heal us; he has wounded us, but he will bandage our wounds, won't he? ² In two or three days he will revive us, and we will live in his presence. ³ Let us try to know the Lord. He will come to us as surely as the day dawns, as surely as the spring rains that water the earth."

4.19 *sacrifices*; some ancient translations *altars*. Verses 17–19 in Hebrew are unclear.
5.2 Probable text *a deep pit at Acacia City*; Hebrew unclear.
5.8 *Bethaven*: See 4.15.
5.11 Probable text *those who had none to give*; Hebrew *command*.

1050

Hosea

Isaiah
Jerem.
Lamen.
Ezekiel
Daniel

HOSEA 6.6

God wants a deep

RELATIONSHIP
– WITH US. –

Whether you know him or
not, on this page

WRITE A SHORT
NOTE TO GOD.

It can be serious,
colourful, funny or just
about your day!

_____

_____

_____

_____

_____

_____

_____

_____

_____

_____

_____

_____

_____

_____

_____

4 But the LORD says, "Israel and Judah, what am I going to do with you? Your love for me disappears as quickly as morning mist; it is like dew, that vanishes early in the day. 5 That is why I have sent my prophets to you with my message of judgement and destruction. What I want from you is plain and clear: 6 I want your constant love, not your animal sacrifices. I would rather have my people know me than burn offerings to me.

7 "But as soon as they entered the land at Adam,* they broke the covenant I had made with them. 8 Gilead is a city full of evil people and murderers. 9 The priests are like a gang of robbers who wait in ambush for someone. Even on the road to the holy place at Shechem they commit murder. And they do all this evil deliberately! 10 I have seen a horrible thing in Israel: my people have defiled themselves by worshipping idols.

11 "And as for you, people of Judah, I have set a time to punish you also for what you are doing.

7 "Whenever I want to heal my people Israel and make them prosperous again, all I can see is their wickedness and the evil they do. They cheat one another; they break into houses and steal; they rob people in the streets. 2 It never enters their heads that I will remember all this evil; but their sins surround them, and I cannot avoid seeing them."

Conspiracy in the Palace

3 The LORD says, "People deceive the king and his officers by their evil plots. 4 They are all treacherous and disloyal. Their hatred smoulders like the fire in an oven, which is not stirred by the baker until the dough is ready to bake. 5 On the day of the king's celebration they made the king and his officials drunk and foolish with wine. 6 Yes, they burned* like an oven with their plotting. All night their anger smouldered, and in the morning it burst into flames.

7 "In the heat of their anger they murdered their rulers. Their kings have been assassinated one after another, but no one prays to me for help."

Israel and the Nations

8 The LORD says, "The people of Israel are like a half-baked loaf of bread. They rely on the nations around them 9 and do not realize that this reliance on foreigners has robbed them of their strength. Their days are numbered, but they don't even know it. 10 The arrogance of the people of Israel cries out against them. In spite of everything that has happened, they have not returned to me, the LORD their God. 11 Israel flits about like a silly pigeon; first her people call on Egypt for help, and then they run to Assyria! 12 But I will spread out a net and catch them like birds as they go by. I will punish them for the evil they have done.*

13 "They are doomed! They have left me and rebelled against me. They will be destroyed. I wanted to save them, but their worship of me was false. 14 They have not prayed to me sincerely, but instead they throw themselves down and wail as the heathen do. When they pray for corn and wine, they gash themselves like pagans. What rebels they are! 15 Even though I was the one who brought them up and made them strong, they plotted against

6.7 Probable text But... at Adam; Hebrew But like Adam.
7.6 One ancient translation burned; Hebrew drew near.
7.12 Probable text the evil they have done; Hebrew the report to their congregation.

HOSEA 7–9

1051

Hosea

⋯⋯⋯⋮

Joel
Amos
Obadiah
Jonah
Micah

me. ¹⁶ They keep on turning away from me to a god that is powerless.* They are as unreliable as a crooked bow. Because their leaders talk arrogantly, they will die a violent death, and the Egyptians will laugh."

The LORD Condemns Israel for Idol Worship

8 The LORD says, "Sound the alarm! Enemies are swooping down on my land like eagles! My people have broken the covenant I made with them and have rebelled against my teaching. ² Even though they call me their God and claim that they are my people and that they know me, ³ they have rejected what is good. Because of this their enemies will pursue them.

⁴ "My people chose kings, but they did it on their own. They appointed leaders, but without my approval. They took their silver and gold and made idols — for their own destruction. ⁵ I hate the gold bull worshipped by the people of the city of Samaria. I am furious with them. How long will it be before they give up their idolatry? ⁶ An Israelite craftsman made the idol, and it is not a god at all! The gold bull worshipped in Samaria will be smashed to pieces! ⁷ When they sow the wind, they will reap a storm! A field of corn that doesn't ripen can never produce any bread. But even if it did, foreigners would eat it up. ⁸ Israel has become like any other nation and is as useless as a broken pot. ⁹ Stubborn as wild donkeys, the people of Israel go their own way. They have gone off to seek help from Assyria, and have paid other nations to protect them. ¹⁰ But now I am going to gather them together and punish them. Soon they will writhe in pain, when the emperor of Assyria oppresses them.

¹¹ "The more altars the people of Israel build for removing sin, the more places they have for sinning! ¹² I write down countless teachings for the people, but they reject them as strange and foreign. ¹³ They offer sacrifices to me and eat the meat of the sacrifices.* But I, the LORD, am not pleased with them, and now I will remember their sin and punish them for it; I will send them back to Egypt!

¹⁴ "The people of Israel have built palaces, but they have forgotten their own Maker. The people of Judah have built fortified cities. But I will send fire that will burn down their palaces and their cities."

Hosea Announces Punishment for Israel

9 People of Israel, stop celebrating your festivals like pagans. You have turned away from your God and have been unfaithful to him. All over the land you have sold yourselves like prostitutes to the god Baal and have loved the corn you thought he paid you with! ² But soon you will not have enough corn and olive oil, and there will be no wine. ³ The people of Israel will not remain in the LORD's land, but will have to go back to Egypt and will have to eat forbidden food* in Assyria. ⁴ In those foreign lands they will not be able to make offerings of wine to the LORD, or bring their sacrifices to him. Their food will defile everyone who eats it, like food eaten at funerals. It will be used only to satisfy their hunger; none of it will be taken as an offering to the LORD's Temple. ⁵ And when the time comes

7.16 Probable text *a god... powerless*; Hebrew unclear.
8.13 *They offer... the sacrifices*; Hebrew unclear.
9.3 *forbidden food*: The Law of Moses prohibited the eating of certain foods as being ritually unclean (see Lev 11).

1052

Hosea

:·········

Isaiah
Jerem.
Lamen.
Ezekiel
Daniel

HOSEA 9, 10

for the appointed festivals in honour of the LORD, what will they do then? [6]When the disaster comes and the people are scattered, the Egyptians will gather them up — gather them for burial there at Memphis! Their treasures of silver and the places where their homes once stood will be overgrown with weeds and thorn bushes.

[7]The time for punishment has come, the time when people will get what they deserve. When that happens, Israel will know it! "This prophet," you say, "is a fool. This inspired man is insane." You people hate me so much because your sin is so great. [8]God has sent me as a prophet to warn his people Israel. Yet wherever I go, you try to trap me like a bird. Even in God's Temple the people are the prophet's enemies. [9]They are hopelessly evil in what they do, just as they were at Gibeah.* God will remember their sin and punish them for it.

Israel's Sin and its Consequences

[10]The LORD says, "When I first found Israel, it was like finding grapes growing in the desert. When I first saw your ancestors, it was like seeing the first ripe figs of the season. But when they came to Mount Peor, they began to worship Baal, and soon became as disgusting as the gods they loved. [11]Israel's greatness will fly away like a bird, and there will be no more children born to them, no more women pregnant, no more children conceived. [12]But even if they did bring up children, I would take them away and not leave one alive. When I abandon these people, terrible things will happen to them."

[13]LORD, I can see their children being hunted down* and killed. [14]What shall I ask you to do to these people? Make their women barren! Make them unable to nurse their babies!

The LORD's Judgement on Israel

[15]The LORD says, "All their evil-doing began in Gilgal. It was there that I began to hate them. And because of the evil they have done, I will drive them out of my land. I will not love them any more; all their leaders have rebelled against me. [16]The people of Israel are like a plant whose roots have dried up and which bears no fruit. They will have no children, but even if they did, I would kill the children so dear to them."

The Prophet Speaks about Israel

[17]The God I serve will reject his people, because they have not listened to him. They will become wanderers among the nations.

10 The people of Israel were like a grapevine that was full of grapes. The more prosperous they were, the more altars they built. The more productive their land was, the more beautiful they made the sacred stone pillars they worship. [2]The people whose hearts are deceitful must now suffer for their sins. God will break down their altars and destroy their sacred pillars.

[3]These people will soon be saying, "We have no king because we did not fear the LORD. But what could a king do for us anyway?" [4]They utter empty words and make false promises and useless treaties. Justice has become injustice, growing like poisonous weeds in a ploughed field.

....

9.9 *Gibeah*: At this city some Israelites of the tribe of Benjamin raped a Levite's concubine; this caused a civil war that almost wiped out the Benjaminites (see Judg 19—21).
9.13 Probable text *being hunted down*; Hebrew unclear.

Hosea

.........⋮.

Joel
Amos
Obadiah
Jonah
Micah

5 The people who live in the city of Samaria will be afraid and will mourn the loss of the gold bull* at Bethaven*. They and the priests who serve the idol will weep over it. They will wail when it is stripped of its golden splendour. 6 The idol will be carried off to Assyria as tribute to the great emperor. The people of Israel will be disgraced and put to shame because of the advice they followed. 7 Their king will be carried off, like a chip of wood on water. 8 The hilltop shrines of Aven,* where the people of Israel worship idols, will be destroyed. Thorns and weeds will grow up over their altars. The people will call out to the mountains, "Hide us!" and to the hills, "Cover us!"

The LORD Pronounces Judgement on Israel

9 The LORD says, "The people of Israel have not stopped sinning against me since the time of their sin at Gibeah.* So at Gibeah war will catch up with them. 10 I will attack* this sinful people and punish them. Nations will join together against them, and they will be punished for their many sins.

11 "Israel was once like a well-trained young cow, ready and willing to thresh grain. But I decided to put a yoke* on her beautiful neck and to harness her for harder work. I made Judah pull the plough and Israel pull the harrow. 12 I said, 'Plough new ground for yourselves, plant righteousness, and reap the blessings that your devotion to me will produce. It is time for you to turn to me, your LORD, and I will come and pour out blessings upon you.' 13 But instead you planted evil and reaped its harvest. You have eaten the fruit produced by your lies.

"Because you trusted in your chariots* and in the large number of your soldiers, 14 war will come to your people, and all your fortresses will be destroyed. It will be like the day when King Shalman destroyed the city of Betharbel in battle, and mothers and their children were crushed to death. 15 That is what will happen to you, people of Bethel, because of the terrible evil that you have done. As soon as the battle begins, the king of Israel will die."

God's Love for his Rebellious People

11 The LORD says,
"When Israel was a child, I loved him
and called him out of Egypt as my son.*
2 But the more I* called to him,
the more he turned away from me.*
My people sacrificed to Baal;
they burnt incense to idols.
3 Yet I was the one who taught Israel to walk.
I took my people up in my arms,*
but they did not acknowledge that I took care of them.

RIGHTEOUSNESS

PROVERBS 11.30;
HOSEA 10.12;
2 PETER 3.13

DEFINITION: The quality of
being morally right
or justifiable.
(oxforddictionaries.com)

10.5 Some ancient translations *bull*; Hebrew *cows*.
10.5 *Bethaven*: This name means "house of evil" or "house of idolatry" and in this passage refers to the city of Bethel, a name which means "house of God". In verse 8, Bethaven is called Aven. See also 4.15 and 5.8.
10.8 *Aven*: See 10.5.
10.9 *Gibeah*: See 9.9.
10.10 One ancient translation *I will attack*; Hebrew *In my desire*.
10.11 Probable text *put a yoke*; Hebrew *spare*.
10.13 One ancient translation *chariots*; Hebrew *way*.
11.1 *him and called him... son*; or *him; from the time he left Egypt I have called him my son*.
11.2 One ancient translation *I*; Hebrew *they*.
11.2 One ancient translation *me*; Hebrew *them*.
11.3 One ancient translation *I... my arms*; Hebrew *He... his arms*.

1054

Hosea

.·:·.......

Isaiah
Jerem.
Lamen.
Ezekiel
Daniel

HOSEA 11, 12

HOSEA 11.8

MY love FOR you · is too · STRONG

4 I drew them to me with affection and love.
  I picked them up and held them to my cheek;
  I bent down to them and fed them.*

5 "They refuse to return to me, and so they must return to Egypt, and Assyria will rule them. 6 War will sweep through their cities and break down the city gates. It will destroy my people because they do what they themselves think best. 7 They insist on turning away from me. They will cry out because of the yoke that is on them, but no one will lift it from them.*

8 "How can I give you up, Israel?
    How can I abandon you?
  Could I ever destroy you as I did Admah,
    or treat you as I did Zeboiim?
  My heart will not let me do it!
    My love for you is too strong.
9 I will not punish you in my anger;
    I will not destroy Israel again.
  For I am God and not a human being.
    I, the Holy One, am with you.
  I will not come to you in anger.

10 "My people will follow me when I roar like a lion at their enemies. They will hurry to me from the west. 11 They will come from Egypt, as swiftly as birds, and from Assyria, like doves. I will bring them to their homes again. I, the Lord, have spoken."

Israel and Judah are Condemned

12 The Lord says, "The people of Israel have surrounded me with lies and deceit, and the people of Judah are still rebelling against me, the faithful and holy God.

12 Everything that the people of Israel do from morning to night is useless and destructive. Treachery and acts of violence increase among them. They make treaties with Assyria and do business with Egypt."

2 The Lord has an accusation to bring against the people of Judah; he is also going to punish Israel for the way her people act. He will pay them back for what they have done. 3 Their ancestor Jacob struggled with his twin brother Esau while the two of them were still in their mother's womb; when Jacob grew up, he fought against God — 4 he fought against an angel and won. He wept and asked for a blessing. And at Bethel God came to our ancestor Jacob and spoke with him.* 5 This was the Lord God Almighty — the Lord is the name by which he is to be worshipped. 6 So now, descendants of Jacob, trust in your God and return to him. Be loyal and just, and wait patiently for your God to act.

Further Words of Judgement

7 The Lord says, "The people of Israel are as dishonest as the Canaanites; they love to cheat their customers with false scales. 8 'We are rich,' they say. 'We've made a fortune. And no one can accuse us of getting rich dishonestly.' 9 But I, the Lord your God who led you out of Egypt, I will make you live in tents again, as you did when I came to you in the desert.

···

11.4 Verse 4 in Hebrew is unclear.
11.7 Verse 7 in Hebrew is unclear.
12.4 Some ancient translations *him*; Hebrew *us*.

HOSEA 12–14

1055

Hosea
........:

Joel
Amos
Obadiah
Jonah
Micah

¹⁰"I spoke to the prophets and gave them many visions, and through the prophets I gave my people warnings. ¹¹Yet idols are worshipped in Gilead, and those who worship them will die. Bulls are sacrificed in Gilgal, and the altars there will become piles of stone in the open fields."

¹²Our ancestor Jacob had to flee to Mesopotamia, where, in order to get a wife, he worked for another man and took care of his sheep. ¹³The LORD sent a prophet to rescue the people of Israel from slavery in Egypt and to take care of them. ¹⁴The people of Israel have made the LORD bitterly angry; they deserve death for their crimes. Their Lord will punish them for the disgrace they have brought on him.

Final Judgement on Israel

13 In the past, when the tribe of Ephraim spoke, the other tribes of Israel were afraid; they looked up to Ephraim. But the people sinned by worshipping Baal, and for this they will die. ²They still keep on sinning by making metal images to worship — idols of silver, designed by human minds, made by human hands. And then they say, "Offer sacrifices to them!" How can anyone kiss those idols — idols in the shape of bulls!* ³And so these people will disappear like morning mist, like the dew that vanishes early in the day. They will be like chaff which the wind blows from the threshing place, like smoke from a chimney.

⁴The LORD says, "I am the LORD your God, who led you out of Egypt. You have no God but me. I alone am your saviour. ⁵I took care of you in a dry, desert land. ⁶But when you entered the good land, you became full and satisfied, and then you grew proud and forgot me. ⁷So I will attack you like a lion. Like a leopard I will lie in wait along your path. ⁸I will attack you like a bear that has lost her cubs, and I will tear you open. Like a lion I will devour you on the spot, and will tear you to pieces like a wild animal.

⁹"I will destroy you, people of Israel! Then who can help you?* ¹⁰You asked for a king and for leaders, but how can they save the nation?* ¹¹In my anger I have given you kings, and in my fury I have taken them away.

¹²"Israel's sin and guilt are on record, and the records are safely stored away. ¹³Israel has a chance to live, but is too foolish to take it — like a child about to be born, who refuses to come out of the womb. ¹⁴I will not save this people from the world of the dead or rescue them from the power of death. Bring on* your plagues, death! Bring on your destruction, world of the dead! I will no longer have pity for this people. ¹⁵Even though Israel flourishes like weeds,* I will send a hot east wind from the desert, and it will dry up their springs and wells. It will take away everything of value. ¹⁶Samaria must be punished for rebelling against me. Her people will die in war; babies will be dashed to the ground, and pregnant women will be ripped open."

Hosea's Plea to Israel

14 Return to the LORD your God, people of Israel. Your sin has made you stumble and fall. ²Return to the LORD, and let this prayer be your offering to him: "Forgive all our sins and

....

13.2 Probable text *And then they... bulls!*; Hebrew unclear.
13.9 One ancient translation *who can help you?*; Hebrew *in me is your help.*
13.10 Verse 10 in Hebrew is unclear.
13.14 Some ancient translations *Bring on*; Hebrew *I will be.*
13.15 Probable text *like weeds*; Hebrew *among brothers.*

1056

Hosea

⋮⋯⋯⋯

Isaiah
Jerem.
Lamen.
Ezekiel
Daniel

HOSEA 14

accept our prayer, and we will praise you as we have promised. [3] Assyria can never save us, and war horses cannot protect us. We will never again say to our idols that they are our God. O LORD, you show mercy to those who have no one else to turn to."

The LORD Promises New Life for Israel

[4] The LORD says,

"I will bring my people back to me.
I will love them with all my heart;
    no longer am I angry with them.
[5] I will be to the people of Israel
    like rain in a dry land.
They will blossom like flowers;
    they will be firmly rooted
    like the trees of Lebanon.
[6] They will be alive with new growth,
    and beautiful like olive trees.
They will be fragrant
    like the cedars of Lebanon.
[7] Once again they will live under my protection.
They will grow corn
    and be fruitful like a vineyard.
They will be as famous as the wine of Lebanon.
[8] The people of Israel* will have nothing more to do with
        idols;
    I will answer their prayers and take care of them;
Like an evergreen tree I will shelter them;
    I am the source of all their blessings."

Conclusion

[9] May those who are wise understand what is written here, and may they take it to heart. The LORD's ways are right, and righteous people live by following them, but sinners stumble and fall because they ignore them.

14.8 One ancient translation *The people of Israel*; Hebrew *Israel, I.*

THE BOOK OF

JOEL

WRITTEN: SOMETIME BETWEEN 850 AND 400BC

WHY READ IT?

The book of Joel is partly about making sense of a natural disaster brought by God. For those who relied on the land for food, locusts were one of the worst kind of swarms. Joel teaches us how devastating the day will be when God finally answers those who are determined to be his enemies. Like many other prophetic writings, although the book starts with judgement, it ends with some amazing promises of hope. Just read chapter 2 verse 28! It's also an interesting insight into beliefs about the Spirit of God in the Old Testament.

WHAT YOU NEED TO KNOW:

The book of Joel is split into two parts. In chapter 1, Jerusalem has been bombarded by a huge swarm of locusts, followed by a drought. Locusts destroyed crops and caused utter devastation. The second chapter sees the prophet Joel interpret these events as a warning from God of what will happen on the final judgement day. The Israelites saw the day of judgement as the time when they would have victory as God wiped out their enemies. Joel's prophecy was a stern warning that if God's people didn't obey him, the day of judgement would not turn out as they expected.

Can you think of any nations today that have been stripped of resources? Research some online, draw their outlines in <u>this box</u> and pray for them.

835BC →   400BC →

JOEL
FIRST PROPHET OR LAST PROPHET? WE JUST DON'T KNOW!

1058

Joel

Jerem.
Lamen.
Ezekiel
Daniel
Hosea

JOEL 1

1 This is the LORD's message to Joel son of Pethuel.

The People Mourn the Destruction of the Crops

2 Pay attention, you older people;
　　everyone in Judah, listen.
Has anything like this ever happened
　　in your time or the time of your ancestors?
3 Tell your children about it;
　　they will tell their children,
　　who in turn will tell the next generation.

4 Swarm after swarm of locusts settled on the crops;
　　what one swarm left, the next swarm devoured.
5 Wake up and weep, you drunkards;
　　cry, you wine drinkers;
　　the grapes for making new wine have been destroyed.

6 An army of locusts has attacked our land;
　　they are powerful and too many to count;
　　their teeth are as sharp as those of a lion.
7 They have destroyed our grapevines
　　and chewed up our fig trees.
They have stripped off the bark,
　　till the branches are white.

8 Cry, you people, like a young woman who mourns the
　　　death
　　of the man she was going to marry.
9 There is no corn or wine to offer in the Temple;
　　the priests mourn because they have no offerings for
　　　the LORD.
10 The fields are bare;
　the ground mourns
　　because the corn is destroyed,
　　the grapes are dried up,
　　and the olive trees are withered.

11 Grieve, you farmers;
　cry, you that take care of the vineyards,
　　because the wheat, the barley,
　　yes, all the crops are destroyed.
12 The grapevines and fig trees have withered;
　　all the fruit trees have wilted and died.
The joy of the people is gone.
13 Put on sackcloth and weep,
　　you priests who serve at the altar!
Go into the Temple and mourn all night!
There is no corn or wine to offer your God.
14 Give orders for a fast;
　　call an assembly!
Gather the leaders
　　and all the people of Judah
into the Temple of the LORD your God
　　and cry out to him.
15 The day of the LORD is near;
　　the day when the Almighty brings destruction.
　　What terror that day will bring!
16 We look on helpless as our crops are destroyed.
　　There is no joy in the Temple of our God.

1059

Joel
....

Amos
Obadiah
Jonah
Micah
Nahum

17 The seeds die in the dry earth.
  There is no grain to be stored,
    and so the empty granaries are in ruins.
18 The cattle are bellowing in distress
    because there is no pasture for them;
    the flocks of sheep also suffer.
19 I cry out to you, LORD,
    because the pastures and trees are dried up,
    as though a fire had burnt them.
20 Even the wild animals cry out to you
    because the streams have become dry.

The Locusts as a Warning of the Day of the LORD

2 Blow the trumpet; sound the alarm
    on Zion, God's sacred hill.*
  Tremble, people of Judah!
    The day of the LORD is coming soon.
2 It will be a dark and gloomy day,
    a black and cloudy day.
  The great army of locusts advances
    like darkness spreading over the mountains.
  There has never been anything like it,
    and there never will be again.

3 Like fire they eat up the plants.
    In front of them the land is like the Garden of Eden,
    but behind them it is a barren desert.
  Nothing escapes them.
4 They look like horses;
    they run like war horses.
5 As they leap on the tops of the mountains,
    they rattle like chariots;
    they crackle like dry grass on fire.
  They are lined up like a great army ready for battle.
6 As they approach, everyone is terrified;
    every face turns pale.
7 They attack like warriors;
    they climb the walls like soldiers.
  They all keep marching straight ahead
    and do not change direction
8   or get in each other's way.
  They swarm through defences,
    and nothing can stop them.
9 They rush against the city;
    they run over the walls;
    they climb up the houses
    and go in through the windows like thieves.

10 The earth shakes as they advance;
    the sky trembles.
  The sun and the moon grow dark,
    and the stars no longer shine.
11 The LORD thunders commands to his army.
    The troops that obey him
    are many and mighty.
  How terrible is the day of the LORD!
    Who will survive it?

....

2.1 *sacred hill*: Mount Zion.

1060

Joel

Jerem.
Lamen.
Ezekiel
Daniel
Hosea

JOEL 2

JOEL 2.12-32

God often says through his prophets that if his people repent, he will restore them. Repentance means

– CHANGING –

DIREGTION.

Read Joel 2.12-32, then close this book and bring to mind anything you're doing that you know isn't right. How can you change your direction? Ask God to help you.

A Call to Repentance

12 "But even now," says the LORD,
    "repent sincerely and return to me
    with fasting and weeping and mourning.
13 Let your broken heart show your sorrow;
    tearing your clothes is not enough."

Come back to the LORD your God.
    He is kind and full of mercy;
    he is patient and keeps his promise;
    he is always ready to forgive and not punish.
14 Perhaps the LORD your God will change his mind
    and bless you with abundant crops.
    Then you can offer him corn and wine.

15 Blow the trumpet on Mount Zion;
    give orders for a fast and call an assembly!
16 Gather the people together;
    prepare them for a sacred meeting;
    bring the old people;
    gather the children and the babies too.
    Even newly married couples
    must leave their room and come.
17 The priests, serving the LORD
    between the altar and the entrance of the Temple,
    must weep and pray:
    "Have pity on your people, LORD.
    Do not let other nations despise us and mock us
    by saying, 'Where is your God?'"

God Restores Fertility to the Land

18 Then the LORD showed concern for his land;
    he had mercy on his people.
19 He answered them:
    "Now I am going to give you
    corn and wine and olive oil, and you will be satisfied.
    Other nations will no longer despise you.
20 I will remove the locust army that came from the north
    and will drive some of them into the desert.
    Their front ranks will be driven into the Dead Sea,
    their rear ranks into the Mediterranean.
    Their dead bodies will stink.
    I will destroy them because of all they have done to you.

21 "Fields, don't be afraid,
    but be joyful and glad
    because of all the LORD has done for you.
22 Animals, don't be afraid.
    The pastures are green;
    the trees bear their fruit,
    and there are plenty of figs and grapes.

23 "Be glad, people of Zion,
    rejoice at what the LORD your God has done for you.
    He has given you the right amount of autumn rain;*
    he has poured down the winter rain for you
    and the spring rain as before.

2.23 right amount of autumn rain; or autumn rain because he is just.

JOEL 2, 3

1061

Joel
............:.

Amos
Obadiah
Jonah
Micah
Nahum

24 The threshing places will be full of corn;
the pits beside the presses will overflow with wine and
olive oil.
25 I will give you back what you lost
in the years when swarms of locusts ate your crops.
It was I who sent this army against you.
26 Now you will have plenty to eat, and be satisfied.
You will praise the Lord your God,
who has done wonderful things for you.
My people will never be despised again.
27 Then, Israel, you will know that I am among you,
and that I, the Lord, am your God
and there is no other.
My people will never be despised again.

The Day of the Lord

28 "Afterwards I will pour out my Spirit on everyone:
your sons and daughters will proclaim my message;
your old people will have dreams,
and your young people will see visions.
29 At that time I will pour out my Spirit
even on servants, both men and women.

30 "I will give warnings of that day
in the sky and on the earth;
there will be bloodshed, fire, and clouds of smoke.
31 The sun will be darkened,
and the moon will turn red as blood
before the great and terrible day of the Lord comes.
32 But all who ask the Lord for help will be saved.
As the Lord has said,
'Some in Jerusalem will escape;
those whom I choose will survive.'"

God will Judge the Nations

3 The Lord says,
"At that time I will restore
the prosperity of Judah and Jerusalem.
2 I will gather all the nations
and bring them to the Valley of Judgement.
There I will judge them
for all they have done to my people.
They have scattered the Israelites in foreign countries
and divided up Israel, my land.
3 They threw dice to decide
who would get the captives.
They sold boys and girls into slavery
to pay for prostitutes and wine.

4 "What are you trying to do to me, Tyre, Sidon, and all the regions of Philistia? Are you trying to pay me back for something? If you are, I will quickly pay you back! 5 You have taken my silver and gold and carried my rich treasures into your temples. 6 You have taken the people of Judah and Jerusalem far from their own country and sold them to the Greeks. 7 Now I am going to bring them out of the places to which you have sold them. I will do to you what you have done to them. 8 I will let your sons and daughters be sold to the people of Judah; they will sell them to the far-off Sabeans. I, the Lord, have spoken.

1062

Joel

:·.........

Jerem.
Lamen.
Ezekiel
Daniel
Hosea

JOEL 3

9 "Make this announcement among the nations:
  'Prepare for war;
    call your warriors;
    gather all your soldiers and march!
10 Hammer the points of your ploughs into swords
    and your pruning knives into spears.
  Even the weak must fight.
11 Hurry* and come,
    all you surrounding nations,
    and gather in the valley.'"

Send down, O Lord, your army to attack them.

12 "The nations must get ready
    and come to the Valley of Judgement.
  There I, the Lord, will sit to judge
    all the surrounding nations.
13 They are very wicked;
  cut them down like corn
    at harvest time;
  crush them as grapes are crushed
    in a full winepress
    until the wine runs over."

14 Thousands and thousands
    are in the Valley of Judgement.
  It is there that the day of the Lord
    will soon come.
15 The sun and the moon grow dark,
    and the stars no longer shine.

God will Bless his People
16 The Lord roars from Mount Zion;
    his voice thunders from Jerusalem;
    earth and sky tremble.
  But he will defend his people.
17 "Then, Israel, you will know that I am the Lord your God.
    I live on Zion, my sacred hill.
  Jerusalem will be a sacred city;
    foreigners will never conquer it again.

18 "At that time the mountains will be covered with
      vineyards,
    and cattle will be found on every hill;
    there will be plenty of water for all the streams of Judah.
  A stream will flow from the Temple of the Lord,
    and it will water the Valley of Acacia.

19 "Egypt will become a desert,
    and Edom a ruined waste,
  because they attacked the land of Judah
    and killed its innocent people.
20-21 I will avenge* those who were killed;
    I will not spare the guilty.
  But Judah and Jerusalem will be inhabited for ever,
    and I, the Lord, will live on Mount Zion."

....

3.11 Probable text *Hurry*; Hebrew *Help*.
3.20–21 Some ancient translations *avenge*; Hebrew *declare innocent*.

THE BOOK OF

AMOS

WRITTEN: 760-755BC

WHAT YOU NEED TO KNOW:

Amos prophesied at a time of prosperity for the northern kingdom of Israel, before it was destroyed by the Assyrians. Everyone thought they were doing just fine, despite their total rejection of God, so Amos was sent in to deliver a stark warning. Amos brought prophecies of five types of disaster (found in chapters 7 and 8). His prophecies were so offensive to the king of Israel that Amos got kicked out of the temple and wasn't allowed back! That didn't stop him from saying what God had told him to say, though. The last two chapters prophesy the destruction of Israel (which occurred several years after the prophecy was given) but the book ends with a short passage about restoration.

WHY READ IT?

Amos was a very down-to-earth sort of prophet. He wasn't descended from the priestly line; he was a sheep farmer. It's interesting that not only does God use prophets to speak to all kinds of people, he uses all kinds of people to be his prophets. It's also interesting that even though the Israelites were living sinful lives, they were still going to places of worship to fulfil their religious duties, expecting that this would keep them covered. Amos was sent in by God to warn them that God not only didn't approve of these false signs of devotion - he hated them.

God used Amos, a farmer, to

• SPEAK TO A •

NATION

What message do you think God might want you to bring to your nation?

write some thoughts here

ONAH   (760-755BC)   HOSEA   ISAIAH

AMOS   MICAH   HABAKKUK
IN ISRAEL BEFORE EXILE

1064

Amos

·:········

Lamen.
Ezekiel
Daniel
Hosea
Joel

AMOS 1, 2

1 These are the words of Amos, a shepherd from the town of Tekoa. Two years before the earthquake, when Uzziah was king of Judah and Jeroboam son of Jehoash was king of Israel, God revealed to Amos all these things about Israel. [2] Amos said,

"The LORD roars from Mount Zion;
    his voice thunders from Jerusalem.
The pastures dry up,
    and the grass on Mount Carmel turns brown."

God's Judgement on Israel's Neighbours

Syria
[3] The LORD says, "The people of Damascus have sinned again and again, and for this I will certainly punish them. They treated the people of Gilead with savage cruelty. [4] So I will send fire upon the palace built by King Hazael and I will burn down the fortresses of King Benhadad. [5] I will smash the city gates of Damascus and remove the inhabitants of the Valley of Aven and the ruler of Betheden. The people of Syria will be taken away as prisoners to the land of Kir."

Philistia
[6] The LORD says, "The people of Gaza have sinned again and again, and for this I will certainly punish them. They carried off a whole nation and sold them as slaves to the people of Edom. [7] So I will send fire upon the city walls of Gaza and burn down its fortresses. [8] I will remove the rulers of the cities of Ashdod and Ashkelon. I will punish the city of Ekron, and all the Philistines who are left will die."

Tyre
[9] The LORD says, "The people of Tyre have sinned again and again, and for this I will certainly punish them. They carried off a whole nation into exile in the land of Edom, and did not keep the treaty of friendship they had made. [10] So I will send fire upon the city walls of Tyre and burn down its fortresses."

Edom
[11] The LORD says, "The people of Edom have sinned again and again, and for this I will certainly punish them. They hunted down their relatives,* the Israelites, and showed them no mercy. Their anger had no limits, and they never let it die. [12] So I will send fire upon the city of Teman and burn down the fortresses of Bozrah."

Ammon
[13] The LORD says, "The people of Ammon have sinned again and again, and for this I will certainly punish them. In their wars for more territory they even ripped open pregnant women in Gilead. [14] So I will send fire upon the city walls of Rabbah and burn down its fortresses. Then there will be shouts on the day of battle, and the fighting will rage like a storm. [15] Their king and his officers will go into exile."

Moab
2 The LORD says, "The people of Moab have sinned again and again, and for this I will certainly punish them. They

----

1.11 *their relatives*: The Israelites were descended from Jacob, who was the brother of Esau, the ancestor of the Edomites.

AMOS 2, 3

1065

Amos

Obadiah
Jonah
Micah
Nahum
Habak.

dishonoured the bones of the king of Edom by burning them to ashes. [2] I will send fire upon the land of Moab and burn down the fortresses of Kerioth. The people of Moab will die in the noise of battle while soldiers are shouting and trumpets are sounding. [3] I will kill the ruler of Moab and all the leaders of the land."

Judah

[4] The LORD says, "The people of Judah have sinned again and again, and for this I will certainly punish them. They have despised my teachings and have not kept my commands. They have been led astray by the same false gods that their ancestors served. [5] So I will send fire upon Judah and burn down the fortresses of Jerusalem."

God's Judgement on Israel

[6] The LORD says, "The people of Israel have sinned again and again, and for this I will certainly punish them. They sell into slavery honest people who cannot pay their debts, the poor who cannot repay even the price of a pair of sandals. [7] They trample* down the weak and helpless and push the poor out of the way. A man and his father have intercourse with the same slave woman, and so profane my holy name. [8] At every place of worship people sleep on clothing that they have taken from the poor as security for debts. In the temple of their God they drink wine which they have taken from those who owe them money.

[9] "And yet, my people, it was for your sake that I totally destroyed the Amorites, who were as tall as cedar trees and as strong as oaks. [10] I brought you out of Egypt, led you through the desert for forty years, and gave you the land of the Amorites to be your own. [11] I chose some of your sons to be prophets, and some of your young men to be Nazirites.* Isn't this true, people of Israel? I, the LORD, have spoken. [12] But you made the Nazirites drink wine, and ordered the prophets not to speak my message. [13] And now I will crush you to the ground, and you will groan like a cart loaded with corn. [14] Not even fast runners will escape; strong men will lose their strength, and soldiers will not be able to save their own lives. [15] Bowmen will not stand their ground, fast runners will not get away, and men on horses will not escape with their lives. [16] On that day even the bravest soldiers will drop their weapons and run." The LORD has spoken.

3 People of Israel, listen to this message which the LORD has spoken about you, the entire nation that he brought out of Egypt: [2] "Of all the nations on earth, you are the only one I have known and cared for. That is what makes your sins so terrible, and that is why I must punish you for them."

The Prophet's Task

[3] Do two people start travelling together without arranging to meet?

[4] Does a lion roar in the forest unless he has found a victim?
Does a young lion growl in his den unless he has caught something?

[5] Does a bird get caught in a trap if the trap has not been baited?
Does a trap spring unless something sets it off?

[6] Does the war trumpet sound in a city without making the people afraid?

2.7 *trample*; Hebrew unclear.
2.11 *Nazirites*: Israelites who showed their devotion to God by taking vows not to drink wine or beer or cut their hair or touch corpses (see Num 6.1–8).

TURN THESE SHAPES INTO

SOMETHING ELSE.

1066

Amos

:..........

Lamen.
Ezekiel
Daniel
Hosea
Joel

Does disaster strike a city unless the LORD sends it?

[7] The Sovereign LORD never does anything without revealing his plan to his servants, the prophets.

[8] When a lion roars, who can avoid being afraid?

When the Sovereign LORD speaks, who can avoid proclaiming his message?

The Doom of Samaria

[9] Announce to those who live in the palaces of Egypt and Ashdod: "Gather together in the hills surrounding Samaria and see the great disorder and the crimes being committed there."

[10] The LORD says, "These people fill their mansions with things taken by crime and violence. They don't even know how to be honest. [11] And so an enemy will surround their land, destroy their defences, and plunder their mansions."

[12] The LORD says, "As a shepherd recovers only two legs or an ear of a sheep that a lion has eaten, so only a few will survive of Samaria's people, who now recline on luxurious couches.* [13] Listen now, and warn the descendants of Jacob," says the Sovereign LORD Almighty. [14] "On the day when I punish the people of Israel for their sins, I will destroy the altars of Bethel. The corners of every altar will be broken off and will fall to the ground. [15] I will destroy winter houses and summer houses. The houses decorated with ivory will fall in ruins; every large house will be destroyed."

4 Listen to this, you women of Samaria, who grow fat like the well-fed cows of Bashan, who ill-treat the weak, oppress the poor, and demand that your husbands keep you supplied with liquor! [2] As the Sovereign LORD is holy, he has promised, "The days will come when they will drag you away with hooks; every one of you will be like a fish on a hook. [3] You will be dragged to the nearest break in the wall and thrown out."*

Israel's Failure to Learn

[4] The Sovereign LORD says, "People of Israel, go to the holy place in Bethel and sin, if you must! Go to Gilgal and sin with all your might! Go ahead and bring animals to be sacrificed morning after morning, and bring your tithes every third day. [5] Go ahead and offer your bread in thanksgiving to God, and boast about the extra offerings you bring! This is the kind of thing you love to do.

[6] "I was the one who brought famine to all your cities, yet you did not come back to me. [7] I held back the rain when your crops needed it most. I sent rain on one city, but not on another. Rain fell on one field, but another field dried up. [8] Weak with thirst, the people of several cities went to a city where they hoped to find water, but there was not enough to drink. Still you did not come back to me.

[9] "I sent a scorching wind to dry up your crops. The locusts ate up all your gardens and vineyards, your fig trees and olive trees. Still you did not come back to me.

[10] "I sent a plague on you like the one I sent on Egypt. I killed your young men in battle and took your horses away. I filled your nostrils with the stink of dead bodies in your camps. Still you did not come back to me.

[11] "I destroyed some of you as I destroyed Sodom and Gomorrah. Those of you who survived were like a burning stick saved from a fire. Still you did not come back to me," says the LORD. [12] "So

....

3.12 *luxurious couches*; Hebrew unclear.
4.3 Hebrew has an additional word, the meaning of which is unclear.

AMOS 4, 5

1067

Amos

Obadiah
Jonah
Micah
Nahum
Habak.

then, people of Israel, I am going to punish you. And because I am going to do this, get ready to face my judgement!"

13 God is the one who made the mountains
and created the winds.
He makes his thoughts known to people;
he changes day into night.
He walks on the heights of the earth.
This is his name: the LORD God Almighty!

A Call to Repentance

5 Listen, people of Israel, to this funeral song which I sing over you:

2 Virgin Israel has fallen,
Never to rise again!
She lies abandoned on the ground,
And no one helps her up.

3 The Sovereign LORD says, "A city in Israel sends out a thousand soldiers, but only a hundred return; another city sends out a hundred, but only ten come back." 4 The LORD says to the people of Israel, "Come to me, and you will live. 5 Do not go to Beersheba to worship. Do not try to find me at Bethel — Bethel will come to nothing. Do not go to Gilgal — her people are doomed to exile." 6 Go to the LORD, and you will live. If you do not go, he will sweep down like fire on the people of Israel. The fire will burn up the people of Bethel, and no one will be able to put it out. 7 You are doomed, you that twist justice and cheat people out of their rights!

8 The LORD made the stars,
the Pleiades and Orion.
He turns darkness into daylight,
and day into night.
He calls for the waters of the sea
and pours them out on the earth.
His name is the LORD.
9 He brings destruction on the mighty and their
strongholds.

10 You people hate anyone who challenges injustice and speaks the whole truth in court. 11 You have oppressed the poor and robbed them of their grain. And so you will not live in the fine stone houses you build or drink wine from the beautiful vineyards you plant. 12 I know how terrible your sins are and how many crimes you have committed. You persecute good people, take bribes, and prevent the poor from getting justice in the courts. 13 And so, keeping quiet in such evil times is the clever thing to do!

14 Make it your aim to do what is right, not what is evil, so that you may live. Then the LORD God Almighty really will be with you, as you claim he is. 15 Hate what is evil, love what is right, and see that justice prevails in the courts. Perhaps the LORD will be merciful to the people of this nation who are still left alive.

16 And so the Sovereign LORD Almighty says, "There will be wailing and cries of sorrow in the city streets. Even farmers will be called to mourn the dead along with those who are paid to mourn. 17 There will be wailing in all the vineyards. All this will take place because I am coming to punish you." The LORD has spoken.

AMOS 5.4

· COME ·
TO ME,
AND YOU WILL
LIVE

1068

Amos

∴⋯⋯⋯

Lamen.
Ezekiel
Daniel
Hosea
Joel

AMOS 5, 6

[18] How terrible it will be for you who long for the day of the LORD! What good will that day do you? For you it will be a day of darkness and not of light. [19] It will be like someone who runs from a lion and meets a bear! Or like someone who comes home and puts his hand on the wall — only to be bitten by a snake! [20] The day of the LORD will bring darkness and not light; it will be a day of gloom, without any brightness.

[21] The LORD says, "I hate your religious festivals; I cannot stand them! [22] When you bring me burnt offerings and grain offerings, I will not accept them; I will not accept the animals you have fattened to bring me as offerings. [23] Stop your noisy songs; I do not want to listen to your harps. [24] Instead, let justice flow like a stream, and righteousness like a river that never goes dry.

[25] "People of Israel, I did not demand sacrifices and offerings during those forty years that I led you through the desert. [26] But now, because you have worshipped images of Sakkuth, your king god, and of Kaiwan, your star god, you will have to carry those images [27] when I take you into exile in a land beyond Damascus," says the LORD, whose name is Almighty God.

The Destruction of Israel

6 How terrible it will be for you that have such an easy life in Zion and for you that feel safe in Samaria — you great leaders of this great nation Israel, you to whom the people go for help! [2] Go and look at the city of Calneh. Then go on to the great city of Hamath and on down to the Philistine city of Gath. Were they any better than the kingdoms of Judah and Israel? Was their territory larger than yours? [3] You refuse to admit that a day of disaster is coming, but what you do only brings that day closer. [4] How terrible it will be for you that stretch out on your luxurious couches, feasting on veal and lamb! [5] You like to compose songs, as David did, and play them on harps. [6] You drink wine by the bowlful and use the finest perfumes, but you do not mourn over the ruin of Israel. [7] So you will be the first to go into exile. Your feasts and banquets will come to an end.

[8] The Sovereign LORD Almighty has given this solemn warning: "I hate the pride of the people of Israel; I despise their luxurious mansions. I will give their capital city and everything in it to the enemy."

[9] If there are ten men left in a family, they will die. [10] The dead man's relative, the one in charge of the funeral, will take the body out of the house. The relative will call to whoever is still left in the house, "Is anyone else there with you?"

A voice will answer, "No!"

Then the relative will say, "Be quiet! We must be careful not even to mention the LORD's name."*

[11] When the LORD gives the command, houses large and small will be smashed to pieces. [12] Do horses gallop on rocks? Does anyone plough the sea with oxen? Yet you have turned justice into poison, and right into wrong.

[13] You boast about capturing the town of Lodebar.* You boast, "We were strong enough to take Karnaim."*

[14] The LORD God Almighty himself says, "People of Israel, I am going to send a foreign army to occupy your country. It will

6.10 Verse 10 in Hebrew is unclear.
6.13 *Lodebar*: This name sounds like the Hebrew for "nothing".
6.13 *Karnaim*: The name of this small town means "horns", a symbol of strength.

AMOS 6–8

1069

Amos
·········:·

Obadiah
Jonah
Micah
Nahum
Habak.

oppress you from Hamath Pass in the north to the brook of the Arabah in the south."

A Vision of Locusts

7 I had a vision from the Sovereign LORD. In it I saw him create a swarm of locusts just after the king's share of the hay had been cut and the grass was starting to grow again. [2] In my vision I saw the locusts eat up every green thing in the land, and then I said, "Sovereign LORD, forgive your people! How can they survive? They are so small and weak!"

[3] The LORD changed his mind and said, "What you saw will not take place."

A Vision of Fire

[4] I had another vision from the Sovereign LORD. In it I saw him preparing to punish his people with fire. The fire burnt up the great ocean under the earth, and started to burn up the land. [5] Then I said, "Stop, Sovereign LORD! How can your people survive? They are so small and weak!"

[6] The LORD changed his mind again and said, "This will not take place either."

A Vision of a Plumb Line

[7] I had another vision from the Lord. In it I saw him standing beside a wall that had been built with the help of a plumb line, and there was a plumb line in his hand. [8] He asked me, "Amos, what do you see?"

"A plumb line," I answered.

Then he said, "I am using it to show that my people are like a wall that is out of line. I will not change my mind again about punishing them. [9] The places where Isaac's descendants worship will be destroyed. The holy places of Israel will be left in ruins. I will bring the dynasty of King Jeroboam to an end."

Amos and Amaziah

[10] Amaziah, the priest of Bethel, then sent a report to King Jeroboam of Israel: "Amos is plotting against you among the people. His speeches will destroy the country. [11] This is what he says: 'Jeroboam will die in battle, and the people of Israel will be taken away from their land into exile.'"

[12] Amaziah then said to Amos, "That's enough, prophet! Go on back to Judah and do your preaching there. Let *them* pay you for it. [13] Don't prophesy here at Bethel any more. This is the king's place of worship, the national temple."

[14] Amos answered, "I am not the kind of prophet who prophesies for pay. I am a herdsman, and I take care of fig trees. [15] But the LORD took me from my work as a shepherd and ordered me to come and prophesy to his people Israel. [16] So now listen to what the LORD says. You tell me to stop prophesying, to stop raving against the people of Israel. [17] And so, Amaziah, the LORD says to you, 'Your wife will become a prostitute on the streets, and your children will be killed in war. Your land will be divided up and given to others, and you yourself will die in a heathen country. And the people of Israel will certainly be taken away from their own land into exile.'"

A Vision of a Basket of Fruit

8 I had another vision from the Sovereign LORD. In it I saw a basket of fruit. [2] The LORD asked, "Amos, what do you see?"

"A basket of fruit," I answered.

AMOS 7.14-15

God can use ordinary people to do

EXTRAORDINARY
THINGS FOR HIM.

In prayer, ask God to reveal a word or thought for you to give someone. (If you feel God has given you something to share with someone, it might be a good idea to check first with someone you trust, like a youth worker, just to make sure.)

1070

Amos

.·:·‥‥‥‥

Lamen.
Ezekiel
Daniel
Hosea
Joel

AMOS 8, 9

The LORD said to me, "The end* has come for my people Israel. I will not change my mind again about punishing them. ³On that day the songs in the palace will become cries of mourning. There will be dead bodies everywhere. They will be thrown out in silence."*

Israel's Doom

⁴Listen to this, you that trample on the needy and try to destroy the poor of the country. ⁵You say to yourselves, "We can hardly wait for the holy days to be over so that we can sell our corn. When will the Sabbath end, so that we can start selling again? Then we can overcharge, use false measures, and tamper with the scales to cheat our customers. ⁶We can sell worthless wheat at a high price. We'll find a poor person who can't pay his debts, not even the price of a pair of sandals, and we'll buy him as a slave."

⁷The LORD, the God of Israel, has sworn, "I will never forget their evil deeds. ⁸And so the earth will quake, and everyone in the land will be in distress. The whole country will be shaken; it will rise and fall like the River Nile. ⁹The time is coming when I will make the sun go down at noon and the earth grow dark in daytime. I, the Sovereign LORD, have spoken. ¹⁰I will turn your festivals into funerals and change your glad songs into cries of grief. I will make you shave your heads and wear sackcloth, and you will be like parents mourning for their only child. That day will be bitter to the end.

¹¹"The time is coming when I will send famine on the land. People will be hungry, but not for bread; they will be thirsty, but not for water. They will hunger and thirst for a message from the LORD. I, the Sovereign LORD, have spoken. ¹²People will wander from the Dead Sea to the Mediterranean and then on from the north to the east. They will look everywhere for a message from the LORD, but they will not find it. ¹³On that day even healthy young men and women will collapse from thirst. ¹⁴Those who swear by the idols of Samaria, who say, 'By the god of Dan,' or, 'By the god of Beersheba' — those people will fall and not rise again."

The Lord's Judgements

9 I saw the Lord standing by the altar. He gave the command: "Strike the tops of the temple columns so hard that the whole porch will shake. Break them off and let them fall on the heads of the people. I will kill the rest of the people in war. No one will get away; not one will escape. ²Even if they dig their way down to the world of the dead, I will catch them. Even if they climb up to heaven, I will bring them down. ³If they hide on the top of Mount Carmel, I will search for them and catch them. If they hide from me at the bottom of the sea, I will command the sea monster* to bite them. ⁴If they are taken away into captivity by their enemies, I will order them to be put to death. I am determined to destroy them, not to help them."

⁵ The Sovereign LORD Almighty touches the earth,
   and it quakes;
      all who live there mourn.
   The whole world rises and falls like the River Nile.

....

8.2 *end*: The Hebrew words for "end" and "fruit" sound alike.
8.3 *out in silence*; or *out. Silence!*
9.3 *sea monster*: It was believed that the sea was inhabited by a great monster. This creature, like all others, was regarded as under God's control.

Amos

....

Obadiah
Jonah
Micah
Nahum
Habak.

⁶ The LORD builds his home in the heavens,
    and over the earth he puts the dome of the sky.
He calls for the waters of the sea
    and pours them out on the earth.
His name is the LORD!

⁷ The LORD says, "People of Israel, I think as much of the people of Ethiopia as I do of you. I brought the Philistines from Crete and the Syrians from Kir, just as I brought you from Egypt. ⁸ I, the Sovereign LORD, am watching this sinful kingdom of Israel, and I will destroy it from the face of the earth. But I will not destroy all the descendants of Jacob.

⁹ "I will give the command and shake the people of Israel like corn in a sieve. I will shake them among the nations to remove all who are worthless. ¹⁰ The sinners among my people will be killed in war — all those who say, 'God will not let any harm come near us.'"

The Future Restoration of Israel

¹¹ The LORD says, "A day is coming when I will restore the kingdom of David, which is like a house fallen into ruins. I will repair its walls and restore it. I will rebuild it and make it as it was long ago. ¹² And so the people of Israel will conquer what is left of the land of Edom and all the nations that were once mine," says the LORD, who will cause this to happen.

¹³ "The days are coming," says the LORD,
    "when corn will grow faster than it can be harvested,
    and grapes will grow faster than the wine can be made.
The mountains will drip with sweet wine,
    and the hills will flow with it.
¹⁴ I will bring my people back to their land.
    They will rebuild their ruined cities and live there;
    they will plant vineyards and drink the wine;
    they will plant gardens and eat what they grow.
¹⁵ I will plant my people on the land I gave them,
    and they will not be pulled up again."
The LORD your God has spoken.

THE BOOK OF

OBADIAH

WRITTEN: AROUND 600-500BC

WHAT YOU NEED TO KNOW:

Obadiah spoke not to the people of God in either Israel or Judah, but to the Edomites. The Edomites were descendants of Esau (the brother of Jacob - see Genesis 25). The descendants of Jacob (the Israelites) and Esau (the Edomites) had become bitter enemies. During the period in which Obadiah was speaking, the Israelites were suffering some hardships, and the Edomites (who lived just south of Judah) were rejoicing and celebrating their distress. So God sent Obadiah to prophesy judgement on the neighbours of the Israelites.

WHY READ IT?

Though it's the shortest book in the Old Testament, Obadiah is not to be skipped over. We see in Obadiah (and other prophets, not least Jonah and Nahum) how God has something to say even to Israel's enemies. He tells us that gloating and boasting do not pay off!

KEY CHARACTER:

We're not entirely sure who Obadiah was. His book doesn't make reference to his life, and his name (meaning 'servant of the Lord') was quite common. However, one belief is that Obadiah was a convert to Judaism from Edom, which would explain why he prophesied to the Edomites.

SUMMARISE THE MESSAGE OF OBADIAH TO THE EDOMITES IN ONE SENTENCE:

NAHUM

OBADIAH
JUDAH GOES INTO EXILE

EZEKIEL

JEREMIAH

(586BC)

DANIEL

HAGG

OBADIAH

1073

Obadiah
....

Jonah
Micah
Nahum
Habak.
Zephan.

¹This is the prophecy of Obadiah — what the Sovereign Lord said about the nation of Edom.

The Lord will Punish Edom

The Lord has sent his messenger to the nations,
  and we have heard his message:
"Get ready! Let us go to war against Edom!"
² The Lord says to Edom,
  "I will make you weak;
  everyone will despise you.
³ Your pride has deceived you.
  Your capital is a fortress of solid rock;
    your home is high in the mountains,
  and so you say to yourself,
    'Who can ever pull me down?'
⁴ Even though you make your home
    as high as an eagle's nest,
    so that it seems to be among the stars,
  yet I will pull you down.

⁵ "When thieves come at night,
    they take only what they want.
  When people gather grapes,
    they always leave a few.
  But your enemies have wiped you out completely.
⁶ Descendants of Esau, your treasures have been looted.
⁷ Your allies have deceived you;
    they have driven you from your country.
  People who were at peace with you have now conquered
      you.
  Those friends who ate with you have laid a trap for you;
    they say of you, 'Where is all that cleverness he had?'

⁸ "On the day I punish Edom,
    I will destroy their clever men
    and wipe out all their wisdom.
⁹ The fighting men of Teman will be terrified,
    and every soldier in Edom will be killed.

Reasons for Edom's Punishment

¹⁰ "Because you robbed and killed
    your brothers,* the descendants of Jacob,
  you will be destroyed and dishonoured for ever.
¹¹ You stood aside on that day
    when enemies broke down their gates.
  You were as bad as those strangers
    who carried off Jerusalem's wealth
    and divided it among themselves.
¹² You should not have gloated
    over the misfortune of your brothers in Judah.
  You should not have been glad
    on the day of their ruin.
  You should not have laughed at them
    in their distress.
¹³ You should not have entered the city of my people
    to gloat over their suffering

1.10 *your brothers*: The Israelites were descended from Jacob, who was the brother of Esau, the ancestor of the Edomites.

1074

OBADIAH

Obadiah

Ezekiel
Daniel
Hosea
Joel
Amos

and to seize their riches
on the day of their disaster.
¹⁴ You should not have stood at the crossroads
to catch those trying to escape.
You should not have handed them over to the enemy
on the day of their distress.

God will Judge the Nations

¹⁵ "The day is near when I, the LORD,
will judge all nations.
Edom, what you have done
will be done to you.
You will get back what you have given.
¹⁶ My people have drunk a bitter cup of punishment
on my sacred hill.*
But all the surrounding nations will drink
a still more bitter cup of punishment;
they will drink it all and vanish away.

The Victory of Israel

¹⁷ "But on Mount Zion some will escape,
and it will be a sacred place.
The people of Jacob will possess
the land that is theirs by right.
¹⁸ The people of Jacob and of Joseph will be like fire;
they will destroy the people of Esau
as fire burns stubble.
No descendant of Esau will survive.
I, the LORD, have spoken.

¹⁹ "People from southern Judah will occupy Edom;
those from the western foothills will capture Philistia;
Israelites will possess the territory of Ephraim and
Samaria;
the people of Benjamin will take Gilead.
²⁰ The army of exiles from northern Israel
will return and conquer Phoenicia
as far north as Zarephath.
The exiles from Jerusalem who are in Sardis
will capture the towns of southern Judah.
²¹ The victorious men of Jerusalem
will attack Edom and rule over it.
And the LORD himself will be King."

OBADIAH V. 17

'Mount Zion' is a picture
of the place where

GOD LIVES

– WITH HIS –

PEOPLE.

DRAW A MOUNTAIN

on this page and write
some adjectives to
describe what God's
eternal dwelling will be like.

1.16 *sacred hill:* Mount Zion.

THE BOOK OF

JONAH

WRITTEN: SOMETIME BETWEEN 500 AND 300BC

WHAT YOU NEED TO KNOW:

Jonah was a prophet from Israel, sent by God to Nineveh. Nineveh was known as 'the great city' because of its size. It was the capital city of the Assyrians, the fierce enemy of the Israelites. Nineveh was famous for its corruption and evil - so maybe it's not such a wonder that Jonah was reluctant to go there! Unlike most other prophets, who have plenty to say, Jonah only has one line of prophecy from God to deliver (see chapter 3 verse 4). Also unlike most other prophets, Jonah's pleas turned out to be successful, at least for a short while (see also the book of Nahum).

WHY READ IT?

You probably know the story of Jonah pretty well. But have you ever considered what a scary prospect it must have been to deliver a message to Nineveh? Here we learn that God, in his mercy, offers redemption even to the most broken and lost society, like the Assyrians. And, there's a giant fish!

WRITE DOWN THE TOP FIVE
CHARACTERISTICS OF
JONAH
AFTER YOU'VE READ THE STORY.

1. _____
2. _____
3. _____
4. _____
5. _____

Are there any places you would be fearful of going to for God? (Maybe it's even your school, with your own mates!) Write them down here and pray for God's courage.

ONAH
(760BC)

AMOS

HOSEA

MICAH

ISAIAH

HABAKKUK

JONAH 1

Nineveh is in modern-day northern Iraq, near Mosul. At one time it was a stronghold for ISIS. In Jonah's day, it was a major city of the Assyrians, who were seen as

• TOTALLY •

EVIL

and dangerous. A modern-day retelling of Jonah could probably be set in the same place. Imagine Jonah being called to bring God's message straight to ISIS in their stronghold!

Jonah Disobeys the LORD

1 One day the LORD spoke to Jonah son of Amittai. ²He said, "Go to Nineveh, that great city, and speak out against it; I am aware how wicked its people are." ³Jonah, however, set out in the opposite direction in order to get away from the LORD. He went to Joppa, where he found a ship about to go to Spain. He paid his fare and went aboard with the crew to sail to Spain, where he would be away from the LORD. ⁴But the LORD sent a strong wind on the sea, and the storm was so violent that the ship was in danger of breaking up. ⁵The sailors were terrified and cried out for help, each one to his own god. Then, in order to lessen the danger,* they threw the cargo* overboard. Meanwhile, Jonah had gone below and was lying in the ship's hold, sound asleep.

⁶The captain found him there and said to him, "What are you doing asleep? Get up and pray to your god for help. Maybe he will feel sorry for us and spare our lives."

⁷The sailors said to one another, "Let's draw lots and find out who is to blame for getting us into this danger." They did so, and Jonah's name was drawn. ⁸So they said to him: "Now then, tell us! Who is to blame for this? What are you doing here? What country do you come from? What is your nationality?"

⁹"I am a Hebrew," Jonah answered. "I worship the LORD, the God of heaven, who made land and sea." ¹⁰Jonah went on to tell them that he was running away from the LORD.

The sailors were terrified, and said to him, "That was an awful thing to do!"* ¹¹The storm was getting worse all the time, so the sailors asked him, "What should we do to you to stop the storm?"

¹²Jonah answered, "Throw me into the sea, and it will calm down. I know it is my fault that you are caught in this violent storm."

¹³Instead, the sailors tried to get the ship to shore, rowing with all their might. But the storm was getting worse and worse, and they got nowhere. ¹⁴So they cried out to the LORD, "O LORD, we pray, don't punish us with death for taking this man's life! You, O LORD, are responsible for all this; it is your doing." ¹⁵Then they picked Jonah up and threw him into the sea, and it calmed down at once. ¹⁶This made the sailors so afraid of the LORD that they offered a sacrifice and promised to serve him.

¹⁷At the LORD's command a large fish swallowed Jonah, and he was inside the fish for three days and nights.

Jonah's Prayer

2 From deep inside the fish Jonah prayed to the LORD his God:
² "In my distress, O LORD, I called to you,
and you answered me.
From deep in the world of the dead
I cried for help, and you heard me.
³ You threw me down into the depths,
to the very bottom of the sea,
where the waters were all round me,
and all your mighty waves rolled over me.
⁴ I thought I had been banished from your presence
and would never see your holy Temple again.

1.5 *lessen the danger*; or *lighten the ship*.
1.5 *cargo*; or *equipment*.
1.10 *and said… to do!*; or *and asked him, "Why did you have to run away like that?"*

JONAH 2–4

1077

Jonah

....

Micah
Nahum
Habak.
Zephan.
Haggai

⁵ The water came over me and choked me;
   the sea covered me completely,
   and seaweed was wrapped round my head.
⁶ I went down to the very roots of the mountains,
   into the land whose gates lock shut for ever.*
 But you, O LORD my God,
   brought me back from the depths alive.
⁷ When I felt my life slipping away,
   then, O LORD, I prayed to you,
   and in your holy Temple you heard me.
⁸ Those who worship worthless idols
   have abandoned their loyalty to you.
⁹ But I will sing praises to you;
   I will offer you a sacrifice
   and do what I have promised.
 Salvation comes from the LORD!"

¹⁰ Then the LORD ordered the fish to spew Jonah up on the beach, and it did.

Jonah Obeys the LORD

3 Once again the LORD spoke to Jonah. ² He said, "Go to Nineveh, that great city, and proclaim to the people the message I have given you." ³ So Jonah obeyed the LORD and went to Nineveh, a city so large that it took three days to walk through it. ⁴ Jonah started through the city, and after walking a whole day, he proclaimed, "In forty days Nineveh will be destroyed!"

⁵ The people of Nineveh believed God's message. So they decided that everyone should fast, and all the people, from the greatest to the least, put on sackcloth to show that they had repented.

⁶ When the king of Nineveh heard about it, he got up from his throne, took off his robe, put on sackcloth, and sat down in ashes. ⁷ He sent out a proclamation to the people of Nineveh: "This is an order from the king and his officials: no one is to eat anything; all persons, cattle, and sheep are forbidden to eat or drink. ⁸ All persons and animals must wear sackcloth. Everyone must pray earnestly to God and must give up his wicked behaviour and his evil actions. ⁹ Perhaps God will change his mind; perhaps he will stop being angry, and we will not die!"

¹⁰ God saw what they did; he saw that they had given up their wicked behaviour. So he changed his mind and did not punish them as he had said he would.

Jonah's Anger and God's Mercy

4 Jonah was very unhappy about this and became angry. ² So he prayed, "LORD, didn't I say before I left home that this is just what you would do? That's why I did my best to run away to Spain! I knew that you are a loving and merciful God, always patient, always kind, and always ready to change your mind and not punish. ³ Now, LORD, let me die. I am better off dead than alive."

⁴ The LORD answered, "What right have you to be angry?"

⁵ Jonah went out east of the city and sat down. He made a shelter for himself and sat in its shade, waiting to see what would happen to Nineveh. ⁶ Then the LORD God made a plant grow up over Jonah to give him some shade, so that he would be

---

2.6 *the land whose gates lock shut for ever*: A reference to the world of the dead (see 2.2).

1078

Jonah

·:·········

Daniel
Hosea
Joel
Amos
Obadiah

JONAH 4

JONAH 4.11

God cares and
makes time even for
those who seem

- FARTHEST -

AWAY

from him. With some
friends, why not pray
for people around the
world - those who
would even declare
themselves as enemies
of God - asking that
God might change their
minds and hearts.

more comfortable. Jonah was extremely pleased with the plant. [7] But at dawn the next day, at God's command, a worm attacked the plant, and it died. [8] After the sun had risen, God sent a hot east wind, and Jonah was about to faint from the heat of the sun beating down on his head. So he wished he were dead.* "I am better off dead than alive," he said.

[9] But God said to him, "What right have you to be angry about the plant?"

Jonah replied, "I have every right to be angry — angry enough to die!"

[10] The LORD said to him, "This plant grew up in one night and disappeared the next; you didn't do anything for it, and you didn't make it grow — yet you feel sorry for it! [11] How much more, then, should I have pity on Nineveh, that great city. After all, it has more than 120,000 innocent children in it, as well as many animals!"

4.8 *wished he were dead*; or *prayed that he would die.*

THE BOOK OF
MICAH

WRITTEN: 737-696BC
(WITH SOME LATER ADDITIONS)

WHAT YOU NEED TO KNOW:

Micah prophesied around the same time as Isaiah and, like Isaiah, spoke a lot about right living, especially justice. A little like Amos, Micah came from a rural background. Unlike Isaiah, who prophesied in the temples and cities, he went around the towns and villages delivering messages of God's judgement, warnings and, of course, hope for the future.

WHY READ IT?

Micah is one of the most poetic prophets: he writes with a lot of imagery. His book concentrates largely on living as God calls people to live. He recognises that God wants people to ignore corruption and greed and focus on righteousness and caring for others. Micah's warnings and messages have much to say to Western societies today.

Micah's writings are

CREATIVE
AND POETIC

Go through the book of Micah and highlight all the creative picture language he uses.

Why not write a poem right _here_ about the world you live in today.

_____
_____
_____
_____
_____
_____
_____
_____
_____
_____
_____
_____
_____
_____
_____

COLOUR
THESE SHAPES

AMOS   MICAH   HABAKKUK

HOSEA   (737-696BC)   ISAIAH   ZEPHANIAH

1080

Micah

⠂⟨⠂⠂⠂⠂⠂⠂⠂⠂

Hosea
Joel
Amos
Obadiah
Jonah

MICAH 1

1 During the time that Jotham, Ahaz, and Hezekiah were kings of Judah, the LORD gave this message to Micah, who was from the town of Moresheth. The LORD revealed to Micah all these things about Samaria and Jerusalem.

A Lament for Samaria and Jerusalem

² Hear this, all you nations;
  listen to this, all who live on earth!
The Sovereign LORD will testify against you.
  Listen! He speaks from his heavenly temple.
³ The LORD is coming from his holy place;
  he will come down and walk on the tops of the
    mountains.
⁴ Then the mountains will melt under him
  like wax in a fire;
they will pour down into the valleys
  like water pouring down a hill.

⁵ All this will happen because the people of Israel have sinned and rebelled against God. Who is to blame for Israel's rebellion? Samaria, the capital city itself! Who is guilty of idolatry in Judah? Jerusalem itself! ⁶ So the LORD says, "I will make Samaria a pile of ruins in the open country, a place for planting grapevines. I will pour the rubble of the city down into the valley, and will lay bare the city's foundations. ⁷ All its precious idols will be smashed to pieces, everything given to its temple prostitutes will be destroyed by fire, and all its images will become a desolate heap. Samaria acquired these things for its fertility rites, and now her enemies will carry them off for temple prostitutes elsewhere."

⁸ Then Micah said, "Because of this I will mourn and lament. To show my sorrow, I will walk about barefoot and naked. I will howl like a jackal and wail like an ostrich. ⁹ Samaria's wounds cannot be healed, and Judah is about to suffer in the same way; destruction has reached the gates of Jerusalem itself, where my people live."

The Enemy Approaches Jerusalem

¹⁰ Don't tell our enemies in Gath about our defeat; don't let them see you weeping. People of Beth Leaphrah,* show your despair by rolling in the dust! ¹¹ You people of Shaphir, go into exile, naked and ashamed. Those who live in Zaanan dare not come out of their city. When you hear the people of Bethezel mourn, you will know that there is no refuge there. ¹² The people of Maroth wait anxiously for relief, because the LORD has brought disaster close to Jerusalem. ¹³ You that live in Lachish, hitch the horses to the chariots. You imitated the sins of Israel and so caused Jerusalem to sin. ¹⁴ And now, people of Judah, say goodbye to the town of Moresheth Gath. The kings of Israel will get no help from the town of Achzib. ¹⁵ People of Mareshah, the LORD will hand you over to an enemy, who is going to capture your town. The leaders of Israel will go and hide in the cave at Adullam. ¹⁶ People of Judah, cut off your hair in mourning for the children you love. Make yourselves as bald as vultures, because your children will be taken away from you into exile.

1.10 *Beth Leaphrah*: The prophet speaks of outlying towns (verses 10–14) which an enemy army approaching Jerusalem would attack.

Micah

....

Nahum
Habak.
Zephan.
Haggai
Zechar.

The Fate of Those who Oppress the Poor

2 How terrible it will be for those who lie awake and plan evil! When morning comes, as soon as they have the chance, they do the evil they planned. ²When they want fields, they seize them; when they want houses, they take them. No one's family or property is safe.

³And so the LORD says, "I am planning to bring disaster on you, and you will not be able to escape it. You are going to find yourselves in trouble, and then you will not walk so proudly any more. ⁴When that time comes, people will use your story as an example of disaster, and they will sing this song of despair about your experience:

> We are completely ruined!
> The LORD has taken our land away
> And given it to those who took us captive."*

⁵So then, when the time comes for the land to be given back to the LORD's people, there will be no share for any of you.

⁶The people preach at me and say, "Don't preach at us. Don't preach about all that. God is not going to disgrace us. ⁷Do you think the people of Israel are under a curse?* Has the LORD lost his patience? Would he really do such things? Doesn't he* speak kindly to those who do right?"

⁸The LORD replies, "You attack my people* like enemies. Men return from battle, thinking they are safe at home, but there you are, waiting to steal the coats off their backs. ⁹You drive the women of my people out of the homes they love, and you have robbed their children of my blessings for ever. ¹⁰Get up and go; there is no safety here any more. Your sins have doomed this place to destruction.

¹¹"These people want the kind of prophet who goes about full of lies and deceit and says, 'I prophesy that wine and liquor will flow for you.'

¹²"But I will gather you together, all you people of Israel that are left. I will bring you together like sheep returning to the fold. Like a pasture full of sheep, your land will once again be filled with many people."

¹³God will open the way for them and lead them out of exile. They will break out of the city gates and go free. Their king, the LORD himself, will lead them out.

Micah Denounces Israel's Leaders

3 Listen, you rulers of Israel! You are supposed to be concerned about justice, ²yet you hate what is good and you love what is evil. You skin my people alive and tear the flesh off their bones. ³You eat my people up. You strip off their skin, break their bones, and chop them up like meat for the pot. ⁴The time is coming when you will cry out to the LORD, but he will not answer you. He will not listen to your prayers, for you have done evil.

⁵My people are deceived by prophets who promise peace to those who pay them, but threaten war for those who don't. To these prophets the LORD says, ⁶"Prophets, your day is almost

Colour these shapes.

....

2.4 Probable text *those who took us captive*; Hebrew *rebels*.
2.7 Probable text *under a curse*; Hebrew unclear.
2.7 One ancient translation *Doesn't he*; Hebrew *Don't I*.
2.8 Probable text *You attack my people*; Hebrew *Recently my people have attacked*.

over; the sun is going down on you. Because you mislead my people, you will have no more prophetic visions, and you will not be able to predict anything." [7] Those who predict the future will be disgraced by their failure. They will all be humiliated because God does not answer them.

[8] But as for me, the LORD fills me with his Spirit and power, and gives me a sense of justice and the courage to tell the people of Israel what their sins are. [9] Listen to me, you rulers of Israel, you that hate justice and turn right into wrong. [10] You are building God's city, Jerusalem, on a foundation of murder and injustice. [11] The city's rulers govern for bribes, the priests interpret the Law for pay, the prophets give their revelations for money — and they all claim that the LORD is with us. "No harm will come to us," they say. "The LORD is with us."

[12] And so, because of you, Zion will be ploughed like a field, Jerusalem will become a pile of ruins, and the Temple hill will become a forest.

The LORD's Universal Reign of Peace
(Is 2.2–4)

4 In days to come
    the mountain where the Temple stands
    will be the highest one of all,
    towering above all the hills.
 Many nations will come streaming to it,
 [2]   and their people will say,
 "Let us go up the hill of the LORD,*
    to the Temple of Israel's God.
 He will teach us what he wants us to do;
    we will walk in the paths he has chosen.
 For the LORD's teaching comes from Jerusalem;
    from Zion he speaks to his people."

[3] He will settle disputes among the nations,
    among the great powers near and far.
 They will hammer their swords into ploughs
    and their spears into pruning knives.
 Nations will never again go to war,
    never prepare for battle again.
[4] Everyone will live in peace
    among his own vineyards and fig trees,
    and no one will make him afraid.
 The LORD Almighty has promised this.

[5] Each nation worships and obeys its own god, but we will worship and obey the LORD our God for ever and ever.

Israel will Return from Exile

[6] "The time is coming," says the LORD, "when I will gather together the people I punished, those who have suffered in exile. [7] They are crippled and far from home, but I will make a new beginning with those who are left, and they will become a great nation. I will rule over them on Mount Zion from that time on and for ever."

[8] And you, Jerusalem, where God, like a shepherd, watches over his people, will once again be the capital of the kingdom that was yours. [9] Why do you cry out so loudly? Why are you suffering

4.2 *hill of the* LORD: Mount Zion.

MICAH 4–6

1083

Micah

..........:

Nahum
Habak.
Zephan.
Haggai
Zechar.

like a woman in labour? Is it because you have no king, and your counsellors are dead? ¹⁰Twist and groan,* people of Jerusalem, like a woman giving birth, for now you will have to leave the city and live in the open country. You will have to go to Babylon, but there the LORD will save you from your enemies. ¹¹Many nations have gathered to attack you. They say, "Jerusalem must be destroyed! We will see this city in ruins!" ¹²But these nations do not know what is in the LORD's mind. They do not realize that they have been gathered together to be punished in the same way that corn is brought in to be threshed.

¹³The LORD says, "People of Jerusalem, go and punish your enemies! I will make you as strong as a bull with iron horns and bronze hoofs. You will crush many nations, and the wealth they got by violence you will present to me, the Lord of the whole world."

5 People of Jerusalem, gather your forces!* We are besieged! They are attacking the leader of Israel!

God Promises a Ruler from Bethlehem

²The LORD says, "Bethlehem Ephrathah, you are one of the smallest towns in Judah, but out of you I will bring a ruler for Israel, whose family line goes back to ancient times."

³So the LORD will abandon his people to their enemies until the woman who is to give birth has her son. Then those Israelites who are in exile will be reunited with their own people. ⁴When he comes, he will rule his people with the strength that comes from the LORD and with the majesty of the LORD God himself. His people will live in safety because people all over the earth will acknowledge his greatness, ⁵and he will bring peace.

Deliverance and Punishment

When the Assyrians invade our country and break through our defences, we will send our strongest leaders to fight them. ⁶By force of arms they will conquer Assyria, the land of Nimrod, and they* will save us from the Assyrians when they invade our territory.

⁷The people of Israel who survive will be like refreshing dew sent by the LORD for many nations, like showers on growing plants. They will depend on God, not human beings. ⁸Those who are left among the nations will be like a lion hunting for food in a forest or a pasture: it gets in among the sheep, pounces on them, and tears them to pieces — and there is no hope of rescue. ⁹Israel will conquer her enemies and destroy them all.

¹⁰The LORD says, "At that time I will take away your horses and destroy your chariots. ¹¹I will destroy the cities in your land and tear down all your defences. ¹²I will destroy the magic charms you use and leave you without any fortune tellers. ¹³I will destroy your idols and sacred stone pillars; no longer will you worship the things that you yourselves have made. ¹⁴I will pull down the images of the goddess Asherah in your land and destroy your cities. ¹⁵And in my great anger I will take revenge on all nations that have not obeyed me."

The LORD's Case against Israel

6 Listen to the LORD's case against Israel.
Arise, O LORD, and present your case; let the mountains and the hills hear what you say.

....

4.10 Probable text *groan*; Hebrew *bring forth*.
5.1 Probable text *People... forces!*; Hebrew unclear.
5.6 Probable text *they*; Hebrew *he*.

1084

Micah

....

Hosea
Joel
Amos
Obadiah
Jonah

²You mountains, you everlasting foundations of the earth, listen to the LORD's case! The LORD has a case against his people. He is going to bring an accusation against Israel. ³The LORD says, "My people, what have I done to you? How have I been a burden to you? Answer me. ⁴I brought you out of Egypt; I rescued you from slavery; I sent Moses, Aaron, and Miriam to lead you. ⁵My people, remember what King Balak of Moab planned to do to you and how Balaam son of Beor answered him. Remember the things that happened on the way from the camp at Acacia to Gilgal. Remember these things and you will realize what I did in order to save you."

What the LORD Requires

⁶What shall I bring to the LORD, the God of heaven, when I come to worship him? Shall I bring the best calves to burn as offerings to him? ⁷Will the LORD be pleased if I bring him thousands of sheep or endless streams of olive oil? Shall I offer him my firstborn child to pay for my sins? ⁸No, the LORD has told us what is good. What he requires of us is this: to do what is just, to show constant love, and to live in humble fellowship with our God.

⁹It is wise to fear the LORD. He calls to the city, "Listen, you people who assemble in the city!* ¹⁰In the houses of evil people are treasures which they got dishonestly. They use false measures, a thing that I hate.* ¹¹How can I forgive those who use false scales and weights? ¹²Your rich people exploit the poor, and all of you are liars. ¹³So I have already begun* your ruin and destruction because of your sins. ¹⁴You will eat, but not be satisfied — in fact you will still be hungry. You will carry things off, but you will not be able to save them; anything you do save I will destroy in war. ¹⁵You will sow corn, but not harvest the crop. You will press oil from olives, but never be able to use it. You will make wine, but never drink it. ¹⁶This will happen because you have followed the evil practices of King Omri and of his son, King Ahab. You have continued their policies, and so I will bring you to ruin, and everyone will despise you. People* everywhere will treat you with contempt."*

Israel's Moral Corruption

7 It's hopeless! I am like a hungry person who finds no fruit left on the trees and no grapes on the vines. All the grapes and all the tasty figs have been picked. ²There is not an honest person left in the land, no one loyal to God. Everyone is waiting for a chance to commit murder. Everyone hunts down his own people. ³They are all experts at doing evil. Officials and judges ask for bribes. The influential person tells them what he wants, and so they scheme together.* ⁴Even the best and most honest of them are as worthless as weeds.

The day has come when God will punish the people, as he warned them through their watchmen, the prophets. Now they are in confusion. ⁵Don't believe your neighbour or trust your friend. Be careful what you say even to your wife. ⁶In these times sons

MICAH 6.8

JUSTICE, LOVE, HUMILITY

6.9 Probable text *who assemble in the city*; Hebrew *and who appointed it. Yet.*
6.10 Verse 10 in Hebrew is unclear.
6.13 Some ancient translations *begun*; Hebrew *made ill.*
6.16 One ancient translation *People*; Hebrew *My people.*
6.16 *People... contempt;* or *As my people you will everywhere be treated with contempt.*
7.3 *and so they scheme together;* Hebrew unclear.

Micah

Nahum
Habak.
Zephan.
Haggai
Zechar.

treat their fathers like fools, daughters oppose their mothers, and young women quarrel with their mothers-in-law; a person's enemies are the members of his own family.

[7] But I will watch for the LORD; I will wait confidently for God, who will save me. My God will hear me.

The LORD Brings Salvation

[8] Our enemies have no reason to gloat over us. We have fallen, but we will rise again. We are in darkness now, but the LORD will give us light. [9] We have sinned against the LORD, so now we must endure his anger for a while. But in the end he will defend us and right the wrongs that have been done to us. He will bring us out to the light; we will live to see him save us. [10] Then our enemies will see this and be disgraced — the same enemies who taunted us by asking, "Where is the LORD your God?" We will see them defeated, trampled* down like mud in the streets.

[11] People of Jerusalem, the time to rebuild the city walls is coming. At that time your territory will be enlarged. [12] Your people will return to you from everywhere — from Assyria in the east, from Egypt in the south, from the region of the Euphrates, from distant seas and far-off mountains. [13] But the earth will become a desert because of the wickedness of those who live on it.

The LORD's Compassion on Israel

[14] Be a shepherd to your people, LORD, the people you have chosen. Although they live apart in the wilderness, there is fertile land around them. Let them go and feed in the rich pastures of Bashan and Gilead, as they did long ago.

[15] Work miracles for us,* LORD, as you did in the days when you brought us out of Egypt. [16] The nations will see this and be frustrated in spite of all their strength. In dismay they will close their mouths and cover their ears. [17] They will crawl in the dust like snakes; they will come from their fortresses, trembling and afraid. They will turn in fear to the LORD our God.

[18] There is no other god like you, O LORD; you forgive the sins of your people who have survived. You do not stay angry for ever, but you take pleasure in showing us your constant love. [19] You will be merciful to us once again. You will trample our sins underfoot and send them to the bottom of the sea! [20] You will show your faithfulness and constant love to your people, the descendants of Abraham and of Jacob, as you promised our ancestors long ago.

7.10 *We will see... trampled*; or *We will gloat over them as they lie trampled.*
7.15 Probable text *Work miracles for us*; Hebrew *I will work miracles for him.*

THE BOOK OF

NAHUM

WRITTEN: 630-612BC

WHAT YOU NEED TO KNOW:

Only a few decades previously, God had sent Jonah to prophesy to the people of Nineveh, and they changed their ways and turned to God. Sadly, it didn't last long. Within a short time they had once again become evil and corrupt. So God sent Nahum, a no-nonsense prophet who let the Ninevites know what they had done and what would happen as a result. In chapters 2 and 3, Nahum spells out the doom coming to Assyria. The words of Nahum (as well as some prophecies found in Zephaniah) soon came to pass, as the Assyrians were crushed by the Babylonians and the Medes. The city of Nineveh was destroyed in 612BC.

WHY READ IT?

In most prophetic writings, the prophets launch straight into the messages they've received from God. Nahum takes a different approach. He opens the first chapter of his book by unpacking God's character - his goodness toward those who trust in him but his righteous anger for those who turn against him. The main message of Nahum is that evil will not prosper.

Nahum is perhaps the most

STRANGELY NAMED

prophet in the Old Testament. His prophecies are all about destruction or Assyria, yet his name means

'COMFORT'

DRAW YOUR CURRENT VIEW

- whether it's your desk, your bed, out of the window, the cat... whatever!

HABAKKUK

NAHUM
NINEVEH DESTROYED 612BC
(630-612BC)

ZEPHANIAH

JEREMIAH

OBADIAH

DANI

NAHUM 1, 2

1087

Nahum
....
Habak.
Zephan.
Haggai
Zechar.
Malachi

1

This is a message about Nineveh, the account of a vision seen by Nahum, who was from Elkosh.

The Lord's Anger against Nineveh

2 The LORD God tolerates no rivals;
    he punishes those who oppose him.
    In his anger he pays them back.
3 The LORD does not easily become angry,
    but he is powerful and never lets the guilty go unpunished.

Where the LORD walks, storms arise;
    the clouds are the dust raised by his feet!
4 He commands the sea, and it dries up!
    He makes the rivers go dry.
The fields of Bashan wither,
    Mount Carmel turns brown,
    and the flowers of Lebanon fade.
5 Mountains quake in the presence of the LORD;
    hills melt before him.
The earth shakes when the LORD appears;
    the world and all its people tremble.
6 When he is angry, who can survive?
    Who can survive his terrible fury?
He pours out his flaming anger;
    rocks crumble to dust before him.

7 The LORD is good;
    he protects his people in times of trouble;
    he takes care of those who turn to him.
8 Like a great rushing flood he completely destroys his enemies;*
    he sends to their death those who oppose him.
9 What are you plotting against the LORD?
    He will destroy you.
    No one opposes him more than once.
10 Like tangled thorns and dry straw,
    you drunkards will be burnt up!

11 From you, Nineveh, there came someone full of wicked schemes, who plotted against the LORD. 12 This is what the LORD says to his people Israel: "Even though the Assyrians are strong and numerous, they will be destroyed and disappear. My people, I made you suffer, but I will not do it again. 13 I will now end Assyria's power over you and break the chains that bind you."

14 This is what the LORD has decreed about the Assyrians: "They will have no descendants to carry on their name. I will destroy the idols that are in the temples of their gods. I am preparing a grave for the Assyrians — they don't deserve to live!"

15 Look, a messenger is coming over the mountains with good news! He is on his way to announce the victory! People of Judah, celebrate your festivals and give God what you solemnly promised him. The wicked will never invade your land again. They have been totally destroyed!

The Fall of Nineveh

2

Nineveh, you are under attack!
    The power that will shatter you has come.
    Prepare the defences!

1.8 Some ancient translations *his enemies*; Hebrew *its place*.

NAHUM 1

The minor prophets
show us that God is

GOOD
– AND –
LOVING,

but also just.

Read Nahum 1, then

LIST AND COLOUR

the different
characteristics of God.

1088

Nahum

Joel
Amos
Obadiah
Jonah
Micah

FILL THIS SPACE HOWEVER YOU LIKE...

Guard the road!
Prepare for battle!
2 (The LORD is about to restore the glory of Israel, as it was before
her enemies plundered her.)
3 The enemy soldiers carry red shields
and wear uniforms of red.
They are preparing to attack!
Their chariots flash like fire!
Their horses* prance!

4 Chariots dash wildly through the streets,
rushing to and fro through the city squares.
They flash like torches
and dart about like lightning.
5 The officers are summoned;
they stumble as they press forward.

The attackers rush to the wall
and set up the shield for the battering ram.
6 The gates by the river burst open;
the palace is filled with terror.
7 The queen is taken captive;
her servants moan like doves
and beat their breasts in sorrow.
8 Like water from a broken dam
the people rush from Nineveh!*
"Stop! Stop!" the cry rings out —
but no one turns back.

9 Plunder the silver!
Plunder the gold!
The city is full of treasure!

10 Nineveh is destroyed, deserted, desolate!
Hearts melt with fear;
knees tremble, strength is gone;
faces grow pale.

11 Where now is the city
that was like a den of lions,
the place where young lions were fed,
where the lion and the lioness would go
and their cubs would be safe?
12 The lion killed his prey
and tore it to pieces for his mate and her cubs;
he filled his den with torn flesh.

13 "I am your enemy!" says the LORD Almighty. "I will burn up
your chariots. Your soldiers will be killed in war, and I will take
away everything that you took from others. The demands of your
envoys will no longer be heard."

3 Doomed is the lying, murderous city,
full of wealth to be looted and plundered!
2 Listen! The crack of the whip,
the rattle of wheels,

2.3 Some ancient translations *horses*; Hebrew *cypresses*.
2.8 Probable text *Like water... Nineveh*; Hebrew unclear.

Nahum

....

Habak.

Zephan.

Haggai

Zechar.

Malachi

  the gallop of horses,
  the jolting of chariots!
³ Horsemen charge,
  swords flash, spears gleam!
Corpses are piled high,
  dead bodies without number —
  men stumble over them!
⁴ Nineveh the whore is being punished.
  Attractive and full of deadly charms,
  she enchanted nations and enslaved* them.

⁵ The Lord Almighty says,
  "I will punish you, Nineveh!
  I will strip you naked
  and let the nations see you,
  see you in all your shame.
⁶ I will treat you with contempt
  and cover you with filth.
  People will stare at you in horror.
⁷ All who see you will shrink back.
  They will say, 'Nineveh lies in ruins!
  Who has any sympathy for her?
  Who will want to comfort her?'"

⁸ Nineveh, are you any better than Thebes, the capital of Egypt? She too had a river to protect her like a wall — the Nile was her defence. ⁹ She ruled Ethiopia and Egypt, there was no limit to her power; Libya was her ally. ¹⁰ Yet the people of Thebes were carried off into exile. At every street corner their children were beaten to death. Their leading men were carried off in chains and divided among their captors.

¹¹ Nineveh, you too will fall into a drunken stupor! You too will try to escape from your enemies. ¹² All your fortresses will be like fig trees with ripe figs: shake the trees, and the fruit falls right into your mouth! ¹³ Your soldiers are like women, and your country stands defenceless before your enemies. Fire will destroy the bars across your gates. ¹⁴ Draw water to prepare for a siege, and strengthen your fortresses! Trample the clay to make bricks, and get the brick moulds ready! ¹⁵ No matter what you do, you will still be burnt to death or killed in battle. You will be wiped out like crops eaten up by locusts.

  You multiplied like locusts! ¹⁶ You produced more merchants than there are stars in the sky! But now they are gone, like locusts that spread their wings and fly away. ¹⁷ Your officials are like a swarm of locusts that stay in the walls on a cold day. But when the sun comes out, they fly away, and no one knows where they have gone!

¹⁸ Emperor of Assyria, your governors are dead, and your noblemen are asleep for ever! Your people are scattered on the mountains, and there is no one to bring them home again. ¹⁹ There is no remedy for your injuries, and your wounds cannot be healed. All those who hear the news of your destruction clap their hands for joy. Did anyone escape your endless cruelty?

3.4 *enslaved*; or *seduced*.

THE BOOK OF
HABAKKUK

WRITTEN: AROUND 650-600BC

Spend some time in prayer before reading Habakkuk. Give over some time to God, asking him to speak to you through this book.

_____

_____

_____

_____

WITH ONE COLOURED PEN,

UNDERLINE

THE PLACES WHERE HABAKKUK

WRESTLES WITH GOD.

WITH ANOTHER COLOUR,

UNDERLINE

PLACES WHERE HE

PRAISES GOD.

WHAT YOU NEED TO KNOW:

Habakkuk wrote at the same time as Jeremiah and, like Jeremiah, prophesied the destruction of Jerusalem. In its style of writing, though, Habakkuk is closer to the book of Job, as it contains a conversation between a man and God about what is fair and right. In this conversation, God reveals that the Babylonians are going to destroy Jerusalem as punishment, although the Babylonians too will face God's justice in due course. God then gives Habakkuk a revelation to write down, after which Habakkuk sings a song of praise to God. Although, like Jeremiah, Habakkuk is saddened to hear of the upcoming fall of Jerusalem, he chooses to rejoice in God anyway because of God's righteousness.

WHY READ IT?

Habakkuk is a man who (a little like David) is open enough to be honest with God and to ask him what he is doing. Habakkuk's name in Hebrew means 'to wrestle', and that is what Habakkuk does with God. He shows us that there is space to question God, as long as we recognise that, even in the midst of our questioning, God deserves praise.

HABAKKUK
IN JUDAH BEFORE EXILE

MICAH

ISAIAH

(650-600BC)

ZEPHANIAH

NAHUM

JEREMI

1091

Habak.

Zephan.
Haggai
Zechar.
Malachi
Matt.

1
This is the message that the LORD revealed to the prophet Habakkuk.

Habakkuk Complains of Injustice
² O LORD, how long must I call for help before you listen, before you save us from violence? ³ Why do you make me see such trouble? How can you endure to look on such wrongdoing? Destruction and violence are all round me, and there is fighting and quarrelling everywhere. ⁴ The law is weak and useless, and justice is never done. Evil people get the better of the righteous, and so justice is perverted.

The LORD's Reply
⁵ Then the LORD said to his people, "Keep watching the nations round you, and you will be astonished at what you see. I am going to do something that you will not believe when you hear about it. ⁶ I am bringing the Babylonians to power, those fierce, restless people. They are marching out across the world to conquer other lands. ⁷ They spread fear and terror, and in their pride they are a law to themselves.

⁸ "Their horses are faster than leopards, fiercer than hungry wolves. Their horsemen come riding from distant lands; their horses paw the ground. They come swooping down like eagles attacking their prey.

⁹ "Their armies advance in violent conquest, and everyone is terrified as they approach.* Their captives are as numerous as grains of sand. ¹⁰ They treat kings with contempt and laugh at high officials. No fortress can stop them — they pile up earth against it and capture it. ¹¹ Then they sweep on like the wind and are gone, these men whose power is their god."

Habakkuk Complains to the LORD Again
¹² LORD, from the very beginning you are God. You are my God, holy and eternal. LORD, my God and protector, you have chosen the Babylonians and made them strong so that they can punish us. ¹³ But how can you stand these treacherous, evil men? Your eyes are too holy to look at evil, and you cannot stand the sight of people doing wrong. So why are you silent while they destroy people who are more righteous than they are?

¹⁴ How can you treat people like fish or like a swarm of insects that have no ruler to direct them? ¹⁵ The Babylonians catch people with hooks, as though they were fish. They drag them off in nets and shout for joy over their catch! ¹⁶ They even worship their nets and offer sacrifices to them, because their nets provide them with the best of everything.

¹⁷ Are they going to use their swords for ever and keep on destroying nations without mercy?

The LORD's Answer to Habakkuk
2
I will climb my watchtower and wait to see what the LORD will tell me to say and what answer he* will give to my complaint. ² The LORD gave me this answer: "Write down clearly on clay tablets what I reveal to you, so that it can be read at a glance. ³ Put it in writing, because it is not yet time for it to come true. But the time is coming quickly, and what I show you will come

HABAKKUK 1

Habakkuk has a Q and A with God. On this page, write down some of the

BIG
- QUESTIONS -
you would like to ask God, and pray that God will speak to you.

1.9 Probable text *and everyone… approach*; Hebrew unclear.
2.1 One ancient translation *he*; Hebrew *I*

true. It may seem slow in coming, but wait for it; it will certainly take place, and it will not be delayed. [4]And this is the message: 'Those who are evil will not survive,* but those who are righteous will live because they are faithful to God.' "

Doom on the Unrighteous

[5]Wealth is deceitful. Greedy people are proud and restless — like death itself they are never satisfied. That is why they conquer nation after nation for themselves. [6]The conquered people will taunt their conquerors and show their scorn for them. They will say, "You take what isn't yours, but you are doomed! How long will you go on getting rich by forcing your debtors to pay up?"

[7]But before you know it, you that have conquered others will be in debt yourselves and be forced to pay interest. Enemies will come and make you tremble. They will plunder you! [8]You have plundered the people of many nations, but now those who have survived will plunder you because of the murders you have committed and because of your violence against the people of the world and its cities.*

[9]You are doomed! You have made your family rich with what you took by violence, and have tried to make your own home safe from harm and danger! [10]But your schemes have brought shame on your family; by destroying many nations you have only brought ruin on yourself. [11]Even the stones of the walls cry out against you, and the rafters echo the cry.

[12]You are doomed! You founded a city on crime and built it up by murder. [13]The nations you conquered wore themselves out in useless labour, and all they have built goes up in flames. The LORD Almighty has done this. [14]But the earth will be as full of the knowledge of the LORD's glory as the seas are full of water.

[15]You are doomed! In your fury you humiliated and disgraced your neighbours; you made them stagger as though they were drunk. [16]You in turn will be covered with shame instead of honour. You yourself will drink and stagger. The LORD will make you drink your own cup of punishment, and your honour will be turned to disgrace. [17]You have cut down the forests of Lebanon; now you will be cut down. You killed its animals; now animals will terrify you. This will happen because of the murders you have committed and because of your violence against the people of the world and its cities.*

[18]What's the use of an idol? It is only something that a human being has made, and it tells you nothing but lies. What good does it do for its maker to trust it — a god that can't even talk! [19]You are doomed! You say to a piece of wood, "Wake up!" or to a block of stone, "Get up!" Can an idol reveal anything to you? It may be covered with silver and gold, but there is no life in it.

[20]The LORD is in his holy Temple; let everyone on earth be silent in his presence.

A Prayer of Habakkuk

3 This is a prayer of the prophet Habakkuk:*

[2] O LORD, I have heard of what you have done,
    and I am filled with awe.

....

2.4 Probable text *will not survive*; Hebrew unclear.
2.8; 2.17 *the people… cities*; or *the land, the city, and those who live in it.*
3.1 Hebrew has an additional phrase, the meaning of which is unclear.

Habak.
....
Zephan.
Haggai
Zechar.
Malachi
Matt.

Now do again in our times
the great deeds you used to do.
Be merciful, even when you are angry.

3 God is coming again from Edom;
the holy God is coming from the hills of
Paran.
His splendour covers the heavens;
and the earth is full of his praise.
4 He comes with the brightness of lightning;
light flashes from his hand,
there where his power is hidden.
5 He sends disease before him
and commands death to follow him.
6 When he stops, the earth shakes;
at his glance the nations tremble.
The eternal mountains are shattered;
the everlasting hills sink down,
the hills where he walked in ancient times.

7 I saw the people of Cushan afraid
and the people of Midian tremble.
8 Was it the rivers that made you angry, LORD?
Was it the sea that made you furious?
You rode upon the clouds;
the storm cloud was your chariot,
as you brought victory to your people.
9 You got ready to use your bow,
ready to shoot your arrows.*
Your lightning split open the earth.
10 When the mountains saw you, they trembled;
water poured down from the skies.
The waters under the earth roared,
and their waves rose high.
11 At the flash of your speeding arrows
and the gleam of your shining spear,
the sun and the moon stood still.
12 You marched across the earth in anger;
in fury you trampled the nations.
13 You went out to save your people,
to save your chosen king.
You struck down the leader of the wicked
and completely destroyed his followers.*
14 Your arrows pierced the commander of his army
when it came like a storm to scatter us,
gloating like those who secretly oppress the
poor.*
15 You trampled the sea with your horses,
and the mighty waters foamed.

16 I hear all this, and I tremble;
my lips quiver with fear.
My body goes limp,
and my feet stumble* beneath me.

Colour these shapes.

....

3.9 Probable text *ready to shoot your arrows*; Hebrew unclear.
3.13 Probable text *completely... followers*; Hebrew unclear.
3.14 Verse 14 in Hebrew is unclear.
3.16 Probable text *my feet stumble*; Hebrew *I am excited, because.*

Habak.

⋮ ⋯⋯⋯

Amos
Obadiah
Jonah
Micah
Nahum

I will quietly wait for the time to come
    when God will punish those who attack us.

17 Even though the fig trees have no fruit
    and no grapes grow on the vines,
    even though the olive crop fails
    and the fields produce no corn,
    even though the sheep all die
    and the cattle stalls are empty,
18 I will still be joyful and glad,
    because the LORD God is my saviour.
19 The Sovereign LORD gives me strength.
    He makes me sure-footed as a deer,
    and keeps me safe on the mountains.

THE BOOK OF
ZEPHANIAH

WRITTEN: SOMETIME BETWEEN 600 AND 500BC

WHAT YOU NEED TO KNOW:

Zephaniah was the great-great-grandson of King Hezekiah, so he was undoubtedly the poshest Old Testament prophet. He prophesied during the reign of King Josiah. Like many of the other prophetic books, this one starts with judgement on Judah and some of the surrounding nations, but it moves on to bring messages of hope for a great future. Zephaniah was the only prophet, other than Jonah, whose warnings were actually taken on board: it was during Josiah's reign that the Jews turned back to God. Zephaniah had ordered the repair and purification of Solomon's temple, and it was here that the book of the law was found, which moved Josiah to bring his people back to God (see 2 Kings 22-23).

WHY READ IT?

Zephaniah, like Joel, spoke a lot about the 'day of the Lord' - a time when God would come to bring judgement on those who opposed him and to rescue those who trusted him. But Zephaniah's prophecy is less about vengeance and more about the need to seek God. This book is a great way to discover the character of God towards those who choose to trust in him. It teaches us about God's anger, but also his tender good nature.

FIND OUT THE MEANING OF THE NAME ZEPHANIAH, AND WRITE IT <u>HERE</u>:

THE
DAY
OF THE
LORD

ZEPHANIAH
IN JUDAH BEFORE EXILE

...AIAH   JEREMIAH

HABAKKUK   (640-609BC)   NAHUM   OBADIAH

1 This is the message that the LORD gave to Zephaniah during the time that Josiah son of Amon was king of Judah. (Zephaniah was descended from King Hezekiah through Amariah, Gedaliah, and Cushi.)

The Day of the LORD's Judgement

² The LORD said, "I am going to destroy everything on earth, ³ all human beings and animals, birds and fish. I will bring about the downfall of* the wicked. I will destroy the whole human race, and no survivors will be left. I, the LORD, have spoken.

⁴ "I will punish the people of Jerusalem and of all Judah. I will destroy the last trace of the worship of Baal there, and no one will even remember the pagan priests who serve him. ⁵ I will destroy anyone who goes up on the roof and worships the sun, the moon, and the stars. I will also destroy those who worship me and swear loyalty to me, but then take oaths in the name of the god Molech. ⁶ I will destroy those who have turned back and no longer follow me, those who do not come to me or ask me to guide them."

⁷ The day is near when the LORD will sit in judgement; so be silent in his presence. The LORD is preparing to sacrifice his people and has invited enemies to plunder Judah. ⁸ "On that day of slaughter," says the LORD, "I will punish the officials, the king's sons, and all who practise foreign customs. ⁹ I will punish all who worship like pagans and who steal and kill in order to fill their master's house* with loot.

¹⁰ "On that day," says the LORD, "you will hear the sound of crying at the Fish Gate in Jerusalem. You will hear wailing in the newer part of the city and a great crashing sound in the hills. ¹¹ Wail and cry when you hear this, you that live in the lower part of the city, because all the merchants will be dead!

¹² "At that time I will take a lamp and search Jerusalem. I will punish the people who are self-satisfied and confident, who say to themselves, 'The LORD never does anything, one way or the other.' ¹³ Their wealth will be looted and their houses destroyed. They will never live in the houses they are building or drink wine from the vineyards they are planting."

¹⁴ The great day of the LORD is near — very near and coming fast! That will be a bitter day, for even* the bravest soldiers will cry out in despair! ¹⁵ It will be a day of fury, a day of trouble and distress, a day of ruin and destruction, a day of darkness and gloom, a black and cloudy day, ¹⁶ a day filled with the sound of war trumpets and the battle cry of soldiers attacking fortified cities and high towers.

¹⁷ The LORD says, "I will bring such disasters on mankind that everyone will grope about like someone blind. They have sinned against me, and now their blood will be poured out like water, and their dead bodies will lie rotting on the ground."

¹⁸ On the day when the LORD shows his fury, not even all their silver and gold will save them. The whole earth will be destroyed by the fire of his anger. He will put an end — a sudden end — to everyone who lives on earth.

A Plea for Repentance

2 Shameless nation, come to your senses ² before you are driven away like chaff blown by the wind, before the burning anger

---

1.3 Probable text *I will bring about the downfall of*; Hebrew *the stumbling blocks*.
1.9 *their master's house*; or *the temple of their god*.
1.14 *That... even*; or *Listen! That terrible day is coming when even*.

ZEPHANIAH 2, 3

1097

Zephan.

....

Haggai
Zechar.
Malachi
Matt.
Mark

of the LORD comes upon you, before the day when he shows his fury. ³ Turn to the LORD, all you humble people of the land, who obey his commands. Do what is right, and humble yourselves before the LORD. Perhaps you will escape punishment on the day when the LORD shows his anger.

The Doom of the Nations round Israel

⁴ No one will be left in the city of Gaza. Ashkelon will be deserted. The people of Ashdod will be driven out in half a day,* and the people of Ekron will be driven from their city. ⁵ You Philistines are doomed, you people who live along the coast. The LORD has passed sentence on you. He will destroy you, and not one of you will be left. ⁶ Your land by the sea will become open fields with shepherds' huts and sheep pens. ⁷ The people of Judah who survive will occupy your land. They will pasture their flocks there and sleep in the houses of Ashkelon. The LORD their God will be with them and make them prosper again.

⁸ The LORD Almighty says, "I have heard the people of Moab and Ammon insulting and taunting my people, and boasting that they would seize their land. ⁹ As surely as I am the living LORD, the God of Israel, I swear that Moab and Ammon are going to be destroyed like Sodom and Gomorrah. They will become a place of salt pits and everlasting ruin, overgrown with weeds. Those of my people who survive will plunder them and take their land."

¹⁰ That is how the people of Moab and Ammon will be punished for their pride and arrogance and for insulting the people of the LORD Almighty. ¹¹ The LORD will terrify them. He will reduce the gods of the earth to nothing, and then every nation will worship him, each in its own land.

¹² The LORD will also put the people of Ethiopia to death.

¹³ The LORD will use his power to destroy Assyria. He will make the city of Nineveh a deserted ruin, a waterless desert. ¹⁴ It will be a place where flocks, herds, and animals of every kind will lie down. Owls will live among its ruins and hoot from the windows. Crows* will caw on the doorsteps. The cedar wood of her buildings will be stripped away. ¹⁵ That is what will happen to the city that is so proud of its own power and thinks it is safe. Its people think that their city is the greatest in the world. What a desolate place it will become, a place where wild animals will rest! Everyone who passes by will shrink back in horror.

Jerusalem's Sin and Redemption

3 Jerusalem is doomed, that corrupt, rebellious city that oppresses its own people. ² It has not listened to the LORD or accepted his discipline. It has not put its trust in the LORD or asked for his help. ³ Its officials are like roaring lions; its judges are like hungry wolves, too greedy to leave a bone until morning. ⁴ The prophets are irresponsible and treacherous; the priests defile what is sacred, and twist the law of God to their own advantage. ⁵ But the LORD is still in the city; he does what is right and never what is wrong. Every morning without fail, he brings justice to his people. And yet the unrighteous people there keep on doing wrong and are not ashamed.

⁶ The LORD says, "I have wiped out whole nations; I have destroyed their cities and left their walls and towers in ruins. The cities are deserted; the streets are empty — no one is left.

2.4 *in half a day*; or *by a surprise attack at noon.*
2.14 Some ancient translations *Crows*; Hebrew *Desolation.*

REDEMPTION

ZEPHANIAH 3.1

DEFINITION: The action of saving or being saved from sin, error, or evil. (oxforddictionaries.com)

Zephan.

Obadiah
Jonah
Micah
Nahum
Habak.

[7] I thought that then my people would have reverence for me and accept my discipline, that they would never forget* the lesson I taught them. But soon they were behaving as badly as ever.

[8] "Just wait," the LORD says. "Wait for the day when I rise to accuse the nations. I have made up my mind to gather nations and kingdoms, in order to let them feel the force of my anger. The whole earth will be destroyed by the fire of my fury.

[9] "Then I will change the people of the nations, and they will pray to me alone and not to other gods. They will all obey me. [10] Even from distant Ethiopia my scattered people will bring offerings to me. [11] At that time you, my people, will no longer need to be ashamed that you rebelled against me. I will remove everyone who is proud and arrogant, and you will never again rebel against me on my sacred hill.* [12] I will leave there a humble and lowly people, who will come to me for help. [13] The people of Israel who survive will do no wrong to anyone, tell no lies, nor try to deceive. They will be prosperous and secure, afraid of no one."

A Song of Joy

[14] Sing and shout for joy, people of Israel!
  Rejoice with all your heart, Jerusalem!
[15] The LORD has ended your punishment;
  he has removed all your enemies.
The LORD, the king of Israel, is with you;
  there is no reason now to be afraid.
[16] The time is coming when they will say to Jerusalem,
  "Do not be afraid, city of Zion!
  Do not let your hands hang limp!
[17] The LORD your God is with you;
  his power gives you victory.
The LORD will take delight in you,
  and in his love he will give you new life.*
He will sing and be joyful over you,
[18]   as joyful as people at a festival."
The LORD says,
  "I have ended the threat of doom
  and taken away your disgrace.*
[19] The time is coming!
I will punish your oppressors;
  I will rescue all the lame
  and bring the exiles home.
I will turn their shame to honour,
  and all the world will praise them.
[20] The time is coming!
I will bring your scattered people home;
  I will make you famous throughout the world
  and make you prosperous once again."
The LORD has spoken.

ZEPHANIAH 3.17

God takes

DELIGHT
IN YOU

and sings over you!

Play some music you
really love (music without
lyrics might work best)
and sit and reflect on
this passage.

3.7 Some ancient translations *they would never forget*; Hebrew *their dwelling would not be cut off.*
3.11 *sacred hill*: Mount Zion.
3.17 Some ancient translations *give you new life*; Hebrew *be silent.*
3.18 Verse 18 in Hebrew is unclear.

THE BOOK OF

HAGGAI

WRITTEN: AROUND 535-520BC

Haggai kept his focus on God when many other people were

DEFLATED, LAZY OR SCARED

WHAT YOU NEED TO KNOW:

Jerusalem and Solomon's temple had been destroyed, and Haggai was one of the exiles who had been sent to Babylon. He was also one of the Jews who returned to Jerusalem, possibly with Nehemiah. So Haggai prophesied at a time when the Jews returned with a mission - to rebuild the temple. However, God's people were becoming discouraged, partly because of the amount of work needed, and partly because they were facing pressure and opposition from Judah's enemies. Some of the wealthier people even got lazy and concentrated on building their own houses before God's. Haggai's aim was to remind everyone why they were doing what they were doing. His job was to communicate, from God, the priorities and purpose for God's people.

Write down some of the character qualities Haggai must have had, to make him this way.

_____

_____

_____

_____

_____

_____

WHY READ IT?

We don't find many prophecies of destruction in Haggai, mainly because most of the destruction had already taken place. However, we do find punchy language, keeping people focused on God and their mission. Haggai is a great book to read if we are finding the pressures of life a little too much, as it is all about reminding ourselves why we do what we do. If God's people renew their devotion to him and his purposes, they will experience his love and favour.

What are some of the pressures you are facing that might make it hard to focus on God? Write them here.

_____

_____

_____

_____

ADIAH   EZEKIEL   (535-520BC)   ZECHARIAH

DANIEL   HAGGAI   MALACHI
EZRA REBUILDING TEMPLE

1100

Haggai

Jonah
Micah
Nahum
Habak.
Zephan.

HAGGAI 1, 2

The Lord's Command to Rebuild the Temple

1 During the second year that Darius was emperor of Persia, on the first day of the sixth month, the Lord spoke through the prophet Haggai. The message was for the governor of Judah, Zerubbabel son of Shealtiel, and for the High Priest, Joshua son of Jehozadak.

[2] The Lord Almighty said to Haggai, "These people say that this is not the right time to rebuild the Temple." [3] The Lord then gave this message to the people through the prophet Haggai: [4] "My people, why should you be living in well-built houses while my Temple lies in ruins? [5] Don't you see what is happening to you? [6] You have sown much corn, but have harvested very little. You have food to eat, but not enough to make you full. You have wine to drink, but not enough to get drunk on! You have clothing, but not enough to keep you warm. And a worker cannot earn enough to live on. [7] Can't you see why this has happened? [8] Now go up into the hills, get timber, and rebuild the Temple; then I will be pleased and will be worshipped as I should be.

[9] "You hoped for large harvests, but they turned out to be small. And when you brought the harvest home, I blew it away.* Why did I do that? Because my Temple lies in ruins while every one of you is busy working on his own house. [10] That is why there is no rain and nothing can grow. [11] I have brought drought on the land — on its hills, cornfields, vineyards, and olive orchards — on every crop the ground produces, on people and animals, on everything you try to grow."

The People Obey the Lord's Command

[12] Then Zerubbabel and Joshua and all the people who had returned from the exile* in Babylonia, did what the Lord their God told them to do. They were afraid and obeyed the prophet Haggai, the Lord's messenger. [13] Then Haggai gave the Lord's message to the people: "I will be with you — that is my promise." [14] The Lord inspired everyone to work on the Temple: Zerubbabel, the governor of Judah; Joshua, the High Priest, and all the people who had returned from the exile.* They began working on the Temple of the Lord Almighty, their God, [15] on the 24th day of the sixth month of the second year that Darius was emperor.

The Splendour of the New Temple

2 On the 21st day of the seventh month of that same year, the Lord spoke again through the prophet Haggai. [2] He told Haggai to speak to Zerubbabel, the governor of Judah, to Joshua, the High Priest, and to the people, and to say to them, [3] "Is there anyone among you who can still remember how splendid the Temple used to be? How does it look to you now? It must seem like nothing at all. [4] But now don't be discouraged, any of you. Do the work, for I am with you. [5] When you came out of Egypt, I promised that I would always be with you. I am still with you, so do not be afraid.

[6] "Before long I will shake heaven and earth, land and sea. [7] I will overthrow all the nations, and their treasures will be brought here, and the Temple will be filled with wealth. [8] All the silver and gold of the world is mine. [9] The new Temple will be more splendid than the old one, and there I will give my people prosperity and peace." The Lord Almighty has spoken.

1.9 *I blew it away*; or *I spoilt it*.
1.12; 1.14 *who had returned from the exile*; or *who had not gone into exile*.

Haggai

Zechar.
Malachi
Matt.
Mark
Luke

The Prophet Consults the Priests

¹⁰ On the 24th day of the ninth month of the second year that Darius was emperor, the LORD Almighty spoke again to the prophet Haggai. ¹¹ He said, "Ask the priests for a ruling on this question: ¹² Suppose someone takes a piece of consecrated meat from a sacrifice and carries it in a fold of his robe. If he then lets his robe touch any bread, cooked food, wine, olive oil, or any kind of food at all, will it make that food consecrated also?"

When the question was asked, the priests answered, "No."

¹³ Then Haggai asked, "Suppose someone is defiled because he has touched a dead body. If he then touches any of these foods, will that make them defiled too?"

The priests answered, "Yes."

¹⁴ Then Haggai said, "The LORD says that the same thing applies to the people of this nation and to everything they produce; and so everything they offer on the altar is defiled."

The LORD Promises his Blessing

¹⁵ The LORD says, "Can't you see what has happened to you? Before you started to rebuild the Temple, ¹⁶ you would go to a heap of corn expecting to find 200 kilogrammes, but there would be only a hundred. You would go to draw a hundred litres of wine from a vat, but find only forty. ¹⁷ I sent scorching winds and hail to ruin everything you tried to grow, but still you did not repent. ¹⁸ Today is the 24th day of the ninth month, the day that the foundation of the Temple has been completed. See what is going to happen from now on. ¹⁹ Although there is no corn left, and the grapevines, fig trees, pomegranates, and olive trees have not yet produced, yet from now on I will bless you."

The LORD's Promise to Zerubbabel

²⁰ On that same day, the 24th of the month, the LORD gave Haggai a second message ²¹ for Zerubbabel, the governor of Judah: "I am about to shake heaven and earth ²² and overthrow kingdoms and end their power. I will overturn chariots and their drivers; the horses will die, and their riders will kill one another. ²³ On that day I will take you, Zerubbabel my servant, and I will appoint you to rule in my name. You are the one I have chosen." The LORD Almighty has spoken.

HAGGAI 2

The people of Judah have returned from exile and the temple has been rebuilt. God promises to

MAKE
– IT –
SPLENDID.

On this page,
DRAW A TEMPLE
and make it splendid!

THE BOOK OF
ZECHARIAH

WRITTEN: 535-470BC

WHAT YOU NEED TO KNOW:

We don't know loads about Zechariah - only that his grandfather was Iddo, a priest who returned from exile to Judah. Therefore, Zechariah too was likely to have been a Levite and priest. Like Haggai, Zechariah wrote during the time between the Jews' return from exile and the rebuilding of the temple. His writings are quite a bit different from any other minor prophet's. He prophesied largely in visions, and many of the visions are quite difficult to understand. There are eight visions that speak of a world (perhaps our world in the future) where God is in full control and evil meets its end. It is a hope-filled book for people who had returned from exile but were under great pressure to rebuild the temple and withstand their enemies.

WHY READ IT?

Zechariah contains more specific references to the coming Messiah than perhaps any other prophet. The book contains plenty of detailed imagery about a coming king (chapter 9). Zechariah talks not only of the restoration of Israel and Judah but also of the end times when God will come to reign forever. It's a book not only for the future of the Jews who returned from exile, but also for our future.

As well as being one of the most creative prophets, Zechariah was one of the youngest. What we see from all the prophets is that God uses old people, young people, rich people, poor people, royalty and farmers to communicate his messages to his people.

There are
EIGHT 'VISIONS'
in the book of Zechariah.
Make a list of the titles of them here:

1. _____
2. _____
3. _____
4. _____
5. _____
6. _____
7. _____
8. _____

OBADIAH

DANIEL

EZEKIEL

HAGGAI

ZECHARIAH
EZRA REBUILDING TEMPLE

(535-520BC)

MALAC

ZECHARIAH 1, 2

1103

Zechar.

....

Malachi

Matt.

Mark

Luke

John

The Lord Calls his People to Return to him

1 In the eighth month of the second year that Darius was emperor of Persia, the Lord gave this message to the prophet Zechariah, the son of Berechiah and grandson of Iddo. ² The Lord Almighty told Zechariah to say to the people, "I, the Lord, was very angry with your ancestors, ³ but now I say to you, 'Return to me, and I will return to you. ⁴ Do not be like your ancestors. Long ago the prophets gave them my message, telling them not to live evil, sinful lives any longer. But they would not listen to me or obey me. ⁵ Your ancestors and those prophets are no longer alive. ⁶ Through my servants the prophets I gave your ancestors commands and warnings, but they disregarded them and suffered the consequences. Then they repented and acknowledged that I, the Lord Almighty, had punished them as they deserved and as I had determined to do.' "

The Prophet's Vision of the Horses

⁷ In the second year that Darius was emperor, on the 24th day of the eleventh month (the month of Shebat), the Lord gave me a message in a vision at night. ⁸ I saw someone riding a red horse. He had stopped among some myrtle trees in a valley, and behind him were other horses — red, dappled, and white. ⁹ I asked him, "Sir, what do these horses mean?"

He answered, "I will show you what they mean. ¹⁰ The Lord sent them to go and inspect the earth."

¹¹ They reported to the angel: "We have been all over the world and have found that the whole world lies helpless and subdued."

¹² Then the angel said, "Almighty Lord, you have been angry with Jerusalem and the cities of Judah for seventy years now. How much longer will it be before you show them mercy?"

¹³ The Lord answered the angel with comforting words, ¹⁴ and the angel told me to proclaim what the Lord Almighty had said: "I have a deep love and concern for Jerusalem, my holy city, ¹⁵ and I am very angry with the nations that enjoy quiet and peace. For while I was holding back my anger against my people, those nations made the sufferings of my people worse. ¹⁶ So I have come back to Jerusalem to show mercy to the city. My Temple will be restored, and the city will be rebuilt."

¹⁷ The angel also told me to proclaim: "The Lord Almighty says that his cities will be prosperous again and that he will once again help Jerusalem and claim the city as his own."

The Vision of the Horns

¹⁸ In another vision I saw four ox horns. ¹⁹ I asked the angel that had been speaking to me, "What do these horns mean?"

He answered, "They stand for the world powers that have scattered the people of Judah, Israel, and Jerusalem."

²⁰ Then the Lord showed me four workers with hammers. ²¹ I asked, "What have they come to do?"

He answered, "They have come to terrify and overthrow the nations that completely crushed the land of Judah and scattered its people."

The Vision of the Measuring Line

2 In another vision I saw a man with a measuring line in his hand. ² "Where are you going?" I asked.

"To measure Jerusalem," he answered, "to see how long and how wide it is."

1104

Zechar.

⋮⋯⋯⋯

Micah
Nahum
Habak.
Zephan.
Haggai

ZECHARIAH 2, 3

³Then I saw the angel who had been speaking to me step forward, and another angel came to meet him. ⁴The first one said to the other, "Run and tell that young man with the measuring line that there are going to be so many people and so much livestock in Jerusalem that it will be too big to have walls. ⁵The LORD has promised that he himself will be a wall of fire round the city to protect it and that he will live there in all his glory."

The Exiles are Called to Come Home

⁶⁻⁷The LORD said to his people, "I scattered you in all directions. But now, you exiles, escape from Babylonia and return to Jerusalem. ⁸Anyone who strikes you strikes what is most precious to me."

So the LORD Almighty* sent me with this message for the nations that had plundered his people: ⁹"The LORD himself will fight against you, and you will be plundered by the people who were once your servants."

When this happens, everyone will know that the LORD Almighty sent me.

¹⁰The LORD said, "Sing for joy, people of Jerusalem! I am coming to live among you!"

¹¹At that time many nations will come to the LORD and become his people. He will live among you, and you will know that he has sent me to you. ¹²Once again Judah will be the special possession of the LORD in his sacred land, and Jerusalem will be the city he loves most of all.

¹³Be silent, everyone, in the presence of the LORD, for he is coming from his holy dwelling place.

The Prophet's Vision of the High Priest

3 In another vision the LORD showed me the High Priest Joshua standing before the angel of the LORD. And there beside Joshua stood Satan,* ready to bring an accusation against him. ²The angel of the LORD* said to Satan, "May the LORD condemn you, Satan! May the LORD, who loves Jerusalem, condemn you. This man is like a stick snatched from the fire."

³Joshua was standing there, wearing filthy clothes. ⁴The angel said to his heavenly attendants, "Take away the filthy clothes this man is wearing." Then he said to Joshua, "I have taken away your sin and will give you new clothes to wear."

⁵He commanded the attendants to put* a clean turban on Joshua's head. They did so, and then they put the new clothes on him while the angel of the LORD stood there.

⁶Then the angel told Joshua that ⁷the LORD Almighty had said: "If you obey my laws and perform the duties I have assigned to you, then you will continue to be in charge of my Temple and its courts, and I will hear your prayers, just as I hear the prayers of the angels who are in my presence. ⁸Listen then, Joshua, you who are the High Priest; and listen, you fellow-priests of his, you that are the sign of a good future: I will reveal my servant, who is called The Branch! ⁹I am placing in front of Joshua a single stone with seven facets. I will engrave an inscription on it, and in a single day I will take away the sin of this land. ¹⁰When that day

2.8 Hebrew has two additional words, the meaning of which is unclear.
3.1 *Satan*: A supernatural being whose name indicates he was regarded as the opponent of human beings.
3.2 One ancient translation *The angel of the LORD*; Hebrew *The LORD*.
3.5 Some ancient translations *He commanded the attendants to put*; Hebrew *I said, "Let them put.*

ZECHARIAH 3–5

1105

Zechar.

Malachi
Matt.
Mark
Luke
John

comes, each of you will invite his neighbour to come and enjoy peace and security, surrounded by your vineyards and fig trees."

The Vision of the Lampstand

4 The angel who had been speaking to me came again and roused me as if I had been sleeping. [2]"What do you see?" he asked.

"A lampstand made of gold," I answered. "At the top is a bowl for the oil. On the lampstand are seven lamps, each one with places for seven wicks. [3] There are two olive trees beside the lampstand, one on each side of it." [4] Then I asked the angel, "What do these things stand for, sir?"

[5]"Don't you know?" he asked me.

"No, I don't, sir," I replied.*

[10b] The angel said to me, "The seven lamps are the seven eyes of the LORD, which see all over the earth."

[11] Then I asked him, "What do the two olive trees on either side of the lampstand mean? [12] And what is the meaning of the two olive branches beside the two gold pipes from which the olive oil pours?"

[13] He asked me, "Don't you know?"

"No, I don't, sir," I answered.

[14] Then he said, "These are the two men whom God has chosen and anointed to serve him, the Lord of the whole earth."

God's Promise to Zerubbabel

[6] The angel told me to give Zerubbabel this message from the LORD: "You will succeed, not by military might or by your own strength, but by my spirit. [7] Obstacles as great as mountains will disappear before you. You will rebuild the Temple, and as you put the last stone in place, the people will shout, 'Beautiful, beautiful!'"

[8] Another message came to me from the LORD. [9] He said, "Zerubbabel has laid the foundation of the Temple, and he will finish the building. When this happens, my people will know that it is I who sent you to them. [10a] They are disappointed because so little progress is being made. But they will see Zerubbabel continuing to build the Temple, and they will be glad."

The Vision of the Flying Scroll

5 I looked again, and this time I saw a scroll flying through the air. [2] The angel asked me what I saw. I answered, "A scroll flying through the air; it is nine metres long and 4.5 metres wide."

[3] Then he said to me, "On it is written the curse that is to go out over the whole land. On one side of the scroll it says that every thief will be removed from the land; and on the other side it says that everyone who tells lies under oath will also be taken away. [4] The LORD Almighty says that he will send this curse out, and it will enter the house of every thief and the house of everyone who tells lies under oath. It will remain in their houses and leave them in ruins."

The Vision of the Woman in the Basket

[5] The angel appeared again and said, "Look! Something else is coming!"

[6] "What is it?" I asked.

ZECHARIAH 4.7

OBSTACLES
– as great as –
MOUNTAINS
WILL DISAPPEAR
BEFORE YOU

4.5 Verses 10b–14 are moved here from the end of the chapter in order to retain the natural order of the narrative.

1106

Zechar.

.:.........

Micah
Nahum
Habak.
Zephan.
Haggai

ZECHARIAH 5–7

He replied, "It is a basket, and it stands for the sin* of the whole land."

[7] The basket had a lid made of lead. As I watched, the lid was raised, and there in the basket sat a woman!

[8] The angel said, "This woman represents wickedness." Then he pushed her down into the basket and put the lid back down. [9] I looked up and saw two women flying towards me with powerful wings like those of a stork. They picked up the basket and flew off with it.

[10] I asked the angel, "Where are they taking it?"

[11] He answered, "To Babylonia, where they will build a temple for it. When the temple is finished, the basket will be placed there to be worshipped."

The Vision of the Four Chariots

6 I had another vision. This time I saw four chariots coming out from between two bronze mountains. [2] The first chariot was pulled by red horses, the second by black horses, [3] the third by white horses, and the fourth by dappled horses. [4] Then I asked the angel, "Sir, what do these chariots mean?"

[5] He answered, "These are the four winds; they have just come from the presence of the Lord of all the earth."

[6] The chariot pulled by the black horses was going north to Babylonia, the white horses were going to the west, and the dappled horses were going to the country in the south. [7] As the dappled horses came out, they were impatient to go and inspect the earth. The angel said, "Go and inspect the earth!" — and they did. [8] Then the angel cried out to me, "The horses that went north to Babylonia have calmed down the LORD's anger."

The Command to Crown Joshua

[9] The LORD gave me this message. [10] He said, "Take the gifts given by the exiles Heldai, Tobijah, and Jedaiah, and go at once to the home of Josiah son of Zephaniah. All these men have returned from exile in Babylonia. [11] Make a crown out of the silver and gold they have given, and put it on the head of the High Priest, Joshua son of Jehozadak. [12] Tell him that the LORD Almighty says, 'The man who is called The Branch will flourish where he is and rebuild the LORD's Temple. [13] He is the one who will build it and receive the honour due to a king, and he will rule his people. A priest will stand by his throne, and they will work together in peace and harmony.' [14] The crown will be a memorial in the LORD's Temple in honour of Heldai,* Tobijah, Jedaiah, and Josiah."*

[15] Men who live far away will come and help to rebuild the Temple of the LORD. And when it is rebuilt, you will know that the LORD Almighty sent me to you. This will all happen if you fully obey the commands of the LORD your God.

The LORD Condemns Insincere Fasting

7 In the fourth year that Darius was emperor, on the fourth day of the ninth month (the month of Kislev), the LORD gave me a message.

[2] The people of Bethel had sent Sharezer and Regemmelech and their men to the Temple of the LORD Almighty to pray for the LORD's blessing [3] and to ask the priests and the prophets this

---

5.6 Some ancient translations *sin*; Hebrew *eye*.
6.14 One ancient translation *Heldai*; Hebrew *Helem*.
6.14 One ancient translation *Josiah*; Hebrew *Hen*.

ZECHARIAH 7, 8

1107

Zechar.

⋯⋯⋯⋮⋗

Malachi
Matt.
Mark
Luke
John

question: "Should we continue to mourn because of the destruction of the Temple, by fasting in the fifth month as we have done for so many years now?"

[4] This is the message of the LORD that came to me. [5] He said, "Tell the people of the land and the priests that when they fasted and mourned in the fifth and seventh months during these seventy years, it was not in honour of me. [6] And when they ate and drank, it was for their own satisfaction."

[7] This is what the LORD said through the earlier prophets at the time when Jerusalem was prosperous and filled with people and when there were many people living not only in the towns round the city but also in the southern region and in the western foothills.

Disobedience, the Cause of Exile

[8] The LORD gave this message to Zechariah: [9] "Long ago I gave these commands to my people: 'You must see that justice is done, and must show kindness and mercy to one another. [10] Do not oppress widows, orphans, foreigners who live among you, or anyone else in need. And do not plan ways of harming one another.'

[11] "But my people stubbornly refused to listen. They closed their minds [12] and made their hearts as hard as rock. Because they would not listen to the teaching which I sent through the prophets who lived long ago, I became very angry. [13] Because they did not listen when I spoke, I did not answer when they prayed. [14] Like a storm I swept them away to live in foreign countries. This good land was left a desolate place, with no one living in it."

The LORD Promises to Restore Jerusalem

8 The LORD Almighty gave this message to Zechariah: [2] "I have longed to help Jerusalem because of my deep love for her people, a love which has made me angry with her enemies. [3] I will return to Jerusalem, my holy city, and live there. It will be known as the faithful city, and the hill of the LORD Almighty* will be called the sacred hill. [4] Once again old men and women, so old that they use a stick when they walk, will be sitting in the city squares. [5] And the streets will again be full of boys and girls playing.

[6] "This may seem impossible to those of the nation who are now left, but it's not impossible for me. [7] I will rescue my people from the lands where they have been taken, [8] and will bring them back from east and west to live in Jerusalem. They will be my people, and I will be their God, ruling over them faithfully and justly.

[9] "Have courage! You are now hearing the same words the prophets spoke at the time the foundation was being laid for rebuilding my Temple. [10] Before that time no one could afford to hire either men or animals, and no one was safe from his enemies. I turned people against one another. [11] But now I am treating the survivors of this nation differently. [12] They will sow their crops in peace. Their vines will bear grapes, the earth will produce crops, and there will be plenty of rain. I will give all these blessings to the people of my nation who survive. [13] People of Judah and Israel! In the past foreigners have cursed one another by saying, 'May the same disasters fall on you that fell on Judah and Israel!' But I will save you, and then those foreigners will say to one another, 'May you receive the same blessings that came to Judah and Israel!' So have courage and don't be afraid."

[14] The LORD Almighty says, "When your ancestors made me angry, I planned disaster for them and did not change my mind,

⋯⋯⋯⋯⋯⋯⋯⋯⋯⋯⋯⋯⋯⋯⋯⋯⋯⋯⋯⋯⋯⋯⋯⋯⋯⋯⋯⋯⋯⋯⋯⋯⋯⋯

8.3 *hill of the* LORD *almighty*: Mount Zion.

1108

Zechar.

Micah
Nahum
Habak.
Zephan.
Haggai

but carried out my plans. [15] But now I am planning to bless the people of Jerusalem and Judah. So don't be afraid. [16] These are the things you should do: speak the truth to one another. In the courts, give real justice — the kind that brings peace. [17] Do not plan ways of harming one another. Do not give false testimony under oath. I hate lying, injustice, and violence."

[18] The LORD Almighty gave this message to Zechariah: [19] "The fasts held in the fourth, fifth, seventh, and tenth months will become festivals of joy and gladness for the people of Judah. You must love truth and peace."

[20] The LORD Almighty says, "The time is coming when people from many* cities will come to Jerusalem. [21] Those from one city will say to those from another, 'We are going to worship the LORD Almighty and pray for his blessing. Come with us!' [22] Many* peoples and powerful nations will come to Jerusalem to worship the LORD Almighty, and to pray for his blessing. [23] In those days ten foreigners will come to one Jew and say, 'We want to share in your destiny, because we have heard that God is with you.'"

Judgement on Neighbouring Nations

9 This is the LORD's message:

He has decreed punishment for the land of Hadrach and for the city of Damascus. Not only the tribes of Israel, but also the capital of Syria belong to the LORD. [2] Hamath, which borders on Hadrach, also belongs to him, and so do the cities of Tyre and Sidon, with all their skill. [3] Tyre has built fortifications for herself and has piled up so much silver and gold that it is as common as dirt! [4] But the Lord will take away everything she has. He will throw her wealth into the sea, and the city will be burnt to the ground.

[5] The city of Ashkelon will see this and be afraid. The city of Gaza will see it and suffer great pain. So will Ekron, and her hopes will be shattered. Gaza will lose her king, and Ashkelon will be left deserted. [6] People of mixed race will live in Ashdod. The LORD says, "I will humble all these proud Philistines. [7] They will no longer eat meat with blood in it, or other forbidden food. All the survivors will become part of my people and be like a clan in the tribe of Judah. Ekron will become part of my people, as the Jebusites* did. [8] I will guard my land and keep armies from passing through it. I will not allow tyrants to oppress my people any more. I have seen how my people have suffered."

The Future King

[9] Rejoice, rejoice, people of Zion!
   Shout for joy, you people of Jerusalem!
   Look, your king is coming to you!
He comes triumphant and victorious,
   but humble and riding on a donkey —
    on a colt, the foal of a donkey.
[10] The LORD says,
"I will remove the war chariots from Israel
   and take the horses from Jerusalem;
   the bows used in battle will be destroyed.
Your king will make peace among the nations;
   he will rule from sea to sea,
    from the River Euphrates to the ends of the earth."

8.20; 8.22 *many*; or *great*.
9.7 *Jebusites*: The original inhabitants of Jerusalem, who became David's subjects after he captured the city.

ZECHARIAH 9.9

Conservative estimates suggest that Jesus fulfilled over

300

• PROPHECIES •

from the Old Testament, some as obvious as this one here. (Read John 12.14-15 to see it happening.) The fact that he fulfils loads of prophecies from hundreds of years before his birth is a great piece of evidence that Jesus is the Messiah.

ZECHARIAH 9, 10

1109

Zechar.

....

Malachi
Matt.
Mark
Luke
John

The Restoration of God's People

[11] The LORD says,
"Because of my covenant with you
that was sealed by the blood of sacrifices,
I will set your people free —
free from the waterless pit of exile.
[12] Return, you exiles who now have hope;
return to your place of safety.
I tell you now, I will repay you twice over
with blessing for all you have suffered.
[13] I will use Judah like a soldier's bow
and Israel like the arrows.
I will use the men of Zion like a sword,
to fight the men of Greece."

[14] The LORD will appear above his people;
he will shoot his arrows like lightning.
The Sovereign LORD will sound the trumpet;
he will march in the storms from the south.
[15] The LORD Almighty will protect his people,
and they will destroy their enemies.
They will shout in battle like drunken men
and will shed the blood of their enemies;
it will flow like the blood of a sacrifice
poured on the altar from a bowl.*

[16] When that day comes, the LORD will save his people,
as a shepherd saves his flock from danger.
They will shine in his land
like the jewels of a crown.
[17] How good and beautiful the land will be!
The young people will grow strong on its corn and
wine.

The LORD Promises Deliverance

10 Ask the LORD for rain in the spring of the year. It is the LORD who sends rain clouds and showers, making the fields green for everyone. [2] People consult idols and fortune tellers, but the answers they get are lies and nonsense. Some interpret dreams, but only mislead you; the comfort they give is useless. So the people wander about like lost sheep. They are in trouble because they have no leader.

[3] The LORD says, "I am angry with those foreigners who rule my people, and I am going to punish them. The people of Judah are mine, and I, the LORD Almighty, will take care of them. They will be my powerful war horses. [4] From among them will come rulers, leaders, and commanders to govern my people.* [5] The people of Judah will be victorious like soldiers who trample their enemies into the mud of the streets. They will fight because the LORD is with them, and they will defeat even the enemy horsemen.

[6] "I will make the people of Judah strong;
I will rescue the people of Israel.
I will have compassion on them
and bring them all back home.

....

9.15 Verse 15 in Hebrew is unclear.
10.4 *From among... people*; or *All oppressors — rulers, leaders, and commanders — will depart together from Judah.*

Zechar.

··⁝········

Micah
Nahum
Habak.
Zephan.
Haggai

They will be as though I had never rejected them.
I am the LORD their God; I will answer their prayers.
7 The people of Israel will be strong like soldiers,
happy like men who have been drinking wine.
Their descendants will remember this victory
and be glad because of what the LORD has done.

8 "I will call my people
and gather them together.
I will rescue them
and make them as numerous as they used to be.
9 Though I have scattered them among the nations,
yet in far-off places they will remember me.
They and their children will survive
and return home together.
10 From Egypt and Assyria I will bring them home
and settle them in their own country.
I will settle them in Gilead and Lebanon also;
the whole land will be filled with people.
11 When they pass through their sea of trouble,
I, the LORD, will strike the waves,
and the depths of the Nile will go dry.
Proud Assyria will be humbled,
and mighty Egypt will lose her power.
12 I will make my people strong;
they will worship and obey me."
The LORD has spoken.

The Fall of the Tyrants

11 Open your doors, Lebanon,
so that fire can burn down your cedar trees!*
2 Weep and wail, cypress trees —
the cedars have fallen;
those glorious trees have been destroyed!
Weep and wail, oaks of Bashan —
the dense forest has been cut down!
3 The rulers cry out in grief;
their glory is gone!
Listen to the roaring of the lions;
their forest home along the Jordan is destroyed!

The Two Shepherds

4 The LORD my God said to me, "Act the part of the shepherd*
of a flock of sheep that are going to be butchered. 5 Their owners
kill them and go unpunished. They sell the meat and say, 'Praise
the LORD! We are rich!' Even their own shepherds have no pity
on them."

6 (The LORD said, "I will no longer pity anyone on earth. I myself
will put all the people in the power of their rulers. Those rulers
will devastate the earth, and I will not save it from their power.")

7 Those who bought and sold the sheep hired me, and I became
the shepherd of the sheep that were going to be butchered. I took
two sticks: one I called "Favour", and the other "Unity". And I took
care of the flock. 8 I lost patience with three other shepherds, who

....

11.1 *cedar trees*: Trees are used here as symbols of powerful nations or their
kings.
11.4 *shepherd*: Shepherd is used here as a symbol of a king or leader, and
sheep as symbols of his people or followers.

ZECHARIAH 11, 12

1111

Zechar.

.........:

Malachi
Matt.
Mark
Luke
John

hated me, and I got rid of them all in a single month. ⁹Then I said to the flock, "I will not be your shepherd any longer. Let those who are to die, die. Let those who are to be destroyed, be destroyed. Those who are left will destroy one another." ¹⁰Then I took the stick called "Favour" and broke it, to cancel the covenant which the Lord had made with all the nations. ¹¹So the covenant was cancelled on that day. Those who bought and sold the sheep were watching me, and they knew that the Lord was speaking through what I did. ¹²I said to them, "If you are willing, give me my wages. But if not, keep them." So they paid me thirty pieces of silver as my wages.

¹³The Lord said to me, "Put them in the temple treasury."* So I took the thirty pieces of silver — the magnificent sum they thought I was worth — and put them in the temple treasury. ¹⁴Then I broke the second stick, the one called "Unity", and the unity of Judah and Israel was shattered.

¹⁵Then the Lord said to me, "Once again act the part of a shepherd, this time a worthless one. ¹⁶I have put a shepherd in charge of my flock, but he does not help the sheep that are threatened by destruction; nor does he look for the lost, or heal those that are hurt, or feed the healthy. Instead, he eats the meat of the fattest sheep and tears off their hoofs. ¹⁷That worthless shepherd is doomed! He has abandoned his flock. War will totally destroy his power. His arm will wither, and his right eye will go blind."

The Future Deliverance of Jerusalem

12 This is a message about Israel from the Lord, the Lord who spread out the skies, created the earth, and gave life to man. He says, ²"I will make Jerusalem like a cup of wine; the nations round her will drink and stagger like drunken men. And when they besiege Jerusalem, the cities of the rest of Judah will also be besieged. ³But when that time comes, I will make Jerusalem like a heavy stone — any nation that tries to lift it will be hurt. All the nations of the world will join forces to attack her. ⁴At that time I will terrify all their horses and make all their riders go mad. I will watch over the people of Judah, but I will make the horses of their enemies blind. ⁵Then the clans of Judah will say to themselves, 'The Lord God Almighty gives strength to his people who live in Jerusalem.'

⁶"At that time I will make the clans of Judah like a fire in a forest or in a field of ripe corn — they will destroy all the surrounding nations. The people of Jerusalem will remain safe in the city.

⁷"I, the Lord, will give victory to the armies of Judah first, so that the honour which the descendants of David and the people of Jerusalem will receive will be no greater than that of the rest of Judah. ⁸At that time the Lord will protect those who live in Jerusalem, and even the weakest among them will become as strong as David was. The descendants of David will lead them like the angel of the Lord, like God himself. ⁹At that time I will destroy every nation that tries to attack Jerusalem.

¹⁰"I will fill the descendants of David and the other people of Jerusalem with the spirit of mercy and the spirit of prayer. They will look at the one whom they stabbed to death, and they will mourn for him like those who mourn for an only child. They will mourn bitterly, like those who have lost their firstborn son. ¹¹At

---

11.13 Some ancient translations *Put them in the temple treasury*; Hebrew *Give them to the potter.*

Zechar.

Micah
Nahum
Habak.
Zephan.
Haggai

that time the mourning in Jerusalem will be as great as the mourning for Hadad Rimmon* in the plain of Megiddo. 12-14 Each family in the land will mourn by itself: the family descended from David, the family descended from Nathan, the family descended from Levi, the family descended from Shimei, and all the other families. Each family will mourn by itself, and the men of each family will mourn separately from the women.

13 "When that time comes," says the LORD Almighty, "a fountain will be opened to purify the descendants of David and the people of Jerusalem from their sin and idolatry. 2 At that time I will remove the names of the idols from the land, and no one will remember them any more. I will get rid of anyone who claims to be a prophet and will take away the desire to worship idols. 3 Then if anyone still insists on prophesying, his own father and mother will tell him that he must be put to death, because he claimed to speak the LORD's word, but spoke lies instead. When he prophesies, his own father and mother will stab him to death. 4 When that time comes, no prophet will be proud of his visions, or act like a prophet, or wear a prophet's coarse garment in order to deceive people. 5 Instead, he will say, 'I am not a prophet. I am a farmer — I have farmed the land all my life.' 6 Then if someone asks him, 'What are those wounds on your chest?' he will answer, 'I got them at a friend's house.'"

The Command to Kill God's Shepherd

7 The LORD Almighty says, "Wake up, sword, and attack the shepherd* who works for me! Kill him, and the sheep will be scattered. I will attack my people 8 and throughout the land two-thirds of the people will die. 9 And I will test the third that survives and will purify them as silver is purified by fire. I will test them as gold is tested. Then they will pray to me, and I will answer them. I will tell them that they are my people, and they will confess that I am their God."

Jerusalem and the Nations

14 The day when the LORD will sit in judgement is near. Then Jerusalem will be looted, and the loot will be divided up before your eyes. 2 The LORD will bring all the nations together to make war on Jerusalem. The city will be taken, the houses looted, and the women raped. Half the people will go into exile, but the rest of them will not be taken away from the city. 3 Then the LORD will go out and fight against those nations, as he has fought in times past. 4 At that time he will stand on the Mount of Olives, to the east of Jerusalem. Then the Mount of Olives will be split in two from east to west by a large valley. Half the mountain will move northwards and half of it southwards. 5 You will escape through this valley that divides the mountain in two.* You will flee as your ancestors did when the earthquake struck in the time of King Uzziah of Judah. The LORD my God will come, bringing all the angels with him.

6 When that time comes, there will no longer be cold or frost,* 7 nor any darkness. There will always be daylight, even at night-time. When this will happen is known only to the LORD.

TURN THESE
LINES INTO A
PICTURE OF
SOMETHING.

12.11 *Hadad Rimmon*: Probably a name for Baal, the god of vegetation in Canaan and Syria. When the vegetation died each year, the worshippers thought that the god had died too, and they mourned his death.
13.7 *shepherd*: See 11.4.
14.5 Probable text *You will escape… in two*; Hebrew unclear.
14.6 Probable text *cold or frost*; Hebrew unclear.

ZECHARIAH 14

1113

Zechar.

....

Malachi
Matt.
Mark
Luke
John

8 When that day comes, fresh water will flow from Jerusalem, half of it to the Dead Sea and the other half to the Mediterranean. It will flow all the year round, in the dry season as well as the wet. 9 Then the LORD will be king over all the earth; everyone will worship him as God and know him by the same name.

10 The whole region, from Geba in the north to Rimmon in the south, will be made level. Jerusalem will tower above the land round it; the city will reach from the Benjamin Gate to the Corner Gate, where there had been an earlier gate, and from the Tower of Hananel to the royal winepresses. 11 The people will live there in safety, no longer threatened by destruction.

12 The LORD will bring a terrible disease on all the nations that make war on Jerusalem. Their flesh will rot away while they are still alive; their eyes and their tongues will rot away.

13 At that time the LORD will make them so confused and afraid that everyone will seize the man next to him and attack him. 14 The men of Judah will fight to defend Jerusalem. They will take as loot the wealth of all the nations — gold, silver, and clothing in great abundance.

15 A terrible disease will also fall on the horses, the mules, the camels, and the donkeys — on all the animals in the camps of the enemy.

16 Then all the survivors from the nations that have attacked Jerusalem will go there each year to worship the LORD Almighty as king, and to celebrate the Festival of Shelters. 17 If any nation refuses to go and worship the LORD Almighty as king, then rain will not fall on their land. 18 If the Egyptians refuse to celebrate the Festival of Shelters, then they will be struck by the same disease that the LORD will send on every nation that refuses to go. 19 This will be the punishment that will fall on Egypt and on all the other nations if they do not celebrate the Festival of Shelters.

20 At that time even the harness bells of the horses will be inscribed with the words "Dedicated to the LORD". The cooking pots in the Temple will be as sacred as the bowls before the altar. 21 Every cooking pot in Jerusalem and in all Judah will be set apart for use in the worship of the LORD Almighty. The people who offer sacrifices will use them for boiling the meat of the sacrifices. When that time comes, there will no longer be any merchant in the Temple of the LORD Almighty.

THE BOOK OF

MALACHI

WRITTEN: AROUND 450-420BC

WHAT YOU NEED TO KNOW:

The temple and the walls of Jerusalem had been rebuilt and most of the Jews were back in their homeland. (Malachi may have returned from exile in Nehemiah's time.) However, they were still under foreign rule. God's people had begun waiting for a coming Messiah to fulfil all of the prophecies that had been made, but old habits had started creeping back. Malachi, the last prophet in our Old Testament, had a special message for those who insisted on doing religion but rejecting God. Priests were cheating God by not paying tithes (a tenth of their income), but wondered why God wasn't blessing them. Malachi said that God would rather shut down the temple than take false offerings. He encouraged people to focus on God, reminding them that a future king would be coming soon.

WHY READ IT?

Malachi is the perfect book to round off the Old Testament. It speaks of the importance of focusing on God and loving him as a father, and it then prophesies the coming Messiah. The last two chapters focus on this special king, who would not arrive for another 400 years. This book serves as the bridge between Old Testament and New, showing us a loving God who wants to be our Father, while promising that the plan set out from Genesis onwards is close to being fulfilled.

Malachi has an unusual writing style, speaking in questions and answers.

Write down some of the

QUESTIONS
YOU WOULD LIKE TO
ASK GOD

and what you imagine his answers to those questions might be.

OBADIAH · DANIEL · EZEKIEL · HAGGAI · ZECHARIAH · (450-420B · MALAC

1

This is the message that the LORD gave Malachi to tell the people of Israel.

The LORD's Love for Israel

[2] The LORD says to his people, "I have always loved you."

But they reply, "How have you shown your love for us?"

The LORD answers, "Esau and Jacob were brothers, but I have loved Jacob and his descendants, [3] and have hated Esau and his descendants. I have devastated Esau's hill country and abandoned the land to jackals."

[4] If Esau's descendants, the Edomites, say, "Our towns have been destroyed, but we will rebuild them," then the LORD will reply, "Let them rebuild — I will tear them down again. People will call them 'The evil country' and 'The nation with whom the LORD is angry for ever.'"

[5] The people of Israel are going to see this with their own eyes, and they will say, "The LORD is mighty even outside the land of Israel!"

The LORD Reprimands the Priests

[6] The LORD Almighty says to the priests, "A son honours his father, and a servant honours his master. I am your father — why don't you honour me? I am your master — why don't you respect me? You despise me, and yet you ask, 'How have we despised you?' [7] This is how — by offering worthless food on my altar. Then you ask, 'How have we failed to respect you?' I will tell you — by showing contempt for my altar. [8] When you bring a blind or sick or lame animal to sacrifice to me, do you think there's nothing wrong with that? Try giving an animal like that to the governor! Would he be pleased with you or grant you any favours?"

[9] Now, you priests, try asking God to be good to us. He will not answer your prayer, and it will be your fault. [10] The LORD Almighty says, "I wish one of you would close the temple doors so as to prevent you from lighting useless fires on my altar. I am not pleased with you; I will not accept the offerings you bring me. [11] People from one end of the world to the other honour me. Everywhere they burn incense to me and offer acceptable sacrifices. All of them honour me! [12] But you dishonour me when you say that my altar is worthless and when you offer on it food that you despise. [13] You say, 'How tired we are of all this!' and you turn up your nose at me. As your offering to me you bring a stolen animal or one that is lame or sick. Do you think I will accept that from you? [14] A curse on the cheat who sacrifices a worthless animal to me, when he has in his flock a good animal that he promised to give me! For I am a great king, and people of all nations fear me."

2

The LORD Almighty says to the priests, "This command is for you: [2] You must honour me by what you do. If you will not listen to what I say, then I will bring a curse on you. I will put a curse on the things you receive for your support. In fact, I have already put a curse on them, because you do not take my command seriously. [3] I will punish your children and rub your faces in the dung of the animals you sacrifice — and you will be taken out to the dunghill. [4] Then you will know that I have given you this command, so that my covenant with the priests, the descendants of Levi, will not be broken.

[5] "In my covenant I promised them life and well-being, and this is what I gave them, so that they might respect me. In those days they did respect and fear me. [6] They taught what was right,

1116

Malachi

.·:........

Nahum
Habak.
Zephan.
Haggai
Zechar.

MALACHI 2, 3

MALACHI 3.10

Talk with friends or
family about the
things you have and
how you can be

GENEROUS
- WITH THEM. -

Discuss together: what
does God promise in
Malachi 3.10? What do
you think this promise
means for us today? In
what ways can we be
more generous?

not what was wrong. They lived in harmony with me; they not only did what was right themselves, but they also helped many others to stop doing evil. [7]It is the duty of priests to teach the true knowledge of God. People should go to them to learn my will, because they are the messengers of the LORD Almighty.

[8]"But now you priests have turned away from the right path. Your teaching has led many to do wrong. You have broken the covenant I made with you. [9]So I, in turn, will make the people of Israel despise you because you do not obey my will, and when you teach my people, you do not treat everyone alike."

The People's Unfaithfulness to God

[10]Don't we all have the same father? Didn't the same God create us all? Then why do we break our promises to one another, and why do we despise the covenant that God made with our ancestors? [11]The people of Judah have broken their promise to God and done a horrible thing in Jerusalem and all over the country. They have defiled the Temple which the LORD loves. Men have married women who worship foreign gods. [12]May the LORD remove from the community of Israel those who did this, and never again let them participate in the offerings our nation brings to the LORD Almighty.*

[13]This is another thing you do. You drown the LORD's altar with tears, weeping and wailing because he no longer accepts the offerings you bring him. [14]You ask why he no longer accepts them. It is because he knows you have broken your promise to the wife you married when you were young. She was your partner, and you have broken your promise to her, although you promised before God that you would be faithful to her. [15]Didn't God make you one body and spirit with her?* What was his purpose in this? It was that you should have children who are truly God's people. So make sure that none of you breaks his promise to his wife. [16]"I hate divorce," says the LORD God of Israel. "I hate it when one of you does such a cruel thing to his wife. Make sure that you do not break your promise to be faithful to your wife."

The Day of Judgement is Near

[17]You have tired the LORD out with your talk. But you ask, "How have we tired him?" By saying, "The LORD Almighty thinks all evildoers are good; in fact he likes them." Or by asking, "Where is the God who is supposed to be just?"

3 The LORD Almighty answers, "I will send my messenger to prepare the way for me. Then the Lord you are looking for will suddenly come to his Temple. The messenger you long to see will come and proclaim my covenant."

[2]But who will be able to endure the day when he comes? Who will be able to survive when he appears? He will be like strong soap, like a fire that refines metal. [3]He will come to judge like one who refines and purifies silver. As a metalworker refines silver and gold, so the LORD's messenger will purify the priests, so that they will bring to the LORD the right kind of offerings. [4]Then the offerings which the people of Judah and Jerusalem bring to the LORD will be pleasing to him, as they used to be in the past.

[5]The LORD Almighty says, "I will appear among you to judge, and I will testify at once against those who practise magic, against adulterers, against those who give false testimony,

2.12 One ancient translation *May... Almighty*; Hebrew unclear.
2.15 Probable text *Didn't God... her*; Hebrew unclear.

MALACHI 3, 4

1117

Malachi

....

Matt.
Mark
Luke
John
Acts

those who cheat employees out of their wages, and those who take advantage of widows, orphans, and foreigners — against all who do not respect me.

The Payment of Tithes

⁶"I am the LORD, and I do not change. And so you, the descendants of Jacob, are not yet completely lost. ⁷You, like your ancestors before you, have turned away from my laws and have not kept them. Turn back to me, and I will turn to you. But you ask, 'What must we do to turn back to you?' ⁸I ask you, is it right for a person to cheat God? Of course not, yet you are cheating me. 'How?' you ask. In the matter of tithes and offerings. ⁹A curse is on all of you because the whole nation is cheating me. ¹⁰Bring the full amount of your tithes to the Temple, so that there will be plenty of food there. Put me to the test and you will see that I will open the windows of heaven and pour out on you in abundance all kinds of good things. ¹¹I will not let insects destroy your crops, and your grapevines will be loaded with grapes. ¹²Then the people of all nations will call you happy, because your land will be a good place to live in.

God's Promise of Mercy

¹³"You have said terrible things about me," says the LORD. "But you ask, 'What have we said about you?' ¹⁴You have said, 'It's useless to serve God. What's the use of doing what he says or of trying to show the LORD Almighty that we are sorry for what we have done? ¹⁵As we see it, proud people are the ones who are happy. Evil people not only prosper, but they test God's patience with their evil deeds and get away with it.'"

¹⁶Then the people who feared the LORD spoke to one another, and the LORD listened and heard what they said. In his presence, there was written down in a book a record of those who feared the LORD and respected him. ¹⁷"They will be my people," says the LORD Almighty. "On the day when I act, they will be my very own. I will be merciful to them, as a father is merciful to the son who serves him. ¹⁸Once again my people will see the difference between what happens to the righteous and to the wicked, to the person who serves me and the one who does not."

The Day of the LORD is Coming

4 The LORD Almighty says, "The day is coming when all proud and evil people will burn like straw. On that day they will burn up, and there will be nothing left of them. ²But for you who obey me, my saving power will rise on you like the sun and bring healing like the sun's rays. You will be as free and happy as calves let out of a stall. ³On the day when I act, you will overcome the wicked, and they will be like dust under your feet.

⁴"Remember the teachings of my servant Moses, the laws and commands which I gave him at Mount Sinai for all the people of Israel to obey.

⁵"But before the great and terrible day of the LORD comes, I will send you the prophet Elijah. ⁶He will bring fathers and children together again; otherwise I would have to come and destroy your country."

MALACHI 4

Between the Old Testament and the New Testament are 400 years where we don't hear any more prophecy - but God's people are waiting for someone special.

WATCH THIS

FILM

TO LEARN about the years of silence.

Head to gnbyouthedition.co.uk/silence

400 YEARS
OF SILENCE

By the time of the prophet Malachi, the Judeans had been allowed to return home from captivity in Babylonia - but they weren't really free, as the whole area was now under the rule of the Persians. The temple had been rebuilt, but it was a lot smaller than before, and many Jewish people were still scattered around the Persian empire.

During the next 400 years, it seemed as if God was silent because there were no important prophets - but a lot happened. The area of Palestine was conquered many times, by the Greeks, the Egyptians and Syrians, the Maccabees (Jews who rebelled against the Syrians) and then the Romans. The temple was damaged a few different times. Local synagogues - Jewish places of prayer and study - sprang up in towns and villages, where people could go and hear God's law being taught and explained.

IMPORTANT GROUPS OF PEOPLE

There may have been no new prophecy, but the law was still really important to the Jewish people. So they elected scribes, who were professionals at explaining what God's law meant and how it should be lived out. These people became very influential.

The other great power was the Sanhedrin - the Jewish council or law court.
The Great Sanhedrin in Jerusalem was made up of 71 wise men, including the high priest and chief priests. Local Sanhedrins, outside Jerusalem, were smaller than this.

Two groups of leaders, the Pharisees and Sadducees, may have been part of the Sanhedrin. The Pharisees are really important in the Gospels, as the ordinary people looked up to them as experts in Jewish laws and traditions. They had strict beliefs about how the Jews should live according to those laws. However, they sometimes split into smaller groups, based on different views on how to understand the law.

The Sadducees were a smaller group of rulers, made up of the rich and wealthy. Unlike the Pharisees, they did not believe in angels or life after death, and were keen not to upset the Roman authorities. The chief priests and high priests were generally Sadducees, and so the Sadducees tended to control the temple.

Another important group was the Zealots. The Zealots had a slogan, 'No ruler but God', and were political activists in the Jewish community. They were very much opposed to Roman rule and wanted to protect the Jews from Roman traditions.

Then there were the common people - the farmers and fishermen.

All these groups had heard teachings about a coming Messiah, and everyone was waiting for this promised king to arrive.

SSSHHHHHHHHHHHHHH!

Spend five minutes sitting in complete silence and just listen. Write in the space above all of the noises you hear during those five minutes.

Imagine how it would feel if you were used to hearing from God or experiencing his presence,

AND THEN HE JUST

STOPPED

saying anything new to you.

Imagine if that was true for everyone you ever met, and imagine if the silence then stretched on for

400 YEARS.

And what if, the last time God did speak, he made

A REALLY GREAT

PROMISE

...but that was ages ago and there's no sign of the promise being fulfilled?

WRITE YOUR THOUGHTS HERE.

PROPHECIES

ABOUT JESUS

Here's a crazy thing about the life of Jesus - much of it was predicted before he was even born. In the Old Testament we have hundreds of prophecies about a coming saviour, some general and some specific. Many Christians believe that Jesus fulfilled all of them. Let's explore just a few!

In the spaces below, write a summary of each Bible passage. How well do you think the New Testament verses fulfil the prophecies? You could also circle the verses in the New Testament where Jesus fulfils Old Testament prophecies.

PROPHECY	FULFILMENT
Psalm 22.14-18	John 19.23-37
Isaiah 7.14	Luke 1.34-37
Isaiah 53.7	Luke 23.9
Micah 5.2	Matthew 2.1-6
Zechariah 11.12-13	Matthew 27.1-4
Malachi 3.1	Mark 1.1-8

In total, it's possible that Jesus fulfilled well over 300 Old Testament prophecies.

THE GOSPEL OF
MATTHEW

WRITTEN: AROUND AD80

If you met Jesus, what would you do?
What would you want to say to him?

_____

_____

_____

_____

_____

_____

_____

_____

_____

_____

WHO IS JESUS TO YOU?

As you read this Gospel,

SCRIBBLE

IN THE MARGINS

and highlight or circle anything that gets you
thinking about what Jesus is like.

WHAT YOU NEED TO KNOW:

Matthew is one of the four books called 'Gospels' that tell us about the life and teachings of Jesus. This Gospel has a particular focus on Jesus' work and teachings. It begins with his birth, continuing until his resurrection. Matthew wrote his Gospel for the Jews, so this book is full of references to parts of the Old Testament that would have had a lot of meaning for them. He aimed to tell the Jews, through his writing, that Jesus was the Messiah who had been promised to them long ago.

WHY READ IT?

The Old Testament pointed towards Jesus in loads of different ways, and Jesus changed the world by what he did and taught. Read Matthew to find out about the Son of God who was promised long before he was born. It's full of life-changing stuff and tells us about the one who sets us free and enables us to have a relationship with God.

(6BC)
ESUS' BIRTH

HEALING AND TEACHING

DEATH

RESURRECTION
(AD27)

Matt.

Habak.
Zephan.
Haggai
Zechar.
Malachi

The Ancestors of Jesus Christ
(Lk 3.23–38)

1 This is the list of the ancestors of Jesus Christ, a descendant of David, who was a descendant of Abraham.

2-6a From Abraham to King David, the following ancestors are listed: Abraham, Isaac, Jacob, Judah and his brothers; then Perez and Zerah (their mother was Tamar), Hezron, Ram, Amminadab, Nahshon, Salmon, Boaz (his mother was Rahab), Obed (his mother was Ruth), Jesse, and King David.

6b-11 From David to the time when the people of Israel were taken into exile in Babylon, the following ancestors are listed: David, Solomon (his mother was the woman who had been Uriah's wife), Rehoboam, Abijah, Asa, Jehoshaphat, Jehoram, Uzziah, Jotham, Ahaz, Hezekiah, Manasseh, Amon, Josiah, and Jehoiachin and his brothers.

12-16 From the time after the exile in Babylon to the birth of Jesus, the following ancestors are listed: Jehoiachin, Shealtiel, Zerubbabel, Abiud, Eliakim, Azor, Zadok, Achim, Eliud, Eleazar, Matthan, Jacob, and Joseph, who married Mary, the mother of Jesus, who was called the Messiah.

17 So then, there were fourteen generations from Abraham to David, and fourteen from David to the exile in Babylon, and fourteen from then to the birth of the Messiah.

The Birth of Jesus Christ
(Lk 2.1–7)

18 This was how the birth of Jesus Christ took place. His mother Mary was engaged to Joseph, but before they were married, she found out that she was going to have a baby by the Holy Spirit. 19 Joseph was a man who always did what was right, but he did not want to disgrace Mary publicly; so he made plans to break the engagement privately. 20 While he was thinking about this, an angel of the Lord appeared to him in a dream and said, "Joseph, descendant of David, do not be afraid to take Mary to be your wife. For it is by the Holy Spirit that she has conceived. 21 She will have a son, and you will name him Jesus — because he will save his people from their sins."

22 Now all this happened in order to make what the Lord had said through the prophet come true, 23 "A virgin will become pregnant and have a son, and he will be called Immanuel" (which means, "God is with us").

24 So when Joseph woke up, he married Mary, as the angel of the Lord had told him to do. 25 But he had no sexual relations with her before she gave birth to her son. And Joseph named him Jesus.

Visitors from the East

2 Jesus was born in the town of Bethlehem in Judea, during the time when Herod was king. Soon afterwards, some men who studied the stars came from the east to Jerusalem 2 and asked, "Where is the baby born to be the king of the Jews? We saw his star when it came up in the east, and we have come to worship him."

3 When King Herod heard about this, he was very upset, and so was everyone else in Jerusalem. 4 He called together all the chief priests and the teachers of the Law and asked them, "Where will the Messiah be born?"

5 "In the town of Bethlehem in Judea," they answered. "For this is what the prophet wrote:

1125

Matt.

....

Mark
Luke
John
Acts
Romans

6 'Bethlehem in the land of Judah,
    you are by no means the least of the leading cities of
        Judah;
    for from you will come a leader
        who will guide my people Israel.'"

7 So Herod called the visitors from the east to a secret meeting and found out from them the exact time the star had appeared. 8 Then he sent them to Bethlehem with these instructions: "Go and make a careful search for the child, and when you find him, let me know, so that I too may go and worship him."

9-10 And so they left, and on their way they saw the same star they had seen in the east. When they saw it, how happy they were, what joy was theirs! It went ahead of them until it stopped over the place where the child was. 11 They went into the house, and when they saw the child with his mother Mary, they knelt down and worshipped him. They brought out their gifts of gold, frankincense, and myrrh, and presented them to him.

12 Then they returned to their country by another road, since God had warned them in a dream not to go back to Herod.

The Escape to Egypt

13 After they had left, an angel of the Lord appeared in a dream to Joseph and said, "Herod will be looking for the child in order to kill him. So get up, take the child and his mother and escape to Egypt, and stay there until I tell you to leave."

14 Joseph got up, took the child and his mother, and left during the night for Egypt, 15 where he stayed until Herod died. This was done to make what the Lord had said through the prophet come true, "I called my Son out of Egypt."

The Killing of the Children

16 When Herod realized that the visitors from the east had tricked him, he was furious. He gave orders to kill all the boys in Bethlehem and its neighbourhood who were two years old and younger — this was done in accordance with what he had learned from the visitors about the time when the star had appeared.

17 In this way what the prophet Jeremiah had said came true:
18 "A sound is heard in Ramah,
    the sound of bitter weeping.
  Rachel is crying for her children;
    she refuses to be comforted,
    for they are dead."

The Return from Egypt

19 After Herod died, an angel of the Lord appeared in a dream to Joseph in Egypt 20 and said, "Get up, take the child and his mother, and go back to the land of Israel, because those who tried to kill the child are dead." 21 So Joseph got up, took the child and his mother, and went back to Israel.

22 But when Joseph heard that Archelaus had succeeded his father Herod as king of Judea, he was afraid to go there. He was given more instructions in a dream, so he went to the province of Galilee 23 and made his home in a town named Nazareth. And so what the prophets had said came true: "He will be called a Nazarene."

The Preaching of John the Baptist
(Mk 1.1–8; Lk 3.1–18; Jn 1.19–28)

3 At that time John the Baptist came to the desert of Judah and started preaching. 2 "Turn away from your sins," he said,

Matt.

Habak.
Zephan.
Haggai
Zechar.
Malachi

"because the Kingdom of heaven is near!" [3] John was the man the prophet Isaiah was talking about when he said:

"Someone is shouting in the desert,
    'Prepare a road for the Lord;
    make a straight path for him to travel!'"

[4] John's clothes were made of camel's hair; he wore a leather belt round his waist, and his food was locusts and wild honey. [5] People came to him from Jerusalem, from the whole province of Judea, and from all the country near the River Jordan. [6] They confessed their sins, and he baptized them in the Jordan.

[7] When John saw many Pharisees and Sadducees coming to him to be baptized, he said to them, "You snakes — who told you that you could escape from the punishment God is about to send? [8] Do those things that will show that you have turned from your sins. [9] And don't think you can escape punishment by saying that Abraham is your ancestor. I tell you that God can take these stones and make descendants for Abraham! [10] The axe is ready to cut down the trees at the roots; every tree that does not bear good fruit will be cut down and thrown in the fire. [11] I baptize you with water to show that you have repented, but the one who will come after me will baptize you with the Holy Spirit and fire. He is much greater than I am; and I am not good enough even to carry his sandals. [12] He has his winnowing shovel with him to thresh out all the grain. He will gather his wheat into his barn, but he will burn the chaff in a fire that never goes out."

The Baptism of Jesus
(Mk 1.9–11; Lk 3.21–22)

[13] At that time Jesus arrived from Galilee and came to John at the Jordan to be baptized by him. [14] But John tried to make him change his mind. "I ought to be baptized by you," John said, "and yet you have come to me!"

[15] But Jesus answered him, "Let it be so for now. For in this way we shall do all that God requires." So John agreed.

[16] As soon as Jesus was baptized, he came up out of the water. Then heaven was opened to him, and he saw the Spirit of God coming down like a dove and alighting on him. [17] Then a voice said from heaven, "This is my own dear Son, with whom I am pleased."

The Temptation of Jesus
(Mk 1.12–13; Lk 4.1–13)

4 Then the Spirit led Jesus into the desert to be tempted by the Devil. [2] After spending forty days and nights without food, Jesus was hungry. [3] Then the Devil came to him and said, "If you are God's Son, order these stones to turn into bread."

[4] But Jesus answered, "The scripture says, 'Human beings cannot live on bread alone, but need every word that God speaks.'"

[5] Then the Devil took Jesus to Jerusalem, the Holy City, set him on the highest point of the Temple, [6] and said to him, "If you are God's Son, throw yourself down, for the scripture says:

'God will give orders to his angels about you;
    they will hold you up with their hands,
    so that not even your feet will be hurt on the stones.'"

[7] Jesus answered, "But the scripture also says, 'Do not put the Lord your God to the test.'"

[8] Then the Devil took Jesus to a very high mountain and showed him all the kingdoms of the world in all their greatness. [9] "All this I will give you," the Devil said, "if you kneel down and worship me."

MATTHEW 4.1-11

Jesus didn't just resist the temptations of Satan, but he did it by quoting verses from the Old Testament. (Look up Deuteronomy 8.3, Deuteronomy 6.16 and Deuteronomy 6.13 to see what we're talking about.) There is power in knowing the Bible, as it means we can

• REMEMBER •

VERSES

that help us when we face difficult times.

MATTHEW 4, 5

1127

Matt.
....
Mark
Luke
John
Acts
Romans

[10] Then Jesus answered, "Go away, Satan! The scripture says, 'Worship the Lord your God and serve only him!'"

[11] Then the Devil left Jesus; and angels came and helped him.

Jesus Begins his Work in Galilee
(Mk 1.14–15; Lk 4.14–15)

[12] When Jesus heard that John had been put in prison, he went away to Galilee. [13] He did not stay in Nazareth, but went to live in Capernaum, a town by Lake Galilee, in the territory of Zebulun and Naphtali. [14] This was done to make what the prophet Isaiah had said come true:

[15] "Land of Zebulun and land of Naphtali,
　　on the road to the sea, on the other side of the Jordan,
　　Galilee, land of the Gentiles!
[16] The people who live in darkness
　　will see a great light.
　　On those who live in the dark land of death
　　　the light will shine."

[17] From that time Jesus began to preach his message: "Turn away from your sins, because the Kingdom of heaven is near!"

Jesus Calls Four Fishermen
(Mk 1.16–20; Lk 5.1–11)

[18] As Jesus walked along the shore of Lake Galilee, he saw two brothers who were fishermen, Simon (called Peter) and his brother Andrew, catching fish in the lake with a net. [19] Jesus said to them, "Come with me, and I will teach you to catch people." [20] At once they left their nets and went with him.

[21] He went on and saw two other brothers, James and John, the sons of Zebedee. They were in their boat with their father Zebedee, getting their nets ready. Jesus called them, [22] and at once they left the boat and their father, and went with him.

Jesus Teaches, Preaches, and Heals
(Lk 6.17–19)

[23] Jesus went all over Galilee, teaching in the synagogues, preaching the Good News about the Kingdom, and healing people who had all kinds of disease and sickness. [24] The news about him spread through the whole country of Syria, so that people brought to him all those who were sick, suffering from all kinds of diseases and disorders: people with demons, and epileptics, and paralytics — and Jesus healed them all. [25] Large crowds followed him from Galilee and the Ten Towns, from Jerusalem, Judea, and the land on the other side of the Jordan.

The Sermon on the Mount
5.1—7.29

5 Jesus saw the crowds and went up a hill, where he sat down. His disciples gathered round him, [2] and he began to teach them:

True Happiness
(Lk 6.20–23)

[3] "Happy are those who know they are spiritually poor;
　　the Kingdom of heaven belongs to them!
[4] Happy are those who mourn;
　　God will comfort them!
[5] Happy are those who are humble;
　　they will receive what God has promised!

1128

Matt.

Habak.
Zephan.
Haggai
Zechar.
Malachi

MATTHEW 5-7

As you read through the Sermon on the Mount, use different colours to highlight bits that

STAND OUT
TO YOU.

In the margins, use the same colours to write how you can do something practical about each of them in your life.

6 Happy are those whose greatest desire is to do what God requires;
   God will satisfy them fully!
7 Happy are those who are merciful to others;
   God will be merciful to them!
8 Happy are the pure in heart;
   they will see God!
9 Happy are those who work for peace;
   God will call them his children!
10 Happy are those who are persecuted because they do what God requires;
   the Kingdom of heaven belongs to them!
11 "Happy are you when people insult you and persecute you and tell all kinds of evil lies against you because you are my followers. 12 Be happy and glad, for a great reward is kept for you in heaven. This is how the prophets who lived before you were persecuted.

Salt and Light
(Mk 9.50; Lk 14.34–35)

13 "You are like salt for the whole human race. But if salt loses its saltiness, there is no way to make it salty again. It has become worthless, so it is thrown out and people trample on it.
14 "You are like light for the whole world. A city built on a hill cannot be hidden. 15 No one lights a lamp and puts it under a bowl; instead he puts it on the lampstand, where it gives light for everyone in the house. 16 In the same way your light must shine before people, so that they will see the good things you do and praise your Father in heaven.

Teaching about the Law

17 "Do not think that I have come to do away with the Law of Moses and the teachings of the prophets. I have not come to do away with them, but to make their teachings come true. 18 Remember that as long as heaven and earth last, not the least point nor the smallest detail of the Law will be done away with — not until the end of all things.* 19 So then, whoever disobeys even the least important of the commandments and teaches others to do the same, will be least in the Kingdom of heaven. On the other hand, whoever obeys the Law and teaches others to do the same, will be great in the Kingdom of heaven. 20 I tell you, then, that you will be able to enter the Kingdom of heaven only if you are more faithful than the teachers of the Law and the Pharisees in doing what God requires.

Teaching about Anger
(Lk 12.57–59)

21 "You have heard that people were told in the past, 'Do not commit murder; anyone who does will be brought to trial.' 22 But now I tell you: whoever is angry* with his brother will be brought to trial, whoever calls his brother 'You good-for-nothing!' will be brought before the Council, and whoever calls his brother a worthless fool will be in danger of going to the fire of hell. 23 So if you are about to offer your gift to God at the altar and there you remember that your brother has something against

5.18 *the end of all things*; or *all its teachings come true.*
5.22 *whoever is angry*; some manuscripts have *whoever without cause is angry.*

1129

Matt.

....

Mark

Luke

John

Acts

Romans

you, [24] leave your gift there in front of the altar, go at once and make peace with your brother, and then come back and offer your gift to God.

[25] "If someone brings a lawsuit against you and takes you to court, settle the dispute with him while there is time, before you get to court. Once you are there, he will hand you over to the judge, who will hand you over to the police, and you will be put in jail. [26] There you will stay, I tell you, until you pay the last penny of your fine.

Teaching about Adultery

[27] "You have heard that it was said, 'Do not commit adultery.' [28] But now I tell you: anyone who looks at a woman and wants to possess her is guilty of committing adultery with her in his heart. [29] So if your right eye causes you to sin, take it out and throw it away! It is much better for you to lose a part of your body than to have your whole body thrown into hell. [30] If your right hand causes you to sin, cut it off and throw it away! It is much better for you to lose one of your limbs than for your whole body to go to hell.

Teaching about Divorce
(Mt 19.9; Mk 10.11–12; Lk 16.18)

[31] "It was also said, 'Anyone who divorces his wife must give her a written notice of divorce.' [32] But now I tell you: if a man divorces his wife, for any cause other than her unfaithfulness, then he is guilty of making her commit adultery if she marries again; and the man who marries her commits adultery also.

Teaching about Vows

[33] "You have also heard that people were told in the past, 'Do not break your promise, but do what you have vowed to the Lord to do.' [34] But now I tell you: do not use any vow when you make a promise. Do not swear by heaven, for it is God's throne; [35] nor by earth, for it is the resting place for his feet; nor by Jerusalem, for it is the city of the great King. [36] Do not even swear by your head, because you cannot make a single hair white or black. [37] Just say 'Yes' or 'No' — anything else you say comes from the Evil One.

Teaching about Revenge
(Lk 6.29–30)

[38] "You have heard that it was said, 'An eye for an eye, and a tooth for a tooth.' [39] But now I tell you: do not take revenge on someone who wrongs you. If anyone slaps you on the right cheek, let him slap your left cheek too. [40] And if someone takes you to court to sue you for your shirt, let him have your coat as well. [41] And if one of the occupation troops forces you to carry his pack one kilometre, carry it two kilometres. [42] When someone asks you for something, give it to him; when someone wants to borrow something, lend it to him.

Love for Enemies
(Lk 6.27–28, 32–36)

[43] "You have heard that it was said, 'Love your friends, hate your enemies.' [44] But now I tell you: love your enemies and pray for those who persecute you, [45] so that you may become the children of your Father in heaven. For he makes his sun to shine on bad and good people alike, and gives rain to those who do good and

1130

Matt.

⁙········

Habak.
Zephan.
Haggai
Zechar.
Malachi

MATTHEW 5, 6

to those who do evil. ⁴⁶Why should God reward you if you love only the people who love you? Even the tax collectors do that! ⁴⁷And if you speak only to your friends, have you done anything out of the ordinary? Even the pagans do that! ⁴⁸You must be perfect — just as your Father in heaven is perfect!

Teaching about Charity

6 "Make certain you do not perform your religious duties in public so that people will see what you do. If you do these things publicly, you will not have any reward from your Father in heaven.

²"So when you give something to a needy person, do not make a big show of it, as the hypocrites do in the houses of worship and on the streets. They do it so that people will praise them. I assure you, they have already been paid in full. ³But when you help a needy person, do it in such a way that even your closest friend will not know about it. ⁴Then it will be a private matter. And your Father, who sees what you do in private, will reward you.

Teaching about Prayer
(Lk 11.2–4)

⁵"When you pray, do not be like the hypocrites! They love to stand up and pray in the houses of worship and on the street corners, so that everyone will see them. I assure you, they have already been paid in full. ⁶But when you pray, go to your room, close the door, and pray to your Father, who is unseen. And your Father, who sees what you do in private, will reward you.

⁷"When you pray, do not use a lot of meaningless words, as the pagans do, who think that their gods will hear them because their prayers are long. ⁸Do not be like them. Your Father already knows what you need before you ask him. ⁹This, then, is how you should pray:

'Our Father in heaven:
May your holy name be honoured;
10   may your Kingdom come;
may your will be done on earth as it is in heaven.
11   Give us today the food we need.*
12   Forgive us the wrongs we have done,
as we forgive the wrongs that others have done to us.
13   Do not bring us to hard testing,
but keep us safe from the Evil One.'*

¹⁴"If you forgive others the wrongs they have done to you, your Father in heaven will also forgive you. ¹⁵But if you do not forgive others, then your Father will not forgive the wrongs you have done.

Teaching about Fasting

¹⁶"And when you fast, do not put on a sad face as the hypocrites do. They neglect their appearance so that everyone will see that they are fasting. I assure you, they have already been paid in full. ¹⁷When you go without food, wash your face and comb your hair, ¹⁸so that others cannot know that you are fasting — only your Father, who is unseen, will know. And your Father, who sees what you do in private, will reward you.

··

6.11 *we need*; or *for today*; or *for tomorrow*.
6.13 Some manuscripts add *For yours is the kingdom, and the power, and the glory for ever. Amen.*

MATTHEW 6, 7

1131

Matt.
....
Mark
Luke
John
Acts
Romans

Riches in Heaven
(Lk 12.33–34)

[19] "Do not store up riches for yourselves here on earth, where moths and rust destroy, and robbers break in and steal. [20] Instead, store up riches for yourselves in heaven, where moths and rust cannot destroy, and robbers cannot break in and steal. [21] For your heart will always be where your riches are.

The Light of the Body
(Lk 11.34–36)

[22] "The eyes are like a lamp for the body. If your eyes are sound, your whole body will be full of light; [23] but if your eyes are no good, your body will be in darkness. So if the light in you is darkness, how terribly dark it will be!

God and Possessions
(Lk 16.13; 12.22–31)

[24] "No one can be a slave of two masters; he will hate one and love the other; he will be loyal to one and despise the other. You cannot serve both God and money.

[25] "This is why I tell you not to be worried about the food and drink you need in order to stay alive, or about clothes for your body. After all, isn't life worth more than food? And isn't the body worth more than clothes? [26] Look at the birds: they do not sow seeds, gather a harvest and put it in barns; yet your Father in heaven takes care of them! Aren't you worth much more than birds? [27] Can any of you live a bit longer* by worrying about it?

[28] "And why worry about clothes? Look how the wild flowers grow: they do not work or make clothes for themselves. [29] But I tell you that not even King Solomon with all his wealth had clothes as beautiful as one of these flowers. [30] It is God who clothes the wild grass — grass that is here today and gone tomorrow, burnt up in the oven. Won't he be all the more sure to clothe you? How little faith you have!

[31] "So do not start worrying: 'Where will my food come from? or my drink? or my clothes?' [32] (These are the things the pagans are always concerned about.) Your Father in heaven knows that you need all these things. [33] Instead, be concerned above everything else with the Kingdom of God and with what he requires of you, and he will provide you with all these other things. [34] So do not worry about tomorrow; it will have enough worries of its own. There is no need to add to the troubles each day brings.

Judging Others
(Lk 6.37–38, 41–42)

7 "Do not judge others, so that God will not judge you, [2] for God will judge you in the same way as you judge others, and he will apply to you the same rules you apply to others. [3] Why, then, do you look at the speck in your brother's eye, and pay no attention to the log in your own eye? [4] How dare you say to your brother, 'Please, let me take that speck out of your eye,' when you have a log in your own eye? [5] You hypocrite! First take the log out of your own eye, and then you will be able to see clearly to take the speck out of your brother's eye.

6.27 *live a bit longer*; or *grow a bit taller*.

Write
ONE THING
that you will
CHANGE
ABOUT YOUR
LIFE
having read this passage.

1132

Matt.

Habak.
Zephan.
Haggai
Zechar.
Malachi

MATTHEW 7

6 "Do not give what is holy to dogs — they will only turn and attack you. Do not throw your pearls in front of pigs — they will only trample them underfoot.

Ask, Seek, Knock
(Lk 11.9–13)

7 "Ask, and you will receive; seek, and you will find; knock, and the door will be opened to you. 8 For everyone who asks will receive, and anyone who seeks will find, and the door will be opened to those who knock. 9 Would any of you who are fathers give your son a stone when he asks for bread? 10 Or would you give him a snake when he asks for a fish? 11 Bad as you are, you know how to give good things to your children. How much more, then, will your Father in heaven give good things to those who ask him!

12 "Do for others what you want them to do for you: this is the meaning of the Law of Moses and of the teachings of the prophets.

The Narrow Gate
(Lk 13.24)

13 "Go in through the narrow gate, because the gate to hell is wide and the road that leads to it is easy, and there are many who travel it. 14 But the gate to life is narrow and the way that leads to it is hard, and there are few people who find it.

A Tree and its Fruit
(Lk 6.43–44)

15 "Be on your guard against false prophets; they come to you looking like sheep on the outside, but on the inside they are really like wild wolves. 16 You will know them by what they do. Thorn bushes do not bear grapes, and briars do not bear figs. 17 A healthy tree bears good fruit, but a poor tree bears bad fruit. 18 A healthy tree cannot bear bad fruit, and a poor tree cannot bear good fruit. 19 And any tree that does not bear good fruit is cut down and thrown in the fire. 20 So then, you will know the false prophets by what they do.

I Never Knew You
(Lk 13.25–27)

21 "Not everyone who calls me 'Lord, Lord' will enter the Kingdom of heaven, but only those who do what my Father in heaven wants them to do. 22 When Judgement Day comes, many will say to me, 'Lord, Lord! In your name we spoke God's message, by your name we drove out many demons and performed many miracles!' 23 Then I will say to them, 'I never knew you. Get away from me, you wicked people!'

The Two House Builders
(Lk 6.47–49)

24 "So then, anyone who hears these words of mine and obeys them is like a wise man who built his house on rock. 25 The rain poured down, the rivers overflowed, and the wind blew hard against that house. But it did not fall, because it was built on rock.

26 "But anyone who hears these words of mine and does not obey them is like a foolish man who built his house on sand. 27 The rain poured down, the rivers overflowed, the wind blew hard against that house, and it fell. And what a terrible fall that was!"

Matt.

Mark
Luke
John
Acts
Romans

The Authority of Jesus

28 When Jesus finished saying these things, the crowd was amazed at the way he taught. 29 He wasn't like the teachers of the Law; instead, he taught with authority.

Jesus Heals a Man
(Mk 1.40–45; Lk 5.12–16)

8 When Jesus came down from the hill, large crowds followed him. 2 Then a man suffering from a dreaded skin disease came to him, knelt down before him, and said, "Sir, if you want to, you can make me clean."*

3 Jesus stretched out his hand and touched him. "I do want to," he answered. "Be clean!" At once the man was healed of his disease. 4 Then Jesus said to him, "Listen! Don't tell anyone, but go straight to the priest and let him examine you; then in order to prove to everyone that you are cured, offer the sacrifice that Moses ordered."

Jesus Heals a Roman Officer's Servant
(Lk 7.1–10)

5 When Jesus entered Capernaum, a Roman officer met him and begged for help: 6 "Sir, my servant is sick in bed at home, unable to move and suffering terribly."

7 "I will go and make him well," Jesus said.

8 "Oh no, sir," answered the officer. "I do not deserve to have you come into my house. Just give the order, and my servant will get well. 9 I, too, am a man under the authority of superior officers, and I have soldiers under me. I order this one, 'Go!' and he goes; and I order that one, 'Come!' and he comes; and I order my slave, 'Do this!' and he does it."

10 When Jesus heard this, he was surprised and said to the people following him, "I tell you, I have never found anyone in Israel with faith like this. 11 I assure you that many will come from the east and the west and sit down with Abraham, Isaac, and Jacob at the feast in the Kingdom of heaven. 12 But those who should be in the Kingdom will be thrown out into the darkness, where they will cry and grind their teeth." 13 Then Jesus said to the officer, "Go home, and what you believe will be done for you."

And the officer's servant was healed that very moment.

Jesus Heals Many People
(Mk 1.29–34; Lk 4.38–41)

14 Jesus went to Peter's home, and there he saw Peter's mother-in-law sick in bed with a fever. 15 He touched her hand; the fever left her, and she got up and began to wait on him.

16 When evening came, people brought to Jesus many who had demons in them. Jesus drove out the evil spirits with a word and healed all who were sick. 17 He did this to make what the prophet Isaiah had said come true, "He himself took our sickness and carried away our diseases."

The Would-be Followers of Jesus
(Lk 9.57–62)

18 When Jesus noticed the crowd round him, he ordered his disciples to go to the other side of the lake. 19 A teacher of the

8.2 make me clean: This disease was considered to make a person ritually unclean.

1134

Matt.

Habak.
Zephan.
Haggai
Zechar.
Malachi

MATTHEW 8, 9

MATTHEW 8.21-22

Jesus can seem

• A LITTLE •

HARSH

in verse 22. It looks as if the man was just asking to go and bury his father, who had recently died. However, there's a lot going on behind all this.

The man appeared willing to follow Jesus but he actually wanted to get out of his spiritual responsibility. He asked to go and bury his father, but his father may simply have been old and not yet dead. If so, the man was asking to go and be with his father until he died, bury him and then come back (which could have been a long long time). Jesus wanted him to put his spiritual life back in focus.

Law came to him. "Teacher," he said, "I am ready to go with you wherever you go."

20 Jesus answered him, "Foxes have holes, and birds have nests, but the Son of Man has nowhere to lie down and rest."

21 Another man, who was a disciple, said, "Sir, first let me go back and bury my father."

22 "Follow me," Jesus answered, "and let the dead bury their own dead."

Jesus Calms a Storm
(Mk 4.35–41; Lk 8.22–25)

23 Jesus got into a boat, and his disciples went with him. 24 Suddenly a fierce storm hit the lake, and the boat was in danger of sinking. But Jesus was asleep. 25 The disciples went to him and woke him up. "Save us, Lord!" they said. "We are about to die!"

26 "Why are you so frightened?" Jesus answered. "How little faith you have!" Then he got up and ordered the winds and the waves to stop, and there was a great calm.

27 Everyone was amazed. "What kind of man is this?" they said. "Even the winds and the waves obey him!"

Jesus Heals Two Men with Demons
(Mk 5.1–20; Lk 8.26–39)

28 When Jesus came to the territory of Gadara on the other side of the lake, he was met by two men who came out of the burial caves there. These men had demons in them and were so fierce that no one dared travel on that road. 29 At once they screamed, "What do you want with us, you Son of God? Have you come to punish us before the right time?"

30 Not far away there was a large herd of pigs feeding. 31 So the demons begged Jesus, "If you are going to drive us out, send us into that herd of pigs."

32 "Go," Jesus told them; so they left and went off into the pigs. The whole herd rushed down the side of the cliff into the lake and was drowned.

33 The men who had been taking care of the pigs ran away and went into the town, where they told the whole story and what had happened to the men with the demons. 34 So everyone from the town went out to meet Jesus; and when they saw him, they begged him to leave their territory.

Jesus Heals a Paralysed Man
(Mk 2.1–12; Lk 5.17–26)

9 Jesus got into the boat and went back across the lake to his own town,* 2 where some people brought to him a paralysed man, lying on a bed. When Jesus saw how much faith they had, he said to the paralysed man, "Courage, my son! Your sins are forgiven."

3 Then some teachers of the Law said to themselves, "This man is speaking blasphemy!"

4 Jesus perceived what they were thinking, so he said, "Why are you thinking such evil things? 5 Is it easier to say, 'Your sins are forgiven,' or to say, 'Get up and walk'? 6 I will prove to you, then, that the Son of Man has authority on earth to forgive sins." So he said to the paralysed man, "Get up, pick up your bed, and go home!"

9.1 *his own town*: Capernaum (see 4.13).

MATTHEW 9

1135

Matt.
....

Mark
Luke
John
Acts
Romans

[7]The man got up and went home. [8]When the people saw it, they were afraid, and praised God for giving such authority to people.

Jesus Calls Matthew
(Mk 2.13–17; Lk 5.27–32)

[9]Jesus left that place, and as he walked along, he saw a tax collector, named Matthew, sitting in his office. He said to him, "Follow me."

Matthew got up and followed him.

[10]While Jesus was having a meal in Matthew's house,* many tax collectors and other outcasts came and joined Jesus and his disciples at the table. [11]Some Pharisees saw this and asked his disciples, "Why does your teacher eat with such people?"

[12]Jesus heard them and answered, "People who are well do not need a doctor, but only those who are sick. [13]Go and find out what is meant by the scripture that says: 'It is kindness that I want, not animal sacrifices.' I have not come to call respectable people, but outcasts."

The Question about Fasting
(Mk 2.18–22; Lk 5.33–39)

[14]Then the followers of John the Baptist came to Jesus, asking, "Why is it that we and the Pharisees fast often, but your disciples don't fast at all?"

[15]Jesus answered, "Do you expect the guests at a wedding party to be sad as long as the bridegroom is with them? Of course not! But the day will come when the bridegroom will be taken away from them, and then they will fast.

[16]"No one patches up an old coat with a piece of new cloth, for the new patch will shrink and make an even bigger hole in the coat. [17]Nor does anyone pour new wine into used wineskins, for the skins will burst, the wine will pour out, and the skins will be ruined. Instead, new wine is poured into fresh wineskins, and both will keep in good condition."

The Official's Daughter and the Woman who Touched Jesus' Cloak
(Mk 5.21–43; Lk 8.40–56)

[18]While Jesus was saying this, a Jewish official came to him, knelt down before him, and said, "My daughter has just died; but come and place your hands on her, and she will live."

[19]So Jesus got up and followed him, and his disciples went along with him.

[20]A woman who had suffered from severe bleeding for twelve years came up behind Jesus and touched the edge of his cloak. [21]She said to herself, "If I only touch his cloak, I will get well."

[22]Jesus turned round and saw her, and said, "Courage, my daughter! Your faith has made you well." At that very moment the woman became well.

[23]Then Jesus went into the official's house. When he saw the musicians for the funeral and the people all stirred up, [24]he said, "Get out, everybody! The little girl is not dead — she is only sleeping!" Then they all laughed at him. [25]But as soon as the people had been put out, Jesus went into the girl's room and took hold of her hand, and she got up. [26]The news about this spread all over that part of the country.

....

9.10 *in Matthew's house*; or *in his* (that is, Jesus') *house.*

Jesus Heals Two Blind Men

27 Jesus left that place, and as he walked along, two blind men started following him. "Take pity on us, Son of David!" they shouted.

28 When Jesus had gone indoors, the two blind men came to him, and he asked them, "Do you believe that I can heal you?"

"Yes, sir!" they answered.

29 Then Jesus touched their eyes and said, "Let it happen, then, just as you believe!" — 30 and their sight was restored. Jesus spoke sternly to them, "Don't tell this to anyone!"

31 But they left and spread the news about Jesus all over that part of the country.

Jesus Heals a Man who could not Speak

32 As the men were leaving, some people brought to Jesus a man who could not talk because he had a demon. 33 But as soon as the demon was driven out, the man started talking, and everyone was amazed. "We have never seen anything like this in Israel!" they exclaimed.

34 But the Pharisees said, "It is the chief of the demons who gives Jesus the power to drive out demons."

Jesus has Pity for the People

35 Jesus went round visiting all the towns and villages. He taught in the synagogues, preached the Good News about the Kingdom, and healed people with every kind of disease and sickness. 36 As he saw the crowds, his heart was filled with pity for them, because they were worried and helpless, like sheep without a shepherd. 37 So he said to his disciples, "The harvest is large, but there are few workers to gather it in. 38 Pray to the owner of the harvest that he will send out workers to gather in his harvest."

The Twelve Apostles
(Mk 3.13–19; Lk 6.12–16)

10 Jesus called his twelve disciples together and gave them authority to drive out evil spirits and to heal every disease and every sickness. 2 These are the names of the twelve apostles: first, Simon (called Peter) and his brother Andrew; James and his brother John, the sons of Zebedee; 3 Philip and Bartholomew; Thomas and Matthew, the tax collector; James son of Alphaeus, and Thaddaeus; 4 Simon the Patriot, and Judas Iscariot, who betrayed Jesus.

The Mission of the Twelve
(Mk 6.7–13; Lk 9.1–6)

5 These twelve men were sent out by Jesus with the following instructions: "Do not go to any Gentile territory or any Samaritan towns. 6 Instead, you are to go to the lost sheep of the people of Israel. 7 Go and preach, 'The Kingdom of heaven is near!' 8 Heal the sick, bring the dead back to life, heal those who suffer from dreaded skin diseases, and drive out demons. You have received without paying, so give without being paid. 9 Do not carry any gold, silver, or copper money in your pockets; 10 do not carry a beggar's bag for the journey or an extra shirt or shoes or a stick. Workers should be given what they need.

11 "When you come to a town or village, go in and look for someone who is willing to welcome you, and stay with him until you leave that place. 12 When you go into a house, say, 'Peace be with you.' 13 If the people in that house welcome you, let your

greeting of peace remain; but if they do not welcome you, then take back your greeting. [14] And if some home or town will not welcome you or listen to you, then leave that place and shake the dust off your feet. [15] I assure you that on the Judgement Day God will show more mercy to the people of Sodom and Gomorrah than to the people of that town!

Coming Persecutions
(Mk 13.9–13; Lk 21.12–17)

[16] "Listen! I am sending you out just like sheep to a pack of wolves. You must be as cautious as snakes and as gentle as doves. [17] Watch out, for there will be those who will arrest you and take you to court, and they will whip you in the synagogues. [18] For my sake you will be brought to trial before rulers and kings, to tell the Good News to them and to the Gentiles. [19] When they bring you to trial, do not worry about what you are going to say or how you will say it; when the time comes, you will be given what you will say. [20] For the words you will speak will not be yours; they will come from the Spirit of your Father speaking through you.

[21] "Men will hand over their own brothers to be put to death, and fathers will do the same to their children; children will turn against their parents and have them put to death. [22] Everyone will hate you because of me. But whoever holds out to the end will be saved. [23] When they persecute you in one town, run away to another one. I assure you that you will not finish your work in all the towns of Israel before the Son of Man comes.

[24] "No pupil is greater than his teacher; no slave is greater than his master. [25] So a pupil should be satisfied to become like his teacher, and a slave like his master. If the head of the family is called Beelzebul, the members of the family will be called even worse names!

Whom to Fear
(Lk 12.2–7)

[26] "So do not be afraid of people. Whatever is now covered up will be uncovered, and every secret will be made known. [27] What I am telling you in the dark you must repeat in broad daylight, and what you have heard in private you must announce from the housetops. [28] Do not be afraid of those who kill the body but cannot kill the soul; rather be afraid of God, who can destroy both body and soul in hell. [29] For only a penny you can buy two sparrows, yet not one sparrow falls to the ground without your Father's consent. [30] As for you, even the hairs of your head have all been counted. [31] So do not be afraid; you are worth much more than many sparrows!

Confessing and Rejecting Christ
(Lk 12.8–9)

[32] "For those who declare publicly that they belong to me, I will do the same before my Father in heaven. [33] But if anyone rejects me publicly, I will reject him before my Father in heaven.

Not Peace, but a Sword
(Lk 12.51–53; 14.26–27)

[34] "Do not think that I have come to bring peace to the world. No, I did not come to bring peace, but a sword. [35] I came to set sons against their fathers, daughters against their mothers, daughters-in-law against their mothers-in-law; [36] your worst enemies will be the members of your own family.

MAKE NOTES HERE.

Matt.

Mark
Luke
John
Acts
Romans

Matt.

⁘ ╌╌╌╌╌

Habak.

Zephan.

Haggai

Zechar.

Malachi

37"Those who love their father or mother more than me are not fit to be my disciples; those who love their son or daughter more than me are not fit to be my disciples. 38 Those who do not take up their cross and follow in my steps are not fit to be my disciples. 39 Those who try to gain their own life will lose it; but those who lose their life for my sake will gain it.

Rewards
(Mk 9.41)

40"Whoever welcomes you welcomes me; and whoever welcomes me welcomes the one who sent me. 41 Whoever welcomes God's messenger because he is God's messenger, will share in his reward. And whoever welcomes a good man because he is good, will share in his reward. 42 You can be sure that whoever gives even a drink of cold water to one of the least of these my followers because he is my follower, will certainly receive a reward."

The Messengers from John the Baptist
(Lk 7.18–35)

11 When Jesus finished giving these instructions to his twelve disciples, he left that place and went off to teach and preach in the towns near there.

2 When John the Baptist heard in prison about the things that Christ was doing, he sent some of his disciples to him. 3 "Tell us," they asked Jesus, "are you the one John said was going to come, or should we expect someone else?"

4 Jesus answered, "Go back and tell John what you are hearing and seeing: 5 the blind can see, the lame can walk, those who suffer from dreaded skin diseases are made clean,* the deaf hear, the dead are brought back to life, and the Good News is preached to the poor. 6 How happy are those who have no doubts about me!"

7 While John's disciples were leaving, Jesus spoke about him to the crowds: "When you went out to John in the desert, what did you expect to see? A blade of grass bending in the wind? 8 What did you go out to see? A man dressed up in fancy clothes? People who dress like that live in palaces! 9 Tell me, what did you go out to see? A prophet? Yes indeed, but you saw much more than a prophet. 10 For John is the one of whom the scripture says: 'God said, I will send my messenger ahead of you to open the way for you.' 11 I assure you that John the Baptist is greater than anyone who has ever lived. But the one who is least in the Kingdom of heaven is greater than John. 12 From the time John preached his message until this very day the Kingdom of heaven has suffered violent attacks,* and violent men try to seize it. 13 Until the time of John all the prophets and the Law of Moses spoke about the Kingdom; 14 and if you are willing to believe their message, John is Elijah, whose coming was predicted. 15 Listen, then, if you have ears!

16 "Now, to what can I compare the people of this day? They are like children sitting in the market place. One group shouts to the other, 17 'We played wedding music for you, but you wouldn't dance! We sang funeral songs, but you wouldn't cry!' 18 When John came, he fasted and drank no wine, and everyone said, 'He has a demon in him!' 19 When the Son of Man came, he ate and drank, and everyone said, 'Look at this man! He is a glutton and a drinker, a friend of tax collectors and other outcasts!' God's wisdom, however, is shown to be true by its results."

11.5 *made clean*: See 8.2.
11.12 *has suffered violent attacks*; or *has been coming violently.*

Matt.

....

Mark

Luke

John

Acts

Romans

The Unbelieving Towns
(Lk 10.13–15)

20 The people in the towns where Jesus had performed most of his miracles did not turn from their sins, so he reproached those towns. 21 "How terrible it will be for you, Chorazin! How terrible for you too, Bethsaida! If the miracles which were performed in you had been performed in Tyre and Sidon, the people there would long ago have put on sackcloth and sprinkled ashes on themselves, to show that they had turned from their sins! 22 I assure you that on the Judgement Day God will show more mercy to the people of Tyre and Sidon than to you! 23 And as for you, Capernaum! Did you want to lift yourself up to heaven? You will be thrown down to hell! If the miracles which were performed in you had been performed in Sodom, it would still be in existence today! 24 You can be sure that on the Judgement Day God will show more mercy to Sodom than to you!"

Come to Me and Rest
(Lk 10.21–22)

25 At that time Jesus said, "Father, Lord of heaven and earth! I thank you because you have shown to the unlearned what you have hidden from the wise and learned. 26 Yes, Father, this was how you wanted it to happen.

27 "My Father has given me all things. No one knows the Son except the Father, and no one knows the Father except the Son and those to whom the Son chooses to reveal him.

28 "Come to me, all of you who are tired from carrying heavy loads, and I will give you rest. 29 Take my yoke and put it on you, and learn from me, because I am gentle and humble in spirit; and you will find rest. 30 For the yoke I will give you is easy, and the load I will put on you is light."

The Question about the Sabbath
(Mk 2.23–28; Lk 6.1–5)

12 Not long afterwards Jesus was walking through some cornfields on the Sabbath. His disciples were hungry, so they began to pick ears of corn and eat the grain. 2 When the Pharisees saw this, they said to Jesus, "Look, it is against our Law for your disciples to do this on the Sabbath!"

3 Jesus answered, "Have you never read what David did that time when he and his men were hungry? 4 He went into the house of God, and he and his men ate the bread offered to God, even though it was against the Law for them to eat it — only the priests were allowed to eat that bread. 5 Or have you not read in the Law of Moses that every Sabbath the priests in the Temple actually break the Sabbath law, yet they are not guilty? 6 I tell you that there is something here greater than the Temple. 7 The scripture says, 'It is kindness that I want, not animal sacrifices.' If you really knew what this means, you would not condemn people who are not guilty; 8 for the Son of Man is Lord of the Sabbath."

The Man with a Paralysed Hand
(Mk 3.1–6; Lk 6.6–11)

9 Jesus left that place and went to a synagogue, 10 where there was a man who had a paralysed hand. Some people were there who wanted to accuse Jesus of doing wrong, so they asked him, "Is it against our Law to heal on the Sabbath?"

11 Jesus answered, "What if one of you has a sheep and it falls into a deep hole on the Sabbath? Will you not take hold of it

MATTHEW 11.28

I WILL GIVE YOU ·REST·

1140

Matt.

·:·········

Habak.
Zephan.
Haggai
Zechar.
Malachi

MATTHEW 12

and lift it out? [12] And a human being is worth much more than a sheep! So then, our Law does allow us to help someone on the Sabbath." [13] Then he said to the man with the paralysed hand, "Stretch out your hand."

He stretched it out, and it became well again, just like the other one. [14] Then the Pharisees left and made plans to kill Jesus.

God's Chosen Servant

[15] When Jesus heard about the plot against him, he went away from that place; and large crowds followed him. He healed all those who were ill [16] and gave them orders not to tell others about him. [17] He did this so as to make what God had said through the prophet Isaiah come true:

[18] "Here is my servant, whom I have chosen,
    the one I love, and with whom I am pleased.
  I will send my Spirit upon him,
    and he will announce my judgement to the nations.
[19] He will not argue or shout,
    or make loud speeches in the streets.
[20] He will not break off a bent reed,
    or put out a flickering lamp.
  He will persist until he causes justice to triumph,
[21]   and in him all peoples will put their hope."

Jesus and Beelzebul
(Mk 3.20–30; Lk 11.14–23)

[22] Then some people brought to Jesus a man who was blind and could not talk because he had a demon. Jesus healed the man, so that he was able to talk and see. [23] The crowds were all amazed at what Jesus had done. "Could he be the Son of David?" they asked.

[24] When the Pharisees heard this, they replied, "He drives out demons only because their ruler Beelzebul gives him power to do so."

[25] Jesus knew what they were thinking, so he said to them, "Any country that divides itself into groups which fight each other will not last very long. And any town or family that divides itself into groups which fight each other will fall apart. [26] So if one group is fighting another in Satan's kingdom, this means that it is already divided into groups and will soon fall apart! [27] You say that I drive out demons because Beelzebul gives me the power to do so. Well, then, who gives your followers the power to drive them out? What your own followers do proves that you are wrong! [28] No, it is not Beelzebul, but God's Spirit, who gives me the power to drive out demons, which proves that the Kingdom of God has already come upon you.

[29] "No one can break into a strong man's house and take away his belongings unless he first ties up the strong man; then he can plunder his house.

[30] "Anyone who is not for me is really against me; anyone who does not help me gather is really scattering. [31] And so I tell you that people can be forgiven any sin and any evil thing they say;* but whoever says evil things against the Holy Spirit will not be forgiven. [32] Anyone who says something against the Son of Man can be forgiven; but whoever says something against the Holy Spirit will not be forgiven — now or ever.

12.31 evil thing they say; or evil thing they say against God.

MATTHEW 12, 13

1141

Matt.

....

Mark
Luke
John
Acts
Romans

A Tree and its Fruit
(Lk 6.43–45)

33 "To have good fruit you must have a healthy tree; if you have a poor tree, you will have bad fruit. A tree is known by the kind of fruit it bears. 34 You snakes — how can you say good things when you are evil? For the mouth speaks what the heart is full of. 35 A good person brings good things out of a treasure of good things; a bad person brings bad things out of a treasure of bad things.

36 "You can be sure that on Judgement Day everyone will have to give account of every useless word he has ever spoken. 37 Your words will be used to judge you — to declare you either innocent or guilty."

The Demand for a Miracle
(Mk 8.11–12; Lk 11.29–32)

38 Then some teachers of the Law and some Pharisees spoke up. "Teacher," they said, "we want to see you perform a miracle."

39 "How evil and godless are the people of this day!" Jesus exclaimed. "You ask me for a miracle? No! The only miracle you will be given is the miracle of the prophet Jonah. 40 In the same way that Jonah spent three days and nights in the big fish, so will the Son of Man spend three days and nights in the depths of the earth. 41 On Judgement Day the people of Nineveh will stand up and accuse you, because they turned from their sins when they heard Jonah preach; and I tell you that there is something here greater than Jonah! 42 On Judgement Day the Queen of Sheba will stand up and accuse you, because she travelled all the way from her country to listen to King Solomon's wise teaching; and I assure you that there is something here greater than Solomon!

The Return of the Evil Spirit
(Lk 11.24–26)

43 "When an evil spirit goes out of a person, it travels over dry country looking for a place to rest. If it can't find one, 44 it says to itself, 'I will go back to my house.' So it goes back and finds the house empty, clean, and all tidy. 45 Then it goes out and brings along seven other spirits even worse than itself, and they come and live there. So when it is all over, that person is in a worse state than he was at the beginning. This is what will happen to the evil people of this day."

Jesus' Mother and Brothers
(Mk 3.31–35; Lk 8.19–21)

46 Jesus was still talking to the people when his mother and brothers arrived. They stood outside, asking to speak with him. 47 So one of the people there said to him, "Look, your mother and brothers are standing outside, and they want to speak with you."*

48 Jesus answered, "Who is my mother? Who are my brothers?" 49 Then he pointed to his disciples and said, "Look! Here are my mother and my brothers! 50 Whoever does what my Father in heaven wants him to do is my brother, my sister, and my mother."

The Parable of the Sower
(Mk 4.1–9; Lk 8.4–8)

13 That same day Jesus left the house and went to the lakeside, where he sat down to teach. 2 The crowd that

12.47 Some manuscripts do not have verse 47.

1142

Matt.

Habak.
Zephan.
Haggai
Zechar.
Malachi

MATTHEW 13

MATTHEW 13.1-9, 18-23

Read through the parable of the sower and Jesus' explanation of it.

DOODLE
– HERE –

the type of seed that you identify with most.

gathered round him was so large that he got into a boat and sat in it, while the crowd stood on the shore. ³He used parables to tell them many things.

"Once there was a man who went out to sow corn. ⁴As he scattered the seed in the field, some of it fell along the path, and the birds came and ate it up. ⁵Some of it fell on rocky ground, where there was little soil. The seeds soon sprouted, because the soil wasn't deep. ⁶But when the sun came up, it burnt the young plants; and because the roots had not grown deep enough, the plants soon dried up. ⁷Some of the seed fell among thorn bushes, which grew up and choked the plants. ⁸But some seeds fell in good soil, and the plants produced corn; some produced 100 grains, others sixty, and others thirty."

⁹And Jesus concluded, "Listen, then, if you have ears!"

The Purpose of the Parables
(Mk 4.10–12; Lk 8.9–10)

¹⁰Then the disciples came to Jesus and asked him, "Why do you use parables when you talk to the people?"

¹¹Jesus answered, "The knowledge about the secrets of the Kingdom of heaven has been given to you, but not to them. ¹²For the person who has something will be given more, so that he will have more than enough; but the person who has nothing will have taken away from him even the little he has. ¹³The reason I use parables in talking to them is that they look, but do not see, and they listen, but do not hear or understand. ¹⁴So the prophecy of Isaiah applies to them:

'This people will listen and listen, but not
    understand;
  they will look and look, but not see,
¹⁵ because their minds are dull,
    and they have stopped up their ears
    and have closed their eyes.
  Otherwise, their eyes would see,
    their ears would hear,
    their minds would understand,
  and they would turn to me, says God,
    and I would heal them.'

¹⁶"As for you, how fortunate you are! Your eyes see and your ears hear. ¹⁷I assure you that many prophets and many of God's people wanted very much to see what you see, but they could not, and to hear what you hear, but they did not.

Jesus Explains the Parable of the Sower
(Mk 4.13–20; Lk 8.11–15)

¹⁸"Listen, then, and learn what the parable of the sower means. ¹⁹Those who hear the message about the Kingdom but do not understand it are like the seeds that fell along the path. The Evil One comes and snatches away what was sown in them. ²⁰The seeds that fell on rocky ground stand for those who receive the message gladly as soon as they hear it. ²¹But it does not sink deep into them, and they don't last long. So when trouble or persecution comes because of the message, they give up at once. ²²The seeds that fell among thorn bushes stand for those who hear the message; but the worries about this life and the love for riches choke the message, and they don't bear fruit. ²³And the seeds sown in the good soil stand for those who hear the message and understand it: they bear fruit, some as much as 100, others sixty, and others thirty."

MATTHEW 13

1143

Matt.

Mark
Luke
John
Acts
Romans

The Parable of the Weeds

24 Jesus told them another parable: "The Kingdom of heaven is like this. A man sowed good seed in his field. 25 One night, when everyone was asleep, an enemy came and sowed weeds among the wheat and went away. 26 When the plants grew and the ears of corn began to form, then the weeds showed up. 27 The man's servants came to him and said, 'Sir, it was good seed you sowed in your field; where did the weeds come from?' 28 'It was some enemy who did this,' he answered. 'Do you want us to go and pull up the weeds?' they asked him. 29 'No,' he answered, 'because as you gather the weeds you might pull up some of the wheat along with them. 30 Let the wheat and the weeds both grow together until harvest. Then I will tell the harvest workers to pull up the weeds first, tie them in bundles and burn them, and then to gather in the wheat and put it in my barn.' "

The Parable of the Mustard Seed

(Mk 4.30–32; Lk 13.18–19)

31 Jesus told them another parable: "The Kingdom of heaven is like this. A man takes a mustard seed and sows it in his field. 32 It is the smallest of all seeds, but when it grows up, it is the biggest of all plants. It becomes a tree, so that birds come and make their nests in its branches."

The Parable of the Yeast

(Lk 13.20–21)

33 Jesus told them still another parable: "The Kingdom of heaven is like this. A woman takes some yeast and mixes it with forty litres of flour until the whole batch of dough rises."

Jesus' Use of Parables

(Mk 4.33–34)

34 Jesus used parables to tell all these things to the crowds; he would not say a thing to them without using a parable. 35 He did this to make what the prophet had said come true:

"I will use parables when I speak to them;
   I will tell them things unknown since the creation of the
      world."

Jesus Explains the Parable of the Weeds

36 When Jesus had left the crowd and gone indoors, his disciples came to him and said, "Tell us what the parable about the weeds in the field means."

37 Jesus answered, "The man who sowed the good seed is the Son of Man; 38 the field is the world; the good seed is the people who belong to the Kingdom; the weeds are the people who belong to the Evil One; 39 and the enemy who sowed the weeds is the Devil. The harvest is the end of the age, and the harvest workers are angels. 40 Just as the weeds are gathered up and burnt in the fire, so the same thing will happen at the end of the age: 41 the Son of Man will send out his angels to gather up out of his Kingdom all those who cause people to sin and all others who do evil things, 42 and they will throw them into the fiery furnace, where they will cry and grind their teeth. 43 Then God's people will shine like the sun in their Father's Kingdom. Listen, then, if you have ears!

The Parable of the Hidden Treasure

44 "The Kingdom of heaven is like this. A man happens to find a treasure hidden in a field. He covers it up again, and is so happy

Matt.

Habak.
Zephan.
Haggai
Zechar.
Malachi

that he goes and sells everything he has, and then goes back and buys that field.

The Parable of the Pearl

45 "Also, the Kingdom of heaven is like this. A man is looking for fine pearls, 46 and when he finds one that is unusually fine, he goes and sells everything he has, and buys that pearl.

The Parable of the Net

47 "Also, the Kingdom of heaven is like this. Some fishermen throw their net out in the lake and catch all kinds of fish. 48 When the net is full, they pull it to shore and sit down to divide the fish: the good ones go into their buckets, the worthless ones are thrown away. 49 It will be like this at the end of the age: the angels will go out and gather up the evil people from among the good 50 and will throw them into the fiery furnace, where they will cry and grind their teeth.

New Truths and Old

51 "Do you understand these things?" Jesus asked them.

"Yes," they answered.

52 So he replied, "This means, then, that every teacher of the Law who becomes a disciple in the Kingdom of heaven is like the owner of a house who takes new and old things out of his storeroom."

Jesus is Rejected at Nazareth
(Mk 6.1–6; Lk 4.16–30)

53 When Jesus finished telling these parables, he left that place 54 and went back to his home town. He taught in the synagogue, and those who heard him were amazed. "Where did he get such wisdom?" they asked. "And what about his miracles? 55 Isn't he the carpenter's son? Isn't Mary his mother, and aren't James, Joseph, Simon, and Judas his brothers? 56 Aren't all his sisters living here? Where did he get all this?" 57 And so they rejected him.

Jesus said to them, "A prophet is respected everywhere except in his home town and by his own family." 58 Because they did not have faith, he did not perform many miracles there.

The Death of John the Baptist
(Mk 6.14–29; Lk 9.7–9)

14 At that time Herod, the ruler of Galilee, heard about Jesus. 2 "He is really John the Baptist, who has come back to life," he told his officials. "That is why he has this power to perform miracles."

3 For Herod had earlier ordered John's arrest, and he had him chained and put in prison. He had done this because of Herodias, his brother Philip's wife. 4 For some time John the Baptist had told Herod, "It isn't right for you to be married to Herodias!" 5 Herod wanted to kill him, but he was afraid of the Jewish people, because they considered John to be a prophet.

6 On Herod's birthday the daughter of Herodias danced in front of the whole group. Herod was so pleased 7 that he promised her, "I swear that I will give you anything you ask for!"

8 At her mother's suggestion she asked him, "Give me here and now the head of John the Baptist on a dish!"

9 The king was sad, but because of the promise he had made in front of all his guests he gave orders that her wish be granted. 10 So he had John beheaded in prison. 11 The head was brought in

on a dish and given to the girl, who took it to her mother. [12] John's disciples came, carried away his body, and buried it; then they went and told Jesus.

Jesus Feeds a Great Crowd
(Mk 6.30–44; Lk 9.10–17; Jn 6.1–14)

[13] When Jesus heard the news about John, he left there in a boat and went to a lonely place by himself. The people heard about it, so they left their towns and followed him by land. [14] Jesus got out of the boat, and when he saw the large crowd, his heart was filled with pity for them, and he healed those who were ill.

[15] That evening his disciples came to him and said, "It is already very late, and this is a lonely place. Send the people away and let them go to the villages to buy food for themselves."

[16] "They don't have to leave," answered Jesus. "You yourselves give them something to eat!"

[17] "All we have here are five loaves and two fish," they replied.

[18] "Then bring them here to me," Jesus said. [19] He ordered the people to sit down on the grass; then he took the five loaves and the two fish, looked up to heaven, and gave thanks to God. He broke the loaves and gave them to the disciples, and the disciples gave them to the people. [20] Everyone ate and had enough. Then the disciples took up twelve baskets full of what was left over. [21] The number of men who ate was about 5,000, not counting the women and children.

Jesus Walks on the Water
(Mk 6.45–52; Jn 6.15–21)

[22] Then Jesus made the disciples get into the boat and go on ahead to the other side of the lake, while he sent the people away. [23] After sending the people away, he went up a hill by himself to pray. When evening came, Jesus was there alone; [24] and by this time the boat was far out in the lake, tossed about by the waves, because the wind was blowing against it.

[25] Between three and six o'clock in the morning Jesus came to the disciples, walking on the water. [26] When they saw him walking on the water, they were terrified. "It's a ghost!" they said, and screamed with fear.

[27] Jesus spoke to them at once. "Courage!" he said. "It is I. Don't be afraid!"

[28] Then Peter spoke up. "Lord, if it is really you, order me to come out on the water to you."

[29] "Come!" answered Jesus. So Peter got out of the boat and started walking on the water to Jesus. [30] But when he noticed the strong wind, he was afraid and started to sink down in the water. "Save me, Lord!" he cried.

[31] At once Jesus reached out and grabbed hold of him and said, "How little faith you have! Why did you doubt?"

[32] They both got into the boat, and the wind died down. [33] Then the disciples in the boat worshipped Jesus. "Truly you are the Son of God!" they exclaimed.

Jesus Heals the Sick in Gennesaret
(Mk 6.53–56)

[34] They crossed the lake and came to land at Gennesaret, [35] where the people recognized Jesus. So they sent for the sick people in all the surrounding country and brought them to Jesus. [36] They begged him to let those who were ill at least touch the edge of his cloak; and all who touched it were made well.

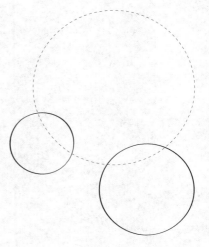

TURN THESE SHAPES INTO

SOMETHING
ELSE.

Matt.

Mark
Luke
John
Acts
Romans

1146

Matt.

Habak.
Zephan.
Haggai
Zechar.
Malachi

MATTHEW 15

The Teaching of the Ancestors
(Mk 7.1–13)

15 Then some Pharisees and teachers of the Law came from Jerusalem to Jesus and asked him, [2] "Why is it that your disciples disobey the teaching handed down by our ancestors? They don't wash their hands in the proper way before they eat!"

[3] Jesus answered, "And why do you disobey God's command and follow your own teaching? [4] For God said, 'Respect your father and your mother,' and 'Whoever curses his father or his mother is to be put to death.' [5] But you teach that if a person has something he could use to help his father or mother, but says, 'This belongs to God,' [6] he does not need to honour his father.* In this way you disregard God's command, in order to follow your own teaching. [7] You hypocrites! How right Isaiah was when he prophesied about you!

[8] 'These people, says God, honour me with their words,
but their heart is really far away from me.
[9] It is no use for them to worship me,
because they teach human rules as though they were
my laws!' "

The Things that Make a Person Unclean
(Mk 7.14–23)

[10] Then Jesus called the crowd to him and said to them, "Listen and understand! [11] It is not what goes into a person's mouth that makes him ritually unclean; rather, what comes out of it makes him unclean."

[12] Then the disciples came to him and said, "Do you know that the Pharisees had their feelings hurt by what you said?"

[13] "Every plant which my Father in heaven did not plant will be pulled up," answered Jesus. [14] "Don't worry about them! They are blind leaders of the blind; and when one blind man leads another, both fall into a ditch."

[15] Peter spoke up, "Explain this saying to us."

[16] Jesus said to them, "You are still no more intelligent than the others. [17] Don't you understand? Anything that goes into a person's mouth goes into his stomach and then on out of his body. [18] But the things that come out of the mouth come from the heart, and these are the things that make a person ritually unclean. [19] For from his heart come the evil ideas which lead him to kill, commit adultery, and do other immoral things; to rob, lie, and slander others. [20] These are the things that make a person unclean. But to eat without washing your hands as they say you should — this doesn't make a person unclean."

A Woman's Faith
(Mk 7.24–30)

[21] Jesus left that place and went off to the territory near the cities of Tyre and Sidon. [22] A Canaanite woman who lived in that region came to him. "Son of David!" she cried out. "Have mercy on me, sir! My daughter has a demon and is in a terrible condition."

[23] But Jesus did not say a word to her. His disciples came to him and begged him, "Send her away! She is following us and making all this noise!"

[24] Then Jesus replied, "I have been sent only to the lost sheep of the people of Israel."

15.6 *his father*; some manuscripts have *his father or mother*.

Matt.

Mark
Luke
John
Acts
Romans

²⁵ At this the woman came and fell at his feet. "Help me, sir!" she said.

²⁶ Jesus answered, "It isn't right to take the children's food and throw it to the dogs."

²⁷ "That's true, sir," she answered; "but even the dogs eat the leftovers that fall from their masters' table."

²⁸ So Jesus answered her, "You are a woman of great faith! What you want will be done for you." And at that very moment her daughter was healed.

Jesus Heals Many People

²⁹ Jesus left there and went along by Lake Galilee. He climbed a hill and sat down. ³⁰ Large crowds came to him, bringing with them the lame, the blind, the crippled, the dumb, and many other sick people, whom they placed at Jesus' feet; and he healed them. ³¹ The people were amazed as they saw the dumb speaking, the crippled made whole, the lame walking, and the blind seeing; and they praised the God of Israel.

Jesus Feeds Another Great Crowd
(Mk 8.1–10)

³² Jesus called his disciples to him and said, "I feel sorry for these people, because they have been with me for three days and now have nothing to eat. I don't want to send them away without feeding them, for they might faint on their way home."

³³ The disciples asked him, "Where will we find enough food in this desert to feed this crowd?"

³⁴ "How much bread have you?" Jesus asked.

"Seven loaves," they answered, "and a few small fish."

³⁵ So Jesus ordered the crowd to sit down on the ground. ³⁶ Then he took the seven loaves and the fish, gave thanks to God, broke them, and gave them to the disciples; and the disciples gave them to the people. ³⁷ They all ate and had enough. Then the disciples took up seven baskets full of pieces left over. ³⁸ The number of men who ate was 4,000, not counting the women and children.

³⁹ Then Jesus sent the people away, got into a boat, and went to the territory of Magadan.

The Demand for a Miracle
(Mk 8.11–13; Lk 12.54–56)

16 Some Pharisees and Sadducees who came to Jesus wanted to trap him, so they asked him to perform a miracle for them, to show that God approved of him. ² But Jesus answered, "When the sun is setting, you say, 'We are going to have fine weather, because the sky is red.' ³ And early in the morning you say, 'It is going to rain, because the sky is red and dark.' You can predict the weather by looking at the sky, but you cannot interpret the signs concerning these times!* ⁴ How evil and godless are the people of this day! You ask me for a miracle? No! The only miracle you will be given is the miracle of Jonah."

So he left them and went away.

The Yeast of the Pharisees and Sadducees
(Mk 8.14–21)

⁵ When the disciples crossed over to the other side of the lake, they forgot to take any bread. ⁶ Jesus said to them, "Take

16.3 Some manuscripts do not have the words of Jesus in verses 2–3.

Matt.

Habak.
Zephan.
Haggai
Zechar.
Malachi

KINGDOM

JOB 25.1-2;
MATTHEW 16.19

Search for the Oxford
or Cambridge Dictionary
definition of 'kingdom'
and write the
definition here. ⟍

⟍
↓

_____

_____

_____

_____

_____

_____

_____

_____

_____

_____

_____

_____

_____

_____

_____

_____

_____

care; be on your guard against the yeast of the Pharisees and Sadducees."

7 They started discussing among themselves, "He says this because we didn't bring any bread."

8 Jesus knew what they were saying, so he asked them, "Why are you discussing among yourselves about not having any bread? How little faith you have! 9 Don't you understand yet? Don't you remember when I broke the five loaves for the 5,000 men? How many baskets did you fill? 10 And what about the seven loaves for the 4,000 men? How many baskets did you fill? 11 How is it that you don't understand that I was not talking to you about bread? Guard yourselves from the yeast of the Pharisees and Sadducees!"

12 Then the disciples understood that he was not warning them to guard themselves from the yeast used in bread but from the teaching of the Pharisees and Sadducees.

Peter's Declaration about Jesus
(Mk 8.27–30; Lk 9.18–21)

13 Jesus went to the territory near the town of Caesarea Philippi, where he asked his disciples, "Who do people say the Son of Man is?"

14 "Some say John the Baptist," they answered. "Others say Elijah, while others say Jeremiah or some other prophet."

15 "What about you?" he asked them. "Who do you say I am?"

16 Simon Peter answered, "You are the Messiah, the Son of the living God."

17 "Good for you, Simon son of John!" answered Jesus. "For this truth did not come to you from any human being, but it was given to you directly by my Father in heaven. 18 And so I tell you, Peter: you are a rock, and on this rock foundation I will build my church, and not even death will ever be able to overcome it. 19 I will give you the keys of the Kingdom of heaven; what you prohibit on earth will be prohibited in heaven, and what you permit on earth will be permitted in heaven."

20 Then Jesus ordered his disciples not to tell anyone that he was the Messiah.

Jesus Speaks about his Suffering and Death
(Mk 8.31—9.1; Lk 9.22–27)

21 From that time on Jesus began to say plainly to his disciples, "I must go to Jerusalem and suffer much from the elders, the chief priests, and the teachers of the Law. I will be put to death, but three days later I will be raised to life."

22 Peter took him aside and began to rebuke him. "God forbid it, Lord!" he said. "That must never happen to you!"

23 Jesus turned around and said to Peter, "Get away from me, Satan! You are an obstacle in my way, because these thoughts of yours don't come from God, but from human nature."

24 Then Jesus said to his disciples, "If anyone wants to come with me, he must forget self, carry his cross, and follow me. 25 For whoever wants to save his own life will lose it; but whoever loses his life for my sake will find it. 26 Will people gain anything if they win the whole world but lose their life? Of course not! There is nothing they can give to regain their life. 27 For the Son of Man is about to come in the glory of his Father with his angels, and then he will reward each one according to his deeds. 28 I assure you that there are some here who will not die until they have seen the Son of Man come as King."

MATTHEW 17

1149

Matt.

Mark
Luke
John
Acts
Romans

The Transfiguration
(Mk 9.2–13; Lk 9.28–36)

17 Six days later Jesus took with him Peter and the brothers James and John and led them up a high mountain where they were alone. [2] As they looked on, a change came over Jesus: his face was shining like the sun, and his clothes were dazzling white. [3] Then the three disciples saw Moses and Elijah talking with Jesus. [4] So Peter spoke up and said to Jesus, "Lord, how good it is that we are here! If you wish, I will make three tents here, one for you, one for Moses, and one for Elijah."

[5] While he was talking, a shining cloud came over them, and a voice from the cloud said, "This is my own dear Son, with whom I am pleased — listen to him!"

[6] When the disciples heard the voice, they were so terrified that they threw themselves face downwards on the ground. [7] Jesus came to them and touched them. "Get up," he said. "Don't be afraid!" [8] So they looked up and saw no one there but Jesus.

[9] As they came down the mountain, Jesus ordered them, "Don't tell anyone about this vision you have seen until the Son of Man has been raised from death."

[10] Then the disciples asked Jesus, "Why do the teachers of the Law say that Elijah has to come first?"

[11] "Elijah is indeed coming first," answered Jesus, "and he will get everything ready. [12] But I tell you that Elijah has already come and people did not recognize him, but treated him just as they pleased. In the same way they will also ill-treat the Son of Man."

[13] Then the disciples understood that he was talking to them about John the Baptist.

Jesus Heals a Boy with a Demon
(Mk 9.14–29; Lk 9.37–43a)

[14] When they returned to the crowd, a man came to Jesus, knelt before him, [15] and said, "Sir, have mercy on my son! He is an epileptic and has such terrible fits that he often falls in the fire or into water. [16] I brought him to your disciples, but they could not heal him."

[17] Jesus answered, "How unbelieving and wrong you people are! How long must I stay with you? How long do I have to put up with you? Bring the boy here to me!" [18] Jesus gave a command to the demon, and it went out of the boy, and at that very moment he was healed.

[19] Then the disciples came to Jesus in private and asked him, "Why couldn't we drive the demon out?"

[20] "It was because you haven't enough faith," answered Jesus. "I assure you that if you have faith as big as a mustard seed, you can say to this hill, 'Go from here to there!' and it will go. You could do anything!"*

Jesus Speaks Again about his Death
(Mk 9.30–32; Lk 9.43b–45)

[22] When the disciples all came together in Galilee, Jesus said to them, "The Son of Man is about to be handed over to people [23] who will kill him; but three days later he will be raised to life."

The disciples became very sad.

17.20 Some manuscripts add verse 21: *But only prayer and fasting can drive this kind out; nothing else can* (see Mk 9.29).

Matt.

....

Habak.
Zephan.
Haggai
Zechar.
Malachi

Payment of the Temple Tax

²⁴ When Jesus and his disciples came to Capernaum, the collectors of the temple tax came to Peter and asked, "Does your teacher pay the temple tax?"

²⁵ "Of course," Peter answered.

When Peter went into the house, Jesus spoke up first, "Simon, what is your opinion? Who pays duties or taxes to the kings of this world? The citizens of the country or the foreigners?"

²⁶ "The foreigners," answered Peter.

"Well, then," replied Jesus, "that means that the citizens don't have to pay. ²⁷ But we don't want to offend these people. So go to the lake and drop in a line. Pull up the first fish you hook, and in its mouth you will find a coin worth enough for my temple tax and yours. Take it and pay them our taxes."

Who is the Greatest?
(Mk 9.33–37; Lk 9.46–48)

18 At that time the disciples came to Jesus, asking, "Who is the greatest in the Kingdom of heaven?"

² So Jesus called a child, made him stand in front of them, ³ and said, "I assure you that unless you change and become like children, you will never enter the Kingdom of heaven. ⁴ The greatest in the Kingdom of heaven is the one who humbles himself and becomes like this child. ⁵ And whoever welcomes in my name one such child as this, welcomes me.

Temptations to Sin
(Mk 9.42–48; Lk 17.1–2)

⁶ "If anyone should cause one of these little ones to lose his faith in me, it would be better for that person to have a large millstone tied round his neck and be drowned in the deep sea. ⁷ How terrible for the world that there are things that make people lose their faith! Such things will always happen — but how terrible for the one who causes them!

⁸ "If your hand or your foot makes you lose your faith, cut it off and throw it away! It is better for you to enter life without a hand or a foot than to keep both hands and both feet and be thrown into the eternal fire. ⁹ And if your eye makes you lose your faith, take it out and throw it away! It is better for you to enter life with only one eye than to keep both eyes and be thrown into the fire of hell.

The Parable of the Lost Sheep
(Lk 15.3–7)

¹⁰ "See that you don't despise any of these little ones. Their angels in heaven, I tell you, are always in the presence of my Father in heaven.*

¹² "What do you think a man does who has 100 sheep and one of them gets lost? He will leave the other 99 grazing on the hillside and go and look for the lost sheep. ¹³ When he finds it, I tell you, he feels far happier over this one sheep than over the 99 that did not get lost. ¹⁴ In just the same way your* Father in heaven does not want any of these little ones to be lost.

....

18.10 Some manuscripts add verse 11: *For the Son of Man came to save the lost* (see Lk 19.10).
18.14 *your*; some manuscripts have *my*.

MATTHEW 18, 19

1151

Matt.
....

Mark
Luke
John
Acts
Romans

A Brother or Sister who Sins

15 "If your brother sins against you,* go to him and show him his fault. But do it privately, just between yourselves. If he listens to you, you have won your brother back. 16 But if he will not listen to you, take one or two other persons with you, so that 'every accusation may be upheld by the testimony of two or more witnesses,' as the scripture says. 17 And if he will not listen to them, then tell the whole thing to the church. Finally, if he will not listen to the church, treat him as though he were a pagan or a tax collector.

Prohibiting and Permitting

18 "And so I tell all of you: what you prohibit on earth will be prohibited in heaven, and what you permit on earth will be permitted in heaven.

19 "And I tell you more: whenever two of you on earth agree about anything you pray for, it will be done for you by my Father in heaven. 20 For where two or three come together in my name, I am there with them."

The Parable of the Unforgiving Servant

21 Then Peter came to Jesus and asked, "Lord, if my brother keeps on sinning against me, how many times do I have to forgive him? Seven times?"

22 "No, not seven times," answered Jesus, "but seventy times seven,* 23 because the Kingdom of heaven is like this. Once there was a king who decided to check on his servants' accounts. 24 He had just begun to do so when one of them was brought in who owed him millions of pounds. 25 The servant did not have enough to pay his debt, so the king ordered him to be sold as a slave, with his wife and his children and all that he had, in order to pay the debt. 26 The servant fell on his knees before the king. 'Be patient with me,' he begged, 'and I will pay you everything!' 27 The king felt sorry for him, so he forgave him the debt and let him go.

28 "Then the man went out and met one of his fellow-servants who owed him a few pounds. He grabbed him and started choking him. 'Pay back what you owe me!' he said. 29 His fellow-servant fell down and begged him, 'Be patient with me, and I will pay you back!' 30 But he refused; instead, he had him thrown into jail until he should pay the debt. 31 When the other servants saw what had happened, they were very upset and went to the king and told him everything. 32 So he called the servant in. 'You worthless slave!' he said. 'I forgave you the whole amount you owed me, just because you asked me to. 33 You should have had mercy on your fellow-servant, just as I had mercy on you.' 34 The king was very angry, and he sent the servant to jail to be punished until he should pay back the whole amount."

35 And Jesus concluded, "That is how my Father in heaven will treat every one of you unless you forgive your brother from your heart."

Jesus Teaches about Divorce
(Mk 10.1–12)

19 When Jesus finished saying these things, he left Galilee and went to the territory of Judea on the other side of the River Jordan. 2 Large crowds followed him, and he healed them there.

....

18.15 Some manuscripts do not have *against you*.
18.22 *seventy times seven*; or *77 times*.

MATTHEW 19.16-30

In the box below, write all of the possessions that mean the most to you. If Jesus asked you to give up or

- GIVE -

AWAY

each one of them, do you think you would? How would you feel? What does this show you about how you value your things, compared with following Jesus?

[3] Some Pharisees came to him and tried to trap him by asking, "Does our Law allow a man to divorce his wife for whatever reason he wishes?"

[4] Jesus answered, "Haven't you read the scripture that says that in the beginning the Creator made people male and female? [5] And God said, 'For this reason a man will leave his father and mother and unite with his wife, and the two will become one.' [6] So they are no longer two, but one. No human being must separate, then, what God has joined together."

[7] The Pharisees asked him, "Why, then, did Moses give the law for a man to hand his wife a divorce notice and send her away?"

[8] Jesus answered, "Moses gave you permission to divorce your wives because you are so hard to teach. But it was not like that at the time of creation. [9] I tell you, then, that any man who divorces his wife for any cause other than her unfaithfulness, commits adultery if he marries some other woman."

[10] His disciples said to him, "If this is how it is between a man and his wife, it is better not to marry."

[11] Jesus answered, "This teaching does not apply to everyone, but only to those to whom God has given it. [12] For there are different reasons why men cannot marry: some, because they were born that way; others, because men made them that way; and others do not marry for the sake of the Kingdom of heaven. Let him who can accept this teaching do so."

Jesus Blesses Little Children
(Mk 10.13–16; Lk 18.15–17)

[13] Some people brought children to Jesus for him to place his hands on them and to pray for them, but the disciples scolded the people. [14] Jesus said, "Let the children come to me and do not stop them, because the Kingdom of heaven belongs to such as these."

[15] He placed his hands on them and then went away.

The Rich Young Man
(Mk 10.17–31; Lk 18.18–30)

[16] Once a man came to Jesus. "Teacher," he asked, "what good thing must I do to receive eternal life?"

[17] "Why do you ask me concerning what is good?" answered Jesus. "There is only One who is good. Keep the commandments if you want to enter life."

[18] "What commandments?" he asked.

Jesus answered, "Do not commit murder; do not commit adultery; do not steal; do not accuse anyone falsely; [19] respect your father and your mother; and love your neighbour as you love yourself."

[20] "I have obeyed all these commandments," the young man replied. "What else do I need to do?"

[21] Jesus said to him, "If you want to be perfect, go and sell all you have and give the money to the poor, and you will have riches in heaven; then come and follow me."

[22] When the young man heard this, he went away sad, because he was very rich.

[23] Jesus then said to his disciples, "I assure you: it will be very hard for rich people to enter the Kingdom of heaven. [24] I repeat: it is much harder for a rich person to enter the Kingdom of God than for a camel to go through the eye of a needle."

[25] When the disciples heard this, they were completely amazed. "Who, then, can be saved?" they asked.

MATTHEW 19, 20

1153

Matt.
....
Mark
Luke
John
Acts
Romans

²⁶ Jesus looked straight at them and answered, "This is impossible for human beings, but for God everything is possible."

²⁷ Then Peter spoke up. "Look," he said, "we have left everything and followed you. What will we have?"

²⁸ Jesus said to them, "You can be sure that when the Son of Man sits on his glorious throne in the New Age, then you twelve followers of mine will also sit on thrones, to rule the twelve tribes of Israel. ²⁹ And everyone who has left houses or brothers or sisters or father or mother or children or fields for my sake, will receive a hundred times more and will be given eternal life. ³⁰ But many who now are first will be last, and many who now are last will be first.

The Workers in the Vineyard

20 "The Kingdom of heaven is like this. Once there was a man who went out early in the morning to hire some men to work in his vineyard. ² He agreed to pay them the regular wage, a silver coin a day, and sent them to work in his vineyard. ³ He went out again to the market place at nine o'clock and saw some men standing there doing nothing, ⁴ so he told them, 'You also go and work in the vineyard, and I will pay you a fair wage.' ⁵ So they went. Then at twelve o'clock and again at three o'clock he did the same thing. ⁶ It was nearly five o'clock when he went to the market place and saw some other men still standing there. 'Why are you wasting the whole day here doing nothing?' he asked them. ⁷ 'No one hired us,' they answered. 'Well, then, you also go and work in the vineyard,' he told them.

⁸ "When evening came, the owner told his foreman, 'Call the workers and pay them their wages, starting with those who were hired last and ending with those who were hired first.' ⁹ The men who had begun to work at five o'clock were paid a silver coin each. ¹⁰ So when the men who were the first to be hired came to be paid, they thought they would get more; but they too were given a silver coin each. ¹¹ They took their money and started grumbling against the employer. ¹² 'These men who were hired last worked only one hour,' they said, 'while we put up with a whole day's work in the hot sun — yet you paid them the same as you paid us!'

¹³ "'Listen, friend,' the owner answered one of them, 'I have not cheated you. After all, you agreed to do a day's work for one silver coin. ¹⁴ Now take your pay and go home. I want to give this man who was hired last as much as I have given you. ¹⁵ Don't I have the right to do as I wish with my own money? Or are you jealous because I am generous?' "

¹⁶ And Jesus concluded, "So those who are last will be first, and those who are first will be last."

Jesus Speaks a Third Time about his Death
(Mk 10.32–34; Lk 18.31–34)

¹⁷ As Jesus was going up to Jerusalem, he took the twelve disciples aside and spoke to them privately, as they walked along. ¹⁸ "Listen," he told them, "we are going up to Jerusalem, where the Son of Man will be handed over to the chief priests and the teachers of the Law. They will condemn him to death ¹⁹ and then hand him over to the Gentiles, who will mock him, whip him, and crucify him; but three days later he will be raised to life."

A Mother's Request
(Mk 10.35–45)

²⁰ Then the wife of Zebedee came to Jesus with her two sons, bowed before him, and asked him a favour.

1154

Matt.

Habak.
Zephan.
Haggai
Zechar.
Malachi

MATTHEW 20, 21

²¹"What do you want?" Jesus asked her.

She answered, "Promise me that these two sons of mine will sit at your right and your left when you are King."

²²"You don't know what you are asking for," Jesus answered the sons. "Can you drink the cup of suffering that I am about to drink?"

"We can," they answered.

²³"You will indeed drink from my cup," Jesus told them, "but I do not have the right to choose who will sit at my right and my left. These places belong to those for whom my Father has prepared them."

²⁴When the other ten disciples heard about this, they became angry with the two brothers. ²⁵So Jesus called them all together and said, "You know that the rulers of the heathen have power over them, and the leaders have complete authority. ²⁶This, however, is not the way it shall be among you. If one of you wants to be great, he must be the servant of the rest; ²⁷and if one of you wants to be first, he must be your slave — ²⁸like the Son of Man, who did not come to be served, but to serve and to give his life to redeem many people."

Jesus Heals Two Blind Men
(Mk 10.46–52; Lk 18.35–43)

²⁹As Jesus and his disciples were leaving Jericho, a large crowd was following. ³⁰Two blind men who were sitting by the road heard that Jesus was passing by, so they began to shout, "Son of David! Take pity on us, sir!"

³¹The crowd scolded them and told them to be quiet. But they shouted even more loudly, "Son of David! Take pity on us, sir!"

³²Jesus stopped and called them. "What do you want me to do for you?" he asked them.

³³"Sir," they answered, "we want you to give us our sight!"

³⁴Jesus had pity on them and touched their eyes; at once they were able to see, and they followed him.

The Triumphant Entry into Jerusalem
(Mk 11.1–11; Lk 19.28–40; Jn 12.12–19)

21 As Jesus and his disciples approached Jerusalem, they came to Bethphage at the Mount of Olives. There Jesus sent two of the disciples on ahead ²with these instructions: "Go to the village there ahead of you, and at once you will find a donkey tied up with her colt beside her. Untie them and bring them to me. ³And if anyone says anything, tell him, 'The Master* needs them'; and then he will let them go at once."

⁴This happened in order to make what the prophet had said come true:

⁵ "Tell the city of Zion,
    Look, your king is coming to you!
  He is humble and rides on a donkey
    and on a colt, the foal of a donkey."

⁶So the disciples went and did what Jesus had told them to do: ⁷they brought the donkey and the colt, threw their cloaks over them, and Jesus got on. ⁸A large crowd of people spread their cloaks on the road while others cut branches from the trees and spread them on the road. ⁹The crowds walking in front of Jesus and those walking behind began to shout, "Praise to David's Son! God bless him who comes in the name of the Lord! Praise God!"

21.3 *The Master*; or *Their owner*.

Matt.
Mark
Luke
John
Acts
Romans

[10] When Jesus entered Jerusalem, the whole city was thrown into an uproar. "Who is he?" the people asked. [11] "This is the prophet Jesus, from Nazareth in Galilee," the crowds answered.

Jesus Goes to the Temple
(Mk 11.15–19; Lk 19.45–48; Jn 2.13–22)

[12] Jesus went into the Temple and drove out all those who were buying and selling there. He overturned the tables of the moneychangers and the stools of those who sold pigeons, [13] and said to them, "It is written in the Scriptures that God said, 'My Temple will be called a house of prayer.' But you are making it a hideout for thieves!"

[14] The blind and the crippled came to him in the Temple, and he healed them. [15] The chief priests and the teachers of the Law became angry when they saw the wonderful things he was doing and the children shouting in the Temple, "Praise to David's Son!" [16] So they asked Jesus, "Do you hear what they are saying?"

"Indeed I do," answered Jesus. "Haven't you ever read this scripture? 'You have trained children and babies to offer perfect praise.'"

[17] Jesus left them and went out of the city to Bethany, where he spent the night.

Jesus Curses the Fig Tree
(Mk 11.12–14, 20–24)

[18] On his way back to the city early next morning, Jesus was hungry. [19] He saw a fig tree by the side of the road and went to it, but found nothing on it except leaves. So he said to the tree, "You will never again bear fruit!" At once the fig tree dried up.

[20] The disciples saw this and were astounded. "How did the fig tree dry up so quickly?" they asked.

[21] Jesus answered, "I assure you that if you believe and do not doubt, you will be able to do what I have done to this fig tree. And not only this, but you will even be able to say to this hill, 'Get up and throw yourself in the sea,' and it will. [22] If you believe, you will receive whatever you ask for in prayer."

The Question about Jesus' Authority
(Mk 11.27–33; Lk 20.1–8)

[23] Jesus came back to the Temple; and as he taught, the chief priests and the elders came to him and asked, "What right have you to do these things? Who gave you this right?"

[24] Jesus answered them, "I will ask you just one question, and if you give me an answer, I will tell you what right I have to do these things. [25] Where did John's right to baptize come from: was it from God or from human beings?"

They started to argue among themselves, "What shall we say? If we answer, 'From God,' he will say to us, 'Why, then, did you not believe John?' [26] But if we say, 'From human beings,' we are afraid of what the people might do, because they are all convinced that John was a prophet." [27] So they answered Jesus, "We don't know."

And he said to them, "Neither will I tell you, then, by what right I do these things.

The Parable of the Two Sons

[28] "Now, what do you think? There was once a man who had two sons. He went to the elder one and said, 'Son, go and work

MATTHEW 21.12-13

Without a bit of

• EXTRA •

INFO,

it can be hard to know why Jesus got so angry here. People would buy their sacrifices within the temple walls, but in order to do so they had to change their money into special currency used within the temple. There were two problems with this.

First, those offering the money-changing services and providing sacrifices were cheating the people and being unfair to them.

Second, this all took place in the only part of the temple that Gentiles (non-Jews) could enter, so their area was overcrowded with stalls - not exactly the place of worship to God that it was meant to be!

1156

Matt.

.:.........

Habak.
Zephan.
Haggai
Zechar.
Malachi

MATTHEW 21, 22

in the vineyard today.' ²⁹'I don't want to,' he answered, but later he changed his mind and went. ³⁰Then the father went to the other son and said the same thing. 'Yes, sir,' he answered, but he did not go. ³¹Which one of the two did what his father wanted?"

"The elder one," they answered.

So Jesus said to them, "I tell you: the tax collectors and the prostitutes are going into the Kingdom of God ahead of you. ³²For John the Baptist came to you showing you the right path to take, and you would not believe him; but the tax collectors and the prostitutes believed him. Even when you saw this, you did not later change your minds and believe him.

The Parable of the Tenants in the Vineyard
(Mk 12.1–12; Lk 20.9–19)

³³"Listen to another parable," Jesus said. "There was once a landowner who planted a vineyard, put a fence around it, dug a hole for the winepress, and built a watchtower. Then he let out the vineyard to tenants and went on a journey. ³⁴When the time came to gather the grapes, he sent his slaves to the tenants to receive his share of the harvest. ³⁵The tenants seized his slaves, beat one, killed another, and stoned another. ³⁶Again the man sent other slaves, more than the first time, and the tenants treated them the same way. ³⁷Last of all he sent his son to them. 'Surely they will respect my son,' he said. ³⁸But when the tenants saw the son, they said to themselves, 'This is the owner's son. Come on, let's kill him, and we will get his property!' ³⁹So they seized him, threw him out of the vineyard, and killed him.

⁴⁰"Now, when the owner of the vineyard comes, what will he do to those tenants?" Jesus asked.

⁴¹"He will certainly kill those evil men," they answered, "and let the vineyard out to other tenants, who will give him his share of the harvest at the right time."

⁴²Jesus said to them, "Haven't you ever read what the Scriptures say?

'The stone which the builders rejected as worthless
turned out to be the most important of all.
This was done by the Lord;
what a wonderful sight it is!'

⁴³"And so I tell you," added Jesus, "the Kingdom of God will be taken away from you and given to a people who will produce the proper fruits."*

⁴⁵The chief priests and the Pharisees heard Jesus' parables and knew that he was talking about them, ⁴⁶so they tried to arrest him. But they were afraid of the crowds, who considered Jesus to be a prophet.

The Parable of the Wedding Feast
(Lk 14.15–24)

22 Jesus again used parables in talking to the people. ²"The Kingdom of heaven is like this. Once there was a king who prepared a wedding feast for his son. ³He sent his servants to tell the invited guests to come to the feast, but they did not want to come. ⁴So he sent other servants with this message for the guests: 'My feast is ready now; my bullocks and prize calves have been butchered, and everything is ready. Come to the wedding feast!'

....

21.43 Some manuscripts add verse 44: *Whoever falls on this stone will be cut to pieces; and if the stone falls on someone, it will crush him to dust* (see Lk 20.18).

MATTHEW 22

1157

Matt.
................:
Mark
Luke
John
Acts
Romans

⁵ But the invited guests paid no attention and went about their business: one went to his farm, another to his shop, ⁶ while others grabbed the servants, beat them, and killed them. ⁷ The king was very angry; so he sent his soldiers, who killed those murderers and burnt down their city. ⁸ Then he called his servants and said to them, 'My wedding feast is ready, but the people I invited did not deserve it. ⁹ Now go to the main streets and invite to the feast as many people as you find.' ¹⁰ So the servants went out into the streets and gathered all the people they could find, good and bad alike; and the wedding hall was filled with people.

¹¹ "The king went in to look at the guests and saw a man who was not wearing wedding clothes. ¹² 'Friend, how did you get in here without wedding clothes?' the king asked him. But the man said nothing. ¹³ Then the king told the servants, 'Tie him up hand and foot, and throw him outside in the dark. There he will cry and grind his teeth.'"

¹⁴ And Jesus concluded, "Many are invited, but few are chosen."

The Question about Paying Taxes
(Mk 12.13–17; Lk 20.20–26)

¹⁵ The Pharisees went off and made a plan to trap Jesus with questions. ¹⁶ Then they sent to him some of their disciples and some members of Herod's party. "Teacher," they said, "we know that you tell the truth. You teach the truth about God's will for people, without worrying about what others think, because you pay no attention to anyone's status. ¹⁷ Tell us, then, what do you think? Is it against our Law to pay taxes to the Roman Emperor, or not?"

¹⁸ Jesus, however, was aware of their evil plan, and so he said, "You hypocrites! Why are you trying to trap me? ¹⁹ Show me the coin for paying the tax!"

They brought him the coin, ²⁰ and he asked them, "Whose face and name are these?"

²¹ "The Emperor's," they answered.

So Jesus said to them, "Well, then, pay the Emperor what belongs to the Emperor, and pay God what belongs to God."

²² When they heard this, they were amazed; and they left him and went away.

The Question about Rising from Death
(Mk 12.18–27; Lk 20.27–40)

²³ That same day some Sadducees came to Jesus and claimed that people will not rise from death. ²⁴ "Teacher," they said, "Moses said that if a man who has no children dies, his brother must marry the widow so that they can have children who will be considered the dead man's children. ²⁵ Now, there were seven brothers who used to live here. The eldest got married and died without having children, so he left his widow to his brother. ²⁶ The same thing happened to the second brother, to the third, and finally to all seven. ²⁷ Last of all, the woman died. ²⁸ Now, on the day when the dead rise to life, whose wife will she be? All of them had married her."

²⁹ Jesus answered them, "How wrong you are! It is because you don't know the Scriptures or God's power. ³⁰ For when the dead rise to life, they will be like the angels in heaven and will not marry. ³¹ Now, as for the dead rising to life: haven't you ever read what God has told you? He said, ³² 'I am the God of Abraham, the God of Isaac, and the God of Jacob.' He is the God of the living, not of the dead."

³³ When the crowds heard this, they were amazed at his teaching.

1158

Matt.

Habak.
Zephan.
Haggai
Zechar.
Malachi

MATTHEW 22, 23

MATTHEW 22.37

LOVE THE
LORD
YOUR GOD
WITH ALL YOUR
heart
WITH ALL YOUR
SOUL
AND
WITH ALL YOUR
mind

The Great Commandment
(Mk 12.28–34; Lk 10.25–28)

³⁴ When the Pharisees heard that Jesus had silenced the Sadducees, they came together, ³⁵ and one of them, a teacher of the Law, tried to trap him with a question. ³⁶ "Teacher," he asked, "which is the greatest commandment in the Law?"

³⁷ Jesus answered, " 'Love the Lord your God with all your heart, with all your soul, and with all your mind.' ³⁸ This is the greatest and the most important commandment. ³⁹ The second most important commandment is like it: 'Love your neighbour as you love yourself.' ⁴⁰ The whole Law of Moses and the teachings of the prophets depend on these two commandments."

The Question about the Messiah
(Mk 12.35–37; Lk 20.41–44)

⁴¹ When some Pharisees gathered together, Jesus asked them, ⁴² "What do you think about the Messiah? Whose descendant is he?"

"He is David's descendant," they answered.

⁴³ "Why, then," Jesus asked, "did the Spirit inspire David to call him 'Lord'? David said,

⁴⁴ 'The Lord said to my Lord:
      Sit here on my right
      until I put your enemies under your feet.'

⁴⁵ If, then, David called him 'Lord', how can the Messiah be David's descendant?"

⁴⁶ No one was able to give Jesus any answer, and from that day on no one dared to ask him any more questions.

Jesus Warns against the Teachers of the Law and the Pharisees
(Mk 12.38–39; Lk 11.43, 46; 20.45–46)

23 Then Jesus spoke to the crowds and to his disciples. ² "The teachers of the Law and the Pharisees are the authorized interpreters of Moses' Law. ³ So you must obey and follow everything they tell you to do; do not, however, imitate their actions, because they don't practise what they preach. ⁴ They tie on to people's backs loads that are heavy and hard to carry, yet they aren't willing even to lift a finger to help them carry those loads. ⁵ They do everything so that people will see them. Look at the straps with scripture verses on them which they wear on their foreheads and arms, and notice how large they are! Notice also how long are the tassels on their cloaks!* ⁶ They love the best places at feasts and the reserved seats in the synagogues; ⁷ they love to be greeted with respect in the market places and to be called 'Teacher'. ⁸ You must not be called 'Teacher', because you are all members of one family and have only one Teacher. ⁹ And you must not call anyone here on earth 'Father', because you have only the one Father in heaven. ¹⁰ Nor should you be called 'Leader', because your one and only leader is the Messiah. ¹¹ The greatest one among you must be your servant. ¹² Whoever makes himself great will be humbled, and whoever humbles himself will be made great.

Jesus Condemns their Hypocrisy
(Mk 12.40; Lk 11.39–42, 44, 52; 20.47)

¹³ "How terrible for you, teachers of the Law and Pharisees! You hypocrites! You lock the door to the Kingdom of heaven in

23.5 tassels on their cloaks: These tassels were worn as a sign of devotion to God (see Num 15.37–41).

Matt.

....

Mark
Luke
John
Acts
Romans

people's faces, and you yourselves don't go in, nor do you allow in those who are trying to enter!*

[15] "How terrible for you, teachers of the Law and Pharisees! You hypocrites! You sail the seas and cross whole countries to win one convert; and when you succeed, you make him twice as deserving of going to hell as you yourselves are!

[16] "How terrible for you, blind guides! You teach, 'If someone swears by the Temple, he isn't bound by his vow; but if he swears by the gold in the Temple, he is bound.' [17] Blind fools! Which is more important, the gold or the Temple which makes the gold holy? [18] You also teach, 'If someone swears by the altar, he isn't bound by his vow; but if he swears by the gift on the altar, he is bound.' [19] How blind you are! Which is the more important, the gift or the altar which makes the gift holy? [20] So then, when a person swears by the altar, he is swearing by it and by all the gifts on it; [21] and when he swears by the Temple, he is swearing by it and by God, who lives there; [22] and when someone swears by heaven, he is swearing by God's throne and by him who sits on it.

[23] "How terrible for you, teachers of the Law and Pharisees! You hypocrites! You give to God a tenth even of the seasoning herbs, such as mint, dill, and cumin, but you neglect to obey the really important teachings of the Law, such as justice and mercy and honesty. These you should practise, without neglecting the others. [24] Blind guides! You strain a fly out of your drink, but swallow a camel!

[25] "How terrible for you, teachers of the Law and Pharisees! You hypocrites! You clean the outside of your cup and plate, while the inside is full of what you have obtained by violence and selfishness. [26] Blind Pharisee! Clean what is inside the cup first, and then the outside will be clean too!

[27] "How terrible for you, teachers of the Law and Pharisees! You hypocrites! You are like whitewashed tombs, which look fine on the outside but are full of bones and decaying corpses on the inside. [28] In the same way, on the outside you appear good to everybody, but inside you are full of hypocrisy and sins.

Jesus Predicts their Punishment
(Lk 11.47–51)

[29] "How terrible for you, teachers of the Law and Pharisees! You hypocrites! You make fine tombs for the prophets and decorate the monuments of those who lived good lives; [30] and you claim that if you had lived during the time of your ancestors, you would not have done what they did and killed the prophets. [31] So you actually admit that you are the descendants of those who murdered the prophets! [32] Go on, then, and finish what your ancestors started! [33] You snakes and children of snakes! How do you expect to escape from being condemned to hell? [34] And so I tell you that I will send you prophets and wise men and teachers; you will kill some of them, crucify others, and whip others in the synagogues and chase them from town to town. [35] As a result, the punishment for the murder of all innocent people will fall on you, from the murder of innocent Abel to the murder of Zechariah son of Berechiah, whom you murdered between the Temple and the

....

23.13 Some manuscripts add verse 14: *How terrible for you, teachers of the Law and Pharisees! You hypocrites! You take advantage of widows and rob them of their homes, and then make a show of saying long prayers! Because of this your punishment will be all the worse!* (see Mk 12.40).

Matt.

·:·········

Habak.
Zephan.
Haggai
Zechar.
Malachi

altar. 36 I tell you indeed: the punishment for all these murders will fall on the people of this day!

Jesus' Love for Jerusalem
(Lk 13.34–35)

37 "Jerusalem, Jerusalem! You kill the prophets and stone the messengers God has sent you! How many times have I wanted to put my arms round all your people, just as a hen gathers her chicks under her wings, but you would not let me! 38 And so your Temple will be abandoned and empty. 39 From now on, I tell you, you will never see me again until you say, 'God bless him who comes in the name of the Lord.'"

Jesus Speaks of the Destruction of the Temple
(Mk 13.1–2; Lk 21.5–6)

24 Jesus left and was going away from the Temple when his disciples came to him to call his attention to its buildings. 2 "Yes," he said, "you may well look at all these. I tell you this: not a single stone here will be left in its place; every one of them will be thrown down."

Troubles and Persecutions
(Mk 13.3–13; Lk 21.7–19)

3 As Jesus sat on the Mount of Olives, the disciples came to him in private. "Tell us when all this will be," they asked, "and what will happen to show that it is the time for your coming and the end of the age."

4 Jesus answered, "Be on your guard, and do not let anyone deceive you. 5 Many men, claiming to speak for me, will come and say, 'I am the Messiah!' and they will deceive many people. 6 You are going to hear the noise of battles close by and the news of battles far away; but do not be troubled. Such things must happen, but they do not mean that the end has come. 7 Countries will fight each other, kingdoms will attack one another. There will be famines and earthquakes everywhere. 8 All these things are like the first pains of childbirth.

9 "Then you will be arrested and handed over to be punished and be put to death. All nations will hate you because of me. 10 Many will give up their faith at that time; they will betray one another and hate one another. 11 Then many false prophets will appear and deceive many people. 12 Such will be the spread of evil that many people's love will grow cold. 13 But whoever holds out to the end will be saved. 14 And this Good News about the Kingdom will be preached through all the world for a witness to all nations; and then the end will come.

The Awful Horror
(Mk 13.14–23; Lk 21.20–24)

15 "You will see 'The Awful Horror' of which the prophet Daniel spoke. It will be standing in the holy place." (Note to the reader: be sure to understand what this means!) 16 "Then those who are in Judea must run away to the hills. 17 Someone who is on the roof of his house must not take the time to go down and get his belongings from the house. 18 Someone who is in the field must not go back to get his cloak. 19 How terrible it will be in those days for women who are pregnant and for mothers with little babies! 20 Pray to God that you will not have to run away during the winter or on a Sabbath! 21 For the trouble at that time will be far more terrible than any there has ever been, from the beginning

MATTHEW 24

1161

Matt.
....
Mark
Luke
John
Acts
Romans

of the world to this very day. Nor will there ever be anything like it again. ²²But God has already reduced the number of days; had he not done so, nobody would survive. For the sake of his chosen people, however, God will reduce the days.

²³"Then, if anyone says to you, 'Look, here is the Messiah!' or 'There he is!' — do not believe it. ²⁴For false Messiahs and false prophets will appear; they will perform great miracles and wonders in order to deceive even God's chosen people, if possible. ²⁵Listen! I have told you this before the time comes.

²⁶"Or, if people should tell you, 'Look, he is out in the desert!' — don't go there; or if they say, 'Look, he is hiding here!' — don't believe it. ²⁷For the Son of Man will come like the lightning which flashes across the whole sky from the east to the west.

²⁸"Wherever there is a dead body, the vultures will gather.

The Coming of the Son of Man
(Mk 13.24–27; Lk 21.25–28)

²⁹"Soon after the trouble of those days, the sun will grow dark, the moon will no longer shine, the stars will fall from heaven, and the powers in space will be driven from their courses. ³⁰Then the sign of the Son of Man will appear in the sky; and all the peoples of earth will weep as they see the Son of Man coming on the clouds of heaven with power and great glory. ³¹The great trumpet will sound, and he will send out his angels to the four corners of the earth, and they will gather his chosen people from one end of the world to the other.

The Lesson of the Fig Tree
(Mk 13.28–31; Lk 21.29–33)

³²"Let the fig tree teach you a lesson. When its branches become green and tender and it starts putting out leaves, you know that summer is near. ³³In the same way, when you see all these things, you will know that the time is near, ready to begin.* ³⁴Remember that all these things will happen before the people now living have all died. ³⁵Heaven and earth will pass away, but my words will never pass away.

No One Knows the Day and Hour
(Mk 13.32–37; Lk 17.26–30, 34–36)

³⁶"No one knows, however, when that day and hour will come — neither the angels in heaven nor the Son;* the Father alone knows. ³⁷The coming of the Son of Man will be like what happened in the time of Noah. ³⁸In the days before the flood people ate and drank, men and women married, up to the very day Noah went into the boat; ³⁹yet they did not realize what was happening until the flood came and swept them all away. That is how it will be when the Son of Man comes. ⁴⁰At that time two men will be working in a field: one will be taken away, the other will be left behind. ⁴¹Two women will be at a mill grinding meal: one will be taken away, the other will be left behind.

⁴²"Be on your guard, then, because you do not know what day your Lord will come. ⁴³If the owner of a house knew the time when the thief would come, you can be sure that he would stay awake and not let the thief break into his house. ⁴⁴So then, you also must always be ready, because the Son of Man will come at an hour when you are not expecting him.

24.33 *the time is near, ready to begin*; or *he is near, ready to come.*
24.36 Some manuscripts do not have *nor the Son.*

1162

MATTHEW 24, 25

Matt.

.∵.········

Habak.
Zephan.
Haggai
Zechar.
Malachi

The Faithful or the Unfaithful Servant
(Lk 12.41–48)

⁴⁵ "Who, then, is a faithful and wise servant? It is the one that his master has placed in charge of the other servants to give them their food at the proper time. ⁴⁶ How happy that servant is if his master finds him doing this when he comes home! ⁴⁷ Indeed, I tell you, the master will put that servant in charge of all his property. ⁴⁸ But if he is a bad servant, he will tell himself that his master will not come back for a long time, ⁴⁹ and he will begin to beat his fellow-servants and to eat and drink with drunkards. ⁵⁰ Then that servant's master will come back one day when the servant does not expect him and at a time he does not know. ⁵¹ The master will cut him in pieces* and make him share the fate of the hypocrites. There he will cry and grind his teeth.

The Parable of the Ten Young Women

25 "At that time the Kingdom of heaven will be like this. Once there were ten young women who took their oil lamps and went out to meet the bridegroom. ² Five of them were foolish, and the other five were wise. ³ The foolish ones took their lamps but did not take any extra oil with them, ⁴ while the wise ones took containers full of oil for their lamps. ⁵ The bridegroom was late in coming, so the women began to nod and fall asleep.

⁶ "It was already midnight when the cry rang out, 'Here is the bridegroom! Come and meet him!' ⁷ The ten women woke up and trimmed their lamps. ⁸ Then the foolish ones said to the wise ones, 'Let us have some of your oil, because our lamps are going out.' ⁹ 'No, indeed,' the wise ones answered, 'there is not enough for you and for us. Go to the shop and buy some for yourselves.' ¹⁰ So the foolish women went off to buy some oil; and while they were gone, the bridegroom arrived. The five who were ready went in with him to the wedding feast, and the door was closed.

¹¹ "Later the other women arrived. 'Sir, sir! Let us in!' they cried out. ¹² 'Certainly not! I don't know you,' the bridegroom answered."

¹³ And Jesus concluded, "Be on your guard, then, because you do not know the day or the hour.

The Parable of the Three Servants
(Lk 19.11–27)

¹⁴ "At that time the Kingdom of heaven will be like this. Once there was a man who was about to go on a journey; he called his servants and put them in charge of his property. ¹⁵ He gave to each one according to his ability: to one he gave 5,000 gold coins, to another he gave 2,000, and to another he gave 1,000. Then he left on his journey. ¹⁶ The servant who had received 5,000 coins went at once and invested his money and earned another 5,000. ¹⁷ In the same way the servant who had received 2,000 coins earned another 2,000. ¹⁸ But the servant who had received 1,000 coins went off, dug a hole in the ground, and hid his master's money.

¹⁹ "After a long time the master of those servants came back and settled accounts with them. ²⁰ The servant who had received 5,000 coins came in and handed over the other 5,000. 'You gave me 5,000 coins, sir,' he said. 'Look! Here are another 5,000 that I have earned.' ²¹ 'Well done, you good and faithful servant!' said his master. 'You have been faithful in managing small amounts,

------

24.51 *cut him in pieces*; or *throw him out*.

MATTHEW 25

1163

Matt.

..........:·

Mark
Luke
John
Acts
Romans

so I will put you in charge of large amounts. Come on in and share my happiness!'

22 "Then the servant who had been given 2,000 coins came in and said, 'You gave me 2,000 coins, sir. Look! Here are another 2,000 that I have earned.' 23 'Well done, you good and faithful servant!' said his master. 'You have been faithful in managing small amounts, so I will put you in charge of large amounts. Come on in and share my happiness!'

24 "Then the servant who had received 1,000 coins came in and said, 'Sir, I know you are a hard man; you reap harvests where you did not sow, and you gather crops where you did not scatter seed. 25 I was afraid, so I went off and hid your money in the ground. Look! Here is what belongs to you.'

26 "'You bad and lazy servant!' his master said. 'You knew, did you, that I reap harvests where I did not sow, and gather crops where I did not scatter seed? 27 Well, then, you should have deposited my money in the bank, and I would have received it all back with interest when I returned. 28 Now, take the money away from him and give it to the one who has 10,000 coins. 29 For to every person who has something, even more will be given, and he will have more than enough; but the person who has nothing, even the little that he has will be taken away from him. 30 As for this useless servant — throw him outside in the darkness; there he will cry and grind his teeth.'

The Final Judgement

31 "When the Son of Man comes as King and all the angels with him, he will sit on his royal throne, 32 and the people of all the nations will be gathered before him. Then he will divide them into two groups, just as a shepherd separates the sheep from the goats. 33 He will put the righteous people on his right and the others on his left. 34 Then the King will say to the people on his right, 'Come, you that are blessed by my Father! Come and possess the kingdom which has been prepared for you ever since the creation of the world. 35 I was hungry and you fed me, thirsty and you gave me a drink; I was a stranger and you received me in your homes, 36 naked and you clothed me; I was sick and you took care of me, in prison and you visited me.'

37 "The righteous will then answer him, 'When, Lord, did we ever see you hungry and feed you, or thirsty and give you a drink? 38 When did we ever see you a stranger and welcome you in our homes, or naked and clothe you? 39 When did we ever see you sick or in prison, and visit you?' 40 The King will reply, 'I tell you, whenever you did this for one of the least important of these members of my family, you did it for me!'

41 "Then he will say to those on his left, 'Away from me, you that are under God's curse! Away to the eternal fire which has been prepared for the Devil and his angels! 42 I was hungry but you would not feed me, thirsty but you would not give me a drink; 43 I was a stranger but you would not welcome me in your homes, naked but you would not clothe me; I was sick and in prison but you would not take care of me.'

44 "Then they will answer him, 'When, Lord, did we ever see you hungry or thirsty or a stranger or naked or sick or in prison, and would not help you?' 45 The King will reply, 'I tell you, whenever you refused to help one of these least important ones, you refused to help me.' 46 These, then, will be sent off to eternal punishment, but the righteous will go to eternal life."

1164

Matt.

Habak.
Zephan.
Haggai
Zechar.
Malachi

MATTHEW 26

WHAT DOES 'GOSPEL' MEAN?
Finish the mindmap below.

The teaching or
revelation of Christ.
(oxforddictionaries.com)

↑

GOSPEL

MATTHEW 26.13;
1 CORINTHIANS 9.14-18

The Plot against Jesus
(Mk 14.1–2; Lk 22.1–2; Jn 11.45–53)

26 When Jesus had finished teaching all these things, he said to his disciples, [2] "In two days, as you know, it will be the Passover Festival, and the Son of Man will be handed over to be crucified."

[3] Then the chief priests and the elders met together in the palace of Caiaphas, the High Priest, [4] and made plans to arrest Jesus secretly and put him to death. [5] "We must not do it during the festival," they said, "or the people will riot."

Jesus is Anointed at Bethany
(Mk 14.3–9; Jn 12.1–8)

[6] Jesus was in Bethany at the house of Simon, a man who had suffered from a dreaded skin disease. [7] While Jesus was eating, a woman came to him with an alabaster jar filled with an expensive perfume, which she poured on his head. [8] The disciples saw this and became angry. "Why all this waste?" they asked. [9] "This perfume could have been sold for a large amount and the money given to the poor!"

[10] Jesus knew what they were saying, so he said to them, "Why are you bothering this woman? It is a fine and beautiful thing that she has done for me. [11] You will always have poor people with you, but you will not always have me. [12] What she did was to pour this perfume on my body to get me ready for burial. [13] Now, I assure you that wherever this gospel is preached all over the world, what she has done will be told in memory of her."

Judas Agrees to Betray Jesus
(Mk 14.10–11; Lk 22.3–6)

[14] Then one of the twelve disciples — the one named Judas Iscariot — went to the chief priests [15] and asked, "What will you give me if I betray Jesus to you?" They counted out thirty silver coins and gave them to him. [16] From then on Judas was looking for a good chance to hand Jesus over to them.

Jesus Eats the Passover Meal with his Disciples
(Mk 14.12–21; Lk 22.7–13, 21–23; Jn 13.21–30)

[17] On the first day of the Festival of Unleavened Bread the disciples came to Jesus and asked him, "Where do you want us to get the Passover meal ready for you?"

[18] "Go to a certain man in the city," he said to them, "and tell him: 'The Teacher says, My hour has come; my disciples and I will celebrate the Passover at your house.'"

[19] The disciples did as Jesus had told them and prepared the Passover meal.

[20] When it was evening, Jesus and the twelve disciples sat down to eat. [21] During the meal Jesus said, "I tell you, one of you will betray me."

[22] The disciples were very upset and began to ask him, one after the other, "Surely, Lord, you don't mean me?"

[23] Jesus answered, "One who dips his bread in the dish with me will betray me. [24] The Son of Man will die as the Scriptures say he will, but how terrible for that man who betrays the Son of Man! It would have been better for that man if he had never been born!"

[25] Judas, the traitor, spoke up. "Surely, Teacher, you don't mean me?" he asked.

Jesus answered, "So you say."

Matt.

....

Mark

Luke

John

Acts

Romans

The Lord's Supper
(Mk 14.22–26; Lk 22.14–20; 1 Cor 11.23–25)

26 While they were eating, Jesus took a piece of bread, gave a prayer of thanks, broke it, and gave it to his disciples. "Take and eat it," he said; "this is my body."

27 Then he took a cup, gave thanks to God, and gave it to them. "Drink it, all of you," he said; 28 "this is my blood, which seals God's covenant, my blood poured out for many for the forgiveness of sins. 29 I tell you, I will never again drink this wine until the day I drink the new wine with you in my Father's Kingdom."

30 Then they sang a hymn and went out to the Mount of Olives.

Jesus Predicts Peter's Denial
(Mk 14.27–31; Lk 22.31–34; Jn 13.36–38)

31 Then Jesus said to them, "This very night all of you will run away and leave me, for the scripture says, 'God will kill the shepherd, and the sheep of the flock will be scattered.' 32 But after I am raised to life, I will go to Galilee ahead of you."

33 Peter spoke up and said to Jesus, "I will never leave you, even though all the rest do!"

34 Jesus said to Peter, "I tell you that before the cock crows tonight, you will say three times that you do not know me."

35 Peter answered, "I will never say that, even if I have to die with you!"

And all the other disciples said the same thing.

Jesus Prays in Gethsemane
(Mk 14.32–42; Lk 22.39–46)

36 Then Jesus went with his disciples to a place called Gethsemane, and he said to them, "Sit here while I go over there and pray." 37 He took with him Peter and the two sons of Zebedee. Grief and anguish came over him, 38 and he said to them, "The sorrow in my heart is so great that it almost crushes me. Stay here and keep watch with me."

39 He went a little farther on, threw himself face downwards on the ground, and prayed, "My Father, if it is possible, take this cup of suffering from me! Yet not what I want, but what you want."

40 Then he returned to the three disciples and found them asleep; and he said to Peter, "How is it that you three were not able to keep watch with me even for one hour? 41 Keep watch and pray that you will not fall into temptation. The spirit is willing, but the flesh is weak."

42 Once more Jesus went away and prayed, "My Father, if this cup of suffering cannot be taken away unless I drink it, your will be done." 43 He returned once more and found the disciples asleep; they could not keep their eyes open.

44 Again Jesus left them, went away, and prayed the third time, saying the same words. 45 Then he returned to the disciples and said, "Are you still sleeping and resting? Look! The hour has come for the Son of Man to be handed over to the power of sinners. 46 Get up, let us go. Look, here is the man who is betraying me!"

The Arrest of Jesus
(Mk 14.43–50; Lk 22.47–53; Jn 18.3–12)

47 Jesus was still speaking when Judas, one of the twelve disciples, arrived. With him was a large crowd armed with swords and clubs and sent by the chief priests and the elders. 48 The traitor had given the crowd a signal: "The man I kiss is the one you want. Arrest him!"

Matt.

Habak.
Zephan.
Haggai
Zechar.
Malachi

[49] Judas went straight to Jesus and said, "Peace be with you, Teacher," and kissed him.

[50] Jesus answered, "Be quick about it, friend!"*

Then they came up, arrested Jesus, and held him tight. [51] One of those who were with Jesus drew his sword and struck at the High Priest's slave, cutting off his ear. [52] "Put your sword back in its place," Jesus said to him. "All who take the sword will die by the sword. [53] Don't you know that I could call on my Father for help, and at once he would send me more than twelve armies of angels? [54] But in that case, how could the Scriptures come true which say that this is what must happen?"

[55] Then Jesus spoke to the crowd, "Did you have to come with swords and clubs to capture me, as though I were an outlaw? Every day I sat down and taught in the Temple, and you did not arrest me. [56] But all this has happened in order to make what the prophets wrote in the Scriptures come true."

Then all the disciples left him and ran away.

Jesus Before the Council
(Mk 14.53–65; Lk 22.54–55, 63–71; Jn 18.13–14, 19–24)

[57] Those who had arrested Jesus took him to the house of Caiaphas, the High Priest, where the teachers of the Law and the elders had gathered together. [58] Peter followed from a distance, as far as the courtyard of the High Priest's house. He went into the courtyard and sat down with the guards to see how it would all come out. [59] The chief priests and the whole Council tried to find some false evidence against Jesus to put him to death; [60] but they could not find any, even though many people came forward and told lies about him. Finally two men stepped up [61] and said, "This man said, 'I am able to tear down God's Temple and three days later build it up again.'"

[62] The High Priest stood up and said to Jesus, "Have you no answer to give to this accusation against you?" [63] But Jesus kept quiet. Again the High Priest spoke to him, "In the name of the living God I now put you on oath: tell us if you are the Messiah, the Son of God."

[64] Jesus answered him, "So you say. But I tell all of you: from this time on you will see the Son of Man sitting on the right of the Almighty and coming on the clouds of heaven!"

[65] At this the High Priest tore his clothes and said, "Blasphemy! We don't need any more witnesses! You have just heard his blasphemy! [66] What do you think?"

They answered, "He is guilty and must die."

[67] Then they spat in his face and beat him; and those who slapped him [68] said, "Prophesy for us, Messiah! Guess who hit you!"

Peter Denies Jesus
(Mk 14.66–72; Lk 22.56–62; Jn 18.15–18, 25–27)

[69] Peter was sitting outside in the courtyard when one of the High Priest's servant women came to him and said, "You, too, were with Jesus of Galilee."

[70] But he denied it in front of them all. "I don't know what you are talking about," he answered, [71] and went on out to the entrance of the courtyard. Another servant woman saw him and said to the men there, "He was with Jesus of Nazareth."

[72] Again Peter denied it and answered, "I swear that I don't know that man!"

. . . .

26.50 *Be quick about it, friend!*; or *Why are you here, friend?*

MATTHEW 26, 27

1167

Matt.
..........:
Mark
Luke
John
Acts
Romans

73 After a little while the men standing there came to Peter. "Of course you are one of them," they said. "After all, the way you speak gives you away!"

74 Then Peter said, "I swear that I am telling the truth! May God punish me if I am not! I do not know that man!"

Just then a cock crowed, 75 and Peter remembered what Jesus had told him: "Before the cock crows, you will say three times that you do not know me." He went out and wept bitterly.

Jesus is Taken to Pilate
(Mk 15.1; Lk 23.1–2; Jn 18.28–32)

27 Early in the morning all the chief priests and the elders made their plans against Jesus to put him to death. 2 They put him in chains, led him off, and handed him over to Pilate, the Roman governor.

The Death of Judas
(Acts 1.18–19)

3 When Judas, the traitor, learnt that Jesus had been condemned, he repented and took back the thirty silver coins to the chief priests and the elders. 4 "I have sinned by betraying an innocent man to death!" he said.

"What do we care about that?" they answered. "That is your business!"

5 Judas threw the coins down in the Temple and left; then he went off and hanged himself.

6 The chief priests picked up the coins and said, "This is blood money, and it is against our Law to put it in the temple treasury." 7 After reaching an agreement about it, they used the money to buy Potter's Field, as a cemetery for foreigners. 8 That is why that field is called "Field of Blood" to this very day.

9 Then what the prophet Jeremiah had said came true: "They took the thirty silver coins, the amount the people of Israel had agreed to pay for him, 10 and used the money to buy the potter's field, as the Lord had commanded me."

Pilate Questions Jesus
(Mk 15.2–5; Lk 23.3–5; Jn 18.33–38)

11 Jesus stood before the Roman governor, who questioned him. "Are you the king of the Jews?" he asked.

"So you say," answered Jesus. 12 But he said nothing in response to the accusations of the chief priests and elders.

13 So Pilate said to him, "Don't you hear all these things they accuse you of?"

14 But Jesus refused to answer a single word, with the result that the Governor was greatly surprised.

Jesus is Sentenced to Death
(Mk 15.6–15; Lk 23.13–25; Jn 18.39—19.16)

15 At every Passover Festival the Roman governor was in the habit of setting free any one prisoner the crowd asked for. 16 At that time there was a well-known prisoner named Jesus Barabbas. 17 So when the crowd gathered, Pilate asked them, "Which one do you want me to set free for you? Jesus Barabbas or Jesus called the Messiah?" 18 He knew very well that the Jewish authorities had handed Jesus over to him because they were jealous.

19 While Pilate was sitting in the judgement hall, his wife sent him a message: "Have nothing to do with that innocent

MATTHEW 27

You may have heard the contents of this chapter many times over, but as you read it, try to

IMAGINE
– THE SCENES –

and what is happening. Who is there? Where are they? How are they feeling? What are they doing? Why do you think they're doing it?

write some thoughts here

man, because in a dream last night I suffered much on account of him."

20 The chief priests and the elders persuaded the crowd to ask Pilate to set Barabbas free and have Jesus put to death. 21 But Pilate asked the crowd, "Which one of these two do you want me to set free for you?"

"Barabbas!" they answered.

22 "What, then, shall I do with Jesus called the Messiah?" Pilate asked them.

"Crucify him!" they all answered.

23 But Pilate asked, "What crime has he committed?"

Then they started shouting at the top of their voices: "Crucify him!"

24 When Pilate saw that it was no use to go on, but that a riot might break out, he took some water, washed his hands in front of the crowd, and said, "I am not responsible for the death of this man! This is your doing!"

25 The whole crowd answered, "Let the responsibility for his death fall on us and our children!"

26 Then Pilate set Barabbas free for them; and after he had Jesus whipped, he handed him over to be crucified.

The Soldiers Mock Jesus
(Mk 15.16–20; Jn 19.2–3)

27 Then Pilate's soldiers took Jesus into the governor's palace, and the whole company gathered round him. 28 They stripped off his clothes and put a scarlet robe on him. 29 Then they made a crown out of thorny branches and placed it on his head, and put a stick in his right hand; then they knelt before him and mocked him. "Long live the King of the Jews!" they said. 30 They spat on him, and took the stick and hit him over the head. 31 When they had finished mocking him, they took the robe off and put his own clothes back on him. Then they led him out to crucify him.

Jesus is Crucified
(Mk 15.21–32; Lk 23.26–43; Jn 19.17–27)

32 As they were going out, they met a man from Cyrene named Simon, and the soldiers forced him to carry Jesus' cross. 33 They came to a place called Golgotha, which means, "The Place of the Skull". 34 There they offered Jesus wine mixed with a bitter substance; but after tasting it, he would not drink it.

35 They crucified him and then divided his clothes among them by throwing dice. 36 After that they sat there and watched him. 37 Above his head they put the written notice of the accusation against him: "This is Jesus, the King of the Jews." 38 Then they crucified two bandits with Jesus, one on his right and the other on his left.

39 People passing by shook their heads and hurled insults at Jesus: 40 "You were going to tear down the Temple and build it up again in three days! Save yourself if you are God's Son! Come on down from the cross!"

41 In the same way the chief priests and the teachers of the Law and the elders jeered at him: 42 "He saved others, but he cannot save himself! Isn't he the king of Israel? If he comes down off the cross now, we will believe in him! 43 He trusts in God and claims to be God's Son. Well, then, let us see if God wants to save him now!"

44 Even the bandits who had been crucified with him insulted him in the same way.

1169

Matt.
............:
Mark
Luke
John
Acts
Romans

The Death of Jesus
(Mk 15.33–41; Lk 23.44–49; Jn 19.28–30)

⁴⁵ At noon the whole country was covered with darkness, which lasted for three hours. ⁴⁶ At about three o'clock Jesus cried out with a loud shout, *"Eli, Eli, lema sabachthani?"* which means, "My God, my God, why did you abandon me?"

⁴⁷ Some of the people standing there heard him and said, "He is calling for Elijah!" ⁴⁸ One of them ran up at once, took a sponge, soaked it in cheap wine, put it on the end of a stick, and tried to make him drink it.

⁴⁹ But the others said, "Wait, let us see if Elijah is coming to save him!"

⁵⁰ Jesus again gave a loud cry and breathed his last.

⁵¹ Then the curtain hanging in the Temple was torn in two from top to bottom. The earth shook, the rocks split apart, ⁵² the graves broke open, and many of God's people who had died were raised to life. ⁵³ They left the graves, and after Jesus rose from death, they went into the Holy City, where many people saw them.

⁵⁴ When the army officer and the soldiers with him who were watching Jesus saw the earthquake and everything else that happened, they were terrified and said, "He really was the Son of God!"

⁵⁵ There were many women there, looking on from a distance, who had followed Jesus from Galilee and helped him. ⁵⁶ Among them were Mary Magdalene, Mary the mother of James and Joseph, and the wife of Zebedee.

The Burial of Jesus
(Mk 15.42–47; Lk 23.50–56; Jn 19.38–42)

⁵⁷ When it was evening, a rich man from Arimathea arrived; his name was Joseph, and he also was a disciple of Jesus. ⁵⁸ He went into the presence of Pilate and asked for the body of Jesus. Pilate gave orders for the body to be given to Joseph. ⁵⁹ So Joseph took it, wrapped it in a new linen sheet, ⁶⁰ and placed it in his own tomb, which he had just recently dug out of solid rock. Then he rolled a large stone across the entrance to the tomb and went away. ⁶¹ Mary Magdalene and the other Mary were sitting there, facing the tomb.

The Guard at the Tomb

⁶² The next day, which was a Sabbath, the chief priests and the Pharisees met with Pilate ⁶³ and said, "Sir, we remember that while that liar was still alive he said, 'I will be raised to life three days later.' ⁶⁴ Give orders, then, for his tomb to be carefully guarded until the third day, so that his disciples will not be able to go and steal the body, and then tell the people that he was raised from death. This last lie would be even worse than the first one."

⁶⁵ "Take a guard," Pilate told them; "go and make the tomb as secure as you can."

⁶⁶ So they left and made the tomb secure by putting a seal on the stone and leaving the guard on watch.

The Resurrection
(Mk 16.1–10; Lk 24.1–12; Jn 20.1–10)

28 After the Sabbath, as Sunday morning was dawning, Mary Magdalene and the other Mary went to look at the tomb. ² Suddenly there was a violent earthquake; an angel of the Lord came down from heaven, rolled the stone away, and sat on it. ³ His appearance was like lightning, and his clothes were

MATTHEW 28.19

Write down three
friends who don't
know Jesus and

PRAY

FOR THEM

every day this week.

1.

2.

3.

white as snow. ⁴The guards were so afraid that they trembled and became like dead men.

⁵The angel spoke to the women. "You must not be afraid," he said. "I know you are looking for Jesus, who was crucified. ⁶He is not here; he has been raised, just as he said. Come here and see the place where he was lying. ⁷Go quickly now, and tell his disciples, 'He has been raised from death, and now he is going to Galilee ahead of you; there you will see him!' Remember what I have told you."

⁸So they left the tomb in a hurry, afraid and yet filled with joy, and ran to tell his disciples.

⁹Suddenly Jesus met them and said, "Peace be with you." They came up to him, took hold of his feet, and worshipped him. ¹⁰"Do not be afraid," Jesus said to them. "Go and tell my brothers to go to Galilee, and there they will see me."

The Report of the Guard

¹¹While the women went on their way, some of the soldiers guarding the tomb went back to the city and told the chief priests everything that had happened. ¹²The chief priests met with the elders and made their plan; they gave a large sum of money to the soldiers ¹³and said, "You are to say that his disciples came during the night and stole his body while you were asleep. ¹⁴And if the Governor should hear of this, we will convince him that you are innocent, and you will have nothing to worry about."

¹⁵The guards took the money and did what they were told to do. And so that is the report spread round by the Jews to this very day.

Jesus Appears to his Disciples
(Mk 16.14–18; Lk 24.36–49; Jn 20.19–23; Acts 1.6–8)

¹⁶The eleven disciples went to the hill in Galilee where Jesus had told them to go. ¹⁷When they saw him, they worshipped him, even though some of them doubted. ¹⁸Jesus drew near and said to them, "I have been given all authority in heaven and on earth. ¹⁹Go, then, to all peoples everywhere and make them my disciples: baptize them in the name of the Father, the Son, and the Holy Spirit, ²⁰and teach them to obey everything I have commanded you. And I will be with you always, to the end of the age."

THE GOSPEL OF
MARK

WRITTEN: AROUND AD70

WHAT YOU NEED TO KNOW:

Mark is the second of the four Gospels in our Bible, but
s thought to have been the first written. This book is a
speedy race through the life of Jesus, starting with his
baptism and focusing on his actions and deeds. Mark
brings to life many of Jesus' miracles, healings and
interactions with others. This book was written for
non-Jews, so Mark takes care to explain Jewish customs.
e also focuses on the incredible things Jesus did as proof
of who he claimed to be.

WHY READ IT?

Mark is short, concise and easy to read if you want to
know all about the actions and life of Jesus. It's also a
great Gospel to read because it was written specifically
for non-Jews (which probably includes you). This book
ighlights that Jesus doesn't just want us to go through
fe following a bunch of rules but that it all comes down
to loving God and loving others (Mark 12.28-31).

KEY CHARACTER:

ip through the four Gospels and piece together who John
the Baptist was and what he was trying to do. (He
ppears mainly in the first few chapters of each Gospel.)

Create a colourful mindmap below
of all the words you would use to

DESCRIBE
· JESUS ·

As you read this Gospel, see if you want
to change or add any words.

JESUS

(AD24)
US' BAPTISM

HEALING AND TEACHING

DEATH

RESURRECTION
(AD27)

1172

Mark

⫶········

Zephan.
Haggai
Zechar.
Malachi
Matt.

MARK 1

The Preaching of John the Baptist
(Mt 3.1–12; Lk 3.1–18; Jn 1.19–28)

1 This is the Good News about Jesus Christ, the Son of God.* ²It began as the prophet Isaiah had written:
"God said, 'I will send my messenger ahead of you
to clear the way for you.'
³ Someone is shouting in the desert,
'Get the road ready for the Lord;
make a straight path for him to travel!' "

⁴So John appeared in the desert, baptizing and preaching.* "Turn away from your sins and be baptized," he told the people, "and God will forgive your sins." ⁵Many people from the province of Judea and the city of Jerusalem went out to hear John. They confessed their sins, and he baptized them in the River Jordan.

⁶John wore clothes made of camel's hair, with a leather belt round his waist, and his food was locusts and wild honey. ⁷He announced to the people, "The man who will come after me is much greater than I am. I am not good enough even to bend down and untie his sandals. ⁸I baptize you with water, but he will baptize you with the Holy Spirit."

The Baptism and Temptation of Jesus
(Mt 3.13—4.11; Lk 3.21–22; 4.1–13)

⁹Not long afterwards Jesus came from Nazareth in the province of Galilee, and was baptized by John in the Jordan. ¹⁰As soon as Jesus came up out of the water, he saw heaven opening and the Spirit coming down on him like a dove. ¹¹And a voice came from heaven, "You are my own dear Son. I am pleased with you."

¹²At once the Spirit made him go into the desert, ¹³where he stayed forty days, being tempted by Satan. Wild animals were there also, but angels came and helped him.

Jesus Calls Four Fishermen
(Mt 4.12–22; Lk 4.14–15; 5.1–11)

¹⁴After John had been put in prison, Jesus went to Galilee and preached the Good News from God. ¹⁵"The right time has come," he said, "and the Kingdom of God is near! Turn away from your sins and believe the Good News!"

¹⁶As Jesus walked along the shore of Lake Galilee, he saw two fishermen, Simon and his brother Andrew, catching fish with a net. ¹⁷Jesus said to them, "Come with me, and I will teach you to catch people." ¹⁸At once they left their nets and went with him.

¹⁹He went a little farther on and saw two other brothers, James and John, the sons of Zebedee. They were in their boat getting their nets ready. ²⁰As soon as Jesus saw them, he called them; they left their father Zebedee in the boat with the hired men and went with Jesus.

A Man with an Evil Spirit
(Lk 4.31–37)

²¹Jesus and his disciples came to the town of Capernaum, and on the next Sabbath Jesus went to the synagogue and began to teach. ²²The people who heard him were amazed at the way he taught, for he wasn't like the teachers of the Law; instead, he taught with authority.

1.1 Some manuscripts do not have *the Son of God*.
1.4 *John appeared in the desert, baptizing and preaching*; some manuscripts have *John the Baptist appeared in the desert, preaching*.

Mark

Luke
John
Acts
Romans
1 Corin.

23 Just then a man with an evil spirit in him came into the synagogue and screamed, 24 "What do you want with us, Jesus of Nazareth? Are you here to destroy us? I know who you are — you are God's holy messenger!"

25 Jesus ordered the spirit, "Be quiet, and come out of the man!"

26 The evil spirit shook the man hard, gave a loud scream, and came out of him. 27 The people were all so amazed that they started saying to one another, "What is this? Is it some kind of new teaching? This man has authority to give orders to the evil spirits, and they obey him!"

28 And so the news about Jesus spread quickly everywhere in the province of Galilee.

Jesus Heals Many People
(Mt 8.14–17; Lk 4.38–41)

29 Jesus and his disciples, including James and John, left the synagogue and went straight to the home of Simon and Andrew. 30 Simon's mother-in-law was sick in bed with a fever, and as soon as Jesus arrived, he was told about her. 31 He went to her, took her by the hand, and helped her up. The fever left her, and she began to wait on them.

32 After the sun had set and evening had come, people brought to Jesus all the sick and those who had demons. 33 All the people of the town gathered in front of the house. 34 Jesus healed many who were sick with all kinds of diseases and drove out many demons. He would not let the demons say anything, because they knew who he was.

Jesus Preaches in Galilee
(Lk 4.42–44)

35 Very early the next morning, long before daylight, Jesus got up and left the house. He went out of the town to a lonely place, where he prayed. 36 But Simon and his companions went out searching for him, 37 and when they found him, they said, "Everyone is looking for you."

38 But Jesus answered, "We must go on to the other villages round here. I have to preach in them also, because that is why I came."

39 So he travelled all over Galilee, preaching in the synagogues and driving out demons.

Jesus Heals a Man
(Mt 8.1–4; Lk 5.12–16)

40 A man suffering from a dreaded skin disease came to Jesus, knelt down, and begged him for help. "If you want to," he said, "you can make me clean."*

41 Jesus was filled with pity,* and stretched out his hand and touched him. "I do want to," he answered. "Be clean!" 42 At once the disease left the man, and he was clean. 43 Then Jesus spoke sternly to him and sent him away at once, 44 after saying to him, "Listen, don't tell anyone about this. But go straight to the priest and let him examine you; then in order to prove to everyone that you are cured, offer the sacrifice that Moses ordered."

45 But the man went away and began to spread the news everywhere. Indeed, he talked so much that Jesus could not go

1.40 make me clean: This disease was considered to make a person ritually unclean.
1.41 pity; some manuscripts have anger.

1174

Mark

Zephan.
Haggai
Zechar.
Malachi
Matt.

MARK 2.1-5

These four men got their friend to Jesus. It is so important to have people around us who

– SUPPORT AND –
ENCOURAGE

us in our faith. Write the names here of friends your age who support you and who you support in return. Maybe you could even arrange to meet them this week?

_____

_____

_____

_____

_____

_____

_____

_____

_____

_____

_____

into a town publicly. Instead, he stayed out in lonely places, and people came to him from everywhere.

Jesus Heals a Paralysed Man
(Mt 9.1–8; Lk 5.17–26)

2 A few days later Jesus went back to Capernaum, and the news spread that he was at home. [2] So many people came together that there was no room left, not even out in front of the door. Jesus was preaching the message to them [3] when four men arrived, carrying a paralysed man to Jesus. [4] Because of the crowd, however, they could not get the man to him. So they made a hole in the roof right above the place where Jesus was. When they had made an opening, they let the man down, lying on his mat. [5] Seeing how much faith they had, Jesus said to the paralysed man, "My son, your sins are forgiven."

[6] Some teachers of the Law who were sitting there thought to themselves, [7]"How does he dare to talk like this? This is blasphemy! God is the only one who can forgive sins!"

[8] At once Jesus knew what they were thinking, so he said to them, "Why do you think such things? [9] Is it easier to say to this paralysed man, 'Your sins are forgiven', or to say, 'Get up, pick up your mat, and walk'? [10] I will prove to you, then, that the Son of Man has authority on earth to forgive sins." So he said to the paralysed man, [11]"I tell you, get up, pick up your mat, and go home!"

[12] While they all watched, the man got up, picked up his mat, and hurried away. They were all completely amazed and praised God, saying, "We have never seen anything like this!"

Jesus Calls Levi
(Mt 9.9–13; Lk 5.27–32)

[13] Jesus went back again to the shore of Lake Galilee. A crowd came to him, and he started teaching them. [14] As he walked along, he saw a tax collector, Levi son of Alphaeus, sitting in his office. Jesus said to him, "Follow me." Levi got up and followed him.

[15] Later on Jesus was having a meal in Levi's house.* A large number of tax collectors and other outcasts were following Jesus, and many of them joined him and his disciples at the table. [16] Some teachers of the Law, who were Pharisees, saw that Jesus was eating with these outcasts and tax collectors, so they asked his disciples, "Why does he eat with such people?"

[17] Jesus heard them and answered, "People who are well do not need a doctor, but only those who are sick. I have not come to call respectable people, but outcasts."

The Question about Fasting
(Mt 9.14–17; Lk 5.33–39)

[18] On one occasion the followers of John the Baptist and the Pharisees were fasting. Some people came to Jesus and asked him, "Why is it that the disciples of John the Baptist and the disciples of the Pharisees fast, but yours do not?"

[19] Jesus answered, "Do you expect the guests at a wedding party to go without food? Of course not! As long as the bridegroom is with them, they will not do that. [20] But the day will come when the bridegroom will be taken away from them, and then they will fast.

[21]"No one uses a piece of new cloth to patch up an old coat, because the new patch will shrink and tear off some of the old

2.15 *in Levi's house*; or *in his* (that is, Jesus') *house*.

MARK 2, 3

1175

Mark

··········⊹

Luke
John
Acts
Romans
1 Corin.

cloth, making an even bigger hole. ²²Nor does anyone pour new wine into used wineskins, because the wine will burst the skins, and both the wine and the skins will be ruined. Instead, new wine must be poured into fresh wineskins."

The Question about the Sabbath
(Mt 12.1–8; Lk 6.1–5)

²³Jesus was walking through some cornfields on the Sabbath. As his disciples walked along with him, they began to pick the ears of corn. ²⁴So the Pharisees said to Jesus, "Look, it is against our Law for your disciples to do that on the Sabbath!"

²⁵Jesus answered, "Have you never read what David did that time when he needed something to eat? He and his men were hungry, ²⁶so he went into the house of God and ate the bread offered to God. This happened when Abiathar was the High Priest. According to our Law only the priests may eat this bread — but David ate it and even gave it to his men."

²⁷And Jesus concluded, "The Sabbath was made for the good of human beings; they were not made for the Sabbath. ²⁸So the Son of Man is Lord even of the Sabbath."

The Man with a Paralysed Hand
(Mt 12.9–14; Lk 6.6–11)

3 Then Jesus went back to the synagogue, where there was a man who had a paralysed hand. ²Some people were there who wanted to accuse Jesus of doing wrong; so they watched him closely to see whether he would heal the man on the Sabbath. ³Jesus said to the man, "Come up here to the front." ⁴Then he asked the people, "What does our Law allow us to do on the Sabbath? To help or to harm? To save someone's life or to destroy it?"

But they did not say a thing. ⁵Jesus was angry as he looked round at them, but at the same time he felt sorry for them, because they were so stubborn and wrong. Then he said to the man, "Stretch out your hand." He stretched it out, and it became well again. ⁶So the Pharisees left the synagogue and met at once with some members of Herod's party, and they made plans to kill Jesus.

A Crowd by the Lake

⁷Jesus and his disciples went away to Lake Galilee, and a large crowd followed him. They had come from Galilee, from Judea, ⁸from Jerusalem, from the territory of Idumea, from the territory on the east side of the Jordan, and from the region round the cities of Tyre and Sidon. All these people came to Jesus because they had heard of the things he was doing. ⁹The crowd was so large that Jesus told his disciples to get a boat ready for him, so that the people would not crush him. ¹⁰He had healed many people, and all those who were ill kept pushing their way to him in order to touch him. ¹¹And whenever the people who had evil spirits in them saw him, they would fall down before him and scream, "You are the Son of God!"

¹²Jesus sternly ordered the evil spirits not to tell anyone who he was.

Jesus Chooses the Twelve Apostles
(Mt 10.1–4; Lk 6.12–16)

¹³Then Jesus went up a hill and called to himself the men he wanted. They came to him, ¹⁴and he chose twelve, whom he

1176

Mark

:· ....

Zephan.
Haggai
Zechar.
Malachi
Matt.

MARK 3, 4

named apostles. "I have chosen you to be with me," he told them. "I will also send you out to preach, [15] and you will have authority to drive out demons."

[16] These are the twelve he chose: Simon (Jesus gave him the name Peter); [17] James and his brother John, the sons of Zebedee (Jesus gave them the name Boanerges, which means "Men of Thunder"); [18] Andrew, Philip, Bartholomew, Matthew, Thomas, James son of Alphaeus, Thaddaeus, Simon the Patriot, [19] and Judas Iscariot, who betrayed Jesus.

Jesus and Beelzebul
(Mt 12.22–32; Lk 11.14–23; 12.10)

[20] Then Jesus went home. Again such a large crowd gathered that Jesus and his disciples had no time to eat. [21] When his family heard about it, they set out to take charge of him, because people were saying, "He's gone mad!"

[22] Some teachers of the Law who had come from Jerusalem were saying, "He has Beelzebul in him! It is the chief of the demons who gives him the power to drive them out."

[23] So Jesus called them to him and spoke to them in parables: "How can Satan drive out Satan? [24] If a country divides itself into groups which fight each other, that country will fall apart. [25] If a family divides itself into groups which fight each other, that family will fall apart. [26] So if Satan's kingdom divides into groups, it cannot last, but will fall apart and come to an end.

[27] "No one can break into a strong man's house and take away his belongings unless he first ties up the strong man; then he can plunder his house.

[28] "I assure you that people can be forgiven all their sins and all the evil things they may say.* [29] But whoever says evil things against the Holy Spirit will never be forgiven, because he has committed an eternal sin." [30] (Jesus said this because some people were saying, "He has an evil spirit in him.")

Jesus' Mother and Brothers
(Mt 12.46–50; Lk 8.19–21)

[31] Then Jesus' mother and brothers arrived. They stood outside the house and sent in a message, asking for him. [32] A crowd was sitting round Jesus, and they said to him, "Look, your mother and your brothers and sisters are outside, and they want you."

[33] Jesus answered, "Who is my mother? Who are my brothers?" [34] He looked at the people sitting round him and said, "Look! Here are my mother and my brothers! [35] Whoever does what God wants him to do is my brother, my sister, my mother."

The Parable of the Sower
(Mt 13.1–9; Lk 8.4–8)

4 Again Jesus began to teach beside Lake Galilee. The crowd that gathered round him was so large that he got into a boat and sat in it. The boat was out in the water, and the crowd stood on the shore at the water's edge. [2] He used parables to teach them many things, saying to them:

[3] "Listen! Once there was a man who went out to sow corn. [4] As he scattered the seed in the field, some of it fell along the path, and the birds came and ate it up. [5] Some of it fell on rocky ground, where there was little soil. The seeds soon sprouted, because the soil wasn't deep. [6] Then, when the sun came up, it

3.28 *evil things they may say*; or *evil things they may say against God.*

MARK 4

1177

Mark

Luke
John
Acts
Romans
1 Corin.

burnt the young plants; and because the roots had not grown deep enough, the plants soon dried up. ⁷Some of the seed fell among thorn bushes, which grew up and choked the plants, and they didn't produce any corn. ⁸But some seeds fell in good soil, and the plants sprouted, grew, and produced corn: some had thirty grains, others sixty, and others 100."

⁹And Jesus concluded, "Listen, then, if you have ears!"

The Purpose of the Parables
(Mt 13.10–17; Lk 8.9–10)

¹⁰When Jesus was alone, some of those who had heard him came to him with the twelve disciples and asked him to explain the parables. ¹¹"You have been given the secret of the Kingdom of God," Jesus answered. "But the others, who are on the outside, hear all things by means of parables, ¹²so that,

'They may look and look,
  yet not see;
they may listen and listen,
  yet not understand.
For if they did, they would turn to God,
  and he would forgive them.' "

Jesus Explains the Parable of the Sower
(Mt 13.18–23; Lk 8.11–15)

¹³Then Jesus asked them, "Don't you understand this parable? How, then, will you ever understand any parable? ¹⁴The sower sows God's message. ¹⁵Some people are like the seeds that fall along the path; as soon as they hear the message, Satan comes and takes it away. ¹⁶Other people are like the seeds that fall on rocky ground. As soon as they hear the message, they receive it gladly. ¹⁷But it does not sink deep into them, and they don't last long. So when trouble or persecution comes because of the message, they give up at once. ¹⁸Other people are like the seeds sown among the thorn bushes. These are the ones who hear the message, ¹⁹but the worries about this life, the love for riches, and all other kinds of desires crowd in and choke the message, and they don't bear fruit. ²⁰But other people are like the seeds sown in good soil. They hear the message, accept it, and bear fruit: some thirty, some sixty, and some 100."

A Lamp under a Bowl
(Lk 8.16–18)

²¹Jesus continued, "Does anyone ever bring in a lamp and put it under a bowl or under the bed? Doesn't he put it on the lampstand? ²²Whatever is hidden away will be brought out into the open, and whatever is covered up will be uncovered. ²³Listen, then, if you have ears!"

²⁴He also said to them, "Pay attention to what you hear! The same rules you use to judge others will be used by God to judge you — but with even greater severity. ²⁵Those who have something will be given more, and those who have nothing will have taken away from them even the little they have."

The Parable of the Growing Seed

²⁶Jesus went on to say, "The Kingdom of God is like this. A man scatters seed in his field. ²⁷He sleeps at night, is up and about during the day, and all the while the seeds are sprouting and growing. Yet he does not know how it happens. ²⁸The soil itself makes the plants grow and bear fruit; first the tender stalk

1178

Mark

·:·········

Zephan.
Haggai
Zechar.
Malachi
Matt.

MARK 4, 5

appears, then the ear, and finally the ear full of corn. ²⁹ When the corn is ripe, the man starts cutting it with his sickle, because harvest time has come.

The Parable of the Mustard Seed
(Mt 13.31–32, 34; Lk 13.18–19)

³⁰ "What shall we say the Kingdom of God is like?" asked Jesus. "What parable shall we use to explain it? ³¹ It is like this. A man takes a mustard seed, the smallest seed in the world, and plants it in the ground. ³² After a while it grows up and becomes the biggest of all plants. It puts out such large branches that the birds come and make their nests in its shade."

³³ Jesus preached his message to the people, using many other parables like these; he told them as much as they could understand. ³⁴ He would not speak to them without using parables, but when he was alone with his disciples, he would explain everything to them.

Jesus Calms a Storm
(Mt 8.23–27; Lk 8.22–25)

³⁵ On the evening of that same day Jesus said to his disciples, "Let us go across to the other side of the lake." ³⁶ So they left the crowd; the disciples got into the boat in which Jesus was already sitting, and they took him with them. Other boats were there too. ³⁷ Suddenly a strong wind blew up, and the waves began to spill over into the boat, so that it was about to fill with water. ³⁸ Jesus was in the back of the boat, sleeping with his head on a pillow. The disciples woke him up and said, "Teacher, don't you care that we are about to die?"

³⁹ Jesus stood up and commanded the wind, "Be quiet!" and he said to the waves, "Be still!" The wind died down, and there was a great calm. ⁴⁰ Then Jesus said to his disciples, "Why are you frightened? Have you still no faith?"

⁴¹ But they were terribly afraid and said to one another, "Who is this man? Even the wind and the waves obey him!"

Jesus Heals a Man with Evil Spirits
(Mt 8.28–34; Lk 8.26–39)

5 Jesus and his disciples arrived on the other side of Lake Galilee, in the territory of Gerasa. ² As soon as Jesus got out of the boat, he was met by a man who came out of the burial caves there. This man had an evil spirit in him ³ and lived among the tombs. Nobody could keep him chained up any more; ⁴ many times his feet and hands had been chained, but every time he broke the chains and smashed the irons on his feet. He was too strong for anyone to control him. ⁵ Day and night he wandered among the tombs and through the hills, screaming and cutting himself with stones.

⁶ He was some distance away when he saw Jesus; so he ran, fell on his knees before him, ⁷ and screamed in a loud voice, "Jesus, Son of the Most High God! What do you want with me? For God's sake, I beg you, don't punish me!" ⁸ (He said this because Jesus was saying, "Evil spirit, come out of this man!")

⁹ So Jesus asked him, "What is your name?"

The man answered, "My name is 'Mob' — there are so many of us!" ¹⁰ And he kept begging Jesus not to send the evil spirits out of that region.

¹¹ There was a large herd of pigs near by, feeding on a hillside. ¹² So the spirits begged Jesus, "Send us to the pigs, and let us

MARK 4.35-41

In Jewish culture, lakes and seas were seen as representations of hell and of evil, so Jews were often wary of large bodies of water. The storm on the lake of Galilee would have been seen as an expression of

EVIL

• FORCES. •

Because of this, when Jesus tells the storm to stop, he is demonstrating his power over darkness and evil.

MARK 5

1179

Mark
..........:.

Luke
John
Acts
Romans
1 Corin.

go into them." [13] He let them go, and the evil spirits went out of the man and entered the pigs. The whole herd — about 2,000 pigs in all — rushed down the side of the cliff into the lake and was drowned.

[14] The men who had been taking care of the pigs ran away and spread the news in the town and among the farms. People went out to see what had happened, [15] and when they came to Jesus, they saw the man who used to have the mob of demons in him. He was sitting there, clothed and in his right mind; and they were all afraid. [16] Those who had seen it told the people what had happened to the man with the demons, and about the pigs.

[17] So they asked Jesus to leave their territory.

[18] As Jesus was getting into the boat, the man who had had the demons begged him, "Let me go with you!"

[19] But Jesus would not let him. Instead, he told him, "Go back home to your family and tell them how much the Lord has done for you and how kind he has been to you."

[20] So the man left and went all through the Ten Towns, telling what Jesus had done for him. And all who heard it were amazed.

Jairus' Daughter and the Woman who Touched Jesus' Cloak
(Mt 9.18–26; Lk 8.40–56)

[21] Jesus went back across to the other side of the lake. There at the lakeside a large crowd gathered round him. [22] Jairus, an official of the local synagogue, arrived, and when he saw Jesus, he threw himself down at his feet [23] and begged him earnestly, "My little daughter is very ill. Please come and place your hands on her, so that she will get well and live!"

[24] Then Jesus started off with him. So many people were going along with Jesus that they were crowding him from every side.

[25] There was a woman who had suffered terribly from severe bleeding for twelve years, [26] even though she had been treated by many doctors. She had spent all her money, but instead of getting better she got worse all the time. [27] She had heard about Jesus, so she came in the crowd behind him, [28] saying to herself, "If I just touch his clothes, I will get well."

[29] She touched his cloak, and her bleeding stopped at once; and she had the feeling inside herself that she was healed of her trouble. [30] At once Jesus knew that power had gone out of him, so he turned round in the crowd and asked, "Who touched my clothes?"

[31] His disciples answered, "You see how the people are crowding you; why do you ask who touched you?"

[32] But Jesus kept looking round to see who had done it. [33] The woman realized what had happened to her, so she came, trembling with fear, knelt at his feet, and told him the whole truth. [34] Jesus said to her, "My daughter, your faith has made you well. Go in peace, and be healed of your trouble."

[35] While Jesus was saying this, some messengers came from Jairus' house and told him, "Your daughter has died. Why bother the Teacher any longer?"

[36] Jesus paid no attention to* what they said, but told him, "Don't be afraid, only believe." [37] Then he did not let anyone else go on with him except Peter and James and his brother John. [38] They arrived at Jairus' house, where Jesus saw the confusion and heard all the loud crying and wailing. [39] He went in and said to them, "Why all this confusion? Why are you crying? The child is not dead — she is only sleeping!"

....

5.36 *paid no attention to*; or *overheard*.

1180

Mark

⁖ ⋯⋯⋯

Zephan.
Haggai
Zechar.
Malachi
Matt.

MARK 5, 6

⁴⁰ They laughed at him, so he put them all out, took the child's father and mother and his three disciples, and went into the room where the child was lying. ⁴¹ He took her by the hand and said to her, *"Talitha, koum,"* which means, "Little girl, I tell you to get up!"

⁴² She got up at once and started walking around. (She was twelve years old.) When this happened, they were completely amazed. ⁴³ But Jesus gave them strict orders not to tell anyone, and he said, "Give her something to eat."

Jesus is Rejected at Nazareth
(Mt 13.53–58; Lk 4.16–30)

6 Jesus left that place and went back to his home town, followed by his disciples. ² On the Sabbath he began to teach in the synagogue. Many people were there; and when they heard him, they were all amazed. "Where did he get all this?" they asked. "What wisdom is this that has been given him? How does he perform miracles? ³ Isn't he the carpenter, the son of Mary, and the brother of James, Joseph, Judas, and Simon? Aren't his sisters living here?" And so they rejected him.

⁴ Jesus said to them, "Prophets are respected everywhere except in their own home town and by their relatives and their family."

⁵ He was not able to perform any miracles there, except that he placed his hands on a few sick people and healed them. ⁶ He was greatly surprised, because the people did not have faith.

Jesus Sends out the Twelve Disciples
(Mt 10.5–15; Lk 9.1–6)

Then Jesus went to the villages round there, teaching the people. ⁷ He called the twelve disciples together and sent them out two by two. He gave them authority over the evil spirits ⁸ and ordered them, "Don't take anything with you on your journey except a stick — no bread, no beggar's bag, no money in your pockets. ⁹ Wear sandals, but don't carry an extra shirt." ¹⁰ He also said, "Wherever you are welcomed, stay in the same house until you leave that place. ¹¹ If you come to a town where people do not welcome you or will not listen to you, leave it and shake the dust off your feet. That will be a warning to them!"

¹² So they went out and preached that people should turn away from their sins. ¹³ They drove out many demons, and rubbed olive oil on many sick people and healed them.

The Death of John the Baptist
(Mt 14.1–12; Lk 9.7–9)

¹⁴ Now King Herod* heard about all this, because Jesus' reputation had spread everywhere. Some people were saying, "John the Baptist has come back to life! That is why he has this power to perform miracles."

¹⁵ Others, however, said, "He is Elijah."

Others said, "He is a prophet, like one of the prophets of long ago."

¹⁶ When Herod heard it, he said, "He is John the Baptist! I had his head cut off, but he has come back to life!" ¹⁷ Herod himself had ordered John's arrest, and he had him chained and put in prison. Herod did this because of Herodias, whom he had married, even though she was the wife of his brother Philip. ¹⁸ John the Baptist kept telling Herod, "It isn't right for you to be married to your brother's wife!"

6.14 *King Herod*: Herod Antipas, ruler of Galilee.

MARK 6

1181

Mark

Luke
John
Acts
Romans
1 Corin.

¹⁹So Herodias held a grudge against John and wanted to kill him, but she could not because of Herod. ²⁰Herod was afraid of John because he knew that John was a good and holy man, and so he kept him safe. He liked to listen to him, even though he became greatly disturbed every time he heard him.

²¹Finally Herodias got her chance. It was on Herod's birthday, when he gave a feast for all the chief government officials, the military commanders, and the leading citizens of Galilee. ²²The daughter of Herodias* came in and danced, and pleased Herod and his guests. So the king said to the girl, "What would you like to have? I will give you anything you want." ²³With many vows he said to her, "I swear that I will give you anything you ask for, even as much as half my kingdom!"

²⁴So the girl went out and asked her mother, "What shall I ask for?"

"The head of John the Baptist," she answered.

²⁵The girl hurried back at once to the king and demanded, "I want you to give me here and now the head of John the Baptist on a dish!"

²⁶This made the king very sad, but he could not refuse her because of the vows he had made in front of all his guests. ²⁷So he sent off a guard at once with orders to bring John's head. The guard left, went to the prison, and cut John's head off; ²⁸then he brought it on a dish and gave it to the girl, who gave it to her mother. ²⁹When John's disciples heard about this, they came and took away his body, and buried it.

Jesus Feeds a Great Crowd
(Mt 14.13–21; Lk 9.10–17; Jn 6.1–14)

³⁰The apostles returned and met with Jesus, and told him all they had done and taught. ³¹There were so many people coming and going that Jesus and his disciples didn't even have time to eat. So he said to them, "Let us go off by ourselves to some place where we will be alone and you can rest for a while." ³²So they started out in a boat by themselves for a lonely place.

³³Many people, however, saw them leave and knew at once who they were; so they went from all the towns and ran ahead by land and arrived at the place ahead of Jesus and his disciples. ³⁴When Jesus got out of the boat, he saw this large crowd, and his heart was filled with pity for them, because they were like sheep without a shepherd. So he began to teach them many things. ³⁵When it was getting late, his disciples came to him and said, "It is already very late, and this is a lonely place. ³⁶Send the people away, and let them go to the nearby farms and villages in order to buy themselves something to eat."

³⁷"You yourselves give them something to eat," Jesus answered.

They asked, "Do you want us to go and spend 200 silver coins* on bread in order to feed them?"

³⁸So Jesus asked them, "How much bread have you got? Go and see."

When they found out, they told him, "Five loaves and also two fish."

³⁹Jesus then told his disciples to make all the people divide into groups and sit down on the green grass. ⁴⁰So the people sat

6.22 *The daughter of Herodias*; some manuscripts have *His daughter Herodias*.
6.37 *silver coins*: A silver coin was the daily wage of a rural worker (see Mt 20.2).

Let a friend you trust
draw something here.

down in rows, in groups of a hundred and groups of fifty. ⁴¹Then Jesus took the five loaves and the two fish, looked up to heaven, and gave thanks to God. He broke the loaves and gave them to his disciples to distribute to the people. He also divided the two fish among them all. ⁴²Everyone ate and had enough. ⁴³Then the disciples took up twelve baskets full of what was left of the bread and the fish. ⁴⁴The number of men who were fed was 5,000.

Jesus Walks on the Water
(Mt 14.22–33; Jn 6.15–21)

⁴⁵At once Jesus made his disciples get into the boat and go ahead of him to Bethsaida, on the other side of the lake, while he sent the crowd away. ⁴⁶After saying goodbye to the people he went away to a hill to pray. ⁴⁷When evening came, the boat was in the middle of the lake, while Jesus was alone on land. ⁴⁸He saw that his disciples were straining at the oars, because they were rowing against the wind; so some time between three and six o'clock in the morning he came to them, walking on the water. He was going to pass them by,* ⁴⁹but they saw him walking on the water. "It's a ghost!" they thought, and screamed. ⁵⁰They were all terrified when they saw him.

Jesus spoke to them at once, "Courage!" he said. "It is I. Don't be afraid!" ⁵¹Then he got into the boat with them, and the wind died down. The disciples were completely amazed, ⁵²because they had not understood the real meaning of the feeding of the 5,000; their minds could not grasp it.

Jesus Heals the Sick in Gennesaret
(Mt 14.34–36)

⁵³They crossed the lake and came to land at Gennesaret, where they tied up the boat. ⁵⁴As they left the boat, people recognized Jesus at once. ⁵⁵So they ran throughout the whole region; and wherever they heard he was, they brought to him sick people lying on their mats. ⁵⁶And everywhere Jesus went, to villages, towns, or farms, people would take those who were ill to the market places and beg him to let them at least touch the edge of his cloak; and all who touched it were made well.

The Teaching of the Ancestors
(Mt 15.1–9)

7 Some Pharisees and teachers of the Law who had come from Jerusalem gathered round Jesus. ²They noticed that some of his disciples were eating their food with hands that were ritually unclean — that is, they had not washed them in the way the Pharisees said people should.

³(For the Pharisees, as well as the rest of the Jews, follow the teaching they received from their ancestors: they do not eat unless they wash their hands in the proper way; ⁴nor do they eat anything that comes from the market unless they wash it first.* And they follow many other rules which they have received, such as the proper way to wash cups, pots, copper bowls, and beds.*)

⁵So the Pharisees and the teachers of the Law asked Jesus, "Why is it that your disciples do not follow the teaching handed down by our ancestors, but instead eat with ritually unclean hands?"

6.48 pass them by; or join them.
7.4 anything that comes from the market unless they wash it first; or anything after they come from the market unless they wash themselves first.
7.4 Some manuscripts do not have and beds.

MARK 7

1183

Mark
.........⟶

Luke
John
Acts
Romans
1 Corin.

6 Jesus answered them, "How right Isaiah was when he prophesied about you! You are hypocrites, just as he wrote:

'These people, says God, honour me with their words,
    but their heart is really far away from me.
7 It is no use for them to worship me,
    because they teach human rules
    as though they were God's laws!'

8 "You put aside God's command and obey human teachings."

9 And Jesus continued, "You have a clever way of rejecting God's law in order to uphold your own teaching. 10 For Moses commanded, 'Respect your father and your mother,' and, 'Whoever curses his father or his mother is to be put to death.' 11 But you teach that if a person has something he could use to help his father or mother, but says, 'This is Corban' (which means, it belongs to God), 12 he is excused from helping his father or mother. 13 In this way the teaching you pass on to others cancels out the word of God. And there are many other things like this that you do."

The Things that Make a Person Unclean
(Mt 15.10–20)

14 Then Jesus called the crowd to him once more and said to them, "Listen to me, all of you, and understand. 15 There is nothing that goes into a person from the outside which can make him ritually unclean. Rather, it is what comes out of a person that makes him unclean."*

17 When he left the crowd and went into the house, his disciples asked him to explain this saying. 18 "You are no more intelligent than the others," Jesus said to them. "Don't you understand? Nothing that goes into a person from the outside can really make him unclean, 19 because it does not go into his heart but into his stomach and then goes on out of the body." (In saying this, Jesus declared that all foods are fit to be eaten.)

20 And he went on to say, "It is what comes out of a person that makes him unclean. 21 For from the inside, from a person's heart, come the evil ideas which lead him to do immoral things, to rob, kill, 22 commit adultery, be greedy, and do all sorts of evil things; deceit, indecency, jealousy, slander, pride, and folly — 23 all these evil things come from inside a person and make him unclean."

A Woman's Faith
(Mt 15.21–28)

24 Then Jesus left and went away to the territory near the city of Tyre. He went into a house and did not want anyone to know he was there, but he could not stay hidden. 25 A woman, whose daughter had an evil spirit in her, heard about Jesus and came to him at once and fell at his feet. 26 The woman was a Gentile, born in the region of Phoenicia in Syria. She begged Jesus to drive the demon out of her daughter. 27 But Jesus answered, "Let us first feed the children. It isn't right to take the children's food and throw it to the dogs."

28 "Sir," she answered, "even the dogs under the table eat the children's leftovers!"

29 So Jesus said to her, "Because of that answer, go back home, where you will find that the demon has gone out of your daughter!"

30 She went home and found her child lying on the bed; the demon had indeed gone out of her.

....

7.15 Some manuscripts add verse 16: *Listen, then, if you have ears!* (see 4.23).

MAKE A NOTE
OF WHEN YOU
ARE GOING TO
SPEND TIME
• WITH GOD •
THIS WEEK

Jesus Heals a Deaf-mute

31 Jesus then left the neighbourhood of Tyre and went on through Sidon to Lake Galilee, going by way of the territory of the Ten Towns. 32 Some people brought him a man who was deaf and could hardly speak, and they begged Jesus to place his hands on him. 33 So Jesus took him off alone, away from the crowd, put his fingers in the man's ears, spat, and touched the man's tongue. 34 Then Jesus looked up to heaven, gave a deep groan, and said to the man, *"Ephphatha,"* which means, "Open up!"

35 At once the man was able to hear, his speech impediment was removed, and he began to talk without any trouble. 36 Then Jesus ordered the people not to speak of it to anyone; but the more he ordered them not to, the more they spoke. 37 And all who heard were completely amazed. "How well he does everything!" they exclaimed. "He even causes the deaf to hear and the dumb to speak!"

Jesus Feeds 4,000 People
(Mt 15.32–39)

8 Not long afterwards another large crowd came together. When the people had nothing left to eat, Jesus called the disciples to him and said, 2 "I feel sorry for these people, because they have been with me for three days and now have nothing to eat. 3 If I send them home without feeding them, they will faint as they go, because some of them have come a long way."

4 His disciples asked him, "Where in this desert can anyone find enough food to feed all these people?"

5 "How much bread have you got?" Jesus asked.

"Seven loaves," they answered.

6 He ordered the crowd to sit down on the ground. Then he took the seven loaves, gave thanks to God, broke them, and gave them to his disciples to distribute to the crowd; and the disciples did so. 7 They also had a few small fish. Jesus gave thanks for these and told the disciples to distribute them too. 8-9 Everybody ate and had enough — there were about 4,000 people. Then the disciples took up seven baskets full of pieces left over. Jesus sent the people away 10 and at once got into a boat with his disciples and went to the district of Dalmanutha.

The Pharisees Ask for a Miracle
(Mt 12.38–42; 16.1–4)

11 Some Pharisees came to Jesus and started to argue with him. They wanted to trap him, so they asked him to perform a miracle to show that God approved of him. 12 But Jesus gave a deep groan and said, "Why do the people of this day ask for a miracle? No, I tell you! No such proof will be given to these people!"

13 He left them, got back into the boat, and started across to the other side of the lake.

The Yeast of the Pharisees and of Herod
(Mt 16.5–12)

14 The disciples had forgotten to bring enough bread and had only one loaf with them in the boat. 15 "Take care," Jesus warned them, "and be on your guard against the yeast of the Pharisees and the yeast of Herod."

16 They started discussing among themselves: "He says this because we haven't any bread."

17 Jesus knew what they were saying, so he asked them, "Why are you discussing about not having any bread? Don't you know or

1185

Mark
..........:.

Luke
John
Acts
Romans
1 Corin.

understand yet? Are your minds so dull? [18] You have eyes — can't you see? You have ears — can't you hear? Don't you remember [19] when I broke the five loaves for the 5,000 people? How many baskets full of leftover pieces did you take up?"

"Twelve," they answered.

[20] "And when I broke the seven loaves for the 4,000 people," asked Jesus, "how many baskets full of leftover pieces did you take up?"

"Seven," they answered.

[21] "And you still don't understand?" he asked them.

Jesus Heals a Blind Man at Bethsaida

[22] They came to Bethsaida, where some people brought a blind man to Jesus and begged him to touch him. [23] Jesus took the blind man by the hand and led him out of the village. After spitting on the man's eyes, Jesus placed his hands on him and asked him, "Can you see anything?"

[24] The man looked up and said, "Yes, I can see people, but they look like trees walking about."

[25] Jesus again placed his hands on the man's eyes. This time the man looked intently, his eyesight returned, and he saw everything clearly. [26] Jesus then sent him home with the order, "Don't go back into the village."

Peter's Declaration about Jesus
(Mt 16.13–20; Lk 9.18–21)

[27] Then Jesus and his disciples went away to the villages near Caesarea Philippi. On the way he asked them, "Tell me, who do people say I am?"

[28] "Some say that you are John the Baptist," they answered; "others say that you are Elijah, while others say that you are one of the prophets."

[29] "What about you?" he asked them. "Who do you say I am?"

Peter answered, "You are the Messiah."

[30] Then Jesus ordered them, "Do not tell anyone about me."

Jesus Speaks about his Suffering and Death
(Mt 16.21–28; Lk 9.22–27)

[31] Then Jesus began to teach his disciples: "The Son of Man must suffer much and be rejected by the elders, the chief priests, and the teachers of the Law. He will be put to death, but three days later he will rise to life." [32] He made this very clear to them. So Peter took him aside and began to rebuke him. [33] But Jesus turned round, looked at his disciples, and rebuked Peter. "Get away from me, Satan," he said. "Your thoughts don't come from God but from human nature!"

[34] Then Jesus called the crowd and his disciples to him. "If anyone wants to come with me," he told them, "he must forget self, carry his cross, and follow me. [35] For whoever wants to save his own life will lose it; but whoever loses his life for me and for the gospel will save it. [36] Do people gain anything if they win the whole world but lose their life? Of course not! [37] There is nothing they can give to regain their life. [38] If a person is ashamed of me and of my teaching in this godless and wicked day, then the Son of Man will be ashamed of him when he comes in the glory of his Father with the holy angels."

9 And he went on to say, "I tell you, there are some here who will not die until they have seen the Kingdom of God come with power."

1186

Mark

⫶⫶⫶⫶⫶⫶⫶⫶

Zephan.
Haggai
Zechar.
Malachi
Matt.

MARK 9

The Transfiguration
(Mt 17.1–13; Lk 9.28–36)

2 Six days later Jesus took with him Peter, James, and John, and led them up a high mountain, where they were alone. As they looked on, a change came over Jesus, 3 and his clothes became shining white — whiter than anyone in the world could wash them. 4 Then the three disciples saw Elijah and Moses talking with Jesus. 5 Peter spoke up and said to Jesus, "Teacher, how good it is that we are here! We will make three tents, one for you, one for Moses, and one for Elijah." 6 He and the others were so frightened that he did not know what to say.

7 Then a cloud appeared and covered them with its shadow, and a voice came from the cloud, "This is my own dear Son — listen to him!" 8 They took a quick look round but did not see anyone else; only Jesus was with them.

9 As they came down the mountain, Jesus ordered them, "Don't tell anyone what you have seen, until the Son of Man has risen from death."

10 They obeyed his order, but among themselves they started discussing the matter, "What does this 'rising from death' mean?" 11 And they asked Jesus, "Why do the teachers of the Law say that Elijah has to come first?"

12 His answer was, "Elijah is indeed coming first in order to get everything ready. Yet why do the Scriptures say that the Son of Man will suffer much and be rejected? 13 I tell you, however, that Elijah has already come and that people treated him just as they pleased, as the Scriptures say about him."

Jesus Heals a Boy with an Evil Spirit
(Mt 17.14–20; Lk 9.37–43a)

14 When they joined the rest of the disciples, they saw a large crowd round them and some teachers of the Law arguing with them. 15 When the people saw Jesus, they were greatly surprised, and ran to him and greeted him. 16 Jesus asked his disciples, "What are you arguing with them about?"

17 A man in the crowd answered, "Teacher, I brought my son to you, because he has an evil spirit in him and cannot talk. 18 Whenever the spirit attacks him, it throws him to the ground, and he foams at the mouth, grits his teeth, and becomes stiff all over. I asked your disciples to drive the spirit out, but they could not."

19 Jesus said to them, "How unbelieving you people are! How long must I stay with you? How long do I have to put up with you? Bring the boy to me!" 20 They brought him to Jesus.

As soon as the spirit saw Jesus, it threw the boy into a fit, so that he fell on the ground and rolled round, foaming at the mouth. 21 "How long has he been like this?" Jesus asked the father.

"Ever since he was a child," he replied. 22 "Many times the evil spirit has tried to kill him by throwing him in the fire and into water. Have pity on us and help us, if you possibly can!"

23 "Yes," said Jesus, "if you yourself can! Everything is possible for the person who has faith."

24 The father at once cried out, "I do have faith, but not enough. Help me to have more!"

25 Jesus noticed that the crowd was closing in on them, so he gave a command to the evil spirit. "Deaf and dumb spirit," he said, "I order you to come out of the boy and never go into him again!"

26 The spirit screamed, threw the boy into a bad fit, and came out. The boy looked like a corpse, and everyone said, "He is

MARK 9

1187

Mark

Luke
John
Acts
Romans
1 Corin.

dead!" [27] But Jesus took the boy by the hand and helped him to rise, and he stood up.

[28] After Jesus had gone indoors, his disciples asked him privately, "Why couldn't we drive the spirit out?"

[29] "Only prayer can drive this kind out," answered Jesus; "nothing else can."

Jesus Speaks Again about his Death
(Mt 17.22–23; Lk 9.43b–45)

[30] Jesus and his disciples left that place and went on through Galilee. Jesus did not want anyone to know where he was, [31] because he was teaching his disciples: "The Son of Man will be handed over to those who will kill him. Three days later, however, he will rise to life."

[32] But they did not understand what this teaching meant, and they were afraid to ask him.

Who is the Greatest?
(Mt 18.1–5; Lk 9.46–48)

[33] They came to Capernaum, and after going indoors Jesus asked his disciples, "What were you arguing about on the road?"

[34] But they would not answer him, because on the road they had been arguing among themselves about who was the greatest. [35] Jesus sat down, called the twelve disciples, and said to them, "Whoever wants to be first must place himself last of all and be the servant of all." [36] Then he took a child and made him stand in front of them. He put his arms round him and said to them, [37] "Whoever welcomes in my name one of these children, welcomes me; and whoever welcomes me, welcomes not only me but also the one who sent me."

Whoever is not Against Us is For Us
(Lk 9.49–50)

[38] John said to him, "Teacher, we saw a man who was driving out demons in your name, and we told him to stop, because he doesn't belong to our group."

[39] "Do not try to stop him," Jesus told them, "because no one who performs a miracle in my name will be able soon afterwards to say evil things about me. [40] For whoever is not against us is for us. [41] I assure you that anyone who gives you a drink of water because you belong to me will certainly receive his reward.

Temptations to Sin
(Mt 18.6–9; Lk 17.1–2)

[42] "If anyone should cause one of these little ones to lose his faith in me, it would be better for that person to have a large millstone tied round his neck and be thrown into the sea. [43] So if your hand makes you lose your faith, cut it off! It is better for you to enter life without a hand than to keep both hands and go off to hell, to the fire that never goes out.* [45] And if your foot makes you lose your faith, cut it off! It is better for you to enter life without a foot than to keep both feet and be thrown into hell.* [47] And if your eye makes you lose your faith, take it out! It is better for you to enter the Kingdom of God with only one eye than to

READ THIS PASSAGE

AGAIN

BUT SLOWER,

taking time to soak
in what is going on.

....

9.43 Some manuscripts add verse 44: *There 'the worms that eat them never die, and the fire that burns them is never put out'* (see verse 48).
9.45 Some manuscripts add verse 46: *There 'the worms that eat them never die, and the fire that burns them is never put out'* (see verse 48).

keep both eyes and be thrown into hell. ⁴⁸There 'the worms that eat them never die, and the fire that burns them is never put out.'

⁴⁹"Everyone will be purified by fire as a sacrifice is purified by salt.

⁵⁰"Salt is good; but if it loses its saltiness, how can you make it salty again?

"Have the salt of friendship among yourselves, and live in peace with one another."

Jesus Teaches about Divorce
(Mt 19.1–12; Lk 16.18)

10 Then Jesus left that place, went to the province of Judea, and crossed the River Jordan. Crowds came flocking to him again, and he taught them, as he always did.

²Some Pharisees came to him and tried to trap him. "Tell us," they asked, "does our Law allow a man to divorce his wife?"

³Jesus answered with a question, "What law did Moses give you?"

⁴Their answer was, "Moses gave permission for a man to write a divorce notice and send his wife away."

⁵Jesus said to them, "Moses wrote this law for you because you are so hard to teach. ⁶But in the beginning, at the time of creation, 'God made them male and female,' as the scripture says. ⁷'And for this reason a man will leave his father and mother and unite with his wife,'* ⁸and the two will become one.' So they are no longer two, but one. ⁹No human being then must separate what God has joined together."

¹⁰When they went back into the house, the disciples asked Jesus about this matter. ¹¹He said to them, "A man who divorces his wife and marries another woman commits adultery against his wife. ¹²In the same way, a woman who divorces her husband and marries another man commits adultery."

Jesus Blesses Little Children
(Mt 19.13–15; Lk 18.15–17)

¹³Some people brought children to Jesus for him to place his hands on them, but the disciples scolded the people. ¹⁴When Jesus noticed this, he was angry and said to his disciples, "Let the children come to me, and do not stop them, because the Kingdom of God belongs to such as these. ¹⁵I assure you that whoever does not receive the Kingdom of God like a child will never enter it." ¹⁶Then he took the children in his arms, placed his hands on each of them, and blessed them.

The Rich Man
(Mt 19.16–30; Lk 18.18–30)

¹⁷As Jesus was starting on his way again, a man ran up, knelt before him, and asked him, "Good Teacher, what must I do to receive eternal life?"

¹⁸"Why do you call me good?" Jesus asked him. "No one is good except God alone. ¹⁹You know the commandments: 'Do not commit murder; do not commit adultery; do not steal; do not accuse anyone falsely; do not cheat; respect your father and your mother.'"

²⁰"Teacher," the man said, "ever since I was young, I have obeyed all these commandments."

²¹Jesus looked straight at him with love and said, "You need only one thing. Go and sell all you have and give the money to the

---

10.7 Some manuscripts do not have *and unite with his wife*.

MARK 10

1189

Mark

Luke
John
Acts
Romans
1 Corin.

poor, and you will have riches in heaven; then come and follow me." ²²When the man heard this, gloom spread over his face, and he went away sad, because he was very rich.

²³Jesus looked round at his disciples and said to them, "How hard it will be for rich people to enter the Kingdom of God!"

²⁴The disciples were shocked at these words, but Jesus went on to say, "My children, how hard it is to enter the Kingdom of God! ²⁵It is much harder for a rich person to enter the Kingdom of God than for a camel to go through the eye of a needle."

²⁶At this the disciples were completely amazed and asked one another, "Who, then, can be saved?"

²⁷Jesus looked straight at them and answered, "This is impossible for human beings, but not for God; everything is possible for God."

²⁸Then Peter spoke up, "Look, we have left everything and followed you."

²⁹"Yes," Jesus said to them, "and I tell you that anyone who leaves home or brothers or sisters or mother or father or children or fields for me and for the gospel, ³⁰will receive much more in this present age. He will receive a hundred times more houses, brothers, sisters, mothers, children and fields — and persecutions as well; and in the age to come he will receive eternal life. ³¹But many who now are first will be last, and many who now are last will be first."

Jesus Speaks a Third Time about his Death
(Mt 20.17–19; Lk 18.31–34)

³²Jesus and his disciples were now on the road going up to Jerusalem. Jesus was going ahead of the disciples, who were filled with alarm; the people who followed behind were afraid. Once again Jesus took the twelve disciples aside and spoke of the things that were going to happen to him. ³³"Listen," he told them, "we are going up to Jerusalem where the Son of Man will be handed over to the chief priests and the teachers of the Law. They will condemn him to death and then hand him over to the Gentiles, ³⁴who will mock him, spit on him, whip him, and kill him; but three days later he will rise to life."

The Request of James and John
(Mt 20.20–28)

³⁵Then James and John, the sons of Zebedee, came to Jesus. "Teacher," they said, "there is something we want you to do for us."

³⁶"What is it?" Jesus asked them.

³⁷They answered, "When you sit on your throne in your glorious Kingdom, we want you to let us sit with you, one at your right and one at your left."

³⁸Jesus said to them, "You don't know what you are asking for. Can you drink the cup of suffering that I must drink? Can you be baptized in the way I must be baptized?"

³⁹"We can," they answered.

Jesus said to them, "You will indeed drink the cup I must drink and be baptized in the way I must be baptized. ⁴⁰But I do not have the right to choose who will sit at my right and my left. It is God who will give these places to those for whom he has prepared them."

⁴¹When the other ten disciples heard about it, they became angry with James and John. ⁴²So Jesus called them all together to him and said, "You know that those who are considered rulers of the heathen have power over them, and the leaders have complete authority. ⁴³This, however, is not the way it is among

1190

Mark

Zephan.
Haggai
Zechar.
Malachi
Matt.

MARK 10, 11

MARK 10.45

He came to
SERVE
• and to •
{ GIVE }
HIS LIFE TO
REDEEM
many people

you. If one of you wants to be great, he must be the servant of the rest; [44] and if one of you wants to be first, he must be the slave of all. [45] For even the Son of Man did not come to be served; he came to serve and to give his life to redeem many people."

Jesus Heals Blind Bartimaeus
(Mt 20.29–34; Lk 18.35–43)

[46] They came to Jericho, and as Jesus was leaving with his disciples and a large crowd, a blind beggar named Bartimaeus son of Timaeus was sitting by the road. [47] When he heard that it was Jesus of Nazareth, he began to shout, "Jesus! Son of David! Take pity on me!"

[48] Many of the people scolded him and told him to be quiet. But he shouted even more loudly, "Son of David, take pity on me!"

[49] Jesus stopped and said, "Call him."

So they called the blind man. "Cheer up!" they said. "Get up, he is calling you."

[50] He threw off his cloak, jumped up, and came to Jesus.

[51] "What do you want me to do for you?" Jesus asked him.

"Teacher," the blind man answered, "I want to see again."

[52] "Go," Jesus told him, "your faith has made you well."

At once he was able to see and followed Jesus on the road.

The Triumphant Entry into Jerusalem
(Mt 21.1–11; Lk 19.28–40; Jn 12.12–19)

11 As they approached Jerusalem, near the towns of Bethphage and Bethany, they came to the Mount of Olives. Jesus sent two of his disciples on ahead [2] with these instructions: "Go to the village there ahead of you. As soon as you get there, you will find a colt tied up that has never been ridden. Untie it and bring it here. [3] And if someone asks you why you are doing that, tell him that the Master* needs it and will send it back at once."

[4] So they went and found a colt out in the street, tied to the door of a house. As they were untying it, [5] some of the bystanders asked them, "What are you doing, untying that colt?"

[6] They answered just as Jesus had told them, and the bystanders let them go. [7] They brought the colt to Jesus, threw their cloaks over the animal, and Jesus got on. [8] Many people spread their cloaks on the road, while others cut branches in the fields and spread them on the road. [9] The people who were in front and those who followed behind began to shout, "Praise God! God bless him who comes in the name of the Lord! [10] God bless the coming kingdom of King David, our father! Praise God!"

[11] Jesus entered Jerusalem, went into the Temple, and looked round at everything. But since it was already late in the day, he went out to Bethany with the twelve disciples.

Jesus Curses the Fig Tree
(Mt 21.18–19)

[12] The next day, as they were coming back from Bethany, Jesus was hungry. [13] He saw in the distance a fig tree covered with leaves, so he went to see if he could find any figs on it. But when he came to it, he found only leaves, because it was not the right time for figs. [14] Jesus said to the fig tree, "No one shall ever eat figs from you again!"

And his disciples heard him.

11.3 *the Master; or its owner.*

MARK 11, 12

1191

Mark
·········⁝·

Luke
John
Acts
Romans
1 Corin.

Jesus Goes to the Temple
(Mt 21.12–17; Lk 19.45–48; Jn 2.13–22)

¹⁵When they arrived in Jerusalem, Jesus went to the Temple and began to drive out all those who were buying and selling. He overturned the tables of the moneychangers and the stools of those who sold pigeons, ¹⁶and he would not let anyone carry anything through the temple courtyards. ¹⁷He then taught the people: "It is written in the Scriptures that God said, 'My Temple will be called a house of prayer for the people of all nations.' But you have turned it into a hideout for thieves!"

¹⁸The chief priests and the teachers of the Law heard of this, so they began looking for some way to kill Jesus. They were afraid of him, because the whole crowd was amazed at his teaching.

¹⁹When evening came, Jesus and his disciples left the city.

The Lesson from the Fig Tree
(Mt 21.20–22)

²⁰Early next morning, as they walked along the road, they saw the fig tree. It was dead all the way down to its roots. ²¹Peter remembered what had happened and said to Jesus, "Look, Teacher, the fig tree you cursed has died!"

²²Jesus answered them, "Have faith in God. ²³I assure you that whoever tells this hill to get up and throw itself in the sea and does not doubt in his heart, but believes that what he says will happen, it will be done for him. ²⁴For this reason I tell you: when you pray and ask for something, believe that you have received it, and you will be given whatever you ask for. ²⁵And when you stand and pray, forgive anything you may have against anyone, so that your Father in heaven will forgive the wrongs you have done."*

The Question about Jesus' Authority
(Mt 21.23–27; Lk 20.1–8)

²⁷They arrived once again in Jerusalem. As Jesus was walking in the Temple, the chief priests, the teachers of the Law, and the elders came to him ²⁸and asked him, "What right have you to do these things? Who gave you this right?"

²⁹Jesus answered them, "I will ask you just one question, and if you give me an answer, I will tell you what right I have to do these things. ³⁰Tell me, where did John's right to baptize come from: was it from God or from human beings?"

³¹They started to argue among themselves: "What shall we say? If we answer, 'From God,' he will say, 'Why, then, did you not believe John?' ³²But if we say, 'From human beings…'" (They were afraid of the people, because everyone was convinced that John had been a prophet.) ³³So their answer to Jesus was, "We don't know."

Jesus said to them, "Neither will I tell you, then, by what right I do these things."

The Parable of the Tenants in the Vineyard
(Mt 21.33–46; Lk 20.9–19)

12 Then Jesus spoke to them in parables: "Once there was a man who planted a vineyard, put a fence round it, dug a hole for the winepress, and built a watchtower. Then he let out the vineyard to tenants and left home on a journey. ²When the time came to gather the grapes, he sent a slave to the tenants to

11.25 Some manuscripts add verse 26: *If you do not forgive others, your Father in heaven will not forgive the wrongs you have done* (see Mt 6.15).

1192

Mark

.:........

Zephan.
Haggai
Zechar.
Malachi
Matt.

MARK 12

receive from them his share of the harvest. ³The tenants seized the slave, beat him, and sent him back without a thing. ⁴Then the owner sent another slave; the tenants beat him over the head and treated him shamefully. ⁵The owner sent another slave, and they killed him; and they treated many others the same way, beating some and killing others. ⁶The only one left to send was the man's own dear son. Last of all, then, he sent his son to the tenants. 'I am sure they will respect my son,' he said. ⁷But those tenants said to one another, 'This is the owner's son. Come on, let's kill him, and his property will be ours!' ⁸So they seized the son and killed him and threw his body out of the vineyard.

⁹"What, then, will the owner of the vineyard do?" asked Jesus. "He will come and kill those tenants and hand the vineyard over to others. ¹⁰Surely you have read this scripture:

'The stone which the builders rejected as worthless
    turned out to be the most important of all.
¹¹ This was done by the Lord;
    what a wonderful sight it is!'"

¹²The Jewish leaders tried to arrest Jesus, because they knew that he had told this parable against them. But they were afraid of the crowd, so they left him and went away.

The Question about Paying Taxes
(Mt 22.15–22; Lk 20.20–26)

¹³Some Pharisees and some members of Herod's party were sent to Jesus to trap him with questions. ¹⁴They came to him and said, "Teacher, we know that you tell the truth, without worrying about what people think. You pay no attention to anyone's status, but teach the truth about God's will for people. Tell us, is it against our Law to pay taxes to the Roman Emperor? Should we pay them or not?"

¹⁵But Jesus saw through their trick and answered, "Why are you trying to trap me? Bring a silver coin, and let me see it."

¹⁶They brought him one, and he asked, "Whose face and name are these?"

"The Emperor's," they answered.

¹⁷So Jesus said, "Well, then, pay the Emperor what belongs to the Emperor, and pay God what belongs to God."

And they were amazed at Jesus.

The Question about Rising from Death
(Mt 22.23–33; Lk 20.27–40)

¹⁸Then some Sadducees, who say that people will not rise from death, came to Jesus and said, ¹⁹"Teacher, Moses wrote this law for us: 'If a man dies and leaves a wife but no children, that man's brother must marry the widow so that they can have children who will be considered the dead man's children.' ²⁰Once there were seven brothers; the eldest got married and died without having children. ²¹Then the second one married the woman, and he also died without having children. The same thing happened to the third brother, ²²and then to the rest: all seven brothers married the woman and died without having children. Last of all, the woman died. ²³Now, when all the dead rise to life on the day of resurrection, whose wife will she be? All seven of them had married her."

²⁴Jesus answered them, "How wrong you are! And do you know why? It is because you don't know the Scriptures or God's power. ²⁵For when the dead rise to life, they will be like the angels in heaven and will not marry. ²⁶Now, as for the dead being raised:

MARK 12

1193

Mark

Luke
John
Acts
Romans
1 Corin.

haven't you ever read in the Book of Moses the passage about the burning bush? There it is written that God said to Moses, 'I am the God of Abraham, the God of Isaac, and the God of Jacob.' [27]He is the God of the living, not of the dead. You are completely wrong!"

The Great Commandment
(Mt 22.34–40; Lk 10.25–28)

[28]A teacher of the Law was there who heard the discussion. He saw that Jesus had given the Sadducees a good answer, so he came to him with a question: "Which commandment is the most important of all?"

[29]Jesus replied, "The most important one is this: 'Listen, Israel! The Lord our God is the only Lord.* [30]Love the Lord your God with all your heart, with all your soul, with all your mind, and with all your strength.' [31]The second most important commandment is this: 'Love your neighbour as you love yourself.' There is no other commandment more important than these two."

[32]The teacher of the Law said to Jesus, "Well done, Teacher! It is true, as you say, that only the Lord is God and that there is no other god but he. [33]And to love God with all your heart and with all your mind and with all your strength, and to love your neighbour as yourself, is more important than to offer animals and other sacrifices to God."

[34]Jesus noticed how wise his answer was, and so he told him, "You are not far from the Kingdom of God."

After this nobody dared to ask Jesus any more questions.

The Question about the Messiah
(Mt 22.41–46; Lk 20.41–44)

[35]As Jesus was teaching in the Temple, he asked the question, "How can the teachers of the Law say that the Messiah will be the descendant of David? [36]The Holy Spirit inspired David to say:

'The Lord said to my Lord:
    Sit here on my right
    until I put your enemies under your feet.'

[37]David himself called him 'Lord'; so how can the Messiah be David's descendant?"

Jesus Warns against the Teachers of the Law
(Mt 23.1–36; Lk 20.45–47)

A large crowd was listening to Jesus gladly. [38]As he taught them, he said, "Watch out for the teachers of the Law, who like to walk around in their long robes and be greeted with respect in the market place, [39]who choose the reserved seats in the synagogues and the best places at feasts. [40]They take advantage of widows and rob them of their homes, and then make a show of saying long prayers. Their punishment will be all the worse!"

The Widow's Offering
(Lk 21.1–4)

[41]As Jesus sat near the temple treasury, he watched the people as they dropped in their money. Many rich men dropped in a lot of money; [42]then a poor widow came along and dropped in two little copper coins, worth about a penny. [43]He called his disciples together and said to them, "I tell you that this poor widow put

....

12.29 *The Lord our God is the only Lord*; or *The Lord is our God, the Lord alone.*

MARK 12.30-31

How do you love God with everything you have? In the space on these pages, write words that
- SUM UP YOUR -

LIFE

and who you are. Write down your personality, things you're good at, your hobbies and all the different areas of your life, like school, home, pocket money - absolutely everything you can think of. Now, fill in the gaps with ideas about how you can love God with all of these things. Use lots of colour. If you run out of space, use sticky notes!

1194

Mark

⁚⋯⋯⋯

Zephan.
Haggai
Zechar.
Malachi
Matt.

MARK 12, 13

more in the offering box than all the others. [44] For the others put in what they had to spare of their riches; but she, poor as she is, put in all she had — she gave all she had to live on."

Jesus Speaks of the Destruction of the Temple
(Mt 24.1–2; Lk 21.5–6)

13 As Jesus was leaving the Temple, one of his disciples said, "Look, Teacher! What wonderful stones and buildings!"

[2] Jesus answered, "You see these great buildings? Not a single stone here will be left in its place; every one of them will be thrown down."

Troubles and Persecutions
(Mt 24.3–14; Lk 21.7–19)

[3] Jesus was sitting on the Mount of Olives, across from the Temple, when Peter, James, John, and Andrew came to him in private. [4] "Tell us when this will be," they said, "and tell us what will happen to show that the time has come for all these things to take place."

[5] Jesus said to them, "Be on guard, and don't let anyone deceive you. [6] Many men, claiming to speak for me, will come and say, 'I am he!' and they will deceive many people. [7] And don't be troubled when you hear the noise of battles close by and news of battles far away. Such things must happen, but they do not mean that the end has come. [8] Countries will fight each other; kingdoms will attack one another. There will be earthquakes everywhere, and there will be famines. These things are like the first pains of childbirth.

[9] "You yourselves must be on guard. You will be arrested and taken to court. You will be beaten in the synagogues; you will stand before rulers and kings for my sake to tell them the Good News. [10] But before the end comes, the gospel must be preached to all peoples. [11] And when you are arrested and taken to court, do not worry beforehand about what you are going to say; when the time comes, say whatever is then given to you. For the words you speak will not be yours; they will come from the Holy Spirit. [12] Men will hand over their own brothers to be put to death, and fathers will do the same to their children. Children will turn against their parents and have them put to death. [13] Everyone will hate you because of me. But whoever holds out to the end will be saved.

The Awful Horror
(Mt 24.15–28; Lk 21.20–24)

[14] "You will see 'The Awful Horror' standing in the place where he should not be." (Note to the reader: be sure to understand what this means!) "Then those who are in Judea must run away to the hills. [15] Someone who is on the roof of his house must not lose time by going down into the house to get anything to take with him. [16] Someone who is in the field must not go back to the house for his cloak. [17] How terrible it will be in those days for women who are pregnant and for mothers with little babies! [18] Pray to God that these things will not happen in the winter! [19] For the trouble of those days will be far worse than any the world has ever known from the very beginning when God created the world until the present time. Nor will there ever be anything like it again. [20] But the Lord has reduced the number of those days; if he had not, nobody would survive. For the sake of his chosen people, however, he has reduced those days.

[21] "Then, if anyone says to you, 'Look, here is the Messiah!' or, 'Look, there he is!' — do not believe him. [22] For false Messiahs and

MARK 13, 14

1195

Mark

Luke
John
Acts
Romans
1 Corin.

false prophets will appear. They will perform miracles and wonders in order to deceive even God's chosen people, if possible. [23] Be on your guard! I have told you everything before the time comes.

The Coming of the Son of Man
(Mt 24.29–31; Lk 21.25–28)

[24] "In the days after that time of trouble the sun will grow dark, the moon will no longer shine, [25] the stars will fall from heaven, and the powers in space will be driven from their courses. [26] Then the Son of Man will appear, coming in the clouds with great power and glory. [27] He will send the angels out to the four corners of the earth to gather God's chosen people from one end of the world to the other.

The Lesson of the Fig Tree
(Mt 24.32–35; Lk 21.29–33)

[28] "Let the fig tree teach you a lesson. When its branches become green and tender and it starts putting out leaves, you know that summer is near. [29] In the same way, when you see these things happening, you will know that the time is near, ready to begin.* [30] Remember that all these things will happen before the people now living have all died. [31] Heaven and earth will pass away, but my words will never pass away.

No one Knows the Day or Hour
(Mt 24.36–44)

[32] "No one knows, however, when that day or hour will come — neither the angels in heaven, nor the Son; only the Father knows. [33] Be on watch, be alert, for you do not know when the time will come. [34] It will be like a man who goes away from home on a journey and leaves his servants in charge, after giving to each one his own work to do and after telling the doorkeeper to keep watch. [35] Be on guard, then, because you do not know when the master of the house is coming — it might be in the evening or at midnight or before dawn or at sunrise. [36] If he comes suddenly, he must not find you asleep. [37] What I say to you, then, I say to all: watch!"

The Plot against Jesus
(Mt 26.1–5; Lk 22.1–2; Jn 11.45–53)

14 It was now two days before the Festival of Passover and Unleavened Bread. The chief priests and the teachers of the Law were looking for a way to arrest Jesus secretly and put him to death. [2] "We must not do it during the festival," they said, "or the people might riot."

Jesus is Anointed at Bethany
(Mt 26.6–13; Jn 12.1–8)

[3] Jesus was in Bethany at the house of Simon, a man who had suffered from a dreaded skin disease. While Jesus was eating, a woman came in with an alabaster jar full of a very expensive perfume made of pure nard. She broke the jar and poured the perfume on Jesus' head. [4] Some of the people there became angry and said to one another, "What was the use of wasting the perfume? [5] It could have been sold for more than 300 silver coins* and the money given to the poor!" And they criticized her harshly.

....

13.29 *the time is near, ready to begin;* or *he is near, ready to come.*
14.5 *silver coins:* See 6.37.

1196

Mark

Zephan.
Haggai
Zechar.
Malachi
Matt.

⁶But Jesus said, "Leave her alone! Why are you bothering her? She has done a fine and beautiful thing for me. ⁷You will always have poor people with you, and any time you want to, you can help them. But you will not always have me. ⁸She did what she could; she poured perfume on my body to prepare it ahead of time for burial. ⁹Now, I assure you that wherever the gospel is preached all over the world, what she has done will be told in memory of her."

Judas Agrees to Betray Jesus
(Mt 26.14–16; Lk 22.3–6)

¹⁰Then Judas Iscariot, one of the twelve disciples, went off to the chief priests in order to betray Jesus to them. ¹¹They were pleased to hear what he had to say, and promised to give him money. So Judas started looking for a good chance to hand Jesus over to them.

Jesus Eats the Passover Meal with his Disciples
(Mt 26.17–25; Lk 22.7–14, 21–23; Jn 13.21–30)

¹²On the first day of the Festival of Unleavened Bread, the day the lambs for the Passover meal were killed, Jesus' disciples asked him, "Where do you want us to go and get the Passover meal ready for you?"

¹³Then Jesus sent two of them with these instructions: "Go into the city, and a man carrying a jar of water will meet you. Follow him ¹⁴to the house he enters, and say to the owner of the house: 'The Teacher says, Where is the room where my disciples and I will eat the Passover meal?' ¹⁵Then he will show you a large upstairs room, prepared and furnished, where you will get everything ready for us."

¹⁶The disciples left, went to the city, and found everything just as Jesus had told them; and they prepared the Passover meal.

¹⁷When it was evening, Jesus came with the twelve disciples. ¹⁸While they were at the table eating, Jesus said, "I tell you that one of you will betray me — one who is eating with me."

¹⁹The disciples were upset and began to ask him, one after the other, "Surely you don't mean me, do you?"

²⁰Jesus answered, "It will be one of you twelve, one who dips his bread in the dish with me. ²¹The Son of Man will die as the Scriptures say he will; but how terrible for that man who betrays the Son of Man! It would have been better for that man if he had never been born!"

The Lord's Supper
(Mt 26.26–30; Lk 22.14–20; 1 Cor 11.23–25)

²²While they were eating, Jesus took a piece of bread, gave a prayer of thanks, broke it, and gave it to his disciples. "Take it," he said, "this is my body."

²³Then he took a cup, gave thanks to God, and handed it to them; and they all drank from it. ²⁴Jesus said, "This is my blood which is poured out for many, my blood which seals God's covenant. ²⁵I tell you, I will never again drink this wine until the day I drink the new wine in the Kingdom of God." ²⁶Then they sang a hymn and went out to the Mount of Olives.

Jesus Predicts Peter's Denial
(Mt 26.31–35; Lk 22.31–34; Jn 13.36–38)

²⁷Jesus said to them, "All of you will run away and leave me, for the scripture says, 'God will kill the shepherd, and the sheep will all be scattered.' ²⁸But after I am raised to life, I will go to Galilee ahead of you."

READ THIS PASSAGE, CLOSE THE BOOK & REFLECT ON WHAT HAPPENED IN THE PASSAGE.

MARK 14

1197

Mark

Luke
John
Acts
Romans
1 Corin.

²⁹Peter answered, "I will never leave you, even though all the rest do!"

³⁰Jesus said to Peter, "I tell you that before the cock crows twice tonight, you will say three times that you do not know me."

³¹Peter answered even more strongly, "I will never say that, even if I have to die with you!"

And all the other disciples said the same thing.

Jesus Prays in Gethsemane
(Mt 26.36–46; Lk 22.39–46)

³²They came to a place called Gethsemane, and Jesus said to his disciples, "Sit here while I pray." ³³He took Peter, James, and John with him. Distress and anguish came over him, ³⁴and he said to them, "The sorrow in my heart is so great that it almost crushes me. Stay here and keep watch."

³⁵He went a little farther on, threw himself on the ground, and prayed that, if possible, he might not have to go through that time of suffering. ³⁶"Father," he prayed, "my Father! All things are possible for you. Take this cup of suffering away from me. Yet not what I want, but what you want."

³⁷Then he returned and found the three disciples asleep. He said to Peter, "Simon, are you asleep? Weren't you able to stay awake even for one hour?" ³⁸And he said to them, "Keep watch, and pray that you will not fall into temptation. The spirit is willing, but the flesh is weak."

³⁹He went away once more and prayed, saying the same words. ⁴⁰Then he came back to the disciples and found them asleep; they could not keep their eyes open. And they did not know what to say to him.

⁴¹When he came back the third time, he said to them, "Are you still sleeping and resting? Enough! The hour has come! Look, the Son of Man is now being handed over to the power of sinners. ⁴²Get up, let us go. Look, here is the man who is betraying me!"

The Arrest of Jesus
(Mt 26.47–56; Lk 22.47–53; Jn 18.3–12)

⁴³Jesus was still speaking when Judas, one of the twelve disciples, arrived. With him was a crowd armed with swords and clubs, and sent by the chief priests, the teachers of the Law, and the elders. ⁴⁴The traitor had given the crowd a signal: "The man I kiss is the one you want. Arrest him and take him away under guard."

⁴⁵As soon as Judas arrived, he went up to Jesus and said, "Teacher!" and kissed him. ⁴⁶So they arrested Jesus and held him tight. ⁴⁷But one of those standing there drew his sword and struck at the High Priest's slave, cutting off his ear. ⁴⁸Then Jesus spoke up and said to them, "Did you have to come with swords and clubs to capture me, as though I were an outlaw? ⁴⁹Day after day I was with you teaching in the Temple, and you did not arrest me. But the Scriptures must come true."

⁵⁰Then all the disciples left him and ran away.

⁵¹A certain young man, dressed only in a linen cloth, was following Jesus. They tried to arrest him, ⁵²but he ran away naked, leaving the cloth behind.

Jesus before the Council
(Mt 26.57–68; Lk 22.54–55, 63–71; Jn 18.13–14, 19–24)

⁵³Then Jesus was taken to the High Priest's house, where all the chief priests, the elders, and the teachers of the Law were

1198

Mark

·⸬·········

Zephan.

Haggai

Zechar.

Malachi

Matt.

MARK 14, 15

gathering. ⁵⁴Peter followed from a distance and went into the courtyard of the High Priest's house. There he sat down with the guards, keeping himself warm by the fire. ⁵⁵The chief priests and the whole Council tried to find some evidence against Jesus in order to put him to death, but they could not find any. ⁵⁶Many witnesses told lies against Jesus, but their stories did not agree.

⁵⁷Then some men stood up and told this lie against Jesus: ⁵⁸"We heard him say, 'I will tear down this Temple which men have made, and after three days I will build one that is not made by men.'" ⁵⁹Not even they, however, could make their stories agree.

⁶⁰The High Priest stood up in front of them all and questioned Jesus, "Have you no answer to the accusation they bring against you?"

⁶¹But Jesus kept quiet and would not say a word. Again the High Priest questioned him, "Are you the Messiah, the Son of the Blessed God?"

⁶²"I am," answered Jesus, "and you will all see the Son of Man seated on the right of the Almighty and coming with the clouds of heaven!"

⁶³The High Priest tore his robes and said, "We don't need any more witnesses! ⁶⁴You heard his blasphemy. What is your decision?"

They all voted against him: he was guilty and should be put to death.

⁶⁵Some of them began to spit on Jesus, and they blindfolded him and hit him. "Guess who hit you!" they said. And the guards took him and slapped him.

Peter Denies Jesus
(Mt 26.69–75; Lk 22.56–62; Jn 18.15–18, 25–27)

⁶⁶Peter was still down in the courtyard when one of the High Priest's servant women came by. ⁶⁷When she saw Peter warming himself, she looked straight at him and said, "You, too, were with Jesus of Nazareth."

⁶⁸But he denied it. "I don't know… I don't understand what you are talking about," he answered, and went out into the passage. Just then a cock crowed.*

⁶⁹The servant woman saw him there and began to repeat to the bystanders, "He is one of them!" ⁷⁰But Peter denied it again.

A little while later the bystanders accused Peter again, "You can't deny that you are one of them, because you, too, are from Galilee."

⁷¹Then Peter said, "I swear that I am telling the truth! May God punish me if I am not! I do not know the man you are talking about!"

⁷²Just then a cock crowed a second time, and Peter remembered how Jesus had said to him, "Before the cock crows twice, you will say three times that you do not know me." And he broke down and cried.

Jesus is Brought before Pilate
(Mt 27.1–2, 11–14; Lk 23.1–5; Jn 18.28–38)

15 Early in the morning the chief priests met hurriedly with the elders, the teachers of the Law, and the whole Council, and made their plans. They put Jesus in chains, led him away, and handed him over to Pilate. ²Pilate questioned him, "Are you the king of the Jews?"

14.68 Some manuscripts do not have *Just then a cock crowed*.

MARK 14.66-72

Count how many times Peter denied Jesus. Now look up John 21.15-19. How many times does Jesus ask Peter the same question? That conversation took place after Jesus had come

• BACK TO •

LIFE.

It symbolises Jesus' offer of forgiveness for Peter's denial.

MARK 15

1199

Mark

...........::

Luke
John
Acts
Romans
1 Corin.

Jesus answered, "So you say."

³ The chief priests were accusing Jesus of many things, ⁴so Pilate questioned him again, "Aren't you going to answer? Listen to all their accusations!"

⁵ Again Jesus refused to say a word, and Pilate was amazed.

Jesus is Sentenced to Death
(Mt 27.15–26; Lk 23.13–25; Jn 18.39—19.16)

⁶ At every Passover Festival Pilate was in the habit of setting free any one prisoner the people asked for. ⁷At that time a man named Barabbas was in prison with the rebels who had committed murder in the riot. ⁸When the crowd gathered and began to ask Pilate for the usual favour, ⁹he asked them, "Do you want me to set free for you the king of the Jews?" ¹⁰He knew very well that the chief priests had handed Jesus over to him because they were jealous.

¹¹ But the chief priests stirred up the crowd to ask, instead, for Pilate to set Barabbas free for them. ¹²Pilate spoke again to the crowd, "What, then, do you want me to do with the one you call the king of the Jews?"

¹³ They shouted back, "Crucify him!"

¹⁴ "But what crime has he committed?" Pilate asked.

They shouted all the louder, "Crucify him!"

¹⁵ Pilate wanted to please the crowd, so he set Barabbas free for them. Then he had Jesus whipped and handed him over to be crucified.

The Soldiers Mock Jesus
(Mt 27.27–31; Jn 19.2–3)

¹⁶ The soldiers took Jesus inside to the courtyard of the governor's palace and called together the rest of the company. ¹⁷They put a purple robe on Jesus, made a crown out of thorny branches, and put it on his head. ¹⁸Then they began to salute him: "Long live the King of the Jews!" ¹⁹They beat him over the head with a stick, spat on him, fell on their knees, and bowed down to him. ²⁰When they had finished mocking him, they took off the purple robe and put his own clothes back on him. Then they led him out to crucify him.

Jesus is Crucified
(Mt 27.32–44; Lk 23.26–43; Jn 19.17–27)

²¹ On the way they met a man named Simon, who was coming into the city from the country, and the soldiers forced him to carry Jesus' cross. (Simon was from Cyrene and was the father of Alexander and Rufus.) ²²They took Jesus to a place called Golgotha, which means "The Place of the Skull". ²³There they tried to give him wine mixed with a drug called myrrh, but Jesus would not drink it. ²⁴Then they crucified him and divided his clothes among themselves, throwing dice to see who would get which piece of clothing. ²⁵It was nine o'clock in the morning when they crucified him. ²⁶The notice of the accusation against him said: "The King of the Jews". ²⁷They also crucified two bandits with Jesus, one on his right and the other on his left.*

²⁹ People passing by shook their heads and hurled insults at Jesus: "Aha! You were going to tear down the Temple and build it up again in three days! ³⁰Now come down from the cross and save yourself!"

....

15.27 Some manuscripts add verse 28: *In this way the scripture came true which says, "He shared the fate of criminals"* (see Lk 22.37).

1200

Mark

∴········

Zephan.
Haggai
Zechar.
Malachi
Matt.

MARK 15, 16

[31] In the same way the chief priests and the teachers of the Law jeered at Jesus, saying to each other, "He saved others, but he cannot save himself! [32] Let us see the Messiah, the king of Israel, come down from the cross now, and we will believe in him!"

And the two who were crucified with Jesus insulted him also.

The Death of Jesus
(Mt 27.45–56; Lk 23.44–49; Jn 19.28–30)

[33] At noon the whole country was covered with darkness, which lasted for three hours. [34] At three o'clock Jesus cried out with a loud shout, *"Eloi, Eloi, lema sabachthani?"* which means, "My God, my God, why did you abandon me?"

[35] Some of the people there heard him and said, "Listen, he is calling for Elijah!" [36] One of them ran up with a sponge, soaked it in cheap wine, and put it on the end of a stick. Then he held it up to Jesus' lips and said, "Wait! Let us see if Elijah is coming to bring him down from the cross!"

[37] With a loud cry Jesus died.

[38] The curtain hanging in the Temple was torn in two, from top to bottom. [39] The army officer who was standing there in front of the cross saw how Jesus had died.* "This man was really the Son of God!" he said.

[40] Some women were there, looking on from a distance. Among them were Mary Magdalene, Mary the mother of the younger James and of Joseph, and Salome. [41] They had followed Jesus while he was in Galilee and had helped him. Many other women who had come to Jerusalem with him were there also.

The Burial of Jesus
(Mt 27.57–61; Lk 23.50–56; Jn 19.38–42)

[42-43] It was towards evening when Joseph of Arimathea arrived. He was a respected member of the Council, who was waiting for the coming of the Kingdom of God. It was Preparation day (that is, the day before the Sabbath), so Joseph went boldly into the presence of Pilate and asked him for the body of Jesus. [44] Pilate was surprised to hear that Jesus was already dead. He called the army officer and asked him if Jesus had been dead a long time. [45] After hearing the officer's report, Pilate told Joseph he could have the body. [46] Joseph bought a linen sheet, took the body down, wrapped it in the sheet, and placed it in a tomb which had been dug out of solid rock. Then he rolled a large stone across the entrance to the tomb. [47] Mary Magdalene and Mary the mother of Joseph were watching and saw where the body of Jesus was placed.

The Resurrection
(Mt 28.1–8; Lk 24.1–12; Jn 20.1–10)

16 After the Sabbath was over, Mary Magdalene, Mary the mother of James, and Salome bought spices to go and anoint the body of Jesus. [2] Very early on Sunday morning, at sunrise, they went to the tomb. [3-4] On the way they said to one another, "Who will roll away the stone for us from the entrance to the tomb?" (It was a very large stone.) Then they looked up and saw that the stone had already been rolled back. [5] So they entered the tomb, where they saw a young man sitting on the right, wearing a white robe — and they were alarmed.

[6] "Don't be alarmed," he said. "I know you are looking for Jesus of Nazareth, who was crucified. He is not here — he has been

---

15.39 *had died*; some manuscripts have *had cried out and died.*

Mark

..........:.

Luke
John
Acts
Romans
1 Corin.

raised! Look, here is the place where they put him. [7]Now go and give this message to his disciples, including Peter: 'He is going to Galilee ahead of you; there you will see him, just as he told you.' "

[8]So they went out and ran from the tomb, distressed and terrified. They said nothing to anyone, because they were afraid.

An Old Ending to the Gospel*
16.9–20

Jesus Appears to Mary Magdalene
(Mt 28.9–10; Jn 20.11–18)

[[9]After Jesus rose from death early on Sunday, he appeared first to Mary Magdalene, from whom he had driven out seven demons. [10]She went and told his companions. They were mourning and crying; [11]and when they heard her say that Jesus was alive and that she had seen him, they did not believe her.

Jesus Appears to Two Disciples
(Lk 24.13–35)

[12]After this, Jesus appeared in a different manner to two of them while they were on their way to the country. [13]They returned and told the others, but they would not believe it.

Jesus Appears to the Eleven
(Mt 28.16–20; Lk 24.36–49; Jn 20.19–23; Acts 1.6–8)

[14]Last of all, Jesus appeared to the eleven disciples as they were eating. He scolded them, because they did not have faith and because they were too stubborn to believe those who had seen him alive. [15]He said to them, "Go throughout the whole world and preach the gospel to the whole human race. [16]Whoever believes and is baptized will be saved; whoever does not believe will be condemned. [17]Believers will be given the power to perform miracles: they will drive out demons in my name; they will speak in strange tongues; [18]if they pick up snakes or drink any poison, they will not be harmed; they will place their hands on sick people, who will get well."

Jesus is Taken Up to Heaven
(Lk 24.50–53; Acts 1.9–11)

[19]After the Lord Jesus had talked with them, he was taken up to heaven and sat at the right side of God. [20]The disciples went and preached everywhere, and the Lord worked with them and proved that their preaching was true by the miracles that were performed.]

Another Old Ending*
16.9–10

[[9]The women went to Peter and his friends and gave them a brief account of all they had been told. [10]After this, Jesus himself sent out through his disciples from the east to the west the sacred and ever-living message of eternal salvation.]

16.9–20 heading Some manuscripts and ancient translations do not have this ending to the Gospel (verses 9–20).

16.9–10 heading Some manuscripts and ancient translations have this shorter ending to the Gospel in addition to the longer ending (verses 9–20).

THE GOSPEL OF
LUKE

WRITTEN: AROUND AD85

WHAT YOU NEED TO KNOW:

Luke, a doctor and friend of Paul, wrote this book about the life of Jesus. Luke set out to make a properly researched case for the claims of Jesus. He was writing specifically for Greek Gentiles (non-Jews), so he focuses on non-Jews in the stories he includes. He fills his pages with accounts of Jesus' interactions with other people, particularly those who weren't very well thought of at the time, including women, lepers and thieves. Luke's account shows that Jesus was on the side of the outcasts, the oppressed, the broken and the poor. The good news that Jesus came to bring is for every single person.

WHY READ IT?

From famous stories like the good Samaritan and the lost son to intriguing accounts of miracles and healings, Luke is full of really great stuff. This Gospel also shows that the hope and freedom that Jesus brings isn't just for a select few, or for those who've got it sorted, but for everyone.

GRAB A COLOURED PEN

or pencil and go through Luke, highlighting all the different people who Jesus interacts with.

Either

LIST OR
DOODLE

below all the different kinds of people you can think of.
Then, as you look through what you've done, reflect on the fact that Jesus died so that each one of those people could have a chance to know him.

(6BC)
JESUS' BIRTH

HEALING AND TEACHING

DEATH

RESURRECTI
(AD27)

LUKE 1

1203

Luke
....
John
Acts
Romans
1 Corin.
2 Corin.

1 Dear Theophilus:

Many people have done their best to write a report of the things that have taken place among us. [2] They wrote what we have been told by those who saw these things from the beginning and who proclaimed the message. [3] And so, your Excellency, because I have carefully studied all these matters from their beginning, I thought it would be good to write an orderly account for you. [4] I do this so that you will know the full truth about everything which you have been taught.

The Birth of John the Baptist is Announced

[5] During the time when Herod was king of Judea,* there was a priest named Zechariah, who belonged to the priestly order of Abijah. His wife's name was Elizabeth; she also belonged to a priestly family. [6] They both lived good lives in God's sight and obeyed fully all the Lord's laws and commands. [7] They had no children because Elizabeth could not have any, and she and Zechariah were both very old.

[8] One day Zechariah was doing his work as a priest in the Temple, taking his turn in the daily service. [9] According to the custom followed by the priests, he was chosen by lot to burn incense on the altar. So he went into the Temple of the Lord, [10] while the crowd of people outside prayed during the hour when the incense was burnt.

[11] An angel of the Lord appeared to him, standing on the right of the altar where the incense was burnt. [12] When Zechariah saw him, he was alarmed and felt afraid. [13] But the angel said to him, "Don't be afraid, Zechariah! God has heard your prayer, and your wife Elizabeth will bear you a son. You are to name him John. [14] How glad and happy you will be, and how happy many others will be when he is born! [15] He will be a great man in the Lord's sight. He must not drink any wine or strong drink. From his very birth he will be filled with the Holy Spirit, [16] and he will bring back many of the people of Israel to the Lord their God. [17] He will go ahead of the Lord, strong and mighty like the prophet Elijah. He will bring fathers and children together again; he will turn disobedient people back to the way of thinking of the righteous; he will get the Lord's people ready for him."

[18] Zechariah said to the angel, "How shall I know if this is so? I am an old man, and my wife is old also."

[19] "I am Gabriel," the angel answered. "I stand in the presence of God, who sent me to speak to you and tell you this good news. [20] But you have not believed my message, which will come true at the right time. Because you have not believed, you will be unable to speak; you will remain silent until the day my promise to you comes true."

[21] In the meantime the people were waiting for Zechariah and wondering why he was spending such a long time in the Temple. [22] When he came out, he could not speak to them, and so they knew that he had seen a vision in the Temple. Unable to say a word, he made signs to them with his hands.

[23] When his period of service in the Temple was over, Zechariah went back home. [24] Some time later his wife Elizabeth became pregnant and did not leave the house for five months. [25] "Now at last the Lord has helped me," she said. "He has taken away my public disgrace!"

1.5 *Judea*: The term here refers to the whole land of Palestine.

1204

Luke

Haggai
Zechar.
Malachi
Matt.
Mark

LUKE 1

STOP RIGHT NOW.

Think of something you're thankful for.

The Birth of Jesus is Announced

26 In the sixth month of Elizabeth's pregnancy God sent the angel Gabriel to a town in Galilee named Nazareth. 27 He had a message for a young woman promised in marriage to a man named Joseph, who was a descendant of King David. Her name was Mary. 28 The angel came to her and said, "Peace be with you! The Lord is with you and has greatly blessed you!"

29 Mary was deeply troubled by the angel's message, and she wondered what his words meant. 30 The angel said to her, "Don't be afraid, Mary; God has been gracious to you. 31 You will become pregnant and give birth to a son, and you will name him Jesus. 32 He will be great and will be called the Son of the Most High God. The Lord God will make him a king, as his ancestor David was, 33 and he will be the king of the descendants of Jacob for ever; his kingdom will never end!"

34 Mary said to the angel, "I am a virgin. How, then, can this be?"

35 The angel answered, "The Holy Spirit will come on you, and God's power will rest upon you. For this reason the holy child will be called the Son of God. 36 Remember your relative Elizabeth. It is said that she cannot have children, but she herself is now six months pregnant, even though she is very old. 37 For there is nothing that God cannot do."

38 "I am the Lord's servant," said Mary; "may it happen to me as you have said." And the angel left her.

Mary Visits Elizabeth

39 Soon afterwards Mary got ready and hurried off to a town in the hill country of Judea. 40 She went into Zechariah's house and greeted Elizabeth. 41 When Elizabeth heard Mary's greeting, the baby moved within her. Elizabeth was filled with the Holy Spirit 42 and said in a loud voice, "You are the most blessed of all women, and blessed is the child you will bear! 43 Why should this great thing happen to me, that my Lord's mother comes to visit me? 44 For as soon as I heard your greeting, the baby within me jumped with gladness. 45 How happy you are to believe that the Lord's message to you will come true!"

Mary's Song of Praise

46 Mary said,
"My heart praises the Lord;
47 my soul is glad because of God my Saviour,
48 for he has remembered me, his lowly servant!
From now on all people will call me happy,
49 because of the great things the Mighty God has done for me.
His name is holy;
50 from one generation to another
he shows mercy to those who honour him.
51 He has stretched out his mighty arm
and scattered the proud with all their plans.
52 He has brought down mighty kings from their thrones,
and lifted up the lowly.
53 He has filled the hungry with good things,
and sent the rich away with empty hands.
54 He has kept the promise he made to our ancestors,
and has come to the help of his servant Israel.
55 He has remembered to show mercy to Abraham
and to all his descendants for ever!"

56 Mary stayed about three months with Elizabeth and then went back home.

LUKE 1, 2

1205

Luke
....

John
Acts
Romans
1 Corin.
2 Corin.

The Birth of John the Baptist

57 The time came for Elizabeth to have her baby, and she gave birth to a son. 58 Her neighbours and relatives heard how wonderfully good the Lord had been to her, and they all rejoiced with her.

59 When the baby was a week old, they came to circumcise him, and they were going to name him Zechariah, after his father. 60 But his mother said, "No! His name is to be John."

61 They said to her, "But you have no relatives with that name!" 62 Then they made signs to his father, asking him what name he would like the boy to have.

63 Zechariah asked for a writing tablet and wrote, "His name is John." How surprised they all were! 64 At that moment Zechariah was able to speak again, and he started praising God. 65 The neighbours were all filled with fear, and the news about these things spread through all the hill country of Judea. 66 Everyone who heard of it thought about it and asked, "What is this child going to be?" For it was plain that the Lord's power was upon him.

Zechariah's Prophecy

67 John's father Zechariah was filled with the Holy Spirit, and he spoke God's message:

68 "Let us praise the Lord, the God of Israel!
He has come to the help of his people and has set them free.
69 He has provided for us a mighty Saviour,
a descendant of his servant David.
70 He promised through his holy prophets long ago
71 that he would save us from our enemies,
from the power of all those who hate us.
72 He said he would show mercy to our ancestors
and remember his sacred covenant.
73-74 With a solemn oath to our ancestor Abraham
he promised to rescue us from our enemies
and allow us to serve him without fear,
75 so that we might be holy and righteous before him
all the days of our life.

76 "You, my child, will be called a prophet of the Most High God.
You will go ahead of the Lord
to prepare his road for him,
77 to tell his people that they will be saved
by having their sins forgiven.
78 Our God is merciful and tender.
He will cause the bright dawn of salvation to rise on us
79 and to shine from heaven on all those who live in the
dark shadow of death,
to guide our steps into the path of peace."

80 The child grew and developed in body and spirit. He lived in the desert until the day when he appeared publicly to the people of Israel.

The Birth of Jesus
(Mt 1.18–25)

2 At that time the Emperor Augustus ordered a census to be taken throughout the Roman Empire. 2 When this first census took place, Quirinius was the governor of Syria. 3 Everyone, then, went to register himself, each to his own town.

WHAT DOES 'SALVATION' MEAN?
Finish the mindmap below.

Deliverance
from sin and
its consequences,
believed by
Christians to be
brought about
by faith in Christ.
(oxforddictionaries.com)

SALVATION

PSALM 70.4; LUKE 1.78

1206

Luke

. : . . . .

Haggai
Zechar.
Malachi
Matt.
Mark

LUKE 2

The chances are that you've heard about the nativity plenty of times before, but there is so much more to this part of the story about the shepherds.

WATCH A SHORT

FILM

ABOUT THIS AT
gnbyouthedition.co.uk/nativity

[4] Joseph went from the town of Nazareth in Galilee to the town of Bethlehem in Judea, the birthplace of King David. Joseph went there because he was a descendant of David. [5] He went to register with Mary, who was promised in marriage to him. She was pregnant, [6] and while they were in Bethlehem, the time came for her to have her baby. [7] She gave birth to her first son, wrapped him in strips of cloth and laid him in a manger — there was no room for them to stay in the inn.

The Shepherds and the Angels

[8] There were some shepherds in that part of the country who were spending the night in the fields, taking care of their flocks. [9] An angel of the Lord appeared to them, and the glory of the Lord shone over them. They were terribly afraid, [10] but the angel said to them, "Don't be afraid! I am here with good news for you, which will bring great joy to all the people. [11] This very day in David's town your Saviour was born — Christ the Lord! [12] And this is what will prove it to you: you will find a baby wrapped in strips of cloth and lying in a manger."

[13] Suddenly a great army of heaven's angels appeared with the angel, singing praises to God:

[14] "Glory to God in the highest heaven,
     and peace on earth to those with whom he is pleased!"

[15] When the angels went away from them back into heaven, the shepherds said to one another, "Let's go to Bethlehem and see this thing that has happened, which the Lord has told us."

[16] So they hurried off and found Mary and Joseph and saw the baby lying in the manger. [17] When the shepherds saw him, they told them what the angel had said about the child. [18] All who heard it were amazed at what the shepherds said. [19] Mary remembered all these things and thought deeply about them. [20] The shepherds went back, singing praises to God for all they had heard and seen; it had been just as the angel had told them.

Jesus is Named

[21] A week later, when the time came for the baby to be circumcised, he was named Jesus, the name which the angel had given him before he had been conceived.

Jesus is Presented in the Temple

[22] The time came for Joseph and Mary to perform the ceremony of purification, as the Law of Moses commanded. So they took the child to Jerusalem to present him to the Lord, [23] as it is written in the law of the Lord: "Every firstborn male is to be dedicated to the Lord." [24] They also went to offer a sacrifice of a pair of doves or two young pigeons, as required by the law of the Lord.

[25] At that time there was a man named Simeon living in Jerusalem. He was a good, God-fearing man and was waiting for Israel to be saved. The Holy Spirit was with him [26] and had assured him that he would not die before he had seen the Lord's promised Messiah. [27] Led by the Spirit, Simeon went into the Temple. When the parents brought the child Jesus into the Temple to do for him what the Law required, [28] Simeon took the child in his arms and gave thanks to God:

[29] "Now, Lord, you have kept your promise,
     and you may let your servant go in peace.
[30] With my own eyes I have seen your salvation,
[31]   which you have prepared in the presence of all
         peoples:

Luke
..........:.

John
Acts
Romans
1 Corin.
2 Corin.

[32] A light to reveal your will to the Gentiles
      and bring glory to your people Israel."

[33] The child's father and mother were amazed at the things Simeon said about him. [34] Simeon blessed them and said to Mary, his mother, "This child is chosen by God for the destruction and the salvation of many in Israel. He will be a sign from God which many people will speak against [35] and so reveal their secret thoughts. And sorrow, like a sharp sword, will break your own heart."

[36-37] There was a very old prophet, a widow named Anna, daughter of Phanuel of the tribe of Asher. She had been married for only seven years and was now 84 years old.* She never left the Temple; day and night she worshipped God, fasting and praying. [38] That very same hour she arrived and gave thanks to God and spoke about the child to all who were waiting for God to set Jerusalem free.

The Return to Nazareth

[39] When Joseph and Mary had finished doing all that was required by the law of the Lord, they returned to their home town of Nazareth in Galilee. [40] The child grew and became strong; he was full of wisdom, and God's blessings were upon him.

The Boy Jesus in the Temple

[41] Every year the parents of Jesus went to Jerusalem for the Passover Festival. [42] When Jesus was twelve years old, they went to the festival as usual. [43] When the festival was over, they started back home, but the boy Jesus stayed in Jerusalem. His parents did not know this; [44] they thought that he was with the group, so they travelled a whole day and then started looking for him among their relatives and friends. [45] They did not find him, so they went back to Jerusalem looking for him. [46] On the third day they found him in the Temple, sitting with the Jewish teachers, listening to them and asking questions. [47] All who heard him were amazed at his intelligent answers. [48] His parents were astonished when they saw him, and his mother said to him, "My son, why have you done this to us? Your father and I have been terribly worried trying to find you."

[49] He answered them, "Why did you have to look for me? Didn't you know that I had to be in my Father's house?" [50] But they did not understand his answer.

[51] So Jesus went back with them to Nazareth, where he was obedient to them. His mother treasured all these things in her heart. [52] Jesus grew both in body and in wisdom, gaining favour with God and people.

The Preaching of John the Baptist
(Mt 3.1–12; Mk 1.1–8; Jn 1.19–28)

3 It was the fifteenth year of the rule of the Emperor Tiberius; Pontius Pilate was governor of Judea, Herod was ruler of Galilee, and his brother Philip was ruler of the territory of Iturea and Trachonitis; Lysanias was ruler of Abilene, [2] and Annas and Caiaphas were high priests. At that time the word of God came to John son of Zechariah in the desert. [3] So John went throughout the whole territory of the River Jordan, preaching, "Turn away from your sins and be baptized, and God will forgive your sins."

[4] As it is written in the book of the prophet Isaiah:
      "Someone is shouting in the desert:

....

2.36–37 was now 84 years old; or had been a widow 84 years.

1208

Luke

·:·········

Haggai
Zechar.
Malachi
Matt.
Mark

'Get the road ready for the Lord;
    make a straight path for him to travel!
5 Every valley must be filled up,
    every hill and mountain levelled off.
The winding roads must be made straight,
    and the rough paths made smooth.
6 The whole human race will see God's salvation!'"

7 Crowds of people came out to John to be baptized by him. "You snakes!" he said to them. "Who told you that you could escape from the punishment God is about to send? 8 Do those things that will show that you have turned from your sins. And don't start saying among yourselves that Abraham is your ancestor. I tell you that God can take these stones and make descendants of Abraham! 9 The axe is ready to cut down the trees at the roots; every tree that does not bear good fruit will be cut down and thrown in the fire."

10 The people asked him, "What are we to do, then?"

11 He answered, "Whoever has two shirts must give one to the man who has none, and whoever has food must share it."

12 Some tax collectors came to be baptized, and they asked him, "Teacher, what are we to do?"

13 "Don't collect more than is legal," he told them.

14 Some soldiers also asked him, "What about us? What are we to do?"

He said to them, "Don't take money from anyone by force or accuse anyone falsely. Be content with your pay."

15 People's hopes began to rise, and they began to wonder whether John perhaps might be the Messiah. 16 So John said to all of them, "I baptize you with water, but someone is coming who is much greater than I am. I am not good enough even to untie his sandals. He will baptize you with the Holy Spirit and fire. 17 He has his winnowing shovel with him, to thresh out all the grain and gather the wheat into his barn; but he will burn the chaff in a fire that never goes out."

18 In many different ways John preached the Good News to the people and urged them to change their ways. 19 But John reprimanded Herod, the governor, because he had married Herodias, his brother's wife, and had done many other evil things. 20 Then Herod did an even worse thing by putting John in prison.

The Baptism of Jesus
(Mt 3.13–17; Mk 1.9–11)

21 After all the people had been baptized, Jesus also was baptized. While he was praying, heaven was opened, 22 and the Holy Spirit came down upon him in bodily form like a dove. And a voice came from heaven, "You are my own dear Son. I am pleased with you."

The Ancestors of Jesus
(Mt 1.1–17)

23 When Jesus began his work, he was about thirty years old. He was the son, so people thought, of Joseph, who was the son of Heli, 24 the son of Matthat, the son of Levi, the son of Melchi, the son of Jannai, the son of Joseph, 25 the son of Mattathias, the son of Amos, the son of Nahum, the son of Esli, the son of Naggai, 26 the son of Maath, the son of Mattathias, the son of Semein, the son of Josech, the son of Joda, 27 the son of Joanan, the son of Rhesa, the son of Zerubbabel, the son of Shealtiel, the son of Neri, 28 the son of Melchi, the son of Addi, the son of

LUKE 3.11

John the Baptist isn't being mysterious here. What do you have that

YOU COULD GIVE

AWAY

or share with others?

Find something you have lots of, and see if you can share it.

LUKE 3, 4

1209

Luke

John
Acts
Romans
1 Corin.
2 Corin.

Cosam, the son of Elmadam, the son of Er, [29]the son of Joshua, the son of Eliezer, the son of Jorim, the son of Matthat, the son of Levi, [30]the son of Simeon, the son of Judah, the son of Joseph, the son of Jonam, the son of Eliakim, [31]the son of Melea, the son of Menna, the son of Mattatha, the son of Nathan, the son of David, [32]the son of Jesse, the son of Obed, the son of Boaz, the son of Salmon, the son of Nahshon, [33]the son of Amminadab, the son of Admin, the son of Arni, the son of Hezron, the son of Perez, the son of Judah, [34]the son of Jacob, the son of Isaac, the son of Abraham, the son of Terah, the son of Nahor, [35]the son of Serug, the son of Reu, the son of Peleg, the son of Eber, the son of Shelah, [36]the son of Cainan, the son of Arphaxad, the son of Shem, the son of Noah, the son of Lamech, [37]the son of Methuselah, the son of Enoch, the son of Jared, the son of Mahalaleel, the son of Kenan, [38]the son of Enosh, the son of Seth, the son of Adam, the son of God.

The Temptation of Jesus
(Mt 4.1–11; Mk 1.12–13)

4 Jesus returned from the Jordan full of the Holy Spirit and was led by the Spirit into the desert, [2]where he was tempted by the Devil for forty days. In all that time he ate nothing, so that he was hungry when it was over.

[3]The Devil said to him, "If you are God's Son, order this stone to turn into bread."

[4]But Jesus answered, "The scripture says, 'Human beings cannot live on bread alone.'"

[5]Then the Devil took him up and showed him in a second all the kingdoms of the world. [6]"I will give you all this power and all this wealth," the Devil told him. "It has all been handed over to me, and I can give it to anyone I choose. [7]All this will be yours, then, if you worship me."

[8]Jesus answered, "The scripture says, 'Worship the Lord your God and serve only him!'"

[9]Then the Devil took him to Jerusalem and set him on the highest point of the Temple, and said to him, "If you are God's Son, throw yourself down from here. [10]For the scripture says, 'God will order his angels to take good care of you.' [11]It also says, 'They will hold you up with their hands so that not even your feet will be hurt on the stones.'"

[12]But Jesus answered, "The scripture says, 'Do not put the Lord your God to the test.'"

[13]When the Devil finished tempting Jesus in every way, he left him for a while.

Jesus Begins his Work in Galilee
(Mt 4.12–17; Mk 1.14–15)

[14]Then Jesus returned to Galilee, and the power of the Holy Spirit was with him. The news about him spread throughout all that territory. [15]He taught in the synagogues and was praised by everyone.

Jesus is Rejected at Nazareth
(Mt 13.53–58; Mk 6.1–6)

[16]Then Jesus went to Nazareth, where he had been brought up, and on the Sabbath he went as usual to the synagogue. He stood up to read the Scriptures [17]and was handed the book of the prophet Isaiah. He unrolled the scroll and found the place where it is written:

1210

Luke

·:········

Haggai
Zechar.
Malachi
Matt.
Mark

LUKE 4.18

HE HAS CHOSEN me to bring GOOD NEWS TO THE POOR. He has sent me to PROCLAIM LIBERTY - to the captives - AND RECOVERY OF SIGHT TO THE BLIND; to set free the OPPRESSED

18 "The Spirit of the Lord is upon me,
    because he has chosen me to bring good news to the poor.
He has sent me to proclaim liberty to the captives
    and recovery of sight to the blind;
to set free the oppressed
19   and announce that the time has come
    when the Lord will save his people."

20 Jesus rolled up the scroll, gave it back to the attendant, and sat down. All the people in the synagogue had their eyes fixed on him, 21 as he said to them, "This passage of scripture has come true today, as you heard it being read."

22 They were all well impressed with him and marvelled at the eloquent words that he spoke. They said, "Isn't he the son of Joseph?"

23 He said to them, "I am sure that you will quote this proverb to me, 'Doctor, heal yourself.' You will also tell me to do here in my home town the same things you heard were done in Capernaum. 24 I tell you this," Jesus added, "prophets are never welcomed in their home town.

25 "Listen to me: it is true that there were many widows in Israel during the time of Elijah, when there was no rain for 3.5 years and a severe famine spread throughout the whole land. 26 Yet Elijah was not sent to anyone in Israel, but only to a widow living in Zarephath in the territory of Sidon. 27 And there were many people suffering from a dreaded skin disease who lived in Israel during the time of the prophet Elisha; yet not one of them was healed, but only Naaman the Syrian."

28 When the people in the synagogue heard this, they were filled with anger. 29 They rose up, dragged Jesus out of the town, and took him to the top of the hill on which their town was built. They meant to throw him over the cliff, 30 but he walked through the middle of the crowd and went his way.

A Man with an Evil Spirit
(Mk 1.21–28)

31 Then Jesus went to Capernaum, a town in Galilee, where he taught the people on the Sabbath. 32 They were all amazed at the way he taught, because he spoke with authority. 33 In the synagogue was a man who had the spirit of an evil demon in him; he screamed out in a loud voice, 34 "Ah! What do you want with us, Jesus of Nazareth? Are you here to destroy us? I know who you are: you are God's holy messenger!"

35 Jesus ordered the spirit, "Be quiet and come out of the man!" The demon threw the man down in front of them and went out of him without doing him any harm.

36 The people were all amazed and said to one another, "What kind of words are these? With authority and power this man gives orders to the evil spirits, and they come out!" 37 And the report about Jesus spread everywhere in that region.

Jesus Heals Many People
(Mt 8.14–17; Mk 1.29–34)

38 Jesus left the synagogue and went to Simon's house. Simon's mother-in-law was sick with a high fever, and they spoke to Jesus about her. 39 He went and stood at her bedside and ordered the fever to leave her. The fever left her, and she got up at once and began to wait on them.

40 After sunset all who had friends who were sick with various diseases brought them to Jesus; he placed his hands on every

LUKE 4, 5

1211

Luke

John
Acts
Romans
1 Corin.
2 Corin.

one of them and healed them all. [41]Demons also went out from many people, screaming, "You are the Son of God!"

Jesus gave the demons an order and would not let them speak, because they knew that he was the Messiah.

Jesus Preaches in the Synagogues
(Mk 1.35–39)

[42]At daybreak Jesus left the town and went off to a lonely place. The people started looking for him, and when they found him, they tried to keep him from leaving. [43]But he said to them, "I must preach the Good News about the Kingdom of God in other towns also, because that is what God sent me to do."

[44]So he preached in the synagogues throughout the country.

Jesus Calls the First Disciples
(Mt 4.18–22; Mk 1.16–20)

5 One day Jesus was standing on the shore of Lake Gennesaret while the people pushed their way up to him to listen to the word of God. [2]He saw two boats pulled up on the beach; the fishermen had left them and were washing the nets. [3]Jesus got into one of the boats — it belonged to Simon — and asked him to push off a little from the shore. Jesus sat in the boat and taught the crowd.

[4]When he finished speaking, he said to Simon, "Push the boat out further to the deep water, and you and your partners let down your nets for a catch."

[5]"Master," Simon answered, "we worked hard all night long and caught nothing. But if you say so, I will let down the nets." [6]They let them down and caught such a large number of fish that the nets were about to break. [7]So they motioned to their partners in the other boat to come and help them. They came and filled both boats so full of fish that the boats were about to sink. [8]When Simon Peter saw what had happened, he fell on his knees before Jesus and said, "Go away from me, Lord! I am a sinful man!"

[9]He and the others with him were all amazed at the large number of fish they had caught. [10]The same was true of Simon's partners, James and John, the sons of Zebedee. Jesus said to Simon, "Don't be afraid; from now on you will be catching people."

[11]They pulled the boats up on the beach, left everything, and followed Jesus.

Jesus Heals a Man
(Mt 8.1–4; Mk 1.40–45)

[12]Once Jesus was in a town where there was a man who was suffering from a dreaded skin disease. When he saw Jesus, he threw himself down and begged him, "Sir, if you want to, you can make me clean!"*

[13]Jesus stretched out his hand and touched him. "I do want to," he answered. "Be clean!" At once the disease left the man. [14]Jesus ordered him, "Don't tell anyone, but go straight to the priest and let him examine you; then to prove to everyone that you are cured, offer the sacrifice as Moses ordered."

[15]But the news about Jesus spread all the more widely, and crowds of people came to hear him and be healed from their diseases. [16]But he would go away to lonely places, where he prayed.

5.12 *make me clean*: This disease was considered to make a person ritually unclean.

1212

Luke

·:·········

Haggai
Zechar.
Malachi
Matt.
Mark

LUKE 5

Jesus Heals a Paralysed Man
(Mt 9.1–8; Mk 2.1–12)

¹⁷One day when Jesus was teaching, some Pharisees and teachers of the Law were sitting there who had come from every town in Galilee and Judea and from Jerusalem. The power of the Lord was present for Jesus to heal the sick. ¹⁸Some men came carrying a paralysed man on a bed, and they tried to take him into the house and put him in front of Jesus. ¹⁹Because of the crowd, however, they could find no way to take him in. So they carried him up on the roof, made an opening in the tiles, and let him down on his bed into the middle of the group in front of Jesus. ²⁰When Jesus saw how much faith they had, he said to the man, "Your sins are forgiven, my friend."

²¹The teachers of the Law and the Pharisees began to say to themselves, "Who is this man who speaks such blasphemy! God is the only one who can forgive sins!"

²²Jesus knew their thoughts and said to them, "Why do you think such things? ²³Is it easier to say, 'Your sins are forgiven you,' or to say, 'Get up and walk'? ²⁴I will prove to you, then, that the Son of Man has authority on earth to forgive sins." So he said to the paralysed man, "I tell you, get up, pick up your bed, and go home!"

²⁵At once the man got up in front of them all, took the bed he had been lying on, and went home, praising God. ²⁶They were all completely amazed! Full of fear, they praised God, saying, "What marvellous things we have seen today!"

Jesus Calls Levi
(Mt 9.9–13; Mk 2.13–17)

²⁷After this, Jesus went out and saw a tax collector named Levi, sitting in his office. Jesus said to him, "Follow me." ²⁸Levi got up, left everything, and followed him.

²⁹Then Levi had a big feast in his house for Jesus, and among the guests was a large number of tax collectors and other people. ³⁰Some Pharisees and some teachers of the Law who belonged to their group complained to Jesus' disciples. "Why do you eat and drink with tax collectors and other outcasts?" they asked.

³¹Jesus answered them, "People who are well do not need a doctor, but only those who are sick. ³²I have not come to call respectable people to repent, but outcasts."

The Question about Fasting
(Mt 9.14–17; Mk 2.18–22)

³³Some people said to Jesus, "The disciples of John fast frequently and offer prayers, and the disciples of the Pharisees do the same; but your disciples eat and drink."

³⁴Jesus answered, "Do you think you can make the guests at a wedding party go without food as long as the bridegroom is with them? Of course not! ³⁵But the day will come when the bridegroom will be taken away from them, and then they will fast."

³⁶Jesus also told them this parable: "No one tears a piece off a new coat to patch up an old coat. If he does, he will have torn the new coat, and the piece of new cloth will not match the old. ³⁷Nor does anyone pour new wine into used wineskins, because the new wine will burst the skins, the wine will pour out, and the skins will be ruined. ³⁸Instead, new wine must be poured into fresh wineskins! ³⁹And no one wants new wine after drinking old wine. 'The old is better,' he says."

The Question about the Sabbath
(Mt 12.1–8; Mk 2.23–28)

6 Jesus was walking through some cornfields on the Sabbath. His disciples began to pick the ears of corn, rub them in their hands, and eat the grain. [2] Some Pharisees asked, "Why are you doing what our Law says you cannot do on the Sabbath?"

[3] Jesus answered them, "Haven't you read what David did when he and his men were hungry? [4] He went into the house of God, took the bread offered to God, ate it, and gave it also to his men. Yet it is against our Law for anyone except the priests to eat that bread."

[5] And Jesus concluded, "The Son of Man is Lord of the Sabbath."

The Man with a Paralysed Hand
(Mt 12.9–14; Mk 3.1–6)

[6] On another Sabbath Jesus went into a synagogue and taught. A man was there whose right hand was paralysed. [7] Some teachers of the Law and some Pharisees wanted a reason to accuse Jesus of doing wrong, so they watched him closely to see if he would heal on the Sabbath. [8] But Jesus knew their thoughts and said to the man, "Stand up and come here to the front." The man got up and stood there. [9] Then Jesus said to them, "I ask you: what does our Law allow us to do on the Sabbath? To help or to harm? To save someone's life or destroy it?" [10] He looked around at them all; then he said* to the man, "Stretch out your hand." He did so, and his hand became well again.

[11] They were filled with rage and began to discuss among themselves what they could do to Jesus.

Jesus Chooses the Twelve Apostles
(Mt 10.1–4; Mk 3.13–19)

[12] At that time Jesus went up a hill to pray and spent the whole night there praying to God. [13] When day came, he called his disciples to him and chose twelve of them, whom he named apostles: [14] Simon (whom he named Peter) and his brother Andrew; James and John, Philip and Bartholomew, [15] Matthew and Thomas, James son of Alphaeus, and Simon (who was called the Patriot), [16] Judas son of James, and Judas Iscariot, who became the traitor.

Jesus Teaches and Heals
(Mt 4.23–25)

[17] When Jesus had come down from the hill with the apostles, he stood on a level place with a large number of his disciples. A large crowd of people was there from all over Judea and from Jerusalem and from the coastal cities of Tyre and Sidon; [18] they had come to hear him and to be healed of their diseases. Those who were troubled by evil spirits also came and were healed. [19] All the people tried to touch him, for power was going out from him and healing them all.

Happiness and Sorrow
(Mt 5.1–12)

[20] Jesus looked at his disciples and said,
    "Happy are you poor;
        the Kingdom of God is yours!
[21] Happy are you who are hungry now;
        you will be filled!

6.10 *said*; some manuscripts have *said angrily*.

APOSTLE

LUKE 6.13;
ACTS 15.6

DEFINITION: An important early Christian teacher or pioneering missionary (oxforddictionaries.com)

The group of early Christians who travelled to different places telling people about Jesus Christ. (dictionary.cambridge.org)

Luke

John
Acts
Romans
1 Corin.
2 Corin.

1214

Luke

·:·········

Haggai
Zechar.
Malachi
Matt.
Mark

LUKE 6

LUKE 6.35

Think of someone you find hard to get along with. Spend some time praying for them, then plan to

DO SOMETHING

KIND

for them this week. In the space below, make a note of what you did.

_____

_____

_____

_____

_____

_____

_____

_____

_____

_____

_____

_____

_____

_____

_____

_____

_____

_____

Happy are you who weep now;
    you will laugh!
22 "Happy are you when people hate you, reject you, insult you, and say that you are evil, all because of the Son of Man! 23 Be glad when that happens, and dance for joy, because a great reward is kept for you in heaven. For their ancestors did the very same things to the prophets.
24 "But how terrible for you who are rich now;
    you have had your easy life!
25 How terrible for you who are full now;
    you will go hungry!
How terrible for you who laugh now;
    you will mourn and weep!
26 "How terrible when all people speak well of you; their ancestors said the very same things about the false prophets.

Love for Enemies
(Mt 5.38–48; 7.12a)

27 "But I tell you who hear me: love your enemies, do good to those who hate you, 28 bless those who curse you, and pray for those who ill-treat you. 29 If anyone hits you on one cheek, let him hit the other one too; if someone takes your coat, let him have your shirt as well. 30 Give to everyone who asks you for something, and when someone takes what is yours, do not ask for it back. 31 Do for others just what you want them to do for you.
32 "If you love only the people who love you, why should you receive a blessing? Even sinners love those who love them! 33 And if you do good only to those who do good to you, why should you receive a blessing? Even sinners do that! 34 And if you lend only to those from whom you hope to get it back, why should you receive a blessing? Even sinners lend to sinners, to get back the same amount! 35 No! Love your enemies and do good to them; lend and expect nothing back. You will then have a great reward, and you will be children of the Most High God. For he is good to the ungrateful and the wicked. 36 Be merciful just as your Father is merciful.

Judging Others
(Mt 7.1–5)

37 "Do not judge others, and God will not judge you; do not condemn others, and God will not condemn you; forgive others, and God will forgive you. 38 Give to others, and God will give to you. Indeed, you will receive a full measure, a generous helping, poured into your hands — all that you can hold. The measure you use for others is the one that God will use for you."
39 And Jesus told them this parable: "One blind man cannot lead another one; if he does, both will fall into a ditch. 40 No pupil is greater than his teacher; but every pupil, when he has completed his training, will be like his teacher.
41 "Why do you look at the speck in your brother's eye, but pay no attention to the log in your own eye? 42 How can you say to your brother, 'Please, brother, let me take that speck out of your eye,' yet cannot even see the log in your own eye? You hypocrite! First take the log out of your own eye, and then you will be able to see clearly to take the speck out of your brother's eye.

A Tree and its Fruit
(Mt 7.16–20; 12.33–35)

43 "A healthy tree does not bear bad fruit, nor does a poor tree bear good fruit. 44 Every tree is known by the fruit it bears; you do

LUKE 6, 7

1215

Luke
....
John
Acts
Romans
1 Corin.
2 Corin.

not pick figs from thorn bushes or gather grapes from bramble bushes. ⁴⁵A good person brings good out of the treasure of good things in his heart; a bad person brings bad out of his treasure of bad things. For the mouth speaks what the heart is full of.

The Two House Builders
(Mt 7.24–27)

⁴⁶"Why do you call me, 'Lord, Lord,' and yet don't do what I tell you? ⁴⁷Anyone who comes to me and listens to my words and obeys them — I will show you what he is like. ⁴⁸He is like a man who, in building his house, dug deep and laid the foundation on rock. The river overflowed and hit that house but could not shake it, because it was well built. ⁴⁹But anyone who hears my words and does not obey them is like a man who built his house without laying a foundation; when the flood hit that house it fell at once — and what a terrible crash that was!"

Jesus Heals a Roman Officer's Servant
(Mt 8.5–13)

7 When Jesus had finished saying all these things to the people, he went to Capernaum. ²A Roman officer there had a servant who was very dear to him; the man was sick and about to die. ³When the officer heard about Jesus, he sent some Jewish elders to ask him to come and heal his servant. ⁴They came to Jesus and begged him earnestly, "This man really deserves your help. ⁵He loves our people and he himself built a synagogue for us."

⁶So Jesus went with them. He was not far from the house when the officer sent friends to tell him, "Sir, don't trouble yourself. I do not deserve to have you come into my house, ⁷neither do I consider myself worthy to come to you in person. Just give the order, and my servant will get well. ⁸I, too, am a man placed under the authority of superior officers, and I have soldiers under me. I order this one, 'Go!' and he goes; I order that one, 'Come!' and he comes; and I order my slave, 'Do this!' and he does it."

⁹Jesus was surprised when he heard this; he turned round and said to the crowd following him, "I tell you, I have never found faith like this, not even in Israel!"

¹⁰The messengers went back to the officer's house and found his servant well.

Jesus Raises a Widow's Son

¹¹Soon afterwards* Jesus went to a town called Nain, accompanied by his disciples and a large crowd. ¹²Just as he arrived at the gate of the town, a funeral procession was coming out. The dead man was the only son of a woman who was a widow, and a large crowd from the town was with her. ¹³When the Lord saw her, his heart was filled with pity for her, and he said to her, "Don't cry." ¹⁴Then he walked over and touched the coffin, and the men carrying it stopped. Jesus said, "Young man! Get up, I tell you!" ¹⁵The dead man sat up and began to talk, and Jesus gave him back to his mother.

¹⁶They all were filled with fear and praised God. "A great prophet has appeared among us!" they said; "God has come to save his people!"

¹⁷This news about Jesus went out through all the country and the surrounding territory.

....

7.11 *Soon afterwards*; some manuscripts have *The next day*.

1216

Luke

·:·········

Haggai
Zechar.
Malachi
Matt.
Mark

LUKE 7

The Messengers from John the Baptist
(Mt 11.2–19)

¹⁸When John's disciples told him about all these things, he called two of them ¹⁹and sent them to the Lord to ask him, "Are you the one John said was going to come, or should we expect someone else?"

²⁰When they came to Jesus, they said, "John the Baptist sent us to ask if you are the one he said was going to come, or if we should expect someone else."

²¹At that very time Jesus cured many people of their sicknesses, diseases, and evil spirits, and gave sight to many blind people. ²²He answered John's messengers, "Go back and tell John what you have seen and heard: the blind can see, the lame can walk, those who suffer from dreaded skin diseases are made clean,* the deaf can hear, the dead are raised to life, and the Good News is preached to the poor. ²³How happy are those who have no doubts about me!"

²⁴After John's messengers had left, Jesus began to speak about him to the crowds: "When you went out to John in the desert, what did you expect to see? A blade of grass bending in the wind? ²⁵What did you go out to see? A man dressed up in fancy clothes? People who dress like that and live in luxury are found in palaces! ²⁶Tell me, what did you go out to see? A prophet? Yes indeed, but you saw much more than a prophet. ²⁷For John is the one of whom the scripture says: 'God said, I will send my messenger ahead of you to open the way for you.' ²⁸I tell you," Jesus added, "John is greater than anyone who has ever lived. But the one who is least in the Kingdom of God is greater than John."

²⁹All the people heard him; they and especially the tax collectors were the ones who had obeyed God's righteous demands and had been baptized by John. ³⁰But the Pharisees and the teachers of the Law rejected God's purpose for themselves and refused to be baptized by John.

³¹Jesus continued, "Now to what can I compare the people of this day? What are they like? ³²They are like children sitting in the market place. One group shouts to the other, 'We played wedding music for you, but you wouldn't dance! We sang funeral songs, but you wouldn't cry!' ³³John the Baptist came, and he fasted and drank no wine, and you said, 'He has a demon in him!' ³⁴The Son of Man came, and he ate and drank, and you said, 'Look at this man! He is a glutton and a drinker, a friend of tax collectors and other outcasts!' ³⁵God's wisdom, however, is shown to be true by all who accept it."

Jesus at the Home of Simon the Pharisee

³⁶A Pharisee invited Jesus to have dinner with him, and Jesus went to his house and sat down to eat. ³⁷In that town was a woman who lived a sinful life. She heard that Jesus was eating in the Pharisee's house, so she brought an alabaster jar full of perfume ³⁸and stood behind Jesus, by his feet, crying and wetting his feet with her tears. Then she dried his feet with her hair, kissed them, and poured the perfume on them. ³⁹When the Pharisee saw this, he said to himself, "If this man really were a prophet, he would know who this woman is who is touching him; he would know what kind of sinful life she lives!"

⁴⁰Jesus spoke up and said to him, "Simon, I have something to tell you."

....

7.22 *made clean*: See 5.12.

Luke

John
Acts
Romans
1 Corin.
2 Corin.

"Yes, Teacher," he said, "tell me."

[41] "There were two men who owed money to a moneylender," Jesus began. "One owed him 500 silver coins, and the other owed him fifty. [42] Neither of them could pay him back, so he cancelled the debts of both. Which one, then, will love him more?"

[43] "I suppose," answered Simon, "that it would be the one who was forgiven more."

"You are right," said Jesus. [44] Then he turned to the woman and said to Simon, "Do you see this woman? I came into your home, and you gave me no water for my feet, but she has washed my feet with her tears and dried them with her hair. [45] You did not welcome me with a kiss, but she has not stopped kissing my feet since I came. [46] You provided no olive oil for my head, but she has covered my feet with perfume. [47] I tell you, then, the great love she has shown proves that her many sins have been forgiven. But whoever has been forgiven little shows only a little love."

[48] Then Jesus said to the woman, "Your sins are forgiven."

[49] The others sitting at the table began to say to themselves, "Who is this, who even forgives sins?"

[50] But Jesus said to the woman, "Your faith has saved you; go in peace."

Women who Accompanied Jesus

8 Some time later Jesus travelled through towns and villages, preaching the Good News about the Kingdom of God. The twelve disciples went with him, [2] and so did some women who had been healed of evil spirits and diseases: Mary (who was called Magdalene), from whom seven demons had been driven out; [3] Joanna, whose husband Chuza was an officer in Herod's court; and Susanna, and many other women who used their own resources to help Jesus and his disciples.

The Parable of the Sower
(Mt 13.1–9; Mk 4.1–9)

[4] People kept coming to Jesus from one town after another; and when a great crowd gathered, Jesus told this parable:

[5] "Once there was a man who went out to sow corn. As he scattered the seed in the field, some of it fell along the path, where it was stepped on, and the birds ate it up. [6] Some of it fell on rocky ground, and when the plants sprouted, they dried up because the soil had no moisture. [7] Some of the seed fell among thorn bushes, which grew up with the plants and choked them. [8] And some seeds fell in good soil; the plants grew and produced corn, a hundred each."

And Jesus concluded, "Listen, then, if you have ears!"

The Purpose of the Parables
(Mt 13.10–17; Mk 4.10–12)

[9] His disciples asked Jesus what this parable meant, [10] and he answered, "The knowledge of the secrets of the Kingdom of God has been given to you, but to the rest it comes by means of parables, so that they may look but not see, and listen but not understand.

Jesus Explains the Parable of the Sower
(Mt 13.18–23; Mk 4.13–20)

[11] "This is what the parable means: the seed is the word of God. [12] The seeds that fell along the path stand for those who hear; but the Devil comes and takes the message away from their

INVITE SOMEONE
— TO WRITE —
SOMETHING
NICE
ABOUT YOU HERE.

1218

Luke

·:········

Haggai
Zechar.
Malachi
Matt.
Mark

LUKE 8

hearts in order to keep them from believing and being saved. 13 The seeds that fell on rocky ground stand for those who hear the message and receive it gladly. But it does not sink deep into them; they believe only for a while but when the time of testing comes, they fall away. 14 The seeds that fell among thorn bushes stand for those who hear; but the worries and riches and pleasures of this life crowd in and choke them, and their fruit never ripens. 15 The seeds that fell in good soil stand for those who hear the message and retain it in a good and obedient heart, and they persist until they bear fruit.

A Lamp under a Bowl
(Mk 4.21–25)

16 "People do not light a lamp and cover it with a bowl or put it under a bed. Instead, they put it on the lampstand, so that people will see the light as they come in.

17 "Whatever is hidden away will be brought out into the open, and whatever is covered up will be found and brought to light.

18 "Be careful, then, how you listen; because those who have something will be given more, but those who have nothing will have taken away from them even the little they think they have."

Jesus' Mother and Brothers
(Mt 12.46–50; Mk 3.31–35)

19 Jesus' mother and brothers came to him, but were unable to join him because of the crowd. 20 Someone said to Jesus, "Your mother and brothers are standing outside and want to see you."

21 Jesus said to them all, "My mother and brothers are those who hear the word of God and obey it."

Jesus Calms a Storm
(Mt 8.23–27; Mk 4.35–41)

22 One day Jesus got into a boat with his disciples and said to them, "Let us go across to the other side of the lake." So they started out. 23 As they were sailing, Jesus fell asleep. Suddenly a strong wind blew down on the lake, and the boat began to fill with water, so that they were all in great danger. 24 The disciples went to Jesus and woke him up, saying, "Master, Master! We are about to die!"

Jesus got up and gave an order to the wind and the stormy water; they died down, and there was a great calm. 25 Then he said to the disciples, "Where is your faith?"

But they were amazed and afraid, and said to one another, "Who is this man? He gives orders to the winds and waves, and they obey him!"

Jesus Heals a Man with Demons
(Mt 8.28–34; Mk 5.1–20)

26 Jesus and his disciples sailed on over to the territory of Gerasa,* which is across the lake from Galilee. 27 As Jesus stepped ashore, he was met by a man from the town who had demons in him. For a long time this man had gone without clothes and would not stay at home, but spent his time in the burial caves. 28 When he saw Jesus, he gave a loud cry, threw himself down at his feet, and shouted, "Jesus, Son of the Most High God! What do you want with me? I beg you, don't punish me!" 29 He said this

8.26 Gerasa; some manuscripts have Gadara (see Mt 8.28); others have Gergesa.

Luke

..........::

John

Acts

Romans

1 Corin.

2 Corin.

because Jesus had ordered the evil spirit to go out of him. Many times it had seized him, and even though he was kept a prisoner, his hands and feet fastened with chains, he would break the chains and be driven by the demon out into the desert.

³⁰ Jesus asked him, "What is your name?"

"My name is 'Mob'," he answered — because many demons had gone into him. ³¹ The demons begged Jesus not to send them into the abyss.*

³² There was a large herd of pigs near by, feeding on a hillside. So the demons begged Jesus to let them go into the pigs, and he let them. ³³ They went out of the man and into the pigs. The whole herd rushed down the side of the cliff into the lake and was drowned.

³⁴ The men who had been taking care of the pigs saw what happened, so they ran off and spread the news in the town and among the farms. ³⁵ People went out to see what had happened, and when they came to Jesus, they found the man from whom the demons had gone out sitting at the feet of Jesus, clothed and in his right mind; and they were all afraid. ³⁶ Those who had seen it told the people how the man had been cured. ³⁷ Then all the people from that territory asked Jesus to go away, because they were terribly afraid. So Jesus got into the boat and left. ³⁸ The man from whom the demons had gone out begged Jesus, "Let me go with you."

But Jesus sent him away, saying, ³⁹ "Go back home and tell what God has done for you."

The man went through the town, telling what Jesus had done for him.

Jairus' Daughter and the Woman who Touched Jesus' Cloak
(Mt 9.18–26; Mk 5.21–43)

⁴⁰ When Jesus returned to the other side of the lake, the people welcomed him, because they had all been waiting for him. ⁴¹ Then a man named Jairus arrived; he was an official in the local synagogue. He threw himself down at Jesus' feet and begged him to go to his home, ⁴² because his only daughter, who was twelve years old, was dying.

As Jesus went along, the people were crowding him from every side. ⁴³ Among them was a woman who had suffered from severe bleeding for twelve years; she had spent all she had on doctors,* but no one had been able to cure her. ⁴⁴ She came up in the crowd behind Jesus and touched the edge of his cloak, and her bleeding stopped at once. ⁴⁵ Jesus asked, "Who touched me?"

Everyone denied it, and Peter said, "Master, the people are all round you and crowding in on you."

⁴⁶ But Jesus said, "Someone touched me, for I knew it when power went out of me." ⁴⁷ The woman saw that she had been found out, so she came trembling and threw herself at Jesus' feet. There in front of everybody, she told him why she had touched him and how she had been healed at once. ⁴⁸ Jesus said to her, "My daughter, your faith has made you well. Go in peace."

⁴⁹ While Jesus was saying this, a messenger came from the official's house. "Your daughter has died," he told Jairus; "don't bother the Teacher any longer."

⁵⁰ But Jesus heard it and said to Jairus, "Don't be afraid; only believe, and she will be well."

....

8.31 *abyss*: It was thought that the demons were to be imprisoned in the depths of the earth until their final punishment.
8.43 Some manuscripts do not have *she had spent all she had on doctors*.

1220

Luke

∴ ·······

Haggai
Zechar.
Malachi
Matt.
Mark

LUKE 8, 9

⁵¹When he arrived at the house, he would not let anyone go in with him except Peter, John, and James, and the child's father and mother. ⁵²Everyone there was crying and mourning for the child. Jesus said, "Don't cry; the child is not dead — she is only sleeping!"

⁵³They all laughed at him, because they knew that she was dead. ⁵⁴But Jesus took her by the hand and called out, "Get up, my child!" ⁵⁵Her life returned, and she got up at once, and Jesus ordered them to give her something to eat. ⁵⁶Her parents were astounded, but Jesus commanded them not to tell anyone what had happened.

Jesus Sends Out the Twelve Disciples
(Mt 10.5–15; Mk 6.7–13)

9 Jesus called the twelve disciples together and gave them power and authority to drive out all demons and to cure diseases. ²Then he sent them out to preach the Kingdom of God and to heal the sick, ³after saying to them, "Take nothing with you for the journey: no stick, no beggar's bag, no food, no money, not even an extra shirt. ⁴Wherever you are welcomed, stay in the same house until you leave that town; ⁵wherever people don't welcome you, leave that town and shake the dust off your feet as a warning to them."

⁶The disciples left and travelled through all the villages, preaching the Good News and healing people everywhere.

Herod's Confusion
(Mt 14.1–12; Mk 6.14–29)

⁷When Herod, the ruler of Galilee, heard about all the things that were happening, he was very confused, because some people were saying that John the Baptist had come back to life. ⁸Others were saying that Elijah had appeared, and still others that one of the prophets of long ago had come back to life. ⁹Herod said, "I had John's head cut off; but who is this man I hear these things about?" And he kept trying to see Jesus.

Jesus Feeds a Great Crowd
(Mt 14.13–21; Mk 6.30–44; Jn 6.1–14)

¹⁰The apostles came back and told Jesus everything they had done. He took them with him, and they went off by themselves to a town called Bethsaida. ¹¹When the crowds heard about it, they followed him. He welcomed them, spoke to them about the Kingdom of God, and healed those who needed it.

¹²When the sun was beginning to set, the twelve disciples came to him and said, "Send the people away so that they can go to the villages and farms round here and find food and lodging, because this is a lonely place."

¹³But Jesus said to them, "You yourselves give them something to eat."

They answered, "All we have are five loaves and two fish. Do you want us to go and buy food for this whole crowd?" ¹⁴(There were about 5,000 men there.)

Jesus said to his disciples, "Make the people sit down in groups of about fifty each."

¹⁵After the disciples had done so, ¹⁶Jesus took the five loaves and two fish, looked up to heaven, thanked God for them, broke them, and gave them to the disciples to distribute to the people. ¹⁷They all ate and had enough, and the disciples took up twelve baskets of what was left over.

Luke

....

John

Acts

Romans

1 Corin.

2 Corin.

Peter's Declaration about Jesus
(Mt 16.13–19; Mk 8.27–29)

18 One day when Jesus was praying alone, the disciples came to him. "Who do the crowds say I am?" he asked them.

19 "Some say that you are John the Baptist," they answered. "Others say that you are Elijah, while others say that one of the prophets of long ago has come back to life."

20 "What about you?" he asked them. "Who do you say I am?"

Peter answered, "You are God's Messiah."

Jesus Speaks about his Suffering and Death
(Mt 16.20–28; Mk 8.30—9.1)

21 Then Jesus gave them strict orders not to tell this to anyone. 22 He also said to them, "The Son of Man must suffer much and be rejected by the elders, the chief priests, and the teachers of the Law. He will be put to death, but three days later he will be raised to life."

23 And he said to them all, "Anyone who wants to come with me must forget self, take up their cross every day, and follow me. 24 For whoever wants to save their own life will lose it, but whoever loses their life for my sake will save it. 25 Will people gain anything if they win the whole world but are themselves lost or defeated? Of course not! 26 If people are ashamed of me and of my teaching, then the Son of Man will be ashamed of them when he comes in his glory and in the glory of the Father and of the holy angels. 27 I assure you that there are some here who will not die until they have seen the Kingdom of God."

The Transfiguration
(Mt 17.1–8; Mk 9.2–8)

28 About a week after he had said these things, Jesus took Peter, John, and James with him and went up a hill to pray. 29 While he was praying, his face changed its appearance, and his clothes became dazzling white. 30 Suddenly two men were there talking with him. They were Moses and Elijah, 31 who appeared in heavenly glory and talked with Jesus about the way in which he would soon fulfil God's purpose by dying in Jerusalem. 32 Peter and his companions were sound asleep, but they woke up and saw Jesus' glory and the two men who were standing with him. 33 As the men were leaving Jesus, Peter said to him, "Master, how good it is that we are here! We will make three tents, one for you, one for Moses, and one for Elijah." (He did not really know what he was saying.)

34 While he was still speaking, a cloud appeared and covered them with its shadow; and the disciples were afraid as the cloud came over them. 35 A voice said from the cloud, "This is my Son, whom I have chosen — listen to him!"

36 When the voice stopped, there was Jesus all alone. The disciples kept quiet about all this, and told no one at that time anything they had seen.

Jesus Heals a Boy with an Evil Spirit
(Mt 17.14–18; Mk 9.14–27)

37 The next day Jesus and the three disciples went down from the hill, and a large crowd met Jesus. 38 A man shouted from the crowd, "Teacher! I beg you, look at my son — my only son! 39 A spirit attacks him with a sudden shout and throws him into a fit, so that he foams at the mouth; it keeps on hurting him and will hardly let him go! 40 I begged your disciples to drive it out, but they couldn't."

LUKE 9.23

FOLLOW
{ME}

1222

Luke

Haggai
Zechar.
Malachi
Matt.
Mark

LUKE 9

[41] Jesus answered, "How unbelieving and wrong you people are! How long must I stay with you? How long do I have to put up with you?" Then he said to the man, "Bring your son here."

[42] As the boy was coming, the demon knocked him to the ground and threw him into a fit. Jesus gave a command to the evil spirit, healed the boy, and gave him back to his father. [43] All the people were amazed at the mighty power of God.

Jesus Speaks Again about his Death
(Mt 17.22–23; Mk 9.30–32)

The people were still marvelling at everything Jesus was doing, when he said to his disciples, [44] "Don't forget what I am about to tell you! The Son of Man is going to be handed over to the power of human beings." [45] But the disciples did not know what this meant. It had been hidden from them so that they could not understand it, and they were afraid to ask him about the matter.

Who is the Greatest?
(Mt 18.1–5; Mk 9.33–37)

[46] An argument broke out among the disciples as to which one of them was the greatest. [47] Jesus knew what they were thinking, so he took a child, stood him by his side, [48] and said to them, "Whoever welcomes this child in my name, welcomes me; and whoever welcomes me, also welcomes the one who sent me. For the one who is least among you all is the greatest."

Whoever is not Against You is For You
(Mk 9.38–40)

[49] John spoke up, "Master, we saw a man driving out demons in your name, and we told him to stop, because he doesn't belong to our group."

[50] "Do not try to stop him," Jesus said to him and to the other disciples, "because whoever is not against you is for you."

A Samaritan Village Refuses to Receive Jesus

[51] As the time drew near when Jesus would be taken up to heaven, he made up his mind and set out on his way to Jerusalem. [52] He sent messengers ahead of him, who went into a village in Samaria to get everything ready for him. [53] But the people there would not receive him, because it was clear that he was on his way to Jerusalem. [54] When the disciples James and John saw this, they said, "Lord, do you want us to call fire down from heaven to destroy them?"*

[55] Jesus turned and rebuked them.* [56] Then Jesus and his disciples went on to another village.

The Would-be Followers of Jesus
(Mt 8.19–22)

[57] As they went on their way, a man said to Jesus, "I will follow you wherever you go."

[58] Jesus said to him, "Foxes have holes, and birds have nests, but the Son of Man has nowhere to lie down and rest."

9.54 Some manuscripts add *as Elijah did.*
9.55 Some manuscripts add *and said, "You don't know what kind of a Spirit you belong to; for the Son of Man did not come to destroy people's lives, but to save them."*

LUKE 9, 10

1223

Luke

..........:

John
Acts
Romans
1 Corin.
2 Corin.

[59] He said to another man, "Follow me."
But that man said, "Sir, first let me go back and bury my father."
[60] Jesus answered, "Let the dead bury their own dead. You go and proclaim the Kingdom of God."
[61] Someone else said, "I will follow you, sir; but first let me go and say goodbye to my family."
[62] Jesus said to him, "Anyone who starts to plough and then keeps looking back is of no use to the Kingdom of God."

Jesus Sends Out the 72

10 After this the Lord chose another 72* men and sent them out two by two, to go ahead of him to every town and place where he himself was about to go. [2] He said to them, "There is a large harvest, but few workers to gather it in. Pray to the owner of the harvest that he will send out workers to gather in his harvest. [3] Go! I am sending you like lambs among wolves. [4] Don't take a purse or a beggar's bag or shoes; don't stop to greet anyone on the road. [5] Whenever you go into a house, first say, 'Peace be with this house.' [6] If a peace-loving person lives there, let your greeting of peace remain on him; if not, take back your greeting of peace. [7] Stay in that same house, eating and drinking whatever they offer you, for workers should be given their pay. Don't move round from one house to another. [8] Whenever you go into a town and are made welcome, eat what is set before you, [9] heal the sick in that town, and say to the people there, 'The Kingdom of God has come near you.' [10] But whenever you go into a town and are not welcomed, go out in the streets and say, [11] 'Even the dust from your town that sticks to our feet we wipe off against you. But remember that the Kingdom of God has come near you!' [12] I assure you that on Judgement Day God will show more mercy to Sodom than to that town!

The Unbelieving Towns
(Mt 11.20–24)

[13] "How terrible it will be for you, Chorazin! How terrible for you too, Bethsaida! If the miracles which were performed in you had been performed in Tyre and Sidon, the people there would long ago have sat down, put on sackcloth, and sprinkled ashes on themselves, to show that they had turned from their sins! [14] God will show more mercy on Judgement Day to Tyre and Sidon than to you. [15] And as for you, Capernaum! Did you want to lift yourself up to heaven? You will be thrown down to hell!"

[16] Jesus said to his disciples, "Whoever listens to you listens to me; whoever rejects you rejects me; and whoever rejects me rejects the one who sent me."

The Return of the 72

[17] The 72* men came back in great joy. "Lord," they said, "even the demons obeyed us when we gave them a command in your name!"

[18] Jesus answered them, "I saw Satan fall like lightning from heaven. [19] Listen! I have given you authority, so that you can walk on snakes and scorpions and overcome all the power of the Enemy, and nothing will hurt you. [20] But don't be glad because the evil spirits obey you; rather be glad because your names are written in heaven."

10.1 *72*; some manuscripts have *seventy*.
10.17 *72*; some manuscripts have *seventy* (see verse 1).

1224

Luke

Haggai
Zechar.
Malachi
Matt.
Mark

LUKE 10

LUKE 10.25-37

There was a good chance that Jesus' listeners had heard a story similar to this before. Jewish teachers often used this tale to teach about serving the poor - except that the third person who helped was a Jew (like them), not a Samaritan. When Jesus changed the third person to a Samaritan, it was

• A BIG •
DEAL.

Why? Because the Samaritans were hated by the Jews. Jesus isn't telling us just to love the poor but to cross boundaries and break down stereotypes in order to love all people.

Jesus Rejoices
(Mt 11.25–27; 13.16–17)

21 At that time Jesus was filled with joy by the Holy Spirit* and said, "Father, Lord of heaven and earth! I thank you because you have shown to the unlearned what you have hidden from the wise and learned. Yes, Father, this was how you wanted it to happen.

22 "My Father has given me all things. No one knows who the Son is except the Father, and no one knows who the Father is except the Son and those to whom the Son chooses to reveal him."

23 Then Jesus turned to the disciples and said to them privately, "How fortunate you are to see the things you see! 24 I tell you that many prophets and kings wanted to see what you see, but they could not, and to hear what you hear, but they did not."

The Parable of the Good Samaritan

25 A teacher of the Law came up and tried to trap Jesus. "Teacher," he asked, "what must I do to receive eternal life?"

26 Jesus answered him, "What do the Scriptures say? How do you interpret them?"

27 The man answered, "'Love the Lord your God with all your heart, with all your soul, with all your strength, and with all your mind'; and 'Love your neighbour as you love yourself.'"

28 "You are right," Jesus replied; "do this and you will live."

29 But the teacher of the Law wanted to justify himself, so he asked Jesus, "Who is my neighbour?"

30 Jesus answered, "There was once a man who was going down from Jerusalem to Jericho when robbers attacked him, stripped him, and beat him up, leaving him half dead. 31 It so happened that a priest was going down that road; but when he saw the man, he walked on by, on the other side. 32 In the same way a Levite also came along, went over and looked at the man, and then walked on by, on the other side. 33 But a Samaritan who was travelling that way came upon the man, and when he saw him, his heart was filled with pity. 34 He went over to him, poured oil and wine on his wounds and bandaged them; then he put the man on his own animal and took him to an inn, where he took care of him. 35 The next day he took out two silver coins and gave them to the innkeeper. 'Take care of him,' he told the innkeeper, 'and when I come back this way, I will pay you whatever else you spend on him.'"

36 And Jesus concluded, "In your opinion, which one of these three acted like a neighbour towards the man attacked by the robbers?"

37 The teacher of the Law answered, "The one who was kind to him."

Jesus replied, "You go, then, and do the same."

Jesus Visits Martha and Mary

38 As Jesus and his disciples went on their way, he came to a village where a woman named Martha welcomed him in her home. 39 She had a sister named Mary, who sat down at the feet of the Lord and listened to his teaching. 40 Martha was upset over all the work she had to do, so she came and said, "Lord, don't you care that my sister has left me to do all the work by myself! Tell her to come and help me!"

10.21 by the Holy Spirit; some manuscripts have by the Spirit; others have in his Spirit.

LUKE 10, 11

1225

Luke

..........:.

John

Acts

Romans

1 Corin.

2 Corin.

⁴¹The Lord answered her, "Martha, Martha! You are worried and troubled over so many things, ⁴²but just one is needed. Mary has chosen the right thing, and it will not be taken away from her."

Jesus' Teaching on Prayer
(Mt 6.9–13; 7.7–11)

11 One day Jesus was praying in a certain place. When he had finished, one of his disciples said to him, "Lord, teach us to pray, just as John taught his disciples."

²Jesus said to them, "When you pray, say this:

> 'Father:
>
> May your holy name be honoured;
> may your Kingdom come.

³ Give us day by day the food we need.*

⁴ Forgive us our sins,
> for we forgive everyone who does us wrong.
> And do not bring us to hard testing.' "

⁵And Jesus said to his disciples, "Suppose one of you should go to a friend's house at midnight and say, 'Friend, let me borrow three loaves of bread. ⁶A friend of mine who is on a journey has just come to my house, and I haven't got any food for him!' ⁷And suppose your friend should answer from inside, 'Don't bother me! The door is already locked, and my children and I are in bed. I can't get up and give you anything.' ⁸Well, what then? I tell you that even if he will not get up and give you the bread because you are his friend, yet he will get up and give you everything you need because you are not ashamed to keep on asking.

⁹"And so I say to you: ask, and you will receive; seek, and you will find; knock, and the door will be opened to you. ¹⁰For all those who ask will receive, and those who seek will find, and the door will be opened to anyone who knocks. ¹¹Would any of you who are fathers give your son a snake when he asks for fish? ¹²Or would you give him a scorpion when he asks for an egg? ¹³Bad as you are, you know how to give good things to your children. How much more, then, will the Father in heaven give the Holy Spirit to those who ask him!"

Jesus and Beelzebul
(Mt 12.22–30; Mk 3.20–27)

¹⁴Jesus was driving out a demon that could not talk; and when the demon went out, the man began to talk. The crowds were amazed, ¹⁵but some of the people said, "It is Beelzebul, the chief of the demons, who gives him the power to drive them out."

¹⁶Others wanted to trap Jesus, so they asked him to perform a miracle to show that God approved of him. ¹⁷But Jesus knew what they were thinking, so he said to them, "Any country that divides itself into groups which fight each other will not last very long; a family divided against itself falls apart. ¹⁸So if Satan's kingdom has groups fighting each other, how can it last? You say that I drive out demons because Beelzebul gives me the power to do so. ¹⁹If this is how I drive them out, how do your followers drive them out? Your own followers prove that you are wrong! ²⁰No, it is rather by means of God's power that I drive out demons, and this proves that the Kingdom of God has already come to you.

²¹"When a strong man, with all his weapons ready, guards his own house, all his belongings are safe. ²²But when a stronger man attacks him and defeats him, he carries away all the weapons the owner was depending on and divides up what he stole.

....

11.3 *the food we need;* or *food for the next day.*

1226

Luke

Haggai
Zechar.
Malachi
Matt.
Mark

LUKE 11

23 "Anyone who is not for me is really against me; anyone who does not help me gather is really scattering.

The Return of the Evil Spirit
(Mt 12.43–45)

24 "When an evil spirit goes out of a person, it travels over dry country looking for a place to rest. If it can't find one, it says to itself, 'I will go back to my house.' 25 So it goes back and finds the house clean and tidy. 26 Then it goes out and brings seven other spirits even worse than itself, and they come and live there. So when it is all over, that person is in a worse state than he was at the beginning."

True Happiness

27 When Jesus had said this, a woman spoke up from the crowd and said to him, "How happy is the woman who bore you and nursed you!"

28 But Jesus answered, "Rather, how happy are those who hear the word of God and obey it!"

The Demand for a Miracle
(Mt 12.38–42)

29 As the people crowded round Jesus, he went on to say, "How evil are the people of this day! They ask for a miracle, but none will be given them except the miracle of Jonah. 30 In the same way that the prophet Jonah was a sign for the people of Nineveh, so the Son of Man will be a sign for the people of this day. 31 On Judgement Day the Queen of Sheba will stand up and accuse the people of today, because she travelled all the way from her country to listen to King Solomon's wise teaching; and I tell you there is something here greater than Solomon. 32 On Judgement Day the people of Nineveh will stand up and accuse you, because they turned from their sins when they heard Jonah preach; and I assure you that there is something here greater than Jonah!

The Light of the Body
(Mt 5.15; 6.22–23)

33 "No one lights a lamp and then hides it or puts it under a bowl;* instead, he puts it on the lampstand, so that people may see the light as they come in. 34 Your eyes are like a lamp for the body. When your eyes are sound, your whole body is full of light; but when your eyes are no good, your whole body will be in darkness. 35 Make certain, then, that the light in you is not darkness. 36 If your whole body is full of light, with no part of it in darkness, it will be bright all over, as when a lamp shines on you with its brightness."

Jesus Accuses the Pharisees and the Teachers of the Law
(Mt 23.1–36; Mk 12.38–40)

37 When Jesus finished speaking, a Pharisee invited him to eat with him; so he went in and sat down to eat. 38 The Pharisee was surprised when he noticed that Jesus had not washed before eating. 39 So the Lord said to him, "Now then, you Pharisees clean the outside of your cup and plate, but inside you are full of violence and evil. 40 Fools! Did not God, who made the outside, also make the inside? 41 But give what is in your cups and plates to the poor, and everything will be ritually clean for you.

....

11.33 Some manuscripts do not have *or puts it under a bowl.*

LUKE 11, 12

1227

Luke

..........:.

John
Acts
Romans
1 Corin.
2 Corin.

⁴²"How terrible for you Pharisees! You give God a tenth of the seasoning herbs, such as mint and rue and all the other herbs, but you neglect justice and love for God. These you should practise, without neglecting the others.

⁴³"How terrible for you Pharisees! You love the reserved seats in the synagogues and to be greeted with respect in the market places. ⁴⁴How terrible for you! You are like unmarked graves which people walk on without knowing it."

⁴⁵One of the teachers of the Law said to him, "Teacher, when you say this, you insult us too!"

⁴⁶Jesus answered, "How terrible also for you teachers of the Law! You put loads on people's backs which are hard to carry, but you yourselves will not stretch out a finger to help them carry those loads. ⁴⁷How terrible for you! You make fine tombs for the prophets — the very prophets your ancestors murdered. ⁴⁸You yourselves admit, then, that you approve of what your ancestors did; they murdered the prophets, and you build their tombs. ⁴⁹For this reason the Wisdom of God said, 'I will send them prophets and messengers; they will kill some of them and persecute others.' ⁵⁰So the people of this time will be punished for the murder of all the prophets killed since the creation of the world, ⁵¹from the murder of Abel to the murder of Zechariah, who was killed between the altar and the Holy Place. Yes, I tell you, the people of this time will be punished for them all!

⁵²"How terrible for you teachers of the Law! You have kept the key that opens the door to the house of knowledge; you yourselves will not go in, and you stop those who are trying to go in!"

⁵³When Jesus left that place, the teachers of the Law and the Pharisees began to criticize him bitterly and ask him questions about many things, ⁵⁴trying to lay traps for him and catch him saying something wrong.

A Warning against Hypocrisy
(Mt 10.26–27)

12 As thousands of people crowded together, so that they were stepping on each other, Jesus said first to his disciples, "Be on guard against the yeast of the Pharisees — I mean their hypocrisy. ²Whatever is covered up will be uncovered, and every secret will be made known. ³So then, whatever you have said in the dark will be heard in broad daylight, and whatever you have whispered in private in a closed room will be shouted from the housetops.

Whom to Fear
(Mt 10.28–31)

⁴"I tell you, my friends, do not be afraid of those who kill the body but cannot afterwards do anything worse. ⁵I will show you whom to fear: fear God, who, after killing, has the authority to throw into hell. Believe me, he is the one you must fear!

⁶"Aren't five sparrows sold for two pennies? Yet not one sparrow is forgotten by God. ⁷Even the hairs of your head have all been counted. So do not be afraid; you are worth much more than many sparrows!

Confessing and Rejecting Christ
(Mt 10.32–33; 12.32; 10.19–20)

⁸"I assure you that for those who declare publicly that they belong to me, the Son of Man will do the same before the angels of God. ⁹But those who reject me publicly, the Son of Man will also reject before the angels of God.

1228

Luke

Haggai
Zechar.
Malachi
Matt.
Mark

LUKE 12

[10] "Whoever says a word against the Son of Man can be forgiven; but those who say evil things against the Holy Spirit will not be forgiven.

[11] "When they bring you to be tried in the synagogues or before governors or rulers, do not be worried about how you will defend yourself or what you will say. [12] For the Holy Spirit will teach you at that time what you should say."

The Parable of the Rich Fool

[13] A man in the crowd said to Jesus, "Teacher, tell my brother to divide with me the property our father left us."

[14] Jesus answered him, "My friend, who gave me the right to judge or to divide the property between you two?" [15] And he went on to say to them all, "Watch out and guard yourselves from every kind of greed; because a person's true life is not made up of the things he owns, no matter how rich he may be."

[16] Then Jesus told them this parable: "There was once a rich man who had land which bore good crops. [17] He began to think to himself, 'I haven't anywhere to keep all my crops. What can I do? [18] This is what I will do,' he told himself; 'I will tear down my barns and build bigger ones, where I will store my corn and all my other goods. [19] Then I will say to myself, Lucky man! You have all the good things you need for many years. Take life easy, eat, drink, and enjoy yourself!' [20] But God said to him, 'You fool! This very night you will have to give up your life; then who will get all these things you have kept for yourself?'"

[21] And Jesus concluded, "This is how it is with those who pile up riches for themselves but are not rich in God's sight."

Trust in God
(Mt 6.25–34)

[22] Then Jesus said to the disciples, "And so I tell you not to worry about the food you need to stay alive or about the clothes you need for your body. [23] Life is much more important than food, and the body much more important than clothes. [24] Look at the crows: they don't sow seeds or gather a harvest; they don't have storerooms or barns; God feeds them! You are worth so much more than birds! [25] Can any of you live a bit longer* by worrying about it? [26] If you can't manage even such a small thing, why worry about the other things? [27] Look how the wild flowers grow: they don't work or make clothes for themselves. But I tell you that not even King Solomon with all his wealth had clothes as beautiful as one of these flowers. [28] It is God who clothes the wild grass — grass that is here today and gone tomorrow, burnt up in the oven. Won't he be all the more sure to clothe you? How little faith you have!

[29] "So don't be all upset, always concerned about what you will eat and drink. [30] (For the pagans of this world are always concerned about all these things.) Your Father knows that you need these things. [31] Instead, be concerned with his Kingdom, and he will provide you with these things.

Riches in Heaven
(Mt 6.19–21)

[32] "Do not be afraid, little flock, for your Father is pleased to give you the Kingdom. [33] Sell all your belongings and give the money

UNDERLINE the bits on THIS PAGE where you feel GOD IS SPEAKING to you.

12.25 *live a bit longer*; or *grow a bit taller*.

LUKE 12

1229

Luke

....

John
Acts
Romans
1 Corin.
2 Corin.

to the poor. Provide for yourselves purses that don't wear out, and save your riches in heaven, where they will never decrease, because no thief can get to them, and no moth can destroy them. [34] For your heart will always be where your riches are.

Watchful Servants

[35] "Be ready for whatever comes, dressed for action and with your lamps lit, [36] like servants who are waiting for their master to come back from a wedding feast. When he comes and knocks, they will open the door for him at once. [37] How happy are those servants whose master finds them awake and ready when he returns! I tell you, he will take off his coat, ask them to sit down, and will wait on them. [38] How happy they are if he finds them ready, even if he should come at midnight or even later! [39] And you can be sure that if the owner of a house knew the time when the thief would come, he would not let the thief break into his house. [40] And you, too, must be ready, because the Son of Man will come at an hour when you are not expecting him."

The Faithful or the Unfaithful Servant
(Mt 24.45–51)

[41] Peter said, "Lord, does this parable apply to us, or do you mean it for everyone?"

[42] The Lord answered, "Who, then, is the faithful and wise servant? He is the one that his master will put in charge, to run the household and give the other servants their share of the food at the proper time. [43] How happy that servant is if his master finds him doing this when he comes home! [44] Indeed, I tell you, the master will put that servant in charge of all his property. [45] But if that servant says to himself that his master is taking a long time to come back and if he begins to beat the other servants, both the men and the women, and eats and drinks and gets drunk, [46] then the master will come back one day when the servant does not expect him and at a time he does not know. The master will cut him in pieces* and make him share the fate of the disobedient.

[47] "The servant who knows what his master wants him to do, but does not get himself ready and do it, will be punished with a heavy whipping. [48] But the servant who does not know what his master wants, and yet does something for which he deserves a whipping, will be punished with a light whipping. Much is required from the person to whom much is given; much more is required from the person to whom much more is given.

Jesus the Cause of Division
(Mt 10.34–36)

[49] "I came to set the earth on fire, and how I wish it were already kindled! [50] I have a baptism to receive, and how distressed I am until it is over! [51] Do you suppose that I came to bring peace to the world? No, not peace, but division. [52] From now on a family of five will be divided, three against two and two against three. [53] Fathers will be against their sons, and sons against their fathers; mothers will be against their daughters, and daughters against their mothers; mothers-in-law will be against their daughters-in-law, and daughters-in-law against their mothers-in-law."

....

12.46 cut him in pieces; or throw him out.

1230

Luke
.｡:........

Haggai
Zechar.
Malachi
Matt.
Mark

LUKE 12, 13

Understanding the Time
(Mt 16.2–3)

54 Jesus said also to the people, "When you see a cloud coming up in the west, at once you say that it is going to rain — and it does. 55 And when you feel the south wind blowing, you say that it is going to get hot — and it does. 56 Hypocrites! You can look at the earth and the sky and predict the weather; why, then, don't you know the meaning of this present time?

Settle with your Opponent
(Mt 5.25–26)

57 "Why do you not judge for yourselves the right thing to do? 58 If someone brings a lawsuit against you and takes you to court, do your best to settle the dispute with them before you get to court. If you don't, they will drag you before the judge, who will hand you over to the police, and you will be put in jail. 59 There you will stay, I tell you, until you pay the last penny of your fine."

Turn from your Sins or Die

13 At that time some people were there who told Jesus about the Galileans whom Pilate had killed while they were offering sacrifices to God. 2 Jesus answered them, "Because those Galileans were killed in that way, do you think it proves that they were worse sinners than all the other Galileans? 3 No indeed! And I tell you that if you do not turn from your sins, you will all die as they did. 4 What about those eighteen people in Siloam who were killed when the tower fell on them? Do you suppose this proves that they were worse than all the other people living in Jerusalem? 5 No indeed! And I tell you that if you do not turn from your sins, you will all die as they did."

The Parable of the Unfruitful Fig Tree

6 Then Jesus told them this parable: "There was once a man who had a fig tree growing in his vineyard. He went looking for figs on it but found none. 7 So he said to his gardener, 'Look, for three years I have been coming here looking for figs on this fig tree, and I haven't found any. Cut it down! Why should it go on using up the soil?' 8 But the gardener answered, 'Leave it alone, sir, just one more year; I will dig round it and put in some manure. 9 Then if the tree bears figs next year, so much the better; if not, then you can have it cut down.'"

Jesus Heals a Crippled Woman on the Sabbath

10 One Sabbath Jesus was teaching in a synagogue. 11 A woman there had an evil spirit that had made her ill for eighteen years; she was bent over and could not straighten up at all. 12 When Jesus saw her, he called out to her, "Woman, you are free from your illness!" 13 He placed his hands on her, and at once she straightened herself up and praised God.

14 The official of the synagogue was angry that Jesus had healed on the Sabbath, so he spoke up and said to the people, "There are six days in which we should work; so come during those days and be healed, but not on the Sabbath!"

15 The Lord answered him, "You hypocrites! Any one of you would untie your ox or your donkey from the stall and take it out to give it water on the Sabbath. 16 Now here is this descendant of Abraham whom Satan has kept bound up for eighteen years; should she not be released on the Sabbath?" 17 His answer made

LUKE 13, 14

1231

Luke

·········:·

John
Acts
Romans
1 Corin.
2 Corin.

his enemies ashamed of themselves, while the people rejoiced over all the wonderful things that he did.

The Parable of the Mustard Seed
(Mt 13.31–32; Mk 4.30–32)

18 Jesus asked, "What is the Kingdom of God like? What shall I compare it with? 19 It is like this. A man takes a mustard seed and sows it in his field. The plant grows and becomes a tree, and the birds make their nests in its branches."

The Parable of the Yeast
(Mt 13.33)

20 Again Jesus asked, "What shall I compare the Kingdom of God with? 21 It is like this. A woman takes some yeast and mixes it with forty litres of flour until the whole batch of dough rises."

The Narrow Door
(Mt 7.13–14, 21–23)

22 Jesus went through towns and villages, teaching the people and making his way towards Jerusalem. 23 Someone asked him, "Sir, will just a few people be saved?"

Jesus answered them, 24 "Do your best to go in through the narrow door; because many people will surely try to go in but will not be able. 25 The master of the house will get up and close the door; then when you stand outside and begin to knock on the door and say, 'Open the door for us, sir!' he will answer you, 'I don't know where you come from!' 26 Then you will answer, 'We ate and drank with you; you taught in our town!' 27 But he will say again, 'I don't know where you come from. Get away from me, all you wicked people!' 28 How you will cry and grind your teeth when you see Abraham, Isaac, and Jacob, and all the prophets in the Kingdom of God, while you are thrown out! 29 People will come from the east and the west, from the north and the south, and sit down at the feast in the Kingdom of God. 30 Then those who are now last will be first, and those who are now first will be last."

Jesus' Love for Jerusalem
(Mt 23.37–39)

31 At that same time some Pharisees came to Jesus and said to him, "You must get out of here and go somewhere else, because Herod wants to kill you."

32 Jesus answered them, "Go and tell that fox: 'I am driving out demons and performing cures today and tomorrow, and on the third day I shall finish my work.' 33 Yet I must be on my way today, tomorrow, and the next day; it is not right for a prophet to be killed anywhere except in Jerusalem.

34 "Jerusalem, Jerusalem! You kill the prophets, you stone the messengers God has sent you! How many times have I wanted to put my arms round all your people, just as a hen gathers her chicks under her wings, but you would not let me! 35 And so your Temple will be abandoned. I assure you that you will not see me until the time comes when you say, 'God bless him who comes in the name of the Lord.' "

Jesus Heals a Sick Man

14 One Sabbath Jesus went to eat a meal at the home of one of the leading Pharisees; and people were watching Jesus closely. 2 A man whose legs and arms were swollen came to

1232

Luke

·:········

Haggai
Zechar.
Malachi
Matt.
Mark

LUKE 14

Jesus, ³and Jesus asked the teachers of the Law and the Pharisees, "Does our Law allow healing on the Sabbath or not?"

⁴But they would not say anything. Jesus took the man, healed him, and sent him away. ⁵Then he said to them, "If any one of you had a son or an ox that happened to fall in a well on a Sabbath, would you not pull them out at once on the Sabbath itself?"

⁶But they were not able to answer him about this.

Humility and Hospitality

⁷Jesus noticed how some of the guests were choosing the best places, so he told this parable to all of them: ⁸"When someone invites you to a wedding feast, do not sit down in the best place. It could happen that someone more important than you has been invited, ⁹and your host, who invited both of you, would have to come and say to you, 'Let him have this place.' Then you would be embarrassed and have to sit in the lowest place. ¹⁰Instead, when you are invited, go and sit in the lowest place, so that your host will come to you and say, 'Come on up, my friend, to a better place.' This will bring you honour in the presence of all the other guests. ¹¹For all those who make themselves great will be humbled, and those who humble themselves will be made great."

¹²Then Jesus said to his host, "When you give a lunch or a dinner, do not invite your friends or your brothers or your relatives or your rich neighbours — for they will invite you back, and in this way you will be paid for what you did. ¹³When you give a feast, invite the poor, the crippled, the lame, and the blind; ¹⁴and you will be blessed, because they are not able to pay you back. God will repay you on the day the good people rise from death."

The Parable of the Great Feast
(Mt 22.1–10)

¹⁵When one of the men sitting at table heard this, he said to Jesus, "How happy are those who will sit down at the feast in the Kingdom of God!"

¹⁶Jesus said to him, "There was once a man who was giving a great feast to which he invited many people. ¹⁷When it was time for the feast, he sent his servant to tell his guests, 'Come, everything is ready!' ¹⁸But they all began, one after another, to make excuses. The first one told the servant, 'I have bought a field and must go and look at it; please accept my apologies.' ¹⁹Another one said, 'I have bought five pairs of oxen and am on my way to try them out; please accept my apologies.' ²⁰Another one said, 'I have just got married, and for that reason I cannot come.'

²¹"The servant went back and told all this to his master. The master was furious and said to his servant, 'Hurry out to the streets and alleys of the town, and bring back the poor, the crippled, the blind, and the lame.' ²²Soon the servant said, 'Your order has been carried out, sir, but there is room for more.' ²³So the master said to the servant, 'Go out to the country roads and lanes and make people come in, so that my house will be full. ²⁴I tell you all that none of those who were invited will taste my dinner!' "

The Cost of Being a Disciple
(Mt 10.37–38)

²⁵Once when large crowds of people were going along with Jesus, he turned and said to them, ²⁶"Those who come to me cannot be my disciples unless they love me more than they love father and mother, wife and children, brothers and sisters, and

LUKE 14, 15

1233

Luke

....

John
Acts
Romans
1 Corin.
2 Corin.

themselves as well. ²⁷Those who do not carry their own cross and come after me cannot be my disciples.

²⁸"If one of you is planning to build a tower, you sit down first and work out what it will cost, to see if you have enough money to finish the job. ²⁹If you don't, you will not be able to finish the tower after laying the foundation; and all who see what happened will laugh at you. ³⁰'This man began to build but can't finish the job!' they will say.

³¹"If a king goes out with 10,000 men to fight another king who comes against him with 20,000 men, he will sit down first and decide if he is strong enough to face that other king. ³²If he isn't, he will send messengers to meet the other king, to ask for terms of peace while he is still a long way off. ³³In the same way," concluded Jesus, "none of you can be my disciple unless you give up everything you have.

Worthless Salt
(Mt 5.13; Mk 9.50)

³⁴"Salt is good, but if it loses its saltiness, there is no way to make it salty again. ³⁵It is no good for the soil or for the manure heap; it is thrown away. Listen, then, if you have ears!"

The Lost Sheep
(Mt 18.12–14)

15 One day when many tax collectors and other outcasts came to listen to Jesus, ²the Pharisees and the teachers of the Law started grumbling, "This man welcomes outcasts and even eats with them!" ³So Jesus told them this parable:

⁴"Suppose one of you has a hundred sheep and loses one of them — what do you do? You leave the other 99 sheep in the pasture and go looking for the one that got lost until you find it. ⁵When you find it, you are so happy that you put it on your shoulders ⁶and carry it back home. Then you call your friends and neighbours together and say to them, 'I am so happy I found my lost sheep. Let us celebrate!' ⁷In the same way, I tell you, there will be more joy in heaven over one sinner who repents than over 99 respectable people who do not need to repent.

The Lost Coin

⁸"Or suppose a woman who has ten silver coins loses one of them — what does she do? She lights a lamp, sweeps her house, and looks carefully everywhere until she finds it. ⁹When she finds it, she calls her friends and neighbours together, and says to them, 'I am so happy I found the coin I lost. Let us celebrate!' ¹⁰In the same way, I tell you, the angels of God rejoice over one sinner who repents."

The Lost Son

¹¹Jesus went on to say, "There was once a man who had two sons. ¹²The younger one said to him, 'Father, give me my share of the property now.' So the man divided his property between his two sons. ¹³After a few days the younger son sold his part of the property and left home with the money. He went to a country far away, where he wasted his money in reckless living. ¹⁴He spent everything he had. Then a severe famine spread over that country, and he was left without a thing. ¹⁵So he went to work for one of the citizens of that country, who sent him out to his farm to take care of the pigs. ¹⁶He wished he could fill himself with the bean pods the pigs ate, but no one gave him anything to eat.

LUKE 15.11-32

In the boxes below, write words to describe what was going on for all

THREE

– CHARACTERS –

in this story. Think about how they felt. What does this show us about God?

THE LOST SON...

THE OLDER SON...

THE FATHER...

1234

Luke

Haggai
Zechar.
Malachi
Matt.
Mark

LUKE 15, 16

¹⁷At last he came to his senses and said, 'All my father's hired workers have more than they can eat, and here I am about to starve! ¹⁸I will get up and go to my father and say, Father, I have sinned against God and against you. ¹⁹I am no longer fit to be called your son; treat me as one of your hired workers.' ²⁰So he got up and started back to his father.

"He was still a long way from home when his father saw him; his heart was filled with pity, and he ran, threw his arms round his son, and kissed him. ²¹'Father,' the son said, 'I have sinned against God and against you. I am no longer fit to be called your son.' ²²But the father called his servants. 'Hurry!' he said. 'Bring the best robe and put it on him. Put a ring on his finger and shoes on his feet. ²³Then go and get the prize calf and kill it, and let us celebrate with a feast! ²⁴For this son of mine was dead, but now he is alive; he was lost, but now he has been found.' And so the feasting began.

²⁵"In the meantime the elder son was out in the field. On his way back, when he came close to the house, he heard the music and dancing. ²⁶So he called one of the servants and asked him, 'What's going on?' ²⁷'Your brother has come back home,' the servant answered, 'and your father has killed the prize calf, because he got him back safe and sound.'

²⁸"The elder brother was so angry that he would not go into the house; so his father came out and begged him to come in. ²⁹But he answered his father, 'Look, all these years I have worked for you like a slave, and I have never disobeyed your orders. What have you given me? Not even a goat for me to have a feast with my friends! ³⁰But this son of yours wasted all your property on prostitutes, and when he comes back home, you kill the prize calf for him!' ³¹'My son,' the father answered, 'you are always here with me, and everything I have is yours. ³²But we had to celebrate and be happy, because your brother was dead, but now he is alive; he was lost, but now he has been found.'"

The Shrewd Manager

16 Jesus said to his disciples, "There was once a rich man who had a servant who managed his property. The rich man was told that the manager was wasting his master's money, ²so he called him in and said, 'What is this I hear about you? Hand in a complete account of your handling of my property, because you cannot be my manager any longer.' ³The servant said to himself, 'My master is going to dismiss me from my job. What shall I do? I am not strong enough to dig ditches, and I am ashamed to beg. ⁴Now I know what I will do! Then when my job is gone, I shall have friends who will welcome me in their homes.'

⁵"So he called in all the people who were in debt to his master. He asked the first one, 'How much do you owe my master?' ⁶'100 barrels of olive oil,' he answered. 'Here is your account,' the manager told him; 'sit down and write fifty.' ⁷Then he asked another one, 'And you — how much do you owe?' 'A thousand sacks of wheat,' he answered. 'Here is your account,' the manager told him; 'write 800.'

⁸"As a result the master of this dishonest manager praised him for doing such a shrewd thing; because the people of this world are much more shrewd in handling their affairs than the people who belong to the light."

⁹And Jesus went on to say, "And so I tell you: make friends for yourselves with worldly wealth, so that when it gives out, you will

LUKE 16

1235

Luke
⋯⋯⋯⋮⋯

John
Acts
Romans
1 Corin.
2 Corin.

be welcomed in the eternal home. [10]Whoever is faithful in small matters will be faithful in large ones; whoever is dishonest in small matters will be dishonest in large ones. [11]If, then, you have not been faithful in handling worldly wealth, how can you be trusted with true wealth? [12]And if you have not been faithful with what belongs to someone else, who will give you what belongs to you?

[13]"No servant can be the slave of two masters; such a servant will hate one and love the other or will be loyal to one and despise the other. You cannot serve both God and money."

Some Sayings of Jesus
(Mt 11.12–13; 5.31–32; Mk 10.11–12)

[14]When the Pharisees heard all this, they sneered at Jesus, because they loved money. [15]Jesus said to them, "You are the ones who make yourselves look right in other people's sight, but God knows your hearts. For the things that are considered of great value by human beings are worth nothing in God's sight.

[16]"The Law of Moses and the writings of the prophets were in effect up to the time of John the Baptist; since then the Good News about the Kingdom of God is being told, and everyone forces their way in. [17]But it is easier for heaven and earth to disappear than for the smallest detail of the Law to be done away with.

[18]"Any man who divorces his wife and marries another woman commits adultery; and the man who marries a divorced woman commits adultery.

The Rich Man and Lazarus

[19]"There was once a rich man who dressed in the most expensive clothes and lived in great luxury every day. [20]There was also a poor man named Lazarus, covered with sores, who used to be brought to the rich man's door, [21]hoping to eat the bits of food that fell from the rich man's table. Even the dogs would come and lick his sores.

[22]"The poor man died and was carried by the angels to sit beside Abraham at the feast in heaven. The rich man died and was buried, [23]and in Hades,* where he was in great pain, he looked up and saw Abraham, far away, with Lazarus at his side. [24]So he called out, 'Father Abraham! Take pity on me, and send Lazarus to dip his finger in some water and cool my tongue, because I am in great pain in this fire!'

[25]"But Abraham said, 'Remember, my son, that in your lifetime you were given all the good things, while Lazarus got all the bad things. But now he is enjoying himself here, while you are in pain. [26]Besides all that, there is a deep pit lying between us, so that those who want to cross over from here to you cannot do so, nor can anyone cross over to us from where you are.' [27]The rich man said, 'Then I beg you, father Abraham, send Lazarus to my father's house, [28]where I have five brothers. Let him go and warn them so that they, at least, will not come to this place of pain.'

[29]"Abraham said, 'Your brothers have Moses and the prophets to warn them; your brothers should listen to what they say.' [30]The rich man answered, 'That is not enough, father Abraham! But if someone were to rise from death and go to them, then they would turn from their sins.' [31]But Abraham said, 'If they will not listen to Moses and the prophets, they will not be convinced even if someone were to rise from death.'"

⋯⋯⋯⋯⋯⋯⋯⋯⋯⋯⋯⋯⋯⋯⋯⋯⋯⋯⋯⋯⋯⋯⋯⋯⋯⋯⋯⋯⋯⋯

16.23 *Hades*: The world of the dead.

1236

Luke

∴

Haggai
Zechar.
Malachi
Matt.
Mark

LUKE 17

Sin
(Mt 18.6–7, 21–22; Mk 9.42)

17 Jesus said to his disciples, "Things that make people fall into sin are bound to happen, but how terrible for the one who makes them happen! ² It would be better for him if a large millstone were tied round his neck and he were thrown into the sea than for him to cause one of these little ones to sin. ³ So watch what you do!

"If your brother sins, rebuke him, and if he repents, forgive him. ⁴ If he sins against you seven times in one day, and each time he comes to you saying, 'I repent,' you must forgive him."

Faith

⁵ The apostles said to the Lord, "Make our faith greater."

⁶ The Lord answered, "If you had faith as big as a mustard seed, you could say to this mulberry tree, 'Pull yourself up by the roots and plant yourself in the sea!' and it would obey you.

A Servant's Duty

⁷ "Suppose one of you has a servant who is ploughing or looking after the sheep. When he comes in from the field, do you tell him to hurry and eat his meal? ⁸ Of course not! Instead, you say to him, 'Get my supper ready, then put on your apron and wait on me while I eat and drink; after that you may have your meal.' ⁹ The servant does not deserve thanks for obeying orders, does he? ¹⁰ It is the same with you; when you have done all you have been told to do, say, 'We are ordinary servants; we have only done our duty.' "

Jesus Heals Ten Men

¹¹ As Jesus made his way to Jerusalem, he went along the border between Samaria and Galilee. ¹² He was going into a village when he was met by ten men suffering from a dreaded skin disease. They stood at a distance ¹³ and shouted, "Jesus! Master! Take pity on us!"

¹⁴ Jesus saw them and said to them, "Go and let the priests examine you."

On the way they were made clean.* ¹⁵ When one of them saw that he was healed, he came back, praising God in a loud voice. ¹⁶ He threw himself to the ground at Jesus' feet and thanked him. The man was a Samaritan. ¹⁷ Jesus said, "There were ten men who were healed; where are the other nine? ¹⁸ Why is this foreigner the only one who came back to give thanks to God?" ¹⁹ And Jesus said to him, "Get up and go; your faith has made you well."

The Coming of the Kingdom
(Mt 24.23–28, 37–41)

²⁰ Some Pharisees asked Jesus when the Kingdom of God would come. His answer was, "The Kingdom of God does not come in such a way as to be seen. ²¹ No one will say, 'Look, here it is!' or, 'There it is!'; because the Kingdom of God is within you."*

²² Then he said to the disciples, "The time will come when you will wish you could see one of the days of the Son of Man, but you will not see it. ²³ There will be those who will say to you, 'Look, over there!' or, 'Look, over here!' But don't go out looking for it. ²⁴ As the lightning flashes across the sky and lights it up from one

17.14 *made clean*: See 5.12.
17.21 *is within you*; or *is among you*, or *will suddenly appear among you*.

1237

Luke

John
Acts
Romans
1 Corin.
2 Corin.

side to the other, so will the Son of Man be in his day. 25 But first he must suffer much and be rejected by the people of this day. 26 As it was in the time of Noah so shall it be in the days of the Son of Man. 27 Everybody kept on eating and drinking, and men and women married, up to the very day Noah went into the boat and the flood came and killed them all. 28 It will be as it was in the time of Lot. Everybody kept on eating and drinking, buying and selling, planting and building. 29 On the day Lot left Sodom, fire and sulphur rained down from heaven and killed them all. 30 That is how it will be on the day the Son of Man is revealed.

31 "On that day someone who is on the roof of his house must not go down into the house to get any belongings; in the same way anyone who is out in the field must not go back to the house. 32 Remember Lot's wife! 33 Whoever tries to save his own life will lose it; whoever loses his life will save it. 34 On that night, I tell you, there will be two people sleeping in the same bed: one will be taken away, the other will be left behind. 35 Two women will be grinding corn together: one will be taken away, the other will be left behind."*

37 The disciples asked him, "Where, Lord?"

Jesus answered, "Wherever there is a dead body, the vultures will gather."

The Parable of the Widow and the Judge

18 Then Jesus told his disciples a parable to teach them that they should always pray and never become discouraged. 2 "In a certain town there was a judge who neither feared God nor respected people. 3 And there was a widow in that same town who kept coming to him and pleading for her rights, saying, 'Help me against my opponent!' 4 For a long time the judge refused to act, but at last he said to himself, 'Even though I don't fear God or respect people, 5 yet because of all the trouble this widow is giving me, I will see to it that she gets her rights. If I don't, she will keep on coming and finally wear me out!' "

6 And the Lord continued, "Listen to what that corrupt judge said. 7 Now, will God not judge in favour of his own people who cry to him day and night for help? Will he be slow to help them? 8 I tell you, he will judge in their favour and do it quickly. But will the Son of Man find faith on earth when he comes?"

The Parable of the Pharisee and the Tax Collector

9 Jesus also told this parable to people who were sure of their own goodness and despised everybody else. 10 "Once there were two men who went up to the Temple to pray: one was a Pharisee, the other a tax collector.

11 "The Pharisee stood apart by himself and prayed,* 'I thank you, God, that I am not greedy, dishonest, or an adulterer, like everybody else. I thank you that I am not like that tax collector over there. 12 I fast two days a week, and I give you a tenth of all my income.'

13 "But the tax collector stood at a distance and would not even raise his face to heaven, but beat on his breast and said, 'God, have pity on me, a sinner!' 14 I tell you," said Jesus, "the tax collector, and not the Pharisee, was in the right with God when he

LUKE 18.1

PRAY
AND NEVER
BECOME
{ DISCOURAGED }

17.35 Some manuscripts add verse 36: *Two men will be working in a field: one will be taken away, the other will be left behind* (see Mt 24.40).
18.11 *stood apart by himself and prayed*; some manuscripts have *stood up and prayed to himself*.

1238

Luke

Haggai
Zechar.
Malachi
Matt.
Mark

LUKE 18

went home. For all who make themselves great will be humbled, and all who humble themselves will be made great."

Jesus Blesses Little Children
(Mt 19.13–15; Mk 10.13–16)

15 Some people brought their babies to Jesus for him to place his hands on them. The disciples saw them and scolded them for doing so, 16 but Jesus called the children to him and said, "Let the children come to me and do not stop them, because the Kingdom of God belongs to such as these. 17 Remember this! Whoever does not receive the Kingdom of God like a child will never enter it."

The Rich Man
(Mt 19.16–30; Mk 10.17–31)

18 A Jewish leader asked Jesus, "Good Teacher, what must I do to receive eternal life?"

19 "Why do you call me good?" Jesus asked him. "No one is good except God alone. 20 You know the commandments: 'Do not commit adultery; do not commit murder; do not steal; do not accuse anyone falsely; respect your father and your mother.'"

21 The man replied, "Ever since I was young, I have obeyed all these commandments."

22 When Jesus heard this, he said to him, "There is still one more thing you need to do. Sell all you have and give the money to the poor, and you will have riches in heaven; then come and follow me." 23 But when the man heard this, he became very sad, because he was very rich.

24 Jesus saw that he was sad and said, "How hard it is for rich people to enter the Kingdom of God! 25 It is much harder for a rich person to enter the Kingdom of God than for a camel to go through the eye of a needle."

26 The people who heard him asked, "Who, then, can be saved?"

27 Jesus answered, "What is humanly impossible is possible for God."

28 Then Peter said, "Look! We have left our homes to follow you."

29 "Yes," Jesus said to them, "and I assure you that anyone who leaves home or wife or brothers or parents or children for the sake of the Kingdom of God 30 will receive much more in this present age and eternal life in the age to come."

Jesus Speaks a Third Time about his Death
(Mt 20.17–19; Mk 10.32–34)

31 Jesus took the twelve disciples aside and said to them, "Listen! We are going to Jerusalem where everything the prophets wrote about the Son of Man will come true. 32 He will be handed over to the Gentiles, who will mock him, insult him, and spit on him. 33 They will whip him and kill him, but three days later he will rise to life."

34 But the disciples did not understand any of these things; the meaning of the words was hidden from them, and they did not know what Jesus was talking about.

Jesus Heals a Blind Beggar
(Mt 20.29–34; Mk 10.46–52)

35 As Jesus was coming near Jericho, there was a blind man sitting by the road, begging. 36 When he heard the crowd passing by, he asked, "What is this?"

37 "Jesus of Nazareth is passing by," they told him.

38 He cried out, "Jesus! Son of David! Take pity on me!"

LUKE 18, 19

1239

Luke
....
John
Acts
Romans
1 Corin.
2 Corin.

³⁹The people in front scolded him and told him to be quiet. But he shouted even more loudly, "Son of David! Take pity on me!"

⁴⁰So Jesus stopped and ordered the blind man to be brought to him. When he came near, Jesus asked him, ⁴¹"What do you want me to do for you?"

"Sir," he answered, "I want to see again."

⁴²Jesus said to him, "Then see! Your faith has made you well." ⁴³At once he was able to see, and he followed Jesus, giving thanks to God. When the crowd saw it, they all praised God.

Jesus and Zacchaeus

19 Jesus went on into Jericho and was passing through. ²There was a chief tax collector there named Zacchaeus, who was rich. ³He was trying to see who Jesus was, but he was a little man and could not see Jesus because of the crowd. ⁴So he ran ahead of the crowd and climbed a sycamore tree to see Jesus, who was going to pass that way. ⁵When Jesus came to that place, he looked up and said to Zacchaeus, "Hurry down, Zacchaeus, because I must stay in your house today."

⁶Zacchaeus hurried down and welcomed him with great joy. ⁷All the people who saw it started grumbling, "This man has gone as a guest to the home of a sinner!"

⁸Zacchaeus stood up and said to the Lord, "Listen, sir! I will give half my belongings to the poor, and if I have cheated anyone, I will pay back four times as much."

⁹Jesus said to him, "Salvation has come to this house today, for this man, also, is a descendant of Abraham. ¹⁰The Son of Man came to seek and to save the lost."

The Parable of the Gold Coins
(Mt 25.14–30)

¹¹While the people were listening to this, Jesus continued and told them a parable. He was now almost at Jerusalem, and they supposed that the Kingdom of God was just about to appear. ¹²So he said, "There was once a man of high rank who was going to a country far away to be made king, after which he planned to come back home. ¹³Before he left, he called his ten servants and gave them each a gold coin and told them, 'See what you can earn with this while I am gone.' ¹⁴Now, his own people hated him, and so they sent messengers after him to say, 'We don't want this man to be our king.'

¹⁵"The man was made king and came back. At once he ordered his servants to appear before him, in order to find out how much they had earned. ¹⁶The first one came and said, 'Sir, I have earned ten gold coins with the one you gave me.' ¹⁷'Well done,' he said; 'you are a good servant! Since you were faithful in small matters, I will put you in charge of ten cities.' ¹⁸The second servant came and said, 'Sir, I have earned five gold coins with the one you gave me.' ¹⁹To this one he said, 'You will be in charge of five cities.'

²⁰"Another servant came and said, 'Sir, here is your gold coin; I kept it hidden in a handkerchief. ²¹I was afraid of you, because you are a hard man. You take what is not yours and reap what you did not sow.' ²²He said to him, 'You bad servant! I will use your own words to condemn you! You know that I am a hard man, taking what is not mine and reaping what I have not sown. ²³Well, then, why didn't you put my money in the bank? Then I would have received it back with interest when I returned.'

²⁴"Then he said to those who were standing there, 'Take the gold coin away from him and give it to the servant who has ten coins.'

LUKE 19.11-27

Grab some coins of different shapes and sizes, and

DRAW

AROUND

– THEM –

on this page.
What are the gifts
God has given you to
use for his glory?
Decorate, write on and
doodle round the shapes to
represent your gifts.

1240

Luke

.·. ········

Haggai
Zechar.
Malachi
Matt.
Mark

LUKE 19, 20

25 But they said to him, 'Sir, he already has ten coins!' 26 'I tell you,' he replied, 'that to all those who have something, even more will be given; but those who have nothing, even the little that they have will be taken away from them. 27 Now, as for those enemies of mine who did not want me to be their king, bring them here and kill them in my presence!' "

The Triumphant Approach to Jerusalem
(Mt 21.1–11; Mk 11.1–11; Jn 12.12–19)

28 After Jesus said this, he went on ahead of them to Jerusalem. 29 As he came near Bethphage and Bethany at the Mount of Olives, he sent two disciples ahead 30 with these instructions: "Go to the village there ahead of you; as you go in, you will find a colt tied up that has never been ridden. Untie it and bring it here. 31 If someone asks you why you are untying it, tell him that the Master* needs it."

32 They went on their way and found everything just as Jesus had told them. 33 As they were untying the colt, its owners said to them, "Why are you untying it?"

34 "The Master* needs it," they answered, 35 and they took the colt to Jesus. Then they threw their cloaks over the animal and helped Jesus get on. 36 As he rode on, people spread their cloaks on the road.

37 When he came near Jerusalem, at the place where the road went down the Mount of Olives, the large crowd of his disciples began to thank God and praise him in loud voices for all the great things that they had seen: 38 "God bless the king who comes in the name of the Lord! Peace in heaven and glory to God!"

39 Then some of the Pharisees in the crowd spoke to Jesus. "Teacher," they said, "command your disciples to be quiet!"

40 Jesus answered, "I tell you that if they keep quiet, the stones themselves will start shouting."

Jesus Weeps over Jerusalem

41 He came closer to the city, and when he saw it, he wept over it, 42 saying, "If you only knew today what is needed for peace! But now you cannot see it! 43 The time will come when your enemies will surround you with barricades, blockade you, and close in on you from every side. 44 They will completely destroy you and the people within your walls; not a single stone will they leave in its place, because you did not recognize the time when God came to save you!"

Jesus Goes to the Temple
(Mt 21.12–17; Mk 11.15–19; Jn 2.13–22)

45 Then Jesus went into the Temple and began to drive out the merchants, 46 saying to them, "It is written in the Scriptures that God said, 'My Temple will be a house of prayer.' But you have turned it into a hideout for thieves!"

47 Every day Jesus taught in the Temple. The chief priests, the teachers of the Law, and the leaders of the people wanted to kill him, 48 but they could not find a way to do it, because all the people kept listening to him, not wanting to miss a single word.

The Question about Jesus' Authority
(Mt 21.23–27; Mk 11.27–33)

20 One day when Jesus was in the Temple teaching the people and preaching the Good News, the chief priests

19.31; 19.34 the Master; or its owner.

LUKE 20

1241

Luke

············

John
Acts
Romans
1 Corin.
2 Corin.

and the teachers of the Law, together with the elders, came [2]and said to him, "Tell us, what right have you to do these things? Who gave you this right?"

[3]Jesus answered them, "Now let me ask you a question. Tell me, [4]did John's right to baptize come from God or from human beings?"

[5]They started to argue among themselves, "What shall we say? If we say, 'From God,' he will say, 'Why, then, did you not believe John?' [6]But if we say 'From human beings,' this whole crowd here will stone us, because they are convinced that John was a prophet." [7]So they answered, "We don't know where it came from."

[8]And Jesus said to them, "Neither will I tell you, then, by what right I do these things."

The Parable of the Tenants in the Vineyard
(Mt 21.33–46; Mk 12.1–12)

[9]Then Jesus told the people this parable: "There was once a man who planted a vineyard, let it out to tenants, and then left home for a long time. [10]When the time came to gather the grapes, he sent a slave to the tenants to receive from them his share of the harvest. But the tenants beat the slave and sent him back without a thing. [11]So he sent another slave; but the tenants beat him also, treated him shamefully, and sent him back without a thing. [12]Then he sent a third slave; the tenants wounded him, too, and threw him out. [13]Then the owner of the vineyard said, 'What shall I do? I will send my own dear son; surely they will respect him!' [14]But when the tenants saw him, they said to one another, 'This is the owner's son. Let's kill him, and his property will be ours!' [15]So they threw him out of the vineyard and killed him.

"What, then, will the owner of the vineyard do to the tenants?" Jesus asked. [16]"He will come and kill those men, and hand the vineyard over to other tenants."

When the people heard this, they said, "Surely not!"

[17]Jesus looked at them and asked, "What, then, does this scripture mean?

'The stone which the builders rejected as worthless
turned out to be the most important of all.'

[18]Everyone who falls on that stone will be cut to pieces; and if that stone falls on someone, it will crush him to dust."

The Question about Paying Taxes
(Mt 22.15–22; Mk 12.13–17)

[19]The teachers of the Law and the chief priests tried to arrest Jesus on the spot, because they knew that he had told this parable against them; but they were afraid of the people. [20]So they looked for an opportunity. They bribed some men to pretend they were sincere, and they sent them to trap Jesus with questions, so that they could hand him over to the authority and power of the Roman Governor. [21]These spies said to Jesus, "Teacher, we know that what you say and teach is right. We know that you pay no attention to anyone's status, but teach the truth about God's will for people. [22]Tell us, is it against our Law for us to pay taxes to the Roman Emperor, or not?"

[23]But Jesus saw through their trick and said to them, [24]"Show me a silver coin. Whose face and name are these on it?"

"The Emperor's," they answered.

1242

LUKE 20, 21

Luke

.:. ....

Haggai
Zechar.
Malachi
Matt.
Mark

²⁵ So Jesus said, "Well, then, pay the Emperor what belongs to the Emperor, and pay God what belongs to God."

²⁶ There before the people they could not catch him out in anything, so they kept quiet, amazed at his answer.

The Question about Rising from Death
(Mt 22.23–33; Mk 12.18–27)

²⁷ Then some Sadducees, who say that people will not rise from death, came to Jesus and said, ²⁸ "Teacher, Moses wrote this law for us: 'If a man dies and leaves a wife but no children, that man's brother must marry the widow so that they can have children who will be considered the dead man's children.' ²⁹ Once there were seven brothers; the eldest got married and died without having children. ³⁰ Then the second one married the woman, ³¹ and then the third. The same thing happened to all seven — they died without having children. ³² Last of all, the woman died. ³³ Now, on the day when the dead rise to life, whose wife will she be? All seven of them had married her."

³⁴ Jesus answered them, "The men and women of this age marry, ³⁵ but the men and women who are worthy to rise from death and live in the age to come will not then marry. ³⁶ They will be like angels and cannot die. They are the children of God, because they have risen from death. ³⁷ And Moses clearly proves that the dead are raised to life. In the passage about the burning bush he speaks of the Lord as 'the God of Abraham, the God of Isaac, and the God of Jacob.' ³⁸ He is the God of the living, not of the dead, for to him all are alive."

³⁹ Some of the teachers of the Law spoke up, "A good answer, Teacher!" ⁴⁰ For they did not dare ask him any more questions.

The Question about the Messiah
(Mt 22.41–46; Mk 12.35–37)

⁴¹ Jesus asked them, "How can it be said that the Messiah will be the descendant of David? ⁴² For David himself says in the book of Psalms,

'The Lord said to my Lord:
  Sit here on my right
⁴³   until I put your enemies as a footstool under your feet.'
⁴⁴ David called him 'Lord'; how, then, can the Messiah be David's descendant?"

Jesus Warns against the Teachers of the Law
(Mt 23.1–36; Mk 12.38–40)

⁴⁵ As all the people listened to him, Jesus said to his disciples, ⁴⁶ "Be on your guard against the teachers of the Law, who like to walk about in their long robes and love to be greeted with respect in the market place; who choose the reserved seats in the synagogues and the best places at feasts; ⁴⁷ who take advantage of widows and rob them of their homes, and then make a show of saying long prayers! Their punishment will be all the worse!"

The Widow's Offering
(Mk 12.41–44)

21 Jesus looked round and saw rich people dropping their gifts in the temple treasury, ² and he also saw a very poor widow dropping in two little copper coins. ³ He said, "I tell you that this poor widow put in more than all the others. ⁴ For the others offered their gifts from what they had to spare of their riches; but she, poor as she is, gave all she had to live on."

1243

Luke
·············
John
Acts
Romans
1 Corin.
2 Corin.

Jesus Speaks of the Destruction of the Temple
(Mt 24.1–2; Mk 13.1–2)

⁵Some of the disciples were talking about the Temple, how beautiful it looked with its fine stones and the gifts offered to God. Jesus said, ⁶"All this you see — the time will come when not a single stone here will be left in its place; every one will be thrown down."

Troubles and Persecutions
(Mt 24.3–14; Mk 13.3–13)

⁷"Teacher," they asked, "when will this be? And what will happen in order to show that the time has come for it to take place?"

⁸Jesus said, "Be on guard; don't be deceived. Many men, claiming to speak for me, will come and say, 'I am he!' and, 'The time has come!' But don't follow them. ⁹Don't be afraid when you hear of wars and revolutions; such things must happen first, but they do not mean that the end is near."

¹⁰He went on to say, "Countries will fight each other; kingdoms will attack one another. ¹¹There will be terrible earthquakes, famines, and plagues everywhere; there will be strange and terrifying things coming from the sky. ¹²Before all these things take place, however, you will be arrested and persecuted; you will be handed over to be tried in synagogues and be put in prison; you will be brought before kings and rulers for my sake. ¹³This will be your chance to tell the Good News. ¹⁴Make up your minds beforehand not to worry about how you will defend yourselves, ¹⁵because I will give you such words and wisdom that none of your enemies will be able to refute or contradict what you say. ¹⁶You will be handed over by your parents, your brothers, your relatives, and your friends; and some of you will be put to death. ¹⁷Everyone will hate you because of me. ¹⁸But not a single hair from your heads will be lost. ¹⁹Stand firm, and you will save yourselves.

Jesus Speaks of the Destruction of Jerusalem
(Mt 24.15–21; Mk 13.14–19)

²⁰"When you see Jerusalem surrounded by armies, then you will know that it will soon be destroyed. ²¹Then those who are in Judea must run away to the hills; those who are in the city must leave, and those who are out in the country must not go into the city. ²²For those will be 'The Days of Punishment', to make all that the Scriptures say come true. ²³How terrible it will be in those days for women who are pregnant and for mothers with little babies! Terrible distress will come upon this land, and God's punishment will fall on this people. ²⁴Some will be killed by the sword, and others will be taken as prisoners to all countries; and the heathen will trample over Jerusalem until their time is up.

The Coming of the Son of Man
(Mt 24.29–31; Mk 13.24–27)

²⁵"There will be strange things happening to the sun, the moon, and the stars. On earth whole countries will be in despair, afraid of the roar of the sea and the raging tides. ²⁶People will faint from fear as they wait for what is coming over the whole earth, for the powers in space will be driven from their courses. ²⁷Then the Son of Man will appear, coming in a cloud with great power and glory. ²⁸When these things begin to happen, stand up and raise your heads, because your salvation is near."

1244

Luke

·:········

Haggai
Zechar.
Malachi
Matt.
Mark

LUKE 21, 22

The Lesson of the Fig Tree
(Mt 24.32–35; Mk 13.28–31)

29 Then Jesus told them this parable: "Think of the fig tree and all the other trees. 30 When you see their leaves beginning to appear, you know that summer is near. 31 In the same way, when you see these things happening, you will know that the Kingdom of God is about to come.

32 "Remember that all these things will take place before the people now living have all died. 33 Heaven and earth will pass away, but my words will never pass away.

The Need to Watch

34 "Be on your guard! Don't let yourselves become occupied with too much feasting and drinking and with the worries of this life, or that Day may suddenly catch you 35 like a trap. For it will come upon all people everywhere on earth. 36 Be on the alert and pray always that you will have the strength to go safely through all those things that will happen and to stand before the Son of Man."

37 Jesus spent those days teaching in the Temple, and when evening came, he would go out and spend the night on the Mount of Olives. 38 Early each morning all the people went to the Temple to listen to him.

The Plot against Jesus
(Mt 26.1–5; Mk 14.1–2; Jn 11.45–53)

22 The time was near for the Festival of Unleavened Bread, which is called the Passover. 2 The chief priests and the teachers of the Law were afraid of the people, and so they were trying to find a way of putting Jesus to death secretly.

Judas Agrees to Betray Jesus
(Mt 26.14–16; Mk 14.10–11)

3 Then Satan entered Judas, called Iscariot, who was one of the twelve disciples. 4 So Judas went off and spoke with the chief priests and the officers of the temple guard about how he could betray Jesus to them. 5 They were pleased and offered to pay him money. 6 Judas agreed to it and started looking for a good chance to hand Jesus over to them without the people knowing about it.

Jesus Prepares to Eat the Passover Meal
(Mt 26.17–25; Mk 14.12–21; Jn 13.21–30)

7 The day came during the Festival of Unleavened Bread when the lambs for the Passover meal were to be killed. 8 Jesus sent off Peter and John with these instructions: "Go and get the Passover meal ready for us to eat."

9 "Where do you want us to get it ready?" they asked him.

10 He answered, "As you go into the city, a man carrying a jar of water will meet you. Follow him into the house that he enters, 11 and say to the owner of the house: 'The Teacher says to you, Where is the room where my disciples and I will eat the Passover meal?' 12 He will show you a large furnished room upstairs, where you will get everything ready."

13 They went off and found everything just as Jesus had told them, and they prepared the Passover meal.

The Lord's Supper
(Mt 26.26–30; Mk 14.22–26; 1 Cor 11.23–25)

14 When the hour came, Jesus took his place at the table with the apostles. 15 He said to them, "I have wanted so much to eat

LUKE 22.14-20

Communion is a
re-enactment of the

- LAST -

SUPPER,

reminding us of what
Jesus has done by
giving up his life for
us. Why not take a few
moments to pause
and reflect on what he
did for you?

LUKE 22

1245

Luke
···········:·
John
Acts
Romans
1 Corin.
2 Corin.

this Passover meal with you before I suffer! [16] For I tell you, I will never eat it until it is given its full meaning in the Kingdom of God."

[17] Then Jesus took a cup, gave thanks to God, and said, "Take this and share it among yourselves. [18] I tell you that from now on I will not drink this wine until the Kingdom of God comes."

[19] Then he took a piece of bread, gave thanks to God, broke it, and gave it to them, saying, "This is my body, which is given for you. Do this in memory of me." [20] In the same way, he gave them the cup after the supper, saying, "This cup is God's new covenant sealed with my blood, which is poured out for you.*

[21] "But, look! The one who betrays me is here at the table with me! [22] The Son of Man will die as God has decided, but how terrible for that man who betrays him!"

[23] Then they began to ask among themselves which one of them it could be who was going to do this.

The Argument about Greatness

[24] An argument broke out among the disciples as to which one of them should be thought of as the greatest. [25] Jesus said to them, "The kings of the pagans have power over their people, and the rulers claim the title 'Friends of the People'. [26] But this is not the way it is with you; rather, the greatest one among you must be like the youngest, and the leader must be like the servant. [27] Who is greater, the one who sits down to eat or the one who serves? The one who sits down, of course. But I am among you as one who serves.

[28] "You have stayed with me all through my trials; [29] and just as my Father has given me the right to rule, so I will give you the same right. [30] You will eat and drink at my table in my Kingdom, and you will sit on thrones to rule over the twelve tribes of Israel.

Jesus Predicts Peter's Denial
(Mt 26.31–35; Mk 14.27–31; Jn 13.36–38)

[31] "Simon, Simon! Listen! Satan has received permission to test all of you, to separate the good from the bad, as a farmer separates the wheat from the chaff. [32] But I have prayed for you, Simon, that your faith will not fail. And when you turn back to me, you must strengthen your brothers."

[33] Peter answered, "Lord, I am ready to go to prison with you and to die with you!"

[34] "I tell you, Peter," Jesus said, "the cock will not crow tonight until you have said three times that you do not know me."

Purse, Bag, and Sword

[35] Then Jesus asked his disciples, "When I sent you out that time without purse, bag, or shoes, did you lack anything?"

"Not a thing," they answered.

[36] "But now," Jesus said, "whoever has a purse or a bag must take it; and whoever has no sword must sell his coat and buy one. [37] For I tell you that the scripture which says, 'He shared the fate of criminals,' must come true about me, because what was written about me is coming true."

[38] The disciples said, "Look! Here are two swords, Lord!"

"That is enough!"* he replied.

22.20 Some manuscripts do not have the words of Jesus after *This is my body* in verse 19, and all of verse 20.
22.38 *That is enough*; or *Enough of this.*

1246

Luke

Haggai
Zechar.
Malachi
Matt.
Mark

LUKE 22

Jesus Prays on the Mount of Olives
(Mt 26.36–46; Mk 14.32–42)

³⁹ Jesus left the city and went, as he usually did, to the Mount of Olives; and the disciples went with him. ⁴⁰ When he arrived at the place, he said to them, "Pray that you will not fall into temptation."

⁴¹ Then he went off from them about the distance of a stone's throw and knelt down and prayed. ⁴²"Father," he said, "if you will, take this cup of suffering away from me. Not my will, however, but your will be done." ⁴³ An angel from heaven appeared to him and strengthened him. ⁴⁴ In great anguish he prayed even more fervently; his sweat was like drops of blood falling to the ground.*

⁴⁵ Rising from his prayer, he went back to the disciples and found them asleep, worn out by their grief. ⁴⁶ He said to them, "Why are you sleeping? Get up and pray that you will not fall into temptation."

The Arrest of Jesus
(Mt 26.47–56; Mk 14.43–50; Jn 18.3–11)

⁴⁷ Jesus was still speaking when a crowd arrived, led by Judas, one of the twelve disciples. He came up to Jesus to kiss him. ⁴⁸ But Jesus said, "Judas, is it with a kiss that you betray the Son of Man?"

⁴⁹ When the disciples who were with Jesus saw what was going to happen, they asked, "Shall we use our swords, Lord?" ⁵⁰ And one of them struck the High Priest's slave and cut off his right ear.

⁵¹ But Jesus said, "Enough of this!" He touched the man's ear and healed him.

⁵² Then Jesus said to the chief priests and the officers of the temple guard and the elders who had come there to get him, "Did you have to come with swords and clubs, as though I were an outlaw? ⁵³ I was with you in the Temple every day, and you did not try to arrest me. But this is your hour to act, when the power of darkness rules."

Peter Denies Jesus
(Mt 26.57–58, 69–75; Mk 14.53–54, 66–72; Jn 18.12–18, 25–27)

⁵⁴ They arrested Jesus and took him away into the house of the High Priest; and Peter followed at a distance. ⁵⁵ A fire had been lit in the centre of the courtyard, and Peter joined those who were sitting round it. ⁵⁶ When one of the servant women saw him sitting there at the fire, she looked straight at him and said, "This man too was with Jesus!"

⁵⁷ But Peter denied it, "Woman, I don't even know him!"

⁵⁸ After a little while a man noticed Peter and said, "You are one of them, too!"

But Peter answered, "Man, I am not!"

⁵⁹ And about an hour later another man insisted strongly, "There isn't any doubt that this man was with Jesus, because he also is a Galilean!"

⁶⁰ But Peter answered, "Man, I don't know what you are talking about!"

At once, while he was still speaking, a cock crowed. ⁶¹ The Lord turned round and looked straight at Peter, and Peter remembered that the Lord had said to him, "Before the cock crows tonight,

---

22.44 Some manuscripts do not have verses 43–44.

LUKE 22, 23

1247

Luke

....

John
Acts
Romans
1 Corin.
2 Corin.

you will say three times that you do not know me." ⁶²Peter went out and wept bitterly.

Jesus is Mocked and Beaten
(Mt 26.67–68; Mk 14.65)

⁶³The men who were guarding Jesus mocked him and beat him. ⁶⁴They blindfolded him and asked him, "Who hit you? Guess!" ⁶⁵And they said many other insulting things to him.

Jesus is Brought before the Council
(Mt 26.59–66; Mk 14.55–64; Jn 18.19–24)

⁶⁶When day came, the elders, the chief priests, and the teachers of the Law met together, and Jesus was brought before the Council. ⁶⁷"Tell us," they said, "are you the Messiah?"

He answered, "If I tell you, you will not believe me; ⁶⁸and if I ask you a question, you will not answer. ⁶⁹But from now on the Son of Man will be seated on the right of Almighty God."

⁷⁰They all said, "Are you, then, the Son of God?"

He answered them, "You say that I am."

⁷¹And they said, "We don't need any witnesses! We ourselves have heard what he said!"

Jesus is Brought before Pilate
(Mt 27.1–2, 11–14; Mk 15.1–5; Jn 18.28–38)

23 The whole group rose up and took Jesus before Pilate, ²where they began to accuse him: "We caught this man misleading our people, telling them not to pay taxes to the Emperor and claiming that he himself is the Messiah, a king."

³Pilate asked him, "Are you the king of the Jews?"

"So you say," answered Jesus.

⁴Then Pilate said to the chief priests and the crowds, "I find no reason to condemn this man."

⁵But they insisted even more strongly, "With his teaching he is starting a riot among the people all through Judea. He began in Galilee and now has come here."

Jesus is Sent to Herod

⁶When Pilate heard this, he asked, "Is this man a Galilean?" ⁷When he learnt that Jesus was from the region ruled by Herod, he sent him to Herod, who was also in Jerusalem at that time. ⁸Herod was very pleased when he saw Jesus, because he had heard about him and had been wanting to see him for a long time. He was hoping to see Jesus perform some miracle. ⁹So Herod asked Jesus many questions, but Jesus made no answer. ¹⁰The chief priests and the teachers of the Law stepped forward and made strong accusations against Jesus. ¹¹Herod and his soldiers mocked Jesus and treated him with contempt; then they put a fine robe on him and sent him back to Pilate. ¹²On that very day Herod and Pilate became friends; before this they had been enemies.

Jesus is Sentenced to Death
(Mt 27.15–26; Mk 15.6–15; Jn 18.39—19.16)

¹³Pilate called together the chief priests, the leaders, and the people, ¹⁴and said to them, "You brought this man to me and said that he was misleading the people. Now, I have examined him here in your presence, and I have not found him guilty of any of the crimes you accuse him of. ¹⁵Nor did Herod find him guilty,

1248

Luke

·:········

Haggai
Zechar.
Malachi
Matt.
Mark

LUKE 23

for he sent him back to us. There is nothing this man has done to deserve death. [16] So I will have him whipped and let him go."*

[18] The whole crowd cried out, "Kill him! Set Barabbas free for us!" [19] (Barabbas had been put in prison for a riot that had taken place in the city, and for murder.)

[20] Pilate wanted to set Jesus free, so he appealed to the crowd again. [21] But they shouted back, "Crucify him! Crucify him!"

[22] Pilate said to them the third time, "But what crime has he committed? I cannot find anything he has done to deserve death! I will have him whipped and set him free."

[23] But they kept on shouting at the top of their voices that Jesus should be crucified, and finally their shouting succeeded. [24] So Pilate passed the sentence on Jesus that they were asking for. [25] He set free the man they wanted, the one who had been put in prison for riot and murder, and he handed Jesus over for them to do as they wished.

Jesus is Crucified
(Mt 27.32–44; Mk 15.21–32; Jn 19.17–27)

[26] The soldiers led Jesus away, and as they were going, they met a man from Cyrene named Simon who was coming into the city from the country. They seized him, put the cross on him, and made him carry it behind Jesus.

[27] A large crowd of people followed him; among them were some women who were weeping and wailing for him. [28] Jesus turned to them and said, "Women of Jerusalem! Don't cry for me, but for yourselves and your children. [29] For the days are coming when people will say, 'How lucky are the women who never had children, who never bore babies, who never nursed them!' [30] That will be the time when people will say to the mountains, 'Fall on us!' and to the hills, 'Hide us!' [31] For if such things as these are done when the wood is green, what will happen when it is dry?"

[32] Two other men, both of them criminals, were also led out to be put to death with Jesus. [33] When they came to the place called "The Skull", they crucified Jesus there, and the two criminals, one on his right and the other on his left. [34] Jesus said, "Forgive them, Father! They don't know what they are doing."*

They divided his clothes among themselves by throwing dice. [35] The people stood there watching while the Jewish leaders jeered at him: "He saved others; let him save himself if he is the Messiah whom God has chosen!"

[36] The soldiers also mocked him: they came up to him and offered him cheap wine, [37] and said, "Save yourself if you are the king of the Jews!"

[38] Above him were written these words: "This is the King of the Jews."

[39] One of the criminals hanging there hurled insults at him: "Aren't you the Messiah? Save yourself and us!"

[40] The other one, however, rebuked him, saying, "Don't you fear God? You received the same sentence he did. [41] Ours, however, is only right, because we are getting what we deserve for what we did; but he has done no wrong." [42] And he said to Jesus, "Remember me, Jesus, when you come as King!"

....

23.16 Some manuscripts add verse 17: *At every Passover Festival Pilate had to set free one prisoner for them* (see Mk 15.6).
23.34 Some manuscripts do not have *Jesus said, "Forgive them, Father! They don't know what they are doing."*

LUKE 23, 24

1249

Luke

John
Acts
Romans
1 Corin.
2 Corin.

43 Jesus said to him, "I promise you that today you will be in Paradise with me."

The Death of Jesus
(Mt 27.45–56; Mk 15.33–41; Jn 19.28–30)

44-45 It was about twelve o'clock when the sun stopped shining and darkness covered the whole country until three o'clock; and the curtain hanging in the Temple was torn in two. 46 Jesus cried out in a loud voice, "Father! In your hands I place my spirit!" He said this and died.

47 The army officer saw what had happened, and he praised God, saying, "Certainly he was a good man!"

48 When the people who had gathered there to watch the spectacle saw what happened, they all went back home, beating their breasts in sorrow. 49 All those who knew Jesus personally, including the women who had followed him from Galilee, stood at a distance to watch.

The Burial of Jesus
(Mt 27.57–61; Mk 15.42–47; Jn 19.38–42)

50-51 There was a man named Joseph from Arimathea, a town in Judea. He was a good and honourable man, who was waiting for the coming of the Kingdom of God. Although he was a member of the Council, he had not agreed with their decision and action. 52 He went into the presence of Pilate and asked for the body of Jesus. 53 Then he took the body down, wrapped it in a linen sheet, and placed it in a tomb which had been dug out of solid rock and which had never been used. 54 It was Friday, and the Sabbath was about to begin.

55 The women who had followed Jesus from Galilee went with Joseph and saw the tomb and how Jesus' body was placed in it. 56 Then they went back home and prepared the spices and perfumes for the body.

On the Sabbath they rested, as the Law commanded.

The Resurrection
(Mt 28.1–10; Mk 16.1–8; Jn 20.1–10)

24 Very early on Sunday morning the women went to the tomb, carrying the spices they had prepared. 2 They found the stone rolled away from the entrance to the tomb, 3 so they went in; but they did not find the body of the Lord Jesus. 4 They stood there puzzled about this, when suddenly two men in bright shining clothes stood by them. 5 Full of fear, the women bowed down to the ground, as the men said to them, "Why are you looking among the dead for one who is alive? 6 He is not here; he has been raised. Remember what he said to you while he was in Galilee: 7 'The Son of Man must be handed over to sinners, be crucified, and three days later rise to life.' "

8 Then the women remembered his words, 9 returned from the tomb, and told all these things to the eleven disciples and all the rest. 10 The women were Mary Magdalene, Joanna, and Mary the mother of James; they and the other women with them told these things to the apostles. 11 But the apostles thought that what the women said was nonsense, and they did not believe them. 12 But Peter got up and ran to the tomb; he bent down and saw the linen wrappings but nothing else. Then he went back home amazed at what had happened.*

24.12 Some manuscripts do not have verse 12.

LUKE 24

The resurrection signifies Jesus' victory over death, giving us freedom and a relationship with God.

THIS IS
– TO BE –

CELEBRATED!

DO SOMETHING TO CELEBRATE.

Turn on your favourite music, grab a snack and stick things on these pages that remind you of celebrating. Think balloons, glitter, colour, wrapping paper - anything!

1250

LUKE 24

Luke

Haggai
Zechar.
Malachi
Matt.
Mark

The Walk to Emmaus
(Mk 16.12–13)

¹³ On that same day two of Jesus' followers were going to a village named Emmaus, about eleven kilometres from Jerusalem, ¹⁴ and they were talking to each other about all the things that had happened. ¹⁵ As they talked and discussed, Jesus himself drew near and walked along with them; ¹⁶ they saw him, but somehow did not recognize him. ¹⁷ Jesus said to them, "What are you talking about to each other, as you walk along?"

They stood still, with sad faces. ¹⁸ One of them, named Cleopas, asked him, "Are you the only visitor in Jerusalem who doesn't know the things that have been happening there these last few days?"

¹⁹ "What things?" he asked.

"The things that happened to Jesus of Nazareth," they answered. "This man was a prophet and was considered by God and by all the people to be powerful in everything he said and did. ²⁰ Our chief priests and rulers handed him over to be sentenced to death, and he was crucified. ²¹ And we had hoped that he would be the one who was going to set Israel free! Besides all that, this is now the third day since it happened. ²² Some of the women of our group surprised us; they went at dawn to the tomb, ²³ but could not find his body. They came back saying they had seen a vision of angels who told them that he is alive. ²⁴ Some of our group went to the tomb and found it exactly as the women had said, but they did not see him."

²⁵ Then Jesus said to them, "How foolish you are, how slow you are to believe everything the prophets said! ²⁶ Was it not necessary for the Messiah to suffer these things and then to enter his glory?" ²⁷ And Jesus explained to them what was said about himself in all the Scriptures, beginning with the books of Moses and the writings of all the prophets.

²⁸ As they came near the village to which they were going, Jesus acted as if he were going farther; ²⁹ but they held him back, saying, "Stay with us; the day is almost over and it is getting dark." So he went in to stay with them. ³⁰ He sat down to eat with them, took the bread, and said the blessing; then he broke the bread and gave it to them. ³¹ Then their eyes were opened and they recognized him, but he disappeared from their sight. ³² They said to each other, "Wasn't it like a fire burning in us when he talked to us on the road and explained the Scriptures to us?"

³³ They got up at once and went back to Jerusalem, where they found the eleven disciples gathered together with the others ³⁴ and saying, "The Lord is risen indeed! He has appeared to Simon!"

³⁵ The two then explained to them what had happened on the road, and how they had recognized the Lord when he broke the bread.

Jesus Appears to his Disciples
(Mt 28.16–20; Mk 16.14–18; Jn 20.19–23; Acts 1.6–8)

³⁶ While the two were telling them this, suddenly the Lord himself stood among them and said to them, "Peace be with you."*

³⁷ They were terrified, thinking that they were seeing a ghost. ³⁸ But he said to them, "Why are you alarmed? Why are these doubts coming up in your minds? ³⁹ Look at my hands and my feet, and see that it is I myself. Feel me, and you will know, for a ghost doesn't have flesh and bones, as you can see I have."

......

24.36 Some manuscripts do not have *and said to them, "Peace be with you."*

LUKE 24

1251

Luke

John
Acts
Romans
1 Corin.
2 Corin.

⁴⁰He said this and showed them his hands and his feet.* ⁴¹They still could not believe, they were so full of joy and wonder; so he asked them, "Have you anything here to eat?" ⁴²They gave him a piece of cooked fish, ⁴³which he took and ate in their presence.

⁴⁴Then he said to them, "These are the very things I told you about while I was still with you: everything written about me in the Law of Moses, the writings of the prophets, and the Psalms had to come true."

⁴⁵Then he opened their minds to understand the Scriptures, ⁴⁶and said to them, "This is what is written: the Messiah must suffer and must rise from death three days later, ⁴⁷and in his name the message about repentance and the forgiveness of sins must be preached to all nations, beginning in Jerusalem. ⁴⁸You are witnesses of these things. ⁴⁹And I myself will send upon you what my Father has promised. But you must wait in the city until the power from above comes down upon you."

Jesus is Taken Up to Heaven
(Mk 16.19–20; Acts 1.9–11)

⁵⁰Then he led them out of the city as far as Bethany, where he raised his hands and blessed them. ⁵¹As he was blessing them, he departed from them and was taken up into heaven.* ⁵²They worshipped him and went back into Jerusalem, filled with great joy, ⁵³and spent all their time in the Temple giving thanks to God.

24.40 Some manuscripts do not have verse 40.
24.51 Some manuscripts do not have and was taken up into heaven.

THE GOSPEL OF
JOHN

WRITTEN: AD90-100

WHY READ IT?

The book of John shows the incredible nature of Jesus as fully God, but also as God in human form. Jesus experienced human life and knows what it is like to feel emotions, to struggle, and to experience loss, excitement and joy. He is a God who understands everything we go through.

WHAT YOU NEED TO KNOW:

The Gospel of John is the last of the four Gospels. This one is quite different from the other three. It starts not with a factual account of some part of Jesus' life, but at the beginning of time, using symbolic language to represent who Jesus is. There are no parables in this book but there's plenty of imagery, as well as seven of Jesus' miracles and seven 'I am' statements describing who he is. John shows Jesus as both fully God and fully man - God in human form.

JESUS WAS BOTH FULLY MAN & FULLY GOD

As you read John's Gospel, write a list of things in it that show that Jesus was fully man. Then, write a list of things that show Jesus was also fully God.

_____
_____
_____
_____
_____
_____
_____
_____
_____
_____
_____
_____
_____

TURN THESE SHAPES INTO
SOMETHING ↘
ELSE

JESUS' BAPTISM (AD24)

HEALING AND TEACHING

DEATH

RESURRECTIO (AD27)

JOHN 1

1253

John
·········⋮·
Acts
Romans
1 Corin.
2 Corin.
Galat.

The Word of Life

1 In the beginning the Word already existed; the Word was with God, and the Word was God. ²From the very beginning the Word was with God. ³Through him God made all things; not one thing in all creation was made without him. ⁴The Word was the source of life,* and this life brought light to humanity. ⁵The light shines in the darkness, and the darkness has never put it out.

⁶God sent his messenger, a man named John, ⁷who came to tell people about the light, so that all should hear the message and believe. ⁸He himself was not the light; he came to tell about the light. ⁹This was the real light — the light that comes into the world and shines on everyone.

¹⁰The Word was in the world, and though God made the world through him, yet the world did not recognize him. ¹¹He came to his own country, but his own people did not receive him. ¹²Some, however, did receive him and believed in him; so he gave them the right to become God's children. ¹³They did not become God's children by natural means, that is, by being born as the children of a human father; God himself was their Father.

¹⁴The Word became a human being and, full of grace and truth, lived among us. We saw his glory, the glory which he received as the Father's only Son.

¹⁵John spoke about him. He cried out, "This is the one I was talking about when I said, 'He comes after me, but he is greater than I am, because he existed before I was born.' "

¹⁶Out of the fullness of his grace he has blessed us all, giving us one blessing after another. ¹⁷God gave the Law through Moses, but grace and truth came through Jesus Christ. ¹⁸No one has ever seen God. The only Son, who is the same as God and is at the Father's side, he has made him known.

John the Baptist's Message
(Mt 3.1–12; Mk 1.1–8; Lk 3.1–18)

¹⁹The Jewish authorities in Jerusalem sent some priests and Levites to John, to ask him, "Who are you?"

²⁰John did not refuse to answer, but spoke out openly and clearly, saying: "I am not the Messiah."

²¹"Who are you, then?" they asked. "Are you Elijah?"

"No, I am not," John answered.

"Are you the Prophet?"* they asked.

"No," he replied.

²²"Then tell us who you are," they said. "We have to take an answer back to those who sent us. What do you say about yourself?"

²³John answered by quoting the prophet Isaiah:
"I am 'the voice of someone shouting in the desert:
Make a straight path for the Lord to travel!' "

²⁴The messengers, who had been sent by the Pharisees, ²⁵then* asked John, "If you are not the Messiah nor Elijah nor the Prophet, why do you baptize?"

²⁶John answered, "I baptize with water, but among you stands the one you do not know. ²⁷He is coming after me, but I am not good enough even to untie his sandals."

1.4 *The Word was the source of life*; or *What was made had life in union with the Word.*
1.21 *the Prophet*: The one who was expected to appear and announce the coming of the Messiah.
1.24–25 *The messengers, who had been sent by the Pharisees,* ²⁵ *then*; or *Those who had been sent were Pharisees; they.*

1254

John

.·:.........

Zechar.
Malachi
Matt.
Mark
Luke

JOHN 1

28 All this happened in Bethany on the east side of the River Jordan, where John was baptizing.

The Lamb of God

29 The next day John saw Jesus coming to him, and said, "There is the Lamb of God, who takes away the sin of the world! 30 This is the one I was talking about when I said, 'A man is coming after me, but he is greater than I am, because he existed before I was born.' 31 I did not know who he would be, but I came baptizing with water in order to make him known to the people of Israel."

32 And John gave this testimony: "I saw the Spirit come down like a dove from heaven and stay on him. 33 I still did not know that he was the one, but God, who sent me to baptize with water, had said to me, 'You will see the Spirit come down and stay on a man; he is the one who baptizes with the Holy Spirit.' 34 I have seen it," said John, "and I tell you that he is the Son of God."

The First Disciples of Jesus

35 The next day John was standing there again with two of his disciples, 36 when he saw Jesus walking by. "There is the Lamb of God!" he said.

37 The two disciples heard him say this and went with Jesus. 38 Jesus turned, saw them following him, and asked, "What are you looking for?"

They answered, "Where do you live, Rabbi?" (This word means "Teacher".)

39 "Come and see," he answered. (It was then about four o'clock in the afternoon.) So they went with him and saw where he lived, and spent the rest of that day with him.

40 One of them was Andrew, Simon Peter's brother. 41 At once he found his brother Simon and told him, "We have found the Messiah." (This word means "Christ".) 42 Then he took Simon to Jesus.

Jesus looked at him and said, "Your name is Simon son of John, but you will be called Cephas." (This is the same as Peter and means "a rock".)

Jesus Calls Philip and Nathanael

43 The next day Jesus decided to go to Galilee. He found Philip and said to him, "Come with me!" 44 (Philip was from Bethsaida, the town where Andrew and Peter lived.) 45 Philip found Nathanael and told him, "We have found the one whom Moses wrote about in the book of the Law and whom the prophets also wrote about. He is Jesus son of Joseph, from Nazareth."

46 "Can anything good come from Nazareth?" Nathanael asked.

"Come and see," answered Philip.

47 When Jesus saw Nathanael coming to him, he said about him, "Here is a real Israelite; there is nothing false in him!"

48 Nathanael asked him, "How do you know me?"

Jesus answered, "I saw you when you were under the fig tree before Philip called you."

49 "Teacher," answered Nathanael, "you are the Son of God! You are the King of Israel!"

50 Jesus said, "Do you believe just because I told you I saw you when you were under the fig tree? You will see much greater things than this!" 51 And he said to them, "I am telling you the truth: you will see heaven open and God's angels going up and coming down on the Son of Man."

JOHN 2, 3

1255

John

Acts
Romans
1 Corin.
2 Corin.
Galat.

The Wedding in Cana

2 Two days later there was a wedding in the town of Cana in Galilee. Jesus' mother was there, [2] and Jesus and his disciples had also been invited to the wedding. [3] When the wine had given out, Jesus' mother said to him, "They have no wine left."

[4] "You must not tell me what to do," Jesus replied. "My time has not yet come."

[5] Jesus' mother then told the servants, "Do whatever he tells you."

[6] The Jews have rules about ritual washing, and for this purpose six stone water jars were there, each one large enough to hold about a hundred litres. [7] Jesus said to the servants, "Fill these jars with water." They filled them to the brim, [8] and then he told them, "Now draw some water out and take it to the man in charge of the feast." They took him the water, [9] which now had turned into wine, and he tasted it. He did not know where this wine had come from (but, of course, the servants who had drawn out the water knew); so he called the bridegroom [10] and said to him, "Everyone else serves the best wine first, and after the guests have had plenty to drink, he serves the ordinary wine. But you have kept the best wine until now!"

[11] Jesus performed this first miracle in Cana in Galilee; there he revealed his glory, and his disciples believed in him.

[12] After this, Jesus and his mother, brothers, and disciples went to Capernaum and stayed there a few days.

Jesus Goes to the Temple

(Mt 21.12–13; Mk 11.15–17; Lk 19.45–46)

[13] It was almost time for the Passover Festival, so Jesus went to Jerusalem. [14] There in the Temple he found people selling cattle, sheep, and pigeons, and also the moneychangers sitting at their tables. [15] So he made a whip from cords and drove all the animals out of the Temple, both the sheep and the cattle; he overturned the tables of the moneychangers and scattered their coins; [16] and he ordered those who sold the pigeons, "Take them out of here! Stop making my Father's house a market place!" [17] His disciples remembered that the scripture says, "My devotion to your house, O God, burns in me like a fire."

[18] The Jewish authorities replied with a question, "What miracle can you perform to show us that you have the right to do this?"

[19] Jesus answered, "Tear down this Temple, and in three days I will build it again."

[20] "Are you going to build it again in three days?" they asked him. "It has taken 46 years to build this Temple!"

[21] But the temple Jesus was speaking about was his body. [22] So when he was raised from death, his disciples remembered that he had said this, and they believed the scripture and what Jesus had said.

Jesus' Knowledge of Human Nature

[23] While Jesus was in Jerusalem during the Passover Festival, many believed in him as they saw the miracles he performed. [24] But Jesus did not trust himself to them, because he knew them all. [25] There was no need for anyone to tell him about them, because he himself knew what was in their hearts.

Jesus and Nicodemus

3 There was a Jewish leader named Nicodemus, who belonged to the party of the Pharisees. [2] One night he went to Jesus

JOHN 2.19-22

In the Old Testament, it was believed that

• GOD'S •

PRESENCE

lived in the temple. When Jesus described himself as the temple, he was signalling the presence of God walking, and living, among the people.

1256

John

·:········

Zechar.
Malachi
Matt.
Mark
Luke

JOHN 3

and said to him, "Rabbi, we know that you are a teacher sent by God. No one could perform the miracles you are doing unless God were with him."

3 Jesus answered, "I am telling you the truth: no one can see the Kingdom of God without being born again."*

4 "How can a grown man be born again?" Nicodemus asked. "He certainly cannot enter his mother's womb and be born a second time!"

5 "I am telling you the truth," replied Jesus. "No one can enter the Kingdom of God without being born of water and the Spirit. 6 A person is born physically of human parents, but is born spiritually of the Spirit. 7 Do not be surprised because I tell you that you must all be born again.* 8 The wind blows wherever it wishes; you hear the sound it makes, but you do not know where it comes from or where it is going. It is like that with everyone who is born of the Spirit."

9 "How can this be?" asked Nicodemus.

10 Jesus answered, "You are a great teacher in Israel, and you don't know this? 11 I am telling you the truth: we speak of what we know and report what we have seen, yet none of you is willing to accept our message. 12 You do not believe me when I tell you about the things of this world; how will you ever believe me, then, when I tell you about the things of heaven? 13 And no one has ever gone up to heaven except the Son of Man, who came down from heaven."*

14 As Moses lifted up the bronze snake on a pole in the desert, in the same way the Son of Man must be lifted up, 15 so that everyone who believes in him may have eternal life. 16 For God loved the world so much that he gave his only Son, so that everyone who believes in him may not die but have eternal life. 17 For God did not send his Son into the world to be its judge, but to be its saviour.

18 Those who believe in the Son are not judged; but those who do not believe have already been judged, because they have not believed in God's only Son. 19 This is how the judgement works: the light has come into the world, but people love the darkness rather than the light, because their deeds are evil. 20 All those who do evil things hate the light and will not come to the light, because they do not want their evil deeds to be shown up. 21 But those who do what is true come to the light in order that the light may show that what they did was in obedience to God.

Jesus and John

22 After this, Jesus and his disciples went to the province of Judea, where he spent some time with them and baptized. 23 John also was baptizing in Aenon, not far from Salim, because there was plenty of water in that place. People were going to him, and he was baptizing them. 24 (This was before John had been put in prison.)

25 Some of John's disciples began arguing with a Jew* about the matter of ritual washing. 26 So they went to John and said, "Teacher, you remember the man who was with you on the east side of the Jordan, the one you spoke about? Well, he is baptizing now, and everyone is going to him!"

27 John answered, "No one can have anything unless God gives it to him. 28 You yourselves are my witnesses that I said, 'I am not the Messiah, but I have been sent ahead of him.'

3.3; 3.7 *again*; or *from above*.
3.13 The quotation may continue through verse 21.
3.25 *a Jew*; some manuscripts have *some Jews*.

John

....

Acts
Romans
1 Corin.
2 Corin.
Galat.

29 The bridegroom is the one to whom the bride belongs; but the bridegroom's friend, who stands by and listens, is glad when he hears the bridegroom's voice. This is how my own happiness is made complete. 30 He must become more important while I become less important."

He who Comes from Heaven

31 He who comes from above is greater than all. He who is from the earth belongs to the earth and speaks about earthly matters, but he who comes from heaven is above all. 32 He tells what he has seen and heard, yet no one accepts his message. 33 But whoever accepts his message confirms by this that God is truthful. 34 The one whom God has sent speaks God's words, because God gives him the fullness of his Spirit. 35 The Father loves his Son and has put everything in his power. 36 Whoever believes in the Son has eternal life; whoever disobeys the Son will not have life, but will remain under God's punishment.

Jesus and the Samaritan Woman

4 The Pharisees heard that Jesus was winning and baptizing more disciples than John. 2 (Actually, Jesus himself did not baptize anyone; only his disciples did.) 3 So when Jesus heard what was being said, he left Judea and went back to Galilee; 4 on his way there he had to go through Samaria.

5 In Samaria he came to a town named Sychar, which was not far from the field that Jacob had given to his son Joseph. 6 Jacob's well was there, and Jesus, tired out by the journey, sat down by the well. It was about noon.

7 A Samaritan woman came to draw some water, and Jesus said to her, "Give me a drink of water." 8 (His disciples had gone into town to buy food.)

9 The woman answered, "You are a Jew, and I am a Samaritan — so how can you ask me for a drink?" (Jews will not use the same cups and bowls that Samaritans use.)*

10 Jesus answered, "If only you knew what God gives and who it is that is asking you for a drink, you would ask him, and he would give you life-giving water."

11 "Sir," the woman said, "you haven't got a bucket, and the well is deep. Where would you get that life-giving water? 12 It was our ancestor Jacob who gave us this well; he and his sons and his flocks all drank from it. You don't claim to be greater than Jacob, do you?"

13 Jesus answered, "All those who drink this water will be thirsty again, 14 but whoever drinks the water that I will give him will never be thirsty again. The water that I will give him will become in him a spring which will provide him with life-giving water and give him eternal life."

15 "Sir," the woman said, "give me that water! Then I will never be thirsty again, nor will I have to come here to draw water."

16 "Go and call your husband," Jesus told her, "and come back."

17 "I haven't got a husband," she answered.

Jesus replied, "You are right when you say you haven't got a husband. 18 You have been married to five men, and the man you live with now is not really your husband. You have told me the truth."

19 "I see you are a prophet, sir," the woman said. 20 "My Samaritan ancestors worshipped God on this mountain, but you Jews say that Jerusalem is the place where we should worship God."

4.9 Jews will not use the same cups and bowls that Samaritans use; or Jews will have nothing to do with Samaritans.

1258

John
....
Zechar.
Malachi
Matt.
Mark
Luke

JOHN 4

JOHN 4.28-30, 39

This woman shared her story with others and they then believed for themselves. There is

POWER IN OUR STORIES!

Spend some time writing down the story of what Jesus has done in your life, and look for an opportunity to share it.

21 Jesus said to her, "Believe me, woman, the time will come when people will not worship the Father either on this mountain or in Jerusalem. 22 You Samaritans do not really know whom you worship; but we Jews know whom we worship, because it is from the Jews that salvation comes. 23 But the time is coming and is already here, when by the power of God's Spirit people will worship the Father as he really is, offering him the true worship that he wants. 24 God is Spirit, and only by the power of his Spirit can people worship him as he really is."

25 The woman said to him, "I know that the Messiah will come, and when he comes, he will tell us everything."

26 Jesus answered, "I am he, I who am talking with you."

27 At that moment Jesus' disciples returned, and they were greatly surprised to find him talking with a woman. But none of them said to her, "What do you want?" or asked him, "Why are you talking with her?"

28 Then the woman left her water jar, went back to the town, and said to the people there, 29 "Come and see the man who told me everything I have ever done. Could he be the Messiah?" 30 So they left the town and went to Jesus.

31 In the meantime the disciples were begging Jesus, "Teacher, have something to eat!"

32 But he answered, "I have food to eat that you know nothing about."

33 So the disciples started asking among themselves, "Could somebody have brought him food?"

34 "My food," Jesus said to them, "is to obey the will of the one who sent me and to finish the work he gave me to do. 35 You have a saying, 'Four more months and then the harvest.' But I tell you, take a good look at the fields; the crops are now ripe and ready to be harvested! 36 The one who reaps the harvest is being paid and gathers the crops for eternal life; so another who sows and the one who reaps will be glad together. 37 The saying is true, 'One sows, another reaps.' 38 I have sent you to reap a harvest in a field where you did not work; others worked there, and you profit from their work."

39 Many of the Samaritans in that town believed in Jesus because the woman had said, "He told me everything I have ever done." 40 So when the Samaritans came to him, they begged him to stay with them, and Jesus stayed there two days.

41 Many more believed because of his message, 42 and they said to the woman, "We believe now, not because of what you said, but because we ourselves have heard him, and we know that he really is the Saviour of the world."

Jesus Heals an Official's Son

43 After spending two days there, Jesus left and went to Galilee. 44 For he himself had said, "A prophet is not respected in his own country." 45 When he arrived in Galilee, the people there welcomed him, because they had gone to the Passover Festival in Jerusalem and had seen everything that he had done during the festival.

46 Then Jesus went back to Cana in Galilee, where he had turned the water into wine. A government official was there whose son was ill in Capernaum. 47 When he heard that Jesus had come from Judea to Galilee, he went to him and asked him to go to Capernaum and heal his son, who was about to die. 48 Jesus said to him, "None of you will ever believe unless you see miracles and wonders."

49 "Sir," replied the official, "come with me before my child dies."

1259

John

Acts
Romans
1 Corin.
2 Corin.
Galat.

50 Jesus said to him, "Go, your son will live!"

The man believed Jesus' words and went. 51 On his way home his servants met him with the news, "Your boy is going to live!" 52 He asked them what time it was when his son got better, and they answered, "It was one o'clock yesterday afternoon when the fever left him." 53 Then the father remembered it was at that very hour that Jesus had told him, "Your son will live." So he and all his family believed.

54 This was the second miracle that Jesus performed after coming from Judea to Galilee.

The Healing at the Pool

5 After this, Jesus went to Jerusalem for a religious festival. 2 Near the Sheep Gate in Jerusalem there is a pool* with five porches; in Hebrew it is called Bethzatha.* 3 A large crowd of sick people were lying in the porches — the blind, the lame, and the paralysed.* 5 A man was there who had been ill for 38 years. 6 Jesus saw him lying there, and he knew that the man had been ill for such a long time; so he asked him, "Do you want to get well?"

7 The sick man answered, "Sir, I have no one here to put me in the pool when the water is stirred up; while I am trying to get in, somebody else gets there first."

8 Jesus said to him, "Get up, pick up your mat, and walk." 9 Immediately the man got well; he picked up his mat and started walking.

The day this happened was a Sabbath, 10 so the Jewish authorities told the man who had been healed, "This is a Sabbath, and it is against our Law for you to carry your mat."

11 He answered, "The man who made me well told me to pick up my mat and walk."

12 They asked him, "Who is the man who told you to do this?"

13 But the man who had been healed did not know who Jesus was, for there was a crowd in that place, and Jesus had slipped away.

14 Afterwards, Jesus found him in the Temple and said, "Listen, you are well now; so stop sinning or something worse may happen to you."

15 Then the man left and told the Jewish authorities that it was Jesus who had healed him. 16 So they began to persecute Jesus, because he had done this healing on a Sabbath. 17 Jesus answered them, "My Father is always working, and I too must work."

18 This saying made the Jewish authorities all the more determined to kill him; not only had he broken the Sabbath law, but he had said that God was his own Father and in this way had made himself equal with God.

The Authority of the Son

19 So Jesus answered them, "I am telling you the truth: the Son can do nothing on his own; he does only what he sees his Father doing. What the Father does, the Son also does. 20 For the Father loves the Son and shows him all that he himself is doing. He will show him even greater things to do than this, and you will all be amazed. 21 Just as the Father raises the dead and gives them life,

5.2 Near the Sheep Gate... a pool; or Near the Sheep Pool... a place.
5.2 Bethzatha; some manuscripts have Bethesda.
5.3 Some manuscripts add verses 3b–4: They were waiting for the water to move, 4 because every now and then an angel of the Lord went down into the pool and stirred up the water. The first sick person to go into the pool after the water was stirred up was healed from whatever disease he had.

1260

John

·:········

Zechar.

Malachi

Matt.

Mark

Luke

JOHN 5, 6

in the same way the Son gives life to those he wants to. 22 Nor does the Father himself judge anyone. He has given his Son the full right to judge, 23 so that all will honour the Son in the same way as they honour the Father. Whoever does not honour the Son does not honour the Father who sent him.

24 "I am telling you the truth: those who hear my words and believe in him who sent me have eternal life. They will not be judged, but have already passed from death to life. 25 I am telling you the truth: the time is coming — the time has already come — when the dead will hear the voice of the Son of God, and those who hear it will come to life. 26 Just as the Father is himself the source of life, in the same way he has made his Son to be the source of life. 27 And he has given the Son the right to judge, because he is the Son of Man. 28 Do not be surprised at this; the time is coming when all the dead will hear his voice 29 and come out of their graves: those who have done good will rise and live, and those who have done evil will rise and be condemned.

Witnesses to Jesus

30 "I can do nothing on my own authority; I judge only as God tells me, so my judgement is right, because I am not trying to do what I want, but only what he who sent me wants.

31 "If I testify on my own behalf, what I say is not to be accepted as real proof. 32 But there is someone else who testifies on my behalf, and I know that what he says about me is true. 33 John is the one to whom you sent your messengers, and he spoke on behalf of the truth. 34 It is not that I must have a human witness; I say this only in order that you may be saved. 35 John was like a lamp, burning and shining, and you were willing for a while to enjoy his light. 36 But I have a witness on my behalf which is even greater than the witness that John gave: what I do, that is, the deeds my Father gave me to do, these speak on my behalf and show that the Father has sent me. 37 And the Father, who sent me, also testifies on my behalf. You have never heard his voice or seen his face, 38 and you do not keep his message in your hearts, for you do not believe in the one whom he sent. 39 You study the Scriptures, because you think that in them you will find eternal life. And these very Scriptures speak about me! 40 Yet you are not willing to come to me in order to have life.

41 "I am not looking for human praise. 42 But I know what kind of people you are, and I know that you have no love for God in your hearts. 43 I have come with my Father's authority, but you have not received me; when, however, someone comes with his own authority, you will receive him. 44 You like to receive praise from one another, but you do not try to win praise from the one who alone is God; how, then, can you believe me? 45 Do not think, however, that I am the one who will accuse you to my Father. Moses, in whom you have put your hope, is the very one who will accuse you. 46 If you had really believed Moses, you would have believed me, because he wrote about me. 47 But since you do not believe what he wrote, how can you believe what I say?"

Jesus Feeds a Great Crowd
(Mt 14.13–21; Mk 6.30–44; Lk 9.10–17)

6 After this, Jesus went across Lake Galilee (or, Lake Tiberias, as it is also called). 2 A large crowd followed him, because they had seen his miracles of healing those who were ill. 3 Jesus went up a hill and sat down with his disciples. 4 The time for the Passover Festival was near. 5 Jesus looked round and saw that

John
....

Acts
Romans
1 Corin.
2 Corin.
Galat.

a large crowd was coming to him, so he asked Philip, "Where can we buy enough food to feed all these people?" [6] (He said this to test Philip; actually he already knew what he would do.)

[7] Philip answered, "For everyone to have even a little, it would take more than 200 silver coins* to buy enough bread."

[8] Another of his disciples, Andrew, who was Simon Peter's brother, said, [9] "There is a boy here who has five loaves of barley bread and two fish. But they will certainly not be enough for all these people."

[10] "Make the people sit down," Jesus told them. (There was a lot of grass there.) So all the people sat down; there were about 5,000 men. [11] Jesus took the bread, gave thanks to God, and distributed it to the people who were sitting there. He did the same with the fish, and they all had as much as they wanted. [12] When they were all full, he said to his disciples, "Gather the pieces left over; let us not waste any." [13] So they gathered them all up and filled twelve baskets with the pieces left over from the five barley loaves which the people had eaten.

[14] Seeing this miracle that Jesus had performed, the people there said, "Surely this is the Prophet* who was to come into the world!" [15] Jesus knew that they were about to come and seize him in order to make him king by force; so he went off again to the hills by himself.

Jesus Walks on the Water
(Mt 14.22–33; Mk 6.45–52)

[16] When evening came, Jesus' disciples went down to the lake, [17] got into a boat, and went back across the lake towards Capernaum. Night came on, and Jesus still had not come to them. [18] By then a strong wind was blowing and stirring up the water. [19] The disciples had rowed about five or six kilometres when they saw Jesus walking on the water, coming near the boat, and they were terrified. [20] "Don't be afraid," Jesus told them, "it is I!" [21] Then they willingly took him into the boat, and immediately the boat reached land at the place they were heading for.

The People Seek Jesus

[22] Next day the crowd which had stayed on the other side of the lake realized that there had been only one boat there. They knew that Jesus had not gone in it with his disciples, but that they had left without him. [23] Other boats, which were from Tiberias, came to shore near the place where the crowd had eaten the bread after the Lord had given thanks. [24] When the crowd saw that Jesus was not there, nor his disciples, they got into those boats and went to Capernaum, looking for him.

Jesus the Bread of Life

[25] When the people found Jesus on the other side of the lake, they said to him, "Teacher, when did you get here?"

[26] Jesus answered, "I am telling you the truth: you are looking for me because you ate the bread and had all you wanted, not because you understood my miracles. [27] Do not work for food that goes bad; instead, work for the food that lasts for eternal life. This is the food which the Son of Man will give you, because God, the Father, has put his mark of approval on him."

MAKE A NOTE OF WHEN YOU ARE GOING TO **SPEND TIME** • WITH GOD • **THIS WEEK**

6.7 *silver coins*: A silver coin was the daily wage of a rural worker (see Mt 20.2).
6.14 *the Prophet*: See 1.21.

1262

JOHN 6

John

Zechar.
Malachi
Matt.
Mark
Luke

28 So they asked him, "What can we do in order to do what God wants us to do?"

29 Jesus answered, "What God wants you to do is to believe in the one he sent."

30 They replied, "What miracle will you perform so that we may see it and believe you? What will you do? 31 Our ancestors ate manna in the desert, just as the scripture says, 'He gave them bread from heaven to eat.'"

32 "I am telling you the truth," Jesus said. "What Moses gave you was not* the bread from heaven; it is my Father who gives you the real bread from heaven. 33 For the bread that God gives is he who comes down from heaven and gives life to the world."

34 "Sir," they asked him, "give us this bread always."

35 "I am the bread of life," Jesus told them. "Those who come to me will never be hungry; those who believe in me will never be thirsty. 36 Now, I told you that you have seen me but will not believe. 37 Everyone whom my Father gives me will come to me. I will never turn away anyone who comes to me, 38 because I have come down from heaven to do not my own will but the will of him who sent me. 39 And it is the will of him who sent me that I should not lose any of all those he has given me, but that I should raise them all to life on the last day. 40 For what my Father wants is that all who see the Son and believe in him should have eternal life. And I will raise them to life on the last day."

41 The people started grumbling about him, because he said, "I am the bread that came down from heaven." 42 So they said, "This man is Jesus son of Joseph, isn't he? We know his father and mother. How, then, does he now say he came down from heaven?"

43 Jesus answered, "Stop grumbling among yourselves. 44 No one can come to me unless the Father who sent me draws him to me; and I will raise him to life on the last day. 45 The prophets wrote, 'Everyone will be taught by God.' Anyone who hears the Father and learns from him comes to me. 46 This does not mean that anyone has seen the Father; he who is from God is the only one who has seen the Father. 47 I am telling you the truth: he who believes has eternal life. 48 I am the bread of life. 49 Your ancestors ate manna in the desert, but they died. 50 But the bread that comes down from heaven is of such a kind that whoever eats it will not die. 51 I am the living bread that came down from heaven. If anyone eats this bread, he will live for ever. The bread that I will give him is my flesh, which I give so that the world may live."

52 This started an angry argument among them. "How can this man give us his flesh to eat?" they asked.

53 Jesus said to them, "I am telling you the truth: if you do not eat the flesh of the Son of Man and drink his blood, you will not have life in yourselves. 54 Those who eat my flesh and drink my blood have eternal life, and I will raise them to life on the last day. 55 For my flesh is the real food; my blood is the real drink. 56 Those who eat my flesh and drink my blood live in me, and I live in them. 57 The living Father sent me, and because of him I live also. In the same way whoever eats me will live because of me. 58 This, then, is the bread that came down from heaven; it is not like the bread that your ancestors ate. They later died, but those who eat this bread will live for ever."

59 Jesus said this as he taught in the synagogue in Capernaum.

....

6.32 *What Moses gave you was not*; or *It was not Moses who gave you.*

1263

John

Acts
Romans
1 Corin.
2 Corin.
Galat.

The Words of Eternal Life

⁶⁰Many of his followers heard this and said, "This teaching is too hard. Who can listen to it?"

⁶¹Without being told, Jesus knew that they were grumbling about this, so he said to them, "Does this make you want to give up? ⁶²Suppose, then, that you should see the Son of Man go back up to the place where he was before? ⁶³What gives life is God's Spirit; human power is of no use at all. The words I have spoken to you bring God's life-giving Spirit. ⁶⁴Yet some of you do not believe." (Jesus knew from the very beginning who were the ones that would not believe and which one would betray him.) ⁶⁵And he added, "This is the very reason I told you that no one can come to me unless the Father makes it possible for him to do so."

⁶⁶Because of this, many of Jesus' followers turned back and would not go with him any more. ⁶⁷So he asked the twelve disciples, "And you — would you also like to leave?"

⁶⁸Simon Peter answered him, "Lord, to whom would we go? You have the words that give eternal life. ⁶⁹And now we believe and know that you are the Holy One who has come from God."

⁷⁰Jesus replied, "I chose the twelve of you, didn't I? Yet one of you is a devil!" ⁷¹He was talking about Judas, the son of Simon Iscariot. For Judas, even though he was one of the twelve disciples, was going to betray him.

Jesus and his Brothers

7 After this, Jesus travelled in Galilee; he did not want to travel in Judea, because the Jewish authorities there were wanting to kill him. ²The time for the Festival of Shelters was near, ³so Jesus' brothers said to him, "Leave this place and go to Judea, so that your followers will see the things that you are doing. ⁴No one hides what he is doing if he wants to be well known. Since you are doing these things, let the whole world know about you!" ⁵(Not even his brothers believed in him.)

⁶Jesus said to them, "The right time for me has not yet come. Any time is right for you. ⁷The world cannot hate you, but it hates me, because I keep telling it that its ways are bad. ⁸You go on to the festival. I am not going* to this festival, because the right time has not come for me." ⁹He said this, and then stayed on in Galilee.

Jesus at the Festival of Shelters

¹⁰After his brothers had gone to the festival, Jesus also went; however, he did not go openly, but secretly. ¹¹The Jewish authorities were looking for him at the festival. "Where is he?" they asked.

¹²There was much whispering about him in the crowd. "He is a good man," some people said. "No," others said, "he is misleading the people." ¹³But no one talked about him openly, because they were afraid of the Jewish authorities.

¹⁴The festival was nearly half over when Jesus went to the Temple and began teaching. ¹⁵The Jewish authorities were greatly surprised and said, "How does this man know so much when he has never had any training?"

¹⁶Jesus answered, "What I teach is not my own teaching, but it comes from God, who sent me. ¹⁷Whoever is willing to do what God wants will know whether what I teach comes from God or whether I speak on my own authority. ¹⁸A person who speaks on his own authority is trying to gain glory for himself. But he

7.8 *I am not going*; some manuscripts have *I am not yet going*.

1264

John

Zechar.

Malachi

Matt.

Mark

Luke

JOHN 7

who wants glory for the one who sent him is honest, and there is nothing false in him. 19 Moses gave you the Law, didn't he? But not one of you obeys the Law. Why are you trying to kill me?"

20 "You have a demon in you!" the crowd answered. "Who is trying to kill you?"

21 Jesus answered, "I performed one miracle, and you were all surprised. 22 Moses ordered you to circumcise your sons (although it was not Moses but your ancestors who started it), and so you circumcise a boy on the Sabbath. 23 If a boy is circumcised on the Sabbath so that Moses' Law is not broken, why are you angry with me because I made a man completely well on the Sabbath? 24 Stop judging by external standards, and judge by true standards."

Is he the Messiah?

25 Some of the people of Jerusalem said, "Isn't this the man the authorities are trying to kill? 26 Look! He is talking in public, and they say nothing against him! Can it be that they really know that he is the Messiah? 27 But when the Messiah comes, no one will know where he is from. And we all know where this man comes from."

28 As Jesus taught in the Temple, he said in a loud voice, "Do you really know me and know where I am from? I have not come on my own authority. He who sent me, however, is truthful. You do not know him, 29 but I know him, because I come from him and he sent me."

30 Then they tried to seize him, but no one laid a hand on him, because his hour had not yet come. 31 But many in the crowd believed in him and said, "When the Messiah comes, will he perform more miracles than this man has?"

Guards are Sent to Arrest Jesus

32 The Pharisees heard the crowd whispering these things about Jesus, so they and the chief priests sent some guards to arrest him. 33 Jesus said, "I shall be with you a little while longer, and then I shall go away to him who sent me. 34 You will look for me, but you will not find me, because you cannot go where I will be."

35 The Jewish authorities said among themselves, "Where is he about to go so that we shall not find him? Will he go to the Greek cities where our people live, and teach the Greeks? 36 He says that we will look for him but will not find him, and that we cannot go where he will be. What does he mean?"

Streams of Life-giving Water

37 On the last and most important day of the festival Jesus stood up and said in a loud voice, "Whoever is thirsty should come to me, and 38 whoever believes in me should drink. As the scripture says, 'Streams of life-giving water will pour out from his side.'"*
39 Jesus said this about the Spirit, which those who believed in him were going to receive. At that time the Spirit had not yet been given, because Jesus had not been raised to glory.

Division among the People

40 Some of the people in the crowd heard him say this and said, "This man is really the Prophet!"*

READ THIS PASSAGE OUT

~LOUD.~

7.38 Jesus' words in verses 37–38 may be translated: *"Whoever is thirsty should come to me and drink.* 38 *As the scripture says, 'Streams of life-giving water will pour out from within anyone who believes in me.'"*
7.40 the Prophet: See 1.21.

JOHN 7, 8

1265

John

....

Acts
Romans
1 Corin.
2 Corin.
Galat.

⁴¹Others said, "He is the Messiah!"

But others said, "The Messiah will not come from Galilee! ⁴²The scripture says that the Messiah will be a descendant of King David and will be born in Bethlehem, the town where David lived." ⁴³So there was a division in the crowd because of Jesus. ⁴⁴Some wanted to seize him, but no one laid a hand on him.

The Unbelief of the Jewish Authorities

⁴⁵When the guards went back, the chief priests and Pharisees asked them, "Why did you not bring him?"

⁴⁶The guards answered, "Nobody has ever talked like this man!"

⁴⁷"Did he fool you, too?" the Pharisees asked them. ⁴⁸"Have you ever known one of the authorities or one Pharisee to believe in him? ⁴⁹This crowd does not know the Law of Moses, so they are under God's curse!"

⁵⁰One of the Pharisees there was Nicodemus, the man who had gone to see Jesus before. He said to the others, ⁵¹"According to our Law we cannot condemn anyone before hearing him and finding out what he has done."

⁵²"Well," they answered, "are you also from Galilee? Study the Scriptures and you will learn that no prophet ever comes* from Galilee."

The Woman Caught in Adultery

8 [Then everyone went home, but Jesus went to the Mount of Olives. ²Early the next morning he went back to the Temple. All the people gathered round him, and he sat down and began to teach them. ³The teachers of the Law and the Pharisees brought in a woman who had been caught committing adultery, and they made her stand before them all. ⁴"Teacher," they said to Jesus, "this woman was caught in the very act of committing adultery. ⁵In our Law Moses commanded that such a woman must be stoned to death. Now, what do you say?" ⁶They said this to trap Jesus, so that they could accuse him. But he bent over and wrote on the ground with his finger.

⁷As they stood there asking him questions, he straightened himself up and said to them, "Whichever one of you has committed no sin may throw the first stone at her." ⁸Then he bent over again and wrote on the ground. ⁹When they heard this, they all left, one by one, the older ones first. Jesus was left alone, with the woman still standing there. ¹⁰He straightened himself up and said to her, "Where are they? Is there no one left to condemn you?"

¹¹"No one, sir," she answered.

"Well, then," Jesus said, "I do not condemn you either. Go, but do not sin again."]*

Jesus the Light of the World

¹²Jesus spoke to the Pharisees again. "I am the light of the world," he said. "Whoever follows me will have the light of life and will never walk in darkness."

¹³The Pharisees said to him, "Now you are testifying on your own behalf; what you say proves nothing."

¹⁴"No," Jesus answered, "even though I do testify on my own behalf, what I say is true, because I know where I came from and

---

7.52 *no prophet ever comes*; one manuscript has *the Prophet will not come*.
8.11 Many manuscripts and early translations do not have this passage (8.1–11); others have it after Jn 21.24; others have it after Lk 21.38; one manuscript has it after Jn 7.36.

1266

John
·: ········

Zechar.
Malachi
Matt.
Mark
Luke

JOHN 8

where I am going. You do not know where I came from or where I am going. [15] You make judgements in a purely human way; I pass judgement on no one. [16] But if I were to do so, my judgement would be true, because I am not alone in this; the Father who sent me is with me. [17] It is written in your Law that when two witnesses agree, what they say is true. [18] I testify on my own behalf, and the Father who sent me also testifies on my behalf."

[19] "Where is your father?" they asked him.

"You know neither me nor my Father," Jesus answered. "If you knew me, you would know my Father also."

[20] Jesus said all this as he taught in the Temple, in the room where the offering boxes were placed. And no one arrested him, because his hour had not come.

You cannot Go Where I am Going

[21] Again Jesus said to them, "I will go away; you will look for me, but you will die in your sins. You cannot go where I am going."

[22] So the Jewish authorities said, "He says that we cannot go where he is going. Does this mean that he will kill himself?"

[23] Jesus answered, "You belong to this world here below, but I come from above. You are from this world, but I am not from this world. [24] That is why I told you that you will die in your sins. And you will die in your sins if you do not believe that 'I Am Who I Am'."

[25] "Who are you?" they asked him.

Jesus answered, "What I have told you from the very beginning.* [26] I have much to say about you, much to condemn you for. The one who sent me, however, is truthful, and I tell the world only what I have heard from him."

[27] They did not understand that Jesus was talking to them about the Father. [28] So he said to them, "When you lift up the Son of Man, you will know that 'I Am Who I Am'; then you will know that I do nothing on my own authority, but I say only what the Father has instructed me to say. [29] And he who sent me is with me; he has not left me alone, because I always do what pleases him."

[30] Many who heard Jesus say these things believed in him.

The Truth will Set you Free

[31] So Jesus said to those who believed in him, "If you obey my teaching, you are really my disciples; [32] you will know the truth, and the truth will set you free."

[33] "We are the descendants of Abraham," they answered, "and we have never been anybody's slaves. What do you mean, then, by saying, 'You will be free'?"

[34] Jesus said to them, "I am telling you the truth: everyone who sins is a slave of sin. [35] A slave does not belong to a family permanently, but a son belongs there for ever. [36] If the Son sets you free, then you will be really free. [37] I know you are Abraham's descendants. Yet you are trying to kill me, because you will not accept my teaching. [38] I talk about what my Father has shown me, but you do what your father has told you."

[39] They answered him, "Our father is Abraham."

"If you really were Abraham's children," Jesus replied, "you would do* the same things that he did. [40] All I have ever done is to tell you the truth I heard from God, yet you are trying to kill

---

8.25 *What I have told you from the very beginning*; or *Why should I speak to you at all?*
8.39 *If you really were... you would do*; some manuscripts have *If you are... do.*

JOHN 8, 9

1267

John

....

Acts
Romans
1 Corin.
2 Corin.
Galat.

me. Abraham did nothing like this! ⁴¹ You are doing what your father did."

"God himself is the only Father we have," they answered, "and we are his true children."

⁴² Jesus said to them, "If God really were your Father, you would love me, because I came from God and now I am here. I did not come on my own authority, but he sent me. ⁴³ Why do you not understand what I say? It is because you cannot bear to listen to my message. ⁴⁴ You are the children of your father, the Devil, and you want to follow your father's desires. From the very beginning he was a murderer and has never been on the side of truth, because there is no truth in him. When he tells a lie, he is only doing what is natural to him, because he is a liar and the father of all lies. ⁴⁵ But I tell the truth, and that is why you do not believe me. ⁴⁶ Which one of you can prove that I am guilty of sin? If I tell the truth, then why do you not believe me? ⁴⁷ He who comes from God listens to God's words. You, however, are not from God, and that is why you will not listen."

Jesus and Abraham

⁴⁸ They asked Jesus, "Were we not right in saying that you are a Samaritan and have a demon in you?"

⁴⁹ "I have no demon," Jesus answered. "I honour my Father, but you dishonour me. ⁵⁰ I am not seeking honour for myself. But there is one who is seeking it and who judges in my favour. ⁵¹ I am telling you the truth: whoever obeys my teaching will never die."

⁵² They said to him, "Now we are certain that you have a demon! Abraham died, and the prophets died, yet you say that whoever obeys your teaching will never die. ⁵³ Our father Abraham died; you do not claim to be greater than Abraham, do you? And the prophets also died. Who do you think you are?"

⁵⁴ Jesus answered, "If I were to honour myself, that honour would be worth nothing. The one who honours me is my Father — the very one you say is your God. ⁵⁵ You have never known him, but I know him. If I were to say that I do not know him, I would be a liar like you. But I do know him, and I obey his word. ⁵⁶ Your father Abraham rejoiced that he was to see the time of my coming; he saw it and was glad."

⁵⁷ They said to him, "You are not even fifty years old — and you have seen Abraham?"*

⁵⁸ "I am telling you the truth," Jesus replied. "Before Abraham was born, 'I Am'."

⁵⁹ Then they picked up stones to throw at him, but Jesus hid himself and left the Temple.

Jesus Heals a Man Born Blind

9 As Jesus was walking along, he saw a man who had been born blind. ² His disciples asked him, "Teacher, whose sin caused him to be born blind? Was it his own or his parents' sin?"

³ Jesus answered, "His blindness has nothing to do with his sins or his parents' sins. He is blind so that God's power might be seen at work in him. ⁴ As long as it is day, we must keep on doing the work of him who sent me; night is coming when no one can work. ⁵ While I am in the world, I am the light for the world."

⁶ After he said this, Jesus spat on the ground and made some mud with the spittle; he rubbed the mud on the man's eyes ⁷ and

8.57 *you have seen Abraham?*; some manuscripts have *has Abraham seen you?*

1268

John

Zechar.
Malachi
Matt.
Mark
Luke

JOHN 9

said, "Go and wash your face in the Pool of Siloam." (This name means "Sent".) So the man went, washed his face, and came back seeing.

8 His neighbours, then, and the people who had seen him begging before this, asked, "Isn't this the man who used to sit and beg?"

9 Some said, "He is the one," but others said, "No he isn't; he just looks like him."

So the man himself said, "I am the man."

10 "How is it that you can now see?" they asked him.

11 He answered, "The man called Jesus made some mud, rubbed it on my eyes, and told me to go to Siloam and wash my face. So I went, and as soon as I washed, I could see."

12 "Where is he?" they asked.

"I don't know," he answered.

The Pharisees Investigate the Healing

13 Then they took to the Pharisees the man who had been blind. 14 The day that Jesus made the mud and cured him of his blindness was a Sabbath. 15 The Pharisees, then, asked the man again how he had received his sight. He told them, "He put some mud on my eyes; I washed my face, and now I can see."

16 Some of the Pharisees said, "The man who did this cannot be from God, for he does not obey the Sabbath law."

Others, however, said, "How could a man who is a sinner perform such miracles as these?" And there was a division among them.

17 So the Pharisees asked the man once more, "You say he cured you of your blindness — well, what do you say about him?"

"He is a prophet," the man answered.

18 The Jewish authorities, however, were not willing to believe that he had been blind and could now see, until they called his parents 19 and asked them, "Is this your son? You say that he was born blind; how is it, then, that he can now see?"

20 His parents answered, "We know that he is our son, and we know that he was born blind. 21 But we do not know how it is that he is now able to see, nor do we know who cured him of his blindness. Ask him; he is old enough, and he can answer for himself!" 22 His parents said this because they were afraid of the Jewish authorities, who had already agreed that anyone who said he believed that Jesus was the Messiah would be expelled from the synagogue. 23 That is why his parents said, "He is old enough; ask him!"

24 A second time they called back the man who had been born blind, and said to him, "Promise before God that you will tell the truth! We know that this man who cured you is a sinner."

25 "I do not know if he is a sinner or not," the man replied. "One thing I do know: I was blind, and now I see."

26 "What did he do to you?" they asked. "How did he cure you of your blindness?"

27 "I have already told you," he answered, "and you would not listen. Why do you want to hear it again? Maybe you, too, would like to be his disciples?"

28 They cursed him and said, "You are that fellow's disciple; but we are Moses' disciples. 29 We know that God spoke to Moses; as for that fellow, however, we do not even know where he comes from!"

30 The man answered, "What a strange thing that is! You do not know where he comes from, but he cured me of my blindness! 31 We know that God does not listen to sinners; he does listen to people who respect him and do what he wants them to do. 32 Since the

beginning of the world nobody has ever heard of anyone giving sight to a person born blind. [33] Unless this man came from God, he would not be able to do a thing."

[34] They answered, "You were born and brought up in sin — and you are trying to teach us?" And they expelled him from the synagogue.

Spiritual Blindness

[35] When Jesus heard what had happened, he found the man and asked him, "Do you believe in the Son of Man?"

[36] The man answered, "Tell me who he is, sir, so that I can believe in him!"

[37] Jesus said to him, "You have already seen him, and he is the one who is talking with you now."

[38] "I believe, Lord!" the man said, and knelt down before Jesus.

[39] Jesus said, "I came to this world to judge, so that the blind should see and those who see should become blind."

[40] Some Pharisees who were there with him heard him say this and asked him, "Surely you don't mean that we are blind, too?"

[41] Jesus answered, "If you were blind, then you would not be guilty; but since you claim that you can see, this means that you are still guilty."

The Parable of the Shepherd

10 Jesus said, "I am telling you the truth: the man who does not enter the sheepfold by the gate, but climbs in some other way, is a thief and a robber. [2] The man who goes in through the gate is the shepherd of the sheep. [3] The gatekeeper opens the gate for him; the sheep hear his voice as he calls his own sheep by name, and he leads them out. [4] When he has brought them out, he goes ahead of them, and the sheep follow him, because they know his voice. [5] They will not follow someone else; instead, they will run away from such a person, because they do not know his voice."

[6] Jesus told them this parable, but they did not understand what he meant.

Jesus the Good Shepherd

[7] So Jesus said again, "I am telling you the truth: I am the gate for the sheep. [8] All others who came before me are thieves and robbers, but the sheep did not listen to them. [9] I am the gate. Whoever comes in by me will be saved; they will come in and go out and find pasture. [10] The thief comes only in order to steal, kill, and destroy. I have come in order that you might have life — life in all its fullness.

[11] "I am the good shepherd, who is willing to die for the sheep. [12] When the hired man, who is not a shepherd and does not own the sheep, sees a wolf coming, he leaves the sheep and runs away; so the wolf snatches the sheep and scatters them. [13] The hired man runs away because he is only a hired man and does not care about the sheep. [14-15] I am the good shepherd. As the Father knows me and I know the Father, in the same way I know my sheep and they know me. And I am willing to die for them. [16] There are other sheep which belong to me that are not in this sheepfold. I must bring them, too; they will listen to my voice, and they will become* one flock with one shepherd.

[17] "The Father loves me because I am willing to give up my life, in order that I may receive it back again. [18] No one takes my life

10.16 *they will become*; some manuscripts have *there will be*.

JOHN 10.10

FINISH THE

- MINDMAP -

BELOW.

WHAT DOES THE WORD 'LIFE' MEAN TO YOU?

1270

John

Zechar.
Malachi
Matt.
Mark
Luke

JOHN 10, 11

away from me. I give it up of my own free will. I have the right to give it up, and I have the right to take it back. This is what my Father has commanded me to do."

19 Again there was a division among the people because of these words. 20 Many of them were saying, "He has a demon! He is mad! Why do you listen to him?"

21 But others were saying, "A man with a demon could not talk like this! How could a demon give sight to blind people?"

Jesus is Rejected

22 It was winter, and the Festival of the Dedication of the Temple was being celebrated in Jerusalem. 23 Jesus was walking in Solomon's Porch in the Temple, 24 when the people gathered round him and asked, "How long are you going to keep us in suspense? Tell us the plain truth: are you the Messiah?"

25 Jesus answered, "I have already told you, but you would not believe me. The things I do by my Father's authority speak on my behalf; 26 but you will not believe, for you are not my sheep. 27 My sheep listen to my voice; I know them, and they follow me. 28 I give them eternal life, and they shall never die. No one can snatch them away from me. 29 What my Father has given me is greater* than everything, and no one can snatch them away from the Father's care. 30 The Father and I are one."

31 Then the people again picked up stones to throw at him. 32 Jesus said to them, "I have done many good deeds in your presence which the Father gave me to do; for which one of these do you want to stone me?"

33 They replied, "We do not want to stone you because of any good deeds, but because of your blasphemy! You are only a man, but you are trying to make yourself God!"

34 Jesus answered, "It is written in your own Law that God said, 'You are gods.' 35 We know that what the scripture says is true for ever; and God called those people gods, the people to whom his message was given. 36 As for me, the Father chose me and sent me into the world. How, then, can you say that I blaspheme because I said that I am the Son of God? 37 Do not believe me, then, if I am not doing the things my Father wants me to do. 38 But if I do them, even though you do not believe me, you should at least believe my deeds, in order that you may know once and for all that the Father is in me and that I am in the Father."

39 Once more they tried to seize Jesus, but he slipped out of their hands.

40 Jesus then went back again across the River Jordan to the place where John had been baptizing, and he stayed there. 41 Many people came to him. "John performed no miracles," they said, "but everything he said about this man was true." 42 And many people there believed in him.

The Death of Lazarus

11 A man named Lazarus, who lived in Bethany, was ill. Bethany was the town where Mary and her sister Martha lived. 2 (This Mary was the one who poured the perfume on the Lord's feet and wiped them with her hair; it was her brother Lazarus who was ill.) 3 The sisters sent Jesus a message: "Lord, your dear friend is ill."

10.29 What my Father has given me is greater; some manuscripts have My Father, who gave them to me, is greater.

John

Acts
Romans
1 Corin.
2 Corin.
Galat.

⁴When Jesus heard it, he said, "The final result of this illness will not be the death of Lazarus; this has happened in order to bring glory to God, and it will be the means by which the Son of God will receive glory."

⁵Jesus loved Martha and her sister and Lazarus. ⁶Yet when he received the news that Lazarus was ill, he stayed where he was for two more days. ⁷Then he said to the disciples, "Let us go back to Judea."

⁸"Teacher," the disciples answered, "just a short time ago the people there wanted to stone you; and are you planning to go back?"

⁹Jesus said, "A day has twelve hours, hasn't it? So whoever walks in broad daylight does not stumble, for they see the light of this world. ¹⁰But if they walk during the night they stumble, because they have no light." ¹¹Jesus said this and then added, "Our friend Lazarus has fallen asleep, but I will go and wake him up."

¹²The disciples answered, "If he is asleep, Lord, he will get well."

¹³Jesus meant that Lazarus had died, but they thought he meant natural sleep. ¹⁴So Jesus told them plainly, "Lazarus is dead, ¹⁵but for your sake I am glad that I was not with him, so that you will believe. Let us go to him."

¹⁶Thomas (called the Twin) said to his fellow-disciples, "Let us all go with the Teacher, so that we may die with him!"

Jesus the Resurrection and the Life

¹⁷When Jesus arrived, he found that Lazarus had been buried four days before. ¹⁸Bethany was less than three kilometres from Jerusalem, ¹⁹and many Judeans had come to see Martha and Mary to comfort them over their brother's death.

²⁰When Martha heard that Jesus was coming, she went out to meet him, but Mary stayed in the house. ²¹Martha said to Jesus, "If you had been here, Lord, my brother would not have died! ²²But I know that even now God will give you whatever you ask him for."

²³"Your brother will rise to life," Jesus told her.

²⁴"I know," she replied, "that he will rise to life on the last day."

²⁵Jesus said to her, "I am the resurrection and the life. Those who believe in me will live, even though they die; ²⁶and all those who live and believe in me will never die. Do you believe this?"

²⁷"Yes, Lord!" she answered. "I do believe that you are the Messiah, the Son of God, who was to come into the world."

Jesus Weeps

²⁸After Martha said this, she went back and called her sister Mary privately. "The Teacher is here," she told her, "and is asking for you." ²⁹When Mary heard this, she got up and hurried out to meet him. ³⁰(Jesus had not yet arrived in the village, but was still in the place where Martha had met him.) ³¹The people who were in the house with Mary, comforting her, followed her when they saw her get up and hurry out. They thought that she was going to the grave to weep there.

³²Mary arrived where Jesus was, and as soon as she saw him, she fell at his feet. "Lord," she said, "if you had been here, my brother would not have died!"

³³Jesus saw her weeping, and he saw how the people who were with her were weeping also; his heart was touched, and he was deeply moved. ³⁴"Where have you buried him?" he asked them.

"Come and see, Lord," they answered.

1272

John

·:·········

Zechar.

Malachi

Matt.

Mark

Luke

JOHN 11, 12

³⁵ Jesus wept. ³⁶ "See how much he loved him!" the people said. ³⁷ But some of them said, "He gave sight to the blind man, didn't he? Could he not have kept Lazarus from dying?"

Lazarus is Brought to Life

³⁸ Deeply moved once more, Jesus went to the tomb, which was a cave with a stone placed at the entrance. ³⁹ "Take the stone away!" Jesus ordered.

Martha, the dead man's sister, answered, "There will be a bad smell, Lord. He has been buried four days!"

⁴⁰ Jesus said to her, "Didn't I tell you that you would see God's glory if you believed?" ⁴¹ They took the stone away. Jesus looked up and said, "I thank you, Father, that you listen to me. ⁴² I know that you always listen to me, but I say this for the sake of the people here, so that they will believe that you sent me." ⁴³ After he had said this, he called out in a loud voice, "Lazarus, come out!" ⁴⁴ He came out, his hands and feet wrapped in grave clothes, and with a cloth round his face. "Untie him," Jesus told them, "and let him go."

The Plot against Jesus
(Mt 26.1–5; Mk 14.1–2; Lk 22.1–2)

⁴⁵ Many of the people who had come to visit Mary saw what Jesus did, and they believed in him. ⁴⁶ But some of them returned to the Pharisees and told them what Jesus had done. ⁴⁷ So the Pharisees and the chief priests met with the Council and said, "What shall we do? Look at all the miracles this man is performing! ⁴⁸ If we let him go on in this way, everyone will believe in him, and the Roman authorities will take action and destroy our Temple and our nation!"

⁴⁹ One of them, named Caiaphas, who was High Priest that year, said, "What fools you are! ⁵⁰ Don't you realize that it is better for you to let one man die for the people, instead of having the whole nation destroyed?" ⁵¹ Actually, he did not say this of his own accord; rather, as he was High Priest that year, he was prophesying that Jesus was going to die for the Jewish people, ⁵² and not only for them, but also to bring together into one body all the scattered people of God.

⁵³ From that day on the Jewish authorities made plans to kill Jesus. ⁵⁴ So Jesus did not travel openly in Judea, but left and went to a place near the desert, to a town named Ephraim, where he stayed with the disciples.

⁵⁵ The time for the Passover Festival was near, and many people went up from the country to Jerusalem to perform the ritual of purification before the festival. ⁵⁶ They were looking for Jesus, and as they gathered in the Temple, they asked one another, "What do you think? Surely he will not come to the festival, will he?" ⁵⁷ The chief priests and the Pharisees had given orders that if anyone knew where Jesus was, he must report it, so that they could arrest him.

Jesus is Anointed at Bethany
(Mt 26.6–13; Mk 14.3–9)

12 Six days before the Passover, Jesus went to Bethany, the home of Lazarus, the man he had raised from death. ² They prepared a dinner for him there, which Martha helped to serve; Lazarus was one of those who were sitting at the table with Jesus. ³ Then Mary took half a litre of a very expensive perfume made of pure nard, poured it on Jesus' feet, and wiped them with her hair.

John

.........:.

Acts
Romans
1 Corin.
2 Corin.
Galat.

The sweet smell of the perfume filled the whole house. [4]One of Jesus' disciples, Judas Iscariot — the one who was going to betray him — said, [5]"Why wasn't this perfume sold for 300 silver coins* and the money given to the poor?" [6]He said this, not because he cared about the poor, but because he was a thief. He carried the money bag and would help himself from it.

[7]But Jesus said, "Leave her alone! Let her keep what she has for the day of my burial. [8]You will always have poor people with you, but you will not always have me."

The Plot against Lazarus

[9]A large number of people heard that Jesus was in Bethany, so they went there, not only because of Jesus but also to see Lazarus, whom Jesus had raised from death. [10]So the chief priests made plans to kill Lazarus too, [11]because on his account many Jews were rejecting them and believing in Jesus.

The Triumphant Entry into Jerusalem
(Mt 21.1–11; Mk 11.1–11; Lk 19.28–40)

[12]The next day the large crowd that had come to the Passover Festival heard that Jesus was coming to Jerusalem. [13]So they took branches of palm trees and went out to meet him, shouting, "Praise God! God bless him who comes in the name of the Lord! God bless the King of Israel!"

[14]Jesus found a donkey and rode on it, just as the scripture says,
[15] "Do not be afraid, city of Zion!
    Here comes your king,
        riding on a young donkey."

[16]His disciples did not understand this at the time; but when Jesus had been raised to glory, they remembered that the scripture said this about him and that they had done this for him.

[17]The people who had been with Jesus when he called Lazarus out of the grave and raised him from death had reported what had happened. [18]That was why the crowd met him — because they heard that he had performed this miracle. [19]The Pharisees then said to one another, "You see, we are not succeeding at all! Look, the whole world is following him!"

Some Greeks Seek Jesus

[20]Some Greeks were among those who had gone to Jerusalem to worship during the festival. [21]They went to Philip (he was from Bethsaida in Galilee) and said, "Sir, we want to see Jesus."

[22]Philip went and told Andrew, and the two of them went and told Jesus. [23]Jesus answered them, "The hour has now come for the Son of Man to receive great glory. [24]I am telling you the truth: a grain of wheat remains no more than a single grain unless it is dropped into the ground and dies. If it does die, then it produces many grains. [25]Those who love their own life will lose it; those who hate their own life in this world will keep it for life eternal. [26]Whoever wants to serve me must follow me, so that my servant will be with me where I am. And my Father will honour anyone who serves me.

Jesus Speaks about his Death

[27]"Now my heart is troubled — and what shall I say? Shall I say, 'Father, do not let this hour come upon me'? But that is why I came — so that I might go through this hour of suffering. [28]Father, bring glory to your name!"

....

12.5 *silver coins*: See 6.7.

1274

John

⁝⁝⁝⁝⁝⁝⁝⁝

Zechar.

Malachi

Matt.

Mark

Luke

JOHN 12, 13

JOHN 13.34

Jesus did a lot of
great things for his
disciples because

HE LOVED

THEM.

List three ways you can
demonstrate your love to
your friends this week.

(1.)

(2.)

(3.)

Then a voice spoke from heaven, "I have brought glory to it, and I will do so again."

29 The crowd standing there heard the voice, and some of them said it was thunder, while others said, "An angel spoke to him!" 30 But Jesus said to them, "It was not for my sake that this voice spoke, but for yours. 31 Now is the time for this world to be judged; now the ruler of this world will be overthrown. 32 When I am lifted up from the earth, I will draw everyone to me." 33 (In saying this he indicated the kind of death he was going to suffer.)

34 The crowd answered, "Our Law tells us that the Messiah will live for ever. How, then, can you say that the Son of Man must be lifted up? Who is this Son of Man?"

35 Jesus answered, "The light will be among you a little longer. Continue on your way while you have the light, so that the darkness will not come upon you; for the one who walks in the dark does not know where he is going. 36 Believe in the light, then, while you have it, so that you will be the people of the light."

The Unbelief of the People

After Jesus said this, he went off and hid himself from them. 37 Even though he had performed all these miracles in their presence, they did not believe in him, 38 so that what the prophet Isaiah had said might come true:

"Lord, who believed the message we told?
To whom did the Lord reveal his power?"

39 And so they were not able to believe, because Isaiah also said:
40 "God has blinded their eyes
and closed their minds,
so that their eyes would not see,
and their minds would not understand,
and they would not turn to me, says God,
for me to heal them."

41 Isaiah said this because he saw Jesus' glory and spoke about him.

42 Even then, many of the Jewish authorities believed in Jesus; but because of the Pharisees they did not talk about it openly, so as not to be expelled from the synagogue. 43 They loved human approval rather than the approval of God.

Judgement by Jesus' Words

44 Jesus said in a loud voice, "Whoever believes in me believes not only in me but also in him who sent me. 45 Whoever sees me sees also him who sent me. 46 I have come into the world as light, so that everyone who believes in me should not remain in the darkness. 47 If anyone hears my message and does not obey it, I will not judge him. I came, not to judge the world, but to save it. 48 Those who reject me and do not accept my message have one who will judge them. The words I have spoken will be their judge on the last day! 49 This is true, because I have not spoken on my own authority, but the Father who sent me has commanded me what I must say and speak. 50 And I know that his command brings eternal life. What I say, then, is what the Father has told me to say."

Jesus Washes his Disciples' Feet

13 It was now the day before the Passover Festival. Jesus knew that the hour had come for him to leave this world and go to the Father. He had always loved those in the world who were his own, and he loved them to the very end.

John

Acts
Romans
1 Corin.
2 Corin.
Galat.

² Jesus and his disciples were at supper. The Devil had already put into the heart of Judas, the son of Simon Iscariot, the thought of betraying Jesus.* ³ Jesus knew that the Father had given him complete power; he knew that he had come from God and was going to God. ⁴ So he rose from the table, took off his outer garment, and tied a towel round his waist. ⁵ Then he poured some water into a basin and began to wash the disciples' feet and dry them with the towel round his waist. ⁶ He came to Simon Peter, who said to him, "Are you going to wash my feet, Lord?"

⁷ Jesus answered him, "You do not understand now what I am doing, but you will understand later."

⁸ Peter declared, "Never at any time will you wash my feet!"

"If I do not wash your feet," Jesus answered, "you will no longer be my disciple."

⁹ Simon Peter answered, "Lord, do not wash only my feet, then! Wash my hands and head, too!"

¹⁰ Jesus said, "Those who have had a bath are completely clean and do not have to wash themselves, except for their feet.* All of you are clean — all except one." ¹¹ (Jesus already knew who was going to betray him; that is why he said, "All of you, except one, are clean.")

¹² After Jesus had washed their feet, he put his outer garment back on and returned to his place at the table. "Do you understand what I have just done to you?" he asked. ¹³ "You call me Teacher and Lord, and it is right that you do so, because that is what I am. ¹⁴ I, your Lord and Teacher, have just washed your feet. You, then, should wash one another's feet. ¹⁵ I have set an example for you, so that you will do just what I have done for you. ¹⁶ I am telling you the truth: slaves are never greater than their master, and messengers are never greater than the one who sent them. ¹⁷ Now that you know this truth, how happy you will be if you put it into practice!

¹⁸ "I am not talking about all of you; I know those I have chosen. But the scripture must come true that says, 'The man who shared my food turned against me.' ¹⁹ I tell you this now before it happens, so that when it does happen, you will believe that 'I Am Who I Am.' ²⁰ I am telling you the truth: whoever receives anyone I send receives me also; and whoever receives me receives him who sent me."

Jesus Predicts his Betrayal
(Mt 26.20–25; Mk 14.17–21; Lk 22.21–23)

²¹ After Jesus had said this, he was deeply troubled and declared openly, "I am telling you the truth: one of you is going to betray me."

²² The disciples looked at one another, completely puzzled about whom he meant. ²³ One of the disciples, the one whom Jesus loved, was sitting next to Jesus. ²⁴ Simon Peter motioned to him and said, "Ask him whom he is talking about."

²⁵ So that disciple moved closer to Jesus' side and asked, "Who is it, Lord?"

²⁶ Jesus answered, "I will dip some bread in the sauce and give it to him; he is the man." So he took a piece of bread, dipped it, and gave it to Judas, the son of Simon Iscariot. ²⁷ As soon as Judas took the bread, Satan entered him. Jesus said to him,

---

13.2 *The Devil… betraying Jesus*; or *The Devil had already decided that Judas, the son of Simon Iscariot, would betray Jesus.*
13.10 Some manuscripts do not have *except for their feet.*

1276

John

∴·········

Zechar.
Malachi
Matt.
Mark
Luke

JOHN 13, 14

"Be quick about what you are doing!" [28] None of the others at the table understood why Jesus said this to him. [29] Since Judas was in charge of the money bag, some of the disciples thought that Jesus had told him to go and buy what they needed for the festival, or to give something to the poor.

[30] Judas accepted the bread and went out at once. It was night.

The New Commandment

[31] After Judas had left, Jesus said, "Now the Son of Man's glory is revealed; now God's glory is revealed through him. [32] And if God's glory is revealed through him, then God will reveal the glory of the Son of Man in himself, and he will do so at once. [33] My children, I shall not be with you very much longer. You will look for me; but I tell you now what I told you, the Jewish authorities, 'You cannot go where I am going.' [34] And now I give you a new commandment: love one another. As I have loved you, so you must love one another. [35] If you have love for one another, then everyone will know that you are my disciples."

Jesus Predicts Peter's Denial
(Mt 26.31–35; Mk 14.27–31; Lk 22.31–34)

[36] "Where are you going, Lord?" Simon Peter asked him.

"You cannot follow me now where I am going," answered Jesus; "but later you will follow me."

[37] "Lord, why can't I follow you now?" asked Peter. "I am ready to die for you!"

[38] Jesus answered, "Are you really ready to die for me? I am telling you the truth: before the cock crows you will say three times that you do not know me.

Jesus the Way to the Father

14 "Do not be worried and upset," Jesus told them. "Believe* in God and believe also in me. [2] There are many rooms in my Father's house, and I am going to prepare a place for you. I would not tell you this if it were not so.* [3] And after I go and prepare a place for you, I will come back and take you to myself, so that you will be where I am. [4] You know the way that leads to the place where I am going."

[5] Thomas said to him, "Lord, we do not know where you are going; so how can we know the way to get there?"

[6] Jesus answered him, "I am the way, the truth, and the life; no one goes to the Father except by me. [7] Now that you have known me," he said to them, "you will know* my Father also, and from now on you do know him and you have seen him."

[8] Philip said to him, "Lord, show us the Father; that is all we need."

[9] Jesus answered, "For a long time I have been with you all; yet you do not know me, Philip? Whoever has seen me has seen the Father. Why, then, do you say, 'Show us the Father'? [10] Do you not believe, Philip, that I am in the Father and the Father is in me? The words that I have spoken to you," Jesus said to his disciples, "do not come from me. The Father, who remains in me, does his own work. [11] Believe me when I say that I am in the Father and the Father is in me. If not, believe because of the things I do.

JOHN 14.6

I AM
• THE •
WAY,
THE
TRUTH,
AND THE
• LIFE •

14.1 *Believe*; or *You believe.*
14.2 *There are… were not so*; or *There are many rooms in my Father's house; if it were not so, would I tell you that I am going to prepare a place for you?*
14.7 *Now that you have known me… you will know*; some manuscripts have *If you had known me… you would know.*

1277

John
..........:

Acts
Romans
1 Corin.
2 Corin.
Galat.

¹² I am telling you the truth: those who believe in me will do what I do — yes, they will do even greater things, because I am going to the Father. ¹³ And I will do whatever you ask for in my name, so that the Father's glory will be shown through the Son. ¹⁴ If you ask me* for anything in my name, I will do it.

The Promise of the Holy Spirit

¹⁵ "If you love me, you will obey my commandments. ¹⁶ I will ask the Father, and he will give you another Helper, who will stay with you for ever. ¹⁷ He is the Spirit who reveals the truth about God. The world cannot receive him, because it cannot see him or know him. But you know him, because he remains with you and is* in you.

¹⁸ "When I go, you will not be left all alone; I will come back to you. ¹⁹ In a little while the world will see me no more, but you will see me; and because I live, you also will live. ²⁰ When that day comes, you will know that I am in my Father and that you are in me, just as I am in you.

²¹ "Those who accept my commandments and obey them are the ones who love me. My Father will love those who love me; I too will love them and reveal myself to them."

²² Judas (not Judas Iscariot) said, "Lord, how can it be that you will reveal yourself to us and not to the world?"

²³ Jesus answered him, "Whoever loves me will obey my teaching. My Father will love him, and my Father and I will come to him and live with him. ²⁴ Whoever does not love me does not obey my teaching. And the teaching you have heard is not mine, but comes from the Father, who sent me.

²⁵ "I have told you this while I am still with you. ²⁶ The Helper, the Holy Spirit, whom the Father will send in my name, will teach you everything and make you remember all that I have told you.

²⁷ "Peace is what I leave with you; it is my own peace that I give you. I do not give it as the world does. Do not be worried and upset; do not be afraid. ²⁸ You heard me say to you, 'I am leaving, but I will come back to you.' If you loved me, you would be glad that I am going to the Father; for he is greater than I. ²⁹ I have told you this now before it all happens, so that when it does happen, you will believe. ³⁰ I cannot talk with you much longer, because the ruler of this world is coming. He has no power over me, ³¹ but the world must know that I love the Father; that is why I do everything as he commands me.

"Come, let us go from this place.

Jesus the Real Vine

15 "I am the real vine, and my Father is the gardener. ² He breaks off every branch in me that does not bear fruit, and he prunes every branch that does bear fruit, so that it will be clean and bear more fruit. ³ You have been made clean already by the teaching I have given you. ⁴ Remain united to me, and I will remain united to you. A branch cannot bear fruit by itself; it can do so only if it remains in the vine. In the same way you cannot bear fruit unless you remain in me.

⁵ "I am the vine, and you are the branches. Those who remain in me, and I in them, will bear much fruit; for you can do nothing without me. ⁶ Whoever does not remain in me is thrown out like a branch and dries up; such branches are gathered up and thrown

14.14 Some manuscripts do not have *me*.
14.17 *is*; some manuscripts have *will be*.

1278

John

·:········

Zechar.
Malachi
Matt.
Mark
Luke

JOHN 15, 16

into the fire, where they are burnt. [7]If you remain in me and my words remain in you, then you will ask for anything you wish, and you shall have it. [8]My Father's glory is shown by your bearing much fruit; and in this way you become my disciples. [9]I love you just as the Father loves me; remain in my love. [10]If you obey my commands, you will remain in my love, just as I have obeyed my Father's commands and remain in his love.

[11]"I have told you this so that my joy may be in you and that your joy may be complete. [12]My commandment is this: love one another, just as I love you. [13]The greatest love a person can have for his friends is to give his life for them. [14]And you are my friends if you do what I command you. [15]I do not call you servants any longer, because servants do not know what their master is doing. Instead, I call you friends, because I have told you everything I have heard from my Father. [16]You did not choose me; I chose you and appointed you to go and bear much fruit, the kind of fruit that endures. And so the Father will give you whatever you ask of him in my name. [17]This, then, is what I command you: love one another.

The World's Hatred

[18]"If the world hates you, just remember that it has hated me first. [19]If you belonged to the world, then the world would love you as its own. But I chose you from this world, and you do not belong to it; that is why the world hates you. [20]Remember what I told you: 'Slaves are not greater than their master.' If people persecuted me, they will persecute you too; if they obeyed my teaching, they will obey yours too. [21]But they will do all this to you because you are mine; for they do not know the one who sent me. [22]They would not have been guilty of sin if I had not come and spoken to them; as it is, they no longer have any excuse for their sin. [23]Whoever hates me hates my Father also. [24]They would not have been guilty of sin if I had not done among them the things that no one else ever did; as it is, they have seen what I did, and they hate both me and my Father. [25]This, however, was bound to happen so that what is written in their Law may come true: 'They hated me for no reason at all.'

[26]"The Helper will come — the Spirit, who reveals the truth about God and who comes from the Father. I will send him to you from the Father, and he will speak about me. [27]And you, too, will speak about me, because you have been with me from the very beginning.

16 [1]"I have told you this, so that you will not give up your faith. [2]You will be expelled from the synagogues, and the time will come when anyone who kills you will think that by doing this he is serving God. [3]People will do these things to you because they have not known either the Father or me. [4]But I have told you this, so that when the time comes for them to do these things, you will remember that I told you.

The Work of the Holy Spirit

"I did not tell you these things at the beginning, for I was with you. [5]But now I am going to him who sent me, yet none of you asks me where I am going. [6]And now that I have told you, your hearts are full of sadness. [7]But I am telling you the truth: it is better for you that I go away, because if I do not go, the Helper will not come to you. But if I do go away, then I will send him to you. [8]And when he comes, he will prove to the people of the world that they are wrong about sin and about what is right and

JOHN 16

1279

John

Acts
Romans
1 Corin.
2 Corin.
Galat.

about God's judgement. [9] They are wrong about sin, because they do not believe in me; [10] they are wrong about what is right, because I am going to the Father and you will not see me any more; [11] and they are wrong about judgement, because the ruler of this world has already been judged.

[12] "I have much more to tell you, but now it would be too much for you to bear. [13] When, however, the Spirit comes, who reveals the truth about God, he will lead you into all the truth. He will not speak on his own authority, but he will speak of what he hears, and will tell you of things to come. [14] He will give me glory, because he will take what I say and tell it to you. [15] All that my Father has is mine; that is why I said that the Spirit will take what I give him and tell it to you.

Sadness and Gladness

[16] "In a little while you will not see me any more, and then a little while later you will see me."

[17] Some of his disciples asked among themselves, "What does this mean? He tells us that in a little while we will not see him, and then a little while later we will see him; and he also says, 'It is because I am going to the Father.' [18] What does this 'a little while' mean? We don't know what he is talking about!"

[19] Jesus knew that they wanted to question him, so he said to them, "I said, 'In a little while you will not see me, and then a little while later you will see me.' Is this what you are asking about among yourselves? [20] I am telling you the truth: you will cry and weep, but the world will be glad; you will be sad, but your sadness will turn into gladness. [21] When a woman is about to give birth, she is sad because her hour of suffering has come; but when the baby is born, she forgets her suffering, because she is happy that a baby has been born into the world. [22] That is how it is with you: now you are sad, but I will see you again, and your hearts will be filled with gladness, the kind of gladness that no one can take away from you.

[23] "When that day comes, you will not ask me for anything. I am telling you the truth: the Father will give you whatever you ask him for in my name.* [24] Until now you have not asked for anything in my name; ask and you will receive, so that your happiness may be complete.

Victory over the World

[25] "I have used figures of speech to tell you these things. But the time will come when I will not use figures of speech, but will speak to you plainly about the Father. [26] When that day comes, you will ask him in my name; and I do not say that I will ask him on your behalf, [27] for the Father himself loves you. He loves you because you love me and have believed that I came from God. [28] I did come from the Father, and I came into the world; and now I am leaving the world and going to the Father."

[29] Then his disciples said to him, "Now you are speaking plainly, without using figures of speech. [30] We know now that you know everything; you do not need someone to ask you questions. This makes us believe that you came from God."

[31] Jesus answered them, "Do you believe now? [32] The time is coming, and is already here, when all of you will be scattered,

....

16.23 *the Father will give you whatever you ask him for in my name*; some manuscripts have *if you ask the Father for anything, he will give it to you in my name*.

GLORY

PSALM 57.11;
EZEKIEL 3.12;
JOHN 17.4

Search for the Oxford
or Cambridge Dictionary
definition of 'glory'
and write the
definition here.

each of you to your own home, and I will be left all alone. But I am not really alone, because the Father is with me. ³³I have told you this so that you will have peace by being united to me. The world will make you suffer. But be brave! I have defeated the world!"

Jesus Prays for his Disciples

17 After Jesus finished saying this, he looked up to heaven and said, "Father, the hour has come. Give glory to your Son, so that the Son may give glory to you. ²For you gave him authority over all humanity, so that he might give eternal life to all those you gave him. ³And eternal life means knowing you, the only true God, and knowing Jesus Christ, whom you sent. ⁴I have shown your glory on earth; I have finished the work you gave me to do. ⁵Father! Give me glory in your presence now, the same glory I had with you before the world was made.

⁶"I have made you known to those you gave me out of the world. They belonged to you, and you gave them to me. They have obeyed your word, ⁷and now they know that everything you gave me comes from you. ⁸I gave them the message that you gave me, and they received it; they know that it is true that I came from you, and they believe that you sent me.

⁹"I pray for them. I do not pray for the world but for those you gave me, for they belong to you. ¹⁰All I have is yours, and all you have is mine; and my glory is shown through them. ¹¹And now I am coming to you; I am no longer in the world, but they are in the world. Holy Father! Keep them safe by the power of your name, the name you gave me,* so that they may be one just as you and I are one. ¹²While I was with them, I kept them safe by the power of your name, the name you gave me.* I protected them, and not one of them was lost, except the man who was bound to be lost — so that the scripture might come true. ¹³And now I am coming to you, and I say these things in the world so that they might have my joy in their hearts in all its fullness. ¹⁴I gave them your message, and the world hated them, because they do not belong to the world, just as I do not belong to the world. ¹⁵I do not ask you to take them out of the world, but I do ask you to keep them safe from the Evil One. ¹⁶Just as I do not belong to the world, they do not belong to the world. ¹⁷Dedicate them to yourself by means of the truth; your word is truth. ¹⁸I sent them into the world, just as you sent me into the world. ¹⁹And for their sake I dedicate myself to you, in order that they, too, may be truly dedicated to you.

²⁰"I pray not only for them, but also for those who believe in me because of their message. ²¹I pray that they may all be one. Father! May they be in us, just as you are in me and I am in you. May they be one, so that the world will believe that you sent me. ²²I gave them the same glory you gave me, so that they may be one, just as you and I are one: ²³I in them and you in me, so that they may be completely one, in order that the world may know that you sent me and that you love them as you love me.

²⁴"Father! You have given them to me, and I want them to be with me where I am, so that they may see my glory, the glory you gave me; for you loved me before the world was made. ²⁵Righteous Father! The world does not know you, but I know you, and these

17.11 *Keep them safe by the power of your name, the name you gave me;* some manuscripts have *By the power of your name keep safe those you have given me.*
17.12 *I kept them safe by the power of your name, the name you gave me;* some manuscripts have *By the power of your name I kept safe those you have given me.*

John

⋯⋯⋯⋮⋮

Acts

Romans

1 Corin.

2 Corin.

Galat.

know that you sent me. ²⁶ I made you known to them, and I will continue to do so, in order that the love you have for me may be in them, and so that I also may be in them."

The Arrest of Jesus
(Mt 26.47–56; Mk 14.43–50; Lk 22.47–53)

18 After Jesus had said this prayer, he left with his disciples and went across the brook called Kidron. There was a garden in that place, and Jesus and his disciples went in. ² Judas, the traitor, knew where it was, because many times Jesus had met there with his disciples. ³ So Judas went to the garden, taking with him a group of Roman soldiers, and some temple guards sent by the chief priests and the Pharisees; they were armed and carried lanterns and torches. ⁴ Jesus knew everything that was going to happen to him, so he stepped forward and asked them, "Who is it you are looking for?"

⁵ "Jesus of Nazareth," they answered.

"I am he," he said.

Judas, the traitor, was standing there with them. ⁶ When Jesus said to them, "I am he," they moved back and fell to the ground. ⁷ Again Jesus asked them, "Who is it you are looking for?"

"Jesus of Nazareth," they said.

⁸ "I have already told you that I am he," Jesus said. "If, then, you are looking for me, let these others go." ⁹ (He said this so that what he had said might come true: "Father, I have not lost even one of those you gave me.")

¹⁰ Simon Peter, who had a sword, drew it and struck the High Priest's slave, cutting off his right ear. The name of the slave was Malchus. ¹¹ Jesus said to Peter, "Put your sword back in its place! Do you think that I will not drink the cup of suffering which my Father has given me?"

Jesus before Annas
¹² Then the Roman soldiers with their commanding officer and the Jewish guards arrested Jesus, bound him, ¹³ and took him first to Annas. He was the father-in-law of Caiaphas, who was High Priest that year. ¹⁴ It was Caiaphas who had advised the Jewish authorities that it was better that one man should die for all the people.

Peter Denies Jesus
(Mt 26.69–70; Mk 14.66–68; Lk 22.55–57)

¹⁵ Simon Peter and another disciple followed Jesus. That other disciple was well known to the High Priest, so he went with Jesus into the courtyard of the High Priest's house, ¹⁶ while Peter stayed outside by the gate. Then the other disciple went back out, spoke to the girl at the gate, and brought Peter inside. ¹⁷ The girl at the gate said to Peter, "Aren't you also one of the disciples of that man?"

"No, I am not," answered Peter.

¹⁸ It was cold, so the servants and guards had built a charcoal fire and were standing round it, warming themselves. So Peter went over and stood with them, warming himself.

The High Priest Questions Jesus
(Mt 26.59–66; Mk 14.55–64; Lk 22.66–71)

¹⁹ The High Priest questioned Jesus about his disciples and about his teaching. ²⁰ Jesus answered, "I have always spoken publicly to everyone; all my teaching was done in the synagogues and in the Temple, where all the people come together. I have never said

1282

John

·:········

Zechar.

Malachi

Matt.

Mark

Luke

JOHN 18

anything in secret. ²¹ Why, then, do you question me? Question the people who heard me. Ask them what I told them — they know what I said."

²² When Jesus said this, one of the guards there slapped him and said, "How dare you talk like that to the High Priest!"

²³ Jesus answered him, "If I have said anything wrong, tell everyone here what it was. But if I am right in what I have said, why do you hit me?"

²⁴ Then Annas sent him, still bound, to Caiaphas the High Priest.

Peter Denies Jesus Again
(Mt 26.71–75; Mk 14.69–72; Lk 22.58–62)

²⁵ Peter was still standing there keeping himself warm. So the others said to him, "Aren't you also one of the disciples of that man?"

But Peter denied it. "No, I am not," he said.

²⁶ One of the High Priest's slaves, a relative of the man whose ear Peter had cut off, spoke up. "Didn't I see you with him in the garden?" he asked.

²⁷ Again Peter said "No" — and at once a cock crowed.

Jesus is Brought before Pilate
(Mt 27.1–2, 11–14; Mk 15.1–5; Lk 23.1–5)

²⁸ Early in the morning Jesus was taken from Caiaphas' house to the governor's palace. The Jewish authorities did not go inside the palace, for they wanted to keep themselves ritually clean, in order to be able to eat the Passover meal. ²⁹ So Pilate went outside to them and asked, "What do you accuse this man of?"

³⁰ Their answer was, "We would not have brought him to you if he had not committed a crime."

³¹ Pilate said to them, "Then you yourselves take him and try him according to your own law."

They replied, "We are not allowed to put anyone to death." ³² (This happened in order to make the words of Jesus come true, the words he used when he indicated the kind of death he would die.)

³³ Pilate went back into the palace and called Jesus. "Are you the King of the Jews?" he asked him.

³⁴ Jesus answered, "Does this question come from you or have others told you about me?"

³⁵ Pilate replied, "Do you think I am a Jew? It was your own people and the chief priests who handed you over to me. What have you done?"

³⁶ Jesus said, "My kingdom does not belong to this world; if my kingdom belonged to this world, my followers would fight to keep me from being handed over to the Jewish authorities. No, my kingdom does not belong here!"

³⁷ So Pilate asked him, "Are you a king, then?"

Jesus answered, "You say that I am a king. I was born and came into the world for this one purpose, to speak about the truth. Whoever belongs to the truth listens to me."

³⁸ "And what is truth?" Pilate asked.

Jesus is Sentenced to Death
(Mt 27.15–31; Mk 15.6–20; Lk 23.13–25)

Then Pilate went back outside to the people and said to them, "I cannot find any reason to condemn him. ³⁹ But according to the custom you have, I always set free a prisoner for you during the Passover. Do you want me to set free for you the King of the Jews?"

JOHN 18, 19

1283

John
....
Acts
Romans
1 Corin.
2 Corin.
Galat.

⁴⁰ They answered him with a shout, "No, not him! We want Barabbas!" (Barabbas was a bandit.)

19 Then Pilate took Jesus and had him whipped. ² The soldiers made a crown out of thorny branches and put it on his head; then they put a purple robe on him ³ and came to him and said, "Long live the King of the Jews!" And they went up and slapped him.

⁴ Pilate went out once more and said to the crowd, "Look, I will bring him out here to you to let you see that I cannot find any reason to condemn him." ⁵ So Jesus came out, wearing the crown of thorns and the purple robe. Pilate said to them, "Look! Here is the man!"

⁶ When the chief priests and the temple guards saw him, they shouted, "Crucify him! Crucify him!"

Pilate said to them, "You take him, then, and crucify him. I find no reason to condemn him."

⁷ The crowd answered back, "We have a law that says he ought to die, because he claimed to be the Son of God."

⁸ When Pilate heard this, he was even more afraid. ⁹ He went back into the palace and asked Jesus, "Where do you come from?"

But Jesus did not answer. ¹⁰ Pilate said to him, "You will not speak to me? Remember, I have the authority to set you free and also to have you crucified."

¹¹ Jesus answered, "You have authority over me only because it was given to you by God. So the man who handed me over to you is guilty of a worse sin."

¹² When Pilate heard this, he tried to find a way to set Jesus free. But the crowd shouted back, "If you set him free, that means that you are not the Emperor's friend! Anyone who claims to be a king is a rebel against the Emperor!"

¹³ When Pilate heard these words, he took Jesus outside and sat down on the judge's seat in the place called "The Stone Pavement". (In Hebrew the name is "Gabbatha".) ¹⁴ It was then almost noon of the day before the Passover. Pilate said to the people, "Here is your king!"

¹⁵ They shouted back, "Kill him! Kill him! Crucify him!"

Pilate asked them, "Do you want me to crucify your king?"

The chief priests answered, "The only king we have is the Emperor!"

¹⁶ Then Pilate handed Jesus over to them to be crucified.

Jesus is Crucified
(Mt 27.32–44; Mk 15.21–32; Lk 23.26–43)

So they took charge of Jesus. ¹⁷ He went out, carrying his cross, and came to "The Place of the Skull", as it is called. (In Hebrew it is called "Golgotha".) ¹⁸ There they crucified him; and they also crucified two other men, one on each side, with Jesus between them. ¹⁹ Pilate wrote a notice and had it put on the cross. "Jesus of Nazareth, the King of the Jews", is what he wrote. ²⁰ Many people read it, because the place where Jesus was crucified was not far from the city. The notice was written in Hebrew, Latin, and Greek. ²¹ The chief priests said to Pilate, "Do not write 'The King of the Jews', but rather, 'This man said, I am the King of the Jews.'"

²² Pilate answered, "What I have written stays written."

²³ After the soldiers had crucified Jesus, they took his clothes and divided them into four parts, one part for each soldier. They also took the robe, which was made of one piece of woven cloth without any seams in it. ²⁴ The soldiers said to one another, "Let's not tear it; let's throw dice to see who will get it." This happened in order to make the scripture come true:

JOHN 19-21

Head to
gnbyouthedition.co.uk/death to
WATCH A SHORT
⇥ FILM ⇤
and unpack the ways these chapters impact your life – right now!

1284

John

∴ ....

Zechar.
Malachi
Matt.
Mark
Luke

JOHN 19, 20

"They divided my clothes among themselves
  and gambled for my robe."
And this is what the soldiers did.

25 Standing close to Jesus' cross were his mother, his mother's sister, Mary the wife of Clopas, and Mary Magdalene. 26 Jesus saw his mother and the disciple he loved standing there; so he said to his mother, "He is your son."

27 Then he said to the disciple, "She is your mother." From that time the disciple took her to live in his home.

The Death of Jesus
(Mt 27.45–56; Mk 15.33–41; Lk 23.44–49)

28 Jesus knew that by now everything had been completed; and in order to make the scripture come true, he said, "I am thirsty."

29 A bowl was there, full of cheap wine; so a sponge was soaked in the wine, put on a stalk of hyssop, and lifted up to his lips. 30 Jesus drank the wine and said, "It is finished!"

Then he bowed his head and died.

Jesus' Side is Pierced

31 Then the Jewish authorities asked Pilate to allow them to break the legs of the men who had been crucified, and to take the bodies down from the crosses. They requested this because it was Friday, and they did not want the bodies to stay on the crosses on the Sabbath, since the coming Sabbath was especially holy. 32 So the soldiers went and broke the legs of the first man and then of the other man who had been crucified with Jesus. 33 But when they came to Jesus, they saw that he was already dead, so they did not break his legs. 34 One of the soldiers, however, plunged his spear into Jesus' side, and at once blood and water poured out. 35 (The one who saw this happen has spoken of it, so that you also may believe.* What he said is true, and he knows that he speaks the truth.) 36 This was done to make the scripture come true: "Not one of his bones will be broken." 37 And there is another scripture that says, "People will look at him whom they pierced."

The Burial of Jesus
(Mt 27.57–61; Mk 15.42–47; Lk 23.50–56)

38 After this, Joseph, who was from the town of Arimathea, asked Pilate if he could take Jesus' body. (Joseph was a follower of Jesus, but in secret, because he was afraid of the Jewish authorities.) Pilate told him he could have the body, so Joseph went and took it away. 39 Nicodemus, who at first had gone to see Jesus at night, went with Joseph, taking with him about thirty kilogrammes of spices, a mixture of myrrh and aloes. 40 The two men took Jesus' body and wrapped it in linen with the spices according to the Jewish custom of preparing a body for burial. 41 There was a garden in the place where Jesus had been put to death, and in it there was a new tomb where no one had ever been buried. 42 Since it was the day before the Sabbath and because the tomb was close by, they placed Jesus' body there.

The Empty Tomb
(Mt 28.1–8; Mk 16.1–8; Lk 24.1–12)

20 Early on Sunday morning, while it was still dark, Mary Magdalene went to the tomb and saw that the stone had been taken away from the entrance. 2 She went running to

....

19.35 *believe*; some manuscripts have *continue to believe.*

John

·········:·

Acts
Romans
1 Corin.
2 Corin.
Galat.

Simon Peter and the other disciple, whom Jesus loved, and told them, "They have taken the Lord from the tomb, and we don't know where they have put him!"

³ Then Peter and the other disciple went to the tomb. ⁴ The two of them were running, but the other disciple ran faster than Peter and reached the tomb first. ⁵ He bent over and saw the linen wrappings, but he did not go in. ⁶ Behind him came Simon Peter, and he went straight into the tomb. He saw the linen wrappings lying there ⁷ and the cloth which had been round Jesus' head. It was not lying with the linen wrappings but was rolled up by itself. ⁸ Then the other disciple, who had reached the tomb first, also went in; he saw and believed. ⁹ (They still did not understand the scripture which said that he must rise from death.) ¹⁰ Then the disciples went back home.

Jesus Appears to Mary Magdalene
(Mt 28.9–10; Mk 16.9–11)

¹¹ Mary stood crying outside the tomb. While she was still crying, she bent over and looked in the tomb ¹² and saw two angels there dressed in white, sitting where the body of Jesus had been, one at the head and the other at the feet. ¹³ "Woman, why are you crying?" they asked her.

She answered, "They have taken my Lord away, and I do not know where they have put him!"

¹⁴ Then she turned round and saw Jesus standing there; but she did not know that it was Jesus. ¹⁵ "Woman, why are you crying?" Jesus asked her. "Who is it that you are looking for?"

She thought he was the gardener, so she said to him, "If you took him away, sir, tell me where you have put him, and I will go and get him."

¹⁶ Jesus said to her, "Mary!"

She turned towards him and said in Hebrew, "Rabboni!" (This means "Teacher".)

¹⁷ "Do not hold on to me," Jesus told her, "because I have not yet gone back up to the Father. But go to my brothers and tell them that I am returning to him who is my Father and their Father, my God and their God."

¹⁸ So Mary Magdalene went and told the disciples that she had seen the Lord and related to them what he had told her.

Jesus Appears to his Disciples
(Mt 28.16–20; Mk 16.14–18; Lk 24.36–49)

¹⁹ It was late that Sunday evening, and the disciples were gathered together behind locked doors, because they were afraid of the Jewish authorities. Then Jesus came and stood among them. "Peace be with you," he said. ²⁰ After saying this, he showed them his hands and his side. The disciples were filled with joy at seeing the Lord. ²¹ Jesus said to them again, "Peace be with you. As the Father sent me, so I send you." ²² Then he breathed on them and said, "Receive the Holy Spirit. ²³ If you forgive people's sins, they are forgiven; if you do not forgive them, they are not forgiven."

Jesus and Thomas

²⁴ One of the twelve disciples, Thomas (called the Twin), was not with them when Jesus came. ²⁵ So the other disciples told him, "We have seen the Lord!"

Thomas said to them, "Unless I see the scars of the nails in his hands and put my finger on those scars and my hand in his side, I will not believe."

1286

John

Zechar.
Malachi
Matt.
Mark
Luke

JOHN 20, 21

26 A week later the disciples were together again indoors, and Thomas was with them. The doors were locked, but Jesus came and stood among them and said, "Peace be with you." 27 Then he said to Thomas, "Put your finger here, and look at my hands; then stretch out your hand and put it in my side. Stop your doubting, and believe!"

28 Thomas answered him, "My Lord and my God!"

29 Jesus said to him, "Do you believe because you see me? How happy are those who believe without seeing me!"

The Purpose of this Book

30 In his disciples' presence Jesus performed many other miracles which are not written down in this book. 31 But these have been written in order that you may believe* that Jesus is the Messiah, the Son of God, and that through your faith in him you may have life.

Jesus Appears to Seven Disciples

21 After this, Jesus appeared once more to his disciples at Lake Tiberias. This is how it happened. 2 Simon Peter, Thomas (called the Twin), Nathanael (the one from Cana in Galilee), the sons of Zebedee, and two other disciples of Jesus were all together. 3 Simon Peter said to the others, "I am going fishing."

"We will come with you," they told him. So they went out in a boat, but all that night they did not catch a thing. 4 As the sun was rising, Jesus stood at the water's edge, but the disciples did not know that it was Jesus. 5 Then he asked them, "Young men, haven't you caught anything?"

"Not a thing," they answered.

6 He said to them, "Throw your net out on the right side of the boat, and you will catch some." So they threw the net out and could not pull it back in, because they had caught so many fish.

7 The disciple whom Jesus loved said to Peter, "It is the Lord!" When Peter heard that it was the Lord, he wrapped his outer garment round him (for he had taken his clothes off) and jumped into the water. 8 The other disciples came to shore in the boat, pulling the net full of fish. They were not very far from land, about a hundred metres away. 9 When they stepped ashore, they saw a charcoal fire there with fish on it and some bread. 10 Then Jesus said to them, "Bring some of the fish you have just caught."

11 Simon Peter went aboard and dragged the net ashore full of big fish, 153 in all; even though there were so many, still the net did not tear. 12 Jesus said to them, "Come and eat." None of the disciples dared ask him, "Who are you?" because they knew it was the Lord. 13 So Jesus went over, took the bread, and gave it to them; he did the same with the fish.

14 This, then, was the third time Jesus appeared to the disciples after he was raised from death.

Jesus and Peter

15 After they had eaten, Jesus said to Simon Peter, "Simon son of John, do you love me more than these others do?"

"Yes, Lord," he answered, "you know that I love you."

Jesus said to him, "Take care of my lambs." 16 A second time Jesus said to him, "Simon son of John, do you love me?"

"Yes, Lord," he answered, "you know that I love you."

Jesus said to him, "Take care of my sheep." 17 A third time Jesus said, "Simon son of John, do you love me?"

20.31 *believe*; some manuscripts have *continue to believe*.

1287

John

.........:

Acts
Romans
1 Corin.
2 Corin.
Galat.

Peter was sad because Jesus asked him the third time, "Do you love me?" so he said to him, "Lord, you know everything; you know that I love you!"

Jesus said to him, "Take care of my sheep. [18] I am telling you the truth: when you were young, you used to get ready and go anywhere you wanted to; but when you are old, you will stretch out your hands and someone else will bind you and take you where you don't want to go." [19] (In saying this, Jesus was indicating the way in which Peter would die and bring glory to God.) Then Jesus said to him, "Follow me!"

Jesus and the Other Disciple

[20] Peter turned round and saw behind him that other disciple, whom Jesus loved — the one who had leaned close to Jesus at the meal and had asked, "Lord, who is going to betray you?" [21] When Peter saw him, he asked Jesus, "Lord, what about this man?"

[22] Jesus answered him, "If I want him to live until I come, what is that to you? Follow me!"

[23] So a report spread among the followers of Jesus that this disciple would not die. But Jesus did not say that he would not die; he said, "If I want him to live until I come, what is that to you?"

[24] He is the disciple who spoke of these things, the one who also wrote them down; and we know that what he said is true.

Conclusion

[25] Now, there are many other things that Jesus did. If they were all written down one by one, I suppose that the whole world could not hold the books that would be written.

Don't compare your
RELATIONSHIP WITH GOD
TO ANYONE ELSE'S.
Everyone's looks a
LITTLE DIFFERENT.

THE BOOK OF

THE ACTS OF THE APOSTLES

WRITTEN: AD85-90

WHAT YOU NEED TO KNOW:

The Acts of the Apostles is the incredible story of how the church started. It records how, after Jesus went into heaven, the Holy Spirit came and equipped the small group of his followers. This small group soon bloomed into thousands, and people's lives were transformed for ever. Through the events recorded in Acts we see the apostles (Jesus' original disciples) and other followers of Jesus spreading the good news, sharing their stories and founding churches. Life was made difficult for the early believers by people from both Jewish and non-Jewish backgrounds. Many of the Christians were put to death (such as Stephen in chapter 7), yet people continued to share the news about Jesus and the church continued to grow.

Draw something to show what 'church' means to you. How similar is this to what the church was like in the early days?

WHY READ IT?

Acts describes loads of amazing things, including the selfless nature of the early believers and their perseverance against all the odds. It shows that the Holy Spirit is active in changing lives, and that Jesus is worth giving everything for. Acts tells us how the church started - so this book is part of your story too.

Read Acts chapter 9 to see how Paul became a Christian. Then flick through the book and look at the chapter headings (in bold type) to see what Paul did after he came to faith.

What was the difference between Paul's life before and Paul's life after he decided to follow Jesus?

(AD27)
JESUS RETURNS TO HEAVEN

PAUL CONVERTED

(AD62)
PAUL IN ROM

PENTECOST

PAUL TRAVELS

ACTS 1

1289

Acts

Romans
1 Corin.
2 Corin.
Galat.
Ephes.

1 Dear Theophilus:

In my first book I wrote about all the things that Jesus did and taught from the time he began his work [2] until the day he was taken up to heaven. Before he was taken up, he gave instructions by the power of the Holy Spirit to the men he had chosen as his apostles. [3] For forty days after his death he appeared to them many times in ways that proved beyond doubt that he was alive. They saw him, and he talked with them about the Kingdom of God. [4] And when they came together,* he gave them this order: "Do not leave Jerusalem, but wait for the gift I told you about, the gift my Father promised. [5] John baptized with water, but in a few days you will be baptized with the Holy Spirit."

Jesus is Taken Up to Heaven
(Mk 16.19–20; Lk 24.50–53)

[6] When the apostles met together with Jesus, they asked him, "Lord, will you at this time give the Kingdom back to Israel?"

[7] Jesus said to them, "The times and occasions are set by my Father's own authority, and it is not for you to know when they will be. [8] But when the Holy Spirit comes upon you, you will be filled with power, and you will be witnesses for me in Jerusalem, in all Judea and Samaria, and to the ends of the earth." [9] After saying this, he was taken up to heaven as they watched him, and a cloud hid him from their sight.

[10] They still had their eyes fixed on the sky as he went away, when two men dressed in white suddenly stood beside them [11] and said, "Galileans, why are you standing there looking up at the sky? This Jesus, who was taken from you into heaven, will come back in the same way that you saw him go to heaven."

Judas' Successor
(Mt 27.3–10)

[12] Then the apostles went back to Jerusalem from the Mount of Olives, which is about a kilometre away from the city. [13] They entered the city and went up to the room where they were staying: Peter, John, James and Andrew, Philip and Thomas, Bartholomew and Matthew, James son of Alphaeus, Simon the Patriot, and Judas son of James. [14] They gathered frequently to pray as a group, together with the women and with Mary the mother of Jesus and with his brothers.

[15] A few days later there was a meeting of the believers, about 120 in all, and Peter stood up to speak. [16] "My fellow-believers," he said, "the scripture had to come true in which the Holy Spirit, speaking through David, made a prediction about Judas, who was the guide for those who arrested Jesus. [17] Judas was a member of our group, for he had been chosen to have a part in our work."

[18] (With the money that Judas got for his evil act he bought a field, where he fell to his death; he burst open and all his bowels spilt out. [19] All the people living in Jerusalem heard about it, and so in their own language they call that field Akeldama, which means "Field of Blood".)

[20] "For it is written in the book of Psalms:

'May his house become empty;
    may no one live in it.'

It is also written:

'May someone else take his place of service.'

1.4 *when they came together*; or *while he was staying with them*; or *while he was eating with them*.

1290

Acts

Malachi
Matt.
Mark
Luke
John

ACTS 1, 2

ACTS 2

Draw what you think

PENTECOST

LOOKED LIKE.

What do you think it would
have felt like to be there?

21-22 "So then, someone must join us as a witness to the resurrection of the Lord Jesus. He must be one of the men who were in our group during the whole time that the Lord Jesus travelled about with us, beginning from the time John preached his message of baptism* until the day Jesus was taken up from us to heaven."

23 So they proposed two men: Joseph, who was called Barsabbas (also known as Justus), and Matthias. 24 Then they prayed, "Lord, you know the thoughts of everyone, so show us which of these two you have chosen 25 to serve as an apostle in the place of Judas, who left to go to the place where he belongs." 26 Then they drew lots to choose between the two men, and the one chosen was Matthias, who was added to the group of eleven apostles.

The Coming of the Holy Spirit

2 When the day of Pentecost came, all the believers were gathered together in one place. 2 Suddenly there was a noise from the sky which sounded like a strong wind blowing, and it filled the whole house where they were sitting. 3 Then they saw what looked like tongues of fire which spread out and touched each person there. 4 They were all filled with the Holy Spirit and began to talk in other languages, as the Spirit enabled them to speak.

5 There were Jews living in Jerusalem, religious people who had come from every country in the world. 6 When they heard this noise, a large crowd gathered. They were all excited, because each one of them heard the believers speaking in his or her own language. 7 In amazement and wonder they exclaimed, "These people who are talking like this are Galileans! 8 How is it, then, that all of us hear them speaking in our own native languages? 9 We are from Parthia, Media, and Elam; from Mesopotamia, Judea, and Cappadocia; from Pontus and Asia, 10 from Phrygia and Pamphylia, from Egypt and the regions of Libya near Cyrene. Some of us are from Rome, 11 both Jews and Gentiles converted to Judaism, and some of us are from Crete and Arabia — yet all of us hear them speaking in our own languages about the great things that God has done!" 12 Amazed and confused, they kept asking each other, "What does this mean?"

13 But others made fun of the believers, saying, "These people are drunk!"

Peter's Message

14 Then Peter stood up with the other eleven apostles and in a loud voice began to speak to the crowd: "Fellow-Jews and all of you who live in Jerusalem, listen to me and let me tell you what this means. 15 These people are not drunk, as you suppose; it is only nine o'clock in the morning. 16 Instead, this is what the prophet Joel spoke about:

17 'This is what I will do in the last days, God says:
   I will pour out my Spirit on everyone.
Your sons and daughters will proclaim my message;
   your young men will see visions,
   and your old men will have dreams.
18 Yes, even on my servants, both men and women,
   I will pour out my Spirit in those days,
   and they will proclaim my message.
19 I will perform miracles in the sky above
   and wonders on the earth below.

1.21–22 John preached his message of baptism; or John baptized him.

ACTS 2

1291

Acts

....

Romans
1 Corin.
2 Corin.
Galat.
Ephes.

There will be blood, fire, and thick smoke;
20   the sun will be darkened,
      and the moon will turn red as blood,
      before the great and glorious Day of the Lord comes.
21 And then, whoever calls out to the Lord for help will be
      saved.'
22 "Listen to these words, fellow-Israelites! Jesus of Nazareth
was a man whose divine authority was clearly proven to you by
all the miracles and wonders which God performed through him.
You yourselves know this, for it happened here among you. 23 In
accordance with his own plan God had already decided that Jesus
would be handed over to you; and you killed him by letting sinful
men crucify him. 24 But God raised him from death, setting him
free from its power, because it was impossible that death should
hold him prisoner. 25 For David said about him:
      'I saw the Lord before me at all times;
         he is near me, and I will not be troubled.
26   And so I am filled with gladness,
         and my words are full of joy.
      And I, mortal though I am,
         will rest assured in hope,
27 because you will not abandon me in the world of the dead;
         you will not allow your faithful servant to rot in the
            grave.
28   You have shown me the paths that lead to life,
         and your presence will fill me with joy.'
29 "My fellow-Israelites, I must speak to you plainly about our
famous ancestor King David. He died and was buried, and his
grave is here with us to this very day. 30 He was a prophet, and
he knew what God had promised him: God had made a vow that
he would make one of David's descendants a king, just as David
was. 31 David saw what God was going to do in the future, and
so he spoke about the resurrection of the Messiah when he said:
      'He was not abandoned in the world of the dead;
         his body did not rot in the grave.'
32 God has raised this very Jesus from death, and we are all
witnesses to this fact. 33 He has been raised to the right-hand side
of God, his Father, and has received from him the Holy Spirit, as
he had promised. What you now see and hear is his gift that he
has poured out on us. 34 For it was not David who went up into
heaven; rather he said:
      'The Lord said to my Lord:
         Sit here at my right
35   until I put your enemies as a footstool under your feet.'
36 "All the people of Israel, then, are to know for sure that this
Jesus, whom you crucified, is the one that God has made Lord
and Messiah!"
37 When the people heard this, they were deeply troubled and
said to Peter and the other apostles, "What shall we do, brothers?"
38 Peter said to them, "Each one of you must turn away from
your sins and be baptized in the name of Jesus Christ, so that
your sins will be forgiven; and you will receive God's gift, the Holy
Spirit. 39 For God's promise was made to you and your children,
and to all who are far away — all whom the Lord our God calls
to himself."
40 Peter made his appeal to them and with many other words
he urged them, saying, "Save yourselves from the punishment
coming on this wicked people!" 41 Many of them believed his
message and were baptized, and about 3,000 people were added

to the group that day. [42] They spent their time in learning from the apostles, taking part in the fellowship, and sharing in the fellowship meals and the prayers.

Life among the Believers

[43] Many miracles and wonders were being done through the apostles, and everyone was filled with awe. [44] All the believers continued together in close fellowship and shared their belongings with one another. [45] They would sell their property and possessions, and distribute the money among all, according to what each one needed. [46] Day after day they met as a group in the Temple, and they had their meals together in their homes, eating with glad and humble hearts, [47] praising God, and enjoying the good will of all the people. And every day the Lord added to their group those who were being saved.

A Lame Man is Healed

3 One day Peter and John went to the Temple at three o'clock in the afternoon, the hour for prayer. [2] There at the Beautiful Gate, as it was called, was a man who had been lame all his life. Every day he was carried to the gate to beg for money from the people who were going into the Temple. [3] When he saw Peter and John going in, he begged them to give him something. [4] They looked straight at him, and Peter said, "Look at us!" [5] So he looked at them, expecting to get something from them. [6] But Peter said to him, "I have no money at all, but I give you what I have: in the name of Jesus Christ of Nazareth I order you to get up and walk!" [7] Then he took him by his right hand and helped him up. At once the man's feet and ankles became strong; [8] he jumped up, stood on his feet, and started walking around. Then he went into the Temple with them, walking and jumping and praising God. [9] The people there saw him walking and praising God, [10] and when they recognized him as the beggar who had sat at the Beautiful Gate, they were all surprised and amazed at what had happened to him.

Peter's Message in the Temple

[11] As the man held on to Peter and John in Solomon's Porch, as it was called, the people were amazed and ran to them. [12] When Peter saw the people, he said to them, "Fellow-Israelites, why are you surprised at this, and why do you stare at us? Do you think that it was by means of our own power or godliness that we made this man walk? [13] The God of Abraham, Isaac, and Jacob, the God of our ancestors, has given divine glory to his Servant Jesus. But you handed him over to the authorities, and you rejected him in Pilate's presence, even after Pilate had decided to set him free. [14] He was holy and good, but you rejected him, and instead you asked Pilate to do you the favour of turning loose a murderer. [15] You killed the one who leads to life, but God raised him from death — and we are witnesses to this. [16] It was the power of his name that gave strength to this lame man. What you see and know was done by faith in his name; it was faith in Jesus that has made him well, as you can all see.

[17] "And now, my fellow-Israelites, I know that what you and your leaders did to Jesus was due to your ignorance. [18] God announced long ago through all the prophets that his Messiah had to suffer; and he made it come true in this way. [19] Repent, then, and turn to God, so that he will forgive your sins. If you do, [20] times of spiritual strength will come from the Lord, and he will

ACTS 3, 4

1293

Acts

...........:

Romans
1 Corin.
2 Corin.
Galat.
Ephes.

send Jesus, who is the Messiah he has already chosen for you. [21] He must remain in heaven until the time comes for all things to be made new, as God announced through his holy prophets who lived long ago. [22] For Moses said, 'The Lord your God will send you a prophet, just as he sent me,* and he will be one of your own people. You are to obey everything that he tells you to do. [23] Anyone who does not obey that prophet shall be separated from God's people and destroyed.' [24] And all the prophets who had a message, including Samuel and those who came after him, also announced what has been happening these days. [25] The promises of God through his prophets are for you, and you share in the covenant which God made with your ancestors. As he said to Abraham, 'Through your descendants I will bless all the people on earth.' [26] And so God chose his Servant and sent him first to you, to bless you by making every one of you turn away from your wicked ways."

Peter and John before the Council

4 Peter and John were still speaking to the people when some priests,* the officer in charge of the temple guards, and some Sadducees arrived. [2] They were annoyed because the two apostles were teaching the people that Jesus had risen from death, which proved that the dead will rise to life. [3] So they arrested them and put them in jail until the next day, since it was already late. [4] But many who heard the message believed; and the number of men grew to about 5,000.

[5] The next day the Jewish leaders, the elders, and the teachers of the Law gathered in Jerusalem. [6] They met with the High Priest Annas and with Caiaphas, John, Alexander, and the others who belonged to the High Priest's family. [7] They made the apostles stand before them and asked them, "How did you do this? What power have you got or whose name did you use?"

[8] Peter, full of the Holy Spirit, answered them, "Leaders of the people and elders: [9] if we are being questioned today about the good deed done to the lame man and how he was healed, [10] then you should all know, and all the people of Israel should know, that this man stands here before you completely well through the power of the name of Jesus Christ of Nazareth — whom you crucified and whom God raised from death. [11] Jesus is the one of whom the scripture says:

'The stone that you the builders despised
   turned out to be the most important of all.'

[12] Salvation is to be found through him alone; in all the world there is no one else whom God has given who can save us."

[13] The members of the Council were amazed to see how bold Peter and John were and to learn that they were ordinary men of no education. They realized then that they had been companions of Jesus. [14] But there was nothing that they could say, because they saw the man who had been healed standing there with Peter and John. [15] So they told them to leave the Council room, and then they started discussing among themselves. [16] "What shall we do with these men?" they asked. "Everyone in Jerusalem knows that this extraordinary miracle has been performed by them, and we cannot deny it. [17] But to keep this matter from spreading any further among the people, let us warn these men never again to speak to anyone in the name of Jesus."

....

3.22 *just as he sent me*; or *like me*.
4.1 *priests*; some manuscripts have *chief priests*.

1294

Acts

┄┄┄┄
Malachi
Matt.
Mark
Luke
John

ACTS 4, 5

ACTS 4.32-35

Get together with

- SOME -

MATES

and chat about this passage. What do you think about it? Do you think living like this is better than the way we live today? Why or why not? Could you see yourself living as part of a society like this?

write some
thoughts here

¹⁸ So they called them back in and told them that on no condition were they to speak or to teach in the name of Jesus. ¹⁹ But Peter and John answered them, "You yourselves judge which is right in God's sight — to obey you or to obey God. ²⁰ For we cannot stop speaking of what we ourselves have seen and heard." ²¹ So the Council warned them even more strongly and then set them free. They saw that it was impossible to punish them, because the people were all praising God for what had happened. ²² The man on whom this miracle of healing had been performed was over forty years old.

The Believers Pray for Boldness
²³ As soon as Peter and John were set free, they returned to their group and told them what the chief priests and the elders had said. ²⁴ When the believers heard it, they all joined together in prayer to God: "Master and Creator of heaven, earth, and sea, and all that is in them! ²⁵ By means of the Holy Spirit you spoke through our ancestor David, your servant, when he said:
  'Why were the Gentiles furious;
    why did people make their useless plots?
²⁶ The kings of the earth prepared themselves,
    and the rulers met together
    against the Lord and his Messiah.'
²⁷ For indeed Herod and Pontius Pilate met together in this city with the Gentiles and the people of Israel against Jesus, your holy Servant, whom you made Messiah. ²⁸ They gathered to do everything that you by your power and will had already decided would happen. ²⁹ And now, Lord, take notice of the threats they have made, and allow us, your servants, to speak your message with all boldness. ³⁰ Stretch out your hand to heal, and grant that wonders and miracles may be performed through the name of your holy Servant Jesus."
³¹ When they finished praying, the place where they were meeting was shaken. They were all filled with the Holy Spirit and began to proclaim God's message with boldness.

The Believers Share their Possessions
³² The group of believers was one in mind and heart. None of them said that any of their belongings were their own, but they all shared with one another everything they had. ³³ With great power the apostles gave witness to the resurrection of the Lord Jesus, and God poured rich blessings on them all. ³⁴ There was no one in the group who was in need. Those who owned fields or houses would sell them, bring the money received from the sale, ³⁵ and hand it over to the apostles; and the money was distributed to each one according to his need.
³⁶ And so it was that Joseph, a Levite born in Cyprus, whom the apostles called Barnabas (which means "One who Encourages"), ³⁷ sold a field he owned, brought the money, and handed it over to the apostles.

Ananias and Sapphira
5 But there was a man named Ananias, who with his wife Sapphira sold some property that belonged to them. ² But with his wife's agreement he kept part of the money for himself and handed the rest over to the apostles. ³ Peter said to him, "Ananias, why did you let Satan take control of you and make you lie to the Holy Spirit by keeping part of the money you received for the property? ⁴ Before you sold the property, it belonged to you; and

ACTS 5

1295

Acts

..........:.

Romans

1 Corin.

2 Corin.

Galat.

Ephes.

after you sold it, the money was yours. Why, then, did you decide to do such a thing? You have not lied to human beings — you have lied to God!" [5] As soon as Ananias heard this, he fell down dead; and all who heard about it were terrified. [6] The young men came in, wrapped up his body, carried him out, and buried him.

[7] About three hours later his wife, not knowing what had happened, came in. [8] Peter asked her, "Tell me, was this the full amount you and your husband received for your property?"

"Yes," she answered, "the full amount."

[9] So Peter said to her, "Why did you and your husband decide to put the Lord's Spirit to the test? The men who buried your husband are now at the door, and they will carry you out too!" [10] At once she fell down at his feet and died. The young men came in and saw that she was dead, so they carried her out and buried her beside her husband. [11] The whole church and all the others who heard of this were terrified.

Miracles and Wonders

[12] Many miracles and wonders were being performed among the people by the apostles. All the believers met together in Solomon's Porch. [13] Nobody outside the group dared to join them, even though the people spoke highly of them. [14] But more and more people were added to the group — a crowd of men and women who believed in the Lord. [15] As a result of what the apostles were doing, sick people were carried out into the streets and placed on beds and mats so that at least Peter's shadow might fall on some of them as he passed by. [16] And crowds of people came in from the towns around Jerusalem, bringing those who were ill or who had evil spirits in them; and they were all healed.

The Apostles are Persecuted

[17] Then the High Priest and all his companions, members of the local party of the Sadducees, became extremely jealous of the apostles; so they decided to take action. [18] They arrested the apostles and put them in the public jail. [19] But that night an angel of the Lord opened the prison gates, led the apostles out, and said to them, [20] "Go and stand in the Temple, and tell the people all about this new life." [21] The apostles obeyed, and at dawn they entered the Temple and started teaching.

The High Priest and his companions called together all the Jewish elders for a full meeting of the Council; then they sent orders to the prison to have the apostles brought before them. [22] But when the officials arrived, they did not find the apostles in prison, so they returned to the Council and reported, [23] "When we arrived at the jail, we found it locked up tight and all the guards on watch at the gates; but when we opened the gates, we found no one inside!" [24] When the chief priests and the officer in charge of the temple guards heard this, they wondered what had happened to the apostles. [25] Then a man came in and said to them, "Listen! The men you put in prison are in the Temple teaching the people!" [26] So the officer went off with his men and brought the apostles back. They did not use force, however, because they were afraid that the people might stone them.

[27] They brought the apostles in, made them stand before the Council, and the High Priest questioned them. [28] "We gave you strict orders not to teach in the name of this man," he said; "but see what you have done! You have spread your teaching all over Jerusalem, and you want to make us responsible for his death!"

²⁹Peter and the other apostles replied, "We must obey God, not men. ³⁰The God of our ancestors raised Jesus from death, after you had killed him by nailing him to a cross. ³¹God raised him to his right-hand side as Leader and Saviour, to give the people of Israel the opportunity to repent and have their sins forgiven. ³²We are witnesses to these things — we and the Holy Spirit, who is God's gift to those who obey him."

³³When the members of the Council heard this, they were so furious that they wanted to have the apostles put to death. ³⁴But one of them, a Pharisee named Gamaliel, who was a teacher of the Law and was highly respected by all the people, stood up in the Council. He ordered the apostles to be taken out for a while, ³⁵and then he said to the Council, "Fellow-Israelites, be careful what you do to these men. ³⁶You remember that Theudas appeared some time ago, claiming to be somebody great, and about 400 men joined him. But he was killed, all his followers were scattered, and his movement died out. ³⁷After that, Judas the Galilean appeared during the time of the census; he drew a crowd after him, but he also was killed, and all his followers were scattered. ³⁸And so in this case, I tell you, do not take any action against these men. Leave them alone! If what they have planned and done is of human origin, it will disappear, ³⁹but if it comes from God, you cannot possibly defeat them. You could find yourselves fighting against God!"

The Council followed Gamaliel's advice. ⁴⁰They called the apostles in, had them whipped, and ordered them never again to speak in the name of Jesus; and then they set them free. ⁴¹As the apostles left the Council, they were happy, because God had considered them worthy to suffer disgrace for the sake of Jesus. ⁴²And every day in the Temple and in people's homes they continued to teach and preach the Good News about Jesus the Messiah.

The Seven Helpers

6 Some time later, as the number of disciples kept growing, there was a quarrel between the Greek-speaking Jews and the native Jews. The Greek-speaking Jews claimed that their widows were being neglected in the daily distribution of funds. ²So the twelve apostles called the whole group of believers together and said, "It is not right for us to neglect the preaching of God's word in order to handle finances. ³So then, brothers and sisters, choose seven men among you who are known to be full of the Holy Spirit and wisdom, and we will put them in charge of this matter. ⁴We ourselves, then, will give our full time to prayer and the work of preaching."

⁵The whole group was pleased with the apostles' proposal, so they chose Stephen, a man full of faith and the Holy Spirit, and Philip, Prochorus, Nicanor, Timon, Parmenas, and Nicolaus, a Gentile from Antioch who had earlier been converted to Judaism. ⁶The group presented them to the apostles, who prayed and placed their hands on them.

⁷And so the word of God continued to spread. The number of disciples in Jerusalem grew larger and larger, and a great number of priests accepted the faith.

The Arrest of Stephen

⁸Stephen, a man richly blessed by God and full of power, performed great miracles and wonders among the people. ⁹But he was opposed by some men who were members of the synagogue

ACTS 6, 7

1297

Acts
....

Romans
1 Corin.
2 Corin.
Galat.
Ephes.

of the Freedmen* (as it was called), which included Jews from Cyrene and Alexandria. They and other Jews from the provinces of Cilicia and Asia started arguing with Stephen. ¹⁰But the Spirit gave Stephen such wisdom that when he spoke, they could not refute him. ¹¹So they bribed some men to say, "We heard him speaking against Moses and against God!" ¹²In this way they stirred up the people, the elders, and the teachers of the Law. They seized Stephen and took him before the Council. ¹³Then they brought in some men to tell lies about him. "This man," they said, "is always talking against our sacred Temple and the Law of Moses. ¹⁴We heard him say that this Jesus of Nazareth will tear down the Temple and change all the customs which have come down to us from Moses!" ¹⁵All those sitting in the Council fixed their eyes on Stephen and saw that his face looked like the face of an angel.

Stephen's Speech

7 The High Priest asked Stephen, "Is this true?"
²Stephen answered, "Brothers and fathers, listen to me! Before our ancestor Abraham had gone to live in Haran, the God of glory appeared to him in Mesopotamia ³and said to him, 'Leave your family and country and go to the land that I will show you.' ⁴And so he left his country and went to live in Haran. After Abraham's father died, God made him move to this land where you now live. ⁵God did not then give Abraham any part of it as his own, not even a square metre of ground, but God promised to give it to him, and that it would belong to him and to his descendants. At the time God made this promise, Abraham had no children. ⁶This is what God said to him: 'Your descendants will live in a foreign country, where they will be slaves and will be badly treated for 400 years. ⁷But I will pass judgement on the people that they will serve, and afterwards your descendants will come out of that country and will worship me in this place.' ⁸Then God gave Abraham the ceremony of circumcision as a sign of the covenant. So Abraham circumcised Isaac a week after he was born; Isaac circumcised his son Jacob, and Jacob circumcised his twelve sons, the famous ancestors of our race.

⁹"Jacob's sons became jealous of their brother Joseph and sold him to be a slave in Egypt. But God was with him ¹⁰and brought him safely through all his troubles. When Joseph appeared before the king of Egypt, God gave him a pleasing manner and wisdom, and the king made Joseph governor over the country and the royal household. ¹¹Then there was a famine all over Egypt and Canaan, which caused much suffering. Our ancestors could not find any food, ¹²and when Jacob heard that there was corn in Egypt, he sent his sons, our ancestors, on their first visit there. ¹³On the second visit Joseph made himself known to his brothers, and the king of Egypt came to know about Joseph's family. ¹⁴So Joseph sent a message to his father Jacob, telling him and the whole family, 75 people in all, to come to Egypt. ¹⁵Then Jacob went to Egypt, where he and his sons died. ¹⁶Their bodies were taken to Shechem, where they were buried in the grave which Abraham had bought from the clan of Hamor for a sum of money.

¹⁷"When the time drew near for God to keep the promise he had made to Abraham, the number of our people in Egypt had grown much larger. ¹⁸At last a king who did not know about Joseph began to rule in Egypt. ¹⁹He tricked our ancestors and was cruel to

ACTS 7.1-50

Stephen summarised a

GOOD CHUNK
– OF THE –
BIBLE

– the story of the Israelites – in his speech. In the space,

SUM IT UP IN YOUR OWN WORDS

or pictures. (You may want to look out for the names of people you might recognise, such as Moses and David.)

6.9 *freedmen*: These were Jews who had been slaves, but had bought or been given their freedom.

1298

Acts

·:·········

Malachi
Matt.
Mark
Luke
John

ACTS 7

them, forcing them to put their babies out of their homes, so that they would die. [20] It was at this time that Moses was born, a very beautiful child. He was cared for at home for three months, [21] and when he was put out of his home, the king's daughter adopted him and brought him up as her own son. [22] He was taught all the wisdom of the Egyptians and became a great man in words and deeds.

[23] "When Moses was forty years old, he decided to find out how his fellow-Israelites were being treated. [24] He saw one of them being ill-treated by an Egyptian, so he went to his help and took revenge on the Egyptian by killing him. [25] (He thought that his own people would understand that God was going to use him to set them free, but they did not understand.) [26] The next day he saw two Israelites fighting, and he tried to make peace between them. 'Listen, men,' he said, 'you are fellow-Israelites; why are you fighting like this?' [27] But the one who was ill-treating the other pushed Moses aside. 'Who made you ruler and judge over us?' he asked. [28] 'Do you want to kill me, just as you killed that Egyptian yesterday?' [29] When Moses heard this, he fled from Egypt and went to live in the land of Midian. There he had two sons.

[30] "After forty years had passed, an angel appeared to Moses in the flames of a burning bush in the desert near Mount Sinai. [31] Moses was amazed by what he saw, and went near the bush to get a better look. But he heard the Lord's voice: [32] 'I am the God of your ancestors, the God of Abraham, Isaac, and Jacob.' Moses trembled with fear and dared not look. [33] The Lord said to him, 'Take your sandals off, for the place where you are standing is holy ground. [34] I have seen the cruel suffering of my people in Egypt. I have heard their groans, and I have come down to set them free. Come now; I will send you to Egypt.'

[35] "Moses is the one who was rejected by the people of Israel. 'Who made you ruler and judge over us?' they asked. He is the one whom God sent to rule the people and set them free with the help of the angel who appeared to him in the burning bush. [36] He led the people out of Egypt, performing miracles and wonders in Egypt and at the Red Sea and for forty years in the desert. [37] Moses is the one who said to the people of Israel, 'God will send you a prophet, just as he sent me,* and he will be one of your own people.' [38] He is the one who was with the people of Israel assembled in the desert; he was there with our ancestors and with the angel who spoke to him on Mount Sinai, and he received God's living messages to pass on to us.

[39] "But our ancestors refused to obey him; they pushed him aside and wished that they could go back to Egypt. [40] So they said to Aaron, 'Make us some gods who will lead us. We do not know what has happened to that man Moses, who brought us out of Egypt.' [41] It was then that they made an idol in the shape of a bull, offered sacrifice to it, and had a feast in honour of what they themselves had made. [42] So God turned away from them and gave them over to worship the stars of heaven, as it is written in the book of the prophets:

'People of Israel! It was not to me
    that you slaughtered and sacrificed animals
      for forty years in the desert.
[43] It was the tent of the god Molech that you carried,
    and the image of Rephan, your star god;
      they were idols that you had made to worship.
And so I will send you into exile beyond Babylon.'

7.37 *just as he sent me*; or *like me*.

1299

Acts

....

Romans
1 Corin.
2 Corin.
Galat.
Ephes.

⁴⁴"Our ancestors had the Tent of God's presence with them in the desert. It had been made as God had told Moses to make it, according to the pattern that Moses had been shown. ⁴⁵Later on, our ancestors who received the tent from their fathers carried it with them when they went with Joshua and took over the land from the nations that God drove out as they advanced. And it stayed there until the time of David. ⁴⁶He won God's favour and asked God to allow him to provide a dwelling place for the God of Jacob.* ⁴⁷But it was Solomon who built him a house.

⁴⁸"But the Most High God does not live in houses built by human hands; as the prophet says:

⁴⁹ 'Heaven is my throne, says the Lord,
   and the earth is my footstool.
   What kind of house would you build for me?
   Where is the place for me to live in?
⁵⁰ Did not I myself make all these things?'

⁵¹"How stubborn you are!" Stephen went on to say. "How heathen your hearts, how deaf you are to God's message! You are just like your ancestors: you too have always resisted the Holy Spirit! ⁵²Was there any prophet that your ancestors did not persecute? They killed God's messengers, who long ago announced the coming of his righteous Servant. And now you have betrayed and murdered him. ⁵³You are the ones who received God's law, that was handed down by angels — yet you have not obeyed it!"

The Stoning of Stephen

⁵⁴As the members of the Council listened to Stephen, they became furious and ground their teeth at him in anger. ⁵⁵But Stephen, full of the Holy Spirit, looked up to heaven and saw God's glory and Jesus standing at the right-hand side of God. ⁵⁶"Look!" he said. "I see heaven opened and the Son of Man standing at the right-hand side of God!"

⁵⁷With a loud cry the members of the Council covered their ears with their hands. Then they all rushed at him at once, ⁵⁸threw him out of the city, and stoned him. The witnesses left their cloaks in the care of a young man named Saul. ⁵⁹They kept on stoning Stephen as he called out to the Lord, "Lord Jesus, receive my spirit!" ⁶⁰He knelt down and cried out in a loud voice, "Lord! Do not remember this sin against them!" He said this and died.

8 And Saul approved of his murder.

Saul Persecutes the Church

That very day the church in Jerusalem began to suffer cruel persecution. All the believers, except the apostles, were scattered throughout the provinces of Judea and Samaria. ²Some devout men buried Stephen, mourning for him with loud cries.

³But Saul tried to destroy the church; going from house to house, he dragged out the believers, both men and women, and threw them into jail.

The Gospel is Preached in Samaria

⁴The believers who were scattered went everywhere, preaching the message. ⁵Philip went to the principal city* in Samaria and preached the Messiah to the people there. ⁶The crowds paid close attention to what Philip said, as they listened to him and saw the miracles that he performed. ⁷Evil spirits came out from many

....

7.46 the God of Jacob; some manuscripts have the people of Israel.
8.5 the principal city; some manuscripts have a city.

1300

Acts

-:-·········

Malachi
Matt.
Mark
Luke
John

ACTS 8

ACTS 8.26-40

Philip used the questions
that the Ethiopian was
struggling with as a
starting-point for
explaining the gospel.

Write down something
faith-related that
a friend is finding
difficult, and pray for
wisdom on their behalf.
Could you

HELP THEM IN THEIR
STRUGGLE?

people with a loud cry, and many paralysed and lame people were healed. [8] So there was great joy in that city.

[9] A man named Simon lived there, who for some time had astounded the Samaritans with his magic. He claimed that he was someone great, [10] and everyone in the city, from all classes of society, paid close attention to him. "He is that power of God known as 'The Great Power'," they said. [11] They paid this attention to him because for such a long time he had astonished them with his magic. [12] But when they believed Philip's message about the good news of the Kingdom of God and about Jesus Christ, they were baptized, both men and women. [13] Simon himself also believed; and after being baptized, he stayed close to Philip and was astounded when he saw the great wonders and miracles that were being performed.

[14] The apostles in Jerusalem heard that the people of Samaria had received the word of God, so they sent Peter and John to them. [15] When they arrived, they prayed for the believers that they might receive the Holy Spirit. [16] For the Holy Spirit had not yet come down on any of them; they had only been baptized in the name of the Lord Jesus. [17] Then Peter and John placed their hands on them, and they received the Holy Spirit.

[18] Simon saw that the Spirit had been given to the believers when the apostles placed their hands on them. So he offered money to Peter and John, [19] and said, "Give this power to me too, so that anyone I place my hands on will receive the Holy Spirit."

[20] But Peter answered him, "May you and your money go to hell, for thinking that you can buy God's gift with money! [21] You have no part or share in our work, because your heart is not right in God's sight. [22] Repent, then, of this evil plan of yours, and pray to the Lord that he will forgive you for thinking such a thing as this. [23] For I see that you are full of bitter envy and are a prisoner of sin."

[24] Simon said to Peter and John, "Please pray to the Lord for me, so that none of these things you spoke of will happen to me."

[25] After they had given their testimony and proclaimed the Lord's message, Peter and John went back to Jerusalem. On their way they preached the Good News in many villages of Samaria.

Philip and the Ethiopian Official
[26] An angel of the Lord said to Philip, "Get ready and go south* to the road that goes from Jerusalem to Gaza." (This road is not used nowadays.)* [27-28] So Philip got ready and went. Now an Ethiopian eunuch, who was an important official in charge of the treasury of the queen of Ethiopia, was on his way home. He had been to Jerusalem to worship God and was going back home in his carriage. As he rode along, he was reading from the book of the prophet Isaiah. [29] The Holy Spirit said to Philip, "Go over to that carriage and stay close to it." [30] Philip ran over and heard him reading from the book of the prophet Isaiah. He asked him, "Do you understand what you are reading?"

[31] The official replied, "How can I understand unless someone explains it to me?" And he invited Philip to climb up and sit in the carriage with him. [32] The passage of scripture which he was reading was this:

"Like a sheep that is taken to be slaughtered,
like a lamb that makes no sound when its wool is cut off,
he did not say a word.

8.26 *south*; or *at midday*.
8.26 *This road is not used nowadays*; or *This is the desert road*.

ACTS 8, 9

1301

Acts

· · · · · · · · · ·⇢

Romans

1 Corin.

2 Corin.

Galat.

Ephes.

³³ He was humiliated, and justice was denied him.
No one will be able to tell about his descendants,
because his life on earth has come to an end."

³⁴ The official asked Philip, "Tell me, of whom is the prophet saying this? Of himself or of someone else?" ³⁵ Then Philip began to speak; starting from this passage of scripture, he told him the Good News about Jesus. ³⁶ As they travelled down the road, they came to a place where there was some water, and the official said, "Here is some water. What is to keep me from being baptized?"*

³⁸ The official ordered the carriage to stop, and both Philip and the official went down into the water, and Philip baptized him. ³⁹ When they came up out of the water, the Spirit of the Lord took Philip away. The official did not see him again, but continued on his way, full of joy. ⁴⁰ Philip found himself in Azotus; he went on to Caesarea, and on the way he preached the Good News in every town.

The Conversion of Saul
(Acts 22.6–16; 26.12–18)

9 In the meantime Saul kept up his violent threats of murder against the followers of the Lord. He went to the High Priest ² and asked for letters of introduction to the synagogues in Damascus, so that if he should find there any followers of the Way of the Lord, he would be able to arrest them, both men and women, and bring them back to Jerusalem.

³ As Saul was coming near the city of Damascus, suddenly a light from the sky flashed round him. ⁴ He fell to the ground and heard a voice saying to him, "Saul, Saul! Why do you persecute me?"

⁵ "Who are you, Lord?" he asked.

"I am Jesus, whom you persecute," the voice said. ⁶ "But get up and go into the city, where you will be told what you must do."

⁷ The men who were travelling with Saul had stopped, not saying a word; they heard the voice but could not see anyone. ⁸ Saul got up from the ground and opened his eyes, but could not see a thing. So they took him by the hand and led him into Damascus. ⁹ For three days he was not able to see, and during that time he did not eat or drink anything.

¹⁰ There was a believer in Damascus named Ananias. He had a vision, in which the Lord said to him, "Ananias!"

"Here I am, Lord," he answered.

¹¹ The Lord said to him, "Get ready and go to Straight Street, and at the house of Judas ask for a man from Tarsus named Saul. He is praying, ¹² and in a vision he has seen a man named Ananias come in and place his hands on him so that he might see again."

¹³ Ananias answered, "Lord, many people have told me about this man and about all the terrible things he has done to your people in Jerusalem. ¹⁴ And he has come to Damascus with authority from the chief priests to arrest all who worship you."

¹⁵ The Lord said to him, "Go, because I have chosen him to serve me, to make my name known to Gentiles and kings and to the people of Israel. ¹⁶ And I myself will show him all that he must suffer for my sake."

¹⁷ So Ananias went, entered the house where Saul was, and placed his hands on him. "Brother Saul," he said, "the Lord has sent me — Jesus himself, who appeared to you on the road as you

---

8.36 Some manuscripts add verse 37: *Philip said to him, "You may be baptized if you believe with all your heart." "I do," he answered; "I believe that Jesus Christ is the Son of God."*

1302

Acts

········

Malachi
Matt.
Mark
Luke
John

ACTS 9

were coming here. He sent me so that you might see again and be filled with the Holy Spirit." [18] At once something like fish scales fell from Saul's eyes, and he was able to see again. He stood up and was baptized; [19] and after he had eaten, his strength came back.

Saul Preaches in Damascus

Saul stayed for a few days with the believers in Damascus. [20] He went straight to the synagogues and began to preach that Jesus was the Son of God.

[21] All who heard him were amazed and asked, "Isn't he the one who in Jerusalem was killing those who worship that man Jesus? And didn't he come here for the very purpose of arresting those people and taking them back to the chief priests?"

[22] But Saul's preaching became even more powerful, and his proofs that Jesus was the Messiah were so convincing that the Jews who lived in Damascus could not answer him.

[23] After many days had gone by, the Jews met together and made plans to kill Saul, [24] but he was told of their plan. Day and night they watched the city gates in order to kill him. [25] But one night Saul's followers took him and let him down through an opening in the wall, lowering him in a basket.

Saul in Jerusalem

[26] Saul went to Jerusalem and tried to join the disciples. But they would not believe that he was a disciple, and they were all afraid of him. [27] Then Barnabas came to his help and took him to the apostles. He explained to them how Saul had seen the Lord on the road and that the Lord had spoken to him. He also told them how boldly Saul had preached in the name of Jesus in Damascus. [28] And so Saul stayed with them and went all over Jerusalem, preaching boldly in the name of the Lord. [29] He also talked and disputed with the Greek-speaking Jews, but they tried to kill him. [30] When the believers found out about this, they took Saul to Caesarea and sent him away to Tarsus.

[31] And so it was that the church throughout Judea, Galilee, and Samaria had a time of peace. Through the help of the Holy Spirit it was strengthened and grew in numbers, as it lived in reverence for the Lord.

Peter in Lydda and Joppa

[32] Peter travelled everywhere, and on one occasion he went to visit God's people who lived in Lydda. [33] There he met a man named Aeneas, who was paralysed and had not been able to get out of bed for eight years. [34] "Aeneas," Peter said to him, "Jesus Christ makes you well. Get up and make your bed." At once Aeneas got up. [35] All the people living in Lydda and Sharon saw him, and they turned to the Lord.

[36] In Joppa there was a woman named Tabitha, who was a believer. (Her name in Greek is Dorcas, meaning "a deer".) She spent all her time doing good and helping the poor. [37] At that time she became ill and died. Her body was washed and laid in a room upstairs. [38] Joppa was not very far from Lydda, and when the believers in Joppa heard that Peter was in Lydda, they sent two men to him with the message, "Please hurry and come to us." [39] So Peter got ready and went with them. When he arrived, he was taken to the room upstairs, where all the widows crowded round him, crying and showing him all the shirts and coats that Dorcas had made while she was alive. [40] Peter put them all out of the room, and knelt down and prayed; then he turned to the

ACTS 9, 10

1303

Acts

....

Romans
1 Corin.
2 Corin.
Galat.
Ephes.

body and said, "Tabitha, get up!" She opened her eyes, and when she saw Peter, she sat up. 41 Peter reached over and helped her get up. Then he called all the believers, including the widows, and presented her alive to them. 42 The news about this spread all over Joppa, and many people believed in the Lord. 43 Peter stayed on in Joppa for many days with a tanner of leather named Simon.

Peter and Cornelius

10 There was a man in Caesarea named Cornelius, who was a captain in the Roman regiment called "The Italian Regiment". 2 He was a religious man; he and his whole family worshipped God. He also did much to help the Jewish poor people and was constantly praying to God. 3 It was about three o'clock one afternoon when he had a vision, in which he clearly saw an angel of God come in and say to him, "Cornelius!"

4 He stared at the angel in fear and said, "What is it, sir?"

The angel answered, "God is pleased with your prayers and works of charity, and is ready to answer you. 5 And now send some men to Joppa for a certain man whose full name is Simon Peter. 6 He is a guest in the home of a tanner of leather named Simon, who lives by the sea." 7 Then the angel went away, and Cornelius called two of his house servants and a soldier, a religious man who was one of his personal attendants. 8 He told them what had happened and sent them off to Joppa.

9 The next day, as they were on their way and coming near Joppa, Peter went up on the roof of the house about noon in order to pray. 10 He became hungry and wanted something to eat; while the food was being prepared, he had a vision. 11 He saw heaven opened and something coming down that looked like a large sheet being lowered by its four corners to the earth. 12 In it were all kinds of animals, reptiles, and wild birds. 13 A voice said to him, "Get up, Peter; kill and eat!"

14 But Peter said, "Certainly not, Lord! I have never eaten anything ritually unclean or defiled."

15 The voice spoke to him again, "Do not consider anything unclean that God has declared clean." 16 This happened three times, and then the thing was taken back up into heaven.

17 While Peter was wondering about the meaning of this vision, the men sent by Cornelius had learnt where Simon's house was, and they were now standing in front of the gate. 18 They called out and asked, "Is there a guest here by the name of Simon Peter?"

19 Peter was still trying to understand what the vision meant, when the Spirit said, "Listen! Three* men are here looking for you. 20 So get ready and go down, and do not hesitate to go with them, for I have sent them." 21 So Peter went down and said to the men, "I am the man you are looking for. Why have you come?"

22 "Captain Cornelius sent us," they answered. "He is a good man who worships God and is highly respected by all the Jewish people. An angel of God told him to invite you to his house, so that he could hear what you have to say." 23 Peter invited the men in and persuaded them to spend the night there.

The next day he got ready and went with them, and some of the believers from Joppa went along with him. 24 The following day he arrived in Caesarea, where Cornelius was waiting for him, together with relatives and close friends that he had invited. 25 As Peter was about to go in, Cornelius met him, fell at his feet, and bowed down before him. 26 But Peter made him rise. "Stand up," he said;

10.19 *Three*; some manuscripts have *Some*; one manuscript has *Two*.

- God can -
& WILL
USE YOU IF YOU
ALLOW
- him to! -

1304

Acts

·:········

Malachi
Matt.
Mark
Luke
John

ACTS 10, 11

"I myself am only a man." ²⁷Peter kept on talking to Cornelius as he went into the house, where he found many people gathered. ²⁸He said to them, "You yourselves know very well that a Jew is not allowed by his religion to visit or associate with Gentiles. But God has shown me that I must not consider any person ritually unclean or defiled. ²⁹And so when you sent for me, I came without any objection. I ask you, then, why did you send for me?"

³⁰Cornelius said, "It was about this time three days ago that I was praying* in my house at three o'clock in the afternoon. Suddenly a man dressed in shining clothes stood in front of me ³¹and said: 'Cornelius! God has heard your prayer and has taken notice of your works of charity. ³²Send someone to Joppa for a man whose full name is Simon Peter. He is a guest in the home of Simon the tanner of leather, who lives by the sea.' ³³And so I sent for you at once, and you have been good enough to come. Now we are all here in the presence of God, waiting to hear anything that the Lord has instructed you to say."

Peter's Speech

³⁴Peter began to speak: "I now realize that it is true that God treats everyone on the same basis. ³⁵Those who worship him and do what is right are acceptable to him, no matter what race they belong to. ³⁶You know the message he sent to the people of Israel, proclaiming the Good News of peace through Jesus Christ, who is Lord of all. ³⁷You know of the great event that took place throughout the land of Israel, beginning in Galilee after John preached his message of baptism. ³⁸You know about Jesus of Nazareth and how God poured out on him the Holy Spirit and power. He went everywhere, doing good and healing all who were under the power of the Devil, for God was with him. ³⁹We are witnesses of everything that he did in the land of Israel and in Jerusalem. Then they put him to death by nailing him to a cross. ⁴⁰But God raised him from death three days later and caused him to appear, ⁴¹not to everyone, but only to the witnesses that God had already chosen, that is, to us who ate and drank with him after he rose from death. ⁴²And he commanded us to preach the gospel to the people and to testify that he is the one whom God has appointed judge of the living and the dead. ⁴³All the prophets spoke about him, saying that all who believe in him will have their sins forgiven through the power of his name."

The Gentiles Receive the Holy Spirit

⁴⁴While Peter was still speaking, the Holy Spirit came down on all those who were listening to his message. ⁴⁵The Jewish believers who had come from Joppa with Peter were amazed that God had poured out his gift of the Holy Spirit on the Gentiles also. ⁴⁶For they heard them speaking in strange tongues and praising God's greatness. Peter spoke up: ⁴⁷"These people have received the Holy Spirit, just as we also did. Can anyone, then, stop them from being baptized with water?" ⁴⁸So he ordered them to be baptized in the name of Jesus Christ. Then they asked him to stay with them for a few days.

Peter's Report to the Church at Jerusalem

11 The apostles and the other believers throughout Judea heard that the Gentiles also had received the word of God. ²When Peter went to Jerusalem, those who were in favour

10.30 *praying*; some manuscripts have *fasting and praying*.

Acts
..........⋮
Romans
1 Corin.
2 Corin.
Galat.
Ephes.

of circumcising Gentiles criticized him, saying, ³"You were a guest in the home of uncircumcised Gentiles, and you even ate with them!" ⁴So Peter gave them a complete account of what had happened from the very beginning:

⁵"While I was praying in the city of Joppa, I had a vision. I saw something coming down that looked like a large sheet being lowered by its four corners from heaven, and it stopped next to me. ⁶I looked closely inside and saw domesticated and wild animals, reptiles, and wild birds. ⁷Then I heard a voice saying to me, 'Get up, Peter; kill and eat!' ⁸But I said, 'Certainly not, Lord! No ritually unclean or defiled food has ever entered my mouth.' ⁹The voice spoke again from heaven, 'Do not consider anything unclean that God has declared clean.' ¹⁰This happened three times, and finally the whole thing was drawn back up into heaven. ¹¹At that very moment three men who had been sent to me from Caesarea arrived at the house where I was* staying. ¹²The Spirit told me to go with them without hesitation. These six fellow-believers from Joppa accompanied me to Caesarea, and we all went into the house of Cornelius. ¹³He told us how he had seen an angel standing in his house, who said to him, 'Send someone to Joppa for a man whose full name is Simon Peter. ¹⁴He will speak words to you by which you and all your family will be saved.' ¹⁵And when I began to speak, the Holy Spirit came down on them just as on us at the beginning. ¹⁶Then I remembered what the Lord had said: 'John baptized with water, but you will be baptized with the Holy Spirit.' ¹⁷It is clear that God gave those Gentiles the same gift that he gave us when we believed in the Lord Jesus Christ; who was I, then, to try to stop God!"

¹⁸When they heard this, they stopped their criticism and praised God, saying, "Then God has given to the Gentiles also the opportunity to repent and live!"

The Church at Antioch

¹⁹Some of the believers who were scattered by the persecution which took place when Stephen was killed went as far as Phoenicia, Cyprus, and Antioch, telling the message to Jews only. ²⁰But other believers, who were from Cyprus and Cyrene, went to Antioch and proclaimed the message to Gentiles* also, telling them the Good News about the Lord Jesus. ²¹The Lord's power was with them, and a great number of people believed and turned to the Lord.

²²The news about this reached the church in Jerusalem, so they sent Barnabas to Antioch. ²³When he arrived and saw how God had blessed the people, he was glad and urged them all to be faithful and true to the Lord with all their hearts. ²⁴Barnabas was a good man, full of the Holy Spirit and faith, and many people were brought to the Lord.

²⁵Then Barnabas went to Tarsus to look for Saul. ²⁶When he found him, he took him to Antioch, and for a whole year the two met with the people of the church and taught a large group. It was at Antioch that the believers were first called Christians.

²⁷About that time some prophets went from Jerusalem to Antioch. ²⁸One of them, named Agabus, stood up and by the power of the Spirit predicted that a severe famine was about to come over all the earth. (It came when Claudius was emperor.) ²⁹The disciples decided that they would each send as much

11.11 *I was*; some manuscripts have *we were*.
11.20 *Gentiles*; some manuscripts have *Greek-speaking Jews* or *Greek-speaking people*.

1306

Acts

:·········

Malachi
Matt.
Mark
Luke
John

ACTS 11, 12

as they could to help their fellow-believers who lived in Judea.
³⁰ They did this, then, and sent the money to the church elders
by Barnabas and Saul.

More Persecution

12 About this time King Herod* began to persecute some
members of the church. ²He had James, the brother of
John, put to death by the sword. ³When he saw that this pleased
the Jews, he went on to arrest Peter. (This happened during the
time of the Festival of Unleavened Bread.) ⁴After his arrest Peter
was put in jail, where he was handed over to be guarded by four
groups of four soldiers each. Herod planned to put him on trial
in public after Passover. ⁵So Peter was kept in jail, but the people
of the church were praying earnestly to God for him.

Peter is Set Free from Prison

⁶The night before Herod was going to bring him out to the
people, Peter was sleeping between two guards. He was tied with
two chains, and there were guards on duty at the prison gate.
⁷Suddenly an angel of the Lord stood there, and a light shone in
the cell. The angel shook Peter by the shoulder, woke him up, and
said, "Hurry! Get up!" At once the chains fell off Peter's hands.
⁸Then the angel said, "Fasten your belt and put on your sandals."
Peter did so, and the angel said, "Put your cloak round you and
come with me." ⁹Peter followed him out of the prison, not knowing,
however, if what the angel was doing was real; he thought he
was seeing a vision. ¹⁰They passed by the first guard post and
then the second, and came at last to the iron gate leading into
the city. The gate opened for them by itself, and they went out.
They walked down a street, and suddenly the angel left Peter.
¹¹Then Peter realized what had happened to him, and said,
"Now I know that it is really true! The Lord sent his angel to rescue
me from Herod's power and from everything the Jewish people
expected to happen."

¹²Aware of his situation, he went to the home of Mary, the
mother of John Mark, where many people had gathered and
were praying. ¹³Peter knocked at the outside door, and a servant
named Rhoda came to answer it. ¹⁴She recognized Peter's voice
and was so happy that she ran back in without opening the
door, and announced that Peter was standing outside. ¹⁵"You
are mad!" they told her. But she insisted that it was true. So they
answered, "It is his angel."

¹⁶Meanwhile Peter kept on knocking. At last they opened the
door, and when they saw him, they were amazed. ¹⁷He motioned
with his hand for them to be quiet, and he explained to them
how the Lord had brought him out of prison. "Tell this to James
and the rest of the believers," he said; then he left and went
somewhere else.

¹⁸When morning came, there was a tremendous confusion
among the guards — what had happened to Peter? ¹⁹Herod
gave orders to search for him, but they could not find him. So he
had the guards questioned and ordered them to be put to death.
After this, Herod left Judea and spent some time in Caesarea.

The Death of Herod

²⁰Herod was very angry with the people of Tyre and Sidon, so
they went in a group to see him. First they convinced Blastus, the

12.1 *King Herod*: Herod Agrippa I, ruler of all Palestine.

ACTS 12, 13

1307

Acts

....

Romans
1 Corin.
2 Corin.
Galat.
Ephes.

man in charge of the palace, that he should help them. Then they went to Herod and asked him for peace, because their country got its food supplies from the king's country.

²¹ On a chosen day Herod put on his royal robes, sat on his throne, and made a speech to the people. ²² "It isn't a man speaking, but a god!" they shouted. ²³ At once the angel of the Lord struck Herod down, because he did not give honour to God. He was eaten by worms and died.

²⁴ Meanwhile the word of God continued to spread and grow.

²⁵ Barnabas and Saul finished their mission and returned from* Jerusalem, taking John Mark with them.

Barnabas and Saul are Chosen and Sent

13 In the church at Antioch there were some prophets and teachers: Barnabas, Simeon (called the Black), Lucius (from Cyrene), Manaen (who had been brought up with Herod* the governor), and Saul. ² While they were serving the Lord and fasting, the Holy Spirit said to them, "Set apart for me Barnabas and Saul, to do the work to which I have called them."

³ They fasted and prayed, placed their hands on them, and sent them off.

In Cyprus

⁴ Having been sent by the Holy Spirit, Barnabas and Saul went to Seleucia and sailed from there to the island of Cyprus. ⁵ When they arrived at Salamis, they preached the word of God in the synagogues. They had John Mark with them to help in the work.

⁶ They went all the way across the island to Paphos, where they met a certain magician named Bar-Jesus, a Jew who claimed to be a prophet. ⁷ He was a friend of the governor of the island, Sergius Paulus, who was an intelligent man. The governor called Barnabas and Saul before him because he wanted to hear the word of God. ⁸ But they were opposed by the magician Elymas (that is his name in Greek), who tried to turn the governor away from the faith. ⁹ Then Saul — also known as Paul — was filled with the Holy Spirit; he looked straight at the magician ¹⁰ and said, "You son of the Devil! You are the enemy of everything that is good. You are full of all kinds of evil tricks, and you always keep trying to turn the Lord's truths into lies! ¹¹ The Lord's hand will come down on you now; you will be blind and will not see the light of day for a time."

At once Elymas felt a dark mist cover his eyes, and he walked about trying to find someone to lead him by the hand. ¹² When the governor saw what had happened, he believed; for he was greatly amazed at the teaching about the Lord.

In Antioch in Pisidia

¹³ Paul and his companions sailed from Paphos and came to Perga, a city in Pamphylia, where John Mark left them and went back to Jerusalem. ¹⁴ They went on from Perga and arrived in Antioch in Pisidia, and on the Sabbath they went into the synagogue and sat down. ¹⁵ After the reading from the Law of Moses and from the writings of the prophets, the officials of the synagogue sent them a message: "Brothers and sisters, we want you to speak to the people if you have a message of encouragement for them." ¹⁶ Paul stood up, motioned with his hand, and began to speak:

....

12.25 *from*; some manuscripts have *to*.
13.1 *herod*: Herod Antipas, ruler of Galilee (see Lk 3.1).

1308

Acts

⁙·········

Malachi

Matt.

Mark

Luke

John

"Fellow-Israelites and all Gentiles here who worship God: hear me! [17] The God of the people of Israel chose our ancestors and made the people a great nation during the time they lived as foreigners in Egypt. God brought them out of Egypt by his great power, [18] and for forty years he endured* them in the desert. [19] He destroyed seven nations in the land of Canaan and made his people the owners of the land. [20] All this took about 450 years.

"After this* he gave them judges until the time of the prophet Samuel. [21] And when they asked for a king, God gave them Saul son of Kish from the tribe of Benjamin, to be their king for forty years. [22] After removing him, God made David their king. This is what God said about him: 'I have found that David son of Jesse is the kind of man I like, a man who will do all I want him to do.' [23] It was Jesus, a descendant of David, whom God made the Saviour of the people of Israel, as he had promised. [24] Before Jesus began his work, John preached to all the people of Israel that they should turn from their sins and be baptized. [25] And as John was about to finish his mission, he said to the people, 'Who do you think I am? I am not the one you are waiting for. But listen! He is coming after me, and I am not good enough to take his sandals off his feet.'

[26] "My fellow-Israelites, descendants of Abraham, and all Gentiles here who worship God: it is to us that this message of salvation has been sent! [27] For the people who live in Jerusalem and their leaders did not know that he is the Saviour, nor did they understand the words of the prophets that are read every Sabbath. Yet they made the prophets' words come true by condemning Jesus. [28] And even though they could find no reason to pass the death sentence on him, they asked Pilate to have him put to death. [29] And after they had done everything that the Scriptures say about him, they took him down from the cross and placed him in a tomb. [30] But God raised him from death, [31] and for many days he appeared to those who had travelled with him from Galilee to Jerusalem. They are now witnesses for him to the people of Israel. [32-33] And we are here to bring the Good News to you: what God promised our ancestors he would do, he has now done for us, who are their descendants, by raising Jesus to life. As it is written in the second Psalm:

'You are my Son;
    today I have become your Father.'
[34] And this is what God said about raising him from death, never to rot away in the grave:

'I will give you the sacred and sure blessings
    that I promised to David.'
[35] As indeed he says in another passage:

'You will not allow your faithful servant to rot in the
    grave.'
[36] For David served God's purposes in his own time, and then he died, was buried with his ancestors, and his body rotted in the grave. [37] But this did not happen to the one whom God raised from death. [38-39] We want you to know, my fellow-Israelites, that it is through Jesus that the message about forgiveness of sins is preached to you; and that everyone who believes in him is set free from all the sins from which the Law of Moses could not set you free. [40] Take care, then, so that what the prophets said may not happen to you:*

ACTS 13.39

EVERYONE
··· who ···
BELIEVES
in him is set
FREE

13.18 he endured; some manuscripts have he took care of.
13.20 All this took about 450 years. "After this; or Some 450 years later.
13.40 Some manuscripts do not have to you.

ACTS 13, 14

1309

Acts

............:

Romans
1 Corin.
2 Corin.
Galat.
Ephes.

[41] 'Look, you scoffers! Be astonished and die!
For what I am doing today
is something that you will not believe,
even when someone explains it to you!' "

[42] As Paul and Barnabas were leaving the synagogue, the people invited them to come back the next Sabbath and tell them more about these things. [43] After the people had left the meeting, Paul and Barnabas were followed by many Jews and by many Gentiles who had been converted to Judaism. The apostles spoke to them and encouraged them to keep on living in the grace of God.

[44] The next Sabbath nearly everyone in the town came to hear the word of the Lord. [45] When the Jews saw the crowds, they were filled with jealousy; they disputed what Paul was saying and insulted him. [46] But Paul and Barnabas spoke out even more boldly: "It was necessary that the word of God should be spoken first to you. But since you reject it and do not consider yourselves worthy of eternal life, we will leave you and go to the Gentiles. [47] For this is the commandment that the Lord has given us:

'I have made you a light for the Gentiles,
so that all the world may be saved.' "

[48] When the Gentiles heard this, they were glad and praised the Lord's message; and those who had been chosen for eternal life became believers.

[49] The word of the Lord spread everywhere in that region. [50] But the Jews stirred up the leading men of the city and the Gentile women of high social standing who worshipped God. They started a persecution against Paul and Barnabas and threw them out of their region. [51] The apostles shook the dust off their feet in protest against them and went on to Iconium. [52] The believers in Antioch were full of joy and the Holy Spirit.

In Iconium

14 The same thing happened in Iconium: Paul and Barnabas went to the synagogue and spoke in such a way that a great number of Jews and Gentiles became believers. [2] But the Jews who would not believe stirred up the Gentiles and turned them against the believers. [3] The apostles stayed there for a long time, speaking boldly about the Lord, who proved that their message about his grace was true by giving them the power to perform miracles and wonders. [4] The people of the city were divided: some were for the Jews, others for the apostles.

[5] Then some Gentiles and Jews, together with their leaders, decided to ill-treat the apostles and stone them. [6] When the apostles learnt about it, they fled to the cities of Lystra and Derbe in Lycaonia and to the surrounding territory. [7] There they preached the Good News.

In Lystra and Derbe

[8] In Lystra there was a man who had been lame from birth and had never been able to walk. [9] He sat there and listened to Paul's words. Paul saw that he believed and could be healed, so he looked straight at him [10] and said in a loud voice, "Stand up straight on your feet!" The man jumped up and started walking around. [11] When the crowds saw what Paul had done, they started shouting in their own Lycaonian language, "The gods have become like men and have come down to us!" [12] They gave Barnabas the name Zeus, and Paul the name Hermes, because he was the chief speaker. [13] The priest of the god Zeus, whose temple stood just outside the town, brought bulls and flowers

WHAT DOES 'GRACE' MEAN?
Finish the mindmap below.

Approval or kindness,
especially (in the
Christian religion)
that is freely
given by God
to all humans.
(dictionary.cambridge.org)

↑

GRACE

ACTS 14.3; ROMANS 5.2;
JUDE v.4

1310

Acts

·:·········

Malachi
Matt.
Mark
Luke
John

to the gate, for he and the crowds wanted to offer sacrifice to the apostles.

14 When Barnabas and Paul heard what they were about to do, they tore their clothes and ran into the middle of the crowd, shouting, 15 "Why are you doing this? We ourselves are only human beings like you! We are here to announce the Good News, to turn you away from these worthless things to the living God, who made heaven, earth, sea, and all that is in them. 16 In the past he allowed all people to go their own way. 17 But he has always given evidence of his existence by the good things he does: he gives you rain from heaven and crops at the right times; he gives you food and fills your hearts with happiness." 18 Even with these words the apostles could hardly keep the crowd from offering a sacrifice to them.

19 Some Jews came from Antioch in Pisidia and from Iconium; they won the crowd over to their side, stoned Paul and dragged him out of the town, thinking that he was dead. 20 But when the believers gathered round him, he got up and went back into the town. The next day he and Barnabas went to Derbe.

The Return to Antioch in Syria

21 Paul and Barnabas preached the Good News in Derbe and won many disciples. Then they went back to Lystra, to Iconium, and on to Antioch in Pisidia. 22 They strengthened the believers and encouraged them to remain true to the faith. "We must pass through many troubles to enter the Kingdom of God," they taught. 23 In each church they appointed elders, and with prayers and fasting they commended them to the Lord, in whom they had put their trust.

24 After going through the territory of Pisidia, they came to Pamphylia. 25 There they preached the message in Perga and then went to Attalia, 26 and from there they sailed back to Antioch, the place where they had been commended to the care of God's grace for the work they had now completed.

27 When they arrived in Antioch, they gathered the people of the church together and told them about all that God had done with them and how he had opened the way for the Gentiles to believe. 28 And they stayed a long time there with the believers.

The Meeting at Jerusalem

15 Some men came from Judea to Antioch and started teaching the believers, "You cannot be saved unless you are circumcised as the Law of Moses requires." 2 Paul and Barnabas got into a fierce argument with them about this, so it was decided that Paul and Barnabas and some of the others in Antioch should go to Jerusalem and see the apostles and elders about this matter.

3 They were sent on their way by the church; and as they went through Phoenicia and Samaria, they reported how the Gentiles had turned to God; this news brought great joy to all the believers. 4 When they arrived in Jerusalem, they were welcomed by the church, the apostles, and the elders, to whom they told all that God had done through them. 5 But some of the believers who belonged to the party of the Pharisees stood up and said, "The Gentiles must be circumcised and told to obey the Law of Moses."

6 The apostles and the elders met together to consider this question. 7 After a long debate Peter stood up and said, "My brothers and sisters, you know that a long time ago God chose me from among you to preach the Good News to the Gentiles, so that they could hear and believe. 8 And God, who knows the

APOSTLE

LUKE 6.13;
ACTS 15.6

DEFINITION: An important early Christian teacher or pioneering missionary (oxforddictionaries.com)

The group of early Christians who travelled to different places telling people about Jesus Christ. (dictionary.cambridge.org)

ACTS 15   1311

Acts
....
Romans
1 Corin.
2 Corin.
Galat.
Ephes.

thoughts of everyone, showed his approval of the Gentiles by giving the Holy Spirit to them, just as he had to us. [9]He made no difference between us and them; he forgave their sins because they believed. [10]So then, why do you now want to put God to the test by laying a load on the backs of the believers which neither our ancestors nor we ourselves were able to carry? [11]No! We believe and are saved by the grace of the Lord Jesus, just as they are."

[12]The whole group was silent as they heard Barnabas and Paul report all the miracles and wonders that God had performed through them among the Gentiles. [13]When they had finished speaking, James spoke up: "Listen to me, my brothers and sisters! [14]Simon has just explained how God first showed his care for the Gentiles by taking from among them a people to belong to him. [15]The words of the prophets agree completely with this. As the scripture says:

[16] 'After this I will return, says the Lord,
    and restore the kingdom of David.
  I will rebuild its ruins
    and make it strong again.
[17] And so all the rest of the human race will come to me,
    all the Gentiles whom I have called to be my own.
[18] So says the Lord, who made this known long ago.'

[19]"It is my opinion," James went on, "that we should not trouble the Gentiles who are turning to God. [20]Instead, we should write a letter telling them not to eat any food that is ritually unclean because it has been offered to idols; to keep themselves from sexual immorality; and not to eat any animal that has been strangled, or any blood. [21]For the Law of Moses has been read for a very long time in the synagogues every Sabbath, and his words are preached in every town."

The Letter to the Gentile Believers

[22]Then the apostles and the elders, together with the whole church, decided to choose some men from the group and send them to Antioch with Paul and Barnabas. They chose two men who were highly respected by the believers, Judas, called Barsabbas, and Silas, [23]and they sent the following letter by them:

"We, the apostles and the elders, your brothers, send greetings to all our brothers of Gentile birth who live in Antioch, Syria, and Cilicia. [24]We have heard that some who went from our group have troubled and upset you by what they said; they had not, however, received any instruction from us. [25]And so we have met together and have all agreed to choose some messengers and send them to you. They will go with our dear friends Barnabas and Paul, [26]who have risked their lives in the service of our Lord Jesus Christ. [27]We send you, then, Judas and Silas, who will tell you in person the same things we are writing. [28]The Holy Spirit and we have agreed not to put any other burden on you besides these necessary rules: [29]eat no food that has been offered to idols; eat no blood; eat no animal that has been strangled; and keep yourselves from sexual immorality. You will do well if you take care not to do these things. With our best wishes."

[30]The messengers were sent off and went to Antioch, where they gathered the whole group of believers and gave them the letter. [31]When the people read it, they were filled with joy by the message of encouragement. [32]Judas and Silas, who were themselves prophets, spoke a long time with them, giving them courage and strength. [33]After spending some time there, they

1312

Acts

·:········

Malachi

Matt.

Mark

Luke

John

ACTS 15, 16

were sent off in peace by the believers and went back to those who had sent them.*

[35] Paul and Barnabas spent some time in Antioch, and together with many others they taught and preached the word of the Lord.

Paul and Barnabas Separate

[36] Some time later Paul said to Barnabas, "Let us go back and visit our brothers and sisters in every town where we preached the word of the Lord, and let us find out how they are getting on." [37] Barnabas wanted to take John Mark with them, [38] but Paul did not think it was right to take him, because he had not stayed with them to the end of their mission, but had turned back and left them in Pamphylia. [39] There was a sharp argument, and they separated: Barnabas took Mark and sailed off for Cyprus, [40] while Paul chose Silas and left, commended by the believers to the care of the Lord's grace. [41] He went through Syria and Cilicia, strengthening the churches.

Timothy Goes with Paul and Silas

16 Paul travelled on to Derbe and Lystra, where a Christian named Timothy lived. His mother, who was also a Christian, was Jewish, but his father was a Greek. [2] All the believers in Lystra and Iconium spoke well of Timothy. [3] Paul wanted to take Timothy along with him, so he circumcised him. He did so because all the Jews who lived in those places knew that Timothy's father was Greek. [4] As they went through the towns, they delivered to the believers the rules decided upon by the apostles and elders in Jerusalem, and told them to obey those rules. [5] So the churches were made stronger in the faith and grew in numbers every day.

In Troas: Paul's Vision

[6] They travelled through the region of Phrygia and Galatia because the Holy Spirit did not let them preach the message in the province of Asia. [7] When they reached the border of Mysia, they tried to go into the province of Bithynia, but the Spirit of Jesus did not allow them. [8] So they travelled right on through* Mysia and went to Troas. [9] That night Paul had a vision in which he saw a Macedonian standing and begging him, "Come over to Macedonia and help us!" [10] As soon as Paul had this vision, we got ready to leave for Macedonia, because we decided that God had called us to preach the Good News to the people there.

In Philippi: the Conversion of Lydia

[11] We left by ship from Troas and sailed straight across to Samothrace, and the next day to Neapolis. [12] From there we went inland to Philippi, a city of the first district of Macedonia;* it is also a Roman colony. We spent several days there. [13] On the Sabbath we went out of the city to the riverside, where we thought there would be a place where Jews gathered for prayer. We sat down and talked to the women who gathered there. [14] One of those who heard us was Lydia from Thyatira, who was a dealer in purple cloth. She was a woman who worshipped God, and the Lord opened her mind to pay attention to what Paul was saying.

··

15.33 Some manuscripts add verse 34: *But Silas decided to stay there.*
16.8 *travelled right on through*; or *passed by.*
16.12 *a city of the first district of Macedonia*; some manuscripts have *a leading city of the district of Macedonia*; or *a leading city of that district in Macedonia.*

Acts

....

Romans
1 Corin.
2 Corin.
Galat.
Ephes.

¹⁵ After she and the people of her house had been baptized, she invited us, "Come and stay in my house if you have decided that I am a true believer in the Lord." And she persuaded us to go.

In Prison at Philippi

¹⁶ One day as we were going to the place of prayer, we were met by a young servant woman who had an evil spirit that enabled her to predict the future. She earned a lot of money for her owners by telling fortunes. ¹⁷ She followed Paul and us, shouting, "These men are servants of the Most High God! They announce to you how you can be saved!" ¹⁸ She did this for many days, until Paul became so upset that he turned round and said to the spirit, "In the name of Jesus Christ I order you to come out of her!" The spirit went out of her that very moment.

¹⁹ When her owners realized that their chance of making money was gone, they seized Paul and Silas and dragged them to the authorities in the public square. ²⁰ They brought them before the Roman officials and said, "These men are Jews, and they are causing trouble in our city. ²¹ They are teaching customs that are against our law; we are Roman citizens, and we cannot accept these customs or practise them." ²² And the crowd joined in the attack against Paul and Silas.

Then the officials tore the clothes off Paul and Silas and ordered them to be whipped. ²³ After a severe beating, they were thrown into jail, and the jailer was ordered to lock them up tight. ²⁴ Upon receiving this order, the jailer threw them into the inner cell and fastened their feet between heavy blocks of wood.

²⁵ About midnight Paul and Silas were praying and singing hymns to God, and the other prisoners were listening to them. ²⁶ Suddenly there was a violent earthquake, which shook the prison to its foundations. At once all the doors opened, and the chains fell off all the prisoners. ²⁷ The jailer woke up, and when he saw the prison doors open, he thought that the prisoners had escaped; so he pulled out his sword and was about to kill himself. ²⁸ But Paul shouted at the top of his voice, "Don't harm yourself! We are all here!"

²⁹ The jailer called for a light, rushed in, and fell trembling at the feet of Paul and Silas. ³⁰ Then he led them out and asked, "Sirs, what must I do to be saved?"

³¹ They answered, "Believe in the Lord Jesus, and you will be saved — you and your family." ³² Then they preached the word of the Lord to him and to all the others in his house. ³³ At that very hour of the night the jailer took them and washed their wounds; and he and all his family were baptized at once. ³⁴ Then he took Paul and Silas up into his house and gave them some food to eat. He and his family were filled with joy, because they now believed in God.

³⁵ The next morning the Roman authorities sent police officers with the order, "Let those men go."

³⁶ So the jailer told Paul, "The officials have sent an order for you and Silas to be released. You may leave, then, and go in peace."

³⁷ But Paul said to the police officers, "We were not found guilty of any crime, yet they whipped us in public — and we are Roman citizens! Then they threw us in prison. And now they want to send us away secretly. Not likely! The Roman officials themselves must come here and let us out."

³⁸ The police officers reported these words to the Roman officials; and when they heard that Paul and Silas were Roman citizens, they were afraid. ³⁹ So they went and apologized to them; then they led

1314

Acts

Malachi
Matt.
Mark
Luke
John

ACTS 16, 17

ACTS 17

Acts records
events happening in all
kinds of places.

GOD WANTS PEOPLE
EVERYWHERE

to have a chance
to know him.

Find any kind of map and
pray over a few places,
asking God to do
something good there.

them out of the prison and asked them to leave the city. [40] Paul and Silas left the prison and went to Lydia's house. There they met the believers, spoke words of encouragement to them, and left.

In Thessalonica

17 Paul and Silas travelled on through Amphipolis and Apollonia and came to Thessalonica, where there was a synagogue. [2] According to his usual habit Paul went to the synagogue. There during three Sabbaths he held discussions with the people, quoting [3] and explaining the Scriptures and proving from them that the Messiah had to suffer and rise from death. "This Jesus whom I announce to you," Paul said, "is the Messiah." [4] Some of them were convinced and joined Paul and Silas; so did many of the leading women and a large group of Greeks who worshipped God.

[5] But some Jews were jealous and gathered worthless loafers from the streets and formed a mob. They set the whole city in an uproar and attacked the home of a man called Jason, in an attempt to find Paul and Silas and bring them out to the people. [6] But when they did not find them, they dragged Jason and some other believers before the city authorities and shouted, "These men have caused trouble everywhere! Now they have come to our city, [7] and Jason has kept them in his house. They are all breaking the laws of the Emperor, saying that there is another king, whose name is Jesus." [8] With these words they threw the crowd and the city authorities into an uproar. [9] The authorities made Jason and the others pay the required amount of money to be released, and then let them go.

In Berea

[10] As soon as night came, the believers sent Paul and Silas to Berea. When they arrived, they went to the synagogue. [11] The people there were more open-minded than the people in Thessalonica. They listened to the message with great eagerness, and every day they studied the Scriptures to see if what Paul said was really true. [12] Many of them believed; and many Greek women of high social standing and many Greek men also believed. [13] But when the Jews in Thessalonica heard that Paul had preached the word of God in Berea also, they came there and started exciting and stirring up the mob. [14] At once the believers sent Paul away to the coast; but both Silas and Timothy stayed in Berea. [15] The men who were taking Paul went with him as far as Athens and then returned to Berea with instructions from Paul that Silas and Timothy should join him as soon as possible.

In Athens

[16] While Paul was waiting in Athens for Silas and Timothy, he was greatly upset when he noticed how full of idols the city was. [17] So he held discussions in the synagogue with the Jews and with the Gentiles who worshipped God, and also in the public square every day with the people who happened to pass by. [18] Certain Epicurean and Stoic teachers also debated with him. Some of them asked, "What is this ignorant show-off trying to say?"

Others answered, "He seems to be talking about foreign gods." They said this because Paul was preaching about Jesus and the resurrection.* [19] So they took Paul, brought him before the city council, the Areopagus, and said, "We would like to know what

17.18 *Jesus and the resurrection*: In Greek, the feminine noun "resurrection" could be understood to be the name of a goddess.

ACTS 17, 18

1315

Acts

....

Romans
1 Corin.
2 Corin.
Galat.
Ephes.

this new teaching is that you are talking about. ²⁰Some of the things we hear you say sound strange to us, and we would like to know what they mean." ²¹(For all the citizens of Athens and the foreigners who lived there liked to spend all their time telling and hearing the latest new thing.)

²²Paul stood up in front of the city council and said, "I see that in every way you Athenians are very religious. ²³For as I walked through your city and looked at the places where you worship, I found an altar on which is written, 'To an Unknown God'. That which you worship, then, even though you do not know it, is what I now proclaim to you. ²⁴God, who made the world and everything in it, is Lord of heaven and earth and does not live in temples made by human hands. ²⁵Nor does he need anything that we can supply by working for him, since it is he himself who gives life and breath and everything else to everyone. ²⁶From one human being he created all races on earth and made them live throughout the whole earth. He himself fixed beforehand the exact times and the limits of the places where they would live. ²⁷He did this so that they would look for him, and perhaps find him as they felt about for him. Yet God is actually not far from any one of us; ²⁸as someone has said,

'In him we live and move and exist.'
It is as some of your poets have said,
'We too are his children.'

²⁹Since we are God's children, we should not suppose that his nature is anything like an image of gold or silver or stone, shaped by human art and skill. ³⁰God has overlooked the times when people did not know him, but now he commands all of them everywhere to turn away from their evil ways. ³¹For he has fixed a day in which he will judge the whole world with justice by means of a man he has chosen. He has given proof of this to everyone by raising that man from death!"

³²When they heard Paul speak about a raising from death, some of them made fun of him, but others said, "We want to hear you speak about this again." ³³And so Paul left the meeting. ³⁴Some men joined him and believed, among whom was Dionysius, a member of the council; there was also a woman named Damaris, and some other people.

In Corinth

18 After this, Paul left Athens and went on to Corinth. ²There he met a Jew named Aquila, born in Pontus, who had recently come from Italy with his wife Priscilla, for the Emperor Claudius had ordered all the Jews to leave Rome. Paul went to see them, ³and stayed and worked with them, because he earned his living by making tents, just as they did. ⁴He held discussions in the synagogue every Sabbath, trying to convince both Jews and Greeks.

⁵When Silas and Timothy arrived from Macedonia, Paul gave his whole time to preaching the message, testifying to the Jews that Jesus is the Messiah. ⁶When they opposed him and said evil things about him, he protested by shaking the dust from his clothes and saying to them, "If you are lost, you yourselves must take the blame for it! I am not responsible. From now on I will go to the Gentiles." ⁷So he left them and went to live in the house of a Gentile named Titius Justus, who worshipped God; his house was next to the synagogue. ⁸Crispus, who was the leader of the synagogue, believed in the Lord, together with all his family; and many other people in Corinth heard the message, believed, and were baptized.

1316

Acts

·:········

Malachi

Matt.

Mark

Luke

John

ACTS 18, 19

[9] One night Paul had a vision in which the Lord said to him, "Do not be afraid, but keep on speaking and do not give up, [10] for I am with you. No one will be able to harm you, for many in this city are my people." [11] So Paul stayed there for a year and a half, teaching the people the word of God.

[12] When Gallio was made the Roman governor of Achaia, Jews there got together, seized Paul, and took him into court. [13] "This man," they said, "is trying to persuade people to worship God in a way that is against the law!"

[14] Paul was about to speak when Gallio said to the Jews, "If this were a matter of some evil crime or wrong that has been committed, it would be reasonable for me to be patient with you Jews. [15] But since it is an argument about words and names and your own law, you yourselves must settle it. I will not be the judge of such things!" [16] And he drove them out of the court. [17] They all seized Sosthenes, the leader of the synagogue, and beat him in front of the court. But that did not bother Gallio a bit.

The Return to Antioch

[18] Paul stayed on with the believers in Corinth for many days, then left them and sailed off with Priscilla and Aquila for Syria. Before sailing from Cenchreae he had his head shaved because of a vow he had taken.* [19] They arrived in Ephesus, where Paul left Priscilla and Aquila. He went into the synagogue and held discussions with the Jews. [20] The people asked him to stay longer, but he would not consent. [21] Instead, he told them as he left, "If it is the will of God, I will come back to you." And so he sailed from Ephesus.

[22] When he arrived at Caesarea, he went to Jerusalem and greeted the church, and then went to Antioch. [23] After spending some time there, he left and went through the region of Galatia and Phrygia, strengthening all the believers.

Apollos in Ephesus and Corinth

[24] At that time a Jew named Apollos, who had been born in Alexandria, came to Ephesus. He was an eloquent speaker and had a thorough knowledge of the Scriptures. [25] He had been instructed in the Way of the Lord, and with great enthusiasm he proclaimed and taught correctly the facts about Jesus. However, he knew only the baptism of John. [26] He began to speak boldly in the synagogue. When Priscilla and Aquila heard him, they took him home with them and explained to him more correctly the Way of God. [27] Apollos then decided to go to Achaia, so the believers in Ephesus helped him by writing to the believers in Achaia, urging them to welcome him. When he arrived, he was a great help to those who through God's grace had become believers. [28] For with his strong arguments he defeated the Jews in public debates by proving from the Scriptures that Jesus is the Messiah.

Paul in Ephesus

19 While Apollos was in Corinth, Paul travelled through the interior of the province and arrived in Ephesus. There he found some disciples [2] and asked them, "Did you receive the Holy Spirit when you became believers?"

"We have not even heard that there is a Holy Spirit," they answered.

18.18 *a vow he had taken*: This refers to the Jewish custom of shaving the head as a sign that a vow has been kept.

³ "Well, then, what kind of baptism did you receive?" Paul asked. "The baptism of John," they answered.

⁴ Paul said, "The baptism of John was for those who turned from their sins; and he told the people of Israel to believe in the one who was coming after him — that is, in Jesus."

⁵ When they heard this, they were baptized in the name of the Lord Jesus. ⁶ Paul placed his hands on them, and the Holy Spirit came upon them; they spoke in strange tongues and also proclaimed God's message. ⁷ They were about twelve men in all.

⁸ Paul went into the synagogue and during three months spoke boldly with the people, holding discussions with them and trying to convince them about the Kingdom of God. ⁹ But some of them were stubborn and would not believe, and before the whole group they said evil things about the Way of the Lord. So Paul left them and took the believers with him, and every day* he held discussions in the lecture hall of Tyrannus. ¹⁰ This went on for two years, so that all the people who lived in the province of Asia, both Jews and Gentiles, heard the word of the Lord.

The Sons of Sceva

¹¹ God was performing unusual miracles through Paul. ¹² Even handkerchiefs and aprons he had used were taken to those who were ill, and their diseases were driven away, and the evil spirits would go out of them. ¹³ Some Jews who travelled round and drove out evil spirits also tried to use the name of the Lord Jesus to do this. They said to the evil spirits, "I command you in the name of Jesus, whom Paul preaches." ¹⁴ Seven brothers, who were the sons of a Jewish High Priest named Sceva, were doing this.

¹⁵ But the evil spirit said to them, "I know Jesus, and I know about Paul; but you — who are you?"

¹⁶ The man who had the evil spirit in him attacked them with such violence that he overpowered them all. They ran away from his house, wounded and with their clothes torn off. ¹⁷ All the Jews and Gentiles who lived in Ephesus heard about this; they were all filled with fear, and the name of the Lord Jesus was given greater honour. ¹⁸ Many of the believers came, publicly admitting and revealing what they had done. ¹⁹ Many of those who had practised magic brought their books together and burnt them in public. They added up the price of the books, and the total came to 50,000 silver coins.* ²⁰ In this powerful way the word of the Lord* kept spreading and growing stronger.

The Riot in Ephesus

²¹ After these things had happened, Paul made up his mind* to travel through Macedonia and Achaia and go on to Jerusalem. "After I go there," he said, "I must also see Rome." ²² So he sent Timothy and Erastus, two of his helpers, to Macedonia, while he spent more time in the province of Asia.

²³ It was at this time that there was serious trouble in Ephesus because of the Way of the Lord. ²⁴ A certain silversmith named Demetrius made silver models of the temple of the goddess Artemis, and his business brought a great deal of profit to the workers. ²⁵ So he called them all together with others whose

DECORATE THESE SHAPES IN RELATION TO YOUR MOOD.

19.9 Some manuscripts add *from 11 a.m. until 4 p.m.*
19.19 *silver coins*: A silver coin was the daily wage of a rural worker (see Mt 20.2).
19.20 *In this… Lord*; or *And so, by the power of the Lord, the message.*
19.21 *Paul made up his mind*; or *Paul, led by the Spirit, decided.*

work was like theirs and said to them, "Men, you know that our prosperity comes from this work. ²⁶ Now, you can see and hear for yourselves what this fellow Paul is doing. He says that gods made by human hands are not gods at all, and he has succeeded in convincing many people, both here in Ephesus and in nearly the whole province of Asia. ²⁷ There is the danger, then, that this business of ours will get a bad name. Not only that, but there is also the danger that the temple of the great goddess Artemis will come to mean nothing and that her greatness will be destroyed — the goddess worshipped by everyone in Asia and in all the world!"

²⁸ As the crowd heard these words, they became furious and started shouting, "Great is Artemis of Ephesus!" ²⁹ The uproar spread throughout the whole city. The mob seized Gaius and Aristarchus, two Macedonians who were travelling with Paul, and rushed with them to the theatre. ³⁰ Paul himself wanted to go before the crowd, but the believers would not let him. ³¹ Some of the provincial authorities, who were his friends, also sent him a message begging him not to show himself in the theatre. ³² Meanwhile the whole meeting was in an uproar: some people were shouting one thing, others were shouting something else, because most of them did not even know why they had come together. ³³ Some of the people concluded that Alexander was responsible, since the Jews made him go up to the front. Then Alexander motioned with his hand for the people to be silent, and he tried to make a speech of defence. ³⁴ But when they recognized that he was a Jew, they all shouted together the same thing for two hours: "Great is Artemis of Ephesus!"

³⁵ At last the town clerk was able to calm the crowd. "Fellow-Ephesians!" he said. "Everyone knows that the city of Ephesus is the keeper of the temple of the great Artemis and of the sacred stone that fell down from heaven. ³⁶ Nobody can deny these things. So then, you must calm down and not do anything reckless. ³⁷ You have brought these men here even though they have not robbed temples or said evil things about our goddess. ³⁸ If Demetrius and his workers have an accusation against anyone, we have the authorities and the regular days for court; charges can be made there. ³⁹ But if there is something more that you want, it will have to be settled in a legal meeting of citizens. ⁴⁰ For after what has happened today, there is the danger that we will be accused of a riot. There is no excuse for all this uproar, and we would not be able to give a good reason for it." ⁴¹ After saying this, he dismissed the meeting.

To Macedonia and Achaia

20 After the uproar died down, Paul called together the believers and with words of encouragement said goodbye to them. Then he left and went on to Macedonia. ² He went through those regions and encouraged the people with many messages. Then he came to Achaia, ³ where he stayed three months. He was getting ready to go to Syria when he discovered that there were Jews plotting against him; so he decided to go back through Macedonia. ⁴ Sopater son of Pyrrhus, from Berea, went with him; so did Aristarchus and Secundus, from Thessalonica; Gaius, from Derbe; Tychicus and Trophimus, from the province of Asia; and Timothy. ⁵ They went ahead and waited for us in Troas. ⁶ We sailed from Philippi after the Festival of Unleavened Bread, and five days later we joined them in Troas, where we spent a week.

1319

Acts

....

Romans

1 Corin.

2 Corin.

Galat.

Ephes.

Paul's Last Visit to Troas

7 On Saturday* evening we gathered together for the fellowship meal. Paul spoke to the people and kept on speaking until midnight, since he was going to leave the next day. 8 Many lamps were burning in the upstairs room where we were meeting. 9 A young man named Eutychus was sitting in the window, and as Paul kept on talking, Eutychus got sleepier and sleepier, until he finally went sound asleep and fell from the third storey to the ground. When they picked him up, he was dead. 10 But Paul went down and threw himself on him and hugged him. "Don't worry," he said, "he is still alive!" 11 Then he went back upstairs, broke bread, and ate. After talking with them for a long time, even until sunrise, Paul left. 12 They took the young man home alive and were greatly comforted.

From Troas to Miletus

13 We went on ahead to the ship and sailed off to Assos, where we were going to take Paul aboard. He had told us to do this, because he was going there by land. 14 When he met us in Assos, we took him aboard and went on to Mitylene. 15 We sailed from there and arrived off Chios the next day. A day later we came to Samos, and the following day we reached Miletus. 16 Paul had decided to sail on past Ephesus, so as not to lose any time in the province of Asia. He was in a hurry to arrive in Jerusalem by the day of Pentecost, if at all possible.

Paul's Farewell Speech to the Elders of Ephesus

17 From Miletus Paul sent a message to Ephesus, asking the elders of the church to meet him. 18 When they arrived, he said to them, "You know how I spent the whole time I was with you, from the first day I arrived in the province of Asia. 19 With all humility and many tears I did my work as the Lord's servant during the hard times that came to me because of the plots of some Jews. 20 You know that I did not hold back anything that would be of help to you as I preached and taught in public and in your homes. 21 To Jews and Gentiles alike I gave solemn warning that they should turn from their sins to God and believe in our Lord Jesus. 22 And now, in obedience to the Holy Spirit I am going to Jerusalem, not knowing what will happen to me there. 23 I only know that in every city the Holy Spirit has warned me that prison and troubles wait for me. 24 But I reckon my own life to be worth nothing to me; I only want to complete my mission and finish the work that the Lord Jesus gave me to do, which is to declare the Good News about the grace of God.

25 "I have gone about among all of you, preaching the Kingdom of God. And now I know that none of you will ever see me again. 26 So I solemnly declare to you this very day: if any of you should be lost, I am not responsible. 27 For I have not held back from announcing to you the whole purpose of God. 28 So keep watch over yourselves and over all the flock which the Holy Spirit has placed in your care. Be shepherds of the church of God,* which he made his own through the blood of his Son.* 29 I know that after I leave, fierce wolves will come among you, and they will not spare the flock. 30 The time will come when some men from your own group will tell lies to lead the believers away after them.

....

20.7 Saturday; or Sunday.
20.28 God; some manuscripts have the Lord.
20.28 through the blood of his Son; or through the sacrificial death of his Son; or through his own blood.

1320

Acts

·⸱········

Malachi
Matt.
Mark
Luke
John

ACTS 20, 21

31 Watch, then, and remember that with many tears, day and night, I taught every one of you for three years.

32 "And now I commend you to the care of God and to the message of his grace, which is able to build you up and give you the blessings God has for all his people. 33 I have not wanted anyone's silver or gold or clothing. 34 You yourselves know that I have worked with these hands of mine to provide everything that my companions and I have needed. 35 I have shown you in all things that by working hard in this way we must help the weak, remembering the words that the Lord Jesus himself said, 'There is more happiness in giving than in receiving.' "

36 When Paul finished, he knelt down with them and prayed. 37 They were all crying as they hugged him and kissed him goodbye. 38 They were especially sad because he had said that they would never see him again. And so they went with him to the ship.

Paul Goes to Jerusalem

21 We said goodbye to them and left. After sailing straight across, we came to Cos; the next day we reached Rhodes, and from there we went on to Patara. 2 There we found a ship that was going to Phoenicia, so we went aboard and sailed away. 3 We came to where we could see Cyprus, and then sailed south of it on to Syria. We went ashore at Tyre, where the ship was going to unload its cargo. 4 There we found some believers and stayed with them a week. By the power of the Spirit they told Paul not to go to Jerusalem. 5 But when our time with them was over, we left and went on our way. All of them, together with their wives and children, went with us out of the city to the beach, where we all knelt and prayed. 6 Then we said goodbye to one another, and we went on board the ship while they went back home.

7 We continued our voyage, sailing from Tyre to Ptolemais, where we greeted the believers and stayed with them for a day. 8 On the following day we left and arrived in Caesarea. There we stayed at the house of Philip the evangelist, one of the seven men who had been chosen as helpers in Jerusalem. 9 He had four unmarried daughters who proclaimed God's message. 10 We had been there for several days when a prophet named Agabus arrived from Judea. 11 He came to us, took Paul's belt, tied up his own feet and hands with it, and said, "This is what the Holy Spirit says: The owner of this belt will be tied up in this way by the Jews in Jerusalem, and they will hand him over to the Gentiles."

12 When we heard this, we and the others there begged Paul not to go to Jerusalem. 13 But he answered, "What are you doing, crying like this and breaking my heart? I am ready not only to be tied up in Jerusalem but even to die there for the sake of the Lord Jesus."

14 We could not convince him, so we gave up and said, "May the Lord's will be done."

15 After spending some time there, we got our things ready and left for Jerusalem. 16 Some of the disciples from Caesarea also went with us and took us to the house of the man we were going to stay with* — Mnason, from Cyprus, who had been a believer since the early days.

Paul Visits James

17 When we arrived in Jerusalem, the believers welcomed us warmly. 18 The next day Paul went with us to see James; and all

······································

21.16 *and took us to the house of the man we were going to stay with*; or *bringing with them the man at whose house we were going to stay.*

ACTS 21

1321

Acts

··········⫶

Romans
1 Corin.
2 Corin.
Galat.
Ephes.

the church elders were present. ¹⁹Paul greeted them and gave a complete report of everything that God had done among the Gentiles through his work. ²⁰After hearing him, they all praised God. Then they said, "Brother Paul, you can see how many thousands of Jews have become believers, and how devoted they all are to the Law. ²¹They have been told that you have been teaching all the Jews who live in Gentile countries to abandon the Law of Moses, telling them not to circumcise their children or follow the Jewish customs. ²²They are sure to hear that you have arrived. What should be done, then? ²³This is what we want you to do. There are four men here who have taken a vow. ²⁴Go along with them and join them in the ceremony of purification and pay their expenses; then they will be able to shave their heads.* In this way everyone will know that there is no truth in any of the things that they have been told about you, but that you yourself live in accordance with the Law of Moses. ²⁵But as for the Gentiles who have become believers, we have sent them a letter telling them we decided that they must not eat any food that has been offered to idols, or any blood, or any animal that has been strangled, and that they must keep themselves from sexual immorality."

²⁶So Paul took the men and the next day performed the ceremony of purification with them. Then he went into the Temple and gave notice of how many days it would be until the end of the period of purification, when a sacrifice would be offered for each one of them.

Paul is Arrested in the Temple

²⁷But just when the seven days were about to come to an end, some Jews from the province of Asia saw Paul in the Temple. They stirred up the whole crowd and seized Paul. ²⁸"Men of Israel!" they shouted. "Help! This is the man who goes everywhere teaching everyone against the people of Israel, the Law of Moses, and this Temple. And now he has even brought some Gentiles into the Temple and defiled this holy place!" ²⁹(They said this because they had seen Trophimus from Ephesus with Paul in the city, and they thought that Paul had taken him into the Temple.)

³⁰Confusion spread through the whole city, and the people all ran together, seized Paul, and dragged him out of the Temple. At once the Temple doors were closed. ³¹The mob was trying to kill Paul, when a report was sent up to the commander of the Roman troops that all Jerusalem was rioting. ³²At once the commander took some officers and soldiers and rushed down to the crowd. When the people saw him with the soldiers, they stopped beating Paul. ³³The commander went over to Paul, arrested him, and ordered him to be bound with two chains. Then he asked, "Who is this man, and what has he done?" ³⁴Some in the crowd shouted one thing, others something else. There was such confusion that the commander could not find out exactly what had happened, so he ordered his men to take Paul up into the fort. ³⁵They got as far as the steps with him, and then the soldiers had to carry him because the mob was so wild. ³⁶They were all coming after him and screaming, "Kill him!"

Paul Defends Himself

³⁷As the soldiers were about to take Paul into the fort, he spoke to the commander: "May I say something to you?"

21.24 *shave their heads*: See 18.18.

1322

Acts

·········

Malachi
Matt.
Mark
Luke
John

ACTS 21, 22

"You speak Greek, do you?" the commander asked. [38]"Then you are not that Egyptian fellow who some time ago started a revolution and led 4,000 armed terrorists out into the desert?"

[39]Paul answered, "I am a Jew, born in Tarsus in Cilicia, a citizen of an important city. Please let me speak to the people."

[40]The commander gave him permission, so Paul stood on the steps and motioned with his hand for the people to be silent. When they were quiet, Paul spoke to them in Hebrew:

22 "My fellow-Jews, listen to me as I make my defence before you!" [2]When they heard him speaking to them in Hebrew, they became even quieter; and Paul went on:

[3]"I am a Jew, born in Tarsus in Cilicia, but brought up here in Jerusalem as a student of Gamaliel. I received strict instruction in the Law of our ancestors and was just as dedicated to God as are all of you who are here today. [4]I persecuted to the death the people who followed this Way. I arrested men and women and threw them into prison. [5]The High Priest and the whole Council can prove that I am telling the truth. I received from them letters written to fellow-Jews in Damascus, so I went there to arrest these people and bring them back in chains to Jerusalem to be punished.

Paul Tells of his Conversion
(Acts 9.1–19; 26.12–18)

[6]"As I was travelling and coming near Damascus, about midday a bright light from the sky flashed suddenly round me. [7]I fell to the ground and heard a voice saying to me, 'Saul, Saul! Why do you persecute me?' [8]'Who are you, Lord?' I asked. 'I am Jesus of Nazareth, whom you persecute,' he said to me. [9]The men with me saw the light, but did not hear the voice of the one who was speaking to me. [10]I asked, 'What shall I do, Lord?' and the Lord said to me, 'Get up and go into Damascus, and there you will be told everything that God has determined for you to do.' [11]I was blind because of the bright light, and so my companions took me by the hand and led me into Damascus.

[12]"In that city was a man named Ananias, a religious man who obeyed our Law and was highly respected by all the Jews living there. [13]He came to me, stood by me, and said, 'Brother Saul, see again!' At that very moment I saw again and looked at him. [14]He said, 'The God of our ancestors has chosen you to know his will, to see his righteous Servant, and to hear him speaking with his own voice. [15]For you will be a witness for him to tell everyone what you have seen and heard. [16]And now, why wait any longer? Get up and be baptized and have your sins washed away by praying to him.'

Paul's Call to Preach to the Gentiles

[17]"I went back to Jerusalem, and while I was praying in the Temple, I had a vision, [18]in which I saw the Lord, as he said to me, 'Hurry and leave Jerusalem quickly, because the people here will not accept your witness about me.' [19]'Lord,' I answered, 'they know very well that I went to the synagogues and arrested and beat those who believe in you. [20]And when your witness Stephen was put to death, I myself was there, approving of his murder and taking care of the cloaks of his murderers.' [21]'Go,' the Lord said to me, 'for I will send you far away to the Gentiles.'"

[22]The people listened to Paul until he said this; but then they started shouting at the top of their voices, "Away with him! Kill him! He's not fit to live!" [23]They were screaming, waving their clothes, and throwing dust up in the air. [24]The Roman commander

Acts

············

Romans
1 Corin.
2 Corin.
Galat.
Ephes.

ordered his men to take Paul into the fort, and he told them to whip him in order to find out why the Jews were screaming like this against him. 25 But when they had tied him up to be whipped, Paul said to the officer standing there, "Is it lawful for you to whip a Roman citizen who hasn't even been tried for any crime?"

26 When the officer heard this, he went to the commander and asked him, "What are you doing? That man is a Roman citizen!"

27 So the commander went to Paul and asked him, "Tell me, are you a Roman citizen?"

"Yes," answered Paul.

28 The commander said, "I became one by paying a large amount of money."

"But I am one by birth," Paul answered.

29 At once the men who were going to question Paul drew back from him; and the commander was frightened when he realized that Paul was a Roman citizen and that he had put him in chains.

Paul before the Council

30 The commander wanted to find out for certain what the Jews were accusing Paul of; so the next day he had Paul's chains taken off and ordered the chief priests and the whole Council to meet. Then he took Paul and made him stand before them.

23 Paul looked straight at the Council and said, "My fellow-Israelites! My conscience is perfectly clear about the way in which I have lived before God to this very day." 2 The High Priest Ananias ordered those who were standing close to Paul to strike him on the mouth. 3 Paul said to him, "God will certainly strike you — you whitewashed wall! You sit there to judge me according to the Law, yet you break the Law by ordering them to strike me!"

4 The men close to Paul said to him, "You are insulting God's High Priest!"

5 Paul answered, "My fellow-Israelites, I did not know that he was the High Priest. The scripture says, 'You must not speak evil of the ruler of your people.'"

6 When Paul saw that some of the group were Sadducees and the others were Pharisees, he called out in the Council, "Fellow-Israelites! I am a Pharisee, the son of Pharisees. I am on trial here because of the hope I have that the dead will rise to life!"

7 As soon as he said this, the Pharisees and Sadducees started to quarrel, and the group was divided. 8 (For the Sadducees say that people will not rise from death and that there are no angels or spirits; but the Pharisees believe in all three.) 9 The shouting became louder, and some of the teachers of the Law who belonged to the party of the Pharisees stood up and protested strongly: "We cannot find anything wrong with this man! Perhaps a spirit or an angel really did speak to him!"

10 The argument became so violent that the commander was afraid that Paul would be torn to pieces. So he ordered his soldiers to go down into the group, get Paul away from them, and take him into the fort.

11 That night the Lord stood by Paul and said, "Don't be afraid! You have given your witness for me here in Jerusalem, and you must also do the same in Rome."

The Plot against Paul's Life

12 The next morning some Jews met together and made a plan. They took a vow that they would not eat or drink anything until they had killed Paul. 13 There were more than forty who planned this together. 14 Then they went to the chief priests and elders and

ACTS 22.1-21

Here Paul

SHARES

– HIS –

STORY,

telling people what he used to be like and what God has done in him since.

Take some time to

WRITE A LETTER TO YOUR YOUNGER SELF,

telling them what God has done in your life and what he has shown you in the last few years.

said, "We have taken a solemn vow together not to eat a thing until we have killed Paul. [15] Now then, you and the Council send word to the Roman commander to bring Paul down to you, pretending that you want to get more accurate information about him. But we will be ready to kill him before he ever gets here."

[16] But the son of Paul's sister heard about the plot; so he went to the fort and told Paul. [17] Then Paul called one of the officers and said to him, "Take this young man to the commander; he has something to tell him." [18] The officer took him, led him to the commander, and said, "The prisoner Paul called me and asked me to bring this young man to you, because he has something to say to you."

[19] The commander took him by the hand, led him off by himself, and asked him, "What have you got to tell me?"

[20] He said, "The Jewish authorities have agreed to ask you tomorrow to take Paul down to the Council, pretending that the Council wants to get more accurate information about him. [21] But don't listen to them, because there are more than forty men who will be hiding and waiting for him. They have taken a vow not to eat or drink until they have killed him. They are now ready to do it and are waiting for your decision."

[22] The commander said, "Don't tell anyone that you have reported this to me." And he sent the young man away.

Paul is Sent to Governor Felix

[23] Then the commander called two of his officers and said, "Get 200 soldiers ready to go to Caesarea, together with seventy horsemen and 200 spearmen, and be ready to leave by nine o'clock tonight. [24] Provide some horses for Paul to ride and get him safely through to the governor Felix." [25] Then the commander wrote a letter that went like this:

[26] "Claudius Lysias to His Excellency, the governor Felix: Greetings. [27] The Jews seized this man and were about to kill him. I learnt that he was a Roman citizen, so I went with my soldiers and rescued him. [28] I wanted to know what they were accusing him of, so I took him down to their Council. [29] I found out that he had not done anything for which he deserved to die or be put in prison; the accusation against him had to do with questions about their own law. [30] And when I was informed that there was a plot against him, at once I decided to send him to you. I have told his accusers to make their charges against him before you."

[31] The soldiers carried out their orders. They got Paul and took him that night as far as Antipatris. [32] The next day the foot soldiers returned to the fort and left the horsemen to go on with him. [33] They took him to Caesarea, delivered the letter to the governor, and handed Paul over to him. [34] The governor read the letter and asked Paul what province he was from. When he found out that he was from Cilicia, [35] he said, "I will hear you when your accusers arrive." Then he gave orders for Paul to be kept under guard in the governor's headquarters.

The Case Against Paul

24 Five days later the High Priest Ananias went to Caesarea with some elders and a lawyer named Tertullus. They appeared before Felix and made their charges against Paul. [2] Then Paul was called in, and Tertullus began to make his accusation, as follows:

"Your Excellency! Your wise leadership has brought us a long period of peace, and many necessary reforms are being made

ACTS 24

1325

Acts

..........:

Romans

1 Corin.

2 Corin.

Galat.

Ephes.

for the good of our country. [3]We welcome this everywhere and at all times, and we are deeply grateful to you. [4]I do not want to take up too much of your time, however, so I beg you to be kind and listen to our brief account. [5]We found this man to be a dangerous nuisance; he starts riots among Jews all over the world and is a leader of the party of the Nazarenes. [6]He also tried to defile the Temple, and we arrested him.* [8]If you question this man, you yourself will be able to learn from him all the things that we are accusing him of." [9]The Jews joined in the accusation and said that all this was true.

Paul's Defence before Felix

[10]The governor then motioned to Paul to speak, and Paul said, "I know that you have been a judge over this nation for many years, and so I am happy to defend myself before you. [11]As you can find out for yourself, it was no more than twelve days ago that I went to Jerusalem to worship. [12]The Jews did not find me arguing with anyone in the Temple, nor did they find me stirring up the people, either in the synagogues or anywhere else in the city. [13]Nor can they give you proof of the accusations they now bring against me. [14]I do admit this to you: I worship the God of our ancestors by following that Way which they say is false. But I also believe in everything written in the Law of Moses and the books of the prophets. [15]I have the same hope in God that these themselves have, namely, that all people, both the good and the bad, will rise from death. [16]And so I do my best always to have a clear conscience before God and human beings.

[17]"After being away from Jerusalem for several years, I went there to take some money to my own people and to offer sacrifices. [18]It was while I was doing this that they found me in the Temple after I had completed the ceremony of purification. There was no crowd with me and no disorder. [19]But some Jews from the province of Asia were there; they themselves ought to come before you and make their accusations if they have anything against me. [20]Or let these who are here tell what crime they found me guilty of when I stood before the Council — [21]except for the one thing I called out when I stood before them: 'I am being tried by you today for believing that the dead will rise to life.'"

[22]Then Felix, who was well informed about the Way, brought the hearing to a close. "When Lysias the commander arrives," he told them, "I will decide your case." [23]He ordered the officer in charge of Paul to keep him under guard, but to give him some freedom and allow his friends to provide for his needs.

Paul before Felix and Drusilla

[24]After some days Felix came with his wife Drusilla, who was Jewish. He sent for Paul and listened to him as he talked about faith in Christ Jesus. [25]But as Paul went on discussing about goodness, self-control, and the coming Day of Judgement, Felix was afraid and said, "You may leave now. I will call you again when I get the chance." [26]At the same time he was hoping that Paul would give him some money; and for this reason he would often send for him and talk with him.

....

24.6 Some manuscripts add verses 6b–8a: *We planned to judge him according to our own law,* [7] *but Lysias the commander came, and with great violence took him from us.* [8] *Then Lysias gave orders that his accusers should come before you.*

1326

Acts

Malachi
Matt.
Mark
Luke
John

ACTS 24, 25

DRAW YOUR CURRENT VIEW

- whether it's your desk, your bed, out of the window, the cat... whatever!

27 After two years had passed, Porcius Festus succeeded Felix as governor. Felix wanted to gain favour with the Jews so he left Paul in prison.

Paul Appeals to the Emperor

25 Three days after Festus arrived in the province, he went from Caesarea to Jerusalem, 2 where the chief priests and the Jewish leaders brought their charges against Paul. They begged Festus 3 to do them the favour of bringing Paul to Jerusalem, for they had made a plot to kill him on the way. 4 Festus answered, "Paul is being kept a prisoner in Caesarea, and I myself will be going back there soon. 5 Let your leaders go to Caesarea with me and accuse the man if he has done anything wrong."

6 Festus spent another eight or ten days with them and then went to Caesarea. On the next day he sat down in the court of judgement and ordered Paul to be brought in. 7 When Paul arrived, the Jews who had come from Jerusalem stood round him and started making many serious charges against him, which they were not able to prove. 8 But Paul defended himself: "I have done nothing wrong against the Law of the Jews or against the Temple or against the Roman Emperor."

9 But Festus wanted to gain favour with the Jews, so he asked Paul, "Would you be willing to go to Jerusalem and be tried on these charges before me there?"

10 Paul said, "I am standing before the Emperor's own court of judgement, where I should be tried. I have done no wrong to the Jews, as you yourself well know. 11 If I have broken the law and done something for which I deserve the death penalty, I do not ask to escape it. But if there is no truth in the charges they bring against me, no one can hand me over to them. I appeal to the Emperor."

12 Then Festus, after conferring with his advisers, answered, "You have appealed to the Emperor, so to the Emperor you will go."

Paul before Agrippa and Bernice

13 Some time later King Agrippa and Bernice came to Caesarea to pay a visit of welcome to Festus. 14 After they had been there several days, Festus explained Paul's situation to the king: "There is a man here who was left a prisoner by Felix; 15 and when I went to Jerusalem, the Jewish chief priests and elders brought charges against him and asked me to condemn him. 16 But I told them that we Romans are not in the habit of handing over anyone accused of a crime before he has met his accusers face to face and has had the chance of defending himself against the accusation. 17 When they came here, then, I lost no time, but on the very next day I sat in the court and ordered the man to be brought in. 18 His opponents stood up, but they did not accuse him of any of the evil crimes that I thought they would. 19 All they had were some arguments with him about their own religion and about a man named Jesus, who has died; but Paul claims that he is alive. 20 I was undecided about how I could get information on these matters, so I asked Paul if he would be willing to go to Jerusalem and be tried there on these charges. 21 But Paul appealed; he asked to be kept under guard and to let the Emperor decide his case. So I gave orders for him to be kept under guard until I could send him to the Emperor."

22 Agrippa said to Festus, "I would like to hear this man myself."

"You will hear him tomorrow," Festus answered.

23 The next day Agrippa and Bernice came with great pomp and ceremony and entered the audience hall with the military chiefs

ACTS 25, 26   1327

Acts
..........:
Romans
1 Corin.
2 Corin.
Galat.
Ephes.

and the leading men of the city. Festus gave the order, and Paul was brought in. ²⁴Festus said, "King Agrippa and all who are here with us: You see this man against whom all the Jewish people, both here and in Jerusalem, have brought complaints to me. They scream that he should not live any longer. ²⁵But I could not find that he had done anything for which he deserved the death sentence. And since he himself made an appeal to the Emperor, I have decided to send him. ²⁶But I have nothing definite about him to write to the Emperor. So I have brought him here before you — and especially before you, King Agrippa! — so that, after investigating his case, I may have something to write. ²⁷For it seems unreasonable to me to send a prisoner without clearly indicating the charges against him."

Paul Defends Himself before Agrippa

26 Agrippa said to Paul, "You have permission to speak on your own behalf." Paul stretched out his hand and defended himself as follows:

²"King Agrippa! I consider myself fortunate that today I am to defend myself before you from all the things these Jews accuse me of, ³particularly since you know so well all the Jewish customs and disputes. I ask you, then, to listen to me with patience.

⁴"All the Jews know how I have lived ever since I was young. They know how I have spent my whole life, at first in my own country and then in Jerusalem. ⁵They have always known, if they are willing to testify, that from the very first I have lived as a member of the strictest party of our religion, the Pharisees. ⁶And now I stand here to be tried because of the hope I have in the promise that God made to our ancestors — ⁷the very thing that the twelve tribes of our people hope to receive, as they worship God day and night. And it is because of this hope, Your Majesty, that I am being accused by these Jews! ⁸Why do you who are here find it impossible to believe that God raises the dead?

⁹"I myself thought that I should do everything I could against the cause of Jesus of Nazareth. ¹⁰That is what I did in Jerusalem. I received authority from the chief priests and put many of God's people in prison; and when they were sentenced to death, I also voted against them. ¹¹Many times I had them punished in the synagogues and tried to make them deny their faith. I was so furious with them that I even went to foreign cities to persecute them.

Paul Tells of his Conversion
(Acts 9.1–19; 22.6–16)

¹²"It was for this purpose that I went to Damascus with authority and orders from the chief priests. ¹³It was on the road at midday, Your Majesty, that I saw a light much brighter than the sun, coming from the sky and shining round me and the men travelling with me. ¹⁴All of us fell to the ground, and I heard a voice say to me in Hebrew, 'Saul, Saul! Why are you persecuting me? You are hurting yourself by hitting back, like an ox kicking against its owner's stick.' ¹⁵'Who are you, Lord?' I asked. And the Lord answered, 'I am Jesus, whom you persecute. ¹⁶But get up and stand on your feet. I have appeared to you to appoint you as my servant. You are to tell others what you have seen of me* today and what I will show you in the future. ¹⁷I will rescue you

26.16 Some manuscripts do not have *of me*.

1328

Acts

Malachi
Matt.
Mark
Luke
John

ACTS 26, 27

ACTS 26.18

FROM THE
DARKNESS
TO THE
LIGHT

from the people of Israel and from the Gentiles to whom I will send you. [18] You are to open their eyes and turn them from the darkness to the light and from the power of Satan to God, so that through their faith in me they will have their sins forgiven and receive their place among God's chosen people.'

Paul Tells of his Work

[19] "And so, King Agrippa, I did not disobey the vision I had from heaven. [20] First in Damascus and in Jerusalem and then in all Judea and among the Gentiles, I preached that they must repent of their sins and turn to God and do the things that would show they had repented. [21] It was for this reason that these Jews seized me while I was in the Temple, and they tried to kill me. [22] But to this very day I have been helped by God, and so I stand here giving my witness to all, to small and great alike. What I say is the very same thing which the prophets and Moses said was going to happen: [23] that the Messiah must suffer and be the first one to rise from death, to announce the light of salvation to the Jews and to the Gentiles."

[24] As Paul defended himself in this way, Festus shouted at him, "You are mad, Paul! Your great learning is driving you mad!"

[25] Paul answered, "I am not mad, Your Excellency! I am speaking the sober truth. [26] King Agrippa! I can speak to you with all boldness, because you know about these things. I am sure that you have taken notice of every one of them, for this thing has not happened hidden away in a corner. [27] King Agrippa, do you believe the prophets? I know that you do!"

[28] Agrippa said to Paul, "In this short time do you think you will make me a Christian?"

[29] "Whether a short time or a long time," Paul answered, "my prayer to God is that you and all the rest of you who are listening to me today might become what I am — except, of course, for these chains!"

[30] Then the king, the governor, Bernice, and all the others got up, [31] and after leaving they said to each other, "This man has not done anything for which he should die or be put in prison." [32] And Agrippa said to Festus, "This man could have been released if he had not appealed to the Emperor."

Paul Sails for Rome

27 When it was decided that we should sail to Italy, they handed Paul and some other prisoners over to Julius, an officer in the Roman regiment called "The Emperor's Regiment". [2] We went aboard a ship from Adramyttium, which was ready to leave for the seaports of the province of Asia, and we sailed away. Aristarchus, a Macedonian from Thessalonica, was with us. [3] The next day we arrived at Sidon. Julius was kind to Paul and allowed him to go and see his friends, to be given what he needed. [4] We went on from there, and because the winds were blowing against us, we sailed on the sheltered side of the island of Cyprus. [5] We crossed over the sea off Cilicia and Pamphylia and came to Myra in Lycia. [6] There the officer found a ship from Alexandria that was going to sail for Italy, so he put us aboard.

[7] We sailed slowly for several days and with great difficulty finally arrived off the town of Cnidus. The wind would not let us go any further in that direction, so we sailed down the sheltered side of the island of Crete, passing by Cape Salmone. [8] We kept close to the coast and with great difficulty came to a place called Safe Harbours, not far from the town of Lasea.

ACTS 27

1329

Acts

....

Romans

1 Corin.

2 Corin.

Galat.

Ephes.

⁹We spent a long time there, until it became dangerous to continue the voyage, for by now the Day of Atonement* was already past. So Paul gave them this advice: ¹⁰"Men, I see that our voyage from here on will be dangerous; there will be great damage to the cargo and to the ship, and loss of life as well." ¹¹But the army officer was convinced by what the captain and the owner of the ship said, and not by what Paul said. ¹²The harbour was not a good one to spend the winter in; so most people were in favour of putting out to sea and trying to reach Phoenix, if possible, in order to spend the winter there. Phoenix is a harbour in Crete that faces south-west and north-west.*

The Storm at Sea

¹³A soft wind from the south began to blow, and the men thought that they could carry out their plan, so they pulled up the anchor and sailed as close as possible along the coast of Crete. ¹⁴But soon a very strong wind — the one called "North-easter" — blew down from the island. ¹⁵It hit the ship, and since it was impossible to keep the ship headed into the wind, we gave up trying and let it be carried along by the wind. ¹⁶We got some shelter when we passed to the south of the little island of Cauda. There, with some difficulty, we managed to make the ship's boat secure. ¹⁷They pulled it aboard and then fastened some ropes tight round the ship. They were afraid that they might run into the sandbanks off the coast of Libya, so they lowered the sail and let the ship be carried by the wind. ¹⁸The violent storm continued, so on the next day they began to throw some of the ship's cargo overboard, ¹⁹and on the following day they threw part of the ship's equipment overboard. ²⁰For many days we could not see the sun or the stars, and the wind kept on blowing very hard. We finally gave up all hope of being saved.

²¹After those on board had gone a long time without food, Paul stood before them and said, "Men, you should have listened to me and not have sailed from Crete; then we would have avoided all this damage and loss. ²²But now I beg you, take heart! Not one of you will lose your life; only the ship will be lost. ²³For last night an angel of the God to whom I belong and whom I worship came to me ²⁴and said, 'Don't be afraid, Paul! You must stand before the Emperor. And God in his goodness to you has spared the lives of all those who are sailing with you.' ²⁵So take heart, men! For I trust in God that it will be just as I was told. ²⁶But we will be driven ashore on some island."

²⁷It was the fourteenth night, and we were being driven about in the Mediterranean by the storm. About midnight the sailors suspected that we were getting close to land. ²⁸So they dropped a line with a weight tied to it and found that the water was forty metres deep; a little later they did the same and found that it was thirty metres deep. ²⁹They were afraid that the ship would go on the rocks, so they lowered four anchors from the back of the ship and prayed for daylight. ³⁰Then the sailors tried to escape from the ship; they lowered the boat into the water and pretended that they were going to put out some anchors from the front of the ship. ³¹But Paul said to the army officer and soldiers, "If the sailors don't stay on board, you have no

....

27.9 *Day of Atonement*: This was celebrated towards the end of September or beginning of October, at which time bad weather made sailing dangerous.
27.12 *south-west and north-west*; or *north-east and south-east*.

1330

Acts

Malachi
Matt.
Mark
Luke
John

ACTS 27, 28

hope of being saved." [32] So the soldiers cut the ropes that held the boat and let it go.

[33] Just before dawn, Paul begged them all to eat some food: "You have been waiting for fourteen days now, and all this time you have not eaten anything. [34] I beg you, then, eat some food; you need it in order to survive. Not even a hair of your heads will be lost." [35] After saying this, Paul took some bread, gave thanks to God before them all, broke it, and began to eat. [36] They took heart, and every one of them also ate some food. [37] There was a total of 276* of us on board. [38] After everyone had eaten enough, they lightened the ship by throwing all the wheat into the sea.

The Shipwreck

[39] When day came, the sailors did not recognize the coast, but they noticed a bay with a beach and decided that, if possible, they would run the ship aground there. [40] So they cut off the anchors and let them sink in the sea, and at the same time they untied the ropes that held the steering oars. Then they raised the sail at the front of the ship so that the wind would blow the ship forward, and we headed for shore. [41] But the ship hit a sandbank and went aground; the front part of the ship got stuck and could not move, while the back part was being broken to pieces by the violence of the waves.

[42] The soldiers made a plan to kill all the prisoners, in order to keep them from swimming ashore and escaping. [43] But the army officer wanted to save Paul, so he stopped them from doing this. Instead, he ordered those who could swim to jump overboard first and swim ashore; [44] the rest were to follow, holding on to the planks or to some broken pieces of the ship. And this was how we all got safely ashore.

In Malta

28 When we were safely ashore, we learnt that the island was called Malta. [2] The natives there were very friendly to us. It had started to rain and was cold, so they lit a fire and made us all welcome. [3] Paul gathered up a bundle of sticks and was putting them on the fire when a snake came out on account of the heat and fastened itself to his hand. [4] The natives saw the snake hanging on Paul's hand and said to one another, "This man must be a murderer, but Fate will not let him live, even though he escaped from the sea." [5] But Paul shook the snake off into the fire without being harmed at all. [6] They were waiting for him to swell up or suddenly fall down dead. But after waiting for a long time and not seeing anything unusual happening to him, they changed their minds and said, "He is a god!"

[7] Not far from that place were some fields that belonged to Publius, the chief official of the island. He welcomed us kindly and for three days we were his guests. [8] Publius' father was in bed, sick with fever and dysentery. Paul went into his room, prayed, placed his hands on him, and healed him. [9] When this happened, all the other sick people on the island came and were healed. [10] They gave us many gifts, and when we sailed, they put on board what we needed for the voyage.

From Malta to Rome

[11] After three months we sailed away on a ship from Alexandria, called "The Twin Gods", which had spent the winter in the island.

27.37 *276*; some manuscripts have *275*; others have *about 76*.

ACTS 28

1331

Acts

Romans
1 Corin.
2 Corin.
Galat.
Ephes.

[12] We arrived in the city of Syracuse and stayed there for three days. [13] From there we sailed on and arrived in the city of Rhegium. The next day a wind began to blow from the south, and in two days we came to the town of Puteoli. [14] We found some believers there who asked us to stay with them a week. And so we came to Rome. [15] The believers in Rome heard about us and came as far as the towns of Market of Appius and Three Inns to meet us. When Paul saw them, he thanked God and was greatly encouraged.

In Rome

[16] When we arrived in Rome, Paul was allowed to live by himself with a soldier guarding him.

[17] After three days Paul called the local Jewish leaders to a meeting. When they had gathered, he said to them, "My fellow-Israelites, even though I did nothing against our people or the customs that we received from our ancestors, I was made a prisoner in Jerusalem and handed over to the Romans. [18] After questioning me, the Romans wanted to release me, because they found that I had done nothing for which I deserved to die. [19] But when the Jews opposed this, I was forced to appeal to the Emperor, even though I had no accusation to make against my own people. [20] That is why I asked to see you and talk with you. As a matter of fact, I am bound in chains like this for the sake of him for whom the people of Israel hope."

[21] They said to him, "We have not received any letters from Judea about you, nor have any of our people come from there with any news or anything bad to say about you. [22] But we would like to hear your ideas, because we know that everywhere people speak against this party to which you belong."

[23] So they fixed a date with Paul, and a large number of them came that day to the place where Paul was staying. From morning till night he explained to them his message about the Kingdom of God, and he tried to convince them about Jesus by quoting from the Law of Moses and the writings of the prophets. [24] Some of them were convinced by his words, but others would not believe. [25] So they left, disagreeing among themselves, after Paul had said this one thing: "How well the Holy Spirit spoke through the prophet Isaiah to your ancestors! [26] For he said,

'Go and say to this people:
You will listen and listen, but not understand;
    you will look and look, but not see,
[27] because this people's minds are dull,
    and they have stopped up their ears
    and closed their eyes.
Otherwise, their eyes would see,
    their ears would hear,
    their minds would understand,
and they would turn to me, says God,
    and I would heal them.' "

[28] And Paul concluded: "You are to know, then, that God's message of salvation has been sent to the Gentiles. They will listen!"*

[30] For two years Paul lived in a place he rented for himself, and there he welcomed all who came to see him. [31] He preached about the Kingdom of God and taught about the Lord Jesus Christ, speaking with all boldness and freedom.

28.28 Some manuscripts add verse 29: *After Paul said this, the Jews left, arguing violently among themselves.*

THE LETTER TO THE
ROMANS

WRITTEN: AROUND AD55-58

SPOTLIGHT:

At this time, Rome was the centre of the Roman world and home to Emperor Nero, the most powerful leader of the time. Rome was rich and multicultural, but Christians were not popular, so it was a dangerous place for the church to be.

WHAT YOU NEED TO KNOW:

Paul wrote this letter to the church in Rome just before he visited them. He wanted to clear up some misunderstandings between the Jewish and non-Jewish (Gentile) members of the church about the effect that Jesus' death has on the way we live out our faith. Romans gives us a strong overview of Paul's whole message about how we are put right with God through believing in Jesus. Christians were persecuted in Rome at this time, so you will also spot advice from Paul on how to behave in the face of an unfriendly society.

WHY READ IT?

There are some amazing chapters in this book that sum up who Jesus is, what he did and the difference that he makes. If you're looking for an overview of the difference that following Jesus makes, this is a brilliant book to read.

In this space, try to write a

SUMMARY
• OF THE •
ENTIRE
LETTER

to the Romans in only
TEN WORDS

(AD30)
PAUL CONVERTED

PAUL WRITES ROMANS
(AD53-57)

(AD62)
PAUL UNDER ARRES
IN ROME

ROMANS 1

1333

Romans
.........:.

1 Corin.
2 Corin.
Galat.
Ephes.
Philipp.

1 From Paul, a servant of Christ Jesus and an apostle chosen and called by God to preach his Good News.
[2] The Good News was promised long ago by God through his prophets, as written in the Holy Scriptures. [3] It is about his Son, our Lord Jesus Christ: as to his humanity, he was born a descendant of David; [4] as to his divine holiness, he was shown with great power to be the Son of God by being raised from death. [5] Through him God gave me the privilege of being an apostle for the sake of Christ, in order to lead people of all nations to believe and obey. [6] This also includes you who are in Rome, whom God has called to belong to Jesus Christ.

[7] And so I write to all of you in Rome whom God loves and has called to be his own people:

May God our Father and the Lord Jesus Christ give you grace and peace.

Prayer of Thanksgiving

[8] First, I thank my God through Jesus Christ for all of you, because the whole world is hearing about your faith. [9] God is my witness that what I say is true — the God whom I serve with all my heart by preaching the Good News about his Son. God knows that I remember you [10] every time I pray. I ask that God in his good will may at last make it possible for me to visit you now. [11] For I want very much to see you, in order to share a spiritual blessing with you to make you strong. [12] What I mean is that both you and I will be helped at the same time, you by my faith and I by yours.

[13] You must remember, my brothers and sisters, that many times I have planned to visit you, but something has always kept me from doing so. I want to win converts among you also, as I have among other Gentiles. [14] For I have an obligation to all peoples, to the civilized and to the savage, to the educated and to the ignorant. [15] So then, I am eager to preach the Good News to you also who live in Rome.

The Power of the Gospel

[16] I have complete confidence in the gospel; it is God's power to save all who believe, first the Jews and also the Gentiles. [17] For the gospel reveals how God puts people right with himself: it is through faith from beginning to end. As the scripture says, "The person who is put right with God through faith shall live."*

The Guilt of the Human Race

[18] God's anger is revealed from heaven against all the sin and evil of the people whose evil ways prevent the truth from being known. [19] God punishes them, because what can be known about God is plain to them, for God himself made it plain. [20] Ever since God created the world, his invisible qualities, both his eternal power and his divine nature, have been clearly seen; they are perceived in the things that God has made. So those people have no excuse at all! [21] They know God, but they do not give him the honour that belongs to him, nor do they thank him. Instead, their thoughts have become complete nonsense, and their empty minds are filled with darkness. [22] They say they are wise, but they are fools; [23] instead of worshipping the immortal God, they worship images made to look like mortal human beings or birds or animals or reptiles.

....

1.17 *put right with God through faith shall live;* or *put right with God shall live through faith.*

1334

Romans

·:·········

Matt.
Mark
Luke
John
Acts

ROMANS 1, 2

²⁴ And so God has given those people over to do the filthy things their hearts desire, and they do shameful things with each other. ²⁵ They exchange the truth about God for a lie; they worship and serve what God has created instead of the Creator himself, who is to be praised for ever! Amen.

²⁶ Because they do this, God has given them over to shameful passions. Even the women pervert the natural use of their sex by unnatural acts. ²⁷ In the same way the men give up natural sexual relations with women and burn with passion for each other. Men do shameful things with each other, and as a result they bring upon themselves the punishment they deserve for their wrongdoing.

²⁸ Because those people refuse to keep in mind the true knowledge about God, he has given them over to corrupted minds, so that they do the things that they should not do. ²⁹ They are filled with all kinds of wickedness, evil, greed, and vice; they are full of jealousy, murder, fighting, deceit, and malice. They gossip ³⁰ and speak evil of one another; they are hateful to God, insolent,* proud, and boastful; they think of more ways to do evil; they disobey their parents; ³¹ they have no conscience; they do not keep their promises, and they show no kindness or pity for others. ³² They know that God's law says that people who live in this way deserve death. Yet, not only do they continue to do these very things, but they even approve of others who do them.

God's Judgement

2 Do you, my friend, pass judgement on others? You have no excuse at all, whoever you are. For when you judge others and then do the same things which they do, you condemn yourself. ² We know that God is right when he judges the people who do such things as these. ³ But you, my friend, do those very things for which you pass judgement on others! Do you think you will escape God's judgement? ⁴ Or perhaps you despise his great kindness, tolerance, and patience. Surely you know that God is kind, because he is trying to lead you to repent. ⁵ But you have a hard and stubborn heart, and so you are making your own punishment even greater on the Day when God's anger and righteous judgements will be revealed. ⁶ For God will reward every person according to what each has done. ⁷ Some people keep on doing good, and seek glory, honour, and immortal life; to them God will give eternal life. ⁸ Other people are selfish and reject what is right, in order to follow what is wrong; on them God will pour out his anger and fury. ⁹ There will be suffering and pain for all those who do what is evil, for the Jews first and also for the Gentiles. ¹⁰ But God will give glory, honour, and peace to all who do what is good, to the Jews first and also to the Gentiles. ¹¹ For God judges everyone by the same standard.

¹² The Gentiles do not have the Law of Moses; they sin and are lost apart from the Law. The Jews have the Law; they sin and are judged by the Law. ¹³ For it is not by hearing the Law that people are put right with God, but by doing what the Law commands. ¹⁴ The Gentiles do not have the Law; but whenever they do by instinct what the Law commands, they are their own law, even though they do not have the Law. ¹⁵ Their conduct shows that what the Law commands is written in their hearts. Their consciences also show that this is true, since their thoughts sometimes accuse them and sometimes defend them. ¹⁶ And so, according to the

....

1.30 *are hateful to God, insolent*; or *hate God, and are insolent.*

ROMANS 2, 3

1335

Romans
............:
1 Corin.
2 Corin.
Galat.
Ephes.
Philipp.

Good News I preach, this is how it will be on that Day when God through Jesus Christ will judge the secret thoughts of all.

The Jews and the Law

¹⁷What about you? You call yourself a Jew; you depend on the Law and boast about God; ¹⁸you know what God wants you to do, and you have learnt from the Law to choose what is right; ¹⁹you are sure that you are a guide for the blind, a light for those who are in darkness, ²⁰an instructor for the foolish, and a teacher for the ignorant. You are certain that in the Law you have the full content of knowledge and of truth. ²¹You teach others — why don't you teach yourself? You preach, "Do not steal" — but do you yourself steal? ²²You say, "Do not commit adultery" — but do you commit adultery? You detest idols — but do you rob temples? ²³You boast about having God's law — but do you bring shame on God by breaking his law? ²⁴The scripture says, "Because of you Jews, the Gentiles speak evil of God."

²⁵If you obey the Law, your circumcision is of value; but if you disobey the Law, you might as well never have been circumcised. ²⁶If the Gentile, who is not circumcised, obeys the commands of the Law, will God not regard him as though he were circumcised? ²⁷And so you Jews will be condemned by the Gentiles because you break the Law, even though you have it written down and are circumcised; but they obey the Law, even though they are not physically circumcised. ²⁸After all, who is a real Jew, truly circumcised? It is not the man who is a Jew on the outside, whose circumcision is a physical thing. ²⁹Rather, the real Jew is the person who is a Jew on the inside, that is, whose heart has been circumcised, and this is the work of God's Spirit, not of the written Law. Such a person receives praise from God, not from human beings.

3 Have the Jews then any advantage over the Gentiles? Or is there any value in being circumcised? ²Much, indeed, in every way! In the first place, God trusted his message to the Jews. ³But what if some of them were not faithful? Does this mean that God will not be faithful? ⁴Certainly not! God must be true, even though every human being is a liar. As the scripture says,

"You must be shown to be right when you speak;
   you must win your case when you are being tried."

⁵But what if our doing wrong serves to show up more clearly God's doing right? Can we say that God does wrong when he punishes us? (This would be the natural question to ask.) ⁶By no means! If God is not just, how can he judge the world? ⁷But what if my untruth serves God's glory by making his truth stand out more clearly? Why should I still be condemned as a sinner? ⁸Why not say, then, "Let us do evil so that good may come"? Some people, indeed, have insulted me by accusing me of saying this very thing! They will be condemned, as they should be.

No one is Righteous

⁹Well then, are we Jews in any better condition than the Gentiles? Not at all!* I have already shown that Jews and Gentiles alike are all under the power of sin. ¹⁰As the Scriptures say:

"There is no one who is righteous,
¹¹   no one who is wise
      or who worships God.

3.9 *any better condition than the Gentiles? Not at all!*; or *any worse condition than the Gentiles? Not altogether.*

1336

Romans

Matt.
Mark
Luke
John
Acts

ROMANS 3, 4

12 All have turned away from God;
  they have all gone wrong;
  no one does what is right, not even one.
13 Their words are full of deadly deceit;
  wicked lies roll off their tongues,
  and dangerous threats, like snake's poison, from their
    lips;
14   their speech is filled with bitter curses.
15 They are quick to hurt and kill;
16   they leave ruin and destruction wherever they go.
17 They have not known the path of peace,
18   nor have they learnt reverence for God."
19 Now we know that everything in the Law applies to those who live under the Law, in order to stop all human excuses and bring the whole world under God's judgement. 20 For no one is put right in God's sight by doing what the Law requires; what the Law does is to make people know that they have sinned.

How We are Put Right with God

21 But now God's way of putting people right with himself has been revealed. It has nothing to do with law, even though the Law of Moses and the prophets gave their witness to it. 22 God puts people right through their faith in Jesus Christ. God does this to all who believe in Christ, because there is no difference at all: 23 everyone has sinned and is far away from God's saving presence. 24 But by the free gift of God's grace all are put right with him through Christ Jesus, who sets them free. 25-26 God offered him, so that by his blood* he should become the means by which people's sins are forgiven through their faith in him. God did this in order to demonstrate that he is righteous. In the past he was patient and overlooked people's sins; but in the present time he deals with their sins, in order to demonstrate his righteousness. In this way God shows that he himself is righteous and that he puts right everyone who believes in Jesus.

27 What, then, can we boast about? Nothing! And what is the reason for this? Is it that we obey the Law? No, but that we believe. 28 For we conclude that a person is put right with God only through faith, and not by doing what the Law commands. 29 Or is God the God of the Jews only? Is he not the God of the Gentiles also? Of course he is. 30 God is one, and he will put the Jews right with himself on the basis of their faith, and will put the Gentiles right through their faith. 31 Does this mean that by this faith we do away with the Law? No, not at all; instead, we uphold the Law.

The Example of Abraham

4 What shall we say, then, of Abraham, the father of our race? What was his experience? 2 If he was put right with God by the things he did, he would have something to boast about — but not in God's sight. 3 The scripture says, "Abraham believed God, and because of his faith God accepted him as righteous." 4 Those who work are paid wages, but they are not regarded as a gift; they are something that has been earned. 5 But those who depend on faith, not on deeds, and who believe in the God who declares the guilty to be innocent, it is this faith that God takes into account in order to put them right with himself. 6 This is what David meant when he spoke of the happiness of the person whom God accepts as righteous, apart from anything that person does:

3.25–26 *by his blood*; or *by his sacrificial death*.

ROMANS 3.21-26

DRAW
- A -
TARGET

on this page. Stand over the page and try to drop your pen so that ink hits the target. We all miss the mark sometimes - but Jesus hit the bull's eye with his life, death and resurrection, and God allows his achievement to count for all of us too. What do you think this says about his nature?

ROMANS 4, 5

1337

Romans
..........⋮.

1 Corin.
2 Corin.
Galat.
Ephes.
Philipp.

7 "Happy are those whose wrongs are forgiven,
   whose sins are pardoned!
8 Happy is the person whose sins the Lord will not keep
   account of!"
9 Does this happiness that David spoke of belong only to those who are circumcised? No indeed! It belongs also to those who are not circumcised. For we have quoted the scripture, "Abraham believed God, and because of his faith God accepted him as righteous." 10 When did this take place? Was it before or after Abraham was circumcised? It was before, not after. 11 He was circumcised later, and his circumcision was a sign to show that because of his faith God had accepted him as righteous before he had been circumcised. And so Abraham is the spiritual father of all who believe in God and are accepted as righteous by him, even though they are not circumcised. 12 He is also the father of those who are circumcised, that is, of those who, in addition to being circumcised, also live the same life of faith that our father Abraham lived before he was circumcised.

God's Promise is Received through Faith

13 When God promised Abraham and his descendants that the world would belong to him, he did so, not because Abraham obeyed the Law, but because he believed and was accepted as righteous by God. 14 For if what God promises is to be given to those who obey the Law, then faith means nothing and God's promise is worthless. 15 The Law brings down God's anger; but where there is no law, there is no disobeying of the law.

16 And so the promise was based on faith, in order that the promise should be guaranteed as God's free gift to all of Abraham's descendants — not just to those who obey the Law, but also to those who believe as Abraham did. For Abraham is the spiritual father of us all; 17 as the scripture says, "I have made you father of many nations." So the promise is good in the sight of God, in whom Abraham believed — the God who brings the dead to life and whose command brings into being what did not exist. 18 Abraham believed and hoped, even when there was no reason for hoping, and so became "the father of many nations." Just as the scripture says, "Your descendants will be as many as the stars." 19 He was then almost 100 years old; but his faith did not weaken when he thought of his body, which was already practically dead, or of the fact that Sarah could not have children. 20 His faith did not leave him, and he did not doubt God's promise; his faith filled him with power, and he gave praise to God. 21 He was absolutely sure that God would be able to do what he had promised. 22 That is why Abraham, through faith, "was accepted as righteous by God". 23 The words "he was accepted as righteous" were not written for him alone. 24 They were written also for us who are to be accepted as righteous, who believe in him who raised Jesus our Lord from death. 25 Because of our sins he was handed over to die, and he was raised to life in order to put us right with God.

Right with God

5 Now that we have been put right with God through faith, we have* peace with God through our Lord Jesus Christ. 2 He has brought us by faith into this experience of God's grace, in which we now live. And so we boast* of the hope we have of sharing

WHAT DOES 'GRACE' MEAN?
Finish the mindmap below.

Approval or kindness, especially (in the Christian religion) that is freely given by God to all humans. (dictionary.cambridge.org)

↖

GRACE

ACTS 14.3; ROMANS 5.2; JUDE v.4

5.1 *we have*; some manuscripts have *let us have*.
5.2 *we boast*; or *let us boast*.

1338

Romans

:·········

Matt.
Mark
Luke
John
Acts

God's glory! ³We also boast* of our troubles, because we know that trouble produces endurance, ⁴endurance brings God's approval, and his approval creates hope. ⁵This hope does not disappoint us, for God has poured out his love into our hearts by means of the Holy Spirit, who is God's gift to us.

⁶For when we were still helpless, Christ died for the wicked at the time that God chose. ⁷It is a difficult thing for someone to die for a righteous person. It may even be that someone might dare to die for a good person. ⁸But God has shown us how much he loves us — it was while we were still sinners that Christ died for us! ⁹By his blood* we are now put right with God; how much more, then, will we be saved by him from God's anger! ¹⁰We were God's enemies, but he made us his friends through the death of his Son. Now that we are God's friends, how much more will we be saved by Christ's life! ¹¹But that is not all; we rejoice because of what God has done through our Lord Jesus Christ, who has now made us God's friends.

Adam and Christ

¹²Sin came into the world through one man, and his sin brought death with it. As a result, death has spread to the whole human race because everyone has sinned. ¹³There was sin in the world before the Law was given; but where there is no law, no account is kept of sins. ¹⁴But from the time of Adam to the time of Moses death ruled over the whole human race, even over those who did not sin in the same way that Adam did when he disobeyed God's command.

Adam was a figure of the one who was to come. ¹⁵But the two are not the same, because God's free gift is not like Adam's sin. It is true that many people died because of the sin of that one man. But God's grace is much greater, and so is his free gift to so many people through the grace of the one man, Jesus Christ. ¹⁶And there is a difference between God's gift and the sin of one man. After the one sin, came the judgement of "Guilty"; but after so many sins, comes the undeserved gift of "Not guilty!" ¹⁷It is true that through the sin of one man death began to rule because of that one man. But how much greater is the result of what was done by the one man, Jesus Christ! All who receive God's abundant grace and are freely put right with him will rule in life through Christ.

¹⁸So then, as the one sin condemned all people, in the same way the one righteous act sets all people free and gives them life. ¹⁹And just as the mass of people were made sinners as the result of the disobedience of one man, in the same way the mass of people will all be put right with God as the result of the obedience of the one man.

²⁰Law was introduced in order to increase wrongdoing; but where sin increased, God's grace increased much more. ²¹So then, just as sin ruled by means of death, so also God's grace rules by means of righteousness, leading us to eternal life through Jesus Christ our Lord.

Dead to Sin but Alive in Union with Christ

6 What shall we say, then? Should we continue to live in sin so that God's grace will increase? ²Certainly not! We have died to sin — how then can we go on living in it? ³For surely you

---

WHAT DOES 'SIN' MEAN?
Finish the mindmap below.

The offence of
breaking, or
the breaking of,
a religious
or moral law
(dictionary.cambridge.org)

SIN

ROMANS 5.12; 1 JOHN 5.17

5.3 *We also boast*; or *Let us also boast*.
5.9 *By his blood*; or *By his sacrificial death*.

Romans

. . . .:

1 Corin.

2 Corin.

Galat.

Ephes.

Philipp.

know that when we were baptized into union with Christ Jesus, we were baptized into union with his death. [4]By our baptism, then, we were buried with him and shared his death, in order that, just as Christ was raised from death by the glorious power of the Father, so also we might live a new life.

[5]For since we have become one with him in dying as he did, in the same way we shall be one with him by being raised to life as he was. [6]And we know that our old being has been put to death with Christ on his cross, in order that the power of the sinful self might be destroyed, so that we should no longer be the slaves of sin. [7]For when people die, they are set free from the power of sin. [8]Since we have died with Christ, we believe that we will also live with him. [9]For we know that Christ has been raised from death and will never die again — death will no longer rule over him. [10]And so, because he died, sin has no power over him; and now he lives his life in fellowship with God. [11]In the same way you are to think of yourselves as dead, so far as sin is concerned, but living in fellowship with God through Christ Jesus.

[12]Sin must no longer rule in your mortal bodies, so that you obey the desires of your natural self. [13]Nor must you surrender any part of yourselves to sin to be used for wicked purposes. Instead, give yourselves to God, as those who have been brought from death to life, and surrender your whole being to him to be used for righteous purposes. [14]Sin must not be your master; for you do not live under law but under God's grace.

Slaves of Righteousness

[15]What, then? Shall we sin, because we are not under law but under God's grace? By no means! [16]Surely you know that when you surrender yourselves as slaves to obey someone, you are in fact the slaves of the master you obey — either of sin, which results in death, or of obedience, which results in being put right with God. [17]But thanks be to God! For though at one time you were slaves to sin, you have obeyed with all your heart the truths found in the teaching you received. [18]You were set free from sin and became the slaves of righteousness. [19](I use everyday language because of the weakness of your natural selves.) At one time you surrendered yourselves entirely as slaves to impurity and wickedness for wicked purposes. In the same way you must now surrender yourselves entirely as slaves of righteousness for holy purposes.

[20]When you were the slaves of sin, you were free from righteousness. [21]What did you gain from doing the things that you are now ashamed of? The result of those things is death! [22]But now you have been set free from sin and are the slaves of God. Your gain is a life fully dedicated to him, and the result is eternal life. [23]For sin pays its wage — death; but God's free gift is eternal life in union with Christ Jesus our Lord.

An Illustration from Marriage

7 Certainly you will understand what I am about to say, my brothers and sisters, because all of you know about law. The law rules over people only as long as they live. [2]A married woman, for example, is bound by the law to her husband as long as he lives; but if he dies, then she is free from the law that bound her to him. [3]So then, if she lives with another man while her husband is alive, she will be called an adulteress; but if her husband dies, she is legally a free woman and does not commit adultery if she marries another man. [4]That is how it is with you, my sisters

1340

Romans

Matt.
Mark
Luke
John
Acts

ROMANS 7, 8

and brothers. As far as the Law is concerned, you also have died because you are part of the body of Christ; and now you belong to him who was raised from death in order that we might be useful in the service of God. [5] For when we lived according to our human nature, the sinful desires stirred up by the Law were at work in our bodies, and all we did ended in death. [6] Now, however, we are free from the Law, because we died to that which once held us prisoners. No longer do we serve in the old way of a written law, but in the new way of the Spirit.

Law and Sin

[7] Shall we say, then, that the Law itself is sinful? Of course not! But it was the Law that made me know what sin is. If the Law had not said, "Do not desire what belongs to someone else," I would not have known such a desire. [8] But by means of that commandment sin found its chance to stir up all kinds of selfish desires in me. Apart from law, sin is a dead thing. [9] I myself was once alive apart from law; but when the commandment came, sin sprang to life, [10] and I died. And the commandment which was meant to bring life, in my case brought death. [11] Sin found its chance, and by means of the commandment it deceived me and killed me.

[12] So then, the Law itself is holy, and the commandment is holy, right, and good. [13] But does this mean that what is good caused my death? By no means! It was sin that did it; by using what is good, sin brought death to me, in order that its true nature as sin might be revealed. And so, by means of the commandment sin is shown to be even more terribly sinful.

The Conflict within Us

[14] We know that the Law is spiritual; but I am unspiritual, sold as a slave to sin. [15] I do not understand what I do; for I don't do what I would like to do, but instead I do what I hate. [16] Since what I do is what I don't want to do, this shows that I agree that the Law is right. [17] So I am not really the one who does this thing; rather it is the sin that lives in me. [18] I know that good does not live in me — that is, in my human nature. For even though the desire to do good is in me, I am not able to do it. [19] I don't do the good I want to do; instead, I do the evil that I do not want to do. [20] If I do what I don't want to do, this means that I am no longer the one who does it; instead, it is the sin that lives in me.

[21] So I find that this law is at work: when I want to do what is good, what is evil is the only choice I have. [22] My inner being delights in the law of God. [23] But I see a different law at work in my body — a law that fights against the law which my mind approves of. It makes me a prisoner to the law of sin which is at work in my body. [24] What an unhappy man I am! Who will rescue me from this body that is taking me to death? [25] Thanks be to God, who does this through our Lord Jesus Christ!

This, then, is my condition: on my own I can serve God's law only with my mind, while my human nature serves the law of sin.

Life in the Spirit

8 There is no condemnation now for those who live in union with Christ Jesus. [2] For the law of the Spirit, which brings us life in union with Christ Jesus, has set me* free from the law of sin and death. [3] What the Law could not do, because human nature was

---

8.2 *me*; some manuscripts have *you*; others have *us*.

ROMANS 8.1

{ NO }

CONDEMNATION

ROMANS 8

Romans

1 Corin.
2 Corin.
Galat.
Ephes.
Philipp.

weak, God did. He condemned sin in human nature by sending his own Son, who came with a nature like sinful human nature, to do away with sin. [4] God did this so that the righteous demands of the Law might be fully satisfied in us who live according to the Spirit, and not according to human nature. [5] Those who live as their human nature tells them to, have their minds controlled by what human nature wants. Those who live as the Spirit tells them to, have their minds controlled by what the Spirit wants. [6] To be controlled by human nature results in death; to be controlled by the Spirit results in life and peace. [7] And so people become enemies of God when they are controlled by their human nature; for they do not obey God's law, and in fact they cannot obey it. [8] Those who obey their human nature cannot please God.

[9] But you do not live as your human nature tells you to; instead, you live as the Spirit tells you to — if, in fact, God's Spirit lives in you. Whoever does not have the Spirit of Christ does not belong to him. [10] But if Christ lives in you, the Spirit is life for you* because you have been put right with God, even though your bodies are going to die because of sin. [11] If the Spirit of God, who raised Jesus from death, lives in you, then he who raised Christ from death will also give life to your mortal bodies by the presence of his Spirit in you.

[12] So then, my brothers and sisters, we have an obligation, but it is not to live as our human nature wants us to. [13] For if you live according to your human nature, you are going to die; but if by the Spirit you put to death your sinful actions, you will live. [14] Those who are led by God's Spirit are God's children. [15] For the Spirit that God has given you does not make you slaves and cause you to be afraid; instead, the Spirit makes you God's children, and by the Spirit's power we cry out to God, "Father! my Father!" [16] God's Spirit joins himself to our spirits to declare that we are God's children. [17] Since we are his children, we will possess the blessings he keeps for his people, and we will also possess with Christ what God has kept for him; for if we share Christ's suffering, we will also share his glory.

The Future Glory

[18] I consider that what we suffer at this present time cannot be compared at all with the glory that is going to be revealed to us. [19] All of creation waits with eager longing for God to reveal his children. [20] For creation was condemned to lose its purpose, not of its own will, but because God willed it to be so. Yet there was the hope [21] that creation itself would one day be set free from its slavery to decay and would share the glorious freedom of the children of God. [22] For we know that up to the present time all of creation groans with pain, like the pain of childbirth. [23] But it is not just creation alone which groans; we who have the Spirit as the first of God's gifts also groan within ourselves, as we wait for God to make us his children and* set our whole being free. [24] For it was by hope that we were saved; but if we see what we hope for, then it is not really hope. For which of us hopes for something we see? [25] But if we hope for what we do not see, we wait for it with patience.

[26] In the same way the Spirit also comes to help us, weak as we are. For we do not know how we ought to pray; the Spirit himself pleads with God for us in groans that words cannot express.

8.10 *the Spirit is life for you*; or *your spirit is alive.*
8.23 Some manuscripts do not have *make us his children and.*

UNDERLINE
THE VERSES
in Romans 8 that say what the Spirit does. Pray and ask God to fill you with His Spirit... then wait and spend some time focusing on God.

1342

Romans

Matt.
Mark
Luke
John
Acts

ROMANS 8, 9

27 And God, who sees into our hearts, knows what the thought of the Spirit is; because the Spirit pleads with God on behalf of his people and in accordance with his will. 28 We know that in all things God works for good with those who love him,* those whom he has called according to his purpose. 29 Those whom God had already chosen he also set apart to become like his Son, so that the Son would be the eldest brother in a large family. 30 And so those whom God set apart, he called; and those he called, he put right with himself, and he shared his glory with them.

God's Love in Christ Jesus

31 In view of all this, what can we say? If God is for us, who can be against us? 32 Certainly not God, who did not even keep back his own Son, but offered him for us all! He gave us his Son — will he not also freely give us all things? 33 Who will accuse God's chosen people? God himself declares them not guilty! 34 Who, then, will condemn them? Not Christ Jesus, who died, or rather, who was raised to life and is at the right-hand side of God, pleading with him for us! 35 Who, then, can separate us from the love of Christ? Can trouble do it, or hardship or persecution or hunger or poverty or danger or death? 36 As the scripture says,

"For your sake we are in danger of death at all times;
we are treated like sheep that are going to be
slaughtered."

37 No, in all these things we have complete victory through him who loved us! 38 For I am certain that nothing can separate us from his love: neither death nor life, neither angels nor other heavenly rulers or powers, neither the present nor the future, 39 neither the world above nor the world below — there is nothing in all creation that will ever be able to separate us from the love of God which is ours through Christ Jesus our Lord.

God and his People

9 I am speaking the truth; I belong to Christ and I do not lie. My conscience, ruled by the Holy Spirit, also assures me that I am not lying 2 when I say how great is my sorrow, how endless the pain in my heart 3 for my people, my own flesh and blood! For their sake I could wish that I myself were under God's curse and separated from Christ. 4 They are God's people; he made them his children and revealed his glory to them; he made his covenants* with them and gave them the Law; they have the true worship; they have received God's promises; 5 they are descended from the famous Hebrew ancestors; and Christ, as a human being, belongs to their race. May God, who rules over all, be praised for ever!* Amen.

6 I am not saying that the promise of God has failed; for not all the people of Israel are the people of God. 7 Nor are all Abraham's descendants the children of God. God said to Abraham, "It is through Isaac that you will have the descendants I promised you." 8 This means that the children born in the usual way* are not the children of God; instead, the children born as a result of

....

8.28 *in all things God works for good with those who love him*; some manuscripts have *all things work for good for those who love God*.
9.4 *covenants*; some manuscripts have *covenant*.
9.5 *May God, who rules over all, be praised for ever!*; or *And may he, who is God ruling over all, be praised for ever!*
9.8 *children born in the usual way*: This refers to the descendants Abraham had through Ishmael, his son by Hagar (see Gal 4.22–23).

ROMANS 9

1343

Romans

..........:.

1 Corin.
2 Corin.
Galat.
Ephes.
Philipp.

God's promise are regarded as the true descendants. ⁹For God's promise was made in these words: "At the right time* I will come back, and Sarah will have a son."

¹⁰And this is not all. For Rebecca's two sons had the same father, our ancestor Isaac. ¹¹⁻¹²But in order that the choice of one son might be completely the result of God's own purpose, God said to her, "The elder will serve the younger." He said this before they were born, before they had done anything either good or bad; so God's choice was based on his call, and not on anything they had done. ¹³As the scripture says, "I loved Jacob, but I hated Esau."

¹⁴Shall we say, then, that God is unjust? Not at all. ¹⁵For he said to Moses, "I will have mercy on anyone I wish; I will take pity on anyone I wish." ¹⁶So then, everything depends, not on what human beings want or do, but only on God's mercy. ¹⁷For the scripture says to the king of Egypt, "I made you king in order to use you to show my power and to spread my fame over the whole world." ¹⁸So then, God has mercy on anyone he wishes, and he makes stubborn anyone he wishes.

God's Anger and Mercy

¹⁹But one of you will say to me, "If this is so, how can God find fault with anyone? Who can resist God's will?" ²⁰But who are you, my friend, to answer God back? A clay pot does not ask the man who made it, "Why did you make me like this?" ²¹After all, the man who makes the pots has the right to use the clay as he wishes, and to make two pots from the same lump of clay, one for special occasions and the other for ordinary use.

²²And the same is true of what God has done. He wanted to show his anger and to make his power known. But he was very patient in enduring those who were the objects of his anger, who were doomed to destruction. ²³And he also wanted to reveal his abundant glory, which was poured out on us who are the objects of his mercy, those of us whom he has prepared to receive his glory. ²⁴For we are the people he called, not only from among the Jews but also from among the Gentiles. ²⁵This is what he says in the book of Hosea:

"The people who were not mine
    I will call 'My People'.
The nation that I did not love
    I will call 'My Beloved'.
²⁶ And in the very place where they were told, 'You are not
        my people,'
    there they will be called the children of the living God."
²⁷And Isaiah exclaims about Israel: "Even if the people of Israel are as many as the grains of sand by the sea, yet only a few of them will be saved; ²⁸for the Lord will quickly settle his full account with the world." ²⁹It is as Isaiah had said before, "If the Lord Almighty had not left us some descendants, we would have become like Sodom, we would have been like Gomorrah."

Paul's Prayer for Israel

³⁰So we say that the Gentiles, who were not trying to put themselves right with God, were put right with him through faith; ³¹while God's people, who were seeking a law that would put them right with God, did not find it. ³²And why not? Because they did not depend on faith but on what they did. And so they stumbled over the "stumbling stone" ³³that the scripture speaks of:

....

9.9 *At the right time*; or *At this time next year.*

1344

Romans

·:········

Matt.
Mark
Luke
John
Acts

ROMANS 9–11

"Look, I place in Zion a stone
that will make people stumble,
a rock that will make them fall.
But whoever believes in him will not be disappointed."

10 My brothers and sisters, how I wish with all my heart that my own people might be saved! How I pray to God for them! [2] I can assure you that they are deeply devoted to God; but their devotion is not based on true knowledge. [3] They have not known the way in which God puts people right with himself, and instead, they have tried to set up their own way; and so they did not submit themselves to God's way of putting people right. [4] For Christ has brought the Law to an end, so that everyone who believes is put right with God.

Salvation is for All

[5] Moses wrote this about being put right with God by obeying the Law: "Whoever obeys the commands of the Law will live." [6] But what the scripture says about being put right with God through faith is this: "You are not to ask yourself, Who will go up into heaven?" (that is, to bring Christ down). [7] "Nor are you to ask, Who will go down into the world below?" (that is, to bring Christ up from death). [8] What it says is this: "God's message is near you, on your lips and in your heart" — that is, the message of faith that we preach. [9] If you confess that Jesus is Lord and believe that God raised him from death, you will be saved. [10] For it is by our faith that we are put right with God; it is by our confession that we are saved. [11] The scripture says, "Whoever believes in him will not be disappointed." [12] This includes everyone, because there is no difference between Jews and Gentiles; God is the same Lord of all and richly blesses all who call to him. [13] As the scripture says, "Everyone who calls out to the Lord for help will be saved."

[14] But how can they call to him for help if they have not believed? And how can they believe if they have not heard the message? And how can they hear if the message is not proclaimed? [15] And how can the message be proclaimed if the messengers are not sent out? As the scripture says, "How wonderful is the coming of messengers who bring good news!" [16] But not all have accepted the Good News. Isaiah himself said, "Lord, who has believed our message?" [17] So then, faith comes from hearing the message, and the message comes through preaching Christ.

[18] But I ask: is it true that they did not hear the message? Of course they did — for as the scripture says:

"The sound of their voice went out to all the world;
their words reached the ends of the earth."

[19] Again I ask: did the people of Israel not understand? Moses himself is the first one to answer:

"I will use a so-called nation
to make my people jealous;
and by means of a nation of fools
I will make my people angry."

[20] And Isaiah is even bolder when he says,

"I was found by those who were not looking for me;
I appeared to those who were not asking for me."

[21] But concerning Israel he says, "All day long I held out my hands to welcome a disobedient and rebellious people."

God's Mercy on Israel

11 I ask, then: did God reject his own people? Certainly not! I myself am an Israelite, a descendant of Abraham,

1345

Romans

···········⋮

1 Corin.
2 Corin.
Galat.
Ephes.
Philipp.

a member of the tribe of Benjamin. [2] God has not rejected his people, whom he chose from the beginning. You know what the scripture says in the passage where Elijah pleads with God against Israel: [3] "Lord, they have killed your prophets and torn down your altars; I am the only one left, and they are trying to kill me." [4] What answer did God give him? "I have kept for myself 7,000 men who have not worshipped the false god Baal." [5] It is the same way now: there is a small number left of those whom God has chosen because of his grace. [6] His choice is based on his grace, not on what they have done. For if God's choice were based on what people do, then his grace would not be real grace.

[7] What then? The people of Israel did not find what they were looking for. It was only the small group that God chose who found it; the rest grew deaf to God's call. [8] As the scripture says, "God made their minds and hearts dull; to this very day they cannot see or hear." [9] And David says:

"May they be caught and trapped at their feasts;
may they fall, may they be punished!
[10] May their eyes be blinded so that they cannot see;
and make them bend under their troubles at all times."

[11] I ask, then: when the Jews stumbled, did they fall to their ruin? By no means! Because they sinned, salvation has come to the Gentiles, to make the Jews jealous of them. [12] The sin of the Jews brought rich blessings to the world, and their spiritual poverty brought rich blessings to the Gentiles. Then, how much greater the blessings will be when the complete number of Jews is included!

The Salvation of the Gentiles

[13] I am speaking now to you Gentiles: as long as I am an apostle to the Gentiles, I will take pride in my work. [14] Perhaps I can make the people of my own race jealous, and so be able to save some of them. [15] For when they were rejected, the human race was changed from God's enemies into his friends. What will it be, then, when they are accepted? It will be life for the dead!

[16] If the first piece of bread is given to God, then the whole loaf is his also; and if the roots of a tree are offered to God, the branches are his also. [17] Some of the branches of the cultivated olive tree have been broken off, and a branch of a wild olive tree has been joined to it. You Gentiles are like that wild olive tree, and now you share the strong spiritual life of the Jews. [18] So then, you must not despise those who were broken off like branches. How can you be proud? You are just a branch; you don't support the roots — the roots support you.

[19] But you will say, "Yes, but the branches were broken off to make room for me." [20] That is true. They were broken off because they did not believe, while you remain in place because you do believe. But do not be proud of it; instead, be afraid. [21] God did not spare the Jews, who are like natural branches; do you think he will spare you? [22] Here we see how kind and how severe God is. He is severe towards those who have fallen, but kind to you — if you continue in his kindness. But if you do not, you too will be broken off. [23] And if the Jews abandon their unbelief, they will be put back in the place where they were; for God is able to do that. [24] You Gentiles are like the branch of a wild olive tree that is broken off and then, contrary to nature, is joined to a cultivated olive tree. The Jews are like this cultivated tree; and it will be much easier for God to join these broken-off branches to their own tree again.

1346

Romans

. . . .

Matt.
Mark
Luke
John
Acts

ROMANS 11, 12

God's Mercy on All

25 There is a secret truth, my brothers and sisters, which I want you to know, for it will keep you from thinking how wise you are. It is that the stubbornness of the people of Israel is not permanent, but will last only until the complete number of Gentiles comes to God. 26 And this is how all Israel will be saved. As the scripture says:

"The Saviour will come from Zion
    and remove all wickedness from the descendants of Jacob.
27 I will make this covenant with them
    when I take away their sins."

28 Because they reject the Good News, the Jews are God's enemies for the sake of you Gentiles. But because of God's choice, they are his friends because of their ancestors. 29 For God does not change his mind about whom he chooses and blesses. 30 As for you Gentiles, you disobeyed God in the past; but now you have received God's mercy because the Jews were disobedient. 31 In the same way, because of the mercy that you have received, the Jews now disobey God, in order that they also may now* receive God's mercy. 32 For God has made all people prisoners of disobedience, so that he might show mercy to them all.

Praise to God

33 How great are God's riches! How deep are his wisdom and knowledge! Who can explain his decisions? Who can understand his ways? 34 As the scripture says:

"Who knows the mind of the Lord?
    Who is able to give him advice?
35 Who has ever given him anything,
    so that he had to pay it back?"

36 For all things were created by him, and all things exist through him and for him. To God be the glory for ever! Amen.

Life in God's Service

12 So then, my brothers and sisters, because of God's great mercy to us I appeal to you: offer yourselves as a living sacrifice to God, dedicated to his service and pleasing to him. This is the true worship that you should offer. 2 Do not conform yourselves to the standards of this world, but let God transform you inwardly by a complete change of your mind. Then you will be able to know the will of God — what is good and is pleasing to him and is perfect.

3 And because of God's gracious gift to me I say to every one of you: do not think of yourself more highly than you should. Instead, be modest in your thinking, and judge yourself according to the amount of faith that God has given you. 4 We have many parts in the one body, and all these parts have different functions. 5 In the same way, though we are many, we are one body in union with Christ, and we are all joined to each other as different parts of one body. 6 So we are to use our different gifts in accordance with the grace that God has given us. If our gift is to speak God's message, we should do it according to the faith that we have; 7 if it is to serve, we should serve; if it is to teach, we should teach; 8 if it is to encourage others, we should do so. Whoever shares with others should do it generously; whoever has authority should work hard; whoever shows kindness to others should do it cheerfully.

9 Love must be completely sincere. Hate what is evil, hold on to what is good. 10 Love one another warmly as Christian brothers and sisters, and be eager to show respect for one another. 11 Work hard

....

11.31 Some manuscripts do not have *now*.

ROMANS 12, 13

1347

Romans

1 Corin.
2 Corin.
Galat.
Ephes.
Philipp.

and do not be lazy. Serve the Lord with a heart full of devotion. [12] Let your hope keep you joyful, be patient in your troubles, and pray at all times. [13] Share your belongings with your needy fellow-Christians, and open your homes to strangers.

[14] Ask God to bless those who persecute you — yes, ask him to bless, not to curse. [15] Be happy with those who are happy, weep with those who weep. [16] Have the same concern for everyone. Do not be proud, but accept humble duties.* Do not think of yourselves as wise.

[17] If someone has done you wrong, do not repay him with a wrong. Try to do what everyone considers to be good. [18] Do everything possible on your part to live in peace with everybody. [19] Never take revenge, my friends, but instead let God's anger do it. For the scripture says, "I will take revenge, I will pay back, says the Lord." [20] Instead, as the scripture says: "If your enemies are hungry, feed them; if they are thirsty, give them a drink; for by doing this you will make them burn with shame." [21] Do not let evil defeat you; instead, conquer evil with good.

Duties towards the State Authorities

13 Everyone must obey the state authorities, because no authority exists without God's permission, and the existing authorities have been put there by God. [2] Whoever opposes the existing authority opposes what God has ordered; and anyone who does so will bring judgement on himself. [3] For rulers are not to be feared by those who do good, but by those who do evil. Would you like to be unafraid of those in authority? Then do what is good, and they will praise you, [4] because they are God's servants working for your own good. But if you do evil, then be afraid of them, because their power to punish is real. They are God's servants and carry out God's punishment on those who do evil. [5] For this reason you must obey the authorities — not just because of God's punishment, but also as a matter of conscience. [6] That is also why you pay taxes, because the authorities are working for God when they fulfil their duties. [7] Pay, then, what you owe them; pay them your personal and property taxes, and show respect and honour for them all.

Duties towards One Another

[8] Be under obligation to no one — the only obligation you have is to love one another. Whoever does this has obeyed the Law. [9] The commandments, "Do not commit adultery; do not commit murder; do not steal; do not desire what belongs to someone else" — all these, and any others besides, are summed up in the one command, "Love your neighbour as you love yourself." [10] If you love someone, you will never do them wrong; to love, then, is to obey the whole Law.

[11] You must do this, because you know that the time has come for you to wake up from your sleep. For the moment when we will be saved is closer now than it was when we first believed. [12] The night is nearly over, day is almost here. Let us stop doing the things that belong to the dark, and let us take up weapons for fighting in the light. [13] Let us conduct ourselves properly, as people who live in the light of day — no orgies or drunkenness, no immorality or indecency, no fighting or jealousy. [14] But take up the weapons of the Lord Jesus Christ, and stop paying attention to your sinful nature and satisfying its desires.

12.16 *accept humble duties*; or *make friends with humble people.*

ROMANS 13.1-7

Make a list of everyone in authority over you (family members, teachers, politicians) and pray for them - whether you

LIKE THEM

OR NOT.

Read Romans 12.9-21 and, with this passage in mind, next time you get a chance, take a moment to chat to them or send them a message to tell them what they are doing well.

1348

Romans

·:·········

Matt.
Mark
Luke
John
Acts

ROMANS 14

Do not Judge One Another

14 Welcome those who are weak in faith, but do not argue with them about their personal opinions. [2]Some people's faith allows them to eat anything, but the person who is weak in the faith eats only vegetables. [3]Those who will eat anything are not to despise those who don't; while those who eat only vegetables are not to pass judgement on those who will eat anything; for God has accepted them. [4]Who are you to judge someone else's servants? It is their own Master who will decide whether they succeed or fail. And they will succeed, because the Lord is able to make them succeed.

[5]Some people think that a certain day is more important than other days, while others think that all days are the same. We should each firmly make up our own minds. [6]Those who think highly of a certain day do so in honour of the Lord; those who will eat anything do so in honour of the Lord, because they give thanks to God for the food. Those who refuse to eat certain things do so in honour of the Lord, and they give thanks to God. [7]None of us lives for himself only, none of us dies for himself only. [8]If we live, it is for the Lord that we live, and if we die, it is for the Lord that we die. So whether we live or die, we belong to the Lord. [9]For Christ died and rose to life in order to be the Lord of the living and of the dead. [10]You then, who eat only vegetables — why do you pass judgement on others? And you who eat anything — why do you despise other believers? All of us will stand before God to be judged by him. [11]For the scripture says:

"As surely as I am the living God, says the Lord,
   everyone will kneel before me,
   and everyone will confess that I am God."

[12]Every one of us, then, will have to give an account of ourselves to God.

Do not Make One Another Fall

[13]So then, let us stop judging one another. Instead, you should decide never to do anything that would make another stumble or fall into sin. [14]My union with the Lord Jesus makes me certain that no food is of itself ritually unclean; but if a person believes that some food is unclean, then it becomes unclean for that person. [15]If you hurt your brother or sister because of something you eat, then you are no longer acting from love. Do not let the food that you eat ruin the person for whom Christ died! [16]Do not let what you regard as good get a bad name. [17]For God's Kingdom is not a matter of eating and drinking, but of the righteousness, peace, and joy which the Holy Spirit gives. [18]And when people serve Christ in this way, they please God and are approved by others.

[19]So then, we must always aim* at those things that bring peace and that help to strengthen one another. [20]Do not, because of food, destroy what God has done. All foods may be eaten, but it is wrong to eat anything that will cause someone else to fall into sin. [21]The right thing to do is to keep from eating meat, drinking wine, or doing anything else that will make your brother or sister fall. [22]Keep what you believe about this matter, then, between yourself and God. Happy are those who do not feel guilty when they do something they judge is right! [23]But if they have doubts about what they eat, God condemns them when they eat it,

14.19 *we must always aim*; some manuscripts have *we always aim*.

because their action is not based on faith. And anything that is not based on faith is sin.

Please Others, not Yourselves

15 We who are strong in the faith ought to help the weak to carry their burdens. We should not please ourselves. ² Instead, we should all please our brothers and sisters for their own good, in order to build them up in the faith. ³ For Christ did not please himself. Instead, as the scripture says, "The insults which are hurled at you have fallen on me." ⁴ Everything written in the Scriptures was written to teach us, in order that we might have hope through the patience and encouragement which the Scriptures give us. ⁵ And may God, the source of patience and encouragement, enable you to have the same point of view among yourselves by following the example of Christ Jesus, ⁶ so that all of you together may praise with one voice the God and Father of our Lord Jesus Christ.

Good News for the Gentiles

⁷ Accept one another, then, for the glory of God, as Christ has accepted you. ⁸ For I tell you that Christ's life of service was on behalf of the Jews, to show that God is faithful, to make his promises to their ancestors come true, ⁹ and to enable even the Gentiles to praise God for his mercy. As the scripture says:

"And so I will praise you among the Gentiles;
I will sing praises to you."
¹⁰ Again it says,
"Rejoice, Gentiles, with God's people!"
¹¹ And again,
"Praise the Lord, all Gentiles;
praise him, all peoples!"
¹² And again, Isaiah says,
"A descendant of Jesse will appear;
he will come to rule the Gentiles,
and they will put their hope in him."
¹³ May God, the source of hope, fill you with all joy and peace by means of your faith in him, so that your hope will continue to grow by the power of the Holy Spirit.

Paul's Reason for Writing so Boldly

¹⁴ My brothers and sisters, I myself feel sure that you are full of goodness, that you have all knowledge, and that you are able to teach one another. ¹⁵ But in this letter I have been quite bold about certain subjects of which I have reminded you. I have been bold because of the privilege God has given me ¹⁶ of being a servant of Christ Jesus to work for the Gentiles. I serve like a priest in preaching the Good News from God, in order that the Gentiles may be an offering acceptable to God, dedicated to him by the Holy Spirit. ¹⁷ In union with Christ Jesus, then, I can be proud of my service for God. ¹⁸ I will be bold and speak only about what Christ has done through me to lead the Gentiles to obey God. He has done this by means of words and deeds, ¹⁹ by the power of miracles and wonders, and by the power of the Spirit of God. And so, in travelling all the way from Jerusalem to Illyricum, I have proclaimed fully the Good News about Christ. ²⁰ My ambition has always been to proclaim the Good News in places where Christ has not been heard of, so as not to build on a foundation laid by someone else. ²¹ As the scripture says:

1350

Romans

Matt.
Mark
Luke
John
Acts

MAKE A LIST OF
PRAYER REQUESTS
FROM OTHER PEOPLE.

_____

_____

_____

_____

_____

_____

_____

_____

_____

_____

_____

_____

_____

_____

_____

_____

_____

_____

_____

_____

_____

_____

_____

"Those who were not told about him will see,
and those who have not heard will understand."

Paul's Plan to Visit Rome

22 And so I have been prevented many times from coming to you. 23 But now that I have finished my work in these regions and since I have been wanting for so many years to come to see you, 24 I hope to do so now. I would like to see you on my way to Spain, and be helped by you to go there, after I have enjoyed visiting you for a while. 25 Just now, however, I am going to Jerusalem in the service of God's people there. 26 For the churches in Macedonia and Achaia have freely decided to give an offering to help the poor among God's people in Jerusalem. 27 That decision was their own; but, as a matter of fact, they have an obligation to help them. Since the Jews shared their spiritual blessings with the Gentiles, the Gentiles ought to use their material blessings to help the Jews. 28 When I have finished this task and have handed over to them all the money that has been raised for them, I shall leave for Spain and visit you on my way there. 29 When I come to you, I know that I shall come with a full measure of the blessing of Christ.

30 I urge you, brothers and sisters, by our Lord Jesus Christ and by the love that the Spirit gives: join me in praying fervently to God for me. 31 Pray that I may be kept safe from the unbelievers in Judea and that my service in Jerusalem may be acceptable to God's people there. 32 And so I will come to you full of joy, if it is God's will, and enjoy a refreshing visit to you. 33 May God, our source of peace, be with all of you. Amen.

Personal Greetings

16 I recommend to you our sister Phoebe, who serves the church at Cenchreae. 2 Receive her in the Lord's name, as God's people should, and give her any help she may need from you; for she herself has been a good friend to many people and also to me.

3 I send greetings to Priscilla and Aquila, my fellow-workers in the service of Christ Jesus; 4 they risked their lives for me. I am grateful to them — not only I, but all the Gentile churches as well. 5 Greetings also to the church that meets in their house.

Greetings to my dear friend Epaenetus, who was the first in the province of Asia to believe in Christ. 6 Greetings to Mary, who has worked so hard for you. 7 Greetings also to Andronicus and Junia,* fellow-Jews who were in prison with me; they are well known among the apostles, and they became Christians before I did.

8 My greetings to Ampliatus, my dear friend in the fellowship of the Lord. 9 Greetings also to Urbanus, our fellow-worker in Christ's service, and to Stachys, my dear friend. 10 Greetings to Apelles, whose loyalty to Christ has been proved. Greetings to those who belong to the family of Aristobulus. 11 Greetings to Herodion, a fellow-Jew, and to the Christians in the family of Narcissus.

12 My greetings to Tryphaena and Tryphosa, who work in the Lord's service, and to my dear friend Persis, who has done so much work for the Lord. 13 I send greetings to Rufus, that outstanding worker in the Lord's service, and to his mother, who has always treated me like a son. 14 My greetings to Asyncritus, Phlegon, Hermes, Patrobas, Hermas, and all the other Christian brothers and sisters with them. 15 Greetings to Philologus and Julia, to

16.7 *Junia;* or *Junias;* some manuscripts have *Julia.*

Nereus and his sister, to Olympas and to all of God's people who are with them.

¹⁶ Greet one another with a holy kiss. All the churches of Christ send you their greetings.

Final Instructions

¹⁷ I urge you, my brothers and sisters: watch out for those who cause divisions and upset people's faith and go against the teaching which you have received. Keep away from them! ¹⁸ For those who do such things are not serving Christ our Lord, but their own appetites. By their fine words and flattering speech they deceive innocent people. ¹⁹ Everyone has heard of your loyalty to the gospel, and for this reason I am happy about you. I want you to be wise about what is good, but innocent in what is evil. ²⁰ And God, our source of peace, will soon crush Satan under your feet.

The grace of our Lord Jesus be with you.*

²¹ Timothy, my fellow-worker, sends you his greetings; and so do Lucius, Jason, and Sosipater, fellow-Jews.

²² I, Tertius, the writer of this letter, send you Christian greetings.

²³ My host Gaius, in whose house the church meets, sends you his greetings; Erastus, the city treasurer, and our brother Quartus send you their greetings.*

Concluding Prayer of Praise

²⁵ Let us give glory to God! He is able to make you stand firm in your faith, according to the Good News I preach about Jesus Christ and according to the revelation of the secret truth which was hidden for long ages in the past. ²⁶ Now, however, that truth has been brought out into the open through the writings of the prophets; and by the command of the eternal God it is made known to all nations, so that all may believe and obey.

²⁷ To the only God, who alone is all-wise, be glory through Jesus Christ for ever! Amen.*

16.20 Some manuscripts omit this sentence.
16.23 Some manuscripts add verse 24: *The grace of our Lord Jesus Christ be with you all. Amen*; others add this after verse 27.
16.27 Some manuscripts have verses 25–27 here and after 14.23; others have them only after 14.23; one has them after 15.33.

THE LETTER OF
1 CORINTHIANS

WRITTEN: AROUND AD50-54

CREATIVELY WRITE
all the adjectives used to
DESCRIBE 'LOVE'
in chapter 13. Write the ones you most desire in bigger letters.

KEY CHARACTER:

Paul, who wrote this letter and many others in the New Testament, once hated Christians and had them killed. He then met Jesus for himself on the way to Damascus (see Acts chapter 9), and his life completely turned around. He went on to start loads of churches and continued to teach the believers after he left, by writing letters to them. What a turnaround in lifestyle!

WHAT YOU NEED TO KNOW:

This letter is the first of two in our Bible written to the church in Corinth. Corinth was a major Roman city in Greece, with a variety of cultures and religions. It was also well known for its low standards of morality. Paul set up the church in Corinth and, soon afterwards, problems emerged. Some hot topics were being debated and causing division, so Paul wrote to the Corinthians to answer their questions and remind them that love wins out over everything else.

WHY READ IT?

There are some meaty topics covered in this book - topics that can cause division, such as sex and marriage, church, the Holy Spirit and the resurrection. Paul reminds us that the Holy Spirit gives us all sorts of gifts, but that love should always be at the centre.

(AD46)
PAUL STARTS MISSIONARY JOURNEYS

VISITS CORINTH

(AD50-54)
WRITES 1 CORINTHIAN

1 CORINTHIANS 1

1353

1 Corin.

·········

2 Corin.
Galat.
Ephes.
Philipp.
Coloss.

1 From Paul, who was called by the will of God to be an apostle of Christ Jesus, and from our brother Sosthenes —
² To the church of God which is in Corinth, to all who are called to be God's holy people, who belong to him in union with Christ Jesus, together with all people everywhere who worship our Lord Jesus Christ, their Lord and ours:
³ May God our Father and the Lord Jesus Christ give you grace and peace.

Blessings in Christ

⁴ I always give thanks to my God for you because of the grace he has given you through Christ Jesus. ⁵ For in union with Christ you have become rich in all things, including all speech and all knowledge. ⁶ The message about Christ has become so firmly established in you ⁷ that you have not failed to receive a single blessing, as you wait for our Lord Jesus Christ to be revealed. ⁸ He will also keep you firm to the end, so that you will be faultless on the Day of our Lord Jesus Christ. ⁹ God is to be trusted, the God who called you to have fellowship with his Son Jesus Christ, our Lord.

Divisions in the Church

¹⁰ By the authority of our Lord Jesus Christ I appeal to all of you, my brothers and sisters, to agree in what you say, so that there will be no divisions among you. Be completely united, with only one thought and one purpose. ¹¹ For some people from Chloe's family have told me quite plainly, my friends, that there are quarrels among you. ¹² Let me put it this way: each one of you says something different. One says, "I follow Paul"; another, "I follow Apollos"; another, "I follow Peter"; and another, "I follow Christ". ¹³ Christ has been divided* into groups! Was it Paul who died on the cross for you? Were you baptized as Paul's disciples?

¹⁴ I thank God that I did not baptize any of you except Crispus and Gaius. ¹⁵ No one can say, then, that you were baptized as my disciples. ¹⁶ (Oh yes, I also baptized Stephanas and his family; but I can't remember whether I baptized anyone else.) ¹⁷ Christ did not send me to baptize. He sent me to tell the Good News, and to tell it without using the language of human wisdom, in order to make sure that Christ's death on the cross is not robbed of its power.

Christ the Power and the Wisdom of God

¹⁸ For the message about Christ's death on the cross is nonsense to those who are being lost; but for us who are being saved it is God's power. ¹⁹ The scripture says:

"I will destroy the wisdom of the wise
and set aside the understanding of the scholars."

²⁰ So then, where does that leave the wise? or the scholars? or the skilful debaters of this world? God has shown that this world's wisdom is foolishness!

²¹ For God in his wisdom made it impossible for people to know him by means of their own wisdom. Instead, by means of the so-called "foolish" message we preach, God decided to save those who believe. ²² Jews want miracles for proof, and Greeks look for wisdom. ²³ As for us, we proclaim the crucified Christ, a message that is offensive to the Jews and nonsense to the Gentiles; ²⁴ but for those whom God has called, both Jews and Gentiles, this message is Christ, who is the power of God and the

···

1.13 *Christ has been divided*; some manuscripts have *Christ cannot be divided*.

1354

1 Corin.

·:········

Mark
Luke
John
Acts
Romans

1 CORINTHIANS 1, 2

wisdom of God. ²⁵ For what seems to be God's foolishness is wiser than human wisdom, and what seems to be God's weakness is stronger than human strength.

²⁶ Now remember what you were, my brothers and sisters, when God called you. From the human point of view few of you were wise or powerful or of high social standing. ²⁷ God purposely chose what the world considers nonsense in order to shame the wise, and he chose what the world considers weak in order to shame the powerful. ²⁸ He chose what the world looks down on and despises, and thinks is nothing, in order to destroy what the world thinks is important. ²⁹ This means that no one can boast in God's presence. ³⁰ But God has brought you into union with Christ Jesus, and God has made Christ to be our wisdom. By him we are put right with God; we become God's holy people and are set free. ³¹ So then, as the scripture says, "Whoever wants to boast must boast of what the Lord has done."

The Message about the Crucified Christ

2 When I came to you, my brothers and sisters, to preach God's secret truth,* I did not use big words and great learning. ² For while I was with you, I made up my mind to forget everything except Jesus Christ and especially his death on the cross. ³ So when I came to you, I was weak and trembled all over with fear, ⁴ and my teaching and message were not delivered with skilful words of human wisdom, but with convincing proof of the power of God's Spirit. ⁵ Your faith, then, does not rest on human wisdom but on God's power.

God's Wisdom

⁶ Yet I do proclaim a message of wisdom to those who are spiritually mature. But it is not the wisdom that belongs to this world or to the powers that rule this world — powers that are losing their power. ⁷ The wisdom I proclaim is God's hidden wisdom, which he had already chosen for our glory even before the world was made. ⁸ None of the rulers of this world knew this wisdom. If they had known it, they would not have crucified the Lord of glory. ⁹ However, as the scripture says:

"What no one ever saw or heard,
    what no one ever thought could happen,
        is the very thing God prepared for those who love him."

¹⁰ But* it was to us that God made known his secret by means of his Spirit. The Spirit searches everything, even the hidden depths of God's purposes. ¹¹ It is only the spirit within people that knows all about them; in the same way, only God's Spirit knows all about God. ¹² We have not received this world's spirit; instead, we have received the Spirit sent by God, so that we may know all that God has given us.

¹³ So then, we do not speak in words taught by human wisdom, but in words taught by the Spirit, as we explain spiritual truths to those who have the Spirit.* ¹⁴ Whoever does not have the Spirit cannot receive the gifts that come from God's Spirit. Such people really do not understand them; they are nonsense to them, because their value can be judged only on a spiritual basis. ¹⁵ Whoever has the Spirit, however, is able to judge the value of everything, but no one is able to judge him. ¹⁶ As the scripture says:

2.1 *God's secret truth*; some manuscripts have *the testimony about God*.
2.10 *But*; some manuscripts have *For*.
2.13 *to those who have the Spirit*; or *with words given by the Spirit*.

1 CORINTHIANS 2–4

1355

1 Corin.

....

2 Corin.
Galat.
Ephes.
Philipp.
Coloss.

"Who knows the mind of the Lord?
Who is able to give him advice?"
We, however, have the mind of Christ.

Servants of God

3 As a matter of fact, my brothers and sisters, I could not talk to you as I talk to people who have the Spirit; I had to talk to you as though you belonged to this world, as children in the Christian faith. [2] I had to feed you with milk, not solid food, because you were not ready for it. And even now you are not ready for it, [3] because you still live as the people of this world live. When there is jealousy among you and you quarrel with one another, doesn't this prove that you belong to this world, living by its standards? [4] When one of you says, "I follow Paul", and another, "I follow Apollos" — aren't you acting like worldly people?

[5] After all, who is Apollos? And who is Paul? We are simply God's servants, by whom you were led to believe. Each one of us does the work which the Lord gave him to do: [6] I sowed the seed, Apollos watered the plant, but it was God who made the plant grow. [7] The one who sows and the one who waters really do not matter. It is God who matters, because he makes the plant grow. [8] There is no difference between the one who sows and the one who waters; God will reward each one according to the work each has done. [9] For we are partners working together for God, and you are God's field.

You are also God's building. [10] Using the gift that God gave me, I did the work of an expert builder and laid the foundation, and someone else is building on it. But each one must be careful how he builds. [11] For God has already placed Jesus Christ as the one and only foundation, and no other foundation can be laid. [12] Some will use gold or silver or precious stones in building on the foundation; others will use wood or grass or straw. [13] And the quality of each person's work will be seen when the Day of Christ exposes it. For on that Day fire will reveal everyone's work; the fire will test it and show its real quality. [14] If what was built on the foundation survives the fire, the builder will receive a reward. [15] But if anyone's work is burnt up, then he will lose it; but he himself will be saved, as if he had escaped through the fire.

[16] Surely you know that you are God's temple and that God's Spirit lives in you! [17] So if anyone destroys God's temple, God will destroy him. For God's temple is holy, and you yourselves are his temple.

[18] No one should fool himself. If anyone among you thinks that he is wise by this world's standards, he should become a fool, in order to be really wise. [19] For what this world considers to be wisdom is nonsense in God's sight. As the scripture says, "God traps the wise in their cleverness"; [20] and another scripture says, "The Lord knows that the thoughts of the wise are worthless." [21] No one, then, should boast about what human beings can do. Actually everything belongs to you: [22] Paul, Apollos, and Peter; this world, life and death, the present and the future — all these are yours, [23] and you belong to Christ, and Christ belongs to God.

Apostles of Christ

4 You should think of us as Christ's servants, who have been put in charge of God's secret truths. [2] The one thing required of such servants is that they be faithful to their master. [3] Now, I am not at all concerned about being judged by you or by any human standard; I don't even pass judgement on myself. [4] My

1 CORINTHIANS 3.16

Here is an

EMPTY

• TIMELINE •

of where God's presence has been found on earth: God's presence was first in the garden of Eden (draw), then in the Covenant Box (draw), then in the temple (draw), then in Jesus (draw). But now God's presence is found in you (draw).

GARDEN OF EDEN

COVENANT BOX

TEMPLE

JESUS

YOU

conscience is clear, but that does not prove that I am really innocent. The Lord is the one who passes judgement on me. [5]So you should not pass judgement on anyone before the right time comes. Final judgement must wait until the Lord comes; he will bring to light the dark secrets and expose the hidden purposes of people's minds. And then all will receive from God the praise they deserve.

[6]For your sake, my brothers and sisters, I have applied all this to Apollos and me, using the two of us as an example, so that you may learn what the saying means, "Observe the proper rules." None of you should be proud of one person and despise another. [7]Who made you superior to others? Didn't God give you everything you have? Well, then, how can you boast, as if what you have were not a gift?

[8]Do you already have everything you need? Are you already rich? Have you become kings, even though we are not? Well, I wish you really were kings, so that we could be kings together with you. [9]For it seems to me that God has given the very last place to us apostles, like people condemned to die in public as a spectacle for the whole world of angels and of humanity. [10]For Christ's sake we are fools; but you are wise in union with Christ! We are weak, but you are strong! We are despised, but you are honoured! [11]To this very moment we go hungry and thirsty; we are clothed in rags; we are beaten; we wander from place to place; [12]we wear ourselves out with hard work. When we are cursed, we bless; when we are persecuted, we endure; [13]when we are insulted, we answer with kind words. We are no more than this world's refuse; we are the scum of the earth to this very moment!

[14]I write this to you, not because I want to make you feel ashamed, but to instruct you as my own dear children. [15]For even if you have 10,000 guardians in your Christian life, you have only one father. For in your life in union with Christ Jesus I have become your father by bringing the Good News to you. [16]I beg you, then, to follow my example. [17]For this purpose I am sending to you Timothy, who is my own dear and faithful son in the Christian life. He will remind you of the principles which I follow in the new life in union with Christ Jesus and which I teach in all the churches everywhere.

[18]Some of you have become proud because you have thought that I would not be coming to visit you. [19]If the Lord is willing, however, I will come to you soon, and then I will find out for myself the power which these proud people have, and not just what they say. [20]For the Kingdom of God is not a matter of words but of power. [21]Which do you prefer? Shall I come to you with a whip, or in a spirit of love and gentleness?

Immorality in the Church

5 Now, it is actually being said that there is sexual immorality among you so terrible that not even the heathen would be guilty of it. I am told that a man is sleeping with his stepmother! [2]How, then, can you be proud? On the contrary, you should be filled with sadness, and the man who has done such a thing should be expelled from your fellowship. [3-4]And even though I am far away from you in body, still I am there with you in spirit; and as though I were there with you, I have in the name of our Lord Jesus already passed judgement on the man who has done this terrible thing. As you meet together, and I meet with you in my spirit, by the power of our Lord Jesus present with us, [5]you are to hand this man over to Satan for his body to be destroyed, so that his spirit may be saved in the Day of the Lord.

1 CORINTHIANS 5, 6

1357

1 Corin.

....

2 Corin.
Galat.
Ephes.
Philipp.
Coloss.

[6] It is not right for you to be proud! You know the saying, "A little bit of yeast makes the whole batch of dough rise." [7] You must remove the old yeast of sin so that you will be entirely pure. Then you will be like a new batch of dough without any yeast, as indeed I know you actually are. For our Passover Festival is ready, now that Christ, our Passover lamb, has been sacrificed. [8] Let us celebrate our Passover, then, not with bread having the old yeast of sin and wickedness, but with the bread that has no yeast, the bread of purity and truth.

[9] In the letter that I wrote you I told you not to associate with immoral people. [10] Now I did not mean pagans who are immoral or greedy or are thieves or who worship idols. To avoid them you would have to get out of the world completely. [11] What I meant was that you should not associate with a person who calls himself a believer but is immoral or greedy or worships idols or is a slanderer or a drunkard or a thief. Don't even sit down to eat with such a person.

[12-13] After all, it is none of my business to judge outsiders. God will judge them. But should you not judge the members of your own fellowship? As the scripture says, "Remove the evil person from your group."

Lawsuits against Fellow-Christians

6 If any of you have a dispute with another Christian, how dare you go before heathen judges instead of letting God's people settle the matter? [2] Don't you know that God's people will judge the world? Well, then, if you are to judge the world, aren't you capable of judging small matters? [3] Do you not know that we shall judge the angels? How much more, then, the things of this life! [4] If such matters come up, are you going to take them to be settled by people who have no standing in the church? [5] Shame on you! Surely there is at least one wise person in your fellowship who can settle a dispute between fellow-Christians. [6] Instead, one Christian goes to court against another and lets unbelievers judge the case!

[7] The very fact that you have legal disputes among yourselves shows that you have failed completely. Would it not be better for you to be wronged? Would it not be better for you to be robbed? [8] Instead, you yourselves wrong one another and rob one another, even your own brothers and sisters! [9] Surely you know that the wicked will not possess God's Kingdom. Do not fool yourselves; people who are immoral or who worship idols or are adulterers or homosexual perverts [10] or who steal or are greedy or are drunkards or who slander others or are thieves — none of these will possess God's Kingdom. [11] Some of you were like that. But you have been purified from sin; you have been dedicated to God; you have been put right with God by the Lord Jesus Christ and by the Spirit of our God.

Use your Bodies for God's Glory

[12] Someone will say, "I am allowed to do anything." Yes; but not everything is good for you. I could say that I am allowed to do anything, but I am not going to let anything make me its slave. [13] Someone else will say, "Food is for the stomach, and the stomach is for food." Yes; but God will put an end to both. The body is not to be used for sexual immorality, but to serve the Lord; and the Lord provides for the body. [14] God raised the Lord from death, and he will also raise us by his power.

[15] You know that your bodies are parts of the body of Christ. Shall I take a part of Christ's body and make it part of the body of a prostitute? Impossible! [16] Or perhaps you don't know that the

1358

1 Corin.

⋮⋮⋮⋮⋮⋮⋮

Mark
Luke
John
Acts
Romans

1 CORINTHIANS 6, 7

On a scale

FROM 1 TO 10,

how easy are you
finding it to read the
Bible currently?

Think of one way you
can go up a number on
the scale.

10
9 8
7 8
5 6
4
3
1 2

man who joins his body to a prostitute becomes physically one with her? The scripture says quite plainly, "The two will become one body." [17]But he who joins himself to the Lord becomes spiritually one with him.

[18]Avoid immorality. Any other sin a man commits does not affect his body; but the man who is guilty of sexual immorality sins against his own body. [19]Don't you know that your body is the temple of the Holy Spirit, who lives in you and who was given to you by God? You do not belong to yourselves but to God; [20]he bought you for a price. So use your bodies for God's glory.

Questions about Marriage

7 Now, to deal with the matters you wrote about.
A man does well not to marry.* [2]But because there is so much immorality, every man should have his own wife, and every woman should have her own husband. [3]A man should fulfil his duty as a husband, and a woman should fulfil her duty as a wife, and each should satisfy the other's needs. [4]A wife is not the master of her own body, but her husband is; in the same way a husband is not the master of his own body, but his wife is. [5]Do not deny yourselves to each other, unless you first agree to do so for a while in order to spend your time in prayer; but then resume normal marital relations. In this way you will be kept from giving in to Satan's temptation because of your lack of self-control.

[6]I tell you this not as an order, but simply as a concession. [7]Actually I would prefer that all of you were as I am; but each one has a special gift from God, one person this gift, another one that gift.

[8]Now, to the unmarried and to the widows I say that it would be better for you to continue to live alone as I do. [9]But if you cannot restrain your desires, go ahead and marry — it is better to marry than to burn with passion.

[10]For married people I have a command which is not my own but the Lord's: a wife must not leave her husband; [11]but if she does, she must remain single or else be reconciled to her husband; and a husband must not divorce his wife.

[12]To the others I say (I, myself, not the Lord): if a Christian man has a wife who is an unbeliever and she agrees to go on living with him, he must not divorce her. [13]And if a Christian woman is married to a man who is an unbeliever and he agrees to go on living with her, she must not divorce him. [14]For the unbelieving husband is made acceptable to God by being united to his wife, and the unbelieving wife is made acceptable to God by being united to her Christian husband. If this were not so, their children would be like pagan children; but as it is, they are acceptable to God. [15]However, if the one who is not a believer wishes to leave the Christian partner, let it be so. In such cases the Christian partner, whether husband or wife, is free to act. God has called you to live in peace. [16]How can you be sure, Christian wife, that you will not save* your husband? Or how can you be sure, Christian husband, that you will not save your wife?

Live as God Called You

[17]Each of you should go on living according to the Lord's gift to you, and as you were when God called you. This is the rule I teach

---

7.1 *A man does well not to marry*; or *You say that a man does well not to marry*.
7.16 *How can you be sure… that you will not save*; or *How do you know… that you will save*.

1 CORINTHIANS 7

1359

1 Corin.

.........:.

2 Corin.
Galat.
Ephes.
Philipp.
Coloss.

in all the churches. ¹⁸ If a circumcised man has accepted God's call, he should not try to remove the marks of circumcision; if an uncircumcised man has accepted God's call, he should not get circumcised. ¹⁹ For whether or not a man is circumcised means nothing; what matters is to obey God's commandments. ²⁰ Each of you should remain as you were when you accepted God's call. ²¹ Were you a slave when God called you? Well, never mind; but if you have a chance to become free, use it.* ²² For a slave who has been called by the Lord is free for the Lord; in the same way a free person who has been called by Christ is his slave. ²³ God bought you for a price; so do not become slaves of human beings. ²⁴ My friends, each of you should remain in fellowship with God in the same condition as you were when you were called.

Questions about the Unmarried and the Widows

²⁵ Now, concerning what you wrote about unmarried people: I do not have a command from the Lord, but I give my opinion as one who by the Lord's mercy is worthy of trust.

²⁶ Considering the present distress, I think it is better for a man to stay as he is. ²⁷ Have you got a wife? Then don't try to get rid of her. Are you unmarried? Then don't look for a wife. ²⁸ But if you do marry, you haven't committed a sin; and if an unmarried woman marries, she hasn't committed a sin. But I would rather spare you the everyday troubles that married people will have.

²⁹ What I mean, my friends, is this: there is not much time left, and from now on married men should live as though they were not married; ³⁰ those who weep, as though they were not sad; those who laugh, as though they were not happy; those who buy, as though they did not own what they bought; ³¹ those who deal in material goods, as though they were not fully occupied with them. For this world, as it is now, will not last much longer.

³² I would like you to be free from worry. An unmarried man concerns himself with the Lord's work, because he is trying to please the Lord. ³³ But a married man concerns himself with worldly matters, because he wants to please his wife; ³⁴ and so he is pulled in two directions. An unmarried woman or a virgin concerns herself with the Lord's work, because she wants to be dedicated both in body and spirit; but a married woman concerns herself with worldly matters, because she wants to please her husband.

³⁵ I am saying this because I want to help you. I am not trying to put restrictions on you. Instead, I want you to do what is right and proper, and to give yourselves completely to the Lord's service without any reservation.

³⁶ In the case of an engaged couple who have decided not to marry: if the man feels that he is not acting properly towards the young woman and if his passions are too strong and he feels that they ought to marry, then they should get married, as he wants to.* There is no sin in this. ³⁷ But if a man, without being forced to do so, has firmly made up his mind not to marry,* and if he has his will under complete control and has already decided in his own mind what to do — then he does well not to marry the

---

7.21 *but if you have a chance to become free, use it;* or *but even if you have a chance to become free, choose rather to make the best of your condition as a slave.*
7.36 *an engaged couple... as he wants to;* or *a man and his unmarried daughter: if he feels that he is not acting properly towards her, and if she is at the right age to marry, then he should do as he wishes and let her get married.*
7.37 *not to marry;* or *not to let his daughter get married.*

1360

1 Corin.

·:········

Mark
Luke
John
Acts
Romans

1 CORINTHIANS 7–9

WHAT DOES 'GOSPEL' MEAN?
Finish the mindmap below.

The teaching or
revelation of Christ.
(oxforddictionaries.com)

↑

GOSPEL

MATTHEW 26.13;
1 CORINTHIANS 9.14-18

young woman.* [38] So the man who marries* does well, but the one who doesn't marry* does even better.

[39] A married woman is not free as long as her husband lives; but if her husband dies, then she is free to be married to any man she wishes, but only if he is a Christian. [40] She will be happier, however, if she stays as she is. That is my opinion, and I think that I too have God's Spirit.

The Question about Food Offered to Idols

8 Now, concerning what you wrote about food offered to idols. It is true, of course, that "all of us have knowledge", as they say. Such knowledge, however, puffs a person up with pride; but love builds up. [2] Those who think they know something really don't know as they ought to know. [3] But the person who loves God is known by him.

[4] So then, about eating the food offered to idols: we know that an idol stands for something that does not really exist; we know that there is only the one God. [5] Even if there are so-called "gods", whether in heaven or on earth, and even though there are many of these "gods" and "lords", [6] yet there is for us only one God, the Father, who is the Creator of all things and for whom we live; and there is only one Lord, Jesus Christ, through whom all things were created and through whom we live.

[7] But not everyone knows this truth. Some people have been so used to idols that to this day when they eat such food they still think of it as food that belongs to an idol; their conscience is weak, and they feel they are defiled by the food. [8] Food, however, will not improve our relations with God; we shall not lose anything if we do not eat, nor shall we gain anything if we do eat.

[9] Be careful, however, not to let your freedom of action make those who are weak in the faith fall into sin. [10] Suppose a person whose conscience is weak in this matter sees you, who have so-called "knowledge", eating in the temple of an idol; will not this encourage him to eat food offered to idols? [11] And so this weak person, your brother for whom Christ died, will perish because of your "knowledge"! [12] And in this way you will be sinning against Christ by sinning against your Christian brothers and sisters and wounding their weak conscience. [13] So then, if food makes my brother or sister sin, I will never eat meat again, so as not to make my brother or sister fall into sin.

Rights and Duties of an Apostle

9 Am I not a free man? Am I not an apostle? Haven't I seen Jesus our Lord? And aren't you the result of my work for the Lord? [2] Even if others do not accept me as an apostle, surely you do! Because of your life in union with the Lord you yourselves are proof of the fact that I am an apostle.

[3] When people criticize me, this is how I defend myself: [4] Haven't I the right to be given food and drink for my work? [5] Haven't I the right to follow the example of the other apostles and the Lord's brothers and Peter, by taking a Christian wife with me on my travels? [6] Or are Barnabas and I the only ones who have to work for our living? [7] What soldier ever has to pay his own expenses in the army? What farmer does not eat the grapes from his own vineyard? What shepherd does not use the milk from his own sheep?

7.37 *marry the young woman*; or *let her get married.*
7.38 *marries*; or *lets his daughter get married.*
7.38 *doesn't marry*; or *doesn't let her get married.*

1 CORINTHIANS 9, 10

1361

1 Corin.

2 Corin.
Galat.
Ephes.
Philipp.
Coloss.

[8] I don't have to limit myself to these everyday examples, because the Law says the same thing. [9] We read in the Law of Moses, "Do not muzzle an ox when you are using it to thresh corn." Now, is God concerned about oxen? [10] Didn't he really mean us when he said that? Of course that was written for us. The one who ploughs and the one who reaps should do their work in the hope of getting a share of the crop. [11] We have sown spiritual seed among you. Is it too much if we reap material benefits from you? [12] If others have the right to expect this from you, haven't we an even greater right?

But we haven't made use of this right. Instead, we have endured everything in order not to put any obstacle in the way of the Good News about Christ. [13] Surely you know that the men who work in the Temple get their food from the Temple and that those who offer the sacrifices on the altar get a share of the sacrifices. [14] In the same way, the Lord has ordered that those who preach the gospel should get their living from it.

[15] But I haven't made use of any of these rights, nor am I writing this now in order to claim such rights for myself. I would rather die first! Nobody is going to turn my rightful boast into empty words! [16] I have no right to boast just because I preach the gospel. After all, I am under orders to do so. And how terrible it would be for me if I did not preach the gospel! [17] If I did my work as a matter of free choice, then I could expect to be paid; but I do it as a matter of duty, because God has entrusted me with this task. [18] What pay do I get, then? It is the privilege of preaching the Good News without charging for it, without claiming my rights in my work for the gospel.

[19] I am a free man, nobody's slave; but I make myself everybody's slave in order to win as many people as possible. [20] While working with the Jews, I live like a Jew in order to win them; and even though I myself am not subject to the Law of Moses, I live as though I were when working with those who are, in order to win them. [21] In the same way, when working with Gentiles, I live like a Gentile, outside the Jewish Law, in order to win Gentiles. This does not mean that I don't obey God's law; I am really under Christ's law. [22] Among the weak in faith I become weak like one of them, in order to win them. So I become all things to all people, that I may save some of them by whatever means are possible.

[23] All this I do for the gospel's sake, in order to share in its blessings. [24] Surely you know that many runners take part in a race, but only one of them wins the prize. Run, then, in such a way as to win the prize. [25] Every athlete in training submits to strict discipline, in order to be crowned with a wreath that will not last; but we do it for one that will last for ever. [26] That is why I run straight for the finishing line; that is why I am like a boxer who does not waste his punches. [27] I harden my body with blows and bring it under complete control, to keep myself from being disqualified after having called others to the contest.

Warnings against Idols

10 I want you to remember, my brothers and sisters, what happened to our ancestors who followed Moses. They were all under the protection of the cloud, and all passed safely through the Red Sea. [2] In the cloud and in the sea they were all baptized as followers of Moses. [3] All ate the same spiritual bread [4] and drank the same spiritual drink. They drank from the spiritual rock that went with them; and that rock was Christ himself. [5] But

1 CORINTHIANS 9.24

RUN, THEN, IN SUCH A WAY AS TO WIN THE PRIZE

even then God was not pleased with most of them, and so their dead bodies were scattered over the desert.

6 Now, all this is an example for us, to warn us not to desire evil things, as they did, 7 nor to worship idols, as some of them did. As the scripture says, "The people sat down to a feast which turned into an orgy of drinking and sex." 8 We must not be guilty of sexual immorality, as some of them were — and in one day 23,000 of them fell dead. 9 We must not put the Lord* to the test, as some of them did — and they were killed by snakes. 10 We must not complain, as some of them did — and they were destroyed by the Angel of Death.

11 All these things happened to them as examples for others, and they were written down as a warning for us. For we live at a time when the end is about to come.

12 Those who think they are standing firm had better be careful that they do not fall. 13 Every test that you have experienced is the kind that normally comes to people. But God keeps his promise, and he will not allow you to be tested beyond your power to remain firm; at the time you are put to the test, he will give you the strength to endure it, and so provide you with a way out.

14 So then, my dear friends, keep away from the worship of idols. 15 I speak to you as sensible people; judge for yourselves what I say. 16 The cup we use in the Lord's Supper and for which we give thanks to God: when we drink from it, we are sharing in the blood of Christ. And the bread we break: when we eat it, we are sharing in the body of Christ. 17 Because there is the one loaf of bread, all of us, though many, are one body, for we all share the same loaf.

18 Consider the people of Israel; those who eat what is offered in sacrifice share in the altar's service to God. 19 Do I imply, then, that an idol or the food offered to it really amounts to anything? 20 No! What I am saying is that what is sacrificed on pagan altars is offered to demons, not to God. And I do not want you to be partners with demons. 21 You cannot drink from the Lord's cup and also from the cup of demons; you cannot eat at the Lord's table and also at the table of demons. 22 Or do we want to make the Lord jealous? Do we think that we are stronger than he?

23 "We are allowed to do anything," so they say. That is true, but not everything is good. "We are allowed to do anything" — but not everything is helpful. 24 None of you should be looking to your own interests, but to the interests of others.

25 You are free to eat anything sold in the meat market, without asking any questions because of your conscience. 26 For, as the scripture says, "The earth and everything in it belong to the Lord."

27 If an unbeliever invites you to a meal and you decide to go, eat what is set before you, without asking any questions because of your conscience. 28 But if someone says to you, "This food was offered to idols," then do not eat that food, for the sake of the one who told you and for conscience' sake — 29 that is, not your own conscience, but the other person's conscience.

"Well, then," someone asks, "why should my freedom to act be limited by another person's conscience? 30 If I thank God for my food, why should anyone criticize me about food for which I give thanks?"

31 Well, whatever you do, whether you eat or drink, do it all for God's glory. 32 Live in such a way as to cause no trouble either to Jews or Gentiles or to the church of God. 33 Just do as I do; I try

10.9 the Lord; some manuscripts have Christ.

1 CORINTHIANS 10, 11

1363

1 Corin.

2 Corin.
Galat.
Ephes.
Philipp.
Coloss.

to please everyone in all that I do, not thinking of my own good, but of the good of all, so that they might be saved. **11** Imitate me, then, just as I imitate Christ.

Covering the Head in Worship

² I praise you because you always remember me and follow the teachings that I have handed on to you. ³ But I want you to understand that Christ is supreme over every man, the husband is supreme over his wife, and God is supreme over Christ. ⁴ So a man who prays or proclaims God's message in public worship with his head covered disgraces Christ. ⁵ And any woman who prays or proclaims God's message in public worship with nothing on her head disgraces her husband; there is no difference between her and a woman whose head has been shaved. ⁶ If the woman does not cover her head, she might as well cut her hair. And since it is a shameful thing for a woman to shave her head or cut her hair, she should cover her head. ⁷ A man has no need to cover his head, because he reflects the image and glory of God. But woman reflects the glory of man; ⁸ for man was not created from woman, but woman from man. ⁹ Nor was man created for woman's sake, but woman was created for man's sake. ¹⁰ On account of the angels, then, a woman should have a covering over her head to show that she is under her husband's authority. ¹¹ In our life in the Lord, however, woman is not independent of man, nor is man independent of woman. ¹² For as woman was made from man, in the same way man is born of woman; and it is God who brings everything into existence.

¹³ Judge for yourselves whether it is proper for a woman to pray to God in public worship with nothing on her head. ¹⁴ Why, nature itself teaches you that long hair on a man is a disgrace, ¹⁵ but on a woman it is a thing of beauty. Her long hair has been given her to serve as a covering. ¹⁶ But if anyone wants to argue about it, all I have to say is that neither we nor the churches of God have any other custom in worship.

The Lord's Supper
(Mt 26.26–29; Mk 14.22–25; Lk 22.14–20)

¹⁷ In the following instructions, however, I do not praise you, because your meetings for worship actually do more harm than good. ¹⁸ In the first place, I have been told that there are opposing groups in your meetings; and this I believe is partly true. ¹⁹ (No doubt there must be divisions among you so that the ones who are in the right may be clearly seen.) ²⁰ When you meet together as a group, it is not the Lord's Supper that you eat. ²¹ For as you eat, you each go ahead with your own meal, so that some are hungry while others get drunk. ²² Haven't you got your own homes in which to eat and drink? Or would you rather despise the church of God and put to shame the people who are in need? What do you expect me to say to you about this? Shall I praise you? Of course I don't!

²³ For I received from the Lord the teaching that I passed on to you: that the Lord Jesus, on the night he was betrayed, took a piece of bread, ²⁴ gave thanks to God, broke it, and said, "This is my body, which is for you. Do this in memory of me." ²⁵ In the same way, after the supper he took the cup and said, "This cup is God's new covenant, sealed with my blood. Whenever you drink it, do so in memory of me."

²⁶ This means that every time you eat this bread and drink from this cup you proclaim the Lord's death until he comes. ²⁷ It follows

1 CORINTHIANS 11.1-16

When you read this chapter, keep in mind that the **CULTURE** – IN CORINTH – at that time was different from ours today. However, what do you think of these passages? How do you think authority should work in a loving relationship? Do you think it is harder to have authority over someone or to be under authority?

1364

1 Corin.

∴ ⋯⋯

Mark
Luke
John
Acts
Romans

1 CORINTHIANS 11, 12

that if anyone eats the Lord's bread or drinks from his cup in a way that dishonours him, he or she is guilty of sin against the Lord's body and blood. [28] So then, you should all examine yourselves first, and then eat the bread and drink from the cup. [29] For if people do not recognize the meaning of the Lord's body when they eat the bread and drink from the cup, they bring judgement on themselves as they eat and drink. [30] That is why many of you are weak and ill, and several have died. [31] If we would examine ourselves first, we would not come under God's judgement. [32] But we are judged and punished by the Lord, so that we shall not be condemned together with the world.

[33] So then, my brothers and sisters, when you gather together to eat the Lord's Supper, wait for one another. [34] Anyone who is hungry should eat at home, so that you will not come under God's judgement as you meet together. As for the other matters, I will settle them when I come.

Gifts from the Holy Spirit

12 Now, concerning what you wrote about the gifts from the Holy Spirit.

I want you to know the truth about them, my brothers and sisters. [2] You know that while you were still heathen, you were led astray in many ways to the worship of lifeless idols. [3] I want you to know that no one who is led by God's Spirit can say "A curse on Jesus!" and no one can confess "Jesus is Lord", without being guided by the Holy Spirit.

[4] There are different kinds of spiritual gifts, but the same Spirit gives them. [5] There are different ways of serving, but the same Lord is served. [6] There are different abilities to perform service, but the same God gives ability to all for their particular service. [7] The Spirit's presence is shown in some way in each person for the good of all. [8] The Spirit gives one person a message full of wisdom, while to another person the same Spirit gives a message full of knowledge. [9] One and the same Spirit gives faith to one person, while to another person he gives the power to heal. [10] The Spirit gives one person the power to work miracles; to another, the gift of speaking God's message; and to yet another, the ability to tell the difference between gifts that come from the Spirit and those that do not. To one person he gives the ability to speak in strange tongues, and to another he gives the ability to explain what is said. [11] But it is one and the same Spirit who does all this; as he wishes, he gives a different gift to each person.

One Body with Many Parts

[12] Christ is like a single body, which has many parts; it is still one body, even though it is made up of different parts. [13] In the same way, all of us, whether Jews or Gentiles, whether slaves or free, have been baptized into the one body by the same Spirit, and we have all been given the one Spirit to drink.

[14] For the body itself is not made up of only one part, but of many parts. [15] If the foot were to say, "Because I am not a hand, I don't belong to the body," that would not keep it from being a part of the body. [16] And if the ear were to say, "Because I am not an eye, I don't belong to the body," that would not keep it from being a part of the body. [17] If the whole body were just an eye, how could it hear? And if it were only an ear, how could it smell? [18] As it is, however, God put every different part in the body just as he wanted it to be. [19] There would not be a body if it were all only one part! [20] As it is, there are many parts but one body.

1 Corin.

2 Corin.
Galat.
Ephes.
Philipp.
Coloss.

²¹ So then, the eye cannot say to the hand, "I don't need you!" Nor can the head say to the feet, "Well, I don't need you!" ²² On the contrary, we cannot do without the parts of the body that seem to be weaker; ²³ and those parts that we think aren't worth very much are the ones which we treat with greater care; while the parts of the body which don't look very nice are treated with special modesty, ²⁴ which the more beautiful parts do not need. God himself has put the body together in such a way as to give greater honour to those parts that need it. ²⁵ And so there is no division in the body, but all its different parts have the same concern for one another. ²⁶ If one part of the body suffers, all the other parts suffer with it; if one part is praised, all the other parts share its happiness.

²⁷ All of you are Christ's body, and each one is a part of it. ²⁸ In the church God has put all in place: in the first place apostles, in the second place prophets, and in the third place teachers; then those who perform miracles, followed by those who are given the power to heal or to help others or to direct them or to speak in strange tongues. ²⁹ They are not all apostles or prophets or teachers. Not everyone has the power to work miracles ³⁰ or to heal diseases or to speak in strange tongues or to explain what is said. ³¹ Set your hearts, then, on the more important gifts.

Best of all, however, is the following way.

Love

13 I may be able to speak the languages of human beings and even of angels, but if I have no love, my speech is no more than a noisy gong or a clanging bell. ² I may have the gift of inspired preaching; I may have all knowledge and understand all secrets; I may have all the faith needed to move mountains — but if I have no love, I am nothing. ³ I may give away everything I have, and even give up my body to be burnt* — but if I have no love, this does me no good.

⁴ Love is patient and kind; it is not jealous or conceited or proud; ⁵ love is not ill-mannered or selfish or irritable; love does not keep a record of wrongs; ⁶ love is not happy with evil, but is happy with the truth. ⁷ Love never gives up; and its faith, hope, and patience never fail.

⁸ Love is eternal. There are inspired messages, but they are temporary; there are gifts of speaking in strange tongues, but they will cease; there is knowledge, but it will pass. ⁹ For our gifts of knowledge and of inspired messages are only partial; ¹⁰ but when what is perfect comes, then what is partial will disappear.

¹¹ When I was a child, my speech, feelings, and thinking were all those of a child; now that I have grown up, I have no more use for childish ways. ¹² What we see now is like a dim image in a mirror; then we shall see face to face. What I know now is only partial; then it will be complete — as complete as God's knowledge of me.

¹³ Meanwhile these three remain: faith, hope, and love; and the greatest of these is love.

More about Gifts from the Spirit

14 It is love, then, that you should strive for. Set your hearts on spiritual gifts, especially the gift of proclaiming God's message. ² Those who speak in strange tongues do not speak to others but to God, because no one understands them. They are speaking secret truths by the power of the Spirit. ³ But those who

READ THIS PASSAGE OUT

⁌LOUD.⁍

13.3 *to be burnt*; some manuscripts have *in order to boast*.

proclaim God's message speak to people and give them help, encouragement, and comfort. ⁴Those who speak in strange tongues help only themselves, but those who proclaim God's message help the whole church.

⁵I would like all of you to speak in strange tongues; but I would rather that you had the gift of proclaiming God's message. For the person who proclaims God's message is of greater value than the one who speaks in strange tongues — unless there is someone present who can explain what is said, so that the whole church may be helped. ⁶So when I come to you, my brothers and sisters, what use will I be to you if I speak in strange tongues? Not a bit, unless I bring you some revelation from God or some knowledge or some inspired message, or some teaching.

⁷Take such lifeless musical instruments as the flute or the harp — how will anyone know the tune that is being played unless the notes are sounded distinctly? ⁸And if the one who plays the bugle does not sound a clear call, who will prepare for battle? ⁹In the same way, how will anyone understand what you are talking about if your message given in strange tongues is not clear? Your words will vanish in the air! ¹⁰There are many different languages in the world, yet none of them is without meaning. ¹¹But if I do not know the language being spoken, those who use it will be foreigners to me and I will be a foreigner to them. ¹²Since you are eager to have the gifts of the Spirit, you must try above everything else to make greater use of those which help to build up the church.

¹³The person who speaks in strange tongues, then, must pray for the gift to explain what is said. ¹⁴For if I pray in this way, my spirit prays indeed, but my mind has no part in it. ¹⁵What should I do, then? I will pray with my spirit, but I will pray also with my mind; I will sing with my spirit, but I will sing also with my mind. ¹⁶When you give thanks to God in spirit only, how can ordinary people taking part in the meeting say "Amen" to your prayer of thanksgiving? They have no way of knowing what you are saying. ¹⁷Even if your prayer of thanks to God is quite good, other people are not helped at all.

¹⁸I thank God that I speak in strange tongues much more than any of you. ¹⁹But in church worship I would rather speak five words that can be understood, in order to teach others, than speak thousands of words in strange tongues.

²⁰Do not be like children in your thinking, my brothers and sisters; be children so far as evil is concerned, but be grown-up in your thinking. ²¹In the Scriptures it is written:

"By means of people speaking strange languages
I will speak to my people, says the Lord.
I will speak through lips of foreigners,
but even then my people will not listen to me."

²²So then, the gift of speaking in strange tongues is proof for unbelievers, not for believers, while the gift of proclaiming God's message is proof for believers, not for unbelievers.

²³If, then, the whole church meets together and everyone starts speaking in strange tongues — and if some ordinary people or unbelievers come in, won't they say that you are all crazy? ²⁴But if everyone is proclaiming God's message when some unbelievers or ordinary people come in, they will be convinced of their sin by what they hear. They will be judged by all they hear, ²⁵their secret thoughts will be brought into the open, and they will bow down and worship God, confessing, "Truly God is here among you!"

1 CORINTHIANS 14, 15

1367

1 Corin.

....

2 Corin.
Galat.
Ephes.
Philipp.
Coloss.

Order in the Church

26 This is what I mean, my brothers and sisters. When you meet for worship, one person has a hymn, another a teaching, another a revelation from God, another a message in strange tongues, and still another the explanation of what is said. Everything must be of help to the church. 27 If someone is going to speak in strange tongues, two or three at the most should speak, one after the other, and someone else must explain what is being said. 28 But if no one is there who can explain, then the one who speaks in strange tongues must be quiet and speak only to himself and to God. 29 Two or three who are given God's message should speak, while the others are to judge what they say. 30 But if someone sitting in the meeting receives a message from God, the one who is speaking should stop. 31 All of you may proclaim God's message, one by one, so that everyone will learn and be encouraged. 32 The gift of proclaiming God's message should be under the speaker's control, 33 because God does not want us to be in disorder but in harmony and peace.

As in all the churches of God's people, 34 the women should keep quiet in the meetings. They are not allowed to speak; as the Jewish Law says, they must not be in charge. 35 If they want to find out about something, they should ask their husbands at home. It is a disgraceful thing for a woman to speak in church.

36 Or could it be that the word of God came from you? Or are you the only ones to whom it came? 37 If anyone supposes he is God's messenger or has a spiritual gift, he must realize that what I am writing to you is the Lord's command. 38 But if he does not pay attention to this, pay no attention to him.

39 So then, my brothers and sisters, set your hearts on proclaiming God's message, but do not forbid the speaking in strange tongues. 40 Everything must be done in a proper and orderly way.

The Resurrection of Christ

15 And now I want to remind you, my brothers and sisters, of the Good News which I preached to you, which you received, and on which your faith stands firm. 2 That is the gospel, the message that I preached to you. You are saved by the gospel if you hold firmly to it — unless it was for nothing that you believed.

3 I passed on to you what I received, which is of the greatest importance: that Christ died for our sins, as written in the Scriptures; 4 that he was buried and that he was raised to life three days later, as written in the Scriptures; 5 that he appeared to Peter and then to all twelve apostles. 6 Then he appeared to more than 500 of his followers at once, most of whom are still alive, although some have died. 7 Then he appeared to James, and afterwards to all the apostles.

8 Last of all he appeared also to me — even though I am like someone whose birth was abnormal.* 9 For I am the least of all the apostles — I do not even deserve to be called an apostle, because I persecuted God's church. 10 But by God's grace I am what I am, and the grace that he gave me was not without effect. On the contrary, I have worked harder than any of the other apostles, although it was not really my own doing, but God's grace working with me. 11 So then, whether it came from me or from them, this is what we all preach, and this is what you believe.

....

15.8 *whose birth was abnormal*; or *who was born at the wrong time.*

1368

1 Corin.

.:........

Mark
Luke
John
Acts
Romans

1 CORINTHIANS 15

Our Resurrection

12 Now, since our message is that Christ has been raised from death, how can some of you say that the dead will not be raised to life? 13 If that is true, it means that Christ was not raised; 14 and if Christ has not been raised from death, then we have nothing to preach and you have nothing to believe. 15 More than that, we are shown to be lying about God, because we said that he raised Christ from death — but if it is true that the dead are not raised to life, then he did not raise Christ. 16 For if the dead are not raised, neither has Christ been raised. 17 And if Christ has not been raised, then your faith is a delusion and you are still lost in your sins. 18 It would also mean that the believers in Christ who have died are lost. 19 If our hope in Christ is good for this life only and no more,* then we deserve more pity than anyone else in all the world.

20 But the truth is that Christ has been raised from death, as the guarantee that those who sleep in death will also be raised. 21 For just as death came by means of a man, in the same way the rising from death comes by means of a man. 22 For just as all people die because of their union with Adam, in the same way all will be raised to life because of their union with Christ. 23 But each one will be raised in the right order: Christ, first of all; then, at the time of his coming, those who belong to him. 24 Then the end will come; Christ will overcome all spiritual rulers, authorities, and powers, and will hand over the Kingdom to God the Father. 25 For Christ must rule until God defeats all enemies and puts them under his feet. 26 The last enemy to be defeated will be death. 27 For the scripture says, "God put *all* things under his feet." It is clear, of course, that the words "all things" do not include God himself, who puts all things under Christ. 28 But when all things have been placed under Christ's rule, then he himself, the Son, will place himself under God, who placed all things under him; and God will rule completely over all.

29 Now, what about those people who are baptized for the dead? What do they hope to accomplish? If it is true, as some claim, that the dead are not raised to life, why are those people being baptized for the dead? 30 And as for us — why would we run the risk of danger every hour? 31 My brothers and sisters, I face death every day! The pride I have in you, in our life in union with Christ Jesus our Lord, makes me declare this. 32 If I have, as it were, fought "wild beasts" here in Ephesus simply from human motives, what have I gained? But if the dead are not raised to life, then, as the saying goes, "Let us eat and drink, for tomorrow we will die."

33 Do not be fooled. "Bad companions ruin good character." 34 Come back to your right senses and stop your sinful ways. I declare to your shame that some of you do not know God.

The Resurrection Body

35 Someone will ask, "How can the dead be raised to life? What kind of body will they have?" 36 You fool! When you sow a seed in the ground, it does not sprout to life unless it dies. 37 And what you sow is a bare seed, perhaps a grain of wheat or some other grain, not the full-bodied plant that will later grow up. 38 God provides that seed with the body he wishes; he gives each seed its own proper body.

39 And the flesh of living beings is not all the same kind of flesh; human beings have one kind of flesh, animals another, birds another, and fish another.

....

15.19 *If our hope in Christ is good for this life only and no more*; or *If all we have in this life is our hope in Christ.*

1 CORINTHIANS 15, 16

1369

1 Corin.

2 Corin.
Galat.
Ephes.
Philipp.
Coloss.

40 And there are heavenly bodies and earthly bodies; the beauty that belongs to heavenly bodies is different from the beauty that belongs to earthly bodies. 41 The sun has its own beauty, the moon another beauty, and the stars a different beauty; and even among stars there are different kinds of beauty.

42 This is how it will be when the dead are raised to life. When the body is buried, it is mortal; when raised, it will be immortal. 43 When buried, it is ugly and weak; when raised, it will be beautiful and strong. 44 When buried, it is a physical body; when raised, it will be a spiritual body. There is, of course, a physical body, so there has to be a spiritual body. 45 For the scripture says, "The first man, Adam, was created a living being"; but the last Adam is the life-giving Spirit. 46 It is not the spiritual that comes first, but the physical, and then the spiritual. 47 The first Adam, made of earth, came from the earth; the second Adam came from heaven. 48 Those who belong to the earth are like the one who was made of earth; those who are of heaven are like the one who came from heaven. 49 Just as we wear the likeness of the man made of earth, so we will wear* the likeness of the Man from heaven.

50 What I mean, brothers and sisters, is that what is made of flesh and blood cannot share in God's Kingdom, and what is mortal cannot possess immortality.

51-52 Listen to this secret truth: we shall not all die, but when the last trumpet sounds, we shall all be changed in an instant, as quickly as the blinking of an eye. For when the trumpet sounds, the dead will be raised, never to die again, and we shall all be changed. 53 For what is mortal must be changed into what is immortal; what will die must be changed into what cannot die. 54 So when this takes place, and the mortal has been changed into the immortal, then the scripture will come true: "Death is destroyed; victory is complete!"

55 "Where, Death, is your victory?
    Where, Death, is your power to hurt?"
56 Death gets its power to hurt from sin, and sin gets its power from the Law. 57 But thanks be to God who gives us the victory through our Lord Jesus Christ!

58 So then, my dear brothers and sisters, stand firm and steady. Keep busy always in your work for the Lord, since you know that nothing you do in the Lord's service is ever useless.

The Offering for Fellow-believers

16 Now, concerning what you wrote about the money to be raised to help God's people in Judea. You must do what I told the churches in Galatia to do. 2 Every Sunday each of you must put aside some money, in proportion to what you have earned, and save it up, so that there will be no need to collect money when I come. 3 After I come, I shall give letters of introduction to those you have approved, and send them to take your gift to Jerusalem. 4 If it seems worthwhile for me to go, then they can go along with me.

Paul's Plans

5 I shall come to you after I have gone through Macedonia — for I have to go through Macedonia. 6 I shall probably spend some time with you, perhaps the whole winter, and then you can help me to continue my journey, wherever it is I shall go next. 7 I want

15.49 *we will wear*; some manuscripts have *let us wear*.

1 CORINTHIANS 16.1-4

Paul wanted the Corinthians to give money to

PEOPLE IN
NEED.

If you would like to do the same, get three jars, and label one 'spend', one 'save' and one 'give'. For any money that you get in the next few months, split it between these jars, putting money in the 'give' jar first.

to see you more than just briefly in passing; I hope to spend quite a long time with you, if the Lord allows.

[8] I will stay here in Ephesus until the day of Pentecost. [9] There is a real opportunity here for great and worthwhile work, even though there are many opponents.

[10] If Timothy comes your way, be sure to make him feel welcome among you, because he is working for the Lord, just as I am. [11] No one should look down on him, but you must help him to continue his trip in peace, so that he will come back to me; for I am expecting him back with the brothers and sisters.

[12] Now, about brother Apollos. I have often encouraged him to visit you with the other believers, but he is not completely convinced* that he should go at this time. When he gets the chance, however, he will go.

Final Words

[13] Be alert, stand firm in the faith, be brave, be strong. [14] Do all your work in love.

[15] You know about Stephanas and his family; they are the first Christian converts in Achaia and have given themselves to the service of God's people. I beg you, my brothers and sisters, [16] to follow the leadership of such people as these, and of anyone else who works and serves with them.

[17] I am happy about the coming of Stephanas, Fortunatus, and Achaicus; they have made up for your absence [18] and have cheered me up, just as they cheered you up. Such men as these deserve notice.

[19] The churches in the province of Asia send you their greetings; Aquila and Priscilla and the church that meets in their house send warm Christian greetings. [20] All the believers here send greetings. Greet one another with a holy kiss.

[21] With my own hand I write this: *Greetings from Paul.*

[22] Whoever does not love the Lord — a curse on him! *Marana tha* — Our Lord, come!

[23] The grace of the Lord Jesus be with you.

[24] My love be with you all in Christ Jesus.

16.12 *he is not completely convinced;* or *it is not at all God's will.*

THE LETTER OF
2 CORINTHIANS

WRITTEN: AROUND AD54-56

WHAT YOU NEED TO KNOW:

This is at least the second letter that Paul wrote to the Corinthians (there may have been others that are not in our Bible). In this letter, Paul is defending himself against accusations from people who are calling him and his teaching false. As Paul writes, he uses a lot of Roman imagery, in order to connect with the audience who will be reading his words.

WHY READ IT?

In this letter, Paul recaps some of the major themes of Christian belief. He also gives insights into the way he stood up for himself in a culture where he was criticised for his faith.

SPOTLIGHT:

Corinth was a coastal city and a port, so there were people of different cultures coming in and out of it on a regular basis. The temple of Aphrodite, the Greek goddess of love, was at the centre of Corinthian life, and its priests dictated many of the values and morals of the city.

As you read through this letter, highlight verses that show how Paul dealt with criticism. Also write on this page how you deal with criticism, either positively or negatively.

(AD48)
PAUL'S 2ND MISSIONARY JOURNEY

VISITS CORINTH

(AD54-56)
WRITES 2 CORINTHIANS

1372

2 Corin.

.·:········

Luke
John
Acts
Romans
1 Corin.

2 CORINTHIANS 1

1 From Paul, an apostle of Christ Jesus by God's will, and from our brother Timothy —

To the church of God in Corinth, and to all God's people throughout Achaia:

2 May God our Father and the Lord Jesus Christ give you grace and peace.

Paul Gives Thanks to God

3 Let us give thanks to the God and Father of our Lord Jesus Christ, the merciful Father, the God from whom all help comes! 4 He helps us in all our troubles, so that we are able to help others who have all kinds of troubles, using the same help that we ourselves have received from God. 5 Just as we have a share in Christ's many sufferings, so also through Christ we share in God's great help. 6 If we suffer, it is for your help and salvation; if we are helped, then you too are helped and given the strength to endure with patience the same sufferings that we also endure. 7 So our hope in you is never shaken; we know that just as you share in our sufferings, you also share in the help we receive.

8 We want to remind you, brothers and sisters, of the trouble we had in the province of Asia. The burdens laid upon us were so great and so heavy that we gave up all hope of staying alive. 9 We felt that the death sentence had been passed on us. But this happened so that we should rely, not on ourselves, but only on God, who raises the dead. 10 From such terrible dangers of death* he saved us, and will save us; and we have placed our hope in him that he will save us again, 11 as you help us by means of your prayers for us. So it will be that the many prayers for us will be answered, and God will bless us; and many will raise their voices to him in thanksgiving for us.

The Change in Paul's Plans

12 We are proud that our conscience assures us that our lives in this world, and especially our relations with you, have been ruled by God-given frankness* and sincerity, by the power of God's grace, and not by human wisdom. 13-14 We write to you only what you can read and understand. But even though you now understand us only in part, I hope that you will come to understand us completely, so that in the Day of our Lord Jesus you can be as proud of us as we shall be of you.

15 I was so sure of all this that I made plans at first to visit you, in order that you might be blessed twice. 16 For I planned to visit you on my way to Macedonia and again on my way back, in order to get help from you for my journey to Judea. 17 In planning this, did I appear fickle? When I make my plans, do I make them from selfish motives, ready to say "Yes, yes" and "No, no" at the same time? 18 As surely as God speaks the truth, my promise to you was not a "Yes" and a "No". 19 For Jesus Christ, the Son of God, who was preached among you by Silas, Timothy, and myself, is not one who is "Yes" and "No". On the contrary, he is God's "Yes"; 20 for it is he who is the "Yes" to all God's promises. This is why through Jesus Christ our "Amen" is said to the glory of God. 21 It is God himself who makes us, together with you, sure of our life in union with Christ; it is God himself who has set us apart, 22 who has placed his mark of ownership upon us, and who has given us the Holy Spirit in our hearts as the guarantee of all that he has in store for us.

....

1.10 *terrible dangers of death*; some manuscripts have *terrible death*.
1.12 *frankness*; some manuscripts have *holiness*.

2 Corin.

....

Galat.
Ephes.
Philipp.
Coloss.
1 Thess.

²³ I call God as my witness — he knows my heart! It was in order to spare you that I decided not to go to Corinth. ²⁴ We are not trying to dictate to you what you must believe; we know that you stand firm in the faith. Instead, we are working with you for your own happiness.

2 So I made up my mind not to come to you again to make you sad. ² For if I were to make you sad, who would be left to cheer me up? Only the very persons I had made sad. ³ That is why I wrote that letter to you — I did not want to come to you and be made sad by the very people who should make me glad. For I am convinced that when I am happy, then all of you are happy too. ⁴ I wrote to you with a greatly troubled and distressed heart and with many tears; my purpose was not to make you sad, but to make you realize how much I love you all.

Forgiveness for the Offender

⁵ Now, if anyone has made somebody sad, he has not done it to me but to all of you — in part at least. (I say this because I do not want to be too hard on him.) ⁶ It is enough that this person has been punished in this way by most of you. ⁷ Now, however, you should forgive him and encourage him, in order to keep him from becoming so sad as to give up completely. ⁸ And so I beg you to let him know that you really do love him. ⁹ I wrote you that letter because I wanted to find out how well you had stood the test and whether you are always ready to obey my instructions. ¹⁰ When you forgive someone for what he or she has done, I forgive them too. For when I forgive — if, indeed, I need to forgive anything — I do it in Christ's presence because of you, ¹¹ in order to keep Satan from getting the upper hand of us; for we know what his plans are.

Paul's Anxiety in Troas

¹² When I arrived in Troas to preach the Good News about Christ, I found that the Lord had opened the way for the work there. ¹³ But I was deeply worried, because I could not find our brother Titus. So I said goodbye to the people there and went on to Macedonia.

Victory through Christ

¹⁴ But thanks be to God! For in union with Christ we are always led by God as prisoners in Christ's victory procession. God uses us to make the knowledge about Christ spread everywhere like a sweet fragrance. ¹⁵ For we are like a sweet-smelling incense offered by Christ to God, which spreads among those who are being saved and those who are being lost. ¹⁶ For those who are being lost, it is a deadly stench that kills; but for those who are being saved, it is a fragrance that brings life. Who, then, is capable of such a task? ¹⁷ We are not like so many others, who handle God's message as if it were cheap merchandise; but because God has sent us, we speak with sincerity in his presence, as servants of Christ.

Servants of the New Covenant

3 Does this sound as if we were again boasting about ourselves? Could it be that, like some other people, we need letters of recommendation to you or from you? ² You yourselves are the letter we have, written on our hearts for everyone to know and read. ³ It is clear that Christ himself wrote this letter and sent it by us. It is written, not with ink but with the Spirit of the living God, and not on stone tablets but on human hearts.

1374

2 Corin.

Luke
John
Acts
Romans
1 Corin.

2 CORINTHIANS 3, 4

4 We say this because we have confidence in God through Christ. 5 There is nothing in us that allows us to claim that we are capable of doing this work. The capacity we have comes from God; 6 it is he who made us capable of serving the new covenant, which consists not of a written law but of the Spirit. The written law brings death, but the Spirit gives life.

7 The Law was carved in letters on stone tablets, and God's glory appeared when it was given. Even though the brightness on Moses' face was fading, it was so strong that the people of Israel could not keep their eyes fixed on him. If the Law, which brings death when it is in force, came with such glory, 8 how much greater is the glory that belongs to the activity of the Spirit! 9 The system which brings condemnation was glorious; how much more glorious is the activity which brings salvation! 10 We may say that because of the far brighter glory now the glory that was so bright in the past is gone. 11 For if there was glory in that which lasted for a while, how much more glory is there in that which lasts for ever!

12 Because we have this hope, we are very bold. 13 We are not like Moses, who had to put a veil over his face so that the people of Israel would not see the brightness fade and disappear. 14 Their minds, indeed, were closed; and to this very day their minds are covered with the same veil as they read the books of the old covenant. The veil is removed only when a person is joined to Christ. 15 Even today, whenever they read the Law of Moses, the veil still covers their minds. 16 But it can be removed, as the scripture says about Moses: "His veil was removed when he turned to the Lord."* 17 Now, "the Lord" in this passage is the Spirit; and where the Spirit of the Lord is present, there is freedom. 18 All of us, then, reflect the glory of the Lord with uncovered faces; and that same glory, coming from the Lord, who is the Spirit, transforms us into his likeness in an ever greater degree of glory.

Spiritual Treasure in Clay Pots

4 God in his mercy has given us this work to do, and so we are not discouraged. 2 We put aside all secret and shameful deeds; we do not act with deceit, nor do we falsify the word of God. In the full light of truth we live in God's sight and try to commend ourselves to everyone's good conscience. 3 For if the gospel we preach is hidden, it is hidden only from those who are being lost. 4 They do not believe, because their minds have been kept in the dark by the evil god of this world. He keeps them from seeing the light shining on them, the light that comes from the Good News about the glory of Christ, who is the exact likeness of God. 5 For it is not ourselves that we preach; we preach Jesus Christ as Lord, and ourselves as your servants for Jesus' sake. 6 The God who said, "Out of darkness the light shall shine!" is the same God who made his light shine in our hearts, to bring us the knowledge of God's glory shining in the face of Christ.

7 Yet we who have this spiritual treasure are like common clay pots, in order to show that the supreme power belongs to God, not to us. 8 We are often troubled, but not crushed; sometimes in doubt, but never in despair; 9 there are many enemies, but we are never without a friend; and though badly hurt at times, we are not destroyed. 10 At all times we carry in our mortal bodies the death of Jesus, so that his life also may be seen in our bodies. 11 Throughout our lives we are always in danger of death for Jesus'

3.16 Verse 16 may be translated: *But the veil is removed whenever someone turns to the Lord.*

2 CORINTHIANS 4, 5

1375

2 Corin.

....

Galat.
Ephes.
Philipp.
Coloss.
1 Thess.

sake, in order that his life may be seen in this mortal body of ours. [12]This means that death is at work in us, but life is at work in you.

[13]The scripture says, "I spoke because I believed." In the same spirit of faith, we also speak because we believe. [14]We know that God, who raised the Lord Jesus to life, will also raise us up with Jesus and take us, together with you, into his presence. [15]All this is for your sake; and as God's grace reaches more and more people, they will offer to the glory of God more prayers of thanksgiving.

Living by Faith

[16]For this reason we never become discouraged. Even though our physical being is gradually decaying, yet our spiritual being is renewed day after day. [17]And this small and temporary trouble we suffer will bring us a tremendous and eternal glory, much greater than the trouble. [18]For we fix our attention, not on things that are seen, but on things that are unseen. What can be seen lasts only for a time, but what cannot be seen lasts for ever.

5 For we know that when this tent we live in — our body here on earth — is torn down, God will have a house in heaven for us to live in, a home he himself has made, which will last for ever. [2]And now we sigh, so great is our desire that our home which comes from heaven should be put on over us; [3]by being clothed with it we shall not be without a body. [4]While we live in this earthly tent, we groan with a feeling of oppression; it is not that we want to get rid of our earthly body, but that we want to have the heavenly one put on over us, so that what is mortal will be transformed by life. [5]God is the one who has prepared us for this change, and he gave us his Spirit as the guarantee of all that he has in store for us.

[6]So we are always full of courage. We know that as long as we are at home in the body we are away from the Lord's home. [7]For our life is a matter of faith, not of sight. [8]We are full of courage and would much prefer to leave our home in the body and be at home with the Lord. [9]More than anything else, however, we want to please him, whether in our home here or there. [10]For all of us must appear before Christ, to be judged by him. We will each receive what we deserve, according to everything we have done, good or bad, in our bodily life.

Friendship with God through Christ

[11]We know what it means to fear the Lord, and so we try to persuade others. God knows us completely, and I hope that in your hearts you know me as well. [12]We are not trying again to recommend ourselves to you; rather, we are trying to give you a good reason to be proud of us, so that you will be able to answer those who boast about people's appearance and not about their character. [13]Are we really insane? It is for God's sake. Or are we sane? Then it is for your sake. [14]We are ruled by the love of Christ, now that we recognize that one man died for everyone, which means that all share in his death. [15]He died for all, so that those who live should no longer live for themselves, but only for him who died and was raised to life for their sake.

[16]No longer, then, do we judge anyone by human standards. Even if at one time we judged Christ according to human standards, we no longer do so. [17]Anyone who is joined to Christ is a new being; the old is gone, the new has come. [18]All this is done by God, who through Christ changed us from enemies into his friends and gave us the task of making others his friends also. [19]Our message is that God was making the whole human race

2 CORINTHIANS 5.17

Find a drawer or cupboard that you can clear out. Put all of the old stuff that you don't use or want in a pile. Consider what Jesus might want to get rid of in your life, and then throw the pile of

OLD STUFF AWAY.

Now take some time to think about the new things that Jesus might want to give you instead of the old (for example, courage, peace, purpose or adventure).

1376

2 Corin.

....

Luke
John
Acts
Romans
1 Corin.

2 CORINTHIANS 5, 6

his friends through Christ.* God did not keep an account of their sins, and he has given us the message which tells how he makes them his friends. [20]Here we are, then, speaking for Christ, as though God himself were making his appeal through us. We plead on Christ's behalf: let God change you from enemies into his friends! [21]Christ was without sin, but for our sake God made him share our sin in order that in union with him we might share the righteousness of God.

6 In our work together with God, then, we beg you who have received God's grace not to let it be wasted. [2]Hear what God says:

"When the time came for me to show you favour
    I heard you;
when the day arrived for me to save you,
    I helped you."

Listen! This is the hour to receive God's favour; today is the day to be saved!

[3]We do not want anyone to find fault with our work, so we try not to put obstacles in anyone's way. [4]Instead, in everything we do we show that we are God's servants by patiently enduring troubles, hardships, and difficulties. [5]We have been beaten, imprisoned, and mobbed; we have been overworked and have gone without sleep or food. [6]By our purity, knowledge, patience, and kindness we have shown ourselves to be God's servants — by the Holy Spirit, by our true love, [7]by our message of truth, and by the power of God. We have righteousness as our weapon, both to attack and to defend ourselves. [8]We are honoured and disgraced; we are insulted and praised. We are treated as liars, yet we speak the truth; [9]as unknown, yet we are known by all; as though we were dead, but, as you see, we live on. Although punished, we are not killed; [10]although saddened, we are always glad; we seem poor, but we make many people rich; we seem to have nothing, yet we really possess everything.

[11]Dear friends in Corinth! We have spoken frankly to you; we have opened our hearts wide. [12]It is not we who have closed our hearts to you; it is you who have closed your hearts to us. [13]I speak now as though you were my children: show us the same feelings that we have for you. Open your hearts wide!

Warning against Pagan Influences

[14]Do not try to work together as equals with unbelievers, for it cannot be done. How can right and wrong be partners? How can light and darkness live together? [15]How can Christ and the Devil agree? What does a believer have in common with an unbeliever? [16]How can God's temple come to terms with pagan idols? For we are the temple of the living God! As God himself has said:

"I will make my home with my people
    and live among them;
I will be their God,
    and they shall be my people."

[17]And so the Lord says,

"You must leave them
    and separate yourselves from them.
Have nothing to do with what is unclean,
    and I will accept you.

5.19 *God was making the whole human race his friends through Christ*; or *God was in Christ making the whole human race his friends.*

2 CORINTHIANS 6–8

1377

2 Corin.

·········

Galat.
Ephes.
Philipp.
Coloss.
1 Thess.

¹⁸ I will be your father,
    and you shall be my sons and daughters,
    says the Lord Almighty."

7 All these promises are made to us, my dear friends. So then, let us purify ourselves from everything that makes body or soul unclean, and let us be completely holy by living in awe of God.

Paul's Joy

² Make room for us in your hearts. We have wronged no one; we have ruined no one, nor tried to take advantage of anyone. ³ I do not say this to condemn you; for, as I have said before, you are so dear to us that we are always together, whether we live or die. ⁴ I am so sure of you; I take such pride in you! In all our troubles I am still full of courage; I am running over with joy.

⁵ Even after we arrived in Macedonia, we had no rest. There were troubles everywhere, quarrels with others, fears in our hearts. ⁶ But God, who encourages the downhearted, encouraged us with the coming of Titus. ⁷ It was not only his coming that cheered us, but also his report of how you encouraged him. He told us how much you want to see me, how sorry you are, how ready you are to defend me; and so I am even happier now.

⁸ For even if that letter of mine made you sad, I am not sorry I wrote it. I could have been sorry when I saw that it made you sad for a while. ⁹ But now I am happy — not because I made you sad, but because your sadness made you change your ways. That sadness was used by God, and so we caused you no harm. ¹⁰ For the sadness that is used by God brings a change of heart that leads to salvation — and there is no regret in that! But sadness that is merely human causes death. ¹¹ See what God did with this sadness of yours: how earnest it has made you, how eager to prove your innocence! Such indignation, such alarm, such feelings, such devotion, such readiness to punish wrongdoing! You have shown yourselves to be without fault in the whole matter.

¹² So, even though I wrote that letter, it was not because of the one who did wrong or the one who was wronged. Instead, I wrote it to make plain to you, in God's sight, how deep your devotion to us really is. ¹³ That is why we were encouraged.

Not only were we encouraged; how happy Titus made us with his happiness over the way in which all of you helped to cheer him up! ¹⁴ I did boast of you to him, and you have not disappointed me. We have always spoken the truth to you, and in the same way the boast we made to Titus has proved true. ¹⁵ And so his love for you grows stronger, as he remembers how all of you were ready to obey his instructions, how you welcomed him with fear and trembling. ¹⁶ How happy I am that I can depend on you completely!

Christian Giving

8 Our brothers and sisters, we want you to know what God's grace has accomplished in the churches in Macedonia. ² They have been severely tested by the troubles they went through; but their joy was so great that they were extremely generous in their giving, even though they are very poor. ³ I can assure you that they gave as much as they could, and even more than they could. Of their own free will ⁴ they begged us and pleaded for the privilege of having a part in helping God's people in Judea. ⁵ It was more than we could have hoped for! First they gave themselves to the Lord; and then, by God's will they gave themselves to us as well. ⁶ So we urged Titus, who began this work, to continue it and help you complete this special service of love. [7]You are so rich in all you have: in faith, speech, and knowledge, in your eagerness to help and in your love for us.* And so we want you to be generous also in this service of love.

[8]I am not laying down any rules. But by showing how eager others are to help, I am trying to find out how real your own love is. [9]You know the grace of our Lord Jesus Christ; rich as he was, he made himself poor for your sake, in order to make you rich by means of his poverty.

[10]My opinion is that it is better for you to finish now what you began last year. You were the first, not only to act, but also to be willing to act. [11]On with it, then, and finish the job! Be as eager to finish it as you were to plan it, and do it with what you now have. [12]If you are eager to give, God will accept your gift on the basis of what you have to give, not on what you haven't.

[13-14]I am not trying to relieve others by putting a burden on you; but since you have plenty at this time, it is only fair that you should help those who are in need. Then, when you are in need and they have plenty, they will help you. In this way both are treated equally. [15]As the scripture says, "The one who gathered much did not have too much, and the one who gathered little did not have too little."

Titus and his Companions

[16]How we thank God for making Titus as eager as we are to help you! [17]Not only did he welcome our request; he was so eager to help that of his own free will he decided to go to you. [18]With him we are sending the brother who is highly respected in all the churches for his work in preaching the gospel. [19]And besides that, he has been chosen and appointed by the churches to travel with us as we carry out this service of love for the sake of the Lord's glory, and in order to show that we want to help.

[20]We are taking care not to stir up any complaints about the way we handle this generous gift. [21]Our purpose is to do what is right, not only in the sight of the Lord, but also in the sight of others.

[22]So we are sending our brother with them; we have tested him many times and found him always very eager to help. And now that he has so much confidence in you, he is all the more eager to help. [23]As for Titus, he is my partner and works with me to help you; as for the other brothers who are going with him, they represent the churches and bring glory to Christ. [24]Show your love to them, so that all the churches will be sure of it and know that we are right in boasting about you.

Help for Fellow-Christians

9 There is really no need for me to write to you about the help being sent to God's people in Judea. [2]I know that you are willing to help, and I have boasted of you to the people in Macedonia. "The brothers and sisters in Achaia," I said, "have been ready to help since last year." Your eagerness has stirred up most of them. [3]Now I am sending these brothers and sisters, so that our boasting about you in this matter may not turn out to be empty words. But, just as I said, you will be ready with your help. [4]However, if the people from Macedonia should come with me and find out that you are not ready, how ashamed we would be — not to speak of your shame — for feeling so sure of you! [5]So I thought it was necessary to urge these brothers and sisters to go to you ahead of me and get ready in advance the gift you

8.7 *your love for us*; some manuscripts have *our love for you.*

2 CORINTHIANS 9, 10

1379

2 Corin.

....

Galat.
Ephes.
Philipp.
Coloss.
1 Thess.

promised to make. Then it will be ready when I arrive, and it will show that you give because you want to, not because you have to.

6 Remember that the person who sows few seeds will have a small crop; the one who sows many seeds will have a large crop. 7 You should each give, then, as you have decided, not with regret or out of a sense of duty; for God loves the one who gives gladly. 8 And God is able to give you more than you need, so that you will always have all you need for yourselves and more than enough for every good cause. 9 As the scripture says:

"He gives generously to the needy;
    his kindness lasts for ever."

10 And God, who supplies seed to sow and bread to eat, will also supply you with all the seed you need and will make it grow and produce a rich harvest from your generosity. 11 He will always make you rich enough to be generous at all times, so that many will thank God for your gifts which they receive from us. 12 For this service you perform not only meets the needs of God's people, but also produces an outpouring of gratitude to God. 13 And because of the proof which this service of yours brings, many will give glory to God for your loyalty to the gospel of Christ, which you profess, and for your generosity in sharing with them and everyone else. 14 And so with deep affection they will pray for you because of the extraordinary grace God has shown you. 15 Let us thank God for his priceless gift!

Paul Defends his Ministry

10 I, Paul, make a personal appeal to you — I who am said to be meek and mild when I am with you, but harsh with you when I am away. By the gentleness and kindness of Christ 2 I beg you not to force me to be harsh when I come; for I am sure I can deal harshly with those who say that we act from worldly motives. 3 It is true that we live in the world, but we do not fight from worldly motives. 4 The weapons we use in our fight are not the world's weapons but God's powerful weapons, which we use to destroy strongholds. We destroy false arguments; 5 we pull down every proud obstacle that is raised against the knowledge of God; we take every thought captive and make it obey Christ. 6 And after you have proved your complete loyalty, we will be ready to punish any act of disloyalty.

7 You are looking at the outward appearance of things. Is there someone there who reckons himself or herself to belong to Christ? Well, let them think again about themselves, because we belong to Christ just as much as they do. 8 For I am not ashamed, even if I have boasted somewhat too much about the authority that the Lord has given us — authority to build you up, not to tear you down. 9 I do not want it to appear that I am trying to frighten you with my letters. 10 Someone will say, "Paul's letters are severe and strong, but when he is with us in person, he is weak, and his words are nothing!" 11 Such a person must understand that there is no difference between what we write in our letters when we are away and what we will do when we are there with you.

12 Of course we would not dare to classify ourselves or compare ourselves with those who rate themselves so highly. How stupid they are! They make up their own standards to measure themselves by, and they judge themselves by their own standards! 13 As for us, however, our boasting will not go beyond certain limits; it will stay within the limits of the work which God has set for us, and this includes our work among you. 14 And since you are within those limits, we were not going beyond them when we came to

1380

2 Corin.

⋮ ⋮⋮⋮⋮⋮⋮

Luke
John
Acts
Romans
1 Corin.

2 CORINTHIANS 10, 11

you, bringing the Good News about Christ. [15] So we do not boast about the work that others have done beyond the limits God set for us. Instead, we hope that your faith may grow and that we may be able to do a much greater work among you, always within the limits that God has set. [16] Then we can preach the Good News in other countries beyond you and shall not have to boast about work already done in someone else's field.

[17] But as the scripture says, "Whoever wants to boast must boast about what the Lord has done." [18] For it is people of whom the Lord thinks well who are really approved, not people who think well of themselves.

Paul and the False Apostles

11 I wish you would tolerate me, even when I am a bit foolish. Please do! [2] I am jealous for you, just as God is; you are like a pure virgin whom I have promised in marriage to one man only, Christ himself. [3] I am afraid that your minds will be corrupted and that you will abandon your full and pure devotion to Christ — in the same way that Eve was deceived by the snake's clever lies. [4] For you gladly tolerate anyone who comes to you and preaches a different Jesus, not the one we preached; and you accept a spirit and a gospel completely different from the Spirit and the gospel you received from us!

[5] I do not think that I am the least bit inferior to those very special so-called "apostles" of yours! [6] Perhaps I am an amateur in speaking, but certainly not in knowledge; we have made this clear to you at all times and in all conditions.

[7] I did not charge you a thing when I preached the Good News of God to you; I humbled myself in order to make you important. Was that wrong of me? [8] While I was working among you, I was paid by other churches. I was robbing them, so to speak, in order to help you. [9] And during the time I was with you I did not bother you for help when I needed money; the brothers and sisters who came from Macedonia brought me everything I needed. As in the past, so in the future: I will never be a burden to you! [10] By Christ's truth in me, I promise that this boast of mine will not be silenced anywhere in all Achaia. [11] Do I say this because I don't love you? God knows I love you!

[12] I will go on doing what I am doing now, in order to keep those other "apostles" from having any reason for boasting and saying that they work in the same way that we do. [13] Those men are not true apostles — they are false apostles, who lie about their work and disguise themselves to look like real apostles of Christ. [14] Well, no wonder! Even Satan can disguise himself to look like an angel of light! [15] So it is no great thing if his servants disguise themselves to look like servants of righteousness. In the end they will get exactly what their actions deserve.

Paul's Sufferings as an Apostle

[16] I repeat: no one should think that I am a fool. But if you do, at least accept me as a fool, so that I will have a little to boast of. [17] Of course what I am saying now is not what the Lord would like me to say; in this matter of boasting I am really talking like a fool. [18] But since there are so many who boast for merely human reasons, I will do the same. [19] You yourselves are so wise, and so you gladly tolerate fools! [20] You tolerate anyone who orders you about or takes advantage of you or traps you or looks down on you or slaps you in the face. [21] I am ashamed to admit that we were too timid to do those things!

2 Corin.

⋯⋯⋯⋮

Galat.
Ephes.
Philipp.
Coloss.
1 Thess.

But if anyone dares to boast about something — I am talking like a fool — I will be just as daring. 22 Are they Hebrews? So am I. Are they Israelites? So am I. Are they Abraham's descendants? So am I. 23 Are they Christ's servants? I sound like a madman — but I am a better servant than they are! I have worked much harder, I have been in prison more times, I have been whipped much more, and I have been near death more often. 24 Five times I was given the 39 lashes by the Jews; 25 three times I was whipped by the Romans; and once I was stoned. I have been in three shipwrecks, and once I spent 24 hours in the water. 26 In my many travels I have been in danger from floods and from robbers, in danger from fellow-Jews and from Gentiles; there have been dangers in the cities, dangers in the wilds, dangers on the high seas, and dangers from false friends. 27 There has been work and toil; often I have gone without sleep; I have been hungry and thirsty; I have often been without enough food, shelter, or clothing. 28 And not to mention other things, every day I am under the pressure of my concern for all the churches. 29 When someone is weak, then I feel weak too; when someone is led into sin, I am filled with distress.

30 If I must boast, I will boast about things that show how weak I am. 31 The God and Father of the Lord Jesus — blessed be his name for ever! — knows that I am not lying. 32 When I was in Damascus, the governor under King Aretas placed guards at the city gates to arrest me. 33 But I was let down in a basket through an opening in the wall and escaped from him.

Paul's Visions and Revelations

12 I have to boast, even though it doesn't do any good. But I will now talk about visions and revelations given me by the Lord. 2 I know a certain Christian man who fourteen years ago was snatched up to the highest heaven (I do not know whether this actually happened or whether he had a vision — only God knows). 3-4 I repeat, I know that this man was snatched to Paradise (again, I do not know whether this actually happened or whether it was a vision — only God knows), and there he heard things which cannot be put into words, things that human lips may not speak. 5 So I will boast about this man — but I will not boast about myself, except the things that show how weak I am. 6 If I wanted to boast, I would not be a fool, because I would be telling the truth. But I will not boast, because I do not want anyone to have a higher opinion of me than he has as a result of what he has seen me do and heard me say.

7 But to keep me from being puffed up with pride because of the many wonderful things I saw, I was given a painful physical ailment, which acts as Satan's messenger to beat me and keep me from being proud. 8 Three times I prayed to the Lord about this and asked him to take it away. 9 But his answer was: "My grace is all you need, for my power is greatest when you are weak." I am most happy, then, to be proud of my weaknesses, in order to feel the protection of Christ's power over me. 10 I am content with weaknesses, insults, hardships, persecutions, and difficulties for Christ's sake. For when I am weak, then I am strong.

Paul's Concern for the Corinthians

11 I am acting like a fool — but you have made me do it. You are the ones who ought to show your approval of me. For even if I am nothing, I am in no way inferior to those very special "apostles" of yours. 12 The many miracles and wonders that prove that I am an apostle were performed among you with much patience. 13 How

2 CORINTHIANS 12

Write down
some of your

- BIGGEST -

WEAKNESSES.

As you look at this list, think about how God might use some of these weaknesses and how they might positively affect your relationship with God.

were you treated any worse than the other churches, except that I did not bother you for financial help? Please forgive me for being so unfair!

[14] This is now the third time that I am ready to come to visit you — and I will not make any demands on you. It is you I want, not your money. After all, children should not have to provide for their parents, but parents should provide for their children. [15] I will be glad to spend all I have, and myself as well, in order to help you. Will you love me less because I love you so much?

[16] You will agree, then, that I was not a burden to you. But someone will say that I was crafty, and trapped you with lies. [17] How? Did I take advantage of you through any of the messengers I sent? [18] I begged Titus to go, and I sent the other Christian brother with him. Would you say that Titus took advantage of you? Do he and I not act from the very same motives and behave in the same way?

[19] Perhaps you think that all along we have been trying to defend ourselves before you. No! We speak as Christ would wish us to speak in the presence of God, and everything we do, dear friends, is done to help you. [20] I am afraid that when I get there I will find you different from what I would like you to be and you will find me different from what you would like me to be. I am afraid that I will find quarrelling and jealousy, hot tempers and selfishness, insults and gossip, pride and disorder. [21] I am afraid that the next time I come my God will humiliate me in your presence, and I shall weep over many who sinned in the past and have not repented of the immoral things they have done — their lust and their sexual sins.

Final Warnings and Greetings

13 This is now the third time that I am coming to visit you. "Any accusation must be upheld by the evidence of two or more witnesses" — as the scripture says. [2] I want to say to those of you who have sinned in the past, and to all the others; I said it before during my second visit to you, but I will say it again now that I am away: the next time I come nobody will escape punishment. [3] You will have all the proof you want that Christ speaks through me. When he deals with you, he is not weak; instead, he shows his power among you. [4] For even though it was in weakness that he was put to death on the cross, it is by God's power that he lives. In union with him we also are weak; but in our relations with you we shall share God's power in his life.

[5] Put yourselves to the test and judge yourselves, to find out whether you are living in faith. Surely you know that Christ Jesus is in you? — unless you have completely failed. [6] I trust you will know that we are not failures. [7] We pray to God that you will do no wrong — not in order to show that we are a success, but so that you may do what is right, even though we may seem to be failures. [8] For we cannot do a thing against the truth, but only for it. [9] We are glad when we are weak but you are strong. And so we also pray that you will become perfect. [10] That is why I write this while I am away from you; it is so that when I arrive I will not have to deal harshly with you in using the authority that the Lord has given me — authority to build you up, not to tear you down.

[11] And now, my brothers and sisters, goodbye! Strive for perfection; listen to my appeals; agree with one another; live in peace. And the God of love and peace will be with you.

[12] Greet one another with a holy kiss.

All God's people send you their greetings.

[13] The grace of the Lord Jesus Christ, the love of God, and the fellowship of the Holy Spirit be with you all.

THE LETTER TO THE

GALATIANS

WRITTEN: AROUND AD48-52

Galatia was a Roman province - a big area that was home to the churches of Antioch, Lystra, Derbe and Iconium. (Read Acts 13-15 to find out about Paul's trips to these places.) Galatia was also the first location of a non-Jewish Christian community.

Have you ever thought how freeing it is to know that we have a relationship with God only because of

JESUS

not because of anything we can do? Spend some time reflecting and praying about this while drawing your own flag of freedom here.

COLOUR IT, STICK SHINY STARS ON IT

- anything you like!

WHAT YOU NEED TO KNOW:

Galatians is a letter to the church in the area of Galatia (modern-day Turkey). Like many other churches at the time, Galatia had been influenced by false teachers who were saying that all Christians, Jewish or Gentile, had to obey Jewish laws, such as not eating certain kinds of meat. Paul wrote this fiery letter to put them straight. He displayed his anger that the way of freedom that Jesus came to bring had been turned back to a message of law-keeping.

WHY READ IT?

Galatians really drives it home that we are not saved (or in a right relationship with God) because we follow rules or laws, but only because of the grace and love of Jesus Christ. It's a big reminder that we are saved by grace, not by anything we do - and that's so freeing!

(AD46)
PAUL'S 1ST MISSIONARY JOURNEY

(AD48-52)
WRITES GALATIANS

VISITS GALATIA

1384

Galat.

GALATIANS 1, 2

1 From Paul, whose call to be an apostle did not come from human beings or by human means, but from Jesus Christ and God the Father, who raised him from death. [2]All the brothers and sisters who are here join me in sending greetings to the churches of Galatia:

[3]May God our Father and the Lord Jesus Christ give you grace and peace.

[4]In order to set us free from this present evil age, Christ gave himself for our sins, in obedience to the will of our God and Father. [5]To God be the glory for ever and ever! Amen.

The One Gospel

[6]I am surprised at you! In no time at all you are deserting the one who called you by the grace of Christ,* and are accepting another gospel. [7]Actually, there is no "other gospel", but I say this because there are some people who are upsetting you and trying to change the gospel of Christ. [8]But even if we or an angel from heaven should preach to you a gospel that is different from the one we preached to you, may he be condemned to hell! [9]We have said it before, and now I say it again: if anyone preaches to you a gospel that is different from the one you accepted, may he be condemned to hell!

[10]Does this sound as if I am trying to win human approval? No indeed! What I want is God's approval! Am I trying to be popular with people? If I were still trying to do so, I would not be a servant of Christ.

How Paul Became an Apostle

[11]Let me tell you, my brothers and sisters, that the gospel I preach is not of human origin. [12]I did not receive it from any human being, nor did anyone teach it to me. It was Jesus Christ himself who revealed it to me.

[13]You have been told how I used to live when I was devoted to the Jewish religion, how I persecuted without mercy the church of God and did my best to destroy it. [14]I was ahead of most fellow-Jews of my age in my practice of the Jewish religion, and was much more devoted to the traditions of our ancestors.

[15]But God in his grace chose me even before I was born, and called me to serve him. And when he decided [16]to reveal his Son to me, so that I might preach the Good News about him to the Gentiles, I did not go to anyone for advice, [17]nor did I go to Jerusalem to see those who were apostles before me. Instead, I went at once to Arabia, and then I returned to Damascus. [18]It was three years later that I went to Jerusalem to obtain information from Peter, and I stayed with him for two weeks. [19]I did not see any other apostle except James,* the Lord's brother.

[20]What I write is true. God knows that I am not lying!

[21]Afterwards I went to places in Syria and Cilicia. [22]At that time the members of the churches in Judea did not know me personally. [23]They knew only what others were saying: "The man who used to persecute us is now preaching the faith that he once tried to destroy!" [24]And so they praised God because of me.

Paul and the Other Apostles

2 Fourteen years later I went back to Jerusalem with Barnabas, taking Titus along with me. [2]I went because God revealed

---

1.6 *by the grace of Christ*; some manuscripts have *by his grace*.
1.19 *any other apostle except James*; or *any other apostle; the only other person I saw was James*.

GALATIANS 2

1385

Galat.

....

Ephes.
Philipp.
Coloss.
1 Thess.
2 Thess.

to me that I should go. In a private meeting with the leaders I explained the gospel message that I preach to the Gentiles. I did not want my work in the past or in the present to be a failure. [3] My companion Titus, even though he is Greek, was not forced to be circumcised, [4] although some wanted it done. Pretending to be fellow-believers, these men slipped into our group as spies, in order to find out about the freedom we have through our union with Christ Jesus. They wanted to make slaves of us, [5] but in order to keep the truth of the gospel safe for you, we did not give in to them for a minute.

[6] But those who seemed to be the leaders — I say this because it makes no difference to me what they were; God does not judge by outward appearances — those leaders, I say, made me no new suggestions to me. [7] On the contrary, they saw that God had given me the task of preaching the gospel to the Gentiles, just as he had given Peter the task of preaching the gospel to the Jews. [8] For by God's power I was made an apostle to the Gentiles, just as Peter was made an apostle to the Jews. [9] James, Peter, and John, who seemed to be the leaders, recognized that God had given me this special task; so they shook hands with Barnabas and me, as a sign that we were all partners. We agreed that Barnabas and I would work among the Gentiles and they among the Jews. [10] All they asked was that we should remember the needy in their group, which is the very thing I have* been eager to do.

Paul Rebukes Peter at Antioch

[11] But when Peter came to Antioch, I opposed him in public, because he was clearly wrong. [12] Before some men who had been sent by James arrived there, Peter had been eating with the Gentile brothers and sisters. But after these men arrived, he drew back and would not eat with the Gentiles, because he was afraid of those who were in favour of circumcising them. [13] The other Jewish brothers and sisters also started acting like cowards along with Peter; and even Barnabas was swept along by their cowardly action. [14] When I saw that they were not walking a straight path in line with the truth of the gospel, I said to Peter in front of them all, "You are a Jew, yet you have been living like a Gentile, not like a Jew. How, then, can you try to force Gentiles to live like Jews?"

Jews and Gentiles are Saved by Faith

[15] Indeed, we are Jews by birth and not "Gentile sinners", as they are called. [16] Yet we know that a person is put right with God only through faith in Jesus Christ, never by doing what the Law requires. We, too, have believed in Christ Jesus in order to be put right with God through our faith in Christ, and not by doing what the Law requires. For no one is put right with God by doing what the Law requires. [17] If, then, as we try to be put right with God by our union with Christ, we are found to be sinners as much as the Gentiles are — does this mean that Christ is serving the cause of sin? By no means! [18] If I start to rebuild the system of Law that I tore down, then I show myself to be someone who breaks the Law. [19] So far as the Law is concerned, however, I am dead — killed by the Law itself — in order that I might live for God. I have been put to death with Christ on his cross, [20] so that it is no longer I who live, but it is Christ who lives in me. This life that I live now, I live by faith in the Son of God, who loved me and gave his life for me. [21] I refuse to reject the grace of God. But

....

2.10 *have*; or *had*.

1386

Galat.

:·········

John
Acts
Romans
1 Corin.
2 Corin.

GALATIANS 2 3

if a person is put right with God through the Law, it means that Christ died for nothing!

Law or Faith

3 You foolish Galatians! Who put a spell on you? Before your very eyes you had a clear description of the death of Jesus Christ on the cross! [2] Tell me this one thing: did you receive God's Spirit by doing what the Law requires or by hearing the gospel and believing it? [3] How can you be so foolish! You began by God's Spirit; do you now want to finish by your own power? [4] Did all your experience mean nothing at all? Surely it meant something! [5] Does God give you the Spirit and work miracles among you because you do what the Law requires or because you hear the gospel and believe it?

[6] Consider the experience of Abraham; as the scripture says, "He believed God, and because of his faith God accepted him as righteous." [7] You should realize then, that the real descendants of Abraham are the people who have faith. [8] The scripture predicted that God would put the Gentiles right with himself through faith. And so the scripture announced the Good News to Abraham: "Through you God will bless the whole human race." [9] Abraham believed and was blessed; so all who believe are blessed as he was.

[10] Those who depend on obeying the Law live under a curse. For the scripture says, "Whoever does not always obey everything that is written in the book of the Law is under God's curse!" [11] Now, it is clear that no one is put right with God by means of the Law, because the scripture says, "Only the person who is put right with God through faith shall live."* [12] But the Law has nothing to do with faith. Instead, as the scripture says, "Whoever *does* everything the Law requires will live."

[13] But by becoming a curse for us Christ has redeemed us from the curse that the Law brings; for the scripture says, "Anyone who is hanged on a tree is under God's curse." [14] Christ did this in order that the blessing which God promised to Abraham might be given to the Gentiles by means of Christ Jesus, so that through faith we might receive the Spirit promised by God.

The Law and the Promise

[15] My brothers and sisters, I am going to use an everyday example: when two people agree on a matter and sign an agreement, no one can break it or add anything to it. [16] Now, God made his promises to Abraham and to his descendant. The scripture does not use the plural "descendants", meaning many people, but the singular "descendant", meaning one person only, namely, Christ. [17] What I mean is that God made a covenant with Abraham and promised to keep it. The Law, which was given 430 years later, cannot break that covenant and cancel God's promise. [18] For if God's gift depends on the Law, then it no longer depends on his promise. However, it was because of his promise that God gave that gift to Abraham.

[19] What, then, was the purpose of the Law? It was added in order to show what wrongdoing is, and it was meant to last until the coming of Abraham's descendant, to whom the promise was made. The Law was handed down by angels, with a man acting as a go-between. [20] But a go-between is not needed when only one person is involved; and God is one.*

3.11 *put right with God through faith shall live*; or *put right with God shall live through faith.*
3.20 *and God is one*; or *and God acts alone.*

GALATIANS 3.19

Can you think of anything from the 'Law'? (Think of books like Leviticus.) If 'Abraham's descendant' means Jesus, what do you think these verses from Galatians mean for you? We don't have to keep the Old Testament laws to be put right with God

(PHEW!),

because we come to faith through Jesus, but they can help us to understand what 'wrongdoing' is.

The Purpose of the Law

²¹ Does this mean that the Law is against God's promises? No, not at all! For if human beings had received a law that could bring life, then everyone could be put right with God by obeying it. ²² But the scripture says that the whole world is under the power of sin; and so the gift which is promised on the basis of faith in Jesus Christ is given to those who believe.

²³ But before the time for faith came, the Law kept us all locked up as prisoners until this coming faith should be revealed. ²⁴ And so the Law was in charge of us until Christ came, in order that we might then be put right with God through faith. ²⁵ Now that the time for faith is here, the Law is no longer in charge of us.

²⁶ It is through faith that all of you are God's children in union with Christ Jesus. ²⁷ You were baptized into union with Christ, and now you are clothed, so to speak, with the life of Christ himself. ²⁸ So there is no difference between Jews and Gentiles, between slaves and free people, between men and women; you are all one in union with Christ Jesus. ²⁹ If you belong to Christ, then you are the descendants of Abraham and will receive what God has promised.

4 But now to continue — the son who will receive his father's property is treated just like a slave while he is young, even though he really owns everything. ² While he is young, there are men who take care of him and manage his affairs until the time set by his father. ³ In the same way, we too were slaves of the ruling spirits of the universe before we reached spiritual maturity. ⁴ But when the right time finally came, God sent his own Son. He came as the son of a human mother and lived under the Jewish Law, ⁵ to redeem those who were under the Law, so that we might become God's sons and daughters.

⁶ To show that you are* his sons and daughters, God sent the Spirit of his Son into our hearts, the Spirit who cries out, "Father, my Father." ⁷ So then, you are no longer a slave but a son or daughter. And since that is what you are, God will give you all that he has for his heirs.

Paul's Concern for the Galatians

⁸ In the past you did not know God, and so you were slaves of beings who are not gods. ⁹ But now that you know God — or, I should say, now that God knows you — how is it that you want to turn back to those weak and pitiful ruling spirits? Why do you want to become their slaves all over again? ¹⁰ You pay special attention to certain days, months, seasons, and years. ¹¹ I am worried about you! Can it be that all my work for you has been for nothing?

¹² I beg you, my brothers and sisters, be like me. After all, I am like you. You have not done me any wrong. ¹³ You remember why I preached the gospel to you the first time; it was because I was ill. ¹⁴ But even though my physical condition was a great trial to you, you did not despise or reject me. Instead, you received me as you would an angel from heaven; you received me as you would Christ Jesus. ¹⁵ You were so happy! What has happened? I myself can say that you would have taken out your own eyes, if you could, and given them to me. ¹⁶ Have I now become your enemy by telling you the truth?

¹⁷ Those other people show a deep interest in you, but their intentions are not good. All they want is to separate you from me,

4.6 *To show that you are*; or *Because you are.*

1388

Galat.

:.........

John
Acts
Romans
1 Corin.
2 Corin.

GALATIANS 4, 5

so that you will have the same interest in them as they have in you. [18] Now, it is good to have such a deep interest if the purpose is good — this is true always, and not merely when I am with you. [19] My dear children! Once again, just like a mother in childbirth, I feel the same kind of pain for you until Christ's nature is formed in you. [20] How I wish I were with you now, so that I could take a different attitude towards you. I am so worried about you!

The Example of Hagar and Sarah

[21] Let me ask those of you who want to be subject to the Law: do you not hear what the Law says? [22] It says that Abraham had two sons, one by a slave woman, the other by a free woman. [23] His son by the slave woman was born in the usual way, but his son by the free woman was born as a result of God's promise. [24] These things can be understood as a figure: the two women represent two covenants. The one whose children are born in slavery is Hagar, and she represents the covenant made at Mount Sinai. [25] Hagar, who stands for Mount Sinai in Arabia, is* a figure of the present city of Jerusalem, in slavery with all its people. [26] But the heavenly Jerusalem is free, and she is our mother. [27] For the scripture says:

> "Be happy, you childless woman!
>   Shout and cry with joy, you who never felt the pains of
>   childbirth!
>   For the woman who was deserted will have more
>   children
>   than the woman whose husband never left her."

[28] Now, you, my brothers and sisters, are God's children as a result of his promise, just as Isaac was. [29] At that time the son who was born in the usual way persecuted the one who was born because of God's Spirit; and it is the same now. [30] But what does the scripture say? It says, "Send the slave woman and her son away; for the son of the slave woman will not have a part of the father's property along with the son of the free woman." [31] So then, my brothers and sisters, we are not the children of a slave woman but of a free woman.

Preserve your Freedom

5 Freedom is what we have — Christ has set us free! Stand, then, as free people, and do not allow yourselves to become slaves again.

[2] Listen! I, Paul, tell you that if you allow yourselves to be circumcised, it means that Christ is of no use to you at all. [3] Once more I warn any man who allows himself to be circumcised that he is obliged to obey the whole Law. [4] Those of you who try to be put right with God by obeying the Law have cut yourselves off from Christ. You are outside God's grace. [5] As for us, our hope is that God will put us right with him; and this is what we wait for by the power of God's Spirit working through our faith. [6] For when we are in union with Christ Jesus, neither circumcision nor the lack of it makes any difference at all; what matters is faith that works through love.

[7] You were doing so well! Who made you stop obeying the truth? How did he persuade you? [8] It was not done by God, who calls you. [9] "It takes only a little yeast to make the whole batch of dough rise," as they say. [10] But I still feel confident about you. Our life in union with the Lord makes me confident that you will

GALATIANS 5.22-23

Colour in the

FRUIT

– OF THE –

SPIRIT

that you see most clearly in yourself. Now, grab a different colour and colour in one that you feel you most need to develop. Pray while you do this.

4.25 *Hagar... is*; some manuscripts have *Sinai is a mountain in Arabia, and it is.*

1389

Galat.

. . . . :

Ephes.
Philipp.
Coloss.
1 Thess.
2 Thess.

not take a different view and that the man who is upsetting you, whoever he is, will be punished by God.

[11] But as for me, my brothers and sisters, if I continue to preach that circumcision is necessary, why am I still being persecuted? If that were true, then my preaching about the cross of Christ would cause no trouble. [12] I wish that the people who are upsetting you would go all the way; let them go on and castrate themselves!

[13] As for you, my brothers and sisters, you were called to be free. But do not let this freedom become an excuse for letting your physical desires control you. Instead, let love make you serve one another. [14] For the whole Law is summed up in one commandment: "Love your neighbour as you love yourself." [15] But if you act like wild animals, hurting and harming each other, then watch out, or you will completely destroy one another.

The Spirit and Human Nature

[16] What I say is this: let the Spirit direct your lives, and you will not satisfy the desires of the human nature. [17] For what our human nature wants is opposed to what the Spirit wants, and what the Spirit wants is opposed to what our human nature wants. These two are enemies, and this means that you cannot do what you want to do. [18] If the Spirit leads you, then you are not subject to the Law.

[19] What human nature does is quite plain. It shows itself in immoral, filthy, and indecent actions; [20] in worship of idols and witchcraft. People become enemies and they fight; they become jealous, angry, and ambitious. They separate into parties and groups; [21] they are envious, get drunk, have orgies, and do other things like these. I warn you now as I have before: those who do these things will not possess the Kingdom of God.

[22] But the Spirit produces love, joy, peace, patience, kindness, goodness, faithfulness, [23] humility, and self-control. There is no law against such things as these. [24] And those who belong to Christ Jesus have put to death their human nature with all its passions and desires. [25] The Spirit has given us life; he must also control our lives. [26] We must not be proud or irritate one another or be jealous of one another.

Bear One Another's Burdens

6 My brothers and sisters, if someone is caught in any kind of wrongdoing, those of you who are spiritual should set him right; but you must do it in a gentle way. And keep an eye on yourselves, so that you will not be tempted, too. [2] Help to carry one another's burdens, and in this way you will obey* the law of Christ. [3] If someone thinks he or she is somebody when really they are nobody, they are only deceiving themselves. [4] You should each judge your own conduct. If it is good, then you can be proud of what you yourself have done, without having to compare it with what someone else has done. [5] For we each have our own load to carry.

[6] Those who are being taught the Christian message should share all the good things they have with their teachers.

[7] Do not deceive yourselves; no one makes a fool of God. People will reap exactly what they sow. [8] If they sow in the field of their natural desires, from it they will gather the harvest of death; if they sow in the field of the Spirit, from the Spirit they will gather

LOVE

PEACE

PATIENCE

HUMILITY

JOY

GOODNESS

KINDNESS

FAITHFULNESS

SELF-CONTROL

6.2 *you will obey*; some manuscripts have *obey*.

the harvest of eternal life. [9] So let us not become tired of doing good; for if we do not give up, the time will come when we will reap the harvest. [10] So then, as often as we have the chance, we should do good to everyone, and especially to those who belong to our family in the faith.

Final Warning and Greeting

[11] See what big letters I make as I write to you now with my own hand! [12] The people who are trying to force you to be circumcised are the ones who want to show off and boast about external matters. They do it, however, only so that they may not be persecuted for the cross of Christ. [13] Even those who practise circumcision do not obey the Law; they want you to be circumcised so that they can boast that you submitted to this physical ceremony. [14] As for me, however, I will boast only about the cross of our Lord Jesus Christ; for by means of his cross the world is dead to me, and I am dead to the world. [15] It does not matter at all whether or not one is circumcised; what does matter is being a new creature. [16] As for those who follow this rule in their lives, may peace and mercy be with them — with them and with all God's people!

[17] To conclude: let no one give me any more trouble, because the scars I have on my body show that I am the slave of Jesus.

[18] May the grace of our Lord Jesus Christ be with you all, my brothers and sisters. Amen.

THE LETTER TO THE
EPHESIANS

WRITTEN: AROUND AD62-64 (OR POSSIBLY LATER)

WHAT YOU NEED TO KNOW:

This letter was written to the church in the city of Ephesus (in modern-day Turkey), possibly while Paul was under house arrest as a prisoner in Rome. The letter to the Ephesians covers many practical issues for Christians and the church, including how to live and work together, being united and recognising God's work through Jesus.

WHY READ IT?

Ephesians gives us a great overview of what God has done through Jesus and what that might mean for the way we live. The people in the church in Ephesus lived in a culture that was pretty messed up, so the letter was teaching them how to live in the midst of this broken world. Even if the brokenness they saw was different to the brokenness we see, Ephesians is packed with good stuff for us to read.

DOODLE HERE...

Write down four
CORE MESSAGES

that you see throughout Ephesians.

1. _____

2. _____

3. _____

4. _____

SPOTLIGHT:

The Ephesians lived in Ephesus - a beautiful, large and impressive city, full of everything you could possibly need. The city was also entrenched in Roman culture. The Romans wanted everyone to know that they were the true world authority, with ultimate power, so they held regular processions of soldiers around the city. This may be why there's a lot in this letter about authority in our relationships with God and other people, as well as the reference to a suit of armour in chapter 6.

(AD48)
PAUL'S 2ND
MISSIONARY JOURNEY

PAUL IN ROME

VISITS EPHESUS

WRITES EPHESIANS
(AD62-64)

Ephes.

Acts
Romans
1 Corin.
2 Corin.
Galat.

1 From Paul, who by God's will is an apostle of Christ Jesus —
To God's people in Ephesus,* who are faithful in their life in union with Christ Jesus:

[2] May God our Father and the Lord Jesus Christ give you grace and peace.

Spiritual Blessings in Christ

[3] Let us give thanks to the God and Father of our Lord Jesus Christ! For in our union with Christ he has blessed us by giving us every spiritual blessing in the heavenly world. [4] Even before the world was made, God had already chosen us to be his through our union with Christ, so that we would be holy and without fault before him.

Because of his love [5] God* had already decided that through Jesus Christ he would make us his sons and daughters — this was his pleasure and purpose. [6] Let us praise God for his glorious grace, for the free gift he gave us in his dear Son! [7] For by the blood* of Christ we are set free, that is, our sins are forgiven. How great is the grace of God, [8] which he gave to us in such large measure!

In all his wisdom and insight [9] God did what he had purposed, and made known to us the secret plan he had already decided to complete by means of Christ. [10] This plan, which God will complete when the time is right, is to bring all creation together, everything in heaven and on earth, with Christ as head.

[11] All things are done according to God's plan and decision; and God chose us to be his own people in union with Christ because of his own purpose, based on what he had decided from the very beginning. [12] Let us, then, who were the first to hope in Christ, praise God's glory!

[13] And you also became God's people when you heard the true message, the Good News that brought you salvation. You believed in Christ, and God put his stamp of ownership on you by giving you the Holy Spirit he had promised. [14] The Spirit is the guarantee that we shall receive what God has promised his people, and this assures us that God will give complete freedom to those who are his. Let us praise his glory!

Paul's Prayer

[15] For this reason, ever since I heard of your faith in the Lord Jesus and your love for all God's people, [16] I have not stopped giving thanks to God for you. I remember you in my prayers [17] and ask the God of our Lord Jesus Christ, the glorious Father, to give you the Spirit, who will make you wise and reveal God to you, so that you will know him. [18] I ask that your minds may be opened to see his light, so that you will know what is the hope to which he has called you, how rich are the wonderful blessings he promises his people, [19] and how very great is his power at work in us who believe. This power working in us is the same as the mighty strength [20] which he used when he raised Christ from death and seated him at his right side in the heavenly world. [21] Christ rules there above all heavenly rulers, authorities, powers, and lords; he has a title superior to all titles of authority in this world and in the next. [22] God put all things under Christ's feet and gave

1.1 Some manuscripts do not have *in Ephesus.*
1.4–5 *before him. Because of his love* [5] *God;* or *before him, and to live in love. God.*
1.7 *by the blood;* or *by the sacrificial death.*

EPHESIANS 1, 2

1393

Ephes.

⋯⋯⋯⋮⋮

Philipp.
Coloss.
1 Thess.
2 Thess.
1 Tim.

him to the church as supreme Lord over all things. [23] The church is Christ's body, the completion of him who himself completes all things everywhere.*

From Death to Life

2 In the past you were spiritually dead because of your disobedience and sins. [2] At that time you followed the world's evil way; you obeyed the ruler of the spiritual powers in space, the spirit who now controls the people who disobey God. [3] Actually all of us were like them and lived according to our natural desires, doing whatever suited the wishes of our own bodies and minds. In our natural condition we, like everyone else, were destined to suffer God's anger.

[4] But God's mercy is so abundant, and his love for us is so great, [5] that while we were spiritually dead in our disobedience he brought us to life with Christ. It is by God's grace that you have been saved. [6] In our union with Christ Jesus he raised us up with him to rule with him in the heavenly world. [7] He did this to demonstrate for all time to come the extraordinary greatness of his grace in the love he showed us in Christ Jesus. [8-9] For it is by God's grace that you have been saved through faith. It is not the result of your own efforts, but God's gift, so that no one can boast about it. [10] God has made us what we are, and in our union with Christ Jesus he has created us for a life of good deeds, which he has already prepared for us to do.

One in Christ

[11] You Gentiles by birth — called "the uncircumcised" by the Jews, who call themselves "the circumcised" (which refers to what men do to their bodies) — remember what you were in the past. [12] At that time you were apart from Christ. You were foreigners and did not belong to God's chosen people. You had no part in the covenants, which were based on God's promises to his people, and you lived in this world without hope and without God. [13] But now, in union with Christ Jesus, you who used to be far away have been brought near by the blood* of Christ. [14] For Christ himself has brought us peace by making Jews and Gentiles one people. With his own body he broke down the wall that separated them and kept them enemies. [15] He abolished the Jewish Law with its commandments and rules, in order to create out of the two races one new people in union with himself, in this way making peace. [16] By his death on the cross Christ destroyed their enmity; by means of the cross he united both races into one body and brought them back to God. [17] So Christ came and preached the Good News of peace to all — to you Gentiles, who were far away from God, and to the Jews, who were near to him. [18] It is through Christ that all of us, Jews and Gentiles, are able to come in the one Spirit into the presence of the Father.

[19] So then, you Gentiles are not foreigners or strangers any longer; you are now fellow-citizens with God's people and members of the family of God. [20] You, too, are built upon the foundation laid by the apostles and prophets,* the cornerstone being Christ Jesus himself. [21] He is the one who holds the whole building together

EPHESIANS 2.4

• His •
LOVE
FOR US
— is so —
GREAT

1.23 *who himself completes all things everywhere*; or *who is himself completely filled with God's fullness.*
2.13 *by the blood of Christ*; or *by the sacrificial death of Christ.*
2.20 *the foundation laid by the apostles and prophets*; or *the foundation, that is, the apostles and prophets.*

1394

Ephes.

:········

Acts
Romans
1 Corin.
2 Corin.
Galat.

EPHESIANS 2–4

and makes it grow into a sacred temple dedicated to the Lord. [22] In union with him you too are being built together with all the others into a place where God lives through his Spirit.

Paul's Work for the Gentiles

3 For this reason I, Paul, the prisoner of Christ Jesus for the sake of you Gentiles, pray to God. [2] Surely you have heard that God in his grace has given me this work to do for your good. [3] God revealed his secret plan and made it known to me. (I have written briefly about this, [4] and if you will read what I have written, you can learn about my understanding of the secret of Christ.) [5] In past times human beings were not told this secret, but God has revealed it now by the Spirit to his holy apostles and prophets. [6] The secret is that by means of the gospel the Gentiles have a part with the Jews in God's blessings; they are members of the same body and share in the promise that God made through Christ Jesus.

[7] I was made a servant of the gospel by God's special gift, which he gave me through the working of his power. [8] I am less than the least of all God's people; yet God gave me this privilege of taking to the Gentiles the Good News about the infinite riches of Christ, [9] and of making all people see how God's secret plan is to be put into effect. God, who is the Creator of all things, kept his secret hidden through all the past ages, [10] in order that at the present time, by means of the church, the angelic rulers and powers in the heavenly world might learn of his wisdom in all its different forms. [11] God did this according to his eternal purpose, which he achieved through Christ Jesus our Lord. [12] In union with Christ and through our faith in him we have the boldness to go into God's presence with all confidence. [13] I beg you, then, not to be discouraged because I am suffering for you; it is all for your benefit.

The Love of Christ

[14] For this reason I fall on my knees before the Father, [15] from whom every family in heaven and on earth receives its true name. [16] I ask God from the wealth of his glory to give you power through his Spirit to be strong in your inner selves, [17] and I pray that Christ will make his home in your hearts through faith. I pray that you may have your roots and foundation in love, [18] so that you, together with all God's people, may have the power to understand how broad and long, how high and deep, is Christ's love. [19] Yes, may you come to know his love — although it can never be fully known — and so be completely filled with the very nature of God.

[20] To him who by means of his power working in us is able to do so much more than we can ever ask for, or even think of: [21] to God be the glory in the church and in Christ Jesus for all time, for ever and ever! Amen.

The Unity of the Body

4 I urge you, then — I who am a prisoner because I serve the Lord: live a life that measures up to the standard God set when he called you. [2] Be always humble, gentle, and patient. Show your love by being tolerant with one another. [3] Do your best to preserve the unity which the Spirit gives by means of the peace that binds you together. [4] There is one body and one Spirit, just as there is one hope to which God has called you. [5] There is one Lord, one faith, one baptism; [6] there is one God and Father of all, who is Lord of all, works through all, and is in all.

EPHESIANS 4

1395

Ephes.

....

Philipp.
Coloss.
1 Thess.
2 Thess.
1 Tim.

[7]Each one of us has received a special gift in proportion to what Christ has given. [8]As the scripture says:

"When he went up to the very heights,
he took many captives with him;
he gave gifts to people."

[9]Now, what does "he went up" mean? It means that first he came down to the lowest depths of the earth.* [10]So the one who came down is the same one who went up, above and beyond the heavens, to fill the whole universe with his presence. [11]It was he who "gave gifts"; he appointed some to be apostles, others to be prophets, others to be evangelists, others to be pastors and teachers. [12]He did this to prepare all God's people for the work of Christian service, in order to build up the body of Christ. [13]And so we shall all come together to that oneness in our faith and in our knowledge of the Son of God; we shall become mature people, reaching to the very height of Christ's full stature. [14]Then we shall no longer be children, carried by the waves and blown about by every shifting wind of the teaching of deceitful people, who lead others into error by the tricks they invent. [15]Instead, by speaking the truth in a spirit of love, we must grow up in every way to Christ, who is the head. [16]Under his control all the different parts of the body fit together, and the whole body is held together by every joint with which it is provided. So when each separate part works as it should, the whole body grows and builds itself up through love.

The New Life in Christ

[17]In the Lord's name, then, I warn you: do not continue to live like the heathen, whose thoughts are worthless [18]and whose minds are in the dark. They have no part in the life that God gives, for they are completely ignorant and stubborn. [19]They have lost all feeling of shame; they give themselves over to vice and do all sorts of indecent things without restraint.

[20]That was not what you learnt about Christ! [21]You certainly heard about him, and as his followers you were taught the truth that is in Jesus. [22]So get rid of your old self, which made you live as you used to — the old self that was being destroyed by its deceitful desires. [23]Your hearts and minds must be made completely new, [24]and you must put on the new self, which is created in God's likeness and reveals itself in the true life that is upright and holy.

[25]No more lying, then! Each of you must tell the truth to one another, because we are all members together in the body of Christ. [26]If you become angry, do not let your anger lead you into sin, and do not stay angry all day. [27]Don't give the Devil a chance. [28]Those who used to rob must stop robbing and start working, in order to earn an honest living for themselves and to be able to help the poor. [29]Do not use harmful words, but only helpful words, the kind that build up and provide what is needed, so that what you say will do good to those who hear you. [30]And do not make God's Holy Spirit sad; for the Spirit is God's mark of ownership on you, a guarantee that the Day will come when God will set you free. [31]Get rid of all bitterness, passion, and anger. No more shouting or insults, no more hateful feelings of any sort. [32]Instead, be kind and tender-hearted to one another, and forgive one another, as God has forgiven you through Christ.

....

4.9 the lowest depths of the earth; or the lower depths, the earth itself.

EPHESIANS 4.32

Forgiveness is counter-cultural and frees us from the grip of resentment and negativity. If God forgives us, through Christ, for all we've ever done wrong, what does it mean for us to

FORGIVE

- ONE ANOTHER -

too? Is there anyone you need to forgive? If so, pray about it now. Don't hold on to it any more.

Living in the Light

5 Since you are God's dear children, you must try to be like him. ² Your life must be controlled by love, just as Christ loved us and gave his life for us as a sweet-smelling offering and sacrifice that pleases God.

³ Since you are God's people, it is not right that any matters of sexual immorality or indecency or greed should even be mentioned among you. ⁴ Nor is it fitting for you to use language which is obscene, profane, or vulgar. Rather you should give thanks to God. ⁵ You may be sure that no one who is immoral, indecent, or greedy (for greed is a form of idolatry) will ever receive a share in the Kingdom of Christ and of God.

⁶ Do not let anyone deceive you with foolish words; it is because of these very things that God's anger will come upon those who do not obey him. ⁷ So have nothing at all to do with such people. ⁸ You yourselves used to be in the darkness, but since you have become the Lord's people, you are in the light. So you must live like people who belong to the light, ⁹ for it is the light* that brings a rich harvest of every kind of goodness, righteousness, and truth. ¹⁰ Try to learn what pleases the Lord. ¹¹ Have nothing to do with the worthless things that people do, things that belong to the darkness. Instead, bring them out to the light. ¹² (It is really too shameful even to talk about the things they do in secret.) ¹³ And when all things are brought out to the light, then their true nature is clearly revealed; ¹⁴ for anything that is clearly revealed becomes light.* That is why it is said:

"Wake up, sleeper,
  and rise from death,
  and Christ will shine on you."

¹⁵ So be careful how you live. Don't live like ignorant people, but like wise people. ¹⁶ Make good use of every opportunity you have, because these are evil days. ¹⁷ Don't be fools, then, but try to find out what the Lord wants you to do.

¹⁸ Do not get drunk with wine, which will only ruin you; instead, be filled with the Spirit. ¹⁹ Speak to one another with the words of psalms, hymns, and sacred songs; sing hymns and psalms to the Lord with praise in your hearts. ²⁰ In the name of our Lord Jesus Christ, always give thanks for everything to God the Father.

Wives and Husbands

²¹ Submit yourselves to one another because of your reverence for Christ.

²² Wives, submit to your husbands as to the Lord. ²³ For a husband has authority over his wife just as Christ has authority over the church; and Christ is himself the Saviour of the church, his body. ²⁴ And so wives must submit completely to their husbands just as the church submits itself to Christ.

²⁵ Husbands, love your wives just as Christ loved the church and gave his life for it. ²⁶ He did this to dedicate the church to God by his word, after making it clean by washing it in water, ²⁷ in order to present the church to himself in all its beauty — pure and faultless, without spot or wrinkle or any other imperfection. ²⁸ Men ought to love their wives just as they love their own bodies. A man who loves his wife loves himself. ²⁹ (People never hate their own bodies. Instead, they feed them

5.9 *the light*; some manuscripts have *the Spirit*.
5.14 *anything that is clearly revealed becomes light*; or *it is light that clearly reveals everything*.

EPHESIANS 5, 6

1397

Ephes.

Philipp.
Coloss.
1 Thess.
2 Thess.
1 Tim.

and take care of them, just as Christ does the church;) [30] for we are members of his body.) [31] As the scripture says, "For this reason a man will leave his father and mother and unite with his wife, and the two will become one." [32] There is a deep secret truth revealed in this scripture, which I understand as applying to Christ and the church. [33] But it also applies to you: every husband must love his wife as himself, and every wife must respect her husband.

Children and Parents

6 Children, it is your Christian duty to* obey your parents, for this is the right thing to do. [2] "Respect your father and mother" is the first commandment that has a promise added: [3] "so that all may go well with you, and you may live a long time in the land."

[4] Parents, do not treat your children in such a way as to make them angry. Instead, bring them up with Christian discipline and instruction.

Slaves and Masters

[5] Slaves, obey your human masters with fear and trembling; and do it with a sincere heart, as though you were serving Christ. [6] Do this not only when they are watching you, because you want to gain their approval; but with all your heart do what God wants, as slaves of Christ. [7] Do your work as slaves cheerfully, as though you served the Lord, and not merely human beings. [8] Remember that the Lord will reward everyone, whether slave or free, for the good work they do.

[9] Masters, behave in the same way towards your slaves and stop using threats. Remember that you and your slaves belong to the same Master in heaven, who judges everyone by the same standard.

The Whole Armour of God

[10] Finally, build up your strength in union with the Lord and by means of his mighty power. [11] Put on all the armour that God gives you, so that you will be able to stand up against the Devil's evil tricks. [12] For we are not fighting against human beings but against the wicked spiritual forces in the heavenly world, the rulers, authorities, and cosmic powers of this dark age. [13] So put on God's armour now! Then when the evil day comes, you will be able to resist the enemy's attacks; and after fighting to the end, you will still hold your ground.

[14] So stand ready, with truth as a belt tight round your waist, with righteousness as your breastplate, [15] and as your shoes the readiness to announce the Good News of peace. [16] At all times carry faith as a shield; for with it you will be able to put out all the burning arrows shot by the Evil One. [17] And accept salvation as a helmet, and the word of God as the sword which the Spirit gives you. [18] Do all this in prayer, asking for God's help. Pray on every occasion, as the Spirit leads. For this reason keep alert and never give up; pray always for all God's people. [19] And pray also for me, that God will give me a message when I am ready to speak, so that I may speak boldly and make known the gospel's secret. [20] For the sake of this gospel I am an ambassador, though now I am in prison. Pray that I may be bold in speaking about the gospel as I should.

6.1 Some manuscripts do not have *it is your Christian duty to.*

EPHESIANS 6.13-17

Read through the

ARMOUR

– OF –

GOD

and make a

QUICK DOODLE

of each piece. (Don't worry - your drawings don't have to be good!) Think about what each part might mean and how you might live out your relationship with Jesus differently if all of these pieces of armour were in place.

Final Greetings

21 Tychicus, our dear brother and faithful servant in the Lord's work, will give you all the news about me, so that you may know how I am getting on. 22 That is why I am sending him to you — to tell you how all of us are getting on, and to encourage you.

23 May God the Father and the Lord Jesus Christ give to all Christian brothers and sisters peace and love with faith. 24 May God's grace be with all those who love our Lord Jesus Christ with undying love.

THE LETTER TO THE

PHILIPPIANS

WRITTEN: AD52-54 OR 58-64

WHAT YOU NEED TO KNOW:

Philippians is a letter of thankfulness, encouragement and joy. Paul wrote it to the church in Philippi while he was a prisoner under house arrest, and he starts by thanking them for their support. It's a deeply loving and friendly letter to the church, but it's challenging too, as he encourages them to keep growing in faith and outlines what growing in faith might look like!

WHY READ IT?

This letter is great at giving us pointers on how to grow in our faith, serve others and spread the good news of Jesus. It's about keeping going in our Christian life, and it challenges us to think about the kind of people God might want us to be.

SPOTLIGHT:

The church in Philippi was set up by Paul on his second missionary journey (see Acts 16), and it was the first church in Europe: Philippi was in northern Greece. It wasn't a huge city, but it was significant. Citizens of Philippi were automatically given Roman citizenship, and they were proud of this. Even though Philippi was over 1,000 miles away from Rome, the people dressed like Romans and spoke Latin, the Romans' language. There was also a strong Roman military and leadership presence. It's no surprise, then, that Paul uses the idea of citizenship to talk about the Christian faith, as this would have made sense to the Philippians.

Fill these boxes with different verses, images and thoughts that stand out to you from Philippians, about how we could aim to live as Christians. When you come back to this page, colour the boxes in while reflecting on what's inside of them.

(AD48)
PAUL'S 2ND MISSIONARY JOURNEY

(AD52-54 OR 58-64)
WRITES PHILIPPIANS

VISITS PHILIPPI

1 From Paul and Timothy, servants of Christ Jesus —
To all God's people in Philippi who are in union with Christ Jesus, including the church leaders and helpers:
² May God our Father and the Lord Jesus Christ give you grace and peace.

Paul's Prayer for his Readers
³ I thank my God for you every time I think of you; ⁴ and every time I pray for you all, I pray with joy ⁵ because of the way in which you have helped me in the work of the gospel from the very first day until now. ⁶ And so I am sure that God, who began this good work in you, will carry it on until it is finished on the Day of Christ Jesus. ⁷ You are always in my heart! And so it is only right for me to feel as I do about you. For you have all shared with me in this privilege that God has given me, both now that I am in prison and also while I was free to defend the gospel and establish it firmly. ⁸ God is my witness that I am telling the truth when I say that my deep feeling for you all comes from the heart of Christ Jesus himself.

⁹ I pray that your love will keep on growing more and more, together with true knowledge and perfect judgement, ¹⁰ so that you will be able to choose what is best. Then you will be free from all impurity and blame on the Day of Christ. ¹¹ Your lives will be filled with the truly good qualities which only Jesus Christ can produce, for the glory and praise of God.

To Live is Christ
¹² I want you to know, my brothers and sisters, that the things that have happened to me have really helped the progress of the gospel. ¹³ As a result, the whole palace guard and all the others here know that I am in prison because I am a servant of Christ. ¹⁴ And my being in prison has given most of the brothers and sisters more confidence in the Lord, so that they grow bolder all the time to preach the message* fearlessly.

¹⁵ Of course some of them preach Christ because they are jealous and quarrelsome, but others from genuine goodwill. ¹⁶ These do so from love, because they know that God has given me the work of defending the gospel. ¹⁷ The others do not proclaim Christ sincerely, but from a spirit of selfish ambition; they think that they will make more trouble for me while I am in prison.

¹⁸ It does not matter! I am happy about it — so long as Christ is preached in every way possible, whether from wrong or right motives. And I will continue to be happy, ¹⁹ because I know that by means of your prayers and the help which comes from the Spirit of Jesus Christ I shall be set free. ²⁰ My deep desire and hope is that I shall never fail in my duty, but that at all times, and especially just now, I shall be full of courage, so that with my whole being I shall bring honour to Christ, whether I live or die. ²¹ For what is life? To me, it is Christ. Death, then, will bring more. ²² But if by continuing to live I can do more worthwhile work, then I am not sure which I should choose. ²³ I am pulled in two directions. I want very much to leave this life and be with Christ, which is a far better thing; ²⁴ but for your sake it is much more important that I remain alive. ²⁵ I am sure of this, and so I know that I will stay on with you all, to add to your progress and joy in the faith, ²⁶ so that when I am with you again, you will have even more reason to be proud of me in your life in union with Christ Jesus.

1.14 *the message*; some manuscripts have *God's message*.

PHILIPPIANS 1, 2

1401

Philipp.

...........:.

Coloss.

1 Thess.

2 Thess.

1 Tim.

2 Tim.

27 Now, the important thing is that your way of life should be as the gospel of Christ requires, so that, whether or not I am able to go and see you, I will hear that you are standing firm with one common purpose and that with only one desire you are fighting together for the faith of the gospel. 28 Don't be afraid of your enemies; always be courageous, and this will prove to them that they will lose and that you will win, because it is God who gives you the victory. 29 For you have been given the privilege of serving Christ, not only by believing in him, but also by suffering for him. 30 Now you can take part with me in the battle. It is the same battle you saw me fighting in the past, and as you hear, the one I am fighting still.

Christ's Humility and Greatness

2 Your life in Christ makes you strong, and his love comforts you. You have fellowship with the Spirit,* and you have kindness and compassion for one another. 2 I urge you, then, to make me completely happy by having the same thoughts, sharing the same love, and being one in soul and mind. 3 Don't do anything from selfish ambition or from a cheap desire to boast, but be humble towards one another, always considering others better than yourselves. 4 And look out for one another's interests, not just for your own. 5 The attitude you should have is the one that Christ Jesus had:

6 He always had the nature of God,
   but he did not think that by force he should try to
      remain* equal with God.
7 Instead of this, of his own free will he gave up all he had,
   and took the nature of a servant.
He became like a human being
   and appeared in human likeness.
8 He was humble and walked the path of obedience all the
      way to death —
   his death on the cross.
9 For this reason God raised him to the highest place above
   and gave him the name that is greater than any other
      name.
10 And so, in honour of the name of Jesus
   all beings in heaven, on earth, and in the world below*
      will fall on their knees,
11 and all will openly proclaim that Jesus Christ is Lord,
   to the glory of God the Father.

Shining as Lights in the World

12 So then, dear friends, as you always obeyed me when I was with you, it is even more important that you obey me now while I am away from you. Keep on working with fear and trembling to complete your salvation, 13 because God is always at work in you to make you willing and able to obey his own purpose.

14 Do everything without complaining or arguing, 15 so that you may be innocent and pure as God's perfect children, who live in a world of corrupt and sinful people. You must shine among them like stars lighting up the sky, 16 as you offer them the message of

2.1 *You have fellowship with the Spirit*; or *The Spirit has brought you into fellowship with one another.*
2.6 *remain*; or *become.*
2.10 *world below*: It was thought that the dead continued to exist in a dark world under the ground.

PHILIPPIANS 2.3-11

Write here what this passage tells you about Jesus. How might it influence the way you
- LIVE YOUR -

LIFE?

1402

Philipp.

⋮........

Romans
1 Corin.
2 Corin.
Galat.
Ephes.

PHILIPPIANS 2, 3

life. If you do so, I shall have reason to be proud of you on the Day of Christ, because it will show that all my effort and work have not been wasted.

17 Perhaps my life's blood is to be poured out like an offering on the sacrifice that your faith offers to God. If that is so, I am glad and share my joy with you all. 18 In the same way, you too must be glad and share your joy with me.

Timothy and Epaphroditus

19 If it is the Lord's will, I hope that I will be able to send Timothy to you soon, so that I may be encouraged by news about you. 20 He is the only one who shares my feelings and who really cares about you. 21 All the others are concerned only with their own affairs, not with the cause of Jesus Christ. 22 And you yourselves know how he has proved his worth, how he and I, like a son and his father, have worked together for the sake of the gospel. 23 So I hope to send him to you as soon as I know how things are going to turn out for me. 24 And I trust in the Lord that I myself will be able to come to you soon.

25 I have thought it necessary to send you our brother Epaphroditus, who has worked and fought by my side and who has served as your messenger in helping me. 26 He is anxious to see you all and is very upset because you had heard that he was ill. 27 Indeed he was ill and almost died. But God had pity on him, and not only on him but on me, too, and spared me an even greater sorrow. 28 I am all the more eager, then, to send him to you, so that you will be glad again when you see him, and my own sorrow will disappear. 29 Receive him, then, with joy, as a brother in the Lord. Show respect to all such people as he, 30 because he risked his life and nearly died for the sake of the work of Christ, in order to give me the help that you yourselves could not give.

The True Righteousness

3 In conclusion, my brothers and sisters, be joyful in your union with the Lord. I don't mind repeating what I have written before, and you will be safer if I do so. 2 Watch out for those who do evil things, those dogs, those who insist on cutting the body. 3 It is we, not they, who have received the true circumcision, for we worship God by means of his Spirit and rejoice in our life in union with Christ Jesus. We do not put any trust in external ceremonies. 4 I could, of course, put my trust in such things. If anyone thinks they can trust in external ceremonies, I have even more reason to feel that way. 5 I was circumcised when I was a week old. I am an Israelite by birth, of the tribe of Benjamin, a pure-blooded Hebrew. As far as keeping the Jewish Law is concerned, I was a Pharisee, 6 and I was so zealous that I persecuted the church. As far as a person can be righteous by obeying the commands of the Law, I was without fault. 7 But all those things that I might count as profit I now reckon as loss for Christ's sake. 8 Not only those things; I reckon everything as complete loss for the sake of what is so much more valuable, the knowledge of Christ Jesus my Lord. For his sake I have thrown everything away; I consider it all as mere refuse, so that I may gain Christ 9 and be completely united with him. I no longer have a righteousness of my own, the kind that is gained by obeying the Law. I now have the righteousness that is given through faith in Christ, the righteousness that comes from God and is based on faith. 10 All I want is to know Christ and to experience the power of his resurrection, to share in his

Philipp.

....

Coloss.

1 Thess.

2 Thess.

1 Tim.

2 Tim.

sufferings and become like him in his death, [11] in the hope that I myself will be raised from death to life.

Running towards the Goal

[12] I do not claim that I have already succeeded or have already become perfect. I keep striving to win the prize for which Christ Jesus has already won me to himself. [13] Of course, my brothers and sisters, I really do not* think that I have already won it; the one thing I do, however, is to forget what is behind me and do my best to reach what is ahead. [14] So I run straight towards the goal in order to win the prize, which is God's call through Christ Jesus to the life above.

[15] All of us who are spiritually mature should have this same attitude. But if some of you have a different attitude, God will make this clear to you. [16] However that may be, let us go forward according to the same rules we have followed until now.

[17] Keep on imitating me, my brothers and sisters. Pay attention to those who follow the right example that we have set for you. [18] I have told you this many times before, and now I repeat it with tears: there are many whose lives make them enemies of Christ's death on the cross. [19] They are going to end up in hell, because their god is their bodily desires. They are proud of what they should be ashamed of, and they think only of things that belong to this world. [20] We, however, are citizens of heaven, and we eagerly wait for our Saviour, the Lord Jesus Christ, to come from heaven. [21] He will change our weak mortal bodies and make them like his own glorious body, using that power by which he is able to bring all things under his rule.

Instructions

4 So then, my brothers and sisters, how dear you are to me and how I miss you! How happy you make me, and how proud I am of you! This then, dear brothers and sisters, is how you should stand firm in your life in the Lord.

[2] Euodia and Syntyche, please, I beg you, try to agree as sisters in the Lord. [3] And you too, my faithful partner, I want you to help these women; for they have worked hard with me to spread the gospel, together with Clement and all my other fellow-workers, whose names are in God's book of the living.

[4] May you always be joyful in your union with the Lord. I say it again: rejoice!

[5] Show a gentle attitude towards everyone. The Lord is coming soon. [6] Don't worry about anything, but in all your prayers ask God for what you need, always asking him with a thankful heart. [7] And God's peace, which is far beyond human understanding, will keep your hearts and minds safe in union with Christ Jesus.

[8] In conclusion, my brothers and sisters, fill your minds with those things that are good and that deserve praise: things that are true, noble, right, pure, lovely, and honourable. [9] Put into practice what you learnt and received from me, both from my words and from my actions. And the God who gives us peace will be with you.

Thanks for the Gift

[10] In my life in union with the Lord it is a great joy to me that after so long a time you once more had the chance of showing that you care for me. I don't mean that you had stopped caring for me — you just had no chance to show it. [11] And I am not saying

3.13 *not*; some manuscripts have *not yet*.

PHILIPPIANS 4.8

TRUE, NOBLE, RIGHT, PURE, { LOVELY, } HONOURABLE

this because I feel neglected, for I have learnt to be satisfied with what I have. [12] I know what it is to be in need and what it is to have more than enough. I have learnt this secret, so that anywhere, at any time, I am content, whether I am full or hungry, whether I have too much or too little. [13] I have the strength to face all conditions by the power that Christ gives me.

[14] But it was very good of you to help me in my troubles. [15] You Philippians know very well that when I left Macedonia in the early days of preaching the Good News, you were the only church to help me; you were the only ones who shared my profits and losses. [16] More than once when I needed help in Thessalonica, you sent it to me. [17] It is not that I just want to receive gifts; rather, I want to see profit added to your account. [18] Here, then, is my receipt for everything you have given me — and it has been more than enough! I have all I need now that Epaphroditus has brought me all your gifts. They are like a sweet-smelling offering to God, a sacrifice which is acceptable and pleasing to him. [19] And with all his abundant wealth through Christ Jesus, my God will supply all your needs. [20] To our God and Father be the glory for ever and ever! Amen.

Final Greetings

[21] Greetings to each one of God's people who belong to Christ Jesus. The brothers and sisters here with me send you their greetings. [22] All God's people here send greetings, especially those who belong to the Emperor's palace.

[23] May the grace of the Lord Jesus Christ be with you all.

THE LETTER TO THE

COLOSSIANS

WRITTEN: AROUND AD62-64 (OR POSSIBLY LATER IN THE FIRST CENTURY)

WHAT YOU NEED TO KNOW:

This letter was written to a church in the city of Colossae (in modern-day Turkey). At the time, the people in the church were hearing and believing a whole bunch of untrue teachings. These teachings included the idea that there was a way to salvation other than Jesus, and that Christians needed to obey Jewish laws and ways of living. They were also beginning to worship angels. As a result, Paul wrote this letter, reminding the believers to focus on Jesus. He explains Jesus' victory over darkness and how we should live, while stamping out the confusion caused by false teaching.

WRITE THE WORD JESUS BELOW

Now look up at the ceiling and try to trace over the top of the letters you've just drawn.

CAN YOU DO IT?

When we take our eyes off Jesus, we can go astray. Pray that God would help you to keep your focus on Jesus.

WHY READ IT?

Colossians is a great letter, full of strong basic truths about the good news of Jesus. It reminds us to keep our focus on him, and it outlines the importance of not just believing the right things but doing the right things too.

SPOTLIGHT:

The Colossians were people from Colossae. Earlier in its history (before this letter was written), Colossae had been a rich city, as it lay on a trade route, so people from all over the world would pass through. All of these people brought with them their own religions, creating a city that was a melting-pot of ideas about faith, with bits and pieces of beliefs that came from all over the place. This is perhaps why Paul felt a need to write to the Colossian church.

DRAW A CITY AS THE BACKGROUND TO THIS SECTION.

(AD48)
PAUL'S 2ND MISSIONARY JOURNEY

(AD62-64)
WRITES COLOSSIANS

UNDER ARREST IN ROME

COLOSSIANS 1.15

Write here what

JESUS

– IS LIKE. –

What does this tell you
about God's character?

_____

_____

_____

_____

_____

_____

_____

_____

_____

_____

_____

_____

_____

_____

_____

_____

_____

_____

_____

_____

1 From Paul, who by God's will is an apostle of Christ Jesus, and from our brother Timothy —

[2] To God's people in Colossae, who are our faithful brothers and sisters in union with Christ:

May God our Father give you grace and peace.

Prayer of Thanksgiving

[3] We always give thanks to God, the Father of our Lord Jesus Christ, when we pray for you. [4] For we have heard of your faith in Christ Jesus and of your love for all God's people. [5] When the true message, the Good News, first came to you, you heard about the hope it offers. So your faith and love are based on what you hope for, which is kept safe for you in heaven. [6] The gospel keeps bringing blessings and is spreading throughout the world, just as it has among you ever since the day you first heard about the grace of God and came to know it as it really is. [7] You learnt of God's grace from Epaphras, our dear fellow-servant, who is Christ's faithful worker on our* behalf. [8] He has told us of the love that the Spirit has given you.

[9] For this reason we have always prayed for you, ever since we heard about you. We ask God to fill you with the knowledge of his will, with all the wisdom and understanding that his Spirit gives. [10] Then you will be able to live as the Lord wants and will always do what pleases him. Your lives will produce all kinds of good deeds, and you will grow in your knowledge of God. [11-12] May you be made strong with all the strength which comes from his glorious power, so that you may be able to endure everything with patience. And with joy give thanks to* the Father, who has made you fit to have your share of what God has reserved for his people in the kingdom of light. [13] He rescued us from the power of darkness and brought us safe into the kingdom of his dear Son, [14] by whom we are set free, that is, our sins are forgiven.

The Person and Work of Christ

[15] Christ is the visible likeness of the invisible God. He is the firstborn Son, superior to all created things. [16] For through him God created everything in heaven and on earth, the seen and the unseen things, including spiritual powers, lords, rulers, and authorities. God created the whole universe through him and for him. [17] Christ existed before all things, and in union with him all things have their proper place. [18] He is the head of his body, the church; he is the source of the body's life. He is the firstborn Son, who was raised from death, in order that he alone might have the first place in all things. [19] For it was by God's own decision that the Son has in himself the full nature of God. [20] Through the Son, then, God decided to bring the whole universe back to himself. God made peace through his Son's blood* on the cross and so brought back to himself all things, both on earth and in heaven.

[21] At one time you were far away from God and were his enemies because of the evil things you did and thought. [22] But now, by means of the physical death of his Son, God has made you his friends, in order to bring you, holy, pure, and faultless, into his presence. [23] You must, of course, continue faithful on a firm and sure foundation, and must not allow yourselves to be shaken

....

1.7 *our*; some manuscripts have *your*.
1.11–12 *with patience. And with joy give thanks to*; or *with patience and joy. And give thanks to*.
1.20 *his Son's blood*; or *his Son's sacrificial death*.

1407

Coloss.
............:

1 Thess.
2 Thess.
1 Tim.
2 Tim.
Titus

from the hope you gained when you heard the gospel. It is of this gospel that I, Paul, became a servant — this gospel which has been preached to everybody in the world.

Paul's Work as a Servant of the Church

24 And now I am happy about my sufferings for you, for by means of my physical sufferings I am helping to complete what still remains of Christ's sufferings on behalf of his body, the church. 25 And I have been made a servant of the church by God, who gave me this task to perform for your good. It is the task of fully proclaiming his message, 26 which is the secret he hid through all past ages from all the human race but has now revealed to his people. 27 God's plan is to make known his secret to his people, this rich and glorious secret which he has for all peoples. And the secret is that Christ is in you, which means that you will share in the glory of God. 28 So we preach Christ to everyone. With all possible wisdom we warn and teach them in order to bring each one into God's presence as a mature individual in union with Christ. 29 To get this done I toil and struggle, using the mighty strength which Christ supplies and which is at work in me.

2 Let me tell you how hard I have worked for you and for the people in Laodicea and for all others who do not know me personally. 2 I do this in order that they may be filled with courage and may be drawn together in love, and so have the full wealth of assurance which true understanding brings. In this way they will know God's secret, which is Christ himself.* 3 He is the key that opens all the hidden treasures of God's wisdom and knowledge.

4 I tell you, then, do not let anyone deceive you with false arguments, no matter how good they seem to be. 5 For even though I am absent in body, yet I am with you in spirit, and I am glad as I see the resolute firmness with which you stand together in your faith in Christ.

Fullness of Life in Christ

6 Since you have accepted Christ Jesus as Lord, live in union with him. 7 Keep your roots deep in him, build your lives on him, and become stronger in your faith, as you were taught. And be filled with thanksgiving.

8 See to it, then, that no one enslaves you by means of the worthless deceit of human wisdom, which comes from the teachings handed down by human beings and from the ruling spirits of the universe, and not from Christ. 9 For the full content of divine nature lives in Christ, in his humanity, 10 and you have been given full life in union with him. He is supreme over every spiritual ruler and authority.

11 In union with Christ you were circumcised, not with the circumcision that is made by human beings, but with the circumcision made by Christ, which consists of being freed from the power of this sinful self. 12 For when you were baptized, you were buried with Christ, and in baptism you were also raised with Christ through your faith in the active power of God, who raised him from death. 13 You were at one time spiritually dead because of your sins and because you were Gentiles without the Law. But God has now brought you to life with Christ. God forgave us all our sins; 14 he cancelled the unfavourable record of our debts with its

2.2 *God's secret, which is Christ himself*; some manuscripts have *God's secret*; others have *the secret of God the Father of Christ*; others have *the secret of the God and Father, and of Christ.*

1408

Coloss.

: ....

1 Corin.
2 Corin.
Galat.
Ephes.
Philipp.

COLOSSIANS 2, 3

binding rules and did away with it completely by nailing it to the cross. [15]And on that cross Christ freed himself from the power of the spiritual rulers and authorities;* he made a public spectacle of them by leading them as captives in his victory procession.

[16]So let no one make rules about what you eat or drink or about holy days or the New Moon Festival or the Sabbath. [17]All such things are only a shadow of things in the future; the reality is Christ. [18]Do not allow yourselves to be condemned by anyone who claims to be superior because of special visions and who insists on false humility and the worship of angels. For no reason at all, such people are all puffed up by their human way of thinking [19]and have stopped holding on to Christ, who is the head of the body. Under Christ's control the whole body is nourished and held together by its joints and ligaments, and it grows as God wants it to grow.

Dying and Living with Christ

[20]You have died with Christ and are set free from the ruling spirits of the universe. Why, then, do you live as though you belonged to this world? Why do you obey such rules as [21]"Don't handle this," "Don't taste that," "Don't touch the other"? [22]All these refer to things which become useless once they are used; they are only human rules and teachings. [23]Of course such rules appear to be based on wisdom in their forced worship of angels, and false humility, and severe treatment of the body; but they have no real value in controlling physical passions.

3 You have been raised to life with Christ, so set your hearts on the things that are in heaven, where Christ sits on his throne at the right-hand side of God. [2]Keep your minds fixed on things there, not on things here on earth. [3]For you have died, and your life is hidden with Christ in God. [4]Your real life is Christ and when he appears, then you too will appear with him and share his glory!

The Old Life and the New

[5]You must put to death, then, the earthly desires at work in you, such as sexual immorality, indecency, lust, evil passions, and greed (for greed is a form of idolatry). [6]Because of such things God's anger will come upon those who do not obey him.* [7]At one time you yourselves used to live according to such desires, when your life was dominated by them.

[8]But now you must get rid of all these things: anger, passion, and hateful feelings. No insults or obscene talk must ever come from your lips. [9]Do not lie to one another, for you have taken off the old self with its habits [10]and have put on the new self. This is the new being which God, its Creator, is constantly renewing in his own image, in order to bring you to a full knowledge of himself. [11]As a result, there is no longer any distinction between Gentiles and Jews, circumcised and uncircumcised, barbarians, savages, slaves, and free, but Christ is all, Christ is in all.

[12]You are the people of God; he loved you and chose you for his own. So then, you must clothe yourselves with compassion, kindness, humility, gentleness, and patience. [13]Be tolerant with one another and forgive one another whenever any of you has a complaint against someone else. You must forgive one another

2.15 *Christ freed himself from the power of the spiritual rulers and authorities*; or *Christ stripped the spiritual rulers and authorities of their power.*
3.6 Some manuscripts do not have *upon those who do not obey him.*

COLOSSIANS 3, 4

1409

Coloss.

....

1 Thess.
2 Thess.
1 Tim.
2 Tim.
Titus

just as the Lord has forgiven you. [14] And to all these qualities add love, which binds all things together in perfect unity. [15] The peace that Christ gives is to guide you in the decisions you make; for it is to this peace that God has called you together in the one body. And be thankful. [16] Christ's message in all its richness must live in your hearts. Teach and instruct each other with all wisdom. Sing psalms, hymns, and sacred songs; sing to God with thanksgiving in your hearts. [17] Everything you do or say, then, should be done in the name of the Lord Jesus, as you give thanks through him to God the Father.

Personal Relations in the New Life

[18] Wives, submit to your husbands, for that is what you should do as Christians.

[19] Husbands, love your wives and do not be harsh with them.

[20] Children, it is your Christian duty to obey your parents always, for that is what pleases God.

[21] Parents, do not irritate your children, or they will become discouraged.

[22] Slaves, obey your human masters in all things, not only when they are watching you because you want to gain their approval; but do it with a sincere heart because of your reverence for the Lord. [23] Whatever you do, work at it with all your heart, as though you were working for the Lord and not for human beings. [24] Remember that the Lord will give you as a reward what he has kept for his people. For Christ is the real Master you serve. [25] And wrongdoers will be repaid for the wrong things they do, because God judges everyone by the same standard.

4 Masters, be fair and just in the way you treat your slaves. Remember that you too have a Master in heaven.

Instructions

[2] Be persistent in prayer, and keep alert as you pray, giving thanks to God. [3] At the same time pray also for us, so that God will give us a good opportunity to preach his message about the secret of Christ. For that is why I am now in prison. [4] Pray, then, that I may speak, as I should, in such a way as to make it clear.

[5] Be wise in the way you act towards those who are not believers, making good use of every opportunity you have. [6] Your speech should always be pleasant and interesting, and you should know how to give the right answer to everyone.

Final Greetings

[7] Our dear brother Tychicus, who is a faithful worker and fellow-servant in the Lord's work, will give you all the news about me. [8] That is why I am sending him to you, in order to cheer you up by telling you how all of us are getting on. [9] With him goes Onesimus, that dear and faithful brother, who belongs to your group. They will tell you everything that is happening here.

[10] Aristarchus, who is in prison with me, sends you greetings, and so does Mark, the cousin of Barnabas. (You have already received instructions to welcome Mark if he comes your way.) [11] Joshua, also called Justus, sends greetings too. These three are the only Jewish believers who work with me for the Kingdom of God, and they have been a great help to me.

[12] Greetings from Epaphras, another member of your group and a servant of Christ Jesus. He always prays fervently for you, asking God to make you stand firm, as mature and fully convinced Christians, in complete obedience to God's will. [13] I can personally

COLOSSIANS 3.23

Have you ever thought about working as if you are

DOING IT FOR GOD?

What difference would this make?

Go and do a task that you don't really enjoy (for example, maybe the washing-up), but do it as if you are working for God. Then think about the difference your motivation made.

testify to his hard work for you and for the people in Laodicea and Hierapolis. [14] Luke, our dear doctor, and Demas send you their greetings.

[15] Give our best wishes to the brothers and sisters in Laodicea and to Nympha and the church that meets in her house.* [16] After you read this letter, make sure that it is read also in the church at Laodicea. At the same time, you are to read the letter that the brothers and sisters in Laodicea will send you. [17] And say to Archippus, "Be sure to finish the task you were given in the Lord's service."

[18] With my own hand I write this: *Greetings from Paul.* Do not forget my chains!

May God's grace be with you.

4.15 *Nympha… her house*; some manuscripts have *Nymphas… his house.*

THE LETTER OF
1 THESSALONIANS

WRITTEN: AD50-51

WHAT YOU NEED TO KNOW:

This letter was written to the church in Thessalonica, in northern Greece. Some theologians think that this is Paul's earliest letter and therefore the oldest book in the New Testament. Lots of people became Christians when Paul visited Thessalonica, but many more people were unhappy about this, so they kicked Paul out of the city. This meant that there were lots of fresh but immature Christians left behind, who needed guidance. Paul wrote this letter in response to questions that the believers were asking about what will happen when Jesus returns, and what happens when we die. He also reminded them to live a holy life meanwhile.

WHY READ IT?

This letter contains discussion about some of life's bigger questions. It reminds us that even though we have questions, we can be sure about what Jesus has done, and we can live for Jesus until he comes again. It's a great read for anyone who has recently become a Christian, as that's the audience it was written for.

SPOTLIGHT:

The city of Thessalonica was one of a number of important places that made up the Roman province of Macedonia (northern Greece). It was the leading seaport of Macedonia and the second biggest city in Greece.

In this letter, Paul talks about living a life that pleases God.

DRAW A TIMELINE

of your day and plot out some of the things you have done or been a part of, that you think were pleasing to God.

(AD48)
PAUL'S 2ND MISSIONARY JOURNEY

(AD50-51)
WRITES 1 THESSALONIANS

VISITS THESSALONICA

1412

1 Thess.

2 Corin.
Galat.
Ephes.
Philipp.
Coloss.

1 THESSALONIANS 1, 2

1 From Paul, Silas, and Timothy —
To the people of the church in Thessalonica, who belong to God the Father and the Lord Jesus Christ:
May grace and peace be yours.

The Life and Faith of the Thessalonians

2 We always thank God for you all and always mention you in our prayers. 3 For we remember before our God and Father how you put your faith into practice, how your love made you work so hard, and how your hope in our Lord Jesus Christ is firm. 4 Our brothers and sisters, we know that God loves you and has chosen you to be his own. 5 For we brought the Good News to you, not with words only, but also with power and the Holy Spirit, and with complete conviction of its truth. You know how we lived when we were with you; it was for your own good. 6 You imitated us and the Lord; and even though you suffered much, you received the message with the joy that comes from the Holy Spirit. 7 So you became an example to all believers in Macedonia and Achaia. 8 For not only did the message about the Lord go out from you throughout Macedonia and Achaia, but the news about your faith in God has gone everywhere. There is nothing, then, that we need to say. 9 All those people speak about how you received us when we visited you, and how you turned away from idols to God, to serve the true and living God 10 and to wait for his Son to come from heaven — his Son Jesus, whom he raised from death and who rescues us from God's anger that is coming.

Paul's Work in Thessalonica

2 Our brothers and sisters, you yourselves know that our visit to you was not a failure. 2 You know how we had already been ill-treated and insulted in Philippi before we came to you in Thessalonica. And even though there was much opposition, our God gave us courage to tell you the Good News that comes from him. 3 Our appeal to you is not based on error or impure motives, nor do we try to trick anyone. 4 Instead, we always speak as God wants us to, because he has judged us worthy to be entrusted with the Good News. We do not try to please people, but to please God, who tests our motives. 5 You know very well that we did not come to you with flattering talk, nor did we use words to cover up greed — God is our witness! 6 We did not try to get praise from anyone, either from you or from others, 7 even though as apostles of Christ we could have made demands on you. But we were gentle when we were with you, like a mother* taking care of her children. 8 Because of our love for you we were ready to share with you not only the Good News from God but even our own lives. You were so dear to us! 9 Surely you remember, our brothers and sisters, how we worked and toiled! We worked day and night so that we would not be any trouble to you as we preached to you the Good News from God.

10 You are our witnesses, and so is God, that our conduct towards you who believe was pure, right, and without fault. 11 You know that we treated each one of you just as a father treats his own children. 12 We encouraged you, we comforted you, and we kept urging you to live the kind of life that pleases God, who calls you to share in his own Kingdom and glory.

13 And there is another reason why we always give thanks to God. When we brought you God's message, you heard it and

---

2.7 we were gentle when we were with you, like a mother; some manuscripts have we were like children when we were with you; we were like a mother.

1 THESSALONIANS 2–4

1413

1 Thess.

2 Thess.
1 Tim.
2 Tim.
Titus
Philem.

accepted it, not as a message from human beings but as God's message, which indeed it is. For God is at work in you who believe. ¹⁴Our brothers and sisters, the same things happened to you that happened to the churches of God in Judea, to the people there who belong to Christ Jesus. You suffered the same persecutions from your own people that they suffered from the Jews, ¹⁵who killed the Lord Jesus and the prophets, and persecuted us. How displeasing they are to God! How hostile they are to everyone! ¹⁶They even tried to stop us from preaching to the Gentiles the message that would bring them salvation. In this way they have brought to completion all the sins they have always committed. And now God's anger has at last come down on them!

Paul's Desire to Visit them Again

¹⁷As for us, brothers and sisters, when we were separated from you for a little while — not in our thoughts, of course, but only in body — how we missed you and how hard we tried to see you again! ¹⁸We wanted to return to you. I myself tried to go back more than once, but Satan would not let us. ¹⁹After all, it is you — you, no less than others! — who are our hope, our joy, and our reason for boasting of our victory in the presence of our Lord Jesus when he comes. ²⁰Indeed, you are our pride and our joy!

3 Finally, we could not bear it any longer. So we decided to stay on alone in Athens ²while we sent Timothy, our brother who works with us for God in preaching the Good News about Christ. We sent him to strengthen you and help your faith, ³so that none of you should turn back because of these persecutions. You yourselves know that such persecutions are part of God's will for us. ⁴For while we were still with you, we told you beforehand that we were going to be persecuted; and as you well know, that is exactly what happened. ⁵That is why I had to send Timothy. I could not bear it any longer, so I sent him to find out about your faith. Surely it could not be that the Devil had tempted you and all our work had been for nothing!

⁶Now Timothy has come back, and he has brought us the welcome news about your faith and love. He has told us that you always think well of us and that you want to see us just as much as we want to see you. ⁷So, in all our trouble and suffering we have been encouraged about you, brothers and sisters. It was your faith that encouraged us, ⁸because now we really live if you stand firm in your life in union with the Lord. ⁹Now we can give thanks to our God for you. We thank him for the joy we have in his presence because of you. ¹⁰Day and night we ask him with all our heart to let us see you personally and supply what is needed in your faith.

¹¹May our God and Father himself and our Lord Jesus prepare the way for us to come to you! ¹²May the Lord make your love for one another and for all people grow more and more and become as great as our love for you. ¹³In this way he will strengthen you, and you will be perfect and holy in the presence of our God and Father when our Lord Jesus comes with all who belong to him.*

A Life that Pleases God

4 Finally, our brothers and sisters, you learnt from us how you should live in order to please God. This is, of course, how you have been living. And now we beg and urge you in the name of the Lord Jesus to do even more. ²For you know the instructions

3.13 *all who belong to him*; or *all his angels*.

1 THESSALONIANS 4

Write a list of all your different groups of relationships (for example, family, friends, leaders, girl/boyfriend). Next to each group, write down who you

- AIM TO -

PLEASE

in those relationships. Then spend some time imagining what those relationships would look like if your aim were to please God in them all.

1 Thess.
::········

2 Corin.
Galat.
Ephes.
Philipp.
Coloss.

we gave you by the authority of the Lord Jesus. ³God wants you to be holy and completely free from sexual immorality. ⁴Each of you men should know how to live with his wife* in a holy and honourable way, ⁵not with a lustful desire, like the heathen who do not know God. ⁶In this matter, then, no man should do wrong to his fellow-Christian or take advantage of him. We have told you this before, and we strongly warned you that the Lord will punish those who do that. ⁷God did not call us to live in immorality, but in holiness. ⁸So then, whoever rejects this teaching is not rejecting a human being, but God, who gives you his Holy Spirit.

⁹There is no need to write to you about love for your fellow-believers. You yourselves have been taught by God how you should love one another. ¹⁰And you have, in fact, behaved like this towards all the brothers and sisters in all Macedonia. So we beg you, our brothers and sisters, to do even more. ¹¹Make it your aim to live a quiet life, to mind your own business, and to earn your own living, just as we told you before. ¹²In this way you will win the respect of those who are not believers, and you will not have to depend on anyone for what you need.

The Lord's Coming

¹³Our brothers and sisters, we want you to know the truth about those who have died, so that you will not be sad, as are those who have no hope. ¹⁴We believe that Jesus died and rose again, and so we believe that God will take back with Jesus those who have died believing in him.

¹⁵What we are teaching you now is the Lord's teaching: we who are alive on the day the Lord comes will not go ahead of those who have died. ¹⁶There will be the shout of command, the archangel's voice, the sound of God's trumpet, and the Lord himself will come down from heaven. Those who have died believing in Christ will rise to life first; ¹⁷then we who are living at that time will be gathered up along with them in the clouds to meet the Lord in the air. And so we will always be with the Lord. ¹⁸So then, encourage one another with these words.

Be Ready for the Lord's Coming

5 There is no need to write to you, brothers and sisters, about the times and occasions when these things will happen. ²For you yourselves know very well that the Day of the Lord will come as a thief comes at night. ³When people say, "Everything is quiet and safe," then suddenly destruction will hit them! It will come as suddenly as the pains that come upon a woman in labour, and people will not escape. ⁴But you, brothers and sisters, are not in the darkness, and the Day should not take you by surprise like a thief. ⁵All of you are people who belong to the light, who belong to the day. We do not belong to the night or to the darkness. ⁶So then, we should not be sleeping like the others; we should be awake and sober. ⁷It is at night that people sleep; it is at night that they get drunk. ⁸But we belong to the day, and we should be sober. We must wear faith and love as a breastplate, and our hope of salvation as a helmet. ⁹God did not choose us to suffer his anger, but to possess salvation through our Lord Jesus Christ, ¹⁰who died for us in order that we might live together with him, whether we are alive or dead when he comes. ¹¹And so encourage one another and help one another, just as you are now doing.

··

4.4 *live with his wife*; or *control his body.*

Final Instructions and Greetings

¹²We beg you, our brothers and sisters, to pay proper respect to those who work among you, who guide and instruct you in the Christian life. ¹³Treat them with the greatest respect and love because of the work they do. Be at peace among yourselves.

¹⁴We urge you, our brothers and sisters, to warn the idle, encourage the timid, help the weak, be patient with everyone. ¹⁵See that no one pays back wrong for wrong, but at all times make it your aim to do good to one another and to all people.

¹⁶Be joyful always, ¹⁷pray at all times, ¹⁸be thankful in all circumstances. This is what God wants from you in your life in union with Christ Jesus.

¹⁹Do not restrain the Holy Spirit; ²⁰do not despise inspired messages. ²¹Put all things to the test: keep what is good ²²and avoid every kind of evil.

²³May the God who gives us peace make you holy in every way and keep your whole being — spirit, soul, and body — free from every fault at the coming of our Lord Jesus Christ. ²⁴He who calls you will do it, because he is faithful.

²⁵Pray also for us, brothers and sisters.

²⁶Greet all the believers with a holy kiss.

²⁷I urge you by the authority of the Lord to read this letter to all the believers.

²⁸The grace of our Lord Jesus Christ be with you.

THE LETTER OF

2 THESSALONIANS

WRITTEN: AD54-56 (OR POSSIBLY LATER IN THE FIRST CENTURY)

WHAT YOU NEED TO KNOW:

Just like 1 Thessalonians, this letter was written to the church in Thessalonica, and the believers still seem to be struggling with very similar issues - some of them thought that Jesus had already returned and they'd missed it. This letter is written in a more formal style than the first one. Some theologians think this might suggest that it was written by someone other than Paul, although it's possible that Paul is just trying to say things more clearly. As in the previous letter, Paul is trying to make clear some of the basics of the Christian faith to a bunch of relatively new and uncertain Christians.

WHY READ IT?

Some of the Thessalonians were so focused on the end of the world that they had forgotten to live now, so in chapter 3 Paul has to tell them not to be lazy. He reminds us to balance the 'now' with what God promises for the future. Like 1 Thessalonians, it's also a great letter for new Christians (or people just exploring) to read, to learn about some of the fundamentals of Christianity.

READ THROUGH CHAPTER 3.

IN THIS SPACE, CREATE A TO-DO LIST OF THINGS THAT YOU HAVE BEEN PUTTING OFF.

THEN GO AND DO ONE OF THEM

(AD48)
PAUL'S 2ND MISSIONARY JOURNEY

(AD54-56)
WRITES 2 THESSALONIANS

VISITS THESSALONICA

2 THESSALONIANS 1, 2

1417

2 Thess.

....

1 Tim.
2 Tim.
Titus
Philem.
Heb.

1

From Paul, Silas, and Timothy —
To the people of the church in Thessalonica, who belong to God our Father and the Lord Jesus Christ:

[2] May God our Father and the Lord Jesus Christ give you grace and peace.

The Judgement at Christ's Coming

[3] Our brothers and sisters, we must thank God at all times for you. It is right for us to do so, because your faith is growing so much and the love each of you has for the others is becoming greater. [4] That is why we ourselves boast about you in the churches of God. We boast about the way you continue to endure and believe through all the persecutions and sufferings you are experiencing.

[5] All of this proves that God's judgement is just and as a result you will become worthy of his Kingdom, for which you are suffering. [6] God will do what is right: he will bring suffering on those who make you suffer, [7] and he will give relief to you who suffer and to us as well. He will do this when the Lord Jesus appears from heaven with his mighty angels, [8] with a flaming fire, to punish those who reject God and who do not obey the Good News about our Lord Jesus. [9] They will suffer the punishment of eternal destruction, separated from the presence of the Lord and from his glorious might, [10] when he comes on that Day to receive glory from all his people and honour from all who believe. You too will be among them, because you have believed the message that we told you.

[11] That is why we always pray for you. We ask our God to make you worthy of the life he has called you to live. May he fulfil by his power all your desire for goodness and complete your work of faith. [12] In this way the name of our Lord Jesus will receive glory from you, and you from him, by the grace of our God and of the Lord* Jesus Christ.

The Wicked One

2

Concerning the coming of our Lord Jesus Christ and our being gathered together to be with him: I beg you, my brothers and sisters, [2] not to be so easily confused in your thinking or upset by the claim that the Day of the Lord has come. Perhaps it is thought that we said this while prophesying or preaching, or that we wrote it in a letter. [3] Do not let anyone deceive you in any way. For the Day will not come until the final Rebellion takes place and the Wicked One appears, who is destined for hell. [4] He will oppose every so-called god or object of worship and will put himself above them all. He will even go in and sit down in God's Temple and claim to be God.

[5] Don't you remember? I told you all this while I was with you. [6] Yet there is something that keeps this from happening now, and you know what it is. At the proper time, then, the Wicked One will appear. [7] The Mysterious Wickedness is already at work, but what is going to happen will not happen until the one who holds it back is taken out of the way. [8] Then the Wicked One will be revealed, but when the Lord Jesus comes, he will kill him with the breath from his mouth and destroy him with his dazzling presence. [9] The Wicked One will come with the power of Satan and perform all kinds of false miracles and wonders, [10] and use every kind of wicked deceit on those who will perish. They will perish because they did not welcome and love the truth so as to be saved. [11] And so God sends the power of error to work in them so that they believe what

1.12 *our God and of the Lord*; or *our God and Lord*.

2 THESSALONIANS 2.1-12

In this passage Paul writes about an individual who is going to have a really negative impact on the world.

If you follow Jesus, you don't need to be afraid of evil or Satan - you just need to know how to neutralise them. It's like germs - they can be dangerous but not when you know how to kill them off.

Read Ephesians 6.10-17, about the

ARMOUR

OF GOD.

Then go and wash your hands with soap and water and pray for God's protection over you today.

1418

2 Thess.

⁞········

Galat.
Ephes.
Philipp.
Coloss.
1 Thess.

2 THESSALONIANS 2, 3

is false. ¹² The result is that all who have not believed the truth, but have taken pleasure in sin, will be condemned.

You are Chosen for Salvation

¹³ We must thank God at all times for you, brothers and sisters, you whom the Lord loves. For God chose you as the first* to be saved by the Spirit's power to make you his holy people and by your faith in the truth. ¹⁴ God called you to this through the Good News we preached to you; he called you to possess your share of the glory of our Lord Jesus Christ. ¹⁵ So then, our brothers and sisters, stand firm and hold on to those truths which we taught you, both in our preaching and in our letter.

¹⁶ May our Lord Jesus Christ himself and God our Father, who loved us and in his grace gave us unfailing courage and a firm hope, ¹⁷ encourage you and strengthen you always to do and say what is good.

Pray for Us

3 Finally, our brothers and sisters, pray for us, that the Lord's message may continue to spread rapidly and be received with honour, just as it was among you. ² Pray also that God will rescue us from wicked and evil people; for not everyone believes the message.

³ But the Lord is faithful, and he will strengthen you and keep you safe from the Evil One. ⁴ And the Lord gives us confidence in you, and we are sure that you are doing and will continue to do what we tell you.

⁵ May the Lord lead you into a greater understanding of God's love and the endurance that is given by Christ.

The Obligation to Work

⁶ Our brothers and sisters, we command you in the name of our Lord Jesus Christ to keep away from all believers who are living a lazy life and who do not follow the instructions that we gave them. ⁷ You yourselves know very well that you should do just what we did. We were not lazy when we were with you. ⁸ We did not accept anyone's support without paying for it. Instead, we worked and toiled; we kept working day and night so as not to be an expense to any of you. ⁹ We did this, not because we have no right to demand our support; we did it to be an example for you to follow. ¹⁰ While we were with you, we used to say to you, "Whoever refuses to work is not allowed to eat."

¹¹ We say this because we hear that there are some people among you who live lazy lives and who do nothing except meddle in other people's business. ¹² In the name of the Lord Jesus Christ we command these people and warn them to lead orderly lives and work to earn their own living.

¹³ But you, brothers and sisters, must not get tired of doing good. ¹⁴ It may be that someone there will not obey the message we send you in this letter. If so, take note of that person and have nothing to do with him or her, so that they will be ashamed. ¹⁵ But do not treat them as an enemy; instead, warn them as a fellow-believer.

Final Words

¹⁶ May the Lord himself, who is our source of peace, give you peace at all times and in every way. The Lord be with you all.

¹⁷ With my own hand I write this: *Greetings from Paul.* This is the way I sign every letter; this is how I write.

¹⁸ May the grace of our Lord Jesus Christ be with you all.

··

2.13 *as the first*; some manuscripts have *from the beginning.*

THE LETTER OF

1 TIMOTHY

WRITTEN: AD61-64
(OR POSSIBLY LATER IN THE FIRST CENTURY)

WHY READ IT?

Timothy was a young leader, and this letter gives advice for young people about building good character and knowing truth. There is also some great advice on how to lead, both in general terms and specifically about dealing with difficult church situations.

In this space write down some of the main characteristics of

A LEADER
THAT YOU ADMIRE

_____
_____
_____
_____
_____
_____
_____
_____
_____
_____
_____
_____
_____
_____
_____
_____

Once you have done this, read through this letter and underline any significant leadership advice that you find.

WHAT YOU NEED TO KNOW:

This letter is a bit different from the others, as it was written to a person rather than a church. Timothy was a young leader who was put in charge of a church in Ephesus after Paul became concerned about its original leaders - so Timothy was mentored by Paul before going on to lead a church himself. This is a letter in which the wisdom of age is speaking to the passion of youth.

KEY CHARACTER:

Timothy was the son of a Greek father and a Jewish mother. He was mentored by Paul until he was entrusted with the leadership of the church in Ephesus. In the letters that Paul wrote to him, Paul seems to be cheering him on from afar.

(AD48)
PAUL MEETS TIMOTHY

(AD61-64)
PAUL WRITES 1 TIMOTHY

PAUL TRAVELS WITH TIMOTHY

1 From Paul, an apostle of Christ Jesus by order of God our Saviour and Christ Jesus our hope —
² To Timothy, my true son in the faith:

May God the Father and Christ Jesus our Lord give you grace, mercy, and peace.

Warnings against False Teaching

³ I want you to stay in Ephesus, just as I urged you when I was on my way to Macedonia. Some people there are teaching false doctrines, and you must order them to stop. ⁴ Tell them to give up those legends and those long lists of ancestors, which only produce arguments; they do not serve God's plan, which is known by faith. ⁵ The purpose of this order is to arouse the love that comes from a pure heart, a clear conscience, and a genuine faith. ⁶ Some people have turned away from these and have lost their way in foolish discussions. ⁷ They want to be teachers of God's law, but they do not understand their own words or the matters about which they speak with so much confidence.

⁸ We know that the Law is good if it is used as it should be used. ⁹ It must be remembered, of course, that laws are made, not for good people, but for lawbreakers and criminals, for the godless and sinful, for those who are not religious or spiritual, for those who kill their fathers or mothers, for murderers, ¹⁰ for the immoral, for sexual perverts, for kidnappers, for those who lie and give false testimony or who do anything else contrary to sound doctrine. ¹¹ That teaching is found in the gospel that was entrusted to me to announce, the Good News from the glorious and blessed God.

Gratitude for God's Mercy

¹² I give thanks to Christ Jesus our Lord, who has given me strength for my work. I thank him for considering me worthy and appointing me to serve him, ¹³ even though in the past I spoke evil of him and persecuted and insulted him. But God was merciful to me because I did not yet have faith and so did not know what I was doing. ¹⁴ And our Lord poured out his abundant grace on me and gave me the faith and love which are ours in union with Christ Jesus. ¹⁵ This is a true saying, to be completely accepted and believed: Christ Jesus came into the world to save sinners. I am the worst of them, ¹⁶ but God was merciful to me in order that Christ Jesus might show his full patience in dealing with me, the worst of sinners, as an example for all those who would later believe in him and receive eternal life. ¹⁷ To the eternal King, immortal and invisible, the only God — to him be honour and glory for ever and ever! Amen.

¹⁸ Timothy, my child, I entrust to you this command, which is in accordance with the words of prophecy spoken in the past about you. Use those words as weapons in order to fight well, ¹⁹ and keep your faith and a clear conscience. Some people have not listened to their conscience and have made a ruin of their faith. ²⁰ Among them are Hymenaeus and Alexander, whom I have punished by handing them over to the power of Satan; this will teach them to stop their blasphemy.

Church Worship

2 First of all, then, I urge that petitions, prayers, requests, and thanksgivings be offered to God for all people; ² for kings and all others who are in authority, that we may live a quiet and peaceful life with all reverence towards God and with proper

1 TIMOTHY 2, 3

1421

1 Tim.

2 Tim.
Titus
Philem.
Heb.
James

conduct. [3] This is good and it pleases God our Saviour, [4] who wants everyone to be saved and to come to know the truth. [5] For there is one God, and there is one who brings God and human beings together, the man Christ Jesus, [6] who gave himself to redeem everyone. That was the proof at the right time that God wants everyone to be saved, [7] and that is why I was sent as an apostle and teacher of the Gentiles, to proclaim the message of faith and truth. I am not lying; I am telling the truth!

[8] In every church service I want the men to pray, men who are dedicated to God and can lift up their hands in prayer without anger or argument. [9] I also want the women to be modest and sensible about their clothes and to dress properly; not with fancy hair styles or with gold ornaments or pearls or expensive dresses, [10] but with good deeds, as is proper for women who claim to be religious. [11] Women should learn in silence and all humility. [12] I do not allow them to teach or to have authority over men; they must keep quiet. [13] For Adam was created first, and then Eve. [14] And it was not Adam who was deceived; it was the woman who was deceived and broke God's law. [15] But a woman will be saved through having children,* if she perseveres* in faith and love and holiness, with modesty.

Leaders in the Church

3 This is a true saying: if a man is eager to be a church leader, he desires an excellent work. [2] A church leader must be without fault; he must have only one wife,* be sober, self-controlled, and orderly; he must welcome strangers in his home; he must be able to teach; [3] he must not be a drunkard or a violent man, but gentle and peaceful; he must not love money; [4] he must be able to manage his own family well and make his children obey him with all respect. [5] For if a man does not know how to manage his own family, how can he take care of the church of God? [6] He must be mature in the faith, so that he will not swell up with pride and be condemned, as the Devil was. [7] He should be a man who is respected by the people outside the church, so that he will not be disgraced and fall into the Devil's trap.

Helpers in the Church

[8] Church helpers must also have a good character and be sincere; they must not drink too much wine or be greedy for money; [9] they should hold to the revealed truth of the faith with a clear conscience. [10] They should be tested first, and then, if they pass the test, they are to serve. [11] Their wives* also must be of good character and must not gossip; they must be sober and honest in everything. [12] A church helper must have only one wife,* and be able to manage his children and family well. [13] Those helpers who do their work well win for themselves a good standing and are able to speak boldly about their faith in Christ Jesus.

The Great Secret

[14] As I write this letter to you, I hope to come and see you soon. [15] But if I am delayed, this letter will let you know how we should conduct ourselves in God's household, which is the church of the

---

2.15 *will be saved through having children*; or *will be kept safe through childbirth*.
2.15 *if she perseveres*; or *if they persevere*.
3.2 *have only one wife*; or *be married only once*.
3.11 *Their wives*; or *Women helpers*.
3.12 *have only one wife*; or *be married only once*.

---

1 TIMOTHY 3.1-13

You see here that God is bothered about your

INWARD

CHARACTER

rather than your outward appearance.

Read through chapter 3; then use the time you would normally spend on your outward appearance to talk to God about your inward character.

1422

1 Tim.

Ephes.
Philipp.
Coloss.
1 Thess.
2 Thess.

1 TIMOTHY 4.12

Whatever your age,
you are called to

LIVE FOR

GOD.

Next to each of these
words, write down one
practical thing that you
can do to live differently
in that area, and ask
God to help you.

Speech:

Conduct:

Love:

Faith:

Purity:

---

living God, the pillar and support of the truth. ¹⁶ No one can deny how great is the secret of our religion:

He appeared in human form,
was shown to be right by the Spirit,*
and was seen by angels.
He was preached among the nations,
was believed in throughout the world,
and was taken up to heaven.

False Teachers

4 The Spirit says clearly that some people will abandon the faith in later times; they will obey lying spirits and follow the teachings of demons. ² Such teachings are spread by deceitful liars, whose consciences are dead, as if burnt with a hot iron. ³ Such people teach that it is wrong to marry and to eat certain foods. But God created those foods to be eaten, after a prayer of thanks, by those who are believers and have come to know the truth. ⁴ Everything that God has created is good; nothing is to be rejected, but everything is to be received with a prayer of thanks, ⁵ because the word of God and the prayer make it acceptable to God.

A Good Servant of Christ Jesus

⁶ If you give these instructions to the believers, you will be a good servant of Christ Jesus, as you feed yourself spiritually on the words of faith and of the true teaching which you have followed. ⁷ But keep away from those godless legends, which are not worth telling. Keep yourself in training for a godly life. ⁸ Physical exercise has some value, but spiritual exercise is valuable in every way, because it promises life both for the present and for the future. ⁹ This is a true saying, to be completely accepted and believed. ¹⁰ We struggle* and work hard, because we have placed our hope in the living God, who is the Saviour of all and especially of those who believe.

¹¹ Give them these instructions and these teachings. ¹² Do not let anyone look down on you because you are young, but be an example for the believers in your speech, your conduct, your love, faith, and purity. ¹³ Until I come, give your time and effort to the public reading of the Scriptures and to preaching and teaching. ¹⁴ Do not neglect the spiritual gift that is in you, which was given to you when the prophets spoke and the elders laid their hands on you. ¹⁵ Practise these things and devote yourself to them, in order that your progress may be seen by all. ¹⁶ Watch yourself and watch your teaching. Keep on doing these things, because if you do, you will save both yourself and those who hear you.

Responsibilities towards Believers

5 Do not rebuke an older man, but appeal to him as if he were your father. Treat the younger men as your brothers, ² the older women as mothers, and the younger women as sisters, with all purity.

³ Show respect for widows who really are all alone. ⁴ But if a widow has children or grandchildren, they should learn first to carry out their religious duties towards their own family and in this way repay their parents and grandparents, because that is

---

3.16 *was shown to be right by the Spirit*; or *and, in spiritual form, was shown to be right.*
4.10 *struggle*; some manuscripts have *are reviled.*

1 TIMOTHY 5, 6

1423

1 Tim.

..........:.

2 Tim.
Titus
Philem.
Heb.
James

what pleases God. [5] A widow who is all alone, with no one to take care of her, has placed her hope in God and continues to pray and ask him for his help night and day. [6] But a widow who gives herself to pleasure has already died, even though she lives. [7] Give them these instructions, so that no one will find fault with them. [8] But if anyone does not take care of his relatives, especially the members of his own family, he has denied the faith and is worse than an unbeliever.

[9] Do not add any widow to the list of widows unless she is over sixty years of age. In addition, she must have been married only once* [10] and have a reputation for good deeds: a woman who brought up her children well, received strangers in her home, performed humble duties for fellow-Christians, helped people in trouble, and devoted herself to doing good.

[11] But do not include younger widows in the list; because when their desires make them want to marry, they turn away from Christ, [12] and so become guilty of breaking their earlier promise to him. [13] They also learn to waste their time in going round from house to house; but even worse, they learn to be gossips and busybodies, talking of things they should not. [14] So I would prefer that the younger widows get married, have children, and take care of their homes, so as to give our enemies no chance of speaking evil of us. [15] For some widows have already turned away to follow Satan. [16] But if any Christian woman has widows in her family, she must take care of them and not put the burden on the church, so that it may take care of the widows who are all alone.

[17] The elders who do good work as leaders should be considered worthy of receiving double pay, especially those who work hard at preaching and teaching. [18] For the scripture says, "Do not muzzle an ox when you are using it to thresh corn" and "Workers should be given their pay." [19] Do not listen to an accusation against an elder unless it is brought by two or more witnesses. [20] Rebuke publicly all those who commit sins, so that the rest may be afraid.

[21] In the presence of God and of Christ Jesus and of the holy angels I solemnly call upon you to obey these instructions without showing any prejudice or favour to anyone in anything you do. [22] Be in no hurry to lay hands on anyone in dedication to the Lord's service. Take no part in the sins of others; keep yourself pure.

[23] Do not drink water only, but take a little wine to help your digestion, since you are ill so often.

[24] The sins of some people are plain to see, and their sins go ahead of them to judgement; but the sins of others are seen only later. [25] In the same way good deeds are plainly seen, and even those that are not so plain cannot be hidden.

6 Those who are slaves must consider their masters worthy of all respect, so that no one will speak evil of the name of God and of our teaching. [2] Slaves belonging to Christian masters must not despise them, for they are their brothers and sisters. Instead, they are to serve them even better, because those who benefit from their work are believers whom they love.

False Teaching and True Riches

You must teach and preach these things. [3] Whoever teaches a different doctrine and does not agree with the true words of our Lord Jesus Christ and with the teaching of our religion [4] is swollen with pride and knows nothing. He has an unhealthy desire to argue and quarrel about words, and this brings on jealousy,

....

5.9 *married only once*; or *faithful to her husband.*

1424

1 Tim.

Ephes.
Philipp.
Coloss.
1 Thess.
2 Thess.

disputes, insults, evil suspicions, [5] and constant arguments from people whose minds do not function and who no longer have the truth. They think that religion is a way to become rich.

[6] Well, religion does make a person very rich, if he is satisfied with what he has. [7] What did we bring into the world? Nothing! What can we take out of the world? Nothing! [8] So then, if we have food and clothes, that should be enough for us. [9] But those who want to get rich fall into temptation and are caught in the trap of many foolish and harmful desires, which pull them down to ruin and destruction. [10] For the love of money is a source of all kinds of evil. Some have been so eager to have it that they have wandered away from the faith and have broken their hearts with many sorrows.

Personal Instructions

[11] But you, man of God, avoid all these things. Strive for righteousness, godliness, faith, love, endurance, and gentleness. [12] Run your best in the race of faith, and win eternal life for yourself; for it was to this life that God called you when you firmly professed your faith before many witnesses. [13] Before God, who gives life to all things, and before Christ Jesus, who firmly professed his faith before Pontius Pilate, I command you [14] to obey your orders and keep them faithfully until the Day when our Lord Jesus Christ will appear. [15] His appearing will be brought about at the right time by God, the blessed and only Ruler, the King of kings and the Lord of lords. [16] He alone is immortal; he lives in the light that no one can approach. No one has ever seen him; no one can ever see him. To him be honour and eternal dominion! Amen.

[17] Command those who are rich in the things of this life not to be proud, but to place their hope, not in such an uncertain thing as riches, but in God, who generously gives us everything for our enjoyment. [18] Command them to do good, to be rich in good works, to be generous and ready to share with others. [19] In this way they will store up for themselves a treasure which will be a solid foundation for the future. And then they will be able to win the life which is true life.

[20] Timothy, keep safe what has been entrusted to your care. Avoid the profane talk and foolish arguments of what some people wrongly call "Knowledge". [21] For some have claimed to possess it, and as a result they have lost the way of faith.

God's grace be with you all.

1 TIMOTHY 6.11

STRIVE FOR
RIGHTEOUSNESS,
GODLINESS,
FAITH,
LOVE,
ENDURANCE,
&
GENTLENESS

THE LETTER OF
2 TIMOTHY

WRITTEN: AD61-64 (OR POSSIBLY LATER IN THE FIRST CENTURY)

WHY READ IT?

This letter encourages us to push through, even when life seems tough. There are some great themes here about digging deep and keeping going, even when you don't feel like it.

WHAT YOU NEED TO KNOW:

This letter seems to have been written to encourage Timothy to keep going, as there is a theme of endurance throughout. This might also be because the writer himself needs to practise endurance. The dating suggests that this could have been the last letter that Paul wrote before his death. If so, with his last letter he chose to encourage and spur on a young person.

This letter talks about

ENDURANCE,
BEING A SOLDIER,
TRAINING
AND KEEPING GOING.

Before starting to read it, do some sort of exercise.

As you do, pray that God will give you the strength to keep going with him when things get tough.

Colour these shapes.

(AD48)
PAUL MEETS TIMOTHY

(AD61-64)
PAUL WRITES 2 TIMOTHY

PAUL TRAVELS WITH TIMOTHY

1426

2 Tim.

:·········

Philipp.
Coloss.
1 Thess.
2 Thess.
1 Tim.

2 TIMOTHY 1, 2

1 From Paul, an apostle of Christ Jesus by God's will, sent to proclaim the promised life which we have in union with Christ Jesus —

2 To Timothy, my dear son:

May God the Father and Christ Jesus our Lord give you grace, mercy, and peace.

Thanksgiving and Encouragement

3 I give thanks to God, whom I serve with a clear conscience, as my ancestors did. I thank him as I remember you always in my prayers night and day. 4 I remember your tears, and I want to see you very much, so that I may be filled with joy. 5 I remember the sincere faith you have, the kind of faith that your grandmother Lois and your mother Eunice also had. I am sure that you have it also. 6 For this reason I remind you to keep alive the gift that God gave you when I laid my hands on you. 7 For the Spirit that God has given us does not make us timid; instead, his Spirit fills us with power, love, and self-control.

8 Do not be ashamed, then, of witnessing for our Lord; nor be ashamed of me, a prisoner for Christ's sake. Instead, take your part in suffering for the Good News, as God gives you the strength to do it. 9 He saved us and called us to be his own people, not because of what we have done, but because of his own purpose and grace. He gave us this grace by means of Christ Jesus before the beginning of time, 10 but now it has been revealed to us through the coming of our Saviour, Christ Jesus. He has ended the power of death and through the gospel has revealed immortal life.

11 God has appointed me as an apostle and teacher to proclaim the Good News, 12 and it is for this reason that I suffer these things. But I am still full of confidence, because I know whom I have trusted, and I am sure that he is able to keep safe until that Day what he has entrusted to me.* 13 Hold firmly to the true words that I taught you, as the example for you to follow, and remain in the faith and love that are ours in union with Christ Jesus. 14 Through the power of the Holy Spirit, who lives in us, keep the good things that have been entrusted to you.

15 You know that everyone in the province of Asia, including Phygelus and Hermogenes, has deserted me. 16 May the Lord show mercy to the family of Onesiphorus, because he cheered me up many times. He was not ashamed that I am in prison, 17 but as soon as he arrived in Rome, he started looking for me until he found me. 18 May the Lord grant him his mercy on that Day! And you know very well how much he did for me in Ephesus.

A Loyal Soldier of Christ Jesus

2 As for you, my son, be strong through the grace that is ours in union with Christ Jesus. 2 Take the teachings that you heard me proclaim in the presence of many witnesses, and entrust them to reliable people, who will be able to teach others also.

3 Take your part in suffering, as a loyal soldier of Christ Jesus. 4 A soldier on active service wants to please his commanding officer and so does not get mixed up in the affairs of civilian life. 5 An athlete who runs in a race cannot win the prize unless he obeys the rules. 6 The farmer who has done the hard work should have the first share of the harvest. 7 Think about what I am saying, because the Lord will enable you to understand it all.

....

1.12 *what he has entrusted to me*; or *what I have entrusted to him.*

[8] Remember Jesus Christ, who was raised from death, who was a descendant of David, as is taught in the Good News I preach. [9] Because I preach the Good News, I suffer and I am even chained like a criminal. But the word of God is not in chains, [10] and so I endure everything for the sake of God's chosen people, in order that they too may obtain the salvation that comes through Christ Jesus and brings eternal glory. [11] This is a true saying:

"If we have died with him,
    we shall also live with him.
[12] If we continue to endure,
    we shall also rule with him.
If we deny him,
    he also will deny us.
[13] If we are not faithful,
    he remains faithful,
    because he cannot be false to himself."

An Approved Worker

[14] Remind your people of this, and give them a solemn warning in God's presence not to fight over words. It does no good, but only ruins the people who listen. [15] Do your best to win full approval in God's sight, as a worker who is not ashamed of his work, one who correctly teaches the message of God's truth. [16] Keep away from profane and foolish discussions, which only drive people further away from God. [17] Such teaching is like an open sore that eats away the flesh. Two men who have taught such things are Hymenaeus and Philetus. [18] They have left the way of truth and are upsetting the faith of some believers by saying that our resurrection has already taken place. [19] But the solid foundation that God has laid cannot be shaken; and on it are written these words: "The Lord knows those who are his" and "All who say that they belong to the Lord must turn away from wrongdoing."

[20] In a large house there are dishes and bowls of all kinds: some are made of silver and gold, others of wood and clay; some are for special occasions, others for ordinary use. [21] If anyone makes himself or herself clean from all those evil things, they will be used for special purposes, because they are dedicated and useful to their Master, ready to be used for every good deed. [22] Avoid the passions of youth, and strive for righteousness, faith, love, and peace, together with those who with a pure heart call out to the Lord for help. [23] But keep away from foolish and ignorant arguments; you know that they end up in quarrels. [24] As the Lord's servant, you must not quarrel. You must be kind towards all, a good and patient teacher, [25] gentle as you correct your opponents, for it may be that God will give them the opportunity to repent and come to know the truth. [26] And then they will come to their senses and escape from the trap of the Devil, who had caught them and made them obey his will.

The Last Days

3 Remember that there will be difficult times in the last days. [2] People will be selfish, greedy, boastful, and conceited; they will be insulting, disobedient to their parents, ungrateful, and irreligious; [3] they will be unkind, merciless, slanderers, violent, and fierce; they will hate the good; [4] they will be treacherous, reckless, and swollen with pride; they will love pleasure rather than God; [5] they will hold to the outward form of our religion, but reject its real power. Keep away from such people. [6] Some of them go into people's houses and gain control over weak women

2 TIMOTHY 1.7

FOR THE SPIRIT THAT GOD HAS GIVEN US DOES NOT MAKE US TIMID; INSTEAD, HIS SPIRIT • FILLS US WITH • POWER, LOVE, AND SELF-CONTROL

2 Tim.

Titus
Philem.
Heb.
James
1 Peter

1428

2 Tim.

··········

Philipp.
Coloss.
1 Thess.
2 Thess.
1 Tim.

2 TIMOTHY 3, 4

2 TIMOTHY 4.2-4

For the next week,

SET AN

ALARM

for 4.24.

If you follow Jesus, at this time stop and pray for your friends who don't know him, and ask God for an opportunity to tell them about him. If you don't follow Jesus, take this time to pray - maybe for the first time!

who are burdened by the guilt of their sins and driven by all kinds of desires, [7] women who are always trying to learn but who can never come to know the truth. [8] As Jannes and Jambres were opposed to Moses, so also these people are opposed to the truth — people whose minds do not function and who are failures in the faith. [9] But they will not get very far, because everyone will see how stupid they are. That is just what happened to Jannes and Jambres.

Last Instructions

[10] But you have followed my teaching, my conduct, and my purpose in life; you have observed my faith, my patience, my love, my endurance, [11] my persecutions, and my sufferings. You know all that happened to me in Antioch, Iconium, and Lystra, the terrible persecutions I endured! But the Lord rescued me from them all. [12] Everyone who wants to live a godly life in union with Christ Jesus will be persecuted; [13] and evil persons and impostors will keep on going from bad to worse, deceiving others and being deceived themselves. [14] But as for you, continue in the truths that you were taught and firmly believe. You know who your teachers were, [15] and you remember that ever since you were a child, you have known the Holy Scriptures, which are able to give you the wisdom that leads to salvation through faith in Christ Jesus. [16] All Scripture is inspired by God and is useful* for teaching the truth, rebuking error, correcting faults, and giving instruction for right living, [17] so that the person who serves God may be fully qualified and equipped to do every kind of good deed.

4 In the presence of God and of Christ Jesus, who will judge the living and the dead, and because he is coming to rule as King, I solemnly urge you [2] to preach the message, to insist upon proclaiming it (whether the time is right or not), to convince, reproach, and encourage, as you teach with all patience. [3] The time will come when people will not listen to sound doctrine, but will follow their own desires and will collect for themselves more and more teachers who will tell them what they are itching to hear. [4] They will turn away from listening to the truth and give their attention to legends. [5] But you must keep control of yourself in all circumstances; endure suffering, do the work of a preacher of the Good News, and perform your whole duty as a servant of God.

[6] As for me, the hour has come for me to be sacrificed; the time is here for me to leave this life. [7] I have done my best in the race, I have run the full distance, and I have kept the faith.* [8] And now there is waiting for me the victory prize of being put right with God, which the Lord, the righteous Judge, will give me on that Day — and not only to me, but to all those who wait with love for him to appear.

Personal Words

[9] Do your best to come to me soon. [10] Demas fell in love with this present world and has deserted me, going off to Thessalonica. Crescens went to Galatia, and Titus to Dalmatia. [11] Only Luke is with me. Get Mark and bring him with you, because he can help me in the work. [12] I sent Tychicus to Ephesus. [13] When you come, bring my coat that I left in Troas with Carpus; bring the books too, and especially the ones made of parchment.

··

3.16 *All Scripture is inspired by God and is useful*; or *Every scripture inspired by God is also useful.*
4.7 *kept the faith*; or *been true to my promise.*

2 Tim.

Titus
Philem.
Heb.
James
1 Peter

¹⁴ Alexander the metalworker did me much harm; the Lord will reward him according to what he has done. ¹⁵ Be on your guard against him yourself, because he was violently opposed to our message.

¹⁶ No one stood by me the first time I defended myself; all deserted me. May God not count it against them! ¹⁷ But the Lord stayed with me and gave me strength, so that I was able to proclaim the full message for all the Gentiles to hear; and I was rescued from being sentenced to death. ¹⁸ And the Lord will rescue me from all evil and take me safely into his heavenly Kingdom. To him be the glory for ever and ever! Amen.

Final Greetings

¹⁹ I send greetings to Priscilla and Aquila and to the family of Onesiphorus. ²⁰ Erastus stayed in Corinth, and I left Trophimus in Miletus, because he was ill. ²¹ Do your best to come before winter.

Eubulus, Pudens, Linus, and Claudia send their greetings, and so do all the other Christians.

²² The Lord be with your spirit.

God's grace be with you all.

THE LETTER TO
TITUS

WRITTEN: AROUND AD80
(OR POSSIBLY LATER, IN THE SECOND CENTURY)

KEY CHARACTER:

The writer seems to have really liked Titus: he calls him 'my true son' in chapter 1. Titus is also mentioned in Galatians, 2 Timothy and 2 Corinthians. He wasn't Jewish, so he is an example of how Jesus is at work in lots of different types of people, doing lots of different things.

Read through Titus 1.5-9.
On the lines below, write different areas where you

HAVE AUTHORITY
OR WHERE YOU LEAD

(it might be in your friendship group or family).

_____

_____

_____

_____

_____

_____

WHY READ IT?

This letter is all about faith and actions, and how, when we live for Jesus, our lives need to be in sync with his. It includes themes of leadership, living with integrity and following Jesus - things that many of us struggle to get better at. The letter also features a lovely summary of the good news of Jesus (check out Titus 2.11-14).

Now think about how your behaviour might change because of the responsibility that you carry.

WHAT YOU NEED TO KNOW:

This letter was written to Titus. Like Timothy, he was a young leader who had been converted to Christianity by Paul. Titus was based in Crete, leading a church there, but Crete was a tough place in which to lead. He was having a rough time, as the Cretans didn't respect authority and were a bit wild. This letter was written not only to help Titus to address these issues and to persevere, but also to help him communicate the great truths of the gospel.

(AD46)
PAUL'S 1ST MISSIONARY JOURNEY

(AD80)
LETTER TO TITUS WRITTEN

TRAVELS WITH TITUS

1431

Titus
···········›

Philem.
Heb.
James
1 Peter
2 Peter

1 From Paul, a servant of God and an apostle of Jesus Christ. I was chosen and sent to help the faith of God's chosen people and to lead them to the truth taught by our religion, ²which is based on the hope for eternal life. God, who does not lie, promised us this life before the beginning of time, ³and at the right time he revealed it in his message. This was entrusted to me, and I proclaim it by order of God our Saviour.

⁴I write to Titus, my true son in the faith that we have in common.

May God the Father and Christ Jesus our Saviour give you grace and peace.

Titus' Work in Crete

⁵I left you in Crete, so that you could put in order the things that still needed doing and appoint church elders in every town. Remember my instructions: ⁶an elder must be blameless; he must have only one wife,* and his children must be believers and not have the reputation of being wild or disobedient. ⁷For since a church leader is in charge of God's work, he should be blameless. He must not be arrogant or quick-tempered, or a drunkard or violent or greedy for money. ⁸He must be hospitable and love what is good. He must be self-controlled, upright, holy, and disciplined. ⁹He must hold firmly to the message which can be trusted and which agrees with the doctrine. In this way he will be able to encourage others with the true teaching and also to show the error of those who are opposed to it.

¹⁰For there are many, especially converts from Judaism, who rebel and deceive others with their nonsense. ¹¹It is necessary to stop their talk, because they are upsetting whole families by teaching what they should not, and all for the shameful purpose of making money. ¹²⁻¹³It was a Cretan himself, one of their own prophets, who spoke the truth when he said, "Cretans are always liars, wicked beasts, and lazy gluttons." For this reason you must rebuke them sharply, so that they may have a healthy faith ¹⁴and no longer hold on to Jewish legends and to human commandments which come from people who have rejected the truth. ¹⁵Everything is pure to those who are themselves pure; but nothing is pure to those who are defiled and unbelieving, for their minds and consciences have been defiled. ¹⁶They claim that they know God, but their actions deny it. They are hateful and disobedient, not fit to do anything good.

Sound Doctrine

2 But you must teach what agrees with sound doctrine. ²Instruct the older men to be sober, sensible, and self-controlled; to be sound in their faith, love, and endurance. ³In the same way instruct the older women to behave as women should who live a holy life. They must not be slanderers or slaves to wine. They must teach what is good, ⁴in order to train the younger women to love their husbands and children, ⁵to be self-controlled and pure, and to be good housewives who submit to their husbands, so that no one will speak evil of the message that comes from God.

⁶In the same way urge the young men to be self-controlled. ⁷In all things you yourself must be an example of good behaviour. Be sincere and serious in your teaching. ⁸Use sound words that cannot be criticized, so that your enemies may be put to shame by not having anything bad to say about us.

1.6 *have only one wife*; or *be married only once.*

TITUS 3.1-11

Circle any verbs (doing words) in this section.

Which are the

- MOST -

CHALLENGING

to the way you live your life?

Why do you think conduct is important to God, if he loves us whatever we do?

write some thoughts here

9 Slaves are to submit to their masters and please them in all things. They must not answer them back 10 or steal from them. Instead, they must show that they are always good and faithful, so as to bring credit to the teaching about God our Saviour in all they do.

11 For God has revealed his grace for the salvation of the whole human race. 12 That grace instructs us to give up ungodly living and worldly passions, and to live self-controlled, upright, and godly lives in this world, 13 as we wait for the blessed Day we hope for, when the glory of our great God and Saviour Jesus Christ* will appear. 14 He gave himself for us, to rescue us from all wickedness and to make us a pure people who belong to him alone and are eager to do good.

15 Teach these things and use your full authority as you encourage and rebuke your hearers. Let none of them look down on you.

Christian Conduct

3 Remind your people to submit to rulers and authorities, to obey them, and to be ready to do good in every way. 2 Tell them not to speak evil of anyone, but to be peaceful and friendly, and always to show a gentle attitude towards everyone. 3 For we ourselves were once foolish, disobedient, and wrong. We were slaves to passions and pleasures of all kinds. We spent our lives in malice and envy; others hated us and we hated them. 4 But when the kindness and love of God our Saviour was revealed, 5 he saved us. It was not because of any good deeds that we ourselves had done, but because of his own mercy that he saved us, through the Holy Spirit, who gives us new birth and new life by washing us. 6 God poured out the Holy Spirit abundantly on us through Jesus Christ our Saviour, 7 so that by his grace we might be put right with God and come into possession of the eternal life we hope for. 8 This is a true saying.

I want you to give special emphasis to these matters, so that those who believe in God may be concerned with giving their time to doing good deeds, which are good and useful for everyone. 9 But avoid stupid arguments, long lists of ancestors, quarrels, and fights about the Law. They are useless and worthless. 10 Give at least two warnings to those who cause divisions, and then have nothing more to do with them. 11 You know that such people are corrupt, and their sins prove that they are wrong.

Final Instructions

12 When I send Artemas or Tychicus to you, do your best to come to me in Nicopolis, because I have decided to spend the winter there. 13 Do your best to help Zenas the lawyer and Apollos to get started on their travels, and see to it that they have everything they need. 14 Our people must learn to spend their time doing good, in order to provide for real needs; they should not live useless lives.

15 All who are with me send you greetings. Give our greetings to our friends in the faith.

God's grace be with you all.

2.13 our great God and Saviour Jesus Christ; or the great God and our Saviour Jesus Christ.

THE LETTER TO

PHILEMON

WRITTEN: SOMETIME BETWEEN AD55 AND 64

WHY READ IT?

This letter shows Paul's passion for looking after those who were powerless. He does an amazing job of defending Onesimus while addressing Philemon in a respectful and encouraging way. We could learn from this when we are fighting someone else's corner.

Spend some time thinking about people or issues that you

• WANT TO FIGHT FOR •

If you could speak to

SOMEONE WITH INFLUENCE

in that area, what would you want to say to them? Bullet-point your letter here. →

_____

_____

_____

_____

_____

_____

_____

_____

WHAT YOU NEED TO KNOW:

Philemon was a well-known Christian and probably a member of the church at Colossae. He also owned a slave called Onesimus. (Slave ownership was common at the time, and most people wouldn't have seen anything wrong with it.) Onesimus had run away from his master, met Paul and become a believer in Jesus. Paul wrote to Philemon, asking him to welcome Onesimus back as a member of the Christian family.

SPOTLIGHT:

Although Philemon might not seem to have a very deep message, there is treasure in this letter. Names have meanings, and if we look at the names here, we see that:
PAUL MEANS 'SMALL' OR 'HUMBLE'
PHILEMON MEANS 'LOVE'
ONESIMUS MEANS 'USEFUL'

So in the letter to Philemon we have one who is small and humble, appealing to one whose name means 'love', asking for one who is useful to be set free.

(AD48)
PAUL MEETS TIMOTHY

PAUL MEETS ONESIMUS

(AD55-64)
PAUL WRITES TO PHILEMON

1434

Philem.

1 Thess.
2 Thess.
1 Tim.
2 Tim.
Titus

PHILEMON

In this book, Paul is concerned that a slave should be treated well by his master.

SLAVES STILL EXIST TODAY.

Check the labels in the clothes that you are wearing. Where were they made? Why not research workers' rights in those countries? You could even find an online petition to sign, supporting workers' rights.

[1] From Paul, a prisoner for the sake of Christ Jesus, and from our brother Timothy —

To our friend and fellow-worker Philemon, [2] and the church that meets in your house, and our sister Apphia, and our fellow-soldier Archippus:

[3] May God our Father and the Lord Jesus Christ give you grace and peace.

Philemon's Love and Faith

[4] Brother Philemon, every time I pray, I mention you and give thanks to my God. [5] For I hear of your love for all God's people and the faith you have in the Lord Jesus. [6] My prayer is that our fellowship with you as believers will bring about a deeper understanding of every blessing which we have in our life in union with Christ. [7] Your love, dear brother, has brought me great joy and much encouragement! You have cheered the hearts of all God's people.

A Request for Onesimus

[8] For this reason I could be bold enough, as your brother in Christ, to order you to do what should be done. [9] But because I love you, I make a request instead. I do this even though I am Paul, the ambassador of Christ Jesus, and at present also a prisoner for his sake.* [10] So I make a request to you on behalf of Onesimus, who is my own son in Christ; for while in prison I have become his spiritual father. [11] At one time he was of no use to you, but now he is useful* both to you and to me.

[12] I am sending him back to you now, and with him goes my heart. [13] I would like to keep him here with me, while I am in prison for the gospel's sake, so that he could help me in your place. [14] However, I do not want to force you to help me; rather, I would like you to do it of your own free will. So I will not do anything unless you agree.

[15] It may be that Onesimus was away from you for a short time so that you might have him back for all time. [16] And now he is not just a slave, but much more than a slave: he is a dear brother in Christ. How much he means to me! And how much more he will mean to you, both as a slave and as a brother in the Lord!

[17] So, if you think of me as your partner, welcome him back just as you would welcome me. [18] If he has done you any wrong or owes you anything, charge it to my account. [19] Here, I will write this with my own hand: *I, Paul, will pay you back.* (I should not have to remind you, of course, that you owe your very self to me.) [20] So, my brother, please do me this favour for the Lord's sake; as a brother in Christ, cheer me up!

[21] I am sure, as I write this, that you will do what I ask — in fact I know that you will do even more. [22] At the same time, get a room ready for me, because I hope that God will answer the prayers of all of you and give me back to you.

Final Greetings

[23] Epaphras, who is in prison with me for the sake of Christ Jesus, sends you his greetings, [24] and so do my fellow-workers Mark, Aristarchus, Demas, and Luke.

[25] May the grace of the Lord Jesus Christ be with you all.

v.9 the ambassador of Christ Jesus, and at present also a prisoner for his sake; or an old man, and at present a prisoner for the sake of Christ Jesus.
v.11 The Greek name Onesimus means "useful".

THE LETTER TO THE
HEBREWS

WRITTEN: AD85-90

WHY READ IT?

This letter is an encouragement to us to stay strong in our faith. It does a great job of unpacking who Jesus is and explaining the difference he makes not only to our lives but also to our relationship with God. It is a very meaty letter, but it really helps us to match Jesus up with themes in the Old Testament.

Hebrews presents Jesus as both God and man, as a high priest, and as a sacrifice. Take three coloured pens and show here what you learn about Jesus in each of these three areas.

KEY CHARACTER:

Melchizedek (mentioned in chapter 7) is a bit of a mystery. He first appears in Genesis 14, where he's called the king of Salem (or Jerusalem). This means 'king of peace', and the name Melchizedek means 'king of righteousness'. These are both names that can be given to Jesus. He is also mentioned in Psalm 110.4, a verse that some people think is a prophecy about the Messiah.

WHAT YOU NEED TO KNOW:

This book is called 'Hebrews' because the people it was written to were Jews (also known as Hebrews) who had decided to follow Jesus. This decision had made life difficult for them. They were being persecuted not only by the Romans for being Christians, but also by their fellow Jews for abandoning their original faith. So the writer wanted to encourage them to keep going. Hebrews is largely about the person of Jesus, but it also includes a reminder of all the amazing people of faith who stayed strong in the past. The letter focuses on showing how Jesus fulfils all the Old Testament beliefs and customs, and how the uniqueness of Jesus should encourage people to persevere in their faith.

(AD70)
ROMANS DESTROY JERUSALEM

LETTER TO HEBREWS WRITTEN
(AD85-90)

1436

Heb.

2 Thess.
1 Tim.
2 Tim.
Titus
Philem.

HEBREWS 1, 2

God's Word through his Son

1 In the past, God spoke to our ancestors many times and in many ways through the prophets, [2] but in these last days he has spoken to us through his Son. He is the one through whom God created the universe, the one whom God has chosen to possess all things at the end. [3] He reflects the brightness of God's glory and is the exact likeness of God's own being, sustaining the universe with his powerful word. After achieving forgiveness for human sins, he sat down in heaven at the right-hand side of God, the Supreme Power.

The Greatness of God's Son

[4] The Son was made greater than the angels, just as the name that God gave him is greater than theirs. [5] For God never said to any of his angels:

"You are my Son;
    today I have become your Father."

Nor did God say about any angel,

"I will be his Father,
    and he will be my Son."

[6] But when God was about to send his firstborn Son into the world, he said:

"All God's angels must worship him."

[7] But about the angels God said,

"God makes his angels winds,
    and his servants flames of fire."

[8] About the Son, however, God said:

"Your kingdom, O God, will last* for ever and ever!
    You rule over your* people with justice.
[9] You love what is right and hate what is wrong.
That is why God, your God, has chosen you
    and has given you the joy of an honour far greater
    than he gave to your companions."

[10] He also said:

"You, Lord, in the beginning created the earth,
    and with your own hands you made the heavens.
[11] They will disappear, but you will remain;
    they will all wear out like clothes.
[12] You will fold them up like a coat,
    and they will be changed like clothes.
But you are always the same,
    and your life never ends."

[13] God never said to any of his angels:

"Sit here on my right
    until I put your enemies
    as a footstool under your feet."

[14] What are the angels, then? They are spirits who serve God and are sent by him to help those who are to receive salvation.

The Great Salvation

2 That is why we must hold on all the more firmly to the truths we have heard, so that we will not be carried away. [2] The message given to our ancestors by the angels was shown to be true, and all who did not follow it or obey it received the punishment they deserved. [3] How, then, shall we escape if we pay no attention to such a great salvation? The Lord himself first announced this

---

1.8 *Your kingdom, O God, will last;* or *God is your kingdom.*
1.8 *your;* some manuscripts have *his.*

HEBREWS 2, 3

1437

Heb.

⋯⋯:⋮

James
1 Peter
2 Peter
1 John
2 John

salvation, and those who heard him proved to us that it is true. ⁴At the same time God added his witness to theirs by performing all kinds of miracles and wonders and by distributing the gifts of the Holy Spirit according to his will.

The One who Leads us to Salvation

⁵God has not placed the angels as rulers over the new world to come — the world of which we speak. ⁶Instead, as it is said somewhere in the Scriptures:

"What are human beings, O God, that you should think of them;
　mere human beings, that you should care for them?
⁷ You made them for a little while lower than the angels;
　you crowned them with glory and honour,*
⁸　and made them rulers over all things."

It says that God made them "rulers over all things"; this clearly includes everything. We do not, however, see human beings ruling over all things now. ⁹But we do see Jesus, who for a little while was made lower than the angels, so that through God's grace he should die for everyone. We see him now crowned with glory and honour because of the death he suffered. ¹⁰It was only right that God, who creates and preserves all things, should make Jesus perfect through suffering, in order to bring many children to share his glory. For Jesus is the one who leads them to salvation.

¹¹He purifies people from their sins, and both he and those who are made pure all have the same Father. That is why Jesus is not ashamed to call them his family. ¹²He says to God:

"I will tell my people what you have done;
　I will praise you in their meeting."

¹³He also says, "I will put my trust in God." And he also says, "Here I am with the children that God has given me."

¹⁴Since the children, as he calls them, are people of flesh and blood, Jesus himself became like them and shared their human nature. He did this so that through his death he might destroy the Devil, who has the power over death, ¹⁵and in this way set free those who were slaves all their lives because of their fear of death. ¹⁶For it is clear that it is not the angels that he helps. Instead, he helps the descendants of Abraham. ¹⁷This means that he had to become like his brothers and sisters in every way, in order to be their faithful and merciful High Priest in his service to God, so that the people's sins would be forgiven. ¹⁸And now he can help those who are tempted, because he himself was tempted and suffered.

Jesus is Greater than Moses

3 My Christian brothers and sisters, who also have been called by God! Think of Jesus, whom God sent to be the High Priest of the faith we profess. ²He was faithful to God, who chose him to do this work, just as Moses was faithful in his work in God's house. ³A man who builds a house receives more honour than the house itself. In the same way Jesus is worthy of much greater honour than Moses. ⁴Every house, of course, is built by someone — and God is the one who has built all things. ⁵Moses was faithful in God's house as a servant, and he spoke of the things that God would say in the future. ⁶But Christ is faithful as the Son in charge of God's house. We are his house if we keep up our courage and our confidence in what we hope for.

2.7 Many manuscripts add: *You made them rulers over everything you made* (see Ps 8.6).

1438

Heb.

2 Thess.
1 Tim.
2 Tim.
Titus
Philem.

HEBREWS 3, 4

A Rest for God's People

7 So then, as the Holy Spirit says:

"If you hear God's voice today,
8   do not be stubborn, as your ancestors were when they
        rebelled against God,
    as they were that day in the desert
    when they put him to the test.
9 There they put me to the test and tried me, says God,
    although they had seen what I did for forty years.
10 And so I was angry with those people and said,
    'They are always disloyal
    and refuse to obey my commands.'
11 I was angry and made a solemn promise:
    'They will never enter the land where I would have given
        them rest!'"

12 My fellow-believers, be careful that no one among you has a heart so evil and unbelieving as to turn away from the living God. 13 Instead, in order that none of you be deceived by sin and become stubborn, you must help one another every day, as long as the word "Today" in the scripture applies to us. 14 For we are all partners with Christ if we hold firmly to the end the confidence we had at the beginning.

15 This is what the scripture says:

"If you hear God's voice today,
    do not be stubborn, as your ancestors were
    when they rebelled against God."

16 Who were the people who heard God's voice and rebelled against him? All those who were led out of Egypt by Moses. 17 With whom was God angry for forty years? With the people who sinned, who fell down dead in the desert. 18 When God made his solemn promise, "They will never enter the land where I would have given them rest" — of whom was he speaking? Of those who rebelled. 19 We see, then, that they were not able to enter the land, because they did not believe.

4 Now, God has offered us the promise that we may receive that rest he spoke about. Let us take care, then, that none of you will be found to have failed to receive that promised rest. 2 For we have heard the Good News, just as they did. They heard the message, but it did them no good, because when they heard it, they did not accept it with faith. 3 We who believe, then, do receive that rest which God promised. It is just as he said:

"I was angry and made a solemn promise:
    'They will never enter the land where I would have given
        them rest!'"

He said this even though his work had been finished from the time he created the world. 4 For somewhere in the Scriptures this is said about the seventh day: "God rested on the seventh day from all his work." 5 This same matter is spoken of again: "They will never enter that land where I would have given them rest." 6 Those who first heard the Good News did not receive that rest, because they did not believe. There are, then, others who are allowed to receive it. 7 This is shown by the fact that God sets another day, which is called "Today". Many years later he spoke of it through David in the scripture already quoted:

"If you hear God's voice today,
    do not be stubborn."

8 If Joshua had given the people the rest that God had promised, God would not have spoken later about another day. 9 As it is, however, there still remains for God's people a rest like God's

HEBREWS 4–6

1439

Heb.

James
1 Peter
2 Peter
1 John
2 John

resting on the seventh day. [10] For those who receive that rest which God promised will rest from their own work, just as God rested from his. [11] Let us, then, do our best to receive that rest, so that no one of us will fail as they did because of their lack of faith.

[12] The word of God is alive and active, sharper than any double-edged sword. It cuts all the way through, to where soul and spirit meet, to where joints and marrow come together. It judges the desires and thoughts of the heart. [13] There is nothing that can be hidden from God; everything in all creation is exposed and lies open before his eyes. And it is to him that we must all give an account of ourselves.

Jesus the Great High Priest

[14] Let us, then, hold firmly to the faith we profess. For we have a great High Priest who has gone into the very presence of God — Jesus, the Son of God. [15] Our High Priest is not one who cannot feel sympathy for our weaknesses. On the contrary, we have a High Priest who was tempted in every way that we are, but did not sin. [16] Let us have confidence, then, and approach God's throne, where there is grace. There we will receive mercy and find grace to help us just when we need it.

5 Every high priest is chosen from his fellow-men and appointed to serve God on their behalf, to offer sacrifices and offerings for sins. [2] Since he himself is weak in many ways, he is able to be gentle with those who are ignorant and make mistakes. [3] And because he is himself weak, he must offer sacrifices not only for the sins of the people but also for his own sins. [4] No one chooses for himself the honour of being a high priest. It is only by God's call that a man is made a high priest — just as Aaron was.

[5] In the same way, Christ did not take upon himself the honour of being a high priest. Instead, God said to him:

"You are my Son;
    today I have become your Father."
[6] He also said in another place,

"You will be a priest for ever,
    in the priestly order of Melchizedek."*

[7] In his life on earth Jesus made his prayers and requests with loud cries and tears to God, who could save him from death. Because he was humble and devoted, God heard him. [8] But even though he was God's Son, he learnt through his sufferings to be obedient. [9] When he was made perfect, he became the source of eternal salvation for all those who obey him, [10] and God declared him to be high priest, in the priestly order of Melchizedek.*

Warning against Abandoning the Faith

[11] There is much we have to say about this matter, but it is hard to explain to you, because you are so slow to understand. [12] There has been enough time for you to be teachers — yet you still need someone to teach you the first lessons of God's message. Instead of eating solid food, you still have to drink milk. [13] Anyone who has to drink milk is still a child, without any experience in the matter of right and wrong. [14] Solid food, on the other hand, is for adults, who through practice are able to distinguish between good and evil.

6 Let us go forward, then, to mature teaching and leave behind us the first lessons of the Christian message. We should not lay again the foundation of turning away from useless works

5.6; 5.10 *in… Melchizedek*; or *like Melchizedek*; or *in the line of succession to Melchizedek*.

HEBREWS 4.8-12

LIE DOWN
– AND –
REST

for ten minutes.
In your mind, reflect on some of your favourite Bible verses while you rest.

Every two minutes, take some scissors and

SNIP A SMALL CUT

into the side of this page. As we reflect on the word of God, it takes the edges off us and shapes the person we are.

Heb.

∴·········

2 Thess.

1 Tim.

2 Tim.

Titus

Philem.

and believing in God; [2] of the teaching about baptisms* and the laying on of hands; of the resurrection of the dead and the eternal judgement. [3] Let us go forward! And this is what we will do, if God allows.

[4] For how can those who abandon their faith be brought back to repent again? They were once in God's light; they tasted heaven's gift and received their share of the Holy Spirit; [5] they knew from experience that God's word is good, and they had felt the powers of the coming age. [6] And then they abandoned their faith! It is impossible to bring them back to repent again, because they are again crucifying the Son of God and exposing him to public shame.

[7] God blesses the soil which drinks in the rain that often falls on it and which grows plants that are useful to those for whom it is cultivated. [8] But if it grows thorns and weeds, it is worth nothing; it is in danger of being cursed by God and will be destroyed by fire.

[9] But even if we speak like this, dear friends, we feel sure about you. We know that you have the better blessings that belong to your salvation. [10] God is not unfair. He will not forget the work you did or the love you showed for him in the help you gave and are still giving to your fellow-Christians. [11] Our great desire is that each of you keep up your eagerness to the end, so that the things you hope for will come true. [12] We do not want you to become lazy, but to be like those who believe and are patient, and so receive what God has promised.

God's Sure Promise

[13] When God made his promise to Abraham, he made a vow to do what he had promised. Since there was no one greater than himself, he used his own name when he made his vow. [14] He said, "I promise you that I will bless you and give you many descendants." [15] Abraham was patient, and so he received what God had promised. [16] When people make vows, they use the name of someone greater than themselves, and the vow settles all arguments. [17] To those who were to receive what he promised, God wanted to make it very clear that he would never change his purpose; so he added his vow to the promise. [18] There are these two things, then, that cannot change and about which God cannot lie. So we who have found safety with him are greatly encouraged to hold firmly to the hope placed before us. [19] We have this hope as an anchor for our lives. It is safe and sure, and goes through the curtain of the heavenly temple into the inner sanctuary. [20] On our behalf Jesus has gone in there before us, and has become a high priest for ever, in the priestly order of Melchizedek.*

The Priest Melchizedek

7 This Melchizedek was king of Salem and a priest of the Most High God. As Abraham was coming back from the battle in which he defeated the four kings, Melchizedek met him and blessed him, [2] and Abraham gave him a tenth of all he had taken. (The first meaning of Melchizedek's name is "King of Righteousness"; and because he was king of Salem, his name also means "King of Peace".) [3] There is no record of Melchizedek's father or mother or of any of his ancestors; no record of his birth or of his death. He is like the Son of God; he remains a priest for ever.

6.2 *baptisms*; or *purification ceremonies*.
6.20 *in… Melchizedek* (see 5.6).

Heb.

James
1 Peter
2 Peter
1 John
2 John

⁴You see, then, how great he was. Abraham, our famous ancestor, gave him a tenth of all he got in the battle. ⁵And those descendants of Levi who are priests are commanded by the Law to collect a tenth from the people of Israel, that is, from their own people, even though they are also descendants of Abraham. ⁶Melchizedek was not descended from Levi, but he collected a tenth from Abraham and blessed him, the man who received God's promises. ⁷There is no doubt that the one who blesses is greater than the one who is blessed. ⁸In the case of the priests the tenth is collected by men who die; but as for Melchizedek the tenth was collected by one who lives, as the scripture says. ⁹And, so to speak, when Abraham paid the tenth, Levi (whose descendants collect the tenth) also paid it. ¹⁰For Levi had not yet been born, but was, so to speak, in the body of his ancestor Abraham when Melchizedek met him.

¹¹It was on the basis of the levitical priesthood that the Law was given to the people of Israel. Now, if the work of the levitical priests had been perfect, there would have been no need for a different kind of priest to appear, one who is in the priestly order of Melchizedek,* not of Aaron. ¹²For when the priesthood is changed, there also has to be a change in the law. ¹³And our Lord, of whom these things are said, belonged to a different tribe, and no member of his tribe ever served as a priest. ¹⁴It is well known that he was born a member of the tribe of Judah; and Moses did not mention this tribe when he spoke of priests.

Another Priest, like Melchizedek

¹⁵The matter becomes even plainer; a different priest has appeared, who is like Melchizedek. ¹⁶He was made a priest, not by human rules and regulations, but through the power of a life which has no end. ¹⁷For the scripture says, "You will be a priest for ever, in the priestly order of Melchizedek."* ¹⁸The old rule, then, is set aside, because it was weak and useless. ¹⁹For the Law of Moses could not make anything perfect. And now a better hope has been provided through which we come near to God.

²⁰In addition, there is also God's vow. There was no such vow when the others were made priests. ²¹But Jesus became a priest by means of a vow when God said to him:
"The Lord has made a solemn promise
    and will not take it back:
'You will be a priest for ever.'"
²²This difference, then, also makes Jesus the guarantee of a better covenant.

²³There is another difference: there were many of those other priests, because they died and could not continue their work. ²⁴But Jesus lives on for ever, and his work as priest does not pass on to someone else. ²⁵And so he is able, now and always, to save those who come to God through him, because he lives for ever to plead with God for them.

²⁶Jesus, then, is the High Priest that meets our needs. He is holy; he has no fault or sin in him; he has been set apart from sinners and raised above the heavens. ²⁷He is not like other high priests; he does not need to offer sacrifices every day for his own sins first and then for the sins of the people. He offered one sacrifice, once and for all, when he offered himself. ²⁸The Law of Moses appoints men who are imperfect to be high priests;

7.11; 7.17 *in… Melchizedek* (see 5.6).

HEBREWS 7

This chapter is talking about how Jesus has replaced Aaron, who was a priest in the old temple system. (Have a read of Leviticus 9.) This is a different side to Jesus than the one we see in the Gospels. Write down in this space some of the words you might use to

• DESCRIBE •

JESUS

when seeing him in this light.

but God's promise made with the vow, which came later than the Law, appoints the Son, who has been made perfect for ever.

Jesus our High Priest

8 The whole point of what we are saying is that we have such a High Priest, who sits at the right of the throne of the Divine Majesty in heaven. ²He serves as High Priest in the Most Holy Place, that is, in the real tent which was put up by the Lord, not by human hands.

³Every High Priest is appointed to present offerings and animal sacrifices to God, and so our High Priest must also have something to offer. ⁴If he were on earth, he would not be a priest at all, since there are priests who offer the gifts required by the Jewish Law. ⁵The work they do as priests is really only a copy and a shadow of what is in heaven. It is the same as it was with Moses. When he was about to build the Sacred Tent, God said to him, "Be sure to make everything according to the pattern you were shown on the mountain." ⁶But now, Jesus has been given priestly work which is superior to theirs, just as the covenant which he arranged between God and his people is a better one, because it is based on promises of better things.

⁷If there had been nothing wrong with the first covenant, there would have been no need for a second one. ⁸But God finds fault with his people when he says:

"The days are coming, says the Lord,
    when I will draw up a new covenant with the people of
        Israel and with the people of Judah.
⁹ It will not be like the covenant that I made with their
        ancestors
    on the day I took them by the hand and led them out
        of Egypt.
They were not faithful to the covenant I made with them,
    and so I paid no attention to them.
¹⁰ Now, this is the covenant that I will make with the people
        of Israel
    in the days to come, says the Lord:
I will put my laws in their minds
    and write them on their hearts.
I will be their God,
    and they will be my people.
¹¹ None of them will have to teach their fellow-citizens
    or say to their fellow-citizens,
        'Know the Lord.'
For they will all know me,
    from the least to the greatest.
¹² I will forgive their sins
    and will no longer remember their wrongs."

¹³By speaking of a new covenant, God has made the first one old; and anything that becomes old and worn out will soon disappear.

Earthly and Heavenly Worship

9 The first covenant had rules for worship and an earthly place for worship as well. ²A Tent was put up, the outer one, which was called the Holy Place. In it were the lampstand and the table with the bread offered to God. ³Behind the second curtain was the Tent called the Most Holy Place. ⁴In it were the gold altar for the burning of incense and the Covenant Box all covered with gold and containing the gold jar with the manna in it, Aaron's stick that had sprouted leaves, and the two stone tablets with

HEBREWS 9

1443

Heb.
..........:.

James
1 Peter
2 Peter
1 John
2 John

the commandments written on them. [5] Above the Box were the winged creatures representing God's presence, with their wings spread over the place where sins were forgiven. But now is not the time to explain everything in detail.

[6] This is how those things have been arranged. The priests go into the outer Tent every day to perform their duties, [7] but only the High Priest goes into the inner Tent, and he does so only once a year. He takes with him blood which he offers to God on behalf of himself and for the sins which the people have committed without knowing they were sinning. [8] The Holy Spirit clearly teaches from all these arrangements that the way into the Most Holy Place has not yet been opened as long as the outer Tent still stands. [9] This is an illustration which points to the present time. It means that the offerings and animal sacrifices presented to God cannot make the worshipper's heart perfect, [10] since they have to do only with food, drink, and various purification ceremonies. These are all outward rules, which apply only until the time when God will establish the new order.

[11] But Christ has already come as the High Priest of the good things that are already here.* The tent in which he serves is greater and more perfect; it is not a tent made by human hands, that is, it is not a part of this created world. [12] When Christ went through the tent and entered once and for all into the Most Holy Place, he did not take the blood of goats and bulls to offer as a sacrifice; rather, he took his own blood and obtained eternal salvation for us. [13] The blood of goats and bulls and the ashes of a burnt calf are sprinkled on the people who are ritually unclean, and this purifies them by taking away their ritual impurity. [14] Since this is true, how much more is accomplished by the blood of Christ! Through the eternal Spirit he offered himself as a perfect sacrifice to God. His blood will purify our consciences from useless rituals, so that we may serve the living God.

[15] For this reason Christ is the one who arranges a new covenant, so that those who have been called by God may receive the eternal blessings that God has promised. This can be done because there has been a death which sets people free from the wrongs they did while the first covenant was in force.

[16] In the case of a will it is necessary to prove that the person who made it has died, [17] for a will means nothing while the person who made it is alive; it comes into effect only after his death. [18] That is why even the first covenant* came into effect only with the use of blood. [19] First, Moses proclaimed to the people all the commandments as set forth in the Law. Then he took the blood of bulls and goats, mixed it with water, and sprinkled it on the book of the Law and all the people, using a sprig of hyssop and some red wool. [20] He said, "This is the blood which seals the covenant that God has commanded you to obey." [21] In the same way Moses also sprinkled the blood on the Sacred Tent and over all the things used in worship. [22] Indeed, according to the Law almost everything is purified by blood, and sins are forgiven only if blood is poured out.

Christ's Sacrifice Takes Away Sins

[23] Those things, which are copies of the heavenly originals, had to be purified in that way. But the heavenly things themselves require much better sacrifices. [24] For Christ did not go into a Holy

9.11 *already here*; some manuscripts have *coming*.
9.18 *covenant*: In Greek the same word means "will" and "covenant".

1444

Heb.

∴ ┄┄┄┄

2 Thess.
1 Tim.
2 Tim.
Titus
Philem.

HEBREWS 9, 10

COVENANT

GENESIS 9.11;
GENESIS 17.7;
HEBREWS 10.16

Search for the Oxford
or Cambridge Dictionary
definition of 'covenant'
and write the
definition here. ↘

_____

_____

_____

_____

_____

_____

_____

_____

_____

_____

_____

_____

_____

_____

Place made by human hands, which was a copy of the real one. He went into heaven itself, where he now appears on our behalf in the presence of God. 25 The Jewish High Priest goes into the Most Holy Place every year with the blood of an animal. But Christ did not go in to offer himself many times, 26 for then he would have had to suffer many times ever since the creation of the world. Instead, now when all ages of time are nearing the end, he has appeared once and for all, to remove sin through the sacrifice of himself. 27 Everyone must die once, and after that be judged by God. 28 In the same manner Christ also was offered in sacrifice once to take away the sins of many. He will appear a second time, not to deal with sin, but to save those who are waiting for him.

10 The Jewish Law is not a full and faithful model of the real things; it is only a faint outline of the good things to come. The same sacrifices are offered for ever, year after year. How can the Law, then, by means of these sacrifices make perfect the people who come to God? 2 If the people worshipping God had really been purified from their sins, they would not feel guilty of sin any more, and all sacrifices would stop. 3 As it is, however, the sacrifices serve year after year to remind people of their sins. 4 For the blood of bulls and goats can never take away sins.

5 For this reason, when Christ was about to come into the world, he said to God:

"You do not want sacrifices and offerings,
    but you have prepared a body for me.
6 You are not pleased with animals burnt whole on the altar
    or with sacrifices to take away sins.
7 Then I said, 'Here I am,
    to do your will, O God,
    just as it is written of me in the book of the Law.' "

8 First he said, "You neither want nor are you pleased with sacrifices and offerings or with animals burnt on the altar and the sacrifices to take away sins." He said this even though all these sacrifices are offered according to the Law. 9 Then he said, "Here I am, O God, to do your will." So God does away with all the old sacrifices and puts the sacrifice of Christ in their place. 10 Because Jesus Christ did what God wanted him to do, we are all purified from sin by the offering that he made of his own body once and for all.

11 Every Jewish priest performs his services every day and offers the same sacrifices many times; but these sacrifices can never take away sins. 12 Christ, however, offered one sacrifice for sins, an offering that is effective for ever, and then he sat down at the right-hand side of God. 13 There he now waits until God puts his enemies as a footstool under his feet. 14 With one sacrifice, then, he has made perfect for ever those who are purified from sin.

15 And the Holy Spirit also gives us his witness. First he says:
16 "This is the covenant that I will make with them
    in the days to come, says the Lord:
    I will put my laws in their hearts
    and write them on their minds."
17 And then he says, "I will not remember their sins and evil deeds any longer." 18 So when these have been forgiven, an offering to take away sins is no longer needed.

Let us Come Near to God

19 We have, then, my brothers and sisters, complete freedom to go into the Most Holy Place by means of the death of Jesus. 20 He opened for us a new way, a living way, through the curtain — that is, through his own body. 21 We have a great priest in charge of

Heb.
....
James
1 Peter
2 Peter
1 John
2 John

the house of God. ²²So let us come near to God with a sincere heart and a sure faith, with hearts that have been purified from a guilty conscience and with bodies washed with clean water. ²³Let us hold on firmly to the hope we profess, because we can trust God to keep his promise. ²⁴Let us be concerned for one another, to help one another to show love and to do good. ²⁵Let us not give up the habit of meeting together, as some are doing. Instead, let us encourage one another all the more, since you see that the Day of the Lord is coming nearer.

²⁶For there is no longer any sacrifice that will take away sins if we purposely go on sinning after the truth has been made known to us. ²⁷Instead, all that is left is to wait in fear for the coming Judgement and the fierce fire which will destroy those who oppose God! ²⁸Anyone who disobeys the Law of Moses is put to death without any mercy when judged guilty on the evidence of two or more witnesses. ²⁹What, then, of those who despise the Son of God? who treat as a cheap thing the blood of God's covenant which purified them from sin? who insult the Spirit of grace? Just think how much worse is the punishment they will deserve! ³⁰For we know who said, "I will take revenge, I will repay"; and who also said, "The Lord will judge his people." ³¹It is a terrifying thing to fall into the hands of the living God!

³²Remember how it was with you in the past. In those days, after God's light had shone on you, you suffered many things, yet were not defeated by the struggle. ³³You were at times publicly insulted and ill-treated, and at other times you were ready to join those who were being treated in this way. ³⁴You shared the sufferings of prisoners, and when all your belongings were seized, you endured your loss gladly, because you knew that you still possessed something much better, which would last for ever. ³⁵Do not lose your courage, then, because it brings with it a great reward. ³⁶You need to be patient, in order to do the will of God and receive what he promises. ³⁷For, as the scripture says:

"Just a little while longer,
     and he who is coming will come;
     he will not delay.
³⁸ My righteous people, however, will believe and live;
     but if any of them turns back,
     I will not be pleased with him."

³⁹We are not people who turn back and are lost. Instead, we have faith and are saved.

Faith

11 To have faith is to be sure of the things we hope for, to be certain of the things we cannot see. ²It was by their faith that people of ancient times won God's approval.

³It is by faith that we understand that the universe was created by God's word, so that what can be seen was made out of what cannot be seen.

⁴It was faith that made Abel offer to God a better sacrifice than Cain's. Through his faith he won God's approval as a righteous man, because God himself approved of his gifts. By means of his faith Abel still speaks, even though he is dead.

⁵It was faith that kept Enoch from dying. Instead, he was taken up to God, and nobody could find him, because God had taken him up. The scripture says that before Enoch was taken up, he had pleased God. ⁶No one can please God without faith, for whoever comes to God must have faith that God exists and rewards those who seek him.

FAITH

ISAIAH 28.16;
HEBREWS 11.1

What do you
think it means?

What does someone
else think it means?

Now go and look up
the definition.

Heb.
⸭⸽⸱⸱⸱⸱⸱⸱⸱

2 Thess.
1 Tim.
2 Tim.
Titus
Philem.

[7] It was faith that made Noah hear God's warnings about things in the future that he could not see. He obeyed God and built a boat in which he and his family were saved. As a result, the world was condemned, and Noah received from God the righteousness that comes by faith.

[8] It was faith that made Abraham obey when God called him to go out to a country which God had promised to give him. He left his own country without knowing where he was going. [9] By faith he lived as a foreigner in the country that God had promised him. He lived in tents, as did Isaac and Jacob, who received the same promise from God. [10] For Abraham was waiting for the city which God has designed and built, the city with permanent foundations.

[11] It was faith that made Abraham able to become a father, even though he was too old and Sarah herself could not have children. He* trusted God to keep his promise. [12] Though Abraham was practically dead, from this one man came as many descendants as there are stars in the sky, as many as the numberless grains of sand on the seashore.

[13] It was in faith that all these persons died. They did not receive the things God had promised, but from a long way off they saw them and welcomed them, and admitted openly that they were foreigners and refugees on earth. [14] Those who say such things make it clear that they are looking for a country of their own. [15] They did not keep thinking about the country they had left; if they had, they would have had the chance to return. [16] Instead, it was a better country they longed for, the heavenly country. And so God is not ashamed for them to call him their God, because he has prepared a city for them.

[17] It was faith that made Abraham offer his son Isaac as a sacrifice when God put Abraham to the test. Abraham was the one to whom God had made the promise, yet he was ready to offer his only son as a sacrifice. [18] God had said to him, "It is through Isaac that you will have the descendants I promised." [19] Abraham reckoned that God was able to raise Isaac from death — and, so to speak, Abraham did receive Isaac back from death.

[20] It was faith that made Isaac promise blessings for the future to Jacob and Esau.

[21] It was faith that made Jacob bless each of the sons of Joseph just before he died. He leaned on the top of his walking stick and worshipped God.

[22] It was faith that made Joseph, when he was about to die, speak of the departure of the Israelites from Egypt, and leave instructions about what should be done with his body.

[23] It was faith that made the parents of Moses hide him for three months after he was born. They saw that he was a beautiful child, and they were not afraid to disobey the king's order.

[24] It was faith that made Moses, when he had grown up, refuse to be called the son of the king's daughter. [25] He preferred to suffer with God's people rather than to enjoy sin for a little while. [26] He reckoned that to suffer scorn for the Messiah was worth far more than all the treasures of Egypt, for he kept his eyes on the future reward.

[27] It was faith that made Moses leave Egypt without being afraid of the king's anger. As though he saw the invisible God, he refused to turn back. [28] It was faith that made him establish

11.11 *It was faith… children.* He; some manuscripts have *It was faith that made Sarah herself able to conceive, even though she was too old to have children. She.*

the Passover and order the blood to be sprinkled on the doors, so that the Angel of Death would not kill the firstborn sons of the Israelites.

²⁹It was faith that made the Israelites able to cross the Red Sea as if on dry land; when the Egyptians tried to do it, the water swallowed them up.

³⁰It was faith that made the walls of Jericho fall down after the Israelites had marched round them for seven days. ³¹It was faith that kept the prostitute Rahab from being killed with those who disobeyed God, for she gave the Israelite spies a friendly welcome.

³²Should I go on? There isn't enough time for me to speak of Gideon, Barak, Samson, Jephthah, David, Samuel, and the prophets. ³³Through faith they fought whole countries and won. They did what was right and received what God had promised. They shut the mouths of lions, ³⁴put out fierce fires, escaped being killed by the sword. They were weak, but became strong; they were mighty in battle and defeated the armies of foreigners. ³⁵Through faith women received their dead relatives raised back to life.

Others, refusing to accept freedom, died under torture in order to be raised to a better life. ³⁶Some were mocked and whipped, and others were put in chains and taken off to prison. ³⁷They were stoned, they were sawn in two, they were killed by the sword. They went round clothed in skins of sheep or goats — poor, persecuted, and ill-treated. ³⁸The world was not good enough for them! They wandered like refugees in the deserts and hills, living in caves and holes in the ground.

³⁹What a record all of these have won by their faith! Yet they did not receive what God had promised, ⁴⁰because God had decided on an even better plan for us. His purpose was that only in company with us would they be made perfect.

God our Father

12 As for us, we have this large crowd of witnesses round us. So then, let us rid ourselves of everything that gets in the way, and of the sin which holds on to us so tightly, and let us run with determination the race that lies before us. ²Let us keep our eyes fixed on Jesus, on whom our faith depends from beginning to end. He did not give up because of the cross! On the contrary, because of the joy that was waiting for him, he thought nothing of the disgrace of dying on the cross, and he is now seated at the right-hand side of God's throne.

³Think of what he went through; how he put up with so much hatred from sinners! So do not let yourselves become discouraged and give up. ⁴For in your struggle against sin you have not yet had to resist to the point of being killed. ⁵Have you forgotten the encouraging words which God speaks to you as his sons and daughters?

"My child, pay attention when the Lord corrects you,
and do not be discouraged when he rebukes you.
⁶ Because the Lord corrects everyone he loves,
and punishes everyone he accepts as his child."

⁷Endure what you suffer as being a father's punishment; your suffering shows that God is treating you as his children. Was there ever a child who was not punished by his father? ⁸If you are not punished, as all his children are, it means you are not real children, but bastards. ⁹In the case of our human fathers, they punished us and we respected them. How much more, then, should we submit to our spiritual Father and live! ¹⁰Our human fathers punished us for a short time, as it seemed right to them; but God does it

HEBREWS 12.1-2

Write down some of the
- DIFFICULT -
SITUATIONS
that you are in or the
problems that you are
facing. How would these
situations feel different
if your perspective
could be totally fixed
on Jesus? Write 'fix
your eyes' on a note
and stick it to the
back of your bedroom
door to remind yourself.

for our own good, so that we may share his holiness. [11] When we are punished, it seems to us at the time something to make us sad, not glad. Later, however, those who have been disciplined by such punishment reap the peaceful reward of a righteous life.

Instructions and Warnings

[12] Lift up your tired hands, then, and strengthen your trembling knees! [13] Keep walking on straight paths, so that the lame foot may not be disabled, but instead be healed.

[14] Try to be at peace with everyone, and try to live a holy life, because no one will see the Lord without it. [15] Guard against turning back from the grace of God. Let no one become like a bitter plant that grows up and causes many troubles with its poison. [16] Let no one become immoral or unspiritual like Esau, who for a single meal sold his rights as the elder son. [17] Afterwards, you know, he wanted to receive his father's blessing; but he was turned away, because he could not find any way to change what he had done, even though in tears he looked for it.*

[18] You have not come, as the people of Israel came, to what you can feel, to Mount Sinai with its blazing fire, the darkness and the gloom, the storm, [19] the blast of a trumpet, and the sound of a voice. When the people heard the voice, they begged not to hear another word, [20] because they could not bear the order which said, "If even an animal touches the mountain, it must be stoned to death." [21] The sight was so terrifying that Moses said, "I am trembling and afraid!"

[22] Instead, you have come to Mount Zion and to the city of the living God, the heavenly Jerusalem, with its thousands of angels. [23] You have come to the joyful gathering of God's firstborn, whose names are written in heaven. You have come to God, who is the judge of all people, and to the spirits of good people made perfect. [24] You have come to Jesus, who arranged the new covenant, and to the sprinkled blood that promises much better things than does the blood of Abel.

[25] Be careful, then, and do not refuse to hear him who speaks. Those who refused to hear the one who gave the divine message on earth did not escape. How much less shall we escape, then, if we turn away from the one who speaks from heaven! [26] His voice shook the earth at that time, but now he has promised, "I will once more shake not only the earth but heaven as well." [27] The words "once more" plainly show that the created things will be shaken and removed, so that the things that cannot be shaken will remain.

[28] Let us be thankful, then, because we receive a kingdom that cannot be shaken. Let us be grateful and worship God in a way that will please him, with reverence and awe; [29] because our God is indeed a destroying fire.

How to Please God

13 Keep on loving one another as Christian brothers and sisters. [2] Remember to welcome strangers in your homes. There were some who did that and welcomed angels without knowing it. [3] Remember those who are in prison, as though you were in prison with them. Remember those who are suffering, as though you were suffering as they are.

[4] Marriage is to be honoured by all, and husbands and wives must be faithful to each other. God will judge those who are immoral and those who commit adultery.

··

12.17 he looked for it; or he tried to get the blessing.

1449

Heb.

..........:

James
1 Peter
2 Peter
1 John
2 John

[5] Keep your lives free from the love of money, and be satisfied with what you have. For God has said, "I will never leave you; I will never abandon you." [6] Let us be bold, then, and say:

"The Lord is my helper,
I will not be afraid.
What can anyone do to me?"

[7] Remember your former leaders, who spoke God's message to you. Think back on how they lived and died, and imitate their faith. [8] Jesus Christ is the same yesterday, today, and for ever. [9] Do not let all kinds of strange teachings lead you from the right way. It is good to receive inner strength from God's grace, and not by obeying rules about foods; those who obey these rules have not been helped by them.

[10] The priests who serve in the Jewish place of worship have no right to eat any of the sacrifice on our altar. [11] The Jewish High Priest brings the blood of the animals into the Most Holy Place to offer it as a sacrifice for sins; but the bodies of the animals are burnt outside the camp. [12] For this reason Jesus also died outside the city, in order to purify the people from sin with his own blood. [13] Let us, then, go to him outside the camp and share his shame. [14] For there is no permanent city for us here on earth; we are looking for the city which is to come. [15] Let us, then, always offer praise to God as our sacrifice through Jesus, which is the offering presented by lips that confess him as Lord. [16] Do not forget to do good and to help one another, because these are the sacrifices that please God.

[17] Obey your leaders and follow their orders. They watch over your souls without resting, since they must give God an account of their service. If you obey them, they will do their work gladly; if not, they will do it with sadness, and that would be of no help to you.

[18] Keep on praying for us. We are sure we have a clear conscience, because we want to do the right thing at all times. [19] And I beg you even more earnestly to pray that God will send me back to you soon.

Closing Prayer

[20-21] God has raised from death our Lord Jesus, who is the Great Shepherd of the sheep as the result of his blood,* by which the eternal covenant is sealed. May the God of peace provide you with every good thing you need in order to do his will, and may he, through Jesus Christ, do in us what pleases him. And to Christ be the glory for ever and ever! Amen.

Final Words

[22] I beg you, my brothers and sisters, to listen patiently to this message of encouragement; for this letter I have written to you is not very long. [23] I want you to know that our brother Timothy has been let out of prison. If he comes soon enough, I will have him with me when I see you.

[24] Give our greetings to all your leaders and to all God's people. The brothers and sisters from Italy send you their greetings.

[25] May God's grace be with you all.

13.20–21 *his blood*; or *his sacrificial death.*

THE LETTER OF
JAMES

WRITTEN: PROBABLY AROUND AD80

WHAT YOU NEED TO KNOW:

This letter was written by James rather than to him, and it was written to all Christians everywhere rather than in a specific location. James was based in Jerusalem, where politics between the Jews and the Romans had become pretty tense. Yet he makes it very clear that no matter what our situation, if we follow Jesus, we can't live like people who don't.

WHY READ IT?

This is a brilliant letter. It's hugely practical and talks about the importance of living out our faith in the world. It's very direct, but if you want a life that looks more like the life of Jesus, then this letter is for you.

KEY CHARACTER:

The James who wrote this book is thought to have been the half-brother of Jesus. However, he decided that Jesus was who he claimed to be only after he had seen Jesus risen from the dead. James lived in a tough environment in Jerusalem, where he led a church, and he ended up being killed for his faith in his brother Jesus.

Go and spend some time

LOOKING IN A MIRROR,
LOOK AWAY,
AND TRY TO DRAW
WHAT YOU SAW

Then read a chapter of James and write out some of what you learned there. God asks us not only to remember what we read but to do something about it as well.

(AD70)
ROMANS DESTROY JERUSALEM

LETTER OF JAMES WRITTEN
(AD80)

1 From James, a servant of God and of the Lord Jesus Christ:
Greetings to all God's people scattered over the whole world.

Faith and Wisdom

² My brothers and sisters, consider yourselves fortunate when all kinds of trials come your way, ³ for you know that when your faith succeeds in facing such trials, the result is the ability to endure. ⁴ Make sure that your endurance carries you all the way without failing, so that you may be perfect and complete, lacking nothing. ⁵ But if any of you lack wisdom, you should pray to God, who will give it to you; because God gives generously and graciously to all. ⁶ But when you pray, you must believe and not doubt at all. Whoever doubts is like a wave in the sea that is driven and blown about by the wind. ⁷⁻⁸ People like that, unable to make up their minds and undecided in all they do, must not think that they will receive anything from the Lord.

Poverty and Riches

⁹ Those Christians who are poor must be glad when God lifts them up, ¹⁰ and the rich Christians must be glad when God brings them down. For the rich will pass away like the flower of a wild plant. ¹¹ The sun rises with its blazing heat and burns the plant; its flower falls off, and its beauty is destroyed. In the same way the rich will be destroyed while they go about their business.

Testing and Tempting

¹² Happy are those who remain faithful under trials, because when they succeed in passing such a test, they will receive as their reward the life which God has promised to those who love him. ¹³ If people are tempted by such trials, they must not say, "This temptation comes from God." For God cannot be tempted by evil, and he himself tempts no one. ¹⁴ But people are tempted when they are drawn away and trapped by their own evil desires. ¹⁵ Then their evil desires conceive and give birth to sin; and sin, when it is full-grown, gives birth to death.

¹⁶ Do not be deceived, my dear brothers and sisters! ¹⁷ Every good gift and every perfect present comes from heaven; it comes down from God, the Creator of the heavenly lights, who does not change or cause darkness by turning. ¹⁸ By his own will he brought us into being through the word of truth, so that we should have first place among all his creatures.

Hearing and Doing

¹⁹ Remember this, my dear brothers and sisters! Everyone must be quick to listen, but slow to speak and slow to become angry. ²⁰ Human anger does not achieve God's righteous purpose. ²¹ So get rid of every filthy habit and all wicked conduct. Submit to God and accept the word that he plants in your hearts, which is able to save you.

²² Do not deceive yourselves by just listening to his word; instead, put it into practice. ²³ Whoever listens to the word but does not put it into practice is like a man who looks in a mirror and sees himself as he is. ²⁴ He takes a good look at himself and then goes away and at once forgets what he looks like. ²⁵ But those who look closely into the perfect law that sets people free, who keep on paying attention to it and do not simply listen and then forget it, but put it into practice — they will be blessed by God in what they do.

²⁶ Do any of you think you are religious? If you do not control your tongue, your religion is worthless and you deceive yourselves.

JAMES 1.22-26

Re-read your favourite three Bible passages. What might God be asking you to DO through these passages?

WRITE DOWN SOME

ACTIONS

here, and go and do one of them as soon as you have finished reading.

1452

James

1 Tim.
2 Tim.
Titus
Philem.
Heb.

JAMES 1, 2

JAMES 1.27

PURE
• AND •
GENUINE
RELIGION
{ IS THIS: }
TO TAKE
CARE OF
ORPHANS
AND WIDOWS
• IN THEIR •
SUFFERING

[27] What God the Father considers to be pure and genuine religion is this: to take care of orphans and widows in their suffering and to keep oneself from being corrupted by the world.

Warning against Prejudice

2 My brothers and sisters, as believers in our Lord Jesus Christ, the Lord of glory, you must never treat people in different ways according to their outward appearance. [2] Suppose a rich man wearing a gold ring and fine clothes comes to your meeting, and a poor man in ragged clothes also comes. [3] If you show more respect to the well-dressed man and say to him, "Have this best seat here," but say to the poor man, "Stand over there, or sit here on the floor by my feet," [4] then you are guilty of creating distinctions among yourselves and of making judgements based on evil motives.

[5] Listen, my dear brothers and sisters! God chose the poor people of this world to be rich in faith and to possess the kingdom which he promised to those who love him. [6] But you dishonour the poor! Who are the ones who oppress you and drag you before the judges? The rich! [7] They are the ones who speak evil of that good name which has been given to you.

[8] You will be doing the right thing if you obey the law of the Kingdom, which is found in the scripture, "Love your neighbour as you love yourself." [9] But if you treat people according to their outward appearance, you are guilty of sin, and the Law condemns you as a lawbreaker. [10] Whoever breaks one commandment is guilty of breaking them all. [11] For the same one who said, "Do not commit adultery," also said, "Do not commit murder." Even if you do not commit adultery, you have become a lawbreaker if you commit murder. [12] Speak and act as people who will be judged by the law that sets us free. [13] For God will not show mercy when he judges the person who has not been merciful; but mercy triumphs over judgement.

Faith and Actions

[14] My brothers and sisters, what good is it for people to say that they have faith if their actions do not prove it? Can that faith save them? [15] Suppose there are brothers or sisters who need clothes and don't have enough to eat. [16] What good is there in your saying to them, "God bless you! Keep warm and eat well!" — if you don't give them the necessities of life? [17] So it is with faith: if it is alone and includes no actions, then it is dead.

[18] But someone will say, "One person has faith, another has actions." My answer is, "Show me how anyone can have faith without actions. I will show you my faith by my actions." [19] Do you believe that there is only one God? Good! The demons also believe — and tremble with fear. [20] You fool! Do you want to be shown that faith without actions is useless?* [21] How was our ancestor Abraham put right with God? It was through his actions, when he offered his son Isaac on the altar. [22] Can't you see? His faith and his actions worked together; his faith was made perfect through his actions. [23] And the scripture came true that said, "Abraham believed God, and because of his faith God accepted him as righteous." And so Abraham was called God's friend. [24] You see, then, that it is by people's actions that they are put right with God, and not by their faith alone.

2.20 *useless*; some manuscripts have *dead*.

JAMES 2–4

1453

James

.......:.

1 Peter
2 Peter
1 John
2 John
3 John

²⁵ It was the same with the prostitute Rahab. She was put right with God through her actions, by welcoming the Israelite spies and helping them to escape by a different road.

²⁶ So then, as the body without the spirit is dead, so also faith without actions is dead.

The Tongue

3 My brothers and sisters, not many of you should become teachers. As you know, we teachers will be judged with greater strictness than others. ² All of us often make mistakes. But if a person never makes a mistake in what he says, he is perfect and is also able to control his whole being. ³ We put a bit into the mouth of a horse to make it obey us, and we are able to make it go where we want. ⁴ Or think of a ship: big as it is and driven by such strong winds, it can be steered by a very small rudder, and it goes wherever the pilot wants it to go. ⁵ So it is with the tongue: small as it is, it can boast about great things.

Just think how large a forest can be set on fire by a tiny flame! ⁶ And the tongue is like a fire. It is a world of wrong, occupying its place in our bodies and spreading evil through our whole being. It sets on fire the entire course of our existence with the fire that comes to it from hell itself. ⁷ Human beings can tame and have tamed all other creatures — wild animals and birds, reptiles and fish. ⁸ But no one has ever been able to tame the tongue. It is evil and uncontrollable, full of deadly poison. ⁹ We use it to give thanks to our Lord and Father and also to curse other people, who are created in the likeness of God. ¹⁰ Words of thanksgiving and cursing pour out from the same mouth. My brothers and sisters, this should not happen! ¹¹ No spring of water pours out sweet water and bitter water from the same opening. ¹² A fig tree, my brothers and sisters, cannot bear olives; a grapevine cannot bear figs, nor can a salty spring produce sweet water.

The Wisdom from Above

¹³ Are there people among you who are wise and understanding? They are to prove it by their good lives, by their good deeds performed with humility and wisdom. ¹⁴ But if in your heart you are jealous, bitter, and selfish, don't sin against the truth by boasting of your wisdom. ¹⁵ Such wisdom does not come down from heaven; it belongs to the world, it is unspiritual and demonic. ¹⁶ Where there is jealousy and selfishness, there is also disorder and every kind of evil. ¹⁷ But the wisdom from above is pure first of all; it is also peaceful, gentle, and friendly; it is full of compassion and produces a harvest of good deeds; it is free from prejudice and hypocrisy. ¹⁸ And goodness is the harvest that is produced from the seeds the peacemakers plant in peace.

Friendship with the World

4 Where do all the fights and quarrels among you come from? They come from your desires for pleasure, which are constantly fighting within you. ² You want things, but you cannot have them, so you are ready to kill; you strongly desire things, but you cannot get them, so you quarrel and fight. You do not have what you want because you do not ask God for it. ³ And when you ask, you do not receive it, because your motives are bad; you ask for things to use for your own pleasures. ⁴ Unfaithful people! Don't you know that to be the world's friend means to be God's enemy? People who want to be the world's friends make themselves God's enemies. ⁵ Don't think that there is no truth

JAMES 4

Clear your mind and ask God to remind you of any relationships where things aren't right.

PUT DOWN YOUR

BIBLE

and go and do something now to put the relationships right. It might mean sending a message or going to visit someone.

1454

James

⠇⠄⠄⠄⠄⠄⠄⠄

1 Tim.
2 Tim.
Titus
Philem.
Heb.

JAMES 4, 5

in the scripture that says, "The spirit that God placed in us is filled with fierce desires."* [6] But the grace that God gives is even stronger. As the scripture says, "God resists the proud, but gives grace to the humble."

[7] So then, submit to God. Resist the Devil, and he will run away from you. [8] Come near to God, and he will come near to you. Wash your hands, you sinners! Purify your hearts, you hypocrites! [9] Be sorrowful, cry, and weep; change your laughter into crying, your joy into gloom! [10] Humble yourselves before the Lord, and he will lift you up.

Warning against Judging a Fellow-Christian

[11] Do not criticize one another, my brothers and sisters. If you criticize fellow-Christians or judge them, you criticize the Law and judge it. If you judge the Law, then you are no longer one who obeys the Law, but one who judges it. [12] God is the only lawgiver and judge. He alone can save and destroy. Who do you think you are, to judge someone else?

Warning against Boasting

[13] Now listen to me, you that say, "Today or tomorrow we will travel to a certain city, where we will stay a year and go into business and make a lot of money." [14] You don't even know what your life tomorrow will be! You are like a puff of smoke, which appears for a moment and then disappears. [15] What you should say is this: "If the Lord is willing, we will live and do this or that." [16] But now you are proud, and you boast; all such boasting is wrong.

[17] So then, those who do not do the good they know they should do are guilty of sin.

Warning to the Rich

5 And now, you rich people, listen to me! Weep and wail over the miseries that are coming upon you! [2] Your riches have rotted away, and your clothes have been eaten by moths. [3] Your gold and silver are covered with rust, and this rust will be a witness against you and will eat up your flesh like fire. You have piled up riches in these last days. [4] You have not paid any wages to those who work in your fields. Listen to their complaints! The cries of those who gather in your crops have reached the ears of God, the Lord Almighty. [5] Your life here on earth has been full of luxury and pleasure. You have made yourselves fat for the day of slaughter. [6] You have condemned and murdered innocent people, and they do not resist you.*

Patience and Prayer

[7] Be patient, then, my brothers and sisters, until the Lord comes. See how patient a farmer is as he waits for his land to produce precious crops. He waits patiently for the autumn and spring rains. [8] You also must be patient. Keep your hopes high, for the day of the Lord's coming is near.

[9] Do not complain against one another, my brothers and sisters, so that God will not judge you. The Judge is near, ready to appear. [10] My brothers and sisters, remember the prophets who spoke in the name of the Lord. Take them as examples of patient endurance under suffering. [11] We call them happy because they

4.5 *The spirit… fierce desires*; or *God yearns jealously over the spirit that he placed in us.*
5.6 *people, and they do not resist you*; or *people. Will God not resist you?*

endured. You have heard of Job's patience, and you know how the Lord provided for him in the end. For the Lord is full of mercy and compassion.

¹²Above all, my brothers and sisters, do not use an oath when you make a promise. Do not swear by heaven or by earth or by anything else. Say only "Yes" when you mean yes, and "No" when you mean no, and then you will not come under God's judgement.

¹³Are any of you in trouble? You should pray. Are any of you happy? You should sing praises. ¹⁴Are any of you ill? You should send for the church elders, who will pray for them and rub olive oil on them in the name of the Lord. ¹⁵This prayer made in faith will heal the sick; the Lord will restore them to health, and the sins they have committed will be forgiven. ¹⁶So then, confess your sins to one another and pray for one another, so that you will be healed. The prayer of a good person has a powerful effect. ¹⁷Elijah was the same kind of person as we are. He prayed earnestly that there would be no rain, and no rain fell on the land for three and a half years. ¹⁸Once again he prayed, and the sky poured out its rain and the earth produced its crops.

¹⁹My brothers and sisters, if any of you wander away from the truth and another one brings them back again, ²⁰remember this: whoever turns a sinner back from his or her wrong way will save that sinner's soul* from death and bring about the forgiveness of many sins.

5.20 that *sinner's soul*; or *his own soul*.

THE LETTER OF
1 PETER

WRITTEN: PROBABLY TOWARDS THE
END OF THE FIRST CENTURY AD

KEY CHARACTER:

Simon Peter was one of Jesus' 12 disciples, and was an uneducated fisherman from Galilee. 'Peter' means 'rock', and was a nickname given to him by Jesus. We read many stories about him in the four Gospels, including his attempt to walk on water and his denial of Jesus. In the end, Peter stuck to his beliefs and was killed by the Romans for his faith.

PERSECUTION AND THE POOR TREATMENT OF CHRISTIANS STILL HAPPEN AROUND THE WORLD NOW.

Why not jump on to the internet and look up what's going on around the world for some of today's Christians. Here are two keywords to search:

PERSECUTED

CHRISTIANS

WHAT YOU NEED TO KNOW:

This is the first of two letters said to have been written by Peter, a disciple of Jesus. The letter was written to believers suffering severe persecution - which was actually happening wherever there were Christians at the time. Believers were being treated horrendously because of their Christian faith by both the Jews and the Romans. They were oppressed and sometimes even killed. Peter writes about encouragement when facing opposition, to motivate the believers to stand firm and pursue holiness.

Join the dots to make a picture.

WHY READ IT?

1 Peter gives us encouragement in the times when it feels difficult to be a Christian - when we are made fun of, people treat us badly or we feel scared about how people might react to us as Christians. The letter is filled with the recognition that Jesus suffered and said we would have trouble in our lives too, but that Jesus gives us comfort in our struggles.

(AD70)
ROMANS DESTROY JERUSALEM

PETER WRITES 1ST LETTER
(AD80-100)

1 From Peter, apostle of Jesus Christ —
To God's chosen people who live as refugees scattered throughout the provinces of Pontus, Galatia, Cappadocia, Asia, and Bithynia. [2] You were chosen according to the purpose of God the Father and were made a holy people by his Spirit, to obey Jesus Christ and be purified by his blood.

May grace and peace be yours in full measure.

A Living Hope

[3] Let us give thanks to the God and Father of our Lord Jesus Christ! Because of his great mercy he gave us new life by raising Jesus Christ from death. This fills us with a living hope, [4] and so we look forward to possessing the rich blessings that God keeps for his people. He keeps them for you in heaven, where they cannot decay or spoil or fade away. [5] They are for you, who through faith are kept safe by God's power for the salvation which is ready to be revealed at the end of time.

[6] Be glad about this, even though it may now be necessary for you to be sad for a while because of the many kinds of trials you suffer. [7] Their purpose is to prove that your faith is genuine. Even gold, which can be destroyed, is tested by fire; and so your faith, which is much more precious than gold, must also be tested, so that it may endure. Then you will receive praise and glory and honour on the Day when Jesus Christ is revealed. [8] You love him, although you have not seen him, and you believe in him, although you do not now see him. So you rejoice with a great and glorious joy which words cannot express, [9] because you are receiving the salvation of your souls, which is the purpose of your faith in him.

[10] It was concerning this salvation that the prophets made careful search and investigation, and they prophesied about this gift which God would give you. [11] They tried to find out when the time would be and how it would come.* This was the time to which Christ's Spirit in them was pointing, in predicting the sufferings that Christ would have to endure and the glory that would follow. [12] God revealed to these prophets that their work was not for their own benefit, but for yours, as they spoke about those things which you have now heard from the messengers who announced the Good News by the power of the Holy Spirit sent from heaven. These are things which even the angels would like to understand.

A Call to Holy Living

[13] So then, have your minds ready for action. Keep alert and set your hope completely on the blessing which will be given you when Jesus Christ is revealed. [14] Be obedient to God, and do not allow your lives to be shaped by those desires you had when you were still ignorant. [15] Instead, be holy in all that you do, just as God who called you is holy. [16] The scripture says, "Be holy because I am holy."

[17] You call him Father, when you pray to God, who judges all people by the same standard, according to what each one has done; so then, spend the rest of your lives here on earth in reverence for him. [18] For you know what was paid to set you free from the worthless manner of life handed down by your ancestors. It was not something that can be destroyed, such as silver or gold; [19] it was the costly sacrifice of Christ, who was like a lamb without

....

1.11 *when the time would be and how it would come;* or *who the person would be and when he would come.*

1458

1 Peter

:·········

2 Tim.
Titus
Philem.
Heb.
James

1 PETER 1, 2

defect or flaw. [20] He had been chosen by God before the creation of the world and was revealed in these last days for your sake. [21] Through him you believe in God, who raised him from death and gave him glory; and so your faith and hope are fixed on God.

[22] Now that by your obedience to the truth you have purified yourselves and have come to have a sincere love for your fellow-believers, love one another earnestly with all your heart.* [23] For through the living and eternal word of God you have been born again as the children of a parent who is immortal, not mortal. [24] As the scripture says:

"All human beings are like grass,
    and all their glory is like wild flowers.
The grass withers, and the flowers fall,
[25]   but the word of the Lord remains for ever."

This word is the Good News that was proclaimed to you.

The Living Stone and the Holy Nation

2 Rid yourselves, then, of all evil; no more lying or hypocrisy or jealousy or insulting language. [2] Be like newborn babies, always thirsty for the pure spiritual milk, so that by drinking it you may grow up and be saved. [3] As the scripture says, "You have found out for yourselves how kind the Lord is."

[4] Come to the Lord, the living stone rejected by people as worthless but chosen by God as valuable. [5] Come as living stones, and let yourselves be used in building the spiritual temple, where you will serve as holy priests to offer spiritual and acceptable sacrifices to God through Jesus Christ. [6] For the scripture says:

"I chose a valuable stone,
    which I am placing as the cornerstone in Zion;
    and whoever believes in him will never be disappointed."

[7] This stone is of great value for you that believe; but for those who do not believe:

"The stone which the builders rejected as worthless
    turned out to be the most important of all."

[8] And another scripture says:

"This is the stone that will make people stumble,
    the rock that will make them fall."

They stumbled because they did not believe in the word; such was God's will for them.

[9] But you are the chosen race, the King's priests, the holy nation, God's own people, chosen to proclaim the wonderful acts of God, who called you out of darkness into his own marvellous light. [10] At one time you were not God's people, but now you are his people; at one time you did not know God's mercy, but now you have received his mercy.

Slaves of God

[11] I appeal to you, my friends, as strangers and refugees in this world! Do not give in to bodily passions, which are always at war against the soul. [12] Your conduct among the heathen should be so good that when they accuse you of being evildoers, they will have to recognize your good deeds and so praise God on the Day of his coming.

[13] For the sake of the Lord submit to every human authority: to the Emperor, who is the supreme authority, [14] and to the governors, who have been appointed by him to punish the evildoers and to praise those who do good. [15] For God wants you to silence the

1.22 *with all your heart*; some manuscripts have *with a pure heart*.

ignorant talk of foolish people by the good things you do. [16] Live as free people; do not, however, use your freedom to cover up any evil, but live as God's slaves. [17] Respect everyone, love your fellow-believers, honour God, and respect the Emperor.

The Example of Christ's Suffering

[18] You servants must submit to your masters and show them complete respect, not only to those who are kind and considerate, but also to those who are harsh. [19] God will bless you for this, if you endure the pain of undeserved suffering because you are conscious of his will. [20] For what credit is there if you endure the beatings you deserve for having done wrong? But if you endure suffering even when you have done right, God will bless you for it. [21] It was to this that God called you, for Christ himself suffered for you and left you an example, so that you would follow in his steps. [22] He committed no sin, and no one ever heard a lie come from his lips. [23] When he was insulted, he did not answer back with an insult; when he suffered, he did not threaten, but placed his hopes in God, the righteous Judge. [24] Christ himself carried our sins in his body to the cross, so that we might die to sin and live for righteousness. It is by his wounds that you have been healed. [25] You were like sheep that had lost their way, but now you have been brought back to follow the Shepherd and Keeper of your souls.

Wives and Husbands

3 In the same way you wives must submit to your husbands, so that if any of them do not believe God's word, your conduct will win them over to believe. It will not be necessary for you to say a word, [2] because they will see how pure and reverent your conduct is. [3] You should not use outward aids to make yourselves beautiful, such as the way you do your hair, or the jewellery you put on, or the dresses you wear. [4] Instead, your beauty should consist of your true inner self, the ageless beauty of a gentle and quiet spirit, which is of the greatest value in God's sight. [5] For the devout women of the past who placed their hope in God used to make themselves beautiful by submitting to their husbands. [6] Sarah was like that; she obeyed Abraham and called him her master. You are now her daughters if you do good and are not afraid of anything.

[7] In the same way you husbands must live with your wives with the proper understanding that they are weaker than you. Treat them with respect, because they also will receive, together with you, God's gift of life. Do this so that nothing will interfere with your prayers.

Suffering for Doing Right

[8] To conclude: you must all have the same attitude and the same feelings; love one another as brothers and sisters, and be kind and humble with one another. [9] Do not pay back evil with evil or cursing with cursing; instead, pay back with a blessing, because a blessing is what God promised to give you when he called you. [10] As the scripture says:

"Whoever wants to enjoy life
 and wishes to see good times,
 must keep from speaking evil
 and stop telling lies.
[11] They must turn away from evil and do good;
 they must strive for peace with all their heart.

1 PETER 3.15

If someone asked you to

- EXPLAIN YOUR -

HOPE

right now, could you?
Write an answer below
to the question 'Why
are you a Christian?'

_____

_____

_____

_____

_____

_____

_____

_____

_____

_____

_____

_____

_____

12 For the Lord watches over the righteous
and listens to their prayers;
but he opposes those who do evil."
13 Who will harm you if you are eager to do what is good? 14 But
even if you should suffer for doing what is right, how happy you
are! Do not be afraid of anyone, and do not worry. 15 But have
reverence for Christ in your hearts, and honour him as Lord. Be
ready at all times to answer anyone who asks you to explain the
hope you have in you, 16 but do it with gentleness and respect.
Keep your conscience clear, so that when you are insulted, those
who speak evil of your good conduct as followers of Christ will be
ashamed of what they say. 17 For it is better to suffer for doing
good, if this should be God's will, than for doing evil. 18 For Christ
died* for sins once and for all, a good man on behalf of sinners,
in order to lead you to God. He was put to death physically, but
made alive spiritually, 19 and in his spiritual existence he went and
preached to the imprisoned spirits. 20 These were the spirits of
those who had not obeyed God when he waited patiently during
the days that Noah was building his boat. The few people in
the boat — eight in all — were saved by the water, 21 which was
a symbol pointing to baptism, which now saves you. It is not the
washing away of bodily dirt, but the promise made to God from
a good conscience. It saves you through the resurrection of Jesus
Christ, 22 who has gone to heaven and is at the right-hand side of
God, ruling over all angels and heavenly authorities and powers.

Changed Lives

4 Since Christ suffered physically, you too must strengthen
yourselves with the same way of thinking that he had; because
whoever suffers physically is no longer involved with sin. 2 From
now on, then, you must live the rest of your earthly lives controlled
by God's will and not by human desires. 3 You have spent enough
time in the past doing what the heathen like to do. Your lives were
spent in indecency, lust, drunkenness, orgies, drinking parties,
and the disgusting worship of idols. 4 And now the heathen are
surprised when you do not join them in the same wild and reckless
living, and so they insult you. 5 But they will have to give an account
of themselves to God, who is ready to judge the living and the
dead. 6 That is why the Good News was preached also to the
dead, to those who had been judged in their physical existence
as everyone is judged; it was preached to them so that in their
spiritual existence they may live as God lives.

Good Managers of God's Gifts

7 The end of all things is near. You must be self-controlled and
alert, to be able to pray. 8 Above everything, love one another
earnestly, because love covers over many sins. 9 Open your homes to
each other without complaining. 10 Each one, as a good manager of
God's different gifts, must use for the good of others the special gift
he has received from God. 11 Whoever preaches must preach God's
messages; whoever serves must serve with the strength that God
gives, so that in all things praise may be given to God through Jesus
Christ, to whom belong glory and power for ever and ever. Amen.

Suffering as a Christian

12 My dear friends, do not be surprised at the painful test you
are suffering, as though something unusual were happening to

3.18 *died*; many manuscripts have *suffered*.

you. [13] Rather be glad that you are sharing Christ's sufferings, so that you may be full of joy when his glory is revealed. [14] Happy are you if you are insulted because you are Christ's followers; this means that the glorious Spirit, the Spirit of God, is resting on you. [15] If any of you suffer, it must not be because you are a murderer or a thief or a criminal or a meddler in other people's affairs. [16] However, if you suffer because you are a Christian, don't be ashamed of it, but thank God that you bear Christ's name.

[17] The time has come for judgement to begin, and God's own people are the first to be judged. If it starts with us, how will it end with those who do not believe the Good News from God? [18] As the scripture says:

"It is difficult for good people to be saved;
   what, then, will become of godless sinners?"

[19] So then, those who suffer because it is God's will for them, should by their good actions trust themselves completely to their Creator, who always keeps his promise.

The Flock of God

5 I, who am an elder myself, appeal to the church elders among you. I am a witness of Christ's sufferings, and I will share in the glory that will be revealed. I appeal to you [2] to be shepherds of the flock that God gave you and to take care of it willingly, as God wants you to, and not unwillingly. Do your work, not for mere pay, but from a real desire to serve. [3] Do not try to rule over those who have been put in your care, but be examples to the flock. [4] And when the Chief Shepherd appears, you will receive the glorious crown which will never lose its brightness.

[5] In the same way you younger people must submit to your elders. And all of you must put on the apron of humility, to serve one another; for the scripture says, "God resists the proud, but shows favour to the humble." [6] Humble yourselves, then, under God's mighty hand, so that he will lift you up in his own good time. [7] Leave all your worries with him, because he cares for you.

[8] Be alert, be on the watch! Your enemy, the Devil, roams round like a roaring lion, looking for someone to devour. [9] Be firm in your faith and resist him, because you know that your fellow-believers in all the world are going through the same kind of sufferings. [10] But after you have suffered for a little while, the God of all grace, who calls you to share his eternal glory in union with Christ, will himself perfect you and give you firmness, strength, and a sure foundation. [11] To him be the power for ever! Amen.

Final Greetings

[12] I write you this brief letter with the help of Silas, whom I regard as a faithful fellow-Christian. I want to encourage you and give my testimony that this is the true grace of God. Stand firm in it.

[13] Your sister church in Babylon,* also chosen by God, sends you greetings, and so does my son Mark. [14] Greet one another with the kiss of Christian love.

May peace be with all of you who belong to Christ.

1 PETER 5.7

It can be really easy to hold on to our worries, but

GOD

– CARES –

FOR US

and wants us to give them over to him. Grab a piece of paper and

WRITE DOWN ANYTHING THAT IS WORRYING YOU RIGHT NOW.

Scrunch it up and hold it tight in your hands while you pray that God would take care of what you have written. When you finish your prayer, let go of the paper as a sign of handing your worries out of your care and into God's.

5.13 *Babylon*: As in the book of Revelation, this probably refers to Rome.

THE LETTER OF
2 PETER

WRITTEN: EARLY AD60s
(OR THE FIRST HALF OF THE SECOND CENTURY)

WHAT YOU NEED TO KNOW:

This is the second letter said to have been written by Peter. In it he writes to the church about how Jesus transforms lives, and he challenges his readers to be holy. The letter was written in response to some false teachings about the Christian faith. Some people were spreading the belief that salvation was fully experienced in this life, so there would be no eternal life, and there would be no second coming of Jesus. In this letter, the writer voices his concerns about this teaching and speaks against it.

HE IS
PATIENT WITH YOU,
because he does not want
ANYONE
TO BE DESTROYED,
but wants all
TO TURN AWAY FROM
THEIR SINS.

2 PETER 3.9

WHY READ IT?

We live in a culture where everything is fast-paced and where we have access to pretty much anything we want, immediately. This letter reminds us that God's timing is different from ours - he is not part of our 'have it now' culture. Peter spurs us on to keep our eyes fixed on Jesus.

As you read through this letter, summarise what each section says to you in the margins.

FILL THE SPACES WITH COLOUR, NOTES, WORDS AND QUESTIONS!

(AD70)
ROMANS DESTROY JERUSALEM

PETER WRITES 2ND LETTER
(AD100-120)

2 Peter

1 John
2 John
3 John
Jude
Revel.

1 From Simon Peter, a servant and apostle of Jesus Christ —
To those who through the righteousness of our God and Saviour Jesus Christ have been given a faith as precious as ours: ² May grace and peace be yours in full measure through your knowledge of God and of Jesus our Lord.

God's Call and Choice

³ God's divine power has given us everything we need to live a truly religious life through our knowledge of the one who called us to share in his own* glory and goodness. ⁴ In this way he has given us the very great and precious gifts he promised, so that by means of these gifts you may escape from the destructive lust that is in the world, and may come to share the divine nature. ⁵ For this very reason do your best to add goodness to your faith; to your goodness add knowledge; ⁶ to your knowledge add self-control; to your self-control add endurance; to your endurance add godliness; ⁷ to your godliness add Christian affection; and to your Christian affection add love. ⁸ These are the qualities you need, and if you have them in abundance, they will make you active and effective in your knowledge of our Lord Jesus Christ. ⁹ But those who do not have them are so short-sighted that they cannot see and have forgotten that they have been purified from their past sins.

¹⁰ So then, my brothers and sisters, try even harder to make God's call and his choice of you a permanent experience; if you do so, you will never abandon your faith.* ¹¹ In this way you will be given the full right to enter the eternal Kingdom of our Lord and Saviour Jesus Christ.

¹² And so I will always remind you of these matters, even though you already know them and are firmly grounded in the truth you have received. ¹³ I think it only right for me to stir up your memory of these matters as long as I am still alive. ¹⁴ I know that I shall soon put off this mortal body, as our Lord Jesus Christ plainly told me. ¹⁵ I will do my best, then, to provide a way for you to remember these matters at all times after my death.

Eyewitnesses of Christ's Glory

¹⁶ We have not depended on made-up stories in making known to you the mighty coming of our Lord Jesus Christ. With our own eyes we saw his greatness. ¹⁷ We were there when he was given honour and glory by God the Father, when the voice came to him from the Supreme Glory, saying, "This is my own dear Son, with whom I am pleased!" ¹⁸ We ourselves heard this voice coming from heaven, when we were with him on the holy mountain.

¹⁹ So we are even more confident of the message proclaimed by the prophets. You will do well to pay attention to it, because it is like a lamp shining in a dark place until the Day dawns and the light of the morning star shines in your hearts. ²⁰ Above all else, however, remember that no one can explain by himself or herself a prophecy in the Scriptures. ²¹ For no prophetic message ever came just from human will, but people were under the control of the Holy Spirit as they spoke the message that came from God.

False Teachers

2 False prophets appeared in the past among the people, and in the same way false teachers will appear among you.

1.3 *to share in his own*; some manuscripts have *through his.*
1.10 *abandon your faith*; or *fall into sin.*

2 PETER 1.5-8

Read the
— LIST OF —
QUALITIES
in these verses.
Circle the ones you'd
like to see more of in
yourself. Pray that
God's Spirit would help
develop these in you.

1464

2 Peter

....

Titus
Philem.
Heb.
James
1 Peter

They will bring in destructive, untrue doctrines, and will deny the Master who redeemed them, and so they will bring upon themselves sudden destruction. ²Even so, many will follow their immoral ways; and because of what they do, others will speak evil of the Way of truth. ³In their greed these false teachers will make a profit out of telling you made-up stories. For a long time now their Judge has been ready, and their Destroyer has been wide awake!

⁴God did not spare the angels who sinned, but threw them into hell, where they are kept chained in darkness,* waiting for the Day of Judgement. ⁵God did not spare the ancient world, but brought the flood on the world of godless people; the only ones he saved were Noah, who preached righteousness, and seven other people. ⁶God condemned the cities of Sodom and Gomorrah, destroying them with fire, and made them an example of what will happen to the godless. ⁷He rescued Lot, a good man, who was distressed by the immoral conduct of lawless people. ⁸That good man lived among them, and day after day he suffered agony as he saw and heard their evil actions. ⁹And so the Lord knows how to rescue godly people from their trials and how to keep the wicked under punishment for the Day of Judgement, ¹⁰especially those who follow their filthy bodily lusts and despise God's authority.

These false teachers are bold and arrogant, and show no respect for the glorious beings above; instead, they insult them. ¹¹Even the angels, who are so much stronger and mightier than these false teachers, do not accuse them with insults in the presence of the Lord. ¹²But these people act by instinct, like wild animals born to be captured and killed; they attack with insults anything they do not understand. They will be destroyed like wild animals, ¹³and they will be paid with suffering for the suffering they have caused. Pleasure for them is to do anything in broad daylight that will satisfy their bodily appetites; they are a shame and a disgrace as they join you in your meals, all the while enjoying their deceitful ways! ¹⁴They want to look at nothing but immoral women; their appetite for sin is never satisfied. They lead weak people into a trap. Their hearts are trained to be greedy. They are under God's curse! ¹⁵They have left the straight path and have lost their way; they have followed the path taken by Balaam son of Beor, who loved the money he would get for doing wrong ¹⁶and was rebuked for his sin. His donkey spoke with a human voice and stopped the prophet's insane action.

¹⁷These people are like dried-up springs, like clouds blown along by a storm; God has reserved a place for them in the deepest darkness. ¹⁸They make proud and stupid statements, and use immoral bodily lusts to trap those who are just beginning to escape from among people who live in error. ¹⁹They promise them freedom while they themselves are slaves of destructive habits — for a person is a slave of anything that has conquered him. ²⁰If people have escaped from the corrupting forces of the world through their knowledge of our Lord and Saviour Jesus Christ, and then are again caught and conquered by them, such people are in a worse state at the end than they were at the beginning. ²¹It would have been much better for them never to have known the way of righteousness than to know it and then turn away from the sacred command that was given them. ²²What happened to them shows that the proverbs are true: "A dog goes back to what it has vomited" and "A pig that has been washed goes back to roll in the mud."

2 PETER 2.15-16

Peter is talking about a story that you can find in Numbers 22.4-35. Go back and read it to

• GET A •

BETTER

understanding of what he is saying.

2.4 chained in darkness; some manuscripts have in dark pits.

The Promise of the Lord's Coming

3 My dear friends, this is now the second letter I have written to you. In both letters I have tried to arouse pure thoughts in your minds by reminding you of these things. ² I want you to remember the words that were spoken long ago by the holy prophets, and the command from the Lord and Saviour which was given you by your apostles. ³ First of all, you must understand that in these last days some people will appear whose lives are controlled by their own lusts. They will mock you ⁴ and will ask, "He promised to come, didn't he? Where is he? Our ancestors have already died, but everything is still the same as it was since the creation of the world!" ⁵ They purposely ignore the fact that long ago God gave a command, and the heavens and earth were created. The earth was formed out of water and by water, ⁶ and it was also by water, the water of the flood, that the old world was destroyed. ⁷ But the heavens and the earth that now exist are being preserved by the same command of God, in order to be destroyed by fire. They are being kept for the day when godless people will be judged and destroyed.

⁸ But do not forget one thing, my dear friends! There is no difference in the Lord's sight between one day and a thousand years; to him the two are the same. ⁹ The Lord is not slow to do what he has promised, as some think. Instead, he is patient with you, because he does not want anyone to be destroyed, but wants all to turn away from their sins.

¹⁰ But the Day of the Lord will come like a thief. On that Day the heavens will disappear with a shrill noise, the heavenly bodies will burn up and be destroyed, and the earth with everything in it will vanish.* ¹¹ Since all these things will be destroyed in this way, what kind of people should you be? Your lives should be holy and dedicated to God, ¹² as you wait for the Day of God and do your best to make it come soon — the Day when the heavens will burn up and be destroyed, and the heavenly bodies will be melted by the heat. ¹³ But we wait for what God has promised: new heavens and a new earth, where righteousness will be at home.

¹⁴ And so, my friends, as you wait for that Day, do your best to be pure and faultless in God's sight and to be at peace with him. ¹⁵ Look on our Lord's patience as the opportunity he is giving you to be saved, just as our dear brother Paul wrote to you, using the wisdom that God gave him. ¹⁶ This is what he says in all his letters when he writes on the subject. There are some difficult things in his letters which ignorant and unstable people explain falsely, as they do with other passages of the Scriptures. So they bring on their own destruction.

¹⁷ But you, my friends, already know this. Be on your guard, then, so that you will not be led away by the errors of lawless people and fall from your safe position. ¹⁸ But continue to grow in the grace and knowledge of our Lord and Saviour Jesus Christ. To him be the glory, now and for ever! Amen.

RIGHTEOUSNESS

PROVERBS 11.30;
HOSEA 10.12;
2 PETER 3.13

DEFINITION: The quality of
being morally right
or justifiable.
(oxforddictionaries.com)

3.10 *vanish*; some manuscripts have *be found*; others have *be burnt up*; one has *be found destroyed*.

THE LETTER OF

1 JOHN

WRITTEN: AD90s

LET US LOVE ONE ANOTHER, BECAUSE LOVE COMES FROM GOD

1 JOHN 4.7

DOODLE HERE...

WHAT YOU NEED TO KNOW:

This is the first of three letters written by a man called John. In this letter, John can't stop talking about how God is love and how we should love each other. It sums up the whole story of the gospel - God loved his people so much that he sent Jesus to die for them.

AS YOU READ THIS LETTER, CIRCLE EVERY TIME THE WORD 'LOVE' IS USED. EACH TIME, THINK ABOUT WHY IT'S USED - WHO FOR, AND WHAT DOES IT MEAN? DO YOU SEE GOD AS LOVE?

WHY READ IT?

The central theme of this letter is love. It explores a key character trait of God and challenges us about how much love we live out practically. It also reminds us that, as Jesus said, we live in the world but do not 'belong to the world' (see John 17.11-16). It encourages us to remember to live our lives as followers of Jesus.

(AD70)
ROMANS DESTROY JERUSALEM

JOHN WRITES 1ST LETTER
(AD90-100)

The Word of Life

1 We write to you about the Word of life, which has existed from the very beginning. We have heard it, and we have seen it with our eyes; yes, we have seen it, and our hands have touched it. ²When this life became visible, we saw it; so we speak of it and tell you about the eternal life which was with the Father and was made known to us. ³What we have seen and heard we announce to you also, so that you will join with us in the fellowship that we have with the Father and with his Son Jesus Christ. ⁴We write this in order that our* joy may be complete.

God is Light

⁵Now the message that we have heard from his Son and announce is this: God is light, and there is no darkness at all in him. ⁶If, then, we say that we have fellowship with him, yet at the same time live in the darkness, we are lying both in our words and in our actions. ⁷But if we live in the light — just as he is in the light — then we have fellowship with one another, and the blood of Jesus, his Son, purifies us from every sin.

⁸If we say that we have no sin, we deceive ourselves, and there is no truth in us. ⁹But if we confess our sins to God, he will keep his promise and do what is right: he will forgive us our sins and purify us from all our wrongdoing. ¹⁰If we say that we have not sinned, we make God out to be a liar, and his word is not in us.

Christ our Helper

2 I am writing this to you, my children, so that you will not sin; but if anyone does sin, we have someone who pleads with the Father on our behalf — Jesus Christ, the righteous one. ²And Christ himself is the means by which our sins are forgiven, and not our sins only, but also the sins of everyone.

³If we obey God's commands, then we are sure that we know him. ⁴Those who say that they know him, but do not obey his commands, are liars and there is no truth in them. ⁵All those who obey his word are people whose love for God has really been made perfect. This is how we can be sure that we are in union with God: ⁶those who say that they remain in union with God should live just as Jesus Christ did.

The New Command

⁷My dear friends, this command I am writing to you is not new; it is the old command, the one you have had from the very beginning. The old command is the message you have already heard. ⁸However, the command I am now writing to you is new, because its truth is seen in Christ and also in you. For the darkness is passing away, and the real light is already shining.

⁹Those who say that they are in the light, yet hate their brothers and sisters, are in the darkness to this very hour. ¹⁰Those who love their brothers and sisters live in the light, and so there is nothing in them that will cause someone else* to sin. ¹¹But those who hate their brothers and sisters are in the darkness; they walk in it and do not know where they are going, because the darkness has made them blind.

¹²I am writing to you, my children, because your sins are forgiven for the sake of Christ. ¹³I am writing to you, fathers, because you know him who has existed from the beginning.

1.4 *our*; some manuscripts have *your*.
2.10 *someone else*; or *them*.

Write
ONE THING
that you will
CHANGE
ABOUT YOUR
LIFE
having read
this passage.

1468

1 John

:·········

Philem.
Heb.
James
1 Peter
2 Peter

I am writing to you, young people, because you have defeated the Evil One.

14 I am writing to you, my children, because you know the Father. I am writing to you, fathers, because you know him who has existed from the beginning. I am writing to you, young people, because you are strong; the word of God lives in you, and you have defeated the Evil One.

15 Do not love the world or anything that belongs to the world. If you love the world, you do not love the Father. 16 Everything that belongs to the world — what the sinful self desires, what people see and want, and everything in this world that people are so proud of — none of this comes from the Father; it all comes from the world. 17 The world and everything in it that people desire is passing away; but those who do the will of God live for ever.

The Enemy of Christ

18 My children, the end is near! You were told that the Enemy of Christ would come; and now many enemies of Christ have already appeared, and so we know that the end is near. 19 These people really did not belong to our fellowship, and that is why they left us; if they had belonged to our fellowship, they would have stayed with us. But they left so that it might be clear that none of them really belonged to us.

20 But you have had the Holy Spirit poured out on you by Christ, and so all of you know the truth. 21 I am writing to you, then, not because you do not know the truth; instead, it is because you do know it, and you also know that no lie ever comes from the truth.

22 Who, then, is the liar? It is those who say that Jesus is not the Messiah. Such people are the Enemies of Christ — they reject both the Father and the Son. 23 For all those who reject the Son also reject the Father; those who accept the Son have the Father also.

24 Be sure, then, to keep in your hearts the message you heard from the beginning. If you keep that message, then you will always live in union with the Son and the Father. 25 And this is what Christ himself promised to give us — eternal life.

26 I am writing this to you about those who are trying to deceive you. 27 But as for you, Christ has poured out his Spirit on you. As long as his Spirit remains in you, you do not need anyone to teach you. For his Spirit teaches you about everything, and what he teaches is true, not false. Obey the Spirit's teaching, then, and remain in union with Christ.

28 Yes, my children, remain in union with him, so that when he appears we may be full of courage and need not hide in shame from him on the Day he comes. 29 You know that Christ is righteous; you should know, then, that everyone who does what is right is God's child.

Children of God

3 See how much the Father has loved us! His love is so great that we are called God's children — and so, in fact, we are. This is why the world does not know us: it has not known God. 2 My dear friends, we are now God's children, but it is not yet clear what we shall become. But we know that when Christ appears, we shall be like him, because we shall see him as he really is. 3 Everyone who has this hope in Christ keeps himself pure, just as Christ is pure.

4 Whoever sins is guilty of breaking God's law, because sin is a breaking of the law. 5 You know that Christ appeared in order to

1 JOHN 3, 4

1469

1 John
...........:.

2 John
3 John
Jude
Revel.

take away sins,* and that there is no sin in him. ⁶So everyone who lives in union with Christ does not continue to sin; but whoever continues to sin has never seen him or known him.

⁷Let no one deceive you, my children! Whoever does what is right is righteous, just as Christ is righteous. ⁸Whoever continues to sin belongs to the Devil, because the Devil has sinned from the very beginning. The Son of God appeared for this very reason, to destroy what the Devil had done.

⁹None of those who are children of God continue to sin, for God's very nature is in them; and because God is their Father, they cannot continue to sin. ¹⁰This is the clear difference between God's children and the Devil's children: all who do not do what is right or do not love others are not God's children.

Love One Another

¹¹The message you heard from the very beginning is this: we must love one another. ¹²We must not be like Cain; he belonged to the Evil One and murdered his own brother Abel. Why did Cain murder him? Because the things he himself did were wrong, but the things his brother did were right.

¹³So do not be surprised, my brothers and sisters, if the people of the world hate you. ¹⁴We know that we have left death and come over into life; we know it because we love our brothers and sisters. Whoever does not love is still under the power of death. ¹⁵All who hate others are murderers, and you know that murderers have not got eternal life in them. ¹⁶This is how we know what love is: Christ gave his life for us. We too, then, ought to give our lives for our brothers and sisters! ¹⁷Rich people who see a brother or sister in need, yet close their hearts against them, cannot claim that they love God. ¹⁸My children, our love should not be just words and talk; it must be true love, which shows itself in action.

Courage before God

¹⁹This, then, is how we will know that we belong to the truth; this is how we will be confident in God's presence. ²⁰If our conscience condemns us, we know that God is greater than our conscience and that he knows everything. ²¹And so, my dear friends, if our conscience does not condemn us, we have courage in God's presence. ²²We receive from him whatever we ask, because we obey his commands and do what pleases him. ²³What he commands is that we believe in his Son Jesus Christ and love one another, just as Christ commanded us. ²⁴Those who obey God's commands live in union with God and God lives in union with them. And because of the Spirit that God has given us we know that God lives in union with us.

The True Spirit and the False

4 My dear friends, do not believe all who claim to have the Spirit, but test them to find out if the spirit they have comes from God. For many false prophets have gone out everywhere. ²This is how you will be able to know whether it is God's Spirit: anyone who acknowledges that Jesus Christ came as a human being has the Spirit who comes from God. ³But anyone who denies this about Jesus does not have the Spirit from God. The spirit that he has is from the Enemy of Christ; you heard that it would come, and now it is here in the world already.

....

3.5 *sins*; some manuscripts have *our sins*.

1 JOHN 4.18

4 But you belong to God, my children, and have defeated the false prophets, because the Spirit who is in you is more powerful than the spirit in those who belong to the world. 5 Those false prophets speak about matters of the world, and the world listens to them because they belong to the world. 6 But we belong to God. Whoever knows God listens to us; whoever does not belong to God does not listen to us. This, then, is how we can tell the difference between the Spirit of truth and the spirit of error.

God is Love

7 Dear friends, let us love one another, because love comes from God. Whoever loves is a child of God and knows God. 8 Whoever does not love does not know God, for God is love. 9 And God showed his love for us by sending his only Son into the world, so that we might have life through him. 10 This is what love is: it is not that we have loved God, but that he loved us and sent his Son to be the means by which our sins are forgiven.

11 Dear friends, if this is how God loved us, then we should love one another. 12 No one has ever seen God, but if we love one another, God lives in union with us, and his love is made perfect in us.

13 We are sure that we live in union with God and that he lives in union with us, because he has given us his Spirit. 14 And we have seen and tell others that the Father sent his Son to be the Saviour of the world. 15 If anyone declares that Jesus is the Son of God, he lives in union with God and God lives in union with him. 16 And we ourselves know and believe the love which God has for us.

God is love, and those who live in love live in union with God and God lives in union with them. 17 Love is made perfect in us in order that we may have courage on Judgement Day; and we will have it because our life in this world is the same as Christ's. 18 There is no fear in love; perfect love drives out all fear. So then, love has not been made perfect in anyone who is afraid, because fear has to do with punishment.

19 We love because God first loved us. 20 If we say we love God, but hate our brothers and sisters, we are liars. For people cannot love God, whom they have not seen, if they do not love their brothers and sisters, whom they have seen. 21 The command that Christ has given us is this: all who love God must love their brother or sister also.

Our Victory over the World

5 Whoever believes that Jesus is the Messiah is a child of God; and whoever loves a father loves his child also. 2 This is how we know that we love God's children: it is by loving God and obeying his commands. 3 For our love for God means that we obey his commands. And his commands are not too hard for us, 4 because every child of God is able to defeat the world. And we win the victory over the world by means of our faith. 5 Who can defeat the world? Only the person who believes that Jesus is the Son of God.

The Witness about Jesus Christ

6 Jesus Christ is the one who came with the water of his baptism and the blood of his death. He came not only with the water, but with both the water and the blood. And the Spirit himself testifies that this is true, because the Spirit is truth. 7 There are three witnesses: 8 the Spirit, the water, and the blood; and all three give the same testimony. 9 We believe human testimony;

1471

1 John

············

2 John

3 John

Jude

Revel.

but God's testimony is much stronger, and he has given this testimony about his Son. ¹⁰So all who believe in the Son of God have this testimony in their own hearts; but those who do not believe God have made him out to be a liar, because they have not believed what God has said about his Son. ¹¹The testimony is this: God has given us eternal life, and this life has its source in his Son. ¹²Whoever has the Son has this life; whoever does not have the Son of God does not have life.

Eternal Life

¹³I am writing this to you so that you may know that you have eternal life — you that believe in the Son of God. ¹⁴We have courage in God's presence, because we are sure that he hears us if we ask him for anything that is according to his will. ¹⁵He hears us whenever we ask him; and since we know this is true, we know also that he gives us what we ask from him.

¹⁶If you see your brother or sister commit a sin that does not lead to death, you should pray to God, who will give them life. This applies to those whose sins do not lead to death. But there is sin which leads to death, and I do not say that you should pray to God about that. ¹⁷All wrongdoing is sin, but there is sin which does not lead to death.

¹⁸We know that none of God's children keep on sinning, for the Son of God keeps them safe, and the Evil One cannot harm them.

¹⁹We know that we belong to God even though the whole world is under the rule of the Evil One.

²⁰We know that the Son of God has come and has given us understanding, so that we know the true God. We live in union with the true God — in union with his Son Jesus Christ. This is the true God, and this is eternal life.

²¹My children, keep yourselves safe from false gods!

WHAT DOES 'SIN' MEAN?
Finish the mindmap below.

The offence of
breaking, or
the breaking of,
a religious
or moral law
(dictionary.cambridge.org)

↑

SIN

ROMANS 5.12; 1 JOHN 5.17

THE LETTER OF

2 JOHN

WRITTEN: AD90s

WHY READ IT?

This letter shows us that it can be easy to get hold of some wrong ideas about Jesus. It's important for us to stick to what we learn about him from the Gospels and the New Testament letters. John's letter challenges us to hold on to that truth - and to always come back to loving one another.

WHAT YOU NEED TO KNOW:

This letter was written to a 'dear Lady' and her family at a time when the early church was struggling with some serious divisions over beliefs that stemmed from false (untrue) teaching. Some people were teaching that Jesus had not really been human, so John aims to combat these rumours in his letter. As in John's first letter, there is a big emphasis on the command to love one another and to live according to the words of Jesus.

Do you think you would be able to tell if someone was teaching you something about Jesus that was untrue? How might you be able to help yourself to recognise false teaching?

write some
thoughts here

(AD70)
ROMANS DESTROY JERUSALEM

JOHN WRITES 2ND LETTER
(AD90-100)

2 JOHN

1473

2 John

....

3 John

Jude

Revel.

¹From the Elder —

To the dear Lady and to her children,* whom I truly love. And I am not the only one, but all who know the truth love you, ²because the truth remains in us and will be with us for ever.

³May God the Father and Jesus Christ, the Father's Son, give us grace, mercy, and peace; may they be ours in truth and love.

Truth and Love

⁴How happy I was to find that some of your children live in the truth, just as the Father commanded us. ⁵And so I ask you, dear Lady: let us all love one another. This is no new command I am writing to you; it is the command which we have had from the beginning. ⁶This love I speak of means that we must live in obedience to God's commands. The command, as you have all heard from the beginning, is that you must all live in love.

⁷Many deceivers have gone out all over the world, people who do not acknowledge that Jesus Christ came as a human being. Such a person is a deceiver and the Enemy of Christ. ⁸Be on your guard, then, so that you will not lose what we* have worked for, but will receive your reward in full.

⁹Anyone who does not stay with the teaching of Christ, but goes beyond it, does not have God. Whoever does stay with the teaching has both the Father and the Son. ¹⁰So then, if someone comes to you who does not bring this teaching, do not welcome him or her in your homes; do not even say, "Peace be with you." ¹¹For anyone who wishes them peace becomes their partner in the evil things they do.

Final Words

¹²I have so much to tell you, but I would rather not do it with paper and ink; instead, I hope to visit you and talk with you personally, so that we shall be completely happy.

¹³The children of your dear Sister* send you their greetings.

2 JOHN 1.6

LIVE IN LOVE

---

v.1 *lady and... her children*: This probably refers to a church and its members (also in verses 4–5).
v.8 *we*; some manuscripts have *you*.
v.13 *children of your dear sister*: This probably refers to the members of the church to which the writer belonged.

THE LETTER OF

3 JOHN

WRITTEN: AD90s

STOP READING & PRAY FOR ONE MINUTE.

It doesn't matter what it's about - just talk to God!

WRITE A LETTER TO YOURSELF, FULL OF

TIPS & ADVICE

ON HOW TO

IMITATE

WHAT IS GOOD RATHER THAN WHAT IS BAD.

WHAT YOU NEED TO KNOW:

This is a personal letter from John to a Christian man called Gaius, advising him on what to do about a troublemaker in the church. A man called Diotrephes was shaking things up and preventing people in his church from being welcoming, hospitable and kind to other believers.

WHY READ IT?

This short letter is a super-quick read that encourages us to help all our fellow Christians, and to imitate goodness rather than evil. It warns us not to follow the example of people who cause trouble.

(AD70)
ROMANS DESTROY JERUSALEM

JOHN WRITES 3RD LETTER
(AD90-100)

3 JOHN

1475

3 John

........:.

Jude

Revel.

3 JOHN

[1] From the Elder —
To my dear Gaius, whom I truly love.
[2] My dear friend, I pray that everything may go well with you and that you may be in good health — as I know you are well in spirit. [3] I was so happy when some fellow-Christians arrived and told me how faithful you are to the truth — just as you always live in the truth. [4] Nothing makes me happier than to hear that my children live in the truth.

Gaius is Praised

[5] My dear friend, you are so faithful in the work you do for your fellow-Christians, even when they are strangers. [6] They have spoken to the church here about your love. Please help them to continue their journey in a way that will please God. [7] For they set out on their journey in the service of Christ without accepting any help from unbelievers. [8] We Christians, then, must help these people, so that we may share in their work for the truth.

Diotrephes and Demetrius

[9] I wrote a short letter to the church; but Diotrephes, who likes to be their leader, will not pay any attention to what I say. [10] When I come, then, I will call attention to everything he has done: the terrible things he says about us and the lies he tells! But that is not enough for him; he will not receive our fellow-Christians when they come, and even stops those who want to receive them and tries to drive them out of the church!
[11] My dear friend, do not imitate what is bad, but imitate what is good. Whoever does good belongs to God; whoever does what is bad has not seen God.
[12] Everyone speaks well of Demetrius; truth itself speaks well of him. And we add our testimony, and you know that what we say is true.

Final Greetings

[13] I have so much to tell you, but I do not want to do it with pen and ink. [14] I hope to see you soon, and then we will talk personally.
[15] Peace be with you.
All your friends send greetings. Greet all our friends personally.

3 JOHN 1.5

Here, John encourages Gaius with a simple statement.

Send a few friends

A SIMPLE
MESSAGE

to encourage them today.

THE LETTER OF

JUDE

WRITTEN: PROBABLY AROUND AD100-125

WHAT YOU NEED TO KNOW:

This letter was written as a warning against leaders who were teaching things about God that weren't true. People had waited for years for the Messiah to come, but now they were becoming impatient and starting to change their beliefs. This false teaching crept in almost unnoticed, and Jude wanted to put people straight.

WHY READ IT?

This letter is a great encouragement to pray about, and check with the Bible, the things we assume about God. We should not shape our view of God based solely on what we experience, the things we go through, or what other people tell us. Instead we should be checking with the Bible. Jude ends with a brilliant prayer for all Christians.

KEY CHARACTER:

Another of Jesus' half-brothers was named Jude. Like James, he only became a follower of Jesus after Jesus had risen from the dead.

Jude warns against false teaching.

FILL THIS SPACE WITH

TRUE THINGS

THAT YOU KNOW ABOUT GOD.

(AD70)
ROMANS DESTROY JERUSALEM

LETTER OF JUDE WRITTEN
(AD100-125)

¹From Jude, servant of Jesus Christ, and brother of James —
To those who have been called by God, who live in the love of
God the Father and the protection of Jesus Christ:
²May mercy, peace, and love be yours in full measure.

False Teachers

³My dear friends, I was doing my best to write to you about the
salvation we share in common, when I felt the need of writing at
once to encourage you to fight on for the faith which once and for
all God has given to his people. ⁴For some godless people have
slipped in unnoticed among us, persons who distort the message
about the grace of our God in order to excuse their immoral ways,
and who reject Jesus Christ, our only Master and Lord. Long ago
the Scriptures predicted the condemnation they have received.

⁵For even though you know all this, I want to remind you of
how the Lord* once rescued the people of Israel from Egypt, but
afterwards destroyed those who did not believe. ⁶Remember the
angels who did not stay within the limits of their proper authority,
but abandoned their own dwelling place: they are bound with
eternal chains in the darkness below, where God is keeping them
for that great Day on which they will be condemned. ⁷Remember
Sodom and Gomorrah, and the nearby towns, whose people
acted as those angels did and indulged in sexual immorality
and perversion: they suffer the punishment of eternal fire as
a plain warning to all.

⁸In the same way also, these people have visions which make
them sin against their own bodies; they despise God's authority
and insult the glorious beings above. ⁹Not even the chief angel
Michael did this. In his quarrel with the Devil, when they argued
about who would have the body of Moses, Michael did not dare to
condemn the Devil with insulting words, but said, "The Lord rebuke
you!" ¹⁰But these people attack with insults anything they do not
understand; and those things that they know by instinct, like wild
animals, are the very things that destroy them. ¹¹How terrible for
them! They have followed the way that Cain took. For the sake of
money they have given themselves over to the error that Balaam
committed. They have rebelled as Korah rebelled, and like him they
are destroyed. ¹²With their shameless carousing they are like dirty
spots in your fellowship meals. They take care only of themselves.
They are like clouds carried along by the wind, but bringing no rain.
They are like trees that bear no fruit, even in autumn, trees that
have been pulled up by the roots and are completely dead. ¹³They
are like wild waves of the sea, with their shameful deeds showing
up like foam. They are like wandering stars, for whom God has
reserved a place for ever in the deepest darkness.

¹⁴It was Enoch, the seventh* direct descendant from Adam,
who long ago prophesied this about them: "The Lord will come
with many thousands of his holy angels ¹⁵to bring judgement
on all, to condemn them all for the godless deeds they have
performed and for all the terrible words that godless sinners
have spoken against him!"

¹⁶These people are always grumbling and blaming others; they
follow their own evil desires; they boast about themselves and
flatter others in order to get their own way.

WHAT DOES 'GRACE' MEAN?
Finish the mindmap below.

Approval or kindness,
especially (in the
Christian religion)
that is freely
given by God
to all humans.
(dictionary.cambridge.org)

↰

GRACE

ACTS 14.3; ROMANS 5.2;
JUDE v.4

---

v.5 *the Lord*; some manuscripts have *Jesus*, which in Greek is the same as
Joshua.
v.14 *Seventh*: This numbering includes both the first and the last in the
series of seven names from Adam to Enoch.

1478

Jude
....
1 Peter
2 Peter
1 John
2 John
3 John

JUDE

This book is about knowing

TRUTH

– ABOUT –

GOD.

Around these pins write experiences, facts or truths about God that are core to your faith.

Warnings and Instructions

[17] But remember, my friends, what you were told in the past by the apostles of our Lord Jesus Christ. [18] They said to you, "When the last days come, people will appear who will mock you, people who follow their own godless desires." [19] These are the people who cause divisions, who are controlled by their natural desires, who do not have the Spirit. [20] But you, my friends, keep on building yourselves up on your most sacred faith. Pray in the power of the Holy Spirit, [21] and keep yourselves in the love of God, as you wait for our Lord Jesus Christ in his mercy to give you eternal life.

[22] Show mercy towards those who have doubts; [23] save others by snatching them out of the fire; and to others show mercy mixed with fear, but hate their very clothes, stained by their sinful lusts.

Prayer of Praise

[24] To him who is able to keep you from falling, and to bring you faultless and joyful before his glorious presence — [25] to the only God our Saviour, through Jesus Christ our Lord, be glory, majesty, might, and authority, from all ages past, and now, and for ever and ever! Amen.

THE BOOK OF
REVELATION

WRITTEN: SOMETIME BETWEEN AD81 AND 96

WHAT YOU NEED TO KNOW:

This can be a tricky book to get your head around. It is looking forward to a time when death and suffering come to an end, but the imagery can be unusual. It's quite likely that the first readers of the book would have understood the symbolic language better than we do. Revelation starts with a series of letters of encouragement and warning to seven different churches. It then contains visions revealed to John, which all point towards a time when Jesus is completely victorious over Satan and we are with him in a new heaven and new earth.

WHY READ IT?

While this isn't the easiest book to read, it is full of hope for a time when pain ends and everything is made new, both personally and in the wider world. It's an encouragement to the church and all of humanity that God is in control. It also affirms to us that the ongoing story of faith, which we are still part of, ends well.

Turn to the Contents page of this Bible, and circle the books that you have read. Once you have read Revelation, look through the other books you've read and reflect on where you've seen Jesus in different ways in each of them.

SPOTLIGHT:

The first three chapters of this book are written to individual churches.

OUR CHURCHES
• ARE NOT PERFECT •

but they are a key part of God's plan for this world to be made right, until Jesus returns. If you attend a church, write a prayer for it <u>here</u>.

_____

_____

_____

_____

_____

_____

If you don't attend a church, why not check social media for a church in your area that you could visit.

(AD70)
ROMANS DESTROY JERUSALEM

(AD81-96)
JOHN WRITES REVELATION

JOHN EXILED TO PATMOS

1480

Revel.

1 John
2 John
3 John
Jude

REVELATION 1.3

The last book of the Bible is hardcore! Whilst we can't claim to know much about it,

WE DID MAKE A

ABOUT THE BOOK of Revelation.

Head to gnbyouthedition.co.uk/end to watch it.

1 This book is the record of the events that Jesus Christ revealed. God gave him this revelation in order to show his servants what must happen very soon. Christ made these things known to his servant John by sending his angel to him, ²and John has told all that he has seen. This is his report concerning the message from God and the truth revealed by Jesus Christ. ³Happy is the one who reads this book, and happy are those who listen to the words of this prophetic message and obey what is written in this book! For the time is near when all these things will happen.

Greetings to the Seven Churches

⁴From John to the seven churches in the province of Asia:

Grace and peace be yours from God, who is, who was, and who is to come, and from the seven spirits in front of his throne, ⁵and from Jesus Christ, the faithful witness, the first to be raised from death and who is also the ruler of the kings of the world.

He loves us, and by his sacrificial death he has freed us from our sins ⁶and made us a kingdom of priests to serve his God and Father. To Jesus Christ be the glory and power for ever and ever! Amen.

⁷Look, he is coming on the clouds! Everyone will see him, including those who pierced him. All peoples on earth will mourn over him. So shall it be!

⁸"I am the first and the last," says the Lord God Almighty, who is, who was, and who is to come.

A Vision of Christ

⁹I am John, your brother, and as a follower of Jesus I am your partner in patiently enduring the suffering that comes to those who belong to his Kingdom. I was put on the island of Patmos because I had proclaimed God's word and the truth that Jesus revealed. ¹⁰On the Lord's day the Spirit took control of me, and I heard a loud voice, that sounded like a trumpet, speaking behind me. ¹¹It said, "Write down what you see, and send the book to the churches in these seven cities: Ephesus, Smyrna, Pergamum, Thyatira, Sardis, Philadelphia, and Laodicea."

¹²I turned round to see who was talking to me, and I saw seven gold lampstands, ¹³and among them there was what looked like a human being, wearing a robe that reached to his feet, and a gold belt round his chest. ¹⁴His hair was white as wool, or as snow, and his eyes blazed like fire; ¹⁵his feet shone like brass that has been refined and polished, and his voice sounded like a roaring waterfall. ¹⁶He held seven stars in his right-hand, and a sharp two-edged sword came out of his mouth. His face was as bright as the midday sun. ¹⁷When I saw him, I fell down at his feet like a dead man. He placed his right-hand on me and said, "Don't be afraid! I am the first and the last. ¹⁸I am the living one! I was dead, but now I am alive for ever and ever. I have authority over death and the world of the dead. ¹⁹Write, then, the things you see, both the things that are now and the things that will happen afterwards. ²⁰This is the secret meaning of the seven stars that you see in my right-hand, and of the seven gold lampstands: the seven stars are the angels of the seven churches, and the seven lampstands are the seven churches.

The Message to Ephesus

2 "To the angel of the church in Ephesus write:

"This is the message from the one who holds the seven stars in his right-hand and who walks among the seven gold lampstands. ²I know what you have done; I know how hard you have worked and how patient you have been. I know that you cannot tolerate evil people and that you have tested those who say they are apostles but are not, and have found out that they are liars. ³You are patient, you have suffered for my sake, and you have not given up. ⁴But this is what I have against you: you do not love me now as you did at first. ⁵Think how far you have fallen! Turn from your sins and do what you did at first. If you don't turn from your sins, I will come to you and take your lampstand from its place. ⁶But this is what you have in your favour: you hate what the Nicolaitans do, as much as I do.

⁷"If you have ears, then, listen to what the Spirit says to the churches!

"To those who win the victory I will give the right to eat the fruit of the tree of life that grows in the Garden of God.

The Message to Smyrna
⁸"To the angel of the church in Smyrna write:

"This is the message from the one who is the first and the last, who died and lived again. ⁹I know your troubles; I know that you are poor — but really you are rich! I know the evil things said against you by those who claim to be Jews but are not; they are a group that belongs to Satan! ¹⁰Don't be afraid of anything you are about to suffer. Listen! The Devil will put you to the test by having some of you thrown into prison, and your troubles will last ten days. Be faithful to me, even if it means death, and I will give you life as your prize of victory.

¹¹"If you have ears, then, listen to what the Spirit says to the churches!

"Those who win the victory will not be hurt by the second death.

The Message to Pergamum
¹²"To the angel of the church in Pergamum write:

"This is the message from the one who has the sharp two-edged sword. ¹³I know where you live, there where Satan has his throne. You are true to me, and you did not abandon your faith in me even during the time when Antipas, my faithful witness, was killed there where Satan lives. ¹⁴But there are a few things I have against you: there are some among you who follow the teaching of Balaam, who taught Balak how to lead the people of Israel into sin by persuading them to eat food that had been offered to idols and to practise sexual immorality. ¹⁵In the same way you have people among you who follow the teaching of the Nicolaitans. ¹⁶Now turn from your sins! If you don't, I will come to you soon and fight against those people with the sword that comes out of my mouth.

¹⁷"If you have ears, then, listen to what the Spirit says to the churches!

"To those who win the victory I will give some of the hidden manna. I will also give each of them a white stone on which is written a new name that no one knows except the one who receives it.

The Message to Thyatira
¹⁸"To the angel of the church in Thyatira write:

"This is the message from the Son of God, whose eyes blaze like fire, whose feet shine like polished brass. ¹⁹I know what you do. I know your love, your faithfulness, your service, and your patience. I know that you are doing more now than you did at first.

1482

Revel.

1 John
2 John
3 John
Jude

REVELATION 2, 3

REVELATION 3.14-17

Pour yourself a cup of

LUKEWARM WATER

and drink it. As you do, reflect on why God might have been so annoyed about the Laodiceans' apathy. Ask God to show you areas where you have lost your effectiveness or grown complacent.

write some thoughts here

²⁰But this is what I have against you: you tolerate that woman Jezebel, who calls herself a messenger of God. By her teaching she misleads my servants into practising sexual immorality and eating food that has been offered to idols. ²¹I have given her time to repent of her sins, but she does not want to turn from her immorality. ²²And so I will throw her on to a bed where she and those who committed adultery with her will suffer terribly. I will do this now unless they repent of the wicked things they did with her. ²³I will also kill her followers, and then all the churches will know that I am the one who knows everyone's thoughts and wishes. I will repay each of you according to what you have done.

²⁴"But the rest of you in Thyatira have not followed this evil teaching; you have not learnt what the others call 'the deep secrets of Satan'. I say to you that I will not put any other burden on you. ²⁵But until I come, you must hold firmly to what you have. ²⁶⁻²⁸To those who win the victory, who continue to the end to do what I want, I will give the same authority that I received from my Father: I will give them authority over the nations, to rule them with an iron rod and to break them to pieces like clay pots. I will also give them the morning star.

²⁹"If you have ears, then, listen to what the Spirit says to the churches!

The Message to Sardis

3 "To the angel of the church in Sardis write:

"This is the message from the one who has the seven spirits of God and the seven stars. I know what you are doing; I know that you have the reputation of being alive, even though you are dead! ²So wake up, and strengthen what you still have before it dies completely. For I find that what you have done is not yet perfect in the sight of my God. ³Remember, then, what you were taught and what you heard; obey it and turn from your sins. If you do not wake up, I will come upon you like a thief, and you will not even know the time when I will come. ⁴But a few of you there in Sardis have kept your clothes clean. You will walk with me, clothed in white, because you are worthy to do so. ⁵Those who win the victory will be clothed like this in white, and I will not remove their names from the book of the living. In the presence of my Father and of his angels I will declare openly that they belong to me.

⁶"If you have ears, then, listen to what the Spirit says to the churches!

The Message to Philadelphia

⁷"To the angel of the church in Philadelphia write:

"This is the message from the one who is holy and true. He has the key that belonged to David, and when he opens a door, no one can close it, and when he closes it, no one can open it. ⁸I know what you do; I know that you have a little power; you have followed my teaching and have been faithful to me. I have opened a door in front of you, which no one can close. ⁹Listen! As for that group that belongs to Satan, those liars who claim that they are Jews but are not, I will make them come and bow down at your feet. They will all know that I love you. ¹⁰Because you have kept my command to endure, I will also keep you safe from the time of trouble which is coming upon the world to test all the people on earth. ¹¹I am coming soon. Keep safe what you have, so that no one will rob you of your victory prize. ¹²I will make those who are victorious pillars in the temple of my God, and they will never leave it. I will write on them the name of my God and the name of the city of my God, the new Jerusalem, which will come down out of heaven from my God. I will also write on them my new name.

¹³"If you have ears, then, listen to what the Spirit says to the churches!

The Message to Laodicea

¹⁴"To the angel of the church in Laodicea write:

"This is the message from the Amen, the faithful and true witness, who is the origin* of all that God has created. ¹⁵I know what you have done; I know that you are neither cold nor hot. How I wish you were either one or the other! ¹⁶But because you are lukewarm, neither hot nor cold, I am going to spit you out of my mouth! ¹⁷You say, 'I am rich and well off; I have all I need.' But you do not know how miserable and pitiful you are! You are poor, naked, and blind. ¹⁸I advise you, then, to buy gold from me, pure gold, in order to be rich. Buy also white clothing to dress yourself and cover up your shameful nakedness. Buy also some ointment to put on your eyes, so that you may see. ¹⁹I rebuke and punish all whom I love. Be in earnest, then, and turn from your sins. ²⁰Listen! I stand at the door and knock; if anyone hears my voice and opens the door, I will come in and eat with them, and they will eat with me. ²¹To those who win the victory I will give the right to sit beside me on my throne, just as I have been victorious and now sit by my Father on his throne.

²²"If you have ears, then, listen to what the Spirit says to the churches!"

Worship in Heaven

4 At this point I had another vision and saw an open door in heaven. And the voice that sounded like a trumpet, which I had heard speaking to me before, said, "Come up here, and I will show you what must happen after this." ²At once the Spirit took control of me. There in heaven was a throne with someone sitting on it. ³His face gleamed like such precious stones as jasper and carnelian, and all round the throne there was a rainbow the colour of an emerald. ⁴In a circle round the throne were 24 other thrones, on which were seated 24 elders dressed in white and wearing crowns of gold. ⁵From the throne came flashes of lightning, rumblings, and peals of thunder. In front of the throne seven lighted torches were burning, which are the seven spirits of God. ⁶Also in front of the throne there was what looked like a sea of glass, clear as crystal.

Surrounding the throne on each of its sides, were four living creatures covered with eyes in front and behind. ⁷The first one looked like a lion; the second looked like a bull; the third had a face like a human face; and the fourth looked like an eagle in flight. ⁸Each one of the four living creatures had six wings, and they were covered with eyes, inside and out. Day and night they never stop singing:

"Holy, holy, holy, is the Lord God Almighty,
who was, who is, and who is to come."

⁹The four living creatures sing songs of glory and honour and thanks to the one who sits on the throne, who lives for ever and ever. When they do so, ¹⁰the 24 elders fall down before the one who sits on the throne, and worship him who lives for ever and ever. They throw their crowns down in front of the throne and say:

....

3.14 origin; or ruler.

1484

Revel.

⋮·········

1 John
2 John
3 John
Jude

REVELATION 4–6

[11] "Our Lord and God! You are worthy
    to receive glory, honour, and power.
  For you created all things,
    and by your will they were given existence and life."

The Scroll and the Lamb

5 I saw a scroll in the right-hand of the one who sits on the throne; it was covered with writing on both sides and was sealed with seven seals. [2] And I saw a mighty angel, who announced in a loud voice, "Who is worthy to break the seals and open the scroll?" [3] But there was no one in heaven or on earth or in the world below* who could open the scroll and look inside it. [4] I cried bitterly because no one could be found who was worthy to open the scroll or look inside it. [5] Then one of the elders said to me, "Don't cry. Look! The Lion from Judah's tribe, the great descendant of David, has won the victory, and he can break the seven seals and open the scroll."

[6] Then I saw a Lamb standing in the centre of the throne, surrounded by the four living creatures and the elders. The Lamb appeared to have been killed. It had seven horns and seven eyes, which are the seven spirits of God that have been sent throughout the whole earth. [7] The Lamb went and took the scroll from the right-hand of the one who sits on the throne. [8] As he did so, the four living creatures and the 24 elders fell down before the Lamb. Each had a harp and gold bowls filled with incense, which are the prayers of God's people. [9] They sang a new song:
  "You are worthy to take the scroll
    and to break open its seals.
  For you were killed, and by your sacrificial death you
      bought for God
    people from every tribe, language, nation, and race.
  [10] You have made them a kingdom of priests to serve our
      God,
    and they shall rule on earth."

[11] Again I looked, and I heard angels, thousands and millions of them! They stood round the throne, the four living creatures, and the elders, [12] and sang in a loud voice:
  "The Lamb who was killed is worthy
    to receive power, wealth, wisdom, and strength,
    honour, glory, and praise!"

[13] And I heard every creature in heaven, on earth, in the world below, and in the sea — all living beings in the universe — and they were singing:
  "To him who sits on the throne and to the Lamb,
    be praise and honour, glory and might,
    for ever and ever!"

[14] The four living creatures answered, "Amen!" And the elders fell down and worshipped.

The Seals

6 Then I saw the Lamb break open the first of the seven seals, and I heard one of the four living creatures say in a voice that sounded like thunder, "Come!" [2] I looked, and there was a white horse. Its rider held a bow, and he was given a crown. He rode out as a conqueror to conquer.

[3] Then the Lamb broke open the second seal; and I heard the second living creature say, "Come!" [4] Another horse came out,

---

5.3 *world below*: The world of the dead (see 1.18).

a red one. Its rider was given the power to bring war on the earth, so that people should kill each other. He was given a large sword.

[5] Then the Lamb broke open the third seal; and I heard the third living creature say, "Come!" I looked, and there was a black horse. Its rider held a pair of scales in his hand. [6] I heard what sounded like a voice coming from among the four living creatures, which said, "A litre of wheat for a day's wages, and three litres of barley for a day's wages. But do not damage the olive trees and the vineyards!"

[7] Then the Lamb broke open the fourth seal; and I heard the fourth living creature say, "Come!" [8] I looked, and there was a pale-coloured horse. Its rider was named Death, and Hades* followed close behind. They were given authority over a quarter of the earth, to kill by means of war, famine, disease, and wild animals.

[9] Then the Lamb broke open the fifth seal. I saw underneath the altar the souls of those who had been killed because they had proclaimed God's word and had been faithful in their witnessing. [10] They shouted in a loud voice, "Almighty Lord, holy and true! How long will it be until you judge the people on earth and punish them for killing us?" [11] Each of them was given a white robe, and they were told to rest a little while longer, until the complete number of their fellow-servants and fellow-Christians had been killed, as they had been.

[12] And I saw the Lamb break open the sixth seal. There was a violent earthquake, and the sun became black like coarse black cloth, and the moon turned completely red like blood. [13] The stars fell down to the earth, like unripe figs falling from the tree when a strong wind shakes it. [14] The sky disappeared like a scroll being rolled up, and every mountain and island was moved from its place. [15] Then the kings of the earth, the rulers and the military chiefs, the rich and the powerful, and all other people, slave and free, hid themselves in caves and under rocks on the mountains. [16] They called out to the mountains and to the rocks, "Fall on us and hide us from the eyes of the one who sits on the throne and from the anger of the Lamb! [17] The terrible day of their anger is here, and who can stand against it?"

The 144,000 People of Israel

7 After this I saw four angels standing at the four corners of the earth, holding back the four winds so that no wind should blow on the earth or the sea or against any tree. [2] And I saw another angel coming up from the east with the seal of the living God. He called out in a loud voice to the four angels to whom God had given the power to damage the earth and the sea. [3] The angel said, "Do not harm the earth, the sea, or the trees, until we mark the servants of our God with a seal on their foreheads." [4] And I was told that the number of those who were marked with God's seal on their foreheads was 144,000. They were from the twelve tribes of Israel, [5-8] 12,000 from each tribe: Judah, Reuben, Gad, Asher, Naphtali, Manasseh, Simeon, Levi, Issachar, Zebulun, Joseph, and Benjamin.

The Enormous Crowd

[9] After this I looked, and there was an enormous crowd — no one could count all the people! They were from every race, tribe, nation, and language, and they stood in front of the throne and of the Lamb, dressed in white robes and holding palm branches

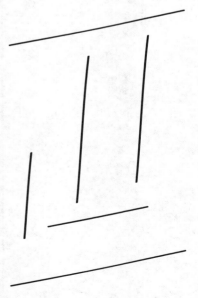

TURN THESE LINES INTO A PICTURE OF SOMETHING.

6.8 *Hades*: The world of the dead (see 1.18).

1486

Revel.

⋮⋯⋯⋯

1 John
2 John
3 John
Jude

REVELATION 7–9

in their hands. [10] They called out in a loud voice: "Salvation comes from our God, who sits on the throne, and from the Lamb!" [11] All the angels stood round the throne, the elders, and the four living creatures. Then they threw themselves face downwards in front of the throne and worshipped God, [12] saying, "Amen! Praise, glory, wisdom, thanksgiving, honour, power, and might belong to our God for ever and ever! Amen!"

[13] One of the elders asked me, "Who are these people dressed in white robes, and where do they come from?"

[14] "I don't know, sir. You do," I answered.

He said to me, "These are the people who have come safely through the terrible persecution. They have washed their robes and made them white with the blood of the Lamb. [15] That is why they stand before God's throne and serve him day and night in his temple. He who sits on the throne will protect them with his presence. [16] Never again will they hunger or thirst; neither sun nor any scorching heat will burn them, [17] because the Lamb, who is in the centre of the throne, will be their shepherd, and he will guide them to springs of life-giving water. And God will wipe away every tear from their eyes."

The Seventh Seal

8 When the Lamb broke open the seventh seal, there was silence in heaven for about half an hour. [2] Then I saw the seven angels who stand before God, and they were given seven trumpets.

[3] Another angel, who had a gold incense burner, came and stood at the altar. He was given a lot of incense to add to the prayers of all God's people and to offer it on the gold altar that stands before the throne. [4] The smoke of the burning incense went up with the prayers of God's people from the hands of the angel standing before God. [5] Then the angel took the incense burner, filled it with fire from the altar, and threw it on the earth. There were rumblings and peals of thunder, flashes of lightning, and an earthquake.

The Trumpets

[6] Then the seven angels with the seven trumpets prepared to blow them.

[7] The first angel blew his trumpet. Hail and fire, mixed with blood, came pouring down on the earth. A third of the earth was burnt up, a third of the trees, and every blade of green grass.

[8] Then the second angel blew his trumpet. Something that looked like a huge mountain on fire was thrown into the sea. A third of the sea was turned into blood, [9] a third of the living creatures in the sea died, and a third of the ships were destroyed.

[10] Then the third angel blew his trumpet. A large star, burning like a torch, dropped from the sky and fell on a third of the rivers and on the springs of water. [11] (The name of the star is "Bitterness".) A third of the water turned bitter, and many people died from drinking the water, because it had turned bitter.

[12] Then the fourth angel blew his trumpet. A third of the sun was struck, and a third of the moon, and a third of the stars, so that their light lost a third of its brightness; there was no light during a third of the day and a third of the night.

[13] Then I looked, and I heard an eagle that was flying high in the air say in a loud voice, "O horror! horror! How horrible it will be for all who live on earth when the sound comes from the trumpets that the other three angels must blow!"

9 Then the fifth angel blew his trumpet. I saw a star which had fallen down to the earth, and it was given the key to

the abyss.* ²The star opened the abyss, and smoke poured out of it, like the smoke from a large furnace; the sunlight and the air were darkened by the smoke from the abyss. ³Locusts came down out of the smoke upon the earth, and they were given the same kind of power that scorpions have. ⁴They were told not to harm the grass or the trees or any other plant; they could harm only the people who did not have the mark of God's seal on their foreheads. ⁵The locusts were not allowed to kill these people, but only to torture them for five months. The pain caused by the torture is like the pain caused by a scorpion's sting. ⁶During those five months they will seek death, but will not find it; they will want to die, but death will flee from them.

⁷The locusts looked like horses ready for battle; on their heads they had what seemed to be crowns of gold, and their faces were like human faces. ⁸Their hair was like women's hair, their teeth were like lions' teeth. ⁹Their chests were covered with what looked like iron breastplates, and the sound made by their wings was like the noise of many horse-drawn chariots rushing into battle. ¹⁰They have tails and stings like those of a scorpion, and it is with their tails that they have the power to hurt people for five months. ¹¹They have a king ruling over them, who is the angel in charge of the abyss. His name in Hebrew is Abaddon; in Greek the name is Apollyon (meaning "The Destroyer").

¹²The first horror is over; after this there are still two more horrors to come.

¹³Then the sixth angel blew his trumpet. I heard a voice coming from the four corners of the gold altar standing before God. ¹⁴The voice said to the sixth angel, "Release the four angels who are bound at the great river Euphrates!" ¹⁵The four angels were released; for this very hour of this very day of this very month and year they had been kept ready to kill a third of all humanity. ¹⁶I was told the number of the mounted troops: it was 200,000,000. ¹⁷And in my vision I saw the horses and their riders: they had breastplates red as fire, blue as sapphire, and yellow as sulphur. The horses' heads were like lions' heads, and from their mouths came out fire, smoke, and sulphur. ¹⁸A third of humanity was killed by those three plagues: the fire, the smoke, and the sulphur coming out of the horses' mouths. ¹⁹For the power of the horses is in their mouths and also in their tails. Their tails are like snakes with heads, and they use them to hurt people.

²⁰The rest of humanity, all those who had not been killed by these plagues, did not turn away from what they themselves had made. They did not stop worshipping demons, nor the idols of gold, silver, bronze, stone, and wood, which cannot see, hear, or walk. ²¹Nor did they repent of their murders, their magic, their sexual immorality, or their stealing.

The Angel and the Little Scroll

10 Then I saw another mighty angel coming down out of heaven. He was wrapped in a cloud and had a rainbow round his head; his face was like the sun, and his legs were like pillars of fire. ²He had a small scroll open in his hand. He put his right foot on the sea and his left foot on the land, ³and called out in a loud voice that sounded like the roar of lions. After he had called out, the seven thunders answered with a roar. ⁴As soon as they spoke, I was about to write. But I heard a voice speak

....

9.1 *abyss:* The place in the depths of the earth where the demons were imprisoned until their final punishment.

1488

Revel.

······

1 John
2 John
3 John
Jude

REVELATION 10, 11

REVELATION 12

John says twice that this vision is 'mysterious', and he's right. The woman might symbolise Eve or the nation of Israel or the Church, but

• NOBODY •

KNOWS

for sure. The dragon could be Satan or it could represent the cruel Roman empire - or both! What's clear, though, is that God wins the fierce battle against evil. Why not grab a bright coloured pencil and <u>underline</u> the verses about God's victory? Then read through the whole chapter and see what God makes stand out to you.

from heaven, "Keep secret what the seven thunders have said; do not write it down!"

[5] Then the angel that I saw standing on the sea and on the land raised his right-hand to heaven [6] and took a vow in the name of God, who lives for ever and ever, who created heaven, earth, and the sea, and everything in them. The angel said, "There will be no more delay! [7] But when the seventh angel blows his trumpet, then God will accomplish his secret plan, as he announced to his servants, the prophets."

[8] Then the voice that I had heard speaking from heaven spoke to me again, saying, "Go and take the open scroll which is in the hand of the angel standing on the sea and on the land."

[9] I went to the angel and asked him to give me the little scroll. He said to me, "Take it and eat it; it will turn sour in your stomach, but in your mouth it will be sweet as honey."

[10] I took the little scroll from his hand and ate it, and it tasted sweet as honey in my mouth. But after I swallowed it, it turned sour in my stomach. [11] Then I was told, "Once again you must proclaim God's message about many nations, races, languages, and kings."

The Two Witnesses

11 I was then given a stick that looked like a measuring rod, and was told, "Go and measure the temple of God and the altar, and count those who are worshipping in the temple. [2] But do not measure the outer courts, because they have been given to the heathen, who will trample on the Holy City for 42 months. [3] I will send my two witnesses dressed in sackcloth, and they will proclaim God's message during those 1,260 days."

[4] The two witnesses are the two olive trees and the two lamps that stand before the Lord of the earth. [5] If anyone tries to harm them, fire comes out of their mouths and destroys their enemies; and in this way, whoever tries to harm them will be killed. [6] They have authority to shut up the sky so that there will be no rain during the time they proclaim God's message. They have authority also over the springs of water, to turn them into blood; they have authority also to strike the earth with every kind of plague as often as they wish.

[7] When they finish proclaiming their message, the beast that comes up out of the abyss will fight against them. He will defeat them and kill them, [8] and their bodies will lie in the street of the great city, where their Lord was crucified. The symbolic name of that city is Sodom, or Egypt. [9] People from all nations, tribes, languages, and races will look at their bodies for three and a half days and will not allow them to be buried. [10] The people of the earth will be happy because of the death of these two. They will celebrate and send presents to each other, because these two prophets brought much suffering upon the earth. [11] After three and a half days a life-giving breath came from God and entered them, and they stood up; and all who saw them were terrified. [12] Then the two prophets heard a loud voice say to them from heaven, "Come up here!" As their enemies watched, they went up into heaven in a cloud. [13] At that very moment there was a violent earthquake; a tenth of the city was destroyed, and 7,000 people were killed. The rest of the people were terrified and praised the greatness of the God of heaven.

[14] The second horror is over, but the third horror will come soon!

The Seventh Trumpet

[15] Then the seventh angel blew his trumpet, and there were loud voices in heaven, saying, "The power to rule over the world

belongs now to our Lord and his Messiah, and he will rule for ever and ever!" [16] Then the 24 elders who sit on their thrones in front of God threw themselves face downwards and worshipped God, [17] saying:

"Lord God Almighty, the one who is and who was!
We thank you that you have taken your great power
and have begun to rule!
[18] The heathen were filled with rage,
because the time for your anger has come,
the time for the dead to be judged.
The time has come to reward your servants, the prophets,
and all your people, all who have reverence for you,
great and small alike.
The time has come to destroy those who destroy the
earth!"

[19] God's temple in heaven was opened, and the Covenant Box was seen there. Then there were flashes of lightning, rumblings and peals of thunder, an earthquake, and heavy hail.

The Woman and the Dragon

12 Then a great and mysterious sight appeared in the sky. There was a woman, whose dress was the sun and who had the moon under her feet and a crown of twelve stars on her head. [2] She was soon to give birth, and the pains and suffering of childbirth made her cry out.

[3] Another mysterious sight appeared in the sky. There was a huge red dragon with seven heads and ten horns and a crown on each of his heads. [4] With his tail he dragged a third of the stars out of the sky and threw them down to the earth. He stood in front of the woman, in order to eat her child as soon as it was born. [5] Then she gave birth to a son, who will rule over all nations with an iron rod. But the child was snatched away and taken to God and his throne. [6] The woman fled to the desert, to a place God had prepared for her, where she will be taken care of for 1,260 days.

[7] Then war broke out in heaven. Michael and his angels fought against the dragon, who fought back with his angels; [8] but the dragon was defeated, and he and his angels were not allowed to stay in heaven any longer. [9] The huge dragon was thrown out — that ancient serpent, called the Devil, or Satan, that deceived the whole world. He was thrown down to earth, and all his angels with him.

[10] Then I heard a loud voice in heaven saying, "Now God's salvation has come! Now God has shown his power as King! Now his Messiah has shown his authority! For the one who stood before our God and accused our brothers and sisters day and night has been thrown out of heaven. [11] Our brothers and sisters won the victory over him by the blood of the Lamb and by the truth which they proclaimed; and they were willing to give up their lives and die. [12] And so be glad, you heavens, and all you that live there! But how terrible for the earth and the sea! For the Devil has come down to you, and he is filled with rage, because he knows that he has only a little time left."

[13] When the dragon realized that he had been thrown down to the earth, he began to pursue the woman who had given birth to the boy. [14] She was given the two wings of a large eagle in order to fly to her place in the desert, where she will be taken care of for three and a half years, safe from the dragon's attack. [15] And then from his mouth the dragon poured out a flood of water after the woman, so that it would carry her away. [16] But the earth helped

1490

Revel.

⋮⋮⋯⋯

1 John
2 John
3 John
Jude

the woman; it opened its mouth and swallowed the water that had come from the dragon's mouth. ¹⁷The dragon was furious with the woman and went off to fight against the rest of her descendants, all those who obey God's commandments and are faithful to the truth revealed by Jesus. ¹⁸And the dragon stood* on the seashore.

The Two Beasts

13 Then I saw a beast coming up out of the sea. It had ten horns and seven heads; on each of its horns there was a crown, and on each of its heads there was a name that was insulting to God. ²The beast looked like a leopard, with feet like a bear's feet and a mouth like a lion's mouth. The dragon gave the beast his own power, his throne, and his vast authority. ³One of the heads of the beast seemed to have been fatally wounded, but the wound had healed. The whole earth was amazed and followed the beast. ⁴Everyone worshipped the dragon because he had given his authority to the beast. They worshipped the beast also, saying, "Who is like the beast? Who can fight against it?"

⁵The beast was allowed to make proud claims which were insulting to God, and it was permitted to have authority for 42 months. ⁶It began to curse God, his name, the place where he lives, and all those who live in heaven. ⁷It was allowed to fight against God's people and to defeat them, and it was given authority over every tribe, nation, language, and race. ⁸All people living on earth will worship it, except those whose names were written before the creation of the world in the book of the living which belongs to the Lamb that was killed.

⁹"Listen, then, if you have ears! ¹⁰Whoever is meant to be captured will surely be captured; whoever is meant to be killed by the sword will surely be killed by the sword. This calls for endurance and faith on the part of God's people."

¹¹Then I saw another beast, which came up out of the earth. It had two horns like a lamb's horns, and it spoke like a dragon. ¹²It used the vast authority of the first beast in its presence. It forced the earth and all who live on it to worship the first beast, whose wound had healed. ¹³This second beast performed great miracles; it made fire come down out of heaven to earth in the sight of everyone. ¹⁴And it deceived all the people living on earth by means of the miracles which it was allowed to perform in the presence of the first beast. The beast told them to build an image in honour of the beast that had been wounded by the sword and yet lived. ¹⁵The second beast was allowed to breathe life into the image of the first beast, so that the image could talk and put to death all those who would not worship it. ¹⁶The beast forced all the people, small and great, rich and poor, slave and free, to have a mark placed on their right hands or on their foreheads. ¹⁷No one could buy or sell without having this mark, that is, the beast's name or the number that stands for the name.

¹⁸This calls for wisdom. Whoever is intelligent can work out the meaning of the number of the beast, because the number stands for a human name. Its number is 666.

The Lamb and his People

14 Then I looked, and there was the Lamb standing on Mount Zion; with him were 144,000 people who have his

12.18 *And the dragon stood*; some manuscripts have *And I stood*, connecting this verse with what follows.

name and his Father's name written on their foreheads. [2] And I heard a voice from heaven that sounded like a roaring waterfall, like a loud peal of thunder. It sounded like the music made by musicians playing their harps. [3] The 144,000 people stood before the throne, the four living creatures, and the elders; they were singing a new song, which only they could learn. They are the only ones who have been redeemed. [4] They are the men who have kept themselves pure by not having sexual relations with women; they are virgins. They follow the Lamb wherever he goes. They have been redeemed from the rest of the human race and are the first ones to be offered to God and to the Lamb. [5] They have never been known to tell lies; they are faultless.

The Three Angels

[6] Then I saw another angel flying high in the air, with an eternal message of Good News to announce to the peoples of the earth, to every race, tribe, language, and nation. [7] He said in a loud voice, "Honour God and praise his greatness! For the time has come for him to judge. Worship him who made heaven, earth, sea, and the springs of water!"

[8] A second angel followed the first one, saying, "She has fallen! Great Babylon has fallen! She made all peoples drink her wine — the strong wine of her immoral lust!"

[9] A third angel followed the first two, saying in a loud voice, "Whoever worships the beast and its image and receives the mark on their forehead or on their hand [10] will themselves drink God's wine, the wine of his fury, which he has poured at full strength into the cup of his anger! All who do this will be tormented in fire and sulphur before the holy angels and the Lamb. [11] The smoke of the fire that torments them goes up for ever and ever. There is no relief day or night for those who worship the beast and its image, for anyone who has the mark of its name."

[12] This calls for endurance on the part of God's people, those who obey God's commandments and are faithful to Jesus.

[13] Then I heard a voice from heaven saying, "Write this: happy are those who from now on die in the service of the Lord!"

"Yes indeed!" answers the Spirit. "They will enjoy rest from their hard work, because the results of their service go with them."

The Harvest of the Earth

[14] Then I looked, and there was a white cloud, and sitting on the cloud was what looked like a human being, with a crown of gold on his head and a sharp sickle in his hand. [15] Then another angel came out from the temple and cried out in a loud voice to the one who was sitting on the cloud, "Use your sickle and reap the harvest, because the time has come; the earth is ripe for the harvest!" [16] Then the one who sat on the cloud swung his sickle on the earth, and the earth's harvest was reaped.

[17] Then I saw another angel come out of the temple in heaven, and he also had a sharp sickle.

[18] Then another angel, who is in charge of the fire, came from the altar. He shouted in a loud voice to the angel who had the sharp sickle, "Use your sickle, and cut the grapes from the vineyard of the earth, because the grapes are ripe!" [19] So the angel swung his sickle on the earth, cut the grapes from the vine, and threw them into the winepress of God's furious anger. [20] The grapes were squeezed out in the winepress outside the city, and blood came out of the winepress in a flood 300 kilometres long and nearly two metres deep.

1492

Revel.

⋮........

1 John
2 John
3 John
Jude

REVELATION 15, 16

The Angels with the Last Plagues

15 Then I saw in the sky another mysterious sight, great and amazing. There were seven angels with seven plagues, which are the last ones, because they are the final expression of God's anger.

[2] Then I saw what looked like a sea of glass mixed with fire. I also saw those who had won the victory over the beast and its image and over the one whose name is represented by a number. They were standing by the sea of glass, holding harps that God had given them [3] and singing the song of Moses, the servant of God, and the song of the Lamb:

"Lord God Almighty,
  how great and wonderful are your deeds!
King of the nations,*
  how right and true are your ways!
[4] Who will not stand in awe of you, Lord?
  Who will refuse to declare your greatness?
  You alone are holy.
All the nations will come
  and worship you,
  because your just actions are seen by all."

[5] After this I saw the temple in heaven open, with the Sacred Tent in it. [6] The seven angels who had the seven plagues came out of the temple, dressed in clean shining linen and with gold belts tied around their chests. [7] Then one of the four living creatures gave the seven angels seven gold bowls full of the anger of God, who lives for ever and ever. [8] The temple was filled with smoke from the glory and power of God, and no one could go into the temple until the seven plagues brought by the seven angels had come to an end.

The Bowls of God's Anger

16 Then I heard a loud voice speaking from the temple to the seven angels: "Go and pour out the seven bowls of God's anger on the earth!"

[2] The first angel went and poured out his bowl on the earth. Terrible and painful sores appeared on those who had the mark of the beast and on those who had worshipped its image.

[3] Then the second angel poured out his bowl on the sea. The water became like the blood of a dead person, and every living creature in the sea died.

[4] Then the third angel poured out his bowl on the rivers and the springs of water, and they turned into blood. [5] I heard the angel in charge of the waters say, "The judgements you have made are just, O Holy One, you who are and who were! [6] They poured out the blood of God's people and of the prophets, and so you have given them blood to drink. They are getting what they deserve!" [7] Then I heard a voice from the altar saying, "Lord God Almighty! True and just indeed are your judgements!"

[8] Then the fourth angel poured out his bowl on the sun, and it was allowed to burn people with its fiery heat. [9] They were burnt by the fierce heat, and they cursed the name of God, who has authority over these plagues. But they would not turn from their sins and praise his greatness.

[10] Then the fifth angel poured out his bowl on the throne of the beast. Darkness fell over the beast's kingdom, and people bit their tongues because of their pain, [11] and they cursed the

15.3 *nations;* some manuscripts have *ages.*

God of heaven for their pains and sores. But they did not turn from their evil ways.

¹²Then the sixth angel poured out his bowl on the great river Euphrates. The river dried up, to provide a way for the kings who come from the east. ¹³Then I saw three unclean spirits that looked like frogs. They were coming out of the mouth of the dragon, the mouth of the beast, and the mouth of the false prophet. ¹⁴They are the spirits of demons that perform miracles. These three spirits go out to all the kings of the world, to bring them together for the battle on the great Day of Almighty God.

¹⁵"Listen! I am coming like a thief! Happy is he who stays awake and guards his clothes, so that he will not walk around naked and be ashamed in public!"

¹⁶Then the spirits brought the kings together in the place that in Hebrew is called Armageddon.

¹⁷Then the seventh angel poured out his bowl in the air. A loud voice came from the throne in the temple, saying, "It is done!" ¹⁸There were flashes of lightning, rumblings and peals of thunder, and a terrible earthquake. There has never been such an earthquake since the creation of the human race; this was the worst earthquake of all! ¹⁹The great city was split into three parts, and the cities of all countries were destroyed. God remembered great Babylon and made her drink the wine from his cup — the wine of his furious anger. ²⁰All the islands disappeared, all the mountains vanished. ²¹Huge hailstones, each weighing as much as fifty kilogrammes, fell from the sky on people, who cursed God on account of the plague of hail, because it was such a terrible plague.

The Famous Prostitute

17 Then one of the seven angels who had the seven bowls came to me and said, "Come, and I will show you how the famous prostitute is to be punished, that great city that is built near many rivers. ²The kings of the earth practised sexual immorality with her, and the people of the world became drunk from drinking the wine of her immorality."

³The Spirit took control of me, and the angel carried me to a desert. There I saw a woman sitting on a red beast that had names insulting to God written all over it; the beast had seven heads and ten horns. ⁴The woman was dressed in purple and scarlet, and covered with gold ornaments, precious stones, and pearls. In her hand she held a gold cup full of obscene and filthy things, the result of her immorality. ⁵On her forehead was written a name that has a secret meaning: "Great Babylon, the mother of all the prostitutes and perverts in the world." ⁶And I saw that the woman was drunk with the blood of God's people and the blood of those who were killed because they had been loyal to Jesus.

When I saw her, I was completely amazed. ⁷"Why are you amazed?" the angel asked me. "I will tell you the secret meaning of the woman and of the beast that carries her, the beast with seven heads and ten horns. ⁸That beast was once alive, but lives no longer; it is about to come up from the abyss and will go off to be destroyed. The people living on earth whose names have not been written before the creation of the world in the book of the living, will all be amazed as they look at the beast. It was once alive; now it no longer lives, but it will reappear.

⁹"This calls for wisdom and understanding. The seven heads are seven hills, on which the woman sits. They are also seven kings: ¹⁰five of them have fallen, one still rules, and the other

Colour these shapes.

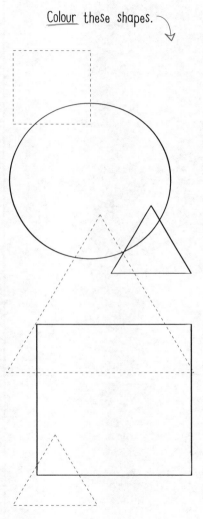

1494

Revel.

.:........

1 John
2 John
3 John
Jude

REVELATION 17, 18

one has not yet come; when he comes, he must rule only a little while. [11] And the beast that was once alive, but lives no longer, is itself an eighth king who is one of the seven and is going off to be destroyed.

[12] "The ten horns you saw are ten kings who have not yet begun to rule, but who will be given authority to rule as kings for one hour with the beast. [13] These ten all have the same purpose, and they give their power and authority to the beast. [14] They will fight against the Lamb; but the Lamb, together with his called, chosen, and faithful followers, will defeat them, because he is Lord of lords and King of kings."

[15] The angel also said to me, "The waters you saw, on which the prostitute is sitting, are nations, peoples, races, and languages. [16] The ten horns you saw, and the beast, will hate the prostitute; they will take away everything she has and leave her naked; they will eat her flesh and destroy her with fire. [17] For God has placed in their hearts the will to carry out his purpose by acting together and giving the beast their power to rule until God's words come true.

[18] "The woman you saw is the great city that rules over the kings of the earth."

The Fall of Babylon

18 After this I saw another angel coming down out of heaven. He had great authority, and his splendour brightened the whole earth. [2] He cried out in a loud voice: "She has fallen! Great Babylon has fallen! She is now haunted by demons and unclean spirits; all kinds of filthy and hateful birds live in her. [3] For all the nations have drunk her wine — the strong wine of her immoral lust. The kings of the earth practised sexual immorality with her, and the merchants of the world grew rich from her unrestrained lust."

[4] Then I heard another voice from heaven, saying:

"Come out, my people! Come out from her!
   You must not take part in her sins;
     you must not share in her punishment!
[5] For her sins are piled up as high as heaven,
    and God remembers her wicked ways.
[6] Treat her exactly as she has treated you;
   pay her back double for all she has done.
Fill her cup with a drink twice as strong
   as the drink she prepared for you.
[7] Give her as much suffering and grief
   as the glory and luxury she gave herself.
For she keeps telling herself:
   'Here I sit, a queen!
   I am no widow,
   I will never know grief!'
[8] Because of this, in one day she will be struck with plagues —
   disease, grief, and famine.
And she will be burnt with fire,
   because the Lord God, who judges her, is mighty."

[9] The kings of the earth who took part in her immorality and lust will cry and weep over the city when they see the smoke from the flames that consume her. [10] They stand a long way off, because they are afraid of sharing in her suffering. They say, "How terrible! How awful! This great and mighty city Babylon! In just one hour you have been punished!"

[11] The merchants of the earth also cry and mourn for her, because no one buys their goods any longer; [12] no one buys their

gold, silver, precious stones, and pearls; their goods of linen, purple cloth, silk, and scarlet cloth; all kinds of rare woods and all kinds of objects made of ivory and of expensive wood, of bronze, iron, and marble; [13] and cinnamon, spice, incense, myrrh, and frankincense; wine and oil, flour and wheat, cattle and sheep, horses and carriages, slaves, and even human lives. [14] The merchants say to her, "All the good things you longed to own have disappeared, and all your wealth and glamour are gone, and you will never find them again!" [15] The merchants, who became rich from doing business in that city, will stand a long way off, because they are afraid of sharing in her suffering. They will cry and mourn, [16] and say, "How terrible! How awful for the great city! She used to dress herself in linen, purple, and scarlet, and cover herself with gold ornaments, precious stones, and pearls! [17] And in one hour she has lost all this wealth!"

All the ships' captains and passengers, the sailors and all others who earn their living on the sea, stood a long way off, [18] and cried out as they saw the smoke from the flames that consumed her: "There never has been another city like this great city!" [19] They threw dust on their heads, they cried and mourned, saying, "How terrible! How awful for the great city! She is the city where all who have ships sailing the seas became rich on her wealth! And in one hour she has lost everything!"

[20] Be glad, heaven, because of her destruction! Be glad, God's people and the apostles and prophets! For God has condemned her for what she did to you!

[21] Then a mighty angel picked up a stone the size of a large millstone and threw it into the sea, saying, "This is how the great city Babylon will be violently thrown down and will never be seen again. [22] The music of harps and of human voices, of players of the flute and the trumpet, will never be heard in you again! No workman in any trade will ever be found in you again; and the sound of the millstone will be heard no more! [23] Never again will the light of a lamp be seen in you; no more will the voices of brides and grooms be heard in you. Your merchants were the most powerful in all the world, and with your false magic you deceived all the peoples of the world!"

[24] Babylon was punished because the blood of prophets and of God's people was found in the city; yes, the blood of all those who have been killed on earth.

19 After this I heard what sounded like the roar of a large crowd of people in heaven, saying, "Praise God! Salvation, glory, and power belong to our God! [2] True and just are his judgements! He has condemned the prostitute who was corrupting the earth with her immorality. God has punished her because she killed his servants." [3] Again they shouted, "Praise God! The smoke from the flames that consume the great city goes up for ever and ever!" [4] The 24 elders and the four living creatures fell down and worshipped God, who was seated on the throne. They said, "Amen! Praise God!"

The Wedding Feast of the Lamb

[5] Then there came from the throne the sound of a voice, saying, "Praise our God, all his servants and all people, both great and small, who have reverence for him!" [6] Then I heard what sounded like a large crowd, like the sound of a roaring waterfall, like loud peals of thunder. I heard them say, "Praise God! For the Lord, our Almighty God, is King! [7] Let us rejoice and be glad; let us praise his greatness! For the time has come for the wedding of the

1496

Revel.

·:·········

1 John
2 John
3 John
Jude

REVELATION 19, 20

Lamb, and his bride has prepared herself for it. [8]She has been given clean shining linen to wear." (The linen is the good deeds of God's people.)

[9]Then the angel said to me, "Write this: happy are those who have been invited to the wedding feast of the Lamb." And the angel added, "These are the true words of God."

[10]I fell down at his feet to worship him, but he said to me, "Don't do it! I am a servant together with you and with your fellow-believers, all those who hold to the truth that Jesus revealed. Worship God!"

For the truth that Jesus revealed is what inspires the prophets.

The Rider on the White Horse

[11]Then I saw heaven open, and there was a white horse. Its rider is called Faithful and True; it is with justice that he judges and fights his battles. [12]His eyes were like a flame of fire, and he wore many crowns on his head. He had a name written on him, but no one except himself knows what it is. [13]The robe he wore was covered with blood. His name is "The Word of God". [14]The armies of heaven followed him, riding on white horses and dressed in clean white linen. [15]Out of his mouth came a sharp sword, with which he will defeat the nations. He will rule over them with a rod of iron, and he will trample out the wine in the winepress of the furious anger of the Almighty God. [16]On his robe and on his thigh was written the name: "King of kings and Lord of lords".

[17]Then I saw an angel standing on the sun. He shouted in a loud voice to all the birds flying in mid air: "Come and gather together for God's great feast! [18]Come and eat the flesh of kings, generals, and soldiers, the flesh of horses and their riders, the flesh of all people, slave and free, great and small!"

[19]Then I saw the beast and the kings of the earth and their armies gathered to fight against the one who was riding the horse and against his army. [20]The beast was taken prisoner, together with the false prophet who had performed miracles in his presence. (It was by those miracles that he had deceived those who had the mark of the beast and those who had worshipped the image of the beast.) The beast and the false prophet were both thrown alive into the lake of fire that burns with sulphur. [21]Their armies were killed by the sword that comes out of the mouth of the one who was riding the horse; and all the birds ate all they could of their flesh.

The Thousand Years

20 Then I saw an angel coming down from heaven, holding in his hand the key of the abyss and a heavy chain. [2]He seized the dragon, that ancient serpent — that is, the Devil, or Satan — and chained him up for a thousand years. [3]The angel threw him into the abyss, locked it, and sealed it, so that he could not deceive the nations any more until the thousand years were over. After that he must be let loose for a little while.

[4]Then I saw thrones, and those who sat on them were given the power to judge. I also saw the souls of those who had been executed because they had proclaimed the truth that Jesus revealed and the word of God. They had not worshipped the beast or its image, nor had they received the mark of the beast on their foreheads or their hands. They came to life and ruled as kings with Christ for a thousand years. [5](The rest of the dead did not come to life until the thousand years were over.) This is the first raising of the dead. [6]Happy and greatly blessed are those who

are included in this first raising of the dead. The second death has no power over them; they shall be priests of God and of Christ, and they will rule with him for a thousand years.

The Defeat of Satan

⁷After the thousand years are over, Satan will be let loose from his prison, ⁸and he will go out to deceive the nations scattered over the whole world, that is, Gog and Magog. Satan will bring them all together for battle, as many as the grains of sand on the seashore. ⁹They spread out over the earth and surrounded the camp of God's people and the city that he loves. But fire came down from heaven and destroyed them. ¹⁰Then the Devil, who deceived them, was thrown into the lake of fire and sulphur, where the beast and the false prophet had already been thrown; and they will be tormented day and night for ever and ever.

The Final Judgement

¹¹Then I saw a great white throne and the one who sits on it. Earth and heaven fled from his presence and were seen no more. ¹²And I saw the dead, great and small alike, standing before the throne. Books were opened, and then another book was opened, the book of the living. The dead were judged according to what they had done, as recorded in the books. ¹³Then the sea gave up its dead. Death and the world of the dead also gave up the dead they held. And all were judged according to what they had done. ¹⁴Then death and the world of the dead were thrown into the lake of fire. (This lake of fire is the second death.) ¹⁵Whoever did not have their names written in the book of the living were thrown into the lake of fire.

The New Heaven and the New Earth

21 Then I saw a new heaven and a new earth. The first heaven and the first earth disappeared, and the sea vanished. ²And I saw the Holy City, the new Jerusalem, coming down out of heaven from God, prepared and ready, like a bride dressed to meet her husband. ³I heard a loud voice speaking from the throne: "Now God's home is with human beings! He will live with them, and they shall be his people. God himself will be with them, and he will be their God. ⁴He will wipe away all tears from their eyes. There will be no more death, no more grief or crying or pain. The old things have disappeared."

⁵Then the one who sits on the throne said, "And now I make all things new!" He also said to me, "Write this, because these words are true and can be trusted." ⁶And he said, "It is done! I am the first and the last, the beginning and the end. To anyone who is thirsty I will give the right to drink from the spring of the water of life without paying for it. ⁷Those who win the victory will receive this from me: I will be their God, and they will be my children. ⁸But cowards, traitors, perverts, murderers, the immoral, those who practise magic, those who worship idols, and all liars — the place for them is the lake burning with fire and sulphur, which is the second death."

The New Jerusalem

⁹One of the seven angels who had the seven bowls full of the seven last plagues came to me and said, "Come, and I will show you the Bride, the wife of the Lamb." ¹⁰The Spirit took control of me, and the angel carried me to the top of a very high mountain. He showed me Jerusalem, the Holy City, coming down out of heaven

REVELATION 21

In this space, draw or write out what you imagine a

NEW

HEAVEN

– AND –

NEW

EARTH

might look like. What might the differences be, compared to what you know now?

1498

Revel.

.:.········

1 John
2 John
3 John
Jude

REVELATION 21, 22

from God [11] and shining with the glory of God. The city shone like a precious stone, like a jasper, clear as crystal. [12] It had a great, high wall with twelve gates and with twelve angels in charge of the gates. On the gates were written the names of the twelve tribes of the people of Israel. [13] There were three gates on each side: three on the east, three on the south, three on the north, and three on the west. [14] The city's wall was built on twelve foundation stones, on which were written the names of the twelve apostles of the Lamb. [15] The angel who spoke to me had a gold measuring rod to measure the city, its gates, and its wall. [16] The city was perfectly square, as wide as it was long. The angel measured the city with his measuring rod: it was 2,400 kilometres long and was as wide and as high as it was long. [17] The angel also measured the wall, and it was sixty metres high,* according to the standard unit of measure which he was using.* [18] The wall was made of jasper, and the city itself was made of pure gold, as clear as glass. [19] The foundation stones of the city wall were adorned with all kinds of precious stones. The first foundation stone was jasper, the second sapphire, the third agate, the fourth emerald, [20] the fifth onyx, the sixth carnelian, the seventh yellow quartz, the eighth beryl, the ninth topaz, the tenth chalcedony, the eleventh turquoise, the twelfth amethyst. [21] The twelve gates were twelve pearls; each gate was made from a single pearl. The street of the city was of pure gold, transparent as glass.

[22] I did not see a temple in the city, because its temple is the Lord God Almighty and the Lamb. [23] The city has no need of the sun or the moon to shine on it, because the glory of God shines on it, and the Lamb is its lamp. [24] The peoples of the world will walk by its light, and the kings of the earth will bring their wealth into it. [25] The gates of the city will stand open all day; they will never be closed, because there will be no night there. [26] The greatness and the wealth of the nations will be brought into the city. [27] But nothing that is impure will enter the city, nor anyone who does shameful things or tells lies. Only those whose names are written in the Lamb's book of the living will enter the city.

22 The angel also showed me the river of the water of life, sparkling like crystal, and coming from the throne of God and of the Lamb [2] and flowing down the middle of the city's street. On each side of the river was the tree of life, which bears fruit twelve times a year, once each month; and its leaves are for the healing of the nations. [3] Nothing that is under God's curse will be found in the city.

The throne of God and of the Lamb will be in the city, and his servants will worship him. [4] They will see his face, and his name will be written on their foreheads. [5] There shall be no more night, and they will not need lamps or sunlight, because the Lord God will be their light, and they will rule as kings for ever and ever.

The Coming of Jesus

[6] Then the angel said to me, "These words are true and can be trusted. And the Lord God, who gives his Spirit to the prophets, has sent his angel to show his servants what must happen very soon."

[7] "Listen!" says Jesus. "I am coming soon! Happy are those who obey the prophetic words in this book!"

[8] I, John, have heard and seen all these things. And when I finished hearing and seeing them, I fell down at the feet of the

---

REVELATION 22.18-21

From the Word of God in Genesis, to the sacrifice of Abraham, to the marriage of Hosea, to the Gospels, to Revelation, this book is all about telling and reflecting

• THE •

STORY

of Jesus, your story, God's story and the reason you were created. It has all been about Jesus.

21.17 *high;* or *thick.*
21.17 In verses 16 and 17 the Greek text speaks of "12,000 furlongs" and "144 cubits" which may have symbolic significance.

angel who had shown me these things, and I was about to worship him. ⁹But he said to me, "Don't do it! I am a servant together with you and with your brothers the prophets and with all those who obey the words in this book. Worship God!" ¹⁰And he said to me, "Do not keep the prophetic words of this book a secret, because the time is near when all this will happen. ¹¹Whoever is evil must go on doing evil, and whoever is filthy must go on being filthy; whoever is good must go on doing good, and whoever is holy must go on being holy."

¹²"Listen!" says Jesus. "I am coming soon! I will bring my rewards with me, to give to each one according to what he has done. ¹³I am the first and the last, the beginning and the end."

¹⁴Happy are those who wash their robes clean and so have the right to eat the fruit from the tree of life and to go through the gates into the city. ¹⁵But outside the city are the perverts and those who practise magic, the immoral and the murderers, those who worship idols and those who are liars both in words and deeds.

¹⁶"I, Jesus, have sent my angel to announce these things to you in the churches. I am descended from the family of David; I am the bright morning star."

¹⁷The Spirit and the Bride say, "Come!"

Everyone who hears this must also say, "Come!"

Come, whoever is thirsty; accept the water of life as a gift, whoever wants it.

Conclusion

¹⁸I, John, solemnly warn everyone who hears the prophetic words of this book: if anyone adds anything to them, God will add to his or her punishment the plagues described in this book. ¹⁹And if anyone takes anything away from the prophetic words of this book, God will take away from them their share of the fruit of the tree of life and of the Holy City, which are described in this book.

²⁰He who gives his testimony to all this says, "Yes indeed! I am coming soon!"

So be it. Come, Lord Jesus!

²¹May the grace of the Lord Jesus be with everyone.*

REVELATION 22.2

Humanity's story began with the tree of life in the garden of Eden and ends with the tree of life here. Our story is being lived out

BETWEEN THE TREES.

Draw all that you can remember of the story of the Bible in between these two trees.

22.21 *everyone*; some manuscripts have *God's people*; others have *all God's people*.

THE BIG ISSUES

AND WHAT THE BIBLE SAYS ABOUT THEM

BULLYING

Have you ever been told that you're not good enough, or that you don't look right or you're not clever enough? Maybe you have been physically pushed around. It hurts us and can really affect our confidence when we get treated this way. It makes us dread going to places where we know we will experience it. Sometimes the words people speak to us can be even more damaging and last with us longer than any physical abuse.

NOBODY DESERVES - TO BE BULLIED -

If you have ever experienced bullying or are currently experiencing it, we suggest that you speak to somebody you trust, like a parent, teacher or youth worker who can help you. The Psalms in the Bible describe the feeling of despair that comes from constant attack by enemies and might be helpful to read, particularly Psalm 13.

Maybe you are the one who has treated another person unkindly. The way we treat people is so important. The Bible has very practical tips on how we can encourage and build each other up, so that nobody has to feel bullied or belittled. It also has prayers and advice for those who are facing difficulties.

KEY BIBLE VERSES: PROVERBS 18.21; EPHESIANS 4.29-32; 1 PETER 3.9; PSALM 13

COMPARISON

KEY BIBLE VERSES: GALATIANS 6.4-5; 1 CORINTHIANS 12; PHILIPPIANS 3.12-14; 1 SAMUEL 18.6-9

Comparing ourselves to other people can be something that pushes us forward and helps us to be better. However, unless we're really secure in who we are, it can be something that piles pressure on to us. When we look at others and only see the ways in which we're not as good as them, it can affect the way we think of our own value. Comparing our looks, exam results, families or social media following to other people's can just increase our feeling of not being good enough. We see this in the story of King Saul and David, when comparison led to jealousy that ruled Saul's life (1 Samuel 18.6-9).

God created us all unique, with different gifts, skills, appearance and, most importantly, purpose. You were created for a purpose that is different from your friends', and the more time you spend trying to be like others, the less time you have to fulfil the purpose you were made for. Don't get so distracted by someone else's race that you forget to run your own! It's about beating your 'personal best', not competing with others.

write some thoughts here

_____

_____

_____

_____

_____

CREATION & THE ENVIRONMENT

KEY BIBLE VERSES: GENESIS 1; LEVITICUS 25.2-7; PSALM 104; MATTHEW 22.39

The Bible tells us that God created the world and everything in it. The earth belongs to him and he gave humankind the responsibility of looking after it. However, it seems like we are messing it up instead. From filling the oceans with plastic that harms sea life to using up fossil fuels just so that we can live comfier lives, it's all got very out of hand.

Think of your most prized possession. Imagine that you give it to a friend to look after, but when you get it back, it's completely trashed. That's a bit what it's like with people and God's earth.

The Bible also tells us to love our neighbours, and a lot of the things we do in our everyday lives have an impact on the places where people live, across the world as well as in our local areas. Loving our neighbours means being careful that the way we live doesn't have a negative impact on them and the places they inhabit.

Research humankind's

IMPACT
• ON THE ENVIRONMENT •
and then write down one thing you will do to make a difference (for example, recycle more).

EVANGELISM

The word 'evangelism' comes from a Greek word that means 'good news' - and it doesn't have to be something big and scary! Very simply, evangelism means sharing with others the good news that Jesus loves us and has plans for our lives, here and eternally.

The Bible says that some people are especially gifted to be evangelists and equip the church to share the gospel. But even if we don't have that particular gift, we can still give it a go. Imagine if there was a really good film at the cinema but you missed out on it because nobody told you about it. Our friends and family won't come to know about the life Jesus gives us if nobody tells them about him.

There are lots of different ways to share our faith. It can be through sharing our own story of what God has done in our lives, or telling people that they are loved by God, or showing them a video about the Christian message. Evangelism can also be done through the way we live our lives - for example, not stealing, not swearing and being different from the world around us.

Evangelism is about being yourself and communicating just a small bit of the amazing news that we are all deeply loved and cared for by Jesus.

KEY BIBLE VERSES: EPHESIANS 4.11; ROMANS 10.14-15; MATTHEW 28.18-19; REVELATION 12.11

WE'VE MADE A FILM ON THIS TOPIC: GO TO GNBYOUTHEDITION.CO.UK/EVANGELISM

FAMILY

God designed the family as a unit for love, acceptance and growing faith, and that's the way many of us experience it.

Everyone's experience of family is different, though. Every family works in a different way, and most families have their own challenges. We are imperfect people, and often our families can bear the brunt of our mistakes and imperfections.

Divorce is becoming more and more common in our society, and it can be hard to handle when stuff like that affects us. Perhaps it affects you.

Whatever our families are like, the Bible talks loads about

– GOD'S FAMILY –

in which he is the father and we are all invited to be his children. It can be a challenge to acknowledge God as a heavenly parent, especially if we don't have a human parent around all the time. But God promises throughout the Bible that he is a good father who will never let us down. Today we are invited to be part of a family of millions round the world, who share one faith and one father.

KEY BIBLE VERSES: EXODUS 20.12; PROVERBS 6.20-21; ISAIAH 63.16; MATTHEW 12.48-50; ROMANS 8.14-17; 1 CORINTHIANS 8.6; EPHESIANS 6.1-4

WE'VE MADE A FILM ON THIS TOPIC: GO TO GNBYOUTHEDITION.CO.UK/FAMILY

HURTING YOURSELF

Some people intentionally hurt themselves in a number of different ways and for a variety of reasons. Often people choose to self-harm as a way of expressing some very difficult feelings that they are struggling to put into words; it can act as an outward expression of inward pain. If you or someone you know is struggling in this way, it is really important that you speak to an adult who you trust.

God loves you deeply and wants to stand with you in your pain. In the Bible we see again and again that people turn to God in their darkest moments. You can do that at any time.

KEY BIBLE VERSES: PSALM 147.2-3; REVELATION 21.3-4; PSALM 23

Go to gnbyouthedition.co.uk/hurting

to watch a

❧ SHORT FILM ❧

we've made on this topic.

IF YOU ARE STRUGGLING WITH THIS TOPIC OR WANT TO KNOW MORE, PLEASE VISIT:
selfharm.co.uk
mind.org.uk (search self harm)
www.nhs.uk/conditions/self-harm

IDENTITY

Part of growing up is about figuring out who we are and the kind of people we hope to become. Loads of things have an influence on our identity, such as where we live, our family and friends, and our interests, but our identity is also tied in with our self-esteem and how we feel about ourselves. Our feelings can be positive ('I am a good friend') or negative ('I'm not good enough').

Our identity can be very 'me' focused, so our feelings about ourselves shift around as we look to ourselves or other people to figure out who we are. But God wants us to focus on him, and to know that we have a secure identity in his love for us. The Bible has loads of verses about how we are loved, accepted and forgiven, and about God's plan for our lives.

READ THE VERSES ABOVE ABOUT IDENTITY.

LET IT SINK IN

that these words are part of

• WHO YOU ARE. •

WRITE OUT THE VERSES THAT

JUMP OUT

to you the most, and stick them somewhere you can see them.

LIVING DIFFERENTLY

Fitting in and being 'normal' can be important, especially when you're growing up. We don't like to be different in case we

- STAND OUT -

in the crowd and others tease us for it. But there are ways in which, as Christians, we might want to live differently from the people around us. The differences can range from what we wear and what music we listen to, to what we do with our boyfriend or girlfriend or going to church on a Sunday instead of playing football.

The world can be a dark place, and God has called us to represent him and bring his light into it, doing good things instead of bad. Fullness of life with Jesus is about freedom, light and love. So it is a privilege to be different, not a disadvantage.

Ultimately, our purpose is to know Jesus and make him known, not to fit in and be like everyone else. We don't need to be the most popular or achieve the most, because our approval comes from God and not the world around us - and that is so liberating!

MAKING WISE DECISIONS

It's hard being a young person! There's loads of pressure on you to behave in certain ways and there are loads of environments, such as parties, where you may not be sure about the wisest move to make. As Christians, we need to think about how to make good choices in those situations. Jesus partied but was perfect!

On motorways you'll see crash barriers in the middle of the road. They are there to prevent you from hitting oncoming traffic. If you hit a crash barrier it's not great, but at least it's not the other side of the road. Making wise decisions when you are partying or under peer pressure can be seen in the same way. Putting barriers in place to make sure you don't cross the line is a good idea.

- BE PROACTIVE! -

Put a limit on how many drinks you'll have before going out; make a choice on what level of banter is inappropriate; decide with your partner how far is too far. Start with what you know: the Bible is clear on some things, like getting smashed, or talking behind people's backs, or sex outside marriage. That's the other side of the motorway, so be wise - put a few barriers in place.

KEY BIBLE VERSES: PROVERBS 3.5-7; PROVERBS 21.5; PROVERBS 23.29-35; JOHN 17.14-16; 1 CORINTHIANS 6.12; 1 CORINTHIANS 15.33; EPHESIANS 5.18; PHILIPPIANS 4.8; 1 PETER 4.1-6

WE'VE MADE A FILM ON THIS TOPIC: GO TO GNBYOUTHEDITION.CO.UK/DECISIONS

MENTAL HEALTH

KEY BIBLE VERSES: PSALM 46.1-3; PSALM 73.26; MATTHEW 11.28-30; PSALM 34.17-20; PHILIPPIANS 4:8

Mental health is something we all have. Positive mental health means being able to cope with day-to-day life, and having a healthy self-esteem and belief in our abilities. Mental ill-health is the opposite - it's when we find everyday demands hard to cope with and lack a positive sense of self. We all have ups and downs, but when our mental health negatively impacts our lives and relationships with others, it can become a problem. This is when someone may have a mental illness.

You've probably heard of some of the more common problems, such as eating disorders, depression and anxiety, but there's a wide range of issues which can look different for each person. Just like someone who's got the flu, people with mental health problems need help and support to get better.

Most importantly, God wants us to know that he's right in the middle of every situation, and it's important for us to talk to God about our issues.

If you, or someone you know, struggles with their mental health, you may want to talk to someone you trust about it. You can also check out some of these websites for guidance:
nhs.uk (search 'youth mental health')
youngminds.org.uk
mind.org.uk

PORN

Pornography is one of those taboo subjects that no one likes to talk about (especially in Christian circles), but in reality many people are struggling with it. One survey showed that two-thirds of 13-17 year olds said they had seen pornography - that is, explicit images of nudity or sex acts.

The thing is, God created sex to be enjoyed, and he gave us a desire for sex - and that in itself isn't a problem. However, pornography

– DAMAGES – RELATIONSHIPS:

it's thought to be a factor in more than half of all divorces. The issue is that porn takes away the real value of human beings and reduces them to nothing more than something we can get pleasure from. It warps what God intended, and it warps our minds and hearts in the process.

Porn isn't healthy - what Jesus says in Matthew 5.28 helps us to see that. Our challenge, as young people, is to keep ourselves pure, knowing that God's plan for us is so much better.

KEY BIBLE VERSES: JOB 31.1; PSALM 119.9-11; PROVERBS 5.15-23; MATTHEW 5.27-30; 1 CORINTHIANS 6.18-20; COLOSSIANS 3.5-8

POVERTY

We live in a world where nearly half of all children live in poverty. There's a big divide between the rich and the poor, and it is clear from the Bible that God cares deeply about this issue. He loves the needy and values them as people. And if we are well off, he wants us to befriend and help those who need our support.

In the Bible, there's loads about helping the poor and how we shouldn't turn a blind eye to them. It's not just people without money who might need help. Some people are poor in relationships - they are lonely or bullied - and some people are poor emotionally because they're unhappy. It doesn't take much for us to look around the world and see that things aren't quite the way they were meant to be.

KEY BIBLE VERSES: PROVERBS 31.8-9; ISAIAH 58.7; MICAH 6.8; LUKE 4.18-19; MATTHEW 25.35-40

Take some time to think about all the kinds of poverty you know about - for example, homelessness and bullying. Now read some of the key Bible verses and, off the back of them, write a sentence outlining what you will commit to do as a result.

I COMMIT TO: _____

_____

_____

_____

_____

_____

SCHOOL & EXAMS

What word would you use to describe your school or college? Perhaps you enjoy it and find certain subjects really interesting. However, maybe for you the best bit is when the bell goes for home time. Or maybe you wonder if you'll ever use equations or knowledge about different types of rocks in the real world. Even if we don't see much point in all the subjects we have to study, our education can benefit us by teaching us how to turn up on time and how to learn new things, which will help us whatever we do in the future.

There can be a lot of pressure to pass exams and do well, which can make us

– REALLY ANXIOUS –

There will be some things you are really good at and other things not so good. God has given us each different gifts, and it's important not to compare ourselves or our grades to the person next to us. Just do the best you can with the gifts and abilities God has given you!

One Bible verse (Colossians 3.23) encourages us to work at everything we do with all our heart, and to imagine we're working for God, not people. This can inspire and motivate us even when we find the teachers annoying!

> KEY BIBLE VERSES: COLOSSIANS 3.23;
> PHILIPPIANS 4.6; LUKE 12.22-31

However well you do at school or college,

– GOD STILL HAS –
PLANS
– FOR YOUR LIFE. –

Write or draw here how you would like God to be using you in 10 years' time.

SEX & RELATIONSHIPS

KEY BIBLE VERSES: 1 THESSALONIANS 4.1-8;
1 CORINTHIANS 6.18-20; GENESIS 2.24-25;
1 CORINTHIANS 7.32-35, SONG OF SONGS 8.6-7

God designed us for relationships. We are created firstly for relationship with him, but also for relationships with each other - whether family, friends or boyfriend or girlfriend. Some Christians feel called to remain single and stay focused completely on God, while others feel called to romantic relationships and one day to marriage. Either way, relationships can be tricky.

Sex is a great gift from God. Many Christians believe that it's not just a physical act. It also has a spiritual element, and is designed to take place within marriage, creating a lasting bond between two people. Not everybody reads the Bible verses about relationships in this way but one thing is for sure - God can help us with pain or hurt or regrets when it comes to sex, as he cares about us and what we do with our bodies.

For more information on this topic, head to gnbyouthedition.co.uk/sex to watch a short

 FILM

WE MADE ABOUT IT.

SOCIAL MEDIA

Social media can be seen as an incredible opportunity to connect with others and impact their lives. How we use this opportunity is massively important, and so is the way we let it affect us. About two-thirds of young people say that social media has a negative influence on the way they feel about themselves, so we need to be on our guard. While Jesus may not have had a social media account, he did say a lot about how we should speak to other people, and this is as true when we're using social media as when we're in face-to-face conversation.

When we look at our timelines, with other people's filtered and staged photos, it can be easy to compare ourselves to them and feel rubbish about ourselves (see 'Comparison'). So how could you

- MAKE THE - EXPERIENCE BETTER

for other people? What would it look like for you to only post images that made people want to do good in the world rather than feel bad about themselves? Could you only write status updates and messages that brought life to those who read them? Or perhaps choose, each week, to raise awareness of something that matters to you and God? You have been given a tool - use it well!

KEY BIBLE VERSES: COLOSSIANS 4.5-6;
EPHESIANS 4.29-32; HEBREWS 10.24

For more information on these two topics, head to gnbyouthedition.co.uk/suffering or gnbyouthedition.co.uk/war to watch a

≽ SHORT FILM ≼

WE MADE ABOUT THEM.

SUFFERING

How can there be a God when there is so much suffering? Great question! Firstly, suffering was never part of God's original plan - the start of Genesis shows us a perfect world going wrong. Secondly, suffering is also not part of God's final plan - the end of Revelation describes a future where there is no more suffering, evil or death. The Bible makes it clear that God is good, so God's nature is not to cause suffering. Much suffering is caused by humans (think about wars, terrorism, inequality and poverty), though not all of it is.

But even if God is not the cause, why does he allow it? Maybe so as not to go against our free will? Perhaps because he can meet us in our suffering? We don't know for definite. Amazingly, though, the God of the Bible never distances himself from suffering. Jesus came to earth and experienced the worst kind of suffering. So we know that Jesus understands our pain, and he promises to be with us through our suffering. Maybe that is more powerful than a one-sentence explanation?

KEY BIBLE VERSES: GENESIS 3.14-19; JOB 5.6-7; ROMANS 8.18-22; 2 CORINTHIANS 1.5; PHILIPPIANS 2.5-11; 1 PETER 2.21; 1 PETER 5.10; REVELATION 21.3-4

WAR & TERRORISM

KEY BIBLE VERSES: PSALM 10.17-18; PSALM 46.1-2, 9-10; PROVERBS 24.10-11; MATTHEW 5.43-48

It feels as if the world we are living in today is increasingly unstable. War is normal, terrorism is normal and they both appear to be happening everywhere. What is the Bible's response?

There is a lot of disagreement about the Christian response to war. Some argue that it can be acceptable to go to war, considering that in the Old Testament, God's people went to war under God's leadership. It's possible that war might prevent something even worse from happening, or protect innocent people. Others would argue that Christians should be pacifists and not take part in war for any reason, considering Jesus' command to love our enemies.

One thing the Bible is clear about is that we're meant to

- LOVE & PRAY -

for those who persecute and cause hurt to us. The people we read about in the news or on social media who have done terrible things - we pray for them and we love them. We don't excuse their actions or hope that they avoid justice, but we pray and we love. Christians are called to bring peace and love in a hurting world.

WORRY & ANXIETY

KEY BIBLE VERSES: MATTHEW 6.25-34; PHILIPPIANS 4.6-7; 1 PETER 5.7; PSALM 23.4

Worry and anxiety are emotions that every single human being experiences. They're normal responses to many situations we face in life, such as exams or loved ones falling ill. However, when worry and anxiety begin to impact our everyday lives, influence our behaviour and take over our thoughts, they can become a problem.

God doesn't want our lives to be ruled by worried thoughts but by things like peace, hope and joy. The Bible says that God cares about us and that we can go to him about every single one of our cares. Even in the times we feel super-overwhelmed and fearful, God is with us.

For more information on this topic, head to gnbyouthedition.co.uk/worry to watch a short

FILM

WE MADE ABOUT IT.

If there is anything that you are

WORRIED

· ABOUT ·

READ PHILIPPIANS 4.6

and bring your situation to God.

VIDEO INDEX

Title	*Code*	*ISBN*
GNB The Youth Edition, Hardback	GNB 073	978-0-564-07037-4

Typesetting and production management by Bible Society Resources Ltd, a wholly-owned subsidiary of The British and Foreign Bible Society

Cover and additional material designed by Becky Vale

BSRL/2019/15M
Printed in China
FT917503

This Bible may be distributed with other covers selected by national Bible Societies who are members of the United Bible Societies. To find out more about the Bible Society in your country visit: www.biblesociety.org

Founded by Billy Graham in 1946, Youth for Christ is about seeing young people's lives changed by Jesus. We do this by showing Jesus in a way which is relevant to every young person in Britain in places like schools, prisons and local communities, using sport, music, the arts and so much more. To find out more about who we are and what we do, visit our website at yfc.co.uk

Across the world, millions of people are not able to engage with the Bible. This is often because the Scriptures aren't available or accessible, or because their significance and value haven't yet been recognised. Working in over 200 countries, Bible Society is a charity and on a global mission to offer the Bible to every man, woman and child. This is because we believe that when people engage with the Bible, lives can be changed, for good.